FOOTBALL YEARBOOK

2006/2007

First published 2006

Data collation by Warner Leach Ltd

ISBN 0-9549819-4-4

Published by Interact Publishing Limited
www.footballyearbook.co.uk

Editor: Terry Pratt

Data interpretation: Tony Warner, Stephen Hall

Production Manager: Stephen Hall

Data management: Peter Watts, Tim Tyler, Andy Salter

Design: Warner Leach Ltd

Programming: Jonathan Proud

Printed and bound in the UK by Butler & Tanner Ltd.

Cover photographs by Getty Images.

By arrangement with the BBC

WORLD STARS ON YOUR DOORSTEP

Did **Andrea Pirlo** have much of an impact on Serie A? What kind of season did Trinidadian **Stern John** have for Coventry? How about the powerful batch of **Ivory Coast** players dotted through the French League? Was **Owen Hargreaves** an important part of Bayern Munich's championship? Did **Beckham's** and **Zidane's** haloes start to slip at Madrid?

Every four years the World Cup reinvents our view of world football. Germany 2006 was a cup of two halves; the exciting Group stages with first-time finalists rocking established football super powers, followed by the tension and caution of the knock-out phase.

Germany came out with most credit, bringing their new-found passion for attack, even to the dreaded third-place play-off. And if 2002 was about the emergence of South Korea and Japan, 2006 gave us two African nations with teams good enough to go toe-to-toe with top sides and match them for attacking power and midfield creativity.

The Premiership has a vested interest in the world game as it is the world's most cosmopolitan league. Increasingly that interest extends to other leagues as we become the new home for their brightest stars. The form of **Andriy Shevchenko**, **Tomas Rosicky** and **Michael Ballack** prior to signing to the Premiership should have fans salivating.

And there are a host of players who didn't get a chance to shine at the World Cup, who are worth looking up in this book:

- Surely Holland must regret leaving the sensational striking of **Klaas Jan Huntelaar** behind!
- And shouldn't van Basten have built his side around the Bundesliga's best midfielder, **Rafael van der Vaart**?
- How much more potent would France have been with **Johan Micoud** and **Ludovic Giuly** in the squad?
- A lot of Premiership clubs have been linked with Lens midfielder **Alou Diarra** but could they handle his disciplinary record?
- Both Man City's **Andy Cole** and Newcastle's **Charles N'Zogbia** show up unexpectedly in our Best in Europe charts

These are just a few tasters. You'll find many more stories and surprises throughout the next 520 pages. This book boils down all performances to an essence that allows you to compare clubs and players across different leagues. We hope you enjoy your discoveries.

As always I'm indebted to Tony Warner, Steve Hall, Peter Watts and Jonathan Proud for all their hard work and knowledge.

Terry Pratt

300

Italian clubs

A goal every 121 minutes in Serie A – Shevchenko leaves the corruption-torn Italian league with his reputation intact

Shevchenko; Premiership bound

342

Dutch clubs

Like Henry and Rooney rolled into one; Dutch youngster tops our European scoring charts –twice!

Huntelaar top at Heerenveen and Ajax

380

German clubs

Hargreaves and Ballack win the Bundesliga Championship and both World Cup heroes have stats to shout about

Owen Hargreaves; top midfielder at Bayern?

418

French clubs

Ivorian and Ghanaian energy and creativity lit up the World Cup. France is the finishing school for emerging African talent

Bonaventure Kalou (PSG) and Aruna Dindane (Lens)

THE CLUBS

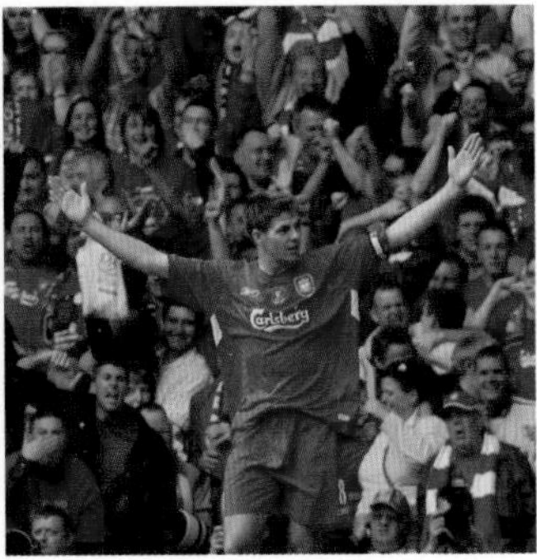

98

FA Cup

From 3-1 down against the Hatters to 3-2 down against the Hammers; Gerrard's scenic route to cup glory

Gerrard sparks another cup comeback

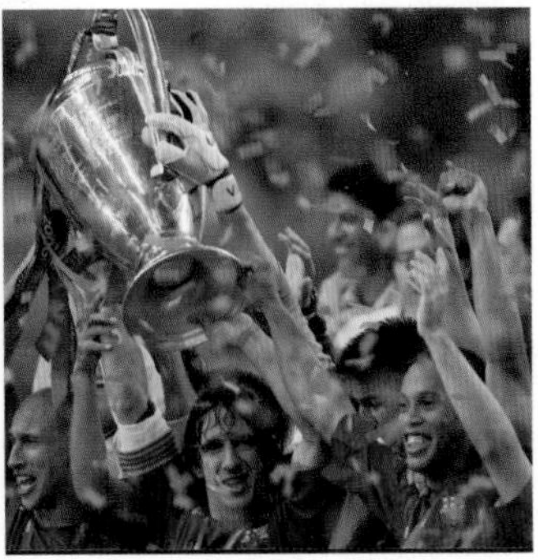

460

Champions League

Ronaldinho crushes Chelsea's expectations and Larsson ends Arsenal's hopes as Barca claim the top club crown

Barcelona; the best side in Europe

476

Uefa Cup

Two nights that will go down in history at the Riverside as Boro and McClaren ride a rollercoaster to the final

Last minute Maccarone

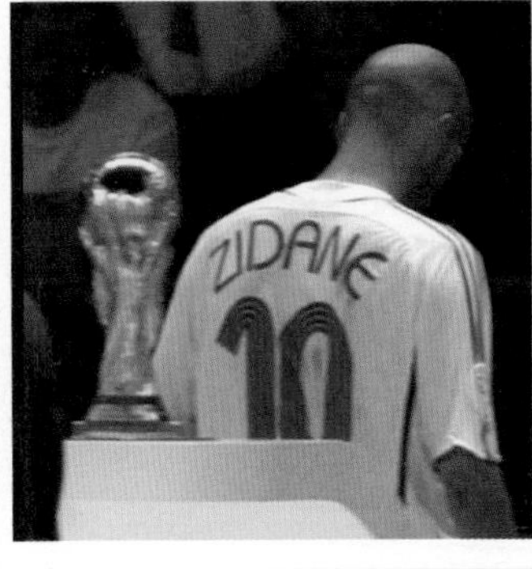

484

World Cup

All the action from Germany in a comprehensive picture, stat and story breakdown of Zidane's World Cup

Zidane turns his back on football

CHARTING PERFORMANCE

Goalkeepers

Bringing the best out of his defence

Good goalkeepers and strong back fours tend to go together. It's rare that you get one without the other as they feed off the mutual confidence that breeds. Edwin van der Sar illustrates the point, last season he picked up rave reviews with United but in the 2004-05 season, he mainly picked up the ball from the back of Fulham's net. We are using his stats as a guide to our goalkeeper charts:

Goals Conceded in the League
The team conceded **33** Goals in van der Sar's 38 league starts.

Goals Conceded in all competitions
Including cups as well he conceded 40 goals in all competitions (51 appearances).

KEY GOALKEEPER

Edwin van der Sar	
Goals Conceded in the League Number of League goals conceded while the player was on the pitch	33
Goals Conceded in all competitions Total number of goals conceded while the player was on the pitch	40
League minutes played Number of minutes played in league matches	3375
Clean Sheets In games when player was on pitch for at least 70 minutesmins	18
Goals to Shots Ratio The average number of shots on target per each League goal conceded	5.9
Defensive Rating Ave mins between League goals conceded while on the pitch	102

Clean Sheets
In the league, Manchester United recorded **18** Clean Sheets in games where van der Sar played for at least 70 minutes and the end of the game finished without a goal being conceded.

Defensive Rating
His Defensive Rating of **102** is arrived at by dividing the number of minutes he played by the number of league goals the team conceded. For van der Sar it is **3375 minutes** divided by **33**.
We use this rating to compare keepers in our Round-up Tables and van der Sar rates fourth-best. Last season he conceded a goal every 58 minutes for Fulham – one of the worst four records in the Premiership.

Goals to Shots Ratio
In the Premiership, we also record a keeper's Goals to Shots Ratio by dividing the number of Shots on Target in his games by the number of goals conceded. It's a good indicator of whether a keeper is out-performing his defence. Last season, van der Sar was the worst performer in the division, saving only 3.7 shots on target for every goal he let in. This season he's second best, level with Petr Cech, saving **5.9** shots on target for each goal conceded. That improvement is worth around 20 goals to United.

Midfielders

He's a box-to-box player

Newcastle hit most goals when Nolberto Solano is on the pitch. The player moved from Villa to a Newcastle midfield that had three star name additions in Parker, Emre and Luque but ultimately became key to their end of season revival. We are using his information to illustrate our midfield charts:

Goals in the League
Solano didn't scored his first goal until their 20th game but finished with **6** league goals. He didn't add any in the cup competitions.

Assists
In the Premiership, we keep a tally of every Assist, where the player has made the final telling pass or header to set up a colleague for a goal. Solano only made **2** Assists, compared to N'Zogbia with 10 Assists on Newcastle's other wing.

Defensive Rating
Midfielders have defensive duties and Solano must protect the team's right flank. His Rating is determined by dividing the number of minutes he played by the number of goals the team conceded during that time. It comes to **82**, which means Newcastle concede just over a goal a game when Solano is on the pitch.

KEY PLAYERS - MIDFIELDERS

Nolberto Solano	
Goals in the League	6
Goals in all competitions	6
Assists League goals scored by a team mate where the player delivered the final pass	2
Defensive Rating Average number of mins between League goals conceded while on the pitch	82
Contribution to Attacking Power Average number of minutes between League team goals while on pitch	55
Scoring Difference Defensive Rating minus Contribution to Attacking Power	27

Contribution to Attacking Power
This shows Solano's real strength. Newcastle score every 55 minutes on average when Solano is on the pitch. This gives him an Attacking Power of **55**. The lower it is the better and Solano is way better than his colleagues – even forwards such as Shearer and Ameobi. The club only score a goal every 173 minutes on average when Solano isn't playing.

Scoring Difference
This measure is a personal goal difference for a player. It is found by taking away their Attacking Power from their Defensive Rating. In Solano's case it's **82** minus **55**, which delivers a Scoring Difference of **+27**. A positive figure means the team are more likely to score than concede when he is on the pitch. A negative figure means the team are move likely to let goals in than score.

Goalscorers

Drogba v Crespo; the Chelsea front line

Didier Drogba and Hernan Crespo shared striking duties at Chelsea with Mourinho usually playing one lead striker with support and goals coming from fast-supporting midfielders. Two very different forwards with almost identical Strike Rates, but Drogba just shades it to earn Chelsea's **Key Goalscorer** slot.

KEY PLAYERS - GOALSCORERS

Didier Drogba	
Goals in the League	12
Goals in all competitions	16
Assists League goals scored by a team mate where the player delivered the final pass	14
Contribution to Attacking Power Average number of minutes between League team goals while on pitch	40
Player Strike Rate Average number of minutes between League goals scored by player	166
Club Strike Rate Average minutes between League goals scored by club	48

Goals in the League

Drogba scored **12** goals in league games and another four in cups to make **16** in all competitions.

Assists

Drogba is a hard-worker and his bustle sets up goals for colleagues in a way Crespo doesn't. As a result, Drogba came third in our Premiership Assists table with **14**.

Contribution to Attacking Power

This measures the potency of the Chelsea attack when a player is on the pitch. With Drogba on the pitch Chelsea averaged a league goal every **40 minutes**. Better than two a game. When Drogba was off, the average dropped to a goal every 65 minutes. Crespo's Attacking Power for the season was 49.

Club Strike Rate

The Club Strike Rate is a measure of Chelsea's average for the league season. 72 goals scored in 3420 league minutes is an average of one every **48 minutes** – slightly better than Crespo.

Player Strike Rate

This measures Drogba's personal Strike Rate. It shows how regularly he scores for Chelsea when he plays – a goal every **166 minutes** on average. This can be compared with other goalscorers in the Premiership (or any other league) even though many will have played more matches than Drogba. The Chelsea man comes fifth in the Premiership chart, just ahead of Crespo, who rated 167 minutes. Lampard may be a midfielder but he was third in the club's Goalscorers Chart, which is based on Strike Rate rather than total goals.

Defenders

Jewell's rock sparkles at the back

Paul Jewell constructed Wigan's Premiership defence around the experience of Stephane Henchoz and the consistency of Arjan De Zeeuw. Pascal Chimbonda's pace won admirers but de Zeeuw earned top place in Wigan's defensive chart.

Goals Conceded in the League

Wigan let in **31** league goals while de Zeeuw was on the pitch, which rose to **38** when you included their cup ties.

League minutes played

He played **2660** minutes in league matches out of a possible 3420.

Clean Sheets

We only measure Clean Sheets in league games where the player has influenced the game for *at least* 70 minutes. These we call **Counting Games**. There were **10** league games when de Zeeuw helped the defence to completely shut out the opposition. You have to have played at least 12 Counting Games to qualify for a club's Key Defenders chart and 17+ Counting Games to get into the Divisional Round-up chart. De Zeeuw is eligible for both with 29 Counting Games.

Defensive Rating

This shows how regularly the team concede a league goal when this player is on the pitch. While de Zeeuw was playing, Wigan conceded a league goal every **86 minutes** so his Defensive Rating is **86**. It's calculated by dividing the minutes played by the league goals conceded. This Rating is used to compare defenders in our Round-up tables and against defenders from other leagues.

KEY PLAYERS - DEFENDERS

Arjan De Zeeuw	
Goals Conceded in the League Number of League goals conceded while the player was on the pitch	31
Goals Conceded in all competitions Total number of goals conceded while the player was on the pitch	38
League minutes played Number of minutes played in league matches	2660
Clean Sheets In games when the player was on pitch for at least 70 minutes	10
Defensive Rating Average number of mins between League goals conceded while on the pitch	86
Club Defensive Rating Average number of mins between League goals conceded by the club this season	66

Club Defensive Rating

This is a quick way to see whether a player is tightening his club's defence or not. It shows the average amount of time between league goals conceded by the club. And over the season Wigan conceded 52 league goals at an average of one every **66 minutes**.

When de Zeeuw was off the pitch, Wigan conceded a league goal every 36 minutes on average.

Squad Appearances

It's not an 11-a-side game anymore

Increasingly managers rotate their team, to rest players, try out different combinations or formations or reverse a poor run. The Squad Appearances table gives a visual impression of how a player has been used.

Squares

A dark green square ■ shows the player was in the starting XI and finished the game. A light green square ■ shows he was on the bench but didn't get subbed on. A blank square shows they didn't make it to the bench.

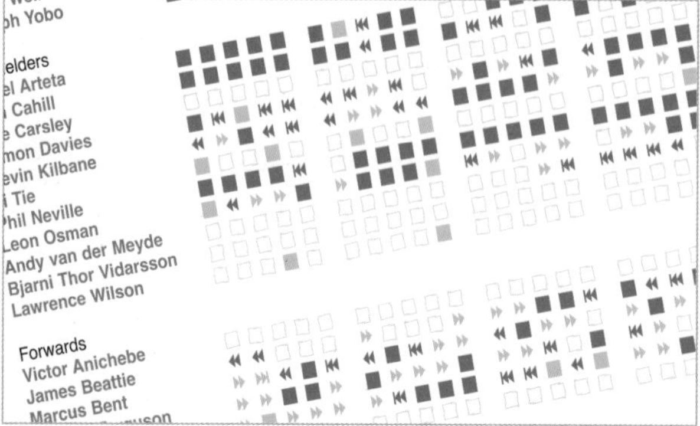

Arrows

A dark green arrow « shows the player started the game but was subbed off or sent off. A light green arrow » shows they started on the bench but were subbed on.

Counting Games

A player earns a Counting Game when they play for more than 70 minutes in a match. Managers often take a view around the 70-minute mark. If the result's a foregone conclusion, they may as well rest players or if they are under pressure, it's time to sacrifice a player to change things around. A dark green arrow with a small line before it |« means they were subbed off *after* 70 minutes and it counts as a Counting Game. A light green arrow with a small line after it means they were subbed on in the first 20 minutes and played a full 70 minutes after that – also a Counting Game.

Competition Key

A quick guide to the Competition, Venue and Result is shown at the top of the Squad Appearances Chart. **H** or **A** in Venue refer to **H**ome and **A**way. The result is W, L or D and shown in the appropriate colour. The Competitions are: **L** = League; **F** = FA Cup; **C** = Champions League; **E** = Uefa Cup; **W** = the League Cup in the English or Scottish divisions; **O** = Other, e.g. a play-off match.

Finally the numbers along the top refer to the game number and can be checked against the Results chart for more details.

There's more information of how squads are used in the Premiership round up pages.

Team of the Season

Selecting the most effective 4-4-2

The club XI

Each club has a team of the season generated by our computer. This ensures that all our own in-built favouritism and subjectivity is factored out. The computer selects first from players who have played at least 12 Counting Games **CG**.

KEY: DR = Defensive Rate, SD = Scoring Difference AP = Attacking Power SR = Strike Rate
CG=Counting games – League games playing at least 70 minutes

Defence

If there is a choice of keeper, it chooses the one with the best (highest) Defensive Rating **DR**. It then selects the best four Defensive Ratings among the club's Defenders. They will be the defence that concedes goals least regularly.

Midfield

It selects the four midfield players with the highest Scoring Difference **SD**. Positive figures mean the side scores more often than it concedes when they play. A midfielder who has seen his side concede a goal a game while he was on the pitch has a Defensive Rating of 90. If they also scored two goals a game while he played, he will have an Attacking Power of 45. Take the 45 away from the 90 and his Scoring Difference is +45. Stevie Gerrard tops the Liverpool charts with +94.

Attack

In most divisions, the computer selects the two best strike rates among the club's forwards. In the Premiership, we give it a little more leeway, if the club plays with a withdrawn forward or an advanced midfield player, we judge them on Attacking Power – Peter Crouch gets in on this basis.

Very rarely, it finds a team that has chopped and changed so much that it can't select a full 4-4-2 who have all played sufficient games. Then we reduce the Counting Games criteria below 12.

Divisional Teams of the Season

The most effective players in each division are sorted into top 15-20 charts of Goalkeepers, Defenders, Midfielders and Goalscorers. We raise the Counting Game barrier to 17 or more Counting Games. The most effective 4-4-2 across a division is selected the same way, with one difference: no team is allowed to have more than one of its players in each position. So the most even Chelsea can put into this XI is four.

Goal Attempts

He's got to at least test the keeper

Shots For

We record goal attempts in Premier League matches. The Goal Attempts For chart details the featured side's attacking prowess. Shots On Target are split into Home and Away totals and the overall figure is also shown as an average per league game. We do the same with Shots Off Target and run both together for the team's complete shots record. Arsenal hit **253** shots at home and **209** away, giving them **462** in total – not particularly high for a top four side.

However, Arsenal have precision in their side and need less shots to score a goal. They scored once for every **4** Shots On Target. And in terms of Accuracy, they have one of the best ratio's in the business, hitting the target **59%** of the time.

GOAL ATTEMPTS

FOR Goal attempts recorded in League games	HOME	AWAY	TOTAL	AVE
shots on target	167	107	274	7.2
shots off target	86	102	188	4.9
TOTAL	253	209	462	12.2
Ratio of goals to shots Average number of shots on target per League goal scored				4
Accuracy rating Average percentage of total goal attempts which were on target				59.3

AGAINST Goal attempts recorded in League games	HOME	AWAY	TOTAL	AVE
shots on target	67	86	153	4
shots off target	63	107	170	4.5
TOTAL	130	193	323	8.5
Ratio of goals to shots Average number of shots on target per League goal scored				4.9
Accuracy rating Average percentage of total goal attempts which were on target				47.4

Shots Against

This is the defensive side of the shots coin, showing how many times opposing teams had a shot at the Arsenal goal. The Ratio of goals to shots is a reflection on the goalkeeper while the Accuracy rating gives a feel for how much pressure the Arsenal defence put the opposing forwards under.

Disciplinary Records

Refs just look at his reputation

Disciplinary records are shown for teams in most of the divisions.

For Bolton the most cards were earned by Kevin Davies, **10** in the league. However, the ever-present Davies doesn't top the Bolton Bookings chart.

Chart position is determined by how regularly the player gets a card of any colour in a league game. El Hadji Diouf earned **6** yellows and **1** red card in the league but he averaged one card for every 200 minutes he was on the pitch. Davies rates fourth place in the chart with an average of a card every 313 minutes.

BOOKINGS

El Hadji Diouf	
League Yellow	6
League Red	1
All competitions Yellow	7
All competitions Red	1
League Average **200** mins between cards	

	PLAYER	LEAGUE Y	LEAGUE R	TOTAL Y	TOTAL R	AVE
1	Diouf	6Y	1R	7Y	1R	200
2	Vaz Te	3	0	3	0	282
3	Ben Haim	9	1	11	1	284
4	Davies	10	0	12	0	313
5	Nakata	3	1	6	1	319
6	Faye	6	0	8	0	333
7	Campo	2	0	2	0	432
8	Nolan	7	0	10	0	444
9	Gardner	3	1	4	1	603
10	Giannakopoulos	4	0	4	0	633
11	O'Brien	2	0	3	0	987
12	N'Gotty	2	0	2	0	1225
13	Jaidi	1	0	1	0	1228
14	Speed	2	0	2	0	1235
15	Hunt	1	0	1	0	1243
	Other	3	0	4	0	
	TOTAL	64	4	80	4	

Top Point Earners

Players who are winners

Average points

Manchester City's Andy Cole made a difference in the games he played. He tops City's Top Points Earners Chart with an average of **1.72** points in the games he influenced for at least 70 minutes.

Club Average Points

Injuries ended Andy Cole's season early and Man City finished dismally. Cole played **18** Counting Games, but City notched 31 points in those games – an average of **1.72**. The club as a whole averaged **1.13** points per game over the whole season.

TOP POINT EARNERS

Andrew Cole	
Counting Games League games when player was on pitch for at least 70 minutes	18
Average points Average League points taken in Counting games	1.72
Club Average points Average points taken in League games	1.13

	PLAYER	GAMES	PTS
1	Andrew Cole	18	1.72
2	Stephen Jordan	18	1.50
3	Claudio Reyna	18	1.44
4	Kiki Musampa	19	1.42
5	Joey Barton	30	1.30
6	Trevor Sinclair	23	1.30
7	Danny Mills	15	1.20
8	David James	38	1.13
9	Sylvain Distin	30	1.10
10	Stephen Ireland	12	1.08

Most Missed Players

If you look at the games Cole missed then City barely averaged half a point a game. In the divisional Round-up tables we chart the most badly missed players, comparing the player's individual average with the club's average and giving a quick guide to the players clubs can't do without. Anything around half a point is significant and Cole is well above that.

THE PREMIERSHIP ROUND-UP

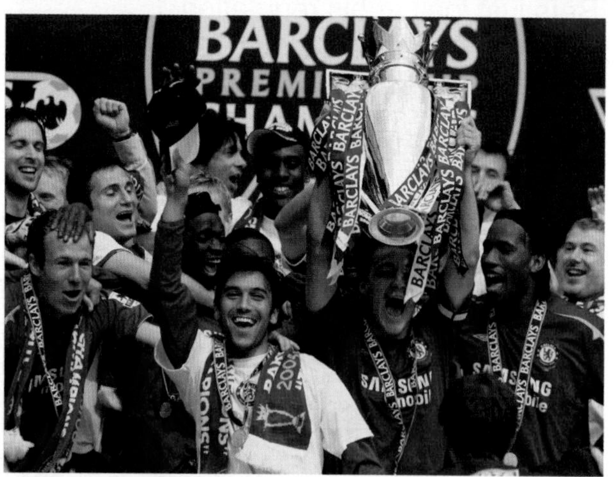

Chelsea retained their Championship by dominating the Defence and Midfield charts again but without setting the Striking table alight. Luckily **Frank Lampard** broke the Premier record for league goals from midfield, while **Didier Drogba** and **Hernan Crespo** finished fifth and sixth in the Strike Rate table with barely a minute separating them.

Topping that table was **Thierry Henry**, who broke a goal every 100 minutes – the first time we have recorded a sub 100-minute Strike Rate in the Premiership – but still found himself well behind the latest Dutch sensation.

Steven Gerrard hit 23 goals in all competitions from midfield and also topped the Assists table.

A special mention for **Thomas Myhre**, who probably started the season as Charlton's third-choice keeper and finished it topping our Shots-to-Goals table. Myhre saved over six shots on target for every goal he let in – better than both **Petr Cech** and **Edwin van der Sar**.

And finally, Arsenal top the Overseas Players charts again – now over 90% of the league action is by non-English nationals.

CLUB STRIKE FORCE

United's Rooney and van Nistelrooy

Goals scored in the League	72
Goals scored in all competitions	106
Shots on target (SoT) Shots on target hit by the team recorded in League games	286

1 Man Utd

Club Strike Rate (CSR) Average number of minutes between League goals scored by club	48.0

	CLUB	LGE	ALL	SoT	CSR
1	Man Utd	72	106	286	48
2	Chelsea	72	96	277	48
3	Arsenal	68	99	274	50
4	Liverpool	57	95	282	60
5	Tottenham	53	55	234	65
6	West Ham	52	70	173	66
7	Blackburn	51	68	183	67
8	Bolton	49	66	198	70
9	Middlesbrough	48	85	219	71
10	Fulham	48	56	178	71
11	Newcastle	47	53	208	73
12	Wigan	45	58	207	76
13	Man City	43	52	212	80
14	Aston Villa	42	57	197	81
15	Charlton	41	58	181	83
16	Portsmouth	37	41	222	92
17	Everton	34	42	203	101
18	West Brom	31	42	161	110
19	Birmingham	28	41	168	122
20	Sunderland	26	31	183	132

CLUB DEFENCES

1 Chelsea

Club Defensive Rate (CDR) Average number of minutes between League goals conceded by club	155

	CLUB	LGE	ALL	CS	SoT	CDR
1	Chelsea	22	34	20	127	155
2	Liverpool	25	43	22	123	137
3	Arsenal	31	44	16	153	110
4	Man Utd	34	44	18	195	101
5	Tottenham	38	42	13	218	90
6	Bolton	41	53	15	191	83
7	Blackburn	42	52	16	174	81
8	Newcastle	42	46	13	210	81
9	Man City	48	54	6	197	71
10	Everton	49	65	13	230	70
11	Birmingham	50	65	10	207	68
12	Wigan	52	63	10	225	66
13	Charlton	55	68	13	263	62
14	Aston Villa	55	65	11	252	62
15	West Ham	55	66	9	263	62
16	Fulham	58	67	10	243	59
17	Middlesbrough	58	81	10	251	59
18	West Brom	58	68	10	254	59
19	Portsmouth	62	67	5	208	55
20	Sunderland	69	74	4	262	50

Gallas and Terry of Chelsea

Goals conceded in the League	22
Goals conceded in all competitions	34
Clean Sheets (CS) Number of league games where no goals were conceded	20
Shots on Target Against (SoT) Shots on Target conceded by team in League games	127

PLAYER NATIONALITIES

Overseas country with the most player appearances in the Premiership - France

In the squad	4855	Percentage of League action	7.38
Appearances in League games	4097	Caps for France this season	50
Most appearances	Chimbonda	Percentage of time on pitch	95.4

	COUNTRY	PLAYERS	IN SQUAD	LGE APP	% LGE ACT	CAPS	MOST APP	APP
	England	270	4855	4097	40.56	159	David James	100.0
1	France	44	882	784	7.38	50	Pascal Chimbonda	95.4
2	Rep of Ireland	34	621	553	5.38	71	Shay Given	100.0
3	Holland	21	461	423	3.88	36	Edwin Van der Sar	98.7
4	Wales	19	378	335	3.34	49	Robbie Savage	87.0
5	Spain	17	373	311	2.92	36	Jose Reina	86.6
6	Scotland	18	381	306	2.77	39	David Weir	84.3
7	Australia	11	265	229	2.28	36	Lucas Neill	91.7
8	Denmark	13	246	194	2.09	31	Thomas Sorensen	94.7
9	N Ireland	7	171	167	1.92	21	Maik Taylor	89.5
10	Portugal	13	214	187	1.82	37	Luis Boa Morte	87.7
11	Finland	8	218	170	1.60	24	Jussi Jaaskelainen	100
12	United States	9	227	152	1.60	15	Brad Friedel	100
13	Nigeria	7	156	146	1.44	19	Joseph Yobo	76.3
14	Senegal	8	158	142	1.32	43	Henri Camara	66.3
15	Czech Republic	9	163	118	1.22	27	Petr Cech	88.2
16	Norway	6	148	119	1.08	21	Morten G Pedersen	82.0
17	Germany	5	124	99	0.99	13	Jens Lehmann	100
18	Ivory Coast	4	109	96	0.95	28	Habib Kolo Toure	86.8
19	Brazil	4	88	82	0.86	5	Gilberto Silva	83.8

CLUB MAKE-UP – HOME AND OVERSEAS PLAYERS

1 Arsenal

Overseas players in the squad	Arsenal	Home country players	7
Percent of overseas players	81.1	Percent of League action	92.62
Most appearances	Lehmann	Appearance percentage	100

	CLUB	OVERSEAS	HOME	% OVERSEAS	% LGE ACT	MOST APP	APP %
1	Arsenal	30	7	81.1	92.62	Jens Lehmann	100
2	Bolton	24	8	75.0	79.14	Jussi Jaaskelainen	100
3	Blackburn	20	9	69.0	78.36	Brad Friedel	100
4	Fulham	23	10	69.7	75.90	Luis Boa Morte	87.7
5	Chelsea	22	8	73.3	72.66	Petr Cech	88.2
6	Wigan	17	13	56.7	67.21	Pascal Chimbonda	95.4
7	Portsmouth	28	7	80.0	66.07	Andy O'Brien	76.3
8	Liverpool	20	10	66.7	64.77	Sami Hyypia	89.6
9	Man Utd	22	14	61.1	61.22	Edwin Van der Sar	98.7
10	Everton	22	12	64.7	57.58	David Weir	84.3
11	Middlesbrough	18	20	47.4	57.19	Ayegbeni Yakubu	75.5
12	Aston Villa	15	13	53.6	52.57	Thomas Sorensen	94.7
13	Newcastle	11	19	36.7	50.61	Shay Given	100
14	Man City	14	15	48.3	48.76	Richard Dunne	81.7
15	Birmingham	15	22	40.5	47.84	Maik Taylor	89.5
16	Charlton	16	14	53.3	46.38	H Hreidarsson	89.5
17	Tottenham	16	16	50.0	44.61	Paul Stalteri	86.8
18	Sunderland	16	16	50.0	44.53	Gary Breen	85.6
19	West Ham	16	19	45.7	38.77	Daniel Gabbidon	79.5
20	West Brom	13	18	41.9	36.84	Mart Albrechtsen	73.5

CLUB STARTING FORMATIONS

1 Wigan	
Most used starting formation	4-4-2
Number of different formations used	3
How often the club used its most frequently used formation	91.7%

	CLUB	Formation	Number	Used %
1	Wigan	4-4-2	3	91.7
2	Tottenham	4-4-2	3	87.5
3	West Ham	4-4-2	3	85.1
4	Aston Villa	4-4-2	6	82.2
5	Man City	4-4-2	3	81.8
6	Newcastle	4-4-2	8	79.2
7	Arsenal	4-4-2	4	77.6
8	West Brom	4-4-2	7	74.4
9	Blackburn	4-1-4-1	3	73.9
10	Man Utd	4-4-2	5	71.4
11	Sunderland	4-4-2	5	67.4
12	Birmingham	4-4-2	5	64.6
13	Portsmouth	4-4-2	8	58.5
14	Middlesbrough	4-4-2	6	54.7
15	Everton	4-4-2	5	44.7
16	Charlton	4-4-2	6	43.5
17	Fulham	4-4-2	7	39.0
18	Liverpool	4-4-2	5	30.5
19	Chelsea	4-3-2-1	6	25.9
20	Bolton	4-4-2	9	20.8

The most commonly quoted formation for Premiership is 4-4-2 with teams starting in that line up in 64% of matches. After that comes 4-4-1-1 used 8% of times and 4-5-1 7%.

Chelsea popularised 4-3-2-1 and only started with 4-4-2 in three games.

Bolton were quoted as using the most different formations with nine different starting line-ups. 17 different formations were tried out. Alain Perrin's 3-3-3-1 is a new one for our records.

Average number of different formations used by Premiership clubs	5.4

FINAL LEAGUE TABLE

		HOME					AWAY					TOTAL			
	P	W	D	L	F	A	W	D	L	F	A	F	A	DIF	PTS
Chelsea	38	18	1	0	47	9	11	3	5	25	13	91	72	22	50
Man Utd	38	13	5	1	37	8	12	3	4	35	26	83	72	34	38
Liverpool	38	15	3	1	32	8	10	4	5	25	17	82	57	25	32
Arsenal	38	14	3	2	48	13	6	4	9	20	18	67	68	31	37
Tottenham	38	12	5	2	31	16	6	6	7	22	22	65	53	38	15
Blackburn	38	13	3	3	31	17	6	3	10	20	25	63	51	42	9
Newcastle	38	11	5	3	28	15	6	2	11	19	27	58	47	42	5
Bolton	38	11	5	3	29	13	4	6	9	20	28	56	49	41	8
West Ham	38	9	3	7	30	25	7	4	8	22	30	55	52	55	-3
Wigan	38	7	3	9	24	26	8	3	8	21	26	51	45	52	-7
Everton	38	8	4	7	22	22	6	4	9	12	27	50	34	49	-15
Fulham	38	13	2	4	31	21	1	4	14	17	37	48	48	58	-10
Charlton	38	8	4	7	22	21	5	4	10	19	34	47	41	55	-14
Middlesbrough	38	7	5	7	28	30	5	4	10	20	28	45	48	58	-10
Man City	38	9	2	8	26	20	4	2	13	17	28	43	43	48	-5
Aston Villa	38	6	6	7	20	20	4	6	9	22	35	42	42	55	-13
Portsmouth	38	5	7	7	17	24	5	1	13	20	38	38	37	62	-25
Birmingham	38	6	5	8	19	20	2	5	12	9	30	34	28	50	-22
West Brom	38	6	2	11	21	24	1	7	11	10	34	30	31	58	-27
Sunderland	38	1	4	14	12	37	2	2	15	14	32	15	26	69	-43

CLUB GOAL ATTEMPTS FOR

On target; Liverpool's Crouch

1 Liverpool	
Total shots	560
Shots on target	282
Shots off target	278
Ratio of shots on target to goals	4.9
Accuracy Rating	50.4

	CLUB	SoT	Soff	Tot	SG	AR
1	Liverpool	282	278	560	4.9	50.4
2	Man Utd	286	269	555	4.0	51.5
3	Chelsea	277	237	514	3.8	53.9
4	Arsenal	274	188	462	4.0	59.3
5	Wigan	207	226	433	4.6	47.8
6	Man City	212	218	430	4.9	49.3
7	Portsmouth	222	189	411	6.0	54
8	Tottenham	234	177	411	4.4	56.9
9	Bolton	198	204	402	4.0	49.3
10	Middlesbrough	219	177	396	4.6	55.3
11	Blackburn	183	201	384	3.6	47.7
12	Aston Villa	197	181	378	4.7	52.1
13	Everton	203	171	374	6.0	54.3
14	Charlton	181	192	373	4.4	48.5
15	Newcastle	208	162	370	4.4	56.2
16	Fulham	178	180	358	3.7	49.7
17	Birmingham	168	186	354	6.0	47.5
18	West Ham	173	181	354	3.3	48.9
19	Sunderland	183	154	337	7.0	54.3
20	West Brom	161	167	328	5.2	49.1

CLUB GOAL ATTEMPTS AGAINST

1 Liverpool	
Total shots against	281
Shots on target against	123
Shots off target against	158
Ratio of shots on target to goals	4.9
Accuracy Rating	43.8

	CLUB	SoT	Soff	Tot	SG	AR
1	Liverpool	123	158	281	4.9	43.8
2	Bolton	191	130	321	4.7	59.5
3	Chelsea	127	194	321	5.8	39.6
4	Arsenal	153	170	323	4.9	47.4
5	Blackburn	174	158	332	4.1	52.4
6	Portsmouth	208	164	372	3.4	55.9
7	Man City	197	180	377	4.1	52.3
8	Birmingham	207	173	380	4.1	54.5
9	Newcastle	210	174	384	5.0	54.7
10	Man Utd	195	190	385	5.7	50.6
11	Tottenham	218	183	401	5.7	54.4
12	Wigan	225	179	404	4.3	55.7
13	Fulham	243	166	409	4.2	59.4
14	West Brom	254	162	416	4.4	61.1
15	Everton	230	193	423	4.7	54.4
16	Sunderland	262	162	424	3.8	61.8
17	Aston Villa	252	183	435	4.6	57.9
18	West Ham	263	181	444	4.8	59.2
19	Middlesbrough	251	199	450	4.3	55.8
20	Charlton	263	198	461	4.8	57.0

Reina makes a save

STADIUM CAPACITY AND HOME CROWDS

	TEAM	CAPACITY	AVE	HIGH	LOW
1	Tottenham	36250	99.51	36247	35427
2	Man Utd*	76000	99.46	73006	67684
3	Newcastle	52326	99.44	52326	50451
4	Arsenal	38500	99.18	38359	37867
5	Chelsea	42449	98.71	42321	40652
6	Portsmouth	20210	98.17	20240	19030
7	Liverpool	45362	97.52	44983	42293
8	Charlton	27116	96.61	27111	23453
9	West Ham	35647	94.66	34970	29582
10	Fulham	22490	91.84	22486	16550
11	Birmingham	30016	91.26	29312	24010
12	Everton	40569	90.86	40158	34333
13	West Brom	28003	90.72	27623	23144
14	Man City	48000	89.28	47192	40256
15	Bolton	28723	87.96	27718	22733
16	Wigan	25000	82.43	25000	16641
17	Middlesbrough	35100	81.09	31908	25971
18	Aston Villa	43275	78.83	42551	26422
19	Sunderland	48300	70.19	44003	28226
20	Blackburn	31367	67	29142	16953

Key: Average. The percentage of each stadium filled in League games over the season (AVE), the stadium capacity and the highest and lowest crowds recorded. * Ground capacity increased during 2006

AWAY ATTENDANCE

	TEAM	AVE	HIGH	LOW
1	Liverpool	95.78	67874	20240
2	Man Utd	94.94	52326	20206
3	Arsenal	93.25	70908	20230
4	Chelsea	92.12	67864	20182
5	Newcastle	92.07	67858	20220
6	Tottenham	91.14	67856	20215
7	Man City	90.86	67839	19556
8	Sunderland	90.36	72519	17223
9	Aston Villa	89.95	67934	17330
10	Blackburn	89.29	67765	20048
11	Everton	89.04	67831	17169
12	West Brom	88.92	67972	17421
13	Portsmouth	88.44	67684	19521
14	West Ham	88.34	69522	18736
15	Wigan	88.27	67793	17149
16	Middlesbrough	87.33	69531	16641
17	Birmingham	87.31	69070	16550
18	Bolton	87.11	67858	18180
19	Charlton	85.99	73006	17074
20	Fulham	85.23	67844	16953

Key: Average. How close each club has come to filling grounds in its away league matches (AVE) and the highest and lowest crowds recorded.

CHART-TOPPING MIDFIELDERS

1 Essien - Chelsea	
Goals scored in the League	2
Assists in all games	2
Defensive Rating Av number of mins between League goals conceded while on the pitch	176
Contribution to Attacking Power Average number of minutes between League team goals while on pitch	42
Scoring Difference Defensive Rating minus Contribution to Attacking Power	134

	PLAYER	CLUB	GOALS	ASS	DEF R	POWER	SCORE DIFF
1	Essien	Chelsea	2	0	176	42	134 mins
2	Robben	Chelsea	6	0	176	55	121 mins
3	Lampard	Chelsea	16	0	158	46	112 mins
4	Makelele	Chelsea	0	0	150	42	108 mins
5	Gerrard	Liverpool	10	0	151	57	94 mins
6	Giggs	Man Utd	2	0	132	46	86 mins
7	Cole, J	Chelsea	5	0	131	46	85 mins
8	Sissoko	Liverpool	0	0	150	67	83 mins
9	Kewell	Liverpool	3	0	134	56	78 mins
10	Hleb	Arsenal	3	0	134	64	70 mins
11	Gilberto Silva	Arsenal	2	0	115	46	69 mins
12	Scholes	Man Utd	2	0	115	49	66 mins
13	Xabi Alonso	Liverpool	3	0	135	70	65 mins
14	Fabregas	Arsenal	3	0	120	56	64 mins
15	Ljungberg	Arsenal	1	0	115	58	57 mins
16	Tugay	Blackburn	1	0	113	58	55 mins
17	Ronaldo	Man Utd	9	0	99	47	52 mins
18	Pires	Arsenal	7	0	98	46	52 mins
19	Park	Man Utd	2	0	105	54	51 mins
20	Flamini	Arsenal	0	0	97	52	45 mins

The Divisional Round-up charts combine the records of chart-topping keepers, defenders, midfield players and forwards, from every club in the division.. The one above is for **the Chart-topping Midfielders**. The players are ranked by their Scoring Difference although other attributes are shown for you to compare.

CHART-TOPPING GOALSCORERS

1 Henry - Arsenal	
Goals scored in the League (GL)	27
Goals scored in all competitions (ALL)	33
Contribution to Attacking Power Average number of minutes between League team goals while on pitch	47
Player Strike Rate (S Rate) Average number of minutes between League goals scored by player	99
Club Strike Rate (CSR) Average minutes between League goals scored by club	50

	PLAYER	CLUB	GOALS: LGE	ALL	POWER	CSR	S RATE
1	Henry	Arsenal	27	33	47	50	99 mins
2	van Nistelrooy	Man Utd	21	24	49	48	124 mins
3	Keane	Tottenham	16	16	62	65	144 mins
4	Bellamy	Blackburn	13	17	67	67	155 mins
5	Drogba	Chelsea	12	16	40	48	166 mins
6	Crespo	Chelsea	10	13	49	48	167 mins
7	Moore, L	Aston Villa	8	8	67	81	185 mins
8	Bent, D	Charlton	17	19	77	83	186 mins
9	Camara	Wigan	12	12	67	76	189 mins
10	Cisse	Liverpool	9	15	62	60	191 mins
11	Mido	Tottenham	11	11	51	65	192 mins
12	Rooney	Man Utd	16	19	48	48	192 mins
13	Cole	Man City	9	10	61	80	196 mins
14	Lampard	Chelsea	16	20	46	48	197 mins
15	Yakubu	Middlesbrough	13	19	74	71	199 mins
16	Harewood	West Ham	14	16	64	66	202 mins
17	Luis Garcia	Liverpool	7	10	55	60	227 mins
18	Ameobi	Newcastle	9	9	67	73	237 mins
19	Kuqi	Blackburn	7	8	59	67	238 mins
20	Viduka	Middlesbrough	7	16	70	71	239 mins

The Chart-topping Goalscorers measures the players by Strike Rate. They are most likely to be Forwards but Midfield players and even Defenders do come through the club tables. It is not a measure of the number of League goals scored - although that is also noted - but how often on average they have scored.

CHART-TOPPING DEFENDERS

1 Ferreira - Chelsea	
Goals Conceded in the League The number of League goals conceded while he was on the pitch	8
Goals Conceded in all competitions The number of goals conceded while he was on the pitch in all competitions	17
Clean Sheets In games when he played at least 70 mins	11
Defensive Rating Average number of minutes between League goals conceded while on pitch	209
Club Defensive Rating Average mins between League goals conceded by the club this season	155

	PLAYER	CLUB	CON: LGE	ALL	CS	CDR	DEF RATE
1	Ferreira	Chelsea	8	17	11	155	209 mins
2	Riise	Liverpool	12	23	16	137	188 mins
3	Del Horno	Chelsea	11	14	13	155	185 mins
4	Terry	Chelsea	20	30	20	155	162 mins
5	Finnan	Liverpool	19	32	21	137	156 mins
6	Gallas	Chelsea	19	26	16	155	154 mins
7	Brown	Man Utd	10	16	10	101	148 mins
8	Carvalho	Chelsea	14	20	11	155	141 mins
9	Hyypia	Liverpool	22	37	20	137	139 mins
10	Carragher	Liverpool	24	38	21	137	135 mins
11	Lauren	Arsenal	16	22	11	110	123 mins
12	O'Shea	Man Utd	24	28	13	101	118 mins
13	Toure	Arsenal	26	32	14	110	114 mins
14	Campbell	Arsenal	16	22	9	110	110 mins
15	Neville, G	Man Utd	20	27	12	101	108 mins
16	Jordan	Man City	15	19	5	71	104 mins
17	Ferdinand	Man Utd	32	40	17	101	103 mins
18	Gardner	Tottenham	14	17	8	90	100 mins
19	Khizanishvili	Blackburn	22	31	11	81	98 mins
20	Senderos	Arsenal	17	25	6	110	98 mins

The Chart-topping Defenders are resolved by their Defensive Rating, how often their team concedes a goal while they are playing. All these rightly favour players at the best performing clubs because good players win matches. However, good players in lower-table clubs will chart where they have lifted the team's performance.

CHART-TOPPING GOALKEEPERS

1 Cech - Chelsea	
Goals conceded in the League	20
Goals conceded in all comps (ALL)	25
Counting Games (CG) League games when he played at least 70 minutes	33
Clean Sheets (CS) In games when he played at least 70 mins	18
Goals to Shots Ratio (GSR) The average number of shots on target per each League goal conceded	5.9
Defensive Rating Average number of minutes between League goals conceded while on pitch	151

	PLAYER	CLUB	CG	CON: LGE	ALL	CS	GSR	DEF RATE
1	Cech	Chelsea	33	20	25	18	5.9	151 mins
2	Reina	Liverpool	33	21	32	20	5.1	141 mins
3	Lehmann	Arsenal	38	31	33	16	4.9	110 mins
4	Van der Sar	Man Utd	38	33	40	18	5.9	102 mins
5	Filan	Wigan	15	13	22	7	5.6	100 mins
6	Robinson	Tottenham	38	38	42	13	5.7	90 mins
7	Jaaskelainen	Bolton	38	41	50	15	4.7	83 mins
8	Friedel	Blackburn	38	42	52	16	4.1	81 mins
9	Given	Newcastle	38	42	46	13	5	81 mins
10	Myhre	Charlton	20	23	32	9	6.1	78 mins
11	Martyn	Everton	20	24	35	8	5.3	73 mins
12	James	Man City	38	48	54	6	4.1	71 mins
13	Taylor, Maik	Birmingham	34	44	56	8	4.3	70 mins
14	Wright	Everton	15	19	20	5	4.5	67 mins
15	Hislop	West Ham	16	21	32	5	5.4	67 mins
16	Kuszczak	West Brom	28	38	41	9	4.8	66 mins
17	Crossley	Fulham	13	17	17	4	4.1	66 mins
18	Sorensen	Aston Villa	36	51	61	11	4.7	64 mins
19	Schwarzer	Middlesbrough	27	38	55	8	4.6	64 mins
20	Carroll	West Ham	19	28	28	3	4.8	61 mins

The Chart-topping Goalkeepers are positioned by their Defensive Rating. We also show Clean Sheets where the team has not conceded and the Keeper has played all or most (at least 70 minutes) of the game. Only the top 20 keepers are included in this chart.

GOALS

	PLAYER	TEAM	LGE	SR
1	Henry	Arsenal	27	99
2	van Nistelrooy	Man Utd	21	124
3	Bent	Charlton	17	186
4	Lampard	Chelsea	16	197
5	Rooney	Man Utd	16	192
6	R Keane	Tottenham	16	144
7	Harewood	West Ham	14	202
8	Bellamy	Blackburn	13	155
9	Yakubu	Middlesboro	13	199
10	Drogba	Chelsea	12	166
11	Camara	Wigan	12	189
12	John	Fulham	11	149
13	Mido	Tottenham	11	192
14	Crespo	Chelsea	10	167
15	Beattie	Everton	10	250
16	Gerrard	Liverpool	10	272
17	Hasselbaink	Middlesboro	10	110
18	Shearer	Newcastle	10	274
19	Pedersen	Blackburn	9	311
20	Giannakopoulos	Bolton	9	281
21	Nolan	Bolton	9	346
22	McBride	Fulham	9	322
23	Cisse	Liverpool	9	191
24	Cole	Man City	9	196
25	Ronaldo	Man Utd	9	254

GOALS - MIDFIELDERS

	PLAYER	TEAM	LGE	SR
1	Lampard	Chelsea	16	197
2	Gerrard	Liverpool	10	272
3	Pedersen	Blackburn	9	311
4	Giannakopoulos	Bolton	9	281
5	Nolan	Bolton	9	346
6	Ronaldo	Man Utd	9	254
7	Pires	Arsenal	7	309
8	Luis Garcia	Liverpool	7	227
9	Robben	Chelsea	6	293
10	McFadden	Everton	6	341
11	Cahill	Everton	6	457
12	Malbranque	Fulham	6	483
13	Boa Morte	Fulham	6	500
14	Barton	Man City	6	455
15	Solano	Newcastle	6	369
16	O'Neil	Portsmouth	6	521

GOALS - DEFENDERS

	PLAYER	TEAM	LGE	SR
1	Ridgewell	Aston Villa	5	546
2	Gallas	Chelsea	5	585
3	Terry	Chelsea	4	810
4	Jaidi	Bolton	3	409
5	Queudrue	Middlesboro	3	718
6	King	Tottenham	3	772
7	Scharner	Wigan	3	436

TEAM OF THE SEASON

CECH
CHELSEA
CG 33 DR 151

FERREIRA
CHELSEA
CG 18 DR 209

LAUREN
ARSENAL
CG 22 DR 123

O'SHEA
MAN UTD
CG 28 DR 118

RIISE
LIVERPOOL
CG 23 DR 188

GERRARD
LIVERPOOL
CG 30 SD +94

ESSIEN
CHELSEA
CG 26 SD +134

GILBERTO SILVA
ARSENAL
CG 31 SD +69

GIGGS
MAN UTD
CG 19 SD +86

HENRY
ARSENAL
CG 28 SR 99

VAN NISTELROOY
MAN UTD
CG 26 SR 124

The Premiership Team of the Season shows a 4-4-2 of the best players in the Premiership based upon the selection criteria used for the chart-toppers. The players selected are taken from the lists for each club except that to get into a Divisional Team of the Season you must have played at least 17 Counting Games in the league (roughly half the league season) and not 12 as is the case in the club lists. The other restriction is that we are only allowing one player from each club in each position. So the maximum number of players one club can have in the divisional team is four.

• **The Divisional team's goalkeeper** is the player with the highest *Defensive Rating*

• **The Divisional team's defenders** are also tested by *Defensive Rating*, i.e. the average number of minutes between league goals conceded while on the pitch.

• **The Divisional team's midfield** are selected on their *Scoring Difference*, i.e.their *Defensive Rating* minus their *Contribution to Attacking Power* (average number of minutes between league goals scored while on the pitch. It takes no account of Assists.

• **The Divisional team strikeforce** is made up of the two strikers with the highest *Strike Rate* (their average number of minutes between league goals scored while on the pitch). Premier teams may include the striker with the best *Attacking Power.*

ASSISTS

	PLAYER	TEAM	LGE	ALL
1	Gerrard	Liverpool	12	13
2	Reyes	Arsenal	11	17
3	Drogba	Chelsea	11	14
4	Henry	Arsenal	9	11
5	Rooney	Man Utd	9	10
5	N'Zogbia	Newcastle	9	10
5	Zamora	West Ham	9	10
8	Lampard	Chelsea	9	9
9	Boa Morte	Fulham	8	10
9	Murphy	(Charlton)	8	10
11	Giggs	Man Utd	8	9
12	Fabregas	Arsenal	8	8
12	Pedersen	Blackburn	8	8
12	Milner	Aston Villa	8	8
15	Ji-Sung Park	Man Utd	7	8
15	Crouch	Liverpool	7	8
15	Viduka	Middlesboro	7	8
15	Vassell	Man City	7	8
15	Pennant	Birmingham	7	8
20	Robben	Chelsea	7	7
20	Ronaldo	Man Utd	7	7
20	Mido	Tottenham	7	7
20	Defoe	Tottenham	7	7
20	Davies	Bolton	7	7
20	Benayoun	West Ham	7	7
20	Downing	Middlesboro	7	7
27	Yakubu	Middlesboro	6	9
28	Kuqi	Blackburn	6	6

SHARE OF GOALS

	PLAYER	TEAM	% LGE GOALS
1	Bent	Charlton	41.46
2	Henry	Arsenal	39.71
3	Keane	Tottenham	30.19
4	Beattie	Everton	29.41
5	van Nistelrooy	Man Utd	29.17
6	Yakubu	Middlesboro	27.08
7	Harewood	West Ham	26.92
8	Camara	Wigan	26.67
9	Bellamy	Blackburn	25.49
10	John	Fulham	22.92
11	Lampard	Chelsea	22.22
12	Rooney	Man Utd	22.22
13	Shearer	Newcastle	21.28
14	Cole	Man City	20.93
15	Hasselbaink	Middlesboro	20.83
16	Mido	Tottenham	20.75
17	Ameobi	Newcastle	19.15
18	Moore	Aston Villa	19.05
19	Baros	Aston Villa	19.05
20	LuaLua	Portsmouth	18.92
21	McBride	Fulham	18.75
22	Vassell	Man City	18.60
23	Giannakopoulos	Bolton	18.37
24	Nolan	Bolton	18.37
25	Roberts	Wigan	17.78

PREMIERSHIP CHART-TOPPING POINT EARNERS

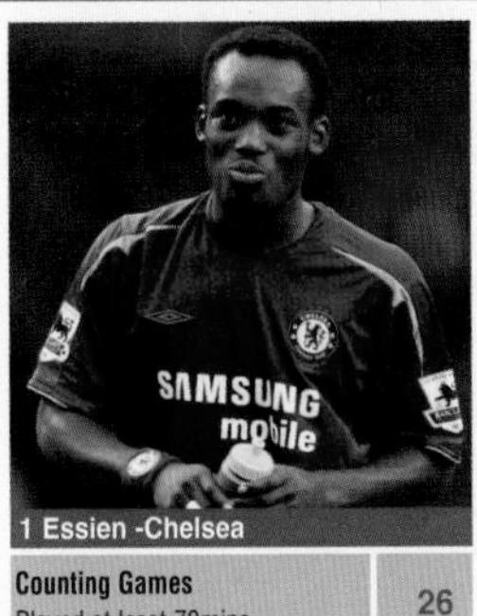

1 Essien -Chelsea

Counting Games Played at least 70mins.	26
Total Points Taken in Counting Games	70
Average Taken in Counting Games	2.69

	PLAYER	TEAM	GAMES	POINTS	AVE
1	Essien	Chelsea	26	70	2.69
2	Del Horno	Chelsea	21	56	2.67
3	Drogba	Chelsea	18	47	2.61
4	Morientes	Liverpool	17	43	2.53
5	Cech	Chelsea	33	82	2.48
6	Park	Man Utd	17	42	2.47
7	Riise	Liverpool	23	54	2.35
8	O'Shea	Man Utd	28	63	2.25
9	Rooney	Man Utd	34	76	2.24
10	Sissoko	Liverpool	20	44	2.20
11	Van der Sar	Man Utd	37	80	2.16
12	Reina	Liverpool	33	70	2.12
13	N'Zogbia	Newcastle	22	45	2.05
14	Khizanishvili	Blackburn	23	46	2.00
15	Mido	Tottenham	22	44	2.00
16	Reyes	Arsenal	18	35	1.94
17	Henry	Arsenal	28	52	1.86
18	Bramble	Newcastle	20	37	1.85
19	Ameobi	Newcastle	20	37	1.85
20	Campbell	Arsenal	19	35	1.84

For the Top Point Earners we have applied the same rule of only allowing one player per position for each club, the same as the Team of the Season. The most one club can have in the top 20 is four players, one keeper, one defender, one midfielder and a forward.

PREMIERSHIP MOST MISSED PLAYERS

	PLAYER	TEAM	AVERAGE	CLUB	DIFF
1	A Cole	Man City	1.72	1.13	0.59
2	N'Zogbia	Newcastle	2.05	1.53	0.52
3	Primus	Portsmouth	1.42	1	0.42
4	Beattie	Everton	1.73	1.32	0.41
5	Morientes	Liverpool	2.53	2.16	0.37
6	Kishishev	Charlton	1.61	1.24	0.37
7	Jordan	Man City	1.5	1.13	0.37
8	Khizanishvili	Blackburn	2	1.66	0.34
9	Bramble	Newcastle	1.85	1.53	0.32
10	Ameobi	Newcastle	1.85	1.53	0.32
11	Reyna	Man City	1.44	1.13	0.31
12	Essien	Chelsea	2.69	2.39	0.30
13	Powell	Charlton	1.54	1.24	0.30
14	Park	Man Utd	2.47	2.18	0.29
15	Mido	Tottenham	2	1.71	0.29
16	Hibbert	Everton	1.61	1.32	0.29
17	Musampa	Man City	1.42	1.13	0.29
18	Del Horno	Chelsea	2.67	2.39	0.28
19	Queudrue	Middlesbrough	1.45	1.18	0.27
20	Riggott	Middlesbrough	1.45	1.18	0.27

The Most Missed Players we have applied the same rule of only allowing one player per position for each club, the same as the Team of the Season. The most one club can have in the top 20 is four players, one keeper, one defender, one midfielder and a forward.

1 Andrew Cole - Man City

Average points	1.72
Club average	1.13
Difference	0.59

MANAGERS - SUBSTITUTIONS USED

Club with the highest percentage of subs used - Chelsea		Jose Mourinho	
Matches where no subs were used	0	Matches where one sub was used	0
Matches where two subs were used	1	Matches where three subs were used	37
Total subs used in season	113	Percentage of possible subs used	99.1

CLUB	MAIN MANAGER	0 SUBS	1 SUB	2 SUBS	3 SUBS	TOTAL	%
Chelsea	Jose Mourinho	0	0	1	37	113	99.1
Liverpool	Rafael Benitez	1	0	7	30	104	91.2
Middlesbrough	Steve McClaren	0	1	8	29	104	91.2
Bolton	Sam Allardyce	0	3	7	28	101	88.6
Charlton	Alan Curbishley	0	2	9	27	101	88.6
Man City	Stuart Pearce	0	1	11	26	101	88.6
West Ham	Alan Pardew	1	0	10	27	101	88.6
Sunderland	Kevin Ball	0	1	12	25	100	87.7
Arsenal	Arsene Wenger	1	2	9	26	98	86.0
Blackburn	Mark Hughes	0	3	10	25	98	86.0
Portsmouth	Harry Redknapp	0	2	13	23	97	85.1
West Brom	Bryan Robson	1	1	12	24	97	85.1
Birmingham	Steve Bruce	0	1	16	21	96	84.2
Man Utd	Sir Alex Ferguson	0	6	9	23	93	81.6
Everton	David Moyes	0	5	17	16	87	76.3
Newcastle	Glenn Roeder	0	7	13	18	87	76.3
Tottenham	Martin Joll	1	5	17	15	84	73.7
Aston Villa	David O'Leary	1	5	19	13	82	71.9
Wigan	Paul Jewell	0	13	14	11	74	64.9
Fulham	Chris Coleman	2	8	20	8	72	63.2

MANAGERS - SUBSTITUTION TIMES

Club with the highest percentage of subs used - Chelsea		Jose Mourinho	
Substitutes made during first half	7	Substitutes made between 46 and 69 minutes (mainly tactical)	61
Substitutes made between 70-85 mins	38		
Substitutes made after 86 mins	7	Total subs used in season	113

CLUB	MANAGER	0-45 MINS	46-69	70-85	86+	TOTAL
Chelsea	Jose Mourinho	7	61	38	7	113
Blackburn	Mark Hughes	5	47	34	12	98
Sunderland	Kevin Ball	9	47	34	10	100
Middlesbrough	Steve McClaren	9	45	40	10	104
West Brom	Bryan Robson	5	44	39	9	97
Charlton	Alan Curbishley	4	42	48	7	101
Liverpool	Rafael Benitez	3	41	49	11	104
Portsmouth	Harry Redknapp	3	41	36	17	97
Man City	Stuart Pearce	3	40	44	14	101
Bolton	Sam Allardyce	9	39	38	15	101
Everton	David Moyes	5	38	37	7	87
Birmingham	Steve Bruce	15	34	34	13	96
Aston Villa	David O'Leary	8	33	37	4	82
Man Utd	Sir Alex Ferguson	3	33	41	16	93
Newcastle	Glenn Roeder	9	32	35	11	87
West Ham	Alan Pardew	7	32	49	13	101
Arsenal	Arsene Wenger	8	29	54	7	98
Tottenham	Martin Joll	4	24	46	10	84
Fulham	Chris Coleman	9	23	35	5	72
Wigan	Paul Jewell	6	21	35	12	74

LEAGUE PENALTY TAKERS

Alan Shearer converts from the spot

Penalties scored - Shearer	4
Penalties saved	0
Penalties missed	0
League total	4
Percentage scored	100
% of all League penalties taken	5.4

1 Lampard - Shearer - Keane

PLAYER	CLUB	TOTAL	Sc	Sa	Mi	%Scored
Lampard	Chelsea	4	4			100%
Shearer	Newcastle	4	4			100%
Keane	Tottenham	4	3	1		75%
Henry	Arsenal	3	3	0	0	100%
Darren Bent	Charlton	3	3			100%
Helguson	Fulham	3	3			100%
Yakubu	Middlesbrough	3	3			100%
Harewood	West Ham	3	3			100%
Beattie	Everton	3	2	1		67%
Gerrard	Liverpool	3	2	1		67%
Van Nistlerooy	Man Utd	3	2	1		67%
Pires	Arsenal	3	1	1	1	33%
Forssell	Birmingham	2	2	0	0	100%
Dickov	Blackburn	2	2	0	0	100%
Speed	Bolton	2	2			100%
Cisse	Liverpool	2	2			100%
Taylor	Portsmouth	2	2			100%
Whitehead	Sunderland	2	2			100%
Baros	Aston Villa	2	1	1	0	50%
Sheringham	West Ham	2	1	1		50%
Barry	Aston Villa	2	0	1	1	0%
Others (17)		17	12	3	2	70.6
TOTALS		74	59	11	4	79.7

CLUB - LEAGUE SQUAD USAGE

1 Liverpool

Players used Total number of players used by the club in the league	24

CLUB	Players used	% by 11	% by 16	Avge
Liverpool	24	66.7	88.7	21.8
Bolton	24	66.7	85.5	21.6
Blackburn	25	66.9	89.3	20.6
Chelsea	25	64.2	89.1	21.2
Man City	26	61.1	80.3	20.0
Man Utd	26	70.1	89.8	19.7
Newcastle	26	64.0	81.8	19.4
Arsenal	27	63.5	85.1	19.1
Aston Villa	27	67.2	86.2	18.5
Wigan	27	69.7	85.4	19.7
Charlton	28	60.9	80.0	18.5
Everton	28	69.1	88.1	18.0
Fulham	28	63.9	80.4	17.5
West Ham	28	65.9	83.4	18.5
Sunderland	29	62.0	79.2	17.9
Tottenham	29	70.7	88.6	17.3
West Brom	29	65.0	84.1	17.8
Birmingham	30	59.3	77.0	17.1
Portsmouth	34	55.0	70.1	15.1
Middlesbrough	37	54.8	72.6	14.1
TOTAL	581			

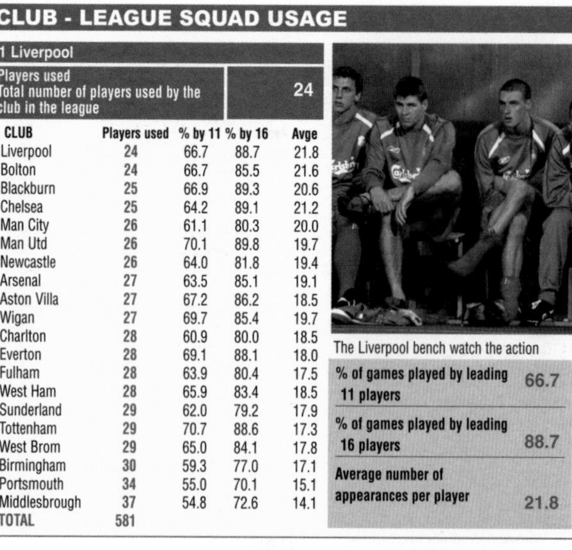
The Liverpool bench watch the action

% of games played by leading 11 players	66.7
% of games played by leading 16 players	88.7
Average number of appearances per player	21.8

LEADING LEAGUE APPEARANCES

DEFENDERS		GAMES	TIME	MIDFIELDERS		GAMES	TIME
	PLAYER				PLAYER		
1	Rio Ferdinand	37	3298 mins	1	Dean Whitehead	37	3329 mins
2	Pascal Chimbonda	37	3261 mins	2	Jonathan Greening	38	3287 mins
3	John Terry	36	3240 mins	3	Frank Lampard	35	3150 mins
4	Jamie Carragher	36	3240 mins	4	Jermaine Pennant	38	3139 mins
5	Paul Konchesky	37	3223 mins	5	Jimmy Bullard	36	3134 mins
6	Lucas Neill	35	3136 mins	6	Gary O'Neil	36	3126 mins
7	Leighton Baines	37	3100 mins	7	Gareth Barry	36	3125 mins
8	Sami Hyypia	35	3063 mins	8	Michael Carrick	35	3122 mins
9	Hermann Hreidarsson	34	3060 mins	9	Kevin Nolan	36	3112 mins
10	Aaron Hughes	35	3018 mins	10	Phil Neville	34	3038 mins
11	Habib Kolo Toure	33	2970 mins	11	Luis Boa Morte	35	3001 mins
12	Curtis Davies	33	2970 mins	12	Robbie Savage	34	2976 mins
13	Paul Stalteri	33	2967 mins	13	Steven Davis	35	2958 mins
14	Steve Finnan	33	2957 mins	14	Hayden Mullins	35	2953 mins
15	William Gallas	34	2927 mins	15	Steed Malbranque	34	2900 mins
16	Gary Breen	35	2926 mins	16	Radostin Kishishev	37	2887 mins
17	Anton Ferdinand	33	2884 mins	17	Gavin McCann	32	2870 mins
18	David Weir	33	2883 mins	18	Gilberto Silva	33	2867 mins

FORWARDS							
1	Darren Bent	36	3160 mins	10	Thierry Henry	32	2670 mins
2	Kevin Davies	37	3132 mins	11	Ruud van Nistelrooy	35	2596 mins
3	Wayne Rooney	36	3073 mins	12	Ayegbeni Yakubu	34	2581 mins
4	Darius Vassell	36	3031 mins	13	James Beattie	32	2503 mins
5	Jason Roberts	34	3009 mins	14	Robbie Keane	36	2302 mins
6	Brian McBride	38	2899 mins	15	Henri Camara	29	2269 mins
7	Marlon Harewood	36	2824 mins	16	Jermain Defoe	36	2213 mins
8	Emile Heskey	34	2815 mins	17	Shola Ameobi	30	2135 mins
9	Alan Shearer	32	2743 mins	18	Peter Crouch	32	2123 mins

FIRST SCORERS

SCORED FIRST					CONCEDED FIRST				
CLUB	MATCHES	WON	DRAWN	LOST	CLUB	MATCHES	WON	DRAWN	LOST
Liverpool	27	25	2	0	Liverpool	7	0	1	6
Chelsea	27	25	2	0	Chelsea	10	4	1	5
Man Utd	24	21	3	0	Man Utd	10	4	1	5
Bolton	22	14	5	3	Bolton	12	1	2	9
Arsenal	21	19	1	1	Arsenal	14	1	3	10
Wigan	20	13	3	4	Blackburn	15	2	1	12
Blackburn	19	17	1	1	Fulham	16	2	0	14
Tottenham	19	14	5	0	Tottenham	16	4	3	9
Everton	19	14	4	1	Everton	17	0	2	15
Fulham	19	12	3	4	Newcastle	17	2	1	14
Newcastle	17	15	2	0	Aston Villa	18	0	4	14
West Ham	15	11	1	3	Wigan	18	2	3	13
Aston Villa	15	10	3	2	Charlton	20	2	2	16
Portsmouth	15	7	3	5	West Ham	20	5	3	12
Man City	13	11	0	2	Man City	22	2	1	19
Middlesbrough	13	10	3	0	Middlesbrough	22	2	3	17
Charlton	12	11	0	1	Portsmouth	22	3	4	15
Birmingham	11	8	1	2	Birmingham	23	0	5	18
Sunderland	11	3	2	6	West Brom	24	1	3	20
West Brom	9	6	1	2	Sunderland	25	0	2	23

CLUB DISCIPLINARY RECORDS

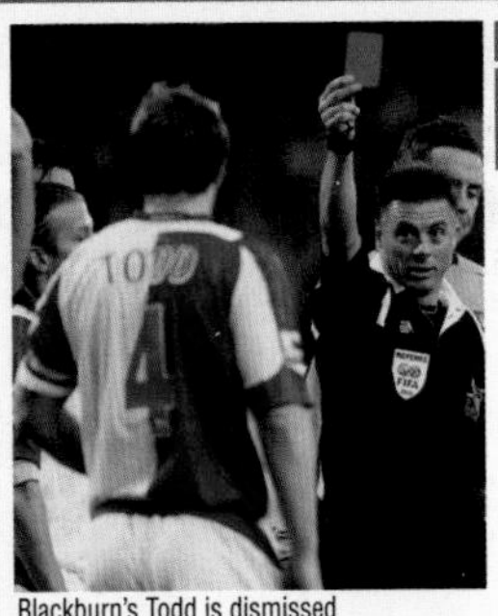
Blackburn's Todd is dismissed

League Yellow	77
League Red	6
League Total	83
All Competitions Yellow	95
All Competitions Red	6
TOTAL	101

1 Blackburn

Cards Average in League
Average number of minutes between a card being shown of either colour — **41**

	CLUB	LEAGUE		TOTAL		AVE
1	Blackburn	77 Y	6 R	95 Y	6 R	41
2	Newcastle	68	8	80	9	45
3	Everton	67	7	80	7	46
4	Man City	71	4	80	6	46
5	Sunderland	70	4	77	5	46
6	Bolton	66	4	82	4	49
7	Chelsea	65	5	93	6	49
8	Fulham	65	2	73	2	51
9	Aston Villa	62	2	70	2	53
10	Birmingham	56	7	70	7	54
11	Man Utd	61	2	97	4	54
12	Tottenham	56	5	57	5	56
13	Middlesbrough	56	3	101	3	58
14	Arsenal	56	2	85	4	59
15	Wigan	54	4	63	4	59
16	Liverpool	53	4	81	4	60
17	Portsmouth	55	1	62	1	61
18	West Ham	50	2	62	2	66
19	West Brom	47	2	52	4	70
20	Charlton	45	2	55	2	73

PLAYER DISCIPLINARY RECORD

1 Taylor - Newcastle

Cards Average in League
Average number of minutes between a card being shown of either colour — **136**

	PLAYER		LEAGUE		TOTAL		AVE
1	Taylor	Newcastle	6Y	1R	8Y	1R	136
2	Thompson	Wigan	4	0	4	0	156
3	Sissoko	Liverpool	10	1	13	1	177
4	Moore	Newcastle	4	0	5	0	180
5	Neville, P	Everton	14	2	14	2	189
6	Cahill	Aston Villa	3	0	3	0	193
7	Diouf	Bolton	6	1	7	1	200
8	Carr	Newcastle	6	2	7	2	201
9	Davids	Tottenham	11	1	11	1	201
10	Christanval	Fulham	4	0	5	0	203
11	Dickov	Blackburn	5	1	7	1	208
12	Diao	Portsmouth	3	0	3	0	219
13	Legwinski	Fulham	4	0	4	0	223
14	Clark	Newcastle	4	0	5	0	224
15	Kyle	Sunderland	4	0	4	0	224
16	Barton	Man City	11	1	12	1	227
17	Hughes	Portsmouth	8	0	9	0	227
18	Brown	Sunderland	4	0	4	0	227
19	Savage	Blackburn	12	1	14	1	228
20	Izzet	Birmingham	3	1	3	1	230

(Playing a minimum of 500 minutes in the League)

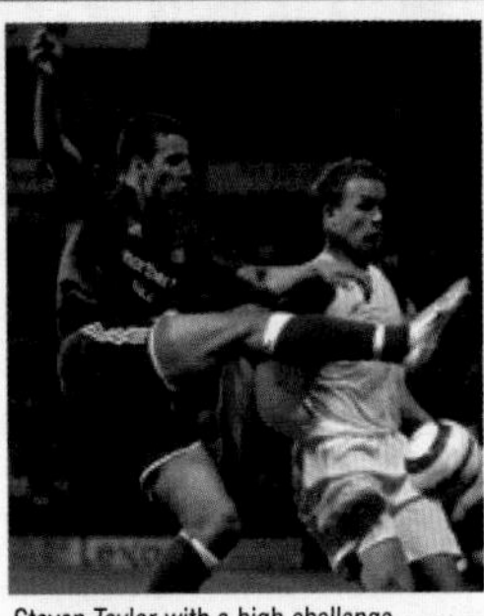
Steven Taylor with a high challenge

League Yellow	6
League Red	1
League Total	7
All Competitions Yellow	8
All Competitions Red	1
TOTAL	9

REFEREES - PENALTIES

1 C.J. Foy

Penalties Average
Average number of minutes between penalties awarded — **248**

	REF	Home	Away	Total	Avge
1	C. J. Foy	6	2	8	248 mins
2	M. A. Riley	5	3	8	315 mins
3	M. L. Dean	3	3	6	345 mins
4	P. Dowd	4	2	6	345 mins
5	U. D. Rennie	5	2	7	347 mins
6	M. Clattenburg	3	1	4	360 mins
7	P. Walton	3	0	3	390 mins
8	S. G. Bennett	3	3	6	450 mins
9	A. G. Wiley	4	2	6	465 mins
10	H. M. Webb	2	3	5	540 mins
11	D. J. Gallagher	2	1	3	600 mins
12	A. Marriner	1	0	1	630 mins
13	M. R. Halsey	3	0	0	630 mins
14	G. Poll	1	2	3	870 mins
15	M. Atkinson	1	0	1	1620 mins
16	R. Styles	0	1	1	2700 mins
	plus				
	A. P. D'Urso	1	0	1	90 mins
	B. Knight	2	0	2	225 mins
	TOTAL	49	25	74	

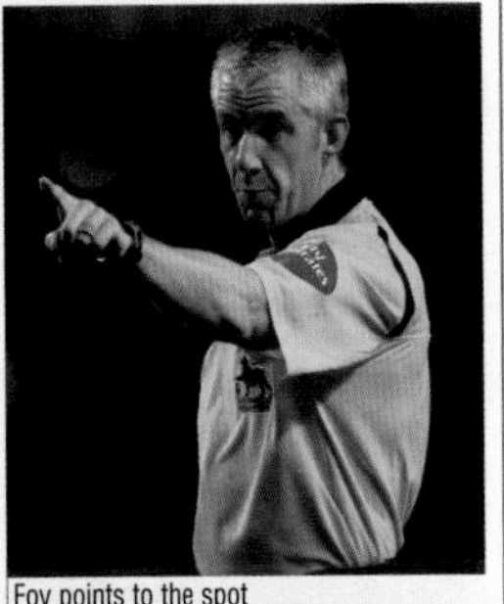
Foy points to the spot

Games	22
Penalties awarded to home side	6
Penalties awarded to away side	2
Total	8

REFEREES - CARDS

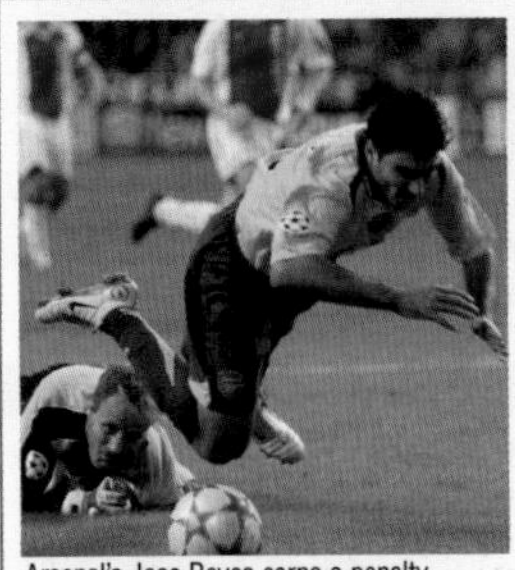
Referee Dowd in action

Games	23
Yellow	101
Yellow/Red	5
Straight reds	2

1 P. Dowd

Cards Average
Average number of cards per match of either colour — **4.70**

	REF	Games	Y	Y/R	R	AVE
1	P. Dowd	23	101	5	2	4.70
2	M. A. Riley	28	118	4	4	4.50
3	S. G. Bennett	30	111	7	3	4.03
4	A. P. D'Urso	1	4	0	0	4.00
5	M. L. Dean	23	78	2	4	3.65
6	G. Poll	29	98	4	1	3.55
7	M. Clattenburg	16	55	0	0	3.44
8	A. G. Wiley	31	99	2	3	3.35
9	R. Styles	30	93	4	3	3.33
10	B. Knight	5	15	0	1	3.20
11	H. M. Webb	30	88	1	4	3.10
12	P. Walton	13	39	0	1	3.08
13	K. Stoud	1	3	0	0	3.00
14	C. J. Foy	22	58	3	3	2.91
15	M. Atkinson	18	49	1	0	2.78
16	L. Mason	3	8	0	0	2.67
17	A. Marriner	7	17	1	0	2.57
18	U. D. Rennie	27	59	0	2	2.26
19	D. J. Gallagher	20	35	3	4	2.10
20	M. R. Halsey	21	37	0	5	2.00
21	R. J. Beeby	2	3	0	0	1.50
	TOTAL	380	1168	37	40	3.28

CLUB - LEAGUE PENALTIES AWARDED

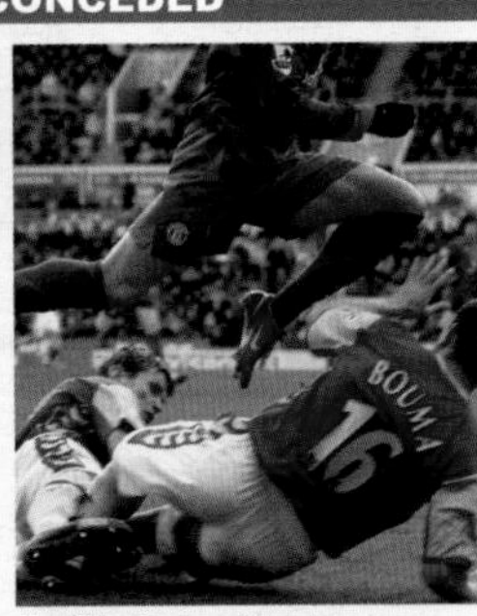
Arsenal's Jose Reyes earns a penalty

Awarded at home - Arsenal	6
Awarded away	0
Number scored	4
Number saved	1
Number missed	1
% of League penalties awarded	8.1
Number of takers	2

1 Arsenal - Liverpool - Tottenham

Penalties Awarded
Total number of penalties awarded to the club in the league — **6**

CLUB	H	A	Total	Sc	Sa	M	%	No
Arsenal	6	0	6	4	1	1	8.1%	2
Liverpool	2	4	6	4	2	0	8.1%	3
Tottenham	4	2	6	4	2	0	8.1%	3
Middlesbrough	4	1	5	5	0	0	6.8%	3
Newcastle	4	1	5	5	0	0	6.8%	2
West Ham	4	1	5	4	1	0	6.8%	2
Aston Villa	2	2	4	1	2	1	5.4%	2
Blackburn	3	1	4	4	0	0	5.4%	3
Bolton	0	4	4	2	1	1	5.4%	3
Charlton	2	2	4	4	0	0	5.4%	2
Chelsea	2	2	4	4	0	0	5.4%	1
Everton	3	1	4	3	1	0	5.4%	2
Fulham	2	2	4	4	0	0	5.4%	2
Man United	2	1	3	2	1	0	4.1%	1
Birmingham	2	0	2	2	0	0	2.7%	1
Portsmouth	1	1	2	2	0	0	2.7%	1
Sunderland	2	0	2	2	0	0	2.7%	1
West Brom	1	1	2	1	0	1	2.7%	2
Man City	1	0	1	1	0	0	1.4%	1
Wigan	1	0	1	1	0	0	1.4%	1
TOTALS	48	26	74	59	11	4		38

CLUB - LEAGUE PENALTIES CONCEDED

1 Aston Villa

Penalties Conceded
Total number of penalties conceded by the club in the league — **8**

CLUB	H	A	Total	Sc	Sa	M	%
Aston Villa	3	5	8	7	1	0	10.8%
West Brom	2	5	7	7	0	0	9.5%
Portsmouth	2	5	7	5	1	1	9.5%
Birmingham	1	5	6	5	1	0	8.1%
Newcastle	2	4	6	4	1	1	8.1%
Bolton	3	2	5	4	0	1	6.8%
Sunderland	1	4	5	3	2	0	6.8%
Everton	3	1	4	4	0	0	5.4%
Wigan	1	3	4	4	0	0	5.4%
Chelsea	2	1	3	3	0	0	4.1%
Man City	1	2	3	2	0	1	4.1%
Middlesbrough	1	2	3	1	2	0	4.1%
Fulham	2	0	2	2	0	0	2.7%
Liverpool	1	1	2	2	0	0	2.7%
Man United	0	2	2	2	0	0	2.7%
West Ham	0	2	2	2	0	0	2.7%
Tottenham	0	2	2	1	1	0	2.7%
Blackburn	0	1	1	1	0	0	1.4%
Arsenal	0	1	1	0	1	0	1.4%
Charlton	1	0	1	0	1	0	1.4%
TOTALS	26	48	74	59	11	4	

Two Villa players go in hard

Conceded at home	3
Conceded away	5
League Total	8
Number scored	7
Number saved or missed	1
% of League penalties conceded	10.8

CHELSEA

Club record signing **Michael Essien** tops our Premier Midfielders chart. Essien only scored twice but the team notched a goal every 42 minutes when he was on the pitch but conceded one only every 176 minutes. He also headed the club's Top Point Earners table.

Only **Didier Drogba** bettered Essien's record of sparking attacks in the Premiership with the club scoring every 40 minutes when he played. He and **Hernan Crespo** were fifth and sixth in the Goalscorers table – only a minute apart on Strike Rate.

The club boasts the top four midfielders on Scoring Difference and **Frank Lampard** claimed the division's record for midfield league goals with 16. His Strike Rate is the best of any midfielder.

Paulo Ferreira kept his crown as the meanest defender with the club only conceding a goal every 209 minutes when he played.

NICKNAME: THE BLUES

KEY: Won Drawn Lost

No	Comp	Opponent	Venue	Res	Score	Scorers
1	facsh	**Arsenal**	H	W	2-1	Drogba 8,57
2	prem	**Wigan**	A	W	1-0	Crespo 90
3	prem	**Arsenal**	H	W	1-0	Drogba 73
4	prem	**West Brom**	H	W	4-0	Lampard 23,80; Cole 43; Drogba 68
5	prem	**Tottenham**	A	W	2-0	Del Horno 39; Duff 71
6	prem	**Sunderland**	H	W	2-0	Geremi 54; Drogba 82
7	ecgpg	**Anderlecht**	H	W	1-0	Lampard 19
8	prem	**Charlton**	A	W	2-0	Crespo 55; Robben 60
9	prem	**Aston Villa**	H	W	2-1	Lampard 45,75 pen
10	ecgpg	**Liverpool**	A	D	0-0	
11	prem	**Liverpool**	A	W	4-1	Lampard 27 pen; Duff 43; Cole 63; Geremi 82
12	prem	**Bolton**	H	W	5-1	Drogba 52,61; Lampard 55,59; Gudjohnsen 74
13	ecgpg	**Real Betis**	H	W	4-0	Drogba 24; Carvalho 44; Cole, J 59; Crespo 64
14	prem	**Everton**	A	D	1-1	Lampard 49
15	ccr3	**Charlton**	H	L	4-5*	Terry 41 (*on penalties)
16	prem	**Blackburn**	H	W	4-2	Drogba 10; Lampard 14 pen,62; Khizanishvili 74 og
17	ecgpg	**Real Betis**	A	L	0-1	
18	prem	**Man Utd**	A	L	0-1	
19	prem	**Newcastle**	H	W	3-0	Cole, J 47; Crespo 51; Duff 90
20	ecgpg	**Anderlecht**	A	W	2-0	Crespo 8; Carvalho 15
21	prem	**Portsmouth**	A	W	2-0	Crespo 27; Lampard 67 pen
22	prem	**Middlesbrough**	H	W	1-0	Terry 62
23	ecgpg	**Liverpool**	H	D	0-0	
24	prem	**Wigan**	H	W	1-0	Terry 67
25	prem	**Arsenal**	A	W	2-0	Robben 39; Cole, J 73
26	prem	**Fulham**	H	W	3-2	Gallas 3; Lampard 24; Crespo 74
27	prem	**Man City**	A	W	1-0	Cole, J 79
28	prem	**Birmingham**	H	W	2-0	Crespo 25; Robben 43
29	prem	**West Ham**	A	W	3-1	Lampard 25; Crespo 61; Drogba 80
30	facr3	**Huddersfield**	H	W	2-1	Cole, C 12; Gudjohnsen 82
31	prem	**Sunderland**	A	W	2-1	Crespo 28; Robben 69
32	prem	**Charlton**	H	D	1-1	Gudjohnsen 18
33	facr4	**Everton**	A	D	1-1	Lampard 73
34	prem	**Aston Villa**	A	D	1-1	Robben 14
35	prem	**Liverpool**	H	W	2-0	Gallas 35; Crespo 68
36	facr4r	**Everton**	H	W	4-1	Robben 22; Lampard 36 pen; Crespo 39; Terry 74
37	prem	**Middlesbrough**	A	L	0-3	
38	facr5	**Colchester**	H	W	3-1	Ferreira 37; Cole, J 79,90
39	eclsl1	**Barcelona**	H	L	1-2	Motta 59 og
40	prem	**Portsmouth**	H	W	2-0	Lampard 65; Robben 78
41	prem	**West Brom**	A	W	2-1	Drogba 51; Cole, J 74
42	eclsl2	**Barcelona**	A	D	1-1	Lampard 90 pen
43	prem	**Tottenham**	H	W	2-1	Essien 14; Gallas 90
44	prem	**Fulham**	A	L	0-1	
45	facqf	**Newcastle**	H	W	1-0	Terry 4
46	prem	**Man City**	H	W	2-0	Drogba 30,33
47	prem	**Birmingham**	A	D	0-0	
48	prem	**West Ham**	H	W	4-1	Drogba 29; Crespo 31; Terry 54; Gallas 69
49	prem	**Bolton**	A	W	2-0	Terry 44; Lampard 59
50	prem	**Everton**	H	W	3-0	Lampard 28; Drogba 62; Essien 74
51	facsf	**Liverpool**	H	L	1-2	Drogba 70
52	prem	**Man Utd**	H	W	3-0	Gallas 5; Cole, J 61; Carvalho 73
53	prem	**Blackburn**	A	L	0-1	
54	prem	**Newcastle**	A	L	0-1	

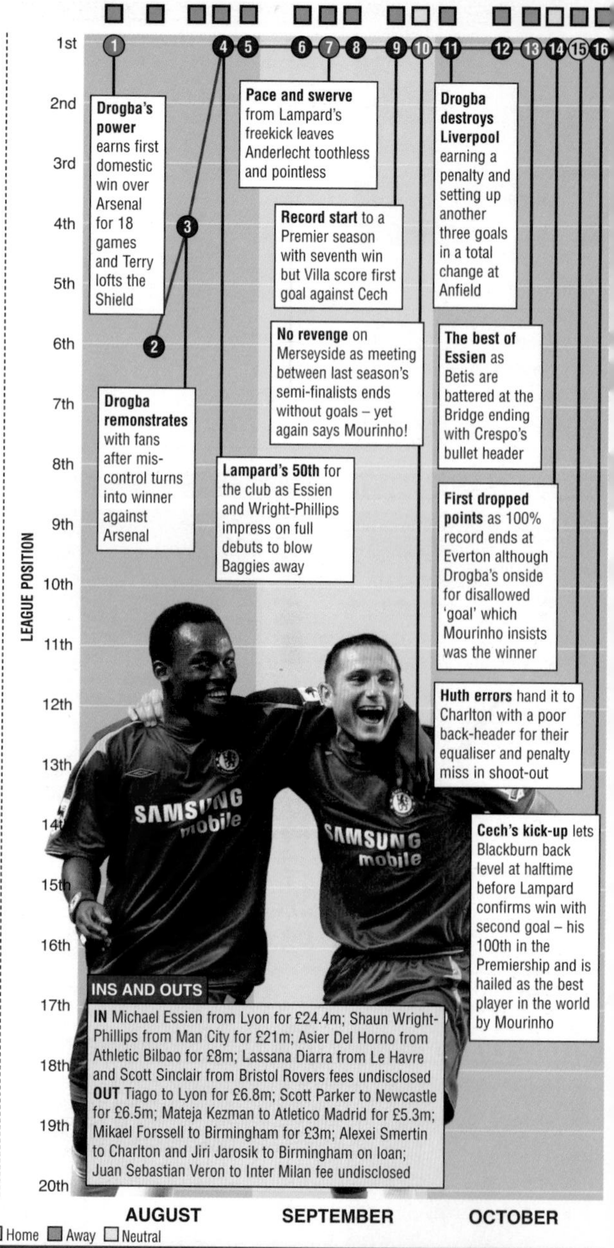

LEAGUE POSITION

1st 2nd 3rd 4th 5th 6th 7th 8th 9th 10th 11th 12th 13th 14th 15th 16th 17th 18th 19th 20th

Drogba's power earns first domestic win over Arsenal for 18 games and Terry lofts the Shield

Drogba remonstrates with fans after mis-control turns into winner against Arsenal

Lampard's 50th for the club as Essien and Wright-Phillips impress on full debuts to blow Baggies away

Pace and swerve from Lampard's freekick leaves Anderlecht toothless and pointless

Record start to a Premier season with seventh win but Villa score first goal against Cech

No revenge on Merseyside as meeting between last season's semi-finalists ends without goals – yet again says Mourinho!

Drogba destroys Liverpool earning a penalty and setting up another three goals in a total change at Anfield

The best of Essien as Betis are battered at the Bridge ending with Crespo's bullet header

First dropped points as 100% record ends at Everton although Drogba's onside for disallowed 'goal' which Mourinho insists was the winner

Huth errors hand it to Charlton with a poor back-header for their equaliser and penalty miss in shoot-out

Cech's kick-up lets Blackburn back level at halftime before Lampard confirms win with second goal – his 100th in the Premiership and is hailed as the best player in the world by Mourinho

INS AND OUTS

IN Michael Essien from Lyon for £24.4m; Shaun Wright-Phillips from Man City for £21m; Asier Del Horno from Athletic Bilbao for £8m; Lassana Diarra from Le Havre and Scott Sinclair from Bristol Rovers fees undisclosed
OUT Tiago to Lyon for £6.8m; Scott Parker to Newcastle for £6.5m; Mateja Kezman to Atletico Madrid for £5.3m; Mikael Forssell to Birmingham for £3m; Alexei Smertin to Charlton and Jiri Jarosik to Birmingham on loan; Juan Sebastian Veron to Inter Milan fee undisclosed

AUGUST SEPTEMBER OCTOBER

Home Away Neutral

ATTENDANCES

HOME GROUND: STAMFORD BRIDGE **CAPACITY:** 42449 **AVERAGE LEAGUE AT HOME:** 41901

No	Opponent	Att	No	Opponent	Att	No	Opponent	Att	No	Opponent	Att
42	Barcelona	98000	40	Portsmouth	42254	23	Liverpool	41598	37	Middlesboro	31037
18	Man Utd	67864	43	Tottenham	42243	16	Blackburn	41553	33	Everton	29742
51	Liverpool	64575	52	Man Utd	42219	32	Charlton	41355	7	Anderlecht	29575
1	Arsenal	58014	15	Charlton	42198	4	West Brom	41201	49	Bolton	27266
17	Real Betis	55000	9	Aston Villa	42146	28	Birmingham	40652	8	Charlton	27111
54	Newcastle	52309	3	Arsenal	42136	39	Barcelona	39521	41	West Brom	26581
27	Man City	46587	24	Wigan	42060	36	Everton	39301	47	Birmingham	26364
11	Liverpool	44235	6	Sunderland	41969	34	Aston Villa	38562	2	Wigan	23575
10	Liverpool	42743	48	West Ham	41919	25	Arsenal	38347	44	Fulham	22486
46	Man City	42321	38	Colchester	41810	13	Real Betis	36457	20	Anderlecht	21070
35	Liverpool	42316	12	Bolton	41775	5	Tottenham	36077	53	Blackburn	20243
26	Fulham	42313	50	Everton	41765	14	Everton	36042	21	Portsmouth	20182
45	Newcastle	42279	22	Middlesboro	41666	29	West Ham	34758			
19	Newcastle	42268	30	Huddersfield	41650	31	Sunderland	32420			

Champions again; next it's Europe...

Final Position: **1st**

KEY: ● League ● Champions Lge ● UEFA Cup ● FA Cup ○ League Cup ● Other

17 18 19 20 21 22 23 24 25 26 27 28 29 30 31 32 33 34 35 36 37 38 39 40 41 42 43 44 45 46 47 48 49 50 51 52 53 54

Undefeated run ends at 40 games – the third longest in league history – as United hang on

Pain in Spain as Betis hand out defeat and only Terry looks committed

Crespo settles it early, scoring one and laying on a goal for Carvalho, to ensure Euro progress

Lampard's record 160th consecutive Premiership start includes an 11th goal to take him top of the scoring charts too

Robben returns to run Boro ragged but it's skipper Terry who scores the vital goal

Essien's tackle makes the headlines in a dull draw as Liverpool finish top of Group G

Terry towers above Wigan to head in another winner as Mourinho praises Cole as his most effective attacker

Lampard's run ends in illness after 164 consecutive league games but Cole's goal is Mourinho's first against City

Red Robben thumps in deflected winner before being sent off for celebrating in the crowd

Carvalho sent off for two yellows as Charlton end 100% home Premiership record

Gallas' 11th goal for the club as rotation takes him to right back and Robben's cheek leads to Reina red

Lampard's cool finish finds a way past Martyn to gain a replay against Everton's battlers

Boro blast as struggling Teessiders inflict Jose's worst defeat

Cole brace kills off Colchester's cup dreams after Carvalho own goal gives them an early lead

Del Horno makes a Messi of it as ugly challenge earns red and Barcelona take revenge

Drogba delights and dismays with fine individual goal and dive which angers Robson after Robben is sent off

Ronaldinho breaks through to earn Barca a quarter-final place as attack fails to spark

Drogba decision rankles with Mourinho as goal is disallowed after Fulham pressurise ref and Gallas' stamp earns club's fifth red in two months

"It was handball" admits Drogba but he nets twice and it could have been a hat-trick as City argue themselves down to ten men

Del Horno sparks offside debate as goal is disallowed after Carvalho is ruled as 'active' by linesman

Double dream bursts with Terry unlucky to concede free kick for Liverpool's first and to be pulled up for foul from netted header

Top midfield scorer in a Premiership season as Lampard claims a record with his 15th league goal

Three penalties refused makes Mourinho glad he didn't need the points or he'd "be suspended forever"

Ballack in town signs up on a Bosman transfer for next season

Champions in style as United are made to look second best by Gallas' reactions, Cole's class and Carvalho's energy

Shevchenko signs for new Premier record of £30.8m

Wenger dossier of Chelsea 'obsession' runs to 120 pages claims Mourinho

Second best player on the planet as Lampard is pipped by Ronaldinho

Keeping constant: Cech signs until 2010, Cudicini to 2009

INS AND OUTS

IN Maniche from Dynamo Moscow on loan
OUT Wayne Bridge to Fulham on loan. Alexei Smertin (from Charlton) to Dynamo Moscow for £100K

MONTH BY MONTH POINTS TALLY

Month	Points	%
AUGUST	12	100%
SEPTEMBER	9	100%
OCTOBER	10	83%
NOVEMBER	6	67%
DECEMBER	18	100%
JANUARY	7	78%
FEBRUARY	7	58%
MARCH	9	75%
APRIL	13	87%
MAY	0	0%

NOVEMBER DECEMBER JANUARY FEBRUARY MARCH APRIL MAY

GOAL ATTEMPTS

FOR – Goal attempts recorded in League games

	HOME	AWAY	TOTAL	AVE
shots on target	143	134	277	7.3
shots off target	118	119	237	6.2
TOTAL	261	253	514	13.5

Ratio of goals to shots Average number of shots on target per League goal scored: **3.8**

Accuracy rating Average percentage of total goal attempts which were on target: **53.9**

AGAINST – Goal attempts recorded in League games

	HOME	AWAY	TOTAL	AVE
shots on target	51	76	127	3.3
shots off target	60	134	194	5.1
TOTAL	111	210	321	8.4

Ratio of goals to shots Average number of shots on target per League goal scored: **5.8**

Accuracy rating Average percentage of total goal attempts which were on target: **39.6**

GOALS

Frank Lampard

League	16
FA Cup	2
League Cup	0
Europe	2
Other	0
TOTAL	20

League Average **197** mins between goals

	PLAYER	LGE	FAC	LC	Euro	TOT	AVE
1	Lampard	16	2	0	2	20	197
2	Drogba	12	1	0	1	16	166
3	Crespo	10	1	0	2	13	167
4	Robben	6	1	0	0	7	293
5	Cole, J	5	2	0	1	8	420
6	Gallas	5	0	0	0	5	585
7	Terry	4	2	1	0	7	810
8	Duff	3	0	0	0	3	529
9	Geremi	2	0	0	0	2	390
10	Gudjohnsen	2	1	0	0	3	774
11	Essien	2	0	0	0	2	1229
12	Del Horno	1	0	0	0	1	2040
13	Carvalho	1	0	0	2	3	1973
14	Cole, C	0	1	0	0	1	
15	Ferreira	0	1	0	0	1	
	Other	3	0	0	1	4	
	TOTAL	72	12	1	9	96	

SQUAD APPEARANCES

Match	1	2	3	4	5	6	7	8	9	10	11	12	13	14	15	16	17	18	19	20	21	22	23	24	25	26	27	28	29	30	31	32	33	34	35	36	37	38	39	40	41	42	43	44	45	46	47	48	49	50	51	52	53
Venue	H	A	H	H	A	H	H	A	H	A	A	H	H	A	H	H	A	A	H	A	A	H	H	H	A	H	A	H	A	H	A	H	A	A	H	H	A	H	H	H	A	A	H	A	H	H	A	H	A	H	H	H	A
Competition	O	L	L	L	L	L	C	L	L	C	L	L	C	L	W	L	C	L	L	C	L	L	C	L	L	L	L	L	L	F	L	L	F	L	L	F	L	F	C	L	L	C	L	L	F	L	L	L	L	L	F	L	L
Result	W	W	W	W	W	W	W	W	W	D	W	W	W	D	L	W	L	L	W	W	W	W	D	W	W	W	W	W	W	W	W	D	D	D	W	W	L	W	L	W	W	D	W	L	W	W	D	W	W	W	L	W	L

Goalkeepers
Petr Cech
Carlo Cudicini
Lenny Pidgeley

Defenders
Wayne Bridge
Ricardo Carvalho
Asier Del Horno
Paulo Ferreira
William Gallas
Robert Huth
Glen Johnson
Nuno Morais
John Terry

Midfielders
Joe Cole
Lassana Diarra
Damien Duff
Michael Essien
Geremi Nitjap
Frank Lampard
Claude Makelele
Maniche
Arjen Robben
Cardoso Tiago
Shaun Wright-Phillips

Forwards
Carlton Cole
Hernan Crespo
Didier Drogba
Eidur Gudjohnsen

KEY: On all match · On bench · Subbed or sent off (Counting game) · Subbed or sent off (playing less than 70 mins) · Subbed on from bench (Counting Game) · Subbed on (playing less than 70 mins) · Subbed on and then subbed or sent off (Counting Game) · Subbed on and then subbed or sent off (playing less than 70 mins) · Not in 16

KEY PLAYERS - GOALSCORERS

Didier Drogba

Goals in the League	12
Goals in all competitions	16
Assists League goals scored by a team mate where the player delivered the final pass	14
Contribution to Attacking Power Average number of minutes between League team goals while on pitch	40
Player Strike Rate Average number of minutes between League goals scored by player	166
Club Strike Rate Average minutes between League goals scored by club	48

	PLAYER	GOALS LGE	GOALS ALL	ASSISTS	POWER	S RATE
1	Didier Drogba	12	16	14	40	166 mins
2	Hernan Crespo	10	13	4	49	167 mins
3	Frank Lampard	16	20	9	46	197 mins
4	Arjen Robben	6	7	7	55	293 mins

KEY PLAYERS - MIDFIELDERS

Michael Essien

Goals in the League	2
Goals in all competitions	2
Assists League goals scored by a team mate where the player delivered the final pass	3
Defensive Rating Average number of mins between League goals conceded while on the pitch	176
Contribution to Attacking Power Average number of minutes between League team goals while on pitch	42
Scoring Difference Defensive Rating minus Contribution to Attacking Power	134

	PLAYER	GOALS LGE	GOALS ALL	ASSISTS	DEF RATE	POWER	SC DIFF
1	Michael Essien	2	2	3	176	42	134 mins
2	Arjen Robben	6	7	7	176	55	121 mins
3	Frank Lampard	16	20	9	158	46	112 mins
4	Claude Makelele	0	0	3	150	42	108 mins

PLAYER APPEARANCES

	AGE (on 01/07/06)	IN NAMED 16	APPEARANCES	COUNTING GAMES	MINUTES ON PITCH	APPEARANCES	MINUTES ON PITCH	THIS SEASON	HOME COUNTRY
Goalkeepers									
Petr Cech	24	36	34	33	3015	42	3735	7	Czech Republic (2)
Carlo Cudicini	32	36	4	3	315	12	1065	-	Italy
Lenny Pidgeley	21	3	1	1	90	1	90	-	England
Defenders									
Wayne Bridge	25	1	0	0	0	2	135	3	England (10)
Ricardo Carvalho	28	27	24	21	1973	35	2963	7	Portugal (7)
Asier Del Horno	25	28	25	21	2040	34	2599	3	Spain (5)
Paulo Ferreira	27	25	21	18	1669	32	2568	7	Portugal (7)
William Gallas	28	34	34	32	2927	45	3917	9	France (8)
Robert Huth	21	23	13	4	536	21	953	6	Germany (19)
Glen Johnson	21	9	4	3	329	8	689	1	England (10)
Nuno Morais	22	0	0	0	0	0	0	-	Portugal
John Terry	25	36	36	36	3240	50	4530	6	England (10)
Midfielders									
Joe Cole	24	34	34	15	2102	47	2836	8	England (10)
Lassana Diarra	21	4	3	2	187	7	365	-	France
Damien Duff	27	29	28	8	1587	40	2333	4	Rep of Ireland (15)
Michael Essien	23	31	31	26	2458	42	3400	4	Ghana (48)
Geremi Nitjap	27	17	15	7	780	21	1127	6	Cameroon (15)
Frank Lampard	28	35	35	35	3150	50	4414	7	England (10)
Claude Makelele	33	31	31	27	2543	41	3428	9	France (8)
Maniche	28	10	8	3	335	11	483	4	Portugal (7)
Arjen Robben	22	28	28	13	1756	40	2618	6	Holland (3)
Cardoso Tiago	25	0	0	0	0	0	0	5	Portugal (7)
Shaun Wright-Phillips	24	29	27	2	1012	38	1540	6	England (10)
Forwards									
Carlton Cole	22	10	9	0	230	13	375	-	England
Hernan Crespo	31	32	30	12	1668	41	2211	6	Argentina (9)
Didier Drogba	28	29	29	18	1989	41	2848	11	Ivory Coast (32)
Eidur Gudjohnsen	27	28	26	11	1548	37	2374	2	Iceland (70)

KEY: LEAGUE ALL COMPS CAPS (MAY FIFA RANKING)

TEAM OF THE SEASON

CECH CG 33 DR 151

FERREIRA CG 18 DR 209

TERRY CG 36 DR 162

GALLAS CG 32 DR 154

DEL HORNO CG 21 DR 185

ESSIEN CG 26 SD +134

LAMPARD CG 35 SD +112

MAKELELE CG 27 SD +108

ROBBEN CG 13 SD +121

J COLE CG 15 AP 46

DROGBA CG 18 SR 166

KEY: DR = Defensive Rate, SD = Scoring Difference AP = Attacking Power SR = Strike Rate, CG=Counting games – League games playing at least 70 minutes

TOP POINT EARNERS

Michael Essien

Counting Games League games when player was on pitch for at least 70 minutes	26
Average points Average League points taken in Counting games	2.69
Club Average points Average points taken in League games	2.39

	PLAYER	GAMES	PTS
1	Michael Essien	26	2.69
2	Asier Del Horno	21	2.67
3	Didier Drogba	18	2.61
4	Claude Makelele	27	2.56
5	John Terry	36	2.53
6	Petr Cech	33	2.48
7	Joe Cole	15	2.47
8	William Gallas	32	2.44
9	Frank Lampard	35	2.43
10	Paulo Ferreira	18	2.39

KEY PLAYERS - DEFENDERS

Paulo Ferreira

Goals Conceded in the League Number of League goals conceded while the player was on the pitch	8
Goals Conceded in all competitions Total number of goals conceded while the player was on the pitch	17
League minutes played Number of minutes played in league matches	1669
Clean Sheets In games when the player was on pitch for at least 70 minutes	11
Defensive Rating Average number of mins between League goals conceded while on the pitch	209
Club Defensive Rating Average number of mins between League goals conceded by the club this season	155

	PLAYER	CON LGE	CON ALL	MINS	C SHEETS	DEF RATE
1	Paulo Ferreira	8	17	1669	11	209 mins
2	Asier Del Horno	11	14	2040	13	185 mins
3	John Terry	20	30	3240	20	162 mins
4	William Gallas	19	26	2927	16	154 mins

KEY GOALKEEPER

Petr Cech

Goals Conceded in the League Number of League goals conceded while the player was on the pitch	20
Goals Conceded in all competitions Total number of goals conceded while the player was on the pitch	25
League minutes played Number of minutes played in league matches	3015
Clean Sheets In games when the player was on pitch for at least 70 minutes	18
Goals to Shots Ratio The average number of shots on target per each League goal conceded	5.9
Defensive Rating Ave mins between League goals conceded while on the pitch	151

BOOKINGS

Robert Huth

League Yellow	3
League Red	0
All competitions Yellow	4
All competitions Red	0

League Average **178** mins between cards

	PLAYER	LEAGUE		TOTAL		AVE
		3Y	0R	4Y	0R	
1	Huth	3Y	0R	4Y	0R	178
2	Carvalho	7	1	8	1	246
3	Drogba	8	0	10	0	248
4	Robben	4	2	6	2	292
5	Makelele	7	0	9	0	363
6	Cole, J	5	0	7	0	420
7	Gallas	5	1	8	1	487
8	Essien	5	0	6	0	491
9	Duff	3	0	4	0	529
10	Gudjohnsen	2	0	2	0	774
11	Geremi	1	0	3	0	780
12	Lampard	4	0	6	0	787
13	Terry	4	0	7	0	810
14	Crespo	1	0	1	0	1668
15	Ferreira	1	0	2	0	1669
	Other	2	0	6	1	
	TOTAL	62	4	89	5	

MANCHESTER UNITED

Wayne Rooney took Wigan apart at Cardiff to earn the first silverware of his career and looked a world-class player for most of the season. A Strike Rate of a league goal every 192 minutes isn't a bad return but not yet world-class.

Ruud van Nistelrooy fell out of favour but still returned a Strike Rate of 124. **Louis Saha** didn't quite play enough to make our charts but 15 goals and a Strike Rate of 164 are impressive.

Ryan Giggs was the best midfielder in the club charts with a Scoring Difference of plus 88. **Cristiano Ronaldo's** Strike Rate of 254 was the second best for a midfielder in the Premiership.

Edwin van der Sar matched Petr Cech with a Goals-to-Shots Ratio of 5.9 shots on target per goal conceded. **Wes Brown's** stats confirmed his return to form with the club's top Defensive Rating.

NICKNAME: RED DEVILS

KEY: Won Drawn Lost

No	Comp	Opponent	Venue	Result	Score	Scorers
1	ec3q1	**Debreceni**	H	W	3-0	Rooney 7; van Nistelrooy 49; Ronaldo 63
2	prem	**Everton**	A	W	2-0	van Nistelrooy 43; Rooney 46
3	prem	**Aston Villa**	H	W	1-0	van Nistelrooy 66
4	ec3q2	**Debreceni**	A	W	3-0	Heinze 20,60; Richardson 65
5	prem	**Newcastle**	A	W	2-0	Rooney 66; van Nistelrooy 90
6	prem	**Man City**	H	D	1-1	van Nistelrooy 45
7	ecgpd	**Villarreal**	A	D	0-0	
8	prem	**Liverpool**	A	D	0-0	
9	prem	**Blackburn**	H	L	1-2	van Nistelrooy 67
10	ecgpd	**Benfica**	H	W	2-1	Giggs 39; van Nistelrooy 85
11	prem	**Fulham**	A	W	3-2	van Nistelrooy 17 pen,45; Rooney 18
12	prem	**Sunderland**	A	W	3-1	Rooney 40; van Nistelrooy 76; Rossi 87
13	ecgpd	**Lille**	H	D	0-0	
14	prem	**Tottenham**	H	D	1-1	Silvestre 7
15	ccr3	**Barnet**	H	W	4-1	Miller 4; Richardson 19; Rossi 51; Ebanks-Blake 89
16	prem	**Middlesbrough**	A	L	1-4	Ronaldo 90
17	ecgpd	**Lille**	A	L	0-1	
18	prem	**Chelsea**	H	W	1-0	Fletcher 31
19	prem	**Charlton**	A	W	3-1	Smith 37; van Nistelrooy 70,85
20	ecgpd	**Villarreal**	H	D	0-0	
21	prem	**West Ham**	A	W	2-1	Rooney 47; O'Shea 56
22	ccr4	**West Brom**	H	W	3-1	Ronaldo 12 pen; Saha 16; O'Shea 56
23	prem	**Portsmouth**	H	W	3-0	Scholes 20; Rooney 80; van Nistelrooy 84
24	ecgpd	**Benfica**	A	L	1-2	Scholes 6
25	prem	**Everton**	H	D	1-1	Giggs 16
26	prem	**Wigan**	H	W	4-0	Ferdinand 30; Rooney 35,55; van Nistelrooy 70 pen
27	prem	**Aston Villa**	A	W	2-0	van Nistelrooy 10; Rooney 51
28	ccqf	**Birmingham**	A	W	3-1	Saha 46,63; Park 50
29	prem	**West Brom**	H	W	3-0	Scholes 35; Ferdinand 45; van Nistelrooy 63
30	prem	**Birmingham**	A	D	2-2	van Nistelrooy 5; Rooney 54
31	prem	**Bolton**	H	W	4-1	N'Gotty 8 og; Saha 44; Ronaldo 68,90
32	prem	**Arsenal**	A	D	0-0	
33	facr3	**Burton**	A	D	0-0	
34	ccsfl1	**Blackburn**	A	D	1-1	Saha 30
35	prem	**Man City**	A	L	1-3	van Nistelrooy 76
36	facr3r	**Burton**	H	W	5-0	Saha 7; Rossi 23,90; Richardson 52; Giggs 68
37	prem	**Liverpool**	H	W	1-0	Ferdinand 90
38	ccsfl2	**Blackburn**	H	W	2-1	van Nistelrooy 8; Saha 51
39	facr4	**Wolves**	A	W	3-0	Richardson 5,52; Saha 45
40	prem	**Blackburn**	A	L	3-4	Saha 37; van Nistelrooy 63,68
41	prem	**Fulham**	H	W	4-2	Park 6; Ronaldo 14,86; Saha 23
42	prem	**Portsmouth**	A	W	3-1	van Nistelrooy 18; Ronaldo 38,45
43	facr5	**Liverpool**	A	L	0-1	
44	ccf	**Wigan**	H	W	4-0	Rooney 33,61; Saha 55; Ronaldo 59
45	prem	**Wigan**	A	W	2-1	Ronaldo 72; Chimbonda 90 og
46	prem	**Newcastle**	H	W	2-0	Rooney 8,12
47	prem	**West Brom**	A	W	2-1	Saha 16,64
48	prem	**Birmingham**	H	W	3-0	Taylor, Maik 3 og; Giggs 15; Rooney 83
49	prem	**West Ham**	H	W	1-0	van Nistelrooy 45
50	prem	**Bolton**	A	W	2-1	Saha 33; van Nistelrooy 79
51	prem	**Arsenal**	H	W	2-0	Rooney 54; Park 78
52	prem	**Sunderland**	H	D	0-0	
53	prem	**Tottenham**	A	W	2-1	Rooney 8,36
54	prem	**Chelsea**	A	L	0-3	
55	prem	**Middlesbrough**	H	D	0-0	
56	prem	**Charlton**	H	W	4-0	Saha 19; Ronaldo 23; Euell 35 og; Richardson 58

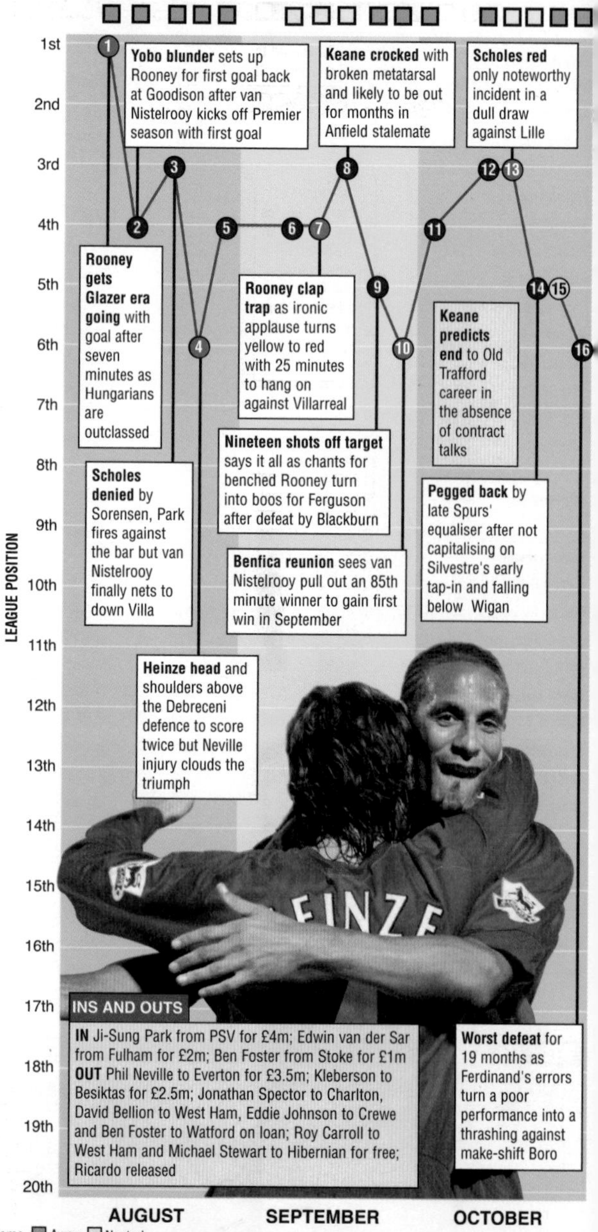

LEAGUE POSITION: 1st–20th — AUGUST, SEPTEMBER, OCTOBER

Yobo blunder sets up Rooney for first goal back at Goodison after van Nistelrooy kicks off Premier season with first goal

Keane crocked with broken metatarsal and likely to be out for months in Anfield stalemate

Scholes red only noteworthy incident in a dull draw against Lille

Rooney gets Glazer era going with goal after seven minutes as Hungarians are outclassed

Rooney clap trap as ironic applause turns yellow to red with 25 minutes to hang on against Villarreal

Keane predicts end to Old Trafford career in the absence of contract talks

Scholes denied by Sorensen, Park fires against the bar but van Nistelrooy finally nets to down Villa

Nineteen shots off target says it all as chants for benched Rooney turn into boos for Ferguson after defeat by Blackburn

Pegged back by late Spurs' equaliser after not capitalising on Silvestre's early tap-in and falling below Wigan

Benfica reunion sees van Nistelrooy pull out an 85th minute winner to gain first win in September

Heinze head and shoulders above the Debreceni defence to score twice but Neville injury clouds the triumph

Worst defeat for 19 months as Ferdinand's errors turn a poor performance into a thrashing against make-shift Boro

INS AND OUTS

IN Ji-Sung Park from PSV for £4m; Edwin van der Sar from Fulham for £2m; Ben Foster from Stoke for £1m **OUT** Phil Neville to Everton for £3.5m; Kleberson to Besiktas for £2.5m; Jonathan Spector to Charlton, David Bellion to West Ham, Eddie Johnson to Crewe and Ben Foster to Watford on loan; Roy Carroll to West Ham and Michael Stewart to Hibernian for free; Ricardo released

Home Away Neutral

ATTENDANCES

HOME GROUND: OLD TRAFFORD **CAPACITY:** 76000 **AVERAGE LEAGUE AT HOME:** 68764

56	Charlton	73006	6	Man City	67839	1	Debreceni	51701	30	Birmingham	28459
52	Sunderland	72519	25	Everton	67831	22	West Brom	48924	39	Wolves	28333
51	Arsenal	70908	26	Wigan	67793	35	Man City	47192	50	Bolton	27718
55	Middlesboro	69531	9	Blackburn	67765	8	Liverpool	44917	47	West Brom	27623
49	West Ham	69522	23	Portsmouth	67684	43	Liverpool	44039	4	Debreceni	27000
48	Birmingham	69070	20	Villarreal	67471	15	Barnet	43673	19	Charlton	26730
29	West Brom	67972	10	Benfica	66112	54	Chelsea	42219	40	Blackburn	25484
3	Aston Villa	67934	17	Lille	65000	12	Sunderland	39085	34	Blackburn	24348
37	Liverpool	67874	38	Blackburn	61637	2	Everton	38610	45	Wigan	23574
18	Chelsea	67864	24	Benfica	61000	32	Arsenal	38313	7	Villarreal	23000
31	Bolton	67858	44	Wigan	60866	27	Aston Villa	37128	11	Fulham	21862
46	Newcastle	67858	13	Lille	60626	53	Tottenham	36141	28	Birmingham	20454
14	Tottenham	67856	36	Burton	53564	21	West Ham	34755	42	Portsmouth	20206
41	Fulham	67844	5	Newcastle	52327	16	Middlesboro	30579	33	Burton	6191

Rooney's Cup glosses over Euro exit

Final Position: 2nd

Y: ● League ● Champions Lge ● UEFA Cup ● FA Cup ○ League Cup ● Other

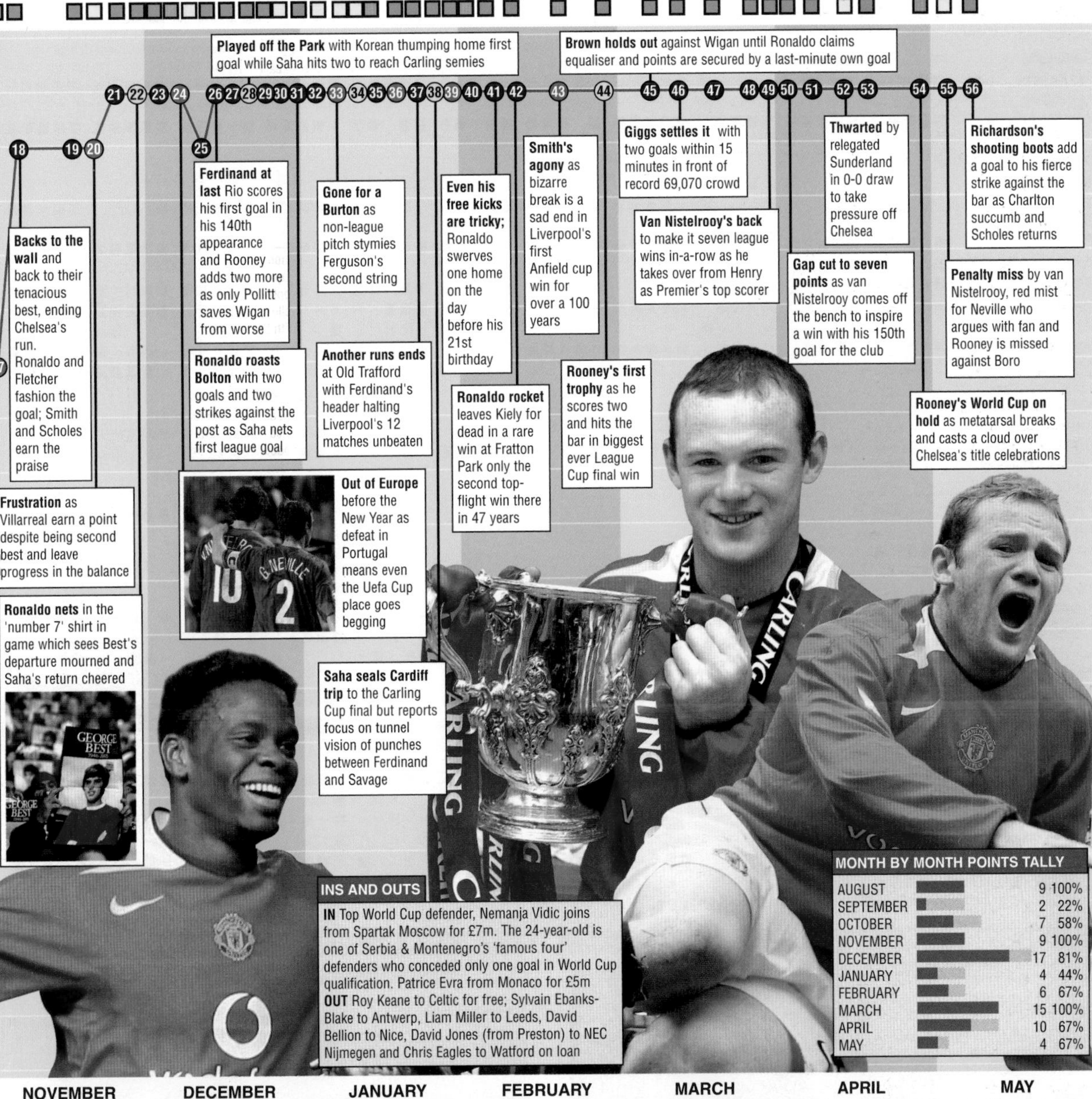

Frustration as Villarreal earn a point despite being second best and leave progress in the balance

Backs to the wall and back to their tenacious best, ending Chelsea's run. Ronaldo and Fletcher fashion the goal; Smith and Scholes earn the praise

Ronaldo nets in the 'number 7' shirt in game which sees Best's departure mourned and Saha's return cheered

Ferdinand at last Rio scores his first goal in his 140th appearance and Rooney adds two more as only Pollitt saves Wigan from worse

Ronaldo roasts Bolton with two goals and two strikes against the post as Saha nets first league goal

Played off the Park with Korean thumping home first goal while Saha hits two to reach Carling semies

Out of Europe before the New Year as defeat in Portugal means even the Uefa Cup place goes begging

Gone for a Burton as non-league pitch stymies Ferguson's second string

Another runs ends at Old Trafford with Ferdinand's header halting Liverpool's 12 matches unbeaten

Saha seals Cardiff trip to the Carling Cup final but reports focus on tunnel vision of punches between Ferdinand and Savage

Even his free kicks are tricky; Ronaldo swerves one home on the day before his 21st birthday

Ronaldo rocket leaves Kiely for dead in a rare win at Fratton Park only the second top-flight win there in 47 years

Smith's agony as bizarre break is a sad end in Liverpool's first Anfield cup win for over a 100 years

Brown holds out against Wigan until Ronaldo claims equaliser and points are secured by a last-minute own goal

Rooney's first trophy as he scores two and hits the bar in biggest ever League Cup final win

Giggs settles it with two goals within 15 minutes in front of record 69,070 crowd

Van Nistelrooy's back to make it seven league wins in-a-row as he takes over from Henry as Premier's top scorer

Gap cut to seven points as van Nistelrooy comes off the bench to inspire a win with his 150th goal for the club

Thwarted by relegated Sunderland in 0-0 draw to take pressure off Chelsea

Rooney's World Cup on hold as metatarsal breaks and casts a cloud over Chelsea's title celebrations

Richardson's shooting boots add a goal to his fierce strike against the bar as Charlton succumb and Scholes returns

Penalty miss by van Nistelrooy, red mist for Neville who argues with fan and Rooney is missed against Boro

INS AND OUTS

IN Top World Cup defender, Nemanja Vidic joins from Spartak Moscow for £7m. The 24-year-old is one of Serbia & Montenegro's 'famous four' defenders who conceded only one goal in World Cup qualification. Patrice Evra from Monaco for £5m
OUT Roy Keane to Celtic for free; Sylvain Ebanks-Blake to Antwerp, Liam Miller to Leeds, David Bellion to Nice, David Jones (from Preston) to NEC Nijmegen and Chris Eagles to Watford on loan

MONTH BY MONTH POINTS TALLY

Month	Points	%
AUGUST	9	100%
SEPTEMBER	2	22%
OCTOBER	7	58%
NOVEMBER	9	100%
DECEMBER	17	81%
JANUARY	4	44%
FEBRUARY	6	67%
MARCH	15	100%
APRIL	10	67%
MAY	4	67%

NOVEMBER DECEMBER JANUARY FEBRUARY MARCH APRIL MAY

GOAL ATTEMPTS

FOR — Goal attempts recorded in League games

	HOME	AWAY	TOTAL	AVE
shots on target	171	115	286	7.5
shots off target	153	116	269	7.1
TOTAL	324	231	555	14.6

Ratio of goals to shots — Average number of shots on target per League goal scored: 4

Accuracy rating — Average percentage of total goal attempts which were on target: 51.5

AGAINST — Goal attempts recorded in League games

	HOME	AWAY	TOTAL	AVE
shots on target	94	101	195	5.1
shots off target	75	115	190	5
TOTAL	169	216	385	10.1

Ratio of goals to shots — Average number of shots on target per League goal scored: 5.7

Accuracy rating — Average percentage of total goal attempts which were on target: 50.6

GOALS

Ruud van Nistelrooy

League	21
FA Cup	0
League Cup	1
Europe	2
Other	0
TOTAL	24

League Average 124 mins between goals

	PLAYER	LGE	FAC	LC	Euro	TOT	AVE
1	van Nistelrooy	21	0	1	2	24	124
2	Rooney	16	0	2	1	19	192
3	Ronaldo	9	0	2	1	12	254
4	Saha	7	2	6	0	15	164
5	Ferdinand	3	0	0	0	3	1099
6	Scholes	2	0	0	1	3	808
7	Giggs	2	1	0	1	4	924
8	Park	2	0	1	0	3	993
9	O'Shea	1	0	1	0	2	2828
10	Fletcher	1	0	0	0	1	1945
11	Rossi	1	2	1	0	4	135
12	Richardson	1	3	1	1	6	1163
13	Silvestre	1	0	0	0	1	2647
14	Smith	1	0	0	0	1	1470
15	Miller	0	0	1	0	1	
	Other	4	0	1	2	7	
	TOTAL	72	8	17	9	106	

SQUAD APPEARANCES

	1–5	6–10	11–15	16–20	21–25	26–30	31–35	36–40	41–45	46–50	51–55
Match	1 2 3 4 5	6 7 8 9 10	11 12 13 14 15	16 17 18 19 20	21 22 23 24 25	26 27 28 29 30	31 32 33 34 35	36 37 38 39 40	41 42 43 44 45	46 47 48 49 50	51 52 53 54 55
Venue	H A H A A	H A A H H	A A H H H	A A H A H	A H H A H	H A A H A	H A A A A	H H H A A	H A A H A	H A H H A	H H A A H
Competition	C L L C L	L C L L C	L L C L W	L C L L C	L W L C L	L L W L L	L L F W L	F L W F L	L L F W L	L L L L L	L L L L L
Result	W W W W W	D D D L W	W W D D W	L L W W D	W W W L D	W W W W D	W D D D L	W W W W L	W W L W W	W W W W W	W D W L D

Goalkeepers
Tim Howard
Luke Steele
Edwin Van der Sar

Defenders
Phillip Bardsley
Wes Brown
Adam Eckersley
Rio Ferdinand
Gabriel Ivan Heinze
Gary Neville
John O'Shea
Gerard Pique
Mikael Silvestre
Nemanja Vidic

Midfielders
Patrice Evra
Darren Fletcher
Quinton Fortune
Darron Gibson
Ryan Giggs
Ritchie Jones
Roy Keane
Lee Martin
Liam Miller
Ji-Sung Park
Keiron Richardson
Cristiano Ronaldo
Paul Scholes
Alan Smith

Forwards
Sylvain Ebanks-Blake
Wayne Rooney
Giuseppe Rossi
Louis Saha
Ole Gunnar Solskjaer
Ruud van Nistelrooy

KEY: On all match | On bench | Subbed or sent off (Counting game) | Subbed or sent off (playing less than 70 mins) | Subbed on from bench (Counting Game) | Subbed on (playing less than 70 mins) | Subbed on and then subbed or sent off (Counting Game) | Subbed on and then subbed or sent off (playing less than 70 mins) | Not in 16

KEY PLAYERS - GOALSCORERS

Ruud van Nistelrooy

Goals in the League	21
Goals in all competitions	24
Assists League goals scored by a team mate where the player delivered the final pass	5
Contribution to Attacking Power Average number of minutes between League team goals while on pitch	49
Player Strike Rate Average number of minutes between League goals scored by player	124
Club Strike Rate Average minutes between League goals scored by club	48

	PLAYER	GOALS LGE	GOALS ALL	ASSISTS	POWER	S RATE
1	Ruud van Nistelrooy	21	24	5	49	124 mins
2	Wayne Rooney	16	19	10	48	192 mins
3	Cristiano Ronaldo	9	12	7	47	254 mins
4	Paul Scholes	2	3	2	49	808 mins

KEY PLAYERS - MIDFIELDERS

Ryan Giggs

Goals in the League	2
Goals in all competitions	4
Assists League goals scored by a team mate where the player delivered the final pass	9
Defensive Rating Average number of mins between League goals conceded while on the pitch	132
Contribution to Attacking Power Average number of minutes between League team goals while on pitch	46
Scoring Difference Defensive Rating minus Contribution to Attacking Power	86

	PLAYER	GOALS LGE	GOALS ALL	ASSISTS	DEF RATE	POWER	SC DIFF
1	Ryan Giggs	2	4	9	132	46	86 mins
2	Paul Scholes	2	3	2	115	49	66 mins
3	Cristiano Ronaldo	9	12	7	99	47	52 mins
4	Ji-Sung Park	2	3	8	105	54	51 mins

PLAYER APPEARANCES

	AGE (on 01/07/06)	IN NAMED 16	APPEARANCES	COUNTING GAMES	MINUTES ON PITCH	APPEARANCES	MINUTES ON PITCH	THIS SEASON	HOME COUNTRY
Goalkeepers									
Tim Howard	27	37	1	0	45	6	495	4	United States (5)
Luke Steele	21	1	0	0	0	0	0	-	England
Edwin Van der Sar	35	38	38	37	3375	51	4545	8	Holland (3)
Defenders									
Phillip Bardsley	21	15	8	2	306	15	829	-	England
Wes Brown	26	24	19	16	1475	31	2466	1	England (10)
Adam Eckersley	20	0	0	0	0	1	90	-	England
Patrice Evra	25	16	11	4	570	14	683	-	France
Rio Ferdinand	27	37	37	36	3298	52	4528	8	England (10)
Gabriel Ivan Heinze	28	6	4	2	231	6	353	3	Argentina (9)
Gary Neville	31	25	25	22	2163	37	3032	3	England (10)
John O'Shea	25	34	34	28	2828	47	3830	5	Rep of Ireland (15)
Gerard Pique	19	10	3	1	97	7	391	-	Spain
Mikael Silvestre	28	34	33	28	2647	48	3834	3	France (8)
Nemanja Vidic	24	15	11	9	861	15	1054	8	Serbia & Mont (44)
Midfielders									
Darren Fletcher	22	31	27	21	1945	41	2992	6	Scotland (85)
Quinton Fortune	29	1	0	0	0	0	0	-	South Africa
Darron Gibson	18	0	0	0	0	1	16	-	N Ireland
Ryan Giggs	32	28	27	19	1848	37	2491	5	Wales (74)
Ritchie Jones	19	1	0	0	0	4	237	-	England
Roy Keane	34	5	5	4	371	6	437	1	Rep of Ireland (15)
Lee Martin	19	0	0	0	0	1	74	-	England
Liam Miller	25	3	1	0	3	92	32	2	Rep of Ireland (15)
Ji-Sung Park	25	34	33	17	1986	44	2450	5	South Korea (29)
Keiron Richardson	21	26	22	9	1163	36	2170	2	England (10)
Cristiano Ronaldo	21	34	33	22	2284	47	3408	6	Portugal (7)
Paul Scholes	31	20	20	17	1615	27	2173	-	England
Alan Smith	25	21	21	15	1470	33	2331	2	England (10)
Forwards									
Sylvain Ebanks-Blake	20	0	0	0	0	1	90	-	England
Wayne Rooney	20	36	36	34	3073	48	4025	6	England (10)
Giuseppe Rossi	19	14	5	1	135	12	520	-	Italy
Louis Saha	27	23	19	11	1148	30	1917	1	France (8)
Ole Gunnar Solskjaer	33	3	3	0	62	5	210	-	Norway
Ruud van Nistelrooy	30	36	35	26	2596	47	3569	6	Holland (3)

KEY: LEAGUE ALL COMPS CAPS (MAY FIFA RANKING)

TEAM OF THE SEASON

VAN DER SAR — CG 37 DR 102

NEVILLE — CG 22 DR 108
FERDINAND — CG 36 DR 103
BROWN — CG 16 DR 148
O'SHEA — CG 28 DR 118

PARK — CG 17 SD +51
SCHOLES — CG 17 SD +66
GIGGS — CG 19 SD +86
RONALDO — CG 22 SD +52

ROONEY — CG 34 AP 48
VAN NISTELROOY — CG 26 SR 124

KEY: DR = Defensive Rate, SD = Scoring Difference AP = Attacking Power SR = Strike Rate, CG=Counting games – League games playing at least 70 minutes

TOP POINT EARNERS

Ji-Sung Park

Counting Games League games when player was on pitch for at least 70 minutes	17
Average points Average League points taken in Counting games	2.47
Club Average points Average points taken in League games	2.18

	PLAYER	GAMES	PTS
1	Ji-Sung Park	17	2.47
2	Wes Brown	16	2.44
3	Cristiano Ronaldo	22	2.36
4	Ryan Giggs	19	2.26
5	John O'Shea	28	2.25
6	Wayne Rooney	34	2.24
7	Darren Fletcher	21	2.19
8	Edwin Van der Sar	37	2.16
9	Gary Neville	22	2.14
10	Rio Ferdinand	36	2.14

KEY PLAYERS - DEFENDERS

Wes Brown

Goals Conceded in the League Number of League goals conceded while the player was on the pitch	10
Goals Conceded in all competitions Total number of goals conceded while the player was on the pitch	16
League minutes played Number of minutes played in league matches	1475
Clean Sheets In games when the player was on pitch for at least 70 minutes	10
Defensive Rating Average number of mins between League goals conceded while on the pitch	148
Club Defensive Rating Average number of mins between League goals conceded by the club this season	101

	PLAYER	CON LGE	CON ALL	MINS	C SHEETS	DEF RATE
1	Wes Brown	10	16	1475	10	148 mins
2	John O'Shea	24	28	2828	13	118 mins
3	Gary Neville	20	27	2163	12	108 mins
4	Rio Ferdinand	32	40	3298	17	103 mins

KEY GOALKEEPER

Edwin Van der Sar

Goals Conceded in the League Number of League goals conceded while the player was on the pitch	33
Goals Conceded in all competitions Total number of goals conceded while the player was on the pitch	40
League minutes played Number of minutes played in league matches	3375
Clean Sheets In games when the player was on pitch for at least 70 minutes	18
Goals to Shots Ratio The average number of shots on target per each League goal conceded	5.9
Defensive Rating Ave mins between League goals conceded while on the pitch	102

BOOKINGS

Cristiano Ronaldo

League Yellow	8
League Red	1
All competitions Yellow	10
All competitions Red	1

League Average **253** mins between cards

	PLAYER	LEAGUE		TOTAL		AVE
1	Ronaldo	8Y	1R	10Y	1R	253
2	Vidic	3	0	5	0	287
3	Richardson	4	0	7	0	290
4	Smith	4	0	9	0	367
5	Rooney	8	0	12	1	384
6	Brown	3	0	3	0	491
7	van Nistelrooy	5	0	6	0	519
8	Scholes	3	0	6	1	538
9	O'Shea	5	0	7	0	565
10	Evra	1	0	1	0	570
11	Giggs	3	0	4	0	616
12	Fletcher	3	0	3	0	648
13	Silvestre	4	0	7	0	661
14	Neville	3	0	6	0	721
15	Ferdinand	2	1	4	1	1099
	Other	0	0	1	0	
	TOTAL	59	2	91	4	

LIVERPOOL

Pepe Reina lived up to Rafael Benitez's billing as the best keeper in Spain. He helped achieve a club record of 11 clean sheets in-a-row and notched 20 in the season – a better total than Petr Cech.

Sami Hyypia matched Reina, while **Steve Finnan** went one better, recording 21 shut-outs in the league. **John Arne Riise** was used in defence and midfield but the club only conceded a goal every 188 minutes when he was on the pitch – the second best Defensive Rating in the league.

The season belonged to **Steven Gerrard**. He hit an astonishing 23 goals in all games and his all-round performance gave him the best Premiership midfield record outside of Chelsea.

There were problems up front but **Djibril Cissé** recorded a Strike Rate of a goal every 191 minutes to sneak into the top ten.

NICKNAME: THE REDS

KEY: Won Drawn Lost

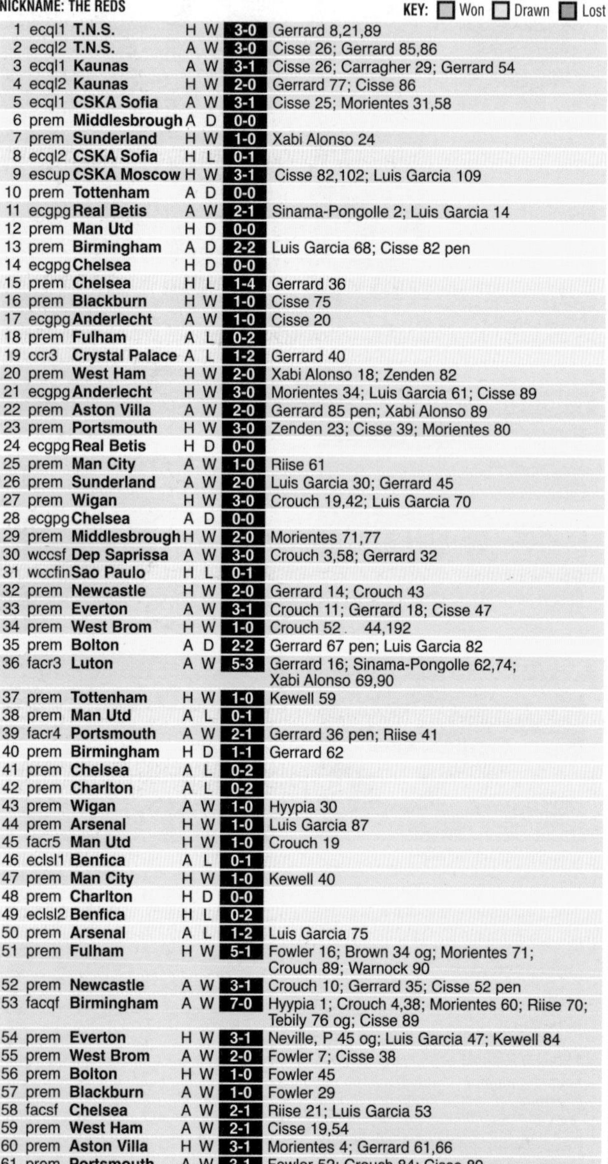

1	ecql1	T.N.S.	H	W	3-0	Gerrard 8,21,89
2	ecql2	T.N.S.	A	W	3-0	Cisse 26; Gerrard 85,86
3	ecql1	Kaunas	A	W	3-1	Cisse 26; Carragher 29; Gerrard 54
4	ecql2	Kaunas	H	W	2-0	Gerrard 77; Cisse 86
5	ecql1	CSKA Sofia	A	W	3-1	Cisse 25; Morientes 31,58
6	prem	Middlesbrough	A	D	0-0	
7	prem	Sunderland	H	W	1-0	Xabi Alonso 24
8	ecql2	CSKA Sofia	H	L	0-1	
9	escup	CSKA Moscow	H	W	3-1	Cisse 82,102; Luis Garcia 109
10	prem	Tottenham	A	D	0-0	
11	ecgpg	Real Betis	A	W	2-1	Sinama-Pongolle 2; Luis Garcia 14
12	prem	Man Utd	H	D	0-0	
13	prem	Birmingham	A	D	2-2	Luis Garcia 68; Cisse 82 pen
14	ecgpg	Chelsea	H	D	0-0	
15	prem	Chelsea	H	L	1-4	Gerrard 36
16	prem	Blackburn	H	W	1-0	Cisse 75
17	ecgpg	Anderlecht	A	W	1-0	Cisse 20
18	prem	Fulham	A	L	0-2	
19	ccr3	Crystal Palace	A	L	1-2	Gerrard 40
20	prem	West Ham	H	W	2-0	Xabi Alonso 18; Zenden 82
21	ecgpg	Anderlecht	H	W	3-0	Morientes 34; Luis Garcia 61; Cisse 89
22	prem	Aston Villa	A	W	2-0	Gerrard 85 pen; Xabi Alonso 89
23	prem	Portsmouth	H	W	3-0	Zenden 23; Cisse 39; Morientes 80
24	ecgpg	Real Betis	H	D	0-0	
25	prem	Man City	A	W	1-0	Riise 61
26	prem	Sunderland	A	W	2-0	Luis Garcia 30; Gerrard 45
27	prem	Wigan	H	W	3-0	Crouch 19,42; Luis Garcia 70
28	ecgpg	Chelsea	A	D	0-0	
29	prem	Middlesbrough	H	W	2-0	Morientes 71,77
30	wccsf	Dep Saprissa	A	W	3-0	Crouch 3,58; Gerrard 32
31	wccfin	Sao Paulo	H	L	0-1	
32	prem	Newcastle	H	W	2-0	Gerrard 14; Crouch 43
33	prem	Everton	A	W	3-1	Crouch 11; Gerrard 18; Cisse 47
34	prem	West Brom	H	W	1-0	Crouch 52. 44,192
35	prem	Bolton	A	D	2-2	Gerrard 67 pen; Luis Garcia 82
36	facr3	Luton	A	W	5-3	Gerrard 16; Sinama-Pongolle 62,74; Xabi Alonso 69,90
37	prem	Tottenham	H	W	1-0	Kewell 59
38	prem	Man Utd	A	L	0-1	
39	facr4	Portsmouth	A	W	2-1	Gerrard 36 pen; Riise 41
40	prem	Birmingham	H	D	1-1	Gerrard 62
41	prem	Chelsea	A	L	0-2	
42	prem	Charlton	A	L	0-2	
43	prem	Wigan	A	W	1-0	Hyypia 30
44	prem	Arsenal	H	W	1-0	Luis Garcia 87
45	facr5	Man Utd	H	W	1-0	Crouch 19
46	eclsl1	Benfica	A	L	0-1	
47	prem	Man City	H	W	1-0	Kewell 40
48	prem	Charlton	H	D	0-0	
49	eclsl2	Benfica	H	L	0-2	
50	prem	Arsenal	A	L	1-2	Luis Garcia 75
51	prem	Fulham	H	W	5-1	Fowler 16; Brown 34 og; Morientes 71; Crouch 89; Warnock 90
52	prem	Newcastle	A	W	3-1	Crouch 10; Gerrard 35; Cisse 52 pen
53	facqf	Birmingham	A	W	7-0	Hyypia 1; Crouch 4,38; Morientes 60; Riise 70; Tebily 76 og; Cisse 89
54	prem	Everton	H	W	3-1	Neville, P 45 og; Luis Garcia 47; Kewell 84
55	prem	West Brom	A	W	2-0	Fowler 7; Cisse 38
56	prem	Bolton	H	W	1-0	Fowler 45
57	prem	Blackburn	A	W	1-0	Fowler 29
58	facsf	Chelsea	A	W	2-1	Riise 21; Luis Garcia 53
59	prem	West Ham	A	W	2-1	Cisse 19,54
60	prem	Aston Villa	H	W	3-1	Morientes 4; Gerrard 61,66
61	prem	Portsmouth	A	W	3-1	Fowler 52; Crouch 84; Cisse 89
62	facf	West Ham	H	W	3-1*	Cisse 32; Gerrard 54,90 (*on penalties)

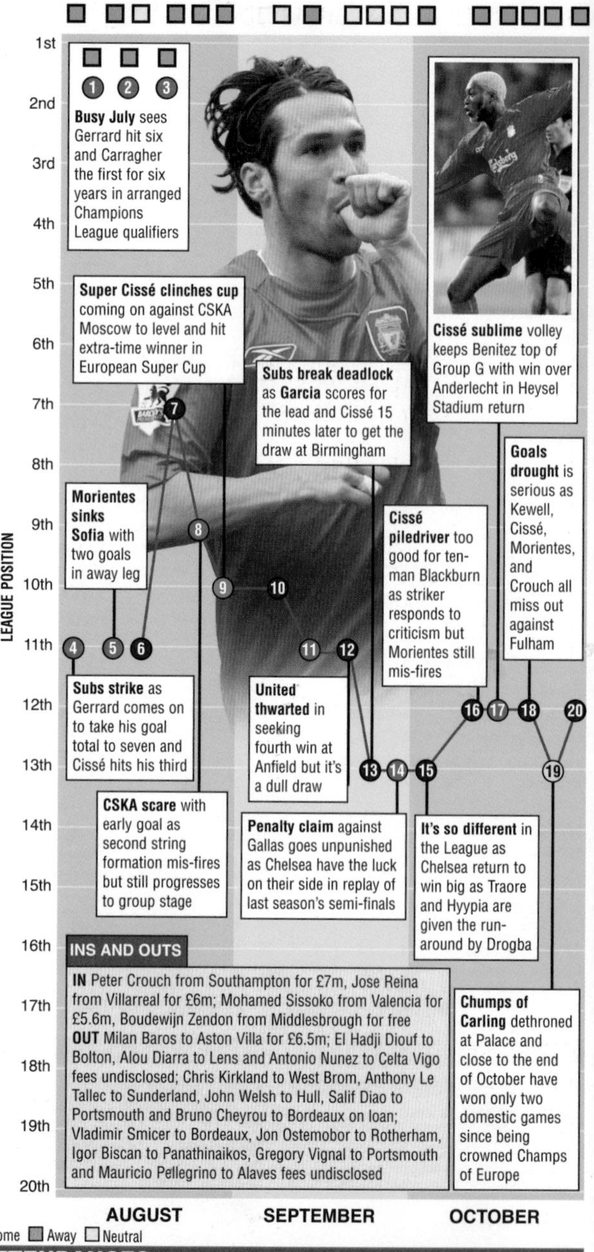

LEAGUE POSITION

1st 2nd 3rd 4th 5th 6th 7th 8th 9th 10th 11th 12th 13th 14th 15th 16th 17th 18th 19th 20th

Busy July sees Gerrard hit six and Carragher the first for six years in arranged Champions League qualifiers

Super Cissé clinches cup coming on against CSKA Moscow to level and hit extra-time winner in European Super Cup

Subs break deadlock as **Garcia** scores for the lead and Cissé 15 minutes later to get the draw at Birmingham

Cissé sublime volley keeps Benitez top of Group G with win over Anderlecht in Heysel Stadium return

Goals drought is serious as Kewell, Cissé, Morientes, and Crouch all miss out against Fulham

Morientes sinks Sofia with two goals in away leg

Cissé piledriver too good for ten-man Blackburn as striker responds to criticism but Morientes still mis-fires

Subs strike as Gerrard comes on to take his goal total to seven and Cissé hits his third

United thwarted in seeking fourth win at Anfield but it's a dull draw

CSKA scare with early goal as second string formation mis-fires but still progresses to group stage

Penalty claim against Gallas goes unpunished as Chelsea have the luck on their side in replay of last season's semi-finals

It's so different in the League as Chelsea return to win big as Traore and Hyypia are given the run-around by Drogba

INS AND OUTS

IN Peter Crouch from Southampton for £7m, Jose Reina from Villarreal for £6m; Mohamed Sissoko from Valencia for £5.6m, Boudewijn Zendon from Middlesbrough for free
OUT Milan Baros to Aston Villa for £6.5m; El Hadji Diouf to Bolton, Alou Diarra to Lens and Antonio Nunez to Celta Vigo fees undisclosed; Chris Kirkland to West Brom, Anthony Le Tallec to Sunderland, John Welsh to Hull, Salif Diao to Portsmouth and Bruno Cheyrou to Bordeaux on loan; Vladimir Smicer to Bordeaux, Jon Ostemobor to Rotherham, Igor Biscan to Panathinaikos, Gregory Vignal to Portsmouth and Mauricio Pellegrino to Alaves fees undisclosed

Chumps of Carling dethroned at Palace and close to the end of October have won only two domestic games since being crowned Champs of Europe

AUGUST SEPTEMBER OCTOBER

Home Away Neutral

ATTENDANCES

HOME GROUND: ANFIELD CAPACITY: 45362 AVERAGE LEAGUE AT HOME: 44236

9	CSKA Mos	80000	60	Aston Villa	44479	14	Chelsea	42743	35	Bolton	27604
62	West Ham	74000	23	Portsmouth	44394	21	Anderlecht	42607	55	West Brom	27576
38	Man Utd	67874	15	Chelsea	44235	22	Aston Villa	42551	53	Birmingham	27378
31	Sao Paulo	66821	32	Newcastle	44197	41	Chelsea	42316	42	Charlton	27111
46	Benfica	65000	56	Bolton	44194	51	Fulham	42293	17	Anderlecht	25000
58	Chelsea	64575	34	West Brom	44192	8	CSKA Sofia	42175	43	Wigan	25000
52	Newcastle	52302	47	Man City	44121	24	Real Betis	42077	18	Fulham	22480
25	Man City	47105	27	Wigan	44098	28	Chelsea	41598	61	Portsmouth	20240
11	Real Betis	45000	44	Arsenal	44065	33	Everton	40158	19	Crystal Palace	19673
37	Tottenham	44983	45	Man Utd	44039	50	Arsenal	38221	39	Portsmouth	17247
54	Everton	44923	30	Dep Saprissa	43902	10	Tottenham	36148	5	CSKA Sofia	16512
12	Man Utd	44917	48	Charlton	43892	59	West Ham	34852	36	Luton	10170
7	Sunderland	44913	40	Birmingham	43851	26	Sunderland	32697	3	Kaunas	8300
1	T.N.S.	44760	4	Kaunas	43717	6	Middlesboro	31908	2	T.N.S.	8009
16	Blackburn	44697	29	Middlesboro	43510	57	Blackburn	29142			
20	West Ham	44537	49	Benfica	42745	13	Birmingham	27733			

Gerrard's still the cup comeback king

Final Position: 3rd

KEY: ● League ● Champions Lge ● UEFA Cup ● FA Cup ○ League Cup ● Other

Clear of Chelsea as rejuvenated Morientes leads the way to a group-topping win over Anderlecht

Crouch at last; a looping deflection starts him scoring and a cool chip follows soon after to end 24 scoreless hours of waiting

'He's big; he's red…' but try as he might the goal eludes Crouch as penalty is saved but Zendon grabs rebound

Riise thumps home first goal of the season to win at Man City

Cissé settles derby with third goal to kill Everton as two in blue see red

Ten on the spin – equals a club record of clean sheets for excellent Reina and Morientes double subdues Boro

Costa Ricans outclassed as Crouch can't stop scoring and 11th clean sheet is recorded in Club World Championships

One-sided final – but Reds somehow lose! 17 corners to nil, three disallowed goals and a hatful of chances for Garcia as Sao Paulo hang on

Riise rocket ends Pompey's cup hopes whizzing exocet-like into the bottom corner

Cissé misses sitter and Kromkamp loses Ferdinand for United to sneak undeserved victory and end 12 game unbeaten run

Alonso from distance; 35 yards, and then from real distance; 60 yards in cup-tie at Luton which has everything

Fowler's overhead flies in to cheers but offside flag denies last-minute dream return

Crouch makes history with first FA Cup win over United at Anfield for over 100 years

Super sub Garcia breaks Lehmann's defiance with a late strike after Gerrard squanders penalty

Reina dismissed in frustration with a wild tackle on Gudjohnsen and a tweak of Robben's cheek

Benfica shake holders with an 85th minute goal as Gerrard is missed in Lisbon and Sissoko suffers eye injury

Simao's killer blow shows holders how to find the net and ends Euro hopes

Floodgates open as **Fowler's** first floors Fulham who are hit for five

Seventh heaven for Benitez's strikers as Birmingham are blitzed with goals from Morientes, Cissé and two for Crouch

Cissé's scintillating form sinks Baggies and Fowler overtakes Dalglish in the all-time scoring list

Gerrard's wild tackle ends in red after 17 minutes but Neville's own goal helps ten men to derby win

Birthday boy Fowler nets winner in one of many happy returns against Bolton over the years

Garcia dents Chelsea hopes again! Striker supplies a sublime finish to put Reds two up to secure FA Cup final spot

Dress rehearsal for FA Cup final ends in Garcia red card costing his place at Cardiff

Cissé's 18th of the season in club record 11th consecutive win but it's only good for third spot

Fowler wins contract extension for next season

Deadly Gerrard salvages FA Cup from the brink of defeat with two stunning strikes before the Hammers succumb to Reina's penalty-saving prowess

Gerrard wins the players' Player of the Year award

NOVEMBER DECEMBER JANUARY FEBRUARY MARCH APRIL MAY

INS AND OUTS

"Leaving was probably one of my biggest regrets." Robbie is back at his spiritual home of Anfield after five years away

IN Robbie Fowler from Man City for free. Jan Kromkamp from Villarreal in swap for Josemi; Daniel Agger from Brondby for £5.8m

OUT Florent Sinama-Pongolle to Blackburn and Neil Mellor to Wigan on loan; Josemi to Villarreal in swap

MONTH BY MONTH POINTS TALLY

Month	Points	%
AUGUST	4	67%
SEPTEMBER	3	33%
OCTOBER	6	50%
NOVEMBER	12	100%
DECEMBER	15	100%
JANUARY	4	44%
FEBRUARY	10	56%
MARCH	10	67%
APRIL	15	100%
MAY	3	100%

GOAL ATTEMPTS

FOR – Goal attempts recorded in League games

	HOME	AWAY	TOTAL	AVE
shots on target	177	105	282	7.4
shots off target	167	111	278	7.3
TOTAL	344	216	560	14.7

Ratio of goals to shots – Average number of shots on target per League goal scored: **4.9**

Accuracy rating – Average percentage of total goal attempts which were on target: **50.4**

AGAINST – Goal attempts recorded in League games

	HOME	AWAY	TOTAL	AVE
shots on target	51	72	123	3.2
shots off target	53	105	158	4.2
TOTAL	104	177	281	7.4

Ratio of goals to shots – Average number of shots on target per League goal scored: **4.9**

Accuracy rating – Average percentage of total goal attempts which were on target: **43.8**

GOALS

Steven Gerrard

League	10
FA Cup	4
League Cup	1
Europe	1
Other	1
TOTAL	17

League Average **272** mins between goals

	PLAYER	LGE	FAC	LC	Euro	TOT	AVE
1	Gerrard	10	4	1	7	23	272
2	Cisse	9	2	0	6	19	191
3	Crouch	8	3	0	0	13	265
4	Luis Garcia	7	1	0	2	11	227
5	Morientes	5	1	0	3	9	366
6	Fowler	5	0	0	0	5	156
7	Xabi Alonso	3	2	0	0	5	857
8	Kewell	3	0	0	0	3	668
9	Zenden	2	0	0	0	2	226
10	Riise	1	3	0	0	4	2261
11	Warnock	1	0	0	0	1	1314
12	Hyypia	1	1	0	0	2	3063
13	Sinama-Pongolle	0	2	0	1	3	
	Other	2	1	0	1	4	
	TOTAL	57	20	1	20	104	

SQUAD APPEARANCES

	1–5	6–10	11–15	16–20	21–25	26–30	31–35	36–40	41–45	46–50	51–55	56–60	61–62
Match	1 2 3 4 5	6 7 8 9 10	11 12 13 14 15	16 17 18 19 20	21 22 23 24 25	26 27 28 29 30	31 32 33 34 35	36 37 38 39 40	41 42 43 44 45	46 47 48 49 50	51 52 53 54 55	56 57 58 59 60	61 62
Venue	H A A H A	A H H H A	A H A H H	H A A A H	H A H H A	A H A H A	H H A H A	A H A A H	A A A H H	A H H H A	H A A H A	H A A A H	A H
Competition	C C C C C	L L C O L	C L L C L	L C L W L	C L L C L	L L C L O	O L L L L	F L L F L	L L L L F	C L L C L	L L F L L	L L F L L	L F
Result	W W W W W	D W L W D	W D D D L	W W L L W	W W W D W	W W D W W	L W W W D	W W L W D	L L W W W	L W D L L	W W W W W	W W W W W	W W

Goalkeepers

Scott Carson
Jerzy Dudek
Jose Reina

Defenders

Daniel Agger
Antonio Barragan
Jamie Carragher
Steve Finnan
Sami Hyypia
Miguel Josemi
Jan Kromkamp
Carl Medjani
David Raven
John Arne Riise
Djimi Traore
Stephen Warnock
Zak Whitbread

Midfielders

Paul Anderson
Steven Gerrard
Dietmar Hamann
Harry Kewell
Darren Potter
Momo Sissoko
Xabi Alonso
Boudewijn Zenden

Forwards

Milan Baros
Djibril Cisse
Peter Crouch
Robbie Fowler
Anthony Le Tallec
Javier Luis Garcia
Fernando Morientes
Florent Sinama-P

KEY: On all match · On bench · Subbed or sent off (Counting game) · Subbed or sent off (playing less than 70 mins) · Subbed on from bench (Counting Game) · Subbed on (playing less than 70 mins) · Subbed on and then subbed or sent off (Counting Game) · Subbed on and then subbed or sent off (playing less than 70 mins) · Not in 16

KEY PLAYERS - GOALSCORERS

Djibril Cisse

Goals in the League	9
Goals in all competitions	19
Assists League goals scored by a team mate where the player delivered the final pass	3
Contribution to Attacking Power Average number of mins between League team goals while on pitch	62
Player Strike Rate Average number of minutes between League goals scored by player	191
Club Strike Rate Average minutes between League goals scored by club	60

	PLAYER	GOALS LGE	GOALS ALL	ASSISTS	POWER	S RATE
1	Djibril Cisse	9	19	3	62	191 mins
2	Javier Luis Garcia	7	11	4	55	227 mins
3	Peter Crouch	8	13	8	52	265 mins
4	Steven Gerrard	10	23	13	57	272 mins

KEY PLAYERS - MIDFIELDERS

Steven Gerrard

Goals in the League	10
Goals in all competitions	23
Assists League goals scored by a team mate where the player delivered the final pass	13
Defensive Rating Average number of mins between League goals conceded while on the pitch	151
Contribution to Attacking Power Average number of minutes between League team goals while on pitch	57
Scoring Difference Defensive Rating minus Contribution to Attacking Power	94

	PLAYER	GOALS LGE	GOALS ALL	ASSISTS	DEF RATE	POWER	SC DIFF
1	Steven Gerrard	10	23	13	151	57	94 mins
2	Momo Sissoko	0	0	2	150	67	83 mins
3	Harry Kewell	3	3	4	134	56	78 mins
4	Xabi Alonso	3	5	5	135	70	65 mins

PLAYER APPEARANCES

	AGE (on 01/07/06)	IN NAMED 16	APPEARANCES	COUNTING GAMES	MINUTES ON PITCH	APPEARANCES	MINUTES ON PITCH	THIS SEASON	HOME COUNTRY
Goalkeepers									
Scott Carson	20	19	0	0	0	4	360	-	England
Jerzy Dudek	33	22	6	5	458	6	458	2	Poland (29)
Jose Reina	23	35	33	33	2962	49	4432	7	Spain (5)
Defenders									
Daniel Agger	21	5	4	4	360	4	360	3	Denmark (19)
Antonio Barragan	18	0	0	0	0	1	12	-	Spain
Jamie Carragher	28	37	36	36	3240	53	4800	7	England (10)
Steve Finnan	30	35	33	33	2957	49	4348	4	Rep of Ireland (31)
Sami Hyypia	32	37	35	34	3063	54	4784	4	Finland (42)
Miguel Josemi	26	12	6	2	264	10	624	-	Spain
Jan Kromkamp	25	14	13	5	608	17	773	5	Holland (3)
David Raven	21	0	0	0	0	1	90	-	England
John Arne Riise	25	34	31	23	2261	47	3555	7	Norway (40)
Djimi Traore	26	24	15	8	812	24	1401	-	France
Stephen Warnock	24	27	20	11	1314	29	1874	-	England
Zak Whitbread	22	1	0	0	0	2	180	-	United States
Midfielders									
Paul Anderson	17	0	0	0	0	0	0	-	England
Steven Gerrard	26	32	32	30	2723	50	4057	7	England (10)
Dietmar Hamann	32	22	17	10	1146	30	1968	1	Germany (19)
Harry Kewell	27	27	27	19	2004	41	2747	2	Australia (42)
Darren Potter	21	1	0	0	0	4	172	-	England
Momo Sissoko	21	28	26	20	1954	43	3334	1	Mali (66)
Xabi Alonso	24	36	35	26	2572	49	3769	5	Spain (5)
Boudewijn Zenden	29	7	7	3	451	13	771	-	Holland
Forwards									
Milan Baros	24	2	2	0	40	2	40	9	Czech Republic (2)
Djibril Cisse	24	34	33	15	1722	50	2644	9	France (8)
Peter Crouch	25	32	32	19	2123	48	3246	5	England (10)
Robbie Fowler	31	15	14	5	781	16	866	-	England
Javier Luis Garcia	28	31	30	12	1587	46	2767	10	Spain (5)
Fernando Morientes	30	30	28	17	1830	43	2723	4	Spain (5)
F. Sinama-Pongolle	21	9	7	1	274	15	481	-	France

KEY: LEAGUE ALL COMPS CAPS (MAY FIFA RANKING)

TEAM OF THE SEASON

REINA — CG 33 DR 141

FINNAN — CG 33 DR 156

HYYPIA — CG 34 DR 139

CARRAGHER — CG 36 DR 135

RIISE — CG 23 DR 188

GERRARD — CG 30 SD +94

ALONSO — CG 26 SD +65

SISSOKO — CG 20 SD +83

KEWELL — CG 19 SD +78

CROUCH — CG 19 AP 52

CISSE — CG 15 SR 191

KEY: DR = Defensive Rate, SD = Scoring Difference AP = Attacking Power SR = Strike Rate, CG=Counting games – League games playing at least 70 minutes

TOP POINT EARNERS

Fernando Morientes

Counting Games League games when player was on pitch for at least 70 minutes	17
Average points Average League points taken in Counting games	2.53
Club Average points Average points taken in League games	2.16

	PLAYER	GAMES	PTS
1	Fernando Morientes	17	2.53
2	John Arne Riise	23	2.35
3	Steve Finnan	33	2.24
4	Momo Sissoko	20	2.20
5	Jamie Carragher	36	2.17
6	Djibril Cisse	15	2.13
7	Steven Gerrard	30	2.13
8	Jose Reina	33	2.12
9	Sami Hyypia	34	2.12
10	Xabi Alonso	26	2.08

KEY PLAYERS - DEFENDERS

John Arne Riise

Goals Conceded in the League Number of League goals conceded while the player was on the pitch	12
Goals Conceded in all competitions Total number of goals conceded while the player was on the pitch	23
League minutes played Number of minutes played in league matches	2261
Clean Sheets In games when the player was on pitch for at least 70 minutes	16
Defensive Rating Average number of mins between League goals conceded while on the pitch	188
Club Defensive Rating Average number of mins between League goals conceded by the club this season	137

	PLAYER	CON LGE	CON ALL	MINS	C SHEETS	DEF RATE
1	John Arne Riise	12	23	2261	16	188 mins
2	Steve Finnan	19	32	2957	21	156 mins
3	Stephen Warnock	9	16	1314	7	146 mins
4	Sami Hyypia	22	37	3063	20	139 mins

KEY GOALKEEPER

Jose Reina

Goals Conceded in the League Number of League goals conceded while the player was on the pitch	21
Goals Conceded in all competitions Total number of goals conceded while the player was on the pitch	32
League minutes played Number of minutes played in league matches	2962
Clean Sheets In games when the player was on pitch for at least 70 minutes	20
Goals to Shots Ratio The average number of shots on target per each League goal conceded	5.1
Defensive Rating Ave mins between League goals conceded while on the pitch	141

BOOKINGS

Momo Sissoko

League Yellow	10
League Red	1
All competitions Yellow	13
All competitions Red	1

League Average 177 mins between cards

	PLAYER	LEAGUE Y	LEAGUE R	TOTAL Y	TOTAL R	AVE
1	Sissoko	10Y	1R	13Y	1R	177
2	Xabi Alonso	8	1	11	1	285
3	Luis Garcia	4	0	6	0	396
4	Dudek	1	0	1	0	458
5	Crouch	4	0	5	0	530
6	Gerrard	4	1	5	1	544
7	Cisse	3	0	4	0	574
8	Carragher	5	0	9	0	648
9	Traore	1	0	2	0	812
10	Kewell	2	0	3	0	1002
11	Hyypia	3	0	4	0	1021
12	Hamann	1	0	5	0	1146
13	Warnock	1	0	2	0	1314
14	Finnan	2	0	2	0	1478
15	Morientes	1	0	1	0	1830
	Other	0	1	3	1	
	TOTAL	50	4	76	4	

ARSENAL

Thierry Henry timed his signing to perfection, dispelling the Champions League disappointment at a stroke. We are used to seeing Henry claim the Premier Golden Boot but this year he also became the club's record scorer and celebrated by finally grabbing a Strike Rate below 100. He scored a league goal every 99 minutes – an average 25 minutes better than rival van Nistelrooy.

After Henry, it was a long way down to **Robert Pires** as the next entry in our charts with a Strike Rate of 309. New signing **Alexander Hleb** snuck into our top ten midfielders on Scoring Difference.

Jens Lehmann was an ever-present in the league and managed a Defensive Rating of a goal conceded every 110 minutes behind an injury hit defence. It was the third best in the division.

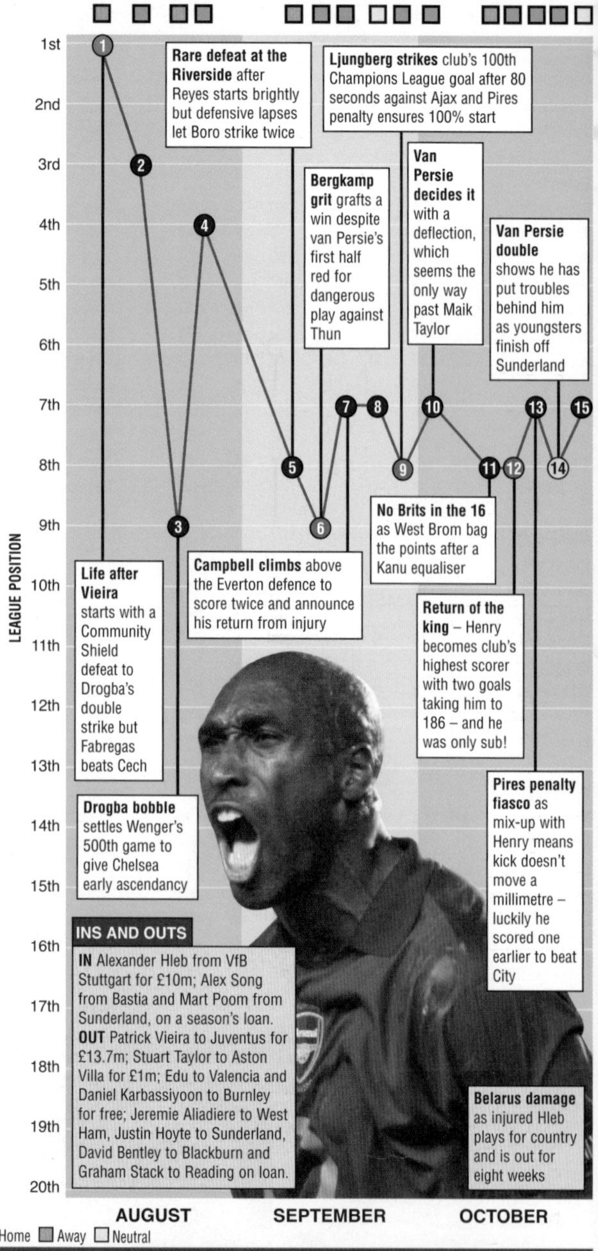

NICKNAME: THE GUNNERS

KEY: Won / Drawn / Lost

1	facsh	**Chelsea**	A	L	1-2	Fabregas 64
2	prem	**Newcastle**	H	W	2-0	Henry 81 pen; van Persie 87
3	prem	**Chelsea**	A	L	0-1	
4	prem	**Fulham**	H	W	4-1	Cygan 32,90; Henry 53,82
5	prem	**Middlesbrough**	A	L	1-2	Reyes 90
6	ecgpb	**FC Thun**	H	W	2-1	Gilberto Silva 51; Bergkamp 90
7	prem	**Everton**	H	W	2-0	Campbell 11,30
8	prem	**West Ham**	A	D	0-0	
9	ecgpb	**Ajax**	A	W	2-1	Ljungberg 2; Pires 69 pen
10	prem	**Birmingham**	H	W	1-0	van Persie 81
11	prem	**West Brom**	A	L	1-2	Senderos 17
12	ecgpb	**Sparta Prague**	A	W	2-0	Henry 21,74
13	prem	**Man City**	H	W	1-0	Pires 61 pen
14	ccr3	**Sunderland**	A	W	3-0	Eboue 61; van Persie 67 pen,87
15	prem	**Tottenham**	A	D	1-1	Pires 77
16	ecgpb	**Sparta Prague**	H	W	3-0	Henry 23; van Persie 81,86
17	prem	**Sunderland**	H	W	3-1	van Persie 12; Henry 36,82
18	prem	**Wigan**	A	W	3-2	van Persie 12; Henry 21,42
19	ecgpb	**FC Thun**	A	W	1-0	Pires 88 pen
20	prem	**Blackburn**	H	W	3-0	Fabregas 4; Henry 45; van Persie 90
21	ccr4	**Reading**	H	W	3-0	Reyes 12; van Persie 42; Lupoli 65
22	prem	**Bolton**	A	L	0-2	
23	ecgpb	**Ajax**	H	D	0-0	
24	prem	**Newcastle**	A	L	0-1	
25	prem	**Chelsea**	H	L	0-2	
26	ccqf	**Doncaster**	A	W	3-1*	Owusu-Abeyie 63; Gilberto Silva 120 (*on penalties)
27	prem	**Charlton**	A	W	1-0	Reyes 58
28	prem	**Portsmouth**	H	W	4-0	Bergkamp 7; Reyes 13; Henry 37,43 pen
29	prem	**Aston Villa**	A	D	0-0	
30	prem	**Man Utd**	H	D	0-0	
31	facr3	**Cardiff**	H	W	2-1	Pires 6,18
32	ccsfl1	**Wigan**	A	L	0-1	
33	prem	**Middlesbrough**	H	W	7-0	Henry 20,30,68; Senderos 22; Pires 45; Gilberto Silva 59; Hleb 84
34	prem	**Everton**	A	L	0-1	
35	ccsfl2	**Wigan**	H	W	2-1	Henry 65; van Persie 107
36	facr4	**Bolton**	A	L	0-1	
37	prem	**West Ham**	H	L	2-3	Henry 45; Pires 88
38	prem	**Birmingham**	A	W	2-0	Adebayor 21; Henry 63
39	prem	**Bolton**	H	D	1-1	Gilberto Silva 90
40	prem	**Liverpool**	A	L	0-1	
41	eclsl1	**Real Madrid**	A	W	1-0	Henry 47
42	prem	**Blackburn**	A	L	0-1	
43	prem	**Fulham**	A	W	4-0	Henry 31,77; Adebayor 35; Fabregas 86
44	eclsl2	**Real Madrid**	H	D	0-0	
45	prem	**Liverpool**	H	W	2-1	Henry 21,83
46	prem	**Charlton**	H	W	3-0	Pires 13; Adebayor 32; Hleb 49
47	ecqfl1	**Juventus**	H	W	2-0	Fabregas 40; Henry 69
48	prem	**Aston Villa**	H	W	5-0	Adebayor 19; Henry 25,46; van Persie 71; Diaby 80
49	ecqfl2	**Juventus**	A	D	0-0	
50	prem	**Man Utd**	A	L	0-2	
51	prem	**Portsmouth**	A	D	1-1	Henry 36
52	prem	**West Brom**	H	W	3-1	Hleb 44; Pires 76; Bergkamp 89
53	ecsfl1	**Villarreal**	H	W	1-0	Toure 41
54	prem	**Tottenham**	H	D	1-1	Henry 83
55	ecsfl2	**Villarreal**	A	D	0-0	
56	prem	**Sunderland**	A	W	3-0	Collins, D 28 og; Fabregas 40; Henry 43
57	prem	**Man City**	A	W	3-1	Ljungberg 30; Reyes 78,84
58	prem	**Wigan**	H	W	4-2	Pires 8; Henry 35,56,76 pen
59	ecfin	**Barcelona**	A	L	1-2	Campbell 37

LEAGUE POSITION
1st
2nd
3rd
4th
5th
6th
7th
8th
9th
10th
11th
12th
13th
14th
15th
16th
17th
18th
19th
20th
Rare defeat at the Riverside after Reyes starts brightly but defensive lapses let Boro strike twice
Ljungberg strikes club's 100th Champions League goal after 80 seconds against Ajax and Pires penalty ensures 100% start
Bergkamp grit grafts a win despite van Persie's first half red for dangerous play against Thun
Van Persie decides it with a deflection, which seems the only way past Maik Taylor
Van Persie double shows he has put troubles behind him as youngsters finish off Sunderland
No Brits in the 16 as West Brom bag the points after a Kanu equaliser
Life after Vieira starts with a Community Shield defeat to Drogba's double strike but Fabregas beats Cech
Campbell climbs above the Everton defence to score twice and announce his return from injury
Return of the king – Henry becomes club's highest scorer with two goals taking him to 186 – and he was only sub!
Drogba bobble settles Wenger's 500th game to give Chelsea early ascendancy
Pires penalty fiasco as mix-up with Henry means kick doesn't move a millimetre – luckily he scored one earlier to beat City
INS AND OUTS
IN Alexander Hleb from VfB Stuttgart for £10m; Alex Song from Bastia and Mart Poom from Sunderland, on a season's loan. **OUT** Patrick Vieira to Juventus for £13.7m; Stuart Taylor to Aston Villa for £1m; Edu to Valencia and Daniel Karbassiyoon to Burnley for free; Jeremie Aliadiere to West Ham, Justin Hoyte to Sunderland, David Bentley to Blackburn and Graham Stack to Reading on loan.
Belarus damage as injured Hleb plays for country and is out for eight weeks
AUGUST
SEPTEMBER
OCTOBER
Home Away Neutral

ATTENDANCES

HOME GROUND: HIGHBURY **CAPACITY:** 38500 **AVERAGE LEAGUE AT HOME:** 38184

41	Real Madrid	80000	30	Man Utd	38313	4	Fulham	37867	5	Middlesboro	28075
59	Barcelona	79500	46	Charlton	38223	29	Aston Villa	37114	27	Charlton	27111
50	Man Utd	70908	28	Portsmouth	38223	34	Everton	36920	38	Birmingham	27075
1	Chelsea	58014	45	Liverpool	38221	31	Cardiff	36552	22	Bolton	26792
24	Newcastle	52297	37	West Ham	38216	21	Reading	36167	11	West Brom	26604
9	Ajax	50000	17	Sunderland	38210	15	Tottenham	36154	18	Wigan	25004
49	Juventus	50000	39	Bolton	38193	44	Real Madrid	35487	55	Villarreal	23000
14	Sunderland	47366	20	Blackburn	38192	47	Juventus	35472	42	Blackburn	22504
40	Liverpool	44065	13	Man City	38189	53	Villarreal	35438	43	Fulham	22397
56	Sunderland	44003	33	Middlesboro	38186	23	Ajax	35376	51	Portsmouth	20230
3	Chelsea	42136	48	Aston Villa	38183	16	Sp Prague	35155	36	Bolton	13326
57	Man City	41875	52	West Brom	38167	8	West Ham	34742	12	Sp Prague	12528
58	Wigan	38359	7	Everton	38121	35	Wigan	34692	32	Wigan	12181
25	Chelsea	38347	2	Newcastle	38072	6	FC Thun	34498	26	Doncaster	10006
54	Tottenham	38326	10	Birmingham	37891	19	FC Thun	32000			

Henry backs Wenger's youngsters

Final Position: 4th

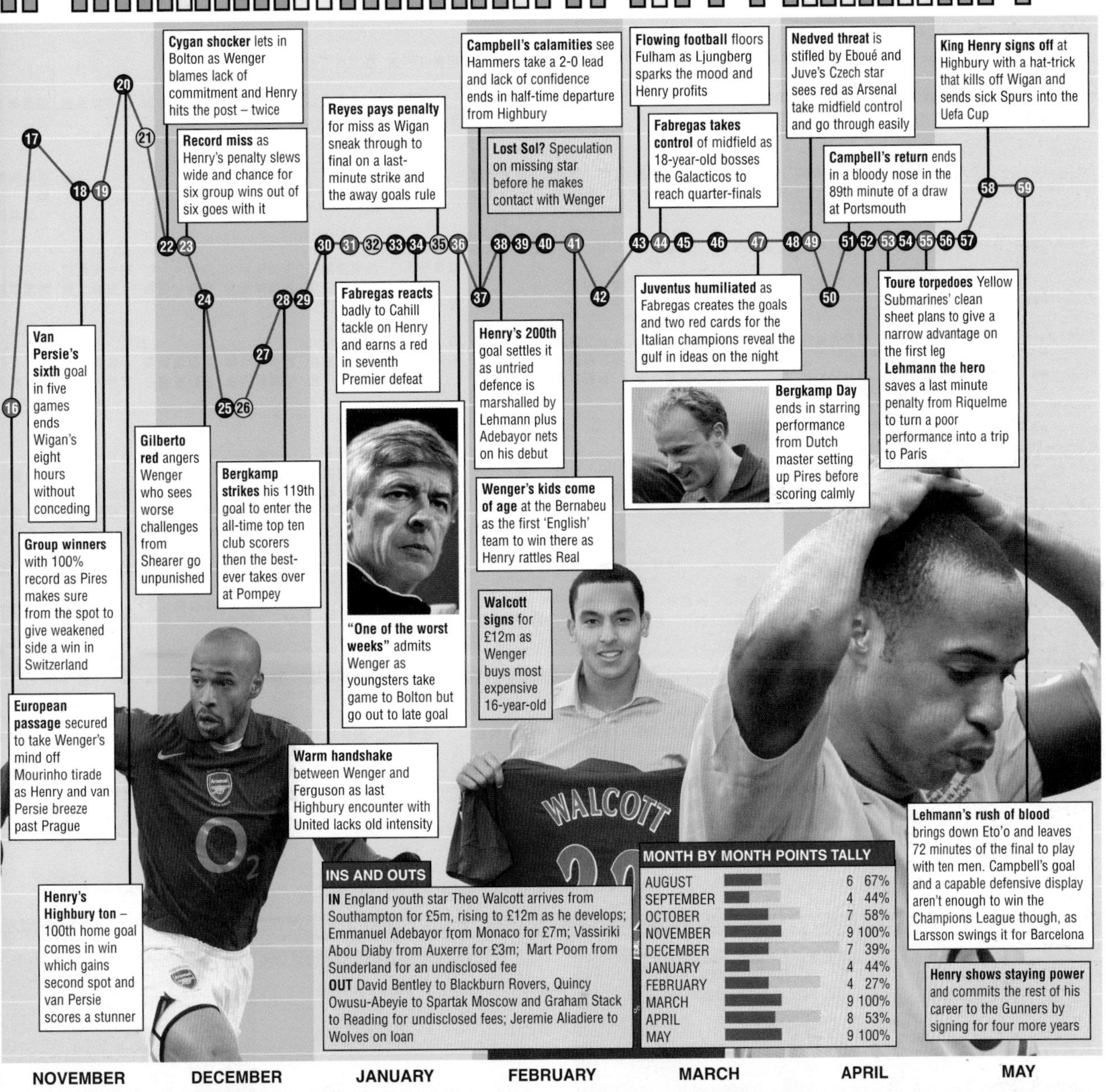
KEY: League Champions Lge UEFA Cup FA Cup League Cup Other
Cygan shocker lets in Bolton as Wenger blames lack of commitment and Henry hits the post – twice
Record miss as Henry's penalty slews wide and chance for six group wins out of six goes with it
Reyes pays penalty for miss as Wigan sneak through to final on a last-minute strike and the away goals rule
Campbell's calamities see Hammers take a 2-0 lead and lack of confidence ends in half-time departure from Highbury
Lost Sol? Speculation on missing star before he makes contact with Wenger
Flowing football floors Fulham as Ljungberg sparks the mood and Henry profits
Fabregas takes control of midfield as 18-year-old bosses the Galacticos to reach quarter-finals
Nedved threat is stifled by Eboué and Juve's Czech star sees red as Arsenal take midfield control and go through easily
Campbell's return ends in a bloody nose in the 89th minute of a draw at Portsmouth
King Henry signs off at Highbury with a hat-trick that kills off Wigan and sends sick Spurs into the Uefa Cup
Van Persie's sixth goal in five games ends Wigan's eight hours without conceding
Fabregas reacts badly to Cahill tackle on Henry and earns a red in seventh Premier defeat
Henry's 200th goal settles it as untried defence is marshalled by Lehmann plus Adebayor nets on his debut
Juventus humiliated as Fabregas creates the goals and two red cards for the Italian champions reveal the gulf in ideas on the night
Toure torpedoes Yellow Submarines' clean sheet plans to give a narrow advantage on the first leg
Lehmann the hero saves a last minute penalty from Riquelme to turn a poor performance into a trip to Paris
Bergkamp Day ends in starring performance from Dutch master setting up Pires before scoring calmly
Gilberto red angers Wenger who sees worse challenges from Shearer go unpunished
Bergkamp strikes his 119th goal to enter the all-time top ten club scorers then the best-ever takes over at Pompey
Wenger's kids come of age at the Bernabeu as the first 'English' team to win there as Henry rattles Real
Group winners with 100% record as Pires makes sure from the spot to give weakened side a win in Switzerland
"One of the worst weeks" admits Wenger as youngsters take game to Bolton but go out to late goal
Walcott signs for £12m as Wenger buys most expensive 16-year-old
European passage secured to take Wenger's mind off Mourinho tirade as Henry and van Persie breeze past Prague
Warm handshake between Wenger and Ferguson as last Highbury encounter with United lacks old intensity
Lehmann's rush of blood brings down Eto'o and leaves 72 minutes of the final to play with ten men. Campbell's goal and a capable defensive display aren't enough to win the Champions League though, as Larsson swings it for Barcelona
Henry's Highbury ton – 100th home goal comes in win which gains second spot and van Persie scores a stunner
Henry shows staying power and commits the rest of his career to the Gunners by signing for four more years
INS AND OUTS
IN England youth star Theo Walcott arrives from Southampton for £5m, rising to £12m as he develops; Emmanuel Adebayor from Monaco for £7m; Vassiriki Abou Diaby from Auxerre for £3m; Mart Poom from Sunderland for an undisclosed fee
OUT David Bentley to Blackburn Rovers, Quincy Owusu-Abeyie to Spartak Moscow and Graham Stack to Reading for undisclosed fees; Jeremie Aliadiere to Wolves on loan
WALCOTT
NOVEMBER
DECEMBER
JANUARY
FEBRUARY
MARCH
APRIL
MAY

MONTH BY MONTH POINTS TALLY

Month	Points	%
AUGUST	6	67%
SEPTEMBER	4	44%
OCTOBER	7	58%
NOVEMBER	9	100%
DECEMBER	7	39%
JANUARY	4	44%
FEBRUARY	4	27%
MARCH	9	100%
APRIL	8	53%
MAY	9	100%

GOAL ATTEMPTS

FOR – Goal attempts recorded in League games

	HOME	AWAY	TOTAL	AVE
shots on target	167	107	274	7.2
shots off target	86	102	188	4.9
TOTAL	253	209	462	12.2

Ratio of goals to shots – Average number of shots on target per League goal scored	4
Accuracy rating – Average percentage of total goal attempts which were on target	59.3

AGAINST – Goal attempts recorded in League games

	HOME	AWAY	TOTAL	AVE
shots on target	67	86	153	4
shots off target	63	107	170	4.5
TOTAL	130	193	323	8.5

Ratio of goals to shots – Average number of shots on target per League goal scored	4.9
Accuracy rating – Average percentage of total goal attempts which were on target	47.4

GOALS

Thierry Henry

League	27
FA Cup	0
League Cup	1
Europe	5
Other	0
TOTAL	33

League Average 99 mins between goals

	PLAYER	LGE	FAC	LC	Euro	TOT	AVE
1	Henry	27	0	1	5	33	99
2	Pires	7	2	0	2	11	309
3	van Persie	6	0	4	2	12	202
4	Reyes	5	0	1	0	6	357
5	Adebayor	4	0	0	0	4	253
6	Fabregas	3	0	0	1	5	883
7	Hleb	3	0	0	0	3	492
8	Campbell	2	0	0	1	3	877
9	Senderos	2	0	0	0	2	837
10	Gilberto Silva	2	0	1	1	4	1434
11	Cygan	2	0	0	0	2	467
12	Bergkamp	2	0	0	1	3	507
13	Ljungberg	1	0	0	1	2	1727
14	Diaby	1	0	0	0	1	795
15	Lupoli	0	0	1	0	1	
	Other	1	0	2	1	4	
	TOTAL	68	2	10	15	96	

SQUAD APPEARANCES

Match: 1 2 3 4 5 | 6 7 8 9 10 | 11 12 13 14 15 | 16 17 18 19 20 | 21 22 23 24 25 | 26 27 28 29 30 | 31 32 33 34 35 | 36 37 38 39 40 | 41 42 43 44 45 | 46 47 48 49 50 | 51 52 53 54 55 | 56 57 58

Venue: A H A H A | H H A A H | A A H A A | H H A A H | H A H A H | A A H A H | H A H A H | A H A H A | A A A H H | H H H A A | A H H H A | A A H

Competition: O L L L L | C L L C L | L C L W L | C L L C L | W L C L L | W L L L L | F W L L W | F L L L L | C L L C L | L C L C L | L L C L C | L L L

Result: L W L W L | W W D W W | L W W W D | W W W W W | W L D L L | W W W D D | W L W L W | L L W D L | W L W D W | W W W D L | D W W D D | W W W

Goalkeepers
- Manuel Almunia
- Mark Howard
- Jens Lehmann
- Mart Poom

Defenders
- Sol Campbell
- Gael Clichy
- Ashley Cole
- Matthew Connolly
- Pascal Cygan
- Johan Djourou
- Emmanuel Eboue
- Kerrea Gilbert
- Justin Hoyte
- Etame Mayer Lauren
- Philippe Senderos
- Habib Kolo Toure

Midfielders
- Patrick Cregg
- Vassiriki Abou Diaby
- Cesc Fabregas
- Mathieu Flamini
- Gilberto Silva
- Alexander Hleb
- Sebastian Larsson
- Fredrik Ljungberg
- Fabrice Muamba
- Robert Pires
- Alexandre Song

Forwards
- Emmanuel Adebayor
- Nicklas Bendtner
- Dennis Bergkamp
- Thierry Henry
- Arturo Lupoli
- Quincy Owusu-Abeyie
- Jose Antonio Reyes
- Anthony Stokes
- Robin van Persie
- Theo Walcott

KEY: On all match | On bench | Subbed or sent off (Counting game) | Subbed or sent off (playing less than 70 mins) | Subbed on from bench (Counting Game) | Subbed on (playing less than 70 mins) | Subbed on and then subbed or sent off (Counting Game) | Subbed on and then subbed or sent off (playing less than 70 mins) | Not in 16

KEY PLAYERS - GOALSCORERS

Thierry Henry	
Goals in the League	27
Goals in all competitions	33
Assists League goals scored by a team mate where the player delivered the final pass	11
Contribution to Attacking Power Average number of minutes between League team goals while on pitch	47
Player Strike Rate Average number of minutes between League goals scored by player	99
Club Strike Rate Average minutes between League goals scored by club	50

	PLAYER	GOALS LGE	GOALS ALL	ASSISTS	POWER	S RATE
1	Thierry Henry	27	33	11	47	99 mins
2	Robert Pires	7	11	5	46	309 mins
3	Jose Antonio Reyes	5	6	17	42	357 mins
4	Alexander Hleb	3	3	1	64	492 mins

KEY PLAYERS - MIDFIELDERS

Alexander Hleb	
Goals in the League	3
Goals in all competitions	3
Assists League goals scored by a team mate where the player delivered the final pass	1
Defensive Rating Average number of mins between League goals conceded while on the pitch	134
Contribution to Attacking Power Average number of minutes between League team goals while on pitch	64
Scoring Difference Defensive Rating minus Contribution to Attacking Power	70

	PLAYER	GOALS LGE	GOALS ALL	ASSISTS	DEF RATE	POWER	SC DIFF
1	Alexander Hleb	3	3	1	134	64	70 mins
2	Gilberto Silva	2	4	0	115	46	69 mins
3	Cesc Fabregas	3	5	8	120	56	64 mins
4	Fredrik Ljungberg	1	2	6	115	58	57 mins

PLAYER APPEARANCES

	AGE (on 01/07/06)	IN NAMED 16	APPEARANCES	COUNTING GAMES	MINUTES ON PITCH	APPEARANCES	MINUTES ON PITCH	THIS SEASON	HOME COUNTRY
Goalkeepers									
Manuel Almunia	29	33	0	0	0	13	1211	-	Spain
Mark Howard	19	0	0	0	0	0	0	-	England
Jens Lehmann	36	38	38	38	3420	47	4158	7	Germany (19)
Mart Poom	34	5	0	0	0	0	0	4	Estonia (61)
Defenders									
Sol Campbell	31	20	20	19	1753	29	2593	3	England (10)
Gael Clichy	20	8	7	5	467	11	732	-	France
Ashley Cole	25	11	11	9	892	15	1252	4	England (10)
Matthew Connolly	0	0	0	0	0	0	0	-	England
Pascal Cygan	32	17	12	10	934	19	1407	-	France
Johan Djourou	19	18	7	6	564	12	1044	3	Switzerland (35)
Emmanuel Eboue	23	23	18	10	1130	32	2267	8	Ivory Coast (32)
Kerrea Gilbert	19	2	2	1	98	9	595	-	England
Justin Hoyte	21	0	0	0	0	0	0	-	England
Etame Mayer Lauren	29	22	22	22	1962	31	2718	-	Cameroon
Philippe Senderos	21	30	20	18	1674	35	3084	10	Switzerland (35)
Habib Kolo Toure	25	33	33	33	2970	46	4140	9	Ivory Coast (32)
Midfielders									
Patrick Cregg	20	0	0	0	0	1	2	-	Rep of Ireland
Vassiriki Abou Diaby	20	13	12	7	795	16	945	-	France
Cesc Fabregas	19	35	35	28	2650	50	3702	1	Spain (5)
Mathieu Flamini	22	33	31	17	1837	49	3287	-	France
Gilberto Silva	29	33	33	31	2867	47	4187	5	Brazil (1)
Alexander Hleb	25	27	25	14	1475	39	2593	-	Belarus
Sebastian Larsson	21	4	3	2	207	9	548	-	Sweden
Fredrik Ljungberg	29	26	25	17	1727	37	2786	4	Sweden (16)
Fabrice Muamba	18	0	0	0	0	2	180	-	Congo DR
Robert Pires	32	35	33	21	2163	48	3041	-	France
Alexandre Song	18	9	5	2	255	9	522	-	Cameroon
Forwards									
Emmanuel Adebayor	22	13	13	10	1012	13	1012	4	Togo (61)
Nicklas Bendtner	18	0	0	0	0	3	97	-	Denmark
Dennis Bergkamp	37	27	24	8	1013	31	1436	-	Holland
Thierry Henry	28	32	32	28	2670	45	3770	8	France (8)
Arturo Lupoli	19	2	1	0	9	5	248	-	Italy
Quincy Owusu-Abeyie	20	5	4	0	47	13	523	-	Holland
Jose Antonio Reyes	22	27	26	18	1785	43	2956	3	Spain (5)
Anthony Stokes	17	0	0	0	0	1	3	-	Rep of Ireland
Robin van Persie	22	26	24	8	1211	37	1881	6	Holland (3)
Theo Walcott	17	1	0	0	0	0	0	1	England (10)

KEY: LEAGUE ALL COMPS CAPS (MAY FIFA RANKING)

TEAM OF THE SEASON

LEHMANN CG 38 DR 110

LAUREN CG 22 DR 123

CAMPBELL CG 19 DR 110

SENDEROS CG 18 DR 98

TOURE CG 33 DR 114

LJUNGBERG CG 17 SD +57

FABREGAS CG 28 SD +64

GILBERTO CG 31 SD +69

HLEB CG 14 SD +70

REYES CG 18 AP 42

HENRY CG 28 SR 99

KEY: DR = Defensive Rate, SD = Scoring Difference AP = Attacking Power SR = Strike Rate, CG=Counting games – League games playing at least 70 minutes

TOP POINT EARNERS

Jose Antonio Reyes

Counting Games League games when player was on pitch for at least 70 minutes	18
Average points Average League points taken in Counting games	1.94
Club Average points Average points taken in League games	1.76

	PLAYER	GAMES	PTS
1	Jose Antonio Reyes	18	1.94
2	Gilberto Silva	31	1.90
3	Thierry Henry	28	1.86
4	Sol Campbell	19	1.84
5	Habib Kolo Toure	33	1.82
6	Cesc Fabregas	28	1.79
7	Jens Lehmann	38	1.76
8	Alexander Hleb	14	1.71
9	Etame Mayer Lauren	22	1.68
10	Robert Pires	21	1.67

KEY PLAYERS - DEFENDERS

Etame Mayer Lauren

Goals Conceded in the League Number of League goals conceded while the player was on the pitch	16
Goals Conceded in all competitions Total number of goals conceded while the player was on the pitch	22
League minutes played Number of minutes played in league matches	1962
Clean Sheets In games when the player was on pitch for at least 70 minutes	11
Defensive Rating Average number of mins between League goals conceded while on the pitch	123
Club Defensive Rating Average number of mins between League goals conceded by the club this season	110

	PLAYER	CON LGE	CON ALL	MINS	C SHEETS	DEF RATE
1	Etame Mayer Lauren	16	22	1962	11	123 mins
2	Habib Kolo Toure	26	32	2970	14	114 mins
3	Sol Campbell	16	22	1753	9	110 mins
4	Philippe Senderos	17	25	1674	6	98 mins

KEY GOALKEEPER

Jens Lehmann

Goals Conceded in the League Number of League goals conceded while the player was on the pitch	31
Goals Conceded in all competitions Total number of goals conceded while the player was on the pitch	33
League minutes played Number of minutes played in league matches	3420
Clean Sheets In games when the player was on pitch for at least 70 minutes	16
Goals to Shots Ratio The average number of shots on target per each League goal conceded	4.9
Defensive Rating Ave mins between League goals conceded while on the pitch	110

BOOKINGS

Pascal Cygan

League Yellow	4
League Red	0
All competitions Yellow	7
All competitions Red	0

League Average **233** mins between cards

	PLAYER	LEAGUE 4Y	LEAGUE 0R	TOTAL 7Y	TOTAL 0R	AVE
1	Cygan	4Y	0R	7Y	0R	233
2	Clichy	2	0	3	0	233
3	Cole	3	0	3	0	297
4	Lauren	6	0	7	0	327
5	Reyes	5	0	10	0	357
6	Diaby	2	0	3	0	397
7	Gilberto Silva	6	1	6	1	409
8	Fabregas	5	1	7	1	441
9	Flamini	4	0	6	0	459
10	Bergkamp	2	0	2	0	506
11	van Persie	2	0	4	1	605
12	Senderos	2	0	4	0	837
13	Ljungberg	2	0	2	0	863
14	Toure	3	0	5	0	990
15	Pires	2	0	2	0	1081
	Other	4	0	9	1	
	TOTAL	54	2	80	4	

TOTTENHAM HOTSPUR

The season ended with a long sick list and a bitter pill to swallow as Arsenal leapt into the last Champions League place. However, having the better of two 1-1 draws against the Gunners and heading them for much of the season, suggests Martin Jol has put together a side that can challenge for a top four spot again.

Robbie Keane has emerged as the fourth best poacher in the division with 16 goals at a Strike Rate of one every 144 minutes. **Mido** weighed in with 11 at a rate of 192 to give the club two in our top 12 strikers chart. Mido also had the best points average.

Aaron Lennon celebrated his England cap by topping the midfielders chart with **Anthony Gardner** enjoying the best Defensive Rating. **Paul Robinson** conceded one goal for every 5.7 shots on target saved, the fourth best record around.

NICKNAME: SPURS

KEY: Won / Drawn / Lost

1	prem	**Portsmouth**	A	W	2-0	Griffin 45 og; Defoe 64
2	prem	**Middlesbrough**	H	W	2-0	Defoe 49; Mido 75
3	prem	**Blackburn**	A	D	0-0	
4	prem	**Chelsea**	H	L	0-2	
5	prem	**Liverpool**	H	D	0-0	
6	prem	**Aston Villa**	A	D	1-1	Keane 78
7	ccr2	**Grimsby**	A	L	0-1	
8	prem	**Fulham**	H	W	1-0	Defoe 7
9	prem	**Charlton**	A	W	3-2	King 51; Mido 64; Keane 80
10	prem	**Everton**	H	W	2-0	Mido 58; Jenas 63
11	prem	**Man Utd**	A	D	1-1	Jenas 72
12	prem	**Arsenal**	H	D	1-1	King 17
13	prem	**Bolton**	A	L	0-1	
14	prem	**West Ham**	H	D	1-1	Mido 16
15	prem	**Wigan**	A	W	2-1	Keane 8; Davids 77
16	prem	**Sunderland**	H	W	3-2	Mido 37; Keane 51; Carrick 77
17	prem	**Portsmouth**	H	W	3-1	King 57; Mido 84 pen; Defoe 89
18	prem	**Middlesbrough**	A	D	3-3	Keane 25; Jenas 63; Mido 83
19	prem	**Birmingham**	H	W	2-0	Keane 58 pen; Defoe 90
20	prem	**West Brom**	A	L	0-2	
21	prem	**Newcastle**	H	W	2-0	Tainio 43; Mido 66
22	prem	**Man City**	A	W	2-0	Mido 31; Keane 83
23	facr3	**Leicester**	A	L	2-3	Jenas 20; Stalteri 41
24	prem	**Liverpool**	A	L	0-1	
25	prem	**Aston Villa**	H	D	0-0	
26	prem	**Fulham**	A	L	0-1	
27	prem	**Charlton**	H	W	3-1	Defoe 14,46; Jenas 41
28	prem	**Sunderland**	A	D	1-1	Keane 38
29	prem	**Wigan**	H	D	2-2	Mido 24; Defoe 68
30	prem	**Blackburn**	H	W	3-2	Keane 9,42; Mido 70
31	prem	**Chelsea**	A	L	1-2	Jenas 45
32	prem	**Birmingham**	A	W	2-0	Lennon 65; Keane 77
33	prem	**West Brom**	H	W	2-1	Keane 67,88 pen
34	prem	**Newcastle**	A	L	1-3	Keane 19
35	prem	**Man City**	H	W	2-1	Stalteri 44; Carrick 49
36	prem	**Everton**	A	W	1-0	Keane 33 pen
37	prem	**Man Utd**	H	L	1-2	Jenas 53
38	prem	**Arsenal**	A	D	1-1	Keane 66
39	prem	**Bolton**	H	W	1-0	Lennon 60
40	prem	**West Ham**	A	L	1-2	Defoe 35

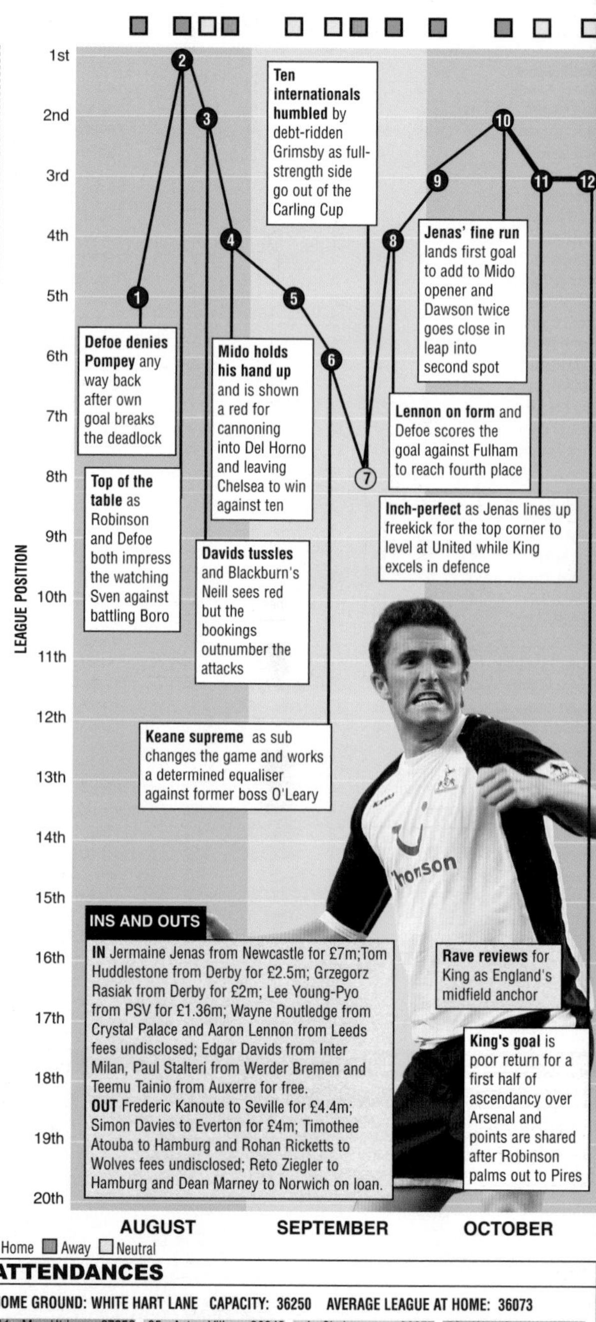

1st
2nd
3rd
4th
5th
6th
7th
8th
9th
10th
11th
12th
13th
14th
15th
16th
17th
18th
19th
20th
LEAGUE POSITION
1
2
3
4
5
6
7
8
9
10
11
12
Ten internationals humbled by debt-ridden Grimsby as full-strength side go out of the Carling Cup
Jenas' fine run lands first goal to add to Mido opener and Dawson twice goes close in leap into second spot
Defoe denies Pompey any way back after own goal breaks the deadlock
Mido holds his hand up and is shown a red for cannoning into Del Horno and leaving Chelsea to win against ten
Lennon on form and Defoe scores the goal against Fulham to reach fourth place
Top of the table as Robinson and Defoe both impress the watching Sven against battling Boro
Inch-perfect as Jenas lines up freekick for the top corner to level at United while King excels in defence
Davids tussles and Blackburn's Neill sees red but the bookings outnumber the attacks
Keane supreme as sub changes the game and works a determined equaliser against former boss O'Leary
INS AND OUTS
IN Jermaine Jenas from Newcastle for £7m;Tom Huddlestone from Derby for £2.5m; Grzegorz Rasiak from Derby for £2m; Lee Young-Pyo from PSV for £1.36m; Wayne Routledge from Crystal Palace and Aaron Lennon from Leeds fees undisclosed; Edgar Davids from Inter Milan, Paul Stalteri from Werder Bremen and Teemu Tainio from Auxerre for free.
OUT Frederic Kanoute to Seville for £4.4m; Simon Davies to Everton for £4m; Timothee Atouba to Hamburg and Rohan Ricketts to Wolves fees undisclosed; Reto Ziegler to Hamburg and Dean Marney to Norwich on loan.
Rave reviews for King as England's midfield anchor
King's goal is poor return for a first half of ascendancy over Arsenal and points are shared after Robinson palms out to Pires
AUGUST
SEPTEMBER
OCTOBER
Home
Away
Neutral

ATTENDANCES

HOME GROUND: WHITE HART LANE CAPACITY: 36250 AVERAGE LEAGUE AT HOME: 36073

11	Man Utd	67856	25	Aston Villa	36243	4	Chelsea	36077	20	West Brom	27510
34	Newcastle	52301	39	Bolton	36179	19	Birmingham	36045	9	Charlton	27111
24	Liverpool	44983	35	Man City	36167	27	Charlton	36034	13	Bolton	26634
31	Chelsea	42243	12	Arsenal	36154	2	Middlesboro	35844	32	Birmingham	26398
22	Man City	40808	14	West Ham	36154	29	Wigan	35676	15	Wigan	22611
36	Everton	39856	33	West Brom	36152	8	Fulham	35427	3	Blackburn	22375
38	Arsenal	38326	5	Liverpool	36148	40	West Ham	34970	26	Fulham	21081
10	Everton	36247	37	Man Utd	36141	28	Sunderland	34700	1	Portsmouth	20215
21	Newcastle	36246	17	Portsmouth	36141	6	Aston Villa	33686	23	Leicester	19844
16	Sunderland	36244	30	Blackburn	36080	18	Middlesboro	27614	7	Grimsby	8206

Sick list means Jol settles for Uefa

Final Position: **5th**

KEY: ● League ● Champions Lge ● UEFA Cup ● FA Cup ○ League Cup ● Other

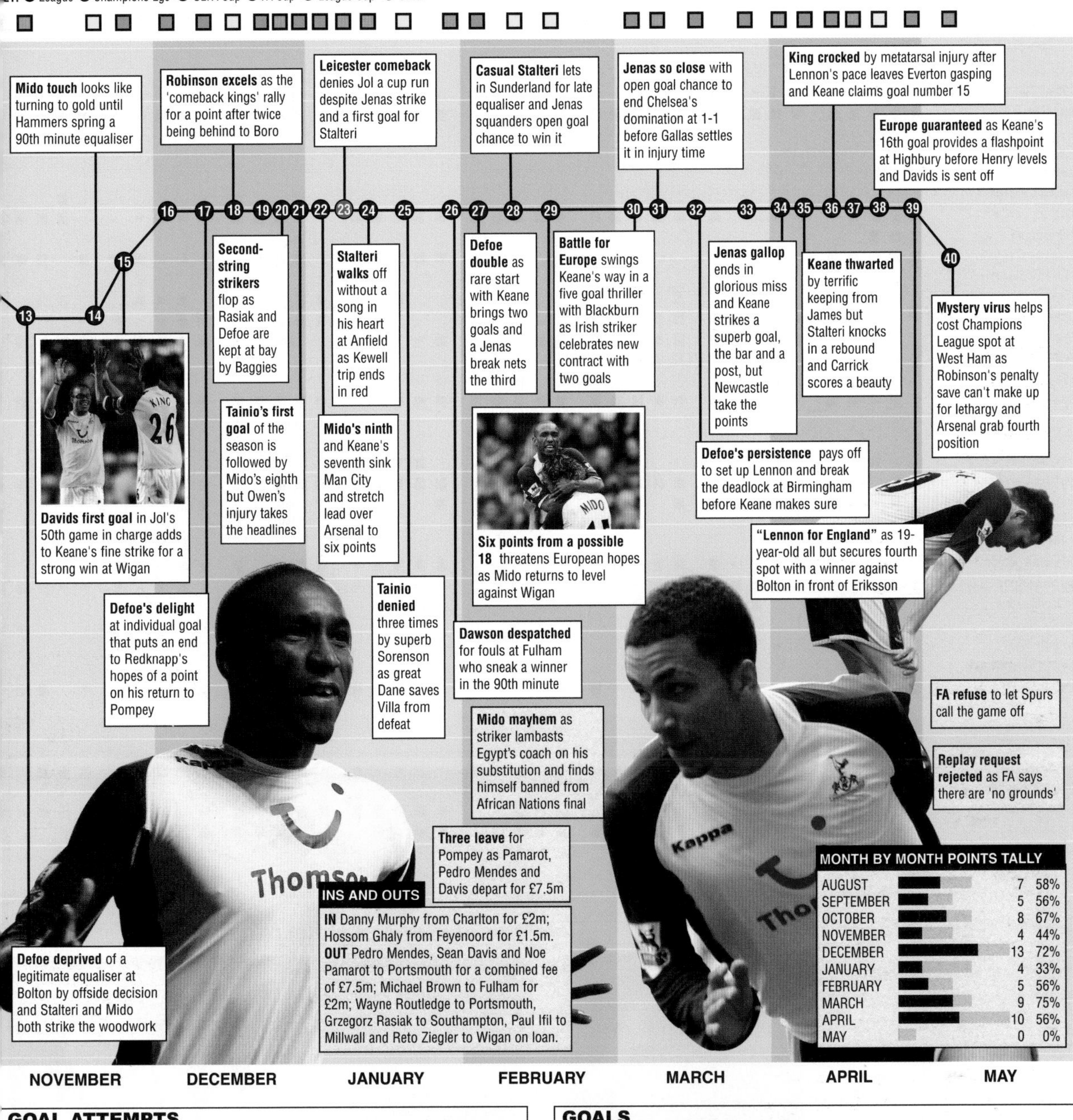

Mido touch looks like turning to gold until Hammers spring a 90th minute equaliser
Robinson excels as the 'comeback kings' rally for a point after twice being behind to Boro
Leicester comeback denies Jol a cup run despite Jenas strike and a first goal for Stalteri
Casual Stalteri lets in Sunderland for late equaliser and Jenas squanders open goal chance to win it
Jenas so close with open goal chance to end Chelsea's domination at 1-1 before Gallas settles it in injury time
King crocked by metatarsal injury after Lennon's pace leaves Everton gasping and Keane claims goal number 15
Europe guaranteed as Keane's 16th goal provides a flashpoint at Highbury before Henry levels and Davids is sent off
13 14 15 16 17 18 19 20 21 22 23 24 25 26 27 28 29 30 31 32 33 34 35 36 37 38 39 40
Second-string strikers flop as Rasiak and Defoe are kept at bay by Baggies
Stalteri walks off without a song in his heart at Anfield as Kewell trip ends in red
Defoe double as rare start with Keane brings two goals and a Jenas break nets the third
Battle for Europe swings Keane's way in a five goal thriller with Blackburn as Irish striker celebrates new contract with two goals
Jenas gallop ends in glorious miss and Keane strikes a superb goal, the bar and a post, but Newcastle take the points
Keane thwarted by terrific keeping from James but Stalteri knocks in a rebound and Carrick scores a beauty
Mystery virus helps cost Champions League spot at West Ham as Robinson's penalty save can't make up for lethargy and Arsenal grab fourth position
Davids first goal in Jol's 50th game in charge adds to Keane's fine strike for a strong win at Wigan
Tainio's first goal of the season is followed by Mido's eighth but Owen's injury takes the headlines
Mido's ninth and Keane's seventh sink Man City and stretch lead over Arsenal to six points
Six points from a possible 18 threatens European hopes as Mido returns to level against Wigan
Defoe's persistence pays off to set up Lennon and break the deadlock at Birmingham before Keane makes sure
"Lennon for England" as 19-year-old all but secures fourth spot with a winner against Bolton in front of Eriksson
Defoe's delight at individual goal that puts an end to Redknapp's hopes of a point on his return to Pompey
Tainio denied three times by superb Sorenson as great Dane saves Villa from defeat
Dawson despatched for fouls at Fulham who sneak a winner in the 90th minute
Mido mayhem as striker lambasts Egypt's coach on his substitution and finds himself banned from African Nations final
FA refuse to let Spurs call the game off
Replay request rejected as FA says there are 'no grounds'
Three leave for Pompey as Pamarot, Pedro Mendes and Davis depart for £7.5m
INS AND OUTS
IN Danny Murphy from Charlton for £2m; Hossom Ghaly from Feyenoord for £1.5m. **OUT** Pedro Mendes, Sean Davis and Noe Pamarot to Portsmouth for a combined fee of £7.5m; Michael Brown to Fulham for £2m; Wayne Routledge to Portsmouth, Grezgorz Rasiak to Southampton, Paul Ifil to Millwall and Reto Ziegler to Wigan on loan.
Defoe deprived of a legitimate equaliser at Bolton by offside decision and Stalteri and Mido both strike the woodwork
NOVEMBER DECEMBER JANUARY FEBRUARY MARCH APRIL MAY

MONTH BY MONTH POINTS TALLY

Month	Points	%
AUGUST	7	58%
SEPTEMBER	5	56%
OCTOBER	8	67%
NOVEMBER	4	44%
DECEMBER	13	72%
JANUARY	4	33%
FEBRUARY	5	56%
MARCH	9	75%
APRIL	10	56%
MAY	0	0%

GOAL ATTEMPTS

FOR – Goal attempts recorded in League games

	HOME	AWAY	TOTAL	AVE
shots on target	136	98	234	6.2
shots off target	110	67	177	4.7
TOTAL	246	165	411	10.8

Ratio of goals to shots – Average number of shots on target per League goal scored	4.4
Accuracy rating – Average percentage of total goal attempts which were on target	56.9

AGAINST – Goal attempts recorded in League games

	HOME	AWAY	TOTAL	AVE
shots on target	91	127	218	5.7
shots off target	85	98	183	4.8
TOTAL	176	225	401	10.6

Ratio of goals to shots – Average number of shots on target per League goal scored	5.7
Accuracy rating – Average percentage of total goal attempts which were on target	54.4

GOALS

Robbie Keane

League	16
FA Cup	0
League Cup	0
Europe	0
Other	0
TOTAL	16

League Average 144 mins between goals

	PLAYER	LGE	FAC	LC	Euro	TOT	AVE
1	Keane	16	0	0	0	16	144
2	Mido	11	0	0	0	11	192
3	Defoe	9	0	0	0	9	246
4	Jenas	6	1	0	0	7	429
5	King	3	0	0	0	3	772
6	Lennon	2	0	0	0	2	904
7	Carrick	2	0	0	0	2	1561
8	Tainio	1	0	0	0	1	1708
9	Stalteri	1	1	0	0	2	2967
10	Davids	1	0	0	0	1	2421
	Other	1	0	0	0	1	
	TOTAL	53	2	0	0	55	

SQUAD APPEARANCES

Match	1	2	3	4	5	6	7	8	9	10	11	12	13	14	15	16	17	18	19	20	21	22	23	24	25	26	27	28	29	30	31	32	33	34	35	36	37	38	39
Venue	A	H	A	H	H	A	A	H	A	H	A	H	A	H	A	H	H	A	H	A	H	A	A	A	H	A	H	A	H	H	A	A	H	A	H	A	H	A	H
Competition	L	L	L	L	L	L	W	L	L	L	L	L	L	L	L	L	L	L	L	L	L	L	F	L	L	L	L	L	L	L	L	L	L	L	L	L	L	L	L
Result	W	W	D	L	D	D	L	W	W	W	D	D	L	D	W	W	W	D	W	L	W	W	L	L	D	L	W	D	D	W	L	W	W	L	W	W	L	D	W

Goalkeepers
Radek Cerny
Paul Robinson

Defenders
Goran Bunjevcevic
Calum Davenport
Michael Dawson
Erik Edman
Anthony Gardner
Tom Huddlestone
Stephen Kelly
Ledley King
Young-Pyo Lee
Noureddine Naybet
Noe Pamarot
Paul Stalteri

Midfielders
Michael Brown
Michael Carrick
Edgar Davids
Sean Davis
Johnnie Jackson
Jermaine Jenas
Aaron Lennon
Pedro Mendes
Danny Murphy
Andrew Reid
Wayne Routledge
Teemu Tainio

Forwards
Lee Barnard
Jermain Defoe
Frederic Kanoute
Robbie Keane
Hossam Mido
Grzegorz Rasiak

KEY: ■ On all match ■ On bench ⏮ Subbed or sent off (Counting game) « Subbed or sent off (playing less than 70 mins) ⏭ Subbed on from bench (Counting Game) » Subbed on (playing less than 70 mins) Subbed on and then subbed or sent off (Counting Game) Subbed on and then subbed or sent off (playing less than 70 mins) □ Not in 16

KEY PLAYERS - GOALSCORERS

Robbie Keane

Goals in the League	16
Goals in all competitions	16
Assists League goals scored by a team mate where the player delivered the final pass	5
Contribution to Attacking Power Average number of minutes between League team goals while on pitch	62
Player Strike Rate Average number of minutes between League goals scored by player	144
Club Strike Rate Average minutes between League goals scored by club	65

	PLAYER	GOALS LGE	GOALS ALL	ASSISTS	POWER	S RATE
1	Robbie Keane	16	16	5	62	144 mins
2	Hossam Mido	11	11	7	51	192 mins
3	Jermain Defoe	9	9	7	63	246 mins
4	Jermaine Jenas	6	7	4	64	429 mins

KEY PLAYERS - MIDFIELDERS

Aaron Lennon

Goals in the League	2
Goals in all competitions	2
Assists League goals scored by a team mate where the player delivered the final pass	3
Defensive Rating Average number of mins between League goals conceded while on the pitch	106
Contribution to Attacking Power Average number of minutes between League team goals while on pitch	65
Scoring Difference Defensive Rating minus Contribution to Attacking Power	41

	PLAYER	GOALS LGE	GOALS ALL	ASSISTS	DEF RATE	POWER	SC DIFF
1	Aaron Lennon	2	2	3	106	65	41 mins
2	Teemu Tainio	1	1	5	100	63	37 mins
3	Michael Carrick	2	2	6	89	64	25 mins
4	Jermaine Jenas	6	7	4	83	64	19 mins

PLAYER APPEARANCES

	AGE (on 01/07/06)	IN NAMED 16	APPEARANCES	COUNTING GAMES	MINUTES ON PITCH	APPEARANCES	MINUTES ON PITCH	THIS SEASON	HOME COUNTRY
Goalkeepers									
Radek Cerny	32	38	0	0	0	0	0	-	Czech Republic
Paul Robinson	26	38	38	38	3420	40	3600	8	England (10)
Defenders									
Goran Bunjevcevic	33	0	0	0	0	0	0	-	Serbia & Montenegro
Calum Davenport	23	7	4	1	108	4	108	-	England
Michael Dawson	22	32	32	30	2752	33	2842	-	England
Erik Edman	27	3	3	3	270	3	270	4	Sweden (16)
Anthony Gardner	25	24	17	15	1405	18	1495	-	England
Tom Huddlestone	19	6	4	0	142	4	142	-	England
Stephen Kelly	22	20	9	8	778	10	868	-	Rep of Ireland
Ledley King	25	26	26	25	2315	27	2405	4	England (10)
Young-Pyo Lee	29	31	31	30	2731	32	2821	4	South Korea (29)
Noureddine Naybet	36	13	3	2	232	4	322	3	Morocco (36)
Noe Pamarot	27	6	2	0	41	2	41	-	France
Paul Stalteri	28	34	33	33	2967	35	3147	-	Canada
Midfielders									
Michael Brown	29	13	9	2	274	11	433	-	England
Michael Carrick	24	36	35	34	3122	37	3278	4	England (10)
Edgar Davids	33	31	31	25	2421	31	2421	2	Holland (3)
Sean Davis	26	0	0	0	0	1	24	-	England
Johnnie Jackson	23	2	1	0	45	1	45	-	England
Jermaine Jenas	23	30	30	27	2575	32	2755	5	England (10)
Aaron Lennon	19	32	27	18	1807	29	1923	-	England
Pedro Mendes	27	8	6	2	267	6	267	-	Portugal
Danny Murphy	29	13	10	2	301	10	301	-	England
Andrew Reid	23	16	13	4	612	14	672	3	Rep of Ireland (15)
Wayne Routledge	21	3	3	1	166	3	166	-	England
Teemu Tainio	26	25	24	16	1708	25	1712	5	Finland (42)
Forwards									
Lee Barnard	21	6	3	0	71	3	71	-	England
Jermain Defoe	23	38	36	23	2213	38	2324	8	England (10)
Frederic Kanoute	28	1	1	0	10	1	10	1	Mali (66)
Robbie Keane	25	37	36	23	2302	38	2482	4	Rep of Ireland (15)
Hossam Mido	23	28	27	22	2108	27	2108	7	Egypt (17)
Grzegorz Rasiak	27	11	8	4	337	9	427	8	Poland (29)

KEY: LEAGUE ALL COMPS CAPS (MAY FIFA RANKING)

TEAM OF THE SEASON

ROBINSON

CG 38 DR 90

STALTERI

CG 33 DR 93

GARDNER

CG 15 DR 100

KING

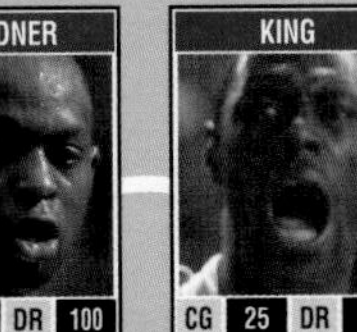

CG 25 DR 89

LEE

CG 30 DR 88

LENNON

CG 18 SD +41

TAINIO

CG 16 SD +37

CARRICK

CG 34 SD +25

JENAS

CG 27 SD +19

MIDO

CG 22 AP 51

KEANE

CG 23 SR 144

KEY: DR = Defensive Rate, SD = Scoring Difference AP = Attacking Power SR = Strike Rate, CG=Counting games – League games playing at least 70 minutes

TOP POINT EARNERS

Hossam Mido

Counting Games League games when player was on pitch for at least 70 minutes	22
Average points Average League points taken in Counting games	2.00
Club Average points Average points taken in League games	1.71

	PLAYER	GAMES	PTS
1	Hossam Mido	22	2.00
2	Anthony Gardner	15	1.80
3	Ledley King	25	1.80
4	Aaron Lennon	18	1.78
5	Paul Stalteri	33	1.76
6	Young-Pyo Lee	30	1.73
7	Paul Robinson	38	1.71
8	Michael Carrick	34	1.71
9	Jermaine Jenas	27	1.70
10	Robbie Keane	23	1.70

KEY PLAYERS - DEFENDERS

Anthony Gardner

Goals Conceded in the League Number of League goals conceded while the player was on the pitch	14
Goals Conceded in all competitions Total number of goals conceded while the player was on the pitch	17
League minutes played Number of minutes played in league matches	1405
Clean Sheets In games when the player was on pitch for at least 70 minutes	8
Defensive Rating Average number of mins between League goals conceded while on the pitch	100
Club Defensive Rating Average number of mins between League goals conceded by the club this season	90

	PLAYER	CON LGE	CON ALL	MINS	C SHEETS	DEF RATE
1	Anthony Gardner	14	17	1405	8	100 mins
2	Paul Stalteri	32	36	2967	11	93 mins
3	Ledley King	26	27	2315	6	89 mins
4	Young-Pyo Lee	31	32	2731	10	88 mins

KEY GOALKEEPER

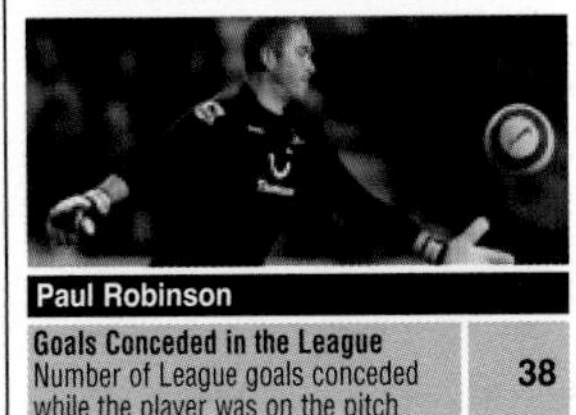

Paul Robinson

Goals Conceded in the League Number of League goals conceded while the player was on the pitch	38
Goals Conceded in all competitions Total number of goals conceded while the player was on the pitch	42
League minutes played Number of minutes played in league matches	3420
Clean Sheets In games when the player was on pitch for at least 70 minutes	13
Goals to Shots Ratio The average number of shots on target per each League goal conceded	5.7
Defensive Rating Ave mins between League goals conceded while on the pitch	90

BOOKINGS

Edgar Davids

League Yellow	11
League Red	1
All competitions Yellow	11
All competitions Red	1

League Average 201 mins between cards

	PLAYER	LEAGUE Y	LEAGUE R	TOTAL Y	TOTAL R	AVE
1	Davids	11Y	1R	11Y	1R	201
2	Dawson	8	2	8	2	275
3	Reid	2	0	2	0	306
4	Mido	4	1	4	1	421
5	Tainio	4	0	4	0	427
6	Stalteri	5	1	5	1	494
7	Gardner	2	0	2	0	702
8	Defoe	3	0	3	0	737
9	King	2	0	2	0	1157
10	Jenas	2	0	2	0	1287
11	Lee, Y-P	2	0	2	0	1365
12	Carrick	2	0	2	0	1561
13	Keane	1	0	1	0	2302
14	Robinson	1	0	1	0	3420
	Other	0	0	0	0	
	TOTAL	49	5	49	5	

BLACKBURN ROVERS

Craig Bellamy made the difference in a season when the defence conceded only one goal less than last year. He hit 17 goals in all competitions and his 13 league goals came at a top five Strike Rate of one every 155 minutes – that's better than Chelsea's strike pair.

Zurab Khizanishvili proved a good acquisition from Rangers and finished as the club's top defender. They only conceded a goal every 98 minutes when he was on the pitch. Reliable **Ryan Nelson** had a Defensive Rating of a goal conceded every 90 minutes.

Kerimoglu Tugay was the pick of the midfield. The club were far less likely to concede (a goal every 113 minutes) and far more likely to score (a goal every 58 minutes) when he was on the pitch.

Keeper **Brad Friedel** had 16 clean sheets in 38 league games.

NICKNAME: ROVERS

KEY: Won Drawn Lost

1	prem	**West Ham**	A	L	1-3	Todd 18
2	prem	**Fulham**	H	W	2-1	Pedersen 15; Tugay 71
3	prem	**Tottenham**	H	D	0-0	
4	prem	**Aston Villa**	A	L	0-1	
5	prem	**Bolton**	A	D	0-0	
6	prem	**Newcastle**	H	L	0-3	
7	ccr2	**Huddersfield**	H	W	3-1	Bellamy 11,84; Khizanishvili 60
8	prem	**Man Utd**	A	W	2-1	Pedersen 33,81
9	prem	**West Brom**	H	W	2-0	Kuqi 80,88
10	prem	**Liverpool**	A	L	0-1	
11	prem	**Birmingham**	H	W	2-0	Dickov 49 pen; Bellamy 81
12	ccr3	**Leeds**	H	W	3-0	Emerton 60; Dickov 76; Neill 89
13	prem	**Chelsea**	A	L	2-4	Bellamy 18 pen,44
14	prem	**Charlton**	H	W	4-1	Emerton 2; Dickov 18; Pedersen 59; Bellamy 90
15	prem	**Man City**	A	D	0-0	
16	prem	**Arsenal**	A	L	0-3	
17	ccr4	**Charlton**	A	W	3-2	Kuqi 75; Thompson 81; Bentley 88
18	prem	**Everton**	H	L	0-2	
19	prem	**West Ham**	H	W	3-2	Dickov 56 pen,57; Kuqi 76
20	prem	**Fulham**	A	L	1-2	Knight 90 og
21	ccqf	**Middlesbrough**	A	W	1-0	Dickov 90
22	prem	**Middlesbrough**	A	W	2-0	Kuqi 38,79
23	prem	**Wigan**	A	W	3-0	Pedersen 15; Reid 53; Bellamy 85
24	prem	**Portsmouth**	H	W	2-1	Pedersen 9; Dickov 38
25	facr3	**QPR**	H	W	3-0	Todd 17; Bellamy 36,85
26	ccsfl1	**Man Utd**	H	D	1-1	Pedersen 35
27	prem	**Bolton**	H	D	0-0	
28	prem	**Newcastle**	A	W	1-0	Pedersen 75
29	ccsfl2	**Man Utd**	A	L	1-2	Reid 32
30	facr4	**West Ham**	A	L	2-4	Bentley 1; Neill 65
31	prem	**Man Utd**	H	W	4-3	Bentley 35,41,56; Neill 45 pen
32	prem	**West Brom**	A	L	0-2	
33	prem	**Everton**	A	L	0-1	
34	prem	**Sunderland**	H	W	2-0	Bellamy 38,63
35	prem	**Arsenal**	H	W	1-0	Pedersen 18
36	prem	**Tottenham**	A	L	2-3	Sinama-Pongolle 44; Bellamy 67
37	prem	**Aston Villa**	H	W	2-0	Todd 49; Bellamy 71
38	prem	**Middlesbrough**	H	W	3-2	Bellamy 11,68; Pedersen 28
39	prem	**Sunderland**	A	W	1-0	Reid 15
40	prem	**Wigan**	H	D	1-1	Kuqi 84
41	prem	**Portsmouth**	A	D	2-2	Bellamy 32,62
42	prem	**Liverpool**	H	L	0-1	
43	prem	**Birmingham**	A	L	1-2	Savage 78
44	prem	**Charlton**	A	W	2-0	Reid 43; Powell 65 og
45	prem	**Chelsea**	H	W	1-0	Reid 43
46	prem	**Man City**	H	W	2-0	Khizanishvili 35; Kuqi 52

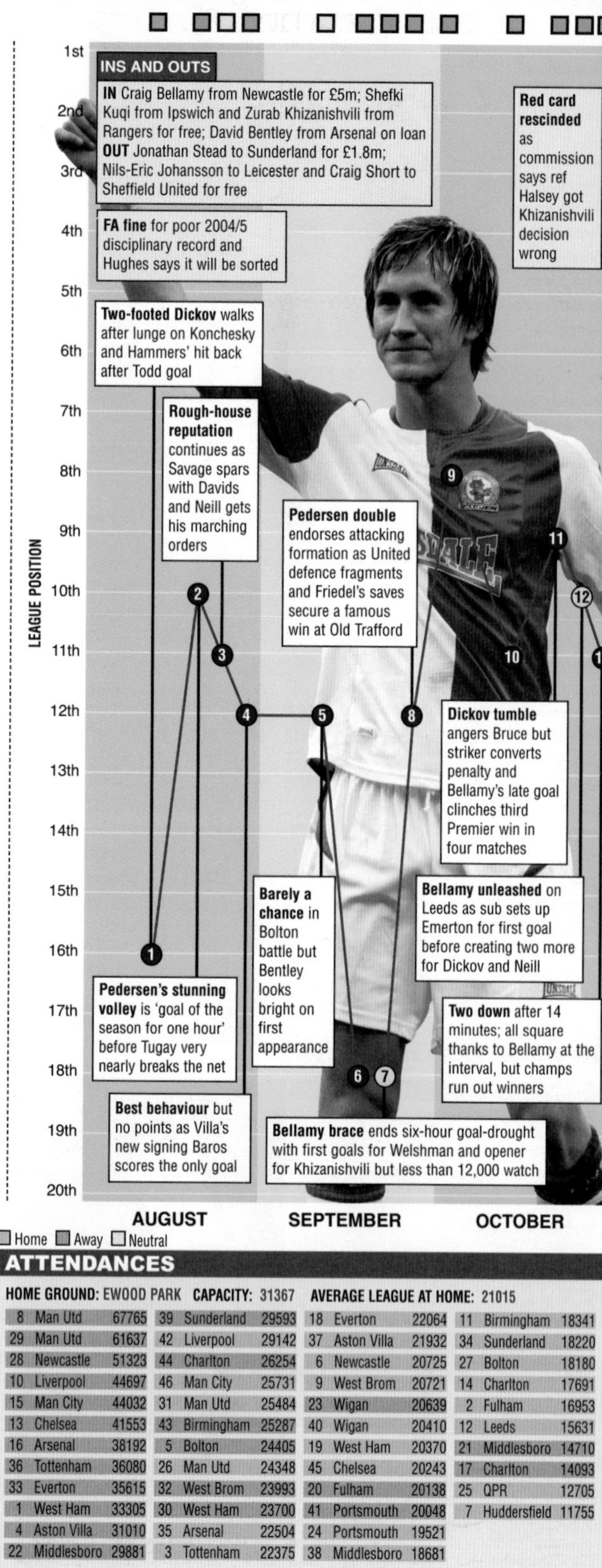

1st
2nd
3rd
4th
5th
6th
7th
8th
9th
10th
11th
12th
13th
14th
15th
16th
17th
18th
19th
20th
LEAGUE POSITION
INS AND OUTS
IN Craig Bellamy from Newcastle for £5m; Shefki Kuqi from Ipswich and Zurab Khizanishvili from Rangers for free; David Bentley from Arsenal on loan OUT Jonathan Stead to Sunderland for £1.8m; Nils-Eric Johansson to Leicester and Craig Short to Sheffield United for free
FA fine for poor 2004/5 disciplinary record and Hughes says it will be sorted
Red card rescinded as commission says ref Halsey got Khizanishvili decision wrong
Two-footed Dickov walks after lunge on Konchesky and Hammers' hit back after Todd goal
Rough-house reputation continues as Savage spars with Davids and Neill gets his marching orders
Pedersen double endorses attacking formation as United defence fragments and Friedel's saves secure a famous win at Old Trafford
Dickov tumble angers Bruce but striker converts penalty and Bellamy's late goal clinches third Premier win in four matches
Bellamy unleashed on Leeds as sub sets up Emerton for first goal before creating two more for Dickov and Neill
Barely a chance in Bolton battle but Bentley looks bright on first appearance
Pedersen's stunning volley is 'goal of the season for one hour' before Tugay very nearly breaks the net
Two down after 14 minutes; all square thanks to Bellamy at the interval, but champs run out winners
Best behaviour but no points as Villa's new signing Baros scores the only goal
Bellamy brace ends six-hour goal-drought with first goals for Welshman and opener for Khizanishvili but less than 12,000 watch
AUGUST
SEPTEMBER
OCTOBER
Home Away Neutral

ATTENDANCES

HOME GROUND: EWOOD PARK **CAPACITY:** 31367 **AVERAGE LEAGUE AT HOME:** 21015

8	Man Utd	67765	39	Sunderland	29593	18	Everton	22064	11	Birmingham	18341
29	Man Utd	61637	42	Liverpool	29142	37	Aston Villa	21932	34	Sunderland	18220
28	Newcastle	51323	44	Charlton	26254	6	Newcastle	20725	27	Bolton	18180
10	Liverpool	44697	46	Man City	25731	9	West Brom	20721	14	Charlton	17691
15	Man City	44032	31	Man Utd	25484	23	Wigan	20639	2	Fulham	16953
13	Chelsea	41553	43	Birmingham	25287	40	Wigan	20410	12	Leeds	15631
16	Arsenal	38192	5	Bolton	24405	19	West Ham	20370	21	Middlesboro	14710
36	Tottenham	36080	26	Man Utd	24348	45	Chelsea	20243	17	Charlton	14093
33	Everton	35615	32	West Brom	23993	20	Fulham	20138	25	QPR	12705
1	West Ham	33305	30	West Ham	23700	41	Portsmouth	20048	7	Huddersfield	11755
4	Aston Villa	31010	35	Arsenal	22504	24	Portsmouth	19521			
22	Middlesboro	29881	3	Tottenham	22375	38	Middlesboro	18681			

Uefa reward for Hughes and Bellamy

Final Position: **6th**

KEY: League, Champions Lge, UEFA Cup, FA Cup, League Cup, Other

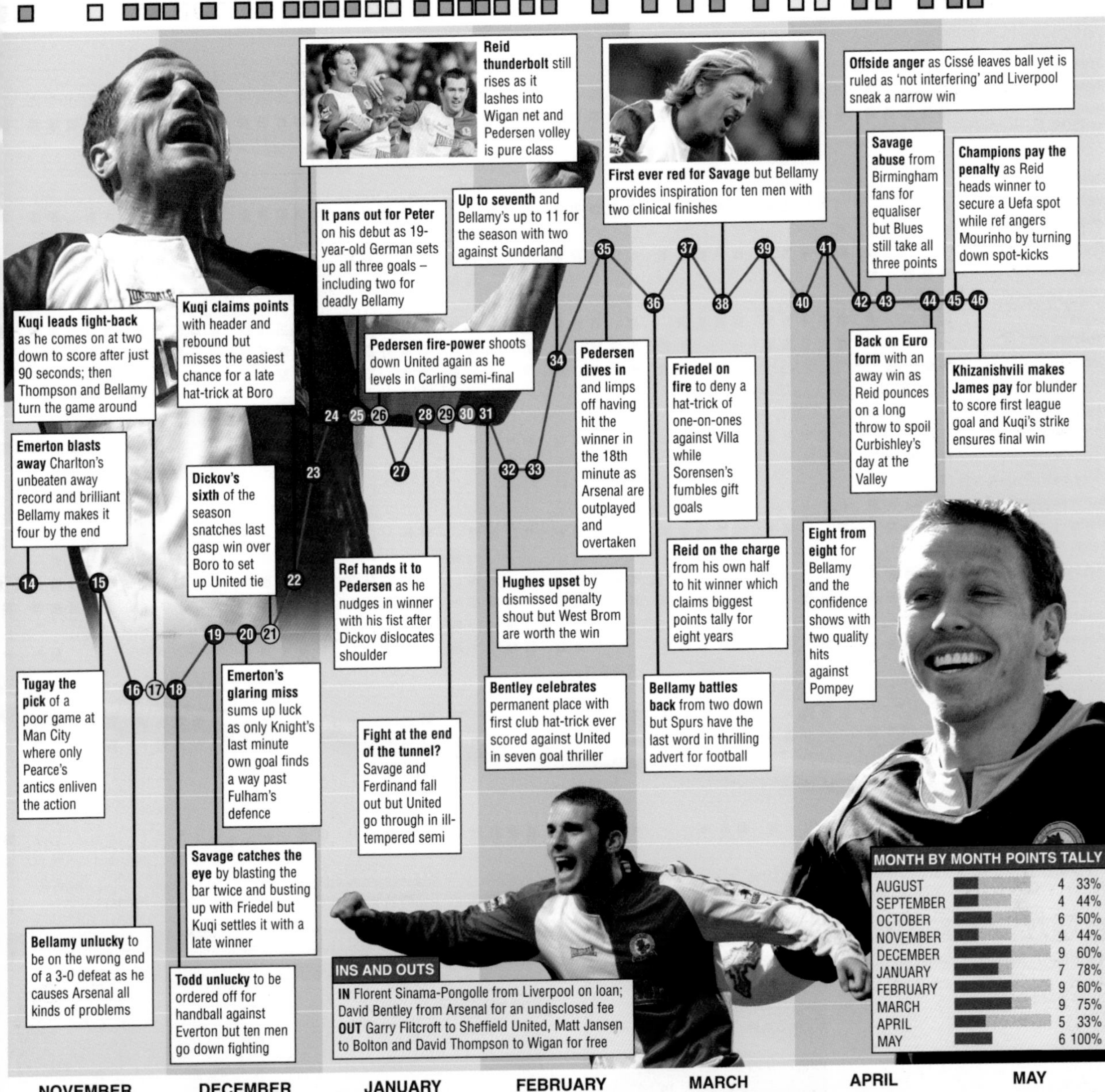

Kuqi leads fight-back as he comes on at two down to score after just 90 seconds; then Thompson and Bellamy turn the game around
Emerton blasts away Charlton's unbeaten away record and brilliant Bellamy makes it four by the end
Tugay the pick of a poor game at Man City where only Pearce's antics enliven the action
Bellamy unlucky to be on the wrong end of a 3-0 defeat as he causes Arsenal all kinds of problems
Kuqi claims points with header and rebound but misses the easiest chance for a late hat-trick at Boro
Dickov's sixth of the season snatches last gasp win over Boro to set up United tie
Emerton's glaring miss sums up luck as only Knight's last minute own goal finds a way past Fulham's defence
Savage catches the eye by blasting the bar twice and busting up with Friedel but Kuqi settles it with a late winner
Todd unlucky to be ordered off for handball against Everton but ten men go down fighting
Reid thunderbolt still rises as it lashes into Wigan net and Pedersen volley is pure class
It pans out for Peter on his debut as 19-year-old German sets up all three goals – including two for deadly Bellamy
Up to seventh and Bellamy's up to 11 for the season with two against Sunderland
Pedersen fire-power shoots down United again as he levels in Carling semi-final
Ref hands it to Pedersen as he nudges in winner with his fist after Dickov dislocates shoulder
Fight at the end of the tunnel? Savage and Ferdinand fall out but United go through in ill-tempered semi
Hughes upset by dismissed penalty shout but West Brom are worth the win
Bentley celebrates permanent place with first club hat-trick ever scored against United in seven goal thriller
Pedersen dives in and limps off having hit the winner in the 18th minute as Arsenal are outplayed and overtaken
First ever red for Savage but Bellamy provides inspiration for ten men with two clinical finishes
Friedel on fire to deny a hat-trick of one-on-ones against Villa while Sorensen's fumbles gift goals
Reid on the charge from his own half to hit winner which claims biggest points tally for eight years
Bellamy battles back from two down but Spurs have the last word in thrilling advert for football
Offside anger as Cissé leaves ball yet is ruled as 'not interfering' and Liverpool sneak a narrow win
Savage abuse from Birmingham fans for equaliser but Blues still take all three points
Champions pay the penalty as Reid heads winner to secure a Uefa spot while ref angers Mourinho by turning down spot-kicks
Back on Euro form with an away win as Reid pounces on a long throw to spoil Curbishley's day at the Valley
Khizanishvili makes James pay for blunder to score first league goal and Kuqi's strike ensures final win
Eight from eight for Bellamy and the confidence shows with two quality hits against Pompey
14 15 16 17 18 19 20 21 22 23 24 25 26 27 28 29 30 31 32 33 34 35 36 37 38 39 40 41 42 43 44 45 46
NOVEMBER DECEMBER JANUARY FEBRUARY MARCH APRIL MAY

INS AND OUTS

IN Florent Sinama-Pongolle from Liverpool on loan; David Bentley from Arsenal for an undisclosed fee
OUT Garry Flitcroft to Sheffield United, Matt Jansen to Bolton and David Thompson to Wigan for free

MONTH BY MONTH POINTS TALLY

Month	Points	%
AUGUST	4	33%
SEPTEMBER	4	44%
OCTOBER	6	50%
NOVEMBER	4	44%
DECEMBER	9	60%
JANUARY	7	78%
FEBRUARY	9	60%
MARCH	9	75%
APRIL	5	33%
MAY	6	100%

GOAL ATTEMPTS

FOR — Goal attempts recorded in League games

	HOME	AWAY	TOTAL	AVE
shots on target	98	85	183	4.8
shots off target	116	85	201	5.3
TOTAL	214	170	384	10.1

Ratio of goals to shots Average number of shots on target per League goal scored: **3.6**

Accuracy rating Average percentage of total goal attempts which were on target: **47.7**

AGAINST — Goal attempts recorded in League games

	HOME	AWAY	TOTAL	AVE
shots on target	67	107	174	4.6
shots off target	73	85	158	4.2
TOTAL	140	192	332	8.7

Ratio of goals to shots Average number of shots on target per League goal scored: **4.1**

Accuracy rating Average percentage of total goal attempts which were on target: **52.4**

GOALS

Craig Bellamy

League	13
FA Cup	2
League Cup	2
Europe	0
Other	0
TOTAL	17

League Average **155** mins between goals

	PLAYER	LGE	FAC	LC	Euro	TOT	AVE
1	Bellamy	13	2	2	0	17	155
2	Pedersen	9	0	1	0	10	311
3	Kuqi	7	0	1	0	8	238
4	Dickov	5	0	2	0	7	250
5	Reid	4	0	1	0	5	704
6	Bentley	3	1	1	0	5	669
7	Todd	2	1	0	0	3	881
8	Savage	1	0	0	0	1	2976
9	Emerton	1	0	1	0	2	1610
10	Sinama-Pongolle	1	0	0	0	1	706
11	Khizanishvili	1	0	1	0	2	2157
12	Tugay	1	0	0	0	1	1810
13	Neill	1	1	1	0	3	3136
14	Thompson	0	0	1	0	1	
	Other	2	0	0	0	2	
	TOTAL	51	5	12	0	68	

SQUAD APPEARANCES

Match	1	2	3	4	5	6	7	8	9	10	11	12	13	14	15	16	17	18	19	20	21	22	23	24	25	26	27	28	29	30	31	32	33	34	35	36	37	38	39	40	41	42	43	44	45
Venue	A	H	H	A	A	H	H	A	H	A	H	H	A	H	A	A	A	H	H	A	A	A	A	H	H	H	H	A	A	A	H	A	A	H	H	A	H	H	A	H	A	H	A	A	H
Competition	L	L	L	L	L	L	W	L	L	L	L	W	L	L	L	L	W	L	L	L	W	L	L	L	F	W	L	L	W	F	L	L	L	L	L	L	L	L	L	L	L	L	L	L	L
Result	L	W	D	L	D	L	W	W	W	L	W	W	L	W	D	L	W	L	W	L	W	W	W	W	W	D	D	W	L	L	W	L	L	W	W	L	W	W	W	D	D	L	L	W	W

Goalkeepers
Peter Enckelman
Brad Friedel
Richard Lee

Defenders
Michael Gray
Vratislav Gresko
Zurab Khizanishvili
Dominic Matteo
James McEveley
Lucas Neill
Ryan Nelsen
Andy Todd

Midfielders
David Bentley
Brett Emerton
Garry Flitcroft
Aaron Mokoena
Morten Gamst Pedersen
Sergio Peter
Steven Reid
Robbie Savage
David Thompson
Kerimoglu Tugay

Forwards
Craig Bellamy
Paul Dickov
Paul Gallagher
Matthew Jansen
Jemal Johnson
Shefki Kuqi
Florent Sinama-Pongolle

KEY: On all match · On bench · Subbed or sent off (Counting game) · Subbed or sent off (playing less than 70 mins) · Subbed on from bench (Counting Game) · Subbed on (playing less than 70 mins) · Subbed on and then subbed or sent off (Counting Game) · Subbed on and then subbed or sent off (playing less than 70 mins) · Not in 16

KEY PLAYERS - GOALSCORERS

Craig Bellamy

Goals in the League	13
Goals in all competitions	17
Assists League goals scored by a team mate where the player delivered the final pass	6
Contribution to Attacking Power Average number of minutes between League team goals while on pitch	67
Player Strike Rate Average number of minutes between League goals scored by player	155
Club Strike Rate Average minutes between League goals scored by club	67

	PLAYER	GOALS LGE	GOALS ALL	ASSISTS	POWER	S RATE
1	Craig Bellamy	13	17	6	67	155 mins
2	Shefki Kuqi	7	8	6	59	238 mins
3	Morten Gamst Pedersen	9	10	8	68	311 mins
4	David Bentley	3	5	0	74	669 mins

KEY PLAYERS - MIDFIELDERS

Kerimoglu Tugay

Goals in the League	1
Goals in all competitions	1
Assists League goals scored by a team mate where the player delivered the final pass	0
Defensive Rating Average number of mins between League goals conceded while on the pitch	113
Contribution to Attacking Power Average number of minutes between League team goals while on pitch	58
Scoring Difference Defensive Rating minus Contribution to Attacking Power	55

	PLAYER	GOALS LGE	GOALS ALL	ASSISTS	DEF RATE	POWER	SC DIFF
1	Kerimoglu Tugay	1	1	0	113	58	55 mins
2	Morten Gamst Pedersen	9	10	8	80	68	12 mins
3	Steven Reid	4	5	1	78	67	11 mins
4	Robbie Savage	1	1	3	78	69	9 mins

PLAYER APPEARANCES

	AGE (on 01/07/06)	IN NAMED 16	APPEARANCES	COUNTING GAMES	MINUTES ON PITCH	APPEARANCES	MINUTES ON PITCH	THIS SEASON	HOME COUNTRY
Goalkeepers									
Peter Enckelman	29	37	0	0	0	0	0	-	Finland
Brad Friedel	35	38	38	38	3420	0	0	-	United States
Richard Lee	23	1	0	0	0	0	0	-	England
Defenders									
Michael Gray	31	30	30	27	2565	3	0	-	England
Vratislav Gresko	28	5	3	1	145	0	0	-	Slovakia
Zurab Khizanishvili	24	29	26	23	2157	3	1	2	Georgia (101)
Dominic Matteo	32	6	6	5	506	2	0	-	Scotland
James McEveley	20	1	0	0	0	0	0	-	England
Lucas Neill	28	35	35	35	3136	12	1	5	Australia (42)
Ryan Nelsen	28	31	31	29	2704	4	0	-	New Zealand
Andy Todd	31	24	22	18	1762	4	1	-	England
Midfielders									
David Bentley	21	32	29	17	2007	7	0	-	England
Brett Emerton	27	32	30	11	1610	2	0	5	Australia (42)
Garry Flitcroft	33	3	2	0	61	0	0	-	England
Aaron Mokoena	25	32	22	2	662	0	0	4	South Africa (53)
M. Gamst Pedersen	24	34	34	29	2803	3	0	6	Norway (40)
Sergio Peter	19	13	8	2	323	2	0	-	Germany
Steven Reid	25	37	34	31	2817	7	0	5	Rep of Ireland (15)
Robbie Savage	31	35	34	32	2976	12	1	-	Wales
David Thompson	28	7	6	1	186	1	0	-	England
Kerimoglu Tugay	35	30	27	14	1810	4	1	-	Turkey
Forwards									
Craig Bellamy	26	27	27	21	2014	5	0	2	Wales (74)
Paul Dickov	33	26	21	8	1250	5	1	-	England
Paul Gallagher	21	2	1	0	11	0	0	-	England
Matthew Jansen	28	6	4	0	103	0	0	-	England
Jemal Johnson	21	5	3	0	15	0	0	-	United States
Shefki Kuqi	29	38	33	14	1665	1	0	3	Finland (42)
F. Sinama-Pongolle	21	12	10	7	706	0	0	-	France

KEY: LEAGUE ALL COMPS CAPS (MAY FIFA RANKING)

TEAM OF THE SEASON

FRIEDEL — CG 38 DR 81

NEILL — CG 35 DR 76

KHIZANISHVILI — CG 23 DR 98

NELSEN — CG 29 DR 90

GRAY — CG 27 DR 88

REID — CG 31 SD +11

SAVAGE — CG 32 SD +9

TUGAY — CG 14 SD +55

PEDERSEN — CG 29 SD +12

KUQI — CG 14 AP 59

BELLAMY — CG 21 SR 155

KEY: DR = Defensive Rate, SD = Scoring Difference AP = Attacking Power SR = Strike Rate, CG=Counting games – League games playing at least 70 minutes

TOP POINT EARNERS

Kerimoglu Tugay

Counting Games League games when player was on pitch for at least 70 minutes	14
Average points Average League points taken in Counting games	2.07
Club Average points Average points taken in League games	1.66

	PLAYER	GAMES	PTS
1	Kerimoglu Tugay	14	2.07
2	Zurab Khizanishvili	23	2.00
3	Shefki Kuqi	14	2.00
4	Michael Gray	27	1.78
5	Morten Gamst Pedersen	29	1.72
6	Lucas Neill	35	1.69
7	Brad Friedel	38	1.66
8	Steven Reid	31	1.65
9	Robbie Savage	32	1.59
10	Ryan Nelsen	29	1.55

KEY PLAYERS - DEFENDERS

Zurab Khizanishvili

Goals Conceded in the League Number of League goals conceded while the player was on the pitch	22
Goals Conceded in all competitions Total number of goals conceded while the player was on the pitch	31
League minutes played Number of minutes played in league matches	2157
Clean Sheets In games when the player was on pitch for at least 70 minutes	11
Defensive Rating Average number of mins between League goals conceded while on the pitch	98
Club Defensive Rating Average number of mins between League goals conceded by the club this season	81

	PLAYER	CON LGE	CON ALL	MINS	C SHEETS	DEF RATE
1	Zurab Khizanishvili	22	31	2157	11	98 mins
2	Ryan Nelsen	30	36	2704	12	90 mins
3	Michael Gray	29	39	2565	13	88 mins
4	Lucas Neill	41	49	3136	14	76 mins

KEY GOALKEEPER

Brad Friedel

Goals Conceded in the League Number of League goals conceded while the player was on the pitch	42
Goals Conceded in all competitions Total number of goals conceded while the player was on the pitch	52
League minutes played Number of minutes played in league matches	3420
Clean Sheets In games when the player was on pitch for at least 70 minutes	16
Goals to Shots Ratio The average number of shots on target per each League goal conceded	4.1
Defensive Rating Ave mins between League goals conceded while on the pitch	81

BOOKINGS

Paul Dickov

League Yellow	5
League Red	1
All competitions Yellow	7
All competitions Red	1

League Average **208** mins between cards

	PLAYER	LEAGUE		TOTAL		AVE
		Y	R	Y	R	
1	Dickov	5	1	7	1	208
2	Savage	12	1	14	1	228
3	Neill	12	1	14	1	241
4	Matteo	2	0	3	0	253
5	Bentley	7	0	8	0	286
6	Todd	4	1	4	1	352
7	Tugay	4	1	7	1	362
8	Reid	7	0	8	0	402
9	Bellamy	5	0	8	0	402
10	Khizanishvili	3	1	3	1	539
11	Nelsen	4	0	4	0	676
12	Emerton	2	0	4	0	805
13	Gray	3	0	3	0	855
14	Pedersen	3	0	4	0	934
15	Kuqi	1	0	1	0	1665
	Other	0	0	0	0	
	TOTAL	74	6	92	6	

NEWCASTLE UNITED

The emergency double act of Glenn Roeder and **Alan Shearer** made managing Newcastle look easy as they guided the club to the verge of a Uefa Cup place. Shearer grabbed Jackie Milburn's record on the way and the turn-around earned Roeder the job full-time and Shearer the chance to go out on a kind of high.

He also claimed the most goals, with ten in the league at a ropey Strike Rate of one every 274 minutes. **Michael Owen** didn't play enough to make our chart but seven goals at a rate of 128 showed what the club was missing.

Nolberto Solano proved the class act he is to top the midfield chart while **Stephen Carr** finished with a fine Defensive Rating of a goal conceded every 95 minutes. **Shay Given** played every game and saved five shots on target for every goal he conceded.

NICKNAME: THE MAGPIES

KEY: Won Drawn Lost

1	etqfl1	**ZTS Dubnica**	A	W	3-1	Chopra 4; Shearer 6; Milner 70
2	etqfl2	**ZTS Dubnica**	H	W	2-0	Shearer 72,90
3	etsfl1	**Deportivo**	A	L	1-2	Bowyer 47
4	etsfl2	**Deportivo**	H	L	1-2	Milner 39
5	prem	**Arsenal**	A	L	0-2	
6	prem	**West Ham**	H	D	0-0	
7	prem	**Bolton**	A	L	0-2	
8	prem	**Man Utd**	H	L	0-2	
9	prem	**Fulham**	H	D	1-1	N'Zogbia 78
10	prem	**Blackburn**	A	W	3-0	Shearer 62; Owen 66; N'Zogbia 85
11	prem	**Man City**	H	W	1-0	Owen 18
12	prem	**Portsmouth**	A	D	0-0	
13	prem	**Wigan**	A	L	0-1	
14	prem	**Sunderland**	H	W	3-2	Ameobi 33,37; Emre Belozoglu 63
15	ccR3	**Grimsby**	A	W	1-0	Shearer 80
16	prem	**West Brom**	A	W	3-0	Owen 46,78; Shearer 80
17	prem	**Birmingham**	H	W	1-0	Emre Belozoglu 78
18	prem	**Chelsea**	A	L	0-3	
19	prem	**Everton**	A	L	0-1	
20	ccR4	**Wigan**	A	L	0-1	
21	prem	**Aston Villa**	H	D	1-1	Shearer 32 pen
22	prem	**Arsenal**	H	W	1-0	Solano 82
23	prem	**West Ham**	A	W	4-2	Owen 5,43,90; Shearer 66
24	prem	**Liverpool**	A	L	0-2	
25	prem	**Tottenham**	A	L	0-2	
26	prem	**Middlesbrough**	H	D	2-2	Solano 27; Clark 90
27	facr3	**Mansfield**	H	W	1-0	Shearer 80
28	prem	**Fulham**	A	L	0-1	
29	prem	**Blackburn**	H	L	0-1	
30	facr4	**Cheltenham**	A	W	2-0	Chopra 41; Parker 43
31	prem	**Man City**	A	L	0-3	
32	prem	**Portsmouth**	H	W	2-0	N'Zogbia 41; Shearer 64
33	prem	**Aston Villa**	A	W	2-1	Ameobi 2; N'Zogbia 29
34	facr5	**Southampton**	H	W	1-0	Dyer 68
35	prem	**Charlton**	H	D	0-0	
36	prem	**Everton**	H	W	2-0	Solano 64,76
37	prem	**Bolton**	H	W	3-1	Solano 33; Shearer 45; Ameobi 70
38	prem	**Man Utd**	A	L	0-2	
39	prem	**Liverpool**	H	L	1-3	Ameobi 41
40	facqf	**Chelsea**	A	L	0-1	
41	prem	**Charlton**	A	L	1-3	Parker 35
42	prem	**Tottenham**	H	W	3-1	Bowyer 2; Ameobi 25; Shearer 30 pen
43	prem	**Middlesbrough**	A	W	2-1	Boateng 29 og; Ameobi 44
44	prem	**Wigan**	H	W	3-1	Shearer 28 pen,66; Bramble 36
45	prem	**Sunderland**	A	W	4-1	Chopra 60; Shearer 61 pen; N'Zogbia 66; Luque 87
46	prem	**West Brom**	H	W	3-0	Solano 30; Ameobi 40 pen,90
47	prem	**Birmingham**	A	D	0-0	
48	prem	**Chelsea**	H	W	1-0	Bramble 73

INS AND OUTS
IN Michael Owen from Real Madrid for £16m, Albert Luque from Deportivo La Coruna for £9.5m; Scott Parker from Chelsea for £6.5m; Emre Belezoglu from Inter Milan for £3.8m; Nolberto Solano from Aston Villa for £1.5m; Lee Clark from Fulham and Craig Moore from Borussia Monchengladbach for free; Tim Krul from Ado Den Haag fee undisclosed
OUT Jermaine Jenas to Tottenham for £7m; Craig Bellamy to Blackburn for £5m; Andy O'Brien to Portsmouth for £2m; Aaron Hughes to Aston Villa for £1.5m; Darren Ambrose to Charlton for £700K; Hugo Viana to Valencia, Laurent Robert to Portsmouth, James Milner to Aston Villa and Nicky Butt to Birmingham on loan; Patrick Kluivert to Valencia for free.
LEAGUE POSITION
1st
2nd
3rd
4th
5th
6th
7th
8th
9th
10th
11th
12th
13th
14th
15th
16th
17th
18th
19th
20th
Busy July sees Dubnica seen off and Bowyer's away goal at Deportivo but Magpies leak two goals in Spain
Near-post predator Owen volleys in the first then darts in for a second before confessing "I was awful in the first half"
Emre and Parker debut but Shearer bows out of European football as Deportivo repeat their first leg win at St James'
A hat-trick of chances but Owen takes just one to score his first home goal and secure a win over City
Owen debut earns free kick for N'Zogbia to level against Fulham but it's a point apiece after Parker's red card
Jenas tackle is reckless claims ref and Arsenal take points from ten men while Souness fumes
'Sack the board' calls from fans who haven't seen a league goal for 465 minutes as Bolton gain first win
Ameobi sparks four goals in eight minutes with two powerful headers but it takes Emre freekick to settle Tyne and Wear derby
Souness relief as striking duo of Shearer and Owen net within four minutes of each other and N'Zogbia adds a third at Blackburn
Stitches can't stop Shearer who takes a blow from Grimsby defender but gets his revenge with 196th club goal
The Geordie 'Galactico' – Owen signs to join up with Shearer at St James'
AUGUST
SEPTEMBER
OCTOBER
Home Away Neutral

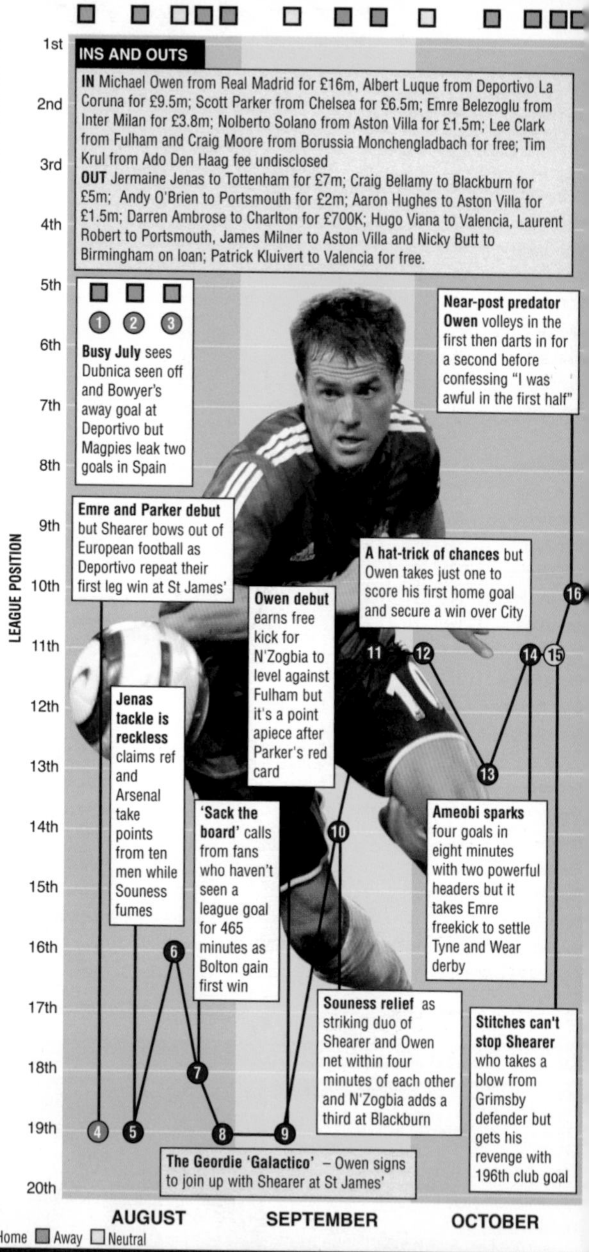

ATTENDANCES

HOME GROUND: ST JAMES' PARK CAPACITY: 52326 AVERAGE LEAGUE AT HOME: 52032

38	Man Utd	67858	9	Fulham	52208	27	Mansfield	41459	16	West Brom	26216
8	Man Utd	52326	17	Birmingham	52191	34	Southampton	40975	7	Bolton	25904
48	Chelsea	52309	37	Bolton	52012	45	Sunderland	40032	2	ZTS Dubnica	25135
26	Middlesboro	52302	36	Everton	51916	5	Arsenal	38072	13	Wigan	22374
14	Sunderland	52302	32	Portsmouth	51627	33	Aston Villa	37140	28	Fulham	21974
44	Wigan	52302	6	West Ham	51620	25	Tottenham	36246	10	Blackburn	20725
39	Liverpool	52302	29	Blackburn	51323	19	Everton	36207	12	Portsmouth	20220
42	Tottenham	52301	35	Charlton	50451	23	West Ham	34836	3	Deportivo	16000
22	Arsenal	52297	24	Liverpool	44197	4	Deportivo	34215	20	Wigan	11574
11	Man City	52280	31	Man City	42413	43	Middlesboro	31202	15	Grimsby	9311
46	West Brom	52272	40	Chelsea	42279	47	Birmingham	28331	30	Cheltenham	7022
21	Aston Villa	52267	18	Chelsea	42268	41	Charlton	27019	1	ZTS Dubnica	6200

Shearer claims record but no trophy

Final Position: 7th

KEY: ● League ● Champions Lge ● UEFA Cup ● FA Cup ○ League Cup ● Other

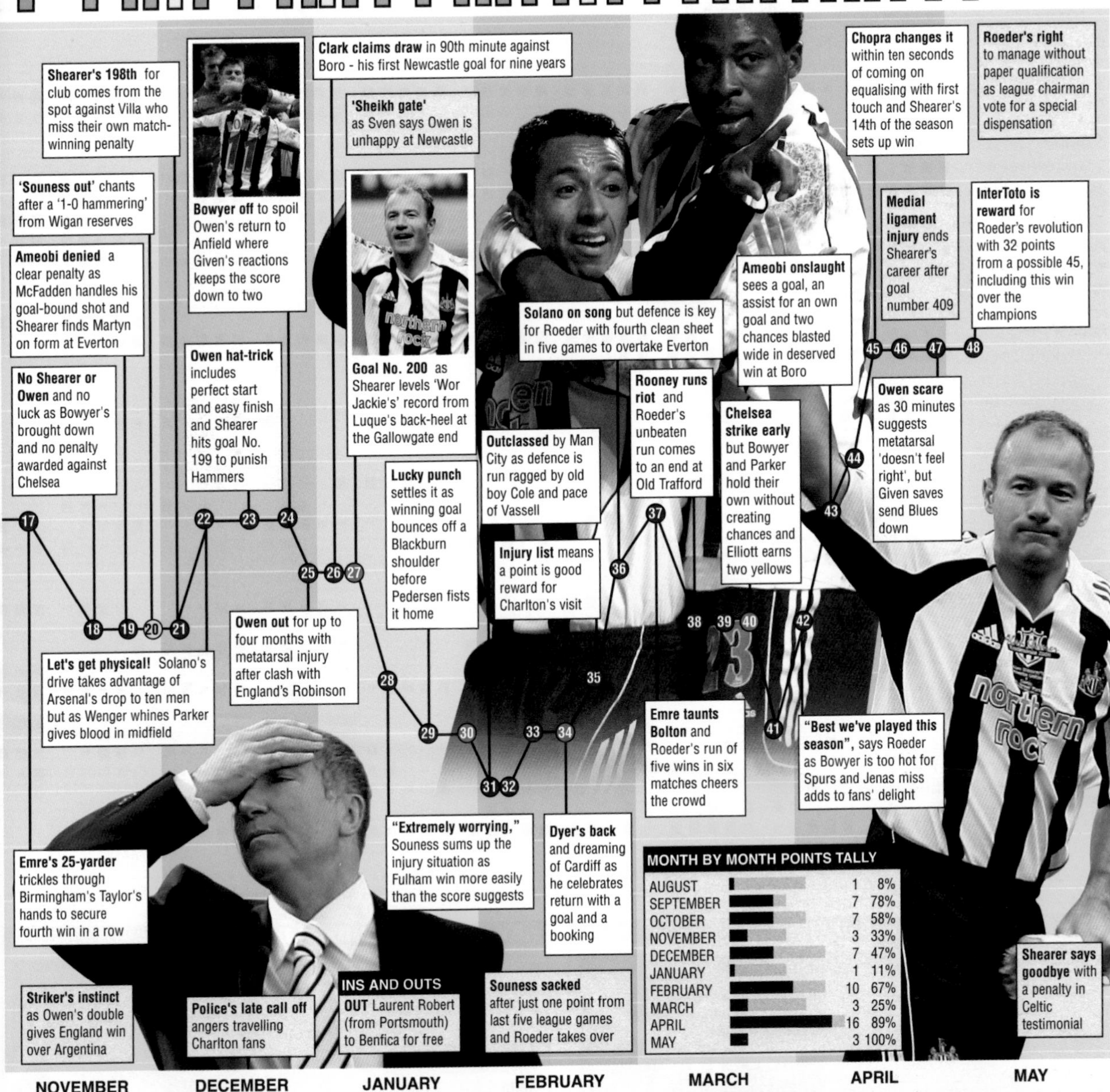

Shearer's 198th for club comes from the spot against Villa who miss their own match-winning penalty
'Souness out' chants after a '1-0 hammering' from Wigan reserves
Ameobi denied a clear penalty as McFadden handles his goal-bound shot and Shearer finds Martyn on form at Everton
No Shearer or Owen and no luck as Bowyer's brought down and no penalty awarded against Chelsea
Bowyer off to spoil Owen's return to Anfield where Given's reactions keeps the score down to two
Owen hat-trick includes perfect start and easy finish and Shearer hits goal No. 199 to punish Hammers
Clark claims draw in 90th minute against Boro - his first Newcastle goal for nine years
'Sheikh gate' as Sven says Owen is unhappy at Newcastle
Goal No. 200 as Shearer levels 'Wor Jackie's' record from Luque's back-heel at the Gallowgate end
Lucky punch settles it as winning goal bounces off a Blackburn shoulder before Pedersen fists it home
Outclassed by Man City as defence is run ragged by old boy Cole and pace of Vassell
Injury list means a point is good reward for Charlton's visit
Solano on song but defence is key for Roeder with fourth clean sheet in five games to overtake Everton
Rooney runs riot and Roeder's unbeaten run comes to an end at Old Trafford
Ameobi onslaught sees a goal, an assist for an own goal and two chances blasted wide in deserved win at Boro
Chelsea strike early but Bowyer and Parker hold their own without creating chances and Elliott earns two yellows
Chopra changes it within ten seconds of coming on equalising with first touch and Shearer's 14th of the season sets up win
Medial ligament injury ends Shearer's career after goal number 409
Roeder's right to manage without paper qualification as league chairman vote for a special dispensation
InterToto is reward for Roeder's revolution with 32 points from a possible 45, including this win over the champions
Owen scare as 30 minutes suggests metatarsal 'doesn't feel right', but Given saves send Blues down
Let's get physical! Solano's drive takes advantage of Arsenal's drop to ten men but as Wenger whines Parker gives blood in midfield
Owen out for up to four months with metatarsal injury after clash with England's Robinson
Emre taunts Bolton and Roeder's run of five wins in six matches cheers the crowd
"Best we've played this season", says Roeder as Bowyer is too hot for Spurs and Jenas miss adds to fans' delight
Emre's 25-yarder trickles through Birmingham's Taylor's hands to secure fourth win in a row
"Extremely worrying," Souness sums up the injury situation as Fulham win more easily than the score suggests
Dyer's back and dreaming of Cardiff as he celebrates return with a goal and a booking
Striker's instinct as Owen's double gives England win over Argentina
Police's late call off angers travelling Charlton fans
INS AND OUTS
OUT Laurent Robert (from Portsmouth) to Benfica for free
Souness sacked after just one point from last five league games and Roeder takes over
Shearer says goodbye with a penalty in Celtic testimonial
NOVEMBER
DECEMBER
JANUARY
FEBRUARY
MARCH
APRIL
MAY

MONTH BY MONTH POINTS TALLY

Month	Points	%
AUGUST	1	8%
SEPTEMBER	7	78%
OCTOBER	7	58%
NOVEMBER	3	33%
DECEMBER	7	47%
JANUARY	1	11%
FEBRUARY	10	67%
MARCH	3	25%
APRIL	16	89%
MAY	3	100%

GOAL ATTEMPTS

FOR – Goal attempts recorded in League games

	HOME	AWAY	TOTAL	AVE
shots on target	127	81	208	5.5
shots off target	96	66	162	4.3
TOTAL	223	147	370	9.7

Ratio of goals to shots – Average number of shots on target per League goal scored: **4.4**

Accuracy rating – Average percentage of total goal attempts which were on target: **56.2**

AGAINST – Goal attempts recorded in League games

	HOME	AWAY	TOTAL	AVE
shots on target	76	134	210	5.5
shots off target	93	81	174	4.6
TOTAL	169	215	384	10.1

Ratio of goals to shots – Average number of shots on target per League goal scored: **5**

Accuracy rating – Average percentage of total goal attempts which were on target: **54.7**

GOALS

Alan Shearer

League	10
FA Cup	1
League Cup	1
Europe	3
Other	0
TOTAL	12

League Average **274** mins between goals

	PLAYER	LGE	FAC	LC	Euro	TOT	AVE
1	Shearer	10	1	1	3	15	274
2	Ameobi	9	0	0	0	9	237
3	Owen	7	0	0	0	7	126
4	Solano	6	0	0	0	6	369
5	N'Zogbia	5	0	0	0	5	463
6	Emre Belozoglu	2	0	0	0	2	795
7	Bramble	2	0	0	0	2	973
8	Chopra	1	1	0	1	3	595
9	Parker	1	1	0	0	2	2302
10	Clark	1	0	0	0	1	897
11	Luque	1	0	0	0	1	653
12	Bowyer	1	0	0	1	1	1627
13	Milner	0	0	0	2	2	
14	Dyer	0	1	0	0	1	
	Other	1	0	0	0	1	
	TOTAL	47	4	1	7	59	

SQUAD APPEARANCES

Match	1	2	3	4	5	6	7	8	9	10	11	12	13	14	15	16	17	18	19	20	21	22	23	24	25	26	27	28	29	30	31	32	33	34	35	36	37	38	39	40	41	42	43	44	45	46	47
Venue	A	H	A	H	A	H	A	H	H	A	H	A	A	H	A	A	H	A	A	A	H	H	A	A	A	H	H	A	H	A	A	H	A	H	H	H	H	A	H	A	A	H	A	H	A	H	A
Competition	O	O	O	O	L	L	L	L	L	L	L	L	L	L	W	L	L	L	L	W	L	L	L	L	L	L	F	L	L	F	L	L	L	F	L	L	L	L	L	F	L	L	L	L	L	L	L
Result	W	W	L	L	L	D	L	L	D	W	W	D	L	W	W	W	W	L	L	L	D	W	W	L	L	D	W	L	L	W	L	W	W	W	D	W	W	L	L	L	L	W	W	W	W	W	D

Goalkeepers
Tony Caig
Shay Given
Steve Harper

Defenders
Celestine Babayaro
Jean-Alain Boumsong
Titus Bramble
Stephen Carr
Robbie Elliott
Kris Gate
Paul Huntington
Craig Moore
Peter Ramage
Steven Taylor

Midfielders
Lee Bowyer
Martin Brittain
Nicky Butt
Lee Clark
Kieron Dyer
Emre Belozoglu
Amdy Faye
Jermaine Jenas
James Milner
Charles N'Zogbia
Alan O'Brien
Scott Parker
Matty Pattison
Nolberto Solano

Forwards
Shola Ameobi
Michael Chopra
Alberto Luque
Michael Owen
Alan Shearer

KEY: On all match | On bench | Subbed or sent off (Counting game) | Subbed or sent off (playing less than 70 mins) | Subbed on from bench (Counting Game) | Subbed on (playing less than 70 mins) | Subbed on and then subbed or sent off (Counting Game) | Subbed on and then subbed or sent off (playing less than 70 mins) | Not in 16

KEY PLAYERS - GOALSCORERS

Shola Ameobi

Goals in the League	9
Goals in all competitions	9
Assists League goals scored by a team mate where the player delivered the final pass	2
Contribution to Attacking Power Average number of minutes between League team goals while on pitch	67
Player Strike Rate **Average number of minutes between League goals scored by player**	**237**
Club Strike Rate Average minutes between League goals scored by club	73

	PLAYER	GOALS LGE	GOALS ALL	ASSISTS	POWER	S RATE
1	Shola Ameobi	9	9	2	67	**237 mins**
2	Alan Shearer	10	12	4	72	**274 mins**
3	Nolberto Solano	6	6	2	55	**369 mins**
4	Charles N'Zogbia	5	5	10	66	**463 mins**

KEY PLAYERS - MIDFIELDERS

Nolberto Solano

Goals in the League	6
Goals in all competitions	6
Assists League goals scored by a team mate where the player delivered the final pass	2
Defensive Rating Average number of mins between League goals conceded while on the pitch	82
Contribution to Attacking Power Average number of minutes between League team goals while on pitch	55
Scoring Difference **Defensive Rating minus Contribution to Attacking Power**	**27**

	PLAYER	GOALS LGE	GOALS ALL	ASSISTS	DEF RATE	POWER	SC DIFF
1	Nolberto Solano	6	6	2	82	55	**27 mins**
2	Charles N'Zogbia	5	5	10	89	66	**23 mins**
3	Amdy Faye	0	0	2	79	61	**18 mins**
4	Emre Belozoglu	2	2	2	69	66	**3 mins**

PLAYER APPEARANCES

	AGE (on 01/07/06)	IN NAMED 16	APPEARANCES	COUNTING GAMES	MINUTES ON PITCH	APPEARANCES	MINUTES ON PITCH	THIS SEASON	HOME COUNTRY
Goalkeepers									
Tony Caig	32	1	0	0	0	0	0	-	England
Shay Given	30	38	38	38	3420	47	4230	5	Rep of Ireland (15)
Steve Harper	32	36	0	0	0	1	90	-	England
Defenders									
Celestine Babayaro	27	28	28	23	2316	35	2907	-	Nigeria
Jean-Alain Boumsong	26	35	33	29	2716	41	3436	9	France (8)
Titus Bramble	24	24	24	20	1946	28	2306	-	England
Stephen Carr	29	19	19	17	1609	24	2026	4	Rep of Ireland (15)
Robbie Elliott	32	32	17	13	1327	22	1777	-	England
Kris Gate	21	1	0	0	0	0	0	-	England
Paul Huntington	18	0	0	0	0	0	0	-	England
Craig Moore	30	10	8	8	720	9	759	1	Australia (42)
Peter Ramage	22	27	23	22	2025	29	2508	-	England
Steven Taylor	20	12	12	10	954	17	1404	-	England
Midfielders									
Lee Bowyer	29	28	28	13	1627	34	2047	-	England
Martin Brittain	21	10	0	0	0	6	192	-	England
Nicky Butt	31	0	0	0	0	2	180	-	England
Lee Clark	33	32	22	7	897	25	1096	-	England
Kieron Dyer	27	11	11	2	452	13	617	-	England
Emre Belozoglu	25	20	20	17	1590	25	1892	3	Turkey (14)
Amdy Faye	29	31	22	13	1343	25	1486	9	Senegal (28)
Jermaine Jenas	23	4	4	2	280	5	370	5	England (10)
James Milner	20	3	3	1	133	7	454	-	England
Charles N'Zogbia	20	34	32	22	2314	41	2957	-	France
Alan O'Brien	21	4	3	0	50	4	55	-	England
Scott Parker	25	26	26	26	2302	32	2827	-	England
Matty Pattison	19	4	3	1	147	3	147	-	South Africa
Nolberto Solano	31	29	29	21	2211	35	2679	-	Peru
Forwards									
Shola Ameobi	24	30	30	20	2135	34	2422	-	England
Michael Chopra	22	18	13	5	595	19	888	-	England
Alberto Luque	28	17	14	4	653	18	830	3	Spain (5)
Michael Owen	26	11	11	9	884	11	884	6	England (10)
Alan Shearer	36	32	32	31	2743	41	3553	-	England

KEY: LEAGUE | ALL COMPS | CAPS | (MAY FIFA RANKING)

TEAM OF THE SEASON

GIVEN — CG 38 DR 81

CARR — CG 17 DR 95
BRAMBLE — CG 20 DR 93
ELLIOTT — CG 13 DR 83
BABAYARO — CG 23 DR 80

SOLANO — CG 21 SD +27
FAYE — CG 13 SD +18
EMRE — CG 17 SD +3
N'ZOGBIA — CG 22 SD +23

SHEARER — CG 31 AP 72
AMEOBI — CG 20 SR 237

KEY: DR = Defensive Rate, SD = Scoring Difference AP = Attacking Power SR = Strike Rate, CG=Counting games – League games playing at least 70 minutes

TOP POINT EARNERS

Charles N'Zogbia

Counting Games League games when player was on pitch for at least 70 minutes	22
Average points Average League points taken in Counting games	2.05
Club Average points Average points taken in League games	1.53

	PLAYER	GAMES	PTS
1	Charles N'Zogbia	22	2.05
2	Amdy Faye	13	1.92
3	Nolberto Solano	21	1.90
4	Titus Bramble	20	1.85
5	Shola Ameobi	20	1.85
6	Robbie Elliott	13	1.77
7	Stephen Carr	17	1.65
8	Emre Belozoglu	17	1.65
9	Shay Given	38	1.53
10	Peter Ramage	22	1.50

KEY PLAYERS - DEFENDERS

Stephen Carr

Goals Conceded in the League Number of League goals conceded while the player was on the pitch	17
Goals Conceded in all competitions Total number of goals conceded while the player was on the pitch	20
League minutes played Number of minutes played in league matches	1609
Clean Sheets In games when the player was on pitch for at least 70 minutes	7
Defensive Rating Average number of mins between League goals conceded while on the pitch	95
Club Defensive Rating Average number of mins between League goals conceded by the club this season	81

	PLAYER	CON LGE	CON ALL	MINS	C SHEETS	DEF RATE
1	Stephen Carr	17	20	1609	7	95 mins
2	Titus Bramble	21	21	1946	7	93 mins
3	Robbie Elliott	16	20	1327	3	83 mins
4	Celestine Babayaro	29	30	2316	10	80 mins

KEY GOALKEEPER

Shay Given

Goals Conceded in the League Number of League goals conceded while the player was on the pitch	42
Goals Conceded in all competitions Total number of goals conceded while the player was on the pitch	46
League minutes played Number of minutes played in league matches	3420
Clean Sheets In games when the player was on pitch for at least 70 minutes	13
Goals to Shots Ratio The average number of shots on target per each League goal conceded	5
Defensive Rating Ave mins between League goals conceded while on the pitch	81

BOOKINGS

Steven Taylor

League Yellow	6
League Red	1
All competitions Yellow	7
All competitions Red	1

League Average **136** mins between cards

	PLAYER	LEAGUE 6Y	LEAGUE 1R	TOTAL 7Y	TOTAL 1R	AVE
1	Taylor	6Y	1R	7Y	1R	136
2	Moore	4	0	5	0	180
3	Carr	6	2	6	2	201
4	Clark	4	0	5	0	224
5	Parker	9	1	10	1	230
6	Emre Belozoglu	4	0	5	0	397
7	Bramble	4	0	4	0	486
8	Ramage	4	0	4	0	506
9	Ameobi	4	0	5	0	533
10	Bowyer	2	1	2	1	542
11	Babayaro	3	1	3	1	579
12	Luque	1	0	1	0	653
13	Elliott	2	0	5	1	663
14	Faye	2	0	2	0	671
15	N'Zogbia	3	0	3	0	771
	Other	9	1	12	1	
	TOTAL	67	7	79	8	

BOLTON

Sam Allardyce missed out on the England vacancy and, more narrowly, on another Uefa-sponsored trip around Europe. He had two very different striking options; the prolific Mexican star **Jared Borgetti** in the squad - and usually on the sidelines - and hard-working **Kevin Davies** on the pitch. Davies' seven league goals came at a Strike Rate of one every 447 minutes. Borgetti also hit seven (mainly in cups) at a Strike Rate of 155.

However, Borgetti didn't see enough league action to be included in our charts so midfielder-cum-striker **Stelios Giannakopoulos** leads the club's Strike Rate charts with scoring goals.

The sixth best defence in the division saw **Bruno N'Gotty** and young **Joey O'Brien** as the stand-out players both recording Defensive Ratings of slightly better than 90 minutes. O'Brien also performed well in the Top Point Earners table.

NICKNAME: THE TROTTERS

KEY: Won / Drawn / Lost

No	Comp	Opponent	H/A	Res	Score	Scorers
1	prem	**Aston Villa**	A	D	2-2	Davies 6; Campo 8
2	prem	**Everton**	H	L	0-1	
3	prem	**Newcastle**	H	W	2-0	Diouf 37; Giannakopoulos 50
4	prem	**West Ham**	A	W	2-1	Nolan 59; Campo 85
5	prem	**Blackburn**	H	D	0-0	
6	uc1rl1	**Loko Plovdiv**	H	W	2-1	Diouf 72; Borgetti 90
7	prem	**Man City**	A	W	1-0	Speed 90 pen
8	prem	**Portsmouth**	H	W	1-0	Nolan 25
9	uc1rl2	**Loko Plovdiv**	A	W	2-1	Tunchev 79 og; Nolan 86
10	prem	**Wigan**	A	L	1-2	Jaidi 68
11	prem	**Chelsea**	A	L	1-5	Giannakopoulos 4
12	ucgph	**Besiktas**	A	D	1-1	Borgetti 29
13	prem	**West Brom**	H	W	2-0	Nakata 81; Nolan 90
14	ccr3	**West Ham**	H	W	1-0	Borgetti 64
15	prem	**Charlton**	A	W	1-0	Nolan 72
16	ucgph	**Z St Petersburg**	H	W	1-0	Nolan 24
17	prem	**Tottenham**	H	W	1-0	Nolan 32
18	ucgph	**Guimaraes**	A	D	1-1	Vaz Te 88
19	prem	**Fulham**	A	L	1-2	Legwinski 90 og
20	ccr4	**Leicester**	H	W	2-1	Borgetti 104; Vaz Te 106
21	prem	**Arsenal**	H	W	2-0	Faye 20; Giannakopoulos 32
22	prem	**Aston Villa**	H	D	1-1	Diouf 82
23	ucgph	**Seville**	H	D	1-1	N'Gotty 65
24	prem	**Everton**	A	W	4-0	Davies 32; Giannakopoulos 75,80; Speed 79 pen
25	ccqf	**Wigan**	A	L	0-2	
26	prem	**Sunderland**	A	D	0-0	
27	prem	**Man Utd**	A	L	1-4	Speed 33
28	prem	**Liverpool**	H	D	2-2	Jaidi 10; Diouf 71
29	facr3	**Watford**	A	W	3-0	Borgetti 11; Giannakopoulos 34; Vaz Te 73
30	prem	**Blackburn**	A	D	0-0	
31	prem	**Man City**	H	W	2-0	Borgetti 37; Nolan 41
32	facr4	**Arsenal**	H	W	1-0	Giannakopoulos 84
33	prem	**Portsmouth**	A	D	1-1	Fadiga 69
34	prem	**Wigan**	H	D	1-1	Giannakopoulos 63
35	prem	**Arsenal**	A	D	1-1	Nolan 12
36	uc3rl1	**Marseille**	H	D	0-0	
37	facr5	**West Ham**	H	D	0-0	
38	uc3rl2	**Marseille**	A	L	1-2	Giannakopoulos 25
39	prem	**Fulham**	H	W	2-1	Helguson 45 og; Nolan 68
40	prem	**Newcastle**	A	L	1-3	Davies 72
41	prem	**West Ham**	H	W	4-1	Giannakopoulos 12,33; Speed 45; Pedersen 81
42	facr5r	**West Ham**	A	L	1-2	Davies 31
43	prem	**Sunderland**	H	W	2-0	Davies 47; Nolan 85
44	prem	**Middlesbrough**	A	L	3-4	Giannakopoulos 3; Okocha 57; Jaidi 81
45	prem	**Man Utd**	H	L	1-2	Davies 26
46	prem	**Birmingham**	A	L	0-1	
47	prem	**Liverpool**	A	L	0-1	
48	prem	**Chelsea**	H	L	0-2	
49	prem	**West Brom**	A	D	0-0	
50	prem	**Charlton**	H	W	4-1	Vaz Te 14; Davies 21,89; Borgetti 31
51	prem	**Tottenham**	A	L	0-1	
52	prem	**Middlesbrough**	H	D	1-1	Vaz Te 51
53	prem	**Birmingham**	H	W	1-0	Vaz Te 65

1st
2nd
3rd
4th
5th
6th
7th
8th
9th
10th
11th
12th
13th
14th
15th
16th
17th
18th
19th
20th
LEAGUE POSITION
AUGUST
SEPTEMBER
OCTOBER
Home Away Neutral
Three penalties denied and late Nolan 'goal' disallowed as ref Riley riles Sam again
Diouf darts in to head Newcastle behind before Stelios scores to add to his list of admirers
Cool Campo settles jitters with 35 yard bar-shaker before linking with Okocha to score winner at West Ham
Own goal salvages Uefa run as Bulgarians' lead is torpedoed by bizarre defensive error before Nolan adds a winner
Borgetti fires home to level Brazilian Ailton's goal in Turkey and injury-hit squad claim a draw
Acrobatic Nolan hits overhead kick winner to move up to third as Nakata's flicks supply the inspiration
Borgetti strikes in stoppage time to give Sam a win after Bulgarians take an early lead
Gardner off after handball but Essien stays on after vicious foul and Chelsea steam back from Stelios' early goal
"Better and better" Allardyce assesses Nakata's form as new signing's freekick despatches West Brom
"We had 17 attempts at goal", Allardyce adds up his efforts, while Everton escape with a 1-0 win
Third in four starts for Borgetti as West Ham fall to in-form Mexican's header
Deflected up to fourth as Faye's shot hits a Charlton defender and Nolan scores from the resulting parry

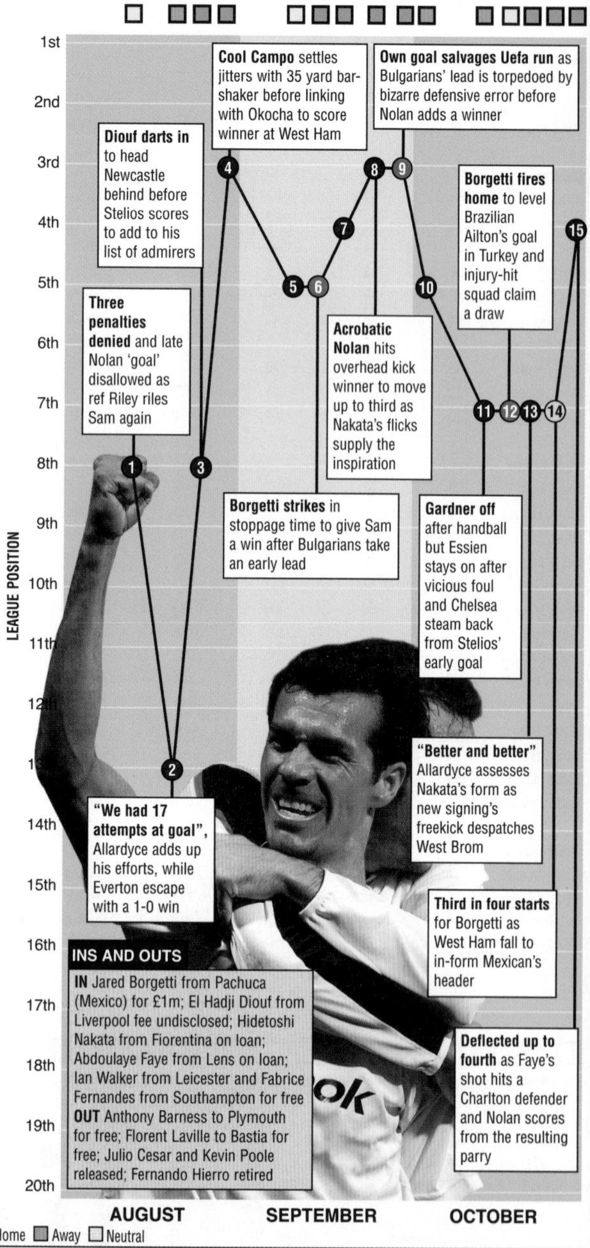

INS AND OUTS

IN Jared Borgetti from Pachuca (Mexico) for £1m; El Hadji Diouf from Liverpool fee undisclosed; Hidetoshi Nakata from Fiorentina on loan; Abdoulaye Faye from Lens on loan; Ian Walker from Leicester and Fabrice Fernandes from Southampton for free **OUT** Anthony Barness to Plymouth for free; Florent Laville to Bastia for free; Julio Cesar and Kevin Poole released; Fernando Hierro retired

ATTENDANCES

HOME GROUND: REEBOK STADIUM CAPACITY: 28723 AVERAGE LEAGUE AT HOME: 25265

27	Man Utd	67858	48	Chelsea	27266	5	Blackburn	24405	33	Portsmouth	19128
40	Newcastle	52012	21	Arsenal	26792	13	West Brom	24151	30	Blackburn	18180
47	Liverpool	44194	17	Tottenham	26634	22	Aston Villa	23646	37	West Ham	17120
7	Man City	43137	46	Birmingham	26493	43	Sunderland	23568	12	Besiktas	17027
11	Chelsea	41775	31	Man City	26466	49	West Brom	23181	16	Z St Peter	15905
38	Marseille	38351	53	Birmingham	26275	8	Portsmouth	23134	23	Seville	15623
35	Arsenal	38193	15	Charlton	26175	39	Fulham	23104	25	Wigan	13401
51	Tottenham	36179	44	Middlesboro	25971	52	Middlesboro	22733	32	Arsenal	13326
24	Everton	34500	3	Newcastle	25904	10	Wigan	20553	29	Watford	13239
1	Aston Villa	33263	34	Wigan	25854	18	Guimaraes	20000	20	Leicester	13067
26	Sunderland	32232	2	Everton	25608	19	Fulham	19768	14	West Ham	10927
4	West Ham	31629	50	Charlton	24713	6	Loko Plovdiv	19723			
45	Man Utd	27718	42	West Ham	24685	9	Loko Plovdiv	19723			
28	Liverpool	27604	41	West Ham	24461	36	Marseille	19288			

No repeat of Uefa adventure for Sam

Final Position: **8th**

KEY: ● League ● Champions Lge ● UEFA Cup ● FA Cup ○ League Cup ● Other

Fifth goal in seven starts for Nolan who thrives in the downpour to score the only goal against Zenit

Cap that! Eriksson's watching as captain Nolan enhances his claim for England call-up with a thunderous shot past Robinson

Back home; Vaz Te returns to his native Portugal to hit vital equaliser against Vitória

Arsenal outplayed and out-fought by Stelios and Faye with sub Vaz Te missing a golden chance for 3-0

Borgetti makes difference as late sub breaks the deadlock after 90 minutes of cup stalemate against Leicester

Diouf mouths off for a red as he leaves the pitch and seven bookings anger Sam at Fulham

Into the last 32 with N'Gotty's first goal for nearly two years enough to progress

Diouf sets up record ninth successive home win but outplayed Villa snatch a draw

Cool Stelios finishes twice and Davies gets first goal since the start of the season as Everton defence self-destructs

"Abysmal" in front of goal says Allardyce as chances go begging and Wigan progress to Carling semis

N'Gotty own goals kick-start Man United who are then unstoppable

Ashton's reward – a run out at the end of game won from Borgetti's 11th minute strike

Allardyce plots an end to Liverpool's winning run with goals from Jaidi and Diouf in ill-tempered draw

Poacher Borgetti nets first Premier goal on second Premier start with a sharp shot before **Nolan** blasts the second

Nakata off as Sam slams Riley's record; five sent off in seven games

Another injury as Fadiga falls badly at Wigan and is out for the season

Stelios stuns holders with diving header – his third in four games against Arsenal – to reach next round

INS AND OUTS

IN Matt Jansen from Blackburn for free; Oscar Perez from Cordoba (Spain) and Ali Al Habsi from Lyn Oslo (Norway) for free **OUT** Martin Djetou and Fabrice Fernandes released

Nolan's exquisite flick leaves Lehmann stranded but Arsenal level late despite Gardner's heroics

Jaaskelainen's clean sheet is Sam's silver lining as crucial save keeps Marseille from an away goal

Stelios denied by linesman's flag and over-elaborate tumble as Hammers escape for a replay

Unlucky Ben Haim turns Marseille winner into his own net

Bankable Nolan is Barclays Player of the Month

Hammers stunned by Stelios, Speed and Pedersen while Okocha is twice denied in a top attacking display

"Dejected" as West Ham turn the tables with a stronger line up and an extra time goal to end silverware chase

Davies breaks the deadlock at Sunderland and Nolan nets his 11th of the season

Stelios misses best chance at Birmingham as home side hang on under pressure

Davies' fine strike only wakes up United, who take all three points with a late onslaught

"Clean sheets eluding us" says Allardyce as shaky Liverpool inflict a fourth defeat

Bloody end to a cracking game as Boro steal it in the last minute after Jaidi levels at 3-3 and Davies falls out with Pogatetz

Vaz Te close as he bundles ball against Chelsea's post but champions prove too strong

Nakata thumps woodwork and Stelios should have earned a penalty but out-played Spurs sneak a win

Vaz Te hooks in a winner for third successive top ten finish but there's no route to Europe

Allardyce to miss out on England job as FA favourite McClaren brings his young side to take a point at the Reebok

MONTH BY MONTH POINTS TALLY

AUGUST	7	58%
SEPTEMBER	7	78%
OCTOBER	6	50%
NOVEMBER	3	50%
DECEMBER	8	53%
JANUARY	5	56%
FEBRUARY	6	50%
MARCH	6	50%
APRIL	4	19%
MAY	4	67%

NOVEMBER DECEMBER JANUARY FEBRUARY MARCH APRIL MAY

GOAL ATTEMPTS

FOR – Goal attempts recorded in League games

	HOME	AWAY	TOTAL	AVE
shots on target	98	85	183	4.8
shots off target	116	85	201	5.3
TOTAL	214	170	384	10.1

Ratio of goals to shots Average number of shots on target per League goal scored	3.6
Accuracy rating Average percentage of total goal attempts which were on target	47.7

AGAINST – Goal attempts recorded in League games

	HOME	AWAY	TOTAL	AVE
shots on target	67	107	174	4.6
shots off target	73	85	158	4.2
TOTAL	140	192	332	8.7

Ratio of goals to shots Average number of shots on target per League goal scored	4.1
Accuracy rating Average percentage of total goal attempts which were on target	52.4

GOALS

Kevin Nolan

League	9
FA Cup	0
League Cup	0
Europe	2
Other	0
TOTAL	11

League Average **346** mins between goals

	PLAYER	LGE	FAC	LC	Euro	TOT	AVE
1	Nolan	9	0	0	2	11	346
2	Giannakopoulos	9	2	0	1	12	281
3	Davies	7	1	0	0	8	447
4	Speed	4	0	0	0	4	618
5	Diouf	3	0	0	1	4	468
6	Jaidi	3	0	0	0	3	409
7	Vaz Te	3	1	1	1	6	282
8	Campo	2	0	0	0	2	433
9	Borgetti	2	1	2	2	7	277
10	Fadiga	1	0	0	0	1	308
11	Faye	1	0	0	0	1	2003
12	Pedersen	1	0	0	0	1	1452
13	Okocha	1	0	0	0	1	1616
14	Nakata	1	0	0	0	1	1276
15	N'Gotty	0	0	0	1	1	
	Other	2	0	0	1	3	
	TOTAL	49	5	3	9	66	

SQUAD APPEARANCES

Match	1	2	3	4	5	6	7	8	9	10	11	12	13	14	15	16	17	18	19	20	21	22	23	24	25	26	27	28	29	30	31	32	33	34	35	36	37	38	39	40	41	42	43	44	45	46	47	48	49	50	51	52	53
Venue	A	H	H	A	H	H	A	H	A	A	A	A	H	H	A	H	H	A	A	H	H	H	H	A	A	A	A	H	A	A	H	H	A	H	A	H	H	A	H	A	H	A	H	A	H	A	A	H	A	H	A	H	H
Competition	L	L	L	L	L	E	L	L	E	L	L	E	L	W	L	E	L	E	L	W	L	L	E	L	W	L	L	L	F	L	L	F	L	L	L	E	F	E	L	L	L	F	L	L	L	L	L	L	L	L	L	L	L
Result	D	L	W	W	D	W	W	W	W	L	L	D	W	W	W	W	W	D	L	W	W	D	D	W	L	D	L	D	W	D	W	W	D	D	D	D	D	L	W	L	W	L	W	L	L	L	L	L	D	W	L	D	W

Goalkeepers
Ali Al Habsi
Sam Ashton
Chris Howarth
Jussi Jaaskelainen
Ian Walker

Defenders
Tal Ben Haim
Jaroslav Fojut
Ricardo Gardner
Nicky Hunt
Radhi Jaidi
Bruno N'Gotty
Joey O'Brien
Robert Sissons

Midfielders
Ivan Campo
Martin Djetou
Khalilou Fadiga
Abdoulaye Faye
Fabrice Fernandes
Stelios Giannakopoulos
Hidetoshi Nakata
Kevin Nolan
Augustine Okocha
Oscar Perez
Gary Speed

Forwards
Jared Echavarria Borgetti
Bedi Buval
Kevin Davies
El Hadji Diouf
Matthew Jansen
Henrik Pedersen
James Sinclair
Ricardo Vaz Te

KEY: On all match · On bench · Subbed or sent off (Counting game) · Subbed or sent off (playing less than 70 mins) · Subbed on from bench (Counting Game) · Subbed on (playing less than 70 mins) · Subbed on and then subbed or sent off (Counting Game) · Subbed on and then subbed or sent off (playing less than 70 mins) · Not in 16

KEY PLAYERS - GOALSCORERS

Stelios Giannakopoulos

Goals in the League	9
Goals in all competitions	12
Assists League goals scored by a team mate where the player delivered the final pass	4
Contribution to Attacking Power Average number of minutes between League team goals while on pitch	70
Player Strike Rate Average number of minutes between League goals scored by player	281
Club Strike Rate Average minutes between League goals scored by club	70

	PLAYER	GOALS LGE	GOALS ALL	ASSISTS	POWER	S RATE
1	Stelios Giannakopoulos	9	12	4	70	**281 mins**
2	Kevin Nolan	9	11	5	69	**346 mins**
3	Radhi Jaidi	3	3	2	53	**409 mins**
4	Kevin Davies	7	8	7	70	**447 mins**

KEY PLAYERS - MIDFIELDERS

Gary Speed

Goals in the League	4
Goals in all competitions	4
Assists League goals scored by a team mate where the player delivered the final pass	3
Defensive Rating Average number of mins between League goals conceded while on the pitch	88
Contribution to Attacking Power Average number of minutes between League team goals while on pitch	65
Scoring Difference Defensive Rating minus Contribution to Attacking Power	23

	PLAYER	GOALS LGE	GOALS ALL	ASSISTS	DEF RATE	POWER	SC DIFF
1	Gary Speed	4	4	3	88	65	**23 mins**
2	Augustine Okocha	1	1	2	85	67	**18 mins**
3	Stelios Giannakopoulos	9	12	4	87	70	**17 mins**
4	Kevin Nolan	9	11	5	82	69	**13 mins**

PLAYER APPEARANCES

	AGE (on 01/07/06)	IN NAMED 16	APPEARANCES	COUNTING GAMES	MINUTES ON PITCH	APPEARANCES	MINUTES ON PITCH	THIS SEASON	HOME COUNTRY
Goalkeepers									
Ali Al Habsi	24	3	0	0	0	0	0	-	Oman
Sam Ashton	19	0	0	0	0	0	0	-	England
Chris Howarth	21	0	0	0	0	0	0	-	
Jussi Jaaskelainen	31	38	38	38	3420	2	0	3	Finland (42)
Ian Walker	34	35	0	0	0	0	0	-	England
Defenders									
Tal Ben Haim	24	36	35	31	2841	9	1	3	Israel (49)
Jaroslav Fojut	-82	3	1	0	5	0	0	-	Poland
Ricardo Gardner	27	30	30	25	2412	3	1	-	Jamaica
Nicky Hunt	22	21	20	11	1243	1	0	-	England
Radhi Jaidi	30	23	16	13	1228	1	0	8	Tunisia (21)
Bruno N'Gotty	35	30	29	26	2451	2	0	-	France
Joey O'Brien	20	23	23	21	1975	2	0	-	Rep of Ireland
Robert Sissons	17	0	0	0	0	0	0	-	England
Midfielders									
Ivan Campo	32	16	15	6	865	2	0	-	Spain
Martin Djetou	31	4	3	0	95	0	0	-	France
Khalilou Fadiga	31	9	8	3	308	2	0	-	Senegal
Abdoulaye Faye	28	30	27	20	2003	6	0	5	Senegal (28)
Fabrice Fernandes	26	1	1	0	16	0	0	-	France
Stelios Giannakop'los	31	36	34	24	2533	4	0	4	Greece (20)
Hidetoshi Nakata	29	30	21	10	1276	3	1	-	Japan
Kevin Nolan	24	36	36	34	3112	7	0	-	England
Augustine Okocha	32	30	26	14	1616	1	0	2	Nigeria (11)
Oscar Perez	24	0	0	0	0	0	0	-	Spain
Gary Speed	36	31	31	27	2471	2	0	-	Wales
Forwards									
Jared Borgetti	32	30	19	2	554	0	0	5	Mexico (4)
Bedi Buval	20	0	0	0	0	0	0	-	France
Kevin Davies	29	37	37	33	3132	10	0	-	England
El Hadji Diouf	25	21	20	14	1405	6	1	5	Senegal (28)
Matthew Jansen	28	6	6	2	271	0	0	-	England
Henrik Pedersen	31	22	21	12	1452	0	0	-	Denmark
James Sinclair	18	0	0	0	0	0	0	-	England
Ricardo Vaz Te	19	26	22	4	847	3	0	-	Portugal

KEY: LEAGUE   ALL COMPS   CAPS   (MAY FIFA RANKING)

TEAM OF THE SEASON

JAASKELAINEN — CG 38 DR 83

O'BRIEN — CG 21 DR 90

BEN HAIM — CG 31 DR 86

N'GOTTY — CG 26 DR 91

GARDNER — CG 25 DR 75

NOLAN — CG 34 SD +13

OKOCHA — CG 14 SD +18

SPEED — CG 27 SD +23

STELIOS — CG 24 SD +17

DIOUF — CG 14 AP 88

DAVIES — CG 33 SR 447

KEY: DR = Defensive Rate, SD = Scoring Difference AP = Attacking Power SR = Strike Rate, CG=Counting games – League games playing at least 70 minutes

TOP POINT EARNERS

Henrik Pedersen

Counting Games League games when player was on pitch for at least 70 minutes	12
Average points Average League points taken in Counting games	1.75
Club Average points Average points taken in League games	1.47

	PLAYER	GAMES	PTS
1	Henrik Pedersen	12	1.75
2	Joey O'Brien	21	1.71
3	El Hadji Diouf	14	1.64
4	Stelios Giannakopoulos	24	1.54
5	Radhi Jaidi	13	1.54
6	Augustine Okocha	14	1.50
7	Kevin Nolan	34	1.50
8	Bruno N'Gotty	26	1.50
9	Jussi Jaaskelainen	38	1.47
10	Tal Ben Haim	31	1.45

KEY PLAYERS - DEFENDERS

Bruno N'Gotty

Goals Conceded in the League Number of League goals conceded while the player was on the pitch	27
Goals Conceded in all competitions Total number of goals conceded while the player was on the pitch	33
League minutes played Number of minutes played in league matches	2451
Clean Sheets In games when the player was on pitch for at least 70 minutes	12
Defensive Rating Average number of mins between League goals conceded while on the pitch	91
Club Defensive Rating Average number of mins between League goals conceded by the club this season	83

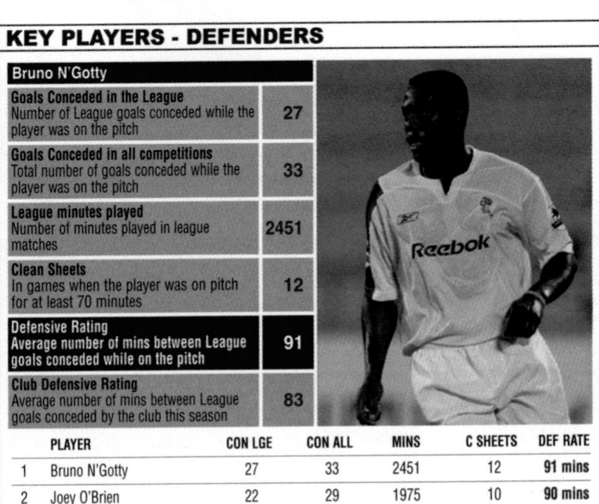

	PLAYER	CON LGE	CON ALL	MINS	C SHEETS	DEF RATE
1	Bruno N'Gotty	27	33	2451	12	91 mins
2	Joey O'Brien	22	29	1975	10	90 mins
3	Tal Ben Haim	33	44	2841	12	86 mins
4	Ricardo Gardner	32	42	2412	8	75 mins

KEY GOALKEEPER

Jussi Jaaskelainen

Goals Conceded in the League Number of League goals conceded while the player was on the pitch	41
Goals Conceded in all competitions Total number of goals conceded while the player was on the pitch	50
League minutes played Number of minutes played in league matches	3420
Clean Sheets In games when the player was on pitch for at least 70 minutes	15
Goals to Shots Ratio The average number of shots on target per each League goal conceded	4.7
Defensive Rating Ave mins between League goals conceded while on the pitch	83

BOOKINGS

El Hadji Diouf

League Yellow	6
League Red	1
All competitions Yellow	7
All competitions Red	1

League Average 200 mins between cards

	PLAYER	LEAGUE Y	LEAGUE R	TOTAL Y	TOTAL R	AVE
1	Diouf	6Y	1R	7Y	1R	200
2	Vaz Te	3	0	3	0	282
3	Ben Haim	9	1	11	1	284
4	Davies	10	0	12	0	313
5	Nakata	3	1	6	1	319
6	Faye	6	0	8	0	333
7	Campo	2	0	2	0	432
8	Nolan	7	0	10	0	444
9	Gardner	3	1	4	1	603
10	Giannakopoulos	4	0	4	0	633
11	O'Brien	2	0	3	0	987
12	N'Gotty	2	0	2	0	1225
13	Jaidi	1	0	1	0	1228
14	Speed	2	0	2	0	1235
15	Hunt	1	0	1	0	1243
	Other	3	0	4	0	
	TOTAL	64	4	80	4	

WEST HAM UNITED

'One of the greatest post-war finals' claimed the commentary. In the season that they lost both Ron Greenwood and John Lyall, the Hammers performed strongly in the top flight and finished with a day to remember.

Marlon Harewood won over the doubters with 14 league goals scored at a Strike Rate of a goal every 202 minutes. **Bobby Zamora** and **Teddy Sheringham** weighed in with goals and **Dean Ashton** looks capable of beating 200 minutes next season.

Yossi Benayoun struck five goals from midfield and finished as the club's top midfielder, while **Daniel Gabbidon** shored up a patchy defence and leads our Top Point Scorers chart. **Shaka Hislop** was a Portsmouth discard but his Goals-to-Shots Ratio of 5.4 shots on target for every goal conceded is one of the better records around.

NICKNAME: THE HAMMERS **KEY:** Won Drawn Lost

1	prem	**Blackburn**	H	W	3-1	Sheringham 46; Reo-Coker 62; Etherington 80
2	prem	**Newcastle**	A	D	0-0	
3	prem	**Bolton**	H	L	1-2	Sheringham 90
4	prem	**Aston Villa**	H	W	4-0	Harewood 24,29,49; Benayoun 88
5	prem	**Fulham**	A	W	2-1	Harewood 46; Warner 52 og
6	ccr2	**Sheff Wed**	A	W	4-2	Zamora 2,63; Dailly 54; Bellion 84
7	prem	**Arsenal**	H	D	0-0	
8	prem	**Sunderland**	A	D	1-1	Benayoun 72
9	prem	**Man City**	A	L	1-2	Zamora 90
10	prem	**Middlesbrough**	H	W	2-1	Sheringham 66; Riggott 74 og
11	ccr3	**Bolton**	A	L	0-1	
12	prem	**Liverpool**	A	L	0-2	
13	prem	**West Brom**	H	W	1-0	Sheringham 57
14	prem	**Tottenham**	A	D	1-1	Ferdinand 90
15	prem	**Man Utd**	H	L	1-2	Harewood 1
16	prem	**Birmingham**	A	W	2-1	Zamora 36; Harewood 45
17	prem	**Blackburn**	A	L	2-3	Zamora 45; Harewood 63
18	prem	**Everton**	A	W	2-1	Weir 19 og; Zamora 67
19	prem	**Newcastle**	H	L	2-4	Solano 20 og; Harewood 73 pen
20	prem	**Portsmouth**	A	D	1-1	Collins 56
21	prem	**Wigan**	H	L	0-2	
22	prem	**Charlton**	A	L	0-2	
23	prem	**Chelsea**	H	L	1-3	Harewood 46
24	facr3	**Norwich**	A	W	2-1	Mullins 6; Zamora 57
25	prem	**Aston Villa**	A	W	2-1	Zamora 51; Harewood 60 pen
26	prem	**Fulham**	H	W	2-1	Ferdinand 17; Benayoun 28
27	facr4	**Blackburn**	H	W	4-2	Sheringham 33 pen; Etherington 37; Khizanishvili 59 og; Zamora 73
28	prem	**Arsenal**	A	W	3-2	Reo-Coker 25; Zamora 32; Etherington 80
29	prem	**Sunderland**	H	W	2-0	Ashton 81; Konchesky 87
30	prem	**Birmingham**	H	W	3-0	Harewood 10,63; Ashton 64
31	facr5	**Bolton**	A	D	0-0	
32	prem	**Everton**	H	D	2-2	Harewood 11; Ashton 23
33	prem	**Bolton**	A	L	1-4	Sheringham 79
34	facr5r	**Bolton**	H	W	2-1	Jaaskelainen 10 og; Harewood 96
35	prem	**Portsmouth**	H	L	2-4	Sheringham 69; Benayoun 90
36	facqf	**Man City**	A	W	2-1	Ashton 41,69
37	prem	**Wigan**	A	W	2-1	Harewood 52; Reo-Coker 90
38	prem	**Man Utd**	A	L	0-1	
39	prem	**Charlton**	H	D	0-0	
40	prem	**Chelsea**	A	L	1-4	Collins 10
41	prem	**Man City**	H	W	1-0	Newton 15
42	prem	**Middlesbrough**	A	L	0-2	
43	facsf	**Middlesbrough**	A	W	1-0	Harewood 78
44	prem	**Liverpool**	H	L	1-2	Reo-Coker 46
45	prem	**West Brom**	A	W	1-0	Reo-Coker 41
46	prem	**Tottenham**	H	W	2-1	Fletcher 10; Benayoun 80
47	facf	**Liverpool**	A	L	1-3*	Carragher 21 og; Ashton 28; Konchesky 64 (*on penalties)

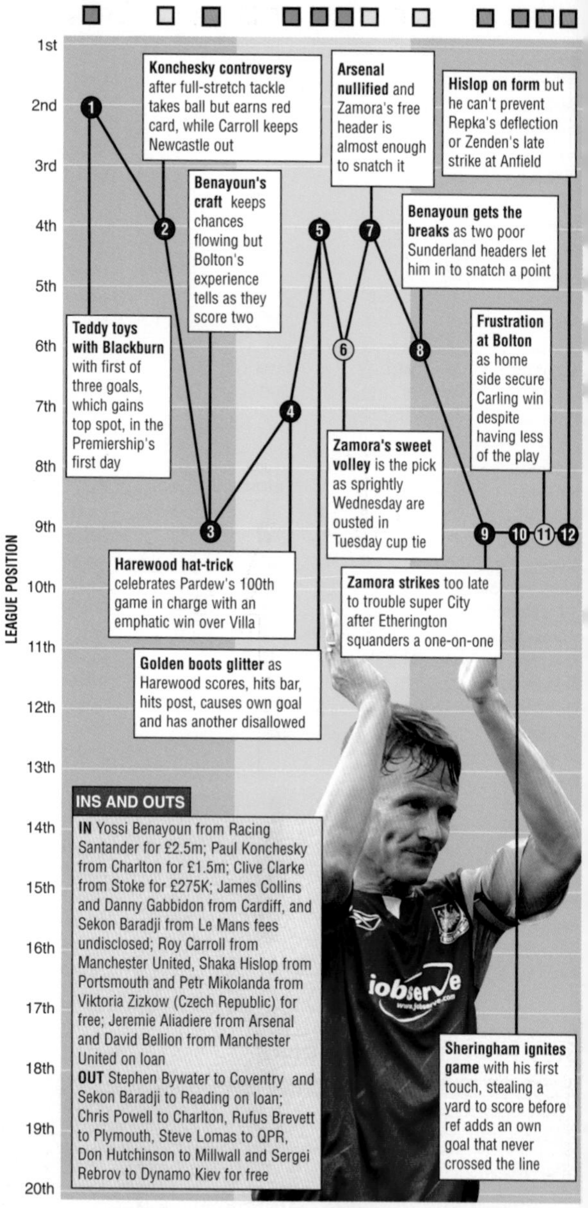

LEAGUE POSITION

1st
2nd
3rd
4th
5th
6th
7th
8th
9th
10th
11th
12th
13th
14th
15th
16th
17th
18th
19th
20th

1 **Teddy toys with Blackburn** with first of three goals, which gains top spot, in the Premiership's first day

2 **Konchesky controversy** after full-stretch tackle takes ball but earns red card, while Carroll keeps Newcastle out

3 **Benayoun's craft** keeps chances flowing but Bolton's experience tells as they score two

4 **Harewood hat-trick** celebrates Pardew's 100th game in charge with an emphatic win over Villa

5 **Golden boots glitter** as Harewood scores, hits bar, hits post, causes own goal and has another disallowed

6 **Zamora's sweet volley** is the pick as sprightly Wednesday are ousted in Tuesday cup tie

7 **Arsenal nullified** and Zamora's free header is almost enough to snatch it

8 **Benayoun gets the breaks** as two poor Sunderland headers let him in to snatch a point

9 **Zamora strikes** too late to trouble super City after Etherington squanders a one-on-one

10 **Sheringham ignites game** with his first touch, stealing a yard to score before ref adds an own goal that never crossed the line

11 **Frustration at Bolton** as home side secure Carling win despite having less of the play

12 **Hislop on form** but he can't prevent Repka's deflection or Zenden's late strike at Anfield

INS AND OUTS

IN Yossi Benayoun from Racing Santander for £2.5m; Paul Konchesky from Charlton for £1.5m; Clive Clarke from Stoke for £275K; James Collins and Danny Gabbidon from Cardiff, and Sekon Baradji from Le Mans fees undisclosed; Roy Carroll from Manchester United, Shaka Hislop from Portsmouth and Petr Mikolanda from Viktoria Zizkow (Czech Republic) for free; Jeremie Aliadiere from Arsenal and David Bellion from Manchester United on loan

OUT Stephen Bywater to Coventry and Sekon Baradji to Reading on loan; Chris Powell to Charlton, Rufus Brevett to Plymouth, Steve Lomas to QPR, Don Hutchinson to Millwall and Sergei Rebrov to Dynamo Kiev for free

AUGUST SEPTEMBER OCTOBER

Home Away Neutral

ATTENDANCES

HOME GROUND: UPTON PARK **CAPACITY:** 35647 **AVERAGE LEAGUE AT HOME:** 33742

47	Liverpool	74000	46	Tottenham	34970	41	Man City	34305	33	Bolton	24461
38	Man Utd	69522	32	Everton	34866	21	Wigan	34131	16	Birmingham	24010
2	Newcastle	51620	44	Liverpool	34852	1	Blackburn	33305	24	Norwich	23968
12	Liverpool	44537	35	Portsmouth	34837	3	Bolton	31629	27	Blackburn	23700
9	Man City	43647	19	Newcastle	34836	30	Birmingham	31294	5	Fulham	21907
40	Chelsea	41919	23	Chelsea	34758	8	Sunderland	31212	17	Blackburn	20370
36	Man City	39357	15	Man Utd	34755	26	Fulham	29812	20	Portsmouth	20168
43	Middlesboro	39148	39	Charlton	34753	4	Aston Villa	29582	37	Wigan	18736
28	Arsenal	38216	29	Sunderland	34745	42	Middlesboro	27658	31	Bolton	17120
25	Aston Villa	36700	7	Arsenal	34742	22	Charlton	25952	6	Sheff Wed	14976
14	Tottenham	36154	10	Middlesboro	34612	34	Bolton	24685	11	Bolton	10927
18	Everton	35704	13	West Brom	34325	45	West Brom	24462			

Strong season builds to classic final

Final Position: 9th

KEY: League, Champions Lge, UEFA Cup, FA Cup, League Cup, Other

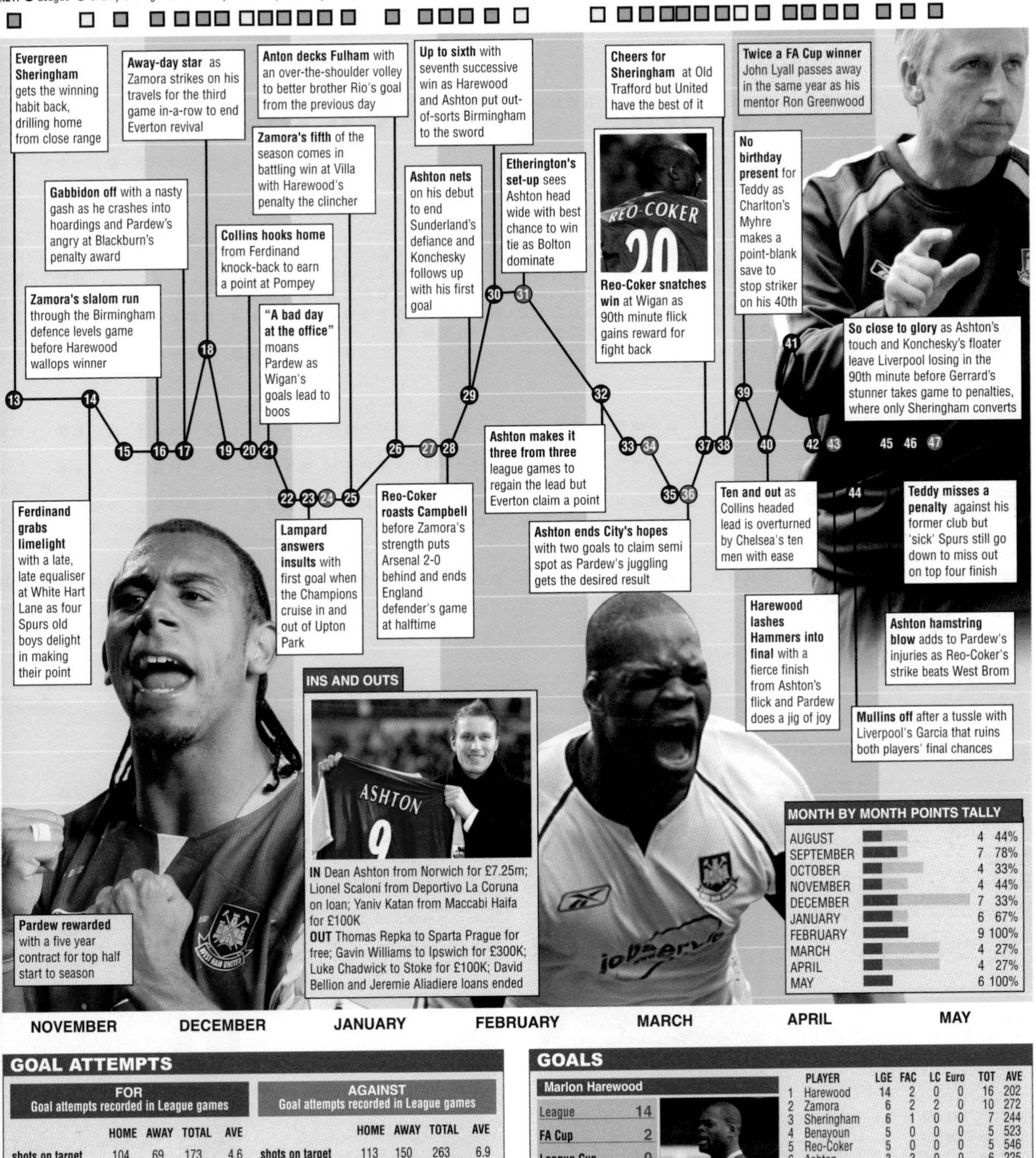

Evergreen Sheringham gets the winning habit back, drilling home from close range
Away-day star as Zamora strikes on his travels for the third game in-a-row to end Everton revival
Anton decks Fulham with an over-the-shoulder volley to better brother Rio's goal from the previous day
Up to sixth with seventh successive win as Harewood and Ashton put out-of-sorts Birmingham to the sword
Cheers for Sheringham at Old Trafford but United have the best of it
Twice a FA Cup winner John Lyall passes away in the same year as his mentor Ron Greenwood
Zamora's fifth of the season comes in battling win at Villa with Harewood's penalty the clincher
Gabbidon off with a nasty gash as he crashes into hoardings and Pardew's angry at Blackburn's penalty award
Ashton nets on his debut to end Sunderland's defiance and Konchesky follows up with his first goal
Etherington's set-up sees Ashton head wide with best chance to win tie as Bolton dominate
REO-COKER 20
Reo-Coker snatches win at Wigan as 90th minute flick gains reward for fight back
No birthday present for Teddy as Charlton's Myhre makes a point-blank save to stop striker on his 40th
Collins hooks home from Ferdinand knock-back to earn a point at Pompey
Zamora's slalom run through the Birmingham defence levels game before Harewood wallops winner
"A bad day at the office" moans Pardew as Wigan's goals lead to boos
So close to glory as Ashton's touch and Konchesky's floater leave Liverpool losing in the 90th minute before Gerrard's stunner takes game to penalties, where only Sheringham converts
13 14 15 16 17 18 19 20 21 22 23 24 25 26 27 28 29 30 31 32 33 34 35 36 37 38 39 40 41 42 43 44 45 46 47
Ashton makes it three from three league games to regain the lead but Everton claim a point
Ferdinand grabs limelight with a late, late equaliser at White Hart Lane as four Spurs old boys delight in making their point
Lampard answers insults with first goal when the Champions cruise in and out of Upton Park
Reo-Coker roasts Campbell before Zamora's strength puts Arsenal 2-0 behind and ends England defender's game at halftime
Ashton ends City's hopes with two goals to claim semi spot as Pardew's juggling gets the desired result
Ten and out as Collins headed lead is overturned by Chelsea's ten men with ease
Teddy misses a penalty against his former club but 'sick' Spurs still go down to miss out on top four finish
Harewood lashes Hammers into final with a fierce finish from Ashton's flick and Pardew does a jig of joy
Ashton hamstring blow adds to Pardew's injuries as Reo-Coker's strike beats West Brom
Mullins off after a tussle with Liverpool's Garcia that ruins both players' final chances
INS AND OUTS
ASHTON 9
IN Dean Ashton from Norwich for £7.25m; Lionel Scaloni from Deportivo La Coruna on loan; Yaniv Katan from Maccabi Haifa for £100K
OUT Thomas Repka to Sparta Prague for free; Gavin Williams to Ipswich for £300K; Luke Chadwick to Stoke for £100K; David Bellion and Jeremie Aliadiere loans ended
Pardew rewarded with a five year contract for top half start to season
MONTH BY MONTH POINTS TALLY
AUGUST 4 44%
SEPTEMBER 7 78%
OCTOBER 4 33%
NOVEMBER 4 44%
DECEMBER 7 33%
JANUARY 6 67%
FEBRUARY 9 100%
MARCH 4 27%
APRIL 4 27%
MAY 6 100%
NOVEMBER DECEMBER JANUARY FEBRUARY MARCH APRIL MAY

GOAL ATTEMPTS

FOR — Goal attempts recorded in League games

	HOME	AWAY	TOTAL	AVE
shots on target	104	69	173	4.6
shots off target	98	83	181	4.8
TOTAL	202	152	354	9.3

Ratio of goals to shots Average number of shots on target per League goal scored: **3.3**

Accuracy rating Average percentage of total goal attempts which were on target: **48.9**

AGAINST — Goal attempts recorded in League games

	HOME	AWAY	TOTAL	AVE
shots on target	113	150	263	6.9
shots off target	112	69	181	4.8
TOTAL	225	219	444	11.7

Ratio of goals to shots Average number of shots on target per League goal scored: **4.8**

Accuracy rating Average percentage of total goal attempts which were on target: **59.2**

GOALS

Marlon Harewood

League	14
FA Cup	2
League Cup	0
Europe	0
Other	0
TOTAL	16

League Average **202** mins between goals

	PLAYER	LGE	FAC	LC	Euro	TOT	AVE
1	Harewood	14	2	0	0	16	202
2	Zamora	6	2	2	0	10	272
3	Sheringham	6	1	0	0	7	244
4	Benayoun	5	0	0	0	5	523
5	Reo-Coker	5	0	0	0	5	546
6	Ashton	3	3	0	0	6	225
7	Collins	2	0	0	0	2	590
8	Etherington	2	1	0	0	3	1377
9	Ferdinand	2	0	0	0	2	1442
10	Fletcher	1	0	0	0	1	627
11	Konchesky	1	1	0	0	2	3223
12	Newton	1	0	0	0	1	904
13	Mullins	0	1	0	0	1	
14	Dailly	0	0	1	0	1	
15	Bellion	0	0	1	0	1	
	Other	4	3	0	0	7	
	TOTAL	52	14	4	0	70	

SQUAD APPEARANCES

Match	Venue	Competition	Result
1	H	L	W
2	A	L	D
3	H	L	L
4	H	L	W
5	A	L	W
6	A	W	W
7	H	L	D
8	A	L	D
9	A	L	L
10	H	L	W
11	A	W	L
12	A	L	L
13	H	L	W
14	A	L	D
15	H	L	L
16	A	L	W
17	A	L	L
18	A	L	W
19	H	L	L
20	A	L	D
21	H	L	L
22	A	L	L
23	H	L	L
24	A	F	W
25	A	L	W
26	H	L	W
27	H	F	W
28	A	L	W
29	H	L	W
30	H	L	W
31	A	F	D
32	H	L	D
33	A	L	L
34	H	F	W
35	H	L	L
36	A	F	W
37	A	L	W
38	A	L	L
39	H	L	D
40	A	L	L
41	H	L	W
42	A	L	L
43	A	F	W
44	H	L	L
45	A	L	W
46	H	L	W

Goalkeepers
Stephen Bywater
Roy Carroll
Shaka Hislop
Matthew Reed
James Walker

Defenders
Chris Cohen
James Collins
Christian Dailly
Anton Ferdinand
Daniel Gabbidon
Paul Konchesky
Tomas Repka
Lionel Scaloni
Elliott Ward

Midfielders
Yossi Benayoun
Clive Clarke
Matthew Etherington
Carl Fletcher
Hayden Mullins
Shaun Newton
Mark Noble
Kyle Reid
Nigel Reo-Coker
Tony Stokes
Gavin Williams

Forwards
Jeremie Aliadiere
Dean Ashton
David Bellion
Hogan Ephraim
Marlon Harewood
Yaniv Katan
Teddy Sheringham
Bobby Zamora

KEY: On all match | On bench | Subbed or sent off (Counting game) | Subbed or sent off (playing less than 70 mins) | Subbed on from bench (Counting Game) | Subbed on (playing less than 70 mins) | Subbed on and then subbed or sent off (Counting Game) | Subbed on and then subbed or sent off (playing less than 70 mins) | Not in 16

KEY PLAYERS - GOALSCORERS

Marlon Harewood

Goals in the League	14
Goals in all competitions	16
Assists League goals scored by a team mate where the player delivered the final pass	4
Contribution to Attacking Power Average number of minutes between League team goals while on pitch	64
Player Strike Rate Average number of minutes between League goals scored by player	202
Club Strike Rate Average minutes between League goals scored by club	66

	PLAYER	GOALS LGE	GOALS ALL	ASSISTS	POWER	S RATE
1	Marlon Harewood	14	16	4	64	202 mins
2	Bobby Zamora	6	10	10	53	272 mins
3	Yossi Benayoun	5	5	7	61	523 mins
4	Nigel Reo-Coker	5	5	4	68	546 mins

KEY PLAYERS - MIDFIELDERS

Yossi Benayoun

Goals in the League	5
Goals in all competitions	5
Assists League goals scored by a team mate where the player delivered the final pass	7
Defensive Rating Average number of mins between League goals conceded while on the pitch	69
Contribution to Attacking Power Average number of minutes between League team goals while on pitch	61
Scoring Difference Defensive Rating minus Contribution to Attacking Power	8

	PLAYER	GOALS LGE	GOALS ALL	ASSISTS	DEF RATE	POWER	SC DIFF
1	Yossi Benayoun	5	5	7	69	61	8 mins
2	Nigel Reo-Coker	5	5	4	70	68	2 mins
3	Matthew Etherington	2	3	5	63	69	-6 mins
4	Hayden Mullins	0	1	1	62	70	-8 mins

PLAYER APPEARANCES

	AGE (on 01/07/06)	IN NAMED 16	APPEARANCES	COUNTING GAMES	MINUTES ON PITCH	APPEARANCES	MINUTES ON PITCH	THIS SEASON	HOME COUNTRY
Goalkeepers									
Stephen Bywater	25	10	1	0	31	1	31	-	England
Roy Carroll	28	19	19	19	1710	19	1710	-	N Ireland
Shaka Hislop	37	37	16	15	1409	25	2279	8	Trinidad & Tob. (47)
Matthew Reed	2007	0	0	0	0	0	0	-	England
James Walker	33	10	3	3	270	3	270	-	England
Defenders									
Chris Cohen	19	0	0	0	0	1	90	-	England
James Collins	22	16	14	13	1180	19	1630	5	Wales (74)
Christian Dailly	32	30	22	7	990	30	1417	6	Scotland (85)
Anton Ferdinand	21	33	33	32	2884	38	3394	-	England
Daniel Gabbidon	26	32	32	30	2718	39	3408	6	Wales (74)
Paul Konchesky	25	37	37	35	3223	45	4003	-	England
Tomas Repka	32	19	19	16	1544	22	1809	-	Czech Republic
Lionel Scaloni	28	14	13	11	1121	17	1472	3	Argentina (9)
Elliott Ward	21	5	4	2	233	6	413	-	England
Midfielders									
Yossi Benayoun	26	34	33	27	2617	39	3201	3	Israel (49)
Clive Clarke	26	9	2	1	120	3	191	-	Rep of Ireland
Matthew Etherington	24	33	33	30	2754	40	3378	-	England
Carl Fletcher	26	14	11	6	627	16	748	7	Wales (74)
Hayden Mullins	27	35	35	33	2953	42	3590	-	England
Shaun Newton	30	29	26	7	904	30	1105	-	England
Mark Noble	19	6	5	3	324	6	414	-	England
Kyle Reid	18	4	2	1	96	2	96	-	England
Nigel Reo-Coker	22	31	31	30	2729	38	3386	-	England
Tony Stokes	19	0	0	0	0	1	5	-	England
Gavin Williams	25	0	0	0	0	1	85	4	Wales (74)
Forwards									
Jeremie Aliadiere	23	11	7	1	178	8	196	-	France
Dean Ashton	22	13	11	7	674	16	1095	-	England
David Bellion	23	14	8	0	221	10	337	-	France
Hogan Ephraim	18	1	0	0	0	1	5	-	England
Marlon Harewood	26	38	36	29	2824	45	3564	-	England
Yaniv Katan	25	9	6	0	151	8	174	-	Israel
Teddy Sheringham	40	29	26	11	1462	31	1671	-	England
Bobby Zamora	25	36	34	12	1630	42	1980	-	England

KEY: LEAGUE ALL COMPS CAPS (MAY FIFA RANKING)

TEAM OF THE SEASON

KEY: DR = Defensive Rate, SD = Scoring Difference AP = Attacking Power SR = Strike Rate, CG=Counting games – League games playing at least 70 minutes

TOP POINT EARNERS

Daniel Gabbidon

Counting Games League games when player was on pitch for at least 70 minutes	30
Average points Average League points taken in Counting games	1.70
Club Average points Average points taken in League games	1.45

	PLAYER	GAMES	PTS
1	Daniel Gabbidon	30	1.70
2	Tomas Repka	16	1.69
3	Shaka Hislop	15	1.60
4	Bobby Zamora	12	1.58
5	Yossi Benayoun	27	1.56
6	Matthew Etherington	30	1.50
7	Nigel Reo-Coker	30	1.50
8	Marlon Harewood	29	1.48
9	Paul Konchesky	35	1.46
10	Anton Ferdinand	32	1.44

KEY PLAYERS - DEFENDERS

Daniel Gabbidon

Goals Conceded in the League Number of League goals conceded while the player was on the pitch	36
Goals Conceded in all competitions Total number of goals conceded while the player was on the pitch	44
League minutes played Number of minutes played in league matches	2718
Clean Sheets In games when the player was on pitch for at least 70 minutes	9
Defensive Rating Average number of mins between League goals conceded while on the pitch	76
Club Defensive Rating Average number of mins between League goals conceded by the club this season	62

	PLAYER	CON LGE	CON ALL	MINS	C SHEETS	DEF RATE
1	Daniel Gabbidon	36	44	2718	9	76 mins
2	Tomas Repka	21	25	1544	4	74 mins
3	Anton Ferdinand	46	52	2884	7	63 mins
4	Paul Konchesky	53	62	3223	7	61 mins

KEY GOALKEEPER

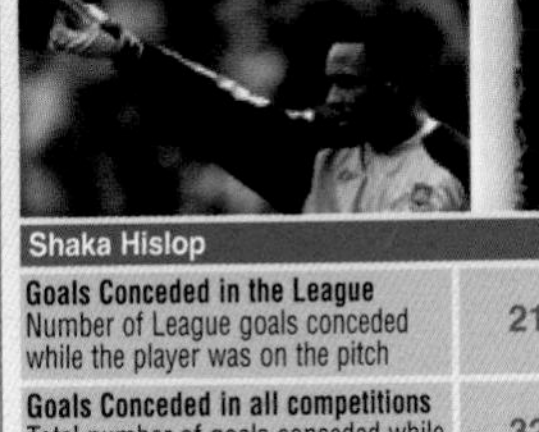

Shaka Hislop

Goals Conceded in the League Number of League goals conceded while the player was on the pitch	21
Goals Conceded in all competitions Total number of goals conceded while the player was on the pitch	32
League minutes played Number of minutes played in league matches	1409
Clean Sheets In games when the player was on pitch for at least 70 minutes	5
Goals to Shots Ratio The average number of shots on target per each League goal conceded	5.4
Defensive Rating Ave mins between League goals conceded while on the pitch	67

BOOKINGS

Christian Dailly

League Yellow	4
League Red	0
All competitions Yellow	7
All competitions Red	0

League Average **247** mins between cards

	PLAYER	LEAGUE 4Y	LEAGUE 0R	TOTAL 7Y	TOTAL 0R	AVE
1	Dailly	4Y	0R	7Y	0R	247
2	Sheringham	5	0	5	0	292
3	Fletcher	2	0	2	0	313
4	Scaloni	3	0	3	0	373
5	Repka	4	0	4	0	386
6	Newton	2	0	2	0	452
7	Harewood	5	0	7	0	564
8	Ferdinand	5	0	5	0	576
9	Konchesky	4	1	4	1	644
10	Carroll	2	0	2	0	855
11	Benayoun	3	0	3	0	872
12	Reo-Coker	3	0	6	0	909
13	Mullins	2	1	2	1	984
14	Gabbidon	2	0	2	0	1359
15	Etherington	1	0	2	0	2754
	Other	0	0	3	0	
	TOTAL	47	2	59	2	

WIGAN ATHLETIC

A season of unexpected success in the Premiership has led to a lot of interest in Paul Jewell's hard-working squad.

Henri Camara's return to the Premiership caught rival's eyes with 12 goals coming at a Strike Rate of one every 189 minutes – the ninth best record in the division. **Jason Roberts'** Strike Rate of 376 minutes puts him 42nd.

Pascal Chimbonda's pace was noted but **Arjan de Zeeuw** has the best Defensive Rating at the club. They conceded a goal every 86 minutes while he was on he pitch – every 36 minutes when he wasn't. **John Filan** enjoyed a better record than **Mike Pollitt** and his Defensive Rating of a goal conceded every 100 minutes puts him fifth in the Premiership Keeper's table. Filan's Goals-to-Shots Ratio of a goal conceded for every 5.6 shots on target is also fifth.

NICKNAME: THE LATICS

KEY: Won Drawn Lost

1	prem	**Chelsea**	H	L	0-1	
2	prem	**Charlton**	A	L	0-1	
3	prem	**Sunderland**	H	W	1-0	Roberts 2 pen
4	prem	**West Brom**	A	W	2-1	Connolly 40; Bullard 90
5	prem	**Middlesbrough**	H	D	1-1	Camara 68
6	ccr2	**Bournemouth**	H	W	1-0	Roberts 86
7	prem	**Everton**	A	W	1-0	Francis 47
8	prem	**Bolton**	H	W	2-1	Camara 48; McCulloch 62
9	prem	**Newcastle**	H	W	1-0	Roberts 40
10	prem	**Aston Villa**	A	W	2-0	Hughes 32 og; Mahon 82
11	ccr3	**Watford**	H	W	3-0	Taylor 98 pen; Johansson 117,120
12	prem	**Fulham**	H	W	1-0	Chimbonda 90
13	prem	**Portsmouth**	A	W	2-0	Chimbonda 48; Roberts 79
14	prem	**Arsenal**	H	L	2-3	Camara 28; Bullard 45
15	prem	**Tottenham**	H	L	1-2	McCulloch 88
16	ccr4	**Newcastle**	H	W	1-0	Connolly 88 pen
17	prem	**Liverpool**	A	L	0-3	
18	prem	**Chelsea**	A	L	0-1	
19	prem	**Man Utd**	A	L	0-4	
20	prem	**Charlton**	H	W	3-0	Camara 9,51,63
21	ccqf	**Bolton**	H	W	2-0	Roberts 40,45
22	prem	**Man City**	H	W	4-3	Roberts 11,45; McCulloch 23; Camara 71
23	prem	**West Ham**	A	W	2-0	Roberts 43; Camara 45
24	prem	**Blackburn**	H	L	0-3	
25	prem	**Birmingham**	A	L	0-2	
26	facr3	**Leeds**	H	D	1-1	Connolly 47
27	ccsfl1	**Arsenal**	H	W	1-0	Scharner 77
28	prem	**West Brom**	H	L	0-1	
29	facr3r	**Leeds**	A	W	4-2*	Johansson 24; Roberts 50,103 (*on penalties)
30	prem	**Middlesbrough**	A	W	3-2	Roberts 2; Thompson 29; Mellor 90
31	ccsfl2	**Arsenal**	A	L	1-2	Roberts 119
32	facr4	**Man City**	A	L	0-1	
33	prem	**Everton**	H	D	1-1	Scharner 45
34	prem	**Bolton**	A	D	1-1	Johansson 77
35	prem	**Liverpool**	H	L	0-1	
36	prem	**Tottenham**	A	D	2-2	Johansson 10,67
37	cccf	**Man Utd**	A	L	0-4	
38	prem	**Man Utd**	H	L	1-2	Scharner 58
39	prem	**Sunderland**	A	W	1-0	Camara 8
40	prem	**Man City**	A	W	1-0	McCulloch 55
41	prem	**West Ham**	H	L	1-2	McCulloch 45
42	prem	**Blackburn**	A	D	1-1	Roberts 52
43	prem	**Birmingham**	H	D	1-1	Johansson 49
44	prem	**Newcastle**	A	L	1-3	Bullard 5
45	prem	**Aston Villa**	H	W	3-2	Bullard 25; Camara 56,60
46	prem	**Fulham**	A	L	0-1	
47	prem	**Portsmouth**	H	L	1-2	Camara 34
48	prem	**Arsenal**	A	L	2-4	Scharner 10; Thompson 33

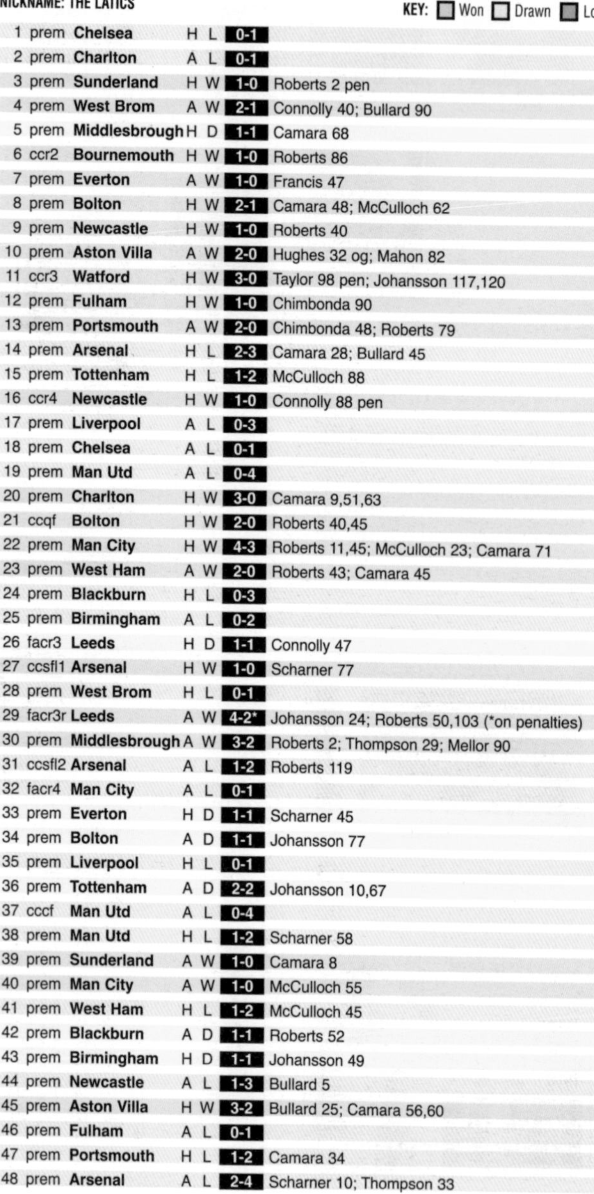

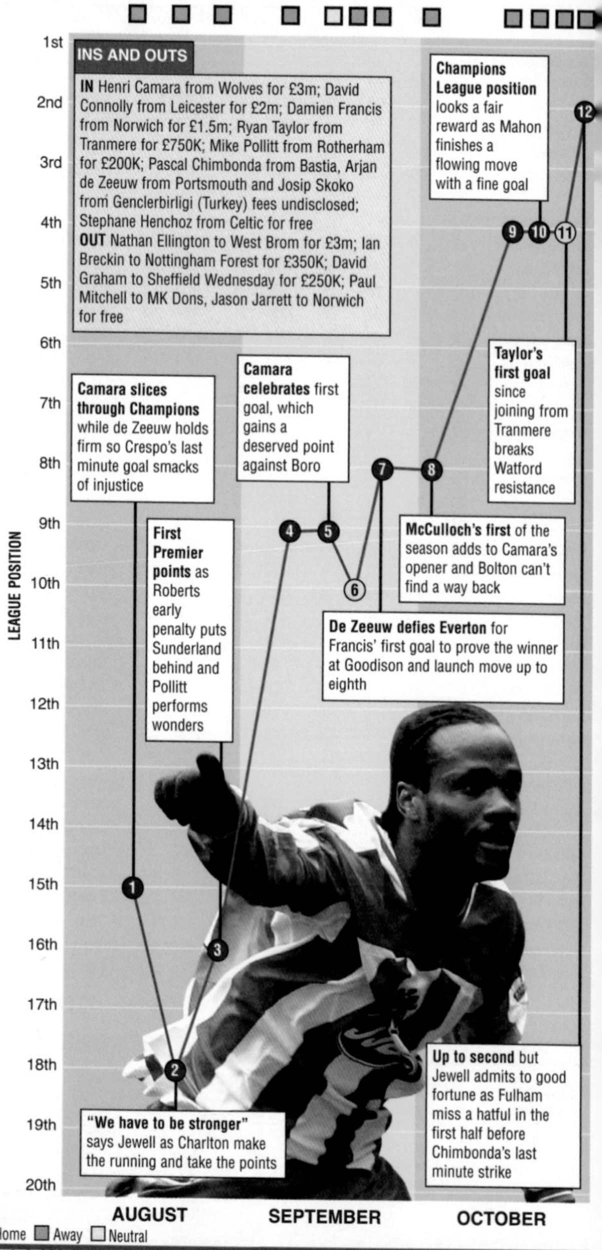

1st
2nd
3rd
4th
5th
6th
7th
8th
9th
10th
11th
12th
13th
14th
15th
16th
17th
18th
19th
20th
LEAGUE POSITION
INS AND OUTS
IN Henri Camara from Wolves for £3m; David Connolly from Leicester for £2m; Damien Francis from Norwich for £1.5m; Ryan Taylor from Tranmere for £750K; Mike Pollitt from Rotherham for £200K; Pascal Chimbonda from Bastia, Arjan de Zeeuw from Portsmouth and Josip Skoko from Genclerbirligi (Turkey) fees undisclosed; Stephane Henchoz from Celtic for free
OUT Nathan Ellington to West Brom for £3m; Ian Breckin to Nottingham Forest for £350K; David Graham to Sheffield Wednesday for £250K; Paul Mitchell to MK Dons, Jason Jarrett to Norwich for free
Champions League position looks a fair reward as Mahon finishes a flowing move with a fine goal
Taylor's first goal since joining from Tranmere breaks Watford resistance
Camara slices through Champions while de Zeeuw holds firm so Crespo's last minute goal smacks of injustice
Camara celebrates first goal, which gains a deserved point against Boro
First Premier points as Roberts early penalty puts Sunderland behind and Pollitt performs wonders
McCulloch's first of the season adds to Camara's opener and Bolton can't find a way back
De Zeeuw defies Everton for Francis' first goal to prove the winner at Goodison and launch move up to eighth
Up to second but Jewell admits to good fortune as Fulham miss a hatful in the first half before Chimbonda's last minute strike
"We have to be stronger" says Jewell as Charlton make the running and take the points
AUGUST
SEPTEMBER
OCTOBER

Home Away Neutral

ATTENDANCES

HOME GROUND: JJB STADIUM **CAPACITY:** 25050 **AVERAGE LEAGUE AT HOME:** 20609

19	Man Utd	67793	39	Sunderland	31194	15	Tottenham	22611	12	Fulham	17266
37	Man Utd	60866	32	Man City	30811	9	Newcastle	22374	3	Sunderland	17223
44	Newcastle	52302	25	Birmingham	29189	33	Everton	21731	46	Fulham	17149
17	Liverpool	44098	30	Middlesboro	27208	47	Portsmouth	21126	20	Charlton	17074
40	Man City	42444	34	Bolton	25854	24	Blackburn	20639	5	Middlesboro	16641
18	Chelsea	42060	4	West Brom	25617	8	Bolton	20553	29	Leeds	15243
48	Arsenal	38359	35	Liverpool	25023	42	Blackburn	20410	21	Bolton	13401
7	Everton	37189	22	Man City	25017	13	Portsmouth	19102	27	Arsenal	12181
36	Tottenham	35676	14	Arsenal	25004	41	West Ham	18736	16	Newcastle	11574
31	Arsenal	34692	1	Chelsea	23575	43	Birmingham	18669	26	Leeds	10980
23	West Ham	34131	38	Man Utd	23574	28	West Brom	17421	11	Watford	4531
10	Aston Villa	32294	2	Charlton	23453	45	Aston Villa	17330	6	Bournemouth	3346

Jewell's heroes sparkle in top flight

Final Position: **10th**

KEY: League, Champions Lge, UEFA Cup, FA Cup, League Cup, Other

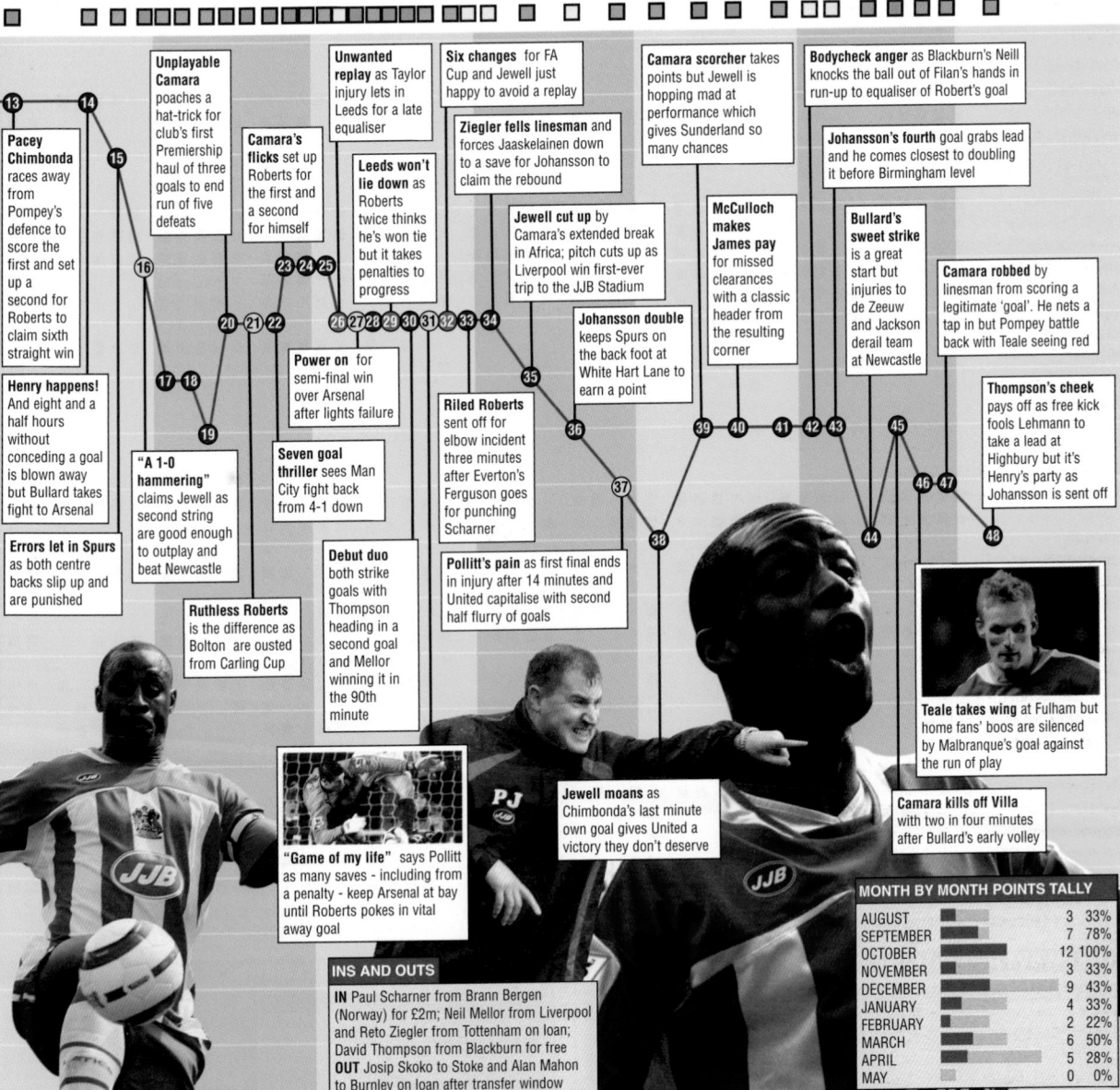

Pacey Chimbonda races away from Pompey's defence to score the first and set up a second for Roberts to claim sixth straight win

Henry happens! And eight and a half hours without conceding a goal is blown away but Bullard takes fight to Arsenal

Errors let in Spurs as both centre backs slip up and are punished

Unplayable Camara poaches a hat-trick for club's first Premiership haul of three goals to end run of five defeats

"A 1-0 hammering" claims Jewell as second string are good enough to outplay and beat Newcastle

Ruthless Roberts is the difference as Bolton are ousted from Carling Cup

Camara's flicks set up Roberts for the first and a second for himself

Seven goal thriller sees Man City fight back from 4-1 down

Unwanted replay as Taylor injury lets in Leeds for a late equaliser

Leeds won't lie down as Roberts twice thinks he's won tie but it takes penalties to progress

Power on for semi-final win over Arsenal after lights failure

Debut duo both strike goals with Thompson heading in a second goal and Mellor winning it in the 90th minute

"Game of my life" says Pollitt as many saves - including from a penalty - keep Arsenal at bay until Roberts pokes in vital away goal

Six changes for FA Cup and Jewell just happy to avoid a replay

Ziegler fells linesman and forces Jaaskelainen down to a save for Johansson to claim the rebound

Riled Roberts sent off for elbow incident three minutes after Everton's Ferguson goes for punching Scharner

Jewell cut up by Camara's extended break in Africa; pitch cuts up as Liverpool win first-ever trip to the JJB Stadium

Johansson double keeps Spurs on the back foot at White Hart Lane to earn a point

Pollitt's pain as first final ends in injury after 14 minutes and United capitalise with second half flurry of goals

Jewell moans as Chimbonda's last minute own goal gives United a victory they don't deserve

Camara scorcher takes points but Jewell is hopping mad at performance which gives Sunderland so many chances

McCulloch makes James pay for missed clearances with a classic header from the resulting corner

Bodycheck anger as Blackburn's Neill knocks the ball out of Filan's hands in run-up to equaliser of Robert's goal

Johansson's fourth goal grabs lead and he comes closest to doubling it before Birmingham level

Bullard's sweet strike is a great start but injuries to de Zeeuw and Jackson derail team at Newcastle

Camara robbed by linesman from scoring a legitimate 'goal'. He nets a tap in but Pompey battle back with Teale seeing red

Thompson's cheek pays off as free kick fools Lehmann to take a lead at Highbury but it's Henry's party as Johansson is sent off

Teale takes wing at Fulham but home fans' boos are silenced by Malbranque's goal against the run of play

Camara kills off Villa with two in four minutes after Bullard's early volley

NOVEMBER DECEMBER JANUARY FEBRUARY MARCH APRIL MAY

INS AND OUTS

IN Paul Scharner from Brann Bergen (Norway) for £2m; Neil Mellor from Liverpool and Reto Ziegler from Tottenham on loan; David Thompson from Blackburn for free
OUT Josip Skoko to Stoke and Alan Mahon to Burnley on loan after transfer window

MONTH BY MONTH POINTS TALLY

Month	Points	%
AUGUST	3	33%
SEPTEMBER	7	78%
OCTOBER	12	100%
NOVEMBER	3	33%
DECEMBER	9	43%
JANUARY	4	33%
FEBRUARY	2	22%
MARCH	6	50%
APRIL	5	28%
MAY	0	0%

GOAL ATTEMPTS

FOR – Goal attempts recorded in League games

	HOME	AWAY	TOTAL	AVE
shots on target	122	85	207	5.4
shots off target	131	95	226	5.9
TOTAL	253	180	433	11.4

Ratio of goals to shots Average number of shots on target per League goal scored: **4.6**

Accuracy rating Average percentage of total goal attempts which were on target: **47.8**

AGAINST – Goal attempts recorded in League games

	HOME	AWAY	TOTAL	AVE
shots on target	107	118	225	5.9
shots off target	94	85	179	4.7
TOTAL	201	203	404	10.6

Ratio of goals to shots Average number of shots on target per League goal scored: **4.3**

Accuracy rating Average percentage of total goal attempts which were on target: **55.7**

GOALS

Henri Camara

League	12
FA Cup	0
League Cup	0
Europe	0
Other	0
TOTAL	12

League Average **189** mins between goals

	PLAYER	LGE	FAC	LC	Euro	TOT	AVE
1	Camara	12	0	0	0	12	189
2	Roberts	8	2	4	0	14	376
3	McCulloch	5	0	0	0	5	471
4	Johansson	4	1	2	0	7	156
5	Bullard	4	0	0	0	4	784
6	Scharner	3	0	1	0	4	436
7	Chimbonda	2	0	0	0	2	1631
8	Thompson	2	0	0	0	2	314
9	Francis	1	0	0	0	1	1475
10	Mellor	1	0	0	0	1	245
11	Connolly	1	1	1	0	3	503
12	Mahon	1	0	0	0	1	380
13	Taylor	0	0	1	0	1	
	Other	1	0	0	0	1	
	TOTAL	45	4	9	0	58	

SQUAD APPEARANCES

Match	1	2	3	4	5	6	7	8	9	10	11	12	13	14	15	16	17	18	19	20	21	22	23	24	25	26	27	28	29	30	31	32	33	34	35	36	37	38	39	40	41	42	43	44	45	46	47	48
Venue	H	A	H	A	H	H	A	H	H	A	H	H	A	H	H	H	A	A	A	H	H	H	A	H	A	H	H	H	A	A	A	A	H	A	H	A	A	H	A	A	H	A	H	A	H	A	H	A
Competition	L	L	L	L	L	W	L	L	L	L	W	L	L	L	L	W	L	L	L	L	W	L	L	L	L	F	W	L	F	L	W	F	L	L	L	L	W	L	L	L	L	L	L	L	L	L	L	L
Result	L	L	W	W	D	W	W	W	W	W	W	W	W	L	L	W	L	L	L	W	W	W	W	L	L	D	W	L	W	W	L	L	D	D	L	D	L	L	W	W	L	D	D	L	W	L	L	L

Goalkeepers
John Filan
Mike Pollitt
Gary Walsh

Defenders
Leighton Baines
Pascal Chimbonda
Arjan De Zeeuw
Stephane Henchoz
Matt Jackson
Steven McMillan
Paul Scharner
Ryan Taylor
Emerson Thome
Joey Waterhouse
David Wright

Midfielders
Jimmy Bullard
Damian Francis
Luke Joyce
Graham Kavanagh
Kevin Lee
Alan Mahon
Lee McCulloch
Josip Skoko
Gary Teale
David Thompson
Reto Ziegler

Forwards
Henri Camara
David Connolly
Andreas Johansson
Neil Mellor
Jason Roberts

KEY: On all match · On bench · Subbed or sent off (Counting game) · Subbed or sent off (playing less than 70 mins) · Subbed on from bench (Counting Game) · Subbed on (playing less than 70 mins) · Subbed on and then subbed or sent off (Counting Game) · Subbed on and then subbed or sent off (playing less than 70 mins) · Not in 16

KEY PLAYERS - GOALSCORERS

Henri Camara

Goals in the League	12
Goals in all competitions	12
Assists League goals scored by a team mate where the player delivered the final pass	0
Contribution to Attacking Power Average number of minutes between League team goals while on pitch	67
Player Strike Rate Average number of minutes between League goals scored by player	189
Club Strike Rate Average minutes between League goals scored by club	76

	PLAYER	GOALS LGE	GOALS ALL	ASSISTS	POWER	S RATE
1	Henri Camara	12	12	0	67	189 mins
2	Jason Roberts	8	14	4	75	376 mins
3	Paul Scharner	3	4	0	77	436 mins
4	Lee McCulloch	5	5	3	74	471 mins

KEY PLAYERS - MIDFIELDERS

Gary Teale

Goals in the League	0
Goals in all competitions	0
Assists League goals scored by a team mate where the player delivered the final pass	4
Defensive Rating Average number of mins between League goals conceded while on the pitch	82
Contribution to Attacking Power Average number of minutes between League team goals while on pitch	66
Scoring Difference Defensive Rating minus Contribution to Attacking Power	16

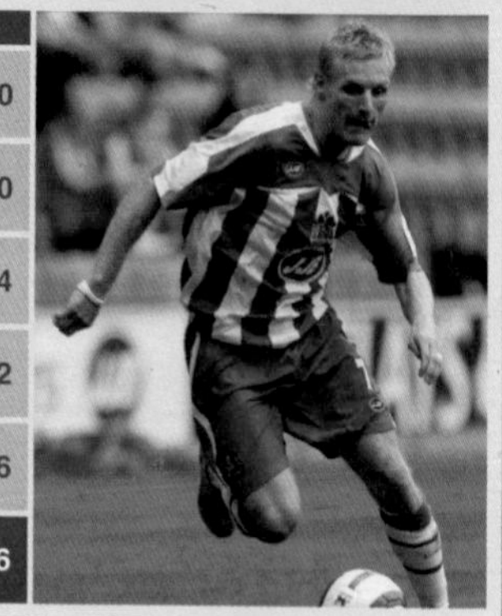

	PLAYER	GOALS LGE	GOALS ALL	ASSISTS	DEF RATE	POWER	SC DIFF
1	Gary Teale	0	0	4	82	66	16 mins
2	Graham Kavanagh	0	0	5	71	70	1 mins
3	Lee McCulloch	5	5	3	69	74	-5 mins
4	Jimmy Bullard	4	4	4	70	76	-6 mins

PLAYER APPEARANCES

	AGE (on 01/07/06)	IN NAMED 16	APPEARANCES	COUNTING GAMES	MINUTES ON PITCH	APPEARANCES	MINUTES ON PITCH	THIS SEASON	HOME COUNTRY
Goalkeepers									
John Filan	36	26	15	14	1305	20	1772	-	Australia
Mike Pollitt	34	35	24	23	2115	30	2638	-	England
Gary Walsh	38	12	0	0	0	0	0	-	England
Defenders									
Leighton Baines	21	37	37	33	3100	43	3655	-	England
Pascal Chimbonda	27	37	37	36	3261	43	3776	2	France (8)
Arjan De Zeeuw	36	31	31	29	2660	35	3050	-	Holland
Stephane Henchoz	31	30	26	25	2290	32	2733	-	Switzerland
Matt Jackson	34	37	16	10	1073	23	1763	-	England
Steven McMillan	30	11	2	0	62	7	494	-	Scotland
Paul Scharner	26	16	16	14	1308	20	1666	2	Austria (73)
Ryan Taylor	21	19	11	4	407	16	882	-	England
Emerson Thome	34	0	0	0	0	3	239	-	Brazil
Joey Waterhouse	18	0	0	0	0	1	3	-	England
David Wright	26	7	2	1	115	4	325	-	England
Midfielders									
Jimmy Bullard	27	36	36	35	3134	42	3573	-	England
Damian Francis	27	28	20	15	1475	24	1821	-	England
Luke Joyce	18	1	0	0	0	1	21	-	England
Graham Kavanagh	32	35	35	30	2786	42	3347	3	Rep of Ireland (15)
Kevin Lee	20	0	0	0	0	0	0	-	England
Alan Mahon	28	13	6	3	380	13	930	-	Rep of Ireland
Lee McCulloch	28	30	30	25	2355	35	2686	2	Scotland (85)
Josip Skoko	30	7	5	1	195	11	734	4	Australia (42)
Gary Teale	27	27	24	17	1723	33	2466	1	Scotland (85)
David Thompson	28	14	10	6	627	10	627	-	England
Reto Ziegler	20	13	10	4	555	13	722	-	Switzerland
Forwards									
Henri Camara	29	29	29	25	2269	32	2471	8	Senegal (28)
David Connolly	29	18	17	3	503	21	738	1	Rep of Ireland (15)
Andreas Johansson	28	22	16	6	622	25	1344	-	Sweden
Neil Mellor	23	3	3	2	245	5	363	-	England
Jason Roberts	28	34	34	33	3009	43	3625	-	Grenada

KEY: LEAGUE ALL COMPS CAPS (MAY FIFA RANKING)

TEAM OF THE SEASON

- FILAN — CG 14 DR 100
- CHIMBONDA — CG 36 DR 65
- DE ZEEUW — CG 29 DR 86
- HENCHOZ — CG 25 DR 72
- BAINES — CG 33 DR 66
- TEALE — CG 17 SD +16
- KAVANAGH — CG 30 SD +1
- MCCULLOCH — CG 25 SD -5
- BULLARD — CG 35 SD -6
- ROBERTS — CG 33 AP 75
- CAMARA — CG 25 SR 189

KEY: DR = Defensive Rate, SD = Scoring Difference AP = Attacking Power SR = Strike Rate, CG=Counting games – League games playing at least 70 minutes

TOP POINT EARNERS

John Filan

Counting Games League games when player was on pitch for at least 70 minutes	14
Average points Average League points taken in Counting games	2.07
Club Average points Average points taken in League games	1.34

	PLAYER	GAMES	PTS
1	John Filan	14	2.07
2	Damian Francis	15	1.87
3	Arjan De Zeeuw	29	1.55
4	Leighton Baines	33	1.48
5	Henri Camara	25	1.48
6	Graham Kavanagh	30	1.47
7	Jimmy Bullard	35	1.46
8	Lee McCulloch	25	1.44
9	Pascal Chimbonda	36	1.33
10	Stephane Henchoz	25	1.32

KEY PLAYERS - DEFENDERS

Arjan De Zeeuw

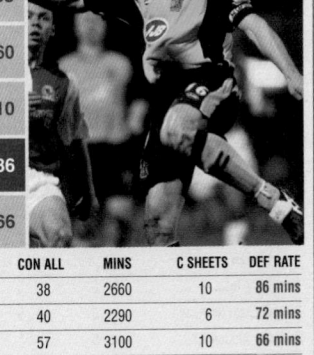

Goals Conceded in the League Number of League goals conceded while the player was on the pitch	31
Goals Conceded in all competitions Total number of goals conceded while the player was on the pitch	38
League minutes played Number of minutes played in league matches	2660
Clean Sheets In games when the player was on pitch for at least 70 minutes	10
Defensive Rating Average number of mins between League goals conceded while on the pitch	86
Club Defensive Rating Average number of mins between League goals conceded by the club this season	66

	PLAYER	CON LGE	CON ALL	MINS	C SHEETS	DEF RATE
1	Arjan De Zeeuw	31	38	2660	10	86 mins
2	Stephane Henchoz	32	40	2290	6	72 mins
3	Leighton Baines	47	57	3100	10	66 mins
4	Pascal Chimbonda	50	60	3261	10	65 mins

KEY GOALKEEPER

John Filan

Goals Conceded in the League Number of League goals conceded while the player was on the pitch	13
Goals Conceded in all competitions Total number of goals conceded while the player was on the pitch	22
League minutes played Number of minutes played in league matches	1305
Clean Sheets In games when the player was on pitch for at least 70 minutes	7
Goals to Shots Ratio The average number of shots on target per each League goal conceded	5.6
Defensive Rating Ave mins between League goals conceded while on the pitch	100

BOOKINGS

David Thompson

League Yellow	4
League Red	0
All competitions Yellow	4
All competitions Red	0

League Average **156** mins between cards

	PLAYER	LEAGUE		TOTAL		AVE
1	Thompson	4Y	0R	4Y	0R	156
2	Scharner	5	0	6	0	261
3	Henchoz	8	0	9	0	286
4	McCulloch	7	1	8	1	294
5	Kavanagh	7	0	9	0	398
6	Chimbonda	6	0	7	0	543
7	Roberts	4	1	4	1	601
8	Johansson	0	1	0	1	622
9	De Zeeuw	4	0	5	0	665
10	Francis	2	0	2	0	737
11	Baines	3	0	3	0	1033
12	Jackson	1	0	1	0	1073
13	Teale	0	1	0	1	1723
	Other	0	0	0	0	
	TOTAL	51	4	58	4	

EVERTON

The poor start reflected shakiness in defence and a lack of goals from midfield. The previous season's Champions League spot was gained on 27 midfield league goals with **Tim Cahill** netting 11. This time Cahill had only scored one by the halfway point and the midfield managed 12 all season.

Alan Stubbs was transferred to Sunderland despite having the club's best Defensive Rating (102 minutes) last year. He returned in January to regain his crown conceding a goal every 80 minutes.

James Beattie only scored ten goals at a disappointing Strike Rate but his return from injury coincided with the end of the losing run - taking the first point off Chelsea - and he finished well ahead in the Top Point Earners chart. **Nigel Martyn** finished with a Defensive Rating ten minutes better than his colleague **Richard Wright**.

NICKNAME: THE TOFFEES

KEY: Won Drawn Lost

1	ec3q1	**Villarreal**	H	L	1-2	Beattie 42
2	prem	**Man Utd**	H	L	0-2	
3	prem	**Bolton**	A	W	1-0	Bent, M 52
4	ec3q2	**Villarreal**	A	L	1-2	Arteta 70
5	prem	**Fulham**	A	L	0-1	
6	prem	**Portsmouth**	H	L	0-1	
7	uc1rl1	**D Bucharest**	A	L	1-5	Yobo 30
8	prem	**Arsenal**	A	L	0-2	
9	prem	**Wigan**	H	L	0-1	
10	uc1rl2	**D Bucharest**	H	W	1-0	Cahill 28
11	prem	**Man City**	A	L	0-2	
12	prem	**Tottenham**	A	L	0-2	
13	prem	**Chelsea**	H	D	1-1	Beattie 36 pen
14	ccr3	**Middlesbrough**	H	L	0-1	
15	prem	**Birmingham**	A	W	1-0	Davies 43
16	prem	**Middlesbrough**	H	W	1-0	Beattie 16
17	prem	**West Brom**	A	L	0-4	
18	prem	**Newcastle**	H	W	1-0	Yobo 46
19	prem	**Blackburn**	A	W	2-0	McFadden 28; Arteta 45
20	prem	**Man Utd**	A	D	1-1	McFadden 7
21	prem	**West Ham**	H	L	1-2	Beattie 9
22	prem	**Bolton**	H	L	0-4	
23	prem	**Aston Villa**	A	L	0-4	
24	prem	**Liverpool**	H	L	1-3	Beattie 42
25	prem	**Sunderland**	A	W	1-0	Cahill 90
26	prem	**Charlton**	H	W	3-1	Beattie 9; Cahill 41,59
27	facr3	**Millwall**	A	D	1-1	Osman 79
28	prem	**Portsmouth**	A	W	1-0	Osman 31
29	facr3r	**Millwall**	H	W	1-0	Cahill 72
30	prem	**Arsenal**	H	W	1-0	Beattie 13
31	facr4	**Chelsea**	H	D	1-1	McFadden 36
32	prem	**Wigan**	A	D	1-1	Thompson 9 og
33	prem	**Man City**	H	W	1-0	Weir 8
34	facr4r	**Chelsea**	A	L	1-4	Arteta 72 pen
35	prem	**Blackburn**	H	W	1-0	Beattie 33
36	prem	**Newcastle**	A	L	0-2	
37	prem	**West Ham**	A	D	2-2	Osman 18; Beattie 71
38	prem	**Fulham**	H	W	3-1	Beattie 14 pen,36; McFadden 55
39	prem	**Aston Villa**	H	W	4-1	McFadden 16; Cahill 22,90; Osman 45
40	prem	**Liverpool**	A	L	1-3	Cahill 61
41	prem	**Sunderland**	H	D	2-2	Osman 5; McFadden 26
42	prem	**Charlton**	A	D	0-0	
43	prem	**Tottenham**	H	L	0-1	
44	prem	**Chelsea**	A	L	0-3	
45	prem	**Birmingham**	H	D	0-0	
46	prem	**Middlesbrough**	A	W	1-0	McFadden 89
47	prem	**West Brom**	H	D	2-2	Anichebe 84; Ferguson 90

1st
2nd
3rd
4th
5th
6th
7th
8th
9th
10th
11th
12th
13th
14th
15th
16th
17th
18th
19th
20th
LEAGUE POSITION
INS AND OUTS
IN Per Kroldrup from Udinese for £5m; Simon Davies from Tottenham for £4m; Phil Neville from Manchester United for £3.5m; Mikel Arteta from Real Sociedad for £2m; Andy van der Meyde from Inter Milan for £1.8m; Nuno Valente from Porto for £1.5m; Matteo Ferrari from Roma on loan
OUT Alan Stubbs to Sunderland and Steve Watson to West Brom for free
1 Riquelme class tells to leave Villarreal in the driving seat despite Beattie's scrambled goal
2 Yobo's comedy defending sets up Rooney for simple goal within 28 seconds of restart and Beattie limps off
3 Ferguson anger at disallowed header that could have taken Villarreal to extra time but Uefa Cup beckons
4 Ferguson header beats Martyn for own goal but it's enough for Portsmouth
5 Neville's first red in the last minute as early season blues extend to a tame defeat by Fulham
In need of a miracle to stay in Europe as Bucharest turn it on after Yobo scores to earn parity at the break
Euro dream over as Cahill's early goal doesn't open the floodgates but at least it's a win!
Sixth defeat out of seven and bottom spot looms as McFadden shows promise but can't breach Wigan
Nightmare continues without a point or even a goal for five league games
First stage fallers go on as Boro dump the Blues out of the Carling Cup
First points off Chelsea for Moyes' target men as Ferguson batters the champs and Beattie converts a penalty
Aerial weakness exposed by Spurs with two headed goals and other close calls
6 7 8 9 10 11 12 13 14 15
AUGUST
SEPTEMBER
OCTOBER
Home Away Neutral

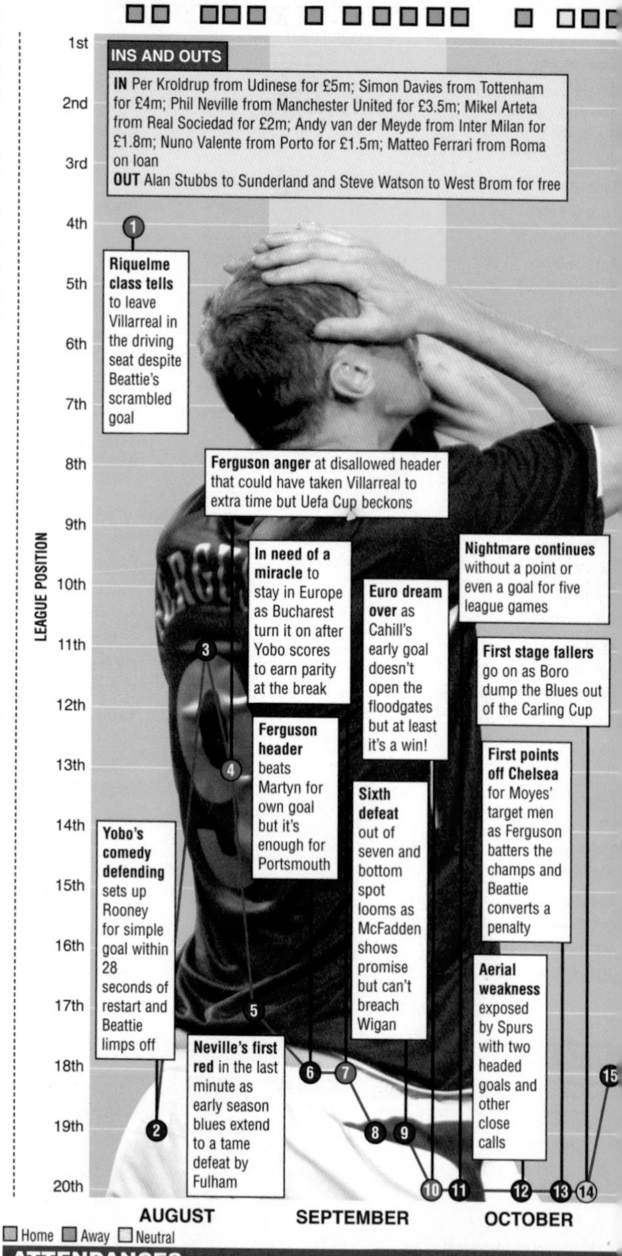

ATTENDANCES

HOME GROUND: GOODISON PARK **CAPACITY:** 40569 **AVERAGE LEAGUE AT HOME:** 36861

20	Man Utd	67831	33	Man City	37827	45	Birmingham	35420	29	Millwall	25800
36	Newcastle	51916	1	Villarreal	37685	37	West Ham	34866	3	Bolton	25608
40	Liverpool	44923	9	Wigan	37189	22	Bolton	34500	17	West Brom	24784
11	Man City	42681	30	Arsenal	36920	16	Middlesboro	34349	19	Blackburn	22064
44	Chelsea	41765	6	Portsmouth	36861	26	Charlton	34333	4	Villarreal	22000
24	Liverpool	40158	38	Fulham	36515	23	Aston Villa	32432	10	D Bucharest	21843
43	Tottenham	39856	39	Aston Villa	36507	25	Sunderland	30576	32	Wigan	21731
47	West Brom	39671	12	Tottenham	36247	31	Chelsea	29742	28	Portsmouth	20094
34	Chelsea	39301	18	Newcastle	36207	46	Middlesboro	29224	5	Fulham	17169
2	Man Utd	38610	13	Chelsea	36042	42	Charlton	26954	27	Millwall	16440
8	Arsenal	38121	21	West Ham	35704	15	Birmingham	26554	7	D Bucharest	11500
41	Sunderland	38093	35	Blackburn	35615	14	Middlesboro	25844			

Awful start as midfield goals dry-up

Final Position: 11th

KEY: ● League ● Champions Lge ● UEFA Cup ● FA Cup ○ League Cup ● Other

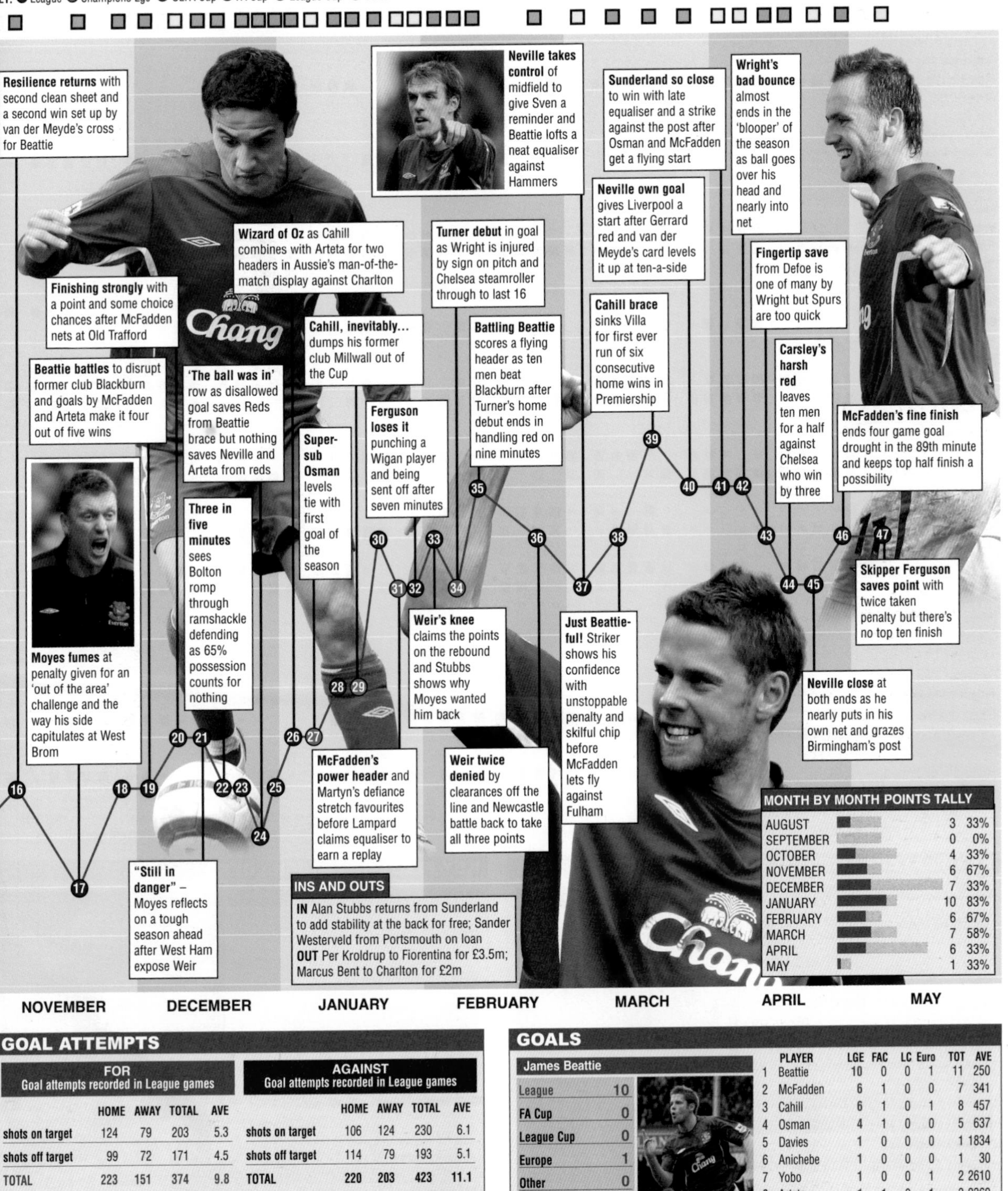

MONTH BY MONTH POINTS TALLY

AUGUST	3	33%
SEPTEMBER	0	0%
OCTOBER	4	33%
NOVEMBER	6	67%
DECEMBER	7	33%
JANUARY	10	83%
FEBRUARY	6	67%
MARCH	7	58%
APRIL	6	33%
MAY	1	33%

INS AND OUTS

IN Alan Stubbs returns from Sunderland to add stability at the back for free; Sander Westerveld from Portsmouth on loan **OUT** Per Kroldrup to Fiorentina for £3.5m; Marcus Bent to Charlton for £2m

GOAL ATTEMPTS

FOR – Goal attempts recorded in League games

	HOME	AWAY	TOTAL	AVE
shots on target	124	79	203	5.3
shots off target	99	72	171	4.5
TOTAL	223	151	374	9.8

Ratio of goals to shots Average number of shots on target per League goal scored: **6**

Accuracy rating Average percentage of total goal attempts which were on target: **54.3**

AGAINST – Goal attempts recorded in League games

	HOME	AWAY	TOTAL	AVE
shots on target	106	124	230	6.1
shots off target	114	79	193	5.1
TOTAL	220	203	423	11.1

Ratio of goals to shots Average number of shots on target per League goal scored: **4.7**

Accuracy rating Average percentage of total goal attempts which were on target: **54.4**

GOALS

James Beattie

League	10
FA Cup	0
League Cup	0
Europe	1
Other	0
TOTAL	11

League Average **250** mins between goals

	PLAYER	LGE	FAC	LC	Euro	TOT	AVE
1	Beattie	10	0	0	1	11	250
2	McFadden	6	1	0	0	7	341
3	Cahill	6	1	0	1	8	457
4	Osman	4	1	0	0	5	637
5	Davies	1	0	0	0	1	1834
6	Anichebe	1	0	0	0	1	30
7	Yobo	1	0	0	1	2	2610
8	Arteta	1	1	0	1	3	2369
9	Bent, M	1	0	0	0	1	816
10	Weir	1	0	0	0	1	2883
11	Ferguson	1	0	0	0	1	978
	Other	1	0	0	0	1	
	TOTAL	34	4	0	4	42	

SQUAD APPEARANCES

Match	1	2	3	4	5	6	7	8	9	10	11	12	13	14	15	16	17	18	19	20	21	22	23	24	25	26	27	28	29	30	31	32	33	34	35	36	37	38	39	40	41	42	43	44	45	46
Venue	H	H	A	A	A	H	A	A	H	H	A	A	H	H	A	H	A	H	A	A	H	H	A	H	A	H	A	A	H	H	H	A	H	A	H	A	A	H	H	A	H	A	H	A	H	A
Competition	C	L	L	C	L	L	E	L	L	E	L	L	L	W	L	L	L	L	L	L	L	L	L	L	L	L	F	L	F	L	F	L	L	F	L	L	L	L	L	L	L	L	L	L	L	L
Result	L	L	W	L	L	L	L	L	L	W	L	L	D	L	W	W	L	W	W	D	L	L	L	L	W	W	D	W	W	W	D	D	W	L	W	L	D	W	W	L	D	D	L	L	D	W

Goalkeepers
Nigel Martyn
John Ruddy
Iain Turner
Sander Westerveld
Richard Wright

Defenders
Patrick Boyle
Matteo Ferrari
Tony Hibbert
Mark Hughes
Per Kroldrup
Gary Naysmith
Nuno Valente
Alessandro Pistone
Alan Stubbs
David Weir
Joseph Yobo

Midfielders
Mikel Arteta
Tim Cahill
Lee Carsley
Simon Davies
Kevin Kilbane
Li Tie
Phil Neville
Leon Osman
Andy van der Meyde
Bjarni Thor Vidarsson
Lawrence Wilson

Forwards
Victor Anichebe
James Beattie
Marcus Bent
Duncan Ferguson
James McFadden
James Vaughan

KEY: On all match · On bench · Subbed or sent off (Counting game) · Subbed or sent off (playing less than 70 mins) · Subbed on from bench (Counting Game) · Subbed on (playing less than 70 mins) · Subbed on and then subbed or sent off (Counting Game) · Subbed on and then subbed or sent off (playing less than 70 mins) · Not in 16

KEY PLAYERS - GOALSCORERS

James Beattie

Goals in the League	10
Goals in all competitions	11
Assists League goals scored by a team mate where the player delivered the final pass	4
Contribution to Attacking Power Average number of minutes between League team goals while on pitch	83
Player Strike Rate Average number of minutes between League goals scored by player	250
Club Strike Rate Average minutes between League goals scored by club	101

	PLAYER	GOALS LGE	GOALS ALL	ASSISTS	POWER	S RATE
1	James Beattie	10	11	4	83	250 mins
2	James McFadden	6	7	2	98	341 mins
3	Tim Cahill	6	8	4	101	457 mins
4	Leon Osman	4	5	4	88	637 mins

KEY PLAYERS - MIDFIELDERS

Leon Osman

Goals in the League	4
Goals in all competitions	5
Assists League goals scored by a team mate where the player delivered the final pass	4
Defensive Rating Average number of mins between League goals conceded while on the pitch	75
Contribution to Attacking Power Average number of minutes between League team goals while on pitch	88
Scoring Difference Defensive Rating minus Contribution to Attacking Power	-13

	PLAYER	GOALS LGE	GOALS ALL	ASSISTS	DEF RATE	POWER	SC DIFF
1	Leon Osman	4	5	4	75	88	-13 mins
2	Mikel Arteta	1	3	6	72	91	-19 mins
3	Tim Cahill	6	8	4	76	101	-25 mins
4	Phil Neville	0	0	1	68	101	-33 mins

PLAYER APPEARANCES

	AGE (on 01/07/06)	IN NAMED 16	APPEARANCES	COUNTING GAMES	MINUTES ON PITCH	APPEARANCES	MINUTES ON PITCH	THIS SEASON	HOME COUNTRY
Goalkeepers									
Nigel Martyn	39	20	20	19	1755	27	2385	-	England
John Ruddy	19	3	1	1	81	1	81	-	England
Iain Turner	22	15	3	1	136	4	226	-	Scotland
Sander Westerveld	31	4	2	2	180	2	180	-	Holland
Richard Wright	28	34	15	13	1268	16	1358	-	England
Defenders									
Patrick Boyle	19	0	0	0	0	0	0	-	Scotland
Matteo Ferrari	26	16	8	4	532	13	932	-	Italy
Tony Hibbert	25	30	29	28	2566	38	3309	-	England
Mark Hughes	19	0	0	0	0	0	0	-	England
Per Kroldrup	26	11	1	1	90	2	148	1	Denmark (19)
Gary Naysmith	27	17	7	7	618	8	655	1	Scotland (85)
Nuno Valente	31	22	20	19	1741	26	2213	3	Portugal (7)
Alessandro Pistone	30	2	2	1	122	3	201	-	Italy
Alan Stubbs	34	15	14	12	1197	14	1197	-	England
David Weir	36	37	33	32	2883	42	3612	6	Scotland (85)
Joseph Yobo	25	32	29	29	2610	34	3060	8	Nigeria (11)
Midfielders									
Mikel Arteta	24	29	29	25	2369	37	3089	-	Spain
Tim Cahill	26	32	32	30	2739	39	3369	5	Australia (42)
Lee Carsley	32	7	5	2	256	6	265	-	Rep of Ireland
Simon Davies	26	36	30	14	1834	36	2284	5	Wales (74)
Kevin Kilbane	29	36	34	15	2004	43	2652	5	Rep of Ireland (15)
Li Tie	28	1	0	0	0	0	0	-	China PR
Phil Neville	29	34	34	33	3038	43	3831	6	England (10)
Leon Osman	25	36	35	25	2547	42	2962	-	England
Andy van der Meyde	26	12	10	3	492	11	521	-	Holland
Bjarni Thor Vidarsson	20	2	0	0	0	0	0	-	Iceland
Lawrence Wilson	19	0	0	0	0	0	0	-	England
Forwards									
Victor Anichebe	18	5	2	0	30	3	32	-	Nigeria
James Beattie	28	32	32	26	2503	38	2845	-	England
Marcus Bent	28	21	18	6	816	24	1155	-	England
Duncan Ferguson	34	27	27	7	978	33	1321	-	Scotland
James McFadden	23	38	32	20	2048	41	2460	5	Scotland (85)
James Vaughan	17	2	1	0	14	1	14	-	England

KEY: LEAGUE ALL COMPS CAPS (MAY FIFA RANKING)

TEAM OF THE SEASON

MARTYN

CG 19 DR 73

HIBBERT

CG 28 DR 78

WEIR

CG 32 DR 70

STUBBS

CG 12 DR 80

VALENTE

CG 19 DR 73

ARTETA

CG 25 SD -19

CAHILL

CG 30 SD -25

NEVILLE

CG 33 SD -33

OSMAN

CG 25 SD -13

MCFADDEN

CG 20 AP 98

BEATTIE

CG 26 SR 250

KEY: DR = Defensive Rate, SD = Scoring Difference AP = Attacking Power SR = Strike Rate, CG=Counting games – League games playing at least 70 minutes

TOP POINT EARNERS

James Beattie

Counting Games League games when player was on pitch for at least 70 minutes	26
Average points Average League points taken in Counting games	1.73
Club Average points Average points taken in League games	1.32

	PLAYER	GAMES	PTS
1	James Beattie	26	1.73
2	Alan Stubbs	12	1.67
3	Tony Hibbert	28	1.61
4	Mikel Arteta	25	1.40
5	Kevin Kilbane	15	1.40
6	Tim Cahill	30	1.37
7	Leon Osman	25	1.36
8	Phil Neville	33	1.33
9	Nuno Valente	19	1.32
10	Nigel Martyn	19	1.32

KEY PLAYERS - DEFENDERS

Alan Stubbs

Goals Conceded in the League Number of League goals conceded while the player was on the pitch	15
Goals Conceded in all competitions Total number of goals conceded while the player was on the pitch	15
League minutes played Number of minutes played in league matches	1197
Clean Sheets In games when the player was on pitch for at least 70 minutes	4
Defensive Rating Average number of mins between League goals conceded while on the pitch	80
Club Defensive Rating Average number of mins between League goals conceded by the club this season	70

	PLAYER	CON LGE	CON ALL	MINS	C SHEETS	DEF RATE
1	Alan Stubbs	15	15	1197	4	80 mins
2	Tony Hibbert	33	49	2566	11	78 mins
3	Nuno Valente	24	34	1741	5	73 mins
4	David Weir	41	57	2883	11	70 mins

KEY GOALKEEPER

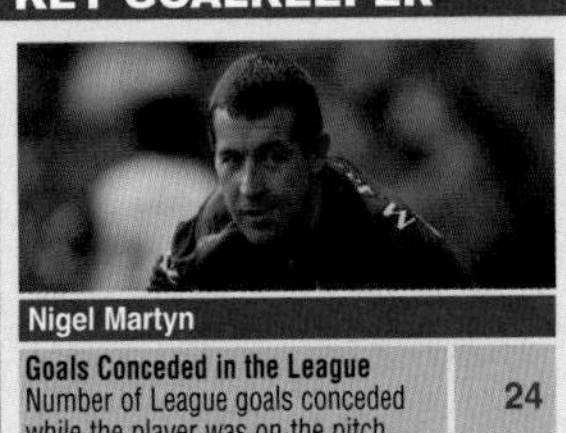

Nigel Martyn

Goals Conceded in the League Number of League goals conceded while the player was on the pitch	24
Goals Conceded in all competitions Total number of goals conceded while the player was on the pitch	35
League minutes played Number of minutes played in league matches	1755
Clean Sheets In games when the player was on pitch for at least 70 minutes	8
Goals to Shots Ratio The average number of shots on target per each League goal conceded	5.3
Defensive Rating Ave mins between League goals conceded while on the pitch	73

BOOKINGS

Phil Neville

League Yellow	14
League Red	2
All competitions Yellow	14
All competitions Red	2

League Average 189 mins between cards

	PLAYER	LEAGUE 14Y	2R	TOTAL 14Y	2R	AVE
1	Neville	14Y	2R	14Y	2R	189
2	van der Meyde	1	1	1	1	246
3	Ferrari	2	0	2	0	266
4	Arteta	7	1	8	1	296
5	Hibbert	8	0	9	0	320
6	Ferguson	2	1	3	1	326
7	Cahill	8	0	10	0	342
8	Kilbane	4	0	5	0	501
9	Stubbs	2	0	2	0	598
10	Naysmith	1	0	1	0	618
11	McFadden	3	0	5	0	682
12	Beattie	3	0	3	0	834
13	Nuno Valente	2	0	4	0	870
14	Davies	2	0	2	0	917
15	Weir	3	0	4	0	961
	Other	3	0	4	0	
	TOTAL	65	5	77	5	

FULHAM

Strong at home but only winning one away game - the second from last – made for an uncertain season. A long flirtation with relegation gave the pundits plenty of chances to suggest Chris Coleman's team were 'too good to go down'. In the end they were and their defeat of Chelsea showed what might have been.

Brian McBride had his best season in the Premiership but nine league goals at a Strike Rate on one every 174 minutes still looks laboured. **Collins John** and **Heidar Helguson** both made good contributions with limited opportunities and finished with Strike Rates under 200. **Papa Bouba Diop** came back from injury to top the midfield chart ahead of **Luis Boa Morte** and **Steed Malbranque**. **Wayne Bridge's** late cameo boosted the points average while warming up for the World Cup.

NICKNAME: THE COTTAGERS

KEY: Won / Drawn / Lost

1	prem	**Birmingham**	H	D	0-0	
2	prem	**Blackburn**	A	L	1-2	McBride 49
3	prem	**Arsenal**	A	L	1-4	Jensen, C 22
4	prem	**Everton**	H	W	1-0	McBride 57
5	prem	**Newcastle**	A	D	1-1	McBride 13
6	prem	**West Ham**	H	L	1-2	Boa Morte 66
7	ccr2	**Lincoln**	H	W	5-4	Rehman 26; Helguson 31; Rosenior 93; Radzinski 95; McBride 120
8	prem	**Tottenham**	A	L	0-1	
9	prem	**Man Utd**	H	L	2-3	John 2; Jensen, C 28
10	prem	**Charlton**	A	D	1-1	John 27
11	prem	**Liverpool**	H	W	2-0	John 30; Boa Morte 90
12	ccr3	**West Brom**	H	L	2-3	Boa Morte 63; Helguson 90
13	prem	**Wigan**	A	L	0-1	
14	prem	**Man City**	H	W	2-1	Malbranque 6,45
15	prem	**Middlesbrough**	A	L	2-3	John 9; Diop 70
16	prem	**Bolton**	H	W	2-1	McBride 4,18
17	prem	**West Brom**	A	D	0-0	
18	prem	**Birmingham**	A	L	0-1	
19	prem	**Blackburn**	H	W	2-1	Diop 45; Boa Morte 52
20	prem	**Chelsea**	A	L	2-3	McBride 29; Helguson 56 pen
21	prem	**Aston Villa**	H	D	3-3	McBride 13,61; Helguson 32 pen
22	prem	**Portsmouth**	A	L	0-1	
23	prem	**Sunderland**	H	W	2-1	John 43,61
24	facr3	**Leyton Orient**	H	L	1-2	John 50
25	prem	**Newcastle**	H	W	1-0	Malbranque 75
26	prem	**West Ham**	A	L	1-2	Helguson 52
27	prem	**Tottenham**	H	W	1-0	Bocanegra 90
28	prem	**Man Utd**	A	L	2-4	McBride 22; Helguson 37
29	prem	**West Brom**	H	W	6-1	Helguson 4,40; Radzinski 48; Davies, C 58 og; John 83,90
30	prem	**Bolton**	A	L	1-2	Helguson 21
31	prem	**Arsenal**	H	L	0-4	
32	prem	**Everton**	A	L	1-3	John 86 pen
33	prem	**Liverpool**	A	L	1-5	John 25
34	prem	**Chelsea**	H	W	1-0	Boa Morte 17
35	prem	**Aston Villa**	A	D	0-0	
36	prem	**Portsmouth**	H	L	1-3	Malbranque 10
37	prem	**Charlton**	H	W	2-1	Boa Morte 15,30
38	prem	**Wigan**	H	W	1-0	Malbranque 45
39	prem	**Man City**	A	W	2-1	John 84; Malbranque 90
40	prem	**Sunderland**	A	L	1-2	Radzinski 76
41	prem	**Middlesbrough**	H	W	1-0	Helguson 84 pen

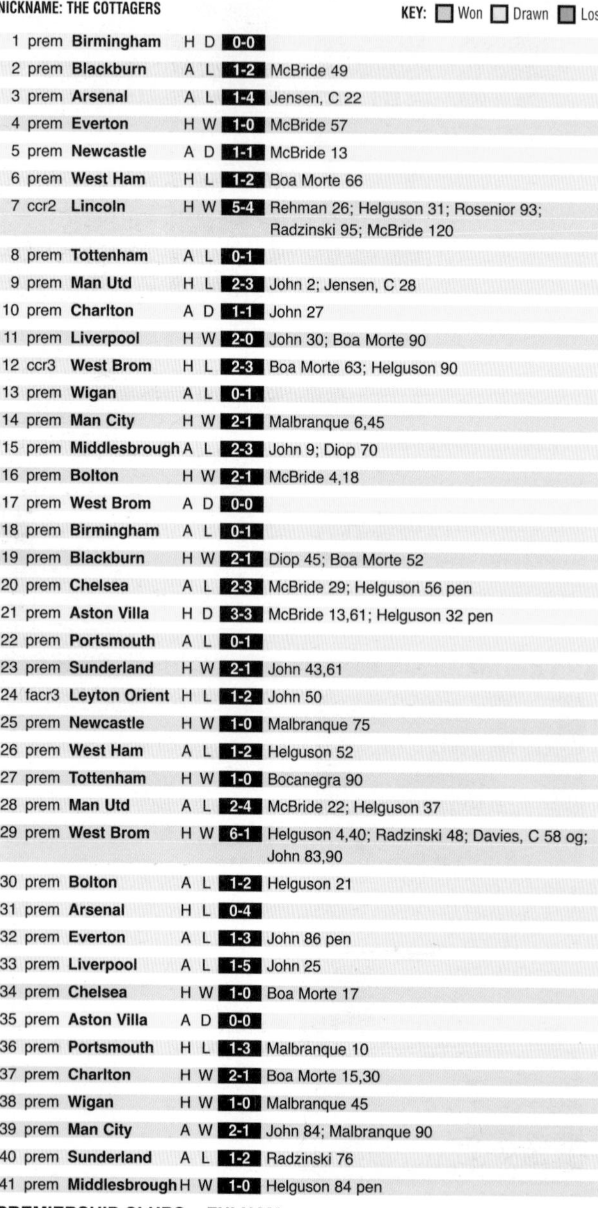

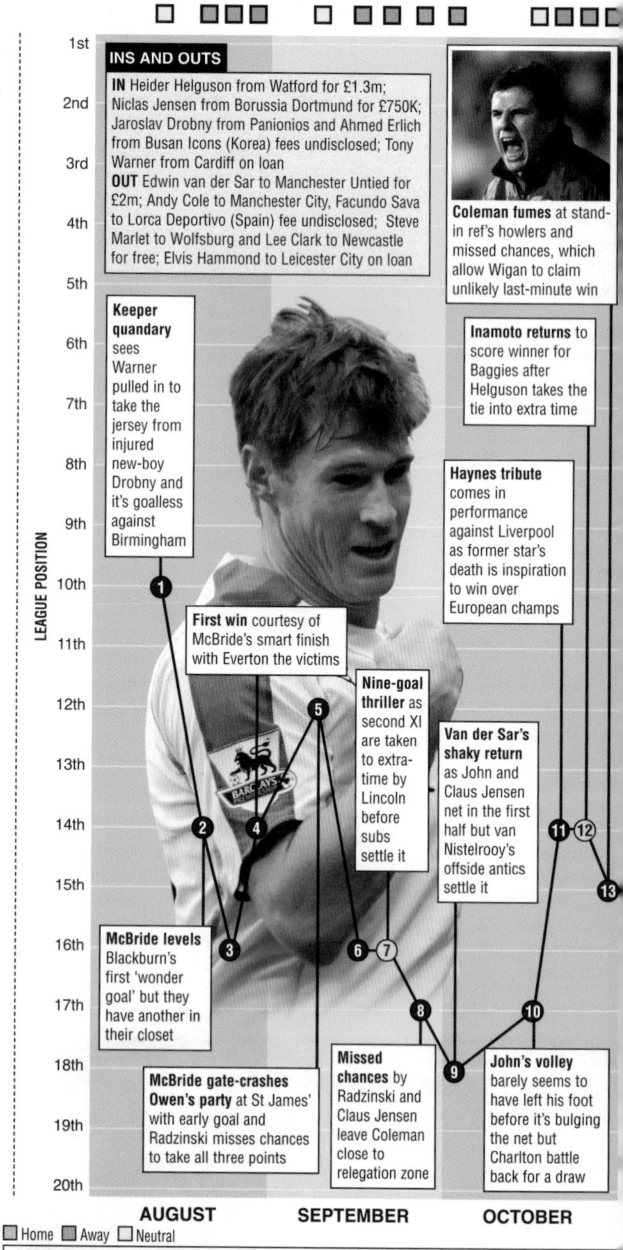

1st
2nd
3rd
4th
5th
6th
7th
8th
9th
10th
11th
12th
13th
14th
15th
16th
17th
18th
19th
20th
LEAGUE POSITION
INS AND OUTS
IN Heider Helguson from Watford for £1.3m; Niclas Jensen from Borussia Dortmund for £750K; Jaroslav Drobny from Panionios and Ahmed Erlich from Busan Icons (Korea) fees undisclosed; Tony Warner from Cardiff on loan
OUT Edwin van der Sar to Manchester Untied for £2m; Andy Cole to Manchester City, Facundo Sava to Lorca Deportivo (Spain) fee undisclosed; Steve Marlet to Wolfsburg and Lee Clark to Newcastle for free; Elvis Hammond to Leicester City on loan
Coleman fumes at stand-in ref's howlers and missed chances, which allow Wigan to claim unlikely last-minute win
Keeper quandary sees Warner pulled in to take the jersey from injured new-boy Drobny and it's goalless against Birmingham
Inamoto returns to score winner for Baggies after Helguson takes the tie into extra time
Haynes tribute comes in performance against Liverpool as former star's death is inspiration to win over European champs
First win courtesy of McBride's smart finish with Everton the victims
Nine-goal thriller as second XI are taken to extra-time by Lincoln before subs settle it
Van der Sar's shaky return as John and Claus Jensen net in the first half but van Nistelrooy's offside antics settle it
McBride levels Blackburn's first 'wonder goal' but they have another in their closet
McBride gate-crashes Owen's party at St James' with early goal and Radzinski misses chances to take all three points
Missed chances by Radzinski and Claus Jensen leave Coleman close to relegation zone
John's volley barely seems to have left his foot before it's bulging the net but Charlton battle back for a draw
AUGUST
SEPTEMBER
OCTOBER
Home
Away
Neutral

ATTENDANCES

HOME GROUND: LOFTUS ROAD CAPACITY: 22480 AVERAGE LEAGUE AT HOME: 20654

28	Man Utd	67844	15	Middlesboro	27599	25	Newcastle	21974	13	Wigan	17266
5	Newcastle	52208	18	Birmingham	27597	6	West Ham	21907	4	Everton	17169
20	Chelsea	42313	10	Charlton	26310	9	Man Utd	21862	38	Wigan	17149
33	Liverpool	42293	17	West Brom	23144	29	West Brom	21508	2	Blackburn	16953
39	Man City	41128	30	Bolton	23104	27	Tottenham	21081	1	Birmingham	16550
3	Arsenal	37867	34	Chelsea	22480	21	Aston Villa	20446	24	Leyton Orient	13394
32	Everton	36515	11	Liverpool	22480	19	Blackburn	20138	12	West Brom	7373
8	Tottenham	35427	41	Middlesboro	22434	16	Bolton	19768	7	Lincoln	5365
35	Aston Villa	32605	31	Arsenal	22397	23	Sunderland	19372			
26	West Ham	29812	36	Portsmouth	22322	37	Charlton	19146			
40	Sunderland	28226	14	Man City	22241	22	Portsmouth	19101			

Late run to 12th for the home boys

Final Position: **12th**

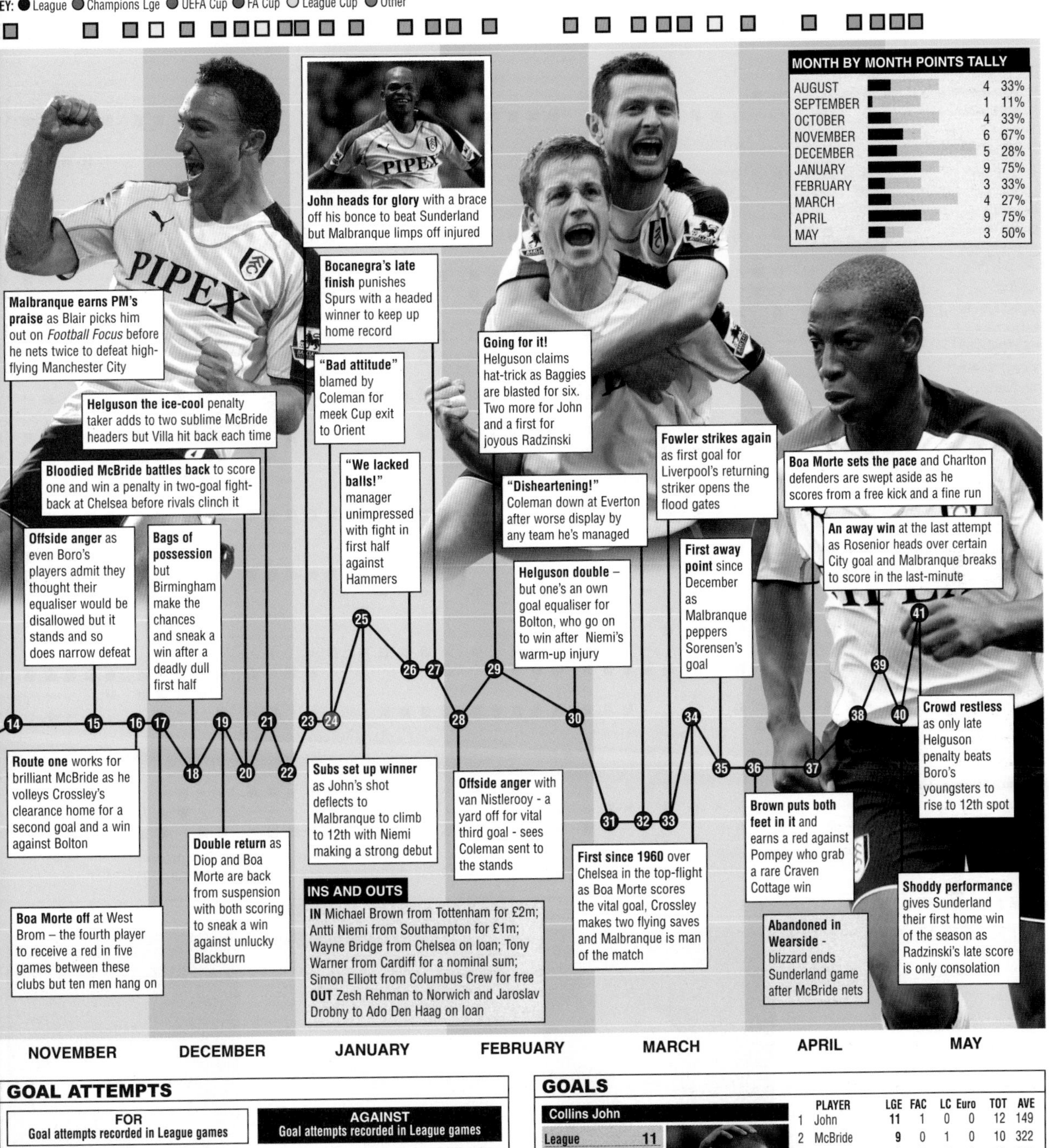

KEY: League Champions Lge UEFA Cup FA Cup League Cup Other
MONTH BY MONTH POINTS TALLY
AUGUST 4 33%
SEPTEMBER 1 11%
OCTOBER 4 33%
NOVEMBER 6 67%
DECEMBER 5 28%
JANUARY 9 75%
FEBRUARY 3 33%
MARCH 4 27%
APRIL 9 75%
MAY 3 50%
John heads for glory with a brace off his bonce to beat Sunderland but Malbranque limps off injured
Malbranque earns PM's praise as Blair picks him out on Football Focus before he nets twice to defeat high-flying Manchester City
Helguson the ice-cool penalty taker adds to two sublime McBride headers but Villa hit back each time
Bloodied McBride battles back to score one and win a penalty in two-goal fight-back at Chelsea before rivals clinch it
Offside anger as even Boro's players admit they thought their equaliser would be disallowed but it stands and so does narrow defeat
Bags of possession but Birmingham make the chances and sneak a win after a deadly dull first half
Bocanegra's late finish punishes Spurs with a headed winner to keep up home record
"Bad attitude" blamed by Coleman for meek Cup exit to Orient
"We lacked balls!" manager unimpressed with fight in first half against Hammers
Going for it! Helguson claims hat-trick as Baggies are blasted for six. Two more for John and a first for joyous Radzinski
"Disheartening!" Coleman down at Everton after worse display by any team he's managed
Helguson double – but one's an own goal equaliser for Bolton, who go on to win after Niemi's warm-up injury
Fowler strikes again as first goal for Liverpool's returning striker opens the flood gates
First away point since December as Malbranque peppers Sorensen's goal
Boa Morte sets the pace and Charlton defenders are swept aside as he scores from a free kick and a fine run
An away win at the last attempt as Rosenior heads over certain City goal and Malbranque breaks to score in the last-minute
Crowd restless as only late Helguson penalty beats Boro's youngsters to rise to 12th spot
Route one works for brilliant McBride as he volleys Crossley's clearance home for a second goal and a win against Bolton
Boa Morte off at West Brom – the fourth player to receive a red in five games between these clubs but ten men hang on
Double return as Diop and Boa Morte are back from suspension with both scoring to sneak a win against unlucky Blackburn
Subs set up winner as John's shot deflects to Malbranque to climb to 12th with Niemi making a strong debut
Offside anger with van Nistlerooy - a yard off for vital third goal - sees Coleman sent to the stands
First since 1960 over Chelsea in the top-flight as Boa Morte scores the vital goal, Crossley makes two flying saves and Malbranque is man of the match
Brown puts both feet in it and earns a red against Pompey who grab a rare Craven Cottage win
Abandoned in Wearside - blizzard ends Sunderland game after McBride nets
Shoddy performance gives Sunderland their first home win of the season as Radzinski's late score is only consolation
INS AND OUTS
IN Michael Brown from Tottenham for £2m; Antti Niemi from Southampton for £1m; Wayne Bridge from Chelsea on loan; Tony Warner from Cardiff for a nominal sum; Simon Elliott from Columbus Crew for free
OUT Zesh Rehman to Norwich and Jaroslav Drobny to Ado Den Haag on loan
NOVEMBER DECEMBER JANUARY FEBRUARY MARCH APRIL MAY

GOAL ATTEMPTS

FOR – Goal attempts recorded in League games

	HOME	AWAY	TOTAL	AVE
shots on target	100	78	178	4.7
shots off target	80	100	180	4.7
TOTAL	180	178	358	9.4

Ratio of goals to shots Average number of shots on target per League goal scored	3.7
Accuracy rating Average percentage of total goal attempts which were on target	49.7

AGAINST – Goal attempts recorded in League games

	HOME	AWAY	TOTAL	AVE
shots on target	97	146	243	6.4
shots off target	88	78	166	4.4
TOTAL	185	224	409	10.8

Ratio of goals to shots Average number of shots on target per League goal scored	4.2
Accuracy rating Average percentage of total goal attempts which were on target	59.4

GOALS

Collins John

League	11
FA Cup	1
League Cup	0
Europe	0
Other	0
TOTAL	12

League Average **149** mins between goals

	PLAYER	LGE	FAC	LC	Euro	TOT	AVE
1	John	11	1	0	0	12	149
2	McBride	9	0	1	0	10	322
3	Helguson	8	0	2	0	10	174
4	Boa Morte	6	0	1	0	7	500
5	Malbranque	6	0	0	0	6	483
6	Jensen, C	2	0	0	0	2	491
7	Diop	2	0	0	0	2	907
8	Radzinski	2	0	1	0	3	1143
9	Bocanegra	1	0	0	0	1	1831
10	Rosenior	0	0	1	0	1	
11	Rehman	0	0	1	0	1	
	Other	1	0	0	0	1	
	TOTAL	48	1	7	0	56	

SQUAD APPEARANCES

Match	1	2	3	4	5	6	7	8	9	10	11	12	13	14	15	16	17	18	19	20	21	22	23	24	25	26	27	28	29	30	31	32	33	34	35	36	37	38	39	40
Venue	H	A	A	H	A	H	H	A	H	A	H	H	A	H	A	H	A	A	H	A	H	A	H	H	H	A	H	A	H	A	H	A	A	H	A	H	H	H	A	A
Competition	L	L	L	L	L	L	W	L	L	L	L	W	L	L	L	L	L	L	L	L	L	L	L	F	L	L	L	L	L	L	L	L	L	L	L	L	L	L	L	L
Result	D	L	L	W	D	L	W	L	L	D	W	L	L	W	L	W	D	L	W	L	D	L	W	L	W	L	W	L	W	L	L	L	L	W	D	L	W	W	W	L

Goalkeepers
Ricardo Batista
Mark Crossley
Jaroslav Drobny
Antti Niemi
Tony Warner

Defenders
Carlos Bocanegra
Wayne Bridge
Philippe Christanval
Alain Goma
Niclas Jensen
Zatyiah Knight
Dean Leacock
Robert Milsom
Ian Pearce
Zeshan Rehman
Liam Rosenior
Moritz Volz

Midfielders
Luis Boa Morte
Michael Brown
Papa Bouba Diop
Simon Elliott
Ahmad Elrich
Sergio Gonzalez Green
Claus Jensen
Sylvain Legwinski
Steed Malbranque
Mark Pembridge
Tomasz Radzinski
Michael Timlin

Forwards
Heidar Helguson
Collins John
Brian McBride

KEY: On all match · On bench · Subbed or sent off (Counting game) · Subbed or sent off (playing less than 70 mins) · Subbed on from bench (Counting Game) · Subbed on (playing less than 70 mins) · Subbed on and then subbed or sent off (Counting Game) · Subbed on and then subbed or sent off (playing less than 70 mins) · Not in 16

KEY PLAYERS - GOALSCORERS

Brian McBride

Goals in the League	9
Goals in all competitions	10
Assists League goals scored by a team mate where the player delivered the final pass	4
Contribution to Attacking Power Average number of minutes between League team goals while on pitch	69
Player Strike Rate Average number of minutes between League goals scored by player	322
Club Strike Rate Average minutes between League goals scored by club	71

	PLAYER	GOALS LGE	GOALS ALL	ASSISTS	POWER	S RATE
1	Brian McBride	9	10	4	69	322 mins
2	Steed Malbranque	6	6	5	74	483 mins
3	Luis Boa Morte	6	7	10	68	500 mins
4	Papa Bouba Diop	2	2	1	76	907 mins

KEY PLAYERS - MIDFIELDERS

Papa Bouba Diop

Goals in the League	2
Goals in all competitions	2
Assists League goals scored by a team mate where the player delivered the final pass	1
Defensive Rating Average number of mins between League goals conceded while on the pitch	73
Contribution to Attacking Power Average number of minutes between League team goals while on pitch	76
Scoring Difference Defensive Rating minus Contribution to Attacking Power	-3

	PLAYER	GOALS LGE	GOALS ALL	ASSISTS	DEF RATE	POWER	SC DIFF
1	Papa Bouba Diop	2	2	1	73	76	-3 mins
2	Luis Boa Morte	6	7	10	60	68	-8 mins
3	Steed Malbranque	6	6	5	59	74	-15 mins
4	Tomasz Radzinski	2	3	6	59	74	-15 mins

PLAYER APPEARANCES

	AGE (on 01/07/06)	IN NAMED 16	APPEARANCES	COUNTING GAMES	MINUTES ON PITCH	APPEARANCES	MINUTES ON PITCH	THIS SEASON	HOME COUNTRY
Goalkeepers									
Ricardo Batista	19	9	0	0	0	1	120	-	Portugal
Mark Crossley	37	21	13	12	1122	13	1122	-	Wales
Jaroslav Drobny	26	2	0	0	0	0	0	-	Czech Republic
Antti Niemi	34	9	9	9	810	9	810	-	Finland
Tony Warner	32	34	18	16	1488	20	1698	-	England
Defenders									
Carlos Bocanegra	27	23	21	20	1831	22	1859	4	United States (5)
Wayne Bridge	25	12	12	12	1080	12	1080	3	England (10)
Philippe Christanval	27	18	15	6	813	16	933	-	France
Alain Goma	33	22	13	13	1170	15	1295	-	France
Niclas Jensen	31	28	16	13	1288	17	1378	5	Denmark (19)
Zatyiah Knight	26	32	30	27	2533	32	2743	-	England
Dean Leacock	22	11	5	4	416	7	598	-	England
Robert Milsom	19	0	0	0	0	0	0	-	England
Ian Pearce	32	18	10	8	821	12	998	-	England
Zeshan Rehman	22	4	2	2	180	3	300	-	England
Liam Rosenior	21	28	24	22	1987	27	2317	-	England
Moritz Volz	23	28	23	23	2049	24	2089	-	Germany
Midfielders									
Luis Boa Morte	28	35	35	32	3001	37	3211	5	Portugal (7)
Michael Brown	29	7	7	5	501	7	501	-	England
Papa Bouba Diop	28	22	22	19	1813	23	1888	8	Senegal (28)
Simon Elliott	32	13	12	10	998	13	1088	-	New Zealand
Ahmad Elrich	25	17	6	1	157	9	394	3	Australia (42)
Claus Jensen	29	11	11	11	981	11	981	4	Denmark (19)
Sylvain Legwinski	32	14	13	9	892	15	1027	-	France
Steed Malbranque	26	34	34	31	2900	35	3020	-	France
Mark Pembridge	35	5	5	5	431	5	431	-	Wales
Tomasz Radzinski	32	36	33	21	2285	35	2433	1	Canada (77)
Michael Timlin	21	-	-	-	0	2	149	-	England
Forwards									
Heidar Helguson	28	35	27	11	1389	29	1629	2	Iceland (99)
Collins John	20	38	35	11	1634	38	1860	-	Holland
Brian McBride	34	38	38	32	2899	39	2947	2	United States (5)

KEY: LEAGUE ALL COMPS CAPS (MAY FIFA RANKING)

TEAM OF THE SEASON

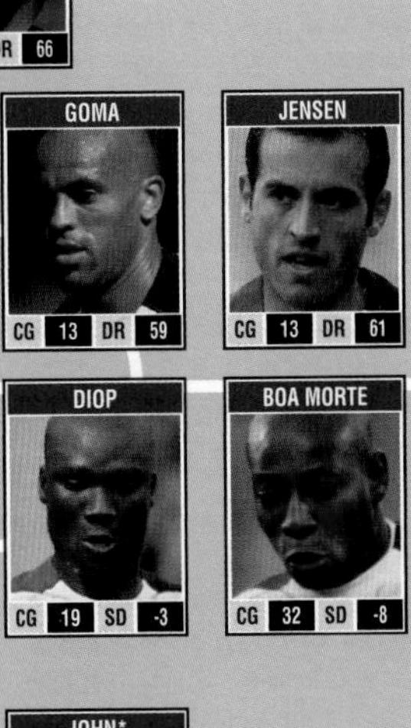

CROSSLEY CG 12 DR 66

VOLZ CG 23 DR 62

BOCANEGRA CG 20 DR 70

GOMA CG 13 DR 59

JENSEN CG 13 DR 61

RADZINSKI CG 21 SD -15

MALBRANQUE CG 31 SD -15

DIOP CG 19 SD -3

BOA MORTE CG 32 SD -8

MCBRIDE CG 32 AP 69

JOHN* CG 11 SR 149

KEY: DR = Defensive Rate, SD = Scoring Difference AP = Attacking Power SR = Strike Rate, CG=Counting games – League games playing at least 70 minutes

TOP POINT EARNERS

Liam Rosenior

Counting Games League games when player was on pitch for at least 70 minutes	22
Average points Average League points taken in Counting games	1.50
Club Average points Average points taken in League games	1.26

	PLAYER	GAMES	PTS
1	Liam Rosenior	22	1.50
2	Wayne Bridge	12	1.50
3	Papa Bouba Diop	19	1.42
4	Brian McBride	32	1.38
5	Luis Boa Morte	32	1.28
6	Carlos Bocanegra	20	1.25
7	Steed Malbranque	31	1.23
8	Zatyiah Knight	27	1.15
9	Moritz Volz	23	1.13
10	Alain Goma	13	1.08

KEY PLAYERS - DEFENDERS

Carlos Bocanegra

Goals Conceded in the League Number of League goals conceded while the player was on the pitch	26
Goals Conceded in all competitions Total number of goals conceded while the player was on the pitch	27
League minutes played Number of minutes played in league matches	1831
Clean Sheets In games when the player was on pitch for at least 70 minutes	5
Defensive Rating Average number of mins between League goals conceded while on the pitch	70
Club Defensive Rating Average number of mins between League goals conceded by the club this season	59

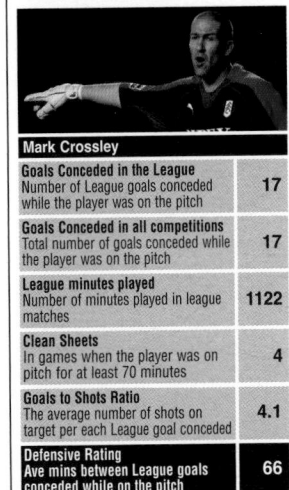

	PLAYER	CON LGE	CON ALL	MINS	C SHEETS	DEF RATE
1	Carlos Bocanegra	26	27	1831	5	70 mins
2	Moritz Volz	33	36	2049	7	62 mins
3	Niclas Jensen	21	23	1288	3	61 mins
4	Alain Goma	20	24	1170	2	59 mins

KEY GOALKEEPER

Mark Crossley

Goals Conceded in the League Number of League goals conceded while the player was on the pitch	17
Goals Conceded in all competitions Total number of goals conceded while the player was on the pitch	17
League minutes played Number of minutes played in league matches	1122
Clean Sheets In games when the player was on pitch for at least 70 minutes	4
Goals to Shots Ratio The average number of shots on target per each League goal conceded	4.1
Defensive Rating Ave mins between League goals conceded while on the pitch	66

BOOKINGS

Michael Brown

League Yellow	2
League Red	1
All competitions Yellow	2
All competitions Red	1

League Average **167** mins between cards

	PLAYER	LEAGUE 2Y	LEAGUE 1R	TOTAL 2Y	TOTAL 1R	AVE
1	Brown	2Y	1R	2Y	1R	167
2	Christanval	4	0	5	0	203
3	Legwinski	4	0	4	0	223
4	Boa Morte	11	1	12	1	250
5	Diop	6	0	7	0	302
6	Helguson	4	0	4	0	347
7	Bocanegra	5	0	5	0	366
8	John	4	0	4	0	408
9	Rosenior	4	0	5	0	496
10	Bridge	2	0	2	0	540
11	Malbranque	4	0	4	0	725
12	Radzinski	3	0	3	0	761
13	Pearce	1	0	3	0	821
14	McBride	3	0	3	0	966
15	Elliott	1	0	1	0	998
	Other	5	0	6	0	
	TOTAL	63	2	70	2	

CHARLTON ATHLETIC

It started with **Darren Bent** banging in the goals but ended with a whimper and the usual slip to lower mid-table. Finally Curbishley had found a goalscorer. Bent finished with the third highest Premiership goals total, 17, scored at the eighth best Strike Rate of one every 186 minutes. No-one else contributed over four goals.

The club used three goalkeepers with **Thomas Myhre** the pick, claiming a Defensive Rating of a goal conceded every 78 minutes when he played. Myhre also had the best Goals-to-Shots Ratio of any keeper in the division. He saved 6.1 shots on target for every goal conceded – ahead of both Cech and van der Sar.

Hermann Hreidarsson was the club's most consistent defender, playing in all but four of the 46 games and recording the best Defensive Rating with a goal conceded every 73 minutes.

NICKNAME: THE ADDICKS

KEY: Won / Drawn / Lost

1	prem	**Sunderland**	A	W	3-1	Bent, D 11,90; Murphy 64
2	prem	**Wigan**	H	W	1-0	Bent, D 42
3	prem	**Middlesbrough**	A	W	3-0	Rommedahl 38; Perry 81; Bent, D 90
4	prem	**Birmingham**	A	W	1-0	Bent, D 15
5	prem	**Chelsea**	H	L	0-2	
6	ccr2	**Hartlepool**	H	W	3-1	Johansson 43 pen; Bent, D 73; Bothroyd 80
7	prem	**West Brom**	A	W	2-1	Murphy 9 pen,31
8	prem	**Tottenham**	H	L	2-3	Bent, D 25,48
9	prem	**Fulham**	H	D	1-1	Murphy 48
10	prem	**Portsmouth**	A	W	2-1	Ambrose 61; Rommedahl 77
11	ccr3	**Chelsea**	A	W	5-4*	Bent, D 45 (*on penalties)
12	prem	**Bolton**	H	L	0-1	
13	prem	**Blackburn**	A	L	1-4	Hughes 36
14	prem	**Man Utd**	H	L	1-3	Ambrose 65
15	prem	**Aston Villa**	A	L	0-1	
16	ccr4	**Blackburn**	H	L	2-3	Ambrose 37; Murphy 50
17	prem	**Man City**	H	L	2-5	Bent, D 36; Bothroyd 73
18	prem	**Sunderland**	H	W	2-0	Bent, D 42; Ambrose 49
19	prem	**Wigan**	A	L	0-3	
20	prem	**Arsenal**	H	L	0-1	
21	prem	**West Ham**	H	W	2-0	Bartlett 21; Bent, D 63
22	prem	**Everton**	A	L	1-3	Holland 18
23	facr3	**Sheff Wed**	A	W	4-2	Rommedahl 13,44; Holland 27; Bent, D 87
24	prem	**Birmingham**	H	W	2-0	Hughes 29; Bent, D 90
25	prem	**Chelsea**	A	D	1-1	Bent, M 59
26	facr4	**Leyton Orient**	H	W	2-1	Fortune 7; Bothroyd 90
27	prem	**West Brom**	H	D	0-0	
28	prem	**Tottenham**	A	L	1-3	Thomas 70
29	prem	**Liverpool**	H	W	2-0	Bent, D 42 pen; Young 45
30	prem	**Man City**	A	L	2-3	Bent, D 50; Bent, M 66
31	facr5	**Brentford**	H	W	3-1	Bent, D 3; Bothroyd 45; Hughes 62
32	prem	**Newcastle**	A	D	0-0	
33	prem	**Aston Villa**	H	D	0-0	
34	prem	**Liverpool**	A	D	0-0	
35	prem	**Middlesbrough**	H	W	2-1	Bent, D 73,86
36	prem	**Arsenal**	A	L	0-3	
37	facqf	**Middlesbrough**	H	D	0-0	
38	prem	**Newcastle**	H	W	3-1	Bent, D 23 pen; Bowyer 37 og; Bothroyd 89
39	prem	**West Ham**	A	D	0-0	
40	prem	**Everton**	H	D	0-0	
41	facqfr	**Middlesbrough**	A	L	2-4	Hughes 13; Southgate 76 og
42	prem	**Fulham**	A	L	1-2	Euell 26
43	prem	**Portsmouth**	H	W	2-1	Hughes 76; Bent, D 83
44	prem	**Bolton**	A	L	1-4	Bent, D 76 pen
45	prem	**Blackburn**	H	L	0-2	
46	prem	**Man Utd**	A	L	0-4	

1st
2nd
3rd
4th
5th
6th
7th
8th
9th
10th
11th
12th
13th
14th
15th
16th
17th
18th
19th
20th
LEAGUE POSITION
Bent double! The debut striker sinks Sunderland with first and last goal despite Ambrose's dismissal
Murphy muscles through to set up Bent for goal that keeps good start going
Bent's fourth in three wins as Boro are overrun in midfield by Smertin and Murphy
Curbishley's 600th league game in charge continues 100% start with Bent adding to goal-a-game tally at Birmingham
Who can stop Chelsea? Hard-fought game between first and second just shows gulf in class
Penalty at last! Murphy grabs his first chance to take a spot kick since his arrival and it helps beat Baggies
Bent impresses Sven with both goals to grab a 2-0 lead but a lucky King strike lets Spurs back in for an unlikely win
Murphy's fourth of the season as he continues his stunning form with an equaliser against Fulham
Ambrose's scoring return to starting line-up with first goal against Pompey before Rommedahl hits the winner
Chelsea's first defeat comes courtesy of Bent's ninth of the season, valiant defence and five-out-of-five penalties
Bothroyd's air-shot best chance to convert performance into points but wicked deflection turns game for Bolton
Eriksson calls up Bent for England friendly but it's Rommedahl who scores for Denmark
Joma
all:sports
AUGUST
SEPTEMBER
OCTOBER
Home / Away / Neutral

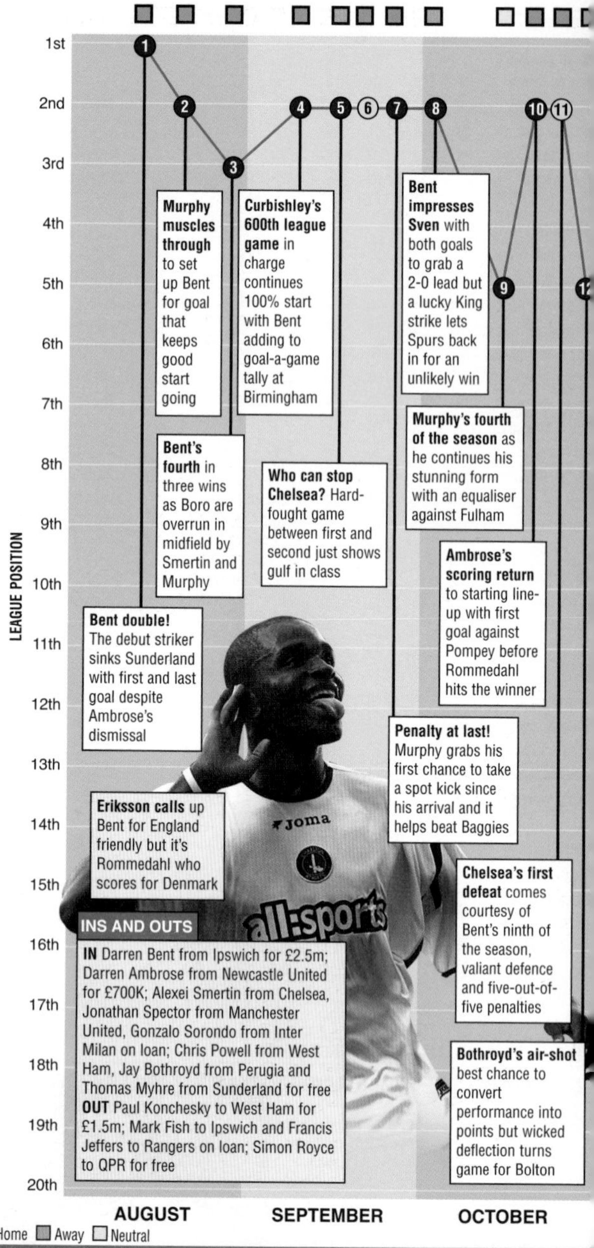

INS AND OUTS

IN Darren Bent from Ipswich for £2.5m; Darren Ambrose from Newcastle United for £700K; Alexei Smertin from Chelsea, Jonathan Spector from Manchester United, Gonzalo Sorondo from Inter Milan on loan; Chris Powell from West Ham, Jay Bothroyd from Perugia and Thomas Myhre from Sunderland for free **OUT** Paul Konchesky to West Ham for £1.5m; Mark Fish to Ipswich and Francis Jeffers to Rangers on loan; Simon Royce to QPR for free

ATTENDANCES

HOME GROUND: THE VALLEY **CAPACITY:** 27116 **AVERAGE LEAGUE AT HOME:** 26195

46	Man Utd	73006	15	Aston Villa	30023	45	Blackburn	26254	2	Wigan	23453
32	Newcastle	50451	5	Chelsea	27111	3	Middlesboro	26206	31	Brentford	22098
34	Liverpool	43892	20	Arsenal	27111	12	Bolton	26175	26	Leyton Orient	22029
11	Chelsea	42198	29	Liverpool	27111	18	Sunderland	26065	42	Fulham	19146
25	Chelsea	41355	8	Tottenham	27111	21	West Ham	25952	10	Portsmouth	19030
30	Man City	41347	38	Newcastle	27019	27	West Brom	25921	13	Blackburn	17691
36	Arsenal	38223	40	Everton	26954	43	Portsmouth	25419	19	Wigan	17074
28	Tottenham	36034	4	Birmingham	26846	17	Man City	25289	23	Sheff Wed	14851
39	West Ham	34753	14	Man Utd	26730	35	Middlesboro	24830	16	Blackburn	14093
1	Sunderland	34446	33	Aston Villa	26594	44	Bolton	24713	6	Hartlepool	10328
22	Everton	34333	24	Birmingham	26312	37	Middlesboro	24187			
41	Middlesboro	30248	9	Fulham	26310	7	West Brom	23909			

Curbishley's era ends in mid-table

Final Position: **13th**

KEY: ● League ● Champions Lge ● UEFA Cup ● FA Cup ○ League Cup ● Other

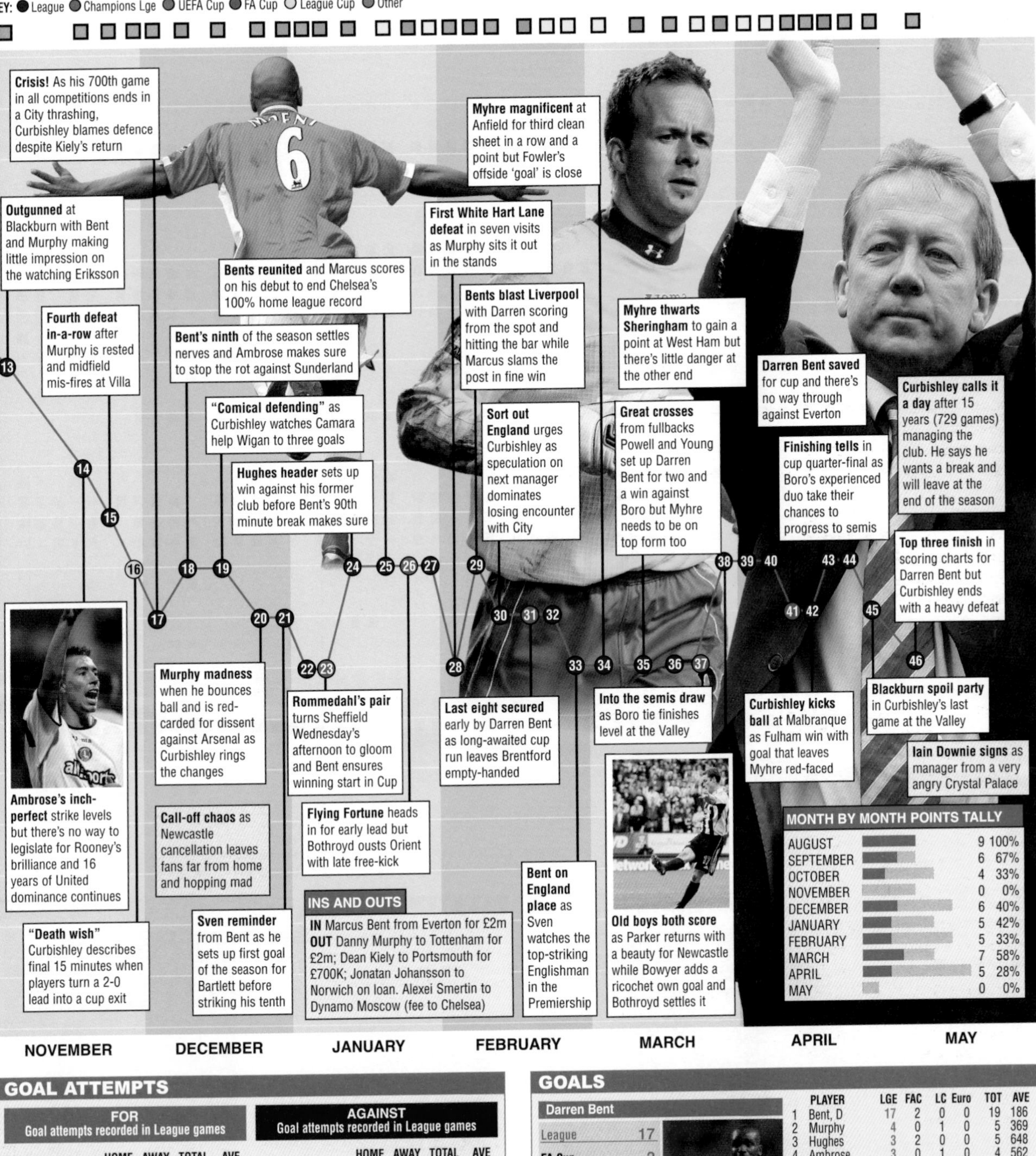

MONTH BY MONTH POINTS TALLY

AUGUST	9	100%
SEPTEMBER	6	67%
OCTOBER	4	33%
NOVEMBER	0	0%
DECEMBER	6	40%
JANUARY	5	42%
FEBRUARY	5	33%
MARCH	7	58%
APRIL	5	28%
MAY	0	0%

GOAL ATTEMPTS

FOR — Goal attempts recorded in League games

	HOME	AWAY	TOTAL	AVE
shots on target	98	83	181	4.8
shots off target	120	72	192	5.1
TOTAL	218	155	373	9.8

Ratio of goals to shots Average number of shots on target per League goal scored: **4.4**

Accuracy rating Average percentage of total goal attempts which were on target: **48.5**

AGAINST — Goal attempts recorded in League games

	HOME	AWAY	TOTAL	AVE
shots on target	110	153	263	6.9
shots off target	115	83	198	5.2
TOTAL	225	236	461	12.1

Ratio of goals to shots Average number of shots on target per League goal scored: **4.8**

Accuracy rating Average percentage of total goal attempts which were on target: **57**

GOALS

Darren Bent

League	17
FA Cup	2
League Cup	0
Europe	0
Other	0
TOTAL	19

League Average **186** mins between goals

	PLAYER	LGE	FAC	LC	Euro	TOT	AVE
1	Bent, D	17	2	0	0	19	186
2	Murphy	4	0	1	0	5	369
3	Hughes	3	2	0	0	5	648
4	Ambrose	3	0	1	0	4	562
5	Bent, M	2	0	0	0	2	489
6	Rommedahl	2	2	0	0	4	702
7	Bothroyd	2	2	1	0	5	287
8	Bartlett	1	0	0	0	1	697
9	Thomas	1	0	0	0	1	1404
10	Young	1	0	0	0	1	2833
11	Euell	1	0	0	0	1	546
12	Holland	1	1	0	0	2	1740
13	Perry	1	0	0	0	1	2438
14	Johansson	0	0	1	0	1	
15	Fortune	0	1	0	0	1	
	Other	2	1	2	0	5	
	TOTAL	41	11	6	0	58	

SQUAD APPEARANCES

Match	1	2	3	4	5	6	7	8	9	10	11	12	13	14	15
Venue	A	H	A	A	H	H	A	H	H	A	A	H	A	H	A
Competition	L	L	L	L	L	W	L	L	L	L	W	L	L	L	L
Result	W	W	W	W	L	W	W	L	D	W	W	L	L	L	L

Match	16	17	18	19	20	21	22	23	24	25	26	27	28	29	30
Venue	H	H	H	A	H	H	A	A	H	A	H	H	A	H	A
Competition	W	L	L	L	L	L	L	F	L	L	F	L	L	L	L
Result	L	L	W	L	L	W	L	W	W	D	W	D	L	W	L

Match	31	32	33	34	35	36	37	38	39	40	41	42	43	44	45
Venue	H	A	H	A	H	A	H	H	A	H	A	A	H	A	H
Competition	F	L	L	L	L	L	F	L	L	L	F	L	L	L	L
Result	W	D	D	D	W	L	D	W	D	D	L	L	W	L	L

Goalkeepers
- Stephen Andersen
- Dean Kiely
- Thomas Myhre
- Darren Randolph

Defenders
- Talal El Karkouri
- Jonathan Fortune
- Hermann Hreidarsson
- Chris Perry
- Chris Powell
- Osei Sankofa
- Gonzalo Sorondo
- Jonathan Spector
- Kelly Youga
- Luke Young

Midfielders
- Darren Ambrose
- Matt Holland
- Bryan Hughes
- Radostin Kishishev
- Danny Murphy
- Dennis Rommedahl
- Lloyd Sam
- Alexei Smertin
- Jerome Thomas

Forwards
- Shaun Bartlett
- Darren Bent
- Marcus Bent
- Jay Bothroyd
- Jason Euell
- Jonatan Johansson
- Kevin Lisbie

KEY: On all match · On bench · Subbed or sent off (Counting game) · Subbed or sent off (playing less than 70 mins) · Subbed on from bench (Counting Game) · Subbed on (playing less than 70 mins) · Subbed on and then subbed or sent off (Counting Game) · Subbed on and then subbed or sent off (playing less than 70 mins) · Not in 16

KEY PLAYERS - GOALSCORERS

Darren Bent

Goals in the League	17
Goals in all competitions	19
Assists League goals scored by a team mate where the player delivered the final pass	5
Contribution to Attacking Power Average number of minutes between League team goals while on pitch	77
Player Strike Rate Average number of minutes between League goals scored by player	186
Club Strike Rate Average minutes between League goals scored by club	83

	PLAYER	GOALS LGE	GOALS ALL	ASSISTS	POWER	S RATE
1	Darren Bent	17	19	5	77	186 mins
2	Danny Murphy	4	5	10	67	369 mins
3	Darren Ambrose	3	4	4	105	562 mins
4	Bryan Hughes	3	5	4	97	648 mins

KEY PLAYERS - MIDFIELDERS

Alexei Smertin

Goals in the League	0
Goals in all competitions	0
Assists League goals scored by a team mate where the player delivered the final pass	1
Defensive Rating Average number of mins between League goals conceded while on the pitch	61
Contribution to Attacking Power Average number of minutes between League team goals while on pitch	66
Scoring Difference Defensive Rating minus Contribution to Attacking Power	-5

	PLAYER	GOALS LGE	GOALS ALL	ASSISTS	DEF RATE	POWER	SC DIFF
1	Alexei Smertin	0	0	1	61	66	-5 mins
2	Radostin Kishishev	0	0	3	70	80	-10 mins
3	Dennis Rommedahl	2	4	4	61	74	-13 mins
4	Danny Murphy	4	5	10	51	67	-16 mins

PLAYER APPEARANCES

	AGE (on 01/07/06)	IN NAMED 16	APPEARANCES	COUNTING GAMES	MINUTES ON PITCH	APPEARANCES	MINUTES ON PITCH	THIS SEASON	HOME COUNTRY
Goalkeepers									
Stephen Andersen	24	33	15	15	1350	16	1470	1	Denmark (19)
Dean Kiely	35	6	3	3	270	4	360	-	Rep of Ireland
Thomas Myhre	32	35	20	20	1800	26	2340	8	Norway (40)
Darren Randolph	19	2	0	0	0	0	0	-	Rep of Ireland
Defenders									
Talal El Karkouri	30	13	10	4	442	12	652	1	Morocco (36)
Jonathan Fortune	25	14	11	7	738	13	918	-	England
Hermann Hreidarsson	31	34	34	34	3060	42	3810	2	Iceland (70)
Chris Perry	33	34	28	27	2438	32	2718	-	England
Chris Powell	36	32	27	24	2212	34	2860	-	England
Osei Sankofa	21	6	4	2	257	4	257	-	England
Gonzalo Sorondo	26	9	7	6	587	8	677	2	Uruguay (22)
Jonathan Spector	20	31	20	12	1252	24	1543	3	United States (5)
Kelly Youga	20	1	0	0	0	0	0	-	France
Luke Young	26	32	32	31	2833	38	3382	6	England (10)
Midfielders									
Darren Ambrose	22	29	28	15	1685	33	1999	-	England
Matt Holland	32	24	23	18	1740	30	2287	-	England
Bryan Hughes	30	35	33	18	1943	40	2474	-	Wales
Radostin Kishishev	31	37	37	28	2887	44	3379	4	Bulgaria (38)
Danny Murphy	29	18	18	16	1476	21	1670	-	England
Dennis Rommedahl	27	23	21	12	1403	25	1630	5	Denmark (19)
Lloyd Sam	21	2	2	0	77	3	167	-	England
Alexei Smertin	31	18	18	16	1519	22	1794	4	Russia (37)
Jerome Thomas	23	26	25	10	1404	31	1791	-	England
Forwards									
Shaun Bartlett	33	18	16	4	697	22	1059	2	South Africa (53)
Darren Bent	22	36	36	35	3160	44	3865	6	England (10)
Marcus Bent	28	13	13	9	977	13	977	-	England
Jay Bothroyd	24	22	18	1	574	25	773	-	England
Jason Euell	29	15	10	4	546	11	559	1	Jamaica (46)
Jonatan Johansson	30	4	4	0	102	6	254	4	Finland (42)
Kevin Lisbie	27	6	6	0	138	7	152	-	Jamaica

KEY: LEAGUE — ALL COMPS — CAPS (MAY FIFA RANKING)

TEAM OF THE SEASON

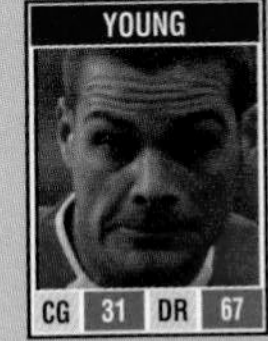

KEY: DR = Defensive Rate, SD = Scoring Difference AP = Attacking Power SR = Strike Rate, CG=Counting games – League games playing at least 70 minutes

TOP POINT EARNERS

Radostin Kishishev

Counting Games League games when player was on pitch for at least 70 minutes	28
Average points Average League points taken in Counting games	1.61
Club Average points Average points taken in League games	1.24

	PLAYER	GAMES	PTS
1	Radostin Kishishev	28	1.61
2	Chris Powell	24	1.54
3	Alexei Smertin	16	1.44
4	Dennis Rommedahl	12	1.42
5	Hermann Hreidarsson	34	1.38
6	Danny Murphy	16	1.38
7	Luke Young	31	1.35
8	Chris Perry	27	1.33
9	Darren Bent	35	1.31
10	Stephen Andersen	15	1.27

KEY PLAYERS - DEFENDERS

Hermann Hreidarsson

Goals Conceded in the League Number of League goals conceded while the player was on the pitch	42
Goals Conceded in all competitions Total number of goals conceded while the player was on the pitch	55
League minutes played Number of minutes played in league matches	3060
Clean Sheets In games when the player was on pitch for at least 70 minutes	13
Defensive Rating Average number of mins between League goals conceded while on the pitch	73
Club Defensive Rating Average number of mins between League goals conceded by the club this season	62

	PLAYER	CON LGE	CON ALL	MINS	C SHEETS	DEF RATE
1	Hermann Hreidarsson	42	55	3060	13	73 mins
2	Luke Young	42	46	2833	11	67 mins
3	Jonathan Spector	19	29	1252	5	66 mins
4	Chris Powell	35	47	2212	8	63 mins

KEY GOALKEEPER

Thomas Myhre

Goals Conceded in the League Number of League goals conceded while the player was on the pitch	23
Goals Conceded in all competitions Total number of goals conceded while the player was on the pitch	32
League minutes played Number of minutes played in league matches	1800
Clean Sheets In games when the player was on pitch for at least 70 minutes	9
Goals to Shots Ratio The average number of shots on target per each League goal conceded	6.1
Defensive Rating Ave mins between League goals conceded while on the pitch	78

BOOKINGS

Gonzalo Sorondo

League Yellow	2
League Red	0
All competitions Yellow	2
All competitions Red	0

League Average **293** mins between cards

	PLAYER	LEAGUE 2Y	LEAGUE 0R	TOTAL 2Y	TOTAL 0R	AVE
1	Sorondo	2	0	2	0	293
2	Murphy	4	1	4	1	295
3	Young	8	0	8	0	354
4	Kishishev	7	0	8	0	412
5	Perry	5	0	6	0	487
6	Ambrose	2	1	2	1	561
7	Hughes	3	0	4	0	647
8	Fortune	1	0	2	0	738
9	Hreidarsson	4	0	4	0	765
10	Powell	2	0	2	0	1106
11	Spector	1	0	2	0	1252
12	Andersen	1	0	1	0	1350
13	Rommedahl	1	0	1	0	1403
14	Thomas	1	0	2	0	1404
15	Bent, D	2	0	2	0	1580
	Other	0	0	4	0	
	TOTAL	44	2	54	2	

MIDDLESBROUGH

Steve McClaren led his team through 64 games, which turned into an endurance race before the Uefa Cup final against Seville. He didn't go out on the high he hoped but he gave the Riverside two classic nights to remember and blooded a new generation of local hopefuls.

The three-pronged strike team didn't always impress but still scored 53 goals between them. **Ayegbeni Yakubu** hit 19 and his league Strike Rate was one every 199 minutes. **Jimmy-Floyd Hasselbaink** somehow didn't achieve enough games to qualify for our charts but ten league goals at a Strike Rate of 110 is class. **Mark Viduka** tuned up for the World Cup with crucial Uefa goals.

George Boateng was easily the most consistent midfield performer. **Franck Queudrue** headed newly crowned manager **Gareth Southgate** in the club's Defensive Rating charts.

NICKNAME: BORO

KEY: Won, Drawn, Lost

1	prem	**Liverpool**	H	D	0-0	
2	prem	**Tottenham**	A	L	0-2	
3	prem	**Birmingham**	A	W	3-0	Viduka 14,45; Queudrue 71
4	prem	**Charlton**	H	L	0-3	
5	prem	**Arsenal**	H	W	2-1	Yakubu 40; Maccarone 59
6	uc1rl1	**Xanthi**	H	W	2-0	Boateng 28; Viduka 83
7	prem	**Wigan**	A	D	1-1	Yakubu 14
8	prem	**Sunderland**	H	L	0-2	
9	uc1rl2	**Xanthi**	A	D	0-0	
10	prem	**Aston Villa**	A	W	3-2	Yakubu 33,88 pen; Boateng 64
11	prem	**Portsmouth**	H	D	1-1	Yakubu 54
12	ucgpd	**Grasshoppers**	A	W	1-0	Hasselbaink 10
13	prem	**West Ham**	A	L	1-2	Queudrue 87
14	ccr3	**Everton**	A	W	1-0	Hasselbaink 38
15	prem	**Man Utd**	H	W	4-1	Mendieta 2,78; Hasselbaink 25; Yakubu 45 pen
16	ucgpd	**Dnipro**	H	W	3-0	Yakubu 36; Viduka 50,56
17	prem	**Everton**	A	L	0-1	
18	prem	**Fulham**	H	W	3-2	Morrison 64; Yakubu 76; Hasselbaink 84
19	ucgpd	**AZ Alkmaar**	A	D	0-0	
20	prem	**West Brom**	H	D	2-2	Viduka 12; Yakubu 66 pen
21	ccr4	**Crystal Palace**	H	W	2-1	Viduka 52; Nemeth 55
22	prem	**Chelsea**	A	L	0-1	
23	prem	**Liverpool**	A	L	0-2	
24	ucgpd	**Liteks Lovetch**	H	W	2-0	Maccarone 80,87
25	prem	**Tottenham**	H	D	3-3	Yakubu 30,43; Queudrue 69
26	ccqf	**Blackburn**	H	L	0-1	
27	prem	**Blackburn**	H	L	0-2	
28	prem	**Man City**	H	D	0-0	
29	prem	**Newcastle**	A	D	2-2	Yakubu 54; Hasselbaink 87
30	facr3	**Nuneaton**	A	D	1-1	Mendieta 15
31	prem	**Arsenal**	A	L	0-7	
32	facr3r	**Nuneaton**	H	W	5-2	Riggott 34; Yakubu 42 pen,58; Parnaby 50; Viduka 63
33	prem	**Wigan**	H	L	2-3	Hasselbaink 56; Yakubu 66
34	facr4	**Coventry**	A	D	1-1	Hasselbaink 46
35	prem	**Sunderland**	A	W	3-0	Pogatetz 19; Parnaby 31; Hasselbaink 71
36	prem	**Aston Villa**	H	L	0-4	
37	facr4r	**Coventry**	H	W	1-0	Hasselbaink 20
38	prem	**Chelsea**	H	W	3-0	Rochemback 2; Downing 45; Yakubu 68
39	uc3rl1	**Stuttgart**	A	W	2-1	Hasselbaink 19; Parnaby 46
40	facr5	**Preston**	A	W	2-0	Yakubu 52,77
41	uc3rl2	**Stuttgart**	H	L	0-1	
42	prem	**West Brom**	A	W	2-0	Hasselbaink 17,44
43	prem	**Birmingham**	H	W	1-0	Viduka 45
44	uc4rl1	**Roma**	H	W	1-0	Yakubu 12 pen
45	prem	**Charlton**	A	L	1-2	Viduka 81
46	uc4rl2	**Roma**	A	L	1-2	Hasselbaink 32
47	prem	**Blackburn**	A	L	2-3	Viduka 16; Rochemback 62
48	facqf	**Charlton**	A	D	0-0	
49	prem	**Bolton**	H	W	4-3	Hasselbaink 8 pen,47; Viduka 30; Parnaby 90
50	ucqfl1	**Basel**	A	L	0-2	
51	prem	**Man City**	A	W	1-0	Cattermole 42
52	ucqfl2	**Basel**	H	W	4-1	Viduka 33,57; Hasselbaink 79; Maccarone 90
53	prem	**Newcastle**	H	L	1-2	Boateng 79
54	facqfr	**Charlton**	H	W	4-2	Rochemback 11; Morrison 26; Hasselbaink 73; Viduka 77
55	prem	**Portsmouth**	A	L	0-1	
56	prem	**West Ham**	H	W	2-0	Hasselbaink 41; Maccarone 57 pen
57	ucsfl1	**St Bucharest**	A	L	0-1	
58	facsf	**West Ham**	H	L	0-1	
59	ucsfl2	**St Bucharest**	H	W	4-2	Maccarone 33,89; Viduka 64; Riggott 73
60	prem	**Everton**	H	L	0-1	
61	prem	**Man Utd**	A	D	0-0	
62	prem	**Bolton**	A	D	1-1	Johnson 47
63	prem	**Fulham**	A	L	0-1	
64	ucfin	**Seville**	H	L	0-4	

LEAGUE POSITION
Viduka double sets up first ever Premier points from St Andrews and Queudrue weighs in with a third
Yakubu opens account and Maccarone adds an unlikely winner as McClaren beats Arsenal with three debutants
Thank goodness for Southgate as Wigan cause problems for new boys Rochembach and Xavier
Yakubu double; he starts scoring and finishes Villa while Boateng executes the 'law of the ex' with a goal to answer boos
Mendieta menace as sub comes on to drive Pompey back and help Yakubu level against his former side
Hasselbaink's first of the season is just enough to snatch a win in Zurich
Last man Ehiogu downs Gerrard to earn a red but Schwarzer stands firm as Liverpool miss chances
"Shock, anger, disappointment", McClaren sees his team booed off the Riverside after being overrun by Charlton
"A wrong decision", fumes McClaren as own goal that didn't cross the line is awarded for Hammers
Schwarzer sickener as ball squeezes under his body while Robinson keeps Hasselbaink at bay
Nightmare start as Sunderland take the lead after just 85 seconds and record first Premier win for 27 matches
One-in-four converted as Hasselbaink misses chances but it's enough to beat Everton
Mendieta pulls the strings as McClaren plots humbling of Fergie yet again
AUGUST
SEPTEMBER
OCTOBER

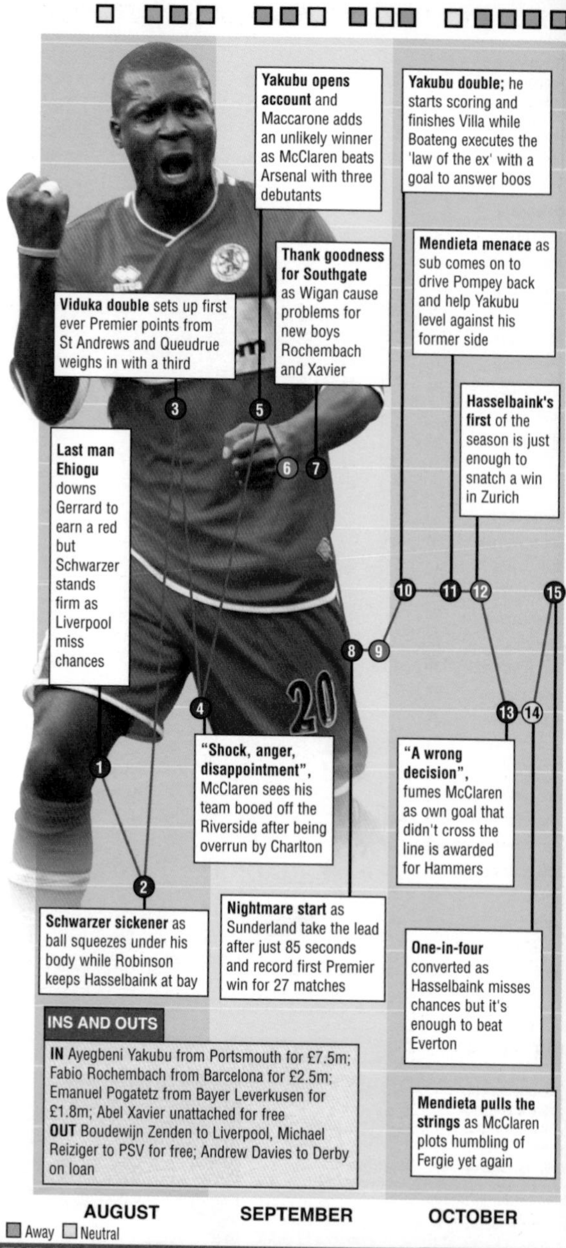

INS AND OUTS

IN Ayegbeni Yakubu from Portsmouth for £7.5m; Fabio Rochembach from Barcelona for £2.5m; Emanuel Pogatetz from Bayer Leverkusen for £1.8m; Abel Xavier unattached for free
OUT Boudewijn Zenden to Liverpool, Michael Reiziger to PSV for free; Andrew Davies to Derby on loan

Home, Away, Neutral

ATTENDANCES

HOME GROUND: RIVERSIDE STADIUM **CAPACITY:** 35100 **AVERAGE LEAGUE AT HOME:** 28463

61	Man Utd	69531	53	Newcastle	31202	36	Aston Villa	27299	63	Fulham	22434
29	Newcastle	52302	38	Chelsea	31037	33	Wigan	27208	39	Stuttgart	21000
23	Liverpool	43510	15	Man Utd	30579	20	West Brom	27041	55	Portsmouth	20204
22	Chelsea	41666	54	Charlton	30248	11	Portsmouth	26551	16	Dnipro	20000
57	St Bucharest	41000	27	Blackburn	29881	32	Nuneaton	26255	40	Preston	19877
51	Man City	40256	10	Aston Villa	29719	4	Charlton	26206	47	Blackburn	18681
58	West Ham	39148	8	Sunderland	29583	49	Bolton	25971	7	Wigan	16641
31	Arsenal	38186	60	Everton	29224	14	Everton	25844	26	Blackburn	14710
64	Seville	36500	43	Birmingham	28141	44	Roma	25354	6	Xanthi	14191
2	Tottenham	35844	34	Coventry	28120	45	Charlton	24830	37	Coventry	14131
59	St Bucharest	34622	5	Arsenal	28075	52	Basel	24521	21	Crystal Palace	10791
13	West Ham	34612	28	Man City	28022	48	Charlton	24187	24	Liteks Lovetch	9436
17	Everton	34349	3	Birmingham	27998	42	West Brom	24061	12	Grasshoppers	8500
46	Roma	32642	56	West Ham	27658	41	Stuttgart	24018	19	AZ Alkmaar	8461
1	Liverpool	31908	25	Tottenham	27614	50	Basel	23639	30	Nuneaton	6000
35	Sunderland	31675	18	Fulham	27599	62	Bolton	22733	9	Xanthi	5013

McClaren's marathon wins England race

Final Position: **14th**

KEY: ● League ● Champions Lge ● UEFA Cup ● FA Cup ○ League Cup ● Other

Empty Riverside echoes to cheers of just 12,000 as Yakubu and Viduka make a winning start

Riggott sees red after two yellows in five minutes as Liverpool claim two late goals

Hasselbaink curses curses as slip sends his shot against the post long before Chelsea eventually find a way past Southgate

Hasselbaink fires home for a 2-1 lead but late Newcastle goal levels it

Easing through to final stages of the Uefa Cup with away draw

Yakubu accidentally scores - again! This time a Morrison shot rebounds home in a six goal draw with Spurs

Euro hangover as Everton hang on

Savaged! Blonde midfielder works himself into a frenzy over 'spitting' incident and hauls Blackburn to win

Rock 'em back! Brazilian stuns Chelsea after 80 seconds before Downing and Yakubu hand out Blues' worst defeat for four years

Distraught fan throws ticket at McClaren as Villa plunder four and Cattermole ends game in tears

Hammered by Henry as Gunners maestro hits a hat-trick in 7-0 thrashing for young defence

Riggott restores order as captain scores first of five against Nuneaton

First league win in ten as Pogatetz heads opener before fine goals by Parnaby and Hasselbain k sink Sunderland

Two-goal Maccarone clinches top spot as Riverside's lowest gate cheers Uefa win over Bulgarians

Schwarzer's agility saves blushes after Viduka misses out on penalty appeal

Roma rocked as Hasselbaink tumbles and Yakubu coolly slots penalty for narrow first leg advantage

Lone forward Hasselbaink takes battle to Germans and Parnaby strikes after halftime to secure first leg victory

Raw nerves on Teesside as Stuttgart grab early goal and McClaren's caution nearly backfires

Yakubu at the double earns quarter-final place

Teesside's greatest evening as last-minute **Maccarone** gets the fourth on the way back from 3-0 down to reach Uefa Cup semis

Nine changes and three teenagers line up at the Valley to give Charlton problems before Bent claims points

Replay to shoehorn in to crowded season but McClaren takes draw to stay in cup

Parnaby slides in for last minute winner

"Guts got us through" says Southgate as Roma are repelled after Hasselbaink's header becomes away goal clincher

Riggott blazes over final chance in injury time after Hammers strike and Schwarzer fractures cheek bone

Damage limitation in Bucharest as Romanians test Schwarzer but only find the net once

Teesside's second greatest evening as last-minute Maccarone does it again, scoring twice on the way back from 3-0 down to claim a Uefa final place against Seville

Viduka's golden chance strikes Seville keeper's legs and the Spanish side romp away with Uefa Cup in the final quarter

All English as 15 of the 16 fielded against Fulham were born within 30 miles of the stadium

"Plenty of entertainment - but very frustrating" McClaren sums up the season after another Riverside rescue act

Nemeth arrows in from a tight angle to claim a place in the Carling last eight

INS AND OUTS

OUT Szilard Nemeth to Strasbourg for a nominal fee; Abel Xavier released

Hasselbaink hot streak runs to eight in 11 games as brace against Baggies lifts relegation worries

Pogatetz injury adds to gloom in Basle as the Austrian defender is stretchered off and Schwarzer is beaten twice

Jones earns a point at Old Trafford with penalty save

Johnson's first goal in tenth start as 11 Englishmen are in line-up for draw at Bolton

NOVEMBER DECEMBER JANUARY FEBRUARY MARCH APRIL MAY

MONTH BY MONTH POINTS TALLY

Month	Points	%
AUGUST	4	33%
SEPTEMBER	4	44%
OCTOBER	7	58%
NOVEMBER	4	44%
DECEMBER	2	13%
JANUARY	4	33%
FEBRUARY	6	67%
MARCH	6	50%
APRIL	6	40%
MAY	2	22%

GOAL ATTEMPTS

FOR – Goal attempts recorded in League games

	HOME	AWAY	TOTAL	AVE
shots on target	120	99	219	5.8
shots off target	91	86	177	4.7
TOTAL	211	185	396	10.4

Ratio of goals to shots Average number of shots on target per League goal scored: **4.6**

Accuracy rating Average percentage of total goal attempts which were on target: **55.3**

AGAINST – Goal attempts recorded in League games

	HOME	AWAY	TOTAL	AVE
shots on target	112	139	251	6.6
shots off target	100	99	199	5.2
TOTAL	212	238	450	11.8

Ratio of goals to shots Average number of shots on target per League goal scored: **4.3**

Accuracy rating Average percentage of total goal attempts which were on target: **55.8**

GOALS

Ayegbeni Yakubu

League	13
FA Cup	4
League Cup	0
Europe	2
Other	0
TOTAL	19

League Average **199** mins between goals

	PLAYER	LGE	FAC	LC	Euro	TOT	AVE
1	Yakubu	13	4	0	2	19	199
2	Hasselbaink	10	3	1	4	18	110
3	Viduka	7	2	1	6	16	239
4	Queudrue	3	0	0	0	3	718
5	Maccarone	2	0	0	5	7	360
6	Rochemback	2	1	0	0	3	922
7	Parnaby	2	1	0	1	4	825
8	Boateng	2	0	0	1	3	1151
9	Mendieta	2	1	0	0	3	607
10	Johnson	1	0	0	0	1	709
11	Morrison	1	1	0	0	2	1678
12	Downing	1	0	0	0	1	984
13	Pogatetz	1	0	0	0	1	1955
14	Cattermole	1	0	0	0	1	990
15	Nemeth	0	0	1	0	1	
	Other	0	1	0	1	2	
	TOTAL	48	14	3	20	85	

SQUAD APPEARANCES

Match	1 2 3 4 5	6 7 8 9 10	11 12 13 14 15	16 17 18 19 20	21 22 23 24 25	26 27 28 29 30	31 32 33 34 35	36 37 38 39 40	41 42 43 44 45	46 47 48 49 50	51 52 53 54 55	56 57 58 59 60	61 62 63
Venue	H A A H H	H A H A A	H A A A H	H A H A H	H A A H H	H H H A A	A H H A A	H H H A A	H A H H A	A A A H A	A H H H A	H A H H H	A A A
Competition	L L L L L	E L L E L	L E L W L	E L L E L	W L L E L	W L L L F	L F L F L	L F L E F	E L L E L	E L F L E	L E L F L	L E F E L	L L L
Result	D L W L W	W D L D W	D W L W W	W L W D D	W L L W D	L L D D D	L W L D W	L W W W W	L W W W L	L L D W L	W W L W L	W L L W L	D D L

Goalkeepers
Bradley Jones
David Knight
Mark Schwarzer
Ross Turnbull

Defenders
Matthew Bates
Colin Cooper
Andrew Davies
Ugo Ehiogu
Anthony McMahon
Stuart Parnaby
Emanuel Pogatetz
Franck Queudrue
Michael Reiziger
Chris Riggott
Gareth Southgate
Andrew Taylor
David Wheater
Abel Xavier

Midfielders
George Boateng
Lee Cattermole
Tom Craddock
Doriva
Stewart Downing
Adam Johnson
Jason Kennedy
Gaizka Mendieta
James Morrison
Ray Parlour
Fabio Rochemback
Josh Walker

Forwards
Malcolm Christie
Danny Graham
Jimmy-Floyd Hasselbaink
Joseph-Desire Job
Massimo Maccarone
Szilard Nemeth
Mark Viduka
Ayegbeni Yakubu

KEY: On all match | On bench | Subbed or sent off (Counting game) | Subbed or sent off (playing less than 70 mins) | Subbed on from bench (Counting Game) | Subbed on (playing less than 70 mins) | Subbed on and then subbed or sent off (Counting Game) | Subbed on and then subbed or sent off (playing less than 70 mins) | Not in 16

KEY PLAYERS - GOALSCORERS

Ayegbeni Yakubu

Goals in the League	13
Goals in all competitions	19
Assists League goals scored by a team mate where the player delivered the final pass	9
Contribution to Attacking Power Average number of minutes between League team goals while on pitch	74
Player Strike Rate Average number of minutes between League goals scored by player	199
Club Strike Rate Average minutes between League goals scored by club	71

	PLAYER	GOALS LGE	GOALS ALL	ASSISTS	POWER	S RATE
1	Ayegbeni Yakubu	13	19	9	74	199 mins
2	Mark Viduka	7	16	8	70	239 mins
3	Franck Queudrue	3	3	2	67	718 mins
4	Stuart Parnaby	2	4	2	59	825 mins

KEY PLAYERS - MIDFIELDERS

George Boateng

Goals in the League	2
Goals in all competitions	3
Assists League goals scored by a team mate where the player delivered the final pass	6
Defensive Rating Average number of mins between League goals conceded while on the pitch	66
Contribution to Attacking Power Average number of minutes between League team goals while on pitch	64
Scoring Difference Defensive Rating minus Contribution to Attacking Power	2

	PLAYER	GOALS LGE	GOALS ALL	ASSISTS	DEF RATE	POWER	SC DIFF
1	George Boateng	2	3	6	66	64	2 mins
2	Fabio Rochemback	2	3	0	51	64	-13 mins
3	James Morrison	1	2	0	49	76	-27 mins
4	Doriva	0	0	2	52	84	-32 mins

PLAYER APPEARANCES

	AGE (on 01/07/06)	IN NAMED 16	APPEARANCES	COUNTING GAMES	MINUTES ON PITCH	APPEARANCES	MINUTES ON PITCH	THIS SEASON	HOME COUNTRY
Goalkeepers									
Bradley Jones	24	32	9	9	810	16	1399	-	United States
David Knight	19	12	0	0	0	0	0	-	England
Mark Schwarzer	33	29	27	27	2430	47	4181	4	Australia (42)
Ross Turnbull	21	2	2	2	180	2	180	-	England
Defenders									
Matthew Bates	19	23	16	11	1049	28	1855	-	England
Colin Cooper	39	1	1	0	6	1	6	-	England
Andrew Davies	21	13	12	5	576	16	891	-	England
Ugo Ehiogu	33	21	18	15	1429	30	2080	-	England
Anthony McMahon	20	4	3	1	160	4	205	-	England
Stuart Parnaby	23	22	20	18	1649	42	3416	-	England
Emanuel Pogatetz	23	26	24	20	1955	41	3407	4	Austria (73)
Franck Queudrue	27	29	29	20	2153	49	3468	-	France
Michael Reiziger	33	4	4	4	360	4	360	-	Holland
Chris Riggott	25	23	22	20	1865	42	3665	-	England
Gareth Southgate	35	24	24	23	2094	42	3569	-	England
Andrew Taylor	19	13	13	7	833	20	1238	-	England
David Wheater	19	9	6	4	395	6	395	-	England
Abel Xavier	33	4	4	4	360	6	540	-	Portugal
Midfielders									
George Boateng	30	26	26	25	2302	44	3904	-	Holland
Lee Cattermole	18	14	14	10	990	24	1678	-	England
Tom Craddock	19	1	1	0	10	1	10	-	England
Doriva	34	33	27	18	1770	41	2959	-	Brazil
Stewart Downing	21	12	12	11	984	26	2224	1	England (10)
Adam Johnson	18	18	13	5	709	18	1035	-	England
Jason Kennedy	19	6	3	1	116	6	247	-	England
Gaizka Mendieta	32	19	17	9	1213	29	2191	-	Spain
James Morrison	20	25	24	16	1678	37	2508	-	England
Ray Parlour	33	13	13	9	961	19	1222	-	England
Fabio Rochemback	24	22	22	19	1843	36	2936	-	Brazil
Josh Walker	17	1	1	0	29	1	29	-	England
Forwards									
Malcolm Christie	27	6	6	1	291	6	291	-	England
Danny Graham	20	4	3	1	100	3	100	-	England
Jimmy-F Hasselbaink	34	24	22	10	1100	44	2871	-	Holland
Joseph-Desire Job	28	1	1	0	13	1	13	-	Cameroon
Massimo Maccarone	26	22	17	4	720	30	1250	-	Italy
Szilard Nemeth	27	5	5	0	196	11	463	-	Hungary
Mark Viduka	30	29	27	13	1671	43	2863	5	Australia (42)
Ayegbeni Yakubu	23	34	34	26	2581	56	3672	1	Nigeria (11)

KEY: LEAGUE — ALL COMPS — CAPS — (MAY FIFA RANKING)

TEAM OF THE SEASON

SCHWARZER

CG 27 DR 64

POGATETZ

CG 20 DR 58

SOUTHGATE

CG 23 DR 63

RIGGOTT

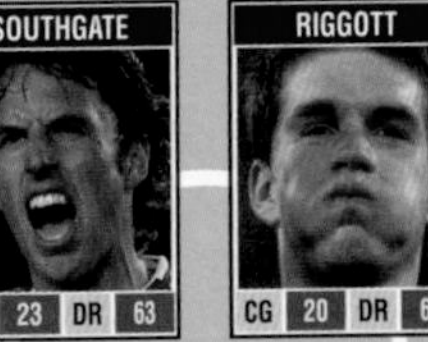

CG 20 DR 62

QUEUDRUE

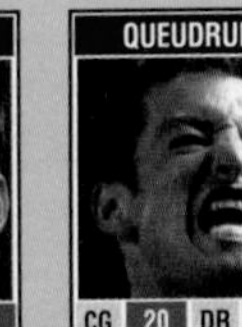

CG 20 DR 65

MORRISON

CG 16 SD -27

DORIVA

CG 18 SD -32

BOATENG

CG 25 SD +2

ROCHEMBACK

CG 19 SD -13

VIDUKA

CG 13 AP 70

YAKUBU

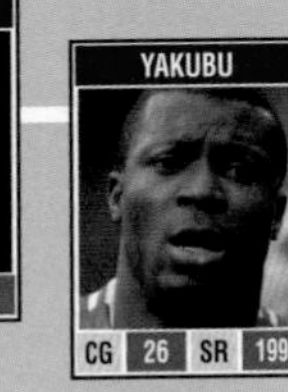

CG 26 SR 199

KEY: DR = Defensive Rate, SD = Scoring Difference AP = Attacking Power SR = Strike Rate, CG=Counting games – League games playing at least 70 minutes

TOP POINT EARNERS

Franck Queudrue

Counting Games League games when player was on pitch for at least 70 minutes	20
Average points Average League points taken in Counting games	1.45
Club Average points Average points taken in League games	1.18

	PLAYER	GAMES	PTS
1	Franck Queudrue	20	1.45
2	Chris Riggott	20	1.45
3	Stuart Parnaby	18	1.44
4	Gareth Southgate	23	1.35
5	George Boateng	25	1.32
6	Emanuel Pogatetz	20	1.30
7	Mark Schwarzer	27	1.26
8	Ayegbeni Yakubu	26	1.23
9	Fabio Rochemback	19	1.16
10	Ugo Ehiogu	15	1.07

KEY PLAYERS - DEFENDERS

Franck Queudrue

Goals Conceded in the League Number of League goals conceded while the player was on the pitch	33
Goals Conceded in all competitions Total number of goals conceded while the player was on the pitch	45
League minutes played Number of minutes played in league matches	2153
Clean Sheets In games when the player was on pitch for at least 70 minutes	6
Defensive Rating Average number of mins between League goals conceded while on the pitch	65
Club Defensive Rating Average number of mins between League goals conceded by the club this season	59

	PLAYER	CON LGE	CON ALL	MINS	C SHEETS	DEF RATE
1	Franck Queudrue	33	45	2153	6	65 mins
2	Gareth Southgate	33	51	2094	7	63 mins
3	Chris Riggott	30	49	1865	7	62 mins
4	Emanuel Pogatetz	34	44	1955	5	58 mins

KEY GOALKEEPER

Mark Schwarzer

Goals Conceded in the League Number of League goals conceded while the player was on the pitch	38
Goals Conceded in all competitions Total number of goals conceded while the player was on the pitch	55
League minutes played Number of minutes played in league matches	2430
Clean Sheets In games when the player was on pitch for at least 70 minutes	8
Goals to Shots Ratio The average number of shots on target per each League goal conceded	4.6
Defensive Rating Ave mins between League goals conceded while on the pitch	64

BOOKINGS

Massimo Maccarone

League Yellow	3
League Red	0
All competitions Yellow	6
All competitions Red	0
League Average 240 mins between cards	

	PLAYER	LEAGUE		TOTAL		AVE
		3Y	0R	6Y	0R	240
1	Maccarone	3Y	0R	6Y	0R	240
2	Cattermole	4	0	7	0	247
3	Doriva	6	1	6	1	252
4	Bates	4	0	6	0	262
5	Hasselbaink	4	0	8	0	275
6	Parlour	3	0	4	0	320
7	Queudrue	6	0	8	0	358
8	Riggott	4	1	7	1	373
9	Pogatetz	5	0	11	0	391
10	Boateng	5	0	9	0	460
11	Rochemback	4	0	7	0	460
12	Mendieta	2	0	3	0	606
13	Southgate	3	0	4	0	698
14	Ehiogu	0	1	0	1	1429
15	Parnaby	1	0	4	0	1649
	Other	0	0	7	0	
	TOTAL	54	3	97	3	

MANCHESTER CITY

Stuart Pearce seemed to have performed miracles with two former England strikers, getting the best from **Andrew Cole** and **Darius Vassell**, but it petered out. Cole started 13 games in the first half of the season, scoring eight goals. Injury left him with one goal from six starts in the second half but overall a strong Strike Rate of a goal every 196 minutes. Vassell's eight goals were more spread out but the Strike Rate of one every 379 minutes wasn't good enough.

Joey Barton weighed in with six goals and was the pick in midfield.

Stephen Jordan finished with a rather good Defensive Rating of a goal conceded every 104 minutes – the 15th best record in the division. It compared to a club average of one conceded every 71 minutes. **David James** played every game but his Goals-to-Shots ratio was poor - a goal conceded for every 4.1 shots on target.

NICKNAME: BLUES/CITIZENS

KEY: Won / Drawn / Lost

1	prem	**West Brom**	H	D	0-0	
2	prem	**Birmingham**	A	W	2-1	Barton 20; Cole 47
3	prem	**Sunderland**	A	W	2-1	Vassell 10; Sinclair 35
4	prem	**Portsmouth**	H	W	2-1	Reyna 66; Cole 69
5	prem	**Man Utd**	A	D	1-1	Barton 76
6	prem	**Bolton**	H	L	0-1	
7	ccr2	**Doncaster**	A	L	0-3*	Vassell 95 pen (*on penalties)
8	prem	**Newcastle**	A	L	0-1	
9	prem	**Everton**	H	W	2-0	Mills 72; Vassell 90
10	prem	**West Ham**	H	W	2-1	Cole 18,56
11	prem	**Arsenal**	A	L	0-1	
12	prem	**Aston Villa**	H	W	3-1	Vassell 4,25; Cole 82
13	prem	**Fulham**	A	L	1-2	Croft 20
14	prem	**Blackburn**	H	D	0-0	
15	prem	**Liverpool**	H	L	0-1	
16	prem	**Charlton**	A	W	5-2	Cole 25,83; Sinclair 37; Barton 69; Vassell 78
17	prem	**West Brom**	A	L	0-2	
18	prem	**Birmingham**	H	W	4-1	Sommeil 1; Barton 14 pen; Sibierski 40; Wright-Phillips, B 70
19	prem	**Wigan**	A	L	3-4	Sibierski 3; Barton 77; Cole 88
20	prem	**Chelsea**	H	L	0-1	
21	prem	**Middlesbrough**	A	D	0-0	
22	prem	**Tottenham**	H	L	0-2	
23	facr3	**Scunthorpe**	H	W	3-1	Fowler 48,56,64 pen
24	prem	**Man Utd**	H	W	3-1	Sinclair 32; Vassell 39; Fowler 90
25	prem	**Bolton**	A	L	0-2	
26	facr4	**Wigan**	H	W	1-0	Cole 84
27	prem	**Newcastle**	H	W	3-0	Riera 14; Cole 38; Vassell 62
28	prem	**Everton**	A	L	0-1	
29	prem	**Charlton**	H	W	3-2	Dunne 22; Samaras 54; Barton 62
30	facr5	**Aston Villa**	A	D	1-1	Richards 90
31	prem	**Liverpool**	A	L	0-1	
32	prem	**Sunderland**	H	W	2-1	Samaras 9,10
33	prem	**Portsmouth**	A	L	1-2	Dunne 83
34	facr5r	**Aston Villa**	H	W	2-1	Samaras 16; Vassell 48
35	prem	**Wigan**	H	L	0-1	
36	facqf	**West Ham**	H	L	1-2	Musampa 85
37	prem	**Chelsea**	A	L	0-2	
38	prem	**Middlesbrough**	H	L	0-1	
39	prem	**Tottenham**	A	L	1-2	Samaras 52
40	prem	**West Ham**	A	L	0-1	
41	prem	**Aston Villa**	A	W	1-0	Vassell 71
42	prem	**Fulham**	H	L	1-2	Dunne 69
43	prem	**Arsenal**	H	L	1-3	Sommeil 39
44	prem	**Blackburn**	A	L	0-2	

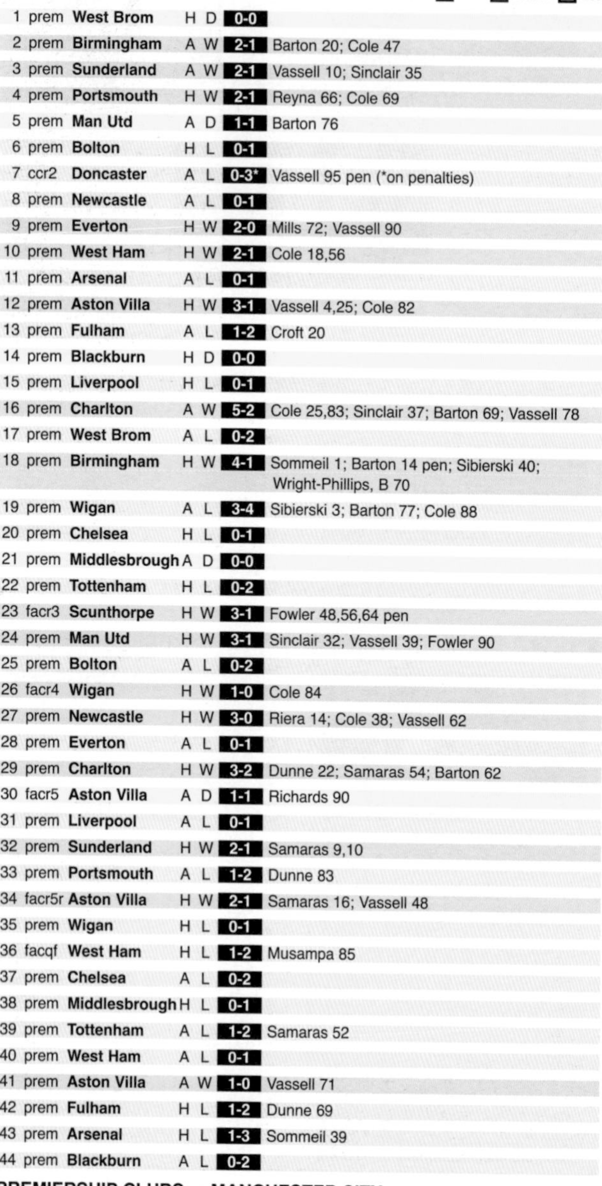

LEAGUE POSITION
1st
2nd
3rd
4th
5th
6th
7th
8th
9th
10th
11th
12th
13th
14th
15th
16th
17th
18th
19th
20th
AUGUST
SEPTEMBER
OCTOBER
Home Away Neutral
Cole finishes with aplomb after setting up Barton to complete fight back over Birmingham for Pearce's tenth game unbeaten
Cole cracker brings the best out of van der Sar as United hang on for a point
Mills' shot sails in from 35 yards to bring the game to life and Vassell's late finish makes sure against sorry Everton
A total travesty as Bolton's woodwork is hit five times before Dunne's handball gives Speed a decisive penalty
Classic Cole scores one of the best team goals of the season as Hammers are torn apart by Musampa and Vassell
Onuoha red (later rescinded) gives Doncaster an edge and their reserve keeper saves twice in penalty shoot-out to claim scalp
Top of the table as Vassell curls in his first goal since transfer and Sinclair pounces to secure win
Don't laugh David; Pires' bizarre penalty takes the headlines but Vassell is close to levelling at Highbury – just ruled offside
Barton wins headlines for the right reasons as he tests out Baggies' keeper but there's no way through
INS AND OUTS
IN Darius Vassell from Aston Villa for £2m; Andy Cole from Fulham for free; Kiki Musampa from Atletico Madrid on loan
OUT Shaun Wright-Phillips to Chelsea for £21m; Paul Bosvelt to Heerenveen for free; Jonathan Macken to Crystal Palace and Christian Negouai to Standard Liege fees undisclosed; Willo Flood to Coventry on loan; Steve McManaman and Kevin Ellegaard released
"Pace, power and passion," Pearce sums up Vassell's two-goal performance against former club Villa
Thomas Cook

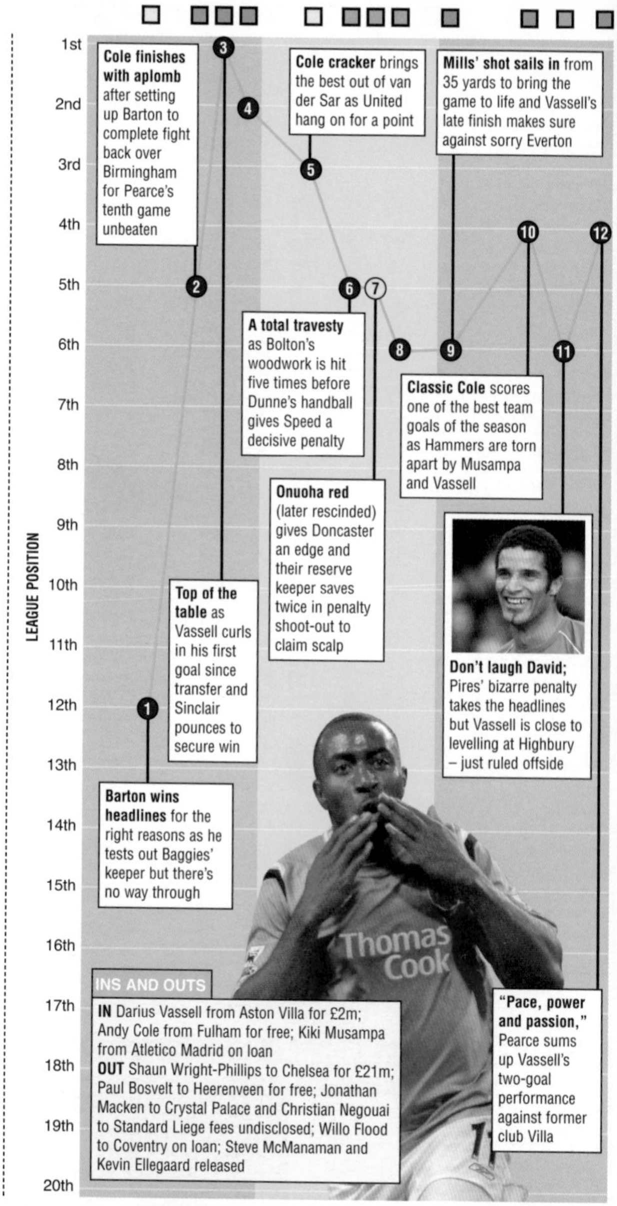

ATTENDANCES

HOME GROUND: CITY OF MANCHESTER STADIUM **CAPACITY:** 48000 **AVE LEAGUE AT HOME:** 42856

5	Man Utd	67839	35	Wigan	42444	38	Middlesboro	40256	25	Bolton	26466
8	Newcastle	52280	27	Newcastle	42413	36	West Ham	39357	41	Aston Villa	26422
24	Man Utd	47192	37	Chelsea	42321	11	Arsenal	38189	2	Birmingham	26366
15	Liverpool	47105	32	Sunderland	42200	28	Everton	37827	44	Blackburn	25731
20	Chelsea	46587	12	Aston Villa	42069	39	Tottenham	36167	17	West Brom	25472
31	Liverpool	44121	43	Arsenal	41875	40	West Ham	34305	16	Charlton	25289
14	Blackburn	44032	29	Charlton	41347	3	Sunderland	33357	19	Wigan	25017
10	West Ham	43647	18	Birmingham	41343	34	Aston Villa	33006	30	Aston Villa	23847
6	Bolton	43137	42	Fulham	41128	26	Wigan	30811	13	Fulham	22241
1	West Brom	42983	4	Portsmouth	41022	21	Middlesboro	28022	33	Portsmouth	19556
9	Everton	42681	22	Tottenham	40808	23	Scunthorpe	27779	7	Doncaster	8228

Pearce fritters away his strong start

Final Position: **15th**

KEY: ● League ● Champions Lge ● UEFA Cup ● FA Cup ○ League Cup ● Other

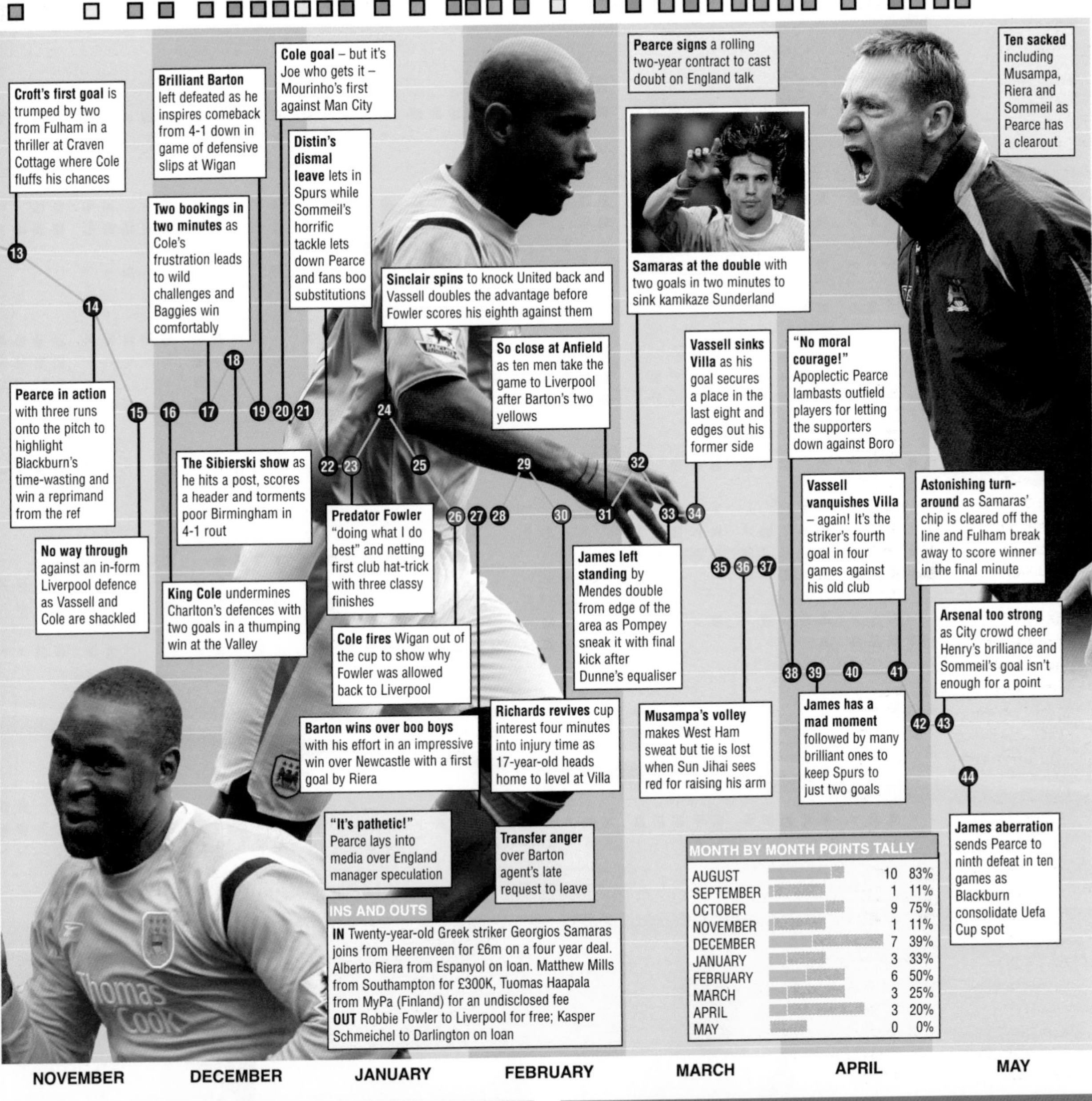

INS AND OUTS

IN Twenty-year-old Greek striker Georgios Samaras joins from Heerenveen for £6m on a four year deal. Alberto Riera from Espanyol on loan. Matthew Mills from Southampton for £300K, Tuomas Haapala from MyPa (Finland) for an undisclosed fee
OUT Robbie Fowler to Liverpool for free; Kasper Schmeichel to Darlington on loan

MONTH BY MONTH POINTS TALLY

AUGUST	10	83%
SEPTEMBER	1	11%
OCTOBER	9	75%
NOVEMBER	1	11%
DECEMBER	7	39%
JANUARY	3	33%
FEBRUARY	6	50%
MARCH	3	25%
APRIL	3	20%
MAY	0	0%

GOAL ATTEMPTS

FOR – Goal attempts recorded in League games

	HOME	AWAY	TOTAL	AVE
shots on target	124	88	212	5.6
shots off target	125	93	218	5.7
TOTAL	249	181	430	11.3

Ratio of goals to shots – Average number of shots on target per League goal scored: **4.9**

Accuracy rating – Average percentage of total goal attempts which were on target: **49.3**

AGAINST – Goal attempts recorded in League games

	HOME	AWAY	TOTAL	AVE
shots on target	83	114	197	5.2
shots off target	92	88	180	4.7
TOTAL	175	202	377	9.9

Ratio of goals to shots – Average number of shots on target per League goal scored: **4.1**

Accuracy rating – Average percentage of total goal attempts which were on target: **52.3**

GOALS

Andrew Cole

League	9
FA Cup	1
League Cup	0
Europe	0
Other	0
TOTAL	10

League Average **196** mins between goals

	PLAYER	LGE	FAC	LC	Euro	TOT	AVE
1	Cole	9	1	0	0	10	196
2	Vassell	8	1	1	0	10	379
3	Barton	6	0	0	0	6	455
4	Samaras	4	1	0	0	5	237
5	Dunne	3	0	0	0	3	931
6	Sinclair	3	0	0	0	3	799
7	Sibierski	2	0	0	0	2	557
8	Sommeil	2	0	0	0	2	598
9	Reyna	1	0	0	0	1	1796
10	Wright-Phillips, B	1	0	0	0	1	337
11	Fowler	1	3	0	0	4	64
12	Riera	1	0	0	0	1	1065
13	Croft	1	0	0	0	1	647
14	Richards	0	1	0	0	1	
15	Musampa	0	1	0	0	1	
	Other	1	0	0	0	1	
	TOTAL	43	8	1	0	52	

SQUAD APPEARANCES

Match	1	2	3	4	5	6	7	8	9	10	11	12	13	14	15	16	17	18	19	20	21	22	23	24	25	26	27	28	29	30	31	32	33	34	35	36	37	38	39	40	41	42	43	44
Venue	H	A	A	H	A	H	A	A	H	H	A	H	A	H	H	A	A	H	A	H	A	H	H	H	A	H	H	A	H	A	A	H	A	H	H	H	A	H	A	A	A	H	H	A
Competition	L	L	L	L	L	L	W	L	L	L	L	L	L	L	L	L	L	L	L	L	L	L	F	L	L	F	L	L	L	F	L	L	L	F	L	F	L	L	L	L	L	L	L	L
Result	D	W	W	W	D	L	L	L	W	W	L	W	L	D	L	W	L	W	L	L	D	L	W	W	L	W	W	L	W	D	L	W	L	W	L	L	L	L	L	L	W	L	L	L

Goalkeepers
Geert De Vlieger
David James
Nicky Weaver

Defenders
Sylvain Distin
Richard Dunne
Stephen Jordan
Danny Mills
Matthew Mills
Nedum Onuoha
Micah Richards
David Sommeil
Sun Jihai
Ben Thatcher

Midfielders
Joey Barton
Willo Flood
Yasser Hussein
Stephen Ireland
Kiki Musampa
Claudio Reyna
Albert Riera
Antoine Sibierski
Trevor Sinclair

Forwards
Andrew Cole
Lee Croft
Robbie Fowler
Ishmael Miller
Georgios Samaras
Darius Vassell
Bradley Wright-Phillips

KEY: On all match | On bench | Subbed or sent off (Counting game) | Subbed or sent off (playing less than 70 mins) | Subbed on from bench (Counting Game) | Subbed on (playing less than 70 mins) | Subbed on and then subbed or sent off (Counting Game) | Subbed on and then subbed or sent off (playing less than 70 mins) | Not in 16

KEY PLAYERS - GOALSCORERS

Andrew Cole

Goals in the League	9
Goals in all competitions	10
Assists League goals scored by a team mate where the player delivered the final pass	5
Contribution to Attacking Power Average number of minutes between League team goals while on pitch	61
Player Strike Rate Average number of minutes between League goals scored by player	196
Club Strike Rate Average minutes between League goals scored by club	80

	PLAYER	GOALS LGE	GOALS ALL	ASSISTS	POWER	S RATE
1	Andrew Cole	9	10	5	61	196 mins
2	Darius Vassell	8	10	8	74	379 mins
3	Joey Barton	6	6	6	68	455 mins
4	Trevor Sinclair	3	3	3	75	799 mins

KEY PLAYERS - MIDFIELDERS

Joey Barton

Goals in the League	6
Goals in all competitions	6
Assists League goals scored by a team mate where the player delivered the final pass	6
Defensive Rating Average number of mins between League goals conceded while on the pitch	70
Contribution to Attacking Power Average number of minutes between League team goals while on pitch	68
Scoring Difference Defensive Rating minus Contribution to Attacking Power	2

	PLAYER	GOALS LGE	GOALS ALL	ASSISTS	DEF RATE	POWER	SC DIFF
1	Joey Barton	6	6	6	70	68	2 mins
2	Trevor Sinclair	3	3	3	75	75	0 mins
3	Kiki Musampa	0	1	1	83	86	-3 mins
4	Claudio Reyna	1	1	1	64	72	-8 mins

PLAYER APPEARANCES

	AGE (on 01/07/06)	IN NAMED 16	APPEARANCES	COUNTING GAMES	MINUTES ON PITCH	APPEARANCES	MINUTES ON PITCH	THIS SEASON	HOME COUNTRY
Goalkeepers									
Geert De Vlieger	34	15	0	0	0	0	0	-	Belgium
David James	35	38	38	38	3420	44	3990	4	England (10)
Nicky Weaver	27	14	0	0	0	0	0	-	England
Defenders									
Sylvain Distin	28	31	31	30	2737	36	3217	-	France
Richard Dunne	26	32	32	30	2793	38	3363	5	Rep of Ireland (15)
Stephen Jordan	24	22	18	18	1561	24	1975	-	England
Danny Mills	29	18	18	15	1480	18	1480	-	England
Matthew Mills	19	2	1	0	7	1	7	-	England
Nedum Onuoha	19	18	10	7	721	12	872	-	England
Micah Richards	18	16	13	11	1009	16	1279	-	England
David Sommeil	31	24	16	10	1196	17	1263	-	France
Sun Jihai	28	32	29	16	1729	34	2174	2	China PR (68)
Ben Thatcher	30	21	18	17	1569	19	1689	-	Wales
Midfielders									
Joey Barton	23	31	31	30	2729	35	3088	-	England
Willo Flood	21	6	5	1	134	5	134	-	Rep of Ireland
Yasser Hussein	22	1	0	0	0	1	64	-	Qatar
Stephen Ireland	17	26	24	12	1280	28	1662	-	Rep of Ireland
Kiki Musampa	28	29	27	19	1984	31	2276	-	Holland
Claudio Reyna	32	22	22	18	1796	23	1885	2	United States (5)
Albert Riera	24	15	15	9	1065	19	1403	-	Spain
Antoine Sibierski	31	32	24	9	1113	29	1434	-	France
Trevor Sinclair	33	31	31	23	2396	34	2666	-	England
Forwards									
Andrew Cole	34	22	22	18	1760	23	1850	-	England
Lee Croft	21	26	21	3	647	25	777	-	England
Robbie Fowler	31	6	4	0	64	5	154	-	England
Ishmael Miller	19	1	1	0	30	1	30	-	England
Georgios Samaras	21	14	14	8	946	16	1081	-	Holland
Darius Vassell	26	36	36	31	3031	41	3468	-	England
Bradley Wright-Phillips	21	27	18	1	337	23	474	-	England

KEY: LEAGUE ALL COMPS CAPS (MAY FIFA RANKING)

TEAM OF THE SEASON

KEY: DR = Defensive Rate, SD = Scoring Difference AP = Attacking Power SR = Strike Rate, CG=Counting games – League games playing at least 70 minutes

TOP POINT EARNERS

Andrew Cole

Counting Games League games when player was on pitch for at least 70 minutes	18
Average points Average League points taken in Counting games	1.72
Club Average points Average points taken in League games	1.13

	PLAYER	GAMES	PTS
1	Andrew Cole	18	1.72
2	Stephen Jordan	18	1.50
3	Claudio Reyna	18	1.44
4	Kiki Musampa	19	1.42
5	Joey Barton	30	1.30
6	Trevor Sinclair	23	1.30
7	Danny Mills	15	1.20
8	David James	38	1.13
9	Sylvain Distin	30	1.10
10	Stephen Ireland	12	1.08

KEY PLAYERS - DEFENDERS

Stephen Jordan

Goals Conceded in the League Number of League goals conceded while the player was on the pitch	15
Goals Conceded in all competitions Total number of goals conceded while the player was on the pitch	19
League minutes played Number of minutes played in league matches	1561
Clean Sheets In games when the player was on pitch for at least 70 minutes	5
Defensive Rating Average number of mins between League goals conceded while on the pitch	104
Club Defensive Rating Average number of mins between League goals conceded by the club this season	71

	PLAYER	CON LGE	CON ALL	MINS	C SHEETS	DEF RATE
1	Stephen Jordan	15	19	1561	5	104 mins
2	Danny Mills	17	17	1480	3	87 mins
3	Richard Dunne	39	45	2793	5	72 mins
4	Sylvain Distin	39	44	2737	5	70 mins

KEY GOALKEEPER

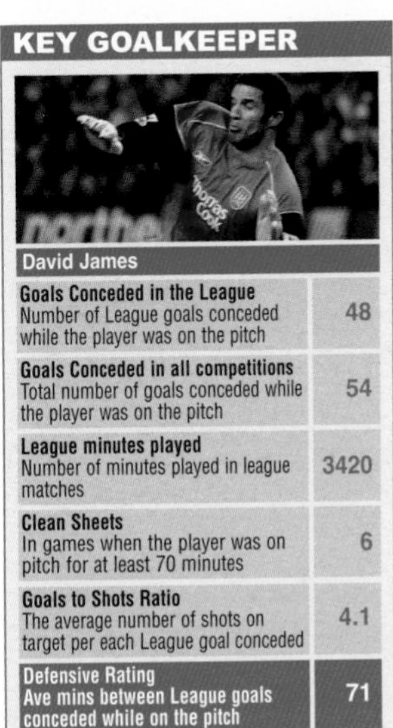

David James

Goals Conceded in the League Number of League goals conceded while the player was on the pitch	48
Goals Conceded in all competitions Total number of goals conceded while the player was on the pitch	54
League minutes played Number of minutes played in league matches	3420
Clean Sheets In games when the player was on pitch for at least 70 minutes	6
Goals to Shots Ratio The average number of shots on target per each League goal conceded	4.1
Defensive Rating Ave mins between League goals conceded while on the pitch	71

BOOKINGS

Joey Barton

League Yellow	11
League Red	1
All competitions Yellow	12
All competitions Red	1
League Average	227 mins between cards

	PLAYER	LEAGUE		TOTAL		AVE
1	Barton	11Y	1R	12Y	1R	227
2	Cole	5	1	5	1	293
3	Jordan	4	1	4	1	312
4	Thatcher	5	0	6	0	313
5	Dunne	8	0	9	0	349
6	Mills, D	4	0	4	0	370
7	Sinclair	5	0	5	0	479
8	Musampa	4	0	5	0	496
9	Richards	2	0	2	0	504
10	Riera	2	0	4	0	532
11	Sun Jihai	3	0	3	1	576
12	Sommeil	2	0	2	0	598
13	Reyna	3	0	3	0	598
14	Croft	1	0	2	0	647
15	Distin	3	1	3	1	684
	Other	7	0	9	1	
	TOTAL	69	4	78	6	

ASTON VILLA

David O'Leary survived and Doug Ellis still holds his stake but the club's lowest Premiership points total has left fans demanding action. Two experienced strikers **Milan Baros** and **Kevin Phillips** signed but were shown up by the increasing promise of 20-year-old **Luke Moore**. He took his fleeting chances to score eight goals and record the seventh best Strike Rate in the division – a league goal every 185 minutes. Baros' eight goals took 254 minutes apiece.

Nolberto Solano returned to Newcastle in a deal which brought in **James Milner** and he tops a poor set of midfield stats ahead of **Gareth Barry**. Barry also recorded 11 yellows and one red card.

Thomas Sorensen struggled behind an unsettled back four. His Defensive Rating of a goal conceded every 64 minutes was worse than the main keepers in two of the relegated clubs.

NICKNAME: THE VILLANS

KEY: Won, Drawn, Lost

1	prem	**Bolton**	H	D	2-2	Phillips 4; Davis 9
2	prem	**Man Utd**	A	L	0-1	
3	prem	**Portsmouth**	A	D	1-1	Hughes 11 og
4	prem	**Blackburn**	H	W	1-0	Baros 11
5	prem	**West Ham**	A	L	0-4	
6	prem	**Tottenham**	H	D	1-1	Milner 4
7	ccr2	**Wycombe**	A	W	8-3	Davis 14,90; Baros 48; Milner 64,86; Easton 69 og; Barry 73 pen,78
8	prem	**Chelsea**	A	L	1-2	Moore 44
9	prem	**Middlesbrough**	H	L	2-3	Moore 50; Davis 90
10	prem	**Birmingham**	A	W	1-0	Phillips 19
11	prem	**Wigan**	H	L	0-2	
12	ccr3	**Burnley**	H	W	1-0	Phillips 22
13	prem	**Man City**	A	L	1-3	Ridgewell 64
14	prem	**Liverpool**	H	L	0-2	
15	prem	**Sunderland**	A	W	3-1	Phillips 55; Barry 82; Baros 83
16	prem	**Charlton**	H	W	1-0	Davis 69
17	ccr4	**Doncaster**	A	L	0-3	
18	prem	**Newcastle**	A	D	1-1	McCann 75
19	prem	**Bolton**	A	D	1-1	Angel 88
20	prem	**Man Utd**	H	L	0-2	
21	prem	**Everton**	H	W	4-0	Baros 35,84; Delaney 48; Angel 82
22	prem	**Fulham**	A	D	3-3	Moore 29; Ridgewell 60,76
23	prem	**Arsenal**	H	D	0-0	
24	prem	**West Brom**	A	W	2-1	Davis 47; Baros 80 pen
25	facr3	**Hull City**	A	W	1-0	Barry 61
26	prem	**West Ham**	H	L	1-2	Hendrie 27
27	prem	**Tottenham**	A	D	0-0	
28	facr4	**Port Vale**	H	W	3-1	Baros 70,74; Davis 90
29	prem	**Chelsea**	H	D	1-1	Moore 70
30	prem	**Middlesbrough**	A	W	4-0	Moore 18,62,64; Phillips 24
31	prem	**Newcastle**	H	L	1-2	Moore 16
32	facr5	**Man City**	H	D	1-1	Baros 72
33	prem	**Charlton**	A	D	0-0	
34	prem	**Portsmouth**	H	W	1-0	Baros 36
35	prem	**Blackburn**	A	L	0-2	
36	facr5r	**Man City**	A	L	1-2	Davis 85
37	prem	**Everton**	A	L	1-4	Agbonlahor 64
38	prem	**Fulham**	H	D	0-0	
39	prem	**Arsenal**	A	L	0-5	
40	prem	**West Brom**	H	D	0-0	
41	prem	**Birmingham**	H	W	3-1	Baros 10,78; Cahill 56
42	prem	**Wigan**	A	L	2-3	Angel 53; Ridgewell 67
43	prem	**Man City**	H	L	0-1	
44	prem	**Liverpool**	A	L	1-3	Barry 58
45	prem	**Sunderland**	H	W	2-1	Barry 43; Ridgewell 78

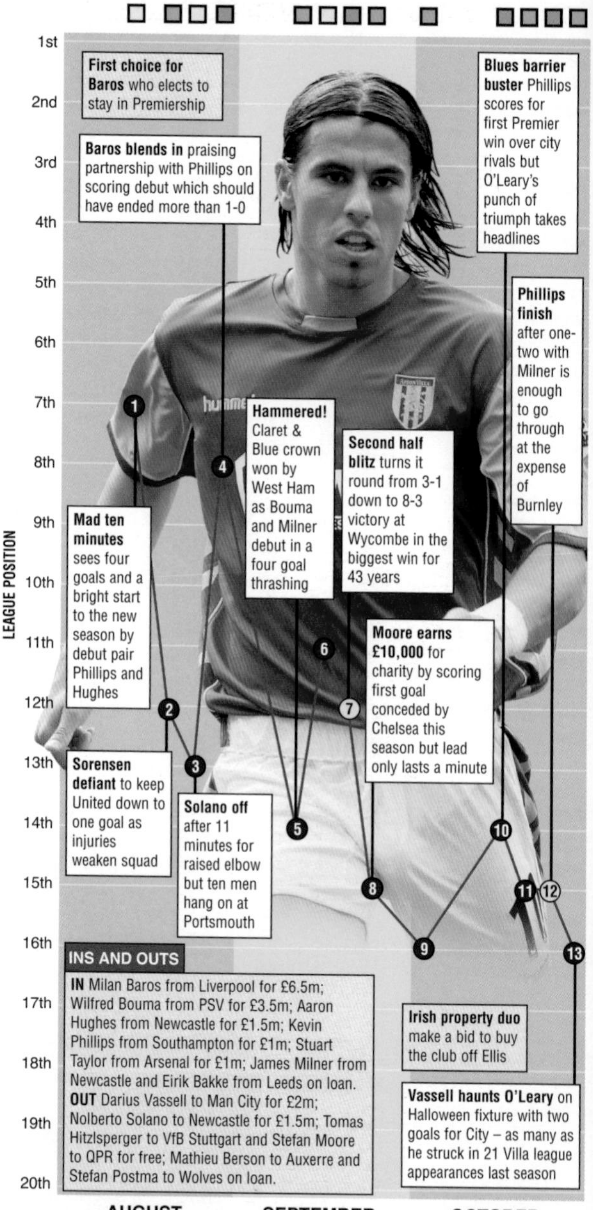

LEAGUE POSITION: 1st – 20th; AUGUST, SEPTEMBER, OCTOBER

First choice for Baros who elects to stay in Premiership

Baros blends in praising partnership with Phillips on scoring debut which should have ended more than 1-0

Blues barrier buster Phillips scores for first Premier win over city rivals but O'Leary's punch of triumph takes headlines

Phillips finish after one-two with Milner is enough to go through at the expense of Burnley

Hammered! Claret & Blue crown won by West Ham as Bouma and Milner debut in a four goal thrashing

Second half blitz turns it round from 3-1 down to 8-3 victory at Wycombe in the biggest win for 43 years

Mad ten minutes sees four goals and a bright start to the new season by debut pair Phillips and Hughes

Moore earns £10,000 for charity by scoring first goal conceded by Chelsea this season but lead only lasts a minute

Sorensen defiant to keep United down to one goal as injuries weaken squad

Solano off after 11 minutes for raised elbow but ten men hang on at Portsmouth

Irish property duo make a bid to buy the club off Ellis

Vassell haunts O'Leary on Halloween fixture with two goals for City – as many as he struck in 21 Villa league appearances last season

INS AND OUTS

IN Milan Baros from Liverpool for £6.5m; Wilfred Bouma from PSV for £3.5m; Aaron Hughes from Newcastle for £1.5m; Kevin Phillips from Southampton for £1m; Stuart Taylor from Arsenal for £1m; James Milner from Newcastle and Eirik Bakke from Leeds on loan.
OUT Darius Vassell to Man City for £2m; Nolberto Solano to Newcastle for £1.5m; Tomas Hitzlsperger to VfB Stuttgart and Stefan Moore to QPR for free; Mathieu Berson to Auxerre and Stefan Postma to Wolves on loan.

Home / Away / Neutral

ATTENDANCES

HOME GROUND: VILLA PARK **CAPACITY:** 43275 **AVERAGE LEAGUE AT HOME:** 34111

2	Man Utd	67934	23	Arsenal	37114	4	Blackburn	31010	32	Man City	23847
18	Newcastle	52267	26	West Ham	36700	28	Port Vale	30434	19	Bolton	23646
44	Liverpool	44479	37	Everton	36507	34	Portsmouth	30194	35	Blackburn	21932
14	Liverpool	42551	27	Tottenham	36243	16	Charlton	30023	22	Fulham	20446
8	Chelsea	42146	45	Sunderland	33820	9	Middlesboro	29719	3	Portsmouth	19778
13	Man City	42069	6	Tottenham	33686	5	West Ham	29582	42	Wigan	17330
41	Birmingham	40158	40	West Brom	33303	10	Birmingham	29312	25	Hull City	17051
15	Sunderland	39707	1	Bolton	33263	30	Middlesboro	27299	17	Doncaster	10590
29	Chelsea	38562	36	Man City	33006	24	West Brom	27073	7	Wycombe	5365
39	Arsenal	38183	38	Fulham	32605	12	Burnley	26872			
31	Newcastle	37140	21	Everton	32432	33	Charlton	26594			
20	Man Utd	37128	11	Wigan	32294	43	Man City	26422			

O'Leary hangs on through uncertainty

Final Position: **16th**

KEY: League, Champions Lge, UEFA Cup, FA Cup, League Cup, Other

MONTH BY MONTH POINTS TALLY

AUGUST	5	42%
SEPTEMBER	1	11%
OCTOBER	3	25%
NOVEMBER	6	67%
DECEMBER	7	39%
JANUARY	4	44%
FEBRUARY	5	42%
MARCH	4	33%
APRIL	4	22%
MAY	3	100%

GOAL ATTEMPTS

FOR – Goal attempts recorded in League games

	HOME	AWAY	TOTAL	AVE
shots on target	108	89	197	5.2
shots off target	104	77	181	4.8
TOTAL	212	166	378	9.9

Ratio of goals to shots – Average number of shots on target per League goal scored: **4.7**

Accuracy rating – Average percentage of total goal attempts which were on target: **52.1**

AGAINST – Goal attempts recorded in League games

	HOME	AWAY	TOTAL	AVE
shots on target	110	142	252	6.6
shots off target	94	89	183	4.8
TOTAL	204	231	435	11.4

Ratio of goals to shots – Average number of shots on target per League goal scored: **4.6**

Accuracy rating – Average percentage of total goal attempts which were on target: **57.9**

GOALS

Luke Moore

League	8
FA Cup	0
League Cup	0
Europe	0
Other	0
TOTAL	8

League Average **185** mins between goals

	PLAYER	LGE	FAC	LC	Euro	TOT	AVE
1	Moore	8	0	0	0	8	185
2	Baros	8	3	1	0	12	254
3	Ridgewell	5	0	0	0	5	546
4	Davis	4	2	2	0	8	740
5	Phillips	4	0	1	0	5	376
6	Barry	3	1	2	0	6	1042
7	Angel	3	0	0	0	3	505
8	Hendrie	1	0	0	0	1	665
9	Milner	1	0	2	0	3	2333
10	Delaney	1	0	0	0	1	1080
11	Cahill	1	0	0	0	1	579
12	McCann	1	0	0	0	1	2870
13	Agbonlahor	1	0	0	0	1	451
	Other	1	0	1	0	2	
	TOTAL	42	6	9	0	57	

SQUAD APPEARANCES

Match	1	2	3	4	5	6	7	8	9	10	11	12	13	14	15	16	17	18	19	20	21	22	23	24	25	26	27	28	29	30	31	32	33	34	35	36	37	38	39	40	41	42	43	44	45
Venue	H	A	A	H	A	H	A	A	H	A	H	H	A	H	A	H	A	A	A	H	H	A	H	A	A	H	A	H	H	A	H	H	A	H	A	A	A	H	A	H	H	A	H	A	H
Competition	L	L	L	L	L	L	W	L	L	L	L	W	L	L	L	L	W	L	L	L	L	L	L	L	F	L	L	F	L	L	L	F	L	L	L	F	L	L	L	L	L	L	L	L	L
Result	D	L	D	W	L	D	W	L	L	W	L	W	L	L	W	W	L	D	D	L	W	D	D	W	W	L	D	W	D	W	L	D	D	W	L	L	L	D	L	D	W	L	L	L	W

Goalkeepers
Wayne Henderson
Thomas Sorensen
Stuart Taylor

Defenders
Wilfred Bouma
Gary Cahill
Ulises De La Cruz
Mark Delaney
Aaron Hughes
Martin Laursen
Olof Mellberg
Liam Ridgewell
Jlloyd Samuel

Midfielders
Eirik Bakke
Gareth Barry
Patrik Berger
Steven Davis
Eric Djemba-Djemba
Craig Gardner
Lee Hendrie
Gavin McCann
James Milner
Nolberto Solano
Peter Whittingham

Forwards
Gabriel Agbonlahor
Juan Pablo Angel
Milan Baros
Luke Moore
Kevin Phillips

KEY: ■ On all match · ■ On bench · ⏮ Subbed or sent off (Counting game) · « Subbed or sent off (playing less than 70 mins) · » Subbed on from bench (Counting Game) · » Subbed on (playing less than 70 mins) · Subbed on and then subbed or sent off (Counting Game) · Subbed on and then subbed or sent off (playing less than 70 mins) · □ Not in 16

KEY PLAYERS - GOALSCORERS

Luke Moore

Goals in the League	8
Goals in all competitions	8
Assists League goals scored by a team mate where the player delivered the final pass	0
Contribution to Attacking Power Average number of minutes between League team goals while on pitch	67
Player Strike Rate Average number of minutes between League goals scored by player	185
Club Strike Rate Average minutes between League goals scored by club	81

	PLAYER	GOALS LGE	GOALS ALL	ASSISTS	POWER	S RATE
1	Luke Moore	8	8	0	67	185 mins
2	Milan Baros	8	12	6	85	254 mins
3	Liam Ridgewell	5	5	0	91	546 mins
4	Steven Davis	4	8	4	85	740 mins

KEY PLAYERS - MIDFIELDERS

James Milner

Goals in the League	1
Goals in all competitions	3
Assists League goals scored by a team mate where the player delivered the final pass	5
Defensive Rating Average number of mins between League goals conceded while on the pitch	67
Contribution to Attacking Power Average number of minutes between League team goals while on pitch	73
Scoring Difference Defensive Rating minus Contribution to Attacking Power	-6

	PLAYER	GOALS LGE	GOALS ALL	ASSISTS	DEF RATE	POWER	SC DIFF
1	James Milner	1	3	5	67	73	-6 mins
2	Gareth Barry	3	6	2	63	76	-13 mins
3	Gavin McCann	1	1	0	65	80	-15 mins
4	Steven Davis	4	8	4	64	85	-21 mins

PLAYER APPEARANCES

	AGE (on 01/07/06)	IN NAMED 16	APPEARANCES	COUNTING GAMES	MINUTES ON PITCH	APPEARANCES	MINUTES ON PITCH	THIS SEASON	HOME COUNTRY
Goalkeepers									
Wayne Henderson	22	1	0	0	0	0	0	-	Rep of Ireland
Thomas Sorensen	30	37	36	36	3240	0	0	5	Denmark (19)
Stuart Taylor	25	38	2	2	180	0	0	-	England
Defenders									
Wilfred Bouma	28	22	20	20	1733	2	0	3	Holland (3)
Gary Cahill	20	16	7	6	579	3	0	-	England
Ulises De La Cruz	31	16	7	2	404	0	0	6	Ecuador (39)
Mark Delaney	30	14	12	12	1080	2	0	1	Wales (74)
Aaron Hughes	26	35	35	32	3018	2	0	2	N Ireland (114)
Martin Laursen	28	1	1	1	90	0	0	-	Denmark
Olof Mellberg	28	27	27	27	2417	5	0	5	Sweden (16)
Liam Ridgewell	21	37	32	30	2730	6	0	-	England
Jlloyd Samuel	25	24	19	11	1223	2	0	-	England
Midfielders									
Eirik Bakke	28	15	14	6	686	1	0	-	Norway
Gareth Barry	25	36	36	33	3125	11	1	-	England
Patrik Berger	32	8	8	2	372	1	0	-	Czech Republic
Steven Davis	21	35	35	32	2958	0	0	7	N Ireland (114)
Eric Djemba-Djemba	25	11	4	1	112	0	0	2	Cameroon (26)
Craig Gardner	19	16	8	0	300	2	0	-	England
Lee Hendrie	29	23	16	5	665	1	0	-	England
Gavin McCann	28	32	32	32	2870	8	0	-	England
James Milner	20	27	27	25	2333	3	0	-	England
Nolberto Solano	31	3	3	1	119	0	1	-	Peru
Peter Whittingham	21	9	4	3	320	1	0	-	England
Forwards									
Gabriel Agbonlahor	19	9	9	3	451	0	0	-	England
Juan Pablo Angel	30	33	31	10	1514	3	0	3	Colombia (36)
Milan Baros	24	25	25	21	2032	7	0	9	Czech Republic (2)
Luke Moore	20	33	27	14	1481	2	0	-	England
Kevin Phillips	32	24	23	11	1502	0	0	-	England

KEY: LEAGUE ALL COMPS CAPS (MAY FIFA RANKING)

TEAM OF THE SEASON

SORENSEN CG 36 DR 64

HUGHES CG 32 DR 67

MELLBERG CG 27 DR 60

RIDGEWELL CG 30 DR 62

DELANEY CG 12 DR 68

MILNER CG 25 SD -6

MCCANN CG 32 SD -15

DAVIS CG 32 SD -21

BARRY CG 33 SD -13

BAROS CG 21 AP 85

MOORE CG 14 SR 185

KEY: DR = Defensive Rate, SD = Scoring Difference AP = Attacking Power SR = Strike Rate, CG=Counting games – League games playing at least 70 minutes

TOP POINT EARNERS

Milan Baros

Counting Games League games when player was on pitch for at least 70 minutes	21
Average points Average League points taken in Counting games	1.29
Club Average points Average points taken in League games	1.11

	PLAYER	GAMES	PTS
1	Milan Baros	21	1.29
2	Aaron Hughes	32	1.28
3	James Milner	25	1.24
4	Wilfred Bouma	20	1.20
5	Gavin McCann	32	1.19
6	Steven Davis	32	1.16
7	Gareth Barry	33	1.15
8	Liam Ridgewell	30	1.10
9	Mark Delaney	12	1.08
10	Thomas Sorensen	36	1.08

KEY PLAYERS - DEFENDERS

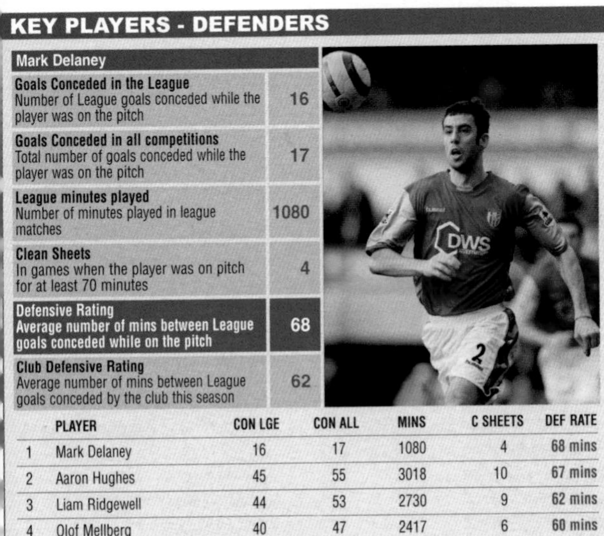

Mark Delaney

Goals Conceded in the League Number of League goals conceded while the player was on the pitch	16
Goals Conceded in all competitions Total number of goals conceded while the player was on the pitch	17
League minutes played Number of minutes played in league matches	1080
Clean Sheets In games when the player was on pitch for at least 70 minutes	4
Defensive Rating Average number of mins between League goals conceded while on the pitch	68
Club Defensive Rating Average number of mins between League goals conceded by the club this season	62

	PLAYER	CON LGE	CON ALL	MINS	C SHEETS	DEF RATE
1	Mark Delaney	16	17	1080	4	68 mins
2	Aaron Hughes	45	55	3018	10	67 mins
3	Liam Ridgewell	44	53	2730	9	62 mins
4	Olof Mellberg	40	47	2417	6	60 mins

KEY GOALKEEPER

Thomas Sorensen

Goals Conceded in the League Number of League goals conceded while the player was on the pitch	51
Goals Conceded in all competitions Total number of goals conceded while the player was on the pitch	61
League minutes played Number of minutes played in league matches	3240
Clean Sheets In games when the player was on pitch for at least 70 minutes	11
Goals to Shots Ratio The average number of shots on target per each League goal conceded	4.7
Defensive Rating Ave mins between League goals conceded while on the pitch	64

BOOKINGS

Gary Cahill

League Yellow	3
League Red	0
All competitions Yellow	3
All competitions Red	0
League Average 193 mins between cards	

	PLAYER	LEAGUE Y	LEAGUE R	TOTAL Y	TOTAL R	AVE
1	Cahill	3	0	3	0	193
2	Barry	11	1	12	1	260
3	Baros	7	0	7	0	290
4	McCann	8	0	9	0	358
5	Ridgewell	6	0	6	0	455
6	Mellberg	5	0	7	0	483
7	Angel	3	0	3	0	504
8	Delaney	2	0	2	0	540
9	Samuel	2	0	4	0	611
10	Hendrie	1	0	1	0	665
11	Bakke	1	0	1	0	686
12	Moore	2	0	2	0	740
13	Milner	3	0	4	0	777
14	Bouma	2	0	2	0	866
15	Hughes	2	0	2	0	1509
	Other	0	0	0	0	
	TOTAL	58	1	65	1	

PORTSMOUTH

Chairman Milan Mandaric realised he had forced out the man who could salvage his Premiership place. Harry Redknapp made an astonishing yo-yo return from their rivals and the loyal Pompey fans swallowed their pride and screamed their team out of the drop zone.

A usual dose of January reinforcements helped but it was **Lomano LuaLua** who ensured the club were always capable of scoring. Stats of seven goals at a Strike Rate of one every 300 minutes would have been bettered if not for the African Cup of Nations and some over celebration.

Pendro Mendes scored a vital winner against Man City and tops the Midfield chart ahead of the hard-working **Gary O'Neil**.

Dejan Stefanovic had the best Defensive Rating.

NICKNAME: POMPEY

KEY: Won / Drawn / Lost

1	prem	**Tottenham**	H	L	0-2	
2	prem	**West Brom**	A	L	1-2	Robert 63
3	prem	**Aston Villa**	H	D	1-1	LuaLua 42
4	prem	**Man City**	A	L	1-2	Viafara 52
5	prem	**Everton**	A	W	1-0	Ferguson 60 og
6	prem	**Birmingham**	H	D	1-1	LuaLua 4
7	ccr2	**Gillingham**	A	L	2-3	O'Neil 24; Taylor 48 pen
8	prem	**Bolton**	A	L	0-1	
9	prem	**Newcastle**	H	D	0-0	
10	prem	**Middlesbrough**	A	D	1-1	O'Neil 46
11	prem	**Charlton**	H	L	1-2	Dario Silva 14
12	prem	**Sunderland**	A	W	4-1	Vukic 48; Taylor 59,67; Dario Silva 74
13	prem	**Wigan**	H	L	0-2	
14	prem	**Liverpool**	A	L	0-3	
15	prem	**Chelsea**	H	L	0-2	
16	prem	**Man Utd**	A	L	0-3	
17	prem	**Tottenham**	A	L	1-3	LuaLua 24
18	prem	**West Brom**	H	W	1-0	Todorov 56
19	prem	**West Ham**	H	D	1-1	O'Neil 17
20	prem	**Arsenal**	A	L	0-4	
21	prem	**Fulham**	H	W	1-0	O'Neil 43
22	prem	**Blackburn**	A	L	1-2	Taylor 3
23	facr3	**Ipswich**	A	W	1-0	Dario Silva 37
24	prem	**Everton**	H	L	0-1	
25	prem	**Birmingham**	A	L	0-5	
26	facr4	**Liverpool**	H	L	1-2	Davis 54
27	prem	**Bolton**	H	D	1-1	Karadas 85
28	prem	**Newcastle**	A	L	0-2	
29	prem	**Man Utd**	H	L	1-3	Taylor 87
30	prem	**Chelsea**	A	L	0-2	
31	prem	**Aston Villa**	A	L	0-1	
32	prem	**Man City**	H	W	2-1	Mendes 60,90
33	prem	**West Ham**	A	W	4-2	LuaLua 19; Davis 25; Mendes 42; Todorov 77
34	prem	**Fulham**	A	W	3-1	O'Neil 1,62; LuaLua 24
35	prem	**Blackburn**	H	D	2-2	LuaLua 41; Todorov 78
36	prem	**Arsenal**	H	D	1-1	LuaLua 66
37	prem	**Middlesbrough**	H	W	1-0	O'Neil 54
38	prem	**Charlton**	A	L	1-2	D'Alessandro 40
39	prem	**Sunderland**	H	W	2-1	Todorov 73; Taylor 88 pen
40	prem	**Wigan**	A	W	2-1	Mwaruwari 63; Taylor 71 pen
41	prem	**Liverpool**	H	L	1-3	Koroman 85

INS AND OUTS

IN Andy O'Brien from Newcastle for £2m; John Viafara from Once Caldas (Columbia) for £1.5m; Collins Mbesuma from Kaizer Chiefs (South Africa) for £500K; Brian Priske from Genk, Frank Songo'o from Barcelona, Zvonimir Vukic from Shakhtar Donetsk and Dario Silva from Seville fees undisclosed; Laurent Robert from Newcastle, Salif Diao from Liverpool and Azar Karadas from Benfica on loan; Sander Westerveld from Real Mallorca and Gregory Vignal from Liverpool for free

OUT Ayegbeni Yakubu to Middlesbrough for £7.5m; Ricardo Fuller to Southampton for £90K; Rowan Vine to Luton for £250K; Patrik Berger to Aston Villa, Shaka Hislop to West Ham and Steve Stone to Leeds for free; David Unsworth to Sheffield United and Arjan de Zeeuw to Wigan fees undisclosed

LEAGUE POSITION: 1st, 2nd, 3rd, 4th, 5th, 6th, 7th, 8th, 9th, 10th, 11th, 12th, 13th, 14th, 15th, 16th, 17th, 18th, 19th, 20th

AUGUST — SEPTEMBER — OCTOBER

Home / Away / Neutral

Griffin's own goal gives Spurs a start against Westerveld and there's no way back

Robert's trademark freekick is the consolation after Westerveld error gives Baggies victory

LuaLua levels as a rampant Robert takes Villa apart but can't clinch the winner

Cruel deflection favours Man City after Viafara's 52nd minute header is overturned by two goals

First win comes away at Goodison courtesy of a battling performance and a Ferguson own goal

Ashdown agony as ball goes in off a post and his arm and Gillingham snatch cup win in extra-time

Perrin sent to stand after outburst at linesman in a poor performance at Bolton

Great Given saves Newcastle from a hiding with two stunning saves from Taylor while LuaLua recovers from Malaria

Perrin makes his point at Boro despite old boy Yakubu levelling O'Neil's strike

Silva reward for shot on the run but gold goes to Charlton who hit back to take points

Taylor's 40-yarder catches out Sunderland as super second half performance has Perrin purring

ATTENDANCES

HOME GROUND: FRATTON PARK CAPACITY: 20210 AVERAGE LEAGUE AT HOME: 19839

16	Man Utd	67684	25	Birmingham	29138	29	Man Utd	20206	6	Birmingham	19319
28	Newcastle	51627	10	Middlesboro	26551	37	Middlesboro	20204	27	Bolton	19128
14	Liverpool	44394	38	Charlton	25419	15	Chelsea	20182	13	Wigan	19102
30	Chelsea	42254	2	West Brom	24404	19	West Ham	20168	21	Fulham	19101
4	Man City	41022	8	Bolton	23134	24	Everton	20094	11	Charlton	19030
20	Arsenal	38223	34	Fulham	22322	39	Sunderland	20078	26	Liverpool	17247
5	Everton	36861	40	Wigan	21126	18	West Brom	20052	23	Ipswich	15593
17	Tottenham	36141	41	Liverpool	20240	35	Blackburn	20048	7	Gillingham	4903
12	Sunderland	34926	36	Arsenal	20230	3	Aston Villa	19778			
33	West Ham	34837	9	Newcastle	20220	32	Man City	19556			
31	Aston Villa	30194	1	Tottenham	20215	22	Blackburn	19521			

Harry 'Houdini' plots his great escape

Final Position: 17th

KEY: ● League ● Champions Lge ● UEFA Cup ● FA Cup ○ League Cup ● Other

MONTH BY MONTH POINTS TALLY

AUGUST	1	8%
SEPTEMBER	4	44%
OCTOBER	5	42%
NOVEMBER	0	0%
DECEMBER	7	39%
JANUARY	0	0%
FEBRUARY	1	8%
MARCH	6	67%
APRIL	14	67%
MAY	0	0%

GOAL ATTEMPTS

FOR – Goal attempts recorded in League games

	HOME	AWAY	TOTAL	AVE
shots on target	135	87	222	5.8
shots off target	112	77	189	5
TOTAL	247	164	411	10.8

Ratio of goals to shots Average number of shots on target per League goal scored: **6.0**

Accuracy rating Average percentage of total goal attempts which were on target: **54.0**

AGAINST – Goal attempts recorded in League games

	HOME	AWAY	TOTAL	AVE
shots on target	79	129	208	5.5
shots off target	77	87	164	4.3
TOTAL	156	216	372	9.8

Ratio of goals to shots Average number of shots on target per League goal scored: **3.4**

Accuracy rating Average percentage of total goal attempts which were on target: **55.9**

GOALS

Lomana LuaLua

League	7
FA Cup	0
League Cup	0
Europe	0
Other	0
TOTAL	7

League Average **300** mins between goals

	PLAYER	LGE	FAC	LC	Euro	TOT	AVE
1	LuaLua	7	0	0	0	7	300
2	O'Neil	6	0	1	0	7	521
3	Taylor	6	0	1	0	7	475
4	Todorov	4	0	0	0	4	257
5	Mendes	3	0	0	0	3	406
6	Dario Silva	2	1	0	0	3	485
7	D'Alessandro	1	0	0	0	1	1074
8	Koroman	1	0	0	0	1	119
9	Viafara	1	0	0	0	1	925
10	Karadas	1	0	0	0	1	496
11	Mwaruwari	1	0	0	0	1	1274
12	Robert	1	0	0	0	1	1149
13	Vukic	1	0	0	0	1	518
14	Davis	1	1	0	0	2	1231
	Other	1	0	0	0	1	
	TOTAL	37	2	2	0	41	

SQUAD APPEARANCES

Match	1	2	3	4	5	6	7	8	9	10	11	12	13	14	15	16	17	18	19	20	21	22	23	24	25	26	27	28	29	30	31	32	33	34	35	36	37	38	39	40
Venue	H	A	H	A	A	H	A	A	H	A	H	A	H	A	H	A	A	H	H	A	H	A	A	H	A	H	H	A	H	A	A	H	A	A	H	H	H	A	H	A
Competition	L	L	L	L	L	L	W	L	L	L	L	L	L	L	L	L	L	L	L	L	L	L	F	L	L	F	L	L	L	L	L	L	L	L	L	L	L	L	L	L
Result	L	L	D	L	W	D	L	L	D	D	L	W	L	L	L	L	L	W	D	L	W	L	W	L	L	L	D	L	L	L	L	W	W	W	D	D	W	L	W	W

Goalkeepers
- Jamie Ashdown
- Andrea Guatelli
- Dean Kiely
- Sander Westerveld

Defenders
- Andrew Griffin
- Andy O'Brien
- Noe Pamarot
- Linvoy Primus
- Brian Priske
- Dejan Stefanovic
- Gregory Vignal

Midfielders
- Aliou Cisse
- Andres D'Alessandro
- Sean Davis
- Salif Diao
- Richard Hughes
- Ognjen Koroman
- Pedro Mendes
- Gary O'Neil
- Laurent Robert
- Wayne Routledge
- Giannis Skopelitis
- Frank Songo'o
- Matthew Taylor
- John Eduis Viafara
- Zvonimir Vukic

Forwards
- Dario Silva
- Azar Karadas
- Lomana LuaLua
- Collins Mbesuma
- Ivica Mornar
- Benjani Mwaruwari
- Emmanuel Olisadebe
- Vincent Pericard
- Svetoslav Todorov

KEY: ■ On all match ■ On bench ⏮ Subbed or sent off (Counting game) « Subbed or sent off (playing less than 70 mins) ⏭ Subbed on from bench (Counting Game) » Subbed on (playing less than 70 mins) Subbed on and then subbed or sent off (Counting Game) Subbed on and then subbed or sent off (playing less than 70 mins) □ Not in 16

KEY PLAYERS - GOALSCORERS

Lomana LuaLua

Goals in the League	7
Goals in all competitions	7
Assists League goals scored by a team mate where the player delivered the final pass	3
Contribution to Attacking Power Average number of minutes between League team goals while on pitch	91
Player Strike Rate Average number of minutes between League goals scored by player	300
Club Strike Rate Average minutes between League goals scored by club	92

	PLAYER	GOALS LGE	GOALS ALL	ASSISTS	POWER	S RATE
1	Lomana LuaLua	7	7	3	91	300 mins
2	Pedro Mendes	3	3	0	76	406 mins
3	Matthew Taylor	6	7	6	89	475 mins
4	Gary O'Neil	6	7	5	87	521 mins

KEY PLAYERS - MIDFIELDERS

Pedro Mendes

Goals in the League	3
Goals in all competitions	3
Assists League goals scored by a team mate where the player delivered the final pass	0
Defensive Rating Average number of mins between League goals conceded while on the pitch	53
Contribution to Attacking Power Average number of minutes between League team goals while on pitch	76
Scoring Difference Defensive Rating minus Contribution to Attacking Power	-23

	PLAYER	GOALS LGE	GOALS ALL	ASSISTS	DEF RATE	POWER	SC DIFF
1	Pedro Mendes	3	3	0	53	76	-23 mins
2	Gary O'Neil	6	7	5	57	87	-30 mins
3	Matthew Taylor	6	7	6	56	89	-33 mins
4	Richard Hughes	0	0	0	61	114	-53 mins

PLAYER APPEARANCES

	AGE (on 01/07/06)	IN NAMED 16	APPEARANCES	COUNTING GAMES	MINUTES ON PITCH	APPEARANCES	MINUTES ON PITCH	THIS SEASON	HOME COUNTRY
Goalkeepers									
Jamie Ashdown	25	36	18	18	1620	19	1740	-	England
Andrea Guatelli	22	3	0	0	0	0	0	-	Italy
Dean Kiely	35	15	15	15	1350	16	1440	-	Rep of Ireland
Sander Westerveld	31	22	5	5	450	6	540	-	Holland
Defenders									
Andrew Griffin	27	25	22	19	1767	22	1767	-	England
Andy O'Brien	27	31	29	29	2610	32	2910	5	Rep of Ireland (15)
Noe Pamarot	27	9	8	4	455	8	455	-	France
Linvoy Primus	32	22	20	19	1724	21	1811	-	England
Brian Priske	29	32	30	27	2433	33	2646	6	Denmark (19)
Dejan Stefanovic	31	28	28	26	2371	31	2671	-	Serbia & Mont.
Gregory Vignal	24	15	14	12	1172	17	1427	-	France
Midfielders									
Aliou Cisse	30	5	3	2	167	3	167	-	Senegal
Andres D'Alessandro	25	14	13	10	1074	13	1074	2	Argentina (9)
Sean Davis	26	17	17	10	1231	18	1321	-	England
Salif Diao	29	11	11	6	659	13	818	-	Senegal
Richard Hughes	27	30	26	18	1817	29	2117	1	Scotland (85)
Ognijen Koroman	27	5	3	0	119	3	119	8	Serbia & Mont. (44)
Pedro Mendes	27	14	14	13	1219	15	1309	-	Portugal
Gary O'Neil	23	36	36	35	3126	39	3426	-	England
Laurent Robert	31	17	17	11	1149	17	1149	-	France
Wayne Routledge	21	15	13	2	444	13	444	-	England
Giannis Skopelitis	28	10	5	0	76	5	76	-	Greece
Frank Songo'o	19	4	2	0	33	3	84	-	France
Matthew Taylor	24	35	34	31	2848	37	3132	-	England
John Eduis Viafara	27	18	14	9	925	15	941	4	Colombia (36)
Zvonimir Vukic	26	11	9	3	518	9	518	7	Serbia & Mont. (44)
Forwards									
Dario Silva	33	13	13	9	969	15	1098	-	Uruguay
Azar Karadas	24	27	17	4	496	20	643	-	Norway
Lomana LuaLua	25	25	25	23	2103	26	2191	5	Congo DR (65)
Collins Mbesuma	22	5	4	0	55	4	55	-	Zambia
Ivica Mornar	32	2	2	0	53	2	53	-	Croatia
Benjani Mwaruwari	27	16	16	10	1274	16	1274	3	Zimbabwe (55)
Emmanuel Olisadebe	27	2	2	0	68	2	68	-	Nigeria
Vincent Pericard	23	7	6	1	210	7	275	-	Cameroon
Svetoslav Todorov	27	29	24	6	1029	27	1155	3	Bulgaria (37)

KEY: LEAGUE ALL COMPS CAPS (MAY FIFA RANKING)

TEAM OF THE SEASON

KIELY

CG 15 DR 59

PRISKE

CG 27 DR 58

PRIMUS

CG 19 DR 62

STEFANOVIC

CG 26 DR 64

VIGNAL

CG 12 DR 59

O'NEIL

CG 35 SD -30

MENDES

CG 13 SD -23

HUGHES

CG 18 SD -53

TAYLOR

CG 31 SD -33

MWARUWARI*

CG 10 AP 70

LUALUA

CG 23 SR 300

KEY: DR = Defensive Rate, SD = Scoring Difference AP = Attacking Power SR = Strike Rate, CG=Counting games – League games playing at least 70 minutes

TOP POINT EARNERS

Linvoy Primus

Counting Games League games when player was on pitch for at least 70 minutes	19
Average points Average League points taken in Counting games	1.42
Club Average points Average points taken in League games	1.00

	PLAYER	GAMES	PTS
1	Linvoy Primus	19	1.42
2	Dean Kiely	15	1.40
3	Brian Priske	27	1.26
4	Pedro Mendes	13	1.15
5	Dejan Stefanovic	26	1.08
6	Matthew Taylor	31	1.06
7	Gary O'Neil	35	1.06
8	Lomana LuaLua	23	0.96
9	Richard Hughes	18	0.94
10	Jamie Ashdown	18	0.89

KEY PLAYERS - DEFENDERS

Dejan Stefanovic

Goals Conceded in the League Number of League goals conceded while the player was on the pitch	37
Goals Conceded in all competitions Total number of goals conceded while the player was on the pitch	42
League minutes played Number of minutes played in league matches	2371
Clean Sheets In games when the player was on pitch for at least 70 minutes	5
Defensive Rating Average number of mins between League goals conceded while on the pitch	64
Club Defensive Rating Average number of mins between League goals conceded by the club this season	55

	PLAYER	CON LGE	CON ALL	MINS	C SHEETS	DEF RATE
1	Dejan Stefanovic	37	42	2371	5	64 mins
2	Linvoy Primus	28	30	1724	2	62 mins
3	Gregory Vignal	20	25	1172	2	59 mins
4	Brian Priske	42	45	2433	4	58 mins

KEY GOALKEEPER

Dean Kiely

Goals Conceded in the League Number of League goals conceded while the player was on the pitch	23
Goals Conceded in all competitions Total number of goals conceded while the player was on the pitch	25
League minutes played Number of minutes played in league matches	1350
Clean Sheets In games when the player was on pitch for at least 70 minutes	1
Goals to Shots Ratio The average number of shots on target per each League goal conceded	3.7
Defensive Rating Ave mins between League goals conceded while on the pitch	59

BOOKINGS

Azar Karadas

League Yellow	4
League Red	0
All competitions Yellow	4
All competitions Red	0

League Average **124** mins between cards

	PLAYER	LEAGUE 4Y	LEAGUE 0R	TOTAL 4Y	TOTAL 0R	AVE
1	Karadas	4	0	4	0	124
2	Diao	3	0	3	0	219
3	Hughes	8	0	9	0	227
4	Viafara	4	0	4	0	231
5	Robert	3	1	3	1	287
6	Griffin	6	0	6	0	294
7	Mendes	4	0	4	0	304
8	Vignal	3	0	4	0	390
9	Stefanovic	5	0	6	0	474
10	Vukic	1	0	1	0	518
11	Taylor	4	0	4	0	712
12	Dario Silva	1	0	2	0	969
13	LuaLua	2	0	2	0	1051
14	Davis	1	0	2	0	1231
15	Mwaruwari	1	0	1	0	1274
	Other	3	0	4	0	
	TOTAL	53	1	59	1	

BIRMINGHAM

Lack of preparation says sacked club captain **Kenny Cunningham**; injuries says **Steve Bruce**. The league table says a lack of goals, with 28 a far worse total than any of last season's relegated clubs. **Emile Heskey** led the line but his four goals were scored at an abysmal Strike Rate of one every 704 minutes.

On loan **Jiri Jarosik** leaves with his reputation intact as the club's top scorer and a respectable midfield Strike Rate of a goal every 332 minutes. **Martin Taylor** recorded defensive stats that shamed his colleagues. The team only conceded a goal every 86 minutes when Taylor played and one every 56 minutes when he didn't.

A Defence Rating of a goal let in every 70 minutes should mean **Maik Taylor** can hold his head up as relegated keepers usually end up with something below 60.

NICKNAME: THE BLUES

KEY: Won / Drawn / Lost

1	prem	**Fulham**	A	D	0-0	
2	prem	**Man City**	H	L	1-2	Butt 7
3	prem	**Middlesbrough**	H	L	0-3	
4	prem	**West Brom**	A	W	3-2	Heskey 10,33; Jarosik 26
5	prem	**Charlton**	H	L	0-1	
6	prem	**Portsmouth**	A	D	1-1	Jarosik 6
7	ccr2	**Scunthorpe**	A	W	2-0	Forssell 15,70 pen
8	prem	**Liverpool**	H	D	2-2	Warnock 72 og; Pandiani 75
9	prem	**Arsenal**	A	L	0-1	
10	prem	**Aston Villa**	H	L	0-1	
11	prem	**Blackburn**	A	L	0-2	
12	ccr3	**Norwich**	H	W	2-1	Pennant 5; Jarosik 86
13	prem	**Everton**	H	L	0-1	
14	prem	**Newcastle**	A	L	0-1	
15	prem	**Sunderland**	A	W	1-0	Gray 68
16	ccr4	**Millwall**	A	W	4-3*	Gray 10; Heskey 102 (*on penalties)
17	prem	**West Ham**	H	L	1-2	Heskey 11
18	prem	**Fulham**	H	W	1-0	Butt 84
19	prem	**Man City**	A	L	1-4	Jarosik 76
20	ccqf	**Man Utd**	H	L	1-3	Jarosik 75
21	prem	**Tottenham**	A	L	0-2	
22	prem	**Man Utd**	H	D	2-2	Clapham 18; Pandiani 78
23	prem	**Chelsea**	A	L	0-2	
24	prem	**Wigan**	H	W	2-0	Pennant 20; Melchiot 33
25	facr3	**Torquay**	A	D	0-0	
26	prem	**Charlton**	A	L	0-2	
27	facr3r	**Torquay**	H	W	2-0	Jarosik 61; Forssell 81
28	prem	**Portsmouth**	H	W	5-0	Jarosik 5; Pennant 37; Upson 55; Forssell 90 pen; Dunn 90
29	facr4	**Reading**	A	D	1-1	Dunn 67
30	prem	**Liverpool**	A	D	1-1	Xabi Alonso 88 og
31	prem	**Arsenal**	H	L	0-2	
32	facr4r	**Reading**	H	W	2-1	Forssell 30; Gray 67
33	prem	**West Ham**	A	L	0-3	
34	facr5	**Stoke**	A	W	1-0	Forssell 47
35	prem	**Sunderland**	H	W	1-0	Heskey 39
36	prem	**Middlesbrough**	A	L	0-1	
37	prem	**West Brom**	H	D	1-1	Forssell 49 pen
38	prem	**Tottenham**	H	L	0-2	
39	facqf	**Liverpool**	H	L	0-7	
40	prem	**Man Utd**	A	L	0-3	
41	prem	**Chelsea**	H	D	0-0	
42	prem	**Bolton**	H	W	1-0	Jarosik 37
43	prem	**Wigan**	A	D	1-1	Dunn 77
44	prem	**Aston Villa**	A	L	1-3	Sutton 25
45	prem	**Blackburn**	H	W	2-1	Butt 62; Forssell 87
46	prem	**Everton**	A	D	0-0	
47	prem	**Newcastle**	H	D	0-0	
48	prem	**Bolton**	A	L	0-1	

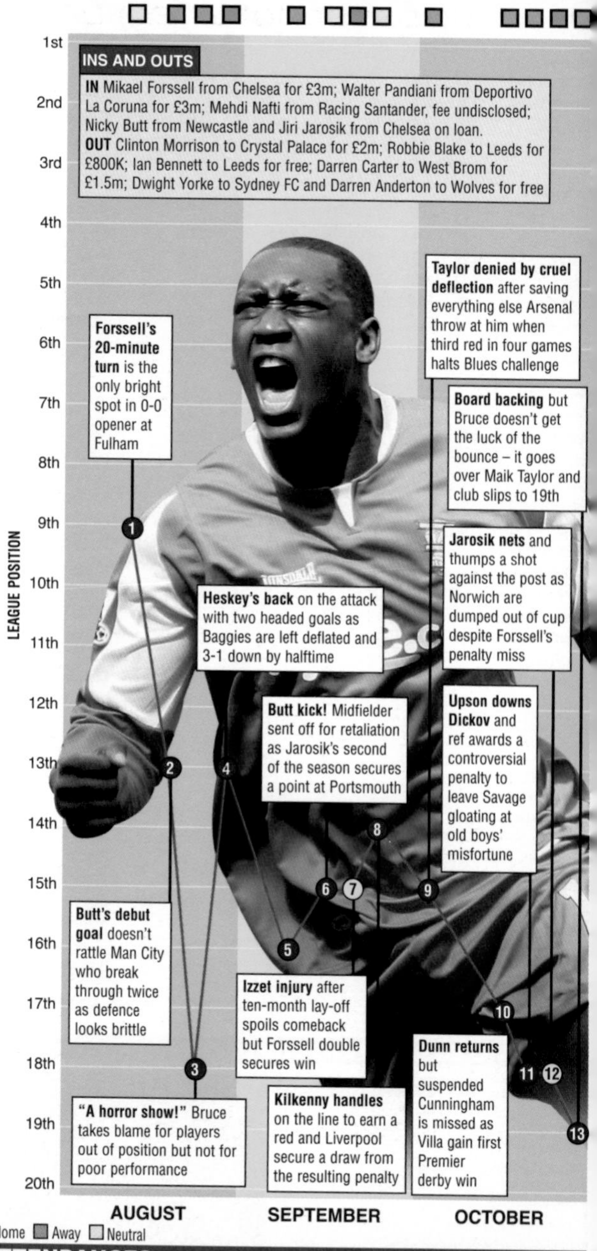

INS AND OUTS

IN Mikael Forssell from Chelsea for £3m; Walter Pandiani from Deportivo La Coruna for £3m; Mehdi Nafti from Racing Santander, fee undisclosed; Nicky Butt from Newcastle and Jiri Jarosik from Chelsea on loan.
OUT Clinton Morrison to Crystal Palace for £2m; Robbie Blake to Leeds for £800K; Ian Bennett to Leeds for free; Darren Carter to West Brom for £1.5m; Dwight Yorke to Sydney FC and Darren Anderton to Wolves for free

1st
2nd
3rd
4th
5th
6th
7th
8th
9th
10th
11th
12th
13th
14th
15th
16th
17th
18th
19th
20th
LEAGUE POSITION
Forssell's 20-minute turn is the only bright spot in 0-0 opener at Fulham
Butt's debut goal doesn't rattle Man City who break through twice as defence looks brittle
"A horror show!" Bruce takes blame for players out of position but not for poor performance
Heskey's back on the attack with two headed goals as Baggies are left deflated and 3-1 down by halftime
Butt kick! Midfielder sent off for retaliation as Jarosik's second of the season secures a point at Portsmouth
Izzet injury after ten-month lay-off spoils comeback but Forssell double secures win
Kilkenny handles on the line to earn a red and Liverpool secure a draw from the resulting penalty
Taylor denied by cruel deflection after saving everything else Arsenal throw at him when third red in four games halts Blues challenge
Board backing but Bruce doesn't get the luck of the bounce – it goes over Maik Taylor and club slips to 19th
Jarosik nets and thumps a shot against the post as Norwich are dumped out of cup despite Forssell's penalty miss
Upson downs Dickov and ref awards a controversial penalty to leave Savage gloating at old boys' misfortune
Dunn returns but suspended Cunningham is missed as Villa gain first Premier derby win
AUGUST
SEPTEMBER
OCTOBER
Home
Away
Neutral

ATTENDANCES

HOME GROUND: ST ANDREWS **CAPACITY:** 30016 **AVERAGE LEAGUE AT HOME:** 27392

40	Man Utd	69070	35	Sunderland	29257	31	Arsenal	27075	4	West Brom	23993
14	Newcastle	52191	24	Wigan	29189	5	Charlton	26846	29	Reading	23762
30	Liverpool	43851	28	Portsmouth	29138	13	Everton	26554	20	Man Utd	20454
19	Man City	41343	12	Norwich	28825	42	Bolton	26493	6	Portsmouth	19319
23	Chelsea	40652	22	Man Utd	28459	38	Tottenham	26398	34	Stoke	18768
44	Aston Villa	40158	47	Newcastle	28331	2	Man City	26366	43	Wigan	18669
9	Arsenal	37891	36	Middlesboro	28141	41	Chelsea	26364	11	Blackburn	18341
21	Tottenham	36045	37	West Brom	28041	26	Charlton	26312	32	Reading	16644
46	Everton	35420	3	Middlesboro	27998	48	Bolton	26275	1	Fulham	16550
15	Sunderland	32442	8	Liverpool	27733	45	Blackburn	25287	16	Millwall	7732
33	West Ham	31294	18	Fulham	27597	27	Torquay	24650	7	Scunthorpe	6109
10	Aston Villa	29312	39	Liverpool	27378	17	West Ham	24010	25	Torquay	5974

Down as Cunningham twists the knife

Final Position: **18th**

KEY: League, Champions Lge, UEFA Cup, FA Cup, League Cup, Other

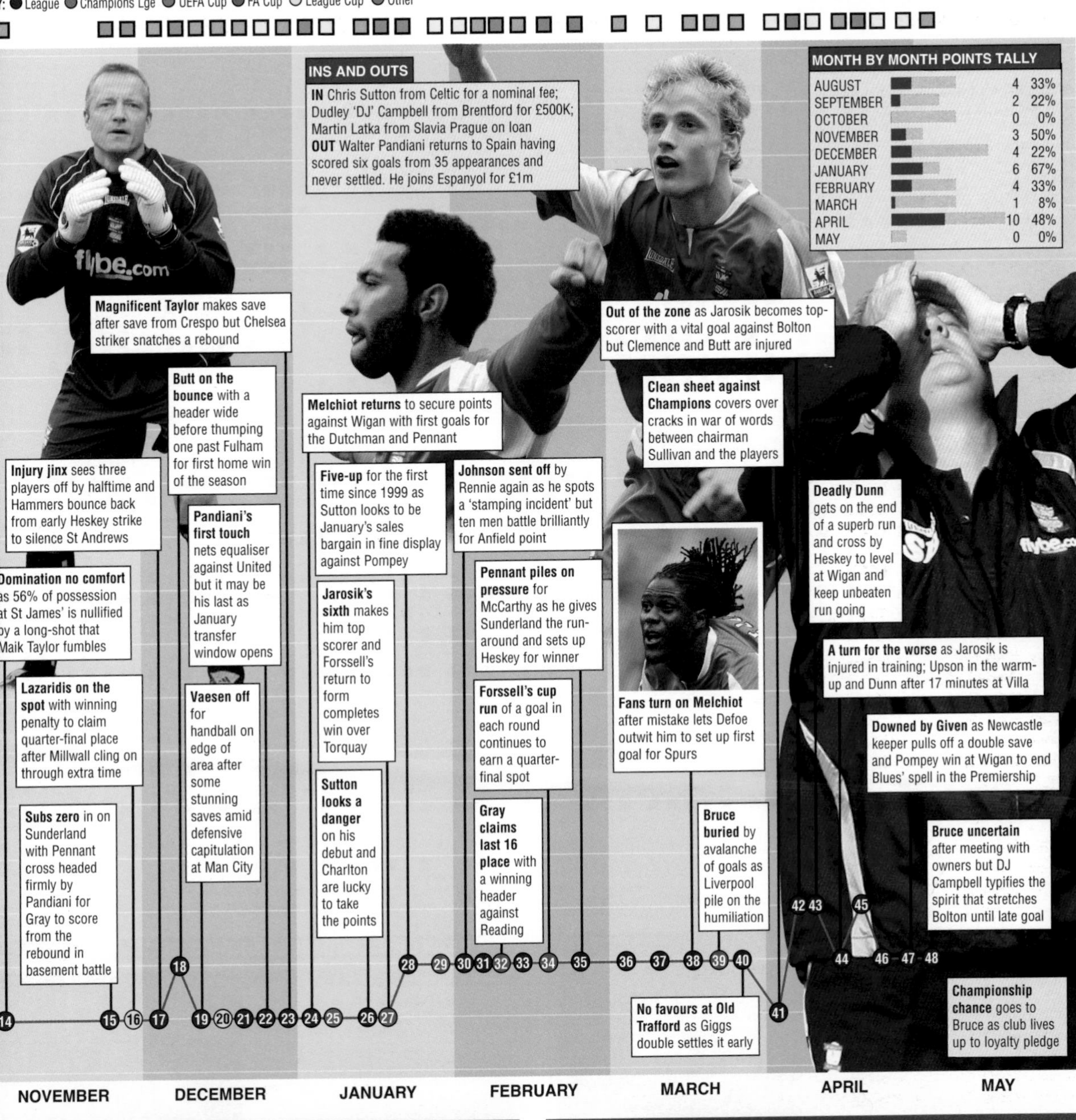

INS AND OUTS
IN Chris Sutton from Celtic for a nominal fee; Dudley 'DJ' Campbell from Brentford for £500K; Martin Latka from Slavia Prague on loan
OUT Walter Pandiani returns to Spain having scored six goals from 35 appearances and never settled. He joins Espanyol for £1m
MONTH BY MONTH POINTS TALLY
AUGUST 4 33%
SEPTEMBER 2 22%
OCTOBER 0 0%
NOVEMBER 3 50%
DECEMBER 4 22%
JANUARY 6 67%
FEBRUARY 4 33%
MARCH 1 8%
APRIL 10 48%
MAY 0 0%
Magnificent Taylor makes save after save from Crespo but Chelsea striker snatches a rebound
Butt on the bounce with a header wide before thumping one past Fulham for first home win of the season
Injury jinx sees three players off by halftime and Hammers bounce back from early Heskey strike to silence St Andrews
Domination no comfort as 56% of possession at St James' is nullified by a long-shot that Maik Taylor fumbles
Pandiani's first touch nets equaliser against United but it may be his last as January transfer window opens
Lazaridis on the spot with winning penalty to claim quarter-final place after Millwall cling on through extra time
Vaesen off for handball on edge of area after some stunning saves amid defensive capitulation at Man City
Subs zero in on Sunderland with Pennant cross headed firmly by Pandiani for Gray to score from the rebound in basement battle
Melchiot returns to secure points against Wigan with first goals for the Dutchman and Pennant
Five-up for the first time since 1999 as Sutton looks to be January's sales bargain in fine display against Pompey
Jarosik's sixth makes him top scorer and Forssell's return to form completes win over Torquay
Sutton looks a danger on his debut and Charlton are lucky to take the points
Johnson sent off by Rennie again as he spots a 'stamping incident' but ten men battle brilliantly for Anfield point
Pennant piles on pressure for McCarthy as he gives Sunderland the run-around and sets up Heskey for winner
Forssell's cup run of a goal in each round continues to earn a quarter-final spot
Gray claims last 16 place with a winning header against Reading
Out of the zone as Jarosik becomes top-scorer with a vital goal against Bolton but Clemence and Butt are injured
Clean sheet against Champions covers over cracks in war of words between chairman Sullivan and the players
Fans turn on Melchiot after mistake lets Defoe outwit him to set up first goal for Spurs
Bruce buried by avalanche of goals as Liverpool pile on the humiliation
No favours at Old Trafford as Giggs double settles it early
Deadly Dunn gets on the end of a superb run and cross by Heskey to level at Wigan and keep unbeaten run going
A turn for the worse as Jarosik is injured in training; Upson in the warm-up and Dunn after 17 minutes at Villa
Downed by Given as Newcastle keeper pulls off a double save and Pompey win at Wigan to end Blues' spell in the Premiership
Bruce uncertain after meeting with owners but DJ Campbell typifies the spirit that stretches Bolton until late goal
Championship chance goes to Bruce as club lives up to loyalty pledge
NOVEMBER
DECEMBER
JANUARY
FEBRUARY
MARCH
APRIL
MAY

GOAL ATTEMPTS

FOR — Goal attempts recorded in League games

	HOME	AWAY	TOTAL	AVE
shots on target	91	77	168	4.4
shots off target	110	76	186	4.9
TOTAL	201	153	354	9.3

Ratio of goals to shots — Average number of shots on target per League goal scored	6
Accuracy rating — Average percentage of total goal attempts which were on target	47.5

AGAINST — Goal attempts recorded in League games

	HOME	AWAY	TOTAL	AVE
shots on target	75	132	207	5.4
shots off target	96	77	173	4.6
TOTAL	171	209	380	10

Ratio of goals to shots — Average number of shots on target per League goal scored	4.1
Accuracy rating — Average percentage of total goal attempts which were on target	54.5

GOALS

Jiri Jarosik

League	5
FA Cup	1
League Cup	2
Europe	0
Other	0
TOTAL	8

League Average 332 mins between goals

	PLAYER	LGE	FAC	LC	Euro	TOT	AVE
1	Jarosik	5	1	2	0	8	332
2	Heskey	4	0	1	0	5	704
3	Forssell	3	3	2	0	8	435
4	Butt	3	0	0	0	3	640
5	Pennant	2	0	1	0	3	1570
6	Dunn	2	1	0	0	3	283
7	Pandiani	2	0	0	0	2	363
8	Gray	1	1	1	0	3	1695
9	Sutton	1	0	0	0	1	829
10	Clapham	1	0	0	0	1	1203
11	Melchiot	1	0	0	0	1	1852
12	Upson	1	0	0	0	1	2078
	Other	2	0	0	0	2	
	TOTAL	28	6	7	0	41	

SQUAD APPEARANCES

Match	1	2	3	4	5	6	7	8	9	10	11	12	13	14	15	16	17	18	19	20	21	22	23	24
Venue	A	H	H	A	H	A	A	H	A	H	A	H	H	A	A	A	H	H	A	H	A	H	A	H
Competition	L	L	L	L	L	L	W	L	L	L	L	W	L	L	L	W	L	L	L	W	L	L	L	L
Result	D	L	L	W	L	D	W	D	L	L	L	W	L	L	W	W	L	W	L	L	L	D	L	W

Match	25	26	27	28	29	30	31	32	33	34	35	36	37	38	39	40	41	42	43	44	45	46	47
Venue	A	A	H	H	A	A	H	H	A	A	H	A	H	H	H	A	H	H	A	A	H	A	H
Competition	F	L	F	L	F	L	L	F	L	F	L	L	L	L	F	L	L	L	L	L	L	L	L
Result	D	L	W	W	D	D	L	W	L	W	W	L	D	L	L	L	D	W	D	L	W	D	D

Goalkeepers
Colin Doyle
Maik Taylor
Nico Vaesen

Defenders
Alex Bruce
Jamie Clapham
Kenny Cunningham
Martin Latka
Mario Melchiot
Samuel Oji
Marcos Painter
Matthew Sadler
Martin Taylor
Olivier Tebily
Matthew Upson

Midfielders
Sam Alsop
Mathew Birley
Nicky Butt
Stephen Clemence
David Dunn
Julian Gray
Mustafa Izzet
Jiri Jarosik
Damien Johnson
Neil Kilkenny
Stan Lazaridis
Mehdi Nafti
Jermaine Pennant
Peter Till

Forwards
Sone Aluko
Dudley Campbell
Mikael Forssell
Emile Heskey
Clinton Morrison
Walter Pandiani
Chris Sutton

KEY: On all match; On bench; Subbed or sent off (Counting game); Subbed or sent off (playing less than 70 mins); Subbed on from bench (Counting Game); Subbed on (playing less than 70 mins); Subbed on and then subbed or sent off (Counting Game); Subbed on and then subbed or sent off (playing less than 70 mins); Not in 16

KEY PLAYERS - GOALSCORERS

Jiri Jarosik

Goals in the League	5
Goals in all competitions	8
Assists League goals scored by a team mate where the player delivered the final pass	0
Contribution to Attacking Power Average number of minutes between League team goals while on pitch	104
Player Strike Rate Average number of minutes between League goals scored by player	332
Club Strike Rate Average minutes between League goals scored by club	122

	PLAYER	GOALS LGE	GOALS ALL	ASSISTS	POWER	S RATE
1	Jiri Jarosik	5	8	0	104	332 mins
2	Nicky Butt	3	3	0	137	640 mins
3	Emile Heskey	4	5	5	122	704 mins
4	Jamie Clapham	1	1	2	120	1203 mins

KEY PLAYERS - MIDFIELDERS

Damien Johnson

Goals in the League	0
Goals in all competitions	0
Assists League goals scored by a team mate where the player delivered the final pass	2
Defensive Rating Average number of mins between League goals conceded while on the pitch	73
Contribution to Attacking Power Average number of minutes between League team goals while on pitch	106
Scoring Difference Defensive Rating minus Contribution to Attacking Power	-33

	PLAYER	GOALS LGE	GOALS ALL	ASSISTS	DEF RATE	POWER	SC DIFF
1	Damien Johnson	0	0	2	73	106	-33 mins
2	Jiri Jarosik	5	8	0	69	104	-35 mins
3	Stan Lazaridis	0	0	0	65	107	-42 mins
4	Jermaine Pennant	2	3	8	70	126	-56 mins

PLAYER APPEARANCES

	AGE (on 01/07/06)	IN NAMED 16	APPEARANCES	COUNTING GAMES	MINUTES ON PITCH	APPEARANCES	MINUTES ON PITCH	THIS SEASON	HOME COUNTRY
Goalkeepers									
Colin Doyle	20	0	0	0	0	0	0	-	England
Maik Taylor	34	38	34	34	3060	41	3690	7	N Ireland (114)
Nico Vaesen	36	38	4	4	360	7	660	-	Belgium
Defenders									
Alex Bruce	21	11	6	3	277	12	645	-	England
Jamie Clapham	30	17	16	12	1203	23	1710	-	England
Kenny Cunningham	35	31	31	30	2665	33	2845	4	Rep of Ireland (15)
Martin Latka	21	8	6	6	520	7	610	-	Czech Republic
Mario Melchiot	29	23	23	19	1852	29	2407	-	Holland
Samuel Oji	20	0	0	0	0	1	1	-	England
Marcos Painter	19	9	4	2	207	9	498	-	England
Matthew Sadler	21	8	8	8	720	9	752	-	England
Martin Taylor	26	24	21	19	1800	28	2406	-	England
Olivier Tebily	30	24	16	10	1047	19	1272	-	Ivory Coast
Matthew Upson	27	25	24	23	2078	29	2558	3	England (10)
Midfielders									
Sam Alsop	21	0	0	0	0	0	0	-	England
Mathew Birley	19	2	1	0	26	3	99	-	England
Nicky Butt	31	26	24	18	1920	29	2376	-	England
Stephen Clemence	28	20	15	8	951	21	1489	-	England
David Dunn	26	15	15	3	566	20	884	-	England
Julian Gray	26	24	21	18	1695	27	2249	-	England
Mustafa Izzet	31	18	16	7	920	18	1001	-	Turkey
Jiri Jarosik	28	25	24	16	1658	32	2165	2	Czech Republic (2)
Damien Johnson	27	31	31	29	2639	38	3253	5	N Ireland (114)
Neil Kilkenny	20	21	18	3	672	25	1019	-	England
Stan Lazaridis	33	21	17	12	1173	20	1369	2	Australia (42)
Mehdi Nafti	27	2	1	1	70	1	70	1	Tunisia (21)
Jermaine Pennant	23	38	38	32	3139	48	4060	-	England
Peter Till	20	0	0	0	0	1	6	-	England
Forwards									
Sone Aluko	17	1	0	0	0	0	0	-	England
Dudley Campbell	25	13	11	3	507	11	507	-	England
Mikael Forssell	25	30	27	9	1306	35	1847	5	Finland (42)
Emile Heskey	28	35	34	28	2815	40	3297	-	England
Clinton Morrison	27	1	1	0	4	1	4	4	Rep of Ireland (15)
Walter Pandiani	30	19	17	5	725	21	966	-	Uruguay
Chris Sutton	33	10	10	8	829	11	919	-	England

KEY: LEAGUE | ALL COMPS | CAPS | (MAY FIFA RANKING)

TEAM OF THE SEASON

TAYLOR — CG 34 DR 70

MELCHIOT — CG 19 DR 71

UPSON — CG 23 DR 65

TAYLOR — CG 19 DR 86

CUNNINGHAM — CG 30 DR 65

PENNANT — CG 32 SD -56

JAROSIK — CG 16 SD -35

JOHNSON — CG 29 SD -33

LAZARIDIS — CG 12 SD -42

HESKEY — CG 28 AP 122

FORSSELL* — CG 9 SR 435

KEY: DR = Defensive Rate, SD = Scoring Difference AP = Attacking Power SR = Strike Rate, CG=Counting games – League games playing at least 70 minutes

TOP POINT EARNERS

Jiri Jarosik

Counting Games League games when player was on pitch for at least 70 minutes	16
Average points Average League points taken in Counting games	1.13
Club Average points Average points taken in League games	0.89

	PLAYER	GAMES	PTS
1	Jiri Jarosik	16	1.13
2	Damien Johnson	29	1.00
3	Kenny Cunningham	30	0.97
4	Emile Heskey	28	0.96
5	Mario Melchiot	19	0.95
6	Martin Taylor	19	0.95
7	Matthew Upson	23	0.87
8	Julian Gray	18	0.83
9	Stan Lazaridis	12	0.83
10	Maik Taylor	34	0.82

KEY PLAYERS - DEFENDERS

Martin Taylor

Goals Conceded in the League Number of League goals conceded while the player was on the pitch	21
Goals Conceded in all competitions Total number of goals conceded while the player was on the pitch	30
League minutes played Number of minutes played in league matches	1800
Clean Sheets In games when the player was on pitch for at least 70 minutes	6
Defensive Rating Average number of mins between League goals conceded while on the pitch	86
Club Defensive Rating Average number of mins between League goals conceded by the club this season	68

	PLAYER	CON LGE	CON ALL	MINS	C SHEETS	DEF RATE
1	Martin Taylor	21	30	1800	6	86 mins
2	Mario Melchiot	26	37	1852	6	71 mins
3	Kenny Cunningham	41	48	2665	9	65 mins
4	Matthew Upson	32	38	2078	5	65 mins

KEY GOALKEEPER

Maik Taylor

Goals Conceded in the League Number of League goals conceded while the player was on the pitch	44
Goals Conceded in all competitions Total number of goals conceded while the player was on the pitch	56
League minutes played Number of minutes played in league matches	3060
Clean Sheets In games when the player was on pitch for at least 70 minutes	8
Goals to Shots Ratio The average number of shots on target per each League goal conceded	4.3
Defensive Rating Ave mins between League goals conceded while on the pitch	70

BOOKINGS

Mustafa Izzet

League Yellow	3
League Red	1
All competitions Yellow	3
All competitions Red	1

League Average **230** mins between cards

	PLAYER	LEAGUE 3Y	LEAGUE 1R	TOTAL 3Y	TOTAL 1R	AVE
1	Izzet	3	1	3	1	230
2	Clemence	4	0	6	0	237
3	Latka	2	0	3	0	260
4	Butt	5	1	6	1	320
5	Tebily	3	0	4	0	349
6	Sutton	2	0	2	0	414
7	Johnson	5	1	7	1	439
8	Cunningham	5	1	5	1	444
9	Heskey	5	1	5	1	469
10	Clapham	2	0	2	0	601
11	Melchiot	3	0	3	0	617
12	Kilkenny	0	1	0	1	672
13	Sadler	1	0	1	0	720
14	Pandiani	1	0	2	0	725
15	Pennant	4	0	4	0	784
	Other	8	0	13	0	
	TOTAL	53	6	66	6	

WEST BROMWICH ALBION

Bryan Robson couldn't repeat the astonishing scenes from the final day of the 2004-05 season. He had a surfeit of strikers after tempting **Nathan Ellington** away from Wigan to join **Kanu**, **Robert Earnshaw**, **Kevin Campbell** and **Geoff Horsfield**, with **Diomansy Kamara** joining in from advanced midfield.

But as they chopped and changed, or were chopped and left, no scoring formula emerged. That Kanu tops the club chart is explained partly by scoring five goals at a Strike Rate of one every 319 minutes, but mostly by playing sufficient games to qualify ahead of Ellington.

Steve Watson played midfield and defence but had the best Defensive Rating at the club. **Tomasz Kuszczak** made the save of the season and his Defensive Rating of a goal conceded every 66 minutes is better than most relegated keepers.

NICKNAME: BAGGIES

KEY: Won Drawn Lost

1	prem	**Man City**	A	D	0-0	
2	prem	**Portsmouth**	H	W	2-1	Horsfield 2,59
3	prem	**Chelsea**	A	L	0-4	
4	prem	**Birmingham**	H	L	2-3	Horsfield 12,64
5	prem	**Wigan**	H	L	1-2	Greening 26
6	prem	**Sunderland**	A	D	1-1	Gera 90
7	ccr2	**Bradford**	H	W	4-1	Ellington 23,72; Kamara 32; Earnshaw 77
8	prem	**Charlton**	H	L	1-2	Davies, C 51
9	prem	**Blackburn**	A	L	0-2	
10	prem	**Arsenal**	H	W	2-1	Kanu 38; Carter 76
11	prem	**Bolton**	A	L	0-2	
12	ccr3	**Fulham**	A	W	3-2	Earnshaw 3; Kanu 88; Inamoto 99
13	prem	**Newcastle**	H	L	0-3	
14	prem	**West Ham**	A	L	0-1	
15	prem	**Everton**	H	W	4-0	Ellington 45 pen,69; Clement 51; Earnshaw 90
16	prem	**Middlesbrough**	A	D	2-2	Ellington 18; Kanu 57
17	ccr4	**Man Utd**	A	L	1-3	Ellington 77
18	prem	**Fulham**	H	D	0-0	
19	prem	**Man City**	H	W	2-0	Kamara 5; Campbell 61
20	prem	**Portsmouth**	A	L	0-1	
21	prem	**Man Utd**	A	L	0-3	
22	prem	**Tottenham**	H	W	2-0	Kanu 23,52
23	prem	**Liverpool**	A	L	0-1	
24	prem	**Aston Villa**	H	L	1-2	Watson 76
25	facr3	**Reading**	H	D	1-1	Gera 82 pen
26	prem	**Wigan**	A	W	1-0	Albrechtsen 56
27	facr3r	**Reading**	A	L	2-3	Chaplow 9,32
28	prem	**Sunderland**	H	L	0-1	
29	prem	**Charlton**	A	D	0-0	
30	prem	**Blackburn**	H	W	2-0	Campbell 6; Greening 32
31	prem	**Fulham**	A	L	1-6	Campbell 85
32	prem	**Middlesbrough**	H	L	0-2	
33	prem	**Chelsea**	H	L	1-2	Kanu 88
34	prem	**Birmingham**	A	D	1-1	Ellington 70
35	prem	**Man Utd**	H	L	1-2	Ellington 78
36	prem	**Tottenham**	A	L	1-2	Davies, C 20
37	prem	**Liverpool**	H	L	0-2	
38	prem	**Aston Villa**	A	D	0-0	
39	prem	**Arsenal**	A	L	1-3	Quashie 72
40	prem	**Bolton**	H	D	0-0	
41	prem	**Newcastle**	A	L	0-3	
42	prem	**West Ham**	H	L	0-1	
43	prem	**Everton**	A	D	2-2	Gera 14; Martinez 47

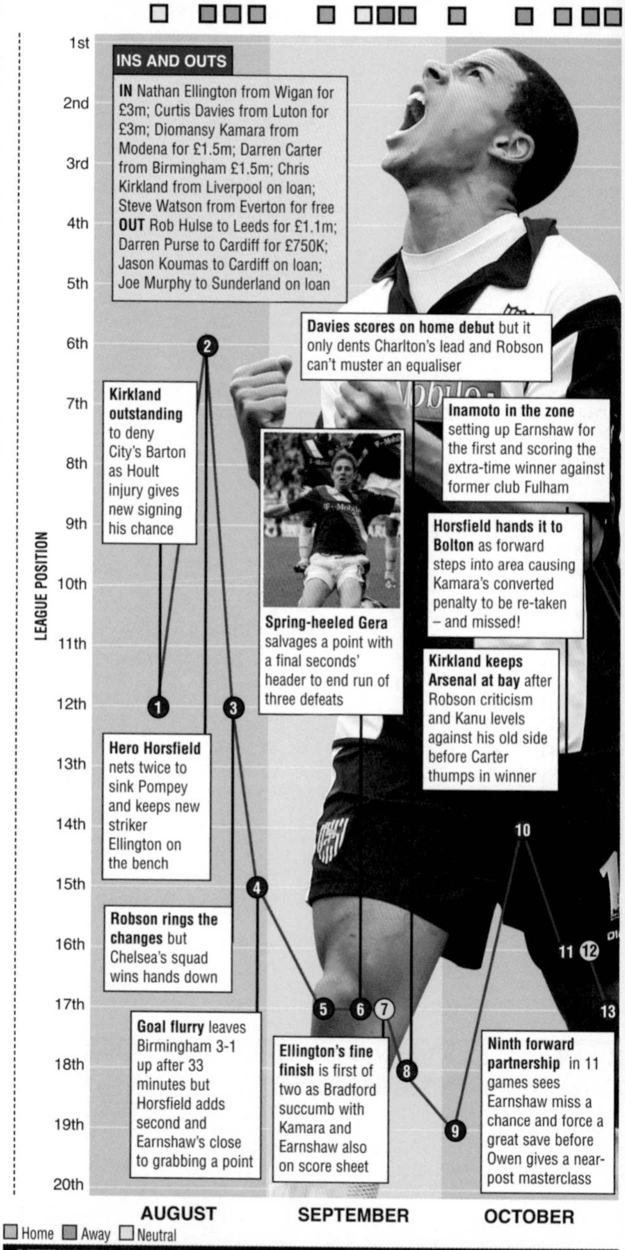

INS AND OUTS

IN Nathan Ellington from Wigan for £3m; Curtis Davies from Luton for £3m; Diomansy Kamara from Modena for £1.5m; Darren Carter from Birmingham £1.5m; Chris Kirkland from Liverpool on loan; Steve Watson from Everton for free
OUT Rob Hulse to Leeds for £1.1m; Darren Purse to Cardiff for £750K; Jason Koumas to Cardiff on loan; Joe Murphy to Sunderland on loan

LEAGUE POSITION: 1st, 2nd, 3rd, 4th, 5th, 6th, 7th, 8th, 9th, 10th, 11th, 12th, 13th, 14th, 15th, 16th, 17th, 18th, 19th, 20th

AUGUST — SEPTEMBER — OCTOBER

1 **Kirkland outstanding** to deny City's Barton as Hoult injury gives new signing his chance

2 **Hero Horsfield** nets twice to sink Pompey and keeps new striker Ellington on the bench

3 **Robson rings the changes** but Chelsea's squad wins hands down

4 **Goal flurry** leaves Birmingham 3-1 up after 33 minutes but Horsfield adds second and Earnshaw's close to grabbing a point

6 **Spring-heeled Gera** salvages a point with a final seconds' header to end run of three defeats

7 **Ellington's fine finish** is first of two as Bradford succumb with Kamara and Earnshaw also on score sheet

8 **Davies scores on home debut** but it only dents Charlton's lead and Robson can't muster an equaliser

9 **Ninth forward partnership** in 11 games sees Earnshaw miss a chance and force a great save before Owen gives a near-post masterclass

10 **Kirkland keeps Arsenal at bay** after Robson criticism and Kanu levels against his old side before Carter thumps in winner

11 **Horsfield hands it to Bolton** as forward steps into area causing Kamara's converted penalty to be re-taken – and missed!

12 **Inamoto in the zone** setting up Earnshaw for the first and scoring the extra-time winner against former club Fulham

Home Away Neutral

ATTENDANCES

HOME GROUND: THE HAWTHORNS CAPACITY: 28003 AVERAGE LEAGUE AT HOME: 25403

21	Man Utd	67972	6	Sunderland	31657	29	Charlton	25921	40	Bolton	23181
41	Newcastle	52272	34	Birmingham	28041	5	Wigan	25617	18	Fulham	23144
17	Man Utd	48924	35	Man Utd	27623	19	Man City	25472	31	Fulham	21508
23	Liverpool	44192	37	Liverpool	27576	15	Everton	24784	9	Blackburn	20721
1	Man City	42983	22	Tottenham	27510	42	West Ham	24462	20	Portsmouth	20052
3	Chelsea	41201	24	Aston Villa	27073	2	Portsmouth	24404	25	Reading	19197
43	Everton	39671	16	Middlesboro	27041	11	Bolton	24151	26	Wigan	17421
39	Arsenal	38167	10	Arsenal	26604	32	Middlesboro	24061	27	Reading	16737
36	Tottenham	36152	33	Chelsea	26581	4	Birmingham	23993	7	Bradford	10792
14	West Ham	34325	28	Sunderland	26464	30	Blackburn	23993	12	Fulham	7373
38	Aston Villa	33303	13	Newcastle	26216	8	Charlton	23909			

Too many strikers spoil the Brom

Final Position: **19th**

KEY: ● League ● Champions Lge ● UEFA Cup ● FA Cup ○ League Cup ● Other

INS AND OUTS

IN Nigel Quashie from Southampton for £1.4m; Jan Kozak from Artmedia Bratislava (Slovakia) and Williams Martinez from Defensor (Uruguay) on loan
OUT Robert Earnshaw to Norwich for £3.5m; Darren Moore to Derby for an undisclosed fee; Riccardo Scimeca to Cardiff City for free

MONTH BY MONTH POINTS TALLY

Month	Points	%
AUGUST	4	33%
SEPTEMBER	1	11%
OCTOBER	3	25%
NOVEMBER	4	44%
DECEMBER	7	39%
JANUARY	4	33%
FEBRUARY	3	33%
MARCH	1	8%
APRIL	2	13%
MAY	1	17%

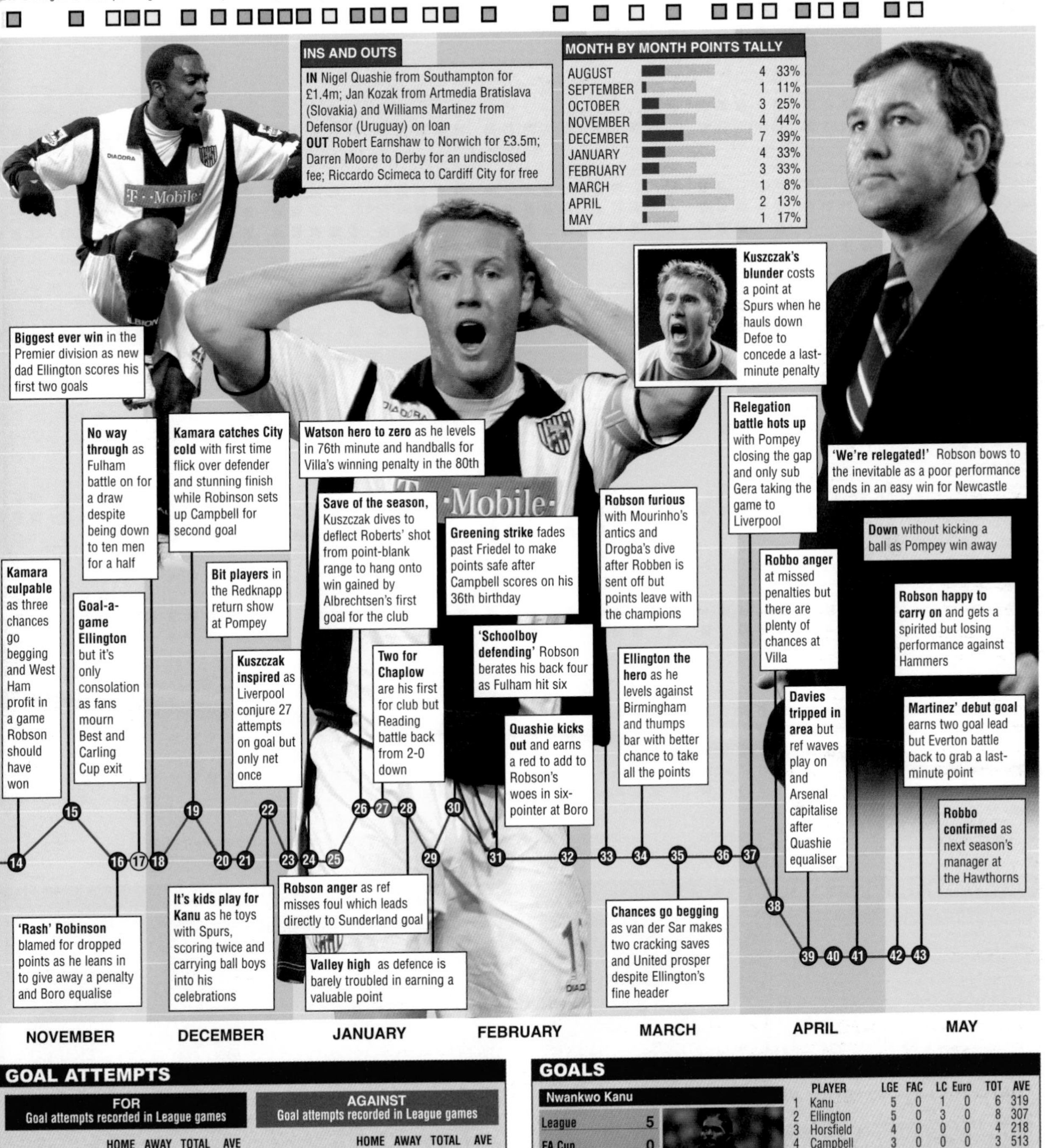

Kuszczak's blunder costs a point at Spurs when he hauls down Defoe to concede a last-minute penalty
Biggest ever win in the Premier division as new dad Ellington scores his first two goals
No way through as Fulham battle on for a draw despite being down to ten men for a half
Kamara catches City cold with first time flick over defender and stunning finish while Robinson sets up Campbell for second goal
Watson hero to zero as he levels in 76th minute and handballs for Villa's winning penalty in the 80th
Relegation battle hots up with Pompey closing the gap and only sub Gera taking the game to Liverpool
'We're relegated!' Robson bows to the inevitable as a poor performance ends in an easy win for Newcastle
Kamara culpable as three chances go begging and West Ham profit in a game Robson should have won
Goal-a-game Ellington but it's only consolation as fans mourn Best and Carling Cup exit
Bit players in the Redknapp return show at Pompey
Save of the season, Kuszczak dives to deflect Roberts' shot from point-blank range to hang onto win gained by Albrechtsen's first goal for the club
Greening strike fades past Friedel to make points safe after Campbell scores on his 36th birthday
Robson furious with Mourinho's antics and Drogba's dive after Robben is sent off but points leave with the champions
Down without kicking a ball as Pompey win away
Robbo anger at missed penalties but there are plenty of chances at Villa
Robson happy to carry on and gets a spirited but losing performance against Hammers
Kuszczak inspired as Liverpool conjure 27 attempts on goal but only net once
Two for Chaplow are his first for club but Reading battle back from 2-0 down
'Schoolboy defending' Robson berates his back four as Fulham hit six
Ellington the hero as he levels against Birmingham and thumps bar with better chance to take all the points
Davies tripped in area but ref waves play on and Arsenal capitalise after Quashie equaliser
Martinez' debut goal earns two goal lead but Everton battle back to grab a last-minute point
Quashie kicks out and earns a red to add to Robson's woes in six-pointer at Boro
Robbo confirmed as next season's manager at the Hawthorns
14 15 16 17 18 19 20 21 22 23 24 25 26 27 28 29 30 31 32 33 34 35 36 37 38 39 40 41 42 43
'Rash' Robinson blamed for dropped points as he leans in to give away a penalty and Boro equalise
It's kids play for Kanu as he toys with Spurs, scoring twice and carrying ball boys into his celebrations
Robson anger as ref misses foul which leads directly to Sunderland goal
Valley high as defence is barely troubled in earning a valuable point
Chances go begging as van der Sar makes two cracking saves and United prosper despite Ellington's fine header
NOVEMBER
DECEMBER
JANUARY
FEBRUARY
MARCH
APRIL
MAY

GOAL ATTEMPTS

FOR — Goal attempts recorded in League games

	HOME	AWAY	TOTAL	AVE
shots on target	92	69	161	4.2
shots off target	95	72	167	4.4
TOTAL	187	141	328	8.6

Ratio of goals to shots — Average number of shots on target per League goal scored: **5.2**

Accuracy rating — Average percentage of total goal attempts which were on target: **49.1**

AGAINST — Goal attempts recorded in League games

	HOME	AWAY	TOTAL	AVE
shots on target	94	160	254	6.7
shots off target	93	69	162	4.3
TOTAL	187	229	416	10.9

Ratio of goals to shots — Average number of shots on target per League goal scored: **4.4**

Accuracy rating — Average percentage of total goal attempts which were on target: **61.1**

GOALS

Nwankwo Kanu

League	5
FA Cup	0
League Cup	1
Europe	0
Other	0
TOTAL	6

League Average **319** mins between goals

	PLAYER	LGE	FAC	LC	Euro	TOT	AVE
1	Kanu	5	0	1	0	6	319
2	Ellington	5	0	3	0	8	307
3	Horsfield	4	0	0	0	4	218
4	Campbell	3	0	0	0	3	513
5	Davies, C	2	0	0	0	2	1485
6	Gera	2	1	0	0	3	543
7	Greening	2	0	0	0	2	1644
8	Carter	1	0	0	0	1	1109
9	Watson	1	0	0	0	1	2309
10	Earnshaw	1	0	2	0	3	415
11	Albrechtsen	1	0	0	0	1	2513
12	Kamara	1	0	1	0	2	1783
13	Martinez	1	0	0	0	1	135
14	Clement	1	0	0	0	1	2673
15	Quashie	1	0	0	0	1	761
	Other	0	2	1	0	3	
	TOTAL	31	3	8	0	42	

SQUAD APPEARANCES

Match	1	2	3	4	5	6	7	8	9	10	11	12	13	14	15	16	17	18	19	20	21	22	23	24	25	26	27	28	29	30	31	32	33	34	35	36	37	38	39	40	41	42
Venue	A	H	A	H	H	A	H	H	A	H	A	A	H	A	H	A	A	H	H	A	A	H	A	H	H	A	A	H	A	H	A	H	H	A	H	A	H	A	A	H	A	H
Competition	L	L	L	L	L	L	W	L	L	L	L	W	L	L	L	L	W	L	L	L	L	L	L	L	F	L	F	L	L	L	L	L	L	L	L	L	L	L	L	L	L	L
Result	D	W	L	L	L	D	W	L	L	W	L	W	L	L	W	D	L	D	W	L	L	W	L	L	D	W	L	L	D	W	L	L	L	D	L	L	L	D	L	D	L	L

Goalkeepers
Russell Hoult
Chris Kirkland
Tomasz Kuszczak

Defenders
Martin Albrechtsen
Neil Clement
Curtis Davies
Thomas Gaardsoe
Jatred Hodgkiss
Williams Martinez
Darren Moore
Paul Robinson
Riccardo Scimeca

Midfielders
Darren Carter
Richard Chaplow
Rob Davies
Lloyd Dyer
Zoltan Gera
Jonathan Greening
Junichi Inamoto
Andy Johnson
Jan Kozak
Nigel Quashie
Ronnie Wallwork
Steve Watson

Forwards
Kevin Campbell
Robert Earnshaw
Nathan Ellington
Geoff Horsfield
Diomansy Mehdi Kamara
Nwankwo Kanu
Stuart Nicholson

KEY: On all match | On bench | Subbed or sent off (Counting game) | Subbed or sent off (playing less than 70 mins) | Subbed on from bench (Counting Game) | Subbed on (playing less than 70 mins) | Subbed on and then subbed or sent off (Counting Game) | Subbed on and then subbed or sent off (playing less than 70 mins) | Not in 16

KEY PLAYERS - GOALSCORERS

Nwankwo Kanu

Goals in the League	5
Goals in all competitions	6
Assists League goals scored by a team mate where the player delivered the final pass	5
Contribution to Attacking Power Average number of minutes between League team goals while on pitch	89
Player Strike Rate Average number of minutes between League goals scored by player	319
Club Strike Rate Average minutes between League goals scored by club	110

	PLAYER	GOALS LGE	GOALS ALL	ASSISTS	POWER	S RATE
1	Nwankwo Kanu	5	6	5	89	319 mins
2	Curtis Davies	2	2	0	114	1485 mins
3	Jonathan Greening	2	2	4	110	1644 mins
4	Diomansy Mehdi Kamara	1	2	0	111	1783 mins

KEY PLAYERS - MIDFIELDERS

Steve Watson

Goals in the League	1
Goals in all competitions	1
Assists League goals scored by a team mate where the player delivered the final pass	3
Defensive Rating Average number of mins between League goals conceded while on the pitch	68
Contribution to Attacking Power Average number of minutes between League team goals while on pitch	96
Scoring Difference Defensive Rating minus Contribution to Attacking Power	-28

	PLAYER	GOALS LGE	GOALS ALL	ASSISTS	DEF RATE	POWER	SC DIFF
1	Steve Watson	1	1	3	68	96	-28 mins
2	Ronnie Wallwork	0	0	3	64	93	-29 mins
3	Junichi Inamoto	0	1	4	64	109	-45 mins
4	Jonathan Greening	2	2	4	61	110	-49 mins

PLAYER APPEARANCES

	AGE (on 01/07/06)	IN NAMED 16	APPEARANCES	COUNTING GAMES	MINUTES ON PITCH	APPEARANCES	MINUTES ON PITCH	THIS SEASON	HOME COUNTRY
Goalkeepers									
Russell Hoult	33	13	1	0	30	2	120	-	England
Chris Kirkland	25	23	10	10	900	12	1110	4	England (10)
Tomasz Kuszczak	24	38	28	27	2490	30	2700	1	Poland (29)
Defenders									
Martin Albrechtsen	26	35	31	26	2513	35	2895	-	Denmark
Neil Clement	27	34	31	29	2673	34	2973	-	England
Curtis Davies	21	34	33	33	2970	35	3180	-	England
Thomas Gaardsoe	26	8	7	5	561	9	637	1	Denmark (19)
Patred Hodgkiss	19	1	1	0	28	1	28	-	England
Williams Martinez	23	5	2	1	135	2	135	1	Uruguay (22)
Darren Moore	32	14	5	2	245	9	590	-	England
Paul Robinson	27	33	33	31	2862	36	3162	8	England (10)
Riccardo Scimeca	31	3	2	2	180	4	345	-	England
Midfielders									
Darren Carter	22	29	20	10	1109	25	1552	-	England
Richard Chaplow	21	14	7	3	374	11	676	-	England
Rob Davies	19	1	0	0	0	1	31	-	Wales
Lloyd Dyer	23	0	0	0	0	2	160	-	England
Zoltan Gera	27	15	15	10	1086	16	1105	4	Hungary (54)
Jonathan Greening	27	38	38	37	3287	41	3496	-	England
Junichi Inamoto	26	25	22	14	1525	26	1876	5	Japan (18)
Andy Johnson	32	8	8	6	644	8	644	-	Wales
Jan Kozak	26	9	6	2	348	6	348	-	Slovakia
Nigel Quashie	27	9	9	8	761	9	761	6	Scotland (85)
Ronnie Wallwork	28	31	31	30	2706	35	3111	-	England
Steve Watson	32	32	30	22	2309	31	2399	-	England
Forwards									
Kevin Campbell	36	29	29	10	1539	31	1599	-	England
Robert Earnshaw	25	17	12	3	415	16	766	7	Wales (74)
Nathan Ellington	25	32	31	11	1535	35	1887	-	England
Geoff Horsfield	32	20	18	7	870	20	973	-	England
Diomansy Kamara	25	27	26	14	1783	29	1995	8	Senegal (28)
Nwankwo Kanu	29	25	25	14	1597	28	1808	8	Nigeria (11)
Stuart Nicholson	19	6	4	0	62	5	77	-	England

KEY: LEAGUE ALL COMPS CAPS (MAY FIFA RANKING)

TEAM OF THE SEASON

KEY: DR = Defensive Rate, SD = Scoring Difference AP = Attacking Power SR = Strike Rate, CG=Counting games – League games playing at least 70 minutes

TOP POINT EARNERS

Junichi Inamoto

Counting Games League games when player was on pitch for at least 70 minutes	14
Average points Average League points taken in Counting games	1.14
Club Average points Average points taken in League games	0.79

	PLAYER	GAMES	PTS
1	Junichi Inamoto	14	1.14
2	Steve Watson	22	0.91
3	Neil Clement	29	0.86
4	Nwankwo Kanu	14	0.86
5	Diomansy Mehdi Kamara	14	0.86
6	Ronnie Wallwork	30	0.83
7	Tomasz Kuszczak	27	0.81
8	Jonathan Greening	37	0.81
9	Curtis Davies	33	0.79
10	Paul Robinson	31	0.74

KEY PLAYERS - DEFENDERS

Paul Robinson

Goals Conceded in the League Number of League goals conceded while the player was on the pitch	44
Goals Conceded in all competitions Total number of goals conceded while the player was on the pitch	50
League minutes played Number of minutes played in league matches	2862
Clean Sheets In games when the player was on pitch for at least 70 minutes	8
Defensive Rating Average number of mins between League goals conceded while on the pitch	65
Club Defensive Rating Average number of mins between League goals conceded by the club this season	59

	PLAYER	CON LGE	CON ALL	MINS	C SHEETS	DEF RATE
1	Paul Robinson	44	50	2862	8	65 mins
2	Curtis Davies	48	52	2970	9	62 mins
3	Neil Clement	44	50	2673	9	61 mins
4	Martin Albrechtsen	45	53	2513	5	56 mins

KEY GOALKEEPER

Tomasz Kuszczak

Goals Conceded in the League Number of League goals conceded while the player was on the pitch	38
Goals Conceded in all competitions Total number of goals conceded while the player was on the pitch	41
League minutes played Number of minutes played in league matches	2490
Clean Sheets In games when the player was on pitch for at least 70 minutes	9
Goals to Shots Ratio The average number of shots on target per each League goal conceded	4.8
Defensive Rating Ave mins between League goals conceded while on the pitch	66

BOOKINGS

Ronnie Wallwork

League Yellow	11
League Red	0
All competitions Yellow	12
All competitions Red	0
League Average **246** mins between cards	

	PLAYER	LEAGUE Y	LEAGUE R	TOTAL Y	TOTAL R	AVE
1	Wallwork	11	0	12	0	246
2	Gaardsoe	2	0	2	0	280
3	Quashie	1	1	1	1	380
4	Robinson	7	0	9	1	408
5	Horsfield	2	0	2	0	435
6	Carter	2	0	3	0	554
7	Watson	4	0	4	0	577
8	Kamara	3	0	3	0	594
9	Johnson	1	0	1	0	644
10	Clement	4	0	4	0	668
11	Gera	1	0	1	0	1086
12	Albrechtsen	2	0	2	1	1256
13	Campbell	1	0	1	0	1539
14	Greening	2	0	2	0	1643
15	Kuszczak	1	0	1	0	2490
	Other	0	0	0	0	
	TOTAL	**44**	**1**	**48**	**3**	

SUNDERLAND

The worst points record in the Premiership again! Mick McCarthy and his side never seemed equipped to even make a pretence at Premiership status. They recorded almost twice as many defeats as they managed points and never found a way to break down opposition defences.

By the time Kevin Ball took over it was already about trying to salvage some hope for the Championship in 2006-07.

Kelvin Davis was the keeper on the receiving end, conceding a goal every 52 minutes. That was the best Defensive Rating in the club as it turned out and only matched by on-loan **Justin Hoyte**.

Poor **Jonathan Stead** played 1689 minutes and only managed one goal. **Anthony Le Tallec** didn't play enough to make the charts but his four goals came at a Strike Rate of one every 311 minutes.

NICKNAME: MACKEMS/BLACKCATS

KEY: Won Drawn Lost

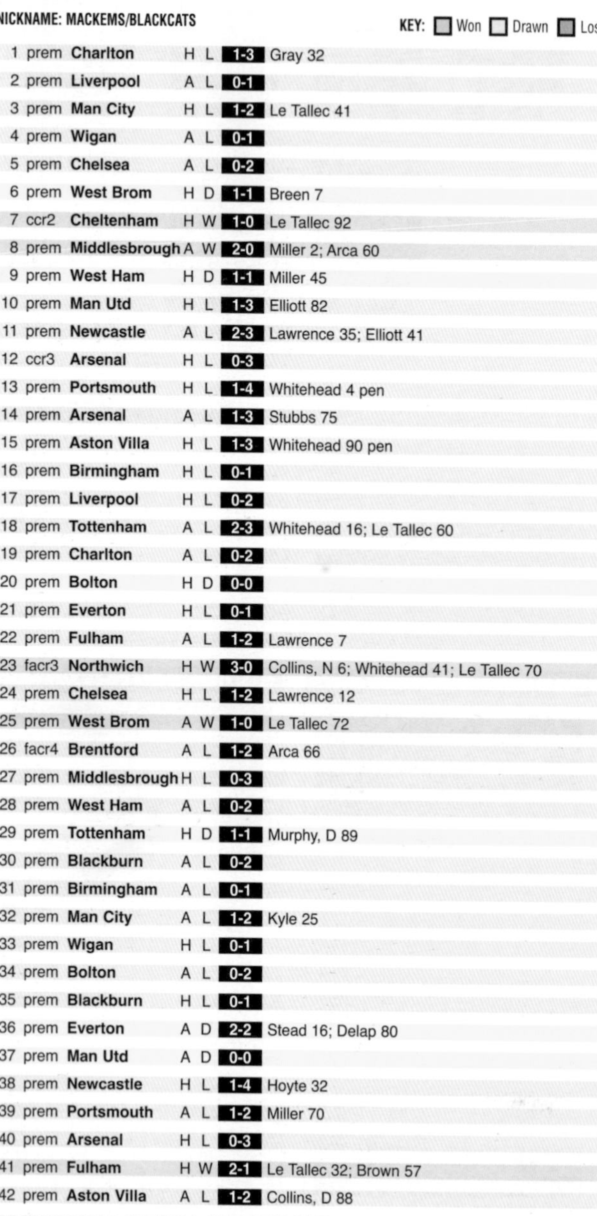

1	prem	**Charlton**	H	L	1-3	Gray 32
2	prem	**Liverpool**	A	L	0-1	
3	prem	**Man City**	H	L	1-2	Le Tallec 41
4	prem	**Wigan**	A	L	0-1	
5	prem	**Chelsea**	A	L	0-2	
6	prem	**West Brom**	H	D	1-1	Breen 7
7	ccr2	**Cheltenham**	H	W	1-0	Le Tallec 92
8	prem	**Middlesbrough**	A	W	2-0	Miller 2; Arca 60
9	prem	**West Ham**	H	D	1-1	Miller 45
10	prem	**Man Utd**	H	L	1-3	Elliott 82
11	prem	**Newcastle**	A	L	2-3	Lawrence 35; Elliott 41
12	ccr3	**Arsenal**	H	L	0-3	
13	prem	**Portsmouth**	H	L	1-4	Whitehead 4 pen
14	prem	**Arsenal**	A	L	1-3	Stubbs 75
15	prem	**Aston Villa**	H	L	1-3	Whitehead 90 pen
16	prem	**Birmingham**	H	L	0-1	
17	prem	**Liverpool**	H	L	0-2	
18	prem	**Tottenham**	A	L	2-3	Whitehead 16; Le Tallec 60
19	prem	**Charlton**	A	L	0-2	
20	prem	**Bolton**	H	D	0-0	
21	prem	**Everton**	H	L	0-1	
22	prem	**Fulham**	A	L	1-2	Lawrence 7
23	facr3	**Northwich**	H	W	3-0	Collins, N 6; Whitehead 41; Le Tallec 70
24	prem	**Chelsea**	H	L	1-2	Lawrence 12
25	prem	**West Brom**	A	W	1-0	Le Tallec 72
26	facr4	**Brentford**	A	L	1-2	Arca 66
27	prem	**Middlesbrough**	H	L	0-3	
28	prem	**West Ham**	A	L	0-2	
29	prem	**Tottenham**	H	D	1-1	Murphy, D 89
30	prem	**Blackburn**	A	L	0-2	
31	prem	**Birmingham**	A	L	0-1	
32	prem	**Man City**	A	L	1-2	Kyle 25
33	prem	**Wigan**	H	L	0-1	
34	prem	**Bolton**	A	L	0-2	
35	prem	**Blackburn**	H	L	0-1	
36	prem	**Everton**	A	D	2-2	Stead 16; Delap 80
37	prem	**Man Utd**	A	D	0-0	
38	prem	**Newcastle**	H	L	1-4	Hoyte 32
39	prem	**Portsmouth**	A	L	1-2	Miller 70
40	prem	**Arsenal**	H	L	0-3	
41	prem	**Fulham**	H	W	2-1	Le Tallec 32; Brown 57
42	prem	**Aston Villa**	A	L	1-2	Collins, D 88

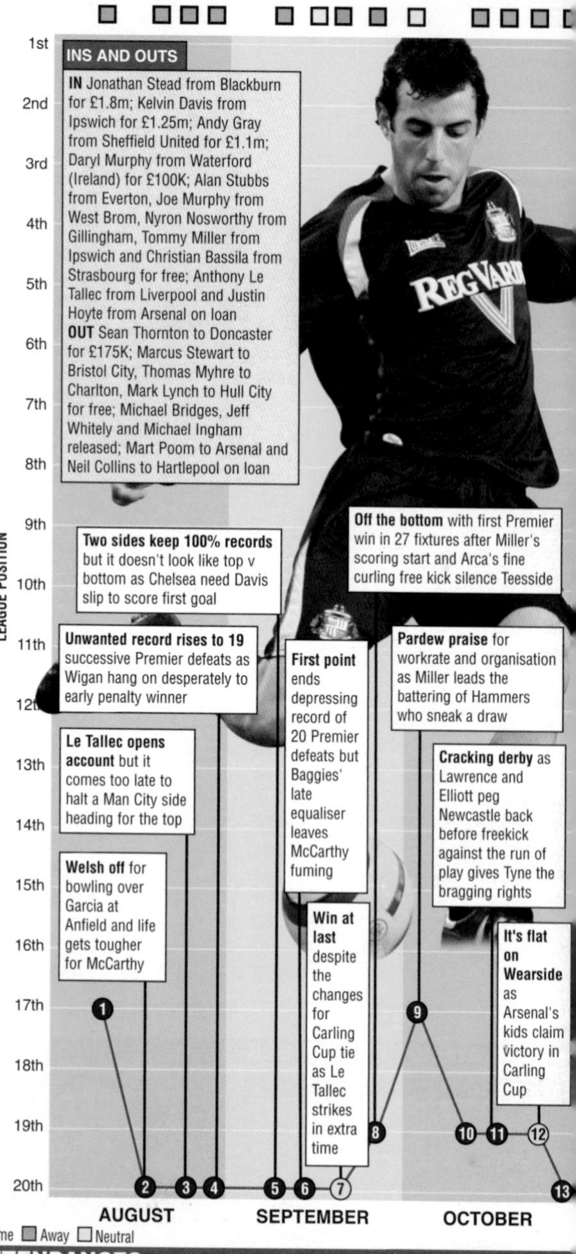

LEAGUE POSITION

1st 2nd 3rd 4th 5th 6th 7th 8th 9th 10th 11th 12th 13th 14th 15th 16th 17th 18th 19th 20th

INS AND OUTS

IN Jonathan Stead from Blackburn for £1.8m; Kelvin Davis from Ipswich for £1.25m; Andy Gray from Sheffield United for £1.1m; Daryl Murphy from Waterford (Ireland) for £100K; Alan Stubbs from Everton, Joe Murphy from West Brom, Nyron Nosworthy from Gillingham, Tommy Miller from Ipswich and Christian Bassila from Strasbourg for free; Anthony Le Tallec from Liverpool and Justin Hoyte from Arsenal on loan

OUT Sean Thornton to Doncaster for £175K; Marcus Stewart to Bristol City, Thomas Myhre to Charlton, Mark Lynch to Hull City for free; Michael Bridges, Jeff Whitely and Michael Ingham released; Mart Poom to Arsenal and Neil Collins to Hartlepool on loan

1 **Welsh off** for bowling over Garcia at Anfield and life gets tougher for McCarthy

2 **Unwanted record rises to 19** successive Premier defeats as Wigan hang on desperately to early penalty winner

3 **Le Tallec opens account** but it comes too late to halt a Man City side heading for the top

4 **Two sides keep 100% records** but it doesn't look like top v bottom as Chelsea need Davis slip to score first goal

6 **First point** ends depressing record of 20 Premier defeats but Baggies' late equaliser leaves McCarthy fuming

7 **Win at last** despite the changes for Carling Cup tie as Le Tallec strikes in extra time

8 **Off the bottom** with first Premier win in 27 fixtures after Miller's scoring start and Arca's fine curling free kick silence Teesside

9 **Pardew praise** for workrate and organisation as Miller leads the battering of Hammers who sneak a draw

11 **Cracking derby** as Lawrence and Elliott peg Newcastle back before freekick against the run of play gives Tyne the bragging rights

12 **It's flat on Wearside** as Arsenal's kids claim victory in Carling Cup

AUGUST SEPTEMBER OCTOBER

Home Away Neutral

ATTENDANCES

HOME GROUND: STADIUM OF LIGHT **CAPACITY:** 48300 **AVERAGE LEAGUE AT HOME:** 33904

37	Man Utd	72519	36	Everton	38093	20	Bolton	32232	19	Charlton	26065
11	Newcastle	52302	18	Tottenham	36244	27	Middlesboro	31675	34	Bolton	23568
12	Arsenal	47366	13	Portsmouth	34926	6	West Brom	31657	39	Portsmouth	20078
2	Liverpool	44913	28	West Ham	34745	9	West Ham	31212	22	Fulham	19372
40	Arsenal	44003	29	Tottenham	34700	33	Wigan	31194	23	Northwich	19323
32	Man City	42200	1	Charlton	34446	21	Everton	30576	30	Blackburn	18220
5	Chelsea	41969	42	Aston Villa	33820	35	Blackburn	29593	4	Wigan	17223
38	Newcastle	40032	3	Man City	33357	8	Middlesboro	29583	7	Cheltenham	11969
15	Aston Villa	39707	17	Liverpool	32697	31	Birmingham	29257	26	Brentford	11698
10	Man Utd	39085	16	Birmingham	32442	41	Fulham	28226			
14	Arsenal	38210	24	Chelsea	32420	25	West Brom	26464			

Dismal season ends in record low

Final Position: 20th

KEY: League, Champions Lge, UEFA Cup, FA Cup, League Cup, Other

INS AND OUTS
IN Rory Delap from Southampton on loan; Kevin Smith from Leeds for free OUT Alan Stubbs to Everton for free; Mart Poom to Arsenal for an undisclosed fee; Carl Robinson to Norwich for £50K; Dan Smith to Huddersfield and Sean Taylor to Blackpool on loan. Neill Collins to Sheffield United for free
McCarthy sacked but players ask "why now?" as Ball takes over in caretaker role with relegation certain
MONTH BY MONTH POINTS TALLY
AUGUST 0 0%
SEPTEMBER 4 44%
OCTOBER 1 8%
NOVEMBER 0 0%
DECEMBER 1 8%
JANUARY 3 25%
FEBRUARY 1 8%
MARCH 0 0%
APRIL 12 17%
MAY 3 33%
Fans boo McCarthy leaving the stadium and rip up tickets as Boro show gulf in class
"Two rubbish teams playing rubbish football", McCarthy condemns lack of effort and ability against Birmingham
Whitehead scorcher of a set piece kick-starts five goals at White Hart Lane with Spurs winning narrowly despite Alnwick's penalty save
Wright exposed twice in Hammers' horror-show, having to pull down players from behind
Davis dents United's hopes on the way down as point at Old Trafford is not enough to avoid the drop
Collins gifts goal to City's Samaras and Breen has a similar moment of madness to get sent off for bizarre handball
Lawrence volley raises hopes before Caldwell's dismissal gives Fulham the advantage
Victorious at last as non-league Northwich are despatched after early goal from Neil Collins
Wenger angry at tackling as Smith's challenge causes injury but Henry still inflicts a defeat
Mixed day for Stubbs whose errors let in Arsenal before scoring to throw club a late lifeline but to no avail
Last-gasp header condemns McCarthy to a dismal New Year as outplayed Everton snatch the point
Davis defiant but Heskey header settles the points for Birmingham and the gap to safety grows
Stead's 1,383 minutes of agony ends in a goal at Everton before Delap adds second equaliser and so nearly claims the winner
Kyle clangers cost points as he breaks clear and misses a one-on-one before handling to give Pompey penalty
Only home win comes in final game as Le Tallec and Brown overcome Fulham to avoid unwanted record
DJ turns tables on McCarthy as second goal from Brentford's DJ Campbell ends cup interest
"We've had enough chances" McCarthy laments lack of good striker at Blackburn but praises the effort
Caldwell caught out after two chances to clear only end up with Charlton netting but Arca takes game to Londoners
A record no-one wanted - 17 home games without a win in the top flight as Phillips scores on first return to Stadium of Light
Penalty shout goes unrewarded as Neill handles for Blackburn and Brown misses one-on-one but crowd cheer performance
Lowest points total by any Premiership team - and the worst in the top-flight in the current points structure – after Villa defeat
Hoyte's gallop rewarded with a goal to take the lead but Newcastle battle to a convincing win
Arca so close to last minute chipped winner but Jaaskelainen tips it away to keep game goalless
First win in 15 gives something to cheer fans as Le Tallec scores via a double deflection
Murphy's law works against Spurs as sub strikes in the 89th minute to grab a point
Davis keeps score down but it's all Bolton and lowest points record looks inevitable
14 15 16 17 18 19 20 21 22 23 24 25 26 27 28 29 30 31 32 33 34 35 36 37 38 39 40 41 42
NOVEMBER DECEMBER JANUARY FEBRUARY MARCH APRIL MAY

GOAL ATTEMPTS

FOR – Goal attempts recorded in League games

	HOME	AWAY	TOTAL	AVE
shots on target	111	72	183	4.8
shots off target	81	73	154	4.1
TOTAL	192	145	337	8.9

Ratio of goals to shots – Average number of shots on target per League goal scored: **7.0**

Accuracy rating – Average percentage of total goal attempts which were on target: **54.3**

AGAINST – Goal attempts recorded in League games

	HOME	AWAY	TOTAL	AVE
shots on target	109	153	262	6.9
shots off target	90	72	162	4.3
TOTAL	199	225	424	11.2

Ratio of goals to shots – Average number of shots on target per League goal scored: **3.8**

Accuracy rating – Average percentage of total goal attempts which were on target: **61.8**

GOALS

Anthony Le Tallec

League	4
FA Cup	1
League Cup	1
Europe	0
Other	0
TOTAL	6

League Average **311** mins between goals

	PLAYER	LGE	FAC	LC	Euro	TOT	AVE
1	Le Tallec	4	1	1	0	6	311
2	Miller	3	0	0	0	3	770
3	Lawrence	3	0	0	0	3	602
4	Whitehead	3	1	0	0	4	1110
5	Elliott	2	0	0	0	2	531
6	Arca	1	1	0	0	2	1978
7	Murphy, D	1	0	0	0	1	604
8	Hoyte	1	0	0	0	1	2373
9	Brown	1	0	0	0	1	910
10	Collins, D	1	0	0	0	1	2000
11	Stead	1	0	0	0	1	1689
12	Kyle	1	0	0	0	1	897
13	Breen	1	0	0	0	1	2926
14	Stubbs	1	0	0	0	1	560
15	Delap	1	0	0	0	1	419
	Other	1	1	0	0	2	
	TOTAL	26	4	1	0	31	

SQUAD APPEARANCES

Match	1	2	3	4	5	6	7	8	9	10	11	12	13	14	15	16	17	18	19	20	21	22	23	24	25	26	27	28	29	30	31	32	33	34	35	36	37	38	39	40	41
Venue	H	A	H	A	A	H	H	A	H	H	A	H	H	A	H	H	H	A	A	H	H	A	H	H	A	A	H	A	H	A	A	A	H	A	H	A	A	H	A	H	H
Competition	L	L	L	L	L	L	W	L	L	L	L	W	L	L	L	L	L	L	L	L	L	L	F	L	L	F	L	L	L	L	L	L	L	L	L	L	L	L	L	L	L
Result	L	L	L	L	L	D	W	W	D	L	L	L	L	L	L	L	L	L	L	D	L	L	W	L	W	L	L	L	D	L	L	L	L	L	L	D	D	L	L	L	W

Goalkeepers
Ben Alnwick
Kelvin Davis
Joe Murphy

Defenders
Gary Breen
Stephen Caldwell
Danny Collins
Neill Collins
Justin Hoyte
George McCartney
Nayron Nosworthy
Dan Smith
Alan Stubbs
Stephen Wright

Midfielders
Julio Arca
Christian Bassila
Rory Delap
Liam Lawrence
Grant Leadbitter
Tommy Miller
Carl Robinson
Andrew Welsh
Dean Whitehead
Martin Woods

Forwards
Chris Brown
Stephen Elliott
Andy Gray
Kevin Kyle
Anthony Le Tallec
Daryl Murphy
Matthew Piper
John Stead

KEY: On all match · On bench · Subbed or sent off (Counting game) · Subbed or sent off (playing less than 70 mins) · Subbed on from bench (Counting Game) · Subbed on (playing less than 70 mins) · Subbed on and then subbed or sent off (Counting Game) · Subbed on and then subbed or sent off (playing less than 70 mins) · Not in 16

KEY PLAYERS - GOALSCORERS

Liam Lawrence

Goals in the League	3
Goals in all competitions	3
Assists League goals scored by a team mate where the player delivered the final pass	1
Contribution to Attacking Power Average number of minutes between League team goals while on pitch	201
Player Strike Rate Average number of minutes between League goals scored by player	602
Club Strike Rate Average minutes between League goals scored by club	132

	PLAYER	GOALS LGE	GOALS ALL	ASSISTS	POWER	S RATE
1	Liam Lawrence	3	3	1	201	602 mins
2	Tommy Miller	3	3	2	116	770 mins
3	Dean Whitehead	3	4	6	133	1110 mins
4	Julio Arca	1	2	2	180	1978 mins

KEY PLAYERS - MIDFIELDERS

Tommy Miller

Goals in the League	3
Goals in all competitions	3
Assists League goals scored by a team mate where the player delivered the final pass	2
Defensive Rating Average number of mins between League goals conceded while on the pitch	49
Contribution to Attacking Power Average number of minutes between League team goals while on pitch	116
Scoring Difference Defensive Rating minus Contribution to Attacking Power	-67

	PLAYER	GOALS LGE	GOALS ALL	ASSISTS	DEF RATE	POWER	SC DIFF
1	Tommy Miller	3	3	2	49	116	-67 mins
2	Dean Whitehead	3	4	6	49	133	-84 mins
3	Julio Arca	1	2	2	62	180	-118 mins
4	Liam Lawrence	3	3	1	50	201	-151 mins

PLAYER APPEARANCES

	AGE (on 01/07/06)	IN NAMED 16	APPEARANCES	COUNTING GAMES	MINUTES ON PITCH	APPEARANCES	MINUTES ON PITCH	THIS SEASON	HOME COUNTRY
Goalkeepers									
Ben Alnwick	19	25	5	5	450	0	0	-	England
Kelvin Davis	29	38	33	33	2970	0	0	-	England
Joe Murphy	25	7	0	0	0	0	0	-	Rep of Ireland
Defenders									
Gary Breen	32	36	35	31	2926	11	1	2	Rep of Ireland (15)
Stephen Caldwell	25	35	24	20	1974	7	1	5	Scotland (85)
Danny Collins	25	28	23	22	2000	0	0	-	Wales
Neill Collins	22	1	0	0	0	0	0	-	Scotland
Justin Hoyte	21	28	27	26	2373	2	0	-	England
George McCartney	25	13	13	12	1091	4	0	-	N Ireland
Nayron Nosworthy	25	32	30	22	2254	5	0	-	England
Dan Smith	19	3	3	0	91	1	0	-	England
Alan Stubbs	34	11	10	7	740	0	0	-	England
Stephen Wright	26	2	2	1	102	3	1	-	England
Midfielders									
Julio Arca	25	24	24	21	1978	5	0	-	Argentina
Christian Bassila	28	16	13	10	980	0	0	-	France
Rory Delap	30	6	6	3	419	2	0	-	Rep of Ireland
Liam Lawrence	24	29	29	13	1805	0	0	-	England
Grant Leadbitter	20	17	12	8	750	2	0	-	England
Tommy Miller	27	29	29	24	2310	4	0	-	England
Carl Robinson	29	9	5	2	276	1	0	7	Wales (74)
Andrew Welsh	22	17	14	9	979	0	1	-	England
Dean Whitehead	24	37	37	37	3329	10	0	-	England
Martin Woods	20	14	7	0	174	1	0	-	England
Forwards									
Chris Brown	21	14	13	9	910	4	0	-	England
Stephen Elliott	22	15	15	10	1062	0	0	5	Rep of Ireland (15)
Andy Gray	28	22	21	7	1125	1	0	-	Scotland
Kevin Kyle	25	15	13	8	897	4	0	-	Scotland
Anthony Le Tallec	21	28	27	8	1242	0	0	-	France
Daryl Murphy	23	27	18	2	604	0	0	-	Rep of Ireland
Matthew Piper	24	0	0	0	0	0	0	-	England
John Stead	23	30	30	11	1689	3	0	-	England

KEY: LEAGUE | ALL COMPS | CAPS | (MAY FIFA RANKING)

TEAM OF THE SEASON

DAVIS — CG 33 DR 52

HOYTE — CG 26 DR 52

BREEN — CG 31 DR 51

D COLLINS — CG 22 DR 51

MCCARTNEY — CG 12 DR 50

MILLER — CG 24 SD -67

WHITEHEAD — CG 37 SD -84

LAWRENCE — CG 13 SD -151

ARCA — CG 21 SD -118

STEAD* — CG 11 AP 154

LA TALLEC* — CG 8 SR 311

KEY: DR = Defensive Rate, SD = Scoring Difference AP = Attacking Power SR = Strike Rate, CG=Counting games – League games playing at least 70 minutes

TOP POINT EARNERS

Justin Hoyte

Counting Games League games when player was on pitch for at least 70 minutes	26
Average points Average League points taken in Counting games	0.58
Club Average points Average points taken in League games	0.39

	PLAYER	GAMES	PTS
1	Justin Hoyte	26	0.58
2	Stephen Caldwell	20	0.55
3	Tommy Miller	24	0.46
4	Liam Lawrence	13	0.46
5	Gary Breen	31	0.45
6	Kelvin Davis	33	0.45
7	Julio Arca	21	0.43
8	George McCartney	12	0.42
9	Nayron Nosworthy	22	0.41
10	Dean Whitehead	37	0.38

KEY PLAYERS - DEFENDERS

Justin Hoyte

Goals Conceded in the League Number of League goals conceded while the player was on the pitch	46
Goals Conceded in all competitions Total number of goals conceded while the player was on the pitch	51
League minutes played Number of minutes played in league matches	2373
Clean Sheets In games when the player was on pitch for at least 70 minutes	4
Defensive Rating Average number of mins between League goals conceded while on the pitch	52
Club Defensive Rating Average number of mins between League goals conceded by the club this season	50

	PLAYER	CON LGE	CON ALL	MINS	C SHEETS	DEF RATE
1	Justin Hoyte	46	51	2373	4	52 mins
2	Gary Breen	57	59	2926	3	51 mins
3	Danny Collins	39	41	2000	3	51 mins
4	George McCartney	22	22	1091	1	50 mins

KEY GOALKEEPER

Kelvin Davis

Goals Conceded in the League Number of League goals conceded while the player was on the pitch	57
Goals Conceded in all competitions Total number of goals conceded while the player was on the pitch	59
League minutes played Number of minutes played in league matches	2970
Clean Sheets In games when the player was on pitch for at least 70 minutes	4
Goals to Shots Ratio The average number of shots on target per each League goal conceded	3.8
Defensive Rating Ave mins between League goals conceded while on the pitch	52

BOOKINGS

Kevin Kyle

League Yellow	4
League Red	0
All competitions Yellow	4
All competitions Red	0

League Average 224 mins between cards

	PLAYER	LEAGUE Y	LEAGUE R	TOTAL Y	TOTAL R	AVE
1	Kyle	4	0	4	0	224
2	Brown	4	0	4	0	227
3	Breen	11	1	11	1	243
4	Caldwell	7	1	7	1	246
5	McCartney	4	0	4	0	272
6	Whitehead	10	0	10	0	332
7	Leadbitter	2	0	2	0	375
8	Arca	5	0	5	0	395
9	Nosworthy	5	0	6	0	450
10	Stead	3	0	3	0	563
11	Miller	4	0	5	0	577
12	Welsh	0	1	0	1	979
13	Gray	1	0	1	0	1125
14	Hoyte	2	0	2	0	1186
	Other	0	0	1	0	
	TOTAL	62	3	65	3	

THE AXA FA CUP

1ST ROUND

Home	Away
Barnet (0) 0 3,545	**Southend** (1) 1 Eastwood 2
Barnsley (1) 1 Hayes 5	**Darlington** (0) 0 6,059
Bournemouth (1) 1 Stock 45	**Tamworth** (1) 2 Ward 29, Storer 82 4,550
Bradford (0) 2 Crooks 56 Windass 59 pen	**Tranmere** (1) 1 Greenacre 6 6,116
Bristol City (0) 0 4,221	**Notts County** (1) 2 Tann 45, Baudet 68
Burnham (0) 1 Miller 88 1,623	**Aldershot** (0) 3 Brough 54, Heald 71 Deen 85
Burscough (1) 3 Bell 10, Cox 89 og Rowan 90	**Gillingham** (0) 2 Jarvis 58, Saunders 77 1,927
Bury (0) 2 Kennedy 52 pen Scott 70	**Scunthorpe** (2) 2 Keogh 6, Baraclough 41 2,940
Cambridge City (0) 0 1,116	**Hereford** (0) 1 Brady 78
Chasetown (1) 1 Day 23 og	**Oldham** (1) 1 D Eyres 31 1,997
Cheltenham (0) 1 McCann 64	**Carlisle** (0) 0 2,405
Chester (0) 2 Branch 55 pen Lowe 71	**Folkestone** (1) 1 Flanagan 10 2,503
Chippenham (0) 1 Harvey 47	**Worcester** (1) 1 Webster 6 2,815
Colchester (2) 9 Halford 39 Brown 44, Iwelumo 48 Cureton 60,71, Watson 64 Yeates 67, Danns 89,90	**Leamington** (0) 1 Adams 72 3,513
Doncaster (1) 4 Heffernan 18,72 McIndoe 53 pen,56 pen	**Blackpool** (0) 1 Clarke 90 pen 4,332
Eastbourne (0) 1 Rowland 90 pen	**Oxford** (0) 1 Basham 70 3,770
Grimsby (0) 1 Jones, G 49	**Bristol Rovers** (1) 2 Agogo 28,87 2,680
Halifax (1) 1 Senior 45	**Rushden & D** (1) 1 Armstrong 2 2,303
Hartlepool (1) 2 Nelson 34 Butler 83	**Dag & Red** (1) 1 Kandol 32 3,655
Histon (1) 4 Jackman 10,58 I Cambridge 50 Nightingale 85	**Hednesford** (0) 0 1,080
Huddersfield (1) 4 Booth 27,69 Schofield 50 pen Holdsworth 81	**Welling** (0) 1 Moore 83 5,518
Kettering (1) 1 Midgley 14 4,548	**Stevenage** (2) 3 Stamp 8, Boyd 43 Elding 69
Leyton Orient (0) 0	**Chesterfield** (0) 0 3,554
Lincoln (1) 1 M Robinson 29	**MK Dons** (1) 1 Edds 45 3,508
Macclesfield (0) 1 Wijnhard 48	**Yeovil** (0) 1 Jevons 81 1,943
Merthyr (1) 1 Williams 29 3,046	**Walsall** (2) 2 Fryatt 17 pen Kinsella 25
Morecambe (0) 1 Carlton 84	**Northwich** (2) 3 Brayson 19,41,67 2,166
Nottm Forest (1) 1 Holt, Gary 39	**Weymouth** (0) 1 Harris 56 10,305
Nuneaton (2) 2 Oddy 15, Staff 34	**Ramsgate** (0) 0 2,153
Peterborough (0) 0	**Burton** (0) 0 3,856
Port Vale (1) 2 Husbands 20 Constantine 65	**Wrexham** (0) 1 McEvilly 63 5,046
Rochdale (0) 0 2,928	**Brentford** (1) 1 O'Connor 45 og
Rotherham (2) 3 McLaren 30,38 Burton 53 4,089	**Mansfield** (2) 4 Brown 28 Coke 37 Barker 75,90
Shrewsbury (3) 4 McMenamin 2 pen Tolley 5, Hope 44 Edwards 55	**Braintree** (0) 1 Quinton 78 2,969
Southport (0) 1 Leadbetter 64	**Woking** (1) 1 Evans 32 1,417
Stockport (1) 2 Easter 41, Briggs 53	**Swansea** (0) 0 2,978
Swindon (1) 2 Gurney 32 Comyn-Platt 87	**Boston** (2) 2 Rusk 26, Talbot 42 3,814
Torquay () 1 Stonebridge 80	**Harrogate** () 1 Holland 20 2,079
Wycombe (0) 1 Burnell 90 3,974	**Northampton** (0) 3 Doig 56, Smith 61 McGleish 80
York (0) 0 3,586	**Grays Ath** (1) 3 Bishop 15 og Slabber 58, Poole 87

FA Cup 1st Round replays

Home	Away
Weymouth () 0 6,500	**Nottm Forest** () 2 Taylor 67,73
Worcester (0) 1 Webster 76	**Chippenham** (0) 0 4,006
Harrogate (0) 0	**Torquay** (0) 0 3,317

Torquay win 6-5 on penalties

Home	Away
MK Dons (2) 2 Platt 14,42	**Lincoln** (1) 1 Mayo 24 pen 4,029
Rushden & D (0) 0	**Halifax** (0) 0 2,133

Rushden & D win 5-4 on penalties

Home	Away
Scunthorpe (0) 1 Johnson 117	**Bury** (0) 0 4,006
Woking (0) 1 McAllister 114	**Southport** (0) 0 2,298
Yeovil (1) 4 Way 23, Terry 73 Johnson 75 Davies 90	**Macclesfield** (0) 0 4,456
Boston (4) 4 Joachim 10,23 Maylett 40 Lee 45	**Swindon** (0) 1 Fallon 83 pen 2,467
Burton (0) 1 Harrad 73	**Peterborough** (0) 0 2,511
Chesterfield (1) 1 Hurst 37 4,895	**Leyton Orient** (2) 2 Mackie 18 Tudor 43
Oldham (1) 4 Warne 31 Porter 56,75 Hall, C 84	**Chasetown** (0) 0 7,235
Oxford (2) 3 Basham 20,45,90 pen	**Eastbourne** (0) 0 4,396

2ND ROUND

Home	Away
Aldershot (0) 0 3,548	**Scunthorpe** (1) 1 Keogh 14
Barnsley () 1 Hayes 43	**Bradford** () 1 Edghill 82 7,051
Boston () 1 Futcher 90 3,995	**Doncaster** () 2 Mulligan 29,58
Burton (3) 4 Gilroy 8,37 Stride 16, Harrad 84	**Burscough** (0) 1 Eaton 60 4,499
Cheltenham (1) 1 Guinan 14	**Oxford** (0) 1 Sabin 52 4,592
Chester (1) 3 Lowe 40 pen,50 Richardson 55	**Nottm Forest** (0) 0 4,732
Hartlepool (0) 1 Llewellyn 52 pen 3,786	**Tamworth** (1) 2 Edwards 33 Redmile 48
Hereford (0) 0 3,620	**Stockport** (1) 2 Easter 3, Wolski 57
Mansfield (2) 3 Barker 13,42 pen Birchall 77	**Grays Ath** (0) 0 2,992
Nuneaton (1) 2 Collins 35 Quailey 52 pen 3,366	**Histon** (2) 2 Barker 36 Knight-Percival 44
Oldham (0) 1 Liddell 57 pen	**Brentford** (0) 1 Sodje 65 4,365
Port Vale (0) 1 Constantine 86	**Bristol Rovers** (0) 1 Gibb 55 4,483
Rushden & D (0) 0 3,245	**Leyton Orient** (0) 1 Steele 66
Shrewsbury () 1 Edwards 45 3,695	**Colchester** () 2 Cureton 23 Iwelumo 52
Southend (0) 1 Eastwood 58 5,267	**MK Dons** (1) 2 McLeod 16 pen Smith 71
Stevenage (1) 2 Boyd 5, Elding 83 3,937	**Northampton** (0) 2 Bojic 67 McGleish 82 pen
Torquay (1) 2 Bedeau 45,69	**Notts County** (0) 1 McMahon 54 2,407
Walsall (1) 2 Fryatt 18 pen, Leitao 83	**Yeovil** (0) 0 4,580
Woking (0) 0	**Northwich** (0) 0 2,462
Worcester (0) 0 4,163	**Huddersfield** (0) 1 Brandon 61

FA Cup 2nd Round replays

Home	Away
Bradford (1) 3 Cooke 34, Bower 67 Wetherall 73 4,738	**Barnsley** (0) 5 Hayes 51,78 Reid 59 Devaney 96,109
Brentford (0) 1 Owusu 78	**Oldham** (0) 0 3,146
Bristol Rovers (0) 0 5,623	**Port Vale** (1) 1 Birchall 22
Histon (0) 1 Bowden 61 3,000	**Nuneaton** (1) 2 Oddy 34 Moore 90
Northampton (2) 2 McGleish 44,45	**Stevenage** (0) 0 4,407
Northwich (1) 2 Elliott 13, Brayson 60	**Woking** (1) 1 Ferguson 45 2,302
Oxford (0) 1 Basham 61 3,455	**Cheltenham** (0) 2 Odejayi 51 Wilson 79

3RD ROUND

Home	Away
Arsenal (2) 2 Pires 6,18 36,552	**Cardiff** (0) 1 Jerome 87
Barnsley (0) 1 Hayes 77 6,884	**Walsall** (0) 1 James 74
Blackburn (2) 3 Todd 17 Bellamy 36,85	**QPR** (0) 0 12,705
Brighton (0) 0 6,734	**Coventry** (0) 1 McSheffrey 50
Burton (0) 0	**Man Utd** (0) 0 6,191

Clough's Burton impress as Brian's son Nigel coaches non-league Albion to hold Manchester United to a draw despite the late introduction of Rooney and Ronaldo for the Reds

Home	Away
Chelsea (1) 2 Cole, C 12 Gudjohnsen 82	**Huddersfield** (0) 1 Taylor-Fletcher 75 41,650
Cheltenham (0) 2 Melligan 59 pen,74 pen 4,741	**Chester** (0) 2 Richardson 80 Drummond 90
Crystal P (2) 4 Hughes 4 McAnuff 37 Johnson 53 pen Freedman 88 pen	**Northampton** (1) 1 Low 12 10,391
Derby (1) 2 Peschisolido 18,67 12,713	**Burnley** (1) 1 O'Connor, G 29
Fulham (0) 1 John 50 13,394	**Leyton Orient** (2) 2 Easton 17 Keith, J 44
Hull City (0) 0 17,051	**Aston Villa** (0) 1 Barry 61
Ipswich (0) 0 15,593	**Portsmouth** (1) 1 Dario Silva 37
Leicester (1) 3 Hammond 44 Hughes 57 de Vries 90	**Tottenham** (2) 2 Jenas 20 Stalteri 41 19,844
Luton (2) 3 Howard 31 Robinson 43 Nicholls 53 pen 10,170	**Liverpool** (1) 5 Gerrard 16 Sinama-Pongolle 62,74 Xabi Alonso 69,90
Man City (0) 3 Fowler 48,56,64 pen 27,779	**Scunthorpe** (1) 1 Keogh 17
Millwall (1) 1 Williams 39 16,440	**Everton** (0) 1 Osman 79

ewcastle (0) **1 Mansfield** (0) **0**
hearer 80 — 41,459

orwich (0) **1 West Ham** (1) **2**
lcVeigh 72 pen — Mullins 6
3,968 — Zamora 57

uneaton (0) **1 Middlesbro** (1) **1**
Murphy 90 pen — Mendieta 15
,000

ort Vale (0) **2 Doncaster** (1) **1**
ogwell 55,73 — Heffernan 27
,923

reston (0) **2 Crewe** (1) **1**
lexander 62 — Jones, B 35
edgwick 86 — 8,380

heff Utd (1) **1 Colchester** (1) **2**
abba 5 — Danns 33
1,820 — Williams 72

heff Wed (1) **2 Charlton** (3) **4**
eckingbottom 16,60 — Rommedahl 13,44
Holland 27
4,851 — Bent, D 87

outhampton (1) **4 MK Dons** (0) **3**
rutton 40 — Lundekvam 59 og
uashie 60 — Rizzo 79
Valcott 66 — Edds 84
enton 88 — 15,908

Walcott scores in a seven goal thriller against MK Dons who fight back to 3-3 before Kenton scores Saints' winner

tockport (1) **2 Brentford** (1) **3**
aster 17 — Owusu 13
riggs 48 — Campbell 65
,078 — Rankin 84

toke (0) **0 Tamworth** (0) **0**
9,366

Sunderland (2) **3 Northwich** (0) **0**
Collins, N 6 — 19,323
Whitehead 41
Le Tallec 70

Torquay (0) **0 Birmingham** (0) **0**
5,974

Watford (0) **0 Bolton** (2) **3**
13,239 — Borgetti 11
Giannakopoulos 34
Vaz Te 73

A rare start for Mexico's top scorer Borgetti sees him make an early impression against Watford with a goal after 11 minutes. Stelios and Vaz Te complete the scoring to leave Watford to concentrate on winning promotion

West Brom (0) **1 Reading** (0) **1**
Gera 82 pen — Doyle 84 pen
19,197

Wigan (0) **1 Leeds** (0) **1**
Connolly 47 — Hulse 88
10,980

Wolves (1) **1 Plymouth** (0) **0**
Clarke 26 — 11,041

FA Cup 3rd Round replays

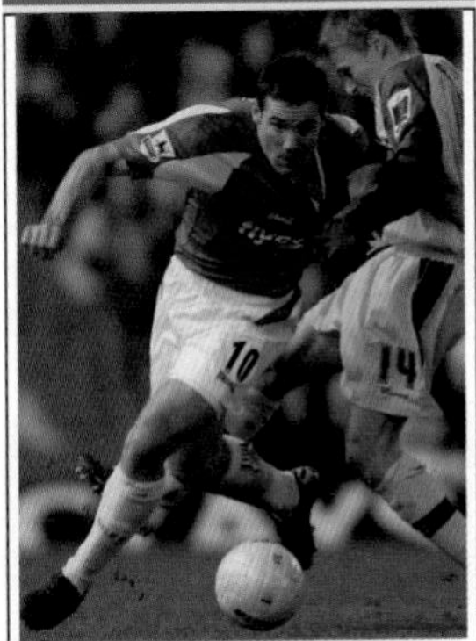

Torquay hold Birmingham goalless at Plainmoor and hold out for 61 minutes at St Andrews before Jarosik breaks the deadlock and Forssell adds a second

Birmingham (0) **2 Torquay** (0) **0**
Jarosik 61 — 24,650
Forssell 81

Chester (0) **0 Cheltenham** (0) **1**
5,096 — Odejayi 52

Everton (0) **1 Millwall** (0) **0**
Cahill 72 — 25,800

Leeds (1) **3 Wigan** (1) **3**
Healy 41,64 pen — Johansson 24
Kelly 116 — Roberts 50,103
15,243
Wigan win 4-2 on penalties

Man Utd (2) **5 Burton** (0) **0**
Saha 7
Rossi 23,90
Richardson 52
Giggs 68 — 53,564

Middlesbro (2) **5 Nuneaton** (0) **2**
Riggott 34 — Murphy 71,86 pen
Yakubu 42 pen,58 — 26,255
Parnaby 50
Viduka 63

Non-league Nuneaton earn their third round draw with Middlesbrough after a last minute penalty from Murphy. He scores twice in the replay but Boro hit form and five goals

Reading (0) **3 West Brom** (2) **2**
Lita 50,65,93 — Chaplow 9,32
16,737

Tamworth (1) **1 Stoke** (0) **1**
Jackson (Tamworth) 42 — Gallagher 80
3,812
Stoke win 5-4 on penalties

Walsall (0) **2 Barnsley** (0) **0**
Leary 68 — 4,074
James 78

4TH ROUND

Aston Villa (0) **3 Port Vale** (0) **1**
Baros 70,74 — Lowndes 85
Davis 90 — 30,434

Bolton (0) **1 Arsenal** (0) **0**
Giannakopoulos 84 — 13,326

Stelios sinks the holders as Bolton strike six minutes from time and hang on against Arsenal's late flurry with Jaaskelainen and Gardner in form

Brentford (0) **2 Sunderland** (0) **1**
Campbell 57,89 — Arca 66
11,698

Charlton (1) **2 Leyton Orient** (0) **1**
Fortune 7 — Steele 53
Bothroyd 90 — 22,029

Cheltenham (0) **0 Newcastle** (2) **2**
7,022 — Chopra 41
Parker 43

Colchester (1) **3 Derby** (0) **1**
Danns 44,52 — Smith 79 pen
Garcia 59 — 5,933

Coventry (0) **1 Middlesbro** (0) **1**
John 54 — Hasselbaink 46
28,120

Everton (1) **1 Chelsea** (0) **1**
McFadden 36 — Lampard 73
29,742

Leicester (0) **0 Southampton** (0) **1**
20,427 — Jones 90

Man City (0) **1 Wigan** (0) **0**
Cole 84 — 30,811

Portsmouth (0) **1 Liverpool** (2) **2**
Davis 54 — Gerrard 36 pen
17,247 — Riise 41

Preston (1) **1 Crystal P** (1) **1**
O'Neil 27 — Johnson 8
9,489

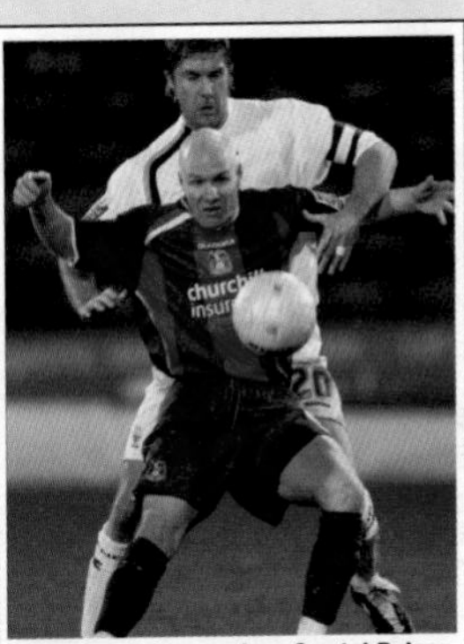

Marksman Johnson gives Crystal Palace a lead at Preston after eight minutes before their Championship rivals battle back with O'Neil heading home from a free kick

Reading (1) **1 Birmingham** (0) **1**
Long 31 — Dunn 67
23,762

Stoke (1) **2 Walsall** (0) **1**
Sidibe 45 — James 51
Chadwick 49 — 8,834

West Ham (2) **4 Blackburn** (1) **2**
Sheringham 33 pen — Bentley 1
Etherington 37 — Neill 65
Khizanishvili 59 og — 23,700
Zamora 73

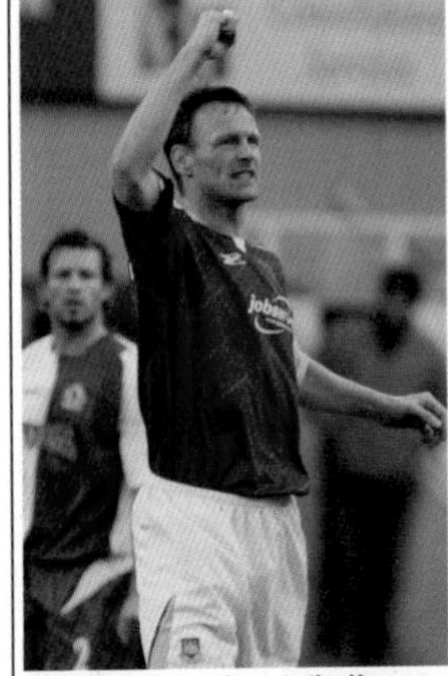

A Sheringham penalty puts the Hammers level, equalising Bentley's first minute goal for Blackburn. Zamora then inspires the home side, scoring the fourth himself in a 4-2 win

Wolves (0) **0 Man Utd** (2) **3**
28,333 — Richardson 5,52
Saha 45

FA Cup 4th Round replays

Birmingham (1) **2 Reading** (0) **1**
Forssell 30 — Hunt 51
Gray 67 — 16,644

Chelsea (3) **4 Everton** (0) **1**
Robben 22 — Arteta 72 pen
Lampard 36 pen — 39,301
Crespo 39
Terry 74

Robben strikes early to make Everton suffer for not hanging onto a lead at home and the replay is wrapped up long before Terry scores Chelsea's fourth goal in a comfortable win

Crystal P (1) **1 Preston** (1) **2**
Ward 26 — Dichio 35,88
7,356

Middlesbro (1) **1 Coventry** (0) **0**
Hasselbaink 20 — 14,131

5TH ROUND

Aston Villa	(0) 1	Man City	(0) 1
Baros 72			Richards 90
23,847			

Richards' late leap grabs the equaliser for Man City in the fourth minute of injury time to keep his side in the competition when they look out of it against Villa

Bolton	(0) 0	West Ham	(0) 0
			17,120

Charlton	(2) 3	Brentford	(0) 1
Bent, D 3			Rankin 83
Bothroyd 45			22,098
Hughes 62			

Chelsea	(1) 3	Colchester	(1) 1
Ferreira 37			Carvalho 28 og
Cole, J 79,90			41,810

Liverpool	(1) 1	Man Utd	(0) 0
Crouch 19			44,039

Out-fought in midfield, Manchester United lose their first FA Cup game to Liverpool for 85 years to a Crouch goal and also lose Smith to a horrific injury

Newcastle	(0) 1	Southampton	(0) 0
Dyer 68			40,975

Preston	(0) 0	Middlesbro	(0) 2
19,877			Yakubu 52,77

Stoke	(0) 0	Birmingham	(0) 1
18,768			Forssell 47

FA Cup 5th Round replays

Man City	(1) 2	Aston Villa	(0) 1
Samaras 16			Davis 85
Vassell 48			33,006

West Ham	(1) 2	Bolton	(1) 1
Jaaskelainen 10 og			Davies 31
Harewood 96			24,685

Bolton have the best of their home tie against West Ham but can't convert their chances and are made to pay after a comical Jaaskelainen own goal and Harewood's 50th in claret and blue

QUARTER-FINALS

Birmingham	(0) 0	Liverpool	(3) 7
27,378			Hyypia 1, Crouch 4,38
			Morientes 60, Riise 70
			Tebily 76, Cisse 89

Strikers in the mood as Birmingham are hit for seven with Hyypia netting in the first minute and Crouch adding two more before halftime. Criticised forwards Morientes and Cissé also get onto the scoresheet in a game that causes Birmingham's Bruce to lose sleep

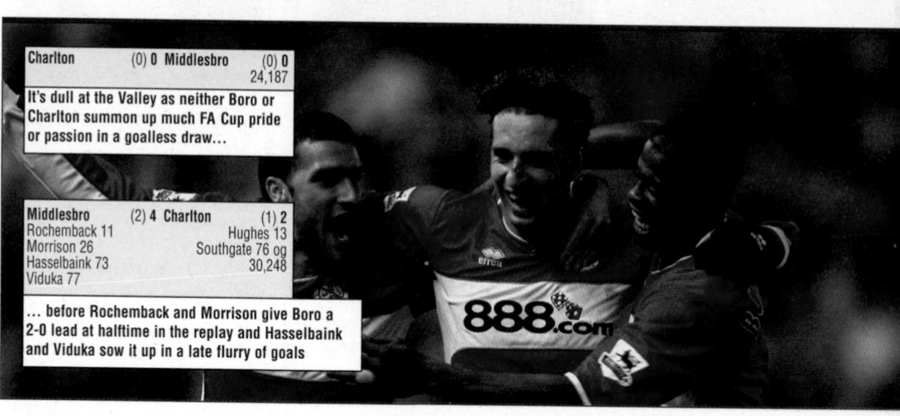

Charlton	(0) 0	Middlesbro	(0) 0
			24,187

It's dull at the Valley as neither Boro or Charlton summon up much FA Cup pride or passion in a goalless draw...

Middlesbro	(2) 4	Charlton	(1) 2
Rochemback 11			Hughes 13
Morrison 26			Southgate 76 og
Hasselbaink 73			30,248
Viduka 77			

... before Rochemback and Morrison give Boro a 2-0 lead at halftime in the replay and Hasselbaink and Viduka sow it up in a late flurry of goals

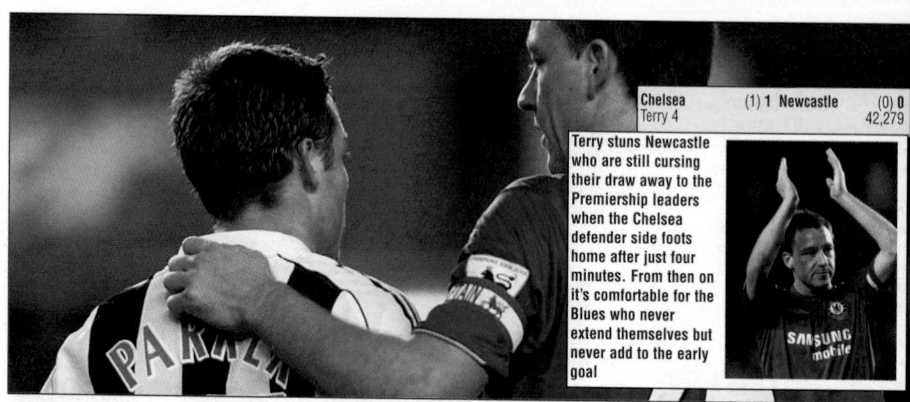

Chelsea	(1) 1	Newcastle	(0) 0
Terry 4			42,279

Terry stuns Newcastle who are still cursing their draw away to the Premiership leaders when the Chelsea defender side foots home after just four minutes. From then on it's comfortable for the Blues who never extend themselves but never add to the early goal

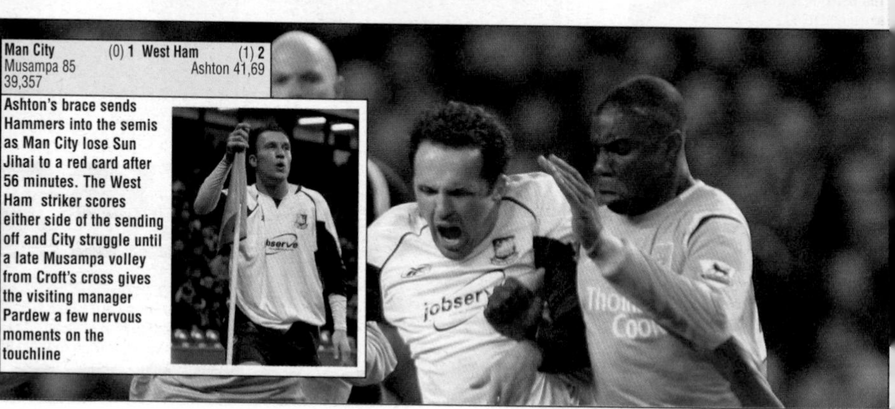

Man City	(0) 1	West Ham	(1) 2
Musampa 85			Ashton 41,69
39,357			

Ashton's brace sends Hammers into the semis as Man City lose Sun Jihai to a red card after 56 minutes. The West Ham striker scores either side of the sending off and City struggle until a late Musampa volley from Croft's cross gives the visiting manager Pardew a few nervous moments on the touchline

SEMI-FINALS

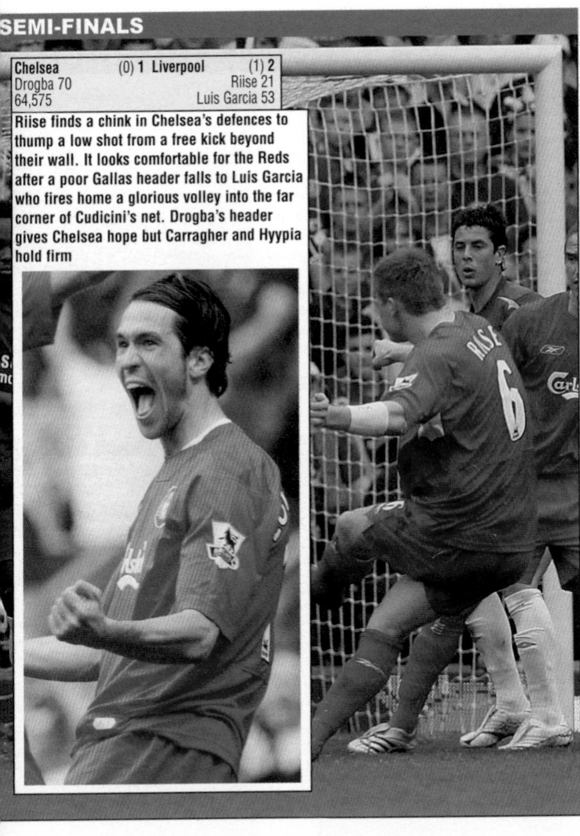

Chelsea	(0) 1	Liverpool	(1) 2
Drogba 70			Riise 21
64,575			Luis Garcia 53

Riise finds a chink in Chelsea's defences to thump a low shot from a free kick beyond their wall. It looks comfortable for the Reds after a poor Gallas header falls to Luis Garcia who fires home a glorious volley into the far corner of Cudicini's net. Drogba's header gives Chelsea hope but Carragher and Hyypia hold firm

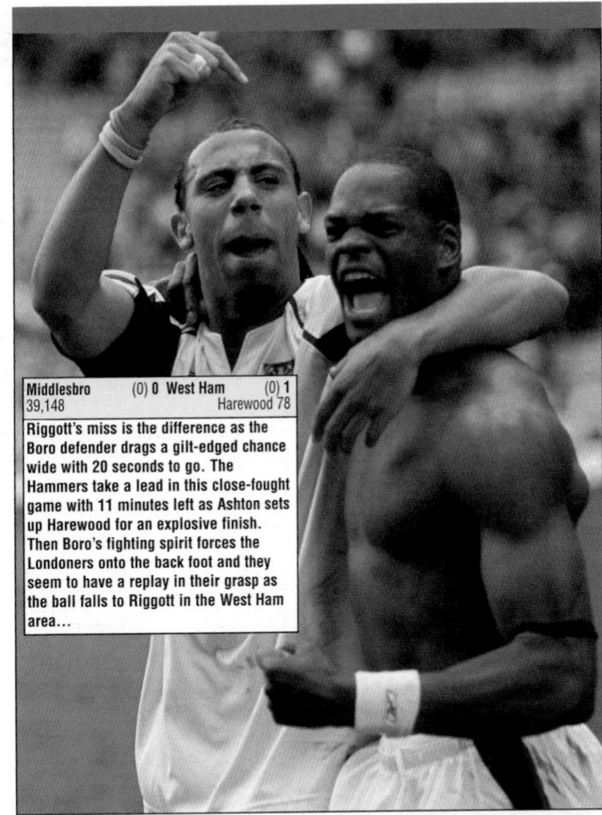

Middlesbro	(0) 0	West Ham	(0) 1
39,148			Harewood 78

Riggott's miss is the difference as the Boro defender drags a gilt-edged chance wide with 20 seconds to go. The Hammers take a lead in this close-fought game with 11 minutes left as Ashton sets up Harewood for an explosive finish. Then Boro's fighting spirit forces the Londoners onto the back foot and they seem to have a replay in their grasp as the ball falls to Riggott in the West Ham area...

FINAL

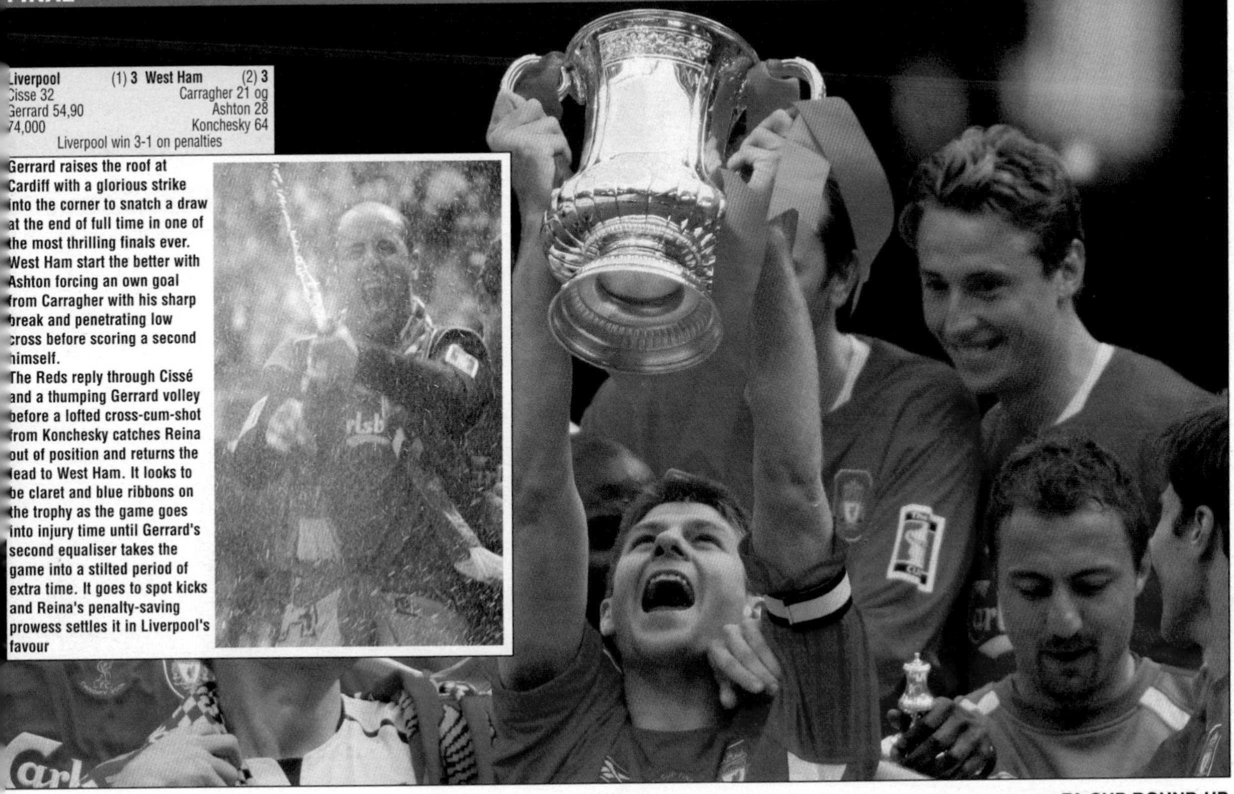

Liverpool	(1) 3	West Ham	(2) 3
Cisse 32			Carragher 21 og
Gerrard 54,90			Ashton 28
74,000			Konchesky 64

Liverpool win 3-1 on penalties

Gerrard raises the roof at Cardiff with a glorious strike into the corner to snatch a draw at the end of full time in one of the most thrilling finals ever. West Ham start the better with Ashton forcing an own goal from Carragher with his sharp break and penetrating low cross before scoring a second himself.

The Reds reply through Cissé and a thumping Gerrard volley before a lofted cross-cum-shot from Konchesky catches Reina out of position and returns the lead to West Ham. It looks to be claret and blue ribbons on the trophy as the game goes into injury time until Gerrard's second equaliser takes the game into a stilted period of extra time. It goes to spot kicks and Reina's penalty-saving prowess settles it in Liverpool's favour

THE CARLING FOOTBALL LEAGUE CUP

1ST ROUND

Blackpool (2) 2 **Hull City** (1) 1
Clarke 29 pen Price 4
Grayson 39 3,819

Bristol City (1) 2 **Barnet** (1) 4
Golbourne 14 Lee 17,53
Bridges 64 Bailey 58
3,383 Roache 81

Burnley (0) 2 **Carlisle** (0) 1
Duff 52 Murray 74
Akinbiyi 90 5,114

Bury (0) 0 **Leicester** (2) 3
2,759 Hamill 37, Stearman 40
Gudjonsson 61 pen

Cheltenham (1) 5 **Brentford** (0) 0
Melligan 5 2,113
Caines 55, Victory 69
McCann 78,81

Chesterfield (1) 2 **Huddersfield** (1) 4
Niven 41 Abbott 9
Hurst 60 Taylor-Fletcher 56,76,90
2,922

Colchester (0) 0 **Cardiff** (2) 2
1,904 Purse 31 pen
Jerome 34

Crystal P (0) 3 **Walsall** (0) 0
Popovic 51 pen 5,508
Granville 83
Hughes 87

Derby (0) 0 **Grimsby** (1) 1
11,756 Jones, G 11

Gillingham (0) 1 **Oxford** (0) 0
Jarvis 83 4,149

Hartlepool (1) 3 **Darlington** (0) 1
Daly 26 Logan 81
Proctor 76,88 6,163

Ipswich (0) 0 **Yeovil** (1) 2
11,299 Way 45, Gall 87

Leeds (2) 2 **Oldham** (0) 0
Ricketts 20 14,970
Richardson 24

Leyton Orient (0) 1 **Luton** (1) 3
McMahon 90 Coyne 45
2,383 Feeney 71
Alexander 76 og

Lincoln (2) 5 **Crewe** (1) 1
Beevers 6 Walker 44
Molango 35, Birch 64,67 2,782
Robinson, M 83

Mansfield (1) 1 **Stoke** (1) 1
Jelleyman 16 Brammer 11 pen
2,799
Mansfield win 3-0 on penalties

Millwall (0) 2 **Bristol Rovers** (0) 0
Hayles 55 3,079
Fangueiro 85

MK Dons (0) 0 **Norwich** (0) 1
4,777 McKenzie 120

Northampton (1) 3 **QPR** (0) 0
Kirk 19, McGleish 62 4,537
Sabin 90 pen

Nottm Forest (1) 2 **Macclesfield** (2) 3
Breckin 9,83 Whitaker 21, Townson 45
5,050 MacKenzie 80

Plymouth (2) 2 **Peterborough** (1) 1
Wotton 35 pen Plummer 22
Taylor 38 5,974

Preston (0) 2 **Barnsley** (0) 2
Dichio 77 Burns 81,108
Alexander 119 pen 3,137
Preston win 5-4 on penalties

Reading (1) 3 **Swansea** (0) 1
Kitson 14,95 Akinfenwa 80
Lita 114 7,603

Rochdale (0) 0 **Bradford** (2) 5
2,820 Windass 7,67,77
Cadamarteri 40
Bridge-Wilkinson 82

Rotherham (1) 3 **Port Vale** (1) 1
Rowland 41 og Cummins 45
Burton 71 2,809
Otsemobor 90

Rushden & D (0) 0 **Coventry** (2) 3
3,240 McSheffrey 10
Heath 41, Morrell 81

Scunthorpe (0) 2 **Tranmere** (0) 1
Ryan 56 Sharps 61
Hinds 82 2,738

Sheff Utd (0) 1 **Boston** (0) 0
Ross 50 6,014

Shrewsbury (1) 3 **Brighton** (1) 2
Stallard 22 McCammon 17
Denny 89,91 Robinson 80
2,141

Southend (0) 0 **Southampton** (2) 3
6,358 Blackstock 44
Dyer 45, Ormerod 89

Stockport (1) 2 **Sheff Wed** (1) 4
Boshell 8 Peacock 15
Le Fondre 108 Partridge 107
3,001 Proudlock 116,120

Swindon (0) 1 **Wycombe** (1) 3
Pook 58 Stonebridge 12
3,976 Tyson 62, Dixon 75

Torquay (0) 0 **Bournemouth** (0) 0
1,876
Bournemouth win 4-3 on penalties

Watford (2) 3 **Notts County** (0) 1
Young 13 Palmer 76
Bouazza 34 pen 7,011
Blizzard 48

Wolves (1) 5 **Chester** (0) 1
Miller 6 Davies 83
Cameron 62,74 9,518
Anderton 72, Ganea 79

Wrexham (0) 0 **Doncaster** (0) 1
2,177 Hughes 86

2ND ROUND

Barnet (1) 2 **Plymouth** (1) 1
King 12 Buzsaky 19
Grazioli 46 1,941

Blackburn (1) 3 **Huddersfield** (0) 1
Bellamy 11,84 Abbott 79
Khizanishvili 60 11,755

Burnley (1) 3 **Barnsley** (0) 0
Lowe 28 4,501
Akinbiyi 52
Spicer 59

Cardiff (0) 2 **Macclesfield** (1) 1
Ledley 50 Bullock 5
Koumas 81 3,849

Charlton (1) 3 **Hartlepool** (1) 1
Johansson 43 pen Daly 40
Bent 73 10,328
Bothroyd 80

Crystal P (0) 1 **Coventry** (0) 0
Reich 67 5,341

Doncaster (0) 1 **Man City** (0) 1
McIndoe 118 pen Vassell 95 pen
8,228
Doncaster win 3-0 on penalties

Fulham (2) 5 **Lincoln** (0) 4
Rehman 26 Green 70
Helguson 31 Volz 82 og
Rosenior 93 Kerr 101
Radzinski 95 Robinson, M 115
McBride 120 5,365

Gillingham (1) 3 **Portsmouth** (1) 2
Byfield 42 O'Neil 24
Ashdown 56 og Taylor 48 pen
Crofts 94 4,903

Grimsby (0) 1 **Tottenham** (0) 0
Kamudimba Kalala 89 8,206

Leicester (1) 2 **Blackpool** (0) 1
de Vries 17,79 Parker 68
7,386

Mansfield (0) 1 **Southampton** (0) 0
Coke 68 3,739

Norwich (1) 2 **Northampton** (0) 0
Huckerby 34 pen 16,766
Ashton 78

Reading (0) 1 **Luton** (0) 0
Oster 80 6,941

Rotherham (0) 0 **Leeds** (2) 2
5,445 Cresswell 19,28

Scunthorpe (0) 0 **Birmingham** (1) 2
6,109 Forssell 15,70 pen

Sheff Wed (0) 2 **West Ham** (1) 4
Coughlan 76 Zamora 2,63
Graham 77 Dailly 54
14,976 Bellion 84

Shrewsbury (0) 0 **Sheff Utd** (0) 0
4,250
Sheff Utd win 4-3 on penalties

Sunderland (0) 1 **Cheltenham** (0) 0
Le Tallec 92 11,969

Watford (1) 2 **Wolves** (1) 1
Carlisle 45,104 Miller 12
9,296

West Brom (2) 4 **Bradford** (1) 1
Ellington 23,72 Schumacher 45
Kamara 32, Earnshaw 77 10,792

Wigan (0) 1 **Bournemouth** (0) 0
Roberts 86 3,346

Wycombe (3) 3 **Aston Villa** (1) 8
Tyson 6 Davis 14,90
Johnson 18 Baros 48, Milner 64,86
Mooney 39 Easton 69 og
5,365 Barry 73 pen,78

Yeovil (0) 1 **Millwall** (0) 2
Davies 87 Dunne 48
5,108 Asaba 53

3RD ROUND

Aston Villa (1) 1 **Burnley** (0) 0
Phillips 22 26,872

Birmingham (1) 2 **Norwich** (1) 1
Pennant 5 Taylor, Martin 41 og
Jarosik 86 28,825

Blackburn (0) 3 **Leeds** (0) 0
Emerton 60 15,631
Dickov 76, Neill 89

Bolton (0) 1 **West Ham** (0) 0
Borgetti 64 10,927

Cardiff (0) 0 **Leicester** (1) 1
8,727 Johansson 10

Chelsea (1) 1 **Charlton** (1) 1
Terry 41 Bent 45
42,198
Charlton win 5-4 on penalties

Mourinho's record goes as he is beaten at home for the first time in 36 games after Bent puts Charlton level and Huth misses penalty in the shoot-out

Crystal P (1) 2 **Liverpool** (1)
Freedman 37 Gerrard 4
Reich 66 19,67

Reich's knockout blow to last season's finalists after Freedman's headed goal is matched by Gerrard's equaliser the German strikes to put Palace through

Doncaster (0) 2 **Gillingham** (0) 0
Heffernan 84,89 6,874

Everton (0) 0 **Middlesbro** (1) 1
25,844 Hasselbaink 3

Fulham (0) 2 **West Brom** (1) 3
Boa Morte 63 Earnshaw
Helguson 90 Kanu 8
7,373 Inamoto 9

Grimsby (0) 0 **Newcastle** (0) 1
9,311 Shearer 8

Mansfield (0) 2 **Millwall** (1) 3
Brown 67 May 2
Barker 68 Robinson, P 6
4,133 Livermore 9

Man Utd (2) 4 **Barnet** (0) 1
Miller 4 Sinclair 74
Richardson 19 43,67
Rossi 51
Ebanks-Blake 89

Reading (0) 2 **Sheff Utd** (0) 0
Kitson 54,75 11,607

Sunderland (0) 0 **Arsenal** (0) 3
47,366 Eboue 61
van Persie 67 pen,8

Wigan (0) 3 **Watford** (0) 0
Taylor 98 pen 4,531
Johansson 117,120

4TH ROUND

Arsenal (2) 3 **Reading** (0) 0
Reyes 12 36,167
van Persie 42
Lupoli 65

Bolton (0) 2 **Leicester** (0) 1
Borgetti 104 Williams 110
Vaz Te 106 13,067

Charlton (1) 2 **Blackburn** (0) 3
Ambrose 37 Kuqi 75
Murphy 50 Thompson 81
14,093 Bentley 88

Doncaster (1) 3 **Aston Villa** (0) 0
McIndoe 20 pen 10,590
Heffernan 53
Thornton 79

Millwall (0) 2 **Birmingham** (1) 2
Dunne 57 Gray 10
Elliott 116 Heskey 102
7,732
Birmingham win 4-3 on penalties

Wigan (0) 1 **Newcastle** (0) 0
Connolly 88 pen 11,574

Man Utd (2) 3 **West Brom** (0) 1
Ronaldo 12 pen Ellington 77
Saha 16, O'Shea 56 48,924

Middlesbro (0) 2 **Crystal P** (1) 1
Viduka 52 Queudrue 31 og
Nemeth 55 10,791

QUARTER-FINALS

rmingham	(0) 1 Man Utd	(0) 3
arosik 75		Saha 46,63
),454		Park 50

Saha strikes twice as Birmingham are blown away in the second half with Park scoring his first United goal

oncaster	(1) 2 Arsenal	(0) 2
lcIndoe 4		Owusu-Abeyie 63
reen 104		Gilberto Silva 120
),006		
Arsenal win 1-3 on penalties		

Doncaster a whisker away from semis when Green's extra time goal leaves Arsenal looking like the Yorkshire club's third Premier victims. Then Gilberto's late strike takes Arsenal level and ultimately through on penalties

Middlesbro	(0) 0 Blackburn	(0) 1
4,710		Dickov 90

Dickov shoots down Boro leaving McClaren angry at his side's limp performance in a half-empty Riverside

Wigan	(2) 2 Bolton	(0) 0
Roberts 40,45		13,401

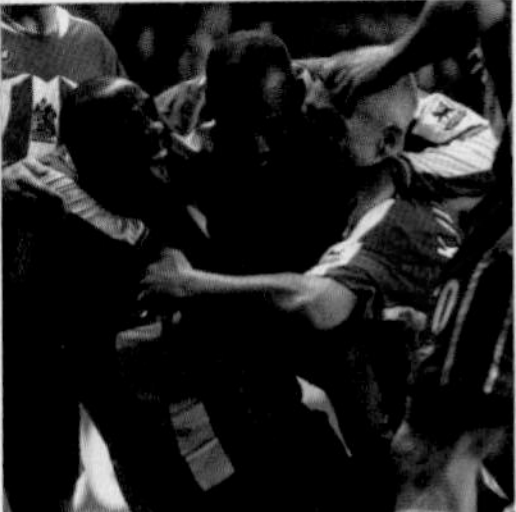

Roberts too hot for Bolton defence to handle as his brace of goals put Wigan into the semi-finals with Pollitt's point blank save from Vaz Te keeping Bolton goalless

SEMI-FINALS

Blackburn	(1) 1 Man Utd	(1) 1
Pedersen 35		Saha 30
24,348		
Man Utd	**(1) 2 Blackburn**	**(1) 1**
van Nistelrooy 8		Reid 32
Saha 51		61,637

Friedel's resistance ends as the Blackburn keeper saves a van Nistelrooy penalty and header before Saha volleys home the winner in a bad tempered second leg. Pedersen and Saha exchanged goals at Ewood Park in the first leg and van Nistelrooy's Old Trafford strike is levelled by Reid before Saha's goal

Wigan	(0) 1 Arsenal	(0) 0
Scharner 77		12,181
Arsenal	**(0) 2 Wigan**	**(0) 1**
Henry 65		Roberts 119
van Persie 107		34,692
Wigan win on the away-goals rule		

Scharner's debut goal lifts Latics in a poor first leg against Arsenal's second XI but Roberts' clinches final spot in last minute of extra time at Highbury. Henry levels scores on aggregate and van Persie's 108th minute free kick gives Arsenal the edge before Roberts slots home the vital away goal

FINAL

Man Utd	(1) 4 Wigan	(0) 0
Rooney 33,61		60,866
Saha 55		
Ronaldo 59		

Rooney's first trophy as he scores first and last in a four goal thrashing of Wigan at Cardiff. The United youngster ends his own goal drought and Ronaldo adds a third with Saha, who is selected ahead of van Nistelrooy, completing the scorers. Saddest sight for Wigan is keeper Pollitt limping off with a hamstring injury in the 14th minute

CHAMPIONSHIP LEAGUE ROUND-UP

FINAL LEAGUE TABLE

		HOME					AWAY					TOTAL			
	P	W	D	L	F	A	W	D	L	F	A	F	A	DIF	PTS
Reading	46	19	3	1	58	14	12	10	1	41	18	99	32	67	106
Sheff Utd	46	15	5	3	43	22	11	7	5	33	24	76	46	30	90
Watford	46	11	7	5	39	24	11	8	4	38	29	77	53	24	81
Preston	46	11	10	2	31	12	9	10	4	28	18	59	30	29	80
Leeds	46	13	7	3	35	18	8	8	7	22	20	57	38	19	78
Crystal Palace	46	13	6	4	39	20	8	6	9	28	28	67	48	19	75
Wolves	46	9	10	4	24	18	7	9	7	26	24	50	42	8	67
Coventry	46	12	7	4	39	22	4	8	11	23	43	62	65	-3	63
Norwich	46	12	4	7	34	25	6	4	13	22	40	56	65	-9	62
Luton	46	11	6	6	45	31	6	4	13	21	36	66	67	-1	61
Cardiff	46	10	7	6	32	24	6	5	12	26	35	58	59	-1	60
Southampton	46	9	10	4	26	17	4	9	10	23	33	49	50	-1	58
Stoke	46	7	5	11	24	32	10	2	11	30	31	54	63	-9	58
Plymouth	46	10	7	6	26	22	3	10	10	13	24	39	46	-7	56
Ipswich	46	8	8	7	28	32	6	6	11	25	34	53	66	-13	56
Leicester	46	8	9	6	30	25	5	6	12	21	34	51	59	-8	54
Burnley	46	11	6	6	34	22	3	6	14	12	32	46	54	-8	54
Hull City	46	8	8	7	24	21	4	8	11	25	34	49	55	-6	52
Sheff Wed	46	7	8	8	22	24	6	5	12	17	28	39	52	-13	52
Derby	46	8	10	5	33	27	2	10	11	20	40	53	67	-14	50
QPR	46	7	7	9	24	26	5	7	11	26	39	50	65	-15	50
Crewe	46	7	7	9	38	40	2	8	13	19	46	57	86	-29	42
Millwall	46	4	8	11	13	27	4	8	11	22	35	35	62	-27	40
Brighton	46	4	8	11	21	34	3	9	11	18	37	39	71	-32	38

CLUB STRIKE FORCE

Leroy Lita of Reading

1 Reading

Goals scored in the League	99
Club Strike Rate (CSR) Average number of minutes between League goals scored by club	42

	CLUB	GOALS	CSR
1	Reading	99	42
2	Sheff Utd	76	54
3	Watford	77	54
4	Crystal Palace	67	62
5	Luton	66	63
6	Coventry	62	67
7	Preston	59	70
8	Cardiff	58	71
9	Crewe	57	73
10	Leeds	57	73
11	Norwich	56	74
12	Stoke	54	77
13	Derby	53	78
14	Ipswich	53	78
15	Leicester	51	81
16	QPR	50	83
17	Wolverhampton	50	83
18	Hull City	49	84
19	Southampton	49	84
20	Burnley	46	90
21	Brighton	39	106
22	Plymouth	39	106
23	Sheff Wed	39	106
24	Millwall	35	118

CLUB DISCIPLINARY RECORDS

Millwall's Robinson dismissed on a stretcher

1 Millwall

League Yellow	95
League Red	12
League Total	107
Cards Average in League Average number of minutes between a card being shown of either colour	39

	CLUB	Y	R	TOTAL	AVE
1	Millwall	95	12	107	39
2	Leicester	85	5	90	46
3	Brighton	84	5	89	47
4	Coventry	84	4	88	47
5	Preston	87	1	88	47
6	Burnley	79	5	84	49
7	Crystal Palace	81	3	84	49
8	QPR	76	7	83	50
9	Leeds	80	1	81	51
10	Cardiff	74	2	76	54
11	Stoke	69	6	75	55
12	Derby	67	6	73	57
13	Southampton	69	4	73	57
14	Wolverhampton	69	2	71	58
15	Luton	64	5	69	60
16	Norwich	66	2	68	60
17	Watford	62	6	68	61
18	Plymouth	66	1	67	62
19	Ipswich	60	6	66	63
20	Sheff Utd	62	2	64	65
21	Sheff Wed	56	1	57	73
22	Hull City	52	3	55	75
23	Reading	38	0	38	109
24	Crewe	34	2	36	115

CLUB DEFENCES

	CLUB	LGE	CS	CDR
1	Preston	30	24	138
2	Reading	32	22	129
3	Leeds	38	17	109
4	Wolverhampton	42	17	99
5	Plymouth	46	14	90
6	Sheff Utd	46	18	90
7	Crystal Palace	48	14	86
8	Southampton	50	18	83
9	Sheff Wed	52	14	80
10	Watford	53	12	78
11	Burnley	54	16	77
12	Hull City	55	13	75
13	Cardiff	59	14	70
14	Leicester	59	10	70
15	Millwall	62	8	67
16	Stoke	63	12	66
17	Coventry	65	11	64
18	Norwich	65	8	64
19	QPR	65	9	64
20	Ipswich	66	8	63
21	Derby	67	9	62
22	Luton	67	10	62
23	Brighton	71	9	58
24	Crewe	86	4	48

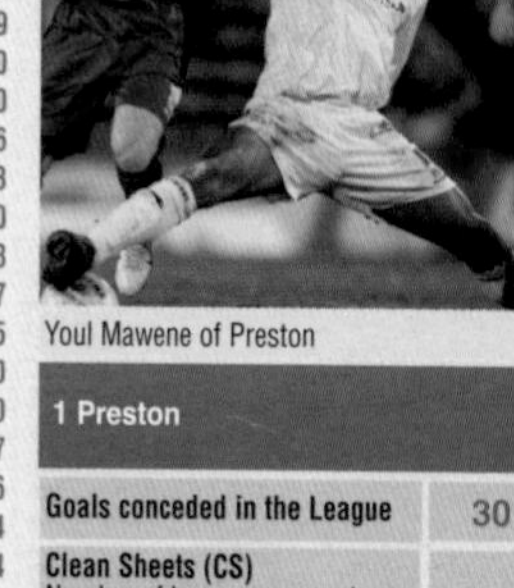

Youl Mawene of Preston

1 Preston

Goals conceded in the League	30
Clean Sheets (CS) Number of league games where no goals were conceded	24
Club Defensive Rate (CDR) Average number of minutes between League goals conceded by club	138

STADIUM CAPACITY AND HOME CROWDS

1	Brighton	7053	96.44	7999	5859
2	Norwich	26034	95.84	27470	23838
3	Luton	9975	91.62	10248	7474
4	Coventry	23627	90.16	26851	16156
5	Reading	24200	83.5	23845	14027
6	Wolverhampton	29400	80.35	27980	21683
7	Ipswich	30300	80.04	29184	22551
8	Hull City	25504	77.8	23486	17698
9	Sheff Utd	30936	76.45	30558	17739
10	Crystal Palace	26309	73.96	23843	17291
11	QPR	18500	72.65	16152	10901
12	Southampton	32551	72.54	30173	19086
13	Derby	33597	71.93	30391	21434
14	Watford	22100	71.72	27419	11358
15	Leicester	32500	68.41	25578	18856
16	Crewe	10066	66.88	8942	5686
17	Plymouth	20922	65.84	17726	10460
18	Preston	22225	65.78	19350	12453
19	Sheff Wed	39859	62.35	33439	20244
20	Cardiff	20000	58.6	16403	8724
21	Leeds	40204	55.6	27843	18353
22	Burnley	22546	55.27	17912	10431
23	Stoke	28218	51.14	20408	10121
24	Millwall	20146	47.3	13209	7108

Key: Average. The percentage of each stadium filled in League games over the season (AVE), the stadium capacity and the highest and lowest crowds recorded.

AWAY ATTENDANCE

1	Leeds	84.68	30173	7220
2	Sheff Wed	78.21	30558	7573
3	Sheff Utd	76.11	33439	6553
4	Southampton	75.06	26688	6588
5	Wolverhampton	75.01	26851	6642
6	Crystal Palace	74.28	27392	6766
7	QPR	73.44	25744	5687
8	Norwich	73.01	30755	6132
9	Leicester	72.9	26801	7053
10	Hull City	72.58	29910	6929
11	Reading	72.54	27980	6484
12	Luton	72.51	26807	6604
13	Cardiff	71.56	27419	5865
14	Derby	71.28	26334	5958
15	Brighton	70.09	27514	5925
16	Burnley	70.05	25204	6267
17	Watford	69.95	25384	6258
18	Ipswich	69.49	25402	5686
19	Stoke	69.22	24223	5859
20	Coventry	69.06	25355	6444
21	Plymouth	68.35	26331	5984
22	Millwall	68.14	25095	5945
23	Preston	67.81	25032	6361
24	Crewe	66.89	25656	6132

Key: Average. How close each club has come to filling grounds in its away league matches (AVE) and the highest and lowest crowds recorded.

CHART-TOPPING MIDFIELDERS

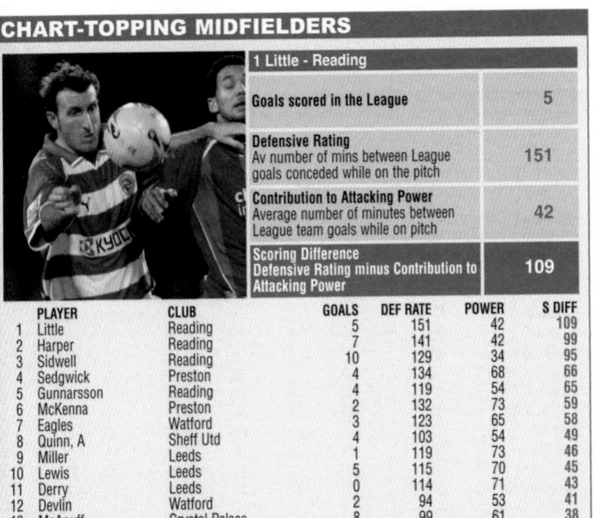

1 Little - Reading	
Goals scored in the League	5
Defensive Rating Av number of mins between League goals conceded while on the pitch	151
Contribution to Attacking Power Average number of minutes between League team goals while on pitch	42
Scoring Difference Defensive Rating minus Contribution to Attacking Power	109

	PLAYER	CLUB	GOALS	DEF RATE	POWER	S DIFF
1	Little	Reading	5	151	42	109
2	Harper	Reading	7	141	42	99
3	Sidwell	Reading	10	129	34	95
4	Sedgwick	Preston	4	134	68	66
5	Gunnarsson	Reading	4	119	54	65
6	McKenna	Preston	2	132	73	59
7	Eagles	Watford	3	123	65	58
8	Quinn, A	Sheff Utd	4	103	54	49
9	Miller	Leeds	1	119	73	46
10	Lewis	Leeds	5	115	70	45
11	Derry	Leeds	0	114	71	43
12	Devlin	Watford	2	94	53	41
13	McAnuff	Crystal Palace	8	99	61	38
14	Douglas	Leeds	5	110	73	37
15	Jones	Preston	3	112	75	37

CHART-TOPPING GOALSCORERS

1 Kitson - Reading	
Goals scored in the League	18
Contribution to Attacking Power Average number of minutes between League team goals while on pitch	43
Club Strike Rate (CSR) Average minutes between League goals scored by club	42
Player Strike Rate Average number of minutes between League goals scored by player	131

	PLAYER	CLUB	GOALS: LGE	POWER	CSR	S RATE
1	Kitson	Reading	18	43	42	131
2	Henderson	Watford	14	55	54	162
3	King	Watford	21	50	54	167
4	Lita	Reading	11	43	42	173
5	Johnson	Crystal Palace	15	66	62	175
6	Vine	Luton	10	67	63	181
7	Nygaard	QPR	9	69	83	185
8	Healy	Leeds	12	62	73	187
9	John	Coventry	10	63	67	189
10	Doyle	Reading	18	43	42	203
11	Cort	Wolverhampton	11	81	83	206
12	Forster	Ipswich	7	78	78	212
13	Morrison	Crystal Palace	13	57	62	214
14	Jerome	Cardiff	18	71	71	216
15	Kabba	Sheff Utd	9	47	54	219

CHART-TOPPING DEFENDERS

1 Davis - Preston	
Goals Conceded in the League The number of League goals conceded while he was on the pitch	19
Clean Sheets In games when he played at least 70 mins	21
Club Defensive Rating Average mins between League goals conceded by the club this season	138
Defensive Rating Average number of minutes between League goals conceded while on pitch	174

	PLAYER	CLUB	CON: LGE	CS	CDR	DEF RATE
1	Davis	Preston	19	21	138	174
2	Mawene	Preston	16	14	138	150
3	Alexander	Preston	23	21	138	149
4	Mears	Preston	17	15	138	149
5	Hill	Preston	15	12	138	138
6	Sonko	Reading	32	22	129	129
7	Ingimarsson	Reading	32	22	129	129
8	Murty	Reading	28	19	129	126
9	Shorey	Reading	28	19	129	126
10	Davidson	Preston	19	12	138	123
11	Unsworth	Sheff Utd	23	14	90	119
12	Crainey	Leeds	18	9	109	118
13	Butler	Leeds	34	16	109	115
14	Kelly	Leeds	35	16	109	111
15	Naylor	Wolverhampton	31	15	99	111

CHART-TOPPING GOALKEEPERS

1 Nash - Preston	
Counting Games Games in which he played at least 70 minutes	46
Goals Conceded in the League The number of League goals conceded while he was on the pitch	30
Clean Sheets In games when he played at least 70 mins	24
Defensive Rating Average number of minutes between League goals conceded while on pitch	138

	PLAYER	CLUB	CG	CONC	CS	DEF RATE
1	Nash	Preston	46	30	24	138
2	Hahnemann	Reading	45	31	22	131
3	Sullivan	Leeds	42	35	14	108
4	Postma	Wolverhampton	29	24	13	107
5	Larrieu	Plymouth	44	43	14	92
6	Kenny	Sheff Utd	46	46	18	90
7	Niemi	Southampton	25	25	11	90
8	Kiraly	Crystal Palace	43	43	14	89
9	Oakes	Wolverhampton	17	17	5	87
10	Jensen	Burnley	39	42	14	82
11	Henderson	Leicester	15	16	4	82
12	Foster	Watford	44	50	11	79
13	Lucas	Sheff Wed	18	21	5	75
14	Myhill	Hull City	45	55	12	73
15	Marshall	Millwall	29	35	5	73

PLAYER DISCIPLINARY RECORD

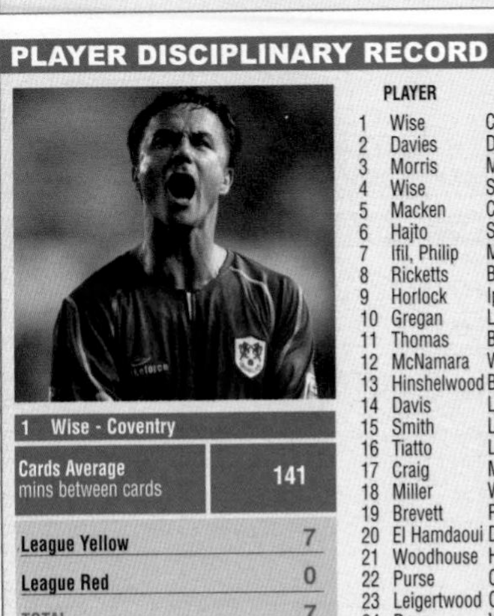

1 Wise - Coventry	
Cards Average mins between cards	141
League Yellow	7
League Red	0
TOTAL	7

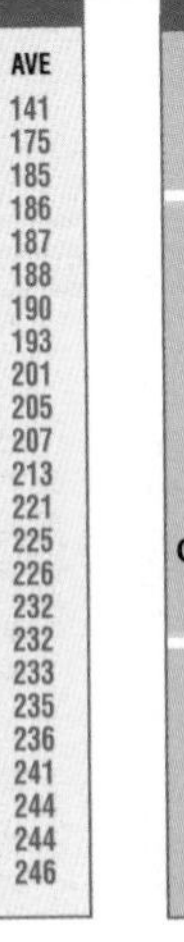

	PLAYER		LY	LR	TOT	AVE
1	Wise	Coventry	7	0	7	141
2	Davies	Derby	8	3	11	175
3	Morris	Millwall	8	2	10	185
4	Wise	Southampton	4	0	4	186
5	Macken	Crystal Palace	5	1	6	187
6	Hajto	Southampton	7	1	8	188
7	Ifil, Philip	Millwall	6	1	7	190
8	Ricketts	Burnley	5	0	5	193
9	Horlock	Ipswich	6	0	6	201
10	Gregan	Leeds	12	0	12	205
11	Thomas	Burnley	3	2	5	207
12	McNamara	Wolverhampton	4	0	4	213
13	Hinshelwood	Brighton	3	1	4	221
14	Davis	Luton	6	1	7	225
15	Smith	Leicester	5	0	5	226
16	Tiatto	Leicester	4	0	4	232
17	Craig	Millwall	8	2	10	232
18	Miller	Wolverhampton	12	0	12	233
19	Brevett	Plymouth	4	0	4	235
20	El Hamdaoui	Derby	2	0	2	236
21	Woodhouse	Hull City	5	0	5	241
22	Purse	Cardiff	12	2	14	244
23	Leigertwood	Crystal Palace	7	0	7	244
24	Ross	Wolverhampton	5	0	5	246

TEAM OF THE SEASON

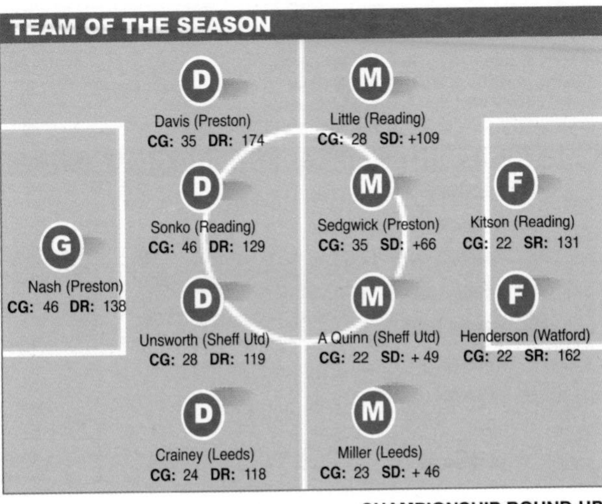

READING

Final Position: **1st**

NICKNAME: THE ROYALS

KEY: ☐Won ☐Drawn ☐Lost

							Attendance
1	div1	Plymouth	H	L	1-2	Lita 54	16,836
2	div1	Brighton	A	W	2-0	Little 15; Kitson 63	6,676
3	div1	Preston	A	W	3-0	Lita 34,46; Little 57	13,154
4	div1	Millwall	H	W	5-0	Convey 6,25; Harper 38; Kitson 43 pen; Sidwell 79	14,225
5	ccr1	Swansea	H	W	3-1	Kitson 14,95; Lita 114	7,603
6	div1	Watford	A	D	0-0		11,358
7	div1	Burnley	H	W	2-1	Lita 7; Doyle 70	14,027
8	div1	Coventry	A	D	1-1	Doyle 68	22,074
9	div1	Crystal Palace	H	W	3-2	Doyle 26; Lita 68; Sonko 87	17,562
10	div1	Crewe	H	W	1-0	Ingimarsson 81	17,668
11	ccr2	Luton	H	W	1-0	Oster 80	6,941
12	div1	Norwich	A	W	1-0	Harper 61	24,850
13	div1	Southampton	A	D	0-0		24,946
14	div1	Sheff Utd	H	W	2-1	Gunnarsson 3,89	22,068
15	div1	Ipswich	H	W	2-0	Naylor 18 og; Doyle 47	17,581
16	div1	Hull City	A	D	1-1	Little 74	17,698
17	div1	Stoke	A	W	1-0	Kitson 77 pen	13,484
18	ccr3	Sheff Utd	H	W	2-0	Kitson 54,75	11,607
19	div1	Leeds	H	D	1-1	Gunnarsson 63	22,012
20	div1	Sheff Wed	H	W	2-0	Whelan 38 og; Kitson 64	16,188
21	div1	QPR	A	W	2-1	Harper 10; Ingimarsson 66	15,347
22	div1	Hull City	H	W	3-1	Convey 7; Doyle 69; Little 70	17,864
23	div1	Ipswich	A	W	3-0	Sidwell 29; Lita 53; Doyle 77	22,621
24	div1	Plymouth	A	W	2-0	Little 20; Doyle 57	14,020
25	ccr4	Arsenal	A	L	0-3		36,167
26	div1	Luton	H	W	3-0	Sidwell 44; Kitson 76; Doyle 88	19,478
27	div1	Brighton	H	W	5-1	Oatway 27 og; Kitson 51 pen,71,90; Hunt 76	18,546
28	div1	Millwall	A	W	2-0	Sidwell 40; Doyle 68	12,920
29	div1	Wolverhampton	A	W	2-0	Kitson 29; Convey 64	27,980
30	div1	Leicester	H	W	2-0	Doyle 60; Gunnarsson 87	22,061
31	div1	Derby	A	D	2-2	Doyle 34; Long 88	21,434
32	div1	Cardiff	H	W	5-1	Sidwell 11,71; Sonko 32; Kitson 51,76 pen	22,061
33	facr3	West Brom	A	D	1-1	Doyle 84 pen	19,197
34	div1	Coventry	H	W	2-0	Kitson 46,78	22,813
35	facr3r	West Brom	H	W	3-2	Lita 50,65,93	16,737
36	div1	Crystal Palace	A	D	1-1	Harper 81	19,888
37	facr4	Birmingham	H	D	1-1	Long 31	23,762
38	div1	Norwich	H	W	4-0	Shorey 6; Sidwell 17; Lita 55; Convey 69	21,442
39	div1	Crewe	A	W	4-3	Shorey 24; Sidwell 26; Lita 43,53	6,484
40	facr4r	Birmingham	A	L	1-2	Hunt 51	16,644
41	div1	Southampton	H	W	2-0	Lita 16; Doyle 38	23,845
42	div1	Sheff Utd	A	D	1-1	Kitson 12	25,011
43	div1	Luton	A	L	2-3	Doyle 1,90	8,705
44	div1	Preston	H	W	2-1	Sidwell 5; Lita 45	23,011
45	div1	Burnley	A	W	3-0	Convey 10; Sonko 55; Kitson 90	12,888
46	div1	Watford	H	D	0-0		23,724
47	div1	Wolverhampton	H	D	1-1	Convey 23	23,502
48	div1	Leicester	A	D	1-1	Doyle 85	25,578
49	div1	Derby	H	W	5-0	Harper 59; Doyle 65; Oster 70; Long 74,83	22,981
50	div1	Cardiff	A	W	5-2	Harper 10,90; Kitson 39; Loovens 52 og; Doyle 87	11,866
51	div1	Leeds	A	D	1-1	Hunt 85	24,535
52	div1	Stoke	H	W	3-1	Sidwell 25; Doyle 56 pen; Halls 62	22,119
53	div1	Sheff Wed	A	D	1-1	Kitson 34	27,307
54	div1	QPR	H	W	2-1	Kitson 40; Murty 84 pen	23,156

LEAGUE APPEARANCES AND BOOKINGS

	AGE (on 01/07/06)	IN NAMED 16	APPEARANCES	COUNTING GAMES	MINUTES ON PITCH	LEAGUE GOALS	Yellow	Red
Goalkeepers								
Adam Federici	21	3	0	0	0	0	0	0
Marcus Hahnemann	34	46	45	45	4050	0	0	0
Graham Stack	24	43	1	1	90	0	0	0
Defenders								
Aaron Brown	23	2	0	0	0	0	0	0
Michael Dobson	25	1	1	0	37	0	0	0
Scott Golbourne	18	1	1	0	27	0	0	0
John Halls	24	3	1	1	90	1	0	0
Ivar Ingimarsson	28	46	46	46	4140	2	1	0
Chris Makin	39	37	12	10	997	0	2	0
Graeme Murty	31	41	40	39	3533	1	3	0
Nicky Shorey	25	40	40	38	3528	2	2	0
Ibrahima Sonko	25	46	46	46	4140	3	1	0
Midfielders								
Sekou Baradji	22	6	1	0	24	0	0	0
Simon Cox	19	3	2	0	21	0	0	0
Brynjar Gunnarsson	30	34	29	18	1788	4	5	0
James Harper	25	45	45	44	3947	7	1	0
Stephen Hunt	24	46	38	3	813	2	1	0
Glen Little	30	35	35	28	2724	5	4	0
Curtis Osano	19	2	0	0	0	0	0	0
John Oster	27	43	33	7	1200	1	2	0
Steven Sidwell	23	34	33	26	2576	10	5	0
Conor Sinnott	20	0	0	0	0	0	0	0
Forwards								
Bobby Convey	23	45	45	39	3589	7	1	0
Kevin Doyle	22	46	45	40	3649	18	4	0
David Kitson	26	35	34	22	2364	18	5	0
Leroy Lita	21	26	26	20	1902	11	1	0
Shane Long	19	14	11	1	264	3	0	0
Eric Obinna	25	12	5	0	47	0	0	0

TEAM OF THE SEASON

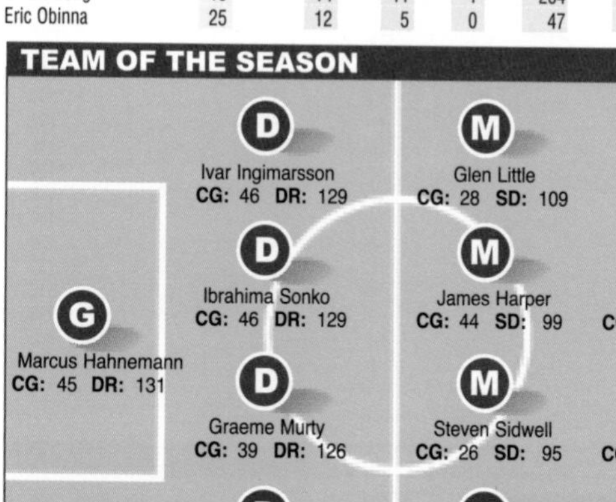

MONTHLY POINTS TALLY

AUGUST	13	72%
SEPTEMBER	11	73%
OCTOBER	11	73%
NOVEMBER	15	100%
DECEMBER	16	89%
JANUARY	10	83%
FEBRUARY	10	67%
MARCH	6	50%
APRIL	14	78%

LEAGUE GOALS

	PLAYER	LGE	FAC	LC	Oth	TOT
1	Kitson	18	0	4	0	22
2	Doyle	18	1	0	0	19
3	Lita	11	3	1	0	15
4	Sidwell	10	0	0	0	10
5	Harper	7	0	0	0	7
6	Convey	7	0	0	0	7
7	Little	5	0	0	0	5
8	Gunnarsson	4	0	0	0	4
9	Sonko	3	0	0	0	3
10	Long	3	1	0	0	4
11	Ingimarsson	2	0	0	0	2
	Other	11	1	1	0	13
	TOTAL	99	6	6	0	111

TOP POINT EARNERS

	PLAYER	GAMES	AV PTS
1	Steven Sidwell	26	2.50
2	Leroy Lita	20	2.45
3	Graeme Murty	39	2.33
4	Glen Little	28	2.32
5	James Harper	44	2.32
6	Bobby Convey	39	2.31
7	Ibrahima Sonko	46	2.30
8	Ivar Ingimarsson	46	2.30
9	Marcus Hahnemann	45	2.29
10	Nicky Shorey	38	2.26
	CLUB AVERAGE:		2.30

DISCIPLINARY RECORDS

	PLAYER	YELLOW	RED	AVE
1	Gunnarsson	5	0	357
2	Kitson	5	0	472
3	Makin	2	0	498
4	Sidwell	5	0	515
5	Oster	2	0	600
6	Little	4	0	681
7	Hunt	1	0	813
8	Doyle	4	0	912
9	Murty	3	0	1177
10	Shorey	2	0	1764
11	Lita	1	0	1902
12	Convey	1	0	3589
13	Harper	1	0	3947
	Other	2	0	
	TOTAL	38	0	

KEY GOALKEEPER

Marcus Hahnemann

Goals Conceded in the League	31	**Counting Games** League games when player was on pitch for at least 70 minutes	45
Goals Conceded in all competitions	31		
Defensive Rating Ave number of mins between League goals conceded while on the pitch	131	**Clean Sheets** In games when player was on pitch for at least 70 minutes	22

KEY PLAYERS - DEFENDERS

Ibrahima Sonko

Goals Conceded in the League	32	**Clean Sheets** In League games when player was on pitch for at least 70 minutes	22
Goals Conceded in all competitions	39		
Defensive Rating Ave number of mins between League goals conceded while on the pitch	129	**Club Defensive Rating** Average number of mins between League goals conceded by the club this season	129

	PLAYER	CON LGE	CON ALL	CLN SHEETS	DEF RATE
1	Ibrahima Sonko	32	39	22	129 mins
2	Ivar Ingimarsson	32	41	22	129 mins
3	Graeme Murty	28	33	19	126 mins
4	Nicky Shorey	28	32	19	126 mins

KEY PLAYERS - MIDFIELDERS

Glen Little

Goals in the League	5	**Contribution to Attacking Power** Average number of minutes between League team goals while on pitch	42
Goals in all competitions	5		
Defensive Rating Average number of mins between League goals conceded while on the pitch	151	**Scoring Difference** Defensive Rating minus Contribution to Attacking Power	109

	PLAYER	GOALS LGE	GOALS ALL	DEF RATE	ATT POWER	SCORE DIFF
1	Glen Little	5	5	151	42	109 mins
2	James Harper	7	7	141	42	99 mins
3	Steven Sidwell	10	10	129	34	95 mins
4	Brynjar Gunnarsson	4	4	119	54	65 mins

KEY PLAYERS - GOALSCORERS

David Kitson

Goals in the League	18	**Player Strike Rate** Average number of minutes between League goals scored by player	131
Goals in all competitions	22		
Contribution to Attacking Power Average number of minutes between League team goals while on pitch	43	**Club Strike Rate** Average number of minutes between League goals scored by club	42

	PLAYER	GOALS LGE	GOALS ALL	POWER	S RATE
1	David Kitson	18	22	43	131 mins
2	Leroy Lita	11	15	43	173 mins
3	Kevin Doyle	18	19	43	203 mins
4	Steven Sidwell	10	10	34	258 mins

Victorious Reading lift the Championship trophy

SQUAD APPEARANCES

Match	1	2	3	4	5	6	7	8	9	10	11	12	13	14	15	16	17	18	19	20	21	22	23	24	25	26	27
Venue	H	A	A	H	H	A	H	A	H	H	H	A	A	H	H	A	A	H	H	H	A	H	A	A	A	H	H
Competition	L	L	L	L	W	L	L	L	L	L	W	L	L	L	L	L	L	W	L	L	L	L	L	L	W	L	L
Result	L	W	W	W	W	D	W	D	W	W	W	W	D	W	W	D	W	W	D	W	W	W	W	W	L	W	W

Match	28	29	30	31	32	33	34	35	36	37	38	39	40	41	42	43	44	45	46	47	48	49	50	51	52	53	54
Venue	A	A	H	A	H	A	H	H	A	H	H	A	A	H	A	A	H	A	H	H	A	H	A	A	H	A	H
Competition	L	L	L	L	L	F	L	F	L	F	L	L	F	L	L	L	L	L	L	L	L	L	L	L	L	L	L
Result	W	W	W	D	W	D	W	W	D	D	W	W	L	W	D	L	W	W	D	D	D	W	W	D	W	D	W

Goalkeepers
Adam Federici
Marcus Hahnemann
Graham Stack

Defenders
Aaron Brown
Michael Dobson
Scott Golbourne
John Halls
Ivar Ingimarsson
Chris Makin
Graeme Murty
Nicky Shorey
Ibrahima Sonko

Midfielders
Sekou Baradji
Simon Cox
Brynjar Gunnarsson
James Harper
Stephen Hunt
Glen Little
Curtis Osano
John Oster
Steven Sidwell
Conor Sinnott

Forwards
Bobby Convey
Kevin Doyle
David Kitson
Leroy Lita
Shane Long
Eric Obinna

KEY: On all match | On bench | Subbed or sent off (Counting game) | Subbed or sent off (playing less than 70 minutes) | Subbed on from bench (Counting Game) | Subbed on (playing less than 70 minutes) | Subbed on and then subbed or sent off (Counting Game) | Subbed on and then subbed or sent off (playing less than 70 minutes) | Not in 16

SHEFFIELD UNITED

Final Position: **2nd**

NICKNAME: THE BLADES

KEY: ☐ Won ☐ Drawn ☐ Lost

No	Comp	Opponent	H/A	Res	Score	Scorers	Attendance
1	div1	Leicester	H	W	4-1	Gray 34 pen; Kabba 81 pen; Ifill, Paul 84; Bromby 90	18,224
2	div1	Burnley	A	W	2-1	Shipperley 5; Morgan 40	11,802
3	div1	QPR	A	L	1-2	Kabba 90	13,497
4	div1	Preston	H	W	2-1	Shipperley 45; Webber 90	20,519
5	ccr1	Boston	H	W	1-0	Ross 50	6,014
6	div1	Coventry	H	W	2-1	Kabba 27; Unsworth 90 pen	17,739
7	div1	Crewe	A	W	3-1	Shipperley 15; Quinn, A 50; Kabba 56	7,501
8	div1	Ipswich	H	W	2-0	Kabba 5,90	21,059
9	div1	Brighton	A	W	1-0	Jagielka 25	6,553
10	div1	Watford	A	W	3-2	Jagielka 56; Ifill, Paul 66; Carlisle 81 og	15,399
11	ccr2	Shrewsbury	A	W	4-3*	(*on penalties)	
12	div1	Derby	H	W	2-1	Unsworth 7; Ifill, Paul 37	22,192
13	div1	Plymouth	H	W	2-0	Shipperley 10; Quinn, A 31	20,111
14	div1	Reading	A	L	1-2	Kabba 15	22,068
15	div1	Wolverhampton	H	W	1-0	Shipperley 16	25,533
16	div1	Millwall	A	W	4-0	Webber 33,73; Pericard 36; Quinn, A 68	9,148
17	div1	Leeds	A	D	1-1	Kabba 69	23,600
18	ccr3	Reading	A	L	0-2		11,607
19	div1	Cardiff	H	D	0-0		25,311
20	div1	Luton	H	W	4-0	Jagielka 34,88; Morgan 50; Pericard 71	22,554
21	div1	Crystal Palace	A	W	3-2	Jagielka 15; Ifill, Paul 45; Shipperley 56	20,344
22	div1	Millwall	H	D	2-2	Unsworth 5; Webber 84	22,292
23	div1	Wolverhampton	A	D	0-0		24,240
24	div1	Leicester	A	L	2-4	Kabba 52; Webber 90	22,382
25	div1	Sheff Wed	H	W	1-0	Quinn, A 24	30,558
26	div1	Burnley	H	W	3-0	Shipperley 29,81; Webber 34	23,118
27	div1	Preston	A	D	0-0		14,378
28	div1	Norwich	H	L	1-3	Jagielka 22	26,505
29	div1	Southampton	A	W	1-0	Shipperley 55	27,443
30	div1	Stoke	H	W	2-1	Montgomery 18; Morgan 90	21,279
31	div1	Hull City	A	W	3-1	Ifill, Paul 31; Webber 45; Armstrong 52	21,929
32	facr3	Colchester	H	L	1-2	Kabba 5	11,820
33	div1	Ipswich	A	D	1-1	Webber 77	23,794
34	div1	Brighton	H	W	3-1	Jagielka 53; Ifill, Paul 64; Tonge 75	27,514
35	div1	Derby	A	W	1-0	Akinbiyi 12	26,275
36	div1	Watford	H	L	1-4	Ifill, Paul 58	20,791
37	div1	Plymouth	A	D	0-0		15,017
38	div1	Reading	H	D	1-1	Dyer 9	25,011
39	div1	Sheff Wed	A	W	2-1	Tonge 37; Akinbiyi 45	33,439
40	div1	QPR	H	L	2-3	Akinbiyi 20; Bircham 28 og	25,360
41	div1	Crewe	H	D	0-0		22,691
42	div1	Coventry	A	L	0-2		23,506
43	div1	Norwich	A	L	1-2	Armstrong 17	25,346
44	div1	Southampton	H	W	3-0	Jagielka 43; Ifill, Paul 46; Shipperley 77	22,824
45	div1	Stoke	A	D	1-1	Webber 83	17,544
46	div1	Hull City	H	W	3-2	Shipperley 36; Ifill, Paul 52; Unsworth 90	26,324
47	div1	Cardiff	A	W	1-0	Webber 76	11,006
48	div1	Leeds	H	D	1-1	Bakke 9 og	29,329
49	div1	Luton	A	D	1-1	Tonge 90	10,248
50	div1	Crystal Palace	H	W	1-0	Morgan 81	27,120

LEAGUE APPEARANCES AND BOOKINGS

	AGE (on 01/07/06)	IN NAMED 16	APPEARANCES	COUNTING GAMES	MINUTES ON PITCH	LEAGUE GOALS	Yellow	Red
Goalkeepers								
Philip Barnes	270	6	0	0	0	0	0	0
Patrick Kenny	27	46	46	46	4140	0	3	0
Defenders								
Chris Armstrong	23	26	24	20	1889	2	3	0
Leigh Bromby	26	35	35	33	3055	1	5	0
Neill Collins	22	2	2	2	180	0	0	0
Simon Francis	21	1	1	0	29	0	0	0
Derek Geary	26	31	20	17	1586	0	5	0
Jon Harley	26	4	4	4	343	0	0	0
Robert Kozluk	28	36	27	19	1939	0	3	0
Chris Lucketti	34	9	3	2	194	0	1	0
Chris Morgan	28	43	39	37	3351	4	7	1
Craig Short	38	24	23	20	1816	0	2	0
David Unsworth	32	34	34	28	2742	4	10	1
Alan Wright	34	8	6	3	342	0	1	0
Midfielders								
Garry Flitcroft	33	9	6	2	218	0	0	0
Keith Gillespie	31	36	30	6	1060	0	1	0
Paul Ifill	26	42	39	20	2356	9	0	0
Philip Jagielka	23	46	46	46	4140	8	2	0
Nick Montgomery	25	43	39	30	2984	1	5	0
Lilian Nalis	34	10	4	3	254	0	0	0
Alan Quinn	27	34	27	22	2052	4	3	0
Stephen Quinn	20	0	0	0	0	0	0	0
Ian Ross	20	0	0	0	0	0	0	0
Michael Tonge	23	42	30	23	2028	3	3	0
Forwards								
Ade Akinbiyi	31	16	15	9	989	3	1	0
Bruce Dyer	31	7	5	1	223	1	1	0
Jonathan Forte	19	1	1	0	45	0	0	0
Andy Gray	28	1	1	1	76	1	0	0
Geoff Horsfield	32	4	3	0	93	0	0	0
Steve Kabba	25	39	34	19	1970	9	2	0
Colin Marrison	20	0	0	0	0	0	0	0
Gary Mulligan	21	0	0	0	0	0	0	0
Vincent Pericard	23	13	11	3	342	2	0	0
Paul Shaw	32	6	1	0	28	0	0	0
Neil Shipperley	31	44	39	26	2724	11	2	0
Danny Webber	24	36	35	24	2270	10	2	0

TEAM OF THE SEASON

G — Patrick Kenny, CG: 46 DR: 90

D — David Unsworth, CG: 28 DR: 119

D — Robert Kozluk, CG: 19 DR: 97

D — Craig Short, CG: 20 DR: 96

D — Chris Armstrong, CG: 20 DR: 94

M — Alan Quinn, CG: 22 SD: 49

M — Paul Ifill, CG: 20 SD: 37

M — Nick Montgomery, CG: 30 SD: 37

M — Philip Jagielka, CG: 46 SD: 36

F — Steve Kabba, CG: 19 SR: 219

F — Danny Webber, CG: 24 SR: 227

MONTHLY POINTS TALLY

Month	Points	%
AUGUST	15	83%
SEPTEMBER	15	100%
OCTOBER	8	53%
NOVEMBER	8	53%
DECEMBER	13	72%
JANUARY	7	78%
FEBRUARY	8	44%
MARCH	4	33%
APRIL	12	67%

LEAGUE GOALS

	PLAYER	LGE	FAC	LC	Oth	TOT
1	Shipperley	11	0	0	0	11
2	Webber	10	0	0	0	10
3	Kabba	9	1	0	0	10
4	Ifill, Paul	9	0	0	0	9
5	Jagielka	8	0	0	0	8
6	Unsworth	4	0	0	0	4
7	Morgan	4	0	0	0	4
8	Quinn, A	4	0	0	0	4
9	Tonge	3	0	0	0	3
10	Akinbiyi	3	0	0	0	3
11	Armstrong	2	0	0	0	2
	Other	9	0	1	0	10
	TOTAL	76	1	1	0	78

TOP POINT EARNERS

	PLAYER	GAMES	AV PTS
1	David Unsworth	28	2.32
2	Steve Kabba	19	2.26
3	Paul Ifill	20	2.25
4	Nick Montgomery	30	2.17
5	Neil Shipperley	26	2.12
6	Leigh Bromby	33	2.12
7	Craig Short	20	2.05
8	Alan Quinn	22	2.05
9	Chris Morgan	37	2.03
10	Robert Kozluk	19	2.00
	CLUB AVERAGE:		1.96

DISCIPLINARY RECORDS

	PLAYER	YELLOW	RED	AVE
1	Unsworth	10	1	249
2	Geary	5	0	317
3	Morgan	7	1	418
4	Montgomery	5	0	596
5	Bromby	5	0	611
6	Armstrong	3	0	629
7	Kozluk	3	0	646
8	Tonge	3	0	676
9	Quinn, A	3	0	684
10	Short	2	0	908
11	Kabba	2	0	985
12	Akinbiyi	1	0	989
13	Gillespie	1	0	1060
	Other	9	0	
	TOTAL	59	2	

KEY GOALKEEPER

Patrick Kenny

Goals Conceded in the League	46	Counting Games League games when player was on pitch for at least 70 minutes	46
Goals Conceded in all competitions	46		
Defensive Rating Ave number of mins between League goals conceded while on the pitch	90	Clean Sheets In games when player was on pitch for at least 70 minutes	18

KEY PLAYERS - DEFENDERS

David Unsworth

Goals Conceded in the League	23	Clean Sheets In League games when player was on pitch for at least 70 minutes	14
Goals Conceded in all competitions	23		
Defensive Rating Ave number of mins between League goals conceded while on the pitch	119	Club Defensive Rating Average number of mins between League goals conceded by the club this season	90

	PLAYER	CON LGE	CON ALL	CLN SHEETS	DEF RATE
1	David Unsworth	23	23	14	119 mins
2	Robert Kozluk	20	22	9	97 mins
3	Craig Short	19	19	9	96 mins
4	Chris Armstrong	20	22	8	94 mins

KEY PLAYERS - MIDFIELDERS

Alan Quinn

Goals in the League	4	Contribution to Attacking Power Average number of minutes between League team goals while on pitch	54
Goals in all competitions	4		
Defensive Rating Average number of mins between League goals conceded while on the pitch	103	Scoring Difference Defensive Rating minus Contribution to Attacking Power	49

	PLAYER	GOALS LGE	GOALS ALL	DEF RATE	ATT POWER	SCORE DIFF
1	Alan Quinn	4	4	103	54	49 mins
2	Nick Montgomery	1	1	90	53	37 mins
3	Paul Ifill	9	9	84	47	37 mins
4	Philip Jagielka	8	8	90	54	36 mins

KEY PLAYERS - GOALSCORERS

Steve Kabba

Goals in the League	9	Player Strike Rate Average number of minutes between League goals scored by player	219
Goals in all competitions	10		
Contribution to Attacking Power Average number of minutes between League team goals while on pitch	47	Club Strike Rate Average number of minutes between League goals scored by club	54

	PLAYER	GOALS LGE	GOALS ALL	POWER	S RATE
1	Steve Kabba	9	10	47	219 mins
2	Danny Webber	10	10	55	227 mins
3	Neil Shipperley	11	11	57	248 mins
4	Paul Ifill	9	9	47	262 mins

Danny Webber and Steven Kabba celebrate promotion

SQUAD APPEARANCES

Match	1	2	3	4	5	6	7	8	9	10	11	12	13	14	15	16	17	18	19	20	21	22	23	24	25
Venue	H	A	A	H	H	H	A	H	A	A	A	H	H	A	H	A	A	A	H	H	A	H	A	A	H
Competition	L	L	L	L	W	L	L	L	L	L	W	L	L	L	L	L	L	W	L	L	L	L	L	L	L
Result	W	W	L	W	W	W	W	W	W	W	W	W	W	L	W	W	D	L	D	W	W	D	D	L	W

Match	26	27	28	29	30	31	32	33	34	35	36	37	38	39	40	41	42	43	44	45	46	47	48	49	50
Venue	H	A	H	A	H	A	H	A	H	A	H	A	H	A	H	H	A	A	H	A	H	A	H	A	H
Competition	L	L	L	L	L	L	F	L	L	L	L	L	L	L	L	L	L	L	L	L	L	L	L	L	L
Result	W	D	L	W	W	W	L	D	W	W	L	D	D	W	L	D	L	L	W	D	W	W	D	D	W

Goalkeepers
Philip Barnes
Patrick Kenny

Defenders
Chris Armstrong
Leigh Bromby
Neill Collins
Simon Francis
Derek Geary
Jon Harley
Robert Kozluk
Chris Lucketti
Chris Morgan
Craig Short
David Unsworth
Alan Wright

Midfielders
Garry Flitcroft
Keith Gillespie
Paul Ifill
Philip Jagielka
Nick Montgomery
Lilian Nalis
Alan Quinn
Stephen Quinn
Ian Ross
Michael Tonge

Forwards
Ade Akinbiyi
Bruce Dyer
Jonathan Forte
Andy Gray
Geoff Horsfield
Steve Kabba
Colin Marrison
Gary Mulligan
Vincent Pericard
Paul Shaw
Neil Shipperley
Danny Webber

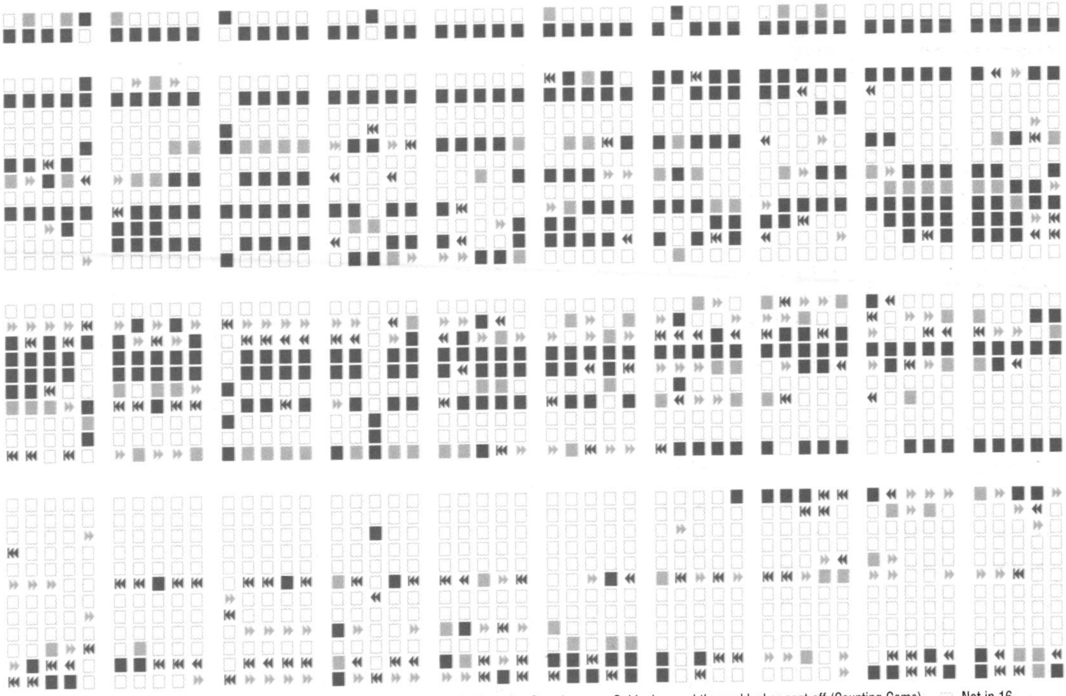

KEY: On all match | On bench | Subbed or sent off (Counting game) | Subbed or sent off (playing less than 70 minutes) | Subbed on from bench (Counting Game) | Subbed on (playing less than 70 minutes) | Subbed on and then subbed or sent off (Counting Game) | Subbed on and then subbed or sent off (playing less than 70 minutes) | Not in 16

WATFORD

PROMOTED VIA THE PLAY-OFFS Final Position: **3rd**

NICKNAME: THE HORNETS

KEY: ☐Won ☐Drawn ☐Lost

#	Comp	Opponent	H/A	Res	Score	Scorers	Attendance
1	div1	Preston	H	L	1-2	Henderson 9	12,597
2	div1	Plymouth	A	D	3-3	King 35; Young 52,61	13,813
3	div1	Cardiff	A	W	3-1	King 7,67; Henderson 52	9,256
4	div1	Burnley	H	W	3-1	King 11; Mahon 30; Spring 83	16,802
5	ccr1	Notts County	H	W	3-1	Young 13; Bouazza 34 pen; Blizzard 48	7,011
6	div1	Reading	H	D	0-0		11,358
7	div1	Derby	A	W	2-1	Spring 67; Carlisle 89	23,664
8	div1	Stoke	A	W	3-0	Devlin 24; Young 67; King 72	14,565
9	div1	Norwich	H	W	2-1	King 13; Young 25	13,502
10	div1	Sheff Utd	H	L	2-3	Henderson 39,53	15,399
11	ccr2	Wolverhampton	H	W	2-1	Carlisle 45,104	9,296
12	div1	Crewe	A	D	0-0		6,258
13	div1	Coventry	A	L	1-3	Young 51	16,978
14	div1	Leeds	H	D	0-0		16,050
15	div1	Leicester	H	L	1-2	Young 49	16,224
16	div1	Sheff Wed	A	D	1-1	Young 86	21,187
17	div1	Ipswich	A	W	1-0	Young 55	24,069
18	ccr3	Wigan	A	L	0-3		4,531
19	div1	Wolverhampton	H	W	3-1	DeMerit 69; King 77; Devlin 80	14,561
20	div1	QPR	H	W	3-1	Spring 39; McNamee 70; Young 76	16,476
21	div1	Hull City	A	W	2-1	Mahon 8; Spring 44	18,444
22	div1	Sheff Wed	H	W	2-1	Carlisle 17; King 24	16,988
23	div1	Leicester	A	D	2-2	King 11; Mackay 85	18,856
24	div1	Preston	A	D	1-1	Spring 11	14,638
25	div1	Brighton	H	D	1-1	King 45	14,455
26	div1	Plymouth	H	D	1-1	King 90	12,884
27	div1	Burnley	A	L	1-4	King 62	13,815
28	div1	Southampton	H	W	3-0	Henderson 28; Carlisle 40; Hajto 47 og	16,972
29	div1	Millwall	A	D	0-0		8,450
30	div1	Crystal Palace	H	L	1-2	Henderson 59	15,856
31	div1	Luton	A	W	2-1	Henderson 9; Mackay 30	10,248
32	facr3	Bolton	H	L	0-3		13,239
33	div1	Stoke	H	W	1-0	Eagles 54	12,247
34	div1	Norwich	A	W	3-2	Henderson 47,65; Spring 90	25,384
35	div1	Crewe	H	W	4-1	Spring 18,26; King 58; Young 62	11,722
36	div1	Sheff Utd	A	W	4-1	Eagles 6; King 47,69; Bouazza 88	20,791
37	div1	Coventry	H	W	4-0	Young 32; King 59; Henderson 78; DeMerit 82	19,842
38	div1	Leeds	A	L	1-2	Young 40	22,007
39	div1	Brighton	A	W	1-0	Eagles 44	6,658
40	div1	Cardiff	H	W	2-1	Mackay 69; King 87	27,419
41	div1	Derby	H	D	2-2	King 35; Bangura 90	16,769
42	div1	Reading	A	D	0-0		23,724
43	div1	Southampton	A	W	3-1	Mahon 3; Henderson 67,72	19,202
44	div1	Millwall	H	L	0-2		16,654
45	div1	Crystal Palace	A	L	1-3	King 28	18,619
46	div1	Luton	H	D	1-1	King 36	15,922
47	div1	Wolverhampton	A	D	1-1	King 65	22,584
48	div1	Ipswich	H	W	2-1	Henderson 33,77	16,721
49	div1	QPR	A	W	2-1	Young 42; Santos 78 og	16,152
50	div1	Hull City	H	D	0-0		17,128
51	d1po1	Crystal Palace	A	W	3-0	King 46; Young 67; Spring 85	22,880
52	d1po2	Crystal Palace	H	D	0-0		
53	d1pof	Leeds	A	W	3-0	DeMerit 25; Sullivan 56 og; Henderson 84 pen	64,736

LEAGUE APPEARANCES AND BOOKINGS

	AGE (on 01/07/06)	IN NAMED 16	APPEARANCES	COUNTING GAMES	MINUTES ON PITCH	LEAGUE GOALS	Yellow	Red
Goalkeepers								
Alec Chamberlain	42	45	3	2	213	0	0	0
Ben Foster	23	44	44	43	3927	0	3	1
Defenders								
Clarke Carlisle	26	41	32	28	2633	3	8	1
James Chambers	25	45	38	24	2497	0	6	0
Jay DeMerit	26	40	31	26	2484	2	3	0
Lloyd Doyley	23	44	44	39	3671	0	2	0
Adam Griffiths	26	0	0	0	0	0	0	0
Malcolm Mackay	34	40	38	34	3150	3	4	1
Adrian Mariappa	19	8	3	1	114	0	0	0
Junior Osborne	18	2	1	0	45	0	1	0
Midfielders								
Alhassan Bangura	18	38	35	10	1412	1	5	0
Dominic Blizzard	22	11	10	6	700	0	0	0
Paul Devlin	34	26	23	16	1694	2	2	0
Toumani Diagouraga	19	5	1	0	45	0	0	0
Chris Eagles	20	18	17	12	1226	3	1	0
Carl Fletcher	26	5	3	3	270	0	1	0
Ben Gill	18	2	0	0	0	0	0	0
Joel Grant	18	11	7	2	308	0	0	0
Gavin Mahon	29	38	38	34	3255	3	4	0
Anthony McNamee	22	45	38	17	2160	1	1	0
Theo Robinson	17	3	1	0	45	0	0	0
Matthew Spring	26	40	39	32	3086	8	6	0
Jordan Stewart	24	46	35	26	2640	0	3	0
Ashley Young	20	39	39	35	3359	13	3	1
Forwards								
Gabriel Agbonlahor	19	4	2	0	109	0	0	0
Trevor Benjamin	27	3	2	1	135	0	0	0
Hameur Bouazza	21	17	14	2	410	1	0	0
Francino Francis	19	3	1	0	26	0	0	0
Darius Henderson	24	31	30	21	2264	14	7	1
Marlon King	26	41	41	37	3506	21	2	1

TEAM OF THE SEASON

G — Ben Foster CG: 43 DR: 79

D — Jay DeMerit CG: 26 DR: 83

D — Malcolm Mackay CG: 34 DR: 81

D — Lloyd Doyley CG: 39 DR: 78

D — James Chambers CG: 24 DR: 76

M — Chris Eagles CG: 12 SD: 58

M — Paul Devlin CG: 16 SD: 41

M — Gavin Mahon CG: 34 SD: 33

M — Matthew Spring CG: 32 SD: 33

F — Darius Henderson CG: 21 SR: 162

F — Marlon King CG: 37 SR: 167

MONTHLY POINTS TALLY

Month	Points	%
AUGUST	11	61%
SEPTEMBER	7	47%
OCTOBER	8	53%
NOVEMBER	11	73%
DECEMBER	6	33%
JANUARY	12	100%
FEBRUARY	12	80%
MARCH	5	33%
APRIL	9	60%

LEAGUE GOALS

	PLAYER	LGE	FAC	LC	Oth	TOT
1	King	21	0	0	1	22
2	Henderson	14	0	0	1	15
3	Young	13	0	1	1	15
4	Spring	8	0	0	1	9
5	Eagles	3	0	0	0	3
6	Mackay	3	0	0	0	3
7	Mahon	3	0	0	0	3
8	Carlisle	3	0	2	0	5
9	Devlin	2	0	0	0	2
10	DeMerit	2	0	0	1	3
11	McNamee	1	0	0	0	1
	Other	4	0	2	1	7
	TOTAL	77	0	5	6	88

TOP POINT EARNERS

	PLAYER	GAMES	AV PTS
1	Jay DeMerit	26	2.00
2	Anthony McNamee	17	1.88
3	Gavin Mahon	34	1.85
4	Matthew Spring	32	1.84
5	James Chambers	24	1.83
6	Chris Eagles	12	1.83
7	Marlon King	37	1.78
8	Ashley Young	35	1.77
9	Malcolm Mackay	34	1.76
10	Paul Devlin	16	1.75
	CLUB AVERAGE:		1.76

DISCIPLINARY RECORDS

	PLAYER	YELLOW	RED	AVE
1	Bangura	5	0	282
2	Henderson	7	1	283
3	Carlisle	8	1	292
4	Chambers, J	6	0	416
5	Spring	6	0	514
6	Mackay	4	1	630
7	Mahon	4	0	813
8	DeMerit	3	0	828
9	Young	3	1	839
10	Devlin	2	0	847
11	Stewart	3	0	880
12	Foster	3	1	981
13	King	2	1	1168
	Other	4	0	
	TOTAL	60	6	

KEY GOALKEEPER

Ben Foster

Goals Conceded in the League	50	**Counting Games** League games when player was on pitch for at least 70 minutes	43
Goals Conceded in all competitions	53		
Defensive Rating Ave number of mins between League goals conceded while on the pitch	79	**Clean Sheets** In games when player was on pitch for at least 70 minutes	11

KEY PLAYERS - DEFENDERS

Jay DeMerit

Goals Conceded in the League	30	**Clean Sheets** In League games when player was on pitch for at least 70 minutes	6
Goals Conceded in all competitions	34		
Defensive Rating Ave number of mins between League goals conceded while on the pitch	83	**Club Defensive Rating** Average number of mins between League goals conceded by the club this season	78

	PLAYER	CON LGE	CON ALL	CLN SHEETS	DEF RATE
1	Jay DeMerit	30	34	6	83 mins
2	Malcolm Mackay	39	45	9	81 mins
3	Lloyd Doyley	47	52	11	78 mins
4	James Chambers	33	37	7	76 mins

KEY PLAYERS - MIDFIELDERS

Chris Eagles

Goals in the League	3	**Contribution to Attacking Power** Average number of minutes between League team goals while on pitch	65
Goals in all competitions	3		
Defensive Rating Average number of mins between League goals conceded while on the pitch	123	**Scoring Difference** Defensive Rating minus Contribution to Attacking Power	58

	PLAYER	GOALS LGE	GOALS ALL	DEF RATE	ATT POWER	SCORE DIFF
1	Chris Eagles	3	3	123	65	58 mins
2	Paul Devlin	2	2	94	53	41 mins
3	Matthew Spring	8	9	88	55	33 mins
4	Gavin Mahon	3	3	86	53	33 mins

KEY PLAYERS - GOALSCORERS

Darius Henderson

Goals in the League	14	**Player Strike Rate** Average number of minutes between League goals scored by player	162
Goals in all competitions	15		
Contribution to Attacking Power Average number of minutes between League team goals while on pitch	55	**Club Strike Rate** Average number of minutes between League goals scored by club	54

	PLAYER	GOALS LGE	GOALS ALL	POWER	S RATE
1	Darius Henderson	14	15	55	162 mins
2	Marlon King	21	22	50	167 mins
3	Ashley Young	13	15	52	258 mins
4	Matthew Spring	8	9	55	386 mins

Watford's Marlon King

SQUAD APPEARANCES

Match	1	2	3	4	5	6	7	8	9	10	11	12	13	14	15	16	17	18	19	20	21	22	23	24	25	26	27
Venue	H	A	A	H	H	H	A	A	H	H	H	A	A	H	H	A	A	A	H	H	A	H	A	A	H	H	A
Competition	L	L	L	L	W	L	L	L	L	L	W	L	L	L	L	L	L	W	L	L	L	L	L	L	L	L	L
Result	L	D	W	W	W	D	W	W	W	L	W	D	L	D	L	D	W	L	W	W	W	W	D	D	D	D	L

Match	28	29	30	31	32	33	34	35	36	37	38	39	40	41	42	43	44	45	46	47	48	49	50	51	52	53
Venue	H	A	H	A	H	H	A	H	A	H	A	A	H	H	A	A	H	A	H	A	H	A	H	A	H	A
Competition	L	L	L	L	F	L	L	L	L	L	L	L	L	L	L	L	L	L	L	L	L	L	L	O	O	O
Result	W	D	L	W	L	W	W	W	W	W	L	W	W	D	D	W	L	L	D	D	W	W	D	W	D	W

Goalkeepers
- Alec Chamberlain
- Ben Foster

Defenders
- Clarke Carlisle
- James Chambers
- Jay DeMerit
- Lloyd Doyley
- Adam Griffiths
- Malcolm Mackay
- Adrian Mariappa
- Junior Osborne

Midfielders
- Alhassan Bangura
- Dominic Blizzard
- Paul Devlin
- Toumani Diagouraga
- Chris Eagles
- Carl Fletcher
- Ben Gill
- Joel Grant
- Gavin Mahon
- Anthony McNamee
- Theo Robinson
- Matthew Spring
- Jordan Stewart
- Ashley Young

Forwards
- Gabriel Agbonlahor
- Trevor Benjamin
- Hameur Bouazza
- Francino Francis
- Darius Henderson
- Marlon King

KEY: On all match; On bench; Subbed or sent off (Counting game); Subbed or sent off (playing less than 70 minutes); Subbed on from bench (Counting Game); Subbed on (playing less than 70 minutes); Subbed on and then subbed or sent off (Counting Game); Subbed on and then subbed or sent off (playing less than 70 minutes); Not in 16

PRESTON NORTH END

Final Position: **4th**

NICKNAME: THE LILYWHITES

KEY: ☐Won ☐Drawn ☐Lost

						Attendance
1 div1	Watford	A	W	2-1	Nugent 22; Etuhu 37	12,597
2 div1	Derby	H	D	1-1	Nugent 15	13,127
3 div1	Reading	H	L	0-3		13,154
4 div1	Sheff Utd	A	L	1-2	McKenna 35	20,519
5 ccr1	Barnsley	H	W	5-4*	Dichio 77; Alexander 119 pen (*on penalties)	3,137
6 div1	Brighton	H	D	0-0		12,461
7 div1	Ipswich	A	W	4-0	Nugent 31,34; Jones 45; Agyemang 85	22,551
8 div1	Millwall	A	W	2-1	Jones 19; Agyemang 77	7,674
9 div1	Burnley	H	D	0-0		17,139
10 div1	Stoke	H	L	0-1		12,453
11 div1	Crystal Palace	A	D	1-1	Lucketti 43	17,291
12 div1	Luton	A	L	0-3		7,815
13 div1	Southampton	H	D	1-1	Agyemang 65	15,263
14 div1	QPR	H	D	1-1	Mawene 90	13,660
15 div1	Cardiff	A	D	2-2	Mears 62; Sedgwick 90	9,574
16 div1	Wolverhampton	A	D	1-1	Etuhu 45	22,802
17 div1	Leicester	H	D	0-0		13,904
18 div1	Hull City	H	W	3-0	Johnson 59; Jones 73; McKenna 76	13,536
19 div1	Leeds	A	D	0-0		22,289
20 div1	Cardiff	H	W	2-1	Sedgwick 22; Agyemang 42	13,904
21 div1	QPR	A	W	2-0	Nugent 60; Davidson 85	10,901
22 div1	Watford	H	D	1-1	Davidson 14	14,638
23 div1	Crewe	A	W	2-0	Davidson 24; Nowland 37	6,364
24 div1	Derby	A	D	1-1	Davis 54	22,740
25 div1	Sheff Utd	H	D	0-0		14,378
26 div1	Sheff Wed	H	D	0-0		18,867
27 div1	Coventry	H	W	3-1	Nowland 26; Alexander 41 pen; Sedgwick 45	12,936
28 div1	Norwich	A	W	3-0	Nowland 45; Alexander 69 pen; Nugent 74	25,032
29 facr3	Crewe	H	W	2-1	Alexander 62; Sedgwick 86	8,380
30 div1	Millwall	H	W	2-0	Agyemang 43; Davis 51	14,165
31 div1	Burnley	A	W	2-0	Nugent 13; Alexander 86 pen	17,220
32 facr4	Crystal Palace	H	D	1-1	O'Neil 27	9,489
33 div1	Crystal Palace	H	W	2-0	Ormerod 13; O'Neil 49	13,867
34 div1	Stoke	A	D	0-0		13,218
35 facr4r	Crystal Palace	A	W	2-1	Dichio 35,88	7,356
36 div1	Luton	H	W	5-1	Neal, L 20; Nugent 53; Mears 84; Sedgwick 90 pen; Davis 90	15,237
37 div1	Southampton	A	D	0-0		19,534
38 facr5	Middlesbrough	H	L	0-2		19,877
39 div1	Reading	A	L	1-2	Davidson 7	23,011
40 div1	Plymouth	A	D	0-0		10,874
41 div1	Brighton	A	D	0-0		6,361
42 div1	Ipswich	H	W	3-1	Nugent 53,62; Agyemang 71	14,507
43 div1	Sheff Wed	A	L	0-2		23,429
44 div1	Plymouth	H	D	0-0		13,925
45 div1	Crewe	H	W	1-0	Ormerod 37	13,170
46 div1	Coventry	A	W	1-0	Whaley 30	21,023
47 div1	Norwich	H	W	2-0	Shackell 20 og; Doherty 38 og	15,714
48 div1	Leicester	A	W	2-1	Whaley 45; Jarrett 49	21,865
49 div1	Wolverhampton	H	W	2-0	Neal, L 42; Ormerod 71	16,885
50 div1	Hull City	A	D	1-1	Whaley 33	19,716
51 div1	Leeds	H	W	2-0	Stock 38; Ormerod 77	19,350
52 d1po1	Leeds	A	D	1-1	Nugent 48	
53 d1po2	Leeds	H	L	0-2		20,383

LEAGUE APPEARANCES AND BOOKINGS

	AGE (on 01/07/06)	IN NAMED 16	APPEARANCES	COUNTING GAMES	MINUTES ON PITCH	LEAGUE GOALS		
Goalkeepers								
Andrew Lonergan	22	4	0	0	0	0	0	0
Carlo Nash	32	46	46	46	4140	0	1	0
Gavin Ward	36	13	0	0	0	0	0	0
Defenders								
Graham Alexander	34	44	40	37	3427	3	3	0
Callum Davidson	30	27	27	25	2329	4	4	0
Claude Davis	27	42	40	35	3304	3	8	0
Matthew Hill	25	28	25	23	2073	0	5	0
Chris Lucketti	34	32	28	22	2151	1	5	0
Youl Mawene	26	38	30	25	2397	1	6	0
Tyrone Mears	23	36	32	27	2529	2	7	0
Brian O'Neil	33	26	25	15	1647	1	5	0
Kelvin Wilson	20	8	6	3	335	0	1	0
Midfielders								
Joe Anyinsah	21	4	3	0	42	0	0	0
Dickson Etuhu	24	15	13	5	712	2	1	0
Jason Jarrett	26	11	10	7	719	1	2	0
David Jones	21	26	24	18	1789	3	3	0
Paul McKenna	28	42	41	35	3421	2	8	0
Lewis Neal	24	38	24	10	1227	2	3	0
Adam Nowland	25	19	13	4	719	3	2	0
Ashley Parillon	-	1	0	0	0	0	0	0
Chris Sedgwick	26	46	46	35	3351	4	4	0
Brian Stock	24	10	6	3	329	1	2	0
Simon Whaley	21	19	16	8	849	3	3	0
Forwards								
Patrick Agyemang	25	44	42	16	2026	6	0	0
Richard Cresswell	28	3	3	3	261	0	1	0
Danny Dichio	31	40	33	13	1600	0	2	1
Dave Hibbert	20	19	11	1	301	0	0	0
Jemal Johnson	21	3	3	1	182	1	1	0
David Nugent	21	32	32	26	2324	10	7	0
Brett Ormerod	29	15	15	11	1084	4	3	0
Marcus Stewart	33	4	4	1	245	0	0	0

TEAM OF THE SEASON

G — Carlo Nash CG: 46 DR: 138

D — Claude Davis CG: 35 DR: 174

D — Youl Mawene CG: 25 DR: 150

D — Graham Alexander CG: 37 DR: 149

D — Tyrone Mears CG: 27 DR: 149

M — Chris Sedgwick CG: 35 SD: 66

M — Paul McKenna CG: 35 SD: 59

M — David Jones CG: 18 SD: 37

M — Lewis Neal CG: 10 SD: 26

F — David Nugent CG: 26 SR: 232

F — Patrick Agyemang CG: 16 SR: 338

MONTHLY POINTS TALLY

AUGUST	8	44%
SEPTEMBER	5	33%
OCTOBER	5	33%
NOVEMBER	11	73%
DECEMBER	9	60%
JANUARY	12	100%
FEBRUARY	5	42%
MARCH	9	50%
APRIL	16	89%
MAY	0	%

LEAGUE GOALS

	PLAYER	LGE	FAC	LC	Oth	TOT
1	Nugent	10	0	0	1	**11**
2	Agyemang	6	0	0	0	**6**
3	Davidson	4	0	0	0	**4**
4	Ormerod	4	0	0	0	**4**
5	Sedgwick	4	1	0	0	**5**
6	Nowland	3	0	0	0	**3**
7	Whaley	3	0	0	0	**3**
8	Davis	3	0	0	0	**3**
9	Jones	3	0	0	0	**3**
10	Alexander	3	1	1	0	**5**
11	Neal, L	2	0	0	0	**2**
	Other	14	3	1	0	18
	TOTAL	**59**	**5**	**2**	**1**	**67**

TOP POINT EARNERS

	PLAYER	GAMES	AV PTS
1	Patrick Agyemang	16	**2.06**
2	Matthew Hill	23	**1.87**
3	Tyrone Mears	27	**1.85**
4	Claude Davis	35	**1.80**
5	Graham Alexander	37	**1.78**
6	Youl Mawene	25	**1.76**
7	Paul McKenna	35	**1.74**
8	Carlo Nash	46	**1.74**
9	Chris Sedgwick	35	**1.71**
10	David Nugent	26	**1.62**
	CLUB AVERAGE:		**1.74**

DISCIPLINARY RECORDS

	PLAYER	YELLOW	RED	AVE
1	Whaley	3	0	**283**
2	O'Neil	5	0	**329**
3	Nugent	7	0	**332**
4	Jarrett	2	0	**359**
5	Nowland	2	0	**359**
6	Mears	7	0	**361**
7	Ormerod	3	0	**361**
8	Mawene	6	0	**399**
9	Neal, L	3	0	**409**
10	Davis	8	0	**413**
11	Hill	5	0	**414**
12	McKenna	8	0	**427**
13	Lucketti	5	0	**430**
	Other	18	1	
	TOTAL	**82**	**1**	

KEY GOALKEEPER

Carlo Nash

Goals Conceded in the League	30	Counting Games League games when player was on pitch for at least 70 minutes	46
Goals Conceded in all competitions	40		
Defensive Rating Ave number of mins between League goals conceded while on the pitch	138	Clean Sheets In games when player was on pitch for at least 70 minutes	24

KEY PLAYERS - GOALSCORERS

David Nugent

Goals in the League	10	Player Strike Rate Average number of minutes between League goals scored by player	232
Goals in all competitions	11		
Contribution to Attacking Power Average number of minutes between League team goals while on pitch	65	Club Strike Rate Average number of minutes between League goals scored by club	70

	PLAYER	GOALS LGE	GOALS ALL	POWER	S RATE
1	David Nugent	10	11	65	232 mins
2	Patrick Agyemang	6	6	65	338 mins
3	Callum Davidson	4	4	75	582 mins
4	David Jones	3	3	75	596 mins

KEY PLAYERS - DEFENDERS

Goals Conceded in the League	19	Clean Sheets In League games when player was on pitch for at least 70 minutes	21
Goals Conceded in all competitions	28		
Defensive Rating Ave number of mins between League goals conceded while on the pitch	174	Club Defensive Rating Average number of mins between League goals conceded by the club this season	138

	PLAYER	CON LGE	CON ALL	CLN SHEETS	DEF RATE
1	Claude Davis	19	28	21	174 mins
2	Youl Mawene	16	24	14	150 mins
3	Graham Alexander	23	30	21	149 mins
4	Tyrone Mears	17	27	15	149 mins

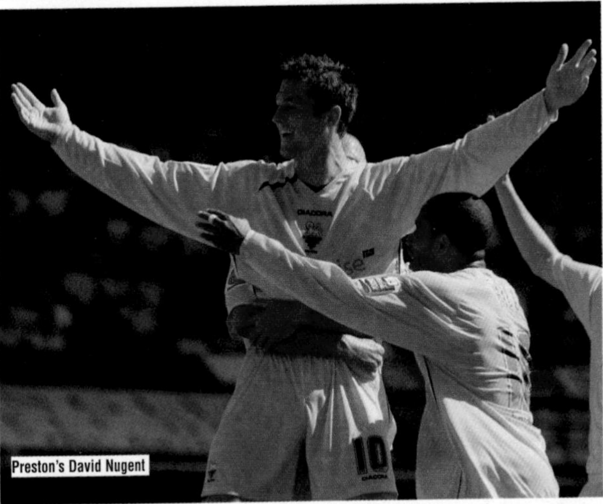

Preston's David Nugent

KEY PLAYERS - MIDFIELDERS

Chris Sedgwick

Goals in the League	4	Contribution to Attacking Power Average number of minutes between League team goals while on pitch	68
Goals in all competitions	5		
Defensive Rating Average number of mins between League goals conceded while on the pitch	134	Scoring Difference Defensive Rating minus Contribution to Attacking Power	66

	PLAYER	GOALS LGE	GOALS ALL	DEF RATE	ATT POWER	SCORE DIFF
1	Chris Sedgwick	4	5	134	68	66 mins
2	Paul McKenna	2	2	132	73	59 mins
3	David Jones	3	3	112	75	37 mins

SQUAD APPEARANCES

Match	1	2	3	4	5	6	7	8	9	10	11	12	13	14	15	16	17	18
Venue	A	H	H	A	H	H	A	A	H	H	A	A	H	H	A	A	H	H
Competition	L	L	L	L	W	L	L	L	L	L	L	L	L	L	L	L	L	L
Result	W	D	L	L	W	D	W	W	D	L	D	L	D	D	D	D	D	W

Match	19	20	21	22	23	24	25	26	27	28	29	30	31	32	33	34	35	36
Venue	A	H	A	H	A	A	H	H	H	A	H	H	A	H	H	A	A	H
Competition	L	L	L	L	L	L	L	L	L	L	F	L	L	F	L	L	F	L
Result	D	W	W	D	W	D	D	D	W	W	W	W	W	D	W	D	W	W

Match	37	38	39	40	41	42	43	44	45	46	47	48	49	50	51	52	53
Venue	A	H	A	A	A	H	A	H	H	A	H	A	H	A	H	A	H
Competition	L	F	L	L	L	L	L	L	L	L	L	L	L	L	L	O	O
Result	D	L	L	D	D	W	L	D	W	W	W	W	W	D	W	D	L

Goalkeepers
- Andrew Lonergan
- Carlo Nash
- Gavin Ward

Defenders
- Graham Alexander
- Callum Davidson
- Claude Davis
- Matthew Hill
- Chris Lucketti
- Youl Mawene
- Tyrone Mears
- Brian O'Neil
- Kelvin Wilson

Midfielders
- Joe Anyinsah
- Dickson Etuhu
- Jason Jarrett
- David Jones
- Paul McKenna
- Lewis Neal
- Adam Nowland
- Ashley Parillon
- Chris Sedgwick
- Brian Stock
- Simon Whaley

Forwards
- Patrick Agyemang
- Richard Cresswell
- Danny Dichio
- Dave Hibbert
- Jemal Johnson
- David Nugent
- Brett Ormerod
- Marcus Stewart

KEY: On all match · On bench · Subbed or sent off (Counting game) · Subbed or sent off (playing less than 70 minutes) · Subbed on from bench (Counting Game) · Subbed on (playing less than 70 minutes) · Subbed on and then subbed or sent off (Counting Game) · Subbed on and then subbed or sent off (playing less than 70 minutes) · Not in 16

LEEDS UNITED

Final Position: **5th**

NICKNAME: UNITED

KEY: ☐Won ☐Drawn ☐Lost

							Attendance
1	div1	Millwall	H	W	2-1	Healy 28,73 pen	20,440
2	div1	Cardiff	A	L	1-2	Blake, R 22	15,231
3	div1	Luton	A	D	0-0		10,102
4	div1	Wolverhampton	H	W	2-0	Lewis 8; Hulse 60	21,229
5	ccr1	Oldham	H	W	2-0	Ricketts 20; Richardson 24	14,970
6	div1	Norwich	A	W	1-0	Hulse 67	25,015
7	div1	Brighton	H	D	3-3	Healy 65,70; Douglas 90	21,212
8	div1	Sheff Wed	A	L	0-1		29,986
9	div1	QPR	A	W	1-0	Hulse 41	15,523
10	ccr2	Rotherham	A	W	2-0	Cresswell 19,28	5,445
11	div1	Ipswich	H	L	0-2		21,676
12	div1	Derby	H	W	3-1	Hulse 32,37,44	18,353
13	div1	Watford	A	D	0-0		16,050
14	div1	Burnley	A	W	2-1	Lewis 71; Hulse 75	16,174
15	div1	Southampton	H	W	2-1	Hulse 11; Blake, R 19	18,881
16	div1	Sheff Utd	H	D	1-1	Richardson 53	23,600
17	ccr3	Blackburn	A	L	0-3		15,631
18	div1	Reading	A	D	1-1	Healy 75	22,012
19	div1	Crewe	A	L	0-1		7,220
20	div1	Preston	H	D	0-0		22,289
21	div1	Southampton	A	W	4-3	Butler 71; Blake, R 77; Healy 84 pen; Miller 86	30,173
22	div1	Burnley	H	W	2-0	Healy 55 pen; Blake, R 70	21,318
23	div1	Millwall	A	W	1-0	May 90 og	8,134
24	div1	Leicester	H	W	2-1	Healy 41; Kilgallon 73	21,402
25	div1	Cardiff	H	L	0-1		20,597
26	div1	Wolverhampton	A	L	0-1		26,821
27	div1	Coventry	H	W	3-1	Douglas 34; Blake, R 61; Cresswell 80	24,291
28	div1	Stoke	A	W	1-0	Lewis 69	20,408
29	div1	Hull City	H	W	2-0	Douglas 45,57	26,387
30	div1	Plymouth	A	W	3-0	Cresswell 53; Blake, R 60; Hulse 86 pen	17,726
31	facr3	Wigan	A	D	1-1	Hulse 88	10,980
32	div1	Brighton	A	L	1-2	Blake, R 38 pen	7,415
33	facr3r	Wigan	H	L	2-4*	Healy 41,64 pen; Kelly 116 (*on penalties)	15,243
34	div1	Sheff Wed	H	W	3-0	Butler 70; Cresswell 82,90	27,843
35	div1	Ipswich	A	D	1-1	Healy 88 pen	25,845
36	div1	QPR	H	W	2-0	Cresswell 39; Butler 84	21,807
37	div1	Derby	A	D	0-0		27,000
38	div1	Watford	H	W	2-1	Blake, R 60 pen,81	22,007
39	div1	Leicester	A	D	1-1	Blake, R 11 pen	25,497
40	div1	Luton	H	W	2-1	Douglas 48; Lewis 53	23,644
41	div1	Crystal Palace	A	W	2-1	Blake, R 33; Hulse 53	23,843
42	div1	Norwich	H	D	2-2	Hulse 20; Lewis 90	24,993
43	div1	Coventry	A	D	1-1	Healy 88 pen	26,643
44	div1	Crystal Palace	H	L	0-1		24,507
45	div1	Stoke	H	D	0-0		21,452
46	div1	Hull City	A	L	0-1		23,486
47	div1	Plymouth	H	D	0-0		20,650
48	div1	Reading	H	D	1-1	Hulse 47	24,535
49	div1	Sheff Utd	A	D	1-1	Healy 41	29,329
50	div1	Crewe	H	W	1-0	Healy 74	21,046
51	div1	Preston	A	L	0-2		19,350
52	d1po1	Preston	H	D	1-1	Lewis 74	
53	d1po2	Preston	A	W	2-0	Hulse 56; Richardson 61	20,383
54	d1pof	Watford	H	L	0-3		64,736

LEAGUE APPEARANCES AND BOOKINGS

	AGE (on 01/07/06)	IN NAMED 16	APPEARANCES	COUNTING GAMES	MINUTES ON PITCH	LEAGUE GOALS		
Goalkeepers								
Ian Bennett	34	44	4	4	360	0	0	0
Neil Sullivan	36	45	42	42	3780	0	1	0
Defenders								
Paul Butler	33	44	44	43	3915	3	7	0
Stephen Crainey	25	25	24	24	2129	0	2	0
Daniel Harding	22	21	20	19	1750	0	2	0
Gary Kelly	32	44	44	43	3884	0	9	0
Matthew Kilgallon	22	38	25	22	2066	1	3	0
Rui Manuel Marques	28	0	0	0	0	0	0	0
Frazer Richardson	23	27	23	9	1163	1	0	0
Midfielders								
Eirik Bakke	28	12	10	6	615	0	0	0
Shaun Derry	28	41	41	40	3636	0	10	0
Jonathan Douglas	24	42	40	31	2973	5	6	0
Gylfi Einarsson	27	21	10	4	527	0	1	0
Sean Gregan	32	35	28	26	2463	0	12	0
Joel Griffiths	26	3	1	0	17	0	0	0
Eddie Lewis	32	43	43	40	3695	5	4	0
Liam Miller	25	28	28	23	2261	1	6	0
Danny Pugh	23	22	12	1	200	0	0	0
Matthew Spring	26	1	0	0	0	0	0	0
Steve Stone	34	2	2	1	120	0	0	0
Simon Walton	18	13	4	3	271	0	3	0
Jermaine Wright	30	4	3	3	224	0	0	0
Forwards								
Jermaine Beckford	22	6	4	0	102	0	0	0
Robbie Blake	30	43	41	22	2611	11	2	0
Richard Cresswell	28	16	16	10	1033	5	0	0
Danny Graham	20	4	3	0	69	0	0	0
David Healy	26	43	42	16	2241	12	6	1
Robert Hulse	26	39	39	31	2831	12	5	0
Ian Moore	29	25	20	3	444	0	1	0
Michael Ricketts	27	4	4	1	135	0	0	0

TEAM OF THE SEASON

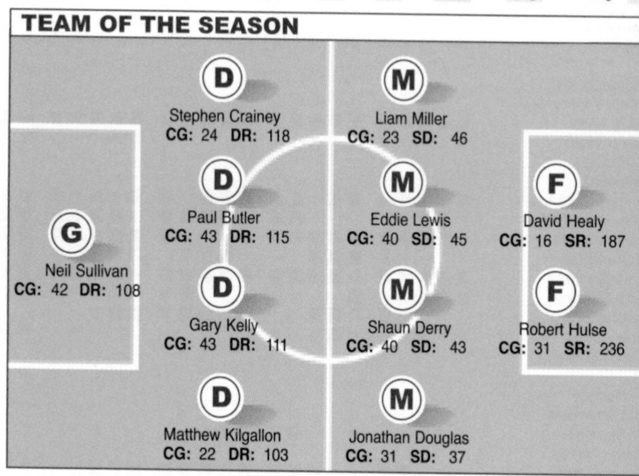

MONTHLY POINTS TALLY

AUGUST	10	67%
SEPTEMBER	7	47%
OCTOBER	9	60%
NOVEMBER	10	67%
DECEMBER	12	67%
JANUARY	7	58%
FEBRUARY	11	73%
MARCH	6	40%
APRIL	6	33%

LEAGUE GOALS

	PLAYER	LGE	FAC	LC	Oth	TOT
1	Hulse	12	1	0	1	14
2	Healy	12	2	0	0	14
3	Blake, R	11	0	0	0	11
4	Cresswell	5	0	2	0	7
5	Lewis	5	0	0	1	6
6	Douglas	5	0	0	0	5
7	Butler	3	0	0	0	3
8	Kilgallon	1	0	0	0	1
9	Miller	1	0	0	0	1
10	Richardson	1	0	1	1	3
11	Kelly	0	1	0	0	1
	Other	1	0	1	0	2
	TOTAL	57	4	4	3	68

TOP POINT EARNERS

	PLAYER	GAMES	AV PTS
1	Daniel Harding	19	2.00
2	David Healy	16	1.94
3	Robbie Blake	22	1.91
4	Gary Kelly	43	1.79
5	Eddie Lewis	40	1.78
6	Liam Miller	23	1.78
7	Paul Butler	43	1.74
8	Sean Gregan	26	1.73
9	Shaun Derry	40	1.70
10	Robert Hulse	31	1.68
	CLUB AVERAGE:		1.70

DISCIPLINARY RECORDS

	PLAYER	YELLOW	RED	AVE
1	Gregan	12	0	205
2	Healy	6	1	320
3	Derry	10	0	363
4	Miller	6	0	376
5	Kelly	9	0	431
6	Douglas	6	0	495
7	Einarsson	1	0	527
8	Butler	7	0	559
9	Hulse	5	0	566
10	Kilgallon	3	0	688
11	Harding	2	0	875
12	Lewis	4	0	923
13	Crainey	2	0	1064
	Other	3	0	
	TOTAL	76	1	

KEY GOALKEEPER

Neil Sullivan			
Goals Conceded in the League	35	Counting Games League games when player was on pitch for at least 70 minutes	42
Goals Conceded in all competitions	46		
Defensive Rating Ave number of mins between League goals conceded while on the pitch	108	Clean Sheets In games when player was on pitch for at least 70 minutes	14

KEY PLAYERS - DEFENDERS

Stephen Crainey			
Goals Conceded in the League	18	Clean Sheets In League games when player was on pitch for at least 70 minutes	9
Goals Conceded in all competitions	23		
Defensive Rating Ave number of mins between League goals conceded while on the pitch	118	Club Defensive Rating Average number of mins between League goals conceded by the club this season	109

	PLAYER	CON LGE	CON ALL	CLN SHEETS	DEF RATE
1	Stephen Crainey	18	23	9	118 mins
2	Paul Butler	34	44	16	115 mins
3	Gary Kelly	35	43	16	111 mins
4	Matthew Kilgallon	20	31	8	103 mins

KEY PLAYERS - MIDFIELDERS

Liam Miller			
Goals in the League	1	Contribution to Attacking Power Average number of minutes between League team goals while on pitch	73
Goals in all competitions	1		
Defensive Rating Average number of mins between League goals conceded while on the pitch	119	Scoring Difference Defensive Rating minus Contribution to Attacking Power	46

	PLAYER	GOALS LGE	GOALS ALL	DEF RATE	ATT POWER	SCORE DIFF
1	Liam Miller	1	1	119	73	46 mins
2	Eddie Lewis	5	6	115	70	45 mins
3	Shaun Derry	0	0	114	71	43 mins
4	Jonathan Douglas	5	5	110	73	37 mins

KEY PLAYERS - GOALSCORERS

David Healy			
Goals in the League	12	Player Strike Rate Average number of minutes between League goals scored by player	187
Goals in all competitions	14		
Contribution to Attacking Power Average number of minutes between League team goals while on pitch	62	Club Strike Rate Average number of minutes between League goals scored by club	73

	PLAYER	GOALS LGE	GOALS ALL	POWER	S RATE
1	David Healy	12	14	62	187 mins
2	Robert Hulse	12	14	79	236 mins
3	Robbie Blake	11	11	65	237 mins
4	Jonathan Douglas	5	5	73	595 mins

Leeds United's Rob Hulse

SQUAD APPEARANCES

Match	1	2	3	4	5	6	7	8	9	10	11	12	13	14	15	16	17	18	19	20	21	22	23	24	25	26	27	28	29	30	31	32	33	34	35	36	37	38	39	40	41	42	43	44	45	46	47	48	49	50	51	52	53	54
Venue	H	A	A	H	H	A	H	A	A	A	H	H	A	A	H	H	A	A	A	H	A	H	A	H	H	A	H	A	H	A	A	A	H	H	A	H	A	H	A	H	A	H	A	H	H	A	H	H	A	H	A	H	A	H
Competition	L	L	L	L	W	L	L	L	L	W	L	L	L	L	L	L	W	L	L	L	L	L	L	L	L	L	L	L	L	L	F	L	F	L	L	L	L	L	L	L	L	L	L	L	L	L	L	L	L	L	L	O	O	O
Result	W	L	D	W	W	W	D	L	W	W	L	W	D	W	W	D	L	D	L	D	W	W	W	W	L	L	W	W	W	W	D	L	L	W	D	W	D	W	D	W	W	D	D	L	D	L	D	D	D	W	L	D	W	L

Goalkeepers
Ian Bennett
Neil Sullivan

Defenders
Paul Butler
Stephen Crainey
Daniel Harding
Gary Kelly
Matthew Kilgallon
Rui Manuel Marques
Frazer Richardson

Midfielders
Eirik Bakke
Shaun Derry
Jonathan Douglas
Gylfi Einarsson
Sean Gregan
Joel Griffiths
Eddie Lewis
Liam Miller
Danny Pugh
Matthew Spring
Steve Stone
Simon Walton
Jermaine Wright

Forwards
Jermaine Beckford
Robbie Blake
Richard Cresswell
Danny Graham
David Healy
Robert Hulse
Ian Moore
Michael Ricketts

KEY: ■ On all match ■ On bench | ◂◂ Subbed or sent off (Counting game) ◂◂ Subbed or sent off (playing less than 70 minutes) | ▸▸ Subbed on from bench (Counting Game) ▸▸ Subbed on (playing less than 70 minutes) | ▸▸ Subbed on and then subbed or sent off (Counting Game) ▸▸ Subbed on and then subbed or sent off (playing less than 70 minutes) | □ Not in 16

CRYSTAL PALACE

Final Position: **6th**

NICKNAME: THE EAGLES

KEY: ☐Won ☐Drawn ☐Lost

						Scorers	Attendance
1	div1	Luton	H	L	1-2	Johnson 52	21,166
2	div1	Wolverhampton	A	L	1-2	McAnuff 42	24,745
3	div1	Norwich	A	D	1-1	Johnson 42	25,102
4	div1	Plymouth	H	W	1-0	Ward 63	18,781
5	ccr1	Walsall	H	W	3-0	Popovic 51 pen; Granville 83; Hughes 87	5,508
6	div1	Stoke	H	W	2-0	Johnson 44,85	17,637
7	div1	Hull City	H	W	2-0	Morrison 27; Johnson 89	18,630
8	div1	Reading	A	L	2-3	Johnson 29; Morrison 47	17,562
9	div1	Cardiff	A	L	0-1		11,647
10	ccr2	Coventry	H	W	1-0	Reich 67	5,341
11	div1	Preston	H	D	1-1	Morrison 90	17,291
12	div1	Sheff Wed	H	W	2-0	Morrison 17; Whelan 57 og	17,413
13	div1	QPR	A	W	3-1	Reich 14,17; Soares 89	13,433
14	div1	Coventry	A	W	4-1	Ward 14; Morrison 45; Watson 58; Macken 90	24,438
15	div1	Brighton	H	L	0-1		22,400
16	div1	Burnley	H	W	2-0	Morrison 38; Freedman 78	20,127
17	ccr3	Liverpool	H	W	2-1	Freedman 37; Reich 66	19,673
18	div1	Crewe	A	D	2-2	Freedman 52; Morrison 65	6,766
19	div1	Sheff Utd	H	L	2-3	Hughes 45; Freedman 85 pen	20,344
20	div1	Brighton	A	W	3-2	Freedman 28,60; McAnuff 90	7,273
21	div1	Coventry	H	W	2-0	Andrews 1; Boyce 34	17,343
22	div1	Luton	A	L	0-2		10,248
23	ccr4	Middlesbrough	A	L	1-2	Queudrue 31 og	10,791
24	div1	Millwall	H	D	1-1	Watson 90	19,571
25	div1	Wolverhampton	H	D	1-1	Johnson 44	19,385
26	div1	Plymouth	A	L	0-2		14,582
27	div1	Ipswich	A	W	2-0	Macken 14; Hughes 61	27,392
28	div1	Derby	H	W	2-0	Morrison 30; Ward 41	18,978
29	div1	Watford	A	W	2-1	Ward 18; Johnson 72 pen	15,856
30	div1	Leicester	H	W	2-0	McAnuff 78; Johnson 90	20,089
31	facr3	Northampton	H	W	4-1	Hughes 4; McAnuff 37; Johnson 53 pen; Freedman 88 pen	10,391
32	div1	Hull City	A	W	2-1	Ward 9; Cort 24 og	18,886
33	div1	Reading	H	D	1-1	Johnson 79 pen	19,888
34	div1	Southampton	A	D	0-0		24,651
35	facr4	Preston	A	D	1-1	Johnson 8	9,489
36	div1	Preston	A	L	0-2		13,867
37	div1	Cardiff	H	W	1-0	Riihilahti 70	17,962
38	facr4r	Preston	H	L	1-2	Ward 26	7,356
39	div1	Sheff Wed	A	D	0-0		24,784
40	div1	QPR	H	W	2-1	Morrison 3; McAnuff 32	17,550
41	div1	Millwall	A	D	1-1	Watson 66	12,296
42	div1	Norwich	H	W	4-1	Johnson 6; Watson 33; Morrison 53; Hall 61	19,066
43	div1	Leeds	H	L	1-2	McAnuff 90	23,843
44	div1	Stoke	A	W	3-1	Sidibe 30 og; McAnuff 48; Johnson 58	10,121
45	div1	Ipswich	H	D	2-2	Riihilahti 10; Morrison 53	22,076
46	div1	Leeds	A	W	1-0	McAnuff 43	24,507
47	div1	Derby	A	L	1-2	Morrison 18	24,857
48	div1	Watford	H	W	3-1	McAnuff 55; Stewart 59 og; DeMerit 86 og	18,619
49	div1	Leicester	A	L	0-2		23,211
50	div1	Crewe	H	D	2-2	Johnson 28,45	18,358
51	div1	Burnley	A	D	0-0		11,449
52	div1	Southampton	H	W	2-1	Johnson 63; Morrison 81	20,995
53	div1	Sheff Utd	A	L	0-1		27,120
54	d1po1	Watford	H	L	0-3		22,880
55	d1po2	Watford	A	D	0-0		

LEAGUE APPEARANCES AND BOOKINGS

	AGE (on 01/07/06)	IN NAMED 16	APPEARANCES	COUNTING GAMES	MINUTES ON PITCH	LEAGUE GOALS	Yellow	Red
Goalkeepers								
Gabor Kiraly	30	46	43	42	3838	0	1	0
Julian Speroni	27	46	4	3	302	0	0	0
Defenders								
Gary Borrowdale	20	32	30	25	2353	0	1	0
Emmerson Boyce	26	42	42	41	3758	1	7	0
Danny Butterfield	26	16	13	8	832	0	1	0
Aaron Fray	19	2	0	0	0	0	0	0
Danny Granville	31	1	0	0	0	0	0	0
Fitz Hall	25	39	39	37	3437	1	11	1
Mark Hudson	24	27	15	8	752	0	2	0
Mikele Leigertwood	23	33	27	17	1708	0	7	0
Tony Popovic	33	18	10	10	887	0	3	0
Darren Ward	27	43	43	42	3757	5	2	0
Glenn Wilson	20	0	0	0	0	0	0	0
Midfielders								
Thomas Black	29	0	0	0	0	0	0	0
Tommy Black	26	3	1	0	3	0	0	0
Anthony Danze	22	0	0	0	0	0	0	0
Michael Hughes	34	41	40	30	2873	2	9	0
Jobi McAnuff	24	41	41	31	3068	8	3	0
Marco Reich	28	23	21	11	1232	2	1	0
Aki Riihilahti	29	17	15	6	755	2	0	0
Tom Soares	19	44	44	34	3313	1	8	0
Sam Togwell	21	1	0	0	0	0	0	0
Ben Watson	20	44	42	34	3364	4	7	1
Forwards								
Wayne Andrews	28	31	24	3	638	1	1	0
Dougie Freedman	31	38	34	17	2013	5	1	0
Lewis Grabban	18	2	0	0	0	0	0	0
Andrew Johnson	25	33	33	27	2621	15	4	0
Joonas Kolkka	31	3	3	1	108	0	0	0
Jonathan Macken	28	28	24	8	1125	2	5	1
Clinton Morrison	27	42	40	27	2781	13	7	0

TEAM OF THE SEASON

G: Gabor Kiraly — CG: 42 DR: 89

D: Mikele Leigertwood — CG: 17 DR: 100

D: Darren Ward — CG: 42 DR: 94

D: Emmerson Boyce — CG: 41 DR: 84

D: Fitz Hall — CG: 37 DR: 84

M: Jobi McAnuff — CG: 31 SD: 38

M: Tom Soares — CG: 34 SD: 22

M: Michael Hughes — CG: 30 SD: 14

M: Ben Watson — CG: 34 SD: 10

F: Andrew Johnson — CG: 27 SR: 175

F: Clinton Morrison — CG: 27 SR: 214

MONTHLY POINTS TALLY

Month	Points	%
AUGUST	7	47%
SEPTEMBER	7	47%
OCTOBER	10	67%
NOVEMBER	6	50%
DECEMBER	11	61%
JANUARY	8	53%
FEBRUARY	11	73%
MARCH	10	56%
APRIL	5	33%

LEAGUE GOALS

	PLAYER	LGE	FAC	LC	Oth	TOT
1	Johnson	15	2	0	0	17
2	Morrison	13	0	0	0	13
3	McAnuff	8	1	0	0	9
4	Ward	5	1	0	0	6
5	Freedman	5	1	1	0	7
6	Watson	4	0	0	0	4
7	Macken	2	0	0	0	2
8	Riihilahti	2	0	0	0	2
9	Hughes	2	1	1	0	4
10	Reich	2	0	2	0	4
11	Hall	1	0	0	0	1
	Other	8	0	3	0	11
	TOTAL	67	6	7	0	80

TOP POINT EARNERS

	PLAYER	GAMES	AV PTS
1	Dougie Freedman	17	1.88
2	Jobi McAnuff	31	1.87
3	Mikele Leigertwood	17	1.82
4	Clinton Morrison	27	1.74
5	Gabor Kiraly	42	1.71
6	Ben Watson	34	1.71
7	Andrew Johnson	27	1.70
8	Fitz Hall	37	1.70
9	Darren Ward	42	1.69
10	Emmerson Boyce	41	1.68
	CLUB AVERAGE:		1.63

DISCIPLINARY RECORDS

	PLAYER	YELLOW	RED	AVE
1	Macken	5	1	187
2	Leigertwood	7	0	244
3	Hall	11	1	286
4	Popovic	3	0	295
5	Hughes	9	0	319
6	Hudson	2	0	376
7	Morrison	7	0	397
8	Soares	8	0	414
9	Watson	7	1	420
10	Boyce	7	0	536
11	Andrews	1	0	638
12	Johnson	4	0	655
13	Butterfield	1	0	832
	Other	9	0	
	TOTAL	81	3	

KEY GOALKEEPER

Gabor Kiraly

Goals Conceded in the League	43	**Counting Games** League games when player was on pitch for at least 70 minutes	42
Goals Conceded in all competitions	50		
Defensive Rating Ave number of mins between League goals conceded while on the pitch	89	**Clean Sheets** In games when player was on pitch for at least 70 minutes	14

KEY PLAYERS - DEFENDERS

Mikele Leigertwood

Goals Conceded in the League	17	**Clean Sheets** In League games when player was on pitch for at least 70 minutes	8
Goals Conceded in all competitions	20		
Defensive Rating Ave number of mins between League goals conceded while on the pitch	100	**Club Defensive Rating** Average number of mins between League goals conceded by the club this season	86

	PLAYER	CON LGE	CON ALL	CLN SHEETS	DEF RATE
1	Mikele Leigertwood	17	20	8	100 mins
2	Darren Ward	40	44	14	94 mins
3	Emmerson Boyce	45	55	13	84 mins
4	Fitz Hall	41	46	12	84 mins

KEY PLAYERS - MIDFIELDERS

Jobi McAnuff

Goals in the League	8	**Contribution to Attacking Power** Average number of minutes between League team goals while on pitch	61
Goals in all competitions	9		
Defensive Rating Average number of mins between League goals conceded while on the pitch	99	**Scoring Difference** Defensive Rating minus Contribution to Attacking Power	38

	PLAYER	GOALS LGE	GOALS ALL	DEF RATE	ATT POWER	SCORE DIFF
1	Jobi McAnuff	8	9	99	61	38 mins
2	Tom Soares	1	1	85	63	22 mins
3	Michael Hughes	2	4	76	62	14 mins
4	Ben Watson	4	4	76	66	10 mins

KEY PLAYERS - GOALSCORERS

Andrew Johnson

Goals in the League	15	**Player Strike Rate** Average number of minutes between League goals scored by player	175
Goals in all competitions	17		
Contribution to Attacking Power Average number of minutes between League team goals while on pitch	66	**Club Strike Rate** Average number of minutes between League goals scored by club	62

	PLAYER	GOALS LGE	GOALS ALL	POWER	S RATE
1	Andrew Johnson	15	17	66	175 mins
2	Clinton Morrison	13	13	57	214 mins
3	Jobi McAnuff	8	9	61	384 mins
4	Dougie Freedman	5	7	58	403 mins

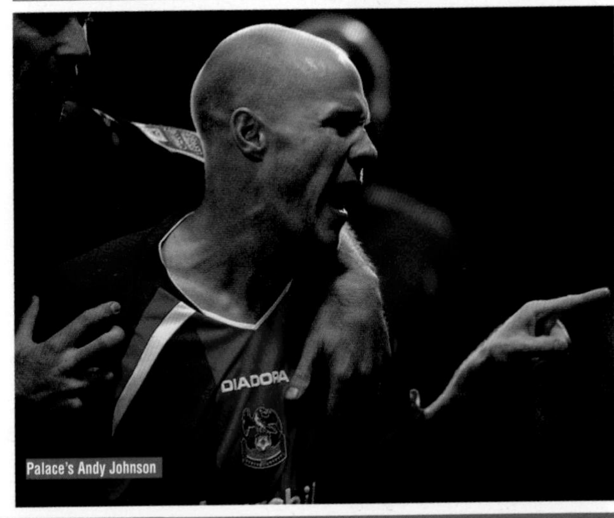

Palace's Andy Johnson

SQUAD APPEARANCES

Match	1	2	3	4	5	6	7	8	9	10	11	12	13	14	15	16	17	18	19	20	21	22	23	24	25	26	27	28	29	30
Venue	H	A	A	H	H	H	H	A	A	H	H	H	A	A	H	H	H	A	H	A	H	A	A	H	H	A	A	H	A	H
Competition	L	L	L	L	W	L	L	L	L	W	L	L	L	L	L	L	W	L	L	L	L	L	W	L	L	L	L	L	L	L
Result	L	L	D	W	W	W	W	L	L	W	D	W	W	W	L	W	W	D	L	W	W	L	L	D	D	L	W	W	W	W

Match	31	32	33	34	35	36	37	38	39	40	41	42	43	44	45	46	47	48	49	50	51	52	53	54	55
Venue	H	A	H	A	A	A	H	H	A	H	A	H	H	A	H	A	A	H	A	H	A	H	A	H	A
Competition	F	L	L	L	F	L	L	F	L	L	L	L	L	L	L	L	L	L	L	L	L	L	L	O	O
Result	W	W	D	D	D	L	W	L	D	W	D	W	L	W	D	W	L	W	L	D	D	W	L	L	D

Goalkeepers
Gabor Kiraly
Julian Speroni

Defenders
Gary Borrowdale
Emmerson Boyce
Danny Butterfield
Aaron Fray
Danny Granville
Fitz Hall
Mark Hudson
Mikele Leigertwood
Tony Popovic
Darren Ward
Glenn Wilson

Midfielders
Thomas Black
Tommy Black
Anthony Danze
Michael Hughes
Jobi McAnuff
Marco Reich
Aki Riihilahti
Tom Soares
Sam Togwell
Ben Watson

Forwards
Wayne Andrews
Dougie Freedman
Lewis Grabban
Andrew Johnson
Joonas Kolkka
Jonathan Macken
Clinton Morrison

KEY: On all match · On bench · Subbed or sent off (Counting game) · Subbed or sent off (playing less than 70 minutes) · Subbed on from bench (Counting Game) · Subbed on (playing less than 70 minutes) · Subbed on and then subbed or sent off (Counting Game) · Subbed on and then subbed or sent off (playing less than 70 minutes) · Not in 16

WOLVERHAMPTON WANDERERS

Final Position: **7th**

NICKNAME: WOLVES

KEY: ☐ Won ☐ Drawn ☐ Lost

							Attendance
1	div1	Southampton	A	D	0-0		24,061
2	div1	Crystal Palace	H	W	2-1	Seol 4; Cort 84	24,745
3	div1	Hull City	H	W	1-0	Delaney 19 og	24,333
4	div1	Leeds	A	L	0-2		21,229
5	ccr1	Chester	H	W	5-1	Miller 6; Cameron 62,74; Anderton 72; Ganea 79	9,518
6	div1	Cardiff	A	D	2-2	Clarke 73; Lescott 90	11,502
7	div1	QPR	H	W	3-1	Cort 8,24,90	22,426
8	div1	Luton	A	D	1-1	Cort 25	10,248
9	div1	Millwall	H	L	1-2	Cort 19	21,897
10	div1	Leicester	H	D	0-0		24,726
11	ccr2	Watford	A	L	1-2	Miller 12	9,296
12	div1	Stoke	A	W	3-1	Cort 42; Miller 48; Naylor 73	18,183
13	div1	Crewe	A	W	4-0	Cort 13,36; Miller 27,34	7,471
14	div1	Burnley	H	L	0-1		21,747
15	div1	Sheff Utd	A	L	0-1		25,533
16	div1	Derby	H	D	1-1	Miller 6	22,914
17	div1	Preston	H	D	1-1	Ganea 59	22,802
18	div1	Watford	A	L	1-3	Seol 90	14,561
19	div1	Brighton	A	D	1-1	Cameron 82	6,642
20	div1	Norwich	H	W	2-0	Seol 2; Ganea 37	23,808
21	div1	Derby	A	W	3-0	Ndah 67; Huddlestone 80; Ganea 86	22,869
22	div1	Sheff Utd	H	D	0-0		24,240
23	div1	Southampton	H	D	0-0		24,628
24	div1	Ipswich	A	D	1-1	Cameron 51	23,563
25	div1	Crystal Palace	A	D	1-1	Seol 19	19,385
26	div1	Leeds	H	W	1-0	Ganea 38	26,821
27	div1	Reading	H	L	0-2		27,980
28	div1	Sheff Wed	A	W	2-0	Anderton 34; Miller 63	24,295
29	div1	Plymouth	H	D	1-1	Cameron 31	22,790
30	div1	Coventry	A	L	0-2		26,851
31	facr3	Plymouth	H	W	1-0	Clarke 26	11,041
32	div1	Luton	H	W	2-1	Davies 57; Ince 88	21,823
33	div1	Millwall	A	D	0-0		9,905
34	facr4	Man Utd	H	L	0-3		28,333
35	div1	Leicester	A	L	0-1		21,358
36	div1	Crewe	H	D	1-1	Kennedy 45	21,683
37	div1	Burnley	A	W	1-0	Ince 15	11,056
38	div1	Ipswich	H	W	1-0	Miller 73 pen	23,561
39	div1	Hull City	A	W	3-2	Aliadiere 27; Miller 58; Cort 88	19,841
40	div1	QPR	A	D	0-0		14,731
41	div1	Stoke	H	D	0-0		22,439
42	div1	Cardiff	H	W	2-0	Rosa 15; Miller 54 pen	23,996
43	div1	Reading	A	D	1-1	Miller 64	23,502
44	div1	Sheff Wed	H	L	1-3	Cort 50	25,161
45	div1	Plymouth	A	L	0-2		15,871
46	div1	Coventry	H	D	2-2	Ince 2; Cameron 22	23,702
47	div1	Watford	H	D	1-1	Aliadiere 17	22,584
48	div1	Preston	A	L	0-2		16,885
49	div1	Brighton	H	W	1-0	Miller 31 pen	22,555
50	div1	Norwich	A	W	2-1	Rosa 45; Kennedy 71	24,081

LEAGUE APPEARANCES AND BOOKINGS

	AGE (on 01/07/06)	IN NAMED 16	APPEARANCES	COUNTING GAMES	MINUTES ON PITCH	LEAGUE GOALS		
Goalkeepers								
Carl Ikeme	20	6	0	0	0	0	0	0
Matt Murray	25	2	1	1	90	0	0	0
Michael Oakes	32	43	17	16	1485	0	0	0
Stefan Postma	29	39	29	28	2565	0	0	0
Defenders								
Jody Craddock	30	29	18	14	1437	0	0	0
Rob Edwards	23	42	42	37	3500	0	2	0
Gabor Gyepes	25	28	20	18	1661	0	4	0
Tom Huddlestone	19	14	13	11	1039	1	2	0
Daniel Jones	19	2	1	0	61	0	0	0
Joleon Lescott	23	46	46	46	4140	1	2	0
Keith Lowe	20	4	3	2	225	0	0	0
Jackie McNamara	32	10	10	9	855	0	4	0
Lee Naylor	26	40	40	38	3454	1	4	0
Maurice Ross	25	23	18	11	1234	0	5	0
Midfielders								
Darren Anderton	34	28	24	11	1472	1	1	0
Colin Cameron	33	30	27	16	1745	4	6	1
Mark Davies	18	22	20	11	1163	1	3	0
Paul Ince	38	19	18	15	1414	3	1	0
Mark Kennedy	30	41	40	37	3394	2	6	0
Seyi Olofinjana	26	23	13	4	655	0	0	0
Rohan Ricketts	23	29	25	12	1596	0	2	0
Denes Rosa	29	12	9	4	521	2	2	0
Forwards								
Jeremie Aliadiere	23	14	14	12	1099	2	3	0
Leon Clarke	21	25	24	5	1023	1	3	0
Carl Cort	28	32	31	23	2270	11	0	0
Tomasz Frankowski	31	16	16	9	970	0	0	0
Ioan Vlorel Ganea	32	21	18	11	1067	4	2	1
Kenny Miller	26	35	35	29	2806	10	12	0
George Ndah	31	15	14	3	580	1	2	0
Ki-Hyeun Seol	27	37	32	17	1975	4	3	0

TEAM OF THE SEASON

G — Stefan Postma, CG: 28 DR: 107

D — Lee Naylor, CG: 38 DR: 111
D — Rob Edwards, CG: 37 DR: 106
D — Joleon Lescott, CG: 46 DR: 99
D — Jody Craddock, CG: 14 DR: 96

M — Rohan Ricketts, CG: 12 SD: 25
M — Colin Cameron, CG: 16 SD: 16
M — Paul Ince, CG: 15 SD: 15
M — Mark Kennedy, CG: 37 SD: 11

F — Carl Cort, CG: 23 SR: 206
F — Kenny Miller, CG: 29 SR: 281

MONTHLY POINTS TALLY

AUGUST	11	61%
SEPTEMBER	8	44%
OCTOBER	2	17%
NOVEMBER	9	60%
DECEMBER	9	50%
JANUARY	4	44%
FEBRUARY	10	67%
MARCH	6	40%
APRIL	8	44%

LEAGUE GOALS

	PLAYER	LGE	FAC	LC	Oth	TOT
1	Cort	11	0	0	0	11
2	Miller	10	0	2	0	12
3	Seol	4	0	0	0	4
4	Ganea	4	0	1	0	5
5	Cameron	4	0	2	0	6
6	Ince	3	0	0	0	3
7	Rosa	2	0	0	0	2
8	Kennedy	2	0	0	0	2
9	Aliadiere	2	0	0	0	2
10	Lescott	1	0	0	0	1
11	Clarke	1	1	0	0	2
	Other	6	0	1	0	7
	TOTAL	50	1	6	0	57

TOP POINT EARNERS

	PLAYER	GAMES	AV PTS
1	Colin Cameron	16	1.75
2	Rohan Ricketts	12	1.75
3	Ki-Hyeun Seol	17	1.59
4	Carl Cort	23	1.57
5	Kenny Miller	29	1.55
6	Lee Naylor	38	1.53
7	Jody Craddock	14	1.50
8	Rob Edwards	37	1.49
9	Paul Ince	15	1.47
10	Joleon Lescott	46	1.46
	CLUB AVERAGE:		1.46

DISCIPLINARY RECORDS

	PLAYER	YELLOW	RED	AVE
1	McNamara	4	0	213
2	Miller	12	0	233
3	Ross	5	0	246
4	Cameron	6	1	249
5	Rosa	2	0	260
6	Ndah	2	0	290
7	Clarke	3	0	341
8	Ganea	2	1	355
9	Aliadiere	3	0	366
10	Davies	3	0	387
11	Gyepes	4	0	415
12	Huddlestone	2	0	519
13	Kennedy	6	0	565
	Other	15	0	
	TOTAL	69	2	

KEY GOALKEEPER

Stefan Postma

Goals Conceded in the League	24	Counting Games League games when player was on pitch for at least 70 minutes	28
Goals Conceded in all competitions	29		
Defensive Rating Ave number of mins between League goals conceded while on the pitch	107	Clean Sheets In games when player was on pitch for at least 70 minutes	13

KEY PLAYERS - DEFENDERS

Lee Naylor

Goals Conceded in the League	31	Clean Sheets In League games when player was on pitch for at least 70 minutes	15
Goals Conceded in all competitions	36		
Defensive Rating Ave number of mins between League goals conceded while on the pitch	111	Club Defensive Rating Average number of mins between League goals conceded by the club this season	99

	PLAYER	CON LGE	CON ALL	CLN SHEETS	DEF RATE
1	Lee Naylor	31	36	15	111 mins
2	Rob Edwards	33	39	15	106 mins
3	Joleon Lescott	42	46	17	99 mins
4	Jody Craddock	15	17	6	96 mins

KEY PLAYERS - MIDFIELDERS

Rohan Ricketts

Goals in the League	0	Contribution to Attacking Power Average number of minutes between League team goals while on pitch	69
Goals in all competitions	0		
Defensive Rating Average number of mins between League goals conceded while on the pitch	94	Scoring Difference Defensive Rating minus Contribution to Attacking Power	25

	PLAYER	GOALS LGE	GOALS ALL	DEF RATE	ATT POWER	SCORE DIFF
1	Rohan Ricketts	0	0	94	69	25 mins
2	Colin Cameron	4	6	92	76	16 mins
3	Paul Ince	3	3	109	94	15 mins
4	Mark Kennedy	2	2	94	83	11 mins

KEY PLAYERS - GOALSCORERS

Carl Cort

Goals in the League	11	Player Strike Rate Average number of minutes between League goals scored by player	206
Goals in all competitions	11		
Contribution to Attacking Power Average number of minutes between League team goals while on pitch	81	Club Strike Rate Average number of minutes between League goals scored by club	83

	PLAYER	GOALS LGE	GOALS ALL	POWER	S RATE
1	Carl Cort	11	11	81	206 mins
2	Kenny Miller	10	12	91	281 mins
3	Colin Cameron	4	6	76	436 mins
4	Paul Ince	3	3	94	471 mins

Wolves' Carl Court

SQUAD APPEARANCES

Match	1	2	3	4	5	6	7	8	9	10	11	12	13	14	15	16	17	18	19	20	21	22	23	24	25
Venue	A	H	H	A	H	A	H	A	H	H	A	A	A	H	A	H	H	A	A	H	A	H	H	A	A
Competition	L	L	L	L	W	L	L	L	L	L	W	L	L	L	L	L	L	L	L	L	L	L	L	L	L
Result	D	W	W	L	W	D	W	D	L	D	L	W	W	L	L	D	D	L	D	W	W	D	D	D	D

Match	26	27	28	29	30	31	32	33	34	35	36	37	38	39	40	41	42	43	44	45	46	47	48	49	50
Venue	H	H	A	H	A	H	H	A	H	A	H	A	H	A	A	H	H	A	H	A	H	H	A	H	A
Competition	L	L	L	L	L	F	L	L	F	L	L	L	L	L	L	L	L	L	L	L	L	L	L	L	L
Result	W	L	W	D	L	W	W	D	L	L	D	W	W	W	D	D	W	D	L	L	D	D	L	W	W

Goalkeepers
Carl Ikeme
Matt Murray
Michael Oakes
Stefan Postma

Defenders
Jody Craddock
Rob Edwards
Gabor Gyepes
Tom Huddlestone
Daniel Jones
Joleon Lescott
Keith Lowe
Jackie McNamara
Lee Naylor
Maurice Ross

Midfielders
Darren Anderton
Colin Cameron
Mark Davies
Paul Ince
Mark Kennedy
Seyi Olofinjana
Rohan Ricketts
Denes Rosa

Forwards
Jeremie Aliadiere
Leon Clarke
Carl Cort
Tomasz Frankowski
Ioan Vlorel Ganea
Kenny Miller
George Ndah
Ki-Hyeun Seol

KEY: On all match | On bench | Subbed or sent off (Counting game) | Subbed or sent off (playing less than 70 minutes) | Subbed on from bench (Counting Game) | Subbed on (playing less than 70 minutes) | Subbed on and then subbed or sent off (Counting Game) | Subbed on and then subbed or sent off (playing less than 70 minutes) | Not in 16

COVENTRY CITY

Final Position: **8th**

NICKNAME: THE SKY BLUES

KEY: ☐Won ☐Drawn ☐Lost

							Attendance
1	div1	Norwich	A	D	1-1	Adebola 65	25,355
2	div1	Millwall	A	D	0-0		8,344
3	div1	Burnley	A	L	0-4		11,683
4	div1	QPR	H	W	3-0	Jorgensen 11; Adebola 24,44	23,000
5	ccr1	Rushden & D	A	W	3-0	McSheffrey 10; Heath 41; Morrell 81	3,240
6	div1	Sheff Utd	A	L	1-2	Scowcroft 24	17,739
7	div1	Southampton	H	D	1-1	Scowcroft 6	23,000
8	div1	Reading	H	D	1-1	Page 87	22,074
9	div1	Derby	A	D	1-1	Adebola 57	21,840
10	div1	Brighton	A	D	2-2	McShane 39 og; Jorgensen 50	6,529
11	ccr2	Crystal Palace	A	L	0-1		5,341
12	div1	Hull City	H	L	0-2		21,161
13	div1	Watford	H	W	3-1	Adebola 2; Flood 20; McSheffrey 86	16,978
14	div1	Sheff Wed	A	L	2-3	McSheffrey 33 pen; Morrell 74	22,732
15	div1	Crystal Palace	H	L	1-4	Heath 45	24,438
16	div1	Ipswich	A	D	2-2	McSheffrey 45; Nalis 56	22,656
17	div1	Leicester	A	L	1-2	McSheffrey 24	22,991
18	div1	Luton	H	W	1-0	Adebola 47	22,228
19	div1	Stoke	H	L	1-2	Nalis 12	16,617
20	div1	Cardiff	A	D	0-0		11,424
21	div1	Ipswich	H	D	1-1	McSheffrey 56	18,316
22	div1	Crystal Palace	A	L	0-2		17,343
23	div1	Norwich	H	D	2-2	McSheffrey 3; Adebola 10	20,433
24	div1	Plymouth	H	W	3-1	Morrell 36; Hutchison 45; McSheffrey 49	18,796
25	div1	Millwall	H	W	1-0	Jorgensen 33	16,156
26	div1	QPR	A	W	1-0	McSheffrey 87	13,556
27	div1	Leeds	A	L	1-3	Hutchison 58	24,291
28	div1	Crewe	H	D	1-1	Hutchison 32	19,045
29	div1	Preston	A	L	1-3	John 59	12,936
30	div1	Wolverhampton	H	W	2-0	Scowcroft 8; Lescott 35 og	26,851
31	facr3	Brighton	A	W	1-0	McSheffrey 50	6,734
32	div1	Reading	A	L	0-2		22,813
33	div1	Derby	H	W	6-1	John 5,47; Wise 59; Adebola 62; McSheffrey 83 pen,90	20,267
34	facr4	Middlesbrough	H	D	1-1	John 54	28,120
35	div1	Hull City	A	W	2-1	Wise 61; John 72	18,381
36	div1	Brighton	H	W	2-0	Wise 43,68	20,541
37	facr4r	Middlesbrough	A	L	0-1		14,131
38	div1	Watford	A	L	0-4		19,842
39	div1	Sheff Wed	H	W	2-1	John 45; McSheffrey 76	20,021
40	div1	Plymouth	A	L	1-3	Wise 83	12,958
41	div1	Burnley	H	W	1-0	Adebola 53	19,641
42	div1	Southampton	A	D	1-1	Hutchison 88 pen	21,980
43	div1	Sheff Utd	H	W	2-0	McSheffrey 5; Adebola 32	23,506
44	div1	Leeds	H	D	1-1	McSheffrey 26	26,643
45	div1	Crewe	A	L	1-4	John 23	6,444
46	div1	Preston	H	L	0-1		21,023
47	div1	Wolverhampton	A	D	2-2	John 25; McSheffrey 60	23,702
48	div1	Luton	A	W	2-1	John 29; McSheffrey 30	8,752
49	div1	Leicester	H	D	1-1	John 11	26,672
50	div1	Stoke	A	W	1-0	Adebola 85	13,385
51	div1	Cardiff	H	W	3-1	John 8; Adebola 65; Wise 90	22,536

LEAGUE APPEARANCES AND BOOKINGS

	AGE (on 01/07/06)	IN NAMED 16	APPEARANCES	COUNTING GAMES	MINUTES ON PITCH	LEAGUE GOALS	Yellow	Red
Goalkeepers								
Stephen Bywater	25	14	14	14	1260	0	0	0
Marton Fulop	23	31	31	31	2790	0	1	0
Clayton Ince	33	39	1	1	90	0	0	0
Defenders								
Richard Duffy	20	34	32	25	2599	0	7	0
Stuart Giddings	20	2	2	1	130	0	0	0
Marcus Hall	30	39	39	37	3402	0	3	0
Matt Heath	25	32	25	21	1977	1	5	1
Andrew Impey	34	21	16	3	494	0	0	0
Ryan Lynch	19	1	0	0	0	0	0	0
Robert Page	31	32	32	32	2880	1	8	0
Richard Shaw	37	30	25	19	1987	0	3	0
Paul Watson	31	6	3	1	119	0	0	0
Andrew Whing	21	38	32	21	2251	0	1	0
Adrian Williams	34	21	14	12	1166	0	4	0
Midfielders								
Liam Davis	19	2	2	0	37	0	0	0
Michael Doyle	24	44	44	42	3850	0	10	1
Willo Flood	21	10	8	4	501	1	2	0
Stephen Hughes	29	20	19	15	1494	0	2	1
Don Hutchison	35	24	24	7	1058	4	4	0
Claus Jorgensen	30	29	27	14	1464	3	2	1
Gary McSheffrey	24	43	43	42	3587	15	10	0
Andy Morrell	31	42	34	8	1260	2	0	0
Lilian Nalis	34	6	6	3	406	2	1	0
Isaac Osbourne	20	16	10	7	638	0	1	0
James Scowcroft	32	41	41	34	3248	3	3	0
Kevin Thornton	19	24	16	2	495	0	2	0
Dennis Wise	39	14	13	10	987	6	7	0
Forwards								
Dele Adebola	31	45	44	34	3277	12	4	0
Stern John	29	25	25	19	1886	10	4	0
Youssef Sofiane	21	1	1	0	45	0	0	0
Neil Wood	23	7	4	0	63	0	0	0

TEAM OF THE SEASON

MONTHLY POINTS TALLY

AUGUST	6	33%
SEPTEMBER	6	40%
OCTOBER	4	27%
NOVEMBER	3	20%
DECEMBER	10	56%
JANUARY	9	75%
FEBRUARY	9	60%
MARCH	5	42%
APRIL	11	61%

LEAGUE GOALS

	PLAYER	LGE	FAC	LC	Oth	TOT
1	McSheffrey	15	1	1	0	17
2	Adebola	12	0	0	0	12
3	John	10	1	0	0	11
4	Wise	6	0	0	0	6
5	Hutchison	4	0	0	0	4
6	Jorgensen	3	0	0	0	3
7	Scowcroft	3	0	0	0	3
8	Nalis	2	0	0	0	2
9	Morrell	2	0	1	0	3
10	Heath	1	0	1	0	2
11	Page	1	0	0	0	1
	Other	3	0	0	0	3
	TOTAL	62	2	3	0	67

TOP POINT EARNERS

	PLAYER	GAMES	AV PTS
1	Andrew Whing	21	1.81
2	Stern John	19	1.74
3	Adrian Williams	12	1.67
4	Marton Fulop	31	1.61
5	Michael Doyle	42	1.45
6	Dele Adebola	34	1.44
7	Robert Page	32	1.41
8	Richard Shaw	19	1.37
9	Claus Jorgensen	14	1.36
10	Marcus Hall	37	1.35
	CLUB AVERAGE:		1.37

DISCIPLINARY RECORDS

	PLAYER	YELLOW	RED	AVE
1	Wise	7	0	141
2	Thornton	2	0	247
3	Flood	2	0	250
4	Hutchison	4	0	264
5	Williams	4	0	291
6	Heath	5	1	329
7	Doyle	10	1	350
8	McSheffrey	10	0	358
9	Page	8	0	360
10	Duffy	7	0	371
11	John	4	0	471
12	Jorgensen	2	1	488
13	Hughes	2	1	498
	Other	16	0	
	TOTAL	83	4	

KEY GOALKEEPER

Marton Fulop

Goals Conceded in the League	39	Counting Games League games when player was on pitch for at least 70 minutes	31
Goals Conceded in all competitions	41		
Defensive Rating Ave number of mins between League goals conceded while on the pitch	72	Clean Sheets In games when player was on pitch for at least 70 minutes	9

KEY PLAYERS - DEFENDERS

Robert Page

Goals Conceded in the League	41	Clean Sheets In League games when player was on pitch for at least 70 minutes	9
Goals Conceded in all competitions	43		
Defensive Rating Ave number of mins between League goals conceded while on the pitch	70	Club Defensive Rating Average number of mins between League goals conceded by the club this season	64

	PLAYER	CON LGE	CON ALL	CLN SHEETS	DEF RATE
1	Robert Page	41	43	9	70 mins
2	Andrew Whing	34	36	6	66 mins
3	Marcus Hall	52	54	9	65 mins
4	Richard Duffy	42	43	7	62 mins

KEY PLAYERS - MIDFIELDERS

Michael Doyle

Goals in the League	0	Contribution to Attacking Power Average number of minutes between League team goals while on pitch	65
Goals in all competitions	0		
Defensive Rating Average number of mins between League goals conceded while on the pitch	65	Scoring Difference Defensive Rating minus Contribution to Attacking Power	0

	PLAYER	GOALS LGE	GOALS ALL	DEF RATE	ATT POWER	SCORE DIFF
1	Michael Doyle	0	0	65	65	0 mins
2	Gary McSheffrey	15	17	64	64	0 mins
3	Claus Jorgensen	3	3	61	70	-9 mins
4	Stephen Hughes	0	0	62	71	-9 mins

KEY PLAYERS - GOALSCORERS

Stern John

Goals in the League	10	Player Strike Rate Average number of minutes between League goals scored by player	189
Goals in all competitions	11		
Contribution to Attacking Power Average number of minutes between League team goals while on pitch	63	Club Strike Rate Average number of minutes between League goals scored by club	67

	PLAYER	GOALS LGE	GOALS ALL	POWER	S RATE
1	Stern John	10	11	63	189 mins
2	Gary McSheffrey	15	17	64	239 mins
3	Dele Adebola	12	12	64	273 mins
4	Claus Jorgensen	3	3	70	488 mins

Coventry's Stern John

SQUAD APPEARANCES

Match	1	2	3	4	5	6	7	8	9	10	11	12	13	14	15	16	17	18	19	20	21	22	23	24	25	26	27	28	29	30	31	32	33	34	35	36	37	38	39	40	41	42	43	44	45	46	47	48	49	50	51
Venue	A	A	A	H	A	A	H	H	A	A	A	H	H	A	H	A	A	H	H	A	H	A	H	H	H	A	A	H	A	H	A	A	H	H	A	H	A	A	H	A	H	A	H	H	A	H	A	A	H	A	H
Competition	L	L	L	L	W	L	L	L	L	L	W	L	L	L	L	L	L	L	L	L	L	L	L	L	L	L	L	L	L	L	F	L	L	F	L	L	F	L	L	L	L	L	L	L	L	L	L	L	L	L	L
Result	D	D	L	W	W	L	D	D	D	D	L	L	W	L	L	D	L	W	L	D	D	L	D	W	W	W	L	D	L	W	W	L	W	D	W	W	L	L	W	L	W	D	W	D	L	L	D	W	D	W	W

Goalkeepers
Stephen Bywater
Marton Fulop
Clayton Ince

Defenders
Richard Duffy
Stuart Giddings
Marcus Hall
Matt Heath
Andrew Impey
Ryan Lynch
Robert Page
Richard Shaw
Paul Watson
Andrew Whing
Adrian Williams

Midfielders
Liam Davis
Michael Doyle
Willo Flood
Stephen Hughes
Don Hutchison
Claus Jorgensen
Gary McSheffrey
Andy Morrell
Lilian Nalis
Isaac Osbourne
James Scowcroft
Kevin Thornton
Dennis Wise

Forwards
Dele Adebola
Stern John
Youssef Sofiane
Neil Wood

KEY: On all match · On bench · Subbed or sent off (Counting game) · Subbed or sent off (playing less than 70 minutes) · Subbed on from bench (Counting Game) · Subbed on (playing less than 70 minutes) · Subbed on and then subbed or sent off (Counting Game) · Subbed on and then subbed or sent off (playing less than 70 minutes) · Not in 16

NORWICH

Final Position: **9th**

NICKNAME: THE CANARIES

KEY: ☐Won ☐Drawn ☐Lost

							Attendance
1	div1	Coventry	H	D	1-1	Ashton 21	25,355
2	div1	Crewe	H	D	1-1	McKenzie 50	25,116
3	div1	Crystal Palace	H	D	1-1	Ashton 6	25,102
4	div1	Southampton	A	L	0-1		23,498
5	ccr1	MK Dons	A	W	1-0	McKenzie 120	4,777
6	div1	Leeds	H	L	0-1		25,015
7	div1	Stoke	A	L	1-3	Ashton 38	14,249
8	div1	Plymouth	H	W	2-0	Doumbe 20 og; Ashton 37	23,981
9	div1	Watford	A	L	1-2	Lisbie 62	13,502
10	div1	Ipswich	A	W	1-0	Huckerby 51	29,184
11	ccr2	Northampton	H	W	2-0	Huckerby 34 pen; Ashton 78	16,766
12	div1	Reading	H	L	0-1		24,850
13	div1	Hull City	H	W	2-1	Safri 15; Doherty 39	27,470
14	div1	Brighton	A	W	3-1	Huckerby 22; McVeigh 41; Henderson 85	6,624
15	div1	Millwall	H	D	1-1	Ashton 52	25,095
16	div1	Luton	A	L	2-4	Ashton 56; Jarrett 85	10,248
17	div1	QPR	A	L	0-3		15,976
18	ccr3	Birmingham	A	L	1-2	Taylor, Martin 41 og	28,825
19	div1	Sheff Wed	H	L	0-1		25,383
20	div1	Cardiff	H	W	1-0	Alexander 77 og	23,838
21	div1	Wolverhampton	A	L	0-2		23,808
22	div1	Luton	H	W	2-0	Hughes 3; Huckerby 25	25,383
23	div1	Millwall	A	L	0-1		7,814
24	div1	Coventry	A	D	2-2	Davenport 40; Fleming 84	20,433
25	div1	Derby	A	L	0-2		23,346
26	div1	Crewe	A	W	2-1	McVeigh 64,85	6,132
27	div1	Southampton	H	W	3-1	Ashton 30,51,66	24,836
28	div1	Sheff Utd	A	W	3-1	McVeigh 33; Ashton 62; Morgan 71 og	26,505
29	div1	Burnley	H	W	2-1	Charlton 16; Huckerby 39	25,204
30	div1	Leicester	A	W	1-0	McVeigh 71	21,072
31	div1	Preston	H	L	0-3		25,032
32	facr3	West Ham	H	L	1-2	McVeigh 72 pen	23,968
33	div1	Plymouth	A	D	1-1	Huckerby 48	13,906
34	div1	Watford	H	L	2-3	McVeigh 44 pen; Thorne 62	25,384
35	div1	Reading	A	L	0-4		21,442
36	div1	Ipswich	H	L	1-2	Johansson 33	25,402
37	div1	Hull City	A	D	1-1	Elliott 87 og	20,527
38	div1	Brighton	H	W	3-0	Huckerby 28; Earnshaw 87,90	24,038
39	div1	Derby	H	W	2-0	Johansson 25; Huckerby 82	24,921
40	div1	Crystal Palace	A	L	1-4	Ward 87 og	19,066
41	div1	Stoke	H	W	2-1	McKenzie 52; Johansson 89	24,223
42	div1	Leeds	A	D	2-2	Hughes 57; McVeigh 75	24,993
43	div1	Sheff Utd	H	W	2-1	McKenzie 33; Earnshaw 45	25,346
44	div1	Burnley	A	L	0-2		11,938
45	div1	Leicester	H	W	2-1	Earnshaw 28; McKenzie 77 pen	24,718
46	div1	Preston	A	L	0-2		15,714
47	div1	Sheff Wed	A	L	0-1		30,755
48	div1	QPR	H	W	3-2	Huckerby 78; Earnshaw 85,90	24,126
49	div1	Cardiff	A	W	1-0	Earnshaw 16	11,590
50	div1	Wolverhampton	H	L	1-2	Earnshaw 73	24,081

LEAGUE APPEARANCES AND BOOKINGS

	AGE (on 01/07/06)	IN NAMED 16	APPEARANCES	COUNTING GAMES	MINUTES ON PITCH	LEAGUE GOALS		
Goalkeepers								
Paul Gallacher	26	24	4	4	360	0	0	0
Robert Green	26	41	41	41	3690	0	0	0
Darren Ward	32	21	0	0	0	0	0	0
Defenders								
Jim Brennan	29	21	17	10	1149	0	0	0
Simon Charlton	34	29	20	16	1513	1	5	0
Jurgen Colin	25	31	24	23	1990	0	3	0
Calum Davenport	23	14	14	13	1207	1	2	1
Gary Doherty	26	43	41	38	3447	1	6	0
Adam Drury	27	39	38	33	3173	0	4	0
Craig Fleming	34	42	36	31	2837	1	4	0
Rossi Jarvis	19	9	4	0	89	0	0	0
Matthieu Louis-Jean	30	5	2	2	180	0	1	0
Zeshan Rehman	22	6	5	5	450	0	1	0
Jason Shackell	22	19	17	15	1415	0	2	0
David Wright	26	5	5	4	377	0	0	0
Midfielders								
Dickson Etuhu	24	25	19	14	1412	0	1	0
Andrew Hughes	28	35	35	25	2645	2	4	0
Jason Jarrett	26	15	11	4	607	1	2	0
Dean Marney	22	13	12	9	903	0	1	0
Paul McVeigh	28	37	35	17	2105	6	5	0
Carl Robinson	29	21	21	16	1582	0	3	0
Youssef Safri	29	30	30	23	2257	1	6	0
Michael Spillane	17	3	2	1	127	0	0	0
Forwards								
Dean Ashton	22	28	28	26	2420	10	2	0
Robert Earnshaw	25	15	15	13	1226	4	0	0
Ian Henderson	21	32	23	7	928	0	1	0
Darren Huckerby	30	42	42	36	3477	7	8	1
Ryan Jarvis	19	7	3	1	144	0	0	0
Jonatan Johansson	30	16	12	5	567	3	0	0
Kevin Lisbie	27	5	5	3	312	1	2	0
Leon McKenzie	28	20	20	8	1030	4	1	0
Peter Thorne	33	23	21	7	885	1	2	0

TEAM OF THE SEASON

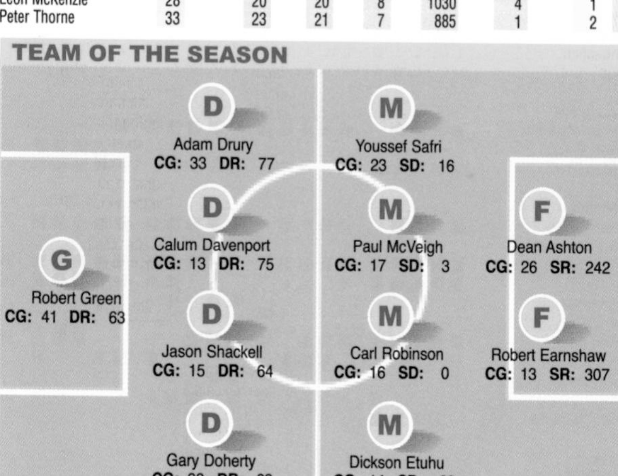

MONTHLY POINTS TALLY

AUGUST	3	17%
SEPTEMBER	9	60%
OCTOBER	4	27%
NOVEMBER	7	47%
DECEMBER	15	83%
JANUARY	1	8%
FEBRUARY	7	47%
MARCH	7	58%
APRIL	9	50%

LEAGUE GOALS

	PLAYER	LGE	FAC	LC	Oth	TOT
1	Ashton	10	0	1	0	11
2	Huckerby	7	0	1	0	8
3	McVeigh	6	1	0	0	7
4	Earnshaw	4	0	0	0	4
5	McKenzie	4	0	1	0	5
6	Johansson	3	0	0	0	3
7	Hughes	2	0	0	0	2
8	Fleming	1	0	0	0	1
9	Doherty	1	0	0	0	1
10	Charlton	1	0	0	0	1
11	Davenport	1	0	0	0	1
	Other	13	0	1	0	14
	TOTAL	53	1	4	0	58

TOP POINT EARNERS

	PLAYER	GAMES	AV PTS
1	Paul McVeigh	17	2.06
2	Youssef Safri	23	1.78
3	Robert Earnshaw	13	1.69
4	Adam Drury	33	1.67
5	Carl Robinson	16	1.63
6	Gary Doherty	38	1.42
7	Jason Shackell	15	1.40
8	Andrew Hughes	25	1.40
9	Darren Huckerby	36	1.36
10	Calum Davenport	13	1.31
	CLUB AVERAGE:		1.35

DISCIPLINARY RECORDS

	PLAYER	YELLOW	RED	AVE
1	Charlton	5	0	302
2	Jarrett	2	0	303
3	Safri	6	0	376
4	Huckerby	8	1	386
5	Davenport	2	1	402
6	McVeigh	5	0	421
7	Thorne	2	0	442
8	Robinson	3	0	527
9	Doherty	6	0	574
10	Hughes	4	0	661
11	Colin	3	0	663
12	Shackell	2	0	707
13	Fleming	4	0	709
	Other	10	0	
	TOTAL	62	2	

KEY GOALKEEPER

Robert Green			
Goals Conceded in the League	59	**Counting Games** League games when player was on pitch for at least 70 minutes	41
Goals Conceded in all competitions	63		
Defensive Rating Ave number of mins between League goals conceded while on the pitch	63	**Clean Sheets** In games when player was on pitch for at least 70 minutes	7

KEY PLAYERS - DEFENDERS

Adam Drury			
Goals Conceded in the League	41	**Clean Sheets** In League games when player was on pitch for at least 70 minutes	8
Goals Conceded in all competitions	43		
Defensive Rating Ave number of mins between League goals conceded while on the pitch	77	**Club Defensive Rating** Average number of mins between League goals conceded by the club this season	63

	PLAYER	CON LGE	CON ALL	CLN SHEETS	DEF RATE
1	Adam Drury	41	43	8	77 mins
2	Calum Davenport	16	18	3	75 mins
3	Jason Shackell	22	22	2	64 mins
4	Gary Doherty	55	59	7	63 mins

KEY PLAYERS - MIDFIELDERS

Youssef Safri			
Goals in the League	1	**Contribution to Attacking Power** Average number of minutes between League team goals while on pitch	78
Goals in all competitions	1		
Defensive Rating Average number of mins between League goals conceded while on the pitch	94	Scoring Difference Defensive Rating minus Contribution to Attacking Power	16

	PLAYER	GOALS LGE	GOALS ALL	DEF RATE	ATT POWER	SCORE DIFF
1	Youssef Safri	1	1	94	78	16 mins
2	Paul McVeigh	6	7	57	54	3 mins
3	Carl Robinson	0	0	57	57	0 mins
4	Dickson Etuhu	0	0	56	78	-22 mins

KEY PLAYERS - GOALSCORERS

Dean Ashton			
Goals in the League	10	Player Strike Rate Average number of minutes between League goals scored by player	242
Goals in all competitions	11		
Contribution to Attacking Power Average number of minutes between League team goals while on pitch	81	**Club Strike Rate** Average number of minutes between League goals scored by club	76

	PLAYER	GOALS LGE	GOALS ALL	POWER	S RATE
1	Dean Ashton	10	11	81	242 mins
2	Robert Earnshaw	4	4	65	307 mins
3	Paul McVeigh	6	7	54	351 mins
4	Darren Huckerby	7	8	72	497 mins

Andy Hughes (top) embraces Darren Huckerby

SQUAD APPEARANCES

Match	1	2	3	4	5	6	7	8	9	10	11	12	13	14	15	16	17	18	19	20	21	22	23	24	25
Venue	H	H	H	A	A	H	A	H	A	A	H	H	H	A	H	A	A	A	H	H	A	H	A	A	A
Competition	L	L	L	L	W	L	L	L	L	L	W	L	L	L	L	L	L	W	L	L	L	L	L	L	L
Result	D	D	D	L	W	L	L	W	L	W	W	L	W	W	D	L	L	L	L	W	L	W	L	D	L

Match	26	27	28	29	30	31	32	33	34	35	36	37	38	39	40	41	42	43	44	45	46	47	48	49	50
Venue	A	H	A	H	A	H	H	A	H	A	H	A	H	H	A	H	A	H	A	H	A	A	H	A	H
Competition	L	L	L	L	L	L	F	L	L	L	L	L	L	L	L	L	L	L	L	L	L	L	L	L	L
Result	W	W	W	W	W	L	L	D	L	L	L	D	W	W	L	W	D	W	L	W	L	L	W	W	L

Goalkeepers
Paul Gallacher
Robert Green
Darren Ward

Defenders
Jim Brennan
Simon Charlton
Jurgen Colin
Calum Davenport
Gary Doherty
Adam Drury
Craig Fleming
Rossi Jarvis
Matthieu Louis-Jean
Zeshan Rehman
Jason Shackell
David Wright

Midfielders
Dickson Etuhu
Andrew Hughes
Jason Jarrett
Dean Marney
Paul McVeigh
Carl Robinson
Youssef Safri
Michael Spillane

Forwards
Dean Ashton
Robert Earnshaw
Ian Henderson
Darren Huckerby
Ryan Jarvis
Jonatan Johansson
Kevin Lisbie
Leon McKenzie
Peter Thorne

KEY: ■ On all match ■ On bench ⏮ Subbed or sent off (Counting game) « Subbed or sent off (playing less than 70 minutes) ⏭ Subbed on from bench (Counting Game) » Subbed on (playing less than 70 minutes) Subbed on and then subbed or sent off (Counting Game) Subbed on and then subbed or sent off (playing less than 70 minutes) □ Not in 16

LUTON TOWN

Final Position: **10th**

NICKNAME: THE HATTERS

KEY: ☐ Won ☐ Drawn ☐ Lost

							Attendance
1	div1	Crystal Palace	A	W	2-1	Howard 44; Brkovic 79	21,166
2	div1	Southampton	H	W	3-2	Nicholls 41; Brkovic 52; Morgan 90	9,447
3	div1	Leeds	H	D	0-0		10,102
4	div1	Stoke	A	L	1-2	Morgan 9	18,653
5	ccr1	Leyton Orient	A	W	3-1	Coyne 45; Feeney 71; Alexander 76 og	2,383
6	div1	Leicester	A	W	2-0	Brkovic 42; Nicholls 90 pen	22,048
7	div1	Millwall	H	W	2-1	Feeney 12; Davies, C 78	8,220
8	div1	Wolverhampton	H	D	1-1	Nicholls 79	10,248
9	div1	QPR	A	L	0-1		13,492
10	div1	Hull City	A	W	1-0	Howard 85	19,184
11	ccr2	Reading	A	L	0-1		6,941
12	div1	Sheff Wed	H	D	2-2	Howard 2,66	8,267
13	div1	Preston	H	W	3-0	Feeney 4; Brkovic 11; Howard 38	7,815
14	div1	Cardiff	A	W	2-1	Morgan 30; Heikkinen 57	14,657
15	div1	Crewe	A	L	1-3	Morgan 29	6,604
16	div1	Norwich	H	W	4-2	Feeney 16; Edwards 27; Holmes 34; Howard 41	10,248
17	div1	Plymouth	H	D	1-1	Feeney 64	8,714
18	div1	Coventry	A	L	0-1		22,228
19	div1	Sheff Utd	A	L	0-4		22,554
20	div1	Burnley	H	L	2-3	Howard 43; Feeney 60	8,518
21	div1	Norwich	A	L	0-2		25,383
22	div1	Crewe	H	W	4-1	Vine 69,72 pen; Morgan 82; Showunmi 89	7,474
23	div1	Crystal Palace	H	W	2-0	Heikkinen 11; Vine 21	10,248
24	div1	Reading	A	L	0-3		19,478
25	div1	Southampton	A	L	0-1		19,086
26	div1	Stoke	H	L	2-3	Brkovic 21; Nicholls 88 pen	8,296
27	div1	Derby	A	D	1-1	Brkovic 80	26,807
28	div1	Brighton	H	W	3-0	Howard 17; Feeney 44; Robinson 62	9,429
29	div1	Ipswich	A	L	0-1		23,957
30	div1	Watford	H	L	1-2	Edwards 49	10,248
31	facr3	Liverpool	H	L	3-5	Howard 31; Robinson 43; Nicholls 53 pen	10,170
32	div1	Wolverhampton	A	L	1-2	Howard 80	21,823
33	div1	QPR	H	W	2-0	Heikkinen 13; Howard 85	9,797
34	div1	Sheff Wed	A	W	2-0	Nicholls 52 pen; Vine 56	23,965
35	div1	Hull City	H	L	2-3	Keane 9; Coyne 86	8,835
36	div1	Preston	A	L	1-5	Mears 82 og	15,237
37	div1	Cardiff	H	D	3-3	Vine 25,26; Barker 60 og	7,826
38	div1	Reading	H	W	3-2	Vine 20,26; Morgan 51	8,705
39	div1	Leeds	A	L	1-2	Howard 82	23,644
40	div1	Millwall	A	L	1-2	Coyne 47	9,871
41	div1	Leicester	H	L	1-2	Howard 53	9,783
42	div1	Derby	H	W	1-0	Howard 72	9,163
43	div1	Brighton	A	D	1-1	Robinson 61	7,139
44	div1	Ipswich	H	W	1-0	Howard 81	9,820
45	div1	Watford	A	D	1-1	Brkovic 73	15,922
46	div1	Coventry	H	L	1-2	Williams 85 og	8,752
47	div1	Plymouth	A	W	2-1	Vine 79; Andrew 88	13,486
48	div1	Sheff Utd	H	D	1-1	Brkovic 72	10,248
49	div1	Burnley	A	D	1-1	Vine 42	12,473

LEAGUE APPEARANCES AND BOOKINGS

	AGE (on 01/07/06)	IN NAMED 16	APPEARANCES	COUNTING GAMES	MINUTES ON PITCH	LEAGUE GOALS	Yellow	Red
Goalkeepers								
Rob Beckwith	21	2	0	0	0	0	0	0
Marlon Beresford	36	41	41	41	3689	0	1	1
Dean Brill	19	44	5	5	450	0	0	0
Dino Seremet	25	3	0	0	0	0	0	0
Defenders								
Leon Barnett	20	30	20	13	1316	0	3	0
Chris Coyne	27	30	30	24	2435	2	4	0
Curtis Davies	21	6	6	6	540	1	1	0
Sol Davis	26	21	21	16	1578	0	6	1
Kevin Foley	21	38	38	35	3224	0	4	0
Markus Heikkinen	27	39	39	37	3376	3	6	0
Russell Perrett	33	26	11	9	852	0	2	1
Paul Underwood	32	29	29	27	2490	0	2	0
Midfielders								
David Bell	22	13	9	1	333	0	0	0
Ahmet Brkovic	31	44	42	33	3252	8	4	0
Carlos Edwards	27	42	42	35	3385	2	1	0
Peter Holmes	25	34	23	14	1399	1	2	0
Keith Keane	19	14	10	5	542	1	1	0
Michael Leary	23	0	0	0	0	0	0	0
Kevin Nicholls	27	33	32	30	2709	5	6	1
Stephen O'Leary	20	0	0	0	0	0	0	0
Steve Robinson	31	27	26	25	2256	2	3	0
Danny Stevens	19	5	1	0	16	0	0	0
Forwards								
Calvin Andrew	19	5	1	0	7	1	0	0
Warren Feeney	25	44	42	21	2516	6	3	0
Steven Howard	30	43	43	39	3573	14	7	1
Dean Morgan	22	41	36	18	2096	6	1	0
Enoch Showunmi	23	45	41	11	1635	1	2	0
Rowan Vine	23	35	31	16	1806	10	5	0

TEAM OF THE SEASON

G — Marlon Beresford, CG: 41 DR: 64

D — Chris Coyne, CG: 24 DR: 72

D — Paul Underwood, CG: 27 DR: 69

D — Sol Davis, CG: 16 DR: 63

D — Markus Heikkinen, CG: 37 DR: 60

M — Steve Robinson, CG: 25 SD: 24

M — Kevin Nicholls, CG: 30 SD: 0

M — Ahmet Brkovic, CG: 33 SD: -3

M — Carlos Edwards, CG: 35 SD: -5

F — Rowan Vine, CG: 16 SR: 181

F — Steven Howard, CG: 39 SR: 255

MONTHLY POINTS TALLY

AUGUST	13	72%
SEPTEMBER	8	53%
OCTOBER	7	47%
NOVEMBER	6	40%
DECEMBER	4	22%
JANUARY	6	50%
FEBRUARY	4	27%
MARCH	4	33%
APRIL	9	50%

LEAGUE GOALS

	PLAYER	LGE	FAC	LC	Oth	TOT
1	Howard	14	1	0	0	15
2	Vine	10	0	0	0	10
3	Brkovic	8	0	0	0	8
4	Feeney	6	0	1	0	7
5	Morgan	6	0	0	0	6
6	Nicholls	5	1	0	0	6
7	Heikkinen	3	0	0	0	3
8	Robinson	2	1	0	0	3
9	Edwards	2	0	0	0	2
10	Coyne	2	0	1	0	3
11	Showunmi	1	0	0	0	1
	Other	7	0	1	0	8
	TOTAL	66	3	3	0	72

TOP POINT EARNERS

	PLAYER	GAMES	AV PTS
1	Dean Morgan	18	2.00
2	Warren Feeney	21	1.76
3	Sol Davis	16	1.63
4	Steve Robinson	25	1.56
5	Ahmet Brkovic	33	1.42
6	Markus Heikkinen	37	1.41
7	Chris Coyne	24	1.33
8	Marlon Beresford	41	1.32
9	Carlos Edwards	35	1.31
10	Kevin Nicholls	30	1.30
	CLUB AVERAGE:		1.33

DISCIPLINARY RECORDS

	PLAYER	YELLOW	RED	AVE
1	Davis	6	1	225
2	Perrett	2	1	284
3	Vine	5	0	361
4	Nicholls	6	1	387
5	Barnett	3	0	438
6	Howard	7	1	446
7	Davies, C	1	0	540
8	Keane	1	0	542
9	Heikkinen	6	0	562
10	Coyne	4	0	608
11	Holmes	2	0	699
12	Robinson	3	0	752
13	Foley	4	0	806
	Other	14	1	
	TOTAL	64	5	

KEY GOALKEEPER

Marlon Beresford

Goals Conceded in the League	58	Counting Games League games when player was on pitch for at least 70 minutes	41
Goals Conceded in all competitions	64		
Defensive Rating Ave number of mins between League goals conceded while on the pitch	64	Clean Sheets In games when player was on pitch for at least 70 minutes	9

KEY PLAYERS - DEFENDERS

Chris Coyne

Goals Conceded in the League	34	Clean Sheets In League games when player was on pitch for at least 70 minutes	7
Goals Conceded in all competitions	40		
Defensive Rating Ave number of mins between League goals conceded while on the pitch	72	Club Defensive Rating Average number of mins between League goals conceded by the club this season	62

	PLAYER	CON LGE	CON ALL	CLN SHEETS	DEF RATE
1	Chris Coyne	34	40	7	72 mins
2	Paul Underwood	36	41	7	69 mins
3	Sol Davis	25	27	4	63 mins
4	Markus Heikkinen	56	59	8	60 mins

KEY PLAYERS - MIDFIELDERS

Steve Robinson

Goals in the League	2	Contribution to Attacking Power Average number of minutes between League team goals while on pitch	63
Goals in all competitions	3		
Defensive Rating Average number of mins between League goals conceded while on the pitch	87	Scoring Difference Defensive Rating minus Contribution to Attacking Power	24

	PLAYER	GOALS LGE	GOALS ALL	DEF RATE	ATT POWER	SCORE DIFF
1	Steve Robinson	2	3	87	63	24 mins
2	Kevin Nicholls	5	6	63	63	0 mins
3	Ahmet Brkovic	8	8	61	64	-3 mins
4	Carlos Edwards	2	2	57	62	-5 mins

KEY PLAYERS - GOALSCORERS

Rowan Vine

Goals in the League	10	Player Strike Rate Average number of minutes between League goals scored by player	181
Goals in all competitions	10		
Contribution to Attacking Power Average number of minutes between League team goals while on pitch	67	Club Strike Rate Average number of minutes between League goals scored by club	63

	PLAYER	GOALS LGE	GOALS ALL	POWER	S RATE
1	Rowan Vine	10	10	67	181 mins
2	Steven Howard	14	15	64	255 mins
3	Dean Morgan	6	6	49	349 mins
4	Ahmet Brkovic	8	8	64	407 mins

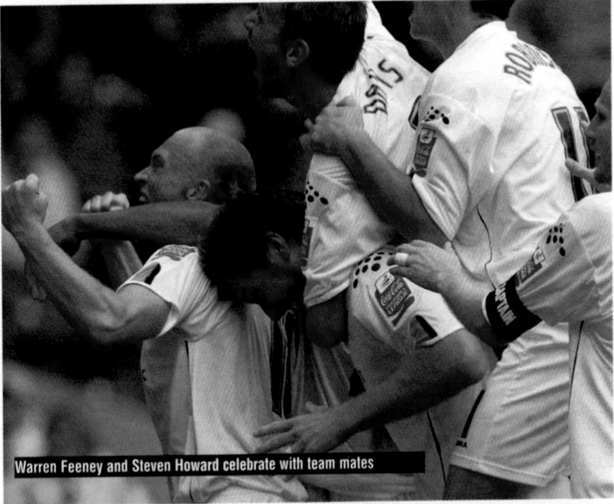

Warren Feeney and Steven Howard celebrate with team mates

SQUAD APPEARANCES

Match	1	2	3	4	5	6	7	8	9	10	11	12	13	14	15	16	17	18	19	20	21	22	23	24	25
Venue	A	H	H	A	A	A	H	H	A	A	A	H	H	A	A	H	H	A	A	H	A	H	H	A	A
Competition	L	L	L	L	W	L	L	L	L	L	W	L	L	L	L	L	L	L	L	L	L	L	L	L	L
Result	W	W	D	L	W	W	W	D	L	W	L	D	W	W	L	W	D	L	L	L	L	W	W	L	L

Match	26	27	28	29	30	31	32	33	34	35	36	37	38	39	40	41	42	43	44	45	46	47	48	49
Venue	H	A	H	A	H	H	A	H	A	H	A	H	H	A	A	H	H	A	H	A	H	A	H	A
Competition	L	L	L	L	L	F	L	L	L	L	L	L	L	L	L	L	L	L	L	L	L	L	L	L
Result	L	D	W	L	L	L	L	W	W	L	L	D	W	L	L	L	W	D	W	D	L	W	D	D

Goalkeepers
Rob Beckwith
Marlon Beresford
Dean Brill
Dino Seremet

Defenders
Leon Barnett
Chris Coyne
Curtis Davies
Sol Davis
Kevin Foley
Markus Heikkinen
Russell Perrett
Paul Underwood

Midfielders
David Bell
Ahmet Brkovic
Carlos Edwards
Peter Holmes
Keith Keane
Michael Leary
Kevin Nicholls
Stephen O'Leary
Steve Robinson
Danny Stevens

Forwards
Calvin Andrew
Warren Feeney
Steven Howard
Dean Morgan
Enoch Showunmi
Rowan Vine

KEY: On all match | On bench | Subbed or sent off (Counting game) | Subbed or sent off (playing less than 70 minutes) | Subbed on from bench (Counting Game) | Subbed on (playing less than 70 minutes) | Subbed on and then subbed or sent off (Counting Game) | Subbed on and then subbed or sent off (playing less than 70 minutes) | Not in 16

CARDIFF CITY

Final Position: **11th**

NICKNAME: THE BLUEBIRDS

KEY: ☐ Won ☐ Drawn ☐ Lost

	Comp	Opponent			Score	Scorers	Attendance
1	div1	Ipswich	A	L	0-1		24,292
2	div1	Leeds	H	W	2-1	Koumas 60; Purse 67 pen	15,231
3	div1	Watford	H	L	1-3	Jerome 80	9,256
4	div1	Derby	A	L	1-2	Jerome 83	23,153
5	ccr1	Colchester	A	W	2-0	Purse 31 pen; Jerome 34	1,904
6	div1	Wolverhampton	H	D	2-2	Jerome 3,49	11,502
7	div1	Burnley	A	D	3-3	Jerome 8; Loovens 45; Purse 72 pen	10,431
8	div1	Leicester	H	W	1-0	Ricketts 8	9,196
9	div1	Crystal Palace	H	W	1-0	Ricketts 26	11,647
10	ccr2	Macclesfield	H	W	2-1	Ledley 50; Koumas 81	3,849
11	div1	Millwall	A	D	0-0		9,254
12	div1	Stoke	A	W	3-0	Jerome 10,43; Purse 12	12,240
13	div1	Luton	H	L	1-2	Ricketts 9	14,657
14	div1	Brighton	A	W	2-1	Koumas 12; Lee 74	6,485
15	div1	Preston	H	D	2-2	Ledley 31; Koumas 80	9,574
16	div1	Crewe	H	W	6-1	Ricketts 18; Ledley 48; Boulding 60; Purse 67 pen; Jerome 68; Koumas 74	10,815
17	ccr3	Leicester	H	L	0-1		8,727
18	div1	Sheff Utd	A	D	0-0		25,311
19	div1	Norwich	A	L	0-1		23,838
20	div1	Coventry	H	D	0-0		11,424
21	div1	Sheff Wed	A	W	3-1	Koumas 9; Jerome 30,38	20,324
22	div1	Preston	A	L	1-2	Loovens 68	13,904
23	div1	Brighton	H	D	1-1	Lee 57	9,595
24	div1	Ipswich	H	W	2-1	Ricketts 30; Koumas 90	8,724
25	div1	Hull City	A	L	0-2		18,364
26	div1	Leeds	A	W	1-0	Koumas 31	20,597
27	div1	Derby	H	D	0-0		12,500
28	div1	Plymouth	H	L	0-2		16,403
29	div1	QPR	A	L	0-1		12,329
30	div1	Southampton	H	W	2-1	Ledley 6; Jerome 9	13,377
31	div1	Reading	A	L	1-5	Jerome 62	22,061
32	facr3	Arsenal	A	L	1-2	Jerome 87	36,552
33	div1	Burnley	H	W	3-0	Thompson 58,60; Koumas 63	10,872
34	div1	Leicester	A	W	2-1	Jerome 13; Koumas 56	20,140
35	div1	Millwall	H	D	1-1	Jerome 28	12,378
36	div1	Crystal Palace	A	L	0-1		17,962
37	div1	Stoke	H	W	3-0	Cooper 18; Cox 30,68	10,780
38	div1	Luton	A	D	3-3	Koumas 55,86; Scimeca 71	7,826
39	div1	Hull City	H	W	1-0	Jerome 21	11,047
40	div1	Watford	A	L	1-2	Whitely 76	27,419
41	div1	Sheff Wed	H	W	1-0	Jerome 19	11,851
42	div1	Wolverhampton	A	L	0-2		23,996
43	div1	Plymouth	A	W	1-0	Thompson 34	13,494
44	div1	QPR	H	D	0-0		14,271
45	div1	Southampton	A	L	2-3	Jerome 54; Purse 90	22,388
46	div1	Reading	H	L	2-5	Jerome 67; Parry 80	11,866
47	div1	Sheff Utd	H	L	0-1		11,006
48	div1	Crewe	A	D	1-1	Koumas 76	5,865
49	div1	Norwich	H	L	0-1		11,590
50	div1	Coventry	A	L	1-3	Thompson 21	22,536

LEAGUE APPEARANCES AND BOOKINGS

	AGE (on 01/07/06)	IN NAMED 16	APPEARANCES	COUNTING GAMES	MINUTES ON PITCH	LEAGUE GOALS		
Goalkeepers								
Neil Alexander	28	46	46	46	4140	0	2	0
Martyn Margetson	34	39	0	0	0	0	0	0
Tony Warner	32	2	0	0	0	0	0	0
Lee Worgan	22	2	0	0	0	0	0	0
Defenders								
Chris Barker	26	45	41	41	3657	0	4	0
Neil Cox	34	46	27	20	2048	2	3	0
Jermaine Darlington	32	12	9	6	596	0	1	0
Joe Jacobson	19	1	1	0	10	0	0	0
Glenn Loovens	22	40	33	29	2805	2	5	0
Darren Purse	29	39	39	37	3417	5	12	2
Riccardo Scimeca	31	18	18	17	1544	1	2	0
Rhys Weston	25	37	30	24	2325	0	4	0
Midfielders								
Neal Ardley	33	43	30	22	2073	0	0	0
Darcy Blake	17	2	1	0	4	0	0	0
Willie Boland	30	24	15	9	984	0	3	0
Kevin Cooper	31	39	36	22	2469	1	3	0
Toni Koskela	23	0	0	0	0	0	0	0
Jason Koumas	26	44	44	42	3841	12	4	0
Joe Ledley	19	42	42	42	3780	3	4	0
Curtis McDonald	18	1	1	0	29	0	0	0
Phillip Mulryne	28	13	4	0	68	0	0	0
Paul Parry	25	30	27	8	1172	1	1	0
Jeff Whitley	31	39	34	30	2877	1	7	0
Forwards								
Andrea Ferretti	19	7	4	0	43	0	1	0
Stuart Fleetwood	20	0	0	0	0	0	0	0
Cameron Jerome	19	44	44	43	3884	18	7	0
Alan Lee	27	28	25	6	876	2	3	0
Guylain Ndumbu-Nsungu	23	18	11	2	317	0	2	0
Michael Ricketts	27	20	17	14	1327	5	5	0
Steven Thompson	27	15	14	13	1213	4	1	0

TEAM OF THE SEASON

G — Neil Alexander CG: 46 DR: 70

D — Chris Barker CG: 41 DR: 81

D — Rhys Weston CG: 24 DR: 75

D — Darren Purse CG: 37 DR: 74

D — Glenn Loovens CG: 29 DR: 70

M — Kevin Cooper CG: 22 SD: 7

M — Jeff Whitley CG: 30 SD: 6

M — Joe Ledley CG: 42 SD: 3

M — Jason Koumas CG: 42 SD: 0

F — Cameron Jerome CG: 43 SR: 216

F — Michael Ricketts CG: 14 SR: 265

MONTHLY POINTS TALLY

Month	Points	%
AUGUST	4	27%
SEPTEMBER	11	73%
OCTOBER	8	53%
NOVEMBER	8	44%
DECEMBER	7	39%
JANUARY	7	58%
FEBRUARY	7	47%
MARCH	7	58%
APRIL	1	6%

LEAGUE GOALS

	PLAYER	LGE	FAC	LC	Oth	TOT
1	Jerome	18	1	1	0	**20**
2	Koumas	12	0	1	0	**13**
3	Purse	5	0	1	0	**6**
4	Ricketts	5	0	0	0	**5**
5	Thompson	4	0	0	0	**4**
6	Ledley	3	0	1	0	**4**
7	Cox	2	0	0	0	**2**
8	Loovens	2	0	0	0	**2**
9	Lee	2	0	0	0	**2**
10	Whitley	1	0	0	0	**1**
11	Parry	1	0	0	0	**1**
	Other	3	0	0	0	3
	TOTAL	**58**	**1**	**4**	**0**	**63**

TOP POINT EARNERS

	PLAYER	GAMES	AV PTS
1	Michael Ricketts	14	**1.64**
2	Kevin Cooper	22	**1.55**
3	Jeff Whitley	30	**1.50**
4	Neil Cox	20	**1.50**
5	Rhys Weston	24	**1.50**
6	Chris Barker	41	**1.41**
7	Cameron Jerome	43	**1.37**
8	Joe Ledley	42	**1.36**
9	Darren Purse	37	**1.35**
10	Neil Alexander	46	**1.30**
	CLUB AVERAGE:		**1.30**

DISCIPLINARY RECORDS

	PLAYER	YELLOW	RED	AVE
1	Purse	12	2	**244**
2	Ricketts	5	0	**265**
3	Lee	3	0	**292**
4	Boland	3	0	**328**
5	Whitley	7	0	**411**
6	Jerome	7	0	**554**
7	Loovens	5	0	**561**
8	Weston	4	0	**581**
9	Darlington	1	0	**596**
10	Cox	3	0	**682**
11	Scimeca	2	0	**772**
12	Cooper	3	0	**823**
13	Barker	4	0	**914**
	Other	12	0	
	TOTAL	**71**	**2**	

KEY GOALKEEPER

Neil Alexander

Goals Conceded in the League	59	Counting Games League games when player was on pitch for at least 70 minutes	46
Goals Conceded in all competitions	61		
Defensive Rating Ave number of mins between League goals conceded while on the pitch	70	Clean Sheets In games when player was on pitch for at least 70 minutes	14

KEY PLAYERS - DEFENDERS

Chris Barker

Goals Conceded in the League	45	Clean Sheets In League games when player was on pitch for at least 70 minutes	14
Goals Conceded in all competitions	49		
Defensive Rating Ave number of mins between League goals conceded while on the pitch	81	Club Defensive Rating Average number of mins between League goals conceded by the club this season	70

	PLAYER	CON LGE	CON ALL	CLN SHEETS	DEF RATE
1	Chris Barker	45	49	14	81 mins
2	Rhys Weston	31	35	9	75 mins
3	Darren Purse	46	50	13	74 mins
4	Glenn Loovens	40	43	10	70 mins

KEY PLAYERS - MIDFIELDERS

Kevin Cooper

Goals in the League	1	Contribution to Attacking Power Average number of minutes between League team goals while on pitch	75
Goals in all competitions	1		
Defensive Rating Average number of mins between League goals conceded while on the pitch	82	Scoring Difference Defensive Rating minus Contribution to Attacking Power	7

	PLAYER	GOALS LGE	GOALS ALL	DEF RATE	ATT POWER	SCORE DIFF
1	Kevin Cooper	1	1	82	75	7 mins
2	Jeff Whitley	1	1	78	72	6 mins
3	Joe Ledley	3	4	73	70	3 mins
4	Jason Koumas	12	13	70	70	0 mins

KEY PLAYERS - GOALSCORERS

Cameron Jerome

Goals in the League	18	Player Strike Rate Average number of minutes between League goals scored by player	216
Goals in all competitions	20		
Contribution to Attacking Power Average number of minutes between League team goals while on pitch	71	Club Strike Rate Average number of minutes between League goals scored by club	71

	PLAYER	GOALS LGE	GOALS ALL	POWER	S RATE
1	Cameron Jerome	18	20	71	216 mins
2	Michael Ricketts	5	5	74	265 mins
3	Steven Thompson	4	4	87	303 mins
4	Jason Koumas	12	13	70	320 mins

Cameron Jerome

SQUAD APPEARANCES

Match	1	2	3	4	5	6	7	8	9	10	11	12	13	14	15	16	17	18	19	20	21	22	23	24	25
Venue	A	H	H	A	A	H	A	H	H	H	A	A	H	A	H	H	H	A	A	H	A	A	H	H	A
Competition	L	L	L	L	W	L	L	L	L	W	L	L	L	L	L	L	W	L	L	L	L	L	L	L	L
Result	L	W	L	L	W	D	D	W	W	W	D	W	L	W	D	W	L	D	L	D	W	L	D	W	L

Match	26	27	28	29	30	31	32	33	34	35	36	37	38	39	40	41	42	43	44	45	46	47	48	49	50
Venue	A	H	H	A	H	A	A	H	A	H	A	H	A	H	A	H	A	A	H	A	H	H	A	H	A
Competition	L	L	L	L	L	L	F	L	L	L	L	L	L	L	L	L	L	L	L	L	L	L	L	L	L
Result	W	D	L	L	W	L	L	W	W	D	L	W	D	W	L	W	L	W	D	L	L	L	D	L	L

Goalkeepers
Neil Alexander
Martyn Margetson
Tony Warner
Lee Worgan

Defenders
Chris Barker
Neil Cox
Jermaine Darlington
Joe Jacobson
Glenn Loovens
Darren Purse
Riccardo Scimeca
Rhys Weston

Midfielders
Neal Ardley
Darcy Blake
Willie Boland
Kevin Cooper
Toni Koskela
Jason Koumas
Joe Ledley
Curtis McDonald
Phillip Mulryne
Paul Parry
Jeff Whitley

Forwards
Andrea Ferretti
Stuart Fleetwood
Cameron Jerome
Alan Lee
Guylain Ndumbu-Nsungu
Michael Ricketts
Steven Thompson

KEY: On all match | On bench | Subbed or sent off (Counting game) | Subbed or sent off (playing less than 70 minutes) | Subbed on from bench (Counting Game) | Subbed on (playing less than 70 minutes) | Subbed on and then subbed or sent off (Counting Game) | Subbed on and then subbed or sent off (playing less than 70 minutes) | Not in 16

SOUTHAMPTON

Final Position: **12th**

NICKNAME: THE SAINTS

KEY: Won · Drawn · Lost

							Attendance
1	div1	Wolverhampton	H	D	0-0		24,061
2	div1	Luton	A	L	2-3	Oakley 18; Jones 45	9,447
3	div1	Sheff Wed	A	W	1-0	Jones 22	26,688
4	div1	Norwich	H	W	1-0	Quashie 15 pen	23,498
5	ccr1	Southend	A	W	3-0	Blackstock 44; Dyer 45; Ormerod 89	6,358
6	div1	Crewe	H	W	2-0	Belmadi 11; Quashie 66	20,792
7	div1	Coventry	A	D	1-1	Fuller 12	23,000
8	div1	QPR	H	D	1-1	Higginbotham 37	25,744
9	div1	Ipswich	A	D	2-2	Powell 50; Wise 69	22,997
10	div1	Derby	A	D	2-2	Ormerod 58; Fuller 90	22,348
11	ccr2	Mansfield	A	L	0-1		3,739
12	div1	Plymouth	H	D	0-0		26,331
13	div1	Reading	H	D	0-0		24,946
14	div1	Preston	A	D	1-1	Davidson 27 og	15,263
15	div1	Hull City	H	D	1-1	Oakley 44	23,810
16	div1	Leeds	A	L	1-2	Walcott 25	18,881
17	div1	Millwall	A	W	2-0	Walcott 18; Fuller 25	10,759
18	div1	Stoke	H	W	2-0	Walcott 16; Belmadi 90	24,095
19	div1	Leicester	A	D	0-0		21,318
20	div1	Leeds	H	L	3-4	Pahars 27; Quashie 35,45 pen	30,173
21	div1	Hull City	A	D	1-1	Kosowski 6	18,061
22	div1	Wolverhampton	A	D	0-0		24,628
23	div1	Burnley	H	D	1-1	Higginbotham 34 pen	21,592
24	div1	Luton	H	W	1-0	Walcott 23	19,086
25	div1	Norwich	A	L	1-3	Belmadi 9	24,836
26	div1	Watford	A	L	0-3		16,972
27	div1	Sheff Utd	H	L	0-1		27,443
28	div1	Cardiff	A	L	1-2	Blackstock 25	13,377
29	div1	Brighton	H	W	2-1	Blackstock 10,86	24,630
30	facr3	MK Dons	H	W	4-3	Prutton 40; Quashie 60; Walcott 66; Kenton 88	15,908
31	div1	QPR	A	L	0-1		15,494
32	div1	Ipswich	H	L	0-2		22,250
33	div1	Crystal Palace	H	D	0-0		24,651
34	facr4	Leicester	A	W	1-0	Jones 90	20,427
35	div1	Plymouth	A	L	1-2	Surman 70	15,936
36	div1	Derby	H	D	0-0		21,829
37	div1	Reading	A	L	0-2		23,845
38	div1	Preston	H	D	0-0		19,534
39	facr5	Newcastle	A	L	0-1		40,975
40	div1	Sheff Wed	H	W	3-0	Higginbotham 33; Rasiak 48; Jones 54	26,236
41	div1	Coventry	H	D	1-1	Rasiak 81	21,980
42	div1	Crewe	A	D	1-1	Madsen 61	6,588
43	div1	Watford	H	L	1-3	Madsen 85	19,202
44	div1	Sheff Utd	A	L	0-3		22,824
45	div1	Burnley	A	D	1-1	Bardsley 1 og	10,636
46	div1	Cardiff	H	W	3-2	Lundekvam 47; Fuller 70,75	22,388
47	div1	Brighton	A	W	2-0	Fuller 37; Chaplow 63	7,999
48	div1	Stoke	A	W	2-1	Rasiak 24 pen,31	16,501
49	div1	Millwall	H	W	2-0	Jones 13 pen; Fuller 90	22,043
50	div1	Crystal Palace	A	L	1-2	Fuller 69	20,995
51	div1	Leicester	H	W	2-0	Fuller 22; Surman 25	26,801

LEAGUE APPEARANCES AND BOOKINGS

	AGE (on 01/07/06)	IN NAMED 16	APPEARANCES	COUNTING GAMES	MINUTES ON PITCH	LEAGUE GOALS		
Goalkeepers								
Bartosz Bialkowski	19	7	5	5	450	0	0	0
Kevin Miller	37	11	7	7	630	0	0	0
Antti Niemi	34	26	25	25	2250	0	1	0
Paul Smith	26	46	10	9	813	0	0	0
Defenders								
Chris Baird	24	18	17	16	1459	0	4	0
Jim Brennan	29	14	14	13	1204	0	0	0
Martin Cranie	19	26	11	6	655	0	1	0
Tomasz Hajto	33	22	20	14	1505	0	7	1
Danny Higginbotham	27	37	37	37	3330	3	3	0
Darren Kenton	27	15	13	11	1079	0	3	0
Claus Lundekvam	33	34	34	32	2958	1	4	1
Matthew Mills	19	6	4	3	294	0	1	0
Alexander Ostlund	27	12	12	8	860	0	3	0
Darren Powell	30	30	24	21	2027	1	6	0
Michael Svensson	30	7	7	7	630	0	1	0
Midfielders								
Djamel Belmadi	30	26	22	16	1689	3	2	0
Richard Chaplow	21	11	11	9	900	1	0	0
Rory Delap	30	22	16	11	1068	0	2	1
Kamil Kosowski	28	21	18	7	943	1	1	0
Neil McCann	31	15	11	7	697	0	1	0
Matthew Oakley	28	29	29	27	2531	2	2	0
Darren Potter	21	13	10	9	788	0	0	0
David Prutton	24	19	17	13	1291	0	2	0
Nigel Quashie	27	24	24	23	2115	4	6	1
Andrew Surman	19	12	12	11	1011	2	1	0
Dennis Wise	39	15	11	7	745	1	4	0
Jermaine Wright	30	13	13	13	1159	0	1	0
Forwards								
Dextor Blackstock	20	23	18	5	814	3	1	0
Nathan Dyer	18	22	16	9	971	0	1	0
Ricardo Fuller	26	32	30	20	2024	9	5	0
Kenwyne Jones	22	37	34	12	1609	4	0	0
Peter Madsen	28	11	9	6	608	2	1	0
Brett Ormerod	29	22	18	10	1138	1	2	0
Marian Pahars	29	8	8	3	410	1	1	0
Grzegorz Rasiak	27	13	13	12	1077	4	1	0
Theo Walcott	17	22	21	10	1241	4	1	0

TEAM OF THE SEASON

G — Antti Niemi — CG: 25 DR: 90

D — Claus Lundekvam — CG: 32 DR: 110
D — Darren Powell — CG: 21 DR: 97
D — Danny Higginbotham — CG: 37 DR: 83
D — Jim Brennan — CG: 13 DR: 80

M — Djamel Belmadi — CG: 16 SD: 33
M — Jermaine Wright — CG: 13 SD: 25
M — Matthew Oakley — CG: 27 SD: -3
M — Nigel Quashie — CG: 23 SD: -4

F — Ricardo Fuller — CG: 20 SR: 225
F — Grzegorz Rasiak — CG: 12 SR: 269

MONTHLY POINTS TALLY

AUGUST	11	61%
SEPTEMBER	5	33%
OCTOBER	8	53%
NOVEMBER	3	25%
DECEMBER	4	22%
JANUARY	4	27%
FEBRUARY	5	42%
MARCH	3	20%
APRIL	15	83%

LEAGUE GOALS

	PLAYER	LGE	FAC	LC	Oth	TOT
1	Fuller	9	0	0	0	9
2	Walcott	4	1	0	0	5
3	Quashie	4	1	0	0	5
4	Rasiak	4	0	0	0	4
5	Jones	4	1	0	0	5
6	Belmadi	3	0	0	0	3
7	Higginbotham	3	0	0	0	3
8	Blackstock	3	0	1	0	4
9	Surman	2	0	0	0	2
10	Madsen	2	0	0	0	2
11	Oakley	2	0	0	0	2
	Other	9	2	2	0	13
	TOTAL	49	5	3	0	57

TOP POINT EARNERS

	PLAYER	GAMES	AV PTS
1	Djamel Belmadi	16	1.75
2	Jermaine Wright	13	1.69
3	Kenwyne Jones	12	1.58
4	Grzegorz Rasiak	12	1.58
5	Ricardo Fuller	20	1.55
6	Jim Brennan	13	1.54
7	Tomasz Hajto	14	1.43
8	Claus Lundekvam	32	1.41
9	Darren Powell	21	1.38
10	Antti Niemi	25	1.36
	CLUB AVERAGE:		1.26

DISCIPLINARY RECORDS

	PLAYER	YELLOW	RED	AVE
1	Wise	4	0	186
2	Hajto	7	1	188
3	Ostlund	3	0	286
4	Quashie	6	1	302
5	Powell	6	0	337
6	Delap	2	1	356
7	Kenton	3	0	359
8	Baird	4	0	364
9	Fuller	5	0	404
10	Ormerod	2	0	569
11	Lundekvam	4	1	591
12	Madsen	1	0	608
13	Svensson, M	1	0	630
	Other	19	0	
	TOTAL	67	4	

KEY GOALKEEPER

Antti Niemi

Goals Conceded in the League	25	Counting Games League games when player was on pitch for at least 70 minutes	25
Goals Conceded in all competitions	25		
Defensive Rating Ave number of mins between League goals conceded while on the pitch	90	Clean Sheets In games when player was on pitch for at least 70 minutes	11

KEY PLAYERS - DEFENDERS

Claus Lundekvam

Goals Conceded in the League	27	Clean Sheets In League games when player was on pitch for at least 70 minutes	15
Goals Conceded in all competitions	30		
Defensive Rating Ave number of mins between League goals conceded while on the pitch	110	Club Defensive Rating Average number of mins between League goals conceded by the club this season	83

	PLAYER	CON LGE	CON ALL	CLN SHEETS	DEF RATE
1	Claus Lundekvam	27	30	15	110 mins
2	Darren Powell	21	22	9	97 mins
3	Danny Higginbotham	40	40	15	83 mins
4	Jim Brennan	15	16	5	80 mins

KEY PLAYERS - MIDFIELDERS

Djamel Belmadi

Goals in the League	3	Contribution to Attacking Power Average number of minutes between League team goals while on pitch	80
Goals in all competitions	3		
Defensive Rating Average number of mins between League goals conceded while on the pitch	113	Scoring Difference Defensive Rating minus Contribution to Attacking Power	33

	PLAYER	GOALS LGE	GOALS ALL	DEF RATE	ATT POWER	SCORE DIFF
1	Djamel Belmadi	3	3	113	80	33 mins
2	Jermaine Wright	0	0	89	64	25 mins
3	Matthew Oakley	2	2	87	90	-3 mins
4	Nigel Quashie	4	5	81	85	-4 mins

KEY PLAYERS - GOALSCORERS

Ricardo Fuller

Goals in the League	9	Player Strike Rate Average number of minutes between League goals scored by player	225
Goals in all competitions	9		
Contribution to Attacking Power Average number of minutes between League team goals while on pitch	75	Club Strike Rate Average number of minutes between League goals scored by club	84

	PLAYER	GOALS LGE	GOALS ALL	POWER	S RATE
1	Ricardo Fuller	9	9	75	225 mins
2	Grzegorz Rasiak	4	4	60	269 mins
3	Kenwyne Jones	4	5	89	402 mins
4	Nigel Quashie	4	5	85	529 mins

Ricardo Fuller (second left) celebrates a goal

SQUAD APPEARANCES

atch	1	2	3	4	5	6	7	8	9	10	11	12	13	14	15	16	17	18	19	20	21	22	23	24	25	26	27	28	29	30	31	32	33	34	35	36	37	38	39	40	41	42	43	44	45	46	47	48	49	50	51
nue	H	A	A	H	A	H	A	H	A	A	A	H	H	A	H	A	A	H	A	H	A	A	H	H	A	A	H	A	H	H	A	H	H	A	A	H	A	H	A	H	H	A	H	A	A	H	A	A	H	A	H
ompetition	L	L	L	L	W	L	L	L	L	L	W	L	L	L	L	L	L	L	L	L	L	L	L	L	L	L	L	L	L	F	L	L	L	F	L	L	L	L	F	L	L	L	L	L	L	L	L	L	L	L	L
esult	D	L	W	W	W	W	D	D	D	D	L	D	D	D	D	L	W	W	D	L	D	D	D	W	L	L	L	L	W	W	L	L	D	W	L	D	L	D	L	W	D	D	L	L	D	W	W	W	W	L	W

oalkeepers
artosz Bialkowski
evin Miller
ntti Niemi
aul Smith

efenders
hris Baird
m Brennan
artin Cranie
omasz Hajto
anny Higginbotham
arren Kenton
laus Lundekvam
atthew Mills
lexander Ostlund
arren Powell
ichael Svensson

idfielders
jamel Belmadi
ichard Chaplow
ory Delap
amil Kosowski
eil McCann
atthew Oakley
arren Potter
avid Prutton
igel Quashie
ndrew Surman
ennis Wise
ermaine Wright

orwards
extor Blackstock
athan Dyer
icardo Fuller
enwyne Jones
eter Madsen
rett Ormerod
larian Pahars
rzegorz Rasiak
heo Walcott

KEY: On all match · On bench · Subbed or sent off (Counting game) · Subbed or sent off (playing less than 70 minutes) · Subbed on from bench (Counting Game) · Subbed on (playing less than 70 minutes) · Subbed on and then subbed or sent off (Counting Game) · Subbed on and then subbed or sent off (playing less than 70 minutes) · Not in 16

STOKE CITY

Final Position: **13th**

NICKNAME: THE POTTERS

KEY: ☐ Won ☐ Drawn ☐ Lost

#	Comp	Opponent	Venue	Result	Score	Scorers	Attendance
1	div1	Sheff Wed	H	D	0-0		18,744
2	div1	Leicester	A	L	2-4	Broomes 64; Halls 89	20,519
3	div1	Millwall	A	W	1-0	Halls 38	8,668
4	div1	Luton	H	W	2-1	Broomes 63; Brammer 90	18,653
5	ccr1	Mansfield	A	L	0-3*	Brammer 11 pen (*on penalties)	2,799
6	div1	Crystal Palace	A	L	0-2		17,637
7	div1	Norwich	H	W	3-1	Kolar 9; Harper 45; Sidibe 69	14,249
8	div1	Watford	H	L	0-3		14,565
9	div1	Hull City	A	W	1-0	Gallagher 74	18,692
10	div1	Preston	A	W	1-0	Gallagher 76	12,453
11	div1	Wolverhampton	H	L	1-3	Buxton 90	18,183
12	div1	Cardiff	H	L	0-3		12,240
13	div1	Plymouth	A	L	1-2	Chadwick 47	12,604
14	div1	Derby	A	L	1-2	Hoefkens 59	22,229
15	div1	Crewe	H	W	2-0	Bangoura 41; Duberry 64	14,080
16	div1	Reading	H	L	0-1		13,484
17	div1	Southampton	A	L	0-2		24,095
18	div1	Coventry	A	W	2-1	Taggart 37; Gallagher 55	16,617
19	div1	Brighton	H	W	3-0	Bangoura 35,75; Russell 68	15,274
20	div1	Crewe	A	W	2-1	Bangoura 16; Halls 88; Gallagher 89	8,942
21	div1	Derby	H	L	1-2	Bangoura 33	13,205
22	div1	Sheff Wed	A	W	2-0	Bangoura 17; Sidibe 86	21,970
23	div1	QPR	H	L	1-2	Bangoura 26	15,367
24	div1	Leicester	H	W	3-2	Gallagher 36 pen; Sidibe 75; Bangoura 78	11,125
25	div1	Luton	A	W	3-2	Gallagher 45,83; Coyne 90 og	8,296
26	div1	Burnley	A	L	0-1		17,912
27	div1	Leeds	H	L	0-1		20,408
28	div1	Sheff Utd	A	L	1-2	Sidibe 57	21,279
29	div1	Ipswich	H	D	2-2	Russell 27; Sidibe 73	14,493
30	facr3	Tamworth	H	D	0-0		9,366
31	div1	Watford	A	L	0-1		12,247
32	facr3r	Tamworth	A	W	5-4*	Gallagher 80 (*on penalties)	3,812
33	div1	Hull City	H	L	0-3		13,444
34	facr4	Walsall	H	W	2-1	Sidibe 45; Chadwick 49	8,834
35	div1	Preston	H	D	0-0		13,218
36	div1	Cardiff	A	L	0-3		10,780
37	div1	Plymouth	H	D	0-0		10,242
38	facr5	Birmingham	H	L	0-1		18,768
39	div1	Millwall	H	W	2-1	Hoefkens 14 pen; Gallagher 56	11,340
40	div1	Norwich	A	L	1-2	Gallagher 58	24,223
41	div1	Wolverhampton	A	D	0-0		22,439
42	div1	Crystal Palace	H	L	1-3	Skoko 47	10,121
43	div1	Burnley	H	W	1-0	Gallagher 52	12,082
44	div1	Leeds	A	D	0-0		21,452
45	div1	QPR	A	W	2-1	Hoefkens 73 pen; Sigurdsson 79	10,918
46	div1	Sheff Utd	H	D	1-1	Skoko 16	17,544
47	div1	Ipswich	A	W	4-1	Wilnis 51 og; Bangoura 82; Chadwick 90; Russell 90	23,592
48	div1	Southampton	H	L	1-2	Gallagher 83	16,501
49	div1	Reading	A	L	1-3	Rooney 59	22,119
50	div1	Coventry	H	L	0-1		13,385
51	div1	Brighton	A	W	5-1	Rooney 6,22,63; Sidibe 40; Sweeney 82	5,859

LEAGUE APPEARANCES AND BOOKINGS

	AGE (on 01/07/06)	IN NAMED 16	APPEARANCES	COUNTING GAMES	MINUTES ON PITCH	LEAGUE GOALS	Yellow	Red
Goalkeepers								
Ed de Goey	39	45	2	1	110	0	0	0
Steve Simonsen	27	45	45	45	4030	0	1	1
Defenders								
Marlon Broomes	28	41	37	32	3074	2	7	1
Lewis Buxton	22	39	32	26	2479	1	5	0
Carl Dickinson	19	8	5	4	405	0	0	0
Michael Duberry	30	41	41	41	3690	1	6	1
John Halls	24	16	13	12	1115	3	2	1
Clinton Hill	27	14	13	12	1082	0	0	0
Carl Hoefkens	29	44	44	43	3888	3	4	0
Gerry Taggart	35	12	3	2	189	1	0	1
Andy Wilkinson	21	10	6	3	324	0	1	0
Midfielders								
David Brammer	31	40	40	36	3365	1	5	0
Luke Chadwick	25	37	36	27	2691	2	5	0
Thordur Gudjonsson	32	2	0	0	0	0	0	0
Kevin Harper	30	14	14	4	668	1	0	0
Karl Henry	23	32	24	10	1131	0	1	0
Martin Kolar	22	20	14	8	870	1	1	0
Peter Kopteff	27	13	6	0	250	0	0	0
Gabriel Ngalula Mbuyi	24	38	21	13	1387	0	0	1
Darel Russell	25	36	36	31	2949	3	8	0
Josip Skoko	30	9	9	9	791	2	1	0
Peter Sweeney	21	25	17	4	692	1	1	0
Forwards								
Sambegou Bangoura	24	24	24	22	1988	9	6	0
Bruce Dyer	31	13	11	2	340	0	1	0
Paul Gallagher	21	37	37	30	2818	11	10	0
Martin Paterson	19	3	3	1	165	0	0	0
Adam Rooney	19	8	6	3	324	4	1	0
Mamady Sidibe	26	42	41	35	3319	6	2	0
Hans Sigurdsson	23	23	23	9	1146	1	1	0

TEAM OF THE SEASON

G — Steve Simonsen CG: 45 DR: 65

D — Clinton Hill CG: 12 DR: 83

D — John Halls CG: 12 DR: 80

D — Carl Hoefkens CG: 43 DR: 68

D — Michael Duberry CG: 41 DR: 64

M — Darel Russell CG: 31 SD: 0

M — David Brammer CG: 36 SD: -2

M — Luke Chadwick CG: 27 SD: -17

M — Gabriel Ngalula Mbuyi CG: 13 SD: -24

F — Sam Bangoura CG: 22 SR: 221

F — Paul Gallagher CG: 30 SR: 256

MONTHLY POINTS TALLY

Month	Points	%
AUGUST	10	56%
SEPTEMBER	6	40%
OCTOBER	3	20%
NOVEMBER	12	80%
DECEMBER	6	33%
JANUARY	1	11%
FEBRUARY	5	42%
MARCH	8	44%
APRIL	7	39%

LEAGUE GOALS

	PLAYER	LGE	FAC	LC	Oth	TOT
1	Gallagher	11	1	0	0	12
2	Bangoura	9	0	0	0	9
3	Sidibe	6	1	0	0	7
4	Rooney	4	0	0	0	4
5	Hoefkens	3	0	0	0	3
6	Russell	3	0	0	0	3
7	Halls	3	0	0	0	3
8	Skoko	2	0	0	0	2
9	Chadwick	2	1	0	0	3
10	Broomes	2	0	0	0	2
11	Brammer	1	0	1	0	2
	Other	9	0	0	0	9
	TOTAL	55	3	1	0	59

TOP POINT EARNERS

	PLAYER	GAMES	AV PTS
1	John Halls	12	1.58
2	David Brammer	36	1.53
3	Sambegou Bangoura	22	1.36
4	Clinton Hill	12	1.33
5	Lewis Buxton	26	1.31
6	Michael Duberry	41	1.29
7	Carl Hoefkens	43	1.28
8	Paul Gallagher	30	1.23
9	Darel Russell	31	1.23
10	Steve Simonsen	45	1.22
	CLUB AVERAGE:		1.26

DISCIPLINARY RECORDS

	PLAYER	YELLOW	RED	AVE
1	Gallagher	10	0	281
2	Bangoura	6	0	331
3	Russell	8	0	368
4	Halls	2	1	371
5	Broomes	7	1	384
6	Buxton	5	0	495
7	Duberry	6	1	527
8	Chadwick	5	0	538
9	Brammer	5	0	673
10	Sweeney	1	0	692
11	Skoko	1	0	791
12	Kolar	1	0	870
13	Hoefkens	4	0	972
	Other	5	2	
	TOTAL	66	5	

KEY GOALKEEPER

Steve Simonsen

Goals Conceded in the League	62	Counting Games League games when player was on pitch for at least 70 minutes	45
Goals Conceded in all competitions	66		
Defensive Rating Ave number of mins between League goals conceded while on the pitch	65	Clean Sheets In games when player was on pitch for at least 70 minutes	11

KEY PLAYERS - DEFENDERS

Clinton Hill

Goals Conceded in the League	13	Clean Sheets In League games when player was on pitch for at least 70 minutes	4
Goals Conceded in all competitions	14		
Defensive Rating Ave number of mins between League goals conceded while on the pitch	83	Club Defensive Rating Average number of mins between League goals conceded by the club this season	66

	PLAYER	CON LGE	CON ALL	CLN SHEETS	DEF RATE
1	Clinton Hill	13	14	4	83 mins
2	John Halls	14	15	4	80 mins
3	Carl Hoefkens	57	61	12	68 mins
4	Michael Duberry	58	62	11	64 mins

KEY PLAYERS - MIDFIELDERS

Darel Russell

Goals in the League	3	Contribution to Attacking Power Average number of minutes between League team goals while on pitch	69
Goals in all competitions	3		
Defensive Rating Average number of mins between League goals conceded while on the pitch	69	Scoring Difference Defensive Rating minus Contribution to Attacking Power	0

	PLAYER	GOALS LGE	GOALS ALL	DEF RATE	ATT POWER	SCORE DIFF
1	Darel Russell	3	3	69	69	0 mins
2	David Brammer	1	2	70	72	-2 mins
3	Luke Chadwick	2	3	73	90	-17 mins
4	Gabriel Ngalula Mbuyi	0	0	58	82	-24 mins

KEY PLAYERS - GOALSCORERS

Sambegou Bangoura

Goals in the League	9	Player Strike Rate Average number of minutes between League goals scored by player	221
Goals in all competitions	9		
Contribution to Attacking Power Average number of minutes between League team goals while on pitch	69	Club Strike Rate Average number of minutes between League goals scored by club	75

	PLAYER	GOALS LGE	GOALS ALL	POWER	S RATE
1	Sambegou Bangoura	9	9	69	221 mins
2	Paul Gallagher	11	12	74	256 mins
3	John Halls	3	3	66	372 mins
4	Mamady Sidibe	6	7	75	553 mins

Stoke's Sambegou Bangoura

SQUAD APPEARANCES

Match	1	2	3	4	5	6	7	8	9	10	11	12	13	14	15	16	17	18	19	20	21	22	23	24	25	26	27	28	29	30	31	32	33	34	35	36	37	38	39	40	41	42	43	44	45	46	47	48	49	50	51
Venue	H	A	A	H	A	A	H	H	A	A	H	H	A	A	H	H	A	A	H	A	H	A	H	H	A	A	H	A	H	H	A	A	H	H	H	A	H	H	H	A	A	H	H	A	A	H	A	H	A	H	A
Competition	L	L	L	L	W	L	L	L	L	L	L	L	L	L	L	L	L	L	L	L	L	L	L	L	L	L	L	L	L	F	L	F	L	F	L	L	L	F	L	L	L	L	L	L	L	L	L	L	L	L	L
Result	D	L	W	W	L	L	W	L	W	W	L	L	L	L	W	L	L	W	W	W	L	W	L	W	W	L	L	L	D	D	L	W	L	W	D	L	D	L	W	L	D	L	W	D	W	D	W	L	L	L	W

Goalkeepers
Ed de Goey
Steve Simonsen

Defenders
Marlon Broomes
Lewis Buxton
Carl Dickinson
Michael Duberry
John Halls
Clinton Hill
Carl Hoefkens
Gerry Taggart
Andy Wilkinson

Midfielders
David Brammer
Luke Chadwick
Thordur Gudjonsson
Kevin Harper
Carl Henry
Martin Kolar
Peter Kopteff
Gabriel Ngalula Mbuyi
Darel Russell
Josip Skoko
Peter Sweeney

Forwards
Sambegou Bangoura
Bruce Dyer
Paul Gallagher
Martin Paterson
Adam Rooney
Mamady Sidibe
Hans Sigurdsson

KEY: ■ On all match ■ On bench ⏮ Subbed or sent off (Counting game) « Subbed or sent off (playing less than 70 minutes) ⏭ Subbed on from bench (Counting Game) » Subbed on (playing less than 70 minutes) » Subbed on and then subbed or sent off (Counting Game) » Subbed on and then subbed or sent off (playing less than 70 minutes) □ Not in 16

PLYMOUTH ARGYLE

Final Position: **14th**

NICKNAME: THE PILGRIMS

KEY: ☐Won ☐Drawn ☐Lost

							Attendance
1	div1	Reading	A	W	2-1	Evans 21; Chadwick 90	16,836
2	div1	Watford	H	D	3-3	Evans 4; Capaldi 12; Wotton 43	13,813
3	div1	Derby	H	L	0-2		14,279
4	div1	Crystal Palace	A	L	0-1		18,781
5	ccr1	Peterborough	H	W	2-1	Wotton 35 pen; Taylor 38	5,974
6	div1	Hull City	H	L	0-1		12,329
7	div1	Brighton	A	L	0-2		6,238
8	div1	Norwich	A	L	0-2		23,981
9	div1	Crewe	H	D	1-1	Taylor 12	10,460
10	div1	Burnley	H	W	1-0	Evans 46	11,829
11	ccr2	Barnet	A	L	1-2	Buzsaky 19	1,941
12	div1	Southampton	A	D	0-0		26,331
13	div1	Sheff Utd	A	L	0-2		20,111
14	div1	Stoke	H	W	2-1	Russell 50 og; Buzsaky 77	12,604
15	div1	Sheff Wed	H	D	1-1	Wotton 79 pen	16,534
16	div1	QPR	A	D	1-1	Buzsaky 39	11,741
17	div1	Luton	A	D	1-1	Djordjic 90	8,714
18	div1	Millwall	H	D	0-0		11,764
19	div1	Ipswich	A	L	1-3	Buzsaky 51	23,083
20	div1	QPR	H	W	3-1	Wotton 7 pen; Doumbe 37; Chadwick 51	13,213
21	div1	Sheff Wed	A	D	0-0		20,244
22	div1	Reading	H	L	0-2		14,020
23	div1	Coventry	A	L	1-3	Norris 25	18,796
24	div1	Watford	A	D	1-1	Chadwick 48	12,884
25	div1	Crystal Palace	H	W	2-0	Chadwick 1; Capaldi 90	14,582
26	div1	Cardiff	A	W	2-0	Wotton 72 pen; Norris 80 pen	16,403
27	div1	Wolverhampton	A	D	1-1	Ward 22	22,790
28	div1	Leeds	H	L	0-3		17,726
29	facr3	Wolverhampton	A	L	0-1		11,041
30	div1	Norwich	H	D	1-1	Charlton 24 og	13,906
31	div1	Crewe	A	W	2-1	Wotton 3 pen,45	5,984
32	div1	Leicester	H	W	1-0	Wotton 47	12,591
33	div1	Southampton	H	W	2-1	Chadwick 45; Wotton 84 pen	15,936
34	div1	Burnley	A	L	0-1		11,292
35	div1	Sheff Utd	H	D	0-0		15,017
36	div1	Stoke	A	D	0-0		10,242
37	div1	Coventry	H	W	3-1	Pericard 12,40,73	12,958
38	div1	Derby	A	L	0-1		25,170
39	div1	Brighton	H	W	1-0	Nalis 37	13,650
40	div1	Preston	H	D	0-0		10,874
41	div1	Hull City	A	L	0-1		20,137
42	div1	Cardiff	H	L	0-1		13,494
43	div1	Preston	A	D	0-0		13,925
44	div1	Wolverhampton	H	W	2-0	Aljofree 9; Ince 80 og	15,871
45	div1	Leeds	A	D	0-0		20,650
46	div1	Millwall	A	D	1-1	Pericard 10	9,183
47	div1	Luton	H	L	1-2	Buzsaky 70	13,486
48	div1	Leicester	A	L	0-1		22,796
49	div1	Ipswich	H	W	2-1	Capaldi 28; Evans 57	15,921

LEAGUE APPEARANCES AND BOOKINGS

	AGE (on 01/07/06)	IN NAMED 16	APPEARANCES	COUNTING GAMES	MINUTES ON PITCH	LEAGUE GOALS		
Goalkeepers								
Romain Larrieu	29	45	45	45	4050	0	1	0
Luke McCormick	22	45	1	1	90	0	0	0
Defenders								
Hasney Aljofree	27	44	37	33	3134	1	4	0
Anthony Barness	34	38	36	30	2872	0	3	0
Rufus Brevett	36	14	13	9	943	0	4	0
Paul Connolly	22	36	31	25	2413	0	8	1
Mathias Doumbe	26	42	42	41	3733	1	6	0
Nuno Mendes	20	4	2	1	130	0	0	0
Elliott Ward	21	16	16	15	1351	1	0	0
Taribo West	32	5	4	4	360	0	1	0
Paul Wotton	28	45	45	45	4050	8	8	0
Midfielders								
Akos Buzsaky	24	42	34	14	1684	4	2	0
Anthony Capaldi	24	42	41	36	3392	3	7	0
Bojan Djordjic	24	34	22	8	1013	1	3	0
Bjarni Gudjonsson	27	14	10	3	504	0	1	0
Lee Hodges	32	21	14	9	1020	0	0	0
Jason Jarrett	26	7	7	7	630	0	0	0
Keith Lasley	26	15	5	0	85	0	0	0
Lilian Nalis	34	20	20	20	1800	1	3	0
David Norris	25	45	45	44	3960	2	6	0
Anthony Pulis	21	7	5	0	55	0	1	0
Forwards								
Nick Chadwick	23	38	37	20	2230	5	3	0
Leon Clarke	21	5	5	2	322	0	0	0
Matthew Derbyshire	20	16	12	2	281	0	0	0
Micky Evans	33	45	45	32	3205	4	2	0
Vincent Pericard	23	15	15	14	1262	4	1	0
Reuben Reid	18	3	1	0	13	0	0	0
Scott Taylor	30	21	18	6	860	1	2	0
Chris Zebroski	19	9	4	0	80	0	0	0

TEAM OF THE SEASON

G — Romain Larrieu, CG: 45 DR: 92

D — Paul Connolly, CG: 25 DR: 105

D — Hasney Aljofree, CG: 33 DR: 92

D — Paul Wotton, CG: 45 DR: 92

D — Elliott Ward, CG: 15 DR: 90

M — Anthony Capaldi, CG: 36 SD: -3

M — David Norris, CG: 44 SD: -3

M — Akos Buzsaky, CG: 14 SD: -32

M — Lillian Nalis, CG: 20 SD: 25

F — Nick Chadwick, CG: 20 SR: 446

F — Vincent Pericard, CG: 14 SR: 316

MONTHLY POINTS TALLY

AUGUST	4	22%
SEPTEMBER	5	33%
OCTOBER	7	47%
NOVEMBER	4	33%
DECEMBER	8	53%
JANUARY	10	67%
FEBRUARY	5	33%
MARCH	5	33%
APRIL	8	44%

LEAGUE GOALS

	PLAYER	LGE	FAC	LC	Oth	TOT
1	Wotton	8	0	1	0	9
2	Chadwick	5	0	0	0	5
3	Pericard	4	0	0	0	4
4	Evans	4	0	0	0	4
5	Buzsaky	4	0	1	0	5
6	Capaldi	3	0	0	0	3
7	Norris	2	0	0	0	2
8	Taylor	1	0	1	0	2
9	Djordjic	1	0	0	0	1
10	Ward	1	0	0	0	1
11	Doumbe	1	0	0	0	1
	Other	5	0	0	0	5
	TOTAL	39	0	3	0	42

TOP POINT EARNERS

	PLAYER	GAMES	AV PTS
1	Elliott Ward	15	1.53
2	Nick Chadwick	20	1.40
3	Lilian Nalis	20	1.40
4	Hasney Aljofree	33	1.36
5	Anthony Capaldi	36	1.31
6	Micky Evans	32	1.28
7	Mathias Doumbe	41	1.27
8	David Norris	44	1.27
9	Romain Larrieu	44	1.25
10	Paul Wotton	45	1.24
	CLUB AVERAGE:		1.22

DISCIPLINARY RECORDS

	PLAYER	YELLOW	RED	AVE
1	Brevett	4	0	235
2	Connolly	8	1	268
3	Djordjic	3	0	337
4	Taylor	2	0	430
5	Capaldi	7	0	484
6	Gudjonsson	1	0	504
7	Wotton	8	0	506
8	Nalis	3	0	600
9	Doumbe	6	0	622
10	Norris	6	0	660
11	Chadwick	3	0	743
12	Aljofree	4	0	783
13	Buzsaky	2	0	842
	Other	7	0	
	TOTAL	64	1	

KEY GOALKEEPER

Romain Larrieu

Goals Conceded in the League	44	Counting Games League games when player was on pitch for at least 70 minutes	45
Goals Conceded in all competitions	44		
Defensive Rating Ave number of mins between League goals conceded while on the pitch	92	Clean Sheets In games when player was on pitch for at least 70 minutes	14

KEY PLAYERS - DEFENDERS

Paul Connolly

Goals Conceded in the League	23	Clean Sheets In League games when player was on pitch for at least 70 minutes	9
Goals Conceded in all competitions	25		
Defensive Rating Ave number of mins between League goals conceded while on the pitch	105	Club Defensive Rating Average number of mins between League goals conceded by the club this season	90

	PLAYER	CON LGE	CON ALL	CLN SHEETS	DEF RATE
1	Paul Connolly	23	25	9	105 mins
2	Paul Wotton	44	46	14	92 mins
3	Hasney Aljofree	34	35	11	92 mins
4	Elliott Ward	15	15	5	90 mins

KEY PLAYERS - MIDFIELDERS

Lilian Nalis

Goals in the League	1	Contribution to Attacking Power Average number of minutes between League team goals while on pitch	113
Goals in all competitions	1		
Defensive Rating Average number of mins between League goals conceded while on the pitch	138	Scoring Difference Defensive Rating minus Contribution to Attacking Power	25

	PLAYER	GOALS LGE	GOALS ALL	DEF RATE	ATT POWER	SCORE DIFF
1	Lilian Nalis	1	1	138	113	25 mins
2	David Norris	2	2	99	102	-3 mins
3	Anthony Capaldi	3	3	94	97	-3 mins
4	Akos Buzsaky	4	5	73	105	-32 mins

KEY PLAYERS - GOALSCORERS

Vincent Pericard

Goals in the League	4	Player Strike Rate Average number of minutes between League goals scored by player	316
Goals in all competitions	4		
Contribution to Attacking Power Average number of minutes between League team goals while on pitch	126	Club Strike Rate Average number of minutes between League goals scored by club	106

	PLAYER	GOALS LGE	GOALS ALL	POWER	S RATE
1	Vincent Pericard	4	4	126	316 mins
2	Akos Buzsaky	4	5	105	421 mins
3	Nick Chadwick	5	5	83	446 mins
4	Paul Wotton	8	9	104	506 mins

Plymouth's Nick Chadwick

SQUAD APPEARANCES

Match	1	2	3	4	5	6	7	8	9	10	11	12	13	14	15	16	17	18	19	20	21	22	23	24	25
Venue	A	H	H	A	H	H	A	A	H	H	A	A	A	H	H	A	A	H	A	H	A	H	A	A	H
Competition	L	L	L	L	W	L	L	L	L	L	W	L	L	L	L	L	L	L	L	L	L	L	L	L	L
Result	W	D	L	L	W	L	L	L	D	W	L	D	L	W	D	D	D	D	L	W	D	L	L	D	W

Match	26	27	28	29	30	31	32	33	34	35	36	37	38	39	40	41	42	43	44	45	46	47	48	49
Venue	A	A	H	A	H	A	H	H	A	H	A	H	A	H	H	A	H	A	H	A	A	H	A	H
Competition	L	L	L	F	L	L	L	L	L	L	L	L	L	L	L	L	L	L	L	L	L	L	L	L
Result	W	D	L	L	D	W	W	W	L	D	D	W	L	W	D	L	L	D	W	D	D	L	L	W

Goalkeepers
Romain Larrieu
Luke McCormick

Defenders
Hasney Aljofree
Anthony Barness
Rufus Brevett
Paul Connolly
Mathias Doumbe
Nuno Mendes
Elliott Ward
Taribo West
Paul Wotton

Midfielders
Akos Buzsaky
Anthony Capaldi
Bojan Djordjic
Bjarni Gudjonsson
Lee Hodges
Jason Jarrett
Keith Lasley
Lilian Nalis
David Norris
Anthony Pulis

Forwards
Nick Chadwick
Leon Clarke
Matthew Derbyshire
Micky Evans
Vincent Pericard
Reuben Reid
Scott Taylor
Chris Zebroski

KEY: On all match | On bench | Subbed or sent off (Counting game) | Subbed or sent off (playing less than 70 minutes) | Subbed on from bench (Counting Game) | Subbed on (playing less than 70 minutes) | Subbed on and then subbed or sent off (Counting Game) | Subbed on and then subbed or sent off (playing less than 70 minutes) | Not in 16

IPSWICH TOWN

Final Position: **15th**

NICKNAME: TRACTOR BOYS

KEY: ☐Won ☐Drawn ☐Lost

							Attendance
1	div1	Cardiff	H	W	1-0	Forster 64	24,292
2	div1	QPR	A	L	1-2	Parkin 54	14,632
3	div1	Leicester	A	D	0-0		21,879
4	div1	Sheff Wed	H	W	2-1	Naylor 7; Westlake 71	24,238
5	ccr1	Yeovil	H	L	0-2		11,299
6	div1	Millwall	A	W	2-1	Currie 13; Parkin 80	8,277
7	div1	Preston	H	L	0-4		22,551
8	div1	Sheff Utd	A	L	0-2		21,059
9	div1	Southampton	H	D	2-2	Naylor 36; Garvan 61	22,997
10	div1	Norwich	H	L	0-1		29,184
11	div1	Leeds	A	W	2-0	Parkin 29,70	21,676
12	div1	Burnley	A	L	0-3		10,496
13	div1	Crewe	H	W	2-1	Currie 54; Forster 68	23,145
14	div1	Reading	A	L	0-2		17,581
15	div1	Coventry	H	D	2-2	Currie 28; Juan 39	22,656
16	div1	Watford	H	L	0-1		24,069
17	div1	Brighton	A	D	1-1	Parkin 39	6,867
18	div1	Derby	A	D	3-3	Naylor 10; Magilton 42; Richards 83	21,598
19	div1	Plymouth	H	W	3-1	McEveley 23; Juan 31; Richards 56 pen	23,083
20	div1	Coventry	A	D	1-1	Williams, G 50	18,316
21	div1	Reading	H	L	0-3		22,621
22	div1	Cardiff	A	L	1-2	Juan 86	8,724
23	div1	Wolverhampton	H	D	1-1	Richards 60 pen	23,563
24	div1	QPR	H	D	2-2	De Vos 34; Haynes 90	24,628
25	div1	Sheff Wed	A	W	1-0	Forster 87	21,716
26	div1	Crystal Palace	H	L	0-2		27,392
27	div1	Hull City	A	L	0-2		20,124
28	div1	Luton	H	W	1-0	Westlake 69	23,957
29	div1	Stoke	A	D	2-2	De Vos 7; Wilnis 18	14,493
30	facr3	Portsmouth	H	L	0-1		15,593
31	div1	Sheff Utd	H	D	1-1	Juan 54	23,794
32	div1	Southampton	A	W	2-0	Lee 4,89	22,250
33	div1	Leeds	H	D	1-1	Haynes 48	25,845
34	div1	Norwich	A	W	2-1	Juan 38; Doherty 88 og	25,402
35	div1	Burnley	H	W	2-1	Lee 62; Richards 83 pen	24,482
36	div1	Crewe	A	W	2-1	Lee 19; McDonald 52	5,686
37	div1	Wolverhampton	A	L	0-1		23,561
38	div1	Leicester	H	W	2-0	Garvan 51; Fuller 85	24,861
39	div1	Millwall	H	D	1-1	Garvan 6	24,864
40	div1	Preston	A	L	1-3	De Vos 38	14,507
41	div1	Crystal Palace	A	D	2-2	Soares 30 og; Fuller 67	22,076
42	div1	Hull City	H	D	1-1	Currie 23	23,968
43	div1	Luton	A	L	0-1		9,820
44	div1	Stoke	H	L	1-4	Haynes 67	23,592
45	div1	Brighton	H	L	1-2	Forster 90	23,964
46	div1	Watford	A	L	1-2	Forster 57	16,721
47	div1	Derby	H	W	2-0	Forster 46; Currie 65	24,067
48	div1	Plymouth	A	L	1-2	Forster 12	15,921

LEAGUE APPEARANCES AND BOOKINGS

	AGE (on 01/07/06)	IN NAMED 16	APPEARANCES	COUNTING GAMES	MINUTES ON PITCH	LEAGUE GOALS		
Goalkeepers								
Lewis Price	21	45	25	24	2194	0	1	0
Shane Supple	19	46	22	21	1946	0	0	0
Defenders								
Scott Barron	20	18	15	12	1163	0	1	0
Chris Casement	18	6	5	1	224	0	0	0
Aidan Collins	19	4	3	2	195	0	0	0
Jason De Vos	32	41	41	40	3645	3	5	0
Mark Fish	32	1	1	0	45	0	0	0
James McEveley	20	19	19	16	1489	1	4	0
Richard Naylor	29	42	42	40	3633	3	6	2
Matthew Richards	21	41	38	27	2897	4	2	0
Luis Castro Sito	26	41	38	30	2912	0	5	2
Fabian Wilnis	35	42	35	27	2800	1	3	1
Midfielders								
Dean Bowditch	20	24	21	4	1083	0	1	0
Vemund Brekke-Skard	24	9	3	0	104	0	0	0
Darren Currie	31	46	46	37	3624	5	0	0
Owen Garvan	18	36	32	23	2353	3	5	0
Danny Haynes	18	20	19	2	850	3	1	0
Kevin Horlock	33	19	17	11	1210	0	6	0
Jimmy Juan	23	37	34	21	2289	5	5	0
Jim Magilton	37	42	34	13	2032	1	1	0
Dean McDonald	20	25	14	2	615	1	0	0
Jamie Peters	19	18	13	2	487	0	0	0
Ian Westlake	22	27	26	13	1722	2	2	0
Gavin Williams	25	12	12	9	914	1	2	0
Forwards								
Billy Clarke	18	4	2	0	67	0	0	0
Nick Forster	32	20	20	14	1485	7	1	0
Ricardo Fuller	26	3	3	2	223	2	3	1
Alan Lee	27	14	14	13	1179	4	3	0
Sam Parkin	25	20	20	15	1528	5	3	0
Adam Proudlock	25	12	9	1	364	0	0	0

TEAM OF THE SEASON

MONTHLY POINTS TALLY

AUGUST	10	56%
SEPTEMBER	4	27%
OCTOBER	5	33%
NOVEMBER	5	33%
DECEMBER	8	44%
JANUARY	6	50%
FEBRUARY	12	80%
MARCH	3	25%
APRIL	3	17%

LEAGUE GOALS

	PLAYER	LGE	FAC	LC	Oth	TOT
1	Forster	7	0	0	0	7
2	Currie	5	0	0	0	5
3	Juan	5	0	0	0	5
4	Parkin	5	0	0	0	5
5	Lee	4	0	0	0	4
6	Richards	4	0	0	0	4
7	Garvan	3	0	0	0	3
8	Naylor	3	0	0	0	3
9	Haynes	3	0	0	0	3
10	De Vos	3	0	0	0	3
11	Fuller	2	0	0	0	2
	Other	9	0	0	0	9
	TOTAL	53	0	0	0	53

TOP POINT EARNERS

	PLAYER	GAMES	AV PTS
1	Owen Garvan	23	1.70
2	Scott Barron	12	1.67
3	Ian Westlake	13	1.46
4	Matthew Richards	27	1.41
5	Fabian Wilnis	27	1.33
6	Jimmy Juan	21	1.33
7	Richard Naylor	40	1.33
8	Shane Supple	21	1.29
9	Darren Currie	37	1.24
10	Jason De Vos	40	1.23
	CLUB AVERAGE:		1.22

DISCIPLINARY RECORDS

	PLAYER	YELLOW	RED	AVE
1	Horlock	6	0	201
2	McEveley	4	0	372
3	Lee	3	0	393
4	Sito	5	2	416
5	Naylor	6	2	454
6	Juan	5	0	457
7	Williams, G	2	0	457
8	Garvan	5	0	470
9	Parkin	3	0	509
10	Wilnis	3	1	700
11	De Vos	5	0	729
12	Haynes	1	0	850
13	Westlake	2	0	861
	Other	7	0	
	TOTAL	57	5	

KEY GOALKEEPER

Shane Supple

Goals Conceded in the League	27	Counting Games League games when player was on pitch for at least 70 minutes	21
Goals Conceded in all competitions	28		
Defensive Rating Ave number of mins between League goals conceded while on the pitch	72	Clean Sheets In games when player was on pitch for at least 70 minutes	5

KEY PLAYERS - DEFENDERS

Scott Barron

Goals Conceded in the League	15	Clean Sheets In League games when player was on pitch for at least 70 minutes	2
Goals Conceded in all competitions	16		
Defensive Rating Ave number of mins between League goals conceded while on the pitch	78	Club Defensive Rating Average number of mins between League goals conceded by the club this season	63

	PLAYER	CON LGE	CON ALL	CLN SHEETS	DEF RATE
1	Scott Barron	15	16	2	78 mins
2	Richard Naylor	52	55	8	70 mins
3	Fabian Wilnis	44	46	6	64 mins
4	Jason De Vos	57	58	7	64 mins

KEY PLAYERS - MIDFIELDERS

Owen Garvan

Goals in the League	3	Contribution to Attacking Power Average number of minutes between League team goals while on pitch	78
Goals in all competitions	3		
Defensive Rating Average number of mins between League goals conceded while on the pitch	74	Scoring Difference Defensive Rating minus Contribution to Attacking Power	-4

	PLAYER	GOALS LGE	GOALS ALL	DEF RATE	ATT POWER	SCORE DIFF
1	Owen Garvan	3	3	74	78	-4 mins
2	Jimmy Juan	5	5	64	74	-10 mins
3	Ian Westlake	2	2	72	82	-10 mins
4	Darren Currie	5	5	65	77	-12 mins

KEY PLAYERS - GOALSCORERS

Nick Forster

Goals in the League	7	Player Strike Rate Average number of minutes between League goals scored by player	212
Goals in all competitions	7		
Contribution to Attacking Power Average number of minutes between League team goals while on pitch	78	Club Strike Rate Average number of minutes between League goals scored by club	78

	PLAYER	GOALS LGE	GOALS ALL	POWER	S RATE
1	Nick Forster	7	7	78	212 mins
2	Alan Lee	4	4	69	295 mins
3	Sam Parkin	5	5	96	306 mins
4	Jimmy Juan	5	5	74	458 mins

Ipswich's Darren Currie

SQUAD APPEARANCES

atch	enue	ompetition	esult
1	H	L	W
2	A	L	L
3	A	L	D
4	H	L	W
5	H	W	L
6	A	L	W
7	H	L	L
8	A	L	L
9	H	L	D
10	H	L	L
11	A	L	W
12	A	L	L
13	H	L	W
14	A	L	L
15	H	L	D
16	H	L	L
17	A	L	D
18	A	L	D
19	H	L	W
20	A	L	D
21	H	L	L
22	A	L	L
23	H	L	D
24	H	L	D
25	A	L	W
26	H	L	L
27	A	L	L
28	H	L	W
29	A	L	D
30	H	F	L
31	H	L	D
32	A	L	W
33	H	L	D
34	A	L	W
35	H	L	W
36	A	L	W
37	A	L	L
38	H	L	W
39	H	L	D
40	A	L	L
41	A	L	D
42	H	L	D
43	A	L	L
44	H	L	L
45	H	L	L
46	A	L	L
47	H	L	W
48	A	L	L

ɔalkeepers
ewis Price
hane Supple

efenders
cott Barron
hris Casement
idan Collins
ason De Vos
ark Fish
ames McEveley
ichard Naylor
latthew Richards
uis Castro Sito
abian Wilnis

lidfielders
ean Bowditch
emund Brekke-Skard
arren Currie
wen Garvan
anny Haynes
evin Horlock
immy Juan
im Magilton
ean McDonald
amie Peters
n Westlake
avin Williams

orwards
illy Clarke
lick Forster
icardo Fuller
lan Lee
am Parkin
dam Proudlock

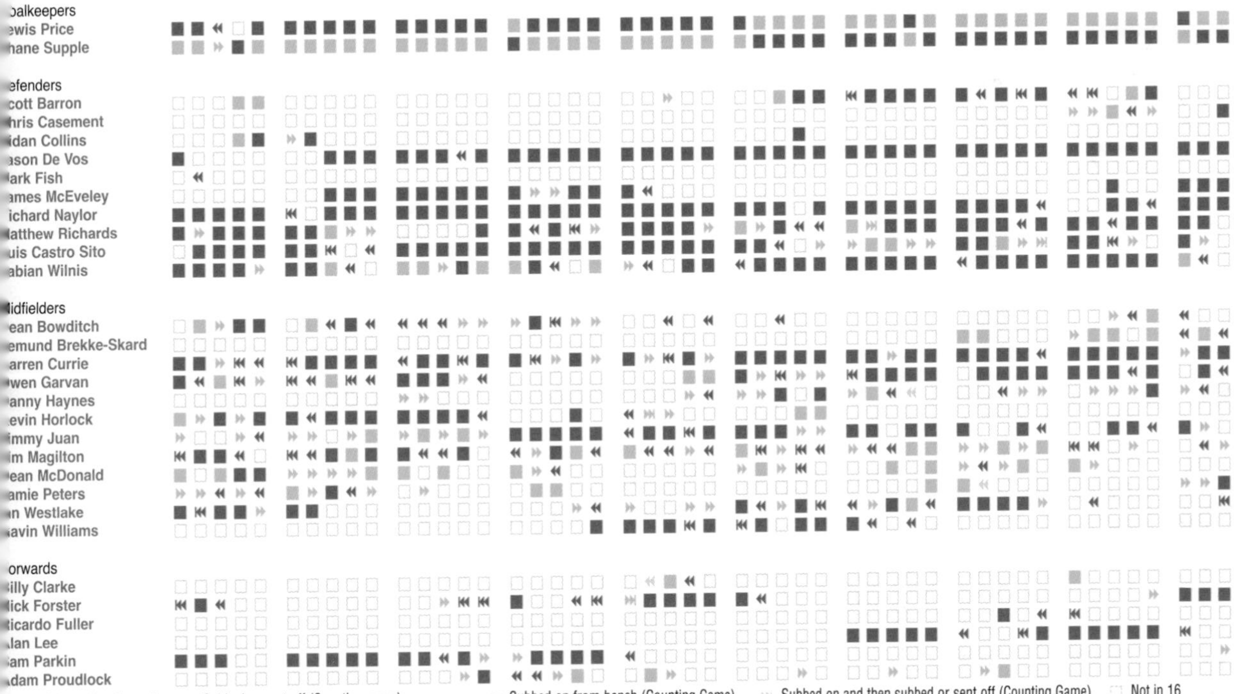

KEY: On all match · On bench · Subbed or sent off (Counting game) · Subbed or sent off (playing less than 70 minutes) · Subbed on from bench (Counting Game) · Subbed on (playing less than 70 minutes) · Subbed on and then subbed or sent off (Counting Game) · Subbed on and then subbed or sent off (playing less than 70 minutes) · Not in 16

LEICESTER CITY

Final Position: **16th**

NICKNAME: THE FOXES

KEY: ☐Won ☐Drawn ☐Lost

							Attendance
1	div1	Sheff Utd	A	L	1-4	Connolly 50	18,224
2	div1	Stoke	H	W	4-2	de Vries 14; Connolly 66,82,90	20,519
3	div1	Ipswich	H	D	0-0		21,879
4	div1	Crewe	A	D	2-2	Tiatto 45; Gudjonsson 50 pen	7,053
5	ccr1	Bury	A	W	3-0	Hamill 37; Stearman 40; Gudjonsson 61 pen	2,759
6	div1	Luton	H	L	0-2		22,048
7	div1	Hull City	A	D	1-1	McCarthy 65	20,192
8	div1	Sheff Wed	H	W	2-0	de Vries 10,12	22,618
9	div1	Cardiff	A	L	0-1		9,196
10	div1	Wolverhampton	A	D	0-0		24,726
11	ccr2	Blackpool	H	W	2-1	de Vries 17,79	7,386
12	div1	QPR	H	L	1-2	Hammond 73	20,148
13	div1	Brighton	H	D	0-0		20,296
14	div1	Derby	A	D	1-1	Hume 85	25,044
15	div1	Watford	A	W	2-1	de Vries 29; Kisnorbo 51	16,224
16	div1	Burnley	H	L	0-1		23,326
17	div1	Coventry	H	W	2-1	de Vries 45,46	22,991
18	ccr3	Cardiff	A	W	1-0	Johansson 10	8,727
19	div1	Preston	A	D	0-0		13,904
20	div1	Southampton	H	D	0-0		21,318
21	div1	Burnley	A	L	0-1		12,592
22	div1	Watford	H	D	2-2	Gudjonsson 38,45 pen	18,856
23	div1	Sheff Utd	H	W	4-2	Hume 12,90; Smith 15; Hammond 74	22,382
24	ccr4	Bolton	A	L	1-2	Williams 110	13,067
25	div1	Leeds	A	L	1-2	Hume 69 pen	21,402
26	div1	Stoke	A	L	2-3	Gudjonsson 21; Hammond 48	11,125
27	div1	Crewe	H	D	1-1	Hume 65	24,873
28	div1	Millwall	H	D	1-1	Gudjonsson 64 pen	22,520
29	div1	Reading	A	L	0-2		22,061
30	div1	Norwich	H	L	0-1		21,072
31	div1	Crystal Palace	A	L	0-2		20,089
32	facr3	Tottenham	H	W	3-2	Hammond 44; Hughes 57; de Vries 90	19,844
33	div1	Sheff Wed	A	L	1-2	Stearman 7	25,398
34	div1	Cardiff	H	L	1-2	Fryatt 41	20,140
35	div1	Plymouth	A	L	0-1		12,591
36	facr4	Southampton	H	L	0-1		20,427
37	div1	QPR	A	W	3-2	Fryatt 10; Stearman 79; Hughes 88	11,785
38	div1	Wolverhampton	H	W	1-0	Fryatt 70	21,358
39	div1	Brighton	A	W	2-1	McCarthy 4; Hume 5	7,187
40	div1	Derby	H	D	2-2	Hume 27; Maybury 55	23,246
41	div1	Leeds	H	D	1-1	Hume 4	25,497
42	div1	Ipswich	A	L	0-2		24,861
43	div1	Hull City	H	W	3-2	Hume 30; Gudjonsson 64,84	22,835
44	div1	Luton	A	W	2-1	Fryatt 16; O'Grady 88	9,783
45	div1	Millwall	A	W	1-0	Hughes 31	10,523
46	div1	Reading	H	D	1-1	Hume 38	25,578
47	div1	Norwich	A	L	1-2	Williams 63	24,718
48	div1	Crystal Palace	H	W	2-0	Welsh 42; Hughes 87	23,211
49	div1	Preston	H	L	1-2	Fryatt 1	21,865
50	div1	Coventry	A	D	1-1	Stearman 9	26,672
51	div1	Plymouth	H	W	1-0	Fryatt 55	22,796
52	div1	Southampton	A	L	0-2		26,801

LEAGUE APPEARANCES AND BOOKINGS

	AGE (on 01/07/06)	IN NAMED 16	APPEARANCES	COUNTING GAMES	MINUTES ON PITCH	LEAGUE GOALS	
Goalkeepers							
Robert Douglas	34	40	32	31	2835	0	3
Paul Henderson	30	34	15	14	1305	0	0
Defenders							
Rufus Brevett	36	7	1	0	3	0	0
Patrik Gerrbrand	25	36	17	14	1337	0	1
Peter Gilbert	22	5	5	3	351	0	0
Nils-Eric Johansson	26	43	39	36	3397	0	7
Patrick Kisnorbo	25	40	37	35	3165	1	5
Alan Maybury	27	41	40	38	3469	1	4
Patrick McCarthy	23	39	38	36	3259	2	11
Alan Sheehan	19	2	2	1	147	0	2
Richard Stearman	18	40	34	28	2691	3	4
Midfielders							
Johannes Gudjonsson	26	42	42	39	3581	7	12
Joe Hamill	22	19	12	6	608	0	0
Stephen Hughes	23	34	34	26	2389	3	5
Ryan Smith	19	19	17	11	1130	1	5
Mohammed Sylla	29	32	28	21	2057	0	5
Danny Tiatto	26	24	18	8	928	1	4
Andrew Welsh	22	10	10	3	425	1	0
James Wesolowski	-1	5	5	3	323	0	0
Jason Wilcox	34	8	6	2	279	0	0
Gareth Williams	24	35	31	22	2289	1	1
Forwards							
David Connolly	29	5	5	5	445	4	0
Mark de Vries	30	29	29	16	1733	6	5
Dion Dublin	37	25	21	14	1446	0	2
Matty Fryatt	20	19	19	17	1530	6	1
Elvis Hammond	25	38	33	11	1471	3	1
Iain Hume	22	39	37	25	2530	10	5
Chris O'Grady	20	18	13	0	198	1	2

TEAM OF THE SEASON

G – Paul Henderson CG: 14 DR: 82

D – Nils-Eric Johansson CG: 36 DR: 74

D – Patrick Kisnorbo CG: 35 DR: 74

D – Patrick McCarthy CG: 36 DR: 72

D – Richard Stearman CG: 28 DR: 66

M – Mohammed Sylla CG: 21 SD: -4

M – Johannes Gudjonsson CG: 39 SD: -6

M – Stephen Hughes CG: 26 SD: -10

M – Gareth Williams CG: 22 SD: -10

F – Iain Hume CG: 25 SR: 253

F – Matty Fryatt CG: 17 SR: 255

MONTHLY POINTS TALLY

AUGUST	6	33%
SEPTEMBER	5	33%
OCTOBER	8	53%
NOVEMBER	5	42%
DECEMBER	2	11%
JANUARY	3	20%
FEBRUARY	8	53%
MARCH	10	83%
APRIL	7	39%

LEAGUE GOALS

	PLAYER	LGE	FAC	LC	Oth	TOT
1	Hume	10	0	0	0	10
2	Gudjonsson	7	0	1	0	8
3	de Vries	6	1	2	0	9
4	Fryatt	6	0	0	0	6
5	Connolly	4	0	0	0	4
6	Stearman	3	0	1	0	4
7	Hughes	3	1	0	0	4
8	Hammond	3	1	0	0	4
9	McCarthy	2	0	0	0	2
10	Kisnorbo	1	0	0	0	1
11	Smith	1	0	0	0	1
	Other	5	0	3	0	8
	TOTAL	51	3	7	0	61

TOP POINT EARNERS

	PLAYER	GAMES	AV PTS
1	Matty Fryatt	17	1.47
2	Iain Hume	25	1.44
3	Paul Henderson	14	1.43
4	Nils-Eric Johansson	36	1.42
5	Johannes Gudjonsson	39	1.28
6	Gareth Williams	22	1.27
7	Stephen Hughes	26	1.23
8	Patrick McCarthy	36	1.22
9	Richard Stearman	28	1.21
10	Patrick Kisnorbo	35	1.20
	CLUB AVERAGE:		1.17

DISCIPLINARY RECORDS

	PLAYER	YELLOW	RED	AVE
1	Smith	5	0	226
2	Tiatto	4	0	232
3	McCarthy	11	2	250
4	Gudjonsson	12	0	298
5	de Vries	5	0	346
6	Sylla	5	0	411
7	Hughes	5	0	477
8	Johansson	7	0	485
9	Hume	5	0	506
10	Kisnorbo	5	1	527
11	Stearman	4	0	672
12	Maybury	4	1	693
13	Dublin	2	0	723
	Other	7	0	
	TOTAL	81	4	

KEY GOALKEEPER

Paul Henderson

Goals Conceded in the League	16	Counting Games League games when player was on pitch for at least 70 minutes	14
Goals Conceded in all competitions	17		
Defensive Rating Ave number of mins between League goals conceded while on the pitch	82	Clean Sheets In games when player was on pitch for at least 70 minutes	4

KEY PLAYERS - DEFENDERS

Patrick Kisnorbo

Goals Conceded in the League	43	Clean Sheets In League games when player was on pitch for at least 70 minutes	7
Goals Conceded in all competitions	44		
Defensive Rating Ave number of mins between League goals conceded while on the pitch	74	Club Defensive Rating Average number of mins between League goals conceded by the club this season	70

	PLAYER	CON LGE	CON ALL	CLN SHEETS	DEF RATE
1	Patrick Kisnorbo	43	44	7	74 mins
2	Nils-Eric Johansson	46	52	10	74 mins
3	Patrick McCarthy	45	51	9	72 mins
4	Richard Stearman	41	47	4	66 mins

KEY PLAYERS - MIDFIELDERS

Mohammed Sylla

Goals in the League	0	Contribution to Attacking Power Average number of minutes between League team goals while on pitch	73
Goals in all competitions	0		
Defensive Rating Average number of mins between League goals conceded while on the pitch	69	Scoring Difference Defensive Rating minus Contribution to Attacking Power	-4

	PLAYER	GOALS LGE	GOALS ALL	DEF RATE	ATT POWER	SCORE DIFF
1	Mohammed Sylla	0	0	69	73	-4 mins
2	Johannes Gudjonsson	7	8	72	78	-6 mins
3	Gareth Williams	1	2	69	79	-10 mins
4	Stephen Hughes	3	4	82	92	-10 mins

KEY PLAYERS - GOALSCORERS

Iain Hume

Goals in the League	10	Player Strike Rate Average number of minutes between League goals scored by player	253
Goals in all competitions	10		
Contribution to Attacking Power Average number of minutes between League team goals while on pitch	82	Club Strike Rate Average number of minutes between League goals scored by club	81

	PLAYER	GOALS LGE	GOALS ALL	POWER	S RATE
1	Iain Hume	10	10	82	253 mins
2	Matty Fryatt	6	6	67	255 mins
3	Mark de Vries	6	9	91	289 mins
4	Johannes Gudjonsson	7	8	78	512 mins

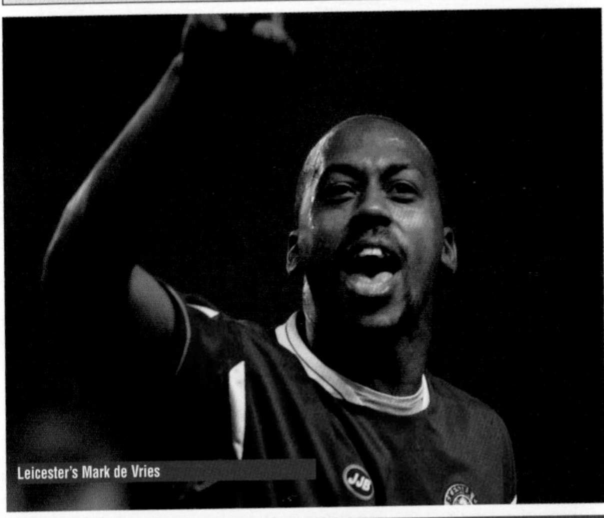

Leicester's Mark de Vries

SQUAD APPEARANCES

Match	1	2	3	4	5	6	7	8	9	10	11	12	13	14	15	16	17	18	19	20	21	22	23	24	25	26
Venue	A	H	H	A	A	H	A	H	A	A	H	H	H	A	A	H	H	A	A	H	A	H	H	A	A	A
Competition	L	L	L	L	W	L	L	L	L	L	W	L	L	L	L	L	L	W	L	L	L	L	L	W	L	L
Result	L	W	D	D	W	L	D	W	L	D	W	L	D	D	W	L	W	W	D	D	L	D	W	L	L	L

Match	27	28	29	30	31	32	33	34	35	36	37	38	39	40	41	42	43	44	45	46	47	48	49	50	51	52
Venue	H	H	A	H	A	H	A	H	A	H	A	H	A	H	H	A	H	A	A	H	A	H	H	A	H	A
Competition	L	L	L	L	L	F	L	L	L	F	L	L	L	L	L	L	L	L	L	L	L	L	L	L	L	L
Result	D	D	L	L	L	W	L	L	L	L	W	W	W	D	D	L	W	W	W	D	L	W	L	D	W	L

Goalkeepers
Robert Douglas
Paul Henderson

Defenders
Rufus Brevett
Patrik Gerrbrand
Peter Gilbert
Nils-Eric Johansson
Patrick Kisnorbo
Alan Maybury
Patrick McCarthy
Alan Sheehan
Richard Stearman

Midfielders
Johannes Gudjonsson
Joe Hamill
Stephen Hughes
Ryan Smith
Mohammed Sylla
Danny Tiatto
Andrew Welsh
James Wesolowski
Jason Wilcox
Gareth Williams

Forwards
David Connolly
Mark de Vries
Dion Dublin
Matty Fryatt
Elvis Hammond
Iain Hume
Chris O'Grady

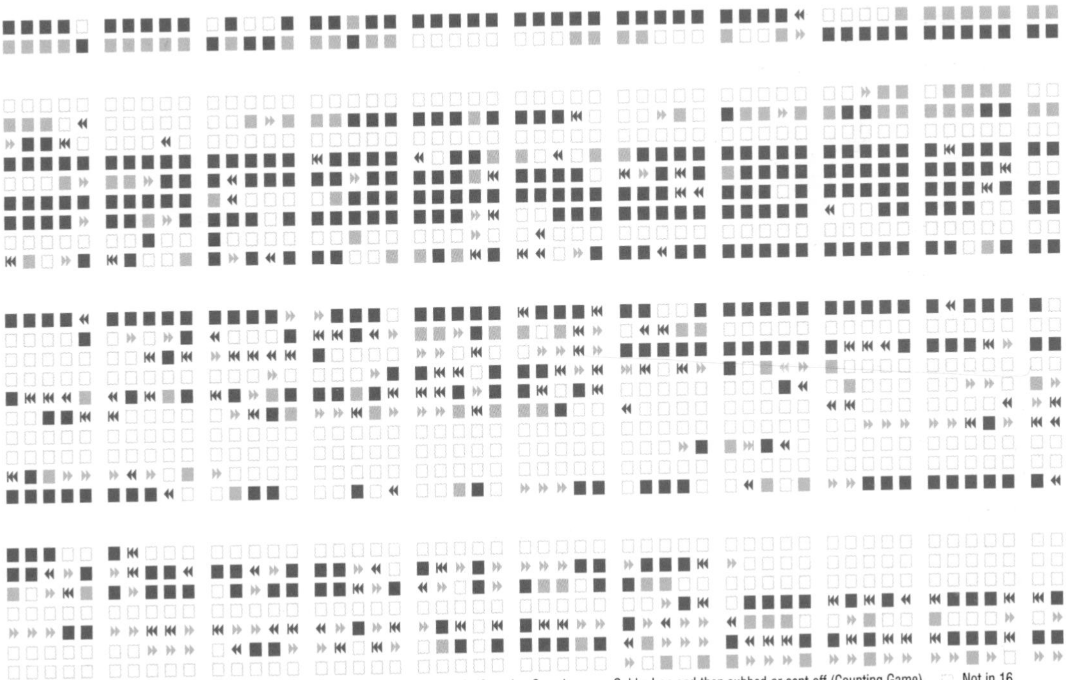

KEY: On all match | On bench | Subbed or sent off (Counting game) | Subbed or sent off (playing less than 70 minutes) | Subbed on from bench (Counting Game) | Subbed on (playing less than 70 minutes) | Subbed on and then subbed or sent off (Counting Game) | Subbed on and then subbed or sent off (playing less than 70 minutes) | Not in 16

BURNLEY

Final Position: **17th**

NICKNAME: THE CLARETS

KEY: ☐ Won ☐ Drawn ☐ Lost

							Attendance
1	div1	Crewe	A	L	1-2	Noel-Williams 67	8,006
2	div1	Sheff Utd	H	L	1-2	Akinbiyi 72	11,802
3	div1	Coventry	H	W	4-0	O'Connor, G 28; Thomas 37; Akinbiyi 87,90	11,683
4	div1	Watford	A	L	1-3	O'Connor, G 16 pen	16,802
5	ccr1	Carlisle	H	W	2-1	Duff 52; Akinbiyi 90	5,114
6	div1	Derby	H	D	2-2	Akinbiyi 46; Noel-Williams 53	12,243
7	div1	Reading	A	L	1-2	Akinbiyi 42	14,027
8	div1	Cardiff	H	D	3-3	Elliott 1,23; O'Connor, J 89	10,431
9	div1	Preston	A	D	0-0		17,139
10	div1	Plymouth	A	L	0-1		11,829
11	ccr2	Barnsley	H	W	3-0	Lowe 28; Akinbiyi 52; Spicer 59	4,501
12	div1	Brighton	H	D	1-1	O'Connor, G 34 pen	11,112
13	div1	Ipswich	H	W	3-0	O'Connor, J 33; O'Connor, G 72; McCann 87	10,496
14	div1	Wolverhampton	A	W	1-0	O'Connor, G 23	21,747
15	div1	Leeds	H	L	1-2	O'Connor, G 60 pen	16,174
16	div1	Leicester	A	W	1-0	Akinbiyi 64	23,326
17	div1	Crystal Palace	A	L	0-2		20,127
18	ccr3	Aston Villa	A	L	0-1		26,872
19	div1	Hull City	H	W	1-0	Akinbiyi 29	11,701
20	div1	Millwall	H	W	2-1	Dyer 76; Elliott 80	10,698
21	div1	Luton	A	W	3-2	Akinbiyi 15,31,54 pen	8,518
22	div1	Leicester	H	W	1-0	Spicer 40	12,592
23	div1	Leeds	A	L	0-2		21,318
24	div1	Crewe	H	W	3-0	Spicer 27,68; Dyer 72	11,151
25	div1	Southampton	A	D	1-1	Akinbiyi 66	21,592
26	div1	Sheff Utd	A	L	0-3		23,118
27	div1	Watford	H	W	4-1	Branch 32; Harley 42,77 pen; O'Connor, J 79	13,815
28	div1	Stoke	H	W	1-0	Akinbiyi 56	17,912
29	div1	Norwich	A	L	1-2	Safri 73 og	25,204
30	div1	Sheff Wed	H	L	1-2	O'Connor, G 84 pen	14,607
31	div1	QPR	A	D	1-1	McCann 10	12,565
32	facr3	Derby	A	L	1-2	O'Connor, G 29	12,713
33	div1	Cardiff	A	L	0-3		10,872
34	div1	Preston	H	L	0-2		17,220
35	div1	Brighton	A	D	0-0		6,267
36	div1	Plymouth	H	W	1-0	Ricketts 24	11,292
37	div1	Ipswich	A	L	1-2	Ricketts 45	24,482
38	div1	Wolverhampton	H	L	0-1		11,056
39	div1	Coventry	A	L	0-1		19,641
40	div1	Reading	H	L	0-3		12,888
41	div1	Derby	A	L	0-3		23,292
42	div1	Stoke	A	L	0-1		12,082
43	div1	Norwich	H	W	2-0	Gray 18; Branch 51	11,938
44	div1	Southampton	H	D	1-1	Gray 9	10,636
45	div1	Sheff Wed	A	D	0-0		24,485
46	div1	QPR	H	W	1-0	Gray 79	11,247
47	div1	Hull City	A	D	0-0		19,926
48	div1	Crystal Palace	H	D	0-0		11,449
49	div1	Millwall	A	L	0-1		7,780
50	div1	Luton	H	D	1-1	Lafferty 78	12,473

LEAGUE APPEARANCES AND BOOKINGS

	AGE (on 01/07/06)	IN NAMED 16	APPEARANCES	COUNTING GAMES	MINUTES ON PITCH	LEAGUE GOALS		
Goalkeepers								
Danny Coyne	27	10	8	6	555	0	0	0
Mark Crossley	18	2	0	0	0	0	0	0
Lee Grant	23	11	1	1	90	0	1	0
Brian Jensen	31	45	39	38	3444	0	1	1
Defenders								
Phillip Bardsley	21	6	6	5	488	0	1	0
Duane Courtney	21	18	7	1	123	0	0	0
Mike Duff	28	44	41	38	3499	0	5	0
Jon Harley	26	41	41	41	3680	2	9	0
Daniel Karbassiyoon	21	26	5	0	98	0	0	0
Keith Lowe	20	18	16	10	1020	0	0	0
John McGreal	34	37	35	30	2831	0	6	0
Martin Reilly	19	0	0	0	0	0	0	0
Frank Sinclair	34	38	37	35	3157	0	11	0
Wayne Thomas	27	17	16	10	1039	1	3	2
Midfielders								
Graham Branch	34	37	37	23	2576	2	5	0
Wade Elliott	27	43	35	19	2034	3	4	0
Micah Hyde	31	44	41	38	3478	0	8	0
Alan Mahon	28	8	8	7	657	0	0	0
Christopher McCann	18	38	23	12	1414	2	3	0
Garreth O'Connor	27	41	29	20	2209	7	5	1
James O'Connor	26	46	46	44	4054	3	4	1
Marc Pugh	19	1	0	0	0	0	0	0
John Spicer	22	41	34	14	1850	3	2	0
Mark Yates	36	3	0	0	0	0	0	0
Forwards								
Ade Akinbiyi	31	29	29	29	2602	11	4	0
Karl Bermingham	20	11	4	1	109	0	0	0
Nathan Dyer	18	8	5	4	395	2	1	0
Andy Gray	28	9	9	9	810	3	0	0
Kyle Lafferty	18	15	11	3	441	1	0	0
Gifton Noel-Williams	26	36	29	16	1808	2	1	0
Michael Ricketts	27	13	13	9	966	2	5	0

TEAM OF THE SEASON

D — Mike Duff — CG: 38 DR: 90

M — Graham Branch — CG: 23 SD: 14

D — Frank Sinclair — CG: 35 DR: 75

M — Garreth O'Connor — CG: 20 SD: 0

F — Gifton Noel-Williams — CG: 16 SR: 904

G — Brian Jensen — CG: 38 DR: 82

D — John McGreal — CG: 30 DR: 66

M — Micah Hyde — CG: 38 SD: -13

F — Ade Akinbiyi — CG: 29 SR: 236

D — Jon Harley — CG: 41 DR: 84

M — James O'Connor — CG: 44 SD: -17

MONTHLY POINTS TALLY

AUGUST	4	22%
SEPTEMBER	9	50%
OCTOBER	6	50%
NOVEMBER	12	80%
DECEMBER	7	39%
JANUARY	2	17%
FEBRUARY	3	25%
MARCH	4	27%
APRIL	7	39%

LEAGUE GOALS

	PLAYER	LGE	FAC	LC	Oth	TOT
1	Akinbiyi	11	0	2	0	13
2	O'Connor, G	7	1	0	0	8
3	Spicer	3	0	1	0	4
4	O'Connor, J	3	0	0	0	3
5	Gray	3	0	0	0	3
6	Elliott	3	0	0	0	3
7	Ricketts	2	0	0	0	2
8	Noel-Williams	2	0	0	0	2
9	McCann	2	0	0	0	2
10	Branch	2	0	0	0	2
11	Dyer	2	0	0	0	2
	Other	6	0	2	0	8
	TOTAL	46	1	5	0	52

TOP POINT EARNERS

	PLAYER	GAMES	AV PTS
1	Garreth O'Connor	20	1.55
2	John Spicer	14	1.43
3	Ade Akinbiyi	29	1.34
4	Wade Elliott	19	1.32
5	Graham Branch	23	1.30
6	Frank Sinclair	35	1.29
7	Jon Harley	41	1.24
8	Mike Duff	38	1.24
9	James O'Connor	44	1.23
10	Brian Jensen	38	1.18
	CLUB AVERAGE:		1.17

DISCIPLINARY RECORDS

	PLAYER	YELLOW	RED	AVE
1	Ricketts	5	0	193
2	Thomas	3	2	207
3	Sinclair	11	0	287
4	O'Connor, G	5	1	368
5	Harley	9	0	408
6	Hyde	8	0	434
7	McCann	3	0	471
8	McGreal	6	0	471
9	Bardsley	1	0	488
10	Elliott	4	0	508
11	Branch	5	0	515
12	Akinbiyi	4	0	650
13	Duff	5	0	699
	Other	8	2	
	TOTAL	77	5	

KEY GOALKEEPER

Brian Jensen

Goals Conceded in the League	42	Counting Games League games when player was on pitch for at least 70 minutes	38
Goals Conceded in all competitions	45		
Defensive Rating Ave number of mins between League goals conceded while on the pitch	82	Clean Sheets In games when player was on pitch for at least 70 minutes	14

KEY PLAYERS - DEFENDERS

Mike Duff

Goals Conceded in the League	39	Clean Sheets In League games when player was on pitch for at least 70 minutes	16
Goals Conceded in all competitions	43		
Defensive Rating Ave number of mins between League goals conceded while on the pitch	90	Club Defensive Rating Average number of mins between League goals conceded by the club this season	77

	PLAYER	CON LGE	CON ALL	CLN SHEETS	DEF RATE
1	Mike Duff	39	43	16	90 mins
2	Jon Harley	44	47	15	84 mins
3	Frank Sinclair	42	45	13	75 mins
4	John McGreal	43	46	9	66 mins

KEY PLAYERS - MIDFIELDERS

Graham Branch

Goals in the League	2	Contribution to Attacking Power Average number of minutes between League team goals while on pitch	89
Goals in all competitions	2		
Defensive Rating Average number of mins between League goals conceded while on the pitch	103	Scoring Difference Defensive Rating minus Contribution to Attacking Power	14

	PLAYER	GOALS LGE	GOALS ALL	DEF RATE	ATT POWER	SCORE DIFF
1	Graham Branch	2	2	103	89	14 mins
2	Garreth O'Connor	7	8	71	71	0 mins
3	Micah Hyde	0	0	70	83	-13 mins
4	James O'Connor	3	3	75	92	-17 mins

KEY PLAYERS - GOALSCORERS

Ade Akinbiyi

Goals in the League	11	Player Strike Rate Average number of minutes between League goals scored by player	237
Goals in all competitions	13		
Contribution to Attacking Power Average number of minutes between League team goals while on pitch	67	Club Strike Rate Average number of minutes between League goals scored by club	90

	PLAYER	GOALS LGE	GOALS ALL	POWER	S RATE
1	Ade Akinbiyi	11	13	67	237 mins
2	Garreth O'Connor	7	8	71	316 mins
3	John Spicer	3	4	103	617 mins
4	Wade Elliott	3	3	102	678 mins

Burnley's Ade Akinbiyi

SQUAD APPEARANCES

Match	1	2	3	4	5	6	7	8	9	10	11	12	13	14	15	16	17	18	19	20	21	22	23	24	25
Venue	A	H	H	A	H	H	A	H	A	A	H	H	H	A	H	A	A	A	H	H	A	H	A	H	A
Competition	L	L	L	L	W	L	L	L	L	L	W	L	L	L	L	L	L	W	L	L	L	L	L	L	L
Result	L	L	W	L	W	D	L	D	D	L	W	D	W	W	L	W	L	L	W	W	W	W	L	W	D

Match	26	27	28	29	30	31	32	33	34	35	36	37	38	39	40	41	42	43	44	45	46	47	48	49	50
Venue	A	H	H	A	H	A	A	A	H	A	H	A	H	A	H	A	A	H	H	A	H	A	H	A	H
Competition	L	L	L	L	L	L	F	L	L	L	L	L	L	L	L	L	L	L	L	L	L	L	L	L	L
Result	L	W	W	L	L	D	L	L	L	D	W	L	L	L	L	L	L	W	D	D	W	D	D	L	D

Goalkeepers
Danny Coyne
Mark Crossley
Lee Grant
Brian Jensen

Defenders
Phillip Bardsley
Duane Courtney
Mike Duff
Jon Harley
Daniel Karbassiyoon
Keith Lowe
John McGreal
Martin Reilly
Frank Sinclair
Wayne Thomas

Midfielders
Graham Branch
Wade Elliott
Micah Hyde
Alan Mahon
Christopher McCann
Garreth O'Connor
James O'Connor
Marc Pugh
John Spicer
Mark Yates

Forwards
Ade Akinbiyi
Karl Bermingham
Nathan Dyer
Andy Gray
Kyle Lafferty
Gifton Noel-Williams
Michael Ricketts

KEY: On all match
On bench
Subbed or sent off (Counting game)
Subbed or sent off (playing less than 70 minutes)
Subbed on from bench (Counting Game)
Subbed on (playing less than 70 minutes)
Subbed on and then subbed or sent off (Counting Game)
Subbed on and then subbed or sent off (playing less than 70 minutes)
Not in 16

HULL CITY

Final Position: **18th**

NICKNAME: THE TIGERS

KEY: ☐Won ☐Drawn ☐Lost

							Attendance
1	div1	QPR	H	D	0-0		22,201
2	div1	Sheff Wed	A	D	1-1	Barmby 23	29,910
3	div1	Wolverhampton	A	L	0-1		24,333
4	div1	Brighton	H	W	2-0	France 40; Burgess 87	18,648
5	ccr1	Blackpool	A	L	1-2	Price 4	3,819
6	div1	Plymouth	A	W	1-0	Elliott 58	12,329
7	div1	Leicester	H	D	1-1	Fagan 51	20,192
8	div1	Crystal Palace	A	L	0-2		18,630
9	div1	Stoke	H	L	0-1		18,692
10	div1	Luton	H	L	0-1		19,184
11	div1	Coventry	A	W	2-0	Welsh 17,74	21,161
12	div1	Norwich	A	L	1-2	Cort 2	27,470
13	div1	Millwall	H	D	1-1	Burgess 81	18,761
14	div1	Southampton	A	D	1-1	Ellison 79	23,810
15	div1	Reading	H	D	1-1	Brown 56	17,698
16	div1	Derby	H	W	2-1	Elliott 11; Green 84 pen	20,661
17	div1	Burnley	A	L	0-1		11,701
18	div1	Preston	A	L	0-3		13,536
19	div1	Watford	H	L	1-2	Barmby 6	18,444
20	div1	Reading	A	L	1-3	Barmby 55	17,864
21	div1	Southampton	H	D	1-1	Barmby 45	18,061
22	div1	QPR	A	D	2-2	France 40; Paynter 50	13,185
23	div1	Cardiff	H	W	2-0	Paynter 70; Fagan 88	18,364
24	div1	Sheff Wed	H	W	1-0	Price 87	21,329
25	div1	Brighton	A	L	1-2	Elliott 4	6,929
26	div1	Crewe	A	D	2-2	Fagan 33; Paynter 80	7,942
27	div1	Ipswich	H	W	2-0	Barmby 56; Fagan 70	20,124
28	div1	Leeds	A	L	0-2		26,387
29	div1	Sheff Utd	H	L	1-3	Price 23	21,929
30	facr3	Aston Villa	H	L	0-1		17,051
31	div1	Crystal Palace	H	L	1-2	Parkin 25	18,886
32	div1	Stoke	A	W	3-0	Russell 7 og; Parkin 55; Duffy 81	13,444
33	div1	Coventry	H	L	1-2	Elliott 31	18,381
34	div1	Luton	A	W	3-2	Elliott 14; Duffy 35; Parkin 38	8,835
35	div1	Norwich	H	D	1-1	Cort 26	20,527
36	div1	Millwall	A	D	1-1	Parkin 78	7,108
37	div1	Cardiff	A	L	0-1		11,047
38	div1	Wolverhampton	H	L	2-3	Cort 50; Edwards 81 pen	19,841
39	div1	Leicester	A	L	2-3	Elliott 35; Green 73	22,835
40	div1	Plymouth	H	W	1-0	Fagan 55	20,137
41	div1	Crewe	H	W	1-0	Green 16	21,163
42	div1	Ipswich	A	D	1-1	Cort 57	23,968
43	div1	Leeds	H	W	1-0	Parkin 76	23,486
44	div1	Sheff Utd	A	L	2-3	Elliott 65; Duffy 70	26,324
45	div1	Burnley	H	D	0-0		19,926
46	div1	Derby	A	D	1-1	Green 33	24,961
47	div1	Preston	H	D	1-1	Mawene 43 og	19,716
48	div1	Watford	A	D	0-0		17,128

LEAGUE APPEARANCES AND BOOKINGS

	AGE (on 01/07/06)	IN NAMED 16	APPEARANCES	COUNTING GAMES	MINUTES ON PITCH	LEAGUE GOALS	Yellow	Red
Goalkeepers								
Matt Duke	28	33	2	1	104	0	0	0
Sergio Leite	26	12	0	0	0	0	0	0
Boaz Myhill	23	45	45	45	4036	0	4	1
Defenders								
Danny Coles	24	9	9	8	728	0	0	0
Sam Collins	29	17	17	16	1485	0	2	0
Leon Cort	26	42	42	42	3780	4	0	0
Andrew Dawson	27	19	18	17	1575	0	2	0
Damien Delaney	24	46	46	45	4114	0	3	0
Roland Edge	27	8	8	6	634	0	0	0
Marc Joseph	29	12	5	2	232	0	1	1
Mark Lynch	24	22	16	9	1040	0	2	1
Rui Manuel Marques	28	1	1	1	90	0	0	0
Alan Rogers	29	9	9	8	765	0	0	0
Alton Thelwell	25	12	9	5	627	0	0	0
Scott Wiseman	20	17	11	8	792	0	0	0
Midfielders								
Keith Andrews	25	28	26	21	2052	0	3	0
Ian Ashbee	29	6	6	6	540	0	1	0
Kevin Ellison	27	29	23	12	1328	1	2	0
Ryan France	25	37	35	27	2681	2	4	0
Russell Fry	20	4	1	0	18	0	0	0
Stuart Green	25	45	38	19	2241	4	1	0
Mark Noble	19	5	5	2	349	0	1	0
Jason Price	29	16	15	6	856	2	1	0
John Welsh	22	33	32	26	2578	2	2	0
Curtis Woodhouse	26	20	18	12	1208	0	5	0
Forwards								
Nick Barmby	32	27	26	9	1628	5	2	0
Chris Brown	21	13	13	7	935	1	2	0
Ben Burgess	24	16	14	2	427	2	0	0
Darryl Duffy	22	18	15	3	619	3	1	0
Stuart Elliott	27	40	40	23	2531	7	5	0
Craig Fagan	23	41	41	23	2636	5	4	0
Stephen McPhee	25	4	4	1	171	0	0	0
Jonathan Parkin	24	18	18	18	1620	5	2	0
William Paynter	21	28	22	7	1025	3	2	0

TEAM OF THE SEASON

G — Boaz Myhill — CG: 45 DR: 73

D — Andrew Dawson — CG: 17 DR: 93

D — Damien Delaney — CG: 45 DR: 75

D — Leon Cort — CG: 42 DR: 71

D — Sam Collins — CG: 16 DR: 62

M — Ryan France — CG: 27 SD: 6

M — John Welsh — CG: 26 SD: -7

M — Curtis Woodhouse — CG: 12 SD: -7

M — Keith Andrews — CG: 21 SD: -8

F — Jonathan Parkin — CG: 18 SR: 324

F — Stuart Elliott — CG: 23 SR: 362

MONTHLY POINTS TALLY

AUGUST	9	50%
SEPTEMBER	4	22%
OCTOBER	5	42%
NOVEMBER	2	13%
DECEMBER	10	56%
JANUARY	3	25%
FEBRUARY	5	33%
MARCH	7	58%
APRIL	7	39%

LEAGUE GOALS

	PLAYER	LGE	FAC	LC	Oth	TOT
1	Elliott	7	0	0	0	7
2	Parkin	5	0	0	0	5
3	Fagan	5	0	0	0	5
4	Barmby	5	0	0	0	5
5	Green	4	0	0	0	4
6	Cort	4	0	0	0	4
7	Duffy	3	0	0	0	3
8	Paynter	3	0	0	0	3
9	Welsh	2	0	0	0	2
10	Burgess	2	0	0	0	2
11	France	2	0	0	0	2
	Other	7	0	1	0	8
	TOTAL	49	0	1	0	50

TOP POINT EARNERS

	PLAYER	GAMES	AV PTS
1	Craig Fagan	23	1.48
2	Andrew Dawson	17	1.29
3	Keith Andrews	21	1.24
4	Jonathan Parkin	18	1.22
5	John Welsh	26	1.19
6	Sam Collins	16	1.19
7	Curtis Woodhouse	12	1.17
8	Ryan France	27	1.15
9	Damien Delaney	45	1.13
10	Stuart Green	19	1.11
	CLUB AVERAGE:		1.13

DISCIPLINARY RECORDS

	PLAYER	YELLOW	RED	AVE
1	Woodhouse	5	0	241
2	Lynch	2	1	346
3	Brown	2	0	467
4	Elliott	5	0	506
5	Paynter	2	0	512
6	Ashbee	1	0	540
7	Duffy	1	0	619
8	Fagan	4	0	659
9	Ellison	2	0	664
10	France	4	0	670
11	Andrews	3	0	684
12	Collins	2	0	742
13	Dawson	2	0	787
	Other	15	1	
	TOTAL	50	2	

KEY GOALKEEPER

Boaz Myhill

Goals Conceded in the League	55	**Counting Games** League games when player was on pitch for at least 70 minutes	45
Goals Conceded in all competitions	56		
Defensive Rating Ave number of mins between League goals conceded while on the pitch	73	**Clean Sheets** In games when player was on pitch for at least 70 minutes	12

KEY PLAYERS - DEFENDERS

Andrew Dawson

Goals Conceded in the League	17	**Clean Sheets** In League games when player was on pitch for at least 70 minutes	7
Goals Conceded in all competitions	17		
Defensive Rating Ave number of mins between League goals conceded while on the pitch	93	**Club Defensive Rating** Average number of mins between League goals conceded by the club this season	75

	PLAYER	CON LGE	CON ALL	CLN SHEETS	DEF RATE
1	Andrew Dawson	17	17	7	93 mins
2	Damien Delaney	55	58	13	75 mins
3	Leon Cort	53	54	11	71 mins
4	Sam Collins	24	25	4	62 mins

KEY PLAYERS - MIDFIELDERS

Ryan France

Goals in the League	2	**Contribution to Attacking Power** Average number of minutes between League team goals while on pitch	71
Goals in all competitions	2		
Defensive Rating Average number of mins between League goals conceded while on the pitch	77	**Scoring Difference** Defensive Rating minus Contribution to Attacking Power	6

	PLAYER	GOALS LGE	GOALS ALL	DEF RATE	ATT POWER	SCORE DIFF
1	Ryan France	2	2	77	71	6 mins
2	Curtis Woodhouse	0	0	86	93	-7 mins
3	John Welsh	2	2	76	83	-7 mins
4	Keith Andrews	0	0	68	76	-8 mins

KEY PLAYERS - GOALSCORERS

Jonathan Parkin

Goals in the League	5	**Player Strike Rate** Average number of minutes between League goals scored by player	324
Goals in all competitions	5		
Contribution to Attacking Power Average number of minutes between League team goals while on pitch	74	**Club Strike Rate** Average number of minutes between League goals scored by club	84

	PLAYER	GOALS LGE	GOALS ALL	POWER	S RATE
1	Jonathan Parkin	5	5	74	324 mins
2	Stuart Elliott	7	7	77	362 mins
3	Craig Fagan	5	5	80	527 mins
4	Stuart Green	4	4	93	560 mins

Hull's Craig Fagan

SQUAD APPEARANCES

Match	1	2	3	4	5	6	7	8	9	10	11	12	13	14	15	16	17	18	19	20	21	22	23	24	25
Venue	H	A	A	H	A	A	H	A	H	H	A	A	H	A	H	H	A	A	H	A	H	A	H	H	A
Competition	L	L	L	L	W	L	L	L	L	L	L	L	L	L	L	L	L	L	L	L	L	L	L	L	L
Result	D	D	L	W	L	W	D	L	L	L	W	L	D	D	D	W	L	L	L	L	D	D	W	W	L

Match	26	27	28	29	30	31	32	33	34	35	36	37	38	39	40	41	42	43	44	45	46	47	48
Venue	A	H	A	H	H	H	A	H	A	H	A	A	H	A	H	H	A	H	A	H	A	H	A
Competition	L	L	L	L	F	L	L	L	L	L	L	L	L	L	L	L	L	L	L	L	L	L	L
Result	D	W	L	L	L	L	W	L	W	D	D	L	L	L	W	W	D	W	L	D	D	D	D

Goalkeepers
Matt Duke
Sergio Leite
Boaz Myhill

Defenders
Danny Coles
Sam Collins
Leon Cort
Andrew Dawson
Damien Delaney
Roland Edge
Marc Joseph
Mark Lynch
Rui Manuel Marques
Alan Rogers
Alton Thelwell
Scott Wiseman

Midfielders
Keith Andrews
Ian Ashbee
Kevin Ellison
Ryan France
Russell Fry
Stuart Green
Mark Noble
Jason Price
John Welsh
Curtis Woodhouse

Forwards
Nick Barmby
Chris Brown
Ben Burgess
Darryl Duffy
Stuart Elliott
Craig Fagan
Stephen McPhee
Jonathan Parkin
William Paynter

KEY: On all match · On bench · Subbed or sent off (Counting game) · Subbed or sent off (playing less than 70 minutes) · Subbed on from bench (Counting Game) · Subbed on (playing less than 70 minutes) · Subbed on and then subbed or sent off (Counting Game) · Subbed on and then subbed or sent off (playing less than 70 minutes) · Not in 16

SHEFFIELD WEDNESDAY

Final Position: **19th**

NICKNAME: THE OWLS

KEY: ☐Won ☐Drawn ☐Lost

						Attendance
1 div1	Stoke	A	D	0-0		18,744
2 div1	Hull City	H	D	1-1	Best 8	29,910
3 div1	Southampton	H	L	0-1		26,688
4 div1	Ipswich	A	L	1-2	Peacock 81	24,238
5 ccr1	Stockport	A	W	4-2	Peacock 15; Partridge 107; Proudlock 116,120	3,001
6 div1	QPR	A	D	0-0		12,131
7 div1	Leicester	A	L	0-2		22,618
8 div1	Leeds	H	W	1-0	Eagles 9	29,986
9 div1	Millwall	H	L	1-2	Coughlan 66	22,446
10 ccr2	West Ham	H	L	2-4	Coughlan 76; Graham 77	14,976
11 div1	Luton	A	D	2-2	Lee 14; Graham 64	8,267
12 div1	Crystal Palace	A	L	0-2		17,413
13 div1	Coventry	H	W	3-2	Coughlan 17; Brunt 43,79 pen	22,732
14 div1	Plymouth	A	D	1-1	Buzsaky 24 og	16,534
15 div1	Watford	H	D	1-1	Brunt 64	21,187
16 div1	Brighton	H	D	1-1	Peacock 55	21,787
17 div1	Norwich	A	W	1-0	Brunt 79	25,383
18 div1	Reading	A	L	0-2		16,188
19 div1	Derby	H	W	2-1	Brunt 69; Graham 74	26,334
20 div1	Cardiff	H	L	1-3	Eagles 65	20,324
21 div1	Watford	A	L	1-2	Whelan 90	16,988
22 div1	Plymouth	H	D	0-0		20,244
23 div1	Stoke	H	L	0-2		21,970
24 div1	Sheff Utd	A	L	0-1		30,558
25 div1	Hull City	A	L	0-1		21,329
26 div1	Ipswich	H	L	0-1		21,716
27 div1	Preston	A	D	0-0		18,867
28 div1	Wolverhampton	H	L	0-2		24,295
29 div1	Burnley	A	W	2-1	Eagles 5; Coughlan 56	14,607
30 div1	Crewe	H	W	3-0	Wood 7; Tudgay 62; McCready 81 og	25,656
31 facr3	Charlton	H	L	2-4	Heckingbottom 16,60	14,851
32 div1	Leicester	H	W	2-1	Brunt 31; Coughlan 40	25,398
33 div1	Leeds	A	L	0-3		27,843
34 div1	Luton	H	L	0-2		23,965
35 div1	Millwall	A	W	1-0	Simek 63	11,896
36 div1	Crystal Palace	H	D	0-0		24,784
37 div1	Coventry	A	L	1-2	Brunt 79	20,021
38 div1	Sheff Utd	H	L	1-2	MacLean 79 pen	33,439
39 div1	Southampton	A	L	0-3		26,236
40 div1	Cardiff	A	L	0-1		11,851
41 div1	QPR	H	D	1-1	Burton 13	22,788
42 div1	Preston	H	W	2-0	Burton 38; O'Brien 51	23,429
43 div1	Wolverhampton	A	W	3-1	Tudgay 45,86; Burton 67	25,161
44 div1	Burnley	H	D	0-0		24,485
45 div1	Crewe	A	L	0-2		8,007
46 div1	Norwich	H	W	1-0	Tudgay 45	30,755
47 div1	Brighton	A	W	2-0	Hart 8 og; O'Brien 69	7,573
48 div1	Reading	H	D	1-1	MacLean 59 pen	27,307
49 div1	Derby	A	W	2-0	Tudgay 5; Best 85	30,391

LEAGUE APPEARANCES AND BOOKINGS

	AGE (on 01/07/06)	IN NAMED 16	APPEARANCES	COUNTING GAMES	MINUTES ON PITCH	LEAGUE GOALS	Yellow	Red
Goalkeepers								
Chris Adamson	27	16	5	5	450	0	0	0
Scott Carson	20	9	9	9	810	0	0	0
David Lucas	28	20	18	17	1573	0	0	0
Nicky Weaver	27	14	14	14	1260	0	1	0
Defenders								
Mikkel Bischoff	24	4	4	3	309	0	1	0
Lee Bullen	35	34	28	11	1369	0	1	0
Patrick Collins	21	7	3	3	270	0	1	0
Graham Coughlan	31	36	33	33	2945	4	1	0
Drissa Diallo	33	15	11	6	712	0	2	0
Peter Gilbert	22	17	17	16	1432	0	4	0
Paul Heckingbottom	28	8	4	4	340	0	0	0
John Hills	28	33	27	25	2253	0	7	1
Graeme Lee	28	20	15	14	1311	1	2	0
Frankie Simek	21	43	43	40	3706	1	8	0
Richard Wood	21	33	30	27	2489	1	2	0
Midfielders								
Steve Adams	25	11	8	3	569	0	0	0
Chris Brunt	21	44	44	34	3354	7	5	0
Chris Eagles	20	26	25	17	1775	3	2	0
Yoann Folly	21	14	14	13	1215	0	1	0
John-Paul McGovern	25	11	7	2	266	0	0	0
Burton O'Brien	25	46	44	34	3235	2	0	0
Ritchie Partridge	25	32	18	2	608	0	0	0
Craig Rocastle	24	24	17	11	1200	0	3	0
Glenn Whelan	22	43	43	37	3520	1	6	0
Forwards								
Gabriel Agbonlahor	19	9	8	2	366	0	0	0
Leon Best	19	17	13	2	530	2	1	0
Deon Burton	29	17	17	14	1344	3	1	0
Barry Corr	21	23	16	4	630	0	1	0
David Graham	27	24	24	11	1428	2	0	0
Steven MacLean	23	14	6	3	360	2	0	0
Daryl Murphy	23	4	4	4	360	0	0	0
Lee Peacock	29	22	22	17	1661	2	1	0
Adam Proudlock	25	6	6	0	214	0	0	0
Marcus Tudgay	23	18	17	12	1190	3	2	0

TEAM OF THE SEASON

G — David Lucas — CG: 17 DR: 75

D — John Hills — CG: 25 DR: 87

D — Peter Gilbert — CG: 16 DR: 84

D — Graham Coughlan — CG: 33 DR: 82

D — Frankie Simek — CG: 40 DR: 77

M — Yoann Folly — CG: 13 SD: 0

M — Burton O'Brien — CG: 34 SD: -23

M — Glenn Whelan — CG: 37 SD: -27

M — Chris Brunt — CG: 34 SD: -33

F — Marcus Tudgay — CG: 12 SR: 397

F — Deon Burton — CG: 14 SR: 448

MONTHLY POINTS TALLY

AUGUST	3	20%
SEPTEMBER	4	27%
OCTOBER	9	60%
NOVEMBER	4	22%
DECEMBER	4	22%
JANUARY	6	50%
FEBRUARY	4	27%
MARCH	7	58%
APRIL	11	61%

LEAGUE GOALS

	PLAYER	LGE	FAC	LC	Oth	TOT
1	Brunt	7	0	0	0	7
2	Coughlan	4	0	1	0	5
3	Eagles	3	0	0	0	3
4	Tudgay	3	0	0	0	3
5	Burton	3	0	0	0	3
6	Graham	2	0	0	0	2
7	MacLean	2	0	0	0	2
8	Best	2	0	0	0	2
9	Peacock	2	0	1	0	3
10	O'Brien	2	0	0	0	2
11	Lee	1	0	0	0	1
	Other	8	2	4	0	14
	TOTAL	**39**	**2**	**6**	**0**	**47**

TOP POINT EARNERS

	PLAYER	GAMES	AV PTS
1	Deon Burton	14	**1.86**
2	John Hills	25	**1.52**
3	Yoann Folly	13	**1.46**
4	Marcus Tudgay	12	**1.42**
5	Chris Eagles	17	**1.18**
6	Graham Coughlan	33	**1.15**
7	Frankie Simek	40	**1.15**
8	Peter Gilbert	16	**1.13**
9	Burton O'Brien	34	**1.12**
10	Chris Brunt	34	**1.12**
	CLUB AVERAGE:		**1.13**

DISCIPLINARY RECORDS

	PLAYER	YELLOW	RED	AVE
1	Hills	7	1	**281**
2	Diallo	2	0	**356**
3	Gilbert	4	0	**358**
4	Rocastle	3	0	**400**
5	Simek	8	0	**463**
6	Best	1	0	**530**
7	Whelan	6	0	**586**
8	Tudgay	2	0	**595**
9	Corr	1	0	**630**
10	Lee	2	0	**655**
11	Brunt	5	0	**670**
12	Eagles	2	0	**887**
13	Folly	1	0	**1215**
	Other	7	0	
	TOTAL	**51**	**1**	

KEY GOALKEEPER

David Lucas

Goals Conceded in the League	21	Counting Games League games when player was on pitch for at least 70 minutes	17
Goals Conceded in all competitions	31		
Defensive Rating Ave number of mins between League goals conceded while on the pitch	75	Clean Sheets In games when player was on pitch for at least 70 minutes	5

KEY PLAYERS - GOALSCORERS

Marcus Tudgay

Goals in the League	3	Player Strike Rate Average number of minutes between League goals scored by player	397
Goals in all competitions	3		
Contribution to Attacking Power Average number of minutes between League team goals while on pitch	85	Club Strike Rate Average number of minutes between League goals scored by club	106

	PLAYER	GOALS LGE	GOALS ALL	POWER	S RATE
1	Marcus Tudgay	3	3	85	397 mins
2	Deon Burton	3	3	79	448 mins
3	Chris Brunt	7	7	108	479 mins
4	Chris Eagles	3	3	118	592 mins

KEY PLAYERS - DEFENDERS

John Hills

Goals Conceded in the League	26	Clean Sheets In League games when player was on pitch for at least 70 minutes	8
Goals Conceded in all competitions	29		
Defensive Rating Ave number of mins between League goals conceded while on the pitch	87	Club Defensive Rating Average number of mins between League goals conceded by the club this season	80

	PLAYER	CON LGE	CON ALL	CLN SHEETS	DEF RATE
1	John Hills	26	29	8	87 mins
2	Peter Gilbert	17	17	5	84 mins
3	Graham Coughlan	36	45	10	82 mins
4	Frankie Simek	48	54	12	77 mins

KEY PLAYERS - MIDFIELDERS

Yoann Folly

Goals in the League	0	Contribution to Attacking Power Average number of minutes between League team goals while on pitch	110
Goals in all competitions	0		
Defensive Rating Average number of mins between League goals conceded while on the pitch	110	Scoring Difference Defensive Rating minus Contribution to Attacking Power	0

	PLAYER	GOALS LGE	GOALS ALL	DEF RATE	ATT POWER	SCORE DIFF
1	Yoann Folly	0	0	110	110	0 mins
2	Burton O'Brien	2	2	75	98	-23 mins
3	Glenn Whelan	1	1	77	104	-27 mins
4	Chris Brunt	7	7	75	108	-33 mins

Wedenesday's Chris Brunt and Richard Wood

SQUAD APPEARANCES

Match	1	2	3	4	5	6	7	8	9	10	11	12	13	14	15	16	17	18	19	20	21	22	23	24	25
Venue	A	H	H	A	A	A	A	H	H	H	A	A	H	A	H	H	A	A	H	H	A	H	H	A	A
Competition	L	L	L	L	W	L	L	L	L	W	L	L	L	L	L	L	L	L	L	L	L	L	L	L	L
Result	D	D	L	L	W	D	L	W	L	L	D	L	W	D	D	D	W	L	W	L	L	D	L	L	L

Match	26	27	28	29	30	31	32	33	34	35	36	37	38	39	40	41	42	43	44	45	46	47	48	49
Venue	H	A	H	A	H	H	H	A	H	A	H	A	H	A	A	H	H	A	H	A	H	A	H	A
Competition	L	L	L	L	L	F	L	L	L	L	L	L	L	L	L	L	L	L	L	L	L	L	L	L
Result	L	D	L	W	W	L	W	L	L	W	D	L	L	L	L	D	W	W	D	L	W	W	D	W

Goalkeepers
Chris Adamson
Scott Carson
David Lucas
Nicky Weaver

Defenders
Mikkel Bischoff
Lee Bullen
Patrick Collins
Graham Coughlan
Drissa Diallo
Peter Gilbert
Paul Heckingbottom
John Hills
Graeme Lee
Frankie Simek
Richard Wood

Midfielders
Steve Adams
Chris Brunt
Chris Eagles
Yoann Folly
John-Paul McGovern
Burton O'Brien
Ritchie Partridge
Craig Rocastle
Glenn Whelan

Forwards
Gabriel Agbonlahor
Leon Best
Deon Burton
Barry Corr
David Graham
Steven MacLean
Daryl Murphy
Lee Peacock
Adam Proudlock
Marcus Tudgay

KEY: On all match · On bench · Subbed or sent off (Counting game) · Subbed or sent off (playing less than 70 minutes) · Subbed on from bench (Counting Game) · Subbed on (playing less than 70 minutes) · Subbed on and then subbed or sent off (Counting Game) · Subbed on and then subbed or sent off (playing less than 70 minutes) · Not in 16

DERBY COUNTY

Final Position: **20th**

NICKNAME: THE RAMS

KEY: ☐ Won ☐ Drawn ☐ Lost

							Attendance
1	div1	Brighton	H	D	1-1	Peschisolido 12	25,292
2	div1	Preston	A	D	1-1	Idiakez 43 pen	13,127
3	div1	Plymouth	A	W	2-0	Rasiak 20; Bisgaard 39	14,279
4	div1	Cardiff	H	W	2-1	Bisgaard 21; Idiakez 45 pen	23,153
5	ccr1	Grimsby	H	L	0-1		11,756
6	div1	Burnley	A	D	2-2	Idiakez 30; Rasiak 90	12,243
7	div1	Watford	H	L	1-2	Bolder 4	23,664
8	div1	Crewe	A	D	1-1	Bisgaard 49	5,958
9	div1	Coventry	H	D	1-1	Bisgaard 14	21,840
10	div1	Southampton	H	D	2-2	Idiakez 80 pen; Davies 85	22,348
11	div1	Sheff Utd	A	L	1-2	Peschisolido 53	22,192
12	div1	Leeds	A	L	1-3	Gregan 74 og	18,353
13	div1	Leicester	H	D	1-1	El Hamdaoui 89	25,044
14	div1	Stoke	H	W	2-1	Idiakez 45; Peschisolido 86	22,229
15	div1	Wolverhampton	A	D	1-1	El Hamdaoui 46	22,914
16	div1	Hull City	A	L	1-2	Idiakez 56 pen	20,661
17	div1	QPR	H	L	1-2	Blackstock 84	24,447
18	div1	Ipswich	H	D	3-3	Blackstock 35,56; Tudgay 38	21,598
19	div1	Sheff Wed	A	L	1-2	Tudgay 42	26,334
20	div1	Wolverhampton	H	L	0-3		22,869
21	div1	Stoke	A	W	2-1	Smith 64; Nyatanga 69	13,205
22	div1	Brighton	A	D	0-0		6,855
23	div1	Norwich	H	W	2-0	Davies 28,52	23,346
24	div1	Preston	H	D	1-1	Smith 81 pen	22,740
25	div1	Cardiff	A	D	0-0		12,500
26	div1	Luton	H	D	1-1	Idiakez 72	26,807
27	div1	Crystal Palace	A	L	0-2		18,978
28	div1	Reading	H	D	2-2	Johnson, Se 32,62	21,434
29	div1	Millwall	A	L	1-2	Johnson, Se 60	9,523
30	facr3	Burnley	H	W	2-1	Peschisolido 18,67	12,713
31	div1	Crewe	H	W	5-1	Peschisolido 11; Johnson, M 21; Smith 53,63; Idiakez 71	22,649
32	div1	Coventry	A	L	1-6	Peschisolido 2	20,267
33	facr4	Colchester	A	L	1-3	Smith 79 pen	5,933
34	div1	Sheff Utd	H	L	0-1		26,275
35	div1	Southampton	A	D	0-0		21,829
36	div1	Leeds	H	D	0-0		27,000
37	div1	Leicester	A	D	2-2	El Hamdaoui 24; Stearman 58 og	23,246
38	div1	Norwich	A	L	0-2		24,921
39	div1	Plymouth	H	W	1-0	Bolder 1	25,170
40	div1	Watford	A	D	2-2	Lisbie 19; Barnes 86	16,769
41	div1	Burnley	H	W	3-0	Smith 19; Idiakez 29; Moore 34	23,292
42	div1	Luton	A	L	0-1		9,163
43	div1	Crystal Palace	H	W	2-1	Idiakez 28,90 pen	24,857
44	div1	Reading	A	L	0-5		22,981
45	div1	Millwall	H	W	1-0	Smith 31	24,415
46	div1	QPR	A	D	1-1	Smith 67	12,606
47	div1	Hull City	H	D	1-1	Smith 89 pen	24,961
48	div1	Ipswich	A	L	0-2		24,067
49	div1	Sheff Wed	H	L	0-2		30,391

LEAGUE APPEARANCES AND BOOKINGS

	AGE (on 01/07/06)	IN NAMED 16	APPEARANCES	COUNTING GAMES	MINUTES ON PITCH	LEAGUE GOALS	Yellow	Red
Goalkeepers								
Lee Camp	21	45	40	40	3600	0	1	0
Kevin Poole	42	40	6	6	540	0	0	0
Lee Grant	23	1	1	1	90	0	0	0
Defenders								
Miles Addison	17	2	2	2	180	0	0	0
Andrew Davies	21	24	23	20	1926	3	8	3
Marc Edworthy	33	34	30	28	2629	0	3	0
Tomasz Hajto	33	6	5	5	450	0	1	0
Richard Jackson	26	34	31	20	2124	0	1	1
Michael Johnson	33	34	31	27	2584	1	5	1
Jeff Kenna	35	17	16	13	1337	0	0	0
Darren Moore	32	14	14	14	1258	1	3	1
Lewin Nyatanga	17	30	24	23	2071	1	1	0
Emerson Thome	34	4	4	3	305	0	1	0
Alan Wright	34	7	7	7	609	0	1	0
Midfielders								
Morten Bisgaard	32	39	33	23	2257	4	5	0
Adam Bolder	25	41	35	22	2316	2	4	0
Nathan Doyle	19	10	4	0	37	0	0	0
Khalilou Fadiga	31	4	4	0	145	0	0	0
Lee Holmes	19	22	18	6	910	0	1	0
Inigo Idiakez	32	42	42	41	3702	11	11	0
Seth Johnson	27	30	30	22	2289	3	7	0
Michael McIndoe	26	8	8	3	506	0	0	0
Paul Thirlwell	27	32	21	11	1362	0	2	0
Peter Whittingham	21	11	11	11	990	0	1	0
Forwards								
Giles Barnes	17	21	19	14	1363	1	2	0
Dextor Blackstock	20	9	9	7	686	3	2	0
Mounir El Hamdaoui	21	9	9	2	473	3	2	0
Danny Graham	20	15	14	10	963	0	0	0
Stern John	29	8	7	3	420	0	0	0
Kevin Lisbie	27	7	7	6	602	1	0	0
Paul Peschisolido	35	38	34	11	1407	5	0	0
Grzegorz Rasiak	27	6	6	6	526	2	0	0
Tommy Smith	26	43	43	40	3708	8	1	0
Marcus Tudgay	23	22	21	8	951	2	3	0

TEAM OF THE SEASON

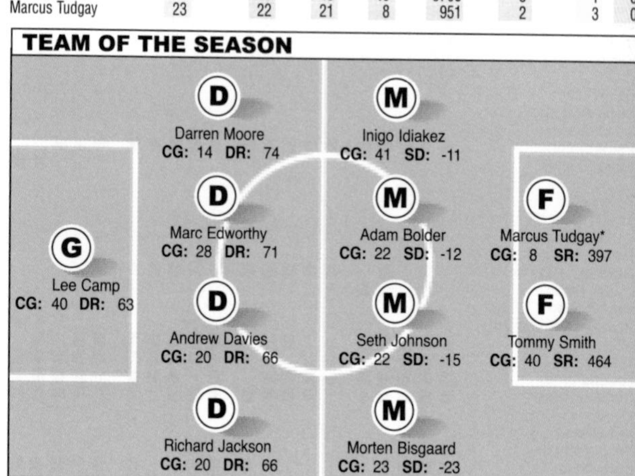

MONTHLY POINTS TALLY

AUGUST	9	50%
SEPTEMBER	3	20%
OCTOBER	5	33%
NOVEMBER	5	33%
DECEMBER	7	39%
JANUARY	3	33%
FEBRUARY	6	33%
MARCH	7	58%
APRIL	5	28%

LEAGUE GOALS

	PLAYER	LGE	FAC	LC	Oth	TOT
1	Idiakez	11	0	0	0	**11**
2	Smith	8	1	0	0	**9**
3	Peschisolido	5	2	0	0	**7**
4	Bisgaard	4	0	0	0	**4**
5	Blackstock	3	0	0	0	**3**
6	El Hamdaoui	3	0	0	0	**3**
7	Davies	3	0	0	0	**3**
8	Johnson, Se	3	0	0	0	**3**
9	Tudgay	2	0	0	0	**2**
10	Bolder	2	0	0	0	**2**
11	Rasiak	2	0	0	0	**2**
	Other	7	0	0	0	7
	TOTAL	**53**	**3**	**0**	**0**	**56**

TOP POINT EARNERS

	PLAYER	GAMES	AV PTS
1	Lewin Nyatanga	23	**1.30**
2	Marc Edworthy	28	**1.29**
3	Tommy Smith	40	**1.23**
4	Adam Bolder	22	**1.23**
5	Darren Moore	14	**1.21**
6	Andrew Davies	20	**1.20**
7	Inigo Idiakez	41	**1.15**
8	Giles Barnes	14	**1.14**
9	Richard Jackson	20	**1.10**
10	Lee Camp	40	**1.10**
	CLUB AVERAGE:		**1.09**

DISCIPLINARY RECORDS

	PLAYER	YELLOW	RED	AVE
1	Davies	8	3	**175**
2	El Hamdaoui	2	0	**236**
3	Moore	3	1	**314**
4	Tudgay	3	0	**317**
5	Johnson, Se	7	0	**327**
6	Idiakez	11	0	**336**
7	Blackstock	2	0	**343**
8	Johnson, M	5	1	**430**
9	Bisgaard	5	0	**451**
10	Bolder	4	0	**579**
11	Wright	1	0	**609**
12	Barnes	2	0	**681**
13	Thirlwell	2	0	**681**
	Other	9	1	
	TOTAL	**64**	**6**	

KEY GOALKEEPER

Lee Camp

Goals Conceded in the League	57	Counting Games League games when player was on pitch for at least 70 minutes	40
Goals Conceded in all competitions	60		
Defensive Rating Ave number of mins between League goals conceded while on the pitch	63	Clean Sheets In games when player was on pitch for at least 70 minutes	9

KEY PLAYERS - DEFENDERS

Darren Moore

Goals Conceded in the League	17	Clean Sheets In League games when player was on pitch for at least 70 minutes	5
Goals Conceded in all competitions	17		
Defensive Rating Ave number of mins between League goals conceded while on the pitch	74	Club Defensive Rating Average number of mins between League goals conceded by the club this season	62

	PLAYER	CON LGE	CON ALL	CLN SHEETS	DEF RATE
1	Darren Moore	17	17	5	74 mins
2	Marc Edworthy	37	38	8	71 mins
3	Richard Jackson	32	33	4	66 mins
4	Andrew Davies	29	32	4	66 mins

KEY PLAYERS - MIDFIELDERS

Inigo Idiakez

Goals in the League	11	Contribution to Attacking Power Average number of minutes between League team goals while on pitch	74
Goals in all competitions	11		
Defensive Rating Average number of mins between League goals conceded while on the pitch	63	Scoring Difference Defensive Rating minus Contribution to Attacking Power	-11

	PLAYER	GOALS LGE	GOALS ALL	DEF RATE	ATT POWER	SCORE DIFF
1	Inigo Idiakez	11	11	63	74	-11 mins
2	Adam Bolder	2	2	68	80	-12 mins
3	Seth Johnson	3	3	59	74	-15 mins
4	Morten Bisgaard	4	4	52	75	-23 mins

KEY PLAYERS - GOALSCORERS

Inigo Idiakez

Goals in the League	11	Player Strike Rate Average number of minutes between League goals scored by player	337
Goals in all competitions	11		
Contribution to Attacking Power Average number of minutes between League team goals while on pitch	74	Club Strike Rate Average number of minutes between League goals scored by club	78

	PLAYER	GOALS LGE	GOALS ALL	POWER	S RATE
1	Inigo Idiakez	11	11	74	337 mins
2	Tommy Smith	8	9	81	464 mins
3	Morten Bisgaard	4	4	75	564 mins
4	Andrew Davies	3	3	77	642 mins

Derby's Lee Camp

SQUAD APPEARANCES

Match	1	2	3	4	5	6	7	8	9	10	11	12	13	14	15	16	17	18	19	20	21	22	23	24	25	26	27	28	29	30	31	32	33	34	35	36	37	38	39	40	41	42	43	44	45	46	47	48	49
Venue	H	A	A	H	H	A	H	A	H	H	A	A	H	H	A	A	H	H	A	H	A	A	H	H	A	H	A	H	A	H	H	A	A	H	A	H	A	A	H	A	H	A	H	A	H	A	H	A	H
Competition	L	L	L	L	W	L	L	L	L	L	L	L	L	L	L	L	L	L	L	L	L	L	L	L	L	L	L	L	L	F	L	L	F	L	L	L	L	L	L	L	L	L	L	L	L	L	L	L	L
Result	D	D	W	W	L	D	L	D	D	D	L	L	D	W	D	L	L	D	L	L	W	D	W	D	D	D	L	D	L	W	W	L	L	L	D	D	D	L	W	D	W	L	W	L	W	D	D	L	L

Goalkeepers
Lee Camp
Kevin Poole
Lee Grant

Defenders
Miles Addison
Andrew Davies
Marc Edworthy
Tomasz Hajto
Richard Jackson
Michael Johnson
Jeff Kenna
Darren Moore
Lewin Nyatanga
Emerson Thome
Alan Wright

Midfielders
Morten Bisgaard
Adam Bolder
Nathan Doyle
Khalilou Fadiga
Lee Holmes
Inigo Idiakez
Seth Johnson
Michael McIndoe
Paul Thirlwell
Peter Whittingham

Forwards
Giles Barnes
Dexter Blackstock
Mounir El Hamdaoui
Danny Graham
Stern John
Kevin Lisbie
Paul Peschisolido
Grzegorz Rasiak
Tommy Smith
Marcus Tudgay

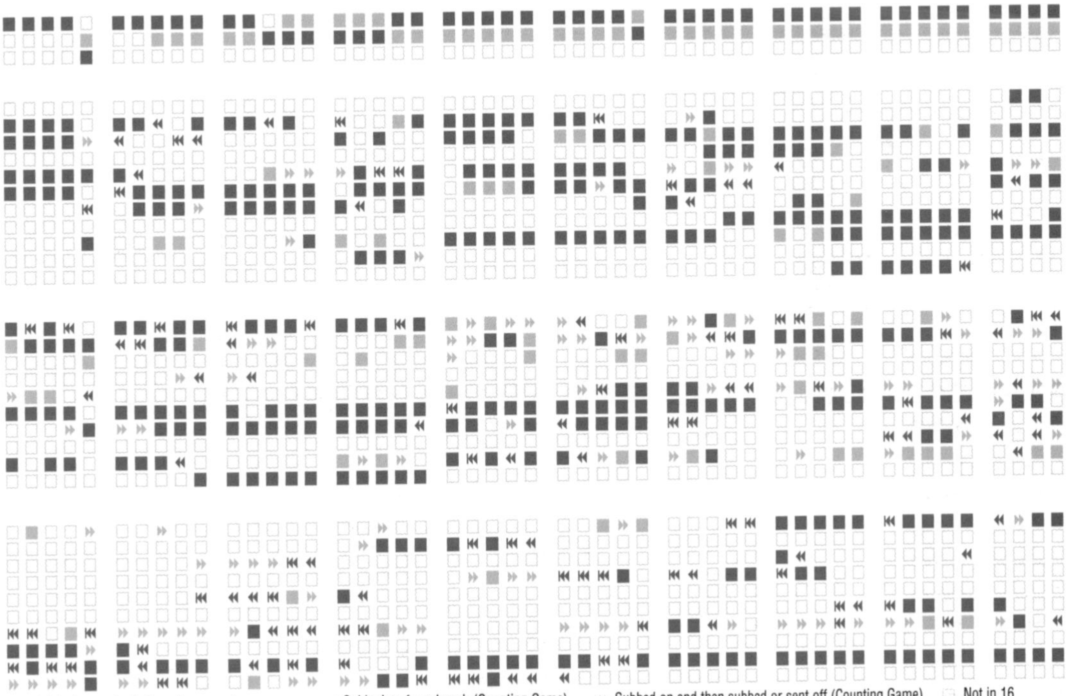

KEY: On all match · On bench · Subbed or sent off (Counting game) · Subbed or sent off (playing less than 70 minutes) · Subbed on from bench (Counting Game) · Subbed on (playing less than 70 minutes) · Subbed on and then subbed or sent off (Counting Game) · Subbed on and then subbed or sent off (playing less than 70 minutes) · Not in 16

QUEENS PARK RANGERS

Final Position: **21th**

NICKNAME: RANGERS

KEY: Won / Drawn / Lost

No	Comp	Opponent	Venue	Result	Score	Scorers	Attendance
1	div1	Hull City	A	D	0-0		22,201
2	div1	Ipswich	H	W	2-1	Gallen 37; Rowlands 45	14,632
3	div1	Sheff Utd	H	W	2-1	Bircham 56; Moore, S 90	13,497
4	div1	Coventry	A	L	0-3		23,000
5	ccr1	Northampton	A	L	0-3		4,537
6	div1	Sheff Wed	H	D	0-0		12,131
7	div1	Wolverhampton	A	L	1-3	Gallen 12	22,426
8	div1	Southampton	A	D	1-1	Shittu 32	25,744
9	div1	Luton	H	W	1-0	Cook 58	13,492
10	div1	Leeds	H	L	0-1		15,523
11	div1	Leicester	A	W	2-1	Nygaard 12; Furlong 86	20,148
12	div1	Millwall	A	D	1-1	Nygaard 25	10,322
13	div1	Crystal Palace	H	L	1-3	Ainsworth 19	13,433
14	div1	Preston	A	D	1-1	Shittu 62	13,660
15	div1	Plymouth	H	D	1-1	Gallen 69 pen	11,741
16	div1	Norwich	H	W	3-0	Nygaard 11; Furlong 18; Santos 42	15,976
17	div1	Derby	A	W	2-1	Ainsworth 30; Gallen 80	24,447
18	div1	Watford	A	L	1-3	Shittu 90	16,476
19	div1	Reading	H	L	1-2	Cook 47	15,347
20	div1	Plymouth	A	L	1-3	Baidoo 61	13,213
21	div1	Preston	H	L	0-2		10,901
22	div1	Hull City	H	D	2-2	Ainsworth 56,66	13,185
23	div1	Stoke	A	W	2-1	Furlong 2; Langley 52 pen	15,367
24	div1	Ipswich	A	D	2-2	Moore, S 26; Furlong 42	24,628
25	div1	Coventry	H	L	0-1		13,556
26	div1	Brighton	A	L	0-1		7,341
27	div1	Cardiff	H	W	1-0	Nygaard 47	12,329
28	div1	Crewe	A	W	4-3	Cook 35; Baidoo 37; Rowlands 57; Langley 81	5,687
29	div1	Burnley	H	D	1-1	Ainsworth 45	12,565
30	facr3	Blackburn	A	L	0-3		12,705
31	div1	Southampton	H	W	1-0	Langley 21 pen	15,494
32	div1	Luton	A	L	0-2		9,797
33	div1	Leicester	H	L	2-3	Ainsworth 6; Shittu 83	11,785
34	div1	Leeds	A	L	0-2		21,807
35	div1	Millwall	H	W	1-0	Nygaard 56	12,355
36	div1	Crystal Palace	A	L	1-2	Furlong 56	17,550
37	div1	Sheff Utd	A	W	3-2	Nygaard 5; Morgan 55 og; Furlong 73	25,360
38	div1	Wolverhampton	H	D	0-0		14,731
39	div1	Sheff Wed	A	D	1-1	Bircham 43	22,788
40	div1	Brighton	H	D	1-1	Ainsworth 13	13,907
41	div1	Cardiff	A	D	0-0		14,271
42	div1	Stoke	H	L	1-2	Nygaard 7	10,918
43	div1	Crewe	H	L	1-2	Ainsworth 90	12,877
44	div1	Burnley	A	L	0-1		11,247
45	div1	Derby	H	D	1-1	Nygaard 59	12,606
46	div1	Norwich	A	L	2-3	Ainsworth 45; Cook 61	24,126
47	div1	Watford	H	L	1-2	Nygaard 39 pen	16,152
48	div1	Reading	A	L	1-2	Furlong 72	23,156

LEAGUE APPEARANCES AND BOOKINGS

	AGE (on 01/07/06)	IN NAMED 16	APPEARANCES	COUNTING GAMES	MINUTES ON PITCH	LEAGUE GOALS	
Goalkeepers							
Paul Jones	39	14	14	13	1215	0	0
Simon Royce	34	35	31	31	2285	0	2
Defenders							
Marcus Bignot	31	44	44	41	3829	0	3
Ian Evatt	24	33	27	21	2010	0	1
Marcin Kus	24	7	3	2	241	0	0
Mauro Milanese	34	35	26	21	1987	0	5
Jonathan Munday	18	2	0	0	0	0	0
Matthew Rose	30	18	15	15	1333	0	1
Georges Santos	35	38	31	21	2184	1	7
Dominic Shimmin	18	11	2	1	111	0	1
Danny Shittu	25	45	45	44	4014	4	7
Andy Taylor	20	4	3	1	111	0	0
Ugo Ukah	22	1	1	0	25	0	0
Midfielders							
Gareth Ainsworth	33	44	43	29	2990	9	5
Stefan Bailey	18	8	5	4	427	0	2
Marcus Bean	21	11	9	2	397	0	3
Marc Bircham	28	27	26	21	1992	2	6
Aaron Brown	26	5	2	0	76	0	0
Lee Cook	23	40	40	31	3077	4	3
Tommy Doherty	27	15	15	9	1080	0	2
Lloyd Dyer	23	15	15	14	1301	0	3
Richard Langley	26	36	33	20	2018	3	3
Steve Lomas	32	22	21	17	1632	0	2
Adam Miller	24	2	1	0	55	0	0
Martin Rowlands	27	14	14	11	1116	2	4
Forwards							
Shabazz Baidoo	26	21	15	5	638	2	2
Leon Clarke	21	1	1	1	90	0	0
Scott Donnelly	18	15	8	2	258	0	0
Paul Furlong	37	38	37	31	2900	7	7
Kevin Gallen	30	18	18	15	1509	4	2
Stefan Moore	22	33	25	11	1294	2	0
Marc Nygaard	29	28	27	13	1665	9	4
Dean Sturridge	32	11	9	2	472	0	1
Sammy Youssouf	29	6	6	1	186	0	0

TEAM OF THE SEASON

G: Paul Jones — CG: 13 DR: 68

D: Mauro Milanese — CG: 21 DR: 74

D: Matthew Rose — CG: 15 DR: 70

D: Marcus Bignot — CG: 41 DR: 64

D: Danny Shittu — CG: 44 DR: 64

M: Marc Bircham — CG: 21 SD: -7

M: Lee Cook — CG: 31 SD: -14

M: Lloyd Dyer — CG: 14 SD: -15

M: Gareth Ainsworth — CG: 29 SD: -19

F: Marc Nygaard — CG: 13 SR: 185

F: Kevin Gallen — CG: 15 SR: 377

MONTHLY POINTS TALLY

Month	Points	%
AUGUST	8	44%
SEPTEMBER	8	53%
OCTOBER	8	53%
NOVEMBER	1	7%
DECEMBER	10	56%
JANUARY	4	33%
FEBRUARY	6	50%
MARCH	4	27%
APRIL	1	6%

LEAGUE GOALS

	PLAYER	LGE	FAC	LC	Oth	TOT
1	Ainsworth	9	0	0	0	9
2	Nygaard	9	0	0	0	9
3	Furlong	7	0	0	0	7
4	Cook	4	0	0	0	4
5	Shittu	4	0	0	0	4
6	Gallen	4	0	0	0	4
7	Langley	3	0	0	0	3
8	Baidoo	2	0	0	0	2
9	Rowlands	2	0	0	0	2
10	Moore, S	2	0	0	0	2
11	Bircham	2	0	0	0	2
	Other	2	0	0	0	2
	TOTAL	50	0	0	0	50

TOP POINT EARNERS

	PLAYER	GAMES	AV PTS
1	Matthew Rose	15	1.53
2	Marc Bircham	21	1.38
3	Simon Royce	30	1.30
4	Paul Furlong	31	1.29
5	Marcus Bignot	41	1.20
6	Georges Santos	21	1.19
7	Richard Langley	20	1.15
8	Kevin Gallen	15	1.13
9	Danny Shittu	44	1.11
10	Lee Cook	31	1.10
	CLUB AVERAGE:		1.09

DISCIPLINARY RECORDS

	PLAYER	YELLOW	RED	AVE
1	Rowlands	4	0	279
2	Santos	7	0	312
3	Baidoo	2	0	319
4	Furlong	7	2	322
5	Bircham	6	0	332
6	Nygaard	4	1	333
7	Doherty	2	1	360
8	Milanese	5	0	397
9	Dyer, L	3	0	433
10	Sturridge	1	0	472
11	Shittu	7	1	501
12	Gallen	2	1	503
13	Ainsworth	5	0	598
	Other	15	1	
	TOTAL	70	7	

KEY GOALKEEPER

Paul Jones			
Goals Conceded in the League	18	Counting Games League games when player was on pitch for at least 70 minutes	13
Goals Conceded in all competitions	18		
Defensive Rating Ave number of mins between League goals conceded while on the pitch	68	Clean Sheets In games when player was on pitch for at least 70 minutes	3

KEY PLAYERS - DEFENDERS

Mauro Milanese			
Goals Conceded in the League	27	Clean Sheets In League games when player was on pitch for at least 70 minutes	5
Goals Conceded in all competitions	33		
Defensive Rating Ave number of mins between League goals conceded while on the pitch	74	Club Defensive Rating Average number of mins between League goals conceded by the club this season	64

	PLAYER	CON LGE	CON ALL	CLN SHEETS	DEF RATE
1	Mauro Milanese	27	33	5	74 mins
2	Matthew Rose	19	22	5	70 mins
3	Marcus Bignot	60	65	9	64 mins
4	Danny Shittu	63	66	9	64 mins

KEY PLAYERS - MIDFIELDERS

Marc Bircham			
Goals in the League	2	Contribution to Attacking Power Average number of minutes between League team goals while on pitch	87
Goals in all competitions	2		
Defensive Rating Average number of mins between League goals conceded while on the pitch	80	Scoring Difference Defensive Rating minus Contribution to Attacking Power	-7

	PLAYER	GOALS LGE	GOALS ALL	DEF RATE	ATT POWER	SCORE DIFF
1	Marc Bircham	2	2	80	87	-7 mins
2	Lee Cook	4	4	65	79	-14 mins
3	Lloyd Dyer	0	0	57	72	-15 mins
4	Gareth Ainsworth	9	9	66	85	-19 mins

KEY PLAYERS - GOALSCORERS

Marc Nygaard			
Goals in the League	9	Player Strike Rate Average number of minutes between League goals scored by player	185
Goals in all competitions	9		
Contribution to Attacking Power Average number of minutes between League team goals while on pitch	69	Club Strike Rate Average number of minutes between League goals scored by club	83

	PLAYER	GOALS LGE	GOALS ALL	POWER	S RATE
1	Marc Nygaard	9	9	69	185 mins
2	Gareth Ainsworth	9	9	85	332 mins
3	Kevin Gallen	4	4	89	377 mins
4	Paul Furlong	7	7	74	414 mins

QPR's Gareth Ainsworth

SQUAD APPEARANCES

Match	1	2	3	4	5	6	7	8	9	10	11	12	13	14	15	16	17	18	19	20	21	22	23	24
Venue	A	H	H	A	A	H	A	A	H	H	A	A	H	A	H	H	A	A	H	A	H	H	A	A
Competition	L	L	L	L	W	L	L	L	L	L	L	L	L	L	L	L	L	L	L	L	L	L	L	L
Result	D	W	W	L	L	D	L	D	W	L	W	D	L	D	D	W	W	L	L	L	L	D	W	D

Match	25	26	27	28	29	30	31	32	33	34	35	36	37	38	39	40	41	42	43	44	45	46	47	48
Venue	H	A	H	A	H	A	H	A	H	A	H	A	A	H	A	H	A	H	H	A	H	A	H	A
Competition	L	L	L	L	L	F	L	L	L	L	L	L	L	L	L	L	L	L	L	L	L	L	L	L
Result	L	L	W	W	D	L	W	L	L	L	W	L	W	D	D	D	D	L	L	L	D	L	L	L

Goalkeepers
Paul Jones
Simon Royce

Defenders
Marcus Bignot
Ian Evatt
Marcin Kus
Mauro Milanese
Jonathan Munday
Matthew Rose
Georges Santos
Dominic Shimmin
Danny Shittu
Andy Taylor
Ugo Ukah

Midfielders
Gareth Ainsworth
Stefan Bailey
Marcus Bean
Marc Bircham
Aaron Brown
Lee Cook
Tommy Doherty
Lloyd Dyer
Richard Langley
Steve Lomas
Adam Miller
Martin Rowlands

Forwards
Shabazz Baidoo
Leon Clarke
Scott Donnelly
Paul Furlong
Kevin Gallen
Stefan Moore
Marc Nygaard
Dean Sturridge
Sammy Youssouf

KEY: On all match / On bench / Subbed or sent off (Counting game) / Subbed or sent off (playing less than 70 minutes) / Subbed on from bench (Counting Game) / Subbed on (playing less than 70 minutes) / Subbed on and then subbed or sent off (Counting Game) / Subbed on and then subbed or sent off (playing less than 70 minutes) / Not in 16

CREWE ALEXANDRA

Final Position: **22th**

NICKNAME: THE RAILWAYMEN

KEY: ☐ Won ☐ Drawn ☐ Lost

							Attendance
1	div1	**Burnley**	H	W	2-1	Jones, B 44; Vaughan 89	8,006
2	div1	**Norwich**	A	D	1-1	Varney 19	25,116
3	div1	**Brighton**	A	D	2-2	Rivers 77; Higdon 83	6,132
4	div1	**Leicester**	H	D	2-2	Varney 1; Rivers 17	7,053
5	ccr1	**Lincoln**	A	L	1-5	Walker 44	2,782
6	div1	**Southampton**	A	L	0-2		20,792
7	div1	**Sheff Utd**	H	L	1-3	Foster 17	7,501
8	div1	**Derby**	H	D	1-1	Rivers 30	5,958
9	div1	**Plymouth**	A	D	1-1	Johnson 8	10,460
10	div1	**Reading**	A	L	0-1		17,668
11	div1	**Watford**	H	D	0-0		6,258
12	div1	**Wolverhampton**	H	L	0-4		7,471
13	div1	**Ipswich**	A	L	1-2	Vaughan 26	23,145
14	div1	**Luton**	H	W	3-1	Jones, B 37; Lunt 88; Varney 90	6,604
15	div1	**Stoke**	A	L	0-2		14,080
16	div1	**Cardiff**	A	L	1-6	Foster 31	10,815
17	div1	**Crystal Palace**	H	D	2-2	Jones, S 7; Higdon 90	6,766
18	div1	**Leeds**	H	W	1-0	Butler 8 og	7,220
19	div1	**Millwall**	A	W	3-1	Jones, S 15,70; Roberts, G 63	8,120
20	div1	**Stoke**	H	L	1-2	Johnson 90	8,942
21	div1	**Luton**	A	L	1-4	Walker 83	7,474
22	div1	**Burnley**	A	L	0-3		11,151
23	div1	**Preston**	H	L	0-2		6,364
24	div1	**Norwich**	H	L	1-2	Jones, B 16	6,132
25	div1	**Leicester**	A	D	1-1	Higdon 40	24,873
26	div1	**Hull City**	H	D	2-2	Johnson 19; Roberts, G 41	7,942
27	div1	**Coventry**	A	D	1-1	Rodgers 90	19,045
28	div1	**QPR**	H	L	3-4	Johnson 15; Varney 39; Jones, B 45	5,687
29	div1	**Sheff Wed**	A	L	0-3		25,656
30	facr3	**Preston**	A	L	1-2	Jones, B 35	8,380
31	div1	**Derby**	A	L	1-5	Vaughan 79	22,649
32	div1	**Plymouth**	H	L	1-2	Rodgers 68	5,984
33	div1	**Watford**	A	L	1-4	Rodgers 81	11,722
34	div1	**Reading**	H	L	3-4	Bell 14; Taylor 51; Lunt 68 pen	6,484
35	div1	**Wolverhampton**	A	D	1-1	Jones, B 6	21,683
36	div1	**Ipswich**	H	L	1-2	Jones, S 15	5,686
37	div1	**Brighton**	H	W	2-1	Bell 58; Foster 64	5,925
38	div1	**Sheff Utd**	A	D	0-0		22,691
39	div1	**Southampton**	H	D	1-1	Rodgers 78	6,588
40	div1	**Hull City**	A	L	0-1		21,163
41	div1	**Coventry**	H	W	4-1	Jones, B 4; Bougherra 17; Rodgers 24; Taylor 61	6,444
42	div1	**Preston**	A	L	0-1		13,170
43	div1	**QPR**	A	W	2-1	Lunt 39; Vaughan 73	12,877
44	div1	**Sheff Wed**	H	W	2-0	Taylor 31,45	8,007
45	div1	**Crystal Palace**	A	D	2-2	Rodgers 68; Lunt 79 pen	18,358
46	div1	**Cardiff**	H	D	1-1	Vaughan 58	5,865
47	div1	**Leeds**	A	L	0-1		21,046
48	div1	**Millwall**	H	W	4-2	Johnson 43; Maynard 46; Varney 59; Jones, S 84	5,945

LEAGUE APPEARANCES AND BOOKINGS

	AGE (on 01/07/06)	IN NAMED 16	APPEARANCES	COUNTING GAMES	MINUTES ON PITCH	LEAGUE GOALS		
Goalkeepers								
Stuart Tomlinson	22	38	2	1	135	0	0	0
Ross Turnbull	21	33	29	28	2559	0	1	0
Ben Williams	23	20	17	16	1446	0	0	0
Defenders								
Paul Bignot	20	7	5	4	396	0	1	0
Madjid Bougherra	23	12	11	10	929	1	0	0
Steve Foster	25	44	39	36	3278	3	7	1
Billy Jones	19	44	44	40	3781	6	5	0
Chris McCready	25	34	25	18	1767	0	0	0
Adrian Moses	31	18	15	10	977	0	0	0
Darren Moss	25	31	31	30	2690	0	4	0
Jon Otsemobor	23	16	16	16	1440	0	1	0
Anthony Tonkin	26	27	27	25	2358	0	1	0
Richard Walker	25	27	18	17	1587	1	1	0
Midfielders								
Lee Bell	22	19	17	12	1225	2	1	0
Justin Cochrane	24	12	4	1	153	0	1	0
Tony Grant	31	11	10	8	819	0	0	0
Michael Higdon	22	33	26	9	1323	3	4	0
Kenny Lunt	26	43	43	43	3870	4	3	1
Ben Rix	22	5	2	0	98	0	0	0
Gary Roberts	19	35	33	24	2445	2	0	0
David Vaughan	23	36	34	26	2552	5	1	0
Forwards								
Eddie Johnson	21	33	22	13	1271	5	1	0
Steve Jones	29	44	41	34	3177	5	1	0
Mark Rivers	30	21	17	9	831	3	0	0
Luke Rodgers	33	31	26	11	1284	6	0	0
Pavol Suhaj	25	9	6	1	179	0	0	0
Gareth Taylor	33	15	15	14	1267	4	0	0
Juan Ugarte	25	2	2	0	37	0	0	0
Luke Varney	23	30	27	15	1556	5	1	0

TEAM OF THE SEASON

G
Ross Turnbull
CG: 28 DR: 54

D
Jon Otsemobor
CG: 16 DR: 63

D
Steve Foster
CG: 36 DR: 53

D
Anthony Tonkin
CG: 25 DR: 51

D
Billy Jones
CG: 40 DR: 50

M
Lee Bell
CG: 12 SD: -6

M
Kenny Lunt
CG: 43 SD: -24

M
David Vaughan
CG: 26 SD: -34

M
Gary Roberts
CG: 24 SD: -37

F
Eddie Johnson
CG: 13 SR: 254

F
Luke Varney
CG: 15 SR: 311

MONTHLY POINTS TALLY

AUGUST	6	33%
SEPTEMBER	3	20%
OCTOBER	4	27%
NOVEMBER	6	40%
DECEMBER	3	17%
JANUARY	0	0%
FEBRUARY	4	33%
MARCH	5	33%
APRIL	11	61%

LEAGUE GOALS

	PLAYER	LGE	FAC	LC	Oth	TOT
1	Rodgers	6	0	0	0	6
2	Jones, B	6	1	0	0	7
3	Jones, S	5	0	0	0	5
4	Varney	5	0	0	0	5
5	Johnson	5	0	0	0	5
6	Vaughan	5	0	0	0	5
7	Lunt	4	0	0	0	4
8	Taylor	4	0	0	0	4
9	Foster	3	0	0	0	3
10	Rivers	3	0	0	0	3
11	Higdon	3	0	0	0	3
	Other	8	0	1	0	9
	TOTAL	57	1	1	0	59

TOP POINT EARNERS

	PLAYER	GAMES	AV PTS
1	Lee Bell	12	1.33
2	Gareth Taylor	14	1.14
3	Jon Otsemobor	16	1.06
4	Anthony Tonkin	25	1.04
5	Steve Jones	34	1.03
6	Ben Williams	16	1.00
7	Luke Varney	15	0.93
8	Billy Jones	40	0.93
9	Kenny Lunt	43	0.93
10	Steve Foster	36	0.92
	CLUB AVERAGE:		0.91

DISCIPLINARY RECORDS

	PLAYER	YELLOW	RED	AVE
1	Higdon	4	0	330
2	Foster	7	1	409
3	Moss	4	0	672
4	Jones, B	5	0	756
5	Lunt	3	1	967
6	Bell	1	0	1225
7	Johnson	1	0	1271
8	Otsemobor	1	0	1440
9	Varney	1	0	1556
10	Walker	1	0	1587
11	Tonkin	1	0	2358
12	Vaughan	1	0	2552
13	Turnbull	1	0	2559
	Other	1	0	
	TOTAL	32	2	

KEY GOALKEEPER

Ross Turnbull

Goals Conceded in the League	47	**Counting Games** League games when player was on pitch for at least 70 minutes	28
Goals Conceded in all competitions	47		
Defensive Rating Ave number of mins between League goals conceded while on the pitch	54	**Clean Sheets** In games when player was on pitch for at least 70 minutes	3

KEY PLAYERS - DEFENDERS

Jon Otsemobor

Goals Conceded in the League	23	**Clean Sheets** In League games when player was on pitch for at least 70 minutes	2
Goals Conceded in all competitions	23		
Defensive Rating Ave number of mins between League goals conceded while on the pitch	63	**Club Defensive Rating** Average number of mins between League goals conceded by the club this season	48

	PLAYER	CON LGE	CON ALL	CLN SHEETS	DEF RATE
1	Jon Otsemobor	23	23	2	63 mins
2	Steve Foster	62	62	4	53 mins
3	Anthony Tonkin	46	51	2	51 mins
4	Billy Jones	76	82	4	50 mins

KEY PLAYERS - MIDFIELDERS

Lee Bell

Goals in the League	2	**Contribution to Attacking Power** Average number of minutes between League team goals while on pitch	64
Goals in all competitions	2		
Defensive Rating Average number of mins between League goals conceded while on the pitch	58	**Scoring Difference** Defensive Rating minus Contribution to Attacking Power	-6

	PLAYER	GOALS LGE	GOALS ALL	DEF RATE	ATT POWER	SCORE DIFF
1	Lee Bell	2	2	58	64	-6 mins
2	Kenny Lunt	4	4	48	72	-24 mins
3	David Vaughan	5	5	46	80	-34 mins
4	Gary Roberts	2	2	39	76	-37 mins

KEY PLAYERS - GOALSCORERS

Eddie Johnson

Goals in the League	5	**Player Strike Rate** Average number of minutes between League goals scored by player	254
Goals in all competitions	5		
Contribution to Attacking Power Average number of minutes between League team goals while on pitch	85	**Club Strike Rate** Average number of minutes between League goals scored by club	73

	PLAYER	GOALS LGE	GOALS ALL	POWER	S RATE
1	Eddie Johnson	5	5	85	254 mins
2	Luke Varney	5	5	65	311 mins
3	Gareth Taylor	4	4	67	317 mins
4	David Vaughan	5	5	80	510 mins

Crewe's Billy Jones

SQUAD APPEARANCES

Match	1	2	3	4	5	6	7	8	9	10	11	12	13	14	15	16	17	18	19	20	21	22	23	24
Venue	H	A	A	H	A	A	H	H	A	A	H	H	A	H	A	A	H	H	A	H	A	A	H	H
Competition	L	L	L	L	W	L	L	L	L	L	L	L	L	L	L	L	L	L	L	L	L	L	L	L
Result	W	D	D	D	L	L	L	D	D	L	D	L	L	W	L	L	D	W	W	L	L	L	L	L

Match	25	26	27	28	29	30	31	32	33	34	35	36	37	38	39	40	41	42	43	44	45	46	47	48
Venue	A	H	A	H	A	A	A	H	A	H	A	H	H	A	H	A	H	A	A	H	A	H	A	H
Competition	L	L	L	L	L	F	L	L	L	L	L	L	L	L	L	L	L	L	L	L	L	L	L	L
Result	D	D	D	L	L	L	L	L	L	L	D	L	W	D	D	L	W	L	W	W	D	D	L	W

Goalkeepers
Stuart Tomlinson
Ross Turnbull
Ben Williams

Defenders
Paul Bignot
Madjid Bougherra
Steve Foster
Billy Jones
Chris McCready
Adrian Moses
Darren Moss
Jon Otsemobor
Anthony Tonkin
Richard Walker

Midfielders
Lee Bell
Justin Cochrane
Tony Grant
Michael Higdon
Kenny Lunt
Ben Rix
Gary Roberts
David Vaughan

Forwards
Eddie Johnson
Steve Jones
Mark Rivers
Luke Rodgers
Pavol Suhaj
Gareth Taylor
Juan Ugarte
Luke Varney

KEY: ■ On all match ■ On bench | ⏮ Subbed or sent off (Counting game) « Subbed or sent off (playing less than 70 minutes) | ⏭ Subbed on from bench (Counting Game) » Subbed on (playing less than 70 minutes) | Subbed on and then subbed or sent off (Counting Game) Subbed on and then subbed or sent off (playing less than 70 minutes) | □ Not in 16

MILLWALL

Final Position: **23th**

NICKNAME: THE LIONS

KEY: ☐ Won ☐ Drawn ☐ Lost

							Attendance
1	div1	Leeds	A	L	1-2	Hutchison 61	20,440
2	div1	Coventry	H	D	0-0		8,344
3	div1	Stoke	H	L	0-1		8,668
4	div1	Reading	A	L	0-5		14,225
5	ccr1	Bristol Rovers	H	W	2-0	Hayles 55; Fangueiro 85	3,079
6	div1	Ipswich	H	L	1-2	May 68	8,277
7	div1	Luton	A	L	1-2	May 46	8,220
8	div1	Preston	H	L	1-2	Hutchison 51	7,674
9	div1	Wolverhampton	A	W	2-1	Wright 27; Hayles 90	21,897
10	div1	Sheff Wed	A	W	2-1	Hayles 50; Asaba 74	22,446
11	ccr2	Yeovil	A	W	2-1	Dunne 48; Asaba 53	5,108
12	div1	Cardiff	H	D	0-0		9,254
13	div1	QPR	H	D	1-1	Hayles 45	10,322
14	div1	Hull City	A	D	1-1	Asaba 61	18,761
15	div1	Norwich	A	D	1-1	Williams 23	25,095
16	div1	Sheff Utd	H	L	0-4		9,148
17	div1	Southampton	H	L	0-2		10,759
18	ccr3	Mansfield	A	W	3-2	May 25; Robinson, P 61; Livermore 90	4,133
19	div1	Plymouth	A	D	0-0		11,764
20	div1	Burnley	A	L	1-2	Wright 1	10,698
21	div1	Crewe	H	L	1-3	Hayles 38 pen	8,120
22	div1	Sheff Utd	A	D	2-2	Dyer 34,55	22,292
23	div1	Norwich	H	W	1-0	Elliott 70	7,814
24	div1	Leeds	H	L	0-1		8,134
25	ccr4	Birmingham	H	L	3-4*	Dunne 57; Elliott 116 (*on penalties)	7,732
26	div1	Crystal Palace	A	D	1-1	May 41	19,571
27	div1	Coventry	A	L	0-1		16,156
28	div1	Reading	H	L	0-2		12,920
29	div1	Leicester	A	D	1-1	McCarthy 28 og	22,520
30	div1	Watford	H	D	0-0		8,450
31	div1	Brighton	A	W	2-1	May 46; Simpson 50	6,847
32	div1	Derby	H	W	2-1	Elliott 73; Williams 78	9,523
33	facr3	Everton	H	D	1-1	Williams 39	16,440
34	div1	Preston	A	L	0-2		14,165
35	facr3r	Everton	A	L	0-1		25,800
36	div1	Wolverhampton	H	D	0-0		9,905
37	div1	Cardiff	A	D	1-1	Powel 60	12,378
38	div1	Sheff Wed	H	L	0-1		11,896
39	div1	QPR	A	L	0-1		12,355
40	div1	Hull City	H	D	1-1	Livermore 80	7,108
41	div1	Crystal Palace	H	D	1-1	May 88	12,296
42	div1	Stoke	A	L	1-2	May 7	11,340
43	div1	Luton	H	W	2-1	May 33; Williams 90	9,871
44	div1	Ipswich	A	D	1-1	Livermore 85	24,864
45	div1	Leicester	H	L	0-1		10,523
46	div1	Watford	A	W	2-0	Asaba 66; May 90	16,654
47	div1	Brighton	H	L	0-2		13,209
48	div1	Derby	A	L	0-1		24,415
49	div1	Plymouth	H	D	1-1	Williams 31	9,183
50	div1	Southampton	A	L	0-2		22,043
51	div1	Burnley	H	W	1-0	Williams 45	7,780
52	div1	Crewe	A	L	2-4	May 15,58	5,945

LEAGUE APPEARANCES AND BOOKINGS

	AGE (on 01/07/06)	IN NAMED 16	APPEARANCES	COUNTING GAMES	MINUTES ON PITCH	LEAGUE GOALS	
Goalkeepers							
Colin Doyle	20	26	14	14	1260	0	0
Paul Jones	39	15	3	3	270	0	0
Andy Marshall	31	32	29	28	2543	0	1
Lenny Pidgeley	21	0	0	0	0	0	0
Defenders							
Tony Craig	21	31	28	25	2322	0	8
Alan Dunne	23	40	39	38	3387	0	11
Philip Ifil	19	20	16	14	1336	0	6
Matt Lawrence	32	30	30	27	2606	0	2
Marcus Phillips	23	26	21	17	1605	0	3
Paul Robinson	24	36	31	26	2544	0	6
Jamie Vincent	31	22	19	15	1522	0	0
Zak Whitbread	22	26	25	23	2174	0	7
Midfielders							
Colin Cameron	33	5	5	5	431	0	1
Barry Cogan	20	20	14	6	705	0	2
Lloyd Dyer	23	7	5	1	253	0	0
Marvin Elliott	21	39	39	32	3049	2	3
Will Hendry	19	9	3	2	191	0	0
Don Hutchison	35	18	11	6	657	2	2
Sam Igoe	30	13	5	2	222	0	0
David Livermore	26	41	41	41	3690	2	9
Jody Morris	27	27	24	18	1858	0	8
Adrian Serioux	27	5	5	1	197	0	2
Josh Simpson	23	20	13	3	597	1	0
Jermaine Wright	30	15	15	15	1345	2	2
Forwards							
Carl Asaba	33	21	21	9	1310	3	1
Kevin Braniff	23	31	15	5	686	0	2
Bruce Dyer	31	11	10	5	673	2	0
Carlos Manuel Fangueiro	29	17	9	0	277	0	1
Barry Hayles	34	23	23	20	1817	4	6
Ben May	22	41	38	20	2364	10	3
Berry Powel	26	12	12	7	792	1	1
Marvin Williams	19	35	33	19	2105	5	8

TEAM OF THE SEASON

MONTHLY POINTS TALLY

AUGUST	1	6%
SEPTEMBER	9	50%
OCTOBER	2	17%
NOVEMBER	4	27%
DECEMBER	6	33%
JANUARY	5	42%
FEBRUARY	2	13%
MARCH	7	58%
APRIL	4	22%

LEAGUE GOALS

	PLAYER	LGE	FAC	LC	Oth	TOT
1	May	10	0	1	0	11
2	Williams	5	1	0	0	6
3	Hayles	4	0	1	0	5
4	Asaba	3	0	1	0	4
5	Elliott	2	0	1	0	3
6	Livermore	2	0	1	0	3
7	Wright	2	0	0	0	2
8	Dyer	2	0	0	0	2
9	Hutchison	2	0	0	0	2
10	Simpson	1	0	0	0	1
11	Powel	1	0	0	0	1
	Other	1	0	4	0	5
	TOTAL	35	1	9	0	45

TOP POINT EARNERS

	PLAYER	GAMES	AV PTS
1	Jermaine Wright	15	1.07
2	Philip Ifil	14	1.00
3	Ben May	20	1.00
4	Marvin Williams	19	1.00
5	Tony Craig	25	0.96
6	Barry Hayles	20	0.95
7	Colin Doyle	14	0.93
8	Jamie Vincent	15	0.93
9	Alan Dunne	38	0.92
10	Paul Robinson	26	0.92
	CLUB AVERAGE:		0.87

DISCIPLINARY RECORDS

	PLAYER	YELLOW	RED	AVE
1	Morris	8	2	185
2	Ifil, Philip	6	1	190
3	Craig	8	2	232
4	Hayles	6	1	259
5	Williams	8	0	263
6	Dunne	11	1	282
7	Whitbread	7	0	310
8	Hutchison	2	0	328
9	Braniff	2	0	343
10	Cogan	2	0	352
11	Robinson, P	6	1	363
12	Livermore	9	0	410
13	Phillips	3	0	535
	Other	13	3	
	TOTAL	91	11	

KEY GOALKEEPER

Andy Marshall

Goals Conceded in the League	35	Counting Games League games when player was on pitch for at least 70 minutes	28
Goals Conceded in all competitions	40		
Defensive Rating Ave number of mins between League goals conceded while on the pitch	73	Clean Sheets In games when player was on pitch for at least 70 minutes	5

KEY PLAYERS - DEFENDERS

Zak Whitbread

Goals Conceded in the League	29	Clean Sheets In League games when player was on pitch for at least 70 minutes	3
Goals Conceded in all competitions	31		
Defensive Rating Ave number of mins between League goals conceded while on the pitch	75	Club Defensive Rating Average number of mins between League goals conceded by the club this season	67

	PLAYER	CON LGE	CON ALL	CLN SHEETS	DEF RATE
1	Zak Whitbread	29	31	3	75 mins
2	Alan Dunne	46	52	7	74 mins
3	Matt Lawrence	36	40	4	72 mins
4	Paul Robinson	36	43	6	71 mins

KEY PLAYERS - MIDFIELDERS

Jermaine Wright

Goals in the League	2	Contribution to Attacking Power Average number of minutes between League team goals while on pitch	103
Goals in all competitions	2		
Defensive Rating Average number of mins between League goals conceded while on the pitch	67	Scoring Difference Defensive Rating minus Contribution to Attacking Power	-36

	PLAYER	GOALS LGE	GOALS ALL	DEF RATE	ATT POWER	SCORE DIFF
1	Jermaine Wright	2	2	67	103	-36 mins
2	David Livermore	2	3	67	119	-52 mins
3	Marvin Elliott	2	3	66	122	-56 mins
4	Jody Morris	0	0	71	169	-98 mins

KEY PLAYERS - GOALSCORERS

Ben May

Goals in the League	10	Player Strike Rate Average number of minutes between League goals scored by player	236
Goals in all competitions	11		
Contribution to Attacking Power Average number of minutes between League team goals while on pitch	107	Club Strike Rate Average number of minutes between League goals scored by club	118

	PLAYER	GOALS LGE	GOALS ALL	POWER	S RATE
1	Ben May	10	11	107	236 mins
2	Marvin Williams	5	6	88	421 mins
3	Barry Hayles	4	5	121	454 mins
4	Jermaine Wright	2	2	103	673 mins

Millwall's Ben May

SQUAD APPEARANCES

'atch	1	2	3	4	5	6	7	8	9	10	11	12	13	14	15	16	17	18	19	20	21	22	23	24	25	26
enue	A	H	H	A	H	H	A	H	A	A	A	H	H	A	A	H	H	A	A	A	H	A	H	H	H	A
ompetition	L	L	L	L	W	L	L	L	L	L	W	L	L	L	L	L	L	W	L	L	L	L	L	L	W	L
esult	L	D	L	L	W	L	L	L	W	W	W	D	D	D	D	L	L	W	D	L	L	D	W	L	L	D

'atch	27	28	29	30	31	32	33	34	35	36	37	38	39	40	41	42	43	44	45	46	47	48	49	50	51	52
enue	A	H	A	H	A	H	H	A	A	H	A	H	A	H	H	A	H	A	H	A	H	A	H	A	H	A
ompetition	L	L	L	L	L	L	F	L	F	L	L	L	L	L	L	L	L	L	L	L	L	L	L	L	L	L
esult	L	L	D	D	W	W	D	L	L	D	D	L	L	D	D	L	W	D	L	W	L	L	D	L	W	L

oalkeepers
olin Doyle
aul Jones
ndy Marshall
enny Pidgeley

efenders
ony Craig
lan Dunne
hilip Ifil
latt Lawrence
larcus Phillips
aul Robinson
amie Vincent
ak Whitbread

lidfielders
olin Cameron
arry Cogan
loyd Dyer
larvin Elliott
Vill Hendry
on Hutchison
am Igoe
avid Livermore
ody Morris
drian Serioux
osh Simpson
ermaine Wright

orwards
arl Asaba
evin Braniff
ruce Dyer
arlos Manuel Fangueiro
arry Hayles
en May
erry Powel
larvin Williams

KEY: On all match · On bench · Subbed or sent off (Counting game) · Subbed or sent off (playing less than 70 minutes) · Subbed on from bench (Counting Game) · Subbed on (playing less than 70 minutes) · Subbed on and then subbed or sent off (Counting Game) · Subbed on and then subbed or sent off (playing less than 70 minutes) · Not in 16

BRIGHTON & HOVE ALBION

Final Position: **24th**

NICKNAME: THE SEAGULLS

KEY: Won / Drawn / Lost

		Opponent			Score	Scorers	Attendance
1	div1	Derby	A	D	1-1	Hammond 7	25,292
2	div1	Reading	H	L	0-2		6,676
3	div1	Crewe	H	D	2-2	Knight 42; Hammond 88	6,132
4	div1	Hull City	A	L	0-2		18,648
5	ccr1	Shrewsbury	A	L	2-3	McCammon 17; Robinson 80	2,141
6	div1	Preston	A	D	0-0		12,461
7	div1	Plymouth	H	W	2-0	Robinson 11; Carpenter 46	6,238
8	div1	Leeds	A	D	3-3	Knight 28; Carole 51; Gregan 83 og	21,212
9	div1	Sheff Utd	H	L	0-1		6,553
10	div1	Coventry	H	D	2-2	Knight 50; Kazim-Richards 56	6,529
11	div1	Burnley	A	D	1-1	McShane 25	11,112
12	div1	Leicester	A	D	0-0		20,296
13	div1	Norwich	H	L	1-3	Frutos 67	6,624
14	div1	Cardiff	H	L	1-2	McShane 61	6,485
15	div1	Crystal Palace	A	W	1-0	McShane 79	22,400
16	div1	Sheff Wed	A	D	1-1	Kazim-Richards 90	21,787
17	div1	Ipswich	H	D	1-1	Hammond 15	6,867
18	div1	Wolverhampton	H	D	1-1	Frutos 40	6,642
19	div1	Stoke	A	L	0-3		15,274
20	div1	Crystal Palace	H	L	2-3	Knight 22,53 pen	7,273
21	div1	Cardiff	A	D	1-1	Kazim-Richards 76	9,595
22	div1	Derby	H	D	0-0		6,855
23	div1	Watford	A	D	1-1	Butters 51	14,455
24	div1	Reading	A	L	1-5	Kazim-Richards 84	18,546
25	div1	Hull City	H	W	2-1	Carole 16; Oatway 45	6,929
26	div1	QPR	H	W	1-0	Butters 7	7,341
27	div1	Luton	A	L	0-3		9,429
28	div1	Millwall	H	L	1-2	Hammond 3	6,847
29	div1	Southampton	A	L	1-2	Mayo 21	24,630
30	facr3	Coventry	H	L	0-1		6,734
31	div1	Leeds	H	W	2-1	Reid 10; Hart 80	7,415
32	div1	Sheff Utd	A	L	1-3	Kazim-Richards 83	27,514
33	div1	Burnley	H	D	0-0		6,267
34	div1	Coventry	A	L	0-2		20,541
35	div1	Leicester	H	L	1-2	Frutos 56	7,187
36	div1	Norwich	A	L	0-3		24,038
37	div1	Watford	H	L	0-1		6,658
38	div1	Crewe	A	L	1-2	Kazim-Richards 10	5,925
39	div1	Plymouth	A	L	0-1		13,650
40	div1	Preston	H	D	0-0		6,361
41	div1	QPR	A	D	1-1	Bignot 80 og	13,907
42	div1	Luton	H	D	1-1	Noel-Williams 18	7,139
43	div1	Millwall	A	W	2-0	Reid 6; McShane 11	13,209
44	div1	Southampton	H	L	0-2		7,999
45	div1	Ipswich	A	W	2-1	Noel-Williams 45; Lynch 73	23,964
46	div1	Sheff Wed	H	L	0-2		7,573
47	div1	Wolverhampton	A	L	0-1		22,555
48	div1	Stoke	H	L	1-5	Loft 84	5,859

LEAGUE APPEARANCES AND BOOKINGS

	AGE (on 01/07/06)	IN NAMED 16	APPEARANCES	COUNTING GAMES	MINUTES ON PITCH	LEAGUE GOALS	
Goalkeepers							
Alan Blayney	24	15	8	8	720	0	0
Florent Chaigneau	22	23	1	1	90	0	0
Wayne Henderson	22	33	32	32	2880	0	2
Michel Kuipers	32	7	5	5	450	0	0
Richard Martin	18	13	0	0	0	0	0
Defenders							
Guy Butters	36	46	45	43	3863	2	2
Jason Dodd	35	12	7	4	465	0	0
Adam El-Abd	21	36	29	22	2163	0	7
Gary Elphick	20	2	2	0	49	0	2
Adam Hinshelwood	22	13	11	9	884	0	3
Joel Lynch	18	17	16	13	1349	1	2
Kerry Mayo	28	28	18	11	1260	1	1
Paul McShane	20	38	38	37	3347	4	11
Paul Reid	27	42	38	33	3160	2	5
Midfielders							
Sebastien Carole	23	41	39	30	2961	2	2
Richard Carpenter	33	32	32	30	2766	1	5
Dean Cox	18	2	1	0	3	0	0
Tommy Elphick	18	11	1	0	18	0	0
Alexandre Frutos	24	37	36	18	2383	3	2
Dean Hammond	23	41	41	40	3625	4	11
Gary Hart	29	36	34	29	2782	1	9
Albert Jarrett	21	11	11	4	657	0	2
Douglas Loft	19	6	3	0	60	1	0
Chris McPhee	23	9	7	2	250	0	0
Alexis Nicolas	23	24	11	4	583	0	2
Charlie Oatway	32	23	18	14	1348	1	1
Forwards							
Joe Gatting	18	14	12	5	519	0	0
Colin Kazim-Richards	19	44	42	21	2580	6	8
Leon Knight	23	25	25	20	1978	3	4
Mark McCammon	27	7	7	2	340	0	1
Gifton Noel-Williams	26	7	7	7	610	2	0
Jake Robinson	19	34	27	7	1192	1	2
Federico Turienzo	23	6	4	0	117	0	0

TEAM OF THE SEASON

G — Wayne Henderson CG: 32 DR: 65

D — Paul McShane CG: 37 DR: 64

D — Paul Reid CG: 33 DR: 63

D — Joel Lynch CG: 13 DR: 59

D — Guy Butters CG: 43 DR: 57

M — Gary Hart CG: 29 SD: -30

M — Dean Hammond CG: 40 SD: -43

M — Charlie Oatway CG: 14 SD: -45

M — Richard Carpenter CG: 30 SD: -46

F — C Kazim-Richards CG: 21 SR: 430

F — Leon Knight CG: 20 SR: 659

MONTHLY POINTS TALLY

AUGUST	6	33%
SEPTEMBER	4	27%
OCTOBER	5	33%
NOVEMBER	3	20%
DECEMBER	7	39%
JANUARY	4	33%
FEBRUARY	0	0%
MARCH	3	25%
APRIL	6	33%

LEAGUE GOALS

	PLAYER	LGE	FAC	LC	Oth	TOT
1	Kazim-Richards	6	0	0	0	6
2	Hammond	4	0	0	0	4
3	McShane	4	0	0	0	4
4	Knight	3	0	0	0	3
5	Frutos	3	0	0	0	3
6	Reid	2	0	0	0	2
7	Carole	2	0	0	0	2
8	Butters	2	0	0	0	2
9	Noel-Williams	2	0	0	0	2
10	Oatway	1	0	0	0	1
11	Robinson	1	0	1	0	2
	Other	9	0	1	0	10
	TOTAL	39	0	2	0	41

TOP POINT EARNERS

	PLAYER	GAMES	AV PTS
1	Paul Reid	33	1.06
2	Charlie Oatway	14	1.00
3	Gary Hart	29	0.97
4	Dean Hammond	40	0.93
5	Colin Kazim-Richards	21	0.90
6	Paul McShane	37	0.86
7	Joel Lynch	13	0.85
8	Leon Knight	20	0.85
9	Sebastien Carole	30	0.83
10	Guy Butters	43	0.81
	CLUB AVERAGE:		0.83

DISCIPLINARY RECORDS

	PLAYER	YELLOW	RED	AVE
1	Hinshelwood	3	1	221
2	Hart	9	1	278
3	Hammond	11	2	278
4	Nicolas	2	0	291
5	McShane	11	0	304
6	El-Abd	7	0	309
7	Kazim-Richards	8	0	322
8	Jarrett	2	0	328
9	Knight	4	0	494
10	Carpenter	5	0	553
11	Robinson	2	0	596
12	Reid	5	0	632
13	Lynch	2	0	674
	Other	10	0	
	TOTAL	81	4	

KEY GOALKEEPER

Wayne Henderson

Goals Conceded in the League	44	Counting Games League games when player was on pitch for at least 70 minutes	32
Goals Conceded in all competitions	44		
Defensive Rating Ave number of mins between League goals conceded while on the pitch	65	Clean Sheets In games when player was on pitch for at least 70 minutes	7

KEY PLAYERS - DEFENDERS

Paul McShane

Goals Conceded in the League	52	Clean Sheets In League games when player was on pitch for at least 70 minutes	8
Goals Conceded in all competitions	56		
Defensive Rating Ave number of mins between League goals conceded while on the pitch	64	Club Defensive Rating Average number of mins between League goals conceded by the club this season	58

	PLAYER	CON LGE	CON ALL	CLN SHEETS	DEF RATE
1	Paul McShane	52	56	8	64 mins
2	Paul Reid	50	53	8	63 mins
3	Joel Lynch	23	23	2	59 mins
4	Guy Butters	68	72	8	57 mins

KEY PLAYERS - MIDFIELDERS

Gary Hart

Goals in the League	1	Contribution to Attacking Power Average number of minutes between League team goals while on pitch	90
Goals in all competitions	1		
Defensive Rating Average number of mins between League goals conceded while on the pitch	60	Scoring Difference Defensive Rating minus Contribution to Attacking Power	-30

	PLAYER	GOALS LGE	GOALS ALL	DEF RATE	ATT POWER	SCORE DIFF
1	Gary Hart	1	1	60	90	-30 mins
2	Dean Hammond	4	4	61	104	-43 mins
3	Charlie Oatway	1	1	59	104	-45 mins
4	Richard Carpenter	1	1	56	102	-46 mins

KEY PLAYERS - GOALSCORERS

Colin Kazim-Richards

Goals in the League	6	Player Strike Rate Average number of minutes between League goals scored by player	430
Goals in all competitions	6		
Contribution to Attacking Power Average number of minutes between League team goals while on pitch	103	Club Strike Rate Average number of minutes between League goals scored by club	106

	PLAYER	GOALS LGE	GOALS ALL	POWER	S RATE
1	Colin Kazim-Richards	6	6	103	430 mins
2	Leon Knight	3	3	94	659 mins
3	Alexandre Frutos	3	3	119	794 mins
4	Paul McShane	4	4	112	837 mins

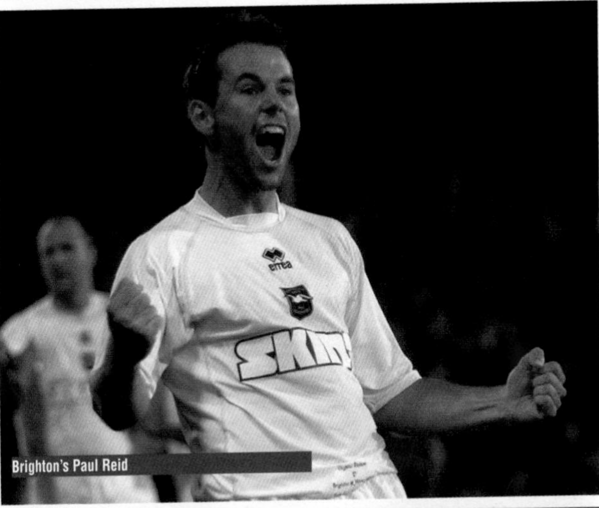

Brighton's Paul Reid

SQUAD APPEARANCES

Match	1	2	3	4	5	6	7	8	9	10	11	12	13	14	15	16	17	18	19	20	21	22	23	24	25
Venue	A	H	H	A	A	A	H	A	H	H	A	A	H	H	A	A	H	H	A	H	A	H	A	A	H
Competition	L	L	L	L	W	L	L	L	L	L	L	L	L	L	L	L	L	L	L	L	L	L	L	L	L
Result	D	L	D	L	L	D	W	D	L	D	D	D	L	L	W	D	D	D	L	L	D	D	D	L	W

Match	26	27	28	29	30	31	32	33	34	35	36	37	38	39	40	41	42	43	44	45	46	47	48
Venue	H	A	H	A	H	H	A	H	A	H	A	H	A	A	H	A	H	A	H	A	H	A	H
Competition	L	L	L	L	F	L	L	L	L	L	L	L	L	L	L	L	L	L	L	L	L	L	L
Result	W	L	L	L	L	W	L	D	L	L	L	L	L	L	D	D	D	W	L	W	L	L	L

Goalkeepers
Alan Blayney
Florent Chaigneau
Wayne Henderson
Michel Kuipers
Richard Martin

Defenders
Guy Butters
Jason Dodd
Adam El-Abd
Gary Elphick
Adam Hinshelwood
Joel Lynch
Kerry Mayo
Paul McShane
Paul Reid

Midfielders
Sebastien Carole
Richard Carpenter
Dean Cox
Tommy Elphick
Alexandre Frutos
Dean Hammond
Gary Hart
Albert Jarrett
Douglas Loft
Chris McPhee
Alexis Nicolas
Charlie Oatway

Forwards
Joe Gatting
Colin Kazim-Richards
Leon Knight
Mark McCammon
Gifton Noel-Williams
Jake Robinson
Federico Turienzo

KEY: On all match · On bench · Subbed or sent off (Counting game) · Subbed or sent off (playing less than 70 minutes) · Subbed on from bench (Counting Game) · Subbed on (playing less than 70 minutes) · Subbed on and then subbed or sent off (Counting Game) · Subbed on and then subbed or sent off (playing less than 70 minutes) · Not in 16

LEAGUE ONE ROUND-UP

FINAL LEAGUE TABLE

	P	HOME W	D	L	F	A	AWAY W	D	L	F	A	TOTAL F	A	DIF	PTS
Southend	46	13	6	4	37	16	10	7	6	35	27	72	43	29	82
Colchester	46	15	4	4	39	21	7	9	7	19	19	58	40	18	79
Brentford	46	10	8	5	35	23	10	8	5	37	29	72	52	20	76
Huddersfield	46	13	6	4	40	25	6	10	7	32	34	72	59	13	73
Barnsley	46	11	11	1	37	19	7	7	9	25	25	62	44	18	72
Swansea	46	11	9	3	42	23	7	8	8	36	32	78	55	23	71
Nottm Forest	46	14	5	4	40	15	5	7	11	27	37	67	52	15	69
Doncaster	46	11	6	6	30	19	9	3	11	25	32	55	51	4	69
Bristol City	46	11	7	5	38	22	7	4	12	28	40	66	62	4	65
Oldham	46	12	4	7	32	24	6	7	10	26	36	58	60	-2	65
Bradford	46	8	9	6	28	25	6	10	7	23	24	51	49	2	61
Scunthorpe	46	8	8	7	36	33	7	7	9	32	40	68	73	-5	60
Port Vale	46	10	5	8	30	26	6	7	10	19	28	49	54	-5	60
Gillingham	46	13	4	6	31	21	3	8	12	19	43	50	64	-14	60
Yeovil	46	8	8	7	27	24	7	3	13	27	38	54	62	-8	56
Chesterfield	46	6	7	10	31	37	8	7	8	32	36	63	73	-10	56
Bournemouth	46	7	11	5	25	20	5	8	10	24	33	49	53	-4	55
Tranmere	46	7	8	8	32	30	6	7	10	18	22	50	52	-2	54
Blackpool	46	9	8	6	33	27	3	9	11	23	37	56	64	-8	53
Rotherham	46	7	9	7	31	26	5	7	11	21	36	52	62	-10	52
Hartlepool	46	6	10	7	28	30	5	7	11	16	29	44	59	-15	50
MK Dons	46	8	8	7	28	25	4	6	13	17	41	45	66	-21	50
Swindon	46	9	5	9	31	31	2	10	11	15	34	46	65	-19	48
Walsall	46	7	7	9	27	34	4	7	12	20	36	47	70	-23	47

CLUB STRIKE FORCE

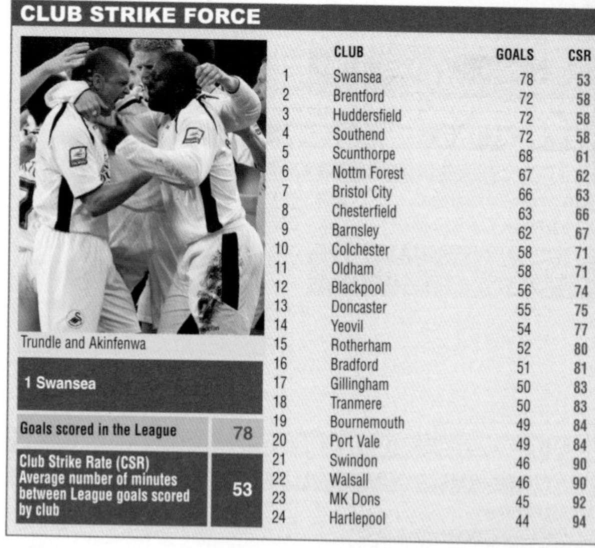

Trundle and Akinfenwa

1 Swansea

Goals scored in the League	78
Club Strike Rate (CSR) Average number of minutes between League goals scored by club	53

	CLUB	GOALS	CSR
1	Swansea	78	53
2	Brentford	72	58
3	Huddersfield	72	58
4	Southend	72	58
5	Scunthorpe	68	61
6	Nottm Forest	67	62
7	Bristol City	66	63
8	Chesterfield	63	66
9	Barnsley	62	67
10	Colchester	58	71
11	Oldham	58	71
12	Blackpool	56	74
13	Doncaster	55	75
14	Yeovil	54	77
15	Rotherham	52	80
16	Bradford	51	81
17	Gillingham	50	83
18	Tranmere	50	83
19	Bournemouth	49	84
20	Port Vale	49	84
21	Swindon	46	90
22	Walsall	46	90
23	MK Dons	45	92
24	Hartlepool	44	94

CLUB DISCIPLINARY RECORDS

Nardiello: 11 cards for Barnsley

1 Barnsley

League Yellow	100
League Red	7
League Total	107
Cards Average in League Average number of minutes between a card being shown of either colour	39

	CLUB	Y	R	TOTAL	AVE
1	Barnsley	100	7	107	39
2	Gillingham	93	8	101	41
3	Walsall	87	5	92	45
4	Swansea	83	7	90	46
5	Blackpool	81	5	86	48
6	Huddersfield	80	6	86	48
7	Swindon	81	5	86	48
8	MK Dons	80	4	84	49
9	Tranmere	78	4	82	50
10	Brentford	75	5	80	52
11	Rotherham	71	9	80	52
12	Hartlepool	69	6	75	55
13	Bradford	68	4	72	58
14	Bristol City	67	3	70	59
15	Port Vale	67	3	70	59
16	Nottm Forest	62	7	69	60
17	Scunthorpe	62	4	66	63
18	Doncaster	59	5	64	65
19	Colchester	59	4	63	66
20	Southend	56	1	57	73
21	Chesterfield	50	2	52	80
22	Oldham	48	2	50	83
23	Yeovil	41	4	45	92
24	Bournemouth	39	3	42	99

CLUB DEFENCES

	CLUB	LGE	CS	CDR
1	Colchester	40	19	104
2	Barnsley	43	20	96
3	Southend	43	16	96
4	Bradford	49	16	84
5	Doncaster	51	16	81
6	Brentford	52	13	80
7	Nottm Forest	52	13	80
8	Tranmere	52	14	80
9	Bournemouth	53	13	78
10	Port Vale	54	11	77
11	Swansea	55	9	75
12	Hartlepool	59	8	70
13	Huddersfield	59	12	70
14	Oldham	60	14	69
15	Bristol City	62	13	67
16	Rotherham	62	14	67
17	Yeovil	62	13	67
18	Blackpool	64	12	65
19	Gillingham	64	13	65
20	Swindon	65	11	64
21	MK Dons	66	9	63
22	Walsall	70	11	59
23	Chesterfield	73	9	57
24	Scunthorpe	73	10	57

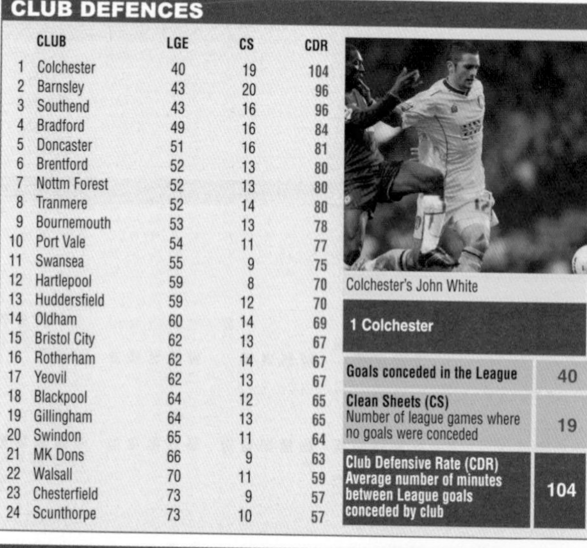

Colchester's John White

1 Colchester

Goals conceded in the League	40
Clean Sheets (CS) Number of league games where no goals were conceded	19
Club Defensive Rate (CDR) Average number of minutes between League goals conceded by club	104

STADIUM CAPACITY AND HOME CROWDS

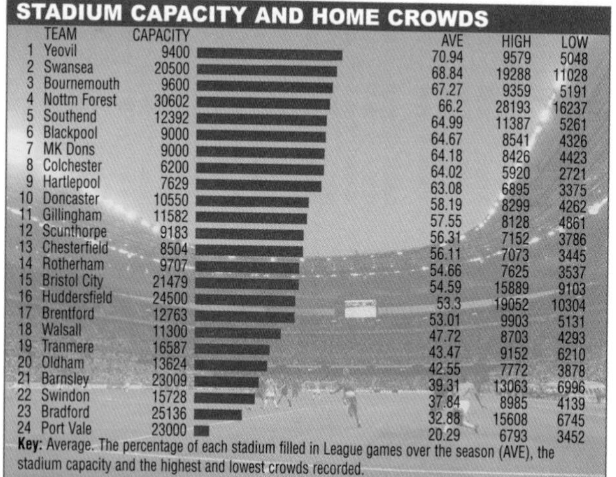

	TEAM	CAPACITY	AVE	HIGH	LOW
1	Yeovil	9400	70.94	9579	5048
2	Swansea	20500	68.84	19288	11028
3	Bournemouth	9600	67.27	9359	5191
4	Nottm Forest	30602	66.2	28193	16237
5	Southend	12392	64.99	11387	5261
6	Blackpool	9000	64.67	8541	4326
7	MK Dons	9000	64.18	8426	4423
8	Colchester	6200	64.02	5920	2721
9	Hartlepool	7629	63.08	6895	3375
10	Doncaster	10550	58.19	8299	4262
11	Gillingham	11582	57.55	8128	4861
12	Scunthorpe	9183	56.31	7152	3786
13	Chesterfield	8504	56.11	7073	3445
14	Rotherham	9707	54.66	7625	3537
15	Bristol City	21479	54.59	15889	9103
16	Huddersfield	24500	53.3	19052	10304
17	Brentford	12763	53.01	9903	5131
18	Walsall	11300	47.72	8703	4293
19	Tranmere	16587	43.47	9152	6210
20	Oldham	13624	42.55	7772	3878
21	Barnsley	23009	39.31	13063	6996
22	Swindon	15728	37.84	8985	4139
23	Bradford	25136	32.88	15608	6745
24	Port Vale	23000	20.29	6793	3452

Key: Average. The percentage of each stadium filled in League games over the season (AVE), the stadium capacity and the highest and lowest crowds recorded.

AWAY ATTENDANCE

	TEAM	AVE	HIGH	LOW
1	Nottm Forest	70.72	18212	5336
2	Huddersfield	58.08	24042	3415
3	Bradford	57.12	17983	4449
4	Bristol City	56.75	16666	3786
5	Doncaster	56.68	23009	2721
6	Rotherham	56.17	20123	4309
7	Barnsley	56.09	19052	2721
8	Swansea	55.85	19132	2950
9	Southend	55.76	19576	3929
10	Yeovil	54.53	28193	3409
11	Gillingham	54.11	19446	3801
12	Swindon	53.57	22444	3537
13	Walsall	53.52	20912	3810
14	Scunthorpe	53.2	19091	3984
15	Port Vale	52.95	17696	3883
16	Brentford	52.91	17234	4121
17	Chesterfield	52.54	21909	3414
18	Tranmere	51.35	22022	3445
19	Oldham	51.14	17807	2742
20	Hartlepool	50.85	17586	3916
21	Blackpool	50.38	17071	3031
22	Colchester	49.88	22680	3375
23	Bournemouth	49.07	26847	3120
24	MK Dons	48.71	18214	3400

Key: Average. How close each club has come to filling grounds in its away league matches (AVE) and the highest and lowest crowds recorded.

CHART-TOPPING MIDFIELDERS

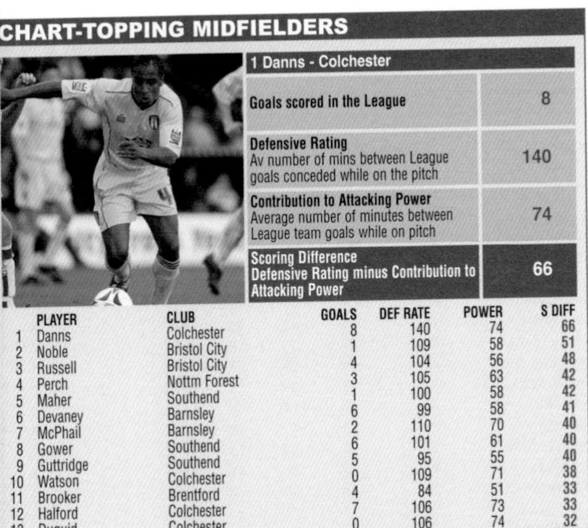

1 Danns - Colchester	
Goals scored in the League	8
Defensive Rating Av number of mins between League goals conceded while on the pitch	140
Contribution to Attacking Power Average number of minutes between League team goals while on pitch	74
Scoring Difference Defensive Rating minus Contribution to Attacking Power	66

	PLAYER	CLUB	GOALS	DEF RATE	POWER	S DIFF
1	Danns	Colchester	8	140	74	66
2	Noble	Bristol City	1	109	58	51
3	Russell	Bristol City	4	104	56	48
4	Perch	Nottm Forest	3	105	63	42
5	Maher	Southend	1	100	58	42
6	Devaney	Barnsley	6	99	58	41
7	McPhail	Barnsley	2	110	70	40
8	Gower	Southend	6	101	61	40
9	Guttridge	Southend	5	95	55	40
10	Watson	Colchester	0	109	71	38
11	Brooker	Brentford	4	84	51	33
12	Halford	Colchester	7	106	73	33
13	Duguid	Colchester	0	106	74	32
14	Bentley	Southend	5	94	62	32
15	Howard	Barnsley	5	91	60	31

CHART-TOPPING GOALSCORERS

1 Sharp - Scunthorpe	
Goals scored in the League	23
Contribution to Attacking Power Average number of minutes between League team goals while on pitch	63
Club Strike Rate (CSR) Average minutes between League goals scored by club	61
Player Strike Rate Average number of minutes between League goals scored by player	132

	PLAYER	CLUB	GOALS: LGE	POWER	CSR	S RATE
1	Sharp	Scunthorpe	23	63	61	132
2	Eastwood	Southend	23	56	58	135
3	Beckett	Oldham	18	76	71	136
4	Graham	Huddersfield	9	57	58	146
5	Trundle	Swansea	20	53	53	150
6	Byfield	Gillingham	14	75	81	170
7	McLeod	MK Dons	17	78	92	174
8	Burton	Rotherham	12	81	80	175
9	Fryatt	Walsall	11	64	88	175
10	Fallon	Swindon	12	88	90	183
11	Brooker	Bristol City	15	59	63	200
12	Abbott	Huddersfield	12	55	58	200
13	Hayter	Bournemouth	20	86	84	207
14	Jevons	Yeovil	15	76	77	208
15	Richards	Barnsley	12	65	67	212

CHART-TOPPING DEFENDERS

Efe Sodje playing for Yeovil

1 Sodje - Southend	
Goals Conceded in the League The number of League goals conceded while he was on the pitch	5
Clean Sheets In games when he played at least 70 mins	9
Club Defensive Rating Average mins between League goals conceded by the club this season	96
Defensive Rating Average number of minutes between League goals conceded while on pitch	226

	PLAYER	CLUB	CON: LGE	CS	CDR	DEF RATE
1	Sodje	Southend	5	9	96	226
2	Baldwin	Colchester	15	9	104	118
3	Fontaine	Bristol City	11	5	67	113
4	Jupp	Southend	23	13	96	110
5	Hassell	Barnsley	20	10	94	109
6	Brown	Colchester	32	15	104	106
7	Sancho	Gillingham	13	6	65	106
8	Marples	Doncaster	11	6	81	105
9	Chilvers	Colchester	29	14	104	102
10	Austin	Barnsley	32	16	94	100
11	White	Colchester	27	12	104	100
12	Prior	Southend	12	6	96	100
13	Stockley	Colchester	21	8	104	99
14	Kay	Barnsley	30	12	94	97
15	Howe	Bournemouth	15	5	78	97

CHART-TOPPING GOALKEEPERS

2 Davison - Colchester	
Counting Games Games in which he played at least 70 minutes	41
Goals Conceded in the League The number of League goals conceded while he was on the pitch	35
Clean Sheets In games when he played at least 70 mins	16
Defensive Rating Average number of minutes between League goals conceded while on pitch	104

	PLAYER	CLUB	CG	CONC	CS	DEF RATE
1	Seremet	Tranmere	13	10	5	117
2	Davison	Colchester	41	35	16	104
3	Blayney	Doncaster	16	14	9	103
4	Colgan	Barnsley	43	39	19	99
5	Flahavan	Southend	43	39	15	99
6	Ricketts	Bradford	36	32	15	98
7	Basso	Bristol City	29	27	9	93
8	Grant, L	Oldham	16	16	5	90
9	Senior	Huddersfield	13	14	5	80
10	Cutler	Rotherham	22	25	8	79
11	Nelson	Brentford	45	51	13	78
12	Stewart	Bournemouth	42	49	12	77
13	Gerrard	Nottm Forest	22	24	6	77
14	Goodlad	Port Vale	46	54	11	77
15	Pedersen	Nottm Forest	18	21	4	75

PLAYER DISCIPLINARY RECORD

Gurney: 14 cards for Swindon

1 Wright - Blackpool	
Cards Average mins between cards	102
League Yellow	7
League Red	1
TOTAL	8

	PLAYER		LY	LR	TOT	AVE
1	Wright	Blackpool	7	1	8	102
2	Nardiello	Barnsley	10	1	11	130
3	Demontagnac	Walsall	7	2	9	149
4	Gurney	Swindon	13	1	14	151
5	Rowland	Port Vale	7	1	8	159
6	Barron	Hartlepool	5	1	6	169
7	Pouton	Gillingham	7	1	8	197
8	Byfield	Gillingham	10	2	12	198
9	Butler	Hartlepool	10	1	11	200
10	Williamson	Rotherham	15	1	16	201
11	Ravenhill	Doncaster	9	1	10	206
12	McGregor	Port Vale	6	0	6	207
13	Lester	Nottm Forest	6	1	7	212
14	Hudson	Huddersfield	9	1	10	215
15	Roper	Walsall	9	1	10	215
16	Clarke, T	Huddersfield	4	2	6	218
17	Ifil	Swindon	11	3	14	221
18	Holloway	Bradford	6	2	8	225
19	McAteer	Tranmere	8	1	9	225
20	Bruce	Tranmere	4	0	4	225
21	Osborn	Walsall	10	0	10	237
22	Tinkler	Hartlepool	3	1	4	238
23	Mills	MK Dons	6	0	6	240
24	Mills	Walsall	5	0	5	243
25	O'Leary	Swansea	2	2	4	246

TEAM OF THE SEASON

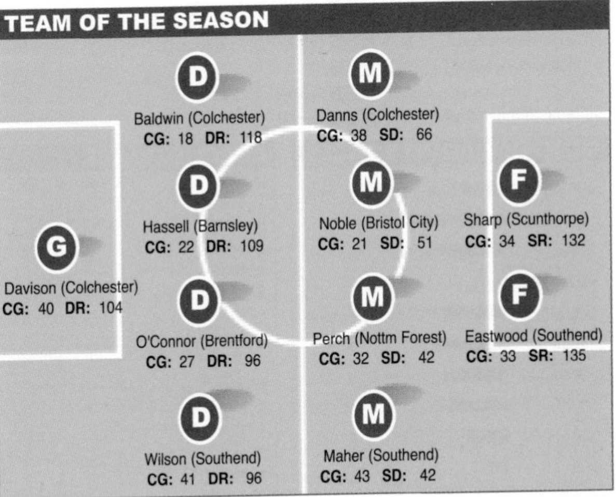

LEAGUE ONE CHAMPIONS

SOUTHEND UNITED

Final Position: **1st**

NICKNAME: THE SHRIMPERS

KEY: ☐Won ☐Drawn ☐Lost

							Attendance
1	div2	Port Vale	H	L	1-2	Gray 72	6,543
2	div2	Bradford	A	W	2-0	Wetherall 15 og; Guttridge 62	8,250
3	div2	Walsall	A	D	2-2	Gray 49; Goater 89	5,569
4	div2	Huddersfield	H	D	1-1	Eastwood 14	5,567
5	ccr1	Southampton	H	L	0-3		6,358
6	div2	Scunthorpe	A	L	0-1		5,569
7	div2	Colchester	H	W	3-1	Goater 3,78; Cole 30	7,344
8	div2	Oldham	H	W	2-1	Lawson 11; Gower 45	5,261
9	div2	Swindon	A	W	2-1	Barrett 2; Gray 88	4,785
10	div2	Tranmere	H	W	3-1	Lawson 16; Goater 33 pen,82	6,691
11	div2	Rotherham	A	W	4-2	Bentley 18; Barrett 26; Gray 84,88 pen	4,259
12	div2	Yeovil	H	W	4-1	Guttridge 60; Gray 69; Eastwood 89,90	6,654
13	div2	Gillingham	A	W	2-1	Bentley 56,70	8,128
14	div2	Nottm Forest	H	W	1-0	Eastwood 81	10,104
15	div2	Doncaster	A	L	0-2		5,899
16	div2	Barnsley	H	D	1-1	Goater 59 pen	6,986
17	div2	Bristol City	A	W	3-0	Eastwood 25,48,76	10,625
18	facr1	Barnet	A	W	1-0	Eastwood 2	3,545
19	div2	Swansea	H	L	1-2	Eastwood 81	11,049
20	div2	Nottm Forest	A	L	0-2		19,576
21	div2	Port Vale	A	L	1-2	Smith 90	3,961
22	facr2	MK Dons	H	L	1-2	Eastwood 58	5,267
23	div2	Chesterfield	H	D	0-0		5,767
24	div2	Bradford	H	D	1-1	Gower 45	7,307
25	div2	Huddersfield	A	D	0-0		11,223
26	div2	MK Dons	H	D	0-0		7,452
27	div2	Hartlepool	A	W	2-1	Eastwood 32; Gray 85 pen	3,929
28	div2	Bournemouth	H	W	2-1	Gray 22 pen; Guttridge 78	6,357
29	div2	Blackpool	A	W	2-1	Bentley 39; Eastwood 89	5,271
30	div2	Oldham	A	D	0-0		5,662
31	div2	Brentford	H	W	4-1	Sodje, E 19; Gower 31; Barrett 63; Wilson 78	10,046
32	div2	Tranmere	A	D	0-0		7,058
33	div2	Swindon	H	W	2-0	Guttridge 31; Gower 32	7,945
34	div2	Yeovil	A	W	2-0	Bentley 36; Goater 75	6,289
35	div2	Rotherham	H	W	2-0	Goater 12; Eastwood 36	7,879
36	div2	Brentford	A	L	0-2		7,022
37	div2	Chesterfield	A	W	4-3	Eastwood 52 pen,56,83; Goater 74	4,527
38	div2	Walsall	H	D	0-0		7,906
39	div2	Colchester	A	W	3-0	Eastwood 11; Maher 21; Wilson 32	5,920
40	div2	Scunthorpe	H	W	3-0	Eastwood 7; Bradbury 54; Goater 75	8,717
41	div2	MK Dons	A	L	1-2	Goater 13	7,071
42	div2	Hartlepool	H	W	3-0	Gower 1; Eastwood 51,71	8,496
43	div2	Bournemouth	A	D	1-1	Eastwood 20	7,638
44	div2	Blackpool	H	W	2-1	Eastwood 60; Guttridge 86	8,180
45	div2	Gillingham	H	L	0-1		11,195
46	div2	Barnsley	A	D	2-2	Gower 52; Eastwood 61	10,663
47	div2	Doncaster	H	L	0-1		10,397
48	div2	Swansea	A	D	2-2	Eastwood 28,63	19,176
49	div2	Bristol City	H	W	1-0	Gray 87	11,387

LEAGUE APPEARANCES, BOOKINGS AND GOALS

	AGE (on 01/07/06)	IN NAMED 16	APPEARANCES	COUNTING GAMES	MINUTES ON PITCH	LEAGUE GOALS		
Goalkeepers								
Darryl Flahavan	27	43	43	43	3870	0	1	0
Bart Griemink	34	14	3	3	270	0	0	0
Defenders								
Adam Barrett	26	45	45	45	4046	3	4	1
Andrew Edwards	34	26	20	19	1717	0	1	0
Lewis Hunt	23	39	30	24	2208	0	1	0
Duncan Jupp	31	32	29	28	2529	0	2	0
Gerard Nash	19	2	0	0	0	0	0	0
Spencer Prior	35	29	17	13	1204	0	3	0
Efetobore Sodje	33	13	13	13	1130	1	1	0
Che Wilson	27	45	44	41	3746	2	4	0
Mark Wright	19	3	0	0	0	0	0	0
Midfielders								
Mark Bentley	28	38	33	18	1975	5	6	0
Jamal Campbell-Ryce	23	13	13	5	613	0	2	0
Mitchell Cole	20	39	29	14	1544	1	0	0
Mark Gower	27	40	40	31	3026	6	4	0
Luke Guttridge	24	41	41	36	3417	5	11	0
Kevin Maher	29	44	44	43	3904	1	9	0
Franck Moussa	-	1	1	0	1	0	0	0
Carl Pettefer	25	28	11	4	432	0	0	0
Jay Smith	24	26	13	2	336	1	0	0
Forwards								
Charles Ademeno	17	5	1	0	4	0	0	0
Lee Bradbury	31	15	15	10	1016	1	1	0
Fredy Eastwood	23	40	40	33	3110	23	4	0
Shaun Goater	36	35	34	26	2372	11	0	0
Wayne Gray	25	39	39	22	2237	9	1	0
James Lawson	19	40	23	6	829	2	1	0

TEAM OF THE SEASON

MONTHLY POINTS TALLY

AUGUST	8	44%
SEPTEMBER	15	100%
OCTOBER	10	67%
NOVEMBER	0	0%
DECEMBER	10	56%
JANUARY	11	73%
FEBRUARY	10	67%
MARCH	9	75%
APRIL	6	33%
MAY	3	100%

LEAGUE GOALS

	PLAYER	LGE	FAC	LC	Oth	TOT
1	Eastwood	23	2	0	0	25
2	Goater	11	0	0	0	11
3	Gray	9	0	0	0	9
4	Gower	6	0	0	0	6
5	Bentley	5	0	0	0	5
6	Guttridge	5	0	0	0	5
7	Barrett	3	0	0	0	3
8	Wilson	2	0	0	0	2
9	Lawson	2	0	0	0	2
10	Bradbury	1	0	0	0	1
11	Smith	1	0	0	0	1
	Other	4	0	0	0	4
	TOTAL	72	2	0	0	74

TOP POINT EARNERS

	PLAYER	GAMES	AV PTS
1	Shaun Goater	26	**2.04**
2	Mitchell Cole	14	**2.00**
3	Luke Guttridge	36	**1.94**
4	Efetobore Sodje	13	**1.92**
5	Andrew Edwards	19	**1.89**
6	Mark Bentley	18	**1.89**
7	Darryl Flahavan	43	**1.84**
8	Duncan Jupp	28	**1.82**
9	Mark Gower	31	**1.81**
10	Kevin Maher	43	**1.81**

DISCIPLINARY RECORDS

	PLAYER	YELLOW	RED	AVE
1	Campbell-Ryce	2	0	**306**
2	Guttridge	11	0	**310**
3	Bentley	6	0	**329**
4	Prior	3	0	**401**
5	Maher	9	0	**433**
6	Gower	4	0	**756**
7	Eastwood	4	0	**777**
8	Barrett	4	1	**809**
9	Lawson	1	0	**829**
10	Wilson	4	0	**936**
11	Bradbury	1	0	**1016**
12	Sodje, E	1	0	**1130**
13	Jupp	2	0	**1264**
	Other	4	0	
	TOTAL	56	1	

KEY GOALKEEPER

Darryl Flahavan

Goals Conceded in the League	39	Counting Games League games when player was on pitch for at least 70 minutes	43
Goals Conceded in all competitions	44		
Defensive Rating Ave number of mins between League goals conceded while on the pitch	99	Clean Sheets In games when player was on pitch for at least 70 minutes	15

KEY PLAYERS - DEFENDERS

Efetobore Sodje

Goals Conceded in the League	5	Clean Sheets In League games when player was on pitch for at least 70 minutes	9
Goals Conceded in all competitions	5		
Defensive Rating Ave number of mins between League goals conceded while on the pitch	226	Club Defensive Rating Average number of mins between League goals conceded by the club this season	96

	PLAYER	CON LGE	CON ALL	CLN SHEETS	DEF RATE
1	Efetobore Sodje	5	5	9	226 mins
2	Duncan Jupp	23	23	13	110 mins
3	Spencer Prior	12	17	6	100 mins
4	Che Wilson	40	45	13	94 mins

KEY PLAYERS - MIDFIELDERS

Kevin Maher

Goals in the League	1	Contribution to Attacking Power Average number of minutes between League team goals while on pitch	58
Goals in all competitions	1		
Defensive Rating Average number of mins between League goals conceded while on the pitch	100	Scoring Difference Defensive Rating minus Contribution to Attacking Power	42

	PLAYER	GOALS LGE	GOALS ALL	DEF RATE	ATT POWER	SCORE DIFF
1	Kevin Maher	1	1	100	58	42 mins
2	Mark Gower	6	6	101	61	40 mins
3	Luke Guttridge	5	5	95	55	40 mins
4	Mark Bentley	5	5	94	62	32 mins

KEY PLAYERS - GOALSCORERS

Fredy Eastwood

Goals in the League	23	Player Strike Rate Average number of minutes between League goals scored by player	135
Goals in all competitions	25		
Contribution to Attacking Power Average number of minutes between League team goals while on pitch	56	Club Strike Rate Average number of minutes between League goals scored by club	58

	PLAYER	GOALS LGE	GOALS ALL	POWER	S RATE
1	Fredy Eastwood	23	25	56	135 mins
2	Shaun Goater	11	11	52	216 mins
3	Wayne Gray	9	9	62	249 mins
4	Mark Bentley	5	5	62	395 mins

Southend captain Kevin Maher with manager Steve Tilson

SQUAD APPEARANCES

Match	1	2	3	4	5	6	7	8	9	10	11	12	13	14	15	16	17	18	19	20	21	22	23	24	25
Venue	H	A	A	H	H	A	H	H	A	H	A	H	A	H	A	H	A	A	H	A	A	H	H	H	A
Competition	L	L	L	L	W	L	L	L	L	L	L	L	L	L	L	L	L	F	L	L	L	F	L	L	L
Result	L	W	D	D	L	L	W	W	W	W	W	W	W	W	L	D	W	W	L	L	L	L	D	D	D

Match	26	27	28	29	30	31	32	33	34	35	36	37	38	39	40	41	42	43	44	45	46	47	48	49
Venue	H	A	H	A	A	H	A	H	A	H	A	A	H	A	H	A	H	A	H	H	A	H	A	H
Competition	L	L	L	L	L	L	L	L	L	L	L	L	L	L	L	L	L	L	L	L	L	L	L	L
Result	D	W	W	W	D	W	D	W	W	W	L	W	D	W	W	L	W	D	W	L	D	L	D	W

Goalkeepers
Darryl Flahavan
Bart Griemink

Defenders
Adam Barrett
Andrew Edwards
Lewis Hunt
Duncan Jupp
Gerard Nash
Spencer Prior
Efetobore Sodje
Che Wilson
Mark Wright

Midfielders
Mark Bentley
Jamal Campbell-Ryce
Mitchell Cole
Mark Gower
Luke Guttridge
Kevin Maher
Franck Moussa
Carl Pettefer
Jay Smith

Forwards
Charles Ademeno
Lee Bradbury
Fredy Eastwood
Shaun Goater
Wayne Gray
James Lawson

KEY: On all match | On bench | Subbed or sent off (Counting game) | Subbed or sent off (playing less than 70 minutes) | Subbed on from bench (Counting Game) | Subbed on (playing less than 70 minutes) | Subbed on and then subbed or sent off (Counting Game) | Subbed on and then subbed or sent off (playing less than 70 minutes) | Not in 16

COLCHESTER UNITED

Final Position: **2nd**

NICKNAME: THE U'S

KEY: ☐ Won ☐ Drawn ☐ Lost

						Scorers	Attendance
1	div2	Gillingham	A	L	1-2	Danns 50	7,293
2	div2	Swansea	H	L	1-2	Halford 67	2,950
3	div2	Barnsley	H	W	1-0	Iwelumo 48	2,721
4	div2	MK Dons	A	D	1-1	Chilvers 79	4,423
5	ccr1	Cardiff	H	L	0-2		1,904
6	div2	Oldham	H	D	0-0		2,742
7	div2	Southend	A	L	1-3	Stockley 19	7,344
8	div2	Bristol City	A	D	0-0		10,180
9	div2	Doncaster	H	W	3-2	Iwelumo 1; McDaid 23 og; Foster 27 og	2,721
10	div2	Port Vale	A	W	1-0	Iwelumo 34	5,166
11	div2	Huddersfield	H	D	1-1	Elokobi 49	3,415
12	div2	Bradford	A	D	1-1	Halford 62	6,891
13	div2	Chesterfield	H	L	1-2	Iwelumo 90	3,414
14	div2	Blackpool	A	W	2-1	Halford 16,90	4,793
15	div2	Bournemouth	H	L	0-1		3,120
16	div2	Tranmere	A	D	0-0		6,612
17	div2	Yeovil	H	W	3-2	Iwelumo 43,90; Cureton 68	3,409
18	facr1	Leamington	H	W	9-1	Halford 39; Brown 44; Iwelumo 48; Cureton 60,71; Watson 64; Yeates 67; Danns 89,90	3,513
19	div2	Rotherham	A	W	2-1	Barker 55 og; Iwelumo 85	3,715
20	div2	Blackpool	H	W	3-2	Iwelumo 34,54 pen; Halford 81	3,031
21	div2	Gillingham	H	W	5-0	Halford 32,52; Cureton 54,66; Brown 70	3,801
22	facr2	Shrewsbury	A	W	2-1	Cureton 23; Iwelumo 52	3,695
23	div2	Hartlepool	A	W	1-0	Cureton 59	3,375
24	div2	Swansea	A	D	1-1	Iwelumo 13	13,230
25	div2	MK Dons	H	W	2-0	Danns 13; Iwelumo 90 pen	3,400
26	div2	Swindon	A	L	0-1		5,531
27	div2	Brentford	A	W	2-0	Yeates 30,86	6,397
28	div2	Nottm Forest	H	W	3-1	Danns 71; Yeates 90; Garcia 90	5,767
29	facr3	Sheff Utd	A	W	2-1	Danns 33; Williams 72	11,820
30	div2	Walsall	A	W	2-0	Danns 76; Iwelumo 88	5,464
31	div2	Bristol City	H	W	3-2	Williams 27; Danns 45,61	4,022
32	div2	Port Vale	H	W	2-1	Garcia 74,87	4,316
33	facr4	Derby	H	W	3-1	Danns 44,52; Garcia 59	5,933
34	div2	Bradford	H	W	3-1	Garcia 41,56; Iwelumo 63	4,503
35	div2	Scunthorpe	H	W	1-0	Iwelumo 45	4,416
36	div2	Huddersfield	A	L	0-2		13,515
37	div2	Walsall	H	D	0-0		3,810
38	facr5	Chelsea	A	L	1-3	Carvalho 28 og	41,810
39	div2	Barnsley	A	L	0-1		9,411
40	div2	Southend	H	L	0-3		5,920
41	div2	Oldham	A	L	0-1		5,822
42	div2	Swindon	H	W	1-0	Iwelumo 14 pen	3,767
43	div2	Doncaster	A	D	0-0		4,262
44	div2	Scunthorpe	A	D	0-0		4,608
45	div2	Brentford	H	D	1-1	Iwelumo 31	5,635
46	div2	Nottm Forest	A	L	0-1		22,680
47	div2	Hartlepool	H	W	2-0	Danns 83,90	3,916
48	div2	Chesterfield	A	D	2-2	Yeates 45; Iwelumo 73	3,649
49	div2	Tranmere	H	W	1-0	Brown 62	4,757
50	div2	Bournemouth	A	W	2-1	Chilvers 5; Vernon 51	6,231
51	div2	Rotherham	H	W	2-0	Barker 29 og; Yeates 53	5,741
52	div2	Yeovil	A	D	0-0		8,785

LEAGUE APPEARANCES, BOOKINGS AND GOALS

	AGE (on 01/07/06)	IN NAMED 16	APPEARANCES	COUNTING GAMES	MINUTES ON PITCH	LEAGUE GOALS	[yellow card]	[red card]
Goalkeepers								
Mark Cousins	-	7	0	0	0	0	0	[illegible]
Aidan Davison	38	41	41	40	3646	0	0	1
Dean Gerken	21	44	7	5	494	0	0	0
Defenders								
Pat Baldwin	23	38	25	18	1770	0	2	0
Wayne Brown	28	41	38	37	3376	2	4	1
Liam Chilvers	24	36	34	33	2972	2	7	0
George Elokobi	20	18	12	8	847	1	3	0
Dean Howell	25	7	4	0	104	0	1	0
Stephen Hunt	21	2	2	0	31	0	0	0
Garry Richards	20	25	14	10	961	0	1	1
Sam Stockley	28	29	28	21	2073	1	2	0
John White	19	41	35	27	2703	0	2	0
Midfielders								
Jamal Campbell-Ryce	23	6	4	1	196	0	1	0
Neil Danns	23	41	41	38	3352	8	6	0
Karl Duguid	28	36	35	26	2444	0	4	0
Richard Garcia	24	23	22	7	929	5	1	0
Greg Halford	21	45	45	45	4019	7	5	0
Kemal Izzet	25	38	33	17	1783	0	4	1
Robbie King	19	7	3	0	20	0	0	0
Kevin Watson	32	46	44	41	3826	0	3	0
Forwards								
Billy Clarke	18	8	6	1	255	0	2	0
Jamie Cureton	30	8	8	7	559	4	0	0
Jamie Guy	18	8	2	0	14	0	0	0
Chris Iwelumo	27	46	46	45	4097	17	3	0
Tony Thorpe	32	14	14	3	502	0	1	0
Scott Vernon	22	11	7	3	323	1	0	0
Gareth Williams	23	27	18	6	682	1	0	0
Mark Yeates	21	44	44	38	3467	5	7	0

TEAM OF THE SEASON

G — Aidan Davison, CG: 40 DR: 104

D — Pat Baldwin, CG: 18 DR: 118

D — Wayne Brown, CG: 37 DR: 106

D — Liam Chilvers, CG: 33 DR: 102

D — John White, CG: 27 DR: 100

M — Neil Danns, CG: 38 SD: 66

M — Kevin Watson, CG: 41 SD: 38

M — Greg Halford, CG: 45 SD: 33

M — Karl Duguid, CG: 26 SD: 32

F — Chris Iwelumo, CG: 45 SR: 241

F — Mark Yeates, CG: 38 SR: 693

MONTHLY POINTS TALLY

Month	Points	%
AUGUST	5	28%
SEPTEMBER	9	60%
OCTOBER	7	47%
NOVEMBER	9	100%
DECEMBER	10	67%
JANUARY	12	100%
FEBRUARY	7	47%
MARCH	5	33%
APRIL	14	67%
MAY	1	33%

LEAGUE GOALS

	PLAYER	LGE	FAC	LC	Oth	TOT
1	Iwelumo	17	2	0	0	19
2	Danns	8	5	0	0	13
3	Halford	7	1	0	0	8
4	Garcia	5	1	0	0	6
5	Yeates	5	1	0	0	6
6	Cureton	4	3	0	0	7
7	Chilvers	2	0	0	0	2
8	Brown	2	1	0	0	3
9	Vernon	1	0	0	0	1
10	Williams	1	1	0	0	2
11	Stockley	1	0	0	0	1
	Other	5	2	0	0	7
	TOTAL	58	17	0	0	75

TOP POINT EARNERS

	PLAYER	GAMES	AV PTS
1	John White	27	2.15
2	Mark Yeates	38	1.84
3	Kevin Watson	41	1.83
4	Neil Danns	38	1.76
5	Liam Chilvers	33	1.73
6	Chris Iwelumo	45	1.73
7	Pat Baldwin	18	1.72
8	Wayne Brown	37	1.70
9	Aidan Davison	40	1.70
10	Greg Halford	45	1.69

DISCIPLINARY RECORDS

	PLAYER	YELLOW	RED	AVE
1	Elokobi	3	0	282
2	Izzet	4	1	356
3	Chilvers	7	0	424
4	Richards	1	1	480
5	Yeates	7	0	495
6	Thorpe	1	0	502
7	Danns	6	0	558
8	Duguid	4	0	611
9	Brown	4	1	675
10	Halford	5	0	803
11	Baldwin	2	0	885
12	Garcia	1	0	929
13	Stockley	2	0	1036
	Other	8	1	
	TOTAL	55	4	

KEY GOALKEEPER

Aidan Davison

Goals Conceded in the League	35	Counting Games League games when player was on pitch for at least 70 minutes	40
Goals Conceded in all competitions	41		
Defensive Rating Ave number of mins between League goals conceded while on the pitch	104	Clean Sheets In games when player was on pitch for at least 70 minutes	16

KEY PLAYERS - DEFENDERS

Pat Baldwin

Goals Conceded in the League	15	Clean Sheets In League games when player was on pitch for at least 70 minutes	9
Goals Conceded in all competitions	22		
Defensive Rating Ave number of mins between League goals conceded while on the pitch	118	Club Defensive Rating Average number of mins between League goals conceded by the club this season	104

	PLAYER	CON LGE	CON ALL	CLN SHEETS	DEF RATE
1	Pat Baldwin	15	22	9	118 mins
2	Wayne Brown	32	40	15	106 mins
3	Liam Chilvers	29	35	14	102 mins
4	John White	27	33	12	100 mins

KEY PLAYERS - MIDFIELDERS

Kevan Hurst

Goals in the League	4	Contribution to Attacking Power Average number of minutes between League team goals while on pitch	53
Goals in all competitions	6		
Defensive Rating Average number of mins between League goals conceded while on the pitch	61	Scoring Difference Defensive Rating minus Contribution to Attacking Power	8

	PLAYER	GOALS LGE	GOALS ALL	DEF RATE	ATT POWER	SCORE DIFF
1	Kevan Hurst	4	6	61	53	8 mins
2	Derek Niven	5	6	62	63	-1 mins
3	Paul Hall	15	15	61	64	-3 mins
4	Mark Allott	3	3	55	65	-10 mins

KEY PLAYERS - GOALSCORERS

Chris Iwelumo

Goals in the League	17	Player Strike Rate Average number of minutes between League goals scored by player	241
Goals in all competitions	19		
Contribution to Attacking Power Average number of minutes between League team goals while on pitch	73	Club Strike Rate Average number of minutes between League goals scored by club	71

	PLAYER	GOALS LGE	GOALS ALL	POWER	S RATE
1	Chris Iwelumo	17	19	73	241 mins
2	Neil Danns	8	13	74	419 mins
3	Greg Halford	7	8	73	574 mins
4	Mark Yeates	5	6	67	693 mins

Dean Gerkin and Greg Halford celebrate

SQUAD APPEARANCES

Match	1	2	3	4	5	6	7	8	9	10	11	12	13	14	15	16	17	18	19	20	21	22	23	24	25	26
Venue	A	H	H	A	H	H	A	A	H	A	H	A	H	A	H	A	H	H	A	H	H	A	A	A	H	A
Competition	L	L	L	L	W	L	L	L	L	L	L	L	L	L	L	L	L	F	L	L	L	F	L	L	L	L
Result	L	L	W	D	L	D	L	D	W	W	D	D	L	W	L	D	W	W	W	W	W	W	W	D	W	L

Match	27	28	29	30	31	32	33	34	35	36	37	38	39	40	41	42	43	44	45	46	47	48	49	50	51	52
Venue	A	H	A	A	H	H	H	H	H	A	H	A	A	H	A	H	A	A	H	A	H	A	H	A	H	A
Competition	L	L	F	L	L	L	F	L	L	L	L	F	L	L	L	L	L	L	L	L	L	L	L	L	L	L
Result	W	W	W	W	W	W	W	W	W	L	D	L	L	L	L	W	D	D	D	L	W	D	W	W	W	D

Goalkeepers
Mark Cousins
Aidan Davison
Dean Gerken

Defenders
Pat Baldwin
Wayne Brown
Liam Chilvers
George Elokobi
Dean Howell
Stephen Hunt
Garry Richards
Sam Stockley
John White

Midfielders
Jamal Campbell-Ryce
Neil Danns
Karl Duguid
Richard Garcia
Greg Halford
Kemal Izzet
Robbie King
Kevin Watson

Forwards
Billy Clarke
Jamie Cureton
Jamie Guy
Chris Iwelumo
Tony Thorpe
Scott Vernon
Gareth Williams
Mark Yeates

KEY: On all match | On bench | Subbed or sent off (Counting game) | Subbed or sent off (playing less than 70 minutes) | Subbed on from bench (Counting Game) | Subbed on (playing less than 70 minutes) | Subbed on and then subbed or sent off (Counting Game) | Subbed on and then subbed or sent off (playing less than 70 minutes) | Not in 16

BRENTFORD

Final Position: **3rd**

NICKNAME: THE BEES

KEY: ☐Won ☐Drawn ☐Lost

							Attendance
1	div2	Scunthorpe	H	W	2-0	Tabb 71; Campbell 81 pen	5,952
2	div2	Chesterfield	A	W	3-1	Sodje 14; Rankin 52,56	4,121
3	div2	Port Vale	A	L	0-1		4,275
4	div2	Tranmere	H	W	2-0	Tabb 23; Hutchinson 50	5,438
5	ccr1	Cheltenham	A	L	0-5		2,113
6	div2	Barnsley	A	D	1-1	Owusu 25	7,462
7	div2	Gillingham	H	D	1-1	Peters 75	6,969
8	div2	Nottm Forest	A	W	2-1	Frampton 23; Pratley 78	17,234
9	div2	MK Dons	H	W	1-0	O'Connor 62 pen	5,862
10	div2	Huddersfield	A	L	2-3	Rankin 23; Campbell 46	11,622
11	div2	Bristol City	H	L	2-3	Brooker 66; Sodje 80	6,413
12	div2	Walsall	A	D	0-0		4,873
13	div2	Rotherham	H	W	2-1	O'Connor 11 pen; Rankin 37	5,901
14	div2	Oldham	A	W	1-0	Fitzgerald, SP 66	5,089
15	div2	Swindon	H	D	0-0		6,969
16	div2	Blackpool	A	D	0-0		5,041
17	div2	Bournemouth	H	L	0-2		6,625
18	facr1	Rochdale	A	W	1-0	O'Connor 45 og	2,928
19	div2	Hartlepool	A	W	2-1	Campbell 22; Owusu 78	4,811
20	div2	Oldham	H	D	3-3	Pratley 17; Campbell 28; Owusu 89	5,450
21	div2	Scunthorpe	A	W	3-1	Pratley 11,24; Brooker 52	4,322
22	facr2	Oldham	A	D	1-1	Sodje 65	4,365
23	div2	Yeovil	H	W	3-2	Jones 6 og; Tabb 13; Turner 88	5,131
24	div2	Chesterfield	H	D	1-1	O'Connor 82	5,628
25	facr2r	Oldham	H	W	1-0	Owusu 78	3,146
26	div2	Tranmere	A	W	4-1	Newman 12; Tabb 14; O'Connor 32 pen; Owusu 53	6,210
27	div2	Swansea	H	W	2-1	O'Connor 26; Hutchinson 35	9,903
28	div2	Colchester	H	L	0-2		6,397
29	div2	Bradford	A	D	3-3	Campbell 4,28 pen; Sodje 58	7,588
30	facr3	Stockport	A	W	3-2	Owusu 13; Campbell 65; Rankin 84	4,078
31	div2	Southend	A	L	1-4	Campbell 65	10,046
32	div2	Nottm Forest	H	D	1-1	Campbell 34	7,859
33	div2	Huddersfield	H	W	2-0	Owusu 25; Campbell 77	7,636
34	facr4	Sunderland	H	W	2-1	Campbell 57,89	11,698
35	div2	Walsall	H	W	5-0	Rankin 7; Newman 11; Brooker 65; Sodje 77; O'Connor 86 pen	5,645
36	div2	Bristol City	A	W	1-0	Owusu 78	10,854
37	div2	Southend	H	W	2-0	Jupp 23 og; Gayle 34	7,022
38	facr5	Charlton	A	L	1-3	Rankin 83	22,098
39	div2	Port Vale	H	L	0-1		7,542
40	div2	Doncaster	A	D	0-0		5,250
41	div2	Yeovil	A	W	2-1	Rankin 12; Rhodes 58	5,137
42	div2	Barnsley	H	W	3-1	Newman 12; Owusu 22,85 pen	7,352
43	div2	Swansea	A	L	1-2	Frampton 30	13,508
44	div2	Gillingham	A	L	2-3	Turner 15; Tabb 79	5,745
45	div2	Doncaster	H	L	0-1		7,323
46	div2	MK Dons	A	W	1-0	Owusu 8	5,592
47	div2	Colchester	A	D	1-1	Tabb 6	5,635
48	div2	Bradford	H	D	1-1	Owusu 43	6,533
49	div2	Rotherham	A	D	2-2	Owusu 68; Rankin 81	5,242
50	div2	Blackpool	H	D	1-1	Owusu 53 pen	7,339
51	div2	Swindon	A	W	3-1	Brooker 27; Gayle 39; Willock 75	6,845
52	div2	Hartlepool	H	D	1-1	O'Connor 84	8,725
53	div2	Bournemouth	A	D	2-2	Sodje 22; Frampton 65	9,359
54	d2po1	Swansea	A	D	1-1	Tabb 29	19,060
55	d2po2	Swansea	H	L	0-2		10,652

LEAGUE APPEARANCES, BOOKINGS AND GOALS

	AGE (on 01/07/06)	IN NAMED 16	APPEARANCES	COUNTING GAMES	MINUTES ON PITCH	LEAGUE GOALS		
Goalkeepers								
Ademola Bankole	36	46	2	2	161	0	1	0
Stuart Nelson	24	46	45	44	3979	0	4	0
Defenders								
Michael Dobson	25	6	6	3	334	0	1	0
Andrew Frampton	26	36	36	33	3067	3	7	1
John Mousinho	20	12	7	1	253	0	0	0
Kevin O'Connor	24	30	30	27	2584	7	2	0
Karleigh Osborne	18	4	1	1	90	0	0	0
Jamie Smith	31	9	7	7	617	0	0	0
Sam Sodje	25	43	43	42	3792	5	9	1
Sam Tillen	21	37	33	20	2201	0	1	0
Michael Turner	22	46	46	46	4140	2	4	0
Ryan Watts	18	0	0	0	0	0	0	0
Midfielders								
Paul Brooker	30	40	36	19	2449	4	3	0
Darius Charles	18	4	2	0	62	0	0	0
Eddie Hutchinson	24	31	27	14	1595	2	4	1
Charlie Ide	18	1	0	0	0	0	0	0
Jo Keenan	23	3	3	0	43	0	0	0
Junior Lewis	32	23	14	9	956	0	1	0
Ricky Newman	35	31	30	24	2442	3	8	1
Darren Pratley	21	32	32	23	2309	4	7	0
Alex Rhodes	24	17	17	4	649	1	1	0
Olafur Ingi Skulason	23	2	2	1	127	0	1	0
Aaron Steele	-	0	0	0	0	0	0	0
Jay Tabb	24	42	42	37	3556	6	9	0
Forwards								
Dudley Campbell	25	26	23	11	1327	9	0	1
Scott P Fitzgerald	26	16	11	0	309	1	1	0
Marcus Gayle	35	40	24	14	1493	2	0	0
Lloyd Owusu	29	42	42	35	3416	12	5	0
Ryan Peters	18	15	10	1	309	1	0	0
Isaiah Rankin	28	39	37	26	2721	7	6	0
Callum Willock	24	17	13	2	436	1	0	0

TEAM OF THE SEASON

G
Stuart Nelson
CG: 44 DR: 78

D
Kevin O'Connor
CG: 27 DR: 96

D
Andrew Frampton
CG: 33 DR: 85

D
Sam Sodje
CG: 42 DR: 84

D
Sam Tillen
CG: 20 DR: 82

M
Paul Brooker
CG: 19 SD: 33

M
Darren Pratley
CG: 23 SD: 28

M
Jay Tabb
CG: 37 SD: 28

M
Eddie Hutchinson
CG: 14 SD: 17

F
Lloyd Owusu
CG: 35 SR: 285

F
Isaiah Rankin
CG: 26 SR: 389

MONTHLY POINTS TALLY

AUGUST	11	61%
SEPTEMBER	7	47%
OCTOBER	8	53%
NOVEMBER	7	78%
DECEMBER	10	67%
JANUARY	5	42%
FEBRUARY	10	67%
MARCH	9	50%
APRIL	8	44%
MAY	1	33%

LEAGUE GOALS

	PLAYER	LGE	FAC	LC	Oth	TOT
1	Owusu	12	2	0	0	14
2	Campbell	9	3	0	0	12
3	Rankin	7	2	0	0	9
4	O'Connor	7	0	0	0	7
5	Tabb	6	0	0	1	7
6	Sodje	5	1	0	0	6
7	Brooker	4	0	0	0	4
8	Pratley	4	0	0	0	4
9	Newman	3	0	0	0	3
10	Frampton	3	0	0	0	3
11	Turner	2	0	0	0	2
	Other	10	1	0	0	11
	TOTAL	72	9	0	1	82

TOP POINT EARNERS

	PLAYER	GAMES	AV PTS
1	Paul Brooker	19	2.26
2	Kevin O'Connor	27	2.07
3	Darren Pratley	23	1.83
4	Eddie Hutchinson	14	1.79
5	Sam Sodje	42	1.79
6	Marcus Gayle	14	1.71
7	Jay Tabb	37	1.70
8	Ricky Newman	24	1.67
9	Lloyd Owusu	35	1.66
10	Michael Turner	46	1.65

DISCIPLINARY RECORDS

	PLAYER	YELLOW	RED	AVE
1	Newman	8	1	271
2	Hutchinson	4	1	319
3	Pratley	7	0	329
4	Sodje	9	1	379
5	Frampton	7	1	383
6	Tabb	9	0	395
7	Rankin	6	0	453
8	Rhodes	1	0	649
9	Owusu	5	0	683
10	Brooker	3	0	816
11	Lewis	1	0	956
12	Nelson	4	0	994
13	Turner	4	0	1035
	Other	3	1	
	TOTAL	71	5	

KEY GOALKEEPER

Stuart Nelson

Goals Conceded in the League	51	Counting Games League games when player was on pitch for at least 70 minutes	44
Goals Conceded in all competitions	65		
Defensive Rating Ave number of mins between League goals conceded while on the pitch	78	Clean Sheets In games when player was on pitch for at least 70 minutes	13

KEY PLAYERS - DEFENDERS

Kevin O'Connor

Goals Conceded in the League	27	Clean Sheets In League games when player was on pitch for at least 70 minutes	9
Goals Conceded in all competitions	38		
Defensive Rating Ave number of mins between League goals conceded while on the pitch	96	Club Defensive Rating Average number of mins between League goals conceded by the club this season	80

	PLAYER	CON LGE	CON ALL	CLN SHEETS	DEF RATE
1	Kevin O'Connor	27	38	9	96 mins
2	Andrew Frampton	36	44	10	85 mins
3	Sam Sodje	45	54	12	84 mins
4	Sam Tillen	27	39	7	82 mins

KEY PLAYERS - MIDFIELDERS

Paul Brooker

Goals in the League	4	Contribution to Attacking Power Average number of minutes between League team goals while on pitch	51
Goals in all competitions	4		
Defensive Rating Average number of mins between League goals conceded while on the pitch	84	Scoring Difference Defensive Rating minus Contribution to Attacking Power	33

	PLAYER	GOALS LGE	GOALS ALL	DEF RATE	ATT POWER	SCORE DIFF
1	Paul Brooker	4	4	84	51	33 mins
2	Jay Tabb	6	7	81	53	28 mins
3	Darren Pratley	4	4	86	58	28 mins
4	Eddie Hutchinson	2	2	76	59	17 mins

KEY PLAYERS - GOALSCORERS

Lloyd Owusu

Goals in the League	12	Player Strike Rate Average number of minutes between League goals scored by player	285
Goals in all competitions	14		
Contribution to Attacking Power Average number of minutes between League team goals while on pitch	59	Club Strike Rate Average number of minutes between League goals scored by club	58

	PLAYER	GOALS LGE	GOALS ALL	POWER	S RATE
1	Lloyd Owusu	12	14	59	285 mins
2	Kevin O'Connor	7	7	54	369 mins
3	Isaiah Rankin	7	9	66	389 mins
4	Darren Pratley	4	4	58	577 mins

Martin Allen

SQUAD APPEARANCES

latch	1	2	3	4	5	6	7	8	9	10	11	12	13	14	15	16	17	18	19	20
enue	H	A	A	H	A	A	H	A	H	A	H	A	H	A	H	A	H	A	A	H
ompetition	L	L	L	L	W	L	L	L	L	L	L	L	L	L	L	L	L	F	L	L
esult	W	W	L	W	L	D	D	W	W	L	L	D	W	W	D	D	L	W	W	D

latch	21	22	23	24	25	26	27	28	29	30	31	32	33	34	35	36	37	38	39	40
enue	A	A	H	H	H	A	H	H	A	A	A	H	H	H	H	A	H	A	H	A
ompetition	L	F	L	L	F	L	L	L	L	F	L	L	L	F	L	L	L	F	L	L
esult	W	D	W	D	W	W	W	L	D	W	L	D	W	W	W	W	W	L	L	D

latch	41	42	43	44	45	46	47	48	49	50	51	52	53	54	55
enue	A	H	A	A	H	A	A	H	A	H	A	H	A	A	H
ompetition	L	L	L	L	L	L	L	L	L	L	L	L	L	O	O
esult	W	W	L	L	L	W	D	D	D	D	W	D	D	D	L

oalkeepers
demola Bankole
tuart Nelson

efenders
lichael Dobson
ndrew Frampton
ohn Mousinho
evin O'Connor
arleigh Osborne
amie Smith
am Sodje
am Tillen
lichael Turner
yan Watts

lidfielders
aul Brooker
arius Charles
ddie Hutchinson
harlie Ide
o Keenan
unior Lewis
icky Newman
arren Pratley
lex Rhodes
lafur Ingi Skulason
aron Steele
ay Tabb

orwards
udley Campbell
cott P Fitzgerald
larcus Gayle
loyd Owusu
yan Peters
saiah Rankin
allum Willock

KEY: On all match — On bench — Subbed or sent off (Counting game) — Subbed or sent off (playing less than 70 minutes) — Subbed on from bench (Counting Game) — Subbed on (playing less than 70 minutes) — Subbed on and then subbed or sent off (Counting Game) — Subbed on and then subbed or sent off (playing less than 70 minutes) — Not in 16

HUDDERSFIELD TOWN

Final Position: **4th**

NICKNAME: THE TERRIERS

KEY: ☐ Won ☐ Drawn ☐ Lost

							Attendance
1	div2	Nottm Forest	A	L	1-2	Abbott 64 pen	24,042
2	div2	Bristol City	H	W	1-0	Abbott 89	11,138
3	div2	Swansea	H	W	3-1	Booth 27; Abbott 41; Schofield 76	10,304
4	div2	Southend	A	D	1-1	Abbott 45	5,567
5	ccr1	Chesterfield	A	W	4-2	Abbott 9; Taylor-Fletcher 56,76,90	2,922
6	div2	Hartlepool	H	W	2-1	Abbott 13; Schofield 18	11,241
7	div2	Doncaster	A	W	2-1	Brandon 2; Worthington 40	7,222
8	div2	Scunthorpe	H	L	1-4	Abbott 66 pen	14,112
9	div2	Oldham	A	W	3-0	Schofield 27; Taylor-Fletcher 37,72	6,803
10	div2	Brentford	H	W	3-2	Abbott 34; Schofield 90; Booth 90	11,622
11	ccr2	Blackburn	A	L	1-3	Abbott 79	11,755
12	div2	Colchester	A	D	1-1	Taylor-Fletcher 65	3,415
13	div2	Tranmere	H	W	1-0	Schofield 87	10,640
14	div2	Bournemouth	H	D	2-2	Schofield 14; Taylor-Fletcher 21	13,522
15	div2	Bradford	A	W	2-1	Hudson 21; Booth 79	12,285
16	div2	Walsall	H	W	3-1	Booth 15; Abbott 34,78	11,642
17	div2	Chesterfield	A	L	3-4	Hudson 80; Worthington 87; Holdsworth 90	6,206
18	div2	Swindon	H	D	1-1	Brandon 54	11,352
19	facr1	Welling	H	W	4-1	Booth 27,69; Schofield 50 pen; Holdsworth 81	5,518
20	div2	Yeovil	A	W	2-1	Booth 11; Hudson 39	6,742
21	div2	Bradford	H	D	0-0		17,331
22	div2	Nottm Forest	H	W	2-1	Schofield 21; Booth 26	17,370
23	facr2	Worcester	A	W	1-0	Brandon 61	4,163
24	div2	MK Dons	A	D	2-2	Abbott 7; Booth 64	4,832
25	div2	Bristol City	A	L	0-2		9,949
26	div2	Southend	H	D	0-0		11,223
27	div2	Rotherham	A	D	1-1	Taylor-Fletcher 90	7,380
28	div2	Port Vale	H	L	0-3		10,824
29	div2	Barnsley	A	D	2-2	Booth 76; Taylor-Fletcher 90	13,063
30	div2	Gillingham	H	D	0-0		11,483
31	facr3	Chelsea	A	L	1-2	Taylor-Fletcher 75	41,650
32	div2	Scunthorpe	A	D	2-2	Schofield 44; McIntosh 90	4,450
33	div2	Blackpool	H	W	2-0	Clarke, T 9; Schofield 73	11,977
34	div2	Brentford	A	L	0-2		7,636
35	div2	Oldham	H	W	3-2	Branston 45 og; Abbott 48; Graham 59	12,973
36	div2	Tranmere	A	L	1-2	Graham 48	8,300
37	div2	Colchester	H	W	2-0	Worthington 14; Graham 68	13,515
38	div2	Blackpool	A	W	1-0	Brandon 43 pen	6,004
39	div2	MK Dons	H	W	5-0	McIntosh 19; Taylor-Fletcher 24; Worthington 36; Mirfin 77; Collins 90	11,423
40	div2	Swansea	A	D	2-2	McIntosh 70; Graham 82	13,110
41	div2	Doncaster	H	D	2-2	McIntosh 8; Graham 40	14,490
42	div2	Hartlepool	A	L	1-3	Graham 22	5,468
43	div2	Rotherham	H	W	4-1	Booth 32,39,82; Taylor-Fletcher 84	15,264
44	div2	Port Vale	A	D	1-1	Booth 81	5,664
45	div2	Barnsley	H	W	1-0	Taylor-Fletcher 55	19,052
46	div2	Gillingham	A	L	0-2		7,014
47	div2	Bournemouth	A	D	1-1	Taylor-Fletcher 71	7,406
48	div2	Chesterfield	H	L	1-2	Graham 12	13,368
49	div2	Walsall	A	W	3-1	Graham 25; Abbott 83; Booth 90	5,554
50	div2	Yeovil	H	L	1-2	Graham 8	14,473
51	div2	Swindon	A	D	0-0		6,353
52	d2po1	Barnsley	A	W	1-0	Taylor-Fletcher 85	16,127
53	d2po2	Barnsley	H	L	1-3	Worthington 65	19,223

LEAGUE APPEARANCES, BOOKINGS AND GOALS

	AGE (on 01/07/06)	IN NAMED 16	APPEARANCES	COUNTING GAMES	MINUTES ON PITCH	LEAGUE GOALS	
Goalkeepers							
Simon Eastwood	17	2	0	0	0	0	0
Paul Rachubka	25	45	34	33	3017	0	1
Phil Senior	23	44	13	12	1123	0	0
Defenders							
Daniel Adams	30	40	40	37	3477	0	7
Nathan Clarke	22	46	46	45	4095	0	7
Tom Clarke	18	36	17	13	1311	1	4
Aaron Hardy	20	1	0	0	0	0	0
Andy Holdsworth	22	42	42	35	3393	1	6
John McCombe	21	16	1	1	90	0	0
Martin McIntosh	35	23	22	18	1691	4	1
David Mirfin	21	33	31	27	2560	1	5
Dan Smith	19	9	8	6	594	0	1
Midfielders							
Adnan Ahmed	22	20	13	4	518	0	2
Chris Brandon	30	40	40	32	3121	3	7
Anthony Carss	30	20	17	8	913	0	2
Michael Collins	20	33	17	8	824	1	2
Mark Hudson	25	33	28	24	2152	3	9
Danny Schofield	26	43	41	35	3332	9	4
John Worthington	23	41	41	41	3645	4	12
Matthew Young	20	5	2	0	46	0	0
Forwards							
Pawel Abbott	24	38	36	24	2404	12	4
Andy Booth	32	36	36	30	2875	13	1
David Graham	27	16	16	15	1314	9	1
Junior Mendes	29	9	5	0	57	0	0
John McAliskey	21	20	9	0	142	0	0
Gary Taylor-Fletcher	25	45	43	23	2773	10	4

TEAM OF THE SEASON

G
Phil Senior
CG: 12 DR: 80

D
Martin McIntosh
CG: 18 DR: 74

D
David Mirfin
CG: 27 DR: 73

D
Nathan Clarke
CG: 45 DR: 69

D
Andy Holdsworth
CG: 35 DR: 69

M
Chris Brandon
CG: 32 SD: 17

M
John Worthington
CG: 41 SD: 11

M
Danny Schofield
CG: 35 SD: 9

M
Mark Hudson
CG: 24 SD: 4

F
David Graham
CG: 15 SR: 146

F
Pawel Abbott
CG: 24 SR: 200

MONTHLY POINTS TALLY

AUGUST	13	72%
SEPTEMBER	10	67%
OCTOBER	8	53%
NOVEMBER	7	78%
DECEMBER	4	22%
JANUARY	8	53%
FEBRUARY	10	67%
MARCH	5	42%
APRIL	7	39%
MAY	1	33%

LEAGUE GOALS

	PLAYER	LGE	FAC	LC	Oth	TOT
1	Booth	13	2	0	0	15
2	Abbott	12	0	2	0	14
3	Taylor-Fletcher	10	1	3	1	15
4	Schofield	9	1	0	0	10
5	Graham	9	0	0	0	9
6	Worthington	4	0	0	1	5
7	McIntosh	4	0	0	0	4
8	Hudson	3	0	0	0	3
9	Brandon	3	1	0	0	4
10	Mirfin	1	0	0	0	1
11	Holdsworth	1	1	0	0	2
	Other	3	0	0	0	3
	TOTAL	72	6	5	2	85

TOP POINT EARNERS

	PLAYER	GAMES	AV PTS
1	Phil Senior	12	1.83
2	Tom Clarke	13	1.77
3	Pawel Abbott	24	1.75
4	Chris Brandon	32	1.72
5	Martin McIntosh	18	1.67
6	Andy Booth	30	1.67
7	John Worthington	41	1.63
8	Danny Schofield	35	1.63
9	Daniel Adams	37	1.62
10	Nathan Clarke	45	1.60

DISCIPLINARY RECORDS

	PLAYER	YELLOW	RED	AVE
1	Hudson	9	1	215
2	Clarke, T	4	2	218
3	Ahmed	2	0	259
4	Worthington	12	0	303
5	Brandon	7	1	390
6	Collins	2	0	412
7	Mirfin	5	1	426
8	Carss	2	0	456
9	Adams	7	0	496
10	Holdsworth	6	0	565
11	Clarke, N	7	0	585
12	Smith	1	0	594
13	Abbott	4	0	601
	Other	12	1	
	TOTAL	80	6	

KEY GOALKEEPER

Phil Senior

Goals Conceded in the League	14	Counting Games League games when player was on pitch for at least 70 minutes	13
Goals Conceded in all competitions	16		
Defensive Rating Ave number of mins between League goals conceded while on the pitch	80	Clean Sheets In games when player was on pitch for at least 70 minutes	5

KEY PLAYERS - DEFENDERS

Martin McIntosh

Goals Conceded in the League	23	Clean Sheets In League games when player was on pitch for at least 70 minutes	5
Goals Conceded in all competitions	27		
Defensive Rating Ave number of mins between League goals conceded while on the pitch	74	Club Defensive Rating Average number of mins between League goals conceded by the club this season	70

	PLAYER	CON LGE	CON ALL	CLN SHEETS	DEF RATE
1	Martin McIntosh	23	27	5	74 mins
2	David Mirfin	35	37	7	73 mins
3	Nathan Clarke	59	70	11	69 mins
4	Andy Holdsworth	49	60	7	69 mins

KEY PLAYERS - MIDFIELDERS

Anthony Sweeney

Goals in the League	5	Contribution to Attacking Power Average number of minutes between League team goals while on pitch	88
Goals in all competitions	5		
Defensive Rating Average number of mins between League goals conceded while on the pitch	71	Scoring Difference Defensive Rating minus Contribution to Attacking Power	-17

	PLAYER	GOALS LGE	GOALS ALL	DEF RATE	ATT POWER	SCORE DIFF
1	Anthony Sweeney	5	5	71	88	-17 mins
2	Thomas Butler	1	2	67	92	-25 mins
3	Lee Bullock	4	4	68	94	-26 mins
4	Richie Humphreys	2	2	70	96	-26 mins

KEY PLAYERS - GOALSCORERS

David Graham

Goals in the League	9	Player Strike Rate Average number of minutes between League goals scored by player	146
Goals in all competitions	9		
Contribution to Attacking Power Average number of minutes between League team goals while on pitch	57	Club Strike Rate Average number of minutes between League goals scored by club	58

	PLAYER	GOALS LGE	GOALS ALL	POWER	S RATE
1	David Graham	9	9	57	146 mins
2	Pawel Abbott	12	14	55	200 mins
3	Andy Booth	13	15	56	221 mins
4	Gary Taylor-Fletcher	10	15	55	277 mins

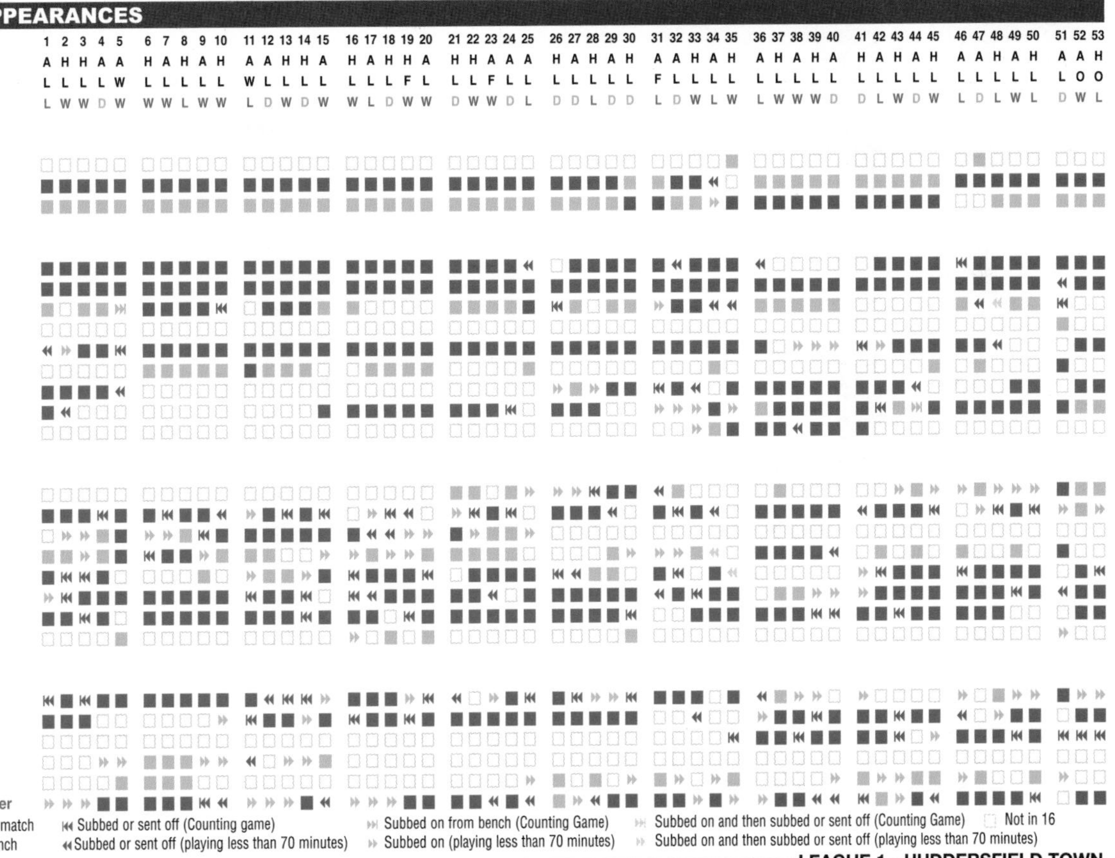

Pawel Abbott

SQUAD APPEARANCES

atch	1	2	3	4	5	6	7	8	9	10	11	12	13	14	15	16	17	18	19	20	21	22	23	24	25	26	27
enue	A	H	H	A	A	H	A	H	A	H	A	A	H	H	A	H	A	H	H	A	H	H	A	A	A	H	A
ompetition	L	L	L	L	W	L	L	L	L	L	W	L	L	L	L	L	L	L	F	L	L	L	F	L	L	L	L
esult	L	W	W	D	W	W	W	L	W	W	L	D	W	D	W	W	L	D	W	W	D	W	W	D	L	D	D

atch	28	29	30	31	32	33	34	35	36	37	38	39	40	41	42	43	44	45	46	47	48	49	50	51	52	53
enue	H	A	H	A	A	H	A	H	A	H	A	H	A	H	A	H	A	H	A	A	H	A	H	A	A	H
ompetition	L	L	L	F	L	L	L	L	L	L	L	L	L	L	L	L	L	L	L	L	L	L	L	L	O	O
esult	L	D	D	L	D	W	L	W	L	W	W	W	D	D	L	W	D	W	L	D	L	W	L	D	W	L

oalkeepers
imon Eastwood
aul Rachubka
hil Senior

efenders
aniel Adams
athan Clarke
om Clarke
aron Hardy
ndy Holdsworth
ohn McCombe
artin McIntosh
avid Mirfin
an Smith

idfielders
dnan Ahmed
hris Brandon
nthony Carss
ichael Collins
ark Hudson
anny Schofield
ohn Worthington
atthew Young

orwards
awel Abbott
ndy Booth
avid Graham
unior Mendes
ohn McAliskey
ary Taylor-Fletcher

KEY: On all match | On bench | Subbed or sent off (Counting game) | Subbed or sent off (playing less than 70 minutes) | Subbed on from bench (Counting Game) | Subbed on (playing less than 70 minutes) | Subbed on and then subbed or sent off (Counting Game) | Subbed on and then subbed or sent off (playing less than 70 minutes) | Not in 16

BARNSLEY

Final Position: **5th**

NICKNAME: THE TYKES

KEY: ☐Won ☐Drawn ☐Lost

							Attendance
1	div2	Swindon	H	W	2-0	Hayes 11; Shuker 47	9,358
2	div2	Scunthorpe	A	L	1-2	Hayes 61	7,152
3	div2	Colchester	A	L	0-1		2,721
4	div2	Yeovil	H	W	1-0	Williams, R 79 pen	8,153
5	ccr1	Preston	A	L	4-5*	Burns 81,108 (*on penalties)	3,137
6	div2	Brentford	H	D	1-1	Turner 24 og	7,462
7	div2	Swansea	A	L	1-3	Burns 35	12,554
8	div2	Nottm Forest	H	W	2-0	Conlon 41; Shuker 46	10,080
9	div2	Gillingham	A	W	3-0	Shuker 40; Hayes 43; Nardiello 85	5,283
10	div2	MK Dons	A	D	0-0		4,620
11	ccr2	Burnley	A	L	0-3		4,501
12	div2	Doncaster	H	L	0-2		12,002
13	div2	Bristol City	A	L	0-3		10,771
14	div2	Oldham	H	W	4-0	Nardiello 8; Devaney 12; Shuker 14,54	8,077
15	div2	Blackpool	H	D	2-2	Richards 81; Howard 84	7,945
16	div2	Southend	A	D	1-1	Richards 61	6,986
17	div2	Rotherham	A	W	1-0	Devaney 73	5,401
18	div2	Walsall	H	W	2-0	Hayes 13; Howard 66	8,145
19	facr1	Darlington	H	W	1-0	Hayes 5	6,059
20	div2	Bradford	A	D	0-0		9,486
21	div2	Rotherham	H	D	1-1	Watt 90	9,894
22	div2	Swindon	A	W	3-0	Devaney 8; Shuker 51,69	5,422
23	facr2	Bradford	H	D	1-1	Hayes 43	7,051
24	div2	Tranmere	H	W	2-1	Devaney 58; Richards 77 pen	6,996
25	div2	Scunthorpe	H	W	5-2	Devaney 2; Hassell 7; Richards 33; Shuker 71; Hayes 90	8,197
26	facr2r	Bradford	A	W	5-3	Hayes 51,78; Reid 59; Devaney 96,109	4,738
27	div2	Yeovil	A	L	1-2	Williams, R 15	5,620
28	div2	Hartlepool	H	D	1-1	Richards 28 pen	9,715
29	div2	Huddersfield	H	D	2-2	Burns 42; Nardiello 81	13,063
30	div2	Chesterfield	A	D	0-0		6,046
31	facr3	Walsall	H	D	1-1	Hayes 77	6,884
32	div2	Gillingham	H	W	1-0	Shuker 15	7,090
33	div2	Port Vale	A	L	2-3	Burns 56; Carbon 67	4,468
34	facr3r	Walsall	A	L	0-2		4,074
35	div2	MK Dons	H	W	2-0	Richards 77; Hassell 79	7,588
36	div2	Nottm Forest	A	W	2-0	Richards 15,31	16,237
37	div2	Bristol City	H	W	2-0	Richards 27,81 pen	8,092
38	div2	Doncaster	A	L	0-2		8,144
39	div2	Port Vale	H	D	1-1	Hayes 56	7,709
40	div2	Tranmere	A	W	1-0	Heckingbottom 16	6,802
41	div2	Colchester	H	W	1-0	Howard 72	9,411
42	div2	Bournemouth	A	D	1-1	McPhail 21	5,191
43	div2	Swansea	H	D	2-2	Nardiello 56; Richards 61 pen	9,743
44	div2	Brentford	A	L	1-3	Wright 68	7,352
45	div2	Hartlepool	A	D	1-1	Kay 36	5,122
46	div2	Bournemouth	H	D	0-0		9,180
47	div2	Huddersfield	A	L	0-1		19,052
48	div2	Chesterfield	H	D	1-1	Howard 31	8,303
49	div2	Oldham	A	W	3-0	Shuker 49; McPhail 62; Devaney 79	7,772
50	div2	Southend	H	D	2-2	Hunt 17 og; Maher 45 og	10,663
51	div2	Blackpool	A	D	1-1	Howard 53	6,912
52	div2	Bradford	H	D	0-0		11,178
53	div2	Walsall	A	W	2-1	Richards 31; Nardiello 83 pen	7,195
54	d2po1	Huddersfield	H	L	0-1		16,127
55	d2po2	Huddersfield	A	W	3-1	Hayes 58; Reid 71; Nardiello 78	19,223
56	d2pof	Swansea	A	W	4-3*	Hayes 19; Nardiello 62 (*on penalties)	55,419

LEAGUE APPEARANCES, BOOKINGS AND GOALS

	AGE (on 01/07/06)	IN NAMED 16	APPEARANCES	COUNTING GAMES	MINUTES ON PITCH	LEAGUE GOALS	
Goalkeepers							
Nick Colgan	32	44	43	43	3870	0	2
Scott Flinders	19	44	3	3	270	0	0
David Scarsella	23	4	0	0	0	0	0
Defenders							
Robert Atkinson	19	1	0	0	0	0	0
Neil Austin	23	39	38	34	3186	0	7
Matthew Carbon	31	26	24	19	1886	1	6
Bobby Hassell	26	31	28	22	2184	2	1
Paul Heckingbottom	28	18	18	17	1516	1	4
Antony Kay	23	36	36	32	2922	1	5
Ryan Laight	20	4	1	0	3	0	0
Paul Reid	24	34	33	32	2874	0	8
Tony Vaughan	30	4	1	0	45	0	0
Steven Watt	21	4	3	2	240	1	3
Robbie Williams	22	37	22	10	1167	2	3
Midfielders							
Jacob Burns	28	33	33	31	2792	3	8
Martin Devaney	26	38	38	27	2766	6	5
Simon Heslop	19	1	0	0	0	0	0
Brian Howard	23	32	31	23	2280	5	8
Richard Kell	26	2	2	0	54	0	0
Anthony McParland	23	10	8	0	133	0	0
Stephen McPhail	26	34	34	29	2739	2	6
Chris Shuker	24	46	46	39	3663	10	5
Dale Tonge	21	27	24	12	1399	0	1
Nicky Wroe	20	24	12	6	645	0	1
Forwards							
Barry Conlon	27	12	11	7	691	1	1
Paul Hayes	22	45	45	29	3207	6	5
Nathan Jarman	19	11	9	0	132	0	0
Nathan Joynes	20	2	0	0	0	0	0
Daniel Nardiello	23	35	34	11	1434	5	10
Marc Richards	23	39	38	25	2548	12	6
Tommy Wright	21	19	17	6	710	1	5

TEAM OF THE SEASON

G — Nick Colgan — CG: 43 DR: 99

D — Bobby Hassell — CG: 22 DR: 109

D — Neil Austin — CG: 34 DR: 100

D — Antony Kay — CG: 32 DR: 97

D — Paul Heckingbottom — CG: 17 DR: 95

M — Martin Devaney — CG: 27 SD: 41

M — Stephen McPhail — CG: 29 SD: 40

M — Brian Howard — CG: 23 SD: 31

M — Jacob Burns — CG: 31 SD: 28

F — Marc Richards — CG: 25 SR: 212

F — Paul Hayes — CG: 29 SR: 535

MONTHLY POINTS TALLY

Month	Points	%
AUGUST	7	39%
SEPTEMBER	7	47%
OCTOBER	11	73%
NOVEMBER	5	56%
DECEMBER	8	53%
JANUARY	10	67%
FEBRUARY	11	61%
MARCH	3	25%
APRIL	7	39%
MAY	3	100%

LEAGUE GOALS

	PLAYER	LGE	FAC	LC	Oth	TOT
1	Richards	12	0	0	0	12
2	Shuker	10	0	0	0	10
3	Devaney	6	2	0	0	8
4	Hayes	6	5	0	2	13
5	Nardiello	5	0	0	2	7
6	Howard	5	0	0	0	5
7	Burns	3	0	2	0	5
8	Williams, R	2	0	0	0	2
9	Hassell	2	0	0	0	2
10	McPhail	2	0	0	0	2
11	Carbon	1	0	0	0	1
	Other	8	1	0	1	10
	TOTAL	62	8	2	5	77

TOP POINT EARNERS

	PLAYER	GAMES	AV PTS
1	Dale Tonge	12	2.00
2	Paul Hayes	29	1.72
3	Neil Austin	34	1.71
4	Bobby Hassell	22	1.68
5	Marc Richards	25	1.68
6	Martin Devaney	27	1.67
7	Jacob Burns	31	1.65
8	Stephen McPhail	29	1.59
9	Nick Colgan	43	1.53
10	Brian Howard	23	1.52

DISCIPLINARY RECORDS

	PLAYER	YELLOW	RED	AVE
1	Nardiello	10	1	130
2	Wright	5	0	142
3	Howard	8	1	253
4	Reid	8	2	287
5	Williams, R	3	1	291
6	Carbon	6	0	314
7	Burns	8	0	349
8	Heckingbottom	4	0	379
9	Austin	7	1	398
10	Richards	6	0	424
11	McPhail	6	0	456
12	Kay	5	1	487
13	Devaney	5	0	553
	Other	16	0	
	TOTAL	97	7	

KEY GOALKEEPER

Nick Colgan

Goals Conceded in the League	39	Counting Games League games when player was on pitch for at least 70 minutes	43
Goals Conceded in all competitions	47		
Defensive Rating Ave number of mins between League goals conceded while on the pitch	99	Clean Sheets In games when player was on pitch for at least 70 minutes	19

KEY PLAYERS - DEFENDERS

Bobby Hassell

Goals Conceded in the League	20	Clean Sheets In League games when player was on pitch for at least 70 minutes	10
Goals Conceded in all competitions	30		
Defensive Rating Ave number of mins between League goals conceded while on the pitch	109	Club Defensive Rating Average number of mins between League goals conceded by the club this season	94

	PLAYER	CON LGE	CON ALL	CLN SHEETS	DEF RATE
1	Bobby Hassell	20	30	10	109 mins
2	Neil Austin	32	41	16	100 mins
3	Antony Kay	30	41	12	97 mins
4	Paul Heckingbottom	16	20	6	95 mins

KEY PLAYERS - MIDFIELDERS

Martin Devaney

Goals in the League	6	Contribution to Attacking Power Average number of minutes between League team goals while on pitch	58
Goals in all competitions	8		
Defensive Rating Average number of mins between League goals conceded while on the pitch	99	Scoring Difference Defensive Rating minus Contribution to Attacking Power	41

	PLAYER	GOALS LGE	GOALS ALL	DEF RATE	ATT POWER	SCORE DIFF
1	Martin Devaney	6	8	99	58	41 mins
2	Stephen McPhail	2	2	110	70	40 mins
3	Brian Howard	5	5	91	60	31 mins
4	Jacob Burns	3	5	93	65	28 mins

KEY PLAYERS - GOALSCORERS

Marc Richards

Goals in the League	12	Player Strike Rate Average number of minutes between League goals scored by player	212
Goals in all competitions	12		
Contribution to Attacking Power Average number of minutes between League team goals while on pitch	65	Club Strike Rate Average number of minutes between League goals scored by club	67

	PLAYER	GOALS LGE	GOALS ALL	POWER	S RATE
1	Marc Richards	12	12	65	212 mins
2	Chris Shuker	10	10	70	366 mins
3	Brian Howard	5	5	60	456 mins
4	Martin Devaney	6	8	58	461 mins

Dale Tonge and Paul Hayes

SQUAD APPEARANCES

atch	1	2	3	4	5	6	7	8	9	10	11	12	13	14	15	16	17	18	19	20	21	22	23	24	25	26	27	28
enue	H	A	A	H	A	H	A	H	A	A	A	H	A	H	H	A	A	H	H	A	H	A	H	H	H	A	A	H
ompetition	L	L	L	L	W	L	L	L	L	L	W	L	L	L	L	L	L	L	F	L	L	L	F	L	L	F	L	L
esult	W	L	L	W	L	D	L	W	W	D	L	L	L	W	D	D	W	W	W	D	D	W	D	W	W	W	L	D

atch	29	30	31	32	33	34	35	36	37	38	39	40	41	42	43	44	45	46	47	48	49	50	51	52	53	54	55	56
enue	H	A	H	H	A	A	H	A	H	A	H	A	H	A	H	A	A	H	A	H	A	H	A	H	A	H	A	A
ompetition	L	L	F	L	L	F	L	L	L	L	L	L	L	L	L	L	L	L	L	L	L	L	L	L	L	O	O	O
esult	D	D	D	W	L	L	W	W	W	L	D	W	W	D	D	L	D	D	L	D	W	D	D	D	W	L	W	W

oalkeepers
ick Colgan
cott Flinders
avid Scarsella

efenders
obert Atkinson
eil Austin
atthew Carbon
obby Hassell
aul Heckingbottom
ntony Kay
yan Laight
aul Reid
ony Vaughan
teven Watt
obbie Williams

idfielders
acob Burns
artin Devaney
imon Heslop
rian Howard
ichard Kell
nthony McParland
tephen McPhail
hris Shuker
ale Tonge
icky Wroe

orwards
arry Conlon
aul Hayes
athan Jarman
athan Joynes
aniel Nardiello
arc Richards
ommy Wright

KEY: On all match — On bench — Subbed or sent off (Counting game) — Subbed or sent off (playing less than 70 minutes) — Subbed on from bench (Counting Game) — Subbed on (playing less than 70 minutes) — Subbed on and then subbed or sent off (Counting Game) — Subbed on and then subbed or sent off (playing less than 70 minutes) — Not in 16

SWANSEA

Final Position: **6th**

NICKNAME: THE SWANS

KEY: ☐ Won ☐ Drawn ☐ Lost

	Comp	Opponent	H/A	Res	Score	Scorers	Attendance
1	div2	Tranmere	H	W	1-0	Akinfenwa 30	16,733
2	div2	Colchester	A	W	2-1	Forbes 35; Trundle 68	2,950
3	div2	Huddersfield	A	L	1-3	Trundle 32 pen	10,304
4	div2	Doncaster	H	L	1-2	McLeod 44	12,744
5	ccr1	Reading	A	L	1-3	Akinfenwa 80	7,603
6	div2	Walsall	A	W	5-2	Martinez 15; Akinfenwa 47; Tudur-Jones 63; McLeod 65; Connor 71	5,745
7	div2	Barnsley	H	W	3-1	McLeod 14,90; Trundle 58	12,554
8	div2	Bristol City	H	W	7-1	McLeod 45,69,87; Akinfenwa 50; Trundle 58 pen,71; Britton 75	13,662
9	div2	MK Dons	A	W	3-1	Trundle 16; Robinson 72,77	4,798
10	div2	Hartlepool	A	D	2-2	Trundle 56,61	4,743
11	div2	Nottm Forest	H	D	1-1	Martinez 84	18,212
12	div2	Bournemouth	A	W	1-0	Trundle 30	5,750
13	div2	Blackpool	H	W	3-2	Trundle 22; Akinfenwa 44; Britton 81	13,911
14	div2	Yeovil	A	L	0-1		7,578
15	div2	Oldham	H	D	0-0		14,029
16	div2	Rotherham	A	D	2-2	Trundle 42; Bean 59	4,056
17	div2	Chesterfield	H	W	5-1	Akinfenwa 7; Trundle 11,28,72; Tudur-Jones 45	13,264
18	facr1	Stockport	A	L	0-2		2,978
19	div2	Southend	A	W	2-1	Trundle 40; Akinfenwa 47	11,049
20	div2	Yeovil	H	W	2-0	Trundle 25 pen,67	19,288
21	div2	Tranmere	A	D	2-2	Tudur-Jones 45; Robinson 88	7,518
22	div2	Scunthorpe	H	W	2-0	Ricketts 53; Forbes 87	13,207
23	div2	Colchester	H	D	1-1	Robinson 30	13,230
24	div2	Doncaster	A	L	1-2	Ricketts 24	7,159
25	div2	Brentford	A	L	1-2	Robinson 90	9,903
26	div2	Swindon	A	D	0-0		8,985
27	div2	Port Vale	H	D	0-0		14,747
28	div2	MK Dons	H	W	3-1	Knight 5,12,27	11,922
29	div2	Bradford	A	D	1-1	Monk 44	7,521
30	div2	Hartlepool	H	D	1-1	Britton 20	13,960
31	div2	Bristol City	A	L	0-1		12,859
32	div2	Gillingham	H	L	1-2	Robinson 84 pen	14,357
33	div2	Bournemouth	H	W	1-0	Robinson 45	12,079
34	div2	Nottm Forest	A	W	2-1	Forbes 27; Trundle 67	19,132
35	div2	Bradford	H	D	1-1	Knight 45	11,028
36	div2	Scunthorpe	A	D	2-2	Robinson 24 pen; Knight 28	4,352
37	div2	Huddersfield	H	D	2-2	Trundle 19; Britton 45	13,110
38	div2	Barnsley	A	D	2-2	Robinson 48; Trundle 64	9,743
39	div2	Walsall	H	D	1-1	Akinfenwa 88	13,262
40	div2	Brentford	H	W	2-1	Akinfenwa 20; Robinson 86	13,508
41	div2	Gillingham	A	L	0-1		6,909
42	div2	Port Vale	A	L	2-3	Akinfenwa 47; Fallon 88	4,850
43	div2	Swindon	H	W	2-1	Robinson 72; Forbes 79	12,465
44	div2	Blackpool	A	L	0-1		6,709
45	div2	Rotherham	H	L	0-2		14,118
46	div2	Oldham	A	D	1-1	O'Leary 68	5,179
47	div2	Southend	H	D	2-2	Fallon 19,34	19,176
48	div2	Chesterfield	A	W	4-0	Knight 5,79,89; Fallon 33	6,294
49	d2po1	Brentford	H	D	1-1	Ricketts 87	19,060
50	d2po2	Brentford	A	W	2-0	Knight 8,15	10,652
51	d2pof	Barnsley	H	L	3-4*	Fallon 28; Robinson 40 (*on penalties)	55,419

LEAGUE APPEARANCES, BOOKINGS AND GOALS

	AGE (on 01/07/06)	IN NAMED 16	APPEARANCES	COUNTING GAMES	MINUTES ON PITCH	LEAGUE GOALS	
Goalkeepers							
Willy Gueret	32	46	46	46	4140	0	2
Brian Murphy	23	31	0	0	0	0	0
Defenders							
Ijah Anderson	30	6	5	0	85	0	0
Kevin Austin	33	33	26	22	2016	0	4
Christian Edwards	30	3	2	1	105	0	0
Andy Gurney	32	1	0	0	0	0	0
Ezomo Iriekpen	24	28	28	26	2467	0	4
Keith Lowe	20	5	4	3	337	0	1
Gary Monk	27	35	33	32	2925	1	7
Samuel Ricketts	24	44	44	42	3849	2	4
Alan Tate	23	43	43	41	3731	0	11
Steven Watt	21	6	2	0	77	0	1
Tommy Williams	25	19	17	13	1236	0	4
Midfielders							
Marcus Bean	21	9	9	8	765	1	3
Leon Britton	23	40	38	29	3022	4	7
Adrian Forbes	27	36	28	9	1298	4	3
Marc Goodfellow	24	22	11	2	510	0	0
Roberto Martinez	32	43	39	29	3009	2	6
Shaun MacDonald	18	13	7	2	245	0	0
Kevin McLeod	25	30	29	20	1924	7	4
Kristian O'Leary	28	25	15	8	986	1	2
Andy Robinson	22	41	39	28	2690	11	3
Owain Tudur-Jones	21	23	21	16	1514	3	2
Darren Way	26	6	5	1	167	0	1
Forwards							
Adebayo Akinfenwa	24	41	34	25	2508	9	7
Paul Connor	27	22	13	4	469	1	0
Rory Fallon	24	18	17	11	1133	4	1
Leon Knight	23	21	17	7	983	8	3
Kevin Nugent	37	1	1	0	39	0	0
Lee Thorpe	30	8	3	1	97	0	0
Lee Trundle	29	37	36	31	3007	20	3

TEAM OF THE SEASON

G Willy Gueret CG: 46 DR: 75

D Ezomo Iriekpen CG: 26 DR: 85

D Gary Monk CG: 32 DR: 77

D Tommy Williams CG: 13 DR: 77

D Alan Tate CG: 41 DR: 76

M Leon Britton CG: 29 SD: 25

M Kevin McLeod CG: 20 SD: 25

M Roberto Martinez CG: 29 SD: 24

M Owain Tudur-Jones CG: 16 SD: 23

F Lee Trundle CG: 31 SR: 150

F Adebayo Akinfenwa CG: 25 SR: 279

MONTHLY POINTS TALLY

Month	Points	%
AUGUST	12	67%
SEPTEMBER	11	73%
OCTOBER	8	53%
NOVEMBER	7	78%
DECEMBER	5	33%
JANUARY	6	33%
FEBRUARY	9	60%
MARCH	5	42%
APRIL	5	28%
MAY	3	100%

LEAGUE GOALS

	PLAYER	LGE	FAC	LC	Oth	TOT
1	Trundle	20	0	0	0	20
2	Robinson	11	0	0	1	12
3	Akinfenwa	9	0	1	0	10
4	Knight	8	0	0	2	10
5	McLeod	7	0	0	0	7
6	Forbes	4	0	0	0	4
7	Britton	4	0	0	0	4
8	Fallon	4	0	0	1	5
9	Tudur-Jones	3	0	0	0	3
10	Martinez	2	0	0	0	2
11	Ricketts	2	0	0	1	3
	Other	4	0	0	0	4
	TOTAL	**78**	**0**	**1**	**5**	**84**

TOP POINT EARNERS

	PLAYER	GAMES	AV PTS
1	Ezomo Iriekpen	26	**1.81**
2	Kevin McLeod	20	**1.80**
3	Adebayo Akinfenwa	25	**1.76**
4	Kevin Austin	22	**1.73**
5	Roberto Martinez	29	**1.72**
6	Samuel Ricketts	42	**1.67**
7	Leon Britton	29	**1.66**
8	Owain Tudur-Jones	16	**1.63**
9	Alan Tate	41	**1.63**
10	Lee Trundle	31	**1.58**

DISCIPLINARY RECORDS

	PLAYER	YELLOW	RED	AVE
1	O'Leary	2	2	**246**
2	Williams, T	4	1	**247**
3	Bean	3	0	**255**
4	Tate	11	1	**310**
5	Knight	3	0	**327**
6	Austin	4	2	**336**
7	Akinfenwa	7	0	**358**
8	Monk	7	0	**417**
9	Britton	7	0	**431**
10	Forbes	3	0	**432**
11	McLeod	4	0	**481**
12	Iriekpen	4	1	**493**
13	Martinez	6	0	**501**
	Other	15	0	
	TOTAL	**80**	**7**	

KEY GOALKEEPER

Willy Gueret

Goals Conceded in the League	55	Counting Games League games when player was on pitch for at least 70 minutes	46
Goals Conceded in all competitions	63		
Defensive Rating Ave number of mins between League goals conceded while on the pitch	75	Clean Sheets In games when player was on pitch for at least 70 minutes	9

KEY PLAYERS - GOALSCORERS

Lee Trundle

Goals in the League	20	Player Strike Rate Average number of minutes between League goals scored by player	150
Goals in all competitions	20		
Contribution to Attacking Power Average number of minutes between League team goals while on pitch	53	Club Strike Rate Average number of minutes between League goals scored by club	53

	PLAYER	GOALS LGE	GOALS ALL	POWER	S RATE
1	Lee Trundle	20	20	53	150 mins
2	Andy Robinson	11	12	63	245 mins
3	Kevin McLeod	7	7	41	275 mins
4	Adebayo Akinfenwa	9	10	47	279 mins

KEY PLAYERS - DEFENDERS

Ezomo Iriekpen

Goals Conceded in the League	29	Clean Sheets In League games when player was on pitch for at least 70 minutes	7
Goals Conceded in all competitions	31		
Defensive Rating Ave number of mins between League goals conceded while on the pitch	85	Club Defensive Rating Average number of mins between League goals conceded by the club this season	75

	PLAYER	CON LGE	CON ALL	CLN SHEETS	DEF RATE
1	Ezomo Iriekpen	29	31	7	85 mins
2	Gary Monk	38	41	6	77 mins
3	Tommy Williams	16	16	1	77 mins
4	Alan Tate	49	57	7	76 mins

Lee Trundle

KEY PLAYERS - MIDFIELDERS

Leon Britton

Goals in the League	4	Contribution to Attacking Power Average number of minutes between League team goals while on pitch	52
Goals in all competitions	4		
Defensive Rating Average number of mins between League goals conceded while on the pitch	77	Scoring Difference Defensive Rating minus Contribution to Attacking Power	25

	PLAYER	GOALS LGE	GOALS ALL	DEF RATE	ATT POWER	SCORE DIFF
1	Leon Britton	4	4	77	52	25 mins
2	Kevin McLeod	7	7	66	41	25 mins
3	Roberto Martinez	2	2	77	53	24 mins
4	Owain Tudur-Jones	3	3	69	46	23 mins

SQUAD APPEARANCES

Match	1	2	3	4	5	6	7	8	9	10	11	12	13	14	15	16	17	18	19	20	21	22	23	24	25
Venue	H	A	A	H	A	A	H	H	A	A	H	A	H	A	H	A	H	A	A	H	A	H	H	A	A
Competition	L	L	L	L	W	L	L	L	L	L	L	L	L	L	L	L	L	F	L	L	L	L	L	L	L
Result	W	W	L	L	L	W	W	W	W	D	D	W	W	L	D	D	W	L	W	W	D	W	D	L	L

Match	26	27	28	29	30	31	32	33	34	35	36	37	38	39	40	41	42	43	44	45	46	47	48	49	50	51
Venue	A	H	H	A	H	A	H	H	A	H	A	H	A	H	H	A	A	H	A	H	A	H	A	H	A	H
Competition	L	L	L	L	L	L	L	L	L	L	L	L	L	L	L	L	L	L	L	L	L	L	L	O	O	O
Result	D	D	W	D	D	L	L	W	W	D	D	D	D	D	W	L	L	W	L	L	D	D	W	D	W	L

Goalkeepers
Willy Gueret
Brian Murphy

Defenders
Ash Anderson
Kevin Austin
Christian Edwards
Andy Gurney
Ezomo Iriekpen
Keith Lowe
Gary Monk
Samuel Ricketts
Alan Tate
Steven Watt
Tommy Williams

Midfielders
Marcus Bean
Leon Britton
Adrian Forbes
Marc Goodfellow
Roberto Martinez
Shaun MacDonald
Kevin McLeod
Kristian O'Leary
Andy Robinson
Owain Tudur-Jones
Darren Way

Forwards
Adebayo Akinfenwa
Paul Connor
Rory Fallon
Leon Knight
Kevin Nugent
Lee Thorpe
Lee Trundle

KEY: On all match; On bench; Subbed or sent off (Counting game); Subbed or sent off (playing less than 70 minutes); Subbed on from bench (Counting Game); Subbed on (playing less than 70 minutes); Subbed on and then subbed or sent off (Counting Game); Subbed on and then subbed or sent off (playing less than 70 minutes); Not in 16

NOTTINGHAM FOREST

Final Position: **7th**

NICKNAME: THE REDS

KEY: ☐ Won ☐ Drawn ☐ Lost

							Attendance
1	div2	Huddersfield	H	W	2-1	Dobie 45; Johnson 87	24,042
2	div2	Walsall	A	L	2-3	Commons 36; Friio 85	8,703
3	div2	Swindon	A	L	1-2	Commons 39	8,108
4	div2	Scunthorpe	H	L	0-1		19,091
5	ccr1	Macclesfield	H	L	2-3	Breckin 9,83	5,050
6	div2	Gillingham	A	W	3-1	Johnson 8; Dobie 44; Weir-Daley 79	7,228
7	div2	Brentford	H	L	1-2	Thompson 48	17,234
8	div2	Barnsley	A	L	0-2		10,080
9	div2	Rotherham	H	W	2-0	Lester 76 pen; Commons 88	20,123
10	div2	Bristol City	H	W	3-1	Lester 25 pen; Perch 27; Commons 55	16,666
11	div2	Swansea	A	D	1-1	Lester 54	18,212
12	div2	Blackpool	H	D	1-1	Breckin 79	17,071
13	div2	Tranmere	H	W	1-0	Taylor 70	22,022
14	div2	Southend	A	L	0-1		10,104
15	div2	Hartlepool	H	W	2-0	Taylor 34; Bopp 90	17,586
16	div2	Yeovil	A	L	0-3		9,072
17	div2	Bradford	H	W	1-0	Johnson 24	17,983
18	facr1	Weymouth	H	D	1-1	Holt, Gary 39	10,305
19	div2	Bournemouth	A	D	1-1	Southall 19	9,222
20	facr1r	Weymouth	A	W	2-0	Taylor 67,73	6,500
21	div2	Southend	H	W	2-0	Wilson 51 og; Southall 70	19,576
22	div2	Huddersfield	A	L	1-2	Lester 46	17,370
23	facr2	Chester	A	L	0-3		4,732
24	div2	Port Vale	H	W	1-0	Tyson 31	17,696
25	div2	Walsall	H	D	1-1	Breckin 35	20,912
26	div2	Scunthorpe	A	L	1-3	Taylor 65 pen	5,857
27	div2	Doncaster	H	W	4-0	Breckin 45; Thompson 50; Southall 53; Taylor 67	23,009
28	div2	Chesterfield	H	D	0-0		21,909
29	div2	Colchester	A	L	1-3	Tyson 90	5,767
30	div2	Oldham	H	W	3-0	Holt, Grant 25; Tyson 63; Southall 67	17,807
31	div2	Brentford	A	D	1-1	Commons 5	7,859
32	div2	Rotherham	A	D	1-1	Tyson 34	7,222
33	div2	Barnsley	H	L	0-2		16,237
34	div2	MK Dons	A	L	0-1		7,670
35	div2	Blackpool	A	D	2-2	Breckin 45; Bennett 90	8,399
36	div2	Swansea	H	L	1-2	Tyson 21	19,132
37	div2	Oldham	A	L	0-3		5,584
38	div2	Port Vale	A	W	2-0	Commons 40; Tyson 90	6,793
39	div2	Swindon	H	W	7-1	Southall 3,51,55; Morgan 17,57; Breckin 29; Lester 90	22,444
40	div2	Bristol City	A	D	1-1	Perch 66	14,397
41	div2	Gillingham	H	D	1-1	Tyson 45	19,446
42	div2	Doncaster	A	W	2-1	Commons 25; Holt, Grant 47	8,299
43	div2	MK Dons	H	W	3-0	McClenahan 20 og; Holt, Grant 34; Breckin 90	18,214
44	div2	Chesterfield	A	W	3-1	Breckin 19; Tyson 29; Thompson 87	7,073
45	div2	Colchester	H	W	1-0	Perch 72	22,680
46	div2	Tranmere	A	W	1-0	Holt, Grant 17	9,152
47	div2	Yeovil	H	W	2-1	Breckin 39; Southall 67	28,193
48	div2	Hartlepool	A	L	2-3	Tyson 15; Commons 67	5,336
49	div2	Bournemouth	H	D	1-1	Tyson 56	26,847
50	div2	Bradford	A	D	1-1	Bennett 88	15,608

LEAGUE APPEARANCES, BOOKINGS AND GOALS

	AGE (on 01/07/06)	IN NAMED 16	APPEARANCES	COUNTING GAMES	MINUTES ON PITCH	LEAGUE GOALS	[yellow card icon]
Goalkeepers							
Patrick Gamble	17	12	0	0	0	0	0
Paul Gerrard	33	35	22	20	1844	0	0
Russell Hoult	33	8	8	8	720	0	0
Rune Pedersen	26	37	18	17	1576	0	0
Defenders							
Julian Bennett	21	18	18	17	1567	2	5
Ian Breckin	30	46	46	45	4109	8	3
Danny Cullip	29	22	11	10	899	0	3
John Curtis	27	29	27	26	2333	0	1
Nicky Eaden	34	29	28	24	2299	0	2
Wes Morgan	22	45	43	38	3588	2	4
Gino Padula	29	5	3	2	200	0	0
John Thompson	25	40	35	29	2636	3	3
Midfielders							
Felix Bastians	18	15	11	2	380	0	1
Eugen Bopp	22	24	12	2	371	1	2
Sammy Clingan	22	17	15	14	1260	0	1
Kristian Commons	22	37	37	32	2973	8	4
David Friio	33	18	17	8	1014	1	2
Ross Gardner	20	29	12	4	543	0	3
Gary Holt	33	30	26	23	2112	0	5
James Perch	20	42	38	32	3042	3	2
Nicky Southall	34	41	40	32	3095	8	4
Forwards							
Eugene Dadi	32	9	5	1	119	0	2
Scott Dobie	27	8	8	6	595	2	0
Neil Harris	28	1	1	0	20	0	0
Grant Holt	25	19	19	17	1513	4	3
David Johnson	29	17	17	9	1026	3	0
Jack Lester	30	39	38	11	1486	5	6
Jon-Paul Pittman	19	2	0	0	0	0	0
Gareth Taylor	33	20	20	14	1438	4	2
Nathan Tyson	24	28	28	28	2486	10	4
Spencer Weir-Daley	20	6	6	0	84	1	0

TEAM OF THE SEASON

G Paul Gerrard CG: 20 DR: 77

D Wes Morgan CG: 38 DR: 83
D Julian Bennett CG: 17 DR: 82
D John Thompson CG: 29 DR: 82
D John Curtis CG: 26 DR: 80

M James Perch CG: 32 SD: 42
M Kristian Commons CG: 32 SD: 29
M Gary Holt CG: 23 SD: 24
M Nicky Southall CG: 32 SD: 17

F Nathan Tyson CG: 28 SR: 249
F Gareth Taylor CG: 14 SR: 360

MONTHLY POINTS TALLY

AUGUST	6	40%
SEPTEMBER	8	44%
OCTOBER	9	60%
NOVEMBER	4	44%
DECEMBER	8	53%
JANUARY	5	28%
FEBRUARY	7	47%
MARCH	8	67%
APRIL	13	72%
MAY	1	33%

LEAGUE GOALS

	PLAYER	LGE	FAC	LC	Oth	TOT
1	Tyson	10	0	0	0	10
2	Southall	8	0	0	0	8
3	Breckin	8	0	2	0	10
4	Commons	8	0	0	0	8
5	Lester	5	0	0	0	5
6	Taylor	4	2	0	0	6
7	Holt, Grant	4	0	0	0	4
8	Perch	3	0	0	0	3
9	Thompson	3	0	0	0	3
10	Johnson	3	0	0	0	3
11	Morgan	2	0	0	0	2
	Other	9	1	0	0	10
	TOTAL	67	3	2	0	72

TOP POINT EARNERS

	PLAYER	GAMES	AV PTS
1	Julian Bennett	17	1.88
2	Grant Holt	17	1.88
3	Rune Pedersen	17	1.76
4	James Perch	32	1.75
5	Kristian Commons	32	1.72
6	Wes Morgan	38	1.68
7	John Curtis	26	1.65
8	Nathan Tyson	28	1.61
9	Gary Holt	23	1.57
10	Ian Breckin	45	1.53

DISCIPLINARY RECORDS

	PLAYER	YELLOW	RED	AVE
1	Gardner	3	0	[illegible]
2	Lester	6	1	[illegible]
3	Bennett	5	1	[illegible]
4	Cullip	3	0	[illegible]
5	Holt, Gary	5	0	[illegible]
6	Taylor	2	1	[illegible]
7	Tyson	4	1	[illegible]
8	Holt, Grant	3	0	[illegible]
9	Friio	2	0	[illegible]
10	Morgan	4	1	[illegible]
11	Commons	4	0	[illegible]
12	Southall	4	0	[illegible]
13	Thompson	3	0	[illegible]
	Other	9	2	
	TOTAL	57	7	

KEY GOALKEEPER

Paul Gerrard

Goals Conceded in the League	24	**Counting Games** League games when player was on pitch for at least 70 minutes	20
Goals Conceded in all competitions	27		
Defensive Rating Ave number of mins between League goals conceded while on the pitch	77	**Clean Sheets** In games when player was on pitch for at least 70 minutes	6

KEY PLAYERS - DEFENDERS

Wes Morgan

Goals Conceded in the League	43	**Clean Sheets** In League games when player was on pitch for at least 70 minutes	12
Goals Conceded in all competitions	50		
Defensive Rating Ave number of mins between League goals conceded while on the pitch	83	**Club Defensive Rating** Average number of mins between League goals conceded by the club this season	80

	PLAYER	CON LGE	CON ALL	CLN SHEETS	DEF RATE
1	Wes Morgan	43	50	12	83 mins
2	John Thompson	32	37	10	82 mins
3	Julian Bennett	19	19	5	82 mins
4	John Curtis	29	32	9	80 mins

KEY PLAYERS - MIDFIELDERS

James Perch

Goals in the League	3	**Contribution to Attacking Power** Average number of minutes between League team goals while on pitch	63
Goals in all competitions	3		
Defensive Rating Average number of mins between League goals conceded while on the pitch	105	**Scoring Difference** Defensive Rating minus Contribution to Attacking Power	42

	PLAYER	GOALS LGE	GOALS ALL	DEF RATE	ATT POWER	SCORE DIFF
1	James Perch	3	3	105	63	42 mins
2	Kristian Commons	8	8	85	56	29 mins
3	Gary Holt	0	1	78	54	24 mins
4	Nicky Southall	8	8	79	62	17 mins

KEY PLAYERS - GOALSCORERS

Nathan Tyson

Goals in the League	10	**Player Strike Rate** Average number of minutes between League goals scored by player	249
Goals in all competitions	10		
Contribution to Attacking Power Average number of minutes between League team goals while on pitch	55	**Club Strike Rate** Average number of minutes between League goals scored by club	62

	PLAYER	GOALS LGE	GOALS ALL	POWER	S RATE
1	Nathan Tyson	10	10	55	249 mins
2	Gareth Taylor	4	6	68	360 mins
3	Kristian Commons	8	8	56	372 mins
4	Grant Holt	4	4	56	378 mins

Nathan Tyson

SQUAD APPEARANCES

Match	1	2	3	4	5	6	7	8	9	10	11	12	13	14	15	16	17	18	19	20	21	22	23	24	25	26	27	28	29	30	31	32	33	34	35	36	37	38	39	40	41	42	43	44	45	46	47	48	49	50
Venue	H	A	A	H	H	A	H	A	H	H	A	H	H	A	H	A	H	H	A	A	H	A	A	H	H	A	H	H	A	H	A	A	H	A	A	H	A	A	H	A	H	A	H	A	H	A	H	A	H	A
Competition	L	L	L	L	W	L	L	L	L	L	L	L	L	L	L	L	L	F	L	F	L	L	F	L	L	L	L	L	L	L	L	L	L	L	L	L	L	L	L	L	L	L	L	L	L	L	L	L	L	L
Result	W	L	L	L	L	W	L	L	W	W	D	D	W	L	W	L	W	D	D	W	W	L	L	W	D	L	W	D	L	W	D	D	L	L	D	L	L	W	W	D	D	W	W	W	W	W	W	L	D	D

Goalkeepers
Patrick Gamble
Paul Gerrard
Russell Hoult
Rune Pedersen

Defenders
Julian Bennett
Ian Breckin
Danny Cullip
John Curtis
Nicky Eaden
Wes Morgan
Gino Padula
John Thompson

Midfielders
Felix Bastians
Eugen Bopp
Sammy Clingan
Kristian Commons
David Friio
Ross Gardner
Gary Holt
James Perch
Nicky Southall

Forwards
Eugene Dadi
Scott Dobie
Neil Harris
Grant Holt
David Johnson
Jack Lester
Jon-Paul Pittman
Gareth Taylor
Nathan Tyson
Spencer Weir-Daley

KEY: On all match; On bench; Subbed or sent off (Counting game); Subbed or sent off (playing less than 70 minutes); Subbed on from bench (Counting Game); Subbed on (playing less than 70 minutes); Subbed on and then subbed or sent off (Counting Game); Subbed on and then subbed or sent off (playing less than 70 minutes); Not in 16

DONCASTER ROVERS

Final Position: **8th**

NICKNAME: ROVERS

KEY: ☐ Won ☐ Drawn ☐ Lost

							Attendance
1	div2	Bristol City	A	D	0-0		15,481
2	div2	MK Dons	H	D	1-1	Heffernan 66	5,232
3	div2	Hartlepool	H	L	0-1		5,061
4	div2	Swansea	A	W	2-1	Mulligan 74; Guy 85	12,744
5	ccr1	Wrexham	A	W	1-0	Hughes 86	2,177
6	div2	Port Vale	A	L	0-2		4,993
7	div2	Huddersfield	H	L	1-2	McIndoe 64 pen	7,222
8	div2	Blackpool	H	L	0-1		5,484
9	div2	Colchester	A	L	2-3	Forte 5; McIndoe 54 pen	2,721
10	div2	Scunthorpe	H	W	3-1	Fortune-West 15; McIndoe 25; Forte 60	6,699
11	ccr2	Man City	H	W	3-0*	McIndoe 118 pen (*on penalties)	8,228
12	div2	Barnsley	A	W	2-0	Green 13; Mulligan 83	12,002
13	div2	Swindon	H	W	1-0	Forte 36	5,282
14	div2	Bradford	H	D	2-2	Ravenhill 55; Fenton 69	6,800
15	div2	Bournemouth	A	L	1-2	Heffernan 7	6,578
16	div2	Southend	H	W	2-0	Ravenhill 77; Forte 88	5,899
17	div2	Walsall	A	L	0-1		5,385
18	ccr3	Gillingham	H	W	2-0	Heffernan 84,89	6,874
19	div2	Tranmere	H	L	0-2		5,542
20	facr1	Blackpool	H	W	4-1	Heffernan 18,72; McIndoe 53 pen,56 pen	4,332
21	div2	Oldham	A	W	1-0	McIndoe 78 pen	5,800
22	div2	Bournemouth	H	W	4-2	Heffernan 41; McIndoe 61 pen; Ravenhill 63; Fenton 85	4,803
23	div2	Bristol City	H	W	2-0	Heffernan 5; Coppinger 68	7,876
24	ccr4	Aston Villa	H	W	3-0	McIndoe 20 pen; Heffernan 53; Thornton 79	10,590
25	facr2	Boston	A	W	2-1	Mulligan 29,58	3,995
26	div2	Gillingham	A	L	0-1		4,861
27	div2	MK Dons	A	W	3-2	Fenton 13; Roberts, S 23; Heffernan 86	5,351
28	div2	Swansea	H	W	2-1	McIndoe 16 pen; Heffernan 84	7,159
29	ccQF	Arsenal	H	L	1-3*	McIndoe 4; Green 104 (*on penalties)	10,006
30	div2	Nottm Forest	A	L	0-4		23,009
31	div2	Rotherham	A	L	0-1		6,761
32	div2	Yeovil	H	L	0-1		5,680
33	facr3	Port Vale	A	L	1-2	Heffernan 27	4,923
34	div2	Chesterfield	H	D	1-1	Heffernan 45	6,528
35	div2	Scunthorpe	A	W	2-1	McIndoe 63; Lee 89	6,978
36	div2	Blackpool	A	L	2-4	McIndoe 26 pen; McCormack 90	4,836
37	div2	Swindon	A	L	1-2	McCormack 64	5,100
38	div2	Barnsley	H	W	2-0	Price 36,59	8,144
39	div2	Chesterfield	A	W	1-0	Price 14	5,719
40	div2	Gillingham	H	W	2-0	Wheater 27; McCormack 45 pen	5,738
41	div2	Hartlepool	A	D	1-1	McCormack 90	5,459
42	div2	Brentford	H	D	0-0		5,250
43	div2	Huddersfield	A	D	2-2	Price 15; Green 57	14,490
44	div2	Port Vale	H	D	1-1	Fortune-West 58	5,511
45	div2	Nottm Forest	H	L	1-2	Coppinger 86 pen	8,299
46	div2	Colchester	H	D	0-0		4,262
47	div2	Brentford	A	W	1-0	Thornton 59	7,323
48	div2	Rotherham	H	W	3-1	Roberts, N 6; Thornton 10; Guy 21	7,542
49	div2	Yeovil	A	L	0-3		5,456
50	div2	Bradford	A	L	1-2	McCormack 68	9,297
51	div2	Walsall	H	W	1-0	Coppinger 42	5,086
52	div2	Southend	A	W	1-0	Coppinger 46	10,397
53	div2	Oldham	H	W	1-0	Coppinger 66	6,104
54	div2	Tranmere	A	W	2-0	Guy 12; Roberts, N 43	8,343

LEAGUE APPEARANCES, BOOKINGS AND GOALS

	AGE (on 01/07/06)	IN NAMED 16	APPEARANCES	COUNTING GAMES	MINUTES ON PITCH	LEAGUE GOALS		
Goalkeepers								
Alan Blayney	24	19	16	16	1440	0	0	0
Jan Budtz	27	35	20	20	1800	0	0	0
Barry Richardson	36	13	0	0	0	0	0	0
Dino Seremet	25	4	1	1	90	0	0	0
Andy Warrington	30	9	9	9	810	0	0	0
Defenders								
Mark Albrighton	30	20	16	15	1412	0	3	0
Nicky Fenton	26	31	25	20	1919	3	4	0
Stephen Foster	31	17	17	17	1530	0	3	0
Graeme Lee	28	20	20	20	1800	1	4	0
Simon Marples	30	18	15	12	1153	0	0	0
Sean McDaid	20	35	35	34	3070	0	3	0
Philip McGuire	26	12	11	9	904	0	1	0
Dave Mulligan	24	33	32	20	2107	2	2	0
Samuel Oji	20	7	4	1	169	0	1	0
Stephen Roberts	26	30	27	19	1987	1	3	0
Tim Ryan	31	7	7	7	609	0	2	0
David Wheater	19	8	7	6	585	1	0	0
Midfielders								
James Coppinger	25	37	36	28	2631	5	0	1
Paul Green	23	35	34	20	2120	2	2	0
Anthony Griffiths	-	6	4	4	359	0	0	0
Kevin Horlock	33	13	13	13	1170	0	3	0
Adam Hughes	23	7	6	3	333	0	1	0
Michael McIndoe	26	33	33	28	2653	8	2	0
Jermaine McSporran	29	2	2	1	153	0	0	0
Uros Predic	32	6	6	3	308	0	0	0
Jason Price	29	11	11	11	947	4	0	0
Ricky Ravenhill	25	36	27	23	2065	3	9	1
Sean Thornton	23	31	29	22	2098	2	4	0
Michael Timlin	21	3	3	2	222	0	0	0
Forwards								
Alun Armstrong	31	10	6	1	169	0	0	0
Jonathan Forte	19	13	13	8	846	4	1	1
Leo Fortune-West	35	40	27	12	1436	2	2	0
Lewis Guy	20	32	31	16	1718	3	5	1
Paul Heffernan	24	28	26	19	1909	7	3	1
Ross McCormack	19	19	19	12	1148	5	0	0
Richard Offiong	22	7	5	1	202	0	0	0
Neil Roberts	28	36	30	15	1502	2	1	0

TEAM OF THE SEASON

G
Alan Blayney
CG: 16 DR: 103

D
Simon Marples
CG: 12 DR: 105

D
Dave Mulligan
CG: 20 DR: 92

D
Graeme Lee
CG: 20 DR: 90

D
Stephen Roberts
CG: 19 DR: 90

M
James Coppinger
CG: 28 SD: 22

M
Kevin Horlock
CG: 13 SD: 20

M
Sean Thornton
CG: 22 SD: 11

M
Michael McIndoe
CG: 28 SD: 8

F
Ross McCormack
CG: 12 SR: 230

F
Paul Heffernan
CG: 19 SR: 273

MONTHLY POINTS TALLY

AUGUST	5	28%
SEPTEMBER	9	60%
OCTOBER	4	27%
NOVEMBER	9	100%
DECEMBER	6	40%
JANUARY	4	33%
FEBRUARY	11	61%
MARCH	6	40%
APRIL	12	67%
MAY	3	100%

LEAGUE GOALS

	PLAYER	LGE	FAC	LC	Oth	TOT
1	McIndoe	8	2	3	0	13
2	Heffernan	7	3	3	0	13
3	McCormack	5	0	0	0	5
4	Coppinger	5	0	0	0	5
5	Price	4	0	0	0	4
6	Forte	4	0	0	0	4
7	Fenton	3	0	0	0	3
8	Guy	3	0	0	0	3
9	Ravenhill	3	0	0	0	3
10	Green	2	0	1	0	3
11	Thornton	2	0	1	0	3
	Other	9	2	1	0	12
	TOTAL	55	7	9	0	71

TOP POINT EARNERS

	PLAYER	GAMES	AV PTS
1	Alan Blayney	16	2.00
2	Leo Fortune-West	12	2.00
3	Stephen Roberts	19	1.95
4	Sean Thornton	22	1.82
5	Lewis Guy	16	1.81
6	Sean McDaid	34	1.76
7	Graeme Lee	20	1.65
8	Dave Mulligan	20	1.65
9	Kevin Horlock	13	1.54
10	James Coppinger	28	1.54

DISCIPLINARY RECORDS

	PLAYER	YELLOW	RED	AVE
1	Ravenhill	9	1	206
2	Guy	5	1	286
3	Ryan	2	0	304
4	Horlock	3	0	390
5	Forte	1	1	423
6	Lee	4	0	450
7	Albrighton	3	0	470
8	Heffernan	3	1	477
9	Fenton	4	0	479
10	Foster	3	0	510
11	Thornton	4	0	524
12	Roberts, S	3	0	662
13	Fortune-West	2	0	718
	Other	11	1	
	TOTAL	57	5	

KEY GOALKEEPER

Alan Blayney

Goals Conceded in the League	14	Counting Games League games when player was on pitch for at least 70 minutes	16
Goals Conceded in all competitions	16		
Defensive Rating Ave number of mins between League goals conceded while on the pitch	103	Clean Sheets In games when player was on pitch for at least 70 minutes	9

KEY PLAYERS - GOALSCORERS

Ross McCormack

Goals in the League	5	Player Strike Rate Average number of minutes between League goals scored by player	230
Goals in all competitions	5		
Contribution to Attacking Power Average number of minutes between League team goals while on pitch	82	Club Strike Rate Average number of minutes between League goals scored by club	75

	PLAYER	GOALS LGE	GOALS ALL	POWER	S RATE
1	Ross McCormack	5	5	82	230 mins
2	Paul Heffernan	7	13	80	273 mins
3	Michael McIndoe	8	13	66	332 mins
4	James Coppinger	5	5	75	526 mins

KEY PLAYERS - DEFENDERS

Simon Marples

Goals Conceded in the League	11	Clean Sheets In League games when player was on pitch for at least 70 minutes	6
Goals Conceded in all competitions	12		
Defensive Rating Ave number of mins between League goals conceded while on the pitch	105	Club Defensive Rating Average number of mins between League goals conceded by the club this season	81

	PLAYER	CON LGE	CON ALL	CLN SHEETS	DEF RATE
1	Simon Marples	11	12	6	105 mins
2	Dave Mulligan	23	27	9	92 mins
3	Stephen Roberts	22	26	9	90 mins
4	Graeme Lee	20	20	9	90 mins

Michael McIndoe

KEY PLAYERS - MIDFIELDERS

James Coppinger

Goals in the League	5	Contribution to Attacking Power Average number of minutes between League team goals while on pitch	75
Goals in all competitions	5		
Defensive Rating Average number of mins between League goals conceded while on the pitch	97	Scoring Difference Defensive Rating minus Contribution to Attacking Power	22

	PLAYER	GOALS LGE	GOALS ALL	DEF RATE	ATT POWER	SCORE DIFF
1	James Coppinger	5	5	97	75	22 mins
2	Kevin Horlock	0	0	98	78	20 mins
3	Sean Thornton	2	3	95	84	11 mins
4	Michael McIndoe	8	13	74	66	8 mins

SQUAD APPEARANCES

Match	1	2	3	4	5	6	7	8	9	10	11	12	13	14	15	16	17	18	19	20	21	22	23	24	25	26	27
Venue	A	H	H	A	A	A	H	H	A	H	H	A	H	H	A	H	A	H	H	H	A	H	H	H	A	A	A
Competition	L	L	L	L	W	L	L	L	L	L	W	L	L	L	L	L	L	W	L	F	L	L	L	W	F	L	L
Result	D	D	L	W	W	L	L	L	L	W	W	W	W	D	L	W	L	W	L	W	W	W	W	W	W	L	W

Match	28	29	30	31	32	33	34	35	36	37	38	39	40	41	42	43	44	45	46	47	48	49	50	51	52	53	54
Venue	H	H	A	A	H	A	H	A	A	A	H	A	H	A	H	A	H	H	H	A	H	A	A	H	A	H	A
Competition	L	W	L	L	L	F	L	L	L	L	L	L	L	L	L	L	L	L	L	L	L	L	L	L	L	L	L
Result	W	L	L	L	L	L	D	W	L	L	W	W	W	D	D	D	D	L	D	W	W	L	L	W	W	W	W

Goalkeepers
Alan Blayney
Jan Budtz
Tonny Nielsen
Barry Richardson
Dino Seremet
Andy Warrington

Defenders
Mark Albrighton
Nicky Fenton
Stephen Foster
Graeme Lee
Simon Marples
Sean McDaid
Philip McGuire
Dave Mulligan
Samuel Oji
Stephen Roberts
Tim Ryan
David Wheater

Midfielders
James Coppinger
Paul Green
Anthony Griffiths
Kevin Horlock
Adam Hughes
Michael McIndoe
Jermaine McSporran
Craig Nelthorpe
Uros Predic
Jason Price
Ricky Ravenhill
Sean Thornton
Michael Timlin

Forwards
Alun Armstrong
Jonathan Forte
Leo Fortune-West
Lewis Guy
Paul Heffernan
Ross McCormack
Richard Offiong
Neil Roberts

KEY: ■ On all match ■ On bench ⏮ Subbed or sent off (Counting game) ⏪ Subbed or sent off (playing less than 70 minutes) ⏭ Subbed on from bench (Counting Game) ⏩ Subbed on (playing less than 70 minutes) Subbed on and then subbed or sent off (Counting Game) Subbed on and then subbed or sent off (playing less than 70 minutes) □ Not in 16

BRISTOL CITY

Final Position: **9th**

NICKNAME: THE ROBINS

KEY: ☐ Won ☐ Drawn ☐ Lost

No.	Comp	Opponent	H/A	Res	Score	Scorers	Attendance
1	div2	Doncaster	H	D	0-0		15,481
2	div2	Huddersfield	A	L	0-1		11,138
3	div2	Bournemouth	A	L	0-2		6,544
4	div2	Port Vale	H	W	4-2	Brooker 4,28; Stewart 7; Murray 14	11,120
5	ccr1	Barnet	H	L	2-4	Golbourne 14; Bridges 64	3,383
6	div2	MK Dons	H	D	2-2	Bridges 53; Heywood 60	10,011
7	div2	Colchester	H	D	0-0		10,180
8	div2	Swansea	A	L	1-7	Cotterill 81	13,662
9	div2	Blackpool	H	D	1-1	Cotterill 85	9,576
10	div2	Nottm Forest	A	L	1-3	Gillespie 15	16,666
11	div2	Brentford	A	W	3-2	Stewart 12; Wilkshire 40; Brooker 74	6,413
12	div2	Barnsley	H	W	3-0	Brooker 23; Stewart 38 pen,44	10,771
13	div2	Hartlepool	H	L	0-1		11,365
14	div2	Tranmere	H	W	1-0	Wilkshire 65	10,495
15	div2	Oldham	A	L	3-4	Brown 48; Quinn 79; Murray 90	5,456
16	div2	Chesterfield	A	L	0-3		5,027
17	div2	Southend	H	L	0-3		10,625
18	facr1	Notts County	H	L	0-2		4,221
19	div2	Swindon	A	L	1-2	Murray 4 pen	7,572
20	div2	Chesterfield	H	L	2-4	Wilkshire 6; Cotterill 85	9,752
21	div2	Doncaster	A	L	0-2		7,876
22	div2	Bradford	H	L	0-1		9,103
23	div2	Huddersfield	H	W	2-0	Murray 5; Cotterill 80	9,949
24	div2	Port Vale	A	W	1-0	Brooker 45	4,214
25	div2	Gillingham	A	D	1-1	Murray 10	7,786
26	div2	Rotherham	H	W	3-1	Brooker 11,77; Murray 48	12,510
27	div2	Yeovil	A	D	1-1	Heywood 50	9,178
28	div2	Walsall	H	W	3-0	Murray 10,30; Wilkshire 88	12,652
29	div2	Scunthorpe	H	D	1-1	Savage 62	11,692
30	div2	Colchester	A	L	2-3	Murray 2; Stewart 90	4,022
31	div2	Blackpool	A	D	1-1	Brooker 26	4,842
32	div2	Swansea	H	W	1-0	Carey 45	12,859
33	div2	Barnsley	A	L	0-2		8,092
34	div2	Brentford	H	L	0-1		10,854
35	div2	Scunthorpe	A	W	2-0	Cotterill 32; Murray 79	3,786
36	div2	Bradford	A	D	1-1	Brooker 16	7,917
37	div2	Bournemouth	H	W	3-1	McCammon 7; Brooker 57,64	11,058
38	div2	Nottm Forest	H	D	1-1	Russell 78	14,397
39	div2	MK Dons	A	W	1-0	Brooker 4	6,855
40	div2	Gillingham	H	W	6-0	Brooker 11; Carey 18,50; Skuse 45 pen; Wilkshire 67; McCammon 90	10,932
41	div2	Rotherham	A	L	1-3	Skuse 80	6,682
42	div2	Yeovil	H	W	2-1	Orr 13; McCammon 21	15,889
43	div2	Walsall	A	W	3-0	Cotterill 44; Russell 51 pen; Keogh 90	5,402
44	div2	Hartlepool	A	W	2-1	Noble 13; Russell 38	5,039
45	div2	Oldham	H	W	2-1	Russell 56 pen; Brooker 75	12,779
46	div2	Tranmere	A	W	3-0	Brooker 17; McCammon 34; Woodman 90 pen	6,288
47	div2	Swindon	H	D	1-1	Cotterill 68	15,632
48	div2	Southend	A	L	0-1		11,387

LEAGUE APPEARANCES, BOOKINGS AND GOALS

	AGE (on 01/07/06)	IN NAMED 16	APPEARANCES	COUNTING GAMES	MINUTES ON PITCH	LEAGUE GOALS	Yellow	Red
Goalkeepers								
Adriano Basso	31	33	29	27	2507	0	0	0
Steve Phillips	28	43	19	17	1607	0	0	0
Defenders								
Louis Carey	29	39	38	36	3335	3	7	1
Liam Fontaine	20	18	15	14	1241	0	0	0
Clayton Fortune	23	10	6	4	445	0	1	0
Scott Golbourne	18	9	5	3	356	0	1	0
Matthew Heywood	26	24	24	21	2008	2	2	0
Marc Joseph	29	8	3	2	230	0	0	0
Richard Keogh	19	22	9	4	416	1	2	0
Bradley Orr	23	40	38	33	3139	1	8	0
David Partridge	27	11	11	10	917	0	3	0
Osei Sankofa	21	8	8	7	655	0	0	1
Jamie Smith	31	12	7	5	462	0	2	0
Craig Woodman	23	37	37	35	3218	1	6	0
Kelly Youga	20	4	4	1	256	0	1	0
Midfielders								
Scott Brown	21	30	29	16	1991	1	5	0
Scott Murray	32	38	37	25	2643	10	2	0
David Noble	24	26	24	21	1956	1	1	0
Alex Russell	33	29	27	20	1976	4	2	0
Cole Skuse	20	40	38	27	2625	2	1	0
Grant Smith	26	14	10	2	418	0	1	0
Luke Wilkshire	24	38	36	17	1907	5	4	1
Forwards								
Calvin Andrew	19	3	3	1	155	0	0	0
Michael Bridges	27	14	11	3	510	1	2	0
Stephen Brooker	25	37	37	32	2996	15	2	0
David Cotterill	18	45	45	32	3262	7	2	0
Stephen Gillespie	22	5	4	1	235	1	1	0
Guy Madjo	22	6	5	1	166	0	0	0
Mark McCammon	27	11	11	7	731	4	3	0
James Quinn	31	4	3	2	233	1	1	0
Basir Savage	24	26	23	11	1289	1	2	0
Marcus Stewart	33	32	27	10	1391	5	5	0

TEAM OF THE SEASON

G — Adriano Basso CG: 27 DR: 93

D — Liam Fontaine CG: 14 DR: 113

D — Craig Woodman CG: 35 DR: 89

D — Louis Carey CG: 36 DR: 88

D — Bradley Orr CG: 33 DR: 77

M — David Noble CG: 21 SD: 51

M — Alex Russell CG: 20 SD: 48

M — Cole Skuse CG: 27 SD: 0

M — Luke Wilkshire CG: 17 SD: 0

F — Stephen Brooker CG: 32 SR: 200

F — David Cotterill CG: 32 SR: 466

MONTHLY POINTS TALLY

Month	Points	%
AUGUST	5	33%
SEPTEMBER	8	44%
OCTOBER	3	20%
NOVEMBER	0	0%
DECEMBER	11	61%
JANUARY	8	53%
FEBRUARY	7	47%
MARCH	7	58%
APRIL	16	89%
MAY	0	0%

LEAGUE GOALS

	PLAYER	LGE	FAC	LC	Oth	TOT
1	Brooker	15	0	0	0	15
2	Murray	10	0	0	0	10
3	Cotterill	7	0	0	0	7
4	Stewart	5	0	0	0	5
5	Wilkshire	5	0	0	0	5
6	McCammon	4	0	0	0	4
7	Russell	4	0	0	0	4
8	Carey	3	0	0	0	3
9	Heywood	2	0	0	0	2
10	Skuse	2	0	0	0	2
11	Noble	1	0	0	0	1
	Other	8	0	2	0	10
	TOTAL	66	0	2	0	68

TOP POINT EARNERS

	PLAYER	GAMES	AV PTS
1	Liam Fontaine	14	2.14
2	Alex Russell	20	1.90
3	Adriano Basso	27	1.78
4	Craig Woodman	35	1.71
5	David Noble	21	1.71
6	Bradley Orr	33	1.70
7	Louis Carey	36	1.64
8	Stephen Brooker	32	1.56
9	David Cotterill	32	1.56
10	Scott Murray	25	1.52

DISCIPLINARY RECORDS

	PLAYER	YELLOW	RED	AVE
1	Smith, J	2	0	231
2	McCammon	3	0	243
3	Bridges	2	0	255
4	Stewart	5	0	278
5	Partridge	3	0	305
6	Wilkshire	4	1	381
7	Orr	8	0	392
8	Brown	5	0	398
9	Carey	7	1	416
10	Woodman	6	0	536
11	Savage	2	0	644
12	Sankofa	0	1	655
13	Russell	2	0	988
	Other	10	0	
	TOTAL	59	3	

KEY GOALKEEPER

Adriano Basso

Goals Conceded in the League	27	Counting Games League games when player was on pitch for at least 70 minutes	27
Goals Conceded in all competitions	27		
Defensive Rating Ave number of mins between League goals conceded while on the pitch	93	Clean Sheets In games when player was on pitch for at least 70 minutes	9

KEY PLAYERS - DEFENDERS

Liam Fontaine

Goals Conceded in the League	11	Clean Sheets In League games when player was on pitch for at least 70 minutes	5
Goals Conceded in all competitions	11		
Defensive Rating Ave number of mins between League goals conceded while on the pitch	113	Club Defensive Rating Average number of mins between League goals conceded by the club this season	67

	PLAYER	CON LGE	CON ALL	CLN SHEETS	DEF RATE
1	Liam Fontaine	11	11	5	113 mins
2	Craig Woodman	36	36	12	89 mins
3	Louis Carey	38	43	12	88 mins
4	Bradley Orr	41	43	11	77 mins

KEY PLAYERS - MIDFIELDERS

David Noble

Goals in the League	1	Contribution to Attacking Power Average number of minutes between League team goals while on pitch	58
Goals in all competitions	1		
Defensive Rating Average number of mins between League goals conceded while on the pitch	109	Scoring Difference Defensive Rating minus Contribution to Attacking Power	51

	PLAYER	GOALS LGE	GOALS ALL	DEF RATE	ATT POWER	SCORE DIFF
1	David Noble	1	1	109	58	51 mins
2	Alex Russell	4	4	104	56	48 mins
3	Cole Skuse	2	2	63	63	0 mins
4	Luke Wilkshire	5	5	60	60	0 mins

KEY PLAYERS - GOALSCORERS

Stephen Brooker

Goals in the League	15	Player Strike Rate Average number of minutes between League goals scored by player	200
Goals in all competitions	15		
Contribution to Attacking Power Average number of minutes between League team goals while on pitch	59	Club Strike Rate Average number of minutes between League goals scored by club	63

	PLAYER	GOALS LGE	GOALS ALL	POWER	S RATE
1	Stephen Brooker	15	15	59	200 mins
2	Scott Murray	10	10	63	264 mins
3	Luke Wilkshire	5	5	60	381 mins
4	David Cotterill	7	7	64	466 mins

David Noble

SQUAD APPEARANCES

Match	1	2	3	4	5	6	7	8	9	10	11	12	13	14	15	16	17	18	19	20	21	22	23	24
Venue	H	A	A	H	H	H	H	A	H	A	A	H	H	H	A	A	H	H	A	H	A	H	H	A
Competition	L	L	L	L	W	L	L	L	L	L	L	L	L	L	L	L	L	F	L	L	L	L	L	L
Result	D	L	L	W	L	D	D	L	D	L	W	W	L	W	L	L	L	L	L	L	L	L	W	W

Match	25	26	27	28	29	30	31	32	33	34	35	36	37	38	39	40	41	42	43	44	45	46	47	48
Venue	A	H	A	H	H	A	A	H	A	H	A	A	H	H	A	H	A	H	A	A	H	A	H	A
Competition	L	L	L	L	L	L	L	L	L	L	L	L	L	L	L	L	L	L	L	L	L	L	L	L
Result	D	W	D	W	D	L	D	W	L	L	W	D	W	D	W	W	L	W	W	W	W	W	D	L

Goalkeepers
Adriano Basso
Steve Phillips

Defenders
Louis Carey
Liam Fontaine
Clayton Fortune
Scott Golbourne
Matthew Heywood
Marc Joseph
Richard Keogh
Bradley Orr
David Partridge
Osei Sankofa
Jamie Smith
Craig Woodman
Kelly Youga

Midfielders
Scott Brown
Scott Murray
David Noble
Alex Russell
Cole Skuse
Grant Smith
Luke Wilkshire

Forwards
Calvin Andrew
Michael Bridges
Stephen Brooker
David Cotterill
Stephen Gillespie
Guy Madjo
Mark McCammon
James Quinn
Basir Savage
Marcus Stewart

KEY: On all match | On bench | Subbed or sent off (Counting game) | Subbed or sent off (playing less than 70 minutes) | Subbed on from bench (Counting Game) | Subbed on (playing less than 70 minutes) | Subbed on and then subbed or sent off (Counting Game) | Subbed on and then subbed or sent off (playing less than 70 minutes) | Not in 16

OLDHAM ATHLETIC

Final Position: **10th**

NICKNAME: THE LATICS

KEY: ☐ Won ☐ Drawn ☐ Lost

							Attendance
1	div2	Yeovil	H	W	2-0	Porter 24; Warne 26	6,979
2	div2	Swindon	A	W	3-2	Scott 13; Liddell 38,51 pen	5,294
3	div2	Tranmere	A	L	0-4		8,466
4	div2	Chesterfield	H	W	4-1	Branston 2; Liddell 4; Warne 57,86	5,347
5	ccr1	Leeds	A	L	0-2		14,970
6	div2	Colchester	A	D	0-0		2,742
7	div2	Rotherham	H	L	0-1		6,950
8	div2	Southend	A	L	1-2	Bonner 69	5,261
9	div2	Huddersfield	H	L	0-3		6,803
10	div2	Gillingham	A	W	1-0	Killen 6	6,259
11	div2	Bournemouth	H	W	1-0	Liddell 62 pen	5,058
12	div2	Port Vale	A	D	2-2	Beckett 15; Killen 81	3,796
13	div2	Barnsley	A	L	0-4		8,077
14	div2	Brentford	H	L	0-1		5,089
15	div2	Swansea	A	D	0-0		14,029
16	div2	Bristol City	H	W	4-3	Hughes 4; Wellens 25; Porter 56; Liddell 87	5,456
17	div2	Scunthorpe	A	L	2-4	Liddell 17,33	5,055
18	facr1	Chasetown	A	D	1-1	Eyres, D 31	1,997
19	div2	Doncaster	H	L	0-1		5,800
20	facr1r	Chasetown	H	W	4-0	Warne 31; Porter 56,75; Hall, C 84	7,235
21	div2	Brentford	A	D	3-3	Porter 11,21,23	5,450
22	div2	Yeovil	A	W	2-0	Warne 39,82	5,852
23	facr2	Brentford	H	D	1-1	Liddell 57 pen	4,365
24	div2	Walsall	H	W	2-1	Porter 34; Warne 72	3,878
25	div2	Swindon	H	D	2-2	Wellens 56; Liddell 71	5,354
26	facr2r	Brentford	A	L	0-1		3,146
27	div2	Chesterfield	A	D	1-1	Warne 47	4,304
28	div2	Bradford	H	W	2-1	Butcher 8; Beckett 13	6,982
29	div2	Hartlepool	H	W	2-1	Beckett 37; Liddell 61	5,047
30	div2	MK Dons	A	W	1-0	Beckett 43	5,082
31	div2	Southend	H	D	0-0		5,662
32	div2	Blackpool	A	L	0-1		5,977
33	div2	Nottm Forest	A	L	0-3		17,807
34	div2	Gillingham	H	W	2-0	Beckett 84,87	5,783
35	div2	Huddersfield	A	L	2-3	Porter 13; Beckett 33	12,973
36	div2	Port Vale	H	L	0-1		5,555
37	div2	Bournemouth	A	D	0-0		5,453
38	div2	Nottm Forest	H	W	3-0	Wellens 53; Butcher 73; Beckett 82	5,584
39	div2	Walsall	A	W	2-0	Beckett 72; Warne 74	5,816
40	div2	Tranmere	H	W	1-0	Wellens 35	5,281
41	div2	Colchester	H	W	1-0	Butcher 90	5,822
42	div2	Rotherham	A	L	0-2		5,823
43	div2	Bradford	A	W	4-1	Warne 16; Beckett 17,82; Butcher 34	7,959
44	div2	Blackpool	H	W	3-1	Beckett 45,55,86 pen	6,480
45	div2	Hartlepool	A	D	1-1	Beckett 45 pen	5,259
46	div2	MK Dons	H	L	1-2	Beckett 28 pen	5,919
47	div2	Barnsley	H	L	0-3		7,772
48	div2	Bristol City	A	L	1-2	Beckett 45	12,779
49	div2	Swansea	H	D	1-1	Beckett 60 pen	5,179
50	div2	Doncaster	A	L	0-1		6,104
51	div2	Scunthorpe	H	D	1-1	Eyres, D 45	5,544

LEAGUE APPEARANCES, BOOKINGS AND GOALS

	AGE (on 01/07/06)	IN NAMED 16	APPEARANCES	COUNTING GAMES	MINUTES ON PITCH	LEAGUE GOALS	Yellow	Red
Goalkeepers								
Lance Cronin	20	14	0	0	0	0	0	0
Chris Day	30	45	30	30	2700	0	0	0
Lee Grant	23	16	16	16	1440	0	0	0
Michael Poke	20	4	0	0	0	0	0	0
Terry Smith	18	10	0	0	0	0	0	0
Defenders								
Guy Branston	27	38	38	37	3339	1	8	0
Neil Eardley	17	1	1	1	90	0	0	0
Terrell Forbes	24	43	39	33	3128	0	0	0
Anthony Grant	19	5	2	1	156	0	0	0
Will Haining	23	17	15	14	1224	0	2	0
Daniel Hall	22	11	10	7	746	0	0	0
Gareth Owen	23	31	17	14	1363	0	0	0
Rob Scott	32	23	21	19	1738	1	4	0
Stefan Stam	29	19	13	9	873	0	0	0
Chris Swailes	35	15	15	12	1232	0	2	0
Marc Tierney	20	34	19	13	1346	0	3	0
Midfielders								
Mark Bonner	32	11	7	4	382	1	0	0
Richard Butcher	25	39	36	30	2845	4	3	0
Paul Edwards	26	39	34	27	2602	0	6	1
David Eyres	42	33	21	14	1378	1	2	0
Mark Hughes	22	37	33	28	2665	1	4	0
Andy Liddell	33	29	29	29	2609	9	0	0
Chris Taylor	19	15	14	9	961	0	0	0
Richard Wellens	26	45	45	42	3916	4	8	0
Forwards								
Luke Beckett	29	38	34	25	2441	18	0	0
Delroy Facey	26	4	3	0	49	0	0	0
Christopher Hall	19	22	17	2	573	0	1	0
Christopher Killen	24	13	12	7	814	2	1	0
Chris Porter	22	37	31	13	1607	7	0	0
Paul Warne	33	40	40	36	3254	9	4	1
Matthew Wolfenden	20	2	1	0	7	0	0	0

TEAM OF THE SEASON

G — Lee Grant, CG: 16 DR: 90

D — Chris Swailes, CG: 12 DR: 88

D — Guy Branston, CG: 37 DR: 76

D — Will Haining, CG: 14 DR: 72

D — Terrell Forbes, CG: 33 DR: 68

M — Mark Hughes, CG: 28 SD: 11

M — Richard Butcher, CG: 30 SD: 10

M — Paul Edwards, CG: 27 SD: 5

M — Richard Wellens, CG: 42 SD: -3

F — Luke Beckett, CG: 25 SR: 136

F — Chris Porter, CG: 13 SR: 230

MONTHLY POINTS TALLY

AUGUST	10	56%
SEPTEMBER	7	47%
OCTOBER	4	27%
NOVEMBER	4	44%
DECEMBER	11	73%
JANUARY	7	39%
FEBRUARY	10	67%
MARCH	10	67%
APRIL	1	7%
MAY	1	33%

LEAGUE GOALS

	PLAYER	LGE	FAC	LC	Oth	TOT
1	Beckett	18	0	0	0	18
2	Liddell	9	1	0	0	10
3	Warne	9	1	0	0	10
4	Porter	7	2	0	0	9
5	Wellens	4	0	0	0	4
6	Butcher	4	0	0	0	4
7	Killen	2	0	0	0	2
8	Branston	1	0	0	0	1
9	Hughes	1	0	0	0	1
10	Scott	1	0	0	0	1
11	Bonner	1	0	0	0	1
	Other	1	2	0	0	3
	TOTAL	58	6	0	0	64

TOP POINT EARNERS

	PLAYER	GAMES	AV PTS
1	Chris Porter	13	2.15
2	Mark Hughes	28	1.68
3	Richard Butcher	30	1.67
4	Guy Branston	37	1.62
5	Paul Edwards	27	1.59
6	Chris Swailes	12	1.58
7	Will Haining	14	1.50
8	Andy Liddell	29	1.48
9	Gareth Owen	14	1.43
10	Chris Day	30	1.43

DISCIPLINARY RECORDS

	PLAYER	YELLOW	RED	AVE
1	Edwards, P	6	1	371
2	Branston	8	0	417
3	Scott	4	0	434
4	Tierney	3	0	448
5	Wellens	8	0	489
6	Hall, C	1	0	573
7	Haining	2	0	612
8	Swailes	2	0	616
9	Warne	4	1	650
10	Hughes	4	0	666
11	Eyres, D	2	0	689
12	Killen	1	0	814
13	Butcher	3	0	948
	Other	0	0	
	TOTAL	48	2	

KEY GOALKEEPER

Lee Grant

Goals Conceded in the League	16	Counting Games League games when player was on pitch for at least 70 minutes	16
Goals Conceded in all competitions			
Defensive Rating Ave number of mins between League goals conceded while on the pitch	90	Clean Sheets In games when player was on pitch for at least 70 minutes	16

KEY PLAYERS - DEFENDERS

Chris Swailes

Goals Conceded in the League	14	Clean Sheets In League games when player was on pitch for at least 70 minutes	6
Goals Conceded in all competitions	14		
Defensive Rating Ave number of mins between League goals conceded while on the pitch	88	Club Defensive Rating Average number of mins between League goals conceded by the club this season	69

	PLAYER	CON LGE	CON ALL	CLN SHEETS	DEF RATE
1	Chris Swailes	14	14	6	88 mins
2	Guy Branston	44	48	13	76 mins
3	Will Haining	17	17	4	72 mins
4	Terrell Forbes	46	50	10	68 mins

KEY PLAYERS - MIDFIELDERS

Mark Hughes

Goals in the League	1	Contribution to Attacking Power Average number of minutes between League team goals while on pitch	70
Goals in all competitions	1		
Defensive Rating Average number of mins between League goals conceded while on the pitch	81	Scoring Difference Defensive Rating minus Contribution to Attacking Power	11

	PLAYER	GOALS LGE	GOALS ALL	DEF RATE	ATT POWER	SCORE DIFF
1	Mark Hughes	1	1	81	70	11 mins
2	Richard Butcher	4	4	75	65	10 mins
3	Paul Edwards	0	0	72	67	5 mins
4	Richard Wellens	4	4	70	73	-3 mins

KEY PLAYERS - GOALSCORERS

Luke Beckett

Goals in the League	18	Player Strike Rate Average number of minutes between League goals scored by player	136
Goals in all competitions	18		
Contribution to Attacking Power Average number of minutes between League team goals while on pitch	76	Club Strike Rate Average number of minutes between League goals scored by club	71

	PLAYER	GOALS LGE	GOALS ALL	POWER	S RATE
1	Luke Beckett	18	18	76	136 mins
2	Chris Porter	7	9	55	230 mins
3	Andy Liddell	9	10	71	290 mins
4	Paul Warne	9	10	69	362 mins

Richard Butcher

SQUAD APPEARANCES

Match	1	2	3	4	5	6	7	8	9	10	11	12	13	14	15	16	17	18	19	20	21	22	23	24	25
Venue	H	A	A	H	A	A	H	A	H	A	H	A	A	H	A	H	A	A	H	H	A	A	H	H	H
Competition	L	L	L	L	W	L	L	L	L	L	L	L	L	L	L	L	L	F	L	F	L	L	F	L	L
Result	W	W	L	W	L	D	L	L	L	W	W	D	L	L	D	W	L	D	L	W	D	W	D	W	D

Match	26	27	28	29	30	31	32	33	34	35	36	37	38	39	40	41	42	43	44	45	46	47	48	49	50	51
Venue	A	A	H	H	A	H	A	A	H	A	H	A	H	A	H	H	A	A	H	A	H	H	A	H	A	H
Competition	F	L	L	L	L	L	L	L	L	L	L	L	L	L	L	L	L	L	L	L	L	L	L	L	L	L
Result	L	D	W	W	W	D	L	L	W	L	L	D	W	W	W	W	L	W	W	D	L	L	L	D	L	D

Goalkeepers
Lance Cronin
Chris Day
Lee Grant
Michael Poke
Terry Smith

Defenders
Guy Branston
Neil Eardley
Terrell Forbes
Anthony Grant
Will Haining
Daniel Hall
Gareth Owen
Rob Scott
Stefan Stam
Chris Swailes
Marc Tierney

Midfielders
Mark Bonner
Richard Butcher
Paul Edwards
David Eyres
Mark Hughes
Andy Liddell
Chris Taylor
Richard Wellens

Forwards
Luke Beckett
Delroy Facey
Christopher Hall
Christopher Killen
Chris Porter
Paul Warne
Matthew Wolfenden

KEY: On all match · On bench · Subbed or sent off (Counting game) · Subbed or sent off (playing less than 70 minutes) · Subbed on from bench (Counting Game) · Subbed on (playing less than 70 minutes) · Subbed on and then subbed or sent off (Counting Game) · Subbed on and then subbed or sent off (playing less than 70 minutes) · Not in 16

BRADFORD CITY

Final Position: **11th**

NICKNAME: THE BANTAMS

KEY: ☐ Won ☐ Drawn ☐ Lost

	Comp	Opponent	Venue	Result	Score	Scorers	Attendance
1	div2	Hartlepool	A	W	2-0	Windass 8; Petta 55	6,271
2	div2	Southend	H	L	0-2		8,250
3	div2	MK Dons	H	W	2-0	Windass 27 pen,52	7,315
4	div2	Rotherham	A	D	1-1	Windass 84	5,222
5	ccr1	Rochdale	A	W	5-0	Windass 7,67,77; Cadamarteri 40; Bridge-Wilkinson 82	2,820
6	div2	Bournemouth	H	L	1-2	Cadamarteri 45	7,621
7	div2	Blackpool	A	L	0-1		6,468
8	div2	Chesterfield	H	W	2-0	Windass 75; Bridge-Wilkinson 81	7,351
9	div2	Tranmere	A	D	2-2	Edghill 21; Wetherall 38	8,225
10	div2	Yeovil	H	D	1-1	Muirhead 64	7,826
11	ccr2	West Brom	A	L	1-4	Schumacher 45	10,792
12	div2	Swindon	A	W	3-2	Windass 34; Claridge 64,72	4,590
13	div2	Colchester	H	D	1-1	Petta 84	6,891
14	div2	Doncaster	A	D	2-2	Kearney 44; Claridge 47	6,800
15	div2	Huddersfield	H	L	1-2	Petta 35	12,285
16	div2	Port Vale	A	W	1-0	Claridge 64	4,892
17	div2	Gillingham	H	W	1-0	Cooke 89	7,729
18	div2	Nottm Forest	A	L	0-1		17,983
19	facr1	Tranmere	H	W	2-1	Crooks 56; Windass 59 pen	6,116
20	div2	Barnsley	H	D	0-0		9,486
21	div2	Huddersfield	A	D	0-0		17,331
22	div2	Hartlepool	H	L	0-1		7,499
23	facr2	Barnsley	A	D	1-1	Edghill 82	7,051
24	div2	Bristol City	A	W	1-0	Carey 79 og	9,103
25	div2	Southend	A	D	1-1	Schumacher 33	7,307
26	facr2r	Barnsley	H	L	3-5	Cooke 34; Bower 67; Wetherall 73	4,738
27	div2	Rotherham	H	L	1-2	Windass 77 pen	7,476
28	div2	Oldham	A	L	1-2	Windass 45 pen	6,982
29	div2	Walsall	H	W	2-0	Bridge-Wilkinson 29; Petta 35	6,745
30	div2	Scunthorpe	A	D	0-0		5,269
31	div2	Brentford	H	D	3-3	Bridge-Wilkinson 44,89 pen; Wetherall 78	7,588
32	div2	Chesterfield	A	L	0-1		4,449
33	div2	Swansea	H	D	1-1	Windass 80	7,521
34	div2	Yeovil	A	W	1-0	Windass 87	6,168
35	div2	Tranmere	H	D	0-0		7,697
36	div2	Colchester	A	L	1-3	Windass 37	4,503
37	div2	Swindon	H	D	1-1	Windass 79	7,283
38	div2	Swansea	A	D	1-1	Wetherall 72	11,028
39	div2	Bristol City	H	D	1-1	Wetherall 52	7,917
40	div2	MK Dons	A	L	1-2	Claridge 64	8,426
41	div2	Bournemouth	A	W	1-0	Stewart 42	5,749
42	div2	Oldham	H	L	1-4	Wilbraham 50	7,959
43	div2	Blackpool	H	W	1-0	Brown 90	7,192
44	div2	Walsall	A	D	2-2	Bower 45; Wetherall 49	4,678
45	div2	Scunthorpe	H	W	4-2	Windass 7,54,60; Bridge-Wilkinson 56	8,409
46	div2	Brentford	A	D	1-1	Symes 36	6,533
47	div2	Doncaster	H	W	2-1	Emanuel 20,27	9,297
48	div2	Gillingham	A	L	1-2	Cadamarteri 74	7,281
49	div2	Port Vale	H	W	1-0	Bower 44	7,139
50	div2	Barnsley	A	D	0-0		11,178
51	div2	Nottm Forest	H	D	1-1	Windass 20	15,608

LEAGUE APPEARANCES, BOOKINGS AND GOALS

	AGE (on 01/07/06)	IN NAMED 16	APPEARANCES	COUNTING GAMES	MINUTES ON PITCH	LEAGUE GOALS	Yellow	Red
Goalkeepers								
Russell Howarth	24	42	11	10	964	0	0	0
Donovan Ricketts	29	36	36	34	3120	0	0	1
Defenders								
Craig Bentham	21	13	7	6	585	0	1	0
Mark Bower	26	45	45	45	4050	2	5	0
Richard Edghill	31	22	19	17	1574	1	2	0
Darren Holloway	28	29	24	19	1800	0	6	2
Damion Stewart	25	39	23	19	1848	1	4	0
John Swift	21	6	5	3	298	0	0	0
Andrew Taylor	19	24	24	24	2160	0	0	0
David Wetherall	35	46	46	46	4140	5	2	0
Jake Wright	20	4	1	0	55	0	0	0
Midfielders								
Marc Bridge-Wilkinson	27	36	36	34	3140	5	4	0
Joe Brown	18	16	13	2	365	1	3	0
Joe Colbeck	19	13	11	5	536	0	0	0
Lee Crooks	28	19	15	13	1264	0	1	0
Lewis Emanuel	22	42	37	22	2429	2	3	0
Thomas Kearney	24	39	15	8	986	1	2	0
Owen Morrison	24	10	10	4	578	0	0	0
Ben Muirhead	23	35	32	18	2156	1	6	1
Thomas Penford	21	11	10	8	787	0	2	0
Bobby Petta	31	29	27	13	1699	4	4	0
Steve Schumacher	22	32	29	21	2170	1	6	0
Forwards								
Danny Cadamarteri	26	43	39	22	2470	2	8	0
Steve Claridge	40	32	26	11	1307	5	1	0
Andrew Cooke	32	23	17	7	891	1	1	0
Kevin Sanasy	21	1	0	0	0	0	0	0
Michael Symes	22	4	3	0	55	1	0	0
Aaron Wilbraham	26	5	5	5	445	1	0	0
Dean Windass	37	40	40	39	3542	16	7	0

TEAM OF THE SEASON

G: Donovan Ricketts — **CG:** 34 **DR:** 98

D: Andrew Taylor — **CG:** 24 **DR:** 90

D: Mark Bower — **CG:** 45 **DR:** 84

D: David Wetherall — **CG:** 46 **DR:** 84

D: Richard Edghill — **CG:** 17 **DR:** 83

M: Lewis Emanuel — **CG:** 22 **SD:** 16

M: Bobby Petta — **CG:** 13 **SD:** 15

M: Marc Bridge-Wilkinson — **CG:** 34 **SD:** 6

M: Ben Muirhead — **CG:** 18 **SD:** 2

F: Dean Windass — **CG:** 39 **SR:** 221

F: Danny Cadamarteri — **CG:** 22 **SR:** 1235

MONTHLY POINTS TALLY

Month	Points	%
AUGUST	7	39%
SEPTEMBER	9	60%
OCTOBER	7	47%
NOVEMBER	2	22%
DECEMBER	8	44%
JANUARY	6	40%
FEBRUARY	3	20%
MARCH	7	58%
APRIL	11	61%
MAY	1	33%

LEAGUE GOALS

	PLAYER	LGE	FAC	LC	Oth	TOT
1	Windass	16	1	3	0	20
2	Bridge-Wilkinson	5	0	1	0	6
3	Wetherall	5	1	0	0	6
4	Claridge	5	0	0	0	5
5	Petta	4	0	0	0	4
6	Cadamarteri	2	0	1	0	3
7	Bower	2	1	0	0	3
8	Emanuel	2	0	0	0	2
9	Muirhead	1	0	0	0	1
10	Kearney	1	0	0	0	1
11	Stewart	1	0	0	0	1
	Other	7	3	1	0	11
	TOTAL	51	6	6	0	63

TOP POINT EARNERS

	PLAYER	GAMES	AV PTS
1	Donovan Ricketts	34	1.44
2	Lewis Emanuel	22	1.41
3	Richard Edghill	17	1.41
4	Andrew Taylor	24	1.38
5	Damion Stewart	19	1.37
6	Dean Windass	39	1.36
7	Mark Bower	45	1.36
8	Steve Schumacher	21	1.33
9	David Wetherall	46	1.33
10	Ben Muirhead	18	1.33

DISCIPLINARY RECORDS

	PLAYER	YELLOW	RED	AVE
1	Holloway	6	2	225
2	Cadamarteri	8	0	308
3	Muirhead	6	1	308
4	Schumacher	6	0	361
5	Penford	2	0	393
6	Petta	4	0	424
7	Stewart	4	0	462
8	Kearney	2	0	493
9	Windass	7	0	506
10	Bentham	1	0	585
11	Bridge-Wilkinson	4	0	785
12	Edghill	2	0	787
13	Emanuel	3	0	809
	Other	10	1	
	TOTAL	65	4	

KEY GOALKEEPER

Donovan Ricketts

Goals Conceded in the League	32	Counting Games League games when player was on pitch for at least 70 minutes	34
Goals Conceded in all competitions	34		
Defensive Rating Ave number of mins between League goals conceded while on the pitch	98	Clean Sheets In games when player was on pitch for at least 70 minutes	15

KEY PLAYERS - DEFENDERS

Andrew Taylor

Goals Conceded in the League	24	Clean Sheets In League games when player was on pitch for at least 70 minutes	9
Goals Conceded in all competitions	24		
Defensive Rating Ave number of mins between League goals conceded while on the pitch	90	Club Defensive Rating Average number of mins between League goals conceded by the club this season	84

	PLAYER	CON LGE	CON ALL	CLN SHEETS	DEF RATE
1	Andrew Taylor	24	24	9	90 mins
2	Mark Bower	48	59	16	84 mins
3	David Wetherall	49	60	16	84 mins
4	Richard Edghill	19	30	5	83 mins

KEY PLAYERS - MIDFIELDERS

Lewis Emanuel

Goals in the League	2	Contribution to Attacking Power Average number of minutes between League team goals while on pitch	90
Goals in all competitions	2		
Defensive Rating Average number of mins between League goals conceded while on the pitch	106	Scoring Difference Defensive Rating minus Contribution to Attacking Power	16

	PLAYER	GOALS LGE	GOALS ALL	DEF RATE	ATT POWER	SCORE DIFF
1	Lewis Emanuel	2	2	106	90	16 mins
2	Bobby Petta	4	4	100	85	15 mins
3	Marc Bridge-Wilkinson	5	6	87	81	6 mins
4	Ben Muirhead	1	1	72	70	2 mins

KEY PLAYERS - GOALSCORERS

Dean Windass

Goals in the League	16	Player Strike Rate Average number of minutes between League goals scored by player	221
Goals in all competitions	20		
Contribution to Attacking Power Average number of minutes between League team goals while on pitch	82	Club Strike Rate Average number of minutes between League goals scored by club	81

	PLAYER	GOALS LGE	GOALS ALL	POWER	S RATE
1	Dean Windass	16	20	82	221 mins
2	Bobby Petta	4	4	85	425 mins
3	Marc Bridge-Wilkinson	5	6	81	628 mins
4	David Wetherall	5	6	81	828 mins

Dean Windass

SQUAD APPEARANCES

Match	1	2	3	4	5	6	7	8	9	10	11	12	13	14	15	16	17	18	19	20	21	22	23	24	25	26	27	28	29	30	31	32	33	34	35	36	37	38	39	40	41	42	43	44	45	46	47	48	49	50	51
Venue	A	H	H	A	A	H	A	H	A	H	A	A	H	A	H	A	H	A	H	H	A	H	A	A	A	H	H	A	H	A	H	A	H	A	H	A	H	A	H	A	A	H	H	A	H	A	H	A	H	A	H
Competition	L	L	L	L	W	L	L	L	L	L	W	L	L	L	L	L	L	L	F	L	L	L	F	L	L	F	L	L	L	L	L	L	L	L	L	L	L	L	L	L	L	L	L	L	L	L	L	L	L	L	L
Result	W	L	W	D	W	L	L	W	D	D	L	W	D	D	L	W	W	L	W	D	D	L	D	W	D	L	L	L	W	D	D	L	D	W	D	L	D	D	D	L	W	L	W	D	W	D	W	L	W	D	D

Goalkeepers
Russell Howarth
Donovan Ricketts

Defenders
Craig Bentham
Mark Bower
Richard Edghill
Darren Holloway
Damion Stewart
John Swift
Andrew Taylor
David Wetherall
Jake Wright

Midfielders
Marc Bridge-Wilkinson
Joe Brown
Joe Colbeck
Lee Crooks
Lewis Emanuel
Thomas Kearney
Owen Morrison
Ben Muirhead
Thomas Penford
Bobby Petta
Steve Schumacher

Forwards
Danny Cadamarteri
Steve Claridge
Andrew Cooke
Kevin Sanasy
Michael Symes
Aaron Wilbraham
Dean Windass

KEY: On all match; On bench; Subbed or sent off (Counting game); Subbed or sent off (playing less than 70 minutes); Subbed on from bench (Counting Game); Subbed on (playing less than 70 minutes); Subbed on and then subbed or sent off (Counting Game); Subbed on and then subbed or sent off (playing less than 70 minutes); Not in 16

SCUNTHORPE UNITED

Final Position: **12th**

NICKNAME: THE IRON

KEY: Won / Drawn / Lost

							Attendance
1	div2	Brentford	A	L	0-2		5,952
2	div2	Barnsley	H	W	2-1	Crosby 28 pen; Taylor 71	7,152
3	div2	Gillingham	H	D	1-1	Hinds 90	5,007
4	div2	Nottm Forest	A	W	1-0	Sharp 71	19,091
5	ccr1	Tranmere	H	W	2-1	Ryan 56; Hinds 82	2,738
6	div2	Southend	H	W	1-0	Baraclough 36	5,569
7	div2	Hartlepool	A	D	3-3	Sharp 9,50; Keogh 65	5,044
8	div2	Huddersfield	A	W	4-1	Beagrie 8 pen; Keogh 46,83; Sparrow 74	14,112
9	div2	Port Vale	H	W	2-0	Hinds 32; Keogh 37	5,694
10	div2	Doncaster	A	L	1-3	Sharp 51	6,699
11	ccr2	Birmingham	H	L	0-2		6,109
12	div2	Walsall	H	L	1-3	Sharp 55	4,973
13	div2	MK Dons	A	L	0-1		4,682
14	div2	Yeovil	H	L	3-4	Keogh 13; Sharp 20,77	4,311
15	div2	Tranmere	A	W	2-0	Keogh 1; Sharp 39	7,522
16	div2	Rotherham	H	D	2-2	Sharp 20,60	6,649
17	div2	Swindon	A	D	1-1	Sparrow 35	4,972
18	div2	Oldham	H	W	4-2	Butler 28; Sharp 31,56; Crosby 52	5,055
19	facr1	Bury	A	D	2-2	Keogh 6; Baraclough 41	2,940
20	div2	Blackpool	A	L	2-5	Sharp 3,35 pen	6,016
21	facr1r	Bury	H	W	1-0	Johnson 117	4,006
22	div2	Tranmere	H	L	1-2	Sharp 68 pen	4,602
23	div2	Brentford	H	L	1-3	Goodwin 8	4,322
24	facr2	Aldershot	A	W	1-0	Keogh 14	3,548
25	div2	Swansea	A	L	0-2		13,207
26	div2	Barnsley	A	L	2-5	Beagrie 89 pen; MacKenzie 90	8,197
27	div2	Nottm Forest	H	W	3-1	Ridley 29; Taylor 72; Byrne 83	5,857
28	div2	Chesterfield	H	D	2-2	Baraclough 65; Johnson 90	5,866
29	div2	Bradford	H	D	0-0		5,269
30	div2	Bournemouth	A	D	1-1	Sharp 6	6,259
31	facr3	Man City	A	L	1-3	Keogh 17	27,779
32	div2	Huddersfield	H	D	2-2	Beagrie 17; Keogh 70	4,450
33	div2	Bristol City	A	D	1-1	Keogh 5	11,692
34	div2	Doncaster	H	L	1-2	Goodwin 48	6,978
35	div2	MK Dons	H	W	2-0	Sharp 3,10 pen	4,631
36	div2	Colchester	A	L	0-1		4,416
37	div2	Walsall	A	D	2-2	Keogh 19; MacKenzie 45	4,911
38	div2	Bristol City	H	L	0-2		3,786
39	div2	Swansea	H	D	2-2	Sharp 6; Torpey 90	4,352
40	div2	Gillingham	A	W	3-1	Sparrow 42; Hinds 59; Keogh 64	6,029
41	div2	Port Vale	A	W	2-1	Sparrow 11; Taylor 59	3,984
42	div2	Southend	A	L	0-3		8,717
43	div2	Hartlepool	H	W	2-0	Baraclough 44; Sparrow 70	4,550
44	div2	Chesterfield	A	W	2-1	Hinds 47; Crosby 63	4,406
45	div2	Colchester	H	D	0-0		4,608
46	div2	Bradford	A	L	2-4	Beagrie 13 pen; Hinds 29	8,409
47	div2	Bournemouth	H	D	2-2	Beagrie 12 pen; Hinds 84	4,136
48	div2	Yeovil	A	W	1-0	Sharp 57	6,759
49	div2	Swindon	H	L	1-2	Sharp 8	5,207
50	div2	Rotherham	A	D	1-1	Keogh 41	5,778
51	div2	Blackpool	H	W	1-0	Sharp 90	5,917
52	div2	Oldham	A	D	1-1	Sharp 88	5,544

LEAGUE APPEARANCES, BOOKINGS AND GOALS

	AGE (on 01/07/06)	IN NAMED 16	APPEARANCES	COUNTING GAMES	MINUTES ON PITCH	LEAGUE GOALS	
Goalkeepers							
Adam Capp	21	10	0	0	0	0	0
Tom Evans	29	36	18	18	1620	0	0
Paul Musselwhite	37	44	28	28	2520	0	1
Defenders							
Andy Butler	22	19	16	13	1313	1	2
Clifford Byrne	24	43	32	24	2403	1	3
Andrew Crosby	33	43	42	35	3346	3	9
Stephen Foster	31	18	18	17	1541	0	3
James Goodwin	24	24	13	6	820	2	4
Richard Hinds	25	42	42	41	3713	6	6
Lee Ridley	23	5	3	2	204	1	0
Michael Rose	23	15	15	14	1305	0	3
Richard Ryan	21	19	13	2	532	0	0
Nathan Stanton	25	34	22	18	1840	0	2
Dean Twibey	19	1	0	0	0	0	0
Marcus Williams	20	34	29	25	2464	0	1
Midfielders							
Ashley Allanson	19	2	1	0	9	0	0
Ian Baraclough	35	38	38	35	3291	3	4
Peter Beagrie	40	32	30	18	1951	5	3
Wayne Corden	30	15	9	2	426	0	0
Neil MacKenzie	30	16	14	9	995	2	1
Andy Parton	22	11	6	1	238	0	0
Rob Smith	-	0	0	0	0	0	0
Matthew Sparrow	22	39	39	28	2756	5	9
Cleveland Taylor	22	46	45	28	3028	3	2
Peter Till	20	9	8	3	463	0	0
Michael Timlin	21	2	1	0	13	0	0
Forwards							
Ismael Ehui	19	6	3	0	43	0	0
Tommy Johnson	35	22	14	2	338	1	2
Andrew Keogh	20	45	45	39	3616	11	3
Billy Sharp	20	37	37	34	3036	23	3
Steve Torpey	35	26	26	14	1567	1	1

TEAM OF THE SEASON

G Tom Evans CG: 18 DR: 65

D Stephen Foster CG: 17 DR: 70

D Michael Rose CG: 14 DR: 62

D Andrew Crosby CG: 35 DR: 59

D Richard Hinds CG: 41 DR: 59

M Ian Baraclough CG: 35 SD: 7

M Peter Beagrie CG: 18 SD: 3

M Matthew Sparrow CG: 28 SD: -1

M Cleveland Taylor CG: 28 SD: -3

F Billy Sharp CG: 34 SR: 132

F Andrew Keogh CG: 39 SR: 329

MONTHLY POINTS TALLY

Month	Points	%
AUGUST	11	61%
SEPTEMBER	6	40%
OCTOBER	8	53%
NOVEMBER	0	0%
DECEMBER	5	33%
JANUARY	3	25%
FEBRUARY	11	52%
MARCH	7	58%
APRIL	8	44%
MAY	1	33%

LEAGUE GOALS

	PLAYER	LGE	FAC	LC	Oth	TOT
1	Sharp	23	0	0	0	23
2	Keogh	11	3	0	0	14
3	Hinds	6	0	1	0	7
4	Sparrow	5	0	0	0	5
5	Beagrie	5	0	0	0	5
6	Taylor	3	0	0	0	3
7	Baraclough	3	1	0	0	4
8	Crosby	3	0	0	0	3
9	Goodwin	2	0	0	0	2
10	MacKenzie	2	0	0	0	2
11	Butler	1	0	0	0	1
	Other	4	1	1	0	6
	TOTAL	68	5	2	0	75

TOP POINT EARNERS

	PLAYER	GAMES	AV PTS
1	Steve Torpey	14	1.93
2	Ian Baraclough	35	1.60
3	Stephen Foster	17	1.53
4	Richard Hinds	41	1.44
5	Cleveland Taylor	28	1.43
6	Matthew Sparrow	28	1.43
7	Paul Musselwhite	28	1.43
8	Marcus Williams	25	1.40
9	Peter Beagrie	18	1.39
10	Andrew Crosby	35	1.37

DISCIPLINARY RECORDS

	PLAYER	YELLOW	RED	AVE
1	Goodwin	4	1	164
2	Sparrow	9	0	306
3	Crosby	9	1	334
4	Rose	3	0	435
5	Foster	3	0	513
6	Ryan	0	1	532
7	Hinds	6	0	618
8	Beagrie	3	0	650
9	Butler	2	0	656
10	Torpey	1	1	783
11	Byrne	3	0	801
12	Baraclough	4	0	822
13	Stanton	2	0	920
	Other	11	0	
	TOTAL	60	4	

KEY GOALKEEPER

Tom Evans

Goals Conceded in the League	25	Counting Games League games when player was on pitch for at least 70 minutes	18
Goals Conceded in all competitions	28		
Defensive Rating Ave number of mins between League goals conceded while on the pitch	65	Clean Sheets In games when player was on pitch for at least 70 minutes	4

KEY PLAYERS - DEFENDERS

Stephen Foster

Goals Conceded in the League	22	Clean Sheets In League games when player was on pitch for at least 70 minutes	5
Goals Conceded in all competitions	22		
Defensive Rating Ave number of mins between League goals conceded while on the pitch	70	Club Defensive Rating Average number of mins between League goals conceded by the club this season	57

	PLAYER	CON LGE	CON ALL	CLN SHEETS	DEF RATE
1	Stephen Foster	22	22	5	70 mins
2	Michael Rose	21	24	3	62 mins
3	Andrew Crosby	57	65	7	59 mins
4	Richard Hinds	63	69	10	59 mins

KEY PLAYERS - MIDFIELDERS

Ian Baraclough

Goals in the League	3	Contribution to Attacking Power Average number of minutes between League team goals while on pitch	59
Goals in all competitions	4		
Defensive Rating Average number of mins between League goals conceded while on the pitch	66	Scoring Difference Defensive Rating minus Contribution to Attacking Power	7

	PLAYER	GOALS LGE	GOALS ALL	DEF RATE	ATT POWER	SCORE DIFF
1	Ian Baraclough	3	4	66	59	7 mins
2	Peter Beagrie	5	5	53	50	3 mins
3	Matthew Sparrow	5	5	63	64	-1 mins
4	Cleveland Taylor	3	3	61	64	-3 mins

KEY PLAYERS - GOALSCORERS

Billy Sharp

Goals in the League	23	Player Strike Rate Average number of minutes between League goals scored by player	132
Goals in all competitions	23		
Contribution to Attacking Power Average number of minutes between League team goals while on pitch	63	Club Strike Rate Average number of minutes between League goals scored by club	61

	PLAYER	GOALS LGE	GOALS ALL	POWER	S RATE
1	Billy Sharp	23	23	63	132 mins
2	Andrew Keogh	11	14	57	329 mins
3	Peter Beagrie	5	5	50	390 mins
4	Matthew Sparrow	5	5	64	551 mins

Billy Sharp

SQUAD APPEARANCES

Match	1	2	3	4	5	6	7	8	9	10	11	12	13	14	15	16	17	18	19	20	21	22	23	24	25	26
Venue	A	H	H	A	H	H	A	A	H	A	H	H	A	H	A	H	A	H	A	A	H	H	H	A	A	A
Competition	L	L	L	L	W	L	L	L	L	L	W	L	L	L	L	L	L	L	F	L	F	L	L	F	L	L
Result	L	W	D	W	W	W	D	W	W	L	L	L	L	L	W	D	D	W	D	L	W	L	L	W	L	L

Match	27	28	29	30	31	32	33	34	35	36	37	38	39	40	41	42	43	44	45	46	47	48	49	50	51	52
Venue	H	H	H	A	A	H	A	H	H	A	A	H	H	A	A	A	H	A	H	A	H	A	H	A	H	A
Competition	L	L	L	L	F	L	L	L	L	L	L	L	L	L	L	L	L	L	L	L	L	L	L	L	L	L
Result	W	D	D	D	L	D	D	L	W	L	D	L	D	W	W	L	W	W	D	L	D	W	L	D	W	D

Goalkeepers
Adam Capp
Tom Evans
Paul Musselwhite

Defenders
Andy Butler
Clifford Byrne
Andrew Crosby
Stephen Foster
James Goodwin
Richard Hinds
Lee Ridley
Michael Rose
Richard Ryan
Nathan Stanton
Dean Twibey
Marcus Williams

Midfielders
Ashley Allanson
Ian Baraclough
Peter Beagrie
Wayne Corden
Neil MacKenzie
Andy Parton
Rob Smith
Matthew Sparrow
Cleveland Taylor
Peter Till
Michael Timlin

Forwards
Ismael Ehui
Tommy Johnson
Andrew Keogh
Billy Sharp
Steve Torpey

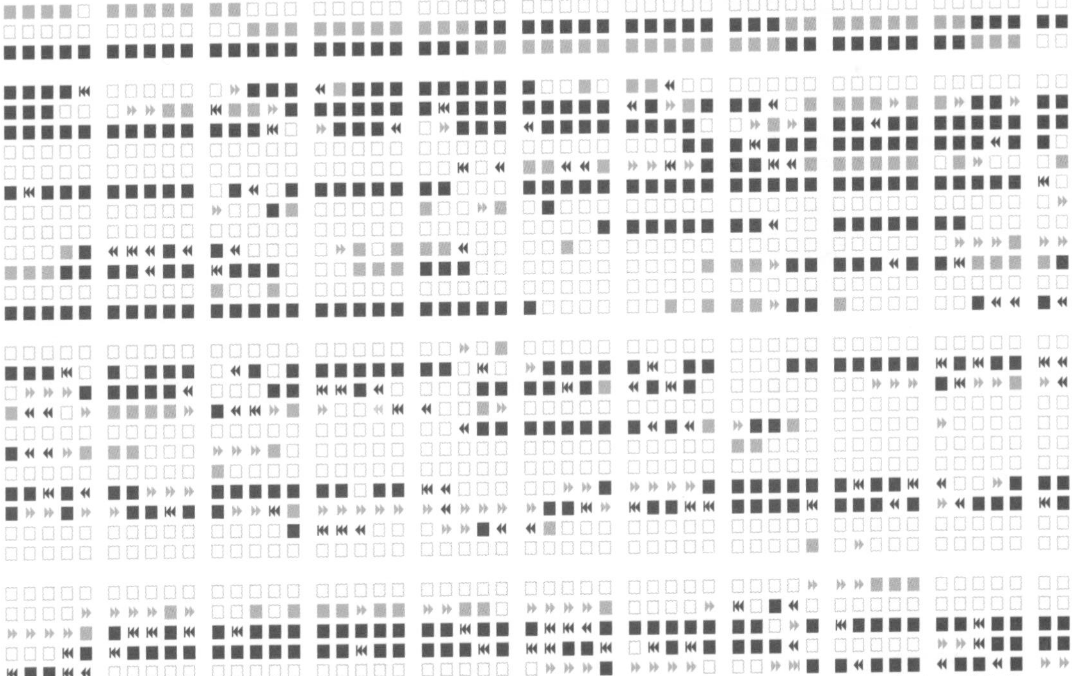

KEY: ■ On all match · ■ On bench · ⏮ Subbed or sent off (Counting game) · « Subbed or sent off (playing less than 70 minutes) · ⏭ Subbed on from bench (Counting Game) · » Subbed on (playing less than 70 minutes) · Subbed on and then subbed or sent off (Counting Game) · Subbed on and then subbed or sent off (playing less than 70 minutes) · □ Not in 16

PORT VALE

Final Position: **13th**

NICKNAME: THE VALIANTS

KEY: ☐Won ☐Drawn ☐Lost

							Attendance
1	div2	Southend	A	W	2-1	Lowndes 12,28	6,543
2	div2	Gillingham	H	D	0-0		4,931
3	div2	Brentford	H	W	1-0	Cummins 53	4,275
4	div2	Bristol City	A	L	2-4	Lowndes 35; Bell 40	11,120
5	ccr1	Rotherham	A	L	1-3	Cummins 45	2,809
6	div2	Doncaster	H	W	2-0	Lowndes 30; Dinning 48	4,993
7	div2	MK Dons	A	D	0-0		4,592
8	div2	Rotherham	H	W	2-0	Lowndes 45; Paynter 90	4,528
9	div2	Scunthorpe	A	L	0-2		5,694
10	div2	Colchester	H	L	0-1		5,166
11	div2	Yeovil	A	L	0-1		5,901
12	div2	Oldham	H	D	2-2	Cornes 71,90	3,796
13	div2	Walsall	H	W	3-2	Birchall 8; Mulligan 55; Cornes 72	5,314
14	div2	Swindon	A	W	2-1	Bell 44; Cornes 53	4,531
15	div2	Bradford	H	L	0-1		4,892
16	div2	Bournemouth	A	W	2-1	Cummins 75; Paynter 86	6,320
17	div2	Hartlepool	H	L	1-2	Cummins 43	4,550
18	facr1	Wrexham	H	W	2-1	Husbands 20; Constantine 65	5,046
19	div2	Chesterfield	A	L	0-2		4,714
20	div2	Swindon	H	D	1-1	Husbands 87	4,108
21	div2	Southend	H	W	2-1	Constantine 18; Husbands 55	3,961
22	facr2	Bristol Rovers	H	D	1-1	Constantine 86	4,483
23	div2	Nottm Forest	A	L	0-1		17,696
24	div2	Gillingham	A	L	0-3		6,210
25	facr2r	Bristol Rovers	A	W	1-0	Birchall 22	5,623
26	div2	Bristol City	H	L	0-1		4,214
27	div2	Blackpool	H	L	1-2	Fortune 58	5,666
28	div2	Huddersfield	A	W	3-0	Constantine 48,65; Dinning 80 pen	10,824
29	div2	Tranmere	H	L	0-2		4,489
30	div2	Swansea	A	D	0-0		14,747
31	facr3	Doncaster	H	W	2-1	Togwell 55,73	4,923
32	div2	Rotherham	A	D	1-1	Husbands 7	3,883
33	div2	Barnsley	H	W	3-2	Sonner 24; Constantine 27; Togwell 73	4,468
34	div2	Colchester	A	L	1-2	Husbands 79 pen	4,316
35	facr4	Aston Villa	A	L	1-3	Lowndes 85	30,434
36	div2	Oldham	A	W	1-0	Constantine 44	5,555
37	div2	Yeovil	H	W	1-0	Constantine 52	4,732
38	div2	Barnsley	A	D	1-1	Cummins 84	7,709
39	div2	Nottm Forest	H	L	0-2		6,793
40	div2	Brentford	A	W	1-0	Smith, J 36	7,542
41	div2	Scunthorpe	H	L	1-2	Cummins 18	3,984
42	div2	Doncaster	A	D	1-1	Constantine 86	5,511
43	div2	Blackpool	A	L	0-1		5,494
44	div2	Huddersfield	H	D	1-1	Cummins 59	5,664
45	div2	Tranmere	A	L	0-3		6,926
46	div2	MK Dons	H	W	3-1	Constantine 13,35 pen; Cummins 45	3,452
47	div2	Swansea	H	W	3-2	Togwell 43; Cummins 58; Constantine 63	4,850
48	div2	Walsall	A	D	1-1	Fortune 86	4,876
49	div2	Bournemouth	H	D	0-0		4,006
50	div2	Bradford	A	L	0-1		7,139
51	div2	Chesterfield	H	W	3-1	Pilkington 5,15; Cummins 81	4,478
52	div2	Hartlepool	A	D	1-1	Cummins 77	6,895

LEAGUE APPEARANCES, BOOKINGS AND GOALS

	AGE (on 01/07/06)	IN NAMED 16	APPEARANCES	COUNTING GAMES	MINUTES ON PITCH	LEAGUE GOALS	
Goalkeepers							
Jonathan Brain	23	46	0	0	0	0	0
Mark Goodlad	26	46	46	46	4140	0	2
Defenders							
George Abbey	27	22	20	17	1620	0	1
Mick Bell	34	20	15	11	1076	2	1
Sam Collins	29	15	15	14	1294	0	1
Clayton Fortune	23	25	25	20	1896	2	1
Mark Innes	27	30	23	13	1487	0	2
Craig James	23	38	34	28	2706	0	10
Mark McGregor	29	17	14	14	1242	0	6
George Pilkington	24	46	46	46	4140	2	3
Steve Rowland	28	25	18	13	1274	0	7
Jason Talbot	20	5	5	2	237	0	0
Michael Walsh	28	7	4	4	343	0	0
Midfielders							
Christopher Birchall	22	31	31	20	2043	1	1
Joe Cardle	19	12	6	2	222	0	1
Michael Cummins	28	39	39	36	3295	10	1
Tony Dinning	31	38	35	30	2848	2	9
Sean Doherty	21	10	6	1	240	0	0
Robin Hulbert	26	2	2	1	146	0	0
Andy Porter	37	4	2	1	154	0	1
Jeff Smith	26	29	27	16	1705	1	1
Danny Sonner	34	33	29	20	2069	1	5
Sam Togwell	21	29	27	25	2318	2	2
Forwards							
Louis Briscoe	18	5	4	0	50	0	0
Leon Constantine	28	30	30	28	2561	10	1
Christopher Cornes	19	12	10	6	609	4	3
Michael Husbands	22	28	24	7	869	4	0
Nathan Lowndes	29	35	35	28	2529	5	4
Gary Mulligan	21	11	10	7	697	1	2
William Paynter	21	16	16	16	1427	2	2
Hector Sam	28	8	4	0	69	0	0

TEAM OF THE SEASON

G — Mark Goodlad CG: 46 DR: 77

D — Mark McGregor CG: 14 DR: 89

D — Craig James CG: 28 DR: 80

D — Steve Rowland CG: 13 DR: 80

D — George Pilkington CG: 46 DR: 77

M — Jeff Smith CG: 16 SD: 9

M — Danny Sonner CG: 20 SD: 3

M — Michael Cummins CG: 36 SD: -2

M — Tony Dinning CG: 30 SD: -3

F — Leon Constantine CG: 28 SR: 256

F — Nathan Lowndes CG: 28 SR: 506

MONTHLY POINTS TALLY

AUGUST	11	61%
SEPTEMBER	4	27%
OCTOBER	9	60%
NOVEMBER	4	44%
DECEMBER	3	17%
JANUARY	5	42%
FEBRUARY	10	56%
MARCH	2	17%
APRIL	11	61%
MAY	1	33%

LEAGUE GOALS

	PLAYER	LGE	FAC	LC	Oth	TOT
1	Constantine	10	2	0	0	12
2	Cummins	10	0	1	0	11
3	Lowndes	5	1	0	0	6
4	Husbands	4	1	0	0	5
5	Cornes	4	0	0	0	4
6	Pilkington	2	0	0	0	2
7	Dinning	2	0	0	0	2
8	Togwell	2	2	0	0	4
9	Paynter	2	0	0	0	2
10	Bell	2	0	0	0	2
11	Fortune	2	0	0	0	2
	Other	4	1	0	0	5
	TOTAL	**49**	**7**	**1**	**0**	**57**

TOP POINT EARNERS

	PLAYER	GAMES	AV PTS
1	Danny Sonner	20	**1.65**
2	Sam Collins	14	**1.64**
3	Jeff Smith	16	**1.50**
4	William Paynter	16	**1.50**
5	Mark Innes	13	**1.46**
6	Mark McGregor	14	**1.43**
7	George Abbey	17	**1.41**
8	Michael Cummins	36	**1.39**
9	Mark Goodlad	46	**1.30**
10	George Pilkington	46	**1.30**

DISCIPLINARY RECORDS

	PLAYER	YELLOW	RED	AVE
1	Rowland	7	1	**159**
2	Cornes	3	0	**203**
3	McGregor	6	0	**207**
4	James	10	0	**270**
5	Dinning	9	1	**284**
6	Mulligan	2	0	**348**
7	Sonner	5	0	**413**
8	Lowndes	4	0	**632**
9	Paynter	2	0	**713**
10	Innes	2	0	**743**
11	Bell	1	0	**1076**
12	Togwell	2	0	**1159**
13	Collins	1	0	**1294**
	Other	11	0	
	TOTAL	**65**	**2**	

KEY GOALKEEPER

Mark Goodlad

Goals Conceded in the League	54	Counting Games League games when player was on pitch for at least 70 minutes	46
Goals Conceded in all competitions	63		
Defensive Rating Ave number of mins between League goals conceded while on the pitch	77	Clean Sheets In games when player was on pitch for at least 70 minutes	11

KEY PLAYERS - DEFENDERS

Mark McGregor

Goals Conceded in the League	14	Clean Sheets In League games when player was on pitch for at least 70 minutes	3
Goals Conceded in all competitions	14		
Defensive Rating Ave number of mins between League goals conceded while on the pitch	89	Club Defensive Rating Average number of mins between League goals conceded by the club this season	77

	PLAYER	CON LGE	CON ALL	CLN SHEETS	DEF RATE
1	Mark McGregor	14	14	3	89 mins
2	Steve Rowland	16	22	2	80 mins
3	Craig James	34	43	7	80 mins
4	George Pilkington	54	63	11	77 mins

KEY PLAYERS - MIDFIELDERS

Jeff Smith

Goals in the League	1	Contribution to Attacking Power Average number of minutes between League team goals while on pitch	81
Goals in all competitions	1		
Defensive Rating Average number of mins between League goals conceded while on the pitch	90	Scoring Difference Defensive Rating minus Contribution to Attacking Power	9

	PLAYER	GOALS LGE	GOALS ALL	DEF RATE	ATT POWER	SCORE DIFF
1	Jeff Smith	1	1	90	81	9 mins
2	Danny Sonner	1	1	77	74	3 mins
3	Michael Cummins	10	11	78	80	-2 mins
4	Tony Dinning	2	2	89	92	-3 mins

KEY PLAYERS - GOALSCORERS

Leon Constantine

Goals in the League	10	Player Strike Rate Average number of minutes between League goals scored by player	256
Goals in all competitions	12		
Contribution to Attacking Power Average number of minutes between League team goals while on pitch	91	Club Strike Rate Average number of minutes between League goals scored by club	84

	PLAYER	GOALS LGE	GOALS ALL	POWER	S RATE
1	Leon Constantine	10	12	91	256 mins
2	Michael Cummins	10	11	80	330 mins
3	Nathan Lowndes	5	6	101	506 mins
4	William Paynter	2	2	75	714 mins

Tony Dinning

SQUAD APPEARANCES

Match	1	2	3	4	5	6	7	8	9	10	11	12	13	14	15	16	17	18	19	20	21	22	23	24	25	26
Venue	A	H	H	A	A	H	A	H	A	H	A	H	H	A	H	A	H	H	A	H	H	H	A	A	A	H
Competition	L	L	L	L	W	L	L	L	L	L	L	L	L	L	L	L	L	F	L	L	L	F	L	L	F	L
Result	W	D	W	L	L	W	D	W	L	L	L	D	W	W	L	W	L	W	L	D	W	D	L	L	W	L

Match	27	28	29	30	31	32	33	34	35	36	37	38	39	40	41	42	43	44	45	46	47	48	49	50	51	52
Venue	H	A	H	A	H	A	H	A	A	A	H	A	H	A	H	A	A	H	A	H	H	A	H	A	H	A
Competition	L	L	L	L	F	L	L	L	F	L	L	L	L	L	L	L	L	L	L	L	L	L	L	L	L	L
Result	L	W	L	D	W	D	W	L	L	W	W	D	L	W	L	D	L	D	L	W	W	D	D	L	W	D

Goalkeepers
- Jonathan Brain
- Mark Goodlad

Defenders
- George Abbey
- Mick Bell
- Sam Collins
- Clayton Fortune
- Mark Innes
- Craig James
- Mark McGregor
- George Pilkington
- Steve Rowland
- Jason Talbot
- Michael Walsh

Midfielders
- Christopher Birchall
- Joe Cardle
- Michael Cummins
- Tony Dinning
- Sean Doherty
- Robin Hulbert
- Andy Porter
- Jeff Smith
- Danny Sonner
- Sam Togwell

Forwards
- Louis Briscoe
- Leon Constantine
- Christopher Cornes
- Michael Husbands
- Nathan Lowndes
- Gary Mulligan
- William Paynter
- Hector Sam

KEY: On all match · On bench · Subbed or sent off (Counting game) · Subbed or sent off (playing less than 70 minutes) · Subbed on from bench (Counting Game) · Subbed on (playing less than 70 minutes) · Subbed on and then subbed or sent off (Counting Game) · Subbed on and then subbed or sent off (playing less than 70 minutes) · Not in 16

GILLINGHAM

Final Position: **14th**

NICKNAME: THE GILLS

KEY: ☐Won ☐Drawn ☐Lost

							Attendance
1	div2	Colchester	H	W	2-1	Crofts 75; Byfield 89	7,293
2	div2	Port Vale	A	D	0-0		4,931
3	div2	Scunthorpe	A	D	1-1	Hessenthaler 61	5,007
4	div2	Bournemouth	H	W	1-0	Browning 39 og	6,568
5	ccr1	Oxford	H	W	1-0	Jarvis 83	4,149
6	div2	Nottm Forest	H	L	1-3	Byfield 78	7,228
7	div2	Brentford	A	D	1-1	Harris 45	6,969
8	div2	Rotherham	A	L	0-3		4,253
9	div2	Barnsley	H	L	0-3		5,283
10	div2	Oldham	H	L	0-1		6,259
11	ccr2	Portsmouth	H	W	3-2	Byfield 42; Ashdown 56 og; Crofts 94	4,903
12	div2	Tranmere	A	D	2-2	Byfield 16,63 pen,63 pen	7,003
13	div2	Chesterfield	H	W	1-0	Sancho 86	7,472
14	div2	Southend	H	L	1-2	Pouton 86	8,128
15	div2	Yeovil	H	D	0-0		6,848
16	div2	Bradford	A	L	0-1		7,729
17	ccr3	Doncaster	A	L	0-2		6,874
18	div2	Blackpool	H	W	2-1	Hope 49; Harris 65	6,300
19	div2	Hartlepool	A	L	1-3	Collin 90	4,522
20	facr1	Burscough	A	L	2-3	Jarvis 58; Saunders 77	1,927
21	div2	Walsall	A	L	0-2		4,785
22	div2	Hartlepool	H	W	1-0	Shields 10	6,092
23	div2	Colchester	A	L	0-5		3,801
24	div2	Doncaster	H	W	1-0	Flynn 18	4,861
25	div2	Port Vale	H	W	3-0	Harris 41; Jarvis 66,82	6,210
26	div2	Bournemouth	A	L	1-2	Harris 62	6,177
27	div2	Bristol City	H	D	1-1	Flynn 61	7,786
28	div2	MK Dons	H	W	3-0	Johnson, L 27; Clohessy 41; Pouton 89	6,012
29	div2	Huddersfield	A	D	0-0		11,483
30	div2	Barnsley	A	L	0-1		7,090
31	div2	Swindon	H	W	3-0	Byfield 20; Flynn 73; Harris 83	7,300
32	div2	Oldham	A	L	0-2		5,783
33	div2	Rotherham	H	D	1-1	Grant 63	6,107
34	div2	Swansea	A	W	2-1	Byfield 18; Harris 71	14,357
35	div2	Chesterfield	A	D	1-1	Black 48	4,652
36	div2	Tranmere	H	D	1-1	Byfield 73	6,803
37	div2	Swindon	A	L	0-1		5,530
38	div2	Doncaster	A	L	0-2		5,738
39	div2	Scunthorpe	H	L	1-3	Cochrane 39	6,029
40	div2	Nottm Forest	A	D	1-1	Bennett 8 og	19,446
41	div2	Bristol City	A	L	0-6		10,932
42	div2	Brentford	H	W	3-2	Sancho 9; Byfield 45 pen,76	5,745
43	div2	Swansea	H	W	1-0	Byfield 54 pen	6,909
44	div2	MK Dons	A	W	2-1	Byfield 59; Black 61	6,432
45	div2	Huddersfield	H	W	2-0	Mulligan 4; Jarvis 90	7,014
46	div2	Southend	A	W	1-0	Black 46	11,195
47	div2	Bradford	H	W	2-1	Black 8; Flynn 53	7,281
48	div2	Yeovil	A	L	3-4	Black 12; Flynn 77; Crofts 88	6,040
49	div2	Walsall	H	L	0-1		7,757
50	div2	Blackpool	A	D	3-3	Byfield 28,52; Flynn 86	8,541

LEAGUE APPEARANCES, BOOKINGS AND GOALS

	AGE (on 01/07/06)	IN NAMED 16	APPEARANCES	COUNTING GAMES	MINUTES ON PITCH	LEAGUE GOALS	(Yellow)
Goalkeepers							
Jason Brown	24	40	39	39	3510	0	2
Tony Bullock	34	8	6	6	540	0	0
Paul Crichton	37	34	1	1	90	0	0
Defenders							
Sean Clohessy	19	20	20	17	1647	1	3
Ian Cox	35	36	36	34	3105	0	8
Andrew Crofts	22	45	45	43	3938	2	10
Chris Hope	33	29	24	19	1836	1	3
Danny Jackman	23	43	42	31	3181	0	2
Richard Rose	23	26	14	13	1235	0	4
Brent Sancho	29	26	19	14	1376	2	1
Tommy Williams	25	13	13	11	1100	0	3
Midfielders							
Thomas Black	29	17	17	15	1312	5	2
Justin Cochrane	24	6	5	5	427	1	3
Michael Flynn	25	39	36	28	2796	6	6
Andy Hessenthaler	40	17	16	10	1063	1	3
Leon Johnson	25	36	28	25	2341	1	8
Alan Pouton	29	27	23	15	1579	2	7
Mark Saunders	35	7	4	3	281	0	1
Paul Smith	34	4	3	2	233	0	0
Daniel Spiller	25	35	32	16	1818	0	1
John Wallis	20	22	17	15	1379	0	4
Forwards							
Moses Ashikodi	19	4	4	0	105	0	3
Darren Byfield	29	29	29	25	2385	14	10
Francis Collin	19	10	6	1	258	1	0
Akwasi Fobi-Edusei	19	6	6	2	367	0	2
Gavin Grant	22	17	10	1	276	1	0
Neil Harris	28	38	36	24	2469	6	5
Steven Hislop	28	10	8	1	229	0	0
Matthew Jarvis	20	35	35	29	2800	3	1
Gary Mulligan	21	14	13	8	853	1	0
Paul Shields	24	20	17	2	627	1	1

TEAM OF THE SEASON

G Jason Brown CG: 39 DR: 68

D Brent Sancho CG: 14 DR: 106

D Danny Jackman CG: 31 DR: 69

D Andrew Crofts CG: 43 DR: 67

D Richard Rose CG: 13 DR: 62

M Thomas Black CG: 15 SD: 5

M John Wallis CG: 15 SD: 4

M Alan Pouton CG: 15 SD: -4

M Michael Flynn CG: 28 SD: -14

F Darren Byfield CG: 25 SR: 170

F Neil Harris CG: 24 SR: 412

MONTHLY POINTS TALLY

AUGUST	9	50%
SEPTEMBER	4	27%
OCTOBER	4	33%
NOVEMBER	3	25%
DECEMBER	10	67%
JANUARY	8	44%
FEBRUARY	2	13%
MARCH	7	58%
APRIL	12	67%
MAY	1	33%

LEAGUE GOALS

	PLAYER	LGE	FAC	LC	Oth	TOT
1	Byfield	14	0	1	0	15
2	Harris	6	0	0	0	6
3	Flynn	6	0	0	0	6
4	Black	5	0	0	0	5
5	Jarvis	3	1	1	0	5
6	Pouton	2	0	0	0	2
7	Crofts	2	0	1	0	3
8	Sancho	2	0	0	0	2
9	Cochrane	1	0	0	0	1
10	Mulligan	1	0	0	0	1
11	Johnson, L	1	0	0	0	1
	Other	8	1	1	0	10
	TOTAL	51	2	4	0	57

TOP POINT EARNERS

	PLAYER	GAMES	AV PTS
1	Brent Sancho	14	1.93
2	Alan Pouton	15	1.73
3	Thomas Black	15	1.67
4	John Wallis	15	1.60
5	Danny Jackman	31	1.55
6	Ian Cox	34	1.41
7	Matthew Jarvis	29	1.41
8	Darren Byfield	25	1.40
9	Jason Brown	39	1.36
10	Andrew Crofts	43	1.33

DISCIPLINARY RECORDS

	PLAYER	YELLOW	RED	AVE
1	Pouton	7	1	197
2	Byfield	10	2	198
3	Johnson, L	8	1	260
4	Rose	4	0	308
5	Wallis	4	0	344
6	Hessenthaler	3	0	354
7	Crofts	10	1	358
8	Williams, T	3	0	366
9	Cox	8	0	388
10	Clohessy	3	1	411
11	Flynn	6	0	466
12	Harris	5	0	493
13	Hope	3	0	612
	Other	10	1	
	TOTAL	84	7	

KEY GOALKEEPER

Jason Brown

Goals Conceded in the League	52	Counting Games League games when player was on pitch for at least 70 minutes	39
Goals Conceded in all competitions	54		
Defensive Rating Ave number of mins between League goals conceded while on the pitch	68	Clean Sheets In games when player was on pitch for at least 70 minutes	11

KEY PLAYERS - DEFENDERS

Brent Sancho

Goals Conceded in the League	13	Clean Sheets In League games when player was on pitch for at least 70 minutes	6
Goals Conceded in all competitions	15		
Defensive Rating Ave number of mins between League goals conceded while on the pitch	106	Club Defensive Rating Average number of mins between League goals conceded by the club this season	65

	PLAYER	CON LGE	CON ALL	CLN SHEETS	DEF RATE
1	Brent Sancho	13	15	6	106 mins
2	Danny Jackman	46	47	10	69 mins
3	Andrew Crofts	59	64	12	67 mins
4	Richard Rose	20	22	4	62 mins

KEY PLAYERS - MIDFIELDERS

Thomas Black

Goals in the League	5	Contribution to Attacking Power Average number of minutes between League team goals while on pitch	77
Goals in all competitions	5		
Defensive Rating Average number of mins between League goals conceded while on the pitch	82	Scoring Difference Defensive Rating minus Contribution to Attacking Power	5

	PLAYER	GOALS LGE	GOALS ALL	DEF RATE	ATT POWER	SCORE DIFF
1	Thomas Black	5	5	82	77	5 mins
2	John Wallis	0	0	77	73	4 mins
3	Alan Pouton	2	2	75	79	-4 mins
4	Michael Flynn	6	6	64	78	-14 mins

KEY PLAYERS - GOALSCORERS

Darren Byfield

Goals in the League	14	Player Strike Rate Average number of minutes between League goals scored by player	170
Goals in all competitions	15		
Contribution to Attacking Power Average number of minutes between League team goals while on pitch	75	Club Strike Rate Average number of minutes between League goals scored by club	81

	PLAYER	GOALS LGE	GOALS ALL	POWER	S RATE
1	Darren Byfield	14	15	75	170 mins
2	Thomas Black	5	5	77	262 mins
3	Neil Harris	6	6	85	412 mins
4	Michael Flynn	6	6	78	466 mins

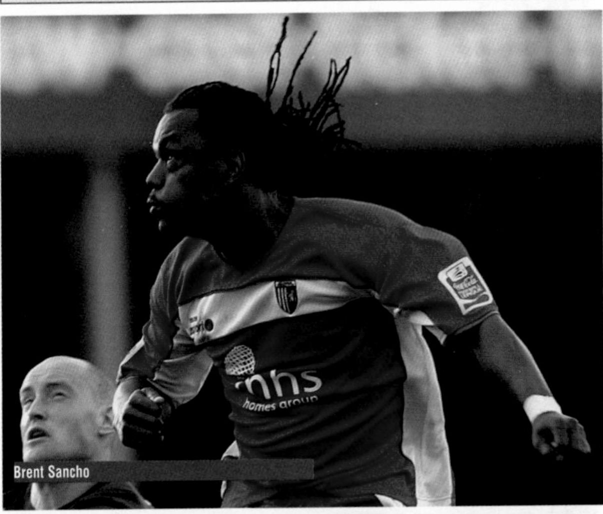

Brent Sancho

SQUAD APPEARANCES

atch	1	2	3	4	5	6	7	8	9	10	11	12	13	14	15	16	17	18	19	20	21	22	23	24	25
enue	H	A	A	H	H	H	A	A	H	H	H	A	H	H	H	A	A	H	A	A	A	H	A	H	H
ompetition	L	L	L	L	W	L	L	L	L	L	W	L	L	L	L	L	W	L	L	F	L	L	L	L	L
esult	W	D	D	W	W	L	D	L	L	L	W	D	W	L	D	L	L	W	L	L	L	W	L	W	W

atch	26	27	28	29	30	31	32	33	34	35	36	37	38	39	40	41	42	43	44	45	46	47	48	49	50
enue	A	H	H	A	A	H	A	H	A	A	H	A	A	H	A	A	H	H	A	H	A	H	A	H	A
ompetition	L	L	L	L	L	L	L	L	L	L	L	L	L	L	L	L	L	L	L	L	L	L	L	L	L
esult	L	D	W	D	L	W	L	D	W	D	D	L	L	L	D	L	W	W	W	W	W	W	L	L	D

oalkeepers
ason Brown
ony Bullock
aul Crichton
efenders
ean Clohessy
n Cox
ndrew Crofts
hris Hope
anny Jackman
ichard Rose
rent Sancho
ommy Williams
idfielders
homas Black
ustin Cochrane
ichael Flynn
ndy Hessenthaler
eon Johnson
lan Pouton
ark Saunders
aul Smith
aniel Spiller
ohn Wallis
orwards
oses Ashikodi
arren Byfield
rancis Collin
kwasi Fobi-Edusei
avin Grant
eil Harris
teven Hislop
atthew Jarvis
ary Mulligan
aul Shields

KEY: On all match · On bench · Subbed or sent off (Counting game) · Subbed or sent off (playing less than 70 minutes) · Subbed on from bench (Counting Game) · Subbed on (playing less than 70 minutes) · Subbed on and then subbed or sent off (Counting Game) · Subbed on and then subbed or sent off (playing less than 70 minutes) · Not in 16

YEOVIL

Final Position: **15th**

NICKNAME: THE GLOVERS

KEY: ☐Won ☐Drawn ☐Lost

							Attendance
1	div2	Oldham	A	L	0-2		6,979
2	div2	Rotherham	H	D	0-0		5,856
3	div2	Blackpool	H	D	1-1	Amankwaah 45	5,698
4	div2	Barnsley	A	L	0-1		8,153
5	ccr1	Ipswich	A	W	2-0	Way 45; Gall 87	11,299
6	div2	Swindon	A	L	2-4	Bastianini 1; Skiverton 87	6,973
7	div2	Chesterfield	H	L	1-3	Alvarez 36	6,079
8	div2	Hartlepool	A	W	1-0	Bastianini 68	4,572
9	div2	Walsall	H	W	2-1	Jevons 65; Gall 70	9,579
10	div2	Bradford	A	D	1-1	Skiverton 6	7,826
11	ccr2	Millwall	H	L	1-2	Davies 87	5,108
12	div2	Port Vale	H	W	1-0	Harrold 85	5,901
13	div2	Southend	A	L	1-4	Jevons 45	6,654
14	div2	Scunthorpe	A	W	4-3	Way 26; Jevons 37; Harrold 59,66	4,311
15	div2	Swansea	H	W	1-0	Skiverton 39	7,578
16	div2	Gillingham	A	D	0-0		6,848
17	div2	Nottm Forest	H	W	3-0	Jevons 6,26; Davies 82	9,072
18	div2	Colchester	A	L	2-3	Bastianini 32; Harrold 51	3,409
19	facr1	Macclesfield	A	D	1-1	Jevons 81	1,943
20	div2	Huddersfield	H	L	1-2	Johnson 47	6,742
21	facr1r	Macclesfield	H	W	4-0	Way 23; Terry 73; Johnson 75; Davies 90	4,456
22	div2	Swansea	A	L	0-2		19,288
23	div2	Oldham	H	L	0-2		5,852
24	facr2	Walsall	A	L	0-2		4,580
25	div2	Brentford	A	L	2-3	Harrold 38; Johnson 68	5,131
26	div2	Rotherham	A	W	2-1	Murdock 32 og; Harrold 36	3,929
27	div2	Barnsley	H	W	2-1	Poole 46; Sodje, E 73	5,620
28	div2	Bournemouth	H	D	1-1	Jevons 80 pen	8,178
29	div2	Tranmere	A	L	1-4	Jevons 32 pen	6,327
30	div2	Bristol City	H	D	1-1	Poole 3	9,178
31	div2	Doncaster	A	W	1-0	Jevons 12	5,680
32	div2	Hartlepool	H	W	2-0	Jevons 26,60	5,480
33	div2	MK Dons	A	D	1-1	Skiverton 13	5,548
34	div2	Bradford	H	L	0-1		6,168
35	div2	Southend	H	L	0-2		6,289
36	div2	Port Vale	A	L	0-1		4,732
37	div2	MK Dons	H	D	1-1	Gall 71	5,048
38	div2	Blackpool	A	L	0-2		5,747
39	div2	Chesterfield	A	W	3-0	Davies 37,90,90	4,843
40	div2	Brentford	H	L	1-2	Skiverton 26	5,137
41	div2	Swindon	H	D	0-0		7,451
42	div2	Bournemouth	A	L	0-1		7,959
43	div2	Walsall	A	W	2-0	Harrold 24; Davies 33	4,464
44	div2	Tranmere	H	D	2-2	Harrold 5,69	5,409
45	div2	Bristol City	A	L	1-2	Davies 64	15,889
46	div2	Doncaster	H	W	3-0	Skiverton 8; Jevons 57; Davies 86	5,456
47	div2	Scunthorpe	H	L	0-1		6,759
48	div2	Nottm Forest	A	L	1-2	Jevons 8	28,193
49	div2	Gillingham	H	W	4-3	Jevons 18 pen; Cohen 36; Terry 52; Davies 56	6,040
50	div2	Huddersfield	A	W	2-1	Jevons 66 pen,72	14,473
51	div2	Colchester	H	D	0-0		8,785

LEAGUE APPEARANCES, BOOKINGS AND GOALS

	AGE (on 01/07/06)	IN NAMED 16	APPEARANCES	COUNTING GAMES	MINUTES ON PITCH	LEAGUE GOALS	
Goalkeepers							
Stephen Collis	25	45	23	21	1951	0	0
Michael Jordan	20	9	0	0	0	0	0
Chris Weale	24	35	25	23	2189	0	0
Defenders							
Kevin Amankwaah	24	39	38	35	3206	1	0
Chris Cohen	19	30	30	29	2617	1	2
Liam Fontaine	20	10	10	7	728	0	0
Scott Guyett	30	26	21	17	1666	0	1
Nathan Jones	33	45	43	36	3373	0	1
Adam Lockwood	24	27	20	18	1644	0	4
Alejandrio Melono	29	1	1	0	59	0	0
Colin Miles	27	36	30	12	1613	0	2
Luke Oliver	21	4	3	0	44	0	0
Michael Rose	23	3	1	0	23	0	1
Terry Skiverton	31	39	36	33	3055	6	3
Efetobore Sodje	33	19	19	16	1475	1	2
Midfielders							
Anthony Barry	20	5	4	3	315	0	0
Lee Johnson	25	26	26	25	2290	2	3
Andrew Lindegaard	25	27	23	13	1415	0	1
David Poole	21	32	25	17	1718	2	2
Craig Rocastle	24	8	8	5	464	0	1
Paul Terry	27	44	42	29	3018	1	5
Darren Way	26	15	15	15	1350	1	1
Marc Wilson	18	5	2	1	100	0	1
Forwards							
Luciano Alvarez	27	7	4	1	248	1	1
Pablo Bastianini	23	23	20	12	1259	3	2
Arron Davies	22	40	39	22	2533	8	0
Kevin Gall	24	41	37	9	1326	2	2
Matt Harrold	22	44	42	25	2591	9	4
Phil Jevons	26	39	38	34	3114	15	2
Daniel Webb	23	7	4	0	39	0	0

TEAM OF THE SEASON

G Stephen Collis CG: 21 DR: 70

D Chris Cohen CG: 29 DR: 73

D Scott Guyett CG: 17 DR: 69

D Adam Lockwood CG: 18 DR: 69

D Terry Skiverton CG: 33 DR: 68

M Andrew Lindegaard CG: 13 SD: 12

M David Poole CG: 17 SD: -7

M Lee Johnson CG: 25 SD: -8

M Paul Terry CG: 29 SD: -19

F Phil Jevons CG: 34 SR: 208

F Matt Harrold CG: 25 SR: 288

MONTHLY POINTS TALLY

AUGUST	2	11%
SEPTEMBER	10	67%
OCTOBER	10	67%
NOVEMBER	0	0%
DECEMBER	8	44%
JANUARY	7	58%
FEBRUARY	1	8%
MARCH	8	44%
APRIL	9	50%
MAY	1	33%

LEAGUE GOALS

	PLAYER	LGE	FAC	LC	Oth	TOT
1	Jevons	15	1	0	0	16
2	Harrold	9	0	0	0	9
3	Davies	8	1	1	0	10
4	Skiverton	6	0	0	0	6
5	Bastianini	3	0	0	0	3
6	Johnson	2	1	0	0	3
7	Poole	2	0	0	0	2
8	Gall	2	0	1	0	3
9	Sodje, E	1	0	0	0	1
10	Amankwaah	1	0	0	0	1
11	Terry	1	1	0	0	2
	Other	4	1	1	0	6
	TOTAL	54	5	3	0	62

TOP POINT EARNERS

	PLAYER	GAMES	AV PTS
1	Scott Guyett	17	1.47
2	Lee Johnson	25	1.44
3	Colin Miles	12	1.42
4	Matt Harrold	25	1.40
5	David Poole	17	1.35
6	Pablo Bastianini	12	1.33
7	Arron Davies	22	1.32
8	Terry Skiverton	33	1.30
9	Stephen Collis	21	1.29
10	Darren Way	15	1.27

DISCIPLINARY RECORDS

	PLAYER	YELLOW	RED	AVE
1	Lockwood	4	0	411
2	Rocastle	1	0	464
3	Sodje, E	2	1	491
4	Johnson	3	1	572
5	Terry	5	0	603
6	Bastianini	2	0	629
7	Harrold	4	0	647
8	Gall	2	0	663
9	Miles	2	0	806
10	Poole	2	0	859
11	Skiverton	3	0	1018
12	Cohen	2	0	1308
13	Way	1	0	1350
	Other	5	1	
	TOTAL	38	3	

KEY GOALKEEPER

Stephen Collis

Goals Conceded in the League	28	Counting Games League games when player was on pitch for at least 70 minutes	21
Goals Conceded in all competitions	28		
Defensive Rating Ave number of mins between League goals conceded while on the pitch	70	Clean Sheets In games when player was on pitch for at least 70 minutes	5

KEY PLAYERS - DEFENDERS

Chris Cohen

Goals Conceded in the League	36	Clean Sheets In League games when player was on pitch for at least 70 minutes	7
Goals Conceded in all competitions	38		
Defensive Rating Ave number of mins between League goals conceded while on the pitch	73	Club Defensive Rating Average number of mins between League goals conceded by the club this season	67

	PLAYER	CON LGE	CON ALL	CLN SHEETS	DEF RATE
1	Chris Cohen	36	38	7	73 mins
2	Scott Guyett	24	24	6	69 mins
3	Adam Lockwood	24	24	5	69 mins
4	Terry Skiverton	45	50	11	68 mins

KEY PLAYERS - MIDFIELDERS

Andrew Lindegaard

Goals in the League	0	Contribution to Attacking Power Average number of minutes between League team goals while on pitch	71
Goals in all competitions	0		
Defensive Rating Average number of mins between League goals conceded while on the pitch	83	Scoring Difference Defensive Rating minus Contribution to Attacking Power	12

	PLAYER	GOALS LGE	GOALS ALL	DEF RATE	ATT POWER	SCORE DIFF
1	Andrew Lindegaard	0	0	83	71	12 mins
2	David Poole	2	2	75	82	-7 mins
3	Lee Johnson	2	3	64	72	-8 mins
4	Paul Terry	1	2	67	86	-19 mins

KEY PLAYERS - GOALSCORERS

Phil Jevons

Goals in the League	15	Player Strike Rate Average number of minutes between League goals scored by player	208
Goals in all competitions	16		
Contribution to Attacking Power Average number of minutes between League team goals while on pitch	76	Club Strike Rate Average number of minutes between League goals scored by club	77

	PLAYER	GOALS LGE	GOALS ALL	POWER	S RATE
1	Phil Jevons	15	16	76	208 mins
2	Matt Harrold	9	9	70	288 mins
3	Arron Davies	8	10	68	317 mins
4	Pablo Bastianini	3	3	70	420 mins

Terry Skiverton

SQUAD APPEARANCES

Match	1	2	3	4	5	6	7	8	9	10	11	12	13	14	15	16	17	18	19	20	21	22	23	24	25
Venue	A	H	H	A	A	A	H	A	H	A	H	H	A	A	H	A	H	A	A	H	H	A	H	A	A
Competition	L	L	L	L	W	L	L	L	L	L	W	L	L	L	L	L	L	L	F	L	F	L	L	F	L
Result	L	D	D	L	W	L	L	W	W	D	L	W	L	W	W	D	W	L	D	L	W	L	L	L	L

Match	26	27	28	29	30	31	32	33	34	35	36	37	38	39	40	41	42	43	44	45	46	47	48	49	50	51
Venue	A	H	H	A	H	A	H	A	H	H	A	H	A	A	H	H	A	A	H	A	H	H	A	H	A	H
Competition	L	L	L	L	L	L	L	L	L	L	L	L	L	L	L	L	L	L	L	L	L	L	L	L	L	L
Result	W	W	D	L	D	W	W	D	L	L	L	D	L	W	L	D	L	W	D	L	W	L	L	W	W	D

Goalkeepers
Stephen Collis
Michael Jordan
Chris Weale
Defenders
Kevin Amankwaah
Chris Cohen
Liam Fontaine
Scott Guyett
Nathan Jones
Adam Lockwood
Alejandrio Melono
Colin Miles
Luke Oliver
Michael Rose
Terry Skiverton
Efetobore Sodje
Midfielders
Anthony Barry
Lee Johnson
Andrew Lindegaard
David Poole
Craig Rocastle
Paul Terry
Darren Way
Marc Wilson
Forwards
Luciano Alvarez
Pablo Bastianini
Arron Davies
Kevin Gall
Matt Harrold
Phil Jevons
Daniel Webb

KEY: On all match / On bench / Subbed or sent off (Counting game) / Subbed or sent off (playing less than 70 minutes) / Subbed on from bench (Counting Game) / Subbed on (playing less than 70 minutes) / Subbed on and then subbed or sent off (Counting Game) / Subbed on and then subbed or sent off (playing less than 70 minutes) / Not in 16

CHESTERFIELD

Final Position: **16th**

NICKNAME: THE SPIREITES

KEY: ☐Won ☐Drawn ☐Lost

							Attendance
1	div2	Blackpool	A	W	3-1	Allison 23; DeBolla 39; Blatherwick 67	6,469
2	div2	Brentford	H	L	1-3	Hall 27	4,121
3	div2	Rotherham	H	L	0-1		5,189
4	div2	Oldham	A	L	1-4	Niven 51	5,347
5	ccr1	Huddersfield	H	L	2-4	Niven 41; Hurst 60	2,922
6	div2	Tranmere	H	L	0-2		3,445
7	div2	Yeovil	A	W	3-1	Hall 44; Smith 53,75	6,079
8	div2	Bradford	A	L	0-2		7,351
9	div2	Bournemouth	H	W	3-0	Larkin 27; Allison 53; Nicholson 79	3,540
10	div2	Walsall	A	W	3-2	Allott 55,68; Allison 77	5,177
11	div2	Hartlepool	H	W	3-1	Larkin 54; Niven 67; Hall 79	4,078
12	div2	Gillingham	A	L	0-1		7,472
13	div2	Colchester	A	W	2-1	Larkin 25; Hall 49	3,414
14	div2	MK Dons	A	D	0-0		5,642
15	div2	Huddersfield	H	W	4-3	Allison 11; Hall 30; Larkin 45; Nicholson 85 pen	6,206
16	div2	Bristol City	H	W	3-0	Allison 57; Nicholson 66,88 pen	5,027
17	div2	Swansea	A	L	1-5	Blatherwick 21	13,264
18	facr1	Leyton Orient	A	D	0-0		3,554
19	div2	Port Vale	H	W	2-0	Allison 31,67	4,714
20	facr1r	Leyton Orient	H	L	1-2	Hurst 37	4,895
21	div2	Bristol City	A	W	4-2	Hall 18,30 pen,61; Hurst 25	9,752
22	div2	Blackpool	H	D	1-1	Clingan 8	4,585
23	div2	Southend	A	D	0-0		5,767
24	div2	Brentford	A	D	1-1	Hall 19	5,628
25	div2	Oldham	H	D	1-1	Allison 69	4,304
26	div2	Scunthorpe	A	D	2-2	Hall 4; Nicholson 58 pen	5,866
27	div2	Swindon	H	D	1-1	Hall 19	4,265
28	div2	Nottm Forest	A	D	0-0		21,909
29	div2	Barnsley	H	D	0-0		6,046
30	div2	Bradford	H	W	1-0	Smith 89	4,449
31	div2	Doncaster	A	D	1-1	Allison 63	6,528
32	div2	Walsall	H	D	2-2	Allison 36; Hurst 80	4,666
33	div2	Bournemouth	A	W	2-1	Allison 25; O'Hara 74	5,837
34	div2	Gillingham	H	D	1-1	Hall 89	4,652
35	div2	Hartlepool	A	L	0-1		4,596
36	div2	Doncaster	H	L	0-1		5,719
37	div2	Southend	H	L	3-4	Larkin 27; Niven 63; Hurst 66	4,527
38	div2	Rotherham	A	W	4-0	Hurst 45; Niven 49; Allott 54; O'Hara 87	6,919
39	div2	Yeovil	H	L	0-3		4,843
40	div2	Tranmere	A	L	1-4	O'Hara 30	6,435
41	div2	Scunthorpe	H	L	1-2	Larkin 15	4,406
42	div2	Swindon	A	L	0-2		5,661
43	div2	Nottm Forest	H	L	1-3	Picken 33	7,073
44	div2	Barnsley	A	D	1-1	Niven 76	8,303
45	div2	Colchester	H	D	2-2	O'Hara 3; Hall 18	3,649
46	div2	Huddersfield	A	W	2-1	Hall 53,67	13,368
47	div2	MK Dons	H	L	1-2	Larkin 50	3,965
48	div2	Port Vale	A	L	1-3	O'Hara 3	4,478
49	div2	Swansea	H	L	0-4		6,294

LEAGUE APPEARANCES, BOOKINGS AND GOALS

	AGE (on 01/07/06)	IN NAMED 16	APPEARANCES	COUNTING GAMES	MINUTES ON PITCH	LEAGUE GOALS	Yellow	Red
Goalkeepers								
Rob Beckwith	21	8	2	2	180	0	0	0
Carl Muggleton	37	33	3	3	270	0	0	0
Barry Roche	24	42	41	41	3690	0	1	0
Defenders								
Alex Bailey	22	19	18	13	1404	0	2	0
Steven Blatherwick	32	30	30	27	2554	2	2	0
Aaron Downes	21	26	22	19	1782	0	1	0
Ashley Foyle	19	2	1	0	21	0	0	0
Reuben Hazell	27	34	33	28	2638	0	5	0
Janos Kovacs	20	19	9	7	723	0	3	1
Shane Nicholson	36	27	25	23	2118	5	3	1
Alan O'Hare	23	36	21	14	1531	0	4	0
Phil Picken	20	34	32	32	2880	1	2	0
Midfielders								
Mark Allott	28	43	43	43	3870	3	9	0
Sammy Clingan	22	22	21	13	1365	1	3	0
Gareth Davies	23	34	20	10	1181	0	1	0
Paul Hall	34	46	45	40	3812	15	2	0
Kevan Hurst	20	38	37	22	2441	4	0	0
Sam Lancaster	20	1	1	0	10	0	0	0
Derek Niven	22	43	42	39	3619	5	6	0
Jamie O'Hara	19	21	20	19	1764	5	0	0
Forwards								
Wayne Allison	37	37	32	23	2355	11	0	0
Mark DeBolla	23	7	4	0	123	1	0	0
Caleb Folan	20	34	27	6	1074	0	1	0
Colin Heath	22	11	4	0	71	0	1	0
Jamie Jackson	19	2	2	0	34	0	0	0
Colin Larkin	24	46	41	26	2696	7	1	0
Tcham N'Toya	22	8	4	1	104	0	2	0
Adam Smith	20	33	26	7	1114	3	1	0

TEAM OF THE SEASON

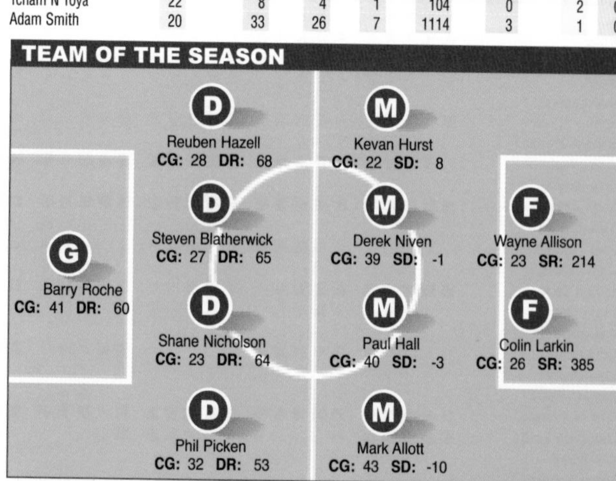

MONTHLY POINTS TALLY

Month	Points	%
AUGUST	6	33%
SEPTEMBER	9	60%
OCTOBER	10	67%
NOVEMBER	7	78%
DECEMBER	6	33%
JANUARY	9	60%
FEBRUARY	4	27%
MARCH	0	0%
APRIL	5	28%
MAY	0	0%

LEAGUE GOALS

	PLAYER	LGE	FAC	LC	Oth	TOT
1	Hall	15	0	0	0	15
2	Allison	11	0	0	0	11
3	Larkin	7	0	0	0	7
4	O'Hara	5	0	0	0	5
5	Niven	5	0	1	0	6
6	Nicholson	5	0	0	0	5
7	Hurst, K	4	1	1	0	6
8	Smith	3	0	0	0	3
9	Allott	3	0	0	0	3
10	Blatherwick	2	0	0	0	2
11	Picken	1	0	0	0	1
	Other	2	0	0	0	2
	TOTAL	63	1	2	0	66

TOP POINT EARNERS

	PLAYER	GAMES	AV PTS
1	Shane Nicholson	23	1.57
2	Reuben Hazell	28	1.57
3	Kevan Hurst	22	1.55
4	Wayne Allison	23	1.52
5	Steven Blatherwick	27	1.44
6	Paul Hall	40	1.35
7	Derek Niven	39	1.33
8	Alex Bailey	13	1.31
9	Barry Roche	41	1.29
10	Colin Larkin	26	1.27

DISCIPLINARY RECORDS

	PLAYER	YELLOW	RED	AVE
1	Kovacs	3	1	180
2	O'Hare	4	0	382
3	Allott	9	0	430
4	Clingan	3	0	455
5	Hazell	5	0	527
6	Nicholson	3	1	529
7	Niven	6	0	603
8	Bailey	2	0	702
9	Folan	1	0	1074
10	Smith	1	0	1114
11	Davies	1	0	1181
12	Blatherwick	2	0	1277
13	Picken	2	0	1440
	Other	5	0	
	TOTAL	47	2	

KEY GOALKEEPER

Barry Roche

Goals Conceded in the League	62	Counting Games League games when player was on pitch for at least 70 minutes	41
Goals Conceded in all competitions	64		
Defensive Rating Ave number of mins between League goals conceded while on the pitch	60	Clean Sheets In games when player was on pitch for at least 70 minutes	8

KEY PLAYERS - DEFENDERS

Reuben Hazell

Goals Conceded in the League	39	Clean Sheets In League games when player was on pitch for at least 70 minutes	8
Goals Conceded in all competitions	41		
Defensive Rating Ave number of mins between League goals conceded while on the pitch	68	Club Defensive Rating Average number of mins between League goals conceded by the club this season	57

	PLAYER	CON LGE	CON ALL	CLN SHEETS	DEF RATE
1	Reuben Hazell	39	41	8	68 mins
2	Steven Blatherwick	39	45	8	65 mins
3	Shane Nicholson	33	39	7	64 mins
4	Phil Picken	54	58	5	53 mins

KEY PLAYERS - MIDFIELDERS

Kevan Hurst

Goals in the League	4	Contribution to Attacking Power Average number of minutes between League team goals while on pitch	53
Goals in all competitions	6		
Defensive Rating Average number of mins between League goals conceded while on the pitch	61	Scoring Difference Defensive Rating minus Contribution to Attacking Power	8

	PLAYER	GOALS LGE	GOALS ALL	DEF RATE	ATT POWER	SCORE DIFF
1	Kevan Hurst	4	6	61	53	8 mins
2	Derek Niven	5	6	62	63	-1 mins
3	Paul Hall	15	15	61	64	-3 mins
4	Mark Allott	3	3	55	65	-10 mins

KEY PLAYERS - GOALSCORERS

Wayne Allison

Goals in the League	11	Player Strike Rate Average number of minutes between League goals scored by player	214
Goals in all competitions	11		
Contribution to Attacking Power Average number of minutes between League team goals while on pitch	57	Club Strike Rate Average number of minutes between League goals scored by club	66

	PLAYER	GOALS LGE	GOALS ALL	POWER	S RATE
1	Wayne Allison	11	11	57	214 mins
2	Paul Hall	15	15	64	254 mins
3	Jamie O'Hara	5	5	77	353 mins
4	Colin Larkin	7	7	63	385 mins

Derek Niven

SQUAD APPEARANCES

Match	1	2	3	4	5	6	7	8	9	10	11	12	13	14	15	16	17	18	19	20	21	22	23	24	25	26	27	28	29	30	31	32	33	34	35	36	37	38	39	40	41	42	43	44	45	46	47	48	49
Venue	A	H	H	A	H	H	A	A	H	A	H	A	A	A	H	H	A	A	H	H	A	H	A	A	H	A	H	A	H	H	A	H	A	H	A	H	H	A	H	A	H	A	H	A	H	A	H	A	H
Competition	L	L	L	L	W	L	L	L	L	L	L	L	L	L	L	L	L	F	L	F	L	L	L	L	L	L	L	L	L	L	L	L	L	L	L	L	L	L	L	L	L	L	L	L	L	L	L	L	L
Result	W	L	L	L	L	L	W	L	W	W	W	L	W	D	W	W	L	D	W	L	W	D	D	D	D	D	D	D	D	W	D	D	W	D	L	L	L	W	L	L	L	L	L	D	D	W	L	L	L

Goalkeepers
Rob Beckwith
Carl Muggleton
Barry Roche

Defenders
Alex Bailey
Steven Blatherwick
Aaron Downes
Ashley Foyle
Reuben Hazell
Janos Kovacs
Shane Nicholson
Alan O'Hare
Phil Picken

Midfielders
Mark Allott
Sammy Clingan
Gareth Davies
Paul Hall
Kevan Hurst
Sam Lancaster
Derek Niven
Jamie O'Hara

Forwards
Wayne Allison
Mark DeBolla
Caleb Folan
Colin Heath
Jamie Jackson
Colin Larkin
Tcham N'Toya
Adam Smith

KEY: On all match | On bench | Subbed or sent off (Counting game) | Subbed or sent off (playing less than 70 minutes) | Subbed on from bench (Counting Game) | Subbed on (playing less than 70 minutes) | Subbed on and then subbed or sent off (Counting Game) | Subbed on and then subbed or sent off (playing less than 70 minutes) | Not in 16

BOURNEMOUTH

Final Position: **17th**

NICKNAME: THE CHERRIES

KEY: ☐Won ☐Drawn ☐Lost

	Comp	Opponent	H/A	Res	Score	Scorers	Attendance
1	div2	MK Dons	A	D	2-2	Hayter 76; Surman 89	5,163
2	div2	Hartlepool	H	D	1-1	Rodrigues 64	5,406
3	div2	Bristol City	H	W	2-0	Stock 20; Hayter 50 pen	6,544
4	div2	Gillingham	A	L	0-1		6,568
5	ccr1	Torquay	A	D	4-3*	(*on penalties)	1,876
6	div2	Bradford	A	W	2-1	Bower 55 og; Surman 64	7,621
7	div2	Walsall	H	D	0-0		5,953
8	div2	Tranmere	H	D	0-0		5,695
9	div2	Chesterfield	A	L	0-3		3,540
10	div2	Swindon	H	W	2-1	Hayter 24 pen,68	7,276
11	ccr2	Wigan	A	L	0-1		3,346
12	div2	Oldham	A	L	0-1		5,058
13	div2	Swansea	H	L	0-1		5,750
14	div2	Huddersfield	A	D	2-2	Hayter 66 pen,70	13,522
15	div2	Doncaster	H	W	2-1	Surman 82; Stock 90	6,578
16	div2	Colchester	A	W	1-0	Keene 90	3,120
17	div2	Port Vale	H	L	1-2	Surman 23	6,320
18	div2	Brentford	A	W	2-0	Keene 26; Hayter 41	6,625
19	facr1	Tamworth	H	L	1-2	Stock 45	4,550
20	div2	Nottm Forest	H	D	1-1	Stock 64	9,222
21	div2	Doncaster	A	L	2-4	Surman 64; Rodrigues 79	4,803
22	div2	MK Dons	H	W	2-0	Foley 36; Cooke 82	5,485
23	div2	Blackpool	A	W	3-1	Hayter 26,27,68 pen	4,326
24	div2	Hartlepool	A	L	1-2	Foley 68	3,755
25	div2	Gillingham	H	W	2-1	Hayter 66; Surman 90	6,177
26	div2	Yeovil	A	D	1-1	Hayter 19 pen	8,178
27	div2	Southend	A	L	1-2	Foley 70	6,357
28	div2	Scunthorpe	H	D	1-1	Hayter 85	6,259
29	div2	Tranmere	A	D	0-0		6,717
30	div2	Rotherham	H	W	2-0	Foley 2; Hayter 11	5,700
31	div2	Swindon	A	L	2-4	Rodrigues 59; Hayter 68 pen	6,092
32	div2	Chesterfield	H	L	1-2	Hayter 66 pen	5,837
33	div2	Swansea	A	L	0-1		12,079
34	div2	Oldham	H	D	0-0		5,453
35	div2	Rotherham	A	L	0-2		4,498
36	div2	Blackpool	H	D	1-1	Pitman 4	5,349
37	div2	Bristol City	A	L	1-3	Hayter 44	11,058
38	div2	Barnsley	H	D	1-1	Griffiths 70	5,191
39	div2	Bradford	H	L	0-1		5,749
40	div2	Yeovil	H	W	1-0	Fletcher 33	7,959
41	div2	Barnsley	A	D	0-0		9,180
42	div2	Southend	H	D	1-1	Hayter 82	7,638
43	div2	Scunthorpe	A	D	2-2	Hayter 33; O'Connor, J 63	4,136
44	div2	Walsall	A	W	1-0	Hayter 17	4,613
45	div2	Huddersfield	H	D	1-1	Fletcher 34	7,406
46	div2	Port Vale	A	D	0-0		4,006
47	div2	Colchester	H	L	1-2	Cooke 8	6,231
48	div2	Nottm Forest	A	D	1-1	Fletcher 48	26,847
49	div2	Brentford	H	D	2-2	Foley 45; Fletcher 90	9,359

LEAGUE APPEARANCES, BOOKINGS AND GOALS

	AGE (on 01/07/06)	IN NAMED 16	APPEARANCES	COUNTING GAMES	MINUTES ON PITCH	LEAGUE GOALS	Yellow	Red
Goalkeepers								
Neil Moss	31	27	4	4	360	0	0	0
Gareth Stewart	26	46	42	42	3780	0	0	0
Defenders								
Karl Broadhurst	26	12	7	4	357	0	1	0
Aaron Brown	23	4	4	3	272	0	1	0
Shaun Cooper	22	39	35	30	2820	0	2	0
Josh Gowling	21	15	13	10	928	0	0	1
Adam Griffiths	26	8	7	6	538	1	3	1
Callum Hart	20	41	39	31	2973	0	4	0
Eddie Howe	28	23	20	16	1460	0	2	0
Shaun Maher	28	9	6	3	318	0	0	0
James O'Connor	21	39	39	35	3279	1	3	0
Stephen Purches	26	30	26	21	1980	0	0	0
Neil Young	32	41	41	40	3618	0	4	1
Midfielders								
Marcus Browning	35	42	42	40	3587	0	5	0
Stephen Cooke	23	35	31	14	1632	2	2	0
James Coutts	19	23	11	0	257	0	0	0
Steve Foley	20	35	35	30	2815	5	0	0
Daryl Fordyce	18	5	3	3	237	0	0	0
Ben Rix	22	15	10	6	588	0	0	0
James Rowe	19	5	2	0	18	0	0	0
John Spicer	22	4	4	4	355	0	0	0
Brian Stock	24	26	26	26	2282	3	2	0
Andrew Surman	19	24	24	23	2063	6	2	0
Jason Tindall	28	20	12	5	533	0	1	0
Forwards								
Curtis Allen	18	1	0	0	0	0	0	0
Steve Fletcher	34	28	27	18	1896	4	2	0
James Hayter	27	46	46	46	4132	20	2	0
Kirk Hudson	19	6	1	0	4	0	0	0
James Keene	20	12	11	6	567	2	2	0
Brett Pitman	18	34	19	3	512	1	1	0
Dani Rodrigues	26	36	29	10	1277	3	0	0

TEAM OF THE SEASON

G — Gareth Stewart — CG: 42 DR: 77

D — Eddie Howe — CG: 16 DR: 97

D — Shaun Cooper — CG: 30 DR: 88

D — James O'Connor — CG: 35 DR: 82

D — Neil Young — CG: 40 DR: 80

M — Brian Stock — CG: 26 SD: 6

M — Stephen Cooke — CG: 14 SD: 0

M — Andrew Surman — CG: 23 SD: 0

M — Steve Foley — CG: 30 SD: -6

F — James Hayter — CG: 46 SR: 207

F — Steve Fletcher — CG: 18 SR: 474

MONTHLY POINTS TALLY

Month	Points	%
AUGUST	9	50%
SEPTEMBER	4	27%
OCTOBER	10	67%
NOVEMBER	4	44%
DECEMBER	7	47%
JANUARY	5	33%
FEBRUARY	3	17%
MARCH	4	44%
APRIL	8	38%
MAY	1	33%

LEAGUE GOALS

	PLAYER	LGE	FAC	LC	Oth	TOT
1	Hayter	20	0	0	0	20
2	Surman	6	0	0	0	6
3	Foley	5	0	0	0	5
4	Fletcher	4	0	0	0	4
5	Stock	3	1	0	0	4
6	Rodrigues	3	0	0	0	3
7	Keene	2	0	0	0	2
8	Cooke	2	0	0	0	2
9	Pitman	1	0	0	0	1
10	Griffiths	1	0	0	0	1
11	O'Connor, J	1	0	0	0	1
	Other	1	0	0	0	1
	TOTAL	49	1	0	0	50

TOP POINT EARNERS

	PLAYER	GAMES	AV PTS
1	Steve Fletcher	18	1.50
2	Andrew Surman	23	1.48
3	Shaun Cooper	30	1.43
4	Brian Stock	26	1.38
5	Steve Foley	30	1.37
6	James O'Connor	35	1.34
7	Neil Young	40	1.28
8	James Hayter	46	1.20
9	Gareth Stewart	42	1.19
10	Marcus Browning	40	1.18

DISCIPLINARY RECORDS

	PLAYER	YELLOW	RED	AVE
1	Griffiths	3	1	134
2	Keene	2	0	283
3	Pitman	1	0	512
4	Tindall	1	0	533
5	Browning	5	0	717
6	Young	4	1	723
7	Howe	2	0	730
8	Hart	4	0	743
9	Cooke	2	0	816
10	Gowling	0	1	928
11	Fletcher	2	0	948
12	Surman	2	0	1031
13	O'Connor, J	3	0	1093
	Other	6	0	
	TOTAL	37	3	

KEY GOALKEEPER

Gareth Stewart

Goals Conceded in the League	49	Counting Games League games when player was on pitch for at least 70 minutes	42
Goals Conceded in all competitions	52		
Defensive Rating Ave number of mins between League goals conceded while on the pitch	77	Clean Sheets In games when player was on pitch for at least 70 minutes	12

KEY PLAYERS - DEFENDERS

Eddie Howe

Goals Conceded in the League	15	Clean Sheets In League games when player was on pitch for at least 70 minutes	5
Goals Conceded in all competitions	15		
Defensive Rating Ave number of mins between League goals conceded while on the pitch	97	Club Defensive Rating Average number of mins between League goals conceded by the club this season	78

	PLAYER	CON LGE	CON ALL	CLN SHEETS	DEF RATE
1	Eddie Howe	15	15	5	97 mins
2	Shaun Cooper	32	35	11	88 mins
3	James O'Connor	40	42	11	82 mins
4	Neil Young	45	48	13	80 mins

KEY PLAYERS - MIDFIELDERS

Brian Stock

Goals in the League	3	Contribution to Attacking Power Average number of minutes between League team goals while on pitch	76
Goals in all competitions	4		
Defensive Rating Average number of mins between League goals conceded while on the pitch	82	Scoring Difference Defensive Rating minus Contribution to Attacking Power	6

	PLAYER	GOALS LGE	GOALS ALL	DEF RATE	ATT POWER	SCORE DIFF
1	Brian Stock	3	4	82	76	6 mins
2	Andrew Surman	6	6	76	76	0 mins
3	Stephen Cooke	2	2	86	86	0 mins
4	Steve Foley	5	5	72	78	-6 mins

KEY PLAYERS - GOALSCORERS

James Hayter

Goals in the League	20	Player Strike Rate Average number of minutes between League goals scored by player	207
Goals in all competitions	20		
Contribution to Attacking Power Average number of minutes between League team goals while on pitch	86	Club Strike Rate Average number of minutes between League goals scored by club	84

	PLAYER	GOALS LGE	GOALS ALL	POWER	S RATE
1	James Hayter	20	20	86	207 mins
2	Andrew Surman	6	6	76	344 mins
3	Steve Fletcher	4	4	68	474 mins
4	Steve Foley	5	5	78	563 mins

Brian Stock

SQUAD APPEARANCES

Match	Venue	Competition	Result
1	A	L	D
2	H	L	D
3	H	L	W
4	A	L	L
5	A	W	D
6	A	L	W
7	H	L	D
8	H	L	D
9	A	L	L
10	H	L	W
11	A	W	L
12	A	L	L
13	H	L	L
14	A	L	D
15	H	L	W
16	A	L	W
17	H	L	L
18	A	L	W
19	H	F	L
20	H	L	D
21	A	L	L
22	H	L	W
23	A	L	W
24	A	L	L
25	H	L	W
26	A	L	D
27	A	L	L
28	H	L	D
29	A	L	D
30	H	L	W
31	A	L	L
32	H	L	L
33	A	L	L
34	H	L	D
35	A	L	L
36	H	L	D
37	A	L	L
38	H	L	D
39	H	L	L
40	H	L	W
41	A	L	D
42	H	L	D
43	A	L	D
44	A	L	W
45	H	L	D
46	A	L	D
47	H	L	L
48	A	L	D
49	H	L	D

Goalkeepers
Neil Moss
Gareth Stewart

Defenders
Karl Broadhurst
Aaron Brown
Shaun Cooper
Josh Gowling
Adam Griffiths
Callum Hart
Eddie Howe
Shaun Maher
James O'Connor
Stephen Purches
Neil Young

Midfielders
Marcus Browning
Stephen Cooke
James Coutts
Steve Foley
Daryl Fordyce
Ben Rix
James Rowe
John Spicer
Brian Stock
Andrew Surman
Tindall

Forwards
Curtis Allen
Steve Fletcher
James Hayter
Kirk Hudson
James Keene
Brett Pitman
Dani Rodrigues

KEY: On all match · On bench · Subbed or sent off (Counting game) · Subbed or sent off (playing less than 70 minutes) · Subbed on from bench (Counting Game) · Subbed on (playing less than 70 minutes) · Subbed on and then subbed or sent off (Counting Game) · Subbed on and then subbed or sent off (playing less than 70 minutes) · Not in 16

TRANMERE ROVERS

Final Position: **18th**

NICKNAME: ROVERS

KEY: ☐Won ☐Drawn ☐Lost

							Attendance
1	div2	Swansea	A	L	0-1		16,733
2	div2	Blackpool	H	D	2-2	Hume 38; Greenacre 45	7,509
3	div2	Oldham	H	W	4-0	Greenacre 45,90 pen; Sharps 54; Roberts 77	8,466
4	div2	Brentford	A	L	0-2		5,438
5	ccr1	Scunthorpe	A	L	1-2	Sharps 61	2,738
6	div2	Chesterfield	A	W	2-0	Jackson 76; Roberts 90	3,445
7	div2	Swindon	H	W	1-0	Greenacre 58	7,557
8	div2	Bournemouth	A	D	0-0		5,695
9	div2	Bradford	H	D	2-2	Facey 24; Greenacre 72	8,225
10	div2	Southend	A	L	1-3	Facey 46	6,691
11	div2	Gillingham	H	D	2-2	Jackson 10; Greenacre 46	7,003
12	div2	Huddersfield	A	L	0-1		10,640
13	div2	Nottm Forest	A	L	0-1		22,022
14	div2	Scunthorpe	H	L	0-2		7,522
15	div2	Bristol City	A	L	0-1		10,495
16	div2	Colchester	H	D	0-0		6,612
17	div2	Doncaster	A	W	2-0	Davies 62; Jennings 90	5,542
18	facr1	Bradford	A	L	1-2	Greenacre 6	6,116
19	div2	MK Dons	H	L	1-2	Jackson 38	6,611
20	div2	Scunthorpe	A	W	2-1	Greenacre 58 pen; Facey 76	4,602
21	div2	Swansea	H	D	2-2	Francis 18; Facey 45	7,518
22	div2	Barnsley	A	L	1-2	Facey 90	6,996
23	div2	Blackpool	A	D	1-1	Facey 81	5,069
24	div2	Brentford	H	L	1-4	Zola 23	6,210
25	div2	Walsall	A	D	0-0		6,476
26	div2	Yeovil	H	W	4-1	Greenacre 50,74,86; Zola 72	6,327
27	div2	Port Vale	A	W	2-0	Harrison 8; Greenacre 90	4,489
28	div2	Rotherham	H	W	3-2	Greenacre 45; Zola 54; Harrison 62	7,361
29	div2	Bournemouth	H	D	0-0		6,717
30	div2	Hartlepool	A	D	0-0		4,181
31	div2	Southend	H	D	0-0		7,058
32	div2	Bradford	A	D	0-0		7,697
33	div2	Huddersfield	H	W	2-1	Tremarco 4; Facey 84	8,300
34	div2	Gillingham	A	D	1-1	O'Leary 48	6,803
35	div2	Hartlepool	H	D	0-0		6,301
36	div2	Barnsley	H	L	0-1		6,802
37	div2	Oldham	A	L	0-1		5,281
38	div2	Swindon	A	W	2-1	Greenacre 21; Aiston 33	4,139
39	div2	Chesterfield	H	W	4-1	Aiston 36,39; Greenacre 45; O'Leary 65	6,435
40	div2	Walsall	H	L	1-2	Greenacre 64	6,615
41	div2	Yeovil	A	D	2-2	Goodison 39; Greenacre 77	5,409
42	div2	Port Vale	H	W	3-0	Zola 28; O'Leary 58; Davies 78	6,926
43	div2	Rotherham	A	L	0-2		4,129
44	div2	Nottm Forest	H	L	0-1		9,152
45	div2	Colchester	A	L	0-1		4,757
46	div2	Bristol City	H	L	0-3		6,288
47	div2	MK Dons	A	W	2-1	Partridge 90 og; Facey 90	7,777
48	div2	Doncaster	H	L	0-2		8,343

LEAGUE APPEARANCES, BOOKINGS AND GOALS

	AGE (on 01/07/06)	IN NAMED 16	APPEARANCES	COUNTING GAMES	MINUTES ON PITCH	LEAGUE GOALS		
Goalkeepers								
John Achterberg	35	19	19	19	1710	0	0	0
Matt Murray	25	2	2	2	180	0	0	0
Philip Palethorpe	19	12	0	0	0	0	0	0
Dino Seremet	25	13	13	13	1170	0	2	0
Steve Wilson	32	42	12	12	1080	0	2	0
Defenders								
Alex Bruce	21	11	11	9	900	0	4	0
Simon Francis	21	17	17	16	1453	1	2	0
Ian Goodison	33	43	38	29	2860	1	7	0
Michael Jackson	32	41	41	39	3602	3	5	1
Paul Linwood	22	20	14	10	1027	0	4	0
David Raven	21	13	11	11	987	0	4	0
Gareth Roberts	28	44	44	43	3915	2	5	0
Ian Sharps	25	39	39	37	3430	1	7	0
Carl Tremarco	20	31	18	9	1128	1	4	0
Midfielders								
Sam Aiston	29	43	36	16	2041	3	2	0
Danny Harrison	23	41	35	26	2501	2	5	0
Oliver James	19	4	1	0	11	0	0	0
Stephen Jennings	21	46	38	22	2424	1	2	0
Gary Jones	31	3	1	1	90	0	0	0
Jason McAteer	35	29	29	18	2026	0	8	1
Stephen O'Leary	20	21	21	15	1499	3	3	1
Mark Rankine	36	31	24	17	1727	0	4	0
Nicky Summerbee	34	6	6	3	338	0	0	0
Theodore Whitmore	33	13	4	0	119	0	0	0
Forwards								
Paul Brown	21	1	0	0	0	0	0	0
Chris Dagnall	21	11	6	0	53	0	0	0
Steve Davies	18	25	22	3	824	2	3	1
Delroy Facey	26	37	37	28	2768	8	1	0
Chris Greenacre	28	45	45	43	3934	16	1	0
Iain Hume	22	6	6	3	409	1	0	0
Calvin Zola	21	25	22	9	1208	4	3	0

TEAM OF THE SEASON

G – Dino Seremet, CG: 13 DR: 117

D – Simon Francis, CG: 16 DR: 97

D – Michael Jackson, CG: 39 DR: 82

D – Ian Sharps, CG: 37 DR: 82

D – Gareth Roberts, CG: 43 DR: 77

M – Sam Aiston, CG: 16 SD: 19

M – Stephen O'Leary, CG: 15 SD: 15

M – Jason McAteer, CG: 18 SD: 5

M – Danny Harrison, CG: 26 SD: -8

F – Chris Greenacre, CG: 43 SR: 246

F – Delroy Facey, CG: 28 SR: 346

MONTHLY POINTS TALLY

Month	Points	%
AUGUST	10	56%
SEPTEMBER	3	20%
OCTOBER	4	27%
NOVEMBER	4	44%
DECEMBER	8	44%
JANUARY	7	47%
FEBRUARY	5	33%
MARCH	10	67%
APRIL	3	20%
MAY	0	0%

LEAGUE GOALS

	PLAYER	LGE	FAC	LC	Oth	TOT
1	Greenacre	16	1	0	0	17
2	Facey	8	0	0	0	8
3	Zola	4	0	0	0	4
4	Jackson	3	0	0	0	3
5	Aiston	3	0	0	0	3
6	O'Leary	3	0	0	0	3
7	Davies	2	0	0	0	2
8	Harrison	2	0	0	0	2
9	Roberts	2	0	0	0	2
10	Goodison	1	0	0	0	1
11	Hume	1	0	0	0	1
	Other	5	0	1	0	6
	TOTAL	**50**	**1**	**1**	**0**	**52**

TOP POINT EARNERS

	PLAYER	GAMES	AV PTS
1	Sam Aiston	16	**1.56**
2	Stephen O'Leary	15	**1.53**
3	Dino Seremet	13	**1.38**
4	Michael Jackson	39	**1.36**
5	Jason McAteer	18	**1.33**
6	Simon Francis	16	**1.31**
7	Danny Harrison	26	**1.31**
8	Ian Sharps	37	**1.30**
9	Chris Greenacre	43	**1.21**
10	Steve Wilson	12	**1.17**

DISCIPLINARY RECORDS

	PLAYER	YELLOW	RED	AVE
1	Davies	3	1	**206**
2	McAteer	8	1	**225**
3	Bruce	4	0	**225**
4	Raven	4	0	**246**
5	Linwood	4	0	**256**
6	Tremarco	4	0	**282**
7	O'Leary	3	1	**374**
8	Zola	3	0	**402**
9	Goodison	7	0	**408**
10	Rankine	4	0	**431**
11	Sharps	7	0	**490**
12	Harrison	5	0	**500**
13	Wilson	2	0	**540**
	Other	20	1	
	TOTAL	**78**	**4**	

KEY GOALKEEPER

Dino Seremet

Goals Conceded in the League	10	Counting Games League games when player was on pitch for at least 70 minutes	13
Goals Conceded in all competitions	10		
Defensive Rating Ave number of mins between League goals conceded while on the pitch	117	Clean Sheets In games when player was on pitch for at least 70 minutes	5

KEY PLAYERS - DEFENDERS

Simon Francis

Goals Conceded in the League	15	Clean Sheets In League games when player was on pitch for at least 70 minutes	7
Goals Conceded in all competitions	15		
Defensive Rating Ave number of mins between League goals conceded while on the pitch	97	Club Defensive Rating Average number of mins between League goals conceded by the club this season	78

	PLAYER	CON LGE	CON ALL	CLN SHEETS	DEF RATE
1	Simon Francis	15	15	7	97 mins
2	Michael Jackson	44	48	14	82 mins
3	Ian Sharps	42	46	12	82 mins
4	Gareth Roberts	51	55	12	77 mins

KEY PLAYERS - MIDFIELDERS

Sam Aiston

Goals in the League	3	Contribution to Attacking Power Average number of minutes between League team goals while on pitch	66
Goals in all competitions	3		
Defensive Rating Average number of mins between League goals conceded while on the pitch	85	Scoring Difference Defensive Rating minus Contribution to Attacking Power	19

	PLAYER	GOALS LGE	GOALS ALL	DEF RATE	ATT POWER	SCORE DIFF
1	Sam Aiston	3	3	85	66	19 mins
2	Stephen O'Leary	3	3	94	79	15 mins
3	Jason McAteer	0	0	70	65	5 mins
4	Danny Harrison	2	2	78	86	-8 mins

KEY PLAYERS - GOALSCORERS

Chris Greenacre

Goals in the League	16	Player Strike Rate Average number of minutes between League goals scored by player	246
Goals in all competitions	17		
Contribution to Attacking Power Average number of minutes between League team goals while on pitch	82	Club Strike Rate Average number of minutes between League goals scored by club	83

	PLAYER	GOALS LGE	GOALS ALL	POWER	S RATE
1	Chris Greenacre	16	17	82	246 mins
2	Delroy Facey	8	8	115	346 mins
3	Stephen O'Leary	3	3	79	500 mins
4	Sam Aiston	3	3	66	680 mins

Gareth Roberts

SQUAD APPEARANCES

Match	1	2	3	4	5	6	7	8	9	10	11	12	13	14	15	16	17	18	19	20	21	22	23	24
Venue	A	H	H	A	A	A	H	A	H	A	H	A	A	H	A	H	A	A	H	A	H	A	A	H
Competition	L	L	L	L	W	L	L	L	L	L	L	L	L	L	L	L	L	F	L	L	L	L	L	L
Result	L	D	W	L	L	W	W	D	D	L	D	L	L	L	L	D	W	L	L	W	D	L	D	L

Match	25	26	27	28	29	30	31	32	33	34	35	36	37	38	39	40	41	42	43	44	45	46	47	48
Venue	A	H	A	H	H	A	H	A	H	A	H	H	A	A	H	H	A	H	A	H	A	H	A	H
Competition	L	L	L	L	L	L	L	L	L	L	L	L	L	L	L	L	L	L	L	L	L	L	L	L
Result	D	W	W	W	D	D	D	D	W	D	D	L	L	W	W	L	D	W	L	L	L	L	W	L

Goalkeepers
John Achterberg
Matt Murray
Philip Palethorpe
Dino Seremet
Steve Wilson

Defenders
Alex Bruce
Simon Francis
Ian Goodison
Michael Jackson
Paul Linwood
David Raven
Gareth Roberts
Ian Sharps
Carl Tremarco

Midfielders
Sam Aiston
Danny Harrison
Oliver James
Stephen Jennings
Gary Jones
Jason McAteer
Stephen O'Leary
Mark Rankine
Nicky Summerbee
Theodore Whitmore

Forwards
Paul Brown
Chris Dagnall
Steve Davies
Delroy Facey
Chris Greenacre
Iain Hume
Calvin Zola

KEY: On all match / On bench / Subbed or sent off (Counting game) / Subbed or sent off (playing less than 70 minutes) / Subbed on from bench (Counting Game) / Subbed on (playing less than 70 minutes) / Subbed on and then subbed or sent off (Counting Game) / Subbed on and then subbed or sent off (playing less than 70 minutes) / Not in 16

BLACKPOOL

Final Position: **19th**

NICKNAME: THE SEASIDERS

KEY: ☐Won ☐Drawn ☐Lost

						Attendance
1 div2	Chesterfield	H	L	1-3	Parker 5	6,469
2 div2	Tranmere	A	D	2-2	Vernon 45; Murphy 69	7,509
3 div2	Yeovil	A	D	1-1	Murphy 15	5,698
4 div2	Swindon	H	D	0-0		4,661
5 ccr1	Hull City	H	W	2-1	Clarke 29 pen; Grayson 39	3,819
6 div2	Rotherham	A	L	0-4		4,384
7 div2	Bradford	H	W	1-0	Wiles 84	6,468
8 div2	Doncaster	A	W	1-0	Donnelly 67	5,484
9 div2	Hartlepool	H	L	1-2	Wright 70	5,494
10 div2	Bristol City	A	D	1-1	Blinkhorn 90	9,576
11 ccr2	Leicester	A	L	1-2	Parker 68	7,386
12 div2	MK Dons	H	W	3-2	Clarke 17 pen; Mills 50 og; Burns 68	4,723
13 div2	Nottm Forest	A	D	1-1	Parker 24	17,071
14 div2	Swansea	A	L	2-3	Parker 36; Donnelly 70	13,911
15 div2	Colchester	H	L	1-2	Wright 90	4,793
16 div2	Barnsley	A	D	2-2	Wiles 29; Wright 68	7,945
17 div2	Brentford	H	D	0-0		5,041
18 div2	Gillingham	A	L	1-2	Parker 23	6,300
19 facr1	Doncaster	A	L	1-4	Clarke 90 pen	4,332
20 div2	Scunthorpe	H	W	5-2	Murphy 18,84; Morris 42,90; Wright 45	6,016
21 div2	Colchester	A	L	2-3	Murphy 67; Wright 90	3,031
22 div2	Chesterfield	A	D	1-1	Harkins 58	4,585
23 div2	Bournemouth	H	L	1-3	Wright 5	4,326
24 div2	Tranmere	H	D	1-1	Clarke 90	5,069
25 div2	Swindon	A	D	0-0		5,766
26 div2	Port Vale	A	W	2-1	Wiles 52; Parker 54	5,666
27 div2	Walsall	A	L	0-2		5,046
28 div2	Southend	H	L	1-2	Parker 75	5,271
29 div2	Oldham	H	W	1-0	Gobern 48	5,977
30 div2	Huddersfield	A	L	0-2		11,977
31 div2	Bristol City	H	D	1-1	Murphy 5	4,842
32 div2	Doncaster	H	W	4-2	Butler 16; Morris 42; Parker 44; Clarke 54	4,836
33 div2	Hartlepool	A	W	3-0	Clarke 28 pen,74 pen; Parker 82	4,421
34 div2	Nottm Forest	H	D	2-2	Bean 16; Fox 47	8,399
35 div2	MK Dons	A	L	0-3		5,691
36 div2	Huddersfield	H	L	0-1		6,004
37 div2	Bournemouth	A	D	1-1	Murphy 61	5,349
38 div2	Yeovil	H	W	2-0	Lindegaard 51 og; Murphy 54	5,747
39 div2	Rotherham	H	D	0-0		5,934
40 div2	Port Vale	H	W	1-0	Williams 66	5,494
41 div2	Bradford	A	L	0-1		7,192
42 div2	Oldham	A	L	1-3	Southern 42	6,480
43 div2	Walsall	H	W	2-0	Williams 49; Southern 57	6,129
44 div2	Southend	A	L	1-2	Williams 32	8,180
45 div2	Swansea	H	W	1-0	Parker 59	6,709
46 div2	Brentford	A	D	1-1	Clarke 88	7,339
47 div2	Barnsley	H	D	1-1	Parker 21	6,912
48 div2	Scunthorpe	A	L	0-1		5,917
49 div2	Gillingham	H	D	3-3	Blinkhorn 13; Parker 56,69	8,541

LEAGUE APPEARANCES, BOOKINGS AND GOALS

	AGE (on 01/07/06)	IN NAMED 16	APPEARANCES	COUNTING GAMES	MINUTES ON PITCH	LEAGUE GOALS	Yellow	Red
Goalkeepers								
Lee Jones	35	41	31	30	2721	0	0	0
Leslie Pogliacomi	30	43	15	15	1350	0	0	0
Defenders								
Chris Armstrong	23	5	5	4	416	0	0	0
Anthony Butler	33	30	24	18	1751	1	4	1
Peter Clarke	24	46	46	46	4134	6	6	0
Danny Coid	24	13	13	11	1032	0	4	0
Rob Edwards	33	34	32	23	2467	0	6	1
Simon Grayson	36	15	12	8	758	0	1	0
Marc Joseph	29	16	16	14	1307	0	3	0
Mark McGregor	29	22	21	16	1534	0	3	0
Sam Stockley	28	8	7	3	345	0	1	0
Sean Taylor	20	4	4	2	277	0	1	0
Andy Taylor	20	3	3	3	270	0	0	0
Danny Warrender	-	18	15	12	1147	0	0	0
Midfielders								
Marcus Bean	21	17	17	17	1530	1	2	0
Jamie Burns	22	7	6	4	410	1	1	0
Ciaran Donnelly	22	27	24	11	1376	2	3	1
John Doolan	32	22	19	11	1233	0	4	0
David Fox	22	9	7	3	347	1	1	0
Lewis Gobern	21	8	8	3	342	0	1	0
Gary Harkins	21	5	4	4	344	1	0	0
Keith Lasley	26	8	8	4	436	0	0	0
Rory Prendergast	28	27	24	14	1619	0	4	0
Keith Southern	22	43	42	36	3342	2	9	0
Jason Wilcox	34	26	26	21	2164	0	2	1
Simon Wiles	21	34	27	14	1552	3	1	0
Forwards								
Matthew Blinkhorn	21	23	15	2	441	2	2	0
Ian Morris	19	32	30	15	1861	3	4	0
John Murphy	29	34	34	25	2552	8	0	0
Keigan Parker	24	40	40	34	3263	12	10	0
Scott Vernon	22	27	17	5	774	1	0	0
Gareth Williams	23	10	9	5	577	3	0	0
Neil Wood	23	9	7	4	524	0	1	0
Tommy Wright	21	15	13	7	820	6	7	1

TEAM OF THE SEASON

G Lee Jones CG: 30 DR: 70

D Marc Joseph CG: 14 DR: 77

D Anthony Butler CG: 18 DR: 67

D Danny Warrender CG: 12 DR: 67

D Peter Clarke CG: 46 DR: 65

M Marcus Bean CG: 17 SD: 6

M Rory Prendergast CG: 14 SD: 2

M Simon Wiles CG: 14 SD: -7

M Jason Wilcox CG: 21 SD: -10

F Keigan Parker CG: 34 SR: 272

F John Murphy CG: 25 SR: 319

MONTHLY POINTS TALLY

AUGUST	6	33%
SEPTEMBER	8	53%
OCTOBER	2	13%
NOVEMBER	4	44%
DECEMBER	5	33%
JANUARY	10	56%
FEBRUARY	5	33%
MARCH	4	33%
APRIL	8	44%
MAY	1	33%

LEAGUE GOALS

	PLAYER	LGE	FAC	LC	Oth	TOT
1	Parker	12	0	1	0	13
2	Murphy	8	0	0	0	8
3	Wright	6	0	0	0	6
4	Clarke	6	1	1	0	8
5	Wiles	3	0	0	0	3
6	Williams	3	0	0	0	3
7	Morris	3	0	0	0	3
8	Blinkhorn	2	0	0	0	2
9	Southern	2	0	0	0	2
10	Donnelly	2	0	0	0	2
11	Bean	1	0	0	0	1
	Other	8	0	1	0	9
	TOTAL	56	1	3	0	60

TOP POINT EARNERS

	PLAYER	GAMES	AV PTS
1	Anthony Butler	18	1.50
2	Ian Morris	15	1.40
3	Marc Joseph	14	1.36
4	Simon Wiles	14	1.36
5	Marcus Bean	17	1.35
6	Jason Wilcox	21	1.33
7	Rory Prendergast	14	1.29
8	Keigan Parker	34	1.26
9	John Murphy	25	1.24
10	Danny Warrender	12	1.17

DISCIPLINARY RECORDS

	PLAYER	YELLOW	RED	AVE
1	Wright	7	1	102
2	Coid	4	0	258
3	Doolan	4	0	308
4	Parker	10	0	326
5	Donnelly	3	1	344
6	Butler	4	1	350
7	Edwards, R	6	1	352
8	Southern	9	0	371
9	Prendergast	4	0	404
10	Joseph	3	0	435
11	Morris	4	0	465
12	McGregor	3	0	511
13	Wood	1	0	524
	Other	12	1	
	TOTAL	74	5	

KEY GOALKEEPER

Lee Jones

Goals Conceded in the League	39	Counting Games League games when player was on pitch for at least 70 minutes	30
Goals Conceded in all competitions	39		
Defensive Rating Ave number of mins between League goals conceded while on the pitch	70	Clean Sheets In games when player was on pitch for at least 70 minutes	8

KEY PLAYERS - DEFENDERS

Marc Joseph

Goals Conceded in the League	17	Clean Sheets In League games when player was on pitch for at least 70 minutes	4
Goals Conceded in all competitions	17		
Defensive Rating Ave number of mins between League goals conceded while on the pitch	77	Club Defensive Rating Average number of mins between League goals conceded by the club this season	65

	PLAYER	CON LGE	CON ALL	CLN SHEETS	DEF RATE
1	Marc Joseph	17	17	4	77 mins
2	Danny Warrender	17	20	4	67 mins
3	Anthony Butler	26	28	6	67 mins
4	Peter Clarke	64	71	12	65 mins

KEY PLAYERS - MIDFIELDERS

Marcus Bean

Goals in the League	1	Contribution to Attacking Power Average number of minutes between League team goals while on pitch	67
Goals in all competitions	1		
Defensive Rating Average number of mins between League goals conceded while on the pitch	73	Scoring Difference Defensive Rating minus Contribution to Attacking Power	6

	PLAYER	GOALS LGE	GOALS ALL	DEF RATE	ATT POWER	SCORE DIFF
1	Marcus Bean	1	1	73	67	6 mins
2	Rory Prendergast	0	0	67	65	2 mins
3	Simon Wiles	3	3	71	78	-7 mins
4	Jason Wilcox	0	0	77	87	-10 mins

KEY PLAYERS - GOALSCORERS

Keigan Parker

Goals in the League	12	Player Strike Rate Average number of minutes between League goals scored by player	272
Goals in all competitions	13		
Contribution to Attacking Power Average number of minutes between League team goals while on pitch	76	Club Strike Rate Average number of minutes between League goals scored by club	74

	PLAYER	GOALS LGE	GOALS ALL	POWER	S RATE
1	Keigan Parker	12	13	76	272 mins
2	John Murphy	8	8	73	319 mins
3	Simon Wiles	3	3	78	517 mins
4	Ian Morris	3	3	56	620 mins

Gareth Williams

SQUAD APPEARANCES

Match	1	2	3	4	5	6	7	8	9	10	11	12	13	14	15	16	17	18	19	20	21	22	23	24	25	26	27	28	29	30	31	32	33	34	35	36	37	38	39	40	41	42	43	44	45	46	47	48	49
Venue	H	A	A	H	H	A	H	A	H	A	A	H	A	A	H	A	H	A	A	H	A	A	H	H	A	A	A	H	H	A	H	H	A	H	A	H	A	H	H	H	A	A	H	A	H	A	H	A	H
Competition	L	L	L	L	W	L	L	L	L	L	W	L	L	L	L	L	L	L	F	L	L	L	L	L	L	L	L	L	L	L	L	L	L	L	L	L	L	L	L	L	L	L	L	L	L	L	L	L	L
Result	L	D	D	D	W	L	W	W	L	D	L	W	D	L	L	D	D	L	L	W	L	D	L	D	D	W	L	L	W	L	D	W	W	D	L	L	D	W	D	W	L	L	W	L	W	D	D	L	D

Goalkeepers
Lee Jones
Leslie Pogliacomi

Defenders
Chris Armstrong
Anthony Butler
Peter Clarke
Danny Coid
Rob Edwards
Simon Grayson
Marc Joseph
Mark McGregor
Sam Stockley
Sean Taylor
Andy Taylor
Danny Warrender

Midfielders
Marcus Bean
Jamie Burns
Ciaran Donnelly
John Doolan
David Fox
Lewis Gobern
Gary Harkins
Keith Lasley
Rory Prendergast
Keith Southern
Jason Wilcox
Simon Wiles

Forwards
Matthew Blinkhorn
Ian Morris
John Murphy
Keigan Parker
Scott Vernon
Gareth Williams
Neil Wood
Tommy Wright

ROTHERHAM UNITED

Final Position: **20th**

NICKNAME: THE MERRY MILLERS

KEY: ☐Won ☐Drawn ☐Lost

						Attendance
1 div2	Walsall	H L	1-2	Butler 42		5,386
2 div2	Yeovil	A D	0-0			5,856
3 div2	Chesterfield	A W	1-0	Butler 59		5,189
4 div2	Bradford	H D	1-1	Burton 81		5,222
5 ccr1	Port Vale	H W	3-1	Rowland 41 og; Burton 71; Otsemobor 90		2,809
6 div2	Blackpool	H W	4-0	Mullin 40; Burton 58 pen,59,86		4,384
7 div2	Oldham	A W	1-0	Burton 80		6,950
8 div2	Port Vale	A L	0-2			4,528
9 div2	Gillingham	H W	3-0	McLaren 46; Burton 81; Butler 90		4,253
10 div2	Nottm Forest	A L	0-2			20,123
11 ccr2	Leeds	H L	0-2			5,445
12 div2	Southend	H L	2-4	Murdock 34; Burton 45 pen		4,259
13 div2	Hartlepool	A D	0-0			4,309
14 div2	Brentford	A L	1-2	Burton 8		5,901
15 div2	Scunthorpe	A D	2-2	Butler 3 og; McLaren 29		6,649
16 div2	Swansea	H D	2-2	Leadbitter 41; Conlon 90		4,056
17 div2	Barnsley	H L	0-1			5,401
18 div2	MK Dons	A D	1-1	Monkhouse 24		5,096
19 facr1	Mansfield	H L	3-4	McLaren 30,38; Burton 53		4,089
20 div2	Colchester	H L	1-2	Burton 23 pen		3,715
21 div2	Barnsley	A D	1-1	Barker 31		9,894
22 div2	Walsall	A L	1-3	Hoskins 78		4,563
23 div2	Swindon	H L	0-1			3,537
24 div2	Yeovil	H L	1-2	Burton 18		3,929
25 div2	Bradford	A W	2-1	Williamson 21; Burton 60		7,476
26 div2	Huddersfield	H D	1-1	Burton 8		7,380
27 div2	Bristol City	A L	1-3	Murdock 26		12,510
28 div2	Doncaster	H W	1-0	Williamson 90		6,761
29 div2	Tranmere	A L	2-3	Barker 14; Hoskins 77		7,361
30 div2	Port Vale	H D	1-1	Hoskins 26		3,883
31 div2	Bournemouth	A L	0-2			5,700
32 div2	Nottm Forest	H D	1-1	Shaw 86		7,222
33 div2	Gillingham	A D	1-1	Williamson 54		6,107
34 div2	Hartlepool	H D	0-0			5,960
35 div2	Southend	A L	0-2			7,879
36 div2	Bournemouth	H W	2-0	Butler 58; Williamson 60		4,498
37 div2	Swindon	A W	3-2	Butler 22,49; Barker 31		7,518
38 div2	Chesterfield	H L	0-4			6,919
39 div2	Blackpool	A D	0-0			5,934
40 div2	Oldham	H W	2-0	Swailes 21 og; McLaren 85		5,823
41 div2	Huddersfield	A L	1-4	Forte 13		15,264
42 div2	Bristol City	H W	3-1	Forte 27,47; Shaw 39		6,682
43 div2	Doncaster	A L	1-3	Forte 15		7,542
44 div2	Tranmere	H W	2-0	Butler 73; Shaw 78		4,129
45 div2	Brentford	H D	2-2	Mullin 43; Shaw 69		5,242
46 div2	Swansea	A W	2-0	Monk 15 og; Robertson 29		14,118
47 div2	Scunthorpe	H D	1-1	Hoskins 83		5,778
48 div2	Colchester	A L	0-2			5,741
49 div2	MK Dons	H D	0-0			7,625

LEAGUE APPEARANCES, BOOKINGS AND GOALS

	AGE (on 01/07/06)	IN NAMED 16	APPEARANCES	COUNTING GAMES	MINUTES ON PITCH	LEAGUE GOALS	
Goalkeepers							
Neil Cutler	29	38	22	22	1980	0	0
Jonathan Hedge	-	8	0	0	0	0	0
Gary Montgomery	23	46	24	24	2160	0	0
Defenders							
Shaun Barker	23	44	43	41	3734	3	7
Stephen Brogan	18	8	3	0	60	0	0
Phil Gilchrist	32	28	11	8	832	0	3
Paul Hurst	31	38	31	27	2567	0	2
Liam King	18	2	0	0	0	0	0
Scott Minto	34	8	6	5	441	0	1
Colin Murdock	31	42	39	38	3460	2	6
Jon Otsemobor	23	24	10	4	427	0	0
Gregor Robertson	22	42	35	26	2641	1	3
David Worrell	28	44	41	38	3475	0	6
Midfielders							
Jamal Campbell-Ryce	23	8	7	3	346	0	0
Sam Duncum	19	4	1	0	59	0	0
Paul Evans	31	4	4	4	350	0	1
Michael Keane	23	29	28	22	2142	0	3
Grant Leadbitter	20	7	5	4	374	1	1
Paul McLaren	29	39	39	32	3016	3	6
Andy Monkhouse	25	23	12	6	663	1	4
John Mullin	30	44	43	38	3545	2	4
Stephen Quinn	20	16	16	15	1413	0	1
Lee Williamson	24	37	37	36	3220	4	15
Forwards							
Deon Burton	29	24	24	23	2095	12	4
Martin Butler	31	41	39	32	3068	7	2
Barry Conlon	27	3	3	1	210	1	1
Jonathan Forte	19	11	11	7	799	4	1
William Hoskins	19	35	23	6	887	4	0
Marc Newsham	19	12	3	0	20	0	0
Paul Shaw	32	17	17	14	1340	4	0
Ryan Taylor	-	4	1	0	10	0	0

TEAM OF THE SEASON

G — Neil Cutler, CG: 22 DR: 79

D — David Worrell, CG: 38 DR: 72

D — Shaun Barker, CG: 41 DR: 70

D — Colin Murdock, CG: 38 DR: 68

D — Gregor Robertson, CG: 26 DR: 66

M — Michael Keane, CG: 22 SD: 10

M — Lee Williamson, CG: 36 SD: -1

M — Stephen Quinn, CG: 15 SD: -4

M — John Mullin, CG: 38 SD: -17

F — Deon Burton, CG: 23 SR: 175

F — Paul Shaw, CG: 14 SR: 335

MONTHLY POINTS TALLY

AUGUST	11	61%
SEPTEMBER	4	27%
OCTOBER	3	20%
NOVEMBER	1	11%
DECEMBER	7	39%
JANUARY	3	20%
FEBRUARY	7	47%
MARCH	7	58%
APRIL	8	44%
MAY	1	33%

LEAGUE GOALS

	PLAYER	LGE	FAC	LC	Oth	TOT
1	Burton	12	1	1	0	14
2	Butler	7	0	0	0	7
3	Williamson	4	0	0	0	4
4	Forte	4	0	0	0	4
5	Hoskins	4	0	0	0	4
6	Shaw	4	0	0	0	4
7	McLaren	3	2	0	0	5
8	Barker	3	0	0	0	3
9	Murdock	2	0	0	0	2
10	Mullin	2	0	0	0	2
11	Monkhouse	1	0	0	0	1
	Other	6	0	2	0	8
	TOTAL	52	3	3	0	58

TOP POINT EARNERS

	PLAYER	GAMES	AV PTS
1	Stephen Quinn	15	1.53
2	Michael Keane	22	1.41
3	Paul Shaw	14	1.29
4	Neil Cutler	22	1.27
5	Gregor Robertson	26	1.27
6	Lee Williamson	36	1.19
7	David Worrell	38	1.18
8	Colin Murdock	38	1.16
9	John Mullin	38	1.16
10	Shaun Barker	41	1.15

DISCIPLINARY RECORDS

	PLAYER	YELLOW	RED	AVE
1	Monkhouse	4	0	165
2	Williamson	15	1	201
3	Gilchrist	3	0	277
4	Barker	7	2	414
5	Burton	4	1	419
6	Keane	3	2	428
7	McLaren	6	1	430
8	Murdock	6	1	494
9	Worrell	6	0	579
10	Forte	1	0	799
11	Robertson	3	0	880
12	Mullin	4	0	886
13	Butler	2	1	1022
	Other	3	0	
	TOTAL	67	9	

KEY GOALKEEPER

Neil Cutler

Goals Conceded in the League	25	Counting Games League games when player was on pitch for at least 70 minutes	22
Goals Conceded in all competitions	28		
Defensive Rating Ave number of mins between League goals conceded while on the pitch	79	Clean Sheets In games when player was on pitch for at least 70 minutes	8

KEY PLAYERS - DEFENDERS

David Worrell

Goals Conceded in the League	48	Clean Sheets In League games when player was on pitch for at least 70 minutes	12
Goals Conceded in all competitions	54		
Defensive Rating Ave number of mins between League goals conceded while on the pitch	72	Club Defensive Rating Average number of mins between League goals conceded by the club this season	67

	PLAYER	CON LGE	CON ALL	CLN SHEETS	DEF RATE
1	David Worrell	48	54	12	72 mins
2	Shaun Barker	53	60	14	70 mins
3	Colin Murdock	51	54	12	68 mins
4	Gregor Robertson	40	43	9	66 mins

KEY PLAYERS - MIDFIELDERS

Michael Keane

Goals in the League	0	Contribution to Attacking Power Average number of minutes between League team goals while on pitch	67
Goals in all competitions	0		
Defensive Rating Average number of mins between League goals conceded while on the pitch	77	Scoring Difference Defensive Rating minus Contribution to Attacking Power	10

	PLAYER	GOALS LGE	GOALS ALL	DEF RATE	ATT POWER	SCORE DIFF
1	Michael Keane	0	0	77	67	10 mins
2	Lee Williamson	4	4	72	73	-1 mins
3	Stephen Quinn	0	0	67	71	-4 mins
4	John Mullin	2	2	67	84	-17 mins

KEY PLAYERS - GOALSCORERS

Deon Burton

Goals in the League	12	Player Strike Rate Average number of minutes between League goals scored by player	175
Goals in all competitions	14		
Contribution to Attacking Power Average number of minutes between League team goals while on pitch	81	Club Strike Rate Average number of minutes between League goals scored by club	80

	PLAYER	GOALS LGE	GOALS ALL	POWER	S RATE
1	Deon Burton	12	14	81	175 mins
2	Paul Shaw	4	4	74	335 mins
3	Martin Butler	7	7	81	438 mins
4	Lee Williamson	4	4	73	805 mins

Paul Hurst

SQUAD APPEARANCES

atch	1	2	3	4	5	6	7	8	9	10	11	12	13	14	15	16	17	18	19	20	21	22	23	24	25
enue	H	A	A	H	H	H	A	A	H	A	H	H	A	A	A	H	H	A	H	H	A	A	H	H	A
ompetition	L	L	L	L	W	L	L	L	L	L	W	L	L	L	L	L	L	L	F	L	L	L	L	L	L
esult	L	D	W	D	W	W	W	L	W	L	L	L	D	L	D	D	L	D	L	L	D	L	L	L	W

atch	26	27	28	29	30	31	32	33	34	35	36	37	38	39	40	41	42	43	44	45	46	47	48	49
enue	H	A	H	A	H	A	H	A	H	A	H	A	H	A	H	A	H	A	H	H	A	H	A	H
ompetition	L	L	L	L	L	L	L	L	L	L	L	L	L	L	L	L	L	L	L	L	L	L	L	L
esult	D	L	W	L	D	L	D	D	D	L	W	W	L	D	W	L	W	L	W	D	W	D	L	D

oalkeepers
eil Cutler
onathan Hedge
ary Montgomery
efenders
haun Barker
tephen Brogan
hil Gilchrist
aul Hurst
iam King
cott Minto
olin Murdock
on Otsemobor
regor Robertson
avid Worrell
idfielders
amal Campbell-Ryce
am Duncum
aul Evans
ichael Keane
rant Leadbitter
aul McLaren
ndy Monkhouse
ohn Mullin
tephen Quinn
ee Williamson
orwards
eon Burton
artin Butler
arry Conlon
onathan Forte
Villiam Hoskins
Aarc Newsham
aul Shaw
yan Taylor

KEY: On all match · On bench · Subbed or sent off (Counting game) · Subbed or sent off (playing less than 70 minutes) · Subbed on from bench (Counting Game) · Subbed on (playing less than 70 minutes) · Subbed on and then subbed or sent off (Counting Game) · Subbed on and then subbed or sent off (playing less than 70 minutes) · Not in 16

HARTLEPOOL

Final Position: **21st**

NICKNAME: THE POOL

KEY: Won Drawn Lost

							Attendance
1	div2	Bradford	H	L	0-2		6,271
2	div2	Bournemouth	A	D	1-1	Bullock 51	5,406
3	div2	Doncaster	A	W	1-0	Daly 45	5,061
4	div2	Walsall	H	D	1-1	Sweeney 63	5,060
5	ccr1	Darlington	H	W	3-1	Daly 26; Proctor 76,88	6,163
6	div2	Huddersfield	A	L	1-2	Boyd 51	11,241
7	div2	Scunthorpe	H	D	3-3	Proctor 6; Williams, E 71; Boyd 90 pen	5,044
8	div2	Yeovil	H	L	0-1		4,572
9	div2	Blackpool	A	W	2-1	Sweeney 86; Istead 90	5,494
10	div2	Swansea	H	D	2-2	Humphreys 25; Sweeney 76	4,743
11	ccR2	Charlton	A	L	1-3	Daly 40	10,328
12	div2	Chesterfield	A	L	1-3	Proctor 11	4,078
13	div2	Rotherham	H	D	0-0		4,309
14	div2	Bristol City	A	W	1-0	Proctor 54	11,365
15	div2	Nottm Forest	A	L	0-2		17,586
16	div2	MK Dons	H	W	2-1	Lewington 50 og; Bullock 84	4,337
17	div2	Port Vale	A	W	2-1	Williams, E 12; Butler 64	4,550
18	div2	Gillingham	H	W	3-1	Daly 15; Sweeney 50; Bullock 86	4,522
19	facr1	Dag & Red	H	W	2-1	Nelson 34; Butler 83	3,655
20	div2	Brentford	H	L	1-2	Sweeney 72	4,811
21	div2	Gillingham	A	L	0-1		6,092
22	div2	Bradford	A	W	1-0	Tinkler 34	7,499
23	facr2	Tamworth	H	L	1-2	Llewellyn 52 pen	3,786
24	div2	Colchester	H	L	0-1		3,375
25	div2	Bournemouth	H	W	2-1	Istead 28; McDonald 39	3,755
26	div2	Walsall	A	L	0-1		4,293
27	div2	Barnsley	A	D	1-1	Williams, E 50	9,715
28	div2	Southend	H	L	1-2	Williams, E 20	3,929
29	div2	Oldham	A	L	1-2	Williams, E 75	5,047
30	div2	Swindon	H	D	1-1	Strachan 36	4,169
31	div2	Yeovil	A	L	0-2		5,480
32	div2	Tranmere	H	D	0-0		4,181
33	div2	Swansea	A	D	1-1	Williams, E 90	13,960
34	div2	Blackpool	H	L	0-3		4,421
35	div2	Rotherham	A	D	0-0		5,960
36	div2	Chesterfield	H	W	1-0	Robson 65	4,596
37	div2	Tranmere	A	D	0-0		6,301
38	div2	Doncaster	H	D	1-1	Boyd 20	5,459
39	div2	Huddersfield	H	W	3-1	Boyd 10; Maidens 53; Porter 82	5,468
40	div2	Scunthorpe	A	L	0-2		4,550
41	div2	Barnsley	H	D	1-1	Porter 9	5,122
42	div2	Southend	A	L	0-3		8,496
43	div2	Oldham	H	D	1-1	Bullock 9	5,259
44	div2	Swindon	A	D	1-1	Humphreys 31	5,225
45	div2	Colchester	A	L	0-2		3,916
46	div2	Bristol City	H	L	1-2	Williams, E 83	5,039
47	div2	MK Dons	A	L	1-2	Proctor 49	6,472
48	div2	Nottm Forest	H	W	3-2	Porter 32; Nelson 59; Proctor 60	5,336
49	div2	Brentford	A	D	1-1	Nelson 90	8,725
50	div2	Port Vale	H	D	1-1	Brown 86	6,895

LEAGUE APPEARANCES, BOOKINGS AND GOALS

	AGE (on 01/07/06)	IN NAMED 16	APPEARANCES	COUNTING GAMES	MINUTES ON PITCH	LEAGUE GOALS	
Goalkeepers							
Tony Davison	-	3	0	0	0	0	0
Demitrios Konstantopoulos	27	46	46	46	4140	0	1
Jim Provett	23	41	0	0	0	0	0
James Winter	20	1	0	0	0	0	0
Defenders							
Michael Barron	31	19	15	9	1014	0	5
John Brackstone	21	8	2	1	135	0	0
Ben Clark	23	37	32	26	2471	0	1
Neill Collins	22	22	22	22	1980	0	1
Darren Craddock	21	8	4	4	360	0	2
Carl Jones	19	9	1	1	90	0	0
Gerard Nash	19	3	3	3	270	0	0
Michael Nelson	24	43	43	42	3837	2	7
Hugh Robertson	31	2	2	2	167	0	0
Matty Robson	21	19	19	11	1274	1	0
Darren Williams	29	44	39	33	3120	0	11
Midfielders							
Lee Bullock	25	32	31	19	1980	4	2
Thomas Butler	25	28	28	22	2206	1	10
Darrell Clarke	28	15	12	3	553	0	2
Richie Humphreys	28	46	46	46	4110	2	2
Steven Istead	20	11	10	4	405	2	0
Michael Maidens	19	23	19	6	949	1	0
Dean McDonald	20	5	5	4	361	1	0
Gavin Strachan	27	12	9	5	503	1	0
Anthony Sweeney	22	35	35	32	2986	5	0
Mark Tinkler	31	21	15	8	955	1	3
Steve Turnbull	19	23	21	13	1382	0	3
Forwards							
Adam Boyd	24	23	21	8	1235	4	0
James Brown	19	5	4	0	50	1	0
Jon Daly	23	31	30	17	1778	2	4
David Foley	18	13	11	0	228	0	1
Chris Llewellyn	26	30	29	18	2002	0	5
Jon-Paul Pittman	19	3	3	2	205	0	1
Joel Porter	27	8	8	5	502	3	0
Mike Proctor	25	27	25	15	1759	5	6
James Walker	18	4	4	0	116	0	0
Eifion Williams	30	36	36	19	2263	7	2

TEAM OF THE SEASON

G — D Konstantopoulos, CG: 46 DR: 70

D — Darren Williams, CG: 33 DR: 76

D — Neill Collins, CG: 22 DR: 71

D — Ben Clark, CG: 26 DR: 69

D — Michael Nelson, CG: 42 DR: 69

M — Anthony Sweeney, CG: 32 SD: -17

M — Thomas Butler, CG: 22 SD: -25

M — Lee Bullock, CG: 19 SD: -26

M — Richie Humphreys, CG: 46 SD: -26

F — Eifion Williams, CG: 19 SR: 323

F — Mike Proctor, CG: 15 SR: 352

MONTHLY POINTS TALLY

AUGUST	6	33%
SEPTEMBER	5	33%
OCTOBER	9	75%
NOVEMBER	6	50%
DECEMBER	4	22%
JANUARY	3	20%
FEBRUARY	6	50%
MARCH	5	33%
APRIL	5	28%
MAY	1	33%

LEAGUE GOALS

	PLAYER	LGE	FAC	LC	Oth	TOT
1	Williams, E	7	0	0	0	7
2	Sweeney	5	0	0	0	5
3	Proctor	5	0	2	0	7
4	Bullock	4	0	0	0	4
5	Boyd	4	0	0	0	4
6	Porter	3	0	0	0	3
7	Daly	2	0	2	0	4
8	Humphreys	2	0	0	0	2
9	Istead	2	0	0	0	2
10	Nelson	2	1	0	0	3
11	Brown	1	0	0	0	1
	Other	7	2	0	0	9
	TOTAL	**44**	**3**	**4**	**0**	**51**

TOP POINT EARNERS

	PLAYER	GAMES	AV PTS
1	Jon Daly	17	**1.47**
2	Chris Llewellyn	18	**1.44**
3	Eifion Williams	19	**1.32**
4	Neill Collins	22	**1.32**
5	Lee Bullock	19	**1.21**
6	Darren Williams	33	**1.21**
7	Anthony Sweeney	32	**1.13**
8	Richie Humphreys	46	**1.09**
9	D Konstantopoulos	46	**1.09**
10	Steve Turnbull	13	**1.08**

DISCIPLINARY RECORDS

	PLAYER	YELLOW	RED	AVE
1	Barron	5	1	**169**
2	Butler	10	1	**200**
3	Tinkler	3	1	**238**
4	Williams, D	11	1	**260**
5	Clarke	2	0	**276**
6	Proctor	6	0	**293**
7	Llewellyn	5	1	**333**
8	Daly	4	0	**444**
9	Turnbull	3	0	**460**
10	Nelson	7	1	**479**
11	Bullock	2	0	**990**
12	Williams, E	2	0	**1131**
13	Collins, N	1	0	**1980**
	Other	4	0	
	TOTAL	**65**	**6**	

KEY GOALKEEPER

Demitrios Konstantopoulos

Goals Conceded in the League	59	Counting Games League games when player was on pitch for at least 70 minutes	46
Goals Conceded in all competitions	66		
Defensive Rating Ave number of mins between League goals conceded while on the pitch	70	Clean Sheets In games when player was on pitch for at least 70 minutes	8

KEY PLAYERS - DEFENDERS

Darren Williams

Goals Conceded in the League	41	Clean Sheets In League games when player was on pitch for at least 70 minutes	7
Goals Conceded in all competitions	48		
Defensive Rating Ave number of mins between League goals conceded while on the pitch	76	Club Defensive Rating Average number of mins between League goals conceded by the club this season	70

	PLAYER	CON LGE	CON ALL	CLN SHEETS	DEF RATE
1	Darren Williams	41	48	7	76 mins
2	Neill Collins	28	32	4	71 mins
3	Michael Nelson	56	63	7	69 mins
4	Ben Clark	36	36	4	69 mins

KEY PLAYERS - MIDFIELDERS

Anthony Sweeney

Goals in the League	5	Contribution to Attacking Power Average number of minutes between League team goals while on pitch	88
Goals in all competitions	5		
Defensive Rating Average number of mins between League goals conceded while on the pitch	71	Scoring Difference Defensive Rating minus Contribution to Attacking Power	-17

	PLAYER	GOALS LGE	GOALS ALL	DEF RATE	ATT POWER	SCORE DIFF
1	Anthony Sweeney	5	5	71	88	-17 mins
2	Thomas Butler	1	2	67	92	-25 mins
3	Lee Bullock	4	4	68	94	-26 mins
4	Richie Humphreys	2	2	70	96	-26 mins

KEY PLAYERS - GOALSCORERS

Eifion Williams

Goals in the League	7	Player Strike Rate Average number of minutes between League goals scored by player	323
Goals in all competitions	7		
Contribution to Attacking Power Average number of minutes between League team goals while on pitch	87	Club Strike Rate Average number of minutes between League goals scored by club	94

	PLAYER	GOALS LGE	GOALS ALL	POWER	S RATE
1	Eifion Williams	7	7	87	323 mins
2	Mike Proctor	5	7	93	352 mins
3	Lee Bullock	4	4	94	495 mins
4	Anthony Sweeney	5	5	88	597 mins

Eifion Williams

SQUAD APPEARANCES

latch	1	2	3	4	5	6	7	8	9	10	11	12	13	14	15	16	17	18	19	20	21	22	23	24	25
enue	H	A	A	H	H	A	H	H	A	H	A	A	H	A	A	H	A	H	H	H	A	A	H	H	H
ompetition	L	L	L	L	W	L	L	L	L	L	W	L	L	L	L	L	L	L	F	L	L	L	F	L	L
esult	L	D	W	D	W	L	D	L	W	D	L	L	D	W	L	W	W	W	W	L	L	W	L	L	W

latch	26	27	28	29	30	31	32	33	34	35	36	37	38	39	40	41	42	43	44	45	46	47	48	49	50
enue	A	A	H	A	H	A	H	A	H	A	H	A	H	H	A	H	A	H	A	A	H	A	H	A	H
ompetition	L	L	L	L	L	L	L	L	L	L	L	L	L	L	L	L	L	L	L	L	L	L	L	L	L
esult	L	D	L	L	D	L	D	D	L	D	W	D	D	W	L	D	L	D	D	L	L	L	W	D	D

oalkeepers
ony Davison
Konstantopoulos
im Provett
ames Winter

efenders
lichael Barron
ohn Brackstone
en Clark
eill Collins
arren Craddock
arl Jones
erard Nash
lichael Nelson
lugh Robertson
latty Robson
arren Williams

lidfielders
ee Bullock
Thomas Butler
Darrell Clarke
Richie Humphreys
Steven Istead
Michael Maidens
Dean McDonald
Gavin Strachan
Anthony Sweeney
Mark Tinkler
Steve Turnbull

Forwards
Adam Boyd
James Brown
Jon Daly
David Foley
Chris Llewellyn
Jon-Paul Pittman
Joel Porter
Mike Proctor
James Walker
Eifion Williams

KEY: On all match · On bench · Subbed or sent off (Counting game) · Subbed or sent off (playing less than 70 minutes) · Subbed on from bench (Counting Game) · Subbed on (playing less than 70 minutes) · Subbed on and then subbed or sent off (Counting Game) · Subbed on and then subbed or sent off (playing less than 70 minutes) · Not in 16

MK DONS

Final Position: **22nd**

NICKNAME: THE DONS/WOMBLES

KEY: ☐Won ☐Drawn ☐Lost

							Attendance
1	div2	Bournemouth	H	D	2-2	McLeod 41,46	5,163
2	div2	Doncaster	A	D	1-1	McLeod 76	5,232
3	div2	Bradford	A	L	0-2		7,315
4	div2	Colchester	H	D	1-1	Wilbraham 23	4,423
5	ccr1	Norwich	H	L	0-1		4,777
6	div2	Bristol City	A	D	2-2	Platt 7,17	10,011
7	div2	Port Vale	H	D	0-0		4,592
8	div2	Brentford	A	L	0-1		5,862
9	div2	Swansea	H	L	1-3	Mills 35	4,798
10	div2	Barnsley	H	D	0-0		4,620
11	div2	Blackpool	A	L	2-3	Rizzo 19 pen; Small 34	4,723
12	div2	Scunthorpe	H	W	1-0	Platt 43	4,682
13	div2	Swindon	H	W	3-1	Kamara 49; Edds 77; McLeod 81	5,536
14	div2	Walsall	A	D	1-1	Edds 72	5,041
15	div2	Chesterfield	H	D	0-0		5,642
16	div2	Hartlepool	A	L	1-2	McLeod 24	4,337
17	div2	Rotherham	H	D	1-1	Kamara 80	5,096
18	facr1	Lincoln	A	D	1-1	Edds 45	3,508
19	div2	Tranmere	A	W	2-1	McLeod 57 pen,58	6,611
20	facr1r	Lincoln	H	W	2-1	Platt 14,42	4,029
21	div2	Walsall	H	W	2-1	McLeod 6; Wilbraham 84	5,506
22	div2	Bournemouth	A	L	0-2		5,485
23	facr2	Southend	A	W	2-1	McLeod 16 pen; Smith 71	5,267
24	div2	Huddersfield	H	D	2-2	Rizzo 81; McLeod 83	4,832
25	div2	Doncaster	H	L	2-3	Smith 73; Wilbraham 87	5,351
26	div2	Colchester	A	L	0-2		3,400
27	div2	Southend	A	D	0-0		7,452
28	div2	Gillingham	A	L	0-3		6,012
29	div2	Oldham	H	L	0-1		5,082
30	facr3	Southampton	A	L	3-4	Lundekvam 59 og; Rizzo 79; Edds 84	15,908
31	div2	Swansea	A	L	1-3	McLeod 81 pen	11,922
32	div2	Yeovil	H	D	1-1	McLeod 74	5,548
33	div2	Barnsley	A	L	0-2		7,588
34	div2	Nottm Forest	H	W	1-0	McLeod 22	7,670
35	div2	Scunthorpe	A	L	0-2		4,631
36	div2	Blackpool	H	W	3-0	McLeod 26,87; Taylor 51	5,691
37	div2	Yeovil	A	D	1-1	Harding 90	5,048
38	div2	Huddersfield	A	L	0-5		11,423
39	div2	Bradford	H	W	2-1	Harding 58; Lewington 89	8,426
40	div2	Bristol City	H	L	0-1		6,855
41	div2	Southend	H	W	2-1	Smith 16; Taylor 78	7,071
42	div2	Nottm Forest	A	L	0-3		18,214
43	div2	Brentford	H	L	0-1		5,592
44	div2	Gillingham	H	L	1-2	Smith 40 pen	6,432
45	div2	Port Vale	A	L	1-3	Platt 28	3,452
46	div2	Oldham	A	W	2-1	McLeod 40,41	5,919
47	div2	Swindon	A	W	1-0	Platt 65	7,273
48	div2	Hartlepool	H	W	2-1	Wilbraham 24; Taylor 89	6,472
49	div2	Chesterfield	A	W	2-1	Platt 13; Edds 86	3,965
50	div2	Tranmere	H	L	1-2	McLeod 90	7,777
51	div2	Rotherham	A	D	0-0		7,625

LEAGUE APPEARANCES, BOOKINGS AND GOALS

	AGE (on 01/07/06)	IN NAMED 16	APPEARANCES	COUNTING GAMES	MINUTES ON PITCH	LEAGUE GOALS	[yellow card]
Goalkeepers							
Matthew Baker	26	40	37	36	3285	0	2
Ricardo Batista	19	10	9	9	810	0	0
David Martin	20	9	0	0	0	0	0
Rob Webb	-	7	0	0	0	0	0
Defenders							
Mirano Carrilho	30	5	3	0	121	0	0
Ben Chorley	23	26	26	24	2242	0	7
Leon Crooks	20	34	23	19	1880	0	1
Malvin Kamara	22	38	23	5	927	2	3
Nathan Koo-Boothe	20	1	0	0	0	0	0
Dean Lewington	22	44	44	41	3867	1	10
Trent McClenahan	21	31	29	21	2153	0	5
Pablo Mills	22	18	16	16	1440	1	6
Craig Morgan	21	45	40	38	3472	0	6
Shola Oyedele	21	4	3	2	197	0	0
David Partridge	27	18	18	16	1549	0	4
Mark Ricketts	21	5	5	3	363	0	0
Midfielders							
Gareth Edds	25	43	41	26	2939	3	1
Ben Harding	21	26	10	7	687	2	0
Nick McKoy	19	24	16	4	643	0	2
Paul Mitchell	24	43	39	33	3177	0	6
Filipe Morais	20	13	13	8	923	0	1
Steve Palmer	38	4	2	1	96	0	0
Jason Puncheon	20	3	1	1	73	0	0
Stephen Quinn	20	16	15	10	1127	0	3
Nicky Rizzo	27	33	29	9	1462	2	1
Wade Small	22	28	28	16	1923	1	7
Gary Smith	22	31	25	14	1599	3	2
Forwards							
Sam Baldock	-	1	0	0	0	0	0
Serge Makofo	19	3	0	0	0	0	0
Izale McLeod	21	39	39	29	2962	17	6
Clive Platt	28	40	40	32	3075	6	3
Scott Taylor	30	19	17	6	866	3	2
Aaron Wilbraham	26	35	31	12	1595	4	2

TEAM OF THE SEASON

G Matthew Baker CG: 36 DR: 62

D Pablo Mills CG: 16 DR: 69

D Leon Crooks CG: 19 DR: 65

D David Partridge CG: 16 DR: 65

D Dean Lewington CG: 41 DR: 63

M Gareth Edds CG: 26 SD: -29

M Gary Smith CG: 14 SD: -29

M Paul Mitchell CG: 33 SD: -38

M Wade Small CG: 16 SD: -80

F Izale McLeod CG: 29 SR: 174

F Aaron Wilbraham CG: 12 SR: 399

MONTHLY POINTS TALLY

AUGUST	5	28%
SEPTEMBER	4	27%
OCTOBER	6	40%
NOVEMBER	6	67%
DECEMBER	2	13%
JANUARY	4	27%
FEBRUARY	7	47%
MARCH	3	25%
APRIL	12	57%
MAY	1	33%

LEAGUE GOALS

	PLAYER	LGE	FAC	LC	Oth	TOT
1	McLeod	17	1	0	0	18
2	Platt	6	2	0	0	8
3	Wilbraham	4	0	0	0	4
4	Edds	3	2	0	0	5
5	Taylor	3	0	0	0	3
6	Smith	3	1	0	0	4
7	Kamara	2	0	0	0	2
8	Harding	2	0	0	0	2
9	Rizzo	2	1	0	0	3
10	Lewington	1	0	0	0	1
11	Small	1	0	0	0	1
	Other	1	1	0	0	2
	TOTAL	45	8	0	0	53

TOP POINT EARNERS

	PLAYER	GAMES	AV PTS
1	David Partridge	16	1.44
2	Gary Smith	14	1.29
3	Dean Lewington	41	1.20
4	Gareth Edds	26	1.19
5	Craig Morgan	38	1.11
6	Paul Mitchell	33	1.09
7	Clive Platt	32	1.09
8	Izale McLeod	29	1.07
9	Pablo Mills	16	1.06
10	Matthew Baker	36	1.06

DISCIPLINARY RECORDS

	PLAYER	YELLOW	RED	AVE
1	Mills	6	0	240
2	Small	7	0	274
3	Chorley	7	1	280
4	Kamara	3	0	309
5	McKoy	2	0	321
6	Lewington	10	1	351
7	Quinn, S	3	0	375
8	Partridge	4	0	387
9	McClenahan	5	0	430
10	Taylor	2	0	433
11	Mitchell	6	1	453
12	McLeod	6	0	493
13	Wilbraham	2	1	531
	Other	17	0	
	TOTAL	80	4	

KEY GOALKEEPER

Matthew Baker

Goals Conceded in the League	53	Counting Games League games when player was on pitch for at least 70 minutes	36
Goals Conceded in all competitions	61		
Defensive Rating Ave number of mins between League goals conceded while on the pitch	62	Clean Sheets In games when player was on pitch for at least 70 minutes	7

KEY PLAYERS - DEFENDERS

Pablo Mills

Goals Conceded in the League	21	Clean Sheets In League games when player was on pitch for at least 70 minutes	4
Goals Conceded in all competitions	21		
Defensive Rating Ave number of mins between League goals conceded while on the pitch	69	Club Defensive Rating Average number of mins between League goals conceded by the club this season	63

	PLAYER	CON LGE	CON ALL	CLN SHEETS	DEF RATE
1	Pablo Mills	21	21	4	69 mins
2	David Partridge	24	24	4	65 mins
3	Leon Crooks	29	34	5	65 mins
4	Dean Lewington	61	67	8	63 mins

KEY PLAYERS - MIDFIELDERS

Gary Smith

Goals in the League	3	Contribution to Attacking Power Average number of minutes between League team goals while on pitch	84
Goals in all competitions	4		
Defensive Rating Average number of mins between League goals conceded while on the pitch	55	Scoring Difference Defensive Rating minus Contribution to Attacking Power	-29

	PLAYER	GOALS LGE	GOALS ALL	DEF RATE	ATT POWER	SCORE DIFF
1	Gary Smith	3	4	55	84	-29 mins
2	Gareth Edds	3	5	63	92	-29 mins
3	Paul Mitchell	0	0	61	99	-38 mins
4	Wade Small	1	1	57	137	-80 mins

KEY PLAYERS - GOALSCORERS

Izale McLeod

Goals in the League	17	Player Strike Rate Average number of minutes between League goals scored by player	174
Goals in all competitions	18		
Contribution to Attacking Power Average number of minutes between League team goals while on pitch	78	Club Strike Rate Average number of minutes between League goals scored by club	92

	PLAYER	GOALS LGE	GOALS ALL	POWER	S RATE
1	Izale McLeod	17	18	78	174 mins
2	Aaron Wilbraham	4	4	80	399 mins
3	Clive Platt	6	8	103	513 mins
4	Gary Smith	3	4	84	533 mins

Wade Small

SQUAD APPEARANCES

Match	1	2	3	4	5	6	7	8	9	10	11	12	13	14	15	16	17	18	19	20	21	22	23	24	25
Venue	H	A	A	H	H	A	H	A	H	H	A	H	H	A	H	A	H	A	A	H	H	A	A	H	H
Competition	L	L	L	L	W	L	L	L	L	L	L	L	L	L	L	L	L	F	L	F	L	L	F	L	L
Result	D	D	L	D	L	D	D	L	L	D	L	W	W	D	D	L	D	D	W	W	W	L	W	D	L

Match	26	27	28	29	30	31	32	33	34	35	36	37	38	39	40	41	42	43	44	45	46	47	48	49	50	51
Venue	A	A	A	H	A	A	H	A	H	A	H	A	A	H	H	H	A	H	H	A	A	A	H	A	H	A
Competition	L	L	L	L	F	L	L	L	L	L	L	L	L	L	L	L	L	L	L	L	L	L	L	L	L	L
Result	L	D	L	L	L	L	D	L	W	L	W	D	L	W	L	W	L	L	L	L	W	W	W	W	L	D

Goalkeepers
Matthew Baker
Ricardo Batista
David Martin
Rob Webb

Defenders
Mirano Carrilho
Ben Chorley
Leon Crooks
Malvin Kamara
Nathan Koo-Boothe
Dean Lewington
Trent McClenahan
Pablo Mills
Craig Morgan
Shola Oyedele
David Partridge
Mark Ricketts

Midfielders
Gareth Edds
Ben Harding
Nick McKoy
Paul Mitchell
Filipe Morais
Steve Palmer
Jason Puncheon
Stephen Quinn
Nicky Rizzo
Wade Small
Gary Smith

Forwards
Sam Baldock
Serge Makofo
Izale McLeod
Clive Platt
Scott Taylor
Aaron Wilbraham

KEY: On all match · On bench · Subbed or sent off (Counting game) · Subbed or sent off (playing less than 70 minutes) · Subbed on from bench (Counting Game) · Subbed on (playing less than 70 minutes) · Subbed on and then subbed or sent off (Counting Game) · Subbed on and then subbed or sent off (playing less than 70 minutes) · Not in 16

SWINDON TOWN

Final Position: **23rd**

NICKNAME: THE ROBINS

KEY: ☐ Won ☐ Drawn ☐ Lost

							Attendance
1	div2	Barnsley	A	L	0-2		9,358
2	div2	Oldham	H	L	2-3	Roberts 79; Thorpe 85	5,294
3	div2	Nottm Forest	H	W	2-1	Fallon 31; O'Hanlon 73	8,108
4	div2	Blackpool	A	D	0-0		4,661
5	ccr1	Wycombe	H	L	1-3	Pook 58	3,976
6	div2	Yeovil	H	W	4-2	Skiverton 24 og; Fallon 50; Heath 66; Roberts 90	6,973
7	div2	Tranmere	A	L	0-1		7,557
8	div2	Walsall	A	L	0-1		5,392
9	div2	Southend	H	L	1-2	Fallon 90	4,785
10	div2	Bournemouth	A	L	1-2	Jenkins 44	7,276
11	div2	Bradford	H	L	2-3	Fallon 19,76	4,590
12	div2	Doncaster	A	L	0-1		5,282
13	div2	MK Dons	A	L	1-3	Fallon 7	5,536
14	div2	Port Vale	H	L	1-2	Fallon 24	4,531
15	div2	Brentford	A	D	0-0		6,969
16	div2	Scunthorpe	H	D	1-1	Roberts 78 pen	4,972
17	div2	Huddersfield	A	D	1-1	Gurney 40 pen	11,352
18	facr1	Boston	H	D	2-2	Gurney 32; Comyn-Platt 87	3,814
19	div2	Bristol City	H	W	2-1	McDermott 12; Fallon 31	7,572
20	facr1r	Boston	A	L	1-4	Fallon 83 pen	2,467
21	div2	Port Vale	A	D	1-1	Bouazza 66	4,108
22	div2	Barnsley	H	L	0-3		5,422
23	div2	Rotherham	A	W	1-0	Fallon 45	3,537
24	div2	Oldham	A	D	2-2	O'Hanlon 12; McDermott 48	5,354
25	div2	Blackpool	H	D	0-0		5,766
26	div2	Colchester	H	W	1-0	Fallon 90	5,531
27	div2	Chesterfield	A	D	1-1	Bouazza 63 pen	4,265
28	div2	Swansea	H	D	0-0		8,985
29	div2	Hartlepool	A	D	1-1	Fallon 78	4,169
30	div2	Gillingham	A	L	0-3		7,300
31	div2	Bournemouth	H	W	4-2	Cureton 37; Miglioranzi 52; Fallon 79; Peacock 90	6,092
32	div2	Southend	A	L	0-2		7,945
33	div2	Walsall	H	W	1-0	Cureton 43	4,597
34	div2	Doncaster	H	W	2-1	Shakes 29; Comyn-Platt 57	5,100
35	div2	Bradford	A	D	1-1	O'Hanlon 90	7,283
36	div2	Gillingham	H	W	1-0	Cureton 27	5,530
37	div2	Rotherham	H	L	2-3	Cureton 20; O'Hanlon 25	7,518
38	div2	Nottm Forest	A	L	1-7	Benjamin 76	22,444
39	div2	Tranmere	H	L	1-2	Cureton 69	4,139
40	div2	Yeovil	A	D	0-0		7,451
41	div2	Colchester	A	L	0-1		3,767
42	div2	Chesterfield	H	W	2-0	Cureton 53,90	5,661
43	div2	Hartlepool	H	D	1-1	Peacock 54	5,225
44	div2	Swansea	A	L	1-2	Shakes 62	12,465
45	div2	MK Dons	H	L	0-1		7,273
46	div2	Scunthorpe	A	W	2-1	Benjamin 25 pen; Shakes 38	5,207
47	div2	Brentford	H	L	1-3	Brown 71	6,845
48	div2	Bristol City	A	D	1-1	Brown 49	15,632
49	div2	Huddersfield	H	D	0-0		6,353

LEAGUE APPEARANCES, BOOKINGS AND GOALS

	AGE (on 01/07/06)	IN NAMED 16	APPEARANCES	COUNTING GAMES	MINUTES ON PITCH	LEAGUE GOALS	Yellow cards	Red cards
Goalkeepers								
Matthew Bulman	19	31	0	0	0	0	0	0
Rhys Evans	24	33	32	32	2880	0	1	0
Tom Heaton	20	19	14	14	1260	0	1	0
Defenders								
Patrick Collins	21	14	13	13	1160	0	2	0
Charlie Comyn-Platt	20	24	22	10	1271	1	3	0
Andy Gurney	32	28	28	20	2116	1	13	1
Leigh Henry	-	1	0	0	0	0	0	0
Jerel Ifil	24	36	36	34	3101	0	11	3
Stephen Jenkins	33	34	24	14	1510	1	5	0
Kyle Lapham	20	1	0	0	0	0	0	0
Andrew Nicholas	22	36	33	30	2805	0	0	0
Nicky Nicolau	22	7	5	3	288	0	0	0
Sean O'Hanlon	23	40	40	37	3431	4	5	0
Alan Reeves	38	2	1	0	14	0	0	0
Jack Smith	22	42	38	34	3239	0	8	0
Midfielders								
Aaron Brown	26	27	27	20	2022	2	3	0
Toumani Diagouraga	19	8	8	5	530	0	3	0
Albert Jarrett	21	7	6	0	213	0	0	0
Neale McDermott	21	15	13	5	785	2	1	0
Chris McPhee	23	8	8	6	545	0	0	0
Stefani Miglioranzi	28	31	27	17	1931	1	3	0
Michael Pook	20	34	30	23	2252	0	3	0
Paul Smith	34	9	9	3	434	0	0	0
David Stroud	18	4	2	1	122	0	0	0
Nicky Summerbee	34	1	1	0	68	0	0	0
Ben Wells	18	8	4	0	83	0	0	0
Gareth Whalley	32	27	24	16	1739	0	1	0
Forwards								
Trevor Benjamin	27	11	8	3	428	2	0	0
Hameur Bouazza	21	13	13	10	989	2	1	0
Jamie Cureton	30	33	30	20	1979	7	1	0
Rory Fallon	24	25	25	24	2195	12	5	1
Colin Heath	22	12	11	4	604	1	2	0
Ashan Holgate	19	8	6	1	234	0	3	0
Lucas Jutkiewicz	-	7	5	3	353	0	1	0
Petr Mikolanda	21	8	5	0	145	0	0	0
Lee Peacock	29	16	15	9	982	2	0	0
Christian Roberts	26	23	21	4	710	3	2	0
Ricky Shakes	21	42	37	23	2461	3	1	0
Tony Thorpe	32	11	7	5	536	1	2	0

TEAM OF THE SEASON

MONTHLY POINTS TALLY

AUGUST	7	39%
SEPTEMBER	0	0%
OCTOBER	3	20%
NOVEMBER	4	44%
DECEMBER	10	56%
JANUARY	7	47%
FEBRUARY	7	47%
MARCH	4	33%
APRIL	5	28%
MAY	1	33%

LEAGUE GOALS

	PLAYER	LGE	FAC	LC	Oth	TOT
1	Fallon	12	1	0	0	13
2	Cureton	7	0	0	0	7
3	O'Hanlon	4	0	0	0	4
4	Shakes	3	0	0	0	3
5	Roberts	3	0	0	0	3
6	Brown	2	0	0	0	2
7	Bouazza	2	0	0	0	2
8	McDermott	2	0	0	0	2
9	Benjamin	2	0	0	0	2
10	Peacock	2	0	0	0	2
11	Heath	1	0	0	0	1
	Other	6	2	1	0	9
	TOTAL	46	3	1	0	50

TOP POINT EARNERS

	PLAYER	GAMES	AV PTS
1	Aaron Brown	20	1.40
2	Jamie Cureton	20	1.25
3	Rhys Evans	32	1.22
4	Ricky Shakes	23	1.22
5	Andrew Nicholas	30	1.17
6	Andy Gurney	20	1.10
7	Jerel Ifil	34	1.09
8	Rory Fallon	24	1.08
9	Jack Smith	34	1.06
10	Stefani Miglioranzi	17	1.06

DISCIPLINARY RECORDS

	PLAYER	YELLOW	RED	AVE
1	Gurney	13	1	151
2	Diagouraga	3	0	176
3	Ifil	11	3	221
4	Thorpe	2	0	268
5	Heath	2	0	302
6	Jenkins	5	0	302
7	Roberts	2	0	355
8	Fallon	5	1	365
9	Smith, J	8	0	404
10	Comyn-Platt	3	0	423
11	Collins	2	0	580
12	Miglioranzi	3	0	643
13	Brown	3	0	674
	Other	15	0	
	TOTAL	77	5	

KEY GOALKEEPER

Rhys Evans

Goals Conceded in the League	42	Counting Games League games when player was on pitch for at least 70 minutes	32
Goals Conceded in all competitions	42		
Defensive Rating Ave number of mins between League goals conceded while on the pitch	69	Clean Sheets In games when player was on pitch for at least 70 minutes	10

KEY PLAYERS - GOALSCORERS

Rory Fallon

Goals in the League	12	Player Strike Rate Average number of minutes between League goals scored by player	183
Goals in all competitions	13		
Contribution to Attacking Power Average number of minutes between League team goals while on pitch	88	Club Strike Rate Average number of minutes between League goals scored by club	90

	PLAYER	GOALS LGE	GOALS ALL	POWER	S RATE
1	Rory Fallon	12	13	88	183 mins
2	Jamie Cureton	7	7	99	283 mins
3	Ricky Shakes	3	3	77	820 mins
4	Sean O'Hanlon	4	4	101	858 mins

KEY PLAYERS - DEFENDERS

Andy Gurney

Goals Conceded in the League	29	Clean Sheets In League games when player was on pitch for at least 70 minutes	5
Goals Conceded in all competitions	35		
Defensive Rating Ave number of mins between League goals conceded while on the pitch	73	Club Defensive Rating Average number of mins between League goals conceded by the club this season	64

	PLAYER	CON LGE	CON ALL	CLN SHEETS	DEF RATE
1	Andy Gurney	29	35	5	73 mins
2	Stephen Jenkins	23	29	1	66 mins
3	Sean O'Hanlon	54	60	9	64 mins
4	Jack Smith	51	58	8	64 mins

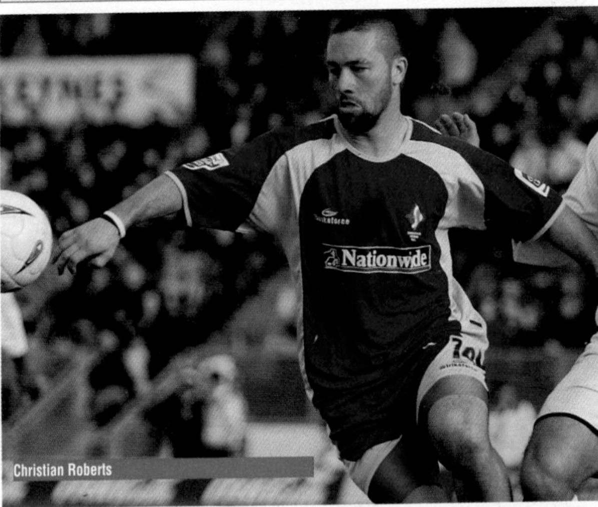

Christian Roberts

KEY PLAYERS - MIDFIELDERS

Aaron Brown

Goals in the League	2	Contribution to Attacking Power Average number of minutes between League team goals while on pitch	101
Goals in all competitions	2		
Defensive Rating Average number of mins between League goals conceded while on the pitch	67	Scoring Difference Defensive Rating minus Contribution to Attacking Power	-34

	PLAYER	GOALS LGE	GOALS ALL	DEF RATE	ATT POWER	SCORE DIFF
1	Aaron Brown	2	2	67	101	-34 mins
2	Gareth Whalley	0	0	67	102	-35 mins
3	Michael Pook	0	1	70	107	-37 mins
4	Stefani Miglioranzi	1	1	52	97	-45 mins

SQUAD APPEARANCES

atch	1	2	3	4	5	6	7	8	9	10	11	12	13	14	15	16	17	18	19	20	21	22	23	24	25	26	27	28	29	30	31	32	33	34	35	36	37	38	39	40	41	42	43	44	45	46	47	48	49
enue	A	H	H	A	H	H	A	A	H	A	H	A	A	H	A	H	A	H	H	A	A	H	A	A	H	H	A	H	A	A	H	A	H	H	A	H	H	A	H	A	A	H	H	A	H	A	H	A	H
ompetition	L	L	L	L	W	L	L	L	L	L	L	L	L	L	L	L	L	F	L	F	L	L	L	L	L	L	L	L	L	L	L	L	L	L	L	L	L	L	L	L	L	L	L	L	L	L	L	L	L
esult	L	L	W	D	L	W	L	L	L	L	L	L	L	L	D	D	D	D	W	L	D	L	W	D	D	W	D	D	D	L	W	L	W	W	D	W	L	L	L	D	L	W	D	L	L	W	L	D	D

oalkeepers
latthew Bulman
hys Evans
om Heaton

efenders
atrick Collins
harlie Comyn-Platt
ndy Gurney
eigh Henry
erel Ifil
tephen Jenkins
yle Lapham
ndrew Nicholas
icky Nicolau
ean O'Hanlon
lan Reeves
ack Smith

lidfielders
aron Brown
oumani Diagouraga
lbert Jarrett
eale McDermott
hris McPhee
tefani Miglioranzi
lichael Pook
aul Smith
avid Stroud
icky Summerbee
en Wells
areth Whalley

orwards
revor Benjamin
lameur Bouazza
amie Cureton
ory Fallon
olin Heath
shan Holgate
ucas Jutkiewicz
etr Mikolanda
ee Peacock
hristian Roberts
icky Shakes
ony Thorpe

KEY: On all match | On bench | Subbed or sent off (Counting game) | Subbed or sent off (playing less than 70 minutes) | Subbed on from bench (Counting Game) | Subbed on (playing less than 70 minutes) | Subbed on and then subbed or sent off (Counting Game) | Subbed on and then subbed or sent off (playing less than 70 minutes) | Not in 16

WALSALL

Final Position: **24th**

NICKNAME: THE SADDLERS

KEY: ☐Won ☐Drawn ☐Lost

							Attendance
1	div2	Rotherham	A	W	2-1	Taylor, K 2; Leitao 90	5,386
2	div2	Nottm Forest	H	W	3-2	Wright 50; Westwood 52; Fryatt 61 pen	8,703
3	div2	Southend	H	D	2-2	Fryatt 65; Leitao 68	5,569
4	div2	Hartlepool	A	D	1-1	Westwood 7	5,060
5	ccr1	Crystal Palace	A	L	0-3		5,508
6	div2	Swansea	H	L	2-5	Fryatt 24 pen; Gueret 51 og	5,745
7	div2	Bournemouth	A	D	0-0		5,953
8	div2	Swindon	H	W	1-0	Fryatt 57	5,392
9	div2	Yeovil	A	L	1-2	Fryatt 34 pen	9,579
10	div2	Chesterfield	H	L	2-3	Leitao 14; Wright 35	5,177
11	div2	Scunthorpe	A	W	3-1	Fryatt 15 pen; Osborn 66,75	4,973
12	div2	Brentford	H	D	0-0		4,873
13	div2	Port Vale	A	L	2-3	Collins 24 og; Demontagnac 36	5,314
14	div2	MK Dons	H	D	1-1	Bennett 90	5,041
15	div2	Huddersfield	A	L	1-3	Smith, P 31	11,642
16	div2	Doncaster	H	W	1-0	Leitao 72	5,385
17	div2	Barnsley	A	L	0-2		8,145
18	facr1	Merthyr	A	W	2-1	Fryatt 17 pen; Kinsella 25	3,046
19	div2	Gillingham	H	W	2-0	Demontagnac 15; Skora 57	4,785
20	div2	MK Dons	A	L	1-2	Skora 13	5,506
21	div2	Rotherham	H	W	3-1	Fryatt 42,45; Leitao 69	4,563
22	facr2	Yeovil	H	W	2-0	Fryatt 18 pen; Leitao 83	4,580
23	div2	Oldham	A	L	1-2	Taylor, K 73	3,878
24	div2	Nottm Forest	A	D	1-1	Fryatt 6	20,912
25	div2	Hartlepool	H	W	1-0	Fryatt 85	4,293
26	div2	Tranmere	H	D	0-0		6,476
27	div2	Bradford	A	L	0-2		6,745
28	div2	Blackpool	H	W	2-0	Constable 46,52	5,046
29	div2	Bristol City	A	L	0-3		12,652
30	facr3	Barnsley	A	D	1-1	James 74	6,884
31	div2	Colchester	H	L	0-2		5,464
32	facr3r	Barnsley	H	W	2-0	Leary 68; James 78	4,074
33	div2	Chesterfield	A	D	2-2	Timm 33; Smith, Grant 50	4,666
34	facr4	Stoke	A	L	1-2	James 51	8,834
35	div2	Swindon	A	L	0-1		4,597
36	div2	Brentford	A	L	0-5		5,645
37	div2	Scunthorpe	H	D	2-2	Keates 30; Barrowman 77	4,911
38	div2	Colchester	A	D	0-0		3,810
39	div2	Oldham	H	L	0-2		5,816
40	div2	Southend	A	D	0-0		7,906
41	div2	Swansea	A	D	1-1	Devlin 17	13,262
42	div2	Tranmere	A	W	2-1	Smith, Grant 41,72	6,615
43	div2	Yeovil	H	L	0-2		4,464
44	div2	Bradford	H	D	2-2	James 17; Westwood 37	4,678
45	div2	Blackpool	A	L	0-2		6,129
46	div2	Bristol City	H	L	0-3		5,402
47	div2	Bournemouth	H	L	0-1		4,613
48	div2	Port Vale	H	D	1-1	Constable 50	4,876
49	div2	Doncaster	A	L	0-1		5,086
50	div2	Huddersfield	H	L	1-3	Leary 90	5,554
51	div2	Gillingham	A	W	1-0	Claridge 56	7,757
52	div2	Barnsley	H	L	1-2	Keates 59 pen	7,195

LEAGUE APPEARANCES, BOOKINGS AND GOALS

	AGE (on 01/07/06)	IN NAMED 16	APPEARANCES	COUNTING GAMES	MINUTES ON PITCH	LEAGUE GOALS	
Goalkeepers							
Rene Gilmartin	19	33	2	2	180	0	0
Joe Murphy	25	14	14	14	1260	0	1
Andy Oakes	29	32	25	24	2205	0	2
John Ruddy	19	6	5	5	450	0	0
Defenders							
Julian Bennett	21	20	19	15	1521	1	3
Daniel Fox	20	33	33	31	2891	0	7
Anthony Gerrard	20	39	34	33	2957	0	10
Pablo Mills	22	14	14	13	1215	0	5
Craig Pead	24	40	39	37	3391	0	5
Ian Roper	29	30	25	24	2153	0	9
Steve Staunton	37	11	7	5	493	0	0
Chris Westwood	29	33	29	25	2364	3	1
Mark Wright	24	33	30	18	2087	2	0
Midfielders							
Joe Broad	23	3	2	1	146	0	0
Ishmel Demontagnac	18	26	24	11	1345	2	7
Paul Devlin	34	9	8	7	672	1	1
Simon Gillett	20	2	2	0	129	0	0
Dean Keates	28	14	14	14	1260	1	0
Mark Kinsella	33	22	10	4	476	0	1
Michael Leary	23	17	15	11	1069	1	2
Paul Merson	38	7	7	5	510	0	0
Simon Osborn	34	36	32	22	2370	2	10
Eric Skora	24	4	4	3	315	2	0
Grant Smith	26	13	13	11	1093	3	2
Paul Smith	34	8	8	6	667	1	1
Michael Standing	25	23	20	5	898	0	0
Daryl Taylor	21	11	11	2	511	0	0
Kris Taylor	22	24	21	11	1364	2	3
Darren Wrack	30	7	7	5	546	0	1
Forwards							
Taiwo Atieno	20	2	2	1	125	0	0
Andrew Barrowman	21	14	13	6	796	1	1
Steve Claridge	40	7	7	7	602	1	1
James Constable	21	21	17	5	761	1	4
Scott P Fitzgerald	26	6	5	0	140	0	0
Matty Fryatt	20	23	23	21	1924	11	3
Kevin James	26	15	15	11	1203	1	0
Ruben Dario Larrosa	-	12	7	2	267	0	0
Jorge Leitao	32	23	23	17	1710	5	4
Alex Nicholls	18	10	8	4	442	0	1
Mads Timm	21	11	9	4	475	1	0

TEAM OF THE SEASON

G: Joe Murphy CG: 14 DR: 74

D: Ian Roper CG: 24 DR: 77

D: Pablo Mills CG: 13 DR: 71

D: Craig Pead CG: 37 DR: 63

D: Julian Bennett CG: 15 DR: 61

M: Simon Osborn CG: 22 SD: -7

M: Dean Keates CG: 14 SD: -105

M: Kris Taylor* CG: 11 SD: -20

M: Ismael Demontagnac* CG: 11 SD: -7

F: Matty Fryatt CG: 21 SR: 175

F: Jorge Leitao CG: 17 SR: 342

MONTHLY POINTS TALLY

AUGUST	9	50%
SEPTEMBER	7	47%
OCTOBER	4	27%
NOVEMBER	6	67%
DECEMBER	8	44%
JANUARY	1	8%
FEBRUARY	3	20%
MARCH	5	42%
APRIL	4	19%
MAY	0	0%

LEAGUE GOALS

	PLAYER	LGE	FAC	LC	Oth	TOT
1	Fryatt	11	2	0	0	13
2	Leitao	5	1	0	0	6
3	Westwood	3	0	0	0	3
4	Smith, Grant	3	0	0	0	3
5	Taylor, K	2	0	0	0	2
6	Demontagnac	2	0	0	0	2
7	Wright	2	0	0	0	2
8	Skora	2	0	0	0	2
9	Osborn	2	0	0	0	2
10	Barrowman	1	0	0	0	1
11	Claridge	1	0	0	0	1
	Other	13	5	0	0	18
	TOTAL	47	8	0	0	55

TOP POINT EARNERS

	PLAYER	GAMES	AV PTS
1	Simon Osborn	22	1.50
2	Matty Fryatt	21	1.48
3	Julian Bennett	15	1.40
4	Joe Murphy	14	1.29
5	Ian Roper	24	1.13
6	Jorge Leitao	17	1.12
7	Mark Wright	18	1.11
8	Craig Pead	37	1.05
9	Daniel Fox	31	1.00
10	Andy Oakes	24	0.96

DISCIPLINARY RECORDS

	PLAYER	YELLOW	RED	AVE
1	Demontagnac	7	2	149
2	Constable	4	0	190
3	Roper	9	1	215
4	Osborn	10	0	237
5	Mills	5	0	243
6	Gerrard	10	0	295
7	Bennett	3	1	380
8	Fox	7	0	413
9	Leitao	4	0	427
10	Taylor, K	3	0	454
11	Kinsella	1	0	476
12	Leary	2	0	534
13	Smith, Grant	2	0	546
	Other	17	1	
	TOTAL	84	5	

KEY GOALKEEPER

Joe Murphy

Goals Conceded in the League	17	Counting Games League games when player was on pitch for at least 70 minutes	14
Goals Conceded in all competitions	17		
Defensive Rating Ave number of mins between League goals conceded while on the pitch	74	Clean Sheets In games when player was on pitch for at least 70 minutes	5

KEY PLAYERS - GOALSCORERS

Matty Fryatt

Goals in the League	11	Player Strike Rate Average number of minutes between League goals scored by player	175
Goals in all competitions	13		
Contribution to Attacking Power Average number of minutes between League team goals while on pitch	64	Club Strike Rate Average number of minutes between League goals scored by club	88

	PLAYER	GOALS LGE	GOALS ALL	POWER	S RATE
1	Matty Fryatt	11	13	64	175 mins
2	Jorge Leitao	5	6	61	342 mins
3	Chris Westwood	3	3	84	788 mins
4	Mark Wright	2	2	77	1044 mins

KEY PLAYERS - DEFENDERS

Ian Roper

Goals Conceded in the League	28	Clean Sheets In League games when player was on pitch for at least 70 minutes	8
Goals Conceded in all competitions	30		
Defensive Rating Ave number of mins between League goals conceded while on the pitch	77	Club Defensive Rating Average number of mins between League goals conceded by the club this season	59

	PLAYER	CON LGE	CON ALL	CLN SHEETS	DEF RATE
1	Ian Roper	28	30	8	77 mins
2	Pablo Mills	17	17	3	71 mins
3	Craig Pead	54	60	10	63 mins
4	Julian Bennett	25	30	4	61 mins

Steve Staunton

KEY PLAYERS - MIDFIELDERS

Simon Osborn

Goals in the League	2	Contribution to Attacking Power Average number of minutes between League team goals while on pitch	79
Goals in all competitions	2		
Defensive Rating Average number of mins between League goals conceded while on the pitch	72	Scoring Difference Defensive Rating minus Contribution to Attacking Power	-7

	PLAYER	GOALS LGE	GOALS ALL	DEF RATE	ATT POWER	SCORE DIFF
1	Simon Osborn	2	2	72	79	-7 mins
2	Dean Keates	1	1	53	158	-105 mins

SQUAD APPEARANCES

Match	1	2	3	4	5	6	7	8	9	10	11	12	13	14	15	16	17	18	19	20	21	22	23	24	25	26
Venue	A	H	H	A	A	H	A	H	A	H	A	H	A	H	A	H	A	A	H	A	H	H	A	A	H	H
Competition	L	L	L	L	W	L	L	L	L	L	L	L	L	L	L	L	L	F	L	L	L	F	L	L	L	L
Result	W	W	D	D	L	L	D	W	L	L	W	D	L	D	L	W	L	W	W	L	W	W	L	D	W	D

Match	27	28	29	30	31	32	33	34	35	36	37	38	39	40	41	42	43	44	45	46	47	48	49	50	51	52
Venue	A	H	A	A	H	H	A	A	A	A	H	A	H	A	A	A	H	H	A	H	H	H	A	H	A	H
Competition	L	L	L	F	L	F	L	F	L	L	L	L	L	L	L	L	L	L	L	L	L	L	L	L	L	L
Result	L	W	L	D	L	W	D	L	L	L	D	D	L	D	D	W	L	D	L	L	L	D	L	L	W	L

Goalkeepers
Rene Gilmartin
Joe Murphy
Andy Oakes
John Ruddy

Defenders
Julian Bennett
Daniel Fox
Anthony Gerrard
Pablo Mills
Craig Pead
Ian Roper
Steve Staunton
Chris Westwood
Mark Wright

Midfielders
Joe Broad
Ishmel Demontagnac
Paul Devlin
Simon Gillett
Dean Keates
Mark Kinsella
Michael Leary
Paul Merson
Simon Osborn
Eric Skora
Grant Smith
Paul Smith
Michael Standing
Daryl Taylor
Kris Taylor
Darren Wrack

Forwards
Taiwo Atieno
Andrew Barrowman
Steve Claridge
James Constable
Scott P Fitzgerald
Matty Fryatt
Kevin James
Ruben Dario Larrosa
Jorge Leitao
Alex Nicholls
Mads Timm

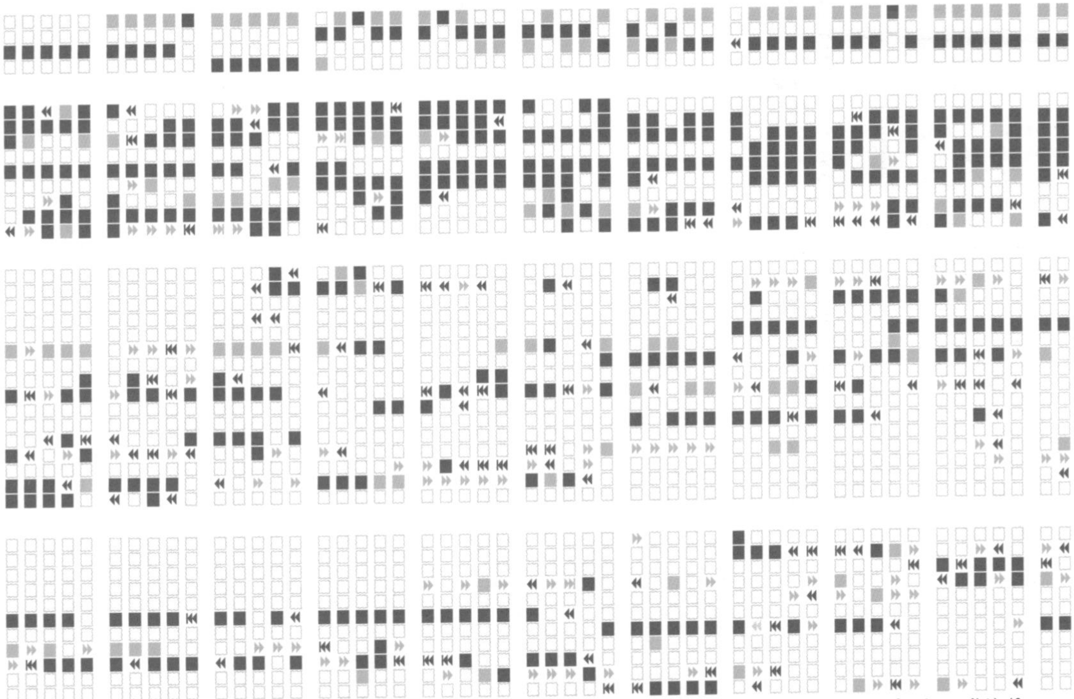

KEY: On all match · On bench · Subbed or sent off (Counting game) · Subbed or sent off (playing less than 70 minutes) · Subbed on from bench (Counting Game) · Subbed on (playing less than 70 minutes) · Subbed on and then subbed or sent off (Counting Game) · Subbed on and then subbed or sent off (playing less than 70 minutes) · Not in 16

LEAGUE TWO ROUND-UP

FINAL LEAGUE TABLE

		HOME					AWAY					TOTAL			
	P	W	D	L	F	A	W	D	L	F	A	F	A	DIF	PTS
Carlisle	46	14	3	6	47	23	11	8	4	37	19	84	42	42	86
Northampton	46	11	8	4	30	15	11	9	3	33	22	63	37	26	83
Leyton Orient	46	11	6	6	29	21	11	9	3	38	30	67	51	16	81
Grimsby	46	13	3	7	37	18	9	9	5	27	26	64	44	20	78
Cheltenham	46	10	7	6	39	31	9	8	6	26	22	65	53	12	72
Wycombe	46	9	9	5	41	29	9	8	6	31	27	72	56	16	71
Lincoln	46	9	11	3	37	21	6	10	7	28	32	65	53	12	66
Darlington	46	10	7	6	32	26	6	8	9	26	26	58	52	6	63
Peterborough	46	9	7	7	28	21	8	4	11	29	28	57	49	8	62
Shrewsbury	46	10	9	4	33	20	6	4	13	22	35	55	55	0	61
Boston	46	11	7	5	34	28	4	9	10	16	32	50	60	-10	61
Bristol Rovers	46	8	6	9	30	29	9	3	11	29	38	59	67	-8	60
Wrexham	46	12	6	5	36	19	3	8	12	25	35	61	54	7	59
Rochdale	46	8	7	8	34	30	6	7	10	32	39	66	69	-3	56
Chester	46	7	6	10	30	29	7	6	10	23	30	53	59	-6	54
Mansfield	46	9	7	7	37	29	4	8	11	22	37	59	66	-7	54
Macclesfield	46	10	9	4	35	27	2	9	12	25	44	60	71	-11	54
Barnet	46	9	8	6	24	22	3	10	10	20	35	44	57	-13	54
Bury	46	6	9	8	22	25	6	8	9	23	32	45	57	-12	53
Torquay	46	7	9	7	33	31	6	4	13	20	35	53	66	-13	52
Notts County	46	7	11	5	30	26	5	5	13	18	37	48	63	-15	52
Stockport	46	7	11	5	34	29	4	8	11	23	49	57	78	-21	52
Oxford	46	7	7	9	25	30	4	9	10	18	27	43	57	-14	49
Rushden & D	46	8	5	10	25	31	3	7	13	19	45	44	76	-32	45

CLUB STRIKE FORCE

Carl Hawley of Carlisle: 22 league goals

1 Carlisle

Goals scored in the League	84
Club Strike Rate (CSR) Average number of minutes between League goals scored by club	49

	CLUB	GOALS	CSR
1	Carlisle	84	49
2	Wycombe	72	58
3	Leyton Orient	67	62
4	Rochdale	66	63
5	Cheltenham	65	64
6	Lincoln	65	64
7	Grimsby	64	65
8	Northampton	63	66
9	Macclesfield	61	68
10	Wrexham	61	68
11	Bristol Rovers	59	70
12	Mansfield	59	70
13	Darlington	58	71
14	Peterborough	57	73
15	Stockport	57	73
16	Shrewsbury	55	75
17	Chester	53	78
18	Torquay	53	78
19	Boston	50	83
20	Notts County	48	86
21	Bury	45	92
22	Barnet	44	94
23	Rushden & D	44	94
24	Oxford	43	96

CLUB DISCIPLINARY RECORDS

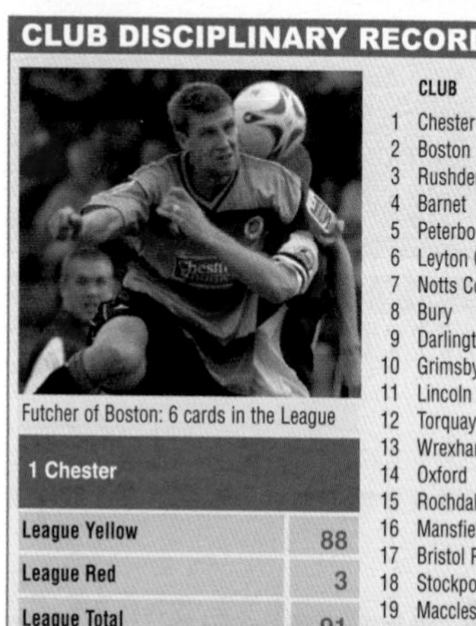

Futcher of Boston: 6 cards in the League

1 Chester

League Yellow	88
League Red	3
League Total	91
Cards Average in League Average number of minutes between a card being shown of either colour	45

	CLUB	Y	R	TOTAL	AVE
1	Chester	88	3	91	45
2	Boston	83	6	89	47
3	Rushden & D	83	5	88	47
4	Barnet	86	0	86	48
5	Peterborough	82	3	85	49
6	Leyton Orient	77	3	80	52
7	Notts County	75	4	79	52
8	Bury	68	3	71	58
9	Darlington	65	7	72	58
10	Grimsby	66	3	69	60
11	Lincoln	61	7	68	61
12	Torquay	61	4	65	64
13	Wrexham	61	4	65	64
14	Oxford	59	5	64	65
15	Rochdale	56	5	61	68
16	Mansfield	51	6	57	73
17	Bristol Rovers	53	3	56	74
18	Stockport	50	4	54	77
19	Macclesfield	52	0	52	80
20	Northampton	48	2	50	83
21	Carlisle	47	2	49	84
22	Cheltenham	46	3	49	84
23	Shrewsbury	47	2	49	84
24	Wycombe	45	1	46	90

CLUB DEFENCES

	CLUB	LGE	CS	CDR
1	Northampton	38	22	109
2	Carlisle	42	20	99
3	Grimsby	44	17	94
4	Peterborough	49	11	84
5	Leyton Orient	51	14	81
6	Darlington	52	13	80
7	Cheltenham	53	12	78
8	Lincoln	53	12	78
9	Wrexham	54	12	77
10	Shrewsbury	55	12	75
11	Wycombe	56	12	74
12	Barnet	57	13	73
13	Bury	57	14	73
14	Oxford	57	12	73
15	Chester	59	11	70
16	Boston	60	13	69
17	Notts County	63	10	66
18	Mansfield	66	13	63
19	Torquay	66	14	63
20	Bristol Rovers	67	7	62
21	Rochdale	69	5	60
22	Macclesfield	71	9	58
23	Rushden & D	76	11	54
24	Stockport	78	7	53

Kevin Gray of Carlisle

1 Northampton

Goals conceded in the League	38
Clean Sheets (CS) Number of league games where no goals were conceded	22
Club Defensive Rate (CDR) Average number of minutes between League goals conceded by club	109

STADIUM CAPACITY AND HOME CROWDS

	TEAM	CAPACITY	AVE	HIGH	LOW
1	Leyton Orient	4989	94.19	6720	3463
2	Northampton	7653	77.55	7114	5012
3	Wycombe	10000	54.45	7134	4166
4	Grimsby	10033	51.34	8458	3658
5	Shrewsbury	8000	49.96	6249	2469
6	Bristol Rovers	12000	49.91	7551	4836
7	Chester	6012	49.38	4801	1806
8	Rushden & D	6441	49.09	5211	2216
9	Torquay	6000	47.52	5697	2010
10	Barnet	5500	46.87	3873	1366
11	Lincoln	10130	46.78	7182	2956
12	Cheltenham	7407	46.62	6005	2531
13	Oxford	12400	43.9	12243	3702
14	Stockport	11000	43.38	10006	3460
15	Carlisle	16651	43.35	13467	5190
16	Boston	6643	37.92	4476	1651
17	Macclesfield	6335	35.91	4553	1576
18	Mansfield	9990	35.64	6444	2357
19	Wrexham	15500	28.89	7240	3195
20	Peterborough	15314	28.5	8637	2833
21	Rochdale	10249	27.4	4439	1769
22	Notts County	20300	26.93	9817	3710
23	Bury	11669	22.23	4276	1673
24	Darlington	27500	15.27	8640	2905

Key: Average. The percentage of each stadium filled in League games over the season (AVE), the stadium capacity and the highest and lowest crowds recorded.

AWAY ATTENDANCE

	TEAM	AVE	HIGH	LOW
1	Carlisle	50.02	10006	1924
2	Grimsby	49.08	10909	1865
3	Northampton	47.77	8637	2010
4	Notts County	47.39	10735	1892
5	Wycombe	47	7206	1869
6	Peterborough	46.71	7486	1810
7	Stockport	46.26	6544	2432
8	Lincoln	44.84	6723	1695
9	Leyton Orient	44.44	12243	1649
10	Rochdale	44.26	7165	2043
11	Boston	44.18	7596	1985
12	Chester	43.37	7240	1651
13	Oxford	43.2	7016	1882
14	Bristol Rovers	42.49	6424	1673
15	Mansfield	42.47	9779	1576
16	Bury	42.24	9817	1796
17	Torquay	41.95	13467	1806
18	Rushden & D	41.77	7036	1777
19	Barnet	41.75	6948	1663
20	Shrewsbury	41.69	7551	1789
21	Darlington	41.53	11182	1769
22	Wrexham	41.5	6249	1616
23	Cheltenham	39.98	6885	1366
24	Macclesfield	37.11	6100	1975

Key: Average. How close each club has come to filling grounds in its away league matches (AVE) and the highest and lowest crowds recorded.

CHART-TOPPING MIDFIELDERS

1 Smith - Northampton	
Goals scored in the League	3
Defensive Rating Av number of mins between League goals conceded while on the pitch	159
Contribution to Attacking Power Average number of minutes between League team goals while on pitch	62
Scoring Difference Defensive Rating minus Contribution to Attacking Power	97

	PLAYER	CLUB	GOALS	DEF RATE	POWER	S DIFF
1	Smith	Northampton	3	159	62	97
2	Low	Northampton	5	128	61	67
3	Kamudimba	Grimsby	5	117	56	61
4	Hunt	Northampton	3	126	65	61
5	Lumsdon	Carlisle	7	90	42	48
6	Murray, A	Carlisle	1	99	55	44
7	Billy	Carlisle	0	95	53	42
8	Taylor	Northampton	7	109	67	42
9	Allen	Stockport	0	118	81	37
10	Jones, G	Grimsby	12	93	61	32
11	Johnson, G	Northampton	1	94	62	32
12	Toner	Grimsby	3	89	59	30
13	Ross	Boston	4	91	62	29
14	Burnell	Wycombe	0	90	63	27
15	Peacock	Darlington	0	96	70	26

CHART-TOPPING GOALSCORERS

1 Tyson - Wycombe	
Goals scored in the League	11
Contribution to Attacking Power Average number of minutes between League team goals while on pitch	45
Club Strike Rate (CSR) Average minutes between League goals scored by club	58
Player Strike Rate Average number of minutes between League goals scored by player	116

	PLAYER	CLUB	GOALS: LGE	POWER	CSR	S RATE
1	Tyson	Wycombe	11	45	58	116
2	Holt, Grant	Rochdale	14	48	63	131
3	Bridges	Carlisle	15	46	49	135
4	Hurst	Notts County	9	74	86	139
5	Derbyshire	Wrexham	10	74	68	141
6	Asamoah	Chester	8	103	78	155
7	Brown	Mansfield	10	54	70	161
8	Lambert	Rochdale	22	64	63	172
9	Hawley	Carlisle	22	52	49	181
10	Crow	Peterborough	15	78	73	182
11	Connell	Torquay	7	99	78	184
12	Kirk	Northampton	9	65	65	194
13	Easter	Stockport	8	63	73	196
14	McGleish	Northampton	17	68	65	200
15	Barker	Mansfield	18	69	70	207

CHART-TOPPING DEFENDERS

1 Bojic - Northampton	
Goals Conceded in the League The number of League goals conceded while he was on the pitch	14
Clean Sheets In games when he played at least 70 mins	9
Club Defensive Rating Average mins between League goals conceded by the club this season	112
Defensive Rating Average number of minutes between League goals conceded while on pitch	131

	PLAYER	CLUB	CON: LGE	CS	CDR	DEF RATE
1	Bojic	Northampton	14	9	112	131
2	Doig	Northampton	26	20	112	124
3	Chambers	Northampton	33	19	112	113
4	Jones, R	Grimsby	31	15	94	108
5	Crowe	Northampton	34	21	112	107
6	Dyche	Northampton	28	14	112	106
7	Murphy	Carlisle	33	16	96	104
8	McDermott	Grimsby	26	11	94	101
9	Arnison	Carlisle	35	14	96	99
10	Whittle	Grimsby	29	13	94	98
11	Roche	Wrexham	15	4	77	98
12	Aranalde	Carlisle	36	16	96	94
13	Croft	Grimsby	26	10	94	93
14	Gray	Carlisle	42	17	96	92
15	Burton	Peterborough	16	4	84	92

CHART-TOPPING GOALKEEPERS

1 Harper - Northampton	
Counting Games Games in which he played at least 70 minutes	44
Goals Conceded in the League The number of League goals conceded while he was on the pitch	37
Clean Sheets In games when he played at least 70 mins	23
Defensive Rating Average number of minutes between League goals conceded while on pitch	112

	PLAYER	CLUB	CG	CONC	CS	DEF RATE
1	Harper	Northampton	44	37	23	112
2	Westwood	Carlisle	35	31	14	102
3	Logan	Boston	12	11	5	98
4	Schmeichel	Bury	15	14	6	96
5	Mildenhall	Grimsby	46	44	17	94
6	Russell, S	Darlington	30	30	9	90
7	MacKenzie	Chester	30	30	11	89
8	Tyler	Peterborough	40	42	10	85
9	Flitney	Barnet	35	39	11	81
10	Higgs	Cheltenham	45	52	12	78
11	Garner	Leyton Orient	43	49	12	78
12	Ingham	Wrexham	40	46	10	77
13	Marriott	Lincoln	43	51	11	76
14	Hart	Shrewsbury	46	55	12	75
15	Turley	Oxford	33	42	8	71

PLAYER DISCIPLINARY RECORD

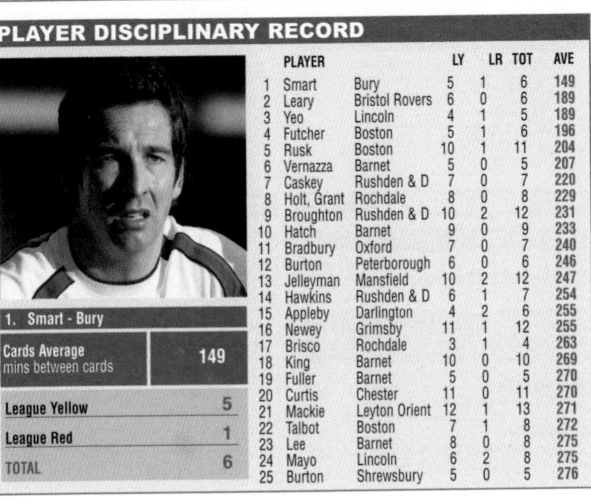

1. Smart - Bury	
Cards Average mins between cards	149
League Yellow	5
League Red	1
TOTAL	6

	PLAYER		LY	LR	TOT	AVE
1	Smart	Bury	5	1	6	149
2	Leary	Bristol Rovers	6	0	6	189
3	Yeo	Lincoln	4	1	5	189
4	Futcher	Boston	5	1	6	196
5	Rusk	Boston	10	1	11	204
6	Vernazza	Barnet	5	0	5	207
7	Caskey	Rushden & D	7	0	7	220
8	Holt, Grant	Rochdale	8	0	8	229
9	Broughton	Rushden & D	10	2	12	231
10	Hatch	Barnet	9	0	9	233
11	Bradbury	Oxford	7	0	7	240
12	Burton	Peterborough	6	0	6	246
13	Jelleyman	Mansfield	10	2	12	247
14	Hawkins	Rushden & D	6	1	7	254
15	Appleby	Darlington	4	2	6	255
16	Newey	Grimsby	11	1	12	255
17	Brisco	Rochdale	3	1	4	263
18	King	Barnet	10	0	10	269
19	Fuller	Barnet	5	0	5	270
20	Curtis	Chester	11	0	11	270
21	Mackie	Leyton Orient	12	1	13	271
22	Talbot	Boston	7	1	8	272
23	Lee	Barnet	8	0	8	275
24	Mayo	Lincoln	6	2	8	275
25	Burton	Shrewsbury	5	0	5	276

TEAM OF THE SEASON

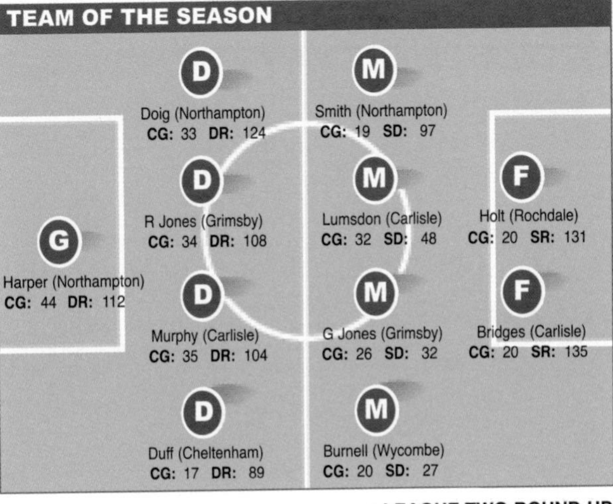

CARLISLE

Final Position: **1st**

NICKNAME: THE FOXES

KEY: ☐Won ☐Drawn ☐Lost

		Opponent	H/A	Result	Score	Scorers	Attendance
1	div3	Wycombe	A	D	1-1	Holmes 17	5,270
2	div3	Peterborough	H	W	1-0	Hawley 17	6,511
3	div3	Barnet	H	L	1-3	Livesey 24	6,650
4	div3	Wrexham	A	W	1-0	McGill 63	4,239
5	ccr1	Burnley	A	L	1-2	Murray 74	5,114
6	div3	Northampton	H	L	0-1		5,730
7	div3	Lincoln	A	D	0-0		4,303
8	div3	Bury	A	W	1-0	Nade 57	3,190
9	div3	Macclesfield	H	W	2-0	Hawley 77; Murray, G 82	5,190
10	div3	Cheltenham	A	W	3-2	Hawley 22,52; Aranalde 79	3,282
11	div3	Leyton Orient	H	L	2-3	McGill 4; Murphy 90	6,584
12	div3	Chester	A	L	0-2		3,394
13	div3	Bristol Rovers	H	L	1-3	O'Brien 7	5,317
14	div3	Oxford	A	L	0-1		5,392
15	div3	Mansfield	H	W	1-0	Hawley 80	5,293
16	div3	Notts County	A	D	0-0		5,347
17	div3	Stockport	H	W	6-0	Hawley 12,77,82; Holmes 36,41; Ikeme 38 og	5,664
18	facr1	Cheltenham	A	L	0-1		2,405
19	div3	Torquay	A	W	4-3	Hawley 3,15,64; Gray 83	2,352
20	div3	Oxford	H	W	2-1	Nade 17; Hawley 57	6,097
21	div3	Wycombe	H	L	0-1		7,033
22	div3	Rushden & D	A	W	4-0	Holmes 19; Hawley 32; Lumsdon 65; Bridges 90	2,216
23	div3	Peterborough	A	D	1-1	Bridges 80	3,689
24	div3	Wrexham	H	W	2-1	Gray 71; Lumsdon 81 pen	6,213
25	div3	Darlington	H	D	1-1	Lumsdon 29 pen	11,182
26	div3	Rochdale	H	W	2-1	Livesey 60; Bridges 80	6,897
27	div3	Grimsby	A	W	2-1	Aranalde 14,76	5,882
28	div3	Bury	H	W	4-0	Grand 10; Aranalde 28; Hawley 46; McGill 84	6,398
29	div3	Shrewsbury	A	L	1-2	Lumsdon 18 pen	4,493
30	div3	Boston	A	W	5-0	Hawley 5,90; Bridges 56,63,80	1,924
31	div3	Cheltenham	H	D	1-1	Bridges 40	6,759
32	div3	Macclesfield	A	L	0-3		4,140
33	div3	Chester	H	W	5-0	Murray 14; Bridges 45; Lumsdon 58 pen; Hawley 64; Murray, G 82	6,581
34	div3	Leyton Orient	A	D	0-0		5,833
35	div3	Shrewsbury	H	D	2-2	Lumsdon 2; Holmes 88	5,568
36	div3	Rushden & D	H	W	5-0	Holmes 2; Hawley 33,49; Hackney 60,61	6,922
37	div3	Barnet	A	W	2-1	Bridges 54; Hackney 75	2,870
38	div3	Northampton	A	W	3-0	Hawley 21; Bridges 74; Livesey 84	7,045
39	div3	Darlington	A	W	5-0	Gray 45; Holmes 60; Bridges 62; Murray, G 88; Grand 90	8,640
40	div3	Boston	H	W	4-2	Lumsdon 2; Hawley 20; Hackney 75,90	7,596
41	div3	Lincoln	H	W	1-0	Bridges 75	6,723
42	div3	Grimsby	H	W	1-0	Bridges 49	10,909
43	div3	Bristol Rovers	A	D	1-1	Hackney 75	6,181
44	div3	Notts County	H	W	2-1	Bridges 45,89	10,735
45	div3	Mansfield	A	D	1-1	Hawley 90	4,488
46	div3	Torquay	H	L	1-2	Aranalde 48	13,467
47	div3	Rochdale	A	W	2-0	Livesey 36; Murphy 44	4,439
48	div3	Stockport	A	D	0-0		10,006

TEAM OF THE SEASON

Pos	Player	Stats
G	Kieren Westwood	CG: 35 DR: 102
D	Peter Murphy	CG: 37 DR: 104
D	Paul Arnison	CG: 37 DR: 99
D	Zigor Aranalde	CG: 36 DR: 94
D	Kevin Gray	CG: 43 DR: 92
M	Chris Lumsdon	CG: 35 SD: 48
M	Adam Murray	CG: 28 SD: 44
M	Chris Billy	CG: 42 SD: 42
M	Brendan McGill	CG: 17 SD: 15
F	Michael Bridges	CG: 23 SR: 135
F	Karl Hawley	CG: 44 SR: 181

KEY PLAYER APPEARANCES

	PLAYER	POS	AGE	APP	MINS ON	GOALS	CARDS(Y)	CARDS(R)
1	Karl Hawley	ATT	24	46	3973	22	3	0
2	Chris Billy	MID	33	45	3897	0	9	0
3	Kevin Gray	DEF	34	44	3845	3	3	1
4	Paul Arnison	DEF	28	41	3471	0	6	0
5	Peter Murphy	DEF	25	44	3427	2	5	0
6	Zigor Aranalde	DEF	33	39	3369	5	6	1
7	Chris Lumsdon	MID	26	38	3225	7	5	0
8	Danny Livesey	DEF	21	36	3171	4	1	0
9	Kieren Westwood	GK	21	35	3150	0	2	0
10	Adam Murray	MID	24	37	2764	1	2	0
11	Derek Holmes	ATT	27	40	2192	7	0	0
12	Michael Bridges	ATT	27	25	2028	15	2	0
13	Brendan McGill	MID	25	26	1711	3	1	0
14	Simon Hackney	MID	22	30	1128	6	1	0
15	Raphael Nade	ATT	25	22	1037	2	0	0
16	Anthony Williams	GK	28	11	990	0	0	0
17	Glenn Murray	ATT	22	26	599	3	0	0
18	David Beharall	DEF	27	6	505	0	0	0

KEY PLAYERS - GOALSCORERS

Michael Bridges

Goals in the League	15
Contribution to Attacking Power Average number of minutes between League team goals while on pitch	46
Player Strike Rate Average number of minutes between League goals scored by player	135
Club Strike Rate Average number of minutes between League goals scored by club	49

	PLAYER	LGE GOALS	POWER	STRIKE RATE
1	Michael Bridges	15	46	135 mins
2	Karl Hawley	22	52	181 mins
3	Derek Holmes	7	44	313 mins
4	Chris Lumsdon	7	42	461 mins

KEY PLAYERS - MIDFIELDERS

Chris Lumsdon

Goals in the League	7
Defensive Rating Average number of mins between League goals conceded while on the pitch	90
Contribution to Attacking Power Average number of minutes between League team goals while on pitch	42
Scoring Difference Defensive Rating minus Contribution to Attacking Power	48

	PLAYER	LGE GOALS	DEF RATE	POWER	SCORE DIFF
1	Chris Lumsdon	7	90	42	48 mins
2	Adam Murray	1	99	55	44 mins
3	Chris Billy	0	95	53	42 mins
4	Brendan McGill	3	74	59	15 mins

KEY PLAYERS - DEFENDERS

Peter Murphy

Goals Conceded when he was on pitch	33
Defensive Rating Ave number of mins between League goals conceded while on the pitch	104
Clean Sheets In games when he played at least 70 minutes	16
Club Defensive Rating Average number of mins between League goals conceded by the club this season.	96

	PLAYER	CON LGE	CLEAN SHEETS	DEF RATE
1	Peter Murphy	33	16	104 mins
2	Paul Arnison	35	14	99 mins
3	Zigor Aranalde	36	16	94 mins
4	Kevin Gray	42	17	92 mins

KEY GOALKEEPER

Kieren Westwood

Goals Conceded in the League	31
Defensive Rating Ave number of mins between League goals conceded while on the pitch.	102
Counting Games Games when he played at least 70 mins	35
Clean Sheets In games when he played at least 70 mins	14

TOP POINT EARNERS

	PLAYER	GAMES	AV PTS
1	Derek Holmes	16	2.25
2	Paul Arnison	37	2.03
3	Chris Lumsdon	35	2.03
4	Michael Bridges	23	2.00
5	Danny Livesey	35	1.97
6	Kieren Westwood	35	1.97
7	Karl Hawley	44	1.86
8	Peter Murphy	37	1.81
9	Chris Billy	42	1.81
10	Adam Murray	28	1.79
	CLUB AVERAGE:		1.87

NORTHAMPTON TOWN

Final Position: **2nd**

NICKNAME: THE COBBLERS

KEY: Won / Drawn / Lost

							Attendance
1	div3	Lincoln	A	D	1-1	Bojic 53	5,397
2	div3	Barnet	H	L	1-2	Dudfield 32	5,817
3	div3	Wrexham	H	D	0-0		5,075
4	div3	Shrewsbury	A	D	1-1	Kirk 80 pen	3,562
5	ccr1	QPR	H	W	3-0	Kirk 19; McGleish 62; Sabin 90 pen	4,537
6	div3	Carlisle	A	W	1-0	Bojic 37	5,730
7	div3	Boston	H	W	3-2	Kirk 22; Taylor 45; Crowe 83	5,012
8	div3	Wycombe	A	D	1-1	Hunt 31	5,650
9	div3	Bury	H	D	1-1	Gilligan 83	5,147
10	div3	Macclesfield	A	W	4-1	McGleish 44 pen,79; Taylor 51; Low 90	2,014
11	ccr2	Norwich	A	L	0-2		16,766
12	div3	Cheltenham	H	L	1-2	Taylor 30	5,407
13	div3	Rushden & D	A	W	3-1	Gilligan 9; Gier 80 og; McGleish 84	5,211
14	div3	Darlington	H	D	0-0		5,182
15	div3	Bristol Rovers	A	D	0-0		6,912
16	div3	Oxford	H	W	1-0	Taylor 74	6,802
17	div3	Stockport	A	L	2-4	Junior Mendes 18; McGleish 31	4,150
18	div3	Grimsby	H	D	0-0		6,067
19	facr1	Wycombe	A	W	3-1	Doig 56; Smith 61; McGleish 80	3,974
20	div3	Chester	A	D	0-0		3,295
21	div3	Bristol Rovers	H	W	4-0	Kirk 34 pen,43; Smith 48; Bojic 89	5,716
22	div3	Lincoln	H	D	1-1	Low 90	5,174
23	facr2	Stevenage	A	D	2-2	Bojic 67; McGleish 82 pen	3,937
24	div3	Torquay	A	D	3-3	McGleish 21,67; Junior Mendes 77	2,010
25	div3	Barnet	A	W	1-0	McGleish 48 pen	2,544
26	facr2r	Stevenage	H	W	2-0	McGleish 44,45	4,407
27	div3	Shrewsbury	H	W	1-0	McGleish 50	5,380
28	div3	Mansfield	H	W	1-0	Hunt 66	6,112
29	div3	Peterborough	H	L	0-1		7,023
30	div3	Rochdale	A	D	1-1	Bojic 49	3,030
31	facr3	Crystal Palace	A	L	1-4	Low 12	10,391
32	div3	Leyton Orient	A	W	2-1	McGleish 35; Doig 54	5,445
33	div3	Macclesfield	H	W	5-1	Taylor 35,89; Kirk 38,90; McGleish 61	5,428
34	div3	Notts County	A	D	2-2	Crowe 69; Jess 77	4,884
35	div3	Bury	A	W	2-0	Parrish 29 og; Kirk 40	2,456
36	div3	Wycombe	H	D	0-0		6,438
37	div3	Rushden & D	H	W	2-0	Hunt 11; McGleish 86	7,036
38	div3	Cheltenham	A	L	1-3	McGleish 90	3,876
39	div3	Leyton Orient	H	D	1-1	Kirk 8	5,552
40	div3	Torquay	H	W	1-0	Taylor 81	5,636
41	div3	Wrexham	A	W	1-0	Gilligan 68	5,012
42	div3	Carlisle	H	L	0-3		7,045
43	div3	Mansfield	A	L	0-1		3,985
44	div3	Boston	A	W	1-0	Johnson, G 79	2,174
45	div3	Notts County	H	W	2-0	Kirk 39; Low 90	6,077
46	div3	Peterborough	A	W	1-0	McGleish 21	8,637
47	div3	Rochdale	H	D	2-2	Low 6; McGleish 35	5,732
48	div3	Darlington	A	W	1-0	McGleish 70	5,220
49	div3	Stockport	H	W	2-0	McGleish 54; Smith 73	6,544
50	div3	Oxford	A	W	3-1	Doig 16; Smith 69; Low 71	8,264
51	div3	Chester	H	W	1-0	McGleish 26	7,114
52	div3	Grimsby	A	D	1-1	Gilligan 90	8,458

TEAM OF THE SEASON

G — Lee Harper — CG: 46 DR: 112

D — Pedj Bojic — CG: 16 DR: 131

D — Chris Doig — CG: 35 DR: 124

D — Luke Chambers — CG: 41 DR: 113

D — Jason Crowe — CG: 40 DR: 107

M — Martin Smith — CG: 19 SD: 97

M — Joshua Low — CG: 26 SD: 67

M — David Hunt — CG: 27 SD: 61

M — Ian Taylor — CG: 33 SD: 42

F — Andy Kirk — CG: 15 SR: 194

F — Scott McGleish — CG: 37 SR: 200

KEY PLAYER APPEARANCES

	PLAYER	POS	AGE	APP	MINS ON	GOALS	CARDS(Y/R)	
1	Lee Harper	GK	34	46	4140	0	0	0
2	Luke Chambers	DEF	20	43	3725	0	4	0
3	Jason Crowe	DEF	27	41	3643	2	6	0
4	Scott McGleish	ATT	32	42	3405	17	1	0
5	Chris Doig	DEF	25	38	3219	2	2	0
6	Sean Dyche	DEF	35	35	2954	0	6	0
7	Ian Taylor	MID	38	33	2950	7	4	0
8	David Hunt	MID	23	40	2909	3	3	1
9	Eoin Jess	MID	35	38	2864	1	2	0
10	Joshua Low	MID	27	35	2562	5	3	0
11	Gavin Johnson	MID	35	24	1976	1	1	0
12	Martin Smith	MID	31	26	1910	3	2	0
13	Pedj Bojic	DEF	22	36	1838	4	0	1
14	Andy Kirk	ATT	27	29	1748	9	6	0
15	David Rowson	MID	29	29	1282	0	3	0
16	Junior Mendes	ATT	29	12	804	2	0	0
17	Jason Lee	ATT	35	11	768	0	2	0
18	Jamie Hand	MID	22	11	729	0	1	0

KEY PLAYERS - GOALSCORERS

Andy Kirk

Goals in the League	9
Contribution to Attacking Power Average number of minutes between League team goals while on pitch	10
Player Strike Rate Average number of minutes between League goals scored by player	194
Club Strike Rate Average number of minutes between League goals scored by club	65

	PLAYER	LGE GOALS		POWER	STRIKE RATE
1	Andy Kirk	9	10	65	194 mins
2	Scott McGleish	17	22	68	200 mins
3	Ian Taylor	7	7	67	421 mins
4	Pedj Bojic	4	5	63	460 mins

KEY PLAYERS - MIDFIELDERS

Martin Smith

Goals in the League	3
Defensive Rating Average number of mins between League goals conceded while on the pitch	159
Contribution to Attacking Power Average number of minutes between League team goals while on pitch	62
Scoring Difference Defensive Rating minus Contribution to Attacking Power	97

	PLAYER	LGE GOALS	DEF RATE	POWER	SCORE DIFF
1	Martin Smith	3	159	62	97 mins
2	Joshua Low	5	128	61	67 mins
3	David Hunt	3	126	65	61 mins
4	Ian Taylor	7	109	67	42 mins

KEY PLAYERS - DEFENDERS

Pedj Bojic

Goals Conceded when he was on pitch	14
Defensive Rating Ave number of mins between League goals conceded while on the pitch	131
Clean Sheets In games when he played at least 70 minutes	9
Club Defensive Rating Average number of mins between League goals conceded by the club this season.	112

	PLAYER	CON LGE	CLEAN SHEETS	DEF RATE
1	Pedj Bojic	14	9	131 mins
2	Chris Doig	26	20	124 mins
3	Luke Chambers	33	19	113 mins
4	Jason Crowe	34	21	107 mins

KEY GOALKEEPER

Lee Harper

Goals Conceded in the League	37
Defensive Rating Ave number of mins between League goals conceded while on the pitch.	112
Counting Games Games when he played at least 70 mins	46
Clean Sheets In games when he played at least 70 mins	23

TOP POINT EARNERS

	PLAYER	GAMES	AV PTS
1	Martin Smith	19	2.21
2	Gavin Johnson	20	1.95
3	Scott McGleish	37	1.92
4	Chris Doig	35	1.89
5	David Hunt	27	1.89
6	Joshua Low	26	1.88
7	Luke Chambers	41	1.83
8	Lee Harper	46	1.80
9	Jason Crowe	40	1.80
10	Sean Dyche	32	1.75
	CLUB AVERAGE:		1.80

LEYTON ORIENT

Final Position: **3rd**

NICKNAME: THE O'S

KEY: ☐Won ☐Drawn ☐Lost

	Comp	Opponent	H/A	Res	Score	Scorers	Attendance
1	div3	Macclesfield	H	W	2-1	Keith, J 2; Echanomi 90	3,600
2	div3	Bury	A	W	2-1	Tudor 21; Zakauni 73	2,053
3	div3	Darlington	A	W	1-0	Lockwood 41 pen	4,021
4	div3	Rochdale	H	L	1-4	Echanomi 76	4,223
5	ccr1	Luton	H	L	1-3	McMahon 90	2,383
6	div3	Cheltenham	A	D	1-1	Mackie 20	3,274
7	div3	Shrewsbury	H	L	0-1		3,742
8	div3	Bristol Rovers	H	L	2-3	Alexander 75; McMahon 89	3,481
9	div3	Barnet	A	W	3-2	Ibehre 40; Alexander 75,89	3,722
10	div3	Wrexham	H	D	1-1	Alexander 80	3,733
11	div3	Carlisle	A	W	3-2	Alexander 10; Lockwood 33 pen; Ibehre 36	6,584
12	div3	Torquay	H	W	2-1	Ibehre 25; Alexander 50	4,091
13	div3	Mansfield	H	W	3-1	Keith, J 16; Alexander 59; Echanomi 76	4,164
14	div3	Stockport	A	D	1-1	Alexander 71	3,901
15	div3	Lincoln	H	D	1-1	Alexander 18	4,837
16	div3	Grimsby	A	W	1-0	Easton 44	4,963
17	div3	Oxford	H	W	1-0	Easton 45	5,268
18	facr1	Chesterfield	H	D	0-0		3,554
19	div3	Peterborough	A	D	1-1	Miller 74	5,341
20	facr1r	Chesterfield	A	W	2-1	Mackie 18; Tudor 43	4,895
21	div3	Stockport	H	D	2-2	Raynes 24 og; Mackie 63	4,997
22	div3	Macclesfield	A	D	0-0		1,649
23	facr2	Rushden & D	A	W	1-0	Steele 66	3,245
24	div3	Chester	H	L	0-1		3,463
25	div3	Bury	H	L	0-1		4,095
26	div3	Rochdale	A	W	4-2	Alexander 10,47; Tudor 35; Mackie 76	2,666
27	div3	Rushden & D	H	W	5-1	Mackie 27; Steele 29,36; Ibehre 74; Easton 87	4,558
28	div3	Wycombe	A	L	2-4	Steele 21; Tudor 68	6,240
29	div3	Notts County	H	W	1-0	Ibehre 45	3,715
30	div3	Boston	A	W	2-1	Ibehre 44; Alexander 58	2,689
31	facr3	Fulham	A	W	2-1	Easton 17; Keith, J 44	13,394
32	div3	Northampton	H	L	1-2	McMahon 86	5,445
33	div3	Wrexham	A	W	2-1	Alexander 4; Lockwood 43 pen	5,031
34	facr4	Charlton	A	L	1-2	Steele 53	22,029
35	div3	Bristol Rovers	A	D	3-3	Ibehre 48,57; Simpson 62	5,966
36	div3	Torquay	A	L	0-2		2,687
37	div3	Carlisle	H	D	0-0		5,833
38	div3	Northampton	A	D	1-1	Mackie 65	5,552
39	div3	Chester	A	W	2-0	Lockwood 35 pen; Connor 72	2,210
40	div3	Darlington	H	W	1-0	Tudor 13	4,767
41	div3	Barnet	H	D	0-0		4,910
42	div3	Shrewsbury	A	D	3-3	Lockwood 19; Connor 26; Tann 47	3,471
43	div3	Cheltenham	H	W	1-0	Connor 23	4,879
44	div3	Rushden & D	A	L	0-1		3,679
45	div3	Wycombe	H	W	1-0	Connor 6	6,720
46	div3	Notts County	A	D	1-1	Corden 48	5,007
47	div3	Boston	H	W	2-0	Lockwood 51 pen; Connor 89	4,391
48	div3	Mansfield	A	W	1-0	Lockwood 75 pen	4,763
49	div3	Grimsby	H	D	0-0		6,582
50	div3	Lincoln	A	D	1-1	Mackie 2	5,660
51	div3	Peterborough	H	W	2-1	Lockwood 15 pen; Corden 70	6,591
52	div3	Oxford	A	W	3-2	Easton 17; Alexander 64; Steele 90	12,243

KEY PLAYER APPEARANCES

	PLAYER	POS	AGE	APP	MINS ON	GOALS	CARDS(Y	/R)
1	Michael Simpson	MID	32	45	3975	1	7	0
2	Glyn Garner	GK	29	43	3829	0	3	0
3	Matthew Lockwood	DEF	29	42	3757	8	4	0
4	Gabriel Zakauni	DEF	20	42	3715	1	5	0
5	Gary Alexander	ATT	26	46	3634	14	6	0
6	John Mackie	DEF	30	40	3526	6	12	1
7	Craig Easton	MID	27	41	3356	4	8	0
8	Joe Keith	MID	27	42	3348	2	4	0
9	Justin Miller	DEF	25	36	3010	1	4	0
10	Shane Tudor	MID	24	32	2443	4	4	1
11	Jabo Ibehre	ATT	23	32	1996	8	6	0
12	Daryl McMahon	MID	23	32	1811	2	2	0
13	Lee Steele	ATT	32	27	1312	4	2	0
14	Donny Barnard	DEF	22	27	1255	0	2	0
15	Paul Connor	ATT	27	16	1221	5	2	1
16	Adam Tann	DEF	24	10	801	1	2	0
17	Wayne Corden	MID	30	8	675	2	1	0
18	Wayne Carlisle	MID	26	12	494	0	0	0

KEY PLAYERS - GOALSCORERS

Jabo Ibehre

Goals in the League	8
Contribution to Attacking Power Average number of minutes between League team goals while on pitch	69
Player Strike Rate Average number of minutes between League goals scored by player	250
Club Strike Rate Average number of minutes between League goals scored by club	62

	PLAYER	LGE GOALS	POWER	STRIKE RATE
1	Jabo Ibehre	8	69	250 mins
2	Gary Alexander	14	60	260 mins
3	Matthew Lockwood	8	60	470 mins
4	John Mackie	6	57	588 mins

KEY PLAYERS - MIDFIELDERS

Craig Easton

Goals in the League	4
Defensive Rating Average number of mins between League goals conceded while on the pitch	86
Contribution to Attacking Power Average number of minutes between League team goals while on pitch	60
Scoring Difference Defensive Rating minus Contribution to Attacking Power	26

	PLAYER	LGE GOALS	DEF RATE	POWER	SCORE DIFF
1	Craig Easton	4	86	60	26 mins
2	Daryl McMahon	2	79	58	21 mins
3	Michael Simpson	1	81	63	18 mins
4	Joe Keith	2	76	63	13 mins

KEY PLAYERS - DEFENDERS

Matthew Lockwood

Goals Conceded when he was on pitch	44
Defensive Rating Ave number of mins between League goals conceded while on the pitch	85
Clean Sheets In games when he played at least 70 minutes	14
Club Defensive Rating Average number of mins between League goals conceded by the club this season.	81

	PLAYER	CON LGE	CLEAN SHEETS	DEF RATE
1	Matthew Lockwood	44	14	85 mins
2	Justin Miller	36	10	84 mins
3	Gabriel Zakauni	46	12	81 mins
4	John Mackie	44	12	80 mins

TEAM OF THE SEASON

G — Glyn Garner CG: 42 DR: 78

D — Matthew Lockwood CG: 41 DR: 85

D — Justin Miller CG: 32 DR: 84

D — Gabriel Zakauni CG: 41 DR: 81

D — John Mackie CG: 38 DR: 80

M — Craig Easton CG: 36 SD: 26

M — Daryl McMahon CG: 16 SD: 21

M — Michael Simpson CG: 43 SD: 18

M — Joe Keith CG: 30 SD: 13

F — Jabo Ibehre CG: 17 SR: 250

F — Gary Alexander CG: 37 SR: 260

KEY GOALKEEPER

Glyn Garner

Goals Conceded in the League	49
Defensive Rating Ave number of mins between League goals conceded while on the pitch.	78
Counting Games Games when he played at least 70 mins	42
Clean Sheets In games when he played at least 70 mins	12

TOP POINT EARNERS

	PLAYER	GAMES	AV PTS
1	Joe Keith	30	2.07
2	John Mackie	38	1.97
3	Jabo Ibehre	17	1.94
4	Gary Alexander	37	1.89
5	Matthew Lockwood	41	1.88
6	Glyn Garner	42	1.83
7	Daryl McMahon	16	1.81
8	Gabriel Zakauni	41	1.78
9	Craig Easton	36	1.78
10	Justin Miller	32	1.78
	CLUB AVERAGE:		1.76

GRIMSBY TOWN

Final Position: **4th**

NICKNAME: THE MARINERS

KEY: Won, Drawn, Lost

							Attendance
1	div3	Oxford	H	D	1-1	Coldicott 62	4,706
2	div3	Bristol Rovers	A	W	2-1	Gritton 75; Jones 88	6,300
3	div3	Darlington	H	L	0-1		3,904
4	ccr1	Derby	A	W	1-0	Jones, G 11	11,756
5	div3	Barnet	A	W	1-0	Andrew 46	2,447
6	div3	Rushden & D	H	W	2-0	McDermott 8; Kamudimba 51 pen	3,774
7	div3	Stockport	H	L	1-3	Jones, G 33	5,381
8	div3	Chester	A	W	2-1	Kamudimba 50 pen; Reddy 80	3,095
9	div3	Peterborough	A	W	1-0	Jones, G 48	4,263
10	div3	Torquay	H	W	3-0	Jones 43; Reddy 66,77	4,026
11	ccr2	Tottenham	H	W	1-0	Kamudimba Kalala 89	8,206
12	div3	Boston	A	D	1-1	Kamudimba 12 pen	4,077
13	div3	Notts County	H	W	4-0	Jones 28; Gritton 45; Kamudimba 46; Cohen 81	5,577
14	div3	Shrewsbury	A	D	0-0		4,607
15	div3	Wycombe	H	L	0-1		7,206
16	div3	Cheltenham	A	W	3-0	Bolland 15; Reddy 65; Cohen 90	3,500
17	div3	Leyton Orient	H	L	0-1		4,963
18	ccr3	Newcastle	H	L	0-1		9,311
19	div3	Northampton	A	D	0-0		6,067
20	facr1	Bristol Rovers	H	L	1-2	Jones, G 49	2,680
21	div3	Macclesfield	H	W	3-1	Jones, G 41; Newey 61; Cohen 80	3,658
22	div3	Wycombe	A	L	1-3	Reddy 37	6,125
23	div3	Oxford	A	W	3-2	Parkinson 3; Bolland 61; Cohen 90	4,323
24	div3	Rochdale	H	W	4-1	Jones, G 67; Cohen 70; Jones 74; Reddy 90	3,896
25	div3	Bristol Rovers	H	L	0-1		4,739
26	div3	Bury	A	W	2-1	Jones, G 29; Cohen 75	3,249
27	div3	Lincoln	H	W	3-0	Toner 9; Reddy 25; Parkinson 44	6,056
28	div3	Wrexham	A	W	2-1	Reddy 52; Downey 84	4,527
29	div3	Carlisle	H	L	1-2	Toner 8	5,882
30	div3	Mansfield	H	W	2-1	Reddy 9; Parkinson 86	4,506
31	div3	Darlington	A	D	0-0		3,924
32	div3	Torquay	A	D	2-2	Parkinson 6; Futcher 81	2,559
33	div3	Stockport	A	L	1-2	Reddy 48	3,860
34	div3	Peterborough	H	L	1-2	Reddy 29	4,462
35	div3	Notts County	A	W	1-0	Reddy 40	6,456
36	div3	Boston	H	W	1-0	Reddy 72	5,028
37	div3	Mansfield	A	L	1-2	Woodhouse 79	3,053
38	div3	Chester	H	W	1-0	Jones, G 42	4,058
39	div3	Rushden & D	A	D	1-1	Futcher 61	3,366
40	div3	Barnet	H	W	3-0	Jones, G 39,41; Bolland 45	5,147
41	div3	Bury	H	W	2-1	Jones, G 14,20	5,196
42	div3	Rochdale	A	D	2-2	Toner 24 pen; Bolland 82	1,865
43	div3	Lincoln	A	L	0-5		7,182
44	div3	Wrexham	H	W	2-0	Jones, G 25; Reddy 88	6,058
45	div3	Carlisle	A	L	0-1		10,909
46	div3	Shrewsbury	H	D	1-1	Goodfellow 66 pen	5,935
47	div3	Leyton Orient	A	D	0-0		6,582
48	div3	Cheltenham	H	W	1-0	Jones, G 69	5,863
49	div3	Macclesfield	A	D	1-1	Jones, G 40	3,849
50	div3	Northampton	H	D	1-1	Kamudimba 75 pen	8,458
51	d3po1	Lincoln	A	W	1-0	Jones, G 22	8,037
52	d3po2	Lincoln	H	W	2-1	Futcher 60; Jones, G 82	8,062
53	d3pof	Cheltenham	H	L	0-1		29,196

TEAM OF THE SEASON

G	Steve Mildenhall	CG: 46 DR: 94
D	Robert Jones	CG: 36 DR: 108
D	John McDermott	CG: 27 DR: 101
D	Justin Whittle	CG: 31 DR: 98
D	Gary Croft	CG: 25 DR: 93
M	Jean-Paul Kamudimba	CG: 12 SD: 61
M	Gary Jones	CG: 27 SD: 32
M	Ciaran Toner	CG: 21 SD: 30
M	Paul Bolland	CG: 42 SD: 23
F	Michael Reddy	CG: 39 SR: 257
F	Gary Cohen	CG: 26 SR: 472

KEY PLAYER APPEARANCES

	PLAYER	POS	AGE	APP	MINS ON	GOALS	CARDS(Y/R)	
1	Steve Mildenhall	GK	28	46	4140	0	2	0
2	Paul Bolland	MID	26	44	3887	3	7	1
3	Michael Reddy	ATT	26	44	3603	14	5	0
4	Robert Jones	DEF	26	40	3355	4	4	0
5	Tom Newey	MID	23	38	3071	1	11	1
6	Gary Jones	MID	31	40	2870	12	5	0
7	Justin Whittle	DEF	35	32	2834	0	1	0
8	Gary Cohen	ATT	22	39	2829	6	5	0
9	Andy Parkinson	MID	27	40	2775	4	2	0
10	John McDermott	DEF	37	32	2621	1	3	0
11	Gary Croft	DEF	32	33	2428	0	5	0
12	Ciaran Toner	MID	25	31	2133	3	2	0
13	Curtis Woodhouse	MID	26	16	1440	1	1	0
14	Jean-Paul Kamudimba	MID	24	21	1406	5	4	0
15	Ben Futcher	DEF	25	15	1155	2	4	0
16	Martin Gritton	ATT	28	26	1036	2	1	0
17	Junior Mendes	ATT	29	15	943	0	1	0
18	Simon Ramsden	DEF	24	12	708	0	1	0

KEY PLAYERS - GOALSCORERS

Gary Jones

Goals in the League	12
Contribution to Attacking Power Average number of minutes between League team goals while on pitch	61
Player Strike Rate Average number of minutes between League goals scored by player	239
Club Strike Rate Average number of minutes between League goals scored by club	65

	PLAYER	LGE GOALS	POWER	STRIKE RATE
1	Gary Jones	12	61	239 mins
2	Michael Reddy	14	64	257 mins
3	Jean-Paul Kamudimba	5	56	281 mins
4	Gary Cohen	6	60	472 mins

KEY PLAYERS - MIDFIELDERS

Jean-Paul Kamudimba

Goals in the League	5
Defensive Rating Average number of mins between League goals conceded while on the pitch	117
Contribution to Attacking Power Average number of minutes between League team goals while on pitch	56
Scoring Difference Defensive Rating minus Contribution to Attacking Power	61

	PLAYER	LGE GOALS	DEF RATE	POWER	SCORE DIFF
1	Jean-Paul Kamudimba	5	117	56	61 mins
2	Gary Jones	12	93	61	32 mins
3	Ciaran Toner	3	89	59	30 mins
4	Paul Bolland	3	88	65	23 mins

KEY PLAYERS - DEFENDERS

Robert Jones

Goals Conceded when he was on pitch	31
Defensive Rating Ave number of mins between League goals conceded while on the pitch	108
Clean Sheets In games when he played at least 70 minutes	15
Club Defensive Rating Average number of mins between League goals conceded by the club this season.	94

	PLAYER	CON LGE	CLEAN SHEETS	DEF RATE
1	Robert Jones	31	15	108 mins
2	John McDermott	26	11	101 mins
3	Justin Whittle	29	13	98 mins
4	Gary Croft	26	10	93 mins

KEY GOALKEEPER

Steve Mildenhall

Goals Conceded in the League	44
Defensive Rating Ave number of mins between League goals conceded while on the pitch.	94
Counting Games Games when he played at least 70 mins	46
Clean Sheets In games when he played at least 70 mins	17

TOP POINT EARNERS

	PLAYER	GAMES	AV PTS
1	Gary Jones	27	2.04
2	Jean-Paul Kamudimba	12	2.00
3	John McDermott	27	1.81
4	Ciaran Toner	21	1.81
5	Justin Whittle	31	1.81
6	Gary Croft	25	1.80
7	Andy Parkinson	24	1.79
8	Gary Cohen	26	1.77
9	Steve Mildenhall	46	1.70
10	Michael Reddy	39	1.67
	CLUB AVERAGE:		1.70

CHELTENHAM

PROMOTED VIA THE PLAY-OFFS Final Position: **5th**

NICKNAME: THE ROBINS

KEY: Won / Drawn / Lost

#	Comp	Opponent	H/A	Res	Score	Scorers	Attendance
1	div3	Bury	H	W	2-1	Odejayi 9; Armstrong 74	2,967
2	div3	Macclesfield	A	D	2-2	Melligan 18; Odejayi 82	1,601
3	div3	Rochdale	A	D	1-1	Spencer 37	2,344
4	div3	Boston	H	W	3-0	Spencer 19; Victory 43; Futcher 45 og	2,680
5	ccr1	Brentford	H	W	5-0	Melligan 5; Caines 55; Victory 69; McCann 78,81	2,113
6	div3	Leyton Orient	H	D	1-1	Finnigan 90	3,274
7	div3	Wycombe	A	D	0-0		5,244
8	div3	Barnet	H	D	1-1	Finnigan 44	3,343
9	div3	Wrexham	A	L	0-2		3,671
10	div3	Carlisle	H	L	2-3	Melligan 19; McCann 87 pen	3,282
11	ccr2	Sunderland	A	L	0-1		11,969
12	div3	Northampton	A	W	2-1	Odejayi 20,45	5,407
13	div3	Peterborough	H	W	2-1	McCann 37; Armstrong 90	2,531
14	div3	Torquay	H	L	0-1		3,578
15	div3	Lincoln	A	W	1-0	Odejayi 76	4,776
16	div3	Grimsby	H	L	0-3		3,500
17	div3	Darlington	A	L	1-3	Connolly 30	3,315
18	div3	Mansfield	H	L	0-2		3,033
19	facr1	Carlisle	H	W	1-0	McCann 64	2,405
20	div3	Notts County	A	W	3-2	Wilson 35; Victory 78; McCann 84	4,903
21	div3	Lincoln	H	W	4-1	Guinan 31; Wilson 64,66; Gillespie 90	3,078
22	div3	Bury	A	W	1-0	Melligan 43	2,251
23	facr2	Oxford	H	D	1-1	Guinan 14	4,592
24	div3	Oxford	H	L	1-2	Guinan 11	2,852
25	div3	Macclesfield	H	D	2-2	Odejayi 85; Caines 90	2,804
26	facr2r	Oxford	A	W	2-1	Odejayi 51; Wilson 79	3,455
27	div3	Boston	A	D	0-0		1,906
28	div3	Chester	H	W	1-0	Wilson 49	3,819
29	div3	Rushden & D	A	W	1-0	McCann 48	2,244
30	div3	Shrewsbury	H	W	1-0	Gillespie 70	3,474
31	div3	Stockport	A	D	2-2	Wilson 69; Finnigan 90	3,777
32	facr3	Chester	H	D	2-2	Melligan 59 pen,74 pen	4,741
33	div3	Barnet	A	D	1-1	Melligan 8	1,366
34	div3	Bristol Rovers	H	L	2-3	Gillespie 70; Odejayi 88	6,005
35	facr3r	Chester	A	W	1-0	Odejayi 52	5,096
36	div3	Carlisle	A	D	1-1	Gray 90 og	6,759
37	facr4	Newcastle	H	L	0-2		7,022
38	div3	Peterborough	A	L	0-1		3,901
39	div3	Northampton	H	W	3-1	Guinan 38; Odejayi 45; Melligan 71 pen	3,876
40	div3	Bristol Rovers	A	W	1-0	Wilson 73	6,885
41	div3	Oxford	A	D	1-1	Gillespie 53	5,232
42	div3	Rochdale	H	D	1-1	Guinan 43	3,184
43	div3	Wycombe	H	W	2-1	Caines 72; Gillespie 90	4,069
44	div3	Leyton Orient	A	L	0-1		4,879
45	div3	Chester	A	W	1-0	Wilson 2	2,281
46	div3	Wrexham	H	D	2-2	McCann 35; Guinan 56	2,737
47	div3	Rushden & D	H	W	3-1	Melligan 7; Wilson 13; Finnigan 33	3,447
48	div3	Shrewsbury	A	L	0-2		3,724
49	div3	Stockport	H	D	3-3	Odejayi 12; Wilson 66; McCann 88 pen	3,525
50	div3	Torquay	A	W	2-1	Spencer 60; Odejayi 70	3,336
51	div3	Darlington	H	D	1-1	McCann 59 pen	3,851
52	div3	Grimsby	A	L	0-1		5,863
53	div3	Notts County	H	W	2-0	Guinan 3; Victory 82	4,518
54	div3	Mansfield	A	W	5-0	Gillespie 34; Vincent 45; McCann 50; Bird 81 pen; Odejayi 85	3,728
55	d3po1	Wycombe	A	W	2-1	Finnigan 43; Guinan 75	5,936
56	d3po2	Wycombe	H	D	0-0		6,813
57	d3pof	Grimsby	A	W	1-0	Guinan 63	29,196

TEAM OF THE SEASON

G — Shane Higgs — CG: 45 DR: 78

D — Shane Duff — CG: 17 DR: 89

D — Jeremy Gill — CG: 41 DR: 83

D — Gavin Caines — CG: 34 DR: 81

D — Jamie Victory — CG: 18 DR: 80

M — John Finnigan — CG: 35 SD: 17

M — Brian Wilson — CG: 40 SD: 15

M — Grant McCann — CG: 33 SD: 14

M — John Melligan — CG: 36 SD: 4

F — Kayode Odejayi — CG: 32 SR: 294

F — Stephen Guinan — CG: 19 SR: 345

KEY PLAYER APPEARANCES

	PLAYER	POS	AGE	APP	MINS ON	GOALS	CARDS(Y/R)	
1	Shane Higgs	GK	29	45	4050	0	0	0
2	Jeremy Gill	DEF	35	42	3645	0	4	0
3	Brian Wilson	MID	23	43	3570	9	5	0
4	John Melligan	MID	25	42	3394	6	2	0
5	John Finnigan	MID	30	39	3262	4	4	0
6	Grant McCann	MID	26	39	3252	8	6	0
7	Kayode Odejayi	ATT	24	41	3231	11	5	0
8	Gavin Caines	DEF	22	39	3154	2	4	0
9	Craig Armstrong	MID	31	34	2693	2	5	0
10	Michael Townsend	DEF	20	31	2668	0	1	1
11	Stephen Guinan	ATT	30	30	2069	6	3	0
12	Damian Spencer	ATT	24	46	2035	3	3	0
13	David Bird	MID	21	36	1906	1	0	0
14	Jamie Victory	DEF	30	22	1763	2	0	0
15	Shane Duff	DEF	24	20	1598	0	3	0
16	Michael Taylor	MID	23	10	860	0	0	0
17	Mick Bell	DEF	34	9	598	0	0	0
18	Steven Gillespie	ATT	21	14	472	5	1	1

KEY PLAYERS - GOALSCORERS

Kayode Odejayi

Goals in the League	11
Contribution to Attacking Power Average number of minutes between League team goals while on pitch	65
Player Strike Rate Average number of minutes between League goals scored by player	294
Club Strike Rate Average number of minutes between League goals scored by club	64

	PLAYER	LGE GOALS	POWER	STRIKE RATE
1	Kayode Odejayi	11	65	294 mins
2	Stephen Guinan	6	74	345 mins
3	Brian Wilson	9	63	397 mins
4	Grant McCann	8	63	407 mins

KEY PLAYERS - MIDFIELDERS

John Finnigan

Goals in the League	4
Defensive Rating Average number of mins between League goals conceded while on the pitch	84
Contribution to Attacking Power Average number of minutes between League team goals while on pitch	67
Scoring Difference Defensive Rating minus Contribution to Attacking Power	17

	PLAYER	LGE GOALS	DEF RATE	POWER	SCORE DIFF
1	John Finnigan	4	84	67	17 mins
2	Brian Wilson	9	78	63	15 mins
3	Grant McCann	8	77	63	14 mins
4	John Melligan	6	75	71	4 mins

KEY PLAYERS - DEFENDERS

Shane Duff

Goals Conceded when he was on pitch	18
Defensive Rating Ave number of mins between League goals conceded while on the pitch	89
Clean Sheets In games when he played at least 70 minutes	8
Club Defensive Rating Average number of mins between League goals conceded by the club this season.	78

	PLAYER	CON LGE	CLEAN SHEETS	DEF RATE
1	Shane Duff	18	8	89 mins
2	Jeremy Gill	44	10	83 mins
3	Gavin Caines	39	10	81 mins
4	Jamie Victory	22	5	80 mins

KEY GOALKEEPER

Shane Higgs

Goals Conceded in the League	52
Defensive Rating Ave number of mins between League goals conceded while on the pitch.	78
Counting Games Games when he played at least 70 mins	45
Clean Sheets In games when he played at least 70 mins	12

TOP POINT EARNERS

	PLAYER	GAMES	AV PTS
1	Stephen Guinan	19	2.11
2	Jamie Victory	18	1.83
3	Shane Duff	17	1.76
4	Gavin Caines	34	1.68
5	Jeremy Gill	41	1.61
6	John Finnigan	35	1.60
7	Shane Higgs	45	1.58
8	Brian Wilson	40	1.58
9	Grant McCann	33	1.55
10	John Melligan	36	1.50
	CLUB AVERAGE:		1.57

WYCOMBE WANDERERS

Final Position: **6th**

NICKNAME: THE CHAIRBOYS

KEY: ☐Won ☐Drawn ☐Lost

						Attendance
1	div3	Carlisle	H	D	1-1 Mooney 37	5,270
2	div3	Rochdale	A	W	2-1 Williamson 7; Bloomfield 23	2,755
3	div3	Oxford	A	D	2-2 Tyson 70,85	6,364
4	div3	Bury	H	W	4-0 Johnson 37; Mooney 68; Tyson 74,80	4,421
5	ccr1	Swindon	A	W	3-1 Stonebridge 12; Tyson 62; Dixon 75	3,976
6	div3	Shrewsbury	A	D	1-1 Tyson 32	3,533
7	div3	Cheltenham	H	D	0-0	5,244
8	div3	Northampton	H	D	1-1 Williamson 58	5,650
9	div3	Stockport	A	D	3-3 Tyson 13,21 pen,53	3,507
10	div3	Barnet	H	W	1-0 Tyson 21	4,994
11	ccr2	Aston Villa	H	L	3-8 Tyson 6; Johnson 18; Mooney 39	5,365
12	div3	Mansfield	A	W	3-2 Betsy 1,15,43	3,237
13	div3	Wrexham	H	W	4-1 Tyson 16,81; Betsy 22; Mooney 58	4,166
14	div3	Chester	H	D	3-3 Mooney 24,50; Johnson 44	5,145
15	div3	Grimsby	A	W	1-0 Mooney 11	7,206
16	div3	Rushden & D	H	D	0-0	5,231
17	div3	Lincoln	A	W	2-1 Williamson 69,90	4,347
18	div3	Peterborough	H	D	2-2 Johnson 74; Easton 80	5,214
19	facr1	Northampton	H	L	1-3 Burnell 90	3,974
20	div3	Darlington	A	D	1-1 Mooney 66	3,928
21	div3	Grimsby	H	W	3-1 Griffin 20; Bloomfield 36; Johnson 78	6,125
22	div3	Carlisle	A	W	1-0 Johnson 88	7,033
23	div3	Boston	H	D	1-1 Bloomfield 71	4,372
24	div3	Rochdale	H	W	3-0 Mooney 9,53; Griffin 85	4,928
25	div3	Bury	A	L	1-2 Betsy 21	2,384
26	div3	Torquay	A	D	2-2 Betsy 71; Lawless 86 og	3,733
27	div3	Leyton Orient	H	W	4-2 Griffin 2; Zakauni 22 og; Bloomfield 50; Oakes 54	6,240
28	div3	Bristol Rovers	A	W	2-1 Mooney 4 pen,46	6,828
29	div3	Macclesfield	H	L	4-5 Mooney 31 pen,61; Martin 71; Morley 76 og	5,364
30	div3	Notts County	H	W	2-0 Collins 58; Torres 72	5,185
31	div3	Barnet	A	D	0-0	3,602
32	div3	Stockport	H	D	1-1 Stonebridge 89	5,512
33	div3	Northampton	A	D	0-0	6,438
34	div3	Wrexham	A	L	0-2	4,311
35	div3	Mansfield	H	D	2-2 Mooney 53; Oakes 77	5,041
36	div3	Notts County	A	W	2-1 Bowditch 32; Stonebridge 76	3,710
37	div3	Boston	A	D	1-1 Betsy 71	2,283
38	div3	Oxford	H	W	2-1 Betsy 17; Mooney 60	7,016
39	div3	Cheltenham	A	L	1-2 Johnson 16	4,069
40	div3	Shrewsbury	H	W	2-0 Bloomfield 15; Martin 73	5,035
41	div3	Torquay	H	L	0-1	7,134
42	div3	Leyton Orient	A	L	0-1	6,720
43	div3	Bristol Rovers	H	L	1-3 Easter 81	6,355
44	div3	Macclesfield	A	L	1-2 Martin 86	1,869
45	div3	Chester	A	L	0-1	2,797
46	div3	Lincoln	H	L	0-3	5,750
47	div3	Rushden & D	A	W	3-1 Mooney 62,88 pen; Johnson 65	3,396
48	div3	Darlington	H	L	0-1	5,840
49	div3	Peterborough	A	W	2-0 Easter 14; Williamson 87	5,376
50	d3po1	Cheltenham	H	L	1-2 Mooney 90	5,936
51	d3po2	Cheltenham	A	D	0-0	6,813

TEAM OF THE SEASON

G — Frank Talia CG: 35 DR: 62

D — Clint Easton CG: 35 DR: 77

D — Danny Senda CG: 44 DR: 76

D — Roger Johnson CG: 45 DR: 72

D — Mike Williamson CG: 38 DR: 72

M — Joe Burnell CG: 21 SD: 27

M — Kevin Betsy CG: 41 SD: 16

M — Stefan Oakes CG: 25 SD: 12

M — Matt Bloomfield CG: 27 SD: 4

F — Nathan Tyson CG: 14 SR: 116

F — Tommy Mooney CG: 44 SR: 231

KEY PLAYER APPEARANCES

	PLAYER	POS	AGE	APP	MINS ON	GOALS	CARDS(Y/R)	
1	Roger Johnson	DEF	23	45	4050	7	6	0
2	Danny Senda	DEF	25	44	3941	0	4	0
3	Tommy Mooney	ATT	34	45	3934	17	2	0
4	Kevin Betsy	MID	28	42	3699	8	3	1
5	Clint Easton	DEF	28	44	3532	1	4	0
6	Mike Williamson	DEF	22	40	3463	5	0	0
7	Frank Talia	GK	33	35	3150	0	1	0
8	Matt Bloomfield	MID	22	39	2945	5	4	0
9	Stefan Oakes	MID	27	37	2633	2	4	0
10	Joe Burnell	MID	25	33	2328	0	3	0
11	Robert Lee	MID	40	32	2067	0	2	0
12	Sergio Torres	MID	22	24	1441	1	1	0
13	Nathan Tyson	ATT	24	15	1273	11	1	0
14	Charlie Griffin	ATT	27	21	1253	3	0	0
15	Russell Martin	MID	20	23	1215	3	2	0
16	Ian Stonebridge	ATT	24	27	1011	2	0	0
17	Jermaine Easter	ATT	24	15	739	2	2	0
18	Dean Bowditch	MID	20	11	721	1	0	0

KEY PLAYERS - GOALSCORERS

Nathan Tyson

Goals in the League	11
Contribution to Attacking Power Average number of minutes between League team goals while on pitch	45
Player Strike Rate Average number of minutes between League goals scored by player	116
Club Strike Rate Average number of minutes between League goals scored by club	58

	PLAYER	LGE GOALS	POWER	STRIKE RATE
1	Nathan Tyson	11	45	116 mins
2	Tommy Mooney	17	56	231 mins
3	Kevin Betsy	8	57	462 mins
4	Roger Johnson	7	58	579 mins

KEY PLAYERS - MIDFIELDERS

Joe Burnell

Goals in the League	0
Defensive Rating Average number of mins between League goals conceded while on the pitch	90
Contribution to Attacking Power Average number of minutes between League team goals while on pitch	63
Scoring Difference Defensive Rating minus Contribution to Attacking Power	27

	PLAYER	LGE GOALS	DEF RATE	POWER	SCORE DIFF
1	Joe Burnell	0	90	63	27 mins
2	Kevin Betsy	8	73	57	16 mins
3	Stefan Oakes	2	66	54	12 mins
4	Matt Bloomfield	5	67	63	4 mins

KEY PLAYERS - DEFENDERS

Clint Easton

Goals Conceded when he was on pitch	46
Defensive Rating Ave number of mins between League goals conceded while on the pitch	77
Clean Sheets In games when he played at least 70 minutes	12
Club Defensive Rating Average number of mins between League goals conceded by the club this season.	74

	PLAYER	CON LGE	CLEAN SHEETS	DEF RATE
1	Clint Easton	46	12	77 mins
2	Danny Senda	52	12	76 mins
3	Roger Johnson	56	11	72 mins
4	Mike Williamson	48	11	72 mins

KEY GOALKEEPER

Frank Talia

Goals Conceded in the League	51
Defensive Rating Ave number of mins between League goals conceded while on the pitch.	62
Counting Games Games when he played at least 70 mins	35
Clean Sheets In games when he played at least 70 mins	5

TOP POINT EARNERS

	PLAYER	GAMES	AV PTS
1	Nathan Tyson	14	1.86
2	Clint Easton	35	1.80
3	Robert Lee	15	1.80
4	Matt Bloomfield	27	1.70
5	Mike Williamson	38	1.58
6	Tommy Mooney	44	1.55
7	Danny Senda	44	1.55
8	Roger Johnson	45	1.51
9	Kevin Betsy	41	1.49
10	Stefan Oakes	25	1.48
	CLUB AVERAGE:		1.54

LINCOLN CITY

Final Position: **7th**

NICKNAME: THE RED IMPS — KEY: Won / Drawn / Lost

	Comp	Opponent	H/A	Res	Score	Scorers	Attendance
1	div3	Northampton	H	D	1-1	Birch 64	5,397
2	div3	Chester	A	D	2-2	Brown 38; Birch 43	2,637
3	div3	Notts County	A	L	1-2	Brown 20	6,153
4	div3	Oxford	H	W	2-1	Birch 62; Asamoah 74	3,724
5	ccr1	Crewe	H	W	5-1	Beevers 6; Molango 35; Birch 64,67; Robinson, M 83	2,782
6	div3	Rushden & D	A	D	1-1	Keates 19	2,860
7	div3	Carlisle	H	D	0-0		4,303
8	div3	Bristol Rovers	A	D	0-0		5,057
9	div3	Wrexham	H	W	2-0	Brown 64; Keates 90	2,956
10	div3	Peterborough	H	L	1-2	Keates 85	5,526
11	ccr2	Fulham	A	L	4-5	Green 70; Volz 82 og; Kerr 101; Robinson, M 115	5,365
12	div3	Torquay	A	L	1-2	McAuley 10	2,281
13	div3	Stockport	H	W	2-0	Birch 53,78	3,508
14	div3	Bury	A	D	1-1	Keates 44	4,118
15	div3	Cheltenham	H	L	0-1		4,776
16	div3	Leyton Orient	A	D	1-1	Butcher 70	4,837
17	div3	Wycombe	H	L	1-2	Robinson, M 52	4,347
18	div3	Rochdale	A	W	2-1	Robinson, M 15; Brown 36	3,420
19	facr1	MK Dons	H	D	1-1	Robinson, M 29	3,508
20	div3	Shrewsbury	H	D	1-1	Brown 51	3,748
21	facr1r	MK Dons	A	L	1-2	Mayo 24 pen	4,029
22	div3	Cheltenham	A	L	1-4	Mayo 60	3,078
23	div3	Northampton	A	D	1-1	Birch 14	5,174
24	div3	Macclesfield	H	D	2-2	McAuley 72; Brown 79	3,171
25	div3	Chester	H	W	3-1	Logan 68; Mayo 70 pen; Asamoah 90	3,563
26	div3	Oxford	A	W	1-0	Logan 80	3,795
27	div3	Boston	H	D	0-0		7,077
28	div3	Grimsby	A	L	0-3		6,056
29	div3	Darlington	H	D	2-2	McAuley 17; Robinson, M 19	4,008
30	div3	Mansfield	A	D	0-0		4,946
31	div3	Wrexham	A	D	1-1	Yeo 63	3,809
32	div3	Barnet	H	W	4-1	Yeo 38; McCombe 63; Robinson, M 81; Kerr 82	4,033
33	div3	Peterborough	A	D	1-1	Yeo 85	6,227
34	div3	Bristol Rovers	H	W	1-0	Birch 73	4,258
35	div3	Stockport	A	W	3-2	Gritton 62; Yeo 69; Frecklington 79	4,506
36	div3	Torquay	H	W	2-0	Kerr 12; Hughes 89	4,454
37	div3	Barnet	A	W	3-2	McCombe 54; Birch 65; Brown 87	1,695
38	div3	Macclesfield	A	D	1-1	Hughes 76	2,268
39	div3	Notts County	H	W	2-1	Green 45; McCombe 79	5,262
40	div3	Rushden & D	H	D	2-2	Yeo 22; McCombe 90	4,383
41	div3	Boston	A	L	1-2	Robinson, M 66	4,476
42	div3	Grimsby	H	W	5-0	Foster 12; Forrester 16; Mayo 38 pen; Robinson, M 44; Beevers 83	7,182
43	div3	Carlisle	A	L	0-1		6,723
44	div3	Darlington	A	L	2-4	Robinson, M 53; Forrester 76	4,028
45	div3	Mansfield	H	D	1-1	Green 53	6,062
46	div3	Bury	H	D	1-1	Frecklington 86	4,439
47	div3	Wycombe	A	W	3-0	Forrester 61,81; Green 73	5,750
48	div3	Leyton Orient	H	D	1-1	Forrester 36	5,660
49	div3	Shrewsbury	A	W	1-0	McAuley 62	5,170
50	div3	Rochdale	H	D	1-1	McAuley 72	7,165
51	d3po1	Grimsby	H	L	0-1		8,037
52	d3po2	Grimsby	A	L	1-2	Robinson, M 27	8,062

TEAM OF THE SEASON

- **G** Alan Marriott — CG: 43 DR: 76
- **D** Paul Morgan — CG: 19 DR: 81
- **D** Jeff Hughes — CG: 18 DR: 80
- **D** Gareth Mcauley — CG: 32 DR: 80
- **D** Jamie McCombe — CG: 38 DR: 78
- **M** Scott Kerr — CG: 40 SD: 15
- **M** Colin Cryan — CG: 36 SD: 13
- **M** Dean Keates — CG: 17 SD: 12
- **M** Nathaniel Brown — CG: 37 SD: 9
- **F** Marvin Robinson — CG: 17 SR: 257
- **F** Gary Birch — CG: 21 SR: 280

KEY PLAYER APPEARANCES

	PLAYER	POS	AGE	APP	MINS ON	GOALS	CARDS(Y)	CARDS(R)
1	Alan Marriott	GK	27	43	3870	0	2	0
2	Scott Kerr	MID	24	41	3595	2	7	0
3	Jamie McCombe	DEF	23	38	3420	4	2	0
4	Nathaniel Brown	MID	25	39	3358	7	6	0
5	Colin Cryan	MID	25	37	3302	0	2	0
6	Gareth Mcauley	DEF	26	35	2893	5	3	0
7	Lee Beevers	DEF	22	33	2509	1	7	1
8	Gary Birch	ATT	24	37	2237	8	1	0
9	Paul Mayo	DEF	24	28	2200	3	6	2
10	Francis Green	ATT	26	28	1927	3	0	0
11	Marvin Robinson	ATT	26	32	1798	7	4	0
12	Derek Asamoah	ATT	25	25	1723	2	1	0
13	Paul Morgan	DEF	27	20	1711	0	0	2
14	Dean Keates	MID	28	21	1655	4	4	1
15	Jeff Hughes	DEF	21	22	1605	2	5	0
16	Luke Foster	DEF	20	16	1207	1	2	0
17	Simon Yeo	ATT	32	12	948	5	4	1
18	Steve Robinson	MID	30	12	889	0	2	0

KEY PLAYERS - GOALSCORERS

Marvin Robinson

Goals in the League	7
Contribution to Attacking Power — Average number of minutes between League team goals while on pitch	53
Player Strike Rate — Average number of minutes between League goals scored by player	257
Club Strike Rate — Average number of minutes between League goals scored by club	64

	PLAYER	LGE GOALS	POWER	STRIKE RATE
1	Marvin Robinson	7	53	257 mins
2	Gary Birch	8	75	280 mins
3	Dean Keates	4	75	414 mins
4	Nathaniel Brown	7	67	480 mins

KEY PLAYERS - MIDFIELDERS

Scott Kerr

Goals in the League	2
Defensive Rating — Average number of mins between League goals conceded while on the pitch	78
Contribution to Attacking Power — Average number of minutes between League team goals while on pitch	63
Scoring Difference — Defensive Rating minus Contribution to Attacking Power	15

	PLAYER	LGE GOALS	DEF RATE	POWER	SCORE DIFF
1	Scott Kerr	2	78	63	15 mins
2	Colin Cryan	0	79	66	13 mins
3	Dean Keates	4	87	75	12 mins
4	Nathaniel Brown	7	76	67	9 mins

KEY PLAYERS - DEFENDERS

Paul Morgan

Goals Conceded when he was on pitch	21
Defensive Rating — Ave number of mins between League goals conceded while on the pitch	81
Clean Sheets — In games when he played at least 70 minutes	5
Club Defensive Rating — Average number of mins between League goals conceded by the club this season.	78

	PLAYER	CON LGE	CLEAN SHEETS	DEF RATE
1	Paul Morgan	21	5	81 min
2	Jeff Hughes	20	5	80 mins
3	Gareth Mcauley	36	8	80 mins
4	Jamie McCombe	44	11	78 mins

KEY GOALKEEPER

Alan Marriott

Goals Conceded in the League	51
Defensive Rating — Ave number of mins between League goals conceded while on the pitch.	76
Counting Games — Games when he played at least 70 mins	43
Clean Sheets — In games when he played at least 70 mins	11

TOP POINT EARNERS

	PLAYER	GAMES	AV PTS
1	Jeff Hughes	18	1.83
2	Francis Green	17	1.71
3	Gareth Mcauley	32	1.63
4	Derek Asamoah	16	1.56
5	Scott Kerr	40	1.53
6	Marvin Robinson	17	1.53
7	Jamie McCombe	38	1.50
8	Alan Marriott	43	1.44
9	Nathaniel Brown	37	1.43
10	Colin Cryan	36	1.42
	CLUB AVERAGE:		1.43

DARLINGTON

Final Position: **8th**

NICKNAME: THE QUAKERS

KEY: Won / Drawn / Lost

	Comp	Opponent	H/A	Result	Score	Scorers	Attendance
1	div3	Rushden & D	A	D	1-1	Wijnhard 58 pen	2,832
2	div3	Stockport	H	W	2-0	Logan 28; Sodje, A 89	4,371
3	div3	Leyton Orient	H	L	0-1		4,021
4	div3	Grimsby	A	W	1-0	Ndumbu-Nsungu 81 pen	3,904
5	ccr1	Hartlepool	A	L	1-3	Logan 81	6,163
6	div3	Chester	A	D	4-4	Johnson, Si 6 pen; Sodje, A 34,49,81	2,469
7	div3	Rochdale	H	W	2-1	Johnson, Si 36; Logan 69	4,318
8	div3	Notts County	H	D	1-1	Ndumbu-Nsungu 80	5,273
9	div3	Mansfield	A	D	2-2	Clarke, M 39; Ndumbu-Nsungu 74	2,803
10	div3	Oxford	H	L	1-2	Webster 79	4,127
11	div3	Bristol Rovers	A	L	0-1		5,652
12	div3	Boston	H	D	0-0		3,115
13	div3	Northampton	A	D	0-0		5,182
14	div3	Macclesfield	H	W	1-0	Johnson, Si 28 pen	3,831
15	div3	Bury	A	L	0-1		2,630
16	div3	Cheltenham	H	W	3-1	Wainwright 75; Dickman 79; Ndumbu-Nsungu 90	3,315
17	div3	Wrexham	A	L	0-1		4,881
18	facr1	Barnsley	A	L	0-1		6,059
19	div3	Wycombe	H	D	1-1	Keogh 36 og	3,928
20	div3	Macclesfield	A	L	0-1		1,769
21	div3	Rushden & D	H	D	1-1	Ndumbu-Nsungu 90 pen	3,209
22	div3	Shrewsbury	A	L	1-3	Stamp 45	2,469
23	div3	Stockport	A	W	3-0	Logan 37; Ndumbu-Nsungu 84; Sodje, A 86	3,502
24	div3	Carlisle	A	D	1-1	Johnson, Si 38	11,182
25	div3	Barnet	H	W	2-1	Ndumbu-Nsungu 44; Johnson, Si 53	2,905
26	div3	Lincoln	A	D	2-2	Kandol 64; Ndumbu-Nsungu 69	4,008
27	div3	Torquay	H	W	3-2	Kandol 14; Ndumbu-Nsungu 76,90 pen	3,785
28	div3	Notts County	A	L	2-3	Lafferty 45; Logan 88	4,244
29	div3	Peterborough	H	W	2-1	Hopkins 77; Lafferty 88	3,822
30	div3	Grimsby	H	D	0-0		3,924
31	div3	Oxford	A	W	2-0	Dickman 47; Johnson, Si 90	4,204
32	div3	Mansfield	H	W	4-0	Lafferty 6; Martis 53; Clarke, M 58; Sodje, A 64	4,282
33	div3	Boston	A	D	0-0		2,268
34	div3	Bristol Rovers	H	D	1-1	Johnson, Si 75 pen	4,579
35	div3	Peterborough	A	L	1-2	Cooke 26	3,960
36	div3	Shrewsbury	H	L	0-1		3,898
37	div3	Leyton Orient	A	L	0-1		4,767
38	div3	Chester	H	W	1-0	Martis 75	3,593
39	div3	Carlisle	H	L	0-5		8,640
40	div3	Barnet	A	L	0-1		2,845
41	div3	Lincoln	H	W	4-2	Bates 48; Clarke, M 57; Johnson 61,71	4,028
42	div3	Rochdale	A	W	2-0	Cooke 34; Johnson 53	1,963
43	div3	Torquay	A	W	2-1	Sodje, A 66; Wainwright 89	2,715
44	div3	Northampton	H	L	0-1		5,220
45	div3	Cheltenham	A	D	1-1	Wainwright 50	3,851
46	div3	Bury	H	L	2-3	Brass 8 og; Sodje, A 80	3,739
47	div3	Wycombe	A	W	1-0	Duke 50	5,840
48	div3	Wrexham	H	D	1-1	Cooke 90	4,648

TEAM OF THE SEASON

G Sam Russell — CG: 30 DR: 90

D David Duke — CG: 14 DR: 90

D Matthew Clarke — CG: 39 DR: 81

D Ryan Valentine — CG: 43 DR: 81

D Shelton Martis — CG: 38 DR: 79

M Anthony Peacock — CG: 14 SD: 26

M Clark Keltie — CG: 21 SD: 13

M Jon Hutchinson — CG: 17 SD: 12

M Neil Wainwright — CG: 19 SD: 12

F Akpo Sodje — CG: 15 SR: 242

F Simon Johnson — CG: 26 SR: 408

KEY PLAYER APPEARANCES

	PLAYER	POS	AGE	APP	MINS ON	GOALS	CARDS(Y)	CARDS(R)
1	Ryan Valentine	DEF	23	43	3870	0	7	0
2	Matthew Clarke	DEF	25	43	3663	3	6	2
3	Shelton Martis	DEF	23	40	3484	2	7	0
4	Jonjo Dickman	MID	27	38	2878	2	2	0
5	Simon Johnson	ATT	23	42	2857	7	5	0
6	Sam Russell	GK	23	30	2700	0	1	0
7	Carlos Logan	MID	20	33	2380	4	2	0
8	Neil Wainwright	MID	28	39	2338	3	0	0
9	Clark Keltie	MID	22	24	2041	0	2	2
10	Akpo Sodje	ATT	26	36	1939	8	1	1
11	Joe Kendrick	DEF	23	21	1782	0	4	0
12	Jon Hutchinson	MID	24	19	1607	0	2	0
13	Anthony Peacock	MID	20	28	1535	0	0	0
14	Matthew Appleby	MID	30	25	1530	0	4	2
15	David Duke	DEF	27	20	1434	1	1	0
16	Guylain Ndumbu-Nsungu	ATT	23	21	1180	10	4	0
17	Andrew Cooke	ATT	32	14	926	2	3	0
18	Bertrand Bossu	GK	25	9	810	0	0	0

KEY PLAYERS - GOALSCORERS

Akpo Sodje

Goals in the League	8
Contribution to Attacking Power — Average number of minutes between League team goals while on pitch	57
Player Strike Rate — Average number of minutes between League goals scored by player	242
Club Strike Rate — Average number of minutes between League goals scored by club	71

	PLAYER	LGE GOALS	POWER	STRIKE RATE
1	Akpo Sodje	8	57	242 mins
2	Simon Johnson	7	82	408 mins
3	Carlos Logan	4	74	595 mins
4	Neil Wainwright	3	63	779 mins

KEY PLAYERS - MIDFIELDERS

Anthony Peacock

Goals in the League	0
Defensive Rating — Average number of mins between League goals conceded while on the pitch	96
Contribution to Attacking Power — Average number of minutes between League team goals while on pitch	70
Scoring Difference — Defensive Rating minus Contribution to Attacking Power	26

	PLAYER	LGE GOALS	DEF RATE	POWER	SCORE DIFF
1	Anthony Peacock	0	96	70	26 mins
2	Clark Keltie	0	79	66	13 mins
3	Neil Wainwright	3	75	63	12 mins
4	Jon Hutchinson	0	85	73	12 mins

KEY PLAYERS - DEFENDERS

David Duke

Goals Conceded when he was on pitch	16
Defensive Rating — Ave number of mins between League goals conceded while on the pitch	90
Clean Sheets — In games when he played at least 70 minutes	5
Club Defensive Rating — Average number of mins between League goals conceded by the club this season.	80

	PLAYER	CON LGE	CLEAN SHEETS	DEF RATE
1	David Duke	16	5	90 mins
2	Matthew Clarke	45	11	81 mins
3	Ryan Valentine	48	13	81 mins
4	Shelton Martis	44	10	79 mins

KEY GOALKEEPER

Sam Russell

Goals Conceded in the League	30
Defensive Rating — Ave number of mins between League goals conceded while on the pitch.	90
Counting Games — Games when he played at least 70 mins	30
Clean Sheets — In games when he played at least 70 mins	9

TOP POINT EARNERS

	PLAYER	GAMES	AV PTS
1	Joe Kendrick	19	1.53
2	David Duke	14	1.43
3	Jon Hutchinson	17	1.41
4	Simon Johnson	26	1.38
5	Matthew Clarke	39	1.38
6	Ryan Valentine	43	1.35
7	Clark Keltie	21	1.33
8	Akpo Sodje	15	1.33
9	Jonjo Dickman	27	1.30
10	Shelton Martis	38	1.26
	CLUB AVERAGE:		1.37

PETERBOROUGH UNITED

Final Position: **9th**

NICKNAME: THE POSH

KEY: ☐Won ☐Drawn ☐Lost

							Attendance
1	div3	Chester	H	L	0-1		4,980
2	div3	Carlisle	A	L	0-1		6,511
3	div3	Bristol Rovers	A	W	3-2	Newton 5; Farrell 23; Logan 73	5,169
4	div3	Mansfield	H	W	2-0	Farrell 50; St Ledger-Hall 60	4,056
5	ccr1	Plymouth	A	L	1-2	Plummer 22	5,974
6	div3	Torquay	H	D	0-0		3,502
7	div3	Stockport	A	D	1-1	Quinn 2	3,774
8	div3	Rushden & D	A	W	2-0	Logan 22; Gain 77	4,403
9	div3	Grimsby	H	L	0-1		4,263
10	div3	Lincoln	A	W	2-1	Quinn 61; Newton 69	5,526
11	div3	Shrewsbury	H	L	0-2		4,274
12	div3	Cheltenham	A	L	1-2	Quinn 75	2,531
13	div3	Boston	A	L	0-1		4,126
14	div3	Macclesfield	A	W	4-0	Crow 47; Farrell 67,70; Willock 71	1,810
15	div3	Rochdale	H	W	3-1	Crow 54,73; Burton 64 pen	4,314
16	div3	Wrexham	H	D	1-1	Farrell 30	4,014
17	div3	Wycombe	A	D	2-2	Crow 33; Benjamin 38	5,214
18	facr1	Burton	H	D	0-0		3,856
19	div3	Leyton Orient	H	D	1-1	Willock 45	5,341
20	facr1r	Burton	A	L	0-1		2,511
21	div3	Wrexham	A	D	1-1	Crow 59	4,480
22	div3	Chester	A	L	1-3	Semple 75	2,701
23	div3	Notts County	H	W	2-0	Semple 41; Willock 57	2,833
24	div3	Carlisle	H	D	1-1	Crow 56	3,689
25	div3	Mansfield	A	D	0-0		3,891
26	div3	Barnet	A	L	1-2	Crow 13	2,715
27	div3	Northampton	A	W	1-0	Plummer 9	7,023
28	div3	Bury	H	W	4-1	Quinn 6; Woodthorpe 40 og; Burton 47; Day 64	3,687
29	div3	Rushden & D	H	W	2-0	Holden 17; Quinn 76 pen	4,613
30	div3	Oxford	H	D	0-0		2,926
31	div3	Darlington	A	L	1-2	Quinn 26	3,822
32	div3	Lincoln	H	D	1-1	Gain (Peterboro) 30	6,227
33	div3	Grimsby	A	W	2-1	Gain 30; Crow 71	4,462
34	div3	Cheltenham	H	W	1-0	Logan 55	3,901
35	div3	Shrewsbury	A	L	1-2	Crow 39 pen	3,295
36	div3	Darlington	H	W	2-1	Arber 43,74	3,960
37	div3	Notts County	A	W	2-1	Crow 40; Purser 58	6,012
38	div3	Bristol Rovers	H	L	1-2	Holden 90	4,292
39	div3	Stockport	H	W	2-0	Holden 70; Semple 88	3,406
40	div3	Torquay	A	L	0-1		2,438
41	div3	Barnet	H	D	2-2	Crow 53; Logan 75	3,983
42	div3	Oxford	A	L	0-1		7,486
43	div3	Northampton	H	L	0-1		8,637
44	div3	Bury	A	W	3-1	Crow 45,90; Newton 62	2,233
45	div3	Boston	H	L	0-1		5,092
46	div3	Rochdale	A	L	0-1		2,318
47	div3	Macclesfield	H	W	3-2	Crow 71,90; Farrell 83	3,002
48	div3	Leyton Orient	A	L	1-2	Opara 85	6,591
49	div3	Wycombe	H	L	0-2		5,376

TEAM OF THE SEASON

G – Mark Tyler, CG: 40 DR: 85

D – Sagi Burton, CG: 16 DR: 92
D – Dean Holden, CG: 33 DR: 89
D – Chris Plummer, CG: 15 DR: 88
D – Sean St Ledger-Hall, CG: 42 DR: 85

M – Paul Carden, CG: 42 SD: 19
M – Jamie Day, CG: 16 SD: 16
M – Dave Farrell, CG: 15 SD: 16
M – Peter Gain, CG: 36 SD: 12

F – Danny Crow, CG: 26 SR: 182
F – James Quinn, CG: 17 SR: 277

KEY PLAYER APPEARANCES

	PLAYER	POS	AGE	APP	MINS ON	GOALS	CARDS(Y/R)	
1	Mark Arber	DEF	28	46	4140	2	5	0
2	Sean St Ledger-Hall	DEF	21	43	3832	1	6	0
3	Paul Carden	MID	27	42	3778	0	12	1
4	Mark Tyler	GK	29	40	3590	0	2	0
5	Peter Gain	MID	29	37	3283	2	5	0
6	Adam Newton	DEF	25	40	3262	3	7	0
7	Dean Holden	DEF	26	35	3018	3	7	1
8	Danny Crow	ATT	20	38	2728	15	4	0
9	Dave Farrell	MID	34	29	1812	6	2	0
10	Jamie Day	MID	21	25	1724	1	0	0
11	James Quinn	ATT	31	24	1664	6	4	0
12	Chris Plummer	DEF	29	22	1502	1	3	0
13	Sagi Burton	DEF	28	19	1477	2	6	0
14	Philip Bolland	DEF	29	17	1452	0	3	0
15	Richard Logan	ATT	24	28	1295	4	3	0
16	Ryan Semple	MID	21	28	1066	3	1	0
17	Peter Kennedy	DEF	32	14	888	0	0	1
18	Callum Willock	ATT	24	15	850	3	1	0

KEY PLAYERS - GOALSCORERS

Danny Crow

Goals in the League	15
Contribution to Attacking Power Average number of minutes between League team goals while on pitch	78
Player Strike Rate Average number of minutes between League goals scored by player	182
Club Strike Rate Average number of minutes between League goals scored by club	73

	PLAYER	LGE GOALS	POWER	STRIKE RATE
1	Danny Crow	15	78	182 mins
2	James Quinn	6	72	277 mins
3	Dave Farrell	6	60	302 mins
4	Sagi Burton	2	70	739 mins

KEY PLAYERS - MIDFIELDERS

Paul Carden

Goals in the League	0
Defensive Rating Average number of mins between League goals conceded while on the pitch	88
Contribution to Attacking Power Average number of minutes between League team goals while on pitch	69
Scoring Difference Defensive Rating minus Contribution to Attacking Power	19

	PLAYER	LGE GOALS	DEF RATE	POWER	SCORE DIFF
1	Paul Carden	0	88	69	19 mins
2	Jamie Day	1	91	75	16 mins
3	Dave Farrell	6	76	60	16 mins
4	Peter Gain	2	82	70	12 mins

KEY PLAYERS - DEFENDERS

Sagi Burton

Goals Conceded when he was on pitch	16
Defensive Rating Ave number of mins between League goals conceded while on the pitch	92
Clean Sheets In games when he played at least 70 minutes	4
Club Defensive Rating Average number of mins between League goals conceded by the club this season.	84

	PLAYER	CON LGE	CLEAN SHEETS	DEF RATE
1	Sagi Burton	16	4	92 mins
2	Dean Holden	34	9	89 mins
3	Chris Plummer	17	6	88 mins
4	Sean St Ledger-Hall	45	11	85 mins

KEY GOALKEEPER

Mark Tyler

Goals Conceded in the League	42
Defensive Rating Ave number of mins between League goals conceded while on the pitch.	85
Counting Games Games when he played at least 70 mins	40
Clean Sheets In games when he played at least 70 mins	10

TOP POINT EARNERS

	PLAYER	GAMES	AV PTS
1	Jamie Day	16	1.56
2	Sagi Burton	16	1.56
3	Chris Plummer	15	1.47
4	James Quinn	17	1.47
5	Paul Carden	42	1.45
6	Peter Gain	36	1.44
7	Dave Farrell	15	1.40
8	Danny Crow	26	1.38
9	Sean St Ledger-Hall	42	1.36
10	Dean Holden	33	1.36
	CLUB AVERAGE:		1.35

SHREWSBURY TOWN

Final Position: **10th**

NICKNAME: THE SHREWS

KEY: Won Drawn Lost

#	Comp	Opponent	H/A	Res	Score	Scorers	Attendance
1	div3	Rochdale	H	L	0-1		4,927
2	div3	Boston	A	D	1-1	Smith 69	2,409
3	div3	Bury	A	L	0-2		2,261
4	div3	Northampton	H	D	1-1	Edwards 6	3,562
5	ccr1	Brighton	H	W	3-2	Stallard 22; Denny 89,91	2,141
6	div3	Wycombe	H	D	1-1	McMenamin 85	3,533
7	div3	Leyton Orient	A	W	1-0	McMenamin 3 pen	3,742
8	div3	Oxford	H	W	2-0	McMenamin 8 pen; Tolley 19	4,073
9	div3	Torquay	A	L	1-2	Langmead 28	2,287
10	div3	Notts County	H	W	2-0	McMenamin 21; Walton 45	4,011
11	ccr2	Sheff Utd	H	L	3-4*	(*on penalties)	
12	div3	Peterborough	A	W	2-0	Sorvel 55; Darby 83	4,274
13	div3	Barnet	H	D	2-2	McMenamin 12; Herd 90	3,628
14	div3	Grimsby	H	D	0-0		4,607
15	div3	Mansfield	A	L	0-4		3,334
16	div3	Stockport	H	D	2-2	Walton 45; Langmead 90	4,316
17	div3	Rushden & D	A	L	0-3		2,954
18	div3	Chester	H	W	3-1	McMenamin 1; Stallard 8; Langmead 58	5,430
19	facr1	Braintree	H	W	4-1	McMenamin 2 pen; Tolley 5; Hope 44; Edwards 55	2,969
20	div3	Lincoln	A	D	1-1	Tolley 18	3,748
21	div3	Rochdale	A	L	3-4	McMenamin 3; Cowan 9; Stallard 42	2,845
22	facr2	Colchester	H	L	1-2	Edwards 45	3,695
23	div3	Darlington	H	W	3-1	Stallard 8; Sorvel 51; Ashton 68	2,469
24	div3	Boston	H	D	1-1	Hope 2	3,376
25	div3	Northampton	A	L	0-1		5,380
26	div3	Bristol Rovers	A	L	1-2	Darby 50	7,551
27	div3	Cheltenham	A	L	0-1		3,474
28	div3	Wrexham	H	W	1-0	Hurst 72	6,249
29	div3	Oxford	A	W	3-0	Langmead 65; Herd 83; Tolley 90	3,702
30	div3	Carlisle	H	W	2-1	McMenamin 32 pen; Sharp 75 pen	4,493
31	div3	Mansfield	H	D	0-0		3,747
32	div3	Notts County	A	L	1-2	Langmead 88	5,438
33	div3	Torquay	H	L	0-1		3,741
34	div3	Macclesfield	H	D	1-1	Burton 50 pen	2,642
35	div3	Barnet	A	L	0-1		1,789
36	div3	Peterborough	H	W	2-1	Sorvel 60; Langmead 87	3,295
37	div3	Carlisle	A	D	2-2	Sorvel 12; Hope 72	5,568
38	div3	Darlington	A	W	1-0	McMenamin 55	3,898
39	div3	Bury	H	L	0-1		3,586
40	div3	Leyton Orient	H	D	3-3	Stallard 39; Edwards 41; Burton 45	3,471
41	div3	Wycombe	A	L	0-2		5,035
42	div3	Bristol Rovers	H	W	1-0	Hurst 73	3,641
43	div3	Macclesfield	A	L	0-2		2,274
44	div3	Cheltenham	H	W	2-0	Langmead 32,75	3,724
45	div3	Wrexham	A	W	2-1	Lawrence 3 og; McMenamin 15 pen	6,310
46	div3	Grimsby	A	D	1-1	Burton 27	5,935
47	div3	Rushden & D	H	W	4-1	Stallard 6,54; Tolley 35; Burton 80	4,239
48	div3	Stockport	A	L	1-3	Hurst 64	5,831
49	div3	Lincoln	H	L	0-1		5,170
50	div3	Chester	A	W	1-0	Langmead 9	3,744

TEAM OF THE SEASON

G: Joe Hart — CG: 46 DR: 75

D: Sagi Burton — CG: 15 DR: 81

D: Ben Herd — CG: 44 DR: 78

D: Kevin Sharp — CG: 26 DR: 78

D: Richard Hope — CG: 41 DR: 75

M: David Edwards — CG: 23 SD: 12

M: Jamie Tolley — CG: 27 SD: 7

M: Neil Ashton — CG: 37 SD: 0

M: Neil Sorvel — CG: 43 SD: 0

F: Kelvin Langmead — CG: 27 SR: 322

F: Mark Stallard — CG: 18 SR: 350

KEY PLAYER APPEARANCES

	PLAYER	POS	AGE	APP	MINS ON	GOALS	CARDS(Y/R)	
1	Joe Hart	GK	19	46	4140	0	1	0
2	Ben Herd	DEF	21	46	3991	2	1	1
3	Neil Sorvel	MID	33	45	3910	4	2	0
4	Richard Hope	DEF	28	42	3735	2	3	0
5	Neil Ashton	MID	21	44	3524	1	9	0
6	Colin McMenamin	ATT	25	43	3505	0	0	0
7	Kelvin Langmead	ATT	21	42	2894	9	1	1
8	Jamie Tolley	MID	23	36	2745	4	5	0
9	Kevin Sharp	DEF	31	30	2427	1	3	0
10	David Edwards	MID	20	30	2382	2	2	0
11	Mark Stallard	ATT	31	37	2099	6	1	0
12	Stuart Whitehead	DEF	29	23	1797	0	0	0
13	Sagi Burton	DEF	28	16	1380	4	5	0
14	David Walton	DEF	33	16	1353	2	1	0
15	Glynn Hurst	ATT	30	16	1204	2	3	0
16	Gavin Cowan	DEF	25	15	837	1	4	0
17	Ben Smith	MID	27	12	782	1	0	0
18	Jay Denny	MID	20	14	761	0	0	0

KEY PLAYERS - GOALSCORERS

Kelvin Langmead

Goals in the League: 9

Contribution to Attacking Power — Average number of minutes between League team goals while on pitch: 69

Player Strike Rate — Average number of minutes between League goals scored by player: 322

Club Strike Rate — Average number of minutes between League goals scored by club: 75

	PLAYER	LGE GOALS	POWER	STRIKE RATE
1	Kelvin Langmead	9	69	322 mins
2	Sagi Burton	4	73	345 mins
3	Mark Stallard	6	70	350 mins
4	Glynn Hurst	2	67	602 mins

KEY PLAYERS - MIDFIELDERS

David Edwards

Goals in the League: 2

Defensive Rating — Average number of mins between League goals conceded while on the pitch: 82

Contribution to Attacking Power — Average number of minutes between League team goals while on pitch: 70

Scoring Difference — Defensive Rating minus Contribution to Attacking Power: 12

	PLAYER	LGE GOALS	DEF RATE	POWER	SCORE DIFF
1	David Edwards	2	82	70	12 mins
2	Jamie Tolley	4	83	76	7 mins
3	Neil Ashton	1	73	73	0 mins
4	Neil Sorvel	4	74	74	0 mins

KEY PLAYERS - DEFENDERS

Sagi Burton

Goals Conceded when he was on pitch: 17

Defensive Rating — Ave number of mins between League goals conceded while on the pitch: 81

Clean Sheets — In games when he played at least 70 minutes: 3

Club Defensive Rating — Average number of mins between League goals conceded by the club this season: 75

	PLAYER	CON LGE	CLEAN SHEETS	DEF RATE
1	Sagi Burton	17	3	81 mins
2	Kevin Sharp	31	8	78 mins
3	Ben Herd	51	11	78 mins
4	Richard Hope	50	12	75 mins

KEY GOALKEEPER

Joe Hart

Goals Conceded in the League: 55

Defensive Rating — Ave number of mins between League goals conceded while on the pitch: 75

Counting Games — Games when he played at least 70 mins: 46

Clean Sheets — In games when he played at least 70 mins: 12

TOP POINT EARNERS

	PLAYER	GAMES	AV PTS
1	Glynn Hurst	12	1.50
2	David Edwards	23	1.48
3	Stuart Whitehead	19	1.47
4	Richard Hope	41	1.44
5	Kelvin Langmead	27	1.41
6	Jamie Tolley	27	1.41
7	Sagi Burton	15	1.40
8	Neil Ashton	37	1.38
9	Colin McMenamin	36	1.36
10	Joe Hart	46	1.33
	CLUB AVERAGE:		1.33

BOSTON UNITED

Final Position: **11th**

NICKNAME: THE PILGRIMS

KEY: ☐Won ☐Drawn ☐Lost

							Attendance
1	div3	Wrexham	A	L	0-2		4,503
2	div3	Shrewsbury	H	D	1-1	Lee 84	2,409
3	div3	Stockport	H	D	2-2	Joachim 50,90	2,432
4	div3	Cheltenham	A	L	0-3		2,680
5	ccr1	Sheff Utd	A	L	0-1		6,014
6	div3	Mansfield	H	D	2-2	Thomas 9; White 34	2,848
7	div3	Northampton	A	L	2-3	White 40; Ross 86	5,012
8	div3	Macclesfield	A	D	2-2	Maylett 48; Whelan 75	2,130
9	div3	Rochdale	H	W	3-2	Whelan 8,58; White 76	2,274
10	div3	Bury	A	D	1-1	Dudfield 82	1,985
11	div3	Grimsby	H	D	1-1	Joachim 90	4,077
12	div3	Darlington	A	D	0-0		3,115
13	div3	Peterborough	H	W	1-0	Ross 63 pen	4,126
14	div3	Notts County	A	W	2-1	Joachim 1; Pipe 11 og	6,632
15	div3	Bristol Rovers	H	W	3-1	Dudfield 10; Ross 52; Joachim 80	2,469
16	div3	Oxford	A	D	0-0		5,084
17	div3	Torquay	H	W	2-0	Ross 21; Joachim 61	2,220
18	facr1	Swindon	A	D	2-2	Rusk 26; Talbot 42	3,814
19	div3	Rushden & D	A	L	0-1		3,205
20	facr1r	Swindon	H	W	4-1	Joachim 10,23; Maylett 40; Lee 45	2,467
21	div3	Notts County	H	L	1-2	Lee 49	2,921
22	div3	Wrexham	H	W	2-1	Joachim 14,66	1,938
23	facr2	Doncaster	H	L	1-2	Futcher 90	3,995
24	div3	Wycombe	A	D	1-1	Green 21	4,372
25	div3	Shrewsbury	A	D	1-1	Whelan 89	3,376
26	div3	Cheltenham	H	D	0-0		1,906
27	div3	Lincoln	A	D	0-0		7,077
28	div3	Barnet	A	L	0-1		2,287
29	div3	Leyton Orient	H	L	1-2	Talbot 49	2,689
30	div3	Macclesfield	H	W	3-1	Talbot 15; Canoville 32; Ellender 81	1,975
31	div3	Chester	A	W	1-0	Rusk 82	2,956
32	div3	Carlisle	H	L	0-5		1,924
33	div3	Bury	H	W	3-1	Joachim 26,31 pen; Till 60	2,018
34	div3	Rochdale	A	D	1-1	Keene 8	2,384
35	div3	Darlington	H	D	0-0		2,268
36	div3	Grimsby	A	L	0-1		5,028
37	div3	Wycombe	H	D	1-1	Joachim 56	2,283
38	div3	Stockport	A	W	1-0	Joachim 67	5,133
39	div3	Mansfield	A	L	0-5		3,121
40	div3	Lincoln	H	W	2-1	Joachim 26; Dudfield 90	4,476
41	div3	Northampton	H	L	0-1		2,174
42	div3	Carlisle	A	L	2-4	Billy 63 og; Rusk 84	7,596
43	div3	Chester	H	L	1-3	Rusk 87	1,651
44	div3	Barnet	H	W	2-1	Dudfield 16; Greaves 35	2,066
45	div3	Leyton Orient	A	L	0-2		4,391
46	div3	Peterborough	A	W	1-0	Clarke 69	5,092
47	div3	Oxford	H	W	1-0	White 6	2,313
48	div3	Bristol Rovers	A	L	1-3	Joachim 60	4,836
49	div3	Rushden & D	H	W	2-0	Dudfield 89; Thomas 90	2,489
50	div3	Torquay	A	D	0-0		5,697

TEAM OF THE SEASON

G — Conrad Logan — CG: 12 DR: 98

D — Mark Greaves — CG: 26 DR: 81

D — Paul Ellender — CG: 25 DR: 78

D — Alan White — CG: 35 DR: 69

D — Austin McCann — CG: 28 DR: 67

M — Ian Ross — CG: 13 SD: 29

M — Brad Maylett — CG: 20 SD: 15

M — Stewart Talbot — CG: 20 SD: -6

M — Chris Holland — CG: 25 SD: -13

F — Julian Joachim — CG: 41 SR: 265

F — Lawrie Dudfield — CG: 17 SR: 386

KEY PLAYER APPEARANCES

	PLAYER	POS	AGE	APP	MINS ON	GOALS	CARDS(Y/R)	
1	Julian Joachim	ATT	31	43	3706	14	0	0
2	Lee Canoville	DEF	25	43	3542	1	5	0
3	Alan White	DEF	30	37	3256	4	5	0
4	Austin McCann	DEF	26	35	2747	0	7	1
5	Mark Greaves	DEF	31	34	2591	1	4	0
6	Chris Holland	MID	30	34	2497	0	2	0
7	Brad Maylett	MID	25	38	2297	1	3	0
8	Simon Rusk	MID	24	34	2253	3	10	1
9	Paul Ellender	DEF	31	25	2250	1	7	0
10	Stewart Talbot	MID	33	30	2183	2	7	1
11	Lawrie Dudfield	ATT	26	36	1931	5	2	0
12	Danny Thomas	MID	25	35	1697	2	2	0
13	Nathan Abbey	GK	27	17	1530	0	2	1
14	Michel Kuipers	GK	32	15	1350	0	3	0
15	Ian Ross	MID	20	14	1179	4	2	0
16	Ben Futcher	DEF	25	14	1176	0	5	1
17	Conrad Logan	GK	20	12	1080	0	0	0
18	Jamie Clarke	DEF	23	15	1068	1	0	0

KEY PLAYERS - GOALSCORERS

Julian Joachim

Goals in the League	14	**Player Strike Rate** Average number of minutes between League goals scored by player	265
Contribution to Attacking Power Average number of minutes between League team goals while on pitch	82	**Club Strike Rate** Average number of minutes between League goals scored by club	83

	PLAYER	LGE GOALS	POWER	STRIKE RATE
1	Julian Joachim	14	82	265 mins
2	Ian Ross	4	62	295 mins
3	Lawrie Dudfield	5	80	386 mins
4	Simon Rusk	3	98	751 mins

KEY PLAYERS - MIDFIELDERS

Ian Ross

Goals in the League	4	**Contribution to Attacking Power** Average number of minutes between League team goals while on pitch	62
Defensive Rating Average number of mins between League goals conceded while on the pitch	91	**Scoring Difference** Defensive Rating minus Contribution to Attacking Power	29

	PLAYER	LGE GOALS	DEF RATE	POWER	SCORE DIFF
1	Ian Ross	4	91	62	29 mins
2	Brad Maylett	1	85	70	15 mins
3	Stewart Talbot	2	75	81	-6 mins
4	Chris Holland	0	83	96	-13 mins

KEY PLAYERS - DEFENDERS

Mark Greaves

Goals Conceded when he was on pitch	32	**Clean Sheets** In games when he played at least 70 minutes	9
Defensive Rating Ave number of mins between League goals conceded while on the pitch	81	**Club Defensive Rating** Average number of mins between League goals conceded by the club this season.	69

	PLAYER	CON LGE	CLEAN SHEETS	DEF RATE
1	Mark Greaves	32	9	81 mins
2	Paul Ellender	29	9	78 mins
3	Alan White	47	12	69 mins
4	Austin McCann	41	7	67 mins

KEY GOALKEEPER

Conrad Logan

Goals Conceded in the League	11
Defensive Rating Ave number of mins between League goals conceded while on the pitch.	98
Counting Games Games when he played at least 70 mins	12
Clean Sheets In games when he played at least 70 mins	5

TOP POINT EARNERS

	PLAYER	GAMES	AV PTS
1	Ian Ross	13	1.77
2	Lawrie Dudfield	17	1.59
3	Brad Maylett	20	1.55
4	Stewart Talbot	20	1.55
5	Alan White	35	1.51
6	Paul Ellender	25	1.48
7	Michel Kuipers	15	1.47
8	Mark Greaves	26	1.35
9	Julian Joachim	41	1.34
10	Austin McCann	28	1.29
	CLUB AVERAGE:		1.33

BRISTOL ROVERS

Final Position: **12th**

NICKNAME: THE PIRATES

KEY: Won / Drawn / Lost

#	Comp	Opponent	H/A	Res	Score	Scorers	Attendance
1	div3	Barnet	A	D	1-1	Agogo 87	3,237
2	div3	Grimsby	H	L	1-2	Agogo 54	6,300
3	div3	Peterborough	H	L	2-3	Walker 45; Elliott 59	5,169
4	div3	Torquay	A	W	3-2	Agogo 74,87; Walker 90	3,964
5	ccr1	Millwall	A	L	0-2		3,079
6	div3	Notts County	A	L	0-2		4,405
7	div3	Leyton Orient	A	W	3-2	Disley 15; Agogo 54 pen,82	3,481
8	div3	Lincoln	H	D	0-0		5,057
9	div3	Oxford	H	D	1-1	Walker 64	5,098
10	div3	Chester	A	L	0-4		2,974
11	div3	Darlington	H	W	1-0	Walker 45	5,652
12	div3	Bury	A	L	0-1		1,673
13	div3	Carlisle	A	W	3-1	Gray 57 og; Aranalde 82 og; Agogo 90	5,317
14	div3	Northampton	H	D	0-0		6,912
15	div3	Boston	A	L	1-3	Walker 12	2,469
16	div3	Wrexham	H	W	2-1	Trollope 88; Walker 90	5,730
17	div3	Macclesfield	A	L	1-2	Disley 55	1,908
18	facr1	Grimsby	A	W	2-1	Agogo 28,87	2,680
19	div3	Rochdale	H	L	1-2	Agogo 38	6,042
20	div3	Northampton	A	L	0-4		5,716
21	div3	Barnet	H	W	2-1	Walker 5,20	5,096
22	facr2	Port Vale	A	D	1-1	Gibb 55	4,483
23	div3	Stockport	A	W	1-0	Walker 35 pen	3,460
24	div3	Grimsby	A	W	1-0	Carruthers 80	4,739
25	facr2r	Port Vale	H	L	0-1		5,623
26	div3	Torquay	H	L	0-1		6,061
27	div3	Shrewsbury	H	W	2-1	Disley 37; Agogo 45 pen	7,551
28	div3	Mansfield	A	D	3-3	Hunt 28; Walker 41 pen,90	2,357
29	div3	Wycombe	H	L	1-2	Walker 61	6,828
30	div3	Rushden & D	A	W	3-2	Campbell 41; Elliott 49; Forrester 90	2,720
31	div3	Cheltenham	A	W	3-2	Forrester 18; Disley 89; Anderson 90	6,005
32	div3	Chester	H	W	2-1	Edwards 10; Disley 42	6,310
33	div3	Lincoln	A	L	0-1		4,258
34	div3	Leyton Orient	H	D	3-3	Agogo 14; Disley 58; Walker 74 pen	5,966
35	div3	Bury	H	W	1-0	Agogo 28	6,027
36	div3	Darlington	A	D	1-1	Agogo 68	4,579
37	div3	Cheltenham	H	L	0-1		6,885
38	div3	Stockport	H	D	2-2	Walker 36,50 pen	5,990
39	div3	Peterborough	A	W	2-1	Agogo 36; Walker 54	4,292
40	div3	Notts County	H	L	1-2	Haldane 53	6,280
41	div3	Oxford	A	L	0-1		6,424
42	div3	Shrewsbury	A	L	0-1		3,641
43	div3	Mansfield	H	W	2-0	Igoe 14; Walker 17	5,253
44	div3	Wycombe	A	W	3-1	Agogo 31,74; Walker 54 pen	6,355
45	div3	Rushden & D	H	L	0-1		6,432
46	div3	Carlisle	H	D	1-1	Disley 55	6,181
47	div3	Wrexham	A	L	0-1		3,749
48	div3	Boston	H	W	3-1	Disley 27; Walker 73 pen; Agogo 77	4,836
49	div3	Rochdale	A	L	0-2		2,649
50	div3	Macclesfield	H	L	2-3	Haldane 12,57	6,100

KEY PLAYER APPEARANCES

	PLAYER	POS	AGE	APP	MINS ON	GOALS	CARDS(Y)	CARDS(R)
1	Scott Shearer	GK	25	45	4050	0	0	0
2	Steve Elliott	DEF	27	45	4050	2	6	0
3	Richard Walker	ATT	28	46	3945	19	5	0
4	James Hunt	MID	29	40	3600	1	6	0
5	Junior Agogo	ATT	26	42	3543	16	2	1
6	Chris Carruthers	MID	22	40	3311	1	2	0
7	Craig Disley	MID	24	42	3260	8	4	0
8	Aaron Lescott	DEF	27	37	3154	0	5	1
9	Craig Hinton	DEF	28	36	3045	0	3	1
10	Stuart Campbell	MID	28	38	2723	1	4	0
11	Alistair Gibb	MID	30	33	1887	0	0	0
12	Lewis Haldane	ATT	20	30	1700	3	4	0
13	Robert Ryan	DEF	29	14	1248	0	2	0
14	Christian Edwards	DEF	30	15	1171	1	1	0
15	Michael Leary	MID	23	13	1134	0	6	0
16	Sam Igoe	MID	30	11	908	1	2	0
17	John Anderson	DEF	33	12	842	1	1	0
18	Jonathan Bass	DEF	30	9	628	0	0	0

KEY PLAYERS - GOALSCORERS

Richard Walker

Goals in the League	19
Contribution to Attacking Power Average number of minutes between League team goals while on pitch	68
Player Strike Rate Average number of minutes between League goals scored by player	208
Club Strike Rate Average number of minutes between League goals scored by club	70

	PLAYER	LGE GOALS	POWER	STRIKE RATE
1	Richard Walker	19	68	208 mins
2	Junior Agogo	16	71	221 mins
3	Craig Disley	8	64	408 mins
4	Lewis Haldane	3	68	567 mins

KEY PLAYERS - MIDFIELDERS

Craig Disley

Goals in the League	8
Defensive Rating Average number of mins between League goals conceded while on the pitch	72
Contribution to Attacking Power Average number of minutes between League team goals while on pitch	64
Scoring Difference Defensive Rating minus Contribution to Attacking Power	8

	PLAYER	LGE GOALS	DEF RATE	POWER	SCORE DIFF
1	Craig Disley	8	72	64	8 mins
2	Chris Carruthers	1	65	72	-7 mins
3	James Hunt	1	62	71	-9 mins
4	Stuart Campbell	1	54	68	-14 mins

KEY PLAYERS - DEFENDERS

Craig Hinton

Goals Conceded when he was on pitch	48
Defensive Rating Ave number of mins between League goals conceded while on the pitch	63
Clean Sheets In games when he played at least 70 minutes	5
Club Defensive Rating Average number of mins between League goals conceded by the club this season.	62

	PLAYER	CON LGE	CLEAN SHEETS	DEF RATE
1	Craig Hinton	48	5	63 mins
2	Aaron Lescott	50	5	63 mins
3	Steve Elliott	65	7	62 mins
4	Robert Ryan	23	3	54 mins

TEAM OF THE SEASON

Pos	Player	Stats
G	Scott Shearer	CG: 45 DR: 62
D	Craig Hinton	CG: 33 DR: 63
D	Aaron Lescott	CG: 35 DR: 63
D	Steve Elliott	CG: 45 DR: 62
D	Robert Ryan	CG: 14 DR: 54
M	Craig Disley	CG: 35 SD: 8
M	Chris Carruthers	CG: 34 SD: -7
M	James Hunt	CG: 40 SD: -9
M	Stuart Campbell	CG: 27 SD: -14
F	Richard Walker	CG: 44 SR: 208
F	Junior Agogo	CG: 39 SR: 221

KEY GOALKEEPER

Scott Shearer

Goals Conceded in the League	65
Defensive Rating Ave number of mins between League goals conceded while on the pitch.	62
Counting Games Games when he played at least 70 mins	45
Clean Sheets In games when he played at least 70 mins	7

TOP POINT EARNERS

	PLAYER	GAMES	AV PTS
1	Alistair Gibb	18	1.67
2	Craig Disley	35	1.46
3	Lewis Haldane	18	1.44
4	Chris Carruthers	34	1.44
5	Craig Hinton	33	1.42
6	Aaron Lescott	35	1.34
7	Scott Shearer	45	1.33
8	James Hunt	40	1.33
9	Junior Agogo	39	1.31
10	Stuart Campbell	27	1.30
	CLUB AVERAGE:		1.30

WREXHAM

Final Position: **13th**

NICKNAME: THE ROBINS

KEY: Won Drawn Lost

							Attendance
1	div3	Boston	H	W	2-0	Jones, Ma 23; Roche 83	4,503
2	div3	Notts County	A	L	0-1		4,382
3	div3	Northampton	A	D	0-0		5,075
4	div3	Carlisle	H	L	0-1		4,239
5	ccr1	Doncaster	H	L	0-1		2,177
6	div3	Bury	A	D	2-2	McEvilly 11; Foy 24	2,468
7	div3	Barnet	H	W	3-1	Jones, Ma 1; Warhurst 32; Foy 59	3,768
8	div3	Cheltenham	H	W	2-0	Holt 8; Walters 69	3,671
9	div3	Lincoln	A	L	0-2		2,956
10	div3	Leyton Orient	A	D	1-1	Ferguson 53	3,733
11	div3	Macclesfield	H	D	1-1	Williams, Danny 65	3,830
12	div3	Wycombe	A	L	1-4	Jones, Ma 54	4,166
13	div3	Stockport	H	W	3-0	Walters 21; Jones, Ma 51,57	4,153
14	div3	Torquay	H	W	4-2	Walters 17,76; Bennett 44; Spender 49	4,301
15	div3	Bristol Rovers	A	L	1-2	Lawrence 57	5,730
16	div3	Peterborough	A	D	1-1	Holt 88	4,014
17	div3	Darlington	H	W	1-0	McEvilly 89 pen	4,881
18	facr1	Port Vale	A	L	1-2	McEvilly 63	5,046
19	div3	Oxford	A	W	3-0	McEvilly 39,58; Jones, Ma 75	4,491
20	div3	Peterborough	H	D	1-1	Burton 69 og	4,480
21	div3	Boston	A	L	1-2	McEvilly 60	1,938
22	div3	Mansfield	H	W	4-1	Williams, Danny 49; McEvilly 53; Walters 61; Jones, Ma 87	3,421
23	div3	Notts County	H	D	1-1	Foy 90	4,726
24	div3	Carlisle	A	L	1-2	Crowell 50 pen	6,213
25	div3	Rochdale	H	W	2-1	Crowell 41 pen; Ferguson 65	5,127
26	div3	Grimsby	H	L	1-2	Jones, Ma 42	4,527
27	div3	Shrewsbury	A	L	0-1		6,249
28	div3	Lincoln	H	D	1-1	Jones, Ma 90	3,809
29	div3	Rushden & D	A	W	2-0	Jones, Ma 36,67	2,617
30	div3	Leyton Orient	H	L	1-2	Bennett 89	5,031
31	div3	Wycombe	H	W	2-0	Lawrence 12; Williams, S 15	4,311
32	div3	Rushden & D	H	W	2-0	Derbyshire 24,36	3,195
33	div3	Mansfield	A	D	2-2	Derbyshire 51,62	3,139
34	div3	Northampton	H	L	0-1		5,012
35	div3	Barnet	A	D	2-2	Jones, Ma 44; Derbyshire 51	2,127
36	div3	Bury	H	D	0-0		4,134
37	div3	Macclesfield	A	L	2-3	Williams, S 9; Holt 33	1,616
38	div3	Rochdale	A	W	1-0	Derbyshire 20	2,856
39	div3	Cheltenham	A	D	2-2	Derbyshire 1,64	2,737
40	div3	Chester	H	W	2-1	Williams, Danny 11; Jones, Ma 36	7,240
41	div3	Grimsby	A	L	0-2		6,058
42	div3	Shrewsbury	H	L	1-2	Derbyshire 78	6,310
43	div3	Chester	A	L	1-2	McEvilly 69	4,801
44	div3	Stockport	A	L	1-2	Spender 38	4,750
45	div3	Bristol Rovers	H	W	1-0	Derbyshire 5	3,749
46	div3	Torquay	A	L	0-1		2,623
47	div3	Oxford	H	D	1-1	Crowell 28	4,575
48	div3	Darlington	A	D	1-1	Williams, D 31	4,648

TEAM OF THE SEASON

G — Michael Ingham CG: 39 DR: 77

D — Lee Roche CG: 16 DR: 98

D — Shaun Pejic CG: 26 DR: 84

D — Andy Holt CG: 32 DR: 80

D — Dennis Lawrence CG: 35 DR: 78

M — Alex Smith CG: 13 SD: 15

M — Dean Bennett CG: 18 SD: 9

M — Mark Jones CG: 40 SD: 9

M — Darren Ferguson CG: 35 SD: 8

F — Matthew Derbyshire CG: 15 SR: 141

F — Jonathan Walters CG: 33 SR: 599

KEY PLAYER APPEARANCES

	PLAYER	POS	AGE	APP	MINS ON	GOALS	CARDS(Y/R)	
1	Danny Williams	MID	26	45	3994	3	7	1
2	Mark Jones	MID	22	42	3615	13	7	0
3	Michael Ingham	GK	25	40	3534	0	1	0
4	Darren Ferguson	MID	34	39	3283	2	6	0
5	Dennis Lawrence	DEF	32	39	3275	2	4	0
6	Andy Holt	DEF	28	36	3037	3	2	0
7	Jonathan Walters	ATT	22	38	2997	5	4	0
8	Shaun Pejic	DEF	23	26	2340	0	1	0
9	Matt Crowell	MID	21	29	2203	3	5	0
10	Dean Bennett	MID	28	33	1928	2	2	1
11	David Bayliss	DEF	30	22	1928	0	4	1
12	Lee Roche	DEF	25	17	1473	1	3	0
13	Matthew Derbyshire	ATT	20	16	1410	10	2	0
14	Simon Spender	DEF	20	19	1399	2	0	1
15	Alex Smith	MID	30	20	1336	0	3	0
16	Lee McEvilly	ATT	24	23	1273	7	1	0
17	Sam Williams	ATT	19	15	1220	2	1	0
18	Robbie Foy	ATT	20	17	798	3	1	0

KEY PLAYERS - GOALSCORERS

Matthew Derbyshire

Goals in the League	10
Contribution to Attacking Power Average number of minutes between League team goals while on pitch	74
Player Strike Rate Average number of minutes between League goals scored by player	141
Club Strike Rate Average number of minutes between League goals scored by club	68

	PLAYER	LGE GOALS	POWER	STRIKE RATE
1	Matthew Derbyshire	10	74	141 mins
2	Mark Jones	13	63	278 mins
3	Jonathan Walters	5	68	599 mins
4	Sam Williams	2	72	610 mins

KEY PLAYERS - MIDFIELDERS

Alex Smith

Goals in the League	0
Defensive Rating Average number of mins between League goals conceded while on the pitch	79
Contribution to Attacking Power Average number of minutes between League team goals while on pitch	64
Scoring Difference Defensive Rating minus Contribution to Attacking Power	15

	PLAYER	LGE GOALS	DEF RATE	POWER	SCORE DIFF
1	Alex Smith	0	79	64	15 mins
2	Dean Bennett	2	71	62	9 mins
3	Mark Jones	13	72	63	9 mins
4	Danny Williams	3	75	67	8 mins

KEY PLAYERS - DEFENDERS

Lee Roche

Goals Conceded when he was on pitch	15
Defensive Rating Ave number of mins between League goals conceded while on the pitch	98
Clean Sheets In games when he played at least 70 minutes	4
Club Defensive Rating Average number of mins between League goals conceded by the club this season.	77

	PLAYER	CON LGE	CLEAN SHEETS	DEF RATE
1	Lee Roche	15	4	98 mins
2	Shaun Pejic	28	8	84 mins
3	Andy Holt	38	9	80 mins
4	Dennis Lawrence	42	9	78 mins

KEY GOALKEEPER

Michael Ingham

Goals Conceded in the League	46
Defensive Rating Ave number of mins between League goals conceded while on the pitch.	77
Counting Games Games when he played at least 70 mins	40
Clean Sheets In games when he played at least 70 mins	10

TOP POINT EARNERS

	PLAYER	GAMES	AV PTS
1	Alex Smith	13	1.62
2	Simon Spender	13	1.46
3	Matt Crowell	23	1.39
4	Sam Williams	14	1.36
5	Dean Bennett	18	1.33
6	Lee Roche	16	1.31
7	David Bayliss	21	1.29
8	Michael Ingham	39	1.28
9	Danny Williams	44	1.27
10	Darren Ferguson	35	1.26
	CLUB AVERAGE:		1.28

ROCHDALE

Final Position: **14th**

NICKNAME: THE DALE

KEY: ☐Won ☐Drawn ☐Lost

							Attendance
1	div3	Shrewsbury	A	W	1-0	Holt, Grant 15	4,927
2	div3	Wycombe	H	L	1-2	Jones 79 pen	2,755
3	div3	Cheltenham	H	D	1-1	Lambert 53	2,344
4	div3	Leyton Orient	A	W	4-1	Holt, Grant 24; Lambert 29,68; Goodall 74	4,223
5	ccr1	Bradford	H	L	0-5		2,820
6	div3	Macclesfield	H	W	3-1	Holt, Grant 31,76; Goodall 33	2,606
7	div3	Darlington	A	L	1-2	Holt, Grant 61 pen	4,318
8	div3	Torquay	H	W	4-1	Lambert 14,67; Warner 22; Holt, Grant 54 pen	2,388
9	div3	Boston	A	L	2-3	Holt, Grant 16; Griffiths 53	2,274
10	div3	Mansfield	H	W	2-0	Sturrock 25; Holt, Grant 83	2,965
11	div3	Barnet	A	D	1-1	Holt, Grant 36	2,338
12	div3	Oxford	H	L	0-1		2,347
13	div3	Rushden & D	H	W	2-1	Sturrock 45; Boardman 90	2,606
14	div3	Chester	A	W	3-2	Jones 40; Holt, Grant 69; Lambert 85	4,327
15	div3	Notts County	H	W	3-0	Lambert 4,12; Cartwright 20	3,348
16	div3	Peterborough	A	L	1-3	Holt, Grant 28 pen	4,314
17	div3	Lincoln	H	L	1-2	Cooksey 54	3,420
18	facr1	Brentford	H	L	0-1		2,928
19	div3	Bristol Rovers	A	W	2-1	Holt, Grant 31 pen; Sturrock 66	6,042
20	div3	Chester	H	D	2-2	Sturrock 69; Lambert 82	3,618
21	div3	Shrewsbury	H	W	4-3	Holt, Grant 6 pen,78; Lambert 47,81	2,845
22	div3	Grimsby	A	L	1-4	Lambert 27	3,896
23	div3	Wycombe	A	L	0-3		4,928
24	div3	Leyton Orient	H	L	2-4	Goodall 24; Sturrock 65	2,666
25	div3	Wrexham	A	L	1-2	Tait 21	5,127
26	div3	Carlisle	A	L	1-2	Sturrock 2	6,897
27	div3	Northampton	H	D	1-1	Low 71 og	3,030
28	div3	Stockport	H	L	0-1		3,520
29	div3	Mansfield	A	L	0-1		3,018
30	div3	Torquay	A	W	3-1	Dagnall 29; Jones 48; Lambert 68	2,043
31	div3	Boston	H	D	1-1	Griffiths 30	2,384
32	div3	Oxford	A	D	1-1	Cooksey 45	3,978
33	div3	Stockport	A	L	0-3		4,312
34	div3	Cheltenham	A	D	1-1	Lambert 82	3,184
35	div3	Bury	H	D	1-1	Lambert 70 pen	3,876
36	div3	Macclesfield	A	W	3-1	McArdle 27; Christie 49; Lambert 83	2,211
37	div3	Wrexham	H	L	0-1		2,856
38	div3	Grimsby	H	D	2-2	Ramsden 52; Lambert 90	1,865
39	div3	Bury	A	L	1-2	Jones 71	4,276
40	div3	Darlington	H	L	0-2		1,963
41	div3	Northampton	A	D	2-2	Lambert 51,90 pen	5,732
42	div3	Rushden & D	A	D	1-1	Dagnall 90	3,135
43	div3	Peterborough	H	W	1-0	Christie 72	2,318
44	div3	Notts County	A	D	1-1	Lambert 81 pen	4,413
45	div3	Barnet	H	D	1-1	Dagnall 23	1,769
46	div3	Bristol Rovers	H	W	2-0	Lambert 45 pen; Cooksey 90	2,649
47	div3	Carlisle	H	L	0-2		4,439
48	div3	Lincoln	A	D	1-1	Lambert 88	7,165

TEAM OF THE SEASON

G — Mathew Gilks CG: 46 DR: 60

D — Simon Ramsden CG: 12 DR: 70

D — Scott Warner CG: 13 DR: 69

D — Gareth Griffiths CG: 26 DR: 62

D — Jonathan Boardman CG: 16 DR: 59

M — Ernie Cooksey CG: 24 SD: 6

M — Lee Cartwright CG: 16 SD: 1

M — Rickie Lambert CG: 41 SD: -2

M — Gary Jones CG: 42 SD: -7

F — Grant Holt CG: 20 SR: 131

F — Blair Sturrock CG: 14 SR: 255

KEY PLAYER APPEARANCES

	PLAYER	POS	AGE	APP	MINS ON	GOALS	CARDS(Y/R)	
1	Mathew Gilks	GK	24	46	4140	0	1	0
2	Rickie Lambert	MID	24	46	3779	22	3	0
3	Gary Jones	MID	37	42	3771	4	6	0
4	Alan Goodall	DEF	24	39	3278	3	4	0
5	Tony Gallimore	DEF	34	34	2838	0	2	0
6	Gareth Griffiths	DEF	36	29	2477	2	4	1
7	Ernie Cooksey	MID	26	34	2459	3	3	0
8	Jamie Clarke	DEF	23	22	1908	0	3	0
9	Grant Holt	ATT	25	21	1836	14	8	0
10	Lee Cartwright	MID	33	27	1783	1	0	0
11	Jonathan Boardman	DEF	25	21	1638	1	1	0
12	Blair Sturrock	ATT	24	31	1527	6	0	0
13	Scott Warner	DEF	22	24	1517	1	0	0
14	Rory McArdle	DEF	19	19	1514	1	2	0
15	Chris Dagnall	ATT	21	21	1438	3	1	0
16	John Doolan	MID	32	18	1384	0	3	0
17	Simon Ramsden	DEF	24	15	1253	1	0	0
18	Neil Brisco	MID	28	16	1054	0	3	1

KEY PLAYERS - GOALSCORERS

Grant Holt

Goals in the League	14	Player Strike Rate Average number of minutes between League goals scored by player	131
Contribution to Attacking Power Average number of minutes between League team goals while on pitch	48	Club Strike Rate Average number of minutes between League goals scored by club	63

	PLAYER	LGE GOALS	POWER	STRIKE RATE
1	Grant Holt	14	48	131 mins
2	Rickie Lambert	22	64	172 mins
3	Blair Sturrock	6	64	255 mins
4	Chris Dagnall	3	76	479 mins

KEY PLAYERS - MIDFIELDERS

Ernie Cooksey

Goals in the League	3	Contribution to Attacking Power Average number of minutes between League team goals while on pitch	60
Defensive Rating Average number of mins between League goals conceded while on the pitch	66	Scoring Difference Defensive Rating minus Contribution to Attacking Power	6

	PLAYER	LGE GOALS	DEF RATE	POWER	SCORE DIFF
1	Ernie Cooksey	3	66	60	6 mins
2	Lee Cartwright	1	59	58	1 mins
3	Rickie Lambert	22	62	64	-2 mins
4	Gary Jones	4	59	66	-7 mins

KEY PLAYERS - DEFENDERS

Simon Ramsden

Goals Conceded when he was on pitch	18	Clean Sheets In games when he played at least 70 minutes	1
Defensive Rating Ave number of mins between League goals conceded while on the pitch	70	Club Defensive Rating Average number of mins between League goals conceded by the club this season.	60

	PLAYER	CON LGE	CLEAN SHEETS	DEF RATE
1	Simon Ramsden	18	1	70 mins
2	Scott Warner	22	2	69 mins
3	Gareth Griffiths	40	5	62 mins
4	Jonathan Boardman	28	2	59 mins

KEY GOALKEEPER

Mathew Gilks

Goals Conceded in the League	69
Defensive Rating Ave number of mins between League goals conceded while on the pitch.	60
Counting Games Games when he played at least 70 mins	46
Clean Sheets In games when he played at least 70 mins	5

TOP POINT EARNERS

	PLAYER	GAMES	AV PTS
1	Lee Cartwright	16	1.69
2	Jamie Clarke	21	1.57
3	Blair Sturrock	14	1.43
4	Grant Holt	20	1.40
5	Scott Warner	13	1.38
6	Alan Goodall	36	1.31
7	Ernie Cooksey	24	1.29
8	Rickie Lambert	41	1.27
9	Tony Gallimore	31	1.26
10	Mathew Gilks	46	1.22
	CLUB AVERAGE:		1.22

CHESTER CITY

Final Position: **15th**

NICKNAME: THE BLUES

KEY: Won / Drawn / Lost

							Attendance
1	div3	Peterborough	A	W	1-0	Drummond 70	4,980
2	div3	Lincoln	H	D	2-2	Davies 50; Branch 90 pen	2,637
3	div3	Rushden & D	A	D	1-1	Lowe 56	2,682
4	ccr1	Wolverhampton	A	L	1-5	Davies 83	9,518
5	div3	Darlington	H	D	4-4	Richardson 47,90; Blundell 55,89	2,469
6	div3	Torquay	A	W	1-0	Lowe 90	2,245
7	div3	Mansfield	H	W	3-1	Blundell 2,60; Lowe 80	3,079
8	div3	Grimsby	H	L	1-2	Lowe 53	3,095
9	div3	Notts County	A	D	1-1	Davies 70	5,404
10	div3	Bristol Rovers	H	W	4-0	Lowe 34; Artell 35; Richardson 45; Blundell 87	2,974
11	div3	Stockport	A	D	0-0		4,873
12	div3	Carlisle	H	W	2-0	Artell 11; Blundell 40	3,394
13	div3	Wycombe	A	D	3-3	Drummond 10; Branch 36,60	5,145
14	div3	Rochdale	H	L	2-3	Drummond 54; Davies 57	4,327
15	div3	Barnet	A	W	3-1	Branch 14; Lowe 44; Curtis 69	2,206
16	div3	Bury	H	D	1-1	Latham 78 pen	3,471
17	div3	Shrewsbury	A	L	1-3	Lowe 35	5,430
18	facr1	Folkestone	H	W	2-1	Branch 55 pen; Lowe 71	2,503
19	div3	Northampton	H	D	0-0		3,295
20	div3	Rochdale	A	D	2-2	Bolland 20; Davies 64	3,618
21	div3	Peterborough	H	W	3-1	Branch 35 pen; Drummond 53; Lowe 66	2,701
22	facr2	Nottm Forest	H	W	3-0	Lowe 40 pen,50; Richardson 55	4,732
23	div3	Leyton Orient	A	W	1-0	Drummond 45	3,463
24	div3	Lincoln	A	L	1-3	Richardson 49	3,563
25	div3	Rushden & D	H	L	1-2	Davies 33 pen	2,265
26	div3	Cheltenham	A	L	0-1		3,819
27	div3	Macclesfield	A	L	0-1		2,910
28	div3	Oxford	H	L	0-1		2,624
29	facr3	Cheltenham	A	D	2-2	Richardson 80; Drummond 90	4,741
30	div3	Boston	H	L	0-1		2,956
31	facr3r	Cheltenham	H	L	0-1		5,096
32	div3	Bristol Rovers	A	L	1-2	Davies 89	6,310
33	div3	Mansfield	A	W	2-1	McNiven 54; Asamoah 69	3,219
34	div3	Notts County	H	L	0-2		2,599
35	div3	Carlisle	A	L	0-5		6,581
36	div3	Stockport	H	L	1-2	Lowe 81	3,446
37	div3	Leyton Orient	H	L	0-2		2,210
38	div3	Grimsby	A	L	0-1		4,058
39	div3	Torquay	H	D	1-1	Blundell 58	1,806
40	div3	Darlington	A	L	0-1		3,593
41	div3	Cheltenham	H	L	0-1		2,281
42	div3	Wrexham	A	L	1-2	Edwards 89	7,240
43	div3	Boston	A	W	3-1	Asamoah 43,50,61	1,651
44	div3	Macclesfield	H	W	2-1	Asamoah 50,90	2,939
45	div3	Oxford	A	W	1-0	Asamoah 19	5,754
46	div3	Wrexham	H	W	2-1	Davies 56 pen; Asamoah 75	4,801
47	div3	Wycombe	H	W	1-0	Drummond 64	2,797
48	div3	Bury	A	D	0-0		3,421
49	div3	Barnet	H	D	0-0		2,367
50	div3	Northampton	A	L	0-1		7,114
51	div3	Shrewsbury	H	L	0-1		3,744

TEAM OF THE SEASON

- G: Chris MacKenzie — CG: 29 DR: 89
- D: Sean Hessey — CG: 17 DR: 89
- D: David Artell — CG: 33 DR: 82
- D: Luke Dimech — CG: 28 DR: 73
- D: Carl Regan — CG: 33 DR: 72
- M: Ben Davies — CG: 42 SD: -4
- M: Ryan Lowe — CG: 28 SD: -5
- M: Stuart Drummond — CG: 37 SD: -8
- M: Tom Curtis — CG: 30 SD: -15
- F: Derek Asamoah — CG: 12 SR: 155
- F: Greg Blundell — CG: 19 SR: 289

KEY PLAYER APPEARANCES

	PLAYER	POS	AGE	APP	MINS ON	GOALS	CARDS(Y/R)	
1	Ben Davies	MID	25	45	3884	7	6	0
2	Scott McNiven	DEF	28	41	3577	1	6	0
3	Stuart Drummond	MID	30	42	3499	6	2	1
4	Carl Regan	DEF	26	41	3316	0	10	0
5	David Artell	DEF	25	37	3022	2	6	1
6	Tom Curtis	MID	33	39	2977	1	11	0
7	Chris MacKenzie	GK	28	30	2657	0	2	0
8	Ryan Lowe	MID	27	32	2653	9	8	1
9	Luke Dimech	DEF	29	30	2549	0	5	0
10	Michael Branch	ATT	27	27	2056	5	5	0
11	Greg Blundell	ATT	30	30	2026	7	2	0
12	Marcus Richardson	ATT	28	34	1808	4	3	0
13	Sean Hessey	DEF	27	19	1601	0	1	0
14	Derek Asamoah	ATT	25	17	1239	8	2	0
15	Justin Walker	MID	30	21	1065	0	3	0
16	Abdelhalim El Kholti	DEF	25	22	1041	0	3	0
17	Philip Bolland	DEF	29	16	1036	1	3	0
18	Mark Albrighton	DEF	30	9	810	0	4	0

KEY PLAYERS - GOALSCORERS

Derek Asamoah

Goals in the League	8
Contribution to Attacking Power Average number of minutes between League team goals while on pitch	103
Player Strike Rate Average number of minutes between League goals scored by player	155
Club Strike Rate Average number of minutes between League goals scored by club	78

	PLAYER	LGE GOALS	POWER	STRIKE RATE
1	Derek Asamoah	8	103	155 mins
2	Greg Blundell	7	88	289 mins
3	Ryan Lowe	9	68	295 mins
4	Michael Branch	5	60	411 mins

KEY PLAYERS - MIDFIELDERS

Ben Davies

Goals in the League	7
Defensive Rating Average number of mins between League goals conceded while on the pitch	8
Contribution to Attacking Power Average number of minutes between League team goals while on pitch	71
Scoring Difference Defensive Rating minus Contribution to Attacking Power	-4

	PLAYER	LGE GOALS	DEF RATE	POWER	SCORE DIFF
1	Ben Davies	7	8	71	-4 mins
2	Ryan Lowe	9	12	63	-5 mins
3	Stuart Drummond	6	7	70	-8 mins
4	Tom Curtis	1	1	73	-15 mins

KEY PLAYERS - DEFENDERS

Sean Hessey

Goals Conceded when he was on pitch	18
Defensive Rating Ave number of mins between League goals conceded while on the pitch	89
Clean Sheets In games when he played at least 70 minutes	5
Club Defensive Rating Average number of mins between League goals conceded by the club this season.	70

	PLAYER	CON LGE	CLEAN SHEETS	DEF RATE
1	Sean Hessey	18	5	89 mins
2	David Artell	37	9	82 mins
3	Luke Dimech	35	8	73 mins
4	Carl Regan	46	9	72 mins

KEY GOALKEEPER

Chris MacKenzie

Goals Conceded in the League	30
Defensive Rating Ave number of mins between League goals conceded while on the pitch.	89
Counting Games Games when he played at least 70 mins	29
Clean Sheets In games when he played at least 70 mins	11

TOP POINT EARNERS

	PLAYER	GAMES	AV PTS
1	Chris MacKenzie	29	1.72
2	Derek Asamoah	12	1.67
3	David Artell	33	1.42
4	Greg Blundell	19	1.37
5	Sean Hessey	17	1.35
6	Ben Davies	42	1.26
7	Scott McNiven	39	1.23
8	Stuart Drummond	37	1.19
9	Luke Dimech	28	1.18
10	Ryan Lowe	28	1.14
	CLUB AVERAGE:		1.17

MANSFIELD TOWN

Final Position: **16th**

CKNAME: THE STAGS — KEY: Won / Drawn / Lost

							Attendance
1	div3	**Stockport**	A	D	2-2	Dawson 22; Birchall 31	4,970
2	div3	**Rushden & D**	H	L	0-1		3,402
3	div3	**Torquay**	H	W	3-0	Rundle 15; Peers 43; Brown 82	2,632
4	div3	**Peterborough**	A	L	0-2		4,056
5	ccr1	**Stoke**	H	W	3-0*	Jelleyman 16 (*on penalties)	2,799
6	div3	**Boston**	A	D	2-2	Barker 26 pen; Brown 69	2,848
7	div3	**Notts County**	H	L	2-3	Barker 15; Jelleyman 60	6,444
8	div3	**Chester**	A	L	1-3	Baptiste 67	3,079
9	div3	**Darlington**	H	D	2-2	Brown 9,64	2,803
10	div3	**Rochdale**	A	L	0-2		2,965
11	ccr2	**Southampton**	H	W	1-0	Coke 68	3,739
12	div3	**Wycombe**	H	L	2-3	Barker 66 pen; Brown 75	3,237
13	div3	**Macclesfield**	A	D	1-1	Birchall 49	1,576
14	div3	**Leyton Orient**	A	L	1-3	Coke 66	4,164
15	div3	**Shrewsbury**	H	W	4-0	Coke 6; Rundle 65; Barker 69; Uhlenbeek 71	3,334
16	div3	**Carlisle**	A	L	0-1		5,293
17	div3	**Barnet**	H	W	4-0	Barker 11 pen,83; Brown 65; Rundle 69	2,809
18	ccr3	**Millwall**	H	L	2-3	Brown 67; Barker 68	4,133
19	div3	**Cheltenham**	A	W	2-0	Barker 29; Brown 68	3,033
20	facr1	**Rotherham**	A	W	4-3	Brown 28; Coke 37; Barker 75,90	4,089
21	div3	**Bury**	H	L	0-3		4,147
22	div3	**Stockport**	H	W	2-1	Peers 26; Barker 31	2,994
23	facr2	**Grays Ath**	H	W	3-0	Barker 13,42 pen; Birchall 77	2,992
24	div3	**Wrexham**	A	L	1-4	Barker 41 pen	3,421
25	div3	**Rushden & D**	A	W	2-1	Brown 19; Coke 50	2,477
26	div3	**Peterborough**	H	D	0-0		3,891
27	div3	**Northampton**	A	L	0-1		6,112
28	div3	**Bristol Rovers**	H	D	3-3	Arnold 14; Rundle 25; Russell 74	2,357
29	div3	**Oxford**	A	W	2-1	Day 61,79	4,005
30	div3	**Lincoln**	H	D	0-0		4,946
31	facr3	**Newcastle**	A	L	0-1		41,459
32	div3	**Grimsby**	A	L	1-2	Barker 79 pen	4,506
33	div3	**Shrewsbury**	A	D	0-0		3,747
34	div3	**Rochdale**	H	W	1-0	Reet (Mans) 40	3,018
35	div3	**Chester**	H	L	1-2	Reet 51	3,219
36	div3	**Darlington**	A	L	0-4		4,282
37	div3	**Macclesfield**	H	D	1-1	Rundle 56	2,901
38	div3	**Wycombe**	A	D	2-2	Hjelde 27; Barker 33	5,041
39	div3	**Grimsby**	H	W	2-1	Barker 19; Coke 40	3,053
40	div3	**Wrexham**	H	D	2-2	Barker 64 pen,67	3,139
41	div3	**Torquay**	A	W	2-0	Reet 11; Brown 83	2,494
42	div3	**Notts County**	A	D	2-2	Wilson 61; Barker 64	9,779
43	div3	**Boston**	H	W	5-0	Barker 43; Greaves 47 og; Reet 51; Uhlenbeek 62; Brown 83 pen	3,121
44	div3	**Northampton**	H	W	1-0	Barker 65	3,985
45	div3	**Bristol Rovers**	A	L	0-2		5,253
46	div3	**Oxford**	H	W	1-0	Reet 84	3,480
47	div3	**Lincoln**	A	D	1-1	Russell 90	6,062
48	div3	**Leyton Orient**	H	L	0-1		4,763
49	div3	**Barnet**	A	L	0-1		2,784
50	div3	**Carlisle**	H	D	1-1	Barker 63	4,488
51	div3	**Bury**	A	D	0-0		3,105
52	div3	**Cheltenham**	H	L	0-5		3,728

TEAM OF THE SEASON

G — Kevin Pressman — CG: 41 DR: 68

D — Jake Buxton — CG: 33 DR: 84

D — Jon Olav Hjelde — CG: 27 DR: 73

D — Gus Uhlenbeek — CG: 24 DR: 66

D — Alex Baptiste — CG: 40 DR: 63

M — Jonathan D'Laryea — CG: 29 SD: 4

M — Adam Rundle — CG: 21 SD: 2

M — Stephen Dawson — CG: 24 SD: 0

M — Lawrence Wilson — CG: 14 SD: -4

F — Simon Brown — CG: 12 SR: 161

F — Richard Barker — CG: 40 SR: 207

KEY PLAYER APPEARANCES

	PLAYER	POS	AGE	APP	MINS ON	GOALS	CARDS(Y/R)	
1	Richard Barker	ATT	31	43	3718	18	3	1
2	Kevin Pressman	GK	38	41	3690	0	0	0
3	Alex Baptiste	DEF	20	41	3617	1	3	0
4	Jake Buxton	DEF	21	39	3270	0	6	0
5	Giles Coke	MID	20	40	3037	4	8	1
6	Gareth Jelleyman	DEF	25	34	2972	1	10	2
7	Stephen Dawson	MID	20	40	2650	1	2	0
8	Gus Uhlenbeek	DEF	35	40	2638	2	3	0
9	Jon Olav Hjelde	DEF	33	31	2624	1	4	1
10	Jonathan D'Laryea	MID	20	29	2585	0	0	0
11	Adam Rundle	MID	21	34	2335	5	0	0
12	Rhys Day	DEF	23	21	1890	2	1	0
13	Simon Brown	ATT	22	29	1610	10	2	0
14	Adam Birchall	ATT	21	31	1601	2	2	0
15	Lawrence Wilson	MID	19	15	1251	1	2	0
16	Danny Reet	ATT	19	18	1123	4	2	1
17	Gavin Peers	DEF	20	13	1042	2	0	0
18	Allan Russell	ATT	25	15	617	2	0	0

KEY PLAYERS - GOALSCORERS

Simon Brown

Goals in the League	10	Player Strike Rate — Average number of minutes between League goals scored by player	161
Contribution to Attacking Power — Average number of minutes between League team goals while on pitch	54	Club Strike Rate — Average number of minutes between League goals scored by club	70

	PLAYER	LGE GOALS	POWER	STRIKE RATE
1	Simon Brown	10	54	161 mins
2	Richard Barker	18	69	207 mins
3	Adam Rundle	5	73	467 mins
4	Giles Coke	4	71	759 mins

KEY PLAYERS - MIDFIELDERS

Jonathan D'Laryea

Goals in the League	0	Contribution to Attacking Power — Average number of minutes between League team goals while on pitch	72
Defensive Rating — Average number of mins between League goals conceded while on the pitch	76	Scoring Difference — Defensive Rating minus Contribution to Attacking Power	4

	PLAYER	LGE GOALS	DEF RATE	POWER	SCORE DIFF
1	Jonathan D'Laryea	0	76	72	4 mins
2	Adam Rundle	5	75	73	2 mins
3	Stephen Dawson	1	72	72	0 mins
4	Lawrence Wilson	1	74	78	-4 mins

KEY PLAYERS - DEFENDERS

Jake Buxton

Goals Conceded when he was on pitch	39	Clean Sheets — In games when he played at least 70 minutes	13
Defensive Rating — Ave number of mins between League goals conceded while on the pitch	84	Club Defensive Rating — Average number of mins between League goals conceded by the club this season.	63

	PLAYER	CON LGE	CLEAN SHEETS	DEF RATE
1	Jake Buxton	39	13	84 mins
2	Jon Olav Hjelde	36	10	73 mins
3	Gus Uhlenbeek	40	8	66 mins
4	Alex Baptiste	57	12	63 mins

KEY GOALKEEPER

Kevin Pressman

Goals Conceded in the League	54
Defensive Rating — Ave number of mins between League goals conceded while on the pitch.	68
Counting Games — Games when he played at least 70 mins	41
Clean Sheets — In games when he played at least 70 mins	12

TOP POINT EARNERS

	PLAYER	GAMES	AV PTS
1	Adam Rundle	21	1.57
2	Jake Buxton	33	1.55
3	Lawrence Wilson	14	1.43
4	Gus Uhlenbeek	24	1.42
5	Jonathan D'Laryea	29	1.41
6	Jon Olav Hjelde	27	1.37
7	Kevin Pressman	41	1.27
8	Alex Baptiste	40	1.23
9	Richard Barker	40	1.23
10	Stephen Dawson	24	1.21
	CLUB AVERAGE:		1.17

MACCLESFIELD

Final Position: **17th**

NICKNAME: THE SILKMEN

KEY: □Won □Drawn □Lost

							Attendance
1	div3	Leyton Orient	A	L	1-2	Harsley 57	3,600
2	div3	Cheltenham	H	D	2-2	MacKenzie 83; Bullock 85	1,601
3	div3	Barnet	A	L	0-1		2,005
4	ccr1	Nottm Forest	A	W	3-2	Whitaker 21; Townson 45; MacKenzie 80	5,050
5	div3	Rochdale	A	L	1-3	Townson 24	2,606
6	div3	Bury	H	W	1-0	Bullock 18	1,965
7	div3	Boston	H	D	2-2	McIntyre 21; Futcher 32 og	2,130
8	div3	Carlisle	A	L	0-2		5,190
9	div3	Rushden & D	H	W	3-1	Bullock 40,86; Harsley 56 pen	2,874
10	div3	Northampton	H	L	1-4	Bullock 62	2,014
11	ccr2	Cardiff	A	L	1-2	Bullock 5	3,849
12	div3	Wrexham	A	D	1-1	Russell 72	3,830
13	div3	Mansfield	H	D	1-1	Russell 36	1,576
14	div3	Notts County	H	D	0-0		1,892
15	div3	Darlington	A	L	0-1		3,831
16	div3	Peterborough	H	L	0-4		1,810
17	div3	Torquay	A	D	1-1	Harsley 49	2,355
18	div3	Bristol Rovers	H	W	2-1	Wijnhard 52; Harsley 65	1,908
19	facr1	Yeovil	H	D	1-1	Wijnhard 48	1,943
20	div3	Grimsby	A	L	1-3	Parkin 43	3,658
21	facr1r	Yeovil	A	L	0-4		4,456
22	div3	Darlington	H	W	1-0	McIntyre 38	1,769
23	div3	Leyton Orient	H	D	0-0		1,649
24	div3	Lincoln	A	D	2-2	Wijnhard 45; Teague 81	3,171
25	div3	Cheltenham	A	D	2-2	Sandwith 58; Parkin 71	2,804
26	div3	Barnet	H	D	1-1	Sandwith 18	1,663
27	div3	Stockport	H	W	6-0	Wijnhard 41,64; Parkin 43,63; Bullock 59; Miles 86	4,553
28	div3	Chester	H	W	1-0	McIntyre 60	2,910
29	div3	Wycombe	A	W	5-4	Wijnhard 3,13; Whitaker 10; Parkin 77,81	5,364
30	div3	Boston	A	L	1-3	Parkin 47	1,975
31	div3	Oxford	H	D	1-1	McIntyre 39	1,972
32	div3	Northampton	A	L	1-5		5,428
33	div3	Carlisle	H	W	3-0	Swailes 6; McIntyre 10; Whitaker 42	4,140
34	div3	Shrewsbury	A	D	1-1	Wijnhard 26	2,642
35	div3	Mansfield	A	D	1-1	Swailes 79	2,901
36	div3	Oxford	A	D	1-1	Sandwith 16	4,331
37	div3	Lincoln	H	D	1-1	Wijnhard 32 pen	2,268
38	div3	Rushden & D	A	L	0-1		2,479
39	div3	Rochdale	H	L	1-3	Miles 56	2,211
40	div3	Wrexham	H	W	3-2	Holt 43 og; Whitaker 74; Briscoe 82	1,616
41	div3	Stockport	A	L	0-2		6,003
42	div3	Shrewsbury	H	W	2-0	McNeil 33; Bullock 61	2,274
43	div3	Chester	A	L	1-2	Townson 75	2,939
44	div3	Bury	A	D	0-0		2,273
45	div3	Wycombe	H	W	2-1	Harsley 39 pen; Whitaker 53	1,869
46	div3	Notts County	A	D	1-1	Harsley 89 pen	4,393
47	div3	Torquay	H	L	0-2		1,808
48	div3	Peterborough	A	L	2-3	Miles 62,89	3,002
49	div3	Grimsby	H	D	1-1	Richardson 43	3,849
50	div3	Bristol Rovers	A	W	3-2	Morley 7; Richardson 29,89	6,100

TEAM OF THE SEASON

G	Alan Fettis	CG: 32	DR: 57
D	Danny Swailes	CG: 38	DR: 64
D	David Morley	CG: 43	DR: 57
D	Andrew Teague	CG: 23	DR: 57
D	Kevin Sandwith	CG: 29	DR: 56
M	Alan Navarro	CG: 24	SD: 2
M	Kevin McIntyre	CG: 40	SD: -4
M	Danny Whitaker	CG: 39	SD: -6
M	Paul Harsley	CG: 44	SD: -11
F	Clyde Wijnhard	CG: 19	SR: 209
F	Martin Bullock*	CG: 37	SR: 484

KEY PLAYER APPEARANCES

	PLAYER	POS	AGE	APP	MINS ON	GOALS	CARDS(Y	R)
1	Paul Harsley	MID	28	45	3973	6	6	0
2	David Morley	DEF	28	45	3946	1	4	0
3	Kevin McIntyre	MID	28	44	3811	5	8	0
4	Danny Whitaker	MID	25	41	3541	4	3	0
5	Danny Swailes	DEF	27	39	3438	2	4	0
6	Martin Bullock	MID	31	40	3387	7	3	0
7	Kevin Sandwith	DEF	28	35	2918	3	3	0
8	Alan Fettis	GK	35	33	2915	0	1	0
9	Alan Navarro	MID	25	27	2327	0	4	0
10	Andrew Teague	DEF	20	25	2098	1	1	0
11	Clyde Wijnhard	ATT	32	19	1670	8	2	0
12	John Miles	ATT	24	24	1162	4	0	0
13	Matthew McNeil	ATT	29	12	1080	1	2	0
14	Michael Briscoe	DEF	23	13	1014	1	2	0
15	Allan Russell	ATT	25	13	998	2	0	0
16	Tommy Lee	GK	20	11	990	0	0	0
17	Ian Brightwell	DEF	38	11	945	0	0	0
18	Jonathan Parkin	ATT	24	11	870	7	3	0

KEY PLAYERS - GOALSCORERS

Clyde Wijnhard

Goals in the League	8
Contribution to Attacking Power Average number of minutes between League team goals while on pitch	56
Player Strike Rate Average number of minutes between League goals scored by player	209
Club Strike Rate Average number of minutes between League goals scored by club	69

	PLAYER	LGE GOALS	POWER	STRIKE RATE
1	Clyde Wijnhard	8	56	209 mins
2	Martin Bullock	7	71	484 mins
3	Paul Harsley	6	69	662 mins
4	Kevin McIntyre	5	69	762 mins

KEY PLAYERS - MIDFIELDERS

Alan Navarro

Goals in the League	0
Defensive Rating Average number of mins between League goals conceded while on the pitch	57
Contribution to Attacking Power Average number of minutes between League team goals while on pitch	55
Scoring Difference Defensive Rating minus Contribution to Attacking Power	2

	PLAYER	LGE GOALS	DEF RATE	POWER	SCORE DIFF
1	Alan Navarro	0	57	55	2 mins
2	Kevin McIntyre	5	65	69	-4 mins
3	Danny Whitaker	4	61	67	-6 mins
4	Paul Harsley	6	58	69	-11 mins

KEY PLAYERS - DEFENDERS

Danny Swailes

Goals Conceded when he was on pitch	54
Defensive Rating Ave number of mins between League goals conceded while on the pitch	64
Clean Sheets In games when he played at least 70 minutes	7
Club Defensive Rating Average number of mins between League goals conceded by the club this season.	58

	PLAYER	CON LGE	CLEAN SHEETS	DEF RATE
1	Danny Swailes	54	7	64 mins
2	Andrew Teague	37	5	57 mins
3	David Morley	69	8	57 mins
4	Kevin Sandwith	52	7	56 mins

KEY GOALKEEPER

Alan Fettis

Goals Conceded in the League	51
Defensive Rating Ave number of mins between League goals conceded while on the pitch.	57
Counting Games Games when he played at least 70 mins	33
Clean Sheets In games when he played at least 70 mins	7

TOP POINT EARNERS

	PLAYER	GAMES	AV PTS
1	Alan Navarro	24	1.50
2	Clyde Wijnhard	19	1.47
3	Kevin McIntyre	40	1.33
4	Danny Whitaker	39	1.33
5	Andrew Teague	23	1.30
6	Matthew McNeil	12	1.25
7	Kevin Sandwith	29	1.21
8	David Morley	43	1.19
9	Martin Bullock	37	1.19
10	Paul Harsley	44	1.16
	CLUB AVERAGE:		1.17

BARNET

Final Position: **18th**

KNAME: THE BEES — KEY: Won / Drawn / Lost

	Comp	Opponent	H/A	Res	Score	Scorers	Attendance
1	div3	Bristol Rovers	H	D	1-1	Graham 77	3,237
2	div3	Northampton	A	W	2-1	Sinclair 56; Bailey 88	5,817
3	div3	Carlisle	A	W	3-1	Grazioli 51; Bailey 60; Sinclair 90	6,650
4	div3	Macclesfield	H	W	1-0	Bailey 26	2,005
5	ccr1	Bristol City	A	W	4-2	Lee 17,53; Bailey 58; Roache 81	3,383
6	div3	Grimsby	H	L	0-1		2,447
7	div3	Wrexham	A	L	1-3	Hendon 45 pen	3,768
8	div3	Cheltenham	A	D	1-1	Lee 56	3,343
9	div3	Leyton Orient	H	L	2-3	Grazioli 1,90	3,722
10	div3	Wycombe	A	L	0-1		4,994
11	ccr2	Plymouth	H	W	2-1	King 12; Grazioli 46	1,941
12	div3	Rochdale	H	D	1-1	Grazioli 87	2,338
13	div3	Shrewsbury	A	D	2-2	Bailey 14 pen; Soares 30	3,628
14	div3	Oxford	H	D	0-0		3,272
15	div3	Torquay	A	D	0-0		2,965
16	div3	Chester	H	L	1-3	Grazioli 78	2,206
17	div3	Mansfield	A	L	0-4		2,809
18	ccr3	Man Utd	A	L	1-4	Sinclair 74	43,673
19	div3	Rushden & D	H	W	2-1	Lee 45; Strevens 74	2,564
20	facr1	Southend	H	L	0-1		3,545
21	div3	Stockport	A	D	1-1	Norville 18	6,056
22	div3	Torquay	H	W	1-0	Bailey 13	2,368
23	div3	Bristol Rovers	A	L	1-2	Strevens 68	5,096
24	div3	Bury	H	D	1-1	Strevens 84	1,796
25	div3	Northampton	H	L	0-1		2,544
26	div3	Macclesfield	A	D	1-1	Bailey 90	1,663
27	div3	Peterborough	H	W	2-1	Yakubu 36; Lee 62	2,715
28	div3	Darlington	A	L	1-2	Strevens 90	2,905
29	div3	Boston	H	W	1-0	Lee 47	2,287
30	div3	Notts County	A	L	0-1		5,249
31	div3	Cheltenham	H	D	1-1	Grazioli 81	1,366
32	div3	Lincoln	A	L	1-4	Grazioli 13	4,033
33	div3	Wycombe	H	D	0-0		3,602
34	div3	Shrewsbury	H	W	1-0	Kandol 29	1,789
35	div3	Lincoln	H	L	2-3	Strevens 21; Kandol 53	1,695
36	div3	Bury	A	D	0-0		2,083
37	div3	Carlisle	H	L	1-2	Holmes 53 og	2,870
38	div3	Leyton Orient	A	D	0-0		4,910
39	div3	Wrexham	H	D	2-2	Norville 30; Kandol 37	2,127
40	div3	Grimsby	A	L	0-3		5,147
41	div3	Peterborough	A	D	2-2	Hessenthaler 10; Fuller 70	3,983
42	div3	Darlington	H	W	1-0	Kandol 80	2,845
43	div3	Boston	A	L	1-2	Roache 73	2,066
44	div3	Notts County	H	W	2-1	Hendon 64 pen,72 pen	2,841
45	div3	Oxford	A	L	0-2		6,948
46	div3	Mansfield	H	W	1-0	Hatch 11	2,784
47	div3	Chester	A	D	0-0		2,367
48	div3	Rochdale	A	D	1-1	Hendon 28 pen	1,769
49	div3	Stockport	H	D	0-0		3,873
50	div3	Rushden & D	A	W	2-1	Hatch 51; Bailey 55	4,174

TEAM OF THE SEASON

		CG	
G	Ross Flitney	CG: 35	DR: 81
D	Simon King	CG: 29	DR: 79
D	Damien Batt	CG: 13	DR: 76
D	Adam Gross	CG: 17	DR: 72
D	Ian Hendon	CG: 33	DR: 71
M	Dwane Lee	CG: 23	SD: -11
M	Nick Bailey	CG: 45	SD: -20
M	Barry Fuller	CG: 15	SD: -21
M	Dean Sinclair	CG: 39	SD: -22
F	Tresor Kandol	CG: 13	SR: 293
F	Guiliano Grazioli	CG: 24	SR: 321

KEY PLAYER APPEARANCES

	PLAYER	POS	AGE	APP	MINS ON	GOALS	CARDS(Y)	CARDS(R)
1	Nick Bailey	MID	22	45	4017	7	7	0
2	Dean Sinclair	MID	21	44	3587	2	4	0
3	Anthony Charles	DEF	25	40	3416	0	6	0
4	Ross Flitney	GK	22	35	3150	0	1	0
5	Ian Hendon	DEF	34	35	3046	4	5	0
6	Simon King	DEF	23	32	2695	0	10	0
7	Ben Strevens	ATT	26	35	2620	5	4	0
8	Guiliano Grazioli	ATT	31	29	2245	7	3	0
9	Dwane Lee	MID	26	27	2201	4	8	0
10	Ishmail Yakubu	DEF	21	26	2186	1	1	0
11	Liam Hatch	ATT	22	35	2097	2	9	0
12	Adam Gross	DEF	20	20	1650	0	4	0
13	Barry Fuller	MID	21	15	1350	1	5	0
14	Damien Batt	DEF	21	21	1298	0	3	0
15	Andy Hessenthaler	MID	40	16	1280	1	2	0
16	Tresor Kandol	ATT	24	13	1170	4	3	0
17	Louie Soares	DEF	21	19	1166	1	1	0
18	Simon Clist	MID	25	14	1123	0	1	0

KEY PLAYERS - GOALSCORERS

Tresor Kandol

Goals in the League	4
Contribution to Attacking Power — Average number of minutes between League team goals while on pitch	98
Player Strike Rate — Average number of minutes between League goals scored by player	293
Club Strike Rate — Average number of minutes between League goals scored by club	94

	PLAYER	LGE GOALS	POWER	STRIKE RATE
1	Tresor Kandol	4	98	293 mins
2	Guiliano Grazioli	7	98	321 mins
3	Ben Strevens	5	94	524 mins
4	Dwane Lee	4	82	550 mins

KEY PLAYERS - MIDFIELDERS

Dwane Lee

Goals in the League	4
Defensive Rating — Average number of mins between League goals conceded while on the pitch	71
Contribution to Attacking Power — Average number of minutes between League team goals while on pitch	82
Scoring Difference — Defensive Rating minus Contribution to Attacking Power	-11

	PLAYER	LGE GOALS	DEF RATE	POWER	SCORE DIFF
1	Dwane Lee	4	71	82	-11 mins
2	Nick Bailey	7	73	93	-20 mins
3	Barry Fuller	1	75	96	-21 mins
4	Dean Sinclair	2	75	97	-22 mins

KEY PLAYERS - DEFENDERS

Simon King

Goals Conceded when he was on pitch	34
Defensive Rating — Ave number of mins between League goals conceded while on the pitch	79
Clean Sheets — In games when he played at least 70 minutes	7
Club Defensive Rating — Average number of mins between League goals conceded by the club this season.	73

	PLAYER	CON LGE	CLEAN SHEETS	DEF RATE
1	Simon King	34	7	79 mins
2	Damien Batt	17	4	76 mins
3	Adam Gross	23	6	72 mins
4	Ian Hendon	43	9	71 mins

KEY GOALKEEPER

Ross Flitney

Goals Conceded in the League	39
Defensive Rating — Ave number of mins between League goals conceded while on the pitch.	81
Counting Games — Games when he played at least 70 mins	35
Clean Sheets — In games when he played at least 70 mins	11

TOP POINT EARNERS

	PLAYER	GAMES	AV PTS
1	Tresor Kandol	13	1.62
2	Andy Hessenthaler	13	1.38
3	Ben Strevens	24	1.33
4	Ian Hendon	33	1.33
5	Adam Gross	17	1.24
6	Barry Fuller	15	1.20
7	Ross Flitney	35	1.20
8	Liam Hatch	20	1.20
9	Nick Bailey	45	1.18
10	Simon King	29	1.17
	CLUB AVERAGE:		1.17

BURY

Final Position: **19th**

NICKNAME: THE SHAKERS

KEY: Won Drawn Lost

					Score	Scorers	Attendance
1	div3	**Cheltenham**	A	L	1-2	Mattis 19	2,967
2	div3	**Leyton Orient**	H	L	1-2	Smart 78	2,053
3	div3	**Shrewsbury**	H	W	2-0	Newby 70; Barry-Murphy 90	2,261
4	div3	**Wycombe**	A	L	0-4		4,421
5	ccr1	**Leicester**	H	L	0-3		2,759
6	div3	**Wrexham**	H	D	2-2	Barry-Murphy 13; Tipton 52	2,468
7	div3	**Macclesfield**	A	L	0-1		1,965
8	div3	**Carlisle**	H	L	0-1		3,190
9	div3	**Northampton**	A	D	1-1	Whaley 26	5,147
10	div3	**Boston**	H	D	1-1	Mattis 38	1,985
11	div3	**Oxford**	A	L	1-2	Kennedy 83	4,198
12	div3	**Bristol Rovers**	H	W	1-0	Scott 42	1,673
13	div3	**Lincoln**	H	D	1-1	Whaley 90	4,118
14	div3	**Rushden & D**	A	W	2-0	Mattis 59; Whaley 69	2,639
15	div3	**Darlington**	H	W	1-0	Adams 35	2,630
16	div3	**Chester**	A	D	1-1	Mattis 10	3,471
17	div3	**Notts County**	H	L	2-3	Kennedy 59 pen; Whaley 81	2,671
18	facr1	**Scunthorpe**	H	D	2-2	Kennedy 52 pen; Scott 70	2,940
19	div3	**Mansfield**	A	W	3-0	Reet 6,75; Whaley 9	4,147
20	facr1r	**Scunthorpe**	A	L	0-1		4,006
21	div3	**Cheltenham**	H	L	0-1		2,251
22	div3	**Barnet**	A	D	1-1	Reet 70	1,796
23	div3	**Leyton Orient**	A	W	1-0	Whaley 54	4,095
24	div3	**Wycombe**	H	W	2-1	Scott 87; Whaley 90	2,384
25	div3	**Grimsby**	H	L	1-2	Reet 13	3,249
26	div3	**Peterborough**	A	L	1-4	Challinor 72	3,687
27	div3	**Carlisle**	A	L	0-4		6,398
28	div3	**Torquay**	H	W	3-2	Hewlett 40 og; Speight 42,49	2,102
29	div3	**Boston**	A	L	1-3	Canoville (Boston) 38 og	2,018
30	div3	**Northampton**	H	L	0-2		2,456
31	div3	**Bristol Rovers**	A	L	0-1		6,027
32	div3	**Rushden & D**	H	D	1-1	Tipton 87	1,777
33	div3	**Torquay**	A	D	0-0		2,129
34	div3	**Barnet**	H	D	0-0		2,083
35	div3	**Shrewsbury**	A	W	1-0	Hope 2 og	3,586
36	div3	**Rochdale**	A	D	1-1	Youngs 61	3,876
37	div3	**Stockport**	H	L	0-1		3,116
38	div3	**Wrexham**	A	D	0-0		4,134
39	div3	**Grimsby**	A	L	1-2	Daly 60	5,196
40	div3	**Oxford**	H	D	1-1	Kennedy 68 pen	1,882
41	div3	**Rochdale**	H	W	2-1	Youngs 33; Gobern 48	4,276
42	div3	**Stockport**	A	W	1-0	Daly 32	6,014
43	div3	**Macclesfield**	H	D	0-0		2,273
44	div3	**Peterborough**	H	L	1-3	Kennedy 76 pen	2,233
45	div3	**Lincoln**	A	D	1-1	Pugh 37	4,439
46	div3	**Chester**	H	D	0-0		3,421
47	div3	**Darlington**	A	W	3-2	Flitcroft 22; Barry-Murphy 85; Tipton 90	3,739
48	div3	**Mansfield**	H	D	0-0		3,105
49	div3	**Notts County**	A	D	2-2	Mattis 41; Youngs 81	9,817

TEAM OF THE SEASON

G — Kasper Schmeichel CG: 15 DR: 96

D — Thomas Kennedy CG: 22 DR: 88
D — John Fitzgerald CG: 21 DR: 85
D — Colin Woodthorpe CG: 30 DR: 78
D — David Challinor CG: 44 DR: 71

M — Simon Whaley CG: 23 SD: -11
M — David Buchanan CG: 19 SD: -19
M — David Flitcroft CG: 38 SD: -24
M — Brian Barry-Murphy CG: 32 SD: -28

F — Matthew Tipton CG: 13 SR: 455
F — Tom Youngs CG: 14 SR: 773

KEY PLAYER APPEARANCES

	PLAYER	POS	AGE	APP	MINS ON	GOALS	CARDS(Y/R)	
1	David Challinor	DEF	30	46	4060	1	5	0
2	David Flitcroft	MID	32	43	3686	1	5	0
3	Paul Scott	DEF	26	41	3598	2	9	0
4	Brian Barry-Murphy	MID	27	40	3094	3	2	0
5	Dwayne Mattis	MID	24	36	2922	5	6	0
6	Colin Woodthorpe	DEF	37	33	2825	0	6	0
7	Thomas Kennedy	DEF	21	33	2363	4	1	0
8	Neil Edwards	GK	35	24	2117	0	3	1
9	Simon Whaley	MID	21	23	2069	7	1	0
10	John Fitzgerald	DEF	22	27	2033	0	1	0
11	David Buchanan	MID	20	23	1936	0	1	0
12	Tom Youngs	ATT	26	30	1545	2	1	0
13	Matthew Tipton	ATT	26	24	1366	3	4	0
14	Kasper Schmeichel	GK	19	15	1350	0	1	0
15	John Hardiker	DEF	24	11	934	0	3	0
16	Allan Smart	ATT	32	13	897	1	5	1
17	Colin Marrison	ATT	20	16	870	0	2	0
18	Jon Daly	ATT	23	11	853	2	2	0

KEY PLAYERS - GOALSCORERS

Simon Whaley

Goals in the League	7
Contribution to Attacking Power Average number of minutes between League team goals while on pitch	80
Player Strike Rate Average number of minutes between League goals scored by player	296
Club Strike Rate Average number of minutes between League goals scored by club	92

	PLAYER	LGE GOALS	POWER	STRIKE RATE
1	Simon Whaley	7	80	296 mins
2	Matthew Tipton	3	124	455 mins
3	Dwayne Mattis	5	108	584 mins
4	Thomas Kennedy	4	79	591 mins

KEY PLAYERS - MIDFIELDERS

Simon Whaley

Goals in the League	7
Defensive Rating Average number of mins between League goals conceded while on the pitch	69
Contribution to Attacking Power Average number of minutes between League team goals while on pitch	80
Scoring Difference Defensive Rating minus Contribution to Attacking Power	-11

	PLAYER	LGE GOALS	DEF RATE	POWER	SCORE DIFF
1	Simon Whaley	7	69	80	-11 mins
2	David Buchanan	0	69	88	-19 mins
3	David Flitcroft	1	71	95	-24 mins
4	Brian Barry-Murphy	3	69	97	-28 mins

KEY PLAYERS - DEFENDERS

Thomas Kennedy

Goals Conceded when he was on pitch	27
Defensive Rating Ave number of mins between League goals conceded while on the pitch	88
Clean Sheets In games when he played at least 70 minutes	9
Club Defensive Rating Average number of mins between League goals conceded by the club this season.	73

	PLAYER	CON LGE	CLEAN SHEETS	DEF RATE
1	Thomas Kennedy	27	9	88 mins
2	John Fitzgerald	24	6	85 mins
3	Colin Woodthorpe	36	11	78 mins
4	David Challinor	57	12	71 mins

KEY GOALKEEPER

Kasper Schmeichel

Goals Conceded in the League	14
Defensive Rating Ave number of mins between League goals conceded while on the pitch.	96
Counting Games Games when he played at least 70 mins	15
Clean Sheets In games when he played at least 70 mins	6

TOP POINT EARNERS

	PLAYER	GAMES	AV PTS
1	Thomas Kennedy	22	1.50
2	David Buchanan	19	1.37
3	Kasper Schmeichel	15	1.33
4	Colin Woodthorpe	30	1.27
5	Brian Barry-Murphy	32	1.22
6	David Flitcroft	38	1.21
7	Simon Whaley	23	1.17
8	David Challinor	44	1.16
9	Paul Scott	40	1.15
10	Neil Edwards	23	1.13
	CLUB AVERAGE:		1.15

TORQUAY

Final Position: **20th**

NICKNAME: THE GULLS

KEY: Won / Drawn / Lost

#	Comp	Opponent	H/A	Res	Score	Scorers	Attendance
1	div3	Notts County	H	D	0-0		3,754
2	div3	Oxford	A	L	0-1		4,820
3	div3	Mansfield	A	L	0-3		2,632
4	div3	Bristol Rovers	H	L	2-3	Constantine 21; Hewlett 58	3,964
5	ccr1	Bournemouth	H	D	3-4*	(*on penalties)	1,876
6	div3	Peterborough	A	D	0-0		3,502
7	div3	Chester	H	L	0-1		2,245
8	div3	Rochdale	A	L	1-4	Connell 16	2,388
9	div3	Shrewsbury	H	W	2-1	Connell 2; Garner 45	2,287
10	div3	Grimsby	A	L	0-3		4,026
11	div3	Lincoln	H	W	2-1	Garner 51; Connell 66	2,281
12	div3	Leyton Orient	A	L	1-2	Kuffour 67	4,091
13	div3	Cheltenham	A	W	1-0	Connell 67	3,578
14	div3	Barnet	H	D	0-0		2,965
15	div3	Wrexham	A	L	2-4	Connell 66; Bedeau 90	4,301
16	div3	Macclesfield	H	D	1-1	Connell 68	2,355
17	div3	Boston	A	L	0-2		2,220
18	facr1	Harrogate	H	D	1-1	Stonebridge 80	2,079
19	div3	Carlisle	H	L	3-4	Robinson, P 13,78 pen; Hill 45	2,352
20	facr1r	Harrogate	A	W	6-5*	(*on penalties)	3,317
21	div3	Barnet	A	L	0-1		2,368
22	div3	Notts County	A	D	2-2	Lockwood 71; Kuffour 90	4,442
23	facr2	Notts County	H	W	2-1	Bedeau 45,69	2,407
24	div3	Northampton	H	D	3-3	Bedeau 56 pen; Kuffour 82; Hill 90	2,010
25	div3	Oxford	H	D	3-3	Lockwood 7; Hill 27,73	2,678
26	div3	Bristol Rovers	A	W	1-0	Sako 88	6,061
27	div3	Wycombe	H	D	2-2	Sako 13; Bedeau 31	3,733
28	div3	Rushden & D	H	W	2-1	Kuffour 2; Hill 33	2,668
29	div3	Darlington	A	L	2-3	Phillips 45; Connell 89	3,785
30	facr3	Birmingham	H	D	0-0		5,974
31	div3	Bury	A	L	2-3	Lockwood 10; Hill 90	2,102
32	facr3r	Birmingham	A	L	0-2		24,650
33	div3	Grimsby	H	D	2-2	Bedeau 34,89	2,559
34	div3	Rochdale	H	L	1-3	Sako 55	2,043
35	div3	Shrewsbury	A	W	1-0	Robinson, P 64	3,741
36	div3	Stockport	A	D	1-1	Bedeau 7	4,455
37	div3	Leyton Orient	H	W	2-0	Phillips 47; Bedeau 62	2,687
38	div3	Lincoln	A	L	0-2		4,454
39	div3	Bury	H	D	0-0		2,129
40	div3	Northampton	A	L	0-1		5,636
41	div3	Mansfield	H	L	0-2		2,494
42	div3	Chester	A	D	1-1	Hill 22	1,806
43	div3	Peterborough	H	W	1-0	Bedeau 65	2,438
44	div3	Wycombe	A	W	1-0	Bedeau 57	7,134
45	div3	Rushden & D	A	L	0-1		3,795
46	div3	Darlington	H	L	1-2	Hill 37	2,715
47	div3	Cheltenham	H	L	1-2	Thorpe 26	3,336
48	div3	Macclesfield	A	W	2-0	Kuffour 54,90	1,808
49	div3	Wrexham	H	W	1-0	Phillips 9	2,623
50	div3	Stockport	H	W	4-0	Thorpe 4,18; Kuffour 23; Hollands 48	3,565
51	div3	Carlisle	A	W	2-1	Hill 8; Kuffour 41	13,467
52	div3	Boston	H	D	0-0		5,697

TEAM OF THE SEASON

G Andy Marriott CG: 46 DR: 63

D Craig Taylor CG: 26 DR: 66

D Matt Hockley CG: 21 DR: 64

D James Sharp CG: 30 DR: 57

D Stephen Woods CG: 33 DR: 57

M Martin Phillips CG: 22 SD: 9

M Anthony Bedeau CG: 19 SD: -9

M Darren Garner CG: 38 SD: -12

M Kevin Hill CG: 37 SD: -12

F Alan Connell CG: 12 SR: 184

F Jonathan Osei Kuffour CG: 32 SR: 396

KEY PLAYER APPEARANCES

	PLAYER	POS	AGE	APP	MINS ON	GOALS	CARDS(Y/R)	
1	Andy Marriott	GK	35	46	4140	0	0	0
2	Darren Garner	MID	34	43	3587	2	11	0
3	Kevin Hill	MID	30	42	3548	9	4	0
4	Jonathan Osei Kuffour	ATT	24	43	3165	8	1	0
5	Stephen Woods	DEF	29	38	3086	0	5	0
6	James Sharp	DEF	30	32	2746	0	6	0
7	Craig Taylor	DEF	32	31	2432	0	2	1
8	Matt Hockley	DEF	24	36	2247	0	4	0
9	Anthony Bedeau	MID	27	31	2128	9	1	1
10	Martin Phillips	MID	30	26	2058	3	1	0
11	Anthony Lloyd	DEF	22	20	1720	0	1	0
12	Matt Hewlett	MID	30	24	1413	1	5	0
13	Alan Connell	ATT	23	22	1289	7	1	0
14	Paul Robinson	ATT	27	21	1170	3	1	0
15	Morike Sako	ATT	24	25	1159	3	3	1
16	Steven Reed	DEF	21	11	990	0	0	0
17	Leon Constantine	ATT	28	15	973	1	3	0
18	Matthew Villis	DEF	22	12	928	0	1	0

KEY PLAYERS - GOALSCORERS

Alan Connell

Goals in the League	7
Contribution to Attacking Power Average number of minutes between League team goals while on pitch	99
Player Strike Rate Average number of minutes between League goals scored by player	184
Club Strike Rate Average number of minutes between League goals scored by club	78

	PLAYER	LGE GOALS	POWER	STRIKE RATE
1	Alan Connell	7	99	184 mins
2	Anthony Bedeau	9	76	236 mins
3	Kevin Hill	9	74	394 mins
4	Jonathan Osei Kuffour	8	75	396 mins

KEY PLAYERS - MIDFIELDERS

Martin Phillips

Goals in the League	3
Defensive Rating Average number of mins between League goals conceded while on the pitch	66
Contribution to Attacking Power Average number of minutes between League team goals while on pitch	57
Scoring Difference Defensive Rating minus Contribution to Attacking Power	9

	PLAYER	LGE GOALS	DEF RATE	POWER	SCORE DIFF
1	Martin Phillips	3	66	57	9 mins
2	Anthony Bedeau	9	67	76	-9 mins
3	Kevin Hill	9	62	74	-12 mins
4	Darren Garner	2	63	75	-12 mins

KEY PLAYERS - DEFENDERS

Craig Taylor

Goals Conceded when he was on pitch	37
Defensive Rating Ave number of mins between League goals conceded while on the pitch	66
Clean Sheets In games when he played at least 70 minutes	9
Club Defensive Rating Average number of mins between League goals conceded by the club this season.	63

	PLAYER	CON LGE	CLEAN SHEETS	DEF RATE
1	Craig Taylor	37	9	66 mins
2	Matt Hockley	35	7	64 mins
3	Stephen Woods	54	9	57 mins
4	James Sharp	48	8	57 mins

KEY GOALKEEPER

Andy Marriott

Goals Conceded in the League	66
Defensive Rating Ave number of mins between League goals conceded while on the pitch.	63
Counting Games Games when he played at least 70 mins	46
Clean Sheets In games when he played at least 70 mins	14

TOP POINT EARNERS

	PLAYER	GAMES	AV PTS
1	Martin Phillips	22	1.59
2	Darren Garner	38	1.32
3	Jonathan Osei Kuffour	32	1.22
4	Kevin Hill	37	1.22
5	Anthony Bedeau	19	1.21
6	Craig Taylor	26	1.19
7	Andy Marriott	46	1.13
8	Matt Hockley	21	1.05
9	James Sharp	30	1.03
10	Anthony Lloyd	19	1.00
	CLUB AVERAGE:		1.13

NOTTS COUNTY

Final Position: **21st**

NICKNAME: THE MAGPIES

KEY: ☐Won ☐Drawn ☐Lost

					Score	Scorers	Attendance
1	div3	Torquay	A	D	0-0		3,754
2	div3	Wrexham	H	W	1-0	Long 90	4,382
3	div3	Lincoln	H	W	2-1	Scoffham 40; Baudet 56	6,153
4	div3	Stockport	A	D	1-1	Williams, A 14 og	3,922
5	ccr1	Watford	A	L	1-3	Palmer 76	7,011
6	div3	Bristol Rovers	H	W	2-0	Hurst 1,79	4,405
7	div3	Mansfield	A	W	3-2	Hurst 18,87; Edwards 82	6,444
8	div3	Darlington	A	D	1-1	White 85	5,273
9	div3	Chester	H	D	1-1	Hurst 56	5,404
10	div3	Shrewsbury	A	L	0-2		4,011
11	div3	Rushden & D	H	D	0-0		5,142
12	div3	Grimsby	A	L	0-4		5,577
13	div3	Macclesfield	A	D	0-0		1,892
14	div3	Boston	H	L	1-2	Edwards 90	6,632
15	div3	Rochdale	A	L	0-3		3,348
16	div3	Carlisle	H	D	0-0		5,347
17	div3	Bury	A	W	3-2	Hurst 35,45,57	2,671
18	facr1	Bristol City	A	W	2-0	Tann 45; Baudet 68	4,221
19	div3	Cheltenham	H	L	2-3	Baudet 45 pen; Edwards 57	4,903
20	div3	Boston	A	W	2-1	Hurst 7; White 82	2,921
21	div3	Torquay	H	D	2-2	Edwards 8; DeBolla 79	4,442
22	facr2	Torquay	A	L	1-2	McMahon 54	2,407
23	div3	Peterborough	A	L	0-2		2,833
24	div3	Wrexham	A	D	1-1	Sheridan 84	4,726
25	div3	Stockport	H	W	2-0	Baudet 40; Friars 73	4,261
26	div3	Oxford	A	L	0-3		5,626
27	div3	Leyton Orient	A	L	0-1		3,715
28	div3	Barnet	H	W	1-0	Martin 10	5,249
29	div3	Darlington	H	W	3-2	Scoffham 55; Martin 82; Baudet 87 pen	4,244
30	div3	Wycombe	A	L	0-2		5,185
31	div3	Shrewsbury	H	W	2-1	Pipe 20; Wilson 37	5,438
32	div3	Northampton	H	D	2-2	Pipe 24; Crooks 75	4,884
33	div3	Chester	A	W	2-0	Baudet 66 pen; Dadi 85 pen	2,599
34	div3	Grimsby	H	L	0-1		6,456
35	div3	Rushden & D	A	L	0-1		3,113
36	div3	Wycombe	H	L	1-2	O'Callaghan 55	3,710
37	div3	Peterborough	H	L	1-2	Dadi 77 pen	6,012
38	div3	Lincoln	A	L	1-2	Edwards 71	5,262
39	div3	Mansfield	H	D	2-2	Palmer 43; Chillingworth 76	9,779
40	div3	Bristol Rovers	A	W	2-1	Chillingworth 5; Scoffham 74	6,280
41	div3	Oxford	H	D	0-0		5,265
42	div3	Northampton	A	L	0-2		6,077
43	div3	Leyton Orient	H	D	1-1	Edwards 74	5,007
44	div3	Barnet	A	L	1-2	Scoffham 46	2,841
45	div3	Macclesfield	H	D	1-1	Edwards 45	4,393
46	div3	Carlisle	A	L	1-2	Scoffham 25	10,735
47	div3	Rochdale	H	D	1-1	Martin 72	4,413
48	div3	Cheltenham	A	L	0-2		4,518
49	div3	Bury	H	D	2-2	Martin 86; Baudet 89 pen	9,817

TEAM OF THE SEASON

G Kevin Pilkington — CG: 45 DR: 65

D Brian O'Callaghan — CG: 26 DR: 67

D Julien Baudet — CG: 42 DR: 66

D Michael Edwards — CG: 45 DR: 66

D Daniel Martin — CG: 12 DR: 66

M Chris Palmer — CG: 22 SD: -8

M Lewis McMahon — CG: 21 SD: -15

M David Pipe — CG: 40 SD: -18

M Lee Crooks — CG: 15 SD: -25

F Glynn Hurst — CG: 12 SR: 139

F Steve Scoffham — CG: 12 SR: 349

KEY PLAYER APPEARANCES

	PLAYER	POS	AGE	APP	MINS ON	GOALS	CARDS(Y	R)
1	Michael Edwards	DEF	26	46	4075	7	3	0
2	Kevin Pilkington	GK	32	45	4050	0	0	0
3	Julien Baudet	DEF	27	42	3779	6	8	1
4	David Pipe	MID	22	43	3734	2	9	0
5	Kelvin Wilson	DEF	20	34	3006	1	6	0
6	Brian O'Callaghan	DEF	25	33	2687	1	1	0
7	Robert Ullathorne	DEF	34	33	2657	0	7	0
8	Chris Palmer	MID	22	29	2211	1	3	0
9	Lewis McMahon	MID	21	29	2049	0	2	1
10	Liam Needham	ATT	20	22	1752	0	1	0
11	Steve Scoffham	ATT	22	30	1744	5	5	1
12	Lee Crooks	MID	28	18	1456	1	5	0
13	Jake Sheridan	MID	19	27	1387	1	5	0
14	Daniel Martin	DEF	19	22	1320	4	2	0
15	Glynn Hurst	ATT	30	18	1252	9	0	0
16	Andy White	ATT	24	26	1156	2	3	0
17	Nathan Doyle	MID	19	12	1035	0	3	0
18	Daniel Chillingworth	ATT	24	13	842	2	1	0

KEY PLAYERS - GOALSCORERS

Glynn Hurst

Goals in the League	9
Contribution to Attacking Power Average number of minutes between League team goals while on pitch	74
Player Strike Rate Average number of minutes between League goals scored by player	139
Club Strike Rate Average number of minutes between League goals scored by club	86

	PLAYER	LGE GOALS	POWER	STRIKE RATE
1	Glynn Hurst	9	74	139 mins
2	Daniel Martin	4	78	330 mins
3	Steve Scoffham	5	97	349 mins
4	Michael Edwards	7	85	582 mins

KEY PLAYERS - MIDFIELDERS

Chris Palmer

Goals in the League	1
Defensive Rating Average number of mins between League goals conceded while on the pitch	74
Contribution to Attacking Power Average number of minutes between League team goals while on pitch	82
Scoring Difference Defensive Rating minus Contribution to Attacking Power	-8

	PLAYER	LGE GOALS	DEF RATE	POWER	SCORE DIFF
1	Chris Palmer	1	74	82	-8 mins
2	Lewis McMahon	0	64	79	-15 mins
3	David Pipe	2	67	85	-18 mins
4	Lee Crooks	1	66	91	-25 mins

KEY PLAYERS - DEFENDERS

Brian O'Callaghan

Goals Conceded when he was on pitch	40
Defensive Rating Ave number of mins between League goals conceded while on the pitch	67
Clean Sheets In games when he played at least 70 minutes	6
Club Defensive Rating Average number of mins between League goals conceded by the club this season.	66

	PLAYER	CON LGE	CLEAN SHEETS	DEF RATE
1	Brian O'Callaghan	40	6	67 mins
2	Michael Edwards	62	10	66 mins
3	Julien Baudet	57	8	66 mins
4	Daniel Martin	20	2	66 mins

KEY GOALKEEPER

Kevin Pilkington

Goals Conceded in the League	62
Defensive Rating Ave number of mins between League goals conceded while on the pitch.	65
Counting Games Games when he played at least 70 mins	45
Clean Sheets In games when he played at least 70 mins	10

TOP POINT EARNERS

	PLAYER	GAMES	AV PTS
1	Steve Scoffham	12	1.50
2	Glynn Hurst	12	1.42
3	Robert Ullathorne	26	1.35
4	Daniel Martin	12	1.33
5	Lewis McMahon	21	1.33
6	Chris Palmer	22	1.27
7	Brian O'Callaghan	26	1.23
8	Julien Baudet	42	1.19
9	Michael Edwards	45	1.16
10	Kelvin Wilson	33	1.15
	CLUB AVERAGE:		1.13

STOCKPORT COUNTY

Final Position: **22nd**

CKNAME: COUNTY | KEY: ☐Won ☐Drawn ☐Lost

						Scorers	Attendance
1	div3	Mansfield	H	D	2-2	Easter 48,66	4,970
2	div3	Darlington	A	L	0-2		4,371
3	div3	Boston	A	D	2-2	Bramble 64; Hamshaw 67	2,432
4	div3	Notts County	H	D	1-1	Easter 35	3,922
5	ccr1	Sheff Wed	H	L	2-4	Boshell 8; Le Fondre 108	3,001
6	div3	Oxford	A	D	1-1	Clare 35	4,329
7	div3	Peterborough	H	D	1-1	St Ledger-Hall 82 og	3,774
8	div3	Grimsby	A	W	3-1	Whittle 56 og; Hamshaw 75; Wolski 79	5,381
9	div3	Wycombe	H	D	3-3	Easter 15,80 pen; Malcolm 45	3,507
10	div3	Rushden & D	A	L	2-3	Gulliver 19 og; Malcolm 61	2,710
11	div3	Chester	H	D	0-0		4,873
12	div3	Lincoln	A	L	0-2		3,508
13	div3	Wrexham	A	L	0-3		4,153
14	div3	Leyton Orient	H	D	1-1	Vaughan 22	3,901
15	div3	Shrewsbury	A	D	2-2	Bramble 32; Malcolm 53	4,316
16	div3	Northampton	H	W	4-2	Bramble 8,62; Singh 54; Briggs 84	4,150
17	div3	Carlisle	A	L	0-6		5,664
18	facr1	Swansea	H	W	2-0	Easter 41; Briggs 53	2,978
19	div3	Barnet	H	D	1-1	Hamshaw 15	6,056
20	div3	Leyton Orient	A	D	2-2	Clare 56; Easter 64	4,997
21	div3	Mansfield	A	L	1-2	Easter 80	2,994
22	facr2	Hereford	A	W	2-0	Easter 3; Wolski 57	3,620
23	div3	Bristol Rovers	H	L	0-1		3,460
24	div3	Darlington	H	L	0-3		3,502
25	div3	Notts County	A	L	0-2		4,261
26	div3	Macclesfield	A	L	0-6		4,553
27	div3	Cheltenham	H	D	2-2	Hamshaw 35; Dickinson 76	3,777
28	facr3	Brentford	H	L	2-3	Easter 17; Briggs 48	4,078
29	div3	Rochdale	A	W	1-0	Easter 8	3,520
30	div3	Rushden & D	H	D	2-2	Griffin 47; Dickinson 90	4,574
31	div3	Grimsby	H	W	2-1	Le Fondre 72,79	3,860
32	div3	Wycombe	A	D	1-1	Hamshaw 38	5,512
33	div3	Torquay	H	D	1-1	Le Fondre 64	4,455
34	div3	Lincoln	H	L	2-3	Briggs 64; Dickinson 83	4,506
35	div3	Chester	A	W	2-1	Dickinson 76,89	3,446
36	div3	Rochdale	H	W	3-0	Boshell 27; Griffin 33; Briggs 88	4,312
37	div3	Bristol Rovers	A	D	2-2	Le Fondre 68,88	5,990
38	div3	Boston	H	L	0-1		5,133
39	div3	Peterborough	A	L	0-2		3,406
40	div3	Bury	A	W	1-0	Dickinson 85	3,116
41	div3	Oxford	H	W	2-1	Bramble 21; Le Fondre 87 pen	4,424
42	div3	Macclesfield	H	W	2-0	Briscoe 12 og; Le Fondre 90	6,003
43	div3	Bury	H	L	0-1		6,014
44	div3	Cheltenham	A	D	3-3	Robinson 34 pen; Briggs 56; Dickinson 90	3,525
45	div3	Wrexham	H	W	2-1	Williams, A 6; Raynes 42	4,750
46	div3	Northampton	A	L	0-2		6,544
47	div3	Shrewsbury	H	W	3-1	Ward 36; O'Connor 54; Robinson 84 pen	5,831
48	div3	Torquay	A	L	0-4		3,565
49	div3	Barnet	A	D	0-0		3,873
50	div3	Carlisle	H	D	0-0		10,006

TEAM OF THE SEASON

G James Spencer — CG: 34 DR: 58

D Adam Griffin — CG: 18 DR: 67

D Ashley Williams — CG: 31 DR: 57

D Keith Briggs — CG: 34 DR: 54

D Mark Robinson — CG: 41 DR: 54

M Damien Allen — CG: 12 SD: 37

M Harpal Singh — CG: 14 SD: -22

M Danny Boshell — CG: 24 SD: -23

M Matthew Hamshaw — CG: 32 SD: -24

F Jermaine Easter — CG: 15 SR: 196

F Tesfaye Bramble — CG: 28 SR: 549

KEY PLAYER APPEARANCES

	PLAYER	POS	AGE	APP	MINS ON	GOALS	CARDS(Y	R)
1	Mark Robinson	DEF	24	44	3837	2	4	0
2	Keith Briggs	DEF	24	41	3306	4	1	0
3	Matthew Hamshaw	MID	24	39	3126	5	0	0
4	James Spencer	GK	21	34	3060	0	1	0
5	Ashley Williams	DEF	21	36	2929	1	6	1
6	Robert Clare	DEF	23	34	2778	2	2	0
7	Tesfaye Bramble	ATT	25	37	2743	5	7	1
8	Danny Boshell	MID	25	33	2447	1	7	0
9	Michael Raynes	DEF	18	25	1943	1	1	0
10	Adam Griffin	DEF	21	25	1938	2	1	0
11	Ross Greenwood	MID	20	22	1655	0	3	0
12	Harpal Singh	MID	24	24	1652	1	2	0
13	Jermaine Easter	ATT	24	19	1567	8	4	0
14	Damien Allen	MID	19	22	1303	0	0	0
15	Mickael Wolski	DEF	27	20	1224	1	2	0
16	Liam Dickinson	ATT	20	21	1203	7	2	0
17	Michael Malcolm	ATT	20	23	1107	3	2	1
18	Tony Vaughan	DEF	30	10	900	1	3	0

KEY PLAYERS - GOALSCORERS

Jermaine Easter

Goals in the League	8
Contribution to Attacking Power Average number of minutes between League team goals while on pitch	63
Player Strike Rate Average number of minutes between League goals scored by player	196
Club Strike Rate Average number of minutes between League goals scored by club	73

	PLAYER	LGE GOALS	POWER	STRIKE RATE
1	Jermaine Easter	8	63	196 mins
2	Tesfaye Bramble	5	72	549 mins
3	Matthew Hamshaw	5	76	625 mins
4	Keith Briggs	4	72	827 mins

KEY PLAYERS - MIDFIELDERS

Damien Allen

Goals in the League	0
Defensive Rating Average number of mins between League goals conceded while on the pitch	118
Contribution to Attacking Power Average number of minutes between League team goals while on pitch	81
Scoring Difference Defensive Rating minus Contribution to Attacking Power	37

	PLAYER	LGE GOALS	DEF RATE	POWER	SCORE DIFF
1	Damien Allen	0	118	81	37 mins
2	Harpal Singh	1	47	69	-22 mins
3	Danny Boshell	1	49	72	-23 mins
4	Matthew Hamshaw	5	52	76	-24 mins

KEY PLAYERS - DEFENDERS

Adam Griffin

Goals Conceded when he was on pitch	29
Defensive Rating Ave number of mins between League goals conceded while on the pitch	67
Clean Sheets In games when he played at least 70 minutes	5
Club Defensive Rating Average number of mins between League goals conceded by the club this season.	53

	PLAYER	CON LGE	CLEAN SHEETS	DEF RATE
1	Adam Griffin	29	5	67 mins
2	Ashley Williams	51	6	57 mins
3	Keith Briggs	61	7	54 mins
4	Mark Robinson	71	6	54 mins

KEY GOALKEEPER

James Spencer

Goals Conceded in the League	53
Defensive Rating Ave number of mins between League goals conceded while on the pitch.	58
Counting Games Games when he played at least 70 mins	34
Clean Sheets In games when he played at least 70 mins	6

TOP POINT EARNERS

	PLAYER	GAMES	AV PTS
1	Damien Allen	12	1.67
2	Adam Griffin	18	1.39
3	Keith Briggs	34	1.35
4	Tesfaye Bramble	28	1.29
5	Michael Raynes	21	1.24
6	Ashley Williams	31	1.23
7	Mark Robinson	41	1.20
8	James Spencer	34	1.18
9	Matthew Hamshaw	32	1.09
10	Robert Clare	28	1.00
	CLUB AVERAGE:		1.13

OXFORD UNITED

Final Position: **23rd**

NICKNAME: THE U'S

KEY: ☐Won ☐Drawn ☐Lost

							Attendance
1	div3	Grimsby	A	D	1-1	Hargreaves 88	4,706
2	div3	Torquay	H	W	1-0	Bradbury 55	4,820
3	div3	Wycombe	H	D	2-2	Hackett 17; Morgan 88	6,364
4	div3	Lincoln	A	L	1-2	Davies 2	3,724
5	ccr1	Gillingham	A	L	0-1		4,149
6	div3	Stockport	H	D	1-1	Roget 21	4,329
7	div3	Shrewsbury	A	L	0-2		4,073
8	div3	Rushden & D	H	D	2-2	Sabin 24; Roget 25	4,189
9	div3	Bristol Rovers	A	D	1-1	Hackett 45	5,098
10	div3	Darlington	A	W	2-1	Sabin 67; Davies 76	4,127
11	div3	Bury	H	W	2-1	Mansell 33; Bradbury 36 pen	4,198
12	div3	Rochdale	A	W	1-0	Quinn 60	2,347
13	div3	Barnet	A	D	0-0		3,272
14	div3	Carlisle	H	W	1-0	Basham 22	5,392
15	div3	Northampton	A	L	0-1		6,802
16	div3	Boston	H	D	0-0		5,084
17	div3	Leyton Orient	A	L	0-1		5,268
18	facr1	Eastbourne	A	D	1-1	Basham 70	3,770
19	div3	Wrexham	H	L	0-3		4,491
20	facr1r	Eastbourne	H	W	3-0	Basham 20,45,90 pen	4,396
21	div3	Carlisle	A	L	1-2	Bradbury 90	6,097
22	div3	Grimsby	H	L	2-3	Fitzgerald, SP 51; Basham 90 pen	4,323
23	facr2	Cheltenham	A	D	1-1	Sabin 52	4,592
24	div3	Cheltenham	A	W	2-1	Basham 9; Sabin 41	2,852
25	div3	Torquay	A	D	3-3	Sabin 5,19; Bradbury 17 pen	2,678
26	facr2r	Cheltenham	H	L	1-2	Basham 61	3,455
27	div3	Lincoln	H	L	0-1		3,795
28	div3	Notts County	H	W	3-0	Basham 63; Sabin 68; Quinn 77	5,626
29	div3	Mansfield	H	L	1-2	Bradbury 38	4,005
30	div3	Chester	A	W	1-0	Basham 75	2,624
31	div3	Shrewsbury	H	L	0-3		3,702
32	div3	Peterborough	A	D	0-0		2,926
33	div3	Macclesfield	A	D	1-1	Basham 47	1,972
34	div3	Darlington	H	L	0-2		4,204
35	div3	Rushden & D	A	L	0-3		3,823
36	div3	Rochdale	H	D	1-1	Ashton 17	3,978
37	div3	Macclesfield	H	D	1-1	E'Beyer 26	4,331
38	div3	Cheltenham	H	D	1-1	Basham 76 pen	5,232
39	div3	Wycombe	A	L	1-2	Obudabe 72	7,016
40	div3	Stockport	A	L	1-2	Sills, T 61	4,424
41	div3	Bristol Rovers	H	W	1-0	Basham 65 pen	6,424
42	div3	Notts County	A	D	0-0		5,265
43	div3	Bury	A	D	1-1	Burgess 71	1,882
44	div3	Peterborough	H	W	1-0	N'Toya 67	7,486
45	div3	Mansfield	A	L	0-1		3,480
46	div3	Chester	H	L	0-1		5,754
47	div3	Barnet	H	W	2-0	N'Toya 1,25	6,948
48	div3	Boston	A	L	0-1		2,313
49	div3	Northampton	H	L	1-3	Willmott 75	8,264
50	div3	Wrexham	A	D	1-1	N'Toya 64 pen	4,575
51	div3	Leyton Orient	H	L	2-3	Sabin 14; Willmott 66	12,243

TEAM OF THE SEASON

- **G** Billy Turley CG: 33 DR: 71
- **D** Christopher Willmott CG: 37 DR: 80
- **D** Leo Roget CG: 32 DR: 78
- **D** Matthew Robinson CG: 44 DR: 75
- **D** Jon Ashton CG: 28 DR: 71
- **M** Chris Hackett CG: 16 SD: -14
- **M** Barry Quinn CG: 42 SD: -20
- **M** Lee Mansell CG: 44 SD: -21
- **M** Chris Hargreaves CG: 33 SD: -35
- **F** Steve Basham CG: 20 SR: 324
- **F** Lee Bradbury CG: 16 SR: 337

KEY PLAYER APPEARANCES

	PLAYER	POS	AGE	APP	MINS ON	GOALS	CARDS(Y	R)
1	Lee Mansell	MID	23	44	3960	1	6	0
2	Matthew Robinson	DEF	31	44	3952	0	7	0
3	Barry Quinn	MID	27	44	3856	2	3	1
4	Christopher Willmott	DEF	28	41	3521	2	3	1
5	Chris Hargreaves	MID	34	35	3060	1	8	1
6	Billy Turley	GK	32	33	2967	0	1	0
7	Leo Roget	DEF	28	33	2887	2	4	0
8	Jon Ashton	DEF	23	33	2638	1	5	0
9	Steve Basham	ATT	28	39	2588	8	0	0
10	Eric Sabin	ATT	31	29	2455	7	2	0
11	Lee Bradbury	ATT	31	22	1685	5	7	0
12	Chris Hackett	MID	23	21	1679	2	1	1
13	Andrew Burgess	MID	24	16	1121	1	0	0
14	Craig Davies	ATT	20	20	1046	2	2	0
15	Chris Tardif	GK	25	11	872	0	0	0
16	Tim Sills	ATT	26	13	833	1	0	0
17	Stuart Gray	MID	32	10	811	0	1	0
18	Adam Griffin	DEF	21	9	704	0	2	0

KEY PLAYERS - GOALSCORERS

Steve Basham

Goals in the League	8	Player Strike Rate Average number of minutes between League goals scored by player	324
Contribution to Attacking Power Average number of minutes between League team goals while on pitch	96	Club Strike Rate Average number of minutes between League goals scored by club	96

	PLAYER	LGE GOALS	POWER	STRIKE RATE
1	Steve Basham	8	96	324 mins
2	Lee Bradbury	5	77	337 mins
3	Eric Sabin	7	94	351 mins
4	Chris Hackett	2	84	840 mins

KEY PLAYERS - MIDFIELDERS

Chris Hackett

Goals in the League	2	Contribution to Attacking Power Average number of minutes between League team goals while on pitch	84
Defensive Rating Average number of mins between League goals conceded while on the pitch	70	Scoring Difference Defensive Rating minus Contribution to Attacking Power	-14

	PLAYER	LGE GOALS	DEF RATE	POWER	SCORE DIFF
1	Chris Hackett	2	70	84	-14 mins
2	Barry Quinn	2	79	99	-20 mins
3	Lee Mansell	1	78	99	-21 mins
4	Chris Hargreaves	1	64	99	-35 mins

KEY PLAYERS - DEFENDERS

Christopher Willmott

Goals Conceded when he was on pitch	44	Clean Sheets In games when he played at least 70 minutes	12
Defensive Rating Ave number of mins between League goals conceded while on the pitch	80	Club Defensive Rating Average number of mins between League goals conceded by the club this season.	73

	PLAYER	CON LGE	CLEAN SHEETS	DEF RATE
1	Christopher Willmott	44	12	80 mins
2	Leo Roget	37	9	78 mins
3	Matthew Robinson	53	12	75 mins
4	Jon Ashton	37	8	71 mins

KEY GOALKEEPER

Billy Turley

Goals Conceded in the League	42
Defensive Rating Ave number of mins between League goals conceded while on the pitch.	71
Counting Games Games when he played at least 70 mins	33
Clean Sheets In games when he played at least 70 mins	8

TOP POINT EARNERS

	PLAYER	GAMES	AV PTS
1	Lee Bradbury	16	1.63
2	Chris Hackett	16	1.31
3	Steve Basham	20	1.25
4	Eric Sabin	26	1.23
5	Christopher Willmott	37	1.19
6	Leo Roget	32	1.16
7	Jon Ashton	28	1.14
8	Barry Quinn	42	1.14
9	Matthew Robinson	44	1.11
10	Billy Turley	33	1.09
	CLUB AVERAGE:		1.07

RUSHDEN & DIAMONDS

Final Position: **24th**

CKNAME: THE DIAMONDS

KEY: ☐Won ☐Drawn ☐Lost

								Attendance
1	div3	Darlington	H	D	1-1	Bell 60		2,832
2	div3	Mansfield	A	W	1-0	Allen 45		3,402
3	div3	Chester	H	D	1-1	O'Grady 61		2,682
4	ccr1	Coventry	H	L	0-3			3,240
5	div3	Lincoln	H	D	1-1	Pearson 64		2,860
6	div3	Grimsby	A	L	0-2			3,774
7	div3	Peterborough	H	L	0-2			4,403
8	div3	Oxford	A	D	2-2	Taylor 54; Grainger 58		4,189
9	div3	Macclesfield	A	L	1-3	Broughton 84		2,874
10	div3	Stockport	H	W	3-2	Gulliver 53; O'Grady 71; Dempster 90		2,710
11	div3	Notts County	A	D	0-0			5,142
12	div3	Northampton	H	L	1-3	Savage 63		5,211
13	div3	Rochdale	A	L	1-2	Okounghae 50		2,606
14	div3	Bury	H	L	0-2			2,639
15	div3	Wycombe	A	D	0-0			5,231
16	div3	Shrewsbury	H	W	3-0	Savage 49; Bell 66; O'Grady 85		2,954
17	div3	Barnet	A	L	1-2	Dempster 65		2,564
18	facr1	Halifax	A	D	1-1	Armstrong 2		2,303
19	div3	Boston	H	W	1-0	Gulliver 90		3,205
20	facr1r	Halifax	H	W	5-4*	(*on penalties)		2,133
21	div3	Darlington	A	D	1-1	Bell 9		3,209
22	facr2	Leyton Orient	H	L	0-1			3,245
23	div3	Carlisle	H	L	0-4			2,216
24	div3	Mansfield	H	L	1-2	Dempster 57		2,477
25	div3	Chester	A	W	2-1	Broughton 11 pen; Bolland 55 og		2,265
26	div3	Leyton Orient	A	L	1-5	Broughton 25		4,558
27	div3	Cheltenham	H	L	0-1			2,244
28	div3	Torquay	A	L	1-2	O'Grady 65		2,668
29	div3	Bristol Rovers	H	L	2-3	Broughton 44,84		2,720
30	div3	Peterborough	A	L	0-2			4,613
31	div3	Wrexham	H	L	0-2			2,617
32	div3	Stockport	A	D	2-2	Gulliver 49; Jackson 68		4,574
33	div3	Oxford	H	W	3-0	Kelly 15,22; Gulliver 20		3,823
34	div3	Northampton	A	L	0-2			7,036
35	div3	Bury	A	D	1-1	Hatswell 82		1,777
36	div3	Notts County	H	W	1-0	Mikolanda 33		3,113
37	div3	Wrexham	A	L	0-2			3,195
38	div3	Carlisle	A	L	0-5			6,922
39	div3	Macclesfield	H	W	1-0	Broughton 81		2,479
40	div3	Grimsby	H	D	1-1	Jackson 72		3,366
41	div3	Lincoln	A	D	2-2	Turner 82; Jackson 84		4,383
42	div3	Leyton Orient	H	W	1-0	Broughton 8		3,679
43	div3	Cheltenham	A	L	1-3	Jackson 53		3,447
44	div3	Torquay	H	W	1-0	Broughton 43		3,795
45	div3	Bristol Rovers	A	W	1-0	Broughton 79		6,432
46	div3	Rochdale	H	D	1-1	Broughton 55		3,135
47	div3	Shrewsbury	A	L	1-4	Caskey 46		4,239
48	div3	Wycombe	H	L	1-3	Kelly 24		3,396
49	div3	Boston	A	L	0-2			2,489
50	div3	Barnet	H	L	1-2	Jackson 86		4,174

TEAM OF THE SEASON

G
Scott Tynan
CG: 13 DR: 62

D
Ronnie Bull
CG: 19 DR: 65

D
Robert Gier
CG: 33 DR: 63

D
Phil Gulliver
CG: 39 DR: 54

D
John Dempster
CG: 13 DR: 53

M
David Bell
CG: 12 SD: -22

M
Marcus Kelly
CG: 38 SD: -30

M
Dave Savage
CG: 25 SD: -33

M
Ashley Nicholls
CG: 22 SD: -35

F
°Drewe Broughton
CG: 27 SR: 278

F
Chris O'Grady
CG: 18 SR: 457

KEY PLAYER APPEARANCES

	PLAYER	POS	AGE	APP	MINS ON	GOALS	CARDS(Y/R)	
1	Marcus Kelly	MID	20	41	3555	3	3	0
2	Phil Gulliver	DEF	23	40	3529	4	3	0
3	Robert Gier	DEF	25	35	2975	0	6	1
4	Drewe Broughton	ATT	27	37	2783	10	10	2
5	Dave Savage	MID	32	32	2502	2	3	0
6	Ashley Nicholls	MID	24	30	2290	0	2	0
7	Chris O'Grady	ATT	20	22	1827	4	2	0
8	Jamie Young	GK	21	20	1791	0	1	0
9	Peter Hawkins	DEF	27	21	1784	0	6	1
10	Ronnie Bull	DEF	25	19	1677	0	5	0
11	Neil McCafferty	MID	21	23	1656	0	5	0
12	Darren Caskey	MID	31	18	1540	0	7	0
13	Wayne Hatswell	DEF	31	17	1514	1	4	0
14	Magnus Okounghae	MID	20	21	1509	1	3	0
15	Tony Stokes	MID	19	19	1451	0	3	0
16	Tyrone Berry	ATT	19	20	1276	0	1	0
17	Scott Tynan	GK	22	14	1231	0	1	0
18	Greg Pearson	ATT	21	22	1206	1	2	0

KEY PLAYERS - GOALSCORERS

Drewe Broughton

Goals in the League	10
Contribution to Attacking Power Average number of minutes between League team goals while on pitch	87
Player Strike Rate Average number of minutes between League goals scored by player	278
Club Strike Rate Average number of minutes between League goals scored by club	94

	PLAYER	LGE GOALS	POWER	STRIKE RATE
1	Drewe Broughton	10	87	278 mins
2	John Dempster	3	72	385 mins
3	David Bell	3	84	394 mins
4	Chris O'Grady	4	91	457 mins

KEY PLAYERS - MIDFIELDERS

David Bell

Goals in the League	3
Defensive Rating Average number of mins between League goals conceded while on the pitch	62
Contribution to Attacking Power Average number of minutes between League team goals while on pitch	84
Scoring Difference Defensive Rating minus Contribution to Attacking Power	-22

	PLAYER	LGE GOALS	DEF RATE	POWER	SCORE DIFF
1	David Bell	3	62	84	-22 mins
2	Marcus Kelly	3	59	89	-30 mins
3	Dave Savage	2	48	81	-33 mins
4	Ashley Nicholls	0	57	92	-35 mins

KEY PLAYERS - DEFENDERS

Ronnie Bull

Goals Conceded when he was on pitch	26
Defensive Rating Ave number of mins between League goals conceded while on the pitch	65
Clean Sheets In games when he played at least 70 minutes	6
Club Defensive Rating Average number of mins between League goals conceded by the club this season.	54

	PLAYER	CON LGE	CLEAN SHEETS	DEF RATE
1	Ronnie Bull	26	6	65 mins
2	Robert Gier	47	11	63 mins
3	Phil Gulliver	65	8	54 mins
4	John Dempster	22	3	53 mins

KEY GOALKEEPER

Scott Tynan

Goals Conceded in the League	20
Defensive Rating Ave number of mins between League goals conceded while on the pitch.	62
Counting Games Games when he played at least 70 mins	13
Clean Sheets In games when he played at least 70 mins	5

TOP POINT EARNERS

	PLAYER	GAMES	AV PTS
1	Drewe Broughton	27	1.22
2	Ronnie Bull	19	1.21
3	Marcus Kelly	38	1.18
4	Scott Tynan	13	1.15
5	John Dempster	13	1.15
6	Darren Caskey	17	1.12
7	Ashley Nicholls	22	1.09
8	David Bell	12	1.08
9	Tony Stokes	12	1.08
10	Robert Gier	33	1.06
	CLUB AVERAGE:		0.98

SCOTTISH PREMIERSHIP ROUND-UP

FINAL LEAGUE TABLE

	HOME						AWAY					TOTAL			
	P	W	D	L	F	A	W	D	L	F	A	F	A	DIF	PTS
Celtic	38	14	4	1	41	15	14	3	2	52	22	93	37	56	91
Hearts	38	15	2	2	43	9	7	6	6	28	22	71	31	40	74
Rangers	38	13	4	2	38	11	8	6	5	29	26	67	37	30	73
Hibernian	38	11	1	7	39	24	6	4	9	22	32	61	56	5	56
Kilmarnock	38	11	3	5	39	29	4	7	8	24	35	63	64	-1	55
Aberdeen	38	8	9	3	30	17	5	6	7	16	23	46	40	6	54
Inverness CT	38	5	6	7	21	21	10	7	3	30	17	51	38	13	58
Motherwell	38	7	5	7	35	31	6	5	8	20	30	55	61	-6	49
Dundee Utd	38	5	8	6	22	28	2	4	13	19	38	41	66	-25	33
Falkirk	38	2	6	11	14	30	6	3	10	21	34	35	64	-29	33
Dunfermline	38	3	5	11	17	39	5	4	10	16	29	33	68	-35	33
Livingston	38	3	4	12	15	33	1	2	16	10	46	25	79	-54	18

CLUB STRIKE FORCE

Celtic's Zurawski: 16 league goals

1 Celtic

Goals scored in the League	93
Club Strike Rate (CSR) Average number of minutes between League goals scored by club	37

	CLUB	GOALS	CSR
1	Celtic	93	37
2	Hearts	71	48
3	Rangers	67	51
4	Kilmarnock	63	54
5	Hibernian	61	56
6	Motherwell	55	62
7	Inverness CT	51	67
8	Aberdeen	46	74
9	Dundee Utd	41	83
10	Falkirk	35	98
11	Dunfermline	33	104
12	Livingston	25	137

CLUB DISCIPLINARY RECORDS

Walker of Livingstone: 13 bookings

1 Livingstone

League Yellow	92
League Red	2
League Total	94
Cards Average in League Average number of minutes between a card being shown of either colour	36

	CLUB	Y	R	TOTAL	AVE
1	Livingston	92	2	94	36
2	Hearts	71	6	77	44
3	Falkirk	73	3	76	45
4	Inverness CT	74	2	76	45
5	Dundee Utd	66	2	68	50
6	Hibernian	64	5	69	50
7	Rangers	63	4	67	51
8	Motherwell	62	2	64	53
9	Dunfermline	50	4	54	63
10	Aberdeen	48	3	51	67
11	Kilmarnock	41	1	42	81
12	Celtic	39	2	41	83

CLUB DEFENCES

	CLUB	LGE	CS	CDR
1	Hearts	31	16	110
2	Celtic	37	15	92
3	Rangers	37	15	92
4	Inverness CT	38	14	90
5	Aberdeen	40	15	86
6	Hibernian	56	7	61
7	Motherwell	61	8	56
8	Falkirk	64	9	53
9	Kilmarnock	64	8	53
10	Dundee Utd	66	4	52
11	Dunfermline	68	6	50
12	Livingston	79	4	43

Goncalves of Hearts

1 Hearts

Goals conceded in the League	31
Clean Sheets (CS) Number of league games where no goals were conceded	16
Club Defensive Rate (CDR) Average number of minutes between League goals conceded by club	110

STADIUM CAPACITY AND HOME CROWDS

	TEAM	CAPACITY	AVE	HIGH	LOW
1	Rangers	50444	97.62	49792	47867
2	Celtic	60832	95.59	60100	48649
3	Hearts	18300	91.62	17379	16139
4	Inverness CT	6280	80.59	7512	3121
5	Hibernian	17500	77.77	17180	10000
6	Falkirk	7550	73.06	6500	4467
7	Dundee Utd	14223	57.64	12404	5034
8	Aberdeen	22199	57.34	18182	9229
9	Dunfermline	12510	49.54	9481	3354
10	Livingston	10024	49.26	9481	2278
11	Motherwell	13742	45.48	11503	3438
12	Kilmarnock	18128	39.01	12426	4644

Key: Average. The percentage of each stadium filled in League games over the season (AVE), the stadium capacity and the highest and lowest crowds recorded.

AWAY ATTENDANCE

	TEAM	AVE	HIGH	LOW
1	Rangers	86.58	59684	6343
2	Celtic	83.47	49788	6459
3	Hearts	79.49	60100	5027
4	Aberdeen	78.95	60018	3724
5	Hibernian	73.51	60047	5732
6	Kilmarnock	64.18	59995	3446
7	Dunfermline	61.18	58203	3621
8	Falkirk	59.11	57782	3121
9	Motherwell	58.91	57388	2283
10	Dundee Utd	58.56	59875	2298
11	Livingston	58.03	57000	3604
12	Inverness CT	52.68	57451	2278

Key: Average. How close each club has come to filling grounds in its away league matches (AVE) and the highest and lowest crowds recorded.

CHART-TOPPING MIDFIELDERS

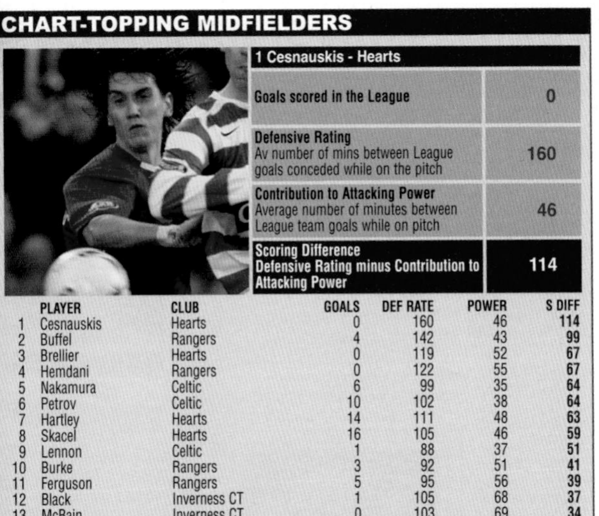

1 Cesnauskis - Hearts	
Goals scored in the League	0
Defensive Rating Av number of mins between League goals conceded while on the pitch	160
Contribution to Attacking Power Average number of minutes between League team goals while on pitch	46
Scoring Difference Defensive Rating minus Contribution to Attacking Power	114

	PLAYER	CLUB	GOALS	DEF RATE	POWER	S DIFF
1	Cesnauskis	Hearts	0	160	46	**114**
2	Buffel	Rangers	4	142	43	**99**
3	Brellier	Hearts	0	119	52	**67**
4	Hemdani	Rangers	0	122	55	**67**
5	Nakamura	Celtic	6	99	35	**64**
6	Petrov	Celtic	10	102	38	**64**
7	Hartley	Hearts	14	111	48	**63**
8	Skacel	Hearts	16	105	46	**59**
9	Lennon	Celtic	1	88	37	**51**
10	Burke	Rangers	3	92	51	**41**
11	Ferguson	Rangers	5	95	56	**39**
12	Black	Inverness CT	1	105	68	**37**
13	McBain	Inverness CT	0	103	69	**34**
14	Ricksen	Rangers	0	82	48	**34**
15	I Murray	Rangers	0	76	45	**31**

CHART-TOPPING GOALSCORERS

1 Boyd - Rangers	
Goals scored in the League	17
Contribution to Attacking Power Average number of minutes between League team goals while on pitch	49
Club Strike Rate (CSR) Average minutes between League goals scored by club	51
Player Strike Rate Average number of minutes between League goals scored by player	74

	PLAYER	CLUB	GOALS: LGE	POWER	CSR	S RATE
1	Boyd	Rangers	17	49	51	**74**
2	Boyd	Kilmarnock	15	45	54	**99**
3	Zurawski	Celtic	16	37	37	**118**
4	Hartson	Celtic	18	39	37	**137**
5	Lovenkrands	Rangers	14	42	51	**152**
6	Dargo	Inverness CT	16	63	67	**153**
7	Riordan	Hibernian	16	56	56	**169**
8	Burchill	Dunfermline	12	89	104	**178**
9	O'Connor	Hibernian	11	58	56	**178**
10	Skacel	Hearts	16	46	48	**183**
11	Duffy	Falkirk	9	86	98	**191**
12	Maloney	Celtic	13	34	37	**199**
13	Wales	Kilmarnock	8	58	54	**203**
14	Wyness	Inverness CT	8	53	67	**211**
15	Naismith	Kilmarnock	13	56	54	**212**

CHART-TOPPING DEFENDERS

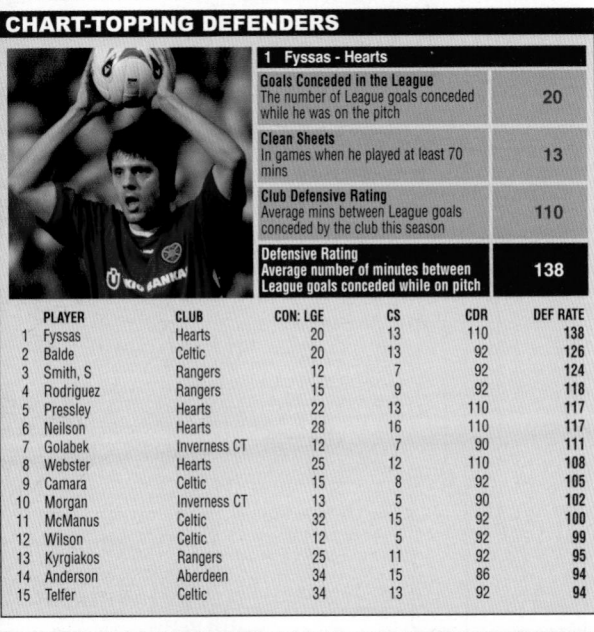

1 Fyssas - Hearts	
Goals Conceded in the League The number of League goals conceded while he was on the pitch	20
Clean Sheets In games when he played at least 70 mins	13
Club Defensive Rating Average mins between League goals conceded by the club this season	110
Defensive Rating Average number of minutes between League goals conceded while on pitch	138

	PLAYER	CLUB	CON: LGE	CS	CDR	DEF RATE
1	Fyssas	Hearts	20	13	110	**138**
2	Balde	Celtic	20	13	92	**126**
3	Smith, S	Rangers	12	7	92	**124**
4	Rodriguez	Rangers	15	9	92	**118**
5	Pressley	Hearts	22	13	110	**117**
6	Neilson	Hearts	28	16	110	**117**
7	Golabek	Inverness CT	12	7	90	**111**
8	Webster	Hearts	25	12	110	**108**
9	Camara	Celtic	15	8	92	**105**
10	Morgan	Inverness CT	13	5	90	**102**
11	McManus	Celtic	32	15	92	**100**
12	Wilson	Celtic	12	5	92	**99**
13	Kyrgiakos	Rangers	25	11	92	**95**
14	Anderson	Aberdeen	34	15	86	**94**
15	Telfer	Celtic	34	13	92	**94**

CHART-TOPPING GOALKEEPERS

1 Gordon - Hearts	
Counting Games Games in which he played at least 70 minutes	35
Goals Conceded in the League The number of League goals conceded while he was on the pitch	26
Clean Sheets In games when he played at least 70 mins	16
Defensive Rating Average number of minutes between League goals conceded while on pitch	122

	PLAYER	CLUB	CG	CONC	CS	DEF RATE
1	Gordon	Hearts	35	26	16	122
2	Langfield	Aberdeen	20	16	10	113
3	Boruc	Celtic	34	30	14	102
4	Brown	Inverness CT	37	38	13	88
5	Waterreus	Rangers	36	37	13	87
6	Esson	Aberdeen	18	24	5	68
7	Smith, G	Motherwell	33	44	8	63
8	Malkowski	Hibernian	32	46	5	61
9	McGregor	Dunfermline	26	40	5	59
10	Combe	Kilmarnock	32	54	8	52
11	Stillie	Dundee Utd	30	53	4	51
12	Glennon	Falkirk	21	42	3	45
13	McKenzie	Livingston	32	70	2	41
14	Halliwell	Dunfermline	12	28	1	39

PLAYER DISCIPLINARY RECORD

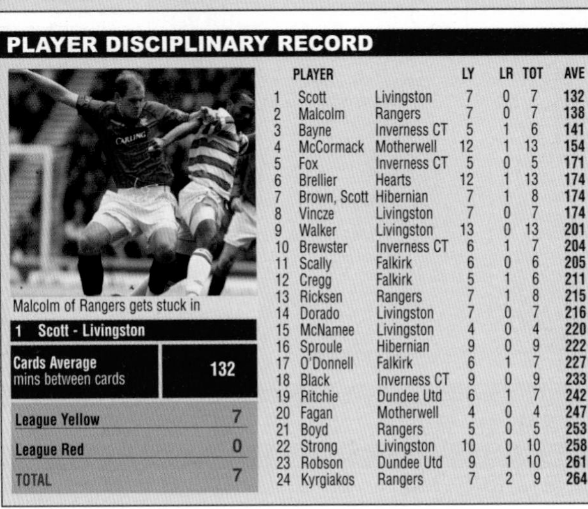

Malcolm of Rangers gets stuck in

1 Scott - Livingston	
Cards Average mins between cards	132
League Yellow	7
League Red	0
TOTAL	7

	PLAYER		LY	LR	TOT	AVE
1	Scott	Livingston	7	0	7	**132**
2	Malcolm	Rangers	7	0	7	**138**
3	Bayne	Inverness CT	5	1	6	**141**
4	McCormack	Motherwell	12	1	13	**154**
5	Fox	Inverness CT	5	0	5	**171**
6	Brellier	Hearts	12	1	13	**174**
7	Brown, Scott	Hibernian	7	1	8	**174**
8	Vincze	Livingston	7	0	7	**174**
9	Walker	Livingston	13	0	13	**201**
10	Brewster	Inverness CT	6	1	7	**204**
11	Scally	Falkirk	6	0	6	**205**
12	Cregg	Falkirk	5	1	6	**211**
13	Ricksen	Rangers	7	1	8	**215**
14	Dorado	Livingston	7	0	7	**216**
15	McNamee	Livingston	4	0	4	**220**
16	Sproule	Hibernian	9	0	9	**222**
17	O'Donnell	Falkirk	6	1	7	**227**
18	Black	Inverness CT	9	0	9	**233**
19	Ritchie	Dundee Utd	6	1	7	**242**
20	Fagan	Motherwell	4	0	4	**247**
21	Boyd	Rangers	5	0	5	**253**
22	Strong	Livingston	10	0	10	**258**
23	Robson	Dundee Utd	9	1	10	**261**
24	Kyrgiakos	Rangers	7	2	9	**264**

TEAM OF THE SEASON

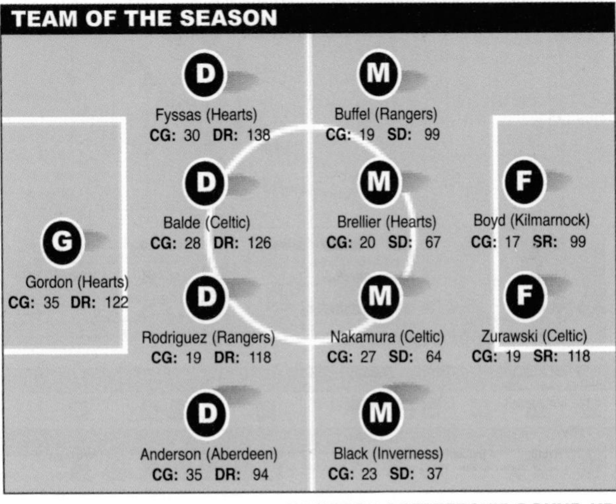

The Story of the Scottish Premiership 2005 - 2006

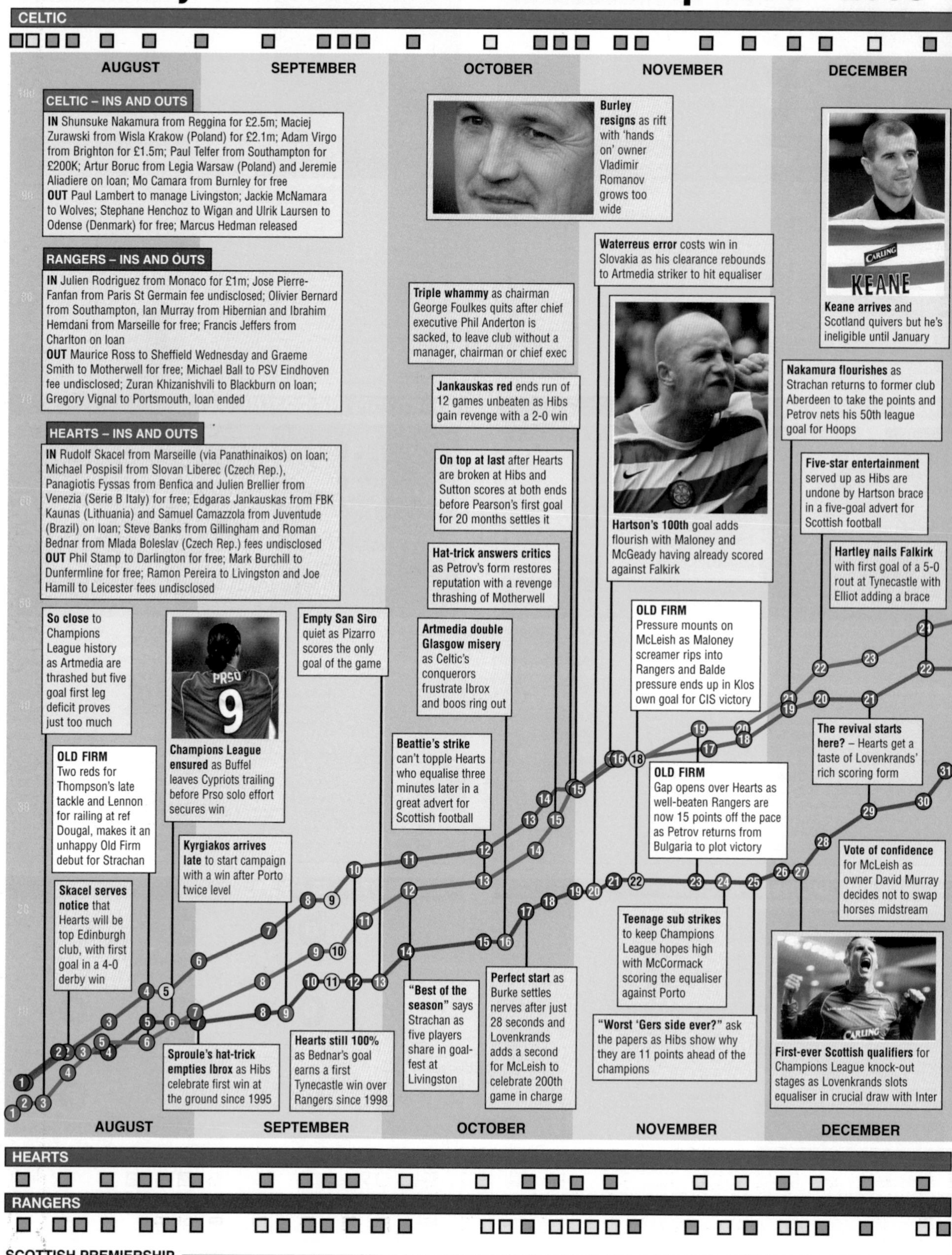

CELTIC
AUGUST
SEPTEMBER
OCTOBER
NOVEMBER
DECEMBER
CELTIC – INS AND OUTS
IN Shunsuke Nakamura from Reggina for £2.5m; Maciej Zurawski from Wisla Krakow (Poland) for £2.1m; Adam Virgo from Brighton for £1.5m; Paul Telfer from Southampton for £200K; Artur Boruc from Legia Warsaw (Poland) and Jeremie Aliadiere on loan; Mo Camara from Burnley for free
OUT Paul Lambert to manage Livingston; Jackie McNamara to Wolves; Stephane Henchoz to Wigan and Ulrik Laursen to Odense (Denmark) for free; Marcus Hedman released
RANGERS – INS AND OUTS
IN Julien Rodriguez from Monaco for £1m; Jose Pierre-Fanfan from Paris St Germain fee undisclosed; Olivier Bernard from Southampton, Ian Murray from Hibernian and Ibrahim Hemdani from Marseille for free; Francis Jeffers from Charlton on loan
OUT Maurice Ross to Sheffield Wednesday and Graeme Smith to Motherwell for free; Michael Ball to PSV Eindhoven fee undisclosed; Zuran Khizanishvili to Blackburn on loan; Gregory Vignal to Portsmouth, loan ended
HEARTS – INS AND OUTS
IN Rudolf Skacel from Marseille (via Panathinaikos) on loan; Michael Pospisil from Slovan Liberec (Czech Rep.), Panagiotis Fyssas from Benfica and Julien Brellier from Venezia (Serie B Italy) for free; Edgaras Jankauskas from FBK Kaunas (Lithuania) and Samuel Camazzola from Juventude (Brazil) on loan; Steve Banks from Gillingham and Roman Bednar from Mlada Boleslav (Czech Rep.) fees undisclosed
OUT Phil Stamp to Darlington for free; Mark Burchill to Dunfermline for free; Ramon Pereira to Livingston and Joe Hamill to Leicester fees undisclosed
Burley resigns as rift with 'hands on' owner Vladimir Romanov grows too wide
Waterreus error costs win in Slovakia as his clearance rebounds to Artmedia striker to hit equaliser
KEANE
Keane arrives and Scotland quivers but he's ineligible until January
Triple whammy as chairman George Foulkes quits after chief executive Phil Anderton is sacked, to leave club without a manager, chairman or chief exec
Jankauskas red ends run of 12 games unbeaten as Hibs gain revenge with a 2-0 win
Nakamura flourishes as Strachan returns to former club Aberdeen to take the points and Petrov nets his 50th league goal for Hoops
On top at last after Hearts are broken at Hibs and Sutton scores at both ends before Pearson's first goal for 20 months settles it
Five-star entertainment served up as Hibs are undone by Hartson brace in a five-goal advert for Scottish football
Hartson's 100th goal adds flourish with Maloney and McGeady having already scored against Falkirk
Hat-trick answers critics as Petrov's form restores reputation with a revenge thrashing of Motherwell
Hartley nails Falkirk with first goal of a 5-0 rout at Tynecastle with Elliot adding a brace
So close to Champions League history as Artmedia are thrashed but five goal first leg deficit proves just too much
PRSO 9
Empty San Siro quiet as Pizarro scores the only goal of the game
Artmedia double Glasgow misery as Celtic's conquerors frustrate Ibrox and boos ring out
OLD FIRM
Pressure mounts on McLeish as Maloney screamer rips into Rangers and Balde pressure ends up in Klos own goal for CIS victory
OLD FIRM
Two reds for Thompson's late tackle and Lennon for railing at ref Dougal, makes it an unhappy Old Firm debut for Strachan
Champions League ensured as Buffel leaves Cypriots trailing before Prso solo effort secures win
Beattie's strike can't topple Hearts who equalise three minutes later in a great advert for Scottish football
The revival starts here? – Hearts get a taste of Lovenkrands' rich scoring form
OLD FIRM
Gap opens over Hearts as well-beaten Rangers are now 15 points off the pace as Petrov returns from Bulgaria to plot victory
Kyrgiakos arrives late to start campaign with a win after Porto twice level
Skacel serves notice that Hearts will be top Edinburgh club, with first goal in a 4-0 derby win
Vote of confidence for McLeish as owner David Murray decides not to swap horses midstream
Teenage sub strikes to keep Champions League hopes high with McCormack scoring the equaliser against Porto
"Best of the season" says Strachan as five players share in goal-fest at Livingston
Perfect start as Burke settles nerves after just 28 seconds and Lovenkrands adds a second for McLeish to celebrate 200th game in charge
"Worst 'Gers side ever?" ask the papers as Hibs show why they are 11 points ahead of the champions
Sproule's hat-trick empties Ibrox as Hibs celebrate first win at the ground since 1995
Hearts still 100% as Bednar's goal earns a first Tynecastle win over Rangers since 1998
First-ever Scottish qualifiers for Champions League knock-out stages as Lovenkrands slots equaliser in crucial draw with Inter
AUGUST
SEPTEMBER
OCTOBER
NOVEMBER
DECEMBER
HEARTS
RANGERS

KEY: League – Celtic, League – Hearts, League – Rangers, Champions Lge, UEFA Cup, Scottish FA Cup, Scottish League Cup, Won, Drawn, Lost

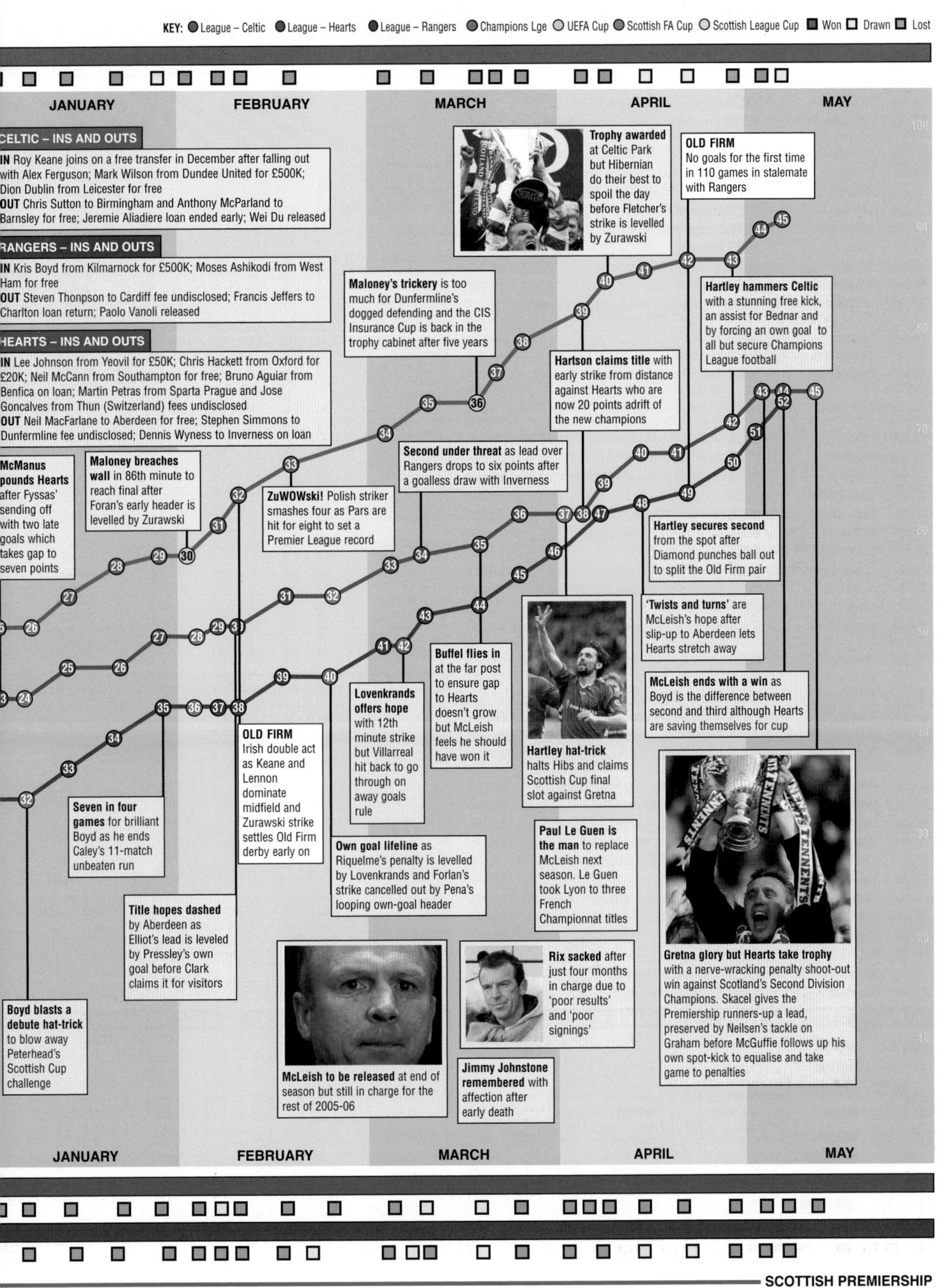

CELTIC – INS AND OUTS

IN Roy Keane joins on a free transfer in December after falling out with Alex Ferguson; Mark Wilson from Dundee United for £500K; Dion Dublin from Leicester for free
OUT Chris Sutton to Birmingham and Anthony McParland to Barnsley for free; Jeremie Aliadiere loan ended early; Wei Du released

RANGERS – INS AND OUTS

IN Kris Boyd from Kilmarnock for £500K; Moses Ashikodi from West Ham for free
OUT Steven Thonpson to Cardiff fee undisclosed; Francis Jeffers to Charlton loan return; Paolo Vanoli released

HEARTS – INS AND OUTS

IN Lee Johnson from Yeovil for £50K; Chris Hackett from Oxford for £20K; Neil McCann from Southampton for free; Bruno Aguiar from Benfica on loan; Martin Petras from Sparta Prague and Jose Goncalves from Thun (Switzerland) fees undisclosed
OUT Neil MacFarlane to Aberdeen for free; Stephen Simmons to Dunfermline fee undisclosed; Dennis Wyness to Inverness on loan

McManus pounds Hearts after Fyssas' sending off with two late goals which takes gap to seven points

Maloney breaches wall in 86th minute to reach final after Foran's early header is levelled by Zurawski

ZuWOWski! Polish striker smashes four as Pars are hit for eight to set a Premier League record

Maloney's trickery is too much for Dunfermline's dogged defending and the CIS Insurance Cup is back in the trophy cabinet after five years

Trophy awarded at Celtic Park but Hibernian do their best to spoil the day before Fletcher's strike is levelled by Zurawski

OLD FIRM
No goals for the first time in 110 games in stalemate with Rangers

Hartley hammers Celtic with a stunning free kick, an assist for Bednar and by forcing an own goal to all but secure Champions League football

Hartson claims title with early strike from distance against Hearts who are now 20 points adrift of the new champions

Second under threat as lead over Rangers drops to six points after a goalless draw with Inverness

Hartley secures second from the spot after Diamond punches ball out to split the Old Firm pair

'Twists and turns' are McLeish's hope after slip-up to Aberdeen lets Hearts stretch away

McLeish ends with a win as Boyd is the difference between second and third although Hearts are saving themselves for cup

Buffel flies in at the far post to ensure gap to Hearts doesn't grow but McLeish feels he should have won it

Lovenkrands offers hope with 12th minute strike but Villarreal hit back to go through on away goals rule

OLD FIRM
Irish double act as Keane and Lennon dominate midfield and Zurawski strike settles Old Firm derby early on

Seven in four games for brilliant Boyd as he ends Caley's 11-match unbeaten run

Own goal lifeline as Riquelme's penalty is levelled by Lovenkrands and Forlan's strike cancelled out by Pena's looping own-goal header

Hartley hat-trick halts Hibs and claims Scottish Cup final slot against Gretna

Paul Le Guen is the man to replace McLeish next season. Le Guen took Lyon to three French Championnat titles

Title hopes dashed by Aberdeen as Elliot's lead is leveled by Pressley's own goal before Clark claims it for visitors

Boyd blasts a debute hat-trick to blow away Peterhead's Scottish Cup challenge

McLeish to be released at end of season but still in charge for the rest of 2005-06

Rix sacked after just four months in charge due to 'poor results' and 'poor signings'

Jimmy Johnstone remembered with affection after early death

Gretna glory but Hearts take trophy with a nerve-wracking penalty shoot-out win against Scotland's Second Division Champions. Skacel gives the Premiership runners-up a lead, preserved by Neilsen's tackle on Graham before McGuffie follows up his own spot-kick to equalise and take game to penalties

CELTIC

Final Position: **1st**

NICKNAME: THE BHOYS

KEY: Won / Drawn / Lost

	Comp	Opponent	H/A	Res	Score	Scorers	Attendance
1	ecql1	Artmedia Brat	A	L	0-5		17,262
2	spl	Motherwell	A	D	4-4	Hartson 14,32,44 pen; Beattie 90	9,903
3	ecql2	Artmedia Brat	H	W	4-0	Thompson 21 pen; Hartson 44; McManus 54; Beattie 82	43,729
4	spl	Dundee Utd	H	W	2-0	Hartson 37; Beattie 88	56,532
5	spl	Falkirk	H	W	3-1	Hartson 49; Thompson 75,90	57,782
6	spl	Rangers	A	L	1-3	Maloney 86 pen	49,699
7	spl	Dunfermline	A	W	4-0	Zurawski 5,74; Hartson 10; Nakamura 58	9,244
8	spl	Aberdeen	H	W	2-0	Zurawski 13; Petrov 61	59,607
9	spl	Hibernian	A	W	1-0	Petrov 5	15,649
10	sccc3	Falkirk	H	W	2-1	Zurawski 62; Hartson 94	24,953
11	spl	Inverness CT	H	W	2-1	Beattie 57,67	57,247
12	spl	Livingston	A	W	5-0	McManus 36; Maloney 45; Zurawski 51; Sutton 62; Beattie 72	9,115
13	spl	Hearts	H	D	1-1	Beattie 13	60,100
14	spl	Kilmarnock	A	W	1-0	Petrov 24	10,544
15	spl	Motherwell	H	W	5-0	Petrov 14,23,79; Maloney 17; Nakamura 67	57,388
16	spl	Dundee Utd	A	W	4-2	Hartson 17; Sutton 28; Archibald 32 og; Pearson 88	11,942
17	spl	Falkirk	A	W	3-0	Maloney 41; McGeady 42; Hartson 69	6,459
18	sccqf	Rangers	H	W	2-0	Maloney 26; Klos 82 og	57,183
19	spl	Rangers	H	W	3-0	Hartson 12; Balde 56; McGeady 61	58,997
20	spl	Dunfermline	H	L	0-1		58,203
21	spl	Aberdeen	A	W	3-1	McGeady 56; Petrov 58; Telfer 64	17,031
22	spl	Hibernian	H	W	3-2	Hartson 40,65; Maloney 57	59,895
23	spl	Inverness CT	A	D	1-1	Hartson 21	7,382
24	spl	Livingston	H	W	2-1	Maloney 39 pen; Nakamura 87	57,000
25	spl	Hearts	A	W	3-2	Pearson 55; McManus 87,90	17,358
26	scr3	Clyde	A	L	1-2	Zurawski 83	8,000
27	spl	Kilmarnock	H	W	4-2	Nakamura 3; Maloney 16 pen; McManus 53; Zurawski 67	59,995
28	spl	Motherwell	A	W	3-1	Zurawski 17; McGeady 71; Hartson 85	11,503
29	spl	Dundee Utd	H	D	3-3	Hartson 9; Zurawski 49; Petrov 67	59,875
30	slc5	Motherwell	A	W	2-1	Zurawski 29; Maloney 88	32,595
31	spl	Falkirk	H	W	2-1	Keane 34; McManus 44	56,672
32	spl	Rangers	A	W	1-0	Zurawski 12	49,788
33	spl	Dunfermline	A	W	8-1	Petrov 3; Hartson 24; Zurawski 32,40,56,88; Maloney 74; Lennon 82	9,015
34	spl	Aberdeen	H	W	3-0	Petrov 66; Maloney 75; Zurawski 89	60,018
35	spl	Hibernian	A	W	2-1	Maloney 36 pen; McManus 60	16,985
36	scccf	Dunfermline	A	W	3-0	Zurawski 43; Maloney 76; Dublin 90	50,090
37	spl	Inverness CT	H	W	2-1	McManus 35; Maloney 79	57,451
38	spl	Livingston	A	W	2-0	Zurawski 47; Maloney 52 pen	7,486
39	spl	Hearts	H	W	1-0	Hartson 4	59,699
40	spl	Kilmarnock	A	W	4-1	Nakamura 8,82; Hartson 64; Dublin 84	10,978
41	spl	Hibernian	H	D	1-1	Zurawski 76	60,047
42	spl	Rangers	H	D	0-0		59,684
43	spl	Hearts	A	L	0-3		16,795
44	spl	Kilmarnock	H	W	2-0	Zurawski 55; Varga 63	48,649
45	spl	Aberdeen	A	D	2-2	Hartson 5; Maloney 61	14,597

LEAGUE APPEARANCES, BOOKINGS AND CAPS

	AGE (on 01/07/06)	IN NAMED 18	APPEARANCES	COUNTING GAMES	MINUTES ON PITCH	YELLOW CARDS	RED CARDS	CAPS THIS SEASON	NATIONAL SIDE
Goalkeepers									
Artur Boruc	26	37	34	34	3060	1	0	7	Poland (29)
David Marshall	21	37	4	4	360	0	0	2	Scotland (85)
Michael McGovern	21	1	0	0	0	0	0	-	Scotland
Defenders									
Didier Agathe	30	9	4	0	33	0	0	-	France
Dianbobo Balde	30	29	28	28	2520	4	0	-	France
Mohammed Camara	31	24	18	17	1569	1	0	-	Guinea
Wei Du	24	3	0	0	0	0	0	1	China PR (68)
Stephen McManus	23	37	36	35	3197	9	0	-	Scotland
Rocco Quinn	19	2	0	0	0	0	0	-	Scotland
Paul Telfer	34	37	36	35	3195	2	0	-	Scotland
Stanislav Varga	33	18	10	10	901	1	0	3	Slovakia (41)
Adam Virgo	23	24	10	2	322	0	0	-	England
Mark Wilson	22	16	14	13	1184	0	0	-	Scotland
Midfielders									
Roy Keane	34	11	10	8	837	1	0	1	Rep of Ireland (15)
Paul Lawson	22	20	3	1	128	0	0	-	Scotland
Neil Lennon	35	33	32	31	2828	4	1	-	N Ireland
Aiden McGeady	20	28	20	9	987	0	0	-	Rep or Ireland
Shunsuke Nakamura	28	34	33	27	2570	1	0	5	Japan (18)
Stephen Pearson	23	32	17	2	462	0	0	-	Scotland
Stilian Petrov	27	37	37	32	3065	5	0	3	Bulgaria (37)
Alan Thompson	32	29	16	7	914	2	1	-	England
Ross Wallace	21	35	11	8	794	0	0	-	Scotland
Forwards									
Jeremie Aliadiere	23	4	0	0	0	0	0	-	France
Craig Beattie	22	13	12	6	646	0	0	3	Scotland (85)
Dion Dublin	37	14	11	3	387	1	0	-	England
Michael Gardyne	20	1	0	0	0	0	0	-	Scotland
John Hartson	31	36	35	23	2465	5	0	5	Wales (74)
Shaun Maloney	23	36	35	26	2588	1	0	4	Scotland (85)
Chris Sutton	33	8	8	7	641	1	0	-	England
Maciej Zurawski	29	24	24	19	1882	0	0	7	Poland (29)

TEAM OF THE SEASON

G — Artur Boruc — CG: 34 DR: 102

D — Dianbobo Balde — CG: 28 DR: 126

D — Mohammed Camara — CG: 17 DR: 105

D — Stephen McManus — CG: 35 DR: 100

D — Paul elfer — CG: 35 DR: 94

M — Shunsuke Nakamura — CG: 27 SD: 64

M — Stilian Petrov — CG: 32 SD: 64

M — Roy Keane* — CG: 8 SD: 42

M — Neil Lennon — CG: 31 SD: 51

F — Maciej Zurawski — CG: 19 SR: 118

F — John Hartson — CG: 23 SR: 137

MONTHLY POINTS TALLY

Month	Points	%
AUGUST	9	75%
SEPTEMBER	9	100%
OCTOBER	13	87%
NOVEMBER	6	67%
DECEMBER	10	83%
JANUARY	10	83%
FEBRUARY	9	100%
MARCH	12	100%
APRIL	8	53%
MAY	4	67%

LEAGUE GOALS

	PLAYER	MINS	GOALS	S RATE
1	Hartson	2465	18	137
2	Zurawski	1882	16	118
3	Maloney	2588	13	199
4	Petrov	3065	10	307
5	McManus	3197	7	457
6	Beattie	646	6	108
7	Nakamura	2570	6	428
8	McGeady	987	4	247
9	Thompson	914	2	457
10	Sutton	641	2	321
11	Pearson	462	2	231
12	Keane	837	1	837
13	Telfer	3195	1	3195
	Other		5	
	TOTAL		93	

TOP POINT EARNERS

	PLAYER	GAMES	AV PTS
1	Zurawski	19	2.68
2	Balde	28	2.64
3	Nakamura	27	2.59
4	Petrov	32	2.50
5	Maloney	26	2.50
6	Boruc	34	2.44
7	Hartson	23	2.43
8	Lennon	31	2.42
9	McManus	35	2.40
10	Telfer	35	2.40
	CLUB AVERAGE:		2.39

DISCIPLINARY RECORDS

	PLAYER	YELLOW	RED	AVE
1	Thompson	2	1	304
2	McManus	9	0	355
3	Hartson	5	0	493
4	Lennon	4	1	565
5	Petrov	5	0	613
6	Balde	4	0	630
7	Sutton	1	0	641
8	Keane	1	0	837
9	Varga	1	0	901
10	Camara	1	0	1569
11	Telfer	2	0	1597
12	Nakamura	1	0	2570
13	Maloney	1	0	2588
	Other	1	0	
	TOTAL	38	2	

KEY GOALKEEPER

Artur Boruc

Goals Conceded in the League	30	**Counting Games** League games when player was on pitch for at least 70 minutes	34
Defensive Rating Ave number of mins between League goals conceded while on the pitch	102	**Clean Sheets** In games when player was on pitch for at least 70 minutes	14

KEY PLAYERS - DEFENDERS

Dianbobo Balde

Goals Conceded Number of League goals conceded while the player was on the pitch	20	**Clean Sheets** In League games when player was on pitch for at least 70 minutes	13
Defensive Rating Ave number of mins between League goals conceded while on the pitch	126	**Club Defensive Rating** Average number of mins between League goals conceded by the club this season	92

	PLAYER	CON LGE	CLEAN SHEETS	DEF RATE
1	Dianbobo Balde	20	13	126 mins
2	Mohammed Camara	15	8	105 mins
3	Stephen McManus	32	15	100 mins
4	Mark Wilson	12	5	99 mins

KEY PLAYERS - MIDFIELDERS

Shunsuke Nakamura

Goals in the League	6	**Contribution to Attacking Power** Average number of minutes between League team goals while on pitch	35
Defensive Rating Average number of mins between League goals conceded while on the pitch	99	**Scoring Difference** Defensive Rating minus Contribution to Attacking Power	64

	PLAYER	LGE GOALS	DEF RATE	POWER	SCORE DIFF
1	Shunsuke Nakamura	6	99	35	64 mins
2	Stilian Petrov	10	102	38	64 mins
3	Paul Telfer	1	94	37	57 mins
4	Neil Lennon	1	88	37	51 mins

KEY PLAYERS - GOALSCORERS

Maciej Zurawski

Goals in the League	16	**Player Strike Rate** Average number of minutes between League goals scored by player	118
Contribution to Attacking Power Average number of minutes between League team goals while on pitch	37	**Club Strike Rate** Average number of minutes between League goals scored by club	37

	PLAYER	LGE GOALS	POWER	STRIKE RATE
1	Maciej Zurawski	16	37	118 mins
2	John Hartson	18	39	137 mins
3	Shaun Maloney	13	34	199 mins
4	Stilian Petrov	10	38	307 mins

John Hartson

SQUAD APPEARANCES

Match	1	2	3	4	5	6	7	8	9	10	11	12	13	14	15	16	17	18	19	20	21	22	23	24	25	26	27	28	29	30	31	32	33	34	35	36	37	38	39	40	41	42	43	44
Venue	A	H	H	H	A	A	H	A	H	H	A	H	A	H	A	A	H	H	H	A	H	A	H	A	A	H	A	H	A	H	A	A	H	A	A	H	A	H	A	H	H	A	H	A
Competition	L	C	L	L	L	L	L	L	W	L	L	L	L	L	L	L	W	L	L	L	L	L	L	L	O	L	L	L	W	L	L	L	L	L	W	L	L	L	L	L	L	L	L	L
Result	D	W	W	W	L	W	W	W	W	W	W	D	W	W	W	W	W	W	L	W	W	D	W	W	L	W	W	D	W	W	W	W	W	W	W	W	W	W	W	D	D	L	W	D

Goalkeepers
Artur Boruc
David Marshall
Michael McGovern

Defenders
Didier Agathe
Dianbobo Balde
Mohammed Camara
Wei Du
Stephen McManus
Rocco Quinn
Paul Telfer
Stanislav Varga
Adam Virgo
Mark Wilson

Midfielders
Roy Keane
Paul Lawson
Neil Lennon
Aiden McGeady
Shunsuke Nakamura
Stephen Pearson
Stilian Petrov
Alan Thompson
Ross Wallace

Forwards
Jeremie Aliadiere
Craig Beattie
Dion Dublin
Michael Gardyne
John Hartson
Shaun Maloney
Chris Sutton
Maciej Zurawski

KEY: On all match | On bench | Subbed or sent off (Counting game) | Subbed or sent off (playing less than 70 minutes) | Subbed on from bench (Counting Game) | Subbed on (playing less than 70 minutes) | Subbed on and then subbed or sent off (Counting Game) | Subbed on and then subbed or sent off (playing less than 70 minutes) | Not in 16

HEART OF MIDLOTHIAN

Final Position: **2nd**

NICKNAME: THE JAM TARTS

KEY: ☐ Won ☐ Drawn ☐ Lost

						Attendance
1 spl	Kilmarnock	A	W	4-2	Skacel 12; Bednar 46; Mikoliunas 61; Hartley 89 pen	7,487
2 spl	Hibernian	H	W	4-0	Skacel 13; Hartley 58 pen; Simmons 71; Mikoliunas 83	16,459
3 spl	Dundee Utd	A	W	3-0	Pressley 6; Bednar 12; Skacel 90	11,654
4 spl	Aberdeen	H	W	2-0	Skacel 20; Pospisil 85	16,139
5 sccc1	Queens Park	A	W	2-0	Jankauskas 15,44	2,429
6 spl	Motherwell	H	W	2-1	Skacel 41; Jankauskas 70	16,213
7 spl	Livingston	A	W	4-1	Skacel 11; Webster 27; Hartley 34,63 pen	8,405
8 spl	Inverness CT	A	W	1-0	Skacel 28	6,704
9 sccc3	Livingston	A	L	0-1		3,805
10 spl	Rangers	H	W	1-0	Bednar 14	17,379
11 spl	Falkirk	A	D	2-2	Pressley 72,90	6,342
12 spl	Celtic	A	D	1-1	Skacel 16	60,100
13 spl	Dunfermline	H	W	2-0	Skacel 21; Pospisil 23	16,500
14 spl	Kilmarnock	H	W	1-0	Jankauskas 34	16,536
15 spl	Hibernian	A	L	0-2		17,180
16 spl	Dundee Utd	H	W	3-0	Hartley 3; Skacel 27; Pospisil 56	16,617
17 spl	Aberdeen	A	D	1-1	Skacel 64	14,901
18 spl	Motherwell	A	D	1-1	Hartley 90 pen	8,131
19 spl	Livingston	H	W	2-1	Skacel 8,15	16,583
20 spl	Inverness CT	H	D	0-0		16,373
21 spl	Rangers	A	L	0-1		49,723
22 spl	Falkirk	H	W	5-0	Hartley 20; Skacel 25; Elliot 41,90; Pospisil 73	16,538
23 spl	Celtic	H	L	2-3	Jankauskas 6; Pressley 8	17,358
24 scr3	Kilmarnock	H	W	2-1	Pressley 23; McAllister 74	12,831
25 spl	Dunfermline	A	W	4-1	Pressley 27; Pospisil 53,66; Skacel 80	8,277
26 spl	Kilmarnock	A	L	0-1		8,811
27 spl	Hibernian	H	W	4-1	Hartley 26,43 pen; Skacel 40; Elliot 49	17,371
28 scr4	Aberdeen	H	W	3-0	Pospisil 20; Elliot 34; Pressley 45 pen	17,353
29 spl	Dundee Utd	A	D	1-1	Hartley 83 pen	10,584
30 spl	Aberdeen	H	L	1-2	Elliot 8	16,895
31 spl	Motherwell	H	W	3-0	Jankauskas 3,13; Elliot 77	16,976
32 Scpqf	Partick	H	W	2-1	Jankauskas 6; Cesnauskis 63	16,365
33 spl	Livingston	A	W	3-2	Aguiar 17; Jankauskas 72; Bednar 87	5,058
34 spl	Inverness CT	A	D	0-0		5,027
35 spl	Rangers	H	D	1-1	Jankauskas 9	17,040
36 spl	Falkirk	A	W	2-1	Hartley 21; Jankauskas 80	5,966
37 SCsf	Hibernian	A	W	4-0	Hartley 28,59,88 pen; Jankauskas 81	43,180
38 spl	Celtic	A	L	0-1		59,699
39 spl	Dunfermline	H	W	4-0	Pospisil 7; Bednar 14; Mikoliunas 25; Makela 58	16,973
40 spl	Kilmarnock	H	W	2-0	Hartley 70; Berra 87	16,497
41 spl	Hibernian	A	L	1-2	Bednar 45	16,654
42 spl	Celtic	H	W	3-0	McManus 7 og; Hartley 9; Bednar 63	16,795
43 spl	Aberdeen	H	W	1-0	Hartley 54 pen	17,327
44 spl	Rangers	A	L	0-2		49,792
45 SCfin	Gretna	H	W	4-2*	Skacel 39 (*on penalties)	51,232

LEAGUE APPEARANCES, BOOKINGS AND CAPS

	AGE (on 01/07/06)	IN NAMED 18	APPEARANCES	COUNTING GAMES	MINUTES ON PITCH	YELLOW CARDS	RED CARDS	CAPS THIS SEASON	NATIONAL SIDE
Goalkeepers									
Steve Banks	34	33	3	2	245	0	0	-	England
Craig Gordon	23	37	36	35	3175	0	1	7	Scotland (85)
Defenders									
Christophe Berra	21	30	12	10	952	0	0	-	Scotland
Panagiotis Fyssas	33	32	32	30	2761	4	1	2	Greece (20)
Jose Goncalves	20	6	4	2	210	0	0	-	Portugal
James McAllister	28	26	17	7	947	1	0	-	Scotland
Robbie Neilson	26	38	37	36	3265	4	0	-	Scotland
Martin Petras	26	10	5	2	290	2	0	-	Slovakia
Steven Pressley	32	29	29	28	2569	6	1	5	Scotland (85)
Ibrahim Tall	30	16	4	3	325	0	0	-	Senegal
Gary Tierney	20	2	0	0	0	0	0	-	Scotland
Andy Webster	24	32	30	30	2700	0	0	7	Scotland (85)
Midfielders									
Bruno Aguiar	25	14	10	9	854	2	0	-	Portugal
Nerijus Barasa	27	5	4	1	160	2	0	-	Lithuania
Mirsad Beslija	27	4	4	2	200	0	0	-	Bosnia and Herz
Julien Brellier	24	32	30	20	2267	12	1	-	France
Samuel Camazzola	23	15	8	5	485	2	0	-	Brazil
Deividas Cesnauskis	25	35	25	14	1436	2	0	-	Lithuania
Chris Hackett	23	2	2	0	75	0	0	-	England
Paul Hartley	29	34	34	33	3008	5	0	5	Scotland (85)
Lee Johnson	25	8	4	1	114	0	0	-	England
Neil MacFarlane	28	6	3	1	133	0	0	-	Scotland
Neil McCann	31	1	1	0	22	0	0	5	Scotland (85)
Stephen Simmons	24	19	11	0	332	0	0	-	Scotland
Rudolf Skacel	26	35	35	31	2926	9	0	4	Czech Republic (2)
Ludek Straceny	29	2	2	1	110	1	0	-	Czech Republic
Lee Wallace	18	29	13	2	440	0	0	-	Scotland
Forwards									
Roman Bednar	23	22	22	17	1598	3	0	-	Czech Republic
Calum Elliot	19	33	28	15	1627	6	0	-	Scotland
Edgaras Jankauskas	31	25	25	18	1929	6	1	-	Lithuania
Juho Makela	23	2	2	0	49	1	0	-	Finland
Saulius Mikoliunas	22	30	23	7	1176	1	1	-	Lithuania
Jamie Mole	18	1	0	0	0	0	0	-	Scotland
Michel Pospisil	27	27	24	9	1112	2	0	-	Czech Republic

TEAM OF THE SEASON

MONTHLY POINTS TALLY

Month	Points	%
AUGUST	12	100%
SEPTEMBER	9	100%
OCTOBER	8	53%
NOVEMBER	5	56%
DECEMBER	7	58%
JANUARY	6	50%
FEBRUARY	4	44%
MARCH	8	67%
APRIL	9	60%
MAY	3	50%

LEAGUE GOALS

	PLAYER	MINS	GOALS	S RATE
1	Skacel	2926	16	183
2	Hartley	3008	14	215
3	Jankauskas	1929	8	241
4	Bednar	1598	7	228
5	Pospisil	1112	7	159
6	Elliot	1627	5	325
7	Pressley	2569	5	514
8	Mikoliunas	1176	3	392
9	Simmons	332	1	332
10	Webster	2700	1	2700
11	Makela	49	1	49
12	Aguiar	854	1	854
13	Berra	952	1	952
	Other		1	
	TOTAL		71	

TOP POINT EARNERS

	PLAYER	GAMES	AV PTS
1	Jankauskas	18	2.39
2	Bednar	17	2.24
3	Pressley	28	2.07
4	Skacel	31	2.06
5	Gordon	35	2.06
6	Fyssas	30	2.03
7	Neilson	36	2.03
8	Brellier	20	2.00
9	Cesnauskis	14	1.93
10	Webster	30	1.93
	CLUB AVERAGE:		1.95

DISCIPLINARY RECORDS

	PLAYER	YELLOW	RED	AVE
1	Brellier	12	1	174
2	Camazzola	2	0	242
3	Elliot	6	0	271
4	Jankauskas	6	1	275
5	Skacel	9	0	325
6	Pressley	6	1	367
7	Aguiar	2	0	427
8	Bednar	3	0	532
9	Fyssas	4	1	552
10	Pospisil	2	0	556
11	Mikoliunas	1	1	588
12	Hartley	5	0	601
13	Cesnauskis	2	0	718
	Other	5	1	
	TOTAL	65	6	

KEY GOALKEEPER

Craig Gordon

Goals Conceded in the League	26	**Counting Games** League games when player was on pitch for at least 70 minutes	35
Defensive Rating Ave number of mins between League goals conceded while on the pitch	122	**Clean Sheets** In League games when player was on pitch for at least 70 minutes	16

KEY PLAYERS - DEFENDERS

Panagiotis Fyssas

Goals Conceded Number of League goals conceded while the player was on the pitch	20	**Clean Sheets** In League games when player was on pitch for at least 70 minutes	13
Defensive Rating Ave number of mins between League goals conceded while on the pitch	138	**Club Defensive Rating** Average number of mins between League goals conceded by the club this season	110

	PLAYER	CON LGE	CLEAN SHEETS	DEF RATE
1	Panagiotis Fyssas	20	13	138 mins
2	Steven Pressley	22	13	117 mins
3	Robbie Neilson	28	16	117 mins
4	Andy Webster	25	12	108 mins

KEY PLAYERS - MIDFIELDERS

Deividas Cesnauskis

Goals in the League	0	**Contribution to Attacking Power** Average number of minutes between League team goals while on pitch	46
Defensive Rating Average number of mins between League goals conceded while on the pitch	160	**Scoring Difference** Defensive Rating minus Contribution to Attacking Power	114

	PLAYER	LGE GOALS	DEF RATE	POWER	SCORE DIFF
1	Deividas Cesnauskis	0	160	46	114 mins
2	Julien Brellier	0	119	52	67 mins
3	Paul Hartley	14	111	48	63 mins
4	Rudolf Skacel	16	105	46	59 mins

KEY PLAYERS - GOALSCORERS

Rudolf Skacel

Goals in the League	16	**Player Strike Rate** Average number of minutes between League goals scored by player	183
Contribution to Attacking Power Average number of minutes between League team goals while on pitch	46	**Club Strike Rate** Average number of minutes between League goals scored by club	48

	PLAYER	LGE GOALS	POWER	STRIKE RATE
1	Rudolf Skacel	16	46	183 mins
2	Paul Hartley	14	48	215 mins
3	Roman Bednar	7	43	228 mins
4	Edgaras Jankauskas	8	49	241 mins

Rudolph Skacel

SQUAD APPEARANCES

Match	1	2	3	4	5	6	7	8	9	10	11	12	13	14	15	16	17	18	19	20	21	22	23	24	25	26	27	28	29	30	31	32	33	34	35	36	37	38	39	40	41	42	43	44	45
Venue	A	H	A	H	A	H	A	A	A	H	A	A	H	H	A	H	A	A	H	H	A	H	H	H	A	A	H	H	A	H	H	H	A	A	H	A	A	A	H	H	A	H	H	A	H
Competition	L	L	L	L	W	L	L	L	W	L	L	L	L	L	L	L	L	L	L	L	L	L	L	O	L	L	L	O	L	L	L	O	L	L	L	L	O	L	L	L	L	L	L	L	O
Result	W	W	W	W	W	W	W	W	L	W	D	D	W	W	L	W	D	D	W	D	L	W	L	W	W	L	W	W	D	L	W	W	W	D	D	W	W	L	W	W	L	W	W	L	W

Goalkeepers
Steve Banks
Craig Gordon

Defenders
Christophe Berra
Panagiotis Fyssas
Jose Goncalves
James McAllister
Robbie Neilson
Martin Petras
Steven Pressley
Ibrahim Tall
Gary Tierney
Andy Webster

Midfielders
Bruno Aguiar
Nerijus Barasa
Mirsad Beslija
Julien Brellier
Samuel Camazzola
Deividas Cesnauskis
Chris Hackett
Paul Hartley
Lee Johnson
Neil MacFarlane
Neil McCann
Stephen Simmons
Rudolf Skacel
Ludek Straceny
Lee Wallace

Forwards
Roman Bednar
Calum Elliot
Edgaras Jankauskas
Juho Makela
Saulius Mikoliunas
Jamie Mole
Michel Pospisil

KEY: On all match | Subbed or sent off (Counting game) | Subbed on from bench (Counting Game) | Subbed on and then subbed or sent off (Counting Game) | Not in 16
On bench | Subbed or sent off (playing less than 70 minutes) | Subbed on (playing less than 70 minutes) | Subbed on and then subbed or sent off (playing less than 70 minutes)

RANGERS

Final Position: **3rd**

NICKNAME: THE GERS KEY: ☐Won ☐Drawn ☐Lost

No	Comp	Opponent	H/A	Res	Score	Scorers	Attendance
1	spl	Livingston	H	W	3-0	Prso 23; Pierre-Fanfan 53; Lovenkrands 90	49,613
2	spl	Inverness CT	A	W	1-0	Ferguson 69	7,512
3	ecql1	A Famagusta	A	W	2-1	Novo 65; Ricksen 70	16,000
4	spl	Aberdeen	A	L	2-3	Prso 39; Lovenkrands 49	18,182
5	spl	Celtic	H	W	3-1	Prso 34; Buffel 51; Novo 88 pen	49,699
6	ecql2	A Famagusta	H	W	2-0	Buffel 39; Prso 58	48,500
7	spl	Hibernian	H	L	0-3		49,754
8	spl	Falkirk	A	D	1-1	Novo 39 pen	6,500
9	ecgph	Porto	H	W	3-2	Lovenkrands 35; Prso 59; Kyrgiakos 85	48,599
10	spl	Kilmarnock	H	W	3-0	Prso 9 pen; Ferguson 67; Greer 82 og	49,076
11	sccc3	Clyde	H	W	5-2	Buffel 5,74; Nieto 98,113; Andrews 111	30,104
12	spl	Hearts	A	L	0-1		17,379
13	ecgph	Inter Milan	A	L	0-1		
14	spl	Dunfermline	H	W	5-1	Buffel 15; Prso 38; Nieto 71; Lovenkrands 75; McCormack 86	48,374
15	spl	Dundee Utd	A	D	0-0		11,696
16	ecgph	Art Bratislava	H	D	0-0		49,018
17	spl	Motherwell	H	W	2-0	Burke 1; Lovenkrands 72	49,215
18	spl	Livingston	A	D	2-2	Ferguson 15; Burke 54	9,481
19	spl	Inverness CT	H	D	1-1	Thompson 54	47,867
20	ecgph	Art Bratislava	A	D	2-2	Prso 3; Thompson 44	6,527
21	spl	Aberdeen	H	D	0-0		49,717
22	sccqf	Celtic	A	L	0-2		57,183
23	spl	Celtic	A	L	0-3		58,997
24	ecgph	Porto	A	D	1-1	McCormack 83	48,000
25	spl	Hibernian	A	L	1-2	Ferguson 59	16,958
26	spl	Falkirk	H	D	2-2	Ireland 31 og; Lovenkrands 56 pen	48,042
27	ecgph	Inter Milan	H	D	1-1	Lovenkrands 38	49,170
28	spl	Kilmarnock	A	W	3-2	Lovenkrands 16,42,72	12,426
29	spl	Hearts	H	W	1-0	Lovenkrands 35	49,723
30	spl	Dunfermline	A	D	3-3	Lovenkrands 22,65 pen; Burke 67	9,481
31	spl	Dundee Utd	H	W	3-0	Buffel 68; Thompson 83; Lovenkrands 86	49,141
32	scr3	Peterhead	H	W	5-0	Kyrgiakos 35; Boyd 50 pen,54,71; McCormack 75	39,870
33	spl	Motherwell	A	W	1-0	Lovenkrands 55	10,689
34	spl	Livingston	H	W	4-1	Boyd 8,56; Prso 89,90	49,211
35	spl	Inverness CT	A	W	3-2	Boyd 6,58 pen; Andrews 27	7,380
36	scr4	Hibernian	H	L	0-3		40,722
37	spl	Aberdeen	A	L	0-2		17,087
38	spl	Celtic	H	L	0-1		49,788
39	spl	Hibernian	H	W	2-0	Boyd 40; Ferguson 74	49,720
40	eclsl1	Villarreal	H	D	2-2	Lovenkrands 22; Pena 82 og	49,372
41	spl	Falkirk	A	W	2-1	Boyd 57; Twaddle 70 og	6,343
42	eclsl2	Villarreal	A	D	1-1	Lovenkrands 12	23,000
43	spl	Kilmarnock	H	W	4-0	Boyd 13; Rodriguez 71; Prso 85 pen; Lovenkrands 87	49,442
44	spl	Hearts	A	D	1-1	Buffel 65	17,040
45	spl	Dunfermline	H	W	1-0	Kyrgiakos 70	49,017
46	spl	Dundee Utd	A	W	4-1	Prso 30; Boyd 31,54,83	11,213
47	spl	Motherwell	H	W	1-0	Boyd 27	49,481
48	spl	Aberdeen	H	D	1-1	Boyd 51	48,987
49	spl	Celtic	A	D	0-0		59,684
50	spl	Kilmarnock	A	W	3-1	Andrews 51,79; Boyd 64	11,583
51	spl	Hibernian	A	W	2-1	Boyd 36,74	10,000
52	spl	Hearts	H	W	2-0	Boyd 36,74	49,792

LEAGUE APPEARANCES, BOOKINGS AND CAPS

	AGE (on 01/07/06)	IN NAMED 18	APPEARANCES	COUNTING GAMES	MINUTES ON PITCH	YELLOW CARDS	RED CARDS	CAPS THIS SEASON	NATIONAL SIDE
Goalkeepers									
Stefan Klos	34	36	2	2	180	0	0	-	Germany
Lee Robinson	20	1	1	0	13	0	0	-	Scotland
Ronald Waterreus	35	37	36	36	3227	0	0	-	Holland
Defenders									
Marvin Andrews	30	36	23	21	1956	2	0	8	Trinidad & Tobago (47)
Michael Ball	26	2	2	2	180	0	0	-	England
Olivier Bernard	26	9	9	8	765	2	0	-	France
Alan Hutton	21	23	19	15	1470	2	0	-	England
Sotirios Kyrgiakos	26	28	28	25	2383	7	2	3	Greece (34)
Alan Lowing	18	6	2	1	104	0	0	-	Scotland
Robert Malcolm	25	22	13	10	970	7	0	-	Scotland
Jose Pierre-Fanfan	30	15	7	7	611	1	0	-	France
Julien Rodriguez	28	22	21	19	1770	1	0	-	France
Steven Smith	20	29	18	15	1487	1	0	-	Scotland
Midfielders									
Thomas Buffel	25	29	29	19	2131	1	0	4	Belgium (42)
Chris Burke	22	29	27	20	2124	4	0	-	Scotland
Barry Ferguson	28	32	32	31	2835	5	1	4	Scotland (85)
Ibrahim Hemdani	28	23	19	17	1583	1	0	-	France
Ian Murray	25	36	30	26	2432	5	0	4	Scotland (85)
Hamed Namouchi	22	17	7	5	500	1	0	-	France
Alex Rae	36	18	9	3	415	1	0	-	Scotland
Gavin Rae	28	11	8	4	410	0	0	-	Scotland
Fernando Ricksen	29	24	21	18	1726	7	1	-	Holland
Forwards									
Kris Boyd	22	17	17	13	1266	5	0	-	Scotland
Francis Jeffers	25	13	8	2	385	0	0	-	England
Peter Lovenkrands	26	34	33	19	2123	2	0	-	Denmark
Ross McCormack	19	21	8	1	252	0	0	-	Scotland
Federico Nieto	22	3	3	0	76	0	0	-	Argentina
Nacho Novo	27	29	24	6	958	3	0	-	Spain
Dado Prso	31	32	32	27	2605	4	0	8	Croatia (23)
Steven Thompson	27	16	14	4	623	1	0	1	Scotland (85)

TEAM OF THE SEASON

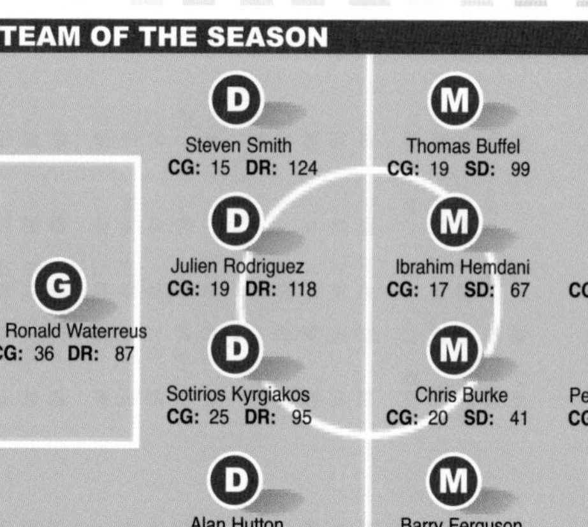

MONTHLY POINTS TALLY

Month	Points	%
AUGUST	6	50%
SEPTEMBER	4	44%
OCTOBER	9	60%
NOVEMBER	1	11%
DECEMBER	11	73%
JANUARY	9	100%
FEBRUARY	3	33%
MARCH	10	83%
APRIL	11	73%
MAY	6	100%

LEAGUE GOALS

	PLAYER	MINS	GOALS	S RATE
1	Boyd	1266	**17**	74
2	Lovenkrands	2123	**14**	152
3	Prso	2605	**9**	289
4	Ferguson	2835	**5**	567
5	Buffel	2131	**4**	533
6	Andrews	1956	**3**	652
7	Burke	2124	**3**	708
8	Novo	958	**2**	479
9	Thompson	623	**2**	312
10	Nieto	76	**1**	76
11	Kyrgiakos	2383	**1**	2383
12	McCormack	252	**1**	252
13	Pierre-Fanfan	611	**1**	611
	Other		4	
	TOTAL		**67**	

TOP POINT EARNERS

	PLAYER	GAMES	AV PTS
1	Boyd	13	**2.69**
2	Buffel	19	**2.42**
3	Smith, S	15	**2.40**
4	Lovenkrands	19	**2.16**
5	Hemdani	17	**2.12**
6	Burke	20	**2.10**
7	Rodriguez	19	**2.05**
8	Kyrgiakos	25	**2.00**
9	Murray, I	26	**1.92**
10	Waterreus	36	**1.92**
	CLUB AVERAGE:		**1.92**

DISCIPLINARY RECORDS

	PLAYER	YELLOW	RED	AVE
1	Malcolm	7	0	**138**
2	Ricksen	7	1	**215**
3	Boyd	5	0	**253**
4	Kyrgiakos	7	2	**264**
5	Novo	3	0	**319**
6	Bernard	2	0	**382**
7	Ferguson	5	1	**472**
8	Murray, I	5	0	**486**
9	Namouchi	1	0	**500**
10	Burke	4	0	**531**
11	Pierre-Fanfan	1	0	**611**
12	Thompson	1	0	**623**
13	Prso	4	0	**651**
	Other	10	0	
	TOTAL	**62**	**4**	

KEY GOALKEEPER

Ronald Waterreus

Goals Conceded in the League	37	**Counting Games** League games when player was on pitch for at least 70 minutes	36
Defensive Rating Ave number of mins between League goals conceded while on the pitch	87	**Clean Sheets** In League games when player was on pitch for at least 70 minutes	13

KEY PLAYERS - DEFENDERS

Steven Smith

Goals Conceded Number of League goals conceded while the player was on the pitch	12	**Clean Sheets** In League games when player was on pitch for at least 70 minutes	7
Defensive Rating Ave number of mins between League goals conceded while on the pitch	124	**Club Defensive Rating** Average number of mins between League goals conceded by the club this season	92

	PLAYER	CON LGE	CLEAN SHEETS	DEF RATE
1	Steven Smith	12	7	124 mins
2	Julien Rodriguez	15	9	118 mins
3	Sotirios Kyrgiakos	25	11	95 mins
4	Alan Hutton	16	6	92 mins

KEY PLAYERS - MIDFIELDERS

Thomas Buffel

Goals in the League	4	**Contribution to Attacking Power** Average number of minutes between League team goals while on pitch	43
Defensive Rating Average number of mins between League goals conceded while on the pitch	142	**Scoring Difference** Defensive Rating minus Contribution to Attacking Power	99

	PLAYER	LGE GOALS	DEF RATE	POWER	SCORE DIFF
1	Thomas Buffel	4	142	43	99 mins
2	Ibrahim Hemdani	0	122	55	67 mins
3	Chris Burke	3	92	51	41 mins
4	Barry Ferguson	5	95	56	39 mins

KEY PLAYERS - GOALSCORERS

Kris Boyd

Goals in the League	17	**Player Strike Rate** Average number of minutes between League goals scored by player	74
Contribution to Attacking Power Average number of minutes between League team goals while on pitch	49	**Club Strike Rate** Average number of minutes between League goals scored by club	51

	PLAYER	LGE GOALS	POWER	STRIKE RATE
1	Kris Boyd	17	49	74 mins
2	Peter Lovenkrands	14	42	152 mins
3	Dado Prso	9	54	289 mins
4	Thomas Buffel	4	43	533 mins

Kris Boyd

SQUAD APPEARANCES

Match	1	2	3	4	5	6	7	8	9	10	11	12	13	14	15	16	17	18	19	20	21	22	23	24	25	26
Venue	H	A	A	A	H	H	H	A	H	H	H	A	A	H	A	H	H	A	H	A	H	A	A	A	A	H
Competition	L	L	C	L	L	C	L	L	C	L	W	L	C	L	L	C	L	L	L	C	L	W	L	C	L	L
Result	W	W	W	L	W	W	L	D	W	W	W	L	L	W	D	D	W	D	D	D	D	L	L	D	L	D

Match	27	28	29	30	31	32	33	34	35	36	37	38	39	40	41	42	43	44	45	46	47	48	49	50	51	52
Venue	H	A	H	A	H	H	A	H	A	H	A	H	H	H	A	A	H	A	H	A	H	H	A	A	A	H
Competition	C	L	L	L	L	O	L	L	L	O	L	L	L	C	L	C	L	L	L	L	L	L	L	L	L	L
Result	D	W	W	D	W	W	W	W	W	L	L	L	W	D	W	D	W	D	W	W	W	D	D	W	W	W

Goalkeepers
Stefan Klos
Lee Robinson
Ronald Waterreus

Defenders
Marvin Andrews
Michael Ball
Olivier Bernard
Alan Hutton
Sotirios Kyrgiakos
Alan Lowing
Robert Malcolm
Jose Karl Pierre-Fanfan
Julien Rodriguez
Steven Smith

Midfielders
Thomas Buffel
Chris Burke
Barry Ferguson
Ibrahim Hemdani
Ian Murray
Hamed Namouchi
Alex Rae
Gavin Rae
Fernando Ricksen

Forwards
Kris Boyd
Francis Jeffers
Peter Lovenkrands
Ross McCormack
Federico Nieto
Nacho Novo
Dado Prso
Steven Thompson

KEY: On all match | Subbed or sent off (Counting game) | Subbed on from bench (Counting Game) | Subbed on and then subbed or sent off (Counting Game) | Not in 16
On bench | Subbed or sent off (playing less than 70 minutes) | Subbed on (playing less than 70 minutes) | Subbed on and then subbed or sent off (playing less than 70 minutes)

HIBERNIAN

Final Position: **4th**

NICKNAME: THE HIBEES

KEY: ☐Won ☐Drawn ☐Lost

							Attendance
1	spl	**Dunfermline**	H	D	1-1	O'Connor 74	13,010
2	spl	**Hearts**	A	L	0-4		16,459
3	spl	**Livingston**	H	W	3-0	Murphy 40; Shiels, D 42; O'Connor 53	11,341
4	spl	**Falkirk**	A	W	2-0	Brown, Sc 36; Riordan 63 pen	6,268
5	spl	**Rangers**	A	W	3-0	Sproule 67,86,90	49,754
6	spl	**Dundee Utd**	H	W	2-1	O'Connor 18 pen; Sproule 70	12,062
7	uc1rl1	**Dnipro**	H	D	0-0		16,861
8	spl	**Celtic**	H	L	0-1		15,649
9	sccc3	**Ayr**	A	W	2-1	Riordan 37,41	2,598
10	spl	**Motherwell**	A	W	3-1	Beuzelin 20; Stewart 68; Riordan 80	6,461
11	uc1rl2	**Dnipro**	A	L	1-5	Riordan 24	
12	spl	**Inverness CT**	H	L	1-2	Fletcher 82	11,683
13	spl	**Kilmarnock**	H	W	4-2	Caldwell 53; Beuzelin 61,80; Riordan 81	11,731
14	spl	**Aberdeen**	A	W	1-0	Riordan 54	13,375
15	spl	**Dunfermline**	A	W	2-1	O'Connor 47,82	6,853
16	spl	**Hearts**	H	W	2-0	Beuzelin 77; O'Connor 79	17,180
17	spl	**Livingston**	A	W	2-1	Shiels, D 82; O'Connor 85	8,390
18	sccqf	**Dunfermline**	A	L	0-3		6,005
19	spl	**Falkirk**	H	L	2-3	Riordan 1,33	13,902
20	spl	**Rangers**	H	W	2-1	Riordan 18; O'Connor 25	16,958
21	spl	**Dundee Utd**	A	L	0-1		7,976
22	spl	**Celtic**	A	L	2-3	Beuzelin 47; Fletcher 53	59,895
23	spl	**Motherwell**	H	W	2-1	Fletcher 3; Riordan 90	11,926
24	spl	**Inverness CT**	A	L	0-2		7,017
25	spl	**Kilmarnock**	A	D	2-2	Hogg 59; O'Connor 84	9,224
26	scr3	**Arbroath**	H	W	6-0	Brown, Scott 40,78; Sproule 45; Stewart 63; O'Connor 74; Fletcher 85	10,523
27	spl	**Aberdeen**	H	L	1-2	Caldwell 90	14,572
28	spl	**Dunfermline**	H	W	3-1	Riordan 16,70; Fletcher 88	13,316
29	spl	**Hearts**	A	L	1-4	O'Connor 57	17,371
30	scr4	**Rangers**	A	W	3-0	O'Connor 50; Sproule 59; Killen 78	40,722
31	spl	**Livingston**	H	W	7-0	Killen 19; Riordan 33 pen,64; O'Connor 48; Mackay 70 og; Fletcher 89,90	12,170
32	spl	**Falkirk**	A	D	0-0		5,937
33	spl	**Rangers**	A	L	0-2		49,720
34	Scpqf	**Falkirk**	A	W	5-1	Riordan 9; O'Connor 67; Sproule 74; Caldwell 77; Fletcher 88	6,259
35	spl	**Dundee Utd**	H	W	3-1	Riordan 5; Archibald 24 og; Killen 32	16,266
36	spl	**Celtic**	H	L	1-2	Riordan 24	16,985
37	spl	**Motherwell**	A	D	2-2	Killen 47; Glass 77	6,724
38	spl	**Inverness CT**	H	L	0-2		12,745
39	SCsf	**Hearts**	H	L	0-4		43,180
40	spl	**Kilmarnock**	H	W	2-1	Riordan 79; Dalglish 86	10,427
41	spl	**Aberdeen**	A	L	0-1		14,110
42	spl	**Celtic**	A	D	1-1	Fletcher 35	60,047
43	spl	**Hearts**	H	W	2-1	Riordan 16; Benjelloun 78	16,654
44	spl	**Aberdeen**	A	L	0-4		10,490
45	spl	**Rangers**	H	L	1-2	Hemdani 72 og	10,000
46	spl	**Kilmarnock**	A	L	1-3	Fletcher 5	5,732

LEAGUE APPEARANCES, BOOKINGS AND CAPS

	AGE (on 01/07/06)	IN NAMED 18	APPEARANCES	COUNTING GAMES	MINUTES ON PITCH	YELLOW CARDS	RED CARDS	CAPS THIS SEASON	NATIONAL SIDE
Goalkeepers									
Simon Brown	29	35	8	6	605	0	1	-	England
Zibigniew Malkowski	28	37	32	31	2816	4	1	-	Poland
Gordon Marshall	42	1	0	0	0	0	0	-	Scotland
Andrew McNeil	19	2	0	0	0	0	0	-	England
Defenders									
Gary Caldwell	25	33	33	32	2887	4	0	4	Scotland (85)
Chris Hogg	21	37	24	19	1992	0	0	-	England
Oumar Konde	26	13	11	6	683	1	0	-	Switzerland
David Murphy	22	31	30	27	2595	2	1	-	England
Humphrey Rudge	28	15	6	4	414	0	0	-	Holland
Gary Smith	35	28	20	18	1690	2	1	-	Scotland
Lewis Stevenson	-	2	0	0	0	0	0	-	
Midfielders									
Guillaume Beuzelin	27	21	21	16	1662	4	0	-	France
Steven Fletcher	19	36	35	10	1726	2	0	-	Scotland
Stephen Glass	30	36	28	20	2093	4	0	-	Scotland
Jamie McCluskey	18	15	3	0	34	0	0	-	Scotland
Kevin McDonald	21	7	2	0	5	0	0	-	Scotland
Antonio Murray	21	8	1	1	90	1	0	-	England
Steven Notman	19	0	0	0	0	0	0	-	Scotland
Jay Shields	21	14	7	7	600	1	0	-	Scotland
Ivan Sproule	25	33	32	14	1998	9	0	6	N Ireland (114)
Michael Stewart	25	26	25	19	1974	2	0	-	Scotland
Kevin Thomson	21	31	31	23	2325	5	0	-	Scotland
Steven Whittaker	22	34	34	33	3021	4	0	-	Scotland
Forwards									
A. Benjelloun	21	5	5	2	283	1	0	-	Morocco
Scott Brown	21	20	19	13	1395	7	1	1	Scotland (85)
Paul Dalglish	29	11	10	1	386	0	0	-	Scotland
Christopher Killen	24	8	7	4	449	1	0	-	New Zealand
Amadou Konte	25	24	13	0	298	2	0	-	England
Sam Morrow	21	23	8	0	148	0	0	-	N Ireland
Garry O'Connor	23	27	27	18	1962	3	0	4	Scotland (85)
Derek Riordan	23	37	37	23	2700	4	0	2	Scotland (85)
Dean Shiels	21	24	17	5	764	1	0	-	Scotland

TEAM OF THE SEASON

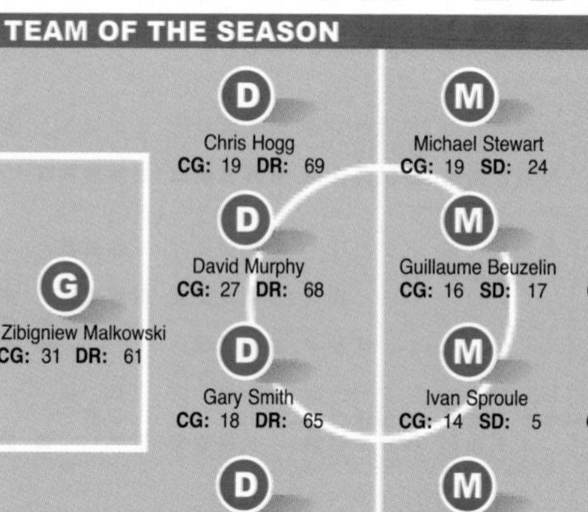

MONTHLY POINTS TALLY

AUGUST	9	75%
SEPTEMBER	6	67%
OCTOBER	12	80%
NOVEMBER	6	67%
DECEMBER	3	25%
JANUARY	4	33%
FEBRUARY	4	44%
MARCH	4	33%
APRIL	7	47%
MAY	0	0%

LEAGUE GOALS

	PLAYER	MINS	GOALS	S RATE
1	Riordan	2700	16	169
2	O'Connor	1962	11	178
3	Fletcher	1726	9	192
4	Beuzelin	1662	5	332
5	Sproule	1998	4	500
6	Killen	449	3	150
7	Caldwell	2887	2	1444
8	Shiels, D	764	2	382
9	Brown, Scott	1395	1	1395
10	Benjelloun	283	1	283
11	Murphy	2595	1	2595
12	Hogg	1992	1	1992
13	Dalglish	386	1	386
	Other		4	
	TOTAL		61	

TOP POINT EARNERS

	PLAYER	GAMES	AV PTS
1	Beuzelin	16	2.06
2	Brown, Scott	13	1.85
3	Hogg	19	1.84
4	Riordan	23	1.74
5	Stewart	19	1.68
6	Smith, G	18	1.67
7	O'Connor	18	1.61
8	Murphy	27	1.48
9	Malkowski	31	1.48
10	Caldwell	32	1.38
	CLUB AVERAGE:		1.47

DISCIPLINARY RECORDS

	PLAYER	YELLOW	RED	AVE
1	Brown, Scott	7	1	174
2	Sproule	9	0	222
3	Beuzelin	4	0	415
4	Thomson	5	0	465
5	Glass	4	0	523
6	Malkowski	4	1	563
7	Smith, G	2	1	563
8	Shields, J	1	0	600
9	Brown, Simon	0	1	605
10	O'Connor	3	0	654
11	Riordan	4	0	675
12	Konde	1	0	683
13	Caldwell	4	0	721
	Other	11	1	
	TOTAL	59	5	

KEY GOALKEEPER

Zibigniew Malkowski

Goals Conceded in the League	46	**Counting Games** League games when player was on pitch for at least 70 minutes	31
Defensive Rating Ave number of mins between League goals conceded while on the pitch	61	**Clean Sheets** In League games when player was on pitch for at least 70 minutes	5

KEY PLAYERS - DEFENDERS

Chris Hogg

Goals Conceded Number of League goals conceded while the player was on the pitch	29	**Clean Sheets** In League games when player was on pitch for at least 70 minutes	5
Defensive Rating Ave number of mins between League goals conceded while on the pitch	69	**Club Defensive Rating** Average number of mins between League goals conceded by the club this season	61

	PLAYER	CON LGE	CLEAN SHEETS	DEF RATE
1	Chris Hogg	29	5	69 mins
2	David Murphy	38	7	68 mins
3	Gary Smith	26	4	65 mins
4	Gary Caldwell	50	4	58 mins

KEY PLAYERS - MIDFIELDERS

Michael Stewart

Goals in the League	1	**Contribution to Attacking Power** Average number of minutes between League team goals while on pitch	52
Defensive Rating Average number of mins between League goals conceded while on the pitch	76	**Scoring Difference** Defensive Rating minus Contribution to Attacking Power	24

	PLAYER	LGE GOALS	DEF RATE	POWER	SCORE DIFF
1	Michael Stewart	1	76	52	24 mins
2	Guillaume Beuzelin	5	72	55	17 mins
3	Ivan Sproule	4	54	49	5 mins
4	Stephen Glass	1	50	52	-2 mins

KEY PLAYERS - GOALSCORERS

Derek Riordan

Goals in the League	16	**Player Strike Rate** Average number of minutes between League goals scored by player	169
Contribution to Attacking Power Average number of minutes between League team goals while on pitch	56	**Club Strike Rate** Average number of minutes between League goals scored by club	56

	PLAYER	LGE GOALS	POWER	STRIKE RATE
1	Derek Riordan	16	56	169 mins
2	Garry O'Connor	11	58	178 mins
3	Guillaume Beuzelin	5	55	332 mins
4	Ivan Sproule	4	49	500 mins

Derek Riordan

SQUAD APPEARANCES

Match	1	2	3	4	5	6	7	8	9	10	11	12	13	14	15	16	17	18	19	20	21	22	23	24	25	26	27	28	29	30	31	32	33	34	35	36	37	38	39	40	41	42	43	44	45	46
Venue	H	A	H	A	A	H	H	H	A	A	A	H	H	A	A	H	A	A	H	H	A	A	H	A	A	H	H	H	A	A	H	A	A	A	H	H	A	H	H	H	A	A	H	A	H	A
Competition	L	L	L	L	L	L	E	L	W	L	E	L	L	L	L	L	L	W	L	L	L	L	L	L	L	O	L	L	L	O	L	L	L	O	L	L	L	L	O	L	L	L	L	L	L	L
Result	D	L	W	W	W	W	D	L	W	W	L	L	W	W	W	W	W	L	L	W	L	L	W	L	D	W	L	W	L	W	W	D	L	W	W	L	D	L	L	W	L	D	W	L	L	L

Goalkeepers
Simon Brown
Zibigniew Malkowski
Gordon Marshall
Andrew McNeil

Defenders
Gary Caldwell
Chris Hogg
Oumar Konde
David Murphy
Humphrey Rudge
Gary Smith
Lewis Stevenson

Midfielders
Guillaume Beuzelin
Steven Fletcher
Stephen Glass
Jamie McCluskey
Kevin McDonald
Antonio Murray
Steven Notman
Jay Shields
Ivan Sproule
Michael Stewart
Kevin Thomson
Steven Whittaker

Forwards
Abdessalam Benjelloun
Scott Brown
Paul Dalglish
Christopher Killen
Amadou Konte
Sam Morrow
Garry O'Connor
Derek Riordan
Dean Shiels

KEY: On all match · On bench · Subbed or sent off (Counting game) · Subbed or sent off (playing less than 70 minutes) · Subbed on from bench (Counting Game) · Subbed on (playing less than 70 minutes) · Subbed on and then subbed or sent off (Counting Game) · Subbed on and then subbed or sent off (playing less than 70 minutes) · Not in 16

KILMARNOCK

Final Position: **5th**

NICKNAME: KILLIE

KEY: ☐ Won ☐ Drawn ☐ Lost

							Attendance
1	spl	**Hearts**	H	L	2-4	Naismith 12; Greer 74	7,487
2	spl	**Aberdeen**	A	W	2-1	Johnston 1; Naismith 72	13,661
3	spl	**Motherwell**	H	W	4-1	Johnston 12; Boyd 19,73; McDonald 61	5,035
4	spl	**Inverness CT**	A	D	2-2	Nish 71; Boyd 74	4,119
5	sccc1	**Stirling**	H	W	4-1	Dodds 42; Invincible 56; Wales 75; Di Giacomo 90	3,124
6	spl	**Livingston**	H	W	3-0	Nish 28,35,43	4,644
7	spl	**Dunfermline**	H	W	3-2	Dodds 8; Boyd 33; Invincible 90	4,737
8	spl	**Rangers**	A	L	0-3		49,076
9	sccc3	**Dunfermline**	H	L	3-4	Boyd 52,90; Wilson, S 72 og	3,191
10	spl	**Falkirk**	H	D	1-1	Boyd 23 pen	5,507
11	spl	**Dundee Utd**	A	D	0-0		6,915
12	spl	**Hibernian**	A	L	2-4	Ford 7; Fowler 40	11,731
13	spl	**Celtic**	H	L	0-1		10,544
14	spl	**Hearts**	A	L	0-1		16,536
15	spl	**Aberdeen**	H	W	4-2	Ford 17; Invincible 18; Boyd 46,56	5,798
16	spl	**Motherwell**	A	D	2-2	Boyd 8,90	4,979
17	spl	**Inverness CT**	H	D	2-2	Boyd 53; Naismith 55	4,708
18	spl	**Livingston**	A	W	3-0	Boyd 25,81; Naismith 28	3,446
19	spl	**Dunfermline**	A	W	1-0	Boyd 41	4,319
20	spl	**Rangers**	H	L	2-3	McDonald 61; Boyd 82	12,426
21	spl	**Falkirk**	A	W	2-1	Fowler 50; Boyd 90	4,804
22	spl	**Dundee Utd**	H	W	2-1	McDonald 38; Wales 90	5,749
23	spl	**Hibernian**	H	D	2-2	Naismith 29; Wales 90	9,224
24	scr3	**Hearts**	A	L	1-2	Nish 85	12,831
25	spl	**Celtic**	A	L	2-4	Naismith 24 pen; Invincible 51	59,995
26	spl	**Hearts**	H	W	1-0	Invincible 46	8,811
27	spl	**Aberdeen**	A	D	2-2	Naismith 30 pen; Lilley 84	10,540
28	spl	**Motherwell**	H	W	2-0	Wales 34,51	5,169
29	spl	**Inverness CT**	A	D	3-3	Naismith 26; Wales 68,84	3,618
30	spl	**Livingston**	H	W	3-1	Wales 21; Naismith 26; Invincible 58	5,266
31	spl	**Dunfermline**	H	W	1-0	Invincible 8	5,507
32	spl	**Rangers**	A	L	0-4		49,442
33	spl	**Falkirk**	H	W	2-1	Invincible 2; Naismith 73	5,443
34	spl	**Dundee Utd**	A	D	2-2	Naismith 12,17	5,830
35	spl	**Hibernian**	A	L	1-2	Wales 18	10,427
36	spl	**Celtic**	H	L	1-4	Nish 89	10,978
37	spl	**Hearts**	A	L	0-2		16,497
38	spl	**Aberdeen**	A	D	0-0		10,634
39	spl	**Rangers**	H	L	1-3	Nish 27	11,583
40	spl	**Celtic**	A	L	0-2		48,649
41	spl	**Hibernian**	H	W	3-1	Naismith 48 pen; Greer 72; Nish 75	5,732

LEAGUE APPEARANCES, BOOKINGS AND CAPS

	AGE (on 01/07/06)	IN NAMED 18	APPEARANCES	COUNTING GAMES	MINUTES ON PITCH	YELLOW CARDS	RED CARDS	CAPS THIS SEASON	NATIONAL SIDE
Goalkeepers									
Cameron Bell	19	18	0	0	0	0	0	-	Scotland
Alan Combe	32	32	32	31	2803	0	1	-	Scotland
Graeme Smith	23	33	7	7	612	0	0	-	Scotland
Defenders									
Shaun Dillon	21	12	0	0	0	0	0	-	Scotland
Simon Ford	24	32	32	31	2841	3	0	-	England
Gordon Greer	25	29	27	26	2405	1	0	-	Scotland
Jamie Hamill	19	4	0	0	0	0	0	-	Scotland
Garry Hay	28	35	35	34	3094	7	0	-	Scotland
David Lilley	28	23	11	6	684	1	0	-	Scotland
Ryan O'Leary	18	2	0	0	0	0	0	-	Rep or Ireland
Lindsay Wilson	27	13	13	9	930	1	0	-	Australia
Fraser Wright	26	28	27	27	2430	1	0	-	
Midfielders									
Rhian Dodds	26	21	10	5	536	1	0	-	England
James Fowler	25	38	38	38	3420	4	0	-	Scotland
Danny Invincible	27	37	37	30	2966	1	0	-	Australia
Peter Leven	22	13	6	2	314	0	0	-	Scotland
Gary Locke	31	19	15	10	950	3	0	-	Scotland
Gary McDonald	24	36	27	14	1487	0	0	-	Scotland
Stephen Murray	23	25	15	1	298	0	0	-	Scotland
Forwards									
Kris Boyd	22	19	19	18	1569	1	0	-	Scotland
Robert Campbell	19	34	2	0	16	0	0	-	Scotland
Paul Di Giacomo	24	22	12	2	300	0	0	-	Scotland
Allan Johnston	32	37	37	36	3225	4	0	-	Scotland
Rory Loy	18	5	0	0	0	0	0	-	Scotland
Steven Naismith	19	37	36	30	2759	9	0	-	Scotland
Colin Nish	25	34	33	24	2355	3	0	-	Scotland
Gary Wales	27	30	30	16	1621	1	0	-	Scotland

TEAM OF THE SEASON

MONTHLY POINTS TALLY

AUGUST	10	83%
SEPTEMBER	4	44%
OCTOBER	4	27%
NOVEMBER	5	56%
DECEMBER	9	75%
JANUARY	5	42%
FEBRUARY	7	78%
MARCH	7	58%
APRIL	1	7%
MAY	3	50%

LEAGUE GOALS

	PLAYER	MINS	GOALS	S RATE
1	Boyd	1479	**15**	99
2	Naismith	2759	**13**	212
3	Wales	1621	**8**	203
4	Nish	2355	**7**	336
5	Invincible	2966	**7**	424
6	McDonald	1487	**3**	496
7	Ford	2841	**2**	1421
8	Greer	2405	**2**	1203
9	Fowler	3420	**2**	1710
10	Johnston	3225	**2**	1613
11	Dodds	536	**1**	536
12	Lilley	684	**1**	684
	Other		**0**	
	TOTAL		**63**	

TOP POINT EARNERS

	PLAYER	GAMES	AV PTS
1	Boyd	17	**1.65**
2	Nish	24	**1.63**
3	Ford	31	**1.61**
4	Invincible	30	**1.53**
5	Hay	34	**1.50**
6	Wright	27	**1.48**
7	Fowler	38	**1.45**
8	Johnston	36	**1.44**
9	Naismith	30	**1.43**
10	Greer	26	**1.42**
	CLUB AVERAGE:		**1.45**

DISCIPLINARY RECORDS

	PLAYER	YELLOW	RED	AVE
1	Naismith	9	0	**306**
2	Locke	3	0	**316**
3	Hay	7	0	**442**
4	Dodds	1	0	**536**
5	Lilley	1	0	**684**
6	Nish	3	0	**785**
7	Johnston	4	0	**806**
8	Fowler	4	0	**855**
9	Wilson	1	0	**930**
10	Ford	3	0	**947**
11	Boyd	1	0	**1479**
12	Wales	1	0	**1621**
13	Greer	1	0	**2405**
	Other	2	1	
	TOTAL	**41**	**1**	

KEY GOALKEEPER

Alan Combe

Goals Conceded in the League	54	Counting Games League games when player was on pitch for at least 70 minutes	31
Defensive Rating Ave number of mins between League goals conceded while on the pitch	52	Clean Sheets In League games when player was on pitch for at least 70 minutes	8

KEY PLAYERS - DEFENDERS

Gordon Greer

Goals Conceded Number of League goals conceded while the player was on the pitch	43	Clean Sheets In League games when player was on pitch for at least 70 minutes	5
Defensive Rating Ave number of mins between League goals conceded while on the pitch	56	Club Defensive Rating Average number of mins between League goals conceded by the club this season	53

	PLAYER	CON LGE	CLEAN SHEETS	DEF RATE
1	Gordon Greer	43	5	56 mins
2	Garry Hay	56	8	55 mins
3	Fraser Wright	45	6	54 mins
4	Simon Ford	54	7	53 mins

KEY PLAYERS - MIDFIELDERS

Danny Invincible

Goals in the League	7	Contribution to Attacking Power Average number of minutes between League team goals while on pitch	57
Defensive Rating Average number of mins between League goals conceded while on the pitch	57	Scoring Difference Defensive Rating minus Contribution to Attacking Power	0

	PLAYER	LGE GOALS	DEF RATE	POWER	SCORE DIFF
1	Danny Invincible	7	57	57	0 mins
2	James Fowler	2	53	54	-1 mins
3	Gary McDonald	3	41	57	-16 mins

KEY PLAYERS - GOALSCORERS

Kris Boyd

Goals in the League	15	Player Strike Rate Average number of minutes between League goals scored by player	99
Contribution to Attacking Power Average number of minutes between League team goals while on pitch	45	Club Strike Rate Average number of minutes between League goals scored by club	54

	PLAYER	LGE GOALS	POWER	STRIKE RATE
1	Kris Boyd	15	45	99 mins
2	Gary Wales	8	58	203 mins
3	Steven Naismith	13	56	212 mins
4	Colin Nish	7	57	336 mins

Alan Combe

SQUAD APPEARANCES

Match	1	2	3	4	5	6	7	8	9	10	11	12	13	14	15	16	17	18	19	20	21	22	23	24	25	26	27	28	29	30	31	32	33	34	35	36	37	38	39	40	41
Venue	H	A	H	A	H	H	H	A	H	H	A	A	H	A	H	A	H	A	A	H	A	H	H	A	A	H	A	H	A	H	H	A	H	A	A	H	A	A	H	A	H
Competition	L	L	L	L	W	L	L	L	W	L	L	L	L	L	L	L	L	L	L	L	L	L	L	O	L	L	L	L	L	L	L	L	L	L	L	L	L	L	L	L	L
Result	L	W	W	D	W	W	W	L	L	D	D	L	L	L	W	D	D	W	W	L	W	W	D	L	L	W	D	W	D	W	W	L	W	D	L	L	L	D	L	L	W

Goalkeepers
Cameron Bell
Alan Combe
Graeme Smith

Defenders
Shaun Dillon
Simon Ford
Gordon Greer
Jamie Hamill
Garry Hay
David Lilley
Ryan O'Leary
Lindsay Wilson
Fraser Wright

Midfielders
Rhian Dodds
James Fowler
Danny Invincible
Peter Leven
Gary Locke
Gary McDonald
Stephen Murray

Forwards
Kris Boyd
Robert Campbell
Paul Di Giacomo
Allan Johnston
Rory Loy
Steven Naismith
Colin Nish
Gary Wales

KEY: On all match | On bench | Subbed or sent off (Counting game) | Subbed or sent off (playing less than 70 minutes) | Subbed on from bench (Counting Game) | Subbed on (playing less than 70 minutes) | Subbed on and then subbed or sent off (Counting Game) | Subbed on and then subbed or sent off (playing less than 70 minutes) | Not in 16

ABERDEEN

Final Position: **6th**

NICKNAME: THE DONS

KEY: Won / Drawn / Lost

	Comp	Opponent	Venue	Result	Score	Scorers	Attendance
1	spl	Dundee Utd	A	D	1-1	Nicholson 48	12,404
2	spl	Kilmarnock	H	L	1-2	Anderson 34	13,661
3	spl	Rangers	H	W	3-2	Anderson 30; Lovell 37; Smith, J 88	18,182
4	spl	Hearts	A	L	0-2		16,139
5	sccc1	Berwick	H	W	3-0	Winter 38; Lovell 52,71	4,398
6	spl	Falkirk	H	W	3-0	Smith, J 3,22; Clark 33	12,249
7	spl	Celtic	A	L	0-2		59,607
8	spl	Dunfermline	A	W	2-0	Crawford 35; Severin 45	6,387
9	sccc3	Stranraer	A	W	2-0	Smith, J 57; Nicholson 67	2,200
10	spl	Livingston	H	D	0-0		12,402
11	spl	Motherwell	H	D	2-2	Mackie 79 pen,85	11,448
12	spl	Inverness CT	A	D	1-1	Smith, J 55	6,809
13	spl	Hibernian	H	L	0-1		13,375
14	spl	Dundee Utd	H	W	2-0	Smith, J 36; Crawford 43	10,720
15	spl	Kilmarnock	A	L	2-4	Anderson 14; Crawford 70	5,798
16	spl	Rangers	A	D	0-0		49,717
17	sccqf	Motherwell	A	L	0-1		3,989
18	spl	Hearts	H	D	1-1	Smith, J 13	14,901
19	spl	Falkirk	A	W	2-1	Ireland 44 og; Anderson 50	5,826
20	spl	Celtic	H	L	1-3	Winter 53	17,031
21	spl	Dunfermline	H	D	0-0		9,881
22	spl	Livingston	A	D	0-0		3,724
23	spl	Motherwell	A	L	1-3	Stewart 90	6,555
24	spl	Inverness CT	H	D	0-0		12,266
25	scr3	Dundee Utd	A	W	3-2	Crawford 63,68; Nicholson 78	8,218
26	spl	Hibernian	A	W	2-1	Crawford 3; Mackie 13	14,572
27	spl	Dundee Utd	A	D	1-1	Mackie 49	9,936
28	spl	Kilmarnock	H	D	2-2	Nicholson 9; Anderson 73	10,540
29	scr4	Hearts	A	L	0-3		17,353
30	spl	Rangers	H	W	2-0	Smith, J 34; Lovell 43	17,087
31	spl	Hearts	A	W	2-1	Pressley 67 og; Clark 86	16,895
32	spl	Falkirk	H	W	1-0	Smith, J 33	11,538
33	spl	Celtic	A	L	0-3		60,018
34	spl	Dunfermline	A	L	0-1		5,308
35	spl	Livingston	H	W	3-0	Anderson 16; Lovell 62; Snoyl 80	9,229
36	spl	Motherwell	H	D	2-2	Lovell 13,22	10,212
37	spl	Inverness CT	A	W	1-0	Lovell 82	7,368
38	spl	Hibernian	H	W	1-0	Severin 21	14,110
39	spl	Rangers	A	D	1-1	Severin 68	48,987
40	spl	Kilmarnock	H	D	0-0		10,634
41	spl	Hibernian	H	W	4-0	Crawford 15; Lovell 30,54; Foster 65	10,490
42	spl	Hearts	A	L	0-1		17,327
43	spl	Celtic	H	D	2-2	Stewart 69,72	14,597

LEAGUE APPEARANCES, BOOKINGS AND CAPS

	AGE (on 01/07/06)	IN NAMED 18	APPEARANCES	COUNTING GAMES	MINUTES ON PITCH	YELLOW CARDS	RED CARDS	CAPS THIS SEASON	NATIONAL SIDE
Goalkeepers									
Ryan Esson	26	31	18	18	1620	1	0	1	Scotland (85)
Greg Kelly	19	8	0	0	0	0	0	-	Scotland
James Langfield	26	37	20	20	1800	0	0	-	Scotland
Defenders									
Russell Anderson	27	36	36	35	3187	4	0	2	Scotland (85)
Richie Byrne	24	20	19	16	1572	2	1	-	Scotland
Andrew Considine	19	25	12	6	716	1	0	-	Scotland
Alexander Diamond	21	33	33	28	2723	5	0	-	Scotland
Daniel Griffin	28	15	10	7	725	0	0	-	N Ireland
Michael Hart	26	4	4	3	315	2	0	-	Scotland
Kevin McNaughton	23	34	34	30	2894	2	0	-	Scotland
Ferne Snoyl	21	12	12	4	719	1	0	-	Holland
Midfielders									
Christopher Clark	25	31	31	29	2699	3	0	-	Scotland
Gary Dempsey	25	37	24	16	1528	2	0	-	Rep of Ireland
Richard Foster	20	37	25	8	1079	2	0	-	Scotland
Kyle Macauley	20	24	5	2	226	0	0	-	Scotland
Neil MacFarlane	28	11	6	2	212	1	0	-	Scotland
Scott Muirhead	21	22	18	8	956	2	1	-	Scotland
Barry Nicholson	27	33	33	31	2807	1	0	-	Scotland
Scott Severin	27	29	28	28	2500	5	1	2	Scotland (85)
Jamie Smith	25	35	35	34	3102	4	0	-	Scotland
Jamie Winter	20	22	7	1	300	0	0	-	Scotland
Forwards									
Steven Craig	25	3	3	0	60	0	0	-	Scotland
Stevie Crawford	32	30	30	25	2299	2	0	-	Scotland
Steve Lovell	25	28	27	14	1706	4	0	-	England
Darren Mackie	24	30	28	8	1384	4	0	-	Scotland
John Stewart	20	32	17	2	425	0	0	-	Scotland

TEAM OF THE SEASON

G James Langfield CG: 20 DR: 113

D Russell Anderson CG: 35 DR: 94

D Kevin McNaughton CG: 30 DR: 93

D Alexander Diamond CG: 28 DR: 83

D Richie Byrne CG: 16 DR: 79

M Jamie Smith CG: 34 SD: 23

M Scott Severin CG: 28 SD: 20

M Gary Dempsey CG: 16 SD: 14

M Barry Nicholson CG: 31 SD: 11

F Steve Lovell CG: 14 SR: 213

F Stevie Crawford CG: 25 SR: 460

MONTHLY POINTS TALLY

Month	Points	%
AUGUST	6	50%
SEPTEMBER	4	44%
OCTOBER	5	33%
NOVEMBER	5	56%
DECEMBER	3	20%
JANUARY	5	56%
FEBRUARY	9	100%
MARCH	4	33%
APRIL	11	73%
MAY	1	17%

LEAGUE GOALS

	PLAYER	MINS	GOALS	S RATE
1	Lovell	1706	8	213
2	Smith, J	3102	8	388
3	Anderson	3187	6	531
4	Crawford	2299	5	460
5	Mackie	1384	4	346
6	Severin	2500	3	833
7	Stewart	425	3	142
8	Clark	2699	2	1350
9	Nicholson	2807	2	1404
10	Winter	300	1	300
11	Snoyl	719	1	719
12	Foster	1079	1	1079
	Other		2	
	TOTAL		46	

TOP POINT EARNERS

	PLAYER	GAMES	AV PTS
1	Lovell	14	1.86
2	Langfield	20	1.60
3	McNaughton	30	1.60
4	Smith, J	34	1.53
5	Clark	29	1.52
6	Anderson	35	1.51
7	Severin	28	1.50
8	Diamond	28	1.46
9	Dempsey	16	1.44
10	Nicholson	31	1.39
	CLUB AVERAGE:		1.42

DISCIPLINARY RECORDS

	PLAYER	YELLOW	RED	AVE
1	Muirhead	2	1	318
2	Mackie	4	0	346
3	Severin	5	1	416
4	Lovell	4	0	426
5	Byrne	2	1	524
6	Foster	2	0	539
7	Diamond	5	0	544
8	Considine	1	0	716
9	Snoyl	1	0	719
10	Dempsey	2	0	764
11	Smith, J	4	0	775
12	Anderson	4	0	796
13	Clark	3	0	899
	Other	6	0	
	TOTAL	45	3	

KEY GOALKEEPER

James Langfield

Goals Conceded in the League	16	Counting Games League games when player was on pitch for at least 70 minutes	20
Defensive Rating Ave number of mins between League goals conceded while on the pitch	113	Clean Sheets In League games when player was on pitch for at least 70 minutes	10

KEY PLAYERS - DEFENDERS

Russell Anderson

Goals Conceded Number of League goals conceded while the player was on the pitch	34	Clean Sheets In League games when player was on pitch for at least 70 minutes	15
Defensive Rating Ave number of mins between League goals conceded while on the pitch	94	Club Defensive Rating Average number of mins between League goals conceded by the club this season	86

	PLAYER	CON LGE	CLEAN SHEETS	DEF RATE
1	Russell Anderson	34	15	94 mins
2	Kevin McNaughton	31	13	93 mins
3	Alexander Diamond	33	11	83 mins
4	Richie Byrne	20	6	79 mins

KEY PLAYERS - MIDFIELDERS

Jamie Smith

Goals in the League	8	Contribution to Attacking Power Average number of minutes between League team goals while on pitch	71
Defensive Rating Average number of mins between League goals conceded while on the pitch	94	Scoring Difference Defensive Rating minus Contribution to Attacking Power	23

	PLAYER	LGE GOALS	DEF RATE	POWER	SCORE DIFF
1	Jamie Smith	8	94	71	23 mins
2	Scott Severin	3	89	69	20 mins
3	Gary Dempsey	0	90	76	14 mins
4	Barry Nicholson	2	85	74	11 mins

KEY PLAYERS - GOALSCORERS

Steve Lovell

Goals in the League	8	Player Strike Rate Average number of minutes between League goals scored by player	213
Contribution to Attacking Power Average number of minutes between League team goals while on pitch	68	Club Strike Rate Average number of minutes between League goals scored by club	74

	PLAYER	LGE GOALS	POWER	STRIKE RATE
1	Steve Lovell	8	68	213 mins
2	Jamie Smith	8	71	388 mins
3	Stevie Crawford	5	77	460 mins
4	Russell Anderson	6	78	531 mins

Jamie Smith

SQUAD APPEARANCES

Match	1	2	3	4	5	6	7	8	9	10	11	12	13	14	15	16	17	18	19	20	21	22	23	24	25	26	27	28	29	30	31	32	33	34	35	36	37	38	39	40	41	42	43
Venue	A	H	H	A	H	H	A	A	A	H	H	A	H	H	A	A	A	H	A	H	H	A	A	H	A	A	A	H	A	H	A	H	A	A	H	H	A	H	A	H	H	A	H
Competition	L	L	L	L	W	L	L	L	W	L	L	L	L	L	L	L	W	L	L	L	L	L	L	L	O	L	L	L	O	L	L	L	L	L	L	L	L	L	L	L	L	L	L
Result	D	L	W	L	W	W	L	W	W	D	D	D	L	W	L	D	L	D	W	L	D	D	L	D	W	W	D	D	L	W	W	W	L	L	W	D	W	W	D	D	W	L	D

Goalkeepers
Ryan Esson
Greg Kelly
James Langfield

Defenders
Russell Anderson
Richie Byrne
Andrew Considine
Alexander Diamond
Daniel Griffin
Michael Hart
Kevin McNaughton
Ferne Snoyl

Midfielders
Christopher Clark
Gary Dempsey
Richard Foster
Kyle Macauley
Neil MacFarlane
Scott Muirhead
Barry Nicholson
Scott Severin
Jamie Smith
Jamie Winter

Forwards
Steven Craig
Stevie Crawford
Steve Lovell
Darren Mackie
John Stewart

KEY: On all match · On bench · Subbed or sent off (Counting game) · Subbed or sent off (playing less than 70 minutes) · Subbed on from bench (Counting Game) · Subbed on (playing less than 70 minutes) · Subbed on and then subbed or sent off (Counting Game) · Subbed on and then subbed or sent off (playing less than 70 minutes) · Not in 16

INVERNESS CALEDONIAN THISTLE

Final Position: **7th**

NICKNAME: CALEY THISTLE

KEY: ☐Won ☐Drawn ☐Lost

		Opponent	Venue	Result	Score	Scorers	Attendance
1	spl	Falkirk	A	W	2-0	Brewster 57,82	4,561
2	spl	Rangers	H	L	0-1		7,512
3	spl	Dunfermline	A	W	1-0	Fox 42	5,005
4	spl	Kilmarnock	H	D	2-2	Brewster 40,72	4,119
5	sccc2	Alloa	H	W	6-1	Wilson 18; Hart 20; McBain 37; Duncan 43; Munro 48; Wyness 87	917
6	spl	Dundee Utd	A	D	1-1	Brewster 84	6,178
7	spl	Motherwell	H	L	1-2	Brewster 25	4,018
8	spl	Hearts	H	L	0-1		6,704
9	sccc3	Dundee Utd	H	W	2-0	Fox 2; Wilson 41	1,919
10	spl	Celtic	A	L	1-2	Wyness 51	57,247
11	spl	Hibernian	A	W	2-1	Proctor 49; Wyness 65	11,683
12	spl	Aberdeen	H	D	1-1	Bayne 73	6,809
13	spl	Livingston	A	D	1-1	Morgan 72	3,372
14	spl	Falkirk	H	L	0-3		3,660
15	spl	Rangers	A	D	1-1	Dargo 26	47,867
16	spl	Dunfermline	H	W	2-1	Black 4; Proctor 8	3,728
17	sccqf	Livingston	A	L	1-2	Dargo 1	1,531
18	spl	Kilmarnock	A	D	2-2	Bayne 29; Dargo 76	4,708
19	spl	Dundee Utd	H	D	1-1	Tokely 20	3,239
20	spl	Motherwell	A	W	2-0	Dargo 63,88	4,103
21	spl	Hearts	A	D	0-0		16,373
22	spl	Celtic	H	D	1-1	Dargo 1	7,382
23	spl	Hibernian	H	W	2-0	Wilson 8; Dargo 11	7,017
24	spl	Aberdeen	A	D	0-0		12,266
25	scr3	Ayr	H	D	1-1	McAllister 51	2,126
26	spl	Livingston	H	W	3-0	Dargo 25,56 pen; Wyness 59	3,604
27	scr3r	Ayr	A	W	2-0	Dargo 38 pen; Wyness 76	2,774
28	spl	Falkirk	A	W	4-1	Wilson 3; Wyness 18; Dargo 38 pen; Tokely 56	4,772
29	spl	Rangers	H	L	2-3	Dargo 13; Wyness 72	7,380
30	scr4	Partick	H	D	2-2	McBain 59; Dargo 77	3,286
31	spl	Dunfermline	A	D	2-2	Dargo 80 pen; Wyness 87	3,354
32	spl	Kilmarnock	H	D	3-3	Wyness 33; Dargo 67; Proctor 85	3,618
33	scr4r	Partick	A	L	2-4*	Wyness 23 (*on penalties)	3,166
34	spl	Dundee Utd	A	W	4-2	Dods 29; Wyness 45; Dargo 48; Morgan 84	6,419
35	spl	Motherwell	H	L	0-1		3,183
36	spl	Hearts	H	D	0-0		5,027
37	spl	Celtic	A	L	1-2	Hart 90	57,451
38	spl	Hibernian	A	W	2-0	Dods 57; Wilson 78 pen	12,745
39	spl	Aberdeen	H	L	0-1		7,368
40	spl	Livingston	A	L	1-2	Tokely 16	2,688
41	spl	Motherwell	A	W	1-0	Dargo 27	3,438
42	spl	Dundee Utd	H	W	1-0	Dargo 90	3,609
43	spl	Livingston	A	W	1-0	Wilson 56	2,278
44	spl	Falkirk	H	W	2-0	Duncan 18; Dargo 30	3,121
45	spl	Dunfermline	A	W	1-0	Morgan 53	5,354

LEAGUE APPEARANCES, BOOKINGS AND CAPS

	AGE (on 01/07/06)	IN NAMED 18	APPEARANCES	COUNTING GAMES	MINUTES ON PITCH	YELLOW CARDS	RED CARDS	CAPS THIS SEASON	NATIONAL SIDE
Goalkeepers									
Mark Brown	25	38	37	37	3330	0	0	-	Scotland
Mike Fraser	22	38	1	1	90	0	0	-	Scotland
Defenders									
Darren Dods	41	37	37	37	3330	6	0	-	Scotland
Stuart Golabek	31	29	17	14	1337	1	0	-	Scotland
Richard Hastings	29	30	27	24	2273	2	0	-	Canada
Stuart McCaffrey	27	23	8	7	632	1	0	-	Scotland
Alan Morgan	22	28	22	12	1330	2	0	-	Scotland
Grant Munro	25	32	32	31	2858	5	0	-	Scotland
Ross Tokely	27	34	34	34	3048	7	0	-	Scotland
Midfielders									
Ian Black	21	29	26	23	2097	9	0	-	Scotland
Russell Duncan	25	37	31	28	2548	3	0	-	Scotland
Liam Fox	22	37	17	7	855	5	0	-	Scotland
Richard Hart	28	34	31	11	1204	3	0	-	Scotland
Roy McBain	31	21	18	15	1444	1	0	-	Scotland
Tom Parratt	-	18	0	0	0	0	0	-	
David Proctor	22	25	17	9	973	1	0	-	Scotland
Alexander Sutherland	-	4	1	1	90	0	0	-	
Barry Wilson	34	35	34	33	2853	8	0	-	Scotland
Forwards									
Graham Bayne	26	25	17	7	849	5	1	-	Scotland
Craig Brewster	39	19	18	14	1430	6	1	-	Scotland
Craig Dargo	28	34	32	26	2455	4	0	-	Scotland
Carricondo Juanjo	27	5	2	0	16	0	0	-	Spain
Liam Keogh	24	10	8	5	488	2	0	-	Scotland
Rory McAllister	-	24	13	2	307	0	0	-	Scotland
Dennis Wyness	29	30	27	16	1691	2	0	-	Scotland

TEAM OF THE SEASON

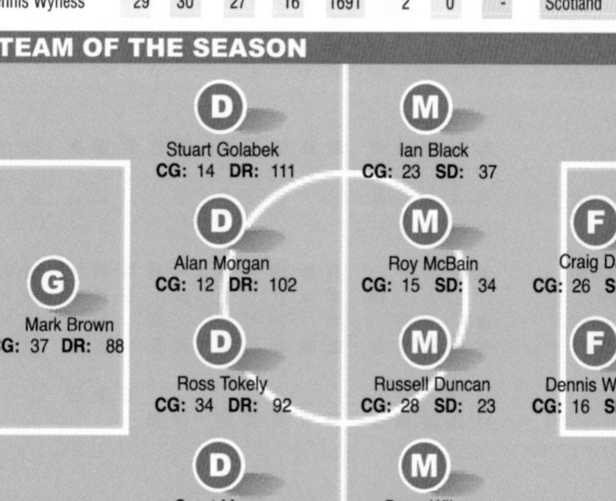

MONTHLY POINTS TALLY

AUGUST	5	42%
SEPTEMBER	0	0%
OCTOBER	6	40%
NOVEMBER	5	56%
DECEMBER	9	60%
JANUARY	6	67%
FEBRUARY	5	56%
MARCH	4	33%
APRIL	9	60%
MAY	6	100%

LEAGUE GOALS

	PLAYER	MINS	GOALS	S RATE
1	Dargo	2455	**16**	153
2	Wyness	1691	**8**	211
3	Brewster	1430	**6**	238
4	Wilson	2853	**4**	713
5	Proctor	973	**3**	324
6	Tokely	3048	**3**	1016
7	Morgan	1330	**3**	443
8	Dods	3330	**2**	1665
9	Bayne	849	**2**	425
10	Duncan	2548	**1**	2548
11	Hart	1204	**1**	1204
12	Fox	855	**1**	855
13	Black	2097	**1**	2097
	Other		**0**	
	TOTAL		**51**	

TOP POINT EARNERS

	PLAYER	GAMES	AV PTS
1	Golabek	14	**1.79**
2	McBain	15	**1.73**
3	Wilson	33	**1.61**
4	Morgan	12	**1.58**
5	Duncan	28	**1.57**
6	Dods	37	**1.54**
7	Tokely	34	**1.50**
8	Hastings	24	**1.50**
9	Brown	37	**1.49**
10	Black	23	**1.43**
	CLUB AVERAGE:		**1.53**

DISCIPLINARY RECORDS

	PLAYER	YELLOW	RED	AVE
1	Bayne	5	1	**141**
2	Fox	5	0	**171**
3	Brewster	6	1	**204**
4	Black	9	0	**233**
5	Keogh	2	0	**244**
6	Wilson	8	0	**356**
7	Hart	3	0	**401**
8	Tokely	7	0	**435**
9	Dods	6	0	**555**
10	Munro	5	0	**571**
11	Dargo	4	0	**613**
12	McCaffrey	1	0	**632**
13	Morgan	2	0	**665**
	Other	10	0	
	TOTAL	**73**	**2**	

KEY GOALKEEPER

Mark Brown

Goals Conceded in the League	38	Counting Games League games when player was on pitch for at least 70 minutes	37
Defensive Rating Ave number of mins between League goals conceded while on the pitch	88	Clean Sheets In League games when player was on pitch for at least 70 minutes	13

KEY PLAYERS - DEFENDERS

Stuart Golabek

Goals Conceded Number of League goals conceded while the player was on the pitch	12	Clean Sheets In League games when player was on pitch for at least 70 minutes	7
Defensive Rating Ave number of mins between League goals conceded while on the pitch	111	Club Defensive Rating Average number of mins between League goals conceded by the club this season	90

	PLAYER	CON LGE	CLEAN SHEETS	DEF RATE
1	Stuart Golabek	12	7	111 mins
2	Alan Morgan	13	5	102 mins
3	Ross Tokely	33	12	92 mins
4	Grant Munro	32	10	89 mins

KEY PLAYERS - MIDFIELDERS

Ian Black

Goals in the League	1	Contribution to Attacking Power Average number of minutes between League team goals while on pitch	68
Defensive Rating Average number of mins between League goals conceded while on the pitch	105	Scoring Difference Defensive Rating minus Contribution to Attacking Power	37

	PLAYER	LGE GOALS	DEF RATE	POWER	SCORE DIFF
1	Ian Black	1	105	68	37 mins
2	Roy McBain	0	103	69	34 mins
3	Barry Wilson	4	84	61	23 mins
4	Russell Duncan	1	85	62	23 mins

KEY PLAYERS - GOALSCORERS

Craig Dargo

Goals in the League	16	Player Strike Rate Average number of minutes between League goals scored by player	153
Contribution to Attacking Power Average number of minutes between League team goals while on pitch	63	Club Strike Rate Average number of minutes between League goals scored by club	67

	PLAYER	LGE GOALS	POWER	STRIKE RATE
1	Craig Dargo	16	63	153 mins
2	Dennis Wyness	8	53	211 mins
3	Craig Brewster	6	79	238 mins
4	Alan Morgan	3	83	443 mins

Darren Dods

SQUAD APPEARANCES

Match	1	2	3	4	5	6	7	8	9	10	11	12	13	14	15
Venue	A	H	A	H	H	A	H	H	H	A	A	H	A	H	A
Competition	L	L	L	L	W	L	L	L	W	L	L	L	L	L	L
Result	W	L	W	D	W	D	L	L	W	L	W	D	D	L	D

Match	16	17	18	19	20	21	22	23	24	25	26	27	28	29	30
Venue	H	A	A	H	A	A	H	H	A	H	H	A	A	H	H
Competition	L	W	L	L	L	L	L	L	L	O	L	O	L	L	O
Result	W	L	D	D	W	D	D	W	D	D	W	W	W	L	D

Match	31	32	33	34	35	36	37	38	39	40	41	42	43	44	45
Venue	A	H	A	A	H	H	A	A	H	A	A	H	A	H	A
Competition	L	L	O	L	L	L	L	L	L	L	L	L	L	L	L
Result	D	D	L	W	L	D	L	W	L	L	W	W	W	W	W

Goalkeepers
- Mark Brown
- Mike Fraser

Defenders
- Darren Dods
- Stuart Golabek
- Richard Hastings
- Stuart McCaffrey
- Alan Morgan
- Grant Munro
- Ross Tokely

Midfielders
- Ian Black
- Russell Duncan
- Liam Fox
- Richard Hart
- Roy McBain
- Tom Parratt
- David Proctor
- Alexander Sutherland
- Barry Wilson

Forwards
- Graham Bayne
- Craig Brewster
- Craig Dargo
- Carricondo Juanjo
- Liam Keogh
- Rory McAllister
- Dennis Wyness

KEY: On all match / On bench / Subbed or sent off (Counting game) / Subbed or sent off (playing less than 70 minutes) / Subbed on from bench (Counting Game) / Subbed on (playing less than 70 minutes) / Subbed on and then subbed or sent off (Counting Game) / Subbed on and then subbed or sent off (playing less than 70 minutes) / Not in 16

MOTHERWELL

Final Position: **8th**

NICKNAME: THE WELL

KEY: ☐Won ☐Drawn ☐Lost

							Attendance
1	spl	Celtic	H	D	4-4	Kerr 20; Hamilton 58; McDonald, S 60; Kinniburgh 84	9,903
2	spl	Dunfermline	H	W	1-0	Hamilton 90	4,649
3	spl	Kilmarnock	A	L	1-4	Clarkson 42	5,035
4	spl	Dundee Utd	H	L	4-5	McCormack 6; McDonald, S 12; Fitzpatrick 49; Hamilton 57	4,706
5	sccc1	Hamilton	H	W	2-1	McDonald, Scott 41 pen; Hamilton 89	4,619
6	spl	Hearts	A	L	1-2	Foran 76 pen	16,213
7	spl	Inverness CT	A	W	2-1	McDonald, S 66; Kinniburgh 70	4,018
8	spl	Falkirk	H	W	5-0	Hamilton 32; Foran 42,46; Fagan 58; McDonald, S 64	5,625
9	sccc3	St Mirren	A	W	2-0	Clarkson 97; Smith, DL 104	3,810
10	spl	Hibernian	H	L	1-3	Foran 83 pen	6,461
11	spl	Aberdeen	A	D	2-2	Clarkson 63,69	11,448
12	spl	Livingston	H	W	1-0	Foran 21	4,507
13	spl	Rangers	A	L	0-2		49,215
14	spl	Celtic	A	L	0-5		57,388
15	spl	Dunfermline	A	W	3-0	Kerr 56; Corrigan 61; Hamilton 79	4,421
16	spl	Kilmarnock	H	D	2-2	McDonald, Scott 24; Kerr 53	4,979
17	sccqf	Aberdeen	H	W	1-0	Kerr 5	3,989
18	spl	Dundee Utd	A	D	1-1	McDonald, Scott 71	6,305
19	spl	Hearts	H	D	1-1	McLean 39	8,131
20	spl	Inverness CT	H	L	0-2		4,103
21	spl	Falkirk	A	W	1-0	Hamilton 58	4,972
22	spl	Hibernian	A	L	1-2	McDonald, Scott 17	11,926
23	spl	Aberdeen	H	W	3-1	McDonald, Scott 9,26; McCormack 53	6,555
24	spl	Livingston	A	W	2-1	Foran 29; McBride 89	4,431
25	scr3	St Mirren	A	L	0-3		6,507
26	spl	Rangers	H	L	0-1		10,689
27	spl	Celtic	H	L	1-3	Hamilton 41	11,503
28	spl	Dunfermline	A	D	1-1	Hamilton 51	4,961
29	slc5	Celtic	H	L	1-2	Foran 11	32,595
30	spl	Kilmarnock	A	L	0-2		5,169
31	spl	Dundee Utd	H	W	2-0	Foran 26,56	5,257
32	spl	Hearts	A	L	0-3		16,976
33	spl	Inverness CT	A	W	1-0	Foran 50 pen	3,183
34	spl	Falkirk	H	W	3-1	McDonald, Scott 31,46; Foran 53	8,179
35	spl	Hibernian	H	D	2-2	O'Donnell 39; Craigan 90	6,724
36	spl	Aberdeen	A	D	2-2	McLean 45; Foran 48 pen	10,212
37	spl	Livingston	H	W	2-1	Hamilton 39; McLean 89	4,458
38	spl	Rangers	A	L	0-1		49,481
39	spl	Inverness CT	H	L	0-1		3,438
40	spl	Falkirk	A	D	1-1	O'Donnell 57	4,467
41	spl	Dunfermline	H	L	2-3	Paterson 7; Craigan 65	3,621
42	spl	Livingston	A	W	1-0	Clarkson 74	2,283
43	spl	Dundee Utd	H	D	1-1	Hamilton 60	5,269

LEAGUE APPEARANCES, BOOKINGS AND CAPS

	AGE (on 01/07/06)	IN NAMED 18	APPEARANCES	COUNTING GAMES	MINUTES ON PITCH	YELLOW CARDS	RED CARDS	CAPS THIS SEASON	NATIONAL SIDE
Goalkeepers									
Gordon Marshall	42	5	1	1	90	0	0	-	Scotland
Alan Martin	17	4	0	0	0	0	0	-	Scotland
Colin Meldrum	30	31	8	7	689	0	0	-	Scotland
Graeme Smith	23	37	33	30	2778	0	0	-	Scotland
Defenders									
Martyn Corrigan	28	29	29	26	2404	3	0	-	Scotland
Stephen Craigan	29	36	36	36	3219	4	0	7	N Ireland (114)
Steven Hammell	24	33	33	31	2838	9	0	-	Scotland
David Keogh	19	9	1	0	45	0	0	-	Scotland
William Kinniburgh	21	30	21	14	1413	3	0	-	Scotland
Brian McLean	21	30	30	27	2462	3	0	-	Scotland
Paul Quinn	21	24	18	16	1461	4	0	-	Scotland
Mark Reynolds	19	10	1	1	79	0	0	-	Scotland
Midfielders									
Kenneth Connolly	19	10	0	0	0	0	0	-	Scotland
Robert Donnelly	-	3	2	1	126	0	0	-	Scotland
Shaun Fagan	22	26	16	10	989	4	0	-	Scotland
Mark Fitzpatrick	20	22	9	1	234	0	0	-	Scotland
Brian Kerr	24	38	36	33	3025	4	0	-	Scotland
Scott Leitch	36	6	1	0	8	0	0	-	Scotland
Kevin McBride	25	23	21	12	1320	4	0	-	Scotland
Alan McCormack	22	24	24	22	2012	12	1	-	Rep of Ireland
Steve McDonald	-	8	2	1	91	0	0	-	
Philip O'Donnell	34	29	29	21	2057	0	0	-	Scotland
Jamie Paterson	26	19	19	6	842	1	0	-	Scotland
Forwards									
David Clarkson	20	32	30	9	1236	0	0	-	Scotland
Adam Coakley	18	10	1	0	2	0	0	-	England
Ritchie Foran	26	32	32	27	2597	5	0	-	Rep of Ireland
Jim Hamilton	30	36	34	24	2480	4	0	-	Scotland
Scott McDonald	22	34	33	27	2578	2	0	-	Australia
Steven McGarry	26	13	9	3	288	0	0	-	Scotland
Andrew Smith	25	6	3	0	91	0	0	1	N Ireland (114)
Darren Lee Smith	-	19	2	1	99	0	0	-	Scotland

TEAM OF THE SEASON

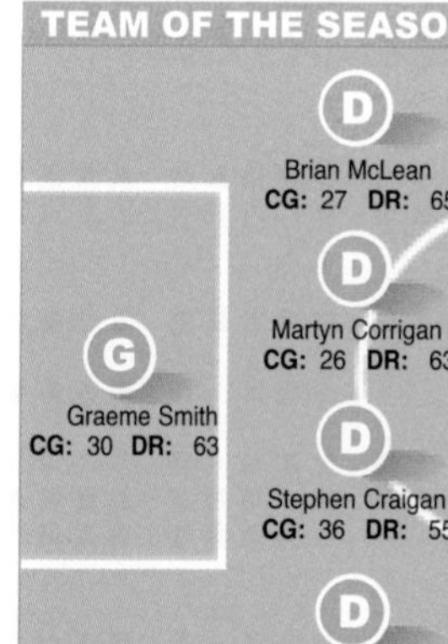

MONTHLY POINTS TALLY

AUGUST	3	25%
SEPTEMBER	6	67%
OCTOBER	7	47%
NOVEMBER	3	33%
DECEMBER	9	60%
JANUARY	1	11%
FEBRUARY	3	33%
MARCH	8	67%
APRIL	4	27%
MAY	4	67%

LEAGUE GOALS

	PLAYER	MINS	GOALS	S RATE
1	Foran	2597	11	236
2	McDonald, Scott	2578	11	234
3	Hamilton	2480	10	248
4	Clarkson	1236	4	309
5	McLean	2462	3	821
6	Kerr	3025	3	1008
7	McCormack	2012	2	1006
8	Kinniburgh	1413	2	707
9	O'Donnell	2057	2	1029
10	Craigan	3219	2	1610
11	McBride	1320	1	1320
12	Fagan	989	1	989
13	Fitzpatrick	234	1	234
	Other		2	
	TOTAL		55	

TOP POINT EARNERS

	PLAYER	GAMES	AV PTS
1	McLean	27	1.44
2	O'Donnell	21	1.43
3	Hamilton	24	1.42
4	Foran	27	1.41
5	Quinn	16	1.31
6	Hammell	31	1.29
7	Kerr	33	1.27
8	Smith, G	30	1.27
9	McCormack	22	1.27
10	McDonald, Scott	27	1.26
	CLUB AVERAGE:		1.29

DISCIPLINARY RECORDS

	PLAYER	YELLOW	RED	AVE
1	McCormack	12	1	154
2	Fagan	4	0	247
3	Hammell	9	0	315
4	McBride	4	0	330
5	Quinn	4	0	365
6	Kinniburgh	3	0	471
7	Foran	5	0	519
8	Hamilton	4	0	620
9	Kerr	4	0	756
10	Corrigan	3	0	801
11	Craigan	4	0	804
12	McLean	3	0	820
13	Paterson	1	0	842
	Other	2	0	
	TOTAL	62	1	

KEY GOALKEEPER

Graeme Smith

Goals Conceded in the League	44	**Counting Games** League games when player was on pitch for at least 70 minutes	30
Defensive Rating Ave number of mins between League goals conceded while on the pitch	63	**Clean Sheets** In League games when player was on pitch for at least 70 minutes	8

KEY PLAYERS - DEFENDERS

Brian McLean

Goals Conceded Number of League goals conceded while the player was on the pitch	38	**Clean Sheets** In League games when player was on pitch for at least 70 minutes	6
Defensive Rating Ave number of mins between League goals conceded while on the pitch	65	**Club Defensive Rating** Average number of mins between League goals conceded by the club this season	56

	PLAYER	CON LGE	CLEAN SHEETS	DEF RATE
1	Brian McLean	38	6	65 mins
2	Martyn Corrigan	38	4	63 mins
3	Stephen Craigan	59	7	55 mins
4	Steven Hammell	53	6	54 mins

KEY PLAYERS - MIDFIELDERS

Philip O'Donnell

Goals in the League	2	**Contribution to Attacking Power** Average number of minutes between League team goals while on pitch	54
Defensive Rating Average number of mins between League goals conceded while on the pitch	54	**Scoring Difference** Defensive Rating minus Contribution to Attacking Power	0

	PLAYER	LGE GOALS	DEF RATE	POWER	SCORE DIFF
1	Philip O'Donnell	2	54	54	0 mins
2	Alan McCormack	2	59	65	-6 mins
3	Kevin McBride	1	63	69	-6 mins
4	Brian Kerr	3	54	63	-9 mins

KEY PLAYERS - GOALSCORERS

Scott McDonald

Goals in the League	11	**Player Strike Rate** Average number of minutes between League goals scored by player	234
Contribution to Attacking Power Average number of minutes between League team goals while on pitch	56	**Club Strike Rate** Average number of minutes between League goals scored by club	62

	PLAYER	LGE GOALS	POWER	STRIKE RATE
1	Scott McDonald	11	56	234 mins
2	Ritchie Foran	11	63	236 mins
3	Jim Hamilton	10	62	248 mins
4	William Kinniburgh	2	67	707 mins

Departing manager Terry Butcher

SQUAD APPEARANCES

atch	1	2	3	4	5	6	7	8	9	10	11	12	13	14	15	16	17	18	19	20	21	22	23	24	25	26	27	28	29	30	31	32	33	34	35	36	37	38	39	40	41	42	43
enue	H	H	A	H	H	A	A	H	A	H	A	H	A	A	A	H	H	A	H	H	A	A	H	A	A	H	H	A	H	A	H	A	A	H	H	A	H	A	H	A	H	A	H
ompetition	L	L	L	L	W	L	L	L	W	L	L	L	L	L	L	L	W	L	L	L	L	L	L	L	O	L	L	L	W	L	L	L	L	L	L	L	L	L	L	L	L	L	L
esult	D	W	L	L	W	L	W	W	W	L	D	W	L	L	W	D	W	D	D	L	W	L	W	W	L	L	L	D	L	L	W	L	W	W	D	D	W	L	L	D	L	W	D

oalkeepers
ordon Marshall
an Martin
olin Meldrum
raeme Smith

efenders
artyn Corrigan
ephen Craigan
even Hammell
avid Keogh
illiam Kinniburgh
rian McLean
aul Quinn
ark Reynolds

dfielders
enneth Connolly
obert Donnelly
haun Fagan
ark Fitzpatrick
rian Kerr
cott Leitch
evin McBride
lan McCormack
teve McDonald
hilip O'Donnell
amie Paterson

orwards
avid Clarkson
dam Coakley
itchie Foran
m Hamilton
cott McDonald
teven McGarry
ndrew Smith
arren Lee Smith

KEY: On all match · On bench · Subbed or sent off (Counting game) · Subbed or sent off (playing less than 70 minutes) · Subbed on from bench (Counting Game) · Subbed on (playing less than 70 minutes) · Subbed on and then subbed or sent off (Counting Game) · Subbed on and then subbed or sent off (playing less than 70 minutes) · Not in 16

DUNDEE UNITED

Final Position: **9th**

NICKNAME: THE TERRORS/ ARABS

KEY: ☐ Won ☐ Drawn ☐ Lost

	Comp	Opponent	H/A	Res	Score	Scorers	Attendance
1	spl	Aberdeen	H	D	1-1	Miller 7	12,404
2	spl	Celtic	A	L	0-2		56,532
3	ucql1	MyPa-47	A	D	0-0		1,820
4	spl	Hearts	H	L	0-3		11,654
5	spl	Motherwell	A	W	5-4	Miller 42,67; Fernandez 53; Brebner 71,74	4,706
6	spl	Inverness CT	H	D	1-1	Miller 66	6,178
7	spl	Hibernian	A	L	1-2	Brebner 14	12,062
8	spl	Livingston	H	W	2-0	Fernandez 34; Canero 76	6,302
9	sccc3	Inverness CT	A	L	0-2		1,919
10	spl	Dunfermline	A	L	1-2	McCracken 41	5,361
11	spl	Kilmarnock	H	D	0-0		6,915
12	spl	Rangers	H	D	0-0		11,696
13	spl	Falkirk	A	W	3-1	Glennon 47 og; Canero 72; Samuel 81	5,316
14	spl	Aberdeen	A	L	0-2		10,720
15	spl	Celtic	H	L	2-4	Sutton 4 og; Samuel 30	11,942
16	spl	Hearts	A	L	0-3		16,617
17	spl	Motherwell	H	D	1-1	McIntyre 67	6,305
18	spl	Inverness CT	A	D	1-1	Miller 7 pen	3,239
19	spl	Hibernian	H	W	1-0	Samuel 61	7,976
20	spl	Livingston	A	L	0-1		3,845
21	spl	Dunfermline	H	W	2-1	Samuel 25; Robson 41	5,889
22	spl	Kilmarnock	A	L	1-2	Samuel 51	5,749
23	spl	Rangers	A	L	0-3		49,141
24	scr3	Aberdeen	H	L	2-3	Fernandez 25,28	8,218
25	spl	Falkirk	H	W	2-1	Fernandez 36; McInnes 89	7,948
26	spl	Aberdeen	H	D	1-1	Archibald 53	9,936
27	spl	Celtic	A	D	3-3	Fernandez 40,86; Miller 82	59,875
28	spl	Hearts	H	D	1-1	Brebner 35	10,584
29	spl	Motherwell	A	L	0-2		5,257
30	spl	Inverness CT	H	L	2-4	Mulgrew 17,39	6,419
31	spl	Dunfermline	A	D	1-1	Kenneth 7	4,694
32	spl	Hibernian	A	L	1-3	Goodwillie 88	16,266
33	spl	Livingston	H	W	3-1	Miller 68,80; Kerr 77	5,730
34	spl	Kilmarnock	H	D	2-2	McCracken 46; McInnes 50	5,830
35	spl	Rangers	H	L	1-4	Samuel 68	11,213
36	spl	Falkirk	A	L	0-1		4,473
37	spl	Livingston	A	L	1-3	Robertson 19	2,298
38	spl	Inverness CT	A	L	0-1		3,609
39	spl	Falkirk	H	L	0-2		5,798
40	spl	Dunfermline	H	L	0-1		5,034
41	spl	Motherwell	A	D	1-1	Samuel 86	5,269

LEAGUE APPEARANCES, BOOKINGS AND CAPS

	AGE (on 01/07/06)	IN NAMED 18	APPEARANCES	COUNTING GAMES	MINUTES ON PITCH	YELLOW CARDS	RED CARDS	CAPS THIS SEASON	NATIONAL SIDE
Goalkeepers									
Euan McLean	20	10	0	0	0	0	0	-	Scotland
Craig Samson	22	34	8	8	720	0	0	-	Scotland
Derek Stillie	32	30	30	30	2700	1	0	-	Scotland
Defenders									
Stuart Abbot	20	11	3	1	129	1	0	-	Scotland
Alan Archibald	28	36	33	33	2955	4	0	-	Scotland
Peter Canero	25	11	11	8	810	2	0	-	Scotland
William Easton	19	6	1	0	19	0	0	-	Scotland
Ross Gardiner	19	15	4	4	343	0	0	-	Scotland
Gary Kenneth	19	38	16	11	1182	0	0	-	Scotland
Lee Mair	25	6	6	5	480	1	0	-	Scotland
David McCracken	24	36	34	34	3060	7	0	-	Scotland
Charles Mulgrew	23	13	13	12	1121	1	0	-	Scotland
Paul Ritchie	30	21	21	16	1697	6	1	-	Scotland
Mark Wilson	22	21	21	20	1809	1	0	-	Scotland
Midfielders									
Grant Brebner	28	26	26	25	2242	6	0	-	Scotland
Greg Cameron	18	29	4	2	236	0	0	-	Scotland
Stuart Duff	24	38	29	23	2147	4	0	-	Scotland
Graeme Holmes	22	2	0	0	0	0	0	-	Scotland
Mark Kerr	24	35	35	34	3117	9	0	-	Scotland
Derek McInnes	35	30	12	7	790	0	0	-	Scotland
David Robertson	19	32	11	5	588	2	0	-	Scotland
Barry Robson	27	31	31	28	2616	9	1	-	Scotland
Forwards									
Craig Brewster	39	1	1	0	27	0	0	-	Scotland
Stevie Crawford	32	5	4	2	305	1	0	-	Scotland
Billy Dodds	37	9	0	0	0	0	0	-	Scotland
David Fernandez	30	32	30	23	2380	3	0	-	Spain
David Goodwillie	17	24	10	0	92	0	0	-	Scotland
James Grady	35	1	0	0	0	0	0	-	Scotland
James McIntyre	34	27	25	17	1718	4	0	-	Scotland
Lee Miller	23	34	34	21	2116	3	0	1	Scotland (85)
Collin Samuel	24	35	35	20	2215	1	0	-	Trinidad & Tobago

TEAM OF THE SEASON

G — Derek Stillie — CG: 30 DR: 51

D — Paul Ritchie — CG: 16 DR: 61

D — Mark Wilson — CG: 19 DR: 55

D — Alan Archibald — CG: 33 DR: 54

D — David McCracken — CG: 34 DR: 53

M — Grant Brebner — CG: 25 SD: -27

M — Mark Kerr — CG: 34 SD: -32

M — Barry Robson — CG: 28 SD: -34

M — Stuart Duff — CG: 23 SD: -50

F — Lee Miller — CG: 21 SR: 265

F — Collin Samuel — CG: 20 SR: 316

MONTHLY POINTS TALLY

Month	Points	%
AUGUST	4	33%
SEPTEMBER	3	33%
OCTOBER	5	33%
NOVEMBER	2	22%
DECEMBER	6	40%
JANUARY	5	56%
FEBRUARY	2	17%
MARCH	4	44%
APRIL	0	0%
MAY	1	17%

LEAGUE GOALS

	PLAYER	MINS	GOALS	S RATE
1	Miller	2116	8	265
2	Samuel	2215	7	316
3	Fernandez	2380	5	476
4	Brebner	2242	4	561
5	McInnes	790	2	395
6	Mulgrew	1121	2	561
7	Canero	731	2	366
8	McCracken	3060	2	1530
9	Goodwillie	92	1	92
10	Robertson	588	1	588
11	Kenneth	1182	1	1182
12	Kerr	3117	1	3117
13	McIntyre	1718	1	1718
	Other		4	
	TOTAL		41	

TOP POINT EARNERS

	PLAYER	GAMES	AV PTS
1	Wilson	19	1.05
2	Fernandez	23	1.04
3	McIntyre	17	1.00
4	Ritchie	16	1.00
5	Stillie	30	0.97
6	Brebner	25	0.92
7	Kerr	34	0.91
8	McCracken	34	0.91
9	Miller	21	0.90
10	Robson	28	0.89
	CLUB AVERAGE:		0.87

DISCIPLINARY RECORDS

	PLAYER	YELLOW	RED	AVE
1	Ritchie	6	1	242
2	Robson	9	1	261
3	Robertson	2	0	294
4	Kerr	9	0	346
5	Brebner	6	0	373
6	McIntyre	4	0	429
7	McCracken	7	0	437
8	Mair	1	0	480
9	Duff	4	0	536
10	Miller	3	0	705
11	Canero	1	0	731
12	Archibald	4	0	738
13	Fernandez	3	0	793
	Other	4	0	
	TOTAL	63	2	

KEY GOALKEEPER

Derek Stillie

Goals Conceded in the League	53	**Counting Games** League games when player was on pitch for at least 70 minutes	30
Defensive Rating Ave number of mins between League goals conceded while on the pitch	51	**Clean Sheets** In League games when player was on pitch for at least 70 minutes	4

KEY PLAYERS - DEFENDERS

Paul Ritchie

Goals Conceded Number of League goals conceded while the player was on the pitch	28	**Clean Sheets** In League games when player was on pitch for at least 70 minutes	4
Defensive Rating Ave number of mins between League goals conceded while on the pitch	61	**Club Defensive Rating** Average number of mins between League goals conceded by the club this season	52

	PLAYER	CON LGE	CLEAN SHEETS	DEF RATE
1	Paul Ritchie	28	4	61 mins
2	Mark Wilson	31	3	55 mins
3	Alan Archibald	55	4	54 mins
4	David McCracken	58	4	53 mins

KEY PLAYERS - MIDFIELDERS

Grant Brebner

Goals in the League	4	**Contribution to Attacking Power** Average number of minutes between League team goals while on pitch	77
Defensive Rating Average number of mins between League goals conceded while on the pitch	50	**Scoring Difference** Defensive Rating minus Contribution to Attacking Power	-27

	PLAYER	LGE GOALS	DEF RATE	POWER	SCORE DIFF
1	Grant Brebner	4	50	77	-27 mins
2	Mark Kerr	1	50	82	-32 mins
3	Barry Robson	1	50	84	-34 mins
4	Stuart Duff	0	48	98	-50 mins

KEY PLAYERS - GOALSCORERS

Lee Miller

Goals in the League	8	**Player Strike Rate** Average number of minutes between League goals scored by player	265
Contribution to Attacking Power Average number of minutes between League team goals while on pitch	73	**Club Strike Rate** Average number of minutes between League goals scored by club	83

	PLAYER	LGE GOALS	POWER	STRIKE RATE
1	Lee Miller	8	73	265 mins
2	Collin Samuel	7	74	316 mins
3	David Fernandez	5	79	476 mins
4	Charles Mulgrew	2	112	561 mins

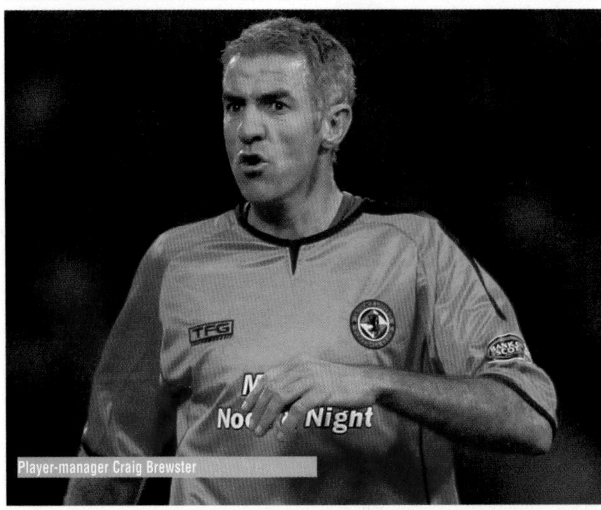

Player-manager Craig Brewster

SQUAD APPEARANCES

Match	1	2	3	4	5	6	7	8	9	10	11	12	13	14	15	16	17	18	19	20	21	22	23	24	25	26	27	28	29	30	31	32	33	34	35	36	37	38	39	40	41
Venue	H	A	A	H	A	H	A	H	A	A	H	H	A	A	H	A	H	A	H	A	H	A	A	H	H	H	A	H	A	H	A	A	H	H	H	A	A	A	H	H	A
Competition	L	L	C	L	L	L	L	L	W	L	L	L	L	L	L	L	L	L	L	L	L	L	L	O	L	L	L	L	L	L	L	L	L	L	L	L	L	L	L	L	L
Result	D	L	D	L	W	D	L	W	L	L	D	D	W	L	L	L	D	D	W	L	W	L	L	L	W	D	D	D	L	L	D	L	W	D	L	L	L	L	L	L	D

Goalkeepers
Euan McLean
Craig Samson
Derek Stillie

Defenders
Stuart Abbot
Alan Archibald
Peter Canero
William Easton
Ross Gardiner
Gary Kenneth
Lee Mair
David McCracken
Charles Mulgrew
Paul Ritchie
Mark Wilson

Midfielders
Grant Brebner
Greg Cameron
Stuart Duff
Graeme Holmes
Mark Kerr
Derek McInnes
David Robertson
Barry Robson

Forwards
Stevie Crawford
Billy Dodds
David Fernandez
David Goodwillie
James McIntyre
Lee Miller
Collin Samuel

KEY: On all match · On bench · Subbed or sent off (Counting game) · Subbed or sent off (playing less than 70 minutes) · Subbed on from bench (Counting Game) · Subbed on (playing less than 70 minutes) · Subbed on and then subbed or sent off (Counting Game) · Subbed on and then subbed or sent off (playing less than 70 minutes) · Not in 16

FALKIRK

Final Position: **10th**

NICKNAME: THE BAIRNS

KEY: ☐Won ☐Drawn ☐Lost

		Opponent	H/A	Result	Score	Scorers	Attendance
1	spl	Inverness CT	H	L	0-2		4,561
2	spl	Livingston	A	W	2-0	Latapy 28; Duffy 72	4,052
3	spl	Celtic	A	L	1-3	Duffy 39 pen	57,782
4	spl	Hibernian	H	L	0-2		6,268
5	sccc1	Partick	H	W	2-1	O'Donnell 10,24	2,575
6	spl	Aberdeen	A	L	0-3		12,249
7	spl	Rangers	H	D	1-1	McBreen 78	6,500
8	spl	Motherwell	A	L	0-5		5,625
9	sccc3	Celtic	A	L	1-2	Gow 54	24,953
10	spl	Kilmarnock	A	D	1-1	Gow 11	5,507
11	spl	Hearts	H	D	2-2	Duffy 27 pen; Pressley 68 og	6,342
12	spl	Dunfermline	A	W	1-0	Duffy 40	7,068
13	spl	Dundee Utd	H	L	1-3	Duffy 3	5,316
14	spl	Inverness CT	A	W	3-0	Thomson, S 21; Duffy 69; Moutinho 90	3,660
15	spl	Livingston	H	D	1-1	Pinxten 19 og	4,786
16	spl	Celtic	H	L	0-3		6,459
17	spl	Hibernian	A	W	3-2	Duffy 48,73; Gow 55	13,902
18	spl	Aberdeen	H	L	1-2	McBreen 82	5,826
19	spl	Rangers	A	D	2-2	Gow 69; Moutinho 71	48,042
20	spl	Motherwell	H	L	0-1		4,972
21	spl	Kilmarnock	H	L	1-2	Milne 74	4,804
22	spl	Hearts	A	L	0-5		16,538
23	spl	Dunfermline	H	L	1-2	Duffy 67	6,235
24	scr3	Brechin	H	W	2-1	Gow 31,63	2,624
25	spl	Dundee Utd	A	L	1-2	McBreen 69	7,948
26	spl	Inverness CT	H	L	1-4	Ireland 10	4,772
27	spl	Livingston	A	W	1-0	O'Donnell 34	4,577
28	scr4	Ross County	H	D	1-1	McBreen 79	3,649
29	spl	Celtic	A	L	1-2	Milne 83	56,672
30	spl	Hibernian	H	D	0-0		5,937
31	scr4r	Ross County	A	W	1-0	Gow 63	2,372
32	spl	Aberdeen	A	L	0-1		11,538
33	Scpqf	Hibernian	H	L	1-5	McBreen 70	6,259
34	spl	Rangers	H	L	1-2	Latapy 66	6,343
35	spl	Motherwell	A	L	1-3	Cregg 55	8,179
36	spl	Kilmarnock	A	L	1-2	McBreen 18	5,443
37	spl	Hearts	H	L	1-2	Gow 45	5,966
38	spl	Dunfermline	A	D	1-1	Ross 20	6,836
39	spl	Dundee Utd	H	W	1-0	Ross 23	4,473
40	spl	Dunfermline	H	D	0-0		5,413
41	spl	Motherwell	H	D	1-1	Gow 15	4,467
42	spl	Dundee Utd	A	W	2-0	Gow 14; McBreen 39	5,798
43	spl	Inverness CT	A	L	0-2		3,121
44	spl	Livingston	H	W	1-0	McBreen 74	5,355

LEAGUE APPEARANCES, BOOKINGS AND CAPS

	AGE (on 01/07/06)	IN NAMED 18	APPEARANCES	COUNTING GAMES	MINUTES ON PITCH	YELLOW CARDS	RED CARDS	CAPS THIS SEASON	NATIONAL SIDE
Goalkeepers									
Allan Ferguson	37	27	9	9	810	0	0	-	Scotland
Mathew Glennon	27	23	21	21	1890	0	0	-	England
Darren Hill	24	11	0	0	0	0	0	-	Scotland
Mark Howard	19	15	8	8	720	0	0	-	England
Defenders									
John Hughes	41	1	1	1	90	0	0	-	Scotland
Craig Ireland	30	23	23	20	1968	1	1	-	Scotland
Andy Lawrie	27	38	29	28	2538	4	0	-	Scotland
Jean-F Lecsinel	19	10	8	6	658	2	0	-	France
Craig McPherson	34	27	18	11	1234	2	0	-	Scotland
T. Jonas Rodrigues	22	36	32	27	2679	8	0	-	Portugal
Midfielders									
Liam Craig	-	16	16	8	921	3	0	-	
Patrick Cregg	20	16	16	14	1270	5	1	-	Rep of Ireland
Kerr Dodds	-	9	9	8	728	2	0	-	
Russell Latapy	37	32	30	22	2158	0	0	7	Trinidad & Tobago (47)
Vitor Santos Lima	26	38	28	20	1985	5	0	-	Portugal
Ken Milne	26	36	33	30	2743	6	0	-	Scotland
Stephen O'Donnell	-	31	27	13	1594	6	1	-	
John O'Neil	35	16	8	3	338	0	0	-	Scotland
Jack Ross	30	21	16	13	1240	3	0	-	Scotland
Neil Scally	27	28	18	11	1230	6	0	-	Scotland
Thomas Scobie	-	3	3	2	194	1	0	-	
Densil Theobald	24	5	0	0	0	0	0	8	Trinidad & Tobago (47)
Steven Thomson	28	31	31	27	2515	6	0	-	Scotland
Mark Twaddle	19	18	6	5	456	1	0	-	Scotland
Forwards									
Darryl Duffy	22	21	21	18	1718	1	0	-	Scotland
Alan Gow	23	35	34	27	2570	1	0	-	Scotland
Daniel McBreen	29	35	32	18	1960	7	0	-	Australia
Ryan McStay	20	15	4	0	119	0	0	-	Scotland
Iain McSween	22	6	1	0	7	0	0	-	Scotland
Pedro Moutinho	26	32	28	6	909	3	0	-	Portugal
Andy Thomson	35	9	5	1	136	0	0	-	Scotland

TEAM OF THE SEASON

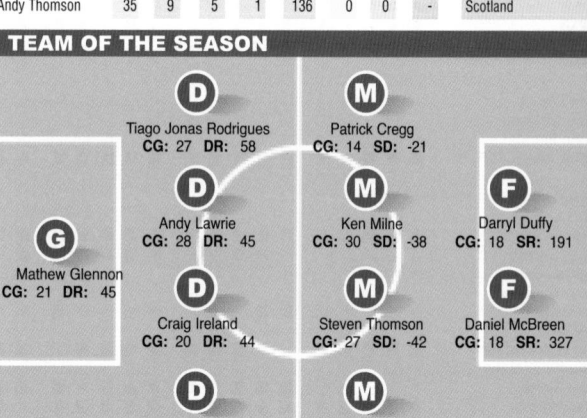

G
Mathew Glennon
CG: 21 DR: 45

D
Tiago Jonas Rodrigues
CG: 27 DR: 58

D
Andy Lawrie
CG: 28 DR: 45

D
Craig Ireland
CG: 20 DR: 44

D
Craig McPerson*
CG: 11 DR: 53

M
Patrick Cregg
CG: 14 SD: -21

M
Ken Milne
CG: 30 SD: -38

M
Steven Thomson
CG: 27 SD: -42

M
Russell Latapy
CG: 22 SD: -49

F
Darryl Duffy
CG: 18 SR: 191

F
Daniel McBreen
CG: 18 SR: 327

MONTHLY POINTS TALLY

Month	Points	%
AUGUST	3	25%
SEPTEMBER	2	22%
OCTOBER	8	53%
NOVEMBER	3	33%
DECEMBER	1	7%
JANUARY	3	33%
FEBRUARY	1	11%
MARCH	0	0%
APRIL	9	60%
MAY	3	50%

LEAGUE GOALS

	PLAYER	MINS	GOALS	S RATE
1	Duffy	1718	**9**	191
2	Gow	2570	**6**	428
3	McBreen	1960	**6**	327
4	Moutinho	909	**2**	455
5	Latapy	2158	**2**	1079
6	Milne	2743	**2**	1372
7	Ross	1240	**2**	620
8	Cregg	1270	**1**	1270
9	Thomson, S	2515	**1**	2515
10	O'Donnell	1594	**1**	1594
11	Ireland	1968	**1**	1968
	Other		**2**	
	TOTAL		**35**	

TOP POINT EARNERS

	PLAYER	GAMES	AV PTS
1	O'Donnell	13	**1.23**
2	Cregg	14	**1.14**
3	Rodrigues	27	**1.11**
4	McBreen	18	**1.06**
5	Milne	30	**1.00**
6	Ross	13	**1.00**
7	Thomson, S	27	**0.93**
8	Duffy	18	**0.89**
9	Glennon	21	**0.81**
10	Lima	20	**0.80**
	CLUB AVERAGE:		**0.87**

DISCIPLINARY RECORDS

	PLAYER	YELLOW	RED	AVE
1	Scally	6	0	**205**
2	Cregg	5	1	**211**
3	O'Donnell	6	1	**227**
4	McBreen	7	0	**280**
5	Moutinho	3	0	**303**
6	Craig	3	0	**307**
7	Lecsinel	2	0	**329**
8	Rodrigues	8	0	**334**
9	Dodds	2	0	**364**
10	Lima	5	0	**397**
11	Ross	3	0	**413**
12	Thomson, S	6	0	**419**
13	Twaddle	1	0	**456**
	Other	15	1	
	TOTAL	**72**	**3**	

KEY GOALKEEPER

Mathew Glennon

Goals Conceded in the League	42	**Counting Games** League games when player was on pitch for at least 70 minutes	21
Defensive Rating Ave number of mins between League goals conceded while on the pitch	45	**Clean Sheets** In League games when player was on pitch for at least 70 minutes	3

KEY PLAYERS - DEFENDERS

Tiago Jonas Rodrigues

Goals Conceded Number of League goals conceded while the player was on the pitch	46	**Clean Sheets** In League games when player was on pitch for at least 70 minutes	8
Defensive Rating Ave number of mins between League goals conceded while on the pitch	58	**Club Defensive Rating** Average number of mins between League goals conceded by the club this season	53

	PLAYER	CON LGE	CLEAN SHEETS	DEF RATE
1	Tiago Jonas Rodrigues	46	8	**58 mins**
2	Andy Lawrie	56	4	**45 mins**
3	Craig Ireland	45	3	**44 mins**

KEY PLAYERS - MIDFIELDERS

Patrick Cregg

Goals in the League	1	**Contribution to Attacking Power** Average number of minutes between League team goals while on pitch	106
Defensive Rating Average number of mins between League goals conceded while on the pitch	85	**Scoring Difference** Defensive Rating minus Contribution to Attacking Power	-21

	PLAYER	LGE GOALS	DEF RATE	POWER	SCORE DIFF
1	Patrick Cregg	1	85	106	**-21 mins**
2	Ken Milne	2	57	95	**-38 mins**
3	Steven Thomson	1	51	93	**-42 mins**
4	Stephen O'Donnell	1	51	100	**-49 mins**

KEY PLAYERS - GOALSCORERS

Darryl Duffy

Goals in the League	9	**Player Strike Rate** Average number of minutes between League goals scored by player	191
Contribution to Attacking Power Average number of minutes between League team goals while on pitch	86	**Club Strike Rate** Average number of minutes between League goals scored by club	98

	PLAYER	LGE GOALS	POWER	STRIKE RATE
1	Darryl Duffy	9	86	**191 mins**
2	Daniel McBreen	6	89	**327 mins**
3	Alan Gow	6	103	**428 mins**
4	Jack Ross	2	124	**620 mins**

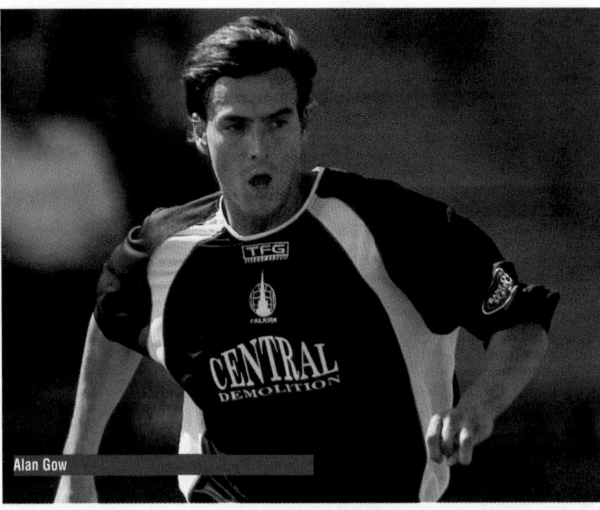

Alan Gow

SQUAD APPEARANCES

Match	1	2	3	4	5	6	7	8	9	10	11	12	13	14	15	16	17	18	19	20	21	22	23	24	25	26	27	28	29	30	31	32	33	34	35	36	37	38	39	40	41	42	43	44
Venue	H	A	A	H	H	A	H	A	A	A	H	A	H	A	H	H	A	H	A	H	H	A	H	H	A	H	A	H	A	H	A	A	H	H	A	A	H	A	H	H	H	A	A	H
Competition	L	L	L	L	W	L	L	L	W	L	L	L	L	L	L	L	L	L	L	L	L	L	L	O	L	L	L	O	L	L	O	L	O	L	L	L	L	L	L	L	L	L	L	L
Result	L	W	L	L	W	L	D	L	L	D	D	W	L	W	D	L	W	L	D	L	L	L	L	W	L	L	W	D	L	D	W	L	L	L	L	L	L	D	W	D	D	W	L	W

Goalkeepers
Allan Ferguson
Mathew Glennon
Darren Hill
Mark Howard

Defenders
John Hughes
Craig Ireland
Andy Lawrie
Jean-Francois Lecsinel
Craig McPherson
Tiago Jonas Rodrigues

Midfielders
Liam Craig
Patrick Cregg
Kerr Dodds
Russell Latapy
Vitor Santos Lima
Ken Milne
Stephen O'Donnell
John O'Neil
Jack Ross
Neil Scally
Thomas Scobie
Densil Theobald
Steven Thomson
Mark Twaddle

Forwards
Darryl Duffy
Alan Gow
Daniel McBreen
Ryan McStay
Iain McSween
Pedro Moutinho
Andy Thomson

KEY: On all match · On bench · Subbed or sent off (Counting game) · Subbed or sent off (playing less than 70 minutes) · Subbed on from bench (Counting Game) · Subbed on (playing less than 70 minutes) · Subbed on and then subbed or sent off (Counting Game) · Subbed on and then subbed or sent off (playing less than 70 minutes) · Not in 16

DUNFERMLINE

Final Position: **11th**

NICKNAME: THE PARS

KEY: ☐Won ☐Drawn ☐Lost

							Attendance
1	spl	Hibernian	A	D	1-1	Shields 12	13,010
2	spl	Motherwell	A	L	0-1		4,649
3	spl	Inverness CT	H	L	0-1		5,005
4	spl	Livingston	A	D	1-1	Makel 44	4,522
5	sccc1	Gretna	A	W	1-0	Burchill 17	1,405
6	spl	Celtic	H	L	0-4		9,244
7	spl	Kilmarnock	A	L	2-3	Burchill 4; Young, Derek 67	4,737
8	spl	Aberdeen	H	L	0-2		6,387
9	sccc3	Kilmarnock	A	W	4-3	McCunnie 7; Young, Derek 8,16,64	3,191
10	spl	Dundee Utd	H	W	2-1	Tod 60; Ross 75	5,361
11	spl	Rangers	A	L	1-5	Hunt 54	48,374
12	spl	Falkirk	H	L	0-1		7,068
13	spl	Hearts	A	L	0-2		16,500
14	spl	Hibernian	H	L	1-2	Mason 86	6,853
15	spl	Motherwell	H	L	0-3		4,421
16	spl	Inverness CT	A	L	1-2	Makel 72	3,728
17	sccqf	Hibernian	H	W	3-0	Burchill 15,45; Mason 90	6,005
18	spl	Livingston	H	L	0-1		6,016
19	spl	Celtic	A	W	1-0	Ross 17	58,203
20	spl	Kilmarnock	H	L	0-1		4,319
21	spl	Aberdeen	A	D	0-0		9,881
22	spl	Dundee Utd	A	L	1-2	Wilson, S 31	5,889
23	spl	Rangers	H	D	3-3	Tod 16; Burchill 23; Young, Darren 90 pen	9,481
24	spl	Falkirk	A	W	2-1	Burchill 44; Hunt 57	6,235
25	scr3	Airdrie	H	L	3-4		
26	spl	Hearts	H	L	1-4	Burchill 57	8,277
27	spl	Hibernian	A	L	1-3	Donnelly 34	13,316
28	slc5	Livingston	H	W	1-0	Young, Darren 37 pen	4,630
29	spl	Motherwell	H	D	1-1	Young, Darren 11	4,961
30	spl	Inverness CT	H	D	2-2	Hunt 8; Burchill 10	3,354
31	spl	Livingston	A	W	1-0	Burchill 11	4,371
32	spl	Celtic	H	L	1-8	Tod 14	9,015
33	spl	Dundee Utd	H	D	1-1	Burchill 14	4,694
34	spl	Kilmarnock	A	L	0-1		5,507
35	spl	Aberdeen	H	W	1-0	Burchill 48	5,308
36	scccf	Celtic	H	L	0-3		50,090
37	spl	Rangers	A	L	0-1		49,017
38	spl	Falkirk	H	D	1-1	Burchill 49	6,836
39	spl	Hearts	A	L	0-4		16,973
40	spl	Falkirk	A	D	0-0		5,413
41	spl	Livingston	H	W	3-2	Burchill 38 pen,78; Hunt 84	5,795
42	spl	Motherwell	A	W	3-2	Campbell, I 21; Burchill 30 pen; Mason 50	3,621
43	spl	Dundee Utd	A	W	1-0	Daquin 78	5,034
44	spl	Inverness CT	H	L	0-1		5,354

LEAGUE APPEARANCES, BOOKINGS AND CAPS

	AGE (on 01/07/06)	IN NAMED 18	APPEARANCES	COUNTING GAMES	MINUTES ON PITCH	YELLOW CARDS	RED CARDS	CAPS THIS SEASON	NATIONAL SIDE
Goalkeepers									
Bryn Halliwell	25	36	12	12	1080	0	0	-	England
Allan McGregor	24	28	26	26	2340	2	0	-	Scotland
Sean Murdoch	19	5	0	0	0	0	0	-	Scotland
Defenders									
Ian Campbell	25	34	17	15	1396	3	0	-	Scotland
Aaron Labonte	22	30	22	19	1774	2	0	-	England
Scott Morrison	21	3	3	3	270	0	0	-	Scotland
Greg Ross	19	34	23	21	1959	0	1	-	Scotland
Greg Shields	29	33	33	32	2914	5	0	-	Scotland
Andrius Skerla	29	3	2	1	120	0	0	-	Lithuania
Scott Thomson	34	26	25	19	1935	1	0	-	Scotland
Andy Tod	34	33	30	24	2314	4	0	-	Scotland
Scott Wilson	29	31	31	27	2610	5	1	-	Scotland
Yannick Zambernardi	28	18	15	11	1068	2	1	-	France
Midfielders									
Simon Donnelly	31	21	13	5	736	0	0	-	Scotland
Lee Makel	33	20	20	16	1668	2	1	-	England
Gary Mason	26	31	29	28	2530	4	0	-	Scotland
Jamie McCunnie	23	30	22	16	1652	1	0	-	Scotland
Scott Muirhead	21	12	12	9	881	0	0	-	Scotland
Nick Phinn	18	16	3	1	138	0	0	-	Scotland
Stephen Simmons	24	8	6	2	287	3	0	-	Scotland
Danny Smith	19	2	0	0	0	0	0	-	Scotland
Darren Young	27	22	21	20	1807	5	0	-	Scotland
Forwards									
Mark Burchill	25	31	31	21	2133	2	0	-	Scotland
Andy Campbell	27	12	5	1	240	0	0	-	England
Frederic Daquin	27	12	9	2	338	0	0	-	France
Gardar Gunnlaugsson	23	1	1	0	17	0	0	-	Iceland
Liam Horsted	20	13	11	4	512	0	0	-	England
Noel Hunt	23	33	32	19	2008	4	0	-	Rep of Ireland
Bartozs Tarachulski	31	33	27	6	1117	4	0	-	Poland
Craig Wilson	20	26	13	5	530	0	0	-	Scotland
Derek Young	26	19	18	8	1124	1	0	-	Scotland

TEAM OF THE SEASON

MONTHLY POINTS TALLY

AUGUST	1	8%
SEPTEMBER	3	33%
OCTOBER	0	0%
NOVEMBER	3	33%
DECEMBER	5	33%
JANUARY	1	11%
FEBRUARY	5	42%
MARCH	3	33%
APRIL	8	53%
MAY	3	50%

LEAGUE GOALS

	PLAYER	MINS	GOALS	S RATE
1	Burchill	2133	12	178
2	Hunt	2008	4	502
3	Tod	2314	3	771
4	Ross	1959	2	980
5	Mason	2530	2	1265
6	Makel	1668	2	834
7	Young, Darren	1807	2	904
8	Wilson, S	2610	1	2610
9	Campbell, I	1396	1	1396
10	Young, Derek	1124	1	1124
11	Shields	2914	1	2914
12	Daquin	338	1	338
13	Donnelly	736	1	736
	Other		0	
	TOTAL		33	

TOP POINT EARNERS

	PLAYER	GAMES	AV PTS
1	Labonte	19	1.21
2	Burchill	21	1.19
3	Hunt	19	1.16
4	Wilson, S	27	1.15
5	Ross	21	1.14
6	McGregor	26	1.00
7	Mason	28	1.00
8	McCunnie	16	1.00
9	Shields	32	0.91
10	Thomson, S M	19	0.89
	CLUB AVERAGE:		0.87

DISCIPLINARY RECORDS

	PLAYER	YELLOW	RED	AVE
1	Tarachulski	4	0	279
2	Zambernardi	2	1	356
3	Young, Darren	5	0	361
4	Wilson, S	5	1	435
5	Campbell, I	3	0	465
6	Hunt	4	0	502
7	Makel	2	1	556
8	Tod	4	0	578
9	Shields	5	0	582
10	Mason	4	0	632
11	Labonte	2	0	887
12	Burchill	2	0	1066
13	Young, Derek	1	0	1124
	Other	4	1	
	TOTAL	47	4	

KEY GOALKEEPER

Allan McGregor

Goals Conceded in the League	40	Counting Games League games when player was on pitch for at least 70 minutes	26
Defensive Rating Ave number of mins between League goals conceded while on the pitch	59	Clean Sheets In League games when player was on pitch for at least 70 minutes	5

KEY PLAYERS - DEFENDERS

Greg Shields

Goals Conceded Number of League goals conceded while the player was on the pitch	46	Clean Sheets In League games when player was on pitch for at least 70 minutes	6
Defensive Rating Ave number of mins between League goals conceded while on the pitch	63	Club Defensive Rating Average number of mins between League goals conceded by the club this season	50

	PLAYER	CON LGE	CLEAN SHEETS	DEF RATE
1	Greg Shields	46	6	63 mins
2	Aaron Labonte	29	5	61 mins
3	Ian Campbell	26	3	54 mins
4	Scott Thomson	39	3	50 mins

KEY PLAYERS - MIDFIELDERS

Gary Mason

Goals in the League	2	Contribution to Attacking Power Average number of minutes between League team goals while on pitch	97
Defensive Rating Average number of mins between League goals conceded while on the pitch	55	Scoring Difference Defensive Rating minus Contribution to Attacking Power	-42

	PLAYER	LGE GOALS	DEF RATE	POWER	SCORE DIFF
1	Gary Mason	2	55	97	-42 mins
2	Darren Young	2	43	106	-63 mins
3	Jamie McCunnie	0	45	110	-65 mins
4	Lee Makel	2	46	128	-82 mins

KEY PLAYERS - GOALSCORERS

Mark Burchill

Goals in the League	12	Player Strike Rate Average number of minutes between League goals scored by player	178
Contribution to Attacking Power Average number of minutes between League team goals while on pitch	89	Club Strike Rate Average number of minutes between League goals scored by club	104

	PLAYER	LGE GOALS	POWER	STRIKE RATE
1	Mark Burchill	12	89	178 mins
2	Noel Hunt	4	96	502 mins
3	Andy Tod	3	122	771 mins
4	Lee Makel	2	128	834 mins

Mark Burchill

SQUAD APPEARANCES

Match	1	2	3	4	5	6	7	8	9	10	11	12	13	14	15	16	17	18	19	20	21	22	23	24	25	26	27	28	29	30	31	32	33	34	35	36	37	38	39	40	41	42	43	44
Venue	A	A	H	A	A	H	A	H	A	H	A	H	A	H	H	A	H	H	A	H	A	A	H	A	H	H	A	H	H	H	A	H	H	A	H	H	A	H	A	A	H	A	A	H
Competition	L	L	L	L	W	L	L	L	W	L	L	L	L	L	L	L	W	L	L	L	L	L	L	L	O	L	L	W	L	L	L	L	L	L	L	W	L	L	L	L	L	L	L	L
Result	D	L	L	D	W	L	L	L	W	W	L	L	L	L	L	L	W	L	W	L	D	L	D	W	L	L	L	W	D	D	W	L	D	L	W	L	L	D	L	D	W	W	W	L

Goalkeepers
Bryn Halliwell
Allan McGregor
Sean Murdoch

Defenders
Ian Campbell
Aaron Labonte
Scott Morrison
Greg Ross
Greg Shields
Andrius Skerla
Scott Thomson
Andy Tod
Scott Wilson
Yannick Zambernardi

Midfielders
Simon Donnelly
Lee Makel
Gary Mason
Jamie McCunnie
Scott Muirhead
Nick Phinn
Stephen Simmons
Danny Smith
Darren Young

Forwards
Mark Burchill
Andy Campbell
Frederic Daquin
Gardar Gunnlaugsson
Liam Horsted
Noel Hunt
Bartozs Tarachulski
Craig Wilson
Derek Young

KEY: On all match · On bench · Subbed or sent off (Counting game) · Subbed or sent off (playing less than 70 minutes) · Subbed on from bench (Counting Game) · Subbed on (playing less than 70 minutes) · Subbed on and then subbed or sent off (Counting Game) · Subbed on and then subbed or sent off (playing less than 70 minutes) · Not in 16

LIVINGSTON

Final Position: **12th**

NICKNAME: THE LIVI' LIONS

KEY: ☐Won ☐Drawn ☐Lost

							Attendance
1	spl	**Rangers**	A	L	0-3		49,613
2	spl	**Falkirk**	H	L	0-2		4,052
3	spl	**Hibernian**	A	L	0-3		11,341
4	spl	**Dunfermline**	H	D	1-1	Pereira 64	4,522
5	sccc1	**Raith**	A	W	2-1	Dair 54; Dalglish 69	2,077
6	spl	**Kilmarnock**	A	L	0-3		4,644
7	spl	**Hearts**	H	L	1-4	Dalglish 45	8,405
8	spl	**Dundee Utd**	A	L	0-2		6,302
9	sccc3	**Hearts**	H	W	1-0	Pereira 54	3,805
10	spl	**Aberdeen**	A	D	0-0		12,402
11	spl	**Celtic**	H	L	0-5		9,115
12	spl	**Motherwell**	A	L	0-1		4,507
13	spl	**Inverness CT**	H	D	1-1	Pinxten 14	3,372
14	spl	**Rangers**	H	D	2-2	Snodgrass 56,64	9,481
15	spl	**Falkirk**	A	D	1-1	Snodgrass 87	4,786
16	spl	**Hibernian**	H	L	1-2	Strong 41	8,390
17	sccqf	**Inverness CT**	H	W	2-1	Mackay 44; Dalglish 117	1,531
18	spl	**Dunfermline**	A	W	1-0	Dalglish 60	6,016
19	spl	**Kilmarnock**	H	L	0-3		3,446
20	spl	**Hearts**	A	L	1-2	Walker 63	16,583
21	spl	**Dundee Utd**	H	W	1-0	Snodgrass 41	3,845
22	spl	**Aberdeen**	H	D	0-0		3,724
23	spl	**Celtic**	A	L	1-2	Dalglish 58	57,000
24	spl	**Motherwell**	H	L	1-2	Pinxten 36	4,431
25	scr3	**Alloa**	A	D	1-1	Brittain 90	1,341
26	scr3r	**Alloa**	H	L	1-2	Dalglish 38 pen	1,508
27	spl	**Inverness CT**	A	L	0-3		3,604
28	spl	**Rangers**	A	L	1-4	Vincze 52	49,211
29	slc5	**Dunfermline**	A	L	0-1		4,630
30	spl	**Falkirk**	H	L	0-1		4,577
31	spl	**Hibernian**	A	L	0-7		12,170
32	spl	**Dunfermline**	H	L	0-1		4,371
33	spl	**Kilmarnock**	A	L	1-3	Hislop 13	5,266
34	spl	**Hearts**	H	L	2-3	Brittain 59; Mackay 77	5,058
35	spl	**Dundee Utd**	A	L	1-3	Morrow 17	5,730
36	spl	**Aberdeen**	A	L	0-3		9,229
37	spl	**Celtic**	H	L	0-2		7,486
38	spl	**Motherwell**	A	L	1-2	Whelan 75	4,458
39	spl	**Inverness CT**	H	W	2-1	Brittain 37; Healy 81	2,688
40	spl	**Dundee Utd**	H	W	3-1	Morrow 8; Pinxten 49; Brittain 90 pen	2,298
41	spl	**Dunfermline**	A	L	2-3	Brittain 9 pen; Healy 63	5,795
42	spl	**Inverness CT**	H	L	0-1		2,278
43	spl	**Motherwell**	H	L	0-1		2,283
44	spl	**Falkirk**	A	L	0-1		5,355

LEAGUE APPEARANCES, BOOKINGS AND CAPS

	AGE (on 01/07/06)	IN NAMED 18	APPEARANCES	COUNTING GAMES	MINUTES ON PITCH	YELLOW CARDS	RED CARDS	CAPS THIS SEASON	NATIONAL SIDE
Goalkeepers									
Roddy McKenzie	30	36	32	32	2880	1	0	-	Scotland
Ludovic Roy	28	33	6	6	540	0	0	-	France
Stephen Woods	36	6	0	0	0	0	0	-	Scotland
Defenders									
Emmanuel Dorado	33	28	21	17	1512	7	0	-	Argentina
David Mackay	26	38	38	38	3420	5	0	-	Scotland
David McNamee	25	14	13	6	880	4	0	-	Scotland
Gary Miller	19	20	4	2	230	1	0	-	Scotland
Harald Pinxten	28	28	26	24	2222	5	0	-	Belgium
Greg Strong	30	34	30	28	2580	10	0	-	England
Midfielders									
Stephen Adam	19	10	2	0	69	1	0	-	Scotland
Neil Barrett	-	8	8	4	540	3	0	-	
Scott Boyd	20	14	4	2	213	0	0	-	Scotland
Richard Brittain	22	35	35	32	2960	3	1	-	Scotland
Jason Dair	32	23	22	16	1638	2	0	-	Scotland
Colin Healy	-	9	9	6	636	0	0	-	
Wesley Hoolahan	-	16	16	10	1158	1	0	-	Rep of Ireland
Paul Lambert	36	7	6	2	355	0	0	-	Scotland
Scott McLaughlin	22	5	3	0	83	0	0	-	Scotland
Martin Scott	-	28	19	7	924	7	0	-	
Dubi Tesevic	-	11	4	1	242	0	0	-	
Paul Tierney	23	33	31	24	2350	7	0	-	England
Gabor Vincze	29	23	18	12	1224	7	0	-	Hungary
Allan Walker	-	35	33	26	2618	13	0	-	Scotland
Forwards									
Derek Adams	31	26	25	16	1715	2	0	-	Scotland
Graham Barrett	24	7	7	5	558	0	0	-	Rep of Ireland
Paul Dalglish	29	18	17	12	1229	2	1	-	Scotland
Graeme Dorrans	-	18	8	2	394	0	0	-	Scotland
Steven Hislop	28	16	13	5	330	1	0	-	Scotland
James McPake	22	18	15	2	553	2	0	-	Scotland
Sam Morrow	21	11	11	10	1280	1	0	-	N Ireland
Ramon Pereira	27	15	11	1	427	3	0	-	Spain
Robert Snodgrass	18	36	26	8	1310	2	0	-	Scotland
Noel Whelan	31	9	8	4	506	2	0	-	England

TEAM OF THE SEASON

G — Roddy McKenzie — CG: 32 DR: 41

D — Harald Pinxten — CG: 24 DR: 48

D — Greg Strong — CG: 28 DR: 44

D — David Mackay — CG: 38 DR: 43

D — Emmanuel Dorado — CG: 17 DR: 38

M — Richard Brittain — CG: 32 SD: -72

M — Allan Walker — CG: 26 SD: -85

M — Paul Tierney — CG: 24 SD: -95

M — Jason Dair — CG: 16 SD: -99

F — Paul Daglish — CG: 12 SR: 380

F — Robert Snodgrass* — CG: 8 SR: 328

MONTHLY POINTS TALLY

AUGUST	1	8%
SEPTEMBER	1	11%
OCTOBER	3	20%
NOVEMBER	3	33%
DECEMBER	4	27%
JANUARY	0	0%
FEBRUARY	0	0%
MARCH	0	0%
APRIL	6	40%
MAY	0	0%

LEAGUE GOALS

	PLAYER	MINS	GOALS	S RATE
1	Brittain	2960	**4**	740
2	Snodgrass	1310	**4**	328
3	Dalglish	1139	**3**	380
4	Pinxten	2222	**3**	741
5	Morrow	1280	**2**	640
6	Healy	636	**2**	318
7	Whelan	506	**1**	506
8	Vincze	1224	**1**	1224
9	Walker	2618	**1**	2618
10	Pereira	427	**1**	427
11	Mackay	3420	**1**	3420
12	Hislop	330	**1**	330
13	Strong	2580	**1**	2580
	Other		**0**	
	TOTAL		**25**	

TOP POINT EARNERS

	PLAYER	GAMES	AV PTS
1	Pinxten	24	**0.67**
2	Walker	26	**0.62**
3	Strong	28	**0.61**
4	Tierney	24	**0.58**
5	Brittain	32	**0.56**
6	Dair	16	**0.50**
7	Mackay	38	**0.47**
8	Vincze	12	**0.42**
9	McKenzie	32	**0.38**
10	Adams	16	**0.25**
	CLUB AVERAGE:		**0.47**

DISCIPLINARY RECORDS

	PLAYER	YELLOW	RED	AVE
1	Scott	7	0	**132**
2	Vincze	7	0	**174**
3	Barrett, N	3	0	**180**
4	Walker	13	0	**201**
5	Dorado	7	0	**216**
6	McNamee	4	0	**220**
7	Whelan	2	0	**253**
8	Strong	10	0	**258**
9	McPake	2	0	**276**
10	Tierney	7	0	**335**
11	Dalglish	2	1	**379**
12	Pinxten	5	0	**444**
13	Snodgrass	2	0	**655**
	Other	15	1	
	TOTAL	**86**	**2**	

KEY GOALKEEPER

Roddy McKenzie

Goals Conceded in the League	**70**	**Counting Games** League games when player was on pitch for at least 70 minutes	**32**
Defensive Rating Ave number of mins between League goals conceded while on the pitch	**41**	**Clean Sheets** In League games when player was on pitch for at least 70 minutes	**2**

KEY PLAYERS - DEFENDERS

Harald Pinxten

Goals Conceded Number of League goals conceded while the player was on the pitch	**46**	**Clean Sheets** In League games when player was on pitch for at least 70 minutes	**3**
Defensive Rating Ave number of mins between League goals conceded while on the pitch	**48**	**Club Defensive Rating** Average number of mins between League goals conceded by the club this season	**43**

	PLAYER	CON LGE	CLEAN SHEETS	DEF RATE
1	Harald Pinxten	46	3	**48 mins**
2	Greg Strong	59	4	**44 mins**
3	David Mackay	79	4	**43 mins**
4	Emmanuel Dorado	40	1	**38 mins**

KEY PLAYERS - MIDFIELDERS

Richard Brittain

Goals in the League	**4**	**Contribution to Attacking Power** Average number of minutes between League team goals while on pitch	**118**
Defensive Rating Average number of mins between League goals conceded while on the pitch	**46**	**Scoring Difference** Defensive Rating minus Contribution to Attacking Power	**-72**

	PLAYER	LGE GOALS	DEF RATE	POWER	SCORE DIFF
1	Richard Brittain	4	46	118	**-72 mins**
2	Allan Walker	1	46	131	**-85 mins**
3	Paul Tierney	0	43	138	**-95 mins**
4	Gabor Vincze	1	37	136	**-99 mins**

KEY PLAYERS - GOALSCORERS

Richard Brittain

Goals in the League	**4**	**Player Strike Rate** Average number of minutes between League goals scored by player	**740**
Contribution to Attacking Power Average number of minutes between League team goals while on pitch	**118**	**Club Strike Rate** Average number of minutes between League goals scored by club	**137**

	PLAYER	LGE GOALS	POWER	STRIKE RATE
1	Richard Brittain	4	118	**740 mins**
2	Harald Pinxten	3	117	**741 mins**
3	Gabor Vincze	1	136	**1224 mins**
4	Greg Strong	1	117	**2580 mins**

Richard Brittain

SQUAD APPEARANCES

Match	1	2	3	4	5	6	7	8	9	10	11	12	13	14	15	16	17	18	19	20	21	22
Venue	A	H	A	H	A	A	H	A	H	A	H	A	H	H	A	H	H	A	H	A	H	H
Competition	L	L	L	L	W	L	L	L	W	L	L	L	L	L	L	L	W	L	L	L	L	L
Result	L	L	L	D	W	L	L	L	W	D	L	L	D	D	D	L	W	W	L	L	W	D

Match	23	24	25	26	27	28	29	30	31	32	33	34	35	36	37	38	39	40	41	42	43	44
Venue	A	H	A	H	A	A	A	H	A	H	A	H	A	A	H	A	H	H	A	H	H	A
Competition	L	L	O	O	L	L	W	L	L	L	L	L	L	L	L	L	L	L	L	L	L	L
Result	L	L	D	L	L	L	L	L	L	L	L	L	L	L	L	L	W	W	L	L	L	L

Goalkeepers
Roddy McKenzie
Ludovic Roy
Stephen Woods

Defenders
Emmanuel Dorado
David Mackay
David McNamee
Gary Miller
Harald Pinxten
Greg Strong

Midfielders
Stephen Adam
Neil Barrett
Scott Boyd
Richard Brittain
Jason Dair
Paul Dalglish
Colin Healy
Wesley Hoolahan
Paul Lambert
Scott McLaughlin
Martin Scott
Dubi Tesevic
Paul Tierney
Gabor Vincze
Allan Walker

Forwards
Derek Adams
Graham Barrett
Paul Dalglish
Graeme Dorrans
Steven Hislop
James McPake
Sam Morrow
Ramon Pereira
Robert Snodgrass
Noel Whelan

KEY: ■ On all match ■ On bench ⏮ Subbed or sent off (Counting game) « Subbed or sent off (playing less than 70 minutes) ⏭ Subbed on from bench (Counting Game) » Subbed on (playing less than 70 minutes) Subbed on and then subbed or sent off (Counting Game) Subbed on and then subbed or sent off (playing less than 70 minutes) □ Not in 16

SPANISH LEAGUE ROUND-UP

FINAL LEAGUE TABLE

		HOME					AWAY					TOTAL			
	P	W	D	L	F	A	W	D	L	F	A	F	A	DIF	PTS
Barcelona	38	15	3	1	45	15	10	4	5	35	20	80	35	45	82
Real Madrid	38	11	4	4	40	21	9	6	4	30	19	70	40	30	70
Valencia	38	10	8	1	34	16	9	4	6	24	17	58	33	25	69
Osasuna	38	12	3	4	28	20	9	2	8	21	23	49	43	6	68
Seville	38	12	5	2	29	15	8	3	8	25	24	54	39	15	68
Celta Vigo	38	13	0	6	25	13	7	4	8	20	20	45	33	12	64
Villarreal	38	9	6	4	28	18	5	9	5	22	21	50	39	11	57
Deportivo	38	6	5	8	19	22	9	5	5	28	23	47	45	2	55
Getafe	38	8	7	4	32	24	7	2	10	22	25	54	49	5	54
Atl Madrid	38	7	6	6	21	18	6	7	6	24	19	45	37	8	52
Real Zaragoza	38	6	6	7	26	26	4	10	5	20	25	46	51	-5	46
Athl Bilbao	38	7	6	6	19	18	4	6	9	21	28	40	46	-6	45
Mallorca	38	6	8	5	21	21	4	5	10	16	30	37	51	-14	43
Real Betis	38	8	5	6	19	19	2	7	10	15	32	34	51	-17	42
Espanyol	38	7	4	8	26	24	3	7	9	10	32	36	56	-20	41
R Santander	38	4	6	9	18	26	5	7	7	18	23	36	49	-13	40
Real Sociedad	38	8	4	7	31	27	3	3	13	17	38	48	65	-17	40
Alaves	38	6	6	7	20	24	3	6	10	15	30	35	54	-19	39
Cadiz	38	4	8	7	22	25	4	4	11	14	27	36	52	-16	36
Malaga	38	3	5	11	16	25	2	4	13	20	43	36	68	-32	24

CLUB STRIKE FORCE

Eto'o, Larsson and Ronaldinho

1 Barcelona

Goals scored in the League	80
Club Strike Rate (CSR) Average number of minutes between League goals scored by club	43

	CLUB	GOALS	CSR
1	Barcelona	80	43
2	Real Madrid	70	49
3	Valencia	58	59
4	Getafe	54	63
5	Seville	54	63
6	Villarreal	50	68
7	Osasuna	49	70
8	Real Sociedad	48	71
9	Deportivo	47	73
10	Real Zaragoza	46	74
11	Atl Madrid	45	76
12	Celta Vigo	45	76
13	Athl Bilbao	40	86
14	Mallorca	37	92
15	Cadiz	36	95
16	Espanyol	36	95
17	Malaga	36	95
18	R Santander	36	95
19	Alaves	35	98
20	Real Betis	34	101

CLUB DISCIPLINARY RECORDS

Oriol of Racing Santander

1 Racing Santander

League Yellow	120
League Red	8
League Total	128
Cards Average in League (AVE) Average number of minutes between a card being shown of either colour	27

	CLUB	Y	R	TOTAL	AVE
1	R Santander	120	8	128	27
2	Atl Madrid	118	9	127	27
3	Malaga	114	11	125	27
4	Deportivo	116	5	121	28
5	Real Madrid	110	10	120	29
6	Osasuna	114	6	120	29
7	Espanyol	105	10	115	30
8	Seville	100	9	109	31
9	Mallorca	102	9	111	32
10	Getafe	99	8	107	32
11	Villarreal	102	5	107	32
12	Real Betis	94	7	101	34
13	Real Zaragoza	94	4	98	35
14	Real Sociedad	84	10	94	36
15	Athl Bilbao	88	6	94	36
16	Cadiz	88	5	93	37
17	Valencia	81	6	87	39
18	Alaves	81	4	85	40
19	Barcelona	74	6	80	43
20	Celta Vigo	77	3	80	43

CLUB DEFENCES

	CLUB	LGE	CS	CDR
1	Celta Vigo	33	14	104
2	Valencia	33	16	104
3	Barcelona	35	17	98
4	Atl Madrid	37	12	92
5	Villarreal	39	9	88
6	Seville	39	16	88
7	Real Madrid	40	15	86
8	Osasuna	43	11	80
9	Deportivo	45	10	76
10	Athl Bilbao	46	11	74
11	Getafe	49	7	70
12	R Santander	49	8	70
13	Real Zaragoza	51	8	67
14	Mallorca	51	9	67
15	Real Betis	51	10	67
16	Cadiz	52	10	66
17	Alaves	54	12	63
18	Espanyol	56	10	61
19	Real Sociedad	65	8	53
20	Malaga	68	5	50

Celta's Angel gets stuck in

1 Celta Vigo

Goals conceded in the League	33
Clean Sheets (CS) Number of league games where no goals were conceded	14
Club Defensive Rate (CDR) Average number of minutes between League goals conceded by club	104

PLAYER NATIONALITIES

Overseas country with the most player appearances in the Spanish League - Argentina

996 league appearances by Argentinian players

	COUNTRY	PLAYERS	IN SQUAD	LGE APP	% LGE ACT	CAPS	MOST APP	APP
1	Spain	433	9066	6727	63.7	91	Francisco Molina	100
2	Argentina	49	1216	996	10.2	70	Mariano Pernia	93.8
3	Brazil	41	1011	897	8.6	26	Anderson Nene	97.5
4	Uruguay	19	394	305	2.6	0	Diego Forlan	79.4
5	Italy	10	217	168	1.6	0	Emiliano Moretti	84.7
6	Portugal	11	218	156	1.6	21	Luis Garcia Miguel	82.9
7	France	12	248	166	1.5	10	Peter Luccin	71
8	Serbia & Montenegro	6	147	134	1.3	23	Savo Milosevic	74.3
9	Cameroon	3	96	82	0.8	8	Samuel Eto'o	88.2
10	Colombia	3	79	58	0.7	4	Luis Perea	89.1
11	Holland	5	116	77	0.6	13	Mark van Bommel	45.5
12	Israel	1	38	37	0.4	0	Dudu Aouate	97.4
13	Venezuela	1	37	37	0.4	0	Juan Arango	94.2
14	England	3	47	40	0.4	13	David Beckham	73.9
15	Bulgaria	2	53	45	0.4	6	Martin Petrov	78.5
16	Chile	2	44	41	0.4	2	Pablo Contreras	59.7
17	Paraguay	3	54	35	0.3	0	Delio Toledo	70.1
18	Romania	2	51	38	0.3	0	Cosmin Contra	61.8
19	Mali	1	32	32	0.3	0	Frederic Kanoute	67.5
20	Australia	1	35	33	0.3	4	John Aloisi	66.7
21	Denmark	2	44	35	0.3	7	Morten Skoubo	40.4

CLUB MAKE-UP – HOME AND OVERSEAS PLAYERS

1 Barcelona

64.4% of appearances by overseas players

	CLUB	OVERSEAS	HOME	% OVERSEAS	% LGE ACT	MOST APP	APP
1	Barcelona	19	14	57.6	64.4	Samuel Eto'o	88.2
2	Villarreal	14	22	38.9	61.2	R Arruabarrena	82.1
3	Mallorca	17	21	44.7	52.5	Juan Arango	94.2
4	Real Madrid	13	27	32.5	52.4	Roberto Carlos	92.2
5	Real Zaragoza	7	19	26.9	50.6	Leonardo Ponzio	90.3
6	Atl Madrid	8	23	25.8	48.7	Luis Perea	89.1
7	Celta Vigo	11	16	40.7	43.1	Fernando Baiano	77.4
8	Seville	12	23	34.3	39.8	Daniel Alves	89.8
9	Alaves	17	15	53.1	39.7	Anderson Nene	97.5
10	Valencia	14	17	45.2	39.5	Emiliano Moretti	84.7
11	Cadiz	11	17	39.3	31.6	Andres Fleurquin	72.9
12	Espanyol	10	21	32.3	31.6	Eduardo Costa	69.6
13	Getafe	7	20	25.9	28.7	Mariano Pernia	93.8
14	R Santander	8	25	24.2	25.2	Dudu Aouate	97.4
15	Deportivo	9	25	26.5	24.0	Aldo Duscher	78.0
16	Malaga	9	27	25.0	22.9	Patricio Edgar	61.5
17	Osasuna	6	21	22.2	22.7	Savo Milosevic	74.3
18	Real Betis	8	26	23.5	21.6	Edu	86.9
19	Real Sociedad	7	27	20.6	19.1	Kahveci Nihat	60.7

CHART-TOPPING MIDFIELDERS

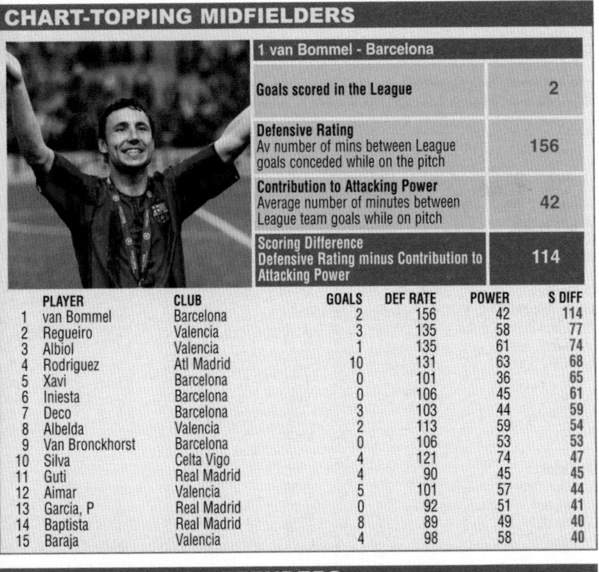

1 van Bommel - Barcelona	
Goals scored in the League	2
Defensive Rating Av number of mins between League goals conceded while on the pitch	156
Contribution to Attacking Power Average number of minutes between League team goals while on pitch	42
Scoring Difference Defensive Rating minus Contribution to Attacking Power	114

	PLAYER	CLUB	GOALS	DEF RATE	POWER	S DIFF
1	van Bommel	Barcelona	2	156	42	114
2	Regueiro	Valencia	3	135	58	77
3	Albiol	Valencia	1	135	61	74
4	Rodriguez	Atl Madrid	10	131	63	68
5	Xavi	Barcelona	0	101	36	65
6	Iniesta	Barcelona	0	106	45	61
7	Deco	Barcelona	3	103	44	59
8	Albelda	Valencia	2	113	59	54
9	Van Bronckhorst	Barcelona	0	106	53	53
10	Silva	Celta Vigo	4	121	74	47
11	Guti	Real Madrid	4	90	45	45
12	Aimar	Valencia	5	101	57	44
13	Garcia, P	Real Madrid	0	92	51	41
14	Baptista	Real Madrid	8	89	49	40
15	Baraja	Valencia	4	98	58	40

CHART-TOPPING GOALSCORERS

1 Eto'o - Barcelona	
Goals scored in the League	26
Contribution to Attacking Power Average number of minutes between League team goals while on pitch	44
Club Strike Rate (CSR) Average minutes between League goals scored by club	43
Player Strike Rate Average number of minutes between League goals scored by player	116

	PLAYER	CLUB	GOALS: LGE	POWER	CSR	S RATE
1	Eto'o	Barcelona	26	44	43	116
2	Villa	Valencia	25	59	59	120
3	Ronaldo	Real Madrid	14	49	49	128
4	Larsson	Barcelona	10	42	43	133
5	Ronaldinho	Barcelona	17	39	43	149
6	Paunovic	Getafe	10	72	63	180
7	Riquelme	Villarreal	12	59	68	181
8	Lobos	Cadiz	7	88	95	188
9	Tristan	Deportivo	12	77	73	192
10	Baiano	Celta Vigo	13	80	76	204
11	Antonito	R Santander	9	77	95	222
12	Rodriguez	Atl Madrid	10	63	76	222
13	Ewerthon	Real Zaragoza	12	73	74	225
14	Saviola	Seville	8	69	63	225
15	Aloisi	Alaves	10	91	98	228

CHART-TOPPING DEFENDERS

1 Edmilson - Barcelona	
Goals Conceded in the League The number of League goals conceded while he was on the pitch	13
Clean Sheets In games when he played at least 70 mins	13
Club Defensive Rating Average mins between League goals conceded by the club this season	98
Defensive Rating Average number of minutes between League goals conceded while on pitch	163

	PLAYER	CLUB	CON: LGE	CS	CDR	DEF RATE
1	Edmilson	Barcelona	13	13	98	163
2	Enrique	Celta Vigo	9	5	104	125
3	Miguel	Valencia	23	15	104	123
4	Lequi	Celta Vigo	19	10	104	122
5	Contreras	Celta Vigo	17	10	104	120
6	Marquez	Barcelona	17	10	98	116
7	Silvinho	Barcelona	17	11	98	114
8	Puyol	Barcelona	28	16	98	112
9	Moretti	Valencia	26	15	104	111
10	Andrade	Deportivo	14	7	76	110
11	Navarro	Seville	18	11	88	106
12	Clavero	Osasuna	17	9	80	102
13	Perea	Atl Madrid	30	11	92	102
14	Pablo Ibanez	Atl Madrid	32	12	92	101
15	Oleguer	Barcelona	27	14	98	101

CHART-TOPPING GOALKEEPERS

1 Pinto - Celta Vigo	
Counting Games Games in which he played at least 70 minutes	36
Goals Conceded in the League The number of League goals conceded while he was on the pitch	28
Clean Sheets In games when he played at least 70 mins	14
Defensive Rating Average number of minutes between League goals conceded while on pitch	117

	PLAYER	CLUB	CG	CONC	CS	DEF RATE
1	Pinto	Celta Vigo	36	28	14	117
2	Valdes	Barcelona	36	28	17	116
3	Canizares	Valencia	36	29	16	112
4	Franco	Atl Madrid	33	29	11	98
5	Contreras	Real Betis	17	15	4	94
6	Palop	Seville	35	35	16	90
7	Casillas	Real Madrid	37	38	15	87
8	Lafuente	Athl Bilbao	20	21	7	86
9	Viera	Villarreal	29	30	6	85
10	Ricardo	Osasuna	31	36	9	78
11	Molina	Deportivo	38	45	10	76
12	Prats	Mallorca	30	36	9	75
13	Calatayud	Getafe	13	16	3	73
14	Aouate	R Santander	37	47	8	71
15	Kameni	Espanyol	17	22	3	70

PLAYER DISCIPLINARY RECORD

1 Amorebieta - Athletic Bilbao	
Cards Average mins between cards	104
League Yellow	10
League Red	1
TOTAL	11

	PLAYER		LY	LR	TOT	AVE
1	Amorebieta	Athl Bilbao	10	1	11	104
2	Garitano	Real Sociedad	10	2	12	122
3	M. Hurtado	Espanyol	9	2	11	124
4	Garcia, P	Real Madrid	11	0	11	125
5	Medina	Cadiz	8	1	9	127
6	Luccin	Atl Madrid	16	2	18	134
7	Estoyanoff	Cadiz	8	1	9	140
8	De Guzman	Deportivo	9	1	10	146
9	Oriol	R Santander	11	0	11	150
10	Oscar Lopez	Real Betis	9	1	10	153
11	Doni	Mallorca	9	1	10	158
12	Farinos	Mallorca	5	1	6	160
13	Edmilson	Barcelona	12	1	13	162
14	Mora	R Santander	12	0	12	165
15	Albelda	Valencia	16	1	17	166

TEAM OF THE SEASON

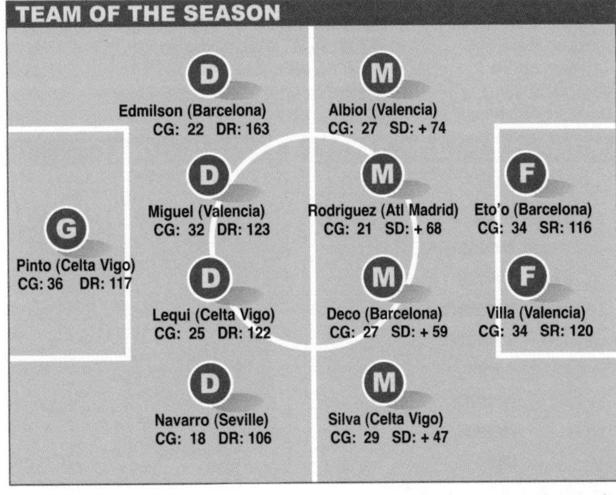

SPANISH LA LIGA CHAMPIONS

BARCELONA

Final Position: **1st**

KEY: ☐ Won ☐ Drawn ☐ Lost

#	Comp	Opponent	H/A	Res	Score	Scorers	Attendance
1	sppr1	**Alaves**	A	D	0-0		16,047
2	sppr1	**Mallorca**	H	W	2-0	Eto'o 27,32	82,000
3	ecgpc	**W Bremen**	A	W	2-0	Deco 13; Ronaldinho 76 pen	37,000
4	sppr1	**Atl Madrid**	A	L	1-2	Eto'o 6	65,000
5	sppr1	**Valencia**	H	D	2-2	Giuly 44; Deco 81	80,000
6	sppr1	**Real Betis**	A	W	4-1	van Bommel 19; Eto'o 58,77; Ezquerro 89	45,000
7	ecgpc	**Udinese**	H	W	4-1	Ronaldinho 13,32,90 pen; Deco 41	65,000
8	sppr1	**Real Zaragoza**	H	D	2-2	Ronaldinho 78 pen; Eto'o 88	81,000
9	sppr1	**Deportivo**	A	D	3-3	Eto'o 41; Ronaldinho 45,52 pen	30,000
10	ecgpc	**Panathinaikos**	A	D	0-0		65,000
11	sppr1	**Osasuna**	H	W	3-0	Eto'o 46,52; Giuly 87	84,000
12	sppr1	**Malaga**	H	W	2-0	Ronaldinho 81 pen; Larsson 88	70,000
13	sppr1	**Real Sociedad**	H	W	5-0	van Bommel 18; Ronaldinho 36,60; Puyol 75; Larsson 86	65,000
14	ecgpc	**Panathinaikos**	H	W	5-0	van Bommel 1; Eto'o 14,40,65; Messi 34	75,000
15	sppr1	**Getafe**	A	W	3-1	Eto'o 2; Giuly 62; Motta 71 fk	14,000
16	sppr1	**Real Madrid**	A	W	3-0	Eto'o 15; Ronaldinho 58,77	80,000
17	ecgpc	**W Bremen**	H	W	3-1	Gabri 14; Ronaldinho 26 fk; Larsson 71	85,000
18	sppr1	**R Santander**	H	W	4-1	Eto'o 31; Messi 52; Ronaldinho 57 pen; Silvinho 66	53,000
19	sppr1	**Villarreal**	A	W	2-0	Pena 24 og; Deco 63	22,000
20	ecgpc	**Udinese**	A	W	2-0	Ezquerro 85; Iniesta 90	38,500
21	sppr1	**Seville**	H	W	2-1	Eto'o 66; Ronaldinho 78	65,000
22	sppr1	**Cadiz**	A	W	3-1	Giuly 32; Eto'o 45 pen,49	20,000
23	sppr1	**Celta Vigo**	H	W	2-0	Eto'o 37,56	65,000
24	sppr1	**Espanyol**	A	W	2-1	Deco 43; Eto'o 46	30,000
25	sppr1	**Athl Bilbao**	H	W	2-1	Ronaldinho 38 pen; Messi 51	72,400
26	sppr1	**Alaves**	H	W	2-0	Larsson 46; Messi 82	72,081
27	sppr1	**Mallorca**	A	W	3-0	Giuly 39; Messi 76,83	23,000
28	sppr1	**Atl Madrid**	H	L	1-3	Larsson 64	83,000
29	sppr1	**Valencia**	A	L	0-1		50,000
30	sppr1	**Real Betis**	H	W	5-1	Larsson 17; Melli 29 og,34 og; Ronaldinho 59; Messi 85	92,500
31	eclsl1	**Chelsea**	A	W	2-1	Terry 71 og; Eto'o 80	39,521
32	sppr1	**Real Zaragoza**	A	W	2-0	Ronaldinho 79 pen; Larsson 82	30,000
33	sppr1	**Deportivo**	H	W	3-2	Ronaldinho 3; Larsson 34; Eto'o 62	77,116
34	eclsl2	**Chelsea**	H	D	1-1	Ronaldinho 78	98,000
35	sppr1	**Osasuna**	A	L	1-2	Larsson 72	18,000
36	sppr1	**Real Sociedad**	A	W	2-0	Larsson 8; Eto'o 52	28,400
37	sppr1	**Getafe**	H	W	3-1	Matellan 21 og; Eto'o 52,69	75,000
38	sppr1	**Malaga**	A	D	0-0		23,000
39	ecqfl1	**Benfica**	A	D	0-0		65,000
40	sppr1	**Real Madrid**	H	D	1-1	Ronaldinho 22 pen	95,000
41	ecqfl2	**Benfica**	H	W	2-0	Ronaldinho 19; Eto'o 88	90,000
42	sppr1	**R Santander**	A	D	2-2	Larsson 17; Eto'o 33	20,600
43	sppr1	**Villarreal**	H	W	1-0	Eto'o 11	76,200
44	ecsfl1	**AC Milan**	A	W	1-0	Giuly 57	85,000
45	ecsfl2	**AC Milan**	H	D	0-0		90,000
46	sppr1	**Cadiz**	H	W	1-0	Ronaldinho 8	85,000
47	sppr1	**Celta Vigo**	A	W	1-0	Eto'o 55	28,500
48	sppr1	**Espanyol**	H	W	2-0	Jarque 19 og; Ronaldinho 51	90,000
49	sppr1	**Seville**	A	L	2-3	Ezquerro 40; Silvinho 42	43,000
50	ecfin	**Arsenal**	H	W	2-1	Eto'o 76; Belletti 80	79,500
51	sppr1	**Athl Bilbao**	A	L	1-3	Eto'o 36	40,000

LEAGUE APPEARANCES, BOOKINGS AND CAPS

	AGE (on 01/07/06)	IN NAMED 18	APPEARANCES	COUNTING GAMES	MINUTES ON PITCH	YELLOW CARDS	RED CARDS	CAPS THIS SEASON	NATIONAL SIDE
Goalkeepers									
Albert Jorquera	27	38	2	2	180	0	0	-	Spain
Victor Valdes	24	38	36	36	3240	3	0	1	Spain (5)
Defenders									
Juliano Belletti	30	31	28	16	1784	9	0	-	Brazil
Abella Damia	24	1	0	0	0	0	0	-	Spain
Edmilson	29	32	27	22	2117	12	1	-	Brazil
Rafael Marquez	27	26	25	19	1979	6	1	4	Mexico (4)
Presas Oleguer	26	36	33	28	2725	1	0	-	Spain
Carlos Puyol	28	35	35	35	3134	7	1	6	Spain (5)
Sergio Rodri	21	5	3	1	166	0	0	-	Spain
Silvinho	32	33	25	20	1933	5	0	-	Brazil
Midfielders									
Anderson Deco	28	30	30	27	2466	7	1	3	Portugal (7)
Garcia Gabri	27	25	11	2	389	1	1	-	Spain
Ludovic Giuly	29	36	29	10	1748	1	0	2	France (8)
Jordi Gomez	21	3	0	0	0	0	0	-	Spain
Andres Iniesta	22	35	33	13	1691	3	0	-	Spain
Lionel Messi	19	18	17	7	909	2	0	7	Argentina (9)
El Diario Montanes	19	2	1	0	20	0	0	-	Spain
Thiago Motta	23	21	15	8	916	2	1	-	Brazil
Olmo	-	1	1	1	90	1	0	-	
Andrea Orlandi	21	1	1	1	74	0	0	-	Spain
Ludovic Sylvestre	22	2	2	1	107	0	0	-	France
Mark van Bommel	29	30	24	12	1556	5	0	2	Holland (3)
Gio Van Bronckhorst	31	33	20	15	1482	3	0	6	Holland (3)
Xavi Hernandez	26	16	16	12	1215	0	0	6	Spain (5)
Forwards									
Hidalgo Cristian	22	2	0	0	0	0	0	-	Spain
Samuel Eto'o	25	34	34	34	3018	1	0	6	Cameroon (26)
Santiago Ezquerro	29	30	12	4	524	0	0	-	Spain
Henrik Larsson	34	35	28	11	1330	0	0	5	Sweden (16)
Maxi Lopez	22	20	5	2	215	0	0	-	Argentina
Ronaldinho	26	30	29	27	2525	5	0	2	Brazil (1)

TEAM OF THE SEASON

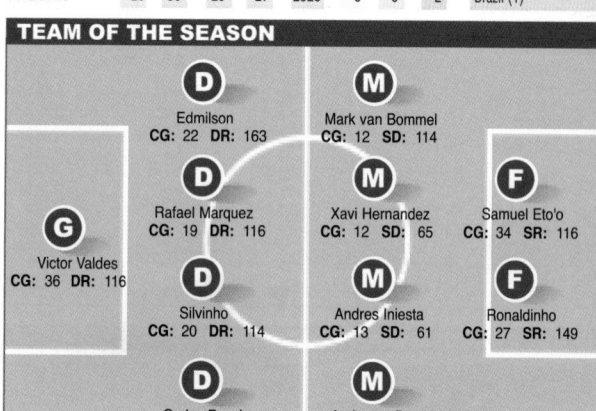

G
Victor Valdes
CG: 36 **DR:** 116

D
Edmilson
CG: 22 **DR:** 163

D
Rafael Marquez
CG: 19 **DR:** 116

D
Silvinho
CG: 20 **DR:** 114

D
Carlos Puyol
CG: 35 **DR:** 112

M
Mark van Bommel
CG: 12 **SD:** 114

M
Xavi Hernandez
CG: 12 **SD:** 65

M
Andres Iniesta
CG: 13 **SD:** 61

M
Anderson Deco
CG: 27 **SD:** 59

F
Samuel Eto'o
CG: 34 **SR:** 116

F
Ronaldinho
CG: 27 **SR:** 149

MONTHLY POINTS TALLY

Month	Points	%
AUGUST	1	33%
SEPTEMBER	7	58%
OCTOBER	11	73%
NOVEMBER	9	100%
DECEMBER	12	100%
JANUARY	12	100%
FEBRUARY	6	50%
MARCH	10	67%
APRIL	8	67%
MAY	6	50%

LEAGUE GOALS

	PLAYER	MINS	GOALS	S RATE
1	Eto'o	3018	**26**	116
2	Ronaldinho	2525	**17**	149
3	Larsson	1330	**10**	133
4	Messi	909	**6**	152
5	Giuly	1748	**5**	350
6	Deco	2466	**3**	822
7	Silvinho	1933	**2**	967
8	van Bommel	1556	**2**	778
9	Ezquerro	524	**2**	262
10	Motta	916	**1**	916
11	Puyol	3134	**1**	3134
	Other		**5**	
	TOTAL		**80**	

TOP POINT EARNERS

	PLAYER	GAMES	AV PTS
1	Edmilson	22	**2.68**
2	Silvinho	20	**2.50**
3	van Bommel	12	**2.42**
4	Ronaldinho	27	**2.41**
5	Marquez	19	**2.32**
6	Oleguer	28	**2.32**
7	Puyol	35	**2.31**
8	Valdes	36	**2.28**
9	Eto'o	34	**2.24**
10	Deco	27	**2.15**
	CLUB AVERAGE:		**2.16**

DISCIPLINARY RECORDS

	PLAYER	YELLOW	RED	AVE
1	Edmilson	12	1	**162**
2	Belletti	9	0	**198**
3	Marquez	6	1	**282**
4	Motta	2	1	**305**
5	Deco	7	1	**308**
6	van Bommel	5	0	**311**
7	Silvinho	5	0	**386**
8	Puyol	7	1	**391**
9	Messi	2	0	**454**
10	Van Bronckhorst	3	0	**494**
11	Ronaldinho	5	0	**505**
12	Iniesta	3	0	**563**
13	Valdes	3	0	**1080**
	Other	3	0	
	TOTAL	**72**	**5**	

KEY GOALKEEPER

Victor Valdes

Goals Conceded in the League	28	**Counting Games** League games when player was on pitch for at least 70 minutes	36
Defensive Rating Ave number of mins between League goals conceded while on the pitch	116	**Clean Sheets** In games when player was on pitch for at least 70 minutes	17

KEY PLAYERS - DEFENDERS

Edmilson

Goals Conceded Number of League goals conceded while the player was on the pitch	13	**Clean Sheets** In League games when player was on pitch for at least 70 minutes	13
Defensive Rating Ave number of mins between League goals conceded while on the pitch	163	**Club Defensive Rating** Average number of mins between League goals conceded by the club this season	98

	PLAYER	CON LGE	CLEAN SHEETS	DEF RATE
1	Edmilson	13	13	163 mins
2	Rafael Marquez	17	10	116 mins
3	Silvinho	17	11	114 mins
4	Carlos Puyol	28	16	112 mins

KEY PLAYERS - MIDFIELDERS

Mark van Bommel

Goals in the League	2	**Contribution to Attacking Power** Average number of minutes between League team goals while on pitch	42
Defensive Rating Average number of mins between League goals conceded while on the pitch	156	**Scoring Difference** Defensive Rating minus Contribution to Attacking Power	114

	PLAYER	LGE GOALS	DEF RATE	POWER	SCORE DIFF
1	Mark van Bommel	2	156	42	114 mins
2	Xavi Hernandez	0	101	36	65 mins
3	Andres Iniesta	0	106	45	61 mins
4	Anderson Deco	3	103	44	59 mins

KEY PLAYERS - GOALSCORERS

Samuel Eto'o

Goals in the League	26	**Player Strike Rate** Average number of minutes between League goals scored by player	116
Contribution to Attacking Power Average number of minutes between League team goals while on pitch	44	**Club Strike Rate** Average number of minutes between League goals scored by club	43

	PLAYER	LGE GOALS	POWER	STRIKE RATE
1	Samuel Eto'o	26	44	116 mins
2	Henrik Larsson*	10	42	133 mins
3	Ronaldinho	17	39	149 mins
4	Mark van Bommel	2	42	778 mins

Ronaldinho is congratulated by his team mates

SQUAD APPEARANCES

Match	1	2	3	4	5	6	7	8	9	10	11	12	13	14	15	16	17	18	19	20	21	22	23	24	25
Venue	A	H	A	A	H	A	H	H	A	A	H	H	H	H	A	A	H	H	A	A	H	A	H	A	H
Competition	L	L	C	L	L	L	C	L	L	C	L	L	L	C	L	L	C	L	L	C	L	L	L	L	L
Result	D	W	W	L	D	W	W	D	D	D	W	W	W	W	W	W	W	W	W	W	W	W	W	W	W

Match	26	27	28	29	30	31	32	33	34	35	36	37	38	39	40	41	42	43	44	45	46	47	48	49	50	51
Venue	H	A	H	A	H	A	A	H	H	A	A	H	A	A	H	H	A	H	A	H	H	A	H	A	H	A
Competition	L	L	L	L	L	C	L	L	C	L	L	L	L	C	L	C	L	L	C	C	L	L	L	L	C	L
Result	W	W	L	L	W	W	W	W	D	L	W	W	D	D	D	W	D	W	W	D	W	W	W	L	W	L

Goalkeepers
Albert Jorquera
Victor Valdes

Defenders
Juliano Belletti
Edmilson
Rafael Marquez
Presas Oleguer
Carlos Puyol
Sergio Rodri
Silvinho

Midfielders
Anderson Deco
Garcia Gabri
Ludovic Giuly
Jordi Gomez
Andres Iniesta
Lionel Messi
El Diario Montanes
Thiago Motta
Olmo
Andrea Orlandi
Ludovic Sylvestre
Mark van Bommel
Giov Van Bronckhorst
Xavi Hernandez

Forwards
Hidalgo Cristian
Samuel Eto'o
Santiago Ezquerro
Henrik Larsson
Maxi Lopez
Ronaldinho

KEY: ■ On all match ■ On bench
⏮ Subbed or sent off (Counting game)
« Subbed or sent off (playing less than 70 minutes)
⏭ Subbed on from bench (Counting Game)
» Subbed on (playing less than 70 minutes)
» Subbed on and then subbed or sent off (Counting Game)
» Subbed on and then subbed or sent off (playing less than 70 minutes)
□ Not in 16

REAL MADRID

Final Position: **2nd**

KEY: ☐ Won ☐ Drawn ☐ Lost

							Attendance
1	sppr1	Cadiz	A	W	2-1	Ronaldo 3; Raul 84	22,000
2	sppr1	Celta Vigo	H	L	2-3	Ronaldo 36 pen; Baptista 43	80,000
3	ecgpf	Lyon	A	L	0-3		40,000
4	sppr1	Espanyol	A	L	0-1		39,000
5	sppr1	Athl Bilbao	H	W	3-1	Robinho 53; Raul 64,68	70,000
6	sppr1	Alaves	A	W	3-0	Ronaldo 60,83; Guti 90	14,596
7	ecgpf	Olympiakos	H	W	2-1	Raul 9; Soldado 86	52,000
8	sppr1	Mallorca	H	W	4-0	Ronaldo 32; Roberto Carlos 44,65; Baptista 78	72,140
9	sppr1	Atl Madrid	A	W	3-0	Ronaldo 9 pen,61; Perea 90 og	56,000
10	ecgpf	Rosenborg BK	H	W	4-1	Woodgate 48; Raul 52; Helguera 68; Beckham 82	69,053
11	sppr1	Valencia	H	L	1-2	Raul 37	77,500
12	sppr1	Deportivo	A	L	1-3	Raul 86	35,000
13	sppr1	Real Betis	A	W	2-0	Robinho 30; Mejia 80	35,000
14	ecgpf	Rosenborg BK	A	W	2-0	Dorsin 26 og; Guti 41	20,122
15	sppr1	Real Zaragoza	H	W	1-0	Roberto Carlos 79 pen	82,000
16	sppr1	Barcelona	H	L	0-3		80,000
17	ecgpf	Lyon	H	D	1-1	Guti 41	59,000
18	sppr1	Real Sociedad	A	D	2-2	Raul Bravo 87; Zidane 88	23,292
19	sppr1	Getafe	H	W	1-0	Ronaldo 17	72,000
20	ecgpf	Olympiakos	A	L	1-2	Sergio 7	31,456
21	sppr1	Malaga	A	W	2-0	Sergio 34; Robinho 38	23,000
22	sppr1	Osasuna	H	D	1-1	Soldado 84	66,110
23	sppr1	R Santander	H	L	1-2	Ronaldo 68	56,210
24	sppr1	Villarreal	A	D	0-0		20,000
25	sppr1	Seville	H	W	4-2	Guti 7; Zidane 57 pen,60,90	58,321
26	sppr1	Cadiz	H	W	3-1	Roberto Carlos 68; Beckham 71; Robinho 83	60,000
27	sppr1	Celta Vigo	A	W	2-1	Robinho 17; Cicinho 57	26,000
28	sppr1	Espanyol	H	W	4-0	Guti 14; Zidane 43,51; Ronaldo 45	72,043
29	sppr1	Athl Bilbao	A	W	2-0	Robinho 5; Raul Bravo 90	40,000
30	sppr1	Alaves	H	W	3-0	Guti 6; Robinho 11; Cicinho 78	69,114
31	eclsl1	Arsenal	H	L	0-1		80,000
32	sppr1	Mallorca	A	L	1-2	Sergio 32	23,000
33	sppr1	Atl Madrid	H	W	2-1	Cassano 3; Baptista 40	82,000
34	eclsl2	Arsenal	A	D	0-0		35,487
35	sppr1	Valencia	A	D	0-0		51,000
36	sppr1	Real Betis	H	D	0-0		72,000
37	sppr1	Real Zaragoza	A	D	1-1	Ronaldo 90	30,000
38	sppr1	Deportivo	H	W	4-0	Hector 9 og; Ronaldo 37; Sergio 60; Baptista 83	70,000
39	sppr1	Barcelona	A	D	1-1	Ronaldo 37	95,000
40	sppr1	Real Sociedad	H	D	1-1	Ronaldo 26	70,000
41	sppr1	Getafe	A	D	1-1	Baptista 61	14,000
42	sppr1	Malaga	H	W	2-1	Zidane 77 pen; Sergio 90	70,000
43	sppr1	Osasuna	A	W	1-0	Baptista 51 pen	18,000
44	sppr1	R Santander	A	W	3-2	Roberto Carlos 34 pen; Soldado 60; Robinho 70	17,300
45	sppr1	Villarreal	H	D	3-3	Baptista 22,88; Zidane 67	79,497
46	sppr1	Seville	A	L	3-4	Beckham 15,25; Zidane 72	50,000

LEAGUE APPEARANCES, BOOKINGS AND CAPS

	AGE (on 01/07/06)	IN NAMED 18	APPEARANCES	COUNTING GAMES	MINUTES ON PITCH	YELLOW CARDS	RED CARDS	CAPS THIS SEASON	NATIONAL SIDE
Goalkeepers									
Iker Casillas	25	37	37	37	3321	4	1	5	Spain (5)
David Cobeno	24	8	0	0	0	0	0	-	Spain
Jordi Codina	24	1	0	0	0	0	0	-	Spain
Lopez Diego	24	30	2	1	98	0	0	-	Spain
Defenders									
Alvaro Arbeloa	23	0	0	0	0	0	0	-	Spain
Cicinho	26	21	19	15	1435	4	0	5	Brazil (1)
Carlos Diogo	22	33	12	5	582	3	0	-	Uruguay
Ivan Helguera	31	25	20	18	1661	5	0	-	Spain
Alvaro Mejia	24	31	18	14	1437	8	0	-	Spain
Oscar Minambres	25	1	0	0	0	0	0	-	Spain
Francisco Pavon	26	27	10	7	699	1	0	-	Spain
Raul Bravo	25	37	13	4	538	1	0	-	Spain
Roberto Carlos	33	36	36	34	3152	7	1	4	Brazil (1)
Ruben	24	1	0	0	0	0	0	-	Spain
Michel Salgado	30	32	27	23	2255	9	0	-	Spain
Ramos Sergio	25	31	31	29	2704	12	2	-	Spain
Jonathan Woodgate	26	14	9	5	607	5	1	-	England
Midfielders									
Julio Baptista	24	32	32	22	2235	1	1	-	Brazil
David Beckham	31	32	31	26	2526	8	2	7	England (10)
Borja Fernandez	25	0	0	0	0	0	0	-	Spain
Pablo Garcia	29	24	22	11	1377	11	0	-	Uruguay
Thomas Gravesen	30	26	17	4	790	7	1	5	Denmark (19)
Jose Guti	29	33	33	26	2614	11	1	-	Spain
David Iglesias	21	1	0	0	0	0	0	-	Spain
Javi Garcia	19	1	0	0	0	0	0	-	Spain
Jose Jurado	20	9	3	0	21	0	0	-	Spain
Roberto Soldado	21	16	11	0	310	1	0	-	Spain
Marcos Ramiro Teba	20	1	0	0	0	0	0	-	Spain
Zinedine Zidane	34	30	29	23	2180	5	0	8	France (8)
Forwards									
Torres David Barral	23	0	0	0	0	0	0	-	Spain
Antonio Cassano	23	18	12	1	389	1	0	-	Italy
Ruben De la Red	21	8	3	0	28	0	0	-	Spain
Michael Owen	26	1	0	0	0	0	0	6	England (10)
Javier Portillo	24	1	0	0	0	0	0	-	Spain
Raul	29	27	26	17	1803	0	0	7	Spain (5)
Robinho	22	37	37	26	2635	5	0	6	Brazil (1)
Ronaldo	29	23	23	18	1798	1	0	4	Brazil (1)

TEAM OF THE SEASON

(G) Iker Casillas CG: 37 DR: 87

(D) Michel Salgado CG: 23 DR: 94

(D) Cicinho CG: 15 DR: 90

(D) Ramos Sergio CG: 29 DR: 85

(D) Ivan Helguera CG: 18 DR: 83

(M) Jose Guti CG: 26 SD: 45

(M) David Beckham CG: 26 SD: 26

(M) Julio Baptista CG: 22 SD: 40

(M) Zinedine Zidane CG: 23 SD: 27

(F) Ronaldo CG: 18 SR: 128

(F) Robinho CG: 26 SR: 329

MONTHLY POINTS TALLY

AUGUST	3	100%
SEPTEMBER	6	50%
OCTOBER	9	60%
NOVEMBER	4	44%
DECEMBER	7	58%
JANUARY	10	83%
FEBRUARY	9	75%
MARCH	9	60%
APRIL	9	60%
MAY	4	44%

LEAGUE GOALS

	PLAYER	MINS	GOALS	S RATE
1	Ronaldo	1798	**14**	128
2	Zidane	2180	**9**	242
3	Baptista	2235	**8**	279
4	Robinho	2635	**8**	329
5	Raul	1803	**5**	361
6	Roberto Carlos	3152	**5**	630
7	Guti	2614	**4**	654
8	Beckham	2526	**3**	842
9	Sergio	2704	**3**	901
10	Raul Bravo	538	**2**	269
11	Soldado	310	**2**	155
12	Cicinho	1435	**2**	718
13	Mejia	1437	**1**	1437
	Other		**4**	
	TOTAL		**70**	

TOP POINT EARNERS

	PLAYER	GAMES	AV PTS
1	Garcia, P	12	**2.17**
2	Beckham	26	**2.04**
3	Guti	26	**2.00**
4	Salgado	23	**1.96**
5	Roberto Carlos	34	**1.88**
6	Mejia	14	**1.86**
7	Baptista	22	**1.86**
8	Robinho	26	**1.85**
9	Helguera	18	**1.83**
10	Ronaldo	18	**1.83**
	CLUB AVERAGE:		**1.84**

DISCIPLINARY RECORDS

	PLAYER	YELLOW	RED	AVE
1	Gravesen	7	1	**98**
2	Woodgate	5	1	**101**
3	Garcia, P	11	0	**125**
4	Mejia	8	0	**179**
5	Sergio	12	2	**193**
6	Diogo	3	0	**194**
7	Guti	11	1	**217**
8	Salgado	9	0	**250**
9	Beckham	8	2	**252**
10	Helguera	5	0	**332**
11	Cicinho	4	0	**358**
12	Roberto Carlos	7	1	**394**
13	Zidane	5	0	**436**
	Other	13	2	
	TOTAL	**108**	**10**	

EY GOALKEEPER

ker Casillas

Goals Conceded in the League	38	**Counting Games** League games when player was on pitch for at least 70 minutes	37
Defensive Rating Ave number of mins between League goals conceded while on the pitch	87	**Clean Sheets** In games when player was on pitch for at least 70 minutes	15

KEY PLAYERS - GOALSCORERS

Ronaldo

Goals in the League	14	**Player Strike Rate** Average number of minutes between League goals scored by player	128
Contribution to Attacking Power Average number of minutes between League team goals while on pitch	49	**Club Strike Rate** Average number of minutes between League goals scored by club	49

	PLAYER	LGE GOALS	POWER	STRIKE RATE
1	Ronaldo	14	49	128 mins
2	Zinedine Zidane	9	46	242 mins
3	Julio Baptista	8	49	279 mins
4	Robson de Souza Robinho	8	52	329 mins

EY PLAYERS - DEFENDERS

Michel Salgado

Goals Conceded Number of League goals conceded while the player was on the pitch	24	**Clean Sheets** In League games when player was on pitch for at least 70 minutes	12
Defensive Rating Ave number of mins between League goals conceded while on the pitch	94	**Club Defensive Rating** Average number of mins between League goals conceded by the club this season	86

	PLAYER	CON LGE	CLEAN SHEETS	DEF RATE
1	Michel Salgado	24	12	94 mins
2	Cicinho	16	5	90 mins
3	Ramos Sergio	32	12	85 mins
4	Ivan Helguera	20	8	83 mins

David Beckham and Ronaldo

EY PLAYERS - MIDFIELDERS

Jose Guti

Goals in the League	4	**Contribution to Attacking Power** Average number of minutes between League team goals while on pitch	45
Defensive Rating Average number of mins between League goals conceded while on the pitch	90	**Scoring Difference** Defensive Rating minus Contribution to Attacking Power	45

	PLAYER	LGE GOALS	DEF RATE	POWER	SCORE DIFF
1	Jose Guti	4	90	45	45 mins
2	Julio Baptista	8	89	49	40 mins
3	Zinedine Zidane	9	73	46	27 mins
4	David Beckham	93	70	44	26 mins

SQUAD APPEARANCES

atch	1	2	3	4	5	6	7	8	9	10	11	12	13	14	15	16	17	18	19	20	21	22	23	24	25	26	27	28	29	30	31	32	33	34	35	36	37	38	39	40	41	42	43	44	45	46
enue	A	H	A	A	H	A	H	H	A	H	H	A	A	A	H	H	H	A	H	A	A	H	H	A	H	H	A	H	A	H	H	A	H	A	A	H	A	H	A	H	A	H	A	A	H	A
ompetition	L	L	C	L	L	L	C	L	L	C	L	L	L	C	L	L	C	L	L	C	L	L	L	L	L	L	L	L	L	L	C	L	L	C	L	L	L	L	L	L	L	L	L	L	L	L
esult	W	L	L	L	W	W	W	W	W	W	L	L	W	W	W	L	D	D	W	L	W	D	L	D	W	W	W	W	W	W	L	L	W	D	D	D	D	W	D	D	D	W	W	W	D	L

oalkeepers
ker Casillas
avid Cobeno
opez Diego

efenders
icinho
arlos Diogo
van Helguera
lvaro Mejia
rancisco Pavon
aul Bravo
oberto Carlos
ichel Salgado
amos Sergio
onathan Woodgate

idfielders
ulio Baptista
avid Beckham
ablo Garcia
homas Gravesen
ose Guti
avid Iglesias
ose Jurado
oberto Soldado
arcos Ramiro Teba
inedine Zidane

orwards
orres David Barral
ntonio Cassano
uben De la Red
ichael Owen
avier Portillo
aul
obson Robinho
onaldo

KEY: On all match | On bench | Subbed or sent off (Counting game) | Subbed or sent off (playing less than 70 minutes) | Subbed on from bench (Counting Game) | Subbed on (playing less than 70 minutes) | Subbed on and then subbed or sent off (Counting Game) | Subbed on and then subbed or sent off (playing less than 70 minutes) | Not in 16

VALENCIA

Final Position: **3rd**

KEY: Won Drawn Lost

	Comp	Opponent			Score	Scorers	Attendance
1	etsfl2	**Roda JC Kerk**	A	D	0-0		8,000
2	etfl1	**Hamburg**	A	L	0-1		48,000
3	etfl2	**Hamburg**	H	D	0-0		32,000
4	sppr1	**Real Betis**	H	W	1-0	Aimar 52	43,000
5	sppr1	**Real Zaragoza**	A	D	2-2	Angulo 2; Villa 82	30,000
6	sppr1	**Deportivo**	H	D	2-2	Villa 51; Miguel 80	44,000
7	sppr1	**Barcelona**	A	D	2-2	Villa 53 pen,54	80,000
8	sppr1	**Real Sociedad**	H	W	2-1	Aimar 34; Villa 46	55,000
9	sppr1	**Getafe**	A	L	1-2	Villa 30	13,000
10	sppr1	**Malaga**	H	W	2-1	Ayala 10; Vicente 67	40,000
11	sppr1	**Real Madrid**	A	W	2-1	Baraja 22; Villa 39 pen	77,500
12	sppr1	**Seville**	H	L	0-2		39,000
13	sppr1	**R Santander**	H	D	1-1	Albelda 13	40,000
14	sppr1	**Villarreal**	A	L	0-1		21,000
15	sppr1	**Cadiz**	A	W	1-0	Vicente 81	20,000
16	sppr1	**Celta Vigo**	H	W	2-0	Villa 74; Aurelio 78	38,000
17	sppr1	**Espanyol**	A	W	3-1	Angulo 15; Villa 43; Aimar 61	25,000
18	sppr1	**Athl Bilbao**	H	D	1-1	Vicente 73	48,000
19	sppr1	**Alaves**	A	W	1-0	Albiol 7	14,000
20	sppr1	**Mallorca**	H	W	3-0	Albelda 46; Villa 65; Aurelio 81	40,000
21	sppr1	**Atl Madrid**	A	D	0-0		35,000
22	sppr1	**Osasuna**	H	W	2-0	Regueiro 45; Villa 52	40,000
23	sppr1	**Real Betis**	A	W	2-0	Villa 35,79	35,000
24	sppr1	**Real Zaragoza**	H	D	2-2	Kluivert 83; Aimar 89	40,000
25	sppr1	**Deportivo**	A	W	1-0	Villa 22	31,400
26	sppr1	**Barcelona**	H	W	1-0	Villa 44	50,000
27	sppr1	**Real Sociedad**	A	W	2-1	Regueiro 68,79	22,000
28	sppr1	**Getafe**	H	D	1-1	Navarro 78	35,000
29	sppr1	**Malaga**	A	D	0-0		22,000
30	sppr1	**Real Madrid**	H	D	0-0		51,000
31	sppr1	**R Santander**	A	L	1-2	Villa 75	13,800
32	sppr1	**Villarreal**	H	D	1-1	Baraja 37	40,000
33	sppr1	**Seville**	A	L	0-1		44,000
34	sppr1	**Cadiz**	H	W	5-3	Villa 1,64; Angulo 33,56; Navarro 35	40,000
35	sppr1	**Celta Vigo**	A	W	1-0	Angulo 30	16,000
36	sppr1	**Espanyol**	H	W	4-0	Villa 40 pen; Ayala 67; Mista 71; Baraja 86	40,000
37	sppr1	**Athl Bilbao**	A	W	3-0	Villa 82,84,87	40,000
38	sppr1	**Alaves**	H	W	3-0	Baraja 23; Aimar 32; Villa 49	40,000
39	sppr1	**Mallorca**	A	L	1-2	Angulo 16	18,000
40	sppr1	**Atl Madrid**	H	D	1-1	Villa 11 pen	50,000
41	sppr1	**Osasuna**	A	L	1-2	Villa 90	19,300

LEAGUE APPEARANCES, BOOKINGS AND CAPS

	AGE (on 01/07/06)	IN NAMED 18	APPEARANCES	COUNTING GAMES	MINUTES ON PITCH	YELLOW CARDS	RED CARDS	CAPS THIS SEASON	NATIONAL SIDE
Goalkeepers									
Ludovic Butelle	23	32	1	1	90	0	0	-	France
Santiago Canizares	36	36	36	36	3240	5	0	-	Spain
Juan Luis Mora	32	8	1	1	90	0	0	-	Spain
Defenders									
Fabio Aurelio	26	27	24	9	1088	3	0	-	Brazil
Roberto Ayala	33	25	23	22	1993	4	1	7	Argentina (9)
Marco Caneira	27	9	5	3	388	1	0	7	Portugal (7)
Amadeo Carboni	41	21	5	3	313	0	0	-	Italy
Curro Torres	29	16	4	1	97	0	0	-	Spain
Carlos Marchena	27	30	24	18	1817	7	1	4	Spain (5)
Luis Garcia Miguel	26	37	32	32	2834	0	0	3	Portugal (7)
Emiliano Moretti	25	35	33	31	2896	5	0	-	Italy
David Navarro	26	21	8	7	651	3	0	-	Spain
Midfielders									
Pablo Aimar	26	33	32	24	2435	2	0	4	Argentina (9)
David Albelda	28	32	32	32	2837	16	1	3	Spain (5)
Raul Albiol	20	31	27	27	2430	5	0	-	Spain
Ruben Baraja	30	32	31	27	2541	5	1	3	Spain (5)
Gonzalo De l. Santos	29	1	0	0	0	0	0	-	Uruguay
Edu	28	9	6	1	198	2	0	-	Brazil
Juanlu	22	0	0	0	0	0	0	-	Spain
Pedro Lopez	22	14	5	1	114	0	0	-	Spain
D. Pablo Hernandez	21	3	1	0	19	0	0	-	Spain
Mario Regueiro	27	31	24	15	1623	2	0	-	Uruguay
Francisco Rufete	29	26	19	5	752	1	0	-	Spain
Hugo Viana	23	32	20	4	651	2	0	3	Portugal (7)
Rodriguez Vicente	24	21	21	17	1620	2	0	7	Spain (5)
Forwards									
Miguel Angulo	29	36	32	22	2343	8	1	-	Spain
Marco Di Vaio	29	8	5	0	161	0	0	-	Italy
Patrick Kluivert	30	11	10	0	203	2	0	-	Holland
Mista	27	31	29	6	1049	3	0	1	Spain (5)
David Villa	24	37	37	34	3004	3	1	4	Spain (5)

TEAM OF THE SEASON

G — Santiago Canizares CG: 36 DR: 112

D — Luis Garcia Miguel CG: 32 DR: 123

D — Emiliano Moretti CG: 31 DR: 111

D — Roberto Ayala CG: 22 DR: 95

D — Carlos Marchena CG: 18 DR: 91

M — Mario Regueiro CG: 15 SD: 77

M — Raul Albiol CG: 27 SD: 74

M — David Albelda CG: 32 SD: 54

M — Pablo Aimar CG: 24 SD: 44

F — David Villa CG: 34 SR: 120

F — Miguel Angulo CG: 22 SR: 391

MONTHLY POINTS TALLY

Month	Points	%
AUGUST	3	100%
SEPTEMBER	6	50%
OCTOBER	9	60%
NOVEMBER	4	44%
DECEMBER	7	58%
JANUARY	10	83%
FEBRUARY	9	75%
MARCH	9	60%
APRIL	9	60%
MAY	4	44%

LEAGUE GOALS

	PLAYER	MINS	GOALS	S RATE
1	Villa	3004	**25**	120
2	Angulo	2343	**6**	391
3	Aimar	2435	**5**	487
4	Baraja	2541	**4**	635
5	Vicente	1620	**3**	540
6	Regueiro	1623	**3**	541
7	Aurelio	1088	**2**	544
8	Albelda	2837	**2**	1419
9	Ayala	1993	**2**	997
10	Navarro	651	**2**	326
11	Albiol	2430	**1**	2430
12	Miguel	2834	**1**	2834
13	Mista	1049	**1**	1049
	Other		**1**	
	TOTAL		**58**	

TOP POINT EARNERS

	PLAYER	GAMES	AV PTS
1	Angulo	22	**2.09**
2	Albelda	32	**2.00**
3	Regueiro	15	**2.00**
4	Moretti	31	**1.97**
5	Miguel	32	**1.91**
6	Canizares	36	**1.89**
7	Vicente	17	**1.88**
8	Baraja	27	**1.81**
9	Albiol	27	**1.81**
10	Aimar	24	**1.79**
	CLUB AVERAGE:		**1.82**

DISCIPLINARY RECORDS

	PLAYER	YELLOW	RED	AVE
1	Albelda	16	1	**166**
2	Navarro	3	0	**217**
3	Marchena	7	1	**227**
4	Angulo	8	1	**260**
5	Viana	2	0	**325**
6	Mista	3	0	**349**
7	Aurelio	3	0	**362**
8	Ayala	4	1	**398**
9	Baraja	5	1	**423**
10	Albiol	5	0	**486**
11	Moretti	5	0	**579**
12	Canizares	5	0	**648**
13	Villa	3	1	**751**
	Other	7	0	
	TOTAL	**76**	**6**	

KEY GOALKEEPER

Santiago Canizares

Goals Conceded in the League	29	**Counting Games** League games when player was on pitch for at least 70 minutes	36
Defensive Rating Ave number of mins between League goals conceded while on the pitch	112	**Clean Sheets** In games when player was on pitch for at least 70 minutes	16

KEY PLAYERS - DEFENDERS

Luis Garcia Miguel

Goals Conceded Number of League goals conceded while the player was on the pitch	23	**Clean Sheets** In League games when player was on pitch for at least 70 minutes	15
Defensive Rating Ave number of mins between League goals conceded while on the pitch	123	**Club Defensive Rating** Average number of mins between League goals conceded by the club this season	104

	PLAYER	CON LGE	CLEAN SHEETS	DEF RATE
1	Luis Garcia Miguel	23	15	123 mins
2	Emiliano Moretti	26	15	111 mins
3	Roberto Ayala	21	7	95 mins
4	Carlos Marchena	20	8	91 mins

KEY PLAYERS - MIDFIELDERS

Mario Regueiro

Goals in the League	3	**Contribution to Attacking Power** Average number of minutes between League team goals while on pitch	58
Defensive Rating Average number of mins between League goals conceded while on the pitch	135	**Scoring Difference** Defensive Rating minus Contribution to Attacking Power	77

	PLAYER	LGE GOALS	DEF RATE	POWER	SCORE DIFF
1	Mario Regueiro	3	135	58	77 mins
2	Raul Albiol	1	135	61	74 mins
3	David Albelda	2	113	59	54 mins
4	Pablo Aimar	5	101	57	44 mins

KEY PLAYERS - GOALSCORERS

David Villa

Goals in the League	25	**Player Strike Rate** Average number of minutes between League goals scored by player	120
Contribution to Attacking Power Average number of minutes between League team goals while on pitch	59	**Club Strike Rate** Average number of minutes between League goals scored by club	59

	PLAYER	LGE GOALS	POWER	STRIKE RATE
1	David Villa	25	59	120 mins
2	Miguel Angulo	6	54	391 mins
3	Pablo Aimar	5	57	487 mins
4	Rodriguez Guillen Vicente	3	65	540 mins

David Villa and David Albelda

SQUAD APPEARANCES

Match	1	2	3	4	5	6	7	8	9	10	11	12	13	14	15	16	17	18	19	20	21	22	23	24	25	26	27	28	29	30	31	32	33	34	35	36	37	38	39	40	41
Venue	A	A	H	H	A	H	A	H	A	H	A	H	H	A	A	H	A	H	A	H	A	H	A	H	A	H	A	H	A	H	A	H	A	H	A	H	A	H	A	H	A
Competition	O	O	O	L	L	L	L	L	L	L	L	L	L	L	L	L	L	L	L	L	L	L	L	L	L	L	L	L	L	L	L	L	L	L	L	L	L	L	L	L	L
Result	D	L	D	W	D	D	D	W	L	W	W	L	D	L	W	W	W	D	W	W	D	W	W	D	W	W	W	D	D	D	L	D	L	W	W	W	W	W	L	D	L

Goalkeepers
Ludovic Butelle
Santiago Canizares
Juan Luis Mora

Defenders
Fabio Aurelio
Roberto Ayala
Marco Caneira
Amadeo Carboni
Curro Torres
Carlos Marchena
Luis Garcia Miguel
Emiliano Moretti
David Navarro

Midfielders
Pablo Aimar
David Albelda
Raul Albiol
Ruben Baraja
Gonzalo De los Santos
Edu
Pedro Lopez
Mario Regueiro
Francisco Rufete
Hugo Viana
Rodriguez Vicente

Forwards
Miguel Angulo
Marco Di Vaio
Patrick Kluivert
Mista
David Villa

KEY: ■ On all match | ■ On bench | ⏮ Subbed or sent off (Counting game) | « Subbed or sent off (playing less than 70 minutes) | ⏭ Subbed on from bench (Counting Game) | » Subbed on (playing less than 70 minutes) | Subbed on and then subbed or sent off (Counting Game) | Subbed on and then subbed or sent off (playing less than 70 minutes) | □ Not in 16

OSASUNA

Final Position: **4th**

KEY: ☐Won ☐Drawn ☐Lost

						Attendance
1	sppr1	**Villarreal**	H	W	2-1	Romeo 27,62	14,000
2	sppr1	**Real Betis**	A	L	0-1		40,000
3	uc1rl1	**Rennes**	A	L	1-3	Milosevic 50	12,000
4	sppr1	**Seville**	H	W	1-0	David Lopez 62	13,712
5	sppr1	**Real Zaragoza**	A	L	1-3	Delporte 89	28,000
6	sppr1	**Cadiz**	H	W	2-0	Lopez 27; Moha 88	13,700
7	uc1rl2	**Rennes**	H	D	0-0		17,000
8	sppr1	**Deportivo**	A	W	1-0	Munoz 19	23,700
9	sppr1	**Celta Vigo**	H	W	2-0	Milosevic 48; Webo 84	14,500
10	sppr1	**Barcelona**	A	L	0-3		84,000
11	sppr1	**Athl Bilbao**	H	W	3-2	Garcia, R 44; Milosevic 61; Webo 92	15,500
12	sppr1	**Espanyol**	H	W	2-0	David Lopez 29; Munoz 71	50,000
13	sppr1	**Real Sociedad**	A	W	2-1	Garcia, R 34; Cuellar 68	25,800
14	sppr1	**Getafe**	A	D	0-0		14,000
15	sppr1	**Alaves**	H	W	3-2	Milosevic 60; Punal 72 pen; Moha 84	15,000
16	sppr1	**Malaga**	A	W	2-1	Webo 23; Valdo 41	22,000
17	sppr1	**Mallorca**	H	W	1-0	Webo 5	14,500
18	sppr1	**Real Madrid**	A	D	1-1	Milosevic 77	66,110
19	sppr1	**Atl Madrid**	H	W	2-1	Garcia, R 29; Romeo 34	14,000
20	sppr1	**R Santander**	H	D	1-1	Delporte 29	15,000
21	sppr1	**Valencia**	A	L	0-2		40,000
22	sppr1	**Villarreal**	A	L	1-2	Garcia, R 27	20,000
23	sppr1	**Real Betis**	H	L	0-2		15,500
24	sppr1	**Seville**	A	W	1-0	Milosevic 60	37,000
25	sppr1	**Real Zaragoza**	H	D	1-1	Milosevic 3	17,000
26	sppr1	**Cadiz**	A	W	3-1	Milosevic 34; Lopez 36; Garcia, R 88	20,000
27	sppr1	**Deportivo**	H	L	1-2	Romeo 42	14,000
28	sppr1	**Celta Vigo**	A	L	0-2		16,677
29	sppr1	**Barcelona**	H	W	2-1	Valdo 20; Punal 59 pen	18,000
30	sppr1	**Espanyol**	A	W	4-2	Lopez 24; Webo 37; Milosevic 38; Munoz 79	18,000
31	sppr1	**Real Sociedad**	H	W	2-0	Munoz 5; Punal 89	17,000
32	sppr1	**Athl Bilbao**	A	L	0-1		40,000
33	sppr1	**Getafe**	H	L	0-4		18,700
34	sppr1	**Alaves**	A	W	2-1	Webo 14; Milosevic 56	16,843
35	sppr1	**Malaga**	H	D	1-1	Punal 30 pen	16,611
36	sppr1	**Mallorca**	A	W	1-0	Delporte 90	15,000
37	sppr1	**Real Madrid**	H	L	0-1		18,000
38	sppr1	**Atl Madrid**	A	W	1-0	Munoz 15	20,000
39	sppr1	**R Santander**	A	L	1-2	Milosevic 56	14,300
40	sppr1	**Valencia**	H	W	2-1	Milosevic 46; Lopez 49	19,300

LEAGUE APPEARANCES, BOOKINGS AND CAPS

	AGE (on 01/07/06)	IN NAMED 18	APPEARANCES	COUNTING GAMES	MINUTES ON PITCH	YELLOW CARDS	RED CARDS	CAPS THIS SEASON	NATIONAL SIDE
Goalkeepers									
Juantxo Elia	36	37	7	7	630	2	0	-	Spain
Gregorio Linares	20	1	0	0	0	0	0	-	Spain
Lopez Ricardo	34	37	31	31	2790	5	0	-	Spain
Roberto	21	1	0	0	0	0	0	-	Spain
Defenders									
Rafael Clavero	29	30	21	19	1738	8	2	-	Spain
Enrique Corrales	24	27	19	18	1651	9	0	-	Spain
Cesar Cruchaga	32	33	20	12	1213	2	0	-	Spain
Carlos Cuellar	34	33	29	27	2452	6	0	-	Spain
Javier Flano	21	32	31	30	2723	6	0	-	Spain
Miguel Flano	21	23	12	8	871	2	1	-	Spain
Jose Izquierdo	25	19	7	5	577	2	0	-	Spain
Jose Romero Josetxo	31	32	29	26	2450	8	0	-	Spain
Antonio Lopez	24	5	5	4	385	0	0	-	Spain
Juan Ortiz	24	19	6	1	200	1	0	-	Spain
Midfielders									
David Lopez	23	31	29	21	2137	1	0	-	Spain
Ludovic Delporte	26	31	28	16	1886	9	1	-	Spain
Francisco Moreno	22	12	8	1	277	1	0	-	Spain
Raul Garcia	19	34	33	28	2489	7	0	-	Spain
El Yaagoubi Moha	28	32	27	10	1354	8	0	-	Morocco
Inaki Munoz	28	34	30	15	1603	6	1	-	Spain
Francisco Punal	30	34	34	30	2784	12	1	-	Spain
Marcelo Sosa	28	20	11	3	422	4	0	-	Uruguay
Valmiro Valdo	25	20	19	10	1090	2	0	-	Brazil
Forwards									
Gorka Brit	28	13	4	0	71	0	0	-	Spain
Savo Milosevic	32	33	32	25	2541	3	0	9	Serbia & Mont (44)
Bernardo Romeo	28	30	23	8	1361	6	0	-	Argentina
Pierre Webo	24	33	31	14	1765	4	0	9	Cameroon (15)

TEAM OF THE SEASON

G — Lopez Ricardo — CG: 31 DR: 78

D — Rafael Clavero — CG: 19 DR: 102

D — Javier Flano — CG: 30 DR: 83

D — Carlos Cuellar — CG: 27 DR: 82

D — Jose Romero Josetxo — CG: 26 DR: 74

M — David Lopez — CG: 21 SD: 19

M — Ludovic Delporte — CG: 16 SD: 13

M — Raul Garcia — CG: 28 SD: 7

M — Inaki Munoz — CG: 15 SD: 6

F — Savo Milosevic — CG: 25 SR: 231

F — Pierre Webo — CG: 14 SR: 294

MONTHLY POINTS TALLY

AUGUST	3	100%
SEPTEMBER	6	50%
OCTOBER	12	80%
NOVEMBER	7	78%
DECEMBER	10	83%
JANUARY	1	8%
FEBRUARY	7	58%
MARCH	9	60%
APRIL	7	47%
MAY	6	67%

LEAGUE GOALS

	PLAYER	MINS	GOALS	S RATE
1	Milosevic	2541	11	231
2	Webo	1765	6	294
3	Munoz	1603	5	321
4	Garcia, R	2489	5	498
5	Romeo	1361	4	340
6	Punal	2784	4	696
7	Delporte	1886	3	629
8	Valdo	1090	2	545
9	Lopez	385	2	193
10	Moha	1354	2	677
11	David Lopez	2137	2	1069
12	Cuellar	2452	1	2452
	Other		2	
	TOTAL		49	

TOP POINT EARNERS

	PLAYER	GAMES	AV PTS
1	Clavero	19	2.11
2	Milosevic	25	2.04
3	Cuellar	27	2.04
4	Flano, J	30	1.97
5	David Lopez	21	1.81
6	Ricardo	31	1.77
7	Munoz	15	1.73
8	Punal	30	1.70
9	Delporte	16	1.69
10	Garcia, R	28	1.68
	CLUB AVERAGE:		1.79

DISCIPLINARY RECORDS

	PLAYER	YELLOW	RED	AVE
1	Moha	8	0	169
2	Clavero	8	2	173
3	Corrales	9	0	183
4	Delporte	9	1	188
5	Punal	12	1	214
6	Romeo	6	0	226
7	Munoz	6	1	229
8	Izquierdo	2	0	288
9	Flano, M	2	1	290
10	Josetxo	8	0	306
11	Elia	2	0	315
12	Garcia, R	7	0	355
13	Cuellar	6	0	408
	Other	23	0	
	TOTAL	108	6	

KEY GOALKEEPER

Lopez Ricardo

Goals Conceded in the League	36	**Counting Games** League games when player was on pitch for at least 70 minutes	31
Defensive Rating Ave number of mins between League goals conceded while on the pitch	78	**Clean Sheets** In League games when player was on pitch for at least 70 minutes	9

KEY PLAYERS - DEFENDERS

Rafael Clavero

Goals Conceded Number of League goals conceded while the player was on the pitch	17	**Clean Sheets** In League games when player was on pitch for at least 70 minutes	9
Defensive Rating Ave number of mins between League goals conceded while on the pitch	102	**Club Defensive Rating** Average number of mins between League goals conceded by the club this season	80

	PLAYER	CON LGE	CLEAN SHEETS	DEF RATE
1	Rafael Clavero	17	9	102 mins
2	Javier Flano	33	8	83 mins
3	Carlos Cuellar	30	7	82 mins
4	Jose Romero Josetxo	33	7	74 mins

KEY PLAYERS - MIDFIELDERS

David Lopez

Goals in the League	2	**Contribution to Attacking Power** Average number of minutes between League team goals while on pitch	74
Defensive Rating Average number of mins between League goals conceded while on the pitch	93	**Scoring Difference** Defensive Rating minus Contribution to Attacking Power	19

	PLAYER	LGE GOALS	DEF RATE	POWER	SCORE DIFF
1	David Lopez	2	93	74	19 mins
2	Ludovic Delporte	3	86	73	13 mins
3	Raul Garcia	5	80	73	7 mins
4	Inaki Munoz	5	76	70	6 mins

KEY PLAYERS - GOALSCORERS

Savo Milosevic

Goals in the League	11	**Player Strike Rate** Average number of minutes between League goals scored by player	231
Contribution to Attacking Power Average number of minutes between League team goals while on pitch	65	**Club Strike Rate** Average number of minutes between League goals scored by club	70

	PLAYER	LGE GOALS	POWER	STRIKE RATE
1	Savo Milosevic	11	65	231 mins
2	Pierre Webo	6	74	294 mins
3	Inaki Munoz	5	70	321 mins
4	Raul Garcia	5	73	498 mins

Savo Milosevic

SQUAD APPEARANCES

'atch	1	2	3	4	5	6	7	8	9	10	11	12	13	14	15	16	17	18	19	20	21	22	23	24	25	26	27	28	29	30	31	32	33	34	35	36	37	38	39	40
enue	H	A	A	H	A	H	H	A	H	A	H	H	A	A	H	A	H	A	H	H	A	A	H	A	H	A	H	A	H	A	H	A	H	A	H	A	H	A	A	H
'ompetition	L	L	E	L	L	L	E	L	L	L	L	L	L	L	L	L	L	L	L	L	L	L	L	L	L	L	L	L	L	L	L	L	L	L	L	L	L	L	L	L
esult	W	L	L	W	L	W	D	W	W	L	W	W	W	D	W	W	W	D	W	D	L	L	L	W	D	W	L	L	W	W	W	L	L	W	D	W	L	W	L	W

ioalkeepers
- uantxo Elia
- regorio Linares
- opez Ricardo
- oberto

efenders
- afael Clavero
- nrique Corrales
- esar Cruchaga
- arlos Cuellar
- avier Flano
- liguel Flano
- ose Izquierdo
- ose Romero Josetxo
- ntonio Lopez
- uan Ortiz

lidfielders
- avid Lopez
- udovic Delporte
- rancisco Fran Moreno
- aul Garcia
- l Yaagoubi Moha
- naki Munoz
- rancisco Punal
- larcelo Sosa
- almiro Valdo

orwards
- iorka Brit
- avo Milosevic
- ernardo Romeo
- ierre Webo

KEY: On all match · On bench · Subbed or sent off (Counting game) · Subbed or sent off (playing less than 70 minutes) · Subbed on from bench (Counting Game) · Subbed on (playing less than 70 minutes) · Subbed on and then subbed or sent off (Counting Game) · Subbed on and then subbed or sent off (playing less than 70 minutes) · Not in 16

FC SEVILLE

Final Position: **5th**

KEY: ☐Won ☐Drawn ☐Lost

No	Comp	Opponent	H/A	Res	Score	Scorers	Attendance
1	sppr1	**R Santander**	H	W	1-0	Blanco-Gonzalez 29	42,000
2	sppr1	**Villarreal**	A	D	1-1	Adriano 41	18,000
3	uc1rl1	**Mainz**	H	D	0-0		44,000
4	sppr1	**Osasuna**	A	L	0-1		13,712
5	sppr1	**Cadiz**	H	D	0-0		45,000
6	sppr1	**Celta Vigo**	A	L	1-2	Maresca 54 pen	15,000
7	uc1rl2	**Mainz**	A	W	2-0	Kanoute 8,39	32,500
8	sppr1	**Espanyol**	H	D	1-1	Jarque 90	40,000
9	sppr1	**Athl Bilbao**	A	W	1-0	Daniel Alves 44	32,000
10	sppr1	**Alaves**	H	W	2-0	Adriano 26; Maresca 72	45,000
11	sppr1	**Valencia**	A	W	2-0	Fabiano 20; Ayala 48 og	39,000
12	sppr1	**Mallorca**	A	D	1-1	Blanco-Gonzalez 37	14,000
13	ucgph	**Besiktas**	H	W	3-0	Saviola 64; Kanoute 65,89	38,500
14	sppr1	**Atl Madrid**	H	D	0-0		35,000
15	sppr1	**Real Betis**	H	W	1-0	Maresca 49 pen	41,000
16	ucgph	**Zen Petersburg**	A	L	1-2	Puerta 90	17,000
17	sppr1	**Real Zaragoza**	A	W	2-0	Saviola 58; Daniel Alves 90	28,000
18	ucgph	**Guimaraes**	H	W	3-1	Saviola 10,27; Adriano 39	35,000
19	sppr1	**Deportivo**	H	L	0-2		38,000
20	sppr1	**Barcelona**	A	L	1-2	Kanoute 63	65,000
21	ucgph	**Bolton**	A	D	1-1	Adriano 74	15,623
22	sppr1	**Real Sociedad**	H	W	3-2	Blanco-Gonzalez 76,89; Kanoute 82	35,000
23	sppr1	**Getafe**	A	L	0-1		9,500
24	sppr1	**Malaga**	H	W	3-1	Maresca 33; Adriano 66; Dragutinovic 69	33,000
25	sppr1	**Real Madrid**	A	L	2-4	Fabiano 51; Aitor Ocio 80	58,321
26	sppr1	**R Santander**	A	W	3-2	Kanoute 12; Maresca 48,54 pen	14,609
27	sppr1	**Villarreal**	H	W	2-0	Fabiano 30; Kanoute 58	28,000
28	sppr1	**Osasuna**	H	L	0-1		37,000
29	sppr1	**Cadiz**	A	W	4-0	Saviola 6; Puerta 71; Blanco-Gonzalez 90; Kanoute 90	22,000
30	uc3rl1	**Loko Moscow**	A	W	1-0	Jordi 75	10,223
31	sppr1	**Celta Vigo**	H	W	1-0	Saviola 11	28,000
32	uc3rl2	**Loko Moscow**	H	W	2-0	Maresca 34; Puerta 90	32,000
33	sppr1	**Espanyol**	A	L	0-5		11,500
34	sppr1	**Athl Bilbao**	H	W	2-1	Maresca 17; Kanoute 60	38,000
35	uc4rl1	**Lille**	A	L	0-1		11,009
36	sppr1	**Alaves**	A	L	1-2	Saviola 11	12,831
37	uc4rl2	**Lille**	H	W	2-0	Kanoute 29; Fabiano 45	41,000
38	sppr1	**Mallorca**	H	D	1-1	Saviola 35	35,000
39	sppr1	**Atl Madrid**	A	W	1-0	Puerta 76	45,000
40	sppr1	**Valencia**	H	W	1-0	Jordi 90	44,000
41	ucqfl1	**Zen Petersburg**	H	W	4-1	Saviola 15,80; Marti 56; Adriano 90	28,633
42	sppr1	**Real Betis**	A	L	1-2	Saviola 29	45,000
43	ucqfl2	**Zen Petersburg**	A	D	1-1	Blanco-Gonzalez 66	18,500
44	sppr1	**Real Zaragoza**	H	D	1-1	Maresca 90	27,000
45	sppr1	**Deportivo**	A	D	0-0		24,500
46	ucsfl1	**Schalke**	A	D	0-0		
47	ucsfl2	**Schalke**	H	W	1-0	Puerta 101	45,000
48	sppr1	**Real Sociedad**	A	W	2-1	Navas, J 57; Marti 68 pen	26,600
49	sppr1	**Getafe**	H	W	3-0	Pulido 21 og; Saviola 31; Fabiano 39	25,000
50	sppr1	**Malaga**	A	W	2-0	Renato 17; Sales 89	7,000
51	ucfin	**Middlesbrough**	A	W	4-0	Fabiano 26; Maresca 78,84; Kanoute 89	36,500
52	sppr1	**Barcelona**	H	W	3-2	Daniel Alves 21; Aitor Ocio 24 pen; Blanco-Gonzalez 76	43,000
53	sppr1	**Real Madrid**	H	W	4-3	Navas, J 28; Saviola 30,34; Fabiano 44	50,000

LEAGUE APPEARANCES, BOOKINGS AND CAPS

	AGE (on 01/07/06)	IN NAMED 18	APPEARANCES	COUNTING GAMES	MINUTES ON PITCH	YELLOW CARDS	RED CARDS	CAPS THIS SEASON	NATIONAL SIDE
Goalkeepers									
Antonio Notario Caro	33	35	2	2	180	0	0	-	Spain
Andres Palop	32	37	35	35	3150	2	0	-	Spain
Pablo Vargas	22	1	0	0	0	0	0	-	
Defenders									
Aitor Ocio	29	30	22	17	1653	7	1	-	Spain
Jose Angel Crespo	19	7	3	2	199	1	0	-	Spain
Daniel Alves	23	35	35	33	3070	12	1	-	Brazil
Castedo David	32	36	33	28	2680	8	1	-	Spain
Ivica Dragutinovic	30	24	21	17	1698	6	1	5	Serbia & Mont (44)
Julien Escude	26	18	16	13	1206	2	0	-	France
Javi Navarro	32	26	25	18	1905	9	2	-	Spain
Pablo Alfaro	37	11	3	0	14	0	0	-	Spain
Ruiz Pablo Barrero	25	3	3	1	132	0	0	-	Spain
David Prieto	23	7	4	3	328	0	0	-	Spain
Ramos Sergio	25	1	1	1	90	0	0	-	Spain
Midfielders									
Claro Adriano Correia	21	34	32	22	2378	9	0	-	Spain
Antonio Lopez	26	3	2	1	135	0	0	-	Spain
Diego Capel	18	4	4	0	99	1	0	-	Spain
Jesuli	28	14	6	0	153	0	0	-	Spain
Lopez Jordi	25	31	21	10	1168	5	0	-	Spain
Enzo Maresca	26	29	28	20	2065	6	2	-	Italy
Jose Luis Marti	31	35	33	26	2628	5	0	-	Spain
Antonio Moreno Vera	19	1	0	0	0	0	0	-	Spain
Jesus Navas	20	33	33	28	2753	5	0	-	Spain
Antonio Puerta	21	32	17	5	848	2	0	-	Spain
Renato	27	24	21	12	1381	3	0	2	Brazil (1)
Forwards									
Kepa Blanco-Gonzalez	22	38	25	6	1090	5	1	-	Spain
Luis Fabiano	25	36	25	6	1289	5	0	-	Brazil
Francisco Gallardo	26	3	0	0	0	0	0	-	Spain
Frederic Kanoute	28	32	32	21	2307	3	0	-	Mali
Ariza Makukula	25	1	1	1	90	0	0	-	Portugal
Fernando Sales	28	27	13	5	764	2	0	-	Spain
Javier Saviola	24	31	28	12	1801	2	0	3	Argentina (9)

TEAM OF THE SEASON

G — Andres Palop — CG: 35 DR: 90

D — Javi Navarro — CG: 18 DR: 106

D — Julien Escude — CG: 13 DR: 93

D — Aitor Ocio — CG: 17 DR: 87

D — Daniel Alves — CG: 33 DR: 85

M — Enzo Maresca — CG: 20 SD: 35

M — Jose Luis Marti — CG: 26 SD: 30

M — Renato — CG: 12 SD: 25

M — Claro Adriano Correia — CG: 22 SD: 22

F — Javier Saviola — CG: 12 SR: 225

F — Frederic Kanoute — CG: 21 SR: 385

MONTHLY POINTS TALLY

Month	Points	%
AUGUST	3	100%
SEPTEMBER	2	17%
OCTOBER	11	73%
NOVEMBER	7	78%
DECEMBER	3	25%
JANUARY	9	75%
FEBRUARY	6	50%
MARCH	10	67%
APRIL	5	42%
MAY	12	100%

LEAGUE GOALS

	PLAYER	MINS	GOALS	S RATE
1	Maresca	2065	8	258
2	Saviola	1801	8	225
3	Kanoute	2307	6	385
4	Blanco-Gonzalez	1090	6	182
5	Fabiano	1289	5	258
6	Daniel Alves	3070	3	1023
7	Adriano Correia	2378	3	793
8	Navas, J	2753	2	1377
9	Aitor Ocio	1653	2	827
10	Puerta	848	2	424
11	Dragutinovic	1698	1	1698
12	Marti	2628	1	2628
13	Renato	1381	1	1381
	Other		6	
	TOTAL		54	

TOP POINT EARNERS

	PLAYER	GAMES	AV PTS
1	Escude	13	2.23
2	Renato	12	2.08
3	Navarro	18	2.00
4	David	28	1.93
5	Kanoute	21	1.90
6	Daniel Alves	33	1.88
7	Saviola	12	1.83
8	Maresca	20	1.80
9	Adriano Correia	22	1.77
10	Aitor Ocio	17	1.76
	CLUB AVERAGE:		1.79

DISCIPLINARY RECORDS

	PLAYER	YELLOW	RED	AVE
1	Navarro	9	2	173
2	Blanco-Gonzalez	5	1	181
3	Aitor Ocio	7	1	206
4	Jordi	5	0	233
5	Daniel Alves	12	1	236
6	Dragutinovic	6	1	242
7	Fabiano	5	0	257
8	Maresca	6	2	258
9	Adriano Correia	9	0	264
10	David	8	1	297
11	Sales	2	0	382
12	Puerta	2	0	424
13	Renato	3	0	460
	Other	19	0	
	TOTAL	98	9	

KEY GOALKEEPER

Andres Palop

Goals Conceded in the League	35	**Counting Games** League games when player was on pitch for at least 70 minutes	35
Defensive Rating Ave number of mins between League goals conceded while on the pitch	90	**Clean Sheets** In League games when player was on pitch for at least 70 minutes	16

KEY PLAYERS - GOALSCORERS

Javier Saviola

Goals in the League	8	**Player Strike Rate** Average number of minutes between League goals scored by player	225
Contribution to Attacking Power Average number of minutes between League team goals while on pitch	69	**Club Strike Rate** Average number of minutes between League goals scored by club	63

	PLAYER	LGE GOALS	POWER	STRIKE RATE
1	Javier Saviola	8	69	225 mins
2	Enzo Maresca	8	63	258 mins
3	Frederic Kanoute	6	66	385 mins
4	Claro Adriano Correia	3	66	793 mins

KEY PLAYERS - DEFENDERS

Javi Navarro

Goals Conceded Number of League goals conceded while the player was on the pitch	18	**Clean Sheets** In League games when player was on pitch for at least 70 minutes	11
Defensive Rating Ave number of mins between League goals conceded while on the pitch	106	**Club Defensive Rating** Average number of mins between League goals conceded by the club this season	88

	PLAYER	CON LGE	CLEAN SHEETS	DEF RATE
1	Javi Navarro	18	11	106 mins
2	Julien Escude	13	6	93 mins
3	Aitor Ocio	19	7	87 mins
4	Daniel Alves	36	14	85 mins

Enzo Maresca

KEY PLAYERS - MIDFIELDERS

Enzo Maresca

Goals in the League	8	**Contribution to Attacking Power** Average number of minutes between League team goals while on pitch	63
Defensive Rating Average number of mins between League goals conceded while on the pitch	98	**Scoring Difference** Defensive Rating minus Contribution to Attacking Power	35

	PLAYER	LGE GOALS	DEF RATE	POWER	SCORE DIFF
1	Enzo Maresca	8	98	63	35 mins
2	Jose Luis Marti	1	94	64	30 mins
3	Renato	1	106	81	25 mins
4	Claro Adriano Correia	3	88	66	22 mins

SQUAD APPEARANCES

Match	1	2	3	4	5	6	7	8	9	10	11	12	13	14	15	16	17	18	19	20	21	22	23	24	25	26	27
Venue	H	A	H	A	H	A	A	H	A	H	A	A	H	H	H	A	A	H	H	A	A	H	A	H	A	A	H
Competition	L	L	E	L	L	L	E	L	L	L	L	L	E	L	L	E	L	E	L	L	E	L	L	L	L	L	L
Result	W	D	D	L	D	L	W	D	W	W	W	D	W	D	W	L	W	W	L	L	D	W	L	W	L	W	W

Match	28	29	30	31	32	33	34	35	36	37	38	39	40	41	42	43	44	45	46	47	48	49	50	51	52	53
Venue	H	A	A	H	H	A	H	A	A	H	H	A	H	H	A	A	H	A	A	H	A	H	A	A	H	H
Competition	L	L	E	L	E	L	L	E	L	E	L	L	L	E	L	E	L	L	E	E	L	L	L	E	L	L
Result	L	W	W	W	W	L	W	L	L	W	D	W	W	W	L	D	D	D	D	W	W	W	W	W	W	W

Goalkeepers
Antonio Notario Caro
Andres Palop

Defenders
Aitor Ocio
Jose Angel Crespo
Daniel Alves
Castedo David
Ivica Dragutinovic
Julien Escude
Javi Navarro
Pablo Alfaro
Ruiz Pablo Barrero
David Prieto
Ramos Sergio

Midfielders
Claro Adriano Correia
Antonio Lopez
Diego Capel
Jesuli
Lopez Jordi
Enzo Maresca
Jose Luis Marti
Antonio Moreno Vera
Jesus Navas
Antonio Puerta
Renato

Forwards
Kepa Blanco-Gonzalez
Luis Fabiano
Francisco Gallardo
Frederic Kanoute
Ariza Makukula
Fernando Sales
Javier Saviola

KEY: On all match; On bench; Subbed or sent off (Counting game); Subbed or sent off (playing less than 70 minutes); Subbed on from bench (Counting Game); Subbed on (playing less than 70 minutes); Subbed on and then subbed or sent off (Counting Game); Subbed on and then subbed or sent off (playing less than 70 minutes); Not in 16

CELTA VIGO

Final Position: **6th**

KEY: ☐Won ☐Drawn ☐Lost

							Attendance
1	sppr1	**Malaga**	H	W	2-0	Gustavo Lopez 12; Baiano 47	14,000
2	sppr1	**Real Madrid**	A	W	3-2	Contreras 7; Nunez 45; Canobbio 76	80,000
3	sppr1	**R Santander**	H	L	0-1		15,000
4	sppr1	**Villarreal**	A	W	2-1	Baiano 26,45	19,000
5	sppr1	**Seville**	H	W	2-1	Baiano 1; Oubina 15	15,000
6	sppr1	**Cadiz**	A	D	1-1	Baiano 25	20,000
7	sppr1	**Osasuna**	A	L	0-2		14,500
8	sppr1	**Espanyol**	H	W	1-0	Silva 83	15,000
9	sppr1	**Mallorca**	A	L	0-1		12,000
10	sppr1	**Athl Bilbao**	A	D	1-1	Angel 59	30,000
11	sppr1	**Alaves**	H	W	2-1	Canobbio 26; Jonathan 66	14,865
12	sppr1	**Atl Madrid**	H	W	2-1	Baiano 27; Canobbio 54	17,000
13	sppr1	**Valencia**	A	L	0-2		38,000
14	sppr1	**Real Betis**	H	W	2-1	Canobbio 5; Baiano 19	15,000
15	sppr1	**Real Zaragoza**	A	L	0-1		30,000
16	sppr1	**Deportivo**	H	L	0-3		28,500
17	sppr1	**Barcelona**	A	L	0-2		65,000
18	sppr1	**Real Sociedad**	H	W	1-0	Canobbio 25	14,989
19	sppr1	**Getafe**	A	D	1-1	Angel 46	12,000
20	sppr1	**Malaga**	A	W	2-0	Nunez 46; Silva 70	20,000
21	sppr1	**Real Madrid**	H	L	1-2	Lequi 40	26,000
22	sppr1	**R Santander**	A	W	1-0	Perera 89	14,300
23	sppr1	**Villarreal**	H	W	1-0	Baiano 38	16,045
24	sppr1	**Seville**	A	L	0-1		28,000
25	sppr1	**Cadiz**	H	W	2-0	Contreras 37; Silva 73	15,000
26	sppr1	**Osasuna**	H	W	2-0	Baiano 5; Canobbio 72	16,677
27	sppr1	**Espanyol**	A	L	0-2		18,500
28	sppr1	**Athl Bilbao**	H	L	0-1		15,000
29	sppr1	**Alaves**	A	L	0-1		13,237
30	sppr1	**Mallorca**	H	W	2-0	Contreras 7; Baiano 21	15,671
31	sppr1	**Atl Madrid**	A	W	3-0	Lequi 70; Baiano 82; de Ridder 90	50,000
32	sppr1	**Valencia**	H	L	0-1		16,000
33	sppr1	**Real Betis**	A	W	2-0	Jorge 18; Perera 88	32,000
34	sppr1	**Real Zaragoza**	H	W	4-0	Canobbio 30,81; Jorge 46; Perera 80	18,000
35	sppr1	**Deportivo**	A	W	2-0	Silva 34; Perera 88	24,500
36	sppr1	**Barcelona**	H	L	0-1		28,500
37	sppr1	**Real Sociedad**	A	D	2-2	Baiano 45 pen,56	25,500
38	sppr1	**Getafe**	H	W	1-0	Contreras 24	25,522

LEAGUE APPEARANCES, BOOKINGS AND CAPS

	AGE (on 01/07/06)	IN NAMED 18	APPEARANCES	COUNTING GAMES	MINUTES ON PITCH	YELLOW CARDS	RED CARDS	CAPS THIS SEASON	NATIONAL SIDE
Goalkeepers									
Andres Esteban	31	38	2	1	156	0	0	-	Spain
Marcos Bermudez	20	1	0	0	0	0	0	-	Spain
Jose Manuel Pinto	30	37	37	36	3265	4	1	-	Spain
Defenders									
Lopez Ruano Angel	25	37	37	37	3322	8	0	-	Spain
Pablo Contreras	27	30	29	21	2042	9	1	-	Chile
Jose Enrique	20	19	14	12	1125	0	0	-	Spain
Matias Lequi	25	30	28	25	2324	9	1	-	Argentina
Sebastian Mendez	29	23	10	1	295	2	0	-	Argentina
Diego Placente	29	30	25	24	2207	5	0	-	Argentina
Sergio	29	26	26	25	2282	9	0	-	Spain
Yago	26	9	0	0	0	0	0	-	Spain
Midfielders									
Everton Giovanella	35	3	2	1	125	0	0	-	Brazil
Pablo Gustavo Lopez	33	23	15	4	634	2	0	-	Argentina
Santos Iriney	25	29	29	24	2327	4	0	-	Brazil
Aspas Jonathan	24	33	15	4	641	1	0	-	Spain
Larena Jorge	24	33	26	3	1252	2	0	-	Spain
Antonio Nunez	27	35	32	21	2209	6	0	-	Spain
Borja Oubina	24	36	36	35	3179	5	0	-	Spain
David Silva	20	34	34	29	2671	2	0	-	Spain
Forwards									
Fernando Baiano	27	33	33	28	2648	4	0	-	Brazil
Fabian Canobbio	26	32	32	28	2593	2	0	-	Uruguay
Daniel de Ridder	22	27	17	4	760	0	0	-	Holland
Javier Guerrero	29	26	19	3	599	0	0	-	Spain
Juan Sanchez	34	5	3	0	55	0	0	-	Spain
Jose Jesus Perera	26	33	17	1	445	0	0	-	Spain
Roberto	21	22	8	1	254	3	0	-	Brazil

TEAM OF THE SEASON

G — Jose Pinto Colorado — **CG:** 36 **DR:** 117

D — Jose Enrique — **CG:** 12 **DR:** 125

D — Matias Emanuel Lequi — **CG:** 25 **DR:** 122

D — Pablo Fica Contreras — **CG:** 21 **DR:** 120

D — Lopez Ruano Angel — **CG:** 37 **DR:** 101

M — David Silva — **CG:** 29 **SD:** 47

M — Borja Melendez Oubina — **CG:** 35 **SD:** 29

M — Santos da Silva Iriney — **CG:** 24 **SD:** 26

M — Antonio Nunez — **CG:** 21 **SD:** 3

F — Fernando Baiano — **CG:** 28 **SR:** 204

F — Fabian Canobbio — **CG:** 28 **SR:** 324

MONTHLY POINTS TALLY

AUGUST	3	100%
SEPTEMBER	9	75%
OCTOBER	5	33%
NOVEMBER	6	67%
DECEMBER	3	25%
JANUARY	7	58%
FEBRUARY	9	75%
MARCH	6	40%
APRIL	12	80%
MAY	4	44%

LEAGUE GOALS

	PLAYER	MINS	GOALS	S RATE
1	Baiano	2648	**13**	204
2	Canobbio	2593	**8**	324
3	Contreras	2042	**4**	511
4	Perera	445	**4**	111
5	Silva	2671	**4**	668
6	Lequi	2324	**2**	1162
7	Nunez	2209	**2**	1105
8	Angel	3322	**2**	1661
9	Jorge	1252	**2**	626
10	Jonathan	641	**1**	641
11	de Ridder	760	**1**	760
12	Oubina	3179	**1**	3179
13	Gustavo Lopez	634	**1**	634
	Other		**0**	
	TOTAL		**45**	

TOP POINT EARNERS

	PLAYER	GAMES	AV PTS
1	Contreras	21	**2.05**
2	Silva	29	**1.86**
3	Nunez	21	**1.86**
4	Placente	24	**1.83**
5	Pinto	36	**1.78**
6	Iriney	24	**1.71**
7	Oubina	35	**1.66**
8	Angel	37	**1.65**
9	Sergio	25	**1.64**
10	Canobbio	28	**1.61**
	CLUB AVERAGE:		**1.68**

DISCIPLINARY RECORDS

	PLAYER	YELLOW	RED	AVE
1	Contreras	9	1	**204**
2	Lequi	9	1	**232**
3	Sergio	9	0	**253**
4	Gustavo Lopez	2	0	**317**
5	Nunez	6	0	**368**
6	Angel	8	0	**415**
7	Placente	5	0	**441**
8	Iriney	4	0	**581**
9	Jorge	2	0	**626**
10	Oubina	5	0	**635**
11	Jonathan	1	0	**641**
12	Pinto	4	1	**653**
13	Baiano	4	0	**662**
	Other	4	0	
	TOTAL	**72**	**3**	

KEY GOALKEEPER

Jose Manuel Pinto Colorado

Goals Conceded in the League	28	Counting Games League games when player was on pitch for at least 70 minutes	36
Defensive Rating Ave number of mins between League goals conceded while on the pitch	117	Clean Sheets In League games when player was on pitch for at least 70 minutes	14

KEY PLAYERS - DEFENDERS

Jose Enrique

Goals Conceded Number of League goals conceded while the player was on the pitch	9	Clean Sheets In League games when player was on pitch for at least 70 minutes	5
Defensive Rating Ave number of mins between League goals conceded while on the pitch	125	Club Defensive Rating Average number of mins between League goals conceded by the club this season	104

	PLAYER	CON LGE	CLEAN SHEETS	DEF RATE
1	Jose Enrique	9	5	125 mins
2	Matias Emanuel Lequi	19	10	122 mins
3	Pablo Andres Fica Contreras	17	10	120 mins
4	Lopez Ruano Angel	33	13	101 mins

KEY PLAYERS - MIDFIELDERS

David Silva

Goals in the League	4	Contribution to Attacking Power Average number of minutes between League team goals while on pitch	74
Defensive Rating Average number of mins between League goals conceded while on the pitch	121	Scoring Difference Defensive Rating minus Contribution to Attacking Power	47

	PLAYER	LGE GOALS	DEF RATE	POWER	SCORE DIFF
1	David Silva	4	121	74	47 mins
2	Borja Melendez Oubina	1	103	74	29 mins
3	Santos da Silva Iriney	0	101	75	26 mins
4	Antonio Nunez	2	88	85	3 mins

KEY PLAYERS - GOALSCORERS

Fernando Baiano

Goals in the League	13	Player Strike Rate Average number of minutes between League goals scored by player	204
Contribution to Attacking Power Average number of minutes between League team goals while on pitch	80	Club Strike Rate Average number of minutes between League goals scored by club	76

	PLAYER	LGE GOALS	POWER	STRIKE RATE
1	Fernando Baiano	13	80	204 mins
2	Fabian Canobbio	8	76	324 mins
3	Pablo Andres Fica Contreras	4	62	511 mins
4	David Silva	4	74	668 mins

Fernando Baiano and Larena Jorge

SQUAD APPEARANCES

Match	1	2	3	4	5	6	7	8	9	10	11	12	13	14	15	16	17	18	19	20	21	22	23	24	25	26	27	28	29	30	31	32	33	34	35	36	37	38
Venue	H	A	H	A	H	A	A	H	A	A	H	H	A	H	A	H	A	H	A	A	H	A	H	A	H	H	A	H	A	H	A	H	A	H	A	H	A	H
Competition	L	L	L	L	L	L	L	L	L	L	L	L	L	L	L	L	L	L	L	L	L	L	L	L	L	L	L	L	L	L	L	L	L	L	L	L	L	L
Result	W	W	L	W	W	D	L	W	L	D	W	W	L	W	L	L	L	W	D	W	L	W	W	L	W	W	L	L	L	W	W	L	W	W	W	L	D	W

Goalkeepers
Andres Esteban
Marcos Bermudez
Jose Manuel Pinto

Defenders
Lopez Ruano Angel
Pablo Contreras
Jose Enrique
Matias Emanuel Lequi
Sebastian Ariel Mendez
Diego Placente
Sergio
Yago

Midfielders
Everton Giovanella
Pablo Gustavo Lopez
Santos da Silva Iriney
Aspas Juncal Jonathan
Larena Jorge
Antonio Nunez
Borja Melendez Oubina
David Silva

Forwards
Fernando Baiano
Fabian Canobbio
Daniel de Ridder
Javier Guerrero
Juan Sanchez
Jose Jesus Perera
Roberto

KEY: On all match | On bench | Subbed or sent off (Counting game) | Subbed or sent off (playing less than 70 minutes) | Subbed on from bench (Counting Game) | Subbed on (playing less than 70 minutes) | Subbed on and then subbed or sent off (Counting Game) | Subbed on and then subbed or sent off (playing less than 70 minutes) | Not in 16

VILLARREAL

Final Position: **7th**

KEY: ☐Won ☐Drawn ☐Lost

	Competition	Opponent	Venue	Result	Score	Scorers	Attendance
1	ecql1	Everton	A	W	2-1	Figueroa 27; Josico 45	37,685
2	ecql2	Everton	H	W	2-1	Sorin 21; Forlan 90	22,000
3	sppr1	Osasuna	A	L	1-2	Forlan 52	14,000
4	sppr1	Seville	H	D	1-1	Figueroa 72	18,000
5	ecgpd	Man Utd	H	D	0-0		23,000
6	sppr1	Cadiz	A	D	1-1	Jose Mari 38	20,000
7	sppr1	Celta Vigo	H	L	1-2	Riquelme 80	19,000
8	sppr1	Espanyol	A	W	2-1	Josico 44; Senna 65	16,550
9	ecgpd	Lille	A	D	0-0		20,000
10	sppr1	Athl Bilbao	H	W	3-1	Riquelme 45; Jose Mari 61; Senna 78	18,000
11	sppr1	Alaves	A	D	1-1	Roger 4	14,000
12	ecgpd	Benfica	H	D	1-1	Riquelme 72 pen	23,000
13	sppr1	Mallorca	H	W	3-0	Riquelme 14; Jose Mari 32; Forlan 45	18,000
14	sppr1	Real Betis	A	W	3-2	Jose Mari 10; Sorin 58; Riquelme 69 pen	32,000
15	sppr1	Atl Madrid	A	D	1-1	Forlan 94	50,000
16	ecgpd	Benfica	A	W	1-0	Senna 81	30,000
17	sppr1	Valencia	H	W	1-0	Figueroa 24	21,000
18	sppr1	Real Zaragoza	H	D	0-0		17,000
19	ecgpd	Man Utd	A	D	0-0		67,471
20	sppr1	Deportivo	A	W	2-0	Riquelme 55 fk; Sorin 78	24,000
21	sppr1	Barcelona	H	L	0-2		22,000
22	ecgpd	Lille	H	W	1-0	Guayre 67	22,500
23	sppr1	Real Sociedad	A	W	3-1	Guayre 36,55; Riquelme 72	16,170
24	sppr1	Getafe	H	W	2-1	Riquelme 45; Forlan 58	19,000
25	sppr1	Malaga	A	D	0-0		20,000
26	sppr1	Real Madrid	H	D	0-0		20,000
27	sppr1	R Santander	A	L	0-1		17,000
28	sppr1	Osasuna	H	W	2-1	Riquelme 70 pen,77 pen	20,000
29	sppr1	Seville	A	L	0-2		28,000
30	sppr1	Cadiz	H	D	1-1	Calleja 62	20,000
31	sppr1	Celta Vigo	A	L	0-1		16,045
32	sppr1	Espanyol	H	W	4-0	Tacchinardi 24; Senna 35; Forlan 38; Font 82	18,000
33	eclsl1	Rangers	A	D	2-2	Riquelme 8 pen; Forlan 35	49,372
34	sppr1	Athl Bilbao	A	D	1-1	Forlan 43	38,000
35	sppr1	Alaves	H	W	3-2	Riquelme 19,64; Franco 82	18,000
36	eclsl2	Rangers	H	D	1-1	Arruabarrena 49	23,000
37	sppr1	Mallorca	A	D	1-1	Jose Mari 23	17,000
38	sppr1	Atl Madrid	H	D	1-1	Forlan 10	19,000
39	sppr1	Valencia	A	D	1-1	Forlan 69	40,000
40	sppr1	Real Betis	H	L	1-2	Sorin 78	18,000
41	eclsl1	Inter Milan	A	L	1-2	Forlan 1	80,000
42	sppr1	Real Zaragoza	A	W	1-0	Roger 45	30,000
43	ecqfl2	Inter Milan	H	W	1-0	Arruabarrena 58	22,500
44	sppr1	Deportivo	H	D	1-1	Franco 74	20,000
45	sppr1	Barcelona	A	L	0-1		76,200
46	ecsfl1	Arsenal	A	L	0-1		35,438
47	sppr1	Real Sociedad	H	L	0-2		16,000
48	ecsfl2	Arsenal	H	D	0-0		23,000
49	sppr1	Getafe	A	D	1-1	Franco 2	11,000
50	sppr1	Malaga	H	W	2-1	Franco 9; Tacchinardi 19	15,000
51	sppr1	Real Madrid	A	D	3-3	Mejia 31 og; Forlan 39,86 pen	79,497
52	sppr1	R Santander	H	W	2-0	Riquelme 30 pen; Xisco 61	16,000

LEAGUE APPEARANCES, BOOKINGS AND CAPS

	AGE (on 01/07/06)	IN NAMED 18	APPEARANCES	COUNTING GAMES	MINUTES ON PITCH	YELLOW CARDS	RED CARDS	CAPS THIS SEASON	NATIONAL SIDE
Goalkeepers									
Mariano Barbosa	21	32	10	9	871	1	0	-	Argentina
Lopez Vallejo	30	9	0	0	0	0	0	-	Spain
Sebastian Viera	22	33	29	28	2549	3	0	-	Uruguay
Defenders									
Carlos Alcantara	21	10	3	3	270	2	0	-	Spain
Quique Alvarez	30	26	21	21	1872	11	0	-	Spain
Rodolfo Arruabarrena	30	34	33	29	2807	12	0	-	Argentina
Javi Venta	30	28	25	24	2213	2	0	-	Spain
Miguel Josemi	26	21	9	8	757	3	0	-	Spain
Jan Kromkamp	25	15	6	6	540	1	0	5	Holland (3)
Martinez Oscar Lopez	22	2	1	1	90	0	0	-	Spain
Juan Manuel Pena	33	32	25	23	2086	10	1	-	Bolivia
Gonzalo Rodriguez	22	30	29	27	2458	8	1	-	Argentina
Juan Pablo Sorin	30	20	20	11	1399	4	0	8	Argentina (9)
Midfielders									
Cesar Amposta Arzo	20	30	10	5	542	2	0	-	Spain
Javier Calleja	28	23	13	0	319	1	0	-	Spain
Santiago Cazorla	21	28	20	9	1083	3	0	-	Spain
Romero Hector Font	22	29	20	6	912	2	1	-	Spain
Rubio Gomez	21	1	1	0	68	0	0	-	Spain
Josico	31	30	27	19	1998	7	1	-	Spain
Garcia Marcos	19	3	3	1	213	0	0	-	Spain
Juan Riquelme	28	25	25	24	2167	4	0	7	Argentina (9)
Garcia Roger	29	32	24	7	915	2	0	-	Spain
Santi Cazorla	21	3	3	1	161	0	0	-	Spain
Marcos Senna	29	30	28	26	2408	4	0	2	Spain (5)
Alessio Tacchinardi	30	24	23	16	1543	7	1	-	Italy
Luis Valencia	20	7	2	1	94	0	0	-	Ecuador
Forwards									
Luciano Figueroa	25	15	12	6	632	1	0	-	Argentina
Diego Forlan	27	34	33	29	2714	3	0	-	Uruguay
Guillermo Franco	29	12	12	6	765	3	0	-	Argentina
Antonio Guayre	26	23	17	6	816	3	0	-	Spain
Jose Mari	27	35	32	20	2118	3	0	-	Spain
Nadal Xisco	20	5	4	0	83	0	0	-	Spain

TEAM OF THE SEASON

G
Sebastian Viera
CG: 28 DR: 85

D
Juan Manuel Pena
CG: 23 DR: 95

D
Gonzalo Rodriguez
CG: 27 DR: 88

D
Quique Alvarez
CG: 21 DR: 85

D
Javi Venta
CG: 24 DR: 85

M
Alessio Tacchinardi
CG: 16 SD: 38

M
Juan Riquelme
CG: 24 SD: 24

M
Marcos Senna
CG: 26 SD: 17

M
Josico
CG: 19 SD: 8

F
Diego Forlan
CG: 29 SR: 271

F
Jose Mari
CG: 20 SR: 424

MONTHLY POINTS TALLY

Month	Points	%
AUGUST	0	0%
SEPTEMBER	5	42%
OCTOBER	11	73%
NOVEMBER	7	78%
DECEMBER	7	58%
JANUARY	4	33%
FEBRUARY	5	42%
MARCH	6	40%
APRIL	5	33%
MAY	7	78%

LEAGUE GOALS

	PLAYER	MINS	GOALS	S RATE
1	Riquelme	2167	**12**	181
2	Forlan	2714	**10**	271
3	Jose Mari	2118	**5**	424
4	Franco	765	**4**	191
5	Senna	2408	**3**	803
6	Sorin	1399	**3**	466
7	Guayre	816	**2**	408
8	Figueroa	632	**2**	316
9	Tacchinardi	1543	**2**	772
10	Roger	915	**2**	458
11	Font	912	**1**	912
12	Xisco	83	**1**	83
13	Josico	1998	**1**	1998
	Other		**2**	
	TOTAL		**50**	

TOP POINT EARNERS

	PLAYER	GAMES	AV PTS
1	Tacchinardi	16	**1.94**
2	Riquelme	24	**1.79**
3	Javi Venta	24	**1.79**
4	Josico	19	**1.68**
5	Forlan	29	**1.62**
6	Pena	23	**1.57**
7	Senna	26	**1.54**
8	Viera	28	**1.54**
9	Alvarez	21	**1.52**
10	Jose Mari	20	**1.50**
	CLUB AVERAGE:		**1.67**

DISCIPLINARY RECORDS

	PLAYER	YELLOW	RED	AVE
1	Alvarez	11	0	**170**
2	Pena	10	1	**189**
3	Tacchinardi	7	1	**192**
4	Arruabarrena	12	0	**233**
5	Josico	7	1	**249**
6	Josemi	3	0	**252**
7	Franco	3	0	**255**
8	Arzo	2	0	**271**
9	Guayre	3	0	**272**
10	Rodriguez, G	8	1	**273**
11	Font	2	1	**304**
12	Sorin	4	0	**349**
13	Cazorla	3	0	**361**
	Other	24	0	
	TOTAL	**99**	**5**	

KEY GOALKEEPER

Sebastian Viera

Goals Conceded in the League	30	**Counting Games** League games when player was on pitch for at least 70 minutes	28
Defensive Rating Ave number of mins between League goals conceded while on the pitch	85	**Clean Sheets** In games when player was on pitch for at least 70 minutes	6

KEY PLAYERS - DEFENDERS

Juan Manuel Pena

Goals Conceded Number of League goals conceded while the player was on the pitch	22	**Clean Sheets** In League games when player was on pitch for at least 70 minutes	7
Defensive Rating Ave number of mins between League goals conceded while on the pitch	95	**Club Defensive Rating** Average number of mins between League goals conceded by the club this season	88

	PLAYER	CON LGE	CLEAN SHEETS	DEF RATE
1	Juan Manuel Pena	22	7	95 mins
2	Gonzalo Rodriguez	28	7	88 mins
3	Quique Alvarez	22	4	85 mins
4	Javi Venta	26	6	85 mins

KEY PLAYERS - MIDFIELDERS

Alessio Tacchinardi

Goals in the League	2	**Contribution to Attacking Power** Average number of minutes between League team goals while on pitch	53
Defensive Rating Average number of mins between League goals conceded while on the pitch	91	**Scoring Difference** Defensive Rating minus Contribution to Attacking Power	38

	PLAYER	LGE GOALS	DEF RATE	POWER	SCORE DIFF
1	Alessio Tacchinardi	2	91	53	38 mins
2	Juan Riquelme	12	83	59	24 mins
3	Marcos Senna	3	86	69	17 mins
4	Josico	1	77	69	8 mins

KEY PLAYERS - GOALSCORERS

Juan Riquelme

Goals in the League	12	**Player Strike Rate** Average number of minutes between League goals scored by player	181
Contribution to Attacking Power Average number of minutes between League team goals while on pitch	59	**Club Strike Rate** Average number of minutes between League goals scored by club	68

	PLAYER	LGE GOALS	POWER	STRIKE RATE
1	Juan Riquelme	12	59	181 mins
2	Diego Forlan	10	62	271 mins
3	Jose Mari	5	71	424 mins
4	Alessio Tacchinardi	2	53	772 mins

Juan Riquelme and Diego Forlan

SQUAD APPEARANCES

Match	1	2	3	4	5	6	7	8	9	10	11	12	13	14	15	16	17	18	19	20	21	22	23	24	25	26
Venue	A	H	A	H	H	A	H	A	A	H	A	H	H	A	A	A	H	H	A	A	H	H	A	H	A	H
Competition	C	C	L	L	C	L	L	L	C	L	L	C	L	L	L	C	L	L	C	L	L	C	L	L	L	L
Result	W	W	L	D	D	D	L	W	D	W	D	D	W	W	D	W	W	D	D	W	L	W	W	W	D	D

Match	27	28	29	30	31	32	33	34	35	36	37	38	39	40	41	42	43	44	45	46	47	48	49	50	51	52
Venue	A	H	A	H	A	H	A	A	H	H	A	H	A	H	A	A	H	H	A	A	H	H	A	H	A	H
Competition	L	L	L	L	L	L	C	L	L	C	L	L	L	L	C	L	C	L	L	C	L	C	L	L	L	L
Result	L	W	L	D	L	W	D	D	W	D	D	D	D	L	L	W	W	D	L	L	L	D	D	W	D	W

Goalkeepers
Mariano Barbosa
Lopez Vallejo
Sebastian Viera

Defenders
Carlos Alcantara
Quique Alvarez
Rodolfo Arruabarrena
Edu Caballer
Javi Venta
Miguel Josemi
Jan Kromkamp
Martinez Oscar Lopez
Juan Manuel Pena
Gonzalo Rodriguez
Juan Pablo Sorin

Midfielders
Cesar Amposta Arzo
Javier Calleja
Santiago Cazorla
Romero Hector Font
Rubio Gomez
Josico
Garcia Marcos
Juan Riquelme
Garcia Roger
Santi Cazorla
Marcos Senna
Alessio Tacchinardi
Luis Valencia Mosquera

Forwards
Luciano Figueroa
Diego Forlan
Guillermo
Antonio Guayre
Jose Mari
Nadal Xisco

KEY: On all match | On bench | Subbed or sent off (Counting game) | Subbed or sent off (playing less than 70 minutes) | Subbed on from bench (Counting Game) | Subbed on (playing less than 70 minutes) | Subbed on and then subbed or sent off (Counting Game) | Subbed on and then subbed or sent off (playing less than 70 minutes) | Not in 16

DEPORTIVO LA CORUNA

Final Position: **8th**

KEY: ☐ Won ☐ Drawn ☐ Lost

	Comp	Opponent	H/A	Res	Score	Scorers	Attendance
1	etsfl2	**Newcastle**	A	W	2-1	Andrade 45; Munitis 47	34,215
2	etfl1	**Marseille**	H	W	2-0	Castro 67; Carril 86	15,400
3	etfl2	**Marseille**	A	L	1-5	Andrade 8	
4	sppr1	**Mallorca**	A	W	1-0	Juanma 18	18,000
5	sppr1	**Atl Madrid**	H	W	1-0	Capdevila 90	27,000
6	sppr1	**Valencia**	A	D	2-2	Tristan 24; Sergio 83	44,000
7	sppr1	**Real Betis**	H	D	1-1	Tristan 45	23,400
8	sppr1	**Real Zaragoza**	A	D	1-1	Tristan 44	30,000
9	sppr1	**Osasuna**	H	L	0-1		23,700
10	sppr1	**Barcelona**	H	D	3-3	Valeron 10; Munitis 72; Castro 87	30,000
11	sppr1	**Real Sociedad**	A	L	0-2		21,000
12	sppr1	**Real Madrid**	H	W	3-1	De Guzman 35; Juanma 45,84	35,000
13	sppr1	**Getafe**	H	W	1-0	Tristan 25	24,300
14	sppr1	**Malaga**	A	D	1-1	Valeron 74	22,000
15	sppr1	**R Santander**	A	W	3-0	Tristan 17; Valeron 52; Taborda 73	12,700
16	sppr1	**Villarreal**	H	L	0-2		24,000
17	sppr1	**Seville**	A	W	2-0	Tristan 26 pen; Victor 41	38,000
18	sppr1	**Cadiz**	H	W	1-0	Tristan 50	26,000
19	sppr1	**Celta Vigo**	A	W	3-0	Tristan 27 pen; Valeron 43; Capdevila 45	28,500
20	sppr1	**Espanyol**	H	L	1-2	Tristan 82	24,300
21	sppr1	**Athl Bilbao**	A	W	2-1	Amorebieta 24 og; Arizmendi 64	32,000
22	sppr1	**Alaves**	H	L	0-2		23,400
23	sppr1	**Mallorca**	H	D	2-2	Valeron 18; Tristan 25 pen	24,300
24	sppr1	**Atl Madrid**	A	L	2-3	Castro 47,59	35,000
25	sppr1	**Valencia**	H	L	0-1		31,400
26	sppr1	**Real Betis**	A	W	1-0	Castro 90	30,000
27	sppr1	**Real Zaragoza**	H	D	1-1	Munitis 54	20,350
28	sppr1	**Osasuna**	A	W	2-1	Sergio 51; Tristan 72	14,000
29	sppr1	**Barcelona**	A	L	2-3	Juanma 15; Andrade 28	77,116
30	sppr1	**Real Sociedad**	H	L	0-1		24,300
31	sppr1	**Getafe**	A	W	2-1	Victor 30; Xisco 73	10,000
32	sppr1	**Malaga**	H	W	2-1	Victor 54,70	23,350
33	sppr1	**Real Madrid**	A	L	0-4		70,000
34	sppr1	**R Santander**	H	W	2-0	Capdevila 18; Iago Iglesias 55	23,234
35	sppr1	**Villarreal**	A	D	1-1	Sergio 72	20,000
36	sppr1	**Seville**	H	D	0-0		24,500
37	sppr1	**Cadiz**	A	D	1-1	Iago Iglesias 8	20,000
38	sppr1	**Celta Vigo**	H	L	0-2		24,500
39	sppr1	**Espanyol**	A	W	2-1	Carril 72; Tristan 89	16,150
40	sppr1	**Athl Bilbao**	H	L	1-2	Arizmendi 18	19,340
41	sppr1	**Alaves**	A	L	0-1		15,337

LEAGUE APPEARANCES, BOOKINGS AND CAPS

	AGE (on 01/07/06)	IN NAMED 18	APPEARANCES	COUNTING GAMES	MINUTES ON PITCH	YELLOW CARDS	RED CARDS	CAPS THIS SEASON	NATIONAL SIDE
Goalkeepers									
Castro Dani Mallo	27	35	0	0	0	0	0	-	Spain
Francisco Molina	35	38	38	38	3420	3	0	-	Spain
Gustavo Munua	28	2	0	0	0	0	0	-	Uruguay
Defenders									
Jorge Andrade	28	18	18	16	1534	8	0	5	Portugal (7)
Joan Capdevila	28	36	36	35	3206	7	0	-	Spain
Martin Cesar	29	14	7	1	202	3	0	-	Spain
Fabricio Coloccini	24	29	26	23	2126	7	2	6	Argentina (9)
Del Pino Hector	31	26	15	14	1279	3	0	-	Spain
Juanma	29	28	23	22	2012	8	0	-	Spain
Manuel Pablo	30	32	29	26	2398	7	1	-	Spain
Pablo Amo	28	3	2	2	180	0	0	-	Spain
Enrique Romero	35	34	20	14	1495	2	0	-	Spain
Lionel Scaloni	28	18	15	5	723	3	0	3	Argentina (9)
Midfielders									
Roberto Acuna	34	19	4	0	56	0	0	-	Paraguay
Ivan Carril	22	15	9	0	268	1	0	-	Spain
Ruben Castro	25	33	23	5	1064	2	0	-	Spain
Marcos Changui	29	1	0	0	0	0	0	-	Spain
Julian De Guzman	25	35	22	11	1468	9	1	1	Canada (77)
Aldo Duscher	27	32	31	30	2669	15	0	-	Argentina
Francisco Gallardo	26	12	7	0	210	2	0	-	Spain
Iago Iglesias	22	15	11	2	660	2	0	-	Spain
Jesus Munoz	30	2	1	0	17	0	0	-	Spain
Jeronimo Momo	23	9	5	0	163	1	0	-	Spain
Gonzalez Sergio	29	37	36	26	2714	6	0	-	Spain
Juan Carlos Valeron	31	20	20	15	1484	0	0	-	Spain
Sanchez Victor	30	23	21	13	1508	6	0	-	Spain
Forwards									
Angel Arizmendi	22	19	17	9	1093	2	0	-	Spain
Pedro Munitis	31	33	33	28	2734	12	1	-	Spain
Sebastian Taborda	25	11	9	0	201	1	0	-	Uruguay
Diego Tristan	30	36	36	16	2299	6	0	-	Spain
Fernando Xisco	20	5	3	0	48	0	0	-	Spain

TEAM OF THE SEASON

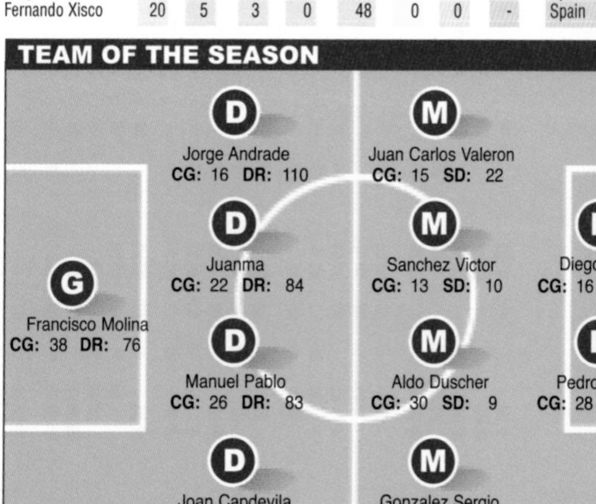

MONTHLY POINTS TALLY

Month	Points	%
AUGUST	3	100%
SEPTEMBER	6	50%
OCTOBER	7	47%
NOVEMBER	4	44%
DECEMBER	9	75%
JANUARY	4	33%
FEBRUARY	7	58%
MARCH	6	40%
APRIL	6	40%
MAY	3	33%

LEAGUE GOALS

	PLAYER	MINS	GOALS	S RATE
1	Tristan	2299	12	192
2	Valeron	1484	5	297
3	Juanma	2012	4	503
4	Castro	1064	4	266
5	Victor	1508	4	377
6	Sergio	2714	3	905
7	Capdevila	3206	3	1069
8	Iago Iglesias	660	2	330
9	Munitis	2734	2	1367
10	Arizmendi	1093	2	547
11	Andrade	1534	1	1534
12	Carril	268	1	268
13	Taborda	201	1	201
	Other		3	
	TOTAL		47	

TOP POINT EARNERS

	PLAYER	GAMES	AV PTS
1	Victor	13	2.00
2	Andrade	16	1.94
3	Valeron	15	1.93
4	Romero	14	1.57
5	Capdevila	35	1.57
6	Duscher	30	1.57
7	Sergio	26	1.54
8	Juanma	22	1.50
9	Manuel Pablo	26	1.46
10	Molina	38	1.45
	CLUB AVERAGE:		1.45

DISCIPLINARY RECORDS

	PLAYER	YELLOW	RED	AVE
1	De Guzman	9	1	146
2	Duscher	15	0	177
3	Andrade	8	0	191
4	Munitis	12	1	210
5	Coloccini	7	2	236
6	Scaloni	3	0	241
7	Juanma	8	0	251
8	Victor	6	0	251
9	Manuel Pablo	7	1	299
10	Iago Iglesias	2	0	330
11	Tristan	6	0	383
12	Hector	3	0	426
13	Sergio	6	0	452
	Other	16	0	
	TOTAL	108	5	

KEY GOALKEEPER

Francisco Molina			
Goals Conceded in the League	45	Counting Games League games when player was on pitch for at least 70 minutes	38
Defensive Rating Ave number of mins between League goals conceded while on the pitch	76	Clean Sheets In League games when player was on pitch for at least 70 minutes	10

KEY PLAYERS - DEFENDERS

Jorge Andrade			
Goals Conceded Number of League goals conceded while the player was on the pitch	14	Clean Sheets In League games when player was on pitch for at least 70 minutes	7
Defensive Rating Ave number of mins between League goals conceded while on the pitch	110	Club Defensive Rating Average number of mins between League goals conceded by the club this season	76

	PLAYER	CON LGE	CLEAN SHEETS	DEF RATE
1	Jorge Andrade	14	7	110 mins
2	Juanma	24	7	84 mins
3	Manuel Pablo	29	8	83 mins
4	Joan Capdevila	41	10	78 mins

KEY PLAYERS - MIDFIELDERS

Juan Carlos Valeron			
Goals in the League	5	Contribution to Attacking Power Average number of minutes between League team goals while on pitch	65
Defensive Rating Average number of mins between League goals conceded while on the pitch	87	Scoring Difference Defensive Rating minus Contribution to Attacking Power	22

	PLAYER	LGE GOALS	DEF RATE	POWER	SCORE DIFF
1	Juan Carlos Valeron	5	87	65	22 mins
2	Sanchez Victor	4	89	79	10 mins
3	Aldo Duscher	0	79	70	9 mins
4	Gonzalez Sergio	3	78	75	3 mins

KEY PLAYERS - GOALSCORERS

Diego Tristan			
Goals in the League	12	Player Strike Rate Average number of minutes between League goals scored by player	192
Contribution to Attacking Power Average number of minutes between League team goals while on pitch	77	Club Strike Rate Average number of minutes between League goals scored by club	73

	PLAYER	LGE GOALS	POWER	STRIKE RATE
1	Diego Tristan	12	77	192 mins
2	Juan Carlos Valeron	5	65	297 mins
3	Sanchez Victor	4	79	377 mins
4	Juanma	4	77	503 mins

Diego Tristan

SQUAD APPEARANCES

Match	1	2	3	4	5	6	7	8	9	10	11	12	13	14	15	16	17	18	19	20	21	22	23	24	25	26	27	28	29	30	31	32	33	34	35	36	37	38	39	40	41
Venue	A	H	A	A	H	A	H	A	H	H	A	H	H	A	A	H	A	H	A	H	A	H	H	A	H	A	H	A	A	H	A	H	A	H	A	H	A	H	A	H	A
Competition	O	O	O	L	L	L	L	L	L	L	L	L	L	L	L	L	L	L	L	L	L	L	L	L	L	L	L	L	L	L	L	L	L	L	L	L	L	L	L	L	L
Result	W	W	L	W	W	D	D	D	L	D	L	W	W	D	W	L	W	W	W	L	W	L	D	L	L	W	D	W	L	L	W	W	L	W	D	D	D	L	W	L	L

Goalkeepers
Castro Dani Mallo
Francisco Molina
Gustavo Munua

Defenders
Jorge Andrade
Joan Capdevila
Martin Cesar
Fabricio Coloccini
Del Pino Hector
Juanma
Manuel Pablo
Pablo Amo
Enrique Romero
Lionel Scaloni

Midfielders
Roberto Acuna
Ivan Carril
Ruben Castro
Marcos Changui
Julian De Guzman
Aldo Duscher
Francisco Gallardo
Iago Iglesias
Jesus Munoz
Jeronimo Momo
Gonzalez Sergio
Juan Carlos Valeron
Sanchez Victor

Forwards
Angel Arizmendi
Pedro Munitis
Sebastian Taborda
Francisco Jimenez Tejada
Diego Tristan
Fernando Xisco

KEY: On all match | Subbed or sent off (Counting game) | Subbed on from bench (Counting Game) | Subbed on and then subbed or sent off (Counting Game) | Not in 16
On bench | Subbed or sent off (playing less than 70 minutes) | Subbed on (playing less than 70 minutes) | Subbed on and then subbed or sent off (playing less than 70 minutes)

GETAFE

Final Position: **9th**

KEY: ☐ Won ☐ Drawn ☐ Lost

#	Comp	Opponent	H/A	Res	Score	Scorers	Attendance
1	sppr1	**Espanyol**	A	W	2-0	Gavilan 53; Riki 60	18,845
2	sppr1	**Athl Bilbao**	H	D	1-1	Guiza 27	14,000
3	sppr1	**Alaves**	A	W	4-3	Belenguer 8; Riki 26,38; Pernia 50 fk	12,347
4	sppr1	**Mallorca**	H	D	1-1	Guiza 7	10,000
5	sppr1	**Atl Madrid**	A	W	1-0	Pernia 70	50,000
6	sppr1	**Valencia**	H	W	2-1	Riki 43; Redondo 89	13,000
7	sppr1	**Real Betis**	A	L	0-1		39,000
8	sppr1	**Real Zaragoza**	H	W	5-2	Paunovic 9; Guiza 22 pen,25; Pulido 37; Redondo 85	14,000
9	sppr1	**Real Sociedad**	A	L	0-3		20,600
10	sppr1	**Deportivo**	A	L	0-1		24,300
11	sppr1	**Barcelona**	H	L	1-3	Pernia 89	14,000
12	sppr1	**Osasuna**	H	D	0-0		14,000
13	sppr1	**Malaga**	H	W	3-2	Paunovic 27,85; Gerardo 39 og	13,000
14	sppr1	**Real Madrid**	A	L	0-1		72,000
15	sppr1	**R Santander**	H	L	1-2	Pernia 43	14,000
16	sppr1	**Villarreal**	A	L	1-2	Riki 20	19,000
17	sppr1	**Seville**	H	W	1-0	Guiza 38	9,500
18	sppr1	**Cadiz**	A	L	0-1		19,000
19	sppr1	**Celta Vigo**	H	D	1-1	Gavilan 42	12,000
20	sppr1	**Espanyol**	H	W	5-0	Guiza 4,65; Pernia 26,76; Gavilan 85	14,000
21	sppr1	**Athl Bilbao**	A	L	0-1		30,000
22	sppr1	**Alaves**	H	D	2-2	Pernia 4; Guiza 90	11,000
23	sppr1	**Mallorca**	A	D	1-1	Dorado 79	17,000
24	sppr1	**Atl Madrid**	H	L	0-3		12,000
25	sppr1	**Valencia**	A	D	1-1	Nano 88	35,000
26	sppr1	**Real Betis**	H	W	1-0	Paunovic 14	14,000
27	sppr1	**Real Zaragoza**	A	W	2-1	Paunovic 39,60	32,000
28	sppr1	**Deportivo**	H	L	1-2	Pachon 58	10,000
29	sppr1	**Barcelona**	A	L	1-3	Nano 4	75,000
30	sppr1	**Real Sociedad**	H	W	2-1	Pernia 19; Guiza 55	11,000
31	sppr1	**Osasuna**	A	W	4-0	Paunovic 34,53; Dorado 37; Pernia 62	18,700
32	sppr1	**Malaga**	A	W	2-1	Paunovic 18,93	11,500
33	sppr1	**Real Madrid**	H	D	1-1	Tena 83	14,000
34	sppr1	**R Santander**	A	W	3-1	Riki 35,61; Pernia 74	18,000
35	sppr1	**Villarreal**	H	D	1-1	Gavilan 1	11,000
36	sppr1	**Seville**	A	L	0-3		25,000
37	sppr1	**Cadiz**	H	W	3-1	Pulido 70; Pachon 81; Riki 90	12,000
38	sppr1	**Celta Vigo**	A	L	0-1		25,522

LEAGUE APPEARANCES, BOOKINGS AND CAPS

	AGE (on 01/07/06)	IN NAMED 18	APPEARANCES	COUNTING GAMES	MINUTES ON PITCH	YELLOW CARDS	RED CARDS	CAPS THIS SEASON	NATIONAL SIDE
Goalkeepers									
Juan Calatayud	26	34	13	13	1170	1	0	-	Spain
Luis Garcia	27	34	25	25	2250	2	0	6	Spain (5)
Alejandro Rebollo	23	5	0	0	0	0	0	-	Spain
Alfonso Monreal Sito	24	3	0	0	0	0	0	-	Spain
Defenders									
David Belenguer	33	31	29	28	2570	8	1	-	Spain
Cosmin Contra	30	25	24	23	2115	7	0	-	Romania
Anibal Matellan	29	24	22	20	1904	10	1	-	Argentina
Javier Paredes	24	19	7	2	254	0	0	-	Spain
Mariano Pernia	32	38	36	36	3208	11	1	-	Argentina
Martin Pulido	27	31	25	18	1805	4	0	-	Spain
Manuel Tena	29	28	17	16	1443	2	0	-	Spain
Midfielders									
Ruiz Alberto	28	17	15	8	867	1	0	-	Spain
Fabio Celestini	30	19	19	16	1512	4	0	-	Switzerland
Jaja Coelho	20	6	2	0	29	0	0	-	Brazil
Mario Cotelo	31	34	28	18	1922	3	2	-	Spain
David Cubillo	28	30	11	5	551	0	0	-	Spain
Diego Rivas	26	33	33	33	2960	15	2	-	Spain
Angel Dorado	29	31	24	11	1489	4	0	-	Spain
Jaime Gavilan	21	34	33	26	2573	7	1	-	Spain
Pablo Redondo	24	32	28	12	1469	3	0	-	Spain
Forwards									
Gheorghe Craioveanu	38	26	14	0	237	0	0	-	Romania
Daniel Guiza	25	35	32	23	2217	8	0	-	Spain
Fernando Nano	24	19	8	2	265	3	0	-	Spain
Valentin Pachon	29	29	22	1	420	2	0	-	Spain
Veljko Paunovic	28	32	30	15	1800	2	0	-	Serbia & Mont
Ivan Riki	25	33	32	27	2491	2	0	-	Spain
Jorge Yordi	31	1	0	0	0	0	0	-	Spain

TEAM OF THE SEASON

MONTHLY POINTS TALLY

Month	Points	%
AUGUST	3	100%
SEPTEMBER	8	67%
OCTOBER	6	40%
NOVEMBER	4	44%
DECEMBER	3	25%
JANUARY	4	33%
FEBRUARY	3	25%
MARCH	9	60%
APRIL	11	73%
MAY	3	33%

LEAGUE GOALS

	PLAYER	MINS	GOALS	S RATE
1	Pernia	3208	10	321
2	Paunovic	1800	10	180
3	Guiza	2217	9	246
4	Riki	2491	8	311
5	Gavilan	2573	4	643
6	Nano	265	2	133
7	Pachon	420	2	210
8	Pulido	1805	2	903
9	Dorado	1489	2	745
10	Redondo	1469	2	735
11	Tena	1443	1	1443
12	Belenguer	2570	1	2570
	Other		1	
	TOTAL		54	

TOP POINT EARNERS

	PLAYER	GAMES	AV PTS
1	Paunovic	15	1.73
2	Cotelo	18	1.72
3	Luis Garcia	25	1.64
4	Tena	16	1.63
5	Guiza	23	1.61
6	Pulido	18	1.61
7	Contra	23	1.57
8	Pernia	36	1.42
9	Gavilan	26	1.42
10	Celestini	16	1.38
	CLUB AVERAGE:		1.42

DISCIPLINARY RECORDS

	PLAYER	YELLOW	RED	AVE
1	Matellan	10	1	173
2	Diego Rivas	15	2	174
3	Pernia	11	1	267
4	Guiza	8	0	277
5	Belenguer	8	1	285
6	Contra	7	0	302
7	Gavilan	7	1	321
8	Dorado	4	0	372
9	Celestini	4	0	378
10	Cotelo	3	2	384
11	Pulido	4	0	451
12	Redondo	3	0	489
13	Tena	2	0	721
	Other	8	0	
	TOTAL	94	8	

KEY GOALKEEPER

Juan Calatayud

Goals Conceded in the League	16	**Counting Games** League games when player was on pitch for at least 70 minutes	13
Defensive Rating Ave number of mins between League goals conceded while on the pitch	73	**Clean Sheets** In League games when player was on pitch for at least 70 minutes	3

KEY PLAYERS - DEFENDERS

Cosmin Contra

Goals Conceded Number of League goals conceded while the player was on the pitch	29	**Clean Sheets** In League games when player was on pitch for at least 70 minutes	4
Defensive Rating Ave number of mins between League goals conceded while on the pitch	73	**Club Defensive Rating** Average number of mins between League goals conceded by the club this season	70

	PLAYER	CON LGE	CLEAN SHEETS	DEF RATE
1	Cosmin Contra	29	4	73 mins
2	Anibal Samuel Matellan	27	5	71 mins
3	Manuel Tena	21	2	69 mins
4	Mariano Pernia	47	7	68 mins

KEY PLAYERS - MIDFIELDERS

Mario Cotelo

Goals in the League	0	**Contribution to Attacking Power** Average number of minutes between League team goals while on pitch	57
Defensive Rating Average number of mins between League goals conceded while on the pitch	66	**Scoring Difference** Defensive Rating minus Contribution to Attacking Power	9

	PLAYER	LGE GOALS	DEF RATE	POWER	SCORE DIFF
1	Mario Cotelo	0	66	57	9 mins
2	Jaime Gavilan	4	70	64	6 mins
3	Fabio Celestini	0	72	66	6 mins
4	Diego Rivas	0	74	72	2 mins

KEY PLAYERS - GOALSCORERS

Veljko Paunovic

Goals in the League	10	**Player Strike Rate** Average number of minutes between League goals scored by player	180
Contribution to Attacking Power Average number of minutes between League team goals while on pitch	72	**Club Strike Rate** Average number of minutes between League goals scored by club	63

	PLAYER	LGE GOALS	POWER	STRIKE RATE
1	Veljko Paunovic	10	72	180 mins
2	Daniel Gonzalez Guiza	9	60	246 mins
3	Ivan Riki	8	66	311 mins
4	Mariano Pernia	10	62	321 mins

Ivan Riki and Manuel Tena

SQUAD APPEARANCES

Match	1	2	3	4	5	6	7	8	9	10	11	12	13	14	15	16	17	18	19
Venue	A	H	A	H	A	H	A	H	A	A	H	H	H	A	H	A	H	A	H
Competition	L	L	L	L	L	L	L	L	L	L	L	L	L	L	L	L	L	L	L
Result	W	D	W	D	W	W	L	W	L	L	L	D	W	L	L	L	W	L	D

Match	20	21	22	23	24	25	26	27	28	29	30	31	32	33	34	35	36	37	38
Venue	H	A	H	A	H	A	H	A	H	A	H	A	A	H	A	H	A	H	A
Competition	L	L	L	L	L	L	L	L	L	L	L	L	L	L	L	L	L	L	L
Result	W	L	D	D	L	D	W	W	L	L	W	W	W	D	W	D	L	W	L

Goalkeepers
Juan Calatayud
Luis Garcia
Alejandro Rebollo
Alfonso Monreal Sito

Defenders
David Belenguer
Cosmin Contra
Anibal Samuel Matellan
Javier Arango Paredes
Mariano Pernia
Martin Pulido
Manuel Tena

Midfielders
Ruiz Alberto
Fabio Celestini
Jaja Coelho
Mario Cotelo
David Cubillo
Diego Rivas
Angel Dorado
Jaime Gavilan
Pablo Redondo

Forwards
Gheorghe Craioveanu
Daniel Gonzalez Guiza
Fernando Nano
Valentin Pachon
Veljko Paunovic
Ivan Riki
Jorge Yordi

KEY: On all match · On bench · Subbed or sent off (Counting game) · Subbed or sent off (playing less than 70 minutes) · Subbed on from bench (Counting Game) · Subbed on (playing less than 70 minutes) · Subbed on and then subbed or sent off (Counting Game) · Subbed on and then subbed or sent off (playing less than 70 minutes) · Not in 16

ATLETICO MADRID

Final Position: **10th**

KEY: ☐Won ☐Drawn ☐Lost

							Attendance
1	sppr1	**Real Zaragoza**	H	D	0-0		50,000
2	sppr1	**Deportivo**	A	L	0-1		27,000
3	sppr1	**Barcelona**	H	W	2-1	Torres 17; Kezman 46	65,000
4	sppr1	**Real Sociedad**	A	L	2-3	Torres 9; Kezman 18	31,300
5	sppr1	**Getafe**	H	L	0-1		50,000
6	sppr1	**Malaga**	A	W	2-0	Torres 66 pen; Kezman 75	21,000
7	sppr1	**Real Madrid**	H	L	0-3		56,000
8	sppr1	**R Santander**	A	W	1-0	Rodriguez 45	15,300
9	sppr1	**Cadiz**	H	W	3-0	Rodriguez 23; Pablo Ibanez 64; Galletti 87	35,000
10	sppr1	**Villarreal**	H	D	1-1	Zahinos 5	50,000
11	sppr1	**Seville**	A	D	0-0		35,000
12	sppr1	**Celta Vigo**	A	L	1-2	Antonio Lopez 61	17,000
13	sppr1	**Espanyol**	H	D	1-1	Luccin 9	35,000
14	sppr1	**Athl Bilbao**	A	D	1-1	Kezman 12	40,000
15	sppr1	**Alaves**	H	D	1-1	Torres 66	30,000
16	sppr1	**Mallorca**	A	D	2-2	Rodriguez 1; Colsa 13	14,000
17	sppr1	**Osasuna**	A	L	1-2	Petrov 25	14,000
18	sppr1	**Valencia**	H	D	0-0		35,000
19	sppr1	**Real Betis**	A	L	0-1		35,000
20	sppr1	**Real Zaragoza**	A	W	2-0	Rodriguez 28; Torres 59	30,000
21	sppr1	**Deportivo**	H	W	3-2	Rodriguez 33,81; Antonio Lopez 54	35,000
22	sppr1	**Barcelona**	A	W	3-1	Torres 32,76; Rodriguez 46	83,000
23	sppr1	**Real Sociedad**	H	W	1-0	Kezman 82	45,000
24	sppr1	**Getafe**	A	W	3-0	Luccin 29; Rodriguez 47; Torres 64	12,000
25	sppr1	**Malaga**	H	W	5-0	Torres 6,10; Rodriguez 40; Valera 67,90	50,000
26	sppr1	**Real Madrid**	A	L	1-2	Kezman 27	82,000
27	sppr1	**R Santander**	H	W	2-1	Torres 65 pen; Pablo Ibanez 74	40,000
28	sppr1	**Villarreal**	A	D	1-1	Torres 58	19,000
29	sppr1	**Seville**	H	L	0-1		45,000
30	sppr1	**Cadiz**	A	D	1-1	Kezman 34	20,000
31	sppr1	**Celta Vigo**	H	L	0-3		50,000
32	sppr1	**Espanyol**	A	D	1-1	Gabi 47	22,850
33	sppr1	**Athl Bilbao**	H	W	1-0	Torres 82	30,000
34	sppr1	**Alaves**	A	W	1-0	Antonio Lopez 23	14,436
35	sppr1	**Mallorca**	H	L	0-1		43,000
36	sppr1	**Osasuna**	H	L	0-1		20,000
37	sppr1	**Valencia**	A	D	1-1	Rodriguez 21	50,000
38	sppr1	**Real Betis**	H	D	1-1	Kezman 24	25,000

LEAGUE APPEARANCES, BOOKINGS AND CAPS

	AGE (on 01/07/06)	IN NAMED 18	APPEARANCES	COUNTING GAMES	MINUTES ON PITCH	YELLOW CARDS	RED CARDS	CAPS THIS SEASON	NATIONAL SIDE
Goalkeepers									
Ivan Cuellar	22	25	0	0	0	0	0	-	Spain
Ismael Gomez Falcon	22	10	6	5	488	0	1	-	Spain
Leonardo Franco	29	33	33	31	2843	2	0	4	Argentina (9)
Francisco Galan	21	4	0	0	0	0	0	-	Spain
Jimenez Gago	20	4	1	1	90	0	0	-	Spain
Defenders									
Antonio Lopez	24	36	36	35	3154	6	1	-	Spain
Antonio Moreno	23	5	1	0	1	0	0	-	Spain
Jose Garcia Calvo	31	36	12	6	574	3	0	-	Spain
Francisco Molinero	20	28	11	10	894	5	0	-	Spain
Pablo Ibanez	24	36	36	35	3217	10	1	6	Spain (5)
Luis Perea	27	34	34	34	3046	11	1	4	Colombia (27)
Pablo Sicillia	24	5	1	0	2	0	0	-	Spain
Juan Velasco	29	29	25	25	2229	8	0	-	Spain
Midfielders									
Gonzalo Colsa	29	29	14	5	591	1	0	-	Spain
Fernandez Gabi	22	36	32	20	1968	9	1	-	Spain
Luciano Galletti	25	33	26	12	1371	5	0	-	Argentina
Ariel Ibagaza	29	30	25	13	1471	8	0	-	Argentina
Peter Luccin	27	30	29	25	2428	16	2	-	France
Maxi Rodriguez	25	29	29	21	2220	4	0	6	Argentina (9)
Mario Suarez Mata	19	11	5	2	203	0	0	-	Spain
Juan Valera	21	30	16	7	775	2	0	-	Spain
Julian Vara Lopez	22	2	2	0	21	0	0	-	Spain
Jose Zahinos	28	29	17	13	1235	5	0	-	Spain
Forwards									
Angel Arizmendi	22	8	1	0	4	0	0	-	Spain
Nobrega Braulio	20	3	1	0	21	0	0	-	Spain
Manu Del Moral	22	13	5	2	207	0	0	-	Spain
Mateja Kezman	27	32	30	24	2264	9	1	9	Serbia & Mont (44)
Fernando Marques	21	10	7	2	238	0	0	-	Spain
Martin Petrov	27	37	35	30	2684	8	1	6	Bulgaria (38)
Segovia Rufino	21	2	1	0	21	0	0	-	Spain
Fernando Torres	22	36	36	35	3192	6	0	7	Spain (5)

TEAM OF THE SEASON

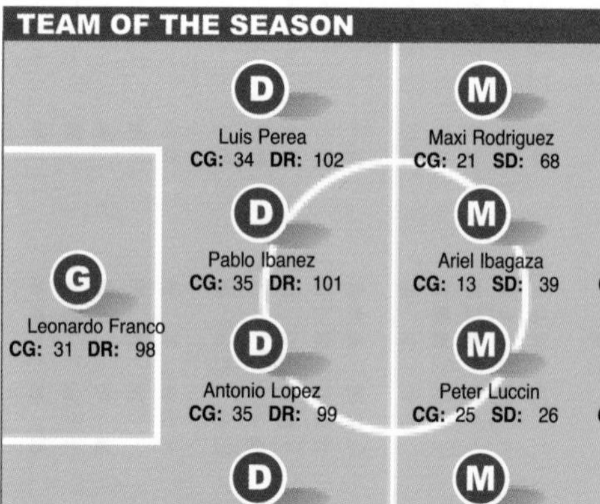

MONTHLY POINTS TALLY

AUGUST	1	33%
SEPTEMBER	3	25%
OCTOBER	10	67%
NOVEMBER	2	22%
DECEMBER	3	25%
JANUARY	7	58%
FEBRUARY	12	100%
MARCH	5	33%
APRIL	7	47%
MAY	2	22%

LEAGUE GOALS

	PLAYER	MINS	GOALS	S RATE
1	Torres	3192	13	246
2	Rodriguez	2220	10	222
3	Kezman	2264	8	283
4	Antonio Lopez	3154	3	1051
5	Luccin	2428	2	1214
6	Pablo Ibanez	3217	2	1609
7	Valera	775	2	388
8	Zahinos	1235	1	1235
9	Gabi	1968	1	1968
10	Galletti	1371	1	1371
11	Colsa	591	1	591
12	Petrov	2684	1	2684
	Other		0	
	TOTAL		45	

TOP POINT EARNERS

	PLAYER	GAMES	AV PTS
1	Rodriguez	21	1.81
2	Franco	31	1.55
3	Kezman	24	1.54
4	Velasco	25	1.52
5	Luccin	25	1.52
6	Petrov	30	1.43
7	Perea	34	1.41
8	Pablo Ibanez	35	1.37
9	Antonio Lopez	35	1.37
10	Galletti	12	1.33
	CLUB AVERAGE:		1.37

DISCIPLINARY RECORDS

	PLAYER	YELLOW	RED	AVE
1	Luccin	16	2	134
2	Molinero	5	0	178
3	Ibagaza	8	0	183
4	Garcia Calvo	3	0	191
5	Gabi	9	1	196
6	Kezman	9	1	226
7	Zahinos	5	0	247
8	Perea	11	1	253
9	Galletti	5	0	274
10	Velasco	8	0	278
11	Pablo Ibanez	10	1	292
12	Petrov	8	1	298
13	Valera	2	0	387
	Other	19	2	
	TOTAL	118	9	

KEY GOALKEEPER

Leonardo Franco

Goals Conceded in the League	29	Counting Games League games when player was on pitch for at least 70 minutes	31
Defensive Rating Ave number of mins between League goals conceded while on the pitch	98	Clean Sheets In League games when player was on pitch for at least 70 minutes	11

KEY PLAYERS - DEFENDERS

Luis Perea

Goals Conceded Number of League goals conceded while the player was on the pitch	30	Clean Sheets In League games when player was on pitch for at least 70 minutes	11
Defensive Rating Ave number of mins between League goals conceded while on the pitch	102	Club Defensive Rating Average number of mins between League goals conceded by the club this season	92

	PLAYER	CON LGE	CLEAN SHEETS	DEF RATE
1	Luis Perea	30	11	102 mins
2	Pablo Ibanez	32	12	101 mins
3	Antonio Lopez	32	11	99 mins
4	Juan Velasco	23	10	97 mins

KEY PLAYERS - MIDFIELDERS

Maxi Rodriguez

Goals in the League	10	Contribution to Attacking Power Average number of minutes between League team goals while on pitch	63
Defensive Rating Average number of mins between League goals conceded while on the pitch	131	Scoring Difference Defensive Rating minus Contribution to Attacking Power	68

	PLAYER	LGE GOALS	DEF RATE	POWER	SCORE DIFF
1	Maxi Rodriguez	10	131	63	68 mins
2	Ariel Ibagaza	0	113	74	39 mins
3	Peter Luccin	2	97	71	26 mins
4	Luciano Galletti	1	105	91	14 mins

KEY PLAYERS - GOALSCORERS

Maxi Rodriguez

Goals in the League	10	Player Strike Rate Average number of minutes between League goals scored by player	222
Contribution to Attacking Power Average number of minutes between League team goals while on pitch	63	Club Strike Rate Average number of minutes between League goals scored by club	76

	PLAYER	LGE GOALS	POWER	STRIKE RATE
1	Maxi Rodriguez	10	63	222 mins
2	Fernando Torres	13	78	246 mins
3	Mateja Kezman	8	67	283 mins
4	Antonio Lopez	3	73	1051 mins

Fernando Torres celebrates

SQUAD APPEARANCES

Match	1	2	3	4	5	6	7	8	9	10	11	12	13	14	15	16	17	18	19	20	21	22	23	24	25	26	27	28	29	30	31	32	33	34	35	36	37	38
Venue	H	A	H	A	H	A	H	A	H	H	A	A	H	A	H	A	A	H	A	A	H	A	H	A	H	A	H	A	H	A	H	A	H	A	H	H	A	H
Competition	L	L	L	L	L	L	L	L	L	L	L	L	L	L	L	L	L	L	L	L	L	L	L	L	L	L	L	L	L	L	L	L	L	L	L	L	L	L
Result	D	L	W	L	L	W	L	W	W	D	D	L	D	D	D	D	L	D	L	W	W	W	W	W	W	L	W	D	L	D	L	D	W	W	L	L	D	D

Goalkeepers
Ivan Cuellar
Ismael Gomez Falcon
Leonardo Franco
Francisco Galan
Roberto Jimenez Gago

Defenders
Antonio Lopez
Antonio Moreno
Jose Garcia Calvo
Francisco Molinero
Pablo Ibanez
Luis Perea
Pablo Sicillia
Juan Velasco

Midfielders
Gonzalo Colsa
Fernandez Gabi
Luciano Galletti
Ariel Ibagaza
Peter Luccin
Maxi Rodriguez
Mario Suarez Mata
Juan Valera
Julian Vara Lopez
Jose Zahinos

Forwards
Angel Arizmendi
Nobrega Braulio
Manu Del Moral
Mateja Kezman
Fernando Marques
Martin Petrov
Segovia Rufino
Fernando Torres

KEY: ■ On all match ■ On bench ⏮ Subbed or sent off (Counting game) « Subbed or sent off (playing less than 70 minutes) ⏭ Subbed on from bench (Counting Game) » Subbed on (playing less than 70 minutes) ⏭ Subbed on and then subbed or sent off (Counting Game) » Subbed on and then subbed or sent off (playing less than 70 minutes) □ Not in 16

REAL ZARAGOZA

Final Position: **11th**

KEY: ☐ Won ☐ Drawn ☐ Lost

						Attendance
1	sppr1	**Atl Madrid**	A	D	0-0		50,000
2	sppr1	**Valencia**	H	D	2-2 Ewerthon 8; Cani 29	30,000
3	sppr1	**Real Betis**	A	D	0-0	44,000
4	sppr1	**Osasuna**	H	W	3-1 Milito 50; Sergio Garcia 80; Savio 82	28,000
5	sppr1	**Deportivo**	H	D	1-1 Milito 13	30,000
6	sppr1	**Barcelona**	A	D	2-2 Milito 47,52	81,000
7	sppr1	**Real Sociedad**	H	L	0-1	29,000
8	sppr1	**Getafe**	A	L	2-5 Movilla 48; Pulido 58 og	14,000
9	sppr1	**R Santander**	H	D	1-1 Milito, D 36	30,000
10	sppr1	**Malaga**	H	D	1-1 Ewerthon 12	25,000
11	sppr1	**Real Madrid**	A	L	0-1	82,000
12	sppr1	**Villarreal**	A	D	0-0	17,000
13	sppr1	**Seville**	H	L	0-2	28,000
14	sppr1	**Cadiz**	A	W	2-1 Cani 69; Ewerthon 70	22,000
15	sppr1	**Celta Vigo**	H	W	1-0 Ewerthon 76	30,000
16	sppr1	**Espanyol**	A	D	2-2 Generelo 51; Milito, D 66	16,190
17	sppr1	**Athl Bilbao**	H	W	3-2 Ewerthon 50 pen,58; Milito, D 76	26,000
18	sppr1	**Alaves**	A	W	2-0 Milito, D 46; Ewerthon 85	12,273
19	sppr1	**Mallorca**	H	W	3-1 Oscar 25; Milito, D 27,80	28,000
20	sppr1	**Atl Madrid**	H	L	0-2	30,000
21	sppr1	**Valencia**	A	D	2-2 Sergio Garcia 45; Ewerthon 64	40,000
22	sppr1	**Real Betis**	H	W	4-3 Milito, D 11,22; Oscar 12; Sergio Garcia 15	33,000
23	sppr1	**Osasuna**	A	D	1-1 Ponzio 41	17,000
24	sppr1	**Deportivo**	A	D	1-1 Milito, D 16	20,350
25	sppr1	**Barcelona**	H	L	0-2	30,000
26	sppr1	**Real Sociedad**	A	W	3-1 Ewerthon 55,69; Oscar 61	19,831
27	sppr1	**Getafe**	H	L	1-2 Milito, D 33	32,000
28	sppr1	**Malaga**	A	W	1-0 Ewerthon 90	16,000
29	sppr1	**Real Madrid**	H	D	1-1 Milito, D 47	30,000
30	sppr1	**R Santander**	A	D	0-0	13,800
31	sppr1	**Villarreal**	H	L	0-1	30,000
32	sppr1	**Seville**	A	D	1-1 Sergio Garcia 46	27,000
33	sppr1	**Cadiz**	H	L	1-2 Savio 20	10,000
34	sppr1	**Celta Vigo**	A	L	0-4	18,000
35	sppr1	**Espanyol**	H	D	1-1 Ewerthon 9	25,000
36	sppr1	**Athl Bilbao**	A	L	0-1	40,000
37	sppr1	**Alaves**	H	W	3-0 Milito, D 59; Savio 69 pen; Oscar 75	20,000
38	sppr1	**Mallorca**	A	L	1-3 Savio 37	12,500

LEAGUE APPEARANCES, BOOKINGS AND CAPS

	AGE (on 01/07/06)	IN NAMED 18	APPEARANCES	COUNTING GAMES	MINUTES ON PITCH	YELLOW CARDS	RED CARDS	CAPS THIS SEASON	NATIONAL SIDE
Goalkeepers									
Sanchez Cesar	34	35	35	34	3090	0	0	-	Spain
Martinez Miguel	24	8	0	0	0	0	0	-	Spain
Raul Valbuena	31	32	5	3	380	1	0	-	Spain
Defenders									
Major Alvaro	29	33	31	30	2740	12	0	-	Brazil
Agustin Aranzabal	33	17	9	2	362	1	0	-	Spain
Manuel Capi	25	30	8	5	528	4	0	-	Spain
Luis Cuartero	31	24	16	7	898	2	0	-	Spain
David Generelo	23	36	30	11	1497	7	1	-	Spain
Jorge Blas Gotor	19	2	0	0	0	0	0	-	Spain
Jesus Maria Chus	22	7	5	3	345	3	1	-	Spain
Cesar Jimenez	28	4	1	0	14	0	0	-	Spain
Gabriel Milito	25	35	34	31	2919	11	0	7	Argentina (9)
Delio Toledo	29	33	31	23	2396	13	1	-	Paraguay
Midfielders									
Ruben Cani	24	30	29	22	2157	4	0	-	Spain
Albert Celades	30	33	26	14	1713	7	1	-	Spain
Miguel Angel Corona	25	11	3	0	47	1	0	-	Spain
Angel Lafita	21	26	13	2	431	0	0	-	Spain
Jose Movilla	31	32	25	15	1616	4	0	-	Spain
Gonzalez Oscar	23	38	36	18	2330	0	0	-	Spain
Leonardo Ponzio	24	36	35	34	3088	11	0	-	Argentina
Alberto Zapater	21	37	35	25	2430	8	0	-	Spain
Forwards									
Juan Camacho	25	1	0	0	0	0	0	-	Spain
Ewerthon	25	38	37	24	2697	2	0	-	Brazil
Diego Milito	27	36	36	30	2929	1	0	-	Argentina
Bortolini Savio	32	31	31	23	2265	1	0	-	Brazil
Sergio Garcia	23	31	18	3	708	1	0	-	Spain

TEAM OF THE SEASON

G Sanchez Cesar CG: 34 DR: 64

D Major Alvaro CG: 30 DR: 72
D Delio Toledo CG: 23 DR: 70
D Gabriel Milito CG: 31 DR: 68
D David Generelo* CG: 11 DR: 78

M Jose Movilla CG: 15 SD: 19
M Ruben Cani CG: 22 SD: 4
M Leonardo Ponzio CG: 34 SD: -2
M Gonzalez Oscar CG: 18 SD: -6

F Ewerthon CG: 24 SR: 225
F Diego Milito CG: 30 SR: 244

MONTHLY POINTS TALLY

AUGUST	1	33%
SEPTEMBER	6	50%
OCTOBER	3	20%
NOVEMBER	1	11%
DECEMBER	10	83%
JANUARY	7	58%
FEBRUARY	5	42%
MARCH	8	53%
APRIL	2	13%
MAY	3	33%

LEAGUE GOALS

	PLAYER	MINS	GOALS	S RATE
1	Ewerthon	2697	12	225
2	Milito, D	2929	12	244
3	Milito, G	2919	4	730
4	Sergio Garcia	708	4	177
5	Oscar	2330	4	583
6	Savio	2265	4	566
7	Cani	2157	2	1079
8	Movilla	1616	1	1616
9	Ponzio	3088	1	3088
10	Generelo	1497	1	1497
	Other		1	
	TOTAL		46	

TOP POINT EARNERS

	PLAYER	GAMES	AV PTS
1	Oscar	18	1.39
2	Ewerthon	24	1.38
3	Cani	22	1.36
4	Movilla	15	1.27
5	Ponzio	34	1.24
6	Alvaro	30	1.23
7	Cesar, S	34	1.18
8	Zapater	25	1.16
9	Milito, G	31	1.13
10	Milito, D	30	1.10
	CLUB AVERAGE:		1.21

DISCIPLINARY RECORDS

	PLAYER	YELLOW	RED	AVE
1	Capi	4	0	132
2	Toledo	13	1	171
3	Generelo	7	1	187
4	Celades	7	1	214
5	Alvaro	12	0	228
6	Milito, G	11	0	265
7	Ponzio	11	0	280
8	Zapater	8	0	303
9	Movilla	4	0	404
10	Cuartero	2	0	449
11	Cani	4	0	539
12	Sergio Garcia	1	0	708
13	Ewerthon	2	0	1348
	Other	2	0	
	TOTAL	88	3	

KEY GOALKEEPER

Sanchez Cesar

Goals Conceded in the League	48	**Counting Games** League games when player was on pitch for at least 70 minutes	34
Defensive Rating Ave number of mins between League goals conceded while on the pitch	64	**Clean Sheets** In League games when player was on pitch for at least 70 minutes	7

KEY PLAYERS - DEFENDERS

Major Alvaro

Goals Conceded Number of League goals conceded while the player was on the pitch	38	**Clean Sheets** In League games when player was on pitch for at least 70 minutes	7
Defensive Rating Ave number of mins between League goals conceded while on the pitch	72	**Club Defensive Rating** Average number of mins between League goals conceded by the club this season	67

	PLAYER	CON LGE	CLEAN SHEETS	DEF RATE
1	Major Alvaro	38	7	72 mins
2	Delio Toledo	34	6	70 mins
3	Gabriel Milito	43	5	68 mins

KEY PLAYERS - MIDFIELDERS

Jose Movilla

Goals in the League	1	**Contribution to Attacking Power** Average number of minutes between League team goals while on pitch	54
Defensive Rating Average number of mins between League goals conceded while on the pitch	73	**Scoring Difference** Defensive Rating minus Contribution to Attacking Power	19

	PLAYER	LGE GOALS	DEF RATE	POWER	SCORE DIFF
1	Jose Movilla	1	73	54	19 mins
2	Ruben Cani	2	74	70	4 mins
3	Leonardo Ponzio	1	72	74	-2 mins
4	Gonzalez Oscar	4	63	69	-6 mins

KEY PLAYERS - GOALSCORERS

Ewerthon

Goals in the League	12	**Player Strike Rate** Average number of minutes between League goals scored by player	225
Contribution to Attacking Power Average number of minutes between League team goals while on pitch	73	**Club Strike Rate** Average number of minutes between League goals scored by club	74

	PLAYER	LGE GOALS	POWER	STRIKE RATE
1	Ewerthon	12	73	225 mins
2	Diego Milito	12	75	244 mins
3	Bortolini Savio	4	84	566 mins
4	Gonzalez Oscar	4	69	583 mins

Diego Milito

SQUAD APPEARANCES

Match	1	2	3	4	5	6	7	8	9	10	11	12	13	14	15	16	17	18	19	20	21	22	23	24	25	26	27	28	29	30	31	32	33	34	35	36	37	38
Venue	A	H	A	H	H	A	H	A	H	H	A	A	H	A	H	A	H	A	H	H	A	H	A	A	H	A	H	A	H	A	H	A	H	A	H	A	H	A
Competition	L	L	L	L	L	L	L	L	L	L	L	L	L	L	L	L	L	L	L	L	L	L	L	L	L	L	L	L	L	L	L	L	L	L	L	L	L	L
Result	D	D	D	W	D	D	L	L	D	D	L	D	L	W	W	D	W	W	W	L	D	W	D	D	L	W	L	W	D	D	L	D	L	L	D	L	W	L

Goalkeepers
Sanchez Cesar
Martinez Miguel
Raul Valbuena

Defenders
Major Alvaro
Agustin Aranzabal
Manuel Capi
Luis Cuartero
David Generelo
Jorge Blas Gotor
Jesus Maria Gomez Chus
Cesar Jimenez
Gabriel Milito
Delio Toledo

Midfielders
Ruben Cani
Albert Celades
Miguel Angel Corona
Angel Lafita
Jose Movilla
Gonzalez Oscar
Leonardo Ponzio
Alberto Zapater

Forwards
Juan Camacho
Ewerthon
Diego Milito
Bortolini Savio
Sergio Garcia

KEY: On all match · On bench · Subbed or sent off (Counting game) · Subbed or sent off (playing less than 70 minutes) · Subbed on from bench (Counting Game) · Subbed on (playing less than 70 minutes) · Subbed on and then subbed or sent off (Counting Game) · Subbed on and then subbed or sent off (playing less than 70 minutes) · Not in 16

ATHLETIC BILBAO

Final Position: **12th**

KEY: ☐ Won ☐ Drawn ☐ Lost

							Attendance
1	sppr1	**Real Sociedad**	H	W	3-0	Yeste 47; Llorente 52; Prieto 81	42,000
2	sppr1	**Getafe**	A	D	1-1	Casas 39	14,000
3	sppr1	**Malaga**	H	L	1-2	Lacruz Gomez 90	32,000
4	sppr1	**Real Madrid**	A	L	1-3	Woodgate 26 og	70,000
5	sppr1	**R Santander**	H	D	0-0		30,000
6	sppr1	**Villarreal**	A	L	1-3	Joseba Etxeberria 20	18,000
7	sppr1	**Seville**	H	L	0-1		32,000
8	sppr1	**Cadiz**	A	L	0-1		20,000
9	sppr1	**Osasuna**	A	L	2-3	Gurpegui 26; Josetxo 81 og	15,500
10	sppr1	**Celta Vigo**	H	D	1-1	Gurpegui 24	30,000
11	sppr1	**Espanyol**	A	D	1-1	Prieto 19	18,500
12	sppr1	**Alaves**	H	L	0-2		40,000
13	sppr1	**Mallorca**	A	W	1-0	Prieto 57	10,000
14	sppr1	**Atl Madrid**	H	D	1-1	Orbaiz 90	40,000
15	sppr1	**Valencia**	A	D	1-1	Joseba Etxeberria 56	48,000
16	sppr1	**Real Betis**	H	W	2-0	Urzaiz 22; Danobeltia 29	30,000
17	sppr1	**Real Zaragoza**	A	L	2-3	Lacruz Gomez 20; Joseba Etxeberria 47	26,000
18	sppr1	**Deportivo**	H	L	1-2	Urzaiz 58	32,000
19	sppr1	**Barcelona**	A	L	1-2	Llorente 16	72,400
20	sppr1	**Real Sociedad**	A	D	3-3	Aduriz 48,67; Iraola 90	22,700
21	sppr1	**Getafe**	H	W	1-0	Orbaiz 73	30,000
22	sppr1	**Malaga**	A	L	1-2	Aduriz 40	22,000
23	sppr1	**Real Madrid**	H	L	0-2		40,000
24	sppr1	**R Santander**	A	W	1-0	Urzaiz 86	17,900
25	sppr1	**Villarreal**	H	D	1-1	Aduriz 41	38,000
26	sppr1	**Seville**	A	L	1-2	Aduriz 21	38,000
27	sppr1	**Cadiz**	H	W	1-0	Tiko 90 pen	38,000
28	sppr1	**Celta Vigo**	A	W	1-0	Aduriz 7	15,000
29	sppr1	**Espanyol**	H	D	1-1	Yeste 90	37,000
30	sppr1	**Osasuna**	H	W	1-0	Prieto 59	40,000
31	sppr1	**Alaves**	A	D	0-0		13,137
32	sppr1	**Mallorca**	H	D	1-1	Yeste 3	37,000
33	sppr1	**Atl Madrid**	A	L	0-1		30,000
34	sppr1	**Valencia**	H	L	0-3		40,000
35	sppr1	**Real Betis**	A	D	1-1	Lacruz Gomez 66	30,000
36	sppr1	**Real Zaragoza**	H	W	1-0	Yeste 74	40,000
37	sppr1	**Deportivo**	A	W	2-1	Casas 70; Orbaiz 88 pen	19,340
38	sppr1	**Barcelona**	H	W	3-1	Iraola 57; Felipe 80; Oleguer 82	40,000

LEAGUE APPEARANCES, BOOKINGS AND CAPS

	AGE (on 01/07/06)	IN NAMED 18	APPEARANCES	COUNTING GAMES	MINUTES ON PITCH	YELLOW CARDS	RED CARDS	CAPS THIS SEASON	NATIONAL SIDE
Goalkeepers									
Daniel Aranzubia	26	38	18	18	1620	0	0	-	Spain
Igor Etxebarrieta	2007	4	0	0	0	0	0	-	Spain
Inaki Lafuente	30	33	20	20	1800	0	0	-	Spain
Defenders									
Fernando Amorebieta	21	18	16	10	1149	10	1	-	Spain
Javier Casas	24	32	24	18	1803	3	1	-	Spain
Unai Exposito	26	30	24	18	1748	5	1	-	Spain
Jesus Lacruz Gomez	28	36	28	20	2041	7	0	-	Spain
Ander Murillo	22	33	27	19	2046	3	0	-	Spain
Luis Prieto	27	36	36	31	2996	5	0	-	Spain
Francisco Tarantino	22	12	3	1	161	3	2	-	Spain
Alde'talora Ustaritz	23	19	18	16	1518	3	0	-	Spain
Midfielders									
Endika Bordas	24	23	3	1	163	0	0	-	Spain
Gurendez Felipe	30	17	2	0	54	0	0	-	Spain
Julen Guerrero	32	30	16	1	418	2	0	-	Spain
Carlos Gurpegui	25	30	30	29	2594	9	0	-	Spain
Felipe Gutierrez	21	10	7	6	547	0	0	-	Spain
Andoni Iraola	24	38	38	33	3129	1	0	-	Spain
Javi Gonzalez	32	11	5	1	218	0	0	-	Spain
Mikel Martins	23	1	0	0	0	0	0	-	Spain
Pablo Orbaiz	27	35	35	35	3138	11	0	-	Spain
Roberto Tiko	29	32	27	3	876	3	0	-	Spain
Francisco Yeste	26	35	35	31	2848	9	0	-	Spain
Forwards									
Aritz Aduriz	25	15	15	11	1117	3	0	-	Spain
Mikel Danobeltia	20	28	22	2	829	2	0	-	Spain
Joseba Etxeberria	28	30	29	18	2019	6	0	-	Spain
Fernando Llorente	21	32	22	6	1100	2	0	-	Spain
Ismael Urzaiz	34	28	25	12	1525	1	1	-	Spain

TEAM OF THE SEASON

G — Inaki Lafuente — CG: 20 DR: 86

D — Aldekoaotalora Ustaritz — CG: 16 DR: 84

D — Luis Prieto — CG: 31 DR: 79

D — Javier Casas — CG: 18 DR: 75

D — Ander Murillo — CG: 19 DR: 73

M — Andoni Iraola — CG: 33 SD: -5

M — Francisco Yeste — CG: 31 SD: -5

M — Pablo Orbaiz — CG: 35 SD: -7

M — Carlos Gurpegui — CG: 29 SD: -17

F — Ismael Urzaiz — CG: 12 SR: 508

F — Joseba Etxeberria — CG: 18 SR: 673

MONTHLY POINTS TALLY

AUGUST	3	100%
SEPTEMBER	2	17%
OCTOBER	1	7%
NOVEMBER	4	44%
DECEMBER	5	42%
JANUARY	4	33%
FEBRUARY	4	33%
MARCH	10	67%
APRIL	3	20%
MAY	9	100%

LEAGUE GOALS

	PLAYER	MINS	GOALS	S RATE
1	Aduriz	1117	6	186
2	Prieto	2996	4	749
3	Yeste	2848	4	712
4	Lacruz Gomez	2041	3	680
5	Orbaiz	3138	3	1046
6	Urzaiz	1525	3	508
7	Etxeberria	2019	3	673
8	Gurpegui	2594	2	1297
9	Casas	1803	2	902
10	Iraola	3129	2	1565
11	Llorente	1100	2	550
12	Tiko	876	1	876
13	Felipe	54	1	54
	Other		4	
	TOTAL		40	

TOP POINT EARNERS

	PLAYER	GAMES	AV PTS
1	Lafuente	20	1.50
2	Ustaritz	16	1.50
3	Urzaiz	12	1.42
4	Prieto	31	1.35
5	Casas	18	1.33
6	Murillo	19	1.32
7	Iraola	33	1.30
8	Yeste	31	1.23
9	Orbaiz	35	1.17
10	Joseba Etxeberria	18	1.17
	CLUB AVERAGE:		1.18

DISCIPLINARY RECORDS

	PLAYER	YELLOW	RED	AVE
1	Amorebieta	10	1	104
2	Orbaiz	11	0	285
3	Gurpegui	9	0	288
4	Exposito	5	1	291
5	Lacruz Gomez	7	0	291
6	Tiko	3	0	292
7	Yeste	9	0	316
8	Joseba Etxeberria	6	0	336
9	Aduriz	3	0	372
10	Danobeltia	2	0	414
11	Casas	3	1	450
12	Ustaritz	3	0	506
13	Llorente	2	0	550
	Other	10	1	
	TOTAL	83	4	

KEY GOALKEEPER

Inaki Lafuente

Goals Conceded in the League	21	**Counting Games** League games when player was on pitch for at least 70 minutes	20
Defensive Rating Ave number of mins between League goals conceded while on the pitch	86	**Clean Sheets** In League games when player was on pitch for at least 70 minutes	7

KEY PLAYERS - DEFENDERS

Aldekoaotalora Ustaritz

Goals Conceded Number of League goals conceded while the player was on the pitch	18	**Clean Sheets** In League games when player was on pitch for at least 70 minutes	5
Defensive Rating Ave number of mins between League goals conceded while on the pitch	84	**Club Defensive Rating** Average number of mins between League goals conceded by the club this season	74

	PLAYER	CON LGE	CLEAN SHEETS	DEF RATE
1	Aldekoaotalora Ustaritz	18	5	84 mins
2	Luis Prieto	38	10	79 mins
3	Javier Casas	24	6	75 mins
4	Ander Murillo	28	6	73 mins

KEY PLAYERS - MIDFIELDERS

Francisco Yeste

Goals in the League	4	**Contribution to Attacking Power** Average number of minutes between League team goals while on pitch	86
Defensive Rating Average number of mins between League goals conceded while on the pitch	81	**Scoring Difference** Defensive Rating minus Contribution to Attacking Power	-5

	PLAYER	LGE GOALS	DEF RATE	POWER	SCORE DIFF
1	Francisco Yeste	4	81	86	-5 mins
2	Andoni Iraola	2	80	85	-5 mins
3	Pablo Orbaiz	3	78	85	-7 mins
4	Carlos Gurpegui	2	72	89	-17 mins

KEY PLAYERS - GOALSCORERS

Ismael Urzaiz

Goals in the League	3	**Player Strike Rate** Average number of minutes between League goals scored by player	508
Contribution to Attacking Power Average number of minutes between League team goals while on pitch	80	**Club Strike Rate** Average number of minutes between League goals scored by club	86

	PLAYER	LGE GOALS	POWER	STRIKE RATE
1	Ismael Urzaiz	3	80	508 mins
2	Joseba Etxeberria	3	88	673 mins
3	Jesus Lacruz Gomez	3	85	680 mins
4	Francisco Yeste	4	86	712 mins

Pablo Orbaiz

SQUAD APPEARANCES

Match	1	2	3	4	5	6	7	8	9	10	11	12	13	14	15	16	17	18	19	20	21	22	23	24	25	26	27	28	29	30	31	32	33	34	35	36	37	38
Venue	H	A	H	A	H	A	H	A	A	H	A	H	A	H	A	H	A	H	A	A	H	A	H	A	H	A	H	A	H	H	A	H	A	H	A	H	A	H
Competition	L	L	L	L	L	L	L	L	L	L	L	L	L	L	L	L	L	L	L	L	L	L	L	L	L	L	L	L	L	L	L	L	L	L	L	L	L	L
Result	W	D	L	L	D	L	L	L	L	D	D	L	W	D	D	W	L	L	L	D	W	L	L	W	D	L	W	W	D	W	D	D	L	L	D	W	W	W

Goalkeepers
Daniel Aranzubia
Igor Etxebarrieta
Inaki Lafuente

Defenders
Fernando Amorebieta
Javier Casas
Unai Exposito
Jesus Lacruz Gomez
Ander Murillo
Luis Prieto
Francisco Tarantino
Aldekoaotalora Ustaritz

Midfielders
Endika Bordas
Gurendez Felipe
Iulen Guerrero
Carlos Gurpegui
Felipe Gutierrez
Andoni Iraola
Javi Gonzalez
Mikel Martins
Pablo Orbaiz
Roberto Tiko
Francisco Yeste

Forwards
Aritz Aduriz
Mikel Danobeltia
Joseba Etxeberria
Fernando Llorente
Ismael Urzaiz

KEY: On all match | On bench | Subbed or sent off (Counting game) | Subbed or sent off (playing less than 70 minutes) | Subbed on from bench (Counting Game) | Subbed on (playing less than 70 minutes) | Subbed on and then subbed or sent off (Counting Game) | Subbed on and then subbed or sent off (playing less than 70 minutes) | Not in 16

MALLORCA

Final Position: **13th**

KEY: ☐Won ☐Drawn ☐Lost

							Attendance
1	sppr1	**Deportivo**	H	L	0-1		18,000
2	sppr1	**Barcelona**	A	L	0-2		82,000
3	sppr1	**Real Sociedad**	H	W	5-2	Yordi 5; Arango 58,59,86; Choutos 90	8,500
4	sppr1	**Getafe**	A	D	1-1	Navarro 87	10,000
5	sppr1	**Malaga**	H	L	1-4	Choutos 78	14,000
6	sppr1	**Real Madrid**	A	L	0-4		72,140
7	sppr1	**R Santander**	H	D	0-0		15,000
8	sppr1	**Villarreal**	A	L	0-3		18,000
9	sppr1	**Celta Vigo**	H	W	1-0	Doni 47	12,000
10	sppr1	**Seville**	H	D	1-1	Victor 34	14,000
11	sppr1	**Cadiz**	A	W	2-1	Victor 26; Arango 84	21,000
12	sppr1	**Espanyol**	A	L	0-2		19,500
13	sppr1	**Athl Bilbao**	H	L	0-1		10,000
14	sppr1	**Alaves**	A	W	3-0	Victor 45,53; Iuliano 66	12,512
15	sppr1	**Osasuna**	A	L	0-1		14,500
16	sppr1	**Atl Madrid**	H	D	2-2	Iuliano 19,84	14,000
17	sppr1	**Valencia**	A	L	0-3		40,000
18	sppr1	**Real Betis**	H	D	1-1	Gutierrez 29	15,000
19	sppr1	**Real Zaragoza**	A	L	1-3	Arango 75	28,000
20	sppr1	**Deportivo**	A	D	2-2	Okubo 51; Arango 54	24,300
21	sppr1	**Barcelona**	H	L	0-3		23,000
22	sppr1	**Real Sociedad**	A	L	1-2	Pisculichi 33	19,000
23	sppr1	**Getafe**	H	D	1-1	Arango 67	17,000
24	sppr1	**Malaga**	A	W	2-0	Pisculichi 55; Campano 90	20,000
25	sppr1	**Real Madrid**	H	W	2-1	Pisculichi 53 pen; Arango 81	23,000
26	sppr1	**R Santander**	A	D	0-0		13,859
27	sppr1	**Villarreal**	H	D	1-1	Pereyra 1	17,000
28	sppr1	**Seville**	A	D	1-1	Okubo 70	35,000
29	sppr1	**Cadiz**	H	W	1-0	Victor 15	15,000
30	sppr1	**Celta Vigo**	A	L	0-2		15,671
31	sppr1	**Espanyol**	H	D	0-0		17,000
32	sppr1	**Athl Bilbao**	A	D	1-1	Arango 24	37,000
33	sppr1	**Alaves**	H	D	0-0		18,000
34	sppr1	**Osasuna**	H	L	0-1		15,000
35	sppr1	**Atl Madrid**	A	W	1-0	Gutierrez 79	43,000
36	sppr1	**Valencia**	H	W	2-1	Arango 8; Doni 46	18,000
37	sppr1	**Real Betis**	A	L	1-2	Yordi 63	45,000
38	sppr1	**Real Zaragoza**	H	W	3-1	Arango 20; Farinos 67; Yordi 86	12,500

LEAGUE APPEARANCES, BOOKINGS AND CAPS

	AGE (on 01/07/06)	IN NAMED 18	APPEARANCES	COUNTING GAMES	MINUTES ON PITCH	YELLOW CARDS	RED CARDS	CAPS THIS SEASON	NATIONAL SIDE
Goalkeepers									
Miguel Moya	22	37	9	8	725	0	0	-	Spain
Antonio Prats	34	37	30	30	2695	2	0	-	Spain
Defenders									
Sergio Ballesteros	30	25	20	19	1665	7	2	-	Spain
Fernandez Borja	25	29	16	7	855	4	0	-	Spain
David Cortez	26	31	27	25	2299	8	0	-	Spain
Mark Iuliano	32	15	13	11	1072	3	0	-	Italy
Jose	21	4	0	0	0	0	0	-	Spain
Francisco Maciel	28	29	18	17	1535	2	0	-	Argentina
Marcos Vales	31	1	0	0	0	0	0	-	Spain
Fernando Navarro	24	32	32	31	2826	12	2	-	Spain
Fernando Nino	31	1	0	0	0	0	0	-	Spain
Jose Nunes	29	17	17	17	1530	2	0	-	Portugal
Alessandro Potenza	22	23	18	16	1485	5	0	-	Italy
Rafael Rafita	23	4	1	0	18	0	0	-	Spain
Eduardo Tuzzio	31	21	10	7	726	5	2	-	Argentina
Midfielders									
Angelos Basinas	30	14	14	12	1161	2	0	4	Greece (34)
Alejandro Campano	27	33	26	9	1107	0	0	-	Spain
Cristiano Doni	33	28	24	13	1583	9	1	-	Italy
Francisco Farinos	28	28	17	8	965	5	1	-	Spain
Jonas Gutierrez	23	30	28	21	2187	5	0	-	Argentina
Txomin Nagore	31	1	1	1	90	0	0	-	Spain
Guillermo Pereyra	26	30	28	23	2196	10	1	-	Argentina
Castano Victor	21	30	28	14	1709	3	0	-	Spain
Forwards									
Juan Arango	26	37	37	35	3222	3	0	-	Venezuela
Bechio Luciano	22	1	1	1	90	1	0	-	Argentina
Toni Munoz	23	1	1	0	10	0	0	-	Spain
Yoshito Okubo	24	31	27	8	1221	4	0	-	Japan
Horacio Peralta	24	15	7	3	394	1	0	-	Uruguay
Pisculichi	22	19	17	9	1100	3	0	-	Argentina
Antoni Tuni	24	38	34	17	2132	5	0	-	Spain
Jorge Yordi	31	23	15	3	620	1	0	-	Spain

TEAM OF THE SEASON

G
Antonio Prats
CG: 30 DR: 75

D
Jose C Araujo Nunes
CG: 17 DR: 96

D
Sergio Ballesteros
CG: 19 DR: 76

D
Fernando Navarro
CG: 31 DR: 69

D
David Cortez
CG: 25 DR: 68

M
Angelos Basinas
CG: 12 SD: 32

M
Castano Victor
CG: 14 SD: -19

M
Guillermo Pereyra
CG: 23 SD: -21

M
Jonas Gutierrez
CG: 21 SD: -26

F
Juan Arango
CG: 35 SR: 293

F
Pisculichi*
CG: 9 SR: 367

MONTHLY POINTS TALLY

AUGUST	0	0%
SEPTEMBER	4	33%
OCTOBER	5	33%
NOVEMBER	3	33%
DECEMBER	4	33%
JANUARY	2	17%
FEBRUARY	7	58%
MARCH	6	40%
APRIL	6	40%
MAY	6	67%

LEAGUE GOALS

	PLAYER	MINS	GOALS	S RATE
1	Arango	3222	11	293
2	Victor	1709	5	342
3	Yordi	620	3	207
4	Pisculichi	1100	3	367
5	Iuliano	1072	3	357
6	Doni	1583	2	792
7	Okubo	1221	2	611
8	Choutos	174	2	87
9	Campano	1107	1	1107
10	Navarro	2826	1	2826
11	Pereyra	2196	1	2196
12	Farinos	965	1	965
13	Gutierrez	2187	1	2187
	Other		2	
	TOTAL		38	

TOP POINT EARNERS

	PLAYER	GAMES	AV PTS
1	Basinas	12	1.75
2	Ballesteros	19	1.32
3	Doni	13	1.31
4	Tuni	17	1.29
5	Nunes	17	1.29
6	Gutierrez	21	1.29
7	Maciel	17	1.29
8	Prats	30	1.27
9	Pereyra	23	1.22
10	Arango	35	1.20
	CLUB AVERAGE:		1.13

DISCIPLINARY RECORDS

	PLAYER	YELLOW	RED	AVE
1	Tuzzio	5	2	103
2	Doni	9	1	158
3	Farinos	5	1	160
4	Ballesteros	7	2	185
5	Pereyra	10	1	199
6	Navarro	12	2	201
7	Borja	4	0	213
8	Cortez	8	0	287
9	Potenza	5	0	297
10	Okubo	4	0	305
11	Iuliano	3	0	357
12	Pisculichi	3	0	366
13	Tuni	5	0	426
	Other	20	0	
	TOTAL	100	9	

KEY GOALKEEPER

Antonio Prats

Goals Conceded in the League	36	Counting Games League games when player was on pitch for at least 70 minutes	30
Defensive Rating Ave number of mins between League goals conceded while on the pitch	75	Clean Sheets In League games when player was on pitch for at least 70 minutes	9

KEY PLAYERS - GOALSCORERS

Juan Arango

Goals in the League	11	Player Strike Rate Average number of minutes between League goals scored by player	293
Contribution to Attacking Power Average number of minutes between League team goals while on pitch	90	Club Strike Rate Average number of minutes between League goals scored by club	92

	PLAYER	LGE GOALS	POWER	STRIKE RATE
1	Juan Arango	11	90	293 mins
2	Castano Victor	5	85	342 mins
3	Cristiano Doni	2	106	792 mins
4	Jonas Gutierrez	1	99	2187 mins

KEY PLAYERS - DEFENDERS

Jose Carlos Araujo Nunes

Goals Conceded Number of League goals conceded while the player was on the pitch	16	Clean Sheets In League games when player was on pitch for at least 70 minutes	6
Defensive Rating Ave number of mins between League goals conceded while on the pitch	96	Club Defensive Rating Average number of mins between League goals conceded by the club this season	68

	PLAYER	CON LGE	CLEAN SHEETS	DEF RATE
1	Jose Carlos Araujo Nunes	16	6	96 mins
2	Sergio Ballesteros	22	5	76 mins
3	Fernando Navarro	41	8	69 mins
4	David Cortez	34	6	68 mins

Juan Arango

KEY PLAYERS - MIDFIELDERS

Angelos Basinas

Goals in the League	0	Contribution to Attacking Power Average number of minutes between League team goals while on pitch	97
Defensive Rating Average number of mins between League goals conceded while on the pitch	129	Scoring Difference Defensive Rating minus Contribution to Attacking Power	32

	PLAYER	LGE GOALS	DEF RATE	POWER	SCORE DIFF
1	Angelos Basinas	0	129	97	32 mins
2	Castano Victor	5	66	85	-19 mins
3	Guillermo Pereyra	1	84	105	-21 mins
4	Jonas Gutierrez	1	73	99	-26 mins

SQUAD APPEARANCES

Match	1	2	3	4	5	6	7	8	9	10	11	12	13	14	15	16	17	18	19	20	21	22	23	24	25	26	27	28	29	30	31	32	33	34	35	36	37	38
Venue	H	A	H	A	H	A	H	A	H	H	A	A	H	A	A	H	A	H	A	A	H	A	H	A	H	A	H	A	H	A	H	A	H	H	A	H	A	H
Competition	L	L	L	L	L	L	L	L	L	L	L	L	L	L	L	L	L	L	L	L	L	L	L	L	L	L	L	L	L	L	L	L	L	L	L	L	L	L
Result	L	L	W	D	L	L	D	L	W	D	W	L	L	W	L	D	L	D	L	D	L	L	D	W	W	D	D	D	W	L	D	D	D	L	W	W	L	W

Goalkeepers
Miguel Moya
Antonio Prats

Defenders
Sergio Ballesteros
Fernandez Borja
David Cortez
Mark Iuliano
Jose
Francisco Maciel
Marcos Vales
Fernando Navarro
Fernando Nino
Jose Carlos Araujo Nunes
Alessandro Potenza
Rafael Rafita
Eduardo Tuzzio

Midfielders
Angelos Basinas
Alejandro Campano
Carlos Carmona
Cristiano Doni
Francisco Farinos
Jonas Gutierrez
Txomin Arbizu Nagore
Guillermo Pereyra
Castano Victor

Forwards
Juan Arango
Lambros Choutos
Bechio Luciano
Toni Munoz
Yoshito Okubo
Horacio Peralta
Pisculichi
Antoni Tuni
Jorge Yordi

KEY: On all match · On bench · Subbed or sent off (Counting game) · Subbed or sent off (playing less than 70 minutes) · Subbed on from bench (Counting Game) · Subbed on (playing less than 70 minutes) · Subbed on and then subbed or sent off (Counting Game) · Subbed on and then subbed or sent off (playing less than 70 minutes) · Not in 16

REAL BETIS

Final Position: **14th**

KEY: ☐Won ☐Drawn ☐Lost

							Attendance
1	ecql1	**AS Monaco**	H	W	1-0	Edu 90	24,000
2	ecql2	**AS Monaco**	A	D	2-2	Oliveira 16,75	13,011
3	sppr1	**Valencia**	A	L	0-1		43,000
4	sppr1	**Osasuna**	H	W	1-0	Oliveira 63 pen	40,000
5	ecgpg	**Liverpool**	H	L	1-2	Arzu 51	45,000
6	sppr1	**Real Zaragoza**	H	D	0-0		44,000
7	sppr1	**Deportivo**	A	D	1-1	Oliveira 28	23,400
8	sppr1	**Barcelona**	H	L	1-4	Juanito 38	45,000
9	ecgpg	**Anderlecht**	A	W	1-0	Oliveira 69	27,500
10	sppr1	**Real Sociedad**	A	D	1-1	Juanito 21	21,000
11	sppr1	**Getafe**	H	W	1-0	Oliveira 18 pen	39,000
12	ecgpg	**Chelsea**	A	L	0-4		36,457
13	sppr1	**Malaga**	A	L	0-5		20,000
14	sppr1	**Villarreal**	H	L	2-3	Oliveira 27; Javi Venta 62 og	32,000
15	sppr1	**Real Madrid**	H	L	0-2		35,000
16	ecgpg	**Chelsea**	H	W	1-0	Dani 28	55,000
17	sppr1	**R Santander**	A	D	1-1	Contreras 22	13,808
18	sppr1	**Seville**	A	L	0-1		41,000
19	ecgpg	**Liverpool**	A	D	0-0		42,077
20	sppr1	**Cadiz**	H	D	1-1	Assuncao 7	37,000
21	sppr1	**Celta Vigo**	A	L	1-2	Edu 89	15,000
22	ecgpg	**Anderlecht**	H	L	0-1		55,259
23	sppr1	**Espanyol**	H	D	0-0		35,000
24	sppr1	**Athl Bilbao**	A	L	0-2		30,000
25	sppr1	**Alaves**	H	W	3-0	Fernando 45; Xisco 65; Joaquin 86	30,000
26	sppr1	**Mallorca**	A	D	1-1	Robert 35	15,000
27	sppr1	**Atl Madrid**	H	W	1-0	Capi 30	35,000
28	sppr1	**Valencia**	H	L	0-2		35,000
29	sppr1	**Osasuna**	A	W	2-0	Luis Fernandez 34; Edu 59	15,500
30	sppr1	**Real Zaragoza**	A	L	3-4	Dani 23,49,60	33,000
31	sppr1	**Deportivo**	H	L	0-1		30,000
32	uc3rl1	**AZ Alkmaar**	H	W	2-0	Tardelli 70; Robert 79	30,000
33	sppr1	**Barcelona**	A	L	1-5	Joaquin 62	92,500
34	uc3rl2	**AZ Alkmaar**	A	L	1-2	Melli 94	8,073
35	sppr1	**Real Sociedad**	H	W	2-0	Dani 32; Robert 90	30,000
36	sppr1	**Getafe**	A	L	0-1		14,000
37	uc4rl1	**S Bucharest**	A	D	0-0		45,023
38	sppr1	**Malaga**	H	D	1-1	Rivas 21	38,000
39	uc4rl2	**S Bucharest**	H	L	0-3		15,851
40	sppr1	**Real Madrid**	A	D	0-0		72,000
41	sppr1	**R Santander**	H	W	1-0	Edu 37	30,000
42	sppr1	**Villarreal**	A	W	2-1	Robert 10,22	18,000
43	sppr1	**Seville**	H	W	2-1	Robert 16 pen; Varela 44	45,000
44	sppr1	**Cadiz**	A	D	1-1	Assuncao 89	20,000
45	sppr1	**Celta Vigo**	H	L	0-2		32,000
46	sppr1	**Espanyol**	A	L	0-2		42,245
47	sppr1	**Athl Bilbao**	H	D	1-1	Robert 26	30,000
48	sppr1	**Alaves**	A	L	0-2		12,431
49	sppr1	**Mallorca**	H	W	2-1	Pereyra 22 og; Robert 35	45,000
50	sppr1	**Atl Madrid**	A	D	1-1	Arzu 76	25,000

LEAGUE APPEARANCES, BOOKINGS AND CAPS

	AGE (on 01/07/06)	IN NAMED 18	APPEARANCES	COUNTING GAMES	MINUTES ON PITCH	YELLOW CARDS	RED CARDS	CAPS THIS SEASON	NATIONAL SIDE
Goalkeepers									
Pedro Contreras	34	31	17	14	1412	0	1	-	Spain
Antonio Doblas	26	38	24	21	2010	3	0	-	Spain
David Relano	24	6	0	0	0	0	0	-	Spain
Defenders									
Paoli Castellini	27	16	7	7	614	2	0	-	Italy
Morales Jaime Perez	24	2	0	0	0	0	0	-	Spain
Juanito	29	37	34	34	3060	6	0	4	Spain (5)
Daniel Lembo	28	11	3	2	181	0	0	-	Uruguay
Luis Fernandez	33	21	18	14	1410	5	0	-	Spain
Victoriano Nano	26	24	13	10	931	5	0	-	Spain
Oscar Lopez	26	20	17	17	1530	9	1	-	Spain
David Rivas	27	31	21	17	1614	6	0	-	Spain
Midfielders									
Arturo Arzu	25	35	30	11	1645	2	0	-	Spain
Juan Jose Canas	34	17	3	0	50	0	0	-	Spain
Jesus Capi	29	30	21	8	1224	4	0	-	Spain
Bascon Israel	19	17	8	0	234	1	0	-	Spain
Sanchez Joaquin	25	35	35	33	3053	3	1	5	Spain (5)
Juande	20	0	0	0	0	0	0	-	Spain
Juan Melli	22	37	33	31	2802	10	1	-	Spain
Miguel Angel	27	17	10	4	520	5	0	-	Spain
Alberto Rivera	28	36	34	28	2700	8	1	1	Spain (5)
Fernando Varela	26	31	26	19	2007	5	1	-	Spain
Forwards									
Marcos Assuncao	29	28	26	18	1856	2	0	-	Brazil
Dani	24	29	26	9	1248	3	0	-	Spain
Edu	27	34	34	32	2973	4	0	-	Brazil
Fernandez Fernando	32	18	13	1	440	0	0	-	Spain
Gomez Isidoro	19	1	0	0	0	0	0	-	Spain
Juanlu	26	11	3	0	95	0	0	-	Spain
Ricardo Oliveira	26	9	9	8	720	2	1	-	Brazil
Robert	25	19	18	10	1136	5	0	-	Brazil
Diego Tardelli Mari	21	16	12	3	630	0	0	-	Brazil
Francisco Xisco	25	30	25	7	1349	4	0	-	Spain

TEAM OF THE SEASON

MONTHLY POINTS TALLY

AUGUST	0	0%
SEPTEMBER	5	42%
OCTOBER	4	27%
NOVEMBER	2	22%
DECEMBER	4	33%
JANUARY	7	58%
FEBRUARY	3	25%
MARCH	8	53%
APRIL	5	33%
MAY	4	44%

LEAGUE GOALS

	PLAYER	MINS	GOALS	S RATE
1	Robert	1136	5	227
2	Dani	1248	4	312
3	Oliveira	720	4	180
4	Edu	2973	3	991
5	Joaquin	3053	2	1527
6	Juanito	3060	2	1530
7	Assuncao	1856	2	928
8	Capi	1224	1	1224
9	Rivas	1614	1	1614
10	Xisco	1349	1	1349
11	Arzu	1645	1	1645
12	Luis Fernandez	1410	1	1410
13	Fernando	440	1	440
	Other		6	
	TOTAL		34	

TOP POINT EARNERS

	PLAYER	GAMES	AV PTS
1	Contreras	14	1.29
2	Rivera	28	1.29
3	Edu	32	1.25
4	Assuncao	18	1.22
5	Varela	19	1.21
6	Rivas	17	1.18
7	Oscar Lopez	17	1.18
8	Joaquin	33	1.15
9	Luis Fernandez	14	1.14
10	Melli	31	1.10
	CLUB AVERAGE:		1.11

DISCIPLINARY RECORDS

	PLAYER	YELLOW	RED	AVE
1	Miguel Angel	5	0	104
2	Oscar Lopez	9	1	153
3	Nano	5	0	186
4	Robert	5	0	227
5	Oliveira	2	1	240
6	Melli	10	1	254
7	Rivas	6	0	269
8	Luis Fernandez	5	0	282
9	Rivera	8	1	300
10	Capi	4	0	306
11	Castellini	2	0	307
12	Varela	5	1	334
13	Xisco	4	0	337
	Other	23	2	
	TOTAL	93	7	

KEY GOALKEEPER

Pedro Contreras

Goals Conceded in the League	15	**Counting Games** League games when player was on pitch for at least 70 minutes	14
Defensive Rating Ave number of mins between League goals conceded while on the pitch	94	**Clean Sheets** In League games when player was on pitch for at least 70 minutes	4

KEY PLAYERS - DEFENDERS

David Rivas

Goals Conceded Number of League goals conceded while the player was on the pitch	22	**Clean Sheets** In League games when player was on pitch for at least 70 minutes	3
Defensive Rating Ave number of mins between League goals conceded while on the pitch	73	**Club Defensive Rating** Average number of mins between League goals conceded by the club this season	67

	PLAYER	CON LGE	CLEAN SHEETS	DEF RATE
1	David Rivas	22	3	73 mins
2	Luis Fernandez	20	5	71 mins
3	Juanito	47	9	65 mins
4	Hernandez Oscar Lopez	25	3	61 mins

KEY PLAYERS - MIDFIELDERS

Fernando Varela

Goals in the League	1	**Contribution to Attacking Power** Average number of minutes between League team goals while on pitch	84
Defensive Rating Average number of mins between League goals conceded while on the pitch	74	**Scoring Difference** Defensive Rating minus Contribution to Attacking Power	-10

	PLAYER	LGE GOALS	DEF RATE	POWER	SCORE DIFF
1	Fernando Varela	1	74	84	-10 mins
2	Sanchez Joaquin	2	66	93	-27 mins
3	Alberto Rivera	0	69	96	-27 mins
4	Juan Melli	0	67	97	-30 mins

KEY PLAYERS - GOALSCORERS

Marcos Assuncao

Goals in the League	2	**Player Strike Rate** Average number of minutes between League goals scored by player	928
Contribution to Attacking Power Average number of minutes between League team goals while on pitch	98	**Club Strike Rate** Average number of minutes between League goals scored by club	101

	PLAYER	LGE GOALS	POWER	STRIKE RATE
1	Marcos Assuncao	2	98	928 mins
2	Edu	3	99	991 mins
3	Luis Fernandez	1	108	1410 mins
4	Pedro Contreras	1	118	1412 mins

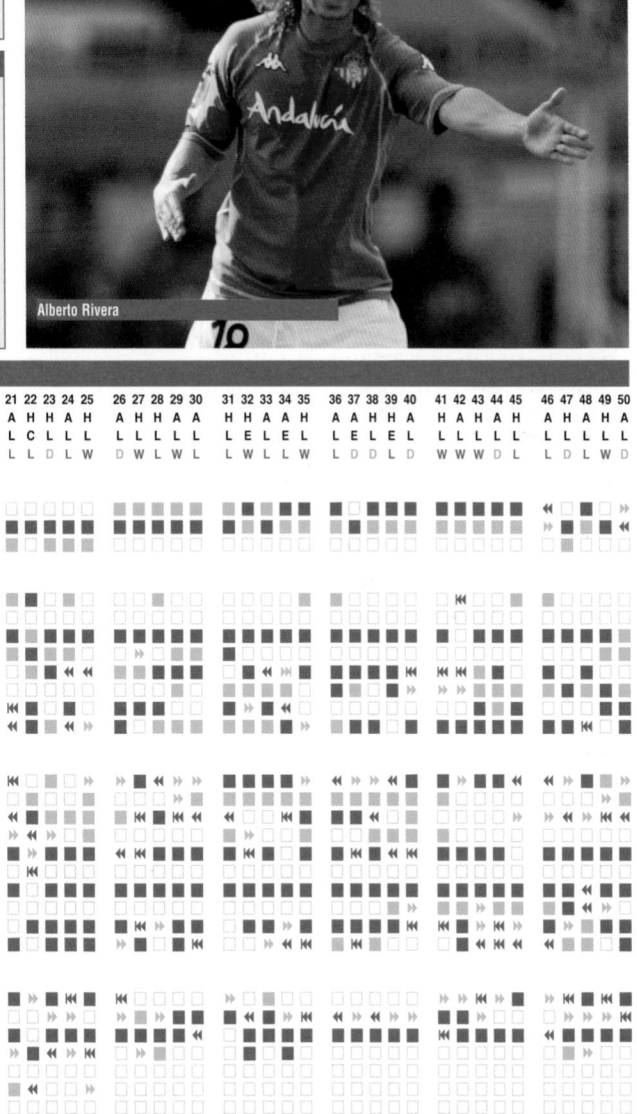

Alberto Rivera

SQUAD APPEARANCES

Match	1	2	3	4	5	6	7	8	9	10	11	12	13	14	15	16	17	18	19	20	21	22	23	24	25
Venue	H	A	A	H	H	H	A	H	A	A	H	A	A	H	H	H	A	A	A	H	A	H	H	A	H
Competition	C	C	L	L	C	L	L	L	C	L	L	C	L	L	L	C	L	L	C	L	L	C	L	L	L
Result	W	D	L	W	L	D	D	L	W	D	W	L	L	L	L	W	D	L	D	D	L	L	D	L	W

Match	26	27	28	29	30	31	32	33	34	35	36	37	38	39	40	41	42	43	44	45	46	47	48	49	50
Venue	A	H	H	A	A	H	H	A	A	H	A	A	H	H	A	H	A	H	A	H	A	H	A	H	A
Competition	L	L	L	L	L	L	E	L	E	L	L	E	L	E	L	L	L	L	L	L	L	L	L	L	L
Result	D	W	L	W	L	L	W	L	L	W	L	D	D	L	D	W	W	W	D	L	L	D	L	W	D

Goalkeepers
Pedro Contreras
Antonio Doblas
David Relano

Defenders
Paoli Castellini
Morales Jaime Perez
Juanito
Daniel Lembo
Luis Fernandez
Victoriano Nano
Hernandez Oscar Lopez
David Rivas

Midfielders
Arturo Arzu
Juan Jose Canas
Jesus Capi
Bascon Israel
Sanchez Joaquin
Juande
Juan Melli
Miguel Angel
Alberto Rivera
Fernando Varela

Forwards
Marcos Assuncao
Dani
Edu
Fernandez Fernando
Gomez Isidoro
Juanlu
Ricardo Oliveira
Robert
Diego Tardelli Mari
Francisco Xisco

KEY: On all match | On bench | Subbed or sent off (Counting game) | Subbed or sent off (playing less than 70 minutes) | Subbed on from bench (Counting Game) | Subbed on (playing less than 70 minutes) | Subbed on and then subbed or sent off (Counting Game) | Subbed on and then subbed or sent off (playing less than 70 minutes) | Not in 16

ESPANYOL

Final Position: **15th**

KEY: ■ Won □ Drawn □ Lost

#	Comp	Opponent	Venue	Res	Score	Scorers	Attendance
1	sppr1	**Getafe**	H	L	0-2		18,845
2	sppr1	**Malaga**	A	W	2-1	Zabaleta 43; Garcia 62	25,000
3	uc1rl1	**FK Teplice**	A	D	1-1	Garcia 82	14,620
4	sppr1	**Real Madrid**	H	W	1-0	Jarque 68	39,000
5	sppr1	**R Santander**	A	L	0-1		10,800
6	sppr1	**Villarreal**	H	L	1-2	Luis Garcia 59	16,550
7	uc1rl2	**FK Teplice**	H	W	2-0	Fredson 79; Jofre 90	9,435
8	sppr1	**Seville**	A	D	1-1	Fredson 16	40,000
9	sppr1	**Cadiz**	H	L	0-2		21,950
10	ucgpb	**Loko Moscow**	A	W	1-0	Tamudo 53	13,718
11	sppr1	**Celta Vigo**	A	L	0-1		15,000
12	sppr1	**Alaves**	A	D	1-1	Luis Garcia 15	10,042
13	sppr1	**Osasuna**	A	L	0-2		50,000
14	sppr1	**Athl Bilbao**	H	D	1-1	Corominas 87	18,500
15	sppr1	**Mallorca**	H	W	2-0	Tamudo 40 pen; Luis Garcia 42	19,500
16	ucgpb	**Palermo**	H	D	1-1	Luis Garcia 90	9,114
17	sppr1	**Atl Madrid**	A	D	1-1	Jarque 11	35,000
18	ucgpb	**Brondby**	A	D	1-1	Tamudo 42	21,399
19	sppr1	**Valencia**	H	L	1-3	Corominas 63	25,000
20	sppr1	**Real Betis**	A	D	0-0		35,000
21	ucgpb	**M Petach-Tikva**	H	W	1-0	Pocchettino 83	5,000
22	sppr1	**Real Zaragoza**	H	D	2-2	Tamudo 49,83	16,190
23	sppr1	**Deportivo**	A	W	2-1	Fredson 75; Sa 81	24,300
24	sppr1	**Barcelona**	H	L	1-2	Tamudo 60	30,000
25	sppr1	**Real Sociedad**	A	W	1-0	Tamudo 90	19,600
26	sppr1	**Getafe**	A	L	0-5		14,000
27	sppr1	**Malaga**	H	W	3-1	Tamudo 10,21; Luis Garcia 33	15,100
28	sppr1	**Real Madrid**	A	L	0-4		72,043
29	sppr1	**R Santander**	H	L	0-2		20,520
30	uc3rl1	**Schalke**	A	L	1-2	Luis Garcia 34	53,642
31	sppr1	**Villarreal**	A	L	0-4		18,000
32	uc3rl2	**Schalke**	H	L	0-3		18,100
33	sppr1	**Seville**	H	W	5-0	Fredson 6; Zabaleta 47; Luis Garcia 54,56,76 pen	11,500
34	sppr1	**Cadiz**	A	L	0-2		18,000
35	sppr1	**Celta Vigo**	H	W	2-0	Tamudo 13; Fredson 39	18,500
36	sppr1	**Osasuna**	H	L	2-4	Tamudo 19; Garcia 66	18,000
37	sppr1	**Athl Bilbao**	A	D	1-1	Juanfran 38	37,000
38	sppr1	**Alaves**	H	D	0-0		18,400
39	sppr1	**Mallorca**	A	D	0-0		17,000
40	sppr1	**Atl Madrid**	H	D	1-1	Pandiani 82	22,850
41	sppr1	**Valencia**	A	L	0-4		40,000
42	sppr1	**Real Betis**	H	W	2-0	Jarque 22; Tamudo 58 pen	42,245
43	sppr1	**Real Zaragoza**	A	D	1-1	Jarque 66	25,000
44	sppr1	**Deportivo**	H	L	1-2	Garcia 43	16,150
45	sppr1	**Barcelona**	A	L	0-2		90,000
46	sppr1	**Real Sociedad**	H	W	1-0	Corominas 90	48,950

LEAGUE APPEARANCES, BOOKINGS AND CAPS

	AGE (on 01/07/06)	IN NAMED 18	APPEARANCES	COUNTING GAMES	MINUTES ON PITCH	YELLOW CARDS	RED CARDS	CAPS THIS SEASON	NATIONAL SIDE
Goalkeepers									
Gabriel Biel	20	9	0	0	0	0	0	-	Spain
Gorka Iraizoz	25	38	21	21	1800	0	0	-	Spain
Carlos Kameni	22	29	17	17	1530	1	0	2	Cameroon (26)
Defenders									
Didier Domi	28	25	17	13	1303	2	0	-	France
David Garcia	25	30	29	27	2514	7	0	-	Spain
Hugo Ibarra	32	1	1	1	90	0	0	-	Argentina
Daniel Jarque	23	33	33	32	2921	8	2	-	Spain
Alberto Lopo	27	33	33	32	2930	9	1	-	Spain
Moises Hurtado	25	27	19	13	1374	9	2	-	Spain
Mauricio Pocchettino	34	20	13	11	1024	4	1	-	Argentina
Miguel Robuste	21	1	0	0	0	0	0	-	Spain
Armando Sa	30	32	20	9	1070	2	2	-	Mozambique
Sergio Sanchez	20	20	10	9	820	4	0	-	Spain
Midfielders									
Eduardo Costa	23	30	30	23	2379	11	2	-	Brazil
Ivan De La Pena	30	34	31	24	2423	9	0	5	Spain (5)
Fredson	25	32	27	9	1509	2	0	-	Brazil
Antonio Ito	31	35	26	17	1831	7	0	-	Spain
Mateu Jofre	26	29	12	1	308	0	0	-	Spain
Juanfran	21	35	30	10	1690	6	0	-	Spain
Miguel Martinez Miki	22	4	2	0	50	0	0	-	Spain
Angel Morales	30	0	0	0	0	0	0	-	Spain
Albert Riera	24	15	7	1	282	1	0	-	Spain
Antonio Velamanzan	29	0	0	0	0	0	0	-	Spain
Pablo Javier Zabaleta	21	34	28	19	2156	7	0	-	Argentina
Forwards									
Ferran Corominas	23	34	32	8	1429	2	0	-	Spain
Fernandez Luis Garcia	25	34	34	24	2607	7	0	-	Spain
Walter Pandiani	30	20	18	2	710	2	0	-	Uruguay
Martin Posse	30	6	4	0	102	0	0	-	Argentina
Jonathan Soriano	20	15	3	0	67	1	0	-	Spain
Raul Tamudo	28	30	30	26	2448	4	0	3	Spain (5)
Alberto Yague	21	3	1	0	1	0	0	-	Spain

TEAM OF THE SEASON

G — Carlos Kameni — CG: 17 DR: 70

D — Didier Domi — CG: 13 DR: 69

D — Daniel Jarque — CG: 32 DR: 68

D — Alberto Lopo — CG: 32 DR: 68

D — David Garcia — CG: 27 DR: 63

M — Eduardo Costa — CG: 23 SD: -25

M — Ivan De La Pena — CG: 24 SD: -31

M — Pablo Javier Zabaleta — CG: 19 SD: -32

M — Antonio Ito — CG: 17 SD: -37

F — Raul Tamudo — CG: 26 SR: 245

F — F Luis Garcia — CG: 24 SR: 372

MONTHLY POINTS TALLY

Month	Points	%
AUGUST	0	0%
SEPTEMBER	6	50%
OCTOBER	2	13%
NOVEMBER	5	56%
DECEMBER	5	42%
JANUARY	6	50%
FEBRUARY	3	25%
MARCH	5	33%
APRIL	6	40%
MAY	3	33%

LEAGUE GOALS

	PLAYER	MINS	GOALS	S RATE
1	Tamudo	2448	10	245
2	Luis Garcia	2607	7	372
3	Fredson	1509	4	377
4	Jarque	2921	4	730
5	Corominas	1429	3	476
6	Garcia	2514	3	838
7	Zabaleta	2156	2	1078
8	Sa	1070	1	1070
9	Juanfran	1690	1	1690
10	Pandiani	710	1	710
	Other		0	
	TOTAL		36	

TOP POINT EARNERS

	PLAYER	GAMES	AV PTS
1	Domi	13	1.46
2	Costa	23	1.30
3	Lopo	32	1.22
4	Zabaleta	19	1.21
5	Tamudo	26	1.19
6	Ito	17	1.18
7	Moises Hurtado	13	1.15
8	Iraizoz	20	1.15
9	Jarque	32	1.09
10	Luis Garcia	24	1.08
	CLUB AVERAGE:		1.08

DISCIPLINARY RECORDS

	PLAYER	YELLOW	RED	AVE
1	Moises Hurtado	9	2	124
2	Costa	11	2	183
3	Pocchettino	4	1	204
4	Sergio Sanchez	4	0	205
5	Ito	7	0	261
6	Sa	2	2	267
7	De La Pena	9	0	269
8	Juanfran	6	0	281
9	Jarque	8	2	292
10	Lopo	9	1	293
11	Zabaleta	7	0	308
12	Pandiani	2	0	355
13	Garcia	7	0	359
	Other	18	0	
	TOTAL	103	10	

KEY GOALKEEPER

Carlos Kameni

Goals Conceded in the League	22	**Counting Games** League games when player was on pitch for at least 70 minutes	17
Defensive Rating Ave number of mins between League goals conceded while on the pitch	70	**Clean Sheets** In League games when player was on pitch for at least 70 minutes	3

KEY PLAYERS - DEFENDERS

Didier Domi

Goals Conceded Number of League goals conceded while the player was on the pitch	19	**Clean Sheets** In League games when player was on pitch for at least 70 minutes	4
Defensive Rating Ave number of mins between League goals conceded while on the pitch	69	**Club Defensive Rating** Average number of mins between League goals conceded by the club this season	61

	PLAYER	CON LGE	CLEAN SHEETS	DEF RATE
1	Didier Domi	19	4	69 mins
2	Alberto Lopo	43	10	68 mins
3	Daniel Jarque	43	8	68 mins
4	David Garcia	40	7	63 mins

KEY PLAYERS - MIDFIELDERS

Eduardo Costa

Goals in the League	0	**Contribution to Attacking Power** Average number of minutes between League team goals while on pitch	95
Defensive Rating Average number of mins between League goals conceded while on the pitch	70	**Scoring Difference** Defensive Rating minus Contribution to Attacking Power	-25

	PLAYER	LGE GOALS	DEF RATE	POWER	SCORE DIFF
1	Eduardo Costa	0	70	95	-25 mins
2	Ivan De La Pena	0	62	93	-31 mins
3	Pablo Javier Zabaleta	2	54	86	-32 mins
4	Antonio Ito	0	59	96	-37 mins

KEY PLAYERS - GOALSCORERS

Raul Tamudo

Goals in the League	10	**Player Strike Rate** Average number of minutes between League goals scored by player	245
Contribution to Attacking Power Average number of minutes between League team goals while on pitch	94	**Club Strike Rate** Average number of minutes between League goals scored by club	95

	PLAYER	LGE GOALS	POWER	STRIKE RATE
1	Raul Tamudo	10	94	245 mins
2	Fernandez Luis Garcia	7	93	372 mins
3	Daniel Jarque	4	89	730 mins
4	David Garcia	3	109	838 mins

Fernandez Luis Garcia

SQUAD APPEARANCES

Match	1	2	3	4	5	6	7	8	9	10	11	12	13	14	15	16	17	18	19	20	21	22	23	24	25	26	27	28	29	30	31	32	33	34	35	36	37	38	39	40	41	42	43	44	45	46
Venue	H	A	A	H	A	H	H	A	H	A	A	A	A	H	H	H	A	A	H	A	H	H	A	H	A	A	H	A	H	A	A	H	H	A	H	H	A	H	A	H	A	H	A	H	A	H
Competition	L	L	E	L	L	L	E	L	L	E	L	L	L	L	L	E	L	E	L	L	E	L	L	L	L	L	L	L	L	E	L	E	L	L	L	L	L	L	L	L	L	L	L	L	L	L
Result	L	W	D	W	L	L	W	D	L	W	L	D	L	D	W	D	D	D	L	D	W	D	W	L	W	L	W	L	L	L	L	L	W	L	W	L	D	D	D	D	L	W	D	L	L	W

Goalkeepers
Gabriel Biel
Gorka Iraizoz
Carlos Kameni

Defenders
Didier Domi
David Garcia
Hugo Ibarra
Daniel Jarque
Alberto Lopo
Moises Hurtado
Mauricio Pocchettino
Miguel Robuste
Armando Sa
Sergio Sanchez

Midfielders
Eduardo Costa
Ivan De La Pena
Fredson
Antonio Ito
Mateu Jofre
Juanfran
Miguel Martinez Miki
Angel Morales
Albert Riera
Antonio Velamanzan
Pablo Javier Zabaleta

Forwards
Ferran Corominas
Fernandez Luis Garcia
Walter Pandiani
Martin Posse
Jonathan Soriano
Raul Tamudo
Alberto Yague

KEY: ■ On all match ■ On bench ⏮ Subbed or sent off (Counting game) « Subbed or sent off (playing less than 70 minutes) ⏭ Subbed on from bench (Counting Game) » Subbed on (playing less than 70 minutes) Subbed on and then subbed or sent off (Counting Game) Subbed on and then subbed or sent off (playing less than 70 minutes) Not in 16

REAL SOCIEDAD

Final Position: **16th**

KEY: ☐Won ☐Drawn ☐Lost

							Attendance
1	sppr1	**Athl Bilbao**	A	L	0-3		42,000
2	sppr1	**Alaves**	H	W	2-1	Barkero 11,34	15,370
3	sppr1	**Mallorca**	A	L	2-5	Novo 20; Prieto 45	8,500
4	sppr1	**Atl Madrid**	H	W	3-2	Kovacevic 55,90; Nihat 82	31,300
5	sppr1	**Valencia**	A	L	1-2	Nihat 61	55,000
6	sppr1	**Real Betis**	H	D	1-1	Kovacevic 49	21,000
7	sppr1	**Real Zaragoza**	A	W	1-0	Prieto 13 pen	29,000
8	sppr1	**Deportivo**	H	W	2-0	Kovacevic 50; Jauregui 68	21,000
9	sppr1	**Getafe**	H	W	3-0	Aramburu 4; Nihat 17; Prieto 41 pen	20,600
10	sppr1	**Barcelona**	A	L	0-5		65,000
11	sppr1	**Osasuna**	H	L	1-2	Prieto 44 pen	25,800
12	sppr1	**Malaga**	A	L	1-3	De Paula 80	21,000
13	sppr1	**Real Madrid**	H	D	2-2	Prieto 44 pen; De Paula 59	23,292
14	sppr1	**R Santander**	A	D	2-2	Novo 21; De Paula 52	20,000
15	sppr1	**Villarreal**	H	L	1-3	Nihat 4	16,170
16	sppr1	**Seville**	A	L	2-3	Labaka 27; Garitano 57	35,000
17	sppr1	**Cadiz**	H	W	2-0	Gabilondo 8; Prieto 75 pen	16,200
18	sppr1	**Celta Vigo**	A	L	0-1		14,989
19	sppr1	**Espanyol**	H	L	0-1		19,600
20	sppr1	**Athl Bilbao**	H	D	3-3	Nihat 7,38; Skoubo 68	22,700
21	sppr1	**Alaves**	A	L	1-3	Stevanovic 90	14,317
22	sppr1	**Mallorca**	H	W	2-1	Skoubo 12; Gonzalez, Mark 83	19,000
23	sppr1	**Atl Madrid**	A	L	0-1		45,000
24	sppr1	**Valencia**	H	L	1-2	Skoubo 1	22,000
25	sppr1	**Real Betis**	A	L	0-2		30,000
26	sppr1	**Real Zaragoza**	H	L	1-3	Nihat 10	19,831
27	sppr1	**Deportivo**	A	W	1-0	Garitano 46	24,300
28	sppr1	**Barcelona**	H	L	0-2		28,400
29	sppr1	**Osasuna**	A	L	0-2		17,000
30	sppr1	**Getafe**	A	L	1-2	Gonzalez, Mark 45	11,000
31	sppr1	**Malaga**	H	W	3-0	Ansotegi 37; Skoubo 69; Prieto 82	29,000
32	sppr1	**Real Madrid**	A	D	1-1	Gonzalez, Mark 63	70,000
33	sppr1	**R Santander**	H	W	1-0	Gonzalez, Mark 75	24,700
34	sppr1	**Villarreal**	A	W	2-0	Alonso 9; Gonzalez, Mark 28	16,000
35	sppr1	**Seville**	H	L	1-2	Jordi 85	26,600
36	sppr1	**Cadiz**	A	D	2-2	Prieto 8; Garitano 47	19,000
37	sppr1	**Celta Vigo**	H	D	2-2	Prieto 7 pen; Skoubo 39	25,500
38	sppr1	**Espanyol**	A	L	0-1		48,950

LEAGUE APPEARANCES, BOOKINGS AND CAPS

	AGE (on 01/07/06)	IN NAMED 18	APPEARANCES	COUNTING GAMES	MINUTES ON PITCH	YELLOW CARDS	RED CARDS	CAPS THIS SEASON	NATIONAL SIDE
Goalkeepers									
Lopez Alberto	37	37	7	6	604	0	0	-	Spain
Asier Riesgo	22	37	32	31	2816	2	0	-	Spain
Mikel Saizar	23	1	0	0	0	0	0	-	Spain
Defenders									
Ion Ansotegi	23	18	13	12	1114	2	0	-	Spain
Sergio Boris	26	20	3	1	135	0	0	-	Spain
Jeremie Brechet	26	3	3	3	270	1	0	-	France
Daniel Cifuentes	25	36	12	9	886	4	1	-	Spain
Javier Garrido	21	37	35	32	3018	8	0	-	Spain
Mikel Gonzalez	20	13	10	9	871	3	0	-	Spain
Mikel Labaka	25	37	32	30	2746	2	0	-	Spain
Lopez Rekarte	30	36	30	28	2612	5	1	-	Spain
Midfielders									
Mikel Alonso	26	31	30	24	2348	2	0	-	Spain
Mikel Aramburu	27	13	13	10	1041	3	1	-	Spain
Jose Barkero	27	22	17	4	633	2	0	-	Spain
Igor Gabilondo	27	24	16	5	695	2	0	-	Spain
Gaizka Garitano	31	20	19	15	1470	10	2	-	Spain
Igor Jauregui	32	25	24	24	2160	4	0	-	Spain
Gorka Larrea	22	22	11	1	226	1	0	-	Spain
Alvaro Novo	28	36	33	22	2340	8	0	-	Spain
Xavier Prieto	22	37	37	26	2697	4	0	-	Spain
Dalibor Stevanovic	21	21	17	6	889	4	0	-	Slovenia
John Eduis Viafara	27	15	10	7	719	3	2	4	Colombia (36)
Forwards									
Oscar De Paula	31	15	6	2	283	0	0	-	Spain
Juan Dominguez	22	4	0	0	0	0	0	-	Spain
Mark Gonzalez	21	16	16	11	1063	3	0	-	South Africa
Darko Kovacevic	32	9	9	9	799	2	0	-	Serbia & Mont
Kahveci Nihat	26	32	32	17	2076	3	1	-	Turkey
Estefania Oskitz	19	1	1	1	90	0	0	-	Spain
Morten Skoubo	26	18	18	14	1382	4	0	2	Denmark (19)
Garikoitz Uranga	26	36	32	12	1407	2	2	-	Spain

TEAM OF THE SEASON

MONTHLY POINTS TALLY

AUGUST	0	0%
SEPTEMBER	6	50%
OCTOBER	10	67%
NOVEMBER	1	11%
DECEMBER	4	33%
JANUARY	1	8%
FEBRUARY	3	25%
MARCH	3	20%
APRIL	10	67%
MAY	2	22%

LEAGUE GOALS

	PLAYER	MINS	GOALS	S RATE
1	Prieto	2697	9	300
2	Nihat	2076	7	297
3	Skoubo	1382	5	276
4	Gonzalez, Mark	1063	5	213
5	Kovacevic	799	4	200
6	Garitano	1470	3	490
7	De Paula	283	3	94
8	Barkero	633	2	317
9	Novo	2340	2	1170
10	Labaka	2746	1	2746
11	Ansotegi	1114	1	1114
12	Stevanovic	889	1	889
13	Aramburu	1041	1	1041
	Other		4	
	TOTAL		48	

TOP POINT EARNERS

	PLAYER	GAMES	AV PTS
1	Nihat	17	1.29
2	Alonso	24	1.25
3	Lopez Rekarte	28	1.21
4	Garitano	15	1.20
5	Prieto	26	1.19
6	Labaka	30	1.17
7	Riesgo	31	1.13
8	Ansotegi	12	1.08
9	Skoubo	14	1.07
10	Garrido	32	1.06
	CLUB AVERAGE:		1.05

DISCIPLINARY RECORDS

	PLAYER	YELLOW	RED	AVE
1	Garitano	10	2	122
2	Viafara	3	2	143
3	Cifuentes	4	1	177
4	Stevanovic	4	0	222
5	Aramburu	3	1	260
6	Gonzalez, Mikel	3	0	290
7	Novo	8	0	292
8	Barkero	2	0	316
9	Skoubo	4	0	345
10	Gabilondo	2	0	347
11	Uranga	2	2	351
12	Gonzalez, Mark	3	0	354
13	Garrido	8	0	377
	Other	26	2	
	TOTAL	82	10	

KEY GOALKEEPER

Asier Riesgo

Goals Conceded in the League	54	**Counting Games** League games when player was on pitch for at least 70 minutes	32
Defensive Rating Ave number of mins between League goals conceded while on the pitch	52	**Clean Sheets** In League games when player was on pitch for at least 70 minutes	7

KEY PLAYERS - DEFENDERS

Javier Garrido

Goals Conceded Number of League goals conceded while the player was on the pitch	53	**Clean Sheets** In League games when player was on pitch for at least 70 minutes	7
Defensive Rating Ave number of mins between League goals conceded while on the pitch	57	**Club Defensive Rating** Average number of mins between League goals conceded by the club this season	53

	PLAYER	CON LGE	CLEAN SHEETS	DEF RATE
1	Javier Garrido	53	7	57 mins
2	Mikel Labaka	49	8	56 mins
3	Ion Gorostola Ansotegi	20	3	56 mins
4	Lopez Rekarte	48	8	54 mins

KEY PLAYERS - MIDFIELDERS

Mikel Alonso

Goals in the League	1	**Contribution to Attacking Power** Average number of minutes between League team goals while on pitch	62
Defensive Rating Average number of mins between League goals conceded while on the pitch	57	**Scoring Difference** Defensive Rating minus Contribution to Attacking Power	-5

	PLAYER	LGE GOALS	DEF RATE	POWER	SCORE DIFF
1	Mikel Alonso	1	57	62	-5 mins
2	Gaizka Garitano	3	70	77	-7 mins
3	Alvaro Novo	2	54	63	-9 mins
4	Xavier Prieto	9	56	67	-11 mins

KEY PLAYERS - GOALSCORERS

Morten Skoubo

Goals in the League	5	**Player Strike Rate** Average number of minutes between League goals scored by player	276
Contribution to Attacking Power Average number of minutes between League team goals while on pitch	69	**Club Strike Rate** Average number of minutes between League goals scored by club	71

	PLAYER	LGE GOALS	POWER	STRIKE RATE
1	Morten Skoubo	5	69	276 mins
2	Kahveci Nihat	7	67	297 mins
3	Xavier Prieto	9	67	300 mins
4	Gaizka Garitano	3	77	490 mins

Mikel Alonso

SQUAD APPEARANCES

Match	1	2	3	4	5	6	7	8	9	10	11	12	13	14	15	16	17	18	19	20	21	22	23	24	25	26	27	28	29	30	31	32	33	34	35	36	37	38
Venue	A	H	A	H	A	H	A	H	H	A	H	A	H	A	H	A	H	A	H	H	A	H	A	H	A	H	A	H	A	A	H	A	H	A	H	A	H	A
Competition	L	L	L	L	L	L	L	L	L	L	L	L	L	L	L	L	L	L	L	L	L	L	L	L	L	L	L	L	L	L	L	L	L	L	L	L	L	L
Result	L	W	L	W	L	D	W	W	W	L	L	L	D	D	L	L	W	L	L	D	L	W	L	L	L	L	W	L	L	L	W	D	W	W	L	D	D	L

Goalkeepers
Lopez Alberto
Asier Riesgo
Mikel Saizar

Defenders
Ion Gorostola Ansotegi
Sergio Gonzalez Boris
Jeremie Brechet
Daniel Alfaro Cifuentes
Javier Garrido
Mikel Gonzalez
Mikel Labaka
Lopez Rekarte

Midfielders
Mikel Alonso
Mikel Aramburu
Jose Barkero
Igor Gabilondo
Gaizka Garitano
Igor Jauregui
Gorka Larrea
Alvaro Novo
Xavier Prieto
Dalibor Stevanovic
John Eduis Viafara

Forwards
Oscar De Paula
Juan Dominguez
Mark Gonzalez
Darko Kovacevic
Kahveci Nihat
Estefania Oskitz
Morten Skoubo
Garikoitz Uranga

KEY: On all match · On bench · Subbed or sent off (Counting game) · Subbed or sent off (playing less than 70 minutes) · Subbed on from bench (Counting Game) · Subbed on (playing less than 70 minutes) · Subbed on and then subbed or sent off (Counting Game) · Subbed on and then subbed or sent off (playing less than 70 minutes) · Not in 16

RACING SANTANDER

Final Position: **17th**

KEY: Won / Drawn / Lost

						Attendance
1	sppr1 **Seville**	A	L	0-1		42,000
2	sppr1 **Cadiz**	H	L	0-1		13,500
3	sppr1 **Celta Vigo**	A	W	1-0	Casquero 60	15,000
4	sppr1 **Espanyol**	H	W	1-0	Antonito 68	10,800
5	sppr1 **Athl Bilbao**	A	D	0-0		30,000
6	sppr1 **Alaves**	H	L	1-2	Juanjo 78	13,832
7	sppr1 **Mallorca**	A	D	0-0		15,000
8	sppr1 **Atl Madrid**	H	L	0-1		15,300
9	sppr1 **Real Zaragoza**	A	D	1-1	Aganzo 71	30,000
10	sppr1 **Valencia**	A	D	1-1	Aganzo 29	40,000
11	sppr1 **Real Betis**	H	D	1-1	Antonito 73	13,808
12	sppr1 **Deportivo**	H	L	0-3		12,700
13	sppr1 **Barcelona**	A	L	1-4	Casquero 71 pen	53,000
14	sppr1 **Real Sociedad**	H	D	2-2	Antonito 68; Alonso 88 og	20,000
15	sppr1 **Getafe**	A	W	2-1	Antonito 19; Aganzo 86	14,000
16	sppr1 **Malaga**	H	D	1-1	Casquero 45	12,800
17	sppr1 **Real Madrid**	A	W	2-1	Ayoze 21; Melo 28	56,210
18	sppr1 **Osasuna**	A	D	1-1	Antonito 44	15,000
19	sppr1 **Villarreal**	H	W	1-0	Matabuena 20	17,000
20	sppr1 **Seville**	H	L	2-3	Juanjo 44; Melo 85	14,609
21	sppr1 **Cadiz**	A	D	1-1	Melo 65	20,000
22	sppr1 **Celta Vigo**	H	L	0-1		14,300
23	sppr1 **Espanyol**	A	W	2-0	Damia 81; Casquero 82	20,520
24	sppr1 **Athl Bilbao**	H	L	0-1		17,900
25	sppr1 **Alaves**	A	D	2-2	Pinilla 27 pen; Dalmat, Wilfried 72	12,824
26	sppr1 **Mallorca**	H	D	0-0		13,859
27	sppr1 **Atl Madrid**	A	L	1-2	Damia 71	40,000
28	sppr1 **Valencia**	H	W	2-1	Damia 16; Ayoze 66	13,800
29	sppr1 **Real Betis**	A	L	0-1		30,000
30	sppr1 **Real Zaragoza**	H	D	0-0		13,800
31	sppr1 **Deportivo**	A	L	0-2		23,234
32	sppr1 **Barcelona**	H	D	2-2	Antonito 19; Serrano 22	20,600
33	sppr1 **Real Sociedad**	A	L	0-1		24,700
34	sppr1 **Getafe**	H	L	1-3	Antonito 38	18,000
35	sppr1 **Malaga**	A	W	3-2	Casquero 17; Antonito 52; Juanjo 79	7,000
36	sppr1 **Real Madrid**	H	L	2-3	Matabuena 76,90	17,300
37	sppr1 **Osasuna**	H	W	2-1	Pablo Alfaro 81 pen; Antonito 89	14,300
38	sppr1 **Villarreal**	A	L	0-2		16,000

LEAGUE APPEARANCES, BOOKINGS AND CAPS

	AGE (on 01/07/06)	IN NAMED 18	APPEARANCES	COUNTING GAMES	MINUTES ON PITCH	YELLOW CARDS	RED CARDS	CAPS THIS SEASON	NATIONAL SIDE
Goalkeepers									
Dudu Aouate	28	38	37	37	3330	2	0	-	Israel
Antonio Tono	26	14	0	0	0	0	0	-	Spain
Juanjo Jose Valencia	34	15	1	1	90	0	0	-	Spain
Defenders									
Abella Damia	24	18	17	13	1331	1	0	-	Spain
Ezequiel Garay	19	14	9	9	810	1	0	-	Argentina
Ho-Jin Lee	23	1	0	0	-1	0	0	-	South Korea
Jose Moraton	26	34	23	22	1986	12	0	-	Spain
Neru	32	26	16	11	1175	2	0	-	Spain
Lozano Oriol	25	28	19	17	1660	11	0	-	Spain
Pablo Alfaro	37	19	17	14	1378	4	1	-	Spain
Pablo Pinillos	32	34	33	31	2836	6	3	-	Spain
San Jose Samuel	22	9	7	6	603	4	0	-	Spain
Midfielders									
Antonio Tomas	21	26	22	11	1246	2	0	-	Spain
Diaz Ayoze	24	31	28	25	2374	7	0	-	Spain
Francisco Casquero	29	28	26	16	1689	5	0	-	Spain
Stephane Dalmat	27	14	11	5	697	1	0	-	France
Juan Jose Juanjo	20	28	22	9	1139	2	0	-	Spain
Jose Marques	21	2	2	0	107	1	0	-	Spain
Sergio Matabuena	27	33	22	12	1346	6	0	-	Spain
Felipe Melo	22	33	33	25	2587	10	1	-	Brazil
Portilla	17	7	3	1	148	0	0	-	Spain
Victor Bermudez	22	35	33	25	2509	11	1	-	Spain
Forwards									
David Aganzo	25	19	17	5	807	3	1	-	Spain
Ramiro Antonito	28	35	32	16	1994	5	0	-	Spain
Wilfried Dalmat	23	21	12	4	643	1	0	-	France
Valle Jonathan	21	24	18	3	811	5	0	-	Spain
Mauricio Pinilla	22	14	12	4	704	1	0	2	Chile (73)
M. del Campo Raul	23	15	12	1	458	0	0	-	Spain
Walid Regragui	30	25	9	7	703	5	0	-	Morocco
Oscar Serrano	24	35	32	18	2174	11	1	-	Spain

TEAM OF THE SEASON

MONTHLY POINTS TALLY

AUGUST	0	0%
SEPTEMBER	7	58%
OCTOBER	3	20%
NOVEMBER	1	11%
DECEMBER	8	67%
JANUARY	5	42%
FEBRUARY	4	33%
MARCH	5	33%
APRIL	4	27%
MAY	3	33%

LEAGUE GOALS

	PLAYER	MINS	GOALS	S RATE
1	Antonito	1994	**9**	222
2	Casquero	1689	**5**	338
3	Matabuena	1346	**3**	449
4	Damia	1331	**3**	444
5	Melo	2587	**3**	862
6	Juanjo	1139	**3**	380
7	Aganzo	807	**3**	269
8	Ayoze	2374	**2**	1187
9	Pablo Alfaro	1378	**1**	1378
10	Serrano	2174	**1**	2174
11	Pinilla	704	**1**	704
12	Dalmat, Wilfried	643	**1**	643
	Other		**1**	
	TOTAL		**36**	

TOP POINT EARNERS

	PLAYER	GAMES	AV PTS
1	Matabuena	12	**1.33**
2	Antonito	16	**1.31**
3	Serrano	18	**1.28**
4	Ayoze	25	**1.24**
5	Oriol	17	**1.18**
6	Mora	22	**1.18**
7	Melo	25	**1.16**
8	Vitolo	25	**1.16**
9	Casquero	16	**1.13**
10	Aouate	37	**1.08**
	CLUB AVERAGE:		**1.05**

DISCIPLINARY RECORDS

	PLAYER	YELLOW	RED	AVE
1	Regragui	5	0	**140**
2	Samuel	4	0	**150**
3	Oriol	11	0	**150**
4	Jonathan	5	0	**162**
5	Mora	12	0	**165**
6	Serrano	11	1	**181**
7	Aganzo	3	1	**201**
8	Vitolo	11	1	**209**
9	Matabuena	6	0	**224**
10	Melo	10	1	**235**
11	Pablo Alfaro	4	1	**275**
12	Pinillos	6	3	**315**
13	Casquero	5	0	**337**
	Other	25	0	
	TOTAL	**118**	**8**	

KEY GOALKEEPER

Dudu Aouate

Goals Conceded in the League	**47**	**Counting Games** League games when player was on pitch for at least 70 minutes	**37**
Defensive Rating Ave number of mins between League goals conceded while on the pitch	**71**	**Clean Sheets** In games when player was on pitch for at least 70 minutes	**8**

KEY PLAYERS - DEFENDERS

Abella Damia

Goals Conceded Number of League goals conceded while the player was on the pitch	**18**	**Clean Sheets** In League games when player was on pitch for at least 70 minutes	**2**
Defensive Rating Ave number of mins between League goals conceded while on the pitch	**74**	**Club Defensive Rating** Average number of mins between League goals conceded by the club this season	**70**

	PLAYER	CON LGE	CLEAN SHEETS	DEF RATE
1	Abella Damia	18	2	**74 mins**
2	Pablo Pinillos	39	6	**73 mins**
3	Pablo Alfaro	19	3	**73 mins**
4	Lozano Oriol	25	3	**66 mins**

KEY PLAYERS - MIDFIELDERS

Sergio Matabuena

Goals in the League	**3**	**Contribution to Attacking Power** Average number of minutes between League team goals while on pitch	**79**
Defensive Rating Average number of mins between League goals conceded while on the pitch	**71**	**Scoring Difference** Defensive Rating minus Contribution to Attacking Power	**-8**

	PLAYER	LGE GOALS	DEF RATE	POWER	SCORE DIFF
1	Sergio Matabuena	3	71	79	**-8 mins**
2	Felipe Melo	3	62	83	**-21 mins**
3	Victor Bermudez	0	78	105	**-27 mins**
4	Diaz Ayoze	2	66	95	**-29 mins**

KEY PLAYERS - GOALSCORERS

Goals in the League	**9**	**Player Strike Rate** Average number of minutes between League goals scored by player	**222**
Contribution to Attacking Power Average number of minutes between League team goals while on pitch	**77**	**Club Strike Rate** Average number of minutes between League goals scored by club	**95**

	PLAYER	LGE GOALS	POWER	STRIKE RATE
1	Ramiro Antonito	9	77	**222 mins**
2	Francisco Casquero	5	106	**338 mins**
3	Abella Damia	3	83	**444 mins**
4	Sergio Matabuena	3	79	**449 mins**

Juan Jose Juanjo and Jose Moraton

SQUAD APPEARANCES

Match	1	2	3	4	5	6	7	8	9	10	11	12	13	14	15	16	17	18	19	20	21	22	23	24	25	26	27	28	29	30	31	32	33	34	35	36	37	38
Venue	A	H	A	H	A	H	A	H	A	A	H	H	A	H	A	H	A	A	H	H	A	H	A	H	A	H	A	H	A	H	A	H	A	H	A	H	H	A
Competition	L	L	L	L	L	L	L	L	L	L	L	L	L	L	L	L	L	L	L	L	L	L	L	L	L	L	L	L	L	L	L	L	L	L	L	L	L	L
Result	L	L	W	W	D	L	D	L	D	D	D	L	L	D	W	D	W	D	W	L	D	L	W	L	D	D	L	W	L	D	L	D	L	L	W	L	W	L

Goalkeepers
Dudu Aouate
Antonio Tono
Juanjo Jose Valencia

Defenders
Abella Damia
Ezequiel Garay
Ho-Jin Lee
Jose Moraton
Neru
Lozano Oriol
Pablo Alfaro
Pablo Pinillos
San Jose Samuel

Midfielders
Antonio Tomas
Diaz Ayoze
Francisco Casquero
Stephane Dalmat
Juan Jose Juanjo
Jose Marques
Sergio Matabuena
Felipe Melo
Portilla
Victor Bermudez

Forwards
David Aganzo
Ramiro Antonito
Wilfried Dalmat
Valle Jonathan
Mauricio Pinilla
Martin del Campo Raul
Walid Regragui
Oscar Serrano

KEY: On all match | On bench | Subbed or sent off (Counting game) | Subbed or sent off (playing less than 70 minutes) | Subbed on from bench (Counting Game) | Subbed on (playing less than 70 minutes) | Subbed on and then subbed or sent off (Counting Game) | Subbed on and then subbed or sent off (playing less than 70 minutes) | Not in 16

ALAVES

Final Position: **18th**

KEY: ☐Won ☐Drawn ☐Lost

							Attendance
1	sppr1	**Barcelona**	H	D	0-0		16,047
2	sppr1	**Real Sociedad**	A	L	1-2	De Lucas 90	15,370
3	sppr1	**Getafe**	H	L	3-4	Nene 6 pen,13,66 pen	12,347
4	sppr1	**Malaga**	A	D	0-0		20,000
5	sppr1	**Real Madrid**	H	L	0-3		14,596
6	sppr1	**R Santander**	A	W	2-1	Wesley 32; Carpintero 90	13,832
7	sppr1	**Villarreal**	H	D	1-1	Nene 13	14,000
8	sppr1	**Seville**	A	L	0-2		45,000
9	sppr1	**Espanyol**	H	D	1-1	Sarriegui 13	10,042
10	sppr1	**Cadiz**	H	D	0-0		14,000
11	sppr1	**Celta Vigo**	A	L	1-2	Astudillo 67	14,865
12	sppr1	**Athl Bilbao**	A	W	2-0	Nene 7; Bodipo 90	40,000
13	sppr1	**Osasuna**	A	L	2-3	Nene 56; Aloisi 90	15,000
14	sppr1	**Mallorca**	H	L	0-3		12,512
15	sppr1	**Atl Madrid**	A	D	1-1	Sarriegui 80	30,000
16	sppr1	**Valencia**	H	L	0-1		14,000
17	sppr1	**Real Betis**	A	L	0-3		30,000
18	sppr1	**Real Zaragoza**	H	L	0-2		12,273
19	sppr1	**Deportivo**	A	W	2-0	Aloisi 21; Bodipo 50	23,400
20	sppr1	**Barcelona**	A	L	0-2		72,081
21	sppr1	**Real Sociedad**	H	W	3-1	Carpintero 34; Aloisi 59,86	14,317
22	sppr1	**Getafe**	A	D	2-2	Aloisi 12; Bodipo 74	11,000
23	sppr1	**Malaga**	H	W	3-2	Cesar Navas 43 og; Aloisi 50; Bodipo 58	13,098
24	sppr1	**Real Madrid**	A	L	0-3		69,114
25	sppr1	**R Santander**	H	D	2-2	Nene 20; Aloisi 35	12,824
26	sppr1	**Villarreal**	A	L	2-3	Aloisi 10; De Lucas 36	18,000
27	sppr1	**Seville**	H	W	2-1	Nene 25; Bodipo 45	12,831
28	sppr1	**Cadiz**	A	D	0-0		18,000
29	sppr1	**Celta Vigo**	H	W	1-0	Aloisi 86	13,237
30	sppr1	**Espanyol**	A	D	0-0		18,400
31	sppr1	**Athl Bilbao**	H	D	0-0		13,137
32	sppr1	**Osasuna**	H	L	1-2	Bodipo 90	16,843
33	sppr1	**Mallorca**	A	D	0-0		18,000
34	sppr1	**Atl Madrid**	H	L	0-1		14,436
35	sppr1	**Valencia**	A	L	0-3		40,000
36	sppr1	**Real Betis**	H	W	2-0	Aloisi 18; Nene 53	12,431
37	sppr1	**Real Zaragoza**	A	L	0-3		20,000
38	sppr1	**Deportivo**	H	W	1-0	Bodipo 79	15,337

LEAGUE APPEARANCES, BOOKINGS AND CAPS

	AGE (on 01/07/06)	IN NAMED 18	APPEARANCES	COUNTING GAMES	MINUTES ON PITCH	YELLOW CARDS	RED CARDS	CAPS THIS SEASON	NATIONAL SIDE
Goalkeepers									
Roberto Bonano	36	28	7	7	630	0	0	-	Argentina
Franco Costanzo	25	33	31	31	2790	5	0	-	Argentina
Defenders									
David Coromina	31	33	28	24	2306	7	0	-	Spain
Edu Alonso	32	36	35	34	3121	2	0	-	Spain
Galvez Gaspar	27	22	21	17	1648	9	0	-	Spain
Jorge Ribeiro	32	9	3	2	189	1	0	-	
Juanito	26	37	36	34	3060	9	1	4	Spain (5)
Mauricio Pellegrino	34	23	14	12	1110	4	0	-	Argentina
Fernandez Poli	29	20	9	7	684	2	0	-	Spain
Josu Sarriegui	27	33	30	29	2673	6	1	-	Spain
Oscar Gomez Tellez	31	8	5	1	210	1	0	-	Spain
Midfielders									
Martin Astudillo	28	34	33	31	2798	9	0	-	Argentina
Santiago Carpintero	29	31	27	18	1881	8	0	-	Spain
Luis Ferrer Carreras	33	5	4	2	232	0	0	-	Spain
Enrique De Lucas	27	23	22	15	1603	4	1	-	Spain
Elton Giovanni	22	14	3	0	53	0	0	-	Brazil
Georgiev	24	16	10	0	248	0	0	-	Bulgaria
Alejandro Fernandez	27	35	33	13	1850	2	0	-	Spain
Mehdi Lacen	22	22	17	8	832	2	0	-	France
Anderson Nene	24	38	38	36	3333	3	0	-	Brazil
Wesley	25	18	10	1	380	2	0	-	Brazil
Forwards									
John Aloisi	30	35	33	22	2280	2	0	4	Australia (42)
H. Arnaud Antchouet	26	6	3	0	57	0	0	-	Gabon
Arthuro Henrique	23	10	6	0	103	0	0	-	Brazil
Rodolfo Diaz Bodipo	28	35	34	21	2246	0	1	-	Spain
Jose Mena	27	17	10	2	354	1	0	-	Spain
Ruben Navarro	28	23	14	4	748	2	0	-	Spain
A D'Agosti Pacheco	30	5	1	1	90	0	0	-	Uruguay

TEAM OF THE SEASON

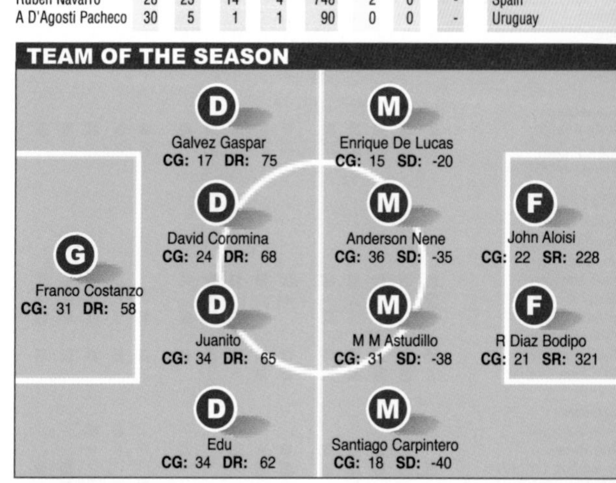

MONTHLY POINTS TALLY

AUGUST	1	33%
SEPTEMBER	1	8%
OCTOBER	6	40%
NOVEMBER	3	33%
DECEMBER	1	8%
JANUARY	6	50%
FEBRUARY	5	42%
MARCH	8	53%
APRIL	2	13%
MAY	6	67%

LEAGUE GOALS

	PLAYER	MINS	GOALS	S RATE
1	Aloisi	2280	**10**	228
2	Nene	3333	**9**	370
3	Bodipo	2246	**7**	321
4	De Lucas	1603	**2**	802
5	Carpintero	1881	**2**	941
6	Sarriegui	2673	**2**	1337
7	Astudillo	2798	**1**	2798
8	Wesley	380	**1**	380
	Other		1	
	TOTAL		**35**	

TOP POINT EARNERS

	PLAYER	GAMES	AV PTS
1	Coromina	24	**1.29**
2	Bodipo	21	**1.24**
3	Carpintero	18	**1.17**
4	Pellegrino	12	**1.17**
5	Sarriegui	29	**1.07**
6	Gaspar	17	**1.06**
7	Nene	36	**1.06**
8	Aloisi	22	**1.05**
9	Edu Alonso	34	**1.00**
10	De Lucas	15	**1.00**
	CLUB AVERAGE:		**1.03**

DISCIPLINARY RECORDS

	PLAYER	YELLOW	RED	AVE
1	Gaspar	9	0	**183**
2	Carpintero	8	0	**235**
3	Pellegrino	4	0	**277**
4	Juanito	9	1	**306**
5	Astudillo	9	0	**310**
6	De Lucas	4	1	**320**
7	Coromina	7	0	**329**
8	Poli	2	0	**342**
9	Navarro	2	0	**374**
10	Sarriegui	6	1	**381**
11	Lacen	2	0	**416**
12	Costanzo	5	0	**558**
13	Jandro	2	0	**925**
	Other	7	1	
	TOTAL	**76**	**4**	

KEY GOALKEEPER

Franco Costanzo

Goals Conceded in the League	48	**Counting Games** League games when player was on pitch for at least 70 minutes	31
Defensive Rating Ave number of mins between League goals conceded while on the pitch	58	**Clean Sheets** In League games when player was on pitch for at least 70 minutes	7

KEY PLAYERS - DEFENDERS

Galvez Gaspar

Goals Conceded Number of League goals conceded while the player was on the pitch	22	**Clean Sheets** In League games when player was on pitch for at least 70 minutes	7
Defensive Rating Ave number of mins between League goals conceded while on the pitch	75	**Club Defensive Rating** Average number of mins between League goals conceded by the club this season	63

	PLAYER	CON LGE	CLEAN SHEETS	DEF RATE
1	Galvez Gaspar	22	7	75 mins
2	David Pararols Coromina	34	8	68 mins
3	Juanito	47	11	65 mins
4	Eduardo Alvarez Edu Alonso	50	11	62 mins

KEY PLAYERS - MIDFIELDERS

Enrique Martinez De Lucas

Goals in the League	2	**Contribution to Attacking Power** Average number of minutes between League team goals while on pitch	84
Defensive Rating Average number of mins between League goals conceded while on the pitch	64	**Scoring Difference** Defensive Rating minus Contribution to Attacking Power	-20

	PLAYER	LGE GOALS	DEF RATE	POWER	SCORE DIFF
1	E Martinez De Lucas	2	64	84	-20 mins
2	Anderson Nene	9	63	98	-35 mins
3	Martin Mauricio Astudillo	1	58	96	-38 mins
4	Santiago Carpintero	2	78	118	-40 mins

KEY PLAYERS - GOALSCORERS

John Aloisi

Goals in the League	10	**Player Strike Rate** Average number of minutes between League goals scored by player	228
Contribution to Attacking Power Average number of minutes between League team goals while on pitch	91	**Club Strike Rate** Average number of minutes between League goals scored by club	98

	PLAYER	LGE GOALS	POWER	STRIKE RATE
1	John Aloisi	10	91	228 mins
2	Rodolfo Diaz Bodipo	7	86	321 mins
3	Anderson Nene	9	98	370 mins
4	Enrique Martinez De Lucas	2	84	802 mins

John Aloisi

SQUAD APPEARANCES

Match	1	2	3	4	5	6	7	8	9	10	11	12	13	14	15	16	17	18	19	20	21	22	23	24	25	26	27	28	29	30	31	32	33	34	35	36	37	38
Venue	H	A	H	A	H	A	H	A	H	H	A	A	A	H	A	H	A	H	A	A	H	A	H	A	H	A	H	A	H	A	H	H	A	H	A	H	A	H
Competition	L	L	L	L	L	L	L	L	L	L	L	L	L	L	L	L	L	L	L	L	L	L	L	L	L	L	L	L	L	L	L	L	L	L	L	L	L	L
Result	D	L	L	D	L	W	D	L	D	D	L	W	L	L	D	L	L	L	W	L	W	D	W	L	D	L	W	D	W	D	D	L	D	L	L	W	L	W

Goalkeepers
- Roberto Bonano
- Franco Costanzo

Defenders
- David Pararols Coromina
- Edu Alonso
- Galvez Gaspar
- Jorge Ribeiro
- Juanito
- Mauricio A. Pellegrino
- Fernandez Poli
- Josu Sarriegui
- Oscar Gomez Tellez

Midfielders
- Martin Mauricio Astudillo
- Santiago Carpintero
- Luis Ferrer Carreras
- Enrique Martinez De Lucas
- Elton Giovanni Machado
- Georgiev
- Alejandro Fernandez
- Mehdi Lacen
- Anderson Nene
- Wesley

Forwards
- John Aloisi
- Henri Arnaud Antchouet
- Arthuro Henrique
- Rodolfo Diaz Bodipo
- Jose Maria Garcia Mena
- Ruben Navarro
- Antonio D'Agosti Pacheco

KEY: On all match · On bench · Subbed or sent off (Counting game) · Subbed or sent off (playing less than 70 minutes) · Subbed on from bench (Counting Game) · Subbed on (playing less than 70 minutes) · Subbed on and then subbed or sent off (Counting Game) · Subbed on and then subbed or sent off (playing less than 70 minutes) · Not in 16

CADIZ

Final Position: **19th**

KEY: ☐Won ☐Drawn ☐Lost

No	Comp	Opponent	Venue	Res	Score	Scorers	Attendance
1	sppr1	**Real Madrid**	H	L	1-2	Pavoni 62	22,000
2	sppr1	**R Santander**	A	W	1-0	Sesma 84	13,500
3	sppr1	**Villarreal**	H	D	1-1	Oli 45	20,000
4	sppr1	**Seville**	A	D	0-0		45,000
5	sppr1	**Osasuna**	A	L	0-2		13,700
6	sppr1	**Celta Vigo**	H	D	1-1	Fleurquin 14	20,000
7	sppr1	**Espanyol**	A	W	2-0	Pavoni 65; Sesma 80	21,950
8	sppr1	**Athl Bilbao**	H	W	1-0	Enrique 13	20,000
9	sppr1	**Atl Madrid**	A	L	0-3		35,000
10	sppr1	**Alaves**	A	D	0-0		14,000
11	sppr1	**Mallorca**	H	L	1-2	Enrique 8	21,000
12	sppr1	**Valencia**	H	L	0-1		20,000
13	sppr1	**Real Betis**	A	D	1-1	Perez 74 pen	37,000
14	sppr1	**Real Zaragoza**	H	L	1-2	Enrique 17	22,000
15	sppr1	**Deportivo**	A	L	0-1		26,000
16	sppr1	**Barcelona**	H	L	1-3	Mirosavljevic 92	20,000
17	sppr1	**Real Sociedad**	A	L	0-2		16,200
18	sppr1	**Getafe**	H	W	1-0	Mirosavljevic 35 pen	19,000
19	sppr1	**Malaga**	A	W	2-0	Medina 14,37	21,000
20	sppr1	**Real Madrid**	A	L	1-3	Medina 54	60,000
21	sppr1	**R Santander**	H	D	1-1	Raul Lopez 74	20,000
22	sppr1	**Villarreal**	A	D	1-1	Medina 1	20,000
23	sppr1	**Seville**	H	L	0-4		22,000
24	sppr1	**Osasuna**	H	L	1-3	Lucas Lobos 15	20,000
25	sppr1	**Celta Vigo**	A	L	0-2		15,000
26	sppr1	**Espanyol**	H	W	2-0	Paz 73; Jonathan 87	18,000
27	sppr1	**Athl Bilbao**	A	L	0-1		38,000
28	sppr1	**Alaves**	H	D	0-0		18,000
29	sppr1	**Mallorca**	A	L	0-1		15,000
30	sppr1	**Atl Madrid**	H	D	1-1	Lucas Lobos 68 pen	20,000
31	sppr1	**Valencia**	A	L	3-5	Enrique 12; Sesma 63,78	40,000
32	sppr1	**Real Betis**	H	D	1-1	Lucas Lobos 69	20,000
33	sppr1	**Real Zaragoza**	A	W	2-1	Lucas Lobos 43 pen; Pavoni 48	10,000
34	sppr1	**Deportivo**	H	D	1-1	Lobos 84	20,000
35	sppr1	**Barcelona**	A	L	0-1		85,000
36	sppr1	**Real Sociedad**	H	D	2-2	Estoyanoff 67; Lobos 90	19,000
37	sppr1	**Getafe**	A	L	1-3	Lobos 21	12,000
38	sppr1	**Malaga**	H	W	5-0	Pavoni 19; Sesma 63,65; Estoyanoff 79; Mirosavljevic 84	18,000

LEAGUE APPEARANCES, BOOKINGS AND CAPS

	AGE (on 01/07/06)	IN NAMED 18	APPEARANCES	COUNTING GAMES	MINUTES ON PITCH	YELLOW CARDS	RED CARDS	CAPS THIS SEASON	NATIONAL SIDE
Goalkeepers									
Armando	35	31	24	24	2160	1	0	-	Spain
Oscar Limia	30	26	14	14	1260	0	0	-	Argentina
Raul Navas	28	19	0	0	0	0	0	-	Spain
Defenders									
Eduardo Berizzo	36	28	15	14	1262	3	0	-	Argentina
Jose De La Cuesta	23	30	14	13	1215	1	0	-	Colombia
Ramon De Quintana	34	32	29	28	2565	2	0	-	Spain
Mario Silva	29	19	7	6	551	1	0	-	Portugal
Abraham Paz	27	26	22	19	1818	4	0	-	Spain
Gonzalez Raul Lopez	29	33	26	26	2288	6	0	-	Spain
Alejandro Varela	32	36	35	32	2970	3	1	-	Spain
Midfielders									
Cadavieco Ivan Ania	28	17	9	2	350	2	0	-	Spain
Benjamin	30	15	14	5	706	2	0	-	Spain
Marc Bertran	24	1	1	1	90	0	0	-	Spain
Juan Jose Bezares	25	33	27	16	1849	10	0	-	Spain
Andres Jose Fleurquin	31	35	30	27	2493	11	0	-	Uruguay
L. Armando Lobos	24	21	19	13	1315	1	0	-	Argentina
Fernando Moran	30	19	14	4	552	2	0	-	Spain
Matias Pavoni	25	30	29	17	2088	3	1	-	Spain
Manolo Perez	29	11	4	0	101	1	0	-	Spain
Roberto Suarez	32	33	23	12	1546	3	0	-	Spain
Luciano German Vella	25	13	10	8	756	3	0	-	Argentina
Forwards									
Carlos Javier Acuna	18	2	0	0	0	0	0	-	Paraguay
Fernando Enrique	29	38	36	19	2314	4	0	-	Spain
Fabian Estoyanoff	23	30	29	6	1260	8	1	-	Uruguay
Alexander Medina	27	21	18	11	1147	8	1	-	Uruguay
Nenad Mirosavljevic	28	17	12	5	622	1	0	-	Serbia & Mont
Jesus Alvarez Oli	34	36	30	11	1549	5	1	-	Spain
Jonathan Sesma	27	36	36	28	2733	3	0	-	Spain

TEAM OF THE SEASON

MONTHLY POINTS TALLY

Month	Points	%
AUGUST	0	0%
SEPTEMBER	5	42%
OCTOBER	8	53%
NOVEMBER	1	11%
DECEMBER	0	0%
JANUARY	7	58%
FEBRUARY	1	8%
MARCH	5	33%
APRIL	5	33%
MAY	4	44%

LEAGUE GOALS

	PLAYER	MINS	GOALS	S RATE
1	Lobos	1315	**7**	188
2	Sesma	2733	**6**	456
3	Medina	1147	**4**	287
4	Enrique	2314	**4**	579
5	Pavoni	2088	**4**	522
6	Mirosavljevic	622	**3**	207
7	Estoyanoff	1260	**2**	630
8	Paz	1818	**1**	1818
9	Raul Lopez	2288	**1**	2288
10	Fleurquin	2493	**1**	2493
11	Perez	101	**1**	101
12	Oli	1549	**1**	1549
	Other		1	
	TOTAL		**36**	

TOP POINT EARNERS

	PLAYER	GAMES	AV PTS
1	Suarez	12	**1.25**
2	De La Cuesta	13	**1.08**
3	Bezares	16	**1.06**
4	Paz	19	**1.00**
5	Limia	14	**1.00**
6	Sesma	28	**1.00**
7	Pavoni	17	**0.94**
8	Varela	32	**0.94**
9	Berizzo	14	**0.93**
10	Armando	24	**0.92**
	CLUB AVERAGE:		**0.95**

DISCIPLINARY RECORDS

	PLAYER	YELLOW	RED	AVE
1	Medina	8	1	**127**
2	Estoyanoff	8	1	**140**
3	Bezares	10	0	**184**
4	Fleurquin	11	0	**226**
5	Vella	3	0	**252**
6	Oli	5	1	**258**
7	Moran	2	0	**276**
8	Benjamin	2	0	**353**
9	Raul Lopez	6	0	**381**
10	Berizzo	3	0	**420**
11	Paz	4	0	**454**
12	Suarez	3	0	**515**
13	Pavoni	3	1	**522**
	Other	17	1	
	TOTAL	**85**	**5**	

KEY GOALKEEPER

Oscar Alejandro Limia

Goals Conceded in the League	19	**Counting Games** League games when player was on pitch for at least 70 minutes	14
Defensive Rating Ave number of mins between League goals conceded while on the pitch	66	**Clean Sheets** In games when player was on pitch for at least 70 minutes	3

KEY PLAYERS - DEFENDERS

Abraham Paz

Goals Conceded Number of League goals conceded while the player was on the pitch	23	**Clean Sheets** In League games when player was on pitch for at least 70 minutes	5
Defensive Rating Ave number of mins between League goals conceded while on the pitch	79	**Club Defensive Rating** Average number of mins between League goals conceded by the club this season	66

	PLAYER	CON LGE	CLEAN SHEETS	DEF RATE
1	Abraham Paz	23	5	**79 mins**
2	Ramon Dalamau De Quintana	38	7	**68 mins**
3	Gonzalez Raul Lopez	35	7	**65 mins**
4	Jose De La Cuesta	19	4	**64 mins**

KEY PLAYERS - MIDFIELDERS

Andres Jose Fleurquin

Goals in the League	1	**Contribution to Attacking Power** Average number of minutes between League team goals while on pitch	100
Defensive Rating Average number of mins between League goals conceded while on the pitch	69	**Scoring Difference** Defensive Rating minus Contribution to Attacking Power	-31

	PLAYER	LGE GOALS	DEF RATE	POWER	SCORE DIFF
1	Andres Jose Fleurquin	1	69	100	**-31 mins**
2	Lucas Armando Lobos	7	53	88	**-35 mins**
3	Juan Jose Bezares	0	60	103	**-43 mins**
4	Matias Pavoni	4	80	123	**-43 mins**

KEY PLAYERS - GOALSCORERS

Lucas Armando Lobos

Goals in the League	7	**Player Strike Rate** Average number of minutes between League goals scored by player	188
Contribution to Attacking Power Average number of minutes between League team goals while on pitch	88	**Club Strike Rate** Average number of minutes between League goals scored by club	95

	PLAYER	LGE GOALS	POWER	STRIKE RATE
1	Lucas Armando Lobos	7	88	**188 mins**
2	Jonathan Sesma	6	88	**456 mins**
3	Matias Pavoni	4	123	**522 mins**
4	Fernando Enrique	4	105	**579 mins**

Jonathan Sesma

SQUAD APPEARANCES

Match	1	2	3	4	5	6	7	8	9	10	11	12	13	14	15	16	17	18	19	20	21	22	23	24	25	26	27	28	29	30	31	32	33	34	35	36	37	38
Venue	H	A	H	A	A	H	A	H	A	A	H	H	A	H	A	H	A	H	A	A	H	A	H	H	A	H	A	H	A	H	A	H	A	H	A	H	A	H
Competition	L	L	L	L	L	L	L	L	L	L	L	L	L	L	L	L	L	L	L	L	L	L	L	L	L	L	L	L	L	L	L	L	L	L	L	L	L	L
Result	L	W	D	D	L	D	W	W	L	D	L	L	D	L	L	L	L	W	W	L	D	D	L	L	L	W	L	D	L	D	L	D	W	D	L	D	L	W

Goalkeepers
Armando
Oscar Alejandro Limia
Raul Navas

Defenders
Eduardo Berizzo
Jose De La Cuesta
Ramon De Quintana
Mario Silva
Abraham Paz
Gonzalez Raul Lopez
Alejandro Varela

Midfielders
Cadavieco Ivan Ania
Benjamin
Marc Bertran
Juan Jose Bezares
Andres Jose Fleurquin
Lucas Armando Lobos
Fernando Moran
Matias Pavoni
Manolo Perez
Roberto Suarez
Luciano German Vella

Forwards
Carlos Javier Acuna
Fernando Enrique
Fabian Estoyanoff
Alexander Medina
Nenad Mirosavljevic
Jesus Alvarez Oli
Jonathan Sesma

KEY: On all match | On bench | Subbed or sent off (Counting game) | Subbed or sent off (playing less than 70 minutes) | Subbed on from bench (Counting Game) | Subbed on (playing less than 70 minutes) | Subbed on and then subbed or sent off (Counting Game) | Subbed on and then subbed or sent off (playing less than 70 minutes) | Not in 16

MALAGA

Final Position: **20th**

KEY: ☐ Won ☐ Drawn ☐ Lost

		Opponent	H/A	Result	Score	Scorers	Attendance
1	sppr1	**Celta Vigo**	A	L	0-2		14,000
2	sppr1	**Espanyol**	H	L	1-2	Gerardo 89 pen	25,000
3	sppr1	**Athl Bilbao**	A	W	2-1	Edgar 85; Hidalgo 90	32,000
4	sppr1	**Alaves**	H	D	0-0		20,000
5	sppr1	**Mallorca**	A	W	4-1	Salva 29; Duda 31,57 fk; Edgar 59	14,000
6	sppr1	**Atl Madrid**	H	L	0-2		21,000
7	sppr1	**Valencia**	A	L	1-2	Salva 75	40,000
8	sppr1	**Real Betis**	H	W	5-0	Salva 8,30; Sanz 51; Counago 63,74	20,000
9	sppr1	**Barcelona**	A	L	0-2		70,000
10	sppr1	**Real Zaragoza**	A	D	1-1	Edgar 41	25,000
11	sppr1	**Deportivo**	H	D	1-1	Nacho 51	22,000
12	sppr1	**Real Sociedad**	H	W	3-1	Cesar Navas 62; Hidalgo 74; Edgar 77	21,000
13	sppr1	**Getafe**	A	L	2-3	Nacho 23; Juan Rodriguez 54	13,000
14	sppr1	**Osasuna**	H	L	1-2	Nacho 37	22,000
15	sppr1	**Real Madrid**	H	L	0-2		23,000
16	sppr1	**R Santander**	A	D	1-1	Navas 39	12,800
17	sppr1	**Villarreal**	H	D	0-0		20,000
18	sppr1	**Seville**	A	L	1-3	Salva 49	33,000
19	sppr1	**Cadiz**	H	L	0-2		21,000
20	sppr1	**Celta Vigo**	H	L	0-2		20,000
21	sppr1	**Espanyol**	A	L	1-3	Ruano 40	15,100
22	sppr1	**Athl Bilbao**	H	W	2-1	Litos 31; Salva 73	22,000
23	sppr1	**Alaves**	A	L	2-3	Duda 70; Hidalgo 90	13,098
24	sppr1	**Mallorca**	H	L	0-2		20,000
25	sppr1	**Atl Madrid**	A	L	0-5		50,000
26	sppr1	**Valencia**	H	D	0-0		22,000
27	sppr1	**Real Betis**	A	D	1-1	Hidalgo 73	38,000
28	sppr1	**Real Zaragoza**	H	L	0-1		16,000
29	sppr1	**Deportivo**	A	L	1-2	Duda 35	23,350
30	sppr1	**Barcelona**	H	D	0-0		23,000
31	sppr1	**Real Sociedad**	A	L	0-3		29,000
32	sppr1	**Getafe**	H	L	1-2	Counago 49	11,500
33	sppr1	**Osasuna**	A	D	1-1	Morales 81	16,611
34	sppr1	**Real Madrid**	A	L	1-2	Bovio 22	70,000
35	sppr1	**R Santander**	H	L	2-3	Ruano 25,30	7,000
36	sppr1	**Villarreal**	A	L	1-2	Gerardo 21	15,000
37	sppr1	**Seville**	H	L	0-2		7,000
38	sppr1	**Cadiz**	A	L	0-5		18,000

LEAGUE APPEARANCES, BOOKINGS AND CAPS

	AGE (on 01/07/06)	IN NAMED 18	APPEARANCES	COUNTING GAMES	MINUTES ON PITCH	YELLOW CARDS	RED CARDS	CAPS THIS SEASON	NATIONAL SIDE
Goalkeepers									
Francesco Arnau	31	36	36	35	3190	0	0	-	Spain
Inaki Goitia	24	37	2	1	140	1	0	-	Spain
Manuel Manolo	21	1	1	1	90	0	0	-	Spain
Javier Arevalo Munoz	24	1	0	0	0	0	0	-	Spain
Defenders									
Ruano Alexis	20	17	17	16	1503	1	0	-	Spain
Cesar Navas	26	21	16	13	1261	3	0	-	Spain
Fernando Sanz	32	20	14	11	1123	2	1	-	Spain
Gabriel Rodrigues	25	18	18	8	1098	1	0	-	Brazil
Garcia Gerardo	31	35	29	28	2542	11	0	-	Spain
Jesus Gamez	21	24	15	9	1063	5	0	-	Spain
Carlos Litos	32	32	8	6	629	4	0	-	Portugal
Cesar Navas	26	12	12	10	980	0	0	-	Spain
Jorge Ribeiro	24	8	4	3	306	1	0	-	Portugal
Fernando Sanz	32	15	15	15	1350	5	0	-	Spain
Vicente Valcarce	31	18	16	15	1365	6	0	-	Spain
Midfielders									
Abel	24	3	0	0	0	0	0	-	Spain
Anderson Silva	23	22	14	6	749	7	2	-	Brazil
Antonio Lopez	26	16	12	7	826	6	1	-	Spain
Ricardo Bovio	24	18	17	14	1332	6	0	-	Brazil
Diego Castro	24	2	2	0	41	0	0	-	Spain
Sergio Duda	26	15	14	11	1074	4	1	-	Portugal
Paco Esteban	24	19	12	1	330	1	0	-	Spain
Antonio Hidalgo	27	37	35	10	1422	4	1	-	Spain
Juan Rodriguez	24	32	27	24	2290	10	2	-	Spain
Sanchez Manu	27	24	12	3	646	0	0	-	Spain
Nacho	26	34	33	28	2701	9	1	-	Spain
Jorge Roldan Pina	23	5	2	0	30	1	0	-	Spain
Marcelo Romero	30	8	3	1	171	0	0	-	Uruguay
Francisco Ruano	31	19	19	16	1605	4	0	-	Spain
Saul	21	2	2	1	135	0	0	-	Spain
Fernando Usero	22	3	2	0	54	1	0	-	Spain
Forwards									
Ador	20	4	2	0	30	0	0	-	Spain
Pablo Counago	26	30	27	10	1460	4	0	-	Spain
Patricio Edgar	28	34	31	19	2105	3	0	-	Angola
Richard Morales	31	28	24	8	1163	4	1	-	Uruguay
Ballesta Salva	31	34	34	28	2589	10	1	-	Spain

TEAM OF THE SEASON

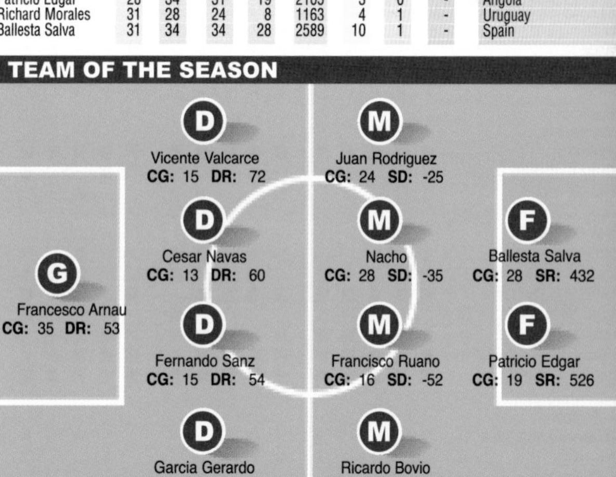

MONTHLY POINTS TALLY

AUGUST	0	0%
SEPTEMBER	7	58%
OCTOBER	4	27%
NOVEMBER	4	44%
DECEMBER	2	17%
JANUARY	0	0%
FEBRUARY	3	25%
MARCH	3	20%
APRIL	1	7%
MAY	0	0%

LEAGUE GOALS

	PLAYER	MINS	GOALS	S RATE
1	Salva	2589	6	432
2	Edgar	2105	4	526
3	Hidalgo	1422	4	356
4	Duda	1074	4	269
5	Counago	1460	3	487
6	Nacho	2701	3	900
7	Ruano	1605	3	535
8	Gerardo	2542	2	1271
9	Cesar Navas	1261	1	1261
10	Bovio	1332	1	1332
11	Juan Rodriguez	2290	1	2290
12	Morales	1163	1	1163
13	Sanz	1350	1	1350
	Other		2	
	TOTAL		36	

TOP POINT EARNERS

	PLAYER	GAMES	AV PTS
1	Edgar	19	0.89
2	Valcarce	15	0.87
3	Cesar Navas	13	0.85
4	Nacho	28	0.79
5	Juan Rodriguez	24	0.71
6	Gerardo	28	0.71
7	Sanz	15	0.67
8	Arnau	35	0.66
9	Salva	28	0.64
10	Ruano	16	0.56
	CLUB AVERAGE:		0.63

DISCIPLINARY RECORDS

	PLAYER	YELLOW	RED	AVE
1	Anderson	7	2	83
2	Antonio Lopez	6	1	118
3	Litos	4	0	157
4	Juan Rodriguez	10	2	190
5	Jesus Gamez	5	0	212
6	Duda	4	1	214
7	Bovio	6	0	222
8	Valcarce	6	0	227
9	Gerardo	11	0	231
10	Morales	4	1	232
11	Salva	10	1	235
12	Nacho	9	1	270
13	Sanz	5	0	270
	Other	22	2	
	TOTAL	109	11	

KEY GOALKEEPER

Francesco Arnau

Goals Conceded in the League	60	**Counting Games** League games when player was on pitch for at least 70 minutes	35
Defensive Rating Ave number of mins between League goals conceded while on the pitch	53	**Clean Sheets** In League games when player was on pitch for at least 70 minutes	4

KEY PLAYERS - DEFENDERS

Vicente Valcarce

Goals Conceded Number of League goals conceded while the player was on the pitch	19	**Clean Sheets** In League games when player was on pitch for at least 70 minutes	3
Defensive Rating Ave number of mins between League goals conceded while on the pitch	72	**Club Defensive Rating** Average number of mins between League goals conceded by the club this season	50

	PLAYER	CON LGE	CLEAN SHEETS	DEF RATE
1	Vicente Valcarce	19	3	72 mins
2	Cesar Navas	21	2	60 mins
3	Fernando Sanz	25	2	54 mins
4	Garcia Gerardo	55	3	46 mins

KEY PLAYERS - MIDFIELDERS

Juan Rodriguez

Goals in the League	1	**Contribution to Attacking Power** Average number of minutes between League team goals while on pitch	85
Defensive Rating Average number of mins between League goals conceded while on the pitch	60	**Scoring Difference** Defensive Rating minus Contribution to Attacking Power	-25

	PLAYER	LGE GOALS	DEF RATE	POWER	SCORE DIFF
1	Juan Rodriguez	1	60	85	-25 mins
2	Nacho	3	55	90	-35 mins
3	Francisco Ruano	3	55	107	-52 mins
4	Ricardo Bovio	1	56	133	-77 mins

KEY PLAYERS - GOALSCORERS

Ballesta Salva

Goals in the League	6	**Player Strike Rate** Average number of minutes between League goals scored by player	432
Contribution to Attacking Power Average number of minutes between League team goals while on pitch	92	**Club Strike Rate** Average number of minutes between League goals scored by club	95

	PLAYER	LGE GOALS	POWER	STRIKE RATE
1	Ballesta Salva	6	92	432 mins
2	Patricio Edgar	4	81	526 mins
3	Francisco Ruano	3	107	535 mins
4	Nacho	3	90	900 mins

Patricio Edgar

SQUAD APPEARANCES

/atch	1	2	3	4	5	6	7	8	9	10	11	12	13	14	15	16	17	18	19	20	21	22	23	24	25	26	27	28	29	30	31	32	33	34	35	36	37	38
/enue	A	H	A	H	A	H	A	H	A	A	H	H	A	H	H	A	H	A	H	H	A	H	A	H	A	H	A	H	A	H	A	H	A	A	H	A	H	A
;ompetition	L	L	L	L	L	L	L	L	L	L	L	L	L	L	L	L	L	L	L	L	L	L	L	L	L	L	L	L	L	L	L	L	L	L	L	L	L	L
ʀesult	L	L	W	D	W	L	L	W	L	D	D	W	L	L	L	D	D	L	L	L	L	W	L	L	L	D	D	L	L	D	L	L	D	L	L	L	L	L

;oalkeepers
'rancesco Arnau
naki Goitia
/lanuel Manolo
avier Arevalo Munoz

)efenders
ʀuano Alexis
;esar Navas
'ernando Sanz
;abriel Rodrigues
;arcia Gerardo
esus Gamez
;arlos Litos
;esar Navas
lorge Ribeiro
'ernando Sanz
/icente Valcarce

/lidfielders
\bel
Anderson Silva
Antonio Lopez
Ricardo Bovio
Diego Castro
Sergio Duda
Paco Esteban
Antonio Hidalgo
Juan Rodriguez
Sanchez Manu
Nacho
Jorge Roldan Pina
Marcelo Romero
Francisco Ruano
Saul
Fernando Usero

Forwards
Ador
Pablo Counago
Patricio Edgar
Richard Morales
Ballesta Salva

KEY: On all match; On bench; Subbed or sent off (Counting game); Subbed or sent off (playing less than 70 minutes); Subbed on from bench (Counting Game); Subbed on (playing less than 70 minutes); Subbed on and then subbed or sent off (Counting Game); Subbed on and then subbed or sent off (playing less than 70 minutes); Not in 16

ITALIAN LEAGUE ROUND-UP

FINAL LEAGUE TABLE

		HOME					AWAY					TOTAL			
	P	W	D	L	F	A	W	D	L	F	A	F	A	DIF	PTS
Juventus	38	14	5	0	33	9	13	5	1	38	15	71	24	47	91
AC Milan	38	18	1	0	50	13	10	3	6	35	18	85	31	54	88
Inter Milan	38	16	1	2	47	13	7	6	6	21	17	68	30	38	76
Fiorentina	38	16	1	2	42	20	6	7	6	24	21	66	41	25	74
Roma	38	11	4	4	35	21	8	8	3	35	21	70	42	28	69
Lazio	38	11	7	1	34	18	5	7	7	23	29	57	47	10	62
Chievo	38	9	8	2	33	19	4	7	8	21	30	54	49	5	54
Palermo	38	9	5	5	31	26	4	8	7	19	26	50	52	-2	52
Livorno	38	8	7	4	22	17	4	6	9	15	27	37	44	-7	49
Parma	38	7	7	5	25	22	5	2	12	21	38	46	60	-14	45
Empoli	38	9	3	7	26	26	4	3	12	20	36	46	62	-16	45
Ascoli	38	7	8	4	27	25	2	8	9	16	28	43	53	-10	43
Udinese	38	6	5	8	19	22	5	5	9	21	32	40	54	-14	43
Sampdoria	38	6	6	7	29	29	4	5	10	18	22	47	51	-4	41
Reggina	38	8	4	7	25	28	3	4	12	14	37	39	65	-26	41
Cagliari	38	6	11	2	23	17	2	4	13	19	38	42	55	-13	39
Siena	38	5	5	9	18	27	4	7	8	24	32	42	59	-17	39
Messina	38	4	9	6	20	24	2	4	13	14	34	34	58	-24	31
Lecce	38	4	7	8	16	22	3	1	15	14	35	30	57	-27	29
Treviso	38	2	4	13	12	26	1	8	10	12	30	24	56	-32	21

CLUB STRIKE FORCE

Milan's Filippo Inzaghi

1 AC Milan

Goals scored in the League	84
Club Strike Rate (CSR) Average number of minutes between League goals scored by club	40

	CLUB	GOALS	CSR
1	AC Milan	84	40
2	Juventus	71	48
3	Roma	70	49
4	Inter Milan	68	50
5	Fiorentina	66	52
6	Lazio	57	60
7	Chievo	54	63
8	Palermo	50	68
9	Sampdoria	47	73
10	Empoli	46	74
10	Parma	46	74
12	Ascoli	43	80
13	Cagliari	42	81
13	Siena	42	81
15	Udinese	40	86
16	Reggina	39	88
17	Livorno	37	92
18	Messina	34	101
19	Lecce	30	114
20	Treviso	24	143

CLUB DISCIPLINARY RECORDS

Lecce's Cassetti: 9 cards

1 Lecce

League Yellow	93
League Red	9
League Total	102
Cards Average in League (AVE) Average number of minutes between a card being shown of either colour	34

	CLUB	Y	R	TOTAL	AVE
1	Lecce	93	9	102	34
2	Udinese	84	12	96	36
3	Messina	89	7	96	36
4	Cagliari	87	8	95	36
5	Reggina	84	9	93	37
6	Siena	85	6	91	38
7	Parma	83	4	87	39
8	Sampdoria	81	4	85	40
9	Ascoli	74	8	82	42
10	Treviso	78	3	81	42
11	Roma	72	7	79	43
12	Chievo	69	8	77	44
13	Palermo	71	5	76	45
14	Lazio	68	3	71	48
15	Inter Milan	66	4	70	49
16	Fiorentina	65	1	66	52
17	Empoli	62	3	65	53
18	Juventus	62	3	65	53
19	Livorno	58	5	63	54
20	AC Milan	53	3	56	61

CLUB DEFENCES

	CLUB	LGE	CS	CDR
1	Juventus	24	17	143
2	Inter Milan	30	19	114
3	AC Milan	31	16	110
4	Fiorentina	41	9	83
5	Roma	42	14	81
6	Livorno	44	17	78
7	Lazio	47	9	73
8	Chievo	49	9	70
9	Sampdoria	51	7	67
10	Palermo	52	11	66
11	Ascoli	53	6	65
12	Udinese	54	10	63
13	Cagliari	55	7	62
14	Treviso	56	4	61
15	Lecce	57	10	60
16	Messina	58	7	59
17	Parma	60	8	57
18	Siena	60	8	57
19	Empoli	62	5	55
20	Reggina	65	9	53

Fabio Cannavaro of Juventus

1 Juventus

Goals conceded in the League	24
Clean Sheets (CS) Number of league games where no goals were conceded	17
Club Defensive Rate (CDR) Average number of minutes between League goals conceded by club	143

PLAYER NATIONALITIES

Overseas country with the most player appearances in the Italian League - Brazil

723 league appearances by Brazilian players

	COUNTRY	PLAYERS	IN SQUAD	LGE APP	% LGE ACT	CAPS	MOST APP	APP
1	Italy	451	9275	7025	68.7	173	Ferdinando Coppola	99.7
2	Brazil	39	872	723	7.2	16	Rodrigo Taddei	95.9
3	Argentina	22	547	443	4.3	21	Sergio Almiron	90.2
4	France	13	288	256	2.6	24	Patrick Vieira	80.9
5	Uruguay	11	223	163	1.5	0	Nelson Abeijon	58.1
6	Serbia & Montenegro	6	130	112	1.1	6	Mirko Vucinic	84.9
7	Portugal	5	139	117	1.0	0	Luis Figo	71.8
8	Croatia	5	133	97	0.9	19	Sasa Bjelanovic	62.4
9	Czech Republic	3	99	91	0.9	17	Tomas Ujfalusi	94.7
10	Nigeria	5	131	109	0.8	0	Christian Obodo	62.9
11	Romania	4	105	87	0.8	0	Christian Chivu	69.5
12	Colombia	5	95	73	0.8	0	Ivan Cordoba	88.8
13	Chile	4	117	82	0.7	4	Jorge Vargas	78.7
14	Australia	3	106	68	0.7	15	Vincenzo Grella	84.6
15	Ivory Coast	3	95	76	0.6	7	Axel Cedric Konan	58.8
16	Holland	2	63	60	0.7	0	Clarence Seedorf	73.7
17	Denmark	3	68	57	0.7	7	Martin Jorgensen	83.5
18	Ghana	3	58	52	0.7	5	Sulley Ali Muntari	66.5
19	Honduras	2	72	55	0.5	0	David Suazo	95.3
20	Albania	2	62	54	0.5	2	Erjon Bogdani	81.7

CLUB MAKE-UP – HOME AND OVERSEAS PLAYERS

1 Inter Milan

86.4% of appearances by overseas players

	CLUB	OVERSEAS	HOME	% OVERSEAS	% LGE ACT	MOST APP	APP
1	Inter Milan	26	8	76.5	86.4	Ivan Cordoba	88.8
2	AC Milan	15	11	57.7	60.1	Nelson Dida	94.7
3	Roma	14	19	42.4	52.6	Rodrigo Taddei	95.9
4	Juventus	13	13	50.0	51.4	Emerson	87.8
5	Udinese	15	25	37.5	45.7	Felipe Dal Belo	92.1
6	Lecce	12	24	33.3	41.6	S Diamoutene	86.7
7	Treviso	15	24	38.5	37.1	Lazzaretti Gustavo	63.3
8	Parma	9	27	25.0	32.4	Simplicio	95.6
9	Fiorentina	10	21	32.3	31.3	Tomas Ujfalusi	94.7
10	Lazio	10	25	28.6	30.8	Emilson	74.3
11	Cagliari	5	20	20.0	24.5	David Suazo	95.3
12	Messina	13	27	32.5	24.2	Rahman Rezaei	89.5
13	Livorno	8	20	28.6	21.7	Jorge Vargas	78.7
14	Siena	7	22	24.1	20.1	Erjon Bogdani	81.7
15	Palermo	6	27	18.2	18.4	Mario Santana	55.6
16	Chievo	5	23	17.9	12.7	Oliveira Amauri	85.0
17	Empoli	2	25	7.4	9.6	Sergio Almiron	90.2
18	Ascoli	8	33	19.5	9.5	Sasa Bjelanovic	62.4
19	Reggina	9	28	24.3	7.2	Carlos Paredes	68.2
20	Sampdoria	4	29	12.1	4.2	Vitaly Kutuzov	43.8

CHART-TOPPING MIDFIELDERS

1 Nedved - Juventus	
Goals scored in the League	5
Defensive Rating Av number of mins between League goals conceded while on the pitch	142
Contribution to Attacking Power Average number of minutes between League team goals while on pitch	45
Scoring Difference Defensive Rating minus Contribution to Attacking Power	97

	PLAYER	CLUB	GOALS	DEF RATE	POWER	S DIFF
1	Nedved	Juventus	5	142	45	97
2	Emerson	Juventus	2	136	48	88
3	Veron	Inter Milan	0	131	47	84
4	Figo	Inter Milan	5	137	53	84
5	Serginho	AC Milan	1	114	38	76
6	Stankovic, D	Inter Milan	2	126	54	72
7	Vieira	Juventus	5	120	50	70
8	Kaka	AC Milan	14	107	39	68
9	Gattuso	AC Milan	3	107	40	67
10	Pirlo	AC Milan	4	105	39	66
11	Seedorf	AC Milan	4	105	41	64
12	Aquilani	Roma	3	109	45	64
13	Camoranesi	Juventus	3	107	48	59
14	Cambiasso	Inter Milan	5	105	52	53
15	Mauri	Lazio	2	90	45	45

CHART-TOPPING GOALSCORERS

1 Trezeguet - Juventus	
Goals scored in the League	23
Contribution to Attacking Power Average number of minutes between League team goals while on pitch	44
Club Strike Rate (CSR) Average minutes between League goals scored by club	48
Player Strike Rate Average number of minutes between League goals scored by player	100

	PLAYER	CLUB	GOALS: LGE	POWER	CSR	S RATE
1	Trezeguet	Juventus	23	44	48	100
2	Toni	Fiorentina	31	52	52	106
3	Cruz	Inter Milan	15	40	50	110
4	Inzaghi	AC Milan	12	38	40	117
5	Shevchenko	AC Milan	18	40	40	121
6	Totti	Roma	15	50	48	136
7	Suazo	Cagliari	22	79	81	148
8	Bonazzoli	Sampdoria	9	58	73	149
9	Del Piero	Juventus	12	50	48	149
10	Tavano	Empoli	19	71	73	150
11	Gilardino	AC Milan	17	41	40	151
12	Lucarelli, C	Livorno	15	102	92	157
13	Pellissier	Chievo	13	65	63	166
14	Adriano	Inter Milan	13	56	50	176
15	Rocchi	Lazio	17	62	59	178

CHART-TOPPING DEFENDERS

1 Zambrotta - Juventus	
Goals Conceded in the League The number of League goals conceded while he was on the pitch	18
Clean Sheets In games when he played at least 70 mins	16
Club Defensive Rating Average mins between League goals conceded by the club this season	137
Defensive Rating Average number of minutes between League goals conceded while on pitch	153

	PLAYER	CLUB	CON: LGE	CS	CDR	DEF RATE
1	Zambrotta	Juventus	18	16	137	153
2	Cannavaro	Juventus	22	17	137	146
3	Balzaretti	Juventus	9	5	137	142
4	Chiellini	Juventus	10	7	137	136
5	Thuram	Juventus	17	9	137	131
6	Kovac, R	Juventus	11	7	137	128
7	Zanetti, J	Inter Milan	19	11	114	118
8	Samuel	Inter Milan	21	14	114	115
9	Materazzi	Inter Milan	14	9	114	113
10	Stam	AC Milan	17	7	110	110
11	Burdisso	Inter Milan	11	4	114	110
12	Cordoba	Inter Milan	28	16	114	108
13	Kaladze	AC Milan	22	11	110	107
14	Nesta	AC Milan	24	11	110	105
15	Bovo	Roma	14	7	81	102

CHART-TOPPING GOALKEEPERS

1 Abbiati - Juventus	
Counting Games Games in which he played at least 70 minutes	18
Goals Conceded in the League The number of League goals conceded while he was on the pitch	10
Clean Sheets In games when he played at least 70 mins	9
Defensive Rating Average number of minutes between League goals conceded while on pitch	161

	PLAYER	CLUB	CG	CONC	CS	DEF RATE
1	Abbiati	Juventus	18	10	9	161
2	Buffon	Juventus	18	12	7	135
3	Cesar, J	Inter Milan	29	23	16	113
4	Dida	AC Milan	36	31	14	105
5	Bucci	Parma	21	19	8	95
6	Doni	Roma	28	29	11	87
7	Frey	Fiorentina	18	19	4	85
8	Benussi	Lecce	15	16	6	78
9	Lobont	Fiorentina	17	19	4	78
10	Amelia	Livorno	36	42	16	77
11	Pavarini	Reggina	18	21	5	74
12	Chimenti	Cagliari	21	26	4	72
13	Fontana	Chievo	29	36	5	70
14	Peruzzi	Lazio	30	38	7	69
15	De Sanctis	Udinese	34	45	9	68

PLAYER DISCIPLINARY RECORD

1. Cristiano - Ascoli	
Cards Average mins between cards	116
League Yellow	7
League Red	1
TOTAL	8

	PLAYER		LY	LR	TOT	AVE
1	Cristiano	Ascoli	7	1	8	116
2	Camorani	Lecce	8	2	10	116
3	Coppola	Messina	12	0	12	156
4	Dacourt	Roma	8	0	8	160
5	Conti	Cagliari	14	1	15	162
6	Tedesco	Reggina	7	2	9	165
7	Obodo	Udinese	11	2	13	165
8	Tosto	Ascoli	5	1	6	169
9	Gastaldello	Siena	9	0	9	170
10	Falsini	Siena	8	1	9	174
11	Materazzi	Inter Milan	9	0	9	175
12	Bega	Cagliari	12	2	14	176
13	Bolano	Parma	6	0	6	179
14	Bizera	Cagliari	6	1	7	182
15	Cristante	Messina	8	1	9	189

TEAM OF THE SEASON

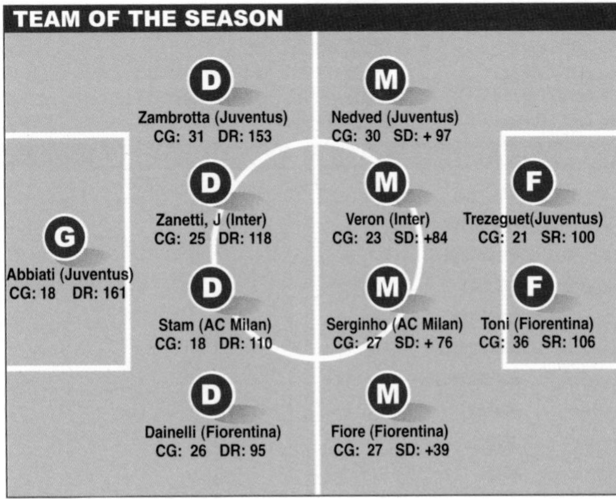

JUVENTUS

Final Position: **1st**

NICKNAME: THE OLD LADY OF TURIN

KEY: ☐Won ☐Drawn ☐Lost

							Attendance
1	itpr1	Chievo	H	W	1-0	Trezeguet 36	24,693
2	itpr1	Empoli	A	W	4-0	Trezeguet 10,59; Vieira 14; Camoranesi 16	10,350
3	ecgpa	Club Brugge	A	W	2-1	Nedved 66; Trezeguet 75	28,000
4	itpr1	Ascoli	H	W	2-1	Del Piero 14 pen,39	27,293
5	itpr1	Udinese	A	W	1-0	Vieira 37	21,780
6	itpr1	Parma	A	W	2-1	Camoranesi 44; Vieira 82	23,116
7	ecgpa	Rapid Vienna	H	W	3-0	Trezeguet 27; Mutu 82; Ibrahimovic 85	49,521
8	itpr1	Inter Milan	H	W	2-0	Trezeguet 22; Nedved 34	33,772
9	itpr1	Messina	H	W	1-0	Del Piero 24	30,097
10	ecgpa	Bayern Munich	A	L	1-2	Ibrahimovic 90	60,000
11	itpr1	Lecce	A	W	3-0	Ibrahimovic 9; Mutu 86; Zalayeta 90	24,941
12	itpr1	Sampdoria	H	W	2-0	Trezeguet 41; Mutu 57	29,977
13	itpr1	AC Milan	A	L	1-3	Trezeguet 76	78,000
14	ecgpa	Bayern Munich	H	W	2-1	Trezeguet 62,85	19,000
15	itpr1	Livorno	H	W	3-0	Ibrahimovic 59; Trezeguet 60; Del Piero 90	29,000
16	itpr1	Roma	A	W	4-1	Nedved 45; Ibrahimovic 56; Trezeguet 58,61	76,000
17	ecgpa	Club Brugge	H	W	1-0	Del Piero 80	35,000
18	itpr1	Treviso	H	W	3-1	Mutu 37; Trezeguet 43; Del Piero 82	27,102
19	itpr1	Fiorentina	A	W	2-1	Trezeguet 8; Camoranesi 88	43,900
20	ecgpa	Rapid Vienna	A	W	3-1	Del Piero 35,45; Ibrahimovic 42	46,500
21	itpr1	Cagliari	H	W	4-0	Nedved 10; Trezeguet 18,52; Vignati 68 og	27,587
22	itpr1	Lazio	A	D	1-1	Trezeguet 26	35,000
23	itpr1	Siena	H	W	2-0	Cannavaro 13; Trezeguet 53	25,587
24	itpr1	Palermo	A	W	2-1	Mutu 15,34	33,149
25	itpr1	Reggina	H	W	1-0	Del Piero 45	25,000
26	itpr1	Chievo	A	D	1-1	Vieira 31	18,673
27	itpr1	Empoli	H	W	2-1	Cannavaro 17,77	26,292
28	itpr1	Ascoli	A	W	3-1	Trezeguet 7,13,18	20,000
29	itpr1	Udinese	H	W	1-0	Del Piero 70	27,501
30	itpr1	Parma	H	D	1-1	Ibrahimovic 45	25,719
31	itpr1	Inter Milan	A	W	2-1	Ibrahimovic 63; Del Piero 85	79,000
32	itpr1	Messina	A	D	2-2	Ibrahimovic 18; Mutu 81	41,000
33	eclsl1	W Bremen	A	L	2-3	Nedved 73; Trezeguet 82	42,000
34	itpr1	Lecce	H	W	3-1	Emerson 18; Kovac, R 44; Del Piero 88 pen	26,721
35	itpr1	Sampdoria	A	W	1-0	Nedved 68	35,369
36	eclsl2	W Bremen	H	W	2-1	Trezeguet 65; Emerson 88	40,000
37	itpr1	AC Milan	H	D	0-0		39,087
38	itpr1	Livorno	A	W	3-1	Trezeguet 3,54; Del Piero 90	15,000
39	itpr1	Roma	H	D	1-1	Emerson 35	29,621
40	ecqfl1	Arsenal	A	L	0-2		35,472
41	itpr1	Treviso	A	D	0-0		6,600
42	ecqfl2	Arsenal	H	D	0-0		50,000
43	itpr1	Fiorentina	H	D	1-1	Del Piero 62	27,666
44	itpr1	Cagliari	A	D	1-1	Cannavaro 90	20,000
45	itpr1	Lazio	H	D	1-1	Trezeguet 86	33,898
46	itpr1	Siena	A	W	3-0	Vieira 3; Trezeguet 7; Mutu 8	15,000
47	itpr1	Palermo	H	W	2-1	Nedved 31; Ibrahimovic 51	56,488
48	itpr1	Reggina	A	W	2-0	Trezeguet 23; Del Piero 90	56,000

LEAGUE APPEARANCES, BOOKINGS AND CAPS

	AGE (on 01/07/06)	IN NAMED 18	APPEARANCES	COUNTING GAMES	MINUTES ON PITCH	YELLOW CARDS	RED CARDS	CAPS THIS SEASON	NATIONAL SIDE
Goalkeepers									
Christian Abbiati	29	35	19	18	1613	1	0	2	Italy (13)
Landry Bonnefoi	22	3	0	0	0	0	0	-	France
Gianluigi Buffon	28	22	18	18	1616	1	0	2	Italy (13)
Antonio Chimenti	36	14	3	2	191	0	0	-	Italy
Defenders									
Federico Balzaretti	24	33	19	12	1278	0	0	-	Italy
Fabio Cannavaro	32	36	36	35	3201	7	1	8	Italy (13)
Giorgio Chiellini	21	26	17	14	1364	5	0	-	Italy
Domenico Criscito	19	1	0	0	0	0	0	-	Italy
Pereira Gladstone	21	1	0	0	0	0	0	-	Brazil
Robert Kovac	32	31	17	15	1409	1	0	6	Croatia (23)
Gianluca Pessotto	35	21	9	6	595	0	0	-	Italy
Lilian Thuram	34	31	27	23	2229	4	1	10	France (8)
Gianluca Zambrotta	29	31	31	30	2749	4	0	6	Italy (13)
Jonathan Zebina	27	12	10	4	487	0	0	1	France (8)
Midfielders									
Manuele Blasi	25	33	13	7	729	3	0	1	Italy (13)
Mauro Camoranesi	29	35	34	20	2247	7	0	8	Italy (13)
Emerson	30	34	34	33	3002	3	0	-	Brazil
Giullano Giannicedda	31	29	15	8	794	1	0	-	Italy
Pavel Nedved	33	33	33	30	2699	7	1	3	Czech Republic (2)
Ruben Olivera	23	11	0	0	0	0	0	-	Uruguay
Patrick Vieira	30	31	31	30	2766	11	0	9	France (8)
Forwards									
Alessandro Del Piero	31	36	33	14	1790	0	0	8	Italy (13)
Zlatan Ibrahimovic	24	35	35	21	2392	4	0	3	Sweden (16)
Adrian Mutu	27	36	32	13	1668	3	0	-	Romania
David Trezeguet	28	34	32	21	2299	0	0	4	France (8)
Marcelo Zalayeta	27	33	16	0	391	0	0	-	Uruguay

TEAM OF THE SEASON

G — Christian Abbiati, CG: 18 DR: 161

D — Gianluca Zambrotta, CG: 30 DR: 153

D — Fabio Cannavaro, CG: 35 DR: 146

D — Federico Balzaretti, CG: 12 DR: 142

D — Giorgio Chiellini, CG: 14 DR: 136

M — Pavel Nedved, CG: 30 SD: 97

M — F de Rosa Emerson, CG: 33 SD: 88

M — Patrick Vieira, CG: 30 SD: 70

M — Mauro Camoranesi, CG: 20 SD: 59

F — David Trezeguet, CG: 21 SR: 100

F — A Del Piero, CG: 14 SR: 149

MONTHLY POINTS TALLY

AUGUST	3	100%
SEPTEMBER	12	100%
OCTOBER	12	80%
NOVEMBER	9	100%
DECEMBER	10	83%
JANUARY	13	87%
FEBRUARY	11	73%
MARCH	8	67%
APRIL	7	47%
MAY	6	100%

LEAGUE GOALS

	PLAYER	MINS	GOALS	S RATE
1	Trezeguet	2299	**23**	100
2	Del Piero	1790	**12**	149
3	Ibrahimovic	2392	**7**	342
4	Mutu	1668	**7**	238
5	Nedved	2699	**5**	540
6	Vieira	2766	**5**	553
7	Cannavaro	3201	**4**	800
8	Camoranesi	2247	**3**	749
9	Emerson	3002	**2**	1501
10	Kovac, R	1409	**1**	1409
11	Zalayeta	391	**1**	391
	Other		1	
	TOTAL		**71**	

TOP POINT EARNERS

	PLAYER	GAMES	AV PTS
1	Abbiati	18	**2.67**
2	Camoranesi	20	**2.60**
3	Del Piero	14	**2.57**
4	Mutu	13	**2.54**
5	Balzaretti	12	**2.50**
6	Emerson	33	**2.48**
7	Kovac, R	15	**2.47**
8	Cannavaro	35	**2.46**
9	Zambrotta	30	**2.43**
10	Chiellini	14	**2.43**
	CLUB AVERAGE:		**2.39**

DISCIPLINARY RECORDS

	PLAYER	YELLOW	RED	AVE
1	Blasi	3	0	**243**
2	Vieira	11	0	**251**
3	Chiellini	5	0	**272**
4	Camoranesi	7	0	**321**
5	Nedved	7	1	**337**
6	Cannavaro	7	1	**400**
7	Thuram	4	1	**445**
8	Mutu	3	0	**556**
9	Ibrahimovic	4	0	**598**
10	Zambrotta	4	0	**687**
11	Giannicedda	1	0	**794**
12	Emerson	3	0	**1000**
13	Kovac, R	1	0	**1409**
	Other	2	0	
	TOTAL	**62**	**3**	

KEY GOALKEEPER

Christian Abbiati

Goals Conceded in the League	10	Counting Games League games when player was on pitch for at least 70 minutes	18
Defensive Rating Ave number of mins between League goals conceded while on the pitch	161	Clean Sheets In games when player was on pitch for at least 70 minutes	9

KEY PLAYERS - DEFENDERS

Gianluca Zambrotta

Goals Conceded Number of League goals conceded while the player was on the pitch	18	Clean Sheets In League games when player was on pitch for at least 70 minutes	16
Defensive Rating Ave number of mins between League goals conceded while on the pitch	153	Club Defensive Rating Average number of mins between League goals conceded by the club this season	137

	PLAYER	CON LGE	CLEAN SHEETS	DEF RATE
1	Gianluca Zambrotta	18	16	153 mins
2	Fabio Cannavaro	22	17	146 mins
3	Federico Balzaretti	9	5	142 mins
4	Giorgio Chiellini	10	7	136 mins

KEY PLAYERS - MIDFIELDERS

Pavel Nedved

Goals in the League	5	Contribution to Attacking Power Average number of minutes between League team goals while on pitch	45
Defensive Rating Average number of mins between League goals conceded while on the pitch	142	Scoring Difference Defensive Rating minus Contribution to Attacking Power	97

	PLAYER	LGE GOALS	DEF RATE	POWER	SCORE DIFF
1	Pavel Nedved	5	142	45	97 mins
2	Fereira de Rosa Emerson	2	136	48	88 mins
3	Patrick Vieira	5	120	50	70 mins
4	Mauro Camoranesi	3	107	48	59 mins

KEY PLAYERS - GOALSCORERS

David Trezeguet

Goals in the League	23	Player Strike Rate Average number of minutes between League goals scored by player	100
Contribution to Attacking Power Average number of minutes between League team goals while on pitch	44	Club Strike Rate Average number of minutes between League goals scored by club	48

	PLAYER	LGE GOALS	POWER	STRIKE RATE
1	David Trezeguet	23	44	100 mins
2	Alessandro Del Piero	12	50	149 mins
3	Adrian Mutu	7	51	238 mins
4	Zlatan Ibrahimovic	7	48	342 mins

Pavel Nedved and David Trezeguet

SQUAD APPEARANCES

Match	1	2	3	4	5	6	7	8	9	10	11	12	13	14	15	16	17	18	19	20	21	22	23	24
Venue	H	A	A	H	A	A	H	H	H	A	A	H	A	H	H	A	H	H	A	A	H	A	H	A
Competition	L	L	C	L	L	L	C	L	L	C	L	L	L	C	L	L	C	L	L	C	L	L	L	L
Result	W	W	W	W	W	W	W	W	W	L	W	W	L	W	W	W	W	W	W	W	W	D	W	W

Match	25	26	27	28	29	30	31	32	33	34	35	36	37	38	39	40	41	42	43	44	45	46	47	48
Venue	H	A	H	A	H	H	A	A	A	H	A	H	H	A	H	A	A	H	H	A	H	A	H	A
Competition	L	L	L	L	L	L	L	L	C	L	L	C	L	L	L	C	L	C	L	L	L	L	L	L
Result	W	D	W	W	W	D	W	D	L	W	W	W	D	W	D	L	D	D	D	D	D	W	W	W

Goalkeepers
Christian Abbiati
Landry Bonnefoi
Gianluigi Buffon
Antonio Chimenti

Defenders
Federico Balzaretti
Fabio Cannavaro
Giorgio Chiellini
Domenico Criscito
Pereira Della Gladstone
Robert Kovac
Gianluca Pessotto
Lilian Thuram
Gianluca Zambrotta
Jonathan Zebina

Midfielders
Manuele Blasi
Mauro Camoranesi
Fereira de Rosa Emerson
Giullano Giannicedda
Pavel Nedved
Ruben Olivera
Patrick Vieira

Forwards
Alessandro Del Piero
Zlatan Ibrahimovic
Adrian Mutu
David Trezeguet
Marcelo Zalayeta

KEY: On all match · On bench · Subbed or sent off (Counting game) · Subbed or sent off (playing less than 70 minutes) · Subbed on from bench (Counting Game) · Subbed on (playing less than 70 minutes) · Subbed on and then subbed or sent off (Counting Game) · Subbed on and then subbed or sent off (playing less than 70 minutes) · Not in 16

AC MILAN

Final Position: **2nd**

NICKNAME: LA ROSSONERI

KEY: ☐ Won ☐ Drawn ☐ Lost

							Attendance
1	itpr1	**Ascoli**	A	D	1-1	Shevchenko 62	20,000
2	itpr1	**Siena**	H	W	3-1	Ambrosini 15; Shevchenko 31; Kaka 81	56,343
3	ecgpe	**Fenerbahce**	H	W	3-1	Kaka 18,87; Shevchenko 89	43,000
4	itpr1	**Sampdoria**	A	L	1-2	Gilardino 18	28,000
5	itpr1	**Lazio**	H	W	2-0	Shevchenko 12; Kaka 14	57,778
6	itpr1	**Treviso**	A	W	2-0	Shevchenko 44 pen; Gilardino 72	9,435
7	ecgpe	**Schalke**	A	D	2-2	Seedorf 1; Shevchenko 59	60,881
8	itpr1	**Reggina**	H	W	2-1	Maldini 5,20	57,538
9	itpr1	**Cagliari**	A	W	2-0	Gilardino 1; Shevchenko 27	18,000
10	ecgpe	**PSV Eindhoven**	H	D	0-0		69,763
11	itpr1	**Palermo**	H	W	2-1	Gattuso 30; Inzaghi 77	65,000
12	itpr1	**Empoli**	A	W	3-1	Gilardino 45,50; Vieri 55	10,000
13	itpr1	**Juventus**	H	W	3-1	Seedorf 14; Kaka 26; Pirlo 45	78,000
14	ecgpe	**PSV Eindhoven**	A	L	0-1		35,500
15	itpr1	**Udinese**	H	W	5-1	Gilardino 25,53; Seedorf 37; Pirlo 45; Kaka 77	58,000
16	itpr1	**Fiorentina**	A	L	1-3	Gilardino 25	44,000
17	ecgpe	**Fenerbahce**	A	W	4-0	Shevchenko 16,52,70,76	50,000
18	itpr1	**Lecce**	H	W	2-1	Pirlo 3; Inzaghi 90	55,129
19	itpr1	**Chievo**	A	L	1-2	Kaladze 22	25,000
20	ecgpe	**Schalke**	H	W	3-2	Pirlo 42; Kaka 52,60	82,000
21	itpr1	**Inter Milan**	A	L	2-3	Shevchenko 39 pen; Stam 83	76,416
22	itpr1	**Messina**	H	W	4-0	Shevchenko 22 pen,47; Pirlo 83; Gilardino 85	60,434
23	itpr1	**Livorno**	A	W	3-0	Gilardino 23,60; Shevchenko 71	14,000
24	itpr1	**Parma**	H	W	4-3	Cardone 27 og; Gilardino 29; Kaka 36; Shevchenko 81	55,000
25	itpr1	**Roma**	A	L	0-1		47,700
26	itpr1	**Ascoli**	H	W	1-0	Inzaghi 4	53,076
27	itpr1	**Siena**	A	W	3-0	Kaka 12,84; Shevchenko 69	13,500
28	itpr1	**Sampdoria**	H	D	1-1	Serginho 13	55,000
29	itpr1	**Lazio**	A	D	0-0		30,000
30	itpr1	**Treviso**	H	W	5-0	Kaka 14; Shevchenko 53,65; Gilardino 62; Inzaghi 73	52,000
31	itpr1	**Reggina**	A	W	4-1	Inzaghi 14,52,90; Gilardino 37	13,000
32	itpr1	**Cagliari**	H	W	1-0	Gilardino 23	55,000
33	eclsl1	**Bayern Munich**	A	D	1-1	Shevchenko 58 pen	66,000
34	itpr1	**Palermo**	A	W	2-0	Inzaghi 72; Shevchenko 83	31,868
35	itpr1	**Empoli**	H	W	3-0	Inzaghi 77,86; Shevchenko 81	54,419
36	eclsl2	**Bayern Munich**	H	W	4-1	Inzaghi 8,47; Shevchenko 25; Kaka 59	71,032
37	itpr1	**Juventus**	A	D	0-0		39,087
38	itpr1	**Udinese**	A	W	4-0	Shevchenko 42,65; Gilardino 61; Seedorf 71	20,000
39	itpr1	**Fiorentina**	H	W	3-1	Shevchenko 20; Kaka 48; Gattuso 60	75,000
40	ecqfl1	**Lyon**	A	D	0-0		40,000
41	itpr1	**Lecce**	A	L	0-1		14,521
42	ecqfl2	**Lyon**	H	W	3-1	Inzaghi 25,88; Shevchenko 90	80,000
43	itpr1	**Chievo**	H	W	4-1	Nesta 28; Kaka 62,70 pen,90	62,627
44	itpr1	**Inter Milan**	H	W	1-0	Kaladze 70	75,000
45	ecsfl1	**Barcelona**	H	L	0-1		85,000
46	itpr1	**Messina**	A	W	3-1	Jankulovski 33; Gattuso 44; Gilardino 90	32,000
47	ecsfl2	**Barcelona**	A	D	0-0		90,000
48	itpr1	**Livorno**	H	W	2-0	Inzaghi 28,65	62,088
49	itpr1	**Parma**	A	W	3-2	Kaka 29 pen; Cafu 43; Seedorf 56	21,920
50	itpr1	**Roma**	H	W	2-1	Kaka 5 pen; Amoroso 90 pen	67,000

LEAGUE APPEARANCES, BOOKINGS AND CAPS

	AGE (on 01/07/06)	IN NAMED 18	APPEARANCES	COUNTING GAMES	MINUTES ON PITCH	YELLOW CARDS	RED CARDS	CAPS THIS SEASON	NATIONAL SIDE
Goalkeepers									
Nelson Dida	32	37	36	36	3240	0	0	4	Brazil (1)
Valerio Fiori	37	1	0	0	0	0	0	-	Italy
Zeljko Kalac	33	36	2	2	180	0	0	5	Australia (42)
Defenders									
Cafu	36	20	19	11	1142	2	0	4	Brazil (1)
Alessandro Costacurta	40	28	15	8	869	0	0	-	Italy
Kakha Kaladze	28	34	28	26	2361	5	0	6	Georgia (84)
Paolo Maldini	38	14	14	12	1141	1	0	-	Italy
Lino Marzoratti	19	4	0	0	0	0	0	-	Italy
Alessandro Nesta	30	32	30	26	2513	8	0	7	Italy (13)
Dario Simic	30	28	15	8	1009	2	0	7	Croatia (23)
Jaap Stam	33	27	25	18	1874	5	1	-	Holland
Midfielders									
Massimo Ambrosini	29	15	14	5	622	1	0	-	Italy
Gennaro Gattuso	28	36	34	28	2663	6	1	7	Italy (13)
Marek Jankulovski	29	29	22	6	831	3	0	5	Czech Republic (2)
Ricardo Kaka	24	36	35	27	2567	1	0	5	Brazil (1)
Andrea Pirlo	27	36	34	31	2848	4	0	8	Italy (13)
Manuel Rui Costa	34	35	26	10	1274	3	0	-	Portugal
Clarence Seedorf	30	36	35	24	2522	3	1	-	Holland
Serginho	35	35	33	27	2614	4	0	-	Brazil
Johann Vogel	29	32	13	7	710	1	0	10	Switzerland (35)
Forwards									
Marcio Amoroso	32	14	4	0	94	0	0	-	Brazil
Alberto Gilardino	24	38	34	27	2571	2	0	8	Italy (13)
Filippo Inzaghi	32	27	23	13	1407	1	0	-	Italy
Andriy Shevchenko	29	31	28	21	2180	0	0	3	Ukraine (45)
Christian Vieri	32	12	8	3	363	1	0	5	Italy (13)

TEAM OF THE SEASON

G
Nelson Dida
CG: 36 DR: 105

D
Jaap Stam
CG: 18 DR: 110

D
Kakha Kaladze
CG: 26 DR: 107

D
Alessandro Nesta
CG: 26 DR: 105

D
Paolo Maldini
CG: 12 DR: 88

M
Serginho
CG: 27 SD: 76

M
Ricardo Kaka
CG: 27 SD: 68

M
Gennaro Gattuso
CG: 28 SD: 67

M
Andrea Pirlo
CG: 31 SD: 66

F
Filippo Inzaghi
CG: 13 SR: 117

F
Andriy Shevchenko
CG: 21 SR: 121

MONTHLY POINTS TALLY

AUGUST	1	33%
SEPTEMBER	9	75%
OCTOBER	15	100%
NOVEMBER	6	67%
DECEMBER	6	50%
JANUARY	10	67%
FEBRUARY	13	87%
MARCH	10	83%
APRIL	12	80%
MAY	6	100%

LEAGUE GOALS

	PLAYER	MINS	GOALS	S RATE
1	Shevchenko	2180	18	121
2	Gilardino	2571	17	151
3	Kaka	2567	14	183
4	Inzaghi	1407	12	117
5	Pirlo	2848	4	712
6	Seedorf	2522	4	631
7	Gattuso	2663	3	888
8	Kaladze	2361	2	1181
9	Maldini	1141	2	571
10	Serginho	2614	1	2614
11	Jankulovski	831	1	831
12	Cafu	1142	1	1142
13	Ambrosini	622	1	622
	Other		5	
	TOTAL		85	

TOP POINT EARNERS

	PLAYER	GAMES	AV PTS
1	Inzaghi	13	3.00
2	Gattuso	28	2.46
3	Seedorf	24	2.38
4	Serginho	27	2.37
5	Nesta	26	2.35
6	Dida	36	2.28
7	Kaka	27	2.26
8	Pirlo	31	2.26
9	Maldini	12	2.25
10	Gilardino	27	2.19
	CLUB AVERAGE:		2.32

DISCIPLINARY RECORDS

	PLAYER	YELLOW	RED	AVE
1	Jankulovski	3	0	277
2	Stam	5	1	312
3	Nesta	8	0	314
4	Gattuso	6	1	380
5	Rui Costa	3	0	424
6	Kaladze	5	0	472
7	Simic	2	0	504
8	Cafu	2	0	571
9	Ambrosini	1	0	622
10	Seedorf	3	1	630
11	Serginho	4	0	653
12	Vogel	1	0	710
13	Pirlo	4	0	712
	Other	5	0	
	TOTAL	52	3	

KEY GOALKEEPER

Nelson Dida

Goals Conceded in the League	31	Counting Games League games when player was on pitch for at least 70 minutes	36
Defensive Rating Ave number of mins between League goals conceded while on the pitch	5	Clean Sheets In games when player was on pitch for at least 70 minutes	14

KEY PLAYERS - DEFENDERS

Jaap Stam

Goals Conceded Number of League goals conceded while the player was on the pitch	17	Clean Sheets In League games when player was on pitch for at least 70 minutes	7
Defensive Rating Ave number of mins between League goals conceded while on the pitch	110	Club Defensive Rating Average number of mins between League goals conceded by the club this season	110

	PLAYER	CON LGE	CLEAN SHEETS	DEF RATE
1	Jaap Stam	17	7	110 mins
2	Kakha Kaladze	22	11	107 mins
3	Alessandro Nesta	24	11	105 mins
4	Paolo Maldini	13	3	88 mins

KEY PLAYERS - MIDFIELDERS

Serginho

Goals in the League	1	Contribution to Attacking Power Average number of minutes between League team goals while on pitch	38
Defensive Rating Average number of mins between League goals conceded while on the pitch	114	Scoring Difference Defensive Rating minus Contribution to Attacking Power	76

	PLAYER	LGE GOALS	DEF RATE	POWER	SCORE DIFF
1	Serginho	1	114	38	76 mins
2	Ricardo Kaka	14	107	39	68 mins
3	Gennaro Gattuso	3	107	40	67 mins
4	Andrea Pirlo	4	105	39	66 mins

KEY PLAYERS - GOALSCORERS

Filippo Inzaghi

Goals in the League	12	Player Strike Rate Average number of minutes between League goals scored by player	117
Contribution to Attacking Power Average number of minutes between League team goals while on pitch	38	Club Strike Rate Average number of minutes between League goals scored by club	40

	PLAYER	LGE GOALS	POWER	STRIKE RATE
1	Filippo Inzaghi	12	38	117 mins
2	Andriy Shevchenko	18	40	121 mins
3	Alberto Gilardino	17	41	151 mins
4	Ricardo Kaka	14	39	183 mins

Ricardo Kaka and Andriy Shevchenko

SQUAD APPEARANCES

Match	1	2	3	4	5	6	7	8	9	10	11	12	13	14	15	16	17	18	19	20	21	22	23	24	25
Venue	A	H	H	A	H	A	A	H	A	H	H	A	H	A	H	A	A	H	A	H	A	H	A	H	A
Competition	L	L	C	L	L	L	C	L	L	C	L	L	L	C	L	L	C	L	L	C	L	L	L	L	L
Result	D	W	W	L	W	W	D	W	W	D	W	W	W	L	W	L	W	W	L	W	L	W	W	W	L

Match	26	27	28	29	30	31	32	33	34	35	36	37	38	39	40	41	42	43	44	45	46	47	48	49	50
Venue	H	A	H	A	H	A	H	A	A	H	H	A	A	H	A	A	H	H	H	H	A	A	H	A	H
Competition	L	L	L	L	L	L	L	C	L	L	C	L	L	L	C	L	C	L	L	C	L	C	L	L	L
Result	W	W	D	D	W	W	W	D	W	W	W	D	W	W	D	L	W	W	W	L	W	D	W	W	W

Goalkeepers
Nelson Dida
Valerio Fiori
Zeljko Kalac

Defenders
Cafu
Alessandro Costacurta
Kakha Kaladze
Paolo Maldini
Lino Marzoratti
Alessandro Nesta
Dario Simic
Jaap Stam

Midfielders
Massimo Ambrosini
Gennaro Gattuso
Marek Jankulovski
Ricardo Kaka
Andrea Pirlo
Manuel Rui Costa
Clarence Seedorf
Serginho
Johann Vogel

Forwards
Marcio Amoroso
Alberto Gilardino
Filippo Inzaghi
Andriy Shevchenko
Christian Vieri

KEY: On all match | On bench | Subbed or sent off (Counting game) | Subbed or sent off (playing less than 70 minutes) | Subbed on from bench (Counting Game) | Subbed on (playing less than 70 minutes) | Subbed on and then subbed or sent off (Counting Game) | Subbed on and then subbed or sent off (playing less than 70 minutes) | Not in 16

INTER MILAN

Final Position: **3rd**

NICKNAME: INTER

KEY: ☐Won ☐Drawn ☐Lost

	Comp	Opponent	H/A	Res	Score	Scorers	Attendance
1	ecql1	Shak Donetsk	A	W	2-0	Martins 68; Adriano 78	32,000
2	ecql2	Shak Donetsk	H	D	1-1	Recoba 12	
3	itpr1	Treviso	H	W	3-0	Adriano 32,68,79	51,542
4	itpr1	Palermo	A	L	2-3	Cruz 85,90	31,309
5	ecgph	Artmedia Brat	A	W	1-0	Cruz 17	28,000
6	itpr1	Lecce	H	W	3-0	Martins 25; Stankovic, D 29; Cruz 84	48,219
7	itpr1	Chievo	A	W	1-0	Samuel 49	12,000
8	itpr1	Fiorentina	H	W	1-0	Martins 7	56,907
9	ecgph	Rangers	H	W	1-0	Pizarro 49	
10	itpr1	Juventus	A	L	0-2		33,772
11	itpr1	Livorno	H	W	5-0	Materazzi 11; Cruz 19; Cambiasso 49; Cordaz 51; Recoba 61	52,000
12	ecgph	Porto	A	L	0-2		25,500
13	itpr1	Udinese	A	W	1-0	Cruz 36	18,000
14	itpr1	Roma	H	L	2-3	Adriano 67,77	50,230
15	itpr1	Sampdoria	A	D	2-2	Cambiasso 31; Cordoba 40	27,500
16	ecgph	Porto	H	W	2-1	Cruz 75 pen,82	37
17	itpr1	Lazio	A	D	0-0		40,000
18	itpr1	Parma	H	W	2-0	Figo 68; Cambiasso 81	47,751
19	ecgph	Artmedia Brat	H	W	4-0	Figo 28; Adriano 41,59,74	
20	itpr1	Messina	A	W	2-1	Recoba 7; Cambiasso 59	40,000
21	itpr1	Ascoli	H	W	1-0	Adriano 24	46,122
22	ecgph	Rangers	A	D	1-1	Adriano 30	49,170
23	itpr1	AC Milan	H	W	3-2	Adriano 24 pen,90; Martins 59	76,416
24	itpr1	Reggina	A	W	4-0	Cordoba 2; Martins 15; Adriano 40; Pizarro 92	23,850
25	itpr1	Empoli	H	W	4-1	Adriano 3; Cruz 45; Figo 66; Martins 85	44,385
26	itpr1	Siena	A	D	0-0		15,000
27	itpr1	Cagliari	H	W	3-2	Martins 10; Adriano 15,58 pen	48,000
28	itpr1	Treviso	A	W	1-0	Cruz 21	9,435
29	itpr1	Palermo	H	W	3-0	Cambiasso 33; Terlizzi 77 og; Figo 80	48,942
30	itpr1	Lecce	A	W	2-0	Figo 72; Stankovic, D 90	15,832
31	itpr1	Chievo	H	W	1-0	Cruz 7	50,000
32	itpr1	Fiorentina	A	L	1-2	Recoba 84	41,000
33	itpr1	Juventus	H	L	1-2	Samuel 74	79,000
34	itpr1	Livorno	A	D	0-0		16,000
35	eclsl1	Ajax	A	D	2-2	Stankovic 49; Cruz 86	51,000
36	itpr1	Udinese	H	W	3-1	Cruz 18,47; Martins 60	45,000
37	itpr1	Roma	A	D	1-1	Materazzi 90	46,500
38	itpr1	Sampdoria	H	W	1-0	Adriano 40	48,826
39	eclsl2	Ajax	H	W	1-0	Stankovic, D 57	45,000
40	itpr1	Lazio	H	W	3-1	Figo 36; Recoba 46,72	46,000
41	itpr1	Parma	A	L	0-1		18,033
42	ecqf1	Villarreal	H	W	2-1	Adriano 7; Martins 54	80,000
43	itpr1	Messina	H	W	3-0	Solari 15,26; Martins 19	46,000
44	ecqfl2	Villarreal	A	L	0-1		22,500
45	itpr1	Ascoli	A	W	2-1	Cruz 51; Mihajlovic 56	18,000
46	itpr1	AC Milan	A	L	0-1		75,000
47	itpr1	Reggina	H	W	4-0	Cruz 16,90; Martins 23; Cesar, R 28	40,000
48	itpr1	Empoli	A	L	0-1		6,500
49	itpr1	Siena	H	D	1-1	Cruz 60	38,000
50	itpr1	Cagliari	A	D	2-2	Cruz 10; Solari 37	15,000

LEAGUE APPEARANCES, BOOKINGS AND CAPS

	AGE (on 01/07/06)	IN NAMED 18	APPEARANCES	COUNTING GAMES	MINUTES ON PITCH	YELLOW CARDS	RED CARDS	CAPS THIS SEASON	NATIONAL SIDE
Goalkeepers									
Julio Cesar	26	35	29	29	2610	0	0	3	Brazil (1)
Paolo Orlandoni	33	3	1	1	90	0	0	-	Italy
Francesco Toldo	34	33	8	8	720	0	0	-	Italy
Defenders									
Marco Andreolli	20	3	2	1	108	0	0	-	Italy
Nicolas Burdisso	25	23	17	12	1215	4	1	2	Argentina (9)
A. Rodrigues Cesar	31	9	8	5	505	1	0	-	Brazil
Ivan Cordoba	29	36	34	33	3037	8	0	-	Colombia
Giuseppe Favalli	34	26	23	19	1886	5	0	-	Italy
Marco Materazzi	32	30	21	17	1583	9	0	9	Italy (13)
Sinisa Mihajlovic	37	17	5	2	270	1	0	-	Serbia & Mont
Walter Samuel	28	31	28	25	2414	5	1	5	Argentina (9)
Pierre Nlend Wome	27	24	12	8	811	1	0	2	Cameroon (26)
Javier Zanetti	32	25	25	25	2250	4	0	1	Argentina (9)
Jose Ze Maria	32	13	8	4	469	1	0	-	Brazil
Midfielders									
Esteban Cambiasso	25	34	34	29	2736	3	0	4	Argentina (9)
Luis Figo	33	34	34	24	2457	3	0	-	Portugal
Domenico Germinale	-	1	1	0	29	0	0	-	
Kily Gonzalez	31	21	15	6	877	2	0	2	Argentina (9)
Daniel Boumsong	19	5	1	0	61	0	0	-	Cameroon
David Marcelo Pizarro	26	37	23	14	1374	1	0	3	Chile (73)
Santiago Solari	29	25	13	7	691	0	0	-	Argentina
Dejan Stankovic	27	24	23	20	1884	4	0	6	Serbia & Mont (44)
Juan Sebastian Veron	31	25	25	23	2098	3	1	-	Argentina
Cristiano Zanetti	29	28	14	6	689	5	0	-	Italy
Forwards									
Adriano	24	30	29	24	2283	1	0	-	Brazil
Julio Cruz	31	36	31	13	1657	2	1	3	Argentina (9)
Obafemi Martins	21	31	28	19	1851	1	0	-	Nigeria
Alvaro Recoba	30	25	20	6	923	2	0	-	Uruguay
Goran Slavkovski	16	1	1	0	8	0	0	-	Sweden

TEAM OF THE SEASON

G
Julio Cesar
CG: 29 **DR:** 113

D
Javier Zanetti
CG: 25 **DR:** 118

D
Walter Samuel
CG: 25 **DR:** 115

D
Marco Materazzi
CG: 17 **DR:** 113

D
Nicolas Burdisso
CG: 12 **DR:** 110

M
Luis Figo
CG: 24 **SD:** 84

M
Juan Sebastian Veron
CG: 23 **SD:** 84

M
Dejan Stankovic
CG: 20 **SD:** 72

M
Esteban Cambiasso
CG: 29 **SD:** 53

F
Julio Cruz
CG: 13 **SR:** 110

F
Adriano
CG: 24 **SR:** 176

MONTHLY POINTS TALLY

Month	Points	%
AUGUST	3	100%
SEPTEMBER	9	75%
OCTOBER	7	47%
NOVEMBER	7	78%
DECEMBER	12	100%
JANUARY	13	87%
FEBRUARY	7	47%
MARCH	7	58%
APRIL	9	60%
MAY	2	33%

LEAGUE GOALS

	PLAYER	MINS	GOALS	S RATE
1	Cruz	1657	**15**	110
2	Adriano	2283	**13**	176
3	Martins	1851	**9**	206
4	Recoba	923	**5**	185
5	Figo	2457	**5**	491
6	Cambiasso	2736	**5**	547
7	Solari	691	**3**	230
8	Cordoba	3037	**2**	1519
9	Samuel	2414	**2**	1207
10	Materazzi	1583	**2**	792
11	Stankovic, D	1884	**2**	942
12	Pizarro	1374	**1**	1374
13	Mihajlovic	270	**1**	270
	Other		3	
	TOTAL		**68**	

TOP POINT EARNERS

	PLAYER	GAMES	AV PTS
1	Veron	23	**2.30**
2	Figo	24	**2.25**
3	Cruz	13	**2.23**
4	Samuel	25	**2.16**
5	Favalli	19	**2.11**
6	Zanetti, J	25	**2.08**
7	Stankovic, D	20	**2.05**
8	Cambiasso	29	**2.03**
9	Cesar, J	29	**2.00**
10	Cordoba	33	**1.94**
	CLUB AVERAGE:		**2.00**

DISCIPLINARY RECORDS

	PLAYER	YELLOW	RED	AVE
1	Zanetti, C	5	0	**137**
2	Materazzi	9	0	**175**
3	Burdisso	4	1	**243**
4	Favalli	5	0	**377**
5	Cordoba	8	0	**379**
6	Samuel	5	1	**402**
7	Kily Gonzalez	2	0	**438**
8	Recoba	2	0	**461**
9	Ze Maria	1	0	**469**
10	Stankovic, D	4	0	**471**
11	Cesar, R	1	0	**505**
12	Veron	3	1	**524**
13	Cruz	2	1	**552**
	Other	14	0	
	TOTAL	**65**	**4**	

KEY GOALKEEPER

Julio Cesar

Goals Conceded in the League	23	Counting Games League games when player was on pitch for at least 70 minutes	29
Defensive Rating Ave number of mins between League goals conceded while on the pitch	113	Clean Sheets In League games when player was on pitch for at least 70 minutes	16

KEY PLAYERS - DEFENDERS

Javier Zanetti

Goals Conceded Number of League goals conceded while the player was on the pitch	19	Clean Sheets In League games when player was on pitch for at least 70 minutes	11
Defensive Rating Ave number of mins between League goals conceded while on the pitch	118	Club Defensive Rating Average number of mins between League goals conceded by the club this season	114

	PLAYER	CON LGE	CLEAN SHEETS	DEF RATE
1	Javier Zanetti	19	11	118 mins
2	Walter Samuel	21	14	115 mins
3	Marco Materazzi	14	9	113 mins
4	Nicolas Burdisso	11	4	110 mins

KEY PLAYERS - MIDFIELDERS

Juan Sebastian Veron

Goals in the League	0	Contribution to Attacking Power Average number of minutes between League team goals while on pitch	47
Defensive Rating Average number of mins between League goals conceded while on the pitch	131	Scoring Difference Defensive Rating minus Contribution to Attacking Power	84

	PLAYER	LGE GOALS	DEF RATE	POWER	SCORE DIFF
1	Juan Sebastian Veron	0	131	47	84 mins
2	Luis Figo	5	137	53	84 mins
3	Dejan Stankovic	2	126	54	72 mins
4	Esteban Cambiasso	5	105	52	53 mins

KEY PLAYERS - GOALSCORERS

Julio Cruz

Goals in the League	15	Player Strike Rate Average number of minutes between League goals scored by player	110
Contribution to Attacking Power Average number of minutes between League team goals while on pitch	40	Club Strike Rate Average number of minutes between League goals scored by club	50

	PLAYER	LGE GOALS	POWER	STRIKE RATE
1	Julio Cruz	15	40	110 mins
2	Adriano	13	56	176 mins
3	Obafemi Martins	9	54	206 mins
4	Luis Figo	5	53	491 mins

Julio Cruz and Esteban Cambiasso

SQUAD APPEARANCES

Match	1	2	3	4	5	6	7	8	9	10	11	12	13	14	15	16	17	18	19	20	21	22	23	24	25
Venue	A	H	H	A	A	H	A	H	H	A	H	A	A	H	A	H	A	H	H	A	H	A	H	A	H
Competition	C	C	L	L	C	L	L	L	C	L	L	C	L	L	L	C	L	L	C	L	L	C	L	L	L
Result	W	D	W	L	W	W	W	W	W	L	W	L	W	L	D	W	D	W	W	W	W	D	W	W	W

Match	26	27	28	29	30	31	32	33	34	35	36	37	38	39	40	41	42	43	44	45	46	47	48	49	50
Venue	A	H	A	H	A	H	A	H	A	A	H	A	H	H	H	A	H	H	A	A	A	H	A	H	A
Competition	L	L	L	L	L	L	L	L	L	C	L	L	L	C	L	L	C	L	C	L	L	L	L	L	L
Result	D	W	W	W	W	W	L	L	D	D	W	D	W	W	W	L	W	W	L	W	L	W	L	D	D

Goalkeepers
- Julio Cesar
- Paolo Orlandoni
- Francesco Toldo

Defenders
- Marco Andreolli
- Nicolas Burdisso
- A. Rodrigues Cesar
- Ivan Cordoba
- Giuseppe Favalli
- Marco Materazzi
- Sinisa Mihajlovic
- Walter Samuel
- Pierre Nlend Wome
- Javier Zanetti
- Jose Ze Maria

Midfielders
- Esteban Cambiasso
- Luis Figo
- Domenico Germinale
- Kily Gonzalez
- Daniel Maa Boumsong
- David Marcelo Pizarro
- Santiago Hernan Solari
- Dejan Stankovic
- Juan Sebastian Veron
- Cristiano Zanetti

Forwards
- Adriano
- Julio Cruz
- Obafemi Martins
- Alvaro Recoba
- Goran Slavkovski

KEY: On all match; On bench; Subbed or sent off (Counting game); Subbed or sent off (playing less than 70 minutes); Subbed on from bench (Counting Game); Subbed on (playing less than 70 minutes); Subbed on and then subbed or sent off (Counting Game); Subbed on and then subbed or sent off (playing less than 70 minutes); Not in 16

FIORENTINA

Final Position: **4th**

NICKNAME: VIOLA

KEY: ☐Won ☐Drawn ☐Lost

							Attendance
1	itpr1	Sampdoria	H	W	2-1	Fiore 13; Toni 30	35,854
2	itpr1	Messina	A	D	2-2	Toni 9; Bojinov 41	23,000
3	itpr1	Udinese	H	W	4-2	Fiore 39; Toni 43,89; Donadel 79	32,000
4	itpr1	Lecce	A	W	3-1	Fiore 48; Bojinov 53; Toni 63	12,775
5	itpr1	Inter Milan	A	L	0-1		56,907
6	itpr1	Livorno	H	W	3-2	Toni 27; Jorgensen 35; Pazzini 60	34,000
7	itpr1	Lazio	A	L	0-1		29,780
8	itpr1	Parma	H	W	4-1	Toni 2,24,60; Fiore 36	30,000
9	itpr1	Siena	A	W	2-0	Toni 2,67	15,000
10	itpr1	Cagliari	H	W	2-1	Toni 53; Jorgensen 82	30,000
11	itpr1	Ascoli	A	W	2-0	Ujfalusi 1; Toni 62	14,000
12	itpr1	AC Milan	H	W	3-1	Toni 10,87; Jorgensen 46	44,000
13	itpr1	Roma	A	D	1-1	Toni 67 pen	38,500
14	itpr1	Juventus	H	L	1-2	Pazzini 39	43,900
15	itpr1	Treviso	H	W	1-0	Fiore 51	43,900
16	itpr1	Empoli	A	D	1-1	Pazzini 70	16,000
17	itpr1	Palermo	H	W	1-0	Jorgensen 40	31,000
18	itpr1	Reggina	A	D	1-1	Jorgensen 13	12,000
19	itpr1	Chievo	H	W	2-1	Toni 35,90	27,000
20	itpr1	Sampdoria	A	L	1-3	Toni 14	22,566
21	itpr1	Messina	H	W	2-0	Toni 45,73	27,840
22	itpr1	Udinese	A	D	0-0		17,000
23	itpr1	Lecce	H	W	1-0	Toni 37	28,700
24	itpr1	Inter Milan	H	W	2-1	Brocchi 10; Jimenez 60	41,000
25	itpr1	Livorno	A	L	0-2		18,000
26	itpr1	Lazio	H	L	1-2	Bojinov 60	30,500
27	itpr1	Parma	A	W	4-2	Bojinov 35,39; Jorgensen 48; Jimenez 68	10,000
28	itpr1	Siena	H	W	2-1	Toni 3; Pazzini 90	31,200
29	itpr1	Ascoli	H	W	3-1	Brocchi 53; Toni 83; Pazzini 89	31,112
30	itpr1	Cagliari	A	D	0-0		10,000
31	itpr1	AC Milan	A	L	1-3	Toni 14	75,000
32	itpr1	Roma	H	D	1-1	Toni 2	40,600
33	itpr1	Juventus	A	D	1-1	Toni 47	27,666
34	itpr1	Treviso	A	W	3-1	Toni 25; Brocchi 49; Montolivo 84	9,435
35	itpr1	Empoli	H	W	2-1	Pasqual 43; Jimenez 59	35,186
36	itpr1	Palermo	A	L	0-1		30,056
37	itpr1	Reggina	H	W	5-2	Fiore 25; Toni 27,64; Jorgensen 35; Bojinov 65	38,534
38	itpr1	Chievo	A	W	2-0	Toni 21; Dainelli 85	30,000

LEAGUE APPEARANCES, BOOKINGS AND CAPS

	AGE (on 01/07/06)	IN NAMED 18	APPEARANCES	COUNTING GAMES	MINUTES ON PITCH	YELLOW CARDS	RED CARDS	CAPS THIS SEASON	NATIONAL SIDE
Goalkeepers									
Gianluca Berti	39	14	1	0	55	0	0	-	Italy
Sebastian Cejas	31	19	3	3	270	0	0	-	Argentina
Sebastian Frey	26	18	18	18	1620	0	0	-	France
Bogdan Lonut Lobont	28	17	17	16	1475	1	0	-	Romania
Marco Roccati	31	6	0	0	0	0	0	-	Italy
Defenders									
Davide Brivio	17	15	1	0	1	0	0	-	Italy
Dario Dainelli	27	34	30	26	2480	8	1	-	Italy
Marco Di Loreto	31	35	19	18	1649	4	0	-	Italy
Alessandro Gamberini	24	26	17	16	1475	2	0	-	Italy
Per Kroldrup	26	17	13	12	1087	0	0	1	Denmark (19)
Cristian Maggio	24	4	3	0	44	0	0	-	Italy
Guiseppe Pancaro	34	37	18	9	1088	4	0	-	Italy
Manuel Pasqual	24	36	35	31	2926	4	0	-	Italy
Tomas Ujfalusi	28	37	36	36	3240	4	0	9	Czech Republic (2)
Midfielders									
Christian Brocchi	30	34	34	31	2878	6	0	-	Italy
Andrea De Falco	20	2	0	0	0	0	0	-	Italy
Marco Donadel	23	35	33	30	2822	10	0	-	Italy
Stefano Fiore	31	38	38	27	2902	3	0	-	Italy
Gianni Guigou	31	13	4	0	46	0	0	-	Uruguay
Antonio Luis Jimenez	22	20	19	9	1105	3	0	-	Italy
Martin Jorgensen	30	37	37	26	2854	2	0	6	Denmark (19)
Enrique Mateo	19	5	0	0	0	0	0	-	Brazil
Riccardo Montolivo	21	37	20	4	842	3	0	-	Italy
Andrea Paolucci	19	4	0	0	0	0	0	-	Italy
Michele Pazienza	23	27	23	8	1132	4	0	-	Italy
Forwards									
Emilov Valeri Bojinov	20	34	27	3	1191	2	0	-	Bulgaria
Samuel Di Carmine	17	1	0	0	0	0	0	-	Italy
Gianpaolo Pazzini	21	34	27	6	1121	2	0	-	Italy
Christian Rigano	32	1	0	0	0	0	0	-	Italy
Luca Toni	29	38	38	36	3293	3	0	9	Italy (13)
Zisis Vryzas	32	1	0	0	0	0	0	2	Greece (34)

TEAM OF THE SEASON

MONTHLY POINTS TALLY

AUGUST	3	100%
SEPTEMBER	7	58%
OCTOBER	12	80%
NOVEMBER	7	78%
DECEMBER	7	58%
JANUARY	8	53%
FEBRUARY	9	60%
MARCH	7	58%
APRIL	8	53%
MAY	6	100%

LEAGUE GOALS

	PLAYER	MINS	GOALS	S RATE
1	Toni	3293	31	106
2	Jorgensen	2854	7	408
3	Bojinov	1191	6	199
4	Fiore	2902	6	484
5	Pazzini	1121	5	224
6	Brocchi	2878	3	959
7	Jimenez	1105	3	368
8	Donadel	2822	1	2822
9	Montolivo	842	1	842
10	Pasqual	2926	1	2926
11	Dainelli	2480	1	2480
12	Ujfalusi	3240	1	3240
	Other		0	
	TOTAL		66	

TOP POINT EARNERS

	PLAYER	GAMES	AV PTS
1	Dainelli	26	2.23
2	Fiore	27	2.22
3	Jorgensen	26	2.12
4	Frey	18	2.06
5	Gamberini	16	2.06
6	Di Loreto	18	2.00
7	Brocchi	31	2.00
8	Ujfalusi	36	1.94
9	Toni	36	1.89
10	Lobont	16	1.88
	CLUB AVERAGE:		1.95

DISCIPLINARY RECORDS

	PLAYER	YELLOW	RED	AVE
1	Pancaro	4	0	272
2	Dainelli	8	1	275
3	Montolivo	3	0	280
4	Donadel	10	0	282
5	Pazienza	4	0	283
6	Jimenez	3	0	368
7	Di Loreto	4	0	412
8	Brocchi	6	0	479
9	Pazzini	2	0	560
10	Bojinov	2	0	595
11	Pasqual	4	0	731
12	Gamberini	2	0	737
13	Ujfalusi	4	0	810
	Other	9	0	
	TOTAL	65	1	

KEY GOALKEEPER

Sebastian Frey

Goals Conceded in the League	19	**Counting Games** League games when player was on pitch for at least 70 minutes	18
Defensive Rating Ave number of mins between League goals conceded while on the pitch	85	**Clean Sheets** In League games when player was on pitch for at least 70 minutes	4

KEY PLAYERS - DEFENDERS

Dario Dainelli

Goals Conceded Number of League goals conceded while the player was on the pitch	26	**Clean Sheets** In League games when player was on pitch for at least 70 minutes	8
Defensive Rating Ave number of mins between League goals conceded while on the pitch	95	**Club Defensive Rating** Average number of mins between League goals conceded by the club this season	81

	PLAYER	CON LGE	CLEAN SHEETS	DEF RATE
1	Dario Dainelli	26	8	**95 mins**
2	Alessandro Gamberini	17	4	**87 mins**
3	Manuel Pasqual	35	8	**84 mins**
4	Marco Di Loreto	21	4	**79 mins**

KEY PLAYERS - MIDFIELDERS

Stefano Fiore

Goals in the League	6	**Contribution to Attacking Power** Average number of minutes between League team goals while on pitch	52
Defensive Rating Average number of mins between League goals conceded while on the pitch	91	**Scoring Difference** Defensive Rating minus Contribution to Attacking Power	39

	PLAYER	LGE GOALS	DEF RATE	POWER	SCORE DIFF
1	Stefano Fiore	6	91	52	**39 mins**
2	Christian Brocchi	3	87	49	**38 mins**
3	Martin Jorgensen	7	82	51	**31 mins**
4	Marco Donadel	1	76	54	**22 mins**

KEY PLAYERS - GOALSCORERS

Luca Toni

Goals in the League	31	**Player Strike Rate** Average number of minutes between League goals scored by player	106
Contribution to Attacking Power Average number of minutes between League team goals while on pitch	52	**Club Strike Rate** Average number of minutes between League goals scored by club	52

	PLAYER	LGE GOALS	POWER	STRIKE RATE
1	Luca Toni	31	52	**106 mins**
2	Martin Jorgensen	7	51	**408 mins**
3	Stefano Fiore	6	52	**484 mins**
4	Christian Brocchi	3	49	**959 mins**

Luca Toni is congratulated by his team mates

SQUAD APPEARANCES

Match	1	2	3	4	5	6	7	8	9	10	11	12	13	14	15	16	17	18	19	20	21	22	23	24	25	26	27	28	29	30	31	32	33	34	35	36	37	38
Venue	H	A	H	A	A	H	A	H	A	H	A	H	A	H	H	A	H	A	H	A	H	A	H	H	A	H	A	H	H	A	A	H	A	A	H	A	H	A
Competition	L	L	L	L	L	L	L	L	L	L	L	L	L	L	L	L	L	L	L	L	L	L	L	L	L	L	L	L	L	L	L	L	L	L	L	L	L	L
Result	W	D	W	W	L	W	L	W	W	W	W	W	D	L	W	D	W	D	W	L	W	D	W	W	L	L	W	W	W	D	L	D	D	W	W	L	W	W

Goalkeepers
Gianluca Berti
Christian Sebastian Cejas
Sebastian Frey
Bogdan Lonut Lobont
Marco Roccati

Defenders
Davide Brivio
Dario Dainelli
Marco Di Loreto
Alessandro Gamberini
Per Kroldrup
Cristian Maggio
Guiseppe Pancaro
Manuel Pasqual
Tomas Ujfalusi

Midfielders
Christian Brocchi
Andrea De Falco
Marco Donadel
Stefano Fiore
Gianni Guigou
Antonio Luis Jimenez
Martin Jorgensen
Enrique Mateo
Riccardo Montolivo
Andrea Paolucci
Michele Pazienza

Forwards
Emilov Valeri Bojinov
Samuel Di Carmine
Gianpaolo Pazzini
Christian Rigano
Luca Toni
Zisis Vryzas

KEY: On all match / On bench / Subbed or sent off (Counting game) / Subbed or sent off (playing less than 70 minutes) / Subbed on from bench (Counting Game) / Subbed on (playing less than 70 minutes) / Subbed on and then subbed or sent off (Counting Game) / Subbed on and then subbed or sent off (playing less than 70 minutes) / Not in 16

ROMA

Final Position: **5th**

NICKNAME: GIALLOROSSI

KEY: ☐Won ☐Drawn ☐Lost

					Scorers	Attendance
1	itpr1	**Reggina**	A	W 3-0	Mancini 30; De Rossi 46; Nonda 90	19,000
2	itpr1	**Udinese**	H	L 0-1		40,000
3	uc1rl1	**Aris**	H	W 5-1	Aquilani 1; Panucci 20,44; Montella 28; Totti 53	11,620
4	itpr1	**Livorno**	A	D 0-0		15,000
5	itpr1	**Parma**	H	W 4-1	Totti 24; Nonda 26,87; Panucci 34	32,500
6	itpr1	**Cagliari**	A	D 0-0		12,550
7	uc1rl2	**Aris**	A	D 0-0		8,500
8	itpr1	**Siena**	H	L 2-3	Taddei 46; Panucci 86	33,000
9	itpr1	**Empoli**	A	L 0-1		8,000
10	ucgpe	**Tromso**	A	W 2-1	Kuffour 35; Cufre 84	5,982
11	itpr1	**Lazio**	H	D 1-1	Totti 40	59,900
12	itpr1	**Inter Milan**	A	W 3-2	Montella 12; Totti 30,47 pen	50,230
13	itpr1	**Ascoli**	H	W 2-1	Panucci 39; Mexes 90	37,681
14	itpr1	**Messina**	A	W 2-0	Mexes 34; Totti 81	30,000
15	itpr1	**Juventus**	H	L 1-4	Totti 65; Perrotta 88	76,000
16	ucgpe	**Strasbourg**	H	D 1-1	Cassano 72	8,500
17	itpr1	**Fiorentina**	H	D 1-1	Tommasi 2; Dacourt 41	38,500
18	ucgpe	**Crvena Zvezda**	A	L 1-3	Nonda 23	35,186
19	itpr1	**Lecce**	A	D 2-2	Cassano 21; Bovo 45	15,000
20	itpr1	**Palermo**	H	L 1-2	Cassano 35	40,000
21	ucgpe	**Basel**	H	W 3-1	Taddei 14; Totti 45; Montella 49	15,000
22	itpr1	**Sampdoria**	A	D 1-1	Totti 15	22,151
23	itpr1	**Chievo**	H	W 4-0	Totti 32 pen,39; Perrotta 65; Taddei 85	30,000
24	itpr1	**Treviso**	A	W 1-0	Aquilani 34	7,500
25	itpr1	**AC Milan**	H	W 1-0	Mancini 81	47,700
26	itpr1	**Reggina**	H	W 3-1	Totti 4,66; Mancini 90	32,000
27	itpr1	**Udinese**	A	W 4-1	Mancini 40 pen,75; De Rossi 62; Chivu 79 pen	16,500
28	itpr1	**Livorno**	H	W 3-0	Totti 31,42 pen; Taddei 62	35,500
29	itpr1	**Parma**	A	W 3-0	Mancini 47,72; Perrotta 77	16,638
30	itpr1	**Cagliari**	H	W 4-3	Perrotta 25; De Rossi 35; Totti 79,90 pen	62,000
31	itpr1	**Siena**	A	W 2-0	De Rossi 70; Mancini 90	14,000
32	uc3rl1	**Club Brugge**	A	W 2-1	Vanaudenaerden 44 og; Perrotta 74	27,138
33	itpr1	**Empoli**	H	W 1-0	Perrotta 15	63,375
34	uc3rl2	**Club Brugge**	H	W 2-1	Mancini 55; Bovo 71	15,209
35	itpr1	**Lazio**	A	W 2-0	Taddei 31; Aquilani 63	60,000
36	itpr1	**Inter Milan**	H	D 1-1	Taddei 9	46,500
37	uc4rl1	**Middlesbrough**	A	L 0-1		25,354
38	itpr1	**Ascoli**	A	L 2-3	Taddei 72; Comotto 75 og	20,000
39	uc4rl2	**Middlesbrough**	H	W 2-1	Mancini 43,66 pen	32,642
40	itpr1	**Messina**	H	W 2-1	Perrotta 7; Aquilani 56	34,000
41	itpr1	**Juventus**	A	D 1-1	Kharja 85	29,621
42	itpr1	**Fiorentina**	A	D 1-1	Cufre 72	40,600
43	itpr1	**Lecce**	H	W 3-1	Mancini 20 pen,73; Chivu 23	13,531
44	itpr1	**Palermo**	A	D 3-3	Taddei 23; Mancini 29,30	27,855
45	itpr1	**Sampdoria**	H	D 0-0		40,000
46	itpr1	**Chievo**	A	D 4-4	De Rossi 4,14; Taddei 25; Dacourt 62	10,500
47	itpr1	**Treviso**	H	W 1-0	Tommasi 36	15,622
48	itpr1	**AC Milan**	A	L 1-2	Mexes 33	67,000

LEAGUE APPEARANCES, BOOKINGS AND CAPS

	AGE (on 01/07/06)	IN NAMED 18	APPEARANCES	COUNTING GAMES	MINUTES ON PITCH	YELLOW CARDS	RED CARDS	CAPS THIS SEASON	NATIONAL SIDE
Goalkeepers									
Gianluca Curci	20	37	10	10	900	0	0	-	Italy
Doni Marangao	26	32	28	28	2520	3	0	-	Brazil
D. Eleftheropoulos	29	1	0	0	0	0	0	-	Greece
Pietro Pipolo	20	3	0	0	0	0	0	-	Italy
Defenders									
Cesare Bovo	23	37	21	14	1423	4	1	-	Italy
Christian Chivu	25	28	27	26	2376	5	2	-	Romania
Leandro Cufre	28	32	30	26	2495	3	0	1	Argentina (9)
Gianluca Freddi	19	4	0	0	0	0	0	-	Italy
Andrea Giacomini	19	1	0	0	0	0	0	-	Italy
Fabrizio Grillo	19	0	0	0	0	0	0	-	Italy
Samuel Osei Kuffour	29	28	22	18	1768	2	0	4	Ghana (48)
Daniele Magliocchetti	20	2	0	0	0	0	0	-	France
Philippe Mexes	24	30	27	23	2167	6	2	-	France
Christian Panucci	33	35	35	35	3137	3	0	-	Italy
Luigi Sartor	31	0	0	0	0	0	0	-	Italy
Midfielders									
E. Reyes Alvarez	26	35	18	2	395	0	0	-	Honduras
Alberto Aquilani	21	27	24	16	1635	8	0	-	Italy
Olivier Dacourt	31	33	26	13	1283	8	0	-	France
Daniele De Rossi	21	35	34	30	2882	9	0	8	Italy (13)
Cristiano Doni	33	2	0	0	0	0	0	-	Italy
Leandro Greco	19	2	1	0	2	0	0	-	Italy
Houssine Kharja	23	24	12	1	238	1	0	-	Morocco
Chuka Stefano Okaka	16	20	7	0	152	0	0	-	Nigeria
Simone Perrotta	28	36	35	33	3048	6	0	2	Italy (13)
Aleandro Rosi	19	24	13	3	453	1	1	-	Italy
Rodrigo Taddei	26	38	38	37	3281	3	0	-	Brazil
Damiano Tommasi	32	33	25	9	1159	0	0	-	Italy
Forwards									
Antonio Cassano	23	6	5	4	354	0	0	-	Italy
Alessio Cerci	18	5	1	0	8	0	0	-	Italy
Alessandro Mancini	25	28	28	27	2357	5	0	-	Brazil
Vincenzo Montella	32	15	12	4	745	1	0	-	Italy
Shabani Nonda	29	17	16	5	749	1	0	-	Burundi
Francesco Totti	29	24	24	22	2039	3	1	4	Italy (13)

TEAM OF THE SEASON

MONTHLY POINTS TALLY

Month	Points	%
AUGUST	3	100%
SEPTEMBER	5	42%
OCTOBER	7	47%
NOVEMBER	4	44%
DECEMBER	5	42%
JANUARY	15	100%
FEBRUARY	15	100%
MARCH	5	42%
APRIL	7	47%
MAY	3	50%

LEAGUE GOALS

	PLAYER	MINS	GOALS	S RATE
1	Totti	2039	15	136
2	Mancini	2357	12	196
3	Taddei	3281	8	410
4	De Rossi	2882	6	480
5	Perrotta	3048	6	508
6	Mexes	2167	3	722
7	Aquilani	1635	3	545
8	Nonda	749	3	250
9	Panucci	3137	3	1046
10	Tommasi	1159	2	580
11	Cassano	354	2	177
12	Chivu	2376	2	1188
13	Dacourt	1283	2	642
	Other		5	
	TOTAL		72	

TOP POINT EARNERS

	PLAYER	GAMES	AV PTS
1	Cufre	26	2.12
2	Bovo	14	2.07
3	Aquilani	16	2.06
4	Doni	28	2.04
5	Mexes	23	1.96
6	Perrotta	33	1.91
7	Mancini	27	1.89
8	De Rossi	30	1.87
9	Totti	22	1.86
10	Chivu	26	1.85
	CLUB AVERAGE:		1.82

DISCIPLINARY RECORDS

	PLAYER	YELLOW	RED	AVE
1	Dacourt	8	0	160
2	Aquilani	8	0	204
3	Rosi	1	1	226
4	Mexes	6	2	270
5	Bovo	4	1	284
6	De Rossi	9	0	320
7	Chivu	5	2	339
8	Mancini	5	0	471
9	Perrotta	6	0	508
10	Totti	3	1	509
11	Montella	1	0	745
12	Nonda	1	0	749
13	Cufre	3	0	831
	Other	11	0	
	TOTAL	71	7	

KEY GOALKEEPER

Donieber Alexander Marangao			
Goals Conceded in the League	29	**Counting Games** League games when player was on pitch for at least 70 minutes	28
Defensive Rating Ave number of mins between League goals conceded while on the pitch	87	**Clean Sheets** In League games when player was on pitch for at least 70 minutes	11

KEY PLAYERS - DEFENDERS

Cesare Bovo			
Goals Conceded Number of League goals conceded while the player was on the pitch	14	**Clean Sheets** In League games when player was on pitch for at least 70 minutes	7
Defensive Rating Ave number of mins between League goals conceded while on the pitch	102	**Club Defensive Rating** Average number of mins between League goals conceded by the club this season	81

	PLAYER	CON LGE	CLEAN SHEETS	DEF RATE
1	Cesare Bovo	14	7	102 mins
2	Christian Chivu	27	10	88 mins
3	Philippe Mexes	25	10	87 mins
4	Christian Panucci	41	12	77 mins

KEY PLAYERS - MIDFIELDERS

Alberto Aquilani			
Goals in the League	3	**Contribution to Attacking Power** Average number of minutes between League team goals while on pitch	45
Defensive Rating Average number of mins between League goals conceded while on the pitch	109	Scoring Difference Defensive Rating minus Contribution to Attacking Power	64

	PLAYER	LGE GOALS	DEF RATE	POWER	SCORE DIFF
1	Alberto Aquilani	3	109	45	64 mins
2	Simone Perrotta	6	82	45	37 mins
3	Rodrigo Taddei	8	80	47	33 mins
4	Daniele De Rossi	6	76	47	29 mins

KEY PLAYERS - GOALSCORERS

Francesco Totti			
Goals in the League	15	Player Strike Rate Average number of minutes between League goals scored by player	136
Contribution to Attacking Power Average number of minutes between League team goals while on pitch	50	**Club Strike Rate** Average number of minutes between League goals scored by club	48

	PLAYER	LGE GOALS	POWER	STRIKE RATE
1	Francesco Totti	15	50	136 mins
2	Alessandro Mancini	12	45	196 mins
3	Rodrigo Taddei	8	47	410 mins
4	Daniele De Rossi	6	47	480 mins

Daniele De Rossi and Francesco Totti

SQUAD APPEARANCES

Match	1	2	3	4	5	6	7	8	9	10	11	12	13	14	15	16	17	18	19	20	21	22	23	24	25
Venue	A	H	H	A	H	A	A	H	A	A	H	A	H	A	H	H	H	A	A	H	H	A	H	A	H
Competition	L	L	E	L	L	L	E	L	L	E	L	L	L	L	L	E	L	E	L	L	E	L	L	L	L
Result	W	L	W	D	W	D	D	L	L	W	D	W	W	W	L	D	D	L	D	L	W	D	W	W	W

Match	26	27	28	29	30	31	32	33	34	35	36	37	38	39	40	41	42	43	44	45	46	47	48
Venue	H	A	H	A	H	A	A	H	H	A	H	A	A	H	H	A	A	H	A	H	A	H	A
Competition	L	L	L	L	L	L	E	L	E	L	L	E	L	E	L	L	L	L	L	L	L	L	L
Result	W	W	W	W	W	W	W	W	W	W	D	L	L	W	W	D	D	W	D	D	D	W	L

Goalkeepers
Gianluca Curci
Doni Marangao
Dimitrios Eleftheropoulos
Pietro Pipolo

Defenders
Cesare Bovo
Christian Chivu
Leandro Cufre
Gianluca Freddi
Andrea Giacomini
Fabrizio Grillo
Samuel Osei Kuffour
Daniele Magliocchetti
Philippe Mexes
Christian Panucci
Luigi Sartor

Midfielders
Edgar Reyes Alvarez
Alberto Aquilani
Olivier Dacourt
Daniele De Rossi
Cristiano Doni
Leandro Greco
Houssine Kharja
Chuka Stefano Okaka
Simone Perrotta
Aleandro Rosi
Rodrigo Taddei
Damiano Tommasi

Forwards
Antonio Cassano
Alessio Cerci
Alessandro Mancini
Vincenzo Montella
Shabani Nonda
Francesco Totti

KEY: On all match; On bench; Subbed or sent off (Counting game); Subbed or sent off (playing less than 70 minutes); Subbed on from bench (Counting Game); Subbed on (playing less than 70 minutes); Subbed on and then subbed or sent off (Counting Game); Subbed on and then subbed or sent off (playing less than 70 minutes); Not in 16

LAZIO

Final Position: **6th**

NICKNAME: BIANCOCELESTI

KEY: ☐ Won ☐ Drawn ☐ Lost

		Opponent			Score	Scorers	Attendance
1	itpr1	Messina	H	W	1-0	Pandev 21	25,000
2	itpr1	Cagliari	A	D	1-1	Siviglia 13	10,000
3	itpr1	Treviso	H	W	3-1	Rocchi 20; Pandev 26; Oddo 86 pen	23,000
4	itpr1	AC Milan	A	L	0-2		57,778
5	itpr1	Palermo	H	W	4-2	Rocchi 58,86; Pandev 60; Manfredini 65	26,000
6	itpr1	Udinese	A	L	0-3		17,000
7	itpr1	Fiorentina	H	W	1-0	Zauri 82	29,780
8	itpr1	Roma	A	D	1-1	Rocchi 57	59,900
9	itpr1	Chievo	H	D	2-2	Rocchi 31; Oddo 90	17,030
10	itpr1	Reggina	A	L	0-1		10,000
11	itpr1	Inter Milan	H	D	0-0		40,000
12	itpr1	Sampdoria	A	L	0-2		22,500
13	itpr1	Empoli	A	W	3-2	Dabo 28; Tare 77; Liverani 80	8,000
14	itpr1	Siena	H	W	3-2	di Canio 42; Cesar, R 61; Tare 80	25,000
15	itpr1	Livorno	A	L	1-2	Pandev 65	15,000
16	itpr1	Juventus	H	D	1-1	Rocchi 16	35,000
17	itpr1	Lecce	A	D	0-0		12,082
18	itpr1	Ascoli	H	W	4-1	di Canio 29; Mudingayi 34; Pandev 73; Tare 81	23,000
19	itpr1	Parma	A	D	1-1	Rocchi 5	13,834
20	itpr1	Messina	A	D	1-1	Manfredini 78	22,000
21	itpr1	Cagliari	H	D	1-1	di Canio 36	26,000
22	itpr1	Treviso	A	W	1-0	Rocchi 87	5,000
23	itpr1	AC Milan	H	D	0-0		30,000
24	itpr1	Palermo	A	L	1-3	Belleri 84	27,074
25	itpr1	Udinese	H	D	1-1	Rocchi 20	20,000
26	itpr1	Fiorentina	A	W	2-1	Behrami 32; Rocchi 49	30,500
27	itpr1	Roma	H	L	0-2		60,000
28	itpr1	Chievo	A	D	2-2	Mauri 32; Oddo 67 pen	8,000
29	itpr1	Reggina	H	W	3-1	di Canio 25; Rocchi 36; Pandev 67	5,000
30	itpr1	Inter Milan	A	L	1-3	Pandev 54	46,000
31	itpr1	Sampdoria	H	W	2-0	Oddo 70,90 pen	22,000
32	itpr1	Empoli	H	D	3-3	Pandev 7; Behrami 8; di Canio 80	20,000
33	itpr1	Siena	A	W	3-2	Mauri 14; Rocchi 22; Dabo 50	9,000
34	itpr1	Livorno	H	W	3-1	Oddo 20; Pandev 56,72	50,000
35	itpr1	Juventus	A	D	1-1	Rocchi 29	33,898
36	itpr1	Lecce	H	W	1-0	Rocchi 57,57	24,000
37	itpr1	Ascoli	A	W	4-1	Stendardo 7; Oddo 11; Pandev 20; Rocchi 57	9,850
38	itpr1	Parma	H	W	1-0	Rocchi 61	36,000

LEAGUE APPEARANCES, BOOKINGS AND CAPS

	AGE (on 01/07/06)	IN NAMED 18	APPEARANCES	COUNTING GAMES	MINUTES ON PITCH	YELLOW CARDS	RED CARDS	CAPS THIS SEASON	NATIONAL SIDE
Goalkeepers									
Marco Ballota	42	29	7	5	514	0	0	-	Italy
Alessio De Angelis	21	2	0	0	0	0	0	-	Italy
Samir Handanovic	21	3	1	1	90	0	0	-	Slovenia
Angelo Peruzzi	36	31	30	29	2625	0	0	5	Italy (13)
Simone Santarelli	17	1	0	0	0	0	0	-	Italy
Matteo Sereni	31	7	2	1	101	0	0	-	Italy
Defenders									
Manuel Belleri	28	34	16	9	974	0	0	-	Italy
A. Rodrigues Cesar	31	11	11	7	748	1	0	-	Brazil
Emilson Sanchez	26	33	29	27	2542	5	0	-	Brazil
Andrea Giallombardo	25	14	5	1	168	0	0	-	Italy
Massimo Oddo	30	35	35	35	3140	5	0	4	Italy (13)
Felice Piccolo	22	6	2	0	38	0	0	-	Italy
Sebastiano Siviglia	33	32	32	31	2820	3	1	-	Italy
Guglielmo Stendardo	25	34	16	14	1346	4	0	-	Italy
Fabio Zaccardi	19	1	0	0	0	0	0	-	Italy
Midfielders									
Roberto Baronio	28	11	7	2	297	3	0	-	Italy
Valon Behrami	21	28	26	21	2118	8	0	-	Serbia & Mont
Massimo Bonanni	24	15	9	1	307	0	0	-	Italy
Ousmane Dabo	29	30	30	25	2356	7	1	-	France
Lorenzo De Silvestri	18	2	0	0	0	0	0	-	Italy
Fabio Firmani	28	10	7	4	473	3	0	-	Italy
Christian Keller	25	14	7	0	253	0	0	-	Denmark
Fabio Liverani	30	31	30	26	2514	4	1	-	Italy
Christian Manfredini	31	32	24	12	1427	6	0	-	Italy
Stefano Mauri	26	16	15	12	1172	1	0	-	Italy
Gaby Mudingayi	25	21	13	8	783	0	0	-	Belgium
Guilherme Siqueira	20	2	0	0	0	0	0	-	Brazil
Francesco Torroni	20	1	0	0	0	0	0	-	Italy
Luciano Zauri	28	37	37	37	3330	5	0	-	Italy
Forwards									
Paolo di Canio	38	32	28	4	1484	3	0	-	Italy
Simone Inzaghi	30	17	6	0	78	0	0	-	Italy
Roberto Muzzi	34	1	1	0	4	0	0	-	Italy
Goran Pandev	22	36	35	15	2026	5	0	-	Macedonia
Tommaso Rocchi	28	38	37	33	3027	3	0	-	Italy
Igli Tare	32	28	20	4	660	2	0	2	Albania (199)

TEAM OF THE SEASON

MONTHLY POINTS TALLY

Month	Points	%
AUGUST	3	100%
SEPTEMBER	7	58%
OCTOBER	5	33%
NOVEMBER	4	44%
DECEMBER	5	42%
JANUARY	9	60%
FEBRUARY	5	33%
MARCH	7	58%
APRIL	11	73%
MAY	6	100%

LEAGUE GOALS

	PLAYER	MINS	GOALS	S RATE
1	Rocchi	3027	17	178
2	Pandev	2026	11	184
3	Oddo	3140	7	449
4	di Canio	1484	5	297
5	Tare	660	3	220
6	Mauri	1172	2	586
7	Manfredini	1427	2	714
8	Behrami	2118	2	1059
9	Dabo	2356	2	1178
10	Cesar, R	748	1	748
11	Stendardo	1346	1	1346
12	Mudingayi	783	1	783
13	Belleri	974	1	974
	Other		3	
	TOTAL		58	

TOP POINT EARNERS

	PLAYER	GAMES	AV PTS
1	Mauri	12	2.25
2	Stendardo	14	1.93
3	Behrami	21	1.76
4	Manfredini	12	1.75
5	Oddo	35	1.69
6	Pandev	15	1.67
7	Liverani	26	1.65
8	Peruzzi	29	1.62
9	Zauri	37	1.59
10	Rocchi	33	1.58
	CLUB AVERAGE:		1.63

DISCIPLINARY RECORDS

	PLAYER	YELLOW	RED	AVE
1	Firmani	3	0	157
2	Manfredini	6	0	237
3	Behrami	8	0	264
4	Dabo	7	1	294
5	Tare	2	0	330
6	Stendardo	4	0	336
7	Pandev	5	0	405
8	di Canio	3	0	494
9	Liverani	4	1	502
10	Cribari	5	0	508
11	Oddo	5	0	628
12	Zauri	5	0	666
13	Siviglia	3	1	705
	Other	5	0	
	TOTAL	65	3	

KEY GOALKEEPER

Angelo Peruzzi

Goals Conceded in the League	38	**Counting Games** League games when player was on pitch for at least 70 minutes	29
Defensive Rating Ave number of mins between League goals conceded while on the pitch	69	**Clean Sheets** In League games when player was on pitch for at least 70 minutes	7

KEY PLAYERS - DEFENDERS

Guglielmo Stendardo

Goals Conceded Number of League goals conceded while the player was on the pitch	17	**Clean Sheets** In League games when player was on pitch for at least 70 minutes	4
Defensive Rating Ave number of mins between League goals conceded while on the pitch	79	**Club Defensive Rating** Average number of mins between League goals conceded by the club this season	73

	PLAYER	CON LGE	CLEAN SHEETS	DEF RATE
1	Guglielmo Stendardo	17	4	79 mins
2	Massimo Oddo	40	9	79 mins
3	Emilson Sanchez Cribari	34	7	75 mins
4	Sebastiano Siviglia	43	6	66 mins

KEY PLAYERS - MIDFIELDERS

Stefano Mauri

Goals in the League	2	**Contribution to Attacking Power** Average number of minutes between League team goals while on pitch	45
Defensive Rating Average number of mins between League goals conceded while on the pitch	90	**Scoring Difference** Defensive Rating minus Contribution to Attacking Power	45

	PLAYER	LGE GOALS	DEF RATE	POWER	SCORE DIFF
1	Stefano Mauri	2	90	45	45 mins
2	Christian Manfredini	2	79	59	20 mins
3	Luciano Zauri	1	72	59	13 mins
4	Fabio Liverani	1	64	53	11 mins

KEY PLAYERS - GOALSCORERS

Tommaso Rocchi

Goals in the League	17	**Player Strike Rate** Average number of minutes between League goals scored by player	178
Contribution to Attacking Power Average number of minutes between League team goals while on pitch	62	**Club Strike Rate** Average number of minutes between League goals scored by club	59

	PLAYER	LGE GOALS	POWER	STRIKE RATE
1	Tommaso Rocchi	17	62	178 mins
2	Goran Pandev	11	51	184 mins
3	Massimo Oddo	7	59	449 mins
4	Stefano Mauri	2	45	586 mins

Tommaso Rocchi

SQUAD APPEARANCES

Match	1	2	3	4	5	6	7	8	9	10	11	12	13	14	15	16	17	18	19	20	21	22	23	24	25	26	27	28	29	30	31	32	33	34	35	36	37	38
Venue	H	A	H	A	H	A	H	A	H	A	H	A	A	H	A	H	A	H	A	A	H	A	H	A	H	A	H	A	H	A	H	H	A	H	A	H	A	H
Competition	L	L	L	L	L	L	L	L	L	L	L	L	L	L	L	L	L	L	L	L	L	L	L	L	L	L	L	L	L	L	L	L	L	L	L	L	L	L
Result	W	D	W	L	W	L	W	D	D	L	D	L	W	W	L	D	D	W	D	D	D	W	D	L	D	W	L	D	W	L	W	D	W	W	D	W	W	W

Goalkeepers
Marco Ballota
Alessio De Angelis
Samir Handanovic
Angelo Peruzzi
Simone Santarelli
Matteo Sereni

Defenders
Manuel Belleri
A. Rodrigues Cesar
Emilson Sanchez Cribari
Andrea Giallombardo
Massimo Oddo
Felice Piccolo
Sebastiano Siviglia
Guglielmo Stendardo
Fabio Zaccardi

Midfielders
Roberto Baronio
Valon Behrami
Massimo Bonanni
Ousmane Dabo
Lorenzo De Silvestri
Fabio Firmani
Christian Keller
Fabio Liverani
Christian Manfredini
Stefano Mauri
Gaby Mudingayi
Guilherme Siqueira
Francesco Torroni
Luciano Zauri

Forwards
Paolo di Canio
Simone Inzaghi
Roberto Muzzi
Goran Pandev
Tommaso Rocchi
Igli Tare

KEY: On all match · On bench · Subbed or sent off (Counting game) · Subbed or sent off (playing less than 70 minutes) · Subbed on from bench (Counting Game) · Subbed on (playing less than 70 minutes) · Subbed on and then subbed or sent off (Counting Game) · Subbed on and then subbed or sent off (playing less than 70 minutes) · Not in 16

CHIEVO VERONA

Final Position: **7th**

NICKNAME: MUSSI VOLANTI

KEY: ☐Won ☐Drawn ☐Lost

							Attendance
1	itpr1	**Juventus**	A	L	0-1		24,693
2	itpr1	**Parma**	H	W	1-0	Mandelli 11	5,580
3	itpr1	**Reggina**	A	W	3-1	Franceschini 19,64; Mandelli 77	12,389
4	itpr1	**Inter Milan**	H	L	0-1		12,000
5	itpr1	**Sampdoria**	A	W	2-1	Franceschini 36; Obinna 60	21,000
6	itpr1	**Treviso**	H	D	0-0		5,304
7	itpr1	**Palermo**	A	D	2-2	Amauri 18,39 pen	27,092
8	itpr1	**Cagliari**	H	W	2-1	D'Anna 71; Obinna 73	10,009
9	itpr1	**Lazio**	A	D	2-2	D'Anna 47; Pellissier 65	17,030
10	itpr1	**Empoli**	H	D	2-2	Semioli 4; Pellissier 62	4,942
11	itpr1	**Siena**	A	W	1-0	Pellissier 10	11,909
12	itpr1	**Ascoli**	H	D	1-1	Pellissier 14	5,113
13	itpr1	**Livorno**	A	D	0-0		10,000
14	itpr1	**AC Milan**	H	W	2-1	Pellissier 45; Tiribocchi 82	25,000
15	itpr1	**Messina**	A	L	0-2		23,000
16	itpr1	**Udinese**	H	W	2-0	Tiribocchi 34; Obinna 64 pen	6,000
17	itpr1	**Roma**	A	L	0-4		30,000
18	itpr1	**Lecce**	H	W	3-1	Pellissier 20,52; Zanchetta 90	8,313
19	itpr1	**Fiorentina**	A	L	1-2	Zanchetta 70	27,000
20	itpr1	**Juventus**	H	D	1-1	Franceschini 21	18,673
21	itpr1	**Parma**	A	L	1-2	Amauri 26	12,447
22	itpr1	**Reggina**	H	W	4-0	Amauri 47,88 pen; Pellissier 74,90	4,853
23	itpr1	**Inter Milan**	A	L	0-1		50,000
24	itpr1	**Sampdoria**	H	D	1-1	Scurto 61	5,005
25	itpr1	**Treviso**	A	W	2-1	Tiribocchi 39,47	4,000
26	itpr1	**Palermo**	H	D	0-0		12,540
27	itpr1	**Cagliari**	A	D	2-2	Tiribocchi 86; Pellissier 90	10,000
28	itpr1	**Lazio**	H	D	2-2	Tiribocchi 42,45	8,000
29	itpr1	**Empoli**	A	L	1-2	Brighi 82	10,000
30	itpr1	**Siena**	H	W	4-1	Obinna 4; Malago 56; Brighi 67; Amauri 82	5,313
31	itpr1	**Ascoli**	A	D	2-2	Amauri 25,90	13,219
32	itpr1	**Livorno**	H	W	2-1	Amauri 14; Obinna 61	6,417
33	itpr1	**AC Milan**	A	L	1-4	Pellissier 13	62,627
34	itpr1	**Messina**	H	W	2-0	Semioli 15; Obinna 90	6,500
35	itpr1	**Udinese**	A	D	1-1	Pellissier 89	15,000
36	itpr1	**Roma**	H	D	4-4	Amauri 8,36; Luciano 49; Pellissier 61	10,500
37	itpr1	**Lecce**	A	D	0-0		8,900
38	itpr1	**Fiorentina**	H	L	0-2		30,000

LEAGUE APPEARANCES, BOOKINGS AND CAPS

	AGE (on 01/07/06)	IN NAMED 18	APPEARANCES	COUNTING GAMES	MINUTES ON PITCH	YELLOW CARDS	RED CARDS	CAPS THIS SEASON	NATIONAL SIDE
Goalkeepers									
Enrico Alfonso	18	7	0	0	0	0	0	-	Italy
Alberto Fontana	39	30	29	27	2529	0	1	-	Italy
Lorenzo Squizzi	32	35	12	9	890	0	0	-	Italy
Defenders									
Lorenzo D'Anna	34	26	26	25	2290	6	2	-	Italy
Salvatore Lanna	29	37	37	37	3315	4	0	-	Italy
Marco Malago	27	31	20	14	1334	3	0	-	Italy
Davide Mandelli	29	33	32	31	2811	7	1	-	Italy
Andrea Mantovani	22	17	4	3	315	0	0	-	Italy
Giovanni Marchese	21	3	0	0	0	0	0	-	Italy
Fabio Moro	30	35	28	27	2415	5	0	-	Italy
Ricky Rickler	19	3	0	0	0	0	0	-	Italy
Giuseppe Scurto	22	31	17	10	1055	4	1	-	Italy
Midfielders									
Filippo Antonelli	27	11	1	0	14	0	0	-	Italy
Matteo Brighi	25	26	26	22	2078	3	0	-	Italy
Daniele Franceschini	30	36	36	31	2989	3	1	-	Italy
Giuseppe Gemiti	25	14	8	1	106	1	0	-	Germany
Federico Giunti	34	28	28	22	2297	6	0	-	Italy
Emiliano Landolina	19	7	0	0	0	0	0	-	Italy
Luciano Siqueira	30	30	18	9	1010	2	1	-	Brazil
Paolo Sammarco	23	26	22	13	1365	6	0	-	Italy
Franco Semioli	26	36	36	33	3034	5	0	-	Italy
Andrea Zanchetta	31	27	15	5	667	2	0	-	Italy
Forwards									
Carvalho Amauri	26	37	37	29	2906	3	0	-	Brazil
Federico Cossato	33	6	5	1	188	2	1	-	Italy
Victor Obinna	19	27	24	5	757	2	0	-	Nigeria
Sergio Pellissier	27	35	34	19	2152	3	0	-	Italy
Simone Tiribocchi	28	33	21	6	917	2	0	-	Italy

TEAM OF THE SEASON

G — Alberto Fontana — CG: 27 DR: 70

D — Lorenzo D'Anna — CG: 25 DR: 82
D — Fabio Moro — CG: 27 DR: 73
D — Salvatore Lanna — CG: 37 DR: 71
D — Davide Mandelli — CG: 31 DR: 69

M — Federico Giunti — CG: 22 SD: 14
M — Paolo Sammarco — CG: 13 SD: 11
M — Franco Semioli — CG: 33 SD: 8
M — Matteo Brighi — CG: 22 SD: 5

F — Sergio Pellissier — CG: 19 SR: 166
F — C De Oliveira — CG: 29 SR: 264

MONTHLY POINTS TALLY

AUGUST	0	0%
SEPTEMBER	9	75%
OCTOBER	7	47%
NOVEMBER	5	56%
DECEMBER	6	50%
JANUARY	7	47%
FEBRUARY	6	40%
MARCH	5	42%
APRIL	8	53%
MAY	1	17%

LEAGUE GOALS

	PLAYER	MINS	GOALS	S RATE
1	Pellissier	2152	13	166
2	Amauri	2906	11	264
3	Tiribocchi	917	7	131
4	Obinna	757	6	126
5	Franceschini	2989	4	747
6	Semioli	3034	2	1517
7	D'Anna	2290	2	1145
8	Zanchetta	667	2	334
9	Brighi	2078	2	1039
10	Mandelli	2811	2	1406
11	Malago	1334	1	1334
12	Luciano Siqueira	1010	1	1010
	Other		1	
	TOTAL		54	

TOP POINT EARNERS

	PLAYER	GAMES	AV PTS
1	D'Anna	25	1.68
2	Giunti	22	1.55
3	Amauri	29	1.52
4	Moro	27	1.52
5	Fontana	27	1.48
6	Pellissier	19	1.47
7	Sammarco	13	1.46
8	Franceschini	31	1.45
9	Lanna	37	1.43
10	Brighi	22	1.41
	CLUB AVERAGE:		1.42

DISCIPLINARY RECORDS

	PLAYER	YELLOW	RED	AVE
1	Scurto	4	1	211
2	Sammarco	6	0	227
3	D'Anna	6	2	286
4	Zanchetta	2	0	333
5	Luciano Siqueira	2	1	336
6	Mandelli	7	1	351
7	Obinna	2	0	378
8	Giunti	6	0	382
9	Malago	3	0	444
10	Tiribocchi	2	0	458
11	Moro	5	0	483
12	Semioli	5	0	606
13	Brighi	3	0	692
	Other	13	2	
	TOTAL	66	7	

KEY GOALKEEPER

Alberto Fontana

Goals Conceded in the League	36	**Counting Games** League games when player was on pitch for at least 70 minutes	27
Defensive Rating Ave number of mins between League goals conceded while on the pitch	70	**Clean Sheets** In games when player was on pitch for at least 70 minutes	5

KEY PLAYERS - DEFENDERS

Lorenzo D'Anna

Goals Conceded Number of League goals conceded while the player was on the pitch	28	**Clean Sheets** In League games when player was on pitch for at least 70 minutes	8
Defensive Rating Ave number of mins between League goals conceded while on the pitch	82	**Club Defensive Rating** Average number of mins between League goals conceded by the club this season	70

	PLAYER	CON LGE	CLEAN SHEETS	DEF RATE
1	Lorenzo D'Anna	28	8	82 mins
2	Fabio Moro	33	7	73 mins
3	Salvatore Lanna	47	9	71 mins
4	Davide Mandelli	41	7	69 mins

KEY PLAYERS - MIDFIELDERS

Federico Giunti

Goals in the League	0	**Contribution to Attacking Power** Average number of minutes between League team goals while on pitch	68
Defensive Rating Average number of mins between League goals conceded while on the pitch	82	**Scoring Difference** Defensive Rating minus Contribution to Attacking Power	14

	PLAYER	LGE GOALS	DEF RATE	POWER	SCORE DIFF
1	Federico Giunti	0	82	68	14 mins
2	Paolo Sammarco	0	91	80	11 mins
3	Franco Semioli	2	71	63	8 mins
4	Matteo Brighi	2	63	58	5 mins

KEY PLAYERS - GOALSCORERS

Sergio Pellissier

Goals in the League	13	**Player Strike Rate** Average number of minutes between League goals scored by player	166
Contribution to Attacking Power Average number of minutes between League team goals while on pitch	65	**Club Strike Rate** Average number of minutes between League goals scored by club	63

	PLAYER	LGE GOALS	POWER	STRIKE RATE
1	Sergio Pellissier	13	65	166 mins
2	Carvalho De Oliveira Amauri	11	68	264 mins
3	Daniele Franceschini	4	68	747 mins
4	Matteo Brighi	2	58	1039 mins

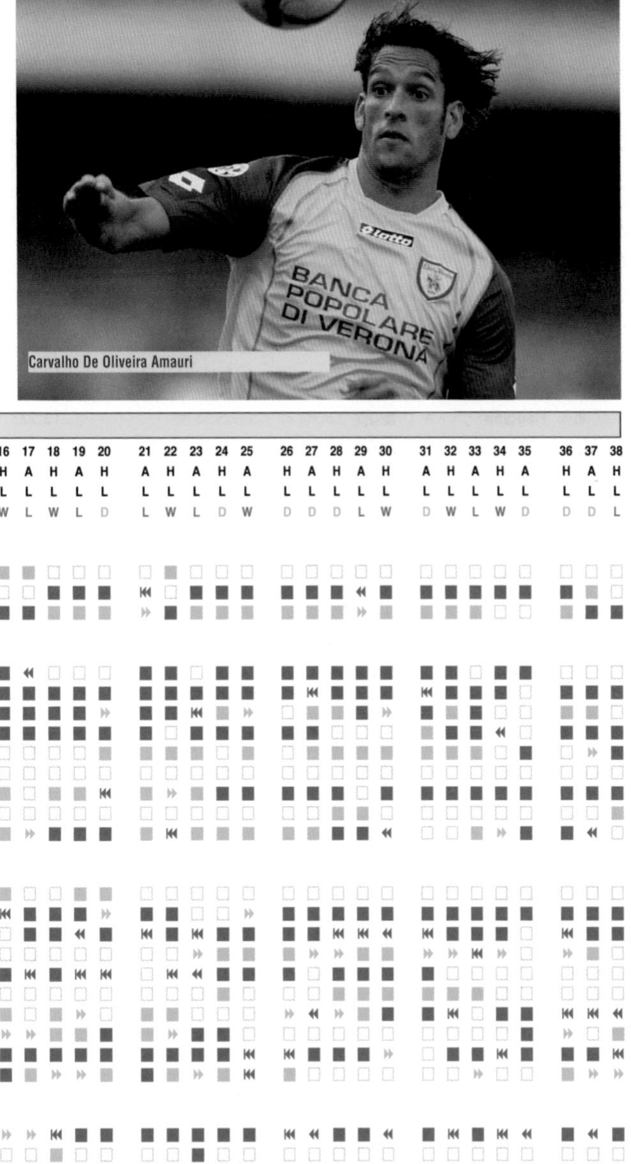

Carvalho De Oliveira Amauri

SQUAD APPEARANCES

latch	1	2	3	4	5	6	7	8	9	10	11	12	13	14	15	16	17	18	19	20	21	22	23	24	25	26	27	28	29	30	31	32	33	34	35	36	37	38
'enue	A	H	A	H	A	H	A	H	A	H	A	H	A	H	A	H	A	H	A	H	A	H	A	H	A	H	A	H	A	H	A	H	A	H	A	H	A	H
;ompetition	L	L	L	L	L	L	L	L	L	L	L	L	L	L	L	L	L	L	L	L	L	L	L	L	L	L	L	L	L	L	L	L	L	L	L	L	L	L
lesult	L	W	W	L	W	D	D	W	D	D	W	D	D	W	L	W	L	W	L	D	L	W	L	D	W	D	D	D	L	W	D	W	L	W	D	D	D	L

ioalkeepers
nrico Alfonso
lberto Fontana
orenzo Squizzi

lefenders
.orenzo D'Anna
ialvatore Lanna
larco Malago
lavide Mandelli
ndrea Mantovani
iiovanni Marchese
'abio Moro
licky Rickler
iiuseppe Scurto

lidfielders
'ilippo Antonelli
latteo Brighi
)aniele Franceschini
iiuseppe Gemiti
'ederico Giunti
Emiliano Landolina
.uciano Siqueira
Paolo Sammarco
'ranco Semioli
Andrea Zanchetta

'orwards
Carvalho De O. Amauri
'ederico Cossato
Victor Obinna
Sergio Pellissier
Simone Tiribocchi

KEY: On all match · On bench · Subbed or sent off (Counting game) · Subbed or sent off (playing less than 70 minutes) · Subbed on from bench (Counting Game) · Subbed on (playing less than 70 minutes) · Subbed on and then subbed or sent off (Counting Game) · Subbed on and then subbed or sent off (playing less than 70 minutes) · Not in 16

PALERMO

Final Position: **8th**

NICKNAME: ROSANERO

KEY: □Won □Drawn □Lost

							Attendance
1	itpr1	**Parma**	A	D	1-1	Terlizzi 36	13,283
2	itpr1	**Inter Milan**	H	W	3-2	Corini 20; Terlizzi 50; Makinwa 72	31,309
3	uc1rl1	**A Famagusta**	H	W	2-1	Corini 6; Brienza 30	13,047
4	itpr1	**Siena**	A	W	2-1	Terlizzi 20; Makinwa 56	7,500
5	itpr1	**Reggina**	H	W	1-0	Terlizzi 66	28,145
6	itpr1	**Lazio**	A	L	2-4	Caracciolo 36; Gonzalez 49	26,000
7	uc1rl2	**A Famagusta**	A	W	4-0	Caracciolo 5; Makinwa 46,68; Santana 53	7,000
8	itpr1	**Empoli**	H	D	2-2	Caracciolo 7; Makinwa 54	26,642
9	itpr1	**Chievo**	H	D	2-2	Corini 15 pen; Caracciolo 90	27,092
10	ucgpb	**M Petach-Tikva**	A	W	2-1	Brienza 11; Terlizzi 77	3,964
11	itpr1	**AC Milan**	A	L	1-2	Caracciolo 28	65,000
12	itpr1	**Lecce**	H	W	3-0	Bonanni 35; Mutarelli 62; Ferri 90	27,084
13	itpr1	**Udinese**	A	D	0-0		16,000
14	ucgpb	**Loko Moscow**	H	D	0-0		20,000
15	itpr1	**Sampdoria**	H	L	0-2		29,087
16	itpr1	**Treviso**	A	D	2-2	Ferri 27; Brienza 69	6,000
17	ucgpb	**Espanyol**	A	D	1-1	Gonzalez 45	9,114
18	itpr1	**Ascoli**	A	D	1-1	Bonanni 35	12,000
19	itpr1	**Cagliari**	H	D	2-2	Caracciolo 20; Makinwa 22	26,209
20	itpr1	**Roma**	A	W	2-1	Biava 21; Caracciolo 78	40,000
21	ucgpb	**Brondby**	H	W	3-0	Makinwa 24; Rinaudo 44,88	4,521
22	itpr1	**Livorno**	H	L	0-2		26,151
23	itpr1	**Fiorentina**	A	L	0-1		31,000
24	itpr1	**Juventus**	H	L	1-2	Terlizzi 12	33,149
25	itpr1	**Messina**	A	D	0-0		28,000
26	itpr1	**Parma**	H	W	4-2	Corini 27; Barzagli 51; Di Michele 53,61	26,990
27	itpr1	**Inter Milan**	A	L	0-3		48,942
28	itpr1	**Siena**	H	L	1-3	Godeas 68	27,428
29	itpr1	**Reggina**	A	D	2-2	Barone 42; Caracciolo 80	13,000
30	itpr1	**Lazio**	H	W	3-1	Gonzalez 12; Tedesco 56; Caracciolo 65	27,074
31	itpr1	**Empoli**	A	W	1-0	Barzagli 90	11,500
32	uc3rl1	**Slavia Prague**	A	L	1-2	Tedesco 42	6,500
33	itpr1	**Chievo**	A	D	0-0		12,540
34	uc3rl2	**Slavia Prague**	H	W	1-0	Godeas 51	8,063
35	itpr1	**AC Milan**	H	L	0-2		31,868
36	itpr1	**Lecce**	A	L	0-2		10,890
37	uc4rl1	**Schalke**	H	W	1-0	Brienza 15	10,581
38	itpr1	**Udinese**	H	W	2-0	Di Michele 53; Tedesco 64	25,792
39	uc4rl2	**Schalke**	A	L	0-3		52,151
40	itpr1	**Sampdoria**	A	W	2-0	Mutarelli 57; Di Michele 66	21,000
41	itpr1	**Treviso**	H	W	1-0	Makinwa 57	26,025
42	itpr1	**Ascoli**	H	D	1-1	Caracciolo 35	26,500
43	itpr1	**Cagliari**	A	D	1-1	Di Michele 90	12,000
44	itpr1	**Roma**	H	D	3-3	Di Michele 50; Barone 52,79	27,855
45	itpr1	**Livorno**	A	L	1-3	Tedesco 90	11,000
46	itpr1	**Fiorentina**	H	W	1-0	Di Michele 52	30,056
47	itpr1	**Juventus**	A	L	1-2	Godeas 62	56,488
48	itpr1	**Messina**	H	W	1-0	Godeas 33	26,588

LEAGUE APPEARANCES, BOOKINGS AND CAPS

	AGE (on 01/07/06)	IN NAMED 18	APPEARANCES	COUNTING GAMES	MINUTES ON PITCH	YELLOW CARDS	RED CARDS	CAPS THIS SEASON	NATIONAL SIDE
Goalkeepers									
Federico Agliardi	23	10	9	9	810	0	0	-	Italy
Mariano G. Andujar	22	29	12	11	999	1	0	-	Argentina
Matteo Guardalben	32	6	6	5	492	0	0	1	Italy (13)
Cristiano Lupatelli	28	15	5	5	441	0	0	-	Italy
Nicola Santoni	27	14	8	7	678	0	0	-	Italy
Defenders									
Pietro Accardi	23	16	6	4	412	0	0	-	Italy
Andrea Barzagli	25	35	35	33	3060	3	0	6	Italy (13)
Guiseppe Biava	29	30	18	15	1474	5	1	-	Italy
Kewullay Conteh	28	16	6	4	461	1	0	-	Sierra Leone
Michele Ferri	25	19	7	2	264	0	1	-	Italy
Leandro Rinaudo	23	28	9	6	643	4	0	-	Italy
Christian Terlizzi	26	24	21	19	1744	6	0	-	Italy
Francesco Velardi	18	1	0	0	0	0	0	-	Italy
Cristian Zaccardo	24	36	36	34	3113	7	0	9	Italy (13)
Midfielders									
Simone Barone	28	36	36	33	3100	4	0	9	Italy (13)
Massimo Bonanni	24	21	18	2	957	2	0	-	Italy
Franco Brienza	27	32	26	6	1269	1	0	-	Italy
Paul Codrea	25	24	11	4	587	5	2	-	Romania
Luca Conean	19	3	0	0	0	0	0	-	Italy
Eugenio Corini	35	28	27	21	2146	4	1	-	Italy
Mariano Gonzalez	25	36	30	13	1713	4	0	-	Argentina
Fabio Grosso	28	33	33	33	2970	5	0	9	Italy (13)
Salvatore Masiello	24	3	2	0	90	0	0	-	Italy
Massimo Mutarelli	28	24	23	13	1474	7	0	-	Italy
Mario Santana	24	29	28	18	1900	6	0	3	Argentina (9)
Giovanni Tedesco	34	14	14	4	686	0	0	-	Italy
Forwards									
Andrea Caracciolo	24	37	35	25	2653	5	0	-	Italy
David Di Michele	30	19	18	13	1414	1	0	-	Italy
Denis Godeas	30	18	12	5	661	0	0	-	Italy
Stephen A. Makinwa	22	25	22	8	1270	0	0	-	Nigeria
Gianluca Palmiteri	18	3	0	0	0	0	0	-	Italy
Simone Pepe	22	12	3	0	94	0	0	-	Italy
Valerio Virga	20	1	0	0	0	0	0	-	Italy

TEAM OF THE SEASON

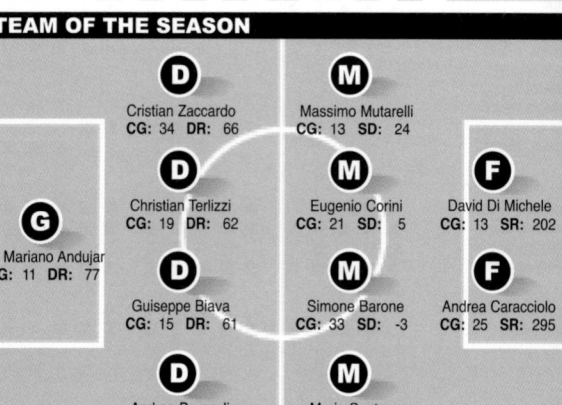

G Mariano Andujar CG: 11 DR: 77

D Cristian Zaccardo CG: 34 DR: 66

D Christian Terlizzi CG: 19 DR: 62

D Guiseppe Biava CG: 15 DR: 61

D Andrea Barzagli CG: 33 DR: 67

M Massimo Mutarelli CG: 13 SD: 24

M Eugenio Corini CG: 21 SD: 5

M Simone Barone CG: 33 SD: -3

M Mario Santana CG: 18 SD: -7

F David Di Michele CG: 13 SR: 202

F Andrea Caracciolo CG: 25 SR: 295

MONTHLY POINTS TALLY

AUGUST	1	33%
SEPTEMBER	9	75%
OCTOBER	6	40%
NOVEMBER	2	22%
DECEMBER	4	33%
JANUARY	4	27%
FEBRUARY	8	53%
MARCH	9	75%
APRIL	6	40%
MAY	3	50%

LEAGUE GOALS

	PLAYER	MINS	GOALS	S RATE
1	Caracciolo	2653	**9**	295
2	Di Michele	1414	**7**	202
3	Terlizzi	1744	**5**	349
4	Makinwa	1270	**5**	254
5	Godeas	661	**3**	220
6	Corini	2146	**3**	715
7	Barone	3100	**3**	1033
8	Tedesco	686	**3**	229
9	Barzagli	3060	**2**	1530
10	Gonzalez	1713	**2**	857
11	Bonanni	957	**2**	479
12	Ferri	264	**2**	132
13	Mutarelli	1474	**2**	737
	Other		**2**	
	TOTAL		**50**	

TOP POINT EARNERS

	PLAYER	GAMES	AV PTS
1	Di Michele	13	**1.62**
2	Mutarelli	13	**1.62**
3	Santana	18	**1.56**
4	Biava	15	**1.53**
5	Corini	21	**1.48**
6	Terlizzi	19	**1.42**
7	Caracciolo	25	**1.40**
8	Barzagli	33	**1.39**
9	Zaccardo	34	**1.24**
10	Barone	33	**1.21**
	CLUB AVERAGE:		**1.37**

DISCIPLINARY RECORDS

	PLAYER	YELLOW	RED	AVE
1	Codrea	5	2	**83**
2	Rinaudo	4	0	**160**
3	Mutarelli	7	0	**210**
4	Biava	5	1	**245**
5	Terlizzi	6	0	**290**
6	Santana	6	0	**316**
7	Gonzalez	4	0	**428**
8	Corini	4	1	**429**
9	Zaccardo	7	0	**444**
10	Conteh	1	0	**461**
11	Bonanni	2	0	**478**
12	Caracciolo	5	0	**530**
13	Grosso	5	0	**594**
	Other	10	0	
	TOTAL	**71**	**4**	

KEY GOALKEEPER

Mariano Andujar

Goals Conceded in the League	13	Counting Games League games when player was on pitch for at least 70 minutes	11
Defensive Rating Ave number of mins between League goals conceded while on the pitch	77	Clean Sheets In League games when player was on pitch for at least 70 minutes	4

KEY PLAYERS - DEFENDERS

Andrea Barzagli

Goals Conceded Number of League goals conceded while the player was on the pitch	46	Clean Sheets In League games when player was on pitch for at least 70 minutes	9
Defensive Rating Ave number of mins between League goals conceded while on the pitch	67	Club Defensive Rating Average number of mins between League goals conceded by the club this season	66

	PLAYER	CON LGE	CLEAN SHEETS	DEF RATE
1	Andrea Barzagli	46	9	67 mins
2	Cristian Zaccardo	47	9	66 mins
3	Christian Terlizzi	28	6	62 mins
4	Guiseppe Biava	24	4	61 mins

KEY PLAYERS - MIDFIELDERS

Massimo Mutarelli

Goals in the League	2	Contribution to Attacking Power Average number of minutes between League team goals while on pitch	74
Defensive Rating Average number of mins between League goals conceded while on the pitch	98	Scoring Difference Defensive Rating minus Contribution to Attacking Power	24

	PLAYER	LGE GOALS	DEF RATE	POWER	SCORE DIFF
1	Massimo Mutarelli	2	98	74	24 mins
2	Eugenio Corini	3	65	60	5 mins
3	Simone Barone	3	66	69	-3 mins
4	Mario Santana	0	61	68	-7 mins

KEY PLAYERS - GOALSCORERS

David Di Michele

Goals in the League	7	Player Strike Rate Average number of minutes between League goals scored by player	202
Contribution to Attacking Power Average number of minutes between League team goals while on pitch	67	Club Strike Rate Average number of minutes between League goals scored by club	68

	PLAYER	LGE GOALS	POWER	STRIKE RATE
1	David Di Michele	7	67	202 mins
2	Andrea Caracciolo	9	65	295 mins
3	Christian Terlizzi	5	65	349 mins
4	Eugenio Corini	3	60	715 mins

Massimo Mutarelli

SQUAD APPEARANCES

Match	1	2	3	4	5	6	7	8	9	10	11	12	13	14	15	16	17	18	19	20	21	22	23	24	25
Venue	A	H	H	A	H	A	A	H	H	A	A	H	A	H	H	A	A	A	H	A	H	H	A	H	A
Competition	L	L	E	L	L	L	E	L	L	E	L	L	L	E	L	L	E	L	L	L	E	L	L	L	L
Result	D	W	W	W	W	L	W	D	D	W	L	W	D	D	L	D	D	D	D	W	W	L	L	L	D

Match	26	27	28	29	30	31	32	33	34	35	36	37	38	39	40	41	42	43	44	45	46	47	48
Venue	H	A	H	A	H	A	A	A	H	H	A	H	H	A	A	H	H	A	H	A	H	A	H
Competition	L	L	L	L	L	L	E	L	E	L	L	E	L	E	L	L	L	L	L	L	L	L	L
Result	W	L	L	D	W	W	L	D	W	L	L	W	W	L	W	W	D	D	D	L	W	L	W

Goalkeepers
- Federico Agliardi
- Mariano Gonzalo Andujar
- Matteo Guardalben
- Cristiano Lupatelli
- Nicola Santoni

Defenders
- Pietro Accardi
- Andrea Barzagli
- Guiseppe Biava
- Kewullay Conteh
- Michele Ferri
- Leandro Rinaudo
- Christian Terlizzi
- Francesco Velardi
- Cristian Zaccardo

Midfielders
- Simone Barone
- Massimo Bonanni
- Franco Brienza
- Paul Codrea
- Luca Conean
- Eugenio Corini
- Mariano Gonzalez
- Fabio Grosso
- Salvatore Masiello
- Massimo Mutarelli
- Mario Santana
- Giovanni Tedesco

Forwards
- Andrea Caracciolo
- David Di Michele
- Denis Godeas
- Stephen Ayodele Makinwa
- Gianluca Palmiteri
- Simone Pepe
- Valerio Virga

KEY: On all match · On bench · Subbed or sent off (Counting game) · Subbed or sent off (playing less than 70 minutes) · Subbed on from bench (Counting Game) · Subbed on (playing less than 70 minutes) · Subbed on and then subbed or sent off (Counting Game) · Subbed on and then subbed or sent off (playing less than 70 minutes) · Not in 16

LIVORNO

Final Position: **9th**

NICKNAME: AMARANTO

KEY: ☐ Won ☐ Drawn ☐ Lost

						Attendance
1 itpr1	Lecce	H	W	2-1	Lucarelli, C 14; Palladino 48	9,000
2 itpr1	Treviso	A	W	1-0	Lucarelli, C 90	5,000
3 itpr1	Roma	H	D	0-0		15,000
4 itpr1	Messina	A	D	0-0		18,000
5 itpr1	Ascoli	H	W	2-0	Palladino 51; Lucarelli, C 78 pen	15,000
6 itpr1	Fiorentina	A	L	2-3	Galante 86; Morrone 88	34,000
7 itpr1	Inter Milan	A	L	0-5		52,000
8 itpr1	Reggina	H	W	1-0	Lucarelli, C 87	15,000
9 itpr1	Cagliari	A	D	1-1	Melara 75	14,000
10 itpr1	Parma	H	W	2-0	Lucarelli, C 16; Morrone 28	12,000
11 itpr1	Juventus	A	L	0-3		29,000
12 itpr1	Empoli	H	W	2-0	Morrone 31; Lucarelli, C 87	15,000
13 itpr1	Chievo	H	D	0-0		10,000
14 itpr1	Udinese	A	W	2-0	Obodo 9 og; Lucarelli, A 73	16,000
15 itpr1	Lazio	H	W	2-1	De Ascentis 59; Lucarelli, C 78	15,000
16 itpr1	Palermo	A	W	2-0	Pfertzel 67; Morrone 93	26,151
17 itpr1	AC Milan	H	L	0-3		14,000
18 itpr1	Sampdoria	A	W	2-0	Lucarelli, C 7,90	23,201
19 itpr1	Siena	H	D	2-2	Morrone 24; Lucarelli, A 54	15,000
20 itpr1	Lecce	A	D	0-0		10,000
21 itpr1	Treviso	H	D	1-1	Galante 90	12,000
22 itpr1	Roma	A	L	0-3		35,500
23 itpr1	Messina	H	D	2-2	Lucarelli, C 54,68	12,000
24 itpr1	Ascoli	A	D	0-0		9,000
25 itpr1	Fiorentina	H	W	2-0	Lucarelli, C 67 pen,76	18,000
26 itpr1	Inter Milan	H	D	0-0		16,000
27 itpr1	Reggina	A	D	1-1	Morrone 46	10,000
28 itpr1	Cagliari	H	L	0-1		12,000
29 itpr1	Parma	A	L	1-2	Bakayoko 45 pen	15,405
30 itpr1	Juventus	H	L	1-3	Pfertzel 52	15,000
31 itpr1	Empoli	A	L	1-2	Lucarelli, C 87 pen	7,000
32 itpr1	Chievo	A	L	1-2	Lucarelli, C 40	6,417
33 itpr1	Udinese	H	L	0-2		11,000
34 itpr1	Lazio	A	L	1-3	Colucci 52	50,000
35 itpr1	Palermo	H	W	3-1	Lucarelli, C 4 pen,41,51	11,000
36 itpr1	AC Milan	A	L	0-2		62,088
37 itpr1	Sampdoria	H	D	0-0		10,000
38 itpr1	Siena	A	D	0-0		7,000

LEAGUE APPEARANCES, BOOKINGS AND CAPS

	AGE (on 01/07/06)	IN NAMED 18	APPEARANCES	COUNTING GAMES	MINUTES ON PITCH	YELLOW CARDS	RED CARDS	CAPS THIS SEASON	NATIONAL SIDE
Goalkeepers									
Paolo Acerbis	25	36	2	2	180	0	0	-	
Marco Amelia	24	38	36	36	3240	1	0	4	Italy (13)
Defenders									
Stefano Argilli	33	15	8	3	465	1	0	-	Italy
David Balleri	37	29	22	11	1148	1	0	-	Italy
Luis Cesar Prates	31	34	28	11	1462	1	0	-	Brazil
Stefano Fanucci	27	20	7	4	471	1	0	-	Italy
Fabio Galante	32	35	35	35	3150	3	0	-	Italy
Andrea Giallombardo	25	1	1	1	90	0	0	-	Italy
Alessandro Grandoni	28	36	35	33	3079	4	0	-	Italy
Alessandro Lucarelli	28	9	9	9	810	0	0	-	Italy
Matteo Melara	27	17	5	4	388	0	0	-	Italy
Marc Pfertzel	25	35	29	21	1997	2	0	-	France
Gennaro Ruotolo	39	31	23	10	1288	5	0	-	Italy
Jorge Vargas	30	33	30	30	2692	12	1	1	Chile (73)
Midfielders									
Luis Fernando Centi	29	13	8	4	367	1	0	-	Italy
Francesco Coco	29	29	27	23	2229	0	1	-	Italy
Giuseppe Colucci	25	28	21	13	1339	4	0	-	Italy
Diego De Ascentis	29	31	29	20	2189	5	1	-	Italy
Nikola Lazetic	28	17	16	9	914	4	0	-	Serbia & Mont
Stefano Morrone	27	35	35	34	3072	5	1	-	Italy
Dario Passoni	32	33	29	23	2291	4	0	-	Italy
Jose Ze Rodolpho	22	1	0	0	0	0	0	-	Brazil
Forwards									
Ibrahim Bakayoko	29	34	20	1	665	0	0	-	Ivory Coast
Cristiano Lucarelli	30	28	27	26	2353	3	1	-	Italy
Raffaele Palladino	22	29	21	9	1274	1	0	-	Italy
Paulinho	19	29	11	1	252	0	0	-	Brazil
Alessandro Stefanini	19	5	0	0	0	0	0	-	Italy

TEAM OF THE SEASON

G
Marco Amelia
CG: 36 DR: 77

D
Jorge Vargas
CG: 30 DR: 77

D
Alessandro Grandoni
CG: 33 DR: 75

D
Fabio Galante
CG: 35 DR: 73

D
Marc Pfertzel
CG: 21 DR: 71

M
Dario Passoni
CG: 23 SD: 4

M
Francesco Coco
CG: 23 SD: -15

M
Diego De Ascentis
CG: 20 SD: -12

M
Giuseppe Colucci
CG: 13 SD: -28

F
Cristiano Lucarelli
CG: 26 SR: 157

F
Stefano Morrone*
CG: 34 SR: 512

MONTHLY POINTS TALLY

AUGUST	3	100%
SEPTEMBER	8	67%
OCTOBER	7	47%
NOVEMBER	4	44%
DECEMBER	9	75%
JANUARY	6	40%
FEBRUARY	7	47%
MARCH	0	0%
APRIL	3	20%
MAY	2	33%

LEAGUE GOALS

	PLAYER	MINS	GOALS	S RATE
1	Lucarelli, C	2353	15	157
2	Morrone	3072	6	512
3	Lucarelli, A	810	2	405
4	Palladino	1274	2	637
5	Pfertzel	1997	2	999
6	Galante	3150	2	1575
7	Melara	388	1	388
8	Bakayoko	665	1	665
9	De Ascentis	2189	1	2189
10	Colucci	1339	1	1339
	Other		4	
	TOTAL		37	

TOP POINT EARNERS

	PLAYER	GAMES	AV PTS
1	Passoni	23	1.43
2	Vargas	30	1.37
3	Amelia	36	1.31
4	Lucarelli, C	26	1.27
5	Grandoni	33	1.27
6	Coco	23	1.26
7	Galante	35	1.26
8	Morrone	34	1.21
9	De Ascentis	20	1.20
10	Colucci	13	1.15
	CLUB AVERAGE:		1.29

DISCIPLINARY RECORDS

	PLAYER	YELLOW	RED	AVE
1	Vargas	12	1	207
2	Lazetic	4	0	228
3	Ruotolo	5	0	257
4	Colucci	4	0	334
5	De Ascentis	5	1	364
6	Argilli	1	0	465
7	Fanucci	1	0	471
8	Morrone	5	1	512
9	Passoni	4	0	572
10	Lucarelli, C	3	1	588
11	Grandoni	4	0	769
12	Pfertzel	2	0	998
13	Galante	3	0	1050
	Other	4	1	
	TOTAL	57	5	

KEY GOALKEEPER

Marco Amelia

Goals Conceded in the League	42	**Counting Games** League games when player was on pitch for at least 70 minutes	36
Defensive Rating Ave number of mins between League goals conceded while on the pitch	77	**Clean Sheets** In League games when player was on pitch for at least 70 minutes	16

KEY PLAYERS - GOALSCORERS

Cristiano Lucarelli

Goals in the League	15	**Player Strike Rate** Average number of minutes between League goals scored by player	157
Contribution to Attacking Power Average number of minutes between League team goals while on pitch	102	**Club Strike Rate** Average number of minutes between League goals scored by club	92

	PLAYER	LGE GOALS	POWER	STRIKE RATE
1	Cristiano Lucarelli	15	102	157 mins
2	Stefano Morrone	6	96	512 mins
3	Marc Pfertzel	2	125	999 mins
4	Giuseppe Colucci	1	112	1339 mins

KEY PLAYERS - DEFENDERS

Jorge Vargas

Goals Conceded Number of League goals conceded while the player was on the pitch	35	**Clean Sheets** In League games when player was on pitch for at least 70 minutes	15
Defensive Rating Ave number of mins between League goals conceded while on the pitch	77	**Club Defensive Rating** Average number of mins between League goals conceded by the club this season	78

	PLAYER	CON LGE	CLEAN SHEETS	DEF RATE
1	Jorge Vargas	35	15	77 mins
2	Alessandro Grandoni	41	14	75 mins
3	Fabio Galante	43	15	73 mins
4	Marc Pfertzel	28	7	71 mins

Fabio Galante

KEY PLAYERS - MIDFIELDERS

Dario Passoni

Goals in the League	0	**Contribution to Attacking Power** Average number of minutes between League team goals while on pitch	88
Defensive Rating Average number of mins between League goals conceded while on the pitch	92	**Scoring Difference** Defensive Rating minus Contribution to Attacking Power	4

	PLAYER	LGE GOALS	DEF RATE	POWER	SCORE DIFF
1	Dario Passoni	0	92	88	4 mins
2	Francesco Coco	0	74	89	-15 mins
3	Stefano Morrone	6	73	96	-23 mins
4	Giuseppe Colucci	1	84	112	-28 mins

SQUAD APPEARANCES

Match	1	2	3	4	5	6	7	8	9	10	11	12	13	14	15	16	17	18	19	20	21	22	23	24	25	26	27	28	29	30	31	32	33	34	35	36	37	38
Venue	H	A	H	A	H	A	A	H	A	H	A	H	H	A	H	A	H	A	H	A	H	A	H	A	H	H	A	H	A	H	A	A	H	A	H	A	H	A
Competition	L	L	L	L	L	L	L	L	L	L	L	L	L	L	L	L	L	L	L	L	L	L	L	L	L	L	L	L	L	L	L	L	L	L	L	L	L	L
Result	W	W	D	D	W	L	L	W	D	W	L	W	D	W	W	W	L	W	D	D	D	L	D	D	W	D	D	L	L	L	L	L	L	L	W	L	D	D

Goalkeepers
Paolo Acerbis
Marco Amelia

Defenders
Stefano Argilli
David Balleri
Luis Cesar Prates
Stefano Fanucci
Fabio Galante
Andrea Giallombardo
Alessandro Grandoni
Alessandro Lucarelli
Matteo Melara
Marc Pfertzel
Gennaro Ruotolo
Jorge Vargas

Midfielders
Luis Fernando Centi
Francesco Coco
Giuseppe Colucci
Diego De Ascentis
Nikola Lazetic
Stefano Morrone
Dario Passoni
Jose Ze Rodolpho

Forwards
Ibrahim Bakayoko
Cristiano Lucarelli
Raffaele Palladino
Paulinho
Alessandro Stefanini

KEY: ■ On all match | ■ On bench | ⏮ Subbed or sent off (Counting game) | « Subbed or sent off (playing less than 70 minutes) | ⏭ Subbed on from bench (Counting Game) | » Subbed on (playing less than 70 minutes) | Subbed on and then subbed or sent off (Counting Game) | Subbed on and then subbed or sent off (playing less than 70 minutes) | □ Not in 16

PARMA

Final Position: **10th**

NICKNAME: CROCIATI

KEY: ☐Won ☐Drawn ☐Lost

							Attendance
1	itpr1	**Palermo**	H	D	1-1	Bresciano 48	13,283
2	itpr1	**Chievo**	A	L	0-1		5,580
3	itpr1	**Empoli**	H	W	1-0	Corradi 17	12,119
4	itpr1	**Roma**	A	L	1-4	Cannavaro 30	32,500
5	itpr1	**Juventus**	H	L	1-2	Delveccio 13	23,116
6	itpr1	**Ascoli**	A	L	1-3	Pisanu 20	9,000
7	itpr1	**Treviso**	H	D	1-1	Simplicio 34	12,259
8	itpr1	**Fiorentina**	A	L	1-4	Grella 66	30,000
9	itpr1	**Messina**	H	D	1-1	Simplicio 36	12,000
10	itpr1	**Livorno**	A	L	0-2		12,000
11	itpr1	**Lecce**	H	W	2-0	Marchionni 31; Morfeo 50	15,499
12	itpr1	**Inter Milan**	A	L	0-2		47,751
13	itpr1	**Udinese**	H	L	1-2	Corradi 89	12,471
14	itpr1	**Reggina**	A	L	1-2	Cardone 13	10,000
15	itpr1	**Sampdoria**	H	D	1-1	Corradi 25	14,242
16	itpr1	**Siena**	A	D	2-2	Corradi 47; Dessena 94	9,500
17	itpr1	**Cagliari**	H	W	1-0	Corradi 23	11,677
18	itpr1	**AC Milan**	A	L	3-4	Cannavaro 24; Marchionni 70,85	55,000
19	itpr1	**Lazio**	H	D	1-1	Corradi 39	13,834
20	itpr1	**Palermo**	A	L	2-4	Simplicio 23; Cannavaro 38	26,990
21	itpr1	**Chievo**	H	W	2-1	Rossi 45; Simplicio 82 pen	12,447
22	itpr1	**Empoli**	A	W	2-1	Marchionni 44; Bresciano 79	8,500
23	itpr1	**Roma**	H	L	0-3		16,638
24	itpr1	**Juventus**	A	D	1-1	Dessena 39	25,719
25	itpr1	**Ascoli**	H	D	0-0		12,854
26	itpr1	**Treviso**	A	W	1-0	Simplicio 14	4,000
27	itpr1	**Fiorentina**	H	L	2-4	Simplicio 3 pen; Bresciano 19	10,000
28	itpr1	**Messina**	A	W	1-0	Bresciano 83	28,000
29	itpr1	**Livorno**	H	W	2-1	Simplicio 37 pen; Bresciano 81	15,405
30	itpr1	**Lecce**	A	W	2-1	Bresciano 53; Simplicio 90	10,334
31	itpr1	**Inter Milan**	H	W	1-0	Simplicio 39	18,033
32	itpr1	**Udinese**	A	L	0-2		15,500
33	itpr1	**Reggina**	H	W	4-0	Bresciano 12; Simplicio 35; Contini 65 pen; Dessena 79	13,531
34	itpr1	**Sampdoria**	A	W	2-1	Corradi 52; Bresciano 90	21,000
35	itpr1	**Siena**	H	D	1-1	Morfeo 64	15,000
36	itpr1	**Cagliari**	A	L	1-3	Corradi 74	15,000
37	itpr1	**AC Milan**	H	L	2-3	Corradi 54,88	21,920
38	itpr1	**Lazio**	A	L	0-1		36,000

LEAGUE APPEARANCES, BOOKINGS AND CAPS

	AGE (on 01/07/06)	IN NAMED 18	APPEARANCES	COUNTING GAMES	MINUTES ON PITCH	YELLOW CARDS	RED CARDS	CAPS THIS SEASON	NATIONAL SIDE
Goalkeepers									
Luca Bucci	37	34	21	20	1804	0	0	-	Italy
Alfonso De Lucia	22	19	4	3	326	0	0	-	Italy
Matteo Guardalben	32	8	7	7	618	0	0	1	Italy (13)
Cristiano Lupatelli	28	12	9	7	672	0	0	-	Italy
Defenders									
Daniele Bonera	25	23	23	21	1955	5	0	2	Italy (13)
Paolo Cannavaro	25	29	29	24	2318	4	0	-	Italy
Giuseppe Cardone	32	28	24	21	1946	6	0	-	Italy
Ferdinand Coly	32	10	8	7	636	2	0	-	Senegal
Matteo Contini	26	34	33	31	2810	9	0	-	Italy
Fernando Couto	36	25	23	15	1571	4	0	-	Portugal
Damiano Ferronetti	22	13	12	10	911	2	0	-	Italy
Filippo Mattiuzzo	19	7	1	0	1	0	0	-	Italy
Giovanni Pasquale	24	27	21	14	1440	5	0	-	Italy
Marco Rossi	18	21	9	3	328	2	1	-	Italy
Midfielders									
Alessandro Bernardini	19	3	0	0	0	0	0	-	Italy
Jorge Bolano	29	21	17	8	1074	6	0	-	Colombia
Ibrahima Camara	21	12	3	2	204	0	0	-	Guinea
Luca Cigarini	20	31	17	3	629	2	0	-	Italy
Daniele Dessena	19	26	17	4	854	5	0	-	Italy
Vincenzo Grella	26	36	34	32	2895	6	0	5	Australia (42)
Matteo Mandorlini	17	2	1	0	6	0	0	-	Italy
Marco Marchionni	25	31	31	30	2627	3	0	-	Italy
Domenico Morfeo	30	26	23	14	1591	3	2	-	Italy
Filippo Savi	19	10	8	1	294	0	0	-	Italy
Fabio Simplicio	26	37	37	36	3271	6	0	-	Brazil
Forwards									
Mark Bresciano	26	34	32	21	2250	2	0	5	Australia (42)
Bernardo Corradi	30	36	36	35	3169	9	1	-	Italy
Zlatko Dedic	21	18	9	1	291	0	0	-	Slovenia
Marco Delveccio	33	10	8	1	397	1	0	-	Italy
Gaetano Grieco	23	1	0	0	0	0	0	-	Italy
Daniele Paponi	18	20	5	0	95	0	0	-	Italy
Andrea Pisanu	24	9	8	3	502	1	0	-	Italy
Francesco Ruopolo	23	15	6	0	111	0	0	-	Italy

TEAM OF THE SEASON

MONTHLY POINTS TALLY

AUGUST	1	33%
SEPTEMBER	3	25%
OCTOBER	2	13%
NOVEMBER	3	33%
DECEMBER	5	42%
JANUARY	7	47%
FEBRUARY	5	33%
MARCH	12	100%
APRIL	7	47%
MAY	0	0%

LEAGUE GOALS

	PLAYER	MINS	GOALS	S RATE
1	Corradi	3169	**10**	317
2	Simplicio	3271	**10**	327
3	Bresciano	2250	**8**	281
4	Marchionni	2627	**4**	657
5	Dessena	854	**3**	285
6	Cannavaro	2318	**3**	773
7	Morfeo	1591	**2**	796
8	Grella	2895	**1**	2895
9	Delveccio	397	**1**	397
10	Pisanu	502	**1**	502
11	Contini	2810	**1**	2810
12	Rossi	328	**1**	328
13	Cardone	1946	**1**	1946
	Other		**0**	
	TOTAL		**46**	

TOP POINT EARNERS

	PLAYER	GAMES	AV PTS
1	Bucci	20	**1.80**
2	Cannavaro	24	**1.63**
3	Bresciano	21	**1.57**
4	Bonera	21	**1.33**
5	Marchionni	30	**1.33**
6	Corradi	35	**1.20**
7	Simplicio	36	**1.19**
8	Grella	32	**1.13**
9	Couto	15	**1.07**
10	Cardone	21	**1.05**
	CLUB AVERAGE:		**1.18**

DISCIPLINARY RECORDS

	PLAYER	YELLOW	RED	AVE
1	Dessena	5	0	**170**
2	Bolano	6	0	**179**
3	Pasquale	5	0	**288**
4	Contini	9	0	**312**
5	Cigarini	2	0	**314**
6	Corradi	9	1	**316**
7	Coly	2	0	**318**
8	Morfeo	3	2	**318**
9	Cardone	6	0	**324**
10	Bonera	5	0	**391**
11	Couto	4	0	**392**
12	Ferronetti	2	0	**455**
13	Grella	6	0	**482**
	Other	16	0	
	TOTAL	**80**	**3**	

KEY GOALKEEPER

Luca Bucci

Goals Conceded in the League	19	**Counting Games** League games when player was on pitch for at least 70 minutes	20
Defensive Rating Ave number of mins between League goals conceded while on the pitch	95	**Clean Sheets** In games when player was on pitch for at least 70 minutes	8

KEY PLAYERS - DEFENDERS

Paolo Cannavaro

Goals Conceded Number of League goals conceded while the player was on the pitch	35	**Clean Sheets** In League games when player was on pitch for at least 70 minutes	7
Defensive Rating Ave number of mins between League goals conceded while on the pitch	66	**Club Defensive Rating** Average number of mins between League goals conceded by the club this season	57

	PLAYER	CON LGE	CLEAN SHEETS	DEF RATE
1	Paolo Cannavaro	35	7	66 mins
2	Daniele Bonera	35	4	56 mins
3	Matteo Contini	52	5	54 mins
4	Fernando Couto	30	4	52 mins

KEY PLAYERS - MIDFIELDERS

Marco Marchionni

Goals in the League	4	**Contribution to Attacking Power** Average number of minutes between League team goals while on pitch	71
Defensive Rating Average number of mins between League goals conceded while on the pitch	58	**Scoring Difference** Defensive Rating minus Contribution to Attacking Power	-13

	PLAYER	LGE GOALS	DEF RATE	POWER	SCORE DIFF
1	Marco Marchionni	4	58	71	-13 mins
2	Vincenzo Grella	1	57	72	-15 mins
3	Fabio Enrico Simplicio	10	55	76	-21 mins
4	Domenico Morfeo	2	50	76	-26 mins

KEY PLAYERS - GOALSCORERS

Mark Bresciano

Goals in the League	8	**Player Strike Rate** Average number of minutes between League goals scored by player	281
Contribution to Attacking Power Average number of minutes between League team goals while on pitch	73	**Club Strike Rate** Average number of minutes between League goals scored by club	74

	PLAYER	LGE GOALS	POWER	STRIKE RATE
1	Mark Bresciano	8	73	281 mins
2	Bernardo Corradi	10	77	317 mins
3	Fabio Enrico Simplicio	10	76	327 mins
4	Marco Marchionni	4	71	657 mins

Vincenzo Grella and Fabio Enrico Simplicio

SQUAD APPEARANCES

Match	1	2	3	4	5	6	7	8	9	10	11	12	13	14	15	16	17	18	19	20	21	22	23	24	25	26	27	28	29	30	31	32	33	34	35	36	37	38
Venue	H	A	H	A	H	A	H	A	H	A	H	A	H	A	H	A	H	A	H	A	H	A	H	A	H	A	H	A	H	A	H	A	H	A	H	A	H	A
Competition	L	L	L	L	L	L	L	L	L	L	L	L	L	L	L	L	L	L	L	L	L	L	L	L	L	L	L	L	L	L	L	L	L	L	L	L	L	L
Result	D	L	W	L	L	L	D	L	D	L	W	L	L	L	D	D	W	L	D	L	W	W	L	D	D	W	L	W	W	W	W	L	W	W	D	L	L	L

Goalkeepers
Luca Bucci
Alfonso De Lucia
Matteo Guardalben
Cristiano Lupatelli

Defenders
Daniele Bonera
Paolo Cannavaro
Giuseppe Cardone
Ferdinand Coly
Matteo Contini
Fernando Couto
Damiano Ferronetti
Filippo Mattiuzzo
Giovanni Pasquale
Marco Rossi

Midfielders
Alessandro Bernardini
Jorge Bolano
Sory Ibrahima Camara
Luca Cigarini
Daniele Dessena
Vincenzo Grella
Matteo Mandorlini
Marco Marchionni
Domenico Morfeo
Filippo Savi
Fabio Enrico Simplicio

Forwards
Mark Bresciano
Bernardo Corradi
Zlatko Dedic
Marco Delveccio
Gaetano Grieco
Daniele Paponi
Andrea Pisanu
Francesco Ruopolo

KEY: On all match · On bench · Subbed or sent off (Counting game) · Subbed or sent off (playing less than 70 minutes) · Subbed on from bench (Counting Game) · Subbed on (playing less than 70 minutes) · Subbed on and then subbed or sent off (Counting Game) · Subbed on and then subbed or sent off (playing less than 70 minutes) · Not in 16

EMPOLI

Final Position: **11th**

KEY: ☐Won ☐Drawn ☐Lost

						Attendance
1	itpr1	**Udinese**	A L	0-1		15,000
2	itpr1	**Juventus**	H L	0-4		10,350
3	itpr1	**Parma**	A L	0-1		12,119
4	itpr1	**Cagliari**	H W	3-1	Tavano 46,64; Almiron 69	9,700
5	itpr1	**Lecce**	H W	1-0	Pozzi 65	6,000
6	itpr1	**Palermo**	A D	2-2	Tavano 9,42	26,642
7	itpr1	**Roma**	H W	1-0	Tavano 59	8,000
8	itpr1	**Treviso**	A W	2-1	Almiron 25; Tavano 80	7,345
9	itpr1	**AC Milan**	H L	1-3	Vannucchi 34	10,000
10	itpr1	**Chievo**	A D	2-2	Rigano 8; Tavano 53	4,942
11	itpr1	**Reggina**	H W	3-0	Busce 7; Tavano 67; Vannucchi 90	8,000
12	itpr1	**Livorno**	A L	0-2		15,000
13	itpr1	**Lazio**	H L	2-3	Bonetto 55; Tavano 59 pen	8,000
14	itpr1	**Sampdoria**	A L	0-2		20,143
15	itpr1	**Siena**	A L	0-1		7,500
16	itpr1	**Fiorentina**	H D	1-1	Vannucchi 73	16,000
17	itpr1	**Inter Milan**	A L	1-4	Vannucchi 64	44,385
18	itpr1	**Messina**	H L	1-3	Almiron 35	8,000
19	itpr1	**Ascoli**	A L	1-3	Almiron 44; Coda 50	8,000
20	itpr1	**Udinese**	H D	1-1	Tavano 52 pen	5,500
21	itpr1	**Juventus**	A L	1-2	Almiron 3	26,292
22	itpr1	**Parma**	H L	1-2	Tavano 59 pen	8,500
23	itpr1	**Cagliari**	A L	1-4	Tavano 60	10,000
24	itpr1	**Lecce**	A W	2-1	Almiron 2; Tavano 41 pen	9,753
25	itpr1	**Palermo**	H L	0-1		11,500
26	itpr1	**Roma**	A L	0-1		63,375
27	itpr1	**Treviso**	H D	1-1	Rigano 90	5,500
28	itpr1	**AC Milan**	A L	0-3		54,419
29	itpr1	**Chievo**	H W	2-1	Rigano 72; Tavano 80	10,000
30	itpr1	**Reggina**	A W	2-0	Pozzi 62; Tavano 82	12,500
31	itpr1	**Livorno**	H W	2-1	Tavano 39; Busce 51	7,000
32	itpr1	**Lazio**	A D	3-3	Tosto 25; Tavano 64; Oddo 90 og	20,000
33	itpr1	**Sampdoria**	H W	2-1	Busce 29,47	6,500
34	itpr1	**Siena**	H W	2-1	Tosto 36; Tavano 39	6,000
35	itpr1	**Fiorentina**	A L	1-2	Rigano 66	35,186
36	itpr1	**Inter Milan**	H W	1-0	Materazzi 90 og	6,500
37	itpr1	**Messina**	A W	2-1	Pozzi 4,70	8,000
38	itpr1	**Ascoli**	H L	1-2	Tavano 25	5,000

LEAGUE APPEARANCES, BOOKINGS AND CAPS

	AGE (on 01/07/06)	IN NAMED 18	APPEARANCES	COUNTING GAMES	MINUTES ON PITCH	YELLOW CARDS	RED CARDS	CAPS THIS SEASON	NATIONAL SIDE
Goalkeepers									
Daniele Balli	38	34	14	14	1260	1	0	-	Italy
Gianluca Berti	39	21	18	18	1620	2	0	-	Italy
C. Sebastian Cejas	31	7	6	6	540	0	0	-	Argentina
Renato Dossena	19	9	0	0	0	0	0	-	Italy
Defenders									
Nicola Ascoli	26	17	11	4	494	4	0	-	Italy
Andrea Coda	21	37	37	36	3252	4	0	-	Italy
Stefano Lucchini	25	31	25	13	1553	6	1	-	Italy
Francesco Pratali	27	31	28	25	2380	6	2	-	Italy
Andrea Raggi	22	31	24	16	1706	3	0	-	Italy
Claudio Scianname	18	1	0	0	0	0	0	-	Italy
Vittorio Tosto	32	10	10	8	764	1	0	-	Italy
Richard Vanigli	35	28	17	11	1075	3	0	-	Italy
Midfielders									
Sergio Almiron	25	38	38	29	3086	2	0	-	Argentina
Riccardo Bonetto	27	18	17	16	1498	3	0	-	Italy
Antonio Busce	30	37	37	37	3330	2	0	-	Italy
Daniele Buzzegoli	23	6	1	0	32	0	0	-	Italy
Fabrizio Ficini	32	35	33	23	2402	7	0	-	Italy
Davide Moro	24	36	31	23	2334	7	0	-	Italy
Ighli Vannucchi	29	36	34	19	2337	2	0	-	Italy
Paolo Zanetti	23	26	8	4	412	2	0	-	Italy
Forwards									
Mirco Gasparetto	26	11	6	0	80	0	0	-	Italy
Francesco Lodi	22	32	16	4	735	0	0	-	Italy
Giorgio Novello	22	1	0	0	0	0	0	-	Italy
Nicola Pozzi	20	30	24	4	897	0	0	-	Italy
Christian Rigano	32	35	33	22	2361	6	0	-	Italy
Matteo Serafini	28	32	13	3	481	1	0	-	Italy
Francesco Tavano	27	37	37	27	2846	0	0	-	Italy

TEAM OF THE SEASON

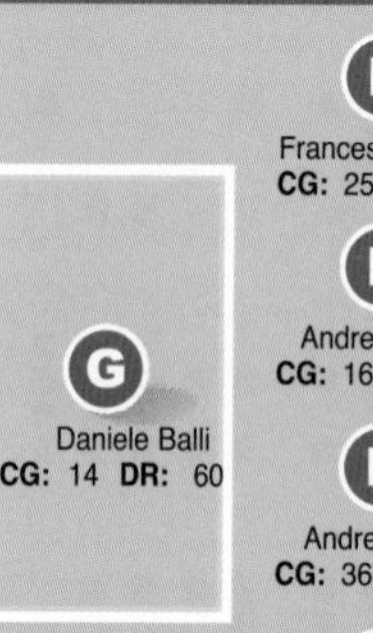

G — Daniele Balli **CG:** 14 **DR:** 60

D — Francesco Pratali **CG:** 25 **DR:** 63

D — Andrea Raggi **CG:** 16 **DR:** 59

D — Andrea Coda **CG:** 36 **DR:** 57

D — Stefano Lucchini **CG:** 13 **DR:** 55

M — Davide Moro **CG:** 23 **SD:** -3

M — Ighli Vannucchi **CG:** 19 **SD:** -11

M — Antonio Busce **CG:** 37 **SD:** -15

M — Sergio Almiron **CG:** 29 **SD:** -18

F — Francesco Tavano **CG:** 27 **SR:** 150

F — Christian Rigano **CG:** 22 **SR:** 590

MONTHLY POINTS TALLY

AUGUST	0	0%
SEPTEMBER	6	50%
OCTOBER	8	53%
NOVEMBER	3	33%
DECEMBER	1	8%
JANUARY	1	7%
FEBRUARY	4	27%
MARCH	9	75%
APRIL	10	67%
MAY	3	50%

LEAGUE GOALS

	PLAYER	MINS	GOALS	S RATE
1	Tavano	2846	**19**	150
2	Almiron	3086	**6**	514
3	Vannucchi	2337	**4**	584
4	Busce	3330	**4**	833
5	Rigano	2361	**4**	590
6	Pozzi	897	**4**	224
7	Tosto	764	**2**	382
8	Bonetto	1498	**1**	1498
9	Coda	3252	**1**	3252
	Other		**2**	
	TOTAL		**47**	

TOP POINT EARNERS

	PLAYER	GAMES	AV PTS
1	Raggi	16	**1.69**
2	Balli	14	**1.64**
3	Pratali	25	**1.44**
4	Moro	23	**1.39**
5	Vannucchi	19	**1.37**
6	Lucchini	13	**1.31**
7	Rigano	22	**1.27**
8	Coda	36	**1.25**
9	Busce	37	**1.22**
10	Bonetto	16	**1.13**
	CLUB AVERAGE:		**1.18**

DISCIPLINARY RECORDS

	PLAYER	YELLOW	RED	AVE
1	Ascoli	4	0	**123**
2	Lucchini	6	1	**221**
3	Pratali	6	2	**297**
4	Moro	7	0	**333**
5	Ficini	7	0	**343**
6	Vanigli	3	0	**358**
7	Rigano	6	0	**393**
8	Serafini	1	0	**481**
9	Bonetto	3	0	**499**
10	Raggi	3	0	**568**
11	Tosto	1	0	**764**
12	Berti	2	0	**810**
13	Coda	4	0	**813**
	Other	7	0	
	TOTAL	**60**	**3**	

KEY GOALKEEPER

Daniele Balli

Goals Conceded in the League	21	Counting Games League games when player was on pitch for at least 70 minutes	14
Defensive Rating Ave number of mins between League goals conceded while on the pitch	60	Clean Sheets In League games when player was on pitch for at least 70 minutes	2

KEY PLAYERS - DEFENDERS

Francesco Pratali

Goals Conceded Number of League goals conceded while the player was on the pitch	38	Clean Sheets In League games when player was on pitch for at least 70 minutes	5
Defensive Rating Ave number of mins between League goals conceded while on the pitch	63	Club Defensive Rating Average number of mins between League goals conceded by the club this season	55

	PLAYER	CON LGE	CLEAN SHEETS	DEF RATE
1	Francesco Pratali	38	5	63 mins
2	Andrea Raggi	29	3	59 mins
3	Andrea Coda	57	5	57 mins
4	Stefano Lucchini	28	2	55 mins

KEY PLAYERS - MIDFIELDERS

Davide Moro

Goals in the League	0	Contribution to Attacking Power Average number of minutes between League team goals while on pitch	60
Defensive Rating Average number of mins between League goals conceded while on the pitch	57	Scoring Difference Defensive Rating minus Contribution to Attacking Power	-3

	PLAYER	LGE GOALS	DEF RATE	POWER	SCORE DIFF
1	Davide Moro	0	57	60	-3 mins
2	Ighli Vannucchi	4	54	65	-11 mins
3	Antonio Busce	4	57	72	-15 mins
4	Sergio Almiron	6	55	73	-18 mins

KEY PLAYERS - GOALSCORERS

Francesco Tavano

Goals in the League	19	Player Strike Rate Average number of minutes between League goals scored by player	150
Contribution to Attacking Power Average number of minutes between League team goals while on pitch	71	Club Strike Rate Average number of minutes between League goals scored by club	73

	PLAYER	LGE GOALS	POWER	STRIKE RATE
1	Francesco Tavano	19	71	150 mins
2	Sergio Almiron	6	73	514 mins
3	Ighli Vannucchi	4	65	584 mins
4	Christian Rigano	4	74	590 mins

Francesco Tavano

SQUAD APPEARANCES

Match	1	2	3	4	5	6	7	8	9	10	11	12	13	14	15	16	17	18	19	20	21	22	23	24	25	26	27	28	29	30	31	32	33	34	35	36	37	38
Venue	A	H	A	H	H	A	H	A	H	A	H	A	H	A	A	H	A	H	A	H	A	H	A	A	H	A	H	A	H	A	H	A	H	H	A	H	A	H
Competition	L	L	L	L	L	L	L	L	L	L	L	L	L	L	L	L	L	L	L	L	L	L	L	L	L	L	L	L	L	L	L	L	L	L	L	L	L	L
Result	L	L	L	W	W	D	W	W	L	D	W	L	L	L	L	D	L	L	L	D	L	L	L	W	L	L	D	L	W	W	W	D	W	W	L	W	W	L

Goalkeepers
Daniele Balli
Gianluca Berti
Christian Sebastian Cejas
Renato Dossena

Defenders
Nicola Ascoli
Andrea Coda
Stefano Lucchini
Francesco Pratali
Andrea Raggi
Claudio Sciannamè
Vittorio Tosto
Richard Vanigli

Midfielders
Sergio Almiron
Riccardo Bonetto
Antonio Busce
Daniele Buzzegoli
Fabrizio Ficini
Davide Moro
Ighli Vannucchi
Paolo Zanetti

Forwards
Mirco Gasparetto
Francesco Lodi
Giorgio Novello
Nicola Pozzi
Christian Rigano
Matteo Serafini
Francesco Tavano

KEY: On all match | On bench | Subbed or sent off (Counting game) | Subbed or sent off (playing less than 70 minutes) | Subbed on from bench (Counting Game) | Subbed on (playing less than 70 minutes) | Subbed on and then subbed or sent off (Counting Game) | Subbed on and then subbed or sent off (playing less than 70 minutes) | Not in 16

ASCOLI

Final Position: **12th**

NICKNAME: PICCHIO

KEY: ☐Won ☐Drawn ☐Lost

							Attendance
1	itpr1	**AC Milan**	H	D	1-1	Cudini 58	20,000
2	itpr1	**Lecce**	A	D	0-0		13,593
3	itpr1	**Juventus**	A	L	1-2	Cariello 32	27,293
4	itpr1	**Siena**	H	D	1-1	Ferrante 58	12,000
5	itpr1	**Livorno**	A	L	0-2		15,000
6	itpr1	**Parma**	H	W	3-1	Bjelanovic 28,78; Foggia 33	9,000
7	itpr1	**Sampdoria**	H	W	2-1	Tosto 45,79	12,000
8	itpr1	**Messina**	A	D	1-1	Comotto 90	15,000
9	itpr1	**Udinese**	H	D	1-1	Fini 18	11,750
10	itpr1	**Roma**	A	L	1-2	Domizzi 83	37,681
11	itpr1	**Fiorentina**	H	L	0-2		14,000
12	itpr1	**Chievo**	A	D	1-1	Comotto 43	5,113
13	itpr1	**Palermo**	H	D	1-1	Ferrante 52	12,000
14	itpr1	**Inter Milan**	A	L	0-1		46,122
15	itpr1	**Reggina**	H	D	1-1	Fini 60	9,000
16	itpr1	**Cagliari**	A	L	1-2	Biso 55	8,000
17	itpr1	**Treviso**	H	W	1-0	Quagliarella 10	7,000
18	itpr1	**Lazio**	A	L	1-4	Guana 14	23,000
19	itpr1	**Empoli**	H	W	3-1	Ferrante 36; Bjelanovic 69; Domizzi 78	8,000
20	itpr1	**AC Milan**	A	L	0-1		53,076
21	itpr1	**Lecce**	H	W	2-0	Ferrante 5; Bjelanovic 36	9,000
22	itpr1	**Juventus**	H	L	1-3	Ferrante 33	20,000
23	itpr1	**Siena**	A	D	1-1	Comotto 38	7,500
24	itpr1	**Livorno**	H	D	0-0		9,000
25	itpr1	**Parma**	A	D	0-0		12,854
26	itpr1	**Sampdoria**	A	W	2-1	Quagliarella 56; Budan 85	20,035
27	itpr1	**Messina**	H	W	1-0	Cariello 90	10,000
28	itpr1	**Udinese**	A	D	1-1	Domizzi 84 pen	15,000
29	itpr1	**Roma**	H	W	3-2	Quagliarella 20; Paci 24; Budan 42	20,000
30	itpr1	**Fiorentina**	A	L	1-3	Domizzi 43	31,112
31	itpr1	**Chievo**	H	D	2-2	Paci 45,62	13,219
32	itpr1	**Palermo**	A	D	1-1	Foggia 71	26,500
33	itpr1	**Inter Milan**	H	L	1-2	Ferrante 21	18,000
34	itpr1	**Reggina**	A	L	0-2		10,000
35	itpr1	**Cagliari**	H	D	2-2	Ferrante 18; Domizzi 78	12,500
36	itpr1	**Treviso**	A	D	2-2	Foggia 12,81	3,463
37	itpr1	**Lazio**	H	L	1-4	Ferrante 30	9,850
38	itpr1	**Empoli**	A	W	2-1	Budan 73,85	5,000

LEAGUE APPEARANCES, BOOKINGS AND CAPS

	AGE (on 01/07/06)	IN NAMED 18	APPEARANCES	COUNTING GAMES	MINUTES ON PITCH	YELLOW CARDS	RED CARDS	CAPS THIS SEASON	NATIONAL SIDE
Goalkeepers									
Alessandro Boccolini	21	13	1	0	11	0	0	-	Italy
Ferdinando Coppola	28	38	38	38	3409	0	0	-	Italy
Carlo Zotti	23	23	0	0	0	0	0	-	Italy
Defenders									
Daniele Adani	31	10	3	1	134	0	0	-	Italy
Francesco Carbone	26	25	11	6	632	0	0	-	Italy
Gianluca Comotto	27	33	31	31	2757	4	1	-	Italy
Ricardo Corallo	26	10	2	1	103	0	0	-	Italy
Mirko Cudini	32	14	11	8	778	0	1	-	
Christiano Del Grosso	23	32	30	24	2421	4	2	-	Italy
Maurizio Domizzi	26	35	34	34	3057	8	1	-	Italy
Maurizio Lauro	25	16	5	3	284	1	0	-	Italy
Massimo Paci	28	33	30	26	2546	6	0	-	Italy
Vittorio Tosto	32	16	14	10	1015	5	1	-	Italy
Midfielders									
Mattia Biso	29	11	9	4	507	2	0	-	Italy
Riccardo Bonetto	27	5	0	0	0	0	0	-	Italy
Alfredo Cariello	26	25	21	1	577	0	0	-	Italy
Nicolas Cordova	27	15	3	0	67	0	0	-	Chile
Domenico Cristiano	30	16	16	8	934	7	1	-	Italy
Ivano Della Morte	31	3	3	0	77	0	0	-	Italy
Michele Fini	32	36	36	32	3012	6	0	-	Italy
Pasquale Foggia	23	34	34	26	2569	4	0	-	Italy
Domenico Giampa	29	13	9	1	287	0	0	-	Italy
Roberto Guana	25	34	33	29	2680	10	1	-	Italy
Alessandro Moro	21	8	2	0	96	0	0	-	Italy
Davide Oresti	20	3	0	0	0	0	0	-	Italy
Andrea Parola	27	32	32	27	2646	7	0	-	Italy
Forwards									
Sasa Bjelanovic	27	34	29	21	2135	4	0	-	Croatia
Igor Budan	26	13	10	4	546	1	0	-	Croatia
Corrado Colombo	26	8	6	1	213	0	0	-	Italy
Marco Ferrante	35	33	28	12	1620	2	0	-	Italy
Fabio Quagliarella	32	34	33	17	1969	2	0	-	Italy
Nicola Zanini	32	11	6	1	244	1	0	-	Italy

TEAM OF THE SEASON

MONTHLY POINTS TALLY

AUGUST	1	33%
SEPTEMBER	2	17%
OCTOBER	8	53%
NOVEMBER	2	22%
DECEMBER	4	33%
JANUARY	6	40%
FEBRUARY	9	60%
MARCH	5	42%
APRIL	3	20%
MAY	3	50%

LEAGUE GOALS

	PLAYER	MINS	GOALS	S RATE
1	Ferrante	1620	**8**	203
2	Domizzi	3057	**5**	611
3	Foggia	2569	**4**	642
4	Bjelanovic	2135	**4**	534
5	Budan	546	**4**	137
6	Comotto	2757	**3**	919
7	Paci	2546	**3**	849
8	Quagliarella	1969	**3**	656
9	Fini	3012	**2**	1506
10	Tosto	1015	**2**	508
11	Cariello	577	**2**	289
12	Guana	2680	**1**	2680
13	Cudini	778	**1**	778
	Other		1	
	TOTAL		**43**	

TOP POINT EARNERS

	PLAYER	GAMES	AV PTS
1	Bjelanovic	21	**1.57**
2	Parola	27	**1.22**
3	Guana	29	**1.21**
4	Foggia	26	**1.19**
5	Comotto	31	**1.19**
6	Paci	26	**1.19**
7	Coppola	38	**1.13**
8	Domizzi	34	**1.09**
9	Fini	32	**1.03**
10	Del Grosso	24	**1.00**
	CLUB AVERAGE:		**1.13**

DISCIPLINARY RECORDS

	PLAYER	YELLOW	RED	AVE
1	Cristiano	7	1	**116**
2	Tosto	5	1	**169**
3	Guana	10	1	**243**
4	Biso	2	0	**253**
5	Domizzi	8	1	**339**
6	Parola	7	0	**378**
7	Del Grosso	4	2	**403**
8	Paci	6	0	**424**
9	Fini	6	0	**502**
10	Bjelanovic	4	0	**533**
11	Budan	1	0	**546**
12	Comotto	4	1	**551**
13	Foggia	4	0	**642**
	Other	4	1	
	TOTAL	**72**	**8**	

KEY GOALKEEPER

Ferdinando Coppola

Goals Conceded in the League	54	Counting Games League games when player was on pitch for at least 70 minutes	38
Defensive Rating Ave number of mins between League goals conceded while on the pitch	63	Clean Sheets In games when player was on pitch for at least 70 minutes	6

KEY PLAYERS - DEFENDERS

Christiano Del Grosso

Goals Conceded Number of League goals conceded while the player was on the pitch	34	Clean Sheets In League games when player was on pitch for at least 70 minutes	3
Defensive Rating Ave number of mins between League goals conceded while on the pitch	71	Club Defensive Rating Average number of mins between League goals conceded by the club this season	63

	PLAYER	CON LGE	CLEAN SHEETS	DEF RATE
1	Christiano Del Grosso	34	3	71 mins
2	Gianluca Comotto	40	5	69 mins
3	Massimo Paci	42	4	61 mins
4	Maurizio Domizzi	50	6	61 mins

KEY PLAYERS - MIDFIELDERS

Pasquale Foggia

Goals in the League	4	Contribution to Attacking Power Average number of minutes between League team goals while on pitch	73
Defensive Rating Average number of mins between League goals conceded while on the pitch	73	Scoring Difference Defensive Rating minus Contribution to Attacking Power	0

	PLAYER	LGE GOALS	DEF RATE	POWER	SCORE DIFF
1	Pasquale Foggia	4	73	73	0 mins
2	Roberto Guana	1	65	74	-9 mins
3	Andrea Parola	0	68	80	-12 mins
4	Michele Fini	2	61	81	-20 mins

KEY PLAYERS - GOALSCORERS

Marco Ferrante

Goals in the League	8	Player Strike Rate Average number of minutes between League goals scored by player	203
Contribution to Attacking Power Average number of minutes between League team goals while on pitch	85	Club Strike Rate Average number of minutes between League goals scored by club	80

	PLAYER	LGE GOALS	POWER	STRIKE RATE
1	Marco Ferrante	8	85	203 mins
2	Sasa Bjelanovic	4	74	534 mins
3	Maurizio Domizzi	5	83	611 mins
4	Pasquale Foggia	4	73	642 mins

Gianluca Comotto

Match	1	2	3	4	5	6	7	8	9	10	11	12	13	14	15	16	17	18	19	20	21	22	23	24	25	26	27	28	29	30	31	32	33	34	35	36	37	38
Venue	H	A	A	H	A	H	H	A	H	A	H	A	H	A	H	A	H	A	H	A	H	H	A	H	A	A	H	A	H	A	H	A	H	A	H	A	H	A
Competition	L	L	L	L	L	L	L	L	L	L	L	L	L	L	L	L	L	L	L	L	L	L	L	L	L	L	L	L	L	L	L	L	L	L	L	L	L	L
Result	D	D	L	D	L	W	W	D	D	L	L	D	D	L	D	L	W	L	W	L	W	L	D	D	D	W	W	D	W	L	D	D	L	L	D	D	L	W
Goalkeepers																																						
Alessandro Boccolini																																						
Ferdinando Coppola																																						
Carlo Zotti																																						
Defenders																																						
Daniele Adani																																						
Francesco Carbone																																						
Gianluca Comotto																																						
Ricardo Corallo																																						
Mirko Cudini																																						
Christiano Del Grosso																																						
Maurizio Domizzi																																						
Maurizio Lauro																																						
Massimo Paci																																						
Vittorio Tosto																																						
Midfielders																																						
Mattia Biso																																						
Riccardo Bonetto																																						
Alfredo Cariello																																						
Nicolas Andrea Cordova																																						
Domenico Cristiano																																						
Ivano Della Morte																																						
Michele Fini																																						
Pasquale Foggia																																						
Domenico Giampa																																						
Roberto Guana																																						
Alessandro Moro																																						
Davide Oresti																																						
Andrea Parola																																						
Forwards																																						
Sasa Bjelanovic																																						
Igor Budan																																						
Corrado Colombo																																						
Marco Ferrante																																						
Fabio Quagliarella																																						
Nicola Zanini																																						

KEY: ■ On all match ■ On bench ⏮ Subbed or sent off (Counting game) « Subbed or sent off (playing less than 70 minutes) ⏭ Subbed on from bench (Counting Game) » Subbed on (playing less than 70 minutes) ⏭ Subbed on and then subbed or sent off (Counting Game) » Subbed on and then subbed or sent off (playing less than 70 minutes) □ Not in 16

UDINESE

Final Position: **13th**

NICKNAME: ZEBRETTE

KEY: ☐Won ☐Drawn ☐Lost

No	Comp	Opponent	H/A	Res	Score	Scorers	Attendance
1	ecql1	Sp Lisbon	A	W	1-0	Iaquinta 29 pen	35,474
2	ecql2	Sp Lisbon	H	W	3-2	Iaquinta 23 pen; Natali 35; Barreto De Souza 90	30,000
3	itpr1	Empoli	H	W	1-0	Muntari 30	15,000
4	itpr1	Roma	A	W	1-0	Muntari 32	40,000
5	ecgpc	Panathinaikos	H	W	3-0	Iaquinta 28,73,76	25,000
6	itpr1	Fiorentina	A	L	2-4	Muntari 28; Iaquinta 90 pen	32,000
7	itpr1	Juventus	H	L	0-1		21,780
8	itpr1	Reggina	A	L	0-2		10,000
9	ecgpc	Barcelona	A	L	1-4	Felipe Dal Belo 24	65,000
10	itpr1	Lazio	H	W	3-0	Iaquinta 51 pen; Di Natale 79; Candela 90	17,000
11	itpr1	Siena	A	W	3-2	Di Michele 26,31,46	7,700
12	ecgpc	W Bremen	H	D	1-1	Di Natale 86	43,952
13	itpr1	Inter Milan	H	L	0-1		18,000
14	itpr1	Ascoli	A	D	1-1	Vidigal 88	11,750
15	itpr1	Palermo	H	D	0-0		16,000
16	ecgpc	W Bremen	A	L	3-4	Di Natale 54,57; Schulz 60 og	35,211
17	itpr1	AC Milan	A	L	1-5	Iaquinta 60	58,000
18	itpr1	Messina	H	W	1-0	Felipe Dal Belo 87	16,000
19	ecgpc	Panathinaikos	A	W	2-1	Iaquinta 81; Candela 83	35,000
20	itpr1	Parma	A	W	2-1	Barreto De Souza 45,48	12,471
21	itpr1	Livorno	H	L	0-2		16,000
22	ecgpc	Barcelona	H	L	0-2		38,500
23	itpr1	Lecce	H	L	1-2	Di Natale 90	15,000
24	itpr1	Chievo	A	L	0-2		6,000
25	itpr1	Sampdoria	H	W	2-0	Zapata 71; Castellini 80 og	16,000
26	itpr1	Cagliari	A	L	1-2	Sensini 23	7,000
27	itpr1	Treviso	H	D	2-2	Motta 13; Di Natale 72 pen	15,000
28	itpr1	Empoli	A	D	1-1	Felipe Dal Belo 55	5,500
29	itpr1	Roma	H	L	1-4	Di Natale 66	16,500
30	itpr1	Fiorentina	H	D	0-0		17,000
31	itpr1	Juventus	A	L	0-1		27,501
32	itpr1	Reggina	H	L	1-2	Iaquinta 15	15,000
33	itpr1	Lazio	A	D	1-1	Iaquinta 27	20,000
34	uc3rl1	Lens	H	W	3-0	Di Natale 36; Barreto De Souza 61,83	8,000
35	itpr1	Siena	H	L	1-2	Iaquinta 38 pen	15,500
36	uc3rl2	Lens	A	L	0-1		26,292
37	itpr1	Inter Milan	A	L	1-3	Iaquinta 83 pen	45,000
38	itpr1	Ascoli	H	D	1-1	Di Natale 77	15,000
39	uc4rl1	Levski Sofia	H	D	0-0		9,000
40	itpr1	Palermo	A	L	0-2		25,792
41	uc4rl2	Levski Sofia	A	L	1-2	Tissone 22,34	37,136
42	itpr1	AC Milan	H	L	0-4		20,000
43	itpr1	Messina	A	D	1-1	Obodo 38	36,000
44	itpr1	Parma	H	W	2-0	Di Natale 20; Felipe Dal Belo 52	15,500
45	itpr1	Livorno	A	W	2-0	Iaquinta 35; Natali 52	11,000
46	itpr1	Lecce	A	W	2-1	Barreto De Souza 25; Di Natale 59	10,476
47	itpr1	Chievo	H	D	1-1	Di Natale 77	15,000
48	itpr1	Sampdoria	A	D	1-1	Di Natale 57	20,644
49	itpr1	Cagliari	H	W	2-0	Iaquinta 15; Barreto De Souza 68	16,000
50	itpr1	Treviso	A	L	1-2	Pieri 15	4,000

LEAGUE APPEARANCES, BOOKINGS AND CAPS

	AGE (on 01/07/06)	IN NAMED 18	APPEARANCES	COUNTING GAMES	MINUTES ON PITCH	YELLOW CARDS	RED CARDS	CAPS THIS SEASON	NATIONAL SIDE
Goalkeepers									
Morgan De Sanctis	29	36	34	34	3060	1	0	7	Italy (13)
Gabriele Paoletti	28	34	4	4	360	1	0	-	Italy
Carlo Sciarrone	22	2	0	0	0	0	0	-	Italy
Defenders									
Valerio Bertotto	33	31	28	21	2062	4	0	-	Italy
Vincent Candela	32	28	26	23	2191	2	1	-	France
Rodrigo Defendi	20	2	2	1	143	0	0	-	Italy
Felipe Dal Belo	21	35	35	35	3150	7	0	-	Brazil
Teixeira Juarez	32	18	5	4	361	2	0	-	Brazil
Marco Motta	20	16	6	4	419	2	0	-	Italy
Cesare Natali	27	19	19	17	1604	4	0	-	Italy
Mirko Pieri	27	24	13	9	913	1	0	-	Italy
Nestor Sensini	33	20	14	14	1260	3	0	-	Argentina
Cristian Zapata	19	27	20	20	1794	5	1	-	Colombia
Midfielders									
Abel Enrique Aguilar	21	9	2	0	77	0	0	-	Colombia
Roberto Baronio	28	13	10	6	683	2	1	-	Italy
Flavio Lazzari	19	2	1	0	2	0	0	-	Italy
Salvatore Masiello	24	2	1	0	28	0	0	-	Italy
Stefano Mauri	26	19	16	9	1062	1	1	-	Italy
Piermario Morosini	20	11	5	0	134	0	0	-	Italy
Sulley Ali Muntari	21	29	29	21	2275	10	2	-	Ghana
Christian Obodo	22	28	28	22	2150	11	2	-	Nigeria
Giampiero Pinzi	25	13	13	8	799	4	2	-	Italy
Fernando Tissone	19	27	24	5	1074	4	0	-	Argentina
Jose Luis Vidigal	33	29	23	9	1286	5	0	-	Portugal
Damiano Zenoni	29	35	32	29	2744	5	0	-	Italy
Forwards									
Paulo Vitor De Souza	20	29	24	15	1543	3	0	-	Brazil
David Di Michele	30	16	15	9	973	1	0	-	Italy
Antonio Di Natale	28	36	35	24	2520	1	0	-	Italy
Vincenzo Iaquinta	26	24	24	18	1906	3	1	8	Italy (13)
Simone Pepe	22	11	5	1	187	0	0	-	Italy
Fausto Rossini	28	20	14	1	514	2	1	-	Italy

TEAM OF THE SEASON

G
Morgan De Sanctis
CG: 34 DR: 68

D
Cristian Eduardo Zapata
CG: 20 DR: 72

D
Cesare Natali
CG: 17 DR: 70

D
Valerio Bertotto
CG: 21 DR: 67

D
Vincent Candela
CG: 23 DR: 66

M
Christian Obodo
CG: 22 SD: 5

M
Sulley Ali Muntari
CG: 21 SD: -10

M
Damiano Zenoni
CG: 29 SD: -14

M
Stefano Mauri*
CG: 9 SD: -42

F
Vincenzo Iaquinta
CG: 18 SR: 212

F
Antonio Di Natale
CG: 24 SR: 252

MONTHLY POINTS TALLY

Month	Points	%
AUGUST	3	100%
SEPTEMBER	3	25%
OCTOBER	8	53%
NOVEMBER	6	67%
DECEMBER	3	25%
JANUARY	3	20%
FEBRUARY	1	7%
MARCH	2	17%
APRIL	11	73%
MAY	3	50%

LEAGUE GOALS

	PLAYER	MINS	GOALS	S RATE
1	Di Natale	2520	**10**	252
2	Iaquinta	1906	**9**	212
3	De Souza	1543	**4**	386
4	Muntari	2275	**3**	758
5	Felipe Dal Belo	3150	**3**	1050
6	Di Michele	973	**3**	324
7	Pieri	913	**1**	913
8	Zapata	1794	**1**	1794
9	Obodo	2150	**1**	2150
10	Sensini	1260	**1**	1260
11	Motta	419	**1**	419
12	Natali	1604	**1**	1604
13	Candela	2191	**1**	2191
	Other		2	
	TOTAL		**41**	

TOP POINT EARNERS

	PLAYER	GAMES	AV PTS
1	Obodo	22	**1.59**
2	Muntari	21	**1.48**
3	De Souza	15	**1.47**
4	Iaquinta	18	**1.39**
5	Zenoni	29	**1.28**
6	De Sanctis	34	**1.24**
7	Zapata	20	**1.20**
8	Natali	17	**1.18**
9	Felipe Dal Belo	35	**1.11**
10	Bertotto	21	**1.10**
	CLUB AVERAGE:		**1.13**

DISCIPLINARY RECORDS

	PLAYER	YELLOW	RED	AVE
1	Pinzi	4	2	**133**
2	Obodo	11	2	**165**
3	Rossini	2	1	**171**
4	Muntari	10	2	**189**
5	Baronio	2	1	**227**
6	Vidigal	5	0	**257**
7	Tissone	4	0	**268**
8	Zapata	5	1	**299**
9	Natali	4	0	**401**
10	Sensini	3	0	**420**
11	Felipe Dal Belo	7	0	**450**
12	Iaquinta	3	1	**476**
13	Barreto De Souza	3	0	**514**
	Other	16	2	
	TOTAL	**79**	**12**	

KEY GOALKEEPER

Morgan De Sanctis

Goals Conceded in the League	45	**Counting Games** League games when player was on pitch for at least 70 minutes	34
Defensive Rating Ave number of mins between League goals conceded while on the pitch	68	**Clean Sheets** In League games when player was on pitch for at least 70 minutes	9

KEY PLAYERS - GOALSCORERS

Vincenzo Iaquinta

Goals in the League	9	**Player Strike Rate** Average number of minutes between League goals scored by player	212
Contribution to Attacking Power Average number of minutes between League team goals while on pitch	73	**Club Strike Rate** Average number of minutes between League goals scored by club	83

	PLAYER	LGE GOALS	POWER	STRIKE RATE
1	Vincenzo Iaquinta	9	73	212 mins
2	Antonio Di Natale	10	74	252 mins
3	Paulo Vitor Barreto De Souza	4	73	386 mins
4	Sulley Ali Muntari	3	81	758 mins

KEY PLAYERS - DEFENDERS

Cristian Eduardo Zapata

Goals Conceded Number of League goals conceded while the player was on the pitch	25	**Clean Sheets** In League games when player was on pitch for at least 70 minutes	6
Defensive Rating Ave number of mins between League goals conceded while on the pitch	72	**Club Defensive Rating** Average number of mins between League goals conceded by the club this season	63

	PLAYER	CON LGE	CLEAN SHEETS	DEF RATE
1	Cristian Eduardo Zapata	25	6	72 mins
2	Cesare Natali	23	6	70 mins
3	Valerio Bertotto	31	5	67 mins
4	Vincent Candela	33	7	66 mins

Jose Luis Vidigal and Vincenzo Iaquinta

KEY PLAYERS - MIDFIELDERS

Christian Obodo

Goals in the League	1	**Contribution to Attacking Power** Average number of minutes between League team goals while on pitch	69
Defensive Rating Average number of mins between League goals conceded while on the pitch	74	**Scoring Difference** Defensive Rating minus Contribution to Attacking Power	5

	PLAYER	LGE GOALS	DEF RATE	POWER	SCORE DIFF
1	Christian Obodo	1	74	69	5 mins
2	Sulley Ali Muntari	3	71	81	-10 mins
3	Damiano Zenoni	0	64	78	-14 mins

SQUAD APPEARANCES

Match	1	2	3	4	5	6	7	8	9	10	11	12	13	14	15	16	17	18	19	20	21	22	23	24	25
Venue	A	H	H	A	H	A	H	A	A	H	A	H	H	A	H	A	A	H	A	A	H	H	H	A	H
Competition	C	C	L	L	C	L	L	L	C	L	L	C	L	L	L	C	L	L	C	L	L	C	L	L	L
Result	W	W	W	W	W	L	L	L	L	W	W	D	L	D	D	L	L	W	W	W	L	L	L	L	W

Match	26	27	28	29	30	31	32	33	34	35	36	37	38	39	40	41	42	43	44	45	46	47	48	49	50
Venue	A	H	A	H	H	A	H	A	H	H	A	A	H	H	A	A	H	A	H	A	A	H	A	H	A
Competition	L	L	L	L	L	L	L	L	E	L	E	L	L	E	L	E	L	L	L	L	L	L	L	L	L
Result	L	D	D	L	D	L	L	D	W	L	L	L	D	D	L	L	L	D	W	W	W	D	D	W	L

Goalkeepers
Morgan De Sanctis
Gabriele Paoletti
Carlo Sciarrone

Defenders
Valerio Bertotto
Vincent Candela
Rodrigo Defendi
Felipe Dal Belo
De Souza Teixeira Juarez
Marco Motta
Cesare Natali
Mirko Pieri
Emanuele Politti
M Rinaldi
Nestor Sensini
Cristian Eduardo Zapata

Midfielders
Abel Enrique Aguilar
Roberto Baronio
Flavio Lazzari
Stefano Mauri
Piermario Morosini
Sulley Ali Muntari
Christian Obodo
Giampiero Pinzi
Fernando Tissone
Jose Luis Vidigal
Damiano Zenoni

Forwards
Paulo Vitor De Souza
David Di Michele
Antonio Di Natale
Vincenzo Iaquinta
Simone Pepe
Fausto Rossini

KEY: On all match · On bench · Subbed or sent off (Counting game) · Subbed or sent off (playing less than 70 minutes) · Subbed on from bench (Counting Game) · Subbed on (playing less than 70 minutes) · Subbed on and then subbed or sent off (Counting Game) · Subbed on and then subbed or sent off (playing less than 70 minutes) · Not in 16

SAMPDORIA

Final Position: **14th**

KEY: ☐Won ☐Drawn ☐Lost

	Comp	Opponent	H/A	Res	Score	Scorers	Attendance
1	itpr1	Fiorentina	A	L	1-2	Diana 74	35,854
2	itpr1	Reggina	H	W	3-2	Bonazzoli 18; Volpi 57; Gasbarroni 85	21,000
3	uc1rl1	Setubal	A	D	1-1	Flachi 14	4,152
4	itpr1	AC Milan	H	W	2-1	Bonazzoli 38; Tonetto 58	28,000
5	itpr1	Treviso	A	W	2-0	Bonazzoli 45,48	5,000
6	itpr1	Chievo	H	L	1-2	Flachi 50	21,000
7	uc1rl2	Setubal	H	W	1-0	Gasbarroni 8	18,558
8	itpr1	Messina	A	W	4-1	Flachi 45; Bonazzoli 63,90; Borriello 75	22,000
9	itpr1	Ascoli	A	L	1-2	Bonazzoli 54	12,000
10	itpr1	Siena	H	D	3-3	Flachi 38 pen; Volpi 54,90 pen	21,000
11	itpr1	Juventus	A	L	0-2		29,977
12	itpr1	Inter Milan	H	D	2-2	Diana 6,35	27,500
13	ucgpc	St Bucharest	H	D	0-0		20,000
14	itpr1	Palermo	A	W	2-0	Gasbarroni 32; Bonazzoli 73	29,087
15	itpr1	Lazio	H	W	2-0	Diana 71; Flachi 73	22,500
16	ucgpc	Halmstad	A	W	3-1	Volpi 31; Diana 67,86; Bonazzoli 86	3,126
17	itpr1	Cagliari	A	L	0-2		8,000
18	ucgpc	Hertha Berlin	H	D	0-0		16,507
19	itpr1	Empoli	H	W	2-0	Borriello 78; Flachi 86	20,143
20	itpr1	Parma	A	D	1-1	Bonazzoli 84	14,242
21	ucgpc	Lens	A	L	1-2	Flachi 23	31,473
22	itpr1	Roma	H	D	1-1	Flachi 56	22,151
23	itpr1	Udinese	A	L	0-2		16,000
24	itpr1	Livorno	H	L	0-2		23,201
25	itpr1	Lecce	A	W	3-0	Diana 22,45; Bazzana 48	12,000
26	itpr1	Fiorentina	H	W	3-1	Palombo 11; Tonetto 24; Flachi 34	22,566
27	itpr1	Reggina	A	L	1-2	Kutuzov 45	12,900
28	itpr1	AC Milan	A	D	1-1	Gasbarroni 36	55,000
29	itpr1	Treviso	H	D	1-1	Kutuzov 30	20,000
30	itpr1	Chievo	A	D	1-1	Kutuzov 30	5,005
31	itpr1	Messina	H	W	4-2	Castellini 19; Volpi 69; Tonetto 80; Foti 90	20,500
32	itpr1	Ascoli	H	L	1-2	Volpi 71	20,035
33	itpr1	Siena	A	L	0-1		7,500
34	itpr1	Juventus	H	L	0-1		35,369
35	itpr1	Inter Milan	A	L	0-1		48,826
36	itpr1	Palermo	H	L	0-2		21,000
37	itpr1	Lazio	A	L	0-2		22,000
38	itpr1	Cagliari	H	D	1-1	Castellini 13	21,000
39	itpr1	Empoli	A	L	1-2	Flachi 60 pen	6,500
40	itpr1	Parma	H	L	1-2	Flachi 39	21,000
41	itpr1	Roma	A	D	0-0		40,000
42	itpr1	Udinese	H	D	1-1	Flachi 61	20,644
43	itpr1	Livorno	A	D	0-0		10,000
44	itpr1	Lecce	H	L	1-3	Flachi 90	21,000

LEAGUE APPEARANCES, BOOKINGS AND CAPS

	AGE (on 01/07/06)	IN NAMED 18	APPEARANCES	COUNTING GAMES	MINUTES ON PITCH	YELLOW CARDS	RED CARDS	CAPS THIS SEASON	NATIONAL SIDE
Goalkeepers									
Francesco Antonioli	36	38	36	36	3240	0	0	-	Italy
Luca Castellazzi	30	36	2	2	180	0	0	-	Italy
Defenders									
Luca Calzolaio	17	3	0	0	0	0	0	-	Italy
Marcello Castellini	33	34	33	32	2925	9	0	-	Italy
Guilio Falcone	32	19	14	12	1158	3	0	-	Italy
Mark Iuliano	32	6	4	3	275	3	1	-	Italy
Simone Pavan	32	32	16	13	1229	2	0	-	Italy
Marco Pisano	24	33	33	31	2791	5	0	-	Italy
Luigi Sala	32	31	23	21	1919	6	0	-	Italy
Marco Zamboni	28	11	1	0	31	0	0	-	Italy
Cristiano Zenoni	29	37	36	29	2875	4	0	-	Italy
Midfielders									
Samuele Dalla Bona	25	36	28	13	1517	1	0	-	Italy
Stefano Aimo Diana	28	30	29	22	2252	10	0	5	Italy (13)
Mark Edusei	29	1	1	0	66	0	0	1	Ghana (48)
Andrea Gasbarroni	24	30	28	8	1530	6	0	-	Italy
Mattia Marchesetti	22	15	8	0	95	0	0	-	Italy
Gionata Mingozzi	19	16	2	0	8	0	0	-	Italy
Angelo Palombo	24	31	31	27	2500	4	1	-	Italy
Max Tonetto	31	35	33	24	2551	4	0	-	Italy
Sergio Volpi	32	35	35	34	3121	9	0	-	Italy
Lamberto Zauli	34	11	8	2	385	1	0	-	Italy
Forwards									
Fabio Bazzani	29	7	6	4	372	2	0	-	Italy
Emiliano Bonazzoli	27	17	17	14	1344	1	0	-	Italy
Marco Borriello	24	17	11	0	282	1	0	-	Italy
Corrado Colombo	26	13	10	3	470	0	0	-	Italy
Francesco Flachi	31	34	33	27	2648	8	2	-	Italy
Salvatore Foti	17	21	12	1	291	0	0	-	Italy
Vitaly Kutuzov	26	34	29	7	1498	2	0	6	Belarus (76)
Danilo Soddimo	18	5	1	0	2	0	0	-	Italy

TEAM OF THE SEASON

MONTHLY POINTS TALLY

Month	Points	%
AUGUST	0	0%
SEPTEMBER	9	75%
OCTOBER	5	33%
NOVEMBER	6	67%
DECEMBER	5	42%
JANUARY	7	47%
FEBRUARY	5	33%
MARCH	0	0%
APRIL	3	20%
MAY	1	17%

LEAGUE GOALS

	PLAYER	MINS	GOALS	S RATE
1	Flachi	2648	11	241
2	Bonazzoli	1344	9	149
3	Diana	2252	6	375
4	Volpi	3121	5	624
5	Gasbarroni	1530	3	510
6	Tonetto	2551	3	850
7	Kutuzov	1498	3	499
8	Castellini	2925	2	1463
9	Borriello	282	2	141
10	Palombo	2500	1	2500
11	Bazzani	372	1	372
	Other		1	
	TOTAL		47	

TOP POINT EARNERS

	PLAYER	GAMES	AV PTS
1	Bonazzoli	14	1.79
2	Dalla Bona	13	1.46
3	Pavan	13	1.31
4	Volpi	34	1.18
5	Zenoni	29	1.14
6	Castellini	32	1.13
7	Antonioli	36	1.11
8	Pisano	31	1.10
9	Sala	21	1.05
10	Palombo	27	0.96
	CLUB AVERAGE:		1.08

DISCIPLINARY RECORDS

	PLAYER	YELLOW	RED	AVE
1	Diana	10	0	225
2	Gasbarroni	6	0	255
3	Flachi	8	2	264
4	Sala	6	0	319
5	Castellini	9	0	325
6	Volpi	9	0	346
7	Falcone	3	0	386
8	Palombo	4	1	500
9	Pisano	5	0	558
10	Pavan	2	0	614
11	Tonetto	4	0	637
12	Zenoni	4	0	718
13	Kutuzov	2	0	749
	Other	2	0	
	TOTAL	74	3	

KEY GOALKEEPER

Francesco Antonioli

Goals Conceded in the League	48	**Counting Games** League games when player was on pitch for at least 70 minutes	36
Defensive Rating Ave number of mins between League goals conceded while on the pitch	68	**Clean Sheets** In League games when player was on pitch for at least 70 minutes	6

KEY PLAYERS - DEFENDERS

Guilio Falcone

Goals Conceded Number of League goals conceded while the player was on the pitch	16	**Clean Sheets** In League games when player was on pitch for at least 70 minutes	3
Defensive Rating Ave number of mins between League goals conceded while on the pitch	72	**Club Defensive Rating** Average number of mins between League goals conceded by the club this season	67

	PLAYER	CON LGE	CLEAN SHEETS	DEF RATE
1	Guilio Falcone	16	3	72 mins
2	Luigi Sala	27	6	71 mins
3	Marco Pisano	40	6	70 mins
4	Cristiano Zenoni	43	5	67 mins

KEY PLAYERS - MIDFIELDERS

Samuele Dalla Bona

Goals in the League	0	**Contribution to Attacking Power** Average number of minutes between League team goals while on pitch	69
Defensive Rating Average number of mins between League goals conceded while on the pitch	72	**Scoring Difference** Defensive Rating minus Contribution to Attacking Power	3

	PLAYER	LGE GOALS	DEF RATE	POWER	SCORE DIFF
1	Samuele Dalla Bona	0	72	69	3 mins
2	Stefano Aimo Diana	6	63	63	0 mins
3	Sergio Volpi	5	69	71	-2 mins
4	Angelo Palombo	1	63	74	-11 mins

KEY PLAYERS - GOALSCORERS

Emiliano Bonazzoli

Goals in the League	9	**Player Strike Rate** Average number of minutes between League goals scored by player	149
Contribution to Attacking Power Average number of minutes between League team goals while on pitch	58	**Club Strike Rate** Average number of minutes between League goals scored by club	73

	PLAYER	LGE GOALS	POWER	STRIKE RATE
1	Emiliano Bonazzoli	9	58	149 mins
2	Francesco Flachi	11	72	241 mins
3	Stefano Aimo Diana	6	63	375 mins
4	Sergio Volpi	5	71	624 mins

Francesco Flachi

SQUAD APPEARANCES

Match	1	2	3	4	5	6	7	8	9	10	11	12	13	14	15	16	17	18	19	20	21	22	23	24	25	26	27	28	29	30	31	32	33	34	35	36	37	38	39	40	41	42	43	44
Venue	A	H	A	H	A	H	H	A	A	H	A	H	H	A	H	A	A	H	H	A	A	H	A	H	A	H	A	A	H	A	H	H	A	H	A	H	A	H	A	H	A	H	A	H
Competition	L	L	E	L	L	L	E	L	L	L	L	L	E	L	L	E	L	E	L	L	E	L	L	L	L	L	L	L	L	L	L	L	L	L	L	L	L	L	L	L	L	L	L	L
Result	L	W	D	W	W	L	W	W	L	D	L	D	D	W	W	W	L	D	W	D	L	D	L	L	W	W	L	D	D	D	W	L	L	L	L	L	L	D	L	L	D	D	D	L

Goalkeepers
Francesco Antonioli
Luca Castellazzi

Defenders
Luca Calzolaio
Marcello Castellini
Guilio Falcone
Mark Iuliano
Simone Pavan
Marco Pisano
Luigi Sala
Marco Zamboni
Cristiano Zenoni

Midfielders
Samuele Dalla Bona
Stefano Aimo Diana
Mark Edusei
Andrea Gasbarroni
Mattia Marchesetti
Gionata Mingozzi
Angelo Palombo
Max Tonetto
Sergio Volpi
Lamberto Zauli

Forwards
Fabio Bazzani
Emiliano Bonazzoli
Marco Borriello
Corrado Colombo
Francesco Flachi
Salvatore Foti
Vitaly Kutuzov
Danilo Soddimo

KEY: On all match | On bench | Subbed or sent off (Counting game) | Subbed or sent off (playing less than 70 minutes) | Subbed on from bench (Counting Game) | Subbed on (playing less than 70 minutes) | Subbed on and then subbed or sent off (Counting Game) | Subbed on and then subbed or sent off (playing less than 70 minutes) | Not in 16

REGGINA

Final Position: **15th**

KEY: ☐ Won ☐ Drawn ☐ Lost

		Opponent	Venue	Result	Score	Scorers	Attendance
1	itpr1	**Roma**	H	L	0-3		19,000
2	itpr1	**Sampdoria**	A	L	2-3	Cozza 28; Missiroli 90	21,000
3	itpr1	**Chievo**	H	L	1-3	Cozza 11	12,389
4	itpr1	**Palermo**	A	L	0-1		28,145
5	itpr1	**Udinese**	H	W	2-0	Cozza 43; Cavalli 76	10,000
6	itpr1	**AC Milan**	A	L	1-2	Cavalli 90	57,538
7	itpr1	**Lecce**	H	W	2-0	Tedesco 13; Cozza 52	10,000
8	itpr1	**Livorno**	A	L	0-1		15,000
9	itpr1	**Treviso**	H	L	1-2	Missiroli 86	12,000
10	itpr1	**Lazio**	H	W	1-0	Zauri 77 og	10,000
11	itpr1	**Empoli**	A	L	0-3		8,000
12	itpr1	**Cagliari**	H	W	3-1	Amoruso 2; Cozza 38 pen; Paredes 80	8,000
13	itpr1	**Siena**	A	D	0-0		7,000
14	itpr1	**Parma**	H	W	2-1	Cozza 9; De Rosa 21	10,000
15	itpr1	**Ascoli**	A	D	1-1	Paredes 88	9,000
16	itpr1	**Inter Milan**	H	L	0-4		23,850
17	itpr1	**Messina**	A	D	1-1	Cozza 86	27,000
18	itpr1	**Fiorentina**	H	D	1-1	Lucarelli, A 12	12,000
19	itpr1	**Juventus**	A	L	0-1		25,000
20	itpr1	**Roma**	A	L	1-3	Franceschini 90	32,000
21	itpr1	**Sampdoria**	H	W	2-1	Paredes 7; Amoruso 45	12,900
22	itpr1	**Chievo**	A	L	0-4		4,853
23	itpr1	**Palermo**	H	D	2-2	De Rosa 45; Paredes 90	13,000
24	itpr1	**Udinese**	A	W	2-1	Amoruso 40,61	15,000
25	itpr1	**AC Milan**	H	L	1-4	Paredes 10	13,000
26	itpr1	**Lecce**	A	D	0-0		12,634
27	itpr1	**Livorno**	H	D	1-1	Cozza 63	10,000
28	itpr1	**Treviso**	A	W	1-0	Amoruso 90	3,000
29	itpr1	**Lazio**	A	L	1-3	Amoruso 69	5,000
30	itpr1	**Empoli**	H	L	0-2		12,500
31	itpr1	**Cagliari**	A	W	2-0	Lucarelli, A 8; Tedesco 20	11,000
32	itpr1	**Siena**	H	D	1-1	Amoruso 51	8,000
33	itpr1	**Parma**	A	L	0-4		13,531
34	itpr1	**Ascoli**	H	W	2-0	De Rosa 10; Amoruso 27	10,000
35	itpr1	**Inter Milan**	A	L	0-4		40,000
36	itpr1	**Messina**	H	W	3-0	Cozza 51; Amoruso 58; Bianchi 76	20,000
37	itpr1	**Fiorentina**	A	L	2-5	Amoruso 81,84 pen	38,534
38	itpr1	**Juventus**	H	L	0-2		56,000

LEAGUE APPEARANCES, BOOKINGS AND CAPS

	AGE (on 01/07/06)	IN NAMED 18	APPEARANCES	COUNTING GAMES	MINUTES ON PITCH	YELLOW CARDS	RED CARDS	CAPS THIS SEASON	NATIONAL SIDE
Goalkeepers									
Nicola Pavarini	32	26	19	17	1554	1	0	-	Italy
Ivan Pelizzoli	25	23	20	19	1759	1	0	-	Italy
Antonino Saviano	22	25	2	1	107	0	0	-	Italy
Defenders									
Jacopo Balestri	31	1	1	1	90	0	0	-	Italy
Juriy Cannarsa	30	12	7	5	573	2	0	-	Italy
Ivan Castiglia	18	4	2	1	110	1	0	-	
Gaetano De Rosa	32	35	35	32	3001	7	0	-	Italy
Ivan Franceschini	29	31	30	26	2479	8	2	-	Italy
Giosa	22	15	6	4	397	2	0	-	Italy
Maurizio Lanzaro	24	31	20	17	1621	2	0	-	Italy
Maurizio Lauro	25	10	5	2	212	2	0	-	Italy
Alessandro Lucarelli	28	33	32	31	2763	6	0	-	Italy
Francesco Modesto	24	38	36	28	2836	2	0	-	Italy
Gaetano Ungaro	18	6	1	0	14	0	0	-	Italy
Midfielders									
Davide Biondini	23	36	27	16	1736	8	1	-	Italy
Filippo Carrobbio	26	36	19	6	722	1	0	-	Italy
Francesco Cozza	32	32	32	25	2561	9	0	-	Italy
Giandomenico Mesto	24	35	35	34	3080	5	2	-	Italy
Carlos Paredes	29	28	28	24	2334	3	2	-	Paraguay
Giacomo Tedesco	30	9	9	8	772	5	0	-	Italy
Giovanni Tedesco	34	18	17	17	1493	7	2	-	Italy
Luca Vigiani	29	37	35	22	2565	6	0	-	Italy
Alessandro Zoppetti	27	1	1	1	70	0	0	-	Italy
Forwards									
Nicola Amoruso	31	31	29	22	2212	3	0	-	Italy
Rolando Bianchi	23	9	9	3	362	0	0	-	Italy
Simone Cavalli	27	17	13	6	706	0	0	-	Italy
Fabio Ceravolo	19	12	5	0	66	0	0	-	Italy
Lambros Choutos	26	15	9	1	233	0	0	-	Greece
Simone Missiroli	20	37	26	6	868	2	0	-	Italy
Luca Rigoni	21	19	4	1	182	1	0	-	Italy

TEAM OF THE SEASON

G — Nicola Pavarini, CG: 17 DR: 74

D — Maurizio Lanzaro, CG: 17 DR: 62

D — Alessandro Lucarelli, CG: 31 DR: 56

D — Gaetano De Rosa, CG: 32 DR: 55

D — Ivan Franceschini, CG: 26 DR: 53

M — Davide Biondini, CG: 16 SD: -23

M — Carlos Paredes, CG: 24 SD: -26

M — Luca Vigiani, CG: 22 SD: -27

M — Giovanni Tedesco, CG: 17 SD: -30

F — Nicola Amoruso, CG: 22 SR: 201

F — Francesco Cozza, CG: 25 SR: 285

MONTHLY POINTS TALLY

Month	Points	%
AUGUST	0	0%
SEPTEMBER	3	25%
OCTOBER	6	40%
NOVEMBER	4	44%
DECEMBER	5	42%
JANUARY	4	27%
FEBRUARY	6	40%
MARCH	6	50%
APRIL	7	47%
MAY	0	0%

LEAGUE GOALS

	PLAYER	MINS	GOALS	S RATE
1	Amoruso	2212	11	201
2	Cozza	2561	9	285
3	Paredes	2334	5	467
4	De Rosa	3001	3	1000
5	Missiroli	868	2	434
6	Cavalli	706	2	353
7	Lucarelli, A	2763	2	1382
8	Tedesco	772	1	772
9	Franceschini	2479	1	2479
10	Bianchi	362	1	362
11	Tedesco	1493	1	1493
	Other		1	
	TOTAL		39	

TOP POINT EARNERS

	PLAYER	GAMES	AV PTS
1	Amoruso	22	1.41
2	Paredes	24	1.38
3	Biondini	16	1.31
4	Vigiani	22	1.27
5	De Rosa	32	1.19
6	Modesto	28	1.14
7	Lucarelli, A	31	1.13
8	Mesto	34	1.12
9	Lanzaro	17	1.12
10	Pavarini	17	1.06
	CLUB AVERAGE:		1.08

DISCIPLINARY RECORDS

	PLAYER	YELLOW	RED	AVE
1	Giovanni Tedesco	5	0	154
2	Giacomo Tedesco	7	2	165
3	Biondini	8	1	192
4	Franceschini	8	2	247
5	Cozza	9	0	284
6	Cannarsa	2	0	286
7	Vigiani	6	0	427
8	De Rosa	7	0	428
9	Missiroli	2	0	434
10	Mesto	5	2	440
11	Lucarelli, A	6	0	460
12	Paredes	3	2	466
13	Carrobbio	1	0	722
	Other	9	0	
	TOTAL	78	9	

KEY GOALKEEPER

Nicola Pavarini

Goals Conceded in the League	21	Counting Games League games when player was on pitch for at least 70 minutes	17
Defensive Rating Ave number of mins between League goals conceded while on the pitch	74	Clean Sheets In League games when player was on pitch for at least 70 minutes	5

KEY PLAYERS - DEFENDERS

Maurizio Lanzaro

Goals Conceded Number of League goals conceded while the player was on the pitch	26	Clean Sheets In League games when player was on pitch for at least 70 minutes	5
Defensive Rating Ave number of mins between League goals conceded while on the pitch	62	Club Defensive Rating Average number of mins between League goals conceded by the club this season	53

	PLAYER	CON LGE	CLEAN SHEETS	DEF RATE
1	Maurizio Lanzaro	26	5	62 mins
2	Alessandro Lucarelli	49	7	56 mins
3	Gaetano De Rosa	55	8	55 mins
4	Ivan Franceschini	47	5	53 mins

KEY PLAYERS - MIDFIELDERS

Davide Biondini

Goals in the League	0	Contribution to Attacking Power Average number of minutes between League team goals while on pitch	79
Defensive Rating Average number of mins between League goals conceded while on the pitch	56	Scoring Difference Defensive Rating minus Contribution to Attacking Power	-23

	PLAYER	LGE GOALS	DEF RATE	POWER	SCORE DIFF
1	Davide Biondini	0	56	79	-23 mins
2	Carlos Humberto Paredes	5	60	86	-26 mins
3	Luca Vigiani	0	53	80	-27 mins
4	Francesco Cozza	9	61	91	-30 mins

KEY PLAYERS - GOALSCORERS

Nicola Amoruso

Goals in the League	11	Player Strike Rate Average number of minutes between League goals scored by player	201
Contribution to Attacking Power Average number of minutes between League team goals while on pitch	76	Club Strike Rate Average number of minutes between League goals scored by club	88

	PLAYER	LGE GOALS	POWER	STRIKE RATE
1	Nicola Amoruso	11	76	201 mins
2	Francesco Cozza	9	91	285 mins
3	Carlos Humberto Paredes	5	86	467 mins
4	Gaetano De Rosa	3	91	1000 mins

Nicola Amoruso

SQUAD APPEARANCES

Match	1	2	3	4	5	6	7	8	9	10	11	12	13	14	15	16	17	18	19	20	21	22	23	24	25	26	27	28	29	30	31	32	33	34	35	36	37	38
Venue	H	A	H	A	H	A	H	A	H	H	A	H	A	H	A	H	A	H	A	A	H	A	H	A	H	A	H	A	A	H	A	H	A	H	A	H	A	H
Competition	L	L	L	L	L	L	L	L	L	L	L	L	L	L	L	L	L	L	L	L	L	L	L	L	L	L	L	L	L	L	L	L	L	L	L	L	L	L
Result	L	L	L	L	W	L	W	L	L	W	L	W	D	W	D	L	D	D	L	L	W	L	D	W	L	D	D	W	L	L	W	D	L	W	L	W	L	L

Goalkeepers
Nicola Pavarini
Ivan Pelizzoli
Antonino Saviano

Defenders
Jacopo Balestri
Juriy Cannarsa
Ivan Castiglia
Gaetano De Rosa
Ivan Franceschini
Giosa
Maurizio Lanzaro
Maurizio Lauro
Alessandro Lucarelli
Francesco Modesto
Gaetano Ungaro

Midfielders
Davide Biondini
Filippo Carrobbio
Francesco Cozza
Giandomenico Mesto
Carlos Humberto Paredes
Giovanni Tedesco
Giacomo Tedesco
Luca Vigiani
Alessandro Zoppetti

Forwards
Nicola Amoruso
Rolando Bianchi
Simone Cavalli
Fabio Ceravolo
Lambros Choutos
Simone Missiroli
Luca Rigoni

KEY: ■ On all match ■ On bench ⏮ Subbed or sent off (Counting game) « Subbed or sent off (playing less than 70 minutes) ⏭ Subbed on from bench (Counting Game) » Subbed on (playing less than 70 minutes) Subbed on and then subbed or sent off (Counting Game) Subbed on and then subbed or sent off (playing less than 70 minutes) □ Not in 16

CAGLIARI

Final Position: **16th**

NICKNAME: ISOLANI

KEY: ☐Won ☐Drawn ☐Lost

							Attendance
1	itpr1	Siena	A	L	1-2	Esposito 10	11,000
2	itpr1	Lazio	H	D	1-1	Suazo 1	10,000
3	itpr1	Messina	H	D	1-1	Suazo 41	12,909
4	itpr1	Empoli	A	L	1-3	Capone 33	9,700
5	itpr1	Roma	H	D	0-0		12,550
6	itpr1	Lecce	A	L	0-3		11,804
7	itpr1	AC Milan	H	L	0-2		18,000
8	itpr1	Chievo	A	L	1-2	Suazo 90	10,009
9	itpr1	Livorno	H	D	1-1	Suazo 51 pen	14,000
10	itpr1	Fiorentina	A	L	1-2	Suazo 23	30,000
11	itpr1	Treviso	H	D	0-0		11,000
12	itpr1	Reggina	A	L	1-3	Abeijon 66	8,000
13	itpr1	Sampdoria	H	W	2-0	Suazo 21,52	8,000
14	itpr1	Palermo	A	D	2-2	Conti 64; Bega 88	26,209
15	itpr1	Juventus	A	L	0-4		27,587
16	itpr1	Ascoli	H	W	2-1	Del Grosso 9 og; Suazo 26 pen	8,000
17	itpr1	Parma	A	L	0-1		11,677
18	itpr1	Udinese	H	W	2-1	Sensini 38 og; Langella 86	7,000
19	itpr1	Inter Milan	A	L	2-3	Esposito 20; Suazo 81	48,000
20	itpr1	Siena	H	W	1-0	Suazo 90	19,800
21	itpr1	Lazio	A	D	1-1	Gobbi 69	26,000
22	itpr1	Messina	A	L	0-1		30,000
23	itpr1	Empoli	H	W	4-1	Abeijon 2; Esposito 19,62; Suazo 37	10,000
24	itpr1	Roma	A	L	3-4	Suazo 12; Langella 19; Conti 55	62,000
25	itpr1	Lecce	H	D	0-0		12,000
26	itpr1	AC Milan	A	L	0-1		55,000
27	itpr1	Chievo	H	D	2-2	Suazo 32; Gobbi 90	10,000
28	itpr1	Livorno	A	W	1-0	Suazo 77	12,000
29	itpr1	Treviso	A	W	2-1	Esposito 10; Suazo 76 pen	3,000
30	itpr1	Fiorentina	H	D	0-0		10,000
31	itpr1	Reggina	H	L	0-2		11,000
32	itpr1	Sampdoria	A	D	1-1	Suazo 67	21,000
33	itpr1	Palermo	H	D	1-1	Suazo 45	12,000
34	itpr1	Juventus	H	D	1-1	Suazo 45	20,000
35	itpr1	Ascoli	A	D	2-2	Suazo 53,74	12,500
36	itpr1	Parma	H	W	3-1	Capone 11; Suazo 31; Esposito 63	15,000
37	itpr1	Udinese	A	L	0-2		16,000
38	itpr1	Inter Milan	H	D	2-2	Capone 8; Suazo 33	15,000

LEAGUE APPEARANCES, BOOKINGS AND CAPS

	AGE (on 01/07/06)	IN NAMED 18	APPEARANCES	COUNTING GAMES	MINUTES ON PITCH	YELLOW CARDS	RED CARDS	CAPS THIS SEASON	NATIONAL SIDE
Goalkeepers									
Andrea Campagnolo	28	34	11	9	875	0	0	-	Italy
Fabian Carini	26	11	11	9	910	0	0	-	Uruguay
Antonio Chimenti	36	21	21	21	1870	1	0	-	Italy
Luca Tomasig	22	12	0	0	0	0	0	-	Italy
Defenders									
Alessandro Agostini	26	36	34	28	2643	3	0	-	Italy
Francesco Bega	31	31	30	25	2467	12	2	-	Italy
Joe Bizera	26	24	16	13	1279	6	1	-	Uruguay
Michele Canini	21	31	29	27	2496	4	1	-	Italy
Michele Ferri	25	16	16	12	1275	2	0	-	Italy
Diego Luis Lopez	31	25	22	17	1771	6	1	-	Uruguay
Francesco Pisano	20	34	22	13	1337	2	0	-	Italy
Fabio Vignati	22	24	1	1	90	0	0	-	Italy
Midfielders									
Nelson Abeijon	32	29	28	19	1986	10	0	-	Uruguay
Alessandro Budel	25	37	28	13	1662	3	0	-	Italy
Daniele Conti	27	30	30	24	2432	14	1	-	Italy
Alessandro Conticchio	32	35	26	9	1226	3	0	-	Italy
Mauro Esposito	27	38	38	35	3265	3	0	1	Italy (13)
Claudio Ferarese	27	13	3	0	67	0	0	-	Italy
Massimo Gobbi	25	35	35	31	2932	6	1	-	Italy
Claudio Pani	20	13	1	0	12	0	0	-	Italy
Forwards									
Andrea Capone	25	37	27	5	1173	3	0	-	Italy
Andrea Cocco	20	17	4	0	138	0	0	-	Italy
Andrea Cossu	26	35	21	2	728	0	0	-	Italy
Antonio Langella	29	25	24	11	1496	6	1	-	Italy
David Suazo	26	37	37	36	3258	3	0	-	Honduras

TEAM OF THE SEASON

MONTHLY POINTS TALLY

AUGUST	0	0%
SEPTEMBER	3	25%
OCTOBER	1	7%
NOVEMBER	4	44%
DECEMBER	4	33%
JANUARY	7	47%
FEBRUARY	5	33%
MARCH	7	58%
APRIL	7	47%
MAY	1	17%

LEAGUE GOALS

	PLAYER	MINS	GOALS	S RATE
1	Suazo	3258	22	148
2	Esposito	3265	6	544
3	Capone	1173	3	391
4	Gobbi	2932	2	1466
5	Langella	1496	2	748
6	Abeijon	1986	2	993
7	Conti	2432	2	1216
8	Bega	2467	1	2467
	Other		2	
	TOTAL		42	

TOP POINT EARNERS

	PLAYER	GAMES	AV PTS
1	Bizera	13	1.38
2	Abeijon	19	1.37
3	Chimenti	21	1.29
4	Conti	24	1.13
5	Suazo	36	1.08
6	Pisano	13	1.08
7	Ferri	12	1.08
8	Esposito	35	1.03
9	Bega	25	1.00
10	Lopez	17	1.00
	CLUB AVERAGE:		1.03

DISCIPLINARY RECORDS

	PLAYER	YELLOW	RED	AVE
1	Conti	14	1	162
2	Bega	12	2	176
3	Bizera	6	1	182
4	Abeijon	10	0	198
5	Langella	6	1	213
6	Lopez	6	1	253
7	Capone	3	0	391
8	Conticchio	3	0	408
9	Gobbi	6	1	418
10	Canini	4	1	499
11	Budel	3	0	554
12	Ferri	2	0	637
13	Pisano	2	0	668
	Other	10	0	
	TOTAL	87	8	

KEY GOALKEEPER

Antonio Chimenti

Goals Conceded in the League	26	**Counting Games** League games when player was on pitch for at least 70 minutes	21
Defensive Rating Ave number of mins between League goals conceded while on the pitch	72	**Clean Sheets** In League games when player was on pitch for at least 70 minutes	4

KEY PLAYERS - DEFENDERS

Francesco Pisano

Goals Conceded Number of League goals conceded while the player was on the pitch	16	**Clean Sheets** In League games when player was on pitch for at least 70 minutes	3
Defensive Rating Ave number of mins between League goals conceded while on the pitch	84	**Club Defensive Rating** Average number of mins between League goals conceded by the club this season	62

	PLAYER	CON LGE	CLEAN SHEETS	DEF RATE
1	Francesco Pisano	16	3	84 mins
2	Francesco Bega	36	6	69 mins
3	Michele Ferri	20	3	64 mins
4	Michele Canini	41	4	61 mins

KEY PLAYERS - MIDFIELDERS

Daniele Conti

Goals in the League	2	**Contribution to Attacking Power** Average number of minutes between League team goals while on pitch	68
Defensive Rating Average number of mins between League goals conceded while on the pitch	59	**Scoring Difference** Defensive Rating minus Contribution to Attacking Power	-9

	PLAYER	LGE GOALS	DEF RATE	POWER	SCORE DIFF
1	Daniele Conti	2	59	68	-9 mins
2	Nelson Abeijon	2	66	76	-10 mins
3	Mauro Esposito	6	64	86	-22 mins
4	Massimo Gobbi	2	57	84	-27 mins

KEY PLAYERS - GOALSCORERS

David Suazo

Goals in the League	22	**Player Strike Rate** Average number of minutes between League goals scored by player	148
Contribution to Attacking Power Average number of minutes between League team goals while on pitch	79	**Club Strike Rate** Average number of minutes between League goals scored by club	81

	PLAYER	LGE GOALS	POWER	STRIKE RATE
1	David Suazo	22	79	148 mins
2	Mauro Esposito	6	86	544 mins
3	Nelson Abeijon	2	76	993 mins
4	Daniele Conti	2	68	1216 mins

Antonio Chimenti

SQUAD APPEARANCES

Match	1	2	3	4	5	6	7	8	9	10	11	12	13	14	15	16	17	18	19	20	21	22	23	24	25	26	27	28	29	30	31	32	33	34	35	36	37	38
Venue	A	H	H	A	H	A	H	A	H	A	H	A	H	A	A	H	A	H	A	H	A	A	H	A	H	A	H	A	A	H	H	A	H	H	A	H	A	H
Competition	L	L	L	L	L	L	L	L	L	L	L	L	L	L	L	L	L	L	L	L	L	L	L	L	L	L	L	L	L	L	L	L	L	L	L	L	L	L
Result	L	D	D	L	D	L	L	L	D	L	D	L	W	D	L	W	L	W	L	W	D	L	W	L	D	L	D	W	W	D	L	D	D	D	D	W	L	D

Goalkeepers
Andrea Campagnolo
Fabian Carini
Antonio Chimenti
Luca Tomasig

Defenders
Alessandro Agostini
Francesco Bega
Joe Bizera
Michele Canini
Michele Ferri
Diego Luis Lopez
Francesco Pisano
Fabio Vignati

Midfielders
Nelson Abeijon
Alessandro Budel
Daniele Conti
Alessandro Conticchio
Mauro Esposito
Claudio Ferarese
Massimo Gobbi
Claudio Pani

Forwards
Andrea Capone
Andrea Cocco
Andrea Cossu
Antonio Langella
David Suazo

KEY: On all match; On bench; Subbed or sent off (Counting game); Subbed or sent off (playing less than 70 minutes); Subbed on from bench (Counting Game); Subbed on (playing less than 70 minutes); Subbed on and then subbed or sent off (Counting Game); Subbed on and then subbed or sent off (playing less than 70 minutes); Not in 16

SIENA

Final Position: **17th**

KEY: Won / Drawn / Lost

							Attendance
1	itpr1	**Cagliari**	H	W	2-1	Chiesa 45 pen,58	11,000
2	itpr1	**AC Milan**	A	L	1-3	Tudor 44	56,343
3	itpr1	**Palermo**	H	L	1-2	Legrottaglie 22	7,500
4	itpr1	**Ascoli**	A	D	1-1	Bogdani 45	12,000
5	itpr1	**Messina**	H	W	4-2	Locatelli 10,46; Chiesa 28,41	7,500
6	itpr1	**Roma**	A	W	3-2	Negro 17; Chiesa 54; Colonnese 90	33,000
7	itpr1	**Udinese**	H	L	2-3	Chiesa 53; Bertotto 67 og	7,700
8	itpr1	**Sampdoria**	A	D	3-3	Locatelli 48; Chiesa 70 pen; Vergassola 82	21,000
9	itpr1	**Fiorentina**	H	L	0-2		15,000
10	itpr1	**Treviso**	A	W	1-0	Chiesa 45	9,435
11	itpr1	**Chievo**	H	L	0-1		11,909
12	itpr1	**Lecce**	A	L	0-3		11,729
13	itpr1	**Reggina**	H	D	0-0		7,000
14	itpr1	**Lazio**	A	L	2-3	Bogdani 52; Peruzzi 90 og	25,000
15	itpr1	**Empoli**	H	W	1-0	Bogdani 2	7,500
16	itpr1	**Parma**	H	D	2-2	Locatelli 52; Chiesa 77	9,500
17	itpr1	**Juventus**	A	L	0-2		25,587
18	itpr1	**Inter Milan**	H	D	0-0		15,000
19	itpr1	**Livorno**	A	D	2-2	Locatelli 8; Chiesa 59 pen	15,000
20	itpr1	**Cagliari**	A	L	0-1		19,800
21	itpr1	**AC Milan**	H	L	0-3		13,500
22	itpr1	**Palermo**	A	W	3-1	Bogdani 29,57,66	27,428
23	itpr1	**Ascoli**	H	D	1-1	Bogdani 50	7,500
24	itpr1	**Messina**	A	D	0-0		16,000
25	itpr1	**Roma**	H	L	0-2		14,000
26	itpr1	**Udinese**	A	W	2-1	Volpato 34,39	15,500
27	itpr1	**Sampdoria**	H	W	1-0	Vergassola 80	7,500
28	itpr1	**Fiorentina**	A	L	1-2	Vergassola 14	31,200
29	itpr1	**Treviso**	H	W	1-0	Bogdani 86	7,500
30	itpr1	**Chievo**	A	L	1-4	Foglio 29	5,313
31	itpr1	**Lecce**	H	L	1-2	Bogdani 85	7,000
32	itpr1	**Reggina**	A	D	1-1	Bogdani 21	8,000
33	itpr1	**Lazio**	H	L	2-3	Vergassola 24; Chiesa 40	9,000
34	itpr1	**Empoli**	A	L	1-2	Bogdani 87	6,000
35	itpr1	**Parma**	A	D	1-1	Guzman 23	15,000
36	itpr1	**Juventus**	H	L	0-3		15,000
37	itpr1	**Inter Milan**	A	D	1-1	Gastaldello 90	38,000
38	itpr1	**Livorno**	H	D	0-0		7,000

LEAGUE APPEARANCES, BOOKINGS AND CAPS

	AGE (on 01/07/06)	IN NAMED 18	APPEARANCES	COUNTING GAMES	MINUTES ON PITCH	YELLOW CARDS	RED CARDS	CAPS THIS SEASON	NATIONAL SIDE
Goalkeepers									
Marco Fortin	32	36	12	12	1080	0	0	-	Italy
Antonio Mirante	22	33	26	26	2340	1	0	-	Italy
Davide Zomer	28	4	0	0	0	0	0	-	Italy
Defenders									
Alberto	31	35	32	21	2201	9	0	-	Brazil
Francesco Colonnese	34	26	14	5	601	0	1	-	Italy
Gianluca Falsini	30	27	24	14	1572	8	1	-	Italy
Paolo Foglio	30	29	20	13	1383	6	0	-	Italy
Daniele Gastaldello	23	30	24	14	1538	9	0	-	Italy
Nicola Legrottaglie	29	34	29	26	2487	7	0	-	Italy
Michele Mignani	34	7	3	2	183	2	0	-	Italy
Cristian Molinaro	22	26	19	10	1075	3	0	-	Italy
Paolo Negro	34	33	30	25	2365	4	0	-	Italy
Daniele Portanova	27	36	28	25	2389	3	0	-	Italy
Igor Tudor	28	27	26	20	1967	8	1	6	Croatia (23)
Midfielders									
Jonathan Bachini	31	7	3	0	76	0	0	-	Italy
Francesco Cozza	32	1	1	1	77	0	0	-	Italy
Roberto D'aversa	30	26	26	24	2197	6	1	-	Italy
Gennaro Esposito	21	2	1	0	2	0	0	-	Italy
Tomas Locatelli	30	28	27	19	1936	1	0	-	Italy
Massimo Marrazina	31	11	8	0	225	0	0	-	Italy
Ricardo Packer	19	6	2	0	10	0	0	-	Brazil
Matteo Paro	23	34	29	22	2206	5	1	-	Italy
Simone Vergassola	30	33	33	32	2938	6	1	-	Italy
Forwards									
Erjon Bogdani	29	34	34	29	2795	3	0	-	Albania
Enrico Chiesa	35	38	38	27	2758	2	0	-	Italy
Tomas Guzman	24	18	10	1	272	0	0	-	Paraguay
Roberto Nanni	24	18	8	0	250	1	0	-	Argentina
Rey Volpato	19	26	13	2	401	1	0	-	Italy

TEAM OF THE SEASON

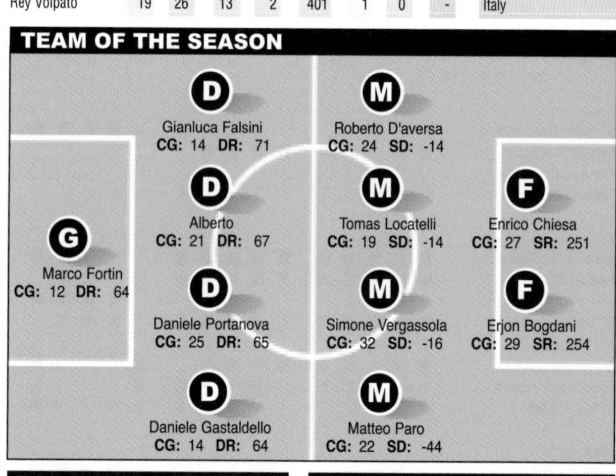

MONTHLY POINTS TALLY

AUGUST	3	100%
SEPTEMBER	4	33%
OCTOBER	7	47%
NOVEMBER	1	11%
DECEMBER	4	33%
JANUARY	5	33%
FEBRUARY	8	53%
MARCH	3	25%
APRIL	2	13%
MAY	2	33%

LEAGUE GOALS

	PLAYER	MINS	GOALS	S RATE
1	Bogdani	2795	**11**	254
2	Chiesa	2758	**11**	251
3	Locatelli	1936	**5**	387
4	Vergassola	2938	**4**	735
5	Volpato	401	**2**	201
6	Guzman	272	**1**	272
7	Gastaldello	1538	**1**	1538
8	Legrottaglie	2487	**1**	2487
9	Tudor	1967	**1**	1967
10	Colonnese	601	**1**	601
11	Foglio	1383	**1**	1383
12	Negro	2365	**1**	2365
	Other		**2**	
	TOTAL		**42**	

TOP POINT EARNERS

	PLAYER	GAMES	AV PTS
1	Falsini	14	**1.36**
2	D'aversa	24	**1.29**
3	Fortin	12	**1.25**
4	Locatelli	19	**1.11**
5	Vergassola	32	**1.09**
6	Legrottaglie	26	**1.08**
7	Portanova	25	**1.08**
8	Gastaldello	14	**1.07**
9	Alberto	21	**1.00**
10	Negro	25	**0.96**
	CLUB AVERAGE:		**1.03**

DISCIPLINARY RECORDS

	PLAYER	YELLOW	RED	AVE
1	Gastaldello	9	0	**170**
2	Falsini	8	1	**174**
3	Tudor	8	1	**218**
4	Foglio	6	0	**230**
5	Alberto	9	0	**244**
6	D'aversa	6	1	**313**
7	Legrottaglie	7	0	**355**
8	Molinaro	3	0	**358**
9	Paro	5	1	**367**
10	Vergassola	6	1	**419**
11	Negro	4	0	**591**
12	Colonnese	0	1	**601**
13	Portanova	3	0	**796**
	Other	7	0	
	TOTAL	**81**	**6**	

KEY GOALKEEPER

Marco Fortin

Goals Conceded in the League	17	Counting Games League games when player was on pitch for at least 70 minutes	12
Defensive Rating Ave number of mins between League goals conceded while on the pitch	64	Clean Sheets In League games when player was on pitch for at least 70 minutes	3

KEY PLAYERS - DEFENDERS

Gianluca Falsini

Goals Conceded Number of League goals conceded while the player was on the pitch	22	Clean Sheets In League games when player was on pitch for at least 70 minutes	4
Defensive Rating Ave number of mins between League goals conceded while on the pitch	71	Club Defensive Rating Average number of mins between League goals conceded by the club this season	57

	PLAYER	CON LGE	CLEAN SHEETS	DEF RATE
1	Gianluca Falsini	22	4	71 mins
2	Alberto	33	6	67 mins
3	Daniele Portanova	37	5	65 mins
4	Daniele Gastaldello	24	5	64 mins

KEY PLAYERS - MIDFIELDERS

Roberto D'aversa

Goals in the League	0	Contribution to Attacking Power Average number of minutes between League team goals while on pitch	69
Defensive Rating Average number of mins between League goals conceded while on the pitch	55	Scoring Difference Defensive Rating minus Contribution to Attacking Power	-14

	PLAYER	LGE GOALS	DEF RATE	POWER	SCORE DIFF
1	Roberto D'aversa	0	55	69	-14 mins
2	Tomas Locatelli	5	55	69	-14 mins
3	Simone Vergassola	4	63	79	-16 mins
4	Matteo Paro	0	61	105	-44 mins

KEY PLAYERS - GOALSCORERS

Enrico Chiesa

Goals in the League	11	Player Strike Rate Average number of minutes between League goals scored by player	251
Contribution to Attacking Power Average number of minutes between League team goals while on pitch	84	Club Strike Rate Average number of minutes between League goals scored by club	81

	PLAYER	LGE GOALS	POWER	STRIKE RATE
1	Enrico Chiesa	11	84	251 mins
2	Erjon Bogdani	11	76	254 mins
3	Tomas Locatelli	5	69	387 mins
4	Simone Vergassola	4	79	735 mins

Igor Tudor

SQUAD APPEARANCES

Match	1	2	3	4	5	6	7	8	9	10	11	12	13	14	15	16	17	18	19
Venue	H	A	H	A	H	A	H	A	H	A	H	A	H	A	H	H	A	H	A
Competition	L	L	L	L	L	L	L	L	L	L	L	L	L	L	L	L	L	L	L
Result	W	L	L	D	W	W	L	D	L	W	L	L	D	L	W	D	L	D	D

Match	20	21	22	23	24	25	26	27	28	29	30	31	32	33	34	35	36	37	38
Venue	A	H	A	H	A	H	A	H	A	H	A	H	A	H	A	A	H	A	H
Competition	L	L	L	L	L	L	L	L	L	L	L	L	L	L	L	L	L	L	L
Result	L	L	W	D	D	L	W	W	L	W	L	L	D	L	L	D	L	D	D

Goalkeepers
Marco Fortin
Antonio Mirante
Davide Zomer

Defenders
Alberto
Francesco Colonnese
Gianluca Falsini
Paolo Foglio
Daniele Gastaldello
Nicola Legrottaglie
Michele Mignani
Cristian Molinaro
Paolo Negro
Daniele Portanova
Igor Tudor

Midfielders
Jonathan Bachini
Francesco Cozza
Roberto D'aversa
Gennaro Esposito
Tomas Locatelli
Massimo Marrazina
Ricardo Packer
Matteo Paro
Simone Vergassola

Forwards
Erjon Bogdani
Enrico Chiesa
Gaetano Tomas Guzman
Roberto Nanni
Rey Volpato

KEY: On all match; On bench; Subbed or sent off (Counting game); Subbed or sent off (playing less than 70 minutes); Subbed on from bench (Counting Game); Subbed on (playing less than 70 minutes); Subbed on and then subbed or sent off (Counting Game); Subbed on and then subbed or sent off (playing less than 70 minutes); Not in 16

MESSINA

Final Position: **18th**

KEY: Won Drawn Lost

		Opponent			Score	Scorers	Attendance
1	itpr1	**Lazio**	A	L	0-1		25,000
2	itpr1	**Fiorentina**	H	D	2-2	Di Napoli 57; Zoro 61	23,000
3	itpr1	**Cagliari**	A	D	1-1	Donati 30	12,909
4	itpr1	**Livorno**	H	D	0-0		18,000
5	itpr1	**Siena**	A	L	2-4	Zoro 12; Di Napoli 67	7,500
6	itpr1	**Sampdoria**	H	L	1-4	D'Agostino 77	22,000
7	itpr1	**Juventus**	A	L	0-1		30,097
8	itpr1	**Ascoli**	H	D	1-1	Zampagna 28	15,000
9	itpr1	**Parma**	A	D	1-1	Muslimovic 77	12,000
10	itpr1	**Lecce**	A	W	2-0	D'Agostino 80,83	11,783
11	itpr1	**Roma**	H	L	0-2		30,000
12	itpr1	**Udinese**	A	L	0-1		16,000
13	itpr1	**Inter Milan**	H	L	1-2	Di Napoli 71	40,000
14	itpr1	**Treviso**	A	D	0-0		5,000
15	itpr1	**Chievo**	H	W	2-0	Di Napoli 17; Zampagna 45 pen	23,000
16	itpr1	**AC Milan**	A	L	0-4		60,434
17	itpr1	**Reggina**	H	D	1-1	Di Napoli 25	27,000
18	itpr1	**Empoli**	A	W	3-1	Muslimovic 7,60; Di Napoli 75	8,000
19	itpr1	**Palermo**	H	D	0-0		28,000
20	itpr1	**Lazio**	H	D	1-1	Rafael 22	22,000
21	itpr1	**Fiorentina**	A	L	0-2		27,840
22	itpr1	**Cagliari**	H	W	1-0	Di Napoli 88	30,000
23	itpr1	**Livorno**	A	D	2-2	Di Napoli 79,90	12,000
24	itpr1	**Siena**	H	D	0-0		16,000
25	itpr1	**Sampdoria**	A	L	2-4	Muslimovic 17; Di Napoli 89	20,500
26	itpr1	**Juventus**	H	D	2-2	Floccari 3,86	41,000
27	itpr1	**Ascoli**	A	L	0-1		10,000
28	itpr1	**Parma**	H	L	0-1		28,000
29	itpr1	**Lecce**	H	W	2-1	Rullo 27 og; Nanni 85	15,000
30	itpr1	**Roma**	A	L	1-2	Di Napoli 68	34,000
31	itpr1	**Udinese**	H	D	1-1	Di Napoli 31	36,000
32	itpr1	**Inter Milan**	A	L	0-3		46,000
33	itpr1	**Treviso**	H	W	3-1	Floccari 14; Sculli 71; Di Napoli 73	21,000
34	itpr1	**Chievo**	A	L	0-2		6,500
35	itpr1	**AC Milan**	H	L	1-3	Sculli 6	32,000
36	itpr1	**Reggina**	A	L	0-3		20,000
37	itpr1	**Empoli**	H	L	1-2	Nocerino 89	8,000
38	itpr1	**Palermo**	A	L	0-1		26,588

LEAGUE APPEARANCES, BOOKINGS AND CAPS

	AGE (on 01/07/06)	IN NAMED 18	APPEARANCES	COUNTING GAMES	MINUTES ON PITCH	YELLOW CARDS	RED CARDS	CAPS THIS SEASON	NATIONAL SIDE
Goalkeepers									
Nicholas Caglioni	23	26	4	2	271	0	0	-	Italy
Andrea Pansera	26	12	1	0	22	0	0	-	Italy
Marco Storari	29	36	35	34	3125	1	1	-	Italy
Defenders									
Salvatore Aronica	28	35	35	33	2994	2	2	-	Italy
Filippo Cristante	29	29	21	18	1704	8	1	-	Italy
Luca Fusco	28	13	2	2	180	1	0	-	Italy
Duccio Innocenti	30	13	6	5	455	0	0	-	Italy
Matthew Orolunleke	22	9	2	0	78	0	0	-	Belgium
Alessandro Parisi	29	13	12	10	931	3	1	-	Italy
Rafael Pereira	26	20	13	5	660	2	0	-	Brazil
Rahman Rezaei	31	35	34	34	3060	7	0	3	Iran (23)
Marco Zanchi	29	29	28	27	2457	12	0	-	Italy
Midfielders									
Filippo Antonelli	27	11	9	3	423	1	0	-	Italy
Domenico Bombara	-	1	1	1	70	0	0	-	
Renato Rafael Bondi	25	14	10	7	663	0	0	-	Brazil
Carmine Coppola	27	23	23	18	1880	12	0	-	Italy
Gaetano D'Agostino	24	25	24	15	1621	6	0	-	Italy
Massimo Donati	25	36	33	29	2761	8	0	-	Italy
Domenico Giampa	29	21	15	7	945	3	0	-	Italy
Jose Mamede	22	16	11	4	526	2	0	-	Portugal
Antonio Nocerino	21	19	11	5	640	3	1	-	Italy
Salvatore Sullo	34	24	14	2	549	2	0	-	Italy
A Tummiolo	22	8	1	0	1	0	0	-	Italy
Marc Zoro	22	27	23	20	1841	3	0	7	Ivory Coast (32)
Forwards									
Arturo Di Napoli	32	35	35	26	2583	3	0	-	Italy
Sergio Floccari	24	19	17	12	1246	1	0	-	Italy
Ivica Iliev	26	10	8	3	464	0	0	-	Serbia & Mont
Zlatan Muslimovic	25	26	25	11	1382	2	0	-	Bosnia
Roberto Nanni	24	14	8	1	233	0	0	-	Argentina
Giuseppe Sculli	25	34	32	28	2512	7	1	-	Italy
Rok Straus	18	1	1	1	90	0	0	-	Italy
Atsushi Yanagisawa	29	11	7	0	96	0	0	-	Japan
Riccardo Zampagna	31	12	12	12	1027	0	0	-	Italy

TEAM OF THE SEASON

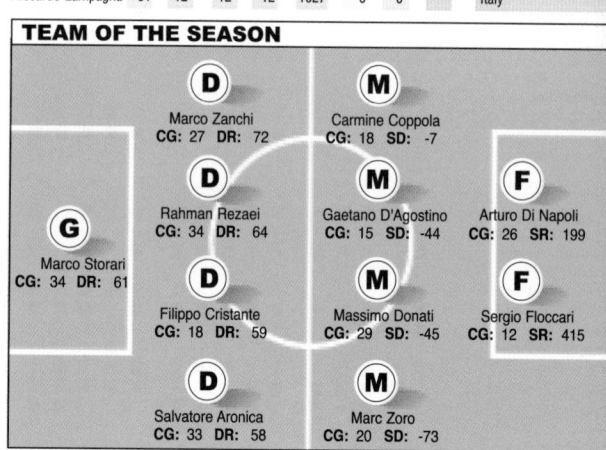

G
Marco Storari
CG: 34 DR: 61

D
Marco Zanchi
CG: 27 DR: 72

D
Rahman Rezaei
CG: 34 DR: 64

D
Filippo Cristante
CG: 18 DR: 59

D
Salvatore Aronica
CG: 33 DR: 58

M
Carmine Coppola
CG: 18 SD: -7

M
Gaetano D'Agostino
CG: 15 SD: -44

M
Massimo Donati
CG: 29 SD: -45

M
Marc Zoro
CG: 20 SD: -73

F
Arturo Di Napoli
CG: 26 SR: 199

F
Sergio Floccari
CG: 12 SR: 415

MONTHLY POINTS TALLY

AUGUST	0	0%
SEPTEMBER	3	25%
OCTOBER	5	33%
NOVEMBER	0	0%
DECEMBER	5	42%
JANUARY	8	53%
FEBRUARY	3	20%
MARCH	4	33%
APRIL	3	20%
MAY	0	0%

LEAGUE GOALS

	PLAYER	MINS	GOALS	S RATE
1	Di Napoli	2583	**13**	199
2	Muslimovic	1382	**4**	346
3	Floccari	1246	**3**	415
4	D'Agostino	1621	**3**	540
5	Sculli	2512	**2**	1256
6	Zampagna	1027	**2**	514
7	Zoro	1841	**2**	921
8	Nocerino	640	**1**	640
9	Rafael	660	**1**	660
10	Nanni	233	**1**	233
11	Donati	2761	**1**	2761
	Other		1	
	TOTAL		**34**	

TOP POINT EARNERS

	PLAYER	GAMES	AV PTS
1	Coppola	18	**1.11**
2	Zanchi	27	**1.07**
3	Donati	29	**0.97**
4	Di Napoli	26	**0.96**
5	Sculli	28	**0.93**
6	Storari	34	**0.88**
7	Rezaei	34	**0.88**
8	Cristante	18	**0.83**
9	Zampagna	12	**0.75**
10	Aronica	33	**0.73**
	CLUB AVERAGE:		**0.82**

DISCIPLINARY RECORDS

	PLAYER	YELLOW	RED	AVE
1	Coppola	12	0	**156**
2	Nocerino	3	1	**160**
3	Cristante	8	1	**189**
4	Zanchi	12	0	**204**
5	Parisi	3	1	**232**
6	Mamede	2	0	**263**
7	D'Agostino	6	0	**270**
8	Sullo	2	0	**274**
9	Sculli	7	1	**314**
10	Giampa	3	0	**315**
11	Rafael	2	0	**330**
12	Donati	8	0	**345**
13	Rezaei	7	0	**437**
	Other	12	3	
	TOTAL	**87**	**7**	

KEY GOALKEEPER

Marco Storari

Goals Conceded in the League	51	Counting Games League games when player was on pitch for at least 70 minutes	34
Defensive Rating Ave number of mins between League goals conceded while on the pitch	61	Clean Sheets In games when player was on pitch for at least 70 minutes	7

KEY PLAYERS - DEFENDERS

Marco Zanchi

Goals Conceded Number of League goals conceded while the player was on the pitch	34	Clean Sheets In League games when player was on pitch for at least 70 minutes	6
Defensive Rating Ave number of mins between League goals conceded while on the pitch	72	Club Defensive Rating Average number of mins between League goals conceded by the club this season	59

	PLAYER	CON LGE	CLEAN SHEETS	DEF RATE
1	Marco Zanchi	34	6	72 mins
2	Rahman Rezaei	48	6	64 mins
3	Filippo Cristante	29	5	59 mins
4	Salvatore Aronica	52	6	58 mins

KEY PLAYERS - MIDFIELDERS

Carmine Coppola

Goals in the League	0	Contribution to Attacking Power Average number of minutes between League team goals while on pitch	85
Defensive Rating Average number of mins between League goals conceded while on the pitch	78	Scoring Difference Defensive Rating minus Contribution to Attacking Power	-7

	PLAYER	LGE GOALS	DEF RATE	POWER	SCORE DIFF
1	Carmine Coppola	0	78	85	-7 mins
2	Gaetano D'Agostino	3	51	95	-44 mins
3	Massimo Donati	1	61	106	-45 mins
4	Marc Zoro	2	50	123	-73 mins

KEY PLAYERS - GOALSCORERS

Arturo Di Napoli

Goals in the League	13	Player Strike Rate Average number of minutes between League goals scored by player	199
Contribution to Attacking Power Average number of minutes between League team goals while on pitch	92	Club Strike Rate Average number of minutes between League goals scored by club	101

	PLAYER	LGE GOALS	POWER	STRIKE RATE
1	Arturo Di Napoli	13	92	199 mins
2	Sergio Floccari	3	104	415 mins
3	Riccardo Zampagna	2	114	514 mins
4	Gaetano D'Agostino	3	95	540 mins

Arturo Di Napoli

Match	1	2	3	4	5	6	7	8	9	10	11	12	13	14	15	16	17	18	19	20	21	22	23	24	25	26	27	28	29	30	31	32	33	34	35	36	37	38
Venue	A	H	A	H	A	H	A	H	A	A	H	A	H	A	H	A	H	A	H	H	A	H	A	H	A	H	A	H	H	A	H	A	H	A	H	A	H	A
Competition	L	L	L	L	L	L	L	L	L	L	L	L	L	L	L	L	L	L	L	L	L	L	L	L	L	L	L	L	L	L	L	L	L	L	L	L	L	L
Result	L	D	D	D	L	L	L	D	D	W	L	L	L	D	W	L	D	W	D	D	L	W	D	D	L	D	L	L	W	L	D	L	W	L	L	L	L	L

Goalkeepers
Nicholas Caglioni
Andrea Pansera
Marco Storari

Defenders
Salvatore Aronica
Filippo Cristante
Luca Fusco
Duccio Innocenti
Matthew Orolunleke
Alessandro Parisi
Rafael Pereira Da Silva
Rahman Rezaei
Marco Zanchi

Midfielders
Filippo Antonelli
Domenico Bombara
Renato Rafael Bondi
Carmine Coppola
Gaetano D'Agostino
Massimo Donati
Domenico Giampa
Jose Mamede
Antonio Nocerino
Salvatore Sullo
A Tummiolo
Marc Zoro

Forwards
Arturo Di Napoli
Sergio Floccari
Ivica Iliev
Zlatan Muslimovic
Roberto Nanni
Giuseppe Sculli
Rok Straus
Atsushi Yanagisawa
Riccardo Zampagna

KEY: On all match / On bench / Subbed or sent off (Counting game) / Subbed or sent off (playing less than 70 minutes) / Subbed on from bench (Counting Game) / Subbed on (playing less than 70 minutes) / Subbed on and then subbed or sent off (Counting Game) / Subbed on and then subbed or sent off (playing less than 70 minutes) / Not in 16

LECCE

Final Position: **19th**

KEY: ☐Won ☐Drawn ☐Lost

#	Comp	Opponent	Venue	Result	Score	Scorers	Attendance
1	itpr1	Livorno	A	L	1-2	Pinardi 39	9,000
2	itpr1	Ascoli	H	D	0-0		13,593
3	itpr1	Inter Milan	A	L	0-3		48,219
4	itpr1	Fiorentina	H	L	1-3	Pinardi 45 pen	12,775
5	itpr1	Empoli	A	L	0-1		6,000
6	itpr1	Cagliari	H	W	3-0	Konan 7; Pinardi 14 pen; Ledesma 67	11,804
7	itpr1	Reggina	A	L	0-2		10,000
8	itpr1	Juventus	H	L	0-3		24,941
9	itpr1	Palermo	A	L	0-3		27,084
10	itpr1	Messina	H	L	0-2		11,783
11	itpr1	Parma	A	L	0-2		15,499
12	itpr1	Siena	H	W	3-0	Vucinic 16; Konan 53; Cozzolino 90	11,729
13	itpr1	AC Milan	A	L	1-2	Konan 67	55,129
14	itpr1	Roma	H	D	2-2	Cozzolino 51; Vucinic 57 pen	15,000
15	itpr1	Udinese	A	W	2-1	Vucinic 41,57	15,000
16	itpr1	Treviso	A	L	1-2	Vucinic 79	4,500
17	itpr1	Lazio	H	D	0-0		12,082
18	itpr1	Chievo	A	L	1-3	Del Vecchio 29	8,313
19	itpr1	Sampdoria	H	L	0-3		12,000
20	itpr1	Livorno	H	D	0-0		10,000
21	itpr1	Ascoli	A	L	0-2		9,000
22	itpr1	Inter Milan	H	L	0-2		15,832
23	itpr1	Fiorentina	A	L	0-1		28,700
24	itpr1	Empoli	H	L	1-2	Ledesma 80 pen	9,753
25	itpr1	Cagliari	A	D	0-0		12,000
26	itpr1	Reggina	H	D	0-0		12,634
27	itpr1	Juventus	A	L	1-3	Del Vecchio 10	26,721
28	itpr1	Palermo	H	W	2-0	Vucinic 63; Giacomazzi 72	10,890
29	itpr1	Messina	A	L	1-2	Babu 44	15,000
30	itpr1	Parma	H	L	1-2	Vucinic 90	10,334
31	itpr1	Siena	A	W	2-1	Giacomazzi 4; Vucinic 71	7,000
32	itpr1	AC Milan	H	W	1-0	Konan 54	14,521
33	itpr1	Roma	A	L	1-3	Del Vecchio 90	13,531
34	itpr1	Udinese	H	L	1-2	Giacomazzi 38	10,476
35	itpr1	Treviso	H	D	1-1	Vucinic 5	8,966
36	itpr1	Lazio	A	L	0-1		24,000
37	itpr1	Chievo	H	D	0-0		8,900
38	itpr1	Sampdoria	A	W	3-1	Del Vecchio 25; Konan 52,85	21,000

LEAGUE APPEARANCES, BOOKINGS AND CAPS

	AGE (on 01/07/06)	IN NAMED 18	APPEARANCES	COUNTING GAMES	MINUTES ON PITCH	YELLOW CARDS	RED CARDS	CAPS THIS SEASON	NATIONAL SIDE
Goalkeepers									
Francesco Benussi	24	36	15	13	1243	0	0	-	Italy
Davide Petrachi	19	4	0	0	0	0	0	-	
Antonio Rosati	23	8	1	0	36	0	0	-	Italy
Vincenzo Sicignano	32	27	24	24	2138	2	1	-	Italy
Defenders									
Giuseppe Abruzzese	25	9	6	5	512	1	0	-	Italy
Mariano Angelo	25	21	12	4	670	1	0	-	Brazil
Alessandro Camisa	21	16	9	7	698	3	0	-	Italy
Marco Cassetti	29	30	29	26	2417	9	0	-	Italy
Gabriel Cichero	22	7	4	1	204	1	0	-	Venezuela
S. Diamoutene	23	35	33	33	2966	7	0	-	Mali
Andrea Esposito	20	6	3	1	136	1	0	-	Italy
Marco Pecorari	28	20	9	5	551	2	0	-	Italy
Tiziano Polenghi	27	11	7	5	555	2	0	-	Italy
Erminio Rullo	22	34	31	26	2535	5	0	-	Italy
Karim Saidi	22	11	9	9	810	1	0	4	Tunisia (21)
Raffaele Schiavi	20	5	1	1	90	0	0	-	Italy
Cristian Silvestri	31	2	2	2	180	0	0	-	Italy
Lorenzo Stovini	29	30	29	28	2565	6	0	-	Italy
Midfielders									
Anderson Babu	25	14	10	3	567	2	0	-	Brazil
Alfonso Camorani	28	29	22	8	1168	8	2	-	Italy
Gennaro Del Vecchio	28	29	29	27	2527	7	1	-	Italy
Aleksei Eremenko Jr	23	11	8	1	335	1	0	-	Finland
Guillermo Giacomazzi	28	15	14	12	1121	3	0	-	Uruguay
Davide Giorgino	21	20	7	2	309	0	0	-	Italy
Cristian Ledesma	27	33	33	27	2640	7	3	-	Argentina
Francesco Marianini	27	32	17	8	1001	0	0	-	Italy
Alex Pinardi	25	28	25	12	1589	6	1	-	Italy
Jaime Zapata Valdes	25	32	26	12	1436	5	0	-	Chile
Forwards									
Giuseppe Cozzolino	20	29	22	4	939	1	0	-	Italy
Axel Konan	23	34	33	16	2011	4	0	-	Ivory Coast
Graziano Pelle	20	15	10	0	287	1	0	-	Italy
Luca Saudati	28	4	4	1	230	1	0	-	Italy
Mirko Vucinic	22	34	34	30	2904	6	1	-	Serbia & Mont

TEAM OF THE SEASON

G — Francesco Benussi, CG: 13 DR: 78

D — S Diamoutene, CG: 33 DR: 67

D — Erminio Rullo, CG: 26 DR: 60

D — Marco Cassetti, CG: 26 DR: 58

D — Lorenzo Stovini, CG: 28 DR: 57

M — Guillermo Giacomazzi, CG: 12 SD: -6

M — Jaime Zapata Valdes, CG: 12 SD: -18

M — Cristian Ledesma, CG: 27 SD: -53

M — Alex Pinardi, CG: 12 SD: -57

F — Mirko Vucinic, CG: 30 SR: 323

F — Axel C Konan, CG: 16 SR: 335

MONTHLY POINTS TALLY

Month	Points	%
AUGUST	0	0%
SEPTEMBER	1	8%
OCTOBER	3	20%
NOVEMBER	3	33%
DECEMBER	5	42%
JANUARY	1	7%
FEBRUARY	2	13%
MARCH	6	50%
APRIL	4	27%
MAY	4	67%

LEAGUE GOALS

	PLAYER	MINS	GOALS	S RATE
1	Vucinic	2904	**9**	323
2	Konan	2011	**6**	335
3	Del Vecchio	2527	**4**	632
4	Giacomazzi	1121	**3**	374
5	Pinardi	1589	**3**	530
6	Ledesma	2640	**2**	1320
7	Cozzolino	939	**2**	470
8	Babu	567	**1**	567
	Other		0	
	TOTAL		**30**	

TOP POINT EARNERS

	PLAYER	GAMES	AV PTS
1	Giacomazzi	12	**1.25**
2	Pinardi	12	**1.00**
3	Valdes	12	**1.00**
4	Diamoutene	33	**0.88**
5	Benussi	13	**0.85**
6	Vucinic	30	**0.83**
7	Stovini	28	**0.82**
8	Ledesma	27	**0.81**
9	Rullo	26	**0.81**
10	Del Vecchio	27	**0.78**
	CLUB AVERAGE:		**0.76**

DISCIPLINARY RECORDS

	PLAYER	YELLOW	RED	AVE
1	Camorani	8	2	**116**
2	Pinardi	6	1	**227**
3	Camisa	3	0	**232**
4	Ledesma	7	3	**264**
5	Cassetti	9	0	**268**
6	Pecorari	2	0	**275**
7	Polenghi	2	0	**277**
8	Babu	2	0	**283**
9	Valdes	5	0	**287**
10	Del Vecchio	7	1	**315**
11	Giacomazzi	3	0	**373**
12	Vucinic	6	1	**414**
13	Diamoutene	7	0	**423**
	Other	21	1	
	TOTAL	**88**	**9**	

KEY GOALKEEPER

Francesco Benussi

Goals Conceded in the League	16	**Counting Games** League games when player was on pitch for at least 70 minutes	13
Defensive Rating Ave number of mins between League goals conceded while on the pitch	78	**Clean Sheets** In League games when player was on pitch for at least 70 minutes	6

KEY PLAYERS - DEFENDERS

Souleymane Diamoutene

Goals Conceded Number of League goals conceded while the player was on the pitch	44	**Clean Sheets** In League games when player was on pitch for at least 70 minutes	10
Defensive Rating Ave number of mins between League goals conceded while on the pitch	67	**Club Defensive Rating** Average number of mins between League goals conceded by the club this season	59

	PLAYER	CON LGE	CLEAN SHEETS	DEF RATE
1	Souleymane Diamoutene	44	10	67 mins
2	Erminio Rullo	42	7	60 mins
3	Marco Cassetti	42	7	58 mins
4	Lorenzo Stovini	45	6	57 mins

KEY PLAYERS - MIDFIELDERS

Guillermo Giacomazzi

Goals in the League	3	**Contribution to Attacking Power** Average number of minutes between League team goals while on pitch	86
Defensive Rating Average number of mins between League goals conceded while on the pitch	80	**Scoring Difference** Defensive Rating minus Contribution to Attacking Power	-6

	PLAYER	LGE GOALS	DEF RATE	POWER	SCORE DIFF
1	Guillermo Giacomazzi	3	80	86	-6 mins
2	Jaime Zapata Valdes	0	72	90	-18 mins
3	Cristian Daniel Ledesma	2	57	110	-53 mins
4	Alex Pinardi	3	57	114	-57 mins

KEY PLAYERS - GOALSCORERS

Mirko Vucinic

Goals in the League	9	**Player Strike Rate** Average number of minutes between League goals scored by player	323
Contribution to Attacking Power Average number of minutes between League team goals while on pitch	112	**Club Strike Rate** Average number of minutes between League goals scored by club	114

	PLAYER	LGE GOALS	POWER	STRIKE RATE
1	Mirko Vucinic	9	112	323 mins
2	Hauillas Axel Cedric Konan	6	106	335 mins
3	Guillermo Giacomazzi	3	86	374 mins
4	Alex Pinardi	3	114	530 mins

Erminio Rullo

SQUAD APPEARANCES

Match	1	2	3	4	5	6	7	8	9	10	11	12	13	14	15	16	17	18	19	20	21	22	23	24	25	26	27	28	29	30	31	32	33	34	35	36	37	38
Venue	A	H	A	H	A	H	A	H	A	H	A	H	A	H	A	A	H	A	H	H	A	H	A	H	A	H	A	H	A	H	A	H	A	H	H	A	H	A
Competition	L	L	L	L	L	L	L	L	L	L	L	L	L	L	L	L	L	L	L	L	L	L	L	L	L	L	L	L	L	L	L	L	L	L	L	L	L	L
Result	L	D	L	L	L	W	L	L	L	L	L	W	L	D	W	L	D	L	L	D	L	L	L	L	D	D	L	W	L	L	W	W	L	L	D	L	D	W

Goalkeepers
Francesco Benussi
Davide Petrachi
Antonio Rosati
Vincenzo Sicignano

Defenders
Giuseppe Abruzzese
Mariano Angelo
Alessandro Camisa
Marco Cassetti
Gabriel Cichero
Souleymane Diamoutene
Andrea Esposito
Marco Pecorari
Tiziano Polenghi
Erminio Rullo
Karim Saidi
Raffaele Schiavi
Cristian Silvestri
Lorenzo Stovini

Midfielders
Anderson Babu
Alfonso Camorani
Gennaro Del Vecchio
Aleksei Eremenko Jr
Guillermo Giacomazzi
Davide Giorgino
Cristian Daniel Ledesma
Francesco Marianini
Alex Pinardi
Jaime Zapata Valdes

Forwards
Giuseppe Cozzolino
Hauillas Axel Konan
Graziano Pelle
Luca Saudati
Mirko Vucinic

KEY: On all match · On bench · Subbed or sent off (Counting game) · Subbed or sent off (playing less than 70 minutes) · Subbed on from bench (Counting Game) · Subbed on (playing less than 70 minutes) · Subbed on and then subbed or sent off (Counting Game) · Subbed on and then subbed or sent off (playing less than 70 minutes) · Not in 16

TREVISO

Final Position: **20th**

KEY: ☐ Won ☐ Drawn ☐ Lost

							Attendance
1	itpr1	Inter Milan	A	L	0-3		51,542
2	itpr1	Livorno	H	L	0-1		5,000
3	itpr1	Lazio	A	L	1-3	Pinga 44	23,000
4	itpr1	Sampdoria	H	L	0-2		5,000
5	itpr1	AC Milan	H	L	0-2		9,435
6	itpr1	Chievo	A	D	0-0		5,304
7	itpr1	Parma	A	D	1-1	Fava 67	12,259
8	itpr1	Empoli	H	L	1-2	Fava 77	7,345
9	itpr1	Reggina	A	W	2-1	Beghetto 18; Parravicini 78	12,000
10	itpr1	Siena	H	L	0-1		9,435
11	itpr1	Cagliari	A	D	0-0		11,000
12	itpr1	Palermo	H	D	2-2	Reginaldo 2,6	6,000
13	itpr1	Juventus	A	L	1-3	Parravicini 25	27,102
14	itpr1	Messina	H	D	0-0		5,000
15	itpr1	Fiorentina	A	L	0-1		43,900
16	itpr1	Lecce	H	W	2-1	Filippini, E 31; Pinga 64	4,500
17	itpr1	Ascoli	A	L	0-1		7,000
18	itpr1	Roma	H	L	0-1		7,500
19	itpr1	Udinese	A	D	2-2	Pinga 33; Dellafiore 58	15,000
20	itpr1	Inter Milan	H	L	0-1		9,435
21	itpr1	Livorno	A	D	1-1	Reginaldo 7	12,000
22	itpr1	Lazio	H	L	0-1		5,000
23	itpr1	Sampdoria	A	D	1-1	Gustavo 63	20,000
24	itpr1	AC Milan	A	L	0-5		52,000
25	itpr1	Chievo	H	L	1-2	Borriello 77	4,000
26	itpr1	Parma	H	L	0-1		4,000
27	itpr1	Empoli	A	D	1-1	Filippini, E 53	5,500
28	itpr1	Reggina	H	L	0-1		3,000
29	itpr1	Siena	A	L	0-1		7,500
30	itpr1	Cagliari	H	L	1-2	Baseggio 23	3,000
31	itpr1	Palermo	A	L	0-1		26,025
32	itpr1	Juventus	H	D	0-0		6,600
33	itpr1	Messina	A	L	1-3	Fava 15	21,000
34	itpr1	Fiorentina	H	L	1-3	Borriello 39	9,435
35	itpr1	Lecce	A	D	1-1	Reginaldo 83	8,966
36	itpr1	Ascoli	H	D	2-2	Reginaldo 14; Borriello 28	3,463
37	itpr1	Roma	A	L	0-1		15,622
38	itpr1	Udinese	H	W	2-1	Borriello 37 pen,77	4,000

LEAGUE APPEARANCES, BOOKINGS AND CAPS

	AGE (on 01/07/06)	IN NAMED 18	APPEARANCES	COUNTING GAMES	MINUTES ON PITCH	YELLOW CARDS	RED CARDS	CAPS THIS SEASON	NATIONAL SIDE
Goalkeepers									
Samir Handanovic	21	20	3	3	270	0	0	-	Slovenia
Matteo Sereni	31	7	7	6	585	0	0	-	Italy
Adriano Zancope	34	37	29	28	2565	2	0	-	Italy
Defenders									
Marcello Cottafava	28	28	26	24	2264	4	0	-	Italy
Herman Dellafiore	21	24	21	20	1805	5	0	-	Argentina
Andrea Dossena	24	22	21	17	1629	7	1	-	
Francesco Galeoto	34	14	11	8	834	3	0	-	Italy
Alberto Giuliatto	32	33	18	11	1143	4	0	-	Italy
Lazzaretti Gustavo	22	27	26	22	2165	3	1	-	Brazil
Stefano Lorenzi	29	10	2	2	180	1	0	-	Italy
Cristian Maggio	24	11	11	10	914	2	0	-	Italy
Marco Mallus	24	3	2	0	55	0	0	-	Italy
Carlos Valdez	23	21	19	14	1437	5	0	-	Uruguay
William Viali	31	27	27	23	2182	4	0	-	Italy
Midfielders									
Walter Baseggio	27	18	17	13	1272	0	1	-	Belgium
Roberto Chiappara	32	16	7	0	162	1	0	-	Italy
Raffaele De Martino	20	26	15	4	684	3	0	-	Italy
Antonio Filipinni	33	34	29	18	2034	4	0	-	Italy
Emanuele Filippini	33	31	31	28	2544	12	0	-	Italy
Fabio Gallo	35	14	14	13	1200	0	0	-	Italy
Gianni Guigou	31	16	13	10	1020	1	0	-	Uruguay
Jehad Muntasser	27	8	4	0	126	0	0	-	Libya
Francesco Parravicini	24	32	29	18	2027	2	0	-	Italy
Andre Luciano Pinga	25	26	23	14	1577	4	0	-	Brazil
Forwards									
Robert Acquafresca	18	15	7	2	307	0	0	-	Italy
Robert Anderson	23	8	1	0	11	0	0	-	Brazil
Luigi Beghetto	33	22	16	2	613	2	0	-	Italy
Marco Borriello	24	20	20	19	1754	5	0	-	Italy
Dino Passaro Fava	29	28	21	11	1364	3	0	-	Italy
Ferreira Reginaldo	32	34	29	13	1765	0	0	-	Brazil
Andrea Russotto	18	6	4	1	144	0	0	-	Italy
Blazej Vascak	22	16	13	8	863	1	0	-	Slovakia

TEAM OF THE SEASON

G — Adriano Zancope CG: 28 DR: 68

D — Marcello Cottafava CG: 24 DR: 69

D — William Viali CG: 23 DR: 68

D — Andrea Dossena CG: 17 DR: 65

D — L de Arujo Gustavo CG: 22 DR: 62

M — Walter Baseggio CG: 13 SD: -63

M — Emanuele Filippini CG: 28 SD: -86

M — Fabio Gallo CG: 13 SD: -87

M — Andre Pinga CG: 14 SD: -89

F — Marco Borriello CG: 19 SR: 351

F — F Reginaldo CG: 13 SR: 353

MONTHLY POINTS TALLY

AUGUST	0	0%
SEPTEMBER	0	0%
OCTOBER	5	33%
NOVEMBER	2	22%
DECEMBER	4	33%
JANUARY	2	13%
FEBRUARY	2	13%
MARCH	0	0%
APRIL	3	20%
MAY	3	50%

LEAGUE GOALS

	PLAYER	MINS	GOALS	S RATE
1	Reginaldo	1765	5	353
2	Borriello	1754	5	351
3	Fava	1364	3	455
4	Pinga	1577	3	526
5	Filippini, E	2544	2	1272
6	Parravicini	2027	2	1014
7	Dellafiore	1805	1	1805
8	Beghetto	613	1	613
9	Gustavo	2165	1	2165
10	Baseggio	1272	1	1272
	Other		0	
	TOTAL		24	

TOP POINT EARNERS

	PLAYER	GAMES	AV PTS
1	Dossena	17	0.71
2	Zancope	28	0.68
3	Filipinni, A	18	0.67
4	Parravicini	18	0.67
5	Baseggio	13	0.62
6	Gallo	13	0.62
7	Gustavo	22	0.59
8	Valdez	14	0.57
9	Filippini, E	28	0.54
10	Borriello	19	0.53
	CLUB AVERAGE:		0.55

DISCIPLINARY RECORDS

	PLAYER	YELLOW	RED	AVE
1	Dossena	7	1	203
2	Filippini, E	12	0	212
3	De Martino	3	0	228
4	Galeoto	3	0	278
5	Giuliatto	4	0	285
6	Valdez	5	0	287
7	Beghetto	2	0	306
8	Borriello	5	0	350
9	Dellafiore	5	0	361
10	Pinga	4	0	394
11	Fava	3	0	454
12	Maggio	2	0	457
13	Filipinni, A	4	0	508
	Other	17	2	
	TOTAL	76	3	

KEY GOALKEEPER

Adriano Zancope

Goals Conceded in the League	**38**	**Counting Games** League games when player was on pitch for at least 70 minutes	**28**
Defensive Rating Ave number of mins between League goals conceded while on the pitch	**68**	**Clean Sheets** In League games when player was on pitch for at least 70 minutes	**4**

KEY PLAYERS - DEFENDERS

Marcello Cottafava

Goals Conceded Number of League goals conceded while the player was on the pitch	**33**	**Clean Sheets** In League games when player was on pitch for at least 70 minutes	**4**
Defensive Rating Ave number of mins between League goals conceded while on the pitch	**69**	**Club Defensive Rating** Average number of mins between League goals conceded by the club this season	**60**

	PLAYER	CON LGE	CLEAN SHEETS	DEF RATE
1	Marcello Cottafava	33	4	**69 mins**
2	William Viali	32	2	**68 mins**
3	Andrea Dossena	25	3	**65 mins**
4	Lazzaretti de Arujo Gustavo	35	1	**62 mins**

KEY PLAYERS - MIDFIELDERS

Walter Baseggio

Goals in the League	**1**	**Contribution to Attacking Power** Average number of minutes between League team goals while on pitch	**116**
Defensive Rating Average number of mins between League goals conceded while on the pitch	**53**	**Scoring Difference** Defensive Rating minus Contribution to Attacking Power	**-63**

	PLAYER	LGE GOALS	DEF RATE	POWER	SCORE DIFF
1	Walter Baseggio	1	53	116	**-63 mins**
2	Emanuele Filippini	2	64	150	**-86 mins**
3	Fabio Gallo	0	63	150	**-87 mins**
4	Andre Luciano Pinga	3	54	143	**-89 mins**

KEY PLAYERS - GOALSCORERS

Marco Borriello

Goals in the League	**5**	**Player Strike Rate** Average number of minutes between League goals scored by player	**351**
Contribution to Attacking Power Average number of minutes between League team goals while on pitch	**135**	**Club Strike Rate** Average number of minutes between League goals scored by club	**143**

	PLAYER	LGE GOALS	POWER	STRIKE RATE
1	Marco Borriello	5	135	**351 mins**
2	Ferreira Da Silva Reginaldo	5	136	**353 mins**
3	Andre Luciano Pinga	3	143	**526 mins**
4	Francesco Parravicini	2	156	**1014 mins**

Herman Paolo Dellafiore, Francesco Parravicini and Fabio Gallo

SQUAD APPEARANCES

Match	1	2	3	4	5	6	7	8	9	10	11	12	13	14	15	16	17	18	19	20	21	22	23	24	25	26	27	28	29	30	31	32	33	34	35	36	37	38
Venue	A	H	A	H	H	A	A	H	A	H	A	H	A	H	A	H	A	H	A	H	A	H	A	A	H	H	A	H	A	H	A	H	A	H	A	H	A	H
Competition	L	L	L	L	L	L	L	L	L	L	L	L	L	L	L	L	L	L	L	L	L	L	L	L	L	L	L	L	L	L	L	L	L	L	L	L	L	L
Result	L	L	L	L	L	D	D	L	W	L	D	D	L	D	L	W	L	L	D	L	D	L	D	L	L	L	D	L	L	L	L	D	L	L	D	D	L	W

Goalkeepers
Samir Handanovic
Matteo Sereni
Adriano Zancope

Defenders
Marcello Cottafava
Herman Paolo Dellafiore
Andrea Dossena
Francesco Galeoto
Alberto Giuliatto
Lazzaretti Gustavo
Stefano Lorenzi
Cristian Maggio
Marco Mallus
Carlos Valdez
William Viali

Midfielders
Walter Baseggio
Roberto Chiappara
Raffaele De Martino
Antonio Filipinni
Emanuele Filippini
Fabio Gallo
Gianni Guigou
Jehad Muntasser
Francesco Parravicini
Andre Luciano Pinga

Forwards
Robert Acquafresca
Robert Anderson
Luigi Beghetto
Marco Borriello
Dino Passaro Fava
Ferreira Reginaldo
Andrea Russotto
Blazej Vascak

KEY: On all match | On bench | Subbed or sent off (Counting game) | Subbed or sent off (playing less than 70 minutes) | Subbed on from bench (Counting Game) | Subbed on (playing less than 70 minutes) | Subbed on and then subbed or sent off (Counting Game) | Subbed on and then subbed or sent off (playing less than 70 minutes) | Not in 16

DUTCH LEAGUE ROUND-UP

FINAL LEAGUE TABLE

		HOME					AWAY					TOTAL			
	P	W	D	L	F	A	W	D	L	F	A	F	A	DIF	PTS
PSV Eindhoven	34	14	3	0	36	8	12	3	2	35	15	71	23	48	84
AZ Alkmaar	34	11	4	2	43	18	12	1	4	35	14	78	32	46	74
Feyenoord	34	13	3	1	47	11	8	5	4	32	23	79	34	45	71
Ajax	34	9	6	2	35	15	9	0	8	31	26	66	41	25	60
Groningen	34	13	3	1	26	9	3	5	9	20	34	46	43	3	56
Utrecht	34	8	4	5	26	22	8	3	6	22	22	48	44	4	55
Heerenveen	34	10	4	3	41	25	4	4	9	22	33	63	58	5	50
Roda JC Kerk	34	9	2	6	30	28	6	3	8	27	26	57	54	3	50
Twente	34	9	1	7	25	17	4	7	6	19	19	44	36	8	47
NEC Nijmegen	34	7	4	6	23	20	6	4	7	20	23	43	43	0	47
Vitesse Arnhem	34	9	2	6	33	27	4	3	10	19	27	52	54	-2	44
RKC Waalwijk	34	7	4	6	29	26	4	2	11	19	32	48	58	-10	39
Heracles	34	6	3	8	19	28	5	3	9	16	30	35	58	-23	39
S Rotterdam	34	8	0	9	25	23	2	7	8	9	27	34	50	-16	37
Den Haag	34	6	3	8	18	22	4	2	11	18	40	36	62	-26	35
NAC Breda	34	6	5	6	24	31	2	4	11	21	35	45	66	-21	33
Willem II Tilb	34	5	4	8	27	29	2	3	12	18	37	45	66	-21	28
Roosendaal	34	1	5	11	14	32	0	1	16	8	58	22	90	-68	9

CLUB STRIKE FORCE

Shota Averladze of Feyenoord

1 Feyenoord

Goals scored in the League	79
Club Strike Rate (CSR) Average number of minutes between League goals scored by club	39

	CLUB	GOALS	CSR
1	Feyenoord	79	39
2	AZ Alkmaar	78	39
3	PSV Eindhoven	71	43
4	Ajax	66	46
5	Heerenveen	63	49
6	Roda JC Kerk	57	54
7	Vitesse Arnhem	52	59
8	RKC Waalwijk	48	64
8	Utrecht	48	64
10	Groningen	46	67
11	NAC Breda	45	68
12	Willem II Tilb	45	68
13	Twente	44	70
14	NEC Nijmegen	43	71
15	Den Haag	36	85
16	Heracles	35	87
17	S Rotterdam	34	90
18	Roosendaal	22	139

CLUB DISCIPLINARY RECORDS

Den Haag's Kum

1 Roosendaal

League Yellow	68
League Red	7
League Total	75
Cards Average in League Average number of minutes between a card being shown of either colour	41

	CLUB	Y	R	TOTAL	AVE
1	Roosendaal	68	7	75	41
2	Den Haag	63	3	66	46
3	S Rotterdam	59	5	64	48
4	Utrecht	59	3	62	49
5	Heracles	61	1	62	49
6	Willem II Tilb	57	4	61	50
7	Groningen	60	1	61	50
8	Roda JC Kerk	52	7	59	52
9	Vitesse Arnhem	55	3	58	53
10	Ajax	51	5	56	55
11	NEC Nijmegen	53	2	55	56
12	Twente	53	1	54	57
13	NAC Breda	51	1	52	59
14	RKC Waalwijk	44	5	49	62
15	AZ Alkmaar	47	2	49	62
16	Heerenveen	36	5	41	75
17	PSV Eindhoven	40	1	41	75
18	Feyenoord	35	1	36	85

CLUB DEFENCES

	CLUB	LGE	CS	CDR
1	PSV Eindhoven	23	17	133
2	AZ Alkmaar	32	14	96
3	Feyenoord	34	11	90
4	Twente	36	12	85
5	Ajax	41	12	75
6	Groningen	43	11	71
7	NEC Nijmegen	43	11	71
8	Utrecht	44	8	70
9	S Rotterdam	50	12	61
10	Vitesse Arnhem	54	6	57
11	Roda JC Kerk	54	7	57
12	RKC Waalwijk	58	5	53
13	Heracles	58	6	53
14	Heerenveen	58	7	53
15	Den Haag	62	5	49
16	NAC Breda	66	3	46
17	Willem II Tilb	66	5	46
18	Roosendaal	90	1	34

Andre Ooijer of PSV

1 PSV Eindhoven

Goals conceded in the League	23
Clean Sheets (CS) Number of league games where no goals were conceded	17
Club Defensive Rate (CDR) Average number of minutes between League goals conceded by club	133

PLAYER NATIONALITIES

Overseas country with the most player appearances in the Dutch League - Belgium

697 league appearances by Belgian players

	COUNTRY	PLAYERS	IN SQUAD	LGE APP	% LGE ACT	CAPS	MOST APP	APP
1	Holland	339	6194	4580	56.0	90	Bas Roorda	100
2	Belgium	48	871	687	8.9	6	Dimitri De Fauw	93.8
3	Sweden	11	294	278	3.6	16	Petter Hansson	97.1
4	Brazil	10	213	198	2.5	2	Andre Bahia	98.5
5	Morocco	10	232	182	1.9	0	Akram Roumani	83.4
6	Hungary	7	144	129	1.8	12	Boldizar Bodor	88.5
7	Serbia & Montenegro	6	151	123	1.6	0	Vladan Kujovic	94.1
8	Ghana	9	173	124	1.6	9	Anthony Obodai	76.9
9	Switzerland	4	127	117	1.3	8	Blaise N'Kufo	91.7
10	Germany	4	107	93	1.3	0	Martin Pieckenhagen	94.1
11	Ivory Coast	4	85	84	1.1	22	Salomon Kalou	94.8
12	Denmark	8	108	88	1.0	6	Kenneth Perez	76.7
13	Finland	7	122	94	1.0	5	Joonas Kolkka	86.6
14	France	7	109	76	0.9	0	Marc-Antoine Fortune	52.7
15	Surinam	3	65	62	0.9	0	Kurt Elshot	97.1
16	Norway	3	81	71	0.8	0	Pa Modou Kah	89.4
17	Australia	7	95	61	0.8	15	Tony Vidmar	55.3
18	Czech Republic	3	58	56	0.8	13	Tomas Galasek	71.4
19	Spain	3	72	62	0.8	0	Alberto Saavedra	72.4
20	Poland	2	58	52	0.7	9	Andrzej Niedzielan	67

CLUB MAKE-UP – HOME AND OVERSEAS PLAYERS

1 Roda JC Kerk

74.5% of appearances by overseas players

	CLUB	OVERSEAS	HOME	% OVERSEAS	% LGE ACT	MOST APP	APP
1	Roda JC Kerk	23	9	71.9	74.5	Vladan Kujovic	84.2
2	Roosendaal	11	18	37.9	55.6	Mark Volders	77.6
3	PSV Eindhoven	22	11	66.7	51.9	Heurelho Gomes	82.9
4	Twente	14	13	51.9	47.6	Blaise N'Kufo	82.0
5	Ajax	20	16	55.6	47.1	Tomas Galasek	63.9
6	NEC Nijmegen	11	18	37.9	42.8	Jonas Olsson	85.0
7	Feyenoord	18	20	47.4	38.9	Andre Bahia	88.2
8	Heerenveen	13	22	37.1	37.2	Petter Hansson	86.8
9	Willem II Tilb	16	22	42.1	36.5	Moussa Dembele	66.6
10	Groningen	8	22	26.7	34.8	Rasmus Lindgren	70.6
11	Heracles	8	17	32.0	32.4	M Pieckenhagen	84.2
12	Den Haag	10	24	29.4	32.0	Joonas Kolkka	77.5
13	Utrecht	9	19	32.1	31.4	Dwight Tiendalli	73.4
14	NAC Breda	10	21	32.3	30.7	Kurt Elshot	86.8
15	Vitesse Arnhem	11	18	37.9	29.0	Gill Swerts	73.8
16	S Rotterdam	8	21	27.6	28.8	Dimitri De Fauw	83.9
17	RKC Waalwijk	10	28	26.3	27.6	Stephan Keller	71.8
18	AZ Alkmaar	8	20	28.6	26.2	Shota Arveladze	70.3

CHART-TOPPING MIDFIELDERS

1 Culina - PSV Eindhoven	
Goals scored in the League	0
Defensive Rating Av number of mins between League goals conceded while on the pitch	201
Contribution to Attacking Power Average number of minutes between League team goals while on pitch	40
Scoring Difference Defensive Rating minus Contribution to Attacking Power	161

	PLAYER	CLUB	GOALS	DEF RATE	POWER	S DIFF
1	Culina	PSV Eindhoven	0	201	40	161
2	Cocu	PSV Eindhoven	10	156	45	111
3	Sibum	Twente	0	143	49	94
4	Simons	PSV Eindhoven	2	132	43	89
5	Ghali	Feyenoord	2	113	36	77
6	Afellay	PSV Eindhoven	2	129	52	77
7	Landzaat	AZ Alkmaar	9	108	40	68
8	Lucius	PSV Eindhoven	0	103	40	63
9	Bosschaart	Feyenoord	0	100	43	57
10	de Zeeuw	AZ Alkmaar	1	87	33	54
11	de Guzman	Feyenoord	4	83	40	43
12	Rosales	Ajax	0	86	46	40
13	Schaars	AZ Alkmaar	1	78	42	36
14	Bakircioglu	Twente	8	98	64	34
15	Lindenbergh	Ajax	0	75	45	30

CHART-TOPPING GOALSCORERS

1 Huntelaar - Heerenveen	
Goals scored in the League	17
Contribution to Attacking Power Average number of minutes between League team goals while on pitch	39
Club Strike Rate (CSR) Average minutes between League goals scored by club	47
Player Strike Rate Average number of minutes between League goals scored by player	72

	PLAYER	CLUB	GOALS: LGE	POWER	CSR	S RATE
1	Huntelaar	Heerenveen	17	39	47	72
2	Huntelaar	Ajax	16	40	46	90
3	Arveladze	AZ Alkmaar	22	42	39	109
4	Farfan	PSV Eindhoven	21	42	43	123
5	Hoogendorp	RKC Waalwijk	12	47	64	133
6	Kuijt	Feyenoord	22	38	39	135
7	Kone	PSV Eindhoven	11	47	43	158
8	Amoah	Vitesse Arnhem	9	56	59	161
9	Cziommer	Roda JC Kerk	8	48	54	163
10	Rosenberg	Ajax	12	48	46	181
11	Ramzi	Utrecht	7	59	64	186
12	Hersi	Vitesse Arnhem	10	56	59	191
13	Kalou	Feyenoord	15	39	39	193
14	Nilsson	Heerenveen	9	56	47	194
15	Hirayama	Heracles	8	58	87	195

CHART-TOPPING DEFENDERS

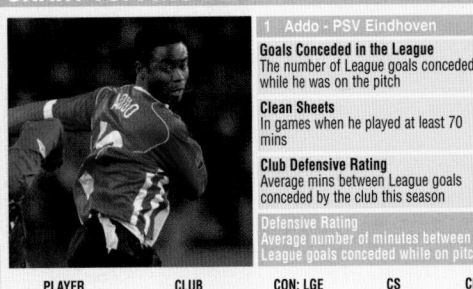

1 Addo - PSV Eindhoven	
Goals Conceded in the League The number of League goals conceded while he was on the pitch	8
Clean Sheets In games when he played at least 70 mins	8
Club Defensive Rating Average mins between League goals conceded by the club this season	133
Defensive Rating Average number of minutes between League goals conceded while on pitch	171

	PLAYER	CLUB	CON: LGE	CS	CDR	DEF RATE
1	Addo	PSV Eindhoven	8	8	133	171
2	Ooijer	PSV Eindhoven	14	14	133	146
3	Alex	PSV Eindhoven	19	14	133	130
4	Lamey	PSV Eindhoven	17	11	133	125
5	Steinsson	AZ Alkmaar	10	5	96	120
6	Mathijsen, J	AZ Alkmaar	21	11	96	106
7	Greene	Feyenoord	27	10	90	103
8	Trabelsi	Ajax	17	10	75	99
9	de Cler	AZ Alkmaar	27	12	96	99
10	Vlaar	Feyenoord	15	6	90	96
11	Jaliens	AZ Alkmaar	27	13	96	96
12	Heubach	Twente	26	10	85	95
13	Bahia	Feyenoord	33	11	90	91
14	Leemans	Roda JC Kerk	14	4	57	89
15	Opdam	AZ Alkmaar	21	7	96	87

CHART-TOPPING GOALKEEPERS

1 Gomes- PSV Eindhoven	
Counting Games Games in which he played at least 70 minutes	31
Goals Conceded in the League The number of League goals conceded while he was on the pitch	21
Clean Sheets In games when he played at least 70 mins	15
Defensive Rating Average number of minutes between League goals conceded while on pitch	135

	PLAYER	CLUB	CG	CONC	CS	DEF RATE
1	Gomes	PSV Eindhoven	31	21	15	135
2	Timmer	AZ Alkmaar	32	30	13	96
3	Lodewijks	Feyenoord	26	24	10	95
4	Boschker	Twente	26	25	11	94
5	Stekelenburg	Ajax	27	30	10	80
6	Babos	NEC Nijmegen	29	36	10	73
7	Roorda	Groningen	34	43	11	71
8	Terol	Utrecht	25	31	6	71
9	Drobny	Den Haag	12	17	2	64
10	Peersman	Willem II Tilb	13	19	2	62
11	Ponk	S Rotterdam	34	50	11	61
12	Kujovic	Roda JC Kerk	32	49	7	59
13	Wapenaar	Vitesse Arnhem	32	49	6	59
14	van Zwam	NAC Breda	17	27	1	57
15	Waterman	Heerenveen	12	18	4	56

PLAYER DISCIPLINARY RECORD

1 Rijaard - Den Haag	
Cards Average mins between cards	144
League Yellow	7
League Red	1
TOTAL	8

	PLAYER		LY	LR	TOT	AVE
1	Rijaard	Den Haag	7	1	8	144
2	Fs Rodriguez	Roosendaal	8	2	10	146
3	Acuna	Roosendaal	11	1	12	167
4	Juanfran	Ajax	5	1	6	172
5	Schenkel	S Rotterdam	6	1	7	179
6	Bodde	Den Haag	5	1	6	207
7	Grygera	Ajax	6	1	7	218
8	Ouedraogo	Twente	8	0	8	221
9	Takak	NEC Nijmegen	5	0	5	225
10	Paap	Roosendaal	4	1	5	229
11	van der Leegte	Den Haag	7	0	7	231
12	Rankovic	Den Haag	9	0	9	233
13	van Dijk, G	Roda JC Kerk	8	2	10	236
14	van der Bergh	S Rotterdam	7	0	7	244
15	Maas	Heracles	9	0	9	247

TEAM OF THE SEASON

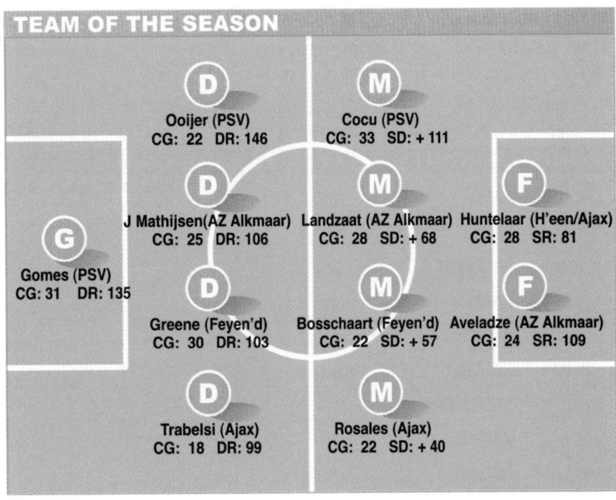

HOLLAND EREDIVISIE CHAMPIONS

PSV EINDHOVEN

Final Position: **1st**

KEY: ☐Won ☐Drawn ☐Lost

							Attendance
1	hosc	**Ajax**	A	L	1-2	Bouma 51	
2	hopr1	**Heracles**	A	D	1-1	Cocu 84	8,500
3	hopr1	**Vitesse Arnhem**	H	W	2-1	Farfan 32 ; Cocu 45	32,600
4	hopr1	**Roda JC Kerk**	A	W	3-0	Farfan 36; Beasley 68; Cocu 86	14,000
5	hopr1	**Utrecht**	H	W	1-0	Kon? 49	32,000
6	ecgpe	**Schalke**	H	W	1-0	Vennegoor 33	30,000
7	hopr1	**Groningen**	A	L	0-1		12,500
8	hopr1	**Roosendaal**	H	W	2-0	Simons 8; Farfan 46	32,000
9	ecgpe	**Fenerbahce**	A	L	0-3		21,895
10	hopr1	**Heerenveen**	A	W	3-2	Kone 37,56,69	21,000
11	hopr1	**AZ Alkmaar**	H	W	3-0	Cocu 43,82; Vennegoor 86	35,000
12	ecgpe	**AC Milan**	A	D	0-0		69,763
13	hopr1	**Ajax**	H	W	1-0	Simons 10 pen	34,700
14	hopr1	**Twente**	A	W	1-0	Afellay 70	13,100
15	ecgpe	**AC Milan**	H	W	1-0	Farfan 12	35,500
16	hopr1	**S Rotterdam**	H	W	3-0	Farfan 34,74; Beasley 35	33,300
17	hopr1	**RKC Waalwijk**	A	D	4-4	Farfan 14,44,51; Robert 89	7,400
18	ecgpe	**Schalke**	A	L	0-3		30,000
19	hopr1	**Den Haag**	H	W	3-0	Vennegoor 60,73; Kone 87	33,000
20	hopr1	**NAC Breda**	H	W	3-0	Vennegoor 53; Farfan 76; Kone 88	32,500
21	ecgpe	**Fenerbahce**	H	W	2-0	Cocu 14; Farfan 85	30,000
22	hopr1	**Feyenoord**	A	L	0-1		45,000
23	hopr1	**Willem II Tilb**	H	W	4-1	Vennegoor 19,42; Farfan 63; Vayrynen 93	32,500
24	hopr1	**NEC Nijmegen**	A	W	2-0	Kone 6; Beasley 89	12,000
25	hopr1	**Twente**	H	D	1-1	Cocu 69	32,500
26	hopr1	**S Rotterdam**	A	W	1-0	Gudelj 75 og	10,000
27	hopr1	**RKC Waalwijk**	H	W	2-0	Farfan 4; Beasley 76	33,000
28	hopr1	**Den Haag**	A	W	2-0	Farfan 55; Cocu 78	8,000
29	hopr1	**Roda JC Kerk**	H	W	3-2	Vennegoor 7 pen,53; Aissati 65	33,100
30	hopr1	**Utrecht**	A	W	2-1	Farfan 21,78	20,000
31	hopr1	**Heracles**	H	W	1-0	Farfan 71	32,900
32	hopr1	**Vitesse Arnhem**	A	W	3-1	Farfan 45,90; Lamey 85	24,000
33	eclsl1	**Lyon**	H	L	0-1		35,000
34	hopr1	**AZ Alkmaar**	A	W	2-1	Vennegoor 3; Kone 6	8,578
35	hopr1	**Heerenveen**	H	W	4-1	Kone 37,83; Cocu 41; Alex 74	33,400
36	eclsl2	**Lyon**	A	L	0-4		41,000
37	hopr1	**Ajax**	A	D	0-0		48,741
38	hopr1	**NEC Nijmegen**	H	W	1-0	Farfan 75	33,000
39	hopr1	**Willem II Tilb**	A	W	3-0	Aissati 5; Addo 45; Kone 46	12,500
40	hopr1	**Roosendaal**	A	W	2-1	Afellay 60; Alex 67	5,000
41	hopr1	**Groningen**	H	D	1-1	Farfan 47	35,000
42	hopr1	**Feyenoord**	H	D	1-1	Cocu 70	35,000
43	hopr1	**NAC Breda**	A	W	6-2	Vennegoor 4,48; Farfan 21,49; Vayrynen 62; Cocu 90	14,950

LEAGUE APPEARANCES, BOOKINGS AND CAPS

	AGE (on 01/07/06)	IN NAMED 18	APPEARANCES	COUNTING GAMES	MINUTES ON PITCH	YELLOW CARDS	RED CARDS	CAPS THIS SEASON	NATIONAL SIDE
Goalkeepers									
Ruud Boffim	18	1	0	0	0	0	0	-	Belgium
Nathan Coe	22	4	0	0	0	0	0	-	Australia
Heurelho Gomes	25	32	32	31	2835	0	0	-	Brazil
Edwin Zoetebier	36	29	3	2	225	0	0	-	Holland
Defenders									
Erik Addo	27	29	20	13	1370	2	0	-	Ghana
Alex	24	28	28	27	2473	2	0	2	Brazil (1)
Michael Ball	26	22	12	8	859	2	0	-	England
Wilfred Bouma	28	3	3	3	270	0	0	3	Holland (3)
Juan Carlos Carizzo	19	1	0	0	0	0	0	-	Argentina
Michael Lamey	26	31	26	21	2122	5	1	-	Holland
Young-Pyo Lee	29	3	3	3	270	0	0	6	South Korea (29)
Andre Ooijer	31	24	24	22	2044	6	0	2	Holland (3)
Michael Reiziger	33	29	13	9	889	2	0	-	Holland
Lindsay Wilson	27	0	0	0	0	0	0	-	Australia
Midfielders									
Ibrahim Afellay	20	27	22	14	1549	4	0	-	Holland
Ismael Aissati	17	31	18	4	690	0	0	-	Morocco
Phillip Cocu	35	33	33	33	2966	3	0	6	Holland (3)
Jason Culina	25	25	22	15	1608	4	0	5	Australia (42)
Guy Dufour	19	1	0	0	0	0	0	-	Belgium
Csaba Feher	30	1	0	0	0	0	0	1	Hungary (54)
Osmar Ferreyra	23	13	1	1	90	0	0	-	Argentina
Theo Lucius	29	28	21	17	1646	4	0	2	Holland (3)
Lee Nguyen	19	3	1	1	91	0	0	-	United States
Timmy Simons	30	33	30	29	2642	1	0	5	Belgium (42)
Mika Vayrynen	24	20	11	3	576	0	0	-	Finland
Forwards									
DaMarcus Beasley	24	28	26	12	1520	0	0	4	United States (5)
Roy Beerens	18	10	2	0	49	0	0	-	Holland
Jefferson Farfan	21	31	31	27	2578	1	0	3	Peru (66)
Arouna Kone	22	21	21	18	1742	2	0	11	Ivory Coast (32)
Robert	25	13	9	0	187	1	0	-	Brazil
Gerald Sibon	32	8	3	1	121	0	0	-	Holland
Archie Thompson	27	7	1	0	6	0	0	-	Australia
Jan Vennegoor	27	32	32	21	2197	1	0	7	Holland (3)

TEAM OF THE SEASON

G
Heurelho Gomes
CG: 31 DR: 135

D
Erik Addo
CG: 13 DR: 171

D
Andre Ooijer
CG: 22 DR: 146

D
Alex
CG: 27 DR: 130

D
Michael Lamey
CG: 21 DR: 125

M
Jason Culina
CG: 15 SD: 161

M
Phillip Cocu
CG: 33 SD: 111

M
Timmy Simons
CG: 29 SD: 89

M
Ibrahim Afellay
CG: 14 SD: 77

F
Jefferson Farfan
CG: 27 SR: 123

F
Arouna Kone
CG: 18 SR: 158

MONTHLY POINTS TALLY

AUGUST	7	78%
SEPTEMBER	6	67%
OCTOBER	12	100%
NOVEMBER	7	78%
DECEMBER	10	67%
JANUARY	9	100%
FEBRUARY	15	100%
MARCH	10	83%
APRIL	8	67%

LEAGUE GOALS

	PLAYER	MINS	GOALS	S RATE
1	Farfan	2578	21	123
2	Vennegoor	2197	11	200
3	Kone	1742	11	158
4	Cocu	2966	10	297
5	Beasley	1520	4	380
6	Aissati	690	2	345
7	Simons	2642	2	1321
8	Vayrynen	576	2	288
9	Afellay	1549	2	775
10	Alex	2473	2	1237
11	Robert	187	1	187
12	Lamey	2122	1	2122
13	Addo	1370	1	1370
	Other		1	
	TOTAL		71	

TOP POINT EARNERS

	PLAYER	GAMES	AV PTS
1	DaMarcus Beasley	12	2.58
2	Ibrahim Afellay	14	2.57
3	Timmy Simons	29	2.55
4	Andre Ooijer	22	2.55
5	Erik Addo	13	2.54
6	Alex	27	2.52
7	Phillip Cocu	33	2.52
8	Jefferson Farfan	27	2.48
9	Michael Lamey	21	2.48
10	Heurelho Gomes	31	2.42
	CLUB AVERAGE:		2.47

DISCIPLINARY RECORDS

	PLAYER	YELLOW	RED	AVE
1	Ooijer	6	0	340
2	Lamey	5	1	353
3	Afellay	4	0	387
4	Culina	4	0	402
5	Lucius	4	0	411
6	Ball	2	0	429
7	Reiziger	2	0	444
8	Addo	2	0	685
9	Kone	2	0	871
10	Cocu	3	0	988
11	Alex	2	0	1236
12	Vennegoor	1	0	2197
13	Farfan	1	0	2578
	Other	1	0	
	TOTAL	39	1	

KEY GOALKEEPER

Heurelho Gomes

Goals Conceded in the League	21	**Counting Games** League games when player was on pitch for at least 70 minutes	31
Defensive Rating Ave number of mins between League goals conceded while on the pitch	135	**Clean Sheets** In games when player was on pitch for at least 70 minutes	15

KEY PLAYERS - DEFENDERS

Erik Addo

Goals Conceded Number of League goals conceded while the player was on the pitch	8	**Clean Sheets** In League games when player was on pitch for at least 70 minutes	8
Defensive Rating Ave number of mins between League goals conceded while on the pitch	171	**Club Defensive Rating** Average number of mins between League goals conceded by the club this season	133

	PLAYER	CON LGE	CLEAN SHEETS	DEF RATE
1	Erik Addo	8	8	171 mins
2	Andre Ooijer	14	14	146 mins
3	Alex	19	14	130 mins
4	Michael Lamey	17	11	125 mins

KEY PLAYERS - MIDFIELDERS

Jason Culina

Goals in the League	0	**Contribution to Attacking Power** Average number of minutes between League team goals while on pitch	40
Defensive Rating Average number of mins between League goals conceded while on the pitch	201	**Scoring Difference** Defensive Rating minus Contribution to Attacking Power	161

	PLAYER	LGE GOALS	DEF RATE	POWER	SCORE DIFF
1	Jason Culina	0	201	40	161 mins
2	Phillip Cocu	10	156	45	111 mins
3	Timmy Simons	2	132	43	89 mins
4	Ibrahim Afellay	2	129	52	77 mins

KEY PLAYERS - GOALSCORERS

Jefferson Farfan

Goals in the League	21	**Player Strike Rate** Average number of minutes between League goals scored by player	123
Contribution to Attacking Power Average number of minutes between League team goals while on pitch	42	**Club Strike Rate** Average number of minutes between League goals scored by club	43

	PLAYER	LGE GOALS	POWER	STRIKE RATE
1	Jefferson Farfan	21	42	123 mins
2	Arouna Kone	11	47	158 mins
3	Jan Vennegoor of Hesselink	11	45	200 mins
4	Phillip Cocu	10	45	297 mins

Jefferson Farfan and Jan Vennegoor of Hesselink

SQUAD APPEARANCES

Match	1	2	3	4	5	6	7	8	9	10	11	12	13	14	15	16	17	18	19	20	21	22	23	24	25	26	27	28	29	30	31	32	33	34	35	36	37	38	39	40	41	42	43
Venue	A	A	H	A	H	H	A	H	A	A	H	A	H	A	H	H	A	A	H	H	H	A	H	A	H	A	H	A	H	A	H	A	H	A	H	A	A	H	A	A	H	H	A
Competition	O	L	L	L	L	C	L	L	C	L	L	C	L	L	C	L	L	C	L	L	C	L	L	L	L	L	L	L	L	L	L	L	C	L	L	C	L	L	L	L	L	L	L
Result	L	D	W	W	W	W	L	W	L	W	W	D	W	W	W	W	D	L	W	W	W	L	W	W	D	W	W	W	W	W	W	W	L	W	W	L	D	W	W	W	D	D	W

Goalkeepers
Ruud Boffim
Nathan Coe
Heurelho Gomes
Edwin Zoetebier

Defenders
Erik Addo
Alex
Michael Ball
Wilfred Bouma
Juan Carlos Carizzo
Michael Lamey
Young-Pyo Lee
Andre Ooijer
Michael Reiziger
Lindsay Wilson

Midfielders
Ibrahim Afellay
Ismael Aissati
Phillip Cocu
Jason Culina
Guy Dufour
Csaba Feher
Osmar Ferreyra
Theo Lucius
Lee Nguyen
Timmy Simons
Mika Vayrynen

Forwards
DaMarcus Beasley
Roy Beerens
Jefferson Farfan
Arouna Kone
Robert
Gerald Sibon
Archie Thompson
Jan Vennegoor

KEY: On all match | On bench | Subbed or sent off (Counting game) | Subbed or sent off (playing less than 70 minutes) | Subbed on from bench (Counting Game) | Subbed on (playing less than 70 minutes) | Subbed on and then subbed or sent off (Counting Game) | Subbed on and then subbed or sent off (playing less than 70 minutes) | Not in 16

AZ ALKMAAR

Final Position: **2nd**

KEY: ☐ Won ☐ Drawn ☐ Lost

	Comp	Opponent	H/A	Res	Score	Scorers	Attendance
1	hopr1	**S Rotterdam**	H	W	3-0	Arveladze 3,47; Sektioui 74	8,523
2	hopr1	**Utrecht**	A	W	2-1	van Galen 48,74	20,000
3	hopr1	**Vitesse Arnhem**	A	W	5-0	Arveladze 30,38; Perez 45,49,90	19,002
4	hopr1	**Roosendaal**	H	W	7-0	Arveladze 29,68,89; Perez 52; Landzaat 63 pen,74; Huysegems 76	8,275
5	uc1rl1	**Krylia Sovetov**	A	L	3-5	Vlaar 18; Perez 55; van Galen 84	
6	hopr1	**Ajax**	H	W	4-2	Arveladze 35,37; Perez 56,58	8,747
7	hopr1	**NAC Breda**	A	L	1-2	Sektioui 12	15,250
8	uc1rl2	**Krylia Sovetov**	H	W	3-1	van Galen 45; Koevermans 80; Landzaat 85 pen	8,095
9	hopr1	**NEC Nijmegen**	H	W	3-2	Perez 20; Sektioui 49; Arveladze 65	8,300
10	hopr1	**PSV Eindhoven**	A	L	0-3		35,000
11	ucgpd	**Dnipro**	A	W	2-1	Arveladze 14; Sektioui 52	12,300
12	hopr1	**Willem II Tilb**	H	W	5-1	Sektioui 3; Landzaat 41 pen; Perez 52; Meerdink 83; Steinsson 88	8,500
13	hopr1	**Den Haag**	A	W	2-0	Sektioui 16; Arveladze 55	7,185
14	hopr1	**Heracles**	H	D	2-2	Sektioui 42; Arveladze 56	8,399
15	hopr1	**Groningen**	A	D	0-0		12,100
16	ucgpd	**Middlesbrough**	H	D	0-0		8,461
17	hopr1	**Roda JC Kerk**	H	W	2-0	Landzaat 34; Koevermans 89	8,377
18	ucgpd	**Liteks Lovetch**	A	W	2-0	van Galen 10; Sektioui 82	4,000
19	hopr1	**Heerenveen**	H	W	2-1	Arveladze 1; Landzaat 74	8,000
20	hopr1	**Twente**	A	W	3-1	Huysegems 65; Koevermans 71; Landzaat 89	13,200
21	ucgpd	**Grasshoppers**	H	W	1-0	Koevermans 70	8,153
22	hopr1	**RKC Waalwijk**	H	W	3-0	de Zeeuw 8; Huysegems 17; Steinsson 64	8,300
23	hopr1	**Feyenoord**	A	L	0-2		45,000
24	hopr1	**Heracles**	A	W	2-0	Landzaat 6; Perez 73	8,500
25	hopr1	**Den Haag**	H	W	3-1	Landzaat 5,60 pen; Ikedia 80	8,349
26	hopr1	**Groningen**	H	D	1-1	Arveladze 60	8,476
27	hopr1	**Roda JC Kerk**	A	W	4-1	Arveladze 2,39,52; Huysegems 48	12,500
28	hopr1	**Vitesse Arnhem**	H	D	1-1	Steinsson 13	8,426
29	hopr1	**Roosendaal**	A	W	5-0	van Galen 12; Meerdink 37; Arveladze 56,66,83	4,500
30	hopr1	**S Rotterdam**	A	W	1-0	Perez 90	11,000
31	uc3rl1	**Real Betis**	A	L	0-2		30,000
32	hopr1	**Utrecht**	H	L	2-3	van Steensel 56 og; Koevermans 62	8,474
33	uc3rl2	**Real Betis**	H	W	2-1	Arveladze 26; Jaliens 35	8,073
34	hopr1	**PSV Eindhoven**	H	L	1-2	Schaars 61	8,578
35	hopr1	**NEC Nijmegen**	A	W	2-0	Medunjanin 49; Koevermans 51	11,750
36	hopr1	**Willem II Tilb**	A	W	3-1	Medunjanin 5; Steinsson 59; Huysegems 87	12,500
37	hopr1	**Feyenoord**	H	W	1-0	Arveladze 58	8,747
38	hopr1	**RKC Waalwijk**	A	W	1-0	Medunjanin 35	7,000
39	hopr1	**NAC Breda**	H	W	3-2	Koevermans 56,66; Arveladze 70	8,500
40	hopr1	**Ajax**	A	L	0-1		48,000
41	hopr1	**Twente**	H	D	0-0		8,500
42	hopr1	**Heerenveen**	A	W	4-2	Koevermans 10,87; Huysegems 43,49	20,800
43	erepo	**Groningen**	A	L	1-3	Jaliens 90	18,500
44	erepo	**Groningen**	H	W	2-1	Koevermans 42; Arveladze 56	8,400

LEAGUE APPEARANCES, BOOKINGS AND CAPS

	AGE (on 01/07/06)	IN NAMED 18	APPEARANCES	COUNTING GAMES	MINUTES ON PITCH	YELLOW CARDS	RED CARDS	CAPS THIS SEASON	NATIONAL SIDE
Goalkeepers									
Henk Timmer	34	34	32	32	2880	0	0	8	Holland (3)
Theo Zwarthoed	23	34	2	2	180	0	0	-	Holland
Defenders									
Tim de Cler	27	30	30	29	2678	5	0	6	Holland (3)
Kew Jaliens	27	31	30	29	2602	7	0	-	Holland
Joris Mathijsen	26	25	25	25	2235	3	0	3	Holland (3)
Barry Opdam	30	26	24	18	1833	4	1	6	Holland (3)
Juha Reini	31	3	1	0	22	0	0	-	Finland
Gretar Rafn Steinsson	24	29	19	12	1198	1	0	4	Iceland (70)
Ron Vlaar	21	12	7	3	371	2	1	3	Holland (3)
Midfielders									
Michael Buskermolen	34	22	6	0	161	1	0	-	Holland
Demy de Zeeuw	23	28	26	17	1918	3	0	-	Holland
Denny Landzaat	30	30	29	28	2581	4	0	8	Holland (3)
Kees Luijckx	20	4	0	0	0	0	0	-	Holland
Danny Mathijssen	23	5	1	0	8	0	0	-	Holland
Haris Medunjanin	21	21	10	3	530	0	0	-	Holland
Martijn Meerdink	29	26	18	6	966	1	0	1	Holland (3)
Rogier Molhoek	24	9	7	5	477	0	0	-	Holland
Stijn Schaars	22	25	24	22	2034	3	0	-	Holland
Barry van Galen	36	30	23	7	1384	3	0	-	Holland
Marien Willemsen	21	1	0	0	0	0	0	-	Holland
Forwards									
Shota Arveladze	33	32	31	24	2403	2	0	1	Georgia (84)
Stein Huysegems	24	34	32	14	1696	0	0	2	Belgium (56)
Pius Ikedia	25	13	12	3	534	1	0	-	Nigeria
Danny Koevermans	27	30	21	6	869	0	0	-	Holland
Jeremain Lens	18	3	1	0	6	0	0	-	Holland
Kenneth Perez	31	32	31	26	2348	5	0	6	Denmark (19)
Adil Ramzi	28	16	8	2	292	2	0	-	Morocco
Tarik Sektioui	29	22	19	12	1362	0	0	2	Morocco (36)

TEAM OF THE SEASON

G — Henk Timmer — CG: 32 DR: 96

D — Gretar Rafn Steinsson — CG: 12 DR: 120

D — Joris Mathijsen — CG: 25 DR: 106

D — Tim de Cler — CG: 29 DR: 99

D — Kew Jaliens — CG: 29 DR: 96

M — Denny Landzaat — CG: 28 SD: 68

M — Demy de Zeeuw — CG: 17 SD: 54

M — Stijn Schaars — CG: 22 SD: 36

M — .Stein Huysegems* — CG: 14 SD: 104

F — Shota Arveladze — CG: 24 SR: 109

F — Tarik Sektioui — CG: 12 SR: 227

MONTHLY POINTS TALLY

Month	Points	%
AUGUST	9	100%
SEPTEMBER	6	67%
OCTOBER	9	75%
NOVEMBER	5	56%
DECEMBER	9	75%
JANUARY	10	83%
FEBRUARY	7	47%
MARCH	12	100%
APRIL	7	58%

LEAGUE GOALS

	PLAYER	MINS	GOALS	S RATE
1	Arveladze	2403	22	109
2	Perez	2348	10	235
3	Landzaat	2581	9	287
4	Koevermans	869	8	109
5	Huysegems	1696	7	242
6	Sektioui	1362	6	227
7	Steinsson	1198	4	300
8	van Galen	1384	3	461
9	Medunjanin	530	3	177
10	Meerdink	966	2	483
11	Ikedia	534	1	534
12	de Zeeuw	1918	1	1918
13	Schaars	2034	1	2034
	Other		1	
	TOTAL		78	

TOP POINT EARNERS

	PLAYER	GAMES	AV PTS
1	Tarik Sektioui	12	2.58
2	Barry Opdam	18	2.39
3	Stein Huysegems	14	2.36
4	Gretar Rafn Steinsson	12	2.33
5	Tim de Cler	29	2.21
6	Henk Timmer	32	2.13
7	Joris Mathijsen	25	2.12
8	Denny Landzaat	28	2.11
9	Kew Jaliens	29	2.10
10	Stijn Schaars	22	2.05
	CLUB AVERAGE:		2.18

DISCIPLINARY RECORDS

	PLAYER	YELLOW	RED	AVE
1	Opdam	4	1	366
2	Jaliens	7	0	371
3	van Galen	3	0	461
4	Perez	5	0	469
5	Ikedia	1	0	534
6	de Cler	5	0	535
7	de Zeeuw	3	0	639
8	Landzaat	4	0	645
9	Schaars	3	0	678
10	Mathijsen, J	3	0	745
11	Meerdink	1	0	966
12	Steinsson	1	0	1198
13	Arveladze	2	0	1201
	Other	0	0	
	TOTAL	42	1	

KEY GOALKEEPER

Henk Timmer

Goals Conceded in the League	30	Counting Games League games when player was on pitch for at least 70 minutes	32
Defensive Rating Ave number of mins between League goals conceded while on the pitch	96	Clean Sheets In League games when player was on pitch for at least 70 minutes	13

KEY PLAYERS - DEFENDERS

Gretar Rafn Steinsson

Goals Conceded Number of League goals conceded while the player was on the pitch	10	Clean Sheets In League games when player was on pitch for at least 70 minutes	5
Defensive Rating Ave number of mins between League goals conceded while on the pitch	120	Club Defensive Rating Average number of mins between League goals conceded by the club this season	96

	PLAYER	CON LGE	CLEAN SHEETS	DEF RATE
1	Gretar Rafn Steinsson	10	5	120 mins
2	Joris Mathijsen	21	11	106 mins
3	Tim de Cler	27	12	99 mins
4	Kew Jaliens	27	13	96 mins

KEY PLAYERS - MIDFIELDERS

Denny Landzaat

Goals in the League	9	Contribution to Attacking Power Average number of minutes between League team goals while on pitch	40
Defensive Rating Average number of mins between League goals conceded while on the pitch	108	Scoring Difference Defensive Rating minus Contribution to Attacking Power	68

	PLAYER	LGE GOALS	DEF RATE	POWER	SCORE DIFF
1	Denny Landzaat	9	108	40	68 mins
2	Demy de Zeeuw	1	87	33	54 mins
3	Stijn Schaars	1	78	42	36 mins

KEY PLAYERS - GOALSCORERS

Shota Arveladze

Goals in the League	22	Player Strike Rate Average number of minutes between League goals scored by player	109
Contribution to Attacking Power Average number of minutes between League team goals while on pitch	42	Club Strike Rate Average number of minutes between League goals scored by club	39

	PLAYER	LGE GOALS	POWER	STRIKE RATE
1	Shota Arveladze	22	42	109 mins
2	Tarik Sektioui	6	40	227 mins
3	Kenneth Perez	10	43	235 mins
4	Stein Huysegems	7	35	242 mins

Shota Aveladze

SQUAD APPEARANCES

Match	1	2	3	4	5	6	7	8	9	10	11	12	13	14	15	16	17	18	19	20	21	22	23	24	25	26	27	28	29	30	31	32	33	34	35	36	37	38	39	40	41	42	43	44
Venue	H	A	A	H	A	H	A	H	H	A	A	H	A	H	A	H	H	A	H	A	H	H	A	A	H	H	A	H	A	A	A	H	H	H	A	A	H	A	H	A	H	A	A	H
Competition	L	L	L	L	E	L	L	E	L	L	E	L	L	L	L	E	L	E	L	L	E	L	L	L	L	L	L	L	L	L	E	L	E	L	L	L	L	L	L	L	L	L	O	O
Result	W	W	W	W	L	W	L	W	W	L	W	W	W	D	D	D	W	W	W	W	W	W	L	W	W	D	W	D	W	W	L	L	W	L	W	W	W	W	W	L	D	W	L	W

Goalkeepers
Henk Timmer
Theo Zwarthoed

Defenders
Tim de Cler
Kew Jaliens
Joris Mathijsen
Barry Opdam
Juha Reini
Gretar Rafn Steinsson
Ron Vlaar

Midfielders
Michael Buskermolen
Demy de Zeeuw
Denny Landzaat
Kees Luijckx
Danny Mathijssen
Haris Medunjanin
Martijn Meerdink
Rogier Molhoek
Stijn Schaars
Barry van Galen
Marien Willemsen

Forwards
Shota Arveladze
Stein Huysegems
Pius Ikedia
Danny Koevermans
Jeremain Lens
Kenneth Perez
Adil Ramzi
Tarik Sektioui

KEY: On all match · On bench · Subbed or sent off (Counting game) · Subbed or sent off (playing less than 70 minutes) · Subbed on from bench (Counting Game) · Subbed on (playing less than 70 minutes) · Subbed on and then subbed or sent off (Counting Game) · Subbed on and then subbed or sent off (playing less than 70 minutes) · Not in 16

FEYENOORD

Final Position: **3rd**

KEY: ☐ Won ☐ Drawn ☐ Lost

							Attendance
1	hopr1	**NAC Breda**	H	W	2-0	Pardo 25 ; Kuijt 72	42,000
2	hopr1	**S Rotterdam**	A	W	3-1	Kuijt 45; Pardo 53; Ghali 57	11,000
3	hopr1	**Ajax**	A	W	2-1	Kalou 16; Kuijt 47	49,567
4	hopr1	**NEC Nijmegen**	H	W	3-0	Kalou 37; Pardo 73; Castelen 90	39,000
5	uc1rl1	**Rap Bucharest**	H	D	1-1	Kuijt 40	15,000
6	hopr1	**Heerenveen**	H	W	5-1	Kuijt 56,73; Bahia 67; Paauwe 76; Kalou 90 pen	36,000
7	hopr1	**Twente**	A	W	3-1	Castelen 26,47; Kuijt 90	13,000
8	uc1rl2	**Rap Bucharest**	A	L	0-1		12,000
9	hopr1	**Utrecht**	A	L	1-3	Keller 39 og	20,041
10	hopr1	**Groningen**	H	W	4-1	Boussaboun 53; Kuijt 66; Kalou 72; Ghali 89	37,500
11	hopr1	**RKC Waalwijk**	A	L	1-2	Castelen 80	6,500
12	hopr1	**Willem II Tilb**	A	W	3-1	de Guzman 9; Castelen 20; Paauwe 60	13,500
13	hopr1	**Vitesse Arnhem**	H	D	0-0		40,000
14	hopr1	**Roda JC Kerk**	A	W	3-2	Kuijt 25; Bahia 33; Biseswar 80	16,000
15	hopr1	**Heracles**	H	W	7-1	Boussaboun 8,60; Greene 19; Kalou 35; Kuijt 76,81; de Guzman 90	38,000
16	hopr1	**Roosendaal**	A	D	2-2	Pardo 21; de Guzman 74	4,800
17	hopr1	**PSV Eindhoven**	H	W	1-0	Kuijt 7	45,000
18	hopr1	**Den Haag**	A	L	1-2	Kalou 66	8,633
19	hopr1	**AZ Alkmaar**	H	W	2-0	Paauwe 3; de Guzman 8	45,000
20	hopr1	**Willem II Tilb**	H	W	6-1	Kuijt 45,75,79; Pardo 50; Kalou 62,69	40,000
21	hopr1	**Vitesse Arnhem**	A	W	1-0	Bahia 28	24,000
22	hopr1	**Roda JC Kerk**	H	D	0-0		40,000
23	hopr1	**Heracles**	A	W	4-0	Kalou 25; Kuijt 36; Castelen 38; Paauwe 75	8,500
24	hopr1	**Ajax**	H	W	3-2	Hofs 21; Castelen 45; Kuijt 48	45,000
25	hopr1	**NEC Nijmegen**	A	W	2-1	Wisgerhof 83 og; Kuijt 90	12,500
26	hopr1	**NAC Breda**	A	D	3-3	Kalou 7,35; Castelen 71	16,385
27	hopr1	**S Rotterdam**	H	W	4-0	Hofs 28,37; Kuijt 52; Boussaboun 88	44,000
28	hopr1	**Groningen**	A	D	1-1	van Hooijdonk 71	19,500
29	hopr1	**Utrecht**	H	W	3-0	Kalou 41,90; Kuijt 49	44,000
30	hopr1	**RKC Waalwijk**	H	D	1-1	van Diemen 34 og	40,000
31	hopr1	**AZ Alkmaar**	A	L	0-1		8,747
32	hopr1	**Den Haag**	H	L	0-2		40,000
33	hopr1	**Twente**	H	W	4-2	Kalou 6,64; Kuijt 23 pen,61	40,000
34	hopr1	**Heerenveen**	A	D	1-1	van Hooijdonk 79	21,500
35	hopr1	**PSV Eindhoven**	A	D	1-1	Castelen 51	35,000
36	hopr1	**Roosendaal**	H	W	2-0	Kuijt 71 pen; van Hooijdonk 83	42,000
37	erepo	**Ajax**	A	L	0-3		34,364
38	erepo	**Ajax**	H	L	2-4	Kuijt 58,87	35,000

LEAGUE APPEARANCES, BOOKINGS AND CAPS

	AGE (on 01/07/06)	IN NAMED 18	APPEARANCES	COUNTING GAMES	MINUTES ON PITCH	YELLOW CARDS	RED CARDS	CAPS THIS SEASON	NATIONAL SIDE
Goalkeepers									
Maikel Aerts	29	28	8	5	559	0	0	-	Holland
Stef Doedee	19	1	0	0	0	0	0	-	Holland
Sherif Ekramy	23	8	3	2	225	0	0	-	Egypt
Jesper Hogedoorn	21	1	0	0	0	0	0	-	Holland
Patrick Lodewijks	39	27	26	25	2276	1	0	-	Holland
Defenders									
Jeffrey Altheer	19	1	0	0	0	0	0	-	Holland
Andre Bahia	22	34	34	33	3015	2	0	-	Brazil
Pieter Collen	26	18	8	5	519	0	0	-	Belgium
Timothy Derijck	19	12	1	0	4	0	0	-	Belgium
Royston Drenthe	19	15	3	0	67	0	0	-	Holland
Serginho Greene	24	32	32	30	2780	4	0	-	Holland
Christian Gyan	27	20	2	1	102	0	0	-	Ghana
Patrick Mtiliga	25	0	0	0	0	0	0	-	Denmark
Alexander Ostlund	27	18	17	15	1445	4	0	6	Sweden (16)
Patrick Paauwe	30	32	30	28	2593	6	0	-	Holland
Karim Saidi	22	11	4	1	141	0	0	4	Tunisia (21)
Ferne Snoyl	21	13	7	5	480	2	1	-	Holland
Ron Vlaar	21	16	16	16	1440	1	0	3	Holland (3)
Midfielders									
Mohammed Abubakari	20	6	0	0	0	0	0	-	Ghana
Pascal Bosschaart	26	32	29	22	2098	4	0	-	Holland
Edwin de Graaf	26	2	2	0	46	0	0	-	Holland
Jonathan de Guzman	18	30	29	27	2502	0	0	-	Canada
Hossam Ghali	24	17	16	14	1353	2	0	4	Egypt (34)
Nick Hofs	23	16	14	10	1063	3	0	-	Holland
Shinji Ono	26	5	4	2	269	1	0	3	Japan (18)
Sebastien Pardo	24	30	21	8	918	1	0	-	Chile
Michel Poldervaart	18	1	0	0	0	0	0	-	Holland
Sammuel	19	1	0	0	0	0	0	-	Brazil
Alfred Schreuder	33	1	1	1	89	0	0	-	Holland
Forwards									
Diego Biseswar	18	14	6	1	282	0	0	-	Holland
Ali Boussaboun	27	31	25	10	1216	2	0	-	Morocco
Romeo Castelen	23	23	23	21	1945	1	0	1	Holland (3)
Salomon Kalou	20	34	34	31	2902	0	0	-	Ivory Coast
Dirk Kuijt	25	33	33	33	2966	1	0	8	Holland (3)
Leonardo	23	1	1	0	21	0	0	-	Brazil
John Owoeri	19	5	1	0	2	0	0	-	Nigeria
Pierre van Hooijdonk	36	14	11	0	253	0	0	-	Holland
Tim Vincken	19	6	3	0	71	0	0	-	Holland

TEAM OF THE SEASON

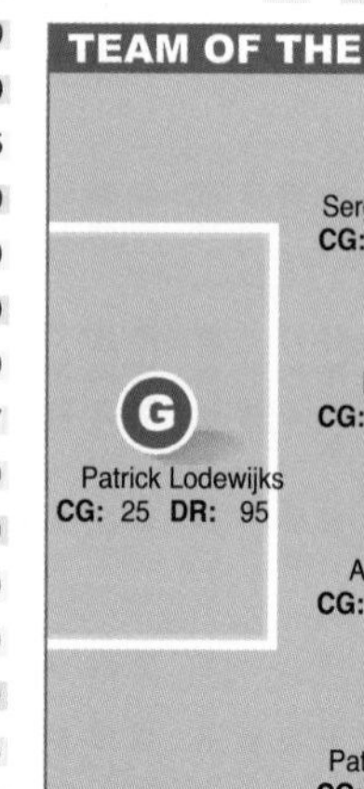

G Patrick Lodewijks CG: 25 DR: 95

D Serginho Greene CG: 30 DR: 103

D Ron Vlaar CG: 16 DR: 96

D Andre Bahia CG: 33 DR: 91

D Patrick Paauwe CG: 28 DR: 86

M Hossam Ghali CG: 14 SD: 77

M Pascal Bosschaart CG: 22 SD: 57

M Jonathan de Guzman CG: 27 SD: 43

M Romeo Castelen* CG: 21 SD: 59

F Dirk Kuijt CG: 33 SR: 135

F Salomon Kalou CG: 31 SR: 193

MONTHLY POINTS TALLY

AUGUST	9	100%
SEPTEMBER	9	100%
OCTOBER	6	50%
NOVEMBER	7	78%
DECEMBER	10	67%
JANUARY	7	78%
FEBRUARY	11	73%
MARCH	4	33%
APRIL	8	67%

LEAGUE GOALS

	PLAYER	MINS	GOALS	S RATE
1	Kuijt	2966	22	135
2	Kalou	2902	15	193
3	Castelen	1945	9	216
4	Pardo	918	5	184
5	de Guzman	2502	4	626
6	Boussaboun	1216	4	304
7	Paauwe	2593	4	648
8	Hofs	1063	3	354
9	Bahia	3015	3	1005
10	van Hooijdonk	253	3	84
11	Ghali	1353	2	677
12	Greene	2780	1	2780
13	Biseswar	282	1	282
	Other		3	
	TOTAL		79	

TOP POINT EARNERS

	PLAYER	GAMES	AV PTS
1	Hossam Ghali	14	2.50
2	Patrick Lodewijks	25	2.44
3	Alexander Ostlund	15	2.33
4	Salomon Kalou	31	2.16
5	Andre Bahia	33	2.15
6	Patrick Paauwe	28	2.14
7	Serginho Greene	30	2.13
8	Dirk Kuijt	33	2.12
9	Pascal Bosschaart	22	1.91
10	Ron Vlaar	16	1.88
	CLUB AVERAGE:		2.09

DISCIPLINARY RECORDS

	PLAYER	YELLOW	RED	AVE
1	Snoyl	2	1	160
2	Hofs	3	0	354
3	Ostlund	4	0	361
4	Paauwe	6	0	432
5	Bosschaart	4	0	524
6	Boussaboun	2	0	608
7	Ghali	2	0	676
8	Greene	4	0	695
9	Pardo	1	0	918
10	Vlaar	1	0	1440
11	Bahia	2	0	1507
12	Castelen	1	0	1945
13	Lodewijks	1	0	2276
	Other	1	0	
	TOTAL	34	1	

KEY GOALKEEPER

Patrick Lodewijks			
Goals Conceded in the League	24	**Counting Games** League games when player was on pitch for at least 70 minutes	25
Defensive Rating Ave number of mins between League goals conceded while on the pitch	95	**Clean Sheets** In League games when player was on pitch for at least 70 minutes	10

KEY PLAYERS - GOALSCORERS

Dirk Kuijt			
Goals in the League	22	**Player Strike Rate** Average number of minutes between League goals scored by player	135
Contribution to Attacking Power Average number of minutes between League team goals while on pitch	38	**Club Strike Rate** Average number of minutes between League goals scored by club	39

	PLAYER	LGE GOALS	POWER	STRIKE RATE
1	Dirk Kuijt	22	38	135 mins
2	Salomon Kalou	15	39	193 mins
3	Romeo Castelen	9	42	216 mins
4	Jonathan de Guzman	4	40	626 mins

KEY PLAYERS - DEFENDERS

Serginho Greene			
Goals Conceded Number of League goals conceded while the player was on the pitch	27	**Clean Sheets** In League games when player was on pitch for at least 70 minutes	10
Defensive Rating Ave number of mins between League goals conceded while on the pitch	103	**Club Defensive Rating** Average number of mins between League goals conceded by the club this season	90

	PLAYER	CON LGE	CLEAN SHEETS	DEF RATE
1	Serginho Greene	27	10	103 mins
2	Ron Vlaar	15	6	96 mins
3	Andre Bahia	33	11	91 mins
4	Patrick Paauwe	30	9	86 mins

Dirk Kuijt

KEY PLAYERS - MIDFIELDERS

Hossam Ghali			
Goals in the League	2	**Contribution to Attacking Power** Average number of minutes between League team goals while on pitch	36
Defensive Rating Average number of mins between League goals conceded while on the pitch	113	**Scoring Difference** Defensive Rating minus Contribution to Attacking Power	77

	PLAYER	LGE GOALS	DEF RATE	POWER	SCORE DIFF
1	Hossam Ghali	2	113	36	77 mins
2	Pascal Bosschaart	0	100	43	57 mins
3	Jonathan de Guzman	4	83	40	43 mins

SQUAD APPEARANCES

Match	1	2	3	4	5	6	7	8	9	10	11	12	13	14	15	16	17	18	19	20	21	22	23	24	25	26	27	28	29	30	31	32	33	34	35	36	37	38
Venue	H	A	A	H	H	H	A	A	A	H	A	A	H	A	H	A	H	A	H	H	A	H	A	H	A	A	H	A	H	H	A	H	H	A	A	H	A	H
Competition	L	L	L	L	E	L	L	E	L	L	L	L	L	L	L	L	L	L	L	L	L	L	L	L	L	L	L	L	L	L	L	L	L	L	L	L	O	O
Result	W	W	W	W	D	W	W	L	L	W	L	W	D	W	W	D	W	L	W	W	W	D	W	W	W	D	W	D	W	D	L	L	W	D	D	W	L	L

Goalkeepers
Maikel Aerts
Sherif Ekramy
Patrick Lodewijks

Defenders
Andre Bahia
Pieter Collen
Timothy Derijck
Royston Drenthe
Serginho Greene
Christian Gyan
Alexander Ostlund
Patrick Paauwe
Karim Saidi
Ferne Snoyl
Ron Vlaar

Midfielders
Mohammed Abubakari
Pascal Bosschaart
Edwin de Graaf
Jonathan de Guzman
Hossam Ghali
Nick Hofs
Shinji Ono
Sebastien Pardo
de Almeida C Sammuel
Alfred Schreuder

Forwards
Diego Biseswar
Ali Boussaboun
Romeo Castelen
Salomon Kalou
Dirk Kuijt
Leonardo
John Oweori
Pierre van Hooijdonk
Tim Vincken

KEY: On all match | On bench | Subbed or sent off (Counting game) | Subbed or sent off (playing less than 70 minutes) | Subbed on from bench (Counting Game) | Subbed on (playing less than 70 minutes) | Subbed on and then subbed or sent off (Counting Game) | Subbed on and then subbed or sent off (playing less than 70 minutes) | Not in 16

AJAX

Final Position: **4th**

KEY: ☐ Won ☐ Drawn ☐ Lost

							Attendance
1	hosc	**PSV Eindhoven**	H	W	2-1	Boukhari 72; Babel 78	
2	ecql1	**Brondby**	A	D	2-2	Rosenberg 31; Babel 74	24,917
3	hopr1	**Roosendaal**	A	W	2-0	Pienaar 59; Rosenberg 85	5,000
4	ecql2	**Brondby**	H	W	3-1	Babel 50; Sneijder 80,88	39,075
5	hopr1	**Feyenoord**	H	L	1-2	Charisteas 79	49,567
6	hopr1	**Willem II Tilb**	A	W	2-0	Galasek 34; Charisteas 86	12,500
7	ecgpb	**Sparta Prague**	A	D	1-1	Sneijder 90	13,500
8	hopr1	**AZ Alkmaar**	A	L	2-4	Sneijder 10,45	8,747
9	hopr1	**Den Haag**	H	D	2-2	Maduro 20; Sneijder 28	52,854
10	hopr1	**Roda JC Kerk**	H	W	4-1	Charisteas 28,40; Pienaar 70; Galasek 84 pen	48,856
11	ecgpb	**Arsenal**	H	L	1-2	Rosenberg 71	50,000
12	hopr1	**S Rotterdam**	A	W	2-1	de Jong 63,77	11,000
13	hopr1	**Heracles**	H	D	0-0		47,650
14	ecgpb	**FC Thun**	H	W	2-0	Anastasiou 36,55	44,772
15	hopr1	**PSV Eindhoven**	A	L	0-1		34,700
16	hopr1	**Heerenveen**	H	D	0-0		47,364
17	ecgpb	**FC Thun**	A	W	4-2	Sneijder 27; Deumi 63 og; de Jong 90; Boukhari 90	31,340
18	hopr1	**NEC Nijmegen**	A	L	0-1		12,000
19	hopr1	**Twente**	H	W	2-0	Majstorovic 70 og; Rosenberg 90	45,120
20	ecgpb	**Sparta Prague**	H	W	2-1	de Jong 68,89	46,158
21	hopr1	**Utrecht**	A	L	0-1		24,500
22	hopr1	**RKC Waalwijk**	H	W	4-1	Maduro 45; Sneijder 48; Rosenberg 84; Babel 86	47,500
23	ecgpb	**Arsenal**	A	D	0-0		35,376
24	hopr1	**Vitesse Arnhem**	A	W	2-0	Galasek 17 pen; Charisteas 75	25,000
25	hopr1	**NAC Breda**	A	W	2-0	Rosenberg 39; Sneijder 80	17,000
26	hopr1	**Groningen**	H	W	3-2	Rosenberg 7; Charisteas 18,67	48,547
27	hopr1	**Heerenveen**	A	L	2-4	Vermaelen 79; Galasek 90 pen	21,000
28	hopr1	**NEC Nijmegen**	H	D	1-1	Rosenberg 12	48,000
29	hopr1	**Twente**	A	W	3-2	Rosenberg 52; Maduro 89; Emanuelson 90	13,250
30	hopr1	**Utrecht**	H	L	1-4	Rosenberg 46	47,650
31	hopr1	**Feyenoord**	A	L	2-3	Rosenberg 23; Huntelaar 90	45,000
32	hopr1	**Willem II Tilb**	H	W	1-0	Rosenberg 55	44,467
33	hopr1	**Den Haag**	A	W	2-1	Grygera 30; Huntelaar 55	9,133
34	hopr1	**Roosendaal**	H	W	6-0	Huntelaar 4,71,78,83; Rosenberg 28,85	46,383
35	eclsl1	**Inter Milan**	H	D	2-2	Huntelaar 16; Rosales 20	51,000
36	hopr1	**Heracles**	A	W	3-1	Huntelaar 45; Timisela 81; Babel 90	7,000
37	hopr1	**S Rotterdam**	H	W	6-0	Boukhari 5,16; Huntelaar 42,56,62; Vermaelen 53	47,476
38	hopr1	**PSV Eindhoven**	H	D	0-0		48,741
39	eclsl2	**Inter Milan**	A	L	0-1		45,000
40	hopr1	**Groningen**	A	L	2-3	Huntelaar 17; Vermaelen 68	19,814
41	hopr1	**NAC Breda**	H	D	1-1	Huntelaar 2	47,700
42	hopr1	**Roda JC Kerk**	A	L	1-2	Huntelaar 18	16,200
43	hopr1	**AZ Alkmaar**	H	W	1-0	Boukhari 33	48,000
44	hopr1	**Vitesse Arnhem**	H	W	2-1	Huntelaar 89; Charisteas 90	45,000
45	hopr1	**RKC Waalwijk**	A	W	4-2	Heitinga 26; Huntelaar 44 pen,87; Boukhari 50	6,000
46	erepo	**Feyenoord**	H	W	3-0	Rosales 27; Heitinga 79; Huntelaar 80	34,364
47	erepo	**Feyenoord**	A	W	4-2	Rosales 34; Huntelaar 40; Boukhari 51; Mitea 81	35,000
48	erepo	**Groningen**	H	W	2-0	Rosenberg 9; Charisteas 68	38,060
49	erepo	**Groningen**	A	L	1-2	Sneijder 88	

LEAGUE APPEARANCES, BOOKINGS AND CAPS

	AGE (on 01/07/06)	IN NAMED 18	APPEARANCES	COUNTING GAMES	MINUTES ON PITCH	YELLOW CARDS	RED CARDS	CAPS THIS SEASON	NATIONAL SIDE
Goalkeepers									
Bogdan Lonut Lobont	28	10	0	0	0	0	0	3	Romania (25)
Maarten Stekelenburg	23	27	27	26	2385	1	0	-	Holland
Hans Vonk	36	31	8	7	675	0	0	-	South Africa
Defenders									
Emanuel Boakye	21	17	6	3	330	1	0	-	Ghana
Urby Emanuelson	20	27	26	22	1985	1	0	2	Holland (3)
Julien Escude	26	6	2	1	120	0	0	-	France
Zdenek Grygera	26	19	18	16	1531	6	1	9	Czech Republic (2)
John Heitinga	22	24	19	13	1397	4	1	1	Holland (3)
Juan Francisco Garcia	29	21	16	10	1034	5	1	-	Spain
Hedwiges Maduro	21	28	28	25	2339	2	0	8	Holland (3)
Robbert Schilder	20	11	4	2	209	0	0	-	Holland
Michael Timisela	20	9	4	2	197	0	0	-	Holland
Hatem Trabelsi	27	24	20	18	1680	4	0	7	Tunisia (21)
Thomas Vermaelen	20	27	24	20	1891	5	1	-	Belgium
Midfielders									
Nigel de Jong	21	18	16	10	1149	1	0	3	Holland (3)
Tomas Galasek	33	27	26	23	2185	2	0	4	Czech Republic (2)
Olaf Lindenbergh	32	31	18	15	1427	3	1	-	Holland
Rasmus Lindgren	21	0	0	0	0	0	0	-	Sweden
Edgar Manucharyan	19	5	4	1	119	0	0	1	Armenia (105)
Anthony Obodai	23	0	0	0	0	0	0	1	Ghana (48)
Steven Pienaar	24	16	15	9	1073	3	0	3	South Africa (53)
Mauro Rosales	25	33	29	22	2161	0	0	-	Argentina
Jeffrey Sarpong	17	14	9	3	450	0	0	-	Holland
Wesley Sneijder	22	19	19	16	1536	5	0	4	Holland (3)
Murat Yildirim	19	2	0	0	0	0	0	-	Turkey
Forwards									
Ioannis Anastasiou	33	14	6	1	284	0	0	-	Greece
Vurnon Anita	17	1	1	1	90	0	0	-	Holland
Ryan Babel	20	33	25	10	1265	0	0	5	Holland (3)
Derk Boerrigter	19	2	0	0	0	0	0	-	Holland
Nourdin Boukhari	26	32	24	17	1592	4	0	2	Morocco (36)
Angelos Charisteas	26	26	17	6	859	2	0	1	Greece (34)
Daniel de Ridder	22	0	0	0	0	0	0	-	Holland
Klaas Jan Huntelaar	22	16	16	16	1435	1	0	-	Holland
Javier Martina	19	1	0	0	0	0	0	-	Holland
Nicolae Mitea	21	3	1	0	1	0	0	-	Romania
Markus Rosenberg	23	34	31	21	2176	1	0	4	Sweden (16)

TEAM OF THE SEASON

G — Maarten Stekelenburg — CG: 26 DR: 80

D — Hatem Trabelsi — CG: 18 DR: 99

D — Zdenek Grygera — CG: 16 DR: 85

D — Hedwiges Maduro — CG: 25 DR: 81

D — John Heitinga — CG: 13 DR: 78

M — Mauro Rosales — CG: 22 SD: 40

M — Olaf Lindenbergh — CG: 15 SD: 30

M — Tomas Galasek — CG: 23 SD: 18

M — Wesley Sneijder — CG: 16 SD: 15

F — Klaas Jan Huntelaar — CG: 16 SR: 90

F — Markus Rosenberg — CG: 21 SR: 181

MONTHLY POINTS TALLY

AUGUST	3	50%
SEPTEMBER	7	58%
OCTOBER	5	42%
NOVEMBER	3	33%
DECEMBER	12	80%
JANUARY	4	44%
FEBRUARY	12	80%
MARCH	5	42%
APRIL	9	75%

LEAGUE GOALS

	PLAYER	MINS	GOALS	S RATE
1	Huntelaar	1435	16	90
2	Rosenberg	2176	12	181
3	Charisteas	859	8	107
4	Sneijder	1536	5	307
5	Galasek	2185	4	546
6	Boukhari	1592	4	398
7	Maduro	2339	3	780
8	Vermaelen	1891	3	630
9	Pienaar	1073	2	537
10	de Jong	1149	2	575
11	Babel	1265	2	633
12	Grygera	1531	1	1531
13	Heitinga	1397	1	1397
	Other		3	
	TOTAL		66	

TOP POINT EARNERS

	PLAYER	GAMES	AV PTS
1	Nourdin Boukhari	17	2.29
2	John Heitinga	13	2.15
3	Markus Rosenberg	21	2.00
4	Klaas Jan Huntelaar	16	1.88
5	Thomas Vermaelen	20	1.85
6	Hedwiges Maduro	25	1.84
7	Mauro Rosales	22	1.73
8	Hatem Trabelsi	18	1.72
9	Maarten Stekelenburg	26	1.69
10	Urby Emanuelson	22	1.68
	CLUB AVERAGE:		1.76

DISCIPLINARY RECORDS

	PLAYER	YELLOW	RED	AVE
1	Juanfran	5	1	172
2	Grygera	6	1	218
3	Heitinga	4	1	279
4	Sneijder	5	0	307
5	Vermaelen	5	1	315
6	Lindenbergh	3	1	356
7	Pienaar	3	0	357
8	Boukhari	4	0	398
9	Trabelsi	4	0	420
10	Charisteas	2	0	429
11	Galasek	2	0	1092
12	de Jong	1	0	1149
13	Maduro	2	0	1169
	Other	4	0	
	TOTAL	50	5	

KEY GOALKEEPER

Maarten Stekelenburg

Goals Conceded in the League	30	**Counting Games** League games when player was on pitch for at least 70 minutes	26
Defensive Rating Ave number of mins between League goals conceded while on the pitch	80	**Clean Sheets** In League games when player was on pitch for at least 70 minutes	10

KEY PLAYERS - DEFENDERS

Hatem Trabelsi

Goals Conceded Number of League goals conceded while the player was on the pitch	17	**Clean Sheets** In League games when player was on pitch for at least 70 minutes	10
Defensive Rating Ave number of mins between League goals conceded while on the pitch	99	**Club Defensive Rating** Average number of mins between League goals conceded by the club this season	75

	PLAYER	CON LGE	CLEAN SHEETS	DEF RATE
1	Hatem Trabelsi	17	10	99 mins
2	Zdenek Grygera	18	5	85 mins
3	Hedwiges Maduro	29	9	81 mins
4	John Heitinga	18	3	78 mins

KEY PLAYERS - MIDFIELDERS

Mauro Rosales

Goals in the League	0	**Contribution to Attacking Power** Average number of minutes between League team goals while on pitch	46
Defensive Rating Average number of mins between League goals conceded while on the pitch	86	**Scoring Difference** Defensive Rating minus Contribution to Attacking Power	40

	PLAYER	LGE GOALS	DEF RATE	POWER	SCORE DIFF
1	Mauro Rosales	0	86	46	40 mins
2	Olaf Lindenbergh	0	75	45	30 mins
3	Tomas Galasek	4	68	50	18 mins
4	Wesley Sneijder	5	70	55	15 mins

KEY PLAYERS - GOALSCORERS

Klaas Jan Huntelaar

Goals in the League	16	**Player Strike Rate** Average number of minutes between League goals scored by player	90
Contribution to Attacking Power Average number of minutes between League team goals while on pitch	40	**Club Strike Rate** Average number of minutes between League goals scored by club	46

	PLAYER	LGE GOALS	POWER	STRIKE RATE
1	Klaas Jan Huntelaar	16	40	90 mins
2	Markus Rosenberg	12	48	181 mins
3	Wesley Sneijder	5	55	307 mins
4	Nourdin Boukhari	4	39	398 mins

Klaas Jan Huntelaar and Nourdin Boukhari

SQUAD APPEARANCES

Match	1	2	3	4	5	6	7	8	9	10	11	12	13	14	15	16	17	18	19	20	21	22	23	24	25	26	27	28	29	30	31	32	33	34	35	36	37	38	39	40	41	42	43	44	45	46	47	48	49
Venue	H	A	A	H	H	A	A	A	H	H	H	A	H	H	A	H	A	A	H	H	A	H	A	A	A	H	A	H	A	H	A	H	A	H	H	A	H	H	A	A	H	A	H	H	A	H	A	H	A
Competition	O	C	L	C	L	L	C	L	L	L	C	L	L	C	L	L	C	L	L	C	L	L	C	L	L	L	L	L	L	L	L	L	L	L	C	L	L	L	C	L	L	L	L	L	L	O	O	O	O
Result	W	D	W	W	L	W	D	L	D	W	L	W	D	W	L	D	W	L	W	W	L	W	D	W	W	W	L	D	W	L	L	W	W	W	D	W	W	D	L	L	D	L	W	W	W	W	W	W	L

Goalkeepers
Bogdan Lonut Lobont
Maarten Stekelenburg
Hans Vonk

Defenders
Emanuel Boakye
Urby Emanuelson
Julien Escude
Zdenek Grygera
John Heitinga
Juan Francisco Garcia
Hedwiges Maduro
Robbert Schilder
Michael Timisela
Hatem Trabelsi
Thomas Vermaelen

Midfielders
Nigel de Jong
Tomas Galasek
Olaf Lindenbergh
Edgar Manucharyan
Steven Pienaar
Mauro Rosales
Jeffrey Sarpong
Wesley Sneijder
Murat Yildirim

Forwards
Ioannis Anastasiou
Vurnon Anita
Ryan Babel
Derk Boerrigter
Nourdin Boukhari
Angelos Charisteas
Klaas Jan Huntelaar
Javier Martina
Nicolae Mitea
Markus Rosenberg

KEY: On all match; On bench; Subbed or sent off (Counting game); Subbed or sent off (playing less than 70 minutes); Subbed on from bench (Counting Game); Subbed on (playing less than 70 minutes); Subbed on and then subbed or sent off (Counting Game); Subbed on and then subbed or sent off (playing less than 70 minutes); Not in 16

FC GRONINGEN

Final Position: **5th**

KEY: ☐ Won ☐ Drawn ☐ Lost

							Attendance
1	hopr1	**Roosendaal**	H	W	1-0	Cornelisse 85	11,200
2	hopr1	**RKC Waalwijk**	A	L	1-2	Lindgren 29	4,600
3	hopr1	**Heracles**	A	L	1-2	Van de Laak 19	7,813
4	hopr1	**S Rotterdam**	H	L	0-1		12,300
5	hopr1	**PSV Eindhoven**	H	W	1-0	Cornelisse 44	12,500
6	hopr1	**Vitesse Arnhem**	A	L	0-2		16,825
7	hopr1	**Willem II Tilb**	H	W	2-0	Luirink 41; Levchenko 45	12,000
8	hopr1	**Feyenoord**	A	L	1-4	Silva 8	37,500
9	hopr1	**Den Haag**	H	W	3-1	Buijs 11,43; Cornelisse 48	11,000
10	hopr1	**Roda JC Kerk**	H	W	1-0	Buijs 79	12,500
11	hopr1	**Heerenveen**	A	L	0-4		21,000
12	hopr1	**AZ Alkmaar**	H	D	0-0		12,100
13	hopr1	**NAC Breda**	A	D	2-2	Cornelisse 18 pen; Salmon 89	14,000
14	hopr1	**Twente**	H	W	1-0	Cornelisse 72	12,500
15	hopr1	**Utrecht**	A	W	2-0	Salmon 81; Cornelisse 90	23,000
16	hopr1	**NEC Nijmegen**	H	W	3-0	Salmon 17,74; Fledderus 90	12,100
17	hopr1	**Ajax**	A	L	2-3	Salmon 80; Levchenko 90	48,547
18	hopr1	**Roda JC Kerk**	A	W	3-1	Buijs 72; Fledderus 82; Nevland 88	12,000
19	hopr1	**Heerenveen**	H	W	2-0	Nevland 24; Buijs 53	20,000
20	hopr1	**AZ Alkmaar**	A	D	1-1	Salmon 16	8,476
21	hopr1	**NAC Breda**	H	W	3-2	Levchenko 18 pen; Salmon 57; Lindgren 90	20,000
22	hopr1	**Heracles**	H	D	0-0		20,000
23	hopr1	**S Rotterdam**	A	L	0-1		8,000
24	hopr1	**Roosendaal**	A	W	2-1	Nevland 42; Cornelisse 77	4,500
25	hopr1	**RKC Waalwijk**	H	W	1-0	Fledderus 22	20,000
26	hopr1	**Feyenoord**	H	D	1-1	Fledderus 12	19,500
27	hopr1	**Willem II Tilb**	A	L	0-5		11,000
28	hopr1	**Den Haag**	A	L	1-2	Nevland 15	6,546
29	hopr1	**Ajax**	H	W	3-2	Levchenko 13 pen; Nevland 45; van der Linden 71	19,814
30	hopr1	**NEC Nijmegen**	A	D	2-2	van de Laak 58; Buijs 80	12,000
31	hopr1	**Vitesse Arnhem**	H	W	2-1	Nevland 38,47	20,000
32	hopr1	**PSV Eindhoven**	A	D	1-1	Nevland 41	35,000
33	hopr1	**Utrecht**	H	W	2-1	van de Laak 50; Lindgren 58	20,000
34	hopr1	**Twente**	A	D	1-1	Cornelisse 78	13,500
35	erepo	**AZ Alkmaar**	H	W	3-1	Cornelisse 55; Fledderus 84; van der Linden 90	18,500
36	erepo	**AZ Alkmaar**	A	L	1-2	Buijs 61	8,400
37	erepo	**Ajax**	A	L	0-2		38,060
38	erepo	**Ajax**	H	W	2-1	Nevland 43; Silva 61	

LEAGUE APPEARANCES, BOOKINGS AND CAPS

	AGE (on 01/07/06)	IN NAMED 18	APPEARANCES	COUNTING GAMES	MINUTES ON PITCH	YELLOW CARDS	RED CARDS	CAPS THIS SEASON	NATIONAL SIDE
Goalkeepers									
Gijs Koopmans	20	8	0	0	0	0	0	-	Holland
Jeroen Lambers	25	26	0	0	0	0	0	-	Holland
Bas Roorda	33	34	34	34	3060	2	0	-	Holland
Defenders									
Danny Buijs	24	34	34	32	2894	4	0	-	Holland
Mathias Floren	29	33	25	14	1530	6	0	-	Sweden
Tieme Klompe	30	3	1	0	20	0	1	-	Holland
Ewald Koster	21	2	0	0	0	0	0	-	Holland
Arnold Kruiswijk	21	24	22	20	1825	5	0	-	Holland
Gijs Luirink	22	21	20	19	1700	5	0	-	Holland
Graham Ramalho	20	1	0	0	0	0	0	-	Canada
Gibril Sankoh	23	33	25	18	1767	0	0	-	Sierra Leone
Bruno Silva	26	23	20	17	1546	5	0	-	Uruguay
Koert Thalen	19	8	1	0	1	0	0	-	Holland
A. van der Linden	30	28	25	22	2102	3	0	-	Holland
Midfielders									
Mark Jan Fledderus	21	28	23	9	1158	3	0	-	Holland
Danny Holla	18	12	0	0	0	0	0	-	Holland
Yevgeniy Levchenko	28	28	28	24	2297	3	0	-	Ukraine
Rasmus Lindgren	21	32	32	25	2414	3	0	-	Sweden
Paul Matthijs	29	29	29	28	2565	6	0	-	Holland
Stefano Seedorf	24	23	19	9	1051	1	0	-	Holland
Koen Van de Laak	23	25	23	16	1626	4	0	-	Holland
Forwards									
Shutlan Axwijk	20	14	0	0	0	0	0	-	Holland
Kiran Bechan	23	14	4	0	43	0	0	-	Holland
Yuri Cornelisse	31	33	33	24	2342	4	0	-	Holland
Robbin Kieft	18	7	2	0	5	0	0	-	Holland
Rogier Krohne	19	5	3	0	21	0	0	-	Holland
Erik Nevland	28	29	29	19	1976	4	0	-	Norway
Marcel Pannekoek	20	9	1	0	2	0	0	-	Holland
Glen Salmon	28	26	24	15	1567	2	0	-	South Africa
Valery Sedoc	20	17	2	1	148	0	0	-	Holland

TEAM OF THE SEASON

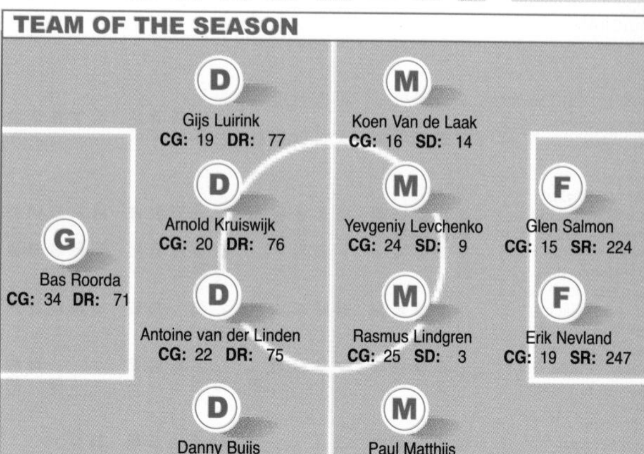

MONTHLY POINTS TALLY

AUGUST	3	33%
SEPTEMBER	3	33%
OCTOBER	9	75%
NOVEMBER	2	22%
DECEMBER	12	80%
JANUARY	7	78%
FEBRUARY	8	53%
MARCH	4	33%
APRIL	8	67%

LEAGUE GOALS

	PLAYER	MINS	GOALS	S RATE
1	Nevland	1976	8	247
2	Cornelisse	2342	8	293
3	Salmon	1567	7	224
4	Buijs	2894	6	482
5	Fledderus	1158	4	290
6	Levchenko	2297	4	574
7	Lindgren	2414	3	805
8	Van de Laak	1626	3	542
9	Luirink	1700	1	1700
10	Silva	1546	1	1546
11	van der Linden	2102	1	2102
	Other		0	
	TOTAL		46	

TOP POINT EARNERS

	PLAYER	GAMES	AV PTS
1	Glen Salmon	15	1.93
2	Antoine van der Linden	22	1.86
3	Arnold Kruiswijk	20	1.80
4	Erik Nevland	19	1.79
5	Gijs Luirink	19	1.79
6	Danny Buijs	32	1.75
7	Yuri Cornelisse	24	1.71
8	Yevgeniy Levchenko	24	1.67
9	Bas Roorda	34	1.65
10	Bruno Silva	17	1.65
	CLUB AVERAGE:		1.65

DISCIPLINARY RECORDS

	PLAYER	YELLOW	RED	AVE
1	Floren	6	0	255
2	Silva	5	0	309
3	Luirink	5	0	340
4	Kruiswijk	5	0	365
5	Fledderus	3	0	386
6	Van de Laak	4	0	406
7	Matthijs	6	0	427
8	Nevland	4	0	494
9	Cornelisse	4	0	585
10	van der Linden	3	0	700
11	Buijs	4	0	723
12	Levchenko	3	0	765
13	Salmon	2	0	783
	Other	6	0	
	TOTAL	60	0	

KEY GOALKEEPER

Bas Roorda

Goals Conceded in the League	43	Counting Games League games when player was on pitch for at least 70 minutes	34
Defensive Rating Ave number of mins between League goals conceded while on the pitch	71	Clean Sheets In games when player was on pitch for at least 70 minutes	11

KEY PLAYERS - DEFENDERS

Gijs Luirink

Goals Conceded Number of League goals conceded while the player was on the pitch	22	Clean Sheets In League games when player was on pitch for at least 70 minutes	6
Defensive Rating Ave number of mins between League goals conceded while on the pitch	77	Club Defensive Rating Average number of mins between League goals conceded by the club this season	71

	PLAYER	CON LGE	CLEAN SHEETS	DEF RATE
1	Gijs Luirink	22	6	77 mins
2	Arnold Kruiswijk	24	10	76 mins
3	Antoine van der Linden	28	6	75 mins
4	Danny Buijs	39	11	74 mins

KEY PLAYERS - MIDFIELDERS

Koen Van de Laak

Goals in the League	3	Contribution to Attacking Power Average number of minutes between League team goals while on pitch	60
Defensive Rating Average number of mins between League goals conceded while on the pitch	74	Scoring Difference Defensive Rating minus Contribution to Attacking Power	14

	PLAYER	LGE GOALS	DEF RATE	POWER	SCORE DIFF
1	Koen Van de Laak	3	74	60	14 mins
2	Yevgeniy Levchenko	4	77	68	9 mins
3	Rasmus Lindgren	3	67	64	3 mins
4	Paul Matthijs	0	71	69	2 mins

KEY PLAYERS - GOALSCORERS

Glen Salmon

Goals in the League	7	Player Strike Rate Average number of minutes between League goals scored by player	224
Contribution to Attacking Power Average number of minutes between League team goals while on pitch	63	Club Strike Rate Average number of minutes between League goals scored by club	67

	PLAYER	LGE GOALS	POWER	STRIKE RATE
1	Glen Salmon	7	63	224 mins
2	Erik Nevland	8	58	247 mins
3	Yuri Cornelisse	8	78	293 mins
4	Danny Buijs	6	67	482 mins

Erik Nevland, Glen Salmon and Koen Van de Laak

SQUAD APPEARANCES

Match	1	2	3	4	5	6	7	8	9	10	11	12	13	14	15	16	17	18	19	20	21	22	23	24	25	26	27	28	29	30	31	32	33	34	35	36	37	38
Venue	H	A	A	H	H	A	H	A	H	H	A	H	A	H	A	H	A	A	H	A	H	H	A	A	H	H	A	A	H	A	H	A	H	A	H	A	A	H
Competition	L	L	L	L	L	L	L	L	L	L	L	L	L	L	L	L	L	L	L	L	L	L	L	L	L	L	L	L	L	L	L	L	L	L	O	O	O	O
Result	W	L	L	L	W	L	W	L	W	W	L	D	D	W	W	W	L	W	W	D	W	D	L	W	W	D	L	L	W	D	W	D	W	D	W	L	L	W

Goalkeepers
Gijs Koopmans
Jeroen Lambers
Bas Roorda

Defenders
Danny Buijs
Mathias Floren
Tieme Klompe
Ewald Koster
Arnold Kruiswijk
Gijs Luirink
Graham Ramalho
Gibril Sankoh
Bruno Silva
Koert Thalen
Antoine van der Linden

Midfielders
Mark Jan Fledderus
Danny Holla
Yevgeniy Levchenko
Rasmus Lindgren
Paul Matthijs
Stefano Seedorf
Koen Van de Laak

Forwards
Shutlan Axwijk
Kiran Bechan
Yuri Cornelisse
Robbin Kieft
Rogier Krohne
Erik Nevland
Marcel Pannekoek
Glen Salmon
Valery Sedoc

KEY: ■ On all match · On bench · ⏮ Subbed or sent off (Counting game) · ◀◀ Subbed or sent off (playing less than 70 minutes) · ⏭ Subbed on from bench (Counting Game) · ▶▶ Subbed on (playing less than 70 minutes) · Subbed on and then subbed or sent off (Counting Game) · Subbed on and then subbed or sent off (playing less than 70 minutes) · Not in 16

UTRECHT

Final Position: **6th**

KEY: ☐ Won ☐ Drawn ☐ Lost

No	Comp	Opponent	Venue	Res	Score	Scorers	Attendance
1	hopr1	**NEC Nijmegen**	A	D	0-0		12,000
2	hopr1	**AZ Alkmaar**	H	L	1-2	Di Tommaso 44	20,000
3	hopr1	**Twente**	H	L	1-3	Somers 89	17,000
4	hopr1	**PSV Eindhoven**	A	L	0-1		32,000
5	hopr1	**Vitesse Arnhem**	H	W	1-0	Somers 35	17,300
6	hopr1	**RKC Waalwijk**	A	W	3-2	van den Bergh 56; Douglas 81; Fortune 90	5,500
7	hopr1	**Feyenoord**	H	W	3-1	Nelisse 7,49,52	20,041
8	hopr1	**Roda JC Kerk**	A	L	1-2	Braafheid 35	13,500
9	hopr1	**Heerenveen**	A	D	1-1	van den Bergh 43	20,500
10	hopr1	**Roosendaal**	H	W	4-1	Maachi 44,65; Broerse 59; Fortune 87	17,500
11	hopr1	**Den Haag**	H	D	1-1	Nelisse 51	17,144
12	hopr1	**NAC Breda**	A	W	1-0	Kruys 37	14,500
13	hopr1	**Ajax**	H	W	1-0	Tiendalli 59	24,500
14	hopr1	**Groningen**	H	L	0-2		23,000
15	hopr1	**Willem II Tilb**	A	W	1-0	Broerse 90	12,500
16	hopr1	**Heracles**	A	D	1-1	Fortune 27	8,254
17	hopr1	**S Rotterdam**	H	D	1-1	van den Bergh 29	20,000
18	hopr1	**Roosendaal**	A	W	2-1	Maachi 30; Tanghe 75	4,500
19	hopr1	**Den Haag**	A	W	3-2	van den Bergh 23; Nelisse 28; Tiendalli 52	6,002
20	hopr1	**NAC Breda**	H	D	2-2	Keller 33; Nelisse 46	17,500
21	hopr1	**Ajax**	A	W	4-1	Ramzi 2,48,87; Nelisse 90 pen	47,650
22	hopr1	**Twente**	A	L	0-3		13,100
23	hopr1	**PSV Eindhoven**	H	L	1-2	Ramzi 48	20,000
24	hopr1	**NEC Nijmegen**	H	D	1-1	Caluwe 22	17,500
25	hopr1	**AZ Alkmaar**	A	W	3-2	van Steensel 3; Ramzi 27; Nelisse 34 pen	8,474
26	hopr1	**Roda JC Kerk**	H	W	2-1	van den Bergh 6; Ramzi 28	18,000
27	hopr1	**Feyenoord**	A	L	0-3		44,000
28	hopr1	**Heerenveen**	H	W	2-0	Nelisse 68; Fortune 90	18,500
29	hopr1	**S Rotterdam**	A	W	1-0	van den Bergh 26	9,000
30	hopr1	**Heracles**	H	W	1-0	Fortune 90	18,000
31	hopr1	**RKC Waalwijk**	H	W	3-1	Braafheid 24; Ramzi 51; Fortune 79	24,500
32	hopr1	**Vitesse Arnhem**	A	L	0-1		19,000
33	hopr1	**Groningen**	A	L	1-2	Caluwe 74	20,000
34	hopr1	**Willem II Tilb**	H	L	1-4	Caluwe 1	24,000
35	erepo	**Twente**	A	L	0-2		10,500
36	erepo	**Twente**	H	L	1-3	Rossini 73	10,000

LEAGUE APPEARANCES, BOOKINGS AND CAPS

	AGE (on 01/07/06)	IN NAMED 18	APPEARANCES	COUNTING GAMES	MINUTES ON PITCH	YELLOW CARDS	RED CARDS	CAPS THIS SEASON	NATIONAL SIDE
Goalkeepers									
Franck Grandel	28	26	11	9	871	0	0	-	France
Daan Huiskamp	20	3	0	0	0	0	0	-	Holland
Andre Krul	19	5	0	0	0	0	0	-	Holland
Joost Terol	26	32	25	24	2189	1	0	-	Holland
Defenders									
Edson Braafheid	23	31	31	29	2700	6	0	-	Holland
David Di Tommaso	26	13	13	13	1170	1	0	-	France
Sander Keller	26	30	30	26	2545	7	0	-	Holland
Erik Pieters	17	1	0	0	0	0	0	-	Holland
Etienne Shew-Atjon	26	27	15	2	440	4	1	-	Holland
Dwight Tiendalli	20	29	29	26	2509	7	1	-	Surinam
Kees van Buuren	19	16	4	3	299	1	0	-	Holland
Leendert van Steensel	22	32	15	4	559	1	0	-	Holland
Midfielders									
Jasper Bolland	20	1	0	0	0	0	0	-	Holland
Joost Broerse	27	30	24	20	1904	4	0	-	Holland
Tom Caluwe	31	15	15	12	1237	1	0	-	Belgium
Tim Cornelisse	28	13	13	11	1116	1	1	-	Holland
Jean-Paul de Jong	35	31	28	22	2123	7	0	-	Holland
Darl Douglas	26	26	25	7	1076	2	0	-	Holland
Rick Kruys	20	34	26	14	1521	3	0	-	Holland
Hans Somers	28	31	30	24	2307	3	0	-	Belgium
Stefaan Tanghe	34	15	11	7	721	2	0	-	Belgium
Forwards									
Adnan Alesic	22	8	1	0	4	0	0	-	Holland
Marc-Antoine Fortune	25	33	31	15	1613	1	0	-	France
Nassir Maachi	20	15	10	6	726	1	0	-	Holland
Robin Nelisse	28	32	32	19	2243	1	0	-	Holland
Adil Ramzi	28	15	15	14	1301	0	0	-	Morocco
Guiseppe Rossini	19	25	8	0	92	0	0	-	Italy
Dave van den Bergh	30	31	30	25	2340	5	0	-	Holland

TEAM OF THE SEASON

G — Joost Terol, CG: 24 DR: 71

D — David Di Tommaso, CG: 13 DR: 84

D — Sander Keller, CG: 26 DR: 75

D — Edson Braafheid, CG: 29 DR: 73

D — Dwight Tiendalli, CG: 26 DR: 66

M — Rick Kruys, CG: 14 SD: 15

M — Hans Somers, CG: 24 SD: 11

M — Joost Broerse, CG: 20 SD: 10

M — Jean-Paul de Jong, CG: 22 SD: 6

F — Adil Ramzi, CG: 14 SR: 186

F — Robin Nelisse, CG: 19 SR: 249

MONTHLY POINTS TALLY

Month	Points	%
AUGUST	1	11%
SEPTEMBER	6	67%
OCTOBER	7	58%
NOVEMBER	7	78%
DECEMBER	8	53%
JANUARY	7	78%
FEBRUARY	7	47%
MARCH	12	80%
APRIL	0	0%

LEAGUE GOALS

	PLAYER	MINS	GOALS	S RATE
1	Nelisse	2243	9	249
2	Ramzi	1301	7	186
3	Fortune	1613	6	269
4	van den Bergh	2340	6	390
5	Maachi	726	3	242
6	Caluwe	1237	3	412
7	Braafheid	2700	2	1350
8	Tiendalli	2509	2	1255
9	Somers	2307	2	1154
10	Broerse	1904	2	952
11	van Steensel	559	1	559
12	Douglas	1076	1	1076
13	Tanghe	721	1	721
	Other		3	
	TOTAL		48	

TOP POINT EARNERS

	PLAYER	GAMES	AV PTS
1	Jean-Paul de Jong	22	1.82
2	Hans Somers	24	1.79
3	Joost Terol	24	1.71
4	Joost Broerse	20	1.65
5	Adil Ramzi	14	1.64
6	Dave van den Bergh	25	1.64
7	David Di Tommaso	13	1.62
8	Sander Keller	26	1.58
9	Dwight Tiendalli	26	1.50
10	Rick Kruys	14	1.50
	CLUB AVERAGE:		1.62

DISCIPLINARY RECORDS

	PLAYER	YELLOW	RED	AVE
1	de Jong	7	0	303
2	Tiendalli	7	1	313
3	Tanghe	2	0	360
4	Keller	7	0	363
5	Braafheid	6	0	450
6	van den Bergh	5	0	468
7	Broerse	4	0	476
8	Kruys	3	0	507
9	Douglas	2	0	538
10	Cornelisse	1	1	558
11	van Steensel	1	0	559
12	Maachi	1	0	726
13	Somers	3	0	769
	Other	5	0	
	TOTAL	54	2	

KEY GOALKEEPER

Joost Terol

Goals Conceded in the League	31	Counting Games League games when player was on pitch for at least 70 minutes	24
Defensive Rating Ave number of mins between League goals conceded while on the pitch	71	Clean Sheets In League games when player was on pitch for at least 70 minutes	6

KEY PLAYERS - DEFENDERS

David Di Tommaso

Goals Conceded Number of League goals conceded while the player was on the pitch	14	Clean Sheets In League games when player was on pitch for at least 70 minutes	4
Defensive Rating Ave number of mins between League goals conceded while on the pitch	84	Club Defensive Rating Average number of mins between League goals conceded by the club this season	70

	PLAYER	CON LGE	CLEAN SHEETS	DEF RATE
1	David Di Tommaso	14	4	84 mins
2	Sander Keller	34	6	75 mins
3	Edson Braafheid	37	7	73 mins
4	Dwight Tiendalli	38	6	66 mins

KEY PLAYERS - MIDFIELDERS

Rick Kruys

Goals in the League	1	Contribution to Attacking Power Average number of minutes between League team goals while on pitch	80
Defensive Rating Average number of mins between League goals conceded while on the pitch	95	Scoring Difference Defensive Rating minus Contribution to Attacking Power	15

	PLAYER	LGE GOALS	DEF RATE	POWER	SCORE DIFF
1	Rick Kruys	1	95	80	15 mins
2	Hans Somers	2	66	55	11 mins
3	Joost Broerse	2	68	58	10 mins
4	Jean-Paul de Jong	0	79	73	6 mins

KEY PLAYERS - GOALSCORERS

Adil Ramzi

Goals in the League	7	Player Strike Rate Average number of minutes between League goals scored by player	186
Contribution to Attacking Power Average number of minutes between League team goals while on pitch	59	Club Strike Rate Average number of minutes between League goals scored by club	64

	PLAYER	LGE GOALS	POWER	STRIKE RATE
1	Adil Ramzi	7	59	186 mins
2	Robin Nelisse	9	62	249 mins
3	Marc-Antoine Fortune	6	85	269 mins
4	Dave van den Bergh	6	62	390 mins

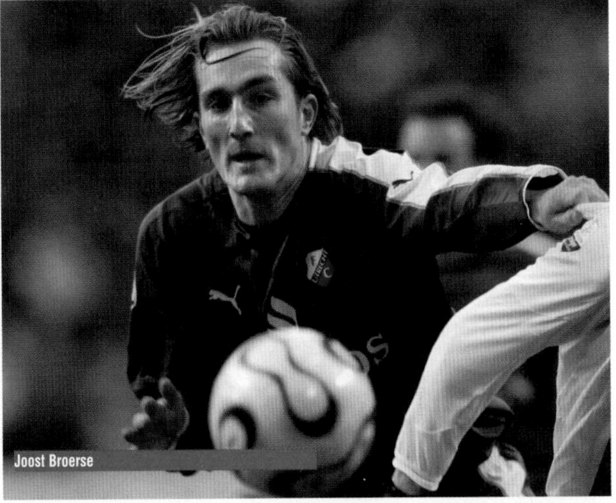
Joost Broerse

SQUAD APPEARANCES

1atch	1	2	3	4	5	6	7	8	9	10	11	12	13	14	15	16	17	18	19	20	21	22	23	24	25	26	27	28	29	30	31	32	33	34	35	36
'enue	A	H	H	A	H	A	H	A	A	H	H	A	H	H	A	A	H	A	A	H	A	A	H	H	A	H	A	H	A	H	H	A	A	H	A	H
;ompetition	L	L	L	L	L	L	L	L	L	L	L	L	L	L	L	L	L	L	L	L	L	L	L	L	L	L	L	L	L	L	L	L	L	L	O	O
Result	D	L	L	L	W	W	W	L	D	W	D	W	W	L	W	D	D	W	W	D	W	L	L	D	W	W	L	W	W	W	W	L	L	L	L	L

Goalkeepers
ranck Grandel
aan Huiskamp
ndre Krul
oost Terol

Defenders
dson Braafheid
avid Di Tommaso
ander Keller
tienne Shew-Atjon
wight Tiendalli
ees van Buuren
eendert van Steensel

Midfielders
oost Broerse
Tom Caluwe
Tim Cornelisse
ean-Paul de Jong
Darl Douglas
Rick Kruys
Hans Somers
Stefaan Tanghe

Forwards
Adnan Alesic
Marc-Antoine Fortune
Nassir Maachi
Robin Nelisse
Adil Ramzi
Guiseppe Rossini
Dave van den Bergh

KEY: On all match | On bench | Subbed or sent off (Counting game) | Subbed or sent off (playing less than 70 minutes) | Subbed on from bench (Counting Game) | Subbed on (playing less than 70 minutes) | Subbed on and then subbed or sent off (Counting Game) | Subbed on and then subbed or sent off (playing less than 70 minutes) | Not in 16

HEERENVEEN

Final Position: **7th**

KEY: ☐Won ☐Drawn ☐Lost

	Comp	Opponent	H/A	Res	Score	Scorers	Attendance
1	hopr1	**Vitesse Arnhem**	A	D	2-2	Huntelaar 66; Hansson 82	18,500
2	hopr1	**Roda JC Kerk**	H	W	5-4	Yildirim 45; Samaras 49; Pranjic 54; Huntelaar 57,76	20,500
3	hopr1	**Den Haag**	A	L	0-1		6,025
4	hopr1	**Heracles**	H	L	1-2	Huntelaar 80 pen	20,500
5	uc1rl1	**Banik Ostrava**	A	L	0-2		10,330
6	hopr1	**Feyenoord**	A	L	1-5	Yildirim 11	36,000
7	hopr1	**NEC Nijmegen**	H	W	2-1	Samaras 1; Pranjic 70	20,400
8	uc1rl2	**Banik Ostrava**	H	W	5-0	Samaras 3; Nilsson 45; Huntelaar 59,66; Yildirim 65	16,500
9	hopr1	**PSV Eindhoven**	H	L	2-3	Bosvelt 16; Tarvajarvi 82	21,000
10	hopr1	**NAC Breda**	A	W	3-0	Huntelaar 5,25,47	14,850
11	ucgpf	**Din Bucharest**	A	D	0-0		10,000
12	hopr1	**Utrecht**	H	D	1-1	Tarvajarvi 90	20,500
13	hopr1	**Ajax**	A	D	0-0		47,364
14	ucgpf	**CSKA Moscow**	H	D	0-0		20,200
15	hopr1	**Groningen**	H	W	4-0	Huntelaar 5,47; Bosvelt 43; Samaras 74	21,000
16	hopr1	**S Rotterdam**	A	W	2-1	Derveld 41; Huntelaar 53	11,000
17	ucgpf	**Marseille**	A	L	0-1		14,777
18	hopr1	**Roosendaal**	H	W	2-0	Bruggink 38; Norrgaard 78	20,200
19	hopr1	**AZ Alkmaar**	A	L	1-2	Samaras 81	8,000
20	hopr1	**Willem II Tilb**	H	D	3-3	Bruggink 40; Huntelaar 65,68	20,000
21	ucgpf	**Levski Sofia**	H	W	2-1	Samaras 54; Hanssen 90	20,025
22	hopr1	**Twente**	H	W	3-1	Huntelaar 13,49 pen; Nilsson 41	20,500
23	hopr1	**RKC Waalwijk**	A	D	2-2	Huntelaar 48,60	6,100
24	hopr1	**Ajax**	H	W	4-2	Samaras 35,76; Huntelaar 38; Hanssen 67	21,000
25	hopr1	**Groningen**	A	L	0-2		20,000
26	hopr1	**S Rotterdam**	H	D	0-0		20,600
27	hopr1	**Roosendaal**	A	W	2-0	Bruggink 31; Hansson 84	4,500
28	hopr1	**Den Haag**	H	W	3-0	Nilsson 3,34,78	20,500
29	hopr1	**Heracles**	A	D	1-1	Nilsson 45	8,500
30	hopr1	**Vitesse Arnhem**	H	W	4-1	Yildirim 20,76; Bosvelt 49; Nilsson 61	20,600
31	uc3rl1	**S Bucharest**	H	L	1-3	Bruggink 24	21,000
32	hopr1	**Roda JC Kerk**	A	L	1-2	Bruggink 17	13,400
33	uc3rl2	**S Bucharest**	A	W	1-0	Bruggink 84	50,000
34	hopr1	**NAC Breda**	H	W	2-1	Norrgaard 2; Pranjic 81	19,000
35	hopr1	**PSV Eindhoven**	A	L	1-4	de Vries 62	33,400
36	hopr1	**Utrecht**	A	L	0-2		18,500
37	hopr1	**RKC Waalwijk**	H	W	2-1	Pranjic 67; Bruggink 89	20,500
38	hopr1	**Twente**	A	W	2-1	Nilsson 17,35	1,300
39	hopr1	**NEC Nijmegen**	A	L	1-4	Nilsson 17; Pothuizen 66 pen	12,000
40	hopr1	**Feyenoord**	H	D	1-1	Tarvajarvi 48	21,500
41	hopr1	**Willem II Tilb**	A	L	3-4	de Vries 44; Bosvelt 59; Bruggink 63	12,000
42	hopr1	**AZ Alkmaar**	H	L	2-4	de Vries 62; Pranjic 72	20,800
43	erepo	**Roda JC Kerk**	A	D	0-0		8,500
44	erepo	**Roda JC Kerk**	H	W	1-0	Lachambre 29 og	10,000
45	erepo	**Twente**	A	W	1-0	Poulsen 87	13,000
46	erepo	**Twente**	H	W	5-0	Bosvelt 12; Nilsson 40,56; Pranjic 71,75 pen	

LEAGUE APPEARANCES, BOOKINGS AND CAPS

	AGE (on 01/07/06)	IN NAMED 18	APPEARANCES	COUNTING GAMES	MINUTES ON PITCH	YELLOW CARDS	RED CARDS	CAPS THIS SEASON	NATIONAL SIDE
Goalkeepers									
Kevin Moeliker	26	16	0	0	0	0	0	-	Holland
Sven Taberima	20	6	0	0	0	0	0	-	Holland
Brian Vandenbussche	24	34	24	24	2142	0	0	-	Belgium
Boy Waterman	22	13	12	12	1008	1	0	-	Holland
Defenders									
Said Bakkati	24	19	8	5	524	0	0	-	Holland
Pim Balkestein	19	1	0	0	0	0	0	-	Holland
Michel Breuer	26	30	30	28	2591	3	0	-	Holland
Fernando Derveld	29	31	17	7	914	3	0	-	Holland
Henrico Drost	19	23	11	4	577	0	0	-	Holland
Jeroen Drost	19	28	24	22	2000	0	0	-	Holland
Petter Hansson	29	33	33	33	2970	2	0	5	Sweden (16)
Robbert Maruanaya	20	4	0	0	0	0	0	-	Holland
Marcel Seip	24	30	28	21	2116	4	2	-	Holland
Midfielders									
Paul Bosvelt	36	30	30	26	2537	7	1	-	Holland
Michael Bradley	18	3	1	1	90	0	0	1	United States (5)
Arnold Bruggink	28	33	31	20	2163	5	0	-	Holland
Andre Hanssen	25	20	10	3	438	1	0	-	Norway
Abdelkarim Kissi	26	15	15	10	1143	2	0	-	Morocco
Hjalte Bo Norregaard	25	31	16	6	842	0	0	-	Denmark
Jakob Poulsen	23	10	7	7	630	0	0	-	Denmark
Thomas Prager	20	24	15	5	644	1	0	-	Austria
Danijel Pranjic	24	32	32	32	2867	3	0	-	Croatia
Oguzhan Turk	20	1	0	0	0	0	0	-	Holland
Ugur Yildirim	24	30	30	26	2459	4	0	-	Holland
Forwards									
Mark de Vries	30	7	6	1	287	0	0	-	Holland
R.Ghoochannejhad	-	3	1	0	7	0	0	-	Holland
Klaas Jan Huntelaar	22	15	15	12	1218	0	1	-	Holland
Ken Ilso Larsen	19	1	1	0	16	0	0	-	Denmark
Lasse Nilsson	24	29	27	16	1744	0	1	-	Sweden
Rawley Rozendaal	18	1	0	0	0	0	0	-	Holland
Georgios Samaras	21	17	15	11	1095	0	0	-	Holland
Lasse Schone	20	1	0	0	0	0	0	-	Denmark
Sebastiaan Steur	22	13	3	0	13	0	0	-	Holland
Niklas Tarvajarvi	23	23	17	2	462	0	0	-	Finland
Joey van de Berg	20	1	1	0	26	0	0	-	Holland

TEAM OF THE SEASON

G — Boy Waterman — CG: 12 DR: 56

D — Michel Breuer — CG: 28 DR: 59

D — Jeroen Drost — CG: 22 DR: 59

D — Petter Hansson — CG: 33 DR: 55

D — Marcel Seip — CG: 21 DR: 53

M — Ugur Yildirim — CG: 26 SD: 9

M — Danijel Pranjic — CG: 32 SD: 8

M — Arnold Bruggink — CG: 20 SD: 6

M — Paul Bosvelt — CG: 26 SD: 4

F — Klaas Jan Huntelaar — CG: 12 SR: 72

F — Lasse Nilsson — CG: 16 SR: 194

MONTHLY POINTS TALLY

Month	Points	%
AUGUST	4	44%
SEPTEMBER	3	33%
OCTOBER	5	42%
NOVEMBER	9	100%
DECEMBER	8	53%
JANUARY	4	44%
FEBRUARY	10	67%
MARCH	6	50%
APRIL	1	8%

LEAGUE GOALS

	PLAYER	MINS	GOALS	S RATE
1	Huntelaar	1218	17	72
2	Nilsson	1744	9	194
3	Bruggink	2163	7	309
4	Samaras	1095	6	183
5	Pranjic	2867	5	573
6	Yildirim	2459	4	615
7	Bosvelt	2537	4	634
8	Tarvajarvi	462	3	154
9	de Vries	287	3	96
10	Hansson	2970	2	1485
11	Norregaard	842	2	421
12	Hanssen	438	1	438
13	Derveld	914	1	914
	Other		1	
	TOTAL		65	

TOP POINT EARNERS

	PLAYER	GAMES	AV PTS
1	Klaas Jan Huntelaar	12	1.83
2	Michel Breuer	28	1.61
3	Brian Vandenbussche	24	1.58
4	Lasse Nilsson	16	1.56
5	Petter Hansson	33	1.52
6	Marcel Seip	21	1.52
7	Jeroen Drost	22	1.50
8	Danijel Pranjic	32	1.47
9	Ugur Yildirim	26	1.46
10	Paul Bosvelt	26	1.42
	CLUB AVERAGE:		1.47

DISCIPLINARY RECORDS

	PLAYER	YELLOW	RED	AVE
1	Derveld	3	0	304
2	Bosvelt	7	1	317
3	Seip	4	2	352
4	Bruggink	5	0	432
5	Kissi	2	0	571
6	Yildirim	4	0	614
7	Prager	1	0	644
8	Breuer	3	0	863
9	Pranjic	3	0	955
10	Waterman	1	0	1008
11	Huntelaar	0	1	1218
12	Hansson	2	0	1485
13	Nilsson	0	1	1744
	Other	0	0	
	TOTAL	35	5	

KEY GOALKEEPER

Boy Waterman			
Goals Conceded in the League	18	Counting Games League games when player was on pitch for at least 70 minutes	12
Defensive Rating Ave number of mins between League goals conceded while on the pitch	56	Clean Sheets In League games when player was on pitch for at least 70 minutes	4

KEY PLAYERS - DEFENDERS

Michel Breuer			
Goals Conceded Number of League goals conceded while the player was on the pitch	44	Clean Sheets In League games when player was on pitch for at least 70 minutes	6
Defensive Rating Ave number of mins between League goals conceded while on the pitch	59	Club Defensive Rating Average number of mins between League goals conceded by the club this season	53

	PLAYER	CON LGE	CLEAN SHEETS	DEF RATE
1	Michel Breuer	44	6	59 mins
2	Jeroen Drost	34	5	59 mins
3	Petter Hansson	54	7	55 mins
4	Marcel Seip	40	6	53 mins

KEY PLAYERS - MIDFIELDERS

Ugur Yildirim			
Goals in the League	4	Contribution to Attacking Power Average number of minutes between League team goals while on pitch	46
Defensive Rating Average number of mins between League goals conceded while on the pitch	55	Scoring Difference Defensive Rating minus Contribution to Attacking Power	9

	PLAYER	LGE GOALS	DEF RATE	POWER	SCORE DIFF
1	Ugur Yildirim	4	55	46	9 mins
2	Danijel Pranjic	5	54	46	8 mins
3	Arnold Bruggink	7	53	47	6 mins
4	Paul Bosvelt	4	51	47	4 mins

KEY PLAYERS - GOALSCORERS

Klaas Jan Huntelaar			
Goals in the League	17	Player Strike Rate Average number of minutes between League goals scored by player	72
Contribution to Attacking Power Average number of minutes between League team goals while on pitch	39	Club Strike Rate Average number of minutes between League goals scored by club	47

	PLAYER	LGE GOALS	POWER	STRIKE RATE
1	Klaas Jan Huntelaar	17	39	72 mins
2	Lasse Nilsson	9	56	194 mins
3	Arnold Bruggink	7	47	309 mins
4	Danijel Pranjic	5	46	573 mins

Lars Nilsson, Niklas Tarvajarvi and Danijel Pranjic

SQUAD APPEARANCES

Match	1	2	3	4	5	6	7	8	9	10	11	12	13	14	15	16	17	18	19	20	21	22	23
Venue	A	H	A	H	A	A	H	H	H	A	A	H	A	H	H	A	A	H	A	H	H	H	A
Competition	L	L	L	L	E	L	L	E	L	L	E	L	L	E	L	L	E	L	L	L	E	L	L
Result	D	W	L	L	L	L	W	W	L	W	D	D	D	D	W	W	L	W	L	D	W	W	D

Match	24	25	26	27	28	29	30	31	32	33	34	35	36	37	38	39	40	41	42	43	44	45	46
Venue	H	A	H	A	H	A	H	H	A	A	H	A	A	H	A	A	H	A	H	A	H	A	H
Competition	L	L	L	L	L	L	L	E	L	E	L	L	L	L	L	L	L	L	L	O	O	O	O
Result	W	L	D	W	W	D	W	L	L	W	W	L	L	W	W	L	D	L	L	D	W	W	W

Goalkeepers
Kevin Moeliker
Sven Taberima
Brian Vandenbussche
Boy Waterman

Defenders
Said Bakkati
Tim Balkestein
Michel Breuer
Fernando Derveld
Henrico Drost
Jeroen Drost
Petter Hansson
Robbert Maruanaya
Marcel Seip

Midfielders
Paul Bosvelt
Michael Bradley
Arnold Bruggink
Andre Hanssen
Abdelkarim Kissi
Hjalte Bo Norregaard
Jakob Poulsen
Thomas Prager
Danijel Pranjic
Oguzhan Turk
Ugur Yildirim

Forwards
Mark de Vries
Reza Ghoochannejhad
Klaas Jan Huntelaar
Ken Ilso Larsen
Lasse Nilsson
Rawley Rozendaal
Georgios Samaras
Lasse Schone
Sebastiaan Steur
Niklas Tarvajarvi
Joey van de Berg

KEY: On all match | On bench | Subbed or sent off (Counting game) | Subbed or sent off (playing less than 70 minutes) | Subbed on from bench (Counting Game) | Subbed on (playing less than 70 minutes) | Subbed on and then subbed or sent off (Counting Game) | Subbed on and then subbed or sent off (playing less than 70 minutes) | Not in 16

RODA JC KERK

Final Position: **8th**

KEY: ☐ Won ☐ Drawn ☐ Lost

		Opponent	H/A	Result	Score	Scorers	Attendance
1	etsfl2	**Valencia**	H	D	0-0		8,000
2	hopr1	**Twente**	H	W	2-0	Sonko 33; Kone 80	11,500
3	hopr1	**Heerenveen**	A	L	4-5	Sonko 15; Kone 44; van Dijk 79 pen; Sergio 82	20,500
4	hopr1	**PSV Eindhoven**	H	L	0-3		14,000
5	hopr1	**RKC Waalwijk**	A	L	0-2		6,800
6	hopr1	**Willem II Tilb**	H	L	0-2		13,200
7	hopr1	**Ajax**	A	L	1-4	Sonko 81	48,856
8	hopr1	**Vitesse Arnhem**	H	W	3-2	Senden 35; Sergio 40; Oper 73	13,000
9	hopr1	**Utrecht**	H	W	2-1	Sergio 54; Oper 58	13,500
10	hopr1	**S Rotterdam**	A	W	3-2	Zoontjes 30 og; Cisse 64; Oper 70	8,212
11	hopr1	**Groningen**	A	L	0-1		12,500
12	hopr1	**NAC Breda**	H	D	3-3	Sergio 25; Oper 45; Bodnar 84	13,500
13	hopr1	**Feyenoord**	H	L	2-3	Sergio 28; Oper 45	16,000
14	hopr1	**AZ Alkmaar**	A	L	0-2		8,377
15	hopr1	**Heracles**	A	W	1-0	Sergio 12	8,153
16	hopr1	**NEC Nijmegen**	H	L	0-1		12,500
17	hopr1	**Roosendaal**	A	W	2-0	Bodnar 20; van Dijk 43	4,600
18	hopr1	**Den Haag**	H	W	3-1	Vicelich 76; Oper 82; Bodor 90	9,500
19	hopr1	**Groningen**	H	L	1-3	Oper 11	12,000
20	hopr1	**NAC Breda**	A	W	4-0	Vicelich 7; van Dijk 61; Oper 76; Cisse 90	13,498
21	hopr1	**Feyenoord**	A	D	0-0		40,000
22	hopr1	**AZ Alkmaar**	H	L	1-4	Voigt 18	12,500
23	hopr1	**PSV Eindhoven**	A	L	2-3	Cziommer 3; Sergio 5	33,100
24	hopr1	**RKC Waalwijk**	H	W	1-0	Cristiano 59	12,500
25	hopr1	**Twente**	A	L	0-1		13,200
26	hopr1	**Heerenveen**	H	W	2-1	van Dijk 53 pen; Cziommer 66	13,400
27	hopr1	**Utrecht**	A	L	1-2	van Dijk 43	18,000
28	hopr1	**Vitesse Arnhem**	A	W	3-1	Cziommer 45; Bodor 80,90	19,000
29	hopr1	**S Rotterdam**	H	D	1-1	Cziommer 57	12,500
30	hopr1	**Den Haag**	A	D	1-1	Sonko 25	6,512
31	hopr1	**Roosendaal**	H	W	5-1	Cziommer 8,24,73; Sonko 29; Rudge 86	13,500
32	hopr1	**Ajax**	H	W	2-1	Lindenbergh 27 og; Sonko 89	16,200
33	hopr1	**Willem II Tilb**	A	D	2-2	Cristiano 19; Rudge 65	12,000
34	hopr1	**NEC Nijmegen**	A	W	3-0	Cristiano 9,66; Cisse 90	11,500
35	hopr1	**Heracles**	H	W	2-1	Cisse 27; Cziommer 38 pen	13,000
36	erepo	**Heerenveen**	H	D	0-0		8,500
37	erepo	**Heerenveen**	A	L	0-1		10,000

LEAGUE APPEARANCES, BOOKINGS AND CAPS

	AGE (on 01/07/06)	IN NAMED 18	APPEARANCES	COUNTING GAMES	MINUTES ON PITCH	YELLOW CARDS	RED CARDS	CAPS THIS SEASON	NATIONAL SIDE
Goalkeepers									
Kevin Begois	24	21	2	2	180	0	0	-	Belgium
Bram Castro	23	9	0	0	0	0	0	-	Belgium
Vladan Kujovic	27	33	32	32	2880	0	0	-	Serbia & Montenegro
Defenders									
Roy Bejas	19	8	0	0	0	0	0	-	Holland
Laszlo Bodnar	27	15	15	14	1234	0	2	6	Hungary (54)
Boldizar Bodor	24	32	32	29	2709	4	0	-	Hungary
Predrag Filipovic	31	18	12	8	786	1	0	-	Serbia & Montenegro
Pa Modou Kah	25	32	32	30	2737	5	2	-	Norway
Vincent Lachambre	25	32	31	28	2579	6	0	-	Belgium
Ken Leemans	23	29	20	12	1248	3	0	-	Belgium
Humprey Rudge	28	11	5	0	89	0	0	-	Holland
Jan-Paul Saeijs	28	11	11	10	954	3	0	-	Holland
Ger Senden	35	29	24	23	2036	6	0	-	Holland
Alexander Voigt	28	29	16	9	948	2	0	-	Germany
Midfielders									
Okan Ayaz	24	2	0	0	0	0	0	-	Belgium
Jerome Colinet	23	17	4	0	56	0	0	-	Belgium
Simon Cziommer	25	15	15	14	1307	3	0	-	Germany
Dirk Jan Derksen	-	14	6	0	191	0	0	-	
Olaf Rompelberg	19	11	0	0	0	0	0	-	Holland
Sergio	25	33	33	31	2874	4	0	-	Brazil
Edrissa Sonko	26	27	19	4	621	0	0	-	Gambia
C. van den Ouweland	24	7	0	0	0	0	0	-	Holland
Kevin van Dessel	27	7	7	1	326	2	0	-	Belgium
Gregoor van Dijk	24	29	28	24	2365	8	2	-	Holland
Ivan Vicelich	30	31	27	22	2115	0	0	-	New Zealand
Forwards									
Sekou Cisse	21	28	27	20	2096	2	1	-	Ivory Coast
Cristiano	25	25	20	7	912	1	0	-	Brazil
Diego Jongen	23	7	1	0	7	0	0	-	Holland
Arouna Kone	22	2	2	2	180	0	0	11	Ivory Coast (32)
Andres Oper	28	24	24	22	2049	2	0	4	Estonia (61)

TEAM OF THE SEASON

G Vladan Kujovic CG: 32 DR: 59

D Ken Leemans CG: 12 DR: 89

D Vincent Lachambre CG: 28 DR: 63

D Boldizar Bodor CG: 29 DR: 56

D Ger Senden CG: 23 DR: 55

M Simon Cziommer CG: 14 SD: 25

M Ivan Vicelich CG: 22 SD: 8

M Gregoor van Dijk CG: 24 SD: -1

M Sergio CG: 31 SD: -2

F Andres Oper CG: 22 SR: 256

F Sekou Cisse CG: 20 SR: 524

MONTHLY POINTS TALLY

AUGUST	3	33%
SEPTEMBER	0	0%
OCTOBER	9	75%
NOVEMBER	1	11%
DECEMBER	9	60%
JANUARY	4	44%
FEBRUARY	6	40%
MARCH	8	67%
APRIL	10	83%

LEAGUE GOALS

	PLAYER	MINS	GOALS	S RATE
1	Cziommer	1307	**8**	163
2	Oper	2049	**8**	256
3	Sergio	2874	**7**	411
4	Sonko	621	**6**	104
5	van Dijk, G	2365	**5**	473
6	Cristiano	912	**4**	228
7	Cisse	2096	**4**	524
8	Kone	180	**2**	90
9	Vicelich	2115	**2**	1058
10	Bodnar	1234	**2**	617
11	Rudge	89	**2**	45
12	Bodor	2709	**2**	1355
13	Voigt	948	**1**	948
	Other		**4**	
	TOTAL		**57**	

TOP POINT EARNERS

	PLAYER	GAMES	AV PTS
1	Simon Cziommer	14	**1.86**
2	Ken Leemans	12	**1.83**
3	Ger Senden	23	**1.57**
4	Vincent Lachambre	28	**1.57**
5	Pa Modou Kah	30	**1.57**
6	Ivan Vicelich	22	**1.55**
7	Sergio	31	**1.52**
8	Gregoor van Dijk	24	**1.50**
9	Sekou Cisse	20	**1.50**
10	Andres Oper	22	**1.50**
	CLUB AVERAGE:		**1.47**

DISCIPLINARY RECORDS

	PLAYER	YELLOW	RED	AVE
1	van Dijk, G	8	2	**236**
2	Saeijs	3	0	**318**
3	Senden	6	0	**339**
4	Kah	5	2	**391**
5	Leemans	3	0	**416**
6	Lachambre	6	0	**429**
7	Cziommer	3	0	**435**
8	Voigt	2	0	**474**
9	Bodnar	0	2	**617**
10	Bodor	4	0	**677**
11	Cisse	2	1	**698**
12	Sergio	4	0	**718**
13	Filipovic	1	0	**786**
	Other	3	0	
	TOTAL	**50**	**7**	

KEY GOALKEEPER

Vladan Kujovic

Goals Conceded in the League	49	**Counting Games** League games when player was on pitch for at least 70 minutes	32
Defensive Rating Ave number of mins between League goals conceded while on the pitch	59	**Clean Sheets** In games when player was on pitch for at least 70 minutes	7

KEY PLAYERS - DEFENDERS

Ken Leemans

Goals Conceded Number of League goals conceded while the player was on the pitch	14	**Clean Sheets** In League games when player was on pitch for at least 70 minutes	4
Defensive Rating Ave number of mins between League goals conceded while on the pitch	89	**Club Defensive Rating** Average number of mins between League goals conceded by the club this season	57

	PLAYER	CON LGE	CLEAN SHEETS	DEF RATE
1	Ken Leemans	14	4	89 mins
2	Vincent Lachambre	41	5	63 mins
3	Boldizar Bodor	48	7	56 mins
4	Ger Senden	37	4	55 mins

KEY PLAYERS - MIDFIELDERS

Simon Cziommer

Goals in the League	8	**Contribution to Attacking Power** Average number of minutes between League team goals while on pitch	48
Defensive Rating Average number of mins between League goals conceded while on the pitch	73	**Scoring Difference** Defensive Rating minus Contribution to Attacking Power	25

	PLAYER	LGE GOALS	DEF RATE	POWER	SCORE DIFF
1	Simon Cziommer	8	73	48	25 mins
2	Ivan Vicelich	2	62	54	8 mins
3	Gregoor van Dijk	5	50	51	-1 mins
4	Sergio	7	57	59	-2 mins

KEY PLAYERS - GOALSCORERS

Simon Cziommer

Goals in the League	8	**Player Strike Rate** Average number of minutes between League goals scored by player	163
Contribution to Attacking Power Average number of minutes between League team goals while on pitch	48	**Club Strike Rate** Average number of minutes between League goals scored by club	54

	PLAYER	LGE GOALS	POWER	STRIKE RATE
1	Simon Cziommer	8	48	163 mins
2	Andres Oper	8	60	256 mins
3	Sergio	7	59	411 mins
4	Gregoor van Dijk	5	51	473 mins

Andres Oper

SQUAD APPEARANCES

Match	1	2	3	4	5	6	7	8	9	10	11	12	13	14	15	16	17	18	19	20	21	22	23	24	25	26	27	28	29	30	31	32	33	34	35	36	37
Venue	H	H	A	H	A	H	A	H	H	A	A	H	H	A	A	H	A	H	H	A	A	H	A	H	A	H	A	A	H	A	H	H	A	A	H	H	A
Competition	O	L	L	L	L	L	L	L	L	L	L	L	L	L	L	L	L	L	L	L	L	L	L	L	L	L	L	L	L	L	L	L	L	L	L	O	O
Result	D	W	L	L	L	L	L	W	W	W	L	D	L	L	W	L	W	W	L	W	D	L	L	W	L	W	L	W	D	D	W	W	D	W	W	D	L

Goalkeepers
Kevin Begois
Bram Castro
Vladan Kujovic

Defenders
Roy Bejas
Laszlo Bodnar
Boldizar Bodor
Predrag Filipovic
Pa Modou Kah
Vincent Lachambre
Ken Leemans
Humprey Rudge
Jan-Paul Saeijs
Ger Senden
Alexander Voigt

Midfielders
Jerome Colinet
Simon Cziommer
Dirk Jan Derksen
Olaf Rompelberg
Sergio
Edrissa Sonko
Charlie van den Ouweland
Kevin van Dessel
Gregoor van Dijk
Ivan Vicelich

Forwards
Sekou Cisse
Cristiano
Diego Jongen
Arouna Kone
Andres Oper

KEY: On all match | On bench | Subbed or sent off (Counting game) | Subbed or sent off (playing less than 70 minutes) | Subbed on from bench (Counting Game) | Subbed on (playing less than 70 minutes) | Subbed on and then subbed or sent off (Counting Game) | Subbed on and then subbed or sent off (playing less than 70 minutes) | Not in 16

TWENTE ENSCHEDE

Final Position: **9th**

KEY: ☐Won ☐Drawn ☐Lost

							Attendance
1	hopr1	**Roda JC Kerk**	A	L	0-2		11,500
2	hopr1	**NEC Nijmegen**	H	L	0-1		13,000
3	hopr1	**Utrecht**	A	W	3-1	Culina 34; N'Kufo 74; Touma 90	17,000
4	hopr1	**Vitesse Arnhem**	H	L	0-1		13,000
5	hopr1	**Den Haag**	A	D	0-0		5,613
6	hopr1	**Feyenoord**	H	L	1-3	Zomer 85	13,000
7	hopr1	**Heracles**	A	W	4-0	Majstorovic 53; Bakircioglu 60; Zomer 83; N'Kufo 90	81,111
8	hopr1	**RKC Waalwijk**	H	W	2-0	Bakircioglu 35,67	13,000
9	hopr1	**NAC Breda**	A	D	1-1	Niemeyer 72	14,150
10	hopr1	**PSV Eindhoven**	H	L	0-1		13,100
11	hopr1	**Willem II Tilb**	H	W	3-1	Afonso 47; N'Kufo 58,81 pen	13,000
12	hopr1	**Ajax**	A	L	0-2		45,120
13	hopr1	**S Rotterdam**	H	W	1-0	Gerritsen 90	13,000
14	hopr1	**Groningen**	A	L	0-1		12,500
15	hopr1	**AZ Alkmaar**	H	L	1-3	Meerdink 32 og	13,200
16	hopr1	**Heerenveen**	A	L	1-3	Gerritsen 77	20,500
17	hopr1	**Roosendaal**	H	W	4-1	Niemeyer 23; Zomer 26,52; Majstorovic 73	12,250
18	hopr1	**PSV Eindhoven**	A	D	1-1	Bakircioglu 40	32,500
19	hopr1	**Willem II Tilb**	A	D	1-1	N'Kufo 57 pen	12,000
20	hopr1	**Ajax**	H	L	2-3	N'Kufo 25,52	13,250
21	hopr1	**S Rotterdam**	A	L	0-1		8,081
22	hopr1	**Utrecht**	H	W	3-0	Bakircioglu 70; Touma 81; N'Kufo 86	13,100
23	hopr1	**Vitesse Arnhem**	A	W	2-1	Gerritsen 90; Touma 90	18,286
24	hopr1	**Roda JC Kerk**	H	W	1-0	Zomer 6	13,200
25	hopr1	**NEC Nijmegen**	A	W	3-0	N'Kufo 15; Bakircioglu 43; Gerritsen 71	11,750
26	hopr1	**RKC Waalwijk**	A	D	0-0		7,000
27	hopr1	**Heracles**	H	W	2-0	Touma 21; Gerritsen 54	13,000
28	hopr1	**NAC Breda**	H	W	1-0	Bakircioglu 67	13,200
29	hopr1	**Roosendaal**	A	D	1-1	Bakircioglu 84	3,500
30	hopr1	**Heerenveen**	H	L	1-2	N'Kufo 26	1,300
31	hopr1	**Feyenoord**	A	L	2-4	Gerritsen 25; N'Kufo 38	40,000
32	hopr1	**Den Haag**	H	W	2-0	Touma 71; N'Kufo 84	13,000
33	hopr1	**AZ Alkmaar**	A	D	0-0		8,500
34	hopr1	**Groningen**	H	D	1-1	Afonso 88	13,500
35	erepo	**Utrecht**	H	W	2-0	N'Kufo 11; Gerritsen 47	10,500
36	erepo	**Utrecht**	A	W	3-1	Touma 68; N'Kufo 82; Gerritsen 84	10,000
37	erepo	**Heerenveen**	H	L	0-1		13,000
38	erepo	**Heerenveen**	A	L	0-5		
39	erepo	**Vitesse Arnhem**	A	D	1-1	N'Kufo 13	10,350
40	erepo	**Vitesse Arnhem**	H	W	2-0	Sibum 69,72	9,250

LEAGUE APPEARANCES, BOOKINGS AND CAPS

	AGE (on 01/07/06)	IN NAMED 18	APPEARANCES	COUNTING GAMES	MINUTES ON PITCH	YELLOW CARDS	RED CARDS	CAPS THIS SEASON	NATIONAL SIDE
Goalkeepers									
Sander Boschker	35	26	26	26	2340	1	0	-	Holland
Remko Pasveer	22	34	8	8	720	0	0	-	Holland
Danny Wintjens	22	7	0	0	0	0	0	-	Holland
Defenders									
Jeroen Heubach	31	28	28	27	2464	5	0	-	Holland
Daniel Majstorovic	29	19	19	19	1710	4	0	1	Sweden (16)
Peter Niemeyer	22	30	30	27	2512	4	0	-	Germany
Resit Schuurman	27	34	10	7	677	1	0	-	Holland
Ramon Zomer	23	31	30	30	2699	4	0	-	Holland
Midfielders									
Kennedy Bakircioglu	25	34	32	26	2541	1	0	-	Sweden
Elbekay Bouchiba	27	18	9	1	235	0	0	-	Morocco
Wout Brama	19	31	29	21	2098	6	0	-	Holland
Jason Culina	25	6	6	6	540	0	0	5	Australia (42)
Karim El Ahmadi	21	24	8	3	499	1	0	-	Holland
Kostant's Loumpoutis	27	24	9	6	589	3	0	-	Greece
Rahim Ouedraogo	25	26	22	19	1772	8	0	-	Burkino Faso
Dmitri Shoukov	30	14	12	6	742	0	0	-	Russia
Bas Sibum	23	27	24	16	1569	4	0	-	Holland
Sharbel Touma	27	28	28	20	2049	0	0	-	Sweden
Karim Touzani	25	15	2	1	95	0	0	-	Holland
Arnar Vidarsson	28	15	9	4	541	0	0	4	Iceland (70)
Niels Wellenberg	23	21	11	8	850	4	0	-	Holland
Forwards									
Guilherme Afonso	20	30	23	4	733	0	0	-	Switzerland
Georgi Gakhokidze	30	15	15	10	1039	3	0	-	Georgia
Anatoli Gerk	21	2	2	0	96	0	0	-	Russia
Patrick Gerritsen	19	25	22	16	1594	2	0	-	Holland
Marcel Kleizen	20	10	6	0	79	0	0	-	Holland
Blaise N'Kufo	31	32	32	31	2806	2	1	-	Switzerland

TEAM OF THE SEASON

G Sander Boschker CG: 26 DR: 94

D Jeroen Heubach CG: 27 DR: 95

D Peter Niemeyer CG: 27 DR: 84

D Ramon Zomer CG: 30 DR: 75

D Daniel Majstorovic CG: 19 DR: 74

M Bas Sibum CG: 16 SD: 94

M Kennedy Bakircioglu CG: 26 SD: 34

M Rahim Ouedraogo CG: 19 SD: 27

M Wout Brama CG: 21 SD: 5

F Blaise N'Kufo CG: 31 SR: 234

F Patrick Gerritsen CG: 16 SR: 266

MONTHLY POINTS TALLY

Month	Points	%
AUGUST	3	33%
SEPTEMBER	1	11%
OCTOBER	7	58%
NOVEMBER	6	67%
DECEMBER	4	27%
JANUARY	1	11%
FEBRUARY	13	87%
MARCH	7	58%
APRIL	5	42%

LEAGUE GOALS

	PLAYER	MINS	GOALS	S RATE
1	N'Kufo	2806	12	234
2	Bakircioglu	2541	8	318
3	Gerritsen	1594	6	266
4	Zomer	2699	5	540
5	Touma	2049	5	410
6	Majstorovic	1710	2	855
7	Afonso	733	2	367
8	Niemeyer	2512	2	1256
9	Culina	540	1	540
	Other		1	
	TOTAL		44	

TOP POINT EARNERS

	PLAYER	GAMES	AV PTS
1	Bas Sibum	16	1.94
2	Patrick Gerritsen	16	1.63
3	Sander Boschker	26	1.62
4	Wout Brama	21	1.57
5	Kennedy Bakircioglu	26	1.54
6	Rahim Ouedraogo	19	1.53
7	Blaise N'Kufo	31	1.52
8	Jeroen Heubach	27	1.48
9	Peter Niemeyer	27	1.37
10	Sharbel Touma	20	1.25
	CLUB AVERAGE:		1.38

DISCIPLINARY RECORDS

	PLAYER	YELLOW	RED	AVE
1	Loumpoutis	3	0	196
2	Wellenberg	4	0	212
3	Ouedraogo	8	0	221
4	Gakhokidze	3	0	346
5	Brama	6	0	349
6	Sibum	4	0	392
7	Majstorovic	4	0	427
8	Heubach	5	0	492
9	El Ahmadi	1	0	499
10	Niemeyer	4	0	628
11	Zomer	4	0	674
12	Schuurman	1	0	677
13	Gerritsen	2	0	797
	Other	4	1	
	TOTAL	53	1	

KEY GOALKEEPER

Sander Boschker

Goals Conceded in the League	25	**Counting Games** League games when player was on pitch for at least 70 minutes	26
Defensive Rating Ave number of mins between League goals conceded while on the pitch	94	**Clean Sheets** In League games when player was on pitch for at least 70 minutes	11

KEY PLAYERS - DEFENDERS

Jeroen Heubach

Goals Conceded Number of League goals conceded while the player was on the pitch	26	**Clean Sheets** In League games when player was on pitch for at least 70 minutes	10
Defensive Rating Ave number of mins between League goals conceded while on the pitch	95	**Club Defensive Rating** Average number of mins between League goals conceded by the club this season	85

	PLAYER	CON LGE	CLEAN SHEETS	DEF RATE
1	Jeroen Heubach	26	10	95 mins
2	Peter Niemeyer	30	9	84 mins
3	Ramon Zomer	36	8	75 mins
4	Daniel Majstorovic	23	4	74 mins

KEY PLAYERS - MIDFIELDERS

Bas Sibum

Goals in the League	0	**Contribution to Attacking Power** Average number of minutes between League team goals while on pitch	49
Defensive Rating Average number of mins between League goals conceded while on the pitch	143	**Scoring Difference** Defensive Rating minus Contribution to Attacking Power	94

	PLAYER	LGE GOALS	DEF RATE	POWER	SCORE DIFF
1	Bas Sibum	0	143	49	94 mins
2	Kennedy Bakircioglu	8	98	64	34 mins
3	Rahim Ouedraogo	0	98	71	27 mins
4	Wout Brama	0	75	70	5 mins

KEY PLAYERS - GOALSCORERS

Blaise N'Kufo

Goals in the League	12	**Player Strike Rate** Average number of minutes between League goals scored by player	234
Contribution to Attacking Power Average number of minutes between League team goals while on pitch	67	**Club Strike Rate** Average number of minutes between League goals scored by club	70

	PLAYER	LGE GOALS	POWER	STRIKE RATE
1	Blaise N'Kufo	12	67	234 mins
2	Patrick Gerritsen	6	55	266 mins
3	Kennedy Bakircioglu	8	64	318 mins
4	Sharbel Touma	5	82	410 mins

Peter Niemeyer

SQUAD APPEARANCES

Match	1	2	3	4	5	6	7	8	9	10	11	12	13	14	15	16	17	18	19	20	21	22	23	24	25	26	27	28	29	30	31	32	33	34	35	36	37	38	39	40
Venue	A	H	A	H	A	H	A	H	A	H	H	A	H	A	H	A	H	A	A	H	A	H	A	H	A	A	H	H	A	H	A	H	A	H	H	A	H	A	A	H
Competition	L	L	L	L	L	L	L	L	L	L	L	L	L	L	L	L	L	L	L	L	L	L	L	L	L	L	L	L	L	L	L	L	L	L	O	O	O	O	O	O
Result	L	L	W	L	D	L	W	W	D	L	W	L	W	L	L	L	W	D	D	L	L	W	W	W	W	D	W	W	D	L	L	W	D	D	W	W	L	L	D	W

Goalkeepers
Sander Boschker
Remko Pasveer
Danny Wintjens

Defenders
Jeroen Heubach
Daniel Majstorovic
Peter Niemeyer
Resit Schuurman
Ramon Zomer

Midfielders
Kennedy Bakircioglu
Elbekay Bouchiba
Wout Brama
Jason Culina
Karim El Ahmadi
Kostantinos Loumpoutis
Rahim Ouedraogo
Dmitri Shoukov
Bas Sibum
Sharbel Touma
Karim Touzani
Arnar Vidarsson
Niels Wellenberg

Forwards
Guilherme Afonso
Georgi Gakhokidze
Anatoli Gerk
Patrick Gerritsen
Marcel Kleizen
Blaise N'Kufo

KEY: On all match | On bench | Subbed or sent off (Counting game) | Subbed or sent off (playing less than 70 minutes) | Subbed on from bench (Counting Game) | Subbed on (playing less than 70 minutes) | Subbed on and then subbed or sent off (Counting Game) | Subbed on and then subbed or sent off (playing less than 70 minutes) | Not in 16

NEC NIJMEGEN

Final Position: **10th**

KEY: Won Drawn Lost

	Comp	Opponent	H/A	Result	Score	Scorers	Attendance
1	hopr1	**Utrecht**	H	D	0-0		12,000
2	hopr1	**Twente**	A	W	1-0	Tininho 81	13,000
3	hopr1	**RKC Waalwijk**	H	L	1-3	Niedzielan 64	11,000
4	hopr1	**Feyenoord**	A	L	0-3		39,000
5	hopr1	**NAC Breda**	H	D	1-1	van der Doelen 79	12,000
6	hopr1	**Heerenveen**	A	L	1-2	Takak 20	20,400
7	hopr1	**AZ Alkmaar**	A	L	2-3	Grot 25; Niedzielan 54	8,300
8	hopr1	**Roosendaal**	H	W	3-1	Denneboom 23; Niedzielan 45; Grot 85	11,750
9	hopr1	**Heracles**	A	W	2-0	Barreto 3; Niedzielan 6	8,250
10	hopr1	**S Rotterdam**	H	D	0-0		12,000
11	hopr1	**Ajax**	H	W	1-0	Denneboom 46	12,000
12	hopr1	**Den Haag**	A	W	1-0	Takak 82	5,938
13	hopr1	**Willem II Tilb**	H	W	2-0	Denneboom 2; Barreto 51	11,000
14	hopr1	**Vitesse Arnhem**	H	W	1-0	Worm 37	12,000
15	hopr1	**Roda JC Kerk**	A	W	1-0	Boutahar 72	12,500
16	hopr1	**Groningen**	A	L	0-3		12,100
17	hopr1	**PSV Eindhoven**	H	L	0-2		12,000
18	hopr1	**Ajax**	A	D	1-1	Wielaert 6	48,000
19	hopr1	**S Rotterdam**	A	W	3-1	Niedzielan 40,47,64	7,500
20	hopr1	**Den Haag**	H	W	5-0	Barreto 53; Jones 58,73; Denneboom 63; Niedzielan 90	11,750
21	hopr1	**Willem II Tilb**	A	D	2-2	Jones 75,84 pen	11,000
22	hopr1	**RKC Waalwijk**	A	W	3-1	Denneboom 42; Boutahar 76; Niedzielan 87	5,500
23	hopr1	**Feyenoord**	H	L	1-2	Denneboom 57	12,500
24	hopr1	**Utrecht**	A	D	1-1	Worm 49	17,500
25	hopr1	**Twente**	H	L	0-3		11,750
26	hopr1	**Roosendaal**	A	L	0-2		4,000
27	hopr1	**AZ Alkmaar**	H	L	0-2		11,750
28	hopr1	**Heracles**	H	W	2-0	Denneboom 4; Jones 56	11,500
29	hopr1	**PSV Eindhoven**	A	L	0-1		33,000
30	hopr1	**Groningen**	H	D	2-2	Tininho 48; Jones 65	12,000
31	hopr1	**Heerenveen**	H	W	4-1	Niedzielan 45; Pothuizen 66 pen; Denneboom 71; Grot 86	12,000
32	hopr1	**NAC Breda**	A	L	1-2	Boutahar 1	14,000
33	hopr1	**Roda JC Kerk**	H	L	0-3		11,500
34	hopr1	**Vitesse Arnhem**	A	D	1-1	Tininho 42 pen	21,250
35	erepo	**Heracles**	A	W	2-0	van der Doelen 66; Boutahar 82	8,500
36	erepo	**Heracles**	H	L	2-3	Worm 43; Denneboom 49	4,000
37	erepo	**Vitesse Arnhem**	A	D	0-0		12,928
38	erepo	**Vitesse Arnhem**	H	L	1-2	Pothuizen 28	12,000

LEAGUE APPEARANCES, BOOKINGS AND CAPS

	AGE (on 01/07/06)	IN NAMED 18	APPEARANCES	COUNTING GAMES	MINUTES ON PITCH	YELLOW CARDS	RED CARDS	CAPS THIS SEASON	NATIONAL SIDE
Goalkeepers									
Gabor Babos	31	29	29	29	2610	2	0	-	Hungary
Dennis de Koning	19	3	0	0	0	0	0	-	Holland
Nicolas Skrever	18	5	0	0	0	0	0	-	Holland
Ferry Thomassen	20	1	0	0	0	0	0	-	Holland
Raymon van Emmerik	26	27	5	5	450	0	0	-	Holland
Defenders									
Bas Bakker	20	8	0	0	0	0	0	-	Holland
Theo Dams	-	0	0	0	0	0	0	-	Holland
Jeffrey Leiwakabessy	25	31	31	31	2764	4	1	-	Holland
Chaimil Mormon	23	3	0	0	0	0	0	-	Surinam
Muslu Nalbantoglu	22	33	17	7	879	0	0	-	Holland
Jonas Olsson	23	34	34	31	2907	3	1	-	Sweden
Patrick Pothuizen	34	29	11	3	528	1	0	-	Holland
Jose Valencia	24	13	2	0	40	0	0	-	Ecuador
Rob Wielaert	27	29	29	27	2505	8	0	-	Holland
Peter Wisgerhof	26	31	31	29	2670	5	0	-	Holland
Midfielders									
Edgar Barreto	21	33	32	28	2684	2	0	3	Paraguay (33)
Said Boutahar	23	32	30	22	2150	1	0	-	Holland
Frank Demouge	24	1	1	1	90	0	0	-	Holland
David Jones	21	17	17	12	1244	2	0	-	England
Jasar Takak	24	27	21	9	1125	5	0	-	Turkey
Tininho	28	32	27	21	2090	3	0	-	Brazil
Bjorn van der Doelen	29	30	29	25	2378	8	0	-	Holland
Forwards									
Romano Denneboom	25	29	29	25	2404	1	0	-	Holland
Guillano Grot	23	33	30	5	998	0	0	-	Holland
Andrzej Niedzielan	27	27	27	20	2051	5	0	2	Poland (29)
Alexander Prent	23	19	5	0	181	0	0	-	Holland
Bart Van den Eede	32	12	8	2	359	2	0	-	Belgium
Sven Werkhoven	22	1	1	0	19	0	0	-	Holland
Rutger Worm	20	25	17	0	507	1	0	-	Holland

TEAM OF THE SEASON

G — Gabor Babos CG: 29 DR: 73

D — Rob Wielaert CG: 27 DR: 76

D — Peter Wisgerhof CG: 29 DR: 76

D — Jeffrey Leiwakabessy CG: 31 DR: 75

D — Jonas Olsson CG: 31 DR: 66

M — Edgar Barreto CG: 28 SD: 0

M — Bjorn van der Doelen CG: 25 SD: -1

M — Tininho CG: 21 SD: -7

M — Said Boutahar CG: 22 SD: -8

F — Andrzej Niedzielan CG: 20 SR: 205

F — R Denneboom CG: 25 SR: 301

MONTHLY POINTS TALLY

Month	Points	%
AUGUST	4	44%
SEPTEMBER	1	11%
OCTOBER	7	58%
NOVEMBER	9	100%
DECEMBER	6	50%
JANUARY	8	67%
FEBRUARY	4	27%
MARCH	4	33%
APRIL	4	33%

LEAGUE GOALS

	PLAYER	MINS	GOALS	S RATE
1	Niedzielan	2051	10	205
2	Denneboom	2404	8	301
3	Jones	1244	6	207
4	Grot	998	3	333
5	Barreto	2684	3	895
6	Boutahar	2150	3	717
7	Tininho	2090	3	697
8	Takak	1125	2	563
9	Worm	507	2	254
10	Pothuizen	528	1	528
11	van der Doelen	2378	1	2378
12	Wielaert	2505	1	2505
	Other		0	
	TOTAL		43	

TOP POINT EARNERS

	PLAYER	GAMES	AV PTS
1	Rob Wielaert	27	1.59
2	Gabor Babos	29	1.52
3	Peter Wisgerhof	29	1.48
4	Jeffrey Leiwakabessy	31	1.48
5	Edgar Barreto	28	1.46
6	Romano Denneboom	25	1.44
7	Bjorn van der Doelen	25	1.40
8	Jonas Olsson	31	1.39
9	Tininho	21	1.38
10	Andrzej Niedzielan	20	1.25
	CLUB AVERAGE:		1.38

DISCIPLINARY RECORDS

	PLAYER	YELLOW	RED	AVE
1	Takak	5	0	225
2	van der Doelen	8	0	297
3	Wielaert	8	0	313
4	Niedzielan	5	0	410
5	Worm	1	0	507
6	Pothuizen	1	0	528
7	Wisgerhof	5	0	534
8	Leiwakabessy	4	1	552
9	Jones	2	0	622
10	Tininho	3	0	696
11	Olsson	3	1	726
12	Babos	2	0	1305
13	Barreto	2	0	1342
	Other	2	0	
	TOTAL	51	2	

KEY GOALKEEPER

Gabor Babos

Goals Conceded in the League	36	**Counting Games** League games when player was on pitch for at least 70 minutes	29
Defensive Rating Ave number of mins between League goals conceded while on the pitch	73	**Clean Sheets** In League games when player was on pitch for at least 70 minutes	10

KEY PLAYERS - DEFENDERS

Peter Wisgerhof

Goals Conceded Number of League goals conceded while the player was on the pitch	35	**Clean Sheets** In League games when player was on pitch for at least 70 minutes	11
Defensive Rating Ave number of mins between League goals conceded while on the pitch	76	**Club Defensive Rating** Average number of mins between League goals conceded by the club this season	70

	PLAYER	CON LGE	CLEAN SHEETS	DEF RATE
1	Peter Wisgerhof	35	11	76 mins
2	Rob Wielaert	33	9	76 mins
3	Jeffrey Leiwakabessy	37	11	75 mins
4	Jonas Olsson	44	9	66 mins

KEY PLAYERS - MIDFIELDERS

Edgar Barreto

Goals in the League	3	**Contribution to Attacking Power** Average number of minutes between League team goals while on pitch	69
Defensive Rating Average number of mins between League goals conceded while on the pitch	69	**Scoring Difference** Defensive Rating minus Contribution to Attacking Power	0

	PLAYER	LGE GOALS	DEF RATE	POWER	SCORE DIFF
1	Edgar Barreto	3	69	69	0 mins
2	Bjorn van der Doelen	1	63	64	-1 mins
3	Tininho	3	80	87	-7 mins
4	Said Boutahar	3	69	77	-8 mins

KEY PLAYERS - GOALSCORERS

Andrzej Niedzielan

Goals in the League	10	**Player Strike Rate** Average number of minutes between League goals scored by player	205
Contribution to Attacking Power Average number of minutes between League team goals while on pitch	60	**Club Strike Rate** Average number of minutes between League goals scored by club	71

	PLAYER	LGE GOALS	POWER	STRIKE RATE
1	Andrzej Niedzielan	10	60	205 mins
2	David Jones	6	59	207 mins
3	Romano Denneboom	8	73	301 mins
4	Tininho	3	87	697 mins

Peter Wisgerhof

SQUAD APPEARANCES

Match	1	2	3	4	5	6	7	8	9	10	11	12	13	14	15	16	17	18	19	20	21	22	23	24	25	26	27	28	29	30	31	32	33	34	35	36	37	38
Venue	H	A	H	A	H	A	A	H	A	H	H	A	H	H	A	A	H	A	A	H	A	A	H	A	H	A	H	H	A	H	H	A	H	A	A	H	A	H
Competition	L	L	L	L	L	L	L	L	L	L	L	L	L	L	L	L	L	L	L	L	L	L	L	L	L	L	L	L	L	L	L	L	L	L	O	O	O	O
Result	D	W	L	L	D	L	L	W	W	D	W	W	W	W	W	L	L	D	W	W	D	W	L	D	L	L	L	W	L	D	W	L	L	D	W	L	D	L

Goalkeepers
Gabor Babos
Dennis de Koning
Nicolas Skrever
Ferry Thomassen
Raymon van Emmerik

Defenders
Bas Bakker
Theo Dams
Jeffrey Leiwakabessy
Chaimil Mormon
Muslu Nalbantoglu
Patrick Pothuizen
Jose Valencia
Rob Wielaert
Peter Wisgerhof

Midfielders
Edgar Barreto
Said Boutahar
Frank Demouge
David Jones
Jonas Olsson
Jasar Takak
Tininho
Bjorn van der Doelen

Forwards
Romano Denneboom
Guillano Grot
Andrzej Niedzielan
Alexander Prent
Bart Van den Eede
Sven Werkhoven
Rutger Worm

KEY: On all match | On bench | Subbed or sent off (Counting game) | Subbed or sent off (playing less than 70 minutes) | Subbed on from bench (Counting Game) | Subbed on (playing less than 70 minutes) | Subbed on and then subbed or sent off (Counting Game) | Subbed on and then subbed or sent off (playing less than 70 minutes) | Not in 16

VITESSE ARNHEM

Final Position: **11th**

KEY: ☐Won ☐Drawn ☐Lost

	Comp	Opponent	H/A	Res	Score	Scorers	Attendance
1	hopr1	**Heerenveen**	H	D	2-2	Esajas 34; Janssen 80	18,500
2	hopr1	**PSV Eindhoven**	A	L	1-2	Alex 21 og	32,600
3	hopr1	**AZ Alkmaar**	H	L	0-5		19,002
4	hopr1	**Twente**	A	W	1-0	Amoah 89	13,000
5	hopr1	**Utrecht**	A	L	0-1		17,300
6	hopr1	**Groningen**	H	W	2-0	Swerts 48; Benson 90	16,825
7	hopr1	**Roda JC Kerk**	A	L	2-3	Janssen 49; Benson 58	13,000
8	hopr1	**Den Haag**	H	W	3-1	Benson 31; Bodde 71 og; Hersi 90	17,265
9	hopr1	**Roosendaal**	A	W	3-0	Janssen 22,87; Hersi 64	4,400
10	hopr1	**Heracles**	H	W	5-1	De Mul 14; Hersi 37,85; Amoah 60,84	17,940
11	hopr1	**Feyenoord**	A	D	0-0		40,000
12	hopr1	**Willem II Tilb**	A	W	4-3	Amoah 9,20,70; Janssen 30	11,000
13	hopr1	**RKC Waalwijk**	H	W	4-2	Janssen 3 ; Amoah 74; Hersi 77,90	19,600
14	hopr1	**NEC Nijmegen**	A	L	0-1		12,000
15	hopr1	**Ajax**	H	L	0-2		25,000
16	hopr1	**S Rotterdam**	A	L	0-1		8,500
17	hopr1	**NAC Breda**	H	W	2-1	Amoah 69,71	18,000
18	hopr1	**Heracles**	A	L	1-3	Benson 75	8,200
19	hopr1	**Feyenoord**	H	L	0-1		24,000
20	hopr1	**Willem II Tilb**	H	W	2-1	Benson 87,89	19,000
21	hopr1	**RKC Waalwijk**	A	W	1-0	Dingsdag 64	5,000
22	hopr1	**AZ Alkmaar**	A	D	1-1	Swerts 40	8,426
23	hopr1	**Twente**	H	L	1-2	Hersi 5	18,286
24	hopr1	**Heerenveen**	A	L	1-4	Junker 7	20,600
25	hopr1	**PSV Eindhoven**	H	L	1-3	Hersi 43	24,000
26	hopr1	**Den Haag**	A	L	0-2		5,033
27	hopr1	**Roda JC Kerk**	H	L	1-3	Blondelle 41	19,000
28	hopr1	**Roosendaal**	H	W	5-1	Junker 6; Knol 8; Hersi 59; Knopper 61; Benson 79	19,000
29	hopr1	**NAC Breda**	A	D	2-2	Knopper 5; Van der Schaaf 90	14,000
30	hopr1	**S Rotterdam**	H	W	3-1	Janssen 57; Junker 65; de Mul 67	19,000
31	hopr1	**Groningen**	A	L	1-2	Knopper 90	20,000
32	hopr1	**Utrecht**	H	W	1-0	Junker 13	19,000
33	hopr1	**Ajax**	A	L	1-2	Hersi 62	45,000
34	hopr1	**NEC Nijmegen**	H	D	1-1	Van der Schaaf 89	21,250
35	erepo	**RKC Waalwijk**	A	D	4-4	Junker 27,39,42; Hersi 45	5,000
36	erepo	**RKC Waalwijk**	H	W	2-0	Junker 87; Hersi 88	10,000
37	erepo	**NEC Nijmegen**	H	D	0-0		12,928
38	erepo	**NEC Nijmegen**	A	W	2-1	Benson 38; Hersi 88	12,000
39	erepo	**Twente**	H	D	1-1	Junker 71	10,350
40	erepo	**Twente**	A	L	0-2		9,250

LEAGUE APPEARANCES, BOOKINGS AND CAPS

	AGE (on 01/07/06)	IN NAMED 18	APPEARANCES	COUNTING GAMES	MINUTES ON PITCH	YELLOW CARDS	RED CARDS	CAPS THIS SEASON	NATIONAL SIDE
Goalkeepers									
Gino Coutinho	23	29	1	1	90	0	0	-	Holland
Piet Veldhuizen	19	5	0	0	0	0	0	-	Holland
Harald Wapenaar	36	32	32	32	2880	0	0	-	Holland
Defenders									
Siebe Blondelle	20	10	3	1	145	3	1	-	Belgium
Michael Dingsdag	23	33	33	32	2941	3	1	-	Holland
Purrel Frankel	29	34	32	23	2220	2	0	-	Holland
Ruud Knol	25	30	27	25	2295	5	0	-	Holland
Giel Neervoort	20	2	0	0	0	0	0	-	Holland
Hesdey Suart	20	1	0	0	0	0	0	-	Holland
Peter van den Berg	34	9	4	2	245	0	0	-	Holland
Paul Verhaegh	22	12	12	12	1080	2	0	-	Holland
Stijn Vreven	32	18	18	18	1602	5	0	-	Belgium
Midfielders									
Tim De Meersman	21	17	1	1	91	0	0	-	Belgium
Youssef Hersi	23	29	25	20	1907	2	0	-	Holland
Theo Janssen	24	30	30	29	2661	6	0	-	Holland
Onur Kaya	20	14	8	3	370	0	0	-	Belgium
Gill Swerts	23	31	30	26	2525	7	0	-	Belgium
R. van der Schaaf	27	27	27	26	2348	7	1	-	Holland
Colin van Mourik	20	4	0	0	0	0	0	-	Holland
Abubakari Yakubu	24	22	21	19	1791	5	0	-	Ghana
Forwards									
Matthew Amoah	25	18	18	14	1448	0	0	7	Ghana (48)
Fred Benson	22	30	27	7	1024	1	0	-	Holland
Tom De Mul	20	30	27	10	1430	3	0	-	Belgium
Etienne Esajas	21	23	11	2	428	0	0	-	Holland
Igor Gluscevic	32	20	7	0	126	0	0	-	Serbia & Montenegro
Mads Junker	25	16	16	15	1374	2	0	-	Denmark
Richard Knopper	28	23	23	22	2032	1	0	-	Holland
Eldridge Rojer	22	33	21	3	548	1	0	-	Holland

TEAM OF THE SEASON

MONTHLY POINTS TALLY

Month	Points	%
AUGUST	1	11%
SEPTEMBER	6	67%
OCTOBER	9	75%
NOVEMBER	7	78%
DECEMBER	3	20%
JANUARY	6	67%
FEBRUARY	1	7%
MARCH	7	58%
APRIL	4	33%

LEAGUE GOALS

	PLAYER	MINS	GOALS	S RATE
1	Hersi	1907	**10**	191
2	Amoah	1448	**9**	161
3	Janssen	2661	**7**	380
4	Benson	1024	**7**	146
5	Junker	1374	**4**	344
6	Knopper	2032	**3**	677
7	De Mul	1430	**2**	715
8	Swerts	2525	**2**	1263
9	Van der Schaaf	2348	**2**	1174
10	Dingsdag	2941	**1**	2941
11	Blondelle	145	**1**	145
12	Esajas	428	**1**	428
13	Knol	2295	**1**	2295
	Other		**2**	
	TOTAL		**52**	

TOP POINT EARNERS

	PLAYER	GAMES	AV PTS
1	Matthew Amoah	14	**1.64**
2	Stijn Vreven	18	**1.61**
3	Remco van der Schaaf	26	**1.58**
4	Theo Janssen	29	**1.41**
5	Youssef Hersi	20	**1.40**
6	Gill Swerts	26	**1.38**
7	Abubakari Yakubu	19	**1.37**
8	Ruud Knol	25	**1.36**
9	Michael Dingsdag	32	**1.31**
10	Harald Wapenaar	32	**1.28**
	CLUB AVERAGE:		**1.29**

DISCIPLINARY RECORDS

	PLAYER	YELLOW	RED	AVE
1	Van der Schaaf	7	1	**293**
2	Vreven	5	0	**320**
3	Yakubu	5	0	**358**
4	Swerts	7	0	**360**
5	Janssen	6	0	**443**
6	Knol	5	0	**459**
7	De Mul	3	0	**476**
8	Verhaegh	2	0	**540**
9	Rojer	1	0	**548**
10	Junker	2	0	**687**
11	Dingsdag	3	1	**735**
12	Hersi	2	0	**953**
13	Benson	1	0	**1024**
	Other	3	0	
	TOTAL	**52**	**2**	

KEY GOALKEEPER

Harald Wapenaar			
Goals Conceded in the League	49	Counting Games League games when player was on pitch for at least 70 minutes	32
Defensive Rating Ave number of mins between League goals conceded while on the pitch	59	Clean Sheets In games when player was on pitch for at least 70 minutes	6

KEY PLAYERS - DEFENDERS

Paul Verhaegh			
Goals Conceded Number of League goals conceded while the player was on the pitch	18	Clean Sheets In League games when player was on pitch for at least 70 minutes	2
Defensive Rating Ave number of mins between League goals conceded while on the pitch	60	Club Defensive Rating Average number of mins between League goals conceded by the club this season	57

	PLAYER	CON LGE	CLEAN SHEETS	DEF RATE
1	Paul Verhaegh	18	2	60 mins
2	Ruud Knol	39	4	59 mins
3	Stijn Vreven	28	4	57 mins
4	Michael Dingsdag	53	6	55 mins

KEY PLAYERS - MIDFIELDERS

Theo Janssen			
Goals in the League	7	Contribution to Attacking Power Average number of minutes between League team goals while on pitch	55
Defensive Rating Average number of mins between League goals conceded while on the pitch	62	Scoring Difference Defensive Rating minus Contribution to Attacking Power	7

	PLAYER	LGE GOALS	DEF RATE	POWER	SCORE DIFF
1	Theo Janssen	7	62	55	7 mins
2	Remco van der Schaaf	2	63	57	6 mins
3	Youssef Hersi	10	62	56	6 mins
4	Gill Swerts	2	65	65	0 mins

KEY PLAYERS - GOALSCORERS

Matthew Amoah			
Goals in the League	9	Player Strike Rate Average number of minutes between League goals scored by player	161
Contribution to Attacking Power Average number of minutes between League team goals while on pitch	56	Club Strike Rate Average number of minutes between League goals scored by club	59

	PLAYER	LGE GOALS	POWER	STRIKE RATE
1	Matthew Amoah	9	56	161 mins
2	Youssef Hersi	10	56	191 mins
3	Mads Junker	4	62	344 mins
4	Theo Janssen	7	55	380 mins

Theo Janssen

SQUAD APPEARANCES

Match	1	2	3	4	5	6	7	8	9	10	11	12	13	14	15	16	17	18	19	20
Venue	H	A	H	A	A	H	A	H	A	H	A	A	H	A	H	A	H	A	H	H
Competition	L	L	L	L	L	L	L	L	L	L	L	L	L	L	L	L	L	L	L	L
Result	D	L	L	W	L	W	L	W	W	W	D	W	W	L	L	L	W	L	L	W

Match	21	22	23	24	25	26	27	28	29	30	31	32	33	34	35	36	37	38	39	40
Venue	A	A	H	A	H	A	H	H	A	H	A	H	A	H	A	H	H	A	H	A
Competition	L	L	L	L	L	L	L	L	L	L	L	L	L	L	O	O	O	O	O	O
Result	W	D	L	L	L	L	L	W	D	W	L	W	L	D	D	W	D	W	D	L

Goalkeepers
Gino Coutinho
Piet Veldhuizen
Harald Wapenaar

Defenders
Siebe Blondelle
Michael Dingsdag
Purrel Frankel
Ruud Knol
Giel Neervoort
Hesdey Suart
Peter van den Berg
Paul Verhaegh
Stijn Vreven

Midfielders
Tim De Meersman
Youssef Hersi
Theo Janssen
Onur Kaya
Gill Swerts
Remco van der Schaaf
Colin van Mourik
Abubakari Yakubu

Forwards
Matthew Amoah
Fred Benson
Tom De Mul
Etienne Esajas
Igor Gluscevic
Mads Junker
Richard Knopper
Eldridge Rojer

KEY: On all match · On bench · Subbed or sent off (Counting game) · Subbed or sent off (playing less than 70 minutes) · Subbed on from bench (Counting Game) · Subbed on (playing less than 70 minutes) · Subbed on and then subbed or sent off (Counting Game) · Subbed on and then subbed or sent off (playing less than 70 minutes) · Not in 16

RKC WAALWIJK

Final Position: **12th**

KEY: ☐ Won ☐ Drawn ☐ Lost

							Attendance
1	hopr1	**Willem II Tilb**	A	W	2-1	Hoogendorp 9,54	10,850
2	hopr1	**Groningen**	H	W	2-1	De Ceulaer 48; Martens 76	4,600
3	hopr1	**NEC Nijmegen**	A	W	3-1	Hoogendorp 13; De Ceulaer 68; Janssen 87	11,000
4	hopr1	**Roda JC Kerk**	H	W	2-0	Hoogendorp 27; Molhoek 74	6,800
5	hopr1	**Heracles**	A	W	2-0	Keller 37; Hoogendorp 74 pen	7,800
6	hopr1	**Utrecht**	H	L	2-3	De Ceulaer 54; Hoogendorp 90 pen	5,500
7	hopr1	**Den Haag**	A	L	1-2	van de Haar 38	6,413
8	hopr1	**Twente**	A	L	0-2		13,000
9	hopr1	**Feyenoord**	H	W	2-1	Martens 32; Teixeira 90	6,500
10	hopr1	**NAC Breda**	H	W	4-1	Hoogendorp 22 pen; Molhoek 55; van de Haar 85; Martens 89	7,000
11	hopr1	**Roosendaal**	A	D	1-1	Keller 57	4,500
12	hopr1	**PSV Eindhoven**	H	D	4-4	De Ceulaer 16; Hoogendorp 64,81; Keller 75	7,400
13	hopr1	**Vitesse Arnhem**	A	L	2-4	De Ceulaer 44; Martens 69	19,600
14	hopr1	**Ajax**	A	L	1-4	Hoogendorp 44	47,500
15	hopr1	**S Rotterdam**	H	W	3-2	Martens 64; Hoogendorp 66; Molhoek 70	6,000
16	hopr1	**AZ Alkmaar**	A	L	0-3		8,300
17	hopr1	**Heerenveen**	H	D	2-2	Zuiverloon 8; Martens 43	6,100
18	hopr1	**NAC Breda**	A	W	2-1	Janssen 39; Hoogendorp 67	12,500
19	hopr1	**Roosendaal**	H	D	1-1	De Ceulaer 4	5,500
20	hopr1	**PSV Eindhoven**	A	L	0-2		33,000
21	hopr1	**Vitesse Arnhem**	H	L	0-1		5,000
22	hopr1	**NEC Nijmegen**	H	L	1-3	Fuchs 12	5,500
23	hopr1	**Roda JC Kerk**	A	L	0-1		12,500
24	hopr1	**Willem II Tilb**	H	W	1-0	Janssen 85	6,800
25	hopr1	**Groningen**	A	L	0-1		20,000
26	hopr1	**Twente**	H	D	0-0		7,000
27	hopr1	**Den Haag**	H	W	3-0	De Ceulaer 30; van Dijk, D 57,73	5,600
28	hopr1	**Feyenoord**	A	D	1-1	Berger 87	40,000
29	hopr1	**Heerenveen**	A	L	1-2	van Dijk, D 35	20,500
30	hopr1	**AZ Alkmaar**	H	L	0-1		7,000
31	hopr1	**Utrecht**	A	L	1-3	van de Haar 52	24,500
32	hopr1	**Heracles**	H	L	0-2		5,000
33	hopr1	**S Rotterdam**	A	L	2-3	van de Haar 45; Olfers 71	9,000
34	hopr1	**Ajax**	H	L	2-4	Lurling 18; Peters 90	6,000
35	erepo	**Vitesse Arnhem**	H	D	4-4	Zuiverloon 46; van Dijk, D 62,84 pen; Mulder 70	5,000
36	erepo	**Vitesse Arnhem**	A	L	0-2		10,000

LEAGUE APPEARANCES, BOOKINGS AND CAPS

	AGE (on 01/07/06)	IN NAMED 18	APPEARANCES	COUNTING GAMES	MINUTES ON PITCH	YELLOW CARDS	RED CARDS	CAPS THIS SEASON	NATIONAL SIDE
Goalkeepers									
Rob van Dijk	37	34	34	34	3060	1	0	-	Holland
Jurgen Wevers	27	32	0	0	0	0	0	-	Holland
Defenders									
Lion Axwijk	22	12	4	1	164	1	0	-	Holland
Tim Bakens	23	17	14	14	1233	1	0	-	Holland
Ryan Donk	20	9	5	4	372	0	0	-	Holland
Cerezo Fung-A-Wing	22	5	2	1	115	0	0	-	Holland
Stephan Keller	27	31	30	26	2456	7	1	-	Switzerland
Tim Peters	21	3	2	0	27	0	0	-	Holland
Randy Rustenberg	22	13	2	0	41	0	0	-	Holland
Sjoerd Schrier	22	7	0	0	0	0	0	-	Holland
Virgilio Teixeira	32	27	25	24	2186	3	0	-	Portugal
David Triantafillidis	20	2	1	0	23	0	0	-	Belgium
Ramon van Haaren	33	27	26	24	2235	3	1	-	Holland
Sjack van Rijsbergen	21	9	1	0	5	0	0	-	Holland
Gianni Zuiverloon	19	32	28	21	2171	4	1	-	Holland
Midfielders									
Robert Fuchs	31	23	21	12	1383	1	0	-	Holland
Michael Krohn-Dehli	23	17	17	10	1071	0	0	-	Denmark
Didi Longuet	24	22	4	1	216	2	0	-	Holland
Anthony Lurling	29	14	14	9	1088	3	0	-	Holland
Maarten Martens	22	21	21	21	1867	2	0	-	Belgium
Danny Mathijssen	23	16	14	11	1065	3	0	-	Holland
Rogier Molhoek	24	16	16	15	1381	3	0	-	Holland
Dustley Mulder	21	13	10	8	771	0	0	-	Holland
Carlos Ramos	19	0	0	0	0	0	0	-	Holland
Patrick van Diemen	34	26	26	25	2293	4	1	-	Holland
Dominique van Dijk	26	30	29	9	1328	1	0	-	Holland
Forwards									
Martijn Barto	21	24	7	0	188	1	0	-	Holland
Ruud Berger	26	15	9	4	563	0	0	-	Holland
Benjamin De Ceulaer	22	25	25	18	1910	2	0	-	Belgium
Anthony Fabri	20	5	0	0	0	0	0	-	France
Rick Hoogendorp	31	18	18	17	1591	1	0	-	Holland
Jochen Janssen	30	23	21	6	851	0	0	-	Belgium
Felino Jardim	20	0	0	0	0	0	0	-	Holland
Toevarno Pinas	-	8	0	0	0	0	0	-	Holland
Eddy Putter	24	2	1	0	4	0	0	-	Holland
Hans van de Haar	31	23	23	18	1809	1	1	-	Holland

TEAM OF THE SEASON

D
Tim Bakens
CG: 14 DR: 59

M
Rogier Molhoek
CG: 15 SD: 7

D
Stephan Keller
CG: 26 DR: 55

M
Maarten Martens
CG: 21 SD: 0

F
Rick Hoogendorp
CG: 17 SR: 133

G
Rob van Dijk
CG: 34 DR: 53

D
Ramon van Haaren
CG: 24 DR: 55

M
Patrick van Diemen
CG: 25 SD: -1

F
Ben De Ceulaer
CG: 18 SR: 273

D
Gianni Zuiverloon
CG: 21 DR: 52

M
Robert Fuchs
CG: 12 SD: -28

MONTHLY POINTS TALLY

AUGUST	9	100%
SEPTEMBER	6	67%
OCTOBER	6	50%
NOVEMBER	2	22%
DECEMBER	4	33%
JANUARY	4	33%
FEBRUARY	4	27%
MARCH	4	27%
APRIL	0	0%

LEAGUE GOALS

	PLAYER	MINS	GOALS	S RATE
1	Hoogendorp	1591	12	133
2	De Ceulaer	1910	7	273
3	Martens	1867	6	311
4	van de Haar	1809	4	452
5	van Dijk, D	1328	3	443
6	Janssen	851	3	284
7	Keller	2456	3	819
8	Molhoek	1381	3	460
9	Peters	27	1	27
10	Berger	563	1	563
11	Zuiverloon	2171	1	2171
12	Fuchs	1383	1	1383
13	Lurling	1088	1	1088
	Other		2	
	TOTAL		48	

TOP POINT EARNERS

	PLAYER	GAMES	AV PTS
1	Rogier Molhoek	15	1.73
2	Rick Hoogendorp	17	1.59
3	Gianni Zuiverloon	21	1.48
4	Maarten Martens	21	1.48
5	Patrick van Diemen	25	1.40
6	Stephan Keller	26	1.35
7	Virgilio Teixeira	24	1.29
8	Rob van Dijk	34	1.15
9	Ramon van Haaren	24	1.13
10	Hans van de Haar	18	1.06
	CLUB AVERAGE:		1.15

DISCIPLINARY RECORDS

	PLAYER	YELLOW	RED	AVE
1	Keller	7	1	307
2	Mathijssen, D	3	0	355
3	Lurling	3	0	362
4	Zuiverloon	4	1	434
5	van Diemen	4	1	458
6	Molhoek	3	0	460
7	van Haaren	3	1	558
8	Teixeira	3	0	728
9	van de Haar	1	1	904
10	Martens	2	0	933
11	De Ceulaer	2	0	955
12	Bakens	1	0	1233
13	van Dijk, D	1	0	1328
	Other	3	0	
	TOTAL	40	5	

KEY GOALKEEPER

Rob van Dijk			
Goals Conceded in the League	58	**Counting Games** League games when player was on pitch for at least 70 minutes	34
Defensive Rating Ave number of mins between League goals conceded while on the pitch	53	**Clean Sheets** In games when player was on pitch for at least 70 minutes	5

KEY PLAYERS - GOALSCORERS

Rick Hoogendorp			
Goals in the League	12	**Player Strike Rate** Average number of minutes between League goals scored by player	133
Contribution to Attacking Power Average number of minutes between League team goals while on pitch	47	**Club Strike Rate** Average number of minutes between League goals scored by club	64

	PLAYER	LGE GOALS	POWER	STRIKE RATE
1	Rick Hoogendorp	12	47	133 mins
2	Benjamin De Ceulaer	7	66	273 mins
3	Maarten Martens	6	52	311 mins
4	Hans van de Haar	4	60	452 mins

KEY PLAYERS - DEFENDERS

Tim Bakens			
Goals Conceded Number of League goals conceded while the player was on the pitch	21	**Clean Sheets** In League games when player was on pitch for at least 70 minutes	3
Defensive Rating Ave number of mins between League goals conceded while on the pitch	59	**Club Defensive Rating** Average number of mins between League goals conceded by the club this season	53

	PLAYER	CON LGE	CLEAN SHEETS	DEF RATE
1	Tim Bakens	21	3	59 mins
2	Ramon van Haaren	41	4	55 mins
3	Stephan Keller	45	4	55 mins
4	Gianni Zuiverloon	42	3	52 mins

Patrick van Diemen

KEY PLAYERS - MIDFIELDERS

Rogier Molhoek			
Goals in the League	3	**Contribution to Attacking Power** Average number of minutes between League team goals while on pitch	46
Defensive Rating Average number of mins between League goals conceded while on the pitch	53	**Scoring Difference** Defensive Rating minus Contribution to Attacking Power	7

	PLAYER	LGE GOALS	DEF RATE	POWER	SCORE DIFF
1	Rogier Molhoek	3	53	46	7 mins
2	Maarten Martens	6	52	52	0 mins
3	Patrick van Diemen	0	49	50	-1 mins
4	Robert Fuchs	1	58	86	-28 mins

SQUAD APPEARANCES

Match	1	2	3	4	5	6	7	8	9	10	11	12	13	14	15	16	17	18	19	20	21	22	23	24	25	26	27	28	29	30	31	32	33	34	35	36
Venue	A	H	A	H	A	H	A	A	H	H	A	H	A	A	H	A	H	A	H	A	H	H	A	H	A	H	H	A	A	H	A	H	A	H	H	A
Competition	L	L	L	L	L	L	L	L	L	L	L	L	L	L	L	L	L	L	L	L	L	L	L	L	L	L	L	L	L	L	L	L	L	L	O	O
Result	W	W	W	W	W	L	L	L	W	W	D	D	L	L	W	L	D	W	D	L	L	L	L	W	L	D	W	D	L	L	L	L	L	L	D	L

Goalkeepers
Rob van Dijk
Jurgen Wevers

Defenders
Lion Axwijk
Tim Bakens
Ryan Donk
Cerezo Fung-A-Wing
Stephan Keller
Tim Peters
Randy Rustenberg
Sjoerd Schrier
Virgilio Teixeira
David Triantafillidis
Ramon van Haaren
Sjack van Rijsbergen
Gianni Zuiverloon

Midfielders
Robert Fuchs
Michael Krohn-Dehli
Didi Longuet
Anthony Lurling
Maarten Martens
Danny Mathijssen
Rogier Molhoek
Dustley Mulder
Patrick van Diemen
Dominique van Dijk

Forwards
Martijn Barto
Ruud Berger
Benjamin De Ceulaer
Rick Hoogendorp
Jochen Janssen
Felino Jardim
Toevarno Pinas
Eddy Putter
Hans van de Haar

KEY: On all match | On bench | Subbed or sent off (Counting game) | Subbed or sent off (playing less than 70 minutes) | Subbed on from bench (Counting Game) | Subbed on (playing less than 70 minutes) | Subbed on and then subbed or sent off (Counting Game) | Subbed on and then subbed or sent off (playing less than 70 minutes) | Not in 16

SC HERACLES

Final Position: **13th**

KEY: ☐Won ☐Drawn ☐Lost

	Comp	Opponent	H/A	Res	Score	Scorers	Attendance
1	hopr1	**PSV Eindhoven**	H	D	1-1	Sluijter 87	8,500
2	hopr1	**Den Haag**	A	W	2-1	Hirayama 77,84	6,000
3	hopr1	**Groningen**	H	W	2-1	Tamerus 74; Quansah 87	7,813
4	hopr1	**Heerenveen**	A	W	2-1	Quansah 48; Tamerus 90	20,500
5	hopr1	**RKC Waalwijk**	H	L	0-2		7,800
6	hopr1	**S Rotterdam**	A	L	0-2		9,000
7	hopr1	**Twente**	H	L	0-4		81,111
8	hopr1	**Ajax**	A	D	0-0		47,650
9	hopr1	**NEC Nijmegen**	H	L	0-2		8,250
10	hopr1	**Vitesse Arnhem**	A	L	1-5	Quansah 18	17,940
11	hopr1	**AZ Alkmaar**	A	D	2-2	Calincov 58; Pieckenhagen 90	8,399
12	hopr1	**Roosendaal**	H	W	3-0	Hellings 9; Calincov 76; Hirayama 86	8,400
13	hopr1	**Feyenoord**	A	L	1-7	Jansen 87	38,000
14	hopr1	**Roda JC Kerk**	H	L	0-1		8,153
15	hopr1	**NAC Breda**	A	L	1-2	Jansen 81	13,699
16	hopr1	**Utrecht**	H	D	1-1	Hirayama 80	8,254
17	hopr1	**Vitesse Arnhem**	H	W	3-1	Hirayama 24; Tamerus 33,39	8,200
18	hopr1	**Willem II Tilb**	A	W	2-1	Sluijter 2; Hirayama 66	11,000
19	hopr1	**AZ Alkmaar**	H	L	0-2		8,500
20	hopr1	**Roosendaal**	A	W	2-1	Hirayama 25; Nurmela 45	4,500
21	hopr1	**Feyenoord**	H	L	0-4		8,500
22	hopr1	**Groningen**	A	D	0-0		20,000
23	hopr1	**Heerenveen**	H	D	1-1	Tanghe 78	8,500
24	hopr1	**PSV Eindhoven**	A	L	0-1		32,900
25	hopr1	**Den Haag**	H	L	1-3	Tanghe 29	8,500
26	hopr1	**Ajax**	H	L	1-3	Sluijter 19	7,000
27	hopr1	**Twente**	A	L	0-2		13,000
28	hopr1	**NEC Nijmegen**	A	L	0-2		11,500
29	hopr1	**Willem II Tilb**	H	W	1-0	Nurmela 7	8,400
30	hopr1	**Utrecht**	A	L	0-1		18,000
31	hopr1	**S Rotterdam**	H	W	1-0	Quansah 43	8,500
32	hopr1	**RKC Waalwijk**	A	W	2-0	Quansah 54; Tamerus 76	5,000
33	hopr1	**NAC Breda**	H	W	4-2	Tamerus 45; Hirayama 54; Tanghe 77; Hocher 90	8,500
34	hopr1	**Roda JC Kerk**	A	L	1-2	Tanghe 76	13,000
35	erepo	**NEC Nijmegen**	H	L	0-2		8,500
36	erepo	**NEC Nijmegen**	A	W	3-2	Smit 34; Sluijter 79,82	4,000

LEAGUE APPEARANCES, BOOKINGS AND CAPS

	AGE (on 01/07/06)	IN NAMED 18	APPEARANCES	COUNTING GAMES	MINUTES ON PITCH	YELLOW CARDS	RED CARDS	CAPS THIS SEASON	NATIONAL SIDE
Goalkeepers									
Martin Pieckenhagen	34	33	32	32	2879	0	1	-	Germany
Brian van Loo	31	31	2	2	180	0	0	-	Holland
Chris Wijnterp	21	1	0	0	0	0	0	-	Holland
Defenders									
Nico-Jan Hoogma	37	31	30	25	2386	2	0	-	Holland
Rudy Jansen	27	29	28	27	2477	2	0	-	Holland
Ragnar Klavan	20	17	14	14	1254	3	0	2	Estonia (61)
Mark Looms	24	25	23	19	1778	2	0	-	Holland
Peter Reekers	25	30	27	19	2020	7	0	-	Holland
Marnix Smit	30	31	14	5	757	3	0	-	Holland
Jan Wuytens	21	24	14	5	639	3	0	-	Belgium
Midfielders									
Remon De Vries	27	33	30	22	2197	4	0	-	Holland
Sergio Hellings	21	30	19	10	1191	3	0	-	Holland
Marc Hocher	21	33	28	20	2121	4	0	-	Holland
Rob Maas	36	26	25	25	2230	9	0	-	Holland
Rob Meijerink	21	4	0	0	0	0	0	-	Holland
Mika Nurmela	34	22	22	20	1813	3	0	-	Finland
Tim Pothast	21	1	0	0	0	0	0	-	Holland
Stefaan Tanghe	34	14	14	14	1260	1	0	-	Belgium
Sander Weenk	20	1	1	0	2	0	0	-	Holland
Forwards									
Denis Calincov	21	15	13	6	723	1	0	-	Moldova
Sota Hirayama	21	33	30	12	1559	2	0	-	Japan
Bernard Hofstede	25	1	1	0	28	1	0	-	Holland
Kwame Quansah	23	33	30	22	2078	5	0	-	Ghana
Thijs Sluijter	26	31	30	25	2337	4	0	-	Holland
Gertjan Tamerus	25	34	33	14	1750	2	0	-	Holland

TEAM OF THE SEASON

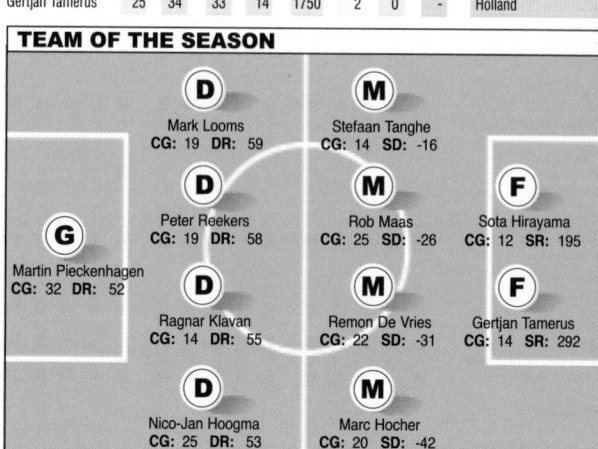

G: Martin Pieckenhagen — CG: 32 DR: 52

D: Mark Looms — CG: 19 DR: 59
D: Peter Reekers — CG: 19 DR: 58
D: Ragnar Klavan — CG: 14 DR: 55
D: Nico-Jan Hoogma — CG: 25 DR: 53

M: Stefaan Tanghe — CG: 14 SD: -16
M: Rob Maas — CG: 25 SD: -26
M: Remon De Vries — CG: 22 SD: -31
M: Marc Hocher — CG: 20 SD: -42

F: Sota Hirayama — CG: 12 SR: 195
F: Gertjan Tamerus — CG: 14 SR: 292

MONTHLY POINTS TALLY

Month	Points	%
AUGUST	7	78%
SEPTEMBER	3	33%
OCTOBER	1	8%
NOVEMBER	4	44%
DECEMBER	4	33%
JANUARY	6	50%
FEBRUARY	2	13%
MARCH	3	25%
APRIL	9	75%

LEAGUE GOALS

	PLAYER	MINS	GOALS	S RATE
1	Hirayama	1559	**8**	195
2	Tamerus	1750	**6**	292
3	Quansah	2078	**5**	416
4	Tanghe	1260	**4**	315
5	Sluijter	2337	**3**	779
6	Calincov	723	**2**	362
7	Jansen	2477	**2**	1239
8	Nurmela	1813	**2**	907
9	Hocher	2121	**1**	2121
10	Hellings	1191	**1**	1191
11	Pieckenhagen	2879	**1**	2879
	Other		**0**	
	TOTAL		**35**	

TOP POINT EARNERS

	PLAYER	GAMES	AV PTS
1	Ragnar Klavan	14	**1.43**
2	Gertjan Tamerus	14	**1.43**
3	Stefaan Tanghe	14	**1.43**
4	Remon De Vries	22	**1.36**
5	Rob Maas	25	**1.36**
6	Peter Reekers	19	**1.32**
7	Thijs Sluijter	25	**1.20**
8	Sota Hirayama	12	**1.17**
9	Kwame Quansah	22	**1.14**
10	Marc Hocher	20	**1.10**
	CLUB AVERAGE:		**1.15**

DISCIPLINARY RECORDS

	PLAYER	YELLOW	RED	AVE
1	Wuytens	3	0	**213**
2	Maas	9	0	**247**
3	Smit	3	0	**252**
4	Reekers	7	0	**288**
5	Hellings	3	0	**397**
6	Quansah	5	0	**415**
7	Klavan	3	0	**418**
8	Hocher	4	0	**530**
9	De Vries	4	0	**549**
10	Sluijter	4	0	**584**
11	Nurmela	3	0	**604**
12	Calincov	1	0	**723**
13	Hirayama	2	0	**779**
	Other	9	1	
	TOTAL	**60**	**1**	

KEY GOALKEEPER

Martin Pieckenhagen

Goals Conceded in the League	55	Counting Games League games when player was on pitch for at least 70 minutes	32
Defensive Rating Ave number of mins between League goals conceded while on the pitch	52	Clean Sheets In games when player was on pitch for at least 70 minutes	6

KEY PLAYERS - DEFENDERS

Mark Looms

Goals Conceded Number of League goals conceded while the player was on the pitch	30	Clean Sheets In League games when player was on pitch for at least 70 minutes	3
Defensive Rating Ave number of mins between League goals conceded while on the pitch	59	Club Defensive Rating Average number of mins between League goals conceded by the club this season	53

	PLAYER	CON LGE	CLEAN SHEETS	DEF RATE
1	Mark Looms	30	3	59 mins
2	Peter Reekers	35	4	58 mins
3	Ragnar Klavan	23	3	55 mins
4	Nico-Jan Hoogma	45	5	53 mins

KEY PLAYERS - MIDFIELDERS

Stefaan Tanghe

Goals in the League	4	Contribution to Attacking Power Average number of minutes between League team goals while on pitch	79
Defensive Rating Average number of mins between League goals conceded while on the pitch	63	Scoring Difference Defensive Rating minus Contribution to Attacking Power	-16

	PLAYER	LGE GOALS	DEF RATE	POWER	SCORE DIFF
1	Stefaan Tanghe	4	63	79	-16 mins
2	Rob Maas	0	60	86	-26 mins
3	Remon De Vries	0	47	78	-31 mins
4	Marc Hocher	1	54	96	-42 mins

KEY PLAYERS - GOALSCORERS

Sota Hirayama

Goals in the League	8	Player Strike Rate Average number of minutes between League goals scored by player	195
Contribution to Attacking Power Average number of minutes between League team goals while on pitch	58	Club Strike Rate Average number of minutes between League goals scored by club	87

	PLAYER	LGE GOALS	POWER	STRIKE RATE
1	Sota Hirayama	8	58	195 mins
2	Gertjan Tamerus	6	76	292 mins
3	Stefaan Tanghe	4	79	315 mins
4	Kwame Quansah	5	99	416 mins

Nico Jan Hoogma

SQUAD APPEARANCES

Match	1	2	3	4	5	6	7	8	9	10	11	12	13	14	15	16	17	18	19	20	21	22	23	24	25	26	27	28	29	30	31	32	33	34	35	36
Venue	H	A	H	A	H	A	H	A	H	A	A	H	A	H	A	H	H	A	H	A	H	A	H	A	H	H	A	A	H	A	H	A	H	A	H	A
Competition	L	L	L	L	L	L	L	L	L	L	L	L	L	L	L	L	L	L	L	L	L	L	L	L	L	L	L	L	L	L	L	L	L	L	O	O
Result	D	W	W	W	L	L	L	D	L	L	D	W	L	L	L	D	W	W	L	W	L	D	D	L	L	L	L	L	W	L	W	W	W	L	L	W

Goalkeepers
Martin Pieckenhagen
Brian van Loo
Chris Wijnterp

Defenders
Nico-Jan Hoogma
Rudy Jansen
Ragnar Klavan
Mark Looms
Peter Reekers
Marnix Smit
Jan Wuytens

Midfielders
Remon De Vries
Sergio Hellings
Marc Hocher
Rob Maas
Rob Meijerink
Mika Nurmela
Tim Pothast
Stefaan Tanghe
Sander Weenk

Forwards
Denis Calincov
Sota Hirayama
Bernard Hofstede
Kwame Quansah
Thijs Sluijter
Gertjan Tamerus

KEY: ■ On all match ■ On bench
⏮ Subbed or sent off (Counting game) « Subbed or sent off (playing less than 70 minutes)
⏭ Subbed on from bench (Counting Game) » Subbed on (playing less than 70 minutes)
Subbed on and then subbed or sent off (Counting Game) Subbed on and then subbed or sent off (playing less than 70 minutes)
□ Not in 16

SPARTA ROTTERDAM

Final Position: **14th**

SPARTA — KEY: ☐ Won ☐ Drawn ☐ Lost

#	Comp	Opponent	H/A	Res	Score	Scorers	Attendance
1	hopr1	AZ Alkmaar	A	L	0-3		8,523
2	hopr1	Feyenoord	H	L	1-3	van der Bergh 20	11,000
3	hopr1	NAC Breda	H	W	1-0	van der Bergh 54	7,000
4	hopr1	Groningen	A	W	1-0	Oost 42 pen	12,300
5	hopr1	Roosendaal	A	D	1-1	Oost 55	4,517
6	hopr1	Heracles	H	W	2-0	van der Bergh 17,60	9,000
7	hopr1	Ajax	H	L	1-2	Polak 52	11,000
8	hopr1	Willem II Tilb	A	D	0-0		13,000
9	hopr1	Roda JC Kerk	H	L	2-3	De Fauw 7; Cvetkov 85	8,212
10	hopr1	NEC Nijmegen	A	D	0-0		12,000
11	hopr1	PSV Eindhoven	A	L	0-3		33,300
12	hopr1	Heerenveen	H	L	1-2	Rose 61	11,000
13	hopr1	Twente	A	L	0-1		13,000
14	hopr1	Den Haag	H	L	2-3	Rose 25,90	10,000
15	hopr1	RKC Waalwijk	A	L	2-3	Polak 45 pen; van der Bergh 90	6,000
16	hopr1	Vitesse Arnhem	H	W	1-0	De Fauw 90	8,500
17	hopr1	Utrecht	A	D	1-1	Cvetkov 90	20,000
18	hopr1	PSV Eindhoven	H	L	0-1		10,000
19	hopr1	NEC Nijmegen	H	L	1-3	Van Tornhout 70	7,500
20	hopr1	Heerenveen	A	D	0-0		20,600
21	hopr1	Twente	H	W	1-0	Oost 3	8,081
22	hopr1	NAC Breda	A	D	0-0		14,000
23	hopr1	Groningen	H	W	1-0	De Fauw 84	8,000
24	hopr1	AZ Alkmaar	H	L	0-1		11,000
25	hopr1	Feyenoord	A	L	0-4		44,000
26	hopr1	Willem II Tilb	H	W	3-2	Rose 8; Obodai 33; Bouaouzan 86	8,000
27	hopr1	Ajax	A	L	0-6		47,476
28	hopr1	Roda JC Kerk	A	D	1-1	Gudde 64	12,500
29	hopr1	Utrecht	H	L	0-1		9,000
30	hopr1	Vitesse Arnhem	A	L	1-3	Oost 34 pen	19,000
31	hopr1	Heracles	A	L	0-1		8,500
32	hopr1	Roosendaal	H	W	5-0	Emnes 33; Cvetkov 46; Rose 59; Oost 65 pen,84	8,000
33	hopr1	RKC Waalwijk	H	W	3-2	Oost 60 pen,79 pen; Cvetkov 83	9,000
34	hopr1	Den Haag	A	W	2-0	van der Bergh 62; Cvetkov 66	10,500

LEAGUE APPEARANCES, BOOKINGS AND CAPS

	AGE (on 01/07/06)	IN NAMED 18	APPEARANCES	COUNTING GAMES	MINUTES ON PITCH	YELLOW CARDS	RED CARDS	CAPS THIS SEASON	NATIONAL SIDE
Goalkeepers									
Frank Kooiman	36	29	0	0	0	0	0	-	Holland
Rene Ponk	34	34	34	34	3060	1	0	-	Holland
Defenders									
Marciano Bruma	22	23	5	3	291	2	1	-	Holland
Dimitri De Fauw	24	32	32	32	2869	5	0	-	Belgium
Wouter Gudde	21	32	26	19	1871	4	0	-	Holland
Nebosja Gudelj	36	33	30	25	2445	3	0	-	Serbia & Montenegro
Steve Olfers	24	22	18	16	1495	1	0	-	Holland
Nathan Rutjes	22	5	2	1	108	0	0	-	Holland
Danny Schenkel	28	16	15	14	1253	6	1	-	Holland
Cees Toet	18	1	0	0	0	0	0	-	Holland
Tom Zoontjes	21	23	16	11	1221	2	0	-	Holland
Midfielders									
Joshua Brard	20	7	0	0	0	0	0	-	Holland
Sani Kaita	20	18	10	6	657	1	0	-	Nigeria
Christophe Kinet	31	7	2	0	66	0	0	-	Belgium
Jan Michels	35	21	21	17	1581	2	1	-	Holland
Anthony Obodai	23	28	27	25	2353	7	0	1	Ghana (48)
Sjaak Polak	30	32	27	21	2100	4	0	-	Holland
Edwin van Bueren	26	28	17	10	1033	2	0	-	Holland
Ricky van der Bergh	25	23	23	17	1713	7	0	-	Holland
Kerem Yilmaz	22	7	3	0	54	0	0	-	Holland
Forwards									
Istvan Bax	20	5	2	0	51	0	0	-	Holland
Rachid Bouaouzan	22	30	30	14	1825	1	0	-	Holland
Ivan Cvetkov	26	34	27	9	1332	0	0	-	Bulgaria
Marvin Emnes	18	19	9	2	324	0	0	-	Holland
Jason Oost	23	30	30	24	2352	2	0	-	Holland
Yuri Rose	27	32	32	28	2712	4	1	-	Holland
Dieter Van Tornhout	21	14	13	7	825	5	1	-	Belgium
Marvin Wijks	22	2	1	0	17	0	0	-	Holland

TEAM OF THE SEASON

G — Rene Ponk — CG: 34 DR: 61

D — Steve Olfers — CG: 16 DR: 75

D — Danny Schenkel — CG: 14 DR: 63

D — Wouter Gudde — CG: 19 DR: 62

D — Dimitri De Fauw — CG: 32 DR: 57

M — Jan Michels — CG: 17 SD: 0

M — Ricky van der Bergh — CG: 17 SD: 0

M — Anthony Obodai — CG: 25 SD: -35

M — Sjaak Polak — CG: 21 SD: -45

F — Jason Oost — CG: 24 SR: 294

F — Yuri Rose — CG: 28 SR: 542

MONTHLY POINTS TALLY

Month	Points	%
AUGUST	3	33%
SEPTEMBER	7	78%
OCTOBER	2	17%
NOVEMBER	0	0%
DECEMBER	4	33%
JANUARY	4	33%
FEBRUARY	7	47%
MARCH	1	8%
APRIL	9	75%

LEAGUE GOALS

	PLAYER	MINS	GOALS	S RATE
1	Oost	2352	8	294
2	van der Bergh	1713	6	286
3	Cvetkov	1332	5	266
4	Rose	2712	5	542
5	De Fauw	2869	3	956
6	Polak	2100	2	1050
7	Emnes	324	1	324
8	Gudde	1871	1	1871
9	Bouaouzan	1825	1	1825
10	Van Tornhout	825	1	825
11	Obodai	2353	1	2353
	Other		0	
	TOTAL		34	

TOP POINT EARNERS

	PLAYER	GAMES	AV PTS
1	Jan Michels	17	1.35
2	Steve Olfers	16	1.31
3	Ricky van der Bergh	17	1.29
4	Danny Schenkel	14	1.29
5	Jason Oost	24	1.21
6	Yuri Rose	28	1.21
7	Rene Ponk	34	1.09
8	Nebosja Gudelj	25	1.08
9	Wouter Gudde	19	1.05
10	Dimitri De Fauw	32	0.97
	CLUB AVERAGE:		1.09

DISCIPLINARY RECORDS

	PLAYER	YELLOW	RED	AVE
1	Van Tornhout	5	1	137
2	Schenkel	6	1	179
3	van der Bergh	7	0	244
4	Obodai	7	0	336
5	Gudde	4	0	467
6	van Bueren	2	0	516
7	Polak	4	0	525
8	Michels	2	1	527
9	Rose	4	1	542
10	De Fauw	5	0	573
11	Zoontjes	2	0	610
12	Kaita	1	0	657
13	Gudelj	3	0	815
	Other	5	0	
	TOTAL	57	4	

KEY GOALKEEPER

Rene Ponk

Goals Conceded in the League	**50**	**Counting Games** League games when player was on pitch for at least 70 minutes	**34**
Defensive Rating Ave number of mins between League goals conceded while on the pitch	**61**	**Clean Sheets** In League games when player was on pitch for at least 70 minutes	**11**

KEY PLAYERS - DEFENDERS

Steve Olfers

Goals Conceded Number of League goals conceded while the player was on the pitch	**20**	**Clean Sheets** In League games when player was on pitch for at least 70 minutes	**6**
Defensive Rating Ave number of mins between League goals conceded while on the pitch	**75**	**Club Defensive Rating** Average number of mins between League goals conceded by the club this season	**60**

	PLAYER	CON LGE	CLEAN SHEETS	DEF RATE
1	Steve Olfers	20	6	75 mins
2	Danny Schenkel	20	5	63 mins
3	Wouter Gudde	30	6	62 mins
4	Dimitri De Fauw	50	9	57 mins

KEY PLAYERS - MIDFIELDERS

Jan Michels

Goals in the League	**0**	**Contribution to Attacking Power** Average number of minutes between League team goals while on pitch	**69**
Defensive Rating Average number of mins between League goals conceded while on the pitch	**69**	**Scoring Difference** Defensive Rating minus Contribution to Attacking Power	**0**

	PLAYER	LGE GOALS	DEF RATE	POWER	SCORE DIFF
1	Jan Michels	0	69	69	0 mins
2	Ricky van der Bergh	6	78	78	0 mins
3	Anthony Obodai	1	56	91	-35 mins
4	Sjaak Polak	2	66	111	-45 mins

KEY PLAYERS - GOALSCORERS

Ricky van der Bergh

Goals in the League	**6**	**Player Strike Rate** Average number of minutes between League goals scored by player	**286**
Contribution to Attacking Power Average number of minutes between League team goals while on pitch	**78**	**Club Strike Rate** Average number of minutes between League goals scored by club	**90**

	PLAYER	LGE GOALS	POWER	STRIKE RATE
1	Ricky van der Bergh	6	78	286 mins
2	Jason Oost	8	90	294 mins
3	Yuri Rose	5	94	542 mins
4	Dimitri De Fauw	3	106	956 mins

Dieter Van Tornhout

SQUAD APPEARANCES

Match	1	2	3	4	5	6	7	8	9	10	11	12	13	14	15	16	17	18	19	20	21	22	23	24	25	26	27	28	29	30	31	32	33	34
Venue	A	H	H	A	A	H	H	A	H	A	A	H	A	H	A	H	A	H	H	A	H	A	H	H	A	H	A	A	H	A	A	H	H	A
Competition	L	L	L	L	L	L	L	L	L	L	L	L	L	L	L	L	L	L	L	L	L	L	L	L	L	L	L	L	L	L	L	L	L	L
Result	L	L	W	W	D	W	L	D	L	D	L	L	L	L	L	W	D	L	L	D	W	D	W	L	L	W	L	D	L	L	L	W	W	W
Goalkeepers																																		
Frank Kooiman																																		
Rene Ponk																																		
Defenders																																		
Marciano Bruma																																		
Dimitri De Fauw																																		
Wouter Gudde																																		
Nebosja Gudelj																																		
Steve Olfers																																		
Nathan Rutjes																																		
Danny Schenkel																																		
Cees Toet																																		
Tom Zoontjes																																		
Midfielders																																		
Joshua Brard																																		
Sani Kaita																																		
Christophe Kinet																																		
Jan Michels																																		
Anthony Obodai																																		
Sjaak Polak																																		
Edwin van Bueren																																		
Ricky van der Bergh																																		
Kerem Yilmaz																																		
Forwards																																		
Istvan Bax																																		
Rachid Bouaouzan																																		
Ivan Cvetkov																																		
Marvin Emnes																																		
Jason Oost																																		
Yuri Rose																																		
Dieter Van Tornhout																																		
Marvin Wijks																																		

KEY: ■ On all match | ■ On bench | ⏮ Subbed or sent off (Counting game) | « Subbed or sent off (playing less than 70 minutes) | ⏭ Subbed on from bench (Counting Game) | » Subbed on (playing less than 70 minutes) | Subbed on and then subbed or sent off (Counting Game) | Subbed on and then subbed or sent off (playing less than 70 minutes) | □ Not in 16

ADO DEN HAAG

Final Position: **15th**

KEY: ☐Won ☐Drawn ☐Lost

							Attendance
1	hopr1	**Heracles**	H	L	1-2	den Ouden 63	6,000
2	hopr1	**Heerenveen**	H	W	1-0	Saeijs 90	6,025
3	hopr1	**NAC Breda**	A	L	1-4	Saeijs 85 pen	13,930
4	hopr1	**Twente**	H	D	0-0		5,613
5	hopr1	**Ajax**	A	D	2-2	Elia 90; Saeijs 90	52,854
6	hopr1	**Willem II Tilb**	A	L	0-1		10,850
7	hopr1	**RKC Waalwijk**	H	W	2-1	den Ouden 15; Stroeve 57	6,413
8	hopr1	**Vitesse Arnhem**	A	L	1-3	Stroeve 42	17,265
9	hopr1	**Groningen**	A	L	1-3	de Graaf 66	11,000
10	hopr1	**AZ Alkmaar**	H	L	0-2		7,185
11	hopr1	**Utrecht**	A	D	1-1	Mols 55	17,144
12	hopr1	**NEC Nijmegen**	H	L	0-1		5,938
13	hopr1	**PSV Eindhoven**	A	L	0-3		33,000
14	hopr1	**S Rotterdam**	A	W	3-2	Kolkka 11; Bodde 44; Verhoek 79	10,000
15	hopr1	**Roosendaal**	H	W	3-0	van der Leegte 6; Kolkka 78,84	6,725
16	hopr1	**Feyenoord**	H	W	2-1	den Ouden 2 pen; Saavedra 79	8,633
17	hopr1	**Roda JC Kerk**	A	L	1-3	Kolkka 86	9,500
18	hopr1	**Utrecht**	H	L	2-3	Mols 59; den Ouden 90 pen	6,002
19	hopr1	**AZ Alkmaar**	A	L	1-3	Stroeve 89	8,349
20	hopr1	**NEC Nijmegen**	A	L	0-5		11,750
21	hopr1	**PSV Eindhoven**	H	L	0-2		8,000
22	hopr1	**Heerenveen**	A	L	0-3		20,500
23	hopr1	**NAC Breda**	H	L	0-3		6,000
24	hopr1	**Ajax**	H	L	1-2	Mols 33	9,133
25	hopr1	**Heracles**	A	W	3-1	Elia 26; de Graaf 82; den Ouden 87	8,500
26	hopr1	**Vitesse Arnhem**	H	W	2-0	Kolkka 10,45	5,033
27	hopr1	**RKC Waalwijk**	A	L	0-3		5,600
28	hopr1	**Groningen**	H	W	2-1	Mols 23; Bodde 66 pen	6,546
29	hopr1	**Roda JC Kerk**	H	D	1-1	Rankovic 68	6,512
30	hopr1	**Feyenoord**	A	W	2-0	Kolkka 37,66	40,000
31	hopr1	**Willem II Tilb**	H	D	1-1	Stroeve 90	9,018
32	hopr1	**Twente**	A	L	0-2		13,000
33	hopr1	**Roosendaal**	A	W	2-1	de Graaf 75; Stroeve 80 pen	4,000
34	hopr1	**S Rotterdam**	H	L	0-2		10,500

LEAGUE APPEARANCES, BOOKINGS AND CAPS

	AGE (on 01/07/06)	IN NAMED 18	APPEARANCES	COUNTING GAMES	MINUTES ON PITCH	YELLOW CARDS	RED CARDS	CAPS THIS SEASON	NATIONAL SIDE
Goalkeepers									
Dorus de Vries	25	28	20	20	1800	0	0	-	Holland
Jaroslav Drobny	26	12	12	12	1080	0	0	-	Czech Republic
Cees Paauwe	28	12	1	1	90	0	0	-	Holland
Arjan van der Kaay	23	3	0	0	0	0	0	-	Holland
Robert Zwinkels	23	13	1	1	90	0	0	-	Holland
Defenders									
Said Bakkati	24	14	12	12	1070	2	0	-	Holland
Youssef El-Akchaoui	25	33	28	25	2335	4	0	-	Holland
Samir El-Moussaoui	19	3	0	0	0	0	0	-	Holland
Cory Gibbs	26	8	5	4	405	1	0	-	United States
Spira Grujic	34	20	16	13	1236	0	0	-	Serbia & Montenegro
Chris Kum	20	14	3	2	203	1	0	-	Holland
John O'Brien	28	3	3	1	218	0	0	2	United States (5)
Danilo Pedrini	20	3	0	0	0	0	0	-	Holland
Raymond Riedewald	19	9	2	2	180	0	0	-	Holland
Daniel Rijaard	29	16	14	12	1153	7	1	-	Holland
Tomasz Rzasa	33	31	25	20	1943	1	0	7	Poland (29)
Alberto Saavedra	24	30	26	24	2216	7	1	-	Spain
Jan-Paul Saeijs	28	15	15	15	1350	4	0	-	Holland
Midfielders									
Ferrie Bodde	24	23	19	11	1246	5	1	-	Holland
Edwin de Graaf	26	24	23	19	1816	1	0	-	Holland
Sean Doherty	21	7	0	0	0	0	0	-	England
Peter Jungschlager	22	30	12	7	742	0	0	-	Holland
Angelo Martha	24	9	1	1	90	1	0	-	Holland
Aleksandar Rankovic	27	27	26	23	2099	9	0	-	Serbia & Montenegro
Roy Stroeve	29	33	27	15	1710	3	0	-	Holland
Tom van der Leegte	29	18	18	18	1620	7	0	-	Holland
Roger Van der Zwan	21	1	0	0	0	0	0	-	Holland
Forwards									
Geert den Ouden	29	29	26	13	1741	3	0	-	Holland
Eljero Elia	19	33	30	12	1509	2	0	-	Holland
Joonas Kolkka	31	31	31	29	2650	2	0	3	Finland (42)
Michael Mols	35	32	29	17	1952	2	0	-	Holland
Paulus Roiha	25	11	9	0	208	0	0	2	Finland (42)
Levi Schwiebbe	19	3	0	0	0	0	0	-	Holland
Wesley Verhoek	19	21	19	5	823	1	0	-	Holland

TEAM OF THE SEASON

G
Jaroslav Drobny
CG: 12 DR: 64

D
Tomasz Rzasa
CG: 20 DR: 57

D
Said Bakkati
CG: 12 DR: 56

D
Daniel Rijaard
CG: 12 DR: 55

D
Jan-Paul Saeijs
CG: 15 DR: 54

M
Roy Stroeve
CG: 15 SD: -26

M
Tom van der Leegte
CG: 18 SD: -36

M
Edwin de Graaf
CG: 19 SD: -44

M
Aleksandar Rankovic
CG: 23 SD: -70

F
Joonas Kolkka
CG: 29 SR: 331

F
Geert den Ouden
CG: 13 SR: 348

MONTHLY POINTS TALLY

AUGUST	3	50%
SEPTEMBER	2	17%
OCTOBER	3	25%
NOVEMBER	1	11%
DECEMBER	9	75%
JANUARY	0	0%
FEBRUARY	6	40%
MARCH	7	58%
APRIL	4	33%

LEAGUE GOALS

	PLAYER	MINS	GOALS	S RATE
1	Kolkka	2650	8	331
2	den Ouden	1741	5	348
3	Stroeve	1710	5	342
4	Mols	1952	4	488
5	de Graaf	1816	3	605
6	Saeijs	1350	3	450
7	Bodde	1246	2	623
8	Elia	1509	2	755
9	Rankovic	2099	1	2099
10	Verhoek	823	1	823
11	Saavedra	2216	1	2216
12	van der Leegte	1620	1	1620
	Other		0	
	TOTAL		36	

TOP POINT EARNERS

	PLAYER	GAMES	AV PTS
1	Eljero Elia	12	1.42
2	Jaroslav Drobny	12	1.42
3	Said Bakkati	12	1.33
4	Michael Mols	17	1.29
5	Alberto Saavedra	24	1.21
6	Daniel Rijaard	12	1.17
7	Youssef El-Akchaoui	25	1.16
8	Geert den Ouden	13	1.15
9	Spira Grujic	13	1.15
10	Tomasz Rzasa	20	1.10
	CLUB AVERAGE:		1.03

DISCIPLINARY RECORDS

	PLAYER	YELLOW	RED	AVE
1	Rijaard	7	1	144
2	Bodde	5	1	207
3	van der Leegte	7	0	231
4	Rankovic	9	0	233
5	Saavedra	7	1	277
6	Saeijs	4	0	337
7	Bakkati	2	0	535
8	Stroeve	3	0	570
9	den Ouden	3	0	580
10	El-Akchaoui	4	0	583
11	Elia	2	0	754
12	Verhoek	1	0	823
13	Mols	2	0	976
	Other	4	0	
	TOTAL	60	3	

KEY GOALKEEPER

Jaroslav Drobny

Goals Conceded in the League	17	**Counting Games** League games when player was on pitch for at least 70 minutes	12
Defensive Rating Ave number of mins between League goals conceded while on the pitch	64	**Clean Sheets** In games when player was on pitch for at least 70 minutes	2

KEY PLAYERS - DEFENDERS

Tomasz Rzasa

Goals Conceded Number of League goals conceded while the player was on the pitch	34	**Clean Sheets** In League games when player was on pitch for at least 70 minutes	4
Defensive Rating Ave number of mins between League goals conceded while on the pitch	57	**Club Defensive Rating** Average number of mins between League goals conceded by the club this season	49

	PLAYER	CON LGE	CLEAN SHEETS	DEF RATE
1	Tomasz Rzasa	34	4	57 mins
2	Said Bakkati	19	2	56 mins
3	Daniel Rijaard	21	3	55 mins
4	Jan-Paul Saeijs	25	3	54 mins

KEY PLAYERS - MIDFIELDERS

Roy Stroeve

Goals in the League	5	**Contribution to Attacking Power** Average number of minutes between League team goals while on pitch	71
Defensive Rating Average number of mins between League goals conceded while on the pitch	45	Scoring Difference Defensive Rating minus Contribution to Attacking Power	-26

	PLAYER	LGE GOALS	DEF RATE	POWER	SCORE DIFF
1	Roy Stroeve	5	45	71	-26 mins
2	Tom van der Leegte	1	45	81	-36 mins
3	Edwin de Graaf	3	47	91	-44 mins
4	Aleksandar Rankovic	1	47	117	-70 mins

KEY PLAYERS - GOALSCORERS

Joonas Kolkka

Goals in the League	8	Player Strike Rate Average number of minutes between League goals scored by player	331
Contribution to Attacking Power Average number of minutes between League team goals while on pitch	85	**Club Strike Rate** Average number of minutes between League goals scored by club	85

	PLAYER	LGE GOALS	POWER	STRIKE RATE
1	Joonas Kolkka	8	85	331 mins
2	Roy Stroeve	5	71	342 mins
3	Geert den Ouden	5	83	348 mins
4	Jan-Paul Saeijs	3	84	450 mins

Joonas Kolkka

SQUAD APPEARANCES

atch	1	2	3	4	5	6	7	8	9	10	11	12	13	14	15	16	17	18	19	20	21	22	23	24	25	26	27	28	29	30	31	32	33	34
enue	H	H	A	H	A	A	H	A	A	H	A	H	A	A	H	H	A	H	A	A	H	A	H	H	A	H	A	H	H	A	H	A	A	H
ompetition	L	L	L	L	L	L	L	L	L	L	L	L	L	L	L	L	L	L	L	L	L	L	L	L	L	L	L	L	L	L	L	L	L	L
esult	L	W	L	D	D	L	W	L	L	L	D	L	L	W	W	W	L	L	L	L	L	L	L	L	W	W	L	W	D	W	D	L	W	L

oalkeepers
orus de Vries
aroslav Drobny
ees Paauwe
rjan van der Kaay
obert Zwinkels

efenders
aid Bakkati
oussef El-Akchaoui
amir El-Moussaoui
ory Gibbs
pira Grujic
hris Kum
ohn O'Brien
anilo Pedrini
aymond Riedewald
aniel Rijaard
omasz Rzasa
lberto Saavedra
an-Paul Saeijs

lidfielders
errie Bodde
dwin de Graaf
ean Doherty
eter Jungschlager
ngelo Martha
leksandar Rankovic
oy Stroeve
om van der Leegte

orwards
eert den Ouden
ljero Elia
oonas Kolkka
lichael Mols
aulus Roiha
evi Schwiebbe
Vesley Verhoek

KEY: On all match / On bench / Subbed or sent off (Counting game) / Subbed or sent off (playing less than 70 minutes) / Subbed on from bench (Counting Game) / Subbed on (playing less than 70 minutes) / Subbed on and then subbed or sent off (Counting Game) / Subbed on and then subbed or sent off (playing less than 70 minutes) / Not in 16

NAC BREDA

Final Position: **16th**

KEY: ☐Won ☐Drawn ☐Lost

	Comp	Opponent	H/A	Res	Score	Scorers	Attendance
1	hopr1	**Feyenoord**	A	L	0-2		42,000
2	hopr1	**Willem II Tilb**	H	W	1-0	Vonlanthen 87	14,000
3	hopr1	**S Rotterdam**	A	L	0-1		7,000
4	hopr1	**Den Haag**	H	W	4-1	Zonneveld 2; Slot 16; Mendes Da Silva 22; Rigters 77	13,930
5	hopr1	**NEC Nijmegen**	A	D	1-1	Jenner 27	12,000
6	hopr1	**AZ Alkmaar**	H	W	2-1	Slot 60; Vonlanthen 77	15,250
7	hopr1	**Roosendaal**	A	W	2-1	Vonlanthen 13; van Hooijdonk 65 pen	5,000
8	hopr1	**Heerenveen**	H	L	0-3		14,850
9	hopr1	**Twente**	H	D	1-1	Vonlanthen 61	14,150
10	hopr1	**RKC Waalwijk**	A	L	1-4	van Hooijdonk 27	7,000
11	hopr1	**Roda JC Kerk**	A	D	3-3	van Hooijdonk 13,90; Penders 65	13,500
12	hopr1	**Utrecht**	H	L	0-1		14,500
13	hopr1	**Groningen**	H	D	2-2	van Hooijdonk 9; Slot 82	14,000
14	hopr1	**PSV Eindhoven**	A	L	0-3		32,500
15	hopr1	**Heracles**	H	W	2-1	Vonlanthen 25; Zwaanswijk 30	13,699
16	hopr1	**Ajax**	H	L	0-2		17,000
17	hopr1	**Vitesse Arnhem**	A	L	1-2	van Gessel 53	18,000
18	hopr1	**RKC Waalwijk**	H	L	1-2	Jenner 46	12,500
19	hopr1	**Roda JC Kerk**	H	L	0-4		13,498
20	hopr1	**Utrecht**	A	D	2-2	Diba 37; Rigters 61	17,500
21	hopr1	**Groningen**	A	L	2-3	van Gessel 56; Leonardo 74	20,000
22	hopr1	**S Rotterdam**	H	D	0-0		14,000
23	hopr1	**Den Haag**	A	W	3-0	Diba 10; van Gessel 52; Leonardo 81	6,000
24	hopr1	**Feyenoord**	H	D	3-3	Diba 24,90; Jenner 90	16,385
25	hopr1	**Willem II Tilb**	A	L	0-2		13,500
26	hopr1	**Heerenveen**	A	L	1-2	Leonardo 6	19,000
27	hopr1	**Roosendaal**	H	W	2-1	Roumani 35 og; Slot 46	14,000
28	hopr1	**Twente**	A	L	0-1		13,200
29	hopr1	**Vitesse Arnhem**	H	D	2-2	Leonardo 12,47	14,000
30	hopr1	**Ajax**	A	D	1-1	Mendes Da Silva 80	47,700
31	hopr1	**AZ Alkmaar**	A	L	2-3	Slot 54; Leonardo 60	8,500
32	hopr1	**NEC Nijmegen**	H	W	2-1	Diba 17; Leonardo 55	14,000
33	hopr1	**Heracles**	A	L	2-4	Leonardo 4; Stam 30	8,500
34	hopr1	**PSV Eindhoven**	H	L	2-6	Vonlanthen 55; Derijck 69	14,950
35	honac	**TOP Oss**	A	D	0-0		3,475
36	honac	**TOP Oss**	H	D	2-2	Diba 56; Stam 58	14,820
37	erepo	**TOP Oss**	A	W	3-1	Diba 55,95,119	4,375
38	honac	**Volendam**	A	W	2-1	Zwaanswijk 56; Diba 86	5,404
39	honac	**Volendam**	H	D	0-0		

LEAGUE APPEARANCES, BOOKINGS AND CAPS

	AGE (on 01/07/06)	IN NAMED 18	APPEARANCES	COUNTING GAMES	MINUTES ON PITCH	YELLOW CARDS	RED CARDS	CAPS THIS SEASON	NATIONAL SIDE
Goalkeepers									
Arjan Cristianen	23	8	0	0	0	0	0	-	Holland
Davy Schollen	30	32	18	17	1539	0	0	-	Belgium
Arno van Zwam	36	27	17	17	1530	0	0	-	Holland
Defenders									
Aykut Demir	17	18	8	4	487	1	0	-	Turkey
Timothy Derijck	19	14	12	10	1004	2	1	-	Belgium
Kurt Elshot	29	33	33	33	2970	4	0	-	Surinam
Arie Jonker	22	12	2	0	9	0	0	-	Holland
Benny Kerstens	23	24	7	4	452	1	0	-	Holland
Wilmer Kousemaker	20	9	1	1	90	0	0	-	Holland
D. Mendes Da Silva	23	26	26	25	2275	5	0	-	Holland
Rob Penders	30	4	4	3	277	1	0	-	Holland
Evandor Sno	19	14	14	13	1178	2	0	-	Holland
Ivo Van Engelen	21	17	4	2	238	1	0	-	Holland
Tony Vidmar	36	21	21	18	1693	2	0	5	Australia (42)
Patrick Zwaanswijk	31	31	31	29	2635	5	0	-	Holland
Midfielders									
Julian Jenner	22	29	28	18	1837	2	0	-	Holland
Tamas Peto	32	16	13	7	879	1	0	-	Hungary
Victor Sikora	28	17	13	5	746	2	0	-	Holland
Arne Slot	27	28	26	20	1971	3	0	-	Holland
Ronnie Stam	22	30	28	19	1856	5	0	-	Holland
Jordi Van Bremen	19	1	0	0	0	0	0	-	Holland
Sander van Gessel	29	31	31	31	2790	3	0	-	Holland
Mike Zonneveld	25	4	4	4	357	1	0	-	Holland
Forwards									
Anouar Diba	23	25	24	13	1514	5	0	-	Holland
Leonardo	23	14	14	10	1007	1	0	-	Brazil
Maceo Rigters	22	29	24	3	833	2	0	-	Holland
Pierre van Hooijdonk	36	18	17	16	1489	1	0	-	Holland
Vincent Vervoort	21	3	0	0	0	0	0	-	Holland
Johan Vonlanthen	20	34	32	17	1954	1	0	8	Switzerland (35)

TEAM OF THE SEASON

G — Arno van Zwam, CG: 17 DR: 57

D — David Mendes Da Silva, CG: 25 DR: 51
D — Patrick Zwaanswijk, CG: 29 DR: 47
D — Kurt Elshot, CG: 33 DR: 46
D — Tony Vidmar, CG: 18 DR: 46

M — Julian Jenner, CG: 18 SD: -19
M — Arne Slot, CG: 20 SD: -19
M — Sander van Gessel, CG: 31 SD: -21
M — Ronnie Stam, CG: 19 SD: -24

F — P van Hooijdonk, CG: 16 SR: 298

F — Anouar Diba, CG: 13 SR: 303

MONTHLY POINTS TALLY

Month	Points	%
AUGUST	3	33%
SEPTEMBER	10	83%
OCTOBER	1	11%
NOVEMBER	2	22%
DECEMBER	3	25%
JANUARY	1	8%
FEBRUARY	5	33%
MARCH	5	42%
APRIL	3	25%

LEAGUE GOALS

	PLAYER	MINS	GOALS	S RATE
1	Leonardo	1007	**8**	126
2	Vonlanthen	1954	**6**	326
3	Slot	1971	**5**	394
4	Diba	1514	**5**	303
5	van Hooijdonk	1489	**5**	298
6	Jenner	1837	**3**	612
7	van Gessel	2790	**3**	930
8	Mendes Da Silva	2275	**2**	1138
9	Rigters	833	**2**	417
10	Derijck	1004	**1**	1004
11	Stam	1856	**1**	1856
12	Zonneveld	357	**1**	357
13	Penders	277	**1**	277
	Other		**2**	
	TOTAL		**45**	

TOP POINT EARNERS

	PLAYER	GAMES	AV PTS
1	Anouar Diba	13	**1.15**
2	Johan Vonlanthen	17	**1.12**
3	Arno van Zwam	17	**1.12**
4	David Mendes Da Silva	25	**1.04**
5	Sander van Gessel	31	**1.03**
6	Arne Slot	20	**1.00**
7	Evandor Sno	13	**1.00**
8	Patrick Zwaanswijk	29	**1.00**
9	Julian Jenner	18	**0.94**
10	Kurt Elshot	33	**0.91**
	CLUB AVERAGE:		**0.97**

DISCIPLINARY RECORDS

	PLAYER	YELLOW	RED	AVE
1	Diba	5	0	**302**
2	Derijck	2	1	**334**
3	Stam	5	0	**371**
4	Sikora	2	0	**373**
5	Rigters	2	0	**416**
6	Kerstens	1	0	**452**
7	Mendes Da Silva	5	0	**455**
8	Demir	1	0	**487**
9	Zwaanswijk	5	0	**527**
10	Sno	2	0	**589**
11	Slot	3	0	**657**
12	Elshot	4	0	**742**
13	Vidmar	2	0	**846**
	Other	9	0	
	TOTAL	**48**	**1**	

KEY GOALKEEPER

Arno van Zwam

Goals Conceded in the League	27	**Counting Games** League games when player was on pitch for at least 70 minutes	17
Defensive Rating Ave number of mins between League goals conceded while on the pitch	57	**Clean Sheets** In games when player was on pitch for at least 70 minutes	1

KEY PLAYERS - DEFENDERS

David Mendes Da Silva

Goals Conceded Number of League goals conceded while the player was on the pitch	45	**Clean Sheets** In League games when player was on pitch for at least 70 minutes	3
Defensive Rating Ave number of mins between League goals conceded while on the pitch	51	**Club Defensive Rating** Average number of mins between League goals conceded by the club this season	46

	PLAYER	CON LGE	CLEAN SHEETS	DEF RATE
1	David Mendes Da Silva	45	3	**51 mins**
2	Patrick Zwaanswijk	56	3	**47 mins**
3	Tony Vidmar	37	3	**46 mins**
4	Kurt Elshot	65	3	**46 mins**

KEY PLAYERS - MIDFIELDERS

Arne Slot

Goals in the League	5	**Contribution to Attacking Power** Average number of minutes between League team goals while on pitch	64
Defensive Rating Average number of mins between League goals conceded while on the pitch	45	**Scoring Difference** Defensive Rating minus Contribution to Attacking Power	-19

	PLAYER	LGE GOALS	DEF RATE	POWER	SCORE DIFF
1	Arne Slot	5	45	64	**-19 mins**
2	Julian Jenner	3	54	73	**-19 mins**
3	Sander van Gessel	3	47	68	**-21 mins**
4	Ronnie Stam	1	38	62	**-24 mins**

KEY PLAYERS - GOALSCORERS

Pierre van Hooijdonk

Goals in the League	5	**Player Strike Rate** Average number of minutes between League goals scored by player	298
Contribution to Attacking Power Average number of minutes between League team goals while on pitch	93	**Club Strike Rate** Average number of minutes between League goals scored by club	68

	PLAYER	LGE GOALS	POWER	STRIKE RATE
1	Pierre van Hooijdonk	5	93	**298 mins**
2	Anouar Diba	5	61	**303 mins**
3	Johan Vonlanthen	6	63	**326 mins**
4	Arne Slot	5	64	**394 mins**

David Mendes Da Silva

SQUAD APPEARANCES

Match	1	2	3	4	5	6	7	8	9	10	11	12	13	14	15	16	17	18	19	20	21	22	23	24	25	26	27	28	29	30	31	32	33	34	35	36	37	38	39
Venue	A	H	A	H	A	H	A	H	H	A	A	H	H	A	H	H	A	H	H	A	A	H	A	H	A	A	H	A	H	A	A	H	A	H	A	H	A	A	H
Competition	L	L	L	L	L	L	L	L	L	L	L	L	L	L	L	L	L	L	L	L	L	L	L	L	L	L	L	L	L	L	L	L	L	L	O	O	O	O	O
Result	L	W	L	W	D	W	W	L	D	L	D	L	D	L	W	L	L	L	L	D	L	D	W	D	L	L	W	L	D	D	L	W	L	L	D	D	W	W	D

Goalkeepers
Arjan Cristianen
Davy Schollen
Arno van Zwam

Defenders
Aykut Demir
Timothy Derijck
Kurt Elshot
Arie Jonker
Benny Kerstens
Wilmer Kousemaker
David Mendes Da Silva
Rob Penders
Evandor Sno
Ivo Van Engelen
Tony Vidmar
Patrick Zwaanswijk

Midfielders
Julian Jenner
Tamas Peto
Victor Sikora
Arne Slot
Ronnie Stam
Jordi Van Bremen
Sander van Gessel
Mike Zonneveld

Forwards
Anouar Diba
Leonardo
Maceo Rigters
Pierre van Hooijdonk
Vincent Vervoort
Johan Vonlanthen

KEY: On all match | On bench | Subbed or sent off (Counting game) | Subbed or sent off (playing less than 70 minutes) | Subbed on from bench (Counting Game) | Subbed on (playing less than 70 minutes) | Subbed on and then subbed or sent off (Counting Game) | Subbed on and then subbed or sent off (playing less than 70 minutes) | Not in 16

WILLEM II TILBURG

Final Position: **17th**

KEY: ☐Won ☐Drawn ☐Lost

	Comp	Opponent	H/A	Res	Score	Scorers	Attendance
1	hopr1	RKC Waalwijk	H	L	1-2	Reuser 57	10,850
2	hopr1	NAC Breda	A	L	0-1		14,000
3	hopr1	Roosendaal	A	D	1-1	Caluwe 83	3,136
4	hopr1	Ajax	H	L	0-2		12,500
5	uc1rl1	AS Monaco	A	L	0-2		8,000
6	hopr1	Roda JC Kerk	A	W	2-0	Kerekes 21; Caluwe 56	13,200
7	hopr1	Den Haag	H	W	1-0	Reuser 90	10,850
8	uc1rl2	AS Monaco	H	L	1-3	Hadouir 84	11,600
9	hopr1	Groningen	A	L	0-2		12,000
10	hopr1	S Rotterdam	H	D	0-0		13,000
11	hopr1	AZ Alkmaar	A	L	1-5	Agustien 17	8,500
12	hopr1	Feyenoord	H	L	1-3	Denissen 90	13,500
13	hopr1	Twente	A	L	1-3	Bobson 69	13,000
14	hopr1	Vitesse Arnhem	H	L	3-4	Smit 10; Feher 73; Reuser 86	11,000
15	hopr1	NEC Nijmegen	A	L	0-2		11,000
16	hopr1	Heerenveen	A	D	3-3	Caluwe 6; Hadouir 12,26	20,000
17	hopr1	Utrecht	H	L	0-1		12,500
18	hopr1	PSV Eindhoven	A	L	1-4	Ceesay 15	32,500
19	hopr1	Feyenoord	A	L	1-6	Reuser 67	40,000
20	hopr1	Heracles	H	L	1-2	Dembele 41	11,000
21	hopr1	Twente	H	D	1-1	Hadouir 8	12,000
22	hopr1	Vitesse Arnhem	A	L	1-2	Dembele 24	19,000
23	hopr1	NEC Nijmegen	H	D	2-2	Dembele 8; van Mosselveld 25	11,000
24	hopr1	Roosendaal	H	W	3-1	Dembele 60; Hadouir 89 pen; Lammens 90 og	11,000
25	hopr1	Ajax	A	L	0-1		44,467
26	hopr1	RKC Waalwijk	A	L	0-1		6,800
27	hopr1	NAC Breda	H	W	2-0	Sno 25; Dembele 27	13,500
28	hopr1	S Rotterdam	A	L	2-3	Redan 81; Agustien 93	8,000
29	hopr1	Groningen	H	W	5-0	Valencia 29; Hadouir 47; Wau 50; Redan 55; Dembele 58	11,000
30	hopr1	AZ Alkmaar	H	L	1-3	Redan 16	12,500
31	hopr1	Heracles	A	L	0-1		8,400
32	hopr1	PSV Eindhoven	H	L	0-3		12,500
33	hopr1	Den Haag	A	D	1-1	Dembele 75	9,018
34	hopr1	Roda JC Kerk	H	D	2-2	Redan 6; Smit 40	12,000
35	hopr1	Heerenveen	H	W	4-3	Dembele 10,71; Redan 20,90	12,000
36	hopr1	Utrecht	A	W	4-1	Redan 17,54; Kerekes 48; Reuser 81	24,000
37	honac	Zwolle	A	W	4-2	Hadouir 9; Redan 65,87; Smit 90	4,850
38	honac	Zwolle	H	W	6-2	Reuser 35,44,75; Kerekes 37; Keenan 75; Hadouir 86	12,500
39	honac	De Graafschap	A	W	1-0	Kerekes 87	10,800
40	honac	De Graafschap	H	W	2-1	Agustien 13; Dembele 79	13,800

LEAGUE APPEARANCES, BOOKINGS AND CAPS

	AGE (on 01/07/06)	IN NAMED 18	APPEARANCES	COUNTING GAMES	MINUTES ON PITCH	YELLOW CARDS	RED CARDS	CAPS THIS SEASON	NATIONAL SIDE
Goalkeepers									
Ahmet Altin	20	7	0	0	0	0	0	-	Turkey
Oscar Moens	33	11	11	10	940	0	1	-	Holland
Tristan Peersman	26	13	13	13	1170	0	0	-	Belgium
Guido van Sant	21	3	0	0	0	0	0	-	Holland
Peter Zois	28	32	11	10	950	0	0	-	Australia
Defenders									
Ryan Holman	19	1	1	0	36	0	0	-	Holland
Jens Janse	20	13	9	8	731	3	0	-	Holland
Michel Kreek	35	7	4	3	314	1	0	-	Holland
Marko Muslin	21	11	5	5	450	0	0	-	France
Mark Obbens	21	1	0	0	0	0	0	-	Holland
Arjan Swinkels	21	10	3	1	92	0	0	-	Holland
Jose Valencia	24	15	15	15	1328	4	0	-	Ecuador
Albert van der Haar	30	31	18	14	1379	0	0	-	Holland
Frank Van der Struijk	21	16	15	12	1178	2	1	-	Holland
Maarten van Lieshout	20	4	1	1	90	0	0	-	Belgium
Frank van Mosselveld	22	16	10	8	746	0	0	-	Holland
Jos van Nieuwstadt	26	25	16	15	1366	3	0	-	Holland
Nuelson Wau	25	29	24	23	2121	2	1	-	Holland
Midfielders									
Kemy Agustien	19	34	34	28	2632	3	0	-	Holland
M. Assou-Ekotto	28	15	14	14	1259	3	0	-	France
Tom Caluwe	31	16	15	10	1152	0	0	-	Belgium
Sven Delanoy	22	10	4	2	218	0	0	-	Belgium
Moussa Dembele	18	33	33	22	2278	2	0	1	Belgium (42)
Csaba Feher	30	23	20	17	1562	6	0	1	Hungary (54)
Joe Keenan	23	13	13	10	964	1	0	-	England
Marko Kolsi	21	12	3	1	170	0	0	-	Finland
Steef Nieuwendaal	20	1	1	0	39	1	0	-	Holland
Martijn Reuser	31	21	20	14	1400	5	0	-	Holland
Arvid Smit	25	22	20	12	1341	3	0	-	Holland
Raymond Victoria	33	26	24	21	1987	6	0	-	Holland
Forwards									
Giorgio Berkleef	20	1	0	0	0	0	0	-	Holland
Kevin Bobson	25	25	22	11	1241	2	1	-	Holland
Jattoo Ceesay	31	12	12	4	549	0	0	-	Gambia
Hans Denissen	22	13	6	0	189	1	0	-	Holland
Anouar Hadouir	23	25	23	12	1508	4	0	-	Holland
Zsombor Kerekes	32	28	20	9	1112	4	0	4	Hungary (54)
Iwan Redan	25	14	11	4	595	1	0	-	Holland
Jonathan Wilmet	20	11	8	5	488	0	0	-	Belgium

TEAM OF THE SEASON

G — Tristan Peersman — CG: 13 DR: 62

D — Jose Valencia — CG: 15 DR: 58

D — Frank Van der Struijk — CG: 12 DR: 49

D — Jos van Nieuwstadt — CG: 15 DR: 46

D — Nuelson Wau — CG: 23 DR: 43

M — Matthieu Assou-Ekotto — CG: 14 SD: 7

M — Raymond Victoria — CG: 21 SD: -11

M — Moussa Dembele — CG: 22 SD: -19

M — Kemy Agustien — CG: 28 SD: -26

F — Anouar Hadouir — CG: 12 SR: 302

F — Zsomber Kerekes* — CG: 10 SR: 556

MONTHLY POINTS TALLY

Month	Points	%
AUGUST	1	11%
SEPTEMBER	6	67%
OCTOBER	1	8%
NOVEMBER	0	0%
DECEMBER	1	8%
JANUARY	2	17%
FEBRUARY	6	40%
MARCH	3	25%
APRIL	8	67%

LEAGUE GOALS

	PLAYER	MINS	GOALS	S RATE
1	Dembele	2278	9	253
2	Redan	595	8	74
3	Hadouir	1508	5	302
4	Reuser	1400	5	280
5	Caluwe	1152	3	384
6	Smit	1341	2	671
7	Kerekes	1112	2	556
8	Agustien	2632	2	1316
9	Wau	2121	1	2121
10	Valencia	1328	1	1328
11	Feher	1562	1	1562
12	Ceesay	549	1	549
13	van Mosselveld	746	1	746
	Other		4	
	TOTAL		45	

TOP POINT EARNERS

	PLAYER	GAMES	AV PTS
1	Matthieu Assou-Ekotto	14	1.29
2	Tristan Peersman	13	1.08
3	Jose Valencia	15	1.07
4	Anouar Hadouir	12	1.00
5	Frank Van der Struijk	12	1.00
6	Raymond Victoria	21	1.00
7	Kemy Agustien	28	0.93
8	Albert van der Haar	14	0.86
9	Moussa Dembele	22	0.82
10	Csaba Feher	17	0.71
	CLUB AVERAGE:		0.82

DISCIPLINARY RECORDS

	PLAYER	YELLOW	RED	AVE
1	Janse	3	0	243
2	Feher	6	0	260
3	Kerekes	4	0	278
4	Reuser	5	0	280
5	Victoria	6	0	331
6	Valencia	4	0	332
7	Hadouir	4	0	377
8	Van der Struijk	2	1	392
9	Bobson	2	1	413
10	Assou-Ekotto	3	0	419
11	Smit	3	0	447
12	van Nieuwstadt	3	0	455
13	Redan	1	0	595
	Other	8	2	
	TOTAL	54	4	

KEY GOALKEEPER

Tristan Peersman

Goals Conceded in the League	19	**Counting Games** League games when player was on pitch for at least 70 minutes	13
Defensive Rating Ave number of mins between League goals conceded while on the pitch	62	**Clean Sheets** In League games when player was on pitch for at least 70 minutes	2

KEY PLAYERS - DEFENDERS

Jose Valencia

Goals Conceded Number of League goals conceded while the player was on the pitch	23	**Clean Sheets** In League games when player was on pitch for at least 70 minutes	2
Defensive Rating Ave number of mins between League goals conceded while on the pitch	58	**Club Defensive Rating** Average number of mins between League goals conceded by the club this season	46

	PLAYER	CON LGE	CLEAN SHEETS	DEF RATE
1	Jose Valencia	23	2	58 mins
2	Frank Van der Struijk	24	2	49 mins
3	Jos van Nieuwstadt	30	2	46 mins
4	Nuelson Wau	49	3	43 mins

KEY PLAYERS - MIDFIELDERS

Matthieu Assou-Ekotto

Goals in the League	0	**Contribution to Attacking Power** Average number of minutes between League team goals while on pitch	48
Defensive Rating Average number of mins between League goals conceded while on the pitch	55	**Scoring Difference** Defensive Rating minus Contribution to Attacking Power	7

	PLAYER	LGE GOALS	DEF RATE	POWER	SCORE DIFF
1	Matthieu Assou-Ekotto	0	55	48	7 mins
2	Raymond Victoria	0	55	66	-11 mins
3	Moussa Dembele	9	44	63	-19 mins
4	Kemy Agustien	2	45	71	-26 mins

KEY PLAYERS - GOALSCORERS

Moussa Dembele

Goals in the League	9	**Player Strike Rate** Average number of minutes between League goals scored by player	253
Contribution to Attacking Power Average number of minutes between League team goals while on pitch	63	**Club Strike Rate** Average number of minutes between League goals scored by club	68

	PLAYER	LGE GOALS	POWER	STRIKE RATE
1	Moussa Dembele	9	63	253 mins
2	Martijn Reuser	5	82	280 mins
3	Anouar Hadouir	5	66	302 mins
4	Arvid Smit	2	103	671 mins

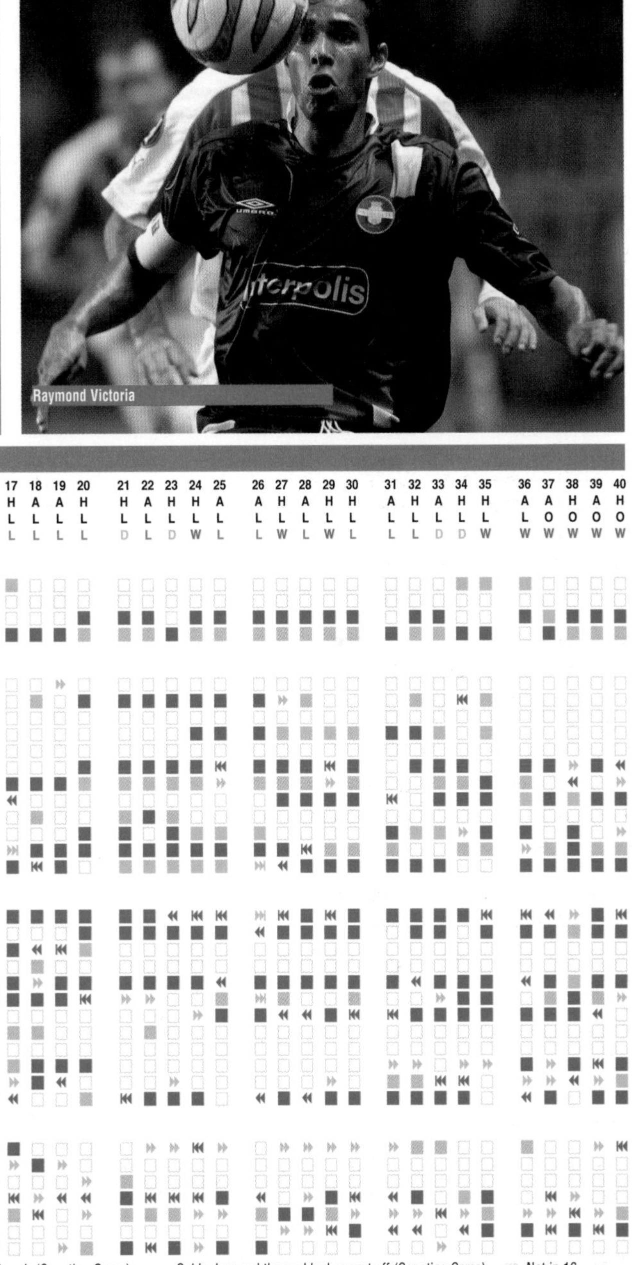

Raymond Victoria

SQUAD APPEARANCES

atch	1	2	3	4	5	6	7	8	9	10	11	12	13	14	15	16	17	18	19	20	21	22	23	24	25	26	27	28	29	30	31	32	33	34	35	36	37	38	39	40
enue	H	A	A	H	A	A	H	H	A	H	A	H	A	H	A	A	H	A	A	H	H	A	H	H	A	A	H	A	H	H	A	H	A	H	H	A	A	H	A	H
ompetition	L	L	L	L	E	L	L	E	L	L	L	L	L	L	L	L	L	L	L	L	L	L	L	L	L	L	L	L	L	L	L	L	L	L	L	L	O	O	O	O
esult	L	L	D	L	L	W	W	L	L	D	L	L	L	L	L	D	L	L	L	L	D	L	D	W	L	L	W	L	W	L	L	L	D	D	W	W	W	W	W	W

oalkeepers
hmet Altin
scar Moens
ristan Peersman
eter Zois

efenders
yan Holman
ens Janse
ichel Kreek
arko Muslin
rjan Swinkels
ose Valencia
lbert van der Haar
rank Van der Struijk
aarten van Lieshout
rank van Mosselveld
os van Nieuwstadt
uelson Wau

idfielders
emy Agustien
atthieu Assou-Ekotto
om Caluwe
ven Delanoy
oussa Dembele
saba Feher
oe Keenan
arko Kolsi
teef Nieuwendaal
artijn Reuser
rvid Smit
aymond Victoria

orwards
evin Bobson
attoo Ceesay
ans Denissen
nouar Hadouir
sombor Kerekes
wan Redan
onathan Wilmet

KEY: On all match | On bench | Subbed or sent off (Counting game) | Subbed or sent off (playing less than 70 minutes) | Subbed on from bench (Counting Game) | Subbed on (playing less than 70 minutes) | Subbed on and then subbed or sent off (Counting Game) | Subbed on and then subbed or sent off (playing less than 70 minutes) | Not in 16

RBC ROOSENDAAL

Final Position: **18th**

KEY: ☐Won ☐Drawn ☐Lost

	Competition	Opponent	Venue	Result	Score	Scorers	Attendance
1	hopr1	**Groningen**	A	L	0-1		11,200
2	hopr1	**Ajax**	H	L	0-2		5,000
3	hopr1	**Willem II Tilb**	H	D	1-1	Lammens 79 pen	3,136
4	hopr1	**AZ Alkmaar**	A	L	0-7		8,275
5	hopr1	**S Rotterdam**	H	D	1-1	Wau 18	4,517
6	hopr1	**PSV Eindhoven**	A	L	0-2		32,000
7	hopr1	**NAC Breda**	H	L	1-2	van Zwam 20 og	5,000
8	hopr1	**NEC Nijmegen**	A	L	1-3	Elkhattabi 45	11,750
9	hopr1	**Vitesse Arnhem**	H	L	0-3		4,400
10	hopr1	**Utrecht**	A	L	1-4	Kpaka 54	17,500
11	hopr1	**RKC Waalwijk**	H	D	1-1	Kpaka 42	4,500
12	hopr1	**Heracles**	A	L	0-3		8,400
13	hopr1	**Heerenveen**	A	L	0-2		20,200
14	hopr1	**Feyenoord**	H	D	2-2	Kpaka 1; Loran 16	4,800
15	hopr1	**Den Haag**	A	L	0-3		6,725
16	hopr1	**Roda JC Kerk**	H	L	0-2		4,600
17	hopr1	**Twente**	A	L	1-4	Sillah 64	12,250
18	hopr1	**Utrecht**	H	L	1-2	Sillah 84	4,500
19	hopr1	**RKC Waalwijk**	A	D	1-1	Daelemans 76	5,500
20	hopr1	**Heracles**	H	L	1-2	Daelemans 59	4,500
21	hopr1	**Heerenveen**	H	L	0-2		4,500
22	hopr1	**Willem II Tilb**	A	L	1-3	Vos 2	11,000
23	hopr1	**AZ Alkmaar**	H	L	0-5		4,500
24	hopr1	**Groningen**	H	L	1-2	Sillah 53	4,500
25	hopr1	**Ajax**	A	L	0-6		46,383
26	hopr1	**NEC Nijmegen**	H	W	2-0	Sillah 62; Kpaka 72	4,000
27	hopr1	**NAC Breda**	A	L	1-2	Daelemans 58	14,000
28	hopr1	**Vitesse Arnhem**	A	L	1-5	Kpaka 78	19,000
29	hopr1	**Twente**	H	D	1-1	Sillah 6	3,500
30	hopr1	**Roda JC Kerk**	A	L	1-5	Fleur 51	13,500
31	hopr1	**PSV Eindhoven**	H	L	1-2	Sillah 31	5,000
32	hopr1	**S Rotterdam**	A	L	0-5		8,000
33	hopr1	**Den Haag**	H	L	1-2	Sillah 52	4,000
34	hopr1	**Feyenoord**	A	L	0-2		42,000

LEAGUE APPEARANCES, BOOKINGS AND CAPS

	AGE (on 01/07/06)	IN NAMED 18	APPEARANCES	COUNTING GAMES	MINUTES ON PITCH	YELLOW CARDS	RED CARDS	CAPS THIS SEASON	NATIONAL SIDE
Goalkeepers									
Erwin Friebel	23	33	5	4	406	0	0	-	Holland
Rodney Ubbergen	20	4	0	0	0	0	0	-	Holland
Mark Volders	29	30	30	29	2655	1	1	-	Belgium
Defenders									
Arjan Ebbinge	31	9	9	7	691	3	1	-	Holland
Melvin Fleur	24	29	26	22	2102	5	0	-	Holland
J. Fortes Rodriguez	34	21	20	14	1468	8	2	-	Spain
Sidney Lammens	29	25	23	19	1842	5	0	-	Belgium
Tyrone Loran	25	28	26	23	2231	2	0	-	Holland
Robert Molenaar	37	16	16	10	1125	2	0	-	Holland
Pauwie Otto	19	1	1	0	2	0	0	-	Holland
Akram Roumani	28	32	30	27	2552	3	0	-	Morocco
A. Van der Smissen	18	6	0	0	0	0	0	-	Holland
Adem Yaran	21	6	1	0	25	0	0	-	Holland
Midfielders									
Jorge Acuna	27	24	24	21	2012	11	1	-	Chile
Richie Basoski	19	6	4	1	138	0	0	-	Holland
Bjorn Daelemans	28	31	28	20	1976	2	0	-	Belgium
Paul de Lange	25	26	26	24	2245	8	1	-	Holland
Danny Guijt	25	4	3	0	81	0	0	-	Holland
Edgar Marcelino	21	29	25	9	1428	3	0	-	Portugal
Frits Paap	19	32	22	9	1147	4	1	-	Holland
Grigor Sahakjan	19	1	0	0	0	0	0	-	Holland
Tim Smolders	25	31	28	13	1658	3	0	-	Belgium
Forwards									
Donny de Groot	26	8	6	2	293	0	0	-	Holland
Ali Elkhattabi	29	20	19	13	1376	0	0	-	Morocco
Paul Kpaka	24	29	29	20	2091	2	0	-	Sierra Leone
Fouad Makhout	21	28	10	1	190	1	0	-	Holland
Ebrima Sillah	26	20	20	20	1764	1	0	-	Gambia
Henk Vos	38	13	13	7	908	2	0	-	Holland
Nyron Wau	22	21	17	10	1076	2	0	-	Holland

TEAM OF THE SEASON

G — Mark Volders, **CG:** 29 **DR:** 34

D — Jose Fortes Rodriguez, **CG:** 14 **DR:** 39

D — Melvin Fleur, **CG:** 22 **DR:** 36

D — Tyrone Loran, **CG:** 23 **DR:** 35

D — Akram Roumani, **CG:** 27 **DR:** 35

M — Jorge Acuna, **CG:** 21 **SD:** -87

M — Paul de Lange, **CG:** 24 **SD:** -89

M — Tim Smolders, **CG:** 13 **SD:** -105

M — Bjorn Daelemans, **CG:** 20 **SD:** -108

F — Ebrima Sillah, **CG:** 20 **SR:** 252

F — Paul Kpaka, **CG:** 20 **SR:** 418

MONTHLY POINTS TALLY

Month	Points	%
AUGUST	1	11%
SEPTEMBER	1	8%
OCTOBER	0	0%
NOVEMBER	1	11%
DECEMBER	1	7%
JANUARY	1	11%
FEBRUARY	3	20%
MARCH	1	8%
APRIL	0	0%

LEAGUE GOALS

	PLAYER	MINS	GOALS	S RATE
1	Sillah	1764	7	252
2	Kpaka	2091	5	418
3	Daelemans	1976	3	659
4	Fleur	2102	1	2102
5	Wau	1076	1	1076
6	Vos	908	1	908
7	Loran	2231	1	2231
8	Lammens	1842	1	1842
9	Elkhattabi	1376	1	1376
	Other		1	
	TOTAL		22	

TOP POINT EARNERS

	PLAYER	GAMES	AV PTS
1	Tyrone Loran	23	0.39
2	Paul de Lange	24	0.38
3	Jose Fortes Rodriguez	14	0.36
4	Paul Kpaka	20	0.35
5	Sidney Lammens	19	0.32
6	Ali Elkhattabi	13	0.31
7	Tim Smolders	13	0.31
8	Akram Roumani	27	0.30
9	Jorge Acuna	21	0.29
10	Mark Volders	29	0.28
	CLUB AVERAGE:		0.26

DISCIPLINARY RECORDS

	PLAYER	YELLOW	RED	AVE
1	Fortes Rodriguez	8	2	146
2	Acuna	11	1	167
3	Ebbinge	3	1	172
4	Paap	4	1	229
5	de Lange	8	1	249
6	Lammens	5	0	368
7	Fleur	5	0	420
8	Vos	2	0	454
9	Marcelino	3	0	476
10	Wau	2	0	538
11	Smolders	3	0	552
12	Molenaar	2	0	562
13	Roumani	3	0	850
	Other	8	1	
	TOTAL	67	7	

KEY GOALKEEPER

Mark Volders

Goals Conceded in the League	79	**Counting Games** League games when player was on pitch for at least 70 minutes	30
Defensive Rating Ave number of mins between League goals conceded while on the pitch	34	**Clean Sheets** In League games when player was on pitch for at least 70 minutes	1

KEY PLAYERS - DEFENDERS

Jose Fortes Rodriguez

Goals Conceded Number of League goals conceded while the player was on the pitch	38	**Clean Sheets** In League games when player was on pitch for at least 70 minutes	1
Defensive Rating Ave number of mins between League goals conceded while on the pitch	39	**Club Defensive Rating** Average number of mins between League goals conceded by the club this season	34

	PLAYER	CON LGE	CLEAN SHEETS	DEF RATE
1	Jose Fortes Rodriguez	38	1	39 mins
2	Melvin Fleur	58	0	36 mins
3	Akram Roumani	73	1	35 mins
4	Tyrone Loran	63	1	35 mins

KEY PLAYERS - MIDFIELDERS

Jorge Acuna

Goals in the League	0	**Contribution to Attacking Power** Average number of minutes between League team goals while on pitch	126
Defensive Rating Average number of mins between League goals conceded while on the pitch	39	**Scoring Difference** Defensive Rating minus Contribution to Attacking Power	-87

	PLAYER	LGE GOALS	DEF RATE	POWER	SCORE DIFF
1	Jorge Acuna	0	39	126	-87 mins
2	Paul de Lange	0	36	125	-89 mins
3	Tim Smolders	0	33	138	-105 mins
4	Bjorn Daelemans	3	33	141	-108 mins

KEY PLAYERS - GOALSCORERS

Ebrima Sillah

Goals in the League	7	**Player Strike Rate** Average number of minutes between League goals scored by player	252
Contribution to Attacking Power Average number of minutes between League team goals while on pitch	136	**Club Strike Rate** Average number of minutes between League goals scored by club	139

	PLAYER	LGE GOALS	POWER	STRIKE RATE
1	Ebrima Sillah	7	136	252 mins
2	Paul Kpaka	5	131	418 mins
3	Bjorn Daelemans	3	141	659 mins
4	Ali Elkhattabi	1	138	1376 mins

Jorges Acuna

SQUAD APPEARANCES

Match	1	2	3	4	5	6	7	8	9	10	11	12	13	14	15	16	17	18	19	20	21	22	23	24	25	26	27	28	29	30	31	32	33	34
Venue	A	H	H	A	H	A	H	A	H	A	H	A	A	H	A	H	A	H	A	H	H	A	H	H	A	H	A	A	H	A	H	A	H	A
Competition	L	L	L	L	L	L	L	L	L	L	L	L	L	L	L	L	L	L	L	L	L	L	L	L	L	L	L	L	L	L	L	L	L	L
Result	L	L	D	L	D	L	L	L	L	L	D	L	L	D	L	L	L	L	D	L	L	L	L	L	L	W	L	L	D	L	L	L	L	L

Goalkeepers
- Erwin Friebel
- Rodney Ubbergen
- Mark Volders

Defenders
- Arjan Ebbinge
- Melvin Fleur
- Jose Fortes Rodriguez
- Sidney Lammens
- Tyrone Loran
- Robert Molenaar
- Pauwie Otto
- Akram Roumani
- Arjan Van der Smissen
- Adem Yaran

Midfielders
- Jorge Acuna
- Richie Basoski
- Bjorn Daelemans
- Paul de Lange
- Danny Guijt
- Edgar Marcelino
- Frits Paap
- Grigor Sahakjan
- Tim Smolders

Forwards
- Donny de Groot
- Ali Elkhattabi
- Paul Kpaka
- Fouad Makhout
- Ebrima Sillah
- Henk Vos
- Nyron Wau

KEY: On all match · On bench · Subbed or sent off (Counting game) · Subbed or sent off (playing less than 70 minutes) · Subbed on from bench (Counting Game) · Subbed on (playing less than 70 minutes) · Subbed on and then subbed or sent off (Counting Game) · Subbed on and then subbed or sent off (playing less than 70 minutes) · Not in 16

GERMAN LEAGUE ROUND-UP

FINAL LEAGUE TABLE

	HOME						AWAY					TOTAL			
	P	W	D	L	F	A	W	D	L	F	A	F	A	DIF	PTS
Bayern Munich	34	14	2	1	42	14	8	7	2	25	18	67	32	35	75
W Bremen	34	12	3	2	50	18	9	4	4	29	19	79	37	42	70
Hamburg	34	10	2	5	26	16	11	3	3	27	14	53	30	23	68
Schalke	34	10	6	1	32	16	6	7	4	15	15	47	31	16	61
B Leverkusen	34	7	6	4	30	23	7	4	6	34	26	64	49	15	52
Hertha Berlin	34	8	5	4	30	22	4	7	6	22	26	52	48	4	48
B Dortmund	34	8	4	5	23	18	3	9	5	22	24	45	42	3	46
Nurnberg	34	9	3	5	31	20	3	5	9	18	31	49	51	-2	44
Stuttgart	34	5	7	5	18	19	4	9	4	19	20	37	39	-2	43
B M'gladbach	34	8	7	2	27	18	2	5	10	15	32	42	50	-8	42
Mainz	34	6	7	4	31	23	3	4	10	15	24	46	47	-1	38
Hannover 96	34	4	9	4	27	24	3	8	6	16	23	43	47	-4	38
Arminia B	34	8	2	7	18	15	2	5	10	14	32	32	47	-15	37
Eintr Frankfurt	34	5	5	7	24	22	4	4	9	18	29	42	51	-9	36
Wolfsburg	34	4	10	3	16	16	3	3	11	17	39	33	55	-22	34
Kaiserslautern	34	5	5	7	26	33	3	4	10	21	38	47	71	-24	33
Cologne	34	5	4	8	24	29	2	5	10	25	42	49	71	-22	30
Duisburg	34	3	9	5	17	23	2	3	12	17	40	34	63	-29	27

CLUB STRIKE FORCE

Bremen's Ivan Klasnic

1 Werder Bremen

Goals scored in the League	79
Club Strike Rate (CSR) Average number of minutes between League goals scored by club	39

	CLUB	GOALS	CSR
1	W Bremen	79	39
2	Bayern Munich	67	46
3	B Leverkusen	64	48
4	Hamburg	53	58
5	Hertha Berlin	52	59
6	Cologne	49	62
7	Nurnberg	49	62
8	Kaiserslautern	47	65
8	Schalke	47	65
10	Mainz	46	67
11	B Dortmund	45	68
12	Hannover 96	43	71
13	B M'gladbach	42	73
13	Eintr Frankfurt	42	73
15	Stuttgart	37	83
16	Duisburg	34	90
17	Wolfsburg	33	93
18	Arminia B	32	96

CLUB DISCIPLINARY RECORDS

Markus Kerth: 9 cards for Duisberg

1 Duisburg

League Yellow	91
League Red	3
League Total	94
Cards Average in League Average number of minutes between a card being shown of either colour	33

	CLUB	Y	R	TOTAL	AVE
1	Duisburg	91	3	94	33
2	Hertha Berlin	82	9	91	34
3	Cologne	81	7	88	35
4	Wolfsburg	81	6	87	35
5	Nurnberg	82	5	87	35
6	B M'gladbach	77	2	79	39
7	Schalke	73	5	78	39
8	Stuttgart	74	2	76	40
9	Hamburg	72	2	74	41
10	W Bremen	69	2	71	43
11	B Leverkusen	62	2	64	48
12	Hannover 96	61	2	63	49
13	Bayern Munich	59	3	62	49
14	Mainz	60	0	60	51
15	Kaiserslautern	57	2	59	52
16	Eintr Frankfurt	57	1	58	53
17	B Dortmund	51	2	53	58
18	Arminia B	48	0	48	64

CLUB DEFENCES

	CLUB	LGE	CS	CDR
1	Hamburg	30	15	102
2	Schalke	31	13	99
3	Bayern Munich	32	12	96
4	W Bremen	37	12	83
5	Stuttgart	39	11	78
6	B Dortmund	42	8	73
7	Mainz	47	7	65
8	Hannover 96	47	8	65
9	Arminia B	47	9	65
10	Hertha Berlin	48	11	64
11	B Leverkusen	49	5	62
12	B M'gladbach	50	7	61
13	Nurnberg	51	5	60
14	Eintr Frankfurt	51	7	60
15	Wolfsburg	55	7	56
16	Duisburg	63	6	49
17	Cologne	71	4	43
18	Kaiserslautern	71	6	43

Hamburg defender Timothee Atouba

1 Hamburg

Goals conceded in the League	30
Clean Sheets (CS) Number of league games where no goals were conceded	15
Club Defensive Rate (CDR) Average number of minutes between League goals conceded by club	102

PLAYER NATIONALITIES

Overseas country with the most player appearances in the German League - Brazil

536 league appearances by Brazilian players

	COUNTRY	PLAYERS	IN SQUAD	LGE APP	% LGE ACT	CAPS	MOST APP	APP
1	Germany	252	4002	3837	46.7	136	Hans-Jorg Butt	100
2	Brazil	25	545	536	7.0	21	Antonio da Silva	95.6
3	Czech Republic	16	291	286	3.4	36	David Jarolim	89.7
4	Switzerland	13	245	237	3.0	74	Mario Cantaluppi	91.1
5	Denmark	14	276	267	2.8	39	Thomas Baelum	77.7
6	Holland	14	230	225	2.8	17	Roy Makaay	86
7	Croatia	13	244	239	2.6	33	Zvonimir Soldo	85.2
8	France	9	207	200	2.5	9	Willy Sagnol	90.8
9	Argentina	6	152	152	2.1	7	Juan Carlos Menseguez	85.8
10	Turkey	9	145	141	1.8	0	Halil Altintop	94.1
11	Serbia & Montenegro	9	146	142	1.7	16	Mladen Krstajic	83.8
12	Belgium	8	156	149	1.6	10	Daniel Van Buyten	78.1
13	Poland	8	126	122	1.5	14	Ebi Smolarek	96.8
14	Portugal	5	128	127	1.4	7	Ze Antonio	98.6
15	Albania	4	90	89	1.2	6	Ervin Skela	97.8
16	Iran	5	103	100	1.0	8	Mehdi Mahdavikia	78.1
17	Macedonia	2	66	66	1.0	0	Aleksandar Vasoki	97.1
18	United States	3	65	65	0.9	8	Kasey Keller	97.1
19	Bulgaria	4	68	66	0.9	4	Dimitar Berbatov	100
20	Bosnia	5	83	81	0.9	11	Sergei Barbarez	94.1

CLUB MAKE-UP – HOME AND OVERSEAS PLAYERS

1 Wolfsburg

66.7% of appearances by overseas players

	CLUB	OVERSEAS	HOME	% OVERSEAS	% LGE ACT	MOST APP	APP
1	Wolfsburg	19	9	67.9	66.7	J-Carlos Menseguez	76.8
2	Schalke	14	12	53.8	63.8	Marcelo Bordon	81.6
3	B M'gladbach	21	9	70.0	63.0	Ze Antonio	88.2
4	Hamburg	15	14	51.7	61.9	Sergei Barbarez	84.2
5	Bayern Munich	14	10	58.3	60.5	Willy Sagnol	81.3
6	Kaiserslautern	16	15	51.6	51.3	Ervin Skela	87.5
7	Hertha Berlin	16	12	57.1	49.9	Marcelinho	80.4
8	Nurnberg	15	15	50.0	49.4	Mario Cantaluppi	81.5
9	Stuttgart	14	11	56.0	48.8	Fernando Meira	83.3
10	B Leverkusen	14	11	56.0	48.1	Dimitar Berbatov	89.4
11	B Dortmund	13	16	44.8	43.9	Ebi Smolarek	86.6
12	Hannover 96	13	16	44.8	40.8	Jiri Stajner	77.4
13	W Bremen	11	14	44.0	39.4	Naldo	81.2
14	Arminia B	15	15	50.0	37.4	Marcio Borges	68.9
15	Eintr Frankfurt	9	18	33.3	37.2	Aleksandar Vasoki	86.8
16	Duisburg	8	21	27.6	33.4	Thomas Baelum	69.5
17	Mainz	11	16	40.7	33.3	Nikolce Noveski	86.4
18	Cologne	14	18	43.8	25.1	Alpay Ozalan	52.1

CHART-TOPPING MIDFIELDERS

1 Van der Vaart - Hamburg	
Goals scored in the League	8
Defensive Rating Av number of mins between League goals conceded while on the pitch	207
Contribution to Attacking Power Average number of minutes between League team goals while on pitch	50
Scoring Difference Defensive Rating minus Contribution to Attacking Power	157

	PLAYER	CLUB	GOALS	DEF RATE	POWER	S DIFF
1	Van der Vaart	Hamburg	8	207	50	157
2	Beinlich	Hamburg	0	141	61	80
3	Hargreaves	Bayern Munich	1	103	40	63
4	Jarolim	Hamburg	2	114	58	56
5	Wicky	Hamburg	1	116	63	53
6	Micoud	W Bremen	8	90	41	49
7	Schulz	W Bremen	0	86	40	46
8	Ze Roberto	Bayern Munich	1	94	48	46
9	Schweinsteiger	Bayern Munich	3	92	48	44
10	Altintop	Schalke	1	113	71	42
11	Kobiashvili	Schalke	1	100	61	39
12	Ballack	Bayern Munich	14	84	46	38
13	Owomoyela	W Bremen	0	76	42	34
14	Frings	W Bremen	3	72	40	32
15	Poulsen	Schalke	2	98	68	30

CHART-TOPPING GOALSCORERS

1 Klose - Werder Bremen	
Goals scored in the League	25
Contribution to Attacking Power Average number of minutes between League team goals while on pitch	33
Club Strike Rate (CSR) Average minutes between League goals scored by club	39
Player Strike Rate Average number of minutes between League goals scored by player	86

	PLAYER	CLUB	GOALS: LGE	POWER	CSR	S RATE
1	Klose	W Bremen	25	33	39	86
2	Klasnic	W Bremen	15	38	39	131
3	Vittek	Nurnberg	16	60	61	134
4	Altintop	Kaiserslautern	20	67	65	144
5	Berbatov	B Leverkusen	21	48	48	146
6	Makaay	Bayern Munich	17	45	46	155
7	Ballack	Bayern Munich	14	46	46	162
8	Klimowicz	Wolfsburg	12	83	93	181
9	Van der Vaart	Hamburg	8	50	58	181
10	Pizarro	Bayern Munich	11	46	46	193
11	Sanogo	Kaiserslautern	10	61	65	194
12	Valdez	W Bremen	9	46	39	198
13	Kiessling	Nurnberg	10	54	61	201
14	Scherz	Cologne	8	54	62	203
15	Zidan	Mainz	9	64	67	205

CHART-TOPPING DEFENDERS

1 Pasanen - Werder Bremen	
Goals Conceded in the League The number of League goals conceded while he was on the pitch	10
Clean Sheets In games when he played at least 70 mins	8
Club Defensive Rating Average mins between League goals conceded by the club this season	83
Defensive Rating Average number of minutes between League goals conceded while on pitch	142

	PLAYER	CLUB	CON: LGE	CS	CDR	DEF RATE
1	Pasanen	W Bremen	10	8	83	142
2	Atouba	Hamburg	22	15	102	126
3	Rodriguez	Schalke	14	10	99	123
4	Demel	Hamburg	16	8	102	109
5	Rafinha	Schalke	23	13	99	106
6	Bordon	Schalke	27	11	99	103
7	Boulahrouz	Hamburg	24	12	102	103
8	Ismael	Bayern Munich	26	11	96	102
9	Fahrenhorst	W Bremen	20	11	83	100
10	Demichelis	Bayern Munich	24	7	96	96
11	Sagnol	Bayern Munich	29	11	96	96
12	Van Buyten	Hamburg	25	10	102	96
13	Lucio	Bayern Munich	28	9	96	93
14	Nowotny	B Leverkusen	12	3	62	92
15	Krstajic	Schalke	29	9	99	88

CHART-TOPPING GOALKEEPERS

1 Wachter - Hamburg	
Counting Games Games in which he played at least 70 minutes	21
Goals Conceded in the League The number of League goals conceded while he was on the pitch	15
Clean Sheets In games when he played at least 70 mins	9
Defensive Rating Average number of minutes between League goals conceded while on pitch	126

	PLAYER	CLUB	CG	CONC	CS	DEF RATE
1	Wachter	Hamburg	21	15	9	126
2	Kahn	Bayern Munich	32	26	11	103
3	Rost	Schalke	32	29	12	99
4	Wiese	W Bremen	15	14	8	92
5	Hildebrand	Stuttgart	31	32	11	87
6	Kirschstein	Hamburg	13	15	6	78
7	Reinke	W Bremen	19	23	4	74
8	Weidenfeller	B Dortmund	25	31	6	73
9	Hain	Arminia B	33	43	9	68
10	Enke	Hannover 96	32	43	8	67
11	Wache	Mainz	20	26	3	66
12	Nikolov	Eintr Frankfurt	30	43	7	63
13	Wetklo	Mainz	15	21	4	63
14	Fiedler	Hertha Berlin	29	42	9	62
15	Butt	B Leverkusen	34	49	5	62

PLAYER DISCIPLINARY RECORD

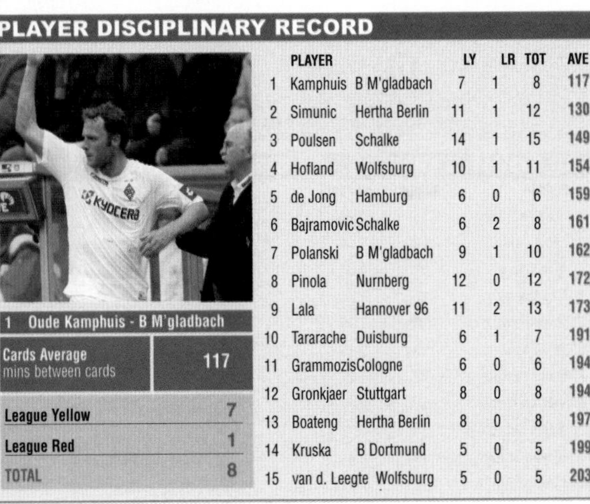

1 Oude Kamphuis - B M'gladbach	
Cards Average mins between cards	117
League Yellow	7
League Red	1
TOTAL	8

	PLAYER		LY	LR	TOT	AVE
1	Kamphuis	B M'gladbach	7	1	8	117
2	Simunic	Hertha Berlin	11	1	12	130
3	Poulsen	Schalke	14	1	15	149
4	Hofland	Wolfsburg	10	1	11	154
5	de Jong	Hamburg	6	0	6	159
6	Bajramovic	Schalke	6	2	8	161
7	Polanski	B M'gladbach	9	1	10	162
8	Pinola	Nurnberg	12	0	12	172
9	Lala	Hannover 96	11	2	13	173
10	Tararache	Duisburg	6	1	7	191
11	Grammozis	Cologne	6	0	6	194
12	Gronkjaer	Stuttgart	8	0	8	194
13	Boateng	Hertha Berlin	8	0	8	197
14	Kruska	B Dortmund	5	0	5	199
15	van d. Leegte	Wolfsburg	5	0	5	203

TEAM OF THE SEASON

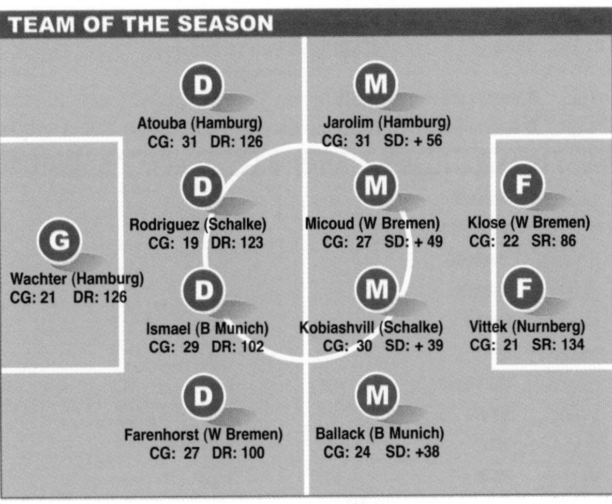

BAYERN MUNICH

Final Position: **1st**

NICKNAME: DIE ROTEN

KEY: ☐Won ☐Drawn ☐Lost

							Attendance
1	gbl	B M'gladbach	H	W	3-0	Hargreaves 28; Makaay 86,89	66,000
2	gbl	B Leverkusen	A	W	5-2	Ballack 3; Makaay 11,57,60; Karimi 35	22,500
3	gbl	Hertha Berlin	H	W	3-0	Ballack 47; Scholl 85; Makaay 87	56,000
4	gbl	Nuremburg	A	W	2-1	Guerrero 21; Ballack 60	47,000
5	ecgpa	Rapid Vienna	A	W	1-0	Guerrero 60	47,000
6	gbl	Hannover 96	H	W	1-0	Demichelis 9	66,000
7	gbl	Eintr Frankfurt	A	W	1-0	Guerrero 72	52,000
8	gbl	Hamburg	A	L	0-2		55,800
9	ecgpa	Club Brugge	H	W	1-0	Demichelis 32	65,527
10	gbl	Wolfsburg	H	W	2-0	Santa Cruz 67; Lucio 90	66,000
11	gbl	Schalke	A	D	1-1	Santa Cruz 19	61,524
12	ecgpa	Juventus	H	W	2-1	Deisler 32; Demichelis 39	60,000
13	gbl	Duisburg	H	W	4-0	Ballack 27; Ze Roberto 33; Santa Cruz 59; Pizarro 90	66,000
14	gbl	Cologne	A	W	2-1	Lucio 55; Ballack 74	50,000
15	ecgpa	Juventus	A	L	1-2	Deisler 66	19,000
16	gbl	W Bremen	H	W	3-1	Schweinsteiger 3; Pizarro 34; Makaay 44	66,000
17	gbl	Arminia B	A	W	2-1	Pizarro 82,90	26,601
18	ecgpa	Rapid Vienna	H	W	4-0	Deisler 21; Karimi 54; Makaay 72,77	66,000
19	gbl	Mainz	H	W	2-1	Pizarro 28,54	66,000
20	gbl	Stuttgart	A	D	0-0		57,000
21	ecgpa	Club Brugge	A	D	1-1	Pizarro 21	27,860
22	gbl	Kaiserslautern	H	W	2-1	Ballack 26; Makaay 54 pen	66,000
23	gbl	B Dortmund	A	W	2-1	Karimi 52; Pizarro 73	81,264
24	gbl	B M'gladbach	A	W	3-1	Makaay 13,69; Ballack 55	54,019
25	gbl	B Leverkusen	H	W	1-0	Ballack 36	69,901
26	gbl	Hertha Berlin	A	D	0-0		66,000
27	gbl	Nuremburg	H	W	2-1	Makaay 27; Ballack 54	69,000
28	gbl	Hannover 96	A	D	1-1	Ballack 89	49,000
29	ecls1	AC Milan	H	D	1-1	Ballack 23	66,000
30	gbl	Eintr Frankfurt	H	W	5-2	Guerrero 21,42; Ballack 33,62; Pizarro 85	69,000
31	gbl	Hamburg	H	L	1-2	Scholl 83	69,000
32	ecls2	AC Milan	A	L	1-4	Ismael 35	71,032
33	gbl	Wolfsburg	A	D	0-0		30,000
34	gbl	Schalke	H	W	3-0	Salihamidzic 48; Pizarro 56; Makaay 89	69,000
35	gbl	Duisburg	A	W	3-1	Salihamidzic 66; Makaay 72; Pizarro 80	31,500
36	gbl	Cologne	H	D	2-2	Sagnol 29; Makaay 39	69,000
37	gbl	W Bremen	A	L	0-3		42,500
38	gbl	Arminia B	H	W	2-0	Ballack 69; Scholl 73	69,000
39	gbl	Mainz	A	D	2-2	Makaay 29,37 pen	20,300
40	gbl	Stuttgart	H	W	3-1	Santa Cruz 11; Pizarro 44; Schweinsteiger 46	69,000
41	gbl	Kaiserslautern	A	D	1-1	Ottl 68	50,574
42	gbl	B Dortmund	H	D	3-3	Makaay 6; Schweinsteiger 48; Ballack 50	69,000

LEAGUE APPEARANCES, BOOKINGS AND CAPS

	AGE (on 01/07/06)	IN NAMED 18	APPEARANCES	COUNTING GAMES	MINUTES ON PITCH	YELLOW CARDS	RED CARDS	CAPS THIS SEASON	NATIONAL SIDE
Goalkeepers									
Bernd Dreher	41	2	1	1	90	0	0	-	Germany
Oliver Kahn	37	32	32	28	2671	2	0	6	Germany (19)
Michael Rensing	22	8	5	2	299	0	0	-	Germany
Defenders									
Martin Demichelis	25	27	27	24	2292	3	1	5	Argentina (9)
Valerien Ismael	30	30	30	29	2652	5	1	-	France
Philipp Lahm	22	20	20	11	1319	1	0	3	Germany (19)
Bixente Lizarazu	36	19	19	8	1271	1	0	-	France
Lucio	28	29	29	29	2610	3	0	6	Brazil (1)
Andreas Ottl	21	9	8	2	310	1	0	-	Germany
Willy Sagnol	29	31	31	31	2780	6	0	9	France (8)
Midfielders									
Michael Ballack	29	26	26	24	2270	10	0	7	Germany (19)
Sebastian Deisler	26	16	16	7	975	3	1	7	Germany (19)
Julio Dos Santos	23	2	1	1	90	0	0	5	Paraguay (33)
Owen Hargreaves	25	17	16	12	1240	5	0	4	England (10)
Jens Jeremies	32	14	12	3	427	0	0	-	Germany
Ali Karimi	27	21	20	5	926	1	0	3	Iran (23)
Hazan Salihamidzic	29	21	21	4	955	3	0	1	Bosnia (63)
Mehmet Scholl	35	19	18	2	535	1	0	-	Germany
B. Schweinsteiger	21	30	30	16	1923	4	0	9	Germany (19)
Jose Ze Roberto	32	27	27	16	1870	3	0	6	Brazil (1)
Forwards									
Jose Paolo Guerrero	22	15	14	4	623	1	0	-	Peru
Roy Makaay	31	31	31	28	2631	2	0	1	Holland (3)
Claudio Pizarro	27	26	26	23	2120	3	0	2	Peru (66)
Roque Santa Cruz	24	13	13	6	685	1	0	2	Paraguay (33)

TEAM OF THE SEASON

G — Oliver Kahn, CG: 28 DR: 103

D — Martin Demichelis, CG: 24 DR: 96

D — Willy Sagnol, CG: 31 DR: 96

D — Lucio, CG: 29 DR: 93

D — Valerien Ismael, CG: 29 DR: 102

M — Owen Hargreaves, CG: 12 SD: 63

M — Jose Ze Roberto, CG: 16 SD: 46

M — Bastian Schweinsteiger, CG: 16 SD: 44

M — Michael Ballack, CG: 24 SD: 38

F — Roy Makaay, CG: 28 SR: 155

F — Claudio Pizarro, CG: 23 SR: 193

MONTHLY POINTS TALLY

AUGUST	9	100%
SEPTEMBER	9	75%
OCTOBER	10	83%
NOVEMBER	9	100%
DECEMBER	7	78%
JANUARY	3	100%
FEBRUARY	11	73%
MARCH	7	58%
APRIL	5	42%
MAY	5	56%

LEAGUE GOALS

	PLAYER	MINS	GOALS	S RATE
1	Makaay	2631	17	155
2	Ballack	2270	14	162
3	Pizarro	2120	11	193
4	Guerrero	623	4	156
5	Santa Cruz	685	4	171
6	Schweinsteiger	1923	3	641
7	Scholl	535	3	178
8	Salihamidzic	955	2	478
9	Karimi	926	2	463
10	Lucio	2610	2	1305
11	Demichelis	2292	1	2292
12	Ottl	310	1	310
13	Hargreaves	1240	1	1240
	Other		2	
	TOTAL		67	

TOP POINT EARNERS

	PLAYER	GAMES	AV PTS
1	Jose Ze Roberto	16	2.69
2	Lucio	29	2.31
3	Willy Sagnol	31	2.26
4	Roy Makaay	28	2.25
5	Owen Hargreaves	12	2.25
6	Oliver Kahn	28	2.25
7	Claudio Pizarro	23	2.22
8	Valerien Ismael	29	2.21
9	Martin Demichelis	24	2.13
10	Bastian Schweinsteiger	16	2.06
	CLUB AVERAGE:		2.21

DISCIPLINARY RECORDS

	PLAYER	YELLOW	RED	AVE
1	Ballack	10	0	227
2	Deisler	3	1	243
3	Hargreaves	5	0	248
4	Salihamidzic	3	0	318
5	Ismael	5	1	442
6	Sagnol	6	0	463
7	Schweinsteiger	4	0	480
8	Scholl	1	0	535
9	Demichelis	3	1	573
10	Guerrero	1	0	623
11	Ze Roberto	3	0	623
12	Santa Cruz	1	0	685
13	Pizarro	3	0	706
	Other	10	0	
	TOTAL	58	3	

KEY GOALKEEPER

Oliver Kahn			
Goals Conceded in the League	26	Counting Games League games when player was on pitch for at least 70 minutes	28
Defensive Rating Ave number of mins between League goals conceded while on the pitch	103	Clean Sheets In games when player was on pitch for at least 70 minutes	11

KEY PLAYERS - DEFENDERS

Valerien Ismael			
Goals Conceded Number of League goals conceded while the player was on the pitch	26	Clean Sheets In League games when player was on pitch for at least 70 minutes	11
Defensive Rating Ave number of mins between League goals conceded while on the pitch	102	Club Defensive Rating Average number of mins between League goals conceded by the club this season	96

	PLAYER	CON LGE	CLEAN SHEETS	DEF RATE
1	Valerien Ismael	26	11	102 mins
2	Martin Demichelis	24	7	96 mins
3	Willy Sagnol	29	11	96 mins
4	Lucio	28	9	93 mins

KEY PLAYERS - MIDFIELDERS

Owen Hargreaves			
Goals in the League	1	Contribution to Attacking Power Average number of minutes between League team goals while on pitch	40
Defensive Rating Average number of mins between League goals conceded while on the pitch	103	Scoring Difference Defensive Rating minus Contribution to Attacking Power	63

	PLAYER	LGE GOALS	DEF RATE	POWER	SCORE DIFF
1	Owen Hargreaves	1	103	40	63 mins
2	Jose Ze Roberto	1	94	48	46 mins
3	Bastian Schweinsteiger	3	92	48	44 mins
4	Michael Ballack	14	84	46	38 mins

KEY PLAYERS - GOALSCORERS

Roy Makaay			
Goals in the League	17	Player Strike Rate Average number of minutes between League goals scored by player	155
Contribution to Attacking Power Average number of minutes between League team goals while on pitch	45	Club Strike Rate Average number of minutes between League goals scored by club	46

	PLAYER	LGE GOALS	POWER	STRIKE RATE
1	Roy Makaay	17	45	155 mins
2	Michael Ballack	14	46	162 mins
3	Claudio Pizarro	11	46	193 mins
4	Bastian Schweinsteiger	3	48	641 mins

Michael Ballack and Roy Makaay

SQUAD APPEARANCES

Match	1	2	3	4	5	6	7	8	9	10	11	12	13	14	15	16	17	18	19	20	21	22	23	24	25	26	27	28	29	30	31	32	33	34	35	36	37	38	39	40	41	42
Venue	H	A	H	A	A	H	A	A	H	H	A	H	H	A	A	H	A	H	H	A	A	H	A	A	H	A	H	A	H	H	H	A	A	H	A	H	A	H	A	H	A	H
Competition	L	L	L	L	C	L	L	L	C	L	L	C	L	L	C	L	L	C	L	L	C	L	L	L	L	L	L	L	C	L	L	C	L	L	L	L	L	L	L	L	L	L
Result	W	W	W	W	W	W	W	L	W	W	D	W	W	W	L	W	W	W	W	D	D	W	W	W	W	D	W	D	D	W	L	L	D	W	W	D	L	W	D	W	D	D

Goalkeepers
Bernd Dreher
Oliver Kahn
Michael Rensing

Defenders
Martin Demichelis
Valerien Ismael
Philipp Lahm
Bixente Lizarazu
Lucio
Andreas Ottl
Willy Sagnol

Midfielders
Michael Ballack
Sebastian Deisler
Julio Dos Santos
Owen Hargreaves
Jens Jeremies
Ali Karimi
Hazan Salihamidzic
Mehmet Scholl
Bastian Schweinsteiger
Jose Ze Roberto

Forwards
Jose Paolo Guerrero
Roy Makaay
Claudio Pizarro
Roque Santa Cruz

KEY: On all match · On bench · Subbed or sent off (Counting game) · Subbed or sent off (playing less than 70 minutes) · Subbed on from bench (Counting Game) · Subbed on (playing less than 70 minutes) · Subbed on and then subbed or sent off (Counting Game) · Subbed on and then subbed or sent off (playing less than 70 minutes) · Not in 16

WERDER BREMEN

Final Position: **2nd**

NICKNAME: FISCHKOPPE

KEY: ☐ Won ☐ Drawn ☐ Lost

		Opponent	H/A	Res	Score	Scorers	Attendance
1	gbl	Arminia B	H	W	5-2	Klose 1,82; Klasnic 18,84; Baumann 36	35,000
2	eq2l1	Basel	A	L	1-2	Klose 73	28,101
3	gbl	Mainz	A	W	2-0	Klasnic 21; Klose 62	22,000
4	eq2l2	Basel	H	W	3-0	Klasnic 64,72; Borowski 67 pen	30,339
5	gbl	Stuttgart	H	D	1-1	Klasnic 41	35,000
6	gbl	Kaiserslautern	A	W	5-1	Micoud 31; Klose 44,78; Frings 45; Vranjes 89	32,851
7	ecgpc	Barcelona	H	L	0-2		37,000
8	gbl	B Dortmund	H	W	3-2	Klose 37; Klasnic 54; Micoud 78	38,000
9	gbl	B M'gladbach	A	L	1-2	van Damme 21	40,251
10	gbl	B Leverkusen	H	W	2-1	Klose 46; Klasnic 77	39,000
11	ecgpc	Panathinaikos	A	L	1-2	Klose 41	50,000
12	gbl	Hertha Berlin	A	W	2-1	Borowski 85; Valdez 89	60,000
13	gbl	Nuremburg	H	W	6-2	Klose 2,34,39; Klasnic 66,85; Borowski 80	40,000
14	ecgpc	Udinese	A	D	1-1	Felipe Dal Belo 64 og	43,952
15	gbl	Hannover 96	A	D	0-0		47,000
16	gbl	Eintr Frankfurt	H	W	4-1	Frings 29; Borowski 52,90; Klose 61	40,000
17	ecgpc	Udinese	H	W	4-3	Klose 15; Baumann 24; Micoud 51,67	35,211
18	gbl	Bayern Munich	A	L	1-3	Klose 1	66,000
19	gbl	Wolfsburg	H	W	6-1	Baumann 5; Borowski 43,52; Klose 60,85; Naldo 72	38,000
20	ecgpc	Barcelona	A	L	1-3	Borowski 22 pen	85,000
21	gbl	Schalke	A	L	1-2	Valdez 56	61,524
22	gbl	Duisburg	H	W	2-0	Valdez 64; Borowski 72	38,000
23	ecgpc	Panathinaikos	H	W	5-1	Micoud 2 pen; Valdez 28,31; Klose 51; Frings 90	38,000
24	gbl	Cologne	A	W	4-1	Naldo 34; Klose 50,90; Micoud 90	47,000
25	gbl	Hamburg	H	D	1-1	Micoud 45	42,500
26	gbl	Arminia B	A	W	1-0	Fahrenhorst 71	24,169
27	gbl	Mainz	H	W	4-2	Valdez 39,69; Micoud 45; Klasnic 45	28,000
28	gbl	Stuttgart	A	D	0-0		50,000
29	gbl	Kaiserslautern	H	L	0-2		38,000
30	gbl	B Dortmund	A	W	1-0	Klasnic 36	68,000
31	eclsl1	Juventus	H	W	3-2	Schulz 39; Borowski 87; Micoud 90	42,000
32	gbl	B M'gladbach	H	W	2-0	Klose 16; Klasnic 27	38,000
33	gbl	B Leverkusen	A	D	1-1	Frings 3 pen	225,000
34	eclsl2	Juventus	A	L	1-2	Micoud 13	40,000
35	gbl	Hertha Berlin	H	L	0-3		40,000
36	gbl	Nuremburg	A	L	1-3	Klose 57	28,000
37	gbl	Hannover 96	H	W	5-0	Valdez 43,52,81; Micoud 45; Klose 53	41,646
38	gbl	Eintr Frankfurt	A	W	1-0	Klose 70 pen	50,000
39	gbl	Bayern Munich	H	W	3-0	Schweinsteiger 33 og; Jensen 79; Borowski 83	42,500
40	gbl	Wolfsburg	A	D	1-1	Valdez 6	27,000
41	gbl	Schalke	H	D	0-0		42,100
42	gbl	Duisburg	A	W	5-3	Micoud 4,16; Klose 31,75; Klasnic 86	17,000
43	gbl	Cologne	H	W	6-0	Borowski 11,25; Klose 19,75; Klasnic 50,69	40,000
44	gbl	Hamburg	A	W	2-1	Klasnic 27; Klose 72	57,000

LEAGUE APPEARANCES, BOOKINGS AND CAPS

	AGE (on 01/07/06)	IN NAMED 18	APPEARANCES	COUNTING GAMES	MINUTES ON PITCH	YELLOW CARDS	RED CARDS	CAPS THIS SEASON	NATIONAL SIDE
Goalkeepers									
Andreas Reinke	45	21	19	19	1709	0	0	-	Germany
Christian Vander	25	3	1	0	62	0	0	-	Germany
Tim Wiese	24	15	15	14	1289	0	0	-	Germany
Defenders									
Leon Andreasen	23	19	18	10	1087	4	0	2	Denmark (19)
Francis Banecki	20	1	0	0	0	0	0	-	Germany
Frank Baumann	30	19	19	16	1550	5	0	-	Germany
Tim Borowski	26	31	31	28	2650	10	0	9	Germany (19)
Frank Fahrenhorst	28	23	23	22	1990	4	1	-	Germany
Naldo	23	32	32	30	2778	3	0	-	Brazil
Petri Pasanen	25	18	18	14	1415	3	0	2	Finland (42)
Jerome Polenz	19	5	3	0	35	0	0	-	Germany
Jelle van Damme	22	10	8	3	337	1	0	3	Belgium (42)
Midfielders									
Torsten Frings	29	28	28	24	2302	8	1	7	Germany (19)
Daniel Jensen	27	27	27	10	1389	1	0	6	Denmark (19)
Pekka Lagerblom	24	5	3	0	54	0	0	4	Finland (42)
Johan Micoud	32	30	30	27	2518	4	0	-	France
Patrick Owomoyela	26	31	31	24	2345	5	0	6	Germany (19)
Christian Schulz	23	30	30	27	2500	9	0	-	Germany
Umit Davala	32	1	1	1	84	0	0	-	Turkey
Jurica Vranjes	26	29	29	11	1417	4	0	5	Croatia (23)
Forwards									
Aaron Hunt	19	7	7	1	234	0	0	-	Germany
Ivan Klasnic	26	30	30	18	1962	1	0	7	Croatia (23)
Miroslav Klose	28	26	26	22	2153	4	0	8	Germany (19)
Marco Stier	22	0	0	0	0	0	0	-	Germany
Nelson Haedo Valdez	22	30	30	15	1783	3	0	4	Paraguay (33)

TEAM OF THE SEASON

G — Tim Wiese, CG: 14 DR: 92

D — Petri Pasanen, CG: 14 DR: 142

D — Frank Fahrenhorst, CG: 22 DR: 100

D — Tim Borowski, CG: 28 DR: 80

D — Naldo, CG: 30 DR: 79

M — Johan Micoud, CG: 27 SD: 49

M — Christian Schulz, CG: 27 SD: 46

M — Patrick Owomoyela, CG: 24 SD: 34

M — Torsten Frings, CG: 24 SD: 32

F — Miroslav Klose, CG: 22 SR: 86

F — Ivan Klasnic, CG: 18 SR: 131

MONTHLY POINTS TALLY

Month	Points	%
AUGUST	7	78%
SEPTEMBER	9	75%
OCTOBER	10	83%
NOVEMBER	3	33%
DECEMBER	7	78%
JANUARY	3	100%
FEBRUARY	10	67%
MARCH	4	33%
APRIL	8	67%
MAY	9	100%

LEAGUE GOALS

	PLAYER	MINS	GOALS	S RATE
1	Klose	2153	25	86
2	Klasnic	1962	15	131
3	Borowski	2650	10	265
4	Valdez	1783	9	198
5	Micoud	2518	8	315
6	Frings	2302	3	767
7	Naldo	2778	2	1389
8	Baumann	1550	2	775
9	van Damme	337	1	337
10	Jensen	1389	1	1389
11	Vranjes	1417	1	1417
12	Fahrenhorst	1990	1	1990
	Other		1	
	TOTAL		79	

TOP POINT EARNERS

	PLAYER	GAMES	AV PTS
1	Petri Pasanen	14	2.29
2	Andreas Reinke	19	2.21
3	Tim Borowski	28	2.21
4	Frank Baumann	16	2.19
5	Johan Micoud	27	2.19
6	Miroslav Klose	22	2.18
7	Naldo	30	2.10
8	Patrick Owomoyela	24	2.08
9	Nelson Haedo Valdez	15	2.07
10	Christian Schulz	27	2.00
	CLUB AVERAGE:		2.06

DISCIPLINARY RECORDS

	PLAYER	YELLOW	RED	AVE
1	Frings	8	1	255
2	Borowski	10	0	265
3	Andreasen	4	0	271
4	Schulz	9	0	277
5	Baumann	5	0	310
6	Vranjes	4	0	354
7	Fahrenhorst	4	1	398
8	Owomoyela	5	0	469
9	Pasanen	3	0	471
10	Klose	4	0	538
11	Valdez	3	0	594
12	Micoud	4	0	629
13	Naldo	3	0	926
	Other	2	0	
	TOTAL	68	2	

KEY GOALKEEPER

Tim Wiese

Goals Conceded in the League	14	Counting Games League games when player was on pitch for at least 70 minutes	14
Defensive Rating Ave number of mins between League goals conceded while on the pitch	92	Clean Sheets In games when player was on pitch for at least 70 minutes	8

KEY PLAYERS - DEFENDERS

Petri Pasanen

Goals Conceded Number of League goals conceded while the player was on the pitch	10	Clean Sheets In League games when player was on pitch for at least 70 minutes	8
Defensive Rating Ave number of mins between League goals conceded while on the pitch	142	Club Defensive Rating Average number of mins between League goals conceded by the club this season	83

	PLAYER	CON LGE	CLEAN SHEETS	DEF RATE
1	Petri Pasanen	10	8	142 mins
2	Frank Fahrenhorst	20	11	100 mins
3	Tim Borowski	33	11	80 mins
4	Naldo	35	11	79 mins

KEY PLAYERS - MIDFIELDERS

Johan Micoud

Goals in the League	8	Contribution to Attacking Power Average number of minutes between League team goals while on pitch	41
Defensive Rating Average number of mins between League goals conceded while on the pitch	90	Scoring Difference Defensive Rating minus Contribution to Attacking Power	49

	PLAYER	LGE GOALS	DEF RATE	POWER	SCORE DIFF
1	Johan Micoud	8	90	41	49 mins
2	Christian Schulz	0	86	40	46 mins
3	Patrick Owomoyela	0	76	42	34 mins
4	Torsten Frings	3	72	40	32 mins

KEY PLAYERS - GOALSCORERS

Miroslav Klose

Goals in the League	25	Player Strike Rate Average number of minutes between League goals scored by player	86
Contribution to Attacking Power Average number of minutes between League team goals while on pitch	33	Club Strike Rate Average number of minutes between League goals scored by club	39

	PLAYER	LGE GOALS	POWER	STRIKE RATE
1	Miroslav Klose	25	33	86 mins
2	Ivan Klasnic	15	38	131 mins
3	Nelson Haedo Valdez	9	46	198 mins
4	Tim Borowski	10	38	265 mins

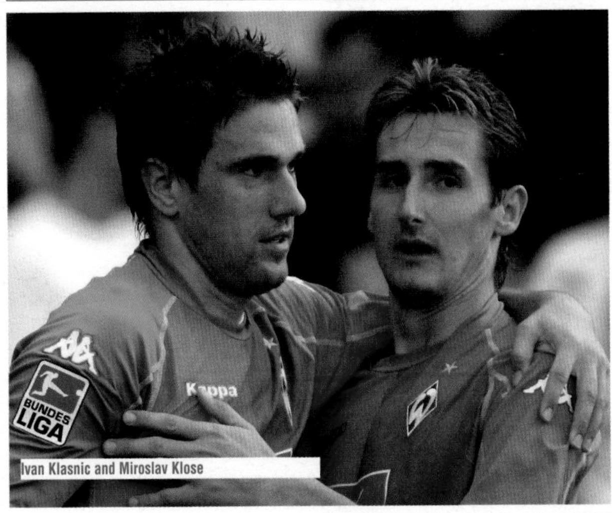

Ivan Klasnic and Miroslav Klose

SQUAD APPEARANCES

Match	1	2	3	4	5	6	7	8	9	10	11	12	13	14	15	16	17	18	19	20	21	22	23	24	25	26	27	28	29	30	31	32	33	34	35	36	37	38	39	40	41	42	43	44
Venue	H	A	A	H	H	A	H	H	A	H	A	A	H	A	A	H	H	A	H	A	A	H	H	A	H	A	H	A	H	A	H	H	A	A	H	A	H	A	H	A	H	A	H	A
Competition	L	C	L	C	L	L	C	L	L	L	C	L	L	C	L	L	C	L	L	C	L	L	C	L	L	L	L	L	L	L	C	L	L	C	L	L	L	L	L	L	L	L	L	L
Result	W	L	W	W	D	W	L	W	L	W	L	W	W	D	D	W	W	L	W	L	L	W	W	W	D	W	W	D	L	W	W	W	D	L	L	L	W	W	W	D	D	W	W	W

Goalkeepers
Andreas Reinke
Christian Vander
Tim Wiese

Defenders
Leon Andreasen
Francis Banecki
Frank Baumann
Tim Borowski
Frank Fahrenhorst
Naldo
Petri Pasanen
Jerome Polenz
Jelle van Damme

Midfielders
Torsten Frings
Daniel Jensen
Pekka Lagerblom
Johan Micoud
Patrick Owomoyela
Christian Schulz
Umit Davala
Jurica Vranjes

Forwards
Aaron Hunt
Ivan Klasnic
Miroslav Klose
Marco Stier
Nelson Haedo Valdez

KEY: On all match | On bench | Subbed or sent off (Counting game) | Subbed or sent off (playing less than 70 minutes) | Subbed on from bench (Counting Game) | Subbed on (playing less than 70 minutes) | Subbed on and then subbed or sent off (Counting Game) | Subbed on and then subbed or sent off (playing less than 70 minutes) | Not in 16

HAMBURG SV

Final Position: **3rd**

NICKNAME: HSV

KEY: ☐Won ☐Drawn ☐Lost

		Opponent			Score	Scorers	Attendance
1	gbl	Nuremburg	H	W	3-0	Mpenza 3; Barbarez 45 pen,60	45,000
2	etfl1	Valencia	H	W	1-0	Barbarez 51	48,000
3	gbl	Arminia B	A	W	2-0	Barbarez 79 pen; Van der Vaart 90	24,000
4	etfl2	Valencia	A	D	0-0		32,000
5	gbl	Hannover 96	H	D	1-1	Mahdavikia 22	48,866
6	gbl	Mainz	A	W	3-1	Wicky 43; Mahdavikia 56; Van der Vaart 71	20,300
7	uc1rl1	Copenhagen	H	D	1-1	Van der Vaart 37	43,085
8	gbl	Eintr Frankfurt	H	D	1-1	Van Buyten 85	45,000
9	gbl	Stuttgart	A	W	2-1	Van der Vaart 32; Jarolim 88	35,000
10	gbl	Bayern Munich	H	W	2-0	Van der Vaart 10; Trochowski 62	55,800
11	uc1rl2	Copenhagen	A	W	1-0	Van der Vaart 90 pen	34,446
12	gbl	Kaiserslautern	A	W	3-0	Van der Vaart 36,82; Barbarez 50	34,775
13	gbl	Wolfsburg	H	L	0-1		54,000
14	ucgpa	CSKA Sofia	A	W	1-0	Van der Vaart 57	22,000
15	gbl	B Dortmund	A	D	1-1	Trochowski 74	76,000
16	gbl	Schalke	H	W	1-0	Mahdavikia 19	55,800
17	ucgpa	Viking	H	W	2-0	Van der Vaart 21; Lauth 66	40,000
18	gbl	B M'gladbach	A	D	0-0		53,466
19	gbl	Duisburg	H	W	2-0	Barbarez 39; Lauth 45	50,000
20	ucgpa	AS Monaco	A	L	0-2		18,000
21	gbl	B Leverkusen	A	W	1-0	Jarolim 82	22,500
22	gbl	Cologne	H	W	3-1	Atouba 43; Lauth 54; Barbarez 73	55,800
23	gbl	Hertha Berlin	H	W	2-1	Van Burik 2 og; Mahdavikia 9 pen	54,149
24	ucgpa	Slavia Prague	H	W	2-0	Barbarez 9; Mpenza 57	46,253
25	gbl	W Bremen	A	D	1-1	Kucukovic 67	42,500
26	gbl	Nuremburg	A	L	1-2	Wiblishauser 65 og	23,928
27	gbl	Arminia B	H	W	2-1	Trochowski 51; Barbarez 73	52,000
28	gbl	Hannover 96	A	L	1-2	Barbarez 81	40,000
29	gbl	Mainz	H	W	1-0	Mahdavikia 6	52,000
30	uc3rl1	FC Thun	A	L	0-1		18,500
31	gbl	Eintr Frankfurt	A	W	2-1	Trochowski 20; Van Buyten 52	50,000
32	uc3rl2	FC Thun	H	W	2-0	Van Buyten 2,33	40,254
33	gbl	Stuttgart	H	L	0-2		51,821
34	gbl	Bayern Munich	A	W	2-1	Demel 16; de Jong 89	69,000
35	uc4rl1	Rap Bucharest	A	L	0-2		15,000
36	gbl	Kaiserslautern	H	W	3-0	Lauth 55; Schonheim 62 og; Van der Vaart 86 pen	44,460
37	uc4rl2	Rap Bucharest	H	W	3-1	Lauth 24; Barbarez 36; Van der Vaart 63	37,866
38	gbl	Wolfsburg	A	W	1-0	Lauth 22	28,095
39	gbl	B Dortmund	H	L	2-4	Lauth 35; Ailton 67	56,000
40	gbl	Schalke	A	W	2-0	Krstajic 57 og; Ailton 80	61,500
41	gbl	B M'gladbach	H	W	2-0	Van der Vaart 34 pen; Takahara 90	56,750
42	gbl	Duisburg	A	W	2-0	Mohrle 24 og; Ailton 30	22,000
43	gbl	B Leverkusen	H	L	0-2		57,000
44	gbl	Cologne	A	W	1-0	Sinkewicz 3 og	50,000
45	gbl	Hertha Berlin	A	L	2-4	Trochowski 9; Lauth 19	74,000
46	gbl	W Bremen	H	L	1-2	Barbarez 59	57,000

LEAGUE APPEARANCES, BOOKINGS AND CAPS

	AGE (on 01/07/06)	IN NAMED 18	APPEARANCES	COUNTING GAMES	MINUTES ON PITCH	YELLOW CARDS	RED CARDS	CAPS THIS SEASON	NATIONAL SIDE
Goalkeepers									
Wolfgang Hesl	20	0	0	0	0	0	0	-	Germany
Sascha Kirschstein	26	17	13	13	1170	1	0	-	Germany
Stefan Wachter	28	22	21	21	1890	0	0	-	Germany
Defenders									
Timothee Atouba	24	31	31	31	2770	7	0	6	Cameroon (26)
Khalid Boulahrouz	24	28	28	27	2468	7	0	7	Holland (3)
Guy Demel	25	22	22	18	1751	3	0	5	Ivory Coast (32)
Rene Klingbeil	25	20	17	6	714	2	0	-	Germany
Bastian Reinhardt	30	14	14	8	769	0	0	-	Germany
Daniel Van Buyten	28	27	27	26	2391	3	1	3	Belgium (42)
Daniel Ziebig	23	1	0	0	0	0	0	-	Germany
Midfielders									
Stefan Beinlich	34	16	16	15	1413	5	0	-	Germany
Collin Benjamin	27	0	0	0	0	0	0	-	Namibia
Nigel de Jong	21	12	12	10	955	6	0	3	Holland (3)
Mario Fillinger	21	3	2	0	21	0	0	-	Germany
David Jarolim	27	31	31	31	2745	10	0	5	Czech Republic (2)
Markus Karl	20	5	3	0	16	0	0	-	Germany
Alexander Laas	22	8	5	1	113	0	0	-	Germany
Charles Takyi	21	2	1	0	19	0	0	-	Germany
Piotr Trochowski	22	33	33	20	2207	1	0	-	Germany
Rafael Van der Vaart	23	19	19	14	1446	4	1	6	Holland (3)
Raphael Wicky	29	19	18	14	1392	5	0	7	Switzerland (35)
Reto Ziegler	20	10	8	0	150	0	0	-	Switzerland
Forwards									
Ailton	32	13	13	8	824	1	0	-	Brazil
Sergei Barbarez	34	33	33	31	2879	9	0	6	Bosnia (72)
Mustafa Kucukovic	19	6	5	0	128	0	0	-	Germany
Benjamin Lauth	24	31	31	14	1915	5	0	-	Germany
Mehdi Mahdavikia	28	30	30	25	2390	3	0	-	Iran
Emile Mpenza	28	10	10	4	447	0	0	2	Belgium (42)
Naohiro Takahara	27	23	21	4	676	0	0	-	Japan

TEAM OF THE SEASON

D — Timothee Atouba — CG: 31 DR: 126

M — Rafael Van der Vaart — CG: 14 SD: 157

D — Guy Demel — CG: 18 DR: 109

M — Stefan Beinlich — CG: 15 SD: 80

F — Benjamin Lauth — CG: 14 SR: 319

G — Stefan Wachter — CG: 21 DR: 126

D — Khalid Boulahrouz — CG: 27 DR: 103

M — David Jarolim — CG: 31 SD: 56

F — Sergei Barbarez — CG: 31 SR: 320

D — Daniel Van Buyten — CG: 26 DR: 96

M — Raphael Wicky — CG: 14 SD: 53

MONTHLY POINTS TALLY

Month	Points	%
AUGUST	7	78%
SEPTEMBER	10	83%
OCTOBER	7	58%
NOVEMBER	7	78%
DECEMBER	7	78%
JANUARY	0	0%
FEBRUARY	9	60%
MARCH	9	75%
APRIL	9	75%
MAY	3	33%

LEAGUE GOALS

	PLAYER	MINS	GOALS	S RATE
1	Barbarez	2879	9	320
2	Van der Vaart	1446	8	181
3	Lauth	1915	6	319
4	Trochowski	2207	5	441
5	Mahdavikia	2390	5	478
6	Ailton	824	3	275
7	Jarolim	2745	2	1373
8	Van Buyten	2391	2	1196
9	Kucukovic	128	1	128
10	Wicky	1392	1	1392
11	Takahara	676	1	676
12	de Jong	955	1	955
13	Atouba	2770	1	2770
	Other		8	
	TOTAL		53	

TOP POINT EARNERS

	PLAYER	GAMES	AV PTS
1	Rafael Van der Vaart	14	2.50
2	Guy Demel	18	2.17
3	Timothee Atouba	31	2.10
4	Sergei Barbarez	31	2.10
5	Stefan Beinlich	15	2.07
6	Stefan Wachter	21	2.05
7	Khalid Boulahrouz	27	2.00
8	David Jarolim	31	2.00
9	Sascha Kirschstein	13	1.92
10	Mehdi Mahdavikia	25	1.92
	CLUB AVERAGE:		2.00

DISCIPLINARY RECORDS

	PLAYER	YELLOW	RED	AVE
1	de Jong	6	0	159
2	Jarolim	10	0	274
3	Wicky	5	0	278
4	Beinlich	5	0	282
5	Van der Vaart	4	1	289
6	Barbarez	9	0	319
7	Boulahrouz	7	0	352
8	Klingbeil	2	0	357
9	Lauth	5	0	383
10	Atouba	7	0	395
11	Demel	3	0	583
12	Van Buyten	3	1	597
13	Mahdavikia	3	0	796
	Other	3	0	
	TOTAL	72	2	

KEY GOALKEEPER

Stefan Wachter

Goals Conceded in the League	15	**Counting Games** League games when player was on pitch for at least 70 minutes	21
Defensive Rating Ave number of mins between League goals conceded while on the pitch	126	**Clean Sheets** In games when player was on pitch for at least 70 minutes	9

KEY PLAYERS - DEFENDERS

Timothee Atouba

Goals Conceded Number of League goals conceded while the player was on the pitch	22	**Clean Sheets** In League games when player was on pitch for at least 70 minutes	15
Defensive Rating Ave number of mins between League goals conceded while on the pitch	126	**Club Defensive Rating** Average number of mins between League goals conceded by the club this season	102

	PLAYER	CON LGE	CLEAN SHEETS	DEF RATE
1	Timothee Atouba	22	15	126 mins
2	Guy Demel	16	8	109 mins
3	Khalid Boulahrouz	24	12	103 mins
4	Daniel Van Buyten	25	10	96 mins

KEY PLAYERS - MIDFIELDERS

Goals in the League	8	**Contribution to Attacking Power** Average number of minutes between League team goals while on pitch	50
Defensive Rating Average number of mins between League goals conceded while on the pitch	207	**Scoring Difference** Defensive Rating minus Contribution to Attacking Power	157

	PLAYER	LGE GOALS	DEF RATE	POWER	SCORE DIFF
1	Rafael Van der Vaart	8	207	50	157 mins
2	Stefan Beinlich	0	141	61	80 mins
3	David Jarolim	2	114	58	56 mins
4	Raphael Wicky	1	116	63	53 mins

KEY PLAYERS - GOALSCORERS

Rafael Van der Vaart

Goals in the League	8	**Player Strike Rate** Average number of minutes between League goals scored by player	181
Contribution to Attacking Power Average number of minutes between League team goals while on pitch	50	**Club Strike Rate** Average number of minutes between League goals scored by club	58

	PLAYER	LGE GOALS	POWER	STRIKE RATE
1	Rafael Van der Vaart	8	50	181 mins
2	Benjamin Lauth	6	56	319 mins
3	Sergei Barbarez	9	56	320 mins
4	Piotr Trochowski	5	63	441 mins

Sergei Barbarez and Rafael Van der Vaart

SQUAD APPEARANCES

Match	1	2	3	4	5	6	7	8	9	10	11	12	13	14	15	16	17	18	19	20	21	22	23
Venue	H	H	A	A	H	A	H	H	A	H	A	A	H	A	A	H	H	A	H	A	A	H	H
Competition	L	O	L	O	L	L	E	L	L	L	E	L	L	E	L	L	E	L	L	E	L	L	L
Result	W	W	W	D	D	W	D	D	W	W	W	W	L	W	D	W	W	D	W	L	W	W	W

Match	24	25	26	27	28	29	30	31	32	33	34	35	36	37	38	39	40	41	42	43	44	45	46
Venue	H	A	A	H	A	H	A	A	H	H	A	A	H	H	A	H	A	H	A	H	A	A	H
Competition	E	L	L	L	L	L	E	L	E	L	L	E	L	E	L	L	L	L	L	L	L	L	L
Result	W	D	L	W	L	W	L	W	W	L	W	L	W	W	W	L	W	W	W	L	W	L	L

Goalkeepers
Wolfgang Hesl
Sascha Kirschstein
Stefan Wachter

Defenders
Timothee Atouba
Khalid Boulahrouz
Guy Demel
Rene Klingbeil
Bastian Reinhardt
Daniel Van Buyten
Daniel Ziebig

Midfielders
Stefan Beinlich
Collin Benjamin
Nigel de Jong
Mario Fillinger
David Jarolim
Markus Karl
Alexander Laas
Charles Takyi
Piotr Trochowski
Rafael Van der Vaart
Raphael Wicky
Reto Ziegler

Forwards
Ailton
Sergei Barbarez
Mustafa Kucukovic
Benjamin Lauth
Mehdi Mahdavikia
Emile Mpenza
Naohiro Takahara

KEY: ■ On all match ■ On bench ⏮ Subbed or sent off (Counting game) ≪ Subbed or sent off (playing less than 70 minutes) ⏭ Subbed on from bench (Counting Game) » Subbed on (playing less than 70 minutes) Subbed on and then subbed or sent off (Counting Game) Subbed on and then subbed or sent off (playing less than 70 minutes) □ Not in 16

SCHALKE 04

Final Position: **4th**

NICKNAME: KONIGSBLAUE

KEY: ☐ Won ☐ Drawn ☐ Lost

						Result	Scorers	Attendance
1	gbl	**Kaiserslautern**	H	W	2-1	Larsen 79; Krstajic 82	61,000
2	gbl	**B Dortmund**	A	W	2-1	Kuranyi 22,58	81,264
3	gbl	**B M'gladbach**	H	D	1-1	Sand 54	61,000
4	gbl	**B Leverkusen**	A	D	1-1	Larsen 85	22,500
5	ecgpe	**PSV Eindhoven**	A	L	0-1		30,000
6	gbl	**Hertha Berlin**	H	D	0-0		60,740
7	gbl	**Nuremburg**	A	D	1-1	Larsen 65	20,000
8	gbl	**Hannover 96**	H	W	2-0	Lincoln 58; Vinicius 66 og	60,000
9	ecgpe	**AC Milan**	H	D	2-2	Larsen 3; Altintop 70	60,881
10	gbl	**Eintr Frankfurt**	A	W	1-0	Larsen 65	35,000
11	gbl	**Bayern Munich**	H	D	1-1	Larsen 90 pen	61,524
12	ecgpe	**Fenerbahce**	A	D	3-3	Lincoln 59,62; Kuranyi 77	50,000
13	gbl	**Wolfsburg**	A	D	0-0		28,000
14	gbl	**Hamburg**	A	L	0-1		55,800
15	ecgpe	**Fenerbahce**	H	W	2-0	Kuranyi 32; Sand 90	59,000
16	gbl	**Duisburg**	H	W	3-0	Kuranyi 13; Meyer 67 og; Rodriguez 86	61,524
17	gbl	**Cologne**	A	D	2-2	Kuranyi 23; Sand 86	50,000
18	ecgpe	**PSV Eindhoven**	H	W	3-0	Kobiashvili 18 pen,72,79 pen	30,000
19	gbl	**W Bremen**	H	W	2-1	Kuranyi 2,64	61,524
20	gbl	**Arminia B**	A	W	1-0	Poulsen 51	26,601
21	ecgpe	**AC Milan**	A	L	2-3	Poulsen 44; Lincoln 66	82,000
22	gbl	**Mainz**	H	W	1-0	Bordon 58	61,000
23	gbl	**Stuttgart**	A	L	0-2		50,000
24	gbl	**Kaiserslautern**	A	W	2-0	Lincoln 12; Kobiashvili 78 pen	35,549
25	gbl	**B Dortmund**	H	D	0-0		61,524
26	gbl	**B M'gladbach**	A	D	0-0		54,000
27	gbl	**B Leverkusen**	H	W	7-4	Larsen 9,63; Krstajic 17; Bajramovic 34; Kuranyi 55; Lincoln 76; Asamoah 81	61,524
28	uc3rl1	**Espanyol**	H	W	2-1	Bordon 67; Ernst 88	53,642
29	gbl	**Hertha Berlin**	A	W	2-1	Asamoah 6; Bajramovic 45	50,000
30	uc3rl2	**Espanyol**	A	W	3-0	Kuranyi 54; Sand 70; Lincoln 73	18,100
31	gbl	**Nuremburg**	H	W	2-0	Kuranyi 58; Lincoln 65	61,524
32	gbl	**Hannover 96**	A	W	2-1	Poulsen 20; Bajramovic 28	47,000
33	uc4rl1	**Palermo**	A	L	0-1		10,581
34	gbl	**Eintr Frankfurt**	H	W	2-0	Larsen 51; Sand 90	61,524
35	uc4rl2	**Palermo**	H	W	3-0	Kobiashvili 44; Larsen 72; Azaouagh 80	52,151
36	gbl	**Bayern Munich**	A	L	0-3		69,000
37	gbl	**Wolfsburg**	H	D	2-2	Kuranyi 7; Lincoln 67	61,524
38	ucqfl1	**Levski Sofia**	A	W	3-1	Varela 48; Lincoln 69; Asamoah 79	38,000
39	gbl	**Hamburg**	H	L	0-2		61,500
40	ucqfl2	**Levski Sofia**	H	D	1-1	Lincoln 57	52,973
41	gbl	**Duisburg**	A	D	1-1	Larsen 85	31,500
42	gbl	**Cologne**	H	D	1-1	Bajramovic 80	61,524
43	ucsfl1	**Seville**	H	D	0-0		
44	gbl	**W Bremen**	A	D	0-0		42,100
45	ucsfl2	**Seville**	A	L	0-1		45,000
46	gbl	**Arminia B**	H	W	3-1	Asamoah 40; Larsen 81; Altintop 88	61,000
47	gbl	**Mainz**	A	L	0-1		20,300
48	gbl	**Stuttgart**	H	W	3-2	Sand 53; Bordon 80; Waldoch 83	61,000

LEAGUE APPEARANCES, BOOKINGS AND CAPS

	AGE (on 01/07/06)	IN NAMED 18	APPEARANCES	COUNTING GAMES	MINUTES ON PITCH	YELLOW CARDS	RED CARDS	CAPS THIS SEASON	NATIONAL SIDE
Goalkeepers									
Ralf Fahrmann	17	1	0	0	0	0	0	-	Germany
Christofer Heimeroth	24	5	2	2	180	0	0	-	Germany
Frank Rost	33	32	32	32	2880	1	0	-	Germany
Defenders									
Sebastian Boenisch	19	3	1	0	7	0	0	-	Germany
Marcelo Jose Bordon	30	32	32	30	2790	4	0	-	Brazil
Thomas Klasener	29	6	4	1	107	0	0	-	Germany
Mladen Krstajic	32	29	29	28	2565	5	0	7	Serbia & Mont (44)
Rafinha	20	29	29	26	2443	4	1	-	Brazil
Dario Rodriguez	31	23	22	19	1715	5	0	-	Uruguay
Tomasz Waldoch	35	3	2	0	27	0	0	-	Poland
Midfielders									
Hamit Altintop	23	22	22	12	1351	5	0	-	Turkey
Mimoun Azaouagh	23	6	4	0	208	0	0	-	Turkey
Zlatan Bajramovic	26	26	25	11	1293	6	2	5	Bosnia (72)
Alex Baumjohann	19	2	1	0	4	0	0	-	Germany
Niko Bungert	19	2	0	0	0	0	0	-	Germany
Simon Cziommer	25	1	0	0	0	0	0	-	Germany
Fabian Ernst	27	32	32	27	2630	7	1	7	Germany (19)
Levan Kobiashvili	28	30	30	30	2700	4	0	5	Georgia (84)
Joseph Laumann	22	1	1	0	1	0	0	-	Germany
Lincoln	27	29	28	27	2464	4	0	-	Brazil
Christian Poulsen	26	28	28	23	2249	14	1	6	Denmark (19)
Gustavo Varela	28	27	27	11	1399	1	0	-	Uruguay
Forwards									
Gerald Asamoah	27	24	23	10	1292	5	0	7	Germany (19)
Kevin Kuranyi	24	30	29	24	2414	5	0	6	Germany (19)
Soren Larsen	24	31	30	9	1345	1	0	6	Denmark (19)
Ebbe Sand	33	30	30	12	1467	2	0	-	Denmark

TEAM OF THE SEASON

MONTHLY POINTS TALLY

Month	Points	%
AUGUST	7	78%
SEPTEMBER	6	50%
OCTOBER	5	42%
NOVEMBER	7	78%
DECEMBER	6	67%
JANUARY	3	100%
FEBRUARY	11	73%
MARCH	7	58%
APRIL	3	25%
MAY	6	67%

LEAGUE GOALS

	PLAYER	MINS	GOALS	S RATE
1	Larsen	1345	**10**	135
2	Kuranyi	2414	**9**	268
3	Lincoln	2464	**5**	493
4	Sand	1467	**4**	367
5	Bajramovic	1293	**4**	323
6	Asamoah	1292	**3**	431
7	Krstajic	2565	**2**	1283
8	Bordon	2790	**2**	1395
9	Poulsen	2249	**2**	1125
10	Altintop	1351	**1**	1351
11	Rodriguez	1715	**1**	1715
12	Kobiashvili	2700	**1**	2700
13	Waldoch	27	**1**	27
	Other		**2**	
	TOTAL		**47**	

TOP POINT EARNERS

	PLAYER	GAMES	AV PTS
1	Ebbe Sand	12	**2.08**
2	Kevin Kuranyi	24	**2.00**
3	Rafinha	26	**1.96**
4	Christian Poulsen	23	**1.91**
5	Fabian Ernst	27	**1.89**
6	Levan Kobiashvili	30	**1.87**
7	Marcelo Jose Bordon	30	**1.80**
8	Dario Rodriguez	19	**1.79**
9	Mladen Krstajic	28	**1.79**
10	Frank Rost	32	**1.78**
	CLUB AVERAGE:		**1.79**

DISCIPLINARY RECORDS

	PLAYER	YELLOW	RED	AVE
1	Poulsen	14	1	**149**
2	Bajramovic	6	2	**161**
3	Asamoah	5	0	**258**
4	Altintop	5	0	**270**
5	Ernst	7	1	**328**
6	Rodriguez	5	0	**343**
7	Kuranyi	5	0	**482**
8	Rafinha	4	1	**488**
9	Krstajic	5	0	**513**
10	Lincoln	4	0	**616**
11	Kobiashvili	4	0	**675**
12	Bordon	4	0	**697**
13	Sand	2	0	**733**
	Other	3	0	
	TOTAL	**73**	**5**	

KEY GOALKEEPER

Frank Rost

Goals Conceded in the League	29	Counting Games League games when player was on pitch for at least 70 minutes	32
Defensive Rating Ave number of mins between League goals conceded while on the pitch	99	Clean Sheets In League games when player was on pitch for at least 70 minutes	12

KEY PLAYERS - DEFENDERS

Dario Rodriguez

Goals Conceded Number of League goals conceded while the player was on the pitch	14	Clean Sheets In League games when player was on pitch for at least 70 minutes	10
Defensive Rating Ave number of mins between League goals conceded while on the pitch	123	Club Defensive Rating Average number of mins between League goals conceded by the club this season	99

	PLAYER	CON LGE	CLEAN SHEETS	DEF RATE
1	Dario Rodriguez	14	10	123 mins
2	Rafinha	23	13	106 mins
3	Marcelo Jose Bordon	27	11	103 mins
4	Mladen Krstajic	29	9	88 mins

KEY PLAYERS - MIDFIELDERS

Hamit Altintop

Goals in the League	1	Contribution to Attacking Power Average number of minutes between League team goals while on pitch	71
Defensive Rating Average number of mins between League goals conceded while on the pitch	113	Scoring Difference Defensive Rating minus Contribution to Attacking Power	42

	PLAYER	LGE GOALS	DEF RATE	POWER	SCORE DIFF
1	Hamit Altintop	1	113	71	42 mins
2	Levan Kobiashvili	1	100	61	39 mins
3	Christian Poulsen	2	98	68	30 mins
4	Fabian Ernst	0	91	66	25 mins

KEY PLAYERS - GOALSCORERS

Kevin Kuranyi

Goals in the League	9	Player Strike Rate Average number of minutes between League goals scored by player	268
Contribution to Attacking Power Average number of minutes between League team goals while on pitch	67	Club Strike Rate Average number of minutes between League goals scored by club	65

	PLAYER	LGE GOALS	POWER	STRIKE RATE
1	Kevin Kuranyi	9	67	268 mins
2	Ebbe Sand	4	59	367 mins
3	Lincoln	5	72	493 mins
4	Christian Poulsen	2	68	1125 mins

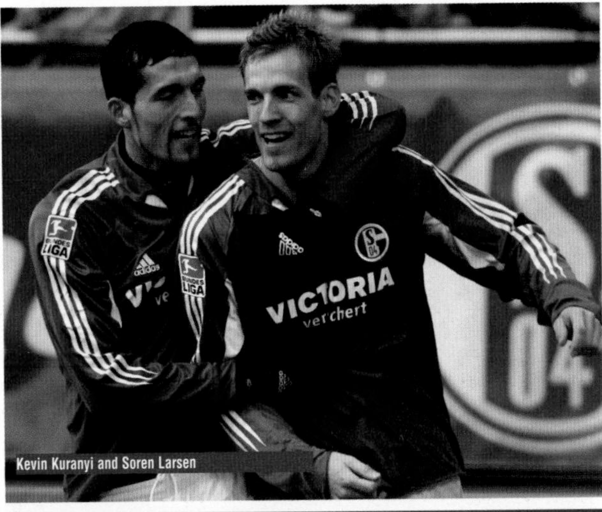

Kevin Kuranyi and Soren Larsen

SQUAD APPEARANCES

Match	1	2	3	4	5	6	7	8	9	10	11	12	13	14	15	16	17	18	19	20	21	22	23	24
Venue	H	A	H	A	A	H	A	H	H	A	H	A	A	A	H	H	A	H	H	A	A	H	A	A
Competition	L	L	L	L	C	L	L	L	C	L	L	C	L	L	C	L	L	C	L	L	C	L	L	L
Result	W	W	D	D	L	D	D	W	D	W	D	D	D	L	W	W	D	W	W	W	L	W	L	W

Match	25	26	27	28	29	30	31	32	33	34	35	36	37	38	39	40	41	42	43	44	45	46	47	48
Venue	H	A	H	H	A	A	H	A	A	H	H	A	H	A	H	H	A	H	H	A	A	H	A	H
Competition	L	L	L	E	L	E	L	L	E	L	E	L	L	E	L	E	L	L	E	L	E	L	L	L
Result	D	D	W	W	W	W	W	W	L	W	W	L	D	W	L	D	D	D	D	D	L	W	L	W

Goalkeepers
Ralf Fahrmann
Christofer Heimeroth
Frank Rost

Defenders
Sebastian Boenisch
Marcelo Jose Bordon
Thomas Klasener
Mladen Krstajic
Rafinha
Dario Rodriguez
Tomasz Waldoch

Midfielders
Hamit Altintop
Mimoun Azaouagh
Zlatan Bajramovic
Alexander Baumjohann
Niko Bungert
Simon Cziommer
Fabian Ernst
Levan Kobiashvili
Joseph Laumann
Lincoln
Christian Poulsen
Gustavo Antonio Varela

Forwards
Gerald Asamoah
Kevin Kuranyi
Soren Larsen
Ebbe Sand

KEY: On all match · On bench · Subbed or sent off (Counting game) · Subbed or sent off (playing less than 70 minutes) · Subbed on from bench (Counting Game) · Subbed on (playing less than 70 minutes) · Subbed on and then subbed or sent off (Counting Game) · Subbed on and then subbed or sent off (playing less than 70 minutes) · Not in 16

BAYER LEVERKUSEN

Final Position: **5th**

NICKNAME: BAYER-LOWEN

KEY: ☐Won ☐Drawn ☐Lost

#	Comp	Opponent	H/A	Res	Score	Scorers	Attendance
1	gbl	Eintr Frankfurt	A	W	4-1	Berbatov 24; Voronin 48; Schneider 56; Krzynowek 59	41,000
2	gbl	Bayern Munich	H	L	2-5	Berbatov 31 pen; Babic 82	22,500
3	gbl	Wolfsburg	A	L	1-2	Berbatov 22	18,201
4	gbl	Schalke	H	D	1-1	Berbatov 73	22,500
5	uc1rl1	CSKA Sofia	H	L	0-1		
6	gbl	Duisburg	A	W	3-1	Juan 37; Berbatov 41; Athirson 89	24,100
7	gbl	Cologne	H	W	2-1	Voronin 24; Rolfes 67	22,500
8	gbl	W Bremen	A	L	1-2	Rolfes 54	39,000
9	uc1rl2	CSKA Sofia	A	L	0-1		22,015
10	gbl	Arminia B	H	D	1-1	Ramelow 85	22,500
11	gbl	Mainz	A	L	1-3	Barnetta 79	20,300
12	gbl	Stuttgart	H	D	1-1	Barnetta 56	20,000
13	gbl	Kaiserslautern	A	D	2-2	Barnetta 39; Voronin 71	30,000
14	gbl	B Dortmund	H	W	2-1	Juan 33; Kringe 86 og	22,500
15	gbl	B M'gladbach	A	D	1-1	Rolfes 5	48,000
16	gbl	Hamburg	H	L	0-1		22,500
17	gbl	Hertha Berlin	H	L	1-2	Berbatov 20	20,000
18	gbl	Nuremburg	A	D	1-1	Schneider 45	20,000
19	gbl	Hannover 96	H	D	0-0		20,000
20	gbl	Eintr Frankfurt	H	W	2-1	Freier 67; Butt 74 pen	22,000
21	gbl	Bayern Munich	A	L	0-1		69,901
22	gbl	Wolfsburg	H	W	4-0	Berbatov 44; Barnetta 55; Schneider 71; Madouni 75	22,500
23	gbl	Schalke	A	L	4-7	Voronin 40,64; Berbatov 50; Krzynowek 70	61,524
24	gbl	Duisburg	H	W	3-2	Freier 7; Barnetta 9; Berbatov 85	22,500
25	gbl	Cologne	A	W	3-0	Berbatov 67; Voronin 70; Krzynowek 83	49,000
26	gbl	W Bremen	H	D	1-1	Berbatov 41	225,000
27	gbl	Arminia B	A	L	0-1		20,000
28	gbl	Mainz	H	L	1-2	Freier 85	21,000
29	gbl	Stuttgart	A	W	2-0	Freier 30; Berbatov 88	38,000
30	gbl	Kaiserslautern	H	W	5-1	Barnetta 9; Berbatov 37 pen,61,90 pen; Fritz 85	22,500
31	gbl	B Dortmund	A	W	2-1	Berbatov 22; Freier 50	75,000
32	gbl	B M'gladbach	H	W	2-1	Rolfes 11,84	22,500
33	gbl	Hamburg	A	W	2-0	Rolfes 8; Freier 77	57,000
34	gbl	Hertha Berlin	A	W	5-1	Juan 5; Berbatov 27,28; Ramelow 63; Schneider 76	50,000
35	gbl	Nuremburg	H	D	2-2	Berbatov 49,89	22,500
36	gbl	Hannover 96	A	D	2-2	Rolfes 16; Berbatov 39	47,387

LEAGUE APPEARANCES, BOOKINGS AND CAPS

	AGE (on 01/07/06)	IN NAMED 18	APPEARANCES	COUNTING GAMES	MINUTES ON PITCH	YELLOW CARDS	RED CARDS	CAPS THIS SEASON	NATIONAL SIDE
Goalkeepers									
Rene Adler	21	1	0	0	0	0	0	-	Germany
Hans-Jorg Butt	32	34	34	34	3060	1	0	-	Germany
Tom Starke	25	2	0	0	0	0	0	-	Germany
Defenders									
Athirson Oliveira	29	18	18	11	1248	3	0	-	Brazil
J. Callsen-Bracker	21	1	1	1	91	0	0	-	Germany
Sascha Dum	20	2	1	0	1	1	0	-	Germany
Juan	27	30	29	27	2516	6	0	5	Brazil (1)
Ahmed Reda Madouni	25	15	13	9	958	1	0	-	France
Jens Nowotny	32	14	14	12	1107	3	0	-	Germany
Roque Junior	29	15	15	13	1219	1	1	3	Brazil (1)
Frederik Stenman	23	15	15	13	1295	2	0	-	Sweden
Midfielders									
Marko Babic	25	26	24	8	1051	4	0	8	Croatia (23)
Tranquillo Barnetta	21	31	31	21	2162	5	0	10	Switzerland (35)
Gonzalo Castro	19	19	19	14	1312	4	0	-	Spain
Paul Freier	26	29	29	15	1870	5	0	-	Germany
Jacek Krzynowek	30	21	20	6	963	0	0	4	Poland (29)
Carsten Ramelow	32	25	25	23	2066	8	1	-	Germany
Simon Rolfes	24	32	32	28	2613	4	0	-	Germany
Bernd Schneider	32	29	29	29	2579	3	0	10	Germany (19)
Forwards									
Dimitar Berbatov	25	34	34	34	3059	3	0	4	Bulgaria (38)
Clemens Fritz	25	30	29	22	2167	2	0	-	Germany
Danko Lazovic	23	10	8	0	127	0	0	-	Serbia & Mont
Michal Papadopoulos	21	6	5	0	57	0	0	-	Czech Republic
Josip Tadic	18	2	1	0	6	0	0	-	Croatia
Andriy Voronin	26	29	28	21	2119	6	0	-	Ukraine

TEAM OF THE SEASON

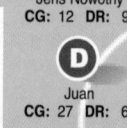

G: Hans-Jorg Butt CG: 34 DR: 62

D: Jens Nowotny CG: 12 DR: 92

D: Juan CG: 27 DR: 65

D: Frederik Stenman CG: 13 DR: 65

D: Roque Junior CG: 13 DR: 49

M: Tranquillo Barnetta CG: 21 SD: 20

M: Simon Rolfes CG: 28 SD: 18

M: Bernd Schneider CG: 29 SD: 17

M: Paul Freier CG: 15 SD: 16

F: Dimitar Berbatov CG: 34 SR: 146

F: Andriy Voronin CG: 21 SR: 353

MONTHLY POINTS TALLY

Month	Points	%
AUGUST	3	33%
SEPTEMBER	7	58%
OCTOBER	3	25%
NOVEMBER	4	44%
DECEMBER	2	22%
JANUARY	3	100%
FEBRUARY	9	60%
MARCH	4	33%
APRIL	12	100%
MAY	5	56%

LEAGUE GOALS

	PLAYER	MINS	GOALS	S RATE
1	Berbatov	3059	21	146
2	Rolfes	2613	7	373
3	Freier	1870	6	312
4	Barnetta	2162	6	360
5	Voronin	2119	6	353
6	Schneider	2579	4	645
7	Juan	2516	3	839
8	Krzynowek	963	2	482
9	Ramelow	2066	2	1033
10	Babic	1051	1	1051
11	Fritz	2167	1	2167
12	Butt	3060	1	3060
13	Athirson	1248	1	1248
	Other		3	
	TOTAL		64	

TOP POINT EARNERS

	PLAYER	GAMES	AV PTS
1	Frederik Stenman	13	2.38
2	Jens Nowotny	12	2.25
3	Clemens Fritz	22	1.82
4	Paul Freier	15	1.80
5	Bernd Schneider	29	1.72
6	Carsten Ramelow	23	1.65
7	Juan	27	1.63
8	Simon Rolfes	28	1.57
9	Hans-Jorg Butt	34	1.53
10	Dimitar Berbatov	34	1.53
	CLUB AVERAGE:		1.53

DISCIPLINARY RECORDS

	PLAYER	YELLOW	RED	AVE
1	Ramelow	8	1	229
2	Babic	4	0	262
3	Castro	4	0	328
4	Voronin	6	0	353
5	Nowotny	3	0	369
6	Freier	5	0	374
7	Athirson	3	0	416
8	Juan	6	0	419
9	Barnetta	5	0	432
10	Roque Junior	1	1	609
11	Stenman	2	0	647
12	Rolfes	4	0	653
13	Schneider	3	0	859
	Other	7	0	
	TOTAL	61	2	

KEY GOALKEEPER

Hans-Jorg Butt

Goals Conceded in the League	49	**Counting Games** League games when player was on pitch for at least 70 minutes	34
Defensive Rating Ave number of mins between League goals conceded while on the pitch	62	**Clean Sheets** In League games when player was on pitch for at least 70 minutes	5

KEY PLAYERS - DEFENDERS

Jens Nowotny

Goals Conceded Number of League goals conceded while the player was on the pitch	12	**Clean Sheets** In League games when player was on pitch for at least 70 minutes	3
Defensive Rating Ave number of mins between League goals conceded while on the pitch	92	**Club Defensive Rating** Average number of mins between League goals conceded by the club this season	62

	PLAYER	CON LGE	CLEAN SHEETS	DEF RATE
1	Jens Nowotny	12	3	92 mins
2	Frederik Stenman	20	4	65 mins
3	Juan	39	5	65 mins
4	Roque Junior	25	0	49 mins

KEY PLAYERS - MIDFIELDERS

Tranquillo Barnetta

Goals in the League	6	**Contribution to Attacking Power** Average number of minutes between League team goals while on pitch	50
Defensive Rating Average number of mins between League goals conceded while on the pitch	70	**Scoring Difference** Defensive Rating minus Contribution to Attacking Power	20

	PLAYER	LGE GOALS	DEF RATE	POWER	SCORE DIFF
1	Tranquillo Barnetta	6	70	50	20 mins
2	Simon Rolfes	7	67	49	18 mins
3	Bernd Schneider	4	63	46	17 mins
4	Paul Freier	6	58	42	16 mins

KEY PLAYERS - GOALSCORERS

Dimitar Berbatov

Goals in the League	21	**Player Strike Rate** Average number of minutes between League goals scored by player	146
Contribution to Attacking Power Average number of minutes between League team goals while on pitch	48	**Club Strike Rate** Average number of minutes between League goals scored by club	48

	PLAYER	LGE GOALS	POWER	STRIKE RATE
1	Dimitar Berbatov	21	48	146 mins
2	Paul Freier	6	42	312 mins
3	Andriy Voronin	6	52	353 mins
4	Tranquillo Barnetta	6	50	360 mins

Dimitar Berbatov

SQUAD APPEARANCES

Match	1	2	3	4	5	6	7	8	9	10	11	12	13	14	15	16	17	18	19	20	21	22	23	24	25	26	27	28	29	30	31	32	33	34	35	36
Venue	A	H	A	H	H	A	H	A	A	H	A	H	A	H	A	H	H	A	H	H	A	H	A	H	A	H	A	H	A	H	A	H	A	A	H	A
Competition	L	L	L	L	E	L	L	L	E	L	L	L	L	L	L	L	L	L	L	L	L	L	L	L	L	L	L	L	L	L	L	L	L	L	L	L
Result	W	L	L	D	L	W	W	L	L	D	L	D	D	W	D	L	L	D	D	W	L	W	L	W	W	D	L	L	W	W	W	W	W	W	D	D

Goalkeepers
- Rene Adler
- Hans-Jorg Butt
- Tom Starke

Defenders
- Athirson Mazolli Oliveira
- Jan Callsen-Bracker
- Sascha Dum
- Juan
- Ahmed Reda Madouni
- Jens Nowotny
- Roque Junior
- Frederik Stenman

Midfielders
- Marko Babic
- Tranquillo Barnetta
- Gonzalo Castro
- Paul Freier
- Jacek Krzynowek
- Carsten Ramelow
- Simon Rolfes
- Bernd Schneider

Forwards
- Dimitar Berbatov
- Clemens Fritz
- Danko Lazovic
- Michal Papadopoulos
- Josip Tadic
- Andriy Voronin

KEY: On all match; On bench; Subbed or sent off (Counting game); Subbed or sent off (playing less than 70 minutes); Subbed on from bench (Counting Game); Subbed on (playing less than 70 minutes); Subbed on and then subbed or sent off (Counting Game); Subbed on and then subbed or sent off (playing less than 70 minutes); Not in 16

HERTHA BERLIN

Final Position: **6th**

NICKNAME: FROSCHE

KEY: ☐ Won ☐ Drawn ☐ Lost

No	Comp	Opponent	Venue	Result	Score	Scorers	Attendance
1	gbl	**Hannover 96**	A	D	2-2	Marcelinho 49 pen; Wichinarek 54	40,473
2	gbl	**Eintr Frankfurt**	H	W	2-0	Schroder 53; Van Lent 78 og	45,000
3	gbl	**Bayern Munich**	A	L	0-3		56,000
4	gbl	**Wolfsburg**	H	W	3-0	Friedrich 70; Pantelic 75; Gilberto 90	40,754
5	uc1rl1	**Apoel Nicosia**	A	W	1-0	Marcelinho 90 pen	6,362
6	gbl	**Schalke**	A	D	0-0		60,740
7	gbl	**Duisburg**	H	W	3-2	Pantelic 6; Marcelinho 72 pen; Rafael 90	30,634
8	gbl	**Cologne**	A	W	1-0	Madlung 52	48,000
9	uc1rl2	**Apoel Nicosia**	H	W	3-1	Marcelinho 15; Rafael 25; Cairo 58	22,612
10	gbl	**W Bremen**	H	L	1-2	Dardai 48	60,000
11	gbl	**Arminia B**	A	L	0-3		20,117
12	ucgpc	**Halmstad**	A	W	1-0	Zecke 67	2,136
13	gbl	**Mainz**	H	W	3-1	Marcelinho 6,34; Pantelic 67	30,000
14	gbl	**Stuttgart**	A	D	3-3	Cairo 8; Rafael 67; Marcelinho 76	40,000
15	gbl	**Kaiserslautern**	H	W	3-0	Marcelinho 6; Pantelic 48; Rafael 52	35,000
16	gbl	**B Dortmund**	A	L	0-2		75,000
17	ucgpc	**Lens**	H	D	0-0		18,510
18	gbl	**B M'gladbach**	H	D	2-2	Basturk 68; Kovac 76	38,438
19	ucgpc	**Sampdoria**	A	D	0-0		16,507
20	gbl	**B Leverkusen**	A	W	2-1	Basturk 58; Marcelinho 64	20,000
21	gbl	**Hamburg**	A	L	1-2	Basturk 76	54,149
22	ucgpc	**S Bucharest**	H	D	0-0		15,603
23	gbl	**Nuremburg**	H	D	1-1	Madlung 86	30,000
24	gbl	**Hannover 96**	H	D	1-1	Van Burik 90	33,000
25	gbl	**Eintr Frankfurt**	A	D	1-1	Boateng 20	35,000
26	gbl	**Bayern Munich**	H	D	0-0		66,000
27	gbl	**Wolfsburg**	A	D	1-1	Marcelinho 32 pen	15,000
28	uc3rl1	**Rap Bucharest**	H	L	0-1		13,430
29	gbl	**Schalke**	H	L	1-2	Madlung 33	50,000
30	uc3rl2	**Rap Bucharest**	A	L	0-2		15,000
31	gbl	**Duisburg**	A	L	1-2	Basturk 68	20,100
32	gbl	**Cologne**	H	L	2-4	Pantelic 56,83	38,000
33	gbl	**W Bremen**	A	W	3-0	Boateng 53; Marcelinho 76; Basturk 83	40,000
34	gbl	**Arminia B**	H	W	1-0	Pantelic 61	48,000
35	gbl	**Mainz**	A	D	2-2	Pantelic 41,89	20,300
36	gbl	**Stuttgart**	H	W	2-0	Marcelinho 46,69 pen	48,000
37	gbl	**Kaiserslautern**	A	W	2-0	Pantelic 14; Gilberto 26	30,000
38	gbl	**B Dortmund**	H	D	0-0		60,000
39	gbl	**B M'gladbach**	A	D	2-2	Basturk 16; Kovac 87	45,000
40	gbl	**B Leverkusen**	H	L	1-5	Marcelinho 41	50,000
41	gbl	**Hamburg**	H	W	4-2	Kirschstein 13 og; Madlung 54; Kovac 69; Pantelic 72	74,000
42	gbl	**Nuremburg**	A	L	1-2	Dardai 41	45,000

LEAGUE APPEARANCES, BOOKINGS AND CAPS

	AGE (on 01/07/06)	IN NAMED 18	APPEARANCES	COUNTING GAMES	MINUTES ON PITCH	YELLOW CARDS	RED CARDS	CAPS THIS SEASON	NATIONAL SIDE
Goalkeepers									
Christian Fiedler	31	29	29	29	2610	1	0	-	Germany
Gerhard Tremmel	27	8	5	5	450	0	0	-	Germany
Defenders									
Sofian Chahed	23	15	15	14	1214	1	0	-	Germany
Malik Fathi	22	26	26	23	2206	3	1	-	Germany
Arne Friedrich	27	31	31	31	2768	3	1	7	Germany (19)
Alexander Madlung	23	21	21	12	1233	4	2	-	Germany
Christopher Samba	22	14	12	3	351	2	0	-	France
Josip Simunic	28	18	18	17	1568	11	1	6	Croatia (23)
Dick Van Burik	32	26	26	22	2093	1	0	-	Holland
Midfielders									
Yildiray Basturk	27	27	27	23	2213	3	0	-	Turkey
Kevin-Prince Boateng	19	21	21	17	1580	8	0	-	Germany
Ante Covic	30	0	0	0	0	0	0	-	Germany
Pal Dardai	30	16	15	7	769	1	0	1	Hungary (54)
Gilberto	29	23	23	20	1868	6	2	1	Brazil (1)
Nico Kovac	34	28	28	19	2017	8	0	7	Croatia (23)
Thorben Marx	25	9	8	2	363	2	0	-	Germany
Andreas Neuendorf	31	25	25	4	896	7	1	-	Germany
Andreas Schmidt	32	1	1	1	90	0	0	-	Germany
Oliver Schroder	26	19	18	10	1165	1	0	-	Germany
Forwards									
Ellery Cairo	27	18	18	11	1111	3	0	-	Holland
Ashkan Dejagah	20	5	3	0	51	0	0	-	Iran
Marcelinho	31	32	32	30	2749	7	1	-	Brazil
Solomon Okoronkwo	19	12	11	1	399	0	0	-	Nigeria
Marko Pantelic	27	28	28	24	2253	5	0	-	Serbia & Mont
Nando Rafael	22	12	12	5	715	2	0	-	Angola
Sejad Salihovic	21	1	0	0	0	0	0	-	Bosnia
Vaclav Sverkos	22	10	10	3	458	3	0	-	Czech Republic
Artur Wichinarek	29	4	3	1	140	0	0	-	Poland

TEAM OF THE SEASON

- **G** Christian Fiedler — CG: 29 DR: 62
- **D** Malik Fathi — CG: 23 DR: 85
- **D** Dick Van Burik — CG: 22 DR: 84
- **D** Sofian Chahed — CG: 14 DR: 76
- **D** Josip Simunic — CG: 17 DR: 68
- **M** Kevin-Prince Boateng — CG: 17 SD: 12
- **M** Gilberto — CG: 20 SD: 9
- **M** Yildiray Basturk — CG: 23 SD: 4
- **M** Nico Kovac — CG: 19 SD: -9
- **F** Marko Pantelic — CG: 24 SR: 205
- **F** Marcelinho — CG: 30 SR: 229

MONTHLY POINTS TALLY

Month	Points	%
AUGUST	4	44%
SEPTEMBER	10	83%
OCTOBER	4	33%
NOVEMBER	4	44%
DECEMBER	4	44%
JANUARY	1	33%
FEBRUARY	3	20%
MARCH	7	58%
APRIL	8	67%
MAY	3	33%

LEAGUE GOALS

	PLAYER	MINS	GOALS	S RATE
1	Marcelinho	2749	**12**	229
2	Pantelic	2253	**11**	205
3	Basturk	2213	**6**	369
4	Madlung	1233	**3**	411
5	Kovac	2017	**3**	672
6	Rafael	715	**3**	238
7	Gilberto	1868	**2**	934
8	Boateng	1580	**2**	790
9	Dardai	769	**2**	385
10	Friedrich	2768	**1**	2768
11	Schroder	1165	**1**	1165
12	Wichinarek	140	**1**	140
13	Cairo	1111	**1**	1111
	Other		**4**	
	TOTAL		**52**	

TOP POINT EARNERS

	PLAYER	GAMES	AV PTS
1	Dick Van Burik	22	**1.77**
2	Josip Simunic	17	**1.71**
3	Malik Fathi	23	**1.70**
4	Gilberto	20	**1.60**
5	Marko Pantelic	24	**1.54**
6	Marcelinho	30	**1.47**
7	Christian Fiedler	29	**1.45**
8	Kevin-Prince Boateng	17	**1.41**
9	Yildiray Basturk	23	**1.39**
10	Nico Kovac	19	**1.37**
	CLUB AVERAGE:		**1.41**

DISCIPLINARY RECORDS

	PLAYER	YELLOW	RED	AVE
1	Neuendorf	7	1	**112**
2	Simunic	11	1	**130**
3	Sverkos	3	0	**152**
4	Boateng	8	0	**197**
5	Madlung	4	2	**205**
6	Gilberto	6	2	**233**
7	Kovac	8	0	**252**
8	Marcelinho	7	1	**343**
9	Rafael	2	0	**357**
10	Cairo	3	0	**370**
11	Pantelic	5	0	**450**
12	Fathi	3	1	**551**
13	Friedrich	3	1	**692**
	Other	8	0	
	TOTAL	**78**	**9**	

KEY GOALKEEPER

Christian Fiedler

Goals Conceded in the League	42	**Counting Games** League games when player was on pitch for at least 70 minutes	29
Defensive Rating Ave number of mins between League goals conceded while on the pitch	62	**Clean Sheets** In games when player was on pitch for at least 70 minutes	9

KEY PLAYERS - DEFENDERS

Malik Fathi

Goals Conceded Number of League goals conceded while the player was on the pitch	26	**Clean Sheets** In League games when player was on pitch for at least 70 minutes	10
Defensive Rating Ave number of mins between League goals conceded while on the pitch	85	**Club Defensive Rating** Average number of mins between League goals conceded by the club this season	64

	PLAYER	CON LGE	CLEAN SHEETS	DEF RATE
1	Malik Fathi	26	10	85 mins
2	Dick Van Burik	25	10	84 mins
3	Sofian Chahed	16	6	76 mins
4	Josip Simunic	23	7	68 mins

KEY PLAYERS - MIDFIELDERS

Kevin-Prince Boateng

Goals in the League	2	**Contribution to Attacking Power** Average number of minutes between League team goals while on pitch	54
Defensive Rating Average number of mins between League goals conceded while on the pitch	66	**Scoring Difference** Defensive Rating minus Contribution to Attacking Power	12

	PLAYER	LGE GOALS	DEF RATE	POWER	SCORE DIFF
1	Kevin-Prince Boateng	2	66	54	12 mins
2	Gilberto	2	64	55	9 mins
3	Yildiray Basturk	6	71	67	4 mins
4	Nico Kovac	3	61	70	-9 mins

KEY PLAYERS - GOALSCORERS

Marko Pantelic

Goals in the League	11	**Player Strike Rate** Average number of minutes between League goals scored by player	205
Contribution to Attacking Power Average number of minutes between League team goals while on pitch	59	**Club Strike Rate** Average number of minutes between League goals scored by club	59

	PLAYER	LGE GOALS	POWER	STRIKE RATE
1	Marko Pantelic	11	59	205 mins
2	Marcelinho	12	58	229 mins
3	Yildiray Basturk	6	67	369 mins
4	Alexander Madlung	3	65	411 mins

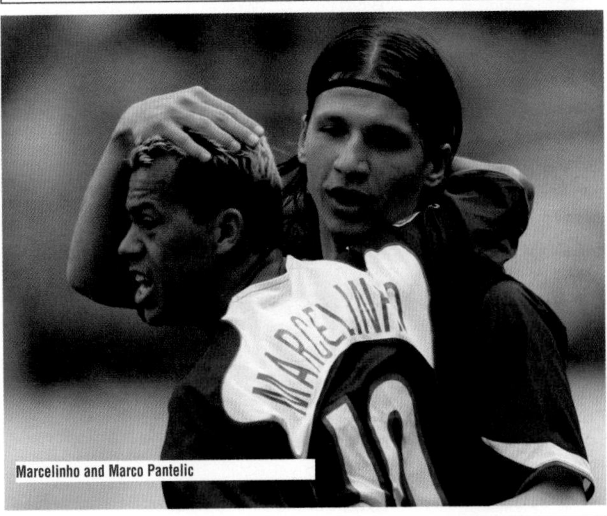

Marcelinho and Marco Pantelic

SQUAD APPEARANCES

Match	1	2	3	4	5	6	7	8	9	10	11	12	13	14	15	16	17	18	19	20	21	22	23	24	25	26	27	28	29	30	31	32	33	34	35	36	37	38	39	40	41	42
Venue	A	H	A	H	A	A	H	A	H	H	A	A	H	A	H	A	H	H	A	A	A	H	H	H	A	H	A	H	H	A	A	H	A	H	A	H	A	H	A	H	H	A
Competition	L	L	L	L	E	L	L	L	E	L	L	E	L	L	L	L	E	L	E	L	L	E	L	L	L	L	L	E	L	E	L	L	L	L	L	L	L	L	L	L	L	L
Result	D	W	L	W	W	D	W	W	W	L	L	W	W	D	W	L	D	D	D	W	L	D	D	D	D	D	D	L	L	L	L	L	W	W	D	W	W	D	D	L	W	L

Goalkeepers
Christian Fiedler
Gerhard Tremmel

Defenders
Sofian Chahed
Malik Fathi
Arne Friedrich
Alexander Madlung
Christopher Samba
Josip Simunic
Dick Van Burik

Midfielders
Yildiray Basturk
Kevin-Prince Boateng
Ante Covic
Pal Dardai
Gilberto
Nico Kovac
Thorben Marx
Andreas Neuendorf
Andreas Schmidt
Oliver Schroder

Forwards
Ellery Cairo
Ashkan Dejagah
Marcelinho
Solomon Okoronkwo
Marko Pantelic
Nando Rafael
Sejad Salihovic
Vaclav Sverkos
Artur Wichinarek

KEY: On all match | On bench | Subbed or sent off (Counting game) | Subbed or sent off (playing less than 70 minutes) | Subbed on from bench (Counting Game) | Subbed on (playing less than 70 minutes) | Subbed on and then subbed or sent off (Counting Game) | Subbed on and then subbed or sent off (playing less than 70 minutes) | Not in 16

BORUSSIA DORTMUND

Final Position: **7th**

NICKNAME: DIE SCHWARZ-GELBEN

KEY: ☐Won ☐Drawn ☐Lost

		Opponent			Score	Scorers	Attendance
1	gbl	Wolfsburg	A	D	2-2	Smolarek 56; Koller 82	22,000
2	gbl	Schalke	H	L	1-2	Smolarek 17	81,264
3	gbl	Duisburg	A	D	1-1	Ricken 61	31,502
4	gbl	Cologne	H	W	2-1	Ricken 25,73	78,000
5	gbl	W Bremen	A	L	2-3	Smolarek 8,69	38,000
6	gbl	Arminia B	H	W	2-0	Koller 27; Smolarek 83	62,100
7	gbl	Mainz	A	D	1-1	Metzelder, C 90	20,300
8	gbl	Stuttgart	H	D	0-0		73,100
9	gbl	Kaiserslautern	A	D	3-3	Smolarek 7,16,40	33,000
10	gbl	Hamburg	H	D	1-1	Metzelder, C 58	76,000
11	gbl	B M'gladbach	H	W	2-1	Kehl 22; Smolarek 90	80,000
12	gbl	B Leverkusen	A	L	1-2	Ricken 69	22,500
13	gbl	Hertha Berlin	H	W	2-0	Smolarek 40,45	75,000
14	gbl	Nuremburg	A	W	2-1	Odonkor 13; Sahin 42	27,500
15	gbl	Hannover 96	H	L	0-2		75,000
16	gbl	Eintr Frankfurt	A	L	0-2		47,000
17	gbl	Bayern Munich	H	L	1-2	Kringe 79	81,264
18	gbl	Wolfsburg	H	W	3-2	Worns 24; Smolarek 32; Gambino 69	65,000
19	gbl	Schalke	A	D	0-0		61,524
20	gbl	Duisburg	H	W	2-0	Brzenska 67; Rosicky 87 pen	65,000
21	gbl	Cologne	A	D	0-0		49,000
22	gbl	W Bremen	H	L	0-1		68,000
23	gbl	Arminia B	A	L	0-1		25,000
24	gbl	Mainz	H	D	1-1	Worns 27	68,000
25	gbl	Stuttgart	A	D	0-0		44,000
26	gbl	Kaiserslautern	H	W	2-1	Dede 25; Kringe 64	68,000
27	gbl	Hamburg	A	W	4-2	Smolarek 25; Rosicky 68,90; Kringe 83	56,000
28	gbl	B M'gladbach	A	L	1-2	Rosicky 16 pen	54,019
29	gbl	B Leverkusen	H	L	1-2	Brzenska 27	75,000
30	gbl	Hertha Berlin	A	D	0-0		60,000
31	gbl	Nuremburg	H	W	2-1	Kringe 19,76	70,000
32	gbl	Hannover 96	A	W	2-1	Rosicky 60; Worns 82	40,000
33	gbl	Eintr Frankfurt	H	D	1-1	Gambino 87	80,000
34	gbl	Bayern Munich	A	D	3-3	Koller 2,76; Degen 64	69,000

LEAGUE APPEARANCES, BOOKINGS AND CAPS

	AGE (on 01/07/06)	IN NAMED 18	APPEARANCES	COUNTING GAMES	MINUTES ON PITCH	YELLOW CARDS	RED CARDS	CAPS THIS SEASON	NATIONAL SIDE
Goalkeepers									
Dennis Gentenaar	30	13	10	10	900	0	0	-	Holland
Roman Weidenfeller	25	25	25	25	2250	2	0	-	Germany
Defenders									
Markus Brzenska	22	22	21	16	1583	6	0	-	Germany
Philipp Degen	23	32	31	25	2388	2	0	11	Switzerland (35)
Uwe Hunemeier	20	4	2	2	181	0	0	-	Germany
Sebastian Kehl	26	29	29	29	2606	5	0	-	Germany
Christoph Metzelder	25	21	20	15	1452	2	0	5	Germany (19)
Malte Metzelder	24	2	2	1	92	0	0	-	Germany
Michael Parensen	20	1	0	0	0	0	0	-	Germany
Sascha Rammel	21	1	0	0	0	0	0	-	Germany
Kosi Saka	20	5	5	0	29	0	1	-	Congo DR
Christian Worns	34	27	27	27	2430	7	0	2	Germany (19)
Midfielders									
Nizamettin Caliskan	19	2	2	1	77	0	0	-	Germany
Leonardo Dede	28	31	31	30	2733	1	0	-	Brazil
Florian Kringe	23	29	29	28	2535	3	0	-	Germany
Marc-Andre Kruska	19	24	24	8	997	5	0	-	Germany
Lars Ricken	29	10	10	3	604	0	0	-	Germany
Tomas Rosicky	25	28	28	25	2311	7	1	5	Czech Republic (2)
Nuri Sahin	17	24	23	20	1864	2	0	-	Turkey
Sahr Senesie	21	1	1	1	90	0	0	-	Sierra Leone
Forwards									
Mehmet Akgun	19	1	0	0	0	0	0	-	Germany
Matthew Amoah	25	8	8	2	401	0	0	7	Ghana (48)
Delron Buckley	28	28	28	11	1545	1	0	1	South Africa (53)
Salvatore Gambino	22	16	15	3	595	1	0	-	Italy
Jan Koller	33	9	9	5	623	0	0	4	Czech Republic (2)
David Odonkor	22	33	33	19	2305	3	0	1	Germany (19)
Ebi Smolarek	25	34	34	32	2963	3	0	7	Poland (29)
Marcus Steegmann	25	4	2	0	19	0	0	-	Germany
Cedric van der Gun	27	3	3	0	69	1	0	-	Holland

TEAM OF THE SEASON

G — Roman Weidenfeller — CG: 25 DR: 73

D — Sebastian Kehl — CG: 29 DR: 81

D — Markus Brzenska — CG: 16 DR: 79

D — Philipp Degen — CG: 25 DR: 75

D — Christian Worns — CG: 27 DR: 74

M — Leonardo Dede — CG: 30 SD: 16

M — Tomas Rosicky — CG: 25 SD: 10

M — Florian Kringe — CG: 28 SD: 2

M — Nuri Sahin — CG: 20 SD: -5

F — Ebi Smolarek — CG: 32 SR: 228

F — David Odonkor — CG: 19 SR: 2305

MONTHLY POINTS TALLY

Month	Points	%
AUGUST	2	22%
SEPTEMBER	7	58%
OCTOBER	6	50%
NOVEMBER	6	67%
DECEMBER	0	0%
JANUARY	3	100%
FEBRUARY	5	33%
MARCH	8	67%
APRIL	4	33%
MAY	5	56%

LEAGUE GOALS

	PLAYER	MINS	GOALS	S RATE
1	Smolarek	2963	**13**	228
2	Rosicky	2311	**5**	462
3	Kringe	2535	**5**	507
4	Koller	623	**4**	156
5	Ricken	604	**4**	151
6	Worns	2430	**3**	810
7	Metzelder, C	1452	**2**	726
8	Brzenska	1583	**2**	792
9	Gambino	595	**2**	298
10	Sahin	1864	**1**	1864
11	Degen	2388	**1**	2388
12	Odonkor	2305	**1**	2305
13	Kehl	2606	**1**	2606
	Other		**1**	
	TOTAL		**45**	

TOP POINT EARNERS

	PLAYER	GAMES	AV PTS
1	Leonardo Dede	30	**1.43**
2	David Odonkor	19	**1.42**
3	Sebastian Kehl	29	**1.41**
4	Ebi Smolarek	32	**1.41**
5	Roman Weidenfeller	25	**1.40**
6	Christian Worns	27	**1.37**
7	Markus Brzenska	16	**1.31**
8	Philipp Degen	25	**1.28**
9	Florian Kringe	28	**1.25**
10	Nuri Sahin	20	**1.25**
	CLUB AVERAGE:		**1.35**

DISCIPLINARY RECORDS

	PLAYER	YELLOW	RED	AVE
1	Kruska	5	0	**199**
2	Brzenska	6	0	**263**
3	Rosicky	7	1	**288**
4	Worns	7	0	**347**
5	Kehl	5	0	**521**
6	Gambino	1	0	**595**
7	Metzelder, C	2	0	**726**
8	Odonkor	3	0	**768**
9	Kringe	3	0	**845**
10	Sahin	2	0	**932**
11	Smolarek	3	0	**987**
12	Weidenfeller	2	0	**1125**
13	Degen	2	0	**1194**
	Other	2	0	
	TOTAL	**50**	**1**	

KEY GOALKEEPER

Roman Weidenfeller			
Goals Conceded in the League	31	**Counting Games** League games when player was on pitch for at least 70 minutes	25
Defensive Rating Ave number of mins between League goals conceded while on the pitch	73	**Clean Sheets** In games when player was on pitch for at least 70 minutes	6

KEY PLAYERS - DEFENDERS

Sebastian Kehl			
Goals Conceded Number of League goals conceded while the player was on the pitch	32	**Clean Sheets** In League games when player was on pitch for at least 70 minutes	8
Defensive Rating Ave number of mins between League goals conceded while on the pitch	81	**Club Defensive Rating** Average number of mins between League goals conceded by the club this season	73

	PLAYER	CON LGE	CLEAN SHEETS	DEF RATE
1	Sebastian Kehl	32	8	81 mins
2	Markus Brzenska	20	6	79 mins
3	Philipp Degen	32	7	75 mins
4	Christian Worns	33	6	74 mins

KEY PLAYERS - MIDFIELDERS

Leonardo Dede			
Goals in the League	1	**Contribution to Attacking Power** Average number of minutes between League team goals while on pitch	62
Defensive Rating Average number of mins between League goals conceded while on the pitch	78	**Scoring Difference** Defensive Rating minus Contribution to Attacking Power	16

	PLAYER	LGE GOALS	DEF RATE	POWER	SCORE DIFF
1	Leonardo Dede	1	78	62	16 mins
2	Tomas Rosicky	5	80	70	10 mins
3	Florian Kringe	5	67	65	2 mins
4	Nuri Sahin	1	64	69	-5 mins

KEY PLAYERS - GOALSCORERS

Ebi Smolarek			
Goals in the League	13	**Player Strike Rate** Average number of minutes between League goals scored by player	228
Contribution to Attacking Power Average number of minutes between League team goals while on pitch	67	**Club Strike Rate** Average number of minutes between League goals scored by club	68

	PLAYER	LGE GOALS	POWER	STRIKE RATE
1	Ebi Smolarek	13	67	228 mins
2	Tomas Rosicky	5	70	462 mins
3	Florian Kringe	5	65	507 mins
4	Christoph Metzelder	2	63	726 mins

Tomas Rosicky, David Odonkor and Ebi Smolarek

SQUAD APPEARANCES

latch	1	2	3	4	5	6	7	8	9	10	11	12	13	14	15	16	17	18	19	20	21	22	23	24	25	26	27	28	29	30	31	32	33	34
enue	A	H	A	H	A	H	A	H	A	H	H	A	H	A	H	A	H	H	A	H	A	H	A	H	A	H	A	A	H	A	H	A	H	A
ompetition	L	L	L	L	L	L	L	L	L	L	L	L	L	L	L	L	L	L	L	L	L	L	L	L	L	L	L	L	L	L	L	L	L	L
esult	D	L	D	W	L	W	D	D	D	D	W	L	W	W	L	L	L	W	D	W	D	L	L	D	D	W	W	L	L	D	W	W	D	D

oalkeepers
ennis Gentenaar
oman Weidenfeller

efenders
larkus Brzenska
hilipp Degen
we Hunemeier
ebastian Kehl
hristoph Metzelder
lalte Metzelder
lichael Parensen
ascha Rammel
osi Saka
hristian Worns

lidfielders
lizamettin Caliskan
eonardo Dede
lorian Kringe
larc-Andre Kruska
ars Ricken
omas Rosicky
luri Sahin
ahr Senesie

orwards
lehmet Akgun
latthew Amoah
elron Buckley
alvatore Gambino
an Koller
avid Odonkor
bi Smolarek
larcus Steegmann
edric van der Gun

KEY: On all match · On bench · Subbed or sent off (Counting game) · Subbed or sent off (playing less than 70 minutes) · Subbed on from bench (Counting Game) · Subbed on (playing less than 70 minutes) · Subbed on and then subbed or sent off (Counting Game) · Subbed on and then subbed or sent off (playing less than 70 minutes) · Not in 16

NUREMBURG

Final Position: **8th**

KEY: □Won □Drawn □Lost

							Attendance
1	gbl	**Hamburg**	A	L	0-3		45,000
2	gbl	**Hannover 96**	H	D	1-1	Mintal 90	35,000
3	gbl	**Eintr Frankfurt**	A	L	0-1		40,000
4	gbl	**Bayern Munich**	H	L	1-2	Pinola 20	47,000
5	gbl	**Wolfsburg**	A	D	1-1	Schroth 88	15,000
6	gbl	**Schalke**	H	D	1-1	Kiessling 21	20,000
7	gbl	**Duisburg**	A	L	0-1		14,000
8	gbl	**Cologne**	H	W	2-1	Kiessling 32,67	23,000
9	gbl	**W Bremen**	A	L	2-6	Kiessling 16; Schroth 57	40,000
10	gbl	**Arminia B**	H	L	2-3	Reinhardt 2; Banovic 83,83	18,000
11	gbl	**Mainz**	A	L	1-4	Kiessling 13	20,300
12	gbl	**Stuttgart**	H	L	0-1		20,000
13	gbl	**Kaiserslautern**	A	W	3-1	Banovic 17; Muller, L 78; Saenko 82	25,000
14	gbl	**B Dortmund**	H	L	1-2	Kiessling 88	27,500
15	gbl	**B M'gladbach**	A	W	1-0	Nikl 62	45,000
16	gbl	**B Leverkusen**	H	D	1-1	Schroth 29	20,000
17	gbl	**Hertha Berlin**	A	D	1-1	Saenko 55	30,000
18	gbl	**Hamburg**	H	W	2-1	Saenko 67; Kiessling 73	23,928
19	gbl	**Hannover 96**	A	D	1-1	Vittek 56	32,000
20	gbl	**Eintr Frankfurt**	H	L	0-1		30,000
21	gbl	**Bayern Munich**	A	L	1-2	Vittek 35	69,000
22	gbl	**Wolfsburg**	H	W	1-0	Saenko 16	22,000
23	gbl	**Schalke**	A	L	0-2		61,524
24	gbl	**Duisburg**	H	W	3-0	Vittek 8,15,86	40,000
25	gbl	**Cologne**	A	W	4-3	Vittek 6 pen,16,22 pen; Saenko 58	47,000
26	gbl	**W Bremen**	H	W	3-1	Vittek 21,69; Schroth 36	28,000
27	gbl	**Arminia B**	A	D	0-0		22,500
28	gbl	**Mainz**	H	W	3-0	Saenko 3; Kiessling 68; Vittek 79	30,000
29	gbl	**Stuttgart**	A	L	0-1		37,000
30	gbl	**Kaiserslautern**	H	W	3-2	Vittek 13,87; Paulus 62	47,250
31	gbl	**B Dortmund**	A	L	1-2	Nikl 29	70,000
32	gbl	**B M'gladbach**	H	W	5-2	Vittek 14,65; Polak 59; Saenko 86; Kiessling 88	42,000
33	gbl	**B Leverkusen**	A	D	2-2	Mnari 35; Kiessling 90	22,500
34	gbl	**Hertha Berlin**	H	W	2-1	Vittek 30; Saenko 86	45,000

LEAGUE APPEARANCES, BOOKINGS AND CAPS

	AGE (on 01/07/06)	IN NAMED 18	APPEARANCES	COUNTING GAMES	MINUTES ON PITCH	YELLOW CARDS	RED CARDS	CAPS THIS SEASON	NATIONAL SIDE
Goalkeepers									
Daniel Klewer	29	3	0	0	0	0	0	-	Germany
Raphael Schafer	27	34	34	33	3015	4	0	-	Germany
Phillip Tschauner	20	1	1	0	45	0	0	-	Germany
Defenders									
Bartosz Bosacki	30	5	4	2	232	0	1	3	Poland (29)
Glauber	22	13	12	8	863	5	1	-	Brazil
Benjamin Lense	27	12	11	7	822	2	0	-	Germany
Sven Muller	26	17	17	8	990	1	0	-	Germany
Marek Nikl	30	27	27	21	2067	6	1	-	Czech Republic
Thomas Paulus	24	19	18	9	1054	2	0	-	Germany
Javier Horacio Pinola	23	25	25	21	2071	12	0	-	Argentina
Dominik Reinhardt	21	24	24	19	1916	3	0	-	Germany
Andreas Wolf	24	20	20	13	1480	7	0	-	Germany
Midfielders									
Ivica Banovic	25	23	23	10	1300	4	1	-	Croatia
Mario Cantaluppi	32	32	32	31	2787	8	0	-	Switzerland
Adel Chedli	29	5	4	0	145	1	0	8	Tunisia (21)
Jan Kristiansen	24	7	7	3	314	0	0	1	Denmark (19)
Marek Mintal	28	4	4	3	275	0	0	2	Slovakia (41)
Jawhar Mnari	29	24	22	17	1691	4	0	8	Tunisia (21)
Lars Muller	30	17	16	9	998	3	0	-	Germany
Sezer Ozturk	20	3	2	1	108	1	0	-	Turkey
Jan Polak	25	32	32	28	2654	6	1	9	Czech Republic (2)
Samuel Slovak	30	1	1	0	24	0	0	-	Slovakia
Sebastian Szikal	19	1	1	0	4	0	0	-	Germany
Maik Wagefeld	25	4	3	0	70	0	0	-	Germany
Forwards									
Pagenburg Chhunly	19	1	1	0	17	0	0	-	Germany
Markus Daun	25	14	13	4	633	0	0	-	Germany
Stefan Kiessling	22	31	31	19	2006	6	0	-	Germany
Ivan Saenko	23	25	25	17	1894	5	0	-	Russia
Markus Schroth	31	29	29	14	1919	1	0	-	Germany
Robert Vittek	24	30	30	21	2148	1	0	7	Slovakia (41)

TEAM OF THE SEASON

G
Raphael Schafer
CG: 33 DR: 62

D
Javier Horacio Pinola
CG: 21 DR: 77

D
Marek Nikl
CG: 21 DR: 71

D
Andreas Wolf
CG: 13 DR: 64

D
Dominik Reinhardt
CG: 19 DR: 58

M
Jawhar Mnari
CG: 17 SD: 2

M
Jan Polak
CG: 28 SD: 0

M
Mario Cantaluppi
CG: 31 SD: -1

M
Ivica Banovic*
CG: 10 SD: -24

F
Robert Vittek
CG: 21 SR: 134

F
Stefan Kiessling
CG: 19 SR: 201

MONTHLY POINTS TALLY

AUGUST	1	11%
SEPTEMBER	2	17%
OCTOBER	3	25%
NOVEMBER	3	33%
DECEMBER	5	56%
JANUARY	3	100%
FEBRUARY	4	27%
MARCH	10	83%
APRIL	6	50%
MAY	7	78%

LEAGUE GOALS

	PLAYER	MINS	GOALS	S RATE
1	Vittek	2148	16	134
2	Kiessling	2006	10	201
3	Saenko	1894	8	237
4	Schroth	1919	4	480
5	Banovic	1300	3	433
6	Nikl	2067	2	1034
7	Reinhardt	1916	1	1916
8	Polak	2654	1	2654
9	Paulus	1054	1	1054
10	Mnari	1691	1	1691
11	Mintal	275	1	275
12	Pinola	2071	1	2071
13	Muller, L	998	1	998
	Other		0	
	TOTAL		50	

TOP POINT EARNERS

	PLAYER	GAMES	AV PTS
1	Markus Schroth	14	1.86
2	Ivan Saenko	17	1.76
3	Robert Vittek	21	1.52
4	Dominik Reinhardt	19	1.47
5	Jawhar Mnari	17	1.47
6	Marek Nikl	21	1.38
7	Raphael Schafer	33	1.33
8	Javier Horacio Pinola	21	1.33
9	Mario Cantaluppi	31	1.29
10	Jan Polak	28	1.29
	CLUB AVERAGE:		1.29

DISCIPLINARY RECORDS

	PLAYER	YELLOW	RED	AVE
1	Glauber	5	1	143
2	Pinola	12	0	172
3	Wolf	7	0	211
4	Banovic	4	1	260
5	Nikl	6	1	295
6	Muller, L	3	0	332
7	Kiessling	6	0	334
8	Cantaluppi	8	0	348
9	Saenko	5	0	378
10	Polak	6	1	379
11	Lense	2	0	411
12	Mnari	4	0	422
13	Paulus	2	0	527
	Other	10	0	
	TOTAL	80	4	

KEY GOALKEEPER

Raphael Schafer

Goals Conceded in the League	49	**Counting Games** League games when player was on pitch for at least 70 minutes	33
Defensive Rating Ave number of mins between League goals conceded while on the pitch	62	**Clean Sheets** In League games when player was on pitch for at least 70 minutes	5

KEY PLAYERS - DEFENDERS

Javier Horacio Pinola

Goals Conceded Number of League goals conceded while the player was on the pitch	27	**Clean Sheets** In League games when player was on pitch for at least 70 minutes	5
Defensive Rating Ave number of mins between League goals conceded while on the pitch	77	**Club Defensive Rating** Average number of mins between League goals conceded by the club this season	60

	PLAYER	CON LGE	CLEAN SHEETS	DEF RATE
1	Javier Horacio Pinola	27	5	77 mins
2	Marek Nikl	29	5	71 mins
3	Andreas Wolf	23	1	64 mins
4	Dominik Reinhardt	33	3	58 mins

KEY PLAYERS - MIDFIELDERS

Jawhar Mnari

Goals in the League	1	**Contribution to Attacking Power** Average number of minutes between League team goals while on pitch	58
Defensive Rating Average number of mins between League goals conceded while on the pitch	60	**Scoring Difference** Defensive Rating minus Contribution to Attacking Power	2

	PLAYER	LGE GOALS	DEF RATE	POWER	SCORE DIFF
1	Jawhar Mnari	1	60	58	2 mins
2	Jan Polak	1	63	63	0 mins
3	Mario Cantaluppi	0	58	59	-1 mins

KEY PLAYERS - GOALSCORERS

Robert Vittek

Goals in the League	16	**Player Strike Rate** Average number of minutes between League goals scored by player	134
Contribution to Attacking Power Average number of minutes between League team goals while on pitch	60	**Club Strike Rate** Average number of minutes between League goals scored by club	61

	PLAYER	LGE GOALS	POWER	STRIKE RATE
1	Robert Vittek	16	60	134 mins
2	Stefan Kiessling	10	54	201 mins
3	Ivan Saenko	8	53	237 mins
4	Markus Schroth	4	62	480 mins

Robert Vittek

SQUAD APPEARANCES

Match	1	2	3	4	5	6	7	8	9	10	11	12	13	14	15	16	17	18	19	20	21	22	23	24	25	26	27	28	29	30	31	32	33	34
Venue	A	H	A	H	A	H	A	H	A	H	A	H	A	H	A	H	A	H	A	H	A	H	A	H	A	H	A	H	A	H	A	H	A	H
Competition	L	L	L	L	L	L	L	L	L	L	L	L	L	L	L	L	L	L	L	L	L	L	L	L	L	L	L	L	L	L	L	L	L	L
Result	L	D	L	L	D	D	L	W	L	L	L	L	W	L	W	D	D	W	D	L	L	W	L	W	W	W	D	W	L	W	L	W	D	W

Goalkeepers
Daniel Klewer
Raphael Schafer
Phillip Tschauner

Defenders
Bartosz Bosacki
Glauber
Benjamin Lense
Sven Muller
Marek Nikl
Thomas Paulus
Javier Horacio Pinola
Dominik Reinhardt
Andreas Wolf

Midfielders
Ivica Banovic
Mario Cantaluppi
Adel Chedli
Jan Kristiansen
Marek Mintal
Jawhar Mnari
Lars Muller
Sezer Ozturk
Jan Polak
Samuel Slovak
Sebastian Szikal
Maik Wagefeld

Forwards
Pagenburg Chhunly
Markus Daun
Stefan Kiessling
Ivan Saenko
Markus Schroth
Robert Vittek

KEY: On all match; On bench; Subbed or sent off (Counting game); Subbed or sent off (playing less than 70 minutes); Subbed on from bench (Counting Game); Subbed on (playing less than 70 minutes); Subbed on and then subbed or sent off (Counting Game); Subbed on and then subbed or sent off (playing less than 70 minutes); Not in 16

VfB STUTTGART

Final Position: **9th**

NICKNAME: DIE SCHWABEN

KEY: ☐Won ☐Drawn ☐Lost

	Comp	Opponent	H/A	Res	Score	Scorers	Attendance
1	gbl	Duisburg	A	D	1-1	Cacau 5	31,500
2	gbl	Cologne	H	L	2-3	Streller 58; Tiffert 69	49,000
3	gbl	W Bremen	A	D	1-1	Tomasson 50	35,000
4	gbl	Arminia B	H	D	1-1	Tomasson 57	30,000
5	uc1rl1	Domzale	H	W	2-0	Tomasson 7; Gentner 89	12,000
6	gbl	Mainz	A	W	2-1	Tomasson 76; Gomez 87	20,000
7	gbl	Hamburg	H	L	1-2	Gomez 53	35,000
8	gbl	Kaiserslautern	H	W	1-0	Tomasson 10	35,000
9	uc1rl2	Domzale	A	L	0-1		2,600
10	gbl	B Dortmund	A	D	0-0		73,100
11	gbl	B M'gladbach	H	D	1-1	Strasser 90 og	45,000
12	ucgpg	Rennes	A	W	2-0	Tomasson 87; Ljuboja 90 pen	22,847
13	gbl	B Leverkusen	A	D	1-1	Ljuboja 72 pen	20,000
14	gbl	Hertha Berlin	H	D	3-3	Ljuboja 52; Cacau 66; Gomez 83	40,000
15	ucgpg	Shak Donetsk	H	L	0-2		15,000
16	gbl	Nuremburg	A	W	1-0	Tiffert 10	20,000
17	gbl	Hannover 96	H	D	2-2	Tomasson 11,67	32,000
18	ucgpg	PAOK Salonika	A	W	2-1	Ljuboja 85,90 pen	35,000
19	gbl	Eintr Frankfurt	A	D	1-1	Ljuboja 63	47,000
20	gbl	Bayern Munich	H	D	0-0		57,000
21	gbl	Wolfsburg	A	W	1-0	Meissner 62	23,696
22	ucgpg	Rap Bucharest	H	W	2-1	Gomez 20,37	14,000
23	gbl	Schalke	H	W	2-0	Gomez 48; Ljuboja 66	50,000
24	gbl	Duisburg	H	L	0-1		35,000
25	gbl	Cologne	A	D	0-0		49,000
26	gbl	W Bremen	H	D	0-0		50,000
27	gbl	Arminia B	A	L	1-2	Magnin 37	20,000
28	uc3rl1	Middlesbrough	H	L	1-2	Ljuboja 85	21,000
29	gbl	Mainz	H	W	2-1	Ljuboja 7; Tiffert 71	25,000
30	uc3rl2	Middlesbrough	A	W	1-0	Tiffert 13	24,018
31	gbl	Hamburg	A	W	2-0	Meissner 43; Gomez 90	51,821
32	gbl	Kaiserslautern	A	D	1-1	Gomez 90	25,000
33	gbl	B Dortmund	H	D	0-0		44,000
34	gbl	B M'gladbach	A	D	1-1	Cacau 75	50,000
35	gbl	B Leverkusen	H	L	0-2		38,000
36	gbl	Hertha Berlin	A	L	0-2		48,000
37	gbl	Nuremburg	H	W	1-0	Tomasson 80	37,000
38	gbl	Hannover 96	A	D	3-3	Ljuboja 52; Hitzlsperger 77; Tomasson 83	36,298
39	gbl	Eintr Frankfurt	H	L	0-2		56,000
40	gbl	Bayern Munich	A	L	1-3	Ljuboja 6	69,000
41	gbl	Wolfsburg	H	W	2-1	Ljuboja 17 pen; Gentner 70	31,000
42	gbl	Schalke	A	L	2-3	Hitzlsperger 33; Cacau 71	61,000

LEAGUE APPEARANCES, BOOKINGS AND CAPS

	AGE (on 01/07/06)	IN NAMED 18	APPEARANCES	COUNTING GAMES	MINUTES ON PITCH	YELLOW CARDS	RED CARDS	CAPS THIS SEASON	NATIONAL SIDE
Goalkeepers									
Dirk Heinen	35	7	3	3	270	0	0	-	Germany
Timo Hildebrand	27	31	31	31	2790	3	0	3	Germany (19)
Michael Langer	21	1	0	0	0	0	0	-	Austria
Defenders									
Markus Babbel	33	16	12	9	922	0	0	-	Germany
Andreas Beck	19	6	5	4	419	1	0	-	Germany
Mathieu Delpierre	25	28	28	27	2475	6	0	-	France
Andreas Hinkel	24	27	26	21	2069	2	0	2	Germany (19)
Ludovic Magnin	27	25	25	22	2115	7	0	8	Switzerland (35)
Fernando Meira	28	32	32	31	2848	5	0	5	Portugal (7)
Martin Stranzl	26	16	15	10	1017	1	0	4	Austria (73)
Boris Zivkovic	30	0	0	0	0	0	0	-	Croatia
Midfielders									
Christian Gentner	20	24	23	11	1381	2	0	-	Germany
Heiko Gerber	33	10	9	7	676	2	0	-	Germany
Jesper Gronkjaer	28	28	25	12	1559	8	0	6	Denmark (19)
Thomas Hitzlsperger	24	26	26	13	1773	4	0	-	Germany
Silvio Meissner	33	25	25	14	1672	8	0	-	Germany
Zvonimir Soldo	38	30	30	28	2607	6	0	-	Croatia
Ivan Stojanov	22	1	1	1	90	0	0	-	Bulgaria
Christian Tiffert	24	28	28	22	2195	9	0	-	Germany
Forwards									
Cacau	25	21	20	4	910	1	1	-	Brazil
Mario Carevic	24	9	7	2	286	0	0	-	Croatia
Mario Gomez	20	30	30	2	1094	2	0	-	Germany
Danijel Ljuboja	28	26	26	21	2092	2	0	8	Serbia & Mont (44)
Marco Streller	25	7	6	2	286	2	0	7	Switzerland (35)
Jon Dahl Tomasson	29	27	26	23	2082	3	1	6	Denmark (19)

TEAM OF THE SEASON

MONTHLY POINTS TALLY

AUGUST	2	22%
SEPTEMBER	7	58%
OCTOBER	4	33%
NOVEMBER	5	56%
DECEMBER	7	78%
JANUARY	0	0%
FEBRUARY	8	53%
MARCH	3	25%
APRIL	4	33%
MAY	3	33%

LEAGUE GOALS

	PLAYER	MINS	GOALS	S RATE
1	Tomasson	2082	8	260
2	Ljuboja	2092	8	262
3	Gomez	1094	6	182
4	Cacau	910	4	228
5	Tiffert	2195	3	732
6	Meissner	1672	2	836
7	Hitzlsperger	1773	2	887
8	Streller	286	1	286
9	Gentner	1381	1	1381
10	Magnin	2115	1	2115
	Other		1	
	TOTAL		37	

TOP POINT EARNERS

	PLAYER	GAMES	AV PTS
1	Thomas Hitzlsperger	13	1.62
2	Zvonimir Soldo	28	1.46
3	Christian Tiffert	22	1.45
4	Danijel Ljuboja	21	1.43
5	Timo Hildebrand	31	1.35
6	Andreas Hinkel	21	1.29
7	Fernando Meira	31	1.29
8	Ludovic Magnin	22	1.27
9	Jesper Gronkjaer	12	1.25
10	Mathieu Delpierre	27	1.22
	CLUB AVERAGE:		1.26

DISCIPLINARY RECORDS

	PLAYER	YELLOW	RED	AVE
1	Gronkjaer	8	0	194
2	Meissner	8	0	209
3	Tiffert	9	0	243
4	Magnin	7	0	302
5	Gerber	2	0	338
6	Delpierre	6	0	412
7	Soldo	6	0	434
8	Hitzlsperger	4	0	443
9	Cacau	1	1	455
10	Tomasson	3	1	520
11	Gomez	2	0	547
12	Meira	5	0	569
13	Gentner	2	0	690
	Other	8	0	
	TOTAL	71	2	

KEY GOALKEEPER

Timo Hildebrand

Goals Conceded in the League	32	Counting Games League games when player was on pitch for at least 70 minutes	31
Defensive Rating Ave number of mins between League goals conceded while on the pitch	87	Clean Sheets In games when player was on pitch for at least 70 minutes	11

KEY PLAYERS - DEFENDERS

Ludovic Magnin

Goals Conceded Number of League goals conceded while the player was on the pitch	26	Clean Sheets In League games when player was on pitch for at least 70 minutes	9
Defensive Rating Ave number of mins between League goals conceded while on the pitch	81	Club Defensive Rating Average number of mins between League goals conceded by the club this season	78

	PLAYER	CON LGE	CLEAN SHEETS	DEF RATE
1	Ludovic Magnin	26	9	81 mins
2	Fernando Meira	35	10	81 mins
3	Mathieu Delpierre	31	9	80 mins
4	Andreas Hinkel	29	6	71 mins

KEY PLAYERS - MIDFIELDERS

Christian Tiffert

Goals in the League	3	Contribution to Attacking Power Average number of minutes between League team goals while on pitch	88
Defensive Rating Average number of mins between League goals conceded while on the pitch	88	Scoring Difference Defensive Rating minus Contribution to Attacking Power	0

	PLAYER	LGE GOALS	DEF RATE	POWER	SCORE DIFF
1	Christian Tiffert	3	88	88	0 mins
2	Zvonimir Soldo	0	93	93	0 mins
3	Thomas Hitzlsperger	2	84	89	-5 mins
4	Silvio Meissner	2	70	80	-10 mins

KEY PLAYERS - GOALSCORERS

Goals in the League	8	Player Strike Rate Average number of minutes between League goals scored by player	260
Contribution to Attacking Power Average number of minutes between League team goals while on pitch	91	Club Strike Rate Average number of minutes between League goals scored by club	83

	PLAYER	LGE GOALS	POWER	STRIKE RATE
1	Jon Dahl Tomasson	8	91	260 mins
2	Danijel Ljuboja	8	84	262 mins
3	Christian Tiffert	3	88	732 mins
4	Silvio Meissner	2	80	836 mins

Danijel Ljuboja

SQUAD APPEARANCES

Match	1	2	3	4	5	6	7	8	9	10	11	12	13	14	15	16	17	18	19	20	21	22	23	24	25	26	27	28	29	30	31	32	33	34	35	36	37	38	39	40	41	42
Venue	A	H	A	H	H	A	H	H	A	A	H	A	A	H	H	A	H	A	A	H	A	H	H	H	A	H	A	H	H	A	A	A	H	A	H	A	H	A	H	A	H	A
Competition	L	L	L	L	E	L	L	L	E	L	L	E	L	L	E	L	L	E	L	L	L	E	L	L	L	L	L	E	L	E	L	L	L	L	L	L	L	L	L	L	L	L
Result	D	L	D	D	W	W	L	W	L	D	D	W	D	D	L	W	D	W	D	D	W	W	W	L	D	D	L	L	W	W	W	D	D	D	L	L	W	D	L	L	W	L

Goalkeepers
Dirk Heinen
Timo Hildebrand
Michael Langer

Defenders
Markus Babbel
Andreas Beck
Mathieu Delpierre
Andreas Hinkel
Ludovic Magnin
Fernando Meira
Martin Stranzl
Boris Zivkovic

Midfielders
Christian Gentner
Heiko Gerber
Jesper Gronkjaer
Thomas Hitzlsperger
Silvio Meissner
Zvonimir Soldo
Ivan Stojanov
Christian Tiffert

Forwards
Cacau
Mario Carevic
Mario Gomez
Danijel Ljuboja
Marco Streller
Jon Dahl Tomasson

KEY: On all match · On bench · Subbed or sent off (Counting game) · Subbed or sent off (playing less than 70 minutes) · Subbed on from bench (Counting Game) · Subbed on (playing less than 70 minutes) · Subbed on and then subbed or sent off (Counting Game) · Subbed on and then subbed or sent off (playing less than 70 minutes) · Not in 16

BORUSSIA MONCHENGLADBACH

Final Position: **10th**

KEY: Won Drawn Lost

							Attendance
1	gbl	Bayern Munich	A	L	0-3		66,000
2	gbl	Wolfsburg	H	D	1-1	Bogelund 90,90	45,000
3	gbl	Schalke	A	D	1-1	Bogelund 41	61,000
4	gbl	Duisburg	H	W	2-1	Neuville 5; Ze Antonio 66	48,854
5	gbl	Cologne	A	L	1-2	Neuville 81	50,000
6	gbl	W Bremen	H	W	2-1	Broich 51; Baumann 60 og	40,251
7	gbl	Arminia B	A	W	2-0	Kluge 32; Neuville 68	23,000
8	gbl	Mainz	H	W	1-0	Ze Antonio 32	42,000
9	gbl	Stuttgart	A	D	1-1	Kluge 17	45,000
10	gbl	Kaiserslautern	H	W	4-1	Strasser 11; El Fakiri 32; Kluge 45; Neuville 86	47,000
11	gbl	B Dortmund	A	L	1-2	Neuville 90	80,000
12	gbl	Hamburg	H	D	0-0		53,466
13	gbl	B Leverkusen	H	D	1-1	Polanski 15	48,000
14	gbl	Hertha Berlin	A	D	2-2	Kahe 7; Friedrich 12 og	38,438
15	gbl	Nuremburg	H	L	0-1		45,000
16	gbl	Hannover 96	A	D	1-1	Kahe 49	38,000
17	gbl	Eintr Frankfurt	H	W	4-3	Jansen 45; Neuville 77,82; Sverkos 88	48,000
18	gbl	Bayern Munich	H	L	1-3	Sonck 56	54,019
19	gbl	Wolfsburg	A	L	0-2		16,000
20	gbl	Schalke	H	D	0-0		54,000
21	gbl	Duisburg	A	D	1-1	Svensson 20	30,000
22	gbl	Cologne	H	W	2-0	Lell 54 og; Neuville 74	54,019
23	gbl	W Bremen	A	L	0-2		38,000
24	gbl	Arminia B	H	W	2-0	Jansen 34; Sonck 65	39,372
25	gbl	Mainz	A	L	0-3		20,300
26	gbl	Stuttgart	H	D	1-1	Fukal 69	50,000
27	gbl	Kaiserslautern	A	L	0-3		26,000
28	gbl	B Dortmund	H	W	2-1	Rafael 6,34	54,019
29	gbl	Hamburg	A	L	0-2		56,750
30	gbl	B Leverkusen	A	L	1-2	Neuville 48	22,500
31	gbl	Hertha Berlin	H	D	2-2	Chahed 10 og; Broich 82	45,000
32	gbl	Nuremburg	A	L	2-5	Ze Antonio 34; Sonck 37	42,000
33	gbl	Hannover 96	H	D	2-2	Jansen 77; Sonck 83	42,000
34	gbl	Eintr Frankfurt	A	W	2-0	Neuville 56; Rafael 90	25,000

LEAGUE APPEARANCES, BOOKINGS AND CAPS

	AGE (on 01/07/06)	IN NAMED 18	APPEARANCES	COUNTING GAMES	MINUTES ON PITCH	YELLOW CARDS	RED CARDS	CAPS THIS SEASON	NATIONAL SIDE
Goalkeepers									
Darius Kampa	29	5	1	1	90	0	0	-	Germany
Kasey Keller	36	33	33	33	2970	1	0	5	United States (5)
Defenders									
Kasper Bogelund	25	16	15	10	1029	4	0	1	Denmark (19)
Marvin Compper	21	7	4	0	106	2	0	-	Germany
Filip Daems	27	25	22	15	1472	6	0	-	Belgium
Max Eberl	32	1	1	0	17	0	0	-	Germany
Milan Fukal	31	25	24	20	1810	8	0	-	Czech Republic
Jeff Strasser	31	26	25	22	2115	9	0	-	Luxembourg
Bo Svensson	26	13	13	12	1092	0	0	1	Denmark (19)
Ze Antonio	29	34	34	33	3018	2	0	-	Portugal
Midfielders									
Jorg Bohme	32	1	1	0	38	0	0	-	Germany
Thomas Broich	25	28	26	15	1634	1	0	-	Germany
Hassan El Fakiri	29	31	31	21	2340	3	0	-	Norway
Robert Flessers	19	3	3	1	149	1	0	-	Germany
Thomas Helveg	35	5	5	3	292	1	0	4	Denmark (19)
Vladimir Ivic	29	1	1	1	90	0	0	1	Serbia & Mont (44)
Marcell Jansen	20	31	31	31	2790	5	0	8	Germany (19)
Peer Kluge	25	28	27	20	1999	5	0	-	Germany
Krisztian Lisztes	30	6	5	0	200	1	0	-	Hungary
Niels Oude Kamphuis	28	12	12	10	937	7	1	-	Holland
Eugen Polanski	20	21	21	17	1620	9	1	-	Poland
Bernd Thijs	28	17	15	7	866	4	0	-	Belgium
Forwards									
Giovane Elber	33	2	2	0	31	0	0	-	Brazil
Marek Heinz	28	3	3	2	244	0	0	7	Czech Republic (2)
Carlos Kahe	23	27	26	14	1598	0	0	-	Brazil
Bekim Kastrati	26	5	4	0	46	0	0	-	Albania
Oliver Neuville	33	34	34	34	2968	3	0	5	Germany (19)
Nando Rafael	22	15	14	4	658	2	0	-	Angola
Wesley Sonck	27	14	14	10	920	1	0	1	Belgium (42)
Vaclav Sverkos	22	14	13	1	352	2	0	-	Czech Republic

TEAM OF THE SEASON

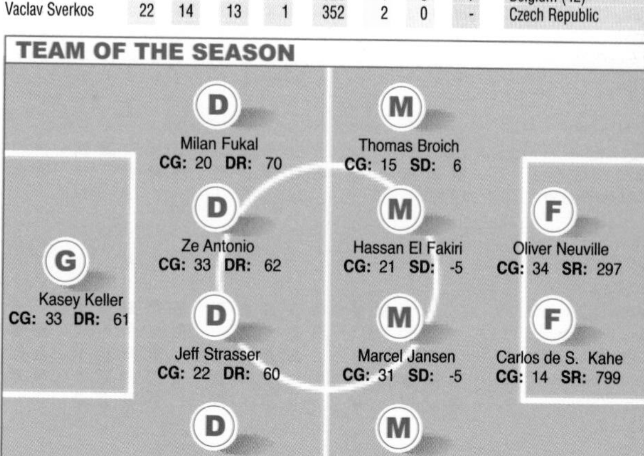

MONTHLY POINTS TALLY

AUGUST	2	22%
SEPTEMBER	9	75%
OCTOBER	7	58%
NOVEMBER	3	33%
DECEMBER	4	44%
JANUARY	0	0%
FEBRUARY	5	33%
MARCH	4	33%
APRIL	4	33%
MAY	4	44%

LEAGUE GOALS

	PLAYER	MINS	GOALS	S RATE
1	Neuville	2968	10	297
2	Sonck	920	4	230
3	Ze Antonio	3018	3	1006
4	Rafael	658	3	219
5	Jansen	2790	3	930
6	Bogelund	1029	3	343
7	Kluge	1999	3	666
8	Broich	1634	2	817
9	Kahe	1598	2	799
10	Sverkos	352	1	352
11	El Fakiri	2340	1	2340
12	Fukal	1810	1	1810
13	Polanski	1620	1	1620
	Other		6	
	TOTAL		43	

TOP POINT EARNERS

	PLAYER	GAMES	AV PTS
1	Thomas Broich	15	1.73
2	Hassan El Fakiri	21	1.52
3	Marcel Jansen	31	1.32
4	Ze Antonio	33	1.27
5	Milan Fukal	20	1.25
6	Oliver Neuville	34	1.24
7	Carlos E de Souza Kahe	14	1.21
8	Filip Daems	15	1.20
9	Jeff Strasser	22	1.18
10	Kasey Keller	33	1.18
	CLUB AVERAGE:		1.24

DISCIPLINARY RECORDS

	PLAYER	YELLOW	RED	AVE
1	Oude Kamphuis	7	1	117
2	Polanski	9	1	162
3	Thijs	4	0	216
4	Fukal	8	0	226
5	Strasser	9	0	235
6	Daems	6	0	245
7	Bogelund	4	0	257
8	Rafael	2	0	329
9	Kluge	5	0	399
10	Jansen	5	0	558
11	El Fakiri	3	0	780
12	Sonck	1	0	920
13	Neuville	3	0	989
	Other	4	0	
	TOTAL	70	2	

KEY GOALKEEPER

Kasey Keller

Goals Conceded in the League	49	Counting Games League games when player was on pitch for at least 70 minutes	33
Defensive Rating Ave number of mins between League goals conceded while on the pitch	61	Clean Sheets In games when player was on pitch for at least 70 minutes	7

KEY PLAYERS - DEFENDERS

Milan Fukal

Goals Conceded Number of League goals conceded while the player was on the pitch	26	Clean Sheets In League games when player was on pitch for at least 70 minutes	4
Defensive Rating Ave number of mins between League goals conceded while on the pitch	70	Club Defensive Rating Average number of mins between League goals conceded by the club this season	61

	PLAYER	CON LGE	CLEAN SHEETS	DEF RATE
1	Milan Fukal	26	4	70 mins
2	Ze Antonio	49	7	62 mins
3	Jeff Strasser	35	3	60 mins
4	Bo Svensson	20	4	55 mins

KEY PLAYERS - MIDFIELDERS

Thomas Broich

Goals in the League	2	Contribution to Attacking Power Average number of minutes between League team goals while on pitch	68
Defensive Rating Average number of mins between League goals conceded while on the pitch	74	Scoring Difference Defensive Rating minus Contribution to Attacking Power	6

	PLAYER	LGE GOALS	DEF RATE	POWER	SCORE DIFF
1	Thomas Broich	2	74	68	6 mins
2	Marcel Jansen	3	61	66	-5 mins
3	Hassan El Fakiri	1	62	67	-5 mins
4	Peer Kluge	3	67	83	-16 mins

KEY PLAYERS - GOALSCORERS

Goals in the League	10	Player Strike Rate Average number of minutes between League goals scored by player	297
Contribution to Attacking Power Average number of minutes between League team goals while on pitch	71	Club Strike Rate Average number of minutes between League goals scored by club	71

	PLAYER	LGE GOALS	POWER	STRIKE RATE
1	Oliver Neuville	10	71	297 mins
2	Peer Kluge	3	83	666 mins
3	Carlos Eduardo de Souza Kahe	2	76	799 mins
4	Thomas Broich	2	68	817 mins

Marcel Jansen

SQUAD APPEARANCES

Match	1	2	3	4	5	6	7	8	9	10	11	12	13	14	15	16	17	18	19	20	21	22	23	24	25	26	27	28	29	30	31	32	33	34
Venue	A	H	A	H	A	H	A	H	A	H	A	H	H	A	H	A	H	H	A	H	A	H	A	H	A	H	A	H	A	A	H	A	H	A
Competition	L	L	L	L	L	L	L	L	L	L	L	L	L	L	L	L	L	L	L	L	L	L	L	L	L	L	L	L	L	L	L	L	L	L
Result	L	D	D	W	L	W	W	W	D	W	L	D	D	D	L	D	W	L	L	D	D	W	L	W	L	D	L	W	L	L	D	L	D	W

Goalkeepers
Darius Kampa
Kasey Keller

Defenders
Kasper Bogelund
Marvin Compper
Filip Daems
Max Eberl
Milan Fukal
Jeff Strasser
Bo Svensson
Ze Antonio

Midfielders
Jorg Bohme
Thomas Broich
Hassan El Fakiri
Robert Flessers
Thomas Helveg
Vladimir Ivic
Marcel Jansen
Peer Kluge
Krisztian Lisztes
Niels Oude Kamphuis
Eugen Polanski
Bernd Thijs

Forwards
Giovane Elber
Marek Heinz
Carlos de Souza Kahe
Bekim Kastrati
Oliver Neuville
Nando Rafael
Wesley Sonck
Vaclav Sverkos

KEY: On all match | On bench | Subbed or sent off (Counting game) | Subbed or sent off (playing less than 70 minutes) | Subbed on from bench (Counting Game) | Subbed on (playing less than 70 minutes) | Subbed on and then subbed or sent off (Counting Game) | Subbed on and then subbed or sent off (playing less than 70 minutes) | Not in 16

MAINZ

Final Position: **11th**

KEY: ☐ Won ☐ Drawn ☐ Lost

							Attendance
1	gbl	Cologne	A	L	0-1		50,374
2	gbl	W Bremen	H	L	0-2		22,000
3	gbl	Arminia B	A	L	0-2		18,300
4	gbl	Hamburg	H	L	1-3	Ruman 69	20,300
5	uc1rl1	Seville	A	D	0-0		44,000
6	gbl	Stuttgart	H	L	1-2	Noveski 77	20,000
7	gbl	Kaiserslautern	A	W	2-0	Thurk 38; Auer 90	40,000
8	gbl	B Dortmund	H	D	1-1	Zidan 64 pen	20,300
9	uc1rl2	Seville	H	L	0-2		32,500
10	gbl	B M'gladbach	A	L	0-1		42,000
11	gbl	B Leverkusen	H	W	3-1	Ruman 57,75; Thurk 61 pen	20,300
12	gbl	Hertha Berlin	A	L	1-3	Friedrich 71	30,000
13	gbl	Nuremburg	H	W	4-1	Paulus 9 og; Auer 11; da Silva 45; Thurk 52	20,300
14	gbl	Hannover 96	A	D	2-2	Friedrich 31; Auer 65	30,000
15	gbl	Eintr Frankfurt	H	D	2-2	Noveski 71; Ruman 90	20,300
16	gbl	Bayern Munich	A	L	1-2	Auer 34	66,000
17	gbl	Wolfsburg	H	W	5-1	Thurk 2 pen,77; Auer 36; Ruman 45; Zidan 51	19,000
18	gbl	Schalke	A	L	0-1		61,000
19	gbl	Duisburg	H	D	1-1	da Silva 27	20,300
20	gbl	Cologne	H	W	4-2	Thurk 5,55; Zidan 61; Auer 87	20,300
21	gbl	W Bremen	A	L	2-4	Zidan 1; Weiland, N 13	28,000
22	gbl	Arminia B	H	D	1-1	Zidan 50 pen	19,500
23	gbl	Hamburg	A	L	0-1		52,000
24	gbl	Stuttgart	A	L	1-2	da Silva 25	25,000
25	gbl	Kaiserslautern	H	L	0-2		20,300
26	gbl	B Dortmund	A	D	1-1	Thurk 53	68,000
27	gbl	B M'gladbach	H	W	3-0	Thurk 62,88; Zidan 68	20,300
28	gbl	B Leverkusen	A	W	2-1	Zidan 34,64	21,000
29	gbl	Hertha Berlin	H	D	2-2	Thurk 52 pen; Casey 78	20,300
30	gbl	Nuremburg	A	L	0-3		30,000
31	gbl	Hannover 96	H	D	0-0		20,300
32	gbl	Eintr Frankfurt	A	D	0-0		49,962
33	gbl	Bayern Munich	H	D	2-2	Zidan 10; Friedrich 13	20,300
34	gbl	Wolfsburg	A	W	3-0	Thurk 5; Auer 81,85	22,000
35	gbl	Schalke	H	W	1-0	Auer 15	20,300
36	gbl	Duisburg	A	D	0-0		28,000

LEAGUE APPEARANCES, BOOKINGS AND CAPS

	AGE (on 01/07/06)	IN NAMED 18	APPEARANCES	COUNTING GAMES	MINUTES ON PITCH	YELLOW CARDS	RED CARDS	CAPS THIS SEASON	NATIONAL SIDE
Goalkeepers									
Dimo Wache	32	20	20	19	1721	0	0	-	Germany
Christian Wetklo	26	17	15	15	1331	2	0	-	Germany
Defenders									
Mathias Abel	25	20	20	16	1527	2	0	-	Germany
Tamas Bodog	35	1	0	0	0	0	0	-	Hungary
Christian Demirtas	22	28	28	21	2148	5	0	-	Germany
Henning Lichte	21	1	0	0	0	0	0	-	Germany
Nikolce Noveski	27	33	33	33	2956	7	0	-	Macedonia
Marko Rose	29	19	19	13	1256	2	0	-	Germany
Benjamin Weigelt	23	23	23	19	1829	4	0	-	Germany
Midfielders									
Otto Addo	31	16	16	4	684	3	0	2	Ghana (48)
Christof Babatz	31	17	17	11	1185	2	0	-	Germany
Antonio da Silva	28	33	33	32	2924	2	0	-	Brazil
Manuel Friedrich	26	34	34	33	2988	3	0	-	Germany
Tom Geissler	22	15	14	0	331	0	0	-	Germany
Fabian Gerber	26	21	21	12	1335	0	0	-	Germany
Milorad Pekovic	28	24	24	21	2043	8	0	-	Serbia
Petr Ruman	29	24	24	13	1435	3	0	-	Czech Republic
Selo	-	1	1	0	8	0	0	-	
Dennis Weiland	31	7	6	0	83	0	0	-	Germany
Niclas Weiland	33	11	11	4	516	2	0	-	Germany
Forwards									
Benjamin Auer	25	29	29	23	2235	2	0	-	Germany
Connor Casey	24	10	10	4	450	2	0	-	United States
Tobias Damm	22	1	1	0	7	0	0	-	Germany
Ranisav Jovanovic	25	2	2	0	18	0	0	-	Serbia & Mont
Romulo	24	8	7	1	170	0	0	-	Brazil
Michael Thurk	30	32	32	29	2638	11	0	-	Germany
Mohamed Zidan	24	27	26	17	1842	0	0	1	Egypt (34)

TEAM OF THE SEASON

MONTHLY POINTS TALLY

AUGUST	0	0%
SEPTEMBER	4	33%
OCTOBER	6	50%
NOVEMBER	2	22%
DECEMBER	4	44%
JANUARY	3	100%
FEBRUARY	1	7%
MARCH	8	67%
APRIL	3	25%
MAY	7	78%

LEAGUE GOALS

	PLAYER	MINS	GOALS	S RATE
1	Thurk	2638	12	220
2	Auer	2235	9	248
3	Zidan	1842	9	205
4	Ruman	1435	5	287
5	Friedrich	2988	3	996
6	da Silva	2924	3	975
7	Noveski	2956	2	1478
8	Weiland, N	516	1	516
9	Casey	450	1	450
	Other		1	
	TOTAL		46	

TOP POINT EARNERS

	PLAYER	GAMES	AV PTS
1	Marko Rose	13	1.46
2	Mohamed Zidan	17	1.41
3	Milorad Pekovic	21	1.33
4	Christian Demirtas	21	1.29
5	Michael Thurk	29	1.24
6	Benjamin Auer	23	1.22
7	Christian Wetklo	15	1.20
8	Antonio da Silva	32	1.16
9	Petr Ruman	13	1.15
10	Nikolce Noveski	33	1.15
	CLUB AVERAGE:		1.12

DISCIPLINARY RECORDS

	PLAYER	YELLOW	RED	AVE
1	Addo	3	0	228
2	Thurk	11	0	239
3	Pekovic	8	0	255
4	Weiland, N	2	0	258
5	Noveski	7	0	422
6	Demirtas	5	0	429
7	Weigelt	4	0	457
8	Ruman	3	0	478
9	Babatz	2	0	592
10	Rose	2	0	628
11	Wetklo	2	0	665
12	Abel	2	0	763
13	Friedrich	3	0	996
	Other	4	0	
	TOTAL	58	0	

KEY GOALKEEPER

Dimo Wache			
Goals Conceded in the League	26	Counting Games League games when player was on pitch for at least 70 minutes	20
Defensive Rating Ave number of mins between League goals conceded while on the pitch	66	Clean Sheets In League games when player was on pitch for at least 70 minutes	3

KEY PLAYERS - DEFENDERS

Marko Rose			
Goals Conceded Number of League goals conceded while the player was on the pitch	16	Clean Sheets In League games when player was on pitch for at least 70 minutes	6
Defensive Rating Ave number of mins between League goals conceded while on the pitch	79	Club Defensive Rating Average number of mins between League goals conceded by the club this season	65

	PLAYER	CON LGE	CLEAN SHEETS	DEF RATE
1	Marko Rose	16	6	79 mins
2	Christian Demirtas	33	4	65 mins
3	Nikolce Noveski	46	7	64 mins
4	Mathias Abel	24	4	64 mins

KEY PLAYERS - MIDFIELDERS

Milorad Pekovic			
Goals in the League	0	Contribution to Attacking Power Average number of minutes between League team goals while on pitch	64
Defensive Rating Average number of mins between League goals conceded while on the pitch	70	Scoring Difference Defensive Rating minus Contribution to Attacking Power	6

	PLAYER	LGE GOALS	DEF RATE	POWER	SCORE DIFF
1	Milorad Pekovic	0	70	64	6 mins
2	Antonio da Silva	3	68	66	2 mins
3	Fabian Gerber	0	74	74	0 mins
4	Manuel Friedrich	3	64	65	-1 mins

KEY PLAYERS - GOALSCORERS

Mohamed Zidan			
Goals in the League	9	Player Strike Rate Average number of minutes between League goals scored by player	205
Contribution to Attacking Power Average number of minutes between League team goals while on pitch	64	Club Strike Rate Average number of minutes between League goals scored by club	67

	PLAYER	LGE GOALS	POWER	STRIKE RATE
1	Mohamed Zidan	9	64	205 mins
2	Michael Thurk	12	64	220 mins
3	Benjamin Auer	9	60	248 mins
4	Petr Ruman	5	65	287 mins

Michael Thurk and Mohamed Zidan

SQUAD APPEARANCES

Match	1	2	3	4	5	6	7	8	9	10	11	12	13	14	15	16	17	18	19	20	21	22	23	24	25	26	27	28	29	30	31	32	33	34	35	36
Venue	A	H	A	H	A	H	A	H	H	A	H	A	H	A	H	A	H	A	H	H	A	H	A	A	H	A	H	A	H	A	H	A	H	A	H	A
Competition	L	L	L	L	E	L	L	L	E	L	L	L	L	L	L	L	L	L	L	L	L	L	L	L	L	L	L	L	L	L	L	L	L	L	L	L
Result	L	L	L	L	D	L	W	D	L	L	W	L	W	D	D	L	W	L	D	W	L	D	L	L	L	D	W	W	D	L	D	D	D	W	W	D
Goalkeepers																																				
Dimo Wache																																				
Christian Wetklo																																				
Defenders																																				
Mathias Abel																																				
Tamas Bodog																																				
Christian Demirtas																																				
Henning Lichte																																				
Nikolce Noveski																																				
Marko Rose																																				
Benjamin Weigelt																																				
Midfielders																																				
Otto Addo																																				
Christof Babatz																																				
Antonio da Silva																																				
Manuel Friedrich																																				
Tom Geissler																																				
Fabian Gerber																																				
Milorad Pekovic																																				
Petr Ruman																																				
Selo																																				
Dennis Weiland																																				
Niclas Weiland																																				
Forwards																																				
Benjamin Auer																																				
Connor Casey																																				
Tobias Damm																																				
Ranisav Jovanovic																																				
Romulo																																				
Michael Thurk																																				
Mohamed Zidan																																				

KEY: ■ On all match | ⏮ Subbed or sent off (Counting game) | « Subbed or sent off (playing less than 70 minutes) | ■ On bench | ⏭ Subbed on from bench (Counting Game) | » Subbed on (playing less than 70 minutes) | Subbed on and then subbed or sent off (Counting Game) | Subbed on and then subbed or sent off (playing less than 70 minutes) | ☐ Not in 16

HANNOVER 96

Final Position: **12th**

KEY: ☐Won ☐Drawn ☐Lost

							Attendance
1	gbl	Hertha Berlin	H	D	2-2	Dabrowski 66; Tarnat 87 fk	40,473
2	gbl	Nuremburg	A	D	1-1	Brdaric 8	35,000
3	gbl	Hamburg	A	D	1-1	Stajner 18	48,866
4	gbl	Eintr Frankfurt	H	W	2-0	Stajner 32; Yankov 64	35,166
5	gbl	Bayern Munich	A	L	0-1		66,000
6	gbl	Wolfsburg	H	L	2-4	Brdaric 30,89	31,517
7	gbl	Schalke	A	L	0-2		60,000
8	gbl	Duisburg	H	D	1-1	Delura 8	27,211
9	gbl	Cologne	A	W	4-1	Stajner 48; Brdaric 53,70; Ricardo Sousa 56 pen	48,000
10	gbl	W Bremen	H	D	0-0		47,000
11	gbl	Arminia B	A	L	1-4	Mertesacker 55	20,000
12	gbl	Mainz	H	D	2-2	Brdaric 86 pen; Tarnat 90	30,000
13	gbl	Stuttgart	A	D	2-2	Hashemian 57; Yankov 68	32,000
14	gbl	Kaiserslautern	H	W	5-1	Tarnat 13,26; Brdaric 62,73; Hashemian 83	32,500
15	gbl	B Dortmund	A	W	2-0	Cherundolo 17; Dabrowski 86	75,000
16	gbl	B M'gladbach	H	D	1-1	Stajner 57	38,000
17	gbl	B Leverkusen	A	D	0-0		20,000
18	gbl	Hertha Berlin	A	D	1-1	Dabrowski 12	33,000
19	gbl	Nuremburg	H	D	1-1	Stajner 74	32,000
20	gbl	Hamburg	H	W	2-1	Zuraw 48; Hashemian 72	40,000
21	gbl	Eintr Frankfurt	A	W	1-0	Yankov 78	29,000
22	gbl	Bayern Munich	H	D	1-1	Brdaric 56	49,000
23	gbl	Wolfsburg	A	L	1-2	Brdaric 17	28,000
24	gbl	Schalke	H	L	1-2	Christiansen 74 pen	47,000
25	gbl	Duisburg	A	D	0-0		18,000
26	gbl	Cologne	H	W	1-0	Hashemian 39	28,000
27	gbl	W Bremen	A	L	0-5		41,646
28	gbl	Arminia B	H	L	0-1		34,361
29	gbl	Mainz	A	D	0-0		20,300
30	gbl	Stuttgart	H	D	3-3	Balitsch 2; Stajner 33; Mertesacker 67	36,298
31	gbl	Kaiserslautern	A	L	0-1		33,000
32	gbl	B Dortmund	H	L	1-2	Mertesacker 45	40,000
33	gbl	B M'gladbach	A	D	2-2	Mertesacker 13; Vinicius 88 og	42,000
34	gbl	B Leverkusen	H	D	2-2	Mertesacker 14; Yankov 52	47,387

LEAGUE APPEARANCES, BOOKINGS AND CAPS

	AGE (on 01/07/06)	IN NAMED 18	APPEARANCES	COUNTING GAMES	MINUTES ON PITCH	YELLOW CARDS	RED CARDS	CAPS THIS SEASON	NATIONAL SIDE
Goalkeepers									
Robert Enke	28	32	32	32	2880	1	0	-	Germany
Morten Jensen	18	2	1	1	90	0	0	-	Germany
Frank Juric	32	5	1	1	90	0	0	-	Australia
Defenders									
Steve Cherundolo	27	22	22	21	1916	2	0	3	United States (5)
Soren Halfar	19	6	5	3	248	0	0	-	Germany
Moritz Marheineke	21	2	0	0	0	0	0	-	Germany
Per Mertesacker	21	30	30	30	2700	1	0	10	Germany (19)
Jonas Troest	21	8	7	2	300	0	0	-	Denmark
Vinicius	25	24	23	12	1349	3	0	-	Brazil
Dariusz Zuraw	33	30	30	29	2636	2	0	-	Poland
Midfielders									
Hanno Balitsch	25	31	31	30	2708	6	0	-	Germany
Christophe Dabrowski	28	32	32	31	2856	11	0	-	Germany
Johannes Dietwald	21	3	1	0	4	0	0	-	Germany
Altin Lala	30	29	29	23	2256	11	2	3	Albania (199)
Silvio Schroter	27	11	11	3	453	0	0	-	Germany
Bastian Schulz	20	1	0	0	0	0	0	-	Germany
Ricardo Sousa	27	13	13	2	543	1	0	-	Portugal
Michael Tarnat	36	29	29	27	2535	6	0	-	Germany
Chavdar Yankov	21	24	22	12	1357	4	0	-	Bulgaria
Forwards									
Thomas Brdaric	31	31	31	26	2493	3	0	-	Germany
Thomas Christiansen	33	6	4	0	66	0	0	-	Spain
Michael Delura	21	25	25	1	863	4	0	-	Germany
Hendrik Hahne	20	10	7	1	243	0	0	-	Germany
Vahid Hashemian	29	29	29	21	2142	4	0	3	Iran (23)
Mohamadou Idrissou	26	4	4	0	61	0	0	-	Cameroon
Fabian Montabell	21	3	2	0	18	0	0	-	Germany
Jiri Stajner	30	33	33	27	2646	2	0	6	Czech Republic (2)
Daniel Stendel	32	5	5	1	110	0	0	-	Germany

TEAM OF THE SEASON

MONTHLY POINTS TALLY

AUGUST	3	33%
SEPTEMBER	3	25%
OCTOBER	5	42%
NOVEMBER	5	56%
DECEMBER	5	56%
JANUARY	1	33%
FEBRUARY	8	53%
MARCH	4	33%
APRIL	2	17%
MAY	2	22%

LEAGUE GOALS

	PLAYER	MINS	GOALS	S RATE
1	Brdaric	2493	10	249
2	Stajner	2646	6	441
3	Mertesacker	2700	5	540
4	Hashemian	2142	4	536
5	Yankov	1357	4	339
6	Tarnat	2535	4	634
7	Dabrowski	2856	3	952
8	Zuraw	2636	1	2636
9	Delura	863	1	863
10	Cherundolo	1916	1	1916
11	Christiansen	66	1	66
12	Balitsch	2708	1	2708
	Other		2	
	TOTAL		43	

TOP POINT EARNERS

	PLAYER	GAMES	AV PTS
1	Chavdar Yankov	12	1.33
2	Vahid Hashemian	21	1.33
3	Michael Tarnat	27	1.30
4	Dariusz Zuraw	29	1.28
5	Hanno Balitsch	30	1.17
6	Steve Cherundolo	21	1.14
7	Robert Enke	32	1.13
8	Christophe Dabrowski	31	1.10
9	Altin Lala	23	1.09
10	Thomas Brdaric	26	1.00
	CLUB AVERAGE:		1.12

DISCIPLINARY RECORDS

	PLAYER	YELLOW	RED	AVE
1	Lala	11	2	173
2	Delura	4	0	215
3	Dabrowski	11	0	259
4	Yankov	4	0	339
5	Tarnat	6	0	422
6	Vinicius	3	0	449
7	Balitsch	6	0	451
8	Hashemian	4	0	535
9	Sousa	1	0	543
10	Brdaric	3	0	831
11	Cherundolo	2	0	958
12	Zuraw	2	0	1318
13	Stajner	2	0	1323
	Other	2	0	
	TOTAL	61	2	

KEY GOALKEEPER

Robert Enke			
Goals Conceded in the League	43	**Counting Games** League games when player was on pitch for at least 70 minutes	32
Defensive Rating Ave number of mins between League goals conceded while on the pitch	67	**Clean Sheets** In League games when player was on pitch for at least 70 minutes	8

KEY PLAYERS - DEFENDERS

Dariusz Zuraw			
Goals Conceded Number of League goals conceded while the player was on the pitch	39	**Clean Sheets** In League games when player was on pitch for at least 70 minutes	8
Defensive Rating Ave number of mins between League goals conceded while on the pitch	68	**Club Defensive Rating** Average number of mins between League goals conceded by the club this season	65

	PLAYER	CON LGE	CLEAN SHEETS	DEF RATE
1	Dariusz Zuraw	39	8	68 mins
2	Vinicius	20	2	67 mins
3	Steve Cherundolo	30	6	64 mins
4	Per Mertesacker	44	7	61 mins

KEY PLAYERS - MIDFIELDERS

Michael Tarnat			
Goals in the League	4	**Contribution to Attacking Power** Average number of minutes between League team goals while on pitch	67
Defensive Rating Average number of mins between League goals conceded while on the pitch	67	**Scoring Difference** Defensive Rating minus Contribution to Attacking Power	0

	PLAYER	LGE GOALS	DEF RATE	POWER	SCORE DIFF
1	Michael Tarnat	4	67	67	0 mins
2	Hanno Balitsch	1	68	69	-1 mins
3	Altin Lala	0	68	71	-3 mins
4	Christophe Dabrowski	3	66	73	-7 mins

KEY PLAYERS - GOALSCORERS

Thomas Brdaric			
Goals in the League	10	**Player Strike Rate** Average number of minutes between League goals scored by player	249
Contribution to Attacking Power Average number of minutes between League team goals while on pitch	71	**Club Strike Rate** Average number of minutes between League goals scored by club	71

	PLAYER	LGE GOALS	POWER	STRIKE RATE
1	Thomas Brdaric	10	71	249 mins
2	Chavdar Yankov	4	71	339 mins
3	Jiri Stajner	6	76	441 mins
4	Vahid Hashemian	4	77	536 mins

Per Mertesacker

SQUAD APPEARANCES

Match	1	2	3	4	5	6	7	8	9	10	11	12	13	14	15	16	17	18	19	20	21	22	23	24	25	26	27	28	29	30	31	32	33	34
Venue	H	A	A	H	A	H	A	H	A	H	A	H	A	H	A	H	A	A	H	H	A	H	A	H	A	H	A	H	A	H	A	H	A	H
Competition	L	L	L	L	L	L	L	L	L	L	L	L	L	L	L	L	L	L	L	L	L	L	L	L	L	L	L	L	L	L	L	L	L	L
Result	D	D	D	W	L	L	L	D	W	D	L	D	D	W	W	D	D	D	D	W	W	D	L	L	D	W	L	L	D	D	L	L	D	D
Goalkeepers																																		
Robert Enke	■	■	■	■	■	■	■	■	■	■	■	■	■	■	■	■	■	■	■	■	■	■	■	■	■	■	■	■	■	■	■	■	□	□
Morten Jensen	□	□	□	□	□	□	□	□	□	□	□	□	□	□	□	□	□	□	□	▒	□	□	□	□	□	□	□	□	□	□	□	□	□	■
Frank Juric	□	□	□	□	□	□	□	□	▒	□	□	▒	□	□	□	□	□	□	▒	□	□	□	□	□	□	□	□	▒	□	□	□	□	■	□
Defenders																																		
Steve Cherundolo	□	□	□	■	■	■	■	□	□	□	□	■	■	■	⏮	□	□	■	□	□	■	■	■	■	■	■	«	□	■	■	■	■	■	■
Soren Halfar	□	□	□	»	»	□	□	□	⏮	⏮	■	▒	□	□	□	□	□	□	□	□	□	□	□	□	□	□	□	□	□	□	□	□	□	□
Moritz Marheineke	□	□	□	□	□	□	□	□	□	□	□	□	□	□	□	□	□	□	▒	▒	□	□	□	□	□	□	□	□	□	□	□	□	□	□
Per Mertesacker	■	■	■	■	■	■	■	■	■	■	■	■	■	■	■	■	■	□	□	□	□	■	■	■	■	■	■	■	■	■	■	■	■	■
Jonas Troest	□	□	□	□	□	□	□	□	□	□	□	□	□	□	□	□	□	□	■	■	»	»	□	«	□	□	□	▒	□	»	□	□	□	»
Vinicius	□	»	□	»	»	»	■	□	»	■	□	▒	»	□	»	□	□	■	■	■	■	■	■	■	»	□	□	⏮	□	■	■	«	»	«
Dariusz Zuraw	■	■	■	■	⏮	«	□	■	■	■	■	■	■	■	■	■	■	■	■	■	■	■	□	■	■	■	■	■	■	□	□	⏭	■	■
Midfielders																																		
Hanno Balitsch	■	■	■	□	□	»	■	■	■	■	■	■	■	■	■	■	⏮	■	■	■	■	■	■	□	■	■	■	■	■	■	■	■	■	■
Christophe Dabrowski	■	■	■	■	■	■	■	■	■	■	■	■	■	«	■	□	■	■	■	■	■	■	■	■	■	■	■	■	■	■	■	□	■	■
Johannes Dietwald	□	»	□	□	□	□	□	□	▒	□	□	□	□	□	□	□	□	□	□	▒	□	□	□	□	□	□	□	□	□	□	□	□	□	□
Altin Lala	■	■	■	■	■	■	■	■	⏮	■	■	«	□	■	■	■	■	«	□	□	□	»	⏮	⏮	⏮	■	⏮	«	■	«	□	■	«	⏮
Silvio Schroter	□	□	□	□	□	□	□	□	□	□	□	□	»	»	»	«	□	□	□	□	□	□	□	□	□	»	»	■	»	⏮	■	«	□	□
Bastian Schulz	□	□	□	□	□	□	□	□	▒	□	□	□	□	□	□	□	□	□	□	□	□	□	□	□	□	□	□	□	□	□	□	□	□	□
Ricardo Sousa	□	□	□	□	□	□	□	⏮	■	«	□	□	□	□	□	»	«	»	»	«	«	□	□	»	□	□	»	»	»	□	□	□	□	□
Michael Tarnat	■	■	■	■	■	⏮	«	■	■	□	□	■	■	■	■	■	■	■	■	■	■	■	⏮	□	«	■	■	□	■	■	■	■	■	□
Chavdar Yankov	■	⏮	■	⏮	«	«	□	»	□	⏭	«	▒	⏮	»	□	«	»	»	▒	⏮	■	□	»	□	□	□	□	□	□	»	■	■	⏮	■
Forwards																																		
Thomas Brdaric	■	■	■	⏮	■	■	⏮	■	⏮	⏮	□	■	□	⏮	■	■	■	«	⏮	»	»	⏮	■	■	■	⏮	■	■	⏮	□	»	■	■	⏮
Thomas Christiansen	□	□	□	□	□	□	□	□	□	□	□	□	□	□	□	□	□	□	»	▒	□	□	□	»	»	»	□	▒	□	□	□	□	□	□
Michael Delura	□	□	□	□	□	□	»	«	»	»	»	»	⏮	«	«	»	»	»	«	»	»	»	»	»	□	□	□	»	»	«	«	»	»	»
Hendrik Hahne	□	□	□	»	»	»	«	□	▒	□	⏮	▒	□	□	□	□	□	□	▒	»	□	□	□	□	□	□	□	□	□	□	□	□	»	□
Vahid Hashemian	■	⏮	■	■	«	■	»	■	»	»	■	»	■	■	⏮	■	■	⏮	■	⏮	⏮	⏮	■	⏮	■	⏮	■	«	«	□	□	□	□	□
Mohamadou Idrissou	□	□	□	□	□	□	□	□	□	□	□	«	»	□	□	»	»	□	□	□	□	□	□	□	□	□	□	□	□	□	□	□	□	□
Fabian Montabell	□	□	□	□	□	□	»	□	▒	□	»	□	□	□	□	□	□	□	□	□	□	□	□	□	□	□	□	□	□	□	□	□	□	□
Jiri Stajner	■	■	■	⏮	■	■	■	»	■	■	■	■	«	»	»	⏮	⏮	«	■	■	⏮	«	■	■	■	⏮	■	■	⏮	⏮	■	■	□	■
Daniel Stendel	□	□	□	□	□	□	□	□	□	□	□	□	□	□	□	□	□	□	□	□	□	□	□	□	□	»	□	»	□	»	□	□	⏮	»

KEY: ■ On all match ▒ On bench ⏮ Subbed or sent off (Counting game) « Subbed or sent off (playing less than 70 minutes) ⏭ Subbed on from bench (Counting Game) » Subbed on (playing less than 70 minutes) Subbed on and then subbed or sent off (Counting Game) Subbed on and then subbed or sent off (playing less than 70 minutes) □ Not in 16

ARMINIA BIELEFELD

Final Position: **13th**

KEY: ☐Won ☐Drawn ☐Lost

							Attendance
1	gbl	W Bremen	A	L	2-5	Krupnikovic 11; Zuma 31	35,000
2	gbl	Hamburg	H	L	0-2		24,000
3	gbl	Mainz	H	W	2-0	Krupnikovic 23,39 pen	18,300
4	gbl	Stuttgart	A	D	1-1	Pinto 79	30,000
5	gbl	Kaiserslautern	H	D	0-0		16,000
6	gbl	B Dortmund	A	L	0-2		62,100
7	gbl	B M'gladbach	H	L	0-2		23,000
8	gbl	B Leverkusen	A	D	1-1	Boakye 58	22,500
9	gbl	Hertha Berlin	H	W	3-0	Borges 14; Westermann 29; Zuma 51	20,117
10	gbl	Nuremburg	A	W	3-2	Fink 35; Leon 88; Zuma 90	18,000
11	gbl	Hannover 96	H	W	4-1	Fink 1; Zuma 53; Boakye 69,84	20,000
12	gbl	Eintr Frankfurt	A	L	0-3		41,000
13	gbl	Bayern Munich	H	L	1-2	Boakye 60	26,601
14	gbl	Wolfsburg	A	D	0-0		20,000
15	gbl	Schalke	H	L	0-1		26,601
16	gbl	Duisburg	A	D	1-1	Vata 52	18,000
17	gbl	Cologne	H	W	3-2	Kobilyk 52; Fink 54,59	26,601
18	gbl	W Bremen	H	L	0-1		24,169
19	gbl	Hamburg	A	L	1-2	Boakye 26	52,000
20	gbl	Mainz	A	D	1-1	Boakye 57	19,500
21	gbl	Stuttgart	H	W	2-1	Boakye 31,50	20,000
22	gbl	Kaiserslautern	A	L	0-2		26,806
23	gbl	B Dortmund	H	W	1-0	Kauf 45	25,000
24	gbl	B M'gladbach	A	L	0-2		39,372
25	gbl	B Leverkusen	H	W	1-0	Djalovic 5	20,000
26	gbl	Hertha Berlin	A	L	0-1		48,000
27	gbl	Nuremburg	H	D	0-0		22,500
28	gbl	Hannover 96	A	W	1-0	Vata 5	34,361
29	gbl	Eintr Frankfurt	H	W	1-0	Westermann 68	22,000
30	gbl	Bayern Munich	A	L	0-2		69,000
31	gbl	Wolfsburg	H	L	0-1		18,000
32	gbl	Schalke	A	L	1-3	Kuntzel 50	61,000
33	gbl	Duisburg	H	L	0-2		15,000
34	gbl	Cologne	A	L	2-4	Kobilyk 46; Djalovic 70	50,000

LEAGUE APPEARANCES, BOOKINGS AND CAPS

	AGE (on 01/07/06)	IN NAMED 18	APPEARANCES	COUNTING GAMES	MINUTES ON PITCH	YELLOW CARDS	RED CARDS	CAPS THIS SEASON	NATIONAL SIDE
Goalkeepers									
Dennis Eilhoff	23	5	2	1	120	0	0	-	Germany
Pascal Formann	23	1	0	0	0	0	0	-	Germany
Mathias Hain	33	33	33	32	2940	2	0	-	Germany
Defenders									
Marcio Borges	33	27	27	26	2355	7	0	-	Brazil
Michael Fink	24	33	33	31	2838	2	0	-	Germany
Petr Gabriel	33	7	6	6	540	0	0	-	Czech Republic
Radim Kucera	32	15	15	10	991	0	0	-	Czech Republic
Tobias Rau	24	16	14	7	784	2	0	-	Germany
Markus Schuler	28	28	28	24	2285	6	0	-	Germany
Heiko Westermann	22	34	34	34	3045	2	0	-	Germany
Midfielders									
Heiner Backhaus	24	1	0	0	0	0	0	-	Germany
Detlev Dammeier	37	14	13	7	800	1	0	-	Germany
Tim Danneberg	20	4	2	1	116	0	0	-	Germany
Ruediger Kauf	31	16	16	15	1367	5	0	-	Germany
David Kobilyk	25	25	25	14	1693	1	0	-	Czech Republic
Bernd Korzynietz	26	34	34	33	2987	2	0	-	Germany
Nebosja Krupnikovic	32	8	8	5	619	0	0	-	Serbia & Mont
Diego Leon	22	4	3	0	38	0	0	-	Spain
Roberto Pinto	27	31	31	3	938	2	0	-	Portugal
Massimiliano Porcello	26	6	6	4	399	2	0	-	Italy
Christian Schwegler	22	2	0	0	0	0	0	-	Switzerland
Kamil Vacek	19	2	1	0	5	0	0	-	Czech Republic
Fatmir Vata	34	22	22	17	1673	4	0	-	Albania
Christian Wieczorek	20	1	1	0	66	0	0	-	Germany
Forwards									
Isaac Boakye	24	25	25	18	1835	0	0	-	Ghana
Radomir Djalovic	23	22	21	5	754	3	0	-	Serbia & Mont
Marco Kuntzel	30	20	19	8	1229	3	0	-	Germany
Ioannis Masmanidis	23	16	16	8	1006	2	0	-	Germany
Artur Wichniarek	29	8	8	2	320	0	0	-	Poland
Sibussio Zuma	31	25	25	21	1917	2	0	-	South Africa

TEAM OF THE SEASON

MONTHLY POINTS TALLY

AUGUST	3	33%
SEPTEMBER	2	17%
OCTOBER	10	83%
NOVEMBER	1	11%
DECEMBER	4	44%
JANUARY	0	0%
FEBRUARY	7	47%
MARCH	4	33%
APRIL	6	50%
MAY	0	0%

LEAGUE GOALS

	PLAYER	MINS	GOALS	S RATE
1	Boakye	1835	8	229
2	Zuma	1917	4	479
3	Fink	2838	4	710
4	Krupnikovic	619	3	206
5	Kobilyk	1693	2	847
6	Vata	1673	2	837
7	Djalovic	754	2	377
8	Westermann	3045	2	1523
9	Pinto	938	1	938
10	Kauf	1367	1	1367
11	Borges	2355	1	2355
12	Leon	38	1	38
13	Kuntzel	1229	1	1229
	Other		0	
	TOTAL		32	

TOP POINT EARNERS

	PLAYER	GAMES	AV PTS
1	Markus Schuler	24	1.42
2	Fatmir Vata	17	1.29
3	Marcio Borges	26	1.19
4	Mathias Hain	32	1.16
5	Sibussio Zuma	21	1.14
6	David Kobilyk	14	1.14
7	Ruediger Kauf	15	1.13
8	Bernd Korzynietz	33	1.12
9	Michael Fink	31	1.10
10	Heiko Westermann	34	1.09
	CLUB AVERAGE:		1.09

DISCIPLINARY RECORDS

	PLAYER	YELLOW	RED	AVE
1	Djalovic	3	0	251
2	Kauf	5	0	273
3	Borges	7	0	336
4	Schuler	6	0	380
5	Rau	2	0	392
6	Kuntzel	3	0	409
7	Vata	4	0	418
8	Pinto	2	0	469
9	Masmanidis	2	0	503
10	Dammeier	1	0	800
11	Zuma	2	0	958
12	Fink	2	0	1419
13	Hain	2	0	1470
	Other	5	0	
	TOTAL	46	0	

KEY GOALKEEPER

Mathias Hain

Goals Conceded in the League	43	Counting Games League games when player was on pitch for at least 70 minutes	32
Defensive Rating Ave number of mins between League goals conceded while on the pitch	68	Clean Sheets In League games when player was on pitch for at least 70 minutes	9

KEY PLAYERS - DEFENDERS

Markus Schuler

Goals Conceded Number of League goals conceded while the player was on the pitch	28	Clean Sheets In League games when player was on pitch for at least 70 minutes	8
Defensive Rating Ave number of mins between League goals conceded while on the pitch	82	Club Defensive Rating Average number of mins between League goals conceded by the club this season	64

	PLAYER	CON LGE	CLEAN SHEETS	DEF RATE
1	Markus Schuler	28	8	82 mins
2	Marcio Borges	35	7	67 mins
3	Michael Fink	43	8	66 mins
4	Heiko Westermann	48	9	63 mins

KEY PLAYERS - MIDFIELDERS

David Kobilyk

Goals in the League	2	Contribution to Attacking Power Average number of minutes between League team goals while on pitch	81
Defensive Rating Average number of mins between League goals conceded while on the pitch	55	Scoring Difference Defensive Rating minus Contribution to Attacking Power	-26

	PLAYER	LGE GOALS	DEF RATE	POWER	SCORE DIFF
1	David Kobilyk	2	55	81	-26 mins
2	Fatmir Vata	2	70	98	-28 mins
3	Bernd Korzynietz	0	65	100	-35 mins
4	Ruediger Kauf	1	80	152	-72 mins

KEY PLAYERS - GOALSCORERS

Isaac Boakye

Goals in the League	8	Player Strike Rate Average number of minutes between League goals scored by player	229
Contribution to Attacking Power Average number of minutes between League team goals while on pitch	87	Club Strike Rate Average number of minutes between League goals scored by club	96

	PLAYER	LGE GOALS	POWER	STRIKE RATE
1	Isaac Boakye	8	87	229 mins
2	Sibussio Zuma	4	87	479 mins
3	Michael Fink	4	89	710 mins
4	Fatmir Vata	2	98	837 mins

Heiko Westermann

SQUAD APPEARANCES

Match	1	2	3	4	5	6	7	8	9	10	11	12	13	14	15	16	17	18	19	20	21	22	23	24	25	26	27	28	29	30	31	32	33	34
Venue	A	H	H	A	H	A	H	A	H	A	H	A	H	A	H	A	H	H	A	A	H	A	H	A	H	A	H	A	H	A	H	A	H	A
Competition	L	L	L	L	L	L	L	L	L	L	L	L	L	L	L	L	L	L	L	L	L	L	L	L	L	L	L	L	L	L	L	L	L	L
Result	L	L	W	D	D	L	L	D	W	W	W	L	L	D	L	D	W	L	L	D	W	L	W	L	W	L	D	W	W	L	L	L	L	L

Goalkeepers
Dennis Eilhoff
Pascal Formann
Mathias Hain

Defenders
Marcio Borges
Michael Fink
Petr Gabriel
Radim Kucera
Tobias Rau
Markus Schuler
Heiko Westermann

Midfielders
Heiner Backhaus
Detlev Dammeier
Tim Danneberg
Ruediger Kauf
David Kobilyk
Bernd Korzynietz
Nebosja Krupnikovic
Diego Leon
Roberto Pinto
Massimiliano Porcello
Christian Schwegler
Kamil Vacek
Fatmir Vata
Christian Wieczorek

Forwards
Isaac Boakye
Radomir Djalovic
Marco Kuntzel
Ioannis Masmanidis
Artur Wichniarek
Sibusio Zuma

KEY: ■ On all match
■ On bench
⏮ Subbed or sent off (Counting game)
« Subbed or sent off (playing less than 70 minutes)
⏭ Subbed on from bench (Counting Game)
» Subbed on (playing less than 70 minutes)
Subbed on and then subbed or sent off (Counting Game)
Subbed on and then subbed or sent off (playing less than 70 minutes)
□ Not in 16

EINTRACHT FRANKFURT

Final Position: **14th**

NICKNAME: DIE EINTRACHT

KEY: □Won □Drawn □Lost

		Opponent	H/A	Res	Score	Scorers	Attendance
1	gbl	B Leverkusen	H	L	1-4	Vasoki 7	41,000
2	gbl	Hertha Berlin	A	L	0-2		45,000
3	gbl	Nuremburg	H	W	1-0	Jones 68	40,000
4	gbl	Hannover 96	A	L	0-2		35,166
5	gbl	Hamburg	A	D	1-1	Cha 90	45,000
6	gbl	Bayern Munich	H	L	0-1		52,000
7	gbl	Wolfsburg	A	L	0-1		17,121
8	gbl	Schalke	H	L	0-1		35,000
9	gbl	Duisburg	A	W	1-0	Meier 27	23,000
10	gbl	Cologne	H	W	6-3	Amanatidis 2; Rehmer 8; Chris 28; Kohler 35; Meier 78; Cha 89,89	45,000
11	gbl	W Bremen	A	L	1-4	Amanatidis 19	40,000
12	gbl	Arminia B	H	W	3-0	Copado 35; Meier 49,55	41,000
13	gbl	Mainz	A	D	2-2	Noveski 3 og,6 og	20,300
14	gbl	Stuttgart	H	D	1-1	Amanatidis 19	47,000
15	gbl	B Dortmund	H	W	2-0	Copado 9; Amanatidis 85	47,000
16	gbl	Kaiserslautern	A	W	2-1	Weissenberger 50; Copado 58	33,000
17	gbl	B M'gladbach	A	L	3-4	Copado 16,21; Chris 90	48,000
18	gbl	B Leverkusen	A	L	1-2	Amanatidis 41	22,000
19	gbl	Hertha Berlin	H	D	1-1	Jones 58	35,000
20	gbl	Nuremburg	A	W	1-0	Amanatidis 43	30,000
21	gbl	Hannover 96	H	L	0-1		29,000
22	gbl	Hamburg	H	L	1-2	Meier 42	50,000
23	gbl	Bayern Munich	A	L	2-5	Preuss 32; Meier 84	69,000
24	gbl	Wolfsburg	H	D	1-1	Amanatidis 65	26,000
25	gbl	Schalke	A	L	0-2		61,524
26	gbl	Duisburg	H	W	5-2	Amanatidis 2,14,58; Kohler 12; Copado 50 pen	32,000
27	gbl	Cologne	A	D	1-1	Rehmer 17	48,000
28	gbl	W Bremen	H	L	0-1		50,000
29	gbl	Arminia B	A	L	0-1		22,000
30	gbl	Mainz	H	D	0-0		49,962
31	gbl	Stuttgart	A	W	2-0	Meier 59; Amanatidis 62 pen	56,000
32	gbl	Kaiserslautern	H	D	2-2	Kohler 50; Amanatidis 69	50,000
33	gbl	B Dortmund	A	D	1-1	Cha 54	80,000
34	gbl	B M'gladbach	H	L	0-2		25,000

LEAGUE APPEARANCES, BOOKINGS AND CAPS

	AGE (on 01/07/06)	IN NAMED 18	APPEARANCES	COUNTING GAMES	MINUTES ON PITCH	YELLOW CARDS	RED CARDS	CAPS THIS SEASON	NATIONAL SIDE
Goalkeepers									
Oka Nikolov	32	30	30	30	2700	0	0	-	Germany
Markus Proll	26	3	2	2	180	0	0	-	Germany
Jan Zimmermann	21	3	2	2	180	0	0	-	Germany
Defenders									
Mounir Chaftar	20	1	1	0	59	1	0	-	Germany
Chris	27	22	22	20	1817	5	0	-	Brazil
Daniyel Cimen	21	14	12	7	770	0	0	-	Germany
Marco Rehmer	34	25	25	21	2025	4	0	-	Germany
Christopher Reinhard	21	7	7	5	476	1	0	-	Germany
Marco Russ	20	10	9	8	734	4	0	-	Germany
Christoph Spycher	28	24	24	24	2140	0	0	9	Switzerland (35)
Aleksandar Vasoki	26	33	33	33	2970	6	0	-	Macedonia
Andre Weidener	36	1	0	0	0	0	0	-	Germany
Midfielders									
Alexander Huber	21	1	1	1	90	0	0	-	Germany
Benjamin Huggel	29	26	26	17	1776	2	0	6	Switzerland (35)
Stefan Lexa	29	14	13	5	598	2	0	-	Austria
Alexander Meier	23	33	33	30	2782	5	0	-	Germany
Patrick Ochs	22	28	28	25	2281	8	0	-	Germany
Christoph Preuss	25	23	23	17	1651	1	0	-	Germany
Alexander Schur	34	2	2	0	32	0	0	-	Germany
M. Weissenberger	31	14	14	4	582	1	0	-	Austria
Forwards									
Ioannis Amanatidis	24	32	32	27	2607	4	0	-	Greece
Doo-Ri Cha	25	27	27	10	1175	1	0	2	South Korea (29)
Francisco Copado	31	24	24	18	1809	1	0	-	Germany
Jermaine Jones	24	20	20	18	1709	8	0	-	Germany
Benjamin Kohler	25	29	29	22	2173	3	1	-	Germany
Dominik Stroh-Engel	20	3	3	0	28	0	0	-	Germany
Arie Van Lent	34	11	11	2	316	0	0	-	Holland

TEAM OF THE SEASON

G — Oka Nikolov — CG: 30 DR: 63

D — Aleksandar Vasoki — CG: 33 DR: 59

D — Marco Rehmer — CG: 21 DR: 55

D — Chris — CG: 20 DR: 53

D — Christoph Spycher — CG: 24 DR: 61

M — Alexander Meier — CG: 30 SD: -5

M — Patrick Ochs — CG: 25 SD: -11

M — Benjamin Huggel — CG: 17 SD: -29

M — Christoph Preuss — CG: 17 SD: -30

F — Ioannis Amanatidis — CG: 27 SR: 217

F — Francisco Copado — CG: 18 SR: 302

MONTHLY POINTS TALLY

Month	Points	%
AUGUST	3	33%
SEPTEMBER	1	8%
OCTOBER	6	50%
NOVEMBER	5	56%
DECEMBER	6	67%
JANUARY	0	0%
FEBRUARY	4	27%
MARCH	5	42%
APRIL	4	33%
MAY	2	22%

LEAGUE GOALS

	PLAYER	MINS	GOALS	S RATE
1	Amanatidis	2607	12	217
2	Meier	2782	7	397
3	Copado	1809	6	302
4	Cha	1175	4	294
5	Kohler	2173	3	724
6	Chris	1817	2	909
7	Rehmer	2025	2	1013
8	Jones	1709	2	855
9	Vasoki	2970	1	2970
10	Weissenberger	582	1	582
11	Preuss	1651	1	1651
	Other		2	
	TOTAL		43	

TOP POINT EARNERS

	PLAYER	GAMES	AV PTS
1	Francisco Copado	18	1.28
2	Benjamin Kohler	22	1.27
3	Ioannis Amanatidis	27	1.22
4	Christoph Spycher	24	1.21
5	Oka Nikolov	30	1.20
6	Marco Rehmer	21	1.14
7	Alexander Meier	30	1.10
8	Christian Maicon Chris	20	1.10
9	Patrick Ochs	25	1.08
10	Jermaine Jones	18	1.06
	CLUB AVERAGE:		1.06

DISCIPLINARY RECORDS

	PLAYER	YELLOW	RED	AVE
1	Russ	4	0	183
2	Jones	8	0	213
3	Ochs	8	0	285
4	Lexa	2	0	299
5	Chris	5	0	363
6	Reinhard	1	0	476
7	Vasoki	6	0	495
8	Rehmer	4	0	506
9	Kohler	3	1	543
10	Meier	5	0	556
11	Weissenberger	1	0	582
12	Amanatidis	4	0	651
13	Huggel	2	0	888
	Other	3	0	
	TOTAL	56	1	

KEY GOALKEEPER

Oka Nikolov

Goals Conceded in the League	43	**Counting Games** League games when player was on pitch for at least 70 minutes	30
Defensive Rating Ave number of mins between League goals conceded while on the pitch	63	**Clean Sheets** In League games when player was on pitch for at least 70 minutes	7

KEY PLAYERS - DEFENDERS

Christoph Spycher

Goals Conceded Number of League goals conceded while the player was on the pitch	35	**Clean Sheets** In League games when player was on pitch for at least 70 minutes	6
Defensive Rating Ave number of mins between League goals conceded while on the pitch	61	**Club Defensive Rating** Average number of mins between League goals conceded by the club this season	60

	PLAYER	CON LGE	CLEAN SHEETS	DEF RATE
1	Christoph Spycher	35	6	61 mins
2	Aleksandar Vasoki	50	7	59 mins
3	Marco Rehmer	37	4	55 mins
4	Chris	34	3	53 mins

KEY PLAYERS - MIDFIELDERS

Alexander Meier

Goals in the League	7	**Contribution to Attacking Power** Average number of minutes between League team goals while on pitch	73
Defensive Rating Average number of mins between League goals conceded while on the pitch	68	**Scoring Difference** Defensive Rating minus Contribution to Attacking Power	-5

	PLAYER	LGE GOALS	DEF RATE	POWER	SCORE DIFF
1	Alexander Meier	7	68	73	-5 mins
2	Patrick Ochs	0	58	69	-11 mins
3	Benjamin Huggel	0	52	81	-29 mins
4	Christoph Preuss	1	49	79	-30 mins

KEY PLAYERS - GOALSCORERS

Ioannis Amanatidis

Goals in the League	12	**Player Strike Rate** Average number of minutes between League goals scored by player	217
Contribution to Attacking Power Average number of minutes between League team goals while on pitch	70	**Club Strike Rate** Average number of minutes between League goals scored by club	71

	PLAYER	LGE GOALS	POWER	STRIKE RATE
1	Ioannis Amanatidis	12	70	217 mins
2	Francisco Copado	6	57	302 mins
3	Alexander Meier	7	73	397 mins
4	Benjamin Kohler	3	64	724 mins

Francisco Copado and Ioannis Amanatidis

SQUAD APPEARANCES

Match	1	2	3	4	5	6	7	8	9	10	11	12	13	14	15	16	17	18	19	20	21	22	23	24	25	26	27	28	29	30	31	32	33	34
Venue	H	A	H	A	A	H	A	H	A	H	A	H	A	H	H	A	A	A	H	A	H	H	A	H	A	H	A	H	A	H	A	H	A	H
Competition	L	L	L	L	L	L	L	L	L	L	L	L	L	L	L	L	L	L	L	L	L	L	L	L	L	L	L	L	L	L	L	L	L	L
Result	L	L	W	L	D	L	L	L	W	W	L	W	D	D	W	W	L	L	D	W	L	L	L	D	L	W	D	L	L	D	W	D	D	L

Goalkeepers
Oka Nikolov
Markus Proll
Jan Zimmermann

Defenders
Mounir Chaftar
Christian Maicon H Chris
Daniyel Cimen
Marco Rehmer
Christopher Reinhard
Marco Russ
Aleksandar Vasoki
Andre Weidener

Midfielders
Alexander Huber
Benjamin Huggel
Stefan Lexa
Alexander Meier
Patrick Ochs
Christoph Preuss
Alexander Schur
Christoph Spycher
Markus Weissenberger

Forwards
Ioannis Amanatidis
Doo-Ri Cha
Francisco Copado
Jermaine Jones
Benjamin Kohler
Dominik Stroh-Engel
Arie Van Lent

KEY: ■ On all match | ■ On bench | ⏮ Subbed or sent off (Counting game) | « Subbed or sent off (playing less than 70 minutes) | ⏭ Subbed on from bench (Counting Game) | » Subbed on (playing less than 70 minutes) | Subbed on and then subbed or sent off (Counting Game) | Subbed on and then subbed or sent off (playing less than 70 minutes) | □ Not in 16

VfL WOLFSBURG

Final Position: **15th**

NICKNAME: DIE WOLFE

KEY: ☐Won ☐Drawn ☐Lost

						Attendance
1	gbl	**B Dortmund**	H D	2-2	Klimowicz 9; Hofland 84	22,000
2	gbl	**B M'gladbach**	A D	1-1	Hanke 41	45,000
3	gbl	**B Leverkusen**	H W	2-1	D'Alessandro 39; Thiam 54	18,201
4	gbl	**Hertha Berlin**	A L	0-3		40,754
5	gbl	**Nuremburg**	H D	1-1	Klimowicz 15	15,000
6	gbl	**Hannover 96**	A W	4-2	Hanke 10,14; Klimowicz 27; D'Alessandro 33	31,517
7	gbl	**Eintr Frankfurt**	H W	1-0	Klimowicz 35	17,121
8	gbl	**Bayern Munich**	A L	0-2		66,000
9	gbl	**Hamburg**	A W	1-0	Klimowicz 19	54,000
10	gbl	**Schalke**	H D	0-0		28,000
11	gbl	**Duisburg**	A L	0-1		20,000
12	gbl	**Cologne**	H D	1-1	Klimowicz 41	19,500
13	gbl	**W Bremen**	A L	1-6	Klimowicz 57	38,000
14	gbl	**Arminia B**	H D	0-0		20,000
15	gbl	**Mainz**	A L	1-5	Klimowicz 3	19,000
16	gbl	**Stuttgart**	H L	0-1		23,696
17	gbl	**Kaiserslautern**	A L	2-3	Klimowicz 47; Hanke 54	25,000
18	gbl	**B Dortmund**	A L	2-3	Hanke 13; Klimowicz 72	65,000
19	gbl	**B M'gladbach**	H W	2-0	Klimowicz 41; Hanke 64	16,000
20	gbl	**B Leverkusen**	A L	0-4		22,500
21	gbl	**Hertha Berlin**	H D	1-1	Hofland 63	15,000
22	gbl	**Nuremburg**	A L	0-1		22,000
23	gbl	**Hannover 96**	H W	2-1	Hanke 9; Menseguez 85	28,000
24	gbl	**Eintr Frankfurt**	A D	1-1	Hanke 58	26,000
25	gbl	**Bayern Munich**	H D	0-0		30,000
26	gbl	**Hamburg**	H L	0-1		28,095
27	gbl	**Schalke**	A D	2-2	Hoogendorp 29; Lamprecht 76	61,524
28	gbl	**Duisburg**	H D	1-1	Marlet 90	16,000
29	gbl	**Cologne**	A L	0-3		40,000
30	gbl	**W Bremen**	H D	1-1	Hristov 22	27,000
31	gbl	**Arminia B**	A W	1-0	Karhan 45	18,000
32	gbl	**Mainz**	H L	0-3		22,000
33	gbl	**Stuttgart**	A L	1-2	Menseguez 5	31,000
34	gbl	**Kaiserslautern**	H D	2-2	Makiadi 66; Klimowicz 69	30,000

LEAGUE APPEARANCES, BOOKINGS AND CAPS

	AGE (on 01/07/06)	IN NAMED 18	APPEARANCES	COUNTING GAMES	MINUTES ON PITCH	YELLOW CARDS	RED CARDS	CAPS THIS SEASON	NATIONAL SIDE
Goalkeepers									
Simon Jentzsch	30	34	34	34	3060	4	0	-	Germany
Andre Lenz	32	4	0	0	0	0	0	-	Germany
Defenders									
Karsten Fischer	22	6	5	2	251	2	0	-	Germany
Maik Franz	24	16	16	12	1188	4	1	-	Germany
Kevin Hofland	27	19	19	19	1697	10	1	-	Holland
Miroslav Karhan	30	30	30	21	2231	2	0	-	Slovakia
Chris. Lamprecht	21	14	14	2	532	3	0	-	Germany
Matthias Langkamp	22	2	1	0	3	0	0	-	Germany
Bojan Neziri	24	20	19	14	1452	1	0	-	Serbia & Mont
Facundo Quiroga	28	28	28	25	2333	3	1	-	Argentina
Stefan Schnoor	35	22	20	10	1062	3	0	-	Germany
Peter van der Heyden	29	24	24	20	1879	4	0	1	Belgium (42)
Midfielders									
Alex	26	18	17	14	1363	4	0	2	Portugal (7)
Andres D'Alessandro	25	13	13	12	1129	4	0	2	Argentina (9)
Marian Hristov	32	9	9	7	659	4	0	-	Bulgaria
Cedric Makiadi	22	12	9	0	247	1	0	-	Congo DR
Hans Sarpei	30	28	27	18	1881	6	0	2	Ghana (48)
Pablo Thiam	32	23	23	15	1635	3	0	4	Guinea (123)
Levan Tskitishvili	29	15	15	12	1201	4	1	-	Georgia
Tom van der Leegte	29	13	13	10	1016	5	0	-	Holland
Patrick Weiser	34	2	2	2	161	0	0	-	Germany
Forwards									
A. Pereira Abuda	20	2	1	0	9	1	0	-	Brazil
Michael Hanke	22	31	31	22	2144	2	0	-	Germany
Rick Hoogendorp	31	13	11	6	669	1	0	-	Holland
Diego F. Klimowicz	32	26	26	23	2169	8	2	-	Argentina
Steve Marlet	32	24	21	5	865	1	0	-	France
Juan C. Menseguez	22	33	33	28	2626	1	0	-	Argentina
Marko Topic	30	2	2	0	19	0	0	-	Bosnia

TEAM OF THE SEASON

MONTHLY POINTS TALLY

AUGUST	5	56%
SEPTEMBER	7	58%
OCTOBER	4	33%
NOVEMBER	2	22%
DECEMBER	0	0%
JANUARY	0	0%
FEBRUARY	7	47%
MARCH	3	25%
APRIL	5	42%
MAY	1	11%

LEAGUE GOALS

	PLAYER	MINS	GOALS	S RATE
1	Klimowicz	2169	12	181
2	Hanke	2144	8	268
3	Hofland	1697	2	849
4	D'Alessandro	1129	2	565
5	Menseguez	2626	2	1313
6	Lamprecht	532	1	532
7	Makiadi	247	1	247
8	Karhan	2231	1	2231
9	Hristov	659	1	659
10	Thiam	1635	1	1635
11	Marlet	865	1	865
12	Hoogendorp	669	1	669
	Other		0	
	TOTAL		33	

TOP POINT EARNERS

	PLAYER	GAMES	AV PTS
1	Alex	14	**1.50**
2	Andres D'Alessandro	12	**1.33**
3	Michael Hanke	22	**1.23**
4	Miroslav Karhan	21	**1.14**
5	Facundo Quiroga	25	**1.12**
6	Bojan Neziri	14	**1.07**
7	Kevin Hofland	19	**1.05**
8	Maik Franz	12	**1.00**
9	Pablo Thiam	15	**1.00**
10	Simon Jentzsch	34	**1.00**
	CLUB AVERAGE:		**1.00**

DISCIPLINARY RECORDS

	PLAYER	YELLOW	RED	AVE
1	Hofland	10	1	**154**
2	Hristov	4	0	**164**
3	Lamprecht	3	0	**177**
4	van der Leegte	5	0	**203**
5	Klimowicz	8	2	**216**
6	Franz	4	1	**237**
7	Tskitishvili	4	1	**240**
8	D'Alessandro	4	0	**282**
9	Sarpei	6	0	**313**
10	Alex	4	0	**340**
11	Schnoor	3	0	**354**
12	van der Heyden	4	0	**469**
13	Thiam	3	0	**545**
	Other	15	1	
	TOTAL	**77**	**6**	

KEY GOALKEEPER

Simon Jentzsch

Goals Conceded in the League	**56**	**Counting Games** League games when player was on pitch for at least 70 minutes	**34**
Defensive Rating Ave number of mins between League goals conceded while on the pitch	**55**	**Clean Sheets** In League games when player was on pitch for at least 70 minutes	**7**

KEY PLAYERS - DEFENDERS

Kevin Hofland

Goals Conceded Number of League goals conceded while the player was on the pitch	**25**	**Clean Sheets** In League games when player was on pitch for at least 70 minutes	**4**
Defensive Rating Ave number of mins between League goals conceded while on the pitch	**68**	**Club Defensive Rating** Average number of mins between League goals conceded by the club this season	**55**

	PLAYER	CON LGE	CLEAN SHEETS	DEF RATE
1	Kevin Hofland	25	4	**68 mins**
2	Peter van der Heyden	30	5	**63 mins**
3	Miroslav Karhan	38	4	**59 mins**
4	Facundo Quiroga	42	6	**56 mins**

KEY PLAYERS - MIDFIELDERS

Alex

Goals in the League	**0**	**Contribution to Attacking Power** Average number of minutes between League team goals while on pitch	**76**
Defensive Rating Average number of mins between League goals conceded while on the pitch	**72**	**Scoring Difference** Defensive Rating minus Contribution to Attacking Power	**-4**

	PLAYER	LGE GOALS	DEF RATE	POWER	SCORE DIFF
1	Alex	0	72	76	**-4 mins**
2	Andres D'Alessandro	2	66	81	**-15 mins**
3	Levan Tskitishvili	0	46	75	**-29 mins**
4	Pablo Thiam	1	51	109	**-58 mins**

KEY PLAYERS - GOALSCORERS

Diego Fernando Klimowicz

Goals in the League	**12**	**Player Strike Rate** Average number of minutes between League goals scored by player	**181**
Contribution to Attacking Power Average number of minutes between League team goals while on pitch	**83**	**Club Strike Rate** Average number of minutes between League goals scored by club	**93**

	PLAYER	LGE GOALS	POWER	STRIKE RATE
1	Diego Fernando Klimowicz	12	83	**181 mins**
2	Michael Hanke	8	79	**268 mins**
3	Andres D'Alessandro	2	81	**565 mins**
4	Kevin Hofland	2	94	**849 mins**

Diego Klimowicz celebrates with his team mates

SQUAD APPEARANCES

Match	1	2	3	4	5	6	7	8	9	10	11	12	13	14	15	16	17	18	19	20	21	22	23	24	25	26	27	28	29	30	31	32	33	34
Venue	H	A	H	A	H	A	H	A	A	H	A	H	A	H	A	H	A	A	H	A	H	A	H	A	H	H	A	H	A	H	A	H	A	H
Competition	L	L	L	L	L	L	L	L	L	L	L	L	L	L	L	L	L	L	L	L	L	L	L	L	L	L	L	L	L	L	L	L	L	L
Result	D	D	W	L	D	W	W	L	W	D	L	D	L	D	L	L	L	L	W	L	D	L	W	D	D	L	D	D	L	D	W	L	L	D

Goalkeepers
Simon Jentzsch
Andre Lenz

Defenders
Karsten Fischer
Maik Franz
Kevin Hofland
Miroslav Karhan
Christopher Lamprecht
Matthias Langkamp
Bojan Neziri
Facundo Quiroga
Stefan Schnoor
Peter van der Heyden

Midfielders
Alex
Andres D'Alessandro
Marian Hristov
Cedric Makiadi
Hans Sarpei
Pablo Thiam
Levan Tskitishvili
Tom van der Leegte
Patrick Weiser

Forwards
Adailson Pereira Abuda
Michael Hanke
Rick Hoogendorp
Diego Fernando Klimowicz
Steve Marlet
Juan Carlos Menseguez
Marko Topic

KEY: On all match | On bench | Subbed or sent off (Counting game) | Subbed or sent off (playing less than 70 minutes) | Subbed on from bench (Counting Game) | Subbed on (playing less than 70 minutes) | Subbed on and then subbed or sent off (Counting Game) | Subbed on and then subbed or sent off (playing less than 70 minutes) | Not in 16

KAISERSLAUTERN

Final Position: **16th**

NICKNAME: DIE ROTEN TEUFEL

KEY: ☐Won ☐Drawn ☐Lost

						Scorers	Attendance
1	gbl	Schalke	A	L	1-2	Altintop 33	61,000
2	gbl	Duisburg	H	W	5-3	Altintop 3,58,81; Lembi 28; Sanogo 68	37,000
3	gbl	Cologne	A	W	3-2	Altintop 19,79; Skela 90	50,000
4	gbl	W Bremen	H	L	1-5	Altintop 84	32,851
5	gbl	Arminia B	A	D	0-0		16,000
6	gbl	Mainz	H	L	0-2		40,000
7	gbl	Stuttgart	A	L	0-1		35,000
8	gbl	Hamburg	H	L	0-3		34,775
9	gbl	B Dortmund	H	D	3-3	Altintop 13,56,78	33,000
10	gbl	B M'gladbach	A	L	1-4	Sanogo 14	47,000
11	gbl	B Leverkusen	H	D	2-2	Engelhardt 32; Goktan 90	30,000
12	gbl	Hertha Berlin	A	L	0-3		35,000
13	gbl	Nuremburg	H	L	1-3	Blank 18	25,000
14	gbl	Hannover 96	A	L	1-5	Sanogo 69	32,500
15	gbl	Bayern Munich	A	L	1-2	Sanogo 39	66,000
16	gbl	Eintr Frankfurt	H	L	1-2	Seitz 85	33,000
17	gbl	Wolfsburg	H	W	3-2	Altintop 45,61,84	25,000
18	gbl	Schalke	H	L	0-2		35,549
19	gbl	Duisburg	A	D	2-2	Halfar 79,83	18,000
20	gbl	Cologne	H	D	2-2	Sanogo 42 pen; Schonheim 76	28,000
21	gbl	W Bremen	A	W	2-0	Sanogo 71; Skela 88	38,000
22	gbl	Arminia B	H	W	2-0	Sanogo 9,88	26,806
23	gbl	Mainz	A	W	2-0	Sanogo 24 pen,26	20,300
24	gbl	Stuttgart	H	D	1-1	Altintop 15	25,000
25	gbl	Hamburg	A	L	0-3		44,460
26	gbl	B Dortmund	A	L	1-2	Skela 45	68,000
27	gbl	B M'gladbach	H	W	3-0	Altintop 32,33; Skela 66	26,000
28	gbl	B Leverkusen	A	L	1-5	Pletsch 63	22,500
29	gbl	Hertha Berlin	H	L	0-2		30,000
30	gbl	Nuremburg	A	L	2-3	Altintop 20,48	47,250
31	gbl	Hannover 96	H	W	1-0	Halfar 39	33,000
32	gbl	Eintr Frankfurt	A	D	2-2	Reinert 16; Ziemer 82	50,000
33	gbl	Bayern Munich	H	D	1-1	Altintop 26	50,574
34	gbl	Wolfsburg	A	D	2-2	Altintop 20; Ziemer 86	30,000

LEAGUE APPEARANCES, BOOKINGS AND CAPS

	AGE (on 01/07/06)	IN NAMED 18	APPEARANCES	COUNTING GAMES	MINUTES ON PITCH	YELLOW CARDS	RED CARDS	CAPS THIS SEASON	NATIONAL SIDE
Goalkeepers									
Thomas Ernst	38	3	3	3	270	0	0	-	Germany
Florian Fromlowitz	20	12	12	11	1037	0	0	-	Germany
Jurgen Macho	28	21	20	19	1753	0	0	2	Austria (73)
Defenders									
Mathieu Beda	24	16	16	15	1395	4	0	-	France
Stefan Blank	29	16	16	11	1189	4	1	-	Germany
Balasz Borbely	26	8	8	1	374	5	0	-	Slovakia
Ingo Hertzsch	28	27	27	22	2129	4	0	-	Germany
Jon Inge Hoiland	28	9	9	6	628	0	0	-	Norway
Hervi Nzelo Lembi	30	29	29	26	2439	5	0	-	Congo DR
Lucien Mettomo	34	9	9	8	757	2	0	-	Cameroon
Marcelo Pletsch	30	23	22	19	1844	3	0	-	Brazil
Torsten Reuter	23	8	8	5	567	0	0	-	Germany
Timo Wenzel	28	4	4	3	315	1	0	-	Germany
Midfielders									
Axel Bellinghausen	23	20	20	12	1498	2	0	-	Germany
Bohl	-	2	2	0	52	0	0	-	
Marco Engelhardt	25	32	32	29	2702	7	0	-	Germany
Daniel Halfar	18	18	18	5	683	4	0	-	Germany
Mihael Mikic	26	20	20	5	835	5	0	-	Croatia
Christian Nerlinger	33	4	4	1	214	3	0	-	Germany
Sebastian Reinert	19	13	13	4	734	0	0	-	Germany
Thomas Riedl	30	11	11	3	575	1	0	-	Germany
Fabian Schonheim	19	18	18	15	1469	0	0	-	Germany
Ciriaco Sforza	36	7	7	4	503	0	1	-	Switzerland
Ervin Skela	29	34	34	32	2993	0	0	3	Albania (199)
Ferydoon Zandi	27	18	18	4	674	1	0	2	Iran (23)
Ziemer	-	2	2	0	31	0	0	-	
Forwards									
Halil Altintop	23	34	34	30	2880	2	0	9	Turkey (14)
Goktan Berkant	25	7	7	1	197	0	0	-	Turkey
Carsten Jancker	31	6	5	2	351	1	0	-	Germany
Boubacar Sanogo	23	24	24	20	1939	1	0	-	Ivory Coast
Jochen Seitz	29	12	11	3	562	2	0	-	Germany

TEAM OF THE SEASON

G — Florian Fromlowitz — CG: 12 DR: 49

D — Hervi Nzelo Lembi — CG: 26 DR: 47

D — Ingo Hertzsch — CG: 22 DR: 43

D — Marcelo Pletsch — CG: 19 DR: 35

D — Matthieu Beda — CG: 15 DR: 63

M — Fabian Schonheim — CG: 15 SD: -3

M — Ervin Skela — CG: 32 SD: -22

M — Marco Engelhardt — CG: 29 SD: -23

M — Axel Bellinghausen — CG: 12 SD: -33

F — Halil Altintop — CG: 30 SR: 144

F — Boubacar Sanogo — CG: 20 SR: 194

MONTHLY POINTS TALLY

Month	Points	%
AUGUST	6	67%
SEPTEMBER	1	8%
OCTOBER	2	17%
NOVEMBER	0	0%
DECEMBER	3	33%
JANUARY	0	0%
FEBRUARY	11	73%
MARCH	4	33%
APRIL	3	25%
MAY	3	33%

LEAGUE GOALS

	PLAYER	MINS	GOALS	S RATE
1	Altintop	2880	20	144
2	Sanogo	1939	10	194
3	Skela	2993	4	748
4	Halfar	683	3	228
5	Ziemer	31	2	16
6	Blank	1189	1	1189
7	Engelhardt	2702	1	2702
8	Pletsch	1844	1	1844
9	Seitz	562	1	562
10	Schonheim	1469	1	1469
11	Reinert	734	1	734
12	Lembi	2439	1	2439
13	Goktan	197	1	197
	Other		0	
	TOTAL		47	

TOP POINT EARNERS

	PLAYER	GAMES	AV PTS
1	Mathieu Beda	15	1.40
2	Fabian Schonheim	15	1.27
3	Hervi Nzelo Lembi	26	1.19
4	Boubacar Sanogo	20	1.15
5	Jurgen Macho	19	1.00
6	Ervin Skela	32	1.00
7	Marco Engelhardt	29	1.00
8	Ingo Hertzsch	22	0.91
9	Halil Altintop	30	0.90
10	Axel Bellinghausen	12	0.83
	CLUB AVERAGE:		0.97

DISCIPLINARY RECORDS

	PLAYER	YELLOW	RED	AVE
1	Mikic	5	0	167
2	Halfar	4	0	170
3	Blank	4	1	237
4	Seitz	2	0	281
5	Beda	4	0	348
6	Mettomo	2	0	378
7	Engelhardt	7	0	386
8	Lembi	5	0	487
9	Sforza	0	1	503
10	Hertzsch	4	0	532
11	Riedl	1	0	575
12	Pletsch	3	0	614
13	Zandi	1	0	674
	Other	5	0	
	TOTAL	47	2	

KEY GOALKEEPER

Florian Fromlowitz

Goals Conceded in the League	21	**Counting Games** League games when player was on pitch for at least 70 minutes	12
Defensive Rating Ave number of mins between League goals conceded while on the pitch	49	**Clean Sheets** In League games when player was on pitch for at least 70 minutes	3

KEY PLAYERS - DEFENDERS

Mathieu Beda

Goals Conceded Number of League goals conceded while the player was on the pitch	22	**Clean Sheets** In League games when player was on pitch for at least 70 minutes	5
Defensive Rating Ave number of mins between League goals conceded while on the pitch	63	**Club Defensive Rating** Average number of mins between League goals conceded by the club this season	43

	PLAYER	CON LGE	CLEAN SHEETS	DEF RATE
1	Mathieu Beda	22	5	63 mins
2	Hervi Nzelo Lembi	52	6	47 mins
3	Ingo Hertzsch	49	4	43 mins
4	Marcelo Pletsch	52	1	35 mins

KEY PLAYERS - MIDFIELDERS

Fabian Schonheim

Goals in the League	1	**Contribution to Attacking Power** Average number of minutes between League team goals while on pitch	64
Defensive Rating Average number of mins between League goals conceded while on the pitch	61	**Scoring Difference** Defensive Rating minus Contribution to Attacking Power	-3

	PLAYER	LGE GOALS	DEF RATE	POWER	SCORE DIFF
1	Fabian Schonheim	1	61	64	-3 mins
2	Ervin Skela	4	43	65	-22 mins
3	Marco Engelhardt	1	41	64	-23 mins
4	Axel Bellinghausen	0	42	75	-33 mins

KEY PLAYERS - GOALSCORERS

Halil Altintop

Goals in the League	20	**Player Strike Rate** Average number of minutes between League goals scored by player	144
Contribution to Attacking Power Average number of minutes between League team goals while on pitch	67	**Club Strike Rate** Average number of minutes between League goals scored by club	65

	PLAYER	LGE GOALS	POWER	STRIKE RATE
1	Halil Altintop	20	67	144 mins
2	Boubacar Sanogo	10	61	194 mins
3	Ervin Skela	4	65	748 mins
4	Fabian Schonheim	1	64	1469 mins

Halil Altintop

SQUAD APPEARANCES

Match	1	2	3	4	5	6	7	8	9	10	11	12	13	14	15	16	17	18	19	20	21	22	23	24	25	26	27	28	29	30	31	32	33	34
Venue	A	H	A	H	A	H	A	H	H	A	H	A	H	A	A	H	H	H	A	H	A	H	A	H	A	A	H	A	H	A	H	A	H	A
Competition	L	L	L	L	L	L	L	L	L	L	L	L	L	L	L	L	L	L	L	L	L	L	L	L	L	L	L	L	L	L	L	L	L	L
Result	L	W	W	L	D	L	L	L	D	L	D	L	L	L	L	L	W	L	D	D	W	W	W	D	L	L	W	L	L	L	W	D	D	D

Goalkeepers
Thomas Ernst
Florian Fromlowitz
Jurgen Macho

Defenders
Mathieu Beda
Stefan Blank
Balasz Borbely
Marco Engelhardt
Ingo Hertzsch
Jon Inge Hoiland
Hervi Nzelo Lembi
Lucien Mettomo
Marcelo Pletsch
Torsten Reuter
Fabian Schonheim
Timo Wenzel

Midfielders
Axel Bellinghausen
Bohl
Daniel Halfar
Mihael Mikic
Christian Nerlinger
Sebastian Reinert
Thomas Riedl
Ciriaco Sforza
Ervin Skela
Ferydoon Zandi
Ziemer

Forwards
Halil Altintop
Goktan Berkant
Carsten Jancker
Boubacar Sanogo
Jochen Seitz

KEY: On all match | On bench | Subbed or sent off (Counting game) | Subbed or sent off (playing less than 70 minutes) | Subbed on from bench (Counting Game) | Subbed on (playing less than 70 minutes) | Subbed on and then subbed or sent off (Counting Game) | Subbed on and then subbed or sent off (playing less than 70 minutes) | Not in 16

COLOGNE

Final Position: **17th**

NICKNAME: GEIBBOCKE

KEY: ☐ Won ☐ Drawn ☐ Lost

							Attendance
1	gbl	Mainz	H	W	1-0	Schlicke 87 pen	50,374
2	gbl	Stuttgart	A	W	3-2	Feulner 9; Streit 47,55	49,000
3	gbl	Kaiserslautern	H	L	2-3	Scherz 81; Niedrig 90	50,000
4	gbl	B Dortmund	A	L	1-2	Scherz 90	78,000
5	gbl	B M'gladbach	H	W	2-1	Podolski 12; Schlicke 30	50,000
6	gbl	B Leverkusen	A	L	1-2	Helmes 77	22,500
7	gbl	Hertha Berlin	H	L	0-1		48,000
8	gbl	Nuremburg	A	L	1-2	Helmes 75	23,000
9	gbl	Hannover 96	H	L	1-4	Streit 47	48,000
10	gbl	Eintr Frankfurt	A	L	3-6	Streit 5; Podolski 54 pen; Alpay 90	45,000
11	gbl	Bayern Munich	H	L	1-2	Scherz 28	50,000
12	gbl	Wolfsburg	A	D	1-1	Epstein 88	19,500
13	gbl	Schalke	H	D	2-2	Benschneider 47; Epstein 57	50,000
14	gbl	Hamburg	A	L	1-3	Schlicke 58	55,800
15	gbl	Duisburg	A	D	1-1	Podolski 30	28,000
16	gbl	W Bremen	H	L	1-4	Szabics 24	47,000
17	gbl	Arminia B	A	L	2-3	Springer 1; Scherz 72	26,601
18	gbl	Mainz	A	L	2-4	Podolski 31 pen; Scherz 49	20,300
19	gbl	Stuttgart	H	D	0-0		49,000
20	gbl	Kaiserslautern	A	D	2-2	Streller 37,74	28,000
21	gbl	B Dortmund	H	D	0-0		49,000
22	gbl	B M'gladbach	A	L	0-2		54,019
23	gbl	B Leverkusen	H	L	0-3		49,000
24	gbl	Hertha Berlin	A	W	4-2	Podolski 53,75; Streller 54; Scherz 87	38,000
25	gbl	Nuremburg	H	L	3-4	Zivkovic 27; Matip 62; Podolski 63	47,000
26	gbl	Hannover 96	A	L	0-1		28,000
27	gbl	Eintr Frankfurt	H	D	1-1	Springer 2	48,000
28	gbl	Bayern Munich	A	D	2-2	Feulner 12; Streit 36	69,000
29	gbl	Wolfsburg	H	W	3-0	Scherz 77; Helmes 78; Sarpei 81 og	40,000
30	gbl	Schalke	A	D	1-1	Podolski 45	61,524
31	gbl	Duisburg	H	W	3-1	Streit 37; Feulner 62; Podolski 80	45,000
32	gbl	Hamburg	H	L	0-1		50,000
33	gbl	W Bremen	A	L	0-6		40,000
34	gbl	Arminia B	H	W	4-2	Podolski 44,84; Scherz 56; Helmes 86	50,000

LEAGUE APPEARANCES, BOOKINGS AND CAPS

	AGE (on 01/07/06)	IN NAMED 18	APPEARANCES	COUNTING GAMES	MINUTES ON PITCH	YELLOW CARDS	RED CARDS	CAPS THIS SEASON	NATIONAL SIDE
Goalkeepers									
Alexander Bade	35	15	13	13	1171	0	0	-	Germany
Stefan Wessels	27	22	21	21	1889	0	0	-	Germany
Defenders									
Alpay Ozalan	33	21	21	19	1782	7	1	-	Turkey
Roland Benschneider	25	13	12	7	705	1	1	-	Germany
Carsten Cullman	30	10	10	9	838	3	0	-	Germany
Aparecido F. Evanilson	30	3	3	1	167	1	0	-	Brazil
Patrick Helmes	22	13	13	3	518	1	0	-	Germany
Christian Lell	21	26	25	19	1881	7	1	-	Germany
Marvin-Job Matip	20	23	22	20	1877	1	0	-	Germany
Bjorn Schlicke	25	15	15	13	1260	4	0	-	Germany
Andrew Sinkala	27	9	9	5	591	3	1	-	Zambia
Lukas Sinkewicz	20	33	33	32	2884	8	0	-	Germany
Boris Zivkovic	30	8	8	7	675	1	0	-	Croatia
Midfielders									
Ricardo Cabanas	27	16	15	15	1347	4	0	9	Switzerland (35)
Denis Epstein	20	10	10	2	424	0	0	-	Germany
Markus Feulner	24	13	13	9	972	2	0	-	Germany
Dimitrios Grammozis	28	19	19	10	1169	6	0	-	Greece
Rolf Guie-Mien	28	8	7	3	402	0	0	-	Congo DR
Anthony Lurling	29	12	12	1	571	3	0	-	Holland
Peter Madsen	-	1	1	1	71	0	0	-	
Youssef Mokhtari	27	13	13	8	899	2	0	-	Morocco
Christian Rahn	27	12	11	5	704	0	0	-	Germany
Matthias Scherz	34	27	27	13	1621	3	1	-	Germany
S. Schindzielorz	27	17	16	7	930	2	0	-	Germany
Christian Springer	34	19	18	8	1076	4	0	-	Germany
Albert Streit	26	30	30	28	2508	5	1	-	Germany
Patrick Weiser	34	1	1	0	45	0	0	-	Germany
Forwards									
Peter Madsen	28	8	8	3	416	0	0	-	Denmark
Lukas Podolski	21	32	32	30	2751	9	0	9	Germany (19)
Marco Streller	25	14	14	10	980	3	0	7	Switzerland (35)
Imre Szabics	25	9	9	2	360	1	1	1	Hungary (54)
Attila Tokoli	30	1	1	0	24	0	0	-	Hungary

TEAM OF THE SEASON

G: Alexander Bade — CG: 13 DR: 45

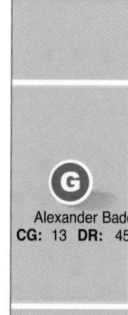

D: Alpay Ozalan — CG: 19 DR: 50

D: Marvin-Job Matip — CG: 20 DR: 47

D: Lukas Sinkewicz — CG: 32 DR: 42

D: Christian Lell — CG: 19 DR: 41

M: Ricardo Cabanas — CG: 15 SD: -7

M: Matthias Scherz — CG: 13 SD: -8

M: Albert Streit — CG: 28 SD: -26

M: D. Grammozis* — CG: 10 SD: -26

F: Lukas Podolski — CG: 30 SR: 250

F: Mario Stroller* — CG: 10 SR: 327

MONTHLY POINTS TALLY

AUGUST	6	67%
SEPTEMBER	3	25%
OCTOBER	0	0%
NOVEMBER	2	33%
DECEMBER	1	8%
JANUARY	0	0%
FEBRUARY	3	20%
MARCH	4	33%
APRIL	8	67%
MAY	3	33%

LEAGUE GOALS

	PLAYER	MINS	GOALS	S RATE
1	Podolski	2751	11	250
2	Scherz	1621	8	203
3	Streit	2508	6	418
4	Helmes	518	4	130
5	Streller	980	3	327
6	Schlicke	1260	3	420
7	Feulner	972	3	324
8	Epstein	424	2	212
9	Springer	1076	2	538
10	Zivkovic	675	1	675
11	Benschneider	705	1	705
12	Alpay	1782	1	1782
13	Matip	1877	1	1877
	Other		3	
	TOTAL		49	

TOP POINT EARNERS

	PLAYER	GAMES	AV PTS
1	Ricardo Cabanas	15	1.20
2	Alexander Bade	13	1.15
3	Marvin-Job Matip	20	1.15
4	Alpay Ozalan	19	1.05
5	Lukas Podolski	30	1.00
6	Lukas Sinkewicz	32	0.91
7	Albert Streit	28	0.86
8	Matthias Scherz	13	0.85
9	Stefan Wessels	21	0.71
10	Christian Lell	19	0.68
	CLUB AVERAGE:		0.88

DISCIPLINARY RECORDS

	PLAYER	YELLOW	RED	AVE
1	Sinkala	3	1	147
2	Grammozis	6	0	194
3	Alpay	7	1	222
4	Lell	7	1	235
5	Lurling	2	0	240
6	Springer	4	0	269
7	Cullman	3	0	279
8	Podolski	9	0	305
9	Schlicke	4	0	315
10	Streller	3	0	326
11	Cabanas	4	0	336
12	Benschneider	1	1	352
13	Sinkewicz	8	0	360
	Other	17	2	
	TOTAL	78	6	

KEY GOALKEEPER

Alexander Bade

Goals Conceded in the League	26	**Counting Games** League games when player was on pitch for at least 70 minutes	13
Defensive Rating Ave number of mins between League goals conceded while on the pitch	45	**Clean Sheets** In League games when player was on pitch for at least 70 minutes	1

KEY PLAYERS - DEFENDERS

Alpay Ozalan

Goals Conceded Number of League goals conceded while the player was on the pitch	36	**Clean Sheets** In League games when player was on pitch for at least 70 minutes	3
Defensive Rating Ave number of mins between League goals conceded while on the pitch	50	**Club Defensive Rating** Average number of mins between League goals conceded by the club this season	43

	PLAYER	CON LGE	CLEAN SHEETS	DEF RATE
1	Alpay Ozalan	36	3	50 mins
2	Marvin-Job Matip	40	3	47 mins
3	Lukas Sinkewicz	68	3	42 mins
4	Christian Lell	46	1	41 mins

KEY PLAYERS - MIDFIELDERS

Ricardo Cabanas

Goals in the League	0	**Contribution to Attacking Power** Average number of minutes between League team goals while on pitch	59
Defensive Rating Average number of mins between League goals conceded while on the pitch	52	**Scoring Difference** Defensive Rating minus Contribution to Attacking Power	-7

	PLAYER	LGE GOALS	DEF RATE	POWER	SCORE DIFF
1	Ricardo Cabanas	0	52	59	-7 mins
2	Matthias Scherz	8	46	54	-8 mins
3	Albert Streit	6	40	66	-26 mins

KEY PLAYERS - GOALSCORERS

Matthias Scherz

Goals in the League	8	**Player Strike Rate** Average number of minutes between League goals scored by player	203
Contribution to Attacking Power Average number of minutes between League team goals while on pitch	54	**Club Strike Rate** Average number of minutes between League goals scored by club	62

	PLAYER	LGE GOALS	POWER	STRIKE RATE
1	Matthias Scherz	8	54	203 mins
2	Lukas Podolski	11	61	250 mins
3	Albert Streit	6	66	418 mins
4	Bjorn Schlicke	3	66	420 mins

Lukas Podolski celebrates with team mates

SQUAD APPEARANCES

Match	1	2	3	4	5	6	7	8	9	10	11	12	13	14	15	16	17	18	19	20	21	22	23	24	25	26	27	28	29	30	31	32	33	34
Venue	H	A	H	A	H	A	H	A	H	A	H	A	H	A	A	H	A	A	H	A	H	A	H	A	H	A	H	A	H	A	H	H	A	H
Competition	L	L	L	L	L	L	L	L	L	L	L	L	L	L	L	L	L	L	L	L	L	L	L	L	L	L	L	L	L	L	L	L	L	L
Result	W	W	L	L	W	L	L	L	L	L	L	D	D	L	D	L	L	L	D	D	D	L	L	W	L	L	D	D	W	D	W	L	L	W

Goalkeepers
Alexander Bade
Stefan Wessels

Defenders
Alpay Ozalan
Roland Benschneider
Carsten Cullman
Aparecido Evanilson
Patrick Helmes
Christian Lell
Marvin-Job Matip
Bjorn Schlicke
Andrew Sinkala
Lukas Sinkewicz
Boris Zivkovic

Midfielders
Ricardo Cabanas
Denis Epstein
Markus Feulner
Dimitrios Grammozis
Rolf-Christel Guie-Mien
Anthony Lurling
Peter Madsen
Youssef Mokhtari
Christian Rahn
Matthias Scherz
Sebastian Schindzielorz
Christian Springer
Albert Streit
Patrick Weiser

Forwards
Peter Madsen
Lukas Podolski
Marco Streller
Imre Szabics
Attila Tokoli

KEY: On all match · On bench · Subbed or sent off (Counting game) · Subbed or sent off (playing less than 70 minutes) · Subbed on from bench (Counting Game) · Subbed on (playing less than 70 minutes) · Subbed on and then subbed or sent off (Counting Game) · Subbed on and then subbed or sent off (playing less than 70 minutes) · Not in 16

DUISBURG

Final Position: **18th**

KEY: Won / Drawn / Lost

					Score	Scorers	Attendance
1	gbl	Stuttgart	H	D	1-1	Ahanfouf 31	31,500
2	gbl	Kaiserslautern	A	L	3-5	Mohrle 23,63; Ahanfouf 66	37,000
3	gbl	B Dortmund	H	D	1-1	Kurth 80	31,502
4	gbl	B M'gladbach	A	L	1-2	Mohrle 9	48,854
5	gbl	B Leverkusen	H	L	1-3	Lavric 31	24,100
6	gbl	Hertha Berlin	A	L	2-3	Grlic 32; Biliskov 53	30,634
7	gbl	Nuremburg	H	W	1-0	Kurth 28	14,000
8	gbl	Hannover 96	A	D	1-1	Ahanfouf 14	27,211
9	gbl	Eintr Frankfurt	H	L	0-1		23,000
10	gbl	Bayern Munich	A	L	0-4		66,000
11	gbl	Wolfsburg	H	W	1-0	Bugera 57	20,000
12	gbl	Schalke	A	L	0-3		61,524
13	gbl	Hamburg	A	L	0-2		50,000
14	gbl	W Bremen	A	L	0-2		38,000
15	gbl	Cologne	H	D	1-1	Ahanfouf 5	28,000
16	gbl	Arminia B	H	D	1-1	Ahanfouf 42	18,000
17	gbl	Mainz	A	D	1-1	Mohrle 86	20,300
18	gbl	Stuttgart	A	W	1-0	Caligiuri 43	35,000
19	gbl	Kaiserslautern	H	D	2-2	Kurth 41; Tararache 62 pen	18,000
20	gbl	B Dortmund	A	L	0-2		65,000
21	gbl	B M'gladbach	H	D	1-1	Lavric 4	30,000
22	gbl	B Leverkusen	A	L	2-3	Lavric 42,65	22,500
23	gbl	Hertha Berlin	H	W	2-1	Tararache 20 pen; Lottner 50	20,100
24	gbl	Nuremburg	A	L	0-3		40,000
25	gbl	Hannover 96	H	D	0-0		18,000
26	gbl	Eintr Frankfurt	A	L	2-5	Bodzek 25; Lavric 33	32,000
27	gbl	Bayern Munich	H	L	1-3	Ahanfouf 40 pen	31,500
28	gbl	Wolfsburg	A	D	1-1	van Houdt 74	16,000
29	gbl	Schalke	H	D	1-1	Poulsen 40 og	31,500
30	gbl	Hamburg	H	L	0-2		22,000
31	gbl	Cologne	A	L	1-3	Ahanfouf 79	45,000
32	gbl	W Bremen	H	L	3-5	Ahn 41; Ahanfouf 45,76	17,000
33	gbl	Arminia B	A	W	2-0	Ahn 59; Caligiuri 80	15,000
34	gbl	Mainz	H	D	0-0		28,000

LEAGUE APPEARANCES, BOOKINGS AND CAPS

	AGE (on 01/07/06)	IN NAMED 18	APPEARANCES	COUNTING GAMES	MINUTES ON PITCH	YELLOW CARDS	RED CARDS	CAPS THIS SEASON	NATIONAL SIDE
Goalkeepers									
Sven Beuckert	32	6	3	0	80	0	0	-	Germany
Georg Koch	34	34	34	31	2980	4	0	-	Germany
Defenders									
Necat Aygun	26	8	8	3	316	0	0	-	Germany
Thomas Baelum	28	29	28	26	2378	7	0	-	Denmark
Marino Biliskov	30	21	21	21	1890	3	0	-	Croatia
Adam Bodzek	20	11	9	5	528	4	0	-	Germany
Alexander Meyer	22	25	25	25	2237	3	0	-	Germany
Uwe Mohrle	26	31	31	31	2790	7	0	-	Germany
Razundara Tjikuzu	26	24	22	17	1746	4	0	-	Namibia
Midfielders									
Markus Anfang	32	14	12	4	651	3	0	-	Germany
Marco Caligiuri	22	14	14	11	1032	3	0	-	Germany
Nasir El Kasmi	23	4	2	0	28	0	0	-	Germany
Ivica Grlic	30	14	13	9	875	5	0	-	Germany
Markus Hausweiler	30	3	3	3	270	2	0	-	Germany
Dirk Lottner	34	20	18	10	1151	2	0	-	Germany
Mike Rietpietsch	32	13	13	1	348	0	0	-	Germany
Mihail Tararache	28	15	15	15	1341	6	1	-	Romania
Andreas Voss	34	1	0	0	0	0	0	-	Germany
Tobias Willi	26	26	25	19	1903	7	1	-	Germany
Carsten Wolters	36	20	18	12	1309	3	0	-	Germany
Forwards									
Abdelaziz Ahanfouf	28	27	27	22	2057	5	0	-	Morocco
Jung Hwan Ahn	30	12	11	1	345	0	0	-	South Korea
Alexander Bugera	27	23	23	20	1888	7	0	-	Germany
Josef Ivanovic	32	1	1	0	14	1	0	-	Germany
Markus Kurth	32	31	31	26	2455	8	1	-	Germany
Klemen Lavric	25	22	21	13	1446	1	0	-	Slovenia
Kai Michalke	30	8	6	1	195	0	0	-	Germany
Niklas Stegmann	19	1	1	0	7	0	0	-	Germany
Peter van Houdt	29	29	29	11	1368	6	0	-	Belgium

TEAM OF THE SEASON

MONTHLY POINTS TALLY

Month	Points	%
AUGUST	2	22%
SEPTEMBER	3	25%
OCTOBER	4	33%
NOVEMBER	0	0%
DECEMBER	3	25%
JANUARY	3	100%
FEBRUARY	5	33%
MARCH	1	8%
APRIL	2	17%
MAY	4	44%

LEAGUE GOALS

	PLAYER	MINS	GOALS	S RATE
1	Ahanfouf	2057	**9**	229
2	Lavric	1446	**5**	289
3	Mohrle	2790	**4**	698
4	Kurth	2455	**3**	818
5	Caligiuri	1032	**2**	516
6	Tararache	1341	**2**	671
7	Ahn	345	**2**	173
8	Biliskov	1890	**1**	1890
9	Grlic	875	**1**	875
10	Lottner	1151	**1**	1151
11	Bodzek	528	**1**	528
12	van Houdt	1368	**1**	1368
13	Bugera	1888	**1**	1888
	Other		**1**	
	TOTAL		**34**	

TOP POINT EARNERS

	PLAYER	GAMES	AV PTS
1	Markus Kurth	26	**1.00**
2	Mihail Tararache	15	**0.93**
3	Klemen Lavric	13	**0.92**
4	Razundara Tjikuzu	17	**0.88**
5	Marino Biliskov	21	**0.86**
6	Alexander Meyer	25	**0.80**
7	Tobias Willi	19	**0.79**
8	Carsten Wolters	12	**0.75**
9	Georg Koch	31	**0.74**
10	Uwe Mohrle	31	**0.74**
	CLUB AVERAGE:		**0.79**

DISCIPLINARY RECORDS

	PLAYER	YELLOW	RED	AVE
1	Bodzek	4	0	**132**
2	Grlic	5	0	**175**
3	Tararache	6	1	**191**
4	Anfang	3	0	**217**
5	van Houdt	6	0	**228**
6	Willi	7	1	**237**
7	Bugera	7	0	**269**
8	Kurth	8	1	**272**
9	Baelum	7	0	**339**
10	Caligiuri	3	0	**344**
11	Mohrle	7	0	**398**
12	Ahanfouf	5	0	**411**
13	Wolters	3	0	**436**
	Other	17	0	
	TOTAL	**88**	**3**	

KEY GOALKEEPER

Georg Koch

Goals Conceded in the League	62	**Counting Games** League games when player was on pitch for at least 70 minutes	31
Defensive Rating Ave number of mins between League goals conceded while on the pitch	48	**Clean Sheets** In games when player was on pitch for at least 70 minutes	6

KEY PLAYERS - DEFENDERS

Marino Biliskov

Goals Conceded Number of League goals conceded while the player was on the pitch	37	**Clean Sheets** In League games when player was on pitch for at least 70 minutes	5
Defensive Rating Ave number of mins between League goals conceded while on the pitch	51	**Club Defensive Rating** Average number of mins between League goals conceded by the club this season	49

	PLAYER	CON LGE	CLEAN SHEETS	DEF RATE
1	Marino Biliskov	37	5	51 mins
2	Razundara Tjikuzu	35	3	50 mins
3	Alexander Meyer	46	4	49 mins
4	Thomas Baelum	49	5	49 mins

KEY PLAYERS - MIDFIELDERS

Mihail Tararache

Goals in the League	2	**Contribution to Attacking Power** Average number of minutes between League team goals while on pitch	84
Defensive Rating Average number of mins between League goals conceded while on the pitch	52	**Scoring Difference** Defensive Rating minus Contribution to Attacking Power	-32

	PLAYER	LGE GOALS	DEF RATE	POWER	SCORE DIFF
1	Mihail Tararache	2	52	84	-32 mins
2	Tobias Willi	0	53	87	-34 mins
3	Carsten Wolters	0	48	94	-46 mins

KEY PLAYERS - GOALSCORERS

Abdelaziz Ahanfouf

Goals in the League	9	**Player Strike Rate** Average number of minutes between League goals scored by player	229
Contribution to Attacking Power Average number of minutes between League team goals while on pitch	98	**Club Strike Rate** Average number of minutes between League goals scored by club	90

	PLAYER	LGE GOALS	POWER	STRIKE RATE
1	Abdelaziz Ahanfouf	9	98	229 mins
2	Klemen Lavric	5	76	289 mins
3	Mihail Tararache	2	84	671 mins
4	Uwe Mohrle	4	90	698 mins

Mihail Tararache and Marino Biliskov

SQUAD APPEARANCES

Match	1	2	3	4	5	6	7	8	9	10	11	12	13	14	15	16	17	18	19	20	21	22	23	24	25	26	27	28	29	30	31	32	33	34
Venue	H	A	H	A	H	A	H	A	H	A	H	A	A	A	H	H	A	A	H	A	H	A	H	A	H	A	H	A	H	H	A	H	A	H
Competition	L	L	L	L	L	L	L	L	L	L	L	L	L	L	L	L	L	L	L	L	L	L	L	L	L	L	L	L	L	L	L	L	L	L
Result	D	L	D	L	L	L	W	D	L	L	W	L	L	L	D	D	D	W	D	L	D	L	W	L	D	L	L	D	D	L	L	L	W	D
Goalkeepers																																		
Sven Beuckert																																		
Georg Koch																																		
Defenders																																		
Necat Aygun																																		
Thomas Baelum																																		
Marino Biliskov																																		
Adam Bodzek																																		
Alexander Meyer																																		
Uwe Mohrle																																		
Razundara Tjikuzu																																		
Midfielders																																		
Markus Anfang																																		
Marco Caligiuri																																		
Nasir El Kasmi																																		
Ivica Grlic																																		
Markus Hausweiler																																		
Dirk Lottner																																		
Mike Rietpietsch																																		
Mihail Tararache																																		
Andreas Voss																																		
Tobias Willi																																		
Carsten Wolters																																		
Forwards																																		
Abdelaziz Ahanfouf																																		
Jung Hwan Ahn																																		
Alexander Bugera																																		
Josef Ivanovic																																		
Markus Kurth																																		
Klemen Lavric																																		
Kai Michalke																																		
Niklas Stegmann																																		
Peter van Houdt																																		

KEY: ■ On all match ■ On bench | ⏮ Subbed or sent off (Counting game) « Subbed or sent off (playing less than 70 minutes) | ⏭ Subbed on from bench (Counting Game) » Subbed on (playing less than 70 minutes) | Subbed on and then subbed or sent off (Counting Game) Subbed on and then subbed or sent off (playing less than 70 minutes) | □ Not in 16

FRENCH LEAGUE ROUND-UP

FINAL LEAGUE TABLE

	HOME						AWAY					TOTAL			
	P	W	D	L	F	A	W	D	L	F	A	F	A	DIF	PTS
Lyon	38	13	4	2	40	18	12	5	2	33	13	73	31	42	84
Bordeaux	38	11	7	1	23	11	7	8	4	20	14	43	25	18	69
Lille	38	12	5	2	33	7	4	9	6	23	24	56	31	25	62
Lens	38	11	7	1	34	14	3	11	5	14	20	48	34	14	60
Marseille	38	10	8	1	28	13	6	4	9	16	22	44	35	9	60
Auxerre	38	13	3	3	33	9	4	5	10	17	30	50	39	11	59
Rennes	38	11	3	5	34	25	7	2	10	14	24	48	49	-1	59
Nice	38	11	4	4	22	12	5	6	8	14	19	36	31	5	58
Paris SG	38	11	3	5	34	20	2	10	7	10	18	44	38	6	52
AS Monaco	38	8	7	4	23	14	5	6	8	19	22	42	36	6	52
Le Mans	38	9	7	3	21	8	4	6	9	12	28	33	36	-3	52
Nancy	38	5	8	6	19	17	7	4	8	16	20	35	37	-2	48
St Etienne	38	6	8	5	18	15	5	6	8	11	24	29	39	-10	47
Nantes	38	7	7	5	22	18	4	5	10	15	23	37	41	-4	45
Sochaux	38	6	7	6	17	19	5	4	10	17	28	34	47	-13	44
Toulouse	38	7	6	6	21	18	3	5	11	15	29	36	47	-11	41
Troyes	38	6	7	6	20	18	3	5	11	17	29	37	47	-10	39
AC Ajaccio	38	6	5	8	15	20	2	4	13	12	33	27	53	-26	33
Strasbourg	38	2	8	9	15	26	3	6	10	18	30	33	56	-23	29
Metz	38	5	4	10	13	24	1	7	11	13	35	26	59	-33	29

CLUB STRIKE FORCE

Lyon's Fred

1 Lyon

Goals scored in the League	73
Club Strike Rate (CSR) Average number of minutes between League goals scored by club	47

	CLUB	GOALS	CSR
1	Lyon	73	47
2	Lille	56	61
3	Auxerre	50	68
4	Lens	48	71
4	Rennes	48	71
6	Marseille	44	78
6	Paris SG	44	78
8	Bordeaux	43	80
8	AS Monaco	42	81
10	Nantes	37	92
10	Troyes	37	92
12	Nice	36	95
12	Toulouse	36	95
13	Nancy	35	98
15	Sochaux	34	101
16	Le Mans	33	104
16	Strasbourg	33	104
18	St Etienne	29	118
19	AC Ajaccio	27	127
20	Metz	26	132

CLUB DISCIPLINARY RECORDS

Alou Diarra of Lens; 15 cards

1 AS Monaco

League Yellow	84
League Red	8
League Total	92
Cards Average in League Average number of minutes between a card being shown of either colour	37

	CLUB	Y	R	TOTAL	AVE
1	AS Monaco	84	8	92	37
2	Nancy	78	7	85	40
3	Paris SG	80	5	85	40
4	Nice	74	3	77	44
5	Lille	74	2	76	45
6	Nantes	72	4	76	45
7	Bordeaux	72	3	75	46
8	Marseille	72	3	75	46
9	Lens	67	7	74	46
10	Troyes	66	3	69	50
11	AC Ajaccio	63	2	65	53
12	Metz	61	4	65	53
13	Rennes	62	3	65	53
14	Strasbourg	59	6	65	53
15	Le Mans	61	3	64	53
16	Lyon	60	1	61	56
17	Sochaux	56	4	60	57
18	Toulouse	56	2	58	59
19	St Etienne	52	4	56	61
20	Auxerre	42	1	43	80

CLUB DEFENCES

	CLUB	LGE	CS	CDR
1	Bordeaux	25	22	137
2	Nice	31	15	110
3	Lyon	31	17	110
4	Lille	31	20	110
5	Lens	34	14	101
6	Marseille	35	14	98
7	AS Monaco	36	13	95
8	Le Mans	36	19	95
9	Nancy	37	16	92
10	Paris SG	38	12	90
11	Auxerre	39	16	88
12	St Etienne	39	17	88
13	Nantes	41	14	83
14	Troyes	47	6	73
15	Toulouse	47	10	73
16	Sochaux	47	12	73
17	Rennes	49	12	70
18	AC Ajaccio	53	10	65
19	Strasbourg	56	8	61
20	Metz	59	11	58

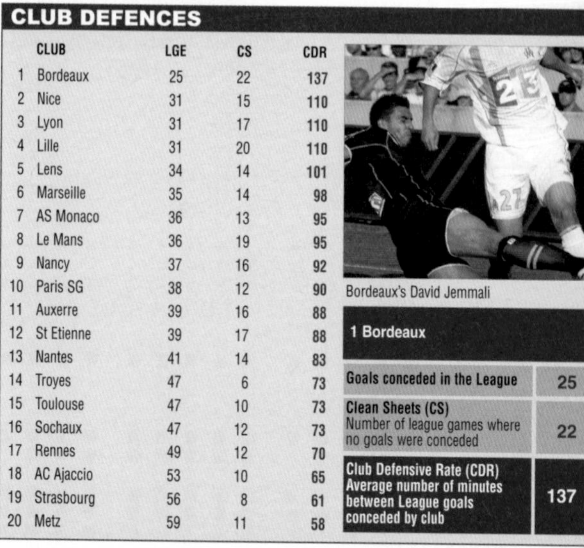

Bordeaux's David Jemmali

1 Bordeaux

Goals conceded in the League	25
Clean Sheets (CS) Number of league games where no goals were conceded	22
Club Defensive Rate (CDR) Average number of minutes between League goals conceded by club	137

PLAYER NATIONALITIES

Overseas country with the most player appearances in the French League - Brazil

707 league appearances by Brazilian players

	COUNTRY	PLAYERS	IN SQUAD	LGE APP	% LGE ACT	CAPS	MOST APP	APP
1	France	373	7603	6215	61.5	97	Stephane Borbiconi	100.0
2	Brazil	31	776	707	7.0	8	Cris	92.5
3	Ivory Coast	18	421	400	3.9	81	Sammy Traore	83.9
4	Senegal	26	389	340	3.3	0	Pape Diakhate	85.8
5	Cameroon	16	272	242	2.5	15	Modeste Mbami	85.8
6	Mali	7	184	179	1.9	0	Adama Coulibaly	88.2
7	Nigeria	6	161	153	1.6	0	Rabiu Afolabi	82.5
8	Sweden	5	150	146	1.5	13	Kim Kallstrom	83.2
9	Switzerland	8	156	142	1.3	34	Stephane Grichting	63.1
10	Morocco	9	143	134	1.3	0	Gharib Amzine	74.2
11	Argentina	9	165	140	1.2	2	Mauro Cetto	76.2
12	Portugal	6	127	107	1.1	18	Pauleta	87.9
13	Guinea	8	126	109	1.1	17	Pascal Feindouno	69.2
14	Czech Republic	4	100	94	1.0	21	David Rozehnal	99.4
15	Tunisia	7	108	98	0.8	13	Karim Haggui	61.9
16	Uruguay	6	116	103	0.8	0	Adrian Sarkisian	58.4
17	Serbia & Montenegro	5	71	59	0.7	2	Dusko Tosic	33.8
18	Italy	5	59	55	0.5	6	Flavio Roma	39.4
19	Greece	2	45	43	0.5	0	Efstathios Tavlaridis	68.0
20	Congo	2	43	43	0.46	0	Herita Nkolongo Ilunga	78.2

CLUB MAKE-UP – HOME AND OVERSEAS PLAYERS

1 Rennes

57.1% of appearances by overseas players

	CLUB	OVERSEAS	HOME	% OVERSEAS	% LGE ACT	MOST APP	APP
1	Rennes	15	14	51.7	57.1	Kim Kallstrom	83.2
2	Marseille	21	23	47.7	54.9	Taye I Taiwo	78.6
3	Lille	13	14	48.1	52.8	Tony Mario Sylva	84.2
4	Sochaux	18	16	52.9	49.5	Rabiu Afolabi	82.5
5	Lyon	9	18	33.3	48.0	Cris	92.5
6	Paris SG	13	16	44.8	44.0	David Rozehnal	99.4
7	Lens	11	15	42.3	43.5	Hilton	89.9
8	Strasbourg	14	22	38.9	42.2	Amara Diane	70.1
9	AS Monaco	12	22	35.3	40.7	Lucas Bernardi	76.1
10	AC Ajaccio	8	22	26.7	37.9	Rodrigo	88.6
11	Nancy	11	18	37.9	35.1	Pape Diakhate	85.8
12	Le Mans	11	19	36.7	33.5	Marko Basa	83.0
13	Bordeaux	10	17	37.0	31.6	Menegazzo	68.7
14	Nice	8	17	32.0	31.6	Sammy Traore	83.9
15	Troyes	9	18	33.3	30.5	Ibrahima Faye	83.7
16	Metz	17	21	44.7	29.1	Herve Tum	46.8
17	St Etienne	9	18	33.3	28.9	Didier Zokora	81.6
18	Nantes	10	21	32.3	28.7	Mauro Cetto	76.2
19	Auxerre	9	18	33.3	28.3	Thom Kahlenberg	71.8
20	Toulouse	6	24	20.0	16.5	Achille Emana	64.0

CHART-TOPPING MIDFIELDERS

1 Debuchy - Lille	
Goals scored in the League	4
Defensive Rating Av number of mins between League goals conceded while on the pitch	171
Contribution to Attacking Power Average number of minutes between League team goals while on pitch	57
Scoring Difference Defensive Rating minus Contribution to Attacking Power	114

	PLAYER	CLUB	GOALS	DEF RATE	POWER	S DIFF
1	Debuchy	Lille	4	171	57	114
2	Diarra	Lyon	3	147	46	101
3	Lachuer	Auxerre	4	146	59	87
4	Juninho	Lyon	9	133	47	86
5	Tiago	Lyon	5	118	45	73
6	Sorlin	Rennes	0	117	51	66
7	Cheyrou	Bordeaux	1	149	84	65
8	Mavuba	Bordeaux	0	138	81	57
9	Menegazzo	Bordeaux	4	131	76	55
10	M'Bia	Rennes	0	118	64	54
11	Dindane	Lens	6	126	76	50
12	Bodmer	Lille	5	108	61	47
13	Cheyrou	Auxerre	2	109	64	45
14	Malouda	Lyon	6	92	48	44
15	Leroy	Lens	0	115	71	44

CHART-TOPPING GOALSCORERS

1 Odemwingie - Lille	
Goals scored in the League	14
Contribution to Attacking Power Average number of minutes between League team goals while on pitch	47
Club Strike Rate (CSR) Average minutes between League goals scored by club	61
Player Strike Rate Average number of minutes between League goals scored by player	114

	PLAYER	CLUB	GOALS: LGE	POWER	CSR	S RATE
1	Odemwingie	Lille	14	47	61	114
2	Fred	Lyon	14	48	46	136
3	Pauleta	Paris SG	21	68	78	143
4	Chevanton	AS Monaco	10	77	81	154
5	Pieroni	Auxerre	11	64	68	168
6	Wiltord	Lyon	13	42	46	181
7	Pagis	Marseille	6	74	76	185
8	Grax	Troyes	9	77	92	196
9	Ilan	Sochaux	11	75	98	197
10	Cousin	Lens	13	67	71	202
11	Niang	Marseille	10	60	76	209
12	Utaka	Rennes	11	60	71	211
13	De Melo	Le Mans	7	94	104	228
14	Diallo	Nantes	10	91	92	237
15	Kalou	Paris SG	9	70	78	240

CHART-TOPPING DEFENDERS

1 Jurietti - Bordeaux	
Goals Conceded in the League The number of League goals conceded while he was on the pitch	13
Clean Sheets In games when he played at least 70 mins	14
Club Defensive Rating Average mins between League goals conceded by the club this season	137
Defensive Rating Average number of minutes between League goals conceded while on pitch	174

	PLAYER	CLUB	CON: LGE	CS	CDR	DEF RATE
1	Jurietti	Bordeaux	13	14	137	174
2	Planus	Bordeaux	17	20	137	168
3	Faubert	Bordeaux	16	18	137	161
4	Evra	AS Monaco	9	9	95	145
5	Afanou	Bordeaux	11	8	137	141
6	Cacapa	Lyon	17	13	110	136
7	Abardonado	Nice	20	14	110	136
8	Assou-Ekotto	Lens	22	11	98	133
9	Mensah	Rennes	8	5	68	133
10	Basa	Le Mans	22	17	92	129
11	Cris	Lyon	25	16	110	126
12	Henrique	Bordeaux	13	11	137	125
13	Fanni	Nice	15	9	110	122
14	Lecluse	Nancy	17	10	92	118
15	Clerc	Lyon	10	5	110	117

CHART-TOPPING GOALKEEPERS

1 Rame - Bordeaux	
Counting Games Games in which he played at least 70 minutes	35
Goals Conceded in the League The number of League goals conceded while he was on the pitch	22
Clean Sheets In games when he played at least 70 mins	20
Defensive Rating Average number of minutes between League goals conceded while on pitch	140

	PLAYER	CLUB	CG	CONC	CS	DEF RATE
1	Rame	Bordeaux	35	22	20	140
2	Coupet	Lyon	37	27	17	122
3	Gregorini	Nice	34	27	14	113
4	Warmuz	AS Monaco	23	19	10	109
5	Sylva	Lille	32	27	17	107
6	Pele	Le Mans	36	30	18	106
7	Letizi	Paris SG	27	22	11	106
8	Barthez	Marseille	24	21	10	103
9	Bracigliano	Nancy	33	29	16	102
10	Itandje	Lens	37	34	12	97
11	Cool	Auxerre	38	35	16	94
12	Landreau	Nantes	36	34	14	92
13	Carasso	Marseille	14	14	4	90
14	Pouplin	Rennes	15	15	5	86
15	Janot	St Etienne	37	39	16	85

PLAYER DISCIPLINARY RECORD

1 Vassillis Zikos - AS Monaco	
Cards Average mins between cards	108
League Yellow	12
League Red	1
TOTAL	14

	PLAYER		LY	LR	TOT	AVE
1	Zikos	AS Monaco	11	1	12	108
2	Cubilier	AS Monaco	5	1	6	154
3	Rool	Nice	14	0	14	177
4	Diarra	Lens	13	2	15	179
5	Cana	Marseille	13	0	13	185
6	Leray	Nantes	7	1	8	189
7	Perez	AS Monaco	7	0	7	190
8	Meniri	Metz	7	2	9	190
9	Jaziri	Troyes	6	0	6	190
10	Tavlaridis	Lille	12	0	12	193
11	Huszti	Metz	6	0	6	194
12	Lecluse	Nancy	8	2	10	200
13	Adailton	Nancy	5	0	5	202
14	Capoue	Nantes	5	1	6	205
15	Bangoura	Le Mans	6	1	7	210
16	Cesar	Marseille	7	0	7	210
17	Cisse	Paris SG	9	2	11	210
18	Matuidi	Troyes	12	0	12	210
19	Briand	Rennes	5	0	5	213
20	Evra	AS Monaco	5	1	6	217

TEAM OF THE SEASON

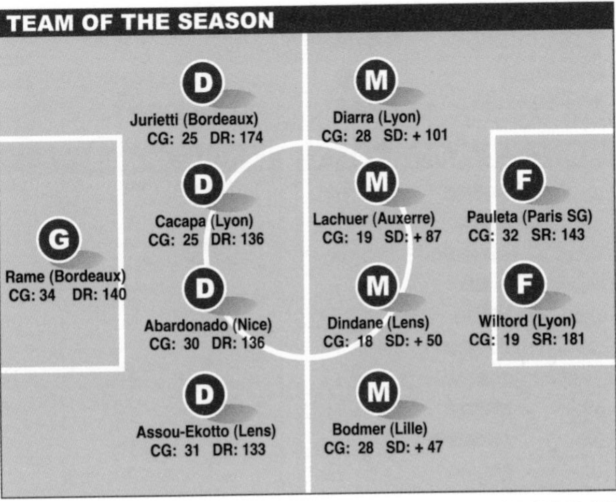

FRENCH LEAGUE CHAMPIONS

LYON

Final Position: **1st**

KEY: ☐ Won ☐ Drawn ☐ Lost

	Comp	Opponent	H/A	Res	Score	Scorers	Attendance
1	frpr1	**Le Mans**	A	W	2-1	Wiltord 36; Carew 58,69	11,000
2	frpr1	**Strasbourg**	H	W	1-0	Carew 26	30,000
3	frpr1	**Marseille**	A	D	1-1	Carew 34	56,000
4	frpr1	**Nancy**	H	W	1-0	Cacapa 93	39,000
5	frpr1	**Auxerre**	A	W	2-0	Diarra 6; Juninho 45	15,000
6	frpr1	**AS Monaco**	H	W	2-1	Fred 5,49	39,043
7	ecgpf	**Real Madrid**	H	W	3-0	Carew 21; Juninho 26; Wiltord 31	40,000
8	frpr1	**Bordeaux**	A	D	1-1	Wiltord 64	32,800
9	frpr1	**Lens**	H	D	1-1	Tiago 37	36,300
10	frpr1	**Nantes**	A	W	1-0	Fred 79	35,500
11	ecgpf	**Rosenborg BK**	A	W	1-0	Cris 45	20,620
12	frpr1	**Rennes**	A	W	3-1	Juninho 52; Tiago 73; Wiltord 87	28,998
13	frpr1	**AC Ajaccio**	H	W	3-2	Fred 29; Juninho 49; Wiltord 68	36,347
14	ecgpf	**Olympiakos**	H	W	2-1	Juninho 4; Govou 89	40,000
15	frpr1	**Metz**	A	W	4-0	Carew 22; Juninho 35; Wiltord 44; Malouda 50	19,333
16	frpr1	**Sochaux**	H	W	1-0	Malouda 53	38,000
17	ecgpf	**Olympiakos**	A	W	4-1	Juninho 41; Carew 44,57; Diarra 55	29,555
18	frpr1	**Toulouse**	A	W	1-0	Govou 9	26,254
19	frpr1	**Troyes**	H	W	2-1	Cris 27,75	37,940
20	ecgpf	**Real Madrid**	A	D	1-1	Carew 72	59,000
21	frpr1	**Nice**	A	D	1-1	Govou 75	12,849
22	frpr1	**Paris SG**	H	W	2-0	Fred 5; Carew 90	38,200
23	ecgpf	**Rosenborg BK**	H	W	2-1	Benzema 33; Fred 90	40,000
24	frpr1	**St Etienne**	A	D	0-0		35,352
25	frpr1	**Lille**	H	L	1-3	Govou 68	36,000
26	frpr1	**Strasbourg**	A	W	4-0	Wiltord 5,55,73; Berthod 41	19,735
27	frpr1	**Marseille**	H	W	2-1	Tiago 54; Govou 83	38,912
28	frpr1	**Nancy**	A	W	2-0	Cacapa 49; Fred 83	20,000
29	frpr1	**Auxerre**	H	D	1-1	Diarra 43	37,958
30	frpr1	**Bordeaux**	H	D	0-0		39,354
31	frpr1	**Lens**	A	D	1-1	Wiltord 91	40,037
32	frpr1	**Nantes**	H	W	3-1	Juninho 8; Diarra 34; Fred 56	37,328
33	eclsl1	**PSV Eindhoven**	A	W	1-0	Juninho 65 fk	35,000
34	frpr1	**Rennes**	H	L	1-4	Juninho 37	29,168
35	frpr1	**AC Ajaccio**	A	W	3-1	Juninho 61; Fred 77; Benzema 87	4,000
36	eclsl2	**PSV Eindhoven**	H	W	4-0	Tiago 26,45; Wiltord 71; Fred 90	41,000
37	frpr1	**Metz**	H	W	4-0	Malouda 11,32; Carew 15; Muller 90	37,000
38	frpr1	**Sochaux**	A	W	4-0	Wiltord 26,52; Pedretti 45; Malouda 58	18,777
39	frpr1	**Toulouse**	H	D	1-1	Carew 48	37,994
40	ecqfl1	**AC Milan**	H	D	0-0		40,000
41	frpr1	**Troyes**	A	W	1-0	Tiago 76	17,835
42	ecqfl2	**AC Milan**	A	L	1-3	Diarra 31	80,000
43	frpr1	**Nice**	H	W	2-1	Fred 21; Malouda 50	30,000
44	frpr1	**Paris SG**	A	W	1-0	Fred 24	43,508
45	frpr1	**AS Monaco**	A	L	1-2	Carew 90	12,357
46	frpr1	**St Etienne**	H	W	4-0	Wiltord 7; Fred 38; Juninho 55 pen; Pedretti 81	39,000
47	frpr1	**Lille**	A	L	0-4		17,000
48	frpr1	**Le Mans**	H	W	8-1	Fred 18,38,75; Cris 26; Wiltord 29; Juninho 42; Govou 87; Tiago 88	44,410

LEAGUE APPEARANCES, BOOKINGS AND CAPS

	AGE (on 01/07/06)	IN NAMED 18	APPEARANCES	COUNTING GAMES	MINUTES ON PITCH	YELLOW CARDS	RED CARDS	CAPS THIS SEASON	NATIONAL SIDE
Goalkeepers									
Gregory Coupet	33	38	37	36	3307	1	0	10	France (8)
Johan Hartock	19	0	0	0	0	0	0	-	France
Remi Vercoutre	26	36	2	1	113	0	0	-	France
Defenders									
Eric Abidal	26	14	14	14	1206	1	0	4	France (8)
Jeremie Berthod	22	16	16	11	1074	3	0	-	France
Cacapa	30	27	26	25	2310	2	0	-	Brazil
Francois Clerc	23	15	14	12	1168	1	0	1	France (8)
Cris	29	36	36	34	3162	3	0	-	Brazil
Lamine Diatta	31	20	13	5	689	2	1	-	Senegal
Yohann Gomez	24	1	1	1	90	0	0	-	France
Sylvain Monsoreau	25	25	19	12	1208	2	0	-	France
Anthony Reveillere	26	22	20	17	1700	3	0	5	France (8)
Midfielders									
Romain Beynie	19	0	0	0	0	0	0	-	France
Jeremie Clement	21	23	16	5	636	1	0	-	France
Mahamadou Diarra	25	31	31	28	2640	6	0	-	Mali
P. Juninho	31	32	32	28	2659	5	0	6	Brazil (1)
Florent Malouda	26	31	31	20	2208	5	0	10	France (8)
Patrick Muller	29	12	12	9	875	0	0	10	Switzerland (35)
Benoit Pedretti	25	30	21	11	1255	3	0	-	France
Cardoso Tiago	25	29	29	21	2240	8	0	5	Portugal (7)
Forwards									
Hatem Benarfa	19	16	11	2	459	0	0	-	France
Karim Benzema	18	14	13	2	536	1	0	-	France
John Alieu Carew	26	29	26	10	1560	4	0	-	Norway
Pierre-Alain Frau	26	7	4	0	157	1	0	-	France
Fred	22	31	31	17	1909	5	0	2	Brazil (1)
Sydney Govou	26	35	34	15	2111	3	0	4	France (8)
Sylvain Wiltord	32	35	35	19	2347	0	0	10	France (8)

TEAM OF THE SEASON

G — Gregory Coupet — CG: 36 DR: 122

D — Cacapa — CG: 25 DR: 136

D — Cris — CG: 34 DR: 126

D — Francois Clerc — CG: 12 DR: 117

D — Sylvain Monsoreau — CG: 12 DR: 110

M — Mahamadou Diarra — CG: 28 SD: 101

M — P Juninho — CG: 28 SD: 86

M — Cardoso Tiago — CG: 21 SD: 73

M — Florent Malouda — CG: 20 SD: 44

F — Fred — CG: 17 SR: 136

F — Sylvain Wiltord — CG: 19 SR: 181

MONTHLY POINTS TALLY

Month	Points	%
AUGUST	10	83%
SEPTEMBER	8	67%
OCTOBER	12	100%
NOVEMBER	7	78%
DECEMBER	4	44%
JANUARY	10	83%
FEBRUARY	5	42%
MARCH	10	83%
APRIL	12	80%
MAY	3	50%

LEAGUE GOALS

	PLAYER	MINS	GOALS	S RATE
1	Fred	1909	14	136
2	Wiltord	2347	13	181
3	Carew	1560	9	173
4	Juninho	2659	9	295
5	Malouda	2208	6	368
6	Tiago	2240	5	448
7	Govou	2111	5	422
8	Cris	3162	3	1054
9	Diarra	2640	3	880
10	Cacapa	2310	2	1155
11	Pedretti	1255	2	628
12	Benzema	536	1	536
13	Muller	875	1	875
	Other		1	
	TOTAL		74	

TOP POINT EARNERS

	PLAYER	GAMES	AV PTS
1	Clerc	12	2.50
2	Cacapa	25	2.44
3	Diarra	28	2.43
4	Wiltord	19	2.37
5	Coupet	36	2.25
6	Fred	17	2.24
7	Cris	34	2.21
8	Abidal	14	2.21
9	Reveillere	17	2.18
10	Tiago	21	2.14
	CLUB AVERAGE:		2.67

DISCIPLINARY RECORDS

	PLAYER	YELLOW	RED	AVE
1	Diatta	2	1	229
2	Tiago	8	0	280
3	Berthod	3	0	358
4	Fred	5	0	381
5	Carew	4	0	390
6	Pedretti	3	0	418
7	Diarra	6	0	440
8	Malouda	5	0	441
9	Juninho	5	0	531
10	Benzema	1	0	536
11	Reveillere	3	0	566
12	Monsoreau	2	0	604
13	Clement	1	0	636
	Other	11	0	
	TOTAL	59	1	

KEY GOALKEEPER

Gregory Coupet

Goals Conceded in the League	27	Counting Games League games when player was on pitch for at least 70 minutes	36
Defensive Rating Ave number of mins between League goals conceded while on the pitch	122	Clean Sheets In games when player was on pitch for at least 70 minutes	17

KEY PLAYERS - DEFENDERS

Cacapa

Goals Conceded Number of League goals conceded while the player was on the pitch	17	Clean Sheets In League games when player was on pitch for at least 70 minutes	13
Defensive Rating Ave number of mins between League goals conceded while on the pitch	136	Club Defensive Rating Average number of mins between League goals conceded by the club this season	110

	PLAYER	CON LGE	CLEAN SHEETS	DEF RATE
1	Cacapa	17	13	136 mins
2	Cris	25	16	126 mins
3	Francois Clerc	10	5	117 mins
4	Sylvain Monsoreau	11	5	110 mins

KEY PLAYERS - MIDFIELDERS

Mahamadou Diarra

Goals in the League	3	Contribution to Attacking Power Average number of minutes between League team goals while on pitch	46
Defensive Rating Average number of mins between League goals conceded while on the pitch	147	Scoring Difference Defensive Rating minus Contribution to Attacking Power	101

	PLAYER	LGE GOALS	DEF RATE	POWER	SCORE DIFF
1	Mahamadou Diarra	3	147	46	101 mins
2	Pernambucano Juninho	9	133	47	86 mins
3	Cardoso Tiago	5	118	45	73 mins
4	Florent Malouda	6	92	48	44 mins

KEY PLAYERS - GOALSCORERS

Fred

Goals in the League	14	Player Strike Rate Average number of minutes between League goals scored by player	136
Contribution to Attacking Power Average number of minutes between League team goals while on pitch	48	Club Strike Rate Average number of minutes between League goals scored by club	46

	PLAYER	LGE GOALS	POWER	STRIKE RATE
1	Fred	14	48	136 mins
2	Sylvain Wiltord	13	42	181 mins
3	Pernambucano Juninho	9	47	295 mins
4	Florent Malouda	6	48	368 mins

Lyon's Brazilian forward Fred

SQUAD APPEARANCES

Match	1	2	3	4	5	6	7	8	9	10	11	12	13	14	15	16	17	18	19	20	21	22	23	24
Venue	A	H	A	H	A	H	H	A	H	A	A	A	H	H	A	H	A	A	H	A	A	H	H	A
Competition	L	L	L	L	L	L	C	L	L	L	C	L	L	C	L	L	C	L	L	C	L	L	C	L
Result	W	W	D	W	W	W	W	D	D	W	W	W	W	W	W	W	W	W	W	D	D	W	W	D

Match	25	26	27	28	29	30	31	32	33	34	35	36	37	38	39	40	41	42	43	44	45	46	47	48
Venue	H	A	H	A	H	H	A	H	A	H	A	H	H	A	H	H	A	A	H	A	A	H	A	H
Competition	L	L	L	L	L	L	L	L	C	L	L	C	L	L	L	C	L	C	L	L	L	L	L	L
Result	L	W	W	W	D	D	D	W	W	L	W	W	W	W	D	D	W	L	W	W	L	W	L	W

Goalkeepers
- Gregory Coupet
- Johan Hartock
- Remi Vercoutre

Defenders
- Eric Abidal
- Jeremie Berthod
- Cacapa
- Francois Clerc
- Cris
- Lamine Diatta
- Yohann Gomez
- Sylvain Monsoreau
- Anthony Reveillere

Midfielders
- Romain Beynie
- Jeremie Clement
- Mahamadou Diarra
- Pernambucano Juninho
- Florent Malouda
- Patrick Muller
- Benoit Pedretti
- Cardoso Tiago

Forwards
- Hatem Benarfa
- Karim Benzema
- John Alieu Carew
- Pierre-Alain Frau
- Fred
- Sydney Govou
- Sylvain Wiltord

KEY: On all match · On bench · Subbed or sent off (Counting game) · Subbed or sent off (playing less than 70 minutes) · Subbed on from bench (Counting Game) · Subbed on (playing less than 70 minutes) · Subbed on and then subbed or sent off (Counting Game) · Subbed on and then subbed or sent off (playing less than 70 minutes) · Not in 16

BORDEAUX

Final Position: **2nd**

NICKNAME: GIRONDINS

KEY: ☐ Won ☐ Drawn ☐ Lost

							Attendance
1	frpr1	Marseille	A	W	2-0	Faubert 16; Ducasse 87	57,000
2	frpr1	Nancy	H	W	1-0	Chamakh 1	25,428
3	frpr1	Auxerre	A	L	0-1		18,000
4	frpr1	AS Monaco	H	W	1-0	Cheyrou 57 fk	25,000
5	frpr1	Strasbourg	A	D	0-0		20,411
6	frpr1	Lens	A	D	1-1	Chamakh 27	30,650
7	frpr1	Lyon	H	D	1-1	Smicer 6	32,800
8	frpr1	Rennes	A	D	2-2	Smicer 4; Chamakh 51	24,661
9	frpr1	AC Ajaccio	H	W	1-0	Darcheville 30	19,400
10	frpr1	Metz	A	W	1-0	Menegazzo 47	15,263
11	frpr1	Sochaux	H	D	1-1	Alonso 90	21,895
12	frpr1	Toulouse	A	D	1-1	Francia 57	25,468
13	frpr1	Troyes	H	W	2-0	Darcheville 7,55	19,581
14	frpr1	Nice	A	W	1-0	Laslandes 47	11,382
15	frpr1	Paris SG	H	L	0-2		32,000
16	frpr1	St Etienne	A	D	1-1	Faubert 74	34,089
17	frpr1	Lille	H	W	1-0	Menegazzo 81	19,252
18	frpr1	Le Mans	A	L	0-1		12,530
19	frpr1	Nantes	H	D	0-0		21,606
20	frpr1	Nancy	A	D	0-0		15,000
21	frpr1	Auxerre	H	W	1-0	Alonso 86	17,965
22	frpr1	AS Monaco	A	W	1-0	Denilson 69	11,476
23	frpr1	Strasbourg	H	W	2-1	Menegazzo 36; Faubert 90	18,208
24	frpr1	Lens	H	W	1-0	Laslandes 27	21,575
25	frpr1	Lyon	A	D	0-0		39,354
26	frpr1	Rennes	H	W	2-0	Menegazzo 39; Smicer 67	20,133
27	frpr1	AC Ajaccio	A	W	2-0	Chamakh 31; Denilson 57	3,500
28	frpr1	Metz	H	D	3-3	Chamakh 17,18; Alonso 70	22,461
29	frpr1	Toulouse	H	W	2-0	Henrique 63; Laslandes 84	24,110
30	frpr1	Troyes	A	D	1-1	Darcheville 30	11,524
31	frpr1	Nice	H	W	1-0	Denilson 1	22,533
32	frpr1	Paris SG	A	L	1-3	Perea 22	43,218
33	frpr1	St Etienne	H	D	0-0		32,000
34	frpr1	Lille	A	L	2-3	Darcheville 15 pen; Faubert 61	20,000
35	frpr1	Sochaux	A	W	3-0	Faubert 18; Jemmali 26; Darcheville 54	15,057
36	frpr1	Le Mans	H	D	2-2	Chamakh 40 pen; Darcheville 52	27,374
37	frpr1	Nantes	A	W	1-0	Darcheville 76	37,000
38	frpr1	Marseille	H	D	1-1	Menegazzo 87	32,765

LEAGUE APPEARANCES, BOOKINGS AND CAPS

	AGE (on 01/07/06)	IN NAMED 18	APPEARANCES	COUNTING GAMES	MINUTES ON PITCH	YELLOW CARDS	RED CARDS	CAPS THIS SEASON	NATIONAL SIDE
Goalkeepers									
Ulrich Rame	33	37	35	34	3080	2	0	-	France
Frederick Roux	33	28	4	4	340	0	0	-	France
Mathieu Valverde	23	7	0	0	0	0	0	-	France
Defenders									
Kodjo Afanou	28	18	18	16	1553	2	0	-	France
Paul Baysse	18	1	0	0	0	0	0	-	France
Roberto Luis Beto	30	7	5	4	407	0	0	-	Portugal
Julien Faubert	22	34	34	26	2575	5	0	-	France
Carlos Henrique	23	24	18	18	1620	7	0	-	Brazil
David Jemmali	31	35	32	30	2782	6	0	-	France
Franck Jurietti	31	26	26	25	2257	4	0	4	France (8)
Florian Marange	20	17	14	14	1253	0	0	-	France
Marc Planus	24	32	32	31	2858	6	0	-	France
Midfielders									
Alejandro Alonso	24	24	19	6	832	3	0	-	Argentina
Bruno Cheyrou	28	31	26	20	1933	7	0	-	France
Denilson	28	31	31	14	1785	7	0	-	Brazil
Pierre Ducasse	19	8	5	1	183	1	0	-	France
Juan-Pablo Francia	21	23	16	5	691	0	0	-	Argentina
Ted Lavie	20	2	2	1	98	0	0	-	France
Rio Mavuba	22	38	36	27	2754	1	0	-	France
Fernando Menegazzo	25	33	31	26	2440	6	1	-	Brazil
Vladimir Smicer	33	26	25	11	1504	1	0	7	Czech Republic (2)
Forwards									
Maromane Chamakh	22	29	29	19	1951	4	1	-	Morocco
Jean-C Darcheville	30	35	34	26	2532	5	1	-	France
Lilian Laslandes	34	31	27	12	1415	2	0	-	France
Laurent Leroy	30	5	2	0	41	1	0	-	France
Edixon Perea	22	25	19	3	666	2	0	-	Colombia

TEAM OF THE SEASON

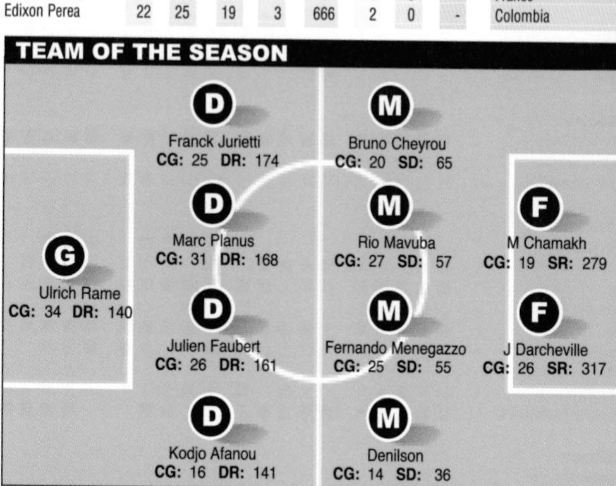

MONTHLY POINTS TALLY

AUGUST	7	58%
SEPTEMBER	6	50%
OCTOBER	8	67%
NOVEMBER	4	44%
DECEMBER	4	44%
JANUARY	13	87%
FEBRUARY	8	67%
MARCH	7	78%
APRIL	5	33%
MAY	4	67%

LEAGUE GOALS

	PLAYER	MINS	GOALS	S RATE
1	Darcheville	2532	8	317
2	Chamakh	1951	7	279
3	Faubert	2575	5	515
4	Menegazzo	2350	4	588
5	Denilson	1785	3	595
6	Laslandes	1415	3	472
7	Alonso	832	3	277
8	Smicer	1504	3	501
9	Henrique	1620	1	1620
10	Francia	691	1	691
11	Ducasse	183	1	183
12	Jemmali	2782	1	2782
13	Cheyrou	1933	1	1933
	Other		2	
	TOTAL		43	

TOP POINT EARNERS

	PLAYER	GAMES	AV PTS
1	Laslandes	12	2.25
2	Denilson	14	2.21
3	Faubert	26	2.04
4	Planus	31	1.97
5	Henrique	18	1.89
6	Menegazzo	25	1.88
7	Jurietti	25	1.88
8	Mavuba	27	1.78
9	Afanou	16	1.75
10	Cheyrou	20	1.75
	CLUB AVERAGE:		1.82

DISCIPLINARY RECORDS

	PLAYER	YELLOW	RED	AVE
1	Henrique	7	0	231
2	Denilson	7	0	255
3	Cheyrou	7	0	276
4	Alonso	3	0	277
5	Perea	2	0	333
6	Menegazzo	6	1	335
7	Chamakh	4	1	390
8	Darcheville	5	1	422
9	Jemmali	6	0	463
10	Planus	6	0	476
11	Faubert	5	0	515
12	Jurietti	4	0	564
13	Laslandes	2	0	707
	Other	6	0	
	TOTAL	70	3	

KEY GOALKEEPER

Ulrich Rame

Goals Conceded in the League	22	Counting Games League games when player was on pitch for at least 70 minutes	34
Defensive Rating Ave number of mins between League goals conceded while on the pitch	140	Clean Sheets In League games when player was on pitch for at least 70 minutes	20

KEY PLAYERS - DEFENDERS

Franck Jurietti

Goals Conceded Number of League goals conceded while the player was on the pitch	13	Clean Sheets In League games when player was on pitch for at least 70 minutes	14
Defensive Rating Ave number of mins between League goals conceded while on the pitch	174	Club Defensive Rating Average number of mins between League goals conceded by the club this season	137

	PLAYER	CON LGE	CLEAN SHEETS	DEF RATE
1	Franck Jurietti	13	14	174 mins
2	Marc Planus	17	20	168 mins
3	Julien Faubert	16	18	161 mins
4	Kodjo Afanou	11	8	141 mins

KEY PLAYERS - MIDFIELDERS

Bruno Cheyrou

Goals in the League	1	Contribution to Attacking Power Average number of minutes between League team goals while on pitch	84
Defensive Rating Average number of mins between League goals conceded while on the pitch	149	Scoring Difference Defensive Rating minus Contribution to Attacking Power	65

	PLAYER	LGE GOALS	DEF RATE	POWER	SCORE DIFF
1	Bruno Cheyrou	1	149	84	65 mins
2	Rio Mavuba	0	138	81	57 mins
3	Fernando Menegazzo	4	131	76	55 mins
4	Denilson	3	105	69	36 mins

KEY PLAYERS - GOALSCORERS

Maromane Chamakh

Goals in the League	7	Player Strike Rate Average number of minutes between League goals scored by player	279
Contribution to Attacking Power Average number of minutes between League team goals while on pitch	72	Club Strike Rate Average number of minutes between League goals scored by club	80

	PLAYER	LGE GOALS	POWER	STRIKE RATE
1	Maromane Chamakh	7	72	279 mins
2	Jean-Claude Darcheville	8	79	317 mins
3	Lilian Laslandes	3	83	472 mins
4	Julien Faubert	5	76	515 mins

Bordeaux's David Jemmali celebrates with Jean-Claude Darcheville

SQUAD APPEARANCES

atch	1	2	3	4	5	6	7	8	9	10	11	12	13	14	15	16	17	18	19	20	21	22	23	24	25	26	27	28	29	30	31	32	33	34	35	36	37	38
enue	A	H	A	H	A	A	H	A	H	A	H	A	H	A	H	A	H	A	H	A	H	A	H	H	A	H	A	H	H	A	H	A	H	A	A	H	A	H
ompetition	L	L	L	L	L	L	L	L	L	L	L	L	L	L	L	L	L	L	L	L	L	L	L	L	L	L	L	L	L	L	L	L	L	L	L	L	L	L
esult	W	W	L	W	D	D	D	D	W	W	D	D	W	W	L	D	W	L	D	D	W	W	W	W	D	W	W	D	W	D	W	L	D	L	W	D	W	D

oalkeepers
lrich Rame
rederick Roux
lathieu Valverde

efenders
odjo Afanou
aul Baysse
oberto Luis Beto
ulien Faubert
arlos Henrique
avid Jemmali
ranck Jurietti
lorian Marange
larc Planus

lidfielders
lejandro Alonso
runo Cheyrou
enilson
ierre Ducasse
ernando Menegazzo
uan-Pablo Francia
ed Lavie
tio Mavuba
ernando Menegazzo
ladimir Smicer

orwards
laromane Chamakh
ean-Claude Darcheville
ilian Laslandes
aurent Leroy
dixon Perea

KEY: On all match · On bench · Subbed or sent off (Counting game) · Subbed or sent off (playing less than 70 minutes) · Subbed on from bench (Counting Game) · Subbed on (playing less than 70 minutes) · Subbed on and then subbed or sent off (Counting Game) · Subbed on and then subbed or sent off (playing less than 70 minutes) · Not in 16

LILLE

Final Position: **3rd**

KEY: ☐Won ☐Drawn ☐Lost

	Comp	Opponent	H/A	Res	Score	Scorers	Attendance
1	frpr1	**Rennes**	H	W	1-0	Makoun 38	14,000
2	frpr1	**AC Ajaccio**	A	D	3-3	Makoun 19; Gygax 39; Debuchy 91	5,000
3	frpr1	**Troyes**	H	L	1-2	Debuchy 68	11,746
4	frpr1	**Sochaux**	A	D	0-0		13,153
5	frpr1	**Toulouse**	H	D	0-0		12,525
6	frpr1	**Metz**	A	W	2-0	Odemwingie 49,59	18,550
7	ecgpd	**Benfica**	A	L	0-1		30,000
8	frpr1	**Nice**	H	W	4-0	Makoun 5; Acimovic 77; Odemwingie 81; Gygax 85	8,000
9	frpr1	**Paris SG**	A	L	1-2	Fauverge 3	35,189
10	frpr1	**St Etienne**	H	W	2-0	Moussilou 25; Aboucherouane 65	13,510
11	ecgpd	**Villarreal**	H	D	0-0		20,000
12	frpr1	**AS Monaco**	H	L	0-1		12,000
13	frpr1	**Le Mans**	A	D	1-1	Moussilou 8	10,057
14	ecgpd	**Man Utd**	A	D	0-0		60,626
15	frpr1	**Nantes**	H	W	2-0	Makoun 21; Moussilou 89	11,868
16	frpr1	**Marseille**	A	D	1-1	Acimovic 51	50,000
17	ecgpd	**Man Utd**	H	W	1-0	Acimovic 38	65,000
18	frpr1	**Strasbourg**	H	W	2-0	Odemwingie 5; Lichtsteiner 65	13,360
19	frpr1	**Auxerre**	A	L	2-3	Bodmer 6 pen; Cabaye 23	15,000
20	ecgpd	**Benfica**	H	D	0-0		60,000
21	frpr1	**Nancy**	H	W	1-0	Aboucherouane 53	11,140
22	frpr1	**Bordeaux**	A	L	0-1		19,252
23	ecgpd	**Villarreal**	A	L	0-1		22,500
24	frpr1	**Lens**	H	D	0-0		16,000
25	frpr1	**Lyon**	A	W	3-1	Odemwingie 8; Debuchy 60; Dumont 69	36,000
26	frpr1	**AC Ajaccio**	H	W	2-0	Odemwingie 36; Gygax 90	11,000
27	frpr1	**Troyes**	A	L	0-1		10,212
28	frpr1	**Sochaux**	H	W	3-0	Moussilou 1; Pitau 45 og; Gygax 55	12,286
29	frpr1	**Toulouse**	A	D	0-0		15,416
30	frpr1	**Metz**	H	W	3-1	Keita 3; Wimbee 52 og; Tavlaridis 64	12,104
31	frpr1	**Nice**	A	L	0-2		9,701
32	frpr1	**Paris SG**	H	D	0-0		17,000
33	uc3rl1	**S Donetsk**	H	W	3-2	Fauverge 19; Dernis 57; Odemwingie 77	19,880
34	frpr1	**St Etienne**	A	W	2-0	Debuchy 42; Keita 62	24,655
35	uc3rl2	**S Donetsk**	A	D	0-0		23,250
36	frpr1	**AS Monaco**	A	W	1-0	Odemwingie 57	6,791
37	frpr1	**Le Mans**	H	W	4-0	Odemwingie 16; Bodmer 38; Schmitz 53; Mirallas 75	16,000
38	uc4rl1	**Seville**	H	W	1-0	Dernis 24	11,009
39	frpr1	**Nantes**	A	D	1-1	Keita 84	25,000
40	uc4rl2	**Seville**	A	L	0-2		41,000
41	frpr1	**Marseille**	H	D	0-0		15,468
42	frpr1	**Strasbourg**	A	D	2-2	Keita 8,79	22,000
43	frpr1	**Auxerre**	H	D	1-1	Odemwingie 21	12,000
44	frpr1	**Nancy**	A	D	0-0		18,000
45	frpr1	**Bordeaux**	H	W	3-2	Bodmer 1; Odemwingie 5,30	20,000
46	frpr1	**Lens**	A	L	2-4	Odemwingie 51; Keita 69	44,991
47	frpr1	**Lyon**	H	W	4-0	Dernis 32; Odemwingie 49,51; Makoun 85	17,000
48	frpr1	**Rennes**	A	D	2-2	Bodmer 77,85	30,000

LEAGUE APPEARANCES, BOOKINGS AND CAPS

	AGE (on 01/07/06)	IN NAMED 18	APPEARANCES	COUNTING GAMES	MINUTES ON PITCH	YELLOW CARDS	RED CARDS	CAPS THIS SEASON	NATIONAL SIDE
Goalkeepers									
Gregory Malicki	32	31	6	6	540	0	0	-	France
Laurent Pichon	25	9	0	0	0	0	0	-	France
Tony Mario Sylva	31	32	32	32	2880	1	0	-	Senegal
Defenders									
Mathieu Chalme	25	32	29	23	2171	5	0	-	France
Santos Dante	22	2	2	2	180	0	0	-	Brazil
Stefan Lichtsteiner	22	31	30	18	1897	5	0	-	Switzerland
Nicolas Plestan	25	24	15	15	1350	1	0	-	France
Rafael Schmitz	25	30	27	26	2397	2	0	-	Brazil
Gregory Tafforeau	29	32	32	31	2823	4	0	-	France
Efstathios Tavlaridis	26	26	26	26	2325	12	0	-	Greece
Milivoje Vitakic	29	20	13	10	1025	3	0	-	Serbia & Montenegro
Midfielders									
Milenko Acimovic	29	12	12	6	800	5	0	-	Slovenia
Mathieu Bodmer	23	36	36	28	2698	3	0	-	France
Yohan Cabaye	20	29	27	16	1755	2	0	-	France
Mathieu Debuchy	20	27	27	16	1876	5	0	-	France
Stephane Dumont	23	11	9	8	761	1	0	-	France
Peter Franquart	21	8	3	1	120	0	0	-	France
Daniel Gygax	24	26	23	7	1071	0	0	10	Switzerland (35)
Jean Makoun	23	31	31	28	2615	5	1	6	Cameroon (26)
Forwards									
H. Aboucherouane	25	13	11	8	786	3	0	-	Morroco
Geoffrey Dernis	25	29	22	14	1580	3	0	-	France
Nicolas Fauverge	21	18	16	4	771	2	0	-	France
Abdel Kader Keita	24	27	27	19	1865	7	0	-	Ivory Coast
Kevin Mirallas	18	17	14	2	407	1	1	-	Belgium
Matt Moussilou	24	27	25	10	1231	1	0	-	France
Peter Odemwingie	24	26	25	14	1600	3	0	-	Nigeria
Larsen Toure	21	3	2	0	56	0	0	-	France

TEAM OF THE SEASON

G
Tony Mario Sylva
CG: 32 DR: 107

D
Rafael Schmitz
CG: 26 DR: 114

D
Nicolas Plestan
CG: 15 DR: 113

D
Gregory Tafforeau
CG: 31 DR: 113

D
Stefan Lichtsteiner
CG: 18 DR: 100

M
Mathieu Debuchy
CG: 16 SD: 114

M
Mathieu Bodmer
CG: 28 SD: 47

M
Jean Makoun
CG: 28 SD: 42

M
Yohan Cabaye
CG: 16 SD: 31

F
Peter Odemwingie
CG: 14 SR: 114

F
Abdel Kader Keita
CG: 19 SR: 311

MONTHLY POINTS TALLY

Month	Points	%
AUGUST	3	25%
SEPTEMBER	9	75%
OCTOBER	5	42%
NOVEMBER	6	67%
DECEMBER	4	44%
JANUARY	10	67%
FEBRUARY	7	58%
MARCH	6	50%
APRIL	5	42%
MAY	4	67%

LEAGUE GOALS

	PLAYER	MINS	GOALS	S RATE
1	Odemwingie	1600	14	114
2	Keita	1865	6	311
3	Makoun	2615	5	523
4	Bodmer	2698	5	540
5	Moussilou	1231	4	308
6	Gygax	1071	4	268
7	Debuchy	1876	4	469
8	Aboucherouane	786	2	393
9	Acimovic	800	2	400
10	Dumont	761	1	761
11	Cabaye	1755	1	1755
12	Mirallas	407	1	407
13	Fauverge	771	1	771
	Other		6	
	TOTAL		56	

TOP POINT EARNERS

	PLAYER	GAMES	AV PTS
1	Chalme	23	1.96
2	Tafforeau	31	1.87
3	Odemwingie	14	1.79
4	Tavlaridis	26	1.69
5	Debuchy	16	1.69
6	Sylva	32	1.69
7	Keita	19	1.68
8	Schmitz	26	1.65
9	Bodmer	28	1.64
10	Makoun	28	1.61
	CLUB AVERAGE:		1.00

DISCIPLINARY RECORDS

	PLAYER	YELLOW	RED	AVE
1	Acimovic	5	0	160
2	Tavlaridis	12	0	193
3	Aboucherouane	3	0	262
4	Keita	7	0	266
5	Vitakic	3	0	341
6	Debuchy	5	0	375
7	Lichtsteiner	5	0	379
8	Fauverge	2	0	385
9	Chalme	5	0	434
10	Makoun	5	1	435
11	Dernis	3	0	526
12	Odemwingie	3	0	533
13	Tafforeau	4	0	705
	Other	11	0	
	TOTAL	73	1	

KEY GOALKEEPER

Tony Mario Sylva

Goals Conceded in the League	27	**Counting Games** League games when player was on pitch for at least 70 minutes	32
Defensive Rating Ave number of mins between League goals conceded while on the pitch	107	**Clean Sheets** In League games when player was on pitch for at least 70 minutes	17

KEY PLAYERS - DEFENDERS

Rafael Schmitz

Goals Conceded Number of League goals conceded while the player was on the pitch	21	**Clean Sheets** In League games when player was on pitch for at least 70 minutes	13
Defensive Rating Ave number of mins between League goals conceded while on the pitch	114	**Club Defensive Rating** Average number of mins between League goals conceded by the club this season	107

	PLAYER	CON LGE	CLEAN SHEETS	DEF RATE
1	Rafael Schmitz	21	13	114 mins
2	Nicolas Plestan	12	9	113 mins
3	Gregory Tafforeau	25	17	113 mins
4	Stefan Lichtsteiner	19	7	100 mins

KEY PLAYERS - MIDFIELDERS

Mathieu Debuchy

Goals in the League	4	**Contribution to Attacking Power** Average number of minutes between League team goals while on pitch	57
Defensive Rating Average number of mins between League goals conceded while on the pitch	171	**Scoring Difference** Defensive Rating minus Contribution to Attacking Power	114

	PLAYER	LGE GOALS	DEF RATE	POWER	SCORE DIFF
1	Mathieu Debuchy	4	171	57	114 mins
2	Mathieu Bodmer	5	108	61	47 mins
3	Jean Makoun	5	109	67	42 mins
4	Yohan Cabaye	1	92	61	31 mins

KEY PLAYERS - GOALSCORERS

Peter Odemwingie

Goals in the League	14	**Player Strike Rate** Average number of minutes between League goals scored by player	114
Contribution to Attacking Power Average number of minutes between League team goals while on pitch	47	**Club Strike Rate** Average number of minutes between League goals scored by club	61

	PLAYER	LGE GOALS	POWER	STRIKE RATE
1	Peter Odemwingie	14	47	114 mins
2	Abdel Kader Keita	6	72	311 mins
3	Mathieu Debuchy	4	57	469 mins
4	Jean Makoun	5	67	523 mins

Lille's Geoffrey Dernis and Peter Odemwingie

SQUAD APPEARANCES

Match	1	2	3	4	5	6	7	8	9	10	11	12	13	14	15	16	17	18	19	20	21	22	23	24
Venue	H	A	H	A	H	A	A	H	A	H	H	H	A	A	H	A	H	H	A	H	H	A	A	H
Competition	L	L	L	L	L	L	C	L	L	L	C	L	L	C	L	L	C	L	L	C	L	L	C	L
Result	W	D	L	D	D	W	L	W	L	W	D	L	D	D	W	D	W	W	L	D	W	L	L	D

Match	25	26	27	28	29	30	31	32	33	34	35	36	37	38	39	40	41	42	43	44	45	46	47	48
Venue	A	H	A	H	A	H	A	H	H	A	A	A	H	H	A	A	H	A	H	A	H	A	H	A
Competition	L	L	L	L	L	L	L	L	E	L	E	L	L	E	L	E	L	L	L	L	L	L	L	L
Result	W	W	L	W	D	W	L	D	W	W	D	W	W	W	D	L	D	D	D	D	W	L	W	D

Goalkeepers
Gregory Malicki
Laurent Pichon
Tony Mario Sylva

Defenders
Mathieu Chalme
Bonfim Costa Dante
Stefan Lichtsteiner
Nicolas Plestan
Rafael Schmitz
Gregory Tafforeau
Efstathios Tavlaridis
Milivoje Vitakic

Midfielders
Milenko Acimovic
Mathieu Bodmer
Yohan Cabaye
Mathieu Debuchy
Stephane Dumont
Peter Franquart
Daniel Gygax
Jean Makoun

Forwards
Hicham Aboucherouane
Geoffrey Dernis
Nicolas Fauverge
Abdel Kader Keita
Kevin Mirallas
Matt Moussilou
Peter Odemwingie
Larsen Toure

KEY: ■ On all match | ■ On bench | ⏮ Subbed or sent off (Counting game) | « Subbed or sent off (playing less than 70 minutes) | ⏭ Subbed on from bench (Counting Game) | » Subbed on (playing less than 70 minutes) | Subbed on and then subbed or sent off (Counting Game) | Subbed on and then subbed or sent off (playing less than 70 minutes) | □ Not in 16

LENS

Final Position: **4th**

KEY: ☐Won ☐Drawn ☐Lost

							Attendance
1	frpr1	Nantes	A	L	0-2		34,000
2	frpr1	Marseille	H	W	2-0	Keita 37; Hilton 61	39,260
3	etfl1	Cluj-Napoca	A	D	1-1	Lachor 23	
4	frpr1	Nancy	A	W	2-1	Diarra 14; Dindane 19	19,500
5	frpr1	Auxerre	H	W	7-0	Cousin 11,56; Thomert 13,37; Jussie 67,74; Demont 72	30,500
6	etfl2	Cluj-Napoca	H	W	3-1	Hilton 38; Coulibaly 76; Cousin 78 pen	
7	frpr1	AS Monaco	A	D	0-0		11,882
8	frpr1	Bordeaux	H	D	1-1	Cousin 29	30,650
9	uc1rl1	G Dyskobolia	H	D	1-1	Hilton 12	20,194
10	frpr1	Strasbourg	A	D	1-1	Dindane 42	18,321
11	frpr1	Lyon	A	D	1-1	Coulibaly 5	36,300
12	frpr1	Rennes	H	D	0-0		29,206
13	uc1rl2	G Dyskobolia	A	W	4-2	Cousin 23,54; Dindane 29; Lachor 90	6,000
14	frpr1	Nice	H	D	2-2	Diarra 46; Thomert 57	29,365
15	ucgpc	S Bucharest	A	L	0-4		20,000
16	frpr1	Troyes	A	D	1-1	Cousin 21	12,000
17	frpr1	Toulouse	H	W	1-0	Cousin 24	29,174
18	ucgpc	Halmstad	H	W	5-0	Cousin 15,22,46; Barul 72; Lachor 90	25,000
19	frpr1	Sochaux	A	D	1-1	Cousin 59	14,499
20	frpr1	AC Ajaccio	A	D	0-0		4,000
21	frpr1	Metz	H	D	0-0		31,926
22	ucgpc	Hertha Berlin	A	D	0-0		18,510
23	frpr1	Paris SG	A	W	4-3	Thomert 2; Dindane 32,68; Jussie 41	40,895
24	frpr1	St Etienne	H	W	2-1	Thomert 33; Cousin 63	30,000
25	frpr1	Lille	A	D	0-0		16,000
26	ucgpc	Sampdoria	H	W	2-1	Thomert 10; Jomaa 90	31,473
27	frpr1	Le Mans	H	W	2-0	Dindane 31; Cousin 90	39,314
28	frpr1	Marseille	A	D	1-1	Hilton 76	50,000
29	frpr1	Nancy	H	L	1-2	Frau 36	32,000
30	frpr1	Auxerre	A	L	0-1		8,000
31	frpr1	AS Monaco	H	D	1-1	Gillet 45	33,796
32	frpr1	Bordeaux	A	L	0-1		21,575
33	frpr1	Strasbourg	H	W	2-1	Cousin 77; Khiter 82	30,922
34	frpr1	Lyon	H	D	1-1	Jussie 55	40,037
35	uc3rl1	Udinese	A	L	0-3		8,000
36	frpr1	Rennes	A	L	1-4	Cousin 90	21,501
37	uc3rl2	Udinese	H	W	1-0	Frau 55	26,292
38	frpr1	AC Ajaccio	H	W	1-0	Cousin 17	36,482
39	frpr1	Nice	A	D	0-0		10,365
40	frpr1	Troyes	H	W	1-0	Cousin 43	35,098
41	frpr1	Toulouse	A	D	1-1	Frau 68	12,941
42	frpr1	Sochaux	H	W	2-1	Keita 20; Frau 35	32,966
43	frpr1	Metz	A	W	1-0	Frau 26 pen	17,957
44	frpr1	Paris SG	H	D	1-1	Jussie 89 pen	39,513
45	frpr1	St Etienne	A	L	0-2		34,938
46	frpr1	Lille	H	W	4-2	Thomert 8; Cousin 39; Keita 42; Frau 52	44,991
47	frpr1	Le Mans	A	D	0-0		12,827
48	frpr1	Nantes	H	W	3-1	Jussie 19; Dindane 21; Coulibaly 85	36,868

LEAGUE APPEARANCES, BOOKINGS AND CAPS

	AGE (on 01/07/06)	IN NAMED 18	APPEARANCES	COUNTING GAMES	MINUTES ON PITCH	YELLOW CARDS	RED CARDS	CAPS THIS SEASON	NATIONAL SIDE
Goalkeepers									
Arnaud Brocard	19	0	0	0	0	0	0	-	France
Sebastien Chabbert	27	35	2	1	136	0	0	-	France
Charles-Hubert Itandje	23	38	37	36	3284	1	1	-	France
Defenders									
Benoit Assou-Ekotto	22	34	34	31	2933	9	1	-	France
Patrick Barul	28	33	20	7	779	0	0	-	France
Adama Coulibaly	25	35	35	33	3016	1	0	-	Mali
Nicholas Gillet	29	34	15	9	976	3	0	-	France
Hilton	28	35	35	33	3075	2	0	-	Brazil
Yoann Lachor	30	14	5	4	340	2	0	-	France
Guillermo Rodiguez	22	3	2	0	73	0	0	-	Uruguay
Kamil Zayatte	21	2	0	0	0	0	0	-	Guinea
Midfielders									
Eric Carriere	33	35	26	11	1372	0	0	-	France
Yohan Demont	28	36	35	35	3147	5	1	-	France
Mounir Diane	24	0	0	0	0	0	0	-	Morocco
Alou Diarra	24	32	32	28	2689	13	2	10	France (8)
Aruna Dindane	25	29	28	18	1889	5	1	5	Ivory Coast (32)
Simon Feindouno	20	0	0	0	0	0	0	-	Guinea
Seydou Keita	26	35	35	33	3008	5	0	-	Mali
Jonathan Lacourt	19	18	10	5	586	3	0	-	France
Jerome Leroy	31	16	15	14	1270	3	0	-	France
Forwards									
Daniel Cousin	29	34	33	28	2622	9	1	-	Gabon
Pierre-Alain Frau	26	20	19	13	1277	0	0	-	France
Issam Jemaa	22	10	6	1	178	0	0	-	Tunisia
Jussie	22	35	34	27	2508	2	0	-	Brazil
Seid Khiter	21	10	7	0	120	0	0	-	France
Olivier Thomert	26	29	29	21	2136	4	0	-	France

TEAM OF THE SEASON

G — Charles-Hubert Itandje — CG: 36 DR: 97

D — Benoit Assou-Ekotto — CG: 31 DR: 133

D — Adama Coulibaly — CG: 33 DR: 108

D — Hilton — CG: 33 DR: 96

D — Nicholas Gillet* — CG: 9 DR: 88

M — Aruna Dindane — CG: 18 SD: 50

M — Jerome Leroy — CG: 14 SD: 44

M — Seydou Keita — CG: 33 SD: 32

M — Yohan Demont — CG: 35 SD: 31

F — Daniel Cousin — CG: 28 SR: 202

F — Pierre-Alain Frau — CG: 13 SR: 255

MONTHLY POINTS TALLY

AUGUST	10	83%
SEPTEMBER	4	33%
OCTOBER	5	56%
NOVEMBER	6	50%
DECEMBER	7	78%
JANUARY	2	13%
FEBRUARY	7	58%
MARCH	8	67%
APRIL	7	58%
MAY	4	67%

LEAGUE GOALS

	PLAYER	MINS	GOALS	S RATE
1	Cousin	2622	13	202
2	Dindane	1889	6	315
3	Jussie	2508	6	418
4	Thomert	2136	6	356
5	Frau	1277	5	255
6	Keita	3008	3	1003
7	Coulibaly	3016	2	1508
8	Diarra	2689	2	1345
9	Hilton	3075	2	1538
10	Gillet	976	1	976
11	Demont	3147	1	3147
	Other		1	
	TOTAL		48	

TOP POINT EARNERS

	PLAYER	GAMES	AV PTS
1	Dindane	18	1.89
2	Keita	33	1.70
3	Diarra	28	1.68
4	Demont	35	1.66
5	Assou-Ekotto	31	1.65
6	Cousin	28	1.61
7	Hilton	33	1.58
8	Thomert	21	1.57
9	Itandje	36	1.56
10	Frau	13	1.54
	CLUB AVERAGE:		1.58

DISCIPLINARY RECORDS

	PLAYER	YELLOW	RED	AVE
1	Diarra	13	2	179
2	Lacourt	3	0	195
3	Cousin	9	1	262
4	Assou-Ekotto	9	1	293
5	Dindane	5	1	314
6	Gillet	3	0	325
7	Leroy	3	0	423
8	Demont	5	1	524
9	Thomert	4	0	534
10	Keita	5	0	601
11	Jussie	2	0	1254
12	Hilton	2	0	1537
13	Itandje	1	1	1642
	Other	1	0	
	TOTAL	65	7	

KEY GOALKEEPER

Charles-Hubert Itandje

Goals Conceded in the League	34	**Counting Games** League games when player was on pitch for at least 70 minutes	36
Defensive Rating Ave number of mins between League goals conceded while on the pitch	97	**Clean Sheets** In League games when player was on pitch for at least 70 minutes	12

KEY PLAYERS - DEFENDERS

Benoit Assou-Ekotto

Goals Conceded Number of League goals conceded while the player was on the pitch	22	**Clean Sheets** In League games when player was on pitch for at least 70 minutes	11
Defensive Rating Ave number of mins between League goals conceded while on the pitch	133	**Club Defensive Rating** Average number of mins between League goals conceded by the club this season	98

	PLAYER	CON LGE	CLEAN SHEETS	DEF RATE
1	Benoit Assou-Ekotto	22	11	133 mins
2	Adama Coulibaly	28	11	108 mins
3	Hilton	32	10	96 mins

KEY PLAYERS - MIDFIELDERS

Aruna Dindane

Goals in the League	6	**Contribution to Attacking Power** Average number of minutes between League team goals while on pitch	76
Defensive Rating Average number of mins between League goals conceded while on the pitch	126	**Scoring Difference** Defensive Rating minus Contribution to Attacking Power	50

	PLAYER	LGE GOALS	DEF RATE	POWER	SCORE DIFF
1	Aruna Dindane	6	126	76	50 mins
2	Jerome Leroy	0	115	71	44 mins
3	Seydou Keita	3	100	68	32 mins
4	Yohan Demont	1	98	67	31 mins

KEY PLAYERS - GOALSCORERS

Daniel Cousin

Goals in the League	13	**Player Strike Rate** Average number of minutes between League goals scored by player	202
Contribution to Attacking Power Average number of minutes between League team goals while on pitch	67	**Club Strike Rate** Average number of minutes between League goals scored by club	71

	PLAYER	LGE GOALS	POWER	STRIKE RATE
1	Daniel Cousin	13	67	202 mins
2	Pierre-Alain Frau	5	67	255 mins
3	Aruna Dindane	6	76	315 mins
4	Olivier Thomert	6	61	356 mins

Lens' Hilton and Daniel Cousin celebrate

SQUAD APPEARANCES

Match	1	2	3	4	5	6	7	8	9	10	11	12	13	14	15	16	17	18	19	20	21	22	23	24
Venue	A	H	A	A	H	H	A	H	H	A	A	H	A	H	A	A	H	H	A	A	H	A	A	H
Competition	L	L	O	L	L	O	L	L	E	L	L	L	E	L	E	L	L	E	L	L	L	E	L	L
Result	L	W	D	W	W	W	D	D	D	D	D	D	W	D	L	D	W	W	D	D	D	D	W	W

Match	25	26	27	28	29	30	31	32	33	34	35	36	37	38	39	40	41	42	43	44	45	46	47	48
Venue	A	H	H	A	H	A	H	A	H	H	A	A	H	H	A	H	A	H	A	H	A	H	A	H
Competition	L	E	L	L	L	L	L	L	L	L	E	L	E	L	L	L	L	L	L	L	L	L	L	L
Result	D	W	W	D	L	L	D	L	W	D	L	L	W	W	D	W	D	W	W	D	L	W	D	W

Goalkeepers
- Arnaud Brocard
- Sebastien Chabbert
- Charles-Hubert Itandje

Defenders
- Benoit Assou-Ekotto
- Patrick Barul
- Adama Coulibaly
- Nicholas Gillet
- Hilton
- Yoann Lachor
- Guillermo Rodiguez
- Kamil Zayatte

Midfielders
- Eric Carriere
- Yohan Demont
- Mounir Diane
- Alou Diarra
- Aruna Dindane
- Simon Feindouno
- Seydou Keita
- Jonathan Lacourt
- Jerome Leroy

Forwards
- Daniel Cousin
- Pierre-Alain Frau
- Issam Jemaa
- Jussie
- Seid Khiter
- Olivier Thomert

KEY: On all match | On bench | Subbed or sent off (Counting game) | Subbed or sent off (playing less than 70 minutes) | Subbed on from bench (Counting Game) | Subbed on (playing less than 70 minutes) | Subbed on and then subbed or sent off (Counting Game) | Subbed on and then subbed or sent off (playing less than 70 minutes) | Not in 16

MARSEILLE

Final Position: **5th**

KEY: ☐Won ☐Drawn ☐Lost

	Comp	Opponent	H/A	Res	Score	Scorers	Attendance
1	frpr1	Bordeaux	H	L	0-2		57,000
2	frpr1	Lens	A	L	0-2		39,260
3	etfl1	Deportivo	A	L	0-2		15,400
4	frpr1	Lyon	H	D	1-1	Taiwo 6	56,000
5	frpr1	Rennes	A	L	2-3	Niang 1; Lamouchi 31,70	29,490
6	etfl2	Deportivo	H	W	5-1	Ribery 4; Meite 65; Niang 73,88; Oruma 90	
7	frpr1	AC Ajaccio	H	D	1-1	Gimenez 59	50,000
8	frpr1	Sochaux	A	W	1-0	Oruma 65	18,493
9	uc1rl1	Beerschot	A	D	0-0		12,000
10	frpr1	Troyes	H	W	2-1	Ribery 22; Lamouchi 34	48,000
11	frpr1	Toulouse	A	L	0-1		28,070
12	frpr1	Metz	H	W	3-1	Dehu 25; Ribery 47; Niang 68	48,000
13	uc1rl2	Beerschot	H	W	4-1*	(*on penalties)	22,068
14	frpr1	Nice	A	W	1-0	Ribery 74	14,923
15	frpr1	Paris SG	H	W	1-0	Cana 78	58,000
16	ucgpf	CSKA Moscow	A	W	2-1	Lamouchi 23; Niang 38	12,000
17	frpr1	St Etienne	A	L	1-2	Ribery 35	35,123
18	frpr1	Lille	H	D	1-1	Koke 28	50,000
19	frpr1	Le Mans	A	L	0-3		16,531
20	frpr1	Nantes	H	W	2-1	Oruma 27; Ribery 72	48,000
21	ucgpf	Heerenveen	H	W	1-0	Taiwo 90 pen	14,777
22	frpr1	AS Monaco	H	W	2-1	Oruma 63; Lamouchi 75	52,000
23	ucgpf	Levski Sofia	A	L	0-1		17,000
24	frpr1	Nancy	A	D	1-1	Niang 59	30,000
25	frpr1	Auxerre	H	W	1-0	Niang 2	51,000
26	ucgpf	Din Bucharest	H	W	2-1	Cesar 39; Delfim 45	15,909
27	frpr1	Strasbourg	A	W	1-0	Niang 60	27,786
28	frpr1	Lens	H	D	1-1	Beye 3	50,000
29	frpr1	Lyon	A	L	1-2	Lamouchi 19	38,912
30	frpr1	Rennes	H	W	1-0	Pagis 64	45,211
31	frpr1	AC Ajaccio	A	L	1-3	Pagis 45	5,500
32	frpr1	Sochaux	H	D	0-0		21,000
33	frpr1	Troyes	A	W	1-0	Lamouchi 7	18,860
34	frpr1	Toulouse	H	D	0-0		43,000
35	uc3rl1	Bolton	A	D	0-0		19,288
36	frpr1	Metz	A	L	0-1		22,689
37	uc3rl2	Bolton	H	W	2-1	Ribery 45; Ben Haim 68 og	38,351
38	frpr1	Nice	H	W	1-0	Maoulida 65	47,000
39	frpr1	Paris SG	A	D	0-0		43,000
40	uc4rl1	Z St Petersburg	H	L	0-1		25,500
41	frpr1	St Etienne	H	W	2-0	Pagis 16,18	56,263
42	uc4rl2	Z St Petersburg	A	D	1-1	Taiwo 74	21,000
43	frpr1	Lille	A	D	0-0		15,468
44	frpr1	Le Mans	H	D	1-1	Maoulida 22	49,593
45	frpr1	Nantes	A	W	3-1	Niang 22,72; Maoulida 52	33,000
46	frpr1	AS Monaco	A	L	0-1		17,594
47	frpr1	Nancy	H	W	6-0	Niang 12,33; Oruma 52; Maoulida 64; Pagis 88,90	50,000
48	frpr1	Auxerre	A	W	2-1	Niang 16; Civelli 67	28,085
49	frpr1	Strasbourg	H	D	2-2	Nasri 47; Ribery 72	57,680
50	frpr1	Bordeaux	A	D	1-1	Maoulida 75	32,765

LEAGUE APPEARANCES, BOOKINGS AND CAPS

	AGE (on 01/07/06)	IN NAMED 18	APPEARANCES	COUNTING GAMES	MINUTES ON PITCH	YELLOW CARDS	RED CARDS	CAPS THIS SEASON	NATIONAL SIDE
Goalkeepers									
Fabien Barthez	35	24	24	24	2155	2	0	4	France (8)
Cedric Carasso	24	34	15	14	1265	1	0	-	France
Defenders									
Garcia Andre Luis	26	19	14	9	891	1	0	-	Brazil
Habib Beye	29	31	29	24	2296	3	0	-	Senegal
Jerome Bonnissel	33	5	5	4	402	1	0	-	France
Alain Cantareil	22	10	6	2	241	0	0	-	France
Bostjan Cesar	23	18	17	16	1476	7	0	-	Slovenia
Renato Civelli	22	11	11	10	948	2	0	-	Argentina
Demetrius Ferreira	32	30	23	13	1392	2	0	-	Brazil
Abdoulaye Meite	25	20	13	11	1059	2	1	8	Ivory Coast (32)
Koji Nakata	26	7	4	3	257	2	0	-	Japan
Alexis Pradie	19	1	1	1	90	0	0	-	France
Taye Ismaila Taiwo	21	30	30	30	2687	4	0	-	Nigeria
Midfielders									
Laurent Battles	30	4	4	1	159	1	0	-	France
Garry Bocaly	18	1	1	1	90	1	0	-	Martinique
Fabien Camus	21	1	1	1	90	0	0	-	France
Lorik Cana	22	27	27	27	2415	13	0	-	Bosnia
Frederic Dehu	33	30	30	28	2605	0	1	-	France
Jose Rola Delfim	29	26	13	7	846	1	0	-	Portugal
Vincent Gastine	24	2	1	0	61	0	0	-	France
Sabri Lamouchi	34	32	32	27	2630	9	1	-	France
Samir Nasri	19	30	30	11	1421	1	0	-	France
Salomon Olembe	25	2	2	1	135	0	0	7	Cameroon (26)
Wilson Oruma	29	30	29	23	2220	4	0	-	Nigeria
Franck Ribery	23	35	35	33	3042	6	0	2	France (8)
Forwards									
Rakhmane Barry	19	2	1	0	45	0	0	-	France
Mohamed Dennoun	25	1	1	0	52	0	0	-	France
Christian Gimenez	31	28	21	7	901	0	0	-	Argentina
Sergio Koke	23	12	9	2	420	0	0	-	Spain
Peguy Luyindula	27	2	2	1	134	0	0	-	France
Toifilou Maoulida	27	16	16	15	1370	4	0	-	France
Andres Mendoza	28	12	11	1	394	1	0	-	Peru
Mame N'Diaye	19	1	1	1	90	0	0	-	Senegal
Mamadou Niang	26	28	28	23	2089	1	0	-	Senegal
Michael Pagis	32	13	13	13	1109	3	0	-	France

TEAM OF THE SEASON

G — Fabien Barthez — CG: 24 DR: 103

D — Habib Beye — CG: 24 DR: 104

D — Demetrius Ferreira — CG: 13 DR: 99

D — Bostjan Cesar — CG: 16 DR: 98

D — Taye Ismaila Taiwo — CG: 30 DR: 93

M — Frederic Dehu — CG: 28 SD: 35

M — Wilson Oruma — CG: 23 SD: 32

M — Lorik Cana — CG: 27 SD: 28

M — Sabri Lamouchi — CG: 27 SD: 19

F — Michael Pagis — CG: 13 SR: 185

F — Mamadou Niang — CG: 23 SR: 209

MONTHLY POINTS TALLY

Month	Points	%
AUGUST	2	17%
SEPTEMBER	9	75%
OCTOBER	7	58%
NOVEMBER	6	67%
DECEMBER	7	78%
JANUARY	5	33%
FEBRUARY	7	58%
MARCH	6	50%
APRIL	6	67%
MAY	5	56%

LEAGUE GOALS

	PLAYER	MINS	GOALS	S RATE
1	Niang	2089	10	209
2	Pagis	1109	6	185
3	Ribery	3042	6	507
4	Lamouchi	2630	6	438
5	Maoulida	1370	5	274
6	Oruma	2220	4	555
7	Cana	2415	1	2415
8	Beye	2296	1	2296
9	Civelli	948	1	948
10	Koke	420	1	420
11	Dehu	2605	1	2605
12	Taiwo	2687	1	2687
13	Nasri	1421	1	1421
	Other		1	
	TOTAL		45	

TOP POINT EARNERS

	PLAYER	GAMES	AV PTS
1	Ferreira	13	2.23
2	Niang	23	1.87
3	Cesar	16	1.75
4	Cana	27	1.74
5	Maoulida	15	1.73
6	Dehu	28	1.71
7	Pagis	13	1.69
8	Barthez	24	1.67
9	Ribery	33	1.58
10	Beye	24	1.54
	CLUB AVERAGE:		1.58

DISCIPLINARY RECORDS

	PLAYER	YELLOW	RED	AVE
1	Cana	13	0	185
2	Cesar	7	0	210
3	Lamouchi	9	1	263
4	Maoulida	4	0	342
5	Meite	2	1	353
6	Pagis	3	0	369
7	Civelli	2	0	474
8	Ribery	6	0	507
9	Oruma	4	0	555
10	Taiwo	4	0	671
11	Ferreira	2	0	696
12	Beye	3	0	765
13	Delfim	1	0	846
	Other	6	1	
	TOTAL	66	3	

KEY GOALKEEPER

Fabien Barthez

Goals Conceded in the League	21	**Counting Games** League games when player was on pitch for at least 70 minutes	24
Defensive Rating Ave number of mins between League goals conceded while on the pitch	103	**Clean Sheets** In games when player was on pitch for at least 70 minutes	10

KEY PLAYERS - DEFENDERS

Habib Beye

Goals Conceded Number of League goals conceded while the player was on the pitch	22	**Clean Sheets** In League games when player was on pitch for at least 70 minutes	7
Defensive Rating Ave number of mins between League goals conceded while on the pitch	104	**Club Defensive Rating** Average number of mins between League goals conceded by the club this season	98

	PLAYER	CON LGE	CLEAN SHEETS	DEF RATE
1	Habib Beye	22	7	104 mins
2	Demetrius Ferreira	14	7	99 mins
3	Bostjan Cesar	15	7	98 mins
4	Taye Ismaila Taiwo	29	9	93 mins

KEY PLAYERS - MIDFIELDERS

Frederic Dehu

Goals in the League	1	**Contribution to Attacking Power** Average number of minutes between League team goals while on pitch	69
Defensive Rating Average number of mins between League goals conceded while on the pitch	104	**Scoring Difference** Defensive Rating minus Contribution to Attacking Power	35

	PLAYER	LGE GOALS	DEF RATE	POWER	SCORE DIFF
1	Frederic Dehu	1	104	69	35 mins
2	Wilson Oruma	4	106	74	32 mins
3	Lorik Cana	1	101	73	28 mins
4	Sabri Lamouchi	6	88	69	19 mins

KEY PLAYERS - GOALSCORERS

Michael Pagis

Goals in the League	6	**Player Strike Rate** Average number of minutes between League goals scored by player	185
Contribution to Attacking Power Average number of minutes between League team goals while on pitch	74	**Club Strike Rate** Average number of minutes between League goals scored by club	76

	PLAYER	LGE GOALS	POWER	STRIKE RATE
1	Michael Pagis	6	74	185 mins
2	Mamadou Niang	10	60	209 mins
3	Toifilou Maoulida	5	62	274 mins
4	Sabri Lamouchi	6	69	438 mins

Marseille's Lorik Cana and Mamadou Niang

SQUAD APPEARANCES

Match	1	2	3	4	5	6	7	8	9	10	11	12	13	14	15	16	17	18	19	20	21	22	23	24	25
Venue	H	A	A	H	A	H	H	A	A	H	A	H	H	A	H	A	A	H	A	H	H	H	A	A	H
Competition	L	L	O	L	L	O	L	L	E	L	L	L	E	L	L	E	L	L	L	L	E	L	E	L	L
Result	L	L	L	D	L	W	D	W	D	W	L	W	W	W	W	W	L	D	L	W	W	W	L	D	W

Match	26	27	28	29	30	31	32	33	34	35	36	37	38	39	40	41	42	43	44	45	46	47	48	49	50
Venue	H	A	H	A	H	A	H	A	H	A	A	H	H	A	H	H	A	A	H	A	A	H	A	H	A
Competition	E	L	L	L	L	L	L	L	L	E	L	E	L	L	E	L	E	L	L	L	L	L	L	L	L
Result	W	W	D	L	W	L	D	W	D	D	L	W	W	D	L	W	D	D	D	W	L	W	W	D	D

Goalkeepers
Fabien Barthez
Cedric Carasso

Defenders
Garcia Andre Luis
Habib Beye
Jerome Bonnissel
Alain Cantareil
Bostjan Cesar
Renato Civelli
Demetrius Ferreira
Abdoulaye Meite
Koji Nakata
Alexis Pradie
Taye Ismaila Taiwo

Midfielders
Laurent Battles
Garry Bocaly
Fabien Camus
Lorik Cana
Frederic Dehu
Jose Rola Delfim
Vincent Gastine
Sabri Lamouchi
Sylvain N'Diaye
Samir Nasri
Salomon Olembe
Wilson Oruma
Franck Ribery

Forwards
Rakhmane Barry
Mohamed Dennoun
Christian Gimenez
Sergio Koke
Peguy Luyindula
Toifilou Maoulida
Andres Mendoza
Mame N'Diaye
Mamadou Niang
Michael Pagis

KEY: On all match | On bench | Subbed or sent off (Counting game) | Subbed or sent off (playing less than 70 minutes) | Subbed on from bench (Counting Game) | Subbed on (playing less than 70 minutes) | Subbed on and then subbed or sent off (Counting Game) | Subbed on and then subbed or sent off (playing less than 70 minutes) | Not in 16

AUXERRE

Final Position: **6th**

KEY: □Won □Drawn □Lost

							Attendance
1	frpr1	**Strasbourg**	A	D	0-0		18,224
2	frpr1	**AS Monaco**	A	W	2-0	Violeau 25; Pieroni 77	15,748
3	frpr1	**Bordeaux**	H	W	1-0	Pieroni 36	18,000
4	frpr1	**Lens**	A	L	0-7		30,500
5	frpr1	**Lyon**	H	L	0-2		15,000
6	frpr1	**Rennes**	A	L	1-3	Diaby 68	27,982
7	uc1rl1	**Levski Sofia**	H	W	2-1	Poyet 53; Pieroni 80	6,000
8	frpr1	**AC Ajaccio**	H	W	2-0	Akale 75; Luyindula 84	5,000
9	frpr1	**Metz**	A	W	2-1	Mignot 34; Luyindula 88	13,630
10	frpr1	**Sochaux**	H	W	3-0	Luyindula 19; Kahlenberg 41; Cheyrou 52	10,000
11	uc1rl2	**Levski Sofia**	A	L	0-1		15,000
12	frpr1	**Toulouse**	A	L	0-2		18,641
13	frpr1	**Troyes**	H	W	3-0	Lachuer 25; Luyindula 78; Benjani 83	12,000
14	frpr1	**Nice**	A	L	0-1		6,000
15	frpr1	**Paris SG**	H	W	2-0	Cisse 52 og; Pieroni 85	22,000
16	frpr1	**St Etienne**	A	D	1-1	Mignot 80	33,005
17	frpr1	**Lille**	H	W	3-2	Lachuer 18; Pieroni 66 pen,73	15,000
18	frpr1	**Le Mans**	A	W	2-0	Pieroni 19; Lachuer 66	10,347
19	frpr1	**Nantes**	H	W	4-0	Luyindula 1,39; Delhommeau 29 og; Cheyrou 90	7,385
20	frpr1	**Marseille**	A	L	0-1		51,000
21	frpr1	**Nancy**	H	L	0-1		7,000
22	frpr1	**AS Monaco**	H	W	2-1	Luyindula 34; Kahlenberg 57	15,000
23	frpr1	**Bordeaux**	A	L	0-1		17,965
24	frpr1	**Lens**	H	W	1-0	Luyindula 44	8,000
25	frpr1	**Lyon**	A	D	1-1	Luyindula 88	37,958
26	frpr1	**Rennes**	H	W	2-0	Pieroni 68; Kahlenberg 79	6,000
27	frpr1	**AC Ajaccio**	A	L	0-1		5,000
28	frpr1	**Metz**	H	D	1-1	Pieroni 75	5,000
29	frpr1	**Sochaux**	A	L	0-1		11,468
30	frpr1	**Toulouse**	H	W	2-0	Akale 20; Kahlenberg 68	5,000
31	frpr1	**Troyes**	A	D	1-1	Kahlenberg 59	11,000
32	frpr1	**Nice**	H	W	2-0	Akale 53; Bolf 76	8,000
33	frpr1	**Paris SG**	A	L	1-4	Mathis 59	35,528
34	frpr1	**St Etienne**	H	D	0-0		20,000
35	frpr1	**Lille**	A	D	1-1	Luyindula 27	12,000
36	frpr1	**Le Mans**	H	D	0-0		10,500
37	frpr1	**Nantes**	A	L	2-3	Akale 59; Kahlenberg 67	30,000
38	frpr1	**Marseille**	H	L	1-2	Mignot 74	28,085
39	frpr1	**Nancy**	A	W	3-1	Pieroni 18; Lachuer 40; Kahlenberg 90	17,000
40	frpr1	**Strasbourg**	H	W	4-0	Kahlenberg 19; Pieroni 43,47; Mathis 83	10,000

LEAGUE APPEARANCES, BOOKINGS AND CAPS

	AGE (on 01/07/06)	IN NAMED 18	APPEARANCES	COUNTING GAMES	MINUTES ON PITCH	YELLOW CARDS	RED CARDS	CAPS THIS SEASON	NATIONAL SIDE
Goalkeepers									
Baptiste Chabert	23	6	0	0	0	0	0	-	France
Fabien Cool	33	38	38	36	3296	0	0	-	France
Sebastien Hamel	30	29	2	1	124	0	0	-	France
Defenders									
Rene Bolf	32	15	10	8	771	2	0	2	Czech Republic (2)
Mamoutou Coulibaly	22	3	0	0	0	0	0	-	Mali
Stephane Grichting	27	28	25	23	2158	4	0	5	Switzerland (35)
Jean-Sebastien Jaures	28	21	18	16	1438	1	0	-	France
Omar Kaalabane	25	16	8	7	670	0	1	-	Guinea
Younes Kaboul	20	11	10	8	725	0	0	-	France
Baptiste Martin	21	21	15	8	932	1	0	-	France
Jean Pascal Mignot	25	30	28	28	2520	7	0	-	France
Johan Radet	29	33	33	26	2632	1	0	-	France
Bacary Sagna	23	23	23	22	2023	2	0	-	France
Midfielders									
Kanga Akale	25	31	31	18	1945	0	0	7	Ivory Coast (32)
Mathieu Berson	26	30	27	19	1856	3	0	-	France
Benoit Cheyrou	25	35	34	34	3049	3	0	-	France
Vassiriki Abou Diaby	20	5	5	3	308	0	0	-	France
Thomas Kahlenberg	23	37	37	23	2454	1	0	4	Denmark (19)
Yann Lachuer	34	27	26	19	1898	1	0	-	France
Lionel Mathis	24	23	22	10	1095	5	0	-	France
Philippe Violeau	35	33	30	24	2337	6	0	-	France
Forwards									
Ludovic Genest	18	2	1	0	3	0	0	-	France
Peguy Luyindula	27	34	33	25	2409	0	0	-	France
Benjani Mwaruwari	27	15	11	8	813	1	0	3	Zimbabwe (55)
Luigi Pieroni	25	36	33	15	1853	3	0	5	Belgium (42)
Romain Poyet	25	18	12	1	261	1	0	-	France

TEAM OF THE SEASON

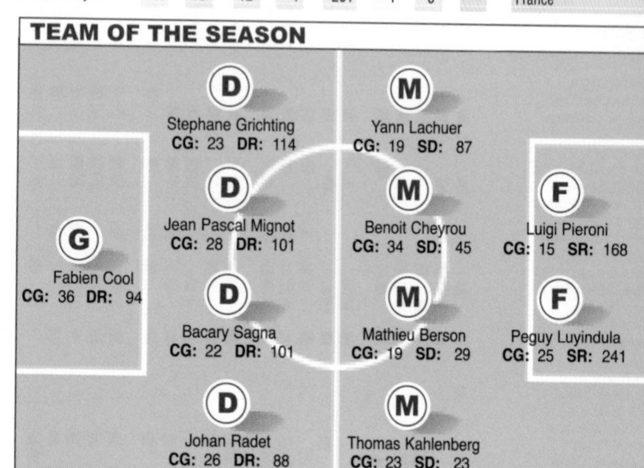

MONTHLY POINTS TALLY

AUGUST	6	50%
SEPTEMBER	9	75%
OCTOBER	6	50%
NOVEMBER	7	78%
DECEMBER	3	33%
JANUARY	10	67%
FEBRUARY	4	33%
MARCH	5	42%
APRIL	2	22%
MAY	6	67%

LEAGUE GOALS

	PLAYER	MINS	GOALS	S RATE
1	Pieroni	1853	11	168
2	Luyindula	2409	10	241
3	Kahlenberg	2454	8	307
4	Lachuer	1898	4	475
5	Akale	1945	4	486
6	Mignot	2520	3	840
7	Mathis	1095	2	548
8	Cheyrou	3049	2	1525
9	Benjani	813	1	813
10	Violeau	2337	1	2337
11	Bolf	771	1	771
12	Diaby	308	1	308
	Other		2	
	TOTAL		50	

TOP POINT EARNERS

	PLAYER	GAMES	AV PTS
1	Lachuer	19	1.89
2	Akale	18	1.83
3	Radet	26	1.77
4	Pieroni	15	1.67
5	Cheyrou	34	1.65
6	Cool	36	1.64
7	Violeau	24	1.63
8	Mignot	28	1.61
9	Sagna	22	1.59
10	Berson	19	1.53
	CLUB AVERAGE:		1.55

DISCIPLINARY RECORDS

	PLAYER	YELLOW	RED	AVE
1	Mathis	5	0	219
2	Mignot	7	0	360
3	Bolf	2	0	385
4	Violeau	6	0	389
5	Grichting	4	0	539
6	Pieroni	3	0	617
7	Berson	3	0	618
8	Kaalabane	0	1	670
9	Benjani	1	0	813
10	Martin	1	0	932
11	Sagna	2	0	1011
12	Cheyrou	3	0	1016
13	Jaures	1	0	1438
	Other	3	0	
	TOTAL	41	1	

KEY GOALKEEPER

Fabien Cool

Goals Conceded in the League	35	Counting Games League games when player was on pitch for at least 70 minutes	36
Defensive Rating Ave number of mins between League goals conceded while on the pitch	94	Clean Sheets In games when player was on pitch for at least 70 minutes	16

KEY PLAYERS - DEFENDERS

Stephane Grichting

Goals Conceded Number of League goals conceded while the player was on the pitch	19	Clean Sheets In League games when player was on pitch for at least 70 minutes	9
Defensive Rating Ave number of mins between League goals conceded while on the pitch	114	Club Defensive Rating Average number of mins between League goals conceded by the club this season	88

	PLAYER	CON LGE	CLEAN SHEETS	DEF RATE
1	Stephane Grichting	19	9	114 mins
2	Bacary Sagna	20	10	101 mins
3	Jean Pascal Mignot	25	13	101 mins
4	Johan Radet	30	12	88 mins

KEY PLAYERS - MIDFIELDERS

Yann Lachuer

Goals in the League	4	Contribution to Attacking Power Average number of minutes between League team goals while on pitch	59
Defensive Rating Average number of mins between League goals conceded while on the pitch	146	Scoring Difference Defensive Rating minus Contribution to Attacking Power	87

	PLAYER	LGE GOALS	DEF RATE	POWER	SCORE DIFF
1	Yann Lachuer	4	146	59	87 mins
2	Benoit Cheyrou	2	109	64	45 mins
3	Mathieu Berson	0	98	69	29 mins
4	Thomas Kahlenberg	8	91	68	23 mins

KEY PLAYERS - GOALSCORERS

Luigi Pieroni

Goals in the League	11	Player Strike Rate Average number of minutes between League goals scored by player	168
Contribution to Attacking Power Average number of minutes between League team goals while on pitch	64	Club Strike Rate Average number of minutes between League goals scored by club	68

	PLAYER	LGE GOALS	POWER	STRIKE RATE
1	Luigi Pieroni	11	64	168 mins
2	Peguy Luyindula	10	73	241 mins
3	Thomas Kahlenberg	8	68	307 mins
4	Yann Lachuer	4	59	475 mins

Auxerre's Yann Lachuer and Luigi Pieroni

SQUAD APPEARANCES

Match	1	2	3	4	5	6	7	8	9	10	11	12	13	14	15	16	17	18	19	20	21	22	23	24	25	26	27	28	29	30	31	32	33	34	35	36	37	38	39	40
Venue	A	A	H	A	H	A	H	H	A	H	A	A	H	A	H	A	H	A	H	A	H	H	A	H	A	H	A	H	A	H	A	H	A	H	A	H	A	H	A	H
Competition	L	L	L	L	L	L	E	L	L	L	E	L	L	L	L	L	L	L	L	L	L	L	L	L	L	L	L	L	L	L	L	L	L	L	L	L	L	L	L	L
Result	D	W	W	L	L	L	W	W	W	W	L	L	W	L	W	D	W	W	W	L	L	W	L	W	D	W	L	D	L	W	D	W	L	D	D	D	L	L	W	W

Goalkeepers
- Baptiste Chabert
- Fabien Cool
- Sebastien Hamel

Defenders
- Rene Bolf
- Mamoutou Coulibaly
- Stephane Grichting
- Jean-Sebastien Jaures
- Omar Kaalabane
- Younes Kaboul
- Baptiste Martin
- Jean Pascal Mignot
- Johan Radet
- Bacary Sagna

Midfielders
- Kanga Akale
- Mathieu Berson
- Benoit Cheyrou
- Vassiriki Abou Diaby
- Thomas Kahlenberg
- Yann Lachuer
- Lionel Mathis
- Philippe Violeau

Forwards
- Ludovic Genest
- Peguy Luyindula
- Mwaruwari Benjani
- Luigi Pieroni
- Romain Poyet

KEY: On all match; On bench; Subbed or sent off (Counting game); Subbed or sent off (playing less than 70 minutes); Subbed on from bench (Counting Game); Subbed on (playing less than 70 minutes); Subbed on and then subbed or sent off (Counting Game); Subbed on and then subbed or sent off (playing less than 70 minutes); Not in 16

RENNES

Final Position: **7th**

KEY: ☐Won ☐Drawn ☐Lost

							Attendance
1	frpr1	**Lille**	A	L	0-1		14,000
2	frpr1	**Nantes**	H	L	0-3		29,344
3	frpr1	**Le Mans**	A	L	0-4		10,732
4	frpr1	**Marseille**	H	W	3-2	Utaka 8; Frei 39; Kallstrom 54	29,490
5	frpr1	**Nancy**	A	L	0-6		16,200
6	frpr1	**Auxerre**	H	W	3-1	Hadji 47,73; Monterrubio 57	27,982
7	uc1rl1	**Osasuna**	H	W	3-1	Frei 26,74; Hadji 83	12,000
8	frpr1	**AS Monaco**	A	W	2-0	Kallstrom 36; Gourcuff 59	8,626
9	frpr1	**Bordeaux**	H	D	2-2	Kallstrom 28; Monterrubio 60	24,661
10	frpr1	**Lens**	A	D	0-0		29,206
11	uc1rl2	**Osasuna**	A	D	0-0		17,000
12	frpr1	**Lyon**	H	L	1-3	Kallstrom 10	28,998
13	frpr1	**Strasbourg**	A	W	1-0	Briand 30	15,000
14	ucgpg	**Stuttgart**	H	L	0-2		22,847
15	frpr1	**AC Ajaccio**	A	W	1-0	Frei 41	3,500
16	frpr1	**Metz**	H	W	2-1	Utaka 17; Frei 56	27,600
17	ucgpg	**Rap Bucharest**	A	L	0-2		16,000
18	frpr1	**Troyes**	A	L	1-2	Gourcuff 16	8,000
19	frpr1	**Toulouse**	H	W	4-1	Gourcuff 28; Ouaddou 49; Frei 56; Monterrubio 90 pen	20,094
20	frpr1	**Sochaux**	A	L	0-1		15,932
21	ucgpg	**S Donetsk**	H	L	0-1		18,727
22	frpr1	**Nice**	H	W	1-0	Frei 62	23,081
23	frpr1	**Paris SG**	A	L	0-2		43,000
24	ucgpg	**PAOK Salonika**	A	L	1-5	Briand 70	3,000
25	frpr1	**St Etienne**	H	L	0-1		28,221
26	frpr1	**Nantes**	A	W	2-0	Didot 29; Utaka 69	30,000
27	frpr1	**Le Mans**	H	W	1-0	Briand 53	20,684
28	frpr1	**Marseille**	A	L	0-1		45,211
29	frpr1	**Nancy**	H	L	0-2		24,142
30	frpr1	**Auxerre**	A	L	0-2		6,000
31	frpr1	**AS Monaco**	H	L	1-3	Mvuemba 23	25,965
32	frpr1	**Bordeaux**	A	L	0-2		20,133
33	frpr1	**Lens**	H	W	4-1	Utaka 37,45,79; Monterrubio 73	21,501
34	frpr1	**Lyon**	A	W	4-1	Utaka 19,51,72; Gourcuff 31	29,168
35	frpr1	**Strasbourg**	H	W	2-1	Kallstrom 62; Briand 66	23,172
36	frpr1	**AC Ajaccio**	H	W	3-0	Gourcuff 50; Monterrubio 81; Hadji 83	22,063
37	frpr1	**Metz**	A	W	1-0	Gourcuff 27	16,591
38	frpr1	**Troyes**	H	W	2-0	Utaka 25; Mensah 52	25,195
39	frpr1	**Toulouse**	A	W	1-0	Aubey 73 og	15,350
40	frpr1	**Sochaux**	H	W	2-1	Kallstrom 4,80 pen	22,612
41	frpr1	**Nice**	A	L	1-2	Utaka 45	11,466
42	frpr1	**Paris SG**	H	D	1-1	Gourcuff 69 pen	28,085
43	frpr1	**St Etienne**	A	D	0-0		32,522
44	frpr1	**Lille**	H	D	2-2	Frei 35,64	30,000

LEAGUE APPEARANCES, BOOKINGS AND CAPS

	AGE (on 01/07/06)	IN NAMED 18	APPEARANCES	COUNTING GAMES	MINUTES ON PITCH	YELLOW CARDS	RED CARDS	CAPS THIS SEASON	NATIONAL SIDE
Goalkeepers									
Gardien Douard	21	5	0	0	0	0	0	-	France
Andreas Isaksson	24	24	24	23	2130	2	0	5	Sweden (16)
Simon Pouplin	21	32	15	14	1290	0	0	-	France
Defenders									
Dos Santos Adailton	22	26	19	17	1528	5	0	-	Brazil
Gregory Bourillon	22	32	32	28	2625	1	0	-	France
Erik Edman	27	27	27	27	2424	5	0	4	Sweden (16)
Jacques Faty	22	26	22	16	1483	5	0	-	France
John Mensah	23	12	12	12	1062	2	0	8	Ghana (48)
Abdeslam Ouaddou	27	20	19	18	1664	2	0	-	Morocco
J-N Perrier Doumbe	27	30	29	27	2489	3	0	-	Cameroon
Alain Rochat	23	10	9	3	339	1	0	-	Switzerland
Laszlo Sepsi	20	0	0	0	0	0	0	-	Romania
Midfielders									
Cedric Barbosa	30	17	11	2	355	2	0	-	France
Jimmy Briand	21	33	26	9	1069	5	0	-	France
Etienne Didot	22	21	19	14	1397	1	0	-	France
Yoann Gourcuff	19	37	36	26	2508	3	0	-	France
Youssouf Hadji	26	22	21	13	1278	3	1	-	Morocco
Cyril Jeunechamp	30	14	13	12	1061	3	1	-	France
Kim Kallstrom	23	34	34	30	2846	7	0	4	Sweden (16)
Stephane M'Bia	20	27	21	15	1417	5	0	-	Cameroon
Arnold Mvuemba	21	25	14	2	409	0	0	-	France
Stephane N'Guema	21	9	5	1	126	0	0	-	Gabon
Oliver N'Siabamfumu	20	1	0	0	0	0	0	-	France
Oliver Sorlin	27	14	13	13	1165	1	0	-	France
Forwards									
Alexander Frei	26	25	24	20	1867	3	0	9	Switzerland (35)
Olivier Monterrubio	29	36	32	26	2522	0	1	-	France
Makhtar N'Diaye	24	14	0	0	0	0	0	-	Senegal
Moussa Sow	20	6	6	0	143	0	0	-	France
John Utaka	24	28	28	25	2325	3	0	-	Nigeria

TEAM OF THE SEASON

MONTHLY POINTS TALLY

AUGUST	3	25%
SEPTEMBER	8	67%
OCTOBER	9	75%
NOVEMBER	3	33%
DECEMBER	3	33%
JANUARY	6	40%
FEBRUARY	6	50%
MARCH	12	100%
APRIL	6	67%
MAY	3	33%

LEAGUE GOALS

	PLAYER	MINS	GOALS	S RATE
1	Utaka	2325	11	211
2	Kallstrom	2846	7	407
3	Frei	1867	7	267
4	Gourcuff	2508	7	358
5	Monterrubio	2522	5	504
6	Hadji	1278	3	426
7	Briand	1069	3	356
8	Didot	1397	1	1397
9	Mensah	1062	1	1062
10	Ouaddou	1664	1	1664
	Other		2	
	TOTAL		48	

TOP POINT EARNERS

	PLAYER	GAMES	AV PTS
1	Mensah	12	2.25
2	Hadji	13	2.15
3	Sorlin	13	2.08
4	M'Bia	15	1.93
5	Gourcuff	26	1.81
6	Didot	14	1.79
7	Edman	27	1.74
8	Utaka	25	1.72
9	Monterrubio	26	1.58
10	Kallstrom	30	1.57
	CLUB AVERAGE:		1.55

DISCIPLINARY RECORDS

	PLAYER	YELLOW	RED	AVE
1	Briand	5	0	213
2	Jeunechamp	3	1	265
3	M'Bia	5	0	283
4	Faty	5	0	296
5	Adailton	5	0	305
6	Hadji	3	1	319
7	Kallstrom	7	0	406
8	Edman	5	0	484
9	Mensah	2	0	531
10	Frei	3	0	622
11	Utaka	3	0	775
12	Perrier Doumbe	3	0	829
13	Ouaddou	2	0	832
	Other	8	1	
	TOTAL	59	3	

KEY GOALKEEPER

Simon Pouplin

Goals Conceded in the League	15	**Counting Games** League games when player was on pitch for at least 70 minutes	14
Defensive Rating Ave number of mins between League goals conceded while on the pitch	86	**Clean Sheets** In League games when player was on pitch for at least 70 minutes	5

KEY PLAYERS - DEFENDERS

John Mensah

Goals Conceded Number of League goals conceded while the player was on the pitch	8	**Clean Sheets** In League games when player was on pitch for at least 70 minutes	5
Defensive Rating Ave number of mins between League goals conceded while on the pitch	133	**Club Defensive Rating** Average number of mins between League goals conceded by the club this season	68

	PLAYER	CON LGE	CLEAN SHEETS	DEF RATE
1	John Mensah	8	5	133 mins
2	Erik Edman	26	10	93 mins
3	Jean-Noel Perrier Doumbe	35	9	71 mins
4	Gregory Bourillon	39	10	67 mins

KEY PLAYERS - MIDFIELDERS

Oliver Sorlin

Goals in the League	0	**Contribution to Attacking Power** Average number of minutes between League team goals while on pitch	51
Defensive Rating Average number of mins between League goals conceded while on the pitch	117	**Scoring Difference** Defensive Rating minus Contribution to Attacking Power	66

	PLAYER	LGE GOALS	DEF RATE	POWER	SCORE DIFF
1	Oliver Sorlin	0	117	51	66 mins
2	Stephane M'Bia	0	118	64	54 mins
3	Youssouf Hadji	3	91	53	38 mins
4	Yoann Gourcuff	7	76	63	13 mins

KEY PLAYERS - GOALSCORERS

John Utaka

Goals in the League	11	**Player Strike Rate** Average number of minutes between League goals scored by player	211
Contribution to Attacking Power Average number of minutes between League team goals while on pitch	60	**Club Strike Rate** Average number of minutes between League goals scored by club	71

	PLAYER	LGE GOALS	POWER	STRIKE RATE
1	John Utaka	11	60	211 mins
2	Alexander Frei	7	98	267 mins
3	Yoann Gourcuff	7	63	358 mins
4	Kim Kallstrom	7	71	407 mins

Rennes' Alexander Frei and John Utaka celebrate

SQUAD APPEARANCES

Match	1	2	3	4	5	6	7	8	9	10	11	12	13	14	15	16	17	18	19	20	21	22	23	24	25	26	27	28	29	30	31	32	33	34	35	36	37	38	39	40	41	42	43	44
Venue	A	H	A	H	A	H	H	A	H	A	A	H	A	H	A	H	A	A	H	A	H	H	A	A	H	A	H	A	H	A	H	A	H	A	H	H	A	H	A	H	A	H	A	H
Competition	L	L	L	L	L	L	E	L	L	L	E	L	L	E	L	L	E	L	L	L	E	L	L	E	L	L	L	L	L	L	L	L	L	L	L	L	L	L	L	L	L	L	L	L
Result	L	L	L	W	L	W	W	W	D	D	D	L	W	L	W	W	L	L	W	L	L	W	L	L	L	W	W	L	L	L	L	L	W	W	W	W	W	W	W	W	L	D	D	D

Goalkeepers
Gardien Douard
Andreas Isaksson
Simon Pouplin

Defenders
Dos Santos Adailton
Gregory Bourillon
Erik Edman
Jacques Faty
John Mensah
Abdeslam Ouaddou
Jean-N. Perrier Doumbe
Alain Rochat
Laszlo Sepsi

Midfielders
Cedric Barbosa
Jimmy Briand
Etienne Didot
Yoann Gourcuff
Youssouf Hadji
Cyril Jeunechamp
Kim Kallstrom
Stephane M'Bia
Arnold Mvuemba
Stephane N'Guema
Oliver N'Siabamfumu
Oliver Sorlin

Forwards
Alexander Frei
Olivier Monterrubio
Makhtar N'Diaye
Moussa Sow
John Utaka

KEY: On all match | On bench | Subbed or sent off (Counting game) | Subbed or sent off (playing less than 70 minutes) | Subbed on from bench (Counting Game) | Subbed on (playing less than 70 minutes) | Subbed on and then subbed or sent off (Counting Game) | Subbed on and then subbed or sent off (playing less than 70 minutes) | Not in 16

NICE

Final Position: **8th**

KEY: ☐ Won ☐ Drawn ☐ Lost

#	Comp	Opponent	H/A	Res	Score	Scorers	Attendance
1	frpr1	Troyes	H	D	1-1	Vahirua 34,34	15,050
2	frpr1	Toulouse	A	W	2-0	Kone 17; Traore 29	18,620
3	frpr1	Sochaux	H	L	1-2	Traore 43	13,555
4	frpr1	Nantes	H	D	1-1	Bagayoko 6	13,440
5	frpr1	Paris SG	A	W	2-1	Traore 72; Bagayoko 89	42,000
6	frpr1	St Etienne	H	L	0-1		13,425
7	frpr1	Lille	A	L	0-4		8,000
8	frpr1	Le Mans	H	W	1-0	Bagayoko 21	9,405
9	frpr1	AS Monaco	A	D	0-0		14,185
10	frpr1	Marseille	H	L	0-1		14,923
11	frpr1	Lens	A	D	2-2	Roudet 29; Camara 84	29,365
12	frpr1	Auxerre	H	W	1-0	Vahirua 34	6,000
13	frpr1	Nancy	A	D	0-0		22,000
14	frpr1	Bordeaux	H	L	0-1		11,382
15	frpr1	Strasbourg	A	D	0-0		14,966
16	frpr1	Lyon	H	D	1-1	Bagayoko 21	12,849
17	frpr1	Rennes	A	L	0-1		23,081
18	frpr1	AC Ajaccio	H	W	1-0	Kone 47	9,627
19	frpr1	Metz	A	L	0-1		12,186
20	frpr1	Toulouse	H	W	2-1	Kone 8; Vahirua 25	8,776
21	frpr1	Sochaux	A	D	1-1	Roudet 13	11,885
22	frpr1	Nantes	A	D	0-0		25,000
23	frpr1	Paris SG	H	W	1-0	Traore 87	11,941
24	frpr1	Lille	H	W	2-0	Vahirua 19; Roudet 39	9,701
25	frpr1	Le Mans	A	L	0-2		9,241
26	frpr1	St Etienne	A	W	1-0	Bellion 37	22,440
27	frpr1	AS Monaco	H	W	2-0	Bellion 8; Kone 76	11,366
28	frpr1	Marseille	A	L	0-1		47,000
29	frpr1	Lens	H	D	0-0		10,365
30	frpr1	Auxerre	A	L	0-2		8,000
31	frpr1	Nancy	H	W	1-0	Kone 55	9,710
32	frpr1	Bordeaux	A	L	0-1		22,533
33	frpr1	Strasbourg	H	W	3-1	Jarjat 61; Bagayoko 62; Traore 90	9,913
34	frpr1	Lyon	A	L	1-2	Ederson 37	30,000
35	frpr1	Rennes	H	W	2-1	Bellion 3; Abardonado 90	11,466
36	frpr1	AC Ajaccio	A	W	3-0	Bellion 3; Kone 32,76	2,000
37	frpr1	Metz	H	W	2-1	Traore 56; Bellion 64	13,000
38	frpr1	Troyes	A	W	2-1	Vahirua 18; Ederson 86	18,013

LEAGUE APPEARANCES, BOOKINGS AND CAPS

	AGE (on 01/07/06)	IN NAMED 18	APPEARANCES	COUNTING GAMES	MINUTES ON PITCH	YELLOW CARDS	RED CARDS	CAPS THIS SEASON	NATIONAL SIDE
Goalkeepers									
Damien Gregorini	27	37	34	34	3060	0	0	-	France
Hugo Lloris	19	29	4	4	360	0	0	-	France
Jeremie Moreau	25	5	0	0	0	0	0	-	France
Defenders									
Jacques Abardonado	28	36	32	30	2710	4	0	-	France
Rod Fanni	24	21	21	20	1830	3	0	-	France
Francois Grenet	31	3	2	1	91	0	0	-	France
Florian Jarjat	26	19	15	10	944	2	0	-	France
Bill Tchato	31	25	24	16	1759	3	2	-	Cameroon
Cedric Varrault	26	28	27	22	2213	5	0	-	France
Anthar Yahia	24	31	21	16	1569	3	0	-	France
Midfielders									
Florent Balmont	26	37	37	37	3310	7	1	-	France
Yohann Bigne	28	25	15	2	542	1	0	-	France
Roberto Bisconti	32	8	8	4	536	1	0	2	Belgium (42)
Olivier Echouafni	33	33	32	25	2434	3	0	-	France
Honorato Ederson	20	22	20	8	924	2	0	-	Brazil
Cyril Rool	31	29	29	28	2484	14	0	-	France
Sebastien Roudet	25	32	26	9	1404	3	0	-	France
Sammy Traore	24	32	32	32	2871	9	0	-	Ivory Coast
Forwards									
Mamadou Bagayoko	27	33	31	23	2334	5	0	-	Mali
David Bellion	23	16	14	10	993	4	0	-	France
Souleymane Camara	23	17	14	1	427	1	0	-	Senegal
Bakary Diakite	25	8	5	3	305	0	0	-	Germany
Pablo Franco Dolci	22	6	2	0	69	0	0	-	France
Bakari Kone	24	32	31	31	2718	2	0	-	Ivory Coast
Marama Vahirua	26	35	31	10	1651	2	0	-	France

TEAM OF THE SEASON

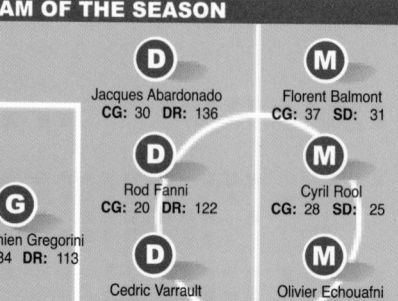

G – Damien Gregorini – CG: 34 DR: 113

D – Jacques Abardonado – CG: 30 DR: 136

D – Rod Fanni – CG: 20 DR: 122

D – Cedric Varrault – CG: 22 DR: 105

D – Bill Tchato – CG: 16 DR: 103

M – Florent Balmont – CG: 37 SD: 31

M – Cyril Rool – CG: 28 SD: 25

M – Olivier Echouafni – CG: 25 SD: 22

M – Sammy Traore – CG: 32 SD: 22

F – Bakari Kone – CG: 31 SR: 388

F – M Bagayoko – CG: 23 SR: 467

MONTHLY POINTS TALLY

Month	Points	%
AUGUST	7	58%
SEPTEMBER	4	33%
OCTOBER	5	42%
NOVEMBER	2	22%
DECEMBER	3	33%
JANUARY	8	67%
FEBRUARY	9	60%
MARCH	4	33%
APRIL	9	75%
MAY	6	100%

LEAGUE GOALS

	PLAYER	MINS	GOALS	S RATE
1	Kone	2718	7	388
2	Traore	2871	6	479
3	Vahirua	1651	6	275
4	Bellion	993	5	199
5	Bagayoko	2334	5	467
6	Roudet	1404	3	468
7	Ederson	924	2	462
8	Camara	427	1	427
9	Abardonado	2710	1	2710
10	Jarjat	944	1	944
	Other		1	
	TOTAL		38	

TOP POINT EARNERS

	PLAYER	GAMES	AV PTS
1	Varrault	22	1.82
2	Fanni	20	1.80
3	Abardonado	30	1.67
4	Rool	28	1.64
5	Echouafni	25	1.60
6	Balmont	37	1.57
7	Tchato	16	1.50
8	Traore	32	1.50
9	Bagayoko	23	1.48
10	Gregorini	34	1.44
	CLUB AVERAGE:		1.53

DISCIPLINARY RECORDS

	PLAYER	YELLOW	RED	AVE
1	Rool	14	0	177
2	Bellion	4	0	248
3	Traore	9	0	319
4	Tchato	3	2	351
5	Balmont	7	1	413
6	Varrault	5	0	442
7	Ederson	2	0	462
8	Bagayoko	5	0	466
9	Roudet	3	0	468
10	Jarjat	2	0	472
11	Yahia	3	0	523
12	Bisconti	1	0	536
13	Bigne	1	0	542
	Other	14	0	
	TOTAL	73	3	

KEY GOALKEEPER

Damien Gregorini

Goals Conceded in the League	27	Counting Games League games when player was on pitch for at least 70 minutes	34
Defensive Rating Ave number of mins between League goals conceded while on the pitch	113	Clean Sheets In League games when player was on pitch for at least 70 minutes	14

KEY PLAYERS - DEFENDERS

Jacques Abardonado

Goals Conceded Number of League goals conceded while the player was on the pitch	20	Clean Sheets In League games when player was on pitch for at least 70 minutes	14
Defensive Rating Ave number of mins between League goals conceded while on the pitch	136	Club Defensive Rating Average number of mins between League goals conceded by the club this season	110

	PLAYER	CON LGE	CLEAN SHEETS	DEF RATE
1	Jacques Abardonado	20	14	136 mins
2	Rod Fanni	15	9	122 mins
3	Cedric Varrault	21	8	105 mins
4	Bill Tchato	17	6	103 mins

KEY PLAYERS - MIDFIELDERS

Florent Balmont

Goals in the League	0	Contribution to Attacking Power Average number of minutes between League team goals while on pitch	87
Defensive Rating Average number of mins between League goals conceded while on the pitch	118	Scoring Difference Defensive Rating minus Contribution to Attacking Power	31

	PLAYER	LGE GOALS	DEF RATE	POWER	SCORE DIFF
1	Florent Balmont	0	118	87	31 mins
2	Cyril Rool	0	108	83	25 mins
3	Sammy Traore	6	125	103	22 mins
4	Olivier Echouafni	0	116	94	22 mins

KEY PLAYERS - GOALSCORERS

Bakari Kone

Goals in the League	7	Player Strike Rate Average number of minutes between League goals scored by player	388
Contribution to Attacking Power Average number of minutes between League team goals while on pitch	91	Club Strike Rate Average number of minutes between League goals scored by club	90

	PLAYER	LGE GOALS	POWER	STRIKE RATE
1	Bakari Kone	7	91	388 mins
2	Mamadou Bagayoko	5	93	467 mins
3	Sammy Traore	6	103	479 mins
4	Jacques Abardonado	1	87	2710 mins

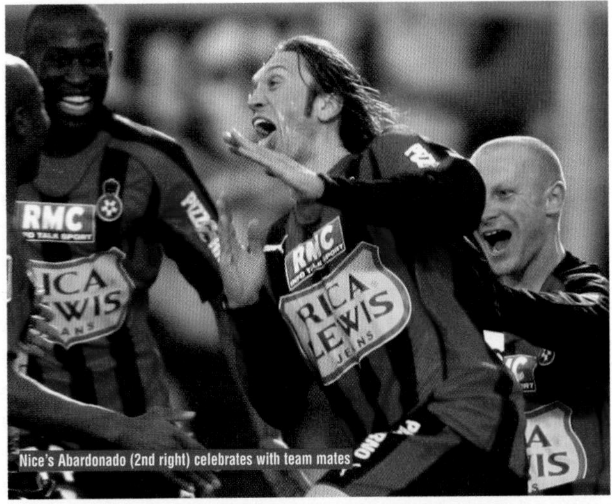

Nice's Abardonado (2nd right) celebrates with team mates

SQUAD APPEARANCES

Match	1	2	3	4	5	6	7	8	9	10	11	12	13	14	15	16	17	18	19	20	21	22	23	24	25	26	27	28	29	30	31	32	33	34	35	36	37	38
Venue	H	A	H	H	A	H	A	H	A	H	A	H	A	H	A	H	A	H	A	H	A	A	H	H	A	A	H	A	H	A	H	A	H	A	H	A	H	A
Competition	L	L	L	L	L	L	L	L	L	L	L	L	L	L	L	L	L	L	L	L	L	L	L	L	L	L	L	L	L	L	L	L	L	L	L	L	L	L
Result	D	W	L	D	W	L	L	W	D	L	D	W	D	L	D	D	L	W	L	W	D	D	W	W	L	W	W	L	D	L	W	L	W	L	W	W	W	W

Goalkeepers
Damien Gregorini
Hugo Lloris
Jeremie Moreau

Defenders
Jacques Abardonado
Rod Fanni
Francois Grenet
Florian Jarjat
Bill Tchato
Cedric Varrault
Anthar Yahia

Midfielders
Florent Balmont
Yohann Bigne
Roberto Bisconti
Olivier Echouafni
Honorato Ederson
Cyril Rool
Sebastien Roudet
Sammy Traore

Forwards
Mamadou Bagayoko
David Bellion
Souleymane Camara
Bakary Diakite
Pablo Franco Dolci
Bakari Kone
Marama Vahirua

KEY: On all match; On bench; Subbed or sent off (Counting game); Subbed or sent off (playing less than 70 minutes); Subbed on from bench (Counting Game); Subbed on (playing less than 70 minutes); Subbed on and then subbed or sent off (Counting Game); Subbed on and then subbed or sent off (playing less than 70 minutes); Not in 16

PARIS St GERMAIN

Final Position: **9th**

KEY: ☐Won ☐Drawn ☐Lost

							Attendance
1	frpr1	**Metz**	H	W	4-1	Kalou 5; Cisse 37; Rothen 49; Landrin 80	43,000
2	frpr1	**Sochaux**	A	W	1-0	Cisse 51	17,543
3	frpr1	**Toulouse**	H	W	2-0	Pauleta 43,61	41,341
4	frpr1	**Troyes**	A	D	1-1	Pauleta 36	17,500
5	frpr1	**Nice**	H	L	1-2	Pauleta 1	42,000
6	frpr1	**Strasbourg**	H	W	1-0	Kalou 28	40,748
7	frpr1	**St Etienne**	A	L	0-3		27,771
8	frpr1	**Lille**	H	W	2-1	Pauleta 12,54	35,189
9	frpr1	**Le Mans**	A	D	0-0		15,182
10	frpr1	**Nantes**	H	W	2-0	Yepes 66; Pauleta 74	42,164
11	frpr1	**Marseille**	A	L	0-1		58,000
12	frpr1	**Nancy**	H	W	1-0	Kalou 52	35,000
13	frpr1	**Auxerre**	A	L	0-2		22,000
14	frpr1	**AS Monaco**	H	D	0-0		43,555
15	frpr1	**Bordeaux**	A	W	2-0	Yepes 35; Pauleta 50	32,000
16	frpr1	**Lens**	H	L	3-4	Pauleta 6,88; Landrin 90	40,895
17	frpr1	**Lyon**	A	L	0-2		38,200
18	frpr1	**Rennes**	H	W	2-0	Pauleta 38,64	43,000
19	frpr1	**AC Ajaccio**	A	D	1-1	Kalou 41	4,500
20	frpr1	**Sochaux**	H	W	3-1	Landrin 27; Pancrate 58; Pauleta 74	36,806
21	frpr1	**Toulouse**	A	L	0-1		20,321
22	frpr1	**Troyes**	H	W	2-1	Pauleta 45 pen; Pancrate 90	35,118
23	frpr1	**Nice**	A	L	0-1		11,941
24	frpr1	**St Etienne**	H	D	2-2	Pauleta 33; Pancrate 84	43,026
25	frpr1	**Strasbourg**	A	D	1-1	Pauleta 31	16,000
26	frpr1	**Lille**	A	D	0-0		17,000
27	frpr1	**Le Mans**	H	L	0-1		39,655
28	frpr1	**Nantes**	A	D	0-0		31,000
29	frpr1	**Marseille**	H	D	0-0		43,000
30	frpr1	**Nancy**	A	D	1-1	Kalou 76	20,000
31	frpr1	**Auxerre**	H	W	4-1	Kalou 26,57; Bolf 37 og; Pauleta 54	35,528
32	frpr1	**AS Monaco**	A	D	1-1	Paulo C?sar 15	11,659
33	frpr1	**Bordeaux**	H	W	3-1	Pauleta 6,38,43	43,218
34	frpr1	**Lens**	A	D	1-1	Kalou 76	39,513
35	frpr1	**Lyon**	H	L	0-1		43,508
36	frpr1	**Rennes**	A	D	1-1	Kalou 89	28,085
37	frpr1	**AC Ajaccio**	H	L	2-4	Yepes 30; Pauleta 51	41,000
38	frpr1	**Metz**	A	L	0-1		15,827

LEAGUE APPEARANCES, BOOKINGS AND CAPS

	AGE (on 01/07/06)	IN NAMED 18	APPEARANCES	COUNTING GAMES	MINUTES ON PITCH	YELLOW CARDS	RED CARDS	CAPS THIS SEASON	NATIONAL SIDE
Goalkeepers									
Jerome Alonzo	33	33	13	11	1080	0	0	-	France
Mohamed Benhamou	26	4	0	0	0	0	0	-	France
Nicolas Cousin	20	4	0	0	0	0	0	-	France
Lionel Letizi	33	32	27	25	2340	2	0	-	France
Defenders									
Sylvain Armand	25	34	34	33	2977	7	2	-	France
Jean H Bilayi Ateba	24	3	2	1	155	0	0	-	Cameroon
Jean-Michel Badiane	23	12	3	2	200	0	0	-	France
Boukari Drame	20	7	4	1	129	0	0	-	France
Ahmed Kantari	21	1	0	0	0	0	0	-	Morocco
Bernard Mendy	24	37	35	31	2856	7	0	-	France
Paulo Cesar	27	10	9	7	692	0	0	-	Brazil
Stephane Pichot	29	34	20	13	1283	2	0	-	France
David Rozehnal	26	38	38	38	3400	6	0	9	Czech Republic (2)
Mario Yepes	30	32	32	31	2832	5	1	2	Colombia (36)
Midfielders									
Lorik Cana	22	4	2	0	52	2	0	-	Bosnia
Edouard Cisse	28	31	29	23	2313	9	2	-	France
Vikash Dhorasoo	32	34	34	28	2609	5	0	9	France (8)
Rudy Haddad	21	11	5	2	229	0	0	-	France
Christophe Landrin	29	31	25	13	1542	1	0	-	France
Modeste Mbami	23	36	35	31	2935	9	0	-	Cameroon
Ragued	-	1	1	0	60	0	0	-	
Cristian Rodriguez	20	12	11	3	423	1	0	-	Uruguay
Jerome Rothen	28	29	28	20	2137	5	0	3	France (8)
Sergei Semak	30	16	12	3	510	2	0	-	Russia
Forwards									
Carlos Bueno	26	17	12	1	334	2	0	-	Uruguay
Franck Dja-Djedje	20	3	2	0	45	0	0	-	France
Bonaventure Kalou	28	28	28	22	2156	9	0	11	Ivory Coast (32)
Fabrice Pancrate	26	34	28	10	1227	1	0	-	France
Pauleta	33	36	36	32	3006	5	0	7	Portugal (7)

TEAM OF THE SEASON

G
Lionel Letizi
CG: 25 **DR:** 106

D
Sylvain Armand
CG: 33 **DR:** 93

D
Stephane Pichot
CG: 13 **DR:** 92

D
David Rozehnal
CG: 38 **DR:** 89

D
Mario Yepes
CG: 31 **DR:** 89

M
Jerome Rothen
CG: 20 **SD:** 37

M
Modeste Mbami
CG: 31 **SD:** 16

M
Vikash Dhorasoo
CG: 28 **SD:** 13

M
Edouard Cisse
CG: 23 **SD:** 4

F
Pauleta
CG: 32 **SR:** 143

F
Bonaventure Kalou
CG: 22 **SR:** 240

MONTHLY POINTS TALLY

AUGUST	7	58%
SEPTEMBER	7	58%
OCTOBER	6	50%
NOVEMBER	4	44%
DECEMBER	4	44%
JANUARY	6	50%
FEBRUARY	4	27%
MARCH	6	50%
APRIL	4	44%
MAY	1	11%

LEAGUE GOALS

	PLAYER	MINS	GOALS	S RATE
1	Pauleta	3006	**21**	143
2	Kalou	2156	**9**	240
3	Yepes	2832	**3**	944
4	Pancrate	1227	**3**	409
5	Landrin	1542	**3**	514
6	Cisse	2313	**2**	1157
7	Rothen	2137	**1**	2137
8	Paulo Cesar	692	**1**	692
	Other		**1**	
	TOTAL		**44**	

TOP POINT EARNERS

	PLAYER	GAMES	AV PTS
1	Dhorasoo	28	**1.64**
2	Rothen	20	**1.60**
3	Letizi	25	**1.60**
4	Kalou	22	**1.55**
5	Pauleta	32	**1.50**
6	Mendy	31	**1.48**
7	Armand	33	**1.45**
8	Cisse	23	**1.43**
9	Rozehnal	38	**1.37**
10	Yepes	31	**1.35**
	CLUB AVERAGE:		**1.37**

DISCIPLINARY RECORDS

	PLAYER	YELLOW	RED	AVE
1	Cisse	9	2	**210**
2	Kalou	9	0	**239**
3	Semak	2	0	**255**
4	Mbami	9	0	**326**
5	Armand	7	2	**330**
6	Mendy	7	0	**408**
7	Rothen	5	0	**427**
8	Yepes	5	1	**472**
9	Dhorasoo	5	0	**521**
10	Rozehnal	6	0	**566**
11	Pauleta	5	0	**601**
12	Pichot	2	0	**641**
13	Letizi	2	0	**1170**
	Other	2	0	
	TOTAL	**75**	**5**	

KEY GOALKEEPER

Lionel Letizi

Goals Conceded in the League	22	**Counting Games** League games when player was on pitch for at least 70 minutes	25
Defensive Rating Ave number of mins between League goals conceded while on the pitch	106	**Clean Sheets** In League games when player was on pitch for at least 70 minutes	11

KEY PLAYERS - DEFENDERS

Sylvain Armand

Goals Conceded Number of League goals conceded while the player was on the pitch	32	**Clean Sheets** In League games when player was on pitch for at least 70 minutes	10
Defensive Rating Ave number of mins between League goals conceded while on the pitch	93	**Club Defensive Rating** Average number of mins between League goals conceded by the club this season	90

	PLAYER	CON LGE	CLEAN SHEETS	DEF RATE
1	Sylvain Armand	32	10	93 mins
2	Stephane Pichot	14	5	92 mins
3	David Rozehnal	38	12	89 mins
4	Mario Yepes	32	10	89 mins

KEY PLAYERS - MIDFIELDERS

Jerome Rothen

Goals in the League	1	**Contribution to Attacking Power** Average number of minutes between League team goals while on pitch	65
Defensive Rating Average number of mins between League goals conceded while on the pitch	102	**Scoring Difference** Defensive Rating minus Contribution to Attacking Power	37

	PLAYER	LGE GOALS	DEF RATE	POWER	SCORE DIFF
1	Jerome Rothen	1	102	65	37 mins
2	Modeste Mbami	0	95	79	16 mins
3	Vikash Dhorasoo	0	77	64	13 mins
4	Edouard Cisse	2	93	89	4 mins

KEY PLAYERS - GOALSCORERS

Pauleta

Goals in the League	21	**Player Strike Rate** Average number of minutes between League goals scored by player	143
Contribution to Attacking Power Average number of minutes between League team goals while on pitch	68	**Club Strike Rate** Average number of minutes between League goals scored by club	78

	PLAYER	LGE GOALS	POWER	STRIKE RATE
1	Pauleta	21	68	143 mins
2	Bonaventure Kalou	9	70	240 mins
3	Christophe Landrin	3	119	514 mins
4	Mario Yepes	3	81	944 mins

PSG's Jerome Rothen congratulates Pauleta

SQUAD APPEARANCES

Match	1	2	3	4	5	6	7	8	9	10	11	12	13	14	15	16	17	18	19	20	21	22	23	24	25	26	27	28	29	30	31	32	33	34	35	36	37	38
Venue	H	A	H	A	H	H	A	H	A	H	A	H	A	H	A	H	A	H	A	H	A	H	A	H	A	A	H	A	H	A	H	A	H	A	H	A	H	A
Competition	L	L	L	L	L	L	L	L	L	L	L	L	L	L	L	L	L	L	L	L	L	L	L	L	L	L	L	L	L	L	L	L	L	L	L	L	L	L
Result	W	W	W	D	L	W	L	W	D	W	L	W	L	D	W	L	L	W	D	W	L	W	L	D	D	D	L	D	D	D	W	D	W	D	L	D	L	L

Goalkeepers
Jerome Alonzo
Mohamed Benhamou
Nicolas Cousin
Lionel Letizi

Defenders
Sylvain Armand
Jean-Hughes Bilayi Ateba
Jean-Michel Badiane
Boukari Drame
Ahmed Kantari
Bernard Mendy
Paulo Cesar
Stephane Pichot
David Rozehnal
Mario Yepes

Midfielders
Lorik Cana
Edouard Cisse
Vikash Dhorasoo
Rudy Haddad
Christophe Landrin
Modeste Mbami
Ragued
Cristian Rodriguez
Jerome Rothen
Sergei Semak

Forwards
Carlos Bueno
Franck Dja-Djedje
Bonaventure Kalou
Fabrice Pancrate
Pauleta

KEY: On all match · On bench · Subbed or sent off (Counting game) · Subbed or sent off (playing less than 70 minutes) · Subbed on from bench (Counting Game) · Subbed on (playing less than 70 minutes) · Subbed on and then subbed or sent off (Counting Game) · Subbed on and then subbed or sent off (playing less than 70 minutes) · Not in 16

MONACO

Final Position: **10th**

KEY: ☐ Won ☐ Drawn ☐ Lost

		Opponent			Score	Scorers	Attendance
1	frpr1	Nancy	A	W	1-0	Kapo Obou 68	20,000
2	frpr1	Auxerre	H	L	0-2		15,748
3	ecql1	Real Betis	A	L	0-1		24,000
4	frpr1	Strasbourg	A	W	2-1	Squillaci 48; Chevanton 79	20,000
5	frpr1	Bordeaux	A	L	0-1		25,000
6	ecql2	Real Betis	H	D	2-2	Gerard 33; Maoulida 63	13,011
7	frpr1	Lens	H	D	0-0		11,882
8	frpr1	Lyon	A	L	1-2	Gigliotti 79	39,043
9	uc1rl1	Willem II Tilb	H	W	2-0	Kapo Obou 23; Adebayor 46	8,000
10	frpr1	Rennes	H	L	0-2		8,626
11	frpr1	Troyes	A	W	2-1	Adebayor 57; Givet 76	12,214
12	frpr1	Nice	H	D	0-0		14,185
13	uc1rl2	Willem II Tilb	A	W	3-1	Maicon 48; Adebayor 58; Chevanton 89	11,600
14	frpr1	Lille	A	W	1-0	Kapo Obou 58	12,000
15	frpr1	Metz	H	W	3-0	Gigliotti 61; Zikos 65; Meriem 71	10,000
16	ucgpa	Viking	A	L	0-1		9,684
17	frpr1	Sochaux	A	L	1-2	Maicon 90	15,020
18	frpr1	AC Ajaccio	H	W	3-0	Chevanton 37; Givet 68; Plasil 75	6,000
19	frpr1	Paris SG	A	D	0-0		43,555
20	frpr1	St Etienne	H	W	1-0	Meriem 55	16,234
21	ucgpa	Hamburg	H	W	2-0	Adebayor 44; Veigneau 90	18,000
22	frpr1	Marseille	A	L	1-2	Meriem 19	52,000
23	ucgpa	Slavia Prague	A	W	2-0	Maoulida 11,71	12,540
24	frpr1	Le Mans	H	W	2-0	Modesto 11; Sorlin 42	9,000
25	frpr1	Nantes	A	D	0-0		28,000
26	ucgpa	CSKA Sofia	H	W	2-1	Kapo Obou 50; Squillaci 75	9,000
27	frpr1	Toulouse	H	W	1-0	Kapo Obou 84 pen	9,107
28	frpr1	Auxerre	A	L	1-2	Di Vaio 29	15,000
29	frpr1	Strasbourg	H	D	1-1	Kapo Obou 72	8,000
30	frpr1	Bordeaux	H	L	0-1		11,476
31	frpr1	Lens	A	D	1-1	Gakpe 6	33,796
32	frpr1	Rennes	A	W	3-1	Vieri 57,67; Veigneau 90	25,965
33	frpr1	Troyes	H	D	1-1	Vieri 15	7,681
34	uc3rl1	Basel	A	L	0-1		14,143
35	frpr1	Nice	A	L	0-2		11,366
36	uc3rl2	Basel	H	D	1-1	Vieri 21 pen	11,335
37	frpr1	Lille	H	L	0-1		6,791
38	frpr1	Metz	A	L	1-2	Di Vaio 37	16,757
39	frpr1	Sochaux	H	W	4-1	Chevanton 8; Di Vaio 17,62; Kapo Obou 46	5,903
40	frpr1	AC Ajaccio	A	L	0-1		4,000
41	frpr1	Paris SG	H	D	1-1	Chevanton 51	11,659
42	frpr1	St Etienne	A	D	1-1	Chevanton 56	33,683
43	frpr1	Marseille	H	W	1-0	Chevanton 27	17,594
44	frpr1	Le Mans	A	D	0-0		13,212
45	frpr1	Lyon	H	W	2-1	Chevanton 32; Di Vaio 57	12,357
46	frpr1	Nantes	H	D	1-1	Chevanton 89	10,061
47	frpr1	Toulouse	A	D	3-3	Gakpe 38; Dos Santos 40; Chevanton 56	20,158
48	frpr1	Nancy	H	D	2-2	Chevanton 63; Modesto 66	9,990

LEAGUE APPEARANCES, BOOKINGS AND CAPS

	AGE (on 01/07/06)	IN NAMED 18	APPEARANCES	COUNTING GAMES	MINUTES ON PITCH	YELLOW CARDS	RED CARDS	CAPS THIS SEASON	NATIONAL SIDE
Goalkeepers									
Andre Biancarelli	36	29	1	0	4	0	0	-	France
Flavio Roma	32	16	15	15	1346	1	0	1	Italy (13)
Guillaume Warmuz	35	30	23	23	2070	1	0	-	France
Defenders									
Eric Cubilier	27	19	13	8	926	5	1	-	France
Manuel Dos Santos	32	16	15	14	1273	1	0	-	France
Patrice Evra	25	15	15	14	1304	5	1	-	France
Gael Givet	24	32	31	28	2649	5	0	6	France (8)
Arnaud Lescure	20	6	2	1	112	1	0	-	France
Douglas Maicon	25	28	28	27	2458	9	0	-	Brazil
Thomas Mangani	19	0	0	0	0	0	0	-	France
Francois Modesto	27	33	27	19	1983	4	0	-	France
Marko Muslin	21	2	0	0	0	0	0	-	France
Julien Rodriguez	28	1	0	0	0	0	0	-	France
Sebastien Squillaci	25	27	27	24	2323	0	1	5	France (8)
Olivier Veigneau	20	26	19	11	1190	0	0	-	France
Midfielders									
Lucas Bernardi	28	32	32	28	2604	8	1	2	Argentina (9)
Serge Gakpe	19	13	12	5	570	1	0	-	France
Lopez Segurra Gerard	27	8	7	4	499	3	1	-	Spain
Malaury Martin	17	1	1	0	53	0	0	-	France
Camel Meriem	26	32	31	24	2390	1	0	-	France
Diego Fernando Perez	26	25	22	13	1335	7	0	-	Uruguay
Jaroslav Plasil	24	21	21	15	1535	2	0	3	Czech Republic (2)
Oliver Sorlin	27	22	20	15	1570	2	0	-	France
Vassilis Zikos	32	19	17	13	1304	11	1	-	Greece
Forwards									
Emmanuel Adebayor	22	13	13	9	944	0	1	-	Togo
Souleymane Camara	23	3	2	0	61	0	0	-	Senegal
Ernesto Chevanton	25	25	23	13	1540	2	0	-	Uruguay
Marco Di Vaio	29	15	14	14	1250	3	0	-	Italy
David Gigliotti	21	22	15	3	557	4	0	-	France
Olivier Kapo Obou	25	29	25	14	1699	4	1	-	France
Alexandre Licata	22	1	0	0	0	0	0	-	France
Toifilou Maoulida	27	17	16	3	717	3	0	-	France
Nicolas Maurice-Belay	21	21	13	5	707	0	0	-	France
Christian Vieri	32	7	7	4	433	1	0	5	Italy (13)

TEAM OF THE SEASON

G — Guillaume Warmuz — CG: 23 DR: 109

D — Patrice Evra — CG: 14 DR: 145

D — Douglas S Maicon — CG: 27 DR: 102

D — Francois Modesto — CG: 19 DR: 99

D — Gael Givet — CG: 28 DR: 98

M — Camel Meriem — CG: 24 SD: 43

M — Vassilis Zikos — CG: 13 SD: 43

M — Lucas Bernardi — CG: 28 SD: 27

M — D Fernando Perez — CG: 13 SD: 9

F — Ernesto Chevanton — CG: 13 SR: 154

F — Marco Di Vaio — CG: 14 SR: 250

MONTHLY POINTS TALLY

Month	Points	%
AUGUST	4	33%
SEPTEMBER	4	33%
OCTOBER	9	75%
NOVEMBER	4	44%
DECEMBER	7	78%
JANUARY	2	17%
FEBRUARY	4	33%
MARCH	4	33%
APRIL	9	60%
MAY	2	33%

LEAGUE GOALS

	PLAYER	MINS	GOALS	S RATE
1	Chevanton	1540	10	154
2	Kapo Obou	1699	5	340
3	Di Vaio	1250	5	250
4	Vieri	433	3	144
5	Meriem	2390	3	797
6	Givet	2649	2	1325
7	Gigliotti	557	2	279
8	Modesto	1983	2	992
9	Gakpe	570	2	285
10	Adebayor	944	1	944
11	Veigneau	1190	1	1190
12	Maicon	2458	1	2458
13	Zikos	1304	1	1304
	Other		4	
	TOTAL		42	

TOP POINT EARNERS

	PLAYER	GAMES	AV PTS
1	Meriem	24	1.71
2	Zikos	13	1.69
3	Chevanton	13	1.69
4	Evra	14	1.57
5	Plasil	15	1.47
6	Bernardi	28	1.46
7	Kapo Obou	14	1.43
8	Givet	28	1.43
9	Modesto	19	1.42
10	Sorlin	15	1.40
	CLUB AVERAGE:		1.37

DISCIPLINARY RECORDS

	PLAYER	YELLOW	RED	AVE
1	Zikos	11	1	108
2	Gerard	3	1	124
3	Gigliotti	4	0	139
4	Cubilier	5	1	154
5	Perez	7	0	190
6	Evra	5	1	217
7	Maoulida	3	0	239
8	Maicon	9	0	273
9	Bernardi	8	1	289
10	Kapo Obou	4	1	339
11	Di Vaio	3	0	416
12	Modesto	4	0	495
13	Givet	5	0	529
	Other	11	2	
	TOTAL	82	8	

KEY GOALKEEPER

Guillaume Warmuz

Goals Conceded in the League	19	**Counting Games** League games when player was on pitch for at least 70 minutes	23
Defensive Rating Ave number of mins between League goals conceded while on the pitch	**109**	**Clean Sheets** In League games when player was on pitch for at least 70 minutes	10

KEY PLAYERS - DEFENDERS

Patrice Evra

Goals Conceded Number of League goals conceded while the player was on the pitch	9	**Clean Sheets** In League games when player was on pitch for at least 70 minutes	9
Defensive Rating Ave number of mins between League goals conceded while on the pitch	**145**	**Club Defensive Rating** Average number of mins between League goals conceded by the club this season	95

	PLAYER	CON LGE	CLEAN SHEETS	DEF RATE
1	Patrice Evra	9	9	145 mins
2	Douglas Sisenando Maicon	24	9	102 mins
3	Francois Modesto	20	9	99 mins
4	Gael Givet	27	10	98 mins

KEY PLAYERS - MIDFIELDERS

Camel Meriem

Goals in the League	3	**Contribution to Attacking Power** Average number of minutes between League team goals while on pitch	77
Defensive Rating Average number of mins between League goals conceded while on the pitch	120	**Scoring Difference** Defensive Rating minus Contribution to Attacking Power	**43**

	PLAYER	LGE GOALS	DEF RATE	POWER	SCORE DIFF
1	Camel Meriem	3	120	77	43 mins
2	Vassilis Zikos	1	130	87	43 mins
3	Lucas Bernardi	0	104	77	27 mins
4	Diego Fernando Perez	0	79	70	9 mins

KEY PLAYERS - GOALSCORERS

Ernesto Chevanton

Goals in the League	10	**Player Strike Rate** Average number of minutes between League goals scored by player	**154**
Contribution to Attacking Power Average number of minutes between League team goals while on pitch	77	**Club Strike Rate** Average number of minutes between League goals scored by club	81

	PLAYER	LGE GOALS	POWER	STRIKE RATE
1	Ernesto Chevanton	10	77	154 mins
2	Marco Di Vaio	5	96	250 mins
3	Narcisse Olivier Kapo Obou	5	100	340 mins
4	Camel Meriem	3	77	797 mins

Monaco's Olivier Kapo Obou and Camel Meriem

SQUAD APPEARANCES

Match	1	2	3	4	5	6	7	8	9	10	11	12	13	14	15	16	17	18	19	20	21	22	23	24
Venue	A	H	A	A	A	H	H	A	H	H	A	H	A	A	H	A	A	H	A	H	H	A	A	H
Competition	L	L	C	L	L	C	L	L	E	L	L	L	E	L	L	E	L	L	L	L	E	L	E	L
Result	W	L	L	W	L	D	D	L	W	L	W	D	W	W	W	L	L	W	D	W	W	L	W	W

Match	25	26	27	28	29	30	31	32	33	34	35	36	37	38	39	40	41	42	43	44	45	46	47	48
Venue	A	H	H	A	H	H	A	A	H	A	A	H	H	A	H	A	H	A	H	A	H	H	A	H
Competition	L	E	L	L	L	L	L	L	L	E	L	E	L	L	L	L	L	L	L	L	L	L	L	L
Result	D	W	W	L	D	L	D	W	D	L	L	D	L	L	W	L	D	D	W	D	W	D	D	D

Goalkeepers
Andre Biancarelli
Flavio Roma
Guillaume Warmuz

Defenders
Eric Cubilier
Manuel Dos Santos
Patrice Evra
Gael Givet
Arnaud Lescure
Douglas Maicon
Thomas Mangani
Francois Modesto
Marko Muslin
Julien Rodriguez
Sebastien Squillaci
Olivier Veigneau

Midfielders
Lucas Bernardi
Serge Gakpe
Lopez Segurra Gerard
Malaury Martin
Camel Meriem
Diego Fernando Perez
Jaroslav Plasil
Oliver Sorlin
Vassilis Zikos

Forwards
Emmanuel Adebayor
Souleymane Camara
Ernesto Chevanton
Marco Di Vaio
David Gigliotti
Olivier Kapo Obou
Alexandre Licata
Toifilou Maoulida
Nicolas Maurice-Belay
Christian Vieri

KEY: On all match | On bench | Subbed or sent off (Counting game) | Subbed or sent off (playing less than 70 minutes) | Subbed on from bench (Counting Game) | Subbed on (playing less than 70 minutes) | Subbed on and then subbed or sent off (Counting Game) | Subbed on and then subbed or sent off (playing less than 70 minutes) | Not in 16

LE MANS

Final Position: **11th**

KEY: Won / Drawn / Lost

No	Comp	Opponent	H/A	Result	Score	Scorers	Attendance
1	frpr1	Lyon	H	L	1-2	De Melo 56	11,000
2	frpr1	Metz	A	D	0-0		18,130
3	frpr1	Rennes	H	W	4-0	De Melo 8,33; Lucau 56; Bangoura 78	10,732
4	frpr1	AC Ajaccio	A	D	0-0		27,000
5	frpr1	Troyes	H	W	1-0	Thomas, F 41	11,000
6	frpr1	Toulouse	A	W	2-0	Lucau 12; Hautcoeur 86	14,814
7	frpr1	Sochaux	H	W	2-1	Hautcoeur 29; De Melo 68	10,867
8	frpr1	Nice	A	L	0-1		9,405
9	frpr1	Paris SG	H	D	0-0		15,182
10	frpr1	St Etienne	A	L	0-3		27,614
11	frpr1	Lille	H	D	1-1	Thomas, F 7	10,057
12	frpr1	Strasbourg	H	W	2-0	Hautcoeur 1; Matsui 42	10,337
13	frpr1	Nantes	A	L	0-1		29,500
14	frpr1	Marseille	H	W	3-0	Chiumiento 5; Fanchone 60; Bangoura 75	16,531
15	frpr1	Nancy	A	L	0-1		15,010
16	frpr1	Auxerre	H	L	0-2		10,347
17	frpr1	AS Monaco	A	L	0-2		9,000
18	frpr1	Bordeaux	H	W	1-0	Bangoura 43	12,530
19	frpr1	Lens	A	L	0-2		39,314
20	frpr1	Metz	H	W	2-0	De Melo 61,90	10,000
21	frpr1	Rennes	A	L	0-1		20,684
22	frpr1	AC Ajaccio	H	W	1-0	Carlos 90 og	8,611
23	frpr1	Troyes	A	W	3-1	Matsui 30,34; Faure 79	12,000
24	frpr1	Toulouse	H	D	1-1	De Melo 22	8,496
25	frpr1	Sochaux	A	D	0-0		12,884
26	frpr1	Nice	H	W	2-0	Fanchone 61; Bangoura 65	9,241
27	frpr1	Paris SG	A	W	1-0	Faure 5	39,655
28	frpr1	St Etienne	H	L	0-1		13,704
29	frpr1	Lille	A	L	0-4		16,000
30	frpr1	Strasbourg	A	W	2-1	Bangoura 57; Grafite 90	1,780
31	frpr1	Nantes	H	D	0-0		12,941
32	frpr1	Marseille	A	D	1-1	Fanchone 34	49,593
33	frpr1	Nancy	H	D	0-0		10,401
34	frpr1	Auxerre	A	D	0-0		10,500
35	frpr1	AS Monaco	H	D	0-0		13,212
36	frpr1	Bordeaux	A	D	2-2	Bangoura 19; Grafite 80	27,374
37	frpr1	Lens	H	D	0-0		12,827
38	frpr1	Lyon	A	L	1-8	Grafite 14	44,410

LEAGUE APPEARANCES, BOOKINGS AND CAPS

Player	AGE (on 01/07/06)	IN NAMED 18	APPEARANCES	COUNTING GAMES	MINUTES ON PITCH	YELLOW CARDS	RED CARDS	CAPS THIS SEASON	NATIONAL SIDE
Goalkeepers									
Thibault Ferrand	20	1	0	0	0	0	0	-	France
Yohann Pele	23	37	36	35	3184	2	0	-	France
Rodolphe Roche	27	33	3	2	236	0	0	-	France
Defenders									
Marko Basa	23	32	32	31	2840	5	1	-	Serbia
Laurent Bonnart	26	35	35	34	3110	4	0	-	France
Gregory Cerdan	23	28	21	15	1447	5	0	-	France
Yannick Fischer	31	27	12	5	716	2	0	-	France
Clement Pinault	21	8	3	2	215	0	0	-	France
Yohann Poulard	30	31	26	25	2288	4	0	-	France
Olivier Thomas	31	36	36	34	3138	5	0	-	France
Midfielders									
Davide Chiumiento	21	20	18	3	842	2	0	-	Italy
Jeremy Choplin	21	5	2	0	24	0	0	-	France
Vinicius De Melo	21	24	23	14	1595	6	1	-	Brazil
Martin Douillard	21	13	10	2	378	1	0	-	France
Kowel Ekhousuehi	22	11	9	1	250	0	0	-	Nigeria
Jacque Ferya	-	1	1	1	90	0	0	-	France
Sebastien Gormond	24	6	3	1	162	1	0	-	France
Grafite	27	13	10	5	656	0	0	-	Brazil
Yohan Hautcoeur	24	35	35	30	2866	4	0	-	France
Luigi Lavecchia	24	1	1	0	6	0	0	-	Italy
Guillaume Loriot	20	7	7	2	272	0	0	-	France
Daisuke Matsui	25	33	33	23	2373	7	0	-	Japan
Bertrand N'Dzomo	21	1	0	0	0	0	0	-	France
Desire Periatambee	30	15	10	2	415	0	0	-	Mauritius
Ndri Romaric	23	21	21	13	1395	3	0	-	Ivory Coast
Frederic Thomas	25	38	38	36	3318	2	0	-	France
Forwards									
Ismael Bangoura	21	24	21	14	1473	6	1	3	Guinea (123)
James Fanchone	26	36	35	24	2552	1	0	-	France
Cedric Faure	27	15	14	9	918	0	0	-	France
Chigury Lucau	21	13	13	7	770	1	0	-	Congo

TEAM OF THE SEASON

G Yohann Pele CG: 35 DR: 106

D Marko Basa CG: 31 DR: 129

D Olivier Thomas CG: 34 DR: 90

D Laurent Bonnart CG: 34 DR: 89

D Yohann Poulard CG: 25 DR: 85

M Vinicius De Melo CG: 14 SD: 12

M Daisuke Matsui CG: 23 SD: 8

M Frederic Thomas CG: 36 SD: 0

M Yohan Hautcoeur CG: 30 SD: -2

F Ismael Bangoura CG: 14 SR: 246

F James Fanchone CG: 24 SR: 851

MONTHLY POINTS TALLY

AUGUST	8	67%
SEPTEMBER	7	58%
OCTOBER	4	33%
NOVEMBER	3	33%
DECEMBER	3	33%
JANUARY	10	67%
FEBRUARY	7	58%
MARCH	5	42%
APRIL	4	33%
MAY	1	17%

LEAGUE GOALS

	PLAYER	MINS	GOALS	S RATE
1	De Melo	1595	7	228
2	Bangoura	1473	6	246
3	Hautcoeur	2866	3	955
4	Fanchone	2552	3	851
5	Grafite	656	3	219
6	Matsui	2373	3	791
7	Faure	918	2	459
8	Lucau	770	2	385
9	Thomas, F	3318	2	1659
10	Chiumiento	842	1	842
	Other		1	
	TOTAL		33	

TOP POINT EARNERS

	PLAYER	GAMES	AV PTS
1	Matsui	23	1.61
2	Hautcoeur	30	1.57
3	Fanchone	24	1.54
4	De Melo	14	1.50
5	Thomas, F	36	1.42
6	Basa	31	1.39
7	Pele	35	1.37
8	Poulard	25	1.36
9	Bangoura	14	1.36
10	Bonnart	34	1.32
	CLUB AVERAGE:		1.37

DISCIPLINARY RECORDS

	PLAYER	YELLOW	RED	AVE
1	Bangoura	6	1	210
2	De Melo	6	1	227
3	Cerdan	5	0	289
4	Matsui	7	0	339
5	Fischer	2	0	358
6	Chiumiento	2	0	421
7	Romaric	3	0	465
8	Basa	5	1	473
9	Poulard	4	0	572
10	Thomas, O	5	0	627
11	Hautcoeur	4	0	716
12	Lucau	1	0	770
13	Bonnart	4	0	777
	Other	5	0	
	TOTAL	59	3	

KEY GOALKEEPER

Yohann Pele

Goals Conceded in the League	30	**Counting Games** League games when player was on pitch for at least 70 minutes	35
Defensive Rating Ave number of mins between League goals conceded while on the pitch	106	**Clean Sheets** In games when player was on pitch for at least 70 minutes	18

KEY PLAYERS - DEFENDERS

Marko Basa

Goals Conceded Number of League goals conceded while the player was on the pitch	22	**Clean Sheets** In League games when player was on pitch for at least 70 minutes	17
Defensive Rating Ave number of mins between League goals conceded while on the pitch	129	**Club Defensive Rating** Average number of mins between League goals conceded by the club this season	92

	PLAYER	CON LGE	CLEAN SHEETS	DEF RATE
1	Marko Basa	22	17	129 mins
2	Olivier Thomas	35	17	90 mins
3	Laurent Bonnart	35	17	89 mins
4	Yohann Poulard	27	12	85 mins

KEY PLAYERS - MIDFIELDERS

Vinicius De Melo

Goals in the League	7	**Contribution to Attacking Power** Average number of minutes between League team goals while on pitch	94
Defensive Rating Average number of mins between League goals conceded while on the pitch	106	**Scoring Difference** Defensive Rating minus Contribution to Attacking Power	12

	PLAYER	LGE GOALS	DEF RATE	POWER	SCORE DIFF
1	Vinicius De Melo	7	106	94	12 mins
2	Daisuke Matsui	3	99	91	8 mins
3	Frederic Thomas	2	104	104	0 mins
4	Yohan Hautcoeur	3	90	92	-2 mins

KEY PLAYERS - GOALSCORERS

Vinicius De Melo

Goals in the League	7	**Player Strike Rate** Average number of minutes between League goals scored by player	228
Contribution to Attacking Power Average number of minutes between League team goals while on pitch	94	**Club Strike Rate** Average number of minutes between League goals scored by club	104

	PLAYER	LGE GOALS	POWER	STRIKE RATE
1	Vinicius De Melo	7	94	228 mins
2	Ismael Bangoura	6	98	246 mins
3	Daisuke Matsui	3	91	791 mins
4	James Fanchone	3	116	851 mins

Le Mans' James Fanchone

SQUAD APPEARANCES

Match	1	2	3	4	5	6	7	8	9	10	11	12	13	14	15	16	17	18	19	20	21	22	23	24	25	26	27	28	29	30	31	32	33	34	35	36	37	38
Venue	H	A	H	A	H	A	H	A	H	A	H	H	A	H	A	H	A	H	A	H	A	H	A	H	A	H	A	H	A	A	H	A	H	A	H	A	H	A
Competition	L	L	L	L	L	L	L	L	L	L	L	L	L	L	L	L	L	L	L	L	L	L	L	L	L	L	L	L	L	L	L	L	L	L	L	L	L	L
Result	L	D	W	D	W	W	W	L	D	L	D	W	L	W	L	L	L	W	L	W	L	W	W	D	D	W	W	L	L	W	D	D	D	D	D	D	D	L

Goalkeepers
Thibault Ferrand
Yohann Pele
Rodolphe Roche

Defenders
Marko Basa
Laurent Bonnart
Gregory Cerdan
Yannick Fischer
Clement Pinault
Yohann Poulard
Olivier Thomas

Midfielders
Davide Chiumiento
Jeremy Choplin
Vinicius De Melo
Martin Douillard
Edorisi Kowel Ekhousuehi
Jacque Ferya
Sebastien Gormond
Grafite
Yohan Hautcoeur
Luigi Lavecchia
Guillaume Loriot
Daisuke Matsui
Bertrand N'Dzomo
Desire Periatambee
Ndri Romaric
Frederic Thomas

Forwards
Ismael Bangoura
James Fanchone
Cedric Faure
Chigury Lucau

KEY: On all match · On bench · Subbed or sent off (Counting game) · Subbed or sent off (playing less than 70 minutes) · Subbed on from bench (Counting Game) · Subbed on (playing less than 70 minutes) · Subbed on and then subbed or sent off (Counting Game) · Subbed on and then subbed or sent off (playing less than 70 minutes) · Not in 16

NANCY

Final Position: **12th**

KEY: ☐Won ☐Drawn ☐Lost

							Attendance
1	frpr1	**AS Monaco**	H	L	0-1		20,000
2	frpr1	**Bordeaux**	A	L	0-1		25,428
3	frpr1	**Lens**	H	L	1-2	Zerka 46	19,500
4	frpr1	**Lyon**	A	L	0-1		39,000
5	frpr1	**Rennes**	H	W	6-0	Kroupi 15,30,71 pen; Rochat 34 og; Diakhate 48; Puygrenier 85	16,200
6	frpr1	**AC Ajaccio**	A	L	0-1		6,500
7	frpr1	**Metz**	H	D	1-1	Andre Luiz 1	21,840
8	frpr1	**St Etienne**	A	W	2-0	Lecluse 32; Sarkisian 66	26,711
9	frpr1	**Troyes**	H	W	2-1	Curbelo 54,72	15,392
10	frpr1	**Sochaux**	A	W	2-0	Curbelo 88; Kroupi 90	11,732
11	frpr1	**Toulouse**	H	W	2-0	Diakhate 25; Kroupi 49	17,011
12	frpr1	**Paris SG**	A	L	0-1		35,000
13	frpr1	**Nice**	H	D	0-0		22,000
14	frpr1	**Nantes**	A	L	0-3		27,000
15	frpr1	**Le Mans**	H	W	1-0	Kim 75	15,010
16	frpr1	**Lille**	A	L	0-1		11,140
17	frpr1	**Marseille**	H	D	1-1	Zerka 48	30,000
18	frpr1	**Strasbourg**	H	L	1-2	Zerka 47	17,000
19	frpr1	**Auxerre**	A	W	1-0	Zerka 6 pen	7,000
20	frpr1	**Bordeaux**	H	D	0-0		15,000
21	frpr1	**Lens**	A	W	2-1	Zerka 28; Brison 75	32,000
22	frpr1	**Lyon**	H	L	0-2		20,000
23	frpr1	**Rennes**	A	W	2-0	Brison 57; Duchemin 90	24,142
24	frpr1	**AC Ajaccio**	H	D	0-0		12,500
25	frpr1	**St Etienne**	H	W	2-0	Chretien 9; Kroupi 16	16,107
26	frpr1	**Troyes**	A	W	1-0	Zerka 60	11,999
27	frpr1	**Sochaux**	H	L	0-3		12,000
28	frpr1	**Toulouse**	A	D	1-1	Sarkisian 67	13,454
29	frpr1	**Metz**	A	D	0-0		18,324
30	frpr1	**Paris SG**	H	D	1-1	Brison 23	20,000
31	frpr1	**Nice**	A	L	0-1		9,710
32	frpr1	**Nantes**	H	D	0-0		15,000
33	frpr1	**Le Mans**	A	D	0-0		10,401
34	frpr1	**Lille**	H	D	0-0		18,000
35	frpr1	**Marseille**	A	L	0-6		50,000
36	frpr1	**Strasbourg**	A	W	3-1	Kroupi 20,24,32 pen	19,072
37	frpr1	**Auxerre**	H	L	1-3	Andre Luiz 86	17,000
38	frpr1	**AS Monaco**	A	D	2-2	Givet 6 og; Andre Luiz 77	9,990

LEAGUE APPEARANCES, BOOKINGS AND CAPS

	AGE (on 01/07/06)	IN NAMED 18	APPEARANCES	COUNTING GAMES	MINUTES ON PITCH	YELLOW CARDS	RED CARDS	CAPS THIS SEASON	NATIONAL SIDE
Goalkeepers									
Gennaro Bracigliano	26	35	33	33	2970	2	0	-	France
Olivier Sorin	25	36	5	5	450	0	0	-	France
Defenders									
Adailton	26	18	16	7	1014	5	0	-	Brazil
Frederic Biancalani	31	30	30	25	2492	6	0	-	France
Benjamin Brat	20	1	0	0	0	0	0	-	France
Manuel da Costa	20	15	10	7	659	2	0	-	France
Pape Diakhate	22	33	33	32	2935	5	0	-	Senegal
Benjamin Gavanon	25	32	28	23	2152	7	0	-	France
Cedric Lecluse	34	34	26	21	2009	8	2	-	France
Patrick N'Tolla	18	4	1	0	18	0	0	-	Cameroon
Sebastien Puygrenier	24	35	32	24	2445	6	0	-	France
Jeremy Sapina	21	1	0	0	0	0	0	-	France
Midfielders									
Jonathan Brison	23	33	30	18	1867	4	1	-	France
Romain Chouleur	20	6	3	0	57	1	0	-	France
Mickael Chretien	22	32	32	28	2722	5	1	-	France
Gaston Curbelo	30	14	13	11	1047	3	0	-	France
Emmanuel Duchemin	27	26	26	23	2216	1	0	-	France
Abdoulaye Keita	27	3	3	1	183	1	0	-	Senegal
Landry N'Guemo	20	17	14	7	855	0	0	-	Cameroon
Adrian Sarkisian	27	34	33	15	1996	1	0	-	Uruguay
Moncef Zerka	24	27	26	15	1793	5	0	-	France
Forwards									
Andre Luiz	26	33	28	16	1782	5	1	-	Brazil
Dagui Bakari	31	1	1	1	90	0	0	-	France
Pascal Berenguer	25	36	35	28	2716	3	0	-	
Basile Camerling	19	8	4	0	113	0	0	-	France
Kim	26	23	23	14	1570	5	1	-	Brazil
Elie Kroupi	26	24	22	7	1173	2	1	-	France
Gergely Rudolf	21	10	5	1	151	1	0	-	Hungary

TEAM OF THE SEASON

G: Gennaro Bracigliano — CG: 33 DR: 102

D: Cedric Lecluse — CG: 21 DR: 118
D: Sebastien Puygrenier — CG: 24 DR: 111
D: Frederic Biancalani — CG: 25 DR: 104
D: Benjamin Gavanon — CG: 23 DR: 94

M: Adrian Sarkisian — CG: 15 SD: 0
M: Emmanuel Duchemin — CG: 23 SD: -10
M: Jonathan Brison — CG: 18 SD: -17
M: Mickael Chretien — CG: 28 SD: -19

F: Silva Luiz — CG: 16 SR: 594
F: Moncef Zerka — CG: 15 SR: 299

MONTHLY POINTS TALLY

AUGUST	3	25%
SEPTEMBER	7	58%
OCTOBER	7	58%
NOVEMBER	3	33%
DECEMBER	4	44%
JANUARY	8	53%
FEBRUARY	6	67%
MARCH	4	27%
APRIL	5	42%
MAY	1	17%

LEAGUE GOALS

	PLAYER	MINS	GOALS	S RATE
1	Kroupi	1173	**9**	130
2	Zerka	1793	**6**	299
3	Curbelo	1047	**3**	349
4	Andre Luiz	1782	**3**	594
5	Brison	1867	**3**	622
6	Diakhate	2935	**2**	1468
7	Sarkisian	1996	**2**	998
8	Kim	1570	**1**	1570
9	Duchemin	2216	**1**	2216
10	Lecluse	2009	**1**	2009
11	Puygrenier	2445	**1**	2445
12	Chretien	2722	**1**	2722
	Other		**2**	
	TOTAL		**35**	

TOP POINT EARNERS

	PLAYER	GAMES	AV PTS
1	Lecluse	21	**1.62**
2	Brison	18	**1.44**
3	Chretien	28	**1.43**
4	Sarkisian	15	**1.40**
5	Berenguer	28	**1.39**
6	Biancalani	25	**1.36**
7	Bracigliano	33	**1.30**
8	Gavanon	23	**1.30**
9	Duchemin	23	**1.22**
10	Puygrenier	24	**1.21**
	CLUB AVERAGE:		**1.26**

DISCIPLINARY RECORDS

	PLAYER	YELLOW	RED	AVE
1	Lecluse	8	2	**200**
2	Adailton	5	0	**202**
3	Kim	5	1	**261**
4	Andre Luiz	5	1	**297**
5	Gavanon	7	0	**307**
6	da Costa	2	0	**329**
7	Curbelo	3	0	**349**
8	Zerka	5	0	**358**
9	Brison	4	1	**373**
10	Kroupi	2	1	**391**
11	Puygrenier	6	0	**407**
12	Biancalani	6	0	**415**
13	Chretien	5	1	**453**
	Other	12	0	
	TOTAL	**75**	**7**	

KEY GOALKEEPER

Gennaro Bracigliano

Goals Conceded in the League	29	Counting Games League games when player was on pitch for at least 70 minutes	33
Defensive Rating Ave number of mins between League goals conceded while on the pitch	102	Clean Sheets In games when player was on pitch for at least 70 minutes	16

KEY PLAYERS - DEFENDERS

Cedric Lecluse

Goals Conceded Number of League goals conceded while the player was on the pitch	17	Clean Sheets In League games when player was on pitch for at least 70 minutes	10
Defensive Rating Ave number of mins between League goals conceded while on the pitch	118	Club Defensive Rating Average number of mins between League goals conceded by the club this season	92

	PLAYER	CON LGE	CLEAN SHEETS	DEF RATE
1	Cedric Lecluse	17	10	118 mins
2	Sebastien Puygrenier	22	11	111 mins
3	Frederic Biancalani	24	11	104 mins
4	Benjamin Gavanon	23	10	94 mins

KEY PLAYERS - MIDFIELDERS

Adrian Sarkisian

Goals in the League	2	Contribution to Attacking Power Average number of minutes between League team goals while on pitch	105
Defensive Rating Average number of mins between League goals conceded while on the pitch	105	Scoring Difference Defensive Rating minus Contribution to Attacking Power	0

	PLAYER	LGE GOALS	DEF RATE	POWER	SCORE DIFF
1	Adrian Sarkisian	2	105	105	0 mins
2	Emmanuel Duchemin	1	79	89	-10 mins
3	Jonathan Brison	3	81	98	-17 mins
4	Mickael Chretien	1	94	113	-19 mins

KEY PLAYERS - GOALSCORERS

Moncef Zerka

Goals in the League	6	Player Strike Rate Average number of minutes between League goals scored by player	299
Contribution to Attacking Power Average number of minutes between League team goals while on pitch	138	Club Strike Rate Average number of minutes between League goals scored by club	98

	PLAYER	LGE GOALS	POWER	STRIKE RATE
1	Moncef Zerka	6	138	299 mins
2	Silva do Nascimento Andre Luiz	3	99	594 mins
3	Jonathan Brison	3	98	622 mins
4	Adrian Sarkisian	2	105	998 mins

Nancy's Frederic Biancalani

SQUAD APPEARANCES

Match	1	2	3	4	5	6	7	8	9	10	11	12	13	14	15	16	17	18	19	20	21	22	23	24	25	26	27	28	29	30	31	32	33	34	35	36	37	38
Venue	H	A	H	A	H	A	H	A	H	A	H	A	H	A	H	A	H	H	A	H	A	H	A	H	H	A	H	A	A	H	A	H	A	H	A	A	H	A
Competition	L	L	L	L	L	L	L	L	L	L	L	L	L	L	L	L	L	L	L	L	L	L	L	L	L	L	L	L	L	L	L	L	L	L	L	L	L	L
Result	L	L	L	L	W	L	D	W	W	W	W	L	D	L	W	L	D	L	W	D	W	L	W	D	W	W	L	D	D	D	L	D	D	D	L	W	L	D

Goalkeepers
Gennaro Bracigliano
Olivier Sorin

Defenders
Da Silva Santos Adailton
Frederic Biancalani
Benjamin Brat
Manuel da Costa
Pape Diakhate
Benjamin Gavanon
Cedric Lecluse
Patrick N'Tolla
Sebastien Puygrenier
Jeremy Sapina

Midfielders
Jonathan Brison
Romain Chouleur
Mickael Chretien
Gaston Curbelo
Emmanuel Duchemin
Abdoulaye Khouma Keita
Landry N'Guemo
Adrian Sarkisian
Moncef Zerka

Forwards
Andre Luiz
Dagui Bakari
Pascal Berenguer
Basile Camerling
Carlos Henrique Dias Kim
Elie Kroupi
Gergely Rudolf

KEY: On all match · On bench · Subbed or sent off (Counting game) · Subbed or sent off (playing less than 70 minutes) · Subbed on from bench (Counting Game) · Subbed on (playing less than 70 minutes) · Subbed on and then subbed or sent off (Counting Game) · Subbed on and then subbed or sent off (playing less than 70 minutes) · Not in 16

St ETIENNE

Final Position: **13th**

KEY: ☐Won ☐Drawn ☐Lost

						Attendance
1 frpr1	**AC Ajaccio**	H	D	0-0		25,928
2 frpr1	**Troyes**	A	D	0-0		10,006
3 frpr1	**Metz**	H	W	2-0	Piquionne 25,32	28,966
4 frpr1	**Toulouse**	A	D	1-1	Hellebuyck 58	21,906
5 frpr1	**Sochaux**	H	D	0-0		31,322
6 frpr1	**Nice**	A	W	1-0	Piquionne 7	13,425
7 frpr1	**Paris SG**	H	W	3-0	Mendy 36; Piquionne 52; Feindouno 78	27,771
8 frpr1	**Nancy**	H	L	0-2		26,711
9 frpr1	**Lille**	A	L	0-2		13,510
10 frpr1	**Le Mans**	H	W	3-0	Perrin, L 42; Hognon 55; Hellebuyck 78	27,614
11 frpr1	**Nantes**	A	D	1-1	Savinaud 10 og	33,500
12 frpr1	**Marseille**	H	W	2-1	Feindouno 23; Hellebuyck 84	35,123
13 frpr1	**Strasbourg**	A	W	1-0	Gomis 71	23,212
14 frpr1	**Auxerre**	H	D	1-1	Hognon 34	33,005
15 frpr1	**AS Monaco**	A	L	0-1		16,234
16 frpr1	**Bordeaux**	H	D	1-1	Ilunga 1	34,089
17 frpr1	**Lens**	A	L	1-2	Perrin, L 24	30,000
18 frpr1	**Lyon**	H	D	0-0		35,352
19 frpr1	**Rennes**	A	W	1-0	Feindouno 66	28,221
20 frpr1	**Troyes**	H	D	1-1	Hognon 51	25,641
21 frpr1	**Metz**	A	W	1-0	Postiga 16	12,273
22 frpr1	**Sochaux**	A	L	0-4		13,566
23 frpr1	**Toulouse**	H	L	1-3	Diawara 84	24,296
24 frpr1	**Paris SG**	A	D	2-2	Piquionne 16; Postiga 34	43,026
25 frpr1	**Nancy**	A	L	0-2		16,107
26 frpr1	**Nice**	H	L	0-1		22,440
27 frpr1	**Lille**	H	L	0-2		24,655
28 frpr1	**Le Mans**	A	W	1-0	Postiga 56	13,704
29 frpr1	**Nantes**	H	W	1-0	Mazure 89	21,163
30 frpr1	**Marseille**	A	L	0-2		56,263
31 frpr1	**Strasbourg**	H	L	0-2		25,566
32 frpr1	**Auxerre**	A	D	0-0		20,000
33 frpr1	**AS Monaco**	H	D	1-1	Gomis 82	33,683
34 frpr1	**Bordeaux**	A	D	0-0		32,000
35 frpr1	**Lens**	H	W	2-0	Sable 1; Piquionne 36	34,938
36 frpr1	**Lyon**	A	L	0-4		39,000
37 frpr1	**Rennes**	H	D	0-0		32,522
38 frpr1	**AC Ajaccio**	A	L	1-3	Sable 63	4,000

LEAGUE APPEARANCES, BOOKINGS AND CAPS

	AGE (on 01/07/06)	IN NAMED 18	APPEARANCES	COUNTING GAMES	MINUTES ON PITCH	YELLOW CARDS	RED CARDS	CAPS THIS SEASON	NATIONAL SIDE
Goalkeepers									
Jeremie Janot	28	37	37	37	3330	0	0	-	France
Jessy Moulin	20	1	0	0	0	0	0	-	France
Jody Viviani	24	34	1	1	90	0	0	-	France
Defenders									
Bruno Basto	28	13	8	6	579	1	0	-	Portugal
Zoumana Camara	27	36	36	33	3139	4	1	-	France
Fousseni Diawara	25	37	35	32	2886	3	0	-	France
Vincent Hognon	31	30	30	30	2700	1	0	-	France
Herita Ilunga	24	30	30	29	2675	6	1	-	Congo
Abdelaziz Kamara	22	4	3	2	241	0	0	-	France
Damien Perquis	22	29	12	6	620	1	0	-	France
Alledine Yahia	24	20	10	4	505	0	1	-	France
Midfielders									
Mouhamadou Dabo	19	20	16	9	883	2	0	-	Senegal
David Hellebuyck	27	35	35	33	3039	6	0	-	France
Samy Houri	20	7	3	0	36	0	0	-	France
Frederic Mendy	32	18	16	7	848	1	0	-	France
Loic Perrin	20	30	26	17	1607	3	0	-	France
Ignacio Piatti	21	2	1	0	10	0	0	-	Argentina
Julien Sable	25	36	36	36	3200	5	0	-	France
Siaka Tiene	24	9	5	1	161	1	0	4	Ivory Coast (32)
Didier Zokora	25	31	31	31	2791	6	0	11	Ivory Coast (32)
Forwards									
Idriss Ech-Chergui	25	1	0	0	0	0	0	-	France
Pascal Feindouno	25	28	28	25	2365	2	0	5	Guinea (123)
Bafetibis Gomis	20	28	24	6	1004	3	1	-	France
Sebastien Mazure	27	27	19	3	728	0	0	-	France
Frederic Piquionne	27	34	33	30	2622	2	0	-	France
Helder Postiga	23	16	16	13	1164	5	0	6	Portugal (7)
Lamine Sakho	28	9	8	1	258	0	0	-	Senegal

TEAM OF THE SEASON

G — Jeremie Janot, **CG:** 37 **DR:** 85

D — Herita Nkolongo Ilunga, **CG:** 29 **DR:** 96

D — Fousseni Diawara, **CG:** 32 **DR:** 93

D — Vincent Hognon, **CG:** 30 **DR:** 90

D — Zoumana Camara, **CG:** 33 **DR:** 83

M — David Hellebuyck, **CG:** 33 **SD:** -24

M — Julien Sable, **CG:** 36 **SD:** -28

M — Didier Zokora, **CG:** 31 **SD:** -30

M — Loic Perrin, **CG:** 17 **SD:** -37

F — Helder Postiga, **CG:** 13 **SR:** 388

F — Frederic Piquionne, **CG:** 30 **SR:** 437

MONTHLY POINTS TALLY

AUGUST	6	50%
SEPTEMBER	6	50%
OCTOBER	10	83%
NOVEMBER	2	22%
DECEMBER	4	44%
JANUARY	4	44%
FEBRUARY	4	22%
MARCH	4	33%
APRIL	5	42%
MAY	1	17%

LEAGUE GOALS

	PLAYER	MINS	GOALS	S RATE
1	Piquionne	2622	6	437
2	Feindouno	2365	3	788
3	Hellebuyck	3039	3	1013
4	Postiga	1164	3	388
5	Hognon	2700	3	900
6	Perrin, L	1607	2	804
7	Sable	3200	2	1600
8	Gomis	1004	2	502
9	Mazure	728	1	728
10	Diawara	2886	1	2886
11	Mendy	848	1	848
12	Ilunga	2675	1	2675
	Other		1	
	TOTAL		29	

TOP POINT EARNERS

	PLAYER	GAMES	AV PTS
1	Hognon	30	1.33
2	Piquionne	30	1.30
3	Hellebuyck	33	1.30
4	Feindouno	25	1.28
5	Zokora	31	1.26
6	Diawara	32	1.25
7	Janot	37	1.24
8	Ilunga	29	1.24
9	Camara	33	1.24
10	Sable	36	1.22
	CLUB AVERAGE:		1.24

DISCIPLINARY RECORDS

	PLAYER	YELLOW	RED	AVE
1	Postiga	5	0	232
2	Gomis	3	1	251
3	Ilunga	6	1	382
4	Dabo	2	0	441
5	Zokora	6	0	465
6	Yahia	0	1	505
7	Hellebuyck	6	0	506
8	Perrin, L	3	0	535
9	Basto	1	0	579
10	Perquis	1	0	620
11	Camara	4	1	627
12	Sable	5	0	640
13	Mendy	1	0	848
	Other	8	0	
	TOTAL	51	4	

KEY GOALKEEPER

Jeremie Janot

Goals Conceded in the League	39	**Counting Games** League games when player was on pitch for at least 70 minutes	37
Defensive Rating Ave number of mins between League goals conceded while on the pitch	85	**Clean Sheets** In League games when player was on pitch for at least 70 minutes	16

KEY PLAYERS - DEFENDERS

Herita Nkolongo Ilunga

Goals Conceded Number of League goals conceded while the player was on the pitch	28	**Clean Sheets** In League games when player was on pitch for at least 70 minutes	13
Defensive Rating Ave number of mins between League goals conceded while on the pitch	96	**Club Defensive Rating** Average number of mins between League goals conceded by the club this season	88

	PLAYER	CON LGE	CLEAN SHEETS	DEF RATE
1	Herita Nkolongo Ilunga	28	13	96 mins
2	Fousseni Diawara	31	14	93 mins
3	Vincent Hognon	30	14	90 mins
4	Zoumana Camara	38	14	83 mins

KEY PLAYERS - MIDFIELDERS

David Hellebuyck

Goals in the League	3	**Contribution to Attacking Power** Average number of minutes between League team goals while on pitch	113
Defensive Rating Average number of mins between League goals conceded while on the pitch	89	**Scoring Difference** Defensive Rating minus Contribution to Attacking Power	-24

	PLAYER	LGE GOALS	DEF RATE	POWER	SCORE DIFF
1	David Hellebuyck	3	89	113	-24 mins
2	Julien Sable	2	91	119	-28 mins
3	Didier Zokora	0	103	133	-30 mins
4	Loic Perrin	2	70	107	-37 mins

KEY PLAYERS - GOALSCORERS

Manuel Marques Helder Postiga

Goals in the League	3	**Player Strike Rate** Average number of minutes between League goals scored by player	388
Contribution to Attacking Power Average number of minutes between League team goals while on pitch	233	**Club Strike Rate** Average number of minutes between League goals scored by club	118

	PLAYER	LGE GOALS	POWER	STRIKE RATE
1	Manuel Marques Helder Postiga	3	233	388 mins
2	Frederic Piquionne	6	114	437 mins
3	Pascal Feindouno	3	148	788 mins
4	Loic Perrin	2	107	804 mins

St Etienne's Julien Sable

SQUAD APPEARANCES

Match	1	2	3	4	5	6	7	8	9	10	11	12	13	14	15	16	17	18	19	20	21	22	23	24	25	26	27	28	29	30	31	32	33	34	35	36	37	38
Venue	H	A	H	A	H	A	H	H	A	H	A	H	A	H	A	H	A	H	A	H	A	A	H	A	A	H	H	A	H	A	H	A	H	A	H	A	H	A
Competition	L	L	L	L	L	L	L	L	L	L	L	L	L	L	L	L	L	L	L	L	L	L	L	L	L	L	L	L	L	L	L	L	L	L	L	L	L	L
Result	D	D	W	D	D	W	W	L	L	W	D	W	W	D	L	D	L	D	W	D	W	L	L	D	L	L	L	W	W	L	L	D	D	D	W	L	D	L

Goalkeepers
Jeremie Janot
Jessy Moulin
Jody Viviani

Defenders
Bruno Basto
Zoumana Camara
Fousseni Diawara
Vincent Hognon
Herita Nkolongo Ilunga
Abdelaziz Kamara
Damien Perquis
Alledine Yahia

Midfielders
Mouhamadou Dabo
David Hellebuyck
Samy Houri
Frederic Mendy
Loic Perrin
Ignacio Piatti
Julien Sable
Siaka Tiene
Didier Zokora

Forwards
Idriss Ech-Chergui
Pascal Feindouno
Bafetibis Gomis
Sebastien Mazure
Frederic Piquionne
Helder Postiga
Lamine Sakho

KEY: ■ On all match | ■ On bench | ⏮ Subbed or sent off (Counting game) | « Subbed or sent off (playing less than 70 minutes) | ⏭ Subbed on from bench (Counting Game) | » Subbed on (playing less than 70 minutes) | Subbed on and then subbed or sent off (Counting Game) | Subbed on and then subbed or sent off (playing less than 70 minutes) | □ Not in 16

NANTES

Final Position: **14th**

KEY: ☐ Won ☐ Drawn ☐ Lost

	Comp	Opponent	H/A	Result	Score	Scorers	Attendance
1	frpr1	**Lens**	H	W	2-0	Yapi Yapo 3; Glombard 7	34,000
2	frpr1	**Rennes**	A	W	3-0	Fae 14; Diallo 78; Bamogo 86	29,344
3	frpr1	**AC Ajaccio**	H	L	0-2		31,500
4	frpr1	**Nice**	A	D	1-1	Fae 46	13,440
5	frpr1	**Metz**	H	D	0-0		27,532
6	frpr1	**Troyes**	A	L	0-1		11,812
7	frpr1	**Toulouse**	H	W	2-0	Diallo 17,32	27,000
8	frpr1	**Sochaux**	A	L	0-1		10,000
9	frpr1	**Lyon**	H	L	0-1		35,500
10	frpr1	**Paris SG**	A	L	0-2		42,164
11	frpr1	**St Etienne**	H	D	1-1	Keseru 2	33,500
12	frpr1	**Lille**	A	L	0-2		11,868
13	frpr1	**Le Mans**	H	W	1-0	Keseru 18 pen	29,500
14	frpr1	**Nancy**	H	W	3-0	Da Rocha 27; Signorio 62; Bamogo 68	27,000
15	frpr1	**Marseille**	A	L	1-2	Bamogo 59	48,000
16	frpr1	**Strasbourg**	H	W	4-3	Delhommeau 48; Bamogo 55; Dimitrijevic 59; Da Rocha 90	26,000
17	frpr1	**Auxerre**	A	L	0-4		7,385
18	frpr1	**AS Monaco**	H	D	0-0		28,000
19	frpr1	**Bordeaux**	A	D	0-0		21,606
20	frpr1	**Rennes**	H	L	0-2		30,000
21	frpr1	**AC Ajaccio**	A	W	2-0	Capoue 13; Diallo 24	3,000
22	frpr1	**Nice**	H	D	0-0		25,000
23	frpr1	**Metz**	A	W	4-1	Guillon 22; Diallo 42,64; Payet 90	12,369
24	frpr1	**Toulouse**	A	L	0-1		15,204
25	frpr1	**Sochaux**	H	W	3-1	Diallo 20,71,73	25,868
26	frpr1	**Troyes**	H	D	1-1	Keseru 77	20,000
27	frpr1	**Lyon**	A	L	1-3	Diallo 73	37,328
28	frpr1	**Paris SG**	H	D	0-0		31,000
29	frpr1	**St Etienne**	A	L	0-1		21,163
30	frpr1	**Lille**	H	D	1-1	Rossi 6	25,000
31	frpr1	**Le Mans**	A	D	0-0		12,941
32	frpr1	**Nancy**	A	D	0-0		15,000
33	frpr1	**Marseille**	H	L	1-3	Oliech 53	33,000
34	frpr1	**Strasbourg**	A	W	1-0	Capoue 29	20,085
35	frpr1	**Auxerre**	H	W	3-2	Oliech 5; Cetto 68; Fae 85	30,000
36	frpr1	**AS Monaco**	A	D	1-1	Capoue 27	10,061
37	frpr1	**Bordeaux**	H	L	0-1		37,000
38	frpr1	**Lens**	A	L	1-3	Fae 8	36,868

LEAGUE APPEARANCES, BOOKINGS AND CAPS

	AGE (on 01/07/06)	IN NAMED 18	APPEARANCES	COUNTING GAMES	MINUTES ON PITCH	YELLOW CARDS	RED CARDS	CAPS THIS SEASON	NATIONAL SIDE
Goalkeepers									
Tony Heurtebis	31	34	3	2	225	0	0	-	France
Mickael Landreau	27	36	36	34	3142	0	1	9	France (8)
Perica Radic	22	2	0	0	0	0	0	-	Serbia & Montenegro
Defenders									
Mauro Cetto	24	29	29	29	2606	8	1	-	Argentina
Pascal Delhommeau	27	24	22	18	1697	4	0	-	France
Stephen Drouin	22	3	0	0	0	0	0	-	France
Karim El Mourabet	19	1	1	0	1	0	0	-	France
David Leray	22	31	22	16	1517	7	1	-	France
Jean-Jacques Pierre	23	17	9	7	680	2	0	-	Haiti
Nicolas Savinaud	30	34	27	25	2329	2	0	-	France
Franck Signorio	24	33	33	33	2970	5	0	-	France
Steven Thicot	19	4	0	0	0	0	0	-	France
Midfielders									
Bocundji Ca	19	23	21	14	1385	4	0	-	France
Aurelien Capoue	24	20	18	11	1231	5	1	-	France
Kevin Das Neves	20	2	2	2	180	0	0	-	France
Mamadou Diallo	24	35	35	23	2372	5	0	-	Mali
Milos Dimitrijevic	22	28	23	17	1642	3	0	-	France
Emerse Fae	22	29	29	24	2307	3	0	8	Ivory Coast (32)
Luigi Glombard	21	16	16	5	769	1	0	-	France
Loic Guillon	24	32	30	26	2467	1	0	-	France
Imed Mhadhbi	30	9	9	3	531	1	0	-	Tunisia
Olivier Quint	34	7	6	3	295	0	0	-	France
Jeremy Toulalan	22	29	29	28	2563	6	0	1	France (8)
Gilles Yapi Yapo	24	13	10	3	477	1	0	9	Ivory Coast (32)
Forwards									
Habib Bamogo	24	31	28	12	1559	3	0	-	France
Frederic Da Rocha	31	37	33	27	2662	8	0	-	France
Claudiu Keseru	19	20	15	4	693	0	0	-	Romania
Dennis Oliech	21	9	9	6	594	2	0	-	Kenya
Dimitri Payet	19	2	2	1	95	0	0	-	France
Gregory Pujol	26	1	1	0	62	0	0	-	France
Julio Hernan Rossi	29	13	11	3	552	1	0	-	Argentina

TEAM OF THE SEASON

MONTHLY POINTS TALLY

Month	Points	%
AUGUST	5	42%
SEPTEMBER	3	25%
OCTOBER	4	33%
NOVEMBER	6	67%
DECEMBER	2	22%
JANUARY	7	58%
FEBRUARY	5	33%
MARCH	3	25%
APRIL	7	58%
MAY	0	0%

LEAGUE GOALS

	PLAYER	MINS	GOALS	S RATE
1	Diallo	2372	10	237
2	Fae	2307	4	577
3	Bamogo	1559	3	520
4	Capoue	1231	3	410
5	Keseru	693	3	231
6	Da Rocha	2662	2	1331
7	Oliech	594	2	297
8	Guillon	2467	1	2467
9	Glombard	769	1	769
10	Signorio	2970	1	2970
11	Dimitrijevic	1642	1	1642
12	Delhommeau	1697	1	1697
13	Cetto	2606	1	2606
	Other		4	
	TOTAL		37	

TOP POINT EARNERS

	PLAYER	GAMES	AV PTS
1	Cetto	29	1.41
2	Savinaud	25	1.40
3	Bamogo	12	1.33
4	Da Rocha	27	1.33
5	Landreau	34	1.32
6	Guillon	26	1.15
7	Signorio	33	1.15
8	Delhommeau	18	1.11
9	Diallo	23	1.09
10	Toulalan	28	1.07
	CLUB AVERAGE:		1.18

DISCIPLINARY RECORDS

	PLAYER	YELLOW	RED	AVE
1	Leray	7	1	189
2	Capoue	5	1	205
3	Cetto	8	1	289
4	Oliech	2	0	297
5	Da Rocha	8	0	332
6	Pierre	2	0	340
7	Ca	4	0	346
8	Delhommeau	4	0	424
9	Toulalan	6	0	427
10	Diallo	5	0	474
11	Yapi Yapo	1	0	477
12	Bamogo	3	0	519
13	Mhadhbi	1	0	531
	Other	16	1	
	TOTAL	72	4	

KEY GOALKEEPER

Mickael Landreau			
Goals Conceded in the League	34	Counting Games League games when player was on pitch for at least 70 minutes	34
Defensive Rating Ave number of mins between League goals conceded while on the pitch	92	Clean Sheets In games when player was on pitch for at least 70 minutes	14

KEY PLAYERS - DEFENDERS

Nicolas Savinaud			
Goals Conceded Number of League goals conceded while the player was on the pitch	22	Clean Sheets In League games when player was on pitch for at least 70 minutes	10
Defensive Rating Ave number of mins between League goals conceded while on the pitch	106	Club Defensive Rating Average number of mins between League goals conceded by the club this season	83

	PLAYER	CON LGE	CLEAN SHEETS	DEF RATE
1	Nicolas Savinaud	22	10	106 mins
2	Mauro Cetto	30	12	87 mins
3	Franck Signorio	36	11	83 mins
4	Pascal Delhommeau	24	7	71 mins

KEY PLAYERS - MIDFIELDERS

Loic Guillon			
Goals in the League	1	Contribution to Attacking Power Average number of minutes between League team goals while on pitch	99
Defensive Rating Average number of mins between League goals conceded while on the pitch	99	Scoring Difference Defensive Rating minus Contribution to Attacking Power	0

	PLAYER	LGE GOALS	DEF RATE	POWER	SCORE DIFF
1	Loic Guillon	1	99	99	0 mins
2	Mamadou Diallo	10	85	91	-6 mins
3	Bocundji Ca	0	66	77	-11 mins
4	Milos Dimitrijevic	1	86	97	-11 mins

KEY PLAYERS - GOALSCORERS

Mamadou Diallo			
Goals in the League	10	Player Strike Rate Average number of minutes between League goals scored by player	237
Contribution to Attacking Power Average number of minutes between League team goals while on pitch	91	Club Strike Rate Average number of minutes between League goals scored by club	92

	PLAYER	LGE GOALS	POWER	STRIKE RATE
1	Mamadou Diallo	10	91	237 mins
2	Habib Bamogo	3	104	520 mins
3	Emerse Fae	4	128	577 mins
4	Frederic Da Rocha	2	83	1331 mins

Nantes' Mamadou Diallo

SQUAD APPEARANCES

Match	1	2	3	4	5	6	7	8	9	10	11	12	13	14	15	16	17	18	19	20	21	22	23	24	25	26	27	28	29	30	31	32	33	34	35	36	37	38
Venue	H	A	H	A	H	A	H	A	H	A	H	A	H	H	A	H	A	H	A	H	A	H	A	A	H	H	A	H	A	H	A	A	H	A	H	A	H	A
Competition	L	L	L	L	L	L	L	L	L	L	L	L	L	L	L	L	L	L	L	L	L	L	L	L	L	L	L	L	L	L	L	L	L	L	L	L	L	L
Result	W	W	L	D	D	L	W	L	L	L	D	L	W	W	L	W	L	D	D	L	W	D	W	L	W	D	L	D	L	D	D	D	L	W	W	D	L	L

Goalkeepers
Tony Heurtebis
Mickael Landreau
Perica Radic

Defenders
Mauro Cetto
Pascal Delhommeau
Stephen Drouin
Karim El Mourabet
David Leray
Jean-Jacques Pierre
Nicolas Savinaud
Franck Signorio
Steven Thicot

Midfielders
Bocundji Ca
Aurelien Capoue
Kevin Das Neves
Mamadou Diallo
Milos Dimitrijevic
Emerse Fae
Luigi Glombard
Loic Guillon
Imed Mhadhbi
Olivier Quint
Jeremy Toulalan
Gilles Yapi Yapo

Forwards
Habib Bamogo
Frederic Da Rocha
Claudiu Andrei Keseru
Dennis Oliech
Dimitri Payet
Gregory Pujol
Julio Hernan Rossi

KEY: On all match · On bench · Subbed or sent off (Counting game) · Subbed or sent off (playing less than 70 minutes) · Subbed on from bench (Counting Game) · Subbed on (playing less than 70 minutes) · Subbed on and then subbed or sent off (Counting Game) · Subbed on and then subbed or sent off (playing less than 70 minutes) · Not in 16

SOCHAUX

Final Position: **15th**

KEY: ☐Won ☐Drawn ☐Lost

#	Comp	Opponent	H/A	Res	Score	Scorers	Attendance
1	frpr1	Toulouse	H	L	0-1		13,234
2	frpr1	Paris SG	H	L	0-1		17,543
3	frpr1	Nice	A	W	2-1	Ilan 79,80	13,555
4	frpr1	Lille	H	D	0-0		13,153
5	frpr1	St Etienne	A	D	0-0		31,322
6	frpr1	Marseille	H	L	0-1		18,493
7	frpr1	Le Mans	A	L	1-2	Ilan 61	10,867
8	frpr1	Nantes	H	W	1-0	Dagano 51	10,000
9	frpr1	Auxerre	A	L	0-3		10,000
10	frpr1	Nancy	H	L	0-2		11,732
11	frpr1	Bordeaux	A	D	1-1	Menez 29	21,895
12	frpr1	AS Monaco	H	W	2-1	Ilan 8; Dagano 39 fk	15,020
13	frpr1	Lyon	A	L	0-1		38,000
14	frpr1	Lens	H	D	1-1	Ilan 10	14,499
15	frpr1	AC Ajaccio	A	W	1-0	Erding 90	5,000
16	frpr1	Rennes	H	W	1-0	Genghini 89	15,932
17	frpr1	Strasbourg	A	D	0-0		20,000
18	frpr1	Metz	H	D	1-1	Isabey 2	11,812
19	frpr1	Troyes	A	L	1-2	Isabey 90	18,585
20	frpr1	Paris SG	A	L	1-3	Sene 56	36,806
21	frpr1	Nice	H	D	1-1	Menez 14	11,885
22	frpr1	Lille	A	L	0-3		12,286
23	frpr1	St Etienne	H	W	4-0	Menez 45 pen; Ilan 52; Dagano 59,90	13,566
24	frpr1	Marseille	A	D	0-0		21,000
25	frpr1	Le Mans	H	D	0-0		12,884
26	frpr1	Nantes	A	L	1-3	Ilan 33	25,868
27	frpr1	Auxerre	H	W	1-0	Dagano 1	11,468
28	frpr1	Nancy	A	W	3-0	Dagano 16; Lecluse 45 og; Ilan 87	12,000
29	frpr1	AS Monaco	A	L	1-4	Ilan 68	5,903
30	frpr1	Lyon	H	L	0-4		18,777
31	frpr1	Lens	A	L	1-2	Ilan 71	32,966
32	frpr1	AC Ajaccio	H	W	3-1	N'Daw 17; Dagano 27; Weldon 90	17,288
33	frpr1	Rennes	A	L	1-2	Diawara 20	22,612
34	frpr1	Strasbourg	H	D	1-1	Ilan 79	16,876
35	frpr1	Bordeaux	H	L	0-3		15,057
36	frpr1	Metz	A	W	1-0	Isabey 57	6,000
37	frpr1	Troyes	H	D	1-1	Afolabi 18	13,977
38	frpr1	Toulouse	A	W	2-1	Weldon 79; Erding 89	23,000

LEAGUE APPEARANCES, BOOKINGS AND CAPS

	AGE (on 01/07/06)	IN NAMED 18	APPEARANCES	COUNTING GAMES	MINUTES ON PITCH	YELLOW CARDS	RED CARDS	CAPS THIS SEASON	NATIONAL SIDE
Goalkeepers									
Jeremy Deichelbohrer	20	2	0	0	0	0	0	-	France
Alexandre Martinovic	31	35	4	2	243	0	0	-	France
Teddy Richert	31	36	36	35	3195	1	0	-	France
Defenders									
Rabiu Afolabi	26	36	32	31	2823	4	1	-	Nigeria
Arnaud Buhler	21	16	12	10	894	1	0	-	Switzerland
Jean Calve	22	21	17	17	1519	0	1	-	France
Omar Daf	29	9	7	7	630	3	0	-	Senegal
Souleymane Diawara	27	21	21	19	1782	6	0	-	Senegal
Maxime Josse	19	8	6	6	540	0	0	-	France
Joao Miranda	21	28	20	17	1622	3	1	-	Brazil
Lionel Potillon	32	11	8	8	710	1	0	-	France
Pape Habib Sow	21	5	1	0	21	0	0	-	Senegal
Dusko Tosic	21	14	14	12	1157	2	0	-	Serbia & Montenegro
Midfielders									
Fabien Boudarene	27	19	19	16	1495	3	0	-	France
Phillipe Brunel	33	20	18	10	1120	1	0	-	France
Ahmed Farag	20	1	0	0	0	0	0	-	Egypt
Benjamin Genghini	20	9	3	1	108	0	0	-	France
Mickael Isabey	31	36	36	33	3034	2	0	-	France
Johan Lonfat	32	8	7	3	404	0	0	-	Switzerland
Mourad Meghni	22	17	15	8	935	2	0	-	France
Valery Mezague	22	17	15	8	887	3	0	-	Cameroon
Guirane N'Daw	22	30	30	30	2700	6	0	-	Senegal
Romain Pitau	28	38	38	37	3302	6	0	-	France
Badara Sene	21	9	3	2	175	0	0	-	Senegal
Forwards									
Moumouni Dagano	25	32	31	26	2467	0	0	1	Burkina Faso (83)
Sigamary Diarra	22	2	2	2	180	0	0	-	France
Mevlut Erding	19	10	8	1	293	0	0	-	France
Araujo Ilan	25	27	27	22	2171	4	1	-	Brazil
Mohamed Kader	27	14	11	2	284	2	0	-	Togo
Jeremy Menez	19	32	30	21	2078	2	0	-	France
Julien Quercia	19	10	6	1	162	0	0	-	France
Marcelo Trapasso	30	3	0	0	0	0	0	-	Argentina
Andrade Weldon	25	11	10	2	316	2	0	-	Brazil
Jaouad Zairi	24	11	9	1	288	2	0	-	Morocco

TEAM OF THE SEASON

G – Teddy Richert CG: 35 DR: 76

D – Dusko Tosic CG: 12 DR: 77
D – Souleymane Diawara CG: 19 DR: 74
D – Rabiu Afolabi CG: 31 DR: 71
D – Joao Miranda CG: 17 DR: 71

M – Fabien Boudarene CG: 16 SD: 0
M – Romain Pitau CG: 37 SD: -28
M – Guirane N'Daw CG: 30 SD: -31
M – Mickael Isabey CG: 33 SD: -41

F – Araujo Ilan CG: 22 SR: 197
F – Moumouni Dagano CG: 26 SR: 352

MONTHLY POINTS TALLY

Month	Points	%
AUGUST	5	42%
SEPTEMBER	3	25%
OCTOBER	4	33%
NOVEMBER	7	78%
DECEMBER	2	22%
JANUARY	5	33%
FEBRUARY	7	58%
MARCH	0	0%
APRIL	7	47%
MAY	4	67%

LEAGUE GOALS

	PLAYER	MINS	GOALS	S RATE
1	Ilan	2171	11	197
2	Dagano	2467	7	352
3	Isabey	3034	4	759
4	Menez	2078	3	693
5	Erding	293	2	147
6	Weldon	316	2	158
7	Diawara	1782	1	1782
8	N'Daw	2700	1	2700
9	Sene	175	1	175
10	Genghini	108	1	108
11	Afolabi	2823	1	2823
	Other		1	
	TOTAL		35	

TOP POINT EARNERS

	PLAYER	GAMES	AV PTS
1	Boudarene	16	1.44
2	Tosic	12	1.33
3	Diawara	19	1.32
4	Dagano	26	1.27
5	Afolabi	31	1.26
6	Isabey	33	1.24
7	Richert	35	1.23
8	N'Daw	30	1.20
9	Pitau	37	1.19
10	Ilan	22	1.18
	CLUB AVERAGE:		1.16

DISCIPLINARY RECORDS

	PLAYER	YELLOW	RED	AVE
1	Daf	3	0	210
2	Mezague	3	0	295
3	Diawara	6	0	297
4	Miranda	3	1	405
5	Ilan	4	1	434
6	N'Daw	6	0	450
7	Meghni	2	0	467
8	Boudarene	3	0	498
9	Pitau	6	0	550
10	Afolabi	4	1	564
11	Tosic	2	0	578
12	Potillon	1	0	710
13	Buhler	1	0	894
	Other	6	1	
	TOTAL	50	4	

KEY GOALKEEPER

Teddy Richert			
Goals Conceded in the League	42	**Counting Games** League games when player was on pitch for at least 70 minutes	35
Defensive Rating Ave number of mins between League goals conceded while on the pitch	76	**Clean Sheets** In games when player was on pitch for at least 70 minutes	12

KEY PLAYERS - DEFENDERS

Dusko Tosic			
Goals Conceded Number of League goals conceded while the player was on the pitch	15	**Clean Sheets** In League games when player was on pitch for at least 70 minutes	5
Defensive Rating Ave number of mins between League goals conceded while on the pitch	77	**Club Defensive Rating** Average number of mins between League goals conceded by the club this season	73

	PLAYER	CON LGE	CLEAN SHEETS	DEF RATE
1	Dusko Tosic	15	5	77 mins
2	Souleymane Diawara	24	7	74 mins
3	Rabiu Afolabi	40	10	71 mins
4	Joao Miranda	23	4	71 mins

KEY PLAYERS - MIDFIELDERS

Fabien Boudarene			
Goals in the League	0	**Contribution to Attacking Power** Average number of minutes between League team goals while on pitch	107
Defensive Rating Average number of mins between League goals conceded while on the pitch	107	**Scoring Difference** Defensive Rating minus Contribution to Attacking Power	0

	PLAYER	LGE GOALS	DEF RATE	POWER	SCORE DIFF
1	Fabien Boudarene	0	107	107	0 mins
2	Romain Pitau	0	72	100	-28 mins
3	Guirane N'Daw	1	69	100	-31 mins
4	Mickael Isabey	4	76	117	-41 mins

KEY PLAYERS - GOALSCORERS

Araujo Ilan			
Goals in the League	11	**Player Strike Rate** Average number of minutes between League goals scored by player	197
Contribution to Attacking Power Average number of minutes between League team goals while on pitch	75	**Club Strike Rate** Average number of minutes between League goals scored by club	98

	PLAYER	LGE GOALS	POWER	STRIKE RATE
1	Araujo Ilan	11	75	197 mins
2	Moumouni Dagano	7	91	352 mins
3	Jeremy Menez	3	130	693 mins
4	Mickael Isabey	4	117	759 mins

Sochaux's Moumouni Dagano

SQUAD APPEARANCES

Match	1	2	3	4	5	6	7	8	9	10	11	12	13	14	15	16	17	18	19	20	21	22	23	24	25	26	27	28	29	30	31	32	33	34	35	36	37	38
Venue	H	H	A	H	A	H	A	H	A	H	A	H	A	H	A	H	A	H	A	A	H	A	H	A	H	A	H	A	A	H	A	H	A	H	H	A	H	A
Competition	L	L	L	L	L	L	L	L	L	L	L	L	L	L	L	L	L	L	L	L	L	L	L	L	L	L	L	L	L	L	L	L	L	L	L	L	L	L
Result	L	L	W	D	D	L	L	W	L	L	D	W	L	D	W	W	D	D	L	L	D	L	W	D	D	L	W	W	L	L	L	W	L	D	L	W	D	W

Goalkeepers
Jeremy Deichelbohrer
Alexandre Martinovic
Teddy Richert

Defenders
Rabiu Afolabi
Arnaud Buhler
Jean Calve
Omar Daf
Souleymane Diawara
Maxime Josse
Joao Miranda
Lionel Potillon
Pape Habib Sow
Dusko Tosic

Midfielders
Fabien Boudarene
Phillipe Brunel
Ahmed Farag
Benjamin Genghini
Mickael Isabey
Johan Lonfat
Mourad Meghni
Valery Mezague
Guirane N'Daw
Romain Pitau
Badara Sene

Forwards
Moumouni Dagano
Sigamary Diarra
Mevlut Erding
Araujo Ilan
Mohamed Kader
Jeremy Menez
Julien Quercia
Marcelo Trapasso
A dos Santos Weldon
Jaouad Zairi

KEY: On all match · On bench · Subbed or sent off (Counting game) · Subbed or sent off (playing less than 70 minutes) · Subbed on from bench (Counting Game) · Subbed on (playing less than 70 minutes) · Subbed on and then subbed or sent off (Counting Game) · Subbed on and then subbed or sent off (playing less than 70 minutes) · Not in 16

TOULOUSE

Final Position: **16th**

KEY: ☐Won ☐Drawn ☐Lost

							Attendance
1	frpr1	Sochaux	A	W	1-0	Santos 15	13,234
2	frpr1	Nice	H	L	0-2		18,620
3	frpr1	Paris SG	A	L	0-2		41,341
4	frpr1	St Etienne	H	D	1-1	Moreira 39	21,906
5	frpr1	Lille	A	D	0-0		12,525
6	frpr1	Le Mans	H	L	0-2		14,814
7	frpr1	Nantes	A	L	0-2		27,000
8	frpr1	Marseille	H	W	1-0	Bergougnoux 12	28,070
9	frpr1	Strasbourg	A	W	4-2	Battles 2; Moreira 7; Dieuze 64; Santos 75	15,000
10	frpr1	Auxerre	H	W	2-0	Emana 46; Bergougnoux 52	18,641
11	frpr1	Nancy	A	L	0-2		17,011
12	frpr1	Bordeaux	H	D	1-1	Moreira 40	25,468
13	frpr1	Lens	A	L	0-1		29,174
14	frpr1	Lyon	H	L	0-1		26,254
15	frpr1	Rennes	A	L	1-4	Congre 82	20,094
16	frpr1	AC Ajaccio	H	W	3-0	Moreira 16; Mathieu 59; Bonnet 90	14,000
17	frpr1	Metz	A	D	2-2	Moreira 40; Santos 89	12,367
18	frpr1	Troyes	H	W	2-1	Bergougnoux 45; Mathieu 90	16,984
19	frpr1	AS Monaco	A	L	0-1		9,107
20	frpr1	Nice	A	L	1-2	Dao 85	8,776
21	frpr1	Paris SG	H	W	1-0	Moreira 86	20,321
22	frpr1	Lille	H	D	0-0		15,416
23	frpr1	Le Mans	A	D	1-1	Akpa-Akpro 10	8,496
24	frpr1	St Etienne	A	W	3-1	Akpa-Akpro 6,70; Arribage 68	24,296
25	frpr1	Nantes	H	W	1-0	Arribage 56	15,204
26	frpr1	Marseille	A	D	0-0		43,000
27	frpr1	Strasbourg	H	L	1-2	Moreira 76	16,883
28	frpr1	Auxerre	A	L	0-2		5,000
29	frpr1	Nancy	H	D	1-1	Emana 74	13,454
30	frpr1	Bordeaux	A	L	0-2		24,110
31	frpr1	Lens	H	D	1-1	Mansare 28	12,941
32	frpr1	Lyon	A	D	1-1	Moreira 43	37,994
33	frpr1	Rennes	H	L	0-1		15,350
34	frpr1	AC Ajaccio	A	L	0-1		5,000
35	frpr1	Metz	H	W	2-0	Santos 17; Moreira 45	15,272
36	frpr1	Troyes	A	L	1-3	Battles 3	13,023
37	frpr1	AS Monaco	H	D	3-3	Dos Santos 31; Moreira 82; Dieuze 88	20,158
38	frpr1	Sochaux	H	L	1-2	Battles 7	23,000

LEAGUE APPEARANCES, BOOKINGS AND CAPS

	AGE (on 01/07/06)	IN NAMED 18	APPEARANCES	COUNTING GAMES	MINUTES ON PITCH	YELLOW CARDS	RED CARDS	CAPS THIS SEASON	NATIONAL SIDE
Goalkeepers									
Benoit Benvegnu	21	8	0	0	0	0	0	-	France
Nicolas Douchez	26	38	13	13	1171	2	0	-	France
Christophe Revault	34	26	25	25	2249	1	0	-	France
Defenders									
Dominique Arribage	35	33	32	30	2756	5	1	-	France
Lucien Aubey	22	33	33	33	2970	1	0	-	France
Daniel Congre	21	16	16	12	1192	0	0	-	France
Albin Ebondo	22	29	29	24	2358	3	0	-	France
Mohamed Fofana	21	6	4	3	300	1	0	-	France
Stephane Lievre	33	9	6	1	242	0	0	-	France
Xavier Pentecote	22	4	4	0	68	0	0	-	France
Midfielders									
Yacine Abdessadki	25	10	9	6	572	2	0	-	Algeria
Jean-L Akpa-Akpro	21	15	13	3	417	1	0	-	France
Laurent Battles	30	31	31	23	2295	5	0	-	France
Henri Bedimo Nsame	22	7	4	3	287	0	0	-	Cameroon
Alexandre Bonnet	19	20	15	2	605	1	0	-	France
Julien Cardy	24	26	20	9	1178	4	0	-	France
Stephane Dalmat	27	1	1	1	90	0	0	-	France
Issou Malia Dao	22	19	16	9	949	2	0	-	France
Achille Emana	24	26	26	23	2190	4	0	2	Cameroon (26)
Thibault Giresse	25	14	9	1	309	1	0	-	France
Jeremy Mathieu	22	35	34	30	2898	4	0	-	France
Daniel Moreira	28	37	37	36	3236	4	0	-	France
Henri Bedimo Nsame	22	6	3	1	123	0	0	-	Cameroon
Francois Sirieix	25	12	8	7	629	2	0	-	France
Nabil Taider	23	17	14	10	1004	0	0	-	France
Forwards									
Bryan Bergougnoux	23	36	34	9	1663	2	1	-	France
Nicolas Dieuze	27	37	35	27	2703	6	0	-	France
Fode Mansare	24	24	23	11	1461	4	0	5	Guinea (123)
Benjamin Psaume	21	1	0	0	0	0	0	-	France
Francileudo Santos	27	27	25	15	1576	1	0	-	Tunisia

TEAM OF THE SEASON

G — Christophe Revault CG: 25 DR: 78

D — Daniel Congre CG: 12 DR: 79

D — Lucien Aubey CG: 33 DR: 78

D — Dominique Arribage CG: 30 DR: 69

D — Albin Ebondo CG: 24 DR: 69

M — Daniel Moreira CG: 36 SD: -11

M — Laurent Battles CG: 23 SD: -30

M — Jeremy Mathieu CG: 30 SD: -35

M — Achille Emana CG: 23 SD: -39

F — Francileudo Santos CG: 15 SR: 394

F — Nicolas Dieuze CG: 27 SR: 1352

MONTHLY POINTS TALLY

AUGUST	2	17%
SEPTEMBER	6	50%
OCTOBER	4	33%
NOVEMBER	3	33%
DECEMBER	4	44%
JANUARY	5	42%
FEBRUARY	7	47%
MARCH	3	25%
APRIL	3	25%
MAY	1	17%

LEAGUE GOALS

	PLAYER	MINS	GOALS	S RATE
1	Moreira	3236	**10**	324
2	Santos	1576	**4**	394
3	Bergougnoux	1663	**3**	554
4	Battles	2295	**3**	765
5	Akpa-Akpro	417	**3**	139
6	Dieuze	2703	**2**	1352
7	Emana	2190	**2**	1095
8	Mathieu	2898	**2**	1449
9	Arribage	2756	**2**	1378
10	Dao	949	**1**	949
11	Congre	1192	**1**	1192
12	Bonnet	605	**1**	605
13	Mansare	1461	**1**	1461
	Other		**1**	
	TOTAL		**36**	

TOP POINT EARNERS

	PLAYER	GAMES	AV PTS
1	Congre	12	**1.50**
2	Revault	25	**1.24**
3	Aubey	33	**1.15**
4	Dieuze	27	**1.15**
5	Moreira	36	**1.14**
6	Battles	23	**1.13**
7	Emana	23	**1.09**
8	Santos	15	**1.07**
9	Arribage	30	**1.03**
10	Ebondo	24	**0.92**
	CLUB AVERAGE:		**1.08**

DISCIPLINARY RECORDS

	PLAYER	YELLOW	RED	AVE
1	Abdessadki	2	0	**286**
2	Cardy	4	0	**294**
3	Sirieix	2	0	**314**
4	Mansare	4	0	**365**
5	Dieuze	6	0	**450**
6	Battles	5	0	**459**
7	Arribage	5	1	**459**
8	Dao	2	0	**474**
9	Emana	4	0	**547**
10	Bergougnoux	2	1	**554**
11	Douchez	2	0	**585**
12	Bonnet	1	0	**605**
13	Mathieu	4	0	**724**
	Other	10	0	
	TOTAL	**53**	**2**	

KEY GOALKEEPER

Christophe Revault

Goals Conceded in the League	29	Counting Games League games when player was on pitch for at least 70 minutes	25
Defensive Rating Ave number of mins between League goals conceded while on the pitch	78	Clean Sheets In games when player was on pitch for at least 70 minutes	7

KEY PLAYERS - DEFENDERS

Daniel Congre

Goals Conceded Number of League goals conceded while the player was on the pitch	15	Clean Sheets In League games when player was on pitch for at least 70 minutes	5
Defensive Rating Ave number of mins between League goals conceded while on the pitch	79	Club Defensive Rating Average number of mins between League goals conceded by the club this season	73

	PLAYER	CON LGE	CLEAN SHEETS	DEF RATE
1	Daniel Congre	15	5	79 mins
2	Lucien Aubey	38	9	78 mins
3	Albin Ebondo	34	6	69 mins
4	Dominique Arribage	40	7	69 mins

KEY PLAYERS - MIDFIELDERS

Daniel Moreira

Goals in the League	10	Contribution to Attacking Power Average number of minutes between League team goals while on pitch	92
Defensive Rating Average number of mins between League goals conceded while on the pitch	81	Scoring Difference Defensive Rating minus Contribution to Attacking Power	-11

	PLAYER	LGE GOALS	DEF RATE	POWER	SCORE DIFF
1	Daniel Moreira	10	81	92	-11 mins
2	Laurent Battles	3	70	100	-30 mins
3	Jeremy Mathieu	2	72	107	-35 mins
4	Achille Emana	2	71	110	-39 mins

KEY PLAYERS - GOALSCORERS

Daniel Moreira

Goals in the League	10	Player Strike Rate Average number of minutes between League goals scored by player	324
Contribution to Attacking Power Average number of minutes between League team goals while on pitch	92	Club Strike Rate Average number of minutes between League goals scored by club	95

	PLAYER	LGE GOALS	POWER	STRIKE RATE
1	Daniel Moreira	10	92	324 mins
2	Francileudo Santos	4	93	394 mins
3	Laurent Battles	3	100	765 mins
4	Achille Emana	2	110	1095 mins

Toulouse's Daniel Moreira and Fode Mansare

SQUAD APPEARANCES

Match	1	2	3	4	5	6	7	8	9	10	11	12	13	14	15	16	17	18	19	20	21	22	23	24	25	26	27	28	29	30	31	32	33	34	35	36	37	38
Venue	A	H	A	H	A	H	A	H	A	H	A	H	A	H	A	H	A	H	A	A	H	H	A	A	H	A	H	A	H	A	H	A	H	A	H	A	H	H
Competition	L	L	L	L	L	L	L	L	L	L	L	L	L	L	L	L	L	L	L	L	L	L	L	L	L	L	L	L	L	L	L	L	L	L	L	L	L	L
Result	W	L	L	D	D	L	L	W	W	W	L	D	L	L	L	W	D	W	L	L	W	D	D	W	W	D	L	L	D	L	D	D	L	L	W	L	D	L

Goalkeepers
Benoit Benvegnu
Nicolas Douchez
Christophe Revault

Defenders
Dominique Arribage
Lucien Aubey
Daniel Congre
Albin Ebondo
Mohamed Fofana
Stephane Lievre
Xavier Pentecote

Midfielders
Yacine Abdessadki
Jean-Louis Akpa-Akpro
Laurent Battles
Henri Bedimo Nsame
Alexandre Bonnet
Julien Cardy
Stephane Dalmat
Issou Malia Dao
Achille Emana
Thibault Giresse
Jeremy Mathieu
Daniel Moreira
Henri Bedimo Nsame
Francois Sirieix
Nabil Taider

Forwards
Bryan Bergougnoux
Nicolas Dieuze
Fode Mansare
Benjamin Psaume
Francileudo Santos

KEY: On all match; On bench; Subbed or sent off (Counting game); Subbed or sent off (playing less than 70 minutes); Subbed on from bench (Counting Game); Subbed on (playing less than 70 minutes); Subbed on and then subbed or sent off (Counting Game); Subbed on and then subbed or sent off (playing less than 70 minutes); Not in 16

TROYES

Final Position: **17th**

KEY: ☐ Won ☐ Drawn ☐ Lost

							Attendance
1	frpr1	Nice	A	D	1-1	Dallet 50	15,050
2	frpr1	St Etienne	H	D	0-0		10,006
3	frpr1	Lille	A	W	2-1	Nivet 2; Dallet 44	11,746
4	frpr1	Paris SG	H	D	1-1	Dallet 48	17,500
5	frpr1	Le Mans	A	L	0-1		11,000
6	frpr1	Nantes	H	W	1-0	Grax 90	11,812
7	frpr1	Marseille	A	L	1-2	Grax 55 pen	48,000
8	frpr1	AS Monaco	H	L	1-2	Grax 32	12,214
9	frpr1	Nancy	A	L	1-2	Grax 27	15,392
10	frpr1	Strasbourg	H	D	1-1	Jaziri 71	10,000
11	frpr1	Auxerre	A	L	0-3		12,000
12	frpr1	Lens	H	D	1-1	Adam 70	12,000
13	frpr1	Bordeaux	A	L	0-2		19,581
14	frpr1	Rennes	H	W	2-1	Jaziri 27; Tourenne 77	8,000
15	frpr1	Lyon	A	L	1-2	Nivet 21	37,940
16	frpr1	Metz	H	D	0-0		10,054
17	frpr1	AC Ajaccio	A	W	1-0	Amzine 79	3,500
18	frpr1	Toulouse	A	L	1-2	Grax 6	16,984
19	frpr1	Sochaux	H	W	2-1	Boucansaud 50; Jaziri 57	18,585
20	frpr1	St Etienne	A	D	1-1	Grax 32	25,641
21	frpr1	Lille	H	W	1-0	Keita 10 og	10,212
22	frpr1	Paris SG	A	L	1-2	Ba 49	35,118
23	frpr1	Le Mans	H	L	1-3	Nivet 59	12,000
24	frpr1	Marseille	H	L	0-1		18,860
25	frpr1	AS Monaco	A	D	1-1	Enza Yamissi 63	7,681
26	frpr1	Nantes	A	D	1-1	Nivet 83	20,000
27	frpr1	Nancy	H	L	0-1		11,999
28	frpr1	Strasbourg	A	L	0-2		20,000
29	frpr1	Auxerre	H	D	1-1	Ba 39	11,000
30	frpr1	Lens	A	L	0-1		35,098
31	frpr1	Bordeaux	H	D	1-1	Nivet 42	11,524
32	frpr1	Rennes	A	L	0-2		25,195
33	frpr1	Lyon	H	L	0-1		17,835
34	frpr1	Metz	A	W	4-2	Medjani 28 og; Dallet 52; Nivet 66 pen; Grax 88	21,027
35	frpr1	AC Ajaccio	H	W	3-0	Tourenne 35; Faye 41; Bangoura 64	19,825
36	frpr1	Toulouse	H	W	3-1	Dallet 48; Grax 79; Jaziri 81	13,023
37	frpr1	Sochaux	A	D	1-1	Grax 90	13,977
38	frpr1	Nice	H	L	1-2	Jaziri 66	18,013

LEAGUE APPEARANCES, BOOKINGS AND CAPS

	AGE (on 01/07/06)	IN NAMED 18	APPEARANCES	COUNTING GAMES	MINUTES ON PITCH	YELLOW CARDS	RED CARDS	CAPS THIS SEASON	NATIONAL SIDE
Goalkeepers									
Ronan Le Crom	31	38	38	38	3404	0	1	-	France
Quentin Westberg	20	34	0	0	0	0	0	-	United States
Defenders									
Frederic Adam	32	14	8	4	527	2	0	-	France
Florian Boucansaud	25	30	30	28	2599	0	0	-	France
Stephen Drouin	22	7	6	5	469	1	0	-	France
Alexandre Dujeux	30	29	20	15	1474	0	0	-	France
Ibrahima Faye	26	32	32	32	2864	4	0	-	Senegal
Auriol Guillaume	26	5	3	2	224	1	0	-	France
Blaise Kouassi	31	27	26	24	2252	5	0	8	Ivory Coast (32)
Jean-Louis Montero	35	30	30	29	2650	4	0	-	France
Gregory Paisley	29	15	12	12	1060	2	0	-	France
Midfielders									
Gharib Amzine	33	35	33	24	2536	5	0	-	Morocco
Branko Boskovic	26	21	19	9	1125	1	0	2	Serbia & Mont (44)
Gael Danic	24	11	10	1	307	0	0	-	France
Cedric Faivre	25	9	4	0	112	1	0	-	France
Blaise Matuidi	19	32	31	26	2520	12	0	-	France
Benjamin Nivet	29	38	38	36	3357	6	0	-	France
Carl Tourenne	34	32	31	21	2356	6	1	-	France
Forwards									
Georges Ba	27	19	19	4	680	0	0	-	Ivory Coast
Ibrahima Bangoura	23	16	14	7	814	0	0	3	Guinea (123)
Sebastien Dallet	32	31	28	18	1858	5	0	-	France
Eloge Enza Yamissi	23	21	17	3	685	1	0	-	France
Nicolas Florentin	28	1	1	0	31	0	0	-	France
Sebastien Grax	22	29	28	13	1760	3	1	-	France
Ziad Jaziri	27	22	20	8	1145	6	0	5	Tunisia (21)
Christian Nade	21	20	17	2	672	1	0	-	France
Ali Zitouni	25	1	1	0	65	0	0	1	Tunisia (21)

TEAM OF THE SEASON

G — Ronan Le Crom
CG: 38 DR: 72

D — Alexandre Dujeux
CG: 15 DR: 82

D — Jean-Louis Montero
CG: 29 DR: 76

D — Gregory Paisley
CG: 12 DR: 76

D — Blaise Kouassi
CG: 24 DR: 75

M — Benjamin Nivet
CG: 36 SD: -20

M — Blaise Matuidi
CG: 26 SD: -23

M — Gharib Amzine
CG: 24 SD: -27

M — Carl Tourenne
CG: 21 SD: -29

F — Sebastien Grax
CG: 13 SR: 196

F — Sebastien Dallet
CG: 18 SR: 372

MONTHLY POINTS TALLY

AUGUST	5	42%
SEPTEMBER	3	25%
OCTOBER	2	17%
NOVEMBER	4	44%
DECEMBER	6	67%
JANUARY	4	33%
FEBRUARY	2	13%
MARCH	2	17%
APRIL	9	75%
MAY	1	17%

LEAGUE GOALS

	PLAYER	MINS	GOALS	S RATE
1	Grax	1760	**9**	196
2	Nivet	3357	**6**	560
3	Dallet	1858	**5**	372
4	Jaziri	1145	**5**	229
5	Tourenne	2356	**2**	1178
6	Ba	680	**2**	340
7	Faye	2864	**1**	2864
8	Boucansaud	2599	**1**	2599
9	Enza Yamissi	685	**1**	685
10	Bangoura	814	**1**	814
11	Adam	527	**1**	527
12	Amzine	2536	**1**	2536
	Other		**2**	
	TOTAL		**37**	

TOP POINT EARNERS

	PLAYER	GAMES	AV PTS
1	Dallet	18	**1.33**
2	Montero	29	**1.28**
3	Kouassi	24	**1.25**
4	Matuidi	26	**1.12**
5	Amzine	24	**1.08**
6	Paisley	12	**1.08**
7	Le Crom	38	**1.03**
8	Grax	13	**1.00**
9	Nivet	36	**1.00**
10	Tourenne	21	**1.00**
	CLUB AVERAGE:		**1.03**

DISCIPLINARY RECORDS

	PLAYER	YELLOW	RED	AVE
1	Jaziri	6	0	**190**
2	Matuidi	12	0	**210**
3	Adam	2	0	**263**
4	Tourenne	6	1	**336**
5	Dallet	5	0	**371**
6	Grax	3	1	**440**
7	Kouassi	5	0	**450**
8	Drouin	1	0	**469**
9	Amzine	5	0	**507**
10	Paisley	2	0	**530**
11	Nivet	6	0	**559**
12	Montero	4	0	**662**
13	Nade	1	0	**672**
	Other	1	1	
	TOTAL	**64**	**3**	

KEY GOALKEEPER

Ronan Le Crom

Goals Conceded in the League	47	Counting Games League games when player was on pitch for at least 70 minutes	38
Defensive Rating Ave number of mins between League goals conceded while on the pitch	72	Clean Sheets In League games when player was on pitch for at least 70 minutes	6

KEY PLAYERS - DEFENDERS

Alexandre Dujeux

Goals Conceded Number of League goals conceded while the player was on the pitch	18	Clean Sheets In League games when player was on pitch for at least 70 minutes	3
Defensive Rating Ave number of mins between League goals conceded while on the pitch	82	Club Defensive Rating Average number of mins between League goals conceded by the club this season	71

	PLAYER	CON LGE	CLEAN SHEETS	DEF RATE
1	Alexandre Dujeux	18	3	82 mins
2	Gregory Paisley	14	1	76 mins
3	Jean-Louis Montero	35	6	76 mins
4	Blaise Kouassi	30	5	75 mins

KEY PLAYERS - MIDFIELDERS

Benjamin Nivet

Goals in the League	6	Contribution to Attacking Power Average number of minutes between League team goals while on pitch	91
Defensive Rating Average number of mins between League goals conceded while on the pitch	71	Scoring Difference Defensive Rating minus Contribution to Attacking Power	-20

	PLAYER	LGE GOALS	DEF RATE	POWER	SCORE DIFF
1	Benjamin Nivet	6	71	91	-20 mins
2	Blaise Matuidi	0	74	97	-23 mins
3	Gharib Amzine	1	67	94	-27 mins
4	Carl Tourenne	2	69	98	-29 mins

KEY PLAYERS - GOALSCORERS

Sebastien Grax

Goals in the League	9	Player Strike Rate Average number of minutes between League goals scored by player	196
Contribution to Attacking Power Average number of minutes between League team goals while on pitch	77	Club Strike Rate Average number of minutes between League goals scored by club	92

	PLAYER	LGE GOALS	POWER	STRIKE RATE
1	Sebastien Grax	9	77	196 mins
2	Sebastien Dallet	5	81	372 mins
3	Benjamin Nivet	6	91	560 mins
4	Carl Tourenne	2	98	1178 mins

Troyes' Sebastien Dallet

SQUAD APPEARANCES

Match	1	2	3	4	5	6	7	8	9	10	11	12	13	14	15	16	17	18	19	20	21	22	23	24	25	26	27	28	29	30	31	32	33	34	35	36	37	38
Venue	A	H	A	H	A	H	A	H	A	H	A	H	A	H	A	H	A	A	H	A	H	A	H	H	A	A	H	A	H	A	H	A	H	A	H	H	A	H
Competition	L	L	L	L	L	L	L	L	L	L	L	L	L	L	L	L	L	L	L	L	L	L	L	L	L	L	L	L	L	L	L	L	L	L	L	L	L	L
Result	D	D	W	D	L	W	L	L	L	D	L	D	L	W	L	D	W	L	W	D	W	L	L	L	D	D	L	L	D	L	D	L	L	W	W	W	D	L

Goalkeepers
Ronan Le Crom
Quentin Westberg

Defenders
Frederic Adam
Florian Boucansaud
Stephen Drouin
Alexandre Dujeux
Ibrahima Faye
Auriol Guillaume
Blaise Kouassi
Jean-Louis Montero
Gregory Paisley

Midfielders
Gharib Amzine
Branko Boskovic
Gael Danic
Cedric Faivre
Blaise Matuidi
Benjamin Nivet
Carl Tourenne

Forwards
Georges Ba
Ibrahima Bangoura
Sebastien Dallet
Eloge Enza Yamissi
Nicolas Florentin
Sebastien Grax
Ziad Jaziri
Christian Nade
Ali Zitouni

KEY: On all match | On bench | Subbed or sent off (Counting game) | Subbed or sent off (playing less than 70 minutes) | Subbed on from bench (Counting Game) | Subbed on (playing less than 70 minutes) | Subbed on and then subbed or sent off (Counting Game) | Subbed on and then subbed or sent off (playing less than 70 minutes) | Not in 16

AC AJACCIO

Final Position: **18th**

KEY: Won / Drawn / Lost

#	Comp	Opponent	Venue	Result	Score	Scorers	Attendance
1	frpr1	St Etienne	A	D	0-0		25,928
2	frpr1	Lille	H	D	3-3	Rocchi 12; Lucas Pereira 27; Saifi 65	5,000
3	frpr1	Nantes	A	W	2-0	Edson 55; Rocchi 72	31,500
4	frpr1	Le Mans	H	D	0-0		27,000
5	frpr1	Marseille	A	D	1-1	Saifi 87 pen	50,000
6	frpr1	Nancy	H	W	1-0	Lucas Pereira 8	6,500
7	frpr1	Auxerre	A	L	0-2		5,000
8	frpr1	Strasbourg	H	D	0-0		5,000
9	frpr1	Bordeaux	A	L	0-1		19,400
10	frpr1	Lyon	A	L	2-3	Diawara 34 pen; Edson 53	36,347
11	frpr1	Rennes	H	L	0-1		3,500
12	frpr1	AS Monaco	A	L	0-3		6,000
13	frpr1	Metz	A	L	0-2		12,592
14	frpr1	Lens	H	D	0-0		4,000
15	frpr1	Sochaux	H	L	0-1		5,000
16	frpr1	Toulouse	A	L	0-3		14,000
17	frpr1	Troyes	H	L	0-1		3,500
18	frpr1	Nice	A	L	0-1		9,627
19	frpr1	Paris SG	H	D	1-1	Rocchi 43	4,500
20	frpr1	Lille	A	L	0-2		11,000
21	frpr1	Nantes	H	L	0-2		3,000
22	frpr1	Le Mans	A	L	0-1		8,611
23	frpr1	Marseille	H	W	3-1	Lucas Pereira 11; Edson 56; N'Diaye 89	5,500
24	frpr1	Nancy	A	D	0-0		12,500
25	frpr1	Auxerre	H	W	1-0	N'Diaye 81	5,000
26	frpr1	Strasbourg	A	D	2-2	N'Diaye 57,62	15,000
27	frpr1	Bordeaux	H	L	0-2		3,500
28	frpr1	Lens	A	L	0-1		36,482
29	frpr1	Lyon	H	L	1-3	Lucas Pereira 83	4,000
30	frpr1	Rennes	A	L	0-3		22,063
31	frpr1	AS Monaco	H	W	1-0	N'Diaye 12	4,000
32	frpr1	Metz	H	L	0-1		3,000
33	frpr1	Sochaux	A	L	1-3	Carlos 63	17,288
34	frpr1	Toulouse	H	W	1-0	Diawara 65	5,000
35	frpr1	Troyes	A	L	0-3		19,825
36	frpr1	Nice	H	L	0-3		2,000
37	frpr1	Paris SG	A	W	4-2	Chafni 20,59; Abnoun 56; Scarpelli 90	41,000
38	frpr1	St Etienne	H	W	3-1	Abnoun 21; Scarpelli 23,26	4,000

LEAGUE APPEARANCES, BOOKINGS AND CAPS

	AGE (on 01/07/06)	IN NAMED 18	APPEARANCES	COUNTING GAMES	MINUTES ON PITCH	YELLOW CARDS	RED CARDS	CAPS THIS SEASON	NATIONAL SIDE
Goalkeepers									
Florian Lucchini	25	4	1	0	35	0	0	-	France
Stephane Porato	32	35	31	29	2711	0	1	-	France
Stephane Trevisan	32	35	8	7	675	1	0	-	France
Defenders									
Anthony Baron	20	4	1	1	90	0	0	-	France
Antonio Carlos	23	28	21	17	1727	2	0	-	Brazil
Xavier Collin	31	36	36	34	3075	5	0	-	France
Frederic Danjou	31	27	22	19	1849	6	0	-	France
Nenad Dzodic	29	14	13	12	1097	2	0	-	Serbia & Mont
Daouda Jabi	25	32	31	29	2668	2	0	-	France
Fabien Laurenti	23	30	30	28	2596	4	0	-	France
J-Toussaint Moretti	26	1	0	0	0	0	0	-	France
Midfielders									
Djamel Abnoun	20	11	7	2	297	0	0	-	France
Andre Luiz	32	25	25	16	1828	2	0	-	Brazil
Christophe Bastien	30	15	9	0	230	1	0	-	France
Kamel Chafni	24	34	34	29	2697	7	0	-	France
Edson	26	27	25	12	1475	4	0	-	Brazil
Azite Franklin	20	1	1	0	5	0	0	-	France
Laurent Merlin	21	3	1	0	1	0	0	-	France
Martial Robin	28	29	23	14	1517	5	0	-	France
Romain Rocchi	24	27	26	18	1977	2	0	-	France
Ramos Rodrigo	25	36	34	34	3030	8	1	-	Brazil
Mathieu Scarpelli	24	19	11	3	483	2	0	-	France
Stephane Ziani	33	8	7	5	532	0	0	-	France
Forwards									
Xavier Becas	27	3	1	0	1	0	0	-	France
Kaba Diawara	30	22	20	9	1270	1	0	-	France
Lucas Pereira	24	32	29	15	1808	5	0	-	Brazil
Christophe Mandrichi	22	21	16	4	600	0	0	-	France
Moussa N'Diaye	27	17	17	17	1523	1	0	-	Senegal
Rafik Saifi	31	27	27	16	1762	3	0	2	Algeria (66)

TEAM OF THE SEASON

G — Stephane Porato, CG: 29 DR: 71

D — Fabien Laurenti, CG: 28 DR: 70

D — Xavier Collin, CG: 34 DR: 68

D — Daouda Jabi, CG: 29 DR: 67

D — Antonio Carlos, CG: 17 DR: 62

M — Martial Robin, CG: 14 SD: -35

M — Edson, CG: 12 SD: -43

M — Kamel Chafni, CG: 29 SD: -45

M — Lacerda Rodrigo, CG: 34 SD: -55

F — Moussa N'Diaye, CG: 17 SR: 305

F — Lucas Pereira, CG: 15 SR: 452

MONTHLY POINTS TALLY

AUGUST	6	50%
SEPTEMBER	4	33%
OCTOBER	0	0%
NOVEMBER	1	8%
DECEMBER	1	11%
JANUARY	4	27%
FEBRUARY	4	33%
MARCH	3	25%
APRIL	3	25%
MAY	6	100%

LEAGUE GOALS

	PLAYER	MINS	GOALS	S RATE
1	N'Diaye	1523	5	305
2	Lucas Pereira	1808	4	452
3	Scarpelli	483	3	161
4	Edson	1475	3	492
5	Rocchi	1977	3	659
6	Diawara	1270	2	635
7	Saifi	1762	2	881
8	Abnoun	297	2	149
9	Chafni	2697	2	1349
10	Carlos	1727	1	1727
	Other		0	
	TOTAL		27	

TOP POINT EARNERS

	PLAYER	GAMES	AV PTS
1	Laurenti	28	1.04
2	Chafni	29	0.97
3	Saifi	16	0.94
4	Collin	34	0.94
5	Edson	12	0.92
6	Rocchi	18	0.89
7	Danjou	19	0.89
8	Andre Luiz	16	0.88
9	Lucas Pereira	15	0.87
10	Robin	14	0.86
	CLUB AVERAGE:		0.87

DISCIPLINARY RECORDS

	PLAYER	YELLOW	RED	AVE
1	Scarpelli	2	0	241
2	Robin	5	0	303
3	Danjou	6	0	308
4	Rodrigo	8	1	336
5	Lucas Pereira	5	0	361
6	Edson	4	0	368
7	Chafni	7	0	385
8	Dzodic	2	0	548
9	Saifi	3	0	587
10	Collin	5	0	615
11	Laurenti	4	0	649
12	Trevisan	1	0	675
13	Carlos	2	0	863
	Other	8	1	
	TOTAL	62	2	

KEY GOALKEEPER

Stephane Porato

Goals Conceded in the League	38	Counting Games League games when player was on pitch for at least 70 minutes	29
Defensive Rating Ave number of mins between League goals conceded while on the pitch	71	Clean Sheets In games when player was on pitch for at least 70 minutes	9

KEY PLAYERS - DEFENDERS

Fabien Laurenti

Goals Conceded Number of League goals conceded while the player was on the pitch	37	Clean Sheets In League games when player was on pitch for at least 70 minutes	9
Defensive Rating Ave number of mins between League goals conceded while on the pitch	70	Club Defensive Rating Average number of mins between League goals conceded by the club this season	65

	PLAYER	CON LGE	CLEAN SHEETS	DEF RATE
1	Fabien Laurenti	37	9	70 mins
2	Xavier Collin	45	10	68 mins
3	Daouda Jabi	40	8	67 mins
4	Antonio Carlos	28	5	62 mins

KEY PLAYERS - MIDFIELDERS

Martial Robin

Goals in the League	0	Contribution to Attacking Power Average number of minutes between League team goals while on pitch	89
Defensive Rating Average number of mins between League goals conceded while on the pitch	54	Scoring Difference Defensive Rating minus Contribution to Attacking Power	-35

	PLAYER	LGE GOALS	DEF RATE	POWER	SCORE DIFF
1	Martial Robin	0	54	89	-35 mins
2	Edson	3	105	148	-43 mins
3	Kamel Chafni	2	63	108	-45 mins
4	Lacerda Ramos Rodrigo	0	66	121	-55 mins

KEY PLAYERS - GOALSCORERS

Moussa N'Diaye

Goals in the League	5	Player Strike Rate Average number of minutes between League goals scored by player	305
Contribution to Attacking Power Average number of minutes between League team goals while on pitch	152	Club Strike Rate Average number of minutes between League goals scored by club	127

	PLAYER	LGE GOALS	POWER	STRIKE RATE
1	Moussa N'Diaye	5	152	305 mins
2	Lucas Pereira	4	113	452 mins
3	Edson	3	148	492 mins
4	Romain Rocchi	3	132	659 mins

Ajaccio's Moussa N'Diaye

SQUAD APPEARANCES

Match	1	2	3	4	5	6	7	8	9	10	11	12	13	14	15	16	17	18	19	20	21	22	23	24	25	26	27	28	29	30	31	32	33	34	35	36	37	38
Venue	A	H	A	H	A	H	A	H	A	A	H	A	A	H	H	A	H	A	H	A	H	A	H	A	H	A	H	A	H	A	H	H	A	H	A	H	A	H
Competition	L	L	L	L	L	L	L	L	L	L	L	L	L	L	L	L	L	L	L	L	L	L	L	L	L	L	L	L	L	L	L	L	L	L	L	L	L	L
Result	D	D	W	D	D	W	L	D	L	L	L	L	L	D	L	L	L	L	D	L	L	L	W	D	W	D	L	L	L	L	W	L	L	W	L	L	W	W

Goalkeepers
Florian Lucchini
Stephane Porato
Stephane Trevisan

Defenders
Anthony Baron
Antonio Carlos
Xavier Collin
Frederic Danjou
Nenad Dzodic
Daouda Jabi
Fabien Laurenti
Jean-Toussaint Moretti

Midfielders
Djamel Abnoun
Andre Luiz
Christophe Bastien
Kamel Chafni
Edson
Azite Franklin
Laurent Merlin
Martial Robin
Romain Rocchi
Lacerda Ramos Rodrigo
Mathieu Scarpelli
Stephane Ziani

Forwards
Xavier Becas
Kaba Diawara
Lucas Pereira
Christophe Mandrichi
Moussa N'Diaye
Rafik Saifi

KEY: On all match · On bench · Subbed or sent off (Counting game) · Subbed or sent off (playing less than 70 minutes) · Subbed on from bench (Counting Game) · Subbed on (playing less than 70 minutes) · Subbed on and then subbed or sent off (Counting Game) · Subbed on and then subbed or sent off (playing less than 70 minutes) · Not in 16

STRASBOURG

Final Position: **19th**

KEY: ☐Won ☐Drawn ☐Lost

	Comp	Opponent	Venue	Result	Score	Scorers	Attendance
1	frpr1	**Auxerre**	H	D	0-0		18,224
2	frpr1	**Lyon**	A	L	0-1		30,000
3	frpr1	**AS Monaco**	H	L	1-2	Le Pen 91	20,000
4	frpr1	**Metz**	A	D	0-0		19,626
5	frpr1	**Bordeaux**	H	D	0-0		20,411
6	frpr1	**Paris SG**	A	L	0-1		40,748
7	uc1rl1	**Liebherr GAK**	A	W	2-0	Pagis 1; Lacour 45	8,000
8	frpr1	**Lens**	H	D	1-1	Pagis 61 pen	18,321
9	frpr1	**AC Ajaccio**	A	D	0-0		5,000
10	frpr1	**Toulouse**	H	L	2-4	Haggui 5,40	15,000
11	uc1rl2	**Liebherr GAK**	H	W	5-0	Haggui 6; Farnerud, A 40; Farnerud, P 51; Le Pen 59; Hosni 68	4,184
12	frpr1	**Troyes**	A	D	1-1	Farnerud, A 42	10,000
13	frpr1	**Rennes**	H	L	0-1		15,000
14	ucgpe	**Basel**	A	W	2-0	Diane 15; Boka 25	21,900
15	frpr1	**Le Mans**	A	L	0-2		10,337
16	frpr1	**St Etienne**	H	L	0-1		23,212
17	ucgpe	**Tromso**	H	W	2-0	Pagis 38; Arrache 67	8,516
18	frpr1	**Lille**	A	L	0-2		13,360
19	frpr1	**Nice**	H	D	0-0		14,966
20	ucgpe	**Roma**	A	D	1-1	Bellaid 51	8,500
21	frpr1	**Nantes**	A	L	3-4	Pagis 38 pen,49; Diane 45	26,000
22	frpr1	**Sochaux**	H	D	0-0		20,000
23	frpr1	**Nancy**	A	W	2-1	Pagis 37 pen; Diane 53	17,000
24	ucgpe	**Crvena Zvezda**	H	D	2-2	Gameiro 79,90	13,416
25	frpr1	**Marseille**	H	L	0-1		27,786
26	frpr1	**Lyon**	H	L	0-4		19,735
27	frpr1	**AS Monaco**	A	D	1-1	Kante 74	8,000
28	frpr1	**Metz**	H	W	2-1	Le Pen 11 pen; Johansen 36	15,000
29	frpr1	**Bordeaux**	A	L	1-2	Le Pen 10 pen	18,208
30	frpr1	**Lens**	A	L	1-2	Gameiro 51	30,922
31	frpr1	**Paris SG**	H	D	1-1	Diane 13	16,000
32	frpr1	**AC Ajaccio**	H	D	2-2	Farnerud, A 2; Diane 59	15,000
33	uc3rl1	**Liteks Lovetch**	A	W	2-0	Le Pen 2; Diane 82	3,000
34	frpr1	**Toulouse**	A	W	2-1	Farnerud, P 5; Abdessadki 60	16,883
35	uc3rl2	**Liteks Lovetch**	H	D	0-0		9,610
36	frpr1	**Troyes**	H	W	2-0	Diane 13; Abdessadki 87	20,000
37	frpr1	**Rennes**	A	L	1-2	Kante 79	23,172
38	uc4rl1	**Basel**	A	L	0-2		22,000
39	frpr1	**Le Mans**	H	L	1-2	Diane 18	1,780
40	uc4rl2	**Basel**	H	D	2-2	Carlier 11; Kante 78	8,115
41	frpr1	**St Etienne**	A	W	2-0	Diane 61; Farnerud, P 76	25,566
42	frpr1	**Lille**	H	D	2-2	Farnerud, A 30; Diane 90	22,000
43	frpr1	**Nice**	A	L	1-3	Johansen 73 pen	9,913
44	frpr1	**Nantes**	H	L	0-1		20,085
45	frpr1	**Sochaux**	A	D	1-1	Farnerud, P 86	16,876
46	frpr1	**Nancy**	H	L	1-3	Diane 16	19,072
47	frpr1	**Marseille**	A	D	2-2	Abdessadki 51; Carlier 67	57,680
48	frpr1	**Auxerre**	A	L	0-4		10,000

LEAGUE APPEARANCES, BOOKINGS AND CAPS

	AGE (on 01/07/06)	IN NAMED 18	APPEARANCES	COUNTING GAMES	MINUTES ON PITCH	YELLOW CARDS	RED CARDS	CAPS THIS SEASON	NATIONAL SIDE
Goalkeepers									
Stephane Cassard	33	32	23	23	2069	1	0	-	France
Regis Gurtner	19	6	0	0	0	0	0	-	France
Nicolas Puydebois	25	36	15	15	1351	1	0	-	France
Defenders									
Habib Bellaid	20	21	15	11	1087	3	0	-	France
Arthur Boka	23	29	27	20	1935	7	1	10	Ivory Coast (32)
Steve Celestini	19	0	0	0	0	0	0	-	France
Jean-C Devaux	31	22	20	13	1382	1	0	-	France
Ricardo Faty	19	11	7	2	329	0	0	-	France
Edgard Gnobela Loue	22	9	8	7	676	1	0	-	Ivory Coast
Karim Haggui	22	25	24	23	2116	1	0	-	Tunisia
Cedric Kante	26	31	30	29	2644	5	0	-	France
Ahmed Farag	24	12	10	7	788	1	1	-	Egypt
Yann Schneider	20	7	4	2	250	3	0	-	France
Jean-C Vergerolle	20	2	1	1	91	0	0	-	France
Midfielders									
Yassine Abdessadki	25	13	13	12	1113	3	0	-	France
Ahmed M Abou	-	4	3	1	170	0	0	-	
Christian Bassila	28	1	1	0	44	0	0	-	France
Yves Deroff	27	35	29	23	2258	9	1	-	France
Alexander Farnerud	22	34	32	18	2120	1	0	-	Sweden
Pontus Farnerud	26	31	29	21	2035	2	1	-	Sweden
Abd Rabo Hosni	21	22	22	19	1800	4	1	-	Egypt
Sidi Yaya Keita	21	12	12	8	874	1	0	-	Mali
Gaetan Krebs	20	7	2	1	92	0	0	-	France
Guillaume Lacour	25	27	27	25	2321	2	0	-	France
Ulrich Le Pen	32	27	25	17	1716	3	0	-	France
Forwards									
Salim Arrache	23	15	13	7	707	0	0	-	France
Rudy Carlier	20	18	11	3	435	0	0	-	France
Amara Diane	23	35	34	21	2396	2	0	-	Ivory Coast
Kevin Gameiro	19	11	8	2	406	0	0	-	France
Haykel Gumemdia	24	14	13	4	620	0	0	7	Tunisia (21)
Pascal Johansen	27	27	26	21	1981	5	0	-	France
Eric Mouloungui	22	2	2	0	34	0	0	-	Gabon
Szilard Nemeth	27	12	7	2	297	0	0	-	Hungary
Michael Pagis	32	16	16	14	1352	2	1	-	France

TEAM OF THE SEASON

G — Stephane Cassard, CG: 23 DR: 61

D — Arthur Boka, CG: 20 DR: 67

D — Karim Haggui, CG: 23 DR: 64

D — Cedric Kante, CG: 29 DR: 63

D — J Devaux, CG: 13 DR: 51

M — Yassine Abdessadki, CG: 12 SD: -18

M — Pontus Farnerud, CG: 21 SD: -18

M — Alexander Farnerud, CG: 18 SD: -33

M — Ulrich Le Pen, CG: 17 SD: -48

F — Amara Diane, CG: 21 SR: 266

F — Michael Pagis, CG: 13 SR: 316

MONTHLY POINTS TALLY

AUGUST	2	17%
SEPTEMBER	2	17%
OCTOBER	1	8%
NOVEMBER	1	11%
DECEMBER	4	44%
JANUARY	4	33%
FEBRUARY	8	53%
MARCH	4	33%
APRIL	1	8%
MAY	1	17%

LEAGUE GOALS

	PLAYER	MINS	GOALS	S RATE
1	Diane	2396	9	266
2	Pagis	1262	4	316
3	Farnerud, A	2120	3	707
4	Farnerud, P	2035	3	678
5	Abdessadki	1113	3	371
6	Le Pen	1716	3	572
7	Haggui	2116	2	1058
8	Kante	2644	2	1322
9	Johansen	1981	2	991
10	Gameiro	406	1	406
11	Carlier	435	1	435
	Other		0	
	TOTAL		33	

TOP POINT EARNERS

	PLAYER	GAMES	AV PTS
1	Puydebois	15	1.13
2	Abdessadki	12	1.08
3	Farnerud, A	18	0.94
4	Le Pen	17	0.94
5	Diane	21	0.86
6	Farnerud, P	21	0.81
7	Johansen	21	0.81
8	Kante	29	0.79
9	Haggui	23	0.74
10	Lacour	25	0.72
	CLUB AVERAGE:		0.76

DISCIPLINARY RECORDS

	PLAYER	YELLOW	RED	AVE
1	Deroff	9	1	225
2	Boka	7	1	241
3	Hosni	4	1	360
4	Bellaid	3	0	362
5	Abdessadki	3	0	371
6	Moslem Farag	1	1	394
7	Johansen	5	0	396
8	Pagis	2	1	420
9	Kante	5	0	528
10	Le Pen	3	0	572
11	Farnerud, P	2	1	678
12	Keita	1	0	874
13	Lacour	2	0	1160
	Other	7	0	
	TOTAL	54	6	

KEY GOALKEEPER

Stephane Cassard

Goals Conceded in the League	34	**Counting Games** League games when player was on pitch for at least 70 minutes	23
Defensive Rating Ave number of mins between League goals conceded while on the pitch	61	**Clean Sheets** In games when player was on pitch for at least 70 minutes	4

KEY PLAYERS - DEFENDERS

Arthur Boka

Goals Conceded Number of League goals conceded while the player was on the pitch	29	**Clean Sheets** In League games when player was on pitch for at least 70 minutes	5
Defensive Rating Ave number of mins between League goals conceded while on the pitch	67	**Club Defensive Rating** Average number of mins between League goals conceded by the club this season	61

	PLAYER	CON LGE	CLEAN SHEETS	DEF RATE
1	Arthur Boka	29	5	67 mins
2	Karim Haggui	33	6	64 mins
3	Cedric Kante	42	5	63 mins
4	Jean-Christophe Devaux	27	1	51 mins

KEY PLAYERS - MIDFIELDERS

Yassine Abdessadki

Goals in the League	3	**Contribution to Attacking Power** Average number of minutes between League team goals while on pitch	74
Defensive Rating Average number of mins between League goals conceded while on the pitch	56	**Scoring Difference** Defensive Rating minus Contribution to Attacking Power	-18

	PLAYER	LGE GOALS	DEF RATE	POWER	SCORE DIFF
1	Yassine Abdessadki	3	56	74	-18 mins
2	Pontus Farnerud	3	60	78	-18 mins
3	Alexander Farnerud	3	73	106	-33 mins
4	Ulrich Le Pen	3	66	114	-48 mins

KEY PLAYERS - GOALSCORERS

Amara Diane

Goals in the League	9	**Player Strike Rate** Average number of minutes between League goals scored by player	266
Contribution to Attacking Power Average number of minutes between League team goals while on pitch	92	**Club Strike Rate** Average number of minutes between League goals scored by club	104

	PLAYER	LGE GOALS	POWER	STRIKE RATE
1	Amara Diane	9	92	266 mins
2	Michael Pagis	4	158	316 mins
3	Yassine Abdessadki	3	74	371 mins
4	Ulrich Le Pen	3	114	572 mins

Strasbourg's Pascal Johansen and Amara Diane

SQUAD APPEARANCES

Match	1	2	3	4	5	6	7	8	9	10	11	12	13	14	15	16	17	18	19	20	21	22	23	24	25
Venue	H	A	H	A	H	A	A	H	A	H	H	A	H	A	A	H	H	A	H	A	A	H	A	H	H
Competition	L	L	L	L	L	L	E	L	L	L	E	L	L	E	L	L	E	L	L	E	L	L	L	E	L
Result	D	L	L	D	D	L	W	D	D	L	W	D	L	W	L	L	W	L	D	D	L	D	W	D	L

Match	26	27	28	29	30	31	32	33	34	35	36	37	38	39	40	41	42	43	44	45	46	47	48
Venue	H	A	H	A	A	H	H	A	A	H	H	A	A	H	H	A	H	A	H	A	H	A	A
Competition	L	L	L	L	L	L	L	E	L	E	L	L	E	L	E	L	L	L	L	L	L	L	L
Result	L	D	W	L	L	D	D	W	W	D	W	L	L	L	D	W	D	L	L	D	L	D	L

Goalkeepers
Stephane Cassard
Regis Gurtner
Nicolas Puydebois

Defenders
Habib Bellaid
Arthur Boka
Steve Celestini
Jean-Christophe Devaux
Ricardo Faty
Edgard Gnobela Loue
Karim Haggui
Cedric Kante
Ahmed A Moslem Farag
Yann Schneider
J Vergerolle

Midfielders
Yassine Abdessadki
Ahmed Moslem Abou
Christian Bassila
Yves Deroff
Alexander Farnerud
Pontus Farnerud
Abd Rabo Hosni
Sidi Yaya Keita
Gaetan Krebs
Guillaume Lacour
Ulrich Le Pen

Forwards
Salim Arrache
Rudy Carlier
Amara Diane
Kevin Gameiro
Haykel Gumemdia
Pascal Johansen
Eric Mouloungui
Szilard Nemeth
Michael Pagis
Mickael Pagis

KEY: On all match · On bench · Subbed or sent off (Counting game) · Subbed or sent off (playing less than 70 minutes) · Subbed on from bench (Counting Game) · Subbed on (playing less than 70 minutes) · Subbed on and then subbed or sent off (Counting Game) · Subbed on and then subbed or sent off (playing less than 70 minutes) · Not in 16

METZ

Final Position: **20th**

KEY: ☐ Won ☐ Drawn ☐ Lost

	Comp	Opponent	H/A	Res	Score	Scorers	Attendance
1	frpr1	Paris SG	A	L	1-4	Ahn 67	43,000
2	frpr1	Le Mans	H	D	0-0		18,130
3	frpr1	St Etienne	A	L	0-2		28,966
4	frpr1	Strasbourg	H	D	0-0		19,626
5	frpr1	Nantes	A	D	0-0		27,532
6	frpr1	Lille	H	L	0-2		18,550
7	frpr1	Nancy	A	D	1-1	Renouard 73	21,840
8	frpr1	Auxerre	H	L	1-2	N'Diaye 90	13,630
9	frpr1	Marseille	A	L	1-3	Renouard 11	48,000
10	frpr1	Bordeaux	H	L	0-1		15,263
11	frpr1	AS Monaco	A	L	0-3		10,000
12	frpr1	Lyon	H	L	0-4		19,333
13	frpr1	Rennes	A	L	1-2	Tum 90	27,600
14	frpr1	AC Ajaccio	H	W	2-0	Gueye 58; Djiba 86	12,592
15	frpr1	Lens	A	D	0-0		31,926
16	frpr1	Troyes	A	D	0-0		10,054
17	frpr1	Toulouse	H	D	2-2	Proment 12 pen,67	12,367
18	frpr1	Sochaux	A	D	1-1	Ahn 9	11,812
19	frpr1	Nice	H	W	1-0	Borbiconi 60	12,186
20	frpr1	Le Mans	A	L	0-2		10,000
21	frpr1	St Etienne	H	L	0-1		12,273
22	frpr1	Strasbourg	A	L	1-2	Tum 87	15,000
23	frpr1	Nantes	H	L	1-4	Proment 26	12,369
24	frpr1	Lille	A	L	1-3	Borbiconi 90	12,104
25	frpr1	Auxerre	A	D	1-1	Obraniak 54	5,000
26	frpr1	Marseille	H	W	1-0	Gueye 87	22,689
27	frpr1	Bordeaux	A	D	3-3	Youla 15; Jemmali 20 og; Contout 43	22,461
28	frpr1	AS Monaco	H	W	2-1	Plasil 71; Tum 81	16,757
29	frpr1	Nancy	H	D	0-0		18,324
30	frpr1	Lyon	A	L	0-4		37,000
31	frpr1	Rennes	H	L	0-1		16,591
32	frpr1	AC Ajaccio	A	W	1-0	Ouadah 71	3,000
33	frpr1	Lens	H	L	0-1		17,957
34	frpr1	Troyes	H	L	2-4	Ouadah 60; Gueye 90	21,027
35	frpr1	Toulouse	A	L	0-2		15,272
36	frpr1	Sochaux	H	L	0-1		6,000
37	frpr1	Nice	A	L	1-2	Agouazi 21	13,000
38	frpr1	Paris SG	H	W	1-0	Huszti 87	15,827

LEAGUE APPEARANCES, BOOKINGS AND CAPS

	AGE (on 01/07/06)	IN NAMED 18	APPEARANCES	COUNTING GAMES	MINUTES ON PITCH	YELLOW CARDS	RED CARDS	CAPS THIS SEASON	NATIONAL SIDE
Goalkeepers									
Kossi Agassa	28	22	1	1	90	0	0	-	Togo
Christophe Marichez	31	18	7	7	630	0	0	-	France
Gregory Wimbee	34	32	30	30	2700	1	0	-	France
Defenders									
Jamal Alioui	24	12	12	8	867	2	0	-	Morocco
Samuel Allegro	28	9	3	2	225	1	0	-	France
Sebastien Bassong	29	33	24	15	1663	1	0	-	France
Franck Beria	23	33	32	28	2614	5	0	-	France
Gaetan Bong	18	5	3	2	225	1	0	-	Cameroon
Stephane Borbiconi	27	38	38	38	3420	0	0	-	France
Jin-Ouk Kang	20	6	4	1	117	0	0	-	South Korea
Sylvain Marchal	26	2	2	2	180	1	0	-	France
Carl Medjani	21	24	22	20	1837	1	0	-	France
Mehdi Meniri	29	23	21	18	1714	7	2	-	France
Stephane Morisot	28	10	5	3	338	2	0	-	France
Gregory Paisley	29	10	8	6	616	3	0	-	France
Midfielders									
Laurent Agouazi	22	9	8	5	533	1	0	-	France
Mamadou Diakite	21	1	1	1	70	1	0	-	France
Dino Djiba	20	15	15	9	1088	1	0	-	Senegal
Szabolcs Huszti	23	22	18	9	1165	6	0	6	Hungary (54)
Gregory Leca	25	3	2	1	91	0	0	-	France
Hemza Mihoubi	20	11	11	11	983	4	0	-	France
Ludovic Obraniak	21	31	31	30	2729	4	1	-	France
Abdelnasser Ouadah	30	28	28	24	2224	5	0	-	France
Gregory Proment	27	35	35	34	3063	6	1	-	France
Sebastien Renouard	22	14	14	3	590	0	0	-	France
Venn Toure	22	1	1	0	54	0	0	-	France
Forwards									
Jung Hwan Ahn	30	16	16	9	1012	1	0	-	South Korea
Mamam Cherif Toure	24	11	9	1	413	2	0	-	Togo
Roy Contout	21	22	17	6	818	3	0	-	France
Babacar Gueye	20	24	21	5	818	0	0	-	Senegal
Momar N'Diaye	18	14	12	5	622	0	0	-	Senegal
Rouslan Pimenov	24	9	8	6	550	0	0	-	Russia
Herve Tum	27	22	21	15	1601	1	0	-	Cameroon
Souleymane Youla	44	16	15	14	1261	1	0	1	Guinea (123)
Marcin Zewlakow	30	16	12	1	469	0	0	-	Poland

TEAM OF THE SEASON

G — Gregory Wimbee CG: 30 DR: 55

D — Sebastien Bassong CG: 15 DR: 62

D — Franck Beria CG: 28 DR: 61

D — Stephane Borbiconi CG: 38 DR: 58

D — Carl Medjani CG: 20 DR: 57

M — Abdelnasser Ouadah CG: 24 SD: -92

M — Gregory Proment CG: 34 SD: -95

M — Ludovic Obraniak CG: 30 SD: -100

M — Hemza Mihoubi* CG: 11 SD: -51

F — Herve Tum CG: 15 SR: 534

F — Souleymane Youla CG: 14 SR: 1261

MONTHLY POINTS TALLY

AUGUST	3	25%
SEPTEMBER	1	8%
OCTOBER	0	0%
NOVEMBER	5	56%
DECEMBER	5	56%
JANUARY	0	0%
FEBRUARY	5	56%
MARCH	7	47%
APRIL	0	0%
MAY	3	50%

LEAGUE GOALS

	PLAYER	MINS	GOALS	S RATE
1	Proment	3063	3	1021
2	Gueye	818	3	273
3	Tum	1601	3	534
4	Borbiconi	3420	2	1710
5	Renouard	590	2	295
6	Ouadah	2224	2	1112
7	Ahn	1012	2	506
8	Youla	1261	1	1261
9	Contout	818	1	818
10	Obraniak	2729	1	2729
11	Djiba	1088	1	1088
12	N'Diaye	622	1	622
13	Huszti	1165	1	1165
	Other		3	
	TOTAL		26	

TOP POINT EARNERS

	PLAYER	GAMES	AV PTS
1	Tum	15	0.93
2	Ouadah	24	0.88
3	Youla	14	0.86
4	Beria	28	0.86
5	Meniri	18	0.83
6	Bassong	15	0.80
7	Obraniak	30	0.80
8	Borbiconi	38	0.76
9	Medjani	20	0.70
10	Proment	34	0.68
	CLUB AVERAGE:		0.76

DISCIPLINARY RECORDS

	PLAYER	YELLOW	RED	AVE
1	Meniri	7	2	190
2	Huszti	6	0	194
3	Paisley	3	0	205
4	Mihoubi	4	0	245
5	Contout	3	0	272
6	Alioui	2	0	433
7	Proment	6	1	437
8	Ouadah	5	0	444
9	Beria	5	0	522
10	Agouazi	1	0	533
11	Obraniak	4	1	545
12	Ahn	1	0	1012
13	Djiba	1	0	1088
	Other	5	0	
	TOTAL	53	4	

KEY GOALKEEPER

Gregory Wimbee

Goals Conceded in the League	49	Counting Games League games when player was on pitch for at least 70 minutes	30
Defensive Rating Ave number of mins between League goals conceded while on the pitch	55	Clean Sheets In League games when player was on pitch for at least 70 minutes	8

KEY PLAYERS - DEFENDERS

Sebastien Bassong

Goals Conceded Number of League goals conceded while the player was on the pitch	27	Clean Sheets In League games when player was on pitch for at least 70 minutes	4
Defensive Rating Ave number of mins between League goals conceded while on the pitch	62	Club Defensive Rating Average number of mins between League goals conceded by the club this season	58

	PLAYER	CON LGE	CLEAN SHEETS	DEF RATE
1	Sebastien Bassong	27	4	62 mins
2	Franck Beria	43	10	61 mins
3	Stephane Borbiconi	59	11	58 mins
4	Carl Medjani	32	5	57 mins

KEY PLAYERS - MIDFIELDERS

Abdelnasser Ouadah

Goals in the League	2	Contribution to Attacking Power Average number of minutes between League team goals while on pitch	159
Defensive Rating Average number of mins between League goals conceded while on the pitch	67	Scoring Difference Defensive Rating minus Contribution to Attacking Power	-92

	PLAYER	LGE GOALS	DEF RATE	POWER	SCORE DIFF
1	Abdelnasser Ouadah	2	67	159	-92 mins
2	Gregory Proment	3	58	153	-95 mins
3	Ludovic Obraniak	1	61	161	-100 mins

KEY PLAYERS - GOALSCORERS

Herve Tum

Goals in the League	3	Player Strike Rate Average number of minutes between League goals scored by player	534
Contribution to Attacking Power Average number of minutes between League team goals while on pitch	123	Club Strike Rate Average number of minutes between League goals scored by club	132

	PLAYER	LGE GOALS	POWER	STRIKE RATE
1	Herve Tum	3	123	534 mins
2	Gregory Proment	3	153	1021 mins
3	Abdelnasser Ouadah	2	159	1112 mins
4	Souleymane Youla	1	115	1261 mins

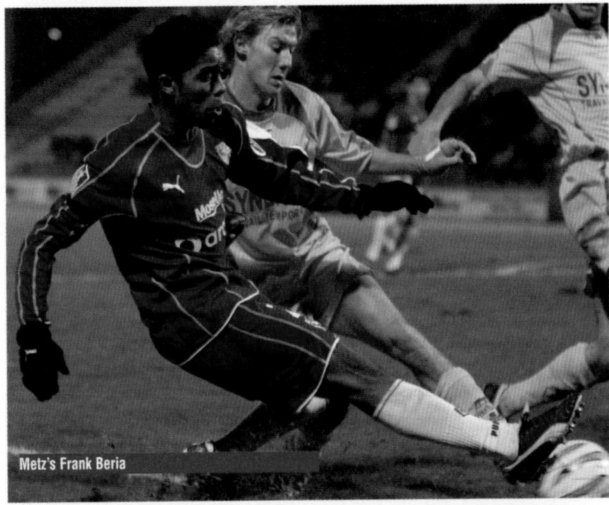
Metz's Frank Beria

SQUAD APPEARANCES

Match	1	2	3	4	5	6	7	8	9	10	11	12	13	14	15	16	17	18	19
Venue	A	H	A	H	A	H	A	H	A	H	A	H	A	H	A	A	H	A	H
Competition	L	L	L	L	L	L	L	L	L	L	L	L	L	L	L	L	L	L	L
Result	L	D	L	D	D	L	D	L	L	L	L	L	L	W	D	D	D	D	W

Match	20	21	22	23	24	25	26	27	28	29	30	31	32	33	34	35	36	37	38
Venue	A	H	A	H	A	A	H	A	H	H	A	H	A	H	H	A	H	A	H
Competition	L	L	L	L	L	L	L	L	L	L	L	L	L	L	L	L	L	L	L
Result	L	L	L	L	L	D	W	D	W	D	L	L	W	L	L	L	L	L	W

Goalkeepers
Kossi Agassa
Christophe Marichez
Gregory Wimbee

Defenders
Jamal Alioui
Samuel Allegro
Sebastien Bassong
Franck Beria
Gaetan Bong
Stephane Borbiconi
Jin-Ouk Kang
Sylvain Marchal
Carl Medjani
Mehdi Meniri
Stephane Morisot
Gregory Paisley

Midfielders
Laurent Agouazi
Mamadou Diakite
Dino Djiba
Szabolcs Huszti
Gregory Leca
Hemza Mihoubi
Ludovic Obraniak
Abdelnasser Ouadah
Gregory Proment
Sebastien Renouard
Venn Toure

Forwards
Jung Hwan Ahn
Mamam Cherif Toure
Roy Contout
Babacar Gueye
Momar N'Diaye
Rouslan Pimenov
Herve Tum
Souleymane Youla
Marcin Zewlakow

KEY: On all match
On bench
Subbed or sent off (Counting game)
Subbed or sent off (playing less than 70 minutes)
Subbed on from bench (Counting Game)
Subbed on (playing less than 70 minutes)
Subbed on and then subbed or sent off (Counting Game)
Subbed on and then subbed or sent off (playing less than 70 minutes)
Not in 16

THE CHAMPIONS LEAGUE

GROUP A

QUALIFYING

Dudelange (1) 1 Rapid Vienna (4) 6
Rapid Vienna (1) 3 Dudelange (2) 2

Rapid Vienna (0) 1 L Moscow (1) 1
L Moscow (0) 0 Rapid Vienna (0) 1

Valerenga (0) 1 Club Brugge (0) 0
Club Brugge (0) 1 Valerenga (0) 0
Club Brugge win 4-3 on penalties

Club Brugge (0) 1 Juventus (0) 2
Matondo 85 — Nedved 66
28,000 — Trezeguet 75

Rapid Vienna (0) 0 Bayern Munich (0) 1
47,000 — Guerrero 60

Bayern Munich (1) 1 Club Brugge (0) 0
Demichelis 32 — 65,527

Juventus (1) 3 Rapid Vienna (0) 0
Trezeguet 27, Mutu 82 — 49,521
Ibrahimovic 85

Bayern Munich (2) 2 Juventus (0) 1
Deisler 32 — Ibrahimovic 90
Demichelis 39 — 60,000

Bayern go top after the first meeting of the two Group A giants. Sebastian Deisler surprises Christian Abbiati with a shot from the right wing before crossing for Martin Demichelis to make it 2-0 before halftime

Rapid Vienna (0) 0 Club Brugge (0) 1
45,000 — Balaban 75

Club Brugge (2) 3 Rapid Vienna (1) 2
Portillo 9 — Kincl 1, Hofmann 81
Balaban 25, Verheyen 63 — 26,000

Juventus (0) 2 Bayern Munich (0) 1
Trezeguet 62,85 — Deisler 66
19,000

Bayern Munich (1) 4 Rapid Vienna (0) 0
Deisler 21, Karimi 54 — 66,000
Makaay 72,77

Juventus (0) 1 Club Brugge (0) 0
Del Piero 80 — 35,000

Club Brugge (1) 1 Bayern Munich (1) 1
Portillo 32 — Pizarro 21
27,860

Rapid Vienna (0) 1 Juventus (3) 3
Kincl 52 — Del Piero 35,45
46,500 — Ibrahimovic 42

Rapid Vienna and Club Brugge are left battling for a Uefa Cup spot from the off as Juventus and Bayern both take six points from their first two games. A scrappy far-post strike by Bosko Balaban gives Brugge a win in Austria and the Belgian club recover from a first-minute goal by Marek Kincl, to win the return game by the odd goal in five

GROUP A TABLE

	P	W	D	L	DIF	PTS
Juventus	6	5	0	1	7	15
Bayern	6	4	1	1	6	13
Club Brugge	6	2	1	3	-1	7
Rapid Vienna	6	0	0	6	-12	0

GROUP B

QUALIFYING

Dynamo Kiev (2) 2 FC Thun (1) 2
FC Thun (0) 1 Dynamo Kiev (0) 0

Malmo (0) 0 FC Thun (1) 1
FC Thun (2) 3 Malmo (0) 0

Brondby (1) 2 Ajax (1) 2
Ajax (0) 3 Brondby (1) 1

Arsenal (0) 2 FC Thun (0) 1
Gilberto Silva 51 — Ferreira 53
Bergkamp 90 — 34,498

Sparta Prague (0) 1 Ajax (0) 1
Matusovic 66 — Sneijder 90 — 13,500

Ajax (0) 1 Arsenal (1) 2
Rosenberg 71 — Ljungberg 2
50,000 — Pires 69 pen

Freddie Ljungberg puts Arsenal firmly in control of Group B on Matchday Two with an away win over their main rivals, Ajax. His early strike is doubled by a Robert Pires penalty before Ajax hit back through Markus Rosenberg

FC Thun (0) 1 Sparta Prague (0) 0
Hodzic 89 — 32,000

Ajax (1) 2 FC Thun (0) 0
Anastasiou 36,55 — 44,772

Sparta Prague (0) 0 Arsenal (1) 2
12,528 — Henry 21,74

Arsenal (1) 3 Sparta Prague (0) 0
Henry 23 — 35,155
van Persie 81,86

FC Thun (0) 2 Ajax (1) 4
Lustrinelli 56 — Sneijder 27
Adriano 75 — Deumi 63 og
31,340 — de Jong 90, Boukhari 90

Ajax (0) 2 Sparta Prague (0) 1
de Jong 68,89 — Petras 90
46,158

FC Thun (0) 0 Arsenal (0) 1
32,000 — Pires 88 pen

Arsenal (0) 0 Ajax (0) 0
35,376

Sparta Prague (0) 0 FC Thun (0) 0
15,000

An away draw with Sparta, followed by a home defeat to Arsenal left Ajax struggling bottom of the table after two games. Home and away wins over Thun get Ajax back on track, but the Stade de Suisse win only comes in injury time with Nigel de Jong scoring in the 91st minute and Nourdin Boukhari netting two minutes later

GROUP B TABLE

	P	W	D	L	DIF	PTS
Arsenal	6	5	1	0	8	16
Ajax	6	3	2	1	4	11
Thun	6	1	1	4	-5	4
Sparta	6	0	2	4	-7	2

GROUP C

QUALIFYING

Wisla Krakow (1) 3 Panathinaikos (1) 1
Panathinaikos (0) 4 Wisla Krakow (0) 1

Sp Lisbon (0) 0 Udinese (1) 1
Udinese (2) 3 Sp Lisbon (1) 2

Basel (1) 2 W Bremen (0) 1
W Bremen (0) 3 Basel (0) 0

Udinese (1) 3 Panathinaikos (0) 0
Iaquinta 28,73,76 — 25,000

Vincenzo Iaquinta gets Udinese's first Champions League group game off to the perfect start with a hat-trick against Panathinaikos in the Friuli Stadium

W Bremen (0) 0 Barcelona (1) 2
37,000 — Deco 13
Ronaldinho 76 pen

Barcelona (3) 4 Udinese (1) 1
Ronaldinho 13,32,90 pen — Felipe Dal Belo 24
Deco 41 — 65,000

Panathinaikos (2) 2 W Bremen (1) 1
Gonzalez 5 pen — Klose 41
Mantzios 8 — 50,000

Panathinaikos (0) 0 Barcelona (0) 0
65,000

Udinese (0) 1 W Bremen (0) 1
Di Natale 86 — Felipe Dal Belo 64 og
43,952

Barcelona (4) 5 Panathinaikos (0) 0
van Bommel 1 — 75,000
Eto'o 14,40,65
Messi 34

W Bremen (2) 4 Udinese (0) 3
Klose 15 — Di Natale 54,57
Baumann 24 — Schulz 60
Micoud 51,67 — 35,211

The battle for the runners-up spot behind Barcelona sees Bremen win a seven goal thriller. The Germans take a three goal lead through in-form stars Miroslav Klose and Johan Micoud, with Frank Baumann adding the third. Udinese reply with three in six minutes then a second Micoud strike settles it

Barcelona (2) 3 W Bremen (1) 1
Gabri 14 — Borowski 22 pen
Ronaldinho 26 — 85,000
Larsson 71

Panathinaikos (1) 1 Udinese (0) 2
Charalambides 45 — Iaquinta 81
35,000 — Candela 83

Udinese (0) 0 Barcelona (0) 2
38,500 — Ezquerro 85, Iniesta 90

W Bremen (3) 5 Panathinaikos (0) 1
Micoud 2 pen — Morris 53
Valdez 28,31 — 38,000
Klose 51, Frings 90

The strike-force of Ronaldinho, Larsson and Eto'o ends up goalless in Greece against Panathinaikos but that draw is the only game where Barcelona drop points. Bremen take four points off Udinese for second place ahead of the Italians on goal difference. It's rough justice on Antonio Di Natale who scores three against Bremen for Udinese

GROUP C TABLE

	P	W	D	L	DIF	PTS
Barcelona	6	5	1	0	14	16
Bremen	6	2	1	3	0	7
Udinese	6	2	1	3	-2	7
Panathinaikos	6	1	1	4	-12	4

GROUP D

QUALIFYING

Man Utd (1) 3 Debreceni (0)
Debreceni (0) 0 Man Utd (1)

Everton (1) 1 Villarreal (2)
Villarreal (1) 2 Everton (0)

Benfica (0) 1 Lille (0)
Miccoli 90 — 30,00

Villarreal (0) 0 Man Utd (0)
23,00

Lille (0) 0 Villarreal (0)
20,00

Man Utd (1) 2 Benfica (0)
Giggs 39 — Simao Sabrosa 5
van Nistelrooy 85 — 66,11

Man Utd (0) 0 Lille (0)
60,62

Villarreal (0) 1 Benfica (0)
Riquelme 72 pen — Manuel Fernandes 7
24,500

Benfica (0) 0 Villarreal (0)
30,000 — Senna 8

Lille (1) 1 Man Utd (0)
Acimovic 38 — 65,00

Lille (0) 0 Benfica (0)
60,00

Man Utd (0) 0 Villarreal (0)
67,47

Benfica (2) 2 Man Utd (1)
Geovanni 16 — Scholes 6
Beto 34 — 61,00

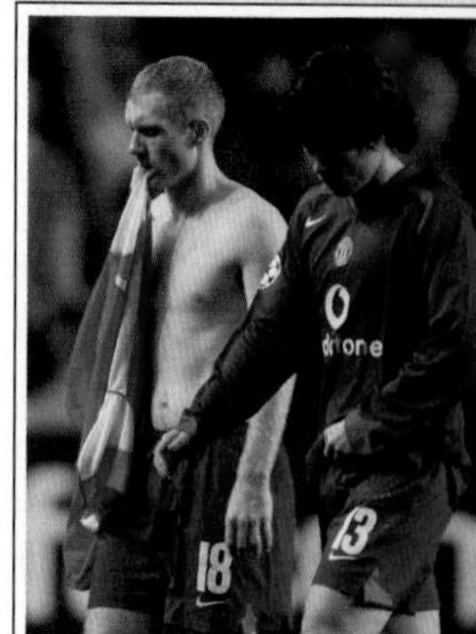

A sixth minute goal from Paul Scholes puts Manchester United ahead in their vital final game and on course for qualification. However, Benfica reply through Giovanni and Beto to take the second spot

Villarreal (0) 1 Lille (0) 0
Guayre 67 — 22,500

Defences rule in Group D with only 12 goals scored in as many games. Six tight draws leave everyone in with a chance of qualifying on the final night but Villarreal's narrow win over Lille and Benfica's home victory over Manchester United are rewarded by qualification. Favourites United finish bottom with Lille taking the Uefa spot

GROUP D TABLE

	P	W	D	L	DIF	PTS
Villarreal	6	2	4	0	2	10
Benfica	6	2	2	2	0	8
Lille	6	1	3	2	-1	6
Man. United	6	1	3	2	-1	6

QUALIFYING AND GROUP STAGES

GROUP E

AC Milan (1) 3 Fenerbahce (0) 1
Kaka 18,87 — Alex 63 pen
Shevchenko 89 — 43,000

PSV Eindhoven (1) 1 Schalke (0) 0
Vennegoor 33 — 30,000

Fenerbahce (1) 3 PSV Eindhoven (0) 0
Alex 40 pen,68 — 21,895
Appiah 90

Schalke (1) 2 AC Milan (1) 2
Larsen 3, Altintop 70 — Seedorf 1
50,881 — Shevchenko 59

Schalke claim a second game draw against in-form Milan. A blistering start sees Clarence Seedorf's first minute goal levelled by Soren Larsen two minutes later. Then Andriy Shevchenko's second half header is countered by sub Hamit Altintrop's rasping strike for the Germans

AC Milan (0) 0 PSV Eindhoven (0) 0
69,763

Fenerbahce (1) 3 Schalke (0) 3
Fabiano 14 — Lincoln 59,62
Marcio 73 — Kuranyi 77
Appiah 79 — 50,000

PSV Eindhoven (1) 1 AC Milan (0) 0
Farfan 12 — 35,500

Milan's only group defeat comes courtesy of Jefferson Farfán who drives home a loose clearance. PSV work hard to hang on to the 11th minute lead from the 21-year-old Peruvian

Schalke (1) 2 Fenerbahce (0) 0
Kuranyi 32 — 59,000
Sand 90

Fenerbahce (0) 0 AC Milan (1) 4
50,000 — Shevchenko 16,52,70,76

Schalke (1) 3 PSV Eindhoven (0) 0
Kobiashvili 18 pen,72,79 pen — 30,000

AC Milan (1) 3 Schalke (1) 2
Pirlo 42. Kaka 52,60 — Poulsen 44
82,000 — Lincoln 66

PSV Eindhoven (1) 2 Fenerbahce (0) 0
Cocu 14 — 30,000
Farfan 85

Last year's classic semi-final clashes between PSV and AC Milan form the backdrop to Group E. PSV gain bragging rights with a win and a draw in the group games. Both sides eventually progress but Schalke run them close, taking points off them at the Arena Aufschalke with Georgian Levan Kobiashvili hitting a hat-trick against PSV

GROUP E TABLE

	P	W	D	L	DIF	PTS
Milan	6	3	2	1	6	11
PSV	6	3	1	2	-2	10
Schalke	6	2	2	2	3	8
Fenerbahçe	6	1	1	4	-7	4

GROUP F

QUALIFYING
S Bucharest (1) 1 Rosenborg BK (0) 1
Rosenborg BK (1) 3 S Bucharest (0) 2

Lyon (3) 3 Real Madrid (0) 0
Carew 21 — 40,000
Juninho 26, Wiltord 31

French champions Lyon are impressive winners over Real Madrid in the opening game. Norway's John Carew opens the scoring in the 21st minute and goals by Brazilian Juninho and French international Sylvain Wiltord finish Madrid before halftime

Olympiakos (1) 1 Rosenborg BK (1) 3
Lago 19 og — Skjelbred 42
31,000 — Mavrogenidis 49 og
Storflor 90

Real Madrid (1) 2 Olympiakos (0) 1
Raul 9 — Kafes 48
Soldado 86 — 52,000

Rosenborg BK (0) 0 Lyon (1) 1
20,620 — Cris 45

Lyon (1) 2 Olympiakos (0) 1
Juninho 4 — Kafes 84
Govou 89 — 40,000

Real Madrid (0) 4 Rosenborg BK (1) 1
Woodgate 48 — Strand 40
Raul 52, Helguera 68 — 69,053
Beckham 82

Olympiakos (1) 1 Lyon (2) 4
Babangida 3 — Juninho 41
29,555 — Carew 44,57, Diarra 55

Rosenborg BK (0) 0 Real Madrid (2) 2
20,122 — Dorsin 26 og
Guti 41

Real Madrid (1) 1 Lyon (0) 1
Guti 41 — Carew 72
59,000

Rosenborg BK (0) 1 Olympiakos (1) 1
Helstad 88 — Rivaldo 25
17,450

Lyon (1) 2 Rosenborg BK (0) 1
Benzema 33 — Braathen 68
Fred 90 — 40,000

Olympiakos (0) 2 Real Madrid (1) 1
Bulut 50 — Sergio 7
Rivaldo 87 — 31,456

Lyon and Real Madrid divide the Group F spoils between them but the French side's form suggests they will do well in the knock-out phase. They hit 13 goals through eight different scorers and win every game apart from a 1-1 draw in the Bernabéu when a John Carew back-heel levels Guti's first half goal. Rosenborg clinch the Uefa spot on goal difference

GROUP F TABLE

	P	W	D	L	DIF	PTS
Lyon	6	5	1	0	9	16
Real Madrid	6	3	1	2	2	10
Rosenborg	6	1	1	4	-5	4
Olympiakos	6	1	1	4	-6	4

GROUP G

QUALIFYING
Liverpool (2) 3 T.N.S. (0) 0
T.N.S. (0) 0 Liverpool (1) 3

Kaunas (0) 1 Liverpool (2) 3
Liverpool (0) 2 Kaunas (0) 0

CSKA Sofia (1) 1 Liverpool (2) 3
Liverpool (0) 0 CSKA Sofia (1) 1

Anderlecht (4) 5 Neftchi (0) 0
Neftchi (1) 1 Anderlecht (0) 0

Anderlecht (2) 2 Slavia Prague (1) 1
Slavia Prague (0) 0 Anderlecht (0) 2

Real Betis (0) 1 AS Monaco (0) 0
AS Monaco (1) 2 Real Betis (1) 2

Chelsea (1) 1 Anderlecht (0) 0
Lampard 19 — 29,575

Real Betis (0) 1 Liverpool (2) 2
Arzu 51 — Sinama-Pongolle 2
45,000 — Luis Garcia 14

Florent Sinama-Pongolle gets the Champions off to a stunning start with the result that ultimately sees Liverpool head Group G above Chelsea

Anderlecht (0) 0 Real Betis (0) 1
27,500 — Oliveira 69

Liverpool (0) 0 Chelsea (0) 0
42,743

Anderlecht (0) 0 Liverpool (1) 1
25,000 — Cisse 20

Chelsea (2) 4 Real Betis (0) 0
Drogba 24 — 36,457
Carvalho 44
Cole, J 59, Crespo 64

Liverpool (1) 3 Anderlecht (0) 0
Morientes 34 — 42,607
Luis Garcia 61
Cisse 89

Real Betis (1) 1 Chelsea (0) 0
Dani 28 — 55,000

After being thumped 4-0 at Stamford Bridge, struggling Real Betis are given little chance of ending Chelsea's unbeaten start to the season. However, sub Dani scores the only goal of the game at the start of the second quarter

Anderlecht (0) 0 Chelsea (2) 2
21,070 — Crespo 8
Carvalho 15

Liverpool (0) 0 Real Betis (0) 0
42,077

Chelsea (0) 0 Liverpool (0) 0
41,598

Real Betis (0) 0 Anderlecht (1) 1
55,259 — Kompany 44

Chelsea and Liverpool's regular battles continue with two goalless stalemates in Group G as the two Premiership sides do their damage against Anderlecht and (to a lesser extent) Betis.
The Belgians are pointless until a meaningless win in the last game away against Betis, who are already sure of the Uefa spot having taken seven points

GROUP G TABLE

	P	W	D	L	DIF	PTS
Liverpool	6	3	3	0	5	12
Chelsea	6	3	2	1	6	11
Betis	6	2	1	3	-4	7
Anderlecht	6	1	0	5	-7	3

GROUP H

QUALIFYING
Kairat Almaty (1) 2 Artmedia B (0) 0
Artmedia B (1) 4 Kairat Almaty (0) 1

Artmedia B (1) 5 Celtic (0) 0
Celtic (2) 4 Artmedia (0) 0

Artmedia B (0) 0 Partizan (0) 0
Partizan (0) 0 Artmedia B (0) 0
Artmedia B win 4-3 on penalties

A Famagusta (0) 1 Rangers (0) 2
Rangers (1) 2 A Famagusta (0) 0

Shakhtar D (0) 0 Inter Milan (0) 2
Inter Milan (1) 1 Shakhtar D (1) 1

Artmedia B (0) 0 Inter Milan (1) 1
28,000 — Cruz 17

Rangers (1) 3 Porto (0) 2
Lovenkrands 35 — Pepe 47,71
Prso 59, Kyrgiakos 85 — 48,599

Porto (2) 2 Artmedia B (1) 3
Lucho Gonzalez 32 — Petras 45
Diego 39 — Kozak 54
48,000 — Borbely 74

Inter Milan (0) 1 Rangers (0) 0
Pizarro 49
Match played behind closed doors

Porto (2) 2 Inter Milan (0) 0
Materazzi 22 og — 25,500
McCarthy 35

Rangers (0) 0 Artmedia B (0) 0
49,018

Artmedia B (1) 2 Rangers (2) 2
Borbely 8, Kozak 59 — Prso 3
6,527 — Thompson 44

Inter Milan (0) 2 Porto (1) 1
Cruz 75 pen,82 — Hugo Almeida 16
Match played behind closed doors

Porto (0) 1 Rangers (0) 1
Lopez, L 60 — McCormack 83
48,000

Inter Milan (2) 4 Artmedia B (0) 0
Figo 28,
Adriano 41,59,74
Match played behind closed doors

Artmedia B (0) 0 Porto (0) 0
9,542

Rangers (1) 1 Inter Milan (1) 1
Lovenkrands 38 — Adriano 30
49,170

Adriano shows his Brazilian striking form to hammer a hat-trick against Artmedia. Luis Figo opens the scoring for an Inter side without an Italian

Inter Milan always looked likely winners of Group H and two early wins confirm their form. A slip against Porto, when Benni McCarthy adds to a Marco Materazzi own goal, is the only blemish and they qualify by the fourth game. The scrap for the second spot is far more even with Rangers only clinching it thanks to two draws in the final games

GROUP H TABLE

	P	W	D	L	DIF	PTS
Internazionale	6	4	1	1	5	13
Rangers	6	1	4	1	0	7
Artmedia	6	1	3	2	-4	6
Porto	6	1	2	3	-1	5

LAST 16

Ajax	(2) 2	Inter Milan	(0) 2
Huntelaar 16		Stankovic 49	
Rosales 20		Cruz 86	
51,000			

Inter Milan	(0) 1	Ajax	(0) 0
Stankovic, D 57		45,000	

Bayern Munich	(1) 1	AC Milan	(0) 1
Ballack 23		Shevchenko 58 pen	
66,000			

AC Milan	(2) 4	Bayern Munich	(1) 1
Inzaghi 8,47		Ismael 35	
Shevchenko 25		71,032	
Kaka 59			

Benfica	(0) 1	Liverpool	(0) 0
Luisao 85		65,000	

Liverpool	(0) 0	Benfica	(1) 2
42,745		Simao Sabrosa 36	
		Miccoli 88	

Chelsea	(0) 1	Barcelona	(0) 2
Motta 59 og		Terry 71 og	
39,521		Eto'o 80	

Barcelona	(0) 1	Chelsea	(0) 1
Ronaldinho 78		Lampard 90 pen	
98,000			

PSV Eindhoven	(0) 0	Lyon	(0) 1
35,000		Juninho 65	

Lyon	(2) 4	PSV Eindhoven	(0) 0
Tiago 26,45		41,000	
Wiltord 71, Fred 90			

Revenge for Lyon as Tiago's scores against the team that knocked them out on penalties last season. PSV captain Cocu is sent off and a second from Tiago and goals from Sylvain Wiltord and Fred complete the rout

Rangers	(1) 2	Villarreal	(2) 2
Lovenkrands 22		Riquelme 8 pen	
Pena 82 og		Forlan 35	
49,372			

Villarreal	(0) 1	Rangers	(1) 1
Arruabarrena 49		Lovenkrands 12	
23,000			

Villarreal qualify on the away goals rule

Peter Lovenkrands' rich vein of goals gives Rangers a 12th minute lead, but Villarreal are the better side and Juan Riquelme releases Diego Forlan to set up Rodolfo Arruabarrena to level and win the tie

Real Madrid	(0) 0	Arsenal	(0) 1
80,000		Henry 47	

Arsenal	(0) 0	Real Madrid	(0) 0
		35,487	

W Bremen	(1) 3	Juventus	(0) 2
Schulz 39		Nedved 73	
Borowski 87		Trezeguet 82	
Micoud 90		42,000	

Juventus	(0) 2	W Bremen	(1) 1
Trezeguet 65		Micoud 13	
Emerson 88		40,000	

Juventus qualify on the away goals rule

QUARTER-FINALS

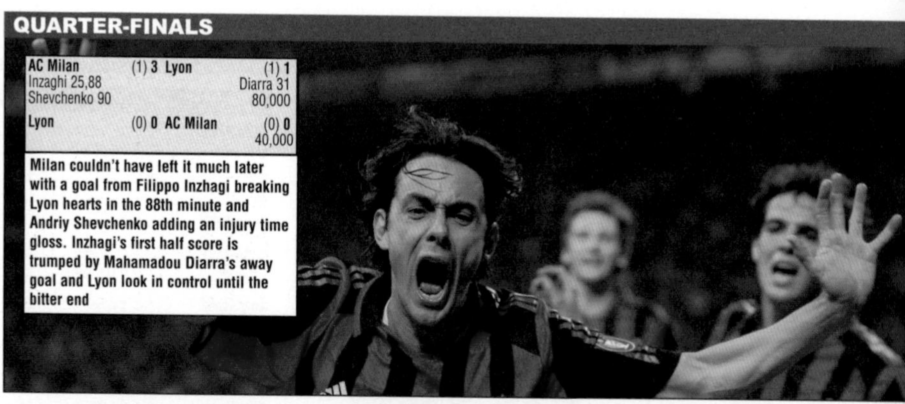

AC Milan	(1) 3	Lyon	(1) 1
Inzaghi 25,88		Diarra 31	
Shevchenko 90		80,000	

Lyon	(0) 0	AC Milan	(0) 0
		40,000	

Milan couldn't have left it much later with a goal from Filippo Inzhagi breaking Lyon hearts in the 88th minute and Andriy Shevchenko adding an injury time gloss. Inzhagi's first half score is trumped by Mahamadou Diarra's away goal and Lyon look in control until the bitter end

Arsenal	(1) 2	Juventus	(0) 0
Fabregas 40		35,472	
Henry 69			

Juventus	(0) 0	Arsenal	(0) 0
		50,000	

A young Arsenal team mugs the Old Lady of Turin in north London in a confident first leg performance which is worth more than the two goals scored by Cesc Fabregas and Thierry Henry. It is billed as 'Fabregas against his mentor' Patrick Vieira and the Spanish youngster is the hands down winner before Juvé's Mauro Camoranesi and Jonathan Zebina are both sent off late in the game

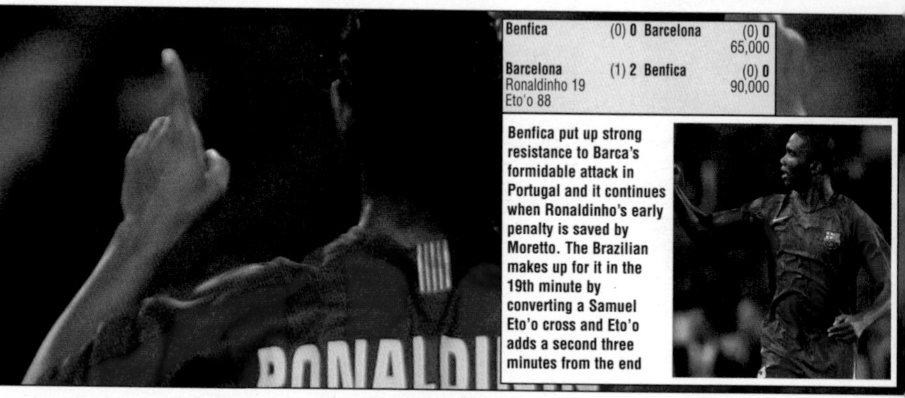

Benfica	(0) 0	Barcelona	(0) 0
		65,000	

Barcelona	(1) 2	Benfica	(0) 0
Ronaldinho 19		90,000	
Eto'o 88			

Benfica put up strong resistance to Barca's formidable attack in Portugal and it continues when Ronaldinho's early penalty is saved by Moretto. The Brazilian makes up for it in the 19th minute by converting a Samuel Eto'o cross and Eto'o adds a second three minutes from the end

Inter Milan	(1) 2	Villarreal	(1) 1
Adriano 7		Forlan 1	
Martins 54		80,000	

Villarreal	(0) 1	Inter Milan	(0) 0
Arruabarrena 58		22,500	

Villarreal win on the away goals rule

Rodolfo Arruabarrena is the Yellow Submarines' unlikely hero for the second tie in-a-row as he heads home the only goal of the second leg against Inter. Juan Riquelme controls the game and Villarreal are not flattered by the win

SEMI-FINALS

Arsenal	(1) 1	Villarreal	(0) 0
Toure 41			35,438
Villarreal	(0) 0	Arsenal	(0) 0
			23,000

Jens Lehmann beats out Juan Riquelme's final minute penalty to avoid extra time and claim Arsenal a place in their first Champions League final. It is a strangely subdued English team, which barely muster an attack in Spain. Villarreal dominate the game but miss what few chances they make as Kolo Toure adds a commanding defensive effort to his decisive goal in the first leg at Highbury

AC Milan	(0) 0	Barcelona	(0) 1
85,000			Giuly 57
Barcelona	(0) 0	AC Milan	(0) 0
			90,000

Ludovic Giuly powers home the vital goal in this tie with a top-corner net-buster from a tight angle to finish off Ronaldinho's imaginative chip. The fact that it is scored in the San Siro makes it doubly important and Barca need only to keep a clean sheet at the Nou Camp to reach the final

FINAL

Barcelona	(0) 2	Arsenal	(1) 1
Eto'o 76			Campbell 37
Belletti 80			79,500

Henrik Larsson comes off the bench to set-up two goals and gain Barcelona the Champions League trophy in his last game for the Spanish club. While Arsenal's semi-final hero, Jens Lehmann, finds himself watching from the stands in Paris after just 18 minutes of the final. The keeper is sent off after bringing down Samuel Eto'o just outside the box as the Barca forward beats the Arsenal offside trap and nudges the ball past Lehmann. Referee Terje Hauge whistles immediately - before Ludovic Giuly follows up to score - and so has to dismiss Lehmann, having disallowed the goal. The pattern of the game then becomes one of Barca pressure and Arsenal counter-attacks

STADIUM CAPACITY AND HOME CROWDS

	CLUB	CAPACITY	AVGE (%)	HIGH	LOW
1	FC Thun	32000	99.31	32000	31340
2	Villarreal	23000	99.13	23000	22500
3	Rangers	50444	97	49170	48599
4	Real Betis	52500	95.24	52500	45000
5	Lyon	42000	95.24	40000	40000
6	Rapid Vienna	48844	94.52	47000	45000
7	Liverpool	45362	93.64	42743	42077
8	Bayern Munich	69060	92.44	66000	60000
9	Olympiakos	33334	92.01	31456	29555
10	Ajax	51324	91.53	50000	44772
11	Anderlecht	26361	91.51	26300	21070
12	Arsenal	38500	91.4	35472	34498
13	Club Brugge	29975	91.03	28000	26000
14	PSV Eindhoven	36500	87.21	35500	30000
15	W Bremen	43000	85.43	38000	35211
16	Man Utd	76000	85.18	67471	60626
17	Chelsea	42449	84.52	41598	29575
18	Udinese	41705	84.09	41705	25000
19	AC Milan	85700	83.96	85000	43000
20	Barcelona	98800	81.98	90000	65000
21	Porto	50106	80.83	48000	25500

Key: Average. The percentage of each stadium filled in Champions League games over the season (AVE), the stadium capacity and the highest and lowest crowds recorded.

AWAY ATTENDANCE

	CLUB	AVGE (%)	HIGH	LOW
1	Man Utd	97.95	65000	23000
2	AC Milan	96.4	90000	35500
3	Sparta Prague	93.75	46158	32000
4	Barcelona	92.97	85000	37000
5	Liverpool	92.85	45000	25000
6	Real Betis	92.8	42077	26300
7	Benfica	92.6	90000	23000
8	Schalke	92.3	82000	30000
9	Juventus	91.91	60000	28000
10	Chelsea	91.39	52500	21070
11	Rosenborg BK	89.2	69053	31000
12	Anderlecht	87.87	52500	29575
13	Real Madrid	87.16	40000	20122
14	Inter Milan	86.55	49170	22500
15	Arsenal	85.75	50000	12528
16	Ajax	85.16	35376	13500
17	W Bremen	84.4	85000	41705
18	Rapid Vienna	84.02	66000	26000
19	FC Thun	83.26	44772	15000
20	Lyon	80.87	80000	20620
21	Club Brugge	78.77	65527	35000

Key: Average. How close each club has come to filling grounds in its away Champions League matches (AVE) and the highest and lowest crowds recorded.

CLUB STRIKE FORCE

	CLUB	GOALS	CSR
1	W Bremen	20	45
2	Schalke	12	45
3	Lyon	19	47
4	Barcelona	24	49
5	Udinese	14	51
6	Ajax	17	53
7	AC Milan	20	54
8	Juventus	16	56
9	Bayern Munich	12	60
10	Liverpool	20	63
11	Inter Milan	17	64
12	Rangers	14	64
13	Porto	8	68
14	Real Madrid	10	72
15	Rosenborg BK	10	72
16	Fenerbahce	7	77
17	Olympiakos	7	77
18	Arsenal	15	78
19	Chelsea	9	80
20	Man Utd	9	80
21	Panathinaikos	9	83
22	FC Thun	8	90
23	Artmedia Bratislava	10	93
24	Villarreal	12	105
25	Club Brugge	7	107
26	Benfica	8	113
27	Real Betis	6	120
28	Anderlecht	5	144
29	Rapid Vienna	5	144
30	PSV Eindhoven	4	180
31	Sparta Prague	2	270
32	Lille	1	540

Johan Micoud and Miroslav Klose

1 Werder Bremen

Goals in the Champions League	20
Club Strike Rate (CSR) Average number of minutes between League goals scored by club	45

CLUB DEFENCE

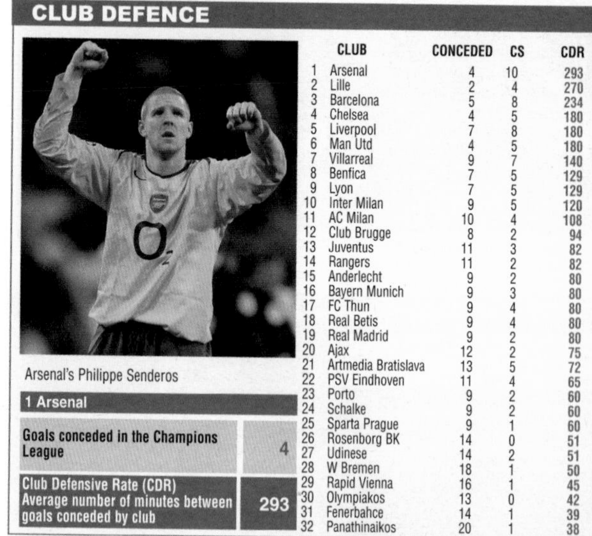

Arsenal's Philippe Senderos

1 Arsenal

Goals conceded in the Champions League	4
Club Defensive Rate (CDR) Average number of minutes between goals conceded by club	293

	CLUB	CONCEDED	CS	CDR
1	Arsenal	4	10	293
2	Lille	2	4	270
3	Barcelona	5	8	234
4	Chelsea	4	5	180
5	Liverpool	7	8	180
6	Man Utd	4	5	180
7	Villarreal	9	7	140
8	Benfica	7	5	129
9	Lyon	7	5	129
10	Inter Milan	9	5	120
11	AC Milan	10	4	108
12	Club Brugge	8	2	94
13	Juventus	11	3	82
14	Rangers	11	2	82
15	Anderlecht	9	2	80
16	Bayern Munich	9	3	80
17	FC Thun	9	4	80
18	Real Betis	9	4	80
19	Real Madrid	9	2	80
20	Ajax	12	2	75
21	Artmedia Bratislava	13	5	72
22	PSV Eindhoven	11	4	65
23	Porto	9	2	60
24	Schalke	9	2	60
25	Sparta Prague	9	1	60
26	Rosenborg BK	14	0	51
27	Udinese	14	2	51
28	W Bremen	18	1	50
29	Rapid Vienna	16	1	45
30	Olympiakos	13	0	42
31	Fenerbahce	14	1	39
32	Panathinaikos	20	1	38

CLUB DISCIPLINARY RECORD

Juve's Pavel Nedved is dismissed

1 Juventus

Yellow	29
Red	5
Cards Average Average number of minutes between a card being shown of either colour	26

	CLUB	Y	R	TOT	CA
1	Juventus	29	5	34	26
2	Udinese	21	2	23	31
3	Real Madrid	21	1	22	33
4	Fenerbahce	13	3	16	34
5	Man Utd	19	2	21	34
6	Real Betis	21	0	21	34
7	Inter Milan	26	2	28	39
8	Schalke	14	0	14	39
9	Villarreal	32	0	32	39
10	Chelsea	17	1	18	40
11	FC Thun	15	2	17	42
12	Lille	13	0	13	42
13	Panathinaikos	18	0	18	42
14	Rangers	21	0	21	43
15	Olympiakos	11	1	12	45
16	Lyon	18	1	19	47
17	W Bremen	17	2	19	47
18	Barcelona	23	0	23	51
19	Porto	10	0	10	54
20	Bayern Munich	13	0	13	55
21	PSV Eindhoven	11	2	13	55
22	AC Milan	18	1	19	57
23	Benfica	15	0	15	60
24	Arsenal	17	2	19	62
25	Rapid Vienna	11	0	11	65
26	Club Brugge	11	0	11	68
27	Ajax	13	0	13	69
28	Artmedia Bratislava	13	0	13	72
29	Anderlecht	8	1	9	80
30	Liverpool	15	0	15	84
31	Sparta Prague	5	1	6	90
32	Rosenborg BK	6	0	6	120

PLAYER DISCIPLINARY RECORD

	PLAYER	CLUB	Y	R	TOT	Avge
1	Vieira	Juventus	5	1	6	104
2	Nedved	Juventus	5	1	6	110
3	Camoranesi	Juventus	4	1	5	117
4	Guti	Real Madrid	4	0	4	129
5	Veron	Inter Milan	4	1	5	138
6	Tacchinardi	Villarreal	5	0	5	138
7	Scholes	Man Utd	3	1	4	139
8	Sagnol	Bayern Munich	4	0	4	157
9	Conceicao	Panathinaikos	4	0	4	165
10	Cocu	PSV Eindhoven	3	1	4	165
11	Govou	Lyon	2	1	3	168
12	Klasnic	W Bremen	2	1	3	169
13	Kobiashvili	Schalke	3	0	3	179
14	Seric	Panathinaikos	3	0	3	185
15	Prso	Rangers	3	0	3	195
16	Cordoba	Inter Milan	4	0	4	196
17	Bejbl	Rapid Vienna	3	0	3	204
18	Iaquinta	Udinese	3	0	3	204
19	Zenoni	Udinese	3	0	3	204
20	Ferreira	FC Thun	3	0	3	206
21	Rivera	Real Betis	3	0	3	210
22	Gattuso	AC Milan	4	0	4	213
23	Stam	AC Milan	2	1	3	215
24	Smith	Man Utd	3	0	3	215

1 Vieira

Yellow	5
Red	1
Cards Average Average number of minutes between a card being shown of either colour	104

CHART-TOPPING GOALSCORERS

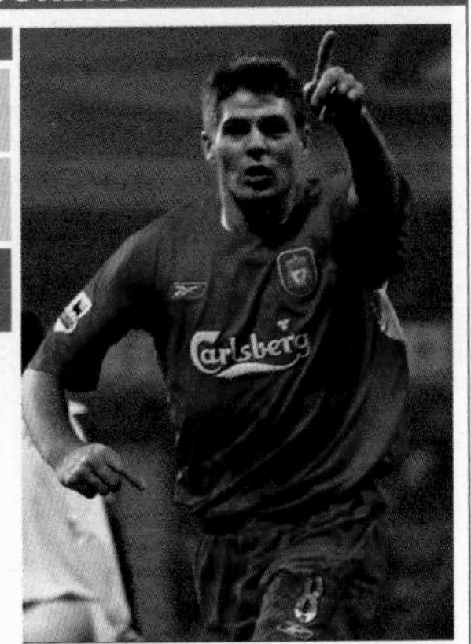

1 Gerrard	
Goals in Chapions League	7
Contribution to Attacking Power (AP) Average number of minutes between League team goals while on pitch	48
Player Strike Rate (SR) Average number of minutes between League goals scored by player	103

	PLAYER	TEAM	G	AP	SR
1	Gerrard	Liverpool	7	48	103
2	Iaquinta	Udinese	6	47	104
3	Shevchenko	AC Milan	9	48	106
4	Cisse	Liverpool	6	49	115
5	Trezeguet	Juventus	6	73	122
6	Sneijder	Ajax	4	54	123
7	Ronaldinho	Barcelona	7	49	154
8	Carew	Lyon	4	48	156
9	Adriano	Inter Milan	6	67	157
10	Eto'o	Barcelona	6	54	163

CHART-TOPPING MIDFIELDERS

1 Essien	
Goals scored in the Champions League	0
Defensive Rating Av number of mins between goals conceded while on the pitch	539
Contribution to Attacking Power Average number of minutes between team goals while on pitch	77
Scoring Difference Defensive Rating minus Contribution to Attacking Power	462

	PLAYER	CLUB	G	DR	AP	SD
1	Essien	Chelsea	0	539	77	462
2	Fabregas	Arsenal	1	472	73	399
3	Pires	Arsenal	2	323	59	264
4	Flamini	Arsenal	0	308	77	231
5	Gilberto Silva	Arsenal	1	300	75	225

CHART-TOPPING DEFENDERS

1 Belletti	
Goals Conceded in the Competition The number of goals conceded while he was on the pitch	1
Clean Sheets In games when he played at least 70 mins	5
Defensive Rating Average number of minutes between goals conceded while on pitch	641
Club Defensive Rating Average mins between goals conceded by the club this season	234

	PLAYER	CLUB	Conc	CS	CDR	DR
1	Belletti	Barcelona	1	5	234	641
2	Eboue	Arsenal	2	8	293	419
3	Gallas	Chelsea	2	5	180	315
4	Toure	Arsenal	4	9	293	270
5	Tafforeau	Lille	2	4	270	270

CHART-TOPPING GOALKEEPERS

1 Valdes	
Goals conceded in the Champions League	5
Counting Games Competition games when he played at least 70 minutes	12
Clean Sheets In games when he played at least 70 mins	7
Defensive Rating Average number of minutes between League goals conceded while on pitch	170

	PLAYER	CLUB	CG	Conc	CS	DR
1	Valdes	Barcelona	12	5	7	216
2	Reina	Liverpool	12	6	7	180
3	Van der Sar	Man Utd	8	4	5	180
4	Barbosa	Villarreal	6	3	3	180
5	Cech	Chelsea	7	4	4	158

TEAM OF THE SEASON

VALDES – BARCELONA – M 1080 DR 216

BELLETTI – BARCELONA – M 641 DR 641

EBOUE – ARSENAL – M 837 DR 419

GALLAS – CHELSEA – M 630 DR 315

TAFFOREAU – LILLE – M 540 DR 270

ESSIEN – CHELSEA – M 539 SD 462

FABREGAS – ARSENAL – M 943 SD 399

FLETCHER – MAN UTD – M 562 SD 201

VAN BOMMEL – BARCELONA – M 513 SD 200

IAQUINTA – UDINESE – M 614 SR 104

SHEVCHENKO – AC MILAN – M 950 SR 106

KEY: DR = Defensive Rate, SD = Scoring Difference AP = Attacking Power SR = Strike Rate, M = Minutes played in Champions League proper.

The Champions League Team of the Season shows a 4-4-2 of the best players in the competition based upon the selection criteria used for the chart-toppers. The players selected are taken from the lists for each 'last 16' club except that to get into the Team of the Season you must have played at least 500 minutes in the competition. The other restriction is that we are only allowing one player from each club in each position. So the maximum number of players one club can have in the divisional team is four.

• **The Champions League team's goalkeeper** is the player with the highest *Defensive Rating*

• **The Champions League team's defenders** are also tested by *Defensive Rating*, i.e. the average number of minutes between league goals conceded while on the pitch.

• **The Champions League team's midfield** are selected on their *Scoring Difference*, i.e.their *Defensive Rating* minus their *Contribution to Attacking Power* (average number of minutes between league goals scored while on the pitch. It takes no account of assists.

• **The Champions League team strikeforce** is made up of the two strikers with the highest *Strike Rate* (their average number of minutes between league goals scored while on the pitch) together with the striker with the highest *Contribution to Attacking Power.*

LEADING CLUB APPEARANCES

CLUB	PLAYER	POS	AGE	APP	MINS ON	GOALS	CARDS(Y/R)		HOME COUNTRY
Barcelona	Van Bronckhorst	MID	31	13	1148	0	0	0	Holland
Villarreal	Senna	MID	29	13	1124	1	2	0	Brazil
Arsenal	Kolo Toure	DEF	25	12	1080	1	2	0	Ivory Coast
AC Milan	Dida	GK	32	12	1058	0	0	0	Brazil
Inter Milan	Adriano	ATT	24	12	941	6	1	0	Brazil
Benfica	Luisao	DEF	25	10	900	1	2	0	Brazil
Liverpool	Hyypia	DEF	32	10	900	0	0	0	Finland
Rangers	Waterreus	GK	35	10	900	0	1	0	Holland
Rangers	Ferguson	MID	28	10	900	0	2	0	Scotland
W Bremen	Frings	MID	29	10	900	1	2	0	Germany
Lyon	Cris	DEF	29	10	855	1	1	0	Brazil
Juventus	Cannavaro	DEF	32	9	810	0	0	0	Italy
Juventus	Emerson	MID	30	9	810	1	0	0	Brazil
Ajax	Pienaar	MID	24	9	783	0	1	0	South Africa
B Munich	Ismael	DEF	30	8	720	1	1	0	France
Chelsea	Carvalho	DEF	28	8	720	2	1	0	Portugal
Chelsea	Terry	DEF	25	8	720	0	2	0	England
Chelsea	Lampard	MID	28	8	720	2	2	0	England

BARCELONA

SPAIN
CHAMPIONS OF EUROPE

	Comp	Opponent	Venue	Res	Score	Scorers	Att
1	ecgpc	**W Bremen**	A	W	2-0	Deco 13; Ronaldinho 76 pen	37,000
2	ecgpc	**Udinese**	H	W	4-1	Ronaldinho 13,32,90 pen; Deco 41	65,000
3	ecgpc	**Panathinaikos**	A	D	0-0		65,000
4	ecgpc	**Panathinaikos**	H	W	5-0	van Bommel 1; Eto'o 14,40,65; Messi 34	75,000
5	ecgpc	**W Bremen**	H	W	3-1	Gabri 14; Ronaldinho 26 fk; Larsson 71	85,000
6	ecgpc	**Udinese**	A	W	2-0	Ezquerro 85; Iniesta 90	38,500
7	eclsl1	**Chelsea**	A	W	2-1	Terry 71 og; Eto'o 80	39,521
8	eclsl2	**Chelsea**	H	D	1-1	Ronaldinho 78	98,000
9	ecqfl1	**Benfica**	A	D	0-0		65,000
10	ecqfl2	**Benfica**	H	W	2-0	Ronaldinho 19; Eto'o 88	90,000
11	ecsfl1	**AC Milan**	A	W	1-0	Giuly 57	85,000
12	ecsfl2	**AC Milan**	H	D	0-0		90,000
13	ecfin	**Arsenal**	H	W	2-1	Eto'o 76; Belletti 80	79,500

1ST GROUP C

	P	W	D	L	F	A	DIF	PTS
Barcelona	6	5	1	0	16	2	14	16
Bremen	6	2	1	3	12	12	0	7
Udinese	6	2	1	3	10	12	-2	7
Panathinaikos	6	1	1	4	4	16	-12	4

PLAYER APPEARANCES

Giovanni van Bronkhorst

Age (on 01/07/06)	31
Appearances in Champions league	13
Total minutes on the pitch	1148
Goals	0
Yellow cards	0
Red cards	0
Home Country	Holland

	PLAYER	POS	AGE	APP	MINS ON	GOALS	CARDS(Y/R)		HOME COUNTRY
1	Gio Van Bronckhorst	MID	31	13	1148	0	0	0	Holland
2	Victor Valdes	GK	24	12	1080	0	1	0	Spain
3	Carlos Puyol	DEF	28	12	1080	0	4	0	Spain
4	Ronaldinho	ATT	26	12	1078	7	0	0	Brazil
5	Samuel Eto'o	ATT	25	11	978	6	1	0	Cameroon
6	Anderson Deco	MID	28	11	969	2	4	0	Portugal
7	Presas Oleguer	DEF	26	11	955	0	2	0	Spain
8	Rafael Marquez	DEF	27	8	703	0	2	0	Mexico
9	Juliano Belletti	DEF	30	10	641	1	1	0	Brazil
10	Edmilson	DEF	29	9	637	0	1	0	Brazil
11	Henrik Larsson	ATT	34	10	560	1	1	0	Sweden
12	Andres Iniesta	MID	22	11	535	1	2	0	Spain
13	Mark van Bommel	MID	29	9	513	1	2	0	Holland
14	Ludovic Giuly	MID	29	8	466	1	0	0	France
15	Thiago Motta	MID	23	7	426	0	1	0	Brazil
16	Lionel Messi	MID	19	6	322	1	0	0	Argentina
17	Xavi Hernandez	MID	26	4	313	0	1	0	Spain
18	Garcia Gabri	MID	27	4	195	1	0	0	Spain

KEY PLAYERS - GOALSCORERS

Ronaldinho

Goals in the Champions League	7
Contribution to Attacking Power Average number of minutes between team goals while on pitch	49
Player Strike Rate The total number of minutes he was on the pitch for every goal scored	154
Club Strike Rate Average number of minutes between goals scored by club	49

	PLAYER	GOALS	ATT POWER	STRIKE RATE
1	Ronaldinho	7	49	154 mins
2	Samuel Eto'o	6	54	163 mins
3	Ludovic Giuly	1	52	466 mins
4	Anderson Deco	2	54	485 mins
5	Mark van Bommel	1	57	513 mins

KEY PLAYERS - MIDFIELDERS

Mark van Bommel

Goals in the Champions League	1
Defensive Rating Average number of mins between goals conceded while on the pitch	257
Contribution to Attacking Power Average number of minutes between team goals while on pitch	57
Scoring Difference Defensive Rating minus Contribution to attacking power	200

	PLAYER	GOALS	DEF RATE	ATT POWER	SCORE DIFF
1	Mark van Bommel	1	257	57	200 mins
2	Ludovic Giuly	1	233	52	181 mins
3	Giovanni Van Bronckhorst	0	230	52	178 mins
4	Anderson Deco	2	194	54	140 mins

KEY PLAYERS - DEFENDERS

Juliano Belletti

Goals Conceded in Champions League	1
Clean Sheets In League games when he played at least than 70 mins	5
Defensive Rating Ave number of mins between goals conceded while on the pitch	641
Club Defensive Rating Average number of mins between goals conceded by the club this season	234

	PLAYER	CONCEDED	CLEAN SHEETS	DEF RATE
1	Juliano Belletti	1	5	641 mins
2	Carlos Puyol	5	7	216 mins
3	Edmilson	3	4	212 mins
4	Presas Oleguer	5	6	191 mins
5	Rafael Marquez	4	4	176 mins

KEY GOALKEEPER

Victor Valdes

Goals Conceded	5
Clean Sheets	7
Counting Games (at least 70mins)	12
Defensive Rating Ave number of mins between goals conceded while on the pitch	216

TOP POINT EARNERS

	PLAYER	GAMES	AV PTS
1	Presas Oleguer	5	3.00
2	Carlos Puyol	6	2.67
3	Gio Van Bronckhorst	6	2.67
4	Victor Valdes	5	2.60
5	Ronaldinho	5	2.60
6	Anderson Deco	5	2.60
7	Samuel Eto'o	4	2.50
8	Xavi Hernandez	4	2.50
9	Juliano Belletti	3	2.33
10	Rafael Marquez	3	2.33
	CLUB AVERAGE:		2.16

Note: Points awarded for knock-out section

ARSENAL

ENGLAND
RUNNERS-UP

NICKNAME: THE GUNNERS

1	ecgpb **FC Thun**	H	W	2-1	Gilberto Silva 51; Bergkamp 90	34,498
2	ecgpb **Ajax**	A	W	2-1	Ljungberg 2; Pires 69 pen	50,000
3	ecgpb **Sparta Prague**	A	W	2-0	Henry 21,74	12,528
4	ecgpb **Sparta Prague**	H	W	3-0	Henry 23; van Persie 81,86	35,155
5	ecgpb **FC Thun**	A	W	1-0	Pires 88 pen	32,000
6	ecgpb **Ajax**	H	D	0-0		35,376
7	eclsl1 **Real Madrid**	A	W	1-0	Henry 47	80,000
8	eclsl2 **Real Madrid**	H	D	0-0		35,487
9	ecqfl1 **Juventus**	H	W	2-0	Fabregas 40; Henry 69	35,472
10	ecqfl2 **Juventus**	A	D	0-0		50,000
11	ecsfl1 **Villarreal**	H	W	1-0	Toure 41	35,438
12	ecsfl2 **Villarreal**	A	D	0-0		23,000
13	ecfin **Barcelona**	A	L	1-2	Campbell 37	79,500

1ST GROUP B

	P	W	D	L	F	A	DIF	PTS
Arsenal	6	5	1	0	10	2	8	16
Ajax	6	3	2	1	10	6	4	11
Thun	6	1	1	4	4	9	-5	4
Sparta	6	0	2	4	2	9	-7	2

PLAYER APPEARANCES

Kolo Toure

Age (on 01/07/06)	25
Appearances in Champions league	12
Total minutes on the pitch	1080
Goals	1
Yellow cards	2
Red cards	0
Home Country	Ivory Coast

	PLAYER	POS	AGE	APP	MINS ON	GOALS	CARDS(Y/R)		HOME COUNTRY
1	Habib Kolo Toure	DEF	25	12	1080	1	2	0	Ivory Coast
2	Cesc Fabregas	MID	19	13	943	1	1	0	Spain
3	Thierry Henry	ATT	28	11	931	5	2	0	France
4	Mathieu Flamini	MID	22	12	925	0	2	0	France
5	Gilberto Silva	MID	29	10	900	1	0	0	Brazil
6	Emmanuel Eboue	DEF	23	11	837	0	1	0	Ivory Coast
7	Fredrik Ljungberg	MID	29	9	789	1	0	0	Sweden
8	Jose Antonio Reyes	ATT	22	12	771	0	3	0	Spain
9	Alexander Hleb	MID	25	10	750	0	1	0	Belarus
10	Jens Lehmann	GK	36	8	648	0	0	1	Germany
11	Robert Pires	MID	32	12	646	2	0	0	France
12	Philippe Senderos	DEF	21	7	630	0	0	0	Switzerland
13	Sol Campbell	DEF	31	6	540	1	0	0	England
14	Manuel Almunia	GK	29	6	521	0	1	0	Spain
15	Etame Mayer Lauren	DEF	29	6	456	0	1	0	Cameroon
16	Robin van Persie	ATT	22	7	279	2	1	1	Holland
17	Ashley Cole	DEF	25	3	270	0	0	0	England
18	Gael Clichy	DEF	20	4	265	0	1	0	France

KEY PLAYERS - GOALSCORERS

Thierry Henry

Goals in the Champions League	5
Contribution to Attacking Power Average number of minutes between team goals while on pitch	116
Player Strike Rate The total number of minutes he was on the pitch for every goal scored	186
Club Strike Rate Average number of minutes between goals scored by club	78

	PLAYER	GOALS	ATT POWER	STRIKE RATE
1	Thierry Henry	5	116	186 mins
2	Robert Pires	2	59	323 mins
3	Sol Campbell	1	60	540 mins
4	Fredrik Ljungberg	1	113	789 mins
5	Gilberto Silva	1	75	900 mins

KEY PLAYERS - MIDFIELDERS

Cesc Fabregas

Goals in the Champions League	1
Defensive Rating Average number of mins between goals conceded while on the pitch	472
Contribution to Attacking Power Average number of minutes between team goals while on pitch	73
Scoring Difference Defensive Rating minus Contribution to attacking power	399

	PLAYER	GOALS	DEF RATE	ATT POWER	SCORE DIFF
1	Cesc Fabregas	1	472	73	399 mins
2	Robert Pires	2	323	59	264 mins
3	Mathieu Flamini	0	308	77	231 mins
4	Gilberto Silva	1	300	75	225 mins
5	Alexander Hleb	0	250	94	156 mins

KEY PLAYERS - DEFENDERS

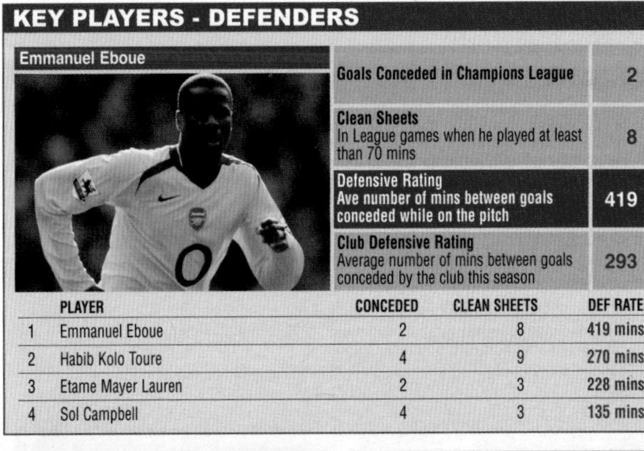

Emmanuel Eboue

Goals Conceded in Champions League	2
Clean Sheets In League games when he played at least than 70 mins	8
Defensive Rating Ave number of mins between goals conceded while on the pitch	419
Club Defensive Rating Average number of mins between goals conceded by the club this season	293

	PLAYER	CONCEDED	CLEAN SHEETS	DEF RATE
1	Emmanuel Eboue	2	8	419 mins
2	Habib Kolo Toure	4	9	270 mins
3	Etame Mayer Lauren	2	3	228 mins
4	Sol Campbell	4	3	135 mins

KEY GOALKEEPER

Manuel Almunia

Goals Conceded	4
Clean Sheets	3
Counting Games (at least 70mins)	6
Defensive Rating Ave number of mins between goals conceded while on the pitch	130

TOP POINT EARNERS

	PLAYER	GAMES	AV PTS
1	Jose Antonio Reyes	4	3.00
1	Robert Pires	4	3.00
1	Sol Campbell	4	3.00
4	Gilberto Silva	3	3.00
4	Cesc Fabregas	3	3.00
4	Fredrik Ljungberg	3	3.00
7	Habib Kolo Toure	5	2.60
7	Mathieu Flamini	5	2.60
7	Manuel Almunia	5	2.60
7	Etame Mayer Lauren	5	2.60
	CLUB AVERAGE:		2.67

Note: Points awarded for knock-out section

VILLARREAL

SPAIN
Losing semi-finalists

1	ecql1	Everton	A	W	2-1	Figueroa 27; Josico 45	37,685
2	ecql2	Everton	H	W	2-1	Sorin 21; Forlan 90	22,000
3	ecgpd	Man Utd	H	D	0-0		23,000
4	ecgpd	Lille	A	D	0-0		20,000
5	ecgpd	Benfica	H	D	1-1	Riquelme 72 pen	23,000
6	ecgpd	Benfica	A	W	1-0	Senna 81	30,000
7	ecgpd	Man Utd	A	D	0-0		67,471
8	ecgpd	Lille	H	W	1-0	Guayre 67	22,500
9	eclsl1	Rangers	A	D	2-2	Riquelme 8 pen; Forlan 35	49,372
10	eclsl2	Rangers	H	D	1-1	Arruabarrena 49	23,000
11	ecqfl1	Inter Milan	A	L	1-2	Forlan 1	80,000
12	ecqfl2	Inter Milan	H	W	1-0	Arruabarrena 58	22,500
13	ecsfl1	Arsenal	A	L	0-1		35,438
14	ecsfl2	Arsenal	H	D	0-0		23,000

KEY PLAYERS - GOALSCORERS

Diego Forlan

Goals in the Champions League	3
Contribution to Attacking Power Average number of minutes between team goals while on pitch	101
Player Strike Rate The total number of minutes he was on the pitch for every goal scored	369
Club Strike Rate Average number of minutes between goals scored by club	105

	PLAYER	GOALS	ATT POWER	STRIKE RATE
1	Diego Forlan	3	101	369 mins
2	Juan Riquelme	2	98	492 mins
3	Rodolfo Arruabarrena	2	109	543 mins
4	Josico	1	83	827 mins

FIRST GROUP D

	P	W	D	L	F	A	DIF	PTS
Villarreal	6	2	4	0	3	1	2	10
Benfica	6	2	2	2	5	5	0	8
Lille	6	1	3	2	1	2	-1	6
Man. United	6	1	3	2	3	4	-1	6

PLAYER APPEARANCES

Marcos Senna

Age (on 01/07/06)	29
Appearances in Champions league	13
Total minutes on the pitch	1124
Goals	1
Yellow cards	2
Red cards	0
Home Country	Spain

	PLAYER	POS	AGE	APP	MINS ON	GOALS	CARDS(Y/R)		HOME COUNTRY
1	Marcos Senna	MID	29	13	1124	1	2	0	Spain
2	Diego Forlan	ATT	27	13	1108	3	2	0	Uruguay
3	Rodolfo Arruabarrena	DEF	30	13	1086	2	3	0	Argentina
4	Juan Riquelme	MID	28	11	983	2	2	0	Argentina
5	Juan Pablo Sorin	DEF	30	13	976	1	2	0	Argentina
6	Gonzalo Rodriguez	DEF	22	11	934	0	3	0	Argentina
7	Josico	MID	31	13	827	1	3	0	Spain
8	Javi Venta	DEF	30	10	779	0	1	0	Spain
9	Juan Manuel Pena	DEF	33	10	723	0	0	0	Bolivia
10	Sebastian Viera	GK	22	8	720	0	3	0	Uruguay
11	Quique Alvarez	DEF	30	9	717	0	1	0	Spain
12	Alessio Tacchinardi	MID	30	10	690	0	5	0	Italy
13	Jose Mari	ATT	27	10	659	0	0	0	Spain
14	Mariano Damian Barbosa	GK	21	6	540	0	0	0	Argentina
15	Jan Kromkamp	DEF	25	5	436	0	1	0	Holland
16	Luciano Figueroa	ATT	25	7	396	1	1	0	Argentina
17	Cesar Amposta Arzo	MID	20	4	240	0	1	0	Spain
18	L. Farcuarson Guillermo	ATT	29	5	199	0	2	0	Argentina

AC MILAN

ITALY
Losing semi-finalists

1	ecgpe	Fenerbahce	H	W	3-1	Kaka 18,87; Shevchenko 89	43,000
2	ecgpe	Schalke	A	D	2-2	Seedorf 1; Shevchenko 59	60,881
3	ecgpe	PSV Eindhoven	H	D	0-0		69,763
4	ecgpe	PSV Eindhoven	A	L	0-1		35,500
5	ecgpe	Fenerbahce	A	W	4-0	Shevchenko 16,52,70,76	50,000
6	ecgpe	Schalke	H	W	3-2	Pirlo 42; Kaka 52,60	82,000
7	eclsl1	Bayern Munich	A	D	1-1	Shevchenko 58 pen	66,000
8	eclsl2	Bayern Munich	H	W	4-1	Inzaghi 8,47; Shevchenko 25; Kaka 59	71,032
9	ecqf1	Lyon	A	D	0-0		40,000
10	ecqfl2	Lyon	H	W	3-1	Inzaghi 25,88; Shevchenko 90	80,000
11	ecsfl1	Barcelona	H	L	0-1		85,000
12	ecsfl2	Barcelona	A	D	0-0		90,000

KEY PLAYERS - GOALSCORERS

Andriy Shevchenko

Goals in the Champions League	9
Contribution to Attacking Power Average number of minutes between team goals while on pitch	48
Player Strike Rate The total number of minutes he was on the pitch for every goal scored	106
Club Strike Rate Average number of minutes between goals scored by club	54

	PLAYER	GOALS	ATT POWER	STRIKE RATE
1	Andriy Shevchenko	9	48	106 mins
2	Ricardo Kaka	5	58	197 mins
3	Clarence Seedorf	1	57	972 mins
4	Andrea Pirlo	1	63	1011 mins

FIRST GROUP E

	P	W	D	L	F	A	DIF	PTS
AC Milan	6	3	2	1	12	6	6	11
PSV	6	3	1	2	4	6	-2	10
Schalke	6	2	2	2	12	9	3	8
Fenerbahçe	6	1	1	4	7	14	-7	4

PLAYER APPEARANCES

Andea Pirlo

Age (on 01/07/06)	27
Appearances in Champions league	12
Total minutes on the pitch	1011
Goals	1
Yellow cards	0
Red cards	0
Home Country	Italy

	PLAYER	POS	AGE	APP	MINS ON	GOALS	CARDS(Y/R)		HOME COUNTRY
1	Nelson Dida	GK	32	12	1058	0	0	0	Brazil
2	Andrea Pirlo	MID	27	12	1011	1	0	0	Italy
3	Ricardo Kaka	MID	24	12	986	5	1	0	Brazil
4	Clarence Seedorf	MID	30	11	972	1	1	0	Holland
5	Andriy Shevchenko	ATT	29	12	950	9	0	0	Ukraine
6	Alessandro Nesta	DEF	30	10	900	0	2	0	Italy
7	Kakha Kaladze	DEF	28	11	868	0	0	0	Georgia
8	Gennaro Gattuso	MID	28	11	855	0	4	0	Italy
9	Serginho	MID	35	11	802	0	1	0	Brazil
10	Jaap Stam	DEF	33	9	647	0	2	1	Holland
11	Paolo Maldini	DEF	38	9	546	0	2	0	Italy
12	Alberto Gilardino	ATT	24	10	507	0	0	0	Italy
13	Filippo Inzaghi	ATT	32	6	396	4	2	0	Italy
14	Cafu	DEF	36	5	297	0	0	0	Brazil
15	Christian Vieri	ATT	32	5	292	0	0	0	Italy
16	Alessandro Costacurta	DEF	40	3	191	0	2	0	Italy
17	Massimo Ambrosini	MID	29	4	141	0	0	0	Italy
18	Dario Simic	DEF	30	2	137	0	0	0	Croatia

BENFICA

PORTUGAL
Quarter-finals

1	ecgpd	**Lille**	H	W	1-0	Miccoli 90	30,000
2	ecgpd	**Man Utd**	A	L	1-2	Simao Sabrosa 59	66,112
3	ecgpd	**Villarreal**	A	D	1-1	Manuel Fernandes 77	23,000
4	ecgpd	**Villarreal**	H	L	0-1		30,000
5	ecgpd	**Lille**	A	D	0-0		60,000
6	ecgpd	**Man Utd**	H	W	2-1	Geovanni 16; Beto 34	61,000
7	eclsl1	**Liverpool**	H	W	1-0	Luisao 85	65,000
8	eclsl2	**Liverpool**	A	W	2-0	Simao Sabrosa 36; Miccoli 88	42,745
9	ecqfl1	**Barcelona**	H	D	0-0		65,000
10	ecqfl2	**Barcelona**	A	L	0-2		90,000

PLAYER APPEARANCES

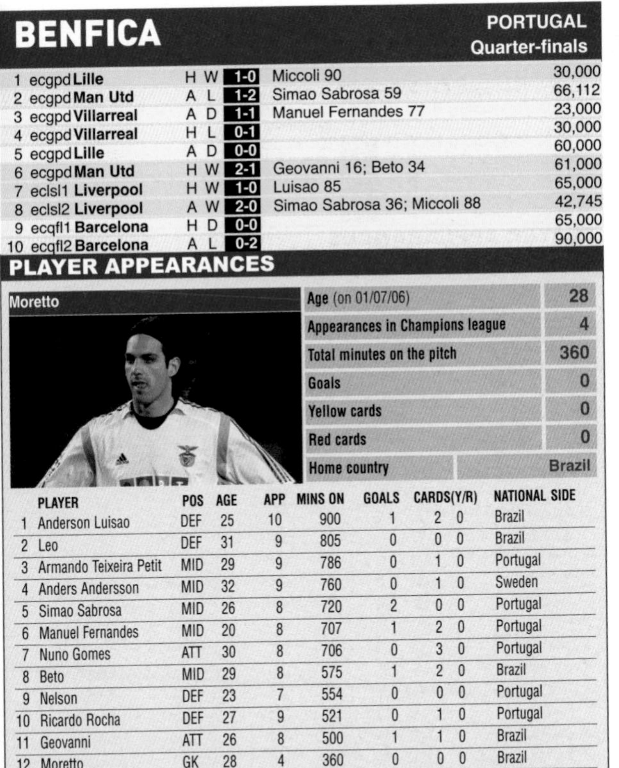

Moretto

Age (on 01/07/06)	28
Appearances in Champions league	4
Total minutes on the pitch	360
Goals	0
Yellow cards	0
Red cards	0
Home country	Brazil

	PLAYER	POS	AGE	APP	MINS ON	GOALS	CARDS(Y/R)		NATIONAL SIDE
1	Anderson Luisao	DEF	25	10	900	1	2	0	Brazil
2	Leo	DEF	31	9	805	0	0	0	Brazil
3	Armando Teixeira Petit	MID	29	9	786	0	1	0	Portugal
4	Anders Andersson	MID	32	9	760	0	1	0	Sweden
5	Simao Sabrosa	MID	26	8	720	2	0	0	Portugal
6	Manuel Fernandes	MID	20	8	707	1	2	0	Portugal
7	Nuno Gomes	ATT	30	8	706	0	3	0	Portugal
8	Beto	MID	29	8	575	1	2	0	Brazil
9	Nelson	DEF	23	7	554	0	0	0	Portugal
10	Ricardo Rocha	DEF	27	9	521	0	1	0	Portugal
11	Geovanni	ATT	26	8	500	1	1	0	Brazil
12	Moretto	GK	28	4	360	0	0	0	Brazil
13	Eduardo Alcides	ATT	21	4	360	0	0	0	Brazil
14	Fabrizio Miccoli	ATT	27	6	360	2	1	0	Italy

JUVENTUS

ITALY
Quarter-finals

1	ecgpa	**Club Brugge**	A	W	2-1	Nedved 66; Trezeguet 75	28,000
2	ecgpa	**Rapid Vienna**	H	W	3-0	Trezeguet 27; Mutu 82; Ibrahimovic 85	49,521
3	ecgpa	**Bayern Munich**	A	L	1-2	Ibrahimovic 90	60,000
4	ecgpa	**Bayern Munich**	H	W	2-1	Trezeguet 62,85	19,000
5	ecgpa	**Club Brugge**	H	W	1-0	Del Piero 80	35,000
6	ecgpa	**Rapid Vienna**	A	W	3-1	Del Piero 35,45; Ibrahimovic 42	46,500
7	eclsl1	**W Bremen**	A	L	2-3	Nedved 73; Trezeguet 82	42,000
8	eclsl2	**W Bremen**	H	W	2-1	Trezeguet 65; Emerson 88	40,000
9	ecqfl1	**Arsenal**	A	L	0-2		35,472
10	ecqfl2	**Arsenal**	H	D	0-0		50,000

PLAYER APPEARANCES

Emerson

Age (on 01/07/06)	30
Appearances in Champions league	9
Total minutes on the pitch	810
Goals	1
Yellow cards	0
Red cards	0
Home country	Brazil

	PLAYER	POS	AGE	APP	MINS ON	GOALS	CARDS(Y/R)		NATIONAL SIDE
1	Fabio Cannavaro	DEF	32	9	810	0	0	0	Italy
2	Fereira de Rosa Emerson	MID	30	9	810	1	0	0	Brazil
3	David Trezeguet	ATT	28	9	732	6	2	0	France
4	Lilian Thuram	DEF	34	8	720	0	2	0	France
5	Gianluca Zambrotta	DEF	29	8	720	0	1	0	Italy
6	Zlatan Ibrahimovic	ATT	24	9	697	3	2	1	Sweden
7	Pavel Nedved	MID	33	8	662	2	5	1	Czech Republic
8	Patrick Vieira	MID	30	7	629	0	5	1	France
9	Mauro Camoranesi	MID	29	9	587	0	4	1	Italy
10	Christian Abbiati	GK	29	6	540	0	0	0	Italy
11	Giorgio Chiellini	DEF	21	6	399	0	1	0	Italy
12	Alessandro Del Piero	ATT	31	7	369	3	1	0	Italy
13	Gianluigi Buffon	GK	28	4	360	0	0	0	Italy
14	Robert Kovac	DEF	32	4	327	0	2	0	Croatia

LYON

FRANCE
Quarter-finals

1	ecgpf	**Real Madrid**	H	W	3-0	Carew 21; Juninho 26; Wiltord 31	40,000
2	ecgpf	**Rosenborg BK**	A	W	1-0	Cris 45	20,620
3	ecgpf	**Olympiakos**	H	W	2-1	Juninho 4; Govou 89	40,000
4	ecgpf	**Olympiakos**	A	W	4-1	Juninho 41; Carew 44,57; Diarra 55	29,555
5	ecgpf	**Real Madrid**	A	D	1-1	Carew 72	59,000
6	ecgpf	**Rosenborg BK**	H	W	2-1	Benzema 33; Fred 90	40,000
7	eclsl1	**PSV Eindhoven**	A	W	1-0	Juninho 65 fk	35,000
8	eclsl2	**PSV Eindhoven**	H	W	4-0	Tiago 26,45; Wiltord 71; Fred 90	41,000
9	ecqf1	**AC Milan**	H	D	0-0		40,000
10	ecqf2	**AC Milan**	A	L	1-3	Diarra 31	80,000

PLAYER APPEARANCES

Mahamadou Diarra

Age (on 01/07/06)	25
Appearances in Champions league	9
Total minutes on the pitch	810
Goals	2
Yellow cards	2
Red cards	0
Home country	Mali

	PLAYER	POS	AGE	APP	MINS ON	GOALS	CARDS(Y/R)		NATIONAL SIDE
1	Cris	DEF	29	10	855	1	1	0	Brazil
2	Mahamadou Diarra	MID	25	9	810	2	2	0	Mali
3	Gregory Coupet	GK	33	9	810	0	1	0	France
4	Florent Malouda	MID	26	9	770	0	0	0	France
5	Pernambucano Juninho	MID	31	8	691	4	3	0	Brazil
6	Cardoso Tiago	MID	25	8	687	2	3	0	Portugal
7	Cacapa	DEF	30	7	630	0	1	0	Brazil
8	John Alieu Carew	ATT	26	10	624	4	1	0	Norway
9	Sylvain Wiltord	ATT	32	10	552	2	1	0	France
10	Eric Abidal	DEF	26	6	540	0	0	0	France
11	Anthony Reveillere	DEF	26	7	540	0	1	0	France
12	Sydney Govou	ATT	26	7	504	1	2	1	France
13	Francois Clerc	DEF	23	5	368	0	0	0	France
14	Fred	ATT	22	9	297	2	0	0	Brazil

INTER MILAN

ITALY
Quarter-finals

1	ecql1	**Shr Donetsk**	A	W	2-0	Martins 68; Adriano 78	32,000
2	ecql2	**Sh Donetsk**	H	D	1-1	Recoba 12	
3	ecgph	**Artmedia Brat**	A	W	1-0	Cruz 17	28,000
4	ecgph	**Rangers**	H	W	1-0	Pizarro 49	
5	ecgph	**Porto**	A	L	0-2		25,500
6	ecgph	**Porto**	H	W	2-1	Cruz 75 pen,82	37,000
7	ecgph	**Artmedia Brat**	H	W	4-0	Figo 28; Adriano 41,59,74	
8	ecgph	**Rangers**	A	D	1-1	Adriano 30	49,170
9	eclsl1	**Ajax**	A	D	2-2	Stankovic 49; Cruz 86	51,000
10	eclsl2	**Ajax**	H	W	1-0	Stankovic, D 57	45,000
11	ecqf1	**Villarreal**	H	W	2-1	Adriano 7; Martins 54	80,000
12	ecqfl2	**Villarreal**	A	L	0-1		22,500

PLAYER APPEARANCES

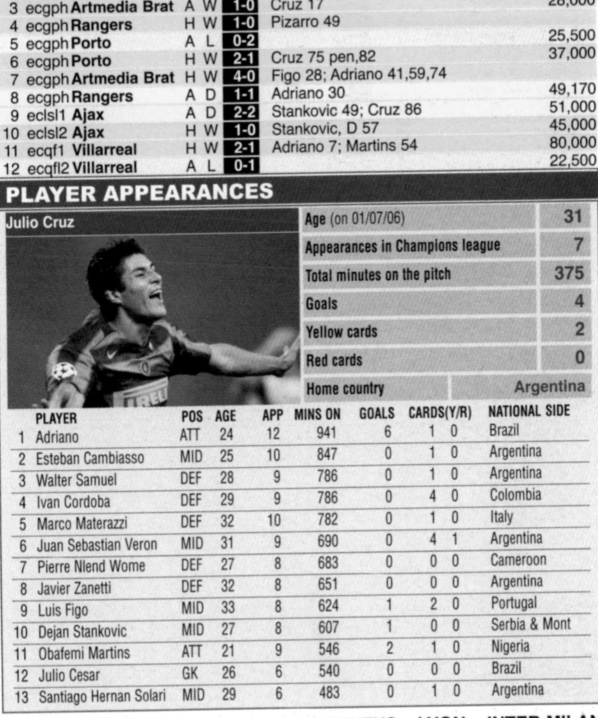

Julio Cruz

Age (on 01/07/06)	31
Appearances in Champions league	7
Total minutes on the pitch	375
Goals	4
Yellow cards	2
Red cards	0
Home country	Argentina

	PLAYER	POS	AGE	APP	MINS ON	GOALS	CARDS(Y/R)		NATIONAL SIDE
1	Adriano	ATT	24	12	941	6	1	0	Brazil
2	Esteban Cambiasso	MID	25	10	847	0	1	0	Argentina
3	Walter Samuel	DEF	28	9	786	0	1	0	Argentina
4	Ivan Cordoba	DEF	29	9	786	0	4	0	Colombia
5	Marco Materazzi	DEF	32	10	782	0	1	0	Italy
6	Juan Sebastian Veron	MID	31	9	690	0	4	1	Argentina
7	Pierre Nlend Wome	DEF	27	8	683	0	0	0	Cameroon
8	Javier Zanetti	DEF	32	8	651	0	0	0	Argentina
9	Luis Figo	MID	33	8	624	1	2	0	Portugal
10	Dejan Stankovic	MID	27	8	607	1	0	0	Serbia & Mont
11	Obafemi Martins	ATT	21	9	546	2	1	0	Nigeria
12	Julio Cesar	GK	26	6	540	0	0	0	Brazil
13	Santiago Hernan Solari	MID	29	6	483	0	1	0	Argentina

CHELSEA

ENGLAND
Last 16

	Comp	Opponent	H/A	Res	Score	Scorers	Att
1	ecgpg	**Anderlecht**	H	W	1-0	Lampard 19	29,575
2	ecgpg	**Liverpool**	A	D	0-0		42,743
3	ecgpg	**Real Betis**	H	W	4-0	Drogba 24; Carvalho 44; Cole, J 59; Crespo 64	36,457
4	ecgpg	**Real Betis**	A	L	0-1		55,000
5	ecgpg	**Anderlecht**	A	W	2-0	Crespo 8; Carvalho 15	21,070
6	ecgpg	**Liverpool**	H	D	0-0		41,598
7	eclsl1	**Barcelona**	H	L	1-2	Motta 59 og	39,521
8	eclsl2	**Barcelona**	A	D	1-1	Lampard 90 pen	98,000

PLAYER APPEARANCES

Ricardo Carvalho

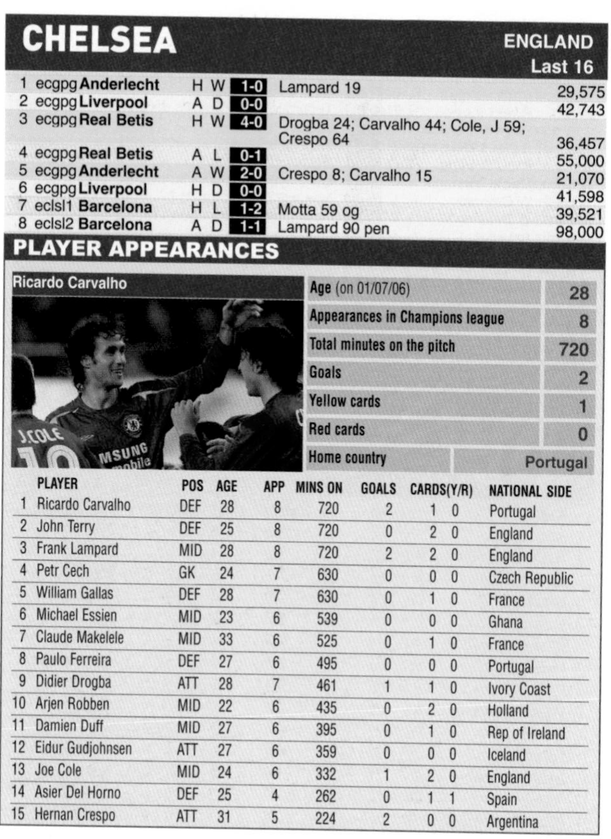

Age (on 01/07/06)	28
Appearances in Champions league	8
Total minutes on the pitch	720
Goals	2
Yellow cards	1
Red cards	0
Home country	Portugal

	PLAYER	POS	AGE	APP	MINS ON	GOALS	CARDS(Y)	CARDS(R)	NATIONAL SIDE
1	Ricardo Carvalho	DEF	28	8	720	2	1	0	Portugal
2	John Terry	DEF	25	8	720	0	2	0	England
3	Frank Lampard	MID	28	8	720	2	2	0	England
4	Petr Cech	GK	24	7	630	0	0	0	Czech Republic
5	William Gallas	DEF	28	7	630	0	1	0	France
6	Michael Essien	MID	23	6	539	0	0	0	Ghana
7	Claude Makelele	MID	33	6	525	0	1	0	France
8	Paulo Ferreira	DEF	27	6	495	0	0	0	Portugal
9	Didier Drogba	ATT	28	7	461	1	1	0	Ivory Coast
10	Arjen Robben	MID	22	6	435	0	2	0	Holland
11	Damien Duff	MID	27	6	395	0	1	0	Rep of Ireland
12	Eidur Gudjohnsen	ATT	27	6	359	0	0	0	Iceland
13	Joe Cole	MID	24	6	332	1	2	0	England
14	Asier Del Horno	DEF	25	4	262	0	1	1	Spain
15	Hernan Crespo	ATT	31	5	224	2	0	0	Argentina

REAL MADRID

SPAIN
Last 16

	Comp	Opponent	H/A	Res	Score	Scorers	Att
1	ecgpf	**Lyon**	A	L	0-3		40,000
2	ecgpf	**Olympiakos**	H	W	2-1	Raul 9; Soldado 86	52,000
3	ecgpf	**Rosenborg BK**	H	W	4-1	Woodgate 48; Raul 52; Helguera 68; Beckham 82	69,053
4	ecgpf	**Rosenborg BK**	A	W	2-0	Dorsin 26 og; Guti 41	20,122
5	ecgpf	**Lyon**	H	D	1-1	Guti 41	59,000
6	ecgpf	**Olympiakos**	A	L	1-2	Sergio 7	31,456
7	eclsl1	**Arsenal**	H	L	0-1		80,000
8	eclsl2	**Arsenal**	A	D	0-0		35,487

PLAYER APPEARANCES

Sergio Ramos

Age (on 01/07/06)	25
Appearances in Champions league	7
Total minutes on the pitch	630
Goals	1
Yellow cards	0
Red cards	1
Home country	Spain

	PLAYER	POS	AGE	APP	MINS ON	GOALS	CARDS(Y)	CARDS(R)	NATIONAL SIDE
1	Sergio Ramos	DEF	25	7	630	1	0	1	Spain
2	Roberto Carlos	DEF	33	7	630	0	2	0	Brazil
3	Iker Casillas	GK	25	7	630	0	1	0	Spain
4	David Beckham	MID	31	7	618	1	2	0	England
5	Robinho	ATT	22	8	598	0	0	0	Brazil
6	Jose Guti	MID	29	7	518	2	4	0	Spain
7	Raul	ATT	29	6	460	2	0	0	Spain
8	Carlos Diogo	DEF	22	5	371	0	2	0	Uruguay
9	Ivan Helguera	DEF	31	4	360	1	0	0	Spain
10	Julio Baptista	MID	24	7	356	0	1	0	Brazil
11	Pablo Garcia	MID	29	4	354	0	3	0	Uruguay
12	Zinedine Zidane	MID	34	4	324	0	0	0	France
13	Thomas Gravesen	MID	30	6	319	0	1	0	Denmark
14	Michel Salgado	DEF	30	5	308	0	1	0	Spain
15	Francisco Pavon	DEF	26	3	270	0	0	0	Spain

BAYERN MUNICH

GERMANY
Last 16

	Comp	Opponent	H/A	Res	Score	Scorers	Att
1	ecgpa	**Rapid Vienna**	A	W	1-0	Guerrero 60	47,000
2	ecgpa	**Club Brugge**	H	W	1-0	Demichelis 32	65,527
3	ecgpa	**Juventus**	H	W	2-1	Deisler 32; Demichelis 39	60,000
4	ecgpa	**Juventus**	A	L	1-2	Deisler 66	19,000
5	ecgpa	**Rapid Vienna**	H	W	4-0	Deisler 21; Karimi 54; Makaay 72,77	66,000
6	ecgpa	**Club Brugge**	A	D	1-1	Pizarro 21	27,860
7	eclsl1	**AC Milan**	H	D	1-1	Ballack 23	66,000
8	eclsl2	**AC Milan**	A	L	1-4	Ismael 35	71,032

PLAYER APPEARANCES

Martin Demichelis

Age (on 01/07/06)	25
Appearances in Champions league	8
Total minutes on the pitch	664
Goals	2
Yellow cards	1
Red cards	0
Home country	Argentina

	PLAYER	POS	AGE	APP	MINS ON	GOALS	CARDS(Y)	CARDS(R)	NATIONAL SIDE
1	Valerien Ismael	DEF	30	8	720	1	1	0	France
2	Martin Demichelis	DEF	25	8	664	2	1	0	Argentina
3	Willy Sagnol	DEF	29	7	630	0	4	0	France
4	Oliver Kahn	GK	37	7	630	0	0	0	Germany
5	Lucio	DEF	28	7	630	0	0	0	Brazil
6	Roy Makaay	ATT	31	8	616	2	0	0	Holland
7	Jose Ze Roberto	MID	32	8	565	0	1	0	Brazil
8	Michael Ballack	MID	29	6	532	1	1	0	Germany
9	Claudio Pizarro	ATT	27	6	501	1	1	0	Peru
10	Bastian Schweinsteiger	MID	21	7	482	0	1	0	Germany
11	Sebastian Deisler	MID	26	6	430	3	0	0	Germany
12	Bixente Lizarazu	DEF	36	6	334	0	0	0	France
13	Jose Paolo Guerrero	ATT	22	7	221	1	2	0	Peru
14	Philipp Lahm	DEF	22	3	208	0	0	0	Germany
15	Mehmet Scholl	MID	35	6	179	0	0	0	Germany
16	Ali Karimi	MID	27	3	160	1	0	0	Iran

RANGERS

SCOTLAND
Last 16

	Comp	Opponent	H/A	Res	Score	Scorers	Att
1	ecql1	**A Famagusta**	A	W	2-1	Novo 65; Ricksen 70	16,000
2	ecql2	**A Famagusta**	H	W	2-0	Buffel 39; Prso 58	48,500
3	ecgph	**Porto**	H	W	3-2	Lovenkrands 35; Prso 59; Kyrgiakos 85	48,599
4	ecgph	**Inter Milan**	A	L	0-1		
5	ecgph	**Artmedia Brat**	H	D	0-0		49,018
6	ecgph	**Artmedia Brat**	A	D	2-2	Prso 3; Thompson 44	6,527
7	ecgph	**Porto**	A	D	1-1	McCormack 83	48,000
8	ecgph	**Inter Milan**	H	D	1-1	Lovenkrands 38	49,170
9	eclsl1	**Villarreal**	H	D	2-2	Lovenkrands 22; Pena 82 og	49,372
10	eclsl2	**Villarreal**	A	D	1-1	Lovenkrands 12	23,000

PLAYER APPEARANCES

Sotirios Kyrgiakos

Age (on 01/07/06)	26
Appearances in Champions league	8
Total minutes on the pitch	688
Goals	1
Yellow cards	2
Red cards	0
Home country	Greece

	PLAYER	POS	AGE	APP	MINS ON	GOALS	CARDS(Y)	CARDS(R)	NATIONAL SIDE
1	Ronald Waterreus	GK	35	10	900	0	1	0	Holland
2	Barry Ferguson	MID	28	10	900	0	2	0	Scotland
3	Peter Lovenkrands	ATT	26	10	779	4	0	0	Denmark
4	Fernando Ricksen	MID	29	8	720	1	1	0	Holland
5	Julien Rodriguez	DEF	28	8	720	0	1	0	France
6	Sotirios Kyrgiakos	DEF	26	8	688	1	2	0	Greece
7	Ian Murray	MID	25	8	618	0	2	0	Scotland
8	Dado Prso	ATT	31	7	586	3	3	0	France
9	Hamed Namouchi	MID	22	7	571	0	0	0	France
10	Ibrahim Hemdani	MID	28	5	450	0	1	0	France
11	Thomas Buffel	MID	25	7	417	1	1	0	Belgium
12	Olivier Bernard	DEF	26	4	359	0	1	0	France
13	Chris Burke	MID	22	6	304	0	1	0	Scotland
14	Marvin Andrews	DEF	30	4	302	0	1	0	Trinidad & Tobago

LIVERPOOL

ENGLAND
Last 16

	Comp	Opponent	Venue	Res	Score	Scorers	Att
1	ecql1	**T.N.S.**	H	W	3-0	Gerrard 8,21,89	44,760
2	ecql2	**T.N.S.**	A	W	3-0	Cisse 26; Gerrard 85,86	8,009
3	ecql1	**Kaunas**	A	W	3-1	Cisse 26; Carragher 29; Gerrard 54	8,300
4	ecql2	**Kaunas**	H	W	2-0	Gerrard 77; Cisse 86	43,717
5	ecql1	**CSKA Sofia**	A	W	3-1	Cisse 25; Morientes 31,58	16,512
6	ecql2	**CSKA Sofia**	H	L	0-1		42,175
7	ecgpg	**Real Betis**	A	W	2-1	Sinama-Pongolle 2; Luis Garcia 14	45,000
8	ecgpg	**Chelsea**	H	D	0-0		42,743
9	ecgpg	**Anderlecht**	A	W	1-0	Cisse 20	25,000
10	ecgpg	**Anderlecht**	H	W	3-0	Morientes 34; Luis Garcia 61; Cisse 89	42,607
11	ecgpg	**Real Betis**	H	D	0-0		42,077
12	ecgpg	**Chelsea**	A	D	0-0		41,598
13	eclsl1	**Benfica**	A	L	0-1		65,000
14	eclsl2	**Benfica**	H	L	0-2		42,745

PLAYER APPEARANCES

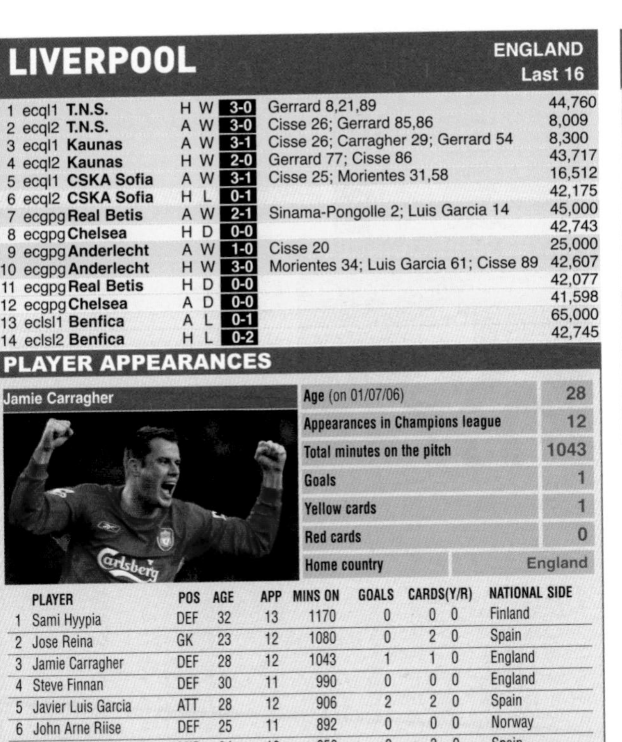

Jamie Carragher

Age (on 01/07/06)	28
Appearances in Champions league	12
Total minutes on the pitch	1043
Goals	1
Yellow cards	1
Red cards	0
Home country	England

	PLAYER	POS	AGE	APP	MINS ON	GOALS	CARDS(Y/R) Y	R	NATIONAL SIDE
1	Sami Hyypia	DEF	32	13	1170	0	0	0	Finland
2	Jose Reina	GK	23	12	1080	0	2	0	Spain
3	Jamie Carragher	DEF	28	12	1043	1	1	0	England
4	Steve Finnan	DEF	30	11	990	0	0	0	England
5	Javier Luis Garcia	ATT	28	12	906	2	2	0	Spain
6	John Arne Riise	DEF	25	11	892	0	0	0	Norway
7	Xabi Alonso	MID	24	10	850	0	3	0	Spain
8	Steven Gerrard	MID	26	12	723	7	1	0	England
9	Dietmar Hamann	MID	32	10	718	0	2	0	Germany
10	Momo Sissoko	MID	21	10	708	0	1	0	France
11	Djibril Cisse	ATT	24	13	692	6	0	0	France

WERDER BREMEN

GERMANY
Last 16

	Comp	Opponent	Venue	Res	Score	Scorers	Att
1	ecql1	**Basel**	A	L	1-2	Klose 73	28,101
2	ecql2	**Basel**	H	W	3-0	Klasnic 64,72; Borowski 67 pen	30,339
3	ecgpc	**Barcelona**	H	L	0-2		37,000
4	ecgpc	**Panathinaikos**	A	L	1-2	Klose 41	50,000
5	ecgpc	**Udinese**	A	D	1-1	Felipe Dal Belo 64 og	43,952
6	ecgpc	**Udinese**	H	W	4-3	Klose 15; Baumann 24; Micoud 51,67	35,211
7	ecgpc	**Barcelona**	A	L	1-3	Borowski 22 pen	85,000
8	ecgpc	**Panathinaikos**	H	W	5-1	Micoud 2 pen; Valdez 28,31; Klose 51; Frings 90	38,000
9	eclsl1	**Juventus**	H	W	3-2	Schulz 39; Borowski 87; Micoud 90	42,000
10	eclsl2	**Juventus**	A	L	1-2	Micoud 13	40,000

PLAYER APPEARANCES

Johan Micoud

Age (on 01/07/06)	32
Appearances in Champions league	10
Total minutes on the pitch	897
Goals	5
Yellow cards	2
Red cards	0
Home country	France

	PLAYER	POS	AGE	APP	MINS ON	GOALS	CARDS(Y/R) Y	R	NATIONAL SIDE
1	Torsten Frings	MID	29	10	900	1	2	0	Germany
2	Johan Micoud	MID	32	10	897	5	2	0	France
3	Patrick Owomoyela	MID	26	10	813	0	0	0	Germany
4	Naldo	DEF	23	9	810	0	0	0	Brazil
5	Tim Borowski	DEF	26	9	810	3	0	0	Germany
6	Christian Schulz	MID	23	10	798	1	1	0	Germany
7	Miroslav Klose	ATT	28	9	743	4	2	1	Germany
8	Andreas Reinke	GK	45	8	720	0	0	0	Germany
9	Frank Baumann	DEF	30	9	670	1	1	0	Germany
10	Ivan Klasnic	ATT	26	6	508	2	2	1	Croatia
11	Nelson Haedo Valdez	ATT	22	9	479	2	1	0	Paraguay
12	Frank Fahrenhorst	DEF	28	5	383	0	1	0	Germany
13	Leon Andreasen	DEF	23	4	360	0	1	0	Denmark

PSV EINDHOVEN

HOLLAND
Last 16

	Comp	Opponent	Venue	Res	Score	Scorers	Att
1	ecgpe	**Schalke**	H	W	1-0	Vennegoor 33	30,000
2	ecgpe	**Fenerbahce**	A	L	0-3		21,895
3	ecgpe	**AC Milan**	A	D	0-0		69,763
4	ecgpe	**AC Milan**	H	W	1-0	Farfan 12	35,500
5	ecgpe	**Schalke**	A	L	0-3		30,000
6	ecgpe	**Fenerbahce**	H	W	2-0	Cocu 14; Farfan 85	30,000
7	eclsl1	**Lyon**	H	L	0-1		35,000
8	eclsl2	**Lyon**	A	L	0-4		41,000

PLAYER APPEARANCES

Phillip Cocu

Age (on 01/07/06)	35
Appearances in Champions league	8
Total minutes on the pitch	663
Goals	1
Yellow cards	3
Red cards	1
Home country	Holland

	PLAYER	POS	AGE	APP	MINS ON	GOALS	CARDS(Y/R) Y	R	NATIONAL SIDE
1	Heurelho Gomes	GK	25	8	720	0	0	0	Brazil
2	Jefferson Farfan	ATT	21	8	680	2	0	0	Peru
3	Timmy Simons	MID	30	8	675	0	1	0	Belgium
4	Phillip Cocu	MID	35	8	663	1	3	1	Holland
5	Andre Ooijer	DEF	31	7	630	0	1	0	Holland
6	Alex	DEF	24	7	615	0	0	0	Brazil
7	Ibrahim Afellay	MID	20	8	602	0	2	0	Holland
8	Michael Reiziger	DEF	33	7	494	0	1	0	Holland
9	Michael Lamey	DEF	26	6	459	0	0	0	Holland
10	Jan Vennegoor	ATT	27	6	445	1	2	1	Holland
11	DaMarcus Beasley	ATT	24	5	394	0	0	0	United States
12	Theo Lucius	MID	29	5	368	0	0	0	Holland
13	Ismael Aissati	MID	17	6	282	0	0	0	Morocco
14	Erik Addo	DEF	27	4	276	0	0	0	Ghana
15	Robert	ATT	25	4	223	0	1	0	Brazil
16	Jason Culina	MID	25	2	109	0	0	0	Australia

AJAX

HOLLAND
Last 16

	Comp	Opponent	Venue	Res	Score	Scorers	Att
1	ecql1	**Brondby**	A	D	2-2	Rosenberg 31; Babel 74	24,917
2	ecql2	**Brondby**	H	W	3-1	Babel 50; Sneijder 80,88	39,075
3	ecgpb	**Sparta Prague**	A	D	1-1	Sneijder 90	13,500
4	ecgpb	**Arsenal**	H	L	1-2	Rosenberg 71	50,000
5	ecgpb	**FC Thun**	H	W	2-0	Anastasiou 36,55	44,772
6	ecgpb	**FC Thun**	A	W	4-2	Sneijder 27; Deumi 63 og; de Jong 90; Boukhari 90	31,340
7	ecgpb	**Sparta Prague**	H	W	2-1	de Jong 68,89	46,158
8	ecgpb	**Arsenal**	A	D	0-0		35,376
9	eclsl1	**Inter Milan**	H	D	2-2	Huntelaar 16; Rosales 20	51,000
10	eclsl2	**Inter Milan**	A	L	0-1		45,000

PLAYER APPEARANCES

Steven Pienaar

Age (on 01/07/06)	24
Appearances in Champions league	9
Total minutes on the pitch	783
Goals	0
Yellow cards	1
Red cards	0
Home country	South Africa

	PLAYER	POS	AGE	APP	MINS ON	GOALS	CARDS(Y/R) Y	R	NATIONAL SIDE
1	Steven Pienaar	MID	24	9	783	0	1	0	South Africa
2	Hedwiges Maduro	DEF	21	9	748	0	1	0	Holland
3	Urby Emanuelson	DEF	20	8	714	0	0	0	Holland
4	Hatem Trabelsi	DEF	27	8	707	0	0	0	Tunisia
5	Zdenek Grygera	DEF	26	8	643	0	1	0	Czech Republic
6	Markus Rosenberg	ATT	23	8	567	2	2	0	Sweden
7	Nourdin Boukhari	ATT	26	9	564	1	0	0	Morocco
8	Nigel de Jong	MID	21	7	550	3	1	0	Holland
9	Maarten Stekelenburg	GK	23	6	540	0	0	0	Holland
10	Ryan Babel	ATT	20	9	491	2	0	0	Holland
11	Wesley Sneijder	MID	22	7	490	4	0	0	Holland
12	Tomas Galasek	MID	33	6	458	0	3	0	Czech Republic
13	Thomas Vermaelen	DEF	20	5	450	0	1	0	Belgium

CLUB BRUGGE

BELGIUM
3rd in Group A

		Opponent				Scorers	Att
1	ecql1	Valerenga	A	L	0-1		13,778
2	ecql2	Valerenga	H	W	4-3*	Balaban 79 (*on penalties)	20,144
3	ecgpa	Juventus	H	L	1-2	Matondo 85	28,000
4	ecgpa	Bayern Munich	A	L	0-1		65,527
5	ecgpa	Rapid Vienna	A	W	1-0	Balaban 75	45,000
6	ecgpa	Rapid Vienna	H	W	3-2	Portillo 9; Balaban 25; Verheyen 63	26,000
7	ecgpa	Juventus	A	L	0-1		35,000
8	ecgpa	Bayern Munich	H	D	1-1	Portillo 32	27,860

PLAYER APPEARANCES

Bosko Balaban

Age (on 01/07/06)	27
Appearances in Champions league	6
Total minutes on the pitch	551
Goals	3
Yellow cards	0
Red cards	0
Home country	Croatia

	PLAYER	POS	AGE	APP	MINS ON	GOALS	CARDS(Y/R)		NATIONAL SIDE
1	Sven Vermant	MID	33	8	743	0	2	0	Belgium
2	Bierger Maertens	MID	26	8	716	0	1	0	Belgium
3	Tomislav Butina	GK	31	7	660	0	0	0	Croatia
4	Bosko Balaban	ATT	27	6	551	3	0	0	Croatia
5	Gaetan Englebert	MID	30	8	541	0	0	0	Belgium
6	Philippe Clement	MID	32	6	530	0	1	0	Belgium
7	Ivan Leko	MID	28	7	505	0	0	0	Croatia
8	Gert Verheyen	ATT	35	6	469	1	2	0	Belgium
9	Marek Spilar	DEF	31	5	450	0	1	0	Slovakia
10	Gunther Vanaudenaerden	DEF	22	6	428	0	0	0	Belgium
11	Javier Portillo	ATT	24	6	413	2	0	0	Spain
12	Jonathan Blondel	MID	22	6	335	0	2	0	Belgium
13	Gregory Dufer	MID	24	5	314	0	0	0	Belgium
14	Joos Valgaeren	DEF	30	3	283	0	0	0	Belgium
15	Olivier De Cock	DEF	30	3	270	0	0	0	Belgium
16	Klukowski	DEF	25	2	210	0	0	0	Canada

UDINESE

ITALY
3rd in Group C

		Opponent				Scorers	Att
1	ecql1	Sp Lisbon	A	W	1-0	Iaquinta 29 pen	35,474
2	ecql2	Sp Lisbon	H	W	3-2	Iaquinta 23 pen; Natali 35; De Souza 90	30,000
3	ecgpc	Panathinaikos	H	W	3-0	Iaquinta 28,73,76	25,000
4	ecgpc	Barcelona	A	L	1-4	Felipe Dal Belo 24	65,000
5	ecgpc	W Bremen	H	D	1-1	Di Natale 86	43,952
6	ecgpc	W Bremen	A	L	3-4	Di Natale 54,57; Schulz 60 og	35,211
7	ecgpc	Panathinaikos	A	W	2-1	Iaquinta 81; Candela 83	35,000
8	ecgpc	Barcelona	H	L	0-2		38,500

PLAYER APPEARANCES

Vincenzo Iaquinta

Age (on 01/07/06)	26
Appearances in Champions league	7
Total minutes on the pitch	614
Goals	6
Yellow cards	3
Red cards	0
Home country	Italy

	PLAYER	POS	AGE	APP	MINS ON	GOALS	CARDS(Y/R)		NATIONAL SIDE
1	Vincent Candela	DEF	32	8	720	1	1	0	France
2	Morgan De Sanctis	GK	29	8	720	0	0	0	Italy
3	Christian Obodo	MID	22	8	697	0	2	0	Nigeria
4	Valerio Bertotto	DEF	33	7	630	0	1	0	Italy
5	Felipe Dal Belo	DEF	21	7	630	1	1	0	Brazil
6	Vincenzo Iaquinta	ATT	26	7	614	6	3	0	Italy
7	Damiano Zenoni	MID	29	8	613	0	3	0	Italy
8	Sulley Ali Muntari	MID	21	8	558	0	0	0	Ghana
9	Antonio Di Natale	ATT	28	8	516	3	1	0	Italy
10	Jose Luis Vidigal	MID	33	5	368	0	3	1	Portugal
11	Nestor Sensini	DEF	33	5	365	0	1	0	Argentina
12	Cesare Natali	DEF	27	4	303	1	1	0	Italy
13	David Di Michele	ATT	30	5	236	0	0	0	Italy
14	De Souza Teixeira Juarez	DEF	32	3	232	0	0	0	Brazil
15	Barreto De Souza	ATT	20	5	201	1	0	0	Brazil
16	Stefano Mauri	MID	26	7	177	0	0	0	Italy

SCHALKE 04

GERMANY
3rd in Group E

		Opponent				Scorers	Att
1	ecgpe	PSV Eindhoven	A	L	0-1		30,000
2	ecgpe	AC Milan	H	D	2-2	Larsen 3; Altintop 70	60,881
3	ecgpe	Fenerbahce	A	D	3-3	Lincoln 59,62; Kuranyi 77	50,000
4	ecgpe	Fenerbahce	H	W	2-0	Kuranyi 32; Sand 90	59,000
5	ecgpe	PSV Eindhoven	H	W	3-0	Kobiashvili 18 pen,72,79 pen	30,000
6	ecgpe	AC Milan	A	L	2-3	Poulsen 44; Lincoln 66	82,000

PLAYER APPEARANCES

Levan Kobiashvilli

Age (on 01/07/06)	28
Appearances in Champions league	6
Total minutes on the pitch	538
Goals	3
Yellow cards	3
Red cards	0
Home country	Georgia

	PLAYER	POS	AGE	APP	MINS ON	GOALS	CARDS(Y/R)		NATIONAL SIDE
1	Lincoln	MID	27	6	540	3	0	0	Brazil
2	Frank Rost	GK	33	6	540	0	0	0	Germany
3	Marcelo Jose Bordon	DEF	30	6	540	0	1	0	Brazil
4	Levan Kobiashvili	MID	28	6	538	3	3	0	Georgia
5	Christian Poulsen	MID	26	6	534	1	1	0	Denmark
6	Mladen Krstajic	DEF	32	6	527	0	1	0	Serbia & Mont
7	Kevin Kuranyi	ATT	24	6	470	2	0	0	Germany
8	Dario Rodriguez	DEF	31	5	450	0	2	0	Uruguay
9	Rafinha	DEF	20	5	450	0	3	0	Brazil
10	Hamit Altintop	MID	23	6	441	1	1	0	Turkey
11	Fabian Ernst	MID	27	5	360	0	1	0	Germany
12	Soren Larsen	ATT	24	4	207	1	0	0	Denmark
13	Ebbe Sand	ATT	33	6	173	1	0	0	Denmark
14	Gustavo Antonio Varela	MID	28	3	94	0	0	0	Uruguay
15	Gerald Asamoah	ATT	27	2	63	0	1	0	Germany
16	Zlatan Bajramovic	MID	26	4	13	0	0	0	Bosnia

REAL BETIS

SPAIN
3rd in Group G

		Opponent				Scorers	Att
1	ecql1	AS Monaco	H	W	1-0	Edu 90	24,000
2	ecql2	AS Monaco	A	D	2-2	Oliveira 16,75	13,011
3	ecgpg	Liverpool	H	L	1-2	Arzu 51	45,000
4	ecgpg	Anderlecht	A	W	1-0	Oliveira 69	27,500
5	ecgpg	Chelsea	A	L	0-4		36,457
6	ecgpg	Chelsea	H	W	1-0	Dani 28	55,000
7	ecgpg	Liverpool	A	D	0-0		42,077
8	ecgpg	Anderlecht	H	L	0-1		55,259

PLAYER APPEARANCES

Ricardo Oliveira

Age (on 01/07/06)	26
Appearances in Champions league	5
Total minutes on the pitch	384
Goals	3
Yellow cards	0
Red cards	0
Home country	Brazil

	PLAYER	POS	AGE	APP	MINS ON	GOALS	CARDS(Y/R)		NATIONAL SIDE
1	Sanchez Joaquin	MID	25	8	640	0	1	0	Spain
2	Antonio Doblas	GK	26	7	630	0	1	0	Spain
3	Alberto Rivera	MID	28	7	630	0	3	0	Spain
4	Juan Melli	MID	22	7	630	0	1	0	Spain
5	David Rivas	DEF	27	7	612	0	2	0	Spain
6	Juanito	DEF	29	7	585	0	1	0	Spain
7	Francisco Xisco	ATT	25	7	417	0	1	0	Spain
8	Hernandez Oscar Lopez	DEF	26	5	405	0	2	0	Spain
9	Fernando Varela	MID	26	5	394	0	4	0	Spain
10	Ricardo Oliveira	ATT	26	5	384	3	0	0	Brazil
11	Marcos Assuncao	ATT	29	7	381	0	0	0	Brazil
12	Edu	ATT	27	4	360	1	0	0	Brazil
13	Fernandez Fernando	ATT	32	6	278	0	1	0	Spain
14	Arturo Arzu	MID	25	4	265	1	0	0	Spain
15	Jesus Capi	MID	29	4	212	0	1	0	Spain
16	Dani	ATT	24	3	185	1	1	0	Spain

FC THUN

SWITZERLAND
3rd in Group B

1	ecql1	Malmo	A W	1-0	Pimenta 34	12,237
2	ecql2	Malmo	H W	3-0	Bernardi 26; Lustrinelli 40,66	31,243
3	ecgpb	Arsenal	A L	1-2	Ferreira 53	34,498
4	ecgpb	Sparta Prague	H W	1-0	Hodzic 89	32,000
5	ecgpb	Ajax	A L	0-2		44,772
6	ecgpb	Ajax	H L	2-4	Lustrinelli 56; Adriano 75	31,340
7	ecgpb	Arsenal	H L	0-1		32,000
8	ecgpb	Sparta Prague	A D	0-0		15,000

PLAYER APPEARANCES

Silvan Aegerter

Age (on 01/07/06)	26
Appearances in Champions league	7
Total minutes on the pitch	630
Goals	0
Yellow cards	1
Red cards	0
Home country	Switzerland

	PLAYER	POS	AGE	APP	MINS ON	GOALS	CARDS(Y)	CARDS(R)	NATIONAL SIDE
1	Eldin Jakupovic	GK	21	8	720	0	0	0	Switzerland
2	Jose Goncalves	DEF	20	8	714	0	2	1	Portugal
3	Mauro Lustrinelli	ATT	30	8	684	3	1	0	Switzerland
4	Selver Hodzic	DEF	27	7	630	1	2	0	Bosnia
5	Silvan Aegerter	MID	26	7	630	0	1	0	Switzerland
6	Nelson Ferreira	MID	24	7	618	1	3	0	Portugal
7	Ljubo Milicevic	DEF	25	7	581	0	2	0	Australia
8	Leandro Vieira	DEF	27	8	554	0	0	0	Brazil
9	Alen Orman	MID	28	6	471	0	0	0	Austria
10	Adriano	MID	23	6	432	1	0	0	Brazil
11	Tiago Bernardi	MID	26	6	430	1	1	0	Brazil
12	Armand Deumi	DEF	27	5	320	0	1	1	Cameroon
13	Andreas Gerber	MID	33	5	294	0	0	0	Switzerland
14	David Pallas	MID	30	2	180	0	0	0	Switzerland
15	Adriano Pimenta	MID	23	2	167	1	0	0	Brazil
16	Gelson	ATT	24	4	133	0	0	0	Brazil

LILLE

FRANCE
3rd in Group D

1	ecgpd	Benfica	A L	0-1		30,000
2	ecgpd	Villarreal	H D	0-0		20,000
3	ecgpd	Man Utd	A D	0-0		60,626
4	ecgpd	Man Utd	H W	1-0	Acimovic 38	65,000
5	ecgpd	Benfica	H D	0-0		60,000
6	ecgpd	Villarreal	A L	0-1		22,500

PLAYER APPEARANCES

Milenco Acimovic

Age (on 01/07/06)	29
Appearances in Champions league	5
Total minutes on the pitch	350
Goals	1
Yellow cards	0
Red cards	0
Home country	Slovenia

	PLAYER	POS	AGE	APP	MINS ON	GOALS	CARDS(Y)	CARDS(R)	NATIONAL SIDE
1	Gregory Tafforeau	DEF	29	6	540	0	2	0	France
2	Jean Makoun	MID	23	6	540	0	2	0	Cameroon
3	Tony Mario Sylva	GK	31	6	540	0	0	0	Senegal
4	Mathieu Bodmer	MID	23	6	495	0	0	0	France
5	Rafael Schmitz	DEF	25	5	450	0	3	0	Brazil
6	Mathieu Chalme	DEF	25	5	428	0	0	0	France
7	Efstathios Tavlaridis	DEF	26	4	360	0	2	0	Greece
8	Geoffrey Dernis	ATT	25	6	359	0	0	0	France
9	Milenko Acimovic	MID	29	5	350	1	0	0	Slovenia
10	Matt Moussilou	ATT	24	6	346	0	0	0	France
11	Mathieu Debuchy	MID	20	4	307	0	0	0	France
12	Stefan Lichtsteiner	DEF	22	4	256	0	0	0	Switzerland
13	Peter Odemwingie	ATT	24	4	255	0	0	0	Nigeria
14	Nicolas Plestan	DEF	25	2	180	0	1	0	France
15	Milivoje Vitakic	DEF	29	2	180	0	1	0	Serbia & Mont
16	Stephane Dumont	MID	23	2	135	0	0	0	France

ROSENBORG BK

NORWAY
3rd in Group F

1	ecql1	St Bucharest	A D	1-1	Helstad 85	12,000
2	ecql2	St Bucharest	H W	3-2	Solli 38; Odegaard 57; Radoi 60 og	13,051
3	ecgpf	Olympiakos	A W	3-1	Skjelbred 42; Mavrogenidis 49 og; Storflor 90	31,000
4	ecgpf	Lyon	H L	0-1		20,620
5	ecgpf	Real Madrid	A L	1-4	Strand 40	69,053
6	ecgpf	Real Madrid	H L	0-2		20,122
7	ecgpf	Olympiakos	H D	1-1	Helstad 88	17,450
8	ecgpf	Lyon	A L	1-2	Braathen 68	40,000

PLAYER APPEARANCES

Oyvind Storflor

Age (on 01/07/06)	26
Appearances in Champions league	8
Total minutes on the pitch	559
Goals	1
Yellow cards	0
Red cards	0
Home country	Norway

	PLAYER	POS	AGE	APP	MINS ON	GOALS	CARDS(Y)	CARDS(R)	NATIONAL SIDE
1	Espen Johnsen	GK	26	8	720	0	1	0	Norway
2	Mikael Dorsin	DEF	24	8	703	0	0	0	Sweden
3	Vidar Riseth	DEF	34	8	626	0	1	0	Norway
4	Jan Gunnar Solli	MID	25	7	616	1	0	0	Norway
5	Christer Basma	DEF	33	7	565	0	0	0	Norway
6	Oyvind Storflor	ATT	26	8	559	1	0	0	Norway
7	Daniel Braathen	ATT	24	8	544	1	0	0	Norway
8	Bjorn Tore Kvarme	DEF	34	6	540	0	0	0	Norway
9	Frode Johnsen	ATT	32	8	512	0	0	0	Norway
10	Roar Strand	MID	36	7	477	1	0	0	Norway
11	Thorstein Helstad	ATT	29	8	451	2	0	0	Norway
12	Orjan Berg	MID	37	4	360	0	1	0	Norway
13	Frederik Winsnes	MID	30	6	354	0	0	0	Norway
14	Per Ciljan Skjelbred	MID	19	5	347	1	0	0	Norway
15	Alejandro Lago	DEF	27	4	315	0	1	0	Uruguay

ARTMEDIA BRATISLAVA

SLOVAKIA
3rd in Group H

1	ecql1	Partizan	H D	0-0		16,127
2	ecql2	Partizan	A W	4-2*	(*on penalties)	31,000
3	ecgph	Inter Milan	H L	0-1		28,000
4	ecgph	Porto	A W	3-2	Petras 45; Kozak 54; Borbely 74	48,000
5	ecgph	Rangers	A D	0-0		49,018
6	ecgph	Rangers	H D	2-2	Borbely 8; Kozak 59	6,527
7	ecgph	Inter Milan	A L	0-4		
8	ecgph	Porto	H D	0-0		9,542

PLAYER APPEARANCES

Juraj Cobej

Age (on 01/07/06)	34
Appearances in Champions league	10
Total minutes on the pitch	930
Goals	0
Yellow cards	0
Red cards	0
Home country	Slovakia

	PLAYER	POS	AGE	APP	MINS ON	GOALS	CARDS(Y)	CARDS(R)	NATIONAL SIDE
1	Juraj Cobej	GK	34	10	930	0	0	0	Slovakia
2	Jan Durica	DEF	24	10	930	0	0	0	Slovakia
3	Branislav Fodrek	MID	25	10	930	0	2	0	Slovakia
4	Jan Kozak	MID	26	10	908	2	1	0	Slovakia
5	Ondrej Debnar	DEF	34	9	840	0	2	0	Slovakia
6	Balazs Borbely	MID	26	9	840	2	2	0	Slovakia
7	Blazej Vascak	MID	22	10	755	1	0	0	Slovakia
8	Juraj Halenar	ATT	23	10	704	3	0	0	Slovakia
9	Peter Petras	MID	27	8	700	1	2	0	Slovakia
10	Branislav Obzera	MID	24	8	510	0	1	0	Slovakia
11	Ales Urbanek	MID	26	6	510	0	1	0	Czech Republic
12	Daniel Tschur	DEF	29	7	371	0	0	0	Czech Republic
13	Pavol Stano	MID	28	9	369	0	2	0	Slovakia
14	Lukas Hartig	ATT	29	5	367	0	0	0	Czech Republic
15	Peter Burak	DEF	27	3	222	0	0	0	Slovakia
16	Jozef Kotula	DEF	29	2	180	0	0	0	Slovakia

RAPID VIENNA

AUSTRIA
4th in Group A

	Comp	Opponent	H/A	Res	Score	Scorers	Att
1	ecql1	Loko Moscow	H	D	1-1	Valachovic 75 pen	17,500
2	ecql2	Loko Moscow	A	W	1-0	Valachovic 85	27,823
3	ecgpa	Bayern Munich	H	L	0-1		47,000
4	ecgpa	Juventus	A	L	0-3		49,521
5	ecgpa	Club Brugge	H	L	0-1		45,000
6	ecgpa	Club Brugge	A	L	2-3	Kincl 1; Hofmann 81	26,000
7	ecgpa	Bayern Munich	A	L	0-4		66,000
8	ecgpa	Juventus	H	L	1-3	Kincl 52	46,500

PLAYER APPEARANCES

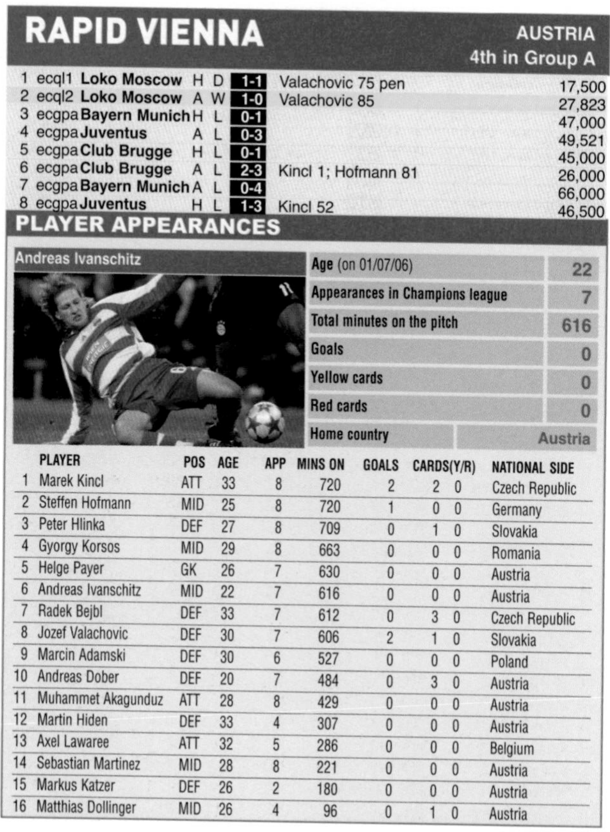

Andreas Ivanschitz

Age (on 01/07/06)	22
Appearances in Champions league	7
Total minutes on the pitch	616
Goals	0
Yellow cards	0
Red cards	0
Home country	Austria

	PLAYER	POS	AGE	APP	MINS ON	GOALS	CARDS(Y)	CARDS(R)	NATIONAL SIDE
1	Marek Kincl	ATT	33	8	720	2	2	0	Czech Republic
2	Steffen Hofmann	MID	25	8	720	1	0	0	Germany
3	Peter Hlinka	DEF	27	8	709	0	1	0	Slovakia
4	Gyorgy Korsos	MID	29	8	663	0	0	0	Romania
5	Helge Payer	GK	26	7	630	0	0	0	Austria
6	Andreas Ivanschitz	MID	22	7	616	0	0	0	Austria
7	Radek Bejbl	DEF	33	7	612	0	3	0	Czech Republic
8	Jozef Valachovic	DEF	30	7	606	2	1	0	Slovakia
9	Marcin Adamski	DEF	30	6	527	0	0	0	Poland
10	Andreas Dober	DEF	20	7	484	0	3	0	Austria
11	Muhammet Akagunduz	ATT	28	8	429	0	0	0	Austria
12	Martin Hiden	DEF	33	4	307	0	0	0	Austria
13	Axel Lawaree	ATT	32	5	286	0	0	0	Belgium
14	Sebastian Martinez	MID	28	8	221	0	0	0	Austria
15	Markus Katzer	DEF	26	2	180	0	0	0	Austria
16	Matthias Dollinger	MID	26	4	96	0	1	0	Austria

PANATHINAIKOS

GREECE
4th in Group C

	Comp	Opponent	H/A	Res	Score	Scorers	Att
1	ecql1	Wisla Krakow	A	L	1-3	Olisadebe 4	15,000
2	ecql2	Wisla Krakow	H	W	4-1	Morris 62; Olisadebe 65; Papadopoulos 87; Kotsios 114	60,000
3	ecgpc	Udinese	A	L	0-3		25,000
4	ecgpc	W Bremen	H	W	2-1	Gonzalez 5 pen; Mantzios 8	50,000
5	ecgpc	Barcelona	H	D	0-0		65,000
6	ecgpc	Barcelona	A	L	0-5		75,000
7	ecgpc	Udinese	H	L	1-2	Charalambides 45	35,000
8	ecgpc	W Bremen	A	L	1-5	Morris 53	38,000

PLAYER APPEARANCES

Ezequiel Gonzalez

Age (on 01/07/06)	25
Appearances in Champions league	6
Total minutes on the pitch	525
Goals	1
Yellow cards	1
Red cards	0
Home country	Argentina

	PLAYER	POS	AGE	APP	MINS ON	GOALS	CARDS(Y)	CARDS(R)	NATIONAL SIDE
1	Mario Galinovic	GK	29	8	750	0	1	0	Croatia
2	Nasief Morris	DEF	25	8	750	2	1	0	South Africa
3	Flavio Conceicao	MID	32	7	660	0	4	0	Brazil
4	Loukas Vintra	DEF	25	6	570	0	2	0	Greece
5	Anthony Seric	MID	27	6	555	0	3	0	Croatia
6	Ezequiel Gonzalez	MID	25	6	525	1	1	0	Argentina
7	Igor Biscan	DEF	28	6	449	0	0	0	Croatia
8	Elias Kotsios	DEF	25	6	448	1	1	0	Greece
9	Mikael Nilsson	MID	28	5	437	0	0	0	Sweden
10	Dimitrios Papadopoulos	ATT	24	6	418	1	0	0	Greece
11	Filipos Darlas	DEF	22	5	401	0	1	0	Greece
12	Sandor Torghelle	ATT	24	5	284	0	2	0	Hungary
13	Costas Charalambides	MID	24	3	279	1	0	0	Cyprus
14	Vaggelis Mantzios	ATT	23	4	270	1	0	0	Greece

FENERBAHCE

TURKEY
4th in Group E

	Comp	Opponent	H/A	Res	Score	Scorers	Att
1	ecgpe	AC Milan	A	L	1-3	Alex 63 pen	43,000
2	ecgpe	PSV Eindhoven	H	W	3-0	Alex 40 pen,68; Appiah 90	21,895
3	ecgpe	Schalke	H	D	3-3	Luciano 14; Nobre 73; Appiah 79	50,000
4	ecgpe	Schalke	A	L	0-2		59,000
5	ecgpe	AC Milan	H	L	0-4		50,000
6	ecgpe	PSV Eindhoven	A	L	0-2		30,000

PLAYER APPEARANCES

Nicolas Anelka

Age (on 01/07/06)	27
Appearances in Champions league	6
Total minutes on the pitch	514
Goals	0
Yellow cards	0
Red cards	0
Home country	France

	PLAYER	POS	AGE	APP	MINS ON	GOALS	CARDS(Y)	CARDS(R)	NATIONAL SIDE
1	Umit Ozat	DEF	29	6	540	0	1	0	Turkey
2	Onder Turaci	DEF	24	6	540	0	1	0	Turkey
3	Serkan Balci	DEF	22	6	540	0	1	0	Turkey
4	Demirel Volkan	GK	25	6	540	0	1	0	Turkey
5	Nicolas Anelka	ATT	27	6	514	0	0	0	France
6	Stephen Appiah	MID	25	6	502	2	0	0	Ghana
7	Fabio Luciano	DEF	31	5	400	1	1	1	Brazil
8	Marco Aurelio	MID	28	5	391	0	3	1	Brazil
9	Selcuk Sahin	MID	25	5	387	0	0	0	Turkey
10	Tuncay Sanli	ATT	24	5	384	0	1	0	Turkey
11	Marcio Nobre	ATT	25	6	383	1	0	0	Brazil
12	Alex De Souza	MID	28	4	356	3	2	1	Brazil
13	Kemal Aslan	MID	24	3	101	0	0	0	Turkey
14	Servet Cetin	DEF	25	1	90	0	0	0	Turkey
15	Deniz Baris	DEF	29	1	90	0	1	0	Turkey
16	Mehmet Yozgatli	MID	27	3	82	0	0	0	Turkey

ANDERLECHT

BELGIUM
4th in Group G

	Comp	Opponent	H/A	Res	Score	Scorers	Att
1	ecql1	Slavia Prague	H	W	2-1	Goor 7; Mpenza 37	17,866
2	ecql2	Slavia Prague	A	W	2-0	Akin 72; Mpenza 84	17,216
3	ecgpg	Chelsea	A	L	0-1		29,575
4	ecgpg	Real Betis	H	L	0-1		27,500
5	ecgpg	Liverpool	H	L	0-1		25,000
6	ecgpg	Liverpool	A	L	0-3		42,607
7	ecgpg	Chelsea	H	L	0-2		21,070
8	ecgpg	Real Betis	A	W	1-0	Kompany 44	55,259

PLAYER APPEARANCES

Gregory Pujol

Age (on 01/07/06)	26
Appearances in Champions league	2
Total minutes on the pitch	111
Goals	0
Yellow cards	0
Red cards	0
Home country	France

	PLAYER	POS	AGE	APP	MINS ON	GOALS	CARDS(Y)	CARDS(R)	NATIONAL SIDE
1	Bart Goor	MID	33	8	720	1	1	0	Belgium
2	Oliver Deschacht	DEF	25	7	614	0	0	0	Belgium
3	Hannu Tihinen	DEF	30	8	600	0	0	0	Finland
4	Mbo Mpenza	ATT	29	7	590	2	0	0	Belgium
5	Anthony Vanden Borre	DEF	18	6	539	0	1	0	Belgium
6	Yves Vanderhaeghe	MID	36	7	528	0	2	0	Belgium
7	Christian Wilhelmsson	MID	26	7	495	0	0	0	Sweden
8	Mark Deman	MID	23	5	450	0	0	0	Belgium
9	Serhat Akin	ATT	25	7	411	1	1	0	Turkey
10	Par Zetterberg	MID	35	7	393	0	0	0	Sweden
11	Vincent Kompany	DEF	20	4	360	1	0	0	Belgium
12	Daniel Zitka	GK	31	4	360	0	0	0	Czech Republic
13	Sylvio Proto	GK	23	4	360	0	0	0	Belgium
14	Michal Zewlakow	DEF	30	5	284	0	0	0	Poland
15	Roland Juhasz	DEF	23	3	270	0	1	0	Hungary
16	Nenad Jestrovic	ATT	30	5	256	0	0	1	Serbia &

SPARTA PRAGUE

CZECH REPUBLIC
4th in Group B

		Opponent	H/A	Res	Score	Scorers	Att
1	ecgpb	**Ajax**	H	D	1-1	Matusovic 66	13,500
2	ecgpb	**FC Thun**	A	L	0-1		32,000
3	ecgpb	**Arsenal**	H	L	0-2		12,528
4	ecgpb	**Arsenal**	A	L	0-3		35,155
5	ecgpb	**Ajax**	A	L	1-2	Petras 90	46,158
6	ecgpb	**FC Thun**	H	D	0-0		15,000

PLAYER APPEARANCES

Karol Kise

Age (on 01/07/06)	29
Appearances in Champions league	3
Total minutes on the pitch	270
Goals	0
Yellow cards	0
Red cards	0
Home country	Slovakia

	PLAYER	POS	AGE	APP	MINS ON	GOALS	CARDS(Y	/R)	NATIONAL SIDE
1	Michal Kadlec	DEF	21	6	540	0	1	0	Czech Republic
2	Zdenek Pospech	DEF	27	6	540	0	0	0	Czech Republic
3	Jaromir Blazek	GK	33	6	540	0	0	0	Czech Republic
4	Tomas Polacek	MID	25	6	528	0	0	0	Czech Republic
5	Martin Petras	DEF	26	6	528	1	1	1	Slovakia
6	Lukas Zelenka	MID	26	6	511	0	0	0	Czech Republic
7	Adam Petrous	DEF	28	5	450	0	1	0	Czech Republic
8	Lukas	DEF	28	4	360	0	1	0	Czech Republic
9	Martin Hasek	MID	36	4	351	0	0	0	Czech Republic
10	Karol Kise	MID	29	3	270	0	0	0	Slovakia
11	Miroslav Slepicka	ATT	24	5	270	0	0	0	Czech Republic
12	Libor Dosek	ATT	28	5	213	0	1	0	Czech Republic
13	Tomas Sivok	MID	22	2	180	0	0	0	Czech Republic
14	Miroslav Matusovic	ATT	25	4	178	1	0	0	Czech Republic
15	Pavel Pergl	MID	28	2	159	0	0	0	Czech Republic
16	Ondoej Herzan	MID	25	3	130	0	0	0	Czech Republic

MANCHESTER UNITED

ENGLAND
4th in Group D

		Opponent	H/A	Res	Score	Scorers	Att
1	ecql1	**Debreceni**	H	W	3-0	Rooney 7; van Nistelrooy 49; Ronaldo 63	51,701
2	ecql2	**Debreceni**	A	W	3-0	Heinze 20,60; Richardson 65	27,000
3	ecgpd	**Villarreal**	A	D	0-0		23,000
4	ecgpd	**Benfica**	H	W	2-1	Giggs 39; van Nistelrooy 85	66,112
5	ecgpd	**Lille**	H	D	0-0		60,626
6	ecgpd	**Lille**	A	L	0-1		65,000
7	ecgpd	**Villarreal**	H	D	0-0		67,471
8	ecgpd	**Benfica**	A	L	1-2	Scholes 6	61,000

PLAYER APPEARANCES

Rio Ferdinand

Age (on 01/07/06)	27
Appearances in Champions league	8
Total minutes on the pitch	720
Goals	0
Yellow cards	2
Red cards	0
Home country	England

	PLAYER	POS	AGE	APP	MINS ON	GOALS	CARDS(Y	/R)	NATIONAL SIDE
1	Edwin Van der Sar	GK	35	8	720	0	0	0	Holland
2	Rio Ferdinand	DEF	27	8	720	0	2	0	England
3	Ruud van Nistelrooy	ATT	30	8	699	2	1	0	Holland
4	Cristiano Ronaldo	MID	21	8	659	1	1	0	Portugal
5	Alan Smith	MID	25	8	645	0	3	0	England
6	John O'Shea	DEF	25	7	624	0	1	0	Rep of Ireland
7	Darren Fletcher	MID	22	7	562	0	0	0	Scotland
8	Paul Scholes	MID	31	7	558	1	3	1	England
9	Mikael Silvestre	DEF	28	6	540	0	2	0	France
10	Wayne Rooney	ATT	20	5	425	1	3	1	England
11	Ryan Giggs	MID	32	5	332	1	0	0	Wales
12	Keiron Richardson	MID	21	5	296	1	1	0	England
13	Wes Brown	DEF	26	3	252	0	0	0	England
14	Phillip Bardsley	DEF	21	3	225	0	0	0	England

OLYMPIAKOS

GREECE
4th in Group F

		Opponent	H/A	Res	Score	Scorers	Att
1	ecgpf	**Rosenborg BK**	H	L	1-3	Lago 19 og	31,000
2	ecgpf	**Real Madrid**	A	L	1-2	Kafes 48	52,000
3	ecgpf	**Lyon**	A	L	1-2	Kafes 84	40,000
4	ecgpf	**Lyon**	H	L	1-4	Babangida 3	29,555
5	ecgpf	**Rosenborg BK**	A	D	1-1	Rivaldo 25	17,450
6	ecgpf	**Real Madrid**	H	W	2-1	Bulut 50; Rivaldo 87	31,456

PLAYER APPEARANCES

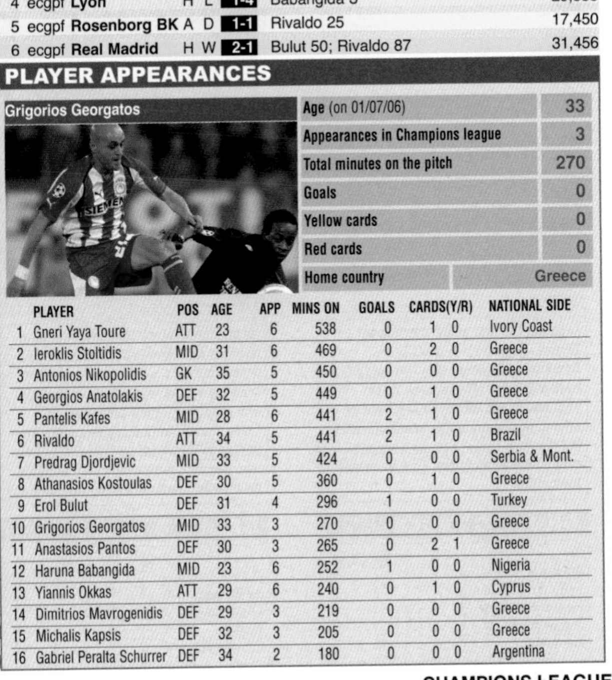

Grigorios Georgatos

Age (on 01/07/06)	33
Appearances in Champions league	3
Total minutes on the pitch	270
Goals	0
Yellow cards	0
Red cards	0
Home country	Greece

	PLAYER	POS	AGE	APP	MINS ON	GOALS	CARDS(Y	/R)	NATIONAL SIDE
1	Gneri Yaya Toure	ATT	23	6	538	0	1	0	Ivory Coast
2	Ieroklis Stoltidis	MID	31	6	469	0	2	0	Greece
3	Antonios Nikopolidis	GK	35	5	450	0	0	0	Greece
4	Georgios Anatolakis	DEF	32	5	449	0	1	0	Greece
5	Pantelis Kafes	MID	28	6	441	2	1	0	Greece
6	Rivaldo	ATT	34	5	441	2	1	0	Brazil
7	Predrag Djordjevic	MID	33	5	424	0	0	0	Serbia & Mont.
8	Athanasios Kostoulas	DEF	30	5	360	0	1	0	Greece
9	Erol Bulut	DEF	31	4	296	1	0	0	Turkey
10	Grigorios Georgatos	MID	33	3	270	0	0	0	Greece
11	Anastasios Pantos	DEF	30	3	265	0	2	1	Greece
12	Haruna Babangida	MID	23	6	252	1	0	0	Nigeria
13	Yiannis Okkas	ATT	29	6	240	0	1	0	Cyprus
14	Dimitrios Mavrogenidis	DEF	29	3	219	0	0	0	Greece
15	Michalis Kapsis	DEF	32	3	205	0	0	0	Greece
16	Gabriel Peralta Schurrer	DEF	34	2	180	0	0	0	Argentina

PORTO

PORTUGAL
4th in Group H

		Opponent	H/A	Res	Score	Scorers	Att
1	ecgph	**Rangers**	A	L	2-3	Pepe 47,71	48,599
2	ecgph	**Artmedia Brat**	H	L	2-3	Lucho Gonzalez 32; Diego 39	48,000
3	ecgph	**Inter Milan**	H	W	2-0	Materazzi 22 og; McCarthy 35	25,500
4	ecgph	**Inter Milan**	A	L	1-2	Hugo Almeida 16	37
5	ecgph	**Rangers**	H	D	1-1	Lopez, L 60	48,000
6	ecgph	**Artmedia Brat**	A	D	0-0		9,542

PLAYER APPEARANCES

Miguel Hugo Almeida

Age (on 01/07/06)	22
Appearances in Champions league	6
Total minutes on the pitch	296
Goals	1
Yellow cards	1
Red cards	0
Home country	Portugal

	PLAYER	POS	AGE	APP	MINS ON	GOALS	CARDS(Y	/R)	NATIONAL SIDE
1	Vitor Manuel Baia	GK	36	6	540	0	0	0	Portugal
2	Luis Oscar Gonzalez	MID	25	6	540	1	1	0	Argentina
3	Jorginho	ATT	29	6	468	0	0	0	Brazil
4	Pepe	DEF	23	5	450	2	1	0	Brazil
5	Ricardo Quaresma	ATT	22	6	448	0	2	0	Portugal
6	Bosingwa	MID	23	5	392	0	2	0	Portugal
7	Cesar Peixoto	ATT	26	4	360	0	1	0	Portugal
8	da Silva Paulo Assuncao	MID	26	4	331	0	0	0	Brazil
9	Pedro Emanuel	DEF	31	5	323	0	1	0	Portugal
10	Miguel Hugo Almeida	ATT	22	6	296	1	1	0	Portugal
11	Ricardo Costa	DEF	25	3	255	0	0	0	Portugal
12	Benni McCarthy	ATT	28	4	254	1	0	0	South Africa
13	Ribas Santos Diego	MID	21	4	248	1	1	0	Brazil
14	Barreto da Silva Ibson	DEF	22	3	181	0	0	0	Brazil
15	Marek Cech	DEF	23	2	180	0	0	0	Slovakia
16	Alan	MID	26	4	155	0	0	0	Brazil

THE UEFA CUP

1ST ROUND

	AGG		LEG1	LEG2
APOEL	1-4	Hertha Berlin	0-1	1-3
Auxerre	2-2	Levski Sofia	2-1	0-1
Levski Sofia win on away goals				
B Leverkusen	0-2	CSKA Sofia	0-1	0-1
Banik Ostrava	2-5	Heerenveen	2-0	0-5
Basel	6-0	Siroki Brijeg	5-0	1-0
Besiktas	4-2	Malmo	0-1	4-1
Bolton	4-2	L Plovdiv	2-1	2-1
Brann	3-5	L Moscow	1-2	2-3
Brondby	3-2	Zurich	2-0	1-2
Crvena Zvezda	1-1	Braga	0-0	1-1
Crvena Zvezda win on away goals				
CSKA Moscow	6-2	Midtjylland	3-1	3-1
D Bucharest	5-2	Everton	5-1	0-1
Feyenoord	1-2	R Bucharest	1-1	0-1
GAK	0-7	Strasbourg	0-2	0-5
G Beerschot	0-0	Marseille	0-0	0-0
Marseille win 4-1 on penalties				
Grasshoppers	4-1	MyPa	1-1	3-0
Guimaraes	4-0	Wisla Krakow	3-0	1-0
Halmstad	4-4	Sporting Lisbon	1-2	3-2
Halmstad win on away goals				
Hamburg	2-1	FC Copenhagen	1-1	1-
Hibernian	1-5	Dnipro	0-0	1-

Everton are blown away by the counter-attacking brilliance of Dinamo Bucharest in Romania. Joseph Yobo levels Claudio Niculescu's goal in the first half but the Premiership side concede four in the second half to make the return leg a formality

Rapid Bucharest see off a free-scoring Feyenoord side with a draw in Holland followed by a Mugarel Buga goal to give them the win in the Romanian capital despite Ono going close to an equaliser

The Ukrainians give a reminder of their improving European club form by thrashing Hibernian 5-1. Dnipro secure a goalless draw in Scotland and hit five at home

GROUP A

CSKA Sofia (0) 0 **Hamburg** (0) 1
22,000 — Van der Vaart 57

Viking (1) 1 **AS Monaco** (0) 0
Nhleko 18 — 9,684

Hamburg (1) 2 **Viking** (0) 0
Van der Vaart 21, Lauth 66 — 40,000

Slavia Prague (2) 4 **CSKA Sofia** (1) 2
Fort 5,75, Vlcek 36, Pitak 56 — Gargorov 10, Sakaliev 58 — 7,171

AS Monaco (1) 2 **Hamburg** (0) 0
Adebayor 44, Veigneau 90 — 18,000

Emmanuel Adebayor fires home a vital goal for Monaco just before half time against Hamburg, who lose defender Khalid Boulahrouz to a red card

Viking (1) 2 **Slavia Prague** (0) 2
Nhleko 26, Gaarde 55 — Vlcek 51, Pitak 83 — 7,941

CSKA Sofia (1) 2 **Viking** (0) 0
Yanev 35 pen, Zadi 47 — 7,000

Slavia Prague (0) 0 **AS Monaco** (1) 2
12,540 — Maoulida 11,71

Hamburg (1) 2 **Slavia Prague** (0) 0
Barbarez 9, Mpenza 57 — 46,253

AS Monaco (0) 2 **CSKA Sofia** (0) 1
Kapo Obou 50, Squillaci 75 — Dimitrov, V 84 — 9,000

Nkosinathi Nhleko surprises AS Monaco with the only goal of the opening game to give Norwegian side Viking an unexpected win. Hamburg beat CSKA Sofia and their strong season continues with a win over Viking before losing at home to AS Monaco. The French and German sides top the group and Czech side Slavia Prague sneak into third spot

GROUP A TABLE

	P	W	D	L	DIF	PTS
AS Monaco	4	3	0	1	4	9
Hamburg	4	3	0	1	3	9
Slavia Prague	4	1	1	2	-2	4
Viking	4	1	1	2	-3	4
CSKA Sofia	4	1	0	3	-2	3

GROUP B

L Moscow (0) 0 **Espanyol** (0) 1
13,718 — Tamudo 53

Macc P-Tikva (1) 1 **Palermo** (1) 2
Golan 45, 3,964 — Brienza 11, Terlizzi 77

Brondby (0) 2 **Macc P-Tikva** (0) 0
Lantz 67, Absalonsen 83 — 12,500

Palermo (0) 0 **L Moscow** (0) 0
20,000

L Moscow (0) 4 **Brondby** (2) 2
Loskov 60,65,84, Lebedenko 62, 8,700 — Retov 11, Skoubo 28

Espanyol (0) 1 **Palermo** (1) 1
Moises 90, 9,114 — Gonzalez 45

Brondby (0) 1 **Espanyol** (1) 1
Skoubo 66, 21,399 — Tamudo 42

Macc P-Tikva (0) 0 **L Moscow** (1) 4
4,000 — Loskov 27 fk, Lebedenko 47,48, Ruopolo 52

Espanyol (0) 1 **Macc P-Tikva** (0) 0
Pocchettino 83 — 5,000

Palermo (2) 3 **Brondby** (0) 0
Makinwa 24, Rinaudo 44,88 — 4,521

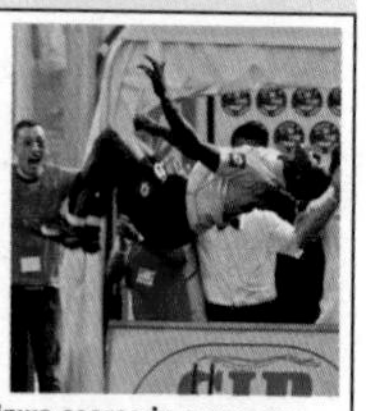

Palermo and Brondby enter the final Group B game knowing that only one can qualify. The Danes start brightly but Stephen Makinwa scores in a one-on-one and Leandro Rinaudo adds two further goals for the Italians

Group B favourites Palermo and Espanyol clash in Spain with the Italians desperate for a win following a goalless draw at home to Locomotive Moscow. Mariano Gonzalez volleys Palermo in front on the stroke of halftime but Espanyol level in the 90th minute as Hurtado Moises heads home. Moscow grab third spot

GROUP B TABLE

	P	W	D	L	DIF	PTS
Palermo	4	2	2	0	4	8
Espanyol	4	2	2	0	2	8
L Moscow	4	2	1	1	5	7
Brondby	4	1	1	2	-3	4
Macca P-Tikva	4	0	0	4	-8	0

GROUP C

Halmstad (0) 0 **Hertha Berlin** (0) 1
2,136 — Zecke 67

Steaua Bucharest (3) 4 **Lens** (0) 0
Iacob 13, Goian 20, Dica 43,63 — 20,000

Romanian league leaders Steaua Bucharest thrash Lens with Victoras Iacob and Dorin Goian giving the home side a two-goal lead. Nicolae Dica adds two more

Lens (2) 5 **Halmstad** (0) 0
Cousin 15,22,46, Barul 72, Lachor 90 — 25,000

Sampdoria (0) 0 **Steaua Bucharest** (0) 0
20,000

Halmstad (1) 1 **Sampdoria** (1) 3
Djuric 18, 3,126 — Volpi 31, Diana 67,86, Bonazzoli 86

Hertha Berlin (0) 0 **Lens** (0) 0
18,510

Sampdoria (0) 0 **Hertha Berlin** (0) 0
16,507

Steaua Bucharest (1) 3 **Halmstad** (0) 0
Radoi 11, Goian 63, Iacob 71 — 25,000

Hertha Berlin (0) 0 **Steaua Bucharest** (0) 0
15,603

Lens (1) 2 **Sampdoria** (1) 1
Thomert 10, Jomaa 90 — Flachi 23 — 31,473

Lens get the first game mauling by Steaua out of their system by hammering Swedish side Halmstad 5-0. Hertha Berlin battle through three goalless draws with their main rivals relying on a narrow win over Halmstad to take third spot. Lens grab second only with a final minute goal to defeat Sampdoria

GROUP C TABLE

	P	W	D	L	DIF	PTS
Steaua B	4	2	2	0	7	8
Lens	4	2	1	1	2	7
Hertha Berlin	4	1	3	0	1	6
Sampdoria	4	1	2	1	1	5
Halmstad	4	0	0	4	-11	0

GROUP D

Dnipro (0) 1 **AZ Alkmaar** (1) 2
Matiukhin 70, 12,300 — Arveladze 14, Sektioui 52

Grasshoppers (0) 0 **Middlesbro** (1) 1
8,500 — Hasselbaink 1

Liteks Lovetch (1) 2 **Grasshoppers** (0) 1
Novakovic 13, Sandrinho 81 — Antonio 9 — 4,000

Middlesbro (1) 3 **Dnipro** (0) 0
Yakubu 36, Viduka 50,56 — 20,000

AZ Alkmaar (0) 0 **Middlesbro** (0) 0
8,46

Dnipro (0) 0 **Liteks Lovetch** (0) 2
3,000 — Novakovic 72, Nazarenko 90 og

Grasshoppers (0) 2 **Dnipro** (1) 3
Toure 85, Renggli 90, 1,808 — Nazarenko 39, Kravchenko 62, Mikhailenko 83

Liteks Lovetch (0) 0 **AZ Alkmaar** (1) 2
4,000 — van Galen 10, Sektioui 82

AZ Alkmaar show their Uefa experience in Bulgaria with Barry Van Galen giving the Dutch side a tenth minute lead. Louis van Gaal's side adds a second through Tarik Sektioui after Liteks Lovetch's Robert Popov is sent off

AZ Alkmaar (0) 1 **Grasshoppers** (0) 0
Koevermans 70 — 8,153

Middlesbro (0) 2 **Liteks Lovetch** (0) 0
Maccarone 80,87 — 9,436

Middlesbrough and last season's semi-finalists AZ Alkmaar both qualify easily from a potentially difficult group after drawing against each-other in Holland and winning all their other games. Experienced Ukrainian side Dnipro are beaten to third spot by Bulgaria's Liteks, who win 2-0 in Ukraine with a Milivoje Novakovic header breaking the deadlock

GROUP D TABLE

	P	W	D	L	DIF	PTS
Middlesboro	4	3	1	0	6	10
AZ Alkmaar	4	3	1	0	4	10
Liteks Lovetch	4	2	0	2	-1	6
Dnipro	4	1	0	3	-5	3
Grasshoppers	4	0	0	4	-4	0

FIRST ROUND AND GROUP STAGE

Krylya Sovetov	6-6	AZ Alkmaar	5-3	1-3
AZ Alkmaar win on away goals				
Lens	5-3	Groclin	1-1	4-2
Liteks Lovetch	3-2	Genk	2-2	1-0
Macc P-Tikva	5-4	Partizan	0-2	5-2
Middlesbrough	2-0	Xanthi	2-0	0-0
Monaco	5-1	Willem II Tilb	2-0	3-1
Palermo	6-1	Anorthosis F	2-1	4-0
PAOK Salonika	3-3	Metalurh Donetsk	1-1	2-2
PAOK Salonika win on away goals				
Rennes	3-1	Osasuna	3-1	0-0

GROUP E

Basel (0) 0 **Strasbourg** (2) 2
21,900 — Diane 15, Boka 25

Tromso (1) 1 **Roma** (1) 2
Arst 42 — Kuffour 35, Cufre 84
5,982

Crvena Zvezda (1) 1 **Basel** (1) 2
Purovic 25 — Delgado 30 pen, Rossi 88
35,000

Strasbourg (1) 2 **Tromso** (0) 0
Pagis 38, Arrache 67 — 8,516

Roma (0) 1 **Strasbourg** (0) 1
Cassano 72 — Bellaid 51
8,500

Tromso (2) 3 **Crvena Zvezda** (1) 1
Bernier 22, Arst 37,74 pen — Zigic 24
4,289

Crvena Zvezda (1) 3 **Roma** (1) 1
Zigic 37,86, Purovic 77 — Nonda 23
35,186

Red Star (Crvena Zvezda) kick-start their Group E hopes against Roma after two surprise defeats. Shabani Nonda gives Roma a 23rd minute lead but 'Serbia's Peter Crouch' Nicola Zigic nets two and Milan Purovic another

Basel (1) 4 **Tromso** (3) 3
Petric 17, Delgardo 61, Chipperfield 67 Degen 75 — Strand 2, 29, Arst 19

Roma (2) 3 **Basel** (0) 1
Taddei 14, Totti 45, Montella 49 — Petric 78
15,000

Strasbourg (0) 2 **Crvena Zvezda** (1) 2
Gameiro 79,90 — Basta 34, Dokaj 64
13,416

Strasbourg gain a vital draw in Rome where Habib Bellaid's goal gives them a lead before Antonio Cassano levels for Roma. A last-minute comeback against Red Star enables Strasbourg to top the group with Kevin Gameiro's goals clawing back a 0-2 scoreline. Basel come from 3-1 down against Tromso to win 4-3 and claim third spot

GROUP E TABLE

	P	W	D	L	DIF	PTS
Strasbourg	4	2	2	0	4	8
Roma	4	2	1	1	1	7
Basel	4	2	0	2	-2	6
Crvena Zvezda	4	1	1	2	-1	4
Tromso	4	1	0	3	-2	3

Roma	5-1	Aris	5-1	0-0
Setubal	1-2	Sampdoria	1-1	0-1

Cristian Panucci scores twice from headers in the first half as Roma show the gulf in class over Thessalonika Aris from Greece, with a 5-1 first leg win

GROUP F

CSKA Moscow (0) 1 **Marseille** (2) 2
Vagner Love 80 — Lamouchi 23, Niang 38
12,000

Marseille put Uefa Cup champions CSKA two behind in Moscow with goals by Sabri Lamouchi and Mamadou Niang in the first half. Vagner Love pulls one back for CSKA in the 80th minute but it is too late

D Bucharest (0) 0 **Heerenveen** (0) 0
10,000

Heerenveen (0) 0 **CSKA Moscow** (0) 0
20,200

Levski Sofia (0) 1 **D Bucharest** (0) 0
Angelov, E. 90 — 20,000

CSKA Moscow (0) 2 **Levski Sofia** (0) 1
Vagner Love 49,73 — Domovchiyski 90
6,000

Marseille (0) 1 **Heerenveen** (0) 0
Taiwo 90 pen — 14,777

D Bucharest (0) 1 **CSKA Moscow** (0) 0
Munteanu 72 — 6,000

Levski Sofia (0) 1 **Marseille** (0) 0
Yovov 56 — 17,000

Heerenveen (0) 2 **Levski Sofia** (0) 1
Samaras 54, Hanssen 90 — Ivanov, G 52
20,025

Marseille (2) 2 **D Bucharest** (0) 1
Cesar 39, Delfim 45 — Niculescu 52
15,909

Bulgaria's strong showing in the Uefa Cup is endorsed by Levski Sofia's narrow win over Marseille to mark their only group defeat as the French team finish top. Levski's second win over Dinamo Bucharest makes them the second Bulgarian side to qualify. Third place goes to Heerenveen after they beat Levski in the final game

GROUP F TABLE

	P	W	D	L	DIF	PTS
Marseille	4	3	0	1	2	9
Levski Sofia	4	2	0	2	0	6
Heerenveen	4	1	2	1	0	5
D Bucharest	4	1	1	2	-1	4
CSKA Moskva	4	1	1	2	-1	4

Seville	2-0	Mainz	0-0	2-0

Frederic Kanouté hits two first half goals for his new club Seville as they beat Bundesliga strugglers Mainz in the second leg to go through

Shakhtar D	6-1	Debrecen	4-1	2-0
Slavia Prague	4-1	Cork City	2-0	2-1

GROUP G

Rennes (0) 0 **Stuttgart** (0) 2
22,847 — Tomasson 87, Ljuboja 90 pen

Shakhtar Donetsk (0) 1 **PAOK Salonika** (0) 0
Brandao 68 pen — 24,650

Rapid Bucharest (1) 2 **Rennes** (0) 0
Niculae 42, Buga 67 — 16,000

Stuttgart (0) 0 **Shakhtar Donetsk** (1) 2
15,000 — Fernandinho 31, Marica 88

Shakhtar Donetsk lead rivals VfB Stuttgart after a Darijo Srna's cross is converted by Fernandinho before an 88th minute goal by sub Ciprian Marica settles it for the Ukrainians

PAOK Salonika (0) 1 **Stuttgart** (0) 2
Megahed 48 — Ljuboja 85,90 pen
35,000

Shakhtar Donetsk (0) 0 **Rapid Bucharest** (0) 1
17,700 — Maldarasanu 87

Rapid Bucharest (1) 1 **PAOK Salonika** (0) 0
Maldarasanu 45 — 12,100

Rennes (0) 0 **Shakhtar Donetsk** (1) 1
18,727 — Elano 38 pen

PAOK Salonika (2) 5 **Rennes** (0) 1
Rochat 4 og, Hristodoulopoulos 38, Yiasoumi 79,89, Salpingidis 83 pen — Briand 70
3,000

Stuttgart (2) 2 **Rapid Bucharest** (0) 1
Gomez 20,37 — Burdujan 80
14,000

Three sides share top spot with nine points as Romanians Rapid beat Shakhtar but suffer their only defeat to two goals by Stuttgart's Mario Gomez. Shakhtar hand Stuttgart their only defeat and the Greek side PAOK and France's disappointing Rennes are the Group G whipping boys. PAOK regain some pride by thumping Rennes 5-1

GROUP G TABLE

	P	W	D	L	DIF	PTS
R Bucharest	4	3	0	1	3	9
Shakhtar D	4	3	0	1	3	9
Stuttgart	4	3	0	1	2	9
PAOK Salonica	4	1	0	3	1	3
Rennes	4	0	0	4	-9	0

Stuttgart	2-1	Domzale	2-0	0-1
Teplice	1-3	Espanyol	1-1	0-2
Tromso	2-1	Galatasaray	1-0	1-1
Valerenga	1-6	Steaua Bucharest	0-3	1-3
Viking	2-2	Austria Magna	1-0	1-2
Viking win on away goals				
Zenit St P	1-0	AEK Athens	0-0	1-0

40 clubs go through to the Group Stage in eight groups of five teams, each playing two home and two away games. The top three clubs in each group go through to the Round of 32, joined by the eight third-placed clubs from the Champions League Group Stage.

GROUP H

Besiktas (1) 1 **Bolton** (1) 1
Ailton 7 — Borgetti 29
17,027

Zenit St P (1) 2 **Guimaraes** (0) 1
Spivak 39 pen, Arshavin 54 — Neca 59
20,500

Bolton (1) 1 **Zenit St P** (0) 0
Nolan 24 — 15,905

Seville (0) 3 **Besiktas** (0) 0
Saviola 64, Kanoute 65,89 — 38,500

Guimaraes (0) 1 **Bolton** (0) 1
Saganowski 85 — Vaz Te 88
20,000

Zenit St P (1) 2 **Seville** (0) 1
Kherzhakov 11,89 — Puerta 90
17,000

Besiktas (1) 1 **Zenit St P** (1) 1
Akin 25 — Hagen 30
16,440

Seville (3) 3 **Guimaraes** (1) 1
Saviola 10,27, Adriano Correia 39 — Bena 44
35,000

Bolton (0) 1 **Seville** (0) 1
N'Gotty 65 — Adriano Correia 74
15,623

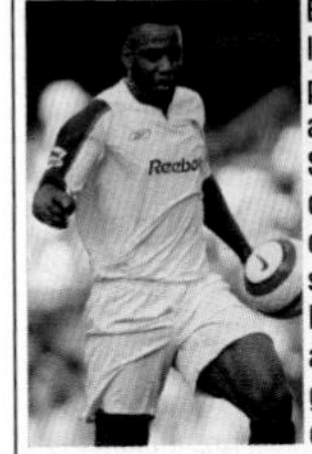

Bolton need at least a draw to progress against already qualified Seville and dominate the chances before substitute Bruno N'Gotty thumps in a 65th minute goal. Seville still earn a point when Adriano Correia's run ends with a neat finish past Ian Walker

Guimaraes (1) 1 **Besiktas** (2) 3
Saganowski 12 — Toraman 9,60, Youla 18
5,000

Seville are early favourites after an impressive win against Besiktas in their first game, courtesy of goals from Javi Saviola and two from Freddie Kanouté. A second win over Portugal's Vitoria Guimaraes ensures qualification despite a defeat to runners-up Zenit in Russia. Bolton manage three draws and beat Zenit to take third spot

GROUP H TABLE

	P	W	D	L	DIF	PTS
Seville	4	2	1	1	4	7
Zenit	4	2	1	1	1	7
Bolton	4	1	3	0	1	6
Besiktas	4	1	2	1	-1	5
Guimarães	4	0	1	3	-5	1

ROUND OF 32

Eight third placed clubs from Champions League Groups join the 24 through from the Group Stage. Artmedia Bratislava, Club Brugge, Lille, Real Betis, Rosenborg, Shalke, Thun, and Udinese join from the Champions League

Artmedia B (0) **0** **Levski Sofia** (1) **1**
5,720 — Angelov, E 9
Levski Sofia (2) **2** **Artmedia B** (0) **0**
Angelov, E 14,27 — 23,441

Basel (0) **1** **AS Monaco** (0) **0**
Degen, D 78 — 14,143
AS Monaco (1) **1** **Basel** (0) **1**
Vieri 21 pen — Majstorovic 56,56
11,335

Bolton (0) **0** **Marseille** (0) **0**
19,288
Marseille (1) **2** **Bolton** (1) **1**
Ribery 45 — Giannakopoulos 25
Ben Haim 68 og — 38,351

Bolton seem victory-bound when Stelios Giannakopoulos scores to earn them a lead and an away goal in the second leg after a 0-0 draw in Lancashire. However, Franck Ribery levels with a header from distance and a Tal Ben Haim own goal gives Marseille the tie

Club Brugge (0) **1** **Roma** (1) **2**
Portillo 61 — Vanaudenaerden 44 og
27,138 — Perrotta 74
Roma (0) **2** **Club Brugge** (0) **1**
Mancini 55 — Verheyen 60
Bovo 71 — 15,209

Roma prove too strong for Club Brugges in both legs of this tie, claiming 2-1 wins home and away. In the second leg Verheyen levels Mancini's opener before Bovo ensures a Roma repeat

Heerenveen (1) **1** **Steaua Bucharest**(1) **3**
Bruggink 24 — Dica 30
21,000 — Goian 76
Paraschiv 78
Steaua Bucharest (0) **0** **Heerenveen** (0) **1**
50,000 — Bruggink 84

Hertha Berlin (0) **0** **Rapid Bucharest** (0) **1**
13,430 — Negru 68 pen
Rapid Bucharest (0) **2** **Hertha Berlin** (0) **0**
Niculae 53 — 15,000
Buga 74

Lille (1) **3** **Shakhtar Donetsk**(0) **2**
Fauverge 19 — Brandao 89
Dernis 57 — Marica 90
Odemwingie 77 — 19,880
Shakhtar Donetsk (0) **0** **Lille** (0) **0**
23,250

Liteks Lovetch (0) **0** **Strasbourg** (1) **2**
3,000 — Le Pen 2
Diane 82
Strasbourg (0) **0** **Liteks Lovetch** (0) **0**
9,610

L Moscow (0) **0** **Seville** (0) **1**
10,223 — Jordi 75
Seville (1) **2** **L Moscow** (0) **0**
Maresca 34 — 32,000
Puerta 90

Real Betis (0) **2** **AZ Alkmaar** (0) **0**
Tardelli 70 — 30,000
Robert 79
AZ Alkmaar (2) **2** **Real Betis** (0) **1**
Arveladze 26 — Melli 94
Jaliens 35 — 8,073

Dutch side AZ fight back from two down in the first leg but are still knocked out by Real Betis. Shoto Arveladze and Kew Jaliens goals pull AZ level. But a missed Denny Landzaat penalty means the tie goes into extra time where Betis win it with a goal from Melli

Rosenborg BK (0) **0** **Zenit St P** (2) **2**
11,082 — Arshavin 22
Kherzhakov 32
Zenit St P (0) **2** **Rosenborg BK** (1) **1**
Kherzhakov 55 — Riseth 45
Denisov 86 — 21,500

Schalke (0) **2** **Espanyol** (1) **1**
Bordon 67 — Luis Garcia 34
Ernst 88 — 53,642
Espanyol (0) **0** **Schalke** (0) **3**
18,100 — Kuranyi 54
Sand 70
Lincoln 73

Espanyol are blown away at home in Spain after a Kevin Kuranyi header gives Schalke a lead to add to their 2-1 win in Germany. Substitute Ebbe Sand adds a second before Lincoln wraps up a three goal win

Slavia Prague (1) **2** **Palermo** (1) **1**
Jarolim 28 — Tedesco 42
Barzagli 49 og — 6,500
Palermo (0) **1** **Slavia Prague** (0) **0**
Godeas 51 — 8,063

Stuttgart (0) **1** **Middlesbro** (1) **2**
Ljuboja 85 — Hasselbaink 19
21,000 — Parnaby 46
Middlesbro (0) **0** **Stuttgart** (1) **1**
24,018 — Tiffert 13

Thun (1) **1** **Hamburg** (0) **0**
Adriano 30 — 18,500
Hamburg (2) **2** **Thun** (0) **0**
Van Buyten 2,33 — 40,254

Udinese (1) **3** **Lens** (0) **0**
Di Natale 36 — 8,000
Barreto De Souza 61,83

Antonio Di Natale shoots Udinese into the driving seat in the first leg of this tie and then sets up 20-year-old Brazilian Paulo Barreto for the first of his two goals. It's too much for Lens to overturn

Lens (0) **1** **Udinese** (0) **0**
Frau 55 — 26,292

LAST 16

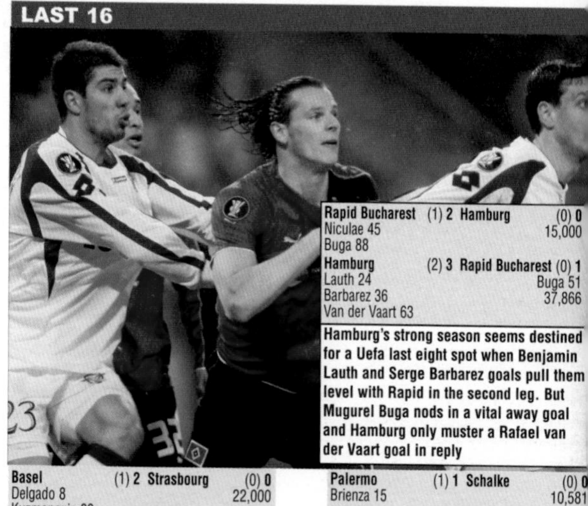

Rapid Bucharest (1) **2** **Hamburg** (0) **0**
Niculae 45 — 15,000
Buga 88
Hamburg (2) **3** **Rapid Bucharest** (0) **1**
Lauth 24 — Buga 51
Barbarez 36 — 37,866
Van der Vaart 63

Hamburg's strong season seems destined for a Uefa last eight spot when Benjamin Lauth and Serge Barbarez goals pull them level with Rapid in the second leg. But Mugurel Buga nods in a vital away goal and Hamburg only muster a Rafael van der Vaart goal in reply

Basel (1) **2** **Strasbourg** (0) **0**
Delgado 8 — 22,000
Kuzmanovic 89
Strasbourg (1) **2** **Basel** (2) **2**
Carlier 11 — Eduardo 7,26
Kante 78 — 8,115

Two goals from Brazilian Eduardo leave Strasbourg with a mountain to climb against their close Swiss neighbours Basel. He strikes after three minutes and again after 26 in the second leg. Strasbourg (already two down from the away leg) twice level but it's too late

Lille (1) **1** **Seville** (0) **0**
Dernis 24 — 11,009
Seville (2) **2** **Lille** (0) **0**
Kanoute 29 — 41,000
Fabiano 45

Lille's forceful midfielder Mathieu Bodmer is sent off for a raised elbow in the first half of the second leg and with him goes their hopes of defending a one goal first leg lead. Freddie Kanouté slots Seville level on aggregate before Luis Fabiano nets the winner

Marseille (0) **0** **Zenit St P** (0) **1**
25,500 — Arshavin 51
Zenit St P (0) **1** **Marseille** (0) **1**
Kherzhakov 69 — Taiwo 74
21,000

Andrei Arshavin's third Uefa goal does the damage in this tie as Zenit claim a first leg away win in Marseille. The Russians also score first in their home leg in St Petersburg with Taiwo's reply being insufficient to take the French side through

Palermo (1) **1** **Schalke** (0) **0**
Brienza 15 — 10,581
Schalke (1) **3** **Palermo** (0) **0**
Kobiashvili 44 — 52,151
Larsen 72, Azaouagh 80

Palermo's Eugenio Corini handles a goal-bound shot to see red in this close-fought tie. The resulting penalty is converted by Georgian Levan Kobiashvili to pull Schalke level on aggregate in the German side's home leg. Dane Soren Larsen puts them ahead in the 72nd minute before Mimoun Azaouagh makes sure

Steaua Bucharest (0) **0** **Real Betis** (0) **0**
45,023
Real Betis (0) **0** **Steaua Bucharest**(0) **3**
15,851 — Nicolita 54,82
Iacob 78

Betis thought they had done the hard work with a 0-0 draw in Romania but Steaua Bucharest's Banel Nicolita has other ideas. He scores twice in Seville as the struggling Betis go down 3-0

Udinese (0) **0** **Levski Sofia** (0) **0**
9,000
Levski Sofia (0) **2** **Udinese** (1) **1**
Borimirov 51 — Tissone 22,34
Tomasic 63 — 37,136

Veteran of the 1994 Bulgarian World Cup side, Daniel Borimirov fires Levski Sofia's comeback against a weakened Udinese side. Fernando Tissone's away goal for Udinese leaves the home side needing to score twice. Borimirov, 36, hits the first and Igor Tomasic heads the winner for the in-form Bulgarians

Middlesbro (1) **1** **Roma** (0) **0**
Yakubu 12 pen — 25,354
Roma (1) **2** **Middlesbro** (1) **1**
Mancini 43,66 pen — Hasselbaink 32
32,642
Middlesbrough win on away goals rule.

A slender one goal advantage from the home leg proves enough for Boro when Jimmy-Floyd Hasselbaink heads them in front in Rome. The rest of the match is about survival as Roma score twice through Mancini but can't get the vital third and go out on away goals

QUARTER-FINALS

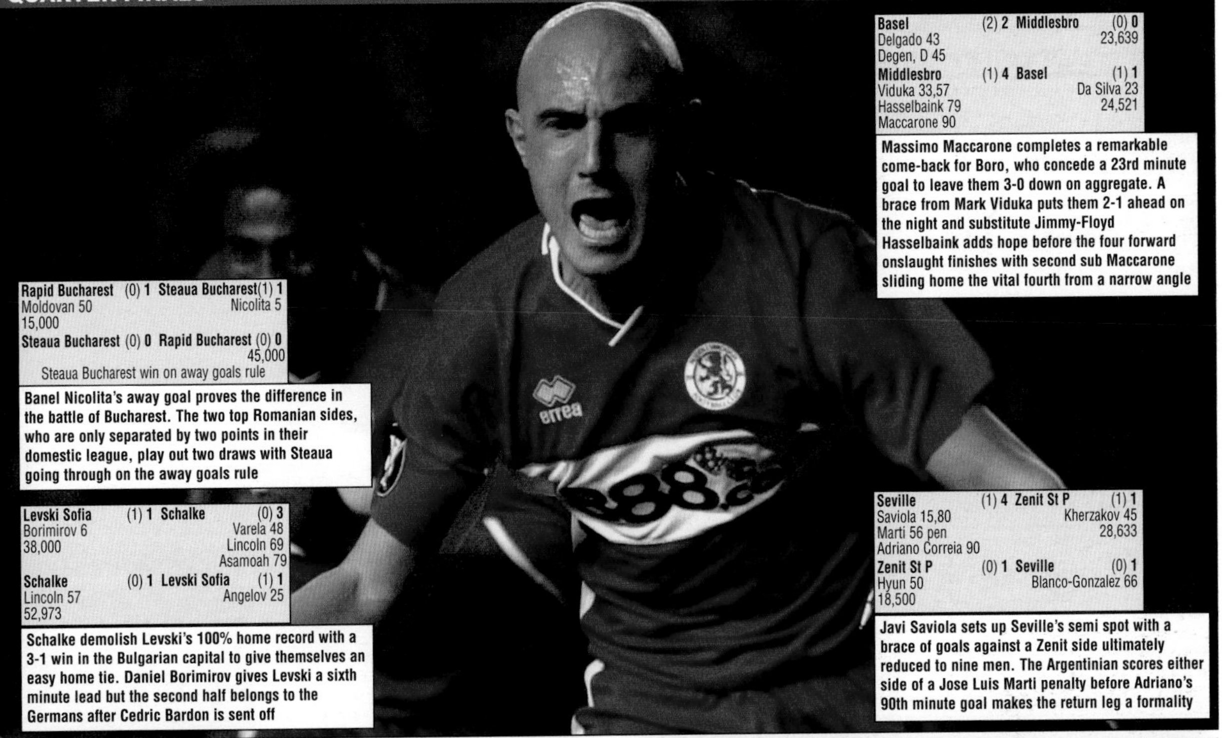

Basel	(2) 2	Middlesbro	(0) 0
Delgado 43			23,639
Degen, D 45			
Middlesbro	(1) 4	**Basel**	(1) 1
Viduka 33,57			Da Silva 23
Hasselbaink 79			24,521
Maccarone 90			

Massimo Maccarone completes a remarkable come-back for Boro, who concede a 23rd minute goal to leave them 3-0 down on aggregate. A brace from Mark Viduka puts them 2-1 ahead on the night and substitute Jimmy-Floyd Hasselbaink adds hope before the four forward onslaught finishes with second sub Maccarone sliding home the vital fourth from a narrow angle

Rapid Bucharest	(0) 1	Steaua Bucharest	(1) 1
Moldovan 50			Nicolita 5
15,000			
Steaua Bucharest	(0) 0	**Rapid Bucharest**	(0) 0
			45,000

Steaua Bucharest win on away goals rule

Banel Nicolita's away goal proves the difference in the battle of Bucharest. The two top Romanian sides, who are only separated by two points in their domestic league, play out two draws with Steaua going through on the away goals rule

Levski Sofia	(1) 1	Schalke	(0) 3
Borimirov 6			Varela 48
38,000			Lincoln 69
			Asamoah 79
Schalke	(0) 1	**Levski Sofia**	(1) 1
Lincoln 57			Angelov 25
52,973			

Schalke demolish Levski's 100% home record with a 3-1 win in the Bulgarian capital to give themselves an easy home tie. Daniel Borimirov gives Levski a sixth minute lead but the second half belongs to the Germans after Cedric Bardon is sent off

Seville	(1) 4	Zenit St P	(1) 1
Saviola 15,80			Kherzakov 45
Marti 56 pen			28,633
Adriano Correia 90			
Zenit St P	(0) 1	**Seville**	(0) 1
Hyun 50			Blanco-Gonzalez 66
18,500			

Javi Saviola sets up Seville's semi spot with a brace of goals against a Zenit side ultimately reduced to nine men. The Argentinian scores either side of a Jose Luis Marti penalty before Adriano's 90th minute goal makes the return leg a formality

SEMI-FINALS

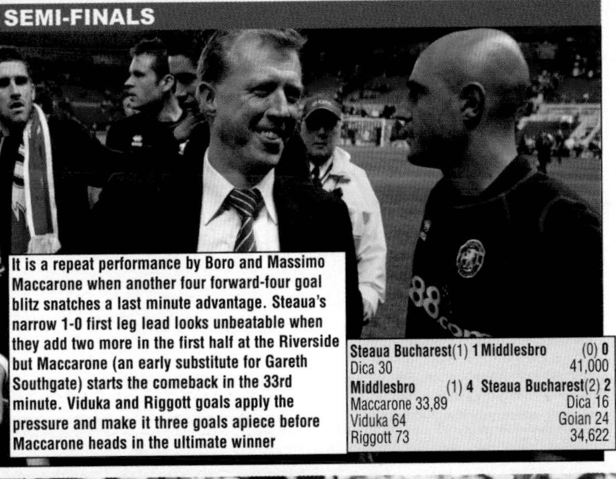

It is a repeat performance by Boro and Massimo Maccarone when another four forward-four goal blitz snatches a last minute advantage. Steaua's narrow 1-0 first leg lead looks unbeatable when they add two more in the first half at the Riverside but Maccarone (an early substitute for Gareth Southgate) starts the comeback in the 33rd minute. Viduka and Riggott goals apply the pressure and make it three goals apiece before Maccarone heads in the ultimate winner

Steaua Bucharest	(1) 1	Middlesbro	(0) 0
Dica 30			41,000
Middlesbro	(1) 4	**Steaua Bucharest**	(2) 2
Maccarone 33,89			Dica 16
Viduka 64			Goian 24
Riggott 73			34,622

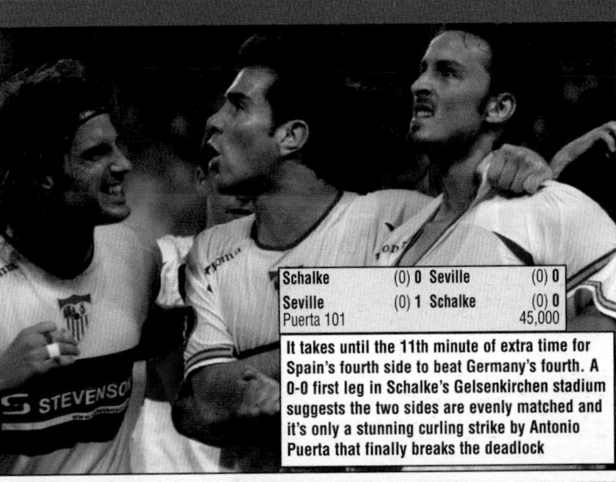

Schalke	(0) 0	Seville	(0) 0
Seville	(0) 1	**Schalke**	(0) 0
Puerta 101			45,000

It takes until the 11th minute of extra time for Spain's fourth side to beat Germany's fourth. A 0-0 first leg in Schalke's Gelsenkirchen stadium suggests the two sides are evenly matched and it's only a stunning curling strike by Antonio Puerta that finally breaks the deadlock

THE FINAL

Enzo Maresca dampens Boro's battling spirit to earn Seville a deserved Uefa Cup victory. The Italian midfielder scores the late second and third goals to ensure this season's trophy belongs to Spain.
Luis Fabiano's clever header gives Seville a first half lead but Boro's comeback exploits in the cup suggest that anything is possible, especially when Massimo Maccarone makes his usual appearance from the subs' bench. The game turns on a save from Andrés Palop to turn away a point-blank volley by Mark Viduka.
However, when Seville substitute Freddie Kanouté's low shot is parried by Schwarzer and Maresca converts the rebound the trophy is destined for Seville. Maresca adds his second before Kanouté turns it into a comprehensive victory in the 89th minute

Middlesbro	(0) 0	Seville	(1) 4
36,500			Fabiano 26
			Maresca 78,84
			Kanoute 89

EUROPEAN LEAGUES ROUND-UP

FINAL PREMIERSHIP LEAGUE TABLE - TOP THREE

		HOME					AWAY					TOTAL			
	P	W	D	L	F	A	W	D	L	F	A	F	A	DIF	PTS
Chelsea	38	18	1	0	47	9	11	3	5	25	13	72	22	50	91
Man Utd	38	13	5	1	37	8	12	3	4	35	26	72	34	38	83
Liverpool	38	15	3	1	32	8	10	4	5	25	17	57	25	32	82

FINAL DUTCH LEAGUE TABLE - TOP THREE

		HOME					AWAY					TOTAL			
	P	W	D	L	F	A	W	D	L	F	A	F	A	DIF	PTS
PSV Eindhoven	34	14	3	0	36	8	12	3	2	35	15	71	23	48	84
AZ Alkmaar	34	11	4	2	43	18	12	1	4	35	14	78	32	46	74
Feyenoord	34	13	3	1	47	11	8	5	4	32	23	79	34	45	71

FINAL FRENCH LEAGUE TABLE - TOP THREE

		HOME					AWAY					TOTAL			
	P	W	D	L	F	A	W	D	L	F	A	F	A	DIF	PTS
Lyon	38	13	4	2	40	18	12	5	2	33	13	73	31	42	84
Bordeaux	38	11	7	1	23	11	7	8	4	20	14	43	25	18	69
Lille	38	12	5	2	33	7	4	9	6	23	24	56	31	25	62

FINAL GERMAN LEAGUE TABLE - TOP THREE

		HOME					AWAY					TOTAL			
	P	W	D	L	F	A	W	D	L	F	A	F	A	DIF	PTS
Bayern Munich	34	14	2	1	42	14	8	7	2	25	18	67	32	35	75
W Bremen	34	12	3	2	50	18	9	4	4	29	19	79	37	42	70
Hamburg	34	10	2	5	26	16	11	3	3	27	14	53	30	23	68

FINAL ITALIAN LEAGUE TABLE - TOP THREE

		HOME					AWAY					TOTAL			
	P	W	D	L	F	A	W	D	L	F	A	F	A	DIF	PTS
Juventus	38	14	5	0	33	9	13	5	1	38	15	71	24	47	91
AC Milan	38	18	1	0	50	13	10	3	6	35	18	85	31	54	88
Inter Milan	38	16	1	2	47	13	7	6	6	21	17	68	30	38	76

FINAL SPANISH LEAGUE TABLE - TOP THREE

		HOME					AWAY					TOTAL			
	P	W	D	L	F	A	W	D	L	F	A	F	A	DIF	PTS
Barcelona	38	15	3	1	45	15	10	4	5	35	20	80	35	45	82
Real Madrid	38	11	4	4	40	21	9	6	4	30	19	70	40	30	70
Valencia	38	10	8	1	34	16	9	4	6	24	17	58	33	25	69

CLUB STRIKE FORCE

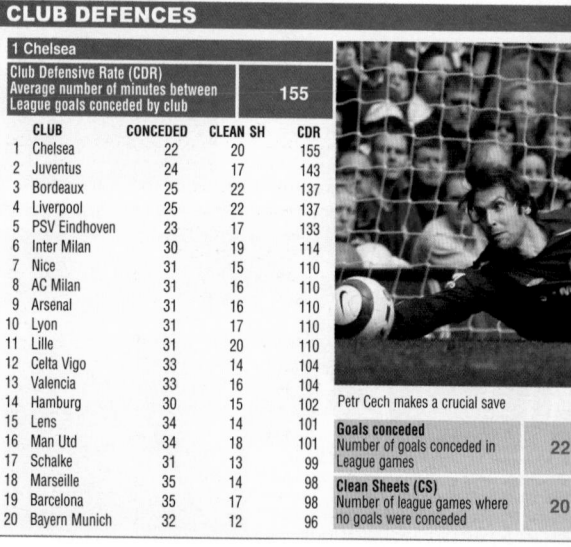

Dirk Kuijt celebrates with team mates

Goals scored in the League	79

1 Feyenoord - W Bremenn

Club Strike Rate (CSR) Average number of minutes between League goals scored by club	39

	CLUB	LEAGUE GOALS	CSR
1	Feyenoord	79	39
1	W Bremen	79	39
3	AZ Alkmaar	78	39
4	AC Milan	84	40
5	Barcelona	80	43
6	PSV Eindhoven	71	43
7	Bayern Munich	67	46
8	Ajax	66	46
9	Lyon	73	47
10	Man Utd	72	48
10	Chelsea	72	48
12	Juventus	71	48
13	B Leverkusen	64	48
14	Roma	70	49
14	Real Madrid	70	49
16	Heerenveen	63	49
17	Inter Milan	68	50
17	Arsenal	68	50
19	Fiorentina	66	52
20	Roda JC Kerk	57	54

CLUB DEFENCES

1 Chelsea

Club Defensive Rate (CDR) Average number of minutes between League goals conceded by club	155

	CLUB	CONCEDED	CLEAN SH	CDR
1	Chelsea	22	20	155
2	Juventus	24	17	143
3	Bordeaux	25	22	137
4	Liverpool	25	22	137
5	PSV Eindhoven	23	17	133
6	Inter Milan	30	19	114
7	Nice	31	15	110
8	AC Milan	31	16	110
9	Arsenal	31	16	110
10	Lyon	31	17	110
11	Lille	31	20	110
12	Celta Vigo	33	14	104
13	Valencia	33	16	104
14	Hamburg	30	15	102
15	Lens	34	14	101
16	Man Utd	34	18	101
17	Schalke	31	13	99
18	Marseille	35	14	98
19	Barcelona	35	17	98
20	Bayern Munich	32	12	96

Petr Cech makes a crucial save

Goals conceded Number of goals conceded in League games	22
Clean Sheets (CS) Number of league games where no goals were conceded	20

PLAYER NATIONALITIES

1 Country with the most player representation across major European leagues - France

Number of players	458	International appearances 04-05	190
Number of occasions in squad	9337	Total minutes played	570083
Actual League appearances	7697	% of European League action	13.54

	COUNTRY	NO OF PLAYERS	CAPS	IN SQUAD	LGE APP	MINS PLAYED	% LGE ACT
1	France	458	190	9337	7697	570093	13.54
2	Italy	476	179	9693	7314	534947	12.70
3	Spain	458	116	9560	7142	507946	12.06
4	Holland	381	156	7064	5365	394311	9.36
5	England	278	176	4978	4195	312591	7.42
6	Germany	263	149	4255	4042	298740	7.09
7	Brazil	150	78	3505	3143	235778	5.60
8	Argentina	94	114	2217	1845	139061	3.30
9	Belgium	64	23	1189	927	65148	1.55
10	Portugal	42	83	882	744	53429	1.27
11	Ivory Coast	32	143	761	702	51836	1.23
12	Czech Republic	35	114	711	645	48588	1.15
13	Denmark	41	94	779	678	47861	1.14
14	Serbia & Montenegro	37	70	704	621	46093	1.09
15	Uruguay	43	0	852	679	43331	1.03
16	Sweden	25	50	612	577	43309	1.03
17	Switzerland	31	139	670	591	42785	1.02
18	Rep of Ireland	34	67	621	553	40467	0.96
19	Senegal	35	0	557	490	35661	0.85
20	Cameroon	31	33	509	434	32609	0.77
	Other (82 countries)	548	643	10896	9249	655210	15.53

CLUB MAKE-UP – HOME AND OVERSEAS PLAYERS

1 Club which used the most overseas players in league action - Arsenal

Overseas players in named 16s	30	Home country players in named 16s	7
Percent of overseas players	81.1	Percent of League action	92.62
Most appearances	Jens Lehmann	% of match time played	100

	CLUB	OVERSEAS	HOME	% OVERSEAS	% LGE ACT	MOST APP	% APP
1	Arsenal	30	7	81.1	92.62	Jens Lehmann	100
2	Inter Milan	26	8	76.5	86.43	Ivan Cordoba	88.8
3	Roda JC Kerk	23	9	71.9	83.27	Vladan Kujovic	94.1
4	Bolton	24	8	75	79.14	Jussi Jaaskelainen	100
5	Blackburn	20	9	69	78.36	Brad Friedel	100
6	Fulham	23	10	69.7	75.9	Luis Boa Morte	87.7
7	Wolfsburg	19	9	67.9	74.51	Juan Menseguez	85.8
8	Chelsea	22	8	73.3	72.66	Petr Cech	88.2
9	Schalke	14	12	53.8	71.35	Marcelo Jose Bordon	91.2
10	B M'gladbach	21	9	70	70.41	Ze Antonio	98.6
11	Hamburg	15	14	51.7	69.17	Sergei Barbarez	94.1
12	Bayern Munich	14	10	58.3	67.57	Willy Sagnol	90.8
13	Wigan	17	13	56.7	67.21	Pascal Chimbonda	95.4
14	Portsmouth	28	7	80	66.07	Andy O'Brien	76.3
15	Liverpool	20	10	66.7	64.77	Sami Hyypia	89.6
16	Barcelona	19	14	57.6	64.4	Samuel Eto'o	88.2
17	Roosendaal	11	18	37.9	61.86	Mark Volders	86.8
18	Villarreal	14	22	38.9	61.23	Rodolfo Arruabarrena	82.1
19	Man Utd	22	14	61.1	61.22	Edwin Van der Sar	98.7
20	AC Milan	15	11	57.7	60.07	Nelson Dida	94.7

CLUB DISCIPLINARY RECORDS

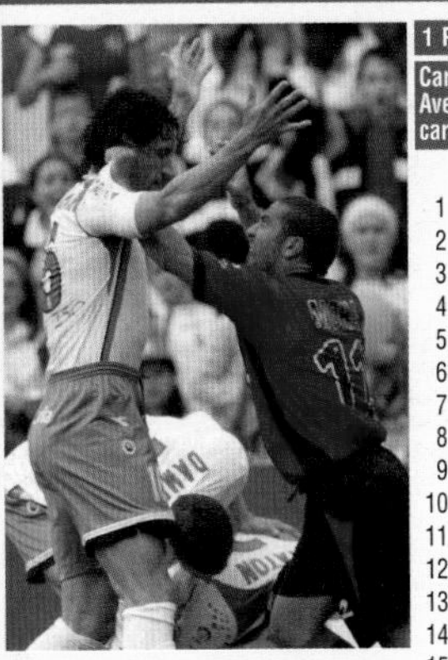
Pablo Alfaro in a ruck with Osasuna's Moha

Yellow cards	120
Red cards	8
Total	128

1 Racing Santander

Cards Average in League Average number of minutes between a card being shown of either colour	26.7

	CLUB	Y	R	TOTAL	AVE
1	R Santander	120	8	128	26.7
2	Atl Madrid	118	9	127	26.9
3	Malaga	114	11	125	27.4
4	Deportivo	116	5	121	28.3
5	Real Madrid	110	10	120	28.5
6	Osasuna	114	6	120	28.5
7	Espanyol	105	10	115	29.7
8	Mallorca	102	9	111	30.8
9	Seville	100	9	109	31.4
10	Getafe	99	8	107	32.0
11	Villarreal	102	5	107	32.0
12	Duisburg	91	3	94	32.6
13	Lecce	93	9	102	33.5
14	Hertha Berlin	82	9	91	33.6
15	Real Betis	94	7	101	33.9
16	Cologne	81	7	88	34.8
17	Real Zaragoza	94	4	98	34.9
18	Wolfsburg	81	6	87	35.2
19	Nurnberg	82	5	87	35.2
20	Udinese	84	12	96	35.6

PLAYER DISCIPLINARY RECORD

1 Amorebieta - Athl Bilbao

Cards Average mins between cards	104
League Yellow	10
League Red	1
TOTAL	11

	PLAYER	LEAGUE	Y	R	TOTAL	AVE
1	Amorebieta	Athl Bilbao	10	1	11	104
2	Zikos	AS Monaco	11	1	12	108
3	Garitano	Real Sociedad	10	2	12	122
4	Garcia, P	Real Madrid	11	0	11	125
5	Simunic	Hertha Berlin	11	1	12	130
6	Luccin	Atl Madrid	16	2	18	134
7	Poulsen	Schalke	14	1	15	149
8	Oriol	R Santander	11	0	11	150
9	Hofland	Wolfsburg	10	1	11	154
10	Coppola	Messina	12	0	12	156
11	Conti	Cagliari	14	1	15	162
12	Edmilson	Barcelona	12	1	13	162
13	Obodo	Udinese	11	2	13	165
14	Mora	R Santander	12	0	12	165
15	Albelda	Valencia	16	1	17	166
16	Acuna	Roosendaal	11	1	12	167
17	Pinola	Nurnberg	12	0	12	172
18	Lala	Hannover 96	11	2	13	173
19	Bega	Cagliari	12	2	14	176
20	Rool	Nice	14	0	14	177

(mimimum of ten cards)

TEAM OF THE SEASON

ABBIATI

JUVENTUS
CG 18 DR 161

ZAMBROTTA

JUVENTUS
CG 31 DR 153

EDMILSON*

BARCELONA
CG 22 DR 163

FERREIRA

CHELSEA
CG 18 DR 209

RIISE*

LIVERPOOL
CG 23 DR 188

NEDVED

JUVENTUS
CG 30 SD +97

GERRARD

LIVERPOOL
CG 30 SD +94

ESSIEN

CHELSEA
CG 26 SD +134

COCU

PSV EINDHOVEN
CG 33 SD +111

HENRY

ARSENAL
CG 28 SR 99

HUNTELAAR

HER/AJAX
CG 28 SR 81

The European Team of the Season shows a 4-4-2 of the best players in the major European Leagues based upon the selection criteria used for the chart-toppers. The players selected are taken from the lists for each club except that to get into this Team of the Season you must have played at least 17 Counting Games in league matches (roughly half the league season) and not 12 as is the case in the club lists. The other restriction is that we are only allowing one player from each club in each position.

- **The Top team's goalkeeper** is the player with the highest *Defensive Rating*
- **The Top team's defenders** are also tested by *Defensive Rating*, i.e. the average number of minutes between league goals conceded while on the pitch.
- **The Top team's midfield** are selected on their *Scoring Difference*, i.e.their *Defensive Rating* minus their *Contribution to Attacking Power* (average number of minutes between league goals scored while on the pitch. It takes no account of assists.
- **The Top team strikeforce** is made up of the two strikers with the highest *Strike Rate* (the average number of minutes between league goals scored while on the pitch).

*Both Edmilson and Riise played in midfield and defence this season.

CHART-TOPPING POINT EARNERS

	PLAYER	TEAM	GAMES	POINTS	AVE
1	Essien	Chelsea	26	70	2.69
2	Edmilson	Barcelona	22	59	2.68
3	Abbiati	Juventus	18	48	2.67
4	Simons	PSV Eindhoven	29	74	2.55
5	Morientes	Liverpool	17	43	2.53
6	Park	Man Utd	17	42	2.47
7	Gattuso	AC Milan	28	69	2.46
8	Cacapa	Lyon	25	61	2.44
9	Lodewijks	Feyenoord	25	61	2.44
10	Diarra	Lyon	28	68	2.43
11	Opdam	AZ Alkmaar	18	43	2.39
12	Stenman	B Leverkusen	13	31	2.38
13	Lucio	Bayern Munich	29	67	2.31
14	Veron	Inter Milan	23	53	2.3
15	Pasanen	W Bremen	14	32	2.29
16	Boukhari	Ajax	17	39	2.29
17	Laslandes	Bordeaux	12	27	2.25
18	Mensah	Rennes	12	27	2.25
19	Mauri	Lazio	12	27	2.25
20	Ferreira	Marseille	13	29	2.23

(Selection limited to top player per club)

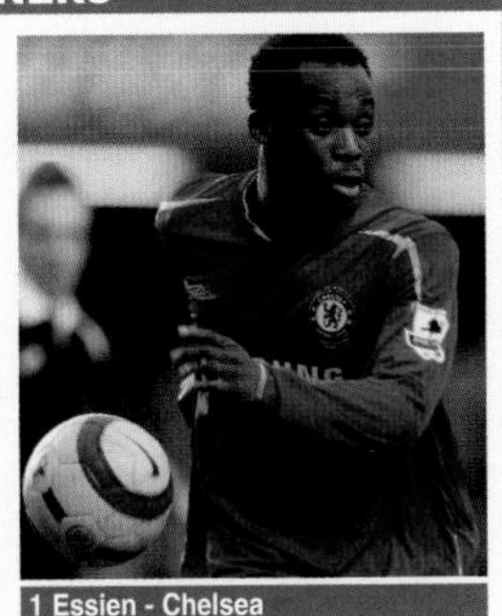

1 Essien - Chelsea

Counting Games Played at least 70mins.	26
Total Points Taken in Counting Games	70
Average points per game Taken in Counting Games	2.69

MOST MISSED PLAYERS

	PLAYER	TEAM	AVERAGE	CLUB	DIFF
1	Bucci	Parma	1.8	1.18	0.62
2	Cole	Man City	1.72	1.13	0.59
3	Boukhari	Ajax	2.29	1.76	0.53
4	N'Zogbia	Newcastle	2.05	1.53	0.52
5	Edmilson	Barcelona	2.68	2.16	0.52
6	Saenko	Nurnberg	1.76	1.29	0.47
7	Obodo	Udinese	1.59	1.13	0.46
8	Cannavaro	Parma	1.63	1.18	0.45
9	Hoogendorp	RKC Waalwijk	1.59	1.15	0.44
10	Bjelanovic	Ascoli	1.57	1.13	0.44
11	Rodriguez	Atl Madrid	1.81	1.37	0.44
12	Primus	Portsmouth	1.42	1	0.42
13	Beattie	Everton	1.73	1.32	0.41
14	Bresciano	Parma	1.57	1.18	0.39
15	Kishishev	Charlton	1.61	1.24	0.37
16	Morientes	Liverpool	2.53	2.16	0.37
17	Jordan	Man City	1.5	1.13	0.37
18	Solano	Newcastle	1.9	1.53	0.37
19	Contreras	Celta Vigo	2.05	1.68	0.37
20	Lecluse	Nancy	1.62	1.26	0.36

(No limit on the number of players per club selected)

1 Bucci - Parma

Average points	1.80
Club average	1.18
Difference	0.62

CHART-TOPPING GOALSCORERS

1 Huntelaar - Heerenveen and Ajax

Goals scored in the League	33
Contribution to Attacking Power Average number of minutes between League team goals while on pitch	40
Player Strike Rate Average number of minutes between League goals scored by player	80
Club Strike Rate (CSR) Average minutes between League goals scored by club	47

	PLAYER	CLUB	GOALS	POWER	CSR	S RATE
1	Huntelaar	Heerenveen/Ajax	33	40	47	80
1	Klose	W Bremen	25	33	39	86
3	Henry	Arsenal	27	47	50	99
4	Trezeguet	Juventus	23	44	48	100
5	Toni	Fiorentina	31	52	52	106
6	Arveladze	AZ Alkmaar	22	42	39	109
7	Eto'o	Barcelona	26	44	43	116
8	Villa	Valencia	25	59	59	120
9	Shevchenko	AC Milan	18	40	40	121
10	Farfan	PSV Eindhoven	21	42	43	123
11	van Nistelrooy	Man Utd	21	49	48	124
12	Ronaldo	Real Madrid	14	49	49	128
13	Klasnic	W Bremen	15	38	39	131
14	Hoogendorp	RKC Waalwijk	12	47	64	133
15	Vittek	Nuremberg	16	60	61	134
16	Kuijt	Feyenoord	22	38	39	135
17	Totti	Roma	15	50	48	136
18	Fred	Lyon	14	48	46	136
19	Pauleta	Paris SG	21	68	78	143
20	Altintop	Kaiserslautern	20	67	65	144

The Chart-topping Goalscorers measures the players by Strike Rate. They are most likely to be Forwards but Midfield players and even Defenders do come through the club tables. It is not a measure of the number of League goals scored - although that is also noted - but how often on average they have scored.

CHART-TOPPING MIDFIELDERS

1 Essien - Chelsea

Goals scored in the League	2
Defensive Rating Av number of mins between League goals conceded while on the pitch	176
Contribution to Attacking Power Average number of minutes between League team goals while on pitch	42
Scoring Difference Defensive Rating minus Contribution to Attacking Power	134

	PLAYER	CLUB	GOALS	DEF R	POWER	SCORE DIFF
1	Essien	Chelsea	2	176	42	134
2	Robben	Chelsea	6	176	55	121
3	Lampard	Chelsea	16	158	46	112
4	Cocu	PSV Eindhoven	10	156	45	111
5	Makelele	Chelsea	0	150	42	108
6	Diarra	Lyon	3	147	46	101
7	Nedved	Juventus	5	142	45	97
8	Gerrard	Liverpool	10	151	57	94
9	Simons	PSV Eindhoven	2	132	43	89
10	Emerson	Juventus	2	136	48	88
11	Lachuer	Auxerre	4	146	59	87
12	Juninho	Lyon	9	133	47	86
13	Giggs	Man Utd	2	132	46	86
14	J Cole	Chelsea	5	131	46	85
15	Veron	Inter Milan	0	131	47	84
16	Figo	Inter Milan	5	137	53	84
17	Sissoko	Liverpool	0	150	67	83
18	Kewell	Liverpool	3	134	56	78
19	Serginho	AC Milan	1	114	38	76
20	Albiol	Valencia	1	135	61	74

The Divisional Round-up charts combine the records of chart-topping keepers, defenders, midfield players and forwards, from every club in the division.. The one above is for **the Chart-topping Midfielders**. The players are ranked by their Scoring Difference although other attributes are shown for you to compare.

TOP LEAGUES IN EUROPE

	UEFA Cup Group Phase	Pts	Champions League Group Phase	Pts	UEFA Cup Round of 32	Pts	Champions League last 16	Pts
Spain	**Espanyol Seville**	2	**Barcelona Villarreal Real Madrid** Real Betis (U)	8	**Seville Real Betis (U)** Espanyol	3	**Barcelona Villarreal** Real Madrid	6
Italy	**Roma Palermo** Sampdoria	3	**AC Milan Juventus Inter Milan** Udinese (U)	8	**Palermo Roma Udinese (U)**	3	**AC Milan Juventus Inter Milan**	6
England	**Middlesbrough Bolton**	2	**Arsenal Chelsea Liverpool** Man Utd	8	**Middlesbrough** Bolton	2	**Arsenal** Liverpool Chelsea	6
France	**Monaco Lens Strasbourg Marseille** Rennes	5	**Lyon** Lille (U)	4	**Strasbourg Lille (U) Marseille** Monaco Lens	5	**Lyon**	2
Germany	**Hamburg Hertha Berlin Stuttgart**	3	**Bayern Munich W Bremen** Schalke (U)	6	**Hamburg Schalke (U)** Hertha Berlin Stuttgart	4	Bayern Munich W Bremen	4
Holland	**AZ Alkmaar Heerenveen**	2	**PSV Ajax**	**4**	AZ Alkmaar Heerenveen	2	PSV Ajax	4
Romania	**Steaua Bucharest Rapid Buch** Dinamo Buch	3			**Steaua Bucharest Rapid Bucharest**	2		
Portugal	Guimaraes	1	**Benfica** FC Porto	4			**Benfica**	2
Switzerland	**Basel** Grasshoppers	2	Thun (U)		**Basel** Thun (U)	2		
Bulgaria	**Levski Sofia Liteks Lovetch** CSKA Sofia	3			**Levski Sofia** Liteks Lovetch	2		
Russia	**L Moscow Zenit St P** CSKA Moscow	3			**Zenit St P** L Moscow	2		
Belgium			Club Brugge (U) Anderlecht	4	Club Brugge (U)	1		
Greece	PAOK Salonica	1	Olympiakos Panathinaikos	4				
Norway	Viking Tromso	2	Rosenborg (U)	2	Rosenborg (U)	1		
Scotland			**Rangers**	2			Rangers	2
Czech Rep	**Slavia Prague**	**1**	Sparta Prague	2	Slavia Prague	1		
Ukraine	**Shakhtar Donetsk** Dnipro	2			Shakhtar Donetsk	1		
Turkey	Besiktas	1	Fenerbache	2				
Slovakia			Artmedia (U)	2	Artmedia (U)	1		
Austria			Rapid Vienna	2				
Serbia & Mont	Crvena Zvezda (Red Star)	1						
Israel	Macca P-Tikva	1						
Sweden	Halmstad	1						
Denmark	Brondby	1						

(U) shows clubs qualifying for Uefa Cup round of 32 from Champions League Group phase

CHART-TOPPING DEFENDERS

1 Ferreira - Chelsea

Goals conceded in the League	8
Clean Sheets In games when he played at least 70 mins	11
Defensive Rating Average number of minutes between League goals conceded while on pitch	209
Club Defensive Rating Average mins between League goals conceded by the club this season	155

	PLAYER	CLUB	CON: LGE	CS	CDR	DEF RATE
1	Ferreira	Chelsea	8	11	155	209
2	Riise	Liverpool	12	16	137	188
3	Del Horno	Chelsea	11	13	155	185
4	Jurietti	Bordeaux	13	14	137	174
5	Planus	Bordeaux	17	20	137	168
6	Edmilson	Barcelona	13	13	98	163
7	Terry	Chelsea	20	20	155	162
8	Faubert	Bordeaux	16	18	137	161
9	Finnan	Liverpool	19	21	137	156
10	Gallas	Chelsea	19	16	155	154
11	Zambrotta	Juventus	18	16	137	153
12	Brown	Man Utd	10	10	101	148
13	Ooijer	PSV Eindhoven	14	14	133	146
14	Cannavaro	Juventus	22	17	137	146
15	Afanou	Bordeaux	11	8	137	141
16	Carvalho	Chelsea	14	11	155	141
17	Hyypia	Liverpool	22	20	137	139
18	Cacapa	Lyon	17	13	110	136
19	Abardonado	Nice	20	14	110	136
20	Carragher	Liverpool	24	21	137	135

The Chart-topping Defenders are resolved by their Defensive Rating, how often their team concedes a goal while they are playing. All these rightly favour players at the best performing clubs because good players win matches. However, good players in lower-table clubs will chart where they have lifted the team's performance.

CHART-TOPPING GOALKEEPERS

1 Abbiati - Juventus

Counting Games Games where he played at least 70 minutes	18
Goals Conceded in the League The number of League goals conceded while he was on the pitch	10
Clean Sheets In games when he played at least 70 mins	9
Defensive Rating Average number of minutes between League goals conceded while on pitch	161

	PLAYER	CLUB	CG	CONC	CS	DEF RATE
1	Abbiati	Juventus	18	10	9	161
2	Cech	Chelsea	34	20	18	151
3	Reina	Liverpool	33	21	20	141
4	Rame	Bordeaux	35	22	20	140
5	Buffon	Juventus	18	12	7	135
6	Gomes	PSV Eindhoven	32	21	15	135
7	Wachter	Hamburg	21	15	9	126
8	Coupet	Lyon	37	27	17	122
9	Pinto	Celta Vigo	37	28	14	117
10	Valdes	Barcelona	36	28	17	116
11	Cesar, J	Inter Milan	29	23	16	113
12	Gregorini	Nice	34	27	14	113
13	Canizares	Valencia	36	29	16	112
14	Lehmann	Arsenal	38	31	16	110
15	Warmuz	AS Monaco	23	19	10	109
16	Sylva	Lille	32	27	17	107
17	Pele	Le Mans	36	30	18	106
18	Letizi	Paris SG	27	22	11	106
19	Dida	AC Milan	36	31	14	105
20	Kahn	Bayern Munich	32	26	11	103

The Chart-topping Goalkeepers are positioned by their Defensive Rating. We also show Clean Sheets where the team has not conceded and the Keeper has played all or most (at least 70 minutes) of the game. Only one keeper is selected from each club unless they have played the requisite number of counting games.

UEFA last 16	Pts	Champ's L. Q-finals	Pts	UEFA Q. finals	Pts	Champ's L.S-finals	Pts	UEFA Semi-finals	Pts	Champ's L.Final Winners	Pts	UEFA Final Winners	Pts
Seville Real Betis	2	**Barcelona Villarreal**	4	**Seville**	1	**Barcelona** Villarreal	4	**Seville**	1	**Barcelona**	4	**Seville**	2
Palermo Roma Udinese	3	**AC Milan** Inter Juventus	6			AC Milan	2						
Middlesbrough	1	**Arsenal**	2	**Middlesbrough**	1	**Arsenal**	2	**Middlesbrough**	1	Arsenal	2	Middlesbrough	1
Strasbourg Lille (U) Marseille	3	Lyon	2										
Schalke (U) Hamburg	2			**Schalke (U)**	1			Schalke (U)	1				
Steaua Buch Rapid Buch	2			**Steaua Buch** Rapid Buch	2			Steaua Bucharest	1				
		Benfica	2										
Basel	1			Basel	1								
Levski Sofia	1			Levski Sofia	1								
Zenit St P	1			Zenit St P	1								

TOTAL		
37	Spain	(3)
31	Italy	(2)
28	England	(1)
21	France	(6)
21	Germany	(=4)
12	Holland	(=4)
10	Romania	(8)
9	Portugal	(=12)
8	Switzerland	(=17)
7	Bulgaria	(=10)
7	Russia	(20)
5	Belgium	(=12)
5	Greece	(=15)
5	Norway	(=17)
4	Scotland	(=21)
4	Czech Rep	(7)
3	Ukraine	(9)
3	Turkey	(=12)
3	Slovakia	(=21)
2	Austria	(=15)
1	Serb & Mon	(=12)
1	Israel	(=17)
1	Sweden	(=21)
1	Denmark	(=21)

Top Leagues in Europe

This chart sees how different country's leagues fared in cross-border rivalries. Picking up from the Champions League and UEFA Cup Group Phases we've noted every surviving club. 24 leagues feature initially and it's gradually whittled down to two winners.

Each league wins one point for every survivor in the UEFA Cup each round and two points in the Champions League.

WORLD CUP GROUP A How the four teams qualified

GERMANY

As host nation Germany did not have to qualify for this World Cup. They played a number of internationals as preparation for the finals during the qualifying period. The results of these were:

1	A	Japan	W	**0 3**
2	A	South Korea	L	**3 1**
3	A	Thailand	W	**1 5**
4	H	Argentina	D	**2 2**
5	A	Slovenia	W	**0 1**
6	A	N Ireland	W	**1 4**
7	H	Russia	D	**2 2**
8	H	Australia	W	**4 3**
9	A	Tunisia	W	**0 3**
10	A	Argentina	D	**2 2**
11	H	Brazil	L	**2 3**
12	H	Mexico	W	**4 3**
13	A	Holland	D	**2 2**
14	A	Slovakia	L	**2 0**
15	H	South Africa	W	**4 2**
16	A	Turkey	L	**2 1**
17	H	China PR	W	**1 0**
18	A	France	D	**0 0**

MICHAEL BALLACK
Coach Jurgan Klinsmann promised a more attack-minded Germany and the pre-tournament friendlies lived up to his promise.
He honed his strike-force, discarding Kuranyi and staying loyal to Bremen's prolific Klose despite an international lean-spell. Another ex-patriot Pole striker Podolski was struggling with Colonge but scoring freely for Germany.
However, the defence was based around Hannover youngster Per Mertesacker, partnered either by the equally inexperienced Huth as other partners were tried and discarded. The midfield, based around 2002 stalwarts, captain Ballack and Schneider looked settled and experienced with Schweinsteiger and Frings enjoying good Champions League performances.

TOP GOALSCORERS
Ballack 9; Podolski 8; Schweinsteiger 4

TOP APPEARANCES
Bernd Schneider 16; Kevin Kuranyi 16; Per Mertesacker 15; Lukas Podolski 14; Michael Ballack 13; Torsten Frings 13

COSTA RICA

16 MATCHES IN QUALIFYING

1	H	Honduras	L	**2 5**
2	A	Guatemala	L	**2 1**
3	H	Canada	W	**1 0**
4	H	Guatemala	W	**5 0**
5	A	Canada	W	**1 3**
6	A	Honduras	D	**0 0**
7	H	Mexico	L	**1 2**
8	H	Panama	W	**2 1**
9	A	Trinidad & Tobago	D	**0 0**
10	A	United States	L	**3 0**
11	H	Guatemala	W	**3 2**
12	A	Mexico	L	**2 0**
13	A	Panama	W	**1 3**
14	H	Trinidad & Tobago	W	**2 0**
15	H	United States	W	**3 0**
16	A	Guatemala	L	**3 1**

PAULO WANCHOPE
Two defeats kicked off the 'Ticos' World Cup and they turned to former coach Alexandre Guimaraes to get them back on track.
He started the Qatar-based striker Wanchope on the bench but brought him on to score the only goal of the game against Canada.
In the next match Wanchope hit a hat-trick in a thrashing of Guatamala and Germany beckoned.
A defeat of the US was the highlight of the second phase with two goals from Hernandez and one from Wanchope ensuring a qualification place above Trinidad and Tobago.

TOP GOALSCORERS
Wanchope 8; Hernandez 5

TOP APPEARANCES
Luis Marin 14; Gilberto Martinez 14; Paulo Wanchope 14; Walter Centeno 13; Alonso Solis 12; Leonardo Ganzalez 11

FINAL QUALIFYING TABLE
N/C AMERICA & CAR STAGE 3

	P	W	D	L	GF	GA	Pts
USA	10	7	1	2	16	6	22
Mexico	10	7	1	2	22	9	22
Costa Rica	10	5	1	4	15	14	16
Trinidad & Tob	10	4	1	5	10	15	13
Guatemala	10	3	2	5	16	18	11
Panama	10	0	2	8	4	21	2

POLAND

10 MATCHES IN QUALIFYING

1	A	N Ireland	W	**0 3**
2	H	England	L	**1 2**
3	A	Austria	W	**1 3**
4	A	Wales	W	**2 3**
5	H	Azerbaijan	W	**8 0**
6	H	N Ireland	W	**1 0**
7	A	Azerbaijan	W	**0 3**
8	H	Austria	W	**3 2**
9	H	Wales	W	**1 0**
10	A	England	L	**2 1**

MACIEJ ZURAWSKI
Poland quickly established themselves as England's main rivals in their qualifying group.
While coach Pawel Janas rang the changes, the goals kept flowing and the Poles easily outscored England. Other British opposition in Northern Ireland and Wales were easily brushed aside and but for two narrow defeats against England the Poles had a 100% record.
The goals came from Celtic's Zurawski who looked sharp throughout, while Frankolowski hit a hat-trick in the 8-0 thrashing of Azerbaijan, and matched Zurawski's total without making a similar impression at Wolves.
Grzegorz Rasiak, then at Spurs, offered other striking options and Poland went into the final qualifying game, topping the group and, despite finishing second, they qualified as one of the best-placed runners-up.

TOP GOALSCORERS
Zurawski 7; Frankolowski 7

TOP APPEARANCES
Maciej Zurawski 8; Tomasz Rzasa 7; Kamil Kosowski 7; Jacek Bak 7; Marcin Baszczynski 7; Tomasz Frankolowski 6

FINAL QUALIFYING TABLE
EUROPE GROUP 6

	P	W	D	L	GF	GA	Pts
England	10	8	1	1	17	5	25
Poland	10	8	0	2	27	9	24
Austria	10	4	3	3	15	12	15
N Ireland	10	2	3	5	10	18	9
Wales	10	2	2	6	10	15	8
Azerbaijan	10	0	3	7	1	21	3

ECUADOR

18 MATCHES IN QUALIFYING

1	H	Venezuela	W	**2 0**
2	A	Brazil	L	**1 0**
3	A	Paraguay	L	**2 1**
4	H	Peru	D	**0 0**
5	A	Argentina	L	**1 0**
6	H	Colombia	W	**2 1**
7	H	Bolivia	W	**3 2**
8	A	Uruguay	L	**1 0**
9	H	Chile	W	**2 0**
10	A	Venezuela	L	**3 1**
11	H	Brazil	W	**1 0**
12	H	Paraguay	W	**5 2**
13	A	Peru	D	**2 2**
14	H	Argentina	W	**2 0**
15	A	Colombia	L	**3 0**
16	A	Bolivia	W	**1 2**
17	H	Uruguay	D	**0 0**
18	A	Chile	D	**0 0**

ULISES DE LA CRUZ
Ecuador made the most of their home advantage by winning seven out of their nine matches in Quito.
The Ecuador capital is at high altitude and both Brazil and Argentina found themselves on the losing side there. The Colombian coach Luis Fernando Suarez took over the side after a poor display at the 2004 Copa America. He built a secure defence around experienced captain Hurtado, Aston Villa defender De La Cruz and Espinoza, who played every qualifying game. Former Southampton striker Delgado is the best source of goals.

TOP GOALSCORERS
Delgado 5; Mendes 5; Valencia 3

TOP APPEARANCES
Giovany Espinoza 18; Ivan Hurtado 17; Ulises De La Cruz 17; Marlon Ayovi 16; Edison Mendes 15; Edwin Tenorio 13

FINAL QUALIFYING TABLE
S AMERICA GROUP

	P	W	D	L	GF	GA	Pts
Brazil	18	9	7	2	35	17	34
Argentina	18	10	4	4	29	17	34
Ecuador	18	8	4	6	23	19	28
Paraguay	18	8	4	6	23	23	28
Uruguay	18	6	7	5	23	28	25
Colombia	18	6	6	6	24	16	24
Chile	18	5	7	6	18	22	22
Venezuela	18	5	3	10	20	28	18
Peru	18	4	6	8	20	28	18
Bolivia	18	4	2	12	20	37	14

WORLD CUP GROUP B How the four teams qualified

ENGLAND

0 MATCHES IN QUALIFYING

1	A	Austria	D	2 2
2	A	Poland	W	1 2
3	H	Wales	W	2 0
4	A	Azerbaijan	W	0 1
5	H	N Ireland	W	4 0
6	H	Azerbaijan	W	2 0
7	A	Wales	W	0 1
8	A	N Ireland	L	1 0
9	H	Austria	W	1 0
10	H	Poland	W	2 1

STEVEN GERRARD

England never looked convincing or lived up to their domestic form in the qualification for the World Cup.

While Gerrard blasted Liverpool to the Champions League, Lampard's goals drove the Chelsea juggernaut to their first Premiership title in 50 years and Beckham was widely seen as one of the top midfielders in the Spanish league, England stuttered.

Rooney didn't score in qualifying, Owen was struggling with fitness and one of the best defences around was breached by Northern Ireland in England's poorest performance. And yet, as ever, coach Sven Goran Eriksson could point to wins when it mattered - over Poland twice - and finishing top of the table.

Other positives were the confirmation of Joe Cole as the left-sided midfield answer and Terry's emergence as a world-class defender.

TOP GOALSCORERS

Lampard 5; Owen 3; Beckham 2

TOP APPEARANCES

Frank Lampard 10; Michael Owen 9; Ashley Cole 8; Rio Ferdinand 8; Wayne Rooney 7; Steven Gerrad 7; Joe Cole 7

FINAL QUALIFYING TABLE
EUROPE GROUP 6

	P	W	D	L	GF	GA	Pts
England	10	8	1	1	17	5	25
Poland	10	8	0	2	27	9	24
Austria	10	4	3	3	15	12	15
N Ireland	10	2	3	5	10	18	9
Wales	10	2	2	6	10	15	8
Azerbaijan	10	0	3	7	1	21	3

PARAGUAY

18 MATCHES IN QUALIFYING

1	A	Peru	L	4 1
2	H	Uruguay	W	4 1
3	H	Ecuador	W	2 1
4	A	Chile	W	0 1
5	H	Brazil	D	0 0
6	A	Bolivia	L	2 1
7	A	Argentina	D	0 0
8	H	Venezuela	W	1 0
9	A	Colombia	D	1 1
10	H	Peru	D	1 1
11	A	Uruguay	L	1 0
12	A	Ecuador	L	5 2
13	H	Chile	W	2 1
14	A	Brazil	L	4 1
15	H	Bolivia	W	4 1
16	H	Argentina	W	1 0
17	A	Venezuela	W	0 1
18	H	Colombia	L	0 1

CARLOS PAREDES

The final South American qualifying berth went to Paraguay with a game to spare after wins over Argentina and Venezuela.

Both the wins were 1-0 with German-based strikers Santa Cruz of Bayern and Bremen's Valdez netting the vital goals. Paredes was in fine form in Serie A and added three goals from midfield for coach Anibal Ruiz's well-drilled mix of local talent and players with top clubs in Europe, Brazil and Argentina.

TOP GOALSCORERS

Cardoza 7; Santa Cruz 4; Paredes 3

TOP APPEARANCES

Jose Cardoza 15; Carlos Gamarra 15; Julio Caceres 15; Justo Villa 15; Paulo Da Silva 14; Carlos Paredes 13.

FINAL QUALIFYING TABLE
S AMERICA GROUP

	P	W	D	L	GF	GA	Pts
Brazil	18	9	7	2	35	17	34
Argentina	18	10	4	4	29	17	34
Ecuador	18	8	4	6	23	19	28
Paraguay	18	8	4	6	23	23	28
Uruguay	18	6	7	5	23	28	25
Colombia	18	6	6	6	24	16	24
Chile	18	5	7	6	18	22	22
Venezuela	18	5	3	10	20	28	18
Peru	18	4	6	8	20	28	18
Bolivia	18	4	2	12	20	37	14

TRINIDAD & TOBAGO

20 MATCHES IN QUALIFYING

1	A	Dom Republic	W	0 2
2	H	Dom Republic	W	4 0
3	A	StVincent/Gren'dines	W	0 2
4	A	St Kitts/Nevis	W	1 2
5	H	Mexico	L	1 3
6	H	St Kitts/Nevis	W	5 1
7	A	Mexico	L	3 0
8	H	StVincent/Gren'dines	W	2 1
9	H	United States	L	1 2
10	A	Guatemala	L	5 1
11	H	Costa Rica	D	0 0
12	H	Panama	W	2 0
13	A	Mexico	L	2 0
14	A	United States	L	1 0
15	H	Guatemala	W	3 2
16	A	Costa Rica	L	2 0
17	A	Panama	W	0 1
18	H	Mexico	W	2 1
19	H	Bahrain	D	1 1
20	A	Bahrain	W	0 1

DWIGHT YORKE

The minnows of the competition's qualifiers came from the one million population of the Caribbean islands of Trinidad and Tobago.

Brilliantly organised by Dutch coach Leo Beenhakker, they used veteran striker Yorke in a deep role, just in front of the back-four. The islanders picked up new talent on the way to a fourth spot in the final phase of the north and central American qualifying group. This gave them a play-off against Bahrain and Port Vale's unlikely recruit Birchall scored in the first leg before Wrexham's lanky defender Lawrence scored the winner in the second. Coventry's John hit ten goals.

TOP GOALSCORERS

John 10; McFarlane 2; Lawrence 2

TOP APPEARANCES

Stern John 16; Marvin Andrews 15; Dennis Lawrence 14; Kenwyne Jones 12; Dwight Yorke 11; Brent Sancho 10

FINAL QUALIFYING TABLE
N/C AMERICA & CAR. STAGE 3

	P	W	D	L	GF	GA	Pts
USA	10	7	1	2	16	6	22
Mexico	10	7	1	2	22	9	22
Costa Rica	10	5	1	4	15	14	16
Trinidad and T	10	4	1	5	10	15	13
Guatemala	10	3	2	5	16	18	11
Panama	10	0	2	8	4	21	2

then beat Bahrain in the CONCACAF and Asia groups play off matches

SWEDEN

10 MATCHES IN QUALIFYING

1	A	Malta	W	0 7
2	H	Croatia	L	0 1
3	H	Hungary	W	3 0
4	A	Iceland	W	1 4
5	A	Bulgaria	W	0 3
6	H	Malta	W	6 0
7	H	Bulgaria	W	3 0
8	A	Hungary	W	0 1
9	A	Croatia	L	1 0
10	H	Iceland	W	3 1

ZLATAN IBRAHIMOVIC

Sweden qualified in one of the best-placed runners-up slots after finishing second to Croatia in their group.

Coach Lars Lagerback was in sole charge, following the retirement of Tommy Soderberg and it was a demanding start, losing at home to the Croats in the second game. The Swedes romped through the rest of their games, scoring freely through Juvetus' star Ibrahimovic and Arsenal's Ljungberg. The evergreen Larsson proved he is still dangerous too. Only anothjer narrow Croatian victory prevented Sweden topping the group.

TOP GOALSCORERS

Ibrahimovic 8; Ljungberg 7; Larsson 5

TOP APPEARANCES

Fredrik Ljungberg 10; Olof Mellberg 10; Andreas Isaksson 10; Tobias Linderoth 10; Teddy Lucic 10; Christian Wilhelmsson 10

FINAL QUALIFYING TABLE
EUROPE GROUP 8

	P	W	D	L	GF	GA	Pts
Croatia	10	7	3	0	21	5	24
Sweden	10	8	0	2	30	4	24
Bulgaria	10	4	3	3	17	17	15
Hungary	10	4	2	4	13	14	14
Iceland	10	1	1	8	14	27	4
Malta	10	0	3	7	4	32	3

WORLD CUP GROUP C How the four teams qualified

ARGENTINA

18 MATCHES IN QUALIFYING

1	H	Chile	D	2 2
2	A	Venezuela	W	0 3
3	H	Bolivia	W	3 0
4	A	Colombia	D	1 1
5	H	Ecuador	W	1 0
6	A	Brazil	L	3 1
7	H	Paraguay	D	0 0
8	A	Peru	W	1 3
9	H	Uruguay	W	4 2
10	A	Chile	D	0 0
11	H	Venezuela	W	3 2
12	A	Bolivia	W	1 2
13	H	Colombia	W	1 0
14	A	Ecuador	L	2 0
15	H	Brazil	W	3 1
16	A	Paraguay	L	1 0
17	H	Peru	W	2 0
18	A	Uruguay	L	1 0

JUAN RIQUELME

Jose Pekerman took over from Marcelo Bielsa in late 2004.

The former youth team coach immediately set about dismantling a side based around Gonzalez, Veron and Aimar in midfield and the aging but still reliable Zanetti and Samual of Inter in defence. Villarreal's Sorin was made skipper and clubmate Riquelme became the midfield playmaker around whom their game pulsed. Ayala and Heinze recovered from injury to secure the defence and there was no shortage of new striking talent to support Crespo - Messi for example.

TOP GOALSCORERS

Crespo 7; Figueroa 3; Riquelme 3

TOP APPEARANCES

Juan Pablo Sorin 13; Javier Zanetti 12; Luiz Gonzalez 12; Hernan Crespo 11; Roberto Ayala 11; Gabriel Heinze 11

FINAL QUALIFYING TABLE
S AMERICA GROUP

	P	W	D	L	GF	GA	Pts
Brazil	18	9	7	2	35	17	34
Argentina	18	10	4	4	29	17	34
Ecuador	18	8	4	6	23	19	28
Paraguay	18	8	4	6	23	23	28
Uruguay	18	6	7	5	23	28	25
Colombia	18	6	6	6	24	16	24
Chile	18	5	7	6	18	22	22
Venezuela	18	5	3	10	20	28	18
Peru	18	4	6	8	20	28	18
Bolivia	18	4	2	12	20	37	14

IVORY COAST

10 MATCHES IN QUALIFYING

1	H	Libya	W	2 0
2	A	Egypt	W	1 2
3	A	Cameroon	L	2 0
4	H	Sudan	W	5 0
5	A	Benin	W	0 1
6	H	Benin	W	3 0
7	A	Libya	D	0 0
8	H	Egypt	W	2 0
9	H	Cameroon	L	2 3
10	A	Sudan	W	1 3

DIDIER DROGBA

The Ivory Coast started as unlikely qualifiers in a group containing African powerhouses Cameroon and emerging Egypt.

However, the emotional Elephants had the talismanic Drogba up front and the hugely experienced Henri Michel as coach. They also had a large number of European based players including skipper Kalou at PSG, leading a massive French contingent. Zokora and Yaya Toure were high-energy midfield players and Kolo Toure and Eboue of Arsenal anchored the defence. The Elephants just made it with Dindane scoring vital goals against Sudan in their final game and despite two defeats to Cameroon.

TOP GOALSCORERS

Drogba 9; Dindane 7

TOP APPEARANCES

Kolo Toure 10; Aruna Dindane 10; Bonaventure Kalou 9; Didier Drogba 9; Cyril Domoraud 9; Didier Zokora 9

FINAL QUALIFYING TABLE
AFRICA GROUP 3

	P	W	D	L	GF	GA	Pts
Ivory Coast	10	7	1	2	20	7	22
Cameroon	10	6	3	1	18	10	21
Egypt	10	5	2	3	26	15	17
Libya	10	3	3	4	8	10	12
Sudan	10	1	3	6	6	22	6
Benin	10	1	2	7	9	23	5

SERBIA & MONT

10 MATCHES IN QUALIFYING

1	A	San Marino	W	0 3
2	A	Bosnia	D	0 0
3	H	San Marino	W	5 0
4	A	Belgium	W	0 2
5	H	Spain	D	0 0
6	H	Belgium	D	0 0
7	H	Lithuania	W	2 0
8	A	Spain	D	1 1
9	A	Lithuania	W	0 2
10	H	Bosnia	W	1 0

DEJAN STANKOVIC

Giants Spain fell victim to the Serbs as the best defence in the qualification process dominated European Group 7.

Master-minded by skipper Krstajic from Schalke 04 in the German Bundesliga supported by solid fullbacks Gavrancic of Kiev and Dragutinovic of Seville, the defence only conceded one goal. It was scored by Raul in Madrid and briefly threatened Serbia and Montenegro's presence at the top of the group, before Kezman equalised.

Coach Ilija Petkovic made the most of limited attacking resources, using veteran Milosevic and former Chelsea striker Kezman with good support coming from midfield star Stankovic of Inter Milan. Keeper Jevric was discarded by Vitesse Arnhem during qualifying but still recorded nine clean sheets.

TOP GOALSCORERS

Kezman 5; Vukic 4; Stankovic 2

TOP APPEARANCES

Dragoslav Jevric 10; Goran Gavrancic 10; Mladen Krstajic 9; Dejan Stankovic 9; Igor Duljaj 9; Ivica Dragutinovic 8

FINAL QUALIFYING TABLE
EUROPE GROUP 7

	P	W	D	L	GF	GA	Pts
Serbia & Mon	10	6	4	0	16	1	22
Spain	10	5	5	0	19	3	20
Bosnia-Herz	10	4	4	2	12	9	16
Belgium	10	3	3	4	16	11	12
Lithuania	10	2	4	4	8	9	10
San Marino	10	0	0	10	2	40	0

HOLLAND

12 MATCHES IN QUALIFYING

1	H	Czech Republic	W	2 0
2	A	Macedonia	D	2 2
3	H	Finland	W	3 1
4	A	Andorra	W	0 3
5	A	Romania	W	0 2
6	H	Armenia	W	2 0
7	H	Romania	W	2 0
8	A	Finland	W	0 4
9	A	Armenia	W	0 1
10	H	Andorra	W	4 0
11	A	Czech Republic	W	0 2
12	H	Macedonia	D	0 0

PHILLIP COCU

Inexperienced coach Marco van Basten left the argumentative old Dutch stars on the shelf and went for youth from the Dutch league.

Seedorf and Davids were left out in favour of unknowns from Ajaz, Feyenoord and AZ, marshalled by the wiles of Cocu from PSV. Kuijt replaced Makaay up front but van Nistelrooy and van der Sar from Manchester United were vital in helping to bed in the new stars in demanding games against the Czech Republic.

TOP GOALSCORERS

Van NIstelrooy 7; Kuijt 3; Cocu 3

TOP APPEARANCES

Edwin van der Sar 12; Dirk Kuijt 11; Ruud van Nistelrooy 10; Denny Landzaat 10; Giovanni van Bronkhorst 10; Rafael van der Vaart 9; Phillip Cocu 8

FINAL QUALIFYING TABLE
EUROPE GROUP 1

	P	W	D	L	GF	GA	Pts
Holland	12	10	2	0	27	3	32
Czech Rep	12	9	0	3	35	12	27
Romania	12	8	1	3	20	10	25
Finland	12	5	1	6	21	19	16
Macedonia	12	2	3	7	11	24	9
Armenia	12	2	1	9	9	25	7
Andorra	12	1	2	9	4	34	5

WORLD CUP GROUP D How the four teams qualified

MEXICO

16 MATCHES IN QUALIFYING

1	A	Trinidad & Tobago	W	1 3
2	H	StVincent/Gren	W	7 0
3	A	StVincent/Gren	W	0 1
4	H	Trinidad & Tobago	W	3 0
5	A	St Kitts/Nevis	W	0 5
6	H	St Kitts/Nevis	W	8 0
7	A	Costa Rica	W	1 2
8	H	United States	W	2 1
9	A	Panama	D	1 1
10	A	Guatemala	W	0 2
11	H	Trinidad & Tobago	W	2 0
12	H	Costa Rica	W	2 0
13	A	United States	L	2 0
14	H	Panama	W	5 0
15	H	Guatemala	W	5 2
16	A	Trinidad & Tobago	L	2 1

JARED BORGETTI

The goal-scoring instinct of Bolton's Borgetti, allied to the defensive excellence of Marquez and strength in depth saw Mexico to Germany.

Qualification is almost a given for Mexico and USA in the CONCACAF group of North and Central America and the Caribbean. However, Mexico looked in fine shape in trouncing minnows Dominica by 18 goals to nil over two legs of a preliminary round. They hit 67 goals in total and only lost to the USA and Trinidad & Tobago once qualification was assured. Argentinian-born coach Ricardo La Volpe rang the changes and earned the wrath of the local press by omitting striker Blanco but he has the best-equipped squad Mexico have sent to a World Cup.

TOP GOALSCORERS

Borgetti 14; Fonseca 10; Lozano 7

TOP APPEARANCES

Carlos Salcido 12; Antonio Naelsen 12; Jared Borgetti 12; Francisco Fonseca 11; Oswaldo Sanchez 11; Luis Perez 11

FINAL QUALIFYING TABLE
N/C AMERICA & CAR STAGE 3

	P	W	D	L	GF	GA	Pts
USA	10	7	1	2	16	6	22
Mexico	10	7	1	2	22	9	22
Costa Rica	10	5	1	4	15	14	16
Trinidad & T	10	4	1	5	10	15	13
Guatemala	10	3	2	5	16	18	11
Panama	10	0	2	8	4	21	2

IRAN

12 MATCHES IN QUALIFYING

1	H	Qatar	W	3 1
2	A	Laos	W	0 7
3	H	Jordan	L	0 1
4	A	Jordan	W	0 2
5	A	Qatar	W	2 3
6	H	Laos	W	7 0
7	A	Bahrain	D	0 0
8	H	Japan	W	2 1
9	A	North Korea	W	0 2
10	H	North Korea	W	1 0
11	H	Bahrain	W	1 0
12	A	Japan	L	2 1

MEHDI MAHDAVIKIA

Iran have emerged as an Asian football power over the last decade and qualified comfortably behind Japan in Asia Group B.

However, Croatian coach Branko Ivankovic claims that a real step up in quality will occur in the next ten years as there is rocketing enthusiasm for football in the country.

Ex-Bundesliga striker Daei admits to 37 years and remains both a leader on the pitch and their main goal threat. He hit nine in qualifying, including four in one game against Laos. Hasherman, who plays for Hannover in the Bundesliga, scored twice in a 2-1 home win over Japan that set up qualification. They could afford to lose the final game against the Japanese as they were already through.

TOP GOALSCORERS

Daei 9; Hasherman 4; Nekoonam 3

TOP APPEARANCES

Hussain Kabei 12; Javad Nekoonam 12; Ali Karimi 11; Yahya Golmohammadi 11; Ebrahim Mirzapour 11; Ali Daei 10

FINAL QUALIFYING TABLE
ASIA STAGE 3 – GROUP B

	P	W	D	L	GF	GA	Pts
Japan	6	5	0	1	9	4	15
Iran	6	4	1	1	7	3	13
Bahrain	6	1	1	4	4	7	4
Korea DPR	6	1	0	5	5	11	3

ANGOLA

10 MATCHES IN QUALIFYING

1	A	Algeria	D	0 0
2	H	Nigeria	W	1 0
3	A	Gabon	D	2 2
4	H	Rwanda	W	1 0
5	H	Zimbabwe	W	1 0
6	A	Zimbabwe	L	2 0
7	H	Algeria	W	2 1
8	A	Nigeria	D	1 1
9	H	Gabon	W	3 0
10	A	Rwanda	W	0 1

PEDRO MANTORRAS

There were plenty of surprises coming through qualifying from Africa but Angola's success was the most unlikely story.

One of the poorest nations on the continent, they began with a preliminary game defeat against Chad and turned to Luis De Oliveira Goncalves as coach to get them out of trouble. They beat Chad in the return and the Portuguese coach built a strong defensive base around Yamba Asha (subsequently suspended for failing a drugs test) Kali and Jamba. Captain Akwa scored in a vital 1-0 home win over favourites Nigeria and Figueiredo levelled in the return leg to give the Angolans the head-to-head advantage when both sides finished on 21 points. Goncalves largely used Angola's pin-up striker Mantorras of Benfica as a substitute both in qualifying and the African Cup of Nations. The two fell out and Mantorras said he would retire after the World Cup.

TOP GOALSCORERS

Akwa 4; Mauro 2

TOP APPEARANCES

Yamba Asha 10; Joao Ricardo 10; Jamba 10; Gilberto 9; Maurito 8; Flavio 8; Ze Kalanga 8; Figueiredo 8; Fabrice Akwa 7

FINAL QUALIFYING TABLE
AFRICA GROUP 4

	P	W	D	L	GF	GA	Pts
Angola	10	6	3	1	12	6	21
Nigeria	10	6	3	1	21	7	21
Zimbabwe	10	4	3	3	13	14	15
Gabon	10	2	4	4	11	13	10
Algeria	10	1	5	4	8	15	8
Rwanda	10	1	2	7	6	16	5

PORTUGAL

12 MATCHES IN QUALIFYING

1	A	Latvia	W	0 2
2	H	Estonia	W	4 0
3	A	Liechtenstein	D	2 2
4	H	Russia	W	7 1
5	A	Luxembourg	W	0 5
6	A	Slovakia	D	1 1
7	H	Slovakia	W	2 0
8	A	Estonia	W	0 1
9	H	Luxembourg	W	6 0
10	A	Russia	D	0 0
11	H	Liechtenstein	W	2 1
12	H	Latvia	W	3 0

LUIS FIGO

The Portuguese romped through qualifying as Europe's highest scorers, hitting 35 goals.

Former World Cup winning coach Luiz Felipe (Big Phil) Scolari used a 4-2-3-1 formation with two defensive midfielders, usually Costinha and Maniche, behind the wonderfully creative trio of Ronaldo, Deco and Figo. Up front Pauleta translated his scoring form in the French league to the international arena, netting 11 times. Estonia, Russia and Luxembourg were all thrashed on the way to the finals and Figo was persuaded out of international retirement to return as captain. The squad also has strength in depth everywhere but up front where Pauleta needs to be in top form.

TOP GOALSCORERS

Pauleta 11; Ronaldo 7; Postiga 3

TOP APPEARANCES

Pauleta 12; Jorge Andrade 12; Maniche 12; Cristiano Ronaldo 12; Deco 11; Pereira Ricardo 11; Paulo Ferreira 9

FINAL QUALIFYING TABLE
EUROPE GROUP 3

	P	W	D	L	GF	GA	Pts
Portugal	12	9	3	0	35	5	30
Slovakia	12	6	5	1	24	8	23
Russia	12	6	5	1	23	12	23
Estonia	12	5	2	5	16	17	17
Latvia	12	4	3	5	18	21	15
Liechtenstein	12	2	2	8	13	23	8
Luxembourg	12	0	0	12	5	48	0

WORLD CUP GROUP E How the four teams qualified

ITALY

10 MATCHES IN QUALIFYING

1	H	Norway	W	2	1
2	A	Moldova	W	0	1
3	A	Slovenia	L	1	0
4	H	Belarus	W	4	3
5	H	Scotland	W	2	0
6	A	Norway	D	0	0
7	A	Scotland	D	1	1
8	A	Belarus	W	1	4
9	H	Slovenia	W	1	0
10	H	Moldova	W	2	1

FRANCESCO TOTTI

Italy had a disruptive run-up to the World Cup. Serie A became embroiled in charges of corruption and their influential striker, Totti, suffered a broken ankle.

Coach Marcello Lippi also mishandled his resources in qualifying, shuffling between the established Azzurri and the new trio of exciting strikers on show in Serie A. The low point was a defeat by tiny neighbours Slovenia and draws that gave hope to Norway and Scotland.

Toni is the scoring sensation of Serie A over the last two seasons and the previously journeyman striker hit five goals in 264 minutes of qualifying action. Gilardino and Iaquinta were also blooded, but Del Piero was still involved and still scoring.

The defence was disrupted by injury to keeper Buffon but remains a strong point with Buffon's Juventus team-mates Cannovaro and Zambrotta allied with AC Milan's Nesta. Midfield experiments ended with a return to the Milan pairing of Gattuso and Pirlo in the centre.

TOP GOALSCORERS

Toni 5; Totti 2; Gilardino 2; Pirlo 2

TOP APPEARANCES

Alberto Gilhardino 8; Gennaro Guttuso 8; Luca Toni 8; Gianluca Zambrotta 8; Daniele De Rossi 8; Alessandro Nesta 7

FINAL QUALIFYING TABLE EUROPE GROUP 5

	P	W	D	L	GF	GA	Pts
Italy	10	7	2	1	17	8	23
Norway	10	5	3	2	12	7	18
Scotland	10	3	4	3	9	7	13
Slovenia	10	3	3	4	10	13	12
Belarus	10	2	4	4	12	14	10
Moldova	10	1	2	7	5	16	5

GHANA

10 MATCHES IN QUALIFYING

1	A	Burkina Faso	L	1	0
2	H	South Africa	W	3	0
3	A	Uganda	D	1	1
4	H	Cape Verde Islands	W	2	0
5	H	Congo DR	D	0	0
6	A	Congo DR	D	1	1
7	H	Burkina Faso	W	2	1
8	A	South Africa	W	0	2
9	H	Uganda	W	2	0
10	A	Cape Verde Islands	W	0	4

SULLEY ALI MUNTARI

The Ghanaians' coach Ratomir Dujkovic joined halfway through qualifying and a finish of four straight wins saw them comfortably top a tricky group.

The Serbian coach began his reign by sacking top defender Kuffour for his critical comments. He then built his team around an exciting midfield trio of Essien, captain Appiah from Fenerbache and Udinese's youngster Muntari. He also recalled the discarded Dutch-based striker Amoah (now with Dortmund) who hit three goals in five appearances.

Group favourites South Africa were beaten home and away, while the dangerous Democratic Republic of Congo (formerly Zaire) were nullified by two draws.

Kuffour was brought back after qualification and after apologising for his remarks.

TOP GOALSCORERS

Amoah 3; Asamoah Gyan 3; Appiah 3

TOP APPEARANCES

Stephen Appiah 9; John Mensah 9; Michael Essien 8; Emmanuel Pappoe 8; Sam Adjei 8; Sulley Ali Muntari 7

FINAL QUALIFYING TABLE AFRICA GROUP 2

	P	W	D	L	GF	GA	Pts
Ghana	10	6	3	1	17	4	21
Congo DR	10	4	4	2	14	10	16
South Africa	10	5	1	4	12	14	16
Burkina Faso	10	4	1	5	14	13	13
Cape Verde	10	3	1	6	8	15	10
Uganda	10	2	2	6	6	15	8

USA

16 MATCHES IN QUALIFYING

1	A	Jamaica	D	1	1
2	H	El Salvador	W	2	0
3	A	Panama	D	1	1
4	A	El Salvador	W	0	2
5	H	Panama	W	6	0
6	H	Jamaica	D	1	1
7	A	Trinidad & Tobago	W	1	2
8	A	Mexico	L	2	1
9	H	Guatemala	W	2	0
10	H	Costa Rica	W	3	0
11	A	Panama	W	0	3
12	H	Trinidad & Tobago	W	1	0
13	H	Mexico	W	2	0
14	A	Guatemala	D	0	0
15	A	Costa Rica	L	3	0
16	H	Panama	W	2	0

BRIAN MCBRIDE

The USA's collection of home and European-based players topped the CONCACAF table alongside Mexico.

Coach Bruce Arena knows his squad well, having managed the side since 1998 and uses his experienced group of strikers Donovan and McBride, captain Reyna and keeper Keller as the spine. Fulham's uncompromising defender Bocanegra has become another regular in the side.

Their only significant qualifying defeat came away against Mexico, a result they reversed in Columbus with second half goals by Beasley and Ralston. The loss to Costa Rica came after qualification was assured and Arena experimented leaving out several regulars.

Highly rated Ghanaian-born youngster Freddy Adu has a host of European suitors but the 17-year-old didn't feature in the qualifying matches.

TOP GOALSCORERS

Johnson 7; Donovan 6; McBride 4

TOP APPEARANCES

Landon Donovan 14; Brian McBride 12; Kasey Keller 12; DaMarcus Beasley 11; Carlos Bocanegra 10; Eddie Lewis 9

FINAL QUALIFYING TABLE N/C AMERICA & CAR. STAGE 3

	P	W	D	L	GF	GA	Pts
USA	10	7	1	2	16	6	22
Mexico	10	7	1	2	22	9	22
Costa Rica	10	5	1	4	15	14	16
Trinidad and T	10	4	1	5	10	15	13
Guatemala	10	3	2	5	16	18	11
Panama	10	0	2	8	4	21	2

CZECH REPUBLIC

14 MATCHES IN QUALIFYING

1	A	Holland	L	2	0
2	H	Romania	W	1	0
3	A	Armenia	W	0	3
4	A	Macedonia	W	0	2
5	H	Finland	W	4	3
6	A	Andorra	W	0	4
7	H	Andorra	W	8	1
8	H	Macedonia	W	6	1
9	A	Romania	L	2	0
10	H	Armenia	W	4	1
11	H	Holland	L	0	2
12	A	Finland	W	0	3
13	A	Norway	W	0	1
14	H	Norway	W	1	0

TOMAS ROSICKY

Two defeats to Holland left the Czech Republic with a play-off against Norway to negotiate.

Goals from Rosicky at home and Smicer away, ensured two 1-0 wins and a place in Germany.

Juventus star Nedved came out of retirement for the play-offs and remains key to the Czech chances. He was the best midfielder in Serie A last season.

Cech kept seven clean sheets behind a settled defence while the tall talismanic striker Koller hit nine goals through qualifying.

Coach Karel Bruckner has a tight squad with a well-balanced midfield unit. Nedved is joined by Rosicky while veteran Poborsky is on the right wing.

TOP GOALSCORERS

Koller 9; Rosicky 7; Baros 5; Lokvenc 5

TOP APPEARANCES

Tomas Ujfalusi 14; Petr Cech 13; Milan Baros 12; Tomas Rosicky 12; Zdenek Grygera 11; Karol Poborsky 11

FINAL QUALIFYING TABLE EUROPE GROUP 1

	P	W	D	L	GF	GA	Pts
Netherlands	12	10	2	0	27	3	32
Czech Rep	12	9	0	3	35	12	27
Romania	12	8	1	3	20	10	25
Finland	12	5	1	6	21	19	16
Macedonia	12	2	3	7	11	24	9
Armenia	12	2	1	9	9	25	7
Andorra	12	1	2	9	4	34	5

European Group Play-offs

Czech Republic beat Norway

WORLD CUP GROUP F How the four teams qualified

BRAZIL

18 MATCHES IN QUALIFYING

1	A	Colombia	W	1 2
2	H	Ecuador	W	1 0
3	A	Peru	D	1 1
4	H	Uruguay	D	3 3
5	A	Paraguay	D	0 0
6	H	Argentina	W	3 1
7	A	Chile	D	1 1
8	H	Bolivia	W	3 1
9	A	Venezuela	W	2 5
10	H	Colombia	D	0 0
11	A	Ecuador	L	1 0
12	H	Peru	W	1 0
13	A	Uruguay	D	1 1
14	H	Paraguay	W	4 1
15	A	Argentina	L	3 1
16	H	Chile	W	5 0
17	A	Bolivia	D	1 1
18	H	Venezuela	W	3 0

RONALDINHO

Only goal difference separated Brazil and Argentina at the top of the South American table.

Three Ronaldo penalties despatched Argentina in the home leg while their rivals gained revenge in Buenos Aires. The only other defeat came at altitude in Ecuador. Ronaldo was one of the mainstays of the team and delivered ten goals despite being off-colour for Madrid. Keeper Dida and veteran fullbacks Roberto Carlos and Cafu also turned out regularly as coach Alberto Parreira stayed loyal to the old guard. He is spoilt for choice up front but is determined to stick with his 'Golden Quartet', of attacking forwards.

TOP GOALSCORERS

Ronaldo 10; Adriano 6; Juninho 5

TOP APPEARANCES

Nelsen Dida 16; Roberto Carlos 15; Ricardo Kaka 15; Ronaldo 15; Cafu 15; Roque Junior 14; Ze Roberto 14

FINAL QUALIFYING TABLE S AMERICA GROUP

	P	W	D	L	GF	GA	Pts
Brazil	18	9	7	2	35	17	34
Argentina	18	10	4	4	29	17	34
Ecuador	18	8	4	6	23	19	28
Paraguay	18	8	4	6	23	23	28
Uruguay	18	6	7	5	23	28	25
Colombia	18	6	6	6	24	16	24
Chile	18	5	7	6	18	22	22
Venezuela	18	5	3	10	20	28	18
Peru	18	4	6	8	20	28	18
Bolivia	18	4	2	12	20	37	14

CROATIA

10 MATCHES IN QUALIFYING

1	H	Hungary	W	3 0
2	A	Sweden	W	0 1
3	H	Bulgaria	D	2 2
4	H	Iceland	W	4 0
5	H	Malta	W	3 0
6	A	Bulgaria	W	1 3
7	A	Iceland	W	1 3
8	A	Malta	D	1 1
9	H	Sweden	W	1 0
10	A	Hungary	D	0 0

DADO PRSO

Croatia edged Sweden off top spot in European Group 8 by doing the double over the Scandanavians.

Wing back Srna scored direct from a free kick to give Croatia a 1-0 win in Sweden. He hit the net again in Zagreb for another narrow win courtesy of his penalty.

Points were dropped to Bulgaria, Hungary and (surprisingly) Malta but Croatia finished unbeaten, only conceding five goals in ten games.

Rangers' Prso led the line selflessly, and scored five goals, while coach Zlatko Kranjcar, selected his son Niko as the deep-lying striker.

The midfield had Srna's energy complemented by the know-how of Bundesliga stalwarts Nico Kovac and Babic. However, the defence was the real strength of the side. It is built around the younger Kovac brother Robert, one of the best central defenders around. Simunic of Hertha Berlin and Siena's Tudor complete an experienced and rugged central defensive trio.

TOP GOALSCORERS

Prso 5; Srna 5; Balaban 2; Tudor 2

TOP APPEARANCES

Marco Babic 9; Niko Kranjcar 9; Darijo Srna 9; Nico Kovac 9; Dado Prso 9; Tomaslav Butina 8; Robert Kovac 8

FINAL QUALIFYING TABLE EUROPE GROUP 8

	P	W	D	L	GF	GA	Pts
Croatia	10	7	3	0	21	5	24
Sweden	10	8	0	2	30	4	24
Bulgaria	10	4	3	3	17	17	15
Hungary	10	4	2	4	13	14	14
Iceland	10	1	1	8	14	27	4
Malta	10	0	3	7	4	32	3

AUSTRALIA

9 MATCHES IN QUALIFYING

1	H	New Zealand	W	1 0
2	H	Tahiti	W	9 0
4	A	Vanuatu	W	0 3
5	A	Solomon Islands	D	2 2
6	H	Solomon Islands	W	7 0
7	A	Solomon Islands	W	1 2
8	A	Uruguay	L	1 0
9	H	Uruguay	W	1 0

HARRY KEWELL

Australia's second qualification for a World Cup came courtesy of two Schwarzer penalty saves in the play-off against Uruguay.

Dutch coach Guus Hiddink was many pundit's choice as the next England manager before the FA process sidelined him. He showed his quality once again by fashioning a spirited Aussie side from exiles in many corners of Europe.

Everton's Cahill provided the scoring catalyst which saw seven put past the Solomon Islands in the Oceania play-offs first leg. Parma-based Bresciano scored the goal that levelled the tie with Uruguay in a 1-0 home win before Schwarzer's saves and Aloisi's spot-kick won through.

TOP GOALSCORERS

Cahill 7; Emerton 4; Aloisi 2; Viduka 2

TOP APPEARANCES

Vincenzo Grella 8; Brett Emerton 8; John Aloisi 7; Tony Vidmar 7; Zeljko Kalac 6; Tim Cahill 6; Scott Chipperfield 6

FINAL QUALIFYING TABLE OCEANIA STAGE 2

	P	W	D	L	GF	GA	Pts
Australia	5	4	1	0	21	3	13
Solomon Is	5	3	1	1	9	6	10
New Zealand	5	3	0	2	17	5	9
Fiji	5	1	1	3	3	10	4
Tahiti	5	1	1	3	2	24	4
Vanuatu	5	1	0	4	5	9	3

Australia beat The Solomon Islands in the group Play-off, then beat Uruguay in the S America and Oceania Play-off

JAPAN

12 MATCHES IN QUALIFYING

1	H	Oman	W	1 0
2	A	Singapore	W	1 2
3	H	India	W	7 0
4	A	India	W	0 4
5	A	Oman	W	0 1
6	H	Singapore	W	1 0
7	H	North Korea	W	2 1
8	A	Iran	L	2 1
9	H	Bahrain	W	1 0
10	A	Bahrain	W	0 1
11	A	North Korea	W	0 2
12	H	Iran	W	2 1

SHUNSUKE NAKAMURA

Japan won every qualification game bar one, a narrow defeat to Iran, on their way to Germany.

They are coached by former Brazilian star Zico but haven't cultivated his attacking instincts with a solid defence being the mainstay of their Asian qualifiers. They also managed without their strong European-based players in midfield for many games. Bolton's Nakata, Celtic's Nakamura and Ono (now back at Urawa Reds in the J-League) are the side's best chance of success in Germany.

The goals were shared around but hard to come by apart from 11 scored against a poor Indian team. Oguro hit three goals in only 156 minutes of play despite just one start in the qualifying games.

TOP GOALSCORERS

Suzuki 3; Fukunishi 3; Oguro 3

TOP APPEARANCES

Tsuneyasu Miyamoto 12; Akira Kaji 11; Alessandro Santos 10; Takayuki Suzuki 9; Keiji Tamada 9; Takashi Fukunishi 9

FINAL QUALIFYING TABLE ASIA STAGE 3 – GROUP B

	P	W	D	L	GF	GA	Pts
Japan	6	5	0	1	9	4	15
Iran	6	4	1	1	7	3	13
Bahrain	6	1	1	4	4	7	4
Korea DPR	6	1	0	5	5	11	3

WORLD CUP GROUP G How the four teams qualified

FRANCE

10 MATCHES IN QUALIFYING

1	H	Israel	D	0 0
2	A	Faroe Islands	W	0 2
3	H	Rep of Ireland	D	0 0
4	A	Cyprus	W	0 2
5	H	Switzerland	D	0 0
6	A	Israel	D	1 1
7	H	Faroe Islands	W	3 0
8	A	Rep of Ireland	W	0 1
9	A	Switzerland	D	1 1
10	H	Cyprus	W	4 0

ZINEDINE ZIDANE

A trio of former stars put France's World Cup qualification back on track when they came out of retirement.

Zidane led Thuram and Makelele back into the French team and to a crucial away win against the Republic of Ireland. Until that late win in France's eighth game, European Qualifying Group 4 had been a stalemate between four countries, Israel, Switzerland, Ireland and France were just notching up draws with each other.

That win in Dublin, courtesy of a Henry goal, nudged France top of the group. Coach Raymond Domenech's selections were muddled until then, with some of the top players in domestic football across Europe failing to gel as a team while lesser players came and went. France's press hailed the returning trio as their saviours.

TOP GOALSCORERS

Cissé 4; Henry 3; Wiltord 3; Giuly 2

TOP APPEARANCES

William Gallas 10; Patrick Vieira 9; Sylvain Wiltord 8; Gael Givet 7; Thierry Henry 6; Gregory Coupet 6; Djibril Cissé 6

FINAL QUALIFYING TABLE
EUROPE GROUP 4

	P	W	D	L	GF	GA	Pts
France	10	5	5	0	14	2	20
Switzerland	10	4	6	0	18	7	18
Israel	10	4	6	0	15	10	18
Rep of Ireland	10	4	5	1	12	5	17
Cyprus	10	1	1	8	8	20	4
Faroe Islands	10	0	1	9	4	27	1

SWITZERLAND

12 MATCHES IN QUALIFYING

1	H	Faroe Islands	W	6 0
2	H	Rep of Ireland	D	1 1
3	A	Israel	D	2 2
4	A	France	D	0 0
5	H	Cyprus	W	1 0
6	A	Faroe Islands	W	1 3
7	H	Israel	D	1 1
8	A	Cyprus	W	1 3
9	H	France	D	1 1
10	A	Rep of Ireland	D	0 0
11	H	Turkey	W	2 0
12	A	Turkey	L	4 2

ALEXANDER FREI

Switzerland emerged from a battlefield of a game in Istanbul as the play-off victors over Turkey.

While FIFA threw sanctions at the disgruntled Turks, the Swiss were battle-hardened and ready for the World Cup. They had emerged narrowly second behind France in the qualifying group. They were level on points with Israel with both teams unbeaten. In the final games, France won in Cyprus but if the Swiss had won in Dublin, they would have finished top and France would have been reduced to a play-off position. The Swiss ran into Ireland's Given in top form and came away with a draw. Coach Jakob Kuhn has built a capable squad based around the tough tackling of AC Milan's Vogel and the goals of Rennes' Frei.

TOP GOALSCORERS

Frei 8; Vonlanthen 4; Rey 3

TOP APPEARANCES

Johann Vogel 12; Pascal Zuberbuehler 12; Patrick Muller 12; Ludovic Magnin 10; Alexander Frei 10; Johan Vonlanthen 10

FINAL QUALIFYING TABLE
EUROPE GROUP 4

	P	W	D	L	GF	GA	Pts
France	10	5	5	0	14	2	20
Switzerland	10	4	6	0	18	7	18
Israel	10	4	6	0	15	10	18
Rep of Ireland	10	4	5	1	12	5	17
Cyprus	10	1	1	8	8	20	4
Faroe Islands	10	0	1	9	4	27	1

Switzerland beat Turkey in the European Group play-offs

SOUTH KOREA

12 MATCHES IN QUALIFYING

1	H	Lebanon	W	2 0
2	A	Maldives	D	0 0
3	H	Vietnam SR	W	2 0
4	A	Vietnam SR	W	1 2
5	A	Lebanon	D	1 1
6	H	Maldives	W	2 0
7	H	Kuwait	W	2 0
8	A	Saudi Arabia	L	2 0
9	H	Uzbekistan	W	2 1
10	A	Uzbekistan	D	1 1
11	A	Kuwait	W	0 4
12	H	Saudi Arabia	L	0 1

JI-SUNG PARK

South Korea used three coaches on route to the World Cup.

First Humberto Coelho was kicked out after a goalless draw with the tiny Maldives. Next, Jo Bonfrere took them to the last eight in Asia but two defeats by Saudi Arabia caused more concern. The percieved lack of style expected by tournament semi-finalists, led to Bonfrere being replaced by fellow Dutchman Dick Advocaat.

The enthusiasm and cheering crowds of the 2002 World Cup on home soil, have been replaced by a number of players who are regulars with top European sides. Former Korean coach Guus Hiddink took Young-Pyo Lee and Ji-Sung Park with him to PSV in Holland before both moved on to the Premiership.

Twenty-year old Chu Young Park of FC Seoul announced himself at the end of qualifying with two goals in three games and was the main threat in the final defeat by Saudi Arabia.

TOP GOALSCORERS

Dong-Gook Lee 5; Chu Young Park 2

TOP APPEARANCES

Woon-Jae Lee 12; Young Pyo-Lee 11; Ki-Hyeon Seol 9; Jung-Hwan Ahn 9; Ji-Sung Park 8; Dong-Gook Lee 8

FINAL QUALIFYING TABLE
ASIA STAGE 3 – GROUP A

	P	W	D	L	GF	GA	Pts
Saudi Arabia	6	4	2	0	10	1	14
South Korea	6	3	1	2	9	5	10
Uzbekistan	6	1	2	3	7	11	5
Kuwait	6	1	1	4	4	13	4

TOGO

10 MATCHES IN QUALIFYING

1	A	Zambia	L	1 0
2	H	Senegal	W	3 1
3	A	Liberia	D	0 0
4	H	Congo	W	2 0
5	H	Mali	W	1 0
6	A	Mali	W	1 2
7	H	Zambia	W	4 1
8	A	Senegal	D	2 2
9	H	Liberia	W	3 0
10	A	Congo	W	2 3

EMMANUEL ADEBAYOR

Senegal were hot favourites to qualify from Africa Group 1.

They had beaten France in the first game of the 2002 World Cup and had players in top clubs around Europe. However, in their second game, they came up against little Togo, who were still smarting from a first game loss to Zambia. Togo's lanky Metz striker, Adebayor scored first and Senaya hit two as Senegal lost 3-1. Adebayor continued to find the net, striking 11 in total to be Africa's highest scorer. The return game in Senegal was a 2-2 draw and Togo finished with two wins to qualify but still sacked coach Stephen Keshi after arguments and disappointment in the African Cup of Nations.

TOP GOALSCORERS

Adebayor 11; Toure 3; Senaya 2

TOP APPEARANCES

Sherif Toure 10; Emmanuel Adebayor 10; Junior Senaya 9; Yao Aziawonou 9; Kossi Agassa 9; Jean-Paul Yaovi Abalo 9

FINAL QUALIFYING TABLE
AFRICA GROUP 1

	P	W	D	L	GF	GA	Pts
Togo	10	7	2	1	20	8	23
Senegal	10	6	3	1	21	8	21
Zambia	10	6	1	3	16	10	19
Congo	10	3	1	6	10	14	10
Mali	10	2	2	6	11	14	8
Liberia	10	1	1	8	3	27	4

WORLD CUP GROUP H How the four teams qualified

SPAIN

12 MATCHES IN QUALIFYING

1	A	Bosnia	D	1 1
2	H	Belgium	W	2 0
3	A	Lithuania	D	0 0
4	H	San Marino	W	5 0
5	A	Serbia & Montenegro	D	0 0
6	H	Lithuania	W	1 0
7	H	Bosnia	D	1 1
8	H	Serbia & Montenegro	D	1 1
9	A	Belgium	W	0 2
10	A	San Marino	W	0 6
11	H	Slovakia	W	5 1
12	A	Slovakia	D	1 1

IKER CASILLAS

Spain were riding high in the Fifa charts on the back of a long unbeaten run but still found themselves in the World Cup play-offs.

Serbia & Montenegro pipped them to the top spot as the Spanish limped to five draws in their ten games. Coach Luis Aragones seemed uncertain of his best midfield, ringing the changes around Puyol in defence and perservering with the struggling Raul as captain. Atletico Madrid striker Torres claimed his place with seven goals in qualifying but the hot domestic form of Valencia's Villa was given little chance to impress.

They had little trouble against Slovakia in the play-offs, who were without their star midfielder Mintel. Spain made sure by crushing them 5-1 in the home leg with Liverpool's Luis Garcia hitting a hat-trick.

TOP GOALSCORERS

Torres 7; Raul 4; Luis Garcia 3

TOP APPEARANCES

Iker Casillas 12; Raul 12; Carlos Puyol 11; Michel Salgardo 10; Fernando Torres 10; Xavi Hernandez 10; David Albelda 9

FINAL QUALIFYING TABLE
EUROPE GROUP 7

	P	W	D	L	GF	GA	Pts
Serbia & Mont	10	6	4	0	16	1	22
Spain	10	5	5	0	19	3	20
Bosnia-Herz	10	4	4	2	12	9	16
Belgium	10	3	3	4	16	11	12
Lithuania	10	2	4	4	8	9	10
San Marino	10	0	0	10	2	40	0

Spain beat Slovakia in the European Group Play-offs

UKRAINE

12 MATCHES IN QUALIFYING

1	A	Denmark	D	1 1
2	A	Kazakhstan	W	1 2
3	H	Greece	D	1 1
4	H	Georgia	W	2 0
5	A	Turkey	W	0 3
6	A	Albania	W	0 2
7	H	Denmark	W	1 0
8	H	Kazakhstan	W	2 0
9	A	Greece	W	0 1
10	A	Georgia	D	1 1
11	H	Turkey	L	0 1
12	H	Albania	D	2 2

ANDRIY SHEVCHENKO

Former striking legend Oleg Blokhin, who won a record 112 caps for the USSR, guided Ukraine to an early qualification success.

With the inspirational Shevchenko leading the side, coach Blokhin surrounded the AC Milan striker with domestic stars from Dinamo Kiev, Dnipro and Shakhtar Donetsk, all of whom were performing regularly in the two European cups. In a tough group with Denmark, Turkey and European champions Greece, Ukraine notched seven draws and two wins and qualified with two games to go after a 1-1 draw in Georgia. They then rested their stars in their only defeat, at home to Turkey, who finished second.

TOP GOALSCORERS

Shevchenko 6; Rotan 3; Husin 3

TOP APPEARANCES

Olekander Shovkovskiy 12; Andrey Rusol 12; Andriy Nesmachniy 11; Andrey Voronin 11; Volodymyr Yeserskiy 10

FINAL QUALIFYING TABLE
EUROPE GROUP 2

	P	W	D	L	GF	GA	Pts
Ukraine	12	7	4	1	18	7	25
Turkey	12	6	5	1	23	9	23
Denmark	12	6	4	2	24	12	22
Greece	12	6	3	3	15	9	21
Albania	12	4	1	7	11	20	13
Georgia	12	2	4	6	14	25	10
Kazakhstan	12	0	1	11	6	29	1

TUNISIA

10 MATCHES IN QUALIFYING

1	H	Botswana	W	4 1
2	A	Guinea	L	2 1
3	A	Morocco	D	1 1
4	A	Malawi	D	2 2
5	H	Malawi	W	7 0
6	A	Botswana	W	1 3
7	H	Guinea	W	2 0
8	H	Kenya	W	1 0
9	A	Kenya	W	0 2
10	H	Morocco	D	2 2

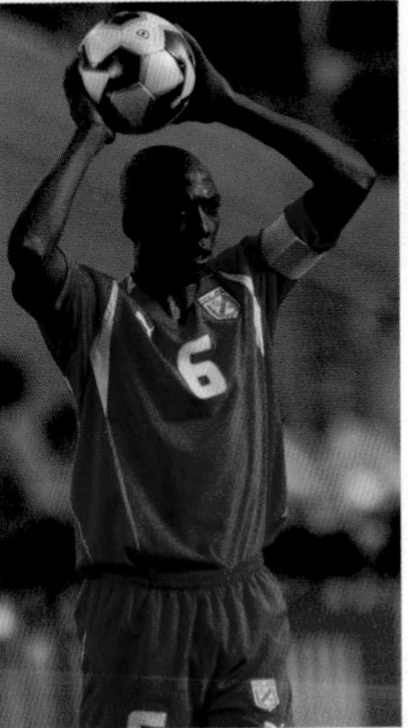

HATEM TRABELSI

Tunisia pipped near neighbours Morocco to the qualification slot in African Group 5.

A lot of attention focussed on Tunisia's ex-patriot Brazilian striker Dos Santos but the return of injured skipper Trabelski at right back was the key to qualification.

Coach Roger Lemerre suffered two draws and a defeat in Tunisia's first four games, before the Ajax player rejoined the side. With Trabelsi, they won the next game by seven goals against Malawi and went on a run of five wins. Going into the final game Tunisia had 20 points and the undefeated Moroccans 19. The two met in that game and Tunisia twice came from behind to draw 2-2 with their rivals and stay a point clear, on their way to Germany.

TOP GOALSCORERS

Dos Santos 6; Clayton 3; Guemamdia 3

TOP APPEARANCES

Rahdi Jaidi 9; Jawhar Mnari 9; Adel Chedii 8; Ali Boumnijel 8; Jose Clayton 7; Francileudo Dos Santos 7 Karim Hagui 7

FINAL QUALIFYING TABLE
AFRICA GROUP 5

	P	W	D	L	GF	GA	Pts
Tunisia	10	6	3	1	25	9	21
Morocco	10	5	5	0	17	7	20
Guinea	10	5	2	3	15	10	17
Kenya	10	3	1	6	8	17	10
Botswana	10	3	0	7	10	18	9
Malawi	10	1	3	6	12	26	6

SAUDI ARABIA

12 MATCHES IN QUALIFYING

1	H	Indonesia	W	3 0
2	A	Sri Lanka	W	0 1
3	H	Turkmenistan	W	3 0
4	A	Turkmenistan	W	0 1
5	A	Indonesia	W	1 3
6	H	Sri Lanka	W	3 0
7	A	Uzbekistan	D	1 1
8	H	South Korea	W	2 0
9	A	Kuwait	D	0 0
10	H	Kuwait	W	3 0
11	H	Uzbekistan	W	3 0
12	A	South Korea	W	0 1

YASSER AL QAHTANI

Saudi Arabia qualified easily from Asia Group A after completing the double over fellow finalists South Korea.

They were unbeaten in their 12 qualifying games and reached their fourth consecutive World Cup finals.

However, coach Marcos Paqueta was the third coach used by the Saudi authorities, who sacked Gerard van der Lem after a poor 2004 Asian Cup campaign and the Argentinian Gabriel Calderon. Brazilian Paqueta knows the domestic game in Saudi and the squad comes entirely from the Saudi league.

They used 60 players in qualifying. Keeper Zaid is one of the few who looks established. Al Qahtani was a recent record £6m Saudi league transfer and shares striking duties with veteran Al Jaber.

TOP GOALSCORERS

Al; Qahtani 4; Khariri 4; Al Jaber 3

TOP APPEARANCES

Hamad Al Montashari 9; Yasser Al Qahtani 9; Mbrouk Zaid 8; Saud Khariri 7; Mohammed Al Shihoub 7

FINAL QUALIFYING TABLE
ASIA STAGE 3 – GROUP A

	P	W	D	L	GF	GA	Pts
Saudi Arabia	6	4	2	0	10	1	14
South Korea	6	3	1	2	9	5	10
Uzbekistan	6	1	2	3	7	11	5
Kuwait	6	1	1	4	4	13	4

WORLD CUP GROUP A

The group stages

MATCH ONE

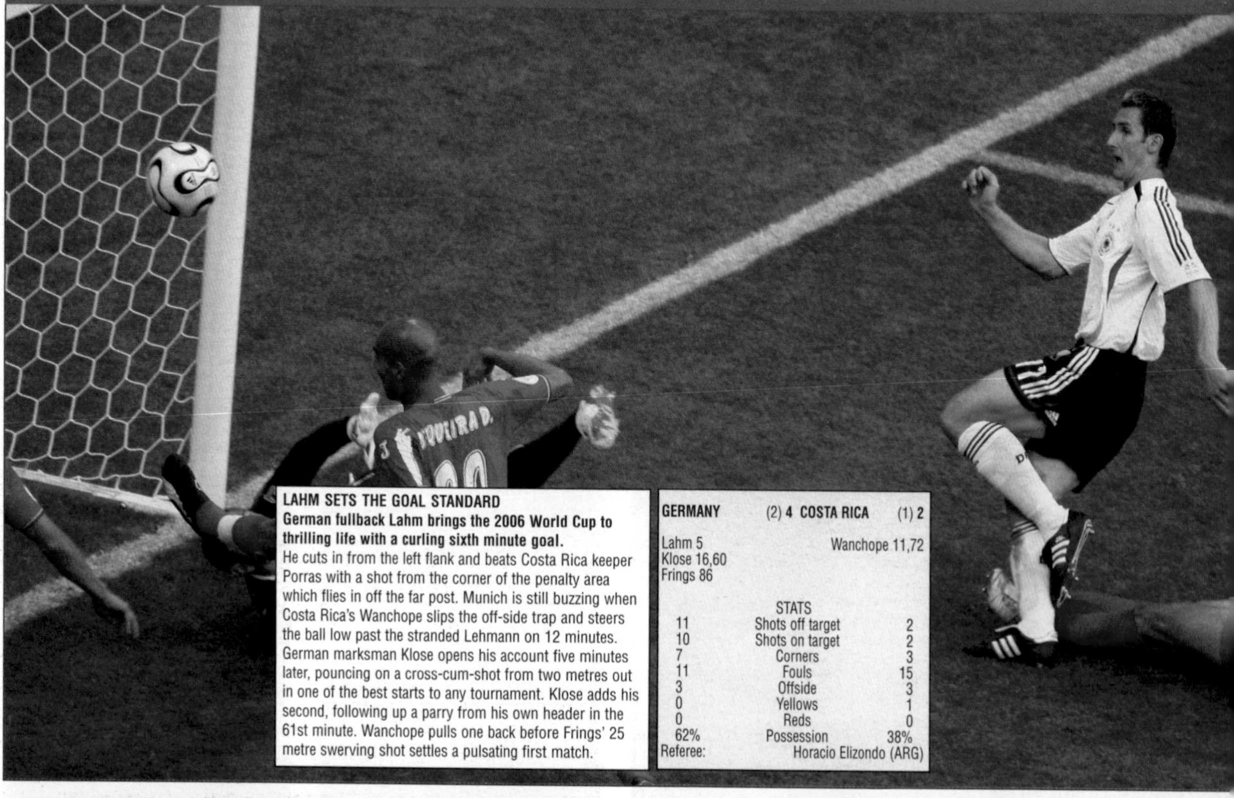

LAHM SETS THE GOAL STANDARD

German fullback Lahm brings the 2006 World Cup to thrilling life with a curling sixth minute goal.

He cuts in from the left flank and beats Costa Rica keeper Porras with a shot from the corner of the penalty area which flies in off the far post. Munich is still buzzing when Costa Rica's Wanchope slips the off-side trap and steers the ball low past the stranded Lehmann on 12 minutes. German marksman Klose opens his account five minutes later, pouncing on a cross-cum-shot from two metres out in one of the best starts to any tournament. Klose adds his second, following up a parry from his own header in the 61st minute. Wanchope pulls one back before Frings' 25 metre swerving shot settles a pulsating first match.

GERMANY (2) 4		COSTA RICA (1) 2
Lahm 5		Wanchope 11,72
Klose 16,60		
Frings 86		
	STATS	
11	Shots off target	2
10	Shots on target	2
7	Corners	3
11	Fouls	15
3	Offside	3
0	Yellows	1
0	Reds	0
62%	Possession	38%
Referee:	Horacio Elizondo (ARG)	

MATCH TWO

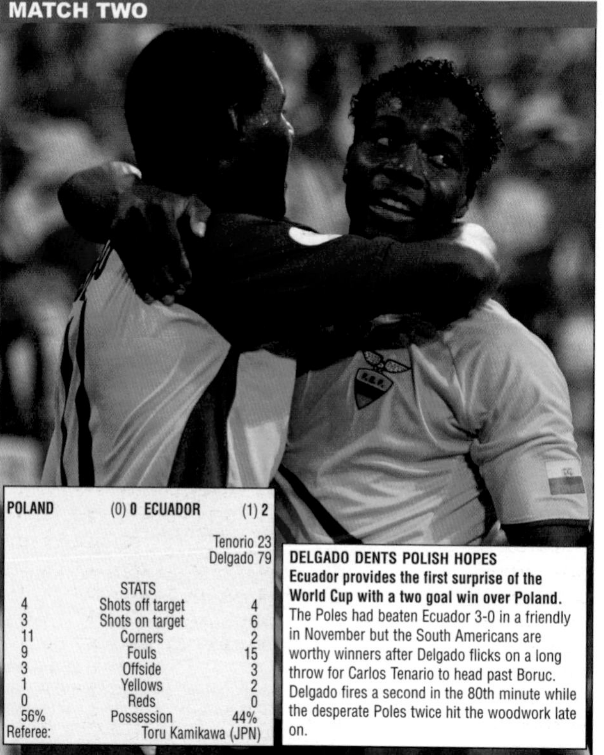

POLAND (0) 0		ECUADOR (1) 2
		Tenorio 23
		Delgado 79
	STATS	
4	Shots off target	4
3	Shots on target	6
11	Corners	2
9	Fouls	15
3	Offside	3
1	Yellows	2
0	Reds	0
56%	Possession	44%
Referee:	Toru Kamikawa (JPN)	

DELGADO DENTS POLISH HOPES

Ecuador provides the first surprise of the World Cup with a two goal win over Poland.

The Poles had beaten Ecuador 3-0 in a friendly in November but the South Americans are worthy winners after Delgado flicks on a long throw for Carlos Tenario to head past Boruc. Delgado fires a second in the 80th minute while the desperate Poles twice hit the woodwork late on.

MATCH THREE

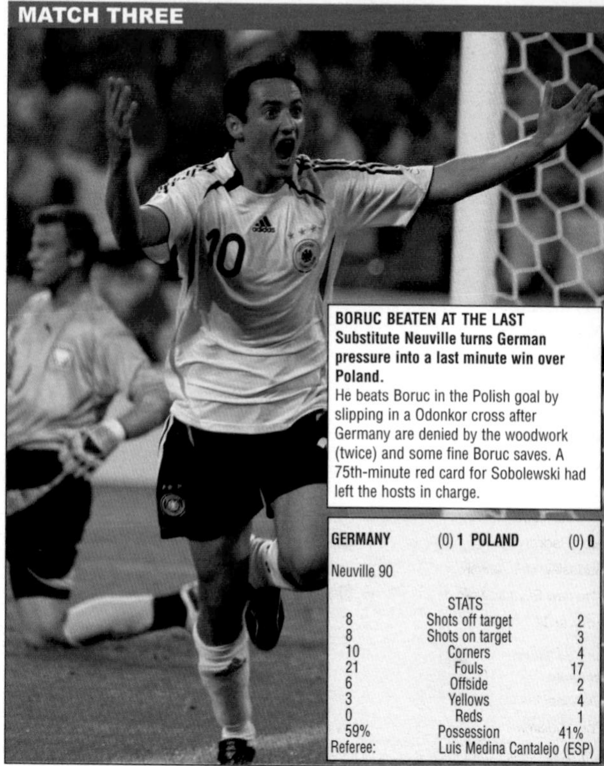

BORUC BEATEN AT THE LAST

Substitute Neuville turns German pressure into a last minute win over Poland.

He beats Boruc in the Polish goal by slipping in a Odonkor cross after Germany are denied by the woodwork (twice) and some fine Boruc saves. A 75th-minute red card for Sobolewski had left the hosts in charge.

GERMANY (0) 1		POLAND (0) 0
Neuville 90		
	STATS	
8	Shots off target	2
8	Shots on target	3
10	Corners	4
21	Fouls	17
6	Offside	2
3	Yellows	4
0	Reds	1
59%	Possession	41%
Referee:	Luis Medina Cantalejo (ESP)	

GERMANY - ECUADOR - POLAND - COSTA RICA

MATCH FOUR

ECUADOR	(1) 3	COSTA RICA	(0) 0
Tenorio 7 Delgado 53 Kaviedes 90			

	STATS	
7	Shots off target	8
7	Shots on target	4
3	Corners	4
18	Fouls	22
3	Offside	2
3	Yellows	2
0	Reds	0
52%	Possession	48%
Referee:	Coffi Codjia (BEN)	

VALENCIA SENDS ECUADOR INTO LAST 16
Costa Rica succumb to a potent Ecuador attack, sparked by winger Valencia.
His cross is headed in by Carlos Tenorio for the first goal and he carries a threat everytime he is on the ball. Delgado adds a second with a fierce shot early in the second half before substitute Kaviedes completes the win in the 80th minute.

MATCH FIVE

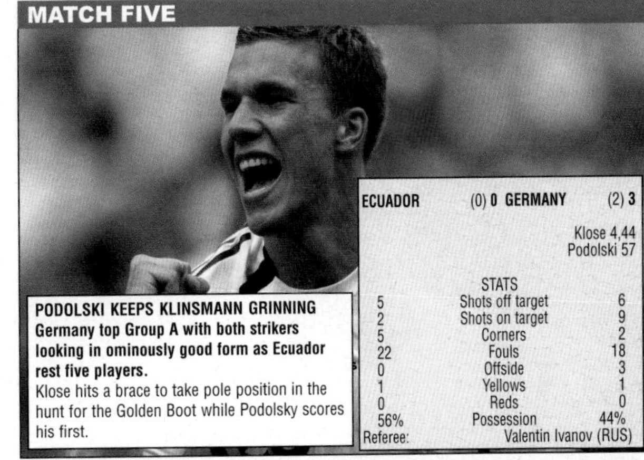

ECUADOR	(0) 0	GERMANY	(2) 3
			Klose 4,44 Podolski 57

	STATS	
5	Shots off target	6
2	Shots on target	9
5	Corners	2
22	Fouls	18
0	Offside	3
1	Yellows	1
0	Reds	0
56%	Possession	44%
Referee:	Valentin Ivanov (RUS)	

PODOLSKI KEEPS KLINSMANN GRINNING
Germany top Group A with both strikers looking in ominously good form as Ecuador rest five players.
Klose hits a brace to take pole position in the hunt for the Golden Boot while Podolsky scores his first.

MATCH SIX

COSTA RICA	(1) 1	POLAND	(1) 2
Gomez 25		Bosacki 33,66	

	STATS	
7	Shots off target	3
5	Shots on target	7
2	Corners	8
12	Fouls	20
4	Offside	1
5	Yellows	5
0	Reds	0
48%	Possession	52%
Referee:	Shamsui Maidin (SIN)	

BOSACKI BRACE ENDS POLISH INTEREST
Poland limp back over the border with a little pride after coming from behind to beat Costa Rica.
Bosacki volleys home an equaliser to Gomez's free kick and heads the winner in an open game.

GROUP A TABLE

	P	W	D	L	F	A	DIF	PTS
Germany	3	3	0	0	8	2	6	9
Ecuador	3	2	0	1	5	3	2	6
Poland	3	1	0	2	2	4	-2	3
Costa Rica	3	0	0	3	3	9	-6	0

POLAND APPEARANCES

Match	1	2	3	Appearances	Started	Subbed on	Subbed off	Mins played	% played	Goals	Yellow	Red
Result	L	L	W									
Goalkeepers												
Artur Boruc	■	■	■	3	3	0	0	270	100.0	0	2	0
Defenders												
Jacek Bak	■	■	■	3	3	0	0	270	100.0	0	1	0
Marcin Baszczynski	■	■	■	3	3	0	0	270	100.0	0	1	0
Bartosz Bosacki	□	■	■	2	2	0	0	180	66.7	2	0	0
Dariusz Dudka	▒	»	▒	1	0	1	0	8	3.0	0	0	0
Mariusz Jop	■	▒	▒	1	1	0	0	90	33.3	0	0	0
Michal Zewlakow	■	«	■	3	3	0	1	262	97.0	0	1	0
Midfielders												
Kamil Kosowski	»	▒	▒	1	0	1	0	13	4.8	0	0	0
Jacek Krzynowek	«	«	■	3	3	0	2	243	90.0	0	1	0
Mariusz Lewandowski	▒	»	»	2	0	2	0	41	15.2	0	0	0
Arek Radomski	■	■	«	3	3	0	1	243	90.0	0	1	0
Radoslaw Sobelewski	«	«	▒	2	2	0	1	141	52.2	0	1	1
Miroslaw Szymkowiak	■	▒	■	2	2	0	0	180	66.7	0	0	0
Forwards												
Pawel Brozek	»	»	»	3	0	3	0	54	20.0	0	0	0
Ireneusz Jelen	»	«	■	3	2	1	1	202	74.8	0	0	0
Grzegorz Rasiak	▒	▒	»	1	0	1	0	6	2.2	0	0	0
Ebi Smolarek	■	■	«	3	3	0	1	264	97.8	0	1	0
Maciej Zurawski	«	■	«	3	3	0	2	217	80.4	0	0	0

COSTA RICA APPEARANCES

Match	1	2	3	Appearances	Started	Subbed on	Subbed off	Mins played	% played	Goals	Yellow	Red
Result	L	L	L									
Goalkeepers												
Jose Porras	■	■	■	3	3	0	0	270	100.0	0	0	0
Defenders												
Jervis Drummond	»	▒	«	2	1	1	1	93	34.4	0	0	0
Leonardo Gonzalez	■	«	■	3	3	0	1	235	87.0	0	1	0
Luis Antonio Marin	■	■	■	3	3	0	0	270	100.0	0	2	0
Gilberto Martinez	«	▒	▒	1	1	0	1	66	24.4	0	0	0
Douglas Sequeira	■	■	▒	2	2	0	0	180	66.7	0	0	0
Michael Umana	■	■	■	3	3	0	0	270	100.0	0	1	0
Harold Wallace	▒	■	»	2	1	1	0	111	41.1	0	0	0
Midfielders												
Randall Azofeifa	»	▒	▒	1	0	1	0	1	0.4	0	0	0
Cristian Badilla	▒	▒	■	1	1	0	0	90	33.3	0	1	0
Kurt Bernard	▒	»	▒	1	0	1	0	7	2.6	0	0	0
Christian Bolanos	»	▒	«	2	1	1	1	90	33.3	0	0	0
Walter Centeno	■	«	■	3	3	0	1	263	97.4	0	0	0
Daniel Fonseca	■	«	▒	2	2	0	1	117	43.3	0	1	0
Carlos Hernandez	▒	»	»	2	0	2	0	44	16.3	0	0	0
Mauricio Solis	«	■	■	3	3	0	1	257	95.2	0	1	0
Forwards												
Ronald Gomez	«	■	«	3	3	0	2	260	96.3	1	1	0
Alvaro Saborio	▒	»	»	2	0	2	0	76	28.1	0	0	0
Paulo Wanchope	■	■	■	3	3	0	0	270	100.0	2	0	0

WORLD CUP GROUP B

MATCH ONE

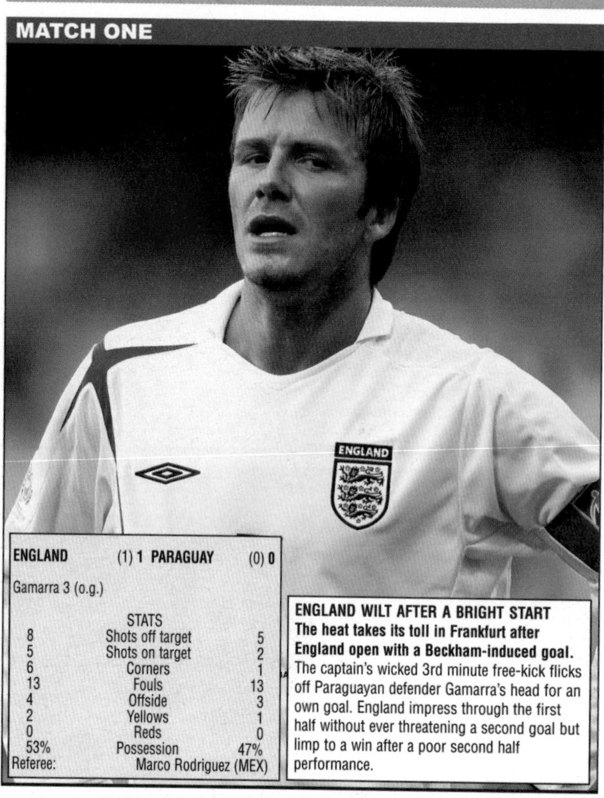

ENGLAND	(1) 1	PARAGUAY	(0) 0
Gamarra 3 (o.g.)			
	STATS		
8	Shots off target		5
5	Shots on target		2
6	Corners		1
13	Fouls		13
4	Offside		3
2	Yellows		1
0	Reds		0
53%	Possession		47%
Referee:	Marco Rodriguez (MEX)		

ENGLAND WILT AFTER A BRIGHT START
The heat takes its toll in Frankfurt after England open with a Beckham-induced goal. The captain's wicked 3rd minute free-kick flicks off Paraguayan defender Gamarra's head for an own goal. England impress through the first half without ever threatening a second goal but limp to a win after a poor second half performance.

MATCH TWO

SOCA WARRIORS HOLD OFF SWEDES
Tiny Trinidad & Tobago frustrate the might of Sweden despite being down to ten men for nearly all the second half. Swedish stars Ibrahimovic, Larsson and Ljungberg can't beat the inspired Hislop - a late substitute in the Trinidad goal - even after Avery John is sent off.

TRINIDAD & TOB	(0) 0	SWEDEN	(0) 0
	STATS		
4	Shots off target		12
2	Shots on target		6
1	Corners		8
10	Fouls		9
1	Offside		2
3	Yellows		1
1	Reds		0
39%	Possession		61%
Referee:	Shamsul Maidin (SIN)		

MATCH THREE

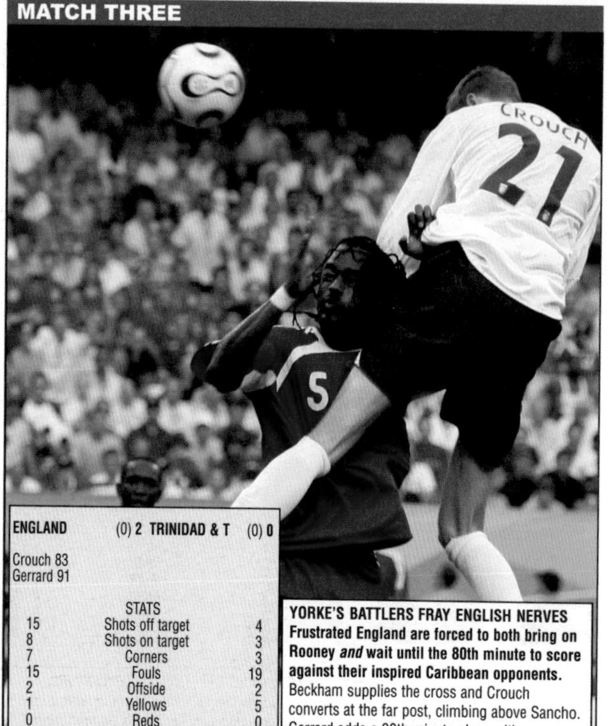

ENGLAND	(0) 2	TRINIDAD & T	(0) 0
Crouch 83			
Gerrard 91			
	STATS		
15	Shots off target		4
8	Shots on target		3
7	Corners		3
15	Fouls		19
2	Offside		2
1	Yellows		5
0	Reds		0
62%	Possession		38%
Referee:	Toru Kamikawa (JPN)		

YORKE'S BATTLERS FRAY ENGLISH NERVES
Frustrated England are forced to both bring on Rooney *and* wait until the 80th minute to score against their inspired Caribbean opponents. Beckham supplies the cross and Crouch converts at the far post, climbing above Sancho. Gerrard adds a 90th minute gloss with a powerful strike into the corner but Trinidad have chances.

MATCH FOUR

SWEDEN	(0) 1	PARAGUAY	(0) 0
Ljungberg 89			
	STATS		
7	Shots off target		13
10	Shots on target		3
6	Corners		3
19	Fouls		15
3	Offside		1
3	Yellows		5
0	Reds		0
58%	Possession		42%
Referee:	Lubos Michel (SVK)		

LJUNGBERG LEAVES IT LATE
A last-minute strike from Arsenal's Ljungberg puts Paraguay out of the World Cup and revives Swedish hopes of progress. Paraguay challenge fiercely and benefit from some poor Swedish finishing, particularly from Ibrahimovic, who is substituted. Finally Ljungberg heads in from close range to win it.

ENGLAND – SWEDEN – PARAGUAY – TRINIDAD AND TOBAGO

PARAGUAY APPEARANCES

Match 1 2 3
Result L L W

Player	Appearances	Started	Subbed on	Subbed off	Mins played	% played	Goals	Yellow	Red
Goalkeepers									
Aldo Bobadilla	3	2	1	0	264	97.8	0	0	0
Justo Villar	1	1	0	1	6	2.2	0	0	0
Defenders									
Julio Cesar Caceres	3	3	0	1	256	94.8	0	0	0
Denis Caniza	3	3	0	1	267	98.9	0	1	0
Paulo Da Silva	1	0	1	0	3	1.1	0	0	0
Carlos Alberto Gamarra	3	3	0	0	270	100.0	0	0	0
Julio Manzur	1	0	1	0	14	5.2	0	0	0
Jorge Nunez	3	2	1	0	190	70.4	0	1	0
Delio Cesar Toledo	1	1	0	1	80	29.6	0	0	0
Midfielders									
Roberto Miguel Acuna	3	3	0	0	270	100.0	0	1	0
Edgar Barreto	2	1	1	0	100	37.0	0	1	0
Carlos Bonet	2	2	0	2	146	54.1	0	0	0
Julio Dos Santos	2	1	1	0	119	44.1	0	1	0
Carlos Paredes	3	3	0	0	270	100.0	0	2	0
Riveros	2	2	0	1	151	55.9	0	0	0
Forwards									
Nelson Cuevas	2	0	2	0	49	18.1	1	0	0
Nelson Haedo Valdez	1	1	0	0	90	33.3	0	1	0
Dante Lopez	1	0	1	0	28	10.4	0	0	0
Roque Santa Cruz	3	3	0	1	242	89.6	0	0	0
Nelson Valdez	2	2	0	1	155	57.4	0	0	0

GROUP B TABLE

	P	W	D	L	F	A	DIF	PTS
England	3	2	1	0	5	2	3	7
Sweden	3	1	2	0	3	2	1	5
Paraguay	3	1	0	2	2	2	0	3
Trinidad and Tobago	3	0	1	2	0	4	-4	1

TRINIDAD AND TOBAGO APPEARANCES

Match 1 2 3
Result D L L

Player	Appearances	Started	Subbed on	Subbed off	Mins played	% played	Goals	Yellow	Red
Goalkeepers									
Shaka Hislop	2	2	0	0	180	66.7	0	1	0
Kelvin Jack	1	1	0	0	90	33.3	0	0	0
Defenders									
Cyd Gray	2	2	0	0	180	66.7	0	1	0
Avery John	2	2	0	1	75	27.8	0	1	1
Dennis Lawrence	3	3	0	0	270	100.0	0	0	0
Brent Sancho	3	3	0	0	270	100.0	0	1	0
Midfielders									
Christopher Birchall	3	3	0	0	270	100.0	0	0	0
Carlos Edwards	3	3	0	1	232	85.9	0	0	0
Kenwyne Jones	2	1	1	1	128	47.4	0	1	0
Russell Latapy	1	0	1	0	24	8.9	0	0	0
Colin Samuel	1	1	0	0	90	33.3	0	0	0
Densil Theobald	3	3	0	2	240	88.9	0	1	0
Aurtis Whitley	3	2	1	1	180	66.7	0	2	0
Evans Wise	2	0	2	0	56	20.7	0	0	0
Forwards									
Cornell Glenn	3	1	2	1	100	37.0	0	0	0
Stern John	3	3	0	0	270	100.0	0	0	0
Dwight Yorke	3	3	0	0	270	100.0	0	1	0

MATCH FIVE

SWEDEN	(0) 2	ENGLAND	(1) 2
Allback 51			Cole 34
Larsson 90			Gerrard 85
	STATS		
3	Shots off target		6
6	Shots on target		8
12	Corners		6
18	Fouls		13
0	Offside		1
2	Yellows		1
0	Reds		0
44%	Possession		56%
Referee:	Masssimo Busacca (SUI)		

SWEDES EXPOSE ENGLAND WEAKNESSES

Owen's World Cup ends one minute into the final Group game as his knee buckles horribly. England enjoy a good first half, with Cole's stunning volley a contender for the tournament highlights. The Swedes strike back with an Allback near-post header and continue to threaten from set-pieces. England sub Gerrard heads home but Larsson completes the scoring, snatching a last minute draw.

MATCH SIX

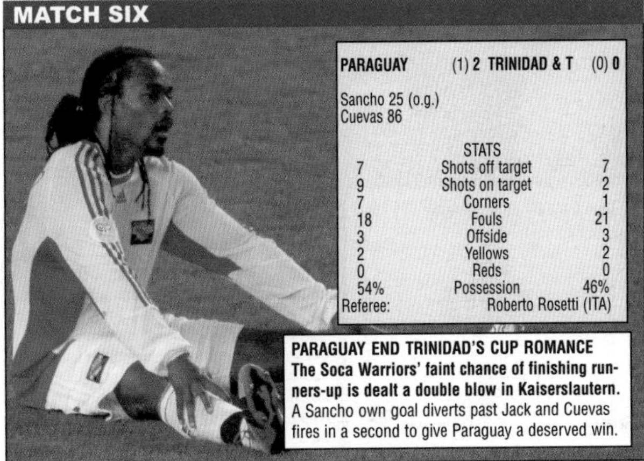

PARAGUAY	(1) 2	TRINIDAD & T	(0) 0
Sancho 25 (o.g.)			
Cuevas 86			
	STATS		
7	Shots off target		7
9	Shots on target		2
7	Corners		1
18	Fouls		21
3	Offside		3
2	Yellows		2
0	Reds		0
54%	Possession		46%
Referee:	Roberto Rosetti (ITA)		

PARAGUAY END TRINIDAD'S CUP ROMANCE

The Soca Warriors' faint chance of finishing runners-up is dealt a double blow in Kaiserslautern. A Sancho own goal diverts past Jack and Cuevas fires in a second to give Paraguay a deserved win.

WORLD CUP GROUP C

The group stages

MATCH ONE

ARGENTINA	(2) 2 IVORY COAST	(0) 1
Crespo 24 Saviola 38		Drogba 82
	STATS	
5	Shots off target	9
4	Shots on target	4
3	Corners	6
15	Fouls	17
6	Offside	0
3	Yellows	2
0	Reds	0
49%	Possession	51%
Referee:	Frank de Bleeckere (BEL)	

CRESPO WINS BATTLE OF CHELSEA STRIKERS

Drogba and Crespo both score in this thrilling game as the excellent Ivory Coast pay for poor early defending.

A clash of styles makes for a fascinating game with the bustle and power of the Elephants being countered by the guile of Riquelme's probing from the Argentinian midfield.

Crespo stabs home in the midst of the confusion caused by Riquelme's free kick for the first goal and Saviola stays onside to steer past Tizie for the second - Riquelme again the provider.

Chances come at both ends in the second half as the Elephants chase the game and gain the reward they are due when the tireless Drogba is twice involved in the move before completing a left-footed finish.

MATCH TWO

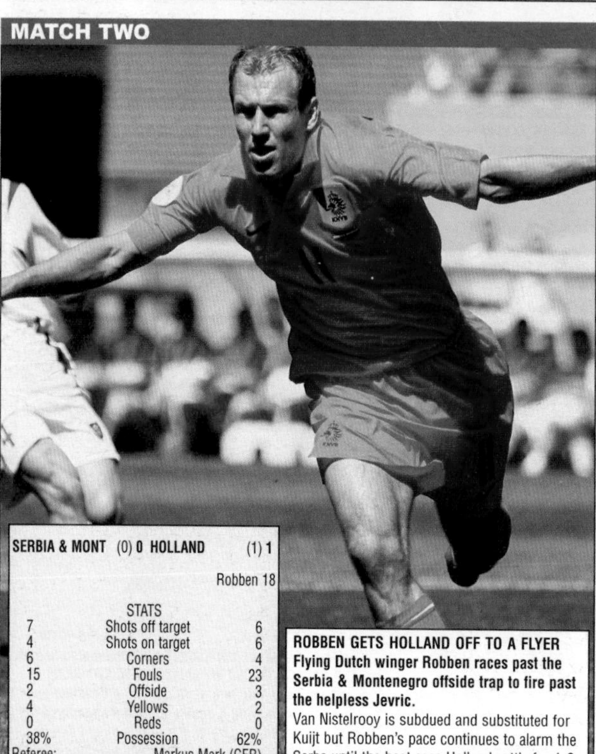

SERBIA & MONT	(0) 0 HOLLAND	(1) 1
		Robben 18
	STATS	
7	Shots off target	6
4	Shots on target	6
6	Corners	4
15	Fouls	23
2	Offside	3
4	Yellows	2
0	Reds	0
38%	Possession	62%
Referee:	Markus Merk (GER)	

ROBBEN GETS HOLLAND OFF TO A FLYER

Flying Dutch winger Robben races past the Serbia & Montenegro offside trap to fire past the helpless Jevric.

Van Nistelrooy is subdued and substituted for Kuijt but Robben's pace continues to alarm the Serbs until the heat sees Holland settle for 1-0.

MATCH THREE

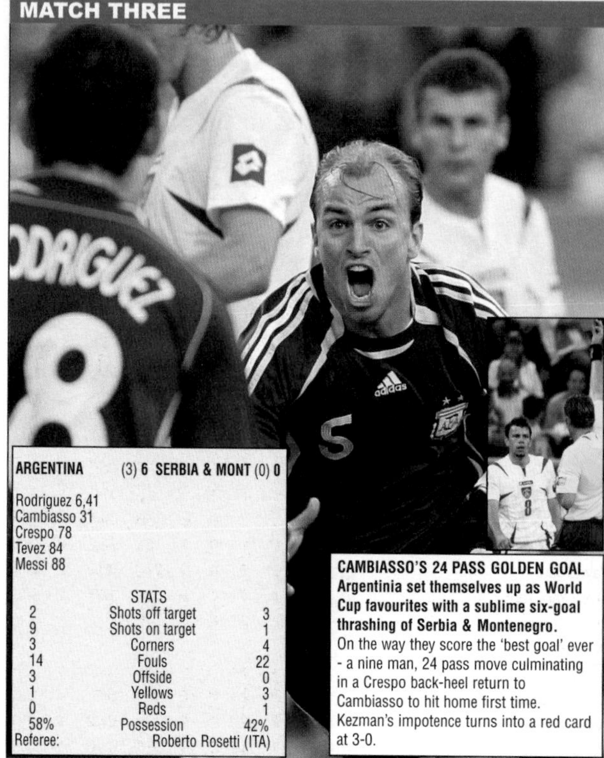

ARGENTINA	(3) 6 SERBIA & MONT	(0) 0
Rodriguez 6,41 Cambiasso 31 Crespo 78 Tevez 84 Messi 88		
	STATS	
2	Shots off target	3
9	Shots on target	1
3	Corners	4
14	Fouls	22
3	Offside	0
1	Yellows	3
0	Reds	1
58%	Possession	42%
Referee:	Roberto Rosetti (ITA)	

CAMBIASSO'S 24 PASS GOLDEN GOAL

Argentinia set themselves up as World Cup favourites with a sublime six-goal thrashing of Serbia & Montenegro.

On the way they score the 'best goal' ever - a nine man, 24 pass move culminating in a Crespo back-heel return to Cambiasso to hit home first time.

Kezman's impotence turns into a red card at 3-0.

ARGENTINA - HOLLAND - IVORY COAST - SERBIA & MONTENEGRO

MATCH FOUR

HOLLAND (2) 2 IVORY COAST (1) 1

van Persie 23, van Nistelrooy 27 — Kone 38

Holland	STATS	Ivory Coast
1	Shots off target	7
8	Shots on target	9
3	Corners	8
24	Fouls	15
6	Offside	4
4	Yellows	3
0	Reds	0
51%	Possession	49%
Referee:	Oscar Ruiz (COL)	

END-TO-END GAME ENDS IN ELEPHANTS' EXIT
Two of the most entertaining attack-minded sides in the competition slug it out but Holland hang on (just !) to progress.
The Ivory Coast look the best team ever to come out of Africa but are undone by early goals from van Persie, a free kick, and van Nistlerooy, converting a Robben pass. Bakary Kone's run and unstoppable shot set up a thrilling second half.

MATCH FIVE

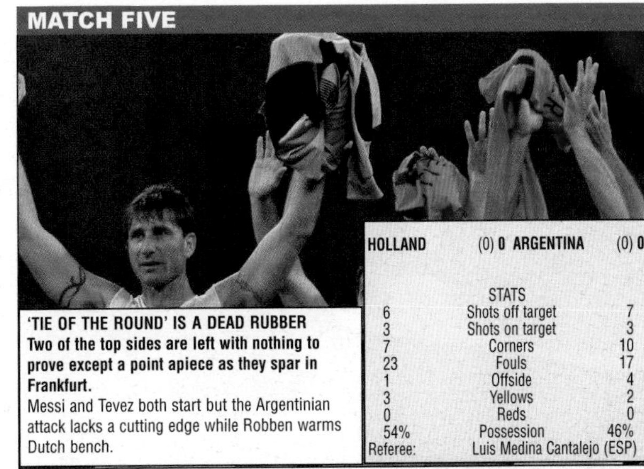

HOLLAND (0) 0 ARGENTINA (0) 0

Holland	STATS	Argentina
6	Shots off target	7
3	Shots on target	3
7	Corners	10
23	Fouls	17
1	Offside	4
3	Yellows	2
0	Reds	0
54%	Possession	46%
Referee:	Luis Medina Cantalejo (ESP)	

'TIE OF THE ROUND' IS A DEAD RUBBER
Two of the top sides are left with nothing to prove except a point apiece as they spar in Frankfurt.
Messi and Tevez both start but the Argentinian attack lacks a cutting edge while Robben warms Dutch bench.

MATCH SIX

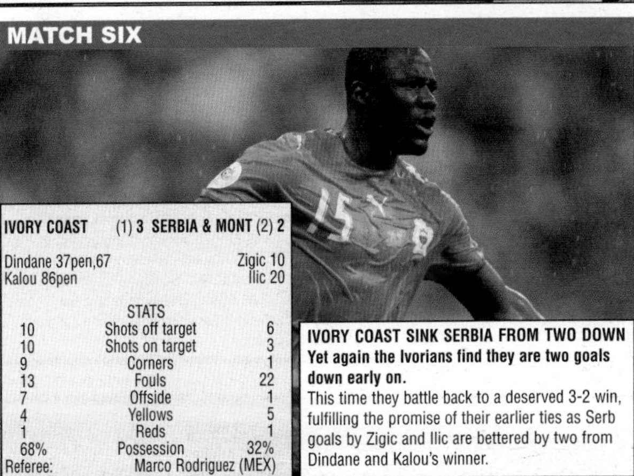

IVORY COAST (1) 3 SERBIA & MONT (2) 2

Dindane 37pen,67, Kalou 86pen — Zigic 10, Ilic 20

Ivory Coast	STATS	Serbia & Mont
10	Shots off target	6
10	Shots on target	3
9	Corners	1
13	Fouls	22
7	Offside	1
4	Yellows	5
1	Reds	1
68%	Possession	32%
Referee:	Marco Rodriguez (MEX)	

IVORY COAST SINK SERBIA FROM TWO DOWN
Yet again the Ivorians find they are two goals down early on.
This time they battle back to a deserved 3-2 win, fulfilling the promise of their earlier ties as Serb goals by Zigic and Ilic are bettered by two from Dindane and Kalou's winner.

GROUP C TABLE

	P	W	D	L	F	A	DIF	PTS
Argentina	3	2	1	0	8	1	7	7
Holland	3	2	1	0	3	1	2	7
Ivory Coast	3	1	0	2	5	6	-1	3
Serbia and Montenegro	3	0	0	3	2	10	-8	0

IVORY COAST APPEARANCES

Match	1	2	3	Appearances	Started	Subbed on	Subbed off	Mins played	% played	Goals	Yellow	Red
Result	L	L	W									
Goalkeepers												
Boubacar Barry				1	1	0	0	90	33.3	0	0	0
Jean Jacques Tizie				2	2	0	0	180	66.7	0	0	0
Defenders												
Arthur Boka				3	3	0	0	270	100.0	0	1	0
Cyril Domoraud				1	1	0	0	89	33.0	0	1	1
Emmanuel Eboue				3	3	0	0	270	100.0	0	1	0
Blaise Kouassi				1	1	0	0	90	33.3	0	0	0
Abdoulaye Meite				2	2	0	0	180	66.7	0	0	0
Habib Kolo Toure				2	2	0	0	180	66.7	0	0	0
Midfielders												
Kanga Akale				3	2	1	2	137	50.7	0	0	0
Bonaventure Kalou				2	1	1	1	73	27.0	1	0	0
Abdulkader Keita				2	2	0	2	148	54.8	0	1	0
Christian Koffi Romaric				1	1	0	1	61	22.6	0	0	0
Yaya Toure				3	3	0	0	270	100.0	0	0	0
Gilles Yapi Yapo				1	0	1	0	29	10.7	0	0	0
Didier Zokora				3	3	0	0	270	100.0	0	1	0
Forwards												
Aruna Dindane				3	1	2	0	154	57.0	2	1	0
Didier Drogba				2	2	0	0	180	66.7	1	2	0
Arouna Kone				3	2	1	1	176	65.2	0	0	0
Bakary Kone				3	1	2	1	122	45.2	1	0	0

SERBIA AND MONTENEGRO APPEARANCES

Match	1	2	3	Appearances	Started	Subbed on	Subbed off	Mins played	% played	Goals	Yellow	Red
Result	L	L	L									
Goalkeepers												
Dragoslav Jevric				3	3	0	0	270	100.0	0	0	0
Defenders												
Nenad Djordjevic				2	2	0	1	132	48.9	0	0	0
Ivica Dragutinovic				1	1	0	0	90	33.3	0	1	0
Milan Dudic				2	2	0	0	180	66.7	0	1	0
Ivan Ergic				2	1	1	0	135	50.0	0	0	0
Goran Gavrancic				3	3	0	0	270	100.0	0	2	0
Mladen Krstajic				3	3	0	1	195	72.2	0	1	0
Albert Nadj				3	2	1	1	164	60.7	0	2	1
Midfielders												
Predrag Djordjevic				3	3	0	0	270	100.0	0	0	0
Igor Duljaj				3	3	0	0	270	100.0	0	1	0
Sasa Ilic				1	1	0	0	90	33.3	1	0	0
Ognjen Koroman				2	1	1	1	95	35.2	0	2	0
Dejan Stankovic				3	3	0	0	270	100.0	0	1	0
Zvonimir Vukic				1	0	1	0	21	7.8	0	0	0
Forwards												
Mateja Kezman				2	2	0	1	130	48.1	0	0	1
Danijel Ljuboja				2	0	2	0	67	24.8	0	0	0
Savo Milosevic				3	2	1	2	139	51.5	0	0	0
Nikola Zigic				2	1	1	1	110	40.7	1	0	0

WORLD CUP GROUP D

The group stages

MATCH ONE

MEXICO	(1) 3 IRAN	(1) 1
Bravo 28,76 Zinha 79		Golmohammadi 36
	STATS	
3	Shots off target	2
4	Shots on target	5
6	Corners	5
25	Fouls	21
1	Offside	2
2	Yellows	1
0	Reds	0
52%	Possession	48%
Referee:	Roberto Rosetti (ITA)	

BRAVO BRACE SHOWS MEXICAN PROMISE
The Mexicans need two late goals to see off Iran but Zinha's final strike shows their flair.
Bravo gives Mexico an early lead, poking home from Franco's nod-on but Iran level through Golmohammadi. Sub Naelsen (known as 'Zinha') then sets up Bravo to regain the Mexican lead before heading home a clever third himself.

MATCH TWO

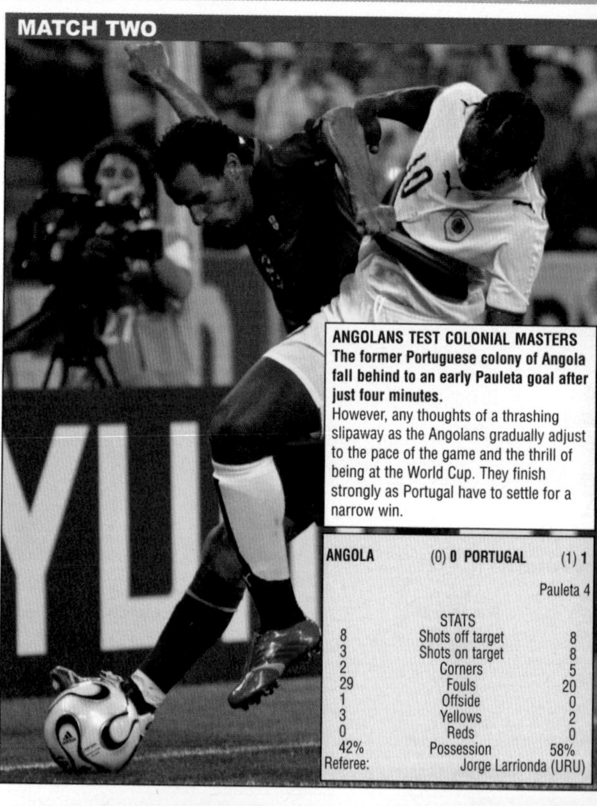

ANGOLANS TEST COLONIAL MASTERS
The former Portuguese colony of Angola fall behind to an early Pauleta goal after just four minutes.
However, any thoughts of a thrashing slipaway as the Angolans gradually adjust to the pace of the game and the thrill of being at the World Cup. They finish strongly as Portugal have to settle for a narrow win.

ANGOLA	(0) 0 PORTUGAL	(1) 1
		Pauleta 4
	STATS	
8	Shots off target	8
3	Shots on target	8
2	Corners	5
29	Fouls	20
1	Offside	0
3	Yellows	2
0	Reds	0
42%	Possession	58%
Referee:	Jorge Larrionda (URU)	

MATCH THREE

MEXICO	(0) 0 ANGOLA	(0) 0
	STATS	
5	Shots off target	7
8	Shots on target	1
6	Corners	5
20	Fouls	22
0	Offside	8
1	Yellows	5
0	Reds	1
54%	Possession	46%
Referee:	Shamsul Maisin (SIN)	

NO WAY THROUGH FOR MEXICO
Angola earn their first World Cup point with a dogged defensive display against Mexico.
The Mexicans are without the injured Borgetti, who is key to their attack, and struggle to turn possession into goal attempts in the first half. They dominate the second half but fail to break through even after Andre is sent off.

MATCH FOUR

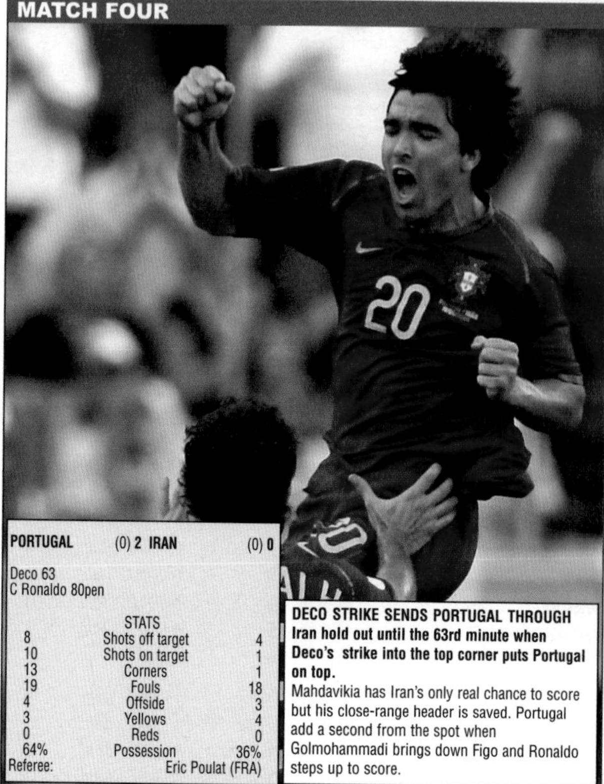

PORTUGAL	(0) 2 IRAN	(0) 0
Deco 63 C Ronaldo 80pen		
	STATS	
8	Shots off target	4
10	Shots on target	1
13	Corners	1
19	Fouls	18
4	Offside	3
3	Yellows	4
0	Reds	0
64%	Possession	36%
Referee:	Eric Poulat (FRA)	

DECO STRIKE SENDS PORTUGAL THROUGH
Iran hold out until the 63rd minute when Deco's strike into the top corner puts Portugal on top.
Mahdavikia has Iran's only real chance to score but his close-range header is saved. Portugal add a second from the spot when Golmohammadi brings down Figo and Ronaldo steps up to score.

ANGOLA APPEARANCES

Match 1 2 3 — Result L D D

Player	Appearances	Started	Subbed on	Subbed off	Mins played	% played	Goals	Yellow	Red
Goalkeepers									
Joao Ricardo	3	3	0	0	270	100.0	0	1	0
Defenders									
Delgado	3	3	0	0	270	100.0	0	1	0
Jamba	3	3	0	0	270	100.0	0	1	0
Kali	3	3	0	0	270	100.0	0	0	0
Loco	3	3	0	0	270	100.0	0	2	0
Rui Manuel Marques	2	0	2	0	36	13.3	0	0	0
Mateus	3	3	0	2	179	66.3	0	0	0
Midfielders									
Andre	2	2	0	0	167	61.9	0	2	1
Edson	1	0	1	0	21	7.8	0	0	0
Figueiredo	3	3	0	3	223	82.6	0	0	0
Antonio Viana Mendonca	3	3	0	0	270	100.0	0	1	0
Miloy	3	1	2	0	109	40.4	0	0	0
Ze Kalanga	3	3	0	2	241	89.3	0	2	0
Forwards									
Fabrice Akwa	3	3	0	2	198	73.3	0	0	0
Flavio	1	0	1	0	40	14.8	1	0	0
Love	1	0	1	0	68	25.2	0	0	0
Mantorras	2	0	2	0	55	20.4	0	0	0

GROUP D TABLE

	P	W	D	L	F	A	DIF	PTS
Portugal	3	3	0	0	5	1	4	9
Mexico	3	1	1	1	4	3	1	4
Angola	3	0	2	1	1	2	-1	2
Iran	3	0	1	2	2	6	-4	1

IRAN APPEARANCES

Match 1 2 3 — Result L L D

Player	Appearances	Started	Subbed on	Subbed off	Mins played	% played	Goals	Yellow	Red
Goalkeepers									
Ebrahim Mirzapour	3	3	0	0	270	100.0	0	0	0
Defenders									
Sohrab Bakhtiarizadeh	2	1	1	0	93	34.4	1	0	0
Yahya Golmohammadi	2	2	0	1	177	65.6	1	1	0
Hossein Kaabi	3	3	0	1	246	91.1	0	1	0
Mohammed Nosrati	3	3	0	2	182	67.4	0	0	0
Rahman Rezaei	3	3	0	0	270	100.0	0	0	0
Midfielders									
Ali Karimi	2	2	0	2	126	46.7	0	0	0
Mehrzad Madanchi	3	2	1	1	183	67.8	0	2	0
Mehdi Mahdavikia	3	3	0	0	270	100.0	0	0	0
Javad Nekoonam	2	2	0	0	180	66.7	0	2	0
Massoud Shojaei	1	0	1	0	78	28.9	0	0	0
Andranik Teymoorian	3	3	0	0	270	100.0	0	1	0
Ferydoon Zandi	2	1	1	0	116	43.0	0	1	0
Forwards									
Arash Borhani	2	0	2	0	34	12.6	0	0	0
Ali Daei	2	2	0	0	180	66.7	0	0	0
Vahid Hashemian	3	3	0	1	218	80.7	0	0	0
Rasoul Paki Khatibi	2	0	2	0	77	28.5	0	0	0

MATCH FIVE

PORTUGAL (2) 2 MEXICO (1) 1

Maniche 6, Simoa Sabrosa 24pen — Fonseca 29

Portugal	STATS	Mexico
6	Shots off target	8
5	Shots on target	6
4	Corners	5
29	Fouls	18
1	Offside	2
4	Yellows	5
0	Reds	1
50%	Possession	50%

Referee: Lubos Michel (SVK)

SCOLARI'S 100% RECORD INTACT
Big Phil Scolari has won every World Cup game as manager and keeps the record going here.
But it's close as Mexico's Bravo misses a penalty after Simao converts one for a 2-0 lead to Portugal. Fonseca's header pulls one back for Mexico who still reach the last 16 but without red-carded Perez.

MATCH SIX

IRAN (0) 1 ANGOLA (0) 1

Bakhtiarizadeh 75 — Flavio 60

Iran	STATS	Angola
5	Shots off target	8
13	Shots on target	7
3	Corners	6
19	Fouls	23
2	Offside	0
3	Yellows	3
0	Reds	0
55%	Possession	45%

Referee: Mark Shield (AUS)

IRAN EQUALISE TO END ANGOLA'S DREAM
Angola's slim hopes of progressing require a good win over Iran and they inch ahead through Flavio.
He heads his 14th international goal after 60 minutes before Bakhtiarizadeh levels for a draw.

WORLD CUP GROUP E

The group stages

MATCH ONE

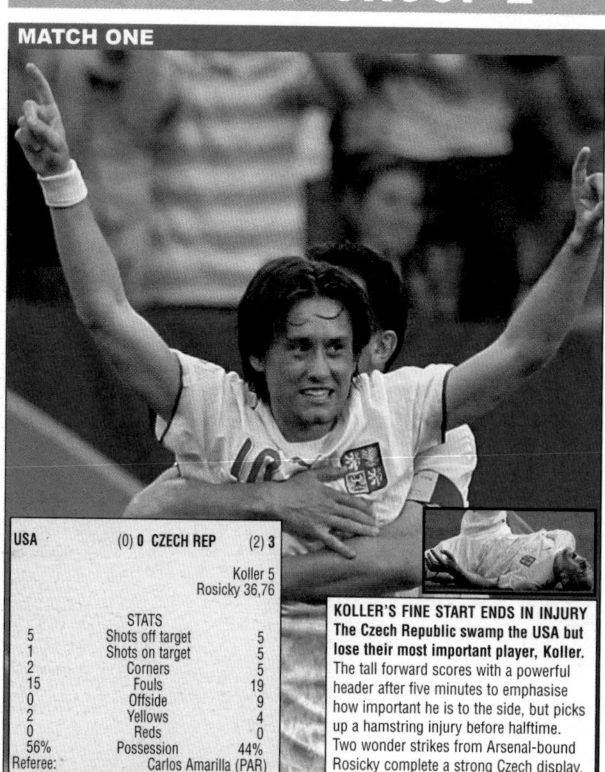

USA	(0) 0	CZECH REP	(2) 3
			Koller 5
			Rosicky 36,76
	STATS		
5	Shots off target		5
1	Shots on target		5
2	Corners		5
15	Fouls		19
0	Offside		9
2	Yellows		4
0	Reds		0
56%	Possession		44%
Referee:			Carlos Amarilla (PAR)

KOLLER'S FINE START ENDS IN INJURY
The Czech Republic swamp the USA but lose their most important player, Koller. The tall forward scores with a powerful header after five minutes to emphasise how important he is to the side, but picks up a hamstring injury before halftime. Two wonder strikes from Arsenal-bound Rosicky complete a strong Czech display.

MATCH TWO

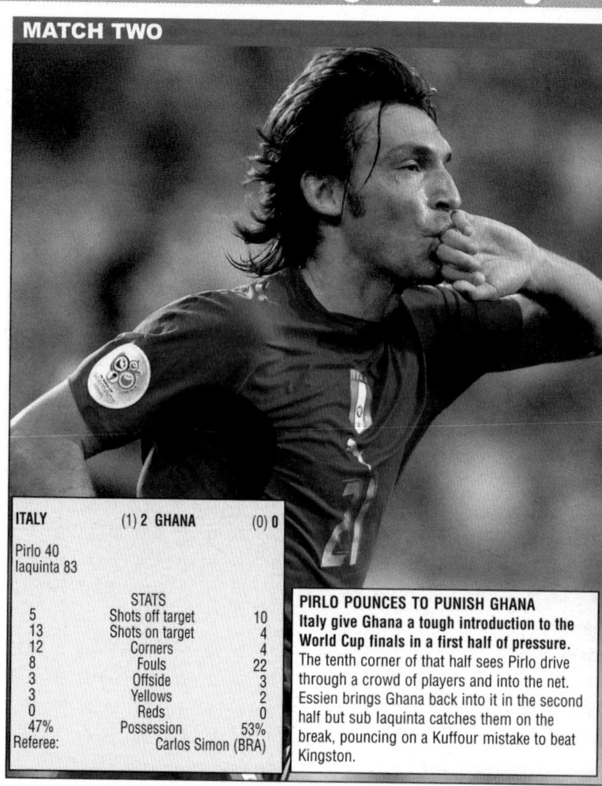

ITALY	(1) 2	GHANA	(0) 0
Pirlo 40			
Iaquinta 83			
	STATS		
5	Shots off target		10
13	Shots on target		4
12	Corners		4
8	Fouls		22
3	Offside		3
3	Yellows		2
0	Reds		0
47%	Possession		53%
Referee:			Carlos Simon (BRA)

PIRLO POUNCES TO PUNISH GHANA
Italy give Ghana a tough introduction to the World Cup finals in a first half of pressure. The tenth corner of that half sees Pirlo drive through a crowd of players and into the net. Essien brings Ghana back into it in the second half but sub Iaquinta catches them on the break, pouncing on a Kuffour mistake to beat Kingston.

MATCH THREE

THE BLACK STARS GAIN AFRICA'S FIRST WIN
Ghana's energy overwhelms an out-of-sorts Czech team in a first win for an African side. The Black Stars (named for their flag's emblem) score after two minutes when captain Appiah finds Asamoah Gyan in the box. Without strikers Koller or Baros, the Czechs struggle to reply and lose Ujfalusi to a red card for a foul in the box. The resulting penalty hits the post but Muntari scores a deserved second with a powerful drive.

CZECH REP	(0) 0	GHANA	(1) 2
			Gyan 2
			Muntari 82
	STATS		
10	Shots off target		12
4	Shots on target		8
6	Corners		7
16	Fouls		22
4	Offside		10
1	Yellows		6
1	Reds		0
49%	Possession		51%
Referee:			Horacio Elizondo (ARG)

MATCH FOUR

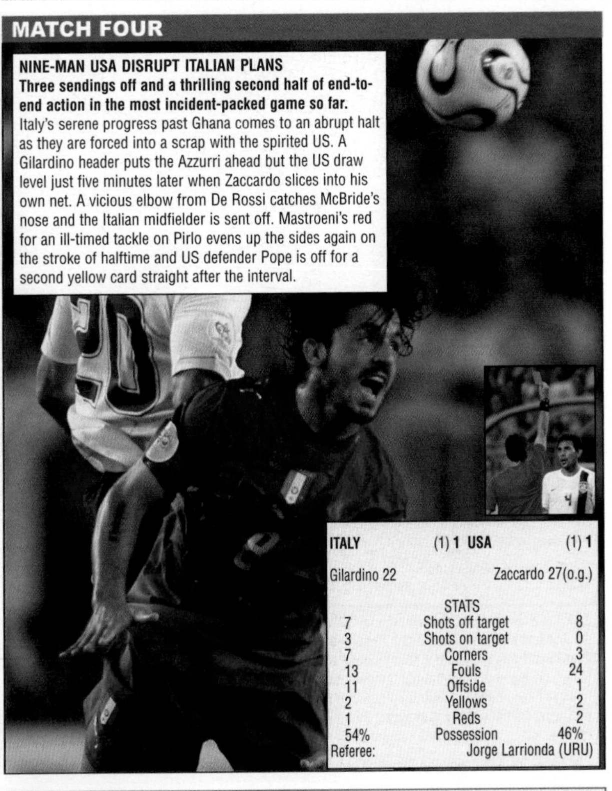

NINE-MAN USA DISRUPT ITALIAN PLANS
Three sendings off and a thrilling second half of end-to-end action in the most incident-packed game so far.
Italy's serene progress past Ghana comes to an abrupt halt as they are forced into a scrap with the spirited US. A Gilardino header puts the Azzurri ahead but the US draw level just five minutes later when Zaccardo slices into his own net. A vicious elbow from De Rossi catches McBride's nose and the Italian midfielder is sent off. Mastroeni's red for an ill-timed tackle on Pirlo evens up the sides again on the stroke of halftime and US defender Pope is off for a second yellow card straight after the interval.

ITALY	(1) 1 USA	(1) 1
Gilardino 22		Zaccardo 27(o.g.)
	STATS	
7	Shots off target	8
3	Shots on target	0
7	Corners	3
13	Fouls	24
11	Offside	1
2	Yellows	2
1	Reds	2
54%	Possession	46%
Referee:	Jorge Larrionda (URU)	

MATCH FIVE

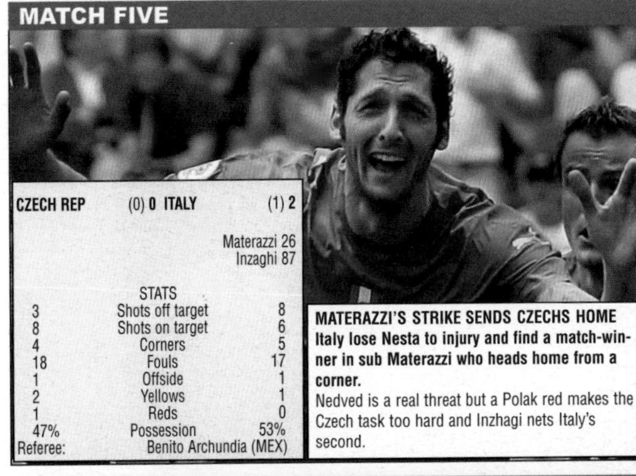

CZECH REP	(0) 0 ITALY	(1) 2
		Materazzi 26
		Inzaghi 87
	STATS	
3	Shots off target	8
8	Shots on target	6
4	Corners	5
18	Fouls	17
1	Offside	1
2	Yellows	1
1	Reds	0
47%	Possession	53%
Referee:	Benito Archundia (MEX)	

MATERAZZI'S STRIKE SENDS CZECHS HOME
Italy lose Nesta to injury and find a match-winner in sub Materazzi who heads home from a corner.
Nedved is a real threat but a Polak red makes the Czech task too hard and Inzhagi nets Italy's second.

MATCH SIX

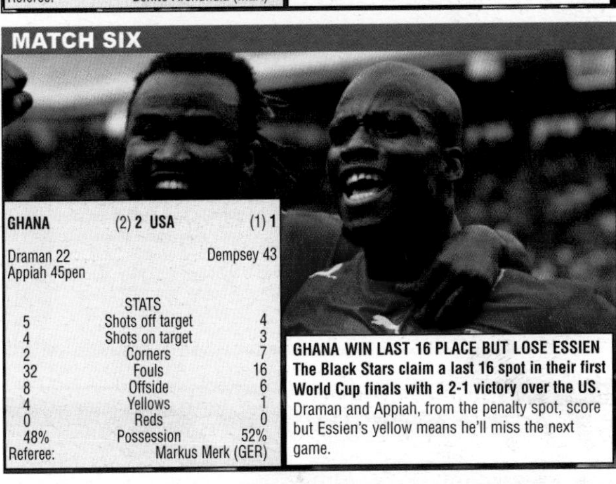

GHANA	(2) 2 USA	(1) 1
Draman 22		Dempsey 43
Appiah 45pen		
	STATS	
5	Shots off target	4
4	Shots on target	3
2	Corners	7
32	Fouls	16
8	Offside	6
4	Yellows	1
0	Reds	0
48%	Possession	52%
Referee:	Markus Merk (GER)	

GHANA WIN LAST 16 PLACE BUT LOSE ESSIEN
The Black Stars claim a last 16 spot in their first World Cup finals with a 2-1 victory over the US.
Draman and Appiah, from the penalty spot, score but Essien's yellow means he'll miss the next game.

GROUP E TABLE

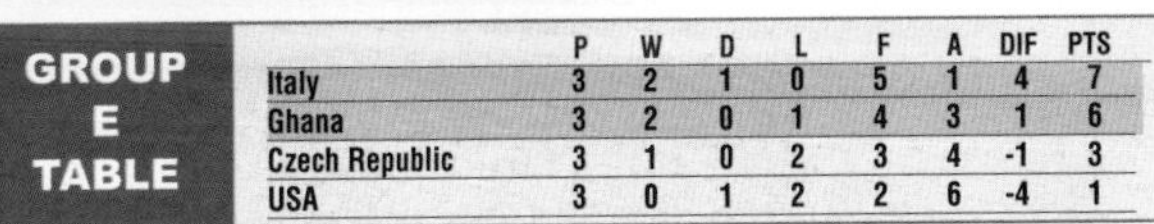

	P	W	D	L	F	A	DIF	PTS
Italy	3	2	1	0	5	1	4	7
Ghana	3	2	0	1	4	3	1	6
Czech Republic	3	1	0	2	3	4	-1	3
USA	3	0	1	2	2	6	-4	1

CZECH REPUBLIC APPEARANCES

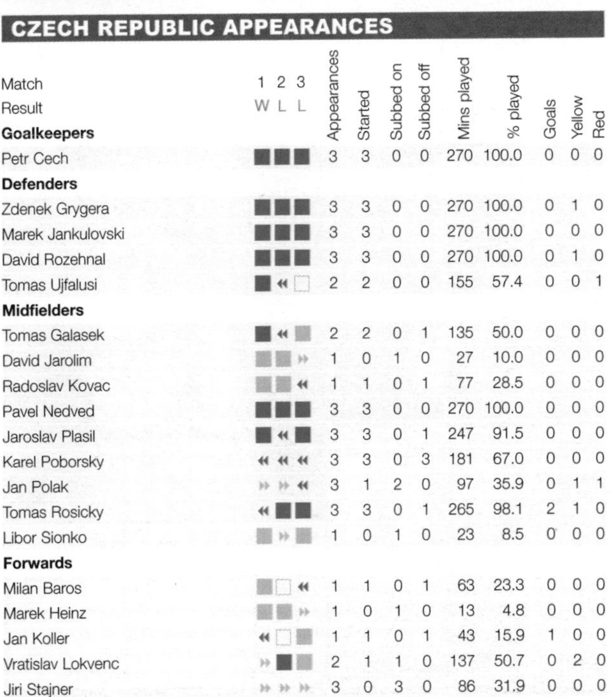

Match	1 2 3	Appearances	Started	Subbed on	Subbed off	Mins played	% played	Goals	Yellow	Red
Result	W L L									
Goalkeepers										
Petr Cech	■ ■ ■	3	3	0	0	270	100.0	0	0	0
Defenders										
Zdenek Grygera	■ ■ ■	3	3	0	0	270	100.0	0	1	0
Marek Jankulovski	■ ■ ■	3	3	0	0	270	100.0	0	0	0
David Rozehnal	■ ■ ■	3	3	0	0	270	100.0	0	1	0
Tomas Ujfalusi	■ « □	2	2	0	0	155	57.4	0	0	1
Midfielders										
Tomas Galasek	■ « ▒	2	2	0	1	135	50.0	0	0	0
David Jarolim	▒ ▒ »	1	0	1	0	27	10.0	0	0	0
Radoslav Kovac	▒ ▒ «	1	1	0	1	77	28.5	0	0	0
Pavel Nedved	■ ■ ■	3	3	0	0	270	100.0	0	0	0
Jaroslav Plasil	■ « ■	3	3	0	1	247	91.5	0	0	0
Karel Poborsky	« « «	3	3	0	3	181	67.0	0	0	0
Jan Polak	» » «	3	1	2	0	97	35.9	0	1	1
Tomas Rosicky	« ■ ■	3	3	0	1	265	98.1	2	1	0
Libor Sionko	▒ » ▒	1	0	1	0	23	8.5	0	0	0
Forwards										
Milan Baros	▒ □ «	1	1	0	1	63	23.3	0	0	0
Marek Heinz	▒ ▒ »	1	0	1	0	13	4.8	0	0	0
Jan Koller	« □ ▒	1	1	0	1	43	15.9	1	0	0
Vratislav Lokvenc	» ■ ▒	2	1	1	0	137	50.7	0	2	0
Jiri Stajner	» » »	3	0	3	0	86	31.9	0	0	0

USA APPEARANCES

Match	1 2 3	Appearances	Started	Subbed on	Subbed off	Mins played	% played	Goals	Yellow	Red
Result	L D L									
Goalkeepers										
Kasey Keller	■ ■ ■	3	3	0	0	270	100.0	0	0	0
Defenders										
Carlos Bocanegra	▒ ■ ■	2	2	0	0	180	66.7	0	0	0
Steve Cherundolo	« ■ «	2	2	0	1	196	72.6	0	0	0
James Conrad	▒ » ■	2	1	1	0	129	47.8	0	0	0
Pablo Mastroeni	« « □	1	1	0	0	90	33.3	0	0	1
John O'Brien	▒ ▒ ▒	0	0	0	0	0	0.0	0	0	0
Oguchi Onyewu	■ ■ ■	3	3	0	0	270	100.0	0	1	0
Eddie George Pope	■ « □	2	2	0	0	136	50.4	0	1	1
Midfielders										
DaMarcus Beasley	■ » ■	3	2	1	0	209	77.4	0	0	0
Bobby Convey	■ « »	3	2	1	1	158	58.5	0	0	0
Clint Dempsey	▒ « ■	2	2	0	1	151	55.9	1	0	0
Eddie Lewis	■ ▒ «	2	2	0	1	163	60.4	0	1	0
Ben Olsen	▒ ▒ »	1	0	1	0	51	18.9	0	0	0
Claudio Reyna	■ ■ «	3	3	0	1	219	81.1	0	1	0
Forwards										
Landon Donovan	■ ■ ■	3	3	0	0	270	100.0	0	0	0
Ed Johnson	▒ ▒ »	1	0	1	0	30	11.1	0	0	0
Brian McBride	« ■ ■	3	3	0	1	256	94.8	0	0	0
Josh Wolff	» ▒ ▒	1	0	1	0	14	5.2	0	0	0

WORLD CUP GROUP F

The group stages

MATCH ONE

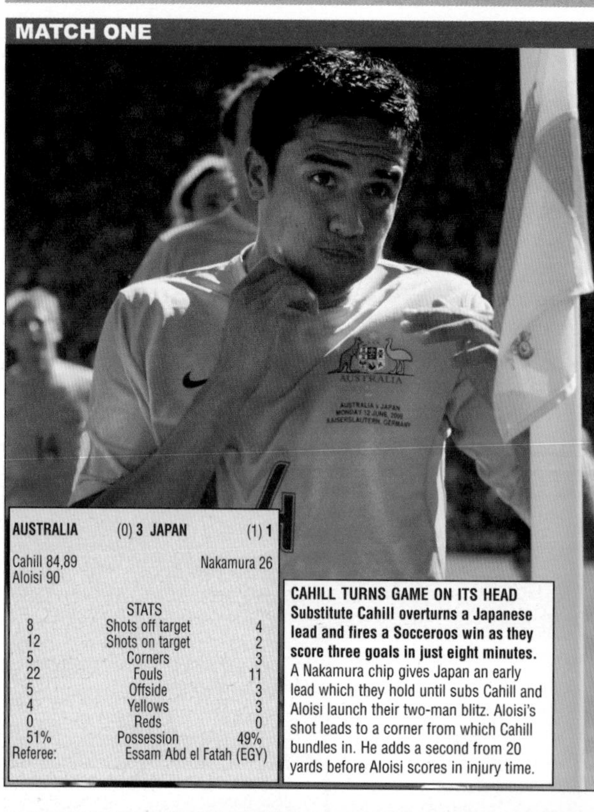

AUSTRALIA	(0) 3 JAPAN	(1) 1
Cahill 84,89 Aloisi 90		Nakamura 26
	STATS	
8	Shots off target	4
12	Shots on target	2
5	Corners	3
22	Fouls	11
5	Offside	3
4	Yellows	3
0	Reds	0
51%	Possession	49%
Referee:	Essam Abd el Fatah (EGY)	

CAHILL TURNS GAME ON ITS HEAD
Substitute Cahill overturns a Japanese lead and fires a Socceroos win as they score three goals in just eight minutes.
A Nakamura chip gives Japan an early lead which they hold until subs Cahill and Aloisi launch their two-man blitz. Aloisi's shot leads to a corner from which Cahill bundles in. He adds a second from 20 yards before Aloisi scores in injury time.

MATCH TWO

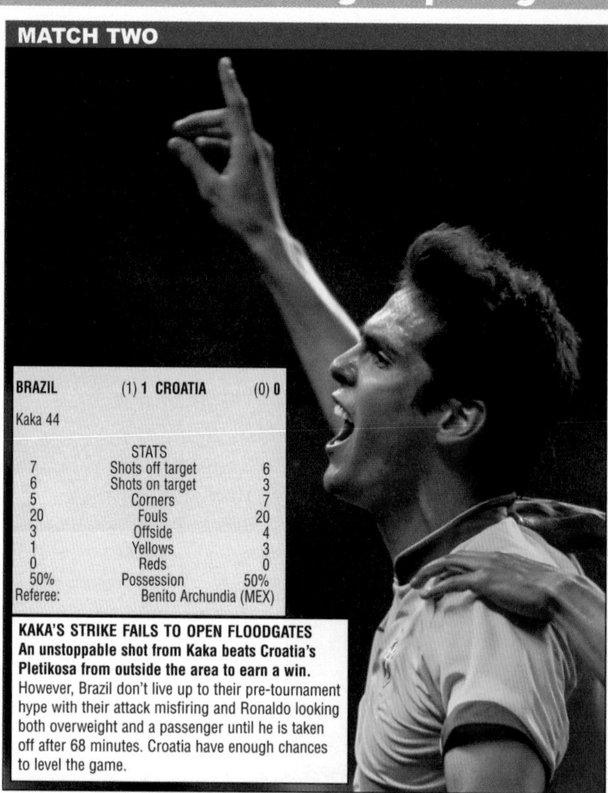

BRAZIL	(1) 1 CROATIA	(0) 0
Kaka 44		
	STATS	
7	Shots off target	6
6	Shots on target	3
5	Corners	7
20	Fouls	20
3	Offside	4
1	Yellows	3
0	Reds	0
50%	Possession	50%
Referee:	Benito Archundia (MEX)	

KAKA'S STRIKE FAILS TO OPEN FLOODGATES
An unstoppable shot from Kaka beats Croatia's Pletikosa from outside the area to earn a win.
However, Brazil don't live up to their pre-tournament hype with their attack misfiring and Ronaldo looking both overweight and a passenger until he is taken off after 68 minutes. Croatia have enough chances to level the game.

MATCH THREE

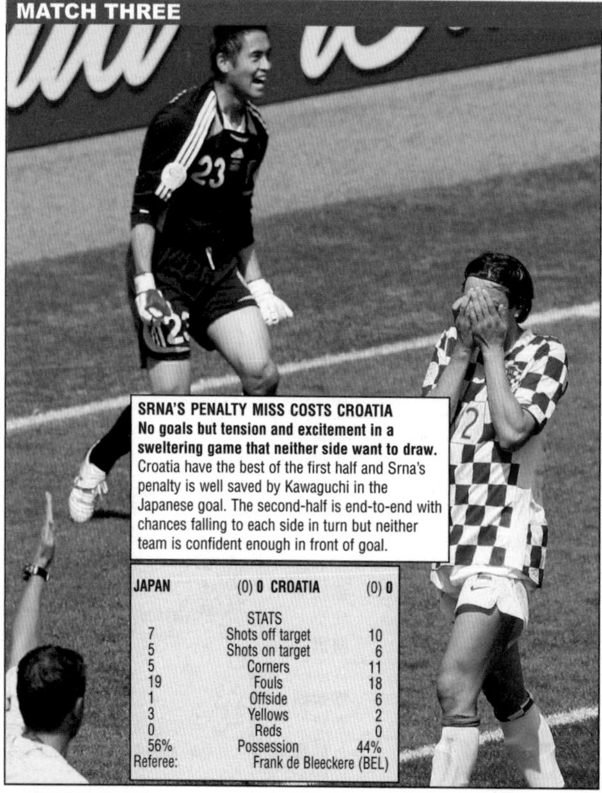

SRNA'S PENALTY MISS COSTS CROATIA
No goals but tension and excitement in a sweltering game that neither side want to draw.
Croatia have the best of the first half and Srna's penalty is well saved by Kawaguchi in the Japanese goal. The second-half is end-to-end with chances falling to each side in turn but neither team is confident enough in front of goal.

JAPAN	(0) 0 CROATIA	(0) 0
	STATS	
7	Shots off target	10
5	Shots on target	6
5	Corners	11
19	Fouls	18
1	Offside	6
3	Yellows	2
0	Reds	0
56%	Possession	44%
Referee:	Frank de Bleeckere (BEL)	

MATCH FOUR

BRAZIL	(0) 2 AUSTRALIA	(0) 0
Adriano 49 Fred 90		
	STATS	
10	Shots off target	10
6	Shots on target	4
7	Corners	4
9	Fouls	25
5	Offside	1
3	Yellows	2
0	Reds	0
53%	Possession	47%
Referee:	Markus Merk (GER)	

BRAZIL THROUGH BUT AUSSIES IMPRESS
Only a 90th minute goal from substitute Fred ends Australia's spirited fight-back against the world champions.
After an even first half, Adriano gives Brazil a lead early in the second but then it's all Australia with Kewell missing a golden chance. Fred nets after Robinho's shot rebounds from a post.

CROATIA APPEARANCES

Match 1 2 3 — Result L D D

	Appearances	Started	Subbed on	Subbed off	Mins played	% played	Goals	Yellow	Red
Goalkeepers									
Stipe Pletikosa	3	3	0	0	270	100.0	0	1	0
Defenders									
Robert Kovac	2	2	0	0	180	66.7	0	2	0
Dario Simic	3	3	0	0	264	97.8	0	1	1
Josip Simunic	3	3	0	0	269	99.6	0	2	1
Stjepan Tomas	1	1	0	1	83	30.7	0	0	0
Igor Tudor	3	3	0	1	249	92.2	0	2	0
Midfielders									
Marko Babic	3	3	0	0	270	100.0	0	0	0
Nico Kovac	3	3	0	1	220	81.5	1	1	0
Jerko Leko	2	0	2	0	76	28.1	0	0	0
Luka Modric	2	0	2	0	30	11.1	0	0	0
Darijo Srna	3	3	0	1	266	98.5	1	1	0
Forwards									
Ivan Bosnjak	1	0	1	0	4	1.5	0	0	0
Ivan Klasnic	3	2	1	1	153	56.7	0	0	0
Niko Kranjcar	3	3	0	2	231	85.6	0	0	0
Ivica Olic	3	1	2	1	128	47.4	0	0	0
Dado Prso	3	3	0	0	270	100.0	0	0	0

GROUP F TABLE

	P	W	D	L	F	A	DIF	PTS
Brazil	3	3	0	0	7	1	6	9
Australia	3	1	1	1	5	5	0	4
Croatia	3	0	2	1	2	3	-1	2
Japan	3	0	1	2	2	7	-5	1

JAPAN APPEARANCES

Match 1 2 3 — Result L D L

	Appearances	Started	Subbed on	Subbed off	Mins played	% played	Goals	Yellow	Red
Goalkeepers									
Yoshikatsu Kawaguchi	3	3	0	0	270	100.0	0	1	0
Defenders									
Alessandro Santos	3	3	0	0	270	100.0	0	1	0
Akira Kaji	2	2	0	0	180	66.7	0	1	0
Yuichi Komano	1	1	0	0	90	33.3	0	0	0
Tsuneyasu Miyamoto	2	2	0	0	180	66.7	0	2	0
Teruyuki Moniwa	1	0	1	1	34	12.6	0	1	0
Yuji Nakazawa	3	3	0	0	270	100.0	0	0	0
Keisuke Tsuboi	2	2	0	1	145	53.7	0	0	0
Midfielders									
Takashi Fukunishi	2	2	0	1	135	50.0	0	0	0
Junichi Inamoto	2	1	1	0	135	50.0	0	0	0
Shunsuke Nakamura	3	3	0	0	270	100.0	1	0	0
Hidetoshi Nakata	3	3	0	0	270	100.0	0	0	0
Koji Nakata	1	0	1	0	35	13.0	0	0	0
Mitsuo Ogasawara	2	2	0	1	145	53.7	0	0	0
Shinji Ono	1	0	1	0	12	4.4	0	0	0
Forwards									
Seiichiro Maki	1	1	0	1	59	21.9	0	0	0
Mashasi Oguro	3	0	3	0	164	60.7	0	0	0
Naohiro Takahara	3	2	1	2	180	66.7	0	1	0
Keiji Tamada	2	1	1	0	119	44.1	1	0	0
Atsushi Yanagisawa	2	2	0	2	139	51.5	0	0	0

MATCH FIVE

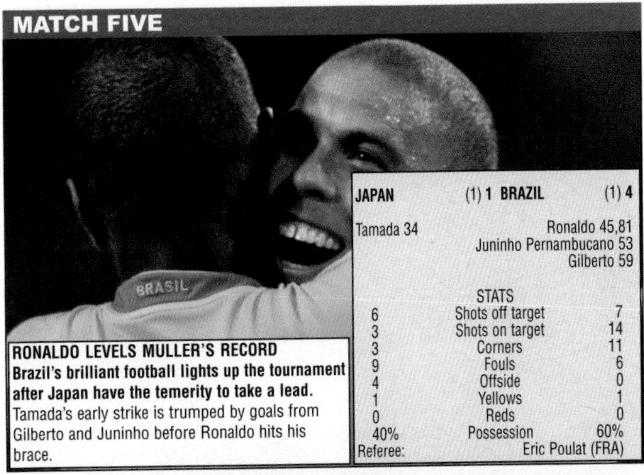

JAPAN (1) 1		BRAZIL (1) 4
Tamada 34		Ronaldo 45,81 Juninho Pernambucano 53 Gilberto 59
	STATS	
6	Shots off target	7
3	Shots on target	14
3	Corners	11
9	Fouls	6
4	Offside	0
1	Yellows	1
0	Reds	0
40%	Possession	60%
Referee:		Eric Poulat (FRA)

RONALDO LEVELS MULLER'S RECORD
Brazil's brilliant football lights up the tournament after Japan have the temerity to take a lead.
Tamada's early strike is trumped by goals from Gilberto and Juninho before Ronaldo hits his brace.

MATCH SIX

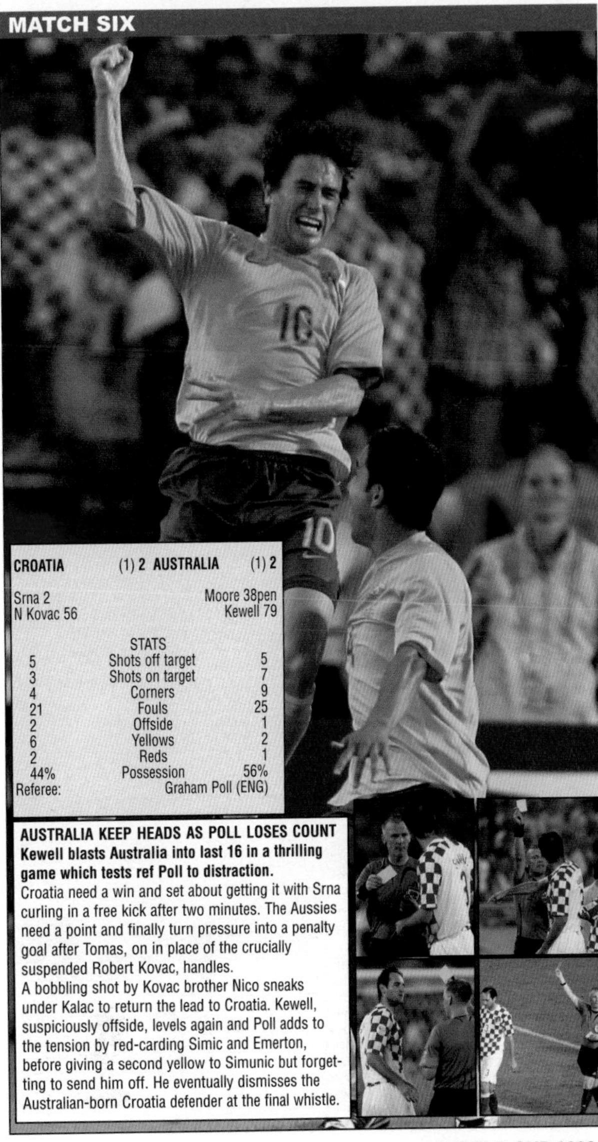

CROATIA (1) 2		AUSTRALIA (1) 2
Srna 2 N Kovac 56		Moore 38pen Kewell 79
	STATS	
5	Shots off target	5
3	Shots on target	7
4	Corners	9
21	Fouls	25
2	Offside	1
6	Yellows	2
2	Reds	1
44%	Possession	56%
Referee:		Graham Poll (ENG)

AUSTRALIA KEEP HEADS AS POLL LOSES COUNT
Kewell blasts Australia into last 16 in a thrilling game which tests ref Poll to distraction.
Croatia need a win and set about getting it with Srna curling in a free kick after two minutes. The Aussies need a point and finally turn pressure into a penalty goal after Tomas, on in place of the crucially suspended Robert Kovac, handles.
A bobbling shot by Kovac brother Nico sneaks under Kalac to return the lead to Croatia. Kewell, suspiciously offside, levels again and Poll adds to the tension by red-carding Simic and Emerton, before giving a second yellow to Simunic but forgetting to send him off. He eventually dismisses the Australian-born Croatia defender at the final whistle.

WORLD CUP GROUP G

MATCH ONE

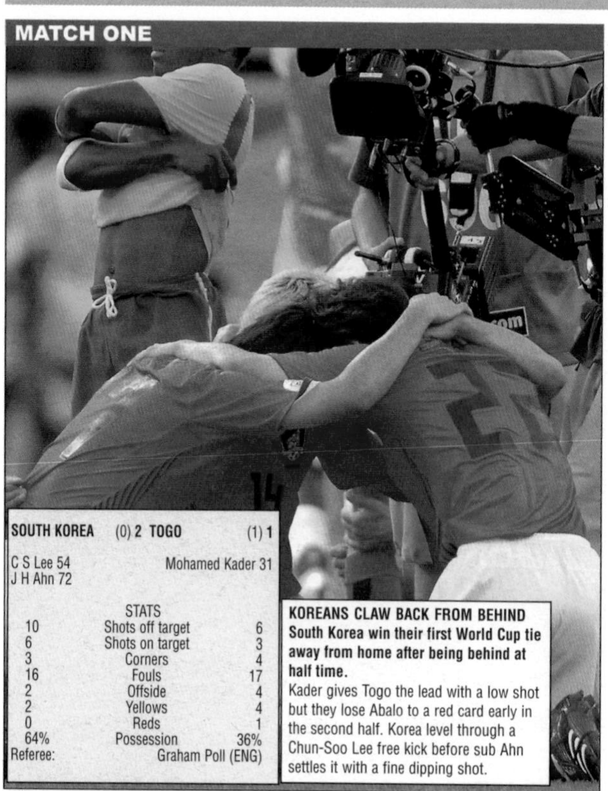

SOUTH KOREA	(0) 2 TOGO	(1) 1
C S Lee 54 J H Ahn 72		Mohamed Kader 31
	STATS	
10	Shots off target	6
6	Shots on target	3
3	Corners	4
16	Fouls	17
2	Offside	4
2	Yellows	4
0	Reds	1
64%	Possession	36%
Referee:		Graham Poll (ENG)

KOREANS CLAW BACK FROM BEHIND

South Korea win their first World Cup tie away from home after being behind at half time.

Kader gives Togo the lead with a low shot but they lose Abalo to a red card early in the second half. Korea level through a Chun-Soo Lee free kick before sub Ahn settles it with a fine dipping shot.

MATCH TWO

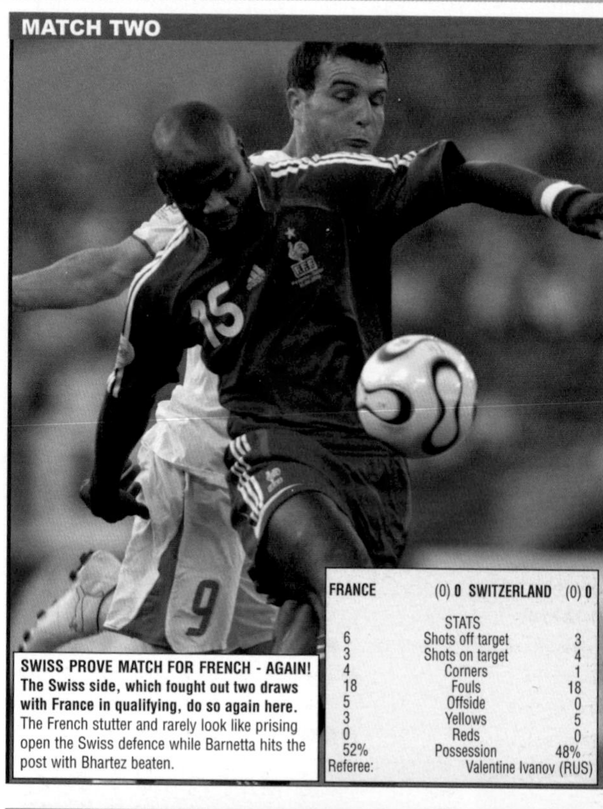

FRANCE	(0) 0 SWITZERLAND	(0) 0
	STATS	
6	Shots off target	3
3	Shots on target	4
4	Corners	1
18	Fouls	18
5	Offside	0
3	Yellows	5
0	Reds	0
52%	Possession	48%
Referee:		Valentine Ivanov (RUS)

SWISS PROVE MATCH FOR FRENCH - AGAIN!

The Swiss side, which fought out two draws with France in qualifying, do so again here.

The French stutter and rarely look like prising open the Swiss defence while Barnetta hits the post with Bhartez beaten.

MATCH THREE

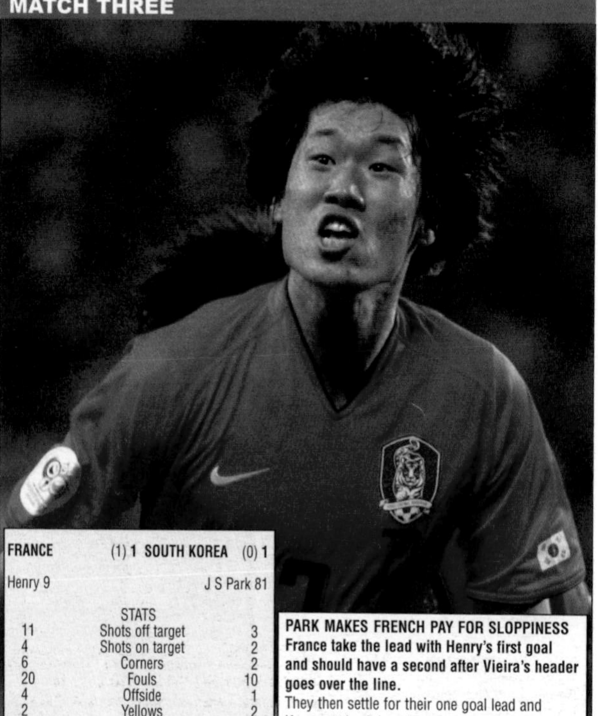

FRANCE	(1) 1 SOUTH KOREA	(0) 1
Henry 9		J S Park 81
	STATS	
11	Shots off target	3
4	Shots on target	2
6	Corners	2
20	Fouls	10
4	Offside	1
2	Yellows	2
0	Reds	0
51%	Possession	49%
Referee:		Benito Archundia (MEX)

PARK MAKES FRENCH PAY FOR SLOPPINESS

France take the lead with Henry's first goal and should have a second after Vieira's header goes over the line.

They then settle for their one goal lead and Korea get back into the game, equalising in the 81st minute after Jae-Jin Cho 's knock down is bundled over the line by Ji-Sung Park.

MATCH FOUR

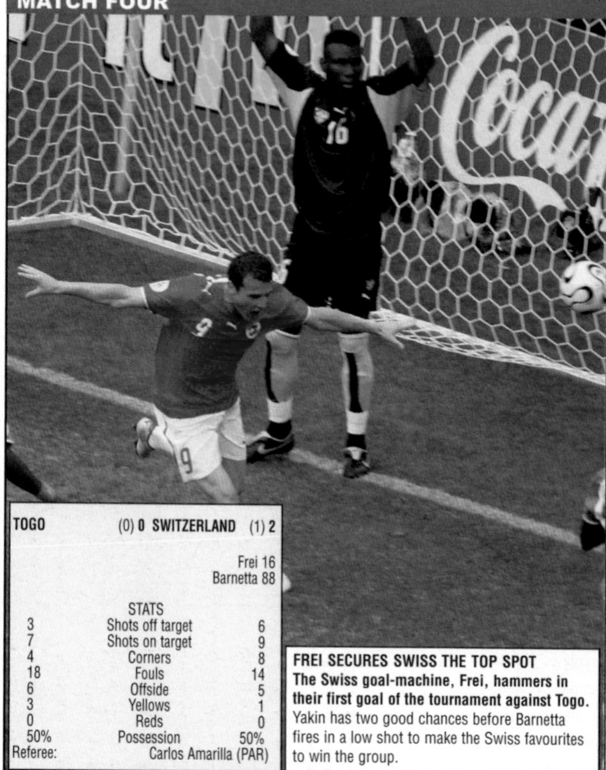

TOGO	(0) 0 SWITZERLAND	(1) 2
		Frei 16 Barnetta 88
	STATS	
3	Shots off target	6
7	Shots on target	9
4	Corners	8
18	Fouls	14
6	Offside	5
3	Yellows	1
0	Reds	0
50%	Possession	50%
Referee:		Carlos Amarilla (PAR)

FREI SECURES SWISS THE TOP SPOT

The Swiss goal-machine, Frei, hammers in their first goal of the tournament against Togo.

Yakin has two good chances before Barnetta fires in a low shot to make the Swiss favourites to win the group.

SOUTH KOREA APPEARANCES

Match 1 2 3 — Result W D L

	Appearances	Started	Subbed on	Subbed off	Mins played	% played	Goals	Yellow	Red
Goalkeepers									
Woon-Jae Lee	3	3	0	0	270	100.0	0	0	0
Defenders									
Jin-Chul Choi	3	3	0	0	270	100.0	0	1	0
Dong-Jin Kim	2	2	0	0	180	66.7	0	1	0
Jin Kyu Kim	2	2	0	1	135	50.0	0	0	0
Young-Pyo Lee	3	3	0	1	242	89.6	0	0	0
Midfielders									
Nam-Il Kim	3	2	1	0	203	75.2	0	0	0
Sang-Sik Kim	2	0	2	0	30	11.1	0	0	0
Young-Chul Kim	2	2	0	0	180	66.7	0	1	0
Eul-Yong Lee	2	2	0	2	112	41.5	0	0	0
Ho Lee	3	3	0	1	248	91.9	0	1	0
Ji-Sung Park	3	3	0	0	270	100.0	1	0	0
Ki-Hyeon Seol	2	0	2	0	70	25.9	0	0	0
Chong-Gug Song	1	1	0	0	90	33.3	0	0	0
Forwards									
Jung-Hwan Ahn	3	0	3	0	92	34.1	1	1	0
Jae-Jin Cho	3	3	0	1	262	97.0	0	0	0
Chung-Soo Lee	3	3	0	1	251	93.0	1	2	0
Chu Young Park	1	1	0	1	65	24.1	0	1	0

GROUP G TABLE

	P	W	D	L	F	A	DIF	PTS
Switzerland	3	2	1	0	4	0	4	7
France	3	1	2	0	3	1	2	5
South Korea	3	1	1	1	3	4	-1	4
Togo	3	0	0	3	1	6	-5	0

TOGO APPEARANCES

Match 1 2 3 — Result L L L

	Appearances	Started	Subbed on	Subbed off	Mins played	% played	Goals	Yellow	Red
Goalkeepers									
Kossi Agassa	3	3	0	0	270	100.0	0	0	0
Defenders									
Jean-Paul Yaovi Abalo	2	2	0	0	142	52.6	0	1	1
Ludovic Assemoassa	1	1	0	1	61	22.6	0	0	0
Dare Nibombe	3	3	0	0	270	100.0	0	0	0
Massamasso Tchangai	3	3	0	0	270	100.0	0	1	0
Assimiou Toure	2	1	1	0	126	46.7	0	0	0
Midfielders									
Kuami Agboh	1	1	0	1	24	8.9	0	0	0
Yao Aziawonou	2	1	1	0	95	35.2	0	1	0
Robert Malm	1	0	1	0	1	0.4	0	0	0
Cherif-Toure Mamam	3	3	0	2	237	87.8	0	1	0
Kader Mohamed	3	3	0	0	270	100.0	1	0	0
Jacques Romao	2	2	0	0	180	66.7	0	2	0
Moustapha Salifou	3	2	1	1	241	89.3	0	2	0
Forwards									
Emmanuel Adebayor	3	3	0	1	254	94.1	0	1	0
Thomas Dossevi	2	1	1	1	84	31.1	0	0	0
Richmond Forson	3	2	1	0	209	77.4	0	0	0
Adekamni Olufade	1	0	1	0	32	11.9	0	0	0
Junior Senaya	3	2	1	1	166	61.5	0	0	0

MATCH FIVE

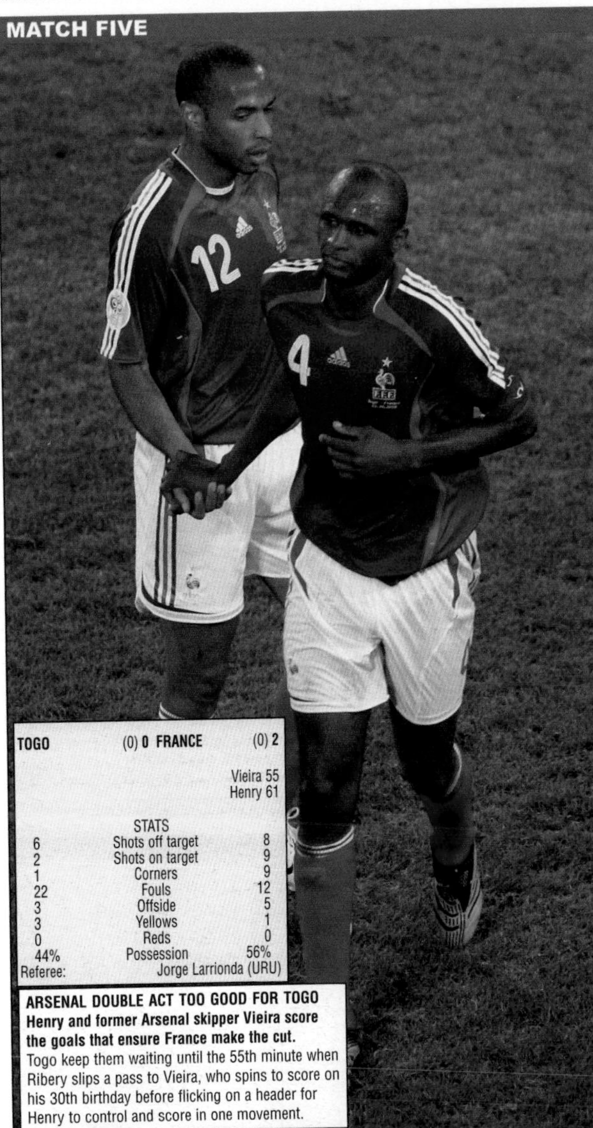

TOGO (0) 0 FRANCE (0) 2

Vieira 55
Henry 61

TOGO	STATS	FRANCE
6	Shots off target	8
2	Shots on target	9
1	Corners	9
22	Fouls	12
3	Offside	5
3	Yellows	1
0	Reds	0
44%	Possession	56%

Referee: Jorge Larrionda (URU)

ARSENAL DOUBLE ACT TOO GOOD FOR TOGO
Henry and former Arsenal skipper Vieira score the goals that ensure France make the cut.
Togo keep them waiting until the 55th minute when Ribery slips a pass to Vieira, who spins to score on his 30th birthday before flicking on a header for Henry to control and score in one movement.

MATCH SIX

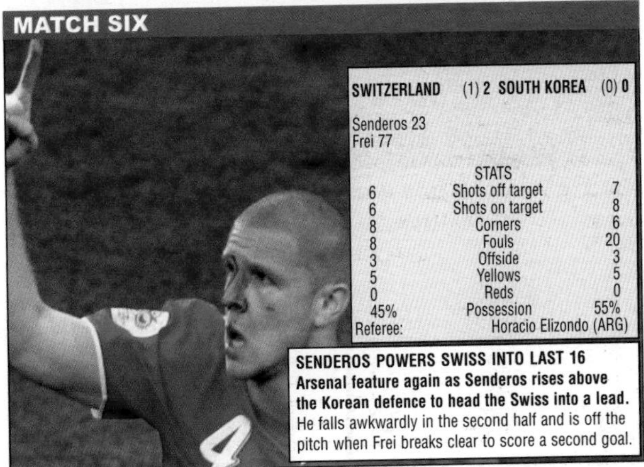

SWITZERLAND (1) 2 SOUTH KOREA (0) 0

Senderos 23
Frei 77

SWITZERLAND	STATS	SOUTH KOREA
6	Shots off target	7
6	Shots on target	8
8	Corners	6
8	Fouls	20
3	Offside	3
5	Yellows	5
0	Reds	0
45%	Possession	55%

Referee: Horacio Elizondo (ARG)

SENDEROS POWERS SWISS INTO LAST 16
Arsenal feature again as Senderos rises above the Korean defence to head the Swiss into a lead.
He falls awkwardly in the second half and is off the pitch when Frei breaks clear to score a second goal.

WORLD CUP GROUP H

The group stages

MATCH ONE

SPAIN	(2) 4 UKRAINE	(0) 0
Alonso 13 Villa 17,48pen Torres 81		
	STATS	
9	Shots off target	3
10	Shots on target	2
7	Corners	1
11	Fouls	14
0	Offside	8
0	Yellows	2
0	Reds	1
55%	Possession	45%
Referee:	Massimo Busacca (SUI)	

VILLA HITS TWO AS ARAGONES FINDS THE RIGHT MIX

Spanish coach Luis Aragones leaves out skipper Raul and sees his side demolish Ukraine by four goals.

The usually nervous Spanish are serenely in control from the moment that Alonso rises to head home a corner in the 13th minute. Villa adds the first of his brace from a free kick four minutes later.

The second half begins with Vashchuk bringing down Torres in the area and the ref red-cards the Dynamo Kiev defender before Villa converts the penalty.

Raul is brought on and Spain complete the rout with a well-constructed fourth goal. Puyol heads into the path of Torres for the Atletico Madrid forward to drive home a first time shot from between two Ukraine defenders.

MATCH TWO

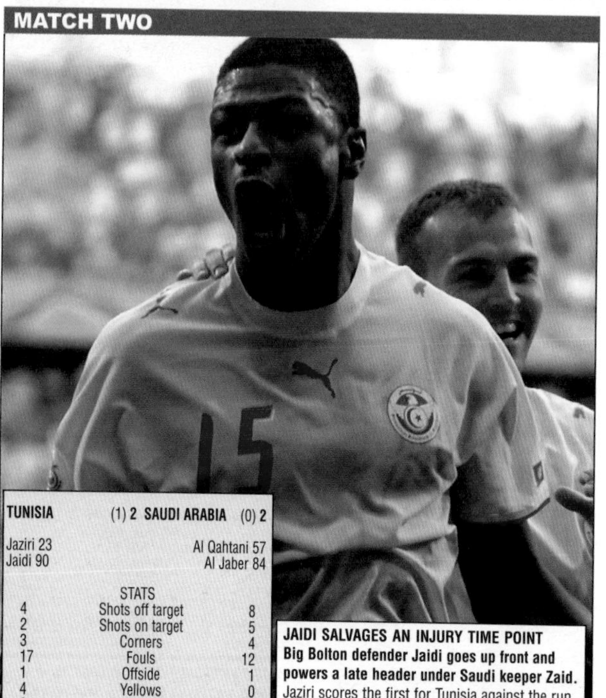

TUNISIA	(1) 2 SAUDI ARABIA	(0) 2
Jaziri 23 Jaidi 90		Al Qahtani 57 Al Jaber 84
	STATS	
4	Shots off target	8
2	Shots on target	5
3	Corners	4
17	Fouls	12
1	Offside	1
4	Yellows	0
0	Reds	0
49%	Possession	51%
Referee:	Mark Shield (AUS)	

JAIDI SALVAGES AN INJURY TIME POINT

Big Bolton defender Jaidi goes up front and powers a late header under Saudi keeper Zaid.

Jaziri scores the first for Tunisia against the run of play. The Saudi's fight back in the second half with goals from both strikers, Al Qahtani and veteran Al Jaber before Jaidi has the last word.

MATCH THREE

EX-KIEV DOUBLE ACT ROUSES UKRAINE

Former Dynamo Kiev shooting stars Shevchenko and Rebrov both score as Ukraine recover from their dreadful opening game.

Saudi, who lost 8-0 to Germany in the last World Cup, fall behind to a Rusol goal after four minutes. Rebrov hits a 30-yard wonder goal before Shevchenko and Kalinichenko get in on the act.

SAUDI ARABIA	(0) 0 UKRAINE	(2) 4
		Rusol 4 Rebrov 36 Shevchenko 46 Kalinichenko 84
	STATS	
6	Shots off target	10
0	Shots on target	9
2	Corners	6
24	Fouls	25
0	Offside	0
3	Yellows	3
0	Reds	0
50%	Possession	50%
Referee:	Graham Poll (ENG)	

MATCH FOUR

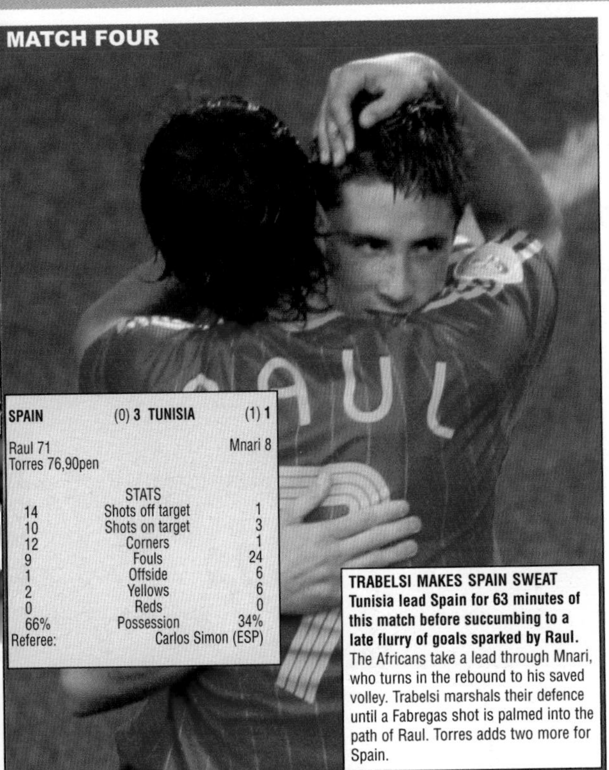

SPAIN	(0) 3	TUNISIA	(1) 1
Raul 71			Mnari 8
Torres 76,90pen			
	STATS		
14	Shots off target		1
10	Shots on target		3
12	Corners		1
9	Fouls		24
1	Offside		6
2	Yellows		6
0	Reds		0
66%	Possession		34%
Referee:	Carlos Simon (ESP)		

TRABELSI MAKES SPAIN SWEAT
Tunisia lead Spain for 63 minutes of this match before succumbing to a late flurry of goals sparked by Raul. The Africans take a lead through Mnari, who turns in the rebound to his saved volley. Trabelsi marshals their defence until a Fabregas shot is palmed into the path of Raul. Torres adds two more for Spain.

MATCH FIVE

SAUDI ARABIA	(0) 0	SPAIN	(1) 1
			Juanito 36
	STATS		
3	Shots off target		6
4	Shots on target		13
4	Corners		10
22	Fouls		22
5	Offside		0
2	Yellows		3
0	Reds		0
40%	Possession		60%
Referee:	Coffi Codjia (BEN)		

ARAGONES' RESERVES TOO GOOD FOR SAUDI
Spain's second string triumph with Juanito's goal. Reyes leads the Spanish in a first half onslaught on the Saudi goal and his free kick is headed home by Juanito. The Saudi's battle back but can't score.

MATCH SIX

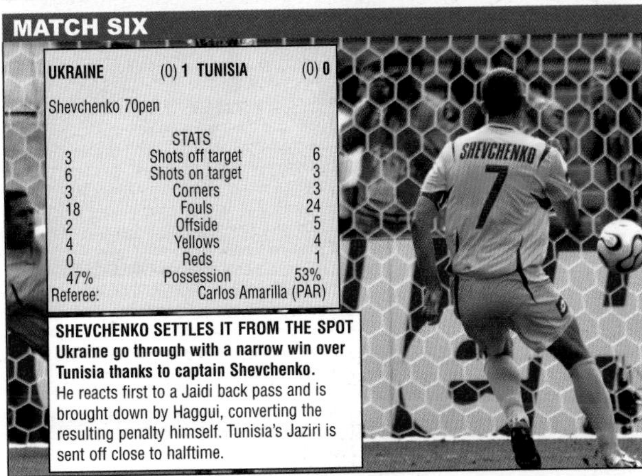

UKRAINE	(0) 1	TUNISIA	(0) 0
Shevchenko 70pen			
	STATS		
3	Shots off target		6
6	Shots on target		3
3	Corners		3
18	Fouls		24
2	Offside		5
4	Yellows		4
0	Reds		1
47%	Possession		53%
Referee:	Carlos Amarilla (PAR)		

SHEVCHENKO SETTLES IT FROM THE SPOT
Ukraine go through with a narrow win over Tunisia thanks to captain Shevchenko. He reacts first to a Jaidi back pass and is brought down by Haggui, converting the resulting penalty himself. Tunisia's Jaziri is sent off close to halftime.

GROUP H TABLE

	P	W	D	L	F	A	DIF	PTS
Spain	3	3	0	0	8	1	7	9
Ukraine	3	2	0	1	5	4	1	6
Tunisia	3	0	1	2	3	6	-3	1
Saudi Arabia	3	0	1	2	2	7	-5	1

TUNISIA APPEARANCES

Match 1 2 3
Result D L L

	Appearances	Started	Subbed on	Subbed off	Mins played	% played	Goals	Yellow	Red
Goalkeepers									
Ali Boumnijel	3	3	0	0	270	100.0	0	0	0
Defenders									
Anis Ayari	2	2	0	1	146	54.1	0	1	0
Kaies Ghodhbane	3	0	3	0	57	21.1	0	0	0
Karim Hagui	3	3	0	0	270	100.0	0	1	0
Radhi Jaidi	3	3	0	0	270	100.0	1	2	0
Hatem Trabelsi	3	3	0	0	270	100.0	0	1	0
Alaeddine Yahia	1	0	1	0	34	12.6	0	0	0
Midfielders									
Riadh Bouazizi	3	3	0	3	189	70.0	0	2	0
Adel Chedli	3	3	0	3	226	83.7	0	1	0
Karim Essediri	1	0	1	0	9	3.3	0	0	0
David Jemmali	1	1	0	0	90	33.3	0	0	0
Jawhar Mnari	3	3	0	0	270	100.0	1	1	0
Mehdi Nafti	3	2	1	1	215	79.6	0	0	0
Hamed Namouchi	3	3	0	0	270	100.0	0	0	0
Forwards									
Chaouki Ben Saada	1	0	1	0	11	4.1	0	0	0
Yassine Chikhaoui	1	1	0	1	81	30.0	0	1	0
Francileudo Dos Santos	1	0	1	0	11	4.1	0	0	0
Haykel Gumemdia	1	0	1	0	11	4.1	0	1	0
Ziad Jaziri	3	3	0	0	224	83.0	1	2	1

SAUDI ARABIA APPEARANCES

Match 1 2 3
Result D L L

	Appearances	Started	Subbed on	Subbed off	Mins played	% played	Goals	Yellow	Red
Goalkeepers									
Mbrouk Zaid	3	3	0	0	270	100.0	0	0	0
Defenders									
Hamad Al Montashari	3	3	0	0	270	100.0	0	0	0
Ahmed Dokhi	3	3	0	1	234	86.7	0	1	0
Abdulaziz Khathran	2	1	1	0	126	46.7	0	0	0
Hussein Sulimani	3	3	0	1	260	96.3	0	0	0
Ridha Tukar	3	3	0	0	270	100.0	0	0	0
Midfielders									
Omar Al Ghamdi	2	2	0	0	180	66.7	0	1	0
Nawaf Al Temyat	2	1	1	1	143	53.0	0	1	0
Moahammed Ameen	2	1	1	1	70	25.9	0	0	0
Khaled Aziz	3	3	0	1	192	71.1	0	0	0
Saud Khariri	3	3	0	0	270	100.0	0	1	0
Mohammed Massad	1	0	1	0	10	3.7	0	0	0
Mohamed Noor	3	3	0	2	240	88.9	0	0	0
Forwards									
Saad Al Harthi	1	1	0	0	90	33.3	0	0	0
Sami Al Jaber	3	1	2	1	90	33.3	1	1	0
Yasser Al Qahtani	2	2	0	1	171	63.3	1	0	0
Malek Mouath	3	0	3	0	84	31.1	0	0	0

WORLD CUP

Second Round

1. GERMANY v SWEDEN

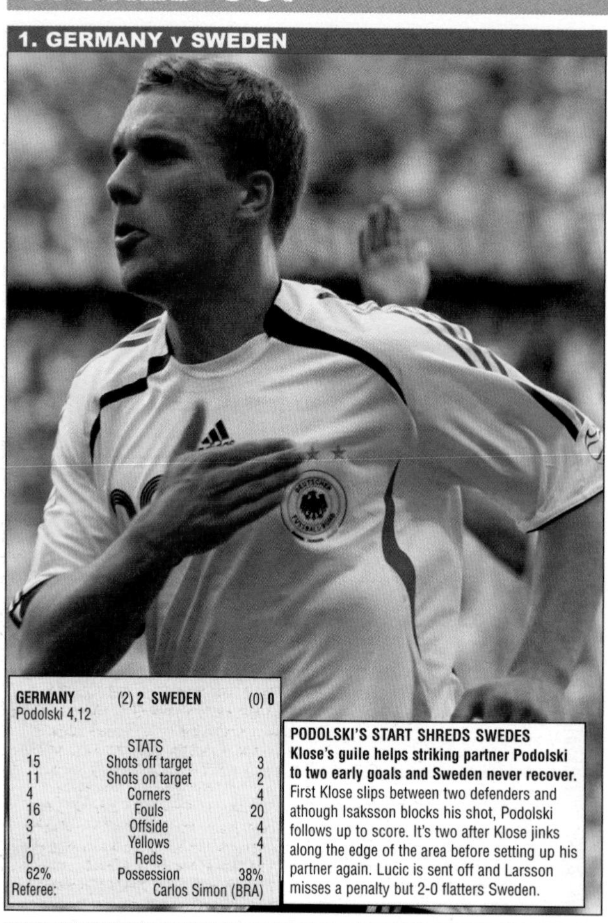

GERMANY (2) **2** **SWEDEN** (0) **0**
Podolski 4,12

GERMANY	STATS	SWEDEN
15	Shots off target	3
11	Shots on target	2
4	Corners	4
16	Fouls	20
3	Offside	4
1	Yellows	4
0	Reds	1
62%	Possession	38%

Referee: Carlos Simon (BRA)

PODOLSKI'S START SHREDS SWEDES

Klose's guile helps striking partner Podolski to two early goals and Sweden never recover. First Klose slips between two defenders and athough Isaksson blocks his shot, Podolski follows up to score. It's two after Klose jinks along the edge of the area before setting up his partner again. Lucic is sent off and Larsson misses a penalty but 2-0 flatters Sweden.

2. ARGENTINA v MEXICO

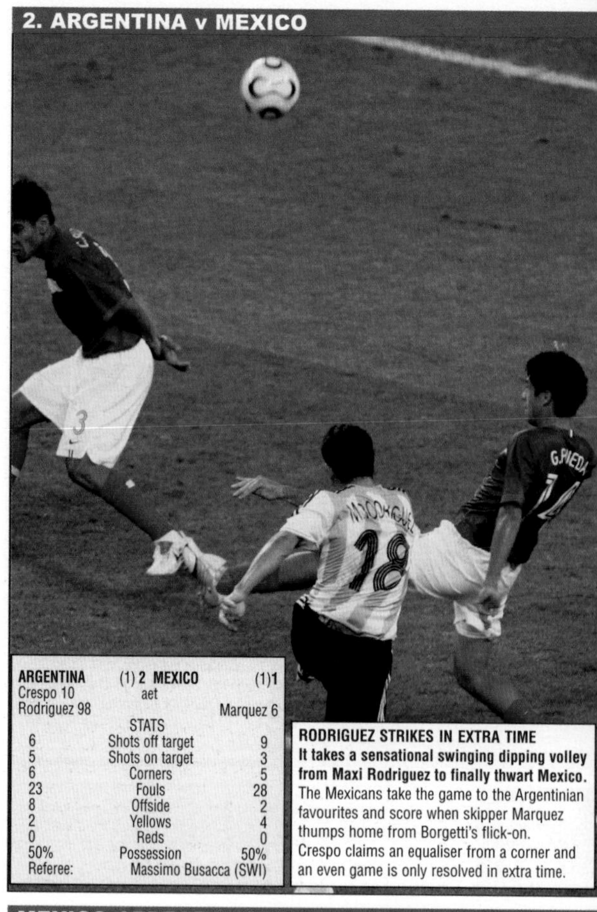

ARGENTINA (1) **2** **MEXICO** (1)**1**
Crespo 10 aet
Rodriguez 98 Marquez 6

ARGENTINA	STATS	MEXICO
6	Shots off target	9
5	Shots on target	3
6	Corners	5
23	Fouls	28
8	Offside	2
2	Yellows	4
0	Reds	0
50%	Possession	50%

Referee: Massimo Busacca (SWI)

RODRIGUEZ STRIKES IN EXTRA TIME

It takes a sensational swinging dipping volley from Maxi Rodriguez to finally thwart Mexico. The Mexicans take the game to the Argentinian favourites and score when skipper Marquez thumps home from Borgetti's flick-on.
Crespo claims an equaliser from a corner and an even game is only resolved in extra time.

SWEDEN APPEARANCES

Match	1 2 3 4	Appearances	Started	Subbed on	Subbed off	Mins played	% played	Goals	Yellow	Red
Result	D W D L									
Goalkeepers										
Andreas Isaksson		3	3	0	0	270	75.0	0	0	0
Rami Shaaban		1	1	0	0	90	25.0	0	0	0
Defenders										
Erik Edman		4	4	0	0	360	100.0	0	0	0
Petter Hansson		1	0	1	0	52	14.4	0	0	0
Teddy Lucic		4	4	0	0	304	84.4	0	2	1
Olof Mellberg		4	4	0	0	360	100.0	0	0	0
Karl Svensson		1	1	0	1	61	16.9	0	0	0
Midfielders										
Niclas Alexandersson		4	4	0	0	360	100.0	0	1	0
Daniel Andersson		1	0	1	0	1	0.3	0	0	0
Mattias Jonson		4	2	2	2	139	38.6	0	1	0
Kim Kallstrom		4	3	1	2	225	62.5	0	0	0
Tobias Linderoth		4	4	0	2	347	96.4	0	1	0
Fredrik Ljungberg		4	4	0	0	360	100.0	1	1	0
Christian Wilhelmsson		4	2	2	2	221	61.4	0	0	0
Forwards										
Marcus Allback		4	1	3	1	166	46.1	1	2	0
Johan Elmander		2	0	2	0	22	6.1	0	0	0
Zlatan Ibrahimovic		3	3	0	2	206	57.2	0	0	0
Henrik Larsson		4	4	0	0	360	100.0	1	1	0

MEXICO APPEARANCES

Match	1 2 3 4	Appearances	Started	Subbed on	Subbed off	Mins played	% played	Goals	Yellow	Red
Result	W D L L									
Goalkeepers										
Oswaldo Sanchez		4	4	0	0	390	100.0	0	0	0
Defenders										
Rafael Marquez		4	4	0	0	390	100.0	1	2	0
Mario Mendez		4	4	0	1	379	97.2	0	0	0
Ricardo Osorio		4	4	0	0	390	100.0	0	0	0
Francisco Rodriguez		1	1	0	1	45	11.5	0	1	0
Carlos Salcido		4	4	0	0	390	100.0	0	1	0
Midfielders										
Castro		1	1	0	0	120	30.8	0	1	0
Guardado		1	1	0	1	65	16.7	0	0	0
Ramon Morales		2	1	1	1	86	22.1	0	0	0
Pavel Pardo		4	4	0	1	307	78.7	0	0	0
Luis Perez		2	1	1	0	105	26.9	0	1	1
Gonzalo Pineda		4	3	1	1	312	80.0	0	1	0
Gerardo Torrado		3	2	1	1	218	55.9	0	2	0
Antonio Naelson Zinha		4	1	3	1	188	48.2	1	1	0
Forwards										
Jesus Arellano		1	0	1	0	39	10.0	0	0	0
Jared Echavarria Borgetti		2	2	0	1	171	43.8	0	0	0
Omar Bravo		3	3	0	0	270	69.2	2	0	0
Fonseca		4	2	2	0	266	68.2	1	1	0
Guillermo Franco		3	2	1	2	129	33.1	0	0	0

3. ENGLAND v ECUADOR

ENGLAND	(0) 1 ECUADOR	(0) 0
Beckham 60		
	STATS	
4	Shots off target	6
4	Shots on target	3
5	Corners	7
13	Fouls	24
3	Offside	6
3	Yellows	3
0	Reds	0
49%	Possession	51%
Referee:	Frank de Bleeckere (BEL)	

BECKHAM'S ACCURACY IS THE DIFFERENCE
A dipping free kick from Beckham slipped into the near post to clinch a game of few chances. Ecuador's Carlos Tenorio has the best of these in the first half as only an Ashley Cole block deflects his shot against the bar. Beckham strikes before Rooney's clever run sets up Lampard but the midfielder fires wide.

4. PORTUGAL v HOLLAND

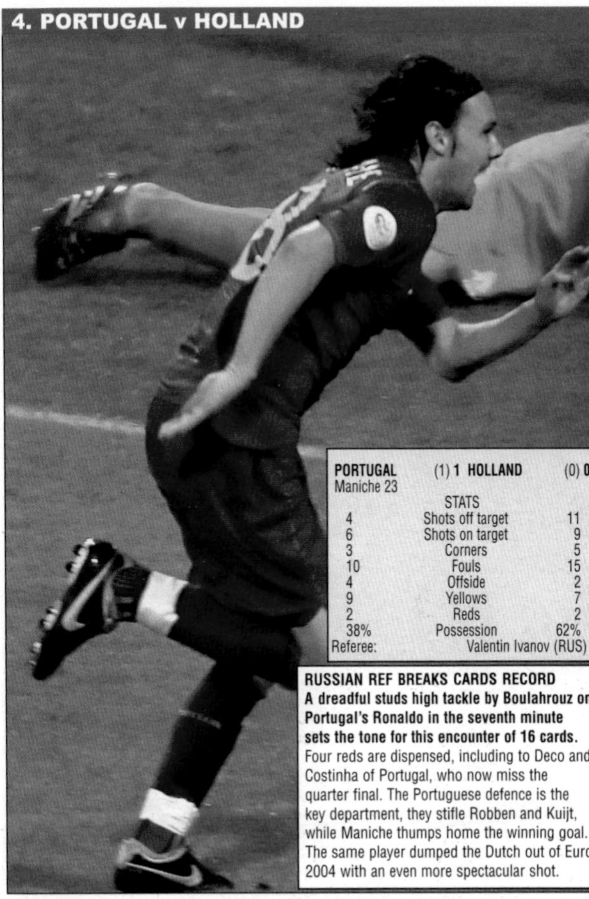

PORTUGAL	(1) 1 HOLLAND	(0) 0
Maniche 23		
	STATS	
4	Shots off target	11
6	Shots on target	9
3	Corners	5
10	Fouls	15
4	Offside	2
9	Yellows	7
2	Reds	2
38%	Possession	62%
Referee:	Valentin Ivanov (RUS)	

RUSSIAN REF BREAKS CARDS RECORD
A dreadful studs high tackle by Boulahrouz on Portugal's Ronaldo in the seventh minute sets the tone for this encounter of 16 cards. Four reds are dispensed, including to Deco and Costinha of Portugal, who now miss the quarter final. The Portuguese defence is the key department, they stifle Robben and Kuijt, while Maniche thumps home the winning goal. The same player dumped the Dutch out of Euro 2004 with an even more spectacular shot.

ECUADOR APPEARANCES

'atch: 1 2 3 4
esult: W W L L

	Appearances	Started	Subbed on	Subbed off	Mins played	% played	Goals	Yellow	Red
oalkeepers									
hristian Mora	4	4	0	0	360	100.0	0	1	0
efenders									
lises De La Cruz	4	4	0	0	360	100.0	0	2	0
ieovanny Espinoza	4	4	0	1	338	93.9	0	0	0
orge Guagua	3	1	2	0	134	37.2	0	0	0
an Angulo Hurtado	3	3	0	1	248	68.9	0	1	0
ano Neicer Reasco	3	3	0	0	270	75.0	0	0	0
lidfielders									
cente Paul Ambrosi	1	1	0	0	90	25.0	0	0	0
arlon Ayovi	1	1	0	1	68	18.9	0	0	0
enitez	1	0	1	0	45	12.5	0	0	0
egundo Castillo	3	3	0	0	270	75.0	0	1	0
dison Mendez	4	4	0	0	360	100.0	0	1	0
dwin Tenorio	4	4	0	1	338	93.9	0	0	0
atricio Urrutia	3	0	3	0	48	13.3	0	0	0
uis Valencia	4	4	0	2	314	87.2	0	2	0
orwards									
elix Borja	1	1	0	1	45	12.5	0	0	0
ugustin Delgado	3	3	0	1	262	72.8	2	0	0
an Kaviedes	4	1	3	0	181	50.3	1	0	0
hristian Lara	2	0	2	0	50	13.9	0	0	0
arlos Tenorio	3	3	0	3	179	49.7	2	1	0

HOLLAND APPEARANCES

Match: 1 2 3 4
Result: W W D L

	Appearances	Started	Subbed on	Subbed off	Mins played	% played	Goals	Yellow	Red
Goalkeepers									
Edwin Van der Sar	4	4	0	0	360	100.0	0	0	0
Defenders									
Khalid Boulahrouz	4	2	2	0	202	56.1	0	1	1
Tim de Cler	1	1	0	0	90	25.0	0	1	0
John Heitinga	3	2	1	1	159	44.2	0	1	0
Jaliens	1	1	0	0	90	25.0	0	0	0
Joris Mathijsen	3	3	0	2	230	63.9	0	1	0
Andre Ooijer	4	4	0	0	360	100.0	0	1	0
Giovanni Van Bronckhorst	3	3	0	0	269	74.7	0	2	1
Midfielders									
Phillip Cocu	4	4	0	1	353	98.1	0	0	0
Denny Landzaat	2	0	2	0	55	15.3	0	1	0
Hedwiges Maduro	1	0	1	0	7	1.9	0	0	0
Arjen Robben	3	3	0	0	270	75.0	1	1	0
Wesley Sneijder	4	4	0	2	312	86.7	0	1	0
Mark van Bommel	3	3	0	2	215	59.7	0	2	0
Rafael van der Vaart	3	1	2	0	166	46.1	0	1	0
Robin van Persie	4	4	0	1	336	93.3	1	0	0
Forwards									
Ryan Babel	1	0	1	0	35	9.7	0	0	0
Dirk Kuijt	3	2	1	0	202	56.1	0	1	0
Ruud van Nistelrooy	2	2	0	2	196	54.4	1	0	0
Jan Vennegoor	1	0	1	0	7	1.9	0	0	0

WORLD CUP

Second Round

5. ITALY v AUSTRALIA

ITALY	(0) 1	AUSTRALIA	(0) 0
Totti 90pen			
	STATS		
5	Shots off target	4	
6	Shots on target	4	
2	Corners	2	
17	Fouls	26	
2	Offside	2	
3	Yellows	3	
1	Reds	0	
41%	Possession	59%	
Referee:	Luis Medina Cantalejo (SPA)		

TOTTI'S LATE PENALTY OUSTS AUSSIES

Italy's centre half Materazzi is sent off soon after half time but their patched-up defence holds firm.

Totti comes on as substitute and converts the controversial penalty (awarded for Neill's tackle on Grosso) four minutes into injury time.

6. SWITZERLAND v UKRAINE

SWITZERLAND	(0) 0	UKRAINE	(0) 0
aet - Ukraine won 3-0 on penalties			
	STATS		
6	Shots off target	8	
6	Shots on target	2	
5	Corners	6	
24	Fouls	20	
0	Offside	1	
1	Yellows	0	
0	Reds	0	
56%	Possession	44%	
Referee:	Benito Archundia (MEX)		

SWISS GO OUT WITHOUT CONCEDING

The unlucky Swiss make World Cup history by being eliminated without a goal being scored against them.

They battle through 120 goalless minutes against the Ukraine but then miss the first three penalties and lose the shoot out 3-0 despite Shevchenko's initial failure from the spot.

AUSTRALIA APPEARANCES

Match 1 2 3 4 / Result W L D L	Appearances	Started	Subbed on	Subbed off	Mins played	% played	Goals	Yellow	Red
Goalkeepers									
Zeljko Kalac	1	1	0	0	90	25.0	0	0	0
Mark Schwarzer	3	3	0	0	270	75.0	0	0	0
Defenders									
Craig Moore	4	4	0	2	308	85.6	1	1	0
Lucas Neill	4	4	0	0	360	100.0	0	0	0
Tony Popovic	1	1	0	1	40	11.1	0	0	0
Midfielders									
Mark Bresciano	4	2	2	1	212	58.9	0	0	0
Tim Cahill	4	3	1	1	273	75.8	2	2	0
Scott Chipperfield	4	4	0	1	344	95.6	0	0	0
Jason Culina	4	4	0	0	360	100.0	0	1	0
Brett Emerton	3	3	0	0	266	73.9	0	2	1
Vincenzo Grella	4	4	0	1	332	92.2	0	2	0
Harry Kewell	3	2	1	0	215	59.7	1	0	0
Luke Wilkshire	2	2	0	1	164	45.6	0	1	0
Forwards									
John Aloisi	4	0	4	0	75	20.8	1	1	0
Joshua Kennedy	2	0	2	0	46	12.8	0	0	0
Mile Sterjovski	3	3	0	2	241	66.9	0	0	0
Mark Viduka	4	4	0	0	360	100.0	0	0	0

SWITZERLAND APPEARANCES

Match 1 2 3 4 / Result D W W L	Appearances	Started	Subbed on	Subbed off	Mins played	% played	Goals	Yellow
Goalkeepers								
Pascal Zuberbuhler	4	4	0	0	390	100.0	0	0
Defenders								
Philipp Degen	2	2	0	0	180	46.2	0	1
Johan Djourou	3	1	2	1	87	22.3	0	1
Stephane Grichting	1	0	1	0	87	22.3	0	0
Ludovic Magnin	3	3	0	0	300	76.9	0	1
Patrick Muller	4	4	0	1	374	95.9	0	0
Philippe Senderos	3	3	0	1	232	59.5	1	1
Midfielders								
Tranquillo Barnetta	4	4	0	0	390	100.0	1	2
Valon Behrami	1	0	1	0	3	0.8	0	0
Ricardo Cabanas	4	4	0	1	378	96.9	0	1
Degen	2	2	0	0	210	53.8	0	0
Daniel Gygax	2	1	1	1	80	20.5	0	0
Xavier Margairaz	2	0	2	0	29	7.4	0	0
Christoph Spycher	1	1	0	0	90	23.1	0	1
Johann Vogel	4	4	0	0	390	100.0	0	1
Raphael Wicky	4	4	0	2	378	96.9	0	1
Forwards								
Alexander Frei	4	4	0	2	383	98.2	2	1
Mauro Lustrinelli	2	0	2	0	7	1.8	0	0
Marco Streller	3	1	2	1	124	31.8	0	0
Hakan Yakin	3	2	1	2	178	45.6	0	1

7. BRAZIL v GHANA

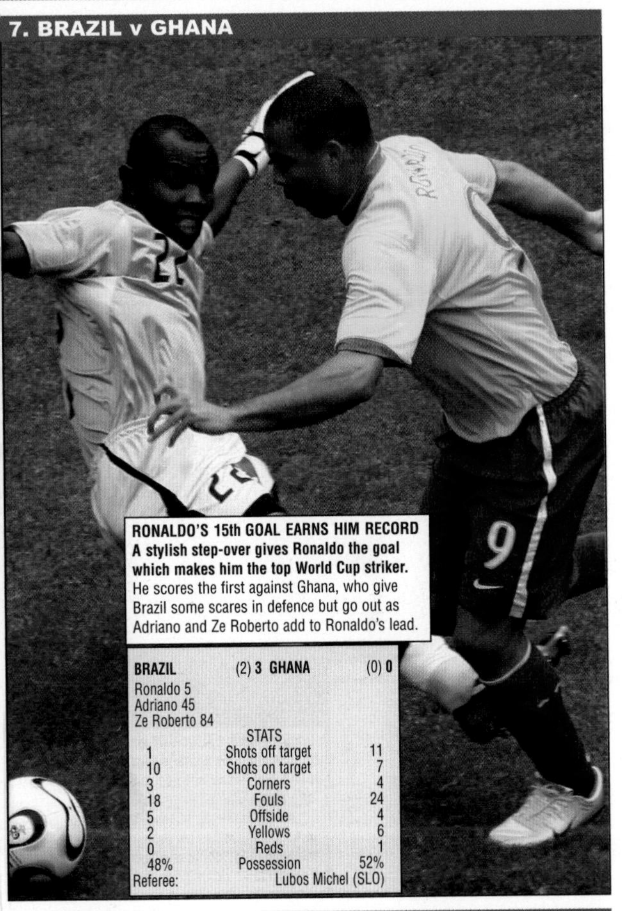

RONALDO'S 15th GOAL EARNS HIM RECORD
A stylish step-over gives Ronaldo the goal which makes him the top World Cup striker. He scores the first against Ghana, who give Brazil some scares in defence but go out as Adriano and Ze Roberto add to Ronaldo's lead.

BRAZIL	(2) 3	GHANA	(0) 0
Ronaldo 5 Adriano 45 Ze Roberto 84			
	STATS		
1	Shots off target	11	
10	Shots on target	7	
3	Corners	4	
18	Fouls	24	
5	Offside	4	
2	Yellows	6	
0	Reds	1	
48%	Possession	52%	
Referee:	Lubos Michel (SLO)		

8. SPAIN v FRANCE

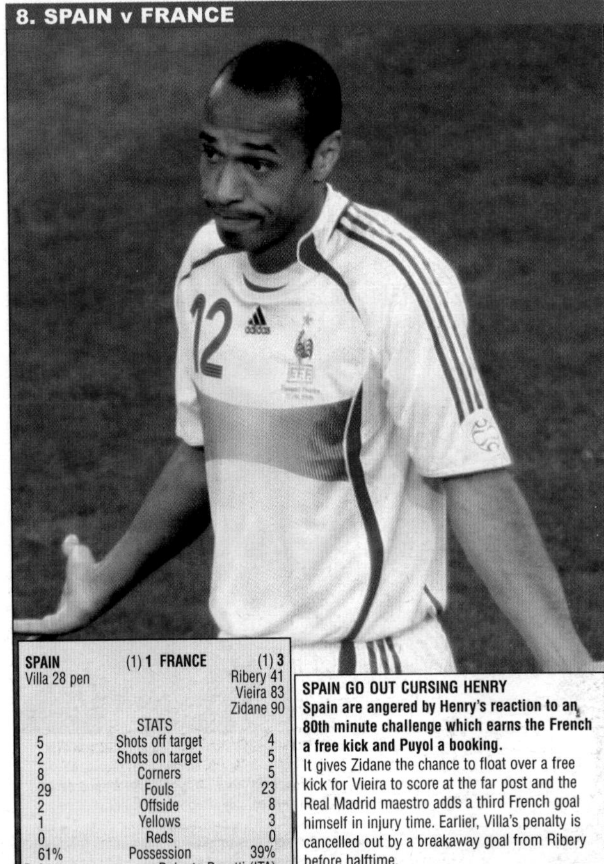

SPAIN	(1) 1	FRANCE	(1) 3
Villa 28 pen			Ribery 41 Vieira 83 Zidane 90
	STATS		
5	Shots off target	4	
2	Shots on target	5	
8	Corners	5	
29	Fouls	23	
2	Offside	8	
1	Yellows	3	
0	Reds	0	
61%	Possession	39%	
Referee:	Roberto Rosetti (ITA)		

SPAIN GO OUT CURSING HENRY
Spain are angered by Henry's reaction to an 80th minute challenge which earns the French a free kick and Puyol a booking. It gives Zidane the chance to float over a free kick for Vieira to score at the far post and the Real Madrid maestro adds a third French goal himself in injury time. Earlier, Villa's penalty is cancelled out by a breakaway goal from Ribery before halftime.

GHANA APPEARANCES

Match 1 2 3 4 — Result L W W L

	Appearances	Started	Subbed on	Subbed off	Mins played	% played	Goals	Yellow	Red
Goalkeepers									
Richard Kingston	4	4	0	0	360	100.0	0	0	0
Defenders									
Eric Adoo	4	2	2	1	192	53.3	0	1	0
Samuel Osei Kuffour	1	1	0	0	90	25.0	0	0	0
John Mensah	4	4	0	0	360	100.0	0	1	0
Habib Mohamed	2	2	0	0	180	50.0	0	1	0
John Pantsil	4	4	0	0	360	100.0	0	1	0
Emmanuel Pappoe	2	2	0	1	135	37.5	0	0	0
Razak Pimpong	3	1	2	0	119	33.1	0	0	0
Illiasu Shilla	4	3	1	0	315	87.5	0	1	0
Midfielders									
Otto Addo	2	1	1	1	90	25.0	0	1	0
Stephen Appiah	4	4	0	0	360	100.0	1	2	0
Haminu Dramini	2	2	0	1	169	46.9	1	0	0
Michael Essien	3	3	0	0	270	75.0	0	2	0
Sulley Muntari	3	3	0	0	270	75.0	1	3	0
Forwards									
Matthew Amoah	4	4	0	4	273	75.8	0	0	0
Derek Boateng	3	1	2	1	121	33.6	0	1	0
Asamoah Gyan	3	3	0	2	252	70.0	1	3	1
Alex Tachie-Mensah	3	0	3	0	34	9.4	0	0	0

SPAIN APPEARANCES

Match 1 2 3 4 — Result W W W L

	Appearances	Started	Subbed on	Subbed off	Mins played	% played	Goals	Yellow	Red
Goalkeepers									
Santiago Ruiz Canizares	1	1	0	0	90	25.0	0	0	0
Iker Casillas	3	3	0	0	270	75.0	0	0	0
Defenders									
Juanito	1	1	0	0	90	25.0	1	0	0
Garcia Diaz Manuel Pablo	3	3	0	0	270	75.0	0	0	0
Carlos Marchena	1	1	0	0	90	25.0	0	1	0
Mariano Pernia	3	3	0	0	270	75.0	0	0	0
Carlos Puyol	3	3	0	0	270	75.0	0	2	0
Michel Fernandez Salgado	1	1	0	0	90	25.0	0	0	0
Sergio Ramos	3	3	0	0	270	75.0	0	0	0
Midfielders									
David Albelda	2	1	1	0	126	35.0	0	1	0
Guerrero Antonio Lopez	1	1	0	0	90	25.0	0	0	0
Cesc Fabregas	4	2	2	1	214	59.4	0	1	0
Sanchez Joaquin	3	1	2	0	162	45.0	0	0	0
Luis Garcia	3	2	1	2	158	43.9	0	0	0
Marcos Senna	3	2	1	1	154	42.8	0	0	0
Xabi Alonso	3	3	0	1	234	65.0	1	0	0
Xavi Hernandez	4	3	1	1	276	76.7	0	0	0
Forwards									
Andres Iniesta	1	1	0	0	90	25.0	0	0	0
Raul	4	2	2	2	179	49.7	1	0	0
Jose Antonio Reyes	1	1	0	1	69	19.2	0	1	0
Fernando Torres	4	3	1	0	291	80.8	3	0	0
David Villa	4	3	1	3	207	57.5	3	0	0

WORLD CUP

GERMANY v ARGENTINA

GERMANY (0) **1** **ARGENTINA** (0) **1**
Klose 80 — Ayala 49
aet - Germany won 4-2 on penalties

Germany	STATS	Argentina
5	Shots off target	7
5	Shots on target	5
4	Corners	6
23	Fouls	32
3	Offside	3
3	Yellows	4
0	Reds	1
43%	Possession	57%

Referee: Lubos Michel (SLO)

HOSTS SHOW PENALTY PROFESSIONALISM
Argentina have the best of this quarter final and take the lead through Ayala from a corner. Germany barely fashion one chance but level through a Klose header. Lehmann is the penalty hero, referring to notes in his sock to make two saves while Germany score four out of four.

ITALY v UKRAINE

ITALY (1) **3** **UKRAINE** (0) **0**
Zambrotta 6
Toni 59,69

Italy	STATS	Ukraine
3	Shots off target	6
7	Shots on target	7
1	Corners	3
15	Fouls	31
2	Offside	2
0	Yellows	3
0	Reds	0
41%	Possession	59%

Referee: Frank de Bleeckere (BEL)

ZAMBROTTA'S EARLY GOAL HAUNTS UKRAINE
Ukraine produce some of their best attacking football of this World Cup in the second half. They should score two or three but either miss or find Buffon in top form. Zambrotta's early strike still separates the sides after Ukraine's onslaught and Toni scores two simple goals from close-in to settle it in Italy's favour.

ARGENTINA APPEARANCES

Match	1	2	3	4	5	Appearances	Started	Subbed on	Subbed off	Mins played	% played	Goals	Yellow	Red
Result	W	W	D	W	L									
Goalkeepers														
Roberto Abbondancieri						5	5	0	1	460	90.2	0	0	0
Leonardo Franco						1	0	1	0	50	9.8	0	0	0
Defenders														
Roberto Ayala						5	5	0	0	510	100.0	1	0	0
Nicolas Burdisso						3	3	0	1	203	39.8	0	0	0
Fabricio Coloccini						2	1	1	0	187	36.7	0	0	0
Leandro Cufre						1	1	0	0	90	17.5	0	0	1
Gabriel Ivan Heinze						4	4	0	0	420	82.4	0	2	0
Gabriel Milito						1	1	0	0	90	17.6	0	0	0
Lionel Scaloni						1	1	0	0	120	23.5	0	0	0
Juan Pablo Sorin						4	4	0	0	420	82.4	0	2	0
Midfielders														
Pablo Aimar						3	0	3	0	58	11.4	0	0	0
Esteban Cambiasso						5	3	2	1	378	74.1	1	1	0
Luis Gonzalez						3	2	1	1	151	29.6	0	1	0
Javier Mascherano						5	5	0	0	510	100.0	0	2	0
Juan Riquelme						5	5	0	3	448	87.8	0	0	0
Maxi Rodriguez						5	5	0	1	493	96.7	3	1	0
Forwards														
Hernan Crespo						4	4	0	3	305	59.8	3	1	0
Julio Cruz						2	0	2	0	64	12.5	0	1	0
Lionel Messi						3	1	2	1	122	23.9	1	0	0
Rodrigo Palacio						1	0	1	0	27	5.3	0	0	0
Javier Saviola						3	3	0	3	215	42.2	1	1	0
Carlos Tevez						4	2	2	0	289	56.7	1	0	0

UKRAINE APPEARANCES

Match	1	2	3	4	5	Appearances	Started	Subbed on	Subbed off	Mins played	% played	Goals	Yellow	Red
Result	L	W	W	W	L									
Goalkeepers														
Oleksander Shovkovskyi						5	5	0	0	480	100.0	0	0	0
Defenders														
Andriy Nesmachniy						5	5	0	0	480	100.0	0	1	0
Andrey Rusol						4	4	0	1	314	65.4	1	2	0
Vyacheslav Sviderskyy						3	3	0	1	199	41.5	0	3	0
Vladyslav Vashchuk						3	2	1	0	212	44.2	0	0	1
Volodymyr Yezerskiy						1	1	0	0	90	18.8	0	1	0
Midfielders														
Oleg Gusev						5	5	0	1	435	90.6	0	0	0
Andriy Husin						1	0	1	0	16	3.3	0	0	0
Husin						4	3	1	1	266	55.4	0	0	0
Maksym Kalinichenko						4	4	0	2	328	68.3	1	2	0
Ruslan Rotan						3	1	2	1	129	26.9	0	0	0
Oleg Shelayev						5	4	1	0	435	90.6	0	1	0
Anatoli Timoshchyuk						5	5	0	0	480	100.0	0	1	0
Forwards														
Oleksiy Byelyk						1	0	1	0	19	4.0	0	0	0
Milevskiy						4	1	3	1	90	18.8	0	1	0
Sergei Rebrov						4	2	2	2	178	37.1	1	0	0
Andriy Shevchenko						5	5	0	2	472	98.3	2	0	0
Andrei Vorobey						4	1	3	1	245	51.0	0	0	0
Andrey Voronin						4	4	0	2	368	76.7	0	0	0

ENGLAND v PORTUGAL

ENGLAND	(0) 0 PORTUGAL	(0) 0
	aet - Portugal won 3-1 on penalties	
	STATS	
5	Shots off target	11
4	Shots on target	9
6	Corners	4
21	Fouls	10
0	Offside	3
2	Yellows	2
1	Reds	0
44%	Possession	56%
Referee:	Horacio Elizondo (ARG)	

RICARDO DENIES ENGLISH YET AGAIN
Portuguese will wins out over English spirit in a tense battle, shaped by Rooney's sending off. Neither side gives the opposing keeper much to do, even when England play 50 minutes with ten men, after Rooney's red for lashing out at Carvalho. Crouch performs wonderfully as sub in England's most cohesive spell of the tournament but Ricardo saves three penalty kicks to ensure it's Portugal who progress.

BRAZIL v FRANCE

BRAZIL	(0) 0 FRANCE	(0) 1
		Henry 57
	STATS	
6	Shots off target	4
1	Shots on target	5
5	Corners	7
22	Fouls	17
2	Offside	5
4	Yellows	3
0	Reds	0
55%	Possession	45%
Referee:	Luis Medina Cantalejo (SPA)	

ZIDANE GIVES BRAZIL A LESSON IN COOL
Zidane's cool control and time on the ball means it's just like watching Brazil - in Bleu! The French defence, effortlessly shielded by Makelele and Vieira, keep Ronaldinho and Kaka quiet and Henry's sharp finish from another Zidane free kick always looks the winning goal.

ENGLAND APPEARANCES

Match	1	2	3	4	5	Appearances	Started	Subbed on	Subbed off	Mins played	% played	Goals	Yellow	Red
Result	W	W	D	W	L									
Goalkeepers														
Paul Robinson						5	5	0	0	480	100.0	0	1	0
Defenders														
Sol Campbell						1	0	1	0	36	7.5	0	0	0
Jamie Carragher						4	2	2	1	280	58.3	0	1	0
Ashley Cole						5	5	0	0	480	100.0	0	0	0
Rio Ferdinand						5	5	0	1	444	92.5	0	0	0
Gary Neville						2	2	0	0	210	43.8	0	0	0
John Terry						5	5	0	0	480	100.0	0	2	0
Midfielders														
David Beckham						5	5	0	2	405	84.4	1	0	0
Michael Carrick						1	1	0	0	90	18.8	0	0	0
Joe Cole						5	5	0	4	383	79.8	1	0	0
Stewart Downing						3	0	3	0	53	11.0	0	0	0
Steven Gerrard						5	4	1	1	411	85.6	2	1	0
Owen Hargreaves						4	3	1	0	309	64.4	0	2	0
Frank Lampard						5	5	0	0	480	100.0	0	1	0
Aaron Lennon						3	0	3	1	106	22.1	0	0	0
Forwards														
Peter Crouch						4	2	2	0	323	67.3	1	1	0
Michael Owen						3	3	0	3	114	23.8	0	0	0
Wayne Rooney						4	3	1	1	252	52.5	0	0	1

BRAZIL APPEARANCES

Match	1	2	3	4	5	Appearances	Started	Subbed on	Subbed off	Mins played	% played	Goals	Yellow	Red
Result	W	W	W	W	L									
Goalkeepers														
Nelson Dida						5	5	0	1	441	98.0	0	0	0
Rogerio Ceni						1	0	1	0	9	2.0	0	0	0
Defenders														
Cafu						4	4	0	1	345	76.7	0	2	0
Cicinho						2	1	1	0	105	23.3	0	0	0
Gilberto						1	1	0	0	90	20.0	1	1	0
Juan						5	5	0	0	450	100.0	0	2	0
Lucio						5	5	0	0	450	100.0	0	1	0
Roberto Carlos						4	4	0	0	360	80.0	0	0	0
Midfielders														
Emerson						3	3	0	2	206	45.8	0	1	0
Gilberto Silva						4	2	2	0	244	54.2	0	0	0
Pernambucano Juninho						3	2	1	1	182	40.4	1	0	0
Ricardo Kaka						5	5	0	3	411	91.3	1	0	0
Jose Ze Roberto						5	4	1	0	380	84.4	1	0	0
Forwards														
Adriano						4	3	1	2	265	58.9	2	1	0
Fred						1	0	1	0	3	0.7	1	0	0
Luis Ricardinho						2	0	2	0	27	6.0	0	0	0
Robinho						4	1	3	0	143	31.8	0	1	0
Ronaldinho						5	5	0	1	430	95.6	0	0	0
Ronaldo						5	5	0	2	409	90.9	3	2	0

WORLD CUP

Semi-finals

GERMANY v ITALY

GERMANY	(0) 0 ITALY	(0) 2
	aet	Grosso 119
		Del Piero 120
	STATS	
11	Shots off target	5
2	Shots on target	10
4	Corners	12
21	Fouls	19
2	Offside	11
2	Yellows	1
0	Reds	0
44%	Possession	56%
Referee:	Benito Archundia (MEX)	

HOSTS DEPART AFTER LAYING ON A STUNNING SEMI

Only two minutes away from the national nightmare of a penalty shoot-out with the Germans, Italy fashion two of the best goals of the World Cup to reach the final.

The standard of passing, midfield creativity and attacking intent of both sides make it the finest game so far. Both sides take turns to dominate, both keepers pull off fine saves and while Italy look defter in possession, Germany have the best chance with Schneider blasting high and wide from Klose's pass. The game's energy barely drops in extra time as both Gilardino and Zambrotta hit the post.

In the 118th minute man-of-the-match Pirlo slips a clever pass to Grosso who finds the perfect curling shot to beat Lehmann. Just before the final whistle Gilardino's reverse pass sets up Del Piero as Italy reap the benefit of Lippi's courage in leaving four forwards on the pitch.

PORTUGAL v FRANCE

PORTUGAL	(0) 0 FRANCE	(1) 1
		Zidane 33 pen
	STATS	
7	Shots off target	1
5	Shots on target	4
8	Corners	3
18	Fouls	11
4	Offside	0
1	Yellows	1
0	Reds	0
58%	Possession	42%
Referee:	Jorge Larrionda (URU)	

ZIDANE HAS EYES ONLY FOR THE FINAL

Portuguese keeper Ricardo claims he can tell which way a player will place a penalty by looking at his eyes.

When Carvalho brings down Henry on the edge of the box for a penalty, Ricardo looks long into Zidane's eyes. He guesses the direction but can't deal with the placement and power and the French skipper gives his side a halftime lead.

France never go close to extending it but only the newly unpopular Ronaldo sparks in the Portuguese attack. When Bhartez flaps at the winger's long range free kick, it rebounds to Figo but the Portuguese heads over and they have blown their best chance of the game. Rival captains, and old Madrid buddies, Figo and Zidane embrace at the end but it's 'Zizou' who endures.

Third place play-off

GERMANY v PORTUGAL

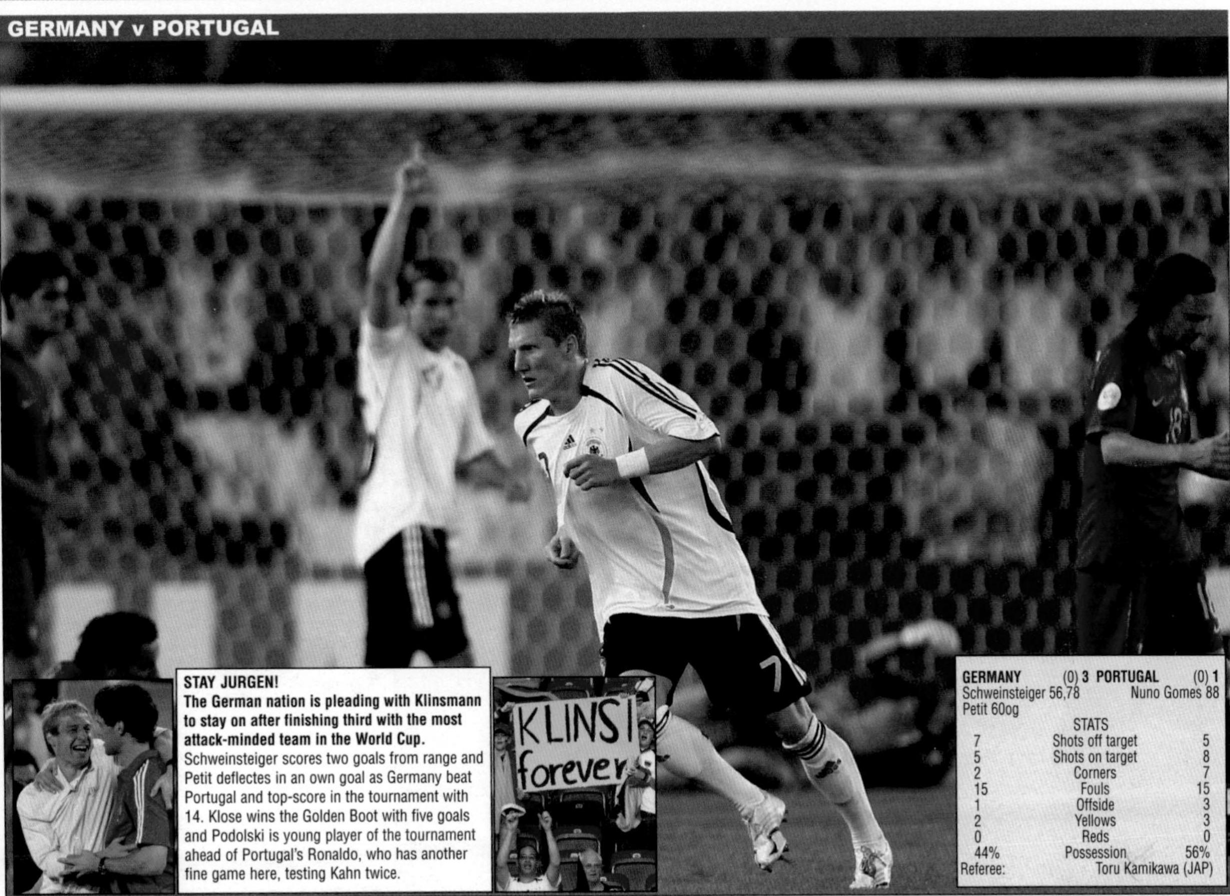

STAY JURGEN!
The German nation is pleading with Klinsmann to stay on after finishing third with the most attack-minded team in the World Cup. Schweinsteiger scores two goals from range and Petit deflectes in an own goal as Germany beat Portugal and top-score in the tournament with 14. Klose wins the Golden Boot with five goals and Podolski is young player of the tournament ahead of Portugal's Ronaldo, who has another fine game here, testing Kahn twice.

GERMANY (0) **3** **PORTUGAL** (0) **1**
Schweinsteiger 56,78 — Nuno Gomes 88
Petit 60og

	STATS	
7	Shots off target	5
5	Shots on target	8
2	Corners	7
15	Fouls	15
1	Offside	3
2	Yellows	3
0	Reds	0
44%	Possession	56%

Referee: Toru Kamikawa (JAP)

GERMANY APPEARANCES

Match 1 2 3 4 5 6 7
Result W W W W W L W

	Appearances	Started	Subbed on	Subbed off	Mins played	% played	Goals	Yellow	Red
Goalkeepers									
Oliver Kahn	1	1	0	0	90	13.0	0	0	0
Jens Lehmann	6	6	0	0	600	87.0	0	0	0
Defenders									
Arne Friedrich	6	6	0	1	572	82.9	0	1	0
Robert Huth	1	1	0	0	90	13.0	0	0	0
Marcell Jansen	1	1	0	0	90	13.0	0	0	0
Philip Lahm	7	7	0	0	690	100.0	1	0	0
Per Mertesacker	6	6	0	0	600	87.0	0	0	0
Christophe Metzelder	6	6	0	0	600	87.0	0	2	0
Jens Nowotny	1	1	0	0	90	13.0	0	0	0
Midfielders									
Michael Ballack	5	5	0	0	510	73.9	0	1	0
Tim Borowski	6	2	4	2	245	35.5	0	2	0
Torsten Frings	6	6	0	2	539	78.1	1	2	0
Mike Hanke	1	0	1	0	20	2.9	0	0	0
Tomas Hitzlsperger	1	0	1	0	12	1.7	0	0	0
Sebastian Kehl	4	2	2	0	236	34.2	0	0	0
Bernd Schneider	7	7	0	4	574	83.2	0	0	0
Bastian Schweinsteiger	7	6	1	4	528	76.5	2	1	0
Forwards									
Gerald Asamoah	1	0	1	0	18	2.6	0	0	0
Miroslav Klose	7	7	0	5	582	84.3	5	0	0
Oliver Neuville	7	0	7	0	146	21.2	1	0	0
Odonkor	4	0	4	0	126	18.3	0	2	0
Lukas Podolski	7	7	0	3	632	91.6	3	1	0

PORTUGAL APPEARANCES

Match 1 2 3 4 5 6 7
Result W W W W W L L

	Appearances	Started	Subbed on	Subbed off	Mins played	% played	Goals	Yellow	Red
Goalkeepers									
Pereira Ricardo	7	7	0	0	660	100.0	0	1	0
Defenders									
Marco Caneira	1	1	0	0	90	13.6	0	0	0
Ricardo Carvalho	6	6	0	0	570	86.4	0	2	0
Paulo Ferreira	2	1	1	0	119	18.0	0	1	0
Fernando Meira	7	7	0	0	660	100.0	0	0	0
Luis Garcia Miguel	6	6	0	1	541	82.0	0	1	0
Nuno Valente	6	6	0	1	548	83.0	0	2	0
Ricardo Costa	1	1	0	0	90	13.6	0	1	0
Midfielders									
Francisco Costinha	5	4	1	2	284	43.0	0	3	1
Anderson Deco	4	4	0	1	336	50.9	1	2	1
Luis Madeira Caeira Figo	7	6	1	4	528	80.0	0	1	0
Maniche	7	6	1	1	565	85.6	2	2	0
Armando Teixeira Petit	6	3	3	1	395	59.8	0	2	0
Cristiano Ronaldo	6	6	0	2	482	73.0	1	1	0
Simao Sabrosa	7	3	4	0	411	62.3	1	0	0
Cardoso Tiago	5	3	2	2	262	39.7	0	0	0
Hugo Viana	2	0	2	0	56	8.5	0	0	0
Forwards									
Luis Boa Morte	1	0	1	0	11	1.7	0	1	0
Nuno Gomes	1	0	1	0	22	3.3	1	0	0
Pauleta	6	6	0	4	430	65.2	1	1	0
Helder Postiga	3	1	2	0	141	21.4	0	0	0

WORLD CUP

ITALY v FRANCE

ITALY	(1) 1	FRANCE	(1) 1
Materazzi 19			Zidane 7 pen

aet - Italy won 5-3 on penalties

ITALY	STATS	FRANCE
2	Shots off target	8
3	Shots on target	5
5	Corners	7
17	Fouls	24
4	Offside	2
1	Yellows	34
0	Reds	1
54%	Possession	46%

Referee: Horacio Elizondo (ARG)

ITALY SURVIVE ZIDANE'S ONSLAUGHT TO TRIUMPH

A final featuring eight players from Serie A's disgraced Juventus club is dominated by its top four defenders.

Thuram excels for France in a first half shaded by Italy before the formidable presence of Buffon, Cannavaro and Zambrotta keep Henry and Zidane at bay through the second half and extra time.

Italy emerge from the penalty shoot out with their fourth trophy but as the second best side in a final. It will be remembered for two powerful uses of Zidane's head: once, sublimely, to finish a move he orchestrated and almost win the cup for France; the second time, inexplicably to tarnish his gilded reputation and almost certainly lose it for them.

Zidane begins the match with a cheeky penalty chip down and in off the bar after Materazzi's awkward challenge on Malouda. Materazzi makes amends by heading home an equaliser powerfully from a Pirlo corner and has an identikit effort disallowed for pushing. Toni hits the bar from another set-piece.

After Zidane is sent off for butting Materazzi in the chest the game goes to penalties. Inevitably the key moment in the penalty shoot out sees Juvé's Trezeguet hit the bar against club-mate Buffon in the only missed spot-kick.

FRANCE APPEARANCES

Match	1	2	3	4	5	6	7	Appearances	Started	Subbed on	Subbed off	Mins played	% played	Goals	Yellow	Red
Result	D	D	W	W	W	W	L									
Goalkeepers																
Fabien Barthez								7	7	0	0	660	100.0	0	0	0
Defenders																
Eric Abidal								6	6	0	0	570	86.4	0	2	0
William Gallas								7	7	0	0	660	100.0	0	0	0
Willy Sagnol								7	7	0	0	660	100.0	0	3	0
Mikael Silvestre								1	1	0	0	90	13.6	0	0	0
Lilian Thuram								7	7	0	0	660	100.0	0	1	0
Midfielders																
Vikash Dhorasoo								2	0	2	0	10	1.5	0	0	0
Alou Diarra								2	0	2	0	75	11.4	0	1	0
Claude Makelele								7	7	0	0	660	100.0	0	1	0
Florent Malouda								6	6	0	5	501	75.9	0	1	0
Franck Ribery								7	6	1	5	512	77.6	1	1	0
Patrick Vieira								7	7	0	2	585	88.6	2	1	0
Zinedine Zidane								6	6	0	1	558	84.5	3	3	1
Forwards																
Sydney Govou								4	0	4	0	64	9.7	0	0	0
Thierry Henry								7	7	0	4	631	95.6	3	0	0
Louis Saha								3	0	3	0	33	5.0	0	2	0
David Trezeguet								3	1	2	0	112	17.0	0	0	0
Sylvain Wiltord								7	2	5	2	208	31.5	0	0	0

ITALY APPEARANCES

Match	1	2	3	4	5	6	7	Appearances	Started	Subbed on	Subbed off	Mins played	% played	Goals	Yellow	Red
Result	W	D	W	W	W	W	W									
Goalkeepers																
Gianluigi Buffon								7	7	0	0	690	100.0	0	0	0
Defenders																
Andrea Barzagli								2	1	1	0	125	18.1	0	0	0
Fabio Cannavaro								7	7	0	0	690	100.0	0	0	0
Fabio Grosso								6	6	0	0	600	87.0	1	1	0
Marco Materazzi								4	3	1	0	363	52.6	2	0	1
Alessandro Nesta								3	3	0	1	196	28.4	0	0	0
Massimo Oddo								1	0	1	0	23	3.3	0	0	0
Cristian Zaccardo								3	2	1	1	157	22.8	0	0	0
Gianluca Zambrotta								6	6	0	0	600	87.0	1	3	0
Midfielders																
Simone Barone								2	0	2	0	40	5.8	0	0	0
Mauro Camoranesi								5	4	1	4	349	50.6	0	2	0
Daniele De Rossi								3	2	1	0	177	25.7	0	1	1
Gennaro Gattuso								6	5	1	1	552	80.0	0	2	0
Simone Perrotta								7	7	0	2	612	88.7	0	0	0
Andrea Pirlo								7	7	0	1	667	96.7	1	0	0
Forwards																
Alessandro Del Piero								5	1	4	1	173	25.1	1	0	0
Alberto Gilardino								5	4	1	3	304	44.1	1	0	0
Vincenzo Iaquinta								5	0	5	0	192	27.8	1	1	0
Filippo Inzaghi								1	0	1	0	31	4.5	1	0	0
Luca Toni								6	6	0	4	480	69.6	2	0	0
Francesco Totti								7	6	1	3	465	67.4	1	1	0

ITALY v FRANCE

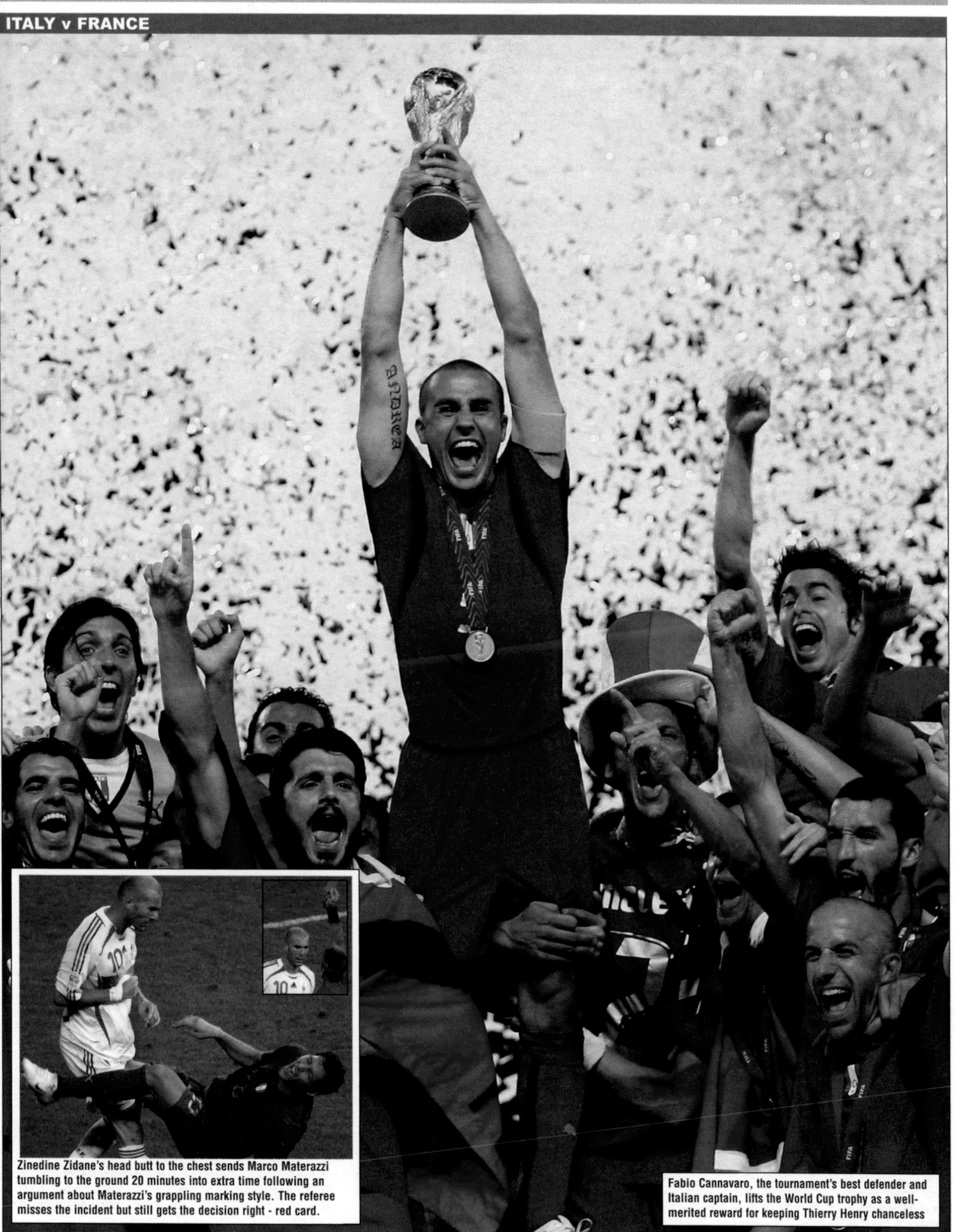

Zinedine Zidane's head butt to the chest sends Marco Materazzi tumbling to the ground 20 minutes into extra time following an argument about Materazzi's grappling marking style. The referee misses the incident but still gets the decision right - red card.

Fabio Cannavaro, the tournament's best defender and Italian captain, lifts the World Cup trophy as a well-merited reward for keeping Thierry Henry chanceless

WORLD CUP

CHART-TOPPING MIDFIELDERS

1 Gattuso - Italy	
Goals scored in the World Cup Finals	0
Assists in all games	0
Defensive Rating Av number of mins between team goals conceded while on the pitch	552
Contribution to Attacking Power Average number of minutes between team goals scored while on pitch	61
Scoring Difference Defensive Rating minus Contribution to Attacking Power	491

	PLAYER	COUNTRY	GOALS	ASS	DEF R	POWER	SCORE DIFF
1	Gattuso	Italy	0	0	552	61	491
2	Gerrard	England	2	0	411	82	329
3	Ze Roberto	Brazil	1	0	380	54	326
4	Camoranesi	Italy	0	0	349	70	279
5	Pirlo	Italy	1	3	334	61	273
6	Perrotta	Italy	0	1	306	61	245
7	Castillo	Ecuador	0	0	270	54	216
8	Tiago	Portugal	0	0	262	66	196
9	Riquelme	Argentina	0	3	224	41	183
10	Lampard	England	0	0	240	80	160
11	Kaka	Brazil	1	1	206	51	155
12	Makelele	France	0	0	220	73	147
13	Beckham	England	1	3	203	68	135
14	Vieira	France	2	2	195	65	130
15	Mascherano	Argentina	0	0	170	46	124
16	Ribery	France	1	1	171	64	107
17	Zidane	France	3	1	186	80	106
18	Xavi	Spain	0	1	138	35	103
19	Rodriguez	Argentina	3	0	164	62	102
20	Figo	Portugal	0	4	176	75	101

(*Switzerland did not concede a goal in the Tournament and so are judged only on attacking power)

The World Cup Round-up charts combine the records of chart-topping keepers, defenders, midfielders and forwards, from every Country in the last 16 of the finals tournament. The one above is for **the Chart-topping Midfielders**. The players are ranked by their Scoring Difference although other attributes are shown.

CHART-TOPPING GOALSCORERS

1 Crespo - Argentina	
Goals scored in the World Cup Finals	3
Contribution to Attacking Power Average number of minutes between team goals while on pitch	31
Player Strike Rate Average number of minutes between goals scored by player	102
Country Strike Rate (CSR) Average minutes between League goals scored by the Country	46

	PLAYER	COUNTRY	GOALS	POWER	CSR	S RATE
1	Crespo	Argentina	3	31	46	102
2	Klose	Germany	5	49	49	116
3	Ronaldo	Brazil	3	45	45	136
4	Rodriguez	Argentina	3	62	46	164
5	Materazzi	Italy	2	73	58	182
6	Zidane	France	3	80	73	186
7	Frei	Switzerland	2	128	98	192
8	Gerrard	England	2	82	80	206
9	Henry	France	3	79	73	210
10	Podolski	Germany	3	53	49	211
11	Shevchenko	Ukraine	2	94	96	236
12	Toni	Italy	2	80	58	240
13	Schweinsteiger	Germany	2	44	49	264
14	Maniche	Portugal	2	113	94	283
15	Vieira	France	2	65	73	293
16	Gilardino	Italy	1	61	58	304
17	Moore	Australia	1	154	72	308
18	Rusol	Ukraine	1	63	96	314
19	Crouch	England	1	65	80	323
20	Kalinichenko	Ukraine	1	66	96	328

The Chart-topping Goalscorers measures the players by Strike Rate. They are most likely to be Forwards but Midfield players and even Defenders can enter the tables. It is not a measure of the number of World Cup Finals goals scored – although that is also noted – but how *often* on average they have scored.

CHART-TOPPING DEFENDERS

1 Magnin - Switzerland	
Goals conceded in the World Cup Finals	0
Clean Sheets In games when he played at least 70 mins	3
Defensive Rating Average number of minutes between goals conceded while on pitch	none conc
Country Defensive Rating Average mins between goals conceded by the Country in the Finals	-

	PLAYER	COUNTRY	CON: WCF	CS	CDR	DEF RATE
1	Magnin	Switzerland	0	3	-	-
2	Muller	Switzerland	0	4	-	-*
3	Grosso	Italy	1	5	315	600
4	Ferdinand	England	1	4	225	444
5	Materazzi	Italy	1	2	315	364
6	Roberto Carlos	Brazil	1	3	225	360
7	Cafu	Brazil	1	3	225	345
8	Cannavaro	Italy	2	5	315	345
9	Zambrotta	Italy	2	4	315	300
10	Carvalho	Portugal	2	4	126	285
11	Thuram	France	2	4	210	285
12	Miguel	Portugal	2	4	126	271
13	Reasco	Ecuador	1	2	90	270
14	Cole, A	England	2	4	225	240
15	Terry	England	2	4	225	240
16	Juan	Brazil	2	3	225	225
17	Lucio	Brazil	2	3	225	225
18	Sagnol	France	3	4	210	220
19	Gallas	France	3	4	210	220
20	Abidal	France	3	3	210	190

(*Switzerland did not concede a goal in the Tournament)

The Chart-topping Defenders are resolved by their Defensive Rating, how often their team concedes a goal while they are playing. All these rightly favour players at the best performing teams because good players win matches. However, good players in other teams may chart where they have lifted the team's performance.

CHART-TOPPING GOALKEEPERS

1 Zuberbuhler - Switzerland	
Counting Games Games where he played at least 70 minutes	4
Goals Conceded in the World Cup Finals	0
Clean Sheets In games when he played at least 70 mins	4
Defensive Rating Average number of minutes between goals conceded while on pitch	none conc

	PLAYER	COUNTRY	CG	CONC WCF	CS	DEF RATE
1	Zuberbuhler	Switzerland	4	0	4	-
2	Buffon	Italy	7	2	5	345
3	Bobadilla	Paraguay	3	1	1	264
4	Robinson	England	5	2	4	240
5	Abbondancieri	Argentina	5	2	2	230
6	Dida	Brazil	5	2	3	221
7	Barthez	France	7	3	4	220
8	Van der Sar	Holland	4	2	2	180
9	Joao Ricardo	Angola	3	2	1	135
10	Ricardo	Portugal	7	5	4	132
11	Lehmann	Germany	6	5	3	120
12	Mora	Ecuador	4	4	2	90
13	Pletikosa	Croatia	3	3	1	90
14	Sanchez, O	Mexico	4	5	1	78
15	Shovkovskyi	Ukraine	5	7	3	69
16	Cech	Czech Republic	3	4	1	68
16	Casillas	Spain	3	4	1	68
18	Schwarzer	Australia	3	4	0	68
18	Boruc	Poland	3	4	0	68
18	Lee, WJ	South Korea	3	4	0	68

The Chart-topping Goalkeepers are positioned by their Defensive Rating. We also show Clean Sheets where the team has not conceded and the Keeper has played all or most (at least 70 minutes) of the game. Only one keeper is selected from each Country – the one with the best performance. All 32 Countries qualify.